ALPINE CLUB LIBRARY CATALOGUE

ALPINE CLUB LIBRARY
CATALOGUE

BOOKS AND PERIODICALS

HEINEMANN · LONDON

Heinemann Educational Books Ltd
22 Bedford Square, London WC1B 3HH

LONDON EDINBURGH MELBOURNE AUCKLAND
HONG KONG SINGAPORE KUALA LUMPUR NEW DELHI
IBADAN NAIROBI JOHANNESBURG
EXETER (NH) KINGSTON PORT OF SPAIN

ISBN 0 435 86050 X
© THE ALPINE CLUB 1982
First published 1982

Reproduced, printed and bound in Great Britain by
Hazell Watson & Viney Ltd, Aylesbury, Bucks.

CONTENTS

FOREWORD

THE ALPINE CLUB LIBRARY

The Alpine Club Library is generally recognised in the mountaineering world to be one of the most important in existence. The Alpine Club itself was founded in 1857 and its records show that it very soon began to buy books; the Club's first Honorary Librarian was appointed in 1861. The first catalogue of the Library was published in 1880 and contained 600 entries. Now there are some 40,000 items housed at the Alpine Club's premises in London.

The Library's collection of nineteenth century publications of early ascents, exploration of mountain areas and related subjects is unique. It contains some books not included in the British Library's catalogue, some on exploration in Asia that are hard to find elsewhere and many early volumes. The oldest bears the imprint 1518; there are others dating from the 16th century and many from the 17th and 18th, mostly illustrated. In addition there are complete runs to the present day of most of the leading mountaineering journals which over the past century have been received by the Alpine Club in exchange for its own Journal. There are already some 4,000 volumes of these and currently over 50 journals are regularly received in half a dozen languages.

The Alpine Club found that managing a library of this size and variety and keeping it fit for research and general use had become a task beyond the resources of voluntary effort. Furthermore, its catalogue was incapable of keeping up with the flow of mountaineering books, periodicals and journals, and a completely new catalogue and classification system were necessary if the riches of the Library were to be readily accessible to readers. The Club therefore set up in 1972 a Trust to which it made over its Library in the hope of drawing upon wider financial resources than a club of 1,000 members could provide in order that a professional Librarian could be engaged to assist the Club's Honorary Librarian in the reorganisation of the Library, to compile a new catalogue, to provide necessary services to readers and to acquire books to fill gaps in the collection. It was realised from the outset that the new catalogue should be published so that it could serve interests wider than those of the Club itself. The Trust has been recognised as a Charity and the task of its Council of Management has been both to direct the work of the Library and to raise the funds necessary for its operation.

The present volume of the new catalogue is the first catalogue of the Library to be published since 1899. It has been compiled to cover all the books, climbing guides, periodicals and club journals held in the Library in March 1979. Further volumes of the catalogue will be published from time to time to cover accessions and a wide variety of material in the Library yet to be catalogued, including collections of letters by eminent mountaineering explorers, diaries of the pioneers, the Führerbücher of many of the early guides, maps, photographs, slides and many volumes of pamphlets and papers in several languages.

The Alpine Club Library is not reserved to members of the Alpine Club, but is open to the public. It is hoped that publication of this first volume of the catalogue will encourage reference to the Library.

Already it has been most encouraging to note the number of visitors
who have made use of it - visitors of many nationalities, some of
whom have come from afar, to check historical records or to plan
expeditions to mountain ranges remote from their homelands or from
London. The Library hopes in this way to preserve the past in an
accessible form, and in particular to give encouragement to the
young. The flow of young British readers has been particularly
stimulating and it would be fair to say that few mountaineering
expeditions based on these Islands now leave our shores without
consulting the Alpine Club Library.

Donations to assist this expensive and lengthy task will be welcomed
by the Hon. Treasurer, Alpine Club Library, 74 South Audley Street,
London W1Y 5FF.

We, the co-signatories of the foreword, wish those who consult the
catalogue good reading, rewarding research and successful exploration in the mountains of the world.

J.H. Emlyn Jones   Douglas Busk
President,   Chairman,
Alpine Club   Alpine Club Library

A WORD OF THANKS

The work of reorganising the Alpine Club Library and preparing the Catalogue has been made possible only because of the generosity of many benefactors and the technical advice so freely given by outside experts.

Many members of the Alpine Club have contributed lavishly, donations have been received from members of the public, and special thanks are due in particular to the following who have given the most generous financial support: Members of the American Alpine Club; Bass Charrington Ltd.; The British Library; Lady Busk; The Grocers' Company; Henry S. Hall, Jr.; Count Guido Monzino of the Italian Alpine Club; The Mount Everest Foundation; The Rayne Foundation; Mrs. I.A.Richards; W.H. Smith and Son Ltd. Very generous gifts of books have been made by members of the Alpine Club, by the late Lucien Devies of the French Alpine Club and by Dr. Albert Eggler of the Swiss Alpine Club.

On the technical side the advice of Miss A.D. Crews of the British Library and of the staff of the London Library has been invaluable, as has the help of the Royal Geographical Society.

The Alpine Club will always be thankful to Lord Chorley, Honorary Treasurer of the Club, who first suggested the formation of the Trust for the Library and did so much of the preliminary work on it, and to the late Lord Tangley who carried out the complicated transactions involved in setting up the Trust.

Thanks are due to successive professional Librarians who have under-taken the task in past years - Thomas Summers, Miss Helen Smith, Mrs. C.R. Ashton, Miss N. Wilson. Mrs. P.E. Johnson, our present Librarian, has been indefatigable in her devotion to the task of cataloguing, of preparing the material for publication and of supervising the compila-tion of the catalogue in page form. She was helped by Mrs. Peronelle Kinnell and Mrs. L.G. Dolan. The laborious and exacting task of producing the catalogue pages has been undertaken by Miss Mary Crawford whose work has been deeply appreciated.

Finally, the Alpine Club wishes to express its thank to past and present members of the Council of the Alpine Club Library who over many years have been untiring in their efforts to raise funds and re-organise and catalogue the Library. The Club owes a quite exceptional debt to Sir Douglas Busk who has led and inspired his team for the past nine years and has by his own efforts raised the greater part of the funds that have made this catalogue possible. The services of Robert Lawford, Honorary Librarian, and Frank Solari, Library Secretary, have been beyond praise and special mention should also be made of the late Robin Fedden who contributed so much to the work.

J.H. Emlyn Jones
President,
Alpine Club

INTRODUCTION

The Catalogue covers all the printed books, climbing guides and periodicals held by the Alpine Club Library in March 1979. It is in two parts. Part 1 contains the Author Catalogue which lists all the books (but not periodicals) in one alphabetical sequence by author, with some title entries. Part 2 consists of three Sections - Section 1 contains the Classified Catalogue of books, Section 2 contains the Classified Catalogue of climbing guides, Section 3 contains the Catalogue of periodicals in one alphabetical sequence.

The entries in the Author Catalogue contain the full bibliographical information pertaining to the books, based on the Anglo-American Cataloguing Rules (British Text) published by the Library Association in 1967. The entries in the Classified Catalogues are abbreviated and these Catalogues should be used in conjunction with the Author Catalogue.

The Classification used in the Library and in this Catalogue was devised specifically for the Alpine Club Library by a former Honorary Librarian, E.C. Pyatt. Basically, geographical location takes precedence where possible, the full system being set out at the beginning of Part 2.

In determining the sequence of the entries in the Catalogue, the German umlaut is treated as if it were a letter 'e' following the vowel to which it is applied. For example, Müller is filed as if it were Mueller, Österreichischer as if it were Oesterreichischer, etc.

PART 1

AUTHOR CATALOGUE

A***, A.
See
ABADIE, A

A., F.E.S.
See
ADAIR, F   E   S

A., T.S.Y.
See
CLARKSON, J   R

ABADIE, A
Itinéraire topographique et historique des
Hautes-Pyrénées, servant de guide aux
établissemens thermaux ..., par A.A.***
[i.e. A. Abadie]. 3e éd. corr. et augm.
Paris: Didier, 1833. 228p., 1 fold. plate,
map. 21cm.

ABADIE, Louis d'
Trente jours de voyage en Suisse par six
écoliers en vacances. Paris: Fabre, Feste,
[18--]. viii, 156p. 19cm. (Bibliothèque
choisie de la jeunesse)

ABBA, Giuseppe Cesare
Le Alpi nostri e il Monferrato [e il
Piemonte, e il Veneto montano, e la Lombardia
montana tra la Sesia e l'Adda, e la Lombardia
montana tra l'Adda e il Mincio]: libro di
lettura par le scuole... Bergamo: Istituto
Italiano d'Arti Grafiche, 1899. 5v., illus.,
maps. 20cm.

ABBATE, Enrico
CLUB ALPINO ITALIANO. Sezione di Roma
Da Brescia a Trento per le Alpi Retiche,
relazione di E. Abbate; illustrata da A. Zoppi.
[Roma]: La Sezione, 1884. 56p., plates, illus.,
maps. 28cm.

ABBATE, Enrico
Guida al Gran Sasso d'Italia. Roma: Club Alpino
Italiano, Sezione di Roma, 1888. vii, 222p.,
plates, illus., maps, plans. 17cm.

ABBATE, Enrico
Guida dell'Abruzzo. Roma: Club Alpino Italiano,
Sezione di Roma, 1903. viii, 558p., maps. 18cm.

PIGEON, Anna and ABBOT, Ellen
Peaks and passes: [particulars of six mountain-
eering tours ... between the years 1869 and 1876].
[The Authors], 1885. 31p. 18cm.

ABBOTT, Jacob
Rollo in Switzerland. Darton, 1854.
197p., plates, illus., map. 18cm. (Rollo's
Tour in Europe, 3)

ABBRUZZI, Luigi Amedeo, of Savoy, Duke of the
See
LUIGI AMEDEO, Duke of the Abruzzi

A'BECKETT, Arthur and SAMBOURNE, Linley
Our holiday in the Scottish highlands. Bradbury,
Agnew, [1876]. 144p., plates, illus.
26 x 41cm.

ABEL, August
Zum Ortler nach Sulden und Tirol ...; Zeich-
nungen von Tony Grubhofer. Meran: F.W.
Ellmenreich, 1898. 159p., illus. 15cm.

ABERCROMBIE, W   R
Alaska, 1899: Copper River exploring expedition.
Washington: Government Printing Office, 1900.
169p., plates (1 fold.), illus., map. 25cm.

GLEN, Edwin F   and ABERCROMBIE, W   R
Reports of explorations in the territory of
Alaska (Cooks Inlet, Sushitna, Copper and Tanana
Rivers) 1898; made under the direction of the
Secretary of War. Washington: Government
Printing Office, 1899. 464p., 1 fold. plate,
map. 25cm.

ABERDARE, Morys George Lyndhurst Bruce, 4th Baron
The Lonsdale book of sporting records, 1937, by
Lord Aberdare [and others]. Seeley, Service
1937. xvi, 457p., plates, illus. 22cm.
(Lonsdale library, 25)

ABERLI, Jean Louis
LONCHAMP, F   C
J.-L. Aberli, 1723-86: son temps, sa vie et son
oeuvre avec un catalogue complet methodique et
raisonné. Paris: Librarie des Bibliophiles,
1927. 3v. in 1., plates, illus. 24cm.

ABETTI, Giorgio
SPEDIZIONE ITALIANA DE FILIPPI, 1913-14
[Relazioni scientifiche della] Spedizione
italiana De Filippi, nell'Himàlaia, Caracorùm
e Turchestàn Cinese (1913-1914). Serie 1.
Geodesia e geofisica ...; sotto la direzione di
Filippo de Filippi. Vol.1. Astronomia geodetica,
geodesia e topografia, [by] G. Abetti [and
others]. Bologna: Zanichelli, 1925. xxxv,
419p., plates (some fold., some col.), illus.
33cm.

ABINGER HIMALAYAN EXPEDITION, 1956
Mountains and memsahibs, by members of the
Abinger Himalayan Expedition 1956; foreword by
Mrs. Pandit. Constable, 1958. x, 198p., plates,
illus., maps. 22cm.
Expedition leader: Joyce Dunsheath.

ABNEY, Sir William de Wyveleslie
The Barnet book of photography: a collection
of practical articles by Capt. W. de W. Abney
[and others]. 3rd ed. Barnet (Herts.): Elliott,
1898. 287p., plates, illus. 22cm.

ABNEY, Sir William de Wyveleslie
ALMER, Christian
[Führerbuch]. A facsimile of Christian Almer's
Führerbuch 1856-1894; reproduced under the
superintendence of C.D. Cunningham and W. de W.
Abney. Sampson Low, Marston, 1896. xxxii,
261p., 1 plate, port. 20cm.

CUNNINGHAM, Carus Dunlop and ABNEY, Sir William
de Wyveleslie
The pioneers of the Alps. Sampson Low, Marston,
Searle, and Rivington, 1887. x, 287p., plates,
illus. 34cm.

- - Large paper ed. 1887.

- - 2nd ed. 1888.

ABRAHAM, Ashley Perry
Beautiful Lakeland ...; illustrations by G.P.
Abraham. Keswick: G.P. Abraham, 1912. 50p.,
plates, illus. 29cm.

ABRAHAM, George Dixon and ABRAHAM, Ashley Perry
Rock-climbing in North Wales. Keswick:
G.P. Abraham, 1906. xxii, 394p., plates,
illus., maps. 24cm.

ABRAHAM, Ashley Perry
Rock-climbing in Skye. Longmans, Green, 1908.
xxii, 330p., plates, illus., map (in pocket).
24cm.

ABRAHAM, Ashley Perry
JONES, Owen Glynne
Rock-climbing in the English Lake District.
2nd ed. with a memoir ... of the author ...
and an appendix by George and Ashley Abraham.
Keswick: G.P. Abraham, 1900. lxiv, 322p.,
plates, illus. 24cm.

ABRAHAM, Ashley Perry
HANKINSON, Alan
Camera on the crags: a portfolio of early
rock climbing photographs by the Abraham
brothers; selected and written by Alan Hankinson.
Heinemann, 1975. 39p., 99 plates, illus., maps
(on lining papers). 29cm.

ABRAHAM, George Dixon
British mountain climbs. Mills & Boon, 1909.
xvi, 448p., plates, illus. 18cm.

- - 2nd ed. 1923.

ABRAHAM, George Dixon
The complete mountaineer. Methuen, 1907.
xv, 493p., plates, illus. 23cm.

- - 2nd ed. 1908.

ABRAHAM, George Dixon
First steps to climbing. Mills & Boon, 1923.
126p., plates, illus. 19cm.

ABRAHAM, George Dixon
Modern mountaineering. Methuen, 1933. ix,
198p., plates, illus. 20cm.

- - 2nd ed. 1945.

- - 3rd ed. rev. 1948.

ABRAHAM, George Dixon
Mountain adventures at home and abroad.
Methuen, 1910. x, 308p., plates, illus.
23cm.

ABRAHAM, George Dixon
On Alpine heights and British crags. Methuen,
1919. xi, 307p., plates, illus. 23cm.

ABRAHAM, George Dixon and ABRAHAM, Ashley Perry
Rock-climbing in North Wales. Keswick: G.P.
Abraham, 1906. xxii, 394p., plates, illus.,
maps. 24cm.

ABRAHAM, George Dixon
JONES, Owen Glynne
Rock-climbing in the English Lake District.
2nd ed. with a memoir ... of the author ...
and an appendix by George and Ashley Abraham.
Keswick: G.P. Abraham, 1900. lxiv, 322p.,
plates, illus. 24cm.

ABRAHAM, George Dixon
Swiss mountain climbs. Mills & Boon, 1911.
xv, 423p., 24 plates, illus. 18cm.

ABRAHAM, George Dixon
HANKINSON, Alan
Camera on the crags: a portfolio of early
rock climbing photographs by the Abraham
brothers; selected and written by Alan Hankinson.
Heinemann, 1975. 39p., 99 plates, illus., maps
(on lining papers). 29cm.

ABRUZZI, Luigi Amedeo, of Savoy, Duke of the
See
LUIGI AMEDEO, Duke of the Abruzzi

ACADEMIC ALPINE CLUB OF KYOTO
Ascent of Noshaq: the Japanese expedition, 1960.
Tokyo: Asahi, 1961. 73p., plates (1 fold.,
some col.), illus., map. 27cm.
In Japanese, with 6p. summary in English.

ACADEMIC ALPINE CLUB OF KYOTO
Chogolisa: the Japanese Chogolisa expedition,
1958. Tokyo: Asahi, 1959. 138p., plates (some
fold., some col.), illus., maps. 27cm.
In Japanese,

ACADEMIC ALPINE CLUB OF KYOTO
Saltoro Kangri: the Japan-Pakistan joint expedition, 1962. Tokyo: Asahi, 1964. xiii, 93p.,
plates (some fold.), illus., maps. 27cm.
In Japanese.

An account of Switzerland, written in the year
1714, [by Abraham Stanyan]. Tonson, 1714.
247p. 20cm.

An account of the principal pleasure tours in
England and Wales. Baldwin, Cradock, & Joy,
1822. viii, 476p., plates (some fold. col.),
illus., maps. 19cm.

ACHARD, Paul
Hommes et chiens du Grand-Saint-Bernard.
Paris: Éditions de France, 1937. 242p.,plates,
illus. 19cm.

ACHLEITNER, Arthur
GRAINER, Franz
Aus freier Wildbahn: Thierstudien aus den
Hochalpen, in Momentaufnahmen von Franz
Grainer; begleittert von Arthur Achleitner.
Berlin: Rud. Schuster, 1898. 1v. (chiefly
illus.). 43cm.

ACHLEITNER, Arthur and UBL, Emil
Tirol and Vorarlberg: neue Schilderung von
Land und Leuten. 2. Aufl. Leipzig: A.H. Payne,
[1905?]. 400p., plates (1 fold., some col.),
illus., map (in pocket). 32cm.

ACKERMANN, Rudolf
A picturesque tour of the English lakes; containing a description of the most romantic
scenery of Cumberland, Westmoreland, and
Lancashire, etc. [R. Ackermann], [1821].
vi, 288p., plates, illus. 27cm.
Preface signed: R. Ackermann.

ACLAND, Hugh Dyke
ARNAUD, Henri
The glorious recovery by the Vaudois of their
valleys, from the original by Henri Arnaud;
with a compendious history of that people,
previous and subsequent to that event, by Hugh
Dyke Acland. Murray, 1827. cxxii, xxv, 239p.,
plates, illus., map. 22cm.

ACLAND, Hugh Dyke
Illustrations of the Vaudois, in a series of
views; engraved by Edward Finden from drawings
by Hugh Dyke Acland; accompanied with descriptions [by H.D. Acland]. C. Tilt, 1831. 34p.,
plates, illus., map. 25cm.
Extract from Arnaud, H. The glorious recovery
by the Vaudois of their valleys. 1827.

Across the Andes, from Buenos Ayres to the
Pacific. Buenos Ayres and Pacific Railway Co.,
[1904]. 44p., 1 fold. plate, illus. (some
fold.), map. 19 x 25cm.

Across the Carpathians, [by Georgina M. Mackenzie
and Adeline P. Irby]. Cambridge, London:
Macmillan, 1862. 299p., 1 fold. plate., map.
20cm.

ADAIR, F E S
Sport in Ladakh: five letters from "The Field",
by F.E.S.A. [i.e. F.E.S. Adair]; illustrated
from photographs by R.S.A. Horace Cox, 1895.
32p., plates, illus. 30cm.

ADAM, Joseph
MACLEOD, Norman
Mountain, loch and glen, illustrating "Our life
in the Highlands" from paintings executed ...
for this work by Joseph Adam; with an essay on
the characteristics of Scottish scenery by
Norman Macleod; prepared under the superintendence of Arthur Helps. 2nd ed. rev. Bell &
Daldy, 1870. 1v. (chiefly illus.). 38cm.

ADAM SMITH, Janet
See
SMITH, Janet Adam

ADAMEC, Ludwig W
Badakhshan Province and northeastern Afghanistan;
edited by Ludwig W. Adamec. Graz: Akademische
Druck-u. Verlagsanstalt, 1972. xiii, 255p.,
plates (some fold.), maps. 28cm. (Historical
and political gazetteer of Afghanistan, v. 1)

ADAMEC, Ludwig W
Farah and southwestern Afghanistan: edited by
Ludwig W. Adamec. Graz: Akademische Druck-u.
Verlagsanstalt, 1973. xv, 375p., plates (some
fold.), geneal. tables, maps. 28cm. (Historical
and political gazetteer of Afghanistan, v. 2)

ADAMS, Andrew Leith
Wanderings of a naturalist in India, the
western Himalayas and Cashmere. Edinburgh:
Edmonston & Douglas, 1867. xi, 333p., plates,
illus. 22cm.

ADAMS, Ansel
Sierra Nevada: the John Muir trail. Berkeley:
Archetype Press, 1938. 1v. of illus. 44cm.

ADAMS, Sir Francis Ottiwell and CUNNINGHAM,
Carus Dunlop
The Swiss Confederation. Macmillan, 1889.
xx, 289p., 1 col. plate, map. 24cm.

ADAMS, Joseph
Ten thousand miles through Canada: the
natural resources, commercial industries, fish
and game, sports and pastimes of the great
dominion. 3rd ed. Methuen, 1913. xx, 310p.,
plates (1 fold. col.), illus., map. 20cm.

ADAMS, W
The modern voyager & traveller through Europe,
Asia, Africa, & America. Vol. 4. Europe.
H. Fisher & P. Jackson, 1828. 458p., plates,
illus., map. 17cm.
Condensed from various contemporary accounts.

ADAMS, William H   Davenport
Alpine adventure; or, Narratives of travel and
research in the Alps, by the author of "The
Mediterranean illustrated" ... [i.e. W.H.D.
Adams]. Nelson, 1878. 237p., illus. 19cm.
Rev. ed. published in 1881 under title: Alpine
climbing: narratives of recent ascents ...

ADAMS, William H   Davenport
Alpine climbing: narratives of recent ascents of
Mont Blanc, the Matterhorn, the Jungfrau, and
other lofty summits of the Alps, by the author
of "The Mediterranean illustrated" ... [i.e.
W.H.D. Adams]. [Rev. ed.] Nelson, 1881. 237p.,
illus. 18cm.
Previous ed. published in 1878 under title:
Alpine adventure; or, Narratives of travel and
research in the Alps.

ADAMS, William H   Davenport
Celebrated women travellers of the nineteenth
century. Swan Sonnenschein, 1883. 459p.,
plates, illus. 19cm.

ADAMS, William H   Davenport
The glacier, iceberg, icefield and avalanche.

See his

Wonders of the physical world.

ADAMS, William H   Davenport
Mountains and mountain-climbing: Records of
adventure and enterprise among the famous moun-
tains of the world, by the author of "The
Mediterranean illustrated" ... [i.e. W.H.D.
Adams]. Nelson, 1883. 415p., illus. 21cm.

ADAMS, William H   Davenport
Wonders of the physical world: the glacier, the
iceberg, the ice-field, and the avalanche, [by
W.H.D. Adams]. Nelson, 1875. 314p., illus.
19cm.

- - Another ed. 1880.

ADDISON, Joseph
Remarks on several parts of Italy, &c. in the
years 1701, 1702, 1703, [by Joseph Addison].
3rd ed. J Tonson, 1726. 312p. 18cm.

AEBY, Christoph
Das Hochgebirge von Grindelwald: Naturbilder
aus der schweizerischen Alpenwelt, von Christoph
Aeby und Edm. von Fellenberg und Pfarrer Gerwer.
Coblenz: Baedeker, 1865. lxv, 151p., plates
(chiefly col., 2 fold.), illus. 28cm.

AELLEN, Hermann
HARDMEYER, J
Locarno und seine Täler; neu bearb. von Hermann
Aellen. 5. Aufl. Zürich: Orell Füssli, [1923]
108p., plates (1 fold.), illus., maps. 20cm.

AENEAS SYLVIUS
See
PIUS II, Pope

AFANASIEFF, Rostislav
100 Kaukasus-Gipfel. München: J.Lindauer, 1913.
x, 192p. 16cm.

BALLIANO, Adolfo and AFFENTRANGER, Irene
La strada è questa ... Bologna: Alfa, 1957.
197p., 16 plates, illus. 21cm. (Semprevivo,2)

AFLALO, F   G
Behind the ranges: parenthesis of travel.
Secker, 1911. 284p., plates, illus. 23cm.

AFLALO, F   G
The cost of sport, by the Earl of Coventry [and
others]; edited by F.G. Aflalo. Murray, 1899.
xiv, 364p. 22cm.

AFLALO, F   G
BAIRNSFATHER, P   R
Sport and nature in the Himalayas; edited by
F.G. Aflalo. Harrison, 1914. xv, 137p.,
illus. 22cm.

AFLALO, F   G
Sport in Europe; edited by F.G. Aflalo. Sands,
1901. xii, 483p., plates, illus. 29cm.

AFLALO, F   G
The sports of the world; edited by F.G. Aflalo.
Cassell, 1903. viii, 416p., illus. 29cm.

AGASSIZ, Elizabeth Cary
Louis Agassiz: his life and correspondence;
edited by Elizabeth Cary Agassiz. Macmillan,
1885. 2 v., plates, illus., port. 21cm.

AGASSIZ, Elizabeth Cary
Louis Agassiz: sa vie et sa correspondence;
traduit ... par Auguste Mayor. Neuchatel; A.G.
Berthoud, 1887. xi, 617p., 1 plate, port. 24cm.

AGASSIZ, Lewis
A journey to Switzerland, and pedestrian tours
in that country, including a sketch of its
history ...Smith, Elder, 1833. vii, 288p.,
1 plate, illus. 23cm.

AGASSIZ, Louis
Études sur les glaciers. Neuchatel; Jent &
Gassmann, 1840. v, 346p. 26cm.

- - Atlas.

AGASSIZ, Louis
[Études sur les glaciers]. Untersuchungen über
die Gletscher. Solothurn; Jent & Gassmann,
1841. xii, 326p. 23cm.

- - Atlas. 1840.

AGASSIZ, Louis
Nouvelles études et expériences sur les glaciers
actuels, leur structure, leur progression et
leur action physique sur le sol. Paris; V.
Masson, 1847. xxi, 598p., plates, illus., bibl.
24cm.

- - Atlas.

AGASSIZ, Louis
AGASSIZ, Elizabeth Carey
Louis Aggasiz: his life and correspondence;
edited by Elizabeth Cary Agassiz. Macmillan,
1885. 2 v. plates, illus., port. 21cm.

AGASSIZ, Louis
AGASSIZ, Elizabeth Cary
  Louis Agassiz: his life and correspondence;
  edited by Elizabeth Cary Agassiz. Macmillan,
  1885. 2v.,plates, illus., port. 21cm.

AGASSIZ, Louis
AGASSIZ, Elizabeth Cary
  Louis Agassiz: sa vie et sa correspondance;
  traduit ... par Auguste Mayor. Neuchatel: A.G.
  Berthoud, 1887. xi, 617p., 1 plate, port. 24cm.

AGASSIZ, Louis
DESOR, Édouard
  L'ascension de la Jungfrau, effectuée le 28
  aout 1841, par MM. Agassiz, Forbes, du
  Chatelier et Desor, précédée du récit de leur
  traversée de la Mer de Glace, du Grimsel à
  Viesch en Valais. [Genève], 1841. 56p.,
  1 plate, illus. 21cm.
  Offprint from Bibliothèque universelle de
  Genève, novembre 1841.

AGASSIZ, Louis
DESOR, Édouard
  Excursions et séjour de M. Agassiz sur la Mer
  de Glace du Lauteraar et du Finsteraar, en
  société de plusieurs naturalistes. [Genève],
  1841. 102p., 2 plates (1 fold., 1 col.),
  illus. 21cm.
  Offprint from Bibliothèque universelle de
  Genève, mars, avril 1841.

AGASSIZ, Louis
DESOR, Édouard
  Récit d'une course faite aux glaciers en hiver,
  par MM. Agassiz et E. Desor. [Genève], 1842.
  36p. 21cm.
  Offprint from Bibliothèque universelle de
  Genève, t.38, 1842.

AGASSIZ, Louis
GOS, Charles,
  L'Hotel des Neuchatelois: un épisode de la conquete des Alpes. Lausanne: Payot, 1928. 170p.,
  plates, illus., map, bibl. 19cm.

AGASSIZ, Louis
VOGT, C.
  Agassiz' und seiner Freunde geologische Alpenreisen in der Schweiz, Savoyen und Piemont...;
  hrsg. von Carl Vogt. 2. stark verm. Aufl.
  Frankfurt am Main: Literarische Anstalt, 1847.
  xxxvi, 672p., 1 fold. col. plate, map. 20cm.

AGNEW, Crispin Hamlyn, of Lochnaw yr.
ARMY EAST GREENLAND EXPEDITION, 1968
  Expedition report, by C.H. Agnew of Lochnaw yr.
  and others. [Glasgow]: The Expedition, [1968?].
  iv, 56p., illus., maps. 30cm.

AGNEW, Crispin Hamlyn, of Lochnaw yr.
JOINT SERVICES EXPEDITION TO CHILEAN PATAGONIA,
1972-73
  The general report, by C.H. Agnew of Lochnaw yr.
  The Expedition Trust Committee, 1974. ix, 70p.,
  1 fold. plate, illus., map, bibl. 30cm.

AGOSTINI, A   M   de
  See
DE AGOSTINI, A   M

AGRESTI, Henri
  Aïr: montagnes de la soif. [Biver]: The Author,
  [1971?]. [17] leaves, illus. 29cm.
  Typescript.

AGRESTI, Henri
  Montagnes arides du Wakhan. [Biver]: The Author,
  [1970]. 38p., illus., maps. 27cm.

AHLES, Mar
  Spemanns goldenes Buch des Sports: eine Hauskunde für jedermann; hrsg. unter Mitwirkung von M.
  Ahles [and others]. Berlin: Spemann, 1910.
  1v. (various pagings), plates, illus. 18cm.

AHLMANN, Hans Wilhelmsson
  Land of Ice and fire; translated from the Swedish
  by Klares and Herbert Lewes. Paul, Trench,
  Trubner, 1938. xi, 271p., plates, illus., map.
  23cm.

AHLUWALIA, Hari Pal Singh
  Higher than Everest: memoirs of a mountaineer;
  foreword by Mrs. Indira Gandhi. Delhi: Vikas,
  1973. ix, plates, illus. 22cm.

AIKIN, Arthur
  Journal of a tour through North Wales and part of
  Shropshire; with observations in mineralogy, and
  other branches of natural history. J. Johnson,
  1797. xvi, 239p., 1 fold. plate, illus. 20cm.

AIMONE, Duke of Spoleto and DESIO, Ardito
  La spedizione geografica italiana al Karakoram
  (1929...): storia del viaggio e risultati geografici. Milano: Arti Grafiche Bertarelli, 1936.
  xxiv, 568, lip., plates, illus., maps. 30cm.

- - Maps (in portfolio).

AIR FRANCE
  Vacationing in five continents: [travel guide...];
  [English texts translated and adapted ... by
  Mostyn Mowbray and Georgianna Pouzzner]. Paris:
  Air France, [1963]. 216p., illus. (some col.),
  maps. 29cm.

AIREY, Alan F
  Irish hill days. Manchester: Open Air Publications, [1937]. 47p., 1 fold. plate, map. 18cm.

AITKEN, Samuel
  Among the Alps: a narrative of personal experiences; the illustrations by Vittorio Sella.
  Northwood: The Author, 1900. 119p., 73 plates,
  illus. 29 x 39cm.

AKADEMISCHER ALPENCLUB BERN
  Clubführer durch die Engelhörner. Bern: G.A.
  Bäschlin, 1914. 104p., plates (1 fold.),
  illus., map, bibl. 19cm.
  Later eds. published under title: Engelhornführer.
- - Nachtrag: Neutouren vom Mai 1914 bis
November 1927. Bern: A.A.C.B.; 1928.

AKADEMISCHER ALPEN-CLUB ZÜRICH
  50 Jahr AACZ, 1896-1946: Festschrift zum fünfzigjährigen Bestehen des Akademischen Alpen-
  club Zürich; [edited by Hans Brun and Carl
  Egger]. Zürich: A.A.C.Z., 1946. 223p., plates,
  illus., bibl. 23cm.

AKADEMISCHER ALPEN-CLUB ZÜRICH
  75 Jahre Akademischer Alpen-Club Zürich, 1896-
  1971. Zürich: A.A.C.Z., 1971. 70p., illus.
  23cm.

AKADEMISCHER ALPEN-CLUB ZÜRICH
  Führer durch die Urner-Alpen. Solothurn:
  Schweizer Alpen-Club, 1905. 2 v., illus.,
  bibl. 17cm. (Clubführer des Schweizer Alpen-
  Club.

- - 3. Aufl. 1930-32.

- - 4. Aufl. of Bd. 1. 1954.

  6. Aufl. of Bd. 2 published in 1966 under title:
  Urner Alpen West.

AKADEMISCHER ALPEN-CLUB ZÜRICH
  Ski-Führer für die Silvretta- und Bernina-
  Gruppe. Chur: Manatschal Ebner, 1913. 122p.,
  illus. 17cm.

AKADEMISCHER ALPEN-CLUB ZÜRICH
  Urner Alpen West. 6 Aufl. Bern: Schweizer
  Alpen-Club, 1966. 292p., illus., maps. 17cm.
  (Clubführer des Schweizer Alpen-Club)
  Previous eds. published as Bd. 2 of: Führer
  durch die Urner Alpen.

AKADEMISCHER ALPENVEREIN MÜNCHEN
Josef Enzensperger: ein Bergsteigerleben; eine
Sammlung von alpinen Schilderungen nebst einem
Anhang Reisebriefe und Kerguelen-Tagebuch;
hrsg. vom Akademischen Alpenverein München.
München: Kommissionsverlag der Vereinigten
Kunstanstalten, 1905. xv, 276p., plates
(2 fold.), illus., maps. 29cm.

AKADEMISCHER ALPENVEREIN MÜNCHEN
WELZENBACH, Willo
Willo Welzenbachs Bergfahrten; unter Mitwirkung von Eugen Allwein, Fritz Bechtold [and
others]; hrsg. vom Akademischen Alpenverein
München. Berlin: Union Deutsche Verlagsgesellschaft, 1935. 260p., plates, illus.,
bibl. 22cm.

AKADEMISCHER SKICLUB MÜNCHEN
Skiführer das bayerische Hochland und angrenzende Gebiete. 2. Aufl. München: J. Lindauer,
1906. viii, 130p. 16cm.

Akademischer Turnverein Graz
Zum 60. Stiftungsfest der A.T.V. Graz von
1914-1924. Graz: A.T.V., [1925]. 123p.,
plates (1 fold.), illus. 24cm.

ALACK, Frank
Guide aspiring; edited by J. Halket Millar.
Auckland: Oswald-Sealy, [1963]. 229p., plates,
illus. 23cm.

ALACK, Frank
A priest wants to live in hell. [Wellington?]:
The Author, [ca 1960]. 3 leaves. 34cm.
Typescript of a broadcast talk on climbing in
the Mahitahi Valley.

ALBANEDER, Joseph Theodor
Der Sauerbrunnen zu Obladis, im Oberinnthal,
k.k. Landgerichts Reid, als Trink- und Bad-
kurort. Innsbruck: Wagner, 1835. 40p., plates,
illus. 19cm.

L'Albanie: guide de montagne. Tirana:
"Albtourist", 1958. 120p., 1 fold. col. plate,
illus., maps. 21cm.

ALBANIS DE BEAUMONT, Jean François
See
BEAUMONT, Jean François Albanis

ALBERT I, King of the Belgians
MALLIEUX, René
Le roi Albert, alpiniste. Brussels: La
Renaissance du livre, 1956. 197p., plates,
illus. 23cm.

ALBERT-MONTÉMONT
See
MONTÉMONT, Albert

ALBERTAS, Sylvia d'
Des Calanques aux faces nord; préface de G.
Winthrop Young. Neuchatel: Attinger, 1948.
206p., plates, illus. 21cm. (Montagne)

ALBERTI, Leandro
Descrittione di tutta l'Italia, et isole per-
tinenti ad essa... Nuovamente ristampata, &
con somma diligenza rev. & corr. Venetia:
Paulo Ugolino, 1596. 495 leaves. 22cm.

ALBERTI, Leandro
Isole appartinenti all' Italia; di nuovo
ricorr... Venetia: Paolo Ugolino, 1596. 95
leaves. 22cm.

Albina: ein Taschenbuch für Wanderer in der sächsischen Schweiz, enthaltend eine Beschreibung
des meissnischen Hochlands ..., [von Wilhelm A.
Lindau]. Pirna: Diller, 1818. iv, 185p.,
plates, illus., map. 13cm.
In slip-case.

ALBINYANA, Josep M   Guilera i
See
GUILERA I ALBINYANA, Josep M

Album des Pyrénées; [drawn by T. Allom]. Pau:
Lafon, [ca 1850]. 1 v. of illus. 23 x 28cm.
Engravings with English captions.

Album d'un alpinista, [da Domenico Vallino].
Biella: G. Amosso, 1878- .
Illus., maps. 22 x 30cm.
Library has pts. 2-3 only.

Album-Panorama suisse. 1re sér. Neuchatel: A.
Spuhler, 1902. 288p., illus. 30 x 41cm.

Album vom Salzburger-Alpenlande. Salzburg: J.
Schoen, [ca 1850]. 1 v. of illus. 34 x 46cm.

Album von Salzburg, Salzkammergut und Berchtesgaden. Salzburg: J. Schoen, [ca 1850]. 1 v.
of illus. 34 x 45cm.

ALDEBERT, Max
Conquête de la haute montagne; presentée par
Max Aldebert. Paris: Jeunes Éditions, 1947.
88p., illus., bibl. 27cm. (Collection
conquête. Les grands thèmes)

ALDROVANDI, Mario
Aosta: le sue valli e i suoi castelli ... =
its valleys and its castles; la raccolta e la
descrizione delle illustrazioni ... dall'Av-
vocato Mario Aldrovandi e le fotografie ...
[da] Luigi Minetti. Torino: S. Lattes, 1930.
183p., plates (1 col.), illus. 35cm.
Text in Italian, French and English.

ALEXANDER, Sir Henry
The Cairngorms; with panoramas by H.C. Dugan,
J.A. Parker and Gordon Wilson. Edinburgh:
Scottish Mountaineering Club, 1928. viii,
218p., plates (some fold.), illus., map, bibl.
23cm. (Scottish Mountaineering Club guides)

- - 2nd ed. with appendix by G.R. Symmers on new
climbs on Lochnager and notes on other ascents.
1938.

- - 3rd ed. rev. by William A. Ewen. 1950.

ALEXANDER, William Lindsay
Switzerland and the Swiss churches, being notes
of a short tour and notices of the principal
religious bodies in that country. Glascow: J.
Maclehose, 1846. xiv, 334p. 18cm.

ALLAIN, Pierre
Alpinisme et compétition; préface d'H. de
Segogne. Paris: Arthaud, 1949. 161p., plates,
illus. 19cm.

ALLAIN, Pierre
L'art de l'alpinisme. Paris: Amiot-Dumont, 1956.
220p., illus. 19cm. (Bibliothèque de
l'alpinisme)

ALLAIS, Émile and GIGNOUX, Paul
Ski français: méthode officielle d'enseignement
de ski de descente de la Fédération Française de
Ski, par Émile Allais et Paul Gignoux en collaboration avec Georges Blanchon; photographies de
A. Figneau. Grenoble: B. Arthaud, 1937. 154p.,
illus. 20cm.

ALLAIS, Giovanni
Le Alpi occidentali nell'antichità: nuove rivelazioni. Torino: V. Bona, 1891. 208p., 1 fold.
plate, map. 25cm.

ALLAN, Alastair
WATKINS MOUNTAINS EXPEDITION, 1969.
Anglo-Danish mountain survey in East Greenland:
preliminary report, [by Alastair Allan]. Cambridge: The Expedition, 1969. 9p., 1 plate, map.
30cm.

ALLAN, John A.
Geology of field map-area, B.C. and Alberta.
Ottawa: Government Printing Bureau, 1914. vii,
312p., plates (1 fold. col.), illus., map. bibl.
26cm. (Canada. Dept. of Mines. Geological Survey.
Memoir, 55; Geological series, no. 46)

ALLASON, Thomas
Picturesque views of the antiquities of Pola in
Istria. Murray, 1819. 67p., plates, illus.,
49cm.

ALLBUT, Robert
The tourist's handbook to Switzerland, with
practical information as to routes, excursions,
railway and diligence fares... Nelson, 1884.
ix, 344p., illus., maps, plans. 19cm.

ALLEN, Edward Frank
A guide to the National Parks of America; compiled and edited by Edward Frank Allen. New
York: McBride, Nast, 1915. 286p., plates
(some fold.), illus., maps. 17cm.

ALLEN, John
MANCHESTER KARAKORUM EXPEDITION, 1968
Report; edited by John Allen. [Manchester]:
The Expedition, [1969?]. 21p., 1 fold.plate,
illus., map, bibl. 25cm.

ALLEN, John
MANCHESTER NEPALESE EXPEDITION, 1970
Report, written by members of the expedition;
edited by John Allen. Manchester: The Expedition, [1971]. 25p., 1 fold. plate, illus.,
map, bibl. 26cm.

ALLEN, Warner
Our Italian front; painted by Martin Hardie;
described by Warner Allen. Black, 1920. ix,
203p., col.plates (1 fold.), illus., map. 23cm.

ALLGÄUER SKIVERBAND
Allgäuer Ski-Touren. Kempten: Allgäuer
Skiverband, 1913. [ca 96p.], illus., maps.
17 x 23cm.

SOPER, N   Jack and ALLINSON, Neil
Buttermere and Newlands area. Stockport: Fell
& Rock Climbing Club, 1970. 151p., 1 col.
plate, illus., maps (on lining papers). 16cm.
(Climbing guides to the English Lake District,
[4th ser.], 4)

ALLIX, André
Observations glaciologiques faites en
Dauphiné jusqu'en 1924, recapitulées et
partiellement editées. Paris: Imprimerie
Nationale, 1927. 179p., plates (some fold.),
illus. 29cm. (France. Ministère de l'agriculture. Direction générale des eaux et
forêts... Études glaciologiques, t. 6)

ALLOM, Thomas
Album des Pyrénées; [drawn by T. Allom]. Pau:
Lafon [ca 1850]. 1 v. of illus. 23 x 28cm.
Engravings with English captions.

ALLOM, Thomas
[Ansichten von Tyrol]. Tombleson's Ansichten
von Tyrol; nach T. Allom's Zeichnungen und
Johanna v. Isser's Skizzen; [Text von Josef
Hormayr]. Tombleson, [ca 1840].127p.,
plates, illus., map. 23cm.

ALLOM, Thomas
[Ansichten von Tyrol]. Views in the Tyrol;
from drawings by T. Allom, after original
sketches by Johanna v. Isser ...; with letterpress descriptions by a companion of Hofer
[i.e. Josef Hormayr]. Black & Armstrong,
[ca 1837]. 72p., plates (1 fold.), illus.,
map. 28cm.
Second title page has title: Forty-six views
of Tyrolese scenery...
Cover title: Tyrolese scenery.

- - Another ed. published under title: Tyrolese
scenery; or, Continental travels. [ca 1840].
Contains different plates.

ALLOM, Thomas
ROSE, Thomas
The British Switzerland; or, Picturesque
rambles in the English Lake District: comprising a series of views ..., by Thomas Allom;
with descriptive letterpress by Thomas Rose.
London Printing and Publishing Co., [1856-60].
2 v., plates (1 fold. col.), illus, map. 28cm.
Covers Westmorland and Cumberland only.

ALLOM, Thomas
Lake and mountain scenery: Westmorland and
Cumberland; from drawings on the spot by T.
Allom and G. Pickering. Jackson, [184-]. 1 v.
of illus. 14 x 23cm.

ALLOM, Thomas
ROSE, Thomas
Westmorland, Cumberland, Durham, and Northum-
berland; illustrated from original drawings by
Thomas Allom ... &c.; with descriptions by T.
Rose. H. Fisher, R. Fisher, & P. Jackson,
1832-[35]. 3 v., plates, illus. 28cm.

ALLSOPP, Allan
Kinder,Roches and northern areas; edited by
Allan Allsopp. Birkenhead: Willmer, 1951.
153p., plates, illus. 16cm. (Climbs on
gritstone, v. 3)

ALLSUP, W
Notes on walking around Shillong. Shillong:
The Author, 1934. 87p. 17cm.

ALMAGIÀ, Roberto
CLUB ALPINO ITALIANO. Sezione di Roma
Tra i monti del Lazio e dell'Abruzzo. 1; a
cura della Sezione di Roma del Club Alpino a
ricordo del cinquantenario della sua fondazione; pubblicazione edita [da] ... Roberto
Almagià [and other]. Roma: La Sezione, 1924.
111p., plates, illus. 26cm.

ALMÁSY, György
Vándor-utam Ázsia Szivébe. Budapest: Kiadja
A.K.M. Természettudományi Társulat, 1903. xii,
737p., plates (some fold., some col.), illus.,
map. 26cm. (Természettudományi Könyvkiadó-
vállalat, 72)

ALMEIDA, P   Camena d'
See
CAMENA D'ALMEIDA, P

ALMER, Christian
[Führerbuch]. A facsimile of Christian Almer's
Führerbuch 1856-1894; reproduced under the
superintendence of C.D. Cunningham and W. de W.
Abney. Sampson Low, Marston, 1896. xxxii,
261p., 1 plate, port. 20cm.

ALMER, Christian
A letter addressed to the members of the Alpine
Club [on the controversy over a leap by
Christian Almer], [by Edward Whymper]. [E.
Whymper], 1900. 16p., plates, illus. 22cm.

Alpenlandschaften: Ansichten aus der deutschen,
oesterreichischen und Schweizer Gebirgswelt,
[text by Julius Meurer]. Leipzig: J.J. Weber,
[1891]. 2v. (chiefly illus.). 42cm.

Alpenröschen: schweizerisches Taschen-Liederbuch:
eine ausgewählte Sammlung der schönsten und
beliebtesten Vaterlands- und Freiheitslieder
... 2 verm. Aufl. Bern: Heuberger,[1897].
416p. 13cm.

Alpenröslein; oder, Vierundzwanzig malarische
Ansichten, [von J.B. Dreseli]; verschiedener
Burgen, Gegenden, Seen u. im Salzkammergute,
dann in den Salzburger-, Berchtesgadener- und
Tyroler-Gebirgen ..., mit erläuterndem
deutschen und französischen Texte... München:
J. Lindauer, 1836. 21p., plates, illus.
21 x 26cm.

ALPEN-SKIVEREIN WIEN
ZDARSKY, Mathias
  Beiträge zur Lawinenkunde; hrsg. vom Alpen-
  Skiverein Wien. Wien: A.B.Z., [1929]. 127p.,
  illus. 16cm.

ALPEN-SKIVEREIN WIEN
ZDARSKY, Mathias
  Skisport: gesammelte Aufsätze; hrsg. vom
  Alpen-Skiverein. Wien: C. Konegen, 1909. vi,
  123p. 17cm.

Les Alpes françaises: Dauphiné, Savoie, Haute
  Savoie, Hautes-Alpes. Paris: Flammarion,
  [n.d.]. 187p., illus., maps, plans. 18cm.

Le Alpi che cingono l'Italia, considerate
  militarmente così nell'antica come nella
  presente loro condizione. Pt. 1a. Torino:
  Mussano, 1845. xv, 935p. 25cm.

Alpine adventure; or, Narratives of travel and
  research in the Alps, by the author of "The
  Mediterranean illustrated" ... [i.e. W.H.D.
  Adams]. Nelson, 1878. 237p., illus. 19cm.
  Rev. ed. published in 1881 under title:Alpine
  climbing: narratives of recent ascents ...

Alpine byways; or, Light leaves gathered in
  1859 and 1860, by a lady [i.e. Mrs. Henry
  Freshfield]. Longman, Green, Longman &
  Roberts, 1861. ix, 232p., plates (some
  col.), maps. 21cm.

ALPINE CLIMBING GROUP
  Selected climbs in the range of Mont Blanc.
  A.C.G., [1953]. 1 v. (loose-leaf), illus. 23cm.

- - Reissue, updated and corrected. [1954]

ALPINE CLIMBING GROUP
  Selected climbs in the range of Mont Blanc;
  translated and adapted by the Alpine Climbing
  Group from the Guide Vallot and other sources;
  edited by E.A. Wrangham. Allen & Unwin, 1957.
  224p., illus., map. 17cm.

Alpine climbing: narratives of recent ascents of
  Mont Blanc, the Matterhorn, the Jungfrau and
  other lofty summits of the Alps, by the author
  of "The Mediterranean illustrated" ... [i.e.
  W.H.D. Adams]. [Rev. ed.]. Nelson, 1881. 18cm.
  Previous ed. published in 1878 under title:
  Alpine adventure; or, Narratives of travel and
  research in the Alps.

ALPINE CLUB
  Alpine Club exhibition: catalogue of a collection
  of mountain paintings and photographs exhibited
  at the XIXth Century Art Gallery ...; with a preliminary note by Douglas W. Freshfield. A.C.,
  1894. 64p. 22cm.

ALPINE CLUB
  The Alpine Club register, 1857-[1890], by A.L.
  Mumm. Arnold, 1923-28. 3 v. 23cm.

ALPINE CLUB
  Catalogue of equipment for mountaineers,
  exhibited at the Alpine Club, December, 1899.
  A.C., 1899. 47p., illus. 23cm.

ALPINE CLUB
BALL, John
  The central Alps. Pt. 1. Including those
  portions of Switzerland to the north of the
  Rhone and the Rhine valleys. New ed.; recon-
  structed and revised on behalf of the Alpine
  Club under the general editorship of A.V.
  Valentine-Richards. Longmans, Green, 1907.
  xxviii, 326p., fold. col. plates, maps. 19cm.
  (Ball's alpine guide, pt. 2)

ALPINE CLUB
BALL, John
  The central Alps. Pt. 2. Including those
  Alpine portions of Switzerland, Italy and
  Austria which lie S. & E. of the Rhone and
  Rhine, S. of the Arlberg, and W. of the Adige.
  New ed.; reconstructed and revised on behalf of
  the Alpine Club under the general editorship of
  George Broke. Longmans, Green, 1911. xix,
  432p., fold. col. plates, maps. 19cm. (Ball's
  alpine guide, pt. 2)

ALPINE CLUB
  Exhibitions of Swiss coloured prints, lent by
  members of the Alpine Club and their friends,
  [at] the Alpine Club, 23, Savile Row ...
  December 1st to 30th, 1924. A.C., 1924. 32p.,
  col. plates, illus. 22cm.
  Catalogue.

ALPINE CLUB
  Guide books.

  Bernese Alps central; compiled by R.G. Collomb.
    1978.
  Bernese Alps east; compiled by R.G. Collomb.
    1978.
  Dolomites east; compiled by J. Brailsford.
    1970.
  Dolomites west; compiled by J. Brailsford.
    1970.
  Mont Blanc range. Vol. 1. Trélatête, Mont Blanc,
    Maudit, Tacul, Brenva; compiled by R.G.
    Collomb, W.H. O'Connor. 1976.
  Mont Blanc range. Vol. 2. Chamonix Aiguilles,
    Rochefort, Jorasses, Leschaux; compiled by
    L.N. Griffin. 1978.
  Mont Blanc range. Vol. 3. Triolet, Verte/Drus,
    Argentière, Chardonnet, Trient; compiled by
    L.N. Griffin. 1980.
  Pennine Alps central; compiled by R.G. Collomb.
    1975.
  Pennine Alps east; compiled by R.G. Collomb.
    1975.
  Pennine Alps west; compiled by R.G. Collomb.
    1979.

ALPINE CLUB
  Guide books; Selected climbs.

  1. Selected climbs in the Mont Blanc range; com-
    piled by R.G. Collomb and P. Crew. 1967.
  2. Selected climbs in the Pennine Alps; edited
    by J. Neill. 1962.
    - - 2nd ed. Vol. 2; compiled by R.G.
    Collomb. 1968.
  3. Selected climbs in the Dolomites; edited by
    P. Crew. 1963.
  4. Selected climbs in the Dauphiné Alps and
    Vercors, by E.A. Wrangham and J. Brailsford.
    1967.
  5. Selected climbs in the Bernese Alps;
    compiled by R.G. Collomb. 1968.

ALPINE CLUB
BALL, John
  Hints and notes practical and scientific for
  travellers in the Alps ..., by John Ball. New
  ed. prepared on behalf of the Alpine Club by
  W.A.B. Coolidge. Longmans, Green & Co., 1899.
  163p., bibl. 19cm.

ALPINE CLUB
  Mountain medicine and physiology: proceedings of
  a symposium for mountaineers, expedition doctors
  and physiologists; sponsored by the Alpine Club;
  edited by Charles Clarke, Michael Ward, Edward
  Williams A.C., 1975. 143p., plates, illus.,
  bibl. 21cm.
  Cover title.

ALPINE CLUB
  Paintings, drawings and sculpture, c. 1800 -
  c. 1920, the properties of the Alpine Club and
  others, which will be sold at auction by Christie,
  Manson & Woods ... on Friday, June 11, 1965.
  Christie, Manson & Woods, 1965. 30p. 25cm.
  Catalogue.

ALPINE CLUB
  Peaks, passes and glaciers: a series of excursions by members of the Alpine Club; edited
  by John Ball. Longman, Brown, Green, Longmans,
  & Roberts, 1859. xvi, 516p., plates (some
  fold., some col.), illus., maps. 22cm.

  - - 2nd ed. 1859.

  - - 4th ed. 1859.

  - - 5th ed. 1860.

ALPINE CLUB
  Peaks, passes, and glaciers; being excursions
  by members of the Alpine Club. 2nd series;
  edited by Edward Shirley Kennedy. Longman,
  Green, Longman, & Roberts, 1862. 2 v., plates
  (some fold., some col.), illus., maps. 22cm.

ALPINE CLUB
  Peaks, passes and glaciers, by members of the
  Alpine Club. 3rd series; edited by A.E.
  Field and Sydney Spencer. Methuen, 1932. xi,
  307p., plates, illus. 23cm.

ALPINE CLUB
  [Peaks, passes and glaciers]. Narratives
  selected from Peaks, passes and glaciers;
  edited with introduction and notes by George
  Wherry. Cambridge: University Press, 1910.
  156p., maps. 18cm.
  Selected from first series.

ALPINE CLUB
  Peaks, passes & glaciers; selected and annotated
  by E.H. Blakeney. Dent, [1926]. xlviii, 317p.
  18cm. (Everyman's library, no. 778)

ALPINE CLUB
  [Peaks, passes and glaciers]. Les grimpeurs
  des Alpes = Peaks, passes and glacies [sic];
  traduit par Él. Dufour. Paris: M. Lévy, 1862.
  347p. 19cm.
  Translation of 1st series; edited by John Ball.
  - - Another ed. 1886.

ALPINE CLUB
  Record of expeditions in 1909 [-1913]. A.C.,
  [1910-14]. 5 pts. in 1. 23cm.

ALPINE CLUB. Library
  Catalogue of books in the Library of the Alpine
  Club. A.C., 1880. 36p. 23cm.

  - - Catalogue of books... 1888.

  - - Catalogue of books... 1889.

  - - [Lists of additions to the Alpine Club
  Library, 1903-17].

  - - [List for Nov. 1932], by A.J. Mackintosh.
  1932.

ALPINE CLUB. Mount Everest Committee
  See
MOUNT EVEREST COMMITTEE

ALPINE CLUB. Special Committee on Equipment
for Mountaineers
  Equipment for mountaineers:[report of the
  Special Committee on Equipment for Mountain-
  eers]. A.C., 1892. 36p., illus. 22cm.

ALPINE CLUB. Special Committee on Equipment
for Mountaineers
  Provisional report of the Special Committee on
  Equipment for Mountaineers. A.C., 1891. 33p.,
  illus. 22cm.

ALPINE CLUB. Special Committee on Ropes, Axes,
and Alpenstocks
  Report of the Special Committee on Ropes, Axes,
  and Alpenstocks, read before the Club on
  July 5, 1864. A.C., 1864. 11p., plates, illus.
  22cm.

ALPINE CLUB
LUNN, Sir Arnold
  A century of mountaineering, 1857-1957: [a cen-
  tenary tribute to the Alpine Club from the
  Swiss Foundation for Alpine Research]. Allen
  & Unwin, 1957. 263p., plates (some col.),
  illus. 25cm.

ALPINE CLUB OF CANADA
  The Alpine Club of Canada in Jasper National
  Park, Alberta, 1926: photographs. [Vancouver]:
  Canadian National Railways, [1926?]. 1 v. of
  illus. 27 x 34cm.
  Album of photographs with explanatory captions.

ALPINE CLUB OF CANADA
CULBERT, Dick
  A climber's guide to the Coastal Ranges of
  British Columbia (International Border to Nass
  River). 2nd ed. Vancouver: A.C.C., 1969.
  vi, 426p., plates (some fold.), illus., maps.
  18cm.

  - - Supplement 1968.

ALPINE GESELLSCHAFT D'VOISTHALER
  Festschrift; hrsg. anlässlich des 25 Jährigen
  bestandes der Gesellschaft. Wien: A.G. D'V.,
  1910. 92p., illus., map. 21cm.

Alpine lyrics, [by W. Bainbridge]. Longman,
  Brown, Green, 1854. vii, 308p. 18cm.

Alpine scrambles and classic rambles: a gipsy
  tour in search of summer snow and winter sun,
  a pocket companion for the unprotected, by the
  author of "Scylla & Charybdis"... J. Nisbet,
  [1882]. 114p. 16cm.
  Preface signed: S.M.H., i.e. Sophia M.
  Holworthy.

Alpine sketches, comprised in a short tour
  through parts of Holland, Flanders, France,
  Savoy, Switzerland and Germany, during the
  summer of 1814, by a member of the University
  of Oxford [i.e. George W. Bridges]. Longman,
  Hurst, Rees, Orme, & Brown, 1814. vii, 312p.
  22cm.

ALPINE SKI CLUB
SKI CLUB OF GREAT BRITAIN
  Handbook on ski-touring and glacier ski-ing.
  Published by the Ski Club of Great Britain in
  conjunction with the Alpine Ski Club and the
  Eagle Ski Club, 1954. 78p. 16cm.

  - - 2nd ed. completely rev. 1961.

An alpine tale, suggested by circumstances which
  occurred towards the commencement of the present
  century, by the author of "Tales from
  Switzerland". Printed for F. Westley, 1823.
  2 v. 20cm.

ALPINI
  See
ITALY. Army. Corpo degli Alpini

ALPINUS
  Alpinus, conteur dauphinois: nouveaux recits;
  précédés d'une Vie d'Alpinus par Raymond Coche.
  [Paris]: Flammarion, 1946. 187p., plates,
  illus. 22cm. (La vie en montagne)

ALPINUS
  La chasse alpestre en Dauphiné: feuilleton du
  Courrier de l'Isère, 1873, [par Alpinus].
  Grenoble: Baratier Frères & Dardelet, 1874.
  viii, 397p. 19cm.

  - - [New ed.] 1925.

UN ALSACIEN
  See
CAMMEL, Gustave Émile

ALTMANN, Johann Georg
Versuch einer historischen und physischen
Beschreibung der helvetischen Eisbergen.
Zürich: Heidegger, 1751. 271p., 2 fold. plates,
illus. 19cm.

ALVER, Joh   L
KONGSBERG TURISTFORENING
Kongsberg, with routes and map; compiled by
Joh. L. Alver; translated by Laura Poulsson.
Kongsberg: K.T., 1890. 59p., map. 16cm.

AMATEUR CAMPING CLUB
The handbook of the Amateur Camping Club. The
Club, [ca 1909]. 104p., illus. 19cm.

AMATI, Giacinto
Peregrinazione al Gran San Bernardo, Losanna,
Friburgo, Ginevra con una corsa a Lione,
Parigi e Londra. Milano: P. Carpano, 1838.
479p., plates, illus, maps. 25cm.

AMATI, Pasquale
Dissertazione ... sopra il passagio dell'Apennino
fatto da Annibale e sopra il Castello Mutilo
degli antichi Galli. Bologna: Longhi, 1776.
180p., map. 26cm.

AN AMERICAN
See
BRUEN, Matthias

AMERICAN ALPINE CLUB
American Alpine Club Annals; [compiled by]
J. Monroe Thorington. [New York, 1947]. 115p.
23cm.
Offprint from American Alpine Journal, vol. 6.,
no. 1., 1946 and no. 3, 1947.

AMERICAN ALPINE CLUB
By-laws and Register of the American Alpine Club,
1919-[1940]. New York: A.A.C., 1919-40. 4v.
18cm.

AMERICAN ALPINE CLUB
BECKEY, Fred
Climber's guide to the Cascade and Olympic
Mountains. [New York]: A.A.C., 1949. iv, 271p.,
plates (1 fold.), illus, maps, bibl. 17cm.

AMERICAN ALPINE CLUB
THORINGTON, James Monroe
A climber's guide to the interior ranges of
British Columbia. New York: A.A.C., 1937.
xii, 149p., 1 plate, map, bibl. 18cm.

- - 2nd ed. 1947.

AMERICAN ALPINE CLUB
PUTNAM, William Lowell
A climber's guide to the interior ranges of
British Columbia. 5th ed. New York: A.A.C.,
1971. 323p., plates, illus., maps, bibl. 17cm.

AMERICAN ALPINE CLUB
PUTNAM, William Lowell
A climber's guide to the interior ranges of
British Columbia north. 6th ed. [New York]:
A.A.C., 1975. 210p., illus., maps. 17cm.

AMERICAN ALPINE CLUB
KRUSZYNA, Robert and PUTNAM, William Lowell
A climber's guide to the interior ranges of
British Columbia south. 6th ed. [New York]:
A.A.C., 1977. 226p., illus., maps. 17cm.

AMERICAN ALPINE CLUB
PALMER, Howard and THORINGTON, James Monroe
A climber's guide to the Rocky Mountains of
Canada. New York: Knickerbocker Press for
A.A.C., 1921. xvii, 183p., plates (some fold.),
illus, maps, bibl. 18cm.

- - 2nd ed. 1930.

- - 3rd ed. 1940.

AMERICAN ALPINE CLUB
THORINGTON, James Monroe
A climber's guide to the Rocky Mountains of
Canada. 6th ed. with the collaboration of
William Lowell Putnam. New York: A.A.C.,
1966. xx, 381p., bibl. 18cm.

AMERICAN ALPINE CLUB
PUTNAM, William Lowell
Climber's guide to the Rocky Mountains of
Canada north 1974, by William L. Putnam, Chris
Jones, Robert Kruszyna. 6th ed. [New York]:
A.A.C., 1974. 289p., illus., maps. 17cm.
Based on previous eds. by James Monroe
Thorington.

AMERICAN ALPINE CLUB
PUTNAM, William Lowell and BOLES, Glen W
Climber's guide to the Rocky Mountains of
Canada south. 6th ed. [New York]: A.A.C.,
1973. 330p., illus., maps. 17cm.
Based on previous eds. by James Monroe
Thorington.

AMERICAN ALPINE CLUB
JONES, Chris
Climbing in North America. Berkeley, London:
University of California Press for the A.A.C.,
1976. xi, 392p., illus., bibl. 22 x 22cm.

AMERICAN ALPINE CLUB
MOUNTAIN RESCUE ASSOCIATION
Mountain rescue equipment and techniques; co-
ordinated by the Mountain Rescue Association.
[New York]: A.A.C., 1967. 15p., illus. 28cm.
(Mountain rescue and safety education program,
article 6)

AMERICAN ALPINE CLUB. Cascade Section
Climber's guide to the Cascade and Olympic
Mountains of Washington, by a committee of the
Cascade Section of the American Alpine Club;
under the Chairmanship of George R. Sainsbury.
[New York]: A.A.C., 1961. xii, 386p., plates
(1 fold. col.), illus., maps. 17cm.
Based on a previous ed. by Fred Becky.

AMERICAN ALPINE CLUB. Research Committee
Surface features of Dinwoody Glacier, Wind
River Mountains, Wyoming; geology by Mark F.
Meier, 1950-1952; sponsored by the Research
Committee, American Alpine Club. New York:
A.A.C., [1953]. Broadsheet, illus., map. 22cm.

AMERICAN GEOGRAPHICAL SOCIETY OF NEW YORK
Memorial volume of the transcontinental excur-
sion of 1912. New York: The Society, 1915.
xi, 407p., plates (1 fold.), illus., maps. 27cm.
Contributions in English, French, German and
Italian.

AMERICAN KARAKORAM EXPEDITION, 1938
Five miles high: the story of an attack on the
second highest mountain in the world, by the
members of the first American Karakoram Expedition; [edited by] Robert H. Bates. New York:
Dodd, Mead, 1939. xiii, 381p., plates (1 fold.),
illus., maps (on lining papers). 23cm.

- - Another ed. 1940.

AMERY, Leopold Stennett
Days of fresh air, being reminiscences of outdoor life. Jarrolds, 1939. 320p., plates,
illus. 23cm.

AMERY, Leopold Stennett
In the rain and sun. Hutchinson, 1946. 251p.,
plates (1 col.), illus. 22cm.
Sequel to: Days of fresh air.

AMERY, Leopold Stennett
The stranger of the Ulysses. Jarrolds, 1934.
163p. 20cm.

AMI, Henry M
North America. Vol. 1. Canada & Newfoundland; edited by Henry M. Ami: 2nd ed., rev. Stanford, 1915. xxviii,1069p., fold. col. plates, illus., maps, bibl. 20cm. (Stanford's compendium of geography and travel)

AMICIS, Edmondo de
See
DE AMICIS, Edmondo

AMICIS, H   de
See
DE AMICIS, Ugo

AMIGUET, Philippe
Technique et poésie de la montagne. Paris: B. Grasset, 1936. 252p., 16 plates, illus. 20cm.

AMORETTI, Carlo
Viaggio da Milano ai tre laghi, Maggiore, di Lugano e di Como, e ne' monti che li circondano. 6a ed. corr... e ... vita dell'autore ... [da] Giovanni Labus. Milano: G. Silvestri, 1824. xl, 373p., port. 18cm.

FICKER, Heinrich von and AMPFERER, Otto
Aus Innsbrucks Bergwelt: Wanderbilder aus Innsbrucks Bergen; mit ... Kunstbeilagen ... nach Originalaufnahmen von Otto Melzer; Text von Heinrich von Ficker und Otto Ampferer. Innsbruck: H. Schwick, 1902. 229p., plates, illus. 30cm.

AMPFERER, Otto
Bergstage: Gewalt und Glück der Höhen. München: Rother, 1930. 270p., plates, illus. 22cm.

AMPLEFORTH COLLEGE HIMALAYAN EXPEDITION, 1977
Report. Ampleforth (Yorks.): Ampleforth College, [1978]. 49p., plates, illus., maps. 21cm.

AMRHEIN, Max
Halt aus oder stirb! München: H.Stock, [1928]. 48p., plates, illus. 19cm.

AMSTUTZ, Eveline
Wiesenblumenfibel; mit Farbenphotos der ... schönsten Wiesenblumen nach der Natur aufgenommen; eingeleitet von Eveline Amstutz; mit botanischen Erläuterungen von W. Rytz. München: F. Bruckmann, 1938. 1 v. (chiefly col. illus.). 11 x 13cm.

AMSTUTZ, Walter
Alpenblumenfibel; mit Farbenphotos der ... schönsten Bergblumen nach der Natur aufgenommen; hrsg. von Walter Amstutz. München: F. Bruckmann, [1936]. 1 v. (chiefly col. illus.). 11 x 13cm.

AMSTUTZ, Walter
Das goldene Buch vom Engadin; hrsg. von Walter Amstutz. München: F. Bruckmann, 1936. 1 v. (chiefly illus.). 32cm.
Cover title: Engiadina terra fina.
Captions in German, French, English and Italian.

AMSTUTZ, Walter
Das Ski-ABC: ein Skischulfilm aus 450 Zeitlupen-Bildern. Zürich: Orell Füssli, 1938. [94p.], illus. 21cm.

AMSTUTZ, Walter
[Das Ski-ABC]. Ski-ing from A-Z: an instructional film of 450 instantaneous movie photographs. Oxford University Press, 1939. [94p.], illus. 20cm.

AMUNDSEN, R
MITTELHOLZER, Walter
Im Flugzeug dem Nordpol entgegen: Junkers'sche Hilfsexpedition für Amundsen nach Spitzbergen 1923; hrsg. von Walter Mittelholzer... Zurich: Orell Füssli, 1924. 106p., plates, illus., maps. 24cm.

AMY, Bernard
La montagne des autres: alpinisme en pays kurde. [Paris]: Arthaud, 1972. 239p., plates, illus., map, bibl. 21cm. (Collection Sempervivum)

AMY, Bernard
Technique de l'alpinisme; sous la direction de Bernard Amy. [Paris]: Arthaud, 1977. 404p., illus, maps, bibl. 25cm.

ANDERSEN, Hans Christian
The ice-maiden; translated from the Danish by Mrs. Bushby; with drawings by Zwecker. R. Bentley, 1836. 173p., illus. 21cm.

ANDERSEN, Hans Christian
Rambles in the romantic regions of the Hartz mountains, Saxon Switzerland, &c.; from the original Danish ... by Charles Beckwith. R. Bentley, 1848. 312p., illus. 21cm.

ANDERSEN, Johannes C
Jubilee history of South Canterbury. Auckland: Whitcombe & Tombs, 1916. xv, 775p., illus, maps. 26cm.

ANDERSON, C   W
To the Pindari Glacier: a sketch book and guide. Calcutta: Thacker, Spink, 1921. 72p., illus. 26cm.

ANDERSON, Sir Charles
An eight week's journal in Norway &c in 1852, with rough outlines. F. & J. Rivington, 1853. viii, 124p., plates, illus., maps. 21cm.

ANDERSON, Eustace
Chamouni and Mont Blanc: a visit to the valley and an ascent of the mountain in the autumn of 1855. Cornish, 1856. 113p., 2 col. plates (1 fold.), illus. 18cm.

ANDERSON, George and ANDERSON, Peter
Guide to the Highlands and Islands of Scotland. Murray,1834. xii, 759p.,plates (1 fold.), maps (1 in pocket), bibl. 18cm.

- - 3rd ed. carefully rev. enl. and remodelled. Edinburgh: Black, 1851.

ANDERSON, J   R   L
The Ulysses factor: the exploring instinct in man. Hodder & Stoughton, 1970. 352p., plates, illus., bibl. 23cm.

ANDERSON, Michael
COLLOMB, Robin Gabriel
Julian Alps: mountain walking and outline climbing guide; compiled by Robin G. Collomb; assisted by M. Anderson. Goring, Reading: West Col, 1978. 136p., illus., maps, bibl. 18cm. (West Col alpine guides)

ANDERSON, Michael
Karwendel. Goring, Reading: West Col, 1971. 56p., illus., map. 19cm. (Pilot alpine guides)

ANDERSON, Michael
Mittel Switzerland. Goring, Reading: West Col, 1974. 51p., illus, maps. 18cm. (Pilot alpine guides)

ANDERSON, George and ANDERSON, Peter
Guide to the Highlands and Islands of Scotland ... Murray, 1834. xii, 759p., plates (1 fold.), maps (1 in pocket), bibl. 18cm.

- - 3rd ed. carefully rev. enl. and remodelled. Edinburgh: Black, 1851.

ANDERSON, Tempest
Volcanic studies in many lands, being reproductions of photographs by the author ... with explanatory notices. Murray, 1903. xxviii, 202p., 105 plates, illus., bibl. 26cm.

- - 2nd series, the text by T.G. Bonney. 1917.

ANDERSON, William
Tales of discovery, enterprise, and adventure
for the young; edited by William Anderson.
Edinburgh, London: Gall & Inglis, [187-]. ii,
250p., plates, illus. 18cm.

ANDRASKO, Kenneth
Alaska crude: visions of the last frontier;
photographs by Marcus Halevi; text by Kenneth
Andrasko. Boston: Little, Brown, 1977. viii,
152p., illus., map. 24cm.

ANDRÉ, August
A guide for Champéry and its surroundings.
Lausanne: A. Trüb, [19--]. 62p., map. 18cm.

ANDRÉ, August
Sur nos monts. Genève: J.G. Fick, 1895. 138p.
17cm.

ANDREA, Silvia
Das Bergell: Wanderungen in der Landschaft
und ihrer Geschichte. Frauenfeld: J Huber,
1901. 121p., plates, illus. 19cm.

ANDREAE, Johann Gerhard Reinhard
Briefe aus der Schweiz nach Hannover geschrieben
in dem Jare 1763. Zürich: Joh. Caspar Füessli,
1776. xxii, 248p., 16 plates (4 fold.), illus.,
map. 29cm.
Preface signed: Andreae.

ANDRÉE, S   A
PALLIN, H   N
Andréegatan. Uppsala: J.A. Lindblad, 1934.
196p., maps. 23cm.

ANDREIS, E
Gran Paradiso: parco nazionale, di E. Andreis,
R. Chabod, M.C. Santi. 2a ed. aggiornata,
completata e illustrata da Renato Chabod.
Milano: Club Alpino Italiano, Touring Club
Italiano, 1963. 662p., plates (1 fold., some
col.), illus., maps, bibl. 17cm. (Guida dei
monti d'Italia)

ANDREW, Ken M and THRIPPLETON, Alan A
The southern Uplands. Edinburgh: Scottish
Mountaineering Trust, 1972. 231p., plates
(1 col.), illus., bibl. 22cm. (Scottish
Mountaineering Club district guide books)

THOMSON, James Merriman Archer and ANDREWS,
Arthur Westlake
The climbs on Lliwedd; issued by the Climbers'
Club. Arnold, 1909. xv, 99p., plates, illus.
16cm.

ANDREWS, Arthur Westlake and PYATT, Edward Charles
Cornwall. Stockport: Climbers' Club, 1950.
164p., plates, illus., maps. 16cm. (Climbing
guides to the Snowdon district and to Cornwall)

ANDREWS, Arthur Westlake
Poems. Vol. 9. St. Ives: The Author, 1943.
138-165p. 26cm.
Typescript.

ANDREWS, Arthur Westlake
Selected poems on West Penrith and Reflections.
Vol. 1. St. Ives: The Author, 1957. 59p. 22cm.

ANDREWS, Arthur Westlake
Selected verse, 1939-1944. Zennor: The Author,
[1944?]. 1 v. (various pagings). 26cm.

ANDREWS, Arthur Westlake
Selected verse, 1940-2. [Zennor]: The Author,
[1942?]. 164p. 26cm.

ANDREWS, Martha
UNIVERSITY OF COLORADO. Institute of Arctic and
Alpine Research
List of publications of the Institute of Arctic
and Alpine Research, 1967-1974; compiled by
Martha Andrews. Boulder (Col.): University of
Colorado, 1975. 45p. 28cm.

ANDREWS, Rodney H
Meteorology and heat balance of the Ablation
area, White Glacier, Canadian Arctic Archipelago - summer 1960. Montreal: McGill
University, 1964. vii, 107p., illus, maps,
bibl. 29cm. (Axel Heiberg Island research
reports, meteorology, no. 1., Jacobsen-McGill
Arctic Research Expedition, 1959-62)

Angelica's ladies library; or, Parental present;
[edited by John Hamilton]. Shakespeare
Library, 1794. vi, 440p. 21cm.

ANGELINI, Giovanni
Civetta per le vie del passato. Bologna:
Nuovi Sentieri, 1977. 363p., illus. (some
col.). 29cm.

ANGELINI, Giovanni
Contributi alla storia dei Monti di Zoldo.
[Venezia?], [1953]. 127p., illus., maps.
25cm. (Monografia de "Le Alpi Venete")
Offprint from Le Alpi Venete, 1949-53.

ANGELINI, Giovanni
La difesa della Valle di Zoldo nel 1848:
memorie e documenti; a cura di Giovanni
Angelini. Padova: Stediv, 1948. 83p., illus.,
map. 25cm.

ANGELINI, Giovanni
Salite in Moiazza. Venezia: Sezioni Trivenete del
C.A.I., 1950. 73p., plates, illus., maps.
25cm. (Monografia de "Le Alpi Venete")

ANGEVILLE, Henriette d'
GAILLARD, Émile
Une ascension romantique en 1838: Henriette
d'Angeville au Mont-Blanc. Chambéry: Éditions
Lire, 1947. 158p., plates, ports. 18cm. (Le
roc et l'eau, 1)

ANGEVILLE, Henriette d'
MEYER, Oskar Erich
Die Braut des Montblanc. Berlin: Union
Deutsche Verlagsgesellschaft, [1933]. 54p.,
illus., bibl. 19cm.

ANGEVILLE, Henriette d'
PAILLON, Mary
L'Album de Mlle d'Angeville. Paris: The
Author, 1909. 8p. 23cm. (Les femmes
alpinistes)
Reprinted with additions from La Montagne, 20
avril 1909.

ANGLO-AMERICAN PATAGONIA EXPEDITION, 1974
See
PATAGONIAN MOUNTAINEERING EXPEDITION, 1974

ANGREVILLE, J   E   d'
La flore vallaisanne. Genève: Mehling, 1862.
viii, 218p. 19cm.

ANGULO, Miguel
Guide des Pyrénées basques: promenades, ascensions, escalades, sur les 2 versants des
Pyrénées. [Pau?]: The Author, 1977. xxvi,
351p., illus., maps, bibl. 16cm.

ANNAN, Noel Gilroy
Leslie Stephen, his thought and character in
relation to his time. Macgibbon and Kee, 1951.
viii, 342p., plates, illus., bibl. 23cm.

Anne of Geierstein, [by Sir Walter Scott].
Edinburgh: A. Black, 1854. 2 v., plates,
illus. 17cm. (Waverley novels, 44-45)

ANNELER, Hedwig
Lötschen, das ist: Landes- u. Volkskunde des
Lötschentales, Text von Hedwig Anneler; Bilder
von Karl Anneler. Bern: Akademische Buchhandlung, 1917. 359p., plates (1 fold., 2 col.),
illus., map. 36cm.

ANNETTE, Barrie M
Limestone climbs on the Dorset coast. 2nd ed.
Southampton: Southampton University Mountain-
eering Club, 1960. 36 leaves, 1 plate, illus.
21cm.
Typescript.

Ansichten aus dem Alpstein, Kanton Appenzell,
Schweiz. St. Gallen: W. Marty, 1863. 1 v. of
illus. 12 x 18cm.

[Ansichten von Tyrol]. Tombleson's Ansichten von
Tyrol; nach T. Allom's Zeichnungen und Johanna
v. Isser's Skizzen; [Text von Josef Hormayr].
Tombleson, [ca 1840]. 127p.,plates, illus.,
map. 23cm.

[Ansichten von Tyrol]. Views in the Tyrol; from
drawings by T. Allom, after original sketches
by Johanna v. Isser ...; with letterpress descriptions by a companion of Hofer [i.e. Josef
Hormayr]. Black and Armstrong, [ca 1837].
72p., plates (1 fold.), illus., map. 28cm.
Second title page has title: Forty-six views of
Tyrolese scenery...
Cover title: Tyrolese scenery.

ANSTED, D   T
Scenery, science and art, being extracts from
the note-book of a geologist and mining engineer.
J. Van Voorst, 1854. viii, 322p., plates,
illus. 23cm.

ANTEVS, Ernst
Alpine zone of Mt. Washington range. Auburn
(Maine): The Author, 1932. viii, 118p., illus.,
maps, bibl. 20cm.

ANTHONIOZ, Charles
Maisons savoyardes; ouvrage illustré ... par
l'auteur; avant-propos de Léandre Vaillat.
Chambéry: Dardel, 1932. ix, 78p., illus. 24cm.

ANUFRIKOV, M   I
Sputnik al'pinista; sostavitel' M.I. Anufrikov.
Moskva: Izd. "Fizkul'tura i Sport", 1970. 336p.,
illus., maps, bibl. 21cm.

ANZIL, Franco
CONVENCIÓN NACIONAL DE TURISMO, 1st, Mérida,
Venezuela, 1961
Itinerarios turísticos-alpinísticos en la Sierra
Nevada de Mérida: trabajo del Club Andino
Venezolano; a cargo de ... Carlos Lacruz y
Franco Anzil. Mérida: C.A.V.,1961. 9 leaves.
35cm.

APPALACHIAN MOUNTAIN CLUB
The A.M.C. Maine mountain guide: a guide to
trails in the mountains of Maine. Boston (Mass.):
A.M.C., 1961. xii, 190p., fold. col. plates,
maps (in pockets). 16cm.

- - 2nd ed. 1968.

APPALACHIAN MOUNTAIN CLUB
The A.M.C. Massachusetts and Rhode Island trail
guide: a guide to hiking trails in Massachusetts
and Rhode Island. Boston (Mass.): A.M.C., 1964.
x, 309p., fold. plates, maps (in pockets). 16cm.

- - 2nd ed. 1967.

APPALACHIAN MOUNTAIN CLUB
The A.M.C. New England canoeing guide: a guide
to the canoeable waterways of New England.
Boston (Mass.): A.M.C., 1965. xvii, 475p., fold.
col. plates, maps (in pockets). 16cm.

- - 2nd ed. 1968.

APPALACHIAN MOUNTAIN CLUB
The A.M.C. White Mountain guide: a guide to paths
in the White Mountains and adjacent regions.
7th ed. Boston (Mass.): A.M.C., 1928. xi,
528p., illus., maps. 16cm.
Previous ed. published in 1925 under title:
Guide to paths in the White Mountains and
adjacent regions.

APPALACHIAN MOUNTAIN CLUB
The A.M.C. White Mountain guide... (Cont.).

- - 8th ed. 1931.

- - 16th ed. 1960.

- - 17th ed. 1963.

- - 18th ed. 1966.

- - 19th ed. 1969.

- - 20th ed. 1972.

APPALACHIAN MOUNTAIN CLUB
Guide to paths in the White Mountains and
adjacent regions. 6th ed. Boston (Mass.):
A.M.C., 1925. xi, 529p., fold. plates (some
col.), illus., maps (1 in pocket). 16cm.
Later eds. published under title: The A.M.C.
White Mountain guide...

APPALACHIAN MOUNTAIN CLUB
Mountain flowers of New England. Boston (Mass.):
A.M.C., 1964. v, 147p., 32 col. plates, illus.
19cm.

APPALACHIAN MOUNTAIN CLUB. Snow-shoe Section
List of excursions, parties, mountain climbs,
1882-1911. [Boston], 1911. 90p. 24cm.

APPLES, H   d'
Croquis chamoniards et le tour du Mont-Blanc.
Genève: Pasche, [19--]. 293p., 1 plate, illus.
22cm.

ARANTHON, Jean d'
La vie de Messire Jean D'Aranthon D'Alex, évêque
et prince de Genève avec son directoire pour
bien mourir... 2e éd. rev. & beaucoup augm...
Lyon: Comba, 1699. 636p., 1 plate, port. 20cm.

ARAGON, Anne Alexandrine
Souvenirs d'un voyage en Suisse. Paris:
Chapelle, 1843. 336p. 22cm.

ARBANERE, Étienne
Tableau des Pyrénées françaises, contenant une
description complète de cette chaîne de montagnes ...   Paris: Treuttel et Würtz, 1828.
2 v. in 1. 23cm.

ARBER, E   A   Newell
Plant life in alpine Switzerland, being an
account in simple language of the natural
history of alpine plants. Murray, 1910. xxiv,
355p., 48 plates, illus., bibl. 21cm.

ARBER, Edward
HOWELL, James
Instructions for forreine travell, 1642;
collated with the 2nd ed. of 1650; carefully
edited by Edward Arber. English Reprints, 1868.
88p. 18cm.

- - Large paper ed. 1869.

ARBEZ, Victor and PORTE, Pierre
Vos premiers pas en ski de fond. [Paris]:
Arthaud, 1975. 72p., illus. 19cm.

ARBUTHNOT, James
A trip to Kashmir. Calcutta: Thacker, Spink,
1900. 104p., plates, illus. 25cm.

ARCHER, Clement Hugh
Climbs in Japan and Korea: a photographic record
and guide. [N.p.]: The Author, [1936]. xi,
221p., plates, illus., maps. 27cm.

ARCHER, Clement Hugh
Coastal climbs in north Devon. Minehead: The
Author, [1961?]. 49p., plates, maps. 25cm.

- - Supplement for 1962.

- - Interim report on 1963.

Archiv kleiner zerstreuter Reisebeschreibungen durch Merkwürdige Gegenden der Schweiz. St. Gallen: Huber, 1796. 2 v. 21cm.

ARCIS, C   Egmond d'
En montagne: récits et souvenirs. Genève: Sonor, [1936]. 205p. 20cm.

ARCIS, C   Egmond d'
Neiges éternelles; avec une préface de Charles Gos. Neuchatel: Attinger, 1945. 173p. 19cm.

ARCONATI VISCONTI, Giammartino
Ascensione al Monte Rosa nell' agosto 1864 fatta da Giammartino Arconati Visconti. Torino, 1872. 23p. 31cm.
Offprint from Giornale delle Alpi.

ARDOUIN-DUMAZET, Victor Eugène
Voyage en France. 2e sér. Anjou, Bas-Maine, Nantes, Basse-Loire, Alpes mancelles, Suisse normande. Paris: Berger-Levrault, 1894. 334p. 19cm.

ARDOUIN-DUMAZET, Victor Eugène
Voyage en France. 7e sér. La région lyonnaise ... 3e éd. Paris: Berger-Levrault, 1911. vii, 575p., fold. plates, maps. 20cm.

ARDOUIN-DUMAZET, Victor Eugène
Voyage en France. 9e sér. Bas-Dauphiné... 2e éd. Paris: Berger-Levrault, 1903. 376p., fold. plates, maps. 19cm.

ARDOUIN-DUMAZET, Victor Eugène
Voyage en France. 10e sér. Les Alpes du Léman a la Durance, nos chasseurs alpins. Paris: Berger-Levrault, 1897. 370p. 19cm.

ARDOUIN-DUMAZET, Victor Eugène
Voyage en France. 12e sér. Alpes de Provence et Alpes maritimes... 2e éd. Paris: Berger-Levrault, 1904. 408p., fold. plates, maps. 19cm.

ARDOUIN-DUMAZET, Victor Eugène
Voyage en France. 39e sér. Pyrénées, partie orientale... Paris: Berger-Levrault, 1904. 339p., fold. plates, maps. 19cm.

ARDOUIN-DUMAZET, Victor Eugène
Voyage en France. 40e sér. Pyrénées centrales ... Paris: Berger-Levrault, 1904. 334p., fold. plates, maps. 19cm.

ARDOUIN-DUMAZET, Victor Eugène
Voyage en France. 41e sè. Pyrénées, partie occidentale... Paris: Berger-Levrault, 1904. 347p., fold. plates, maps. 19cm.

ARGENSON, Antoine Réné de Voyer d', marquis de Paulmy
See
PAULMY, Antoine Réné de Voyer d'Argenson, marquis de

ARGENTIER, Auguste
Courmayeur et Pré-St-Didier, Val d'Aoste: leur bains, leurs eaux & leurs environs. Aoste: D. Lyboz, 1864. 146p. 18cm.

ARGENTINA
Argentine-Chilean Boundary: report presented to the Tribunal appointed by H.B. Majesty's Government ... to justify the Argentine claims for the boundary in the summit of the Cordillera de los Andes... Government of Argentine Republic, 1900. 4 v. (xlix, 1181p.), plates, illus., maps. 34cm.

- - Maps (in portfolio)

ARGENTINA
CHILE
Statement presented on behalf of Chile in reply to the Argentine Report submitted to the Tribunal constituted by H.B. Majesty's Government acting as arbitrator in pursuance of the agreement dated April 17, 1896. Government of Chile, 1901-02. 4 v. in 3, fold. plates, maps. 26cm.

ARGENTINA
CHILE
Statement presented on behalf of Chile ...(cont.)

- - Appendix to the Statement. 1902.

- - Maps (in portfolio)

ARGYLL, John Douglas Sutherland Campbell, 9th Duke of
Canadian pictures, drawn with pen and pencil by the Marquis of Lorne; with numerous illustrations from ... photographs ... and sketches by the Marquis of Lorne ...; engraved by Edward Whymper. Religious Tract Society, [1884?]. viii, 224p., 1 fold. col. plate, illus., map. 29cm.

ARMANDY, André
Terre de suspicion: roman d'aventures. Paris: J. Tallandier, 1926. xii, 255p. 19cm.

ARMENGAUD, André and JOLIS, Agustín
Posets-Maladeta (del Cinca al Noguera Ribagorzana): Cotiella, Bachimala, Perdiguero, Eriste, Aneto, Vallibierna, Forcanada. Barcelona: Centro Excursionista de Cataluna, Club Alpino Catalán, 1958. xxviii, 476p., fold. plates, illus., maps. 16cm.
(Centro Excursionista de Cataluna. Coleccion de guias, 6)

ARMENGAUD, André and JOLIS, Agustín
Posets-Maladeta (du Cinca à la Noguera Ribagorzana): Peña Montañesa, Cotiella, Turbon ...; traduit de l'espagnol par Bernard Clos. Pau: R. Ollivier [pour] Club Alpin Catalan, Centre Excursionniste de Catalogne, 1967. xvi, 307p., fold. plates (1 col.), illus., maps, bibl. 17cm.

ARMENGAUD, André and COMET, François
Pyrénées. T. 4. Guide de la région d'Aure et de Luchon (du Port de Barosa au Val d'Aran); édité sous le patronage de ... F.F.M. Toulouse: Privat, 1953. 360p., fold. col. plates, illus., maps, bibl. 16cm.

ARMSTRONG, Margaret
Field book of western wild flowers, by Margaret Armstrong; in collaboration with J.J. Thornber. New York, London: Putnam, 1915. xx, 596p., col. plates, illus. 18cm.

ARMY EAST GREENLAND EXPEDITION, 1968
Expedition report, by C.H. Agnew of Lochnaw yr. and others. [Glasgow]: The Expedition, [1968?]. iv, 56p., illus., maps. 30cm.

ARMY MOUNTAINEERING ASSOCIATION
BRITISH NEPALESE ARMY ANNAPURNA EXPEDITION, 1970
The ascent of Annapurna, 20th May 1970. Army Mountaineering Association, [1970?]. 5 leaves, 1 plate, maps. 33cm.

ARMY MOUNTAINEERING ASSOCIATION HIMACHAL PRADESH EXPEDITION, 1973
Preliminary report, [by J.W. Fleming]. Aldershot: The Expedition, 1973. [19 leaves]. 30cm.

ARMY MOUNTAINEERING ASSOCIATION HIMACHAL PRADESH EXPEDITION, 1973
Report, [by the leader J.W. Fleming, and other expedition members]. Aldershot: The Expedition, [1974]. xii, 92p., illus., maps. 30cm.

ARNAO, Cesar Morales
See
MORALES ARNAO, Cesar

ARNAUD, F
La vallée de Barcelonnette (l'Ubaye). Grenoble: A. Gratier, 1900. 121p., illus. 25cm. (Les Alpes françaises)

ARNAUD, Henri
    The glorious recovery by the Vaudois of their
    valleys, from the original by Henri Arnaud;
    with a compendious history of that people,
    previous and subsequent to that event, by Hugh
    Dyke Acland. Murray, 1827. cxxii, xxv,
    239p., plates (1 fold.), illus., map. 22cm.

ARNBERGER, Erik
    Die Kartographie im Alpenverein; hrsg. vom
    Deutschen Alpenverein und vom Österreichischen
    Alpenverein. München: D.A.V.; Innsbruck:
    Ö.A.V., 1970. 253p., plates (some fold.),
    illus., maps, bibl. 29cm. (Wissenschaftliche
    Alpenvereinshefte, Heft 22)

ARNOLD, P
    Der Simplon: zur Geschichte des Passes und
    des Dorfes. Eggerberg: Selbstverlag von
    Pfarrer P. Arnold, [1948]. 276p., plates,
    illus., bibl. 23cm.

ARNOLLET, François
    Nos Alpes Isère et Dorons: guide d'excursions
    autour de Brides, Salins... Moutiers: F.
    Ducloz, 1895. xix, 464p., illus. 14cm.

ARNOULD, Joseph
    Hospice of St. Bernard: a prize poem, recited
    in the Theatre, Oxford, June 10, 1834. Oxford:
    J. Vincent, 1834. 19p. 19cm.

AROSA, Hans Roelli
    Schnee: Verse für empfindsame Skileute; Zeich-
    nungen von Karl Hügin. Zürich: "Sport",
    [n.d.]. 42p., illus. 16cm.

ARPS, Louisa Ward
COLORADO MOUNTAIN CLUB
    Front Range panorama; edited by Louisa Ward
    Arps. Denver: C.M.C., 1962. 7 sheets and map
    (in folder). 23 x 32cm.

ARVE, Stéphen d'
    Les fastes du Mont-Blanc: ascensions célèbres
    et catastrophes depuis M. de Saussure jusqu'à
    nos jours. Genève: A. Vérésoff, 1876. 354p.
    22cm.
    New ed. published in 1878 under title:
    Histoire de Mont Blanc ...

ARVE, Stéphen d'
    Histoire du Mont Blanc et de la Vallée de
    Chamonix: ascensions et catastrophes célèbres
    depuis les premières explorations, 1786,
    jusqu'en 1861; préface par Francis Way.
    [Nouv. éd. rev. et augm.]. Paris: Ch.
    Delagrave, 1878. 2 v., plates, illus. 19cm.
    Previous ed. published in 1876 under the title:
    Les fastes du Mont-Blanc ...

ARVE, Stéphen d'
    Le Mont-Blanc: deuxième ascension scientifique
    de ... W. Pitschner, du 30 août au 16 sep-
    tembre 1861: relation sommaire... Annecy: La
    Compagnie des Guides de Chamonix, 1861. 32p.
    22cm.

ARVE, Stéphen d'
    Première acension photographique au sommet du
    Mont-Blanc par MM. Bisson frères, photographes
    de S.M. l'Empereur, sous le direction d'Auguste
    Balmat, le 25 juillet 1861. Annecy: Thésio,
    1861. 15p. 23cm.

Arvendel; or Sketches in Italy and Switzerland,
    [by Gerard T. Noel]. Nisbet, 1826. 123p.
    24cm.
    Essays, verse and verse paraphrases of scrip-
    ture.

ARZANI, Carlo
    I rifugi del Club Alpino Italiano e le stazioni
    del Corpo Nazionale di Soccorso Alpino. 2a ed.
    Lecco: Agielle, 1977. 159p., illus., maps,
    bibl. 21cm.

ASAHI SHIMBUN
    The magnificence of the Himalayas; compiled by
    Asahi Shimbun. Tokyo: Asahi Shimbun, 1978.
    219p. (chiefly col. illus.), map. 27cm.
    Japanese text, introduction and picture cap-
    tions in English.

HARA, Makoto and ASAMI, Masao
    Makalu 1970: Harukanaru mitoono one. Tokyo:
    Meikeido, 1972. 404p., col. plates (some
    fold.), illus., maps, bibl. 27cm.
    The Japanese Makalu Expedition, 1970, organ-
    ised by the Japanese Alpine Club.
    In Japanese with an English summary.

Ascension au Mont Blanc, par MM. Martins,
    Bravais et Lepileur. [Paris?], [1844].
    68-74p., illus. 37cm.
    Offprint from l'Illustration, journal
    universel, no. 84, v. 4, 5 octobre, 1844.

The ascent of the Pieterboth Mountain,
    Mauritius, 13 October, 1864. Mauritius: E.
    Dupuy & P. Dubois, printers, 1864. 15p.,
    plates, illus. 13cm.

ASHBURNER, John
    Cambridge Hindu-Kush Expedition 1966, [by
    John Ashburner, Henry Edmundson and Paul Newby].
    [Cambridge]: The Expedition, [1967?]. 66p.,
    plates (2 fold.), illus., maps. 25cm.

ASHBY, Douglas
    Things seen in Switzerland in summer: a des-
    cription of a wonderful country... Seeley,
    Service, 1928. 158p., plates, illus., map.
    16cm.

ASHENDEN
    The mountains of my life: journeys in Turkey
    and the Alps. Edinburgh: Blackwood, 1954.
    212p., plates, illus. 26cm.

ASHLEY, Clifford W
    The Ashley book of knots. Faber, 1947. x,
    620p., plates, illus., bibl. 30cm.

ASHTON, John R and STOCKS, F. Arnold
    The open air guide, for wayfarers of all kinds.
    Heywood, 1928. 209p., 1 fold. plate, illus.,
    maps. 18cm.

ASSOCIATION OF BRITISH MEMBERS OF THE SWISS
ALPINE CLUB
    [Bergsteigen]. Mountaineering handbook: a
    complete and practical guide for beginner or
    expert. Published for the A.B.M.S.A.C. by
    Paternoster Press, 1950. 168p., illus. 19cm.

ASSOCIATION OF BRITISH MEMBERS OF THE SWISS
ALPINE CLUB
    Inauguration of the Cabane Britannia on the
    Klein Allalinhorne Saas Fee, August 17th, 1912,
    and obituary notices and portrait of Clinton
    Dent. A.B.M.S.A.C., 1913. 52p., plates,
    illus. 22cm.

ASSOCIATION OF BRITISH MEMBERS OF THE SWISS
ALPINE CLUB
    A list and short guide to the huts of the
    Swiss Alpine Club, [with] addenda: Huts belong-
    ing to the Academic Alpine Clubs of Bâle, Bern
    and Zurich and to the French Alpine Club in the
    Mt. Blanc group. A.B.M.S.A.C., [195-?]. 31p.
    16cm.

ASSOCIATION OF BRITISH MEMBERS OF THE SWISS
ALPINE CLUB
    Mountaineering handbook

    See its

    [Bergsteigen]. Mountaineering handbook

ASSOCIATION OF BRITISH MEMBERS OF THE SWISS
ALPINE CLUB
SCHWEIZER ALPEN-CLUB. Sektion Uto
[Technique de l'alpinisme]. The technique of
alpine mountaineering, [by Emil Kern]. English
ed., adapted by members of the Association of
British Members of the Swiss Alpine Club.
A.B.M.S.A.C., [1935]. 74p., illus. 16cm.

ASSOCIATION OF SWISS HOTEL PROPRIETORS AND
MANAGERS
See
SOCIÉTE SUISSE DES HOTELIERS

ASSOCIATION SUISSE DES CLUBS DE SKI
See
SCHWEIZERISCHER SKI-VERBAND

ASSOCIAZIONE NAZIONALE ALPINI
ITALY. Army. Corpo degli Alpini
I Verdi: cinquant'anni di storia alpina,
1872-1922; sotto gli auspici della
Associazione Nazionale Alpini; a cura di Renzo
Boccardi. Roma: Alfieri & Lacroix, [1922].
133p., plates, illus., music. 25cm.

ATKINS, Henry Martin
Ascent to the summit of Mont Blanc, on the
22nd and 23rd of August, 1837. Calkin & Budd,
1838. 51p., 6 plates, illus. 23cm.

ATKINS, Henry Martin
[Ascent to the summit of Mont Blanc...].
Ascension au sommet du Mont-Blanc le 22 et le
23 aout 1837; traduit [par Jourdan] de
l'anglais, avec privilège de l'auteur. Genève,
Londres: Caulkin and Butt [sic], 1838. 63p.
23cm.

ATKINSON, Edwin T
Notes on the history of the Himalaya of the
N.W.P., India. St. Leonards-on-Sea: The Author,
[1883]. 2 v., plates (1 fold.), illus. 25cm.

BARBER, John B and ATKINSON, George
Lakeland passes, including some charming walks
through the District, taken and described by
John B. Barber and George Atkinson. 2nd ed.
Ulverston: J. Atkinson, 1928. 69p., plates
(1 fold.), illus., map. 19cm.

ATKINSON, James
The expedition into Affghanistan: notes and
sketches descriptive of the country contained
in a personal narrative during the campaign of
1839 and 1840, up to the surrender of Dost
Mahomed Khan. Allen, 1842. xx, 428p. 21cm.

ATKINSON, Thomas Witlam
Oriental and western Siberia: a narrative of
seven years' explorations and adventures in
Siberia, Mongolia, the Kirghis steppes, Chinese
Tartary and part of Central Asia. Hurst and
Blackett, 1858. xi, 611p., col. plates (1 fold.),
illus., map. 27cm.

ATKINSON, Thomas Witlam
Travels in the regions of the upper and lower
Amoor and the Russian acquisitions on the
confines of India and China... 2nd ed. Hurst
and Blackett, 1861. xiii, 570p., plates (1
fold. 1 col.), illus., map. 27cm.

ATL, Dr.
Le sinfonie del Popocatepetl: poema messicano;
tradotto in italiano da G.V. Callegari. Milano:
Cristofari, 1930. 76p., plates, illus. 23cm.

Atlas géographique, économique, historique de la
Suisse. Neuchatel: Publications du Dictionnaire
Géographique de la Suisse, [1908]. 48p. of
maps. 30cm.

ATTANOUX, J. Bernard d'
La marche et la pratique du tourisme à pied. 2e
éd. rev. et augm. Paris: Berger-Levrault, 1913.
xiii, 149p. 19cm.

ATWATER, Montgomery M
The avalanche hunters; with an introduction by
Lowell Thomas. Philadelphia: Macrea Smith,
1968. xix, 235p., illus., bibl. 25cm.

ATWOOD, Wallace W
The Rocky Mountains. New York: Vanguard Press,
1945. 324p., plates (1 fold.), illus., maps.
24cm. (American mountain series, v. 3)

ATZWANGER, Peterpaul
SPRINGENSCHMID, Karl
Bauern in den Bergen, in Worten von Karl
Springenschmid; in Bildern von Peterpaul
Atzwanger. München: F. Bruckmann, 1936. 175p.,
illus. 24cm.

Au pay du Mont-Blanc. Genève: Jullien, [1910].
1 v. (chiefly illus.). 22 x 28cm.

AUBERT, Théodore
Émerentienne: roman. Genève; Atar, [1908].
208p. 19cm.

AUBERT, Théodore
L'isole: roman. Genève: Durr, 1908. 267p.
21cm.

AUBIGNÉ, Robert Merle-d'
See
MERLE-D'AUBIGNÉ, Robert

AUDEBRAND, Commandant
Grenoble et le Dauphiné; publié par MM.
Audebrand, Maurice Bergès [and others].
Grenoble: A. Gratier & J. Rey, [1904]. 396p.,
plates, illus., map. 25cm.

AUDEN, Whystan Hugh and ISHERWOOD, Christopher
The ascent of F6: a tragedy in two acts. 2nd
ed. Faber, 1937. 123p. 24cm.

AUDEN, Whystan Hugh
Mountains; illustrated by Edward Bawden.
Faber, 1954. 5p., illus. (1 col.). 22cm.
(Ariel poems)

AUDIBERT, Raoul
Montagnes. Paris: Redier, 1930. 224p. 20cm.
(Collection "la route").

AUDIN, Jean Marie Vincent
See
RICHARD

AUDOUBERT, Louis
Peuterey, fantastique intégrale: récit; préface
de Robert Ollivier. Pau: Marrimpouey, 1975.
99p., plates (1 col.), illus., map. 19cm.

AUER, Harry A
Camp fires in the Yukon. Cincinnati: Stewart
& Kidd, 1916. x, 204p., plates, illus., maps.
22cm.

AUERBACH, Berthold
Auerbach's Dorfgeschichten. 4. Aufl. Mannheim:
Fr. Bassermann, 1848. 512p., plates, illus.
19cm.

AUGIER, Marc Jean Pierre
See
SAINT LOUP

AUGUSTIN FAMILY
Streifzüge durch die norischen Alpen. Wien:
P. Rohrmann, 1840. viii, 253p., 1 plate, map.
20cm.

AUGUSTUS CAESAR, Emperor of Rome
OBERZINER, Giovanni
Le guerre di Augusto contro i popoli alpini.
Roma: E. Loescher, 1900. 2 v. in 1, 5 col.
maps. 34cm.

MIDOWICZ, W   and AUGUSTYNOWICZ, M
Przewodnik Narciarski po beskidzie zachodnim
(Babia Gora, Pasmo Jalowieckie, Beskid
Zywiecki, Beskid Maly ...). Krakow: Oddziele
Polsk. Tow. Tatrz, 1928. 92p., plates (1 fold.)
illus. 14cm.

LHOSTE, Jean Marc and AULARD, Claude
Guide des escalades du Hoggar; avec la collaboration de J. Boissonnas. Paris: Club Alpin
Français, [1962?]. xiv, 154p., illus., maps,
bibl. 28cm.

AULDJO, John
Narrative of an ascent to the summit of Mont
Blanc, on the 8th and 9th August, 1827. Longman,
Rees, Orme, Brown, & Green, 1828. xi, 120p.,
plates (some fold., some col.), illus. 33cm.

- - 2nd ed. 1830.

- - 3rd ed. 1856.

- - 4th ed. 1867.

AULDJO, John
Sketches of Vesuvius with short accounts of its
principal eruptions, from the commencement of
the Christian era to the present time. Naples:
G. Glass, 1832. 96p. 25cm.
Library's copy lacks plates.

- - Another ed. Longman, Rees, Orme, Brown,
Green, & Longman, 1833.

AULDJO, John
THORINGTON, James Monroe
John Auldjo, fortunate traveller: [John Auldjo,
1805-86; collected and arranged for the Alpine
Club by J. Monroe Thorington]. [Philadelphia?]:
The Author, 1953. 1 v. (various pagings). 42cm.

AUSCHER, René
FENDRICH, Anton
Les sports de la neige; adaptation française par
René Auscher. Paris: Hachette, 1912. vii,
134p., illus. 21cm.

AUSSET, Daniel Dollfus-
See
DOLLFUS-AUSSET, Daniel

AUSTIN, J   Allan and VALENTINE, Rodney
Great Langdale, by J.A. Austin and R. Valentine;
illustrated by W. Heaton Cooper. Stockport:
Fell & Rock Climbing Club, 1973. 256p., 1 col.
plate, illus., map (on lining paper). 16cm.
(Climbing guides to the English Lake District,
[4th ser.], 1)

AUSTRIA. Gendarmerie. Zentraldirektion
Alpin-Vorschrift für die österr. Bundesgendarmerie nebst einem Anhang über die Zentralmeldestelle für alpine Unfälle in Wien ...;
Verfasser: G. Bilgeri; Mitarbeiter: Josef
Albert. Wien: Gendarmerie-Zentraldirektion,
[1926?]. vii, 128p., illus. 24cm.

AUSTRIA. Österreichische Bundesbahnen
See
ÖSTERREICHISCHE BUNDESBAHNEN

Austria's just claim to South Tyrol.
[London?]: ["Justice for the Tyrol Committee"],
[1944?]. 84p., plates (some fold., some col.),
illus, maps (1 in pocket). 30cm.

AUSTRIAN ALPINE CLUB
See
ÖSTERREICHISCHER ALPENVEREIN

AUSTRIAN STATE RAILWAYS
See
ÖSTERREICHISCHE BUNDESBAHNEN

Autumn rambles; or, Fireside recollections of
Belgium, the Rhine, the Moselle, German spas,
Switzerland, the Italian lakes, Mont Blanc,
and Paris, written by a lady [i.e. Mrs.
Staley]. Rochdale: Printed by E. Wrigley,
1863. vii, 217p. 19cm.

AUVERGNE, Edmund B   d'
See
D'AUVERGNE, Edmund B

The avalanche; or, The old man of the Alps:
a tale; translated from the French [of Isabelle
de Montolieu]. H.N. Batten, 1829. 78p.,
plates, illus. 18cm.

AVEBURY, John Lubbock, Baron
The beauties of nature and the wonders of the
world we live in. Macmillan, 1892. xiv,
427p., plates, illus., maps. 20cm.

AVEBURY, John Lubbock, Baron
The scenery of Switzerland and the causes to
which it is due. Macmillan, 1896. xxxv,
473p., 1 fold. col. plate, illus., maps, bibl.
20cm.

- - 5th ed. 1913.

Avis aux voyageurs en Suisse, avec une nouvelle
carte des principales routes de la Suisse, où
l'on a marqué les distances d'un endroit à
l'autre, gravée à Berne par M. Eichler, & se
trouve chez l'éditeur J.G. Heinzmann. Berne:
Société Typographique, 1796. 48p., 1 fold.
plate, map. 23cm.

Axel Heiberg Island research reports. Montreal:
McGill University.

Preliminary report, 1961-62. 1963.
The anhydrite diapirs..., by E.W. Hoen. 1964.
Geology of the expedition area..., by P.E.
Fricker. 1963.
Meteorology and heat balance of the Ablation
area..., by R.H. Andrews. 1964.
Pre-Mississippian succession..., by P.E.
Fricker and H.P. Trettin. 1963.

AYMONIN, Monique Keraudren-
See
KERAUDREN-AYMONIN, Monique

AZAN, Paul
Annibal dans les Alpes. Paris: Picard, 1902.
234p., plates, illus, maps, bibl. 27cm.

AZELINE
Carnet d'un touriste. Neuchatel: Delachaux &
Niestlé, 1884. viii, 315p. 20cm.

AZELINE
Par monts et vaux: souvenirs d'un alpiniste.
Paris: Sandoz & Fischbacher, 1879. 247p.
20cm.

AZELINE
Récits d'un montagnard: Alpes et Jura.
Neuchatel: Attinger, 1887. 329p. 18cm.
(Lectures romandes)

AZÉMA, Marc Antonin
La conquête du Fitz-Roy. Paris: Flammarion,
1954. 237p., plates, illus., maps. 23cm.
(Collection "L'aventure vécue")

AZÉMA, Marc Antonin
[La conquête du Fitz-Roy]. The conquest of
Fitzroy; translated by Katharine Chorley and
Nea Morin. Deutsch, 1957. 237p., plates,
illus., maps. 22cm.

B., Mme. D.
Nos Alpes; illustré par Hans Wieland. Genève:
Briquet, [n.d.]. 7p., illus. 25cm.

B., Mr.
Poésies helvétiennes

See

BRIDEL, Philippe Sirice

B., Mr.
Voyage pittoresque aux glacieres de Savoye...

See

BORDIER, André César

B., F.
Le voyageur en Suisse; ou, Manuel instructif
et portatif à l'usage des étrangers qui se proposent de parcourir ce pays; extrait des
meilleurs ouvrages de nos jours. Genève:
L'Auteur, [ca 1816]. 754p. 22cm.
Editor's preface signed: F.B.

B., H.M., C.E. and T.
See
BUXTON, Hannah Maude

B., W.
See
BELLOWS, William

B AND N STEAMSHIP LINE
Sunlit Norway, nature's wonderland. Published
by the B & N Steamship Line and the Norwegian
State Railways, 1912. 205p., illus., maps.
18cm.

BABILLOTTE, A
Führer durch die Vogesen und den elsässischen
Jura. 3. Aufl. Freiburg: P. Lorenz, 1907-08.
100p., maps. 16cm. (Lorenz Reiseführer)

BACCELLI, Alfredo
Vette e ghiacci: impressioni e ricordi. Roma:
Società Editrice Dante Alighieri, 1901. 216p.,
1 plate, illus., port. 21cm. (Biblioteca
dell'Alpinista, v. 1)

EDHOLM, O G and BACHARACH, A L
Exploration medicine, being a practical guide
for those going on expeditions; edited by O.G.
Edholm and A.L. Bacharach; with an introduc-
tion by Sir Raymond Priestly. Bristol: J.
Wright, 1965. xvi, 410p., illus., bibl. 23cm.

BADDELEY, John F
The rugged flanks of Caucasus. Oxford University Press, 1940. 2 v., plates (some fold.),
illus., maps, bibl. 29cm.

BADDELEY, Mountford J B
The English Lake District... 6th ed. rev. and
enl. Dulau, 1891. xxix, 250p., fold. col.
plates, illus., maps. 17cm. (Thorough
guides, 1)

- - 8th ed. thoroughly rev. 1899.

- - 9th ed. thoroughly rev. 1902.

- - 13th ed. rev. Ward, Lock, [1921?].

- - 15th ed. rev. [ca 1930].

Later ed. rev. published under title:The Lake
District.

BADDELEY, Mountford J B and WARD, C S
Ireland. 4th ed. Dulau, 1901. 2 v., col.
plates (some fold.), maps. 17cm. (Thorough
guides, 12 - 13)
Library has pt. 2 only.

- - 5th ed. rev. 1902-09.

BADDELEY, Mountford J B
The Lake District; originally compiled by
M.J.B. Baddeley. 17th ed. rev. Ward, Lock,
[ca 1936]. 315p., fold. col. plates, illus.,
maps. 17cm.
Previous eds. published under title: The
English Lake District.

BADDELEY, Mountford J B and WARD, C S
North Wales. Pt. 1. 7th ed. rev. Dulau,
1902. xxiv, 239p., fold. col. plates, illus.,
maps. 17cm. (Thorough guides, 8)

BADDELEY, Mountford J B
The Peak District of Derbyshire and neighbouring counties... 7th ed. rev. and enl. Dulau,
1899. xvi, 16, 158p., fold. col. plates,
maps. 17cm. (Thorough guides, 4)

BADDELEY, Mountford J B
Scotland. Pt. 1. Edinburgh, Glasgow and the
Highlands... 7th ed. Dulau, 1892. xxxiv,
310p., plates (some fold. col.), maps. 17cm.
(Thorough guides, 2)

WARD, C S and BADDELEY, Mountfield J B
South Wales and the Wye district of Monmouthshire. 4th ed. rev. Dulau, 1901. xvi, 192p.,
plates (some fold. col.), maps. 17cm.
(Thorough guides, 10)

BADDELEY, Mountford J B
Yorkshire... 4th ed. rev. Dulau, 1901-02
[v. 1, 1902]. 2 v. plates, maps, plans. 17cm.
(Thorough guides, 15 - 16)

BADER, H
Der Schnee und seine Metamorphose: erste
Ergebnisse und Andwendungen einer systematischen Untersuchung der alpinen Winterschneedecke... 1934-1938, von H. Bader [and others].
Bern: Kümmerly & Frey, 1939. xxiii, 340p.,
plates (some fold.), illus. 30cm. (Beiträge
zur Geologie der Schweiz. Geotechnische
Serie. Hydrologie, Lfg. 3)

BADER, Paul Louis
Notes sur le Massif des Kerlingarfjöll en
Islande. [Bern], 1917. 10p., 1 plate, illus.
23cm.
Offprint from Echo des Alpes, no. 8, 1917.

BADIN, Adolphe
Grottes et cavernes; ouvrage illustré de ...
vignettes. 2e éd. Paris: Hachette, 1870.
328p., illus. 19cm. (Bibliothèque des
merveilles)

BAEDEKER, Karl
Austria, together with Budapest, Prague,
Karlsbad, Marienbad: handbook for travellers.
12th rev. ed. Leipzig: K. Baedeker, 1929.
lxiv, 518p., illus, maps, plans. 17cm.

BAEDEKER, Karl
Belgium and Holland: handbook for travellers.
7th ed. rev. and augm. Leipsic: K. Baedeker,
1884. lxii, 344p., plates (some fold., some
col.), maps, plans. 17cm.

BAEDEKER, Karl
Dalmatien und die Adria: Westliches Süd-
slawien, Bosnien, Budapest, Istrien, Albanien,
Korfu: Handbuch für Reisende. Leipzig: K.
Baedeker, 1929. 272p., maps, plans. 16cm.

BAEDEKER, Karl
The Dominion of Canada, with Newfoundland
and an excursion to Alaska: handbook for
travellers. 3rd rev. and augm. ed.
Leipzig: K. Baedeker, 1907. lxiv, 331p., col.
plates (some fold.), maps, plans, bibl. 17cm.

- - 4th rev. and augm. ed. 1922.

BAEDEKER, Karl
The eastern Alps including the Bavarian Highlands, Tyrol, Salzburg, Upper and Lower Austria,
Styria, Carinthia and Carniola: handbook for
travellers. 11th ed. rev. and augm. Leipzig:
K. Baedeker, 1907. xxvi, 574p., illus., maps,
plans. 17cm.

BAEDEKER, Karl
Italy from the alps to Naples: abridged handbook for travellers. 3rd rev. ed. Leipzig:
K. Baedeker, 1928. xl, 488p., plates, maps,
plans. 16cm.

BAEDEKER, Karl
Italy: handbook for travellers. Pt. 2. Central
Italy and Rome. 9th rev. ed. Leipsic: K.
Baedeker, 1886. lx, 414p., plates, illus.,
maps, plans. 16cm.

BAEDEKER, Karl
Italy: handbook for travellers. Pt. 3.
Southern Italy and Sicily, with excursions to
the Lipari Islands, Malta, Sardinia, Tunis, and
Corfu. 9th rev. ed. Leipsic: K. Baedeker,
1887. xlviii, 416p., plates, maps, plans.
16cm.

BAEDEKER, Karl
Le midi de la France, depuis l'Auvergne et y
compris les Alpes: manuel du voyageur. 4e
éd. Leipzig: K. Baedeker, 1892. xxx, 482p.,
illus., maps, plans. 16cm.

BAEDEKER, Karl
Northern France from Belgium and the English
Channel to the Loire, excluding Paris and its
environs: handbook for travellers. Leipsic:
K. Baedeker; London: Dulau, 1889. xliii,
395p., maps, plans. 17cm.

BAEDEKER, Karl
Northern Germany, as far as the Bavarian and
Austrian frontiers: handbook for travellers.
15th rev. ed. Leipzig: K. Baedeker, 1910.
xxxviii, 430p., maps, plans. 17cm.

BAEDEKER, Karl
Northern Italy, including Ravenna, Florence,
and Pisa: K. Baedeker, 1930. lxxxii, 704p.,
plates, maps, plans. 16cm.

BAEDEKER, Karl
Norway, Sweden, and Denmark: handbook for
travellers. 6th ed. Leipsic: K. Baedeker,
1895. lxxix, 410, 42p., plates (some fold.,
some col.), maps. 17cm.

- - 8th ed. rev. and augm. 1903.

- - 9th ed. rev. and augm. 1909.

- - 10th ed. rev. and augm. 1912.

BAEDEKER, Karl
Paris and environs with routes from London
to Paris: handbook for travellers. 18th rev.
ed. Leipzig: K. Baedeker, 1913. liv., 491p.,
maps, plans. 17cm.

BAEDEKER, Karl
The Rhine from Rotterdam to Constance: handbook for travellers. 16th rev. ed. Leipzig:
K. Baedeker, 1906. xxxiv, 461p., maps, plans.
17cm.

BAEDEKER, Karl
The Riviera, south-eastern France and Corsica,
the Italian lakes and Lake of Geneva: handbook
for travellers. Leipzig: K. Baedeker, 1931.
xxxvi, 480p., maps, plans. 17cm.

BAEDEKER, Karl
Die Schweiz: Handbüchlein für Reisende; nach
eigener Anschauung und den besten hülfsquellen
bearbeitet. Koblenz: K. Bädeker, 1844. xxxi,
536p., 1 fold. col. plate, map. 16cm.

BAEDEKER, Karl
South-western France from the Loire and the
Rhone to the Spanish frontier: handbook for
travellers. 2nd ed. Leipsic: K. Baedeker,
1895. xxiv, 294p., maps, plans. 16cm.

BAEDEKER, Karl
Southern France from the Loire to the Spanish
and Italian frontiers including Corsica: handbook for travellers. Leipsic: K. Baedeker,
1891. xxvi, 502p., maps, plans. 17cm.

BAEDEKER, Karl
Southern Germany: handbook for travellers.
9th rev. ed. Leipsic: K. Baedeker, 1902.
xxviii, 295p., maps, plans. 16cm.

BAEDEKER, Karl
Spain and Portugal: handbook for travellers.
2nd ed. Leipsic: K. Baedeker; London: Dulau,
1901. lxxxviii, 608p., plates (some fold. some
col.), maps, plans. 17cm.

BAEDEKER, Karl
Le sud-est de la France, du Jura à la Méditerranée y compris la Corse: manuel du voyageur.
9e éd. refondue, augm. et mise à jour. Leipzig:
K. Baedeker, 1910. xxxvi, 547p., illus., maps,
plans. 17cm.

BAEDEKER, Karl
Südbayern Tirol und Salzburg, Ober- und Nieder-
Österreich, Steiermark, Kärnten und Krain:
Handbuck für Reisende. 34. Augl. Leipzig: K.
Baedeker, 1910. xxviii, 676p., illus., maps,
plans. 16cm.

BAEDEKER, Karl
La Suisse et les parties limitrophes de la
Savoie et de l'Italie: manuel du voyageur. 30e
éd. Leipzig: K. Baedeker, 1928. lvi, 632p.,
plates (some fold., some col.), illus., maps,
plans, bibl. 16cm.

BAEDEKER, Karl
La Suisse, les lacs italiens, Milan, Genes,
Turin: manuel du voyageur; traduit de l'allemand
par C.F. Girard. 3e éd. entièrement refondue.
Coblenz: C. Baedeker, 1857. xlv, 396p., plates,
maps, plans. 17cm. (Baedeker's Reisehand-
bucher)

BAEDEKER, Karl
Switzerland together with Chamonix and the
Italian lakes: handbook for travellers. 27th
rev. ed. Leipzig: K. Baedeker, 1928. liv,
618p., plates (some fold., some col.), illus.,
maps, plans, bibl. 16cm.

BAEDEKER, Karl
Tyrol and the Dolomites including the Bavarian
Alps: handbook for travellers. 13th rev. ed.
Leipzig: K. Baedeker, 1927. xxxvi, 612p.,
plates, illus., maps, plans. 17cm.

BAEDEKER, Karl
The United States, with an excursion into Mexico:
handbook for travellers; by Karl Baedeker. 2nd
rev. ed. Leipsic: K. Baedeker; London: Dulau,
1899. c, 579p., fold. col. plates, maps, plans,
bibl. 17cm.

FORREST, Archibald S   and BAGGE, Henry
Switzerland, revisited. Griffiths, [1914].
92p., illus., maps. 22cm.

BAGLEY, Arthur I
Holiday rambles in North Wales. Skeffington,
[1920]. viii, 203p., plates (1 fold.), illus.
20cm.

BAGLEY, Arthur L
Holiday rambles in the English Lake District.
Skeffington, [ca 1925]. 210p., plates, illus.
19cm.

BAGLEY, Arthur L
Walks and scrambles in the Highlands.
Skeffington, 1914. vii, 204p., plates, illus.
20cm.

BAGSHAWE, Thomas Wyatt
Two men in the Antarctic: an expedition to
Graham Land 1920-1922; with a foreword by Frank
Debenham. Cambridge: University Press, 1939.
xxi, 292p., plates (1 fold.), illus., maps (on
lining   papers). 24cm.

BAILEY, E   B
Tectonic essays, mainly alpine. Oxford:
Clarendon Press, 1935. xii, 200p., fold.
plates, illus., maps. 26cm.

BAILEY, Frederick Marshman
Mission to Tashkent. Cape, 1946. 312p.,
plates, illus., map. 21cm.

BAILEY, Frederick Marshman
No passport to Tibet. Hart-Davis, 1957.
294p., plates, illus., maps. 23cm.

DUNSHEATH, Joyce and BAILLIE, Eleanor
Afghan quest: the story of their Abinger
Afghanistan Expedition 1960. Harrap, 1961.
236p., plates, illus., map. 22cm.

BAILLIE, G
Ski-ing simplified for beginners. Selwyn &
Blount, 1923. viii, 93p., plates, illus. 20cm.

BAILLIE, Marianne
First impressions on a tour upon the continent
in the summer of 1818, through parts of France,
Italy, Switzerland, the borders of Germany
and a part of French Flanders. Murray, 1819.
viii, 375p., plates, illus. 23cm.

BAILLIE-GROHMAN, William Adolphus
Camps in the Rockies, being a narrative of life
on the frontier, and sport in the Rocky
Mountains, with an account of the cattle
ranches of the West. New York: Scribner, 1882.
viii, 438p., 1 fold. plate, map. 20cm.

BAILLIE-GROHMAN, William Adolphus
Fifteen years' sport and life in the hunting
grounds of western America and British Columbia.
Cox, 1900. xii, 403p., plates, illus., maps
(fold. col. in pocket), bibl. 26cm.

BAILLIE-GROHMAN, William Adolphus
Gaddings with a primitive people, being a
series of sketches of alpine life and customs.
Remington, 1878. 2v. 19cm.

BAILLIE-GROHMAN, William Adolphus
The land in the mountains, being an account of
the past and present of Tyrol, its people and
its castles; with an introduction by Charles
Landis. Simpkin, Marshall, Hamilton, Kent,
1907. xxxi, 288p., plates (some col.), illus.,
maps. 23cm.

BAILLIE-GROHMAN, William Adolphus
Sport in art: an iconography of sport during
four hundred years from the beginning of the
fifteenth to the end of the eighteenth centuries.
Ballantyne, [1913]. xxiii, 422p., col. plates,
illus. 34cm.

BAILLIE-GROHMAN, William Adolphus
Sport in the Alps in the past and present: an
account of the chase of the chamois, red-deer,
bouquetin ... Black, 1896. xv, 356p., plates,
illus. 24cm.

BAILLIE-GROHMAN, William Adolphus
Tyrol; painted by E. Harrison Compton; described by W.A. Baillie-Grohman. Black, 1908.
x, 208p., col. plates, illus., map. 20cm.

BAILLIE-GROHMAN, William Adolphus
Tyrol and the Tyrolese: the people and the land
in their social, sporting, and mountaineering
aspects. Longmans, Green, 1876. xvi, 278p.,
plates, illus. 20cm.

- - 2nd ed. 1877.

BAILLY, Rosa
Fêtes de la terre. Paris: Éditions de la Forge,
1934-37. 3 v. 19cm.

BAILLY, Rosa
Pastorale de la Maladette. Paris: Éditions de
la Forge, 1939. ii, 172p. 19cm.

BAINBRIDGE, W
Alpine lyrics, [by W. Bainbridge]. Longman,
Brown, Green, 1854. vii, 308p. 18cm.

BAINES, Edward
A companion to the Lakes of Cumberland, Westmorland, and Lancashire, in a descriptive
account of a family tour ... Hurst, Chance,
1829. xii, 271, 48p. 20cm.

- - 3rd ed. Simpkin & Marshall, 1834.

BAINES, Jack
HONG KONG MOUNTAINEERING CLUB EXPEDITION TO THE
SNOW MOUNTAINS OF NEW GUINEA, 1972
[Report], narrative section ..., by Jack Baines.
Hong Kong: The Expedition, [1973]. 27p.,
illus., maps. 26cm.

BAIRNSFATHER, P   R
Sport and nature in the Himalayas; edited by
F.G. Aflalo. Harrison, 1914. xv, 137p.,
illus. 22cm.

BAKER, Ernest Albert
The British highlands with rope & rucksack.
H.F. & G. Witherby, 1933. 236p., plates, illus.,
bibl. 23cm.

BAKER, Ernest Albert
The Highlands with rope and rucksack. H.F. &
G. Witherby, 1923. 253p., plates, illus. 23cm.

BAKER, Ernest Albert
Moors, crags & caves of the High Peak and the
neighbourhood. Manchester, London: Heywood,
[1903]. 207p., plates, illus., maps. 23cm.

BAKER, Ernest Albert and BALCH, Herbert E
The netherworld of Mendip:explorations in the
great caverns of Somerset, Yorkshire, Derbyshire, and elsewhere. Clifton: J. Baker;
London: Simpkin, Marshall, Hamilton, Kent, 1907.
xii, 172p., plates, illus. 24cm.

BAKER, Ernest Albert and ROSS, Francis Edward
The voice of the mountains; edited by Ernest A.
Baker and Francis E. Ross. Routledge, [1905].
xxii, 294p. 17cm.

BAKER, George Percival
Mountaineering memories of the past. [The
Author], 1951. 62p., plates, illus. 23cm.

BAKER, Olaf
Shasta of the wolves; with illustrations by
Charles Livingston Bull. Harrap, 1921. 276p.,
plates, illus. 21cm.

BAKEWELL, R
Travels, comprising observations made during a
residence in the Tarentaise, and various parts
of the Grecian and Pennine Alps, and in
Switzerland and Auvergne, in ... 1820, 1821,
and 1822. Longman, Hurst, Rees, Orme, & Brown,
1823. 2 v., col. plates, illus. 24cm.

BALAVOINE, Hippolyte
Dans les Alpes et le Jura: souvenirs d'un
alpiniste. Paris: Fishbacher, 1911. 295p.
20cm.

BALCH, Edwin Swift
  Mount McKinley and mountain climbers' proofs.
  Philadelphia: Campion, 1914. 142p. 27cm.

BALCH, Edwin Swift
  Mountain exploration; read before the Geo-
  graphical Club, December 9, 1892. [Phila-
  delphia], 1893. 35p., plates, illus. 24cm.
  Offprint from Bulletin of the Geographical
  Club of Philadelphia, v. 1, no. 1.

BAKER, Ernest Albert and BALCH, Herbert E
  The netherworld of Mendip: explorations in the
  great caverns of Somerset, Yorkshire, Derbyshire, and elsewhere. Clifton: J. Baker;
  London: Simpkin, Marshall, Hamilton, Kent, 1907.
  xii, 172p., plates, illus. 24cm.

BALFOUR, John Hutton
  Account of a botanical excursion to Switzerland,
  with pupils, in August 1858. Edinburgh: Printed
  by Neill, 1859. 66p. 24cm.

BALL, Benjamin Lincoln
  Three days on the White Mountains, being the
  perilous adventure of Dr. B.L. Ball on Mount
  Washington. Boston: Lockwood, Brooks, 1877.
  72p. 19cm.

BALL, John
  Le Alpi; traduzione ... [from the Encyclopaedia
  Britannica]... di I. Cremona. Milano: Hoepli,
  1888. vi, 120p. 16cm. (Manuali Hoepli, 76)

BALL, John
  The alpine guide

  For separately published parts in this series
  see his

  The central Alps
  A guide to the eastern Alps
  [etc.]

BALL, John
  The central Alps, including the Bernese Oberland, and all Switzerland excepting the neighbourhood of Monte Rosa and the Great St. Bernard; with
  Lombardy, and the adjoining portion of Tyrol.
  Longman, Green, Longman, Roberts & Green, 1864.
  cxiii, 502p., fold. plates, illus., maps, bibl.
  18cm. (Alpine guide, pt. 2)

  - - New ed. 1876.

  - - New ed. 1882.

BALL, John
  The central Alps. Pt. 1. Including those portions
  of Switzerland to the north of the Rhone and the
  Rhine valleys. New ed.; reconstructed and revised
  on behalf of the Alpine Club under the general
  editorship of A.V. Valentine-Richards. Longmans,
  Green, 1907. xxviii, 326p., fold.col. plates,
  maps. 19cm. (Alpine guide, pt. 2)

BALL, John
  The central Alps. Pt. 2. Including those Alpine
  portions of Switzerland, Italy and Austria which
  lie S. & E. of the Rhone and Rhine, S. of the
  Arlberg, and W. of the Adige. New ed.; reconstructed and revised on behalf of the Alpine
  Club under the general editorship of George Broke.
  Longmans, Green, 1911. xix, 432p., fold. col.
  plates, maps. 19cm. (Alpine guide, pt. 2)

BALL, John
  [The central Alps]. Bernese Alps, including the
  Oberland. Longmans, Green, 1873. 144p., fold.
  plates, maps. 18cm. (Ball's alpine guides)

  - - New ed. 1875.

BALL, John
  [The central Alps]. East Switzerland, including
  the Engadine and Lombard Valleys. Longmans,
  Green, 1873. 347-489p., fold. plates, illus.,
  maps. 18cm. (Ball's alpine guides)

BALL, John
  [The central Alps]. North Switzerland, including the Righi, Zurich and Lucerne. Longmans,
  Green, 1873. 145-244p., fold. plates, maps.
  18cm. (Ball's alpine guides)

BALL, John
  [The central Alps]. The Pass of St. Gothard and
  the Italian lakes. Longmans, Green, 1873.
  245-346p., 1 fold. plate, maps. 18cm. (Ball's
  alpine guides)

BALL, John
  A guide to the eastern Alps. Longmans, Green,
  1868. xxiv, 639p., fold. plates, illus., maps.
  18cm. (Alpine guide, pt. 3)

  - - New ed. 1879.

BALL, John
  [A guide to the eastern Alps]. Central Tyrol,
  including the Gross Glockner. Longmans, Green,
  1873. 139-314p., fold. plates, illus., maps.
  18cm. (Ball's alpine guides)

BALL, John
  [A guide to the eastern Alps]. North Tyrol,
  Bavarian and Salzburg Alps. Longmans, Green,
  1873. 138p., 1 fold. plate, maps. 18cm.
  (Ball's alpine guides)

BALL, John
  [A guide to the eastern Alps]. South Tyrol and
  Venetian or Dolomite Alps. Longmans, Green,
  1873. 399-529p., 1 fold. plate, maps. 18cm.
  (Ball's alpine guides)

BALL, John
  [A guide to the eastern Alps]. Styrian, Carnic
  and Julian Alps. Longmans, Green, 1873.
  315-602p., 1 fold. plate, maps. 18cm. (Ball's
  alpine guides)

BALL, John
  A guide to the western Alps; with an article on
  the geology of the Alps by M.E. Desor. Longman,
  Green, Longman, Roberts & Green, 1863. 377p.,
  fold. col. plates, illus., maps. 18cm. (Alpine
  guide, pt. 1)

  - - New ed. 1870.

  - - New ed. 1877.

  Later ed. published in 1898 under title: The
  estern Alps.

BALL, John
  [A guide to the western Alps]. Pennine Alps,
  including Mont Blanc and Monte Rosa. Longmans,
  Green, 1873. 181-378p., fold. plates, maps.
  19cm. (Ball's alpine guides)

  - - New ed. 1878.

BALL, John
  [A guide to the western Alps]. South-western
  Alps, including Dauphiné and Piedmont from Nice
  to the Little St. Bernard. Longmans, Green,
  1873. 182p., fold. plates, illus, maps. 18cm.
  (Ball's alpine guides)

BALL, John
  Hints and notes practical and scientific for
  travellers in the Alps, being a revision of the
  general Introduction to the 'Alpine guide'.
  New ed. prepared on behalf of the Alpine Club
  by W.A.B. Coolidge. Longmans, Green, 1899.
  clxiv p., bibl. 19cm. (Alpine guide)

BALL, John
  Introduction to 'The Alpine guide'. New ed.
  Longmans, Green, 1873. cxxx p., bibl. 18cm.
  New ed. published in 1899 under title: Hints
  and notes practical and scientific for travellers
  in the Alps...

HOOKER, Sir Joseph Dalton and BALL, John
Journal of a tour in Marocco and the Great
Atlas; with an appendix including A sketch of
the geology of Marocco... Macmillan, 1878. xvi,
499p., plates (some fold.), illus., map. 23cm.

BALL, John
On the cause of the motion of glaciers. [London],
1871. 7p. 22cm.
Offprint from Philosophical Magazine, Feb. 1871.

BALL, John
On the formation of alpine lakes. [London],
1863. 14p., illus. 23cm.
Offprint from Philosophical Magazine, Dec.
1863 (Suppl.).

BALL, John
ALPINE CLUB
Peaks, passes and glaciers: a series of excur-
sions by members of the Alpine Club; edited by
John Ball. Longman, Brown, Green, Longmans, &
Roberts, 1859. xvi, 516p., plates (some fold.,
some col.), illus, maps. 22cm.

- - 2nd ed. 1859.

- - 4th ed. 1859.

- - 5th ed. 1860.

BALL, John
ALPINE CLUB
[Peaks, passes and glaciers]. Les grimpeurs des
Alpes = Peaks, passes and glacies [sic]; traduit
par El. Dufour. Paris: M. Lévy, 1862. 347p.
19cm.
Translation of 1st series; edited by John Ball.

- - Another ed. 1886.

BALL, John
The western Alps. New ed.; reconstructed and
revised on behalf of the Alpine Club by W.A.B.
Coolidge. Longmans, Green, 1898. li, 612p.,
fold. col. plates, illus., maps. 19cm. (Alpine
guide, pt. 1)
Previous eds. published under title: A guide to
the western Alps.

BALL, Sir Robert S
The cause of an ice age. Kegan Paul, Trench,
Trübner, 1891. xv, 180p., plates, illus. 20cm,
(Modern science)

BALLANTYNE, R M
Rivers of ice; a tale illustrative of alpine adventure and glacier action. Nisbet, 1875. vii,
430p., plates, illus. 18cm.

BALLANTYNE, R M
The rover of the Andes: a tale of adventure in
South America. Nisbet, 1885. viii, 431p.,
plates, illus. 20cm.

BALLANTYNE, R M
The world of ice. Nelson, [1915?]. 232p., col.
plates, illus. 20cm.

BALLIANO, Adolfo and AFFENTRANGER, Irene
La strada è questa... Bologna: Alfa, 1957.
197p., plates, illus. 21cm. (Semprevivi, 2)

BALLORE, Fernand, comte de Montessus de
See
MONTESSUS DE BALLORE, Fernand, comte de

BALMAT, Jacques
OXLEY, T Louis
Jacques Balmat; or, The first ascent of Mont
Blanc: a true story. Kerby & Endean, 1881.
38p. 19cm.

BALMAT, Jacques
ROCHAT-CENISE, Charles
Jacques Balmat du Mont-Blanc. Paris: E. Malfère,
1929. 189p. 19cm. (Bibliothèque du hérisson)

BALTARD, Louis Pierre
Journal descriptif en croquis de vues pittoresques faits dans un voyage en Savoye du 10 au
21 août 1837. Lyon: Imprimerie de H. Bruner,
[1837?]. 45p., illus. 36cm.

BALTHASAR, Joseph Anton Felix von
Historische, topographische und oekonomische
Merkwürdigkeit des Kantons Luzern, seinen
Mitbürgern gewidmet, von von Balthasar. Luzern:
J. Salzmann, 1785-89. 3 v. 17cm.

BALTZER, A
Das Berneroberland und Nachbargebiete: ein
geologischer Führer. Berlin: Borntraeger,
1906. xvi, 348p., fold. plates (1 col.),
illus., maps, bibl. 16cm. (Sammlung geologischer Führer, 11)

BALTZER, A
Centralgebiet der Schweiz ...; bearb. von A.
Baltzer, F.J. Kaufmann und C. Moesch. Bern:
Schmid, Francke, 1886-94. 4 v. in 6, plates
(some fold., some col.), illus. 33cm.
(Beiträge zur geologischen Karte der Schweiz,
Lfg.24)
Library lacks v. 2.

BALTZER, A
Der Glärnisch, ein Problem alpinen Gebirgs-
baues: geologische Monographie über einen
Gebirgsstock der östschweizerischen Kalkalpen.
Zürich: Schmidt, 1873. 100p., plates (some
fold., some col.), illus., map. 31cm.

BALTZER, A
Der mechanische Contact von Gneiss und Kalk im
Berner-Oberland. Bern: J. Dalp, 1880. xiv,
255p. 32cm. (Beiträge zur geologischen Karte
der Schweiz, Lfg. 20)

- - Atlas

BANBERGER, E
Sing' ma oans! Alpenliederbuch; hrsg. von E.
Banberger, M. Förderrenther und A. Geiftbeck.
Passau: Rudolf, 1891. vii, 144p. 17cm.

- - 5. Aufl. Passau: Kleiter, 1901.

- - 6. Aufl. [19--].

BANCK, Otto
Alpenbilder: Schilderungen aus Natur und Leben
in der Alpenwelt. Leipzig: Schlicke, 1863.
2 v. 19cm.

- - 2. verm. Aufl. 1869.

BANCROFT, Steve
Recent developments. [Manchester]: The Peak
Committee of the British Mountaineering Council,
1977. 87p., illus. 17cm. (Rock climbs in the
Peak)

BAND, George
Road to Rakaposhi. Hodder & Stoughton, 1955.
192p., plates, illus., maps. 21cm.

BANKS, Mike
Commando climber; foreword by Sir John Hunt ...;
with a frontispiece and drawings in the text by
Lilias Stirling. Dent, 1955. xiii, 240p.,
plates, illus. 22cm.

BANKS, Mike
Greenland. Newton Abbot: David & Charles, 1975.
208p., illus., maps, bibl. 23cm.

BANKS, Mike
High Arctic: the story of the British North
Greenland Expedition; with four chapters by
Angus Erskine; drawings by Lilias Stirling.
Dent, 1957. xii, 276p., plates (1 col.), illus.,
maps. 22cm.

BANKS, Mike
Mountaineering for beginners; with drawings by
Toby Buchan. Seeley, Service, 1977. 92p.,
illus. 23cm.

BANKS, Mike
Rakaposhi; foreword by Sir Gerald Templer.
Secker & Warburg, 1959. 238p., plates (1 col.),
illus., maps. 23cm.

BANKS, Mike
Shockly-Ghastly and others.
(In Blackwood's Magazine, no. 1893, v. 314,
July, 1973, p. 60-68)

BANKS, Mike
Snow commando; illustrated by R. Collomb.
Burke, 1961. 192p., plates, illus. 21cm.

BANNER, H   I   and CREW, Peter
Clogwyn Du'r Arddu; with a geological note by
N.J. Soper; a natural history note by Evan
Roberts; and diagrams by R.B. Evans. Stockport:
Climbers' Club, 1963. ix, 103p., illus., maps
(on lining papers). 16cm. (Climbers' Club
guides to Wales, 6)

BANSE, Ewald
Die Atlasländer (Orient I): eine Länderkunde.
Leipzig: Teubner, 1910. iv, 112p. 1 fold. plate,
illus, maps, bibl. 19cm. (Aus Natur und
Geisteswelt, Bd. 277)

BARA, Jakob
Alpen im Feuer mit den Kärntner Achterjägern an
der italienischen Front. Klagenfurt: A.
Kollitsch, [1918]. 32p. 20cm.

BARBER, John B   and ATKINSON, George
Lakeland passes, including some charming walks
through the District, taken and described by
John B. Barber and George Atkinson. 2nd ed.
Ulverston: Atkinson, 1928. 69p., plates, illus.,
map. 19cm.

BARBEY, Frédéric
La route du Simplon; illustration de Fréd.
Boissonnas. Genève: Atar, 1906. 157p., illus.,
bibl. 34cm.

BARBIER, Andrew
LEICESTER POLYTECHNIC STUDENTS GREENLAND
EXPEDITION, 1972
Kûgssuatsiaq, Søndre Sermilik, Southern Green-
land: [the official report]; edited by Andrew
Barbier. Leicester: City of Leicester Poly-
technic, 1973. v, 159p., plates, illus., maps,
bibl. 30cm.

ZARN, Adolf and BARBLAN, Peter
Der Skifahrer: Ski-Turnen und Ski Fahrtechnik;
mit einem Kapital ... von J.B. Masuger; einem
Vorwort von Sonderegger. Zurich: Bopp, 1920.
246p., illus. 22cm.

ZARN, Adolf and BARBLAN, Peter
[Der Skifahrer]. L'art du ski: gymnastique et
technique du ski; traduction par Felix
Krahnstoever. Zurich: Bopp, 1922. 258p., illus.
21cm.

BARCLAY, Edgar
Mountain life in Algeria; with illustrations by
the author. Kegan Paul, Trench, 1882. xviii,
119p., plates, illus. 26cm.

BARCROFT, Joseph
PERU HIGH-ALTITUDE COMMITTEE
Observations upon the effect of high altitude on
the physiological processes of the human body,
carried out in the Peruvian Andes, chiefly at
Cerro de Pasco: report to the Peru High-Altitude
Committee, 1922, by J. Barcroft [and others].
[London], 1923. 351-480p., plates, illus. 31cm.
Offprint from Philosophical Transactions of the
Royal Society of London, ser. B, v. 211.

BARCROFT, Joseph
The respiratory function of the blood. Pt. 1.
Lessons from high altitudes. [2nd ed.].
Cambridge: University Press, 1925. xi, 207p.,
illus., map. 26cm.

BARETTI, Martino
Aperçu géologique sur la chaîne du Mont Blanc en
rapport avec le trajet probable d'un tunnel pour
une nouvelle ligne de chemin de fer. Turin:
J. Candeletti, 1881. 38p., 3 fold. col. plates,
illus., map. 26cm.

BARETTI, Martino
Geologia della Provincia di Torino. Torino:
Casanova, 1893. 733p. 25cm.

BARETTI, Martino
I ghiacciai antichi e moderni. Torino: [M.
Baretti], 1866. 87p. 28cm.

BARETTI, Martino
Il ghiacciaio del Miage: versante italiano del
gruppo del Monte Bianco (Alpi pennine). Torino,
1880. 37p., 2 col. plates, illus. 31cm.
Offprint from Memorie della Reale Accademia
delle Scienze di Torino, ser. 2, t. 32.

BARETTI, Martino
Relazione sulle condizioni geologiche del
versante destro della Valle della Dora Riparia
tra Chiomonte e Salbertrand. Torino: Camilla
& Bertolero, 1881. 19p., fold. col. plates,
illus. 25cm.

BARETTI, Martino
Studi geologici sul Gruppo del Gran Paradiso,
Roma: L'Accademia, 1877. 122p., 7 plates (some
fold., some col.), illus., maps. 30cm. (Reale
Accademia dei Lincei. Memorie della Classe di
Scienze fisiche ..., ser. 3a, v. 1)

BARETTI, Martino
Studi geologici sulle Alpi Graie settentrionali:
memoria. Roma: L'Accademia, 1879. 104p., 8 col.
plates, illus., maps. 30cm. (Reale Accademia
dei Lincei. Memorie della Classe di Scienze
fisiche ..., ser. 3a, v. 3)

BARETTI, Martino
Sui rilevamenti geologici fatti nelle Alpi
piemontesi durante la compagna 1877: nota. Roma:
L'Accademia, 1878. 12p., 1 col. plate, illus.
30cm. (Reale Accademia dei Lincei. Memorie
della Classe di Scienze fisiche ..., ser. 3a,
v. 2)

BARFORD, John Edward Quintus
Climbing in Britain; edited by J.E.Q. Barford.
Harmondsworth: Penguin, 1946. 160p., plates,
illus., bibl. 18cm. (Pelican books)

EDWARDS, John Menlove and BARFORD, John Edward
Quintus
Clogwyn du'r Arddu. Manchester, 1942. 24p.,
plates, illus., bibl. 22cm.
Offprint from Climbers' Club Journal, 1942.

BARING-GOULD, Sabine
A book of the Cevennes. J. Long, 1907. ix,
308p., plates (some col.), illus., map. 20cm.

BARING-GOULD, Sabine
A book of the Pyrenees. Methuen, 1907. 309p.,
plates, illus., map. 20cm.

BARING-GOULD, Sabine
Iceland: its scenes and sagas. Smith, Elder,
1863. xlviii, plates (1 fold., some col.),
illus, map, bibl. 28cm.

BARKER, Clive S
Bibliography of exploration, mountaineering,
travel, history and nomenclature of the Gilgit-
Hunza River watershed, Haramosh Range and Basha
River watershed in the eastern Hindu-Kush and
western Karakoram. Wellington: The Author,
1965-75. 3 pts. 34cm.
List of periodical articles.
Typescript.

BARKER, Ralph
The last blue mountain; with a foreword by Sir
John Hunt. Chatto & Windus, 1959. 212p.,
plates, illus., maps. 23cm.

- - Another issue. Diadem Books, 1979.

BARKER, Ralph
One man's jungle: a biography of F. Spencer
Chapman, D.S.O. Chatto & Windus, 1975. x,
374p., plates, illus. 23cm.

BARNARD, George
The continental drawing book for the use of
advanced pupils, being views in Switzerland,
the Alps and Italian lakes, drawn from nature
and on stone by George Barnard. Ackermann,
1837. [13 leaves] of illus. 28 x 38cm.

BARNARD, George
Drawing from nature: a series of progressive
instructions in sketching ... with examples
from Switzerland and the Pyrenees... Longmans,
Green, Reader & Dyer, 1865. viii, 348p.,
col. plates, illus. 28cm.

- - New ed. Routledge, 1877.

BARNARD, George
Switzerland: scenes and incidents of travel in
the Bernese Oberland &c. &c., drawn from nature
and on stone by George Barnard. McLean, [1843].
1 v. of illus. 54cm.

BARNARD, George
The theory and practice of landscape painting
in watercolours. New ed. Routledge, 1871.
286p., col. plates, illus. 28cm.

BARNARD, M   R
Sketches of life, scenery, and sport in Norway.
H. Cox, 1871. viii, 312p. 21cm.

BARNARD, M   R
Sport in Norway, and where to find it; together
with ... a list of the Alpine flora of the Dovre
Fjeld and of Norwegian ferns, &c. Chapman &
Hall, 1864. xvi, 334p. 21cm.

BARNEBY, T   P
European alpine flowers in colour; with a foreword by H. Gilbert-Carter. Nelson, 1967. 239p.,
illus. (chiefly col.), maps. 27cm.

BARNES, Malcolm
TENZING NORGAY
After Everest: an autobiography, by Tenzing
Norgay Sherpa; as told to Malcolm Barnes. Allen
& Unwin, 1977. 184p., plates (some col.), illus.,
map. 23cm.

The Barnet book of photography: a collection of
practical articles by Capt. W. de W. Abney [and
others]. 3rd ed. Barnet (Herts.): Elliott,
1898. 287p., plates, illus. 22cm.

BARNS, T   Alexander
The wonderland of the eastern Congo: the region
of snow-crowned volcanoes, the Pygmies, the giant
gorilla and the okapi; introduction by Sir H.H.
Johnston. Putnam, 1922. xxxv, 288p., plates
(1 fold.), illus., map. 27cm.

BARON, A
Pérégrinations en Suisse, en Savoie et sur les
bords du Rhin. 2e éd. Limoges: E. Ardant,
[1867]. 2 v. in 1, plates, illus. 28cm.

BARON, Joseph
All about the English Lakes: a cyclopedia of
places, persons, myths and happenings. Kendal:
Atkinson & Pollitt, 1925. 194p., plates, illus.
22cm.
Reprinted from the Westmorland Gazette.

BARRAUD, Charles D
New Zealand, graphic and descriptive; the illus-
trations by C.D. Barraud; edited by W.T.L.
Travers. Sampson Low, Marston, Searle &
Rivington, 1877. 40p., plates, illus., map.
58cm.

BARRETT, Robert Le Moyne and BARRETT, Katharine
The Himalayan letters of Gipsy Davy and Lady Ba
written on pilgrimage to the high quiet places
among the simple people of an old folk tale.
Cambridge: Heffer, 1927. xii, 280p., fold.
plates, illus. 26cm.

BARROW, Sir John, 1764-1848
A chronological history of voyages into the
Arctic regions; undertaken chiefly for the
purpose of discovering a north-east, north-west,
or polar passage... Murray, 1818. 379, 48p.,
1 fold. plate, illus., map. 22cm.

BARROW, Sir John, 1764-1848
Voyages of discovery and research within the
Arctic regions from the year 1818 to the present
time... Murray, 1846. xiv, 530p., plates (1
fold.), maps, port. 24cm.

BARROW, John, 1808-1898
Excursions in the north of Europe, through parts
of Russia, Finland, Sweden, Denmark, and Norway,
in the years 1830 & 1833. Murray, 1834. viii,
380p., plates (2 fold.), illus., maps. 20cm.

- - New ed. 1835.

BARROW, John, 1808-1898
Expeditions on the glaciers: including an ascent
of Mont Blanc, Monte Rosa, Col du Géant, and
Mont Buet, by a private of the Thirty-Eighth
Artists', and a member of the Alpine Club [i.e.
John Barrow]. Spon, 1864. 122p, plates, illus.
20cm.

BARROW, John, 1808-1898
Mountain ascents in Westmorland and Cumberland.
Sampson Low, Marston, Searle & Rivington, 1886.
viii, 208p., plates, illus., map. 20cm.

- - Rev. and enl. ed. 1888.

BARROW, John, 1808-1898
Tour in Austrian Lombardy, the northern Tyrol,
and Bavaria, in 1840. Murray, 1841. xv, 375p.,
illus. 21cm.

BARROW, John, 1808-1898
Tour on the Continent, by rail and road, in the
summer of 1852, through northern Germany, Austria,
Tyrol, Austrian Lombardy ... Longman, Brown,
Green, & Longmans, 1853. ix, 126p., map. 19cm.
(Traveller's library, 44)

BARRY, Martin
Ascent to the summit of Mont Blanc, 16th - 18th
of 9th Month (Septr), 1834. Earlham: The Author,
[1835]. 40p., 2 plates, illus. 24cm.

- - Another ed. Edinburgh: Blackwood, 1836.

BARSIS, Max
Bottoms up: an unreliable handbook for skiers.
Brattleboro (Vermont): Daye, 1939. [92p.]
(chiefly illus.). 25cm.

BARSIS, Max
Ski whiz! Bottoms up, old and new. New York:
Daye, [1945]. [128p.] (chiefly illus.). 25cm.

BARTH, Hanns
Gröden und seine Berge: ein Buch der Erinnerung
und Dankbarkeit. München: Bruckmann, 1927.
131p., illus. 24cm.

BARTH, Hanns
PURTSCHELLER, Ludwig and HESS, Heinrich
Der Hochtourist in den Ostalpen. 5. Aufl.
begründet von Ludwig Purtscheller und Heinrich
Hess; neu hrsg... von Hanns Barth. Leipzig:
Bibliographisches Institut, 1925-30. 8 v.,
plates, illus., maps. 16cm.

BARTH, Hanns
Nord-Tirol bis zum Brenner und Vorarlberg.
29. Aufl. bearb. von Hanns Barth. Berlin: A.
Goldschmidt, 1922. 163p., 8 maps. 17cm.
(Griebens Reiseführer, 67)

BARTH, Hanns
Tirol und Vorarlberg: praktischer Reiseführer.
27. Aufl. new bearb. von Hanns Barth. Berlin:
A. Goldschmidt, 1911-12. 243p., 11 maps. 17cm.
(Griebens Reiseführer, 67)

BARTH, Hanns
Was fels und Firn mir zugeraunt: Berg-, Zeit-,
und Liebes-Leider eines Alpinisten. München:
J. Lindauer, 1926. 95p. 20cm.

BARTH, Hermann von
Aus den nördlichen Kalkalpen: Ersteigungen und
Erlebnisse in den Gebirgen Berchtesgadens, des
Algäu, des Innthales, des Isar Quellengebietes
und des Wetterstein. Gera: Amthor, 1874. 637p.,
plates (some fold.), illus., maps. 23cm.

BARTH, Hermann von
Aus den nördlichen Kalkalpen: Ersteigungen und
Erlebnisse; mit einer Einleitung und Anmerkungen
hrsg. von R.H. Francé. Leipzig: Theod. Thomas,
[1910]. 2 v. 16cm. (Natur-Bibliothek, Nr.
20/21, 22)

BARTH, Hermann von
Einsame Bergfahrten; [Nachwort von Hans Mertel].
München: A. Langen, [1925]. 230p. 20cm.
(Bücher der Bildung, Bd. 21)

BARTH, Hermann von
Hermann von Barth (eine Auswahl); zusammengestellt vov Anton Ziegler. München, D.u.Ö.A.,
1926. 80p., plates, illus. 20cm.
(Erschliesser der Berge, Bd. 1)

BARTH, L   and PFAUNDLER, L
Die Stubaier Gebirgsgruppe, hypsometrisch und
orografisch bearb. und mit Unterstützung der
kaiserlichen Akademie der Wissenschaften.
Innsbruck: Wagner, 1865. 147p., plates (some
fold., 1 col.), illus, map. 23cm.

BARTHOLDY, Felix Mendelssohn
See
MENDELSSOHN, Felix

BARTLETT, W   H
BEATTIE, William
Switzerland; illustrated in a series of views
taken expressly for this work by W.H. Bartlett.
G. Virtue, 1836. 2 v., plates, illus., map.
28cm.

BARTLETT, W   H
BEATTIE, William
[Switzerland]. La Suisse pittoresque; ornée de
vues dessinées spécialement pour cet ouvrage par
W.H. Bartlett; accompagnée d'un texte par William
Beattie; traduit de l'anglais par L. de Bauclas.
G. Virtue, 1836. 2 v., plates, illus., map.
29cm.

BARTLETT, W   H
BEATTIE, William
[Switzerland]. Die Schweiz nach William Beattie;
mit Stahlstichen versehen nach Original Zeichnungen von W.H. Bartlett ausgeführt... Berlin:
Trowitzsch, [1840]. 2 v., plates, illus., map.
28cm.

BARTLETT, W   H
LA FARINA, Giuseppe
[Switzerland]. La Svizzera storica ed artistica,
descritta da Giuseppe La Farina; ed. illustrata
da una serie di ... incisioni in acciaio [da
W.H. Bartlett]. Firenze: L. Bardi, 1842-43.
2 v., plates, illus. 31cm.
Based on Beattie, William. Switzerland. 1836.

BARTLETT, W   H
KAMPEN, N   G   van
[Switzerland]. Zwitserland en de Alpen van
Savoije; naar afbeeldingen op de plaats zelve
geteekend, [by W.H. Bartlett]; in tafereelen be-
schreven door N.G. van Kampen. Amsterdam: G.J.A.
Beijerinck, [1837]. 2 v. in 1, plates, illus.
28cm.
Based on Beattie, William. Switzerland. 1836.

BARTLETT, W   H
BEATTIE, William
The Waldenses; or, Protestant valleys of Piedmont,
Dauphiny, and the Ban de la Roche; illustrated by
W.H. Bartlett and W. Brockedon. G. Virtue, 1838.
216p., plates (1 fold.), illus., map. 28cm.

BARTLETT, W   H
BEATTIE, William
[The Waldenses ...]. Les vallées vaudoises
pittoresques; ou, vallées protestantes du Piémont, du Dauphiné, et du Ban de la Roche; orné de
gravures par W.H. Bartlett et par W. Brockedon;
traduit par L. de Bauclas. G. Virtue, 1838.
216p., plates (1 fold.), illus., map. 29cm.

BARTOL, C   A
Pictures of Europe, framed in ideas. 2nd ed.
Boston: Crosby, Nichols, 1856. 407p. 21cm.
Also contains: Talbot, I.T. The ascent of Mont
Blanc.

BARTROPP, John
Barbarian: a tale of the Roman wall. Chambers,
1933. 320p. 20cm.

BARY, Alice de
Rochers: poèmes. Paris: Baconnière, 1938.
84p. 20cm.

BASSNETT, S   A
British Army West Greenland Expedition 1971:
final scientific report, [by] S.A. Bassnett and
others. [Donnington?]: The Expedition, 1972.
22p., illus. 30cm.

BASTERFIELD, George
Crags for climbing in and around Great Langdale,
by George Basterfield; and Rock climbing in
Buttermere, by A.R. Thomson. Barrow-in-Furness:
Fell & Rock Climbing Club, [1926]. 68p., plates
(1 fold.), illus., map. 21cm. (Climbers'
guides, [1st ser.], 5)

BASTERFIELD, George
Songs of a cragsman: twelve songs of the hills;
words and music by G. Basterfield; music editor
Oliver Knapton. Barrow-in-Furness: Geo.
Basterfield, 1935. 27p., music. 26cm.

BATE, Dorothea M   A
TREVOR-BATTYE, Aubyn
Camping in Crete, with notes upon the animal and
plant life of the island; including a description
of certain caves and their ancient deposits, by
Dorothea M.A. Bate. Witherby, 1913. xxi, 308p.,
plates, illus., map (fold). 23cm.

BATEMAN, Josiah
The life of the Rev. Henry Venn Elliott; with a
portrait and an appendix containing a short
sketch of the life of the Rev. Julius Elliott.
3rd ed. Macmillan, 1872. xv, 347p. 20cm.

BATENHAM, George
The traveller's companion in an excursion from
Chester through North Wales. Chester: Printed
for G. Batenham by R. Evans, [1827]. 100p.,
plates, illus., map. 17cm.

BATES, E   S
Touring in 1600: a study in the development of
travel as a means of education. Constable, 1911.
xiv, 418p., plates, illus. 23cm.

BATES, Henry Walter
Illustrated travels: a record of discovery,
geography, and adventure; edited by H.W. Bates.
Cassell, Petter & Galpin, [1870?]. viii, 376p.,
illus., maps. 33cm.

BATES, Henry Walter
The naturalist on the River Amazons: a record of
adventures, habits of animals, sketches of
Brazilian and Indian life, and aspects of nature
under the Equator, during eleven years of travel.
2nd ed. Murray, 1864. xii, 466p., 1 fold.
plate, illus., map. 21cm.

BATES, Robert Hicks
AMERICAN KARAKORAM EXPEDITION, 1938
Five miles high: the story of an attack on the
second highest mountain in the world, by the
members of the first American Karakoram Expedition; [edited by] Robert H. Bates. New York:
Dodd, Mead, 1939. xiii, 381p., plates (1 fold.),
illus., maps (on lining papers). 23cm.

- - Another issue. Hale, 1940.

HOUSTON, Charles Sneed and BATES, Robert Hicks
K2: the savage mountain. Collins, 1955. 192p.,
plates, illus., maps. 23cm.

- - Another issue. Diadem Books, 1979.

HOUSTON, Charles Sneed and BATES, Robert Hicks
[K2: the savage mountain]. K2: montagne sans
pitié, par Charles S. Houston, Robert H. Bates
et les membres de la troisième expédition
américaine au Karakorum; traduit par J. et F.
Germain. Paris: Arthaud, 1954. 234p., plates,
illus., map. 22cm.

BATES, Robert Hicks
HOUSTON, Charles Sneed
K2, 8611m: [troisième expédition américaine au
Karakorum], [par] Charles S. Houston, Robert H.
Bates, George I. Bell. Paris: Arthaud, 1954.
100p., 1 fold. plate, illus. (some col.), map.
26cm.

BATSÈRE, B
Excursion dans les Hautes-Pyrénées: souvenirs
historiques, rêveries. 2e éd. Tarbes:
Telmon, 1858. 145p., plates (some col.), illus.
20cm.

BATTAGEL, Arthur
Pyrenees east: a guide to the mountains for
walkers and climbers. Goring, Reading:
Gastons-West Col, 1975. 144p., illus., maps,
bibl. 17cm.

BATTAGEL, Arthur
Pyrenees west: a guide to the mountains for
walkers and climbers. Goring, Reading:
Gastons-West Col, 1975. 136p., illus., maps,
bibl. 17cm.

BATTISTI, Cesare
Guida di Mezolombardo e dintorni: il distretto
di Mezolombardo, da Mezolombardo a Campiglio,
Peio, Rabbi, Mendola, il gruppo de Brenta.
Trento: Società d'Abbellimento di Mezolombardo,
1905. 138p., plates, illus. 17cm.

BATTISTI, Cesare
Il Trentino: cenni geografici, storici, economici;
con un'appendice su l'Alto Adige. Novara:
Istituto Geografico de Agostini, 1915. 54p.,
fold. col. plates, illus., maps. 25cm.

- - 2a ed. 1917.

BATTY, Elizabeth Frances
Italian scenery from drawings made in 1817, by
Miss Batty; [descriptions written by a friend of
the publishers]. Rodwell & Martin, 1820. 197p.,
plates, illus. 27cm.

BATTY, Robert
Welsh scenery, from drawings. Murray, 1823.
1 v. of illus. 29cm.

BATTYE, Aubyn Trevor-
See
TREVOR-BATTYE, Aubyn

BAUD-BOVY, Daniel
À travers les Alpes: [de Brigue à l'Eggishorn et
au glacier d'Aletsch]. Neuchatel: Delachaux &
Niestlé, 1899. xi, 106p., plates, illus. 33cm.

BAUD-BOVY, Daniel
[À travers les Alpes ...]. Wanderungen in den
Alpen: von Brieg auf das Eggischhorn, den
Aletschgletscher und Umgebung ... Basel: Georg,
1899. xi, 106p., plates, illus. 34cm.

BAUD-BOVY, Daniel
La Dent du Midi, Champéry et le Val d'Illiez;
avec la collaboration de H.-F. Montagnier ...;
illustrations d'après les photographies de Fréd.
Boissonnas. Genève: Art Boissonnas, 1923.
173p., plates, illus. 25cm.

BAUD-BOVY, Daniel
La Meije et les Écrins; ouvrage illustré par
Ernest Hareux. Grenoble: Gratier & Rey, [1907].
119p., col. illus. 34cm.

BAUD-BOVY, Daniel
Le Mont-Blanc de près et de loin; illustrations
de Lacombe & Arlaud. Grenoble: Gratier, Rey,
[1903]. 137p., plates, illus., bibl. 34cm.

BAUD-BOVY, Daniel
L'Oberland bernois. Genève: Jeheber, 1926.
180p., plates (1 fold. col.), illus., map, bibl.
25cm. (Collection alpina)

BAUD-BOVY, Daniel
Peasant art in Switzerland; translated by Arthur
Palliser. "The Studio", 1924. xxiv, 76p.,
plates (some col.), illus., bibl. 30cm.

BAUDINO, Carlo
Manuale popolare dell'alpinista. Roma: Morpurgo,
1931. iv, 124p., illus. 17cm. (Biblioteca
dello sport, 3)

BAUER, J   P
Nomina alpium. 1. Alpes valaisanne ouest ...
Alpes valaisannes est ... Massif du Mont Blanc
... Préalpes franco-suisses... Renens: Bauer,
1977. 179p., illus. 21cm.

BAUER, Juliette
Lives of the brothers Humboldt, Alexander and
William; translated and arranged from the German
of Klencke & Schlesier by Juliette Bauer. Ingram,
Cooke, 1852. vii, 431p., 2 plates, ports. 20cm.

BAUER, Paul
Auf Kundfahrt im Himalaja: Siniolchu und Nanga
Parbat - Tat und Schicksal deutscher Bergsteiger;
hrsg. von Paul Bauer. München: Knorr & Hirth,
1937. 170p., plates, illus., maps. 29cm.

BAUER, Paul
[Auf Kundfahrt im Himalaja ...]. Himalayan
quest: the German expeditions to Siniolchum and
Nanga Parbat; edited by Paul Bauer; translated...
by E.G. Hall. Nicholson and Watson, 1938.
150p., plates, illus., maps. 26cm.

BAUER, Paul
Im Kampf um den Himalaja: der erste deutsche
Angriff auf den Kangchendzönga 1929. München:
Knorr & Hirth, 1931. 174p., plates (some fold.,
1 col.), illus., maps, bibl. 24cm.

BAUER, Paul
[Im Kampf um den Himalaja ...]. Himalayan
campaign: The German attack on Kangchenjunga,
the second [sic] highest mountain in the world;
translated by Sumner Austin. Oxford: Blackwell,
1937. 174p., plates, illus., maps. 24cm.
(Blackwell's mountaineering library)
Translation of the Author's Im Kampf um den
Himalaja and um den Kantsch.

BAUER, Paul
[Kampf um den Himalaja]. Kanchenjunga challenge;
foreword by Sir John Hunt. Kimber, 1955. 202p.,
plates, illus., maps (on lining papers). 24cm.

BAUER, Paul
Das Ringen um den Nanga Parbat, 1856-1953:
hundert Jahre bergsteigerischer Geschichte.
München: Süddeutscher Verlag, 1955. 238p.,
plates (2 fold.), illus., maps. 25cm.

BAUER, Paul
[Das Ringen um den Nanga Parbat ...]. The siege
of Nanga Parbat, 1856-1953; translated from the
German by R.W. Rickmers; with a preface by Sir
John Hunt. Hart-Davis, 1956. 211p., plates,
illus., maps. 23cm.

BAUER, Paul
Um den Kantsch: der zweite deutsche Angriff auf
den Kangchendzönga, 1931. München: Knorr &
Hirth, 1933. 192p., plates (1 fold. col.),
illus., maps. 25cm.

BAUER, Walther
ROTHPLETZ, August
Alpine Majestäten und ihr Gefolge: die Gebirgs-
welt der Erde in Bildern ..., Ansichten ... mit
einleitendem Text ... von A. Rothpletz, [Ernest
Platz - Walther Bauer]. München: Vereinigte
Kunstanstalten, 1901-04. 4 v., (chiefly illus.,
maps). 46cm.

BAUGHAN, Blanche Edith
Glimpses of New Zealand scenery. Auckland,
London: Whitcombe & Tombs, [ca 1912]. 323p.,
illus., map. 19cm.

BAULACRE, Léonard
Oeuvres historiques et littéraires de Léonard
Baulacre ...; recueillies et mises en ordre par
Édouard Mallet. Genève: Julien, 1857. 2v. in 1,
plates, illus. 23cm.

BAUM, Vicki
Marion alive. Joseph, 1943. 452p. 21cm.

BAUMANN, F
La Suisse illustrée; [illustrations par F.
Baumann]. Genève: F. Margueron, [1856?]. 1 v.
(chiefly col. illus.). 16 x 23cm.

BAUMBACH, Rudolf
Reise- und Wanderlieder. Stuttgart: Cotta, 1914.
91p. 17cm.

BAUMBACH, Rudolf
Schildereien aus dem Alpenlande; ... Lichtdruck-
bilder nach Gemälden von Carl und Ernst Heyn;
Gedichte von Rudolf Baumbach; Randzeichnungen von
Johann Stauffacher. Leipzig: A.G. Liebeskind,
1882. [84p.], illus. 49cm.

BAUME, Louis Charles
Sivalaya: the 8000-metre peaks of the Himalaya:
a chronicle and bibliography of exploration.
Goring, Reading: Gaston-West Col, 1978. 316p.,
illus., maps, bibl. 24cm.

BAUMEISTER, Georg
Das Bauernhaus des Walgaues und der walserischen
Bergtäler Vorarlbergs einschliesslich des
Montavon: Beiträge zur Hausforschung in
alemannische-romanischem Grenzgebiet. München:
A. Seyfried, 1913. 209p., plates (some col.),
illus., map, plans, bibl. 27cm.

BAUMEISTER, Hans
Jugend in Fels und Eis: ein Ehrenmal gewidmet
dem Helden vom Matterhorn: Toni Schmid von seinen
Kamaraden; bearb. von Hans Baumeister... München:
Alpenkränzchen Berggeist, 1934. 293p., 52
plates, illus. 25cm.

- - 3. Aufl. [ca 1940].

BAUMEISTER, Hans
Menschen im Hochgebirge: Festgabe für Hans Pfann
zum 60 Geburtstage 4. August 1933; bearb. von
Hans Baumeister; hrsg. von der Sektion Bayerland
des Deutschen und Österreichischen Alpenvereins.
München: Alpenvereinsektion Bayerland, 1933.
253p., plates, illus., ports. 25cm.

BAUMGARTNER, Heinrich
Die Gefahren des Bergsteigens; hrsg. vom
Schweizer Alpenclub. Zürich: S.A.C., 1886.
64p. 22cm.

BAUMGARTNER, Heinrich
Tausend Höhenangaben. 3. Aufl. Wr-Neustadt;
Selbstverlag des Verfassers, 1892. [160p.],
illus. 19cm.

BAUMGARTNER, Joseph
Die neuesten und vorzüglichsten Kunst-Strassen
über die Alpen; beschrieben auf einer Reise
durch Östreich, Steyarmark, Kärnthen, Krain und
Tyrol, des Küstenland und die Lombardie, einem
Theil vom Piemont und der südlichen Schweiz.
Wien: F. Ullrich, 1834. x, 332p., 13 fold.
plates, illus. 24cm.

BAURON, Pierre
Autour du Mont-Blanc: étapes de la caravane
minimoise, août 1882. Paris: Delhomme et
Briguet, 1883. 227p., illus. 24cm.
Second ed. published in 1906 under title:
Courses dans les Alpes.

BAURON, Pierre
Courses dans les Alpes. 2e éd. Paris:
Delhomme et Briguet, 1906. xv, 341p., illus.
24cm.
First ed. published in 1883 under title: Autour
du Mont-Blanc ...

BAXTER, George
MACGREGOR, John
The ascent of Mont Blanc: a series of four
views, printed in oil colours by George Baxter;
the original sketches, and the descriptions by
J. Macgregor. [G. Baxter], [1855]. 4p., 4
col. plates, illus. 19 x 27cm.

BAXTER, William Edward
Impressions of central and southern Europe,
being notes of successive journeys in Germany,
Austria, Italy, Switzerland, and the Levant.
Longman, Brown, Green, & Longmans, 1850. xi,
388p. 23cm.

BAXTER, Wynne E
Quiet resting places in the Swiss highlands:
Evolena, Ferpècle, Arolla. Ye Mitre Press,
[1898]. 20p., plates (1 fold.), illus., map.
17cm.

BAYBERGER, Emmeran
Gemsen-Eier: Alpin-Humoristisches in Wort &
Bild. Kempten: Jos. Kösel, 1895-99. 4 v.,
illus. 18cm.
Editor's preface signed: E. Bayberger.

Bayrisches Hochland, Salzburg, Salzkammergut:
praktischer Reiseführer. 27. Aufl. Berlin: A.
Goldschmidt, 1911-12. 244p., 11 maps. 17cm.
(Griebens Reiseführer, 66)

BAZIN, René
Récits de la plaine et de la montagne. 11e
éd. Paris: Calmann-Lévy, [1903?]. 332p.
19cm.

BEAGLEHOLD, J   C
    The discovery of New Zealand. 2nd ed. Oxford
    University Press, 1961. xii, 102p., plates (1
    fold.), illus., maps, bibl. 23cm.

BEAN, Paul
NORTH OF ENGLAND HIMALAYAN EXPEDITION, 1977
    A return to the roof of the world and the story
    of a Himalayan trilogy. [Stockton]: The
    Expedition, 1977. 31p., illus., maps. 30cm.
    At head of title: For the Royal Jubilee.
    Expedition leader: Paul Bean.

BEAN, Paul
NORTH OF ENGLAND HIMALAYAN EXPEDITION, 1975
    The roof of the world: the report of the 1975
    North of England Himalayas Expedition. Stockton:
    The Expedition, 1975. [28p.]. illus., maps.
    30cm.
    Expedition leader: Paul Bean

Beaten tracks; or, Pen and pencil sketches in
    Italy, by the authoress of "Voyage en zigzag"
    [i.e. Elizabeth Tuckett]. Longmans, Green, 1866.
    viii, 278p., plates, illus. 23cm.

BEATTIE, Bob
    My ten secrets of skiing. Barker, 1968. x,
    85p., illus. 25cm.

BEATTIE, William
    Scotland; illustrated in a series of views taken
    expressly for this work, by ... T. Allom [and
    others]. G. Virtue, 1838-42. 2 v., plates,
    illus. 29cm.

BEATTIE, William
    Switzerland; illustrated in a series of views
    taken expressly for this work by W.H. Bartlett.
    G. Virtue, 1836. 2 v., plates, illus., map.
    28cm.

BEATTIE, William
    [Switzerland]. La Suisse pittoresque; ornée de
    vues dessinées spécialement pour cent ouvrage par
    W.H. Bartlett; accompagnée d'un texte par William
    Beattie; traduit de l'anglais par L. de Bauclas.
    G. Virtue, 1836. 2 v., plates, illus., map.
    29cm.

BEATTIE, William
    [Switzerland]. Die Schweiz nach William Beattie;
    mit Stahlstichen versehen nach Original Zeich-
    nungen von W.H. Bartlett ausgeführt... Berlin:
    Trowitzsch, [1840]. 2 v., plates, illus., map.
    28cm.

BEATTIE, William
    [Switzerland]. La Svizzera storica ed artistica,
    descritta da Giuseppe La Farina; ed. illustrata
    da una serie di ... incisioni in acciaio [da
    W.H. Bartlett]. Firenze: L. Bardi, 1842-43.
    2 v., plates, illus. 31cm.
    Based on Beattie, William. Switzerland. 1836.

BEATTIE, William
    [Switzerland]. Zwitserland en de Alpen van
    Savoije; naar afbeeldingen op de plaats zelve
    geteekend, [by W.H. Bartlett]; in tafereelen be-
    schreven door N.G. van Kampen. Amsterdam: G.J.A.
    Beijerinck, [1837]. 2 v. in 1, plates, illus.
    28cm.
    Based on Beattie, William. Switzerland. 1836.

BEATTIE, William
    The Waldenses; or, Protestant valleys of Piedmont,
    Dauphiny, and the Ban de la Roche; illustrated by
    W.H. Bartlett and W. Brockedon. G. Virtue, 1838.
    216p., plates (1 fold.), illus., map. 28cm.

BEATTIE, William
    [The Waldenses ...]. Les vallées vaudoises
    pittoresques; ou, vallées protestantes du Pié-
    mont, du Dauphiné, et du Ban de la Roche; orné de
    gravures par W.H. Bartlett et par W. Brockedon;
    traduit par L. de Bauclas. G. Virtue, 1838.
    216p., plates (1 fold.), illus., map. 29cm.

BEAUCHAMP STRICKLAND, F   de
    See
STRICKLAND, F   de Beauchamp

BEAUCLERK, Lady Diana De Vere
    A summer and winter in Norway. Murray, 1868.
    xii, 148p., 4 plates, illus. 20cm.

BEAUFOY FAMILY
BEAUFOY, Gwendolyn
    Leaves from a beech tree. Oxford: Blackwell,
    1930. ix, 291p., plates, illus. 24cm.

BEAUFOY, Gwendolyn
    Leaves from a beech tree. Oxford: Blackwell,
    1930. ix, 291p., plates, illus. 24cm.

BEAUMONT, Jean François Albanis
    Description des Alpes greques et cottiannes; ou,
    Tableau historique et statistique de la Savoie.
    2e pte. Paris: Renouard, 1806. 2 v., plates,
    illus., map. 32 - 38cm.

BEAUMONT, Jean François Albanis
SAUSSURE, Horace Bénédict de
    Grotte de Balme, située entre Cluse et Maglan sur
    la route de Chamonix = The Grotto of Balme ...;
    [description de Mr. de Saussure ... de Mr.
    Bourrit ... de Mr. J.F. Albanis Beaumont]. Genève:
    les Heritiers J.J. Paschoud, 1827. 34p. 15cm.
    Parallel texts in French and English.

BEAUMONT, Jean François Albanis
    Select views of the antiquities and harbours in
    the South of France; with topographical and his-
    torical descriptions, by the author of the
    Rhaetian Alps [i.e. J.F. Albanis Beaumont].
    Printed by T. Bensley, 1794. 56p., 15 plates,
    maps. 44cm.

BEAUMONT, Jean François Albanis
    Travels from France to Italy, through the
    Lepontine Alps; or, An itinerary of the road from
    Lyons to Turin, by the way of the Pays-de-Vaud,
    the Vallais... G.G. & J. Robinson, 1800. 218p.,
    27 plates, map, plans. 42cm.

- - Another ed. 1806.

BEAUMONT, Jean François Albanis
    Travels through the Maritime Alps, from Italy to
    Lyons... Printed by T. Bensley, 1795. 127p.,
    plates, maps. 44cm.

BEAUMONT, Jean François Albanis
    Travels through the Rhaetian Alps, in the year
    1786, from Italy to Germany, through Tyrol ...;
    with ten large aqua-tinta engravings, from
    original designs, by the author. Printed for the
    Author by C. Clarke, 1792. viii, 82p., 10 plates,
    illus., map. 46cm.

BEAUMONT, Jean François Albanis
    Voyage pittoresque aux Alpes pennines; précédé de
    quelques observations sur les hauteurs des mon-
    tagnes, glaciers... Genève: Bardin, 1787. 20p.,
    12 col. plates, illus. 45cm.

BEAUMONT, Jean François Albanis
    Picturesque tour from Geneva to the Pennine Alps;
    translated from the French [of J.F. Albanis
    Beaumont]. Printed by John Nichols for James
    Bate, 1792. 16p., 12 plates, illus. 53cm.
    Originally published as: Voyage pittoresque aux
    Alpes pennines.

BEAUMONT, L   Élie de
    Notice sur les systèmes de montagnes. Paris: P.
    Bertrand, 1852. 3 v.(xi, 1543p.), 3 fold. plates,
    maps. 15cm.

BEAUVERIE, Jean
HEGI, Gustav and DUNZINGER, Gustav
    [Alpenflora]. Atlas colorié de la flore alpine:
    Jura, Pyrénées, Alpes françaises, Alpes suisses;
    [traduit] par J. Beauverie et L. Faucheron
    d'après Hegi et Dunzinger; préface de R. Gérard.
    Paris: Baillière, 1906. 98p., 30 col. plates,
    illus. 22cm.

BECHER, Gianni Pais
See
PAIS BECHER, Gianni

BECHTOLD, Fritz
Deutsche am Nanga Parbat: der Angriff 1934.
München: Bruckmann, 1935. 68p., illus, maps.
26cm.

BECHTOLD, Fritz
[Deutsche am Nanga Parbat ...]. Nanga Parbat
adventure: a Himalayan expedition; translated
by H.E.G. Tyndale. Murray, 1935. xx, 93p.,
plates, illus., maps. 26cm.

BECKER, Fridolin
Glarnerland mit Walensee und Klausenstrasse;
hrsg. vom Verkehrsverein für den Kanton.Glarus:
J. Bäschlin,[1912?]. 160p., illus., map. 19cm.

BECKER, Fridolin
Über den Klausen: auf neuer Gebirgsstrasse
zwischen Ur- und Ost-Schweiz ...; hrsg. vom
Verkehrsverein für den Kanton Glarus. Glarus:
Bäschlin, 1900. 143p., 1 fold. col. plate,
illus., map. 20cm.

BECKER, Fridolin
SCHWEIZER ALPEN-CLUB. Sektion Uto
Das Unglück an der Jungfrau vom 15. Juli 1887;
auf Veranlassung des Vorstandes der Section
Uto, S.A.C. dargestellt von F. Becker, A.
Fleiner. Zürich: Hofer & Burger, [1887]. 48p.,
col. plates, illus., map. 22cm.

BECKER, Gustav
Die Hochwilde. Stuttgart: Deutsche Verlags-
Anstalt, 1907. 66p., 13 plates, illus., maps.
18cm. (Alpine Gipfelführer, 14)

BECKER, Julius Becker-
See
BECKER-BECKER, Julius

BECKER, R Streiff-
See
STREIFF-BECKER, R

BECKER-BECKER, Julius
SCHWEIZER ALPEN-CLUB
Les cabanes du Club Alpin Suisse, par Julius
Becker-Becker; traduction de A. Bernoud.
Genève: C.A.S., 1892. 63p., 16 plates, illus.,
map. 25 x 34cm.

BECKETT, Samuel J
The fjords and folk of Norway. Methuen, 1915.
xv, 307p., plates, illus., maps. 17cm.

BECKEY, Fred
Challenge of the North Cascades. Seattle: The
Mountaineers, 1969 (1977 reprint). xvi, 280p.,
illus., maps. 21cm.

BECKEY, Fred
Climber's guide to the Cascade and Olympic
Mountains: [New York]: American Alpine Club,
1949. iv, 271p., plates (1 fold.), illus., maps,
bibl. 17cm.

BECKEY, Fred
Columbia River to Stevens Pass. Seattle: The
Mountaineers, 1973. x, 341p., illus., maps.
22cm. (Cascade alpine guide: climbing and high
routes)

BECKEY, Fred
Darrington & Index: rock climbing guide. Seattle:
The Mountaineers, 1976. 63p., illus. 22cm.

BECKEY, Fred and BJORNSTAD, Eric
Guide to Leavenworth rock-climbing areas.
Seattle: The Mountaineers, 1965. 86p., illus.,
maps. 21cm.

BECKEY, Fred
Stevens Pass to Rainy Pass. Seattle: The
Mountaineers, 1977. 352p., plates, illus.,
maps (2 fold. col. as inserts). 22cm. (Cascade
alpine guide: climbing and high routes)

BECKFORD, William
The history of the Caliph Vathek; and European
travels... Ward, Lock, 1891. xxiv, 549p.,
plates, port. 19cm. (Minerva library of famous
books)

BECKFORD, William
Italy, with sketches of Spain and Portugal.
Paris: Baudry's European Library, 1834. vi,
338, 127p. 22cm. (Collection of ancient and
modern British novels and romances, v. 59)
Contains: Vathek: an Arabian tale.

BEER, Dora H de
See
DE BEER, Dora H

BEER, Sir Gavin de
See
DE BEER, Sir Gavin

BEETHAM, Bentley
Borrowdale; with illustrations by W. Heaton
Cooper. Stockport: Fell & Rock Climbing Club,
1953. 173p., 1 plate, illus. 16cm. (Rock-
climbing guides to the English Lake District,
2nd [i.e. 3rd] ser., 5)

BEETHAM, George and MAXWELL, Joseph Prime
The first ascent of Mount Ruapehu, New Zealand,
and a holiday jaunt to Mounts Ruapehu,
Tongariro and Ngauruhoe. Harrison, 1926.
40p., plates, illus. 22cm.

BÉGIN, Émile
Voyage pittoresque en Suisse, en Savoie et sur
les Alpes. Paris: Belin-Leprieur et Morizot,
1852. viii, 560p., plates, illus. 27cm.

BEKE, Charles T
Mount Sinai, a volcano. Tinsley, 1873. 48p.
22cm.

BELCHER, Paul
CITY UNIVERSITY - BRUNEL UNIVERSITY KISHTWAR
HIMALAYA EXPEDITION, 1978
Report ..., written by Paul Belcher; appendices
by Anthony Wheaton. The Expedition, [1979].
54p., plates, illus., map. 31cm.

BELL, Sir Charles
English-Tibetan colloquial dictionary. 2nd ed.
Calcutta: Bengal Secretariat Book Depot, 1920.
xxxvi, 562p. 19cm.

BELL, Sir Charles
Grammar of colloquial Tibetan. 3rd ed. Alipore
(Bengal): Bengal Government Press, 1939. xii,
184p., fold. plates, illus., map (in pocket).
18cm.

BELL, Sir Charles
Portrait of the Dalai Lama. Collins, 1946.
414p., plates (1 col.), illus., maps (on lining
papers). 23cm.

BELL, Sir Charles
The religion of Tibet. Oxford: Clarendon Press,
1931. xvi, 235p., plates (2 fold., 1 col.),
illus., maps. 23cm.

BELL, Sir Charles
Tibet past and present. Oxford. Clarendon
Press, 1924. xiv, 326p., plates (some fold.,
1 col.), illus., 2 maps. 24cm.

BELL, Florence, Lady
BELL, Gertrude
The letters of Gertrude Bell; selected and
edited by Lady Bell. Benn, 1927. 2 v., plates,
illus., maps. 25cm.

BELL, George I
HOUSTON, Charles Sneed
K2, 8611m: [troisième expédition américaine au
Karakorum], [par] Charles S. Houston, Robert H.
Bates, George I. Bell. Paris: Arthaud, 1954.
100p., 1 fold. plate, illus. (some col.), map.
26cm.

BELL, Gertrude
Dauphiné and the Aiguille Méridionale d'Arves:
unpublished letters from ... Gertrude Bell.
London, 1928. 10p., 2 plates, illus. 22cm.
Offprint from Alpine Journal v.40, 1928.

BELL, Gertrude
The letters of Gertrude Bell; selected and
edited by Lady Bell. Benn, 1927. 2 v., plates,
illus., maps. 25cm.

BELL, James Horst Brunnerman
British hills and mountains, by J.H.B. Bell,
E.F. Bozman and J. Fairfax Blakeborough.
Batsford, 1940. viii, 120p., plates (some col.),
illus. 22cm. (British heritage series)

BELL, James Horst Brunnerman
A progress in mountaineering: Scottish hills to
Alpine peaks. Edinburgh, London: Oliver &
Boyd, 1950. xii, 424p., plates, illus., maps,
bibl. 22cm.

BELL, James Mackintosh
The wilds of Maoriland. Macmillan, 1914. xiii,
253p., plates (2 fold. col.), illus., maps.
23cm.

BELL, James Stanislaus
Journal of a residence in Circassia during the
years 1837, 1838 and 1839. Moxon, 1840. 2 v.,
col. plates (1 fold.), illus., map. 23cm.

BELL, William
Mountains beneath the horizon; edited with an
introduction by J. Heath-Stubbs. Faber, 1950.
73p., plates, port. 24cm.

BELLEFON, Patrice de
Excursions et escalades aux Pyrénées. Luchon:
Société de Guides Pyrénées, 1969. 64p., 1 fold.
plate, illus., map, bibl. 16cm.

BELLET, Jean
Le Col du Mont-Cenis; "Porte millenaire des
Alpes": bref historique. Saint-Jean-de-
Maurienne: Société d'histoire et d'archéologie
de Maurienne, 1976. 245p., plates (1 fold.),
illus., maps, bibl. 21cm.

BELLIDO, J   García
See
GARCÍA BELLIDO, J

BELLOC, Hilaire
Many cities. Constable, 1928. xi, 261p.,
plates, illus. 23cm.

BELLOC, Hilaire
The path to Rome. Allen, 1902. xv, 448p., 1
plate, illus. 20cm.

- - Another ed. Nelson, [1910].

BELLOC, Hilaire
The Pyrenees. Methuen, 1909. xi, 340p., plates
(some fold.), illus., maps. 24cm.

BELLONI, Severino
DESIO, Ardito
Results of half-a-century investigation on the
glaciers of the Ortles-Cevedale mountain group
(central Alps) = Risultati ... [by] A. Desio with
the collaboration of S. Belloni [and others].
Roma: Il Consiglio, 1973. 107, 107p., 10 plates
(2 fold.), illus., maps, bibl. 30cm. (Consiglio
Nazionale delle Ricerche. Pubblicazioni, n. 6)

BELLOWS, William
Zermatt and the Matterhorn, by W.B. [i.e.
William Bellows]. Gloucester: The Author, 1925.
19p., plates, illus. 20cm.

BELLOWS, William
[Zermatt and the Matterhorn]. Der Berg meiner
Sehnsucht: Zermatt und das Matterhorn, eine
Traversierung; uebersetzt von Katharine Gericke.
Kilchberg: Wehrli, 1928. 40p., plates, illus.
20cm.

HOLTZ, Mathilda Edith and BEMIS, Katharine Isabel
Glacier National Park: its trails and treasures.
New York. Doran, 1917. 263p., plates, illus.,
map (on lining papers). 21cm.

BENDA, C
GRUBE, A   W
Alpenwanderungen: Fahrten auf hohe und höchste
Alpenspitzen; nach der Originalberichten aus-
gewählt, bearb. und gruppirt für junge und alte
Freunde der Alpenwelt. Leipzig: E. Kummer, 1874.
2 v. in 1, col. plates, illus. 23cm.

- - 3. Aufl. Neu bearb. und ergänzt von C. Benda.
1886.

BENESCH, Erwin
Österreichs Alpenwelt: über Berg und Tal vom
Bodensee bis zum Wienerwald. München: Bruckmann,
1937. 271p., plates (1 fold., 1 col.), illus.,
map (in pocket). 26cm.

BENESCH, Friedrich
See
BENESCH, Fritz

BENESCH, Fritz
Bergfahrten in den Grödner Dolomiten. München:
Bruckmann, 1899. 146p., 29 plates, illus. 33cm.

BENESCH, Fritz
Führer auf den Schneeberg. 5. Aufl. Wien:
Artaria, 1924. vii, 134p., plates, map. 17cm.

BENESCH, Fritz
Führer auf die Karalpe. 8. verm. und verb. Aufl.
Wien: Artaria, 1925. xii, 208p., plates, map.
17cm.

BENESCH, Fritz
Der Semmering und seine Berge: ein Album der
Semmering Landschaft von Gloggnitz bis
Mürzzuschlag; mit ... Abbildungen nach Photo-
graphischen aufnahmen von Fritz Benesch, und einem
Begleitwort von Paul Busson. Wien: Christoph
Reisser, 1913. 88p., col. plates, illus. 25cm.

BENESCH, Fritz
Spezial-Führer auf den Schneeberg. 3 Aufl.
Wien: Artaria, 1913. vii, 148p., plates, illus.,
map. 18cm.

BENESCH, Fritz
Spezialführer auf die Raxalpe. 5. verm. und verb.
Aufl. Wien: Artaria, 1914. xii, 200p., plates,
map. 18cm.

BENGAL. Secretariat
The gazetteer of Sikhim; with an introduction by
H.H. Risley; edited in the Bengal Government
Secretariat. Calcutta: Secretariat Press, 1894.
xxii, 392p., plates (some fold., some col.),
illus., maps (in pocket). 29cm.

BENI, Carlo
Guida illustrata del Casentino. Firenze: Club
Alpino Italiano, Sezione Fierentina, 1881.
209p., plates, map. 16cm.

BENNET, Donald J
Staunings Alps - Greenland: Scoresby Land and
Nathorsts Land. Reading: Gaston's Alpine Books,
West Col Productions, 1972. 120p., plates (2
fold.), illus., maps, bibl. 20cm.

BENNET, E
  Shots and snapshots in British East Africa.
  Longmans, Green, 1914. xii, 312p., plates,
  illus., 2 maps (in pocket). 24cm.

BENNETT, Alfred W
  The flora of the Alps, being a description of
  all ... flowering plants indigenous to
  Switzerland; and of the alpine species of the
  adjacent mountain districts ... including the
  Pyrenees. J.C. Nimmo, 1896. 2 v.,col. plates,
  illus. 21cm.

BENNETT, G J
  The pedestrian's guide through North Wales: a
  tour performed in 1837; with twenty etchings,
  by A. Clint. H. Colburn, [1838]. viii, 391p.,
  plates (some fold.), illus., music. 24cm.

BENSON, Arthur Christopher
  Along the road. Nisbet, 1913. xiii, 383p.,
  plates, port. 21cm.

BENSON, Claude Ernest
  British mountaineering. Routledge, 1909. xi,
  224p., illus. 19cm.

- - 2nd ed. rev. and enl. 1914.

BENSON, Claude Ernest
  Crag and hound in Lakeland. Hurst & Blackett,
  1902. xvi, 313p., illus. 23cm.

BENSON, Claude Ernest
  Mountaineering ventures. T.C. & E.C. Jack,
  [1928?]. 224p., plates, illus. 21cm.

BENSON, Dora
PIGGOTT, Percy J
  Burrow's Guide to North Wales: a practical handbook for the tourist ...; with a special article
  upon mountain walks and rock climbs by Dora
  Benson. Cheltenham, London: Burrow, [ca 1920].
  162p., plates (1 fold., col.), illus., maps.
  19cm.

BENSON, Dora
PIGGOTT, Percy J
  Burrow's Guide to the Lake District: a practical
  handbook for the tourist; with a special
  article upon mountain passes, walks & rock climbs
  by Dora Benson. Cheltenham, London: Burrow,
  [ca 1920]. 120p., plates (1 fold. col.), illus.,
  maps. 19cm.

BENSON, E F
  Winter sports in Switzerland. Allen, 1913. viii,
  197p., plates (some col.), illus. 27cm.

BENSON, Robert Hugh
  The coward. Hutchinson, 1912. 392p. 20cm.

BENT, Allen H
  A bibliography of the White Mountains. Boston:
  Published for the Appalachian Mountain Club by
  Houghton Mifflin, 1911. vii, 114p., plates,
  ports. 23cm.

- - Additions ... [1918].

BENTELI, W
STUDER, Gottlieb
  Panorama vom Mänlichen (Berner Oberland) 2345m,
  aufgenommen von G. Studer; gezeichnet von W.
  Benteli. Bern: J. Dalp,[1874]. 13p., 1 fold.
  col. plate, illus. 29cm.

BENUZZI, Felice
  [Fuga sul Kenya]. No picnic on Mount Kenya. 2nd.
  ed. Kimber, 1952. 231p., plates (1 col.), illus.,
  map (on lining papers), port. 23cm.

BENUZZI, Felice
  [Fuga sul Kenya]. Kenya; ou, La fugue africaine
  ...; traduit ... par Félix Germain. Paris:
  Arthaud, 1950. 310p., plates, illus., bibl. 21cm.

BENZENBERG, J F
  Briefe geschrieben auf einer Reise durch die
  Schweiz im Jahr 1810. Düsseldorf: T.H.C.
  Schreiner, 1811-12. 2 v. in 1. 19cm.

BERALDI, Henri
  Balaïtous et Pelvoux: notes sur les officiers
  de la Carte de France. Paris: The Author,
  1907-10. 2 v., plates (some fold.), maps. 31cm.

BERALDI, Henri
  La carrière posthume de Ramond, 1827-1868:
  notes d'un bibliophile. Paris: The Author, 1927.
  191p. 24cm.

BERALDI, Henri
  Cent ans aux Pyrénées. Paris: The Author,
  1898-1902. 7 v. 27cm.

BERALDI, Henri
  En marge du pyrénéisme: notes d'un bibliophile;
  L'affaire Rilliet-Planta. Paris: The Author,
  1931. 160p. 23cm.

BERALDI, Henri
  Le passé du pyrénéisme: notes d'un bibliophile.
  Paris: The Author, 1911-20. 5 v. 23cm.

BERALDI, Henri
  Le sommet des Pyrénées: notes d'un bibliophile.
  Paris: The Author, 1923-25. 3 v. 24cm.

BÉRARD, Clément
  Au coeur d'un vieux pays: légendes et traditions
  du Valais. 2e éd. Sierre: Walter-Amacker, 1928.
  242p. 20cm.

PARAGOT, Robert and BÉRARDINI, Lucien
  Vingt ans de cordée; préface, Lucien Davies.
  Paris: Flammarion, 1974. 226p., plates, illus.
  22cm. (L'aventure vécue)

BERCHEM, Jacob Pierre Berthoud van
  See
BERTHOUD VAN BERCHEM, Jacob Pierre

BERE, Rennie
  The way to the mountains of the moon. Barker,
  1966. xii, 147p., plates, illus., maps. 23cm.

BERGEAT, Alfred
  Die Vulkane. Breslau: Hirt, 1925. 112p.,
  plates (3 fold.), illus., maps. 20cm.
  (Jedermanns Bucherei: Erdkunde)

BERGEN, J van
  In Italiaansch Zwitserland en Grauwbunderland;
  herinneringen en indrukken ... Baarn: J.F. Van
  de Ven, [19--]. 122p. 20cm.

BERGEN, J van
  In Zwitserland; herinneringen en indrukken...
  Baarn: J.F. Van de Ven, 1908. v, 202p. 18cm.
  (Gids voor Toeristen)

BERGER, Fr
DEUTSCHER UND ÖSTERREICHISCHER ALPENVEREIN.
Sektion Pforzheim
  Ski und Winterführer durch die Münstertaler
  Alpen und angrenzenden Gebiete: Westl. Ortler-
  gruppe, Malser Heide, Unterengadin und Alpen
  von Livigno; unter Mitwirkung des D.u. Oe.
  Alpenvereins; hrsg. von Fr. Berger. München:
  Kommissionsverlag der Deutschen Alpenzeitung,
  1912. 180p., fold. col. plates, maps (in
  pocket). 17cm.

Bergsteigen: Festschrift des Österreichischen
  Alpenklubs zu seiner Hundert-Jahr-Feier, 1878-
  1978; gestaltet von S. Walcher. Wien: Ö.A.V.,
  1979. 231p., ports. 27cm.
  Sonderfolge der Österreichischen Alpenzeitung,
  Jan./Feb. 1979, Folge 1423.

BERLEPSCH, H   E   von
BERLEPSCH, Hermann Alexander von
  Die Alpen, in Natur- und Lebensbildern; dar-
  gestellt von H.A. Berlepsch; mit ... Illus-
  trationen nach Originalzeichnungen von Emil
  Rittmeyer. 4. sehr verm. und verb. Aufl. Jena:
  H. Costenoble, 1871. viii, 511p., 22 plates,
  illus. 24cm.

  - - 5. sehr verm. und verb. Aufl. 2. wohlfeile
  Volksausg.; umgebearb. vermehrt und ergänzt
  vom Sohne des Verfassers, H.E.v. Berlepsch.
  1885.

BERLEPSCH, Hermann Alexander von
  Die Alpen in Natur- und Lebensbildern; dargestellt von H.A. Berlepsch; mit ... Illustrationen nach Originalzeichnungen von Emil
  Rittmeyer. Leipzig: H. Costenoble, 1861.
  viii, 441p., plates, illus. 25cm.

  - - 4. sehr verm. und verb. Aufl. 1871.

  - - 5. sehr verm. und verb. Aufl. 2. wohlfeile
  Volksausg.; umgebearb. vermehrt und ergänzt
  vom Sohne des Verfassers, H.E.v. Berlepsch.
  1885.

BERLEPSCH, Hermann Alexander von
  Die Alpen in Natur- und Lebensbildern: aus-
  gewählte Abschnitte ...; mit einem Bild und
  einer biographischen Skizze von F. v. Berlepsch-
  Valendas; hrsg. von R.H. Francé. Leipzig:
  Theod. Thomas, [1910]. 78p., illus. 16cm.
  (Natur-Bibliothek, Nr. 11)

BERLEPSCH, Hermann Alexander von
  [Die Alpen in Natur- und Lebensbildern]. The
  Alps; or, Sketches of life and nature in the
  mountains; translated by Leslie Stephen; with
  ... plates from designs by Emil Rittmeyer.
  Longman, Green, Longman, & Roberts, 1861. vi,
  407p., 17 col. plates, illus. 23cm.

BERLEPSCH, Hermann Alexander von
  Neuestes Reisehandbuch für die Schweiz.
  Hildburghausen: Verlag des Bibliographischen
  Instituts, 1862. xlvii, 661p., plates, illus.,
  maps, plans. 18cm. (Meyer's Reisebücher, 1)

BERLEPSCH, Hermann Alexander von
  Der Rheinfall, der Zürich-see und der Wallen-
  see: ein Führer für Fremde. Leipzig: J.J.
  Weber, 1858. 89p., illus., map. 17cm.
  (Schweizerische Fremden-Führer, 6)

BERLEPSCH, Hermann Alexander von
  Schweizerkunde: Land, Volk und Staat,
  geographisch-statistisch, übersichtlich-
  vergleichend dargestellt; unter Mitarbeiter-
  schaft der Redaktor Gengel [and others] ...;
  hrsg. von H.A. Berlepsch. Braunschweig: C.A.
  Schwetschke, 1864. xii, 907p. 23cm.

  - - 2. umbearb. Aufl. 1875.

BERLEPSCH, Hermann Alexander von
  Switzerland and the principal parts of
  southern Germany: handbook for travellers by
  Berlepsch and Kohl. Zurich: C. Schmidt, 1874.
  xxiv, 504p., plates, illus., maps, plans.
  16cm.

BERLIN. Gesellschaft für Erdkunde
  See
GESELLSCHAFT FÜR ERDKUNDE ZU BERLIN

BERLIOUX, E   F
  Le Jura. Paris: J. Dumaine, 1880. 140p.,
  2 fold. plates, maps. 26cm. (Lecture de la
  carte de France)

BERN. (Canton). Kantonal-Bernische Natur-
schutzkommission
  See
KANTONAL-BERNISCHE NATURSCHUTZKOMMISSION

BERNARD, A   de
  Les stations d'un touriste. Paris: Hetzel,
  1861. 361p. 18cm.

MOUGIN, P   and BERNARD, C
  Glacier de Tête-Rousse, les avalanches en Savoie.
  Paris: Imprimerie nationale, 1922. 322p.,
  illus., maps, bibl. 29cm. (France. Ministère
  de l'agriculture. Direction générale des eaux et
  forêts. Études glaciologiques, t. 4)

BERNARD, G
  Guide du skieur: fabrication et théorie du ski,
  le ski dans la montagne. Paris: Chapelot, 1910.
  xiii, 122p., plates, illus. 20cm.

BERNARD, M
  Marie-Rose; ou, Le ski sans entraves. Grenoble:
  Didier & Richard, 1931. 180p., illus. 19cm.

BERNARDI, Alfonso
  Fiori del nostro Appennino: primavera, estate,
  autunno nell'Appennino tosco-emiliano; hanno
  collaborato: Alfonso Bernardi [and others].
  Bologna: Club Alpino Italiano, 1964. 48p.,
  col. illus. 21cm.

BERNARDI, Alfonso
  Il Gran Cervino: antologia. Bologna: Zanichelli,
  1963. 320p., plates (some fold., some col.),
  illus., maps. 24cm. (Montagne, 2)

BERNARDI, Alfonso
  La Grande Civetta; a cura di Alfonso Bernardi.
  Bologna: Zanichelli, 1971. 332p., illus. (some
  col.), map (on lining papers). 24cm.

BERNARDI, Alfonso
  Il Monte Bianco, dalle esplorazioni alla conquista (1091-1786): antologia. Bologna:
  Zanichelli, 1965. 317p., plates (some fold.,
  some col.), illus., maps, bibl. 25cm.

BERNARDI, Maziano
  Il Cervino e la sua storia; a cura di Vittorio
  Zumaglino. Torino: S.A. Cervino, 1944. 71p.,
  illus. 29cm.

BERNASCONI, Mario
  Itinerari sciistici della zona Formico-Grioni,
  Prealpi bergamasche, Valle Seriana. Bergamo:
  Club Alpino Italiano, Sezione Bergamo, 1929.
  48p., plates, illus. map. 18cm.

BERNDT, Gustav
  Der Alpenföhn in seinem Einfluss auf Natur- und
  Menschenleben. Gotha: Justus Perthes, 1886.
  66p., 1 fold. col plate, map. 28cm. (Ergänzungsheft zu "Petermanns Mitteilungen", no. 83)

BERNDT, Gustav
  Der Föhn: ein Beitrag zur orographischen Meteorologie und comparative Klimatologie. Göttingen:
  Vandenhoeck & Ruprecht, 1886. viii, 346p.,
  plates (some fold., some col.), maps. 24cm.

BERNE
  See
BERN

BERNHARD, Oscar
  Die erste Hilfe bei Unglücksfällen im Hochgebirge, für Bergführer und Touristen. 5. verm.
  und verb. Aufl. Stuttgart: F. Enke, 1913. viii,
  124p., illus. 19cm.

BERNHARD, Oscar
  [Die erste Hilfe ...]. First aid to the injured,
  with special reference to accidents occuring in
  the mountains: a handbook for guides, climbers
  and travellers; translated by Michael G. Foster.
  Samaden: Tanner, 1896. viii, 136p., illus. 18cm.

BERNOVILLE, Raphaël
  La Souanétie libre: épisode d'un voyage à la
  chaine centrale du Caucase. Paris: Vve A. Morel,
  1875. 173p., plates, illus., map. 37cm.

BERNSTEIN, Jeremy
Profiles: ascending: [biographical article on
American climber Yvon Chouinard].
(In The New Yorker, January 31, 1977. p.36-52,
port.)

BERNT, Ferdinand
Der Bund der Freien: Erzählung. Leipzig: Abel
& Müller, 1910. 352p. 20cm.

BERRET, Paul
Le Dauphiné: choix de textes précédés d'une
étude. Paris: Renouard, 1922. 200p., 1 fold.
plate, illus., map. 25cm. (Les provinces
françaises: anthologies illustrées)

BERTARELLI, L V   and BOEGAN, Eugenio
Duemila grotte: quarant'anni di esplorazioni
nella Venezia Giulia. Milano: Touring Club
Italiano, 1926. 494p., plates, illus., col.
maps (2 fold. in portfolio). 25cm.

BERTARELLI, L V
Southern Italy including Rome, Sicily and
Sardinia; edited by Findlay Muirhead.
Macmillan, 1925. lxxii, 531p., maps, plans.
16cm. (Blue guides)

BERTHOUD, Fritz
Sur la montagne. le ptie. Alpes et Jura.
Neuchatel: Delachaux, 1865. 363p. 20cm.

BERTHOUD VAN BERCHEM, Jacob Pierre
Excursion dans les mines du Haut Faucigny,
et Description de deux nouvelles routes pour
aller sur le Buet & le Breven, avec une notice
sur le Jardin. Lausanne: J.-P. Heubach, 1787.
62p. 21cm.

BERTHOUD VAN BERCHEM, Jacob Pierre
Itinéraire de la Vallée de Chamonix, d'une
partie du Bas-Vallais et des montagnes
avoisinantes. Lausanne: J. Mourer, 1790. 239p.,
2 fold. plates, illus., map. 17cm.

- - [New ed.] Genève: G.J. Manget, 1805.

- - [New ed.] Genève: Manget & Cherbuliez, 1816.

BERTHOUT VAN BERCHEM, Jacob Pierre
See
BERTHOUD VAN BERCHEM

BERTI, Antonio
Le Dolomiti del Cadore: guida alpinistica.
Padova: Drucker, 1908. 166p., plates, illus.,
maps, plans. 18cm.

BERTI, Antonio
Le Dolomiti della Val Talagona e il rifugio
Padova in Prà di Toro: valli, forcelle e cime...
Bassano: S. Pozzato, 1910. 95p., plates, illus.,
maps. 16cm.

BERTI, Antonio
Le Dolomiti Orientali. 3a ed. Milano: Club Alpino
Italiano, Touring Club Italiano, 1950-61. 2 v.,
col. plates (some fold.), illus., maps, bibl.
17cm. (Guida dei monti d'Italia)

BERTI, Antonio
Parlano i monti. Milano: Hoepli, 1948. 552p.
18cm.

BERTINI, Emilio
Guida della Val di Bisenzio, Appennino di Monte-
piano, Toscana. Prato: A. Liei, 1881. 219p.,
map. 16cm.

BERTOLINI, Amilcare und GUGLIERMINA, Giuseppe F
Gruppe Monte Bianco, fra il Colle del Miage, il
Col du Midi e il Col de la Tour Ronde; disegni
Angelo Calegari. Monza: Club Alpino Italiano,
1924. 77p., maps. 18cm. (C.A.I. Sezione
Universitaria. Guida sucai)

BERTOLINI, Amilcare and GUGLIERMINA, Giuseppe F
Gruppo Monte Rosa; schizzi di Angelo Calegari.
Monza: Club Alpino Italiano, 1925. 75p.,
illus. 19cm. (C.A.I. Sezione Universitaria.
Guida Sucai)

BERTOLOTTI, Davide
Viaggio in Savoia; ossia Deserizione degli
Stati oltramontani di S.M. il Re di Sardegna.
Torino: Tipi di G. Favale, 1828. 2 v. in 1.
23cm.

BERTONE, Mario
Aspectos glaciologicos de la zona del Hielo
Continental Patagónico. Buenos Aires:
Instituto Nacional del Hielo Continental
Patagónico, 1972. 121p., plates (some fold.),
illus., maps. 28cm. (Contribucion del
Instituto Nacional del Hielo Continental
Patagónico, 1)

BERTONE, Mario
Inventario de los glaciares existentes en la
vertiente Argentina entre los paralelos 47°
30' y 51° S. Buenos Aires: Instituto Nacional
del Hielo Continental Patagónico, 1960. 103p.,
plates (some fold.), illus., map. 26cm.
(Instituto Nacional del Hielo Continental
Patagónico. Publicacion no. 3)

BERTRAM, Anthony
Pavements and peaks: impressions of travel in
Germany and Austria. Chapman & Hall, 1933.
vii, 263p., plates, illus. 20cm.

BERTRAM, Anthony
To the mountains; with decorations by J.W.
Power. A.A. Knopf, 1929. xiii, 269p., plates,
illus. 20cm.

BERTRAM, Colin
Arctic and Antarctic: the technique of polar
travel. Cambridge: W. Heffer, 1939. xiii,
125p., plates, illus. 25cm.

BERTRAND, E
Le Thevenon; ou, Les journées de la montagne.
Neuchatel: Société Typographique, 1777. 491p.
16cm.

- - Nouv. éd. rev. corr. & augm. 1780.

Beschrijving van Zwitserland, met betrekking
tot deszelts aardrijkskundige ligging, natuurlijke voortbrengsels, oudheden, geschiedenis
en koophandel; uit den Hoogduitsch. Amsterdam:
J.C. van Kesteren, 1824. 2 v., plates, illus.
23cm.

BESOZZI, Manlio
Dallo Stelvio al Tonale: Merano, Bolzano, Dolo-
miti di Brenta; con ... acquarelli originali di
Nino Ramorino. Novara: Istituto Geografico de
Agostini, 1928. 116p., 11 col. plates, illus.
33cm. (Visioni italiche)

BESSE, Eugène
Un voyage au Giétroz, Vallée de Bagnes (Valais,
Suisse) en 1863. Sion: Ch. Steinbach, 1864.
8p. 21cm.

BESSIÈRES, Albert
L'empire de la paix: récits de la montagne
suisse, empire des neiges. Paris: Spes, 1931.
204p. 19cm.

BESSON, H
Manuel pour les savans et les curieux qui
voyagent en Suisse; avec des notes par Mr. W***
[Wyttenbach]. Lausanne: J.-P. Heubach, 1786.
2 v. in 1. 20cm.

BESSONE, Severino
Guide del Monviso; con la collaborazione ...
[di] Felice Burdino. Torino: Club Alpino
Italiano, Sezione di Torino, 1957. xvi, 213p.,
plates (some fold.), illus., maps, bibl. 17cm.

BEST, Allena
Abroad, and how to live there: a narrative of
three years' residence in Germany and Switzerland. Seeley, Jackson & Halliday, 1860. x,
345p., plates, illus. 17cm.

BÉTHA, Pierre Joseph
Valgrisanche: notices historiques. Aoste:
Imprimerie L. Mensio, 1877. 253p. 21cm.

BETHAM-EDWARDS, M
The roof of France; or The Causses of the
Lozère. R. Bentley, 1889. xvi, 327p. 23cm.

BÉTHAZ, Pierre Joseph
See
BÉTHA, Pierre Joseph

BETHELL, Augusta
Helen in Switzerland: a tale for young people;
with illustrations by E. Whymper. Griffith,
Farran, Okeden & Welsh, [1887]. 192p., illus.
17cm.

BETTEX, Gustave and GUILLON, Édouard
Les Alpes suisses dans la littérature et dans
l'art. Lausanne: F. Rouge, 1915. 335p.,
plates, illus. 22cm.

BEVAN, Favell Lee
Near home; or, The countries of Europe described,
with anecdotes and numerous illustrations by the
author of "The peep of day", &c. [i.e. Favell L.
Bevan]. J. Hatchard, 1849. xvi, 386p.,plates,
illus., map. 18cm.

- - 6th ed., carefully rev. Longmans, Green, 1902.

BEVERLEY, William
SMITH, Albert
A hand-book of Mr. Albert Smith's ascent of Mont
Blanc; illustrated by Mr. William Beverley ...;
first represented at the Egyptian Hall, Piccadilly
... March 15, 1852. The Author, 1852. 31p.,
illus. 13 x 21cm.

- - 4th ed. 1853.

- - 5th ed. 1853.

- - 6th ed. 1855.

BEVERLEY, William
SMITH, Albert
[A hand-book of Mr. Albert Smith's ascent of Mont
Blanc]. Exercise in colouring Mont Blanc. [The
Author], [ca 1852]. 1 v. of illus. 16 x 20cm.
Lithographs of William Beverley's drawings for
the Hand-book.

Beyer's guide to western Norway, with the coast-
route to the North Cape and overland routes to
Christiania, by Viljam Olsvig... Bergen: F. Beyer;
London: Philip, [1887]. 199p., fold. col. plates,
illus., maps, bibl. 18cm.

- - Special supplement for 1890.

BEYRER, Magnus Bartholomaeus
Guide des voyageurs dans la ville d'Innsbruck et
des envirens. Innsbruck: Jean-Mahl-Schedl,
[1826]. 235p., plates, illus. 14cm.

BHAGWĀN SHRI HAMSA
See
HAMSA, Bhagwān

BHATTACHARJYA, Bidypati
Mountain sickness. Bristol: J. Wright, 1964.
58p., plates, illus., bibl. 23cm.

GORRET, Amé and BICH, Claude, baron
Guide de la Vallée d'Aoste. Turin: F. Casanova,
1876. x, 443p., illus., map. 20cm.

BICKERSTAFF, Isaac
Love in a village... J. Bell, 1791. 93p. 15cm.

BICKNELL, C
The prehistoric rock engravings in the Italian
Maritime Alps. Bordighera: P. Gibelli, 1902.
74p., 24 plates, illus., map. 27cm.

BICKNELL, Peter
British hills and mountains. Collins, 1947.
48p., col. plates, illus., bibl. 23cm.
(Britain in pictures)

BIDDULPH, M   S
FORESTER, Thomas
Norway in 1848 and 1849, containing Rambles
among the fjelds and fjords of the central and
western districts; and including remarks on its
political, military, ecclesiastical and social
organisation; with extracts from the journals of
Lieut. M.S. Biddulph. Longman, Brown, Green and
Longman, 1850. xv, 484p., plates, illus., maps.
23cm.

BIEL, Stanislaw and WALA, Jerzy
The Polish Hindu Kush and Pamir Expedition, 1971.
[Krakow]: [The Expedition]. [1971?]. 18, 3
leaves, plates, maps. 29cm.

BIENDL, Hans
Die Jungfrau. Stuttgart: Deutsche Verlags-
Anstalt, 1907. 84p., 15 plates, illus., map.
18cm. (Alpine Gipfelführer, 15)

BIENDL, Hans
Der Monte Cristallo. Stuttgart: Deutsche
Verlags-Anstalt, 1906. 64p., plates, illus.,
map. 18cm. (Alpine Gipfelführer, 10)

BIENDL, Hans and RADIO-RADIIS, Alfred von
Schifahrten in den Ostalpen. Bd. 3. Der
Rätikon ... 2. Aufl. im Auftrag des Oesterreichischen Alpenklubs; hrsg. von Hans Biendl
und Alfred Radio-Radiis. Wien: Artaria, 1923.
xv, 160p. 17cm.

BIENDL, Hans and RADIO-RADIIS, Alfred von
Skitouren in den Ostalpen; über Auftrag des
Österreichischen Alpenklubs; hrsg. von Hans
Biendl und Alfred v. Radio-Radiis. Wien: A.
Holzhausen, 1906. 3 v., maps. 17cm.

BIERBAUM, Paul Willi
Streifzüge im Kaukasus und in Hocharmenien,
1912. Zürich: Orell Füssli, 1913. 278p.,
plates, maps. 20cm.

BIESE, Alfred
The development of the feeling for nature in the
middle ages and modern times; [translated from
the German]. Routledge, 1905. vi, 376p. 19cm.

BIGHAM, Hon. Richard
The Caha Mountains. [The Author], 1973. 28
leaves. 34cm.
Typescript.

BIGNAMI-SORMANI, Emilio
CLUB ALPINO ITALIANO. Sezione di Milano
Dizionario alpino italiano. Milano: Hoepli,
1892. xxi, 309p. 16cm. (Manuali Hoepli)
Pt. 1. Vette e valichi italiani; per cura
dell'Ing. Emilio Bignami-Sormani. - Pt. 2.
Valli lombarde e limitrofe alla Lombardia; per
cura dell'Ing. Carlo Scolari.

BILBROUGH, E   Ernest
'Twixt France and Spain; or, A spring in the
Pyrenees; illustrations by Doré and Miss Blunt.
Sampson Low, Marston, 1883. xxiii, 274p.,
plates (1 fold.), illus., map. 20cm.

Bilder-Atlas der Schweiz: Sammlung von Land-
schafts-, Städte-, und Typenbildern aus allen
Kantonen; mit erklärendem Text zusammengestellt durch die Mitarbeiter am Geographischen
Lexicon der Schweiz. Neuenburg: Attinger,
[1910?]. 476p., illus., maps. 31cm.

BILGERI, Georg
AUSTRIA. <u>Gendarmerie.Zentraldirektion</u>
Alpin-Vorschrift für due Österr. Bundes-
gendarmerie nebst einem Anhang über die Zentral-
meldestelle für alpine Unfälle in Wien ...;
Verfasser: G. Bilgeri; Mitarbeiter: Joseph Albert.
Wien: Gendarmerie-Zentraldirektion, [1926?].
vii, 128p., illus. 24cm.

BILGERI, Georg
Der alpine Skilauf. München: Verlag der
deutschen Alpenzeitung, 1910. 103p., plates,
illus. 19cm.

BILGERI, Georg
[Ski-handbuch]. Colonel Bilgeri's handbook on
mountain skiing; translated with notes by Harold
Holme. Chiswick Press, 1929. 110p., illus. 20cm.

BILL, A   F
Davos as a health-resort: a handbook containing
contributions by A.F. Bill [and others]; introduction by W.R. Huggard. Davos: Davos Printing
Co., 1906. iv, 316p., plates, illus. 21cm.

BILLE, Edmond
RAMUZ, C   F
Le village dans la montagne, [text by] C.-F.
Ramuz; [illustrated by] Edm. Bille. Lausanne:
Payot, [1908]. 260p., plates (some col.), illus.
37cm.

BILMA SANDS EXPEDITION, <u>1976</u>
See
BRITISH HOGGAR MOUNTAINS AND BILMA SANDS
EXPEDITION, <u>1976</u>

BINDER, Gottlieb
Der Utliberg und die Albiskette. Zürich: Orell
Fussli [1916]. 66p., 28 plates, illus., map.
20cm. (Wanderbilder, 339, 340)

BING, Walter
Drei Jungens am Seil. Leipzig: Schneider, 1932.
64p., illus. 20cm.

BINGHAM, Hiram
Inca land: explorations in the highlands of Peru.
Boston (Mass.): Houghton Mifflin, 1922. xvii,
365p., plates, illus., maps, bibl. 24cm.

BINGLEY, William
Excursions in North Wales, including Aberystwith
and the Devil's Bridge, intended as a guide to
tourists. 3rd. ed. with corrections and additions
made during excursions in ... 1838, by his son,
W.R. Bingley. Longman, Orme, 1839. xxxi, 355p.,
1 fold. plate, map. 24cm.
Earlier eds.published under titles: A tour round
North Wales; and North Wales.

BINGLEY, William
North Wales, delineated from two excursions
through all the interesting parts ... intended as
a guide to future tourists. 2nd ed. Longman,
Hurst, Rees, Orme, & Brown, 1814. xxiv, 532p.,
plates, illus., fold. col. map. 22cm.
Other eds. published under titles: A tour round
North Wales; and Excursions in North Wales.

BINGLEY, William
North Wales, including its scenery, antiquities,
customs ... delineated from two excursions ...
during the summers of 1798 and 1801. Longman &
Rees, 1804. 2 v., plates, illus., fold. col. map.
24cm.
Other eds. published under titles: A tour round
North Wales; and Excursions in North Wales.

BINGLEY, William
A tour round North Wales, performed during the
summer of 1798... E. Williams, 1800. 2 v., col.
plates, illus., music. 22cm.
Later eds. published under titles: North Wales;
and Excursions in North Wales.

BINGLEY, William
Travels in South America from modern writers,
with remarks and observations, exhibiting a
connected view of the geography and present state
of that quarter of the globe, designed for the
use of young persons. J. Sharpe, 1820. 346p.,
3 plates, illus. 19cm.

BINGLEY, W   R
BINGLEY, William
Excursions in North Wales, including Aberystwith
and the Devil's Bridge, intended as a guide to
tourists. 3rd. ed. with corrections and additions made during excursions in ... 1838, by his
son, W.R. Bingley. Longman, Orme, 1839. xxxi,
355p., 1 fold. plate, map. 24cm.
Earlier eds. published under titles: A tour round
North Wales; and North Wales.

BINNIE, Alfred M
Western Canada in 1933. [London, 1934].
81-88p., plates, illus. 23cm.
Offprint from Alpine Journal, vol. 46, 1934.

BIOLEY, B
Le pont mystérieux du gouffre de la Tête-Noire =
The mysterious bridge on the abyss to be seen
from the Tête-Noire ...; [edited by] B. Bioley.
Martigny-Bourg: Bioley, 1893. 14p., illus. 17cm.

BIRRELL, Francis
BLAIKIE, Thomas
Diary of a Scotch gardener at the French Court
at the end of the eighteenth century; edited
with an introduction by Francis Birrell.
Routledge, 1931. xii, 256p., plates, illus.
23cm.

BIRTLES, Geoff B
Stoney Middleton dale. [N.p.]: The Author, 1966.
[51p.]. 18cm.
Typescript.

BIRTT, W   Bridges
By the roaring Reuss: idylls and stories of the
Alps. Constable, 1898. 184p., plates, illus.
20cm.

BISACCIA, Mario
DEL ZOTTO, Giancarlo
[Alpinismo moderno]. Alpinisme moderne; [collabo-
rateurs: Mario Bisaccia and others]; [sous la
direction de Giancarlo del Zotto]. Paris:
Arthaud, 1971. 235p., plates, illus. 22cm.
(Collection sempervivum, no. 51)

BISCOE, Cecil Earle Tyndale
See
TYNDALE-BISCOE, Cecil Earle

BISSON FRÈRES
CATELIN, Edmond de, <u>vicomte</u>
Première ascension photographique au sommet du
Mont-Blanc par MM. Bisson frères; photographes de
S.M. L'Empereur; sous le direction d'Auguste
Balmat... Annecy: Thésio, 1861. 15p. 23cm.

BITHRAY, Ebenezer
Switzerland and Italy, being personal notes of a
tour via Belgium and Germany, returning home
through France. J.H. Roberts, [1883]. 49p.
25cm.

BIVEN, Peter H   and MCDERMOTT, M   B
Cornwall. Vol. 1; with diagrams by C. Fishwick;
geological notes by M. Springett; notes on mining
and natural history by Ruth Neill; and notes on
birds by J. Braven. Sidcup: Climbers' Club,
1968. xi, 209p., plates (1 fold.), illus., maps.
16cm. (Climbers Club guides)

BECKEY, Fred and <u>BJORNSTAD</u>, Eric
Guide to Leavenworth rock-climbing areas.
Seattle: The Mountaineers, 1965. 86p., illus.,
maps. 21cm.

BLAAS, J
Geologischer Führer durch die Tiroler und
Vorarlberger Alpen. Innsbruck: Wagner, 1902.
7 v., illus., maps. 18cm.
In slip-case.

BLAB, Georg
Aus der Frühzeit der Bergsteigerei. München:
Alpenfreund Verlag, 1926. 116p., plates, illus.
17cm. (Alpenfreund-Bucherei, 15)

BLACHE, Jules
L'homme et la montagne; préface de Raoul
Blanchard. Paris: Gallimard, 1933. 190p., 40
plates, illus. 23cm. (Géographie humaine)

BLACK, C   B
Guide to Switzerland and the Italian lakes.
Sampson Low, Marston, Low & Searle, [n.d.].
170p., maps. 18cm.

Black's picturesque guide through North and South
Wales and Monmouthshire. Edinburgh: Black, 1853.
viii, 406p., plates, illus., fold. maps. 19cm.
Later ed. published in 1872 under title: Black's
picturesque guide to Wales.

Black's picturesque guide to the English Lakes; including an essay on the geology of the district
by John Phillips. 4th ed. Edinburgh: Black, 1850.
xxiv, 240p., plates, illus., maps. 18cm.

- - 17th ed. 1872.

- - 18th ed. 1874.

Black's picturesque guide to Wales. Edinburgh:
Black, 1872. xv, 433p., plates, illus., maps.
18cm.
Previous ed. published in 1853 under title:
Black's picturesque guide through North and South
Wales and Monmouthshire.

Black's picturesque tourist of Scotland. Edinburgh:
Black, 1840. vii, 415p., plates, illus., maps.
18cm.

- - 3rd ed. 1843.

- - 15th ed. 1861.

- - 17th ed. 1865.

BLACKBURN, Henry
Artistic travel in Normandy, Brittany, the
Pyrenees, Spain and Algeria. New ed. Sampson Low,
Marston, 1895. xiii, 320p., plates, illus. 22cm.

BLACKBURN, Henry
The Pyrenees: a description of summer life at
French watering places; ... illustrations by Gustave
Doré. Sampson Low, and Marston, 1867. xvi, 327p.,
1 plate, illus., map. 26cm.

BLACKLER, L   V   Stewart
On secret patrol in High Asia; with an introduction
by Sir George Younghusband. Murray, 1922. xiv,
302p., plates (2 fold., 1 col.), illus., maps.
24cm.

BLACKMAN, M
George Ingle Finch, 1888-1970, elected F.R.S. 1938.
[London, 1972]. 223-239p., 1 plate, port. 26cm.
Offprint from Biographical Memoirs of Fellows of
the Royal Society, v. 18, Nov. 1972.

BLACKSHAW, Alan
Mountaineering, from hill walking to alpine climb-
ing; foreword by Sir John Hunt. Harmondsworth:
Penguin, 1965. 542p., illus., bibl. 18cm.
(Penguin handbooks)
Approved by the British Mountaineering Council and
the Association of Scottish Climbing Clubs.

- - Reprint with revisions. 1968.

- - Rev. ed. 1970.

BLACKWOOD, Algernon
Pan's garden: a volume of nature stories; with
drawings by W. Graham Robertson. Macmillan, 1912.
xi, 531p., illus. 22cm.

BLACKWOOD'S MAGAZINE
Travel, adventure, and sport from Blackwood's
Magazine. Vol. 4. Blackwood, [186-]. 436p.
17cm.

Blätter aus der Walliser Geschichte. 9. Bd., 4.
Jahr. Festschrift zum 75. Geburtstag von Dionys
Imesch; hrsg. vom Geschichtsforschenden Verein
von Oberwallis. Brig: Der Verein, 1943. 327-
506p., plates, illus. 21cm.
Cover title.

BLAIKIE, Thomas
Diary of a Scotch gardener at the French Court
at the end of the eighteenth century; edited
with an introduction by Francis Birrell.
Routledge, 1931. xii, 256p., plates, illus.
23cm.

BLAIKIE, Thomas
[Diary of a Scotch gardener ...]. Journal de
Thomas Blaikie: excursions d'un botaniste
écossais dans les Alpes et le Jura en 1775;
traduit et publié avec une introduction et des
notes par L. Seylaz. Neuchatel: La Baconnière,
1935. 159p., plates, illus. 20cm.
BLAIKIE, Thomas
MONTAGNIER, Henry Fairbanks
Thomas Blaikie and Michel-Gabriel Paccard.
[London], 1933. 34p., 1 col. plate, illus.
23cm.
Offprint from Alpine Journal, v. 45, May 1933.

BLAINVILLE, J   de
Travels through Holland, Germany, Switzerland,
but especially Italy ...; translated from the
author's manuscript ... by Dr. Turnbull, [Mr.
Guthrie, Mr. Lockman and the editor]. J. Noon,
1757. 3 v., maps. 26cm.

BLAKE, J   M
Joy of Tyrol: a human revelation; edited by J.M.
Blake with original drawings... Stanley Paul,
[19--]. 278p., illus. 22cm.

BLAKEBOROUGH, J   Fairfax
BELL, J   H   B
British hills and mountains; by J.H.B. Bell,
E.F. Bozman and J. Fairfax Blakeborough.
Batsford, 1940. viii, 120p., plates (some col.),
illus. 22cm. (British heritage series)

BLAKENEY, Edward Henry
Alpine poems. Winchester: Printed at the
Author's private press, 1929. 38 leaves. 22cm.

BLAKENEY, Edward Henry
Footsteps of autumn and other poems. Ely:
Printed by the Author at his private press,
1912. 58p. 24cm.

BLAKENEY, Edward Henry
ALPINE CLUB
Peaks, passes & glaciers; selected and annotated
by E.H. Blakeney. Dent, [1926]. xlviii, 317p.,
18cm. (Everyman's library, no. 778)

BLAKENEY, Thomas Sydney
A.R. Hinks and the first Everest Expedition,
1921. London, 1970. 333-343p., plates, illus.,
bibl. 25cm.
Offprint from Geographical Journal, v. 136,
pt. 3, September 1970.

BLAKENEY, Thomas Sydney
The Alpine Club. Wiesbaden: F. Steiner, [1964].
256-269p. 18cm.
Offprint from Geographisches Taschenbuch, 1964-65.

BLAKENEY, Thomas Sydney
FRIENDS OF THE NATIONAL LIBRARIES
Thomas Sydney Blakeney: [an obituary].
(In Friends of the National Libraries. Annual
Report, 1976, pp. 5-6)

BLANC, chanoine
Examen de l'apologie des travaux du glacier du
Giétroz. [Lausanne]: [E. Vincent?], 1825. 66p.
19cm.

BLANC, chanoine
Observations sur les travaux que le Gouvernement
du Valais fait exécuter au glacier de Giétroz,
vallée de Bagnes, dans le dessein de prévenir
une nouvelle débacle. Lausanne: E. Vincent,
1825. 24p. 19cm.

BLANC, chanoine
Réflexions sur la réponse de M. l'ingénieur
Venetz à deux lettres concernant les travaux du
glacier Giétroz, Vallée de Bagnes, en Valais,
écrites par le chanoine Blanc à M. Gard, président du Dixain d'Entre-mont, séant en Diète à
Sion, en Décembre 1824. Lausanne: E. Vincent,
1825. 24p. 19cm.

BLANC, chanoine
VENETZ, Ignace
Apologie des travaux du glacier de Giétroz
contre les attaques réitérées de M. le chanoine
Blanc. Sion: A. Advocat, 1825. 23p. 19cm.

BLANC, Pierre and LECOULTRE, Gérald
Ski: 67 itinéraires détaillés, établis par
Pierre Blanc, Gérald Lecoultre en collaboration
avec O. Treyvaud. Lausanne: Payot, 1936. 116p.
17cm. (Les petits guides Schaefer sports)

BLANCHARD, Raoul
Les Alpes françaises. Paris: Colin, 1925.
218p., maps. 18cm. (Collection Armand Colin
(Section de géographie), no. 56)

BLANCHARD, Raoul
Les Alpes françaises à vol d'oiseau, [par] Raoul
Blanchard, F. Seive ...; photographies aériennes
du Capitaine Seive [and others]. Grenoble:
Arthaud, 1928. 187p., illus. 22cm. (Les beaux
pays, 22)

BLANCHARD, Raoul
La Corse. Grenoble: Arthaud, 1927. 149p.,
illus., map. 22cm. (Les beaux pays, 12)

BLANCHET, Émile Robert
Au bout d'un fil: douze ascensions nouvelles dans
les Alpes suisses et françaises. Paris:
Éditions de France, 1937. 217p., plates, illus.
19cm.

BLANCHET, Émile Robert
[Au bout d'un fil ...]. Als Letzter am Seil:
zwölf Erstbesteigungen in den Schweizer und in
den französischen Alpen; ... übertr ... von
Heinrich Erler. Berlin: Union Deutsche Verlagsgesellschaft, [1938]. 162p., plates, illus.
22cm.

BLANCHET, Émile Robert
Hors des chemins battus: ascensions nouvelles
dans les Alpes; préface du général Bruce. Paris:
Éditions de France, 1932. vii, 264p., plates,
illus. 19cm.

BLANCHET, Émile Robert
[Hors des chemins battus ...]. Jenseits be-
gangener Pfade: neue Bergfahrten in den Alpen;
... übertr ... von Heinrich Erler. Berlin: Union
Deutsche Verlagsgesellschaft, [1939?]. 179p.,
plates, illus. 21cm.

BLANCHET, Émile Robert
[Hors des chemins battus ...]. Fuori delle
strade battute; traduzione Matelda Cozzani.
Milano: Eroica, 1935. 246p., plates, illus.
18cm. (Montagna 13)

BLANK, Hans
Illustrirter Führer durch Saalfelden im Pinzgau
und seine Seitenthäler und Berge; mit besonderer
Rücksichtnahme auf das Steinerne Meer. Wien:
A. Hartleben, 1890. viii, 80p., plates, illus.,
maps. 16cm. (Hartleben Illustrirter Führer, 37)

BLASHFORD-SNELL, John and BALLANTINE, Alistair
Expeditions the experts' way; edited by John
Blashford-Snell and Alistair Ballantine. Faber,
1977. 256p., illus., bibl. 21cm.

BLATTL, Josef
Wenn die Lawinen donnern und Anderes: zwanzig
Geschichten aus Tirol. Regensburg: Manz, 1931.
254p. 20cm.

BLAZER, F
Mes souvenirs de montagne. Grenoble: Arthaud,
1929. xv, 238p., plates, illus. 19cm.

BLESSINGTON, Marguerite, Countess of
Heath's book of beauty; with beautifully finished
engravings from drawings by the first artists;
edited by the Countess of Blessington. Longman,
Brown, Green and Longmans, [18--]. vi, 280p.,
plates, illus. 25cm.

BLESSINGTON, Marguerite, Countess of
The keepsake 1846; with ... engravings ... under
the superintendence of Charles Heath; edited by
the Countess of Blessington. Longman, Brown,
Green and Longmans, 1846. iv, 278p., plates,
illus. 25cm.

BLETZACHER, J
Lieder-buch des Deutschen u-Österreichschen
Alpen-Verreines... Hannover: Nagel, 1887. 256p.,
music. 17cm. (Words and music)

BLOBEL, Oscar
Little Herta's Christmas dream: a Christmas
fairy-tale of the mountains; from the German ...
translated by H.M.H.; illustrated by Hugo Grimm.
Sampson Low, Marston, 1911. [48p.], col. illus.
32cm.

BLODIG, Karl
NIEBERL, Franz
Das Gehen auf Eis und Schnee; unter Mitwirkung
von Karl Blodig. München: R. Rother, 1923.
93p., plates, illus. 21cm.

BLODIG, Karl
Die Viertausender der Alpen. München: R.
Rother, 1923. 324p., plates (1 col.), illus.
25cm.

BLODIG, Karl
Zur Erinnerung an Walther Flender, 11. Jan. 1880-
26. Feb. 1902: ein Lebensabriss. Leipzig: [The
Author], [n.d.]. 168p., plates, illus. 24cm.

BLÜMCKE, Adolf and HESS, Hans
Die Nachmessungen am Vernagtferner in den Jahren
1891, 1893 und 1895. Graz: D.u.Ö.A., 1897.
97-112p., 2 col. plates (1 fold.), maps. 29cm.
(Wissenschaftliche Ergänzungshefte zur Zeitschrift
des D.u.Ö Alpenvereins. Bd. 1, Heft 1, Anhang)

BLÜMCKE, Adolf and HESS, Hans
Untersuchungen am Hintereisferner. München:
D.u.Ö.A., 1899. 87p., plates (some fold., 1
col.), illus., maps. 29cm. (Wissenschaftliche
Ergänzungshefte zur Zeitschrift des D.u.Ö. Alpen-
vereins. Bd. 1, Heft 2)

BOADA, J
Picos de Europa: block postal. Madrid: J. Boada,
[19--]. 1 v. of illus. 9 x 15cm.
Sepia postcard views.

BOARDMAN, Peter
1972 Nottingham University Hindu Kush Expedition,
[by Peter D. Boardman]. [Nottingham]: The
Expedition, [1973?]. 37p., plates, illus., maps.
23cm.

BOARDMAN, Peter
The Shining Mountain: two men on Changabang's
West Wall; with material by Joe Tasker. Hodder
and Stoughton, 1978. 192p., plates (some col.),
illus., map. 23cm.

BOBBA, Giovanni
Alpi Marittime. Torino: Club Alpino Italiano,
Sezione di Torino, 1908. xxxi, 416p., plates,
illus., maps. 18cm. (Guida dei monti d'Italia)

BOBBA, Giovanni
MARTELLI, A   E   and VACCARONE, Luigi
Guida delle Alpi occidentali. Torino: Club
Alpino Italiano, Sezione di Torino, 1889-96.
2 v. in 3, fold. plates (some col.), illus.,
maps, bibl. 17cm.
Vol. 2, pt. 2 is by G. Bobba and L. Vaccarone.

BOBBA, Giovanni
Monte Cervino, testo Giovanni Bobba; disegni
Angelo Calegari. 2a ed. Monza: Club Alpino
Italiano, 1924. 72p., illus. 18cm. (Club
Alpino Italiano. Sezione Universitaria. Guida
sucai)

BOBBA, Giovanni
PIUS XI, Pope
Scritti alpinistici ... [di] Achille Ratti
(ora S.S. Pio Papa XI); raccolti e pubblicati
in occasione del cinquantenario della Sezione
di Milano del Club Alpino Italiano ... [da]
Giovanni Bobba e Francesco Mauro. Milano:
Bertieri e Vanzetti, 1923. xxiii, 189p., illus.
26cm.

BOBBA, Giovanni
PIUS XI, Pope
[Scritti alpinistici]. Alpine Schriften des
Priesters Achille Ratti ...; gesammelt und hrsg.
... [von] Giovanni Bobba und Francesco Mauro;
ins Deutsche übertr. von Leopold von Schlözer.
Berlin: R. Mosse, 1925. xxi, 196p., plates,
illus. 26cm.

BOCCARD, François
Histoire du Vallais, avant et sous l'ère chré-
tienne jusqu'à nos jours. Genève: Berthier-
Guers, 1844. 424p. 22cm.

BOCCARDI, Renzo
ITALY. Army. Corpo degli Alpini
I Verdi: cinquant'anni di storia alpina, 1872-
1922; sotto gli auspici della Associazione
Nazionale Alpini; a cura di Renzo Boccardi.
Roma: Alfieri & Lacroix, [1922]. 133p., plates,
illus., music. 25cm.

BODDAM-WHETHAM, J   W
Western wanderings: a record of travel in the
evening land. Bentley, 1874. 364p., plates,
illus. 23cm.

BODDINGTON, Mary
Sketches in the Pyrenees; with some remarks on
Languedoc, Provence, and the Cornice, by the
author of "Slight reminiscences of the Rhine" ...
[i.e. Mary Boddington]. Longman, Rees, Orme,
Brown, Green, & Longman, 1837. 2 v. 21cm.

BODENSTEDT, Friedrich
Eine Königsreise. 3. Aufl. Leipzig: J. Lehmann,
[1883]. 295p. 20cm.

BODENSTEIN, Gustav
Aus der Ostmark: ein Buch von Landschaft und
alpinem Leben, Kultur und Geschichte; geleitet
von Gustav Bodenstein. Wien: Verlag des Wiener
Festausschusses des D.u.Ö. Alpenvereins, 1927.
xii, 319p., plates (some col.), illus. 26cm.

BOECK, Kurt
Durch Indien ins verschlossene Land Nepal:
ethnographische und photographische Studienblätter. Leipzig: F. Hirt, 1903. xvi, 319p.,
plates (1 fold.), illus., map. 25cm.

BOECK, Kurt
Himalaya-Album: 20 photographs of the Indian Alps,
taken by K. Boeck. Baden-Baden: F. Spies, [1894].
1 v. of illus. 42cm.
In portfolio.

BOECK, Kurt
Himalaya: Lieder und Bilder. Rorschacherberg:
Selbstverlag des Verfassers, [1927]. 74p. 35cm.

BOECK, Kurt
Im Banne des Everest: Erlebnisse in Nepal, der
für Weisse verschlossenen Heimat der Gorkhas im
Zentral-Himalaja. Leipzig: Haessel, 1923.
106p., plates (some fold.), illus., map. 25cm.

BOECK, Kurt
Indische Gletscherfahrten: Reisen und Erlebnisse
im Himalaja. Stuttgart: Deutsche Verlags-
Anstalt, 1900. xii, 470p., plates (some fold.,
1 col.), illus., maps. 24cm.

BERTARELLI, L   V   and BOEGAN, Eugenio
Duemila grotte: quarant'anni di esplorazioni nella
Venezia Giulia. Milano: Touring Club Italiano,
1926. 494p., plates, illus., col. maps (2 in
portfolio). 25cm.

BÖHM, August, Edler von Böhmersheim
Führer durch die Hochschwab Gruppe. 2. voll-
standig neu bearb. Aufl. Wien: Lechner [for]
Deutscher und Oesterreichischer Alpenverein,
Section 'Austria', 1896. xv, 154p., plates,
illus. 17cm.

BÖHM, August, Edler von Böhmersheim
Geschichte der Moranenkunde. Wien: Lechner,
1901. viii, 334p., 4 plates, illus., bibl. 29cm.
(Abhandlungen der K. K. Geographischen Gesellschaft in Wien, Bd. 3 no. 4)

BÖHM, Otto and NOSSBERGER, Adolf
Führer durch die Schobergruppe. Wien: Artaria,
1925. xv, 224p., map (in pocket). 17cm.

BOEHM, William D
Glacier Bay. Anchorage: Alaska Northwest Publishing Company, 1975. 134p., 1 fold. col. plate,
illus., map. 22 x 28cm.

BÖHMERSHEIM, August Böhm, Edler von
See
BÖHM, August, Edler von Böhmersheim

BOELL, Jacques
Cimes d'Oisans: récits de courses en Dauphiné;
préface de Lucien Devies. [Paris]: Flammarion,
1937. 137p., 12 plates, illus., maps. 22cm. (La
vie en montagne)

BOELL, Jacques
High heaven; introduction by François Mauriac;
translated[by Dilys Owen]. Elek, 1947. 128p., 32
plates, illus., maps. 22cm.

BOELL, Jacques
S.E.S.: Éclaireurs-Skieurs au combat, 1940 - 1944 -
1945. Grenoble: Arthaud, 1946. 347p., plates,
illus., maps. 19cm. (Collection témoinages, 28)

BÖTTIGER, Carl August
RECKE, Elisa von der
Tagebuch einer Reise durch einen Theil Deutschlands und durch Italien, in den Jahren 1804 bis
1806; hrsg. vom Hofrath Böttiger. Berlin: In der
Nicolaischen Buchhandlung, 1815-17. 4 v., plates,
map. 21cm.

BOFFA, F
SAGLIO, Silvio
Monte Rosa. Milano: Club Alpino Italiano, Touring
Club Italiano, 1960. 575p., plates, illus., map
(on lining papers), bibl. 17cm. (Guida dei monti
d'Italia)

BOGG, Edmund
Two thousand miles of wandering in the border
country, Lakeland and Ribblesdale. Leeds: E. Bogg,
1898. xxii, 263p., illus. 29cm.

BOGLE, George
Narratives of the mission of George Bogle to
Tibet, and of the journey of Thomas Manning to
Lhasa; edited with notes, an introduction and
lives of Mr. Bogle and Mr. Manning by Clements R.
Markham. Trübner, 1876. clxiii, 354p., plates
(some fold., some col.), illus., maps. 23cm.

BOHLIG, F
Die Elmauer Haltspitze. Stuttgart: Deutsche
Verlags-Anstalt, 1905. 54p., plates, illus.,
map. 18cm. (Alpine Gipfelführer, 2)

BOHLIG, F
Der Watzmann. Stuttgart: Deutsche Verlags-
Anstalt, 1906. 66p., plates, illus., maps.
18cm. (Alpine Gipfelführer, 9)

BOILLOT-ROBERT, J
COMPAGNIE DES CHEMINS DE FER JURA-SIMPLON
De Bale à Brigue et Zermatt: guide officiel du
Jura-Simplon, de J. Boillot-Robert. Neuchatel:
F. Wohlgrath, [ca 1893]. 74, 54p., plates
(some fold., some col.), illus., maps. 23 x 32cm.
(Guides illustrés, sér. 3)
"Partie non officielle" contains "Le Jura-Simplon
en dix jours", par Anatole Lediscret; texte
français et anglais.

BOIS-ROBERT, Joseph Lavallée, marquis de
See
LAVALLÉE, Joseph, marquis de Bois-Robert

BOISSON, G
Guide des montagnes des Basses-Pyrénées. T. 1.
Vallée d'Aspe, Chaîne Interaspossaloise.
Bordeaux: Delmas, 1938. 342p., illus., maps.
20cm.

BOISSON, G
Pyrénées occidentales, par Dr. Boisson [and
others]. Pau: R. Olliver [for] Fédération
Française de la Montagne, 1960-63. 2 v., 1 fold.
plate, illus., maps. 17cm.

BOLAND, Henri
Coins de France: Brie, Ardennes, Normandie,
Bretagne, Anjou, Massif Central, Pyrénées.
Paris: Hachette, 1910. 284p., plates, illus.
20cm. (Bibliothèque des voyages illustrés)

BOLAND, Henri
JOANNE, Paul
Itinéraire général de la France: Corse. [Nouv.
éd.; mise à jour par Henri Boland]. Paris:
Hachette, 1892. lxiii, 180p., 4 maps. 18cm.
(Collection des guides-Joanne)

PUTNAM, William Lowell and BOLES, Glen W
Climber's guide to the Rocky Mountains of Canada
South. 5th ed. [New York]: American Alpine
Club, 1973. 330p., illus., maps. 17cm.
Based on earlier eds. by James Monroe Thorington.

BOLLMANN, Louis de
Remarques sur l'état moral, politique et militaire de la Grèce, écrites sur les lieux ...
pendant l'année 1822. Marseille: Carnaud &
Simonin, [1823]. 46p. 20cm.

BOLLMANN, Louis de
Die Schweiz: ein Handbuch zunächt für Reisende,
mit einem Anhang, enthaltend die Beschreibung
der interessanten Punkte der Nachbarlande der
Schweiz. Stuttgart: Hoffmann, 1837. 895p.,
plates, map. 22cm.

BOLLMANN, Louis de
Wegweiser der Schweiz, enthaltend die be-
suchtesten Gegenden des Landes... Bern: J.F.
Wagner, 1836. 213p. 32cm.

BOLT, Niklaus
Svizzero! Die Geschichte einer Jugend; mit 40
Naturstudien von Rud. Münger. Stuttgart: J.F.
Steinkopf, 1913. 245p., illus. 20cm.

BOLZANO. Ente Provinciale per il Turismo
See
Ente Provinciale per il Turismo, Bolzano

BOLZANO. Provinzialverband für den Fremdenverkehr
See
Ente Provinciale per il Turismo, Bolzano

BONACOSSA, Aldo
Regione dell'Ortler. Milano: Club Alpino
Italiano, 1915. xvii, 482p., plates (some fold.,
some col.), illus., maps. 18cm. (Guida dei
monti d'Italia; Alpi centrali)

BONACOSSA, Aldo
Regione Màsino, Bregáglia, Disgrázia. Roma:
Club Alpino Italiano; Milano: Touring Club
Italiano, 1936. 591p., plates (some fold. col.),
illus., maps, bibl. 17cm. (Guida dei monti
d'Italia)

- - 2a ed., di Aldo Bonacossa, Giovanni Rossi.
1977. 2 v.

BONAPARTE, Roland, prince
Le glacier de l'Aletsch et le Lac de Märjelen.
Paris: L'Auteur, 1889. 26p., plates, illus.
28cm.

BONAPARTE, Roland, prince
Le premier établissement des Néerlandais à
Maurice. Paris: L'Auteur, 1890. 60p., plates,
illus., map. 28cm.

BONATTI, Walter
[I giorno grandi]. The great days; translated
by Geoffrey Sutton. Gollancz, 1974. 189p.,
plates, illus. 23cm.

BONATTI, Walter
[Le mie montagne]. On the heights; translated
from the Italian by Lovett F. Edwards. Hart-
Davis, 1964. 248p., plates, illus. 23cm.

- - Another issue. Diadem Books, 1979.

BONATTI, Walter
[Le mie montagne]. À mes montagnes; [traduit
par F. Germain]. [Paris]: Arthaud, 1962. 291p.,
plates, illus., maps. 21cm. (Collection
sempervivum, no. 38)

BONER, Charles
Chamois hunting in the mountains of Bavaria;
with illustrations by Theodore Horschelt.
Chapman & Hall, 1853. viii, 410p., col. plates,
illus. 24cm.

BONER, Charles
Chamois hunting in the mountains of Bavaria and
in the Tyrol; with illustrations by Theodore
Horschelt. New ed. Chapman & Hall, 1860.
xiii, 446p., col. plates, illus. 21cm.
First edition published in 1853 under title:
Chamois hunting in the mountains of Bavaria.

BONER, Charles
Guide for travellers in the plain and on the
mountain. Hardwicke, [1866]. vi, 61p., illus.
17cm.

- - 2nd ed. 1876.

BONER, Charles
Transylvania: its products and its people.
Longmans, Green, Reader, & Dyer, 1865. xiv,
642p., plates (some fold., some col.), illus.,
maps. 22cm.

BONGHI, Ruggiero
In viaggio da Pontresina a Londra: impressioni
dolci, osservazioni amare. 1a ser. Milano:
U. Lombardi, 1889. x, 233p. 19cm.

BONIN, Charles Eudes
Les royaumes des neiges (états himalayens).
Paris: Colin, 1911. x, 306p., plates, illus.,
maps. 20cm.

BONINGTON, Chris
Annapurna South Face. Cassell, 1971. x, 334p.,
plates (1 fold., some col.), illus., maps.
25cm.

- - Another issue. Harmondsworth: Penguin, 1973.

BONINGTON, Chris
[Annapurna South Face]. Annapurna face sud;
traduit de l'anglais par Jeanne et Félix Germain;
préface de Maurice Herzog. [Paris]: Arthaud,
1972. 335p., plates, illus., maps. 21cm.
(Collection sempervivum, no. 54)

BONINGTON, Chris
[Annapurna South Face]. Annapurna Parete Sud;
traduzione ... e introduzione di Luciano Serra;
prefazione di Maurice Herzog. [Milano]:
Dall'Oglio, 1973. 372p., plates (some col.),
illus. 21cm. (Exploits)

BONINGTON, Chris
Changabang, by Chris Bonington [and others];
[edited by Alan Hankinson]. Heinemann, 1975.
118p., col. plates, illus., maps. 26cm.

BONINGTON, Chris
SOUTH WEST FACE BRITISH EVEREST EXPEDITION, 1975
Everest conquered! Expedition fact sheet.
Barclays Bank International, 1975. 4 leaves,
4 illus. (in pocket). 31cm.

BONINGTON, Chris
Everest, South West Face. Hodder & Stoughton,
1973. 352p., plates (some col.), illus., maps.
25cm.

BONINGTON, Chris
[Everest South West Face]. Everest Parete Sud-
Ovest; traduzione ... e introduzione di Luciano
Serra; prefazione di Lord Hunt. [Milano]:
Dall'Oglio, 1975. 311p., plates (some col.),
illus., map. 21cm. (Exploits)

BONINGTON, Chris
Everest the hard way. Hodder & Stoughton, 1976.
239p., col. plates, illus., maps. 26cm.

- - Another issue. Arrow Books, 1977.

BONINGTON, Chris
I chose to climb; with a foreword by Eric Shipton.
Gollancz, 1966. 208p., plates, illus., map.
23cm.

BONINGTON, Chris
The next horizon: autobiography II. Gollancz,
1973. 304p., plates (some col.), illus., maps.
24cm.

BONJOUR, E
A short history of Switzerland, by E. Bonjour,
H.S. Offler and G.R. Potter. Oxford: Clarendon
Press, 1952. 388p., maps, bibl. 23cm.

BONNAMAUX, H   and BONNAMAUX, Ch
Manuel pratique de camping. Paris: Touring Club
de France, [1913]. 181p., illus., bibl. 18cm.

BONNEFOY, A
See
BONNEFOY, J   A

BONNEFOY, J   A
PRIEURÉ DE CHAMONIX
Documents relatifs au Prieuré et a la vallée de
Cahmonix [sic]; recueillis par J.-A. Bonnefoy;
publié et annotés par A. Perrin. Chambéry:
Imprimerie Chatelain, 1879-83. 2 v. 25cm.

BONNEFOY, J   A
PERRIN, André
Le Prieuré de Chamonix: histoire de la vallée et
du Prieuré de Chamonix du Xe au XVIIIe siècle;
d'après les documents recuillis par A. Bonnefoy.
Chambéry: A. Perrin, 1887. 253p., 1 fold. plate,
map. 25cm.

BONNET, Honoré
[Ski à la française]. Ski - the experts' way;
with photographs by Gérald Maurois; English technical adviser Robin Brook-Hollinshead. Newnes,
1966. 237p., illus. 25cm.

BONNEY, Thomas George
The Alpine regions of Switzerland and the
neighbouring countries: a pedestrian's notes
on their physical features, scenery, and natural
history; with illustrations by E. Whymper.
Cambridge: Deighton, Bell; London: Bell & Daldy,
1868. xvi, 351p., plates, illus. 24cm.

BONNEY, Thomas George
WALTON, Elijah
Alpine vignettes; with descriptive text by T.G.
Bonney, 4th ed. W.M. Thompson, 1882. 1 v.
(chiefly col. illus.). 34cm.
First ed. published in 1873 under title:
Vignettes: alpine and eastern.

BONNEY, Thomas George
WALTON, Elijah
The Bernese Oberland: twelve scenes among its
peaks and lakes, by Elijah Walton; with descriptive text by T.G. Bonney. W.M. Thompson, 1874.
1 v. (chiefly col. illus.). 44cm.

BONNEY, Thomas George
The building of the Alps. Unwin, 1912. 384p.,
plates, illus. 24cm.

BONNEY, Thomas George
WALTON, Elijah
The coast of Norway, from Christiania to Hammer-
fest; the descriptive text by T.G. Bonney.
W.M. Thompson, 1871. viii, 24p., 12 plates,
illus. 35 x 44cm.

BONNEY, Thomas George
WALTON, Elijah
English Lake scenery; with descriptive text by
T.G. Bonney. W.M. Thompson, 1876. 1 v.
(chiefly col. illus.). 34cm.

BONNEY, Thomas George
WALTON, Elijah
Flowers from the upper Alps, with glimpses of
their homes; the descriptive text by T.G.
Bonney. W.M. Thompson, 1869. 1 v. (chiefly
col. illus.). 34cm.

- - 5th ed. 1882.

BONNEY, Thomas George
Ice-work present and past. Kegan Paul, Trench,
Trübner, 1896. xiv, 295p., 4 fold. plates,
illus., maps. 20cm.

BONNEY, Thomas George
Lake and mountain scenery from the Swiss Alps;
... photographs from original oil-paintings by
G. Closs and O. Froelicher; ... woodcuts by G.
Roux; with text by T.G. Bonney. Bruckmann,
1874. 148p., illus. 38cm.
Based on a work by H.A. Berlepsch.

BONNEY, Thomas George
Memories of a long life. Cambridge: The Author,
1921. 112, viip. 23cm.

BONNEY, Thomas George
On the formation of "cirques" and their bearing
upon theories attributing the excavation of
alpine valleys mainly to the action of glaciers.
London, 1871. 312-324p., illus. 22cm.
Offprint from the Quarterly journal of the
Geological Society for Aug., 1871.

BONNEY, Thomas George
Outline sketches in the High Alps of Dauphiné.
Longman, Green, Longman, Roberts, & Green, 1865.
xv, 52p., plates (1 col.), illus., map. 26cm.

BONNEY, Thomas George
WALTON, Elijah
The peaks and valleys of the Alps; with descriptive text by T.G. Bonney. Day, 1867. 1 v.
(chiefly col. illus.). 57cm.

- - Another issue. Sampson Low, Son, & Marston,
1868.

BONNEY, Thomas George
WALTON, Elijah
Peaks in pen and pencil for students of alpine
scenery; edited by T.G. Bonney. Longmans, Green,
1872. 26p. (chiefly illus.). 49cm.

BONNEY, Thomas George
The story of our planet. Cassell, 1893. xv,
592p., col. plates, illus., maps. 25cm.

BONNEY, Thomas George
WALTON, Elijah
Vignettes: alpine and eastern; the descriptive
text by T.G. Bonney. W.M. Thompson, 1873. 1 v.
(chiefly col. illus.). 34cm.
Fourth ed. published in 1882 under title: Alpine
vignettes.

BONNEY, Thomas George
ANDERSON, Tempest
Volcanic studies in many lands, being reproductions of photographs by the author ... with explanatory notices. Murray, 1903. xxviii,
202p., 105 plates, illus., bibl. 26cm.

- - 2nd series; the text by T.G. Bonney. 1917.

BONNEY, Thomas George
Volcanoes: their structure and significance.
Murray, 1899. xv, 351p., plates, illus., fold.
map. 23cm.

BONNEY, Thomas George
WALTON, Elijah
Welsh scenery (chiefly in Snowdonia); with
descriptive text by T.G. Bonney. W.M. Thompson,
1875. 1 v. (chiefly illus.). 34cm.

BOSCHI, Luigi, marchese and BONORA, Alfredo
Itinerari dell'Appennino (dal Cimone al Catria).
Bologna: Club Alpino Italiano, Sezione di
Bologna, 1882. 62p., plates, illus., maps.
18cm.

BONPLAND, Aimé
HUMBOLDT, Alexander von,Freiherr
Personal narrative of travels to the equinoctial
regions of America during the years 1799-1804 by
Alexander von Humboldt and Aimé Bonpland,
written in French ...; translated and edited by
Thomasina Ross. Henry G. Bohn, 1852-53. 3 v.
20cm. (Bohn's scientific library)

BONSTETTEN, Ch Victor de
La Scandinavie et les Alpes [et Fragments sur
l'Islande]. Genève: J.J. Paschoud, 1826. xxx,
118, 71p. 21cm.

BONUS, Arthur Rivers
Where Hannibal passed. Methuen, 1925. 88p.,
plates, illus., map. 20cm.

BONVALOT, Gabriel
Du Caucase aux Indes à travers le Pamir; ouvrage
orné de ... dessins et croquis par Albert Pépin.
Paris: Nourrit, 1888. xii, 458p., 1 fold. col.
plate, illus., map. 29cm.

BONVALOT, Gabriel
[Du Caucase aux Indes ...]. Through the heart
of Asia, over the Pamir to India; with ...
illustrations by Albert Pépin; translated by
C.B. Pitman. Chapman & Hall, 1889. 2 v., 1
fold. col. plate, illus., map. 27cm.

BOONE AND CROCKETT CLUB
ROOSEVELT, Theodore
American big-game hunting: the book of the Boone
and Crockett Club; editors, Theodore Roosevelt,
George Bird Grinnell. D. Douglas, 1893. 343p.,
plates, illus. 22cm.

BOONE AND CROCKETT CLUB
ROOSEVELT, Theodore
Hunting in many lands: the book of the Boone
and Crockett Club; editors, Theodore Roosevelt,
George Bird Grinnell. New York: Forest and
Stream Publishing Co., 1895. 447p., plates,
illus. 22cm.

BOOTH, M
Roadside sketches in the South of France and
Spanish Pyrenees, by three wayfarers; with
twenty-four illustrations by Touchstone [i.e.
M. Booth]. Bell & Daldy, 1859. vi, 113p.,
plates, illus. 27cm.

BOOY, T de
EGELER, Cornelius Geoffrey
The untrodden Andes: climbing adventures in the
Cordillera Blanca, Peru, by C.G. Egeler in co-
operation with T. de Booy; translated from the
Dutch by W.E. James. Faber, 1955. 203p.,
plates, illus., maps. 22cm.

BORCHERS, Philipp
Berge und Gletscher im Pamir; mit Beiträgen
von Eugen Allwein [and others]; unter Mitwirkung
des Deutschen und Österreichischen Alpenvereins.
Stuttgart: Strecker und Schröder, 1931. xii,
260p., plates (1 fold. col.), illus., maps. 22cm.

BORCHERS, Philipp and WIEN, Karl
Bergfahrten im Pamir. Innsbruck, 1929. 64-160p.,
1 fold. plate, illus., map. 26cm.
Offprint from Zeitschrift des D.u.Ö.A.V., Bd. 60,
1929.

BORCHERS, Philipp
Die weisse Kordillere; unter Mitarbeit von Wilhelm
Bernard [and others]. Berlin: Scherl, 1935.
396p., plates, illus., map. 24cm.

BORDE, Josef
Achtung Lawine! Ratschläge und Hilfsmittel. 5.
verm. und verb. Aufl. Zürich: J. Borde, 1946.
30p., illus. 15cm.

- - Another issue. Tübingen: Demokrit Verlag, 1966.

BORDE, Josef
Berge und Schnee [und] Achtung Lawine: Ratschläge
und Hilfsmittel. Zürich: J. Borde, 1952. 72p.,
plates, illus. 22cm.

BORDE, Josef and NOSZBERGER, Adolf
Führer für Schneeschuhläufer durch die Ennstaler
Alpen... Wien: Guberner & Hierhammer, 1922.
106p. 16cm.

BORDEAUX, Henry
Aventures en montagne. Neuchatel: Attinger,
1946. 240p. 21cm.

BORDEAUX, Henry
Contes de la montagne; préface de Louis Madelin.
Paris: Collection L'adolescence catholique, 1928.
157p., col. plates, illus. 25cm.

BORDEAUX, Henry
Les fleurs des Alpes; ... planches en dix couleurs d'après les aquarelles de Paul A. Robert;
texte de Henry Bordeaux. Paris: Plon, 1938.
15p., 18 col. plates, illus. 28cm. (Collection
"Iris")

BORDEAUX, Henry
Les jeux dangereux. Paris: Plon-Nourrit, 1926.
286p. 19cm.

BORDEAUX, Henry
[La maison morte]. The house that died;
translated by Harold Harper. Unwin, 1923.
270p. 20cm.

BORDEAUX, Henry
La neige sur les pas: roman. Paris: Plon-
Nourrit, 1912. vii, 348p. 20cm.

BORDEAUX, Henry
[La neige sur les pas]. La neve sulle orme:
romanzo. Firenze: Salani, 1915. 361p., plates,
illus. 17cm.

BORDEAUX, Henry
Paysages romanesques. Paris: Plon-Nourrit,
1906. iii, 358p. 20cm.

BORDEAUX, P   E
À travers les Alpes Militaires: quelques
souvenirs. Grenoble, 1928. 77p. 22cm.
Offprint from Mémoires et Documents de l'Académie
Delphinale.

BORDET, Pierre
Recherches géologiques dans l'Himalaya du Népal,
région du Makalu. Paris: Centre National de la
Recherche Scientfique, 1961. 275p., plates
(some fold.), illus, maps (3 fold. col. in
pocket), bibl. 29cm.
At head of this title: Expéditions françaises à
l'Himalaya 1954-1955...
Summary in English

BORDIER, André César
Voyage pitoresque aux glaciéres de Savoye, fait
en 1772, par Mr. B. [i.e. A.C. Bordier]. Genève:
L.A. Caille, 1773. 303p. 17cm.

BORDIER, Henri L
Le Grütli et Guillaume Tell; ou, Défense de la
tradition vulgaire sur les origines de la Confédération suisse. Genève: H. Georg, 1869.
92p. 23cm.

BORDIER, Henri L
La querelle sur les traditions concernant
l'origine de la Confédération suisse. Genève:
H. Georg, 1869. 31p., bibl. 23cm.

BOREL, Maurice
Atlas cantonal, politique et économique de la
Suisse, par Maurice Borel, cartographe; textes
de H.-A. Jaccard. Neuchatel: Administration des
Publications du Dictionnaire Géographique de la
Suisse, [ca 1912]. iv, 76p., 76 col. plates,
illus., maps. 30cm.

BORGOGNONI, A   and TITTA ROSA, G
Scalatori: le più audaci imprese alpinistiche
da Whymper al "sesto grado", raccontate dai protagonisti; a cura di A. Borgognoni, G. Titta
Rosa. 2a ed. riv. e aggiornata. Milano: Hoepli,
1941. xv, 403p., plates, illus., bibl. 21cmm.

BORIOLI, Ermes
Tessiner und Misoxer Alpen. 3. Aufl., neu bearb.
von Ermes Borioli. Lausanne: Schweizer Alpen-
Club, 1973. 344p., illus., map (on lining
papers). 17cm. (Clubführer des Schweizer Alpen-
Club)

BORTHWICK, Alastair
Always a little further. Glasgow: J. Smith,
1969. viii, 221p. 20cm.

BOSCHI, Luigi, marchese and BONORA, Alfredo
Itinerari dell'Appennino (dal Cimone al Catria).
Bologna: Club Alpino Italiano, Sezione di
Bologna, 1888. 62p., plates, illus., maps.
18cm.

BOSSÉ, Fernand
Géographie de la Suisse. 2e éd. Lausanne:
Pache-Varidel & Bron, 1912. [i.e. 1913]. 109p.,
col.plates, illus., maps. 21cm.

BOSSHARD, Albert
Rundsicht vom Gipfel des Hörnli, 1133m ü.M.;
aufgenommen im Herbst 1895 von Albert Bosshard;
im Auftrag der Direktion der Erziehung und der
Volkwirtschaft des Kantons Zürich. Zürich:
Hofer, 1931. 24cm.
Panorama

BOSSHARD, Walter
Durch Tibet und Turkistan: Reisen im unberührten
Asien. Stuttgard: Strecker und Schröder, 1930.
xv, 246p., plates (1 fold., some col.), illus.,
maps. 23cm.

BOSSOLI, Carlo
Souvenirs de la Suisse: le Mont-Blanc et ses
environs; dessinés d'après nature par Bossoli et
Mottu. Genève: S. Morel, [ca 1860]. 1 v.
(chiefly illus.). 15 x 22cm.

BOSSOLI, E   F
Panorama du Monte Generoso (1740 m.). Milano:
Tensi, [1890]. 24cm.
Originally published in Bollettino del Club
Alpino Italiano, no. 24.

BOSSUS, Pierre
Les Aiguilles Rouges: Perrons,Fis, Massifs de
Colonné et de Platé. [Paris]: Arthaud, 1974.
239p., illus. 17cm.

BOSSUS, Pierre
Guide des Préalpes franco-suisses: chaîne
frontière entre le Valais et la Haute-Savoie.
Genève: Club Alpin Suisse, 1964. xvi, 379p.,
2 fold. col. plates, illus., maps. 17cm.

BOTFIELD, B
Journal of a tour through the Highlands of
Scotland during the summer of 1829, [by B.
Botfield]. Norton Hall: The Author, 1830.
xvi, 376, 23p., plates, illus., map. 18cm.

BOTHMER, Heinrich
Das Schweizerland im Liede: eine anthologie;
zusammengestellt von Heinrich Bothmer. Halle:
O. Hendel, 1892. 190p. 19cm.

BOULNOIS, Helen Mary
Into little Thibet. Simpkin, Marshall, Hamilton,
1923. 256p., plates (some col.), illus. 20cm.

BOURBEL, Raoul, marquis de
Routes in Jammu and Kashmir arranged topo-
graphically with descriptions of routes; distances by stages; and information as to supplies
and transport. Calcutta: Thacker, Spink, 1897.
xvii, 396p., bibl. 26cm.

BOURDILLON, Jennifer and COVERLEY-PRICE, Victor
The Sherpas of Nepal. Oxford University Press,
[1959]. 32p., illus. 21cm. (People of the
world)

BOURDILLON, Jennifer
Visit to the Sherpas. Collins, 1956. 255p.,
plates, illus. 22cm.

MOOSER, R   Aloys and BOURGEOIS, Max
Itinéraires pour skieurs en Haute-Savoie.
Genève: Éditions de la Petite-Fusterie, 1925-29.
2 v., illus. 15cm.

BOURRIT, Marc Théodore
Description des Alpes pennines et rhétiennes.
Genève: J.P. Bonnant, 1781. 2 v., plates,
illus., map. 21cm.

BOURRIT, Marc Théodore
[Description des Alpes pennines et rhétiennes].
Beschreibung der penninischen und rhatischen
Alpen. Zürich: Orell, 1782. 388p., plates,
illus. 19cm.

BOURRIT, Marc Théodore
Description des aspects du Mont-Blanc, du côté
de la Val-d'Aost, des glacieres qui en descendent,
de l'Allée-Blanche ... pour servir de suite à la
description des glacieres, glaciers & amas de
glace du Duché de Savoye. Lausanne: Société
Thypographique, 1776. viii, 160p., 1 fold. plate.
20cm.

- - Reprint. Bologna: Alpina, 1974.

BOURRIT, Marc Théodore
Description des cols; ou, Passages des Alpes.
Genève: G.J. Manget, 1803. 2 v. in 1, plates,
illus. 22cm.

BOURRIT, Marc Théodore
Description des glacieres, glaciers & amas de
glace du Duché de Savoye. Genève: Bonnant, 1773.
xxiv, 137p., 3 plates (2 fold.), illus. 22cm.

BOURRIT, Marc Théodore
[Description des glacieres ...]. A relation of
a journey to the glaciers, in the Dutchy of Savoy;
translated by C. and F. Davy. Norwich: Printed
by Richard Beatniffe, 1775. xxi, 266p., plates,
illus. 18cm.

- - 2nd ed. 1776.

- - 3rd ed. Dublin: R. Cross, 1776.

BOURRIT, Marc Théodore
SAUSSURE, Horace Bénédict de
Grotte de Balme, située entre Cluse et Maglan sur
la route de Chamonix = The Grotte of Balme ...;
[description de Mr. de Saussure ... de Mr.
Bourrit ... de Mr. J.F. Albanis Beaumont].
Genève: Les Heritiers J.J. Paschoud, 1827. 34p.
15cm.
Parallel texts in French & English.

BOURRIT, Marc Théodore
Itinéraire de Genève, Lausanne et Chamouni.
Genève: J.E. Didier, 1791. xiv, 374p., bibl.
16cm.

- - Nouv. éd. rev. corr. et augm. 1792.

- - 3e éd. Genève: J.J. Paschoud, 1808.

BOURRIT, Marc Théodore
Nouvelle description des glacieres, vallées de
glace et glaciers, qui forment la grande chaîne
des Alpes, de Savoye, de Suisse et d'Italie.
Nouv. éd. rev. et corr. Genève: P. Barde, Manget,
1787. 3 v., plates, illus., fold. map. 21cm.

BOURRIT, Marc Théodore
Nouvelle description des vallées de glace et des
hautes montagnes, qui forment la chaîne des Alpes
pennines et rhétiennes. Genève: P. Barde, 1783.
2 v. in 1, plates, illus., map. 21cm.

BOURRIT, Marc Théodore
Nouvelle description générale et particulière
des glaciers, vallées de glace et glaciers, qui
forment la grand chaîne des Alpes de Suisse,
d'Italie & de Savoye. Nouv. éd. corr. & augm.
Genève: P. Barde, 1785. 3 v., plates, illus.,
map. 21cm.

BOURRIT, Marc Théodore
[Nouvelle description générale et particulière
des glacieres ...]. Beschreibung der Savoyischen Eisgeburge; translation of the 2nd 1785
French ed. Zürich: Orell, 1786. 245p. 19cm.

BOUVIER, J   B
SOCIÉTÉ D'HISTOIRE DU HAUT-VALAIS
[Walliser Sagen]. Légendes valaisannes, d'après
les "Walliser Sagen" de la Société d'Histoire du
Haut-Valais; traduction enrichie et illustrée
par J.-B. Bouvier; préface de Jules Gross.
Paris: Attinger, 1931. xviii, 206p., illus.
22cm.

BOVET, Albert
See
AZELINE

BOVET, Mar. Alex
Légendes de la Gruyère; préface de Aug.
Schorderet. Lausanne: Editions "Spes", [1912].
120p., illus. 24cm.

BOVY, Daniel Baud-
See
BAUD-BOVY, Daniel

BOWDEN, J
The naturalist in Norway; or, Notes on the wild
animals, birds, fishes, and plants of that
country, with some account of the principal salmon
rivers. L. Reeve, 1869. xiii, 263p., 8 col.
plates, illus. 20cm.

BOWEN REES, Ioan
See
REES, Ioan Bowen

BOWER, George S
Doe Crags and climbs round Coniston: a climbers'
guide. Barrow-in-Furness: Fell & Rock Climbing
Club, [1922]. 47p., plates, illus. 21cm.
(Climbers' guides, [1st ser.], 1)

BOWER, Hamilton
Diary of a journey across Tibet. Rivington,
Percival, 1894. xvi, 309p., fold. plates (1
col.), illus., map. 23cm.

BOWIE, Mick
BOWIE, Nan
Mick Bowie: the Hermitage years. Wellington:
A.H. & A.W. Reed, 1969. 196p., plates, illus.,
maps. 22cm.

BOWIE, Nan
Mick Bowie: the Hermitage years. Wellington:
A.H. & A.W. Reed, 1969. 196p., plates, illus.,
maps. 22cm.

BOWMAN, Isaiah
The Andes of southern Peru: geographical re-
connaissance along the seventy-third meridian.
New York: H. Holt for the American Geographical
Society, 1916. xi, 336p., plates (some fold.
col.), illus., maps. 26cm.

BOWMAN, W   E
The ascent of Rum Doodle. Parrish, 1956.
141p., plates, illus. 21cm.

BOYD, Louise A
The fiord region of East Greenland, by Louise
A. Boyd; with contributions by J. Harlen Bretz
[and others]. New York: American Geographical
Society, 1935. 2 v., plates (some fold. some
col.), illus., maps. 27cm. (American Geographical Society. Special publications, no.
18)

Boydell's Picturesque scenery of Norway; with
the principal towns from the Naze ... to the
... Swinesund; from original drawings made on
the spot, and engraved by John William Edy;
with remarks and observations made in a tour
through the country, and rev. and corr. by
William Tooke. Hurst, Robinson, 1820. xlvp.,
80 plates, illus. 42cm.

BOYLE, Kay
Avalanche: a novel. Faber, 1944. 154p. 20cm.

BOZANO, Lorenzo
Guida delle Alpi apuane, [da] L. Bozano, E.
Questa, G. Rovereto. Geneva: Club Alpino
Italiano, Sezione Ligure, 1905. x, 370p.,
plates, illus., map. 18cm.

- - 2a ed.; con la collaborazione di Bartholomee
Figari. 1921.

BOZEN. Provinzialverband für den Fremdenverkehr
See
Ente Provinciale per il Turismo, Bolzano

BOZMAN, Ernest Franklin
BELL, James Horst Brunnerman
British hills and mountains, by J.H.B. Bell,
E.F. Bozman and J. Fairfax Blakeborough.
Batsford, 1940. viii, 120p., plates (some
col.), illus. 22cm. (British heritage series)

BOZMAN, Ernest Franklin
Mountain essays by famous climbers; edited by
E.F. Bozman. Dent, [1928]. 256p., illus.,
bibl. 16cm. (Kings treasuries of literature)

BOZMAN, Earnest Franklin
X plus Y: a novel. Dent, 1936. 282p. 20cm.

BRABANT, F   G
The English Lakes; illustrated by Edmund H.
New. Methuen, 1902. x, 379p., plates (some
fold. col.), illus., maps. 16cm.

BRADLEY, Arthur Granville
The English Lakes, described by A.G. Bradley;
pictured by E.W. Haslehust. Blackie, 1910.
56p., col. plates, illus. 24cm. (Beautiful
England)

BRADLEY, Arthur Granville
Highways and byways in North Wales; with illustrations by Joseph Pennell and Hugh Thomson.
Macmillan, 1898 (1905 reprint). xiv, 474p.,
illus., fold. col. map. 21cm.

BRADLEY, Arthur Granville
Highways and byways in the Lake District; with
illustrations by Joseph Pennell. Macmillan,
1901. xii, 332p., illus., fold. map. 20cm.

- - Another issue. (1908 reprint).

- - Pocket ed. 1924.

BRADSHAW, B
B. Bradshaw's dictionary of mineral waters,
climatic health resorts, sea baths, and hydropathic
establishments... Kegan Paul, Trench, Trübner,
1902. xl, 372p., plates, illus., map. 17cm.

BRAHAM, Trevor
Himalayan odyssey. Allen & Unwin, 1974. 243p.,
plates, illus., maps. 25cm.

BRAILSFORD, John
Dolomites East: Civetta, Pelmo, Marmolata, Pala,
Tofana, Cinque Torri, Tre Cime, etc.: selected
climbs; adapted from Italian, German and other
sources and compiled with additional information
by J. Brailsford. Alpine Club, 1970. 247p.,
plates, illus., maps, bibl. 17cm. (Alpine Club
guide books, new series)

BRAILSFORD, John
Dolomites West: Sella, Sassolungo, Geisler,
Catinaccio, Brenta: selected climbs; adapted
from Italian, German and other sources and compiled with additional information by J.
Brailsford. Alpine Club, 1970. 176p., illus.,
maps, bibl. 17cm. (Alpine Club guide books,
new series)

BRAILSFORD, John
LOUGHBOROUGH COLLEGE OF EDUCATION
Loughborough rock climbing series: programmes
1-6, by John Brailsford; editor John Leedham.
Longman, 1969. 6 v., illus. 20cm.

WRANGHAM, E A   and BRAILSFORD, John
Selected climbs in the Dauphiné Alps and Vercors;
translated and adapted from the GHM guide and
other sources by E.A. Wrangham and J. Brailsford.
Alpine Club, 1967. 176p., illus., map. 16cm.
(Alpine Club guide books; selected climbs, 4)

BRAND, Charles
Journal of a voyage to Peru: a passage across
the cordillera of the Andes, in the winter of
1827, performed on foot in the snow; and a
journey across the pampas. Colburn, 1828. xix,
364p., plates, illus. 23cm.

BRANDENSTEIN, Wilhelm
Glocknerfahrten; ausgewählt von Wilhelm
Brandenstein. Leipzig: Franz Deuticke, 1931.
34p., illus., map. 20cm. (Deutsche Lesehefte,
Heft 18)

GRAF, J   H   and BRANDSTETTER, Josef Leop.
Bibliographische Vorarbeiten: Kataloge der
Bibliotheken, Gesellschaftsschriften, Zeitungen
und Kalender; zusammengestellt von J.H. Graf
und J.L. Brandstetter. Bern: K.J. Wyss, 1896.
2 v. in 1. 22cm. (Bibliographie der Schweizerischen Landeskunde, Fasc. 1)

BRANDT, Maurice
KURZ, Marcel
[Clubführer durch die] Walliser Alpen. Bd. 2.
Vom Col Collon zum Theodulpass. 4. Ausg.,
durchgesehen und erweitert von Maurice Brandt.
Zürich: Schweizer Alpen-Club, 1971. 360p.,
illus., maps (on lining papers). 17cm.
(Clubführer des Schweizer Alpen-Club)

BRANDT, Maurice
KURZ, Marcel
[Clubführer durch die] Walliser Alpen. Bd. 3.
Vom Theodulpass zum Monte Moro. 41. Ausg.,
durchgesehen und erweitert von Maurice Brandt.
Zürich: Schweizer Alpen-Club, 1970. 220p.,
illus., maps (on lining papers). 17cm.
(Clubführer des Schweizer Alpen-Club)

BRANDT, Maurice
KURZ, Marcel
[Clubführer durch die] Walliser Alpen. Bd. 4.
Vom Strahlhorn zum Simplon. 4. Ausg., durch-
gesehen und erweitert von Maurice Brandt.
Zürich: Schweizer Alpen-Club, 1970. 339p., 1
fold. plate, illus., maps (on lining papers).
17cm. (Clubführer des Schweizer Alpen-Club)

BRANDT, Maurice
[Clubführer durch die Walliser Alpen]. Alpes
valaisannes. Vol. 1. Du Col Ferret au Col
Collon, elaboré ... par Marcel Kurz. 3e éd.
rev. et augm., par Maurice Brandt. Zurich:
C.A.S., [1977]. 464p., illus., maps (on lining
papers). 17cm. (Guides du Club Alpin Suisse)

BRANDT, Maurice
KURZ, Marcel
[Clubführer durch die Walliser Alpen]. Alpes
valaisannes. Vol. 2. Du Col Collon au Théodulpass. 4e éd. rev. et augm.,par Maurice Brandt.
Zurich: Club Alpin Suisse, 1970. 356p.,
illus., maps (on lining papers). 17cm. (Guides
du Club Alpin Suisse)

BRANDT, Maurice
KURZ, Marcel
[Clubführer durch die Walliser Alpen]. Alpes
valaisannes. Vol. 3. Du Théodulpass au Monte
Moro. 4e éd. rev. et augm., par Maurice Brandt.
Zurich: Club Alpin Suisse, 1970. 236p., illus.,
maps (on lining papers). 17cm. (Guide du Club
Alpin Suisse)

BRANDT, Maurice
KURZ, Marcel
[Clubführer durch die Walliser Alpen]. Alpes
valaisannes. Vol. 4. Du Strahlhorn au Simplon.
4e éd. rev. et augm., par Maurice Brandt.
Zurich: Club Alpin Suisse, 1970. 355p., 1 fold.
plate, illus., maps (on lining papers). (Guides
du Club Alpin Suisse)

BRANDT, Maurice
[Clubführer durch die Walliser Alpen]. Alpes
valaisannes. Vol. 5. Du Simplon à la Furka,
elaboré ... par Maurice Brandt. 2e éd. Lucerne
Club Alpin Suisse, 1976. 300p., illus., maps
(on lining papers). 17cm. (Guides du Club Alpin
Suisse)

BRANDT, Maurice
Guide d'escalades dans le Jura; élaboré pour le
Club Alpin Suisse par Maurice Brandt. Genève:
C.A.S., 1966. 2 v., 1 fold. plate, illus., maps
17cm.
BRANDT, Maurice
Préalpes fribourgeoises: Moléson, Vanil Noir,
Gastlosen, Chemiflue, Gantrisch, Stockhorn.
Lausanne: Club Alpin Suisse, 1972. 260p.,
illus., maps (on lining papers). 17cm. (Guides
du Club Alpin Suisse)

BRANSBY, James, Hews
A description of Llanberis and the Snowdon
district. Carnarvon: Printed by James Rees,
1845. 112p., plates, illus. 19cm.

BRANTSCHEN, Gregor
Gesammelte Lieder im Volkston, [Text und Musik
von G. Brantschen]. Zürich: Hug, [1946]. 80p.,
music. 27cm.

BRANTSCHEN, Gregor
Neue Volkslieder für zwei Singstimmen, Text und
Musik von Gregor Brantschen. Randa, (Wallis):
Ad. Sarbach, 1926. 29p., music. 17cm.

- - 3. verm. Aufl. 1935.

BRASCA, Luigi
Alpi Retiche occidentali. Brescia: Club Alpino
Italiano, 1911. xxxvi, 550p., plates (some fold.,
some col.), illus., maps. 18cm. (Guida dei
monti d'Italia; Alpi centrali, v. 1)

BRASCA, Luigi
Itinerari alpini. Ser. 1. Milano: Club Alpino
Italiano, 1917. 10 leaves. 15cm.
In slip-case.

HUNT, John, Baron Hunt and BRASHER, Christopher
The red snows: an account of the British Caucasus
Expedition, 1958. Hutchinson, 1960. 176p.,
plates (1 col.), illus., map. 22cm.

- - Another issue. Travel Book Club, 1960.

BRATHAY EXPLORATION GROUP
Expedition medicine: a planning guide, by R.N.
Illingworth. Ambleside (Cumbria): Brathay Hall
Trust, 1976. 27p., 1 fold. plate, bibl. 22cm.

BRAUNSCHWEIGER
Promenade durch die Schweiz, [von Braunschweiger].
Hamburg: B.G. Hoffmann, 1793. 270p. 20cm.

BRAUNSTEIN, Josef
Richard Wagner and the Alps; [translated by E.S.
Tattersall]. [N. p.]: [n. pub.], [1929?]. 31p.
21cm.
English translation of an article originally
published in Nachrichten des A.V. Donauland, 1928.

BRAVAIS, Auguste
Ascension au Mont Blanc, par MM. Martins, Bravais
et Lepileur. [Paris?], [1844]. 68-74p., illus.
37cm.
Offprint from L'Illustration, journal universel,
no. 84, v. 4, Octobre, 1844.

BRAVAIS, Auguste
Le Mont Blanc; ou, Description de la vue et des
phénomènes que l'on peut apercevoir du sommet du
Mont Blanc. Paris: Bertrand, [1854]. 38p.,
fold. plate, illus. 18cm.

BRAY, Anna Eliza
The mountains and lakes of Switzerland; with descriptive sketches of other parts of the continent.
Longman, Orme, Brown, Green & Longmans, 1841.
3 v. 21cm.

BRAY, Claude
Ivanda; or, The pilgrim's quest; a tale [of Thibet].
Warne, 1894. 355p., plates, illus. 21cm.

BRAY, Reynold
Five watersheds: a winter journey to Russian
Lapland. Cape, 1935. 289p., plates (1 fold.
col.), illus., map. 22cm.

BREDT, E W
Die Alpen und ihre Maler. Leipzig: Theod. Thomas,
[1910]. 197p., illus., bibl. 27cm.

BRÉGEAULT, Henry
La chaîne du Mont Blanc, par Henry Brégeault [and
others], ouvrage orné de 10 aquarelles en hors-
texte de E. Brun [and others]. Paris: Alpina,
1928. 163p., col. plates, illus., map. 33cm.

BREMER, Fredrika
Two years in Switzerland and Italy; translated by
Mary Howitt. Hurst & Blacket, 1861. 2 v. 21cm.

BREND, William A
The story of ice in the present and past.
Newnes, 1902. 228p., illus. 16cm.

BRENNWALD, Alfred
Vues pittoresques du Lac des Quatre Cantons et de
ses environs, texte par Alfred Brennwald ...;
traduit par Cl. Flamand de Buxy. Lucerne: J. Fr.
Schleicher, [ca 1890]. 81p., col. plates, illus.
15 x 20cm.

BRENTARI, Ottone
Guida del Cadore e della valle di Zoldo. Torino:
Club Alpino Italiano, 1896. 221p., illus., map.
16cm.

BRENTARI, Ottone
Guida del Trentino. Bassano: Pozzato, 1890-1900.
3 v., illus., maps, plans. 17cm. (Società degli
Alpinisti Tridentini. Annuario, 15, 18, 21)

BRENTARI, Ottone
Guida di Monte Baldo. Bassano: Pozzato, 1893.
176p., plates, illus., maps, plans. 17cm.
(Società degli Alpinisti Tridentini. Annuario,
17)

BRESSY, M
Itinerari sciistici di Valle Po e Valle Varaita;
sotto gli auspici dello Sci Club e della Sezione
"Monviso" del C.A.I. Saluzzo: Tipografia
Operaia, 1928. 48p., plates, illus., fold. map.
18cm.

BRETON
Scandinavian sketches; or, A tour in Norway;
intended as the tourist's guide through the
interior of that country. 2nd ed. Bohn, 1837.
vii, 354p., plates, illus., map. 24cm.

BRETON, J B J
Voyage en Piémont: contenant la description topo-
graphique et pittoresque, la statistique et
l'histoire des six départements réunis à la
France, par le Senatus-Consulte de l'an XI. Paris:
Brion, 1803. viii, 247p., map. 23cm.

BREUGEL DOUGLAS, R de
La Dent du Midi; avec ... illustrations ...
aquarelles par C. de Breugel Douglas. La Haye:
W.V. Van Stockum, 1913. 68 leaves, illus. 34cm.

BREWER, William H
Up and down California in 1860-1864: the journal
of William H. Brewer, Professor of Agriculture in
the Sheffield Scientific School from 1864 to 1903;
edited by Francis P. Farquhar; with a preface by
Russell H. Chittenden. New Haven: Yale University
Press; London: Oxford University Press, 1930.
xxx, 601p., plates (1 fold.), illus., map. 24cm.

BRIAN, Alessandro
Guida per escursioni nell' Appennini parmense.
Parma: L. Battei, 1903. 281p., illus., maps.
16cm.

BRIAND, P C
Les jeunes voyageurs en Europe; ou, Description
raisonnées des divers pays compris dans cette
partie due monde... 2e éd. rev. corr. et augm.
Paris: Thieriot, 1827. 2 v., fold. plates, maps.
15cm.

BRIDEL, J P Louis
Kleine Fussreisen durch die Schweiz; aus dem
Französischen der Gebrüder Bridel. Zürich: Orell,
Gessner, Fussli, 1797. 2 v. 17cm.

BRIDEL, J P Louis
BRIDEL, Philippe Sirice
Mélanges helvétiques de 1782 à 1786; [par P.S.
and J.P.L. Bridel]. Lausanne: H. Vincent, 1787.
x, 370p. 15cm.

- - Des années 1787, 1788, 1789, 1790. Basle:
C. Serini, 1791.

BRIDEL, Philippe Sirice
Course à l'éboulement du Glacier de Gétroz et au
Lac de Mauvoisin, au fond de la Vallée de Bagnes,
16 mai 1818, [par Philippe S. Bridel]. Vevey:
Loertscher, [1818]. 16p., 1 fold. plate, illus.
20cm.

BRIDEL, Philippe Sirice
Course de Bâle à Vienne par les vallées du Jura,
[par Philippe S. Bridel]. Bâle: Ch. Aug. Serini,
1789. 256p., 1 plate, map. 17cm.

BRIDEL, Philippe Sirice
Essai statistique sur le Canton de Vallais.
Zurich: Orell Fussli, 1820. 371p., plates (some
fold., 1 col.), illus., map. 14cm.

BRIDEL, Philippe Sirice
BRIDEL, J   P   Louis
Kleine Fussreisen durch die Schweiz; aus dem
Französischen der Gebrüder Bridel. Zürich:
Orell, Gessner, Fussli, 1797. 2 v. 17cm.

BRIDEL, Philippe Sirice
Mélanges helvétiques de 1782 à 1786; [par P.S.
and J.P.L. Bridel]. Lausanne: H. Vincent, 1787.
x, 370p. 15cm.

- - Des années 1787, 1788, 1789, 1790. Basle: C.
A. Serini, 1791.

BRIDEL, Philippe Sirice
Poésie helvétiennes, par Mr. B. [i.e. P.S.
Bridel]. Lausanne: Mourer, 1782. xvi, 248p.,
illus. 20cm.

BRIDEL, Philippe Sirice
Reise durch eine der romantischesten Gegenden
der Schweiz, 1788; [translated by H.A. Reichard].
Gotha: C.W. Ettinger, 1789. 333p., map. 20cm.
BRIDEL, Philippe Sirice
VULLIEMIN, L
Le doyen Bridel: essai biographique. Lausanne:
G. Bridel, 1855. 340p. 19cm.

BRIDGE, George
The mountains of England and Wales: tables of
mountains of two thousand feet and more in altitude; photographs by W.A. Poucher; maps by
George Bridge. Goring, Reading: Gaston's Alpine
Books, West Col Productions, 1973. 1973. 199p.,
illus., maps. 22cm.

BRIDGE, George
Rock climbing in the British Isles, 1894-1970: a
bibliography of guidebooks; compiled by George
Bridge. Goring, Reading: West Col Productions,
1971. 40p., illus. 22cm.

BRIDGES, Sir Egerton
See
BRYDGES, Sir Egerton

BRIDGES, George Windham
Alpine sketches, comprised in a short tour through
parts of Holland, Flanders, France, Savoy,
Switzerland and Germany, during the summer of
1814, by a member of the University of Oxford [i.e.
George W. Bridges]. Longman, Hurst, Rees, Orme,
& Brown, 1814. vii, 312p. 22cm.

BRIDGES, Shirley M
Two in Turkey: a mountain-climbing expedition,
August 1967. [Houston]: The Author, [1967?]. 7
leaves. 28cm.
Typescript.

BRIDGES BIRTT, W
See
BIRTT, W   Bridges

Die brieftasche aus den Alpen. 3 Lfg. St. Gallen:
Reutiner, 1789. 107p. 18cm.

BRIGG, William Anderton
Iter helveticum, being a journal of the doings of
a cabinet ... of five fellow-travellers in
Switzerland, during the last three weeks of
September, 1866 ..., by their Lord Chancellor
[i.e. William A. Brigg] Keighley: Printed
privately by S. Billows, 1887. 89p. 19cm.

BRILEJ, A
Prirocnik za planince: zbirka pravil, navodil in
podaikov ter kratek vodnik po gorah Slovenije.
Ljubljana: J. Moskric, 1950. 312p., col. plates
(1 fold.), illus., maps. 15cm.

BRINCKMAN, Arthur
The rifle in Cashmere: a narrative of shooting
expeditions in Ladak, Cashmere, Punjab, etc.;
with advice on travelling ...; to which are added
notes on army reform and Indian politics. Smith,
Elder, 1862. x, 244p., 2 plates, illus. 21cm.

BRINER, E
ELZINGRE, Ed
Swiss dress: ... colour plates, paintings from
Ed. Elzingre, text by E. Briner. Geneva: "L'Art
en Suisse", 1931. 1 v. (chiefly col. illus.)
28cm. (Éditions de "L'Art en Suisse, no. 7)
Cover title.

BRIQUET, Moise and AQUELIN, L
Ascension du Mont-Rose et du Mont-Blanc en
juillet 1863. Genève, 1864. 36p. 22cm.
Offprint from Journal de Genève.

SCHAUB, Charles and BRIQUET, Moise
Guide pratique de l'ascensionniste sur les montagnes qui entourent le Lac de Genève... 3e éd.
rev. et augm. Genève: J. Jullien, 1893. vi,
240p. 18cm.

BRITISH ARMY AXEL HEIBERG EXPEDITION, 1972
[Report of the] British Army Axel Heiberg Expedition, 1972, [by A.J. Muston and others].
[Donnington]: The Expedition, [1972?]. 1 v.
(various pagings), 1 fold. plate, illus., maps.
30cm.

BRITISH ARMY WEST GREENLAND EXPEDITION, 1971
Report of the British Army West Greenland Expedition, 1971, [by A.J. Muston and others].
[Donnington]: The Expedition, [1971?]. 1 v.
(various pagings), illus., maps. 30cm.

BRITISH BARNAJ HIMALAYAN EXPEDITION, 1977
Expedition report. [Reading?]: The Expedition,
[1978?]. [20p.], maps. 30cm.

BRITISH CAUCASUS EXPEDITION, 1958
[Report of the] British Caucasus Expedition,
1958, [by John Neill]. [The Expedition],
[1958]. 7 leaves. 34cm.
Typescript.

BRITISH CENTRAL SAHARAN EXPEDITION, 1978
Provisional prospectus [for] the British Central
Saharan Expedition, 1978. Belvedere (Kent): The
Expedition, [1977]. [5] leaves, map. 33cm.

BRITISH HOGGAR MOUNTAINS AND BILMA SANDS EXPEDITION,
1976
Technical report. The Expedition, 1977. 69p.,
plates, illus., maps, bibl. 29cm.

BRITISH-INDIAN-NEPALESE SERVICES HIMALAYAN
EXPEDITION, 1960
Oxygen report; [compiled by S. Ward]. Waddington:
The Expedition, 1960. 5p., illus. 33cm.

BRITISH JANNU EXPEDITION, 1978
[Report]. The Expedition, 1978. 11 leaves, map.
29cm.

BRITISH MOUNTAINEERING COUNCIL. Peak Committee
Rock climbs in the Peak.

1. The Sheffield-Stanage area; edited by E.
   Byne. [1963].
2. The Saddleworth-Chew Valley area; edited by
   E. Byne. [1965].
5. The northern limestone area; compiled and
   arranged by Paul Nunn. 1969.
7. The Kinder area; edited by P.J. Nunn.
   [1971].
9. The Staffordshire gritstone area; compiled
   by D. Salt. [1973].

   Recent developments, by S. Bancroft. 1977.

BRITISH MOUNTAINEERING COUNCIL. Safety Sub-
Committee
Mountain hypothermia. B.M.C., 1972. 5p. 21cm.
Cover title.

BRITISH MUSEUM (NATURAL HISTORY)
Checklist of Palaearctic and Indian mammals
1758 to 1946, by J.R. Ellerman and T.C.S.
Morrison-Scott. B.M., 1951. 810p., bibl. 26cm.

BRITISH NEPALESE ARMY ANNAPURNA EXPEDITION, 1970
The ascent of Annapurna, 20th May 1970. Army
Mountaineering Association, [1970?]. 5 leaves,
1 plate, maps. 33cm.

BRITISH SOUTH AMERICA CLIMBING EXPED, 1976-77
See
BRITISH SOUTH AMERICA MOUNTAINEERING EXPEDITION,
1976-77

BRITISH SOUTH AMERICA MOUNTAINEERING EXPEDITION,
1976-77
[Report]. [Sheffield]: The Expedition, [1977].
37 leaves, 1 plate, maps. 30cm.
Expedition leader: Rab Carrington.

BRITISH STANDARDS INSTITUTION
Nylon mountaineering ropes. B.S.I., 1959. 8p.
21cm. (British Standard specification, 3104:
1959)

A Briton abroad, by the author of "Two years abaft
the mast". Remington, 1878. vi, 238p. 20cm.

BROADBENT, Ellinor Lucy
Alpine valleys of Italy, from San Remo to Lake
Orta; with ... illustrations from photographs by
Margaret E. Broadbent. Methuen, 1928. xii,
244p., plates, illus. 20cm.

BROADBENT, Ellinor Lucy
Under the Italian Alps; with a geographical essay
by Marion I. Newbigin. Methuen, 1925. xi, 251p.,
plates (1 fold. col.), illus., map. 20cm.

BROCHEREL, Giulio
Alpinismo. Milano: Hoepli, 1898. vii, 311p.,
bibl. 16cm. (Manuali Hoepli)

BROCHEREL, Giulio
Guida illustrata di Courmayeur e dintorni.
Courmayeur: L'Autore, 1895. viii, 144p., illus.
18cm.

BROCHEREL, Giulio
La Valle d'Aosta. Novara: Istituto Geografico
de Agostini, 1932-33. 2 v., plates, illus. 25cm.

BROCKEDON, William
The hand-book for travellers in Italy, from London
to Naples; illustrated with twenty-five views,
from drawings by Stanfield, Prout, and Brockedon;
engraved by W. and E. Finden. M.A. Nattali, [1831].
189p., plates, illus., maps. 29cm.
Later ed. published in 1835 under title: Road-book
from London to Naples.

BROCKEDON, William
Illustrations of the passes of the Alps, by which
Italy communicates with France, Switzerland, and
Germany. The Author, 1828-29. 2 v., plates,
illus., maps. 30cm.

- - Another ed. Henry G. Bohn, [1877].

BROCKEDON, William
Journals of excursions in the Alps: the Pennine,
Graian, Cottian, Rhetian, Lepontian, and Bernese.
J. Duncan, 1833. xiv, 376p., 1 fold. plate, map.
21cm.

- - 3rd ed. 1845.

BROCKEDON, William
Road-book from London to Naples; illustrated
with twenty-five views, from drawings by
Stanfield, Prout and Brockedon; engraved by W.
and E. Finden. Murray, 1835. vii, 190p., plates,
illus., maps. 24cm.
Originally published in 1831 under title: The
hand-book for travellers in Italy, from London to
Naples.

BROCKEDON, William
BEATTIE, William
The Waldenses; or, Protestant valleys of Piedmont, Dauphiny, and the Ban de la Roche; illustrated by W.H. Bartlett and W. Brockedon. Virtue,
1838. 216p., plates (1 fold.), illus., map.
28cm.

BROCKEDON, William
BEATTIE, William
[The Waldenses ...]. Les Vallées vaudoises
pittoresques; ou, Vallées protestantes du Piémont, du Dauphiné, et du Ban de la Roche; orné
du gravures par W.H. Bartlett et par W. Brockedon;
traduit par L. de Bauclas. G. Virtue, 1838.
216p., plates (1 fold.), illus., map. 29cm.

BROCKLEHURST, Thomas Unett
Mexico to-day: a country with a great future;
and a glance at the prehistoric remains and antiquities of the Montezumas. Murray, 1883. xvi,
259p., plates (some col.), illus., map. 23cm.

BROCKMANN-JEROSCH, Heinrich
Die Flora des Puschlav (Bezirk Bernina, Kanton
Graubünden) und ihre Pflanzengesellschaften.
Leipzig: W. Engelmann, 1907. xii, 438p., plates,
illus., col. fold. map. 27cm. (Die Pflanzen-
gesellschaften der Schweizeralpen, 1 Teil)

BRODBECK, E
L'alpinisme: guide pratique, texte et illustrations de E. Brodbeck. Lausanne: Société
Romande d'Éditions, 1933. 376p., fold. col.
plates, illus., maps. 18cm.

BRØGGER, W C
Norge i det nittende Aarhundrede, tekst og
billeder af Norske Forfattere og Kunstnere;
udgivet af W.C. Brøgger [and others]. Kristiania: Alb. Cammermeyers, 1900. 2 v., plates
(some fold., some col.), illus., maps. 37cm.

BROKE, George
BALL, John
The Central Alps. Pt. 2. Including those
Alpine portions of Switzerland, Italy and Aus-
tria which lie S. & E. of the Rhone and Rhine,
S. of the Arlberg, and W. of the Adige. New ed.,
reconstructed and revised on behalf of the Alpine
Club under the general editorship of George
Broke. Longmans, Green, 1911. xix, 432p., fold.
col. plates, maps. 19cm. (Alpine guide, pt. 2)

BROKE, George
With sack and stock in Alaska. Longmans, Green,
1891. xi, 158p., 2 fold. col. plates, maps.
21cm.

BROOKE, Sir Arthur de Capell
A winter in Lapland and Sweden, with various
observations relating to Finmark and its inhabitants, made during a residence at Hammerfest,
near the North Cape. Murray, [1825]. xvi,
612p., plates (1 fold., some col.), illus., map.
29cm.

BROOKE, N
Voyage à Naples et en Toscane, avant et pendant
l'invasion des Français en Italie; avec ... des
détails sur la terrible explosion du Mont-Vésuve,
pris sur les lieux à minuit, en juin 1794 ...;
traduit de l'anglais. Paris: Nicolle, an 7
[1799]. 275p. 20cm.

BROOKE, T
Comicalities of travel, for the Tarvin Bazaar,
[by T. Brooke]. Chester: J. Seacome, 1836.
126p., plates, illus. 20cm.

BROOKE, Sir Victor
Sir Victor Brooke, sportsman & naturalist: a
memoir of his life and extracts from his letters
and journals; edited by Oscar Leslie Stephen...
Murray, 1894. x, 266p., plates, illus. 22cm.

BROOKS, Phillips
Letters of travel. Macmillan, 1893. 386p.,
plates, illus. 21cm.

BROOMHEAD, Richard
Cheddar: Cheddar Gorge, Brean Down,The Mendips.
Leicester: Cordee, 1977. 96p., illus., maps.
18cm. (Climbs in the South-West)

TAUPIN, D   and BROT, M
Cormot: topo guide d'escalade. Paris: Club
Alpin Français, Section de Paris-Chamonix, 1964.
64p., fold. plates, illus., maps. 22cm.
BROWER, David R
LOVINS, Amory
Eryri, the mountains of longing; with photo-
graphs by Philip Evans; introduction by Sir
Charles Evans; edited with a foreword by David
R. Brower. San Francisco: Friends of the
Earth, [1972]. 176p., illus., map. 36cm.

BROWER, David R
HORNBEIN, Thomas Frederick
Everest: the west ridge; photographs from the
American Mount Everest Expedition and by its
leader, Norman G. Dyhrenfurth; introduction by
William E. Siri; edited by David Brower. San
Francisco: Sierra Club, 1965. 205p., col.
illus. 35cm. (Sierra Club exhibit-format
series, 12)

- - Another issue. Allen & Unwin, 1966.

BROWER, David R
PORTER, Eliot
The place no one knew: Glen Canyon on the
Colorado; edited by David Brower. San Francisco:
Sierra Club, 1963. 170p., illus. 35cm. (Sierra
Club books)

BROWER, David R
KNIGHT, Max
Return to the Alps; photographs by Gerhard
Klammet; edited with a foreword and selection
from Alpine literature by David R. Brower. San
Francisco: Friends of the Earth, [1970]. 160p.,
col. illus., map. 36cm. (Earth's wild places,2)

BROWN, Clare and BROWN, Marshall
Fell walking from Wasdale. Saint Catherine
Press, [1947?]. x, 134p., illus. 17cm.

BROWN, Frederick Augustus Yeats
Family notes. [Rapallo]: [The Author], 1917.
310p. 24cm.

BROWN, Hamish M
Hamish's mountain walk: the first traverse of all
the Scottish Munros in one journey. Gollancz,
1978. 359p., plates, illus., maps, bibl. 24cm.

BROWN, Hamish M
The island of Rhum: a national nature reserve.
Manchester: Cicerone Press, 1972. 64p., illus.,
maps. 17cm. (Cicerone Press guidebooks)

BROWN, Henry Phelps
Sir Alexander Carr-Saunders, 1886-1966. London,
1967. 379-389p., 1 plate, port. 25cm.
Offprint from Proceedings of the British Academy,
v. 53, 1967.

BROWN, Horatio F
John Addington Symonds: a biography; compiled
from his papers and correspondence. 2nd ed.
Smith, Elder, 1908. xxiv, 495p., plates, illus.
21cm.

BROWN, Joe
The hard years: an autobiography. Gollancz,
1967. 256p., 43 plates, illus. 23cm.

BROWN, Clare and BROWN, Marshall
Fell walking from Wasdale. Saint Catherine
Press, [1947?]. x, 134p., illus. 17cm.

BROWN, Percy
Picturesque Nepal. Black, 1912. xvi, 205p.,
plates (4 col.), illus. 22cm.

BROWN, Percy
Tours in Sikhim and the Darjeeling district.
2nd ed. Calcutta: Newman, 1922. xiii, 136p.,
plates (some fold.), illus., map. 19cm.

BROWN, Robert
LINDSAY, W   Lauder
Observations on the lichens collected by Dr.
Robert Brown in West Greenland in 1867   [on
Edward Whymper's expedition]. London, 1869.
305-368p., plates, illus. 31cm.
Offprint from Transactions of the Linnean
Society, v. 27.

BROWN, Stewardson
Alpine flora of the Canadian Rocky Mountains;
illustrated with water-colour drawings and
photographs by Mrs. Charles Schäffer. New York,
London: Putnam, 1907. xxxix, 353p., 80 col.
plates, illus. 20cm.

BROWN, Thomas
The reminiscences of an old traveller throughout different parts of Europe. 2nd ed. greatly
enlarged. Edinburgh: Anderson; London: Simpkin,
Marshall, 1835. viii, 301p. 21cm.

BROWN, Thomas Graham
Brenva. Dent, 1944. xv, 228p., plates, illus.,
maps. 22cm.

BROWN, Thomas Graham and DE BEER, Sir Gavin
The first ascent of Mont Blanc; with a foreword
by Sir John Hunt. Oxford University Press,
1957. 460p., 13 plates (some col.), illus.,
maps., bibl. 23cm.
Published on the occasion of the centenary of the
Alpine Club.

BROWN, Thomas Graham and DE BEER, Sir Gavin
[The first ascent of Mont Blanc]. La prima ascen
sione del Monte Bianco; con una prefazione di
Sir John Hunt. Milano: Martello, 1960. viii,
638p., plates (some col., 1 fold.), illus, maps.,
bibl. 25cm.

BROWNE, Belmore
The conquest of Mount McKinley: the story of thre
expeditions through the Alaskan wilderness to
Mount McKinley ...; appendix by Herschel C.
Parker; with illustrations from original drawings
by the author... New York, London: Putnam, 1913.
xvii, 381p., plates (1 fold., 1 col.), illus.,
maps. 24cm.

- - New ed. Boston: Houghton Mifflin, 1956.

BROWNE, George Forrest
Ice-caves of France and Switzerland: a narrative
of subterranean exploration. Longmans, Green,
1865. ix, 315p., illus. 21cm.

BROWNE, George Forrest
Off the mill: some occasional papers. Smith,
Elder, 1895. viii, 271p., plates, illus. 20cm.

BROWNE, George Forrest
The recollections of a bishop. Smith, Elder,
1915. xi, 427p., plates, illus. 23cm.

BROWNE, J D H
Ten scenes in the last ascent of Mont Blanc,
including five views from the summit. Thos.
McLean, 1853. 13p., plates, illus. 56cm.

BROWNE, Mary A
Mont Blanc and other poems... Hatchard, 1827.
177p. 25cm.

BROWNING, Oscar
WORTHAM, H E
Victorian Eton and Cambridge, being the life of
Oscar Browning. New ed. A. Baker, 1956. viii,
327p., plates, illus. 21cm.

BRUCE, Hon. Charles Granville
The assault on Mount Everest 1922, by Hon. C.G.
Bruce and other members of the expedition.
Arnold, 1923. xi, 339p., plates (2 fold.),
illus., maps. 26cm.

BRUCE, Hon. Charles Granville
[The assault on Mount Everest 1922]. L'assaut
du Mont Everest 1922 ...; traduit par A. de
Gruchy et E. Gaillard. Chambéry: Dardel, [1923].
xx, 304p., plates, illus., maps. 26cm.

BRUCE, Hon. Charles Granville
Himalayan wanderer. A. Maclehose, 1934. 309p.,
plates, illus. 23cm.

BRUCE, Hon. Charles Granville
Kulu and Lahoul. Arnold, 1914. xii, 308p.,
plates (1 fold. col.), maps. 23cm.

BRUCE, Hon. Charles Granville
Twenty years in the Himalaya. Arnold, 1910.
xv., 335p., plates (1 fold. col.), illus., map.
24cm.

BRUCE, Hon. Mrs. Charles Granville
Kashmir. Black, 1911. 95p., col. plates,
illus., map. 21cm. (Peeps at many lands)

BRUCE, Clarence Dalrymple
In the footsteps of Marco Polo, being the account
of a journey overland from Simla to Pekin.
Edinburgh, London: Blackwood, 1907. xiv, 379p.,
plates (1 fold. col.), illus., map. 24cm.

BRUCHET, Max
La Savoie d'après les anciens voyageurs...
Annecy: Hérisson, 1908. vii, 375p. 20cm.

PENCK, Albrecht and BRÜCKNER, Edouard
Die Alpen im Eiseitalter. Leipzig: Tauchnitz,
1909. 3 v. in 1, plates (some fold., 1 col.),
illus., maps (some fold.). 29cm.

BRUEN, Matthias
Essays descriptive and moral, on scenes in Italy,
Switzerland and France, by an American [i.e.
Matthias Bruen]. Edinburgh: Constable, 1823.
xi, 265p. 21cm.

VÁVRA, Karl and BRUNNER, Richard
Skisport: wie wir ihn betreiben; Herausgeber
Sportclub "Die weissen Elf". Wien: Frick, 1910.
vii, 82p., illus. 22cm.

- - 3 Aufl. 1910.

BRUHL, Étienne
Accident à la Meije: roman. Paris: Susse, 1947.
364p., illus., map. 22cm.

BRULLE, Henri
Souvenirs. Toulouse, 1930. 424p., plates,
illus., port. 21cm.
Supplément de textes pyrénéistes du Bulletin
Mensuel de la Section des Pyrénées Centrales du
Club Alpin Français.

BRULLE, Henri
MAURY, Luc
Les ultimes ascensions d'Henri Brulle. [Bordeaux],
1969. 21p., illus. 25cm.
Offprint from Revue pyrénéenne, no. 18, juin 1969
et no. 19, sept. 1969.

BRUN, Friederika
Episoden aus Reisen durch das südliche Deutschland, die westliche Schweiz, Genf und Italien in
den Jahren 1801, 1802, 1803; nebst Anhängen vom
Jahr 1805. Vol. 1. Zürich: Orell Füssli, 1806.
420p. 20cm.

BRUN, Hans
AKADEMISCHER ALPEN-CLUB ZÜRICH
50 Jahre AACZ, 1896-1946: Festschrift zum
fünfzigjährigen Bestehen des Akademischen
Alpenclub Zürich; [edited by Hans Brun und Carl
Egger]. Zürich: A.A.C.Z., 1946. 223p., plates,
illus., bibl. 23cm.

BRUNEL UNIVERSITY KISHTWAR HIMALAYA EXPEDITION,
1978
See
CITY UNIVERSITY - BRUNEL UNIVERSITY KISHTWAR
HIMALAYA EXPEDITION, 1978

BRUNIALTI, Attilio
Il Trentino nella natura, nella storia,
nell'arte e nella vita degli abitanti. Torino:
Unione Tipografico-Editrice Torinese, 1919.
192p., plates (1 fold., 3 col.), illus., map.
27cm. (Le nuove provincie italiane, 1)

BRUNIES, Stephan
Bilder aus dem schweizerischen Nationalpark und
seiner Umgebung. Basel: B. Schwabe, 1919.
29p., 64 plates, illus. 25cm.

BRUNIES, Stephan
Der schweizerische Nationalpark. Basel:
Frobenius, 1914. 211p., plates (2 fold., 1
col.), illus., map, bibl. 22cm.

BRUNIES, Stephan
[Der schweizerische Nationalpark]. Le Parc
national suisse; traduit par Samuel Aubert.
Laussanne: Payot, 1925. 274p., plates (some
fold.), illus., maps, bibl. 22cm.
Translation of 2nd [enl.] German ed.

BRUNNARIUS, Ernest
Ernest Brunnarius, 1857-1901. Paris: Société
d'Éditions Littéraires et Artistiques, 1903.
175p., col. plates, illus. 32cm.

BRUNNER, Giorgio
Un uomo va sui monti. Bologna: Alfa, 1957.
499p., 24 plates, illus., maps. 22cm. (Semprevivo, 3)

BRUNNER, Heinrich
DIRECTION DU DICTIONNAIRE GÉOGRAPHIQUE DE LA SUISSE
Die Schweiz: geographische, demographische,
politische, volkswirtschaftliche und geschichtliche Studie, von Aug. Aeppli [and others];
Redaktion: Heinrich Brunner. Neuenburg: Administration der Bibliothek des Geographischen
Lexikons der Schweiz, 1909. viii, 711p., plate,
illus., maps. 32cm.

BRUNNING, Carl
Rock climbing and mountaineering. Manchester:
Open Air Publications, [1936]. 108p., illus.
19cm.

- - New and rev. ed. 1946.

BRUNTON, Paul
A hermit in the Himalayas. Madras: B.G. Paul,
[ca 1936]. 322p. 22cm.

BRUSONI, Edmondo
Guida alle Alpi centrali italiane e regioni
adiacenti della Svizzera. Domodossola: Club
Alpino Italiano, Sezione di Domodossola e Sezione
di Como, 1892-1908. 3 v., plates, illus., maps,
plans. 19cm.

BRUSONI, Edmondo
Guida ciclo, alpina, itineraria descrittiva della
Valtellina e regioni adiacenti della Svizzera.
Sondrio: Touring Club Italiano, 1906. xxxi,
396p., plates, illus., maps. 20cm.

BRUSONI, Edmondo
Guida delle Alpi ossolane e regioni adiacenti.
Pt. 1. Tra Locarno e il Sempione... Bellinzona:
Società Excursionisti Ossolani, 1901. xi,
191p., plates, illus., maps, plans. 18cm.

BRUSONI, Edmondo
Guida itinerario, alpina, descrittiva di Lecco
... Lecco: Club Alpino Italiano, Sezione di Como
e di Lecco, 1903. xx, 319p., plates, illus.,
maps, plans. 20cm.

BRUSONI, Edmondo
Locarno, seine Umgebung und seine Thäler:
Centovalli, Onsernone, Maggia, di Campo, Bavona,
Lavizzara und Verzasca; zusammengestellt von
Edmund Brusoni. Bellinzona: El. Em. Colombi,
1899. viii, 147p., plates (2 fold. col.),
illus., maps. 18cm.

BRUUN-NEERGAARD, Tønnes Christian
Journal du dernier voyage du Gen. Dolomieu dans
les Alpes. Paris: Solvet, 1802. 154p. 21cm.
Half-title: Journal d'un Danois.

BRYANT, Leslie Vickery
New Zealanders and Everest; with a foreword by
Sir Edmund Hillary. Wellington: Reed, 1953.
48p., illus., map (on lining paper). 23cm.

BRYCE, James, Viscount Bryce
Memories of travel. Macmillan, 1923. xiii,
300p. 23cm.

BRYCE, James, Viscount Bryce
South America: observations and impressions.
Macmillan, 1912. xxv, 611p., col. plates (2
fold.), maps, bibl. 23cm.

BRYCE, James, Viscount Bryce
Transcaucasia and Ararat, being notes of a
vacation tour in the autumn of 1876. Macmillan,
1877. x, 420p., plates, illus., map. 20cm.

BRYCE, James, Viscount Bryce
FISHER, H   A   L
James Bryce, Viscount Bryce of Dechmont.
Macmillan, 1927. 2 v., port. 22cm.

BRYDEN, H   A
SELOUS, Percy
Travel and big game, by Percy Selous with two
chapters by H.A. Bryden... Bellairs, 1897. 195p.,
plates, illus. 26cm.

BRYDGES, Sir Egerton
The lake of Geneva: a poem, moral and descriptive,
in seven books, with notes historical and biographical. Geneva: Printed by A.L. Vignier for
Bossange, 1832. 2 v. in 1, plates, illus., fold.
map. 18cm.

BRYSON, H   Courtney
Rock climbs round London... The Author, 1936.
25p., illus., map. 19cm.

BUCH, Leopold von, Freiherr
Travels through Norway and Lapland during the
years 1806, 1807 and 1808; translated from the
original German by John Black; with notes ... by
Robert Jameson. H. Colburn, 1813. xviii,
466p., plates, maps. 26cm.

BUCH, Leopold von, Freiherr
Voyage en Norvège et en Laponie fait dans les
années 1806, 1807 et 1808; traduit de l'allemand
par J.B.B. Eyriés; précédé d'une introduction par
A. de Humboldt... Paris: Gide, 1816. 2 v. 20cm.

BUCHAN, John
Great hours in sport; edited by John Buchan.
Nelson, 1921. 288p., plates, illus., map. 22cm.
(John Buchan's annual)

BUCHAN, John
The last secrets; The final mysteries of exploration. Nelson, 1923 (1925 reprint). 303p.,
plates, maps. 19cm.

BUCHANAN, John Young
Comptes rendus of observation and reasoning.
Cambridge: University Press, 1917. xl, 452p.,
14 plates, illus. 23cm.

BUCHER, Edwin
Beitrag zu den theoretischen Grundlagen des
Lawinenverbaus. Bern: Kümmerly & Frey, 1948.
113p., illus., bib. 30cm. (Beiträge zur
Geologie der Schweiz, geotechnische Serie,
Hydrologie, Lfg., 6)
Summary in English

BUCHMÜLLER, Julius
Bergsteiger- und Wintersport- Kalender, 1926;
hrsg. von Julius Buchmüller. Wien: Selbstverlag des Herausgebers, 1926. 397p., illus.
16cm.

CHAPMAN, Abel and BUCK, Walter J
Unexplored Spain. Arnold, 1910. xvi, 416p.,
plates, illus. 27cm.

BUCKINGHAM, James Silk
Belgium, the Rhine, Switzerland, and Holland:
an autumnal tour. Jackson, [1848]. 2 v.,
plates, illus. 24cm.

BUCKINGHAM, James Silk
France, Piedmont, Italy, Lombardy, the Tyrol,
and Bavaria: an autumnal tour. Jackson,
[1848]. 2 v., plates, illus. 24cm.

BUCKLAND, William
GORDON, Elizabeth Oke
The life and correspondence of William
Buckland ..., by his daughter Mrs. Gordon.
Murray, 1894. xvi, 288p., plates, illus. 21cm.

BUDDEUS, Aurelio
Schweizerland: Natur und Menschenleben.
Leipzig: Avenarius & Mendelssohn, 1853. 2 v.
in 1. 20cm.

BUDRY, Paul and KÄMPFEN, Werner
Le chemin de Zermatt: petite encyclopédie
pratibornienne à l'usage des touristes curieux;
dessins de Géa Augsbourg; édité par la
Compagnie du Chemin de Fer Viège-Zermatt,
Brigue et Lausanne. Lausanne: La Compagnie,
1941. xvi, 160p., 7 plates, illus. 17cm.

BUDRY, Paul and RIVAZ, Paul de
Villes et régions d'art de la Suisse=Schweizer-
ische Kunststätten. Neuchatel: Éditions de la
Baconnière, [1943]. 3 v., plates, illus. 18cm.

BUDWORTH, Joseph
A fortnight's ramble to the Lakes in Westmorland,
Lancashire, and Cumberland, by a rambler [i.e.
Joseph Budworth]. Hookham & Carpenter, 1792.
xxvii, 267p. 22cm.

- - 2nd ed. J. Nichols, 1795.

- - 3rd ed. J. Nichols, 1810.

BÜDEL, Julius and GLASER, Ulrich
Neue Forschungen im Umkreis der Glocknergruppe;
Schriftleitung: Julius Büdel und Ulrich Glaser.
München: Deutscher Alpenverein, 1969. 321p.,
fold. plates (some col.), illus., maps (5 in
pocket), bibl. 29cm. (Wissenschaftliche Alpenvereinshefte, Heft 21)

BÜHLER, Alfred
Das Meiental im Kanton Uri. Bern: Kümmerly &
Frey, 1928. 156p., plates (3 fold., 2 col.),
illus., maps, bibl. 27cm.

BÜHLER, Fritz
Der Gornergrat und die Walliser Alpenpässe, mit
geschichtlichen Notizen. Luzern: Selbstverlag
des Verfassers, 1894. 107p., fold. col. plates,
illus. 20cm.

BÜHLER, Hermann
Alpine Bibliographie für das Jahr 1931 [-1935];
bearb. von Hermann Bühler; [hrsg. vom Verein der
Freunde der Alpenvereinsbücherei mit Unter-
stützung des Hauptausschusses des Deutschen und
Österreichischen Alpenvereins]. München:
Gesellschaft Alpiner Bücherfreunde, 1932-37.
18cm.
Publisher varies

- - Gesamtregister für die Jahr 1931-1938.
München: Münchner Verlag, 1949.

BUELER, William M
Mountains of the world: a handbook for climbers
& hikers. Seattle: The Mountaineers, 1977.
279p., maps. 18cm.

BUELER, William M
Roof of the Rockies: a history of mountaineering
in Colorado. Boulder: Pruett, 1974. viii,
200p., illus., maps. 23cm.

BÜRLI, J
Taschenbuch für die erste Hülfe bei Unglücks-
fällen und Erkrankungen, mit besonderer
Berücksichtigung der Krankenpflege... Bern:
J. Heuberger, 1903. iii, 124p., illus. 19cm.

BUHAN, Paul
Neiges et sommets pyrénéens: souvenirs d'excursions dans les Pyrénées centrales, [par] Paul
Buhan [and others]. Paris: Les Auteurs, 1911.
141p., illus., fold. map. 33cm.

BUHL, Hermann
Achttausend, drüber und drunter; Vorwort von
Kurt Maix. München: Nymphenburger Verlags-
handlung, 1954. 351p., plates, illus. 24cm.

BUHL, Hermann
[Achttausend, drüber und drunter]. Nanga Parbat
pilgrimage; translated by Hugh Merrick. Hodder
& Stoughton, 1956. 360p., plates, illus., maps.
23cm.

BUHL, Hermann
[Achttausend, drüber und drunter]. Buhl du Nanga
Parbat; traduit de l'allemand par Monique
Bittebierre. [Paris]: Arthaud, 1959. 382p.,
plates, illus. 22cm. (Collection sempervivum,
no. 36)

BUHRER, C
Les observatoires de montagne.
(In Bibliothèque universelle... v. 65, 1895,
p. 328-352)

BULLARD, Fred M
Volcanoes in history, in theory, in eruption.
Austin: University of Texas Press, 1962. xvi,
441p., plates (2 fold., 1 col.), illus., maps,
bibl. 25cm.

BULWER, James Redford
Extracts from my journal, 1852. Norwich: The
Author, 1853. 56p., 4 plates, illus. 24cm.

BUNBURY, Selina
A summer in northern Europe, including sketches
in Sweden, Norway, Finland, the Aland Islands,
Gothland... Hurst & Blackett, 1856. 2 v. in 1.
21cm.

BUNNELL, J   F
Rock climbing guide to Hong Kong. Hong Kong:
Cathay Press, 1959. 65p., plates, illus. 16cm.

BURBAGE, Mike and YOUNG, William
Seafell group. Stockport: Fell & Rock Climbing
Club, 1974. 201p., 1 col. plate, illus., map
(on lining papers). 16cm. (Climbing guides to
the English Lake District, [5th ser.], 7)
BURBERRYS (Firm)
Gabardine in peace and war. Burberrys, [ca
1911]. 142p., illus. 23cm.

BURCH, Lambert van der
Sabaudiae Respublica et historia. Lugd. Batav.:
Ex officina Elzeviriana, 1634. 313p. 12cm.

BURCHARDT, D   B
Fjell i Norge over 2000 m.o.h. = Norwegian
mountains over 2000 metres high: altitudes, locations and first ascents. Oslo, 1950. 201-235p.
25cm.
Offprint from Norsk Geografisk Tidsskrift, Bd. 12,
h. 5.

BURCKHARDT, Alexander
Bergfahrten und Spaziergänge. Vol. 1. Leipzig:
W. Opetz, [1898]. 20cm.
No more published?

BURKHARDT, Carl
Coupe géologique de la Cordillère entre Las
Lajas et Curacautin. La Plata: Museo de La Plata,
1900. vii, 102p., plates, illus., map. 39cm.
(Anales del Museo de La Plata. Sección geologica
y mineralógica, 3)

BURCKHARDT, Carl
Monographie der Kreideketten zwischen Klönthal,
Sihl und Linth. Bern: Schmid, Francke, 1896.
xii, 207p., plates (some fold., some col.),
illus., map, bibl. 33cm. (Beiträge zur geologischen Karte der Schweitz, Lfg. 35, N.F.,
Lfg. 5)

BURCKHARDT, Carl
Profils géologiques transversaux de la Cordillère
argentino-chilienne: stratigraphie et tactonique:
première partie du rapport définitif sur une expédition géologique effectuée par Leo Wehrli et
Carl Burckhardt. La Plata: Museo de La Plata,
1900. vii, 136p., plates (some fold., some col.),
illus., map. 39cm. (Anales del Museo de La
Plata. Sección geológica y mineralógica, 2)

BURDSALL, Richard Lloyd and EMMONS, Arthur Brewster
Men against the clouds: the conquest of Minya
Konka; with contributions by Terris Moore and
Jack Theodore Young. Lane, 1935. xv, 272p.,
plates (some fold.), illus., maps, bibl. 23cm.

BUREAU TOPOGRAPHIQUE FÉDÉRAL
See
SWITZERLAND. Eidgenossisches Topographisches
Bureau

BURFORD, Robert
Description of a view of Mont Blanc, the valley
of Chamounix and the surrounding mountains, now
exhibiting at the Panorama, Leicester Square,
painted by ... Robert Burford from drawings taken
by himself in 1835. Printed by T. Brettell,
1837. 15p., 1 fold. plate, illus. 22cm.

BURFORD, Robert
Description of a view of the Bernese Alps,
taken from the Faulhorn mountain, and part of
Switzerland, now exhibiting at the Panorama,
Leicester Square, painted by ... Robert Burford;
assisted by H.C. Selous, from drawings taken by
himself in 1852. W.J. Golbourn, [1852]. 16p.,
fold. plates, illus. 21cm.

VALSESIA, Teresio and BURGENER, Giuseppe
Macugnaga e il Monte Rosa. Trezzano: A.
Fattorini, 1968. 101p., illus. (some col.),
map (fold.col. in pocket). 28cm.

BURGER-HOFER, H
Panorama vom Gäbris, 1250m. üb. Meer ...; nach
der Natur gezeichnet und autographirt von H.
Burger-Hofer. Zürich: J.J. Hofer, [ca 1880].
18cm.

BURLINGHAM, Frederick
How to become an alpinist. T. Werner Laurie,
[1916?]. xii, 218p., plates. 20cm.

BURMAN, José
A peak to climb: the story of South African
mountaineering; under the auspices of the
Mountain Club of South Africa. Cape Town:
Struik, 1966. 175p., plates (1 fold. some col.),
illus., maps. 25cm.

BURNABY, Fred
On horseback through Asia Minor. Sampson Low,
Marston, Searle, & Rivington, 1877. 2v.,
plates (2 fold. col.), maps, port. 23cm.

BURNABY, Mrs. Fred
See
LE BLOND, Elizabeth

BURNAND, F C
Very much abroad; with illustrations from
"Punch". Bradbury, Agnew, 1890. 436p., illus.
22cm.

BURNAT, Emile and GREMLI, August
Les roses des Alpes maritimes: études sur les
roses qui croissent spontanément dans la
chaîne des Alpes maritimes et le département
français de ce nom. Genève: H. Georg, 1879.
136p., bibl. 23cm.

BURNAT-PROVINS, Marguerite
Petits tableaux valaisans. Vevy: The Author,
1903. 192p., col. plates, illus. 19 x 25cm.
Cover title.

BURNET, Gilbert
Some letters containing an account of what
seemed most remarkable in Switzerland, Italy,
&c. Rotterdam: Printed by Acher, 1686. 307p.
19cm.

BURNET, Gilbert
Some letters containing an account of what
seemed most remarkable in Switzerland, Italy,
&c., written by G. Burnet to T.H.R[obert]
B[oyle]. [N.p.]: [n.pub.], 1687. 225 (i.e.
244)p. 15cm.

BURNS, W C
A short manual of mountaineering training, by
W.C. Burns, F. Shuttleworth and J.E.B. Wright.
6th ed. rev. by P.F. Gentil. Mountaineering
Association, 1964. 80p. 18cm.

BURPEE, Lawrence J
Among the Canadian alps. Lane, Bodley Head,
1915. 239p., plates (some col.), illus., maps,
bibl. 24cm.

BURRARD, Gerald
Big game hunting in the Himalayas and Tibet;
with sections by A.G. Arbuthnot [and others].
H. Jenkins, 1925. 320p., plates (some fold.
col.), illus., maps. 24cm.

BURRARD, Sir Sidney Gerald
The attraction of the Himalaya mountains upon
the plumb-line in India: considerations of
recent data. Dehra Dun: Survey of India, 1901.
ix, 115, xi p., plates (1 fold., some col.),
illus., maps. 29cm. (Survey of India Department. Professional papers, 5)

BURRARD, Sir Sidney Gerald
Completion of the link connecting the triangu-
lations of India and Russia, 1913; prepared
under the direction of Sir S.G. Burrard. Dehra
Dun: Survey of India, 1914. 121p., plates
(some fold.), illus., maps. 33cm. (Records of
the Survey of India, v.6)

BURRARD, Sir Sidney Gerald
Descriptions and co-ordinates of the principal
and secondary stations and other fixed points of
the North-East longitudinal series of triangulation (or Series I of the N.E. Quadrilateral);
prepared under the direction of S.G. Burrard.
Dehra Dun: Survey of India, 1909. 2v., plates,
maps. 31cm. (Synopsis of the results of the
operations of the Great Trigonometrical Survey
of India, v.35)

BURRARD, Sir Sidney Gerald
Explorations in Tibet and neighbouring regions,
1865-[1892]; prepared under the direction of Sir
S.G. Burrard. Dehra Dun: Survey of India, 1915.
2v., plates (some fold), illus., maps (in
pockets). 35cm. (Records of the Survey of
India, v.8)

BURRARD, Sir Sidney Gerald
Investigations of isostasy in Himalayan and
neighbouring regions. Dehra Dun: Survey of
India, 1918. 38p., plates (1 fold. col.),illus.,
maps. 29cm. (Survey of India. Professional
papers, no.17)

BURRARD, Sir Sidney Gerald
Mount Everest and its Tibetan names: a review
of Sir Sven Hedin's book. Dehra Dun: Survey of
India, Geodetic Branch, 1931. 19p., 2 maps.
24cm.

BURRARD, Sir Sidney Gerald
On the origin of the Himalaya mountains: a con-
sideration of the geodetic evidence. Calcutta:
Survey of India, 1912. 2 plates, maps. 29cm.
(Survey of India. Professional papers, no.12)

BURRARD, Sir Sidney Gerald and HAYDEN, Sir Henry
Hubert
A sketch of the geography and geology of the
Himalaya mountains and Tibet. Calcutta: Superintendent Government Printing, India, 1907-1908.
4pts. in 1 (vi, 308p.), plates (some fold.,
some col.), illus., maps. 32cm.

- - 2nd ed. rev., by Sir Sidney Burrard and A.M.
Heron. Delhi: Manager of Publications, 1933-34.

BURROUGHS, John
HARRIMAN ALASKA EXPEDITION, 1899
Alaska, giving the results of the Harriman Alaska
Expedition carried out with the co-operation of
the Washington Academy of Sciences, by John
Burroughs [and others]. Murray, 1902-   .
Plates (some fold., some col.), illus., maps.
27cm.
Vol.1 Narratives, glaciers, natives. 1902.- v.2.
History, geography, resources. 1902.- v.3.
Glaciers and glaciation. New York: Doubleday,
Page, 1904.-

BURTON, John Hill
The Cairngorm mountains. Edinburgh, London:
Blackwood, 1864. 120p., plate, illus. 19cm.

BURTON, Reginald G
Tropics and snows: a record of travel and adventure. Arnold, 1898. xvi, 349p., plates, illus.
24cm.

BURTSCHER, Guido
Die Kämpfe in den Folsen der Tofana: Geschichte
der von Mai 1915 bis November 1917 heiss umstrittenen Kampfabschnitte Travenanzes und
Lagazuoi. Bregenz: J.N. Teutsch, 1933. 232p.,
illus., col. fold. map, bibl. 25cm.

BURY, Charles Kenneth Howard
See
HOWARD-BURY, Charles Kenneth

BUSCAGLIA, Italo
Il sentiero: pagine sulla montagna. Milano:[The
Author], 1934. xi, 133p. 20cm.

BUSCAINI, Gino
Alpi Pennine. Vol.1. Dal Col du Petit Ferret al
Col d'Otemma. Milano: Club Alpino Italiano,
Touring Club Italiano, 1971. 495p., plates (1
fold, some col.), illus., maps. 17cm. (Guida
dei monti d'Italia)

BUSCAINI, Gino
Alpi Pennine. Vol.2. Dal Col d'Otemma al Colle
del Teodulo. Milano: Club Alpino Italiano, Touring Club Italiano, 1970. 610p., plates (some
fold., some col.), illus., maps, bibl. 17cm.
(Guida dei monti d'Italia)

BUSCAINI, Gino and CASTIGLIONI, Ettore
Dolomiti di Brenta. 2a. ed. Milano: Club Alpino
Italiano, Touring Club Italiano, 1977. 510p.,
plates (some col.), illus., maps, bibl. 17cm.
(Guida dei monti d'Italia)

BUSH-ATKINS, Daisy
Through the Alps. Ilfracombe, Devon: Stockwell,
1963. 46p., illus. 19cm.

BUSHNELL, Vivian C   and RAGLE, Richard H
Icefield Ranges Research Project: scientific
results; edited by Vivian C. Bushnell and Richard
H. Ragle; foreword and introduction by Walter A.
Wood. New York: American Geographical Society;
Montreal: Arctic Institute of North America,
1969-72. 3v., fold plates (1 col.), illus., map.
29cm.

BUSINGER, Joseph Maria
Itinéraire du Mont-Righi et du Lac des 4 cantons,
précédé de la description de la ville de Lucerne
et de ses environs; traduit de l'allemand ... par
H. de C*** [i.e. Crousaz]. Lucerne: Xav. Meyer,
1815. vi, 68, 91p., fold. plates, illus., map,
plan. 21cm.

BUSK, Sir Douglas
Armand Charlet: portrait d'un guide; préface de
Lucien Devies; traduit ... par Félix et Jeanne
Germain; illustré ... [par] Bridget Busk. Paris:
Arthaud, 1974. 279p., 10 plates, illus. 20cm.
(Collection sempervivum, no.61)

BUSK, Sir Douglas
The Central Caucasus: the main chain and sub-
sidiary spurs from Elbruz to Kasbek, including
the mountains north of the Shtuluvsek. The
Author, [1948]. 92 leaves. 34cm.
Typescript.

- - Maps.

BUSK, Sir Douglas
The delectable mountains; illustrated by 43 of
the author's own photographs and with maps by the
author; sketches by Bridget Busk. Hodder &
Stoughton, 1946. xi, 274p., plates, illus., fold.
maps. 23cm.

BUSK, Sir Douglas
The fountain of the sun: unfinished journeys in
Ethiopia and the Ruwenzori. Parrish, 1957.
240p., plates (some col.), illus., maps, bibl.
23cm.

BUSK, Sir Douglas
A map of the Central Elburz: note. [London],
1958. 207-208p., map. 22cm.
Offprint from Alpine Journal, v.63, no.297,
Nov. 1958.

BUSK, R   H
The valleys of Tyrol: their traditions and customs, and how to visit them. Longmans, Green,
1874. xxxi, 453p., plates (some fold., 1 col.),
illus., maps. 20cm.

BUSS, Ernst and HEIM, Albert
Der Bergsturz von Elm den 11. September 1881:
Denkschrift. Zürich: J. Wurster, 1881. 163p.,
plates (1 fold., some col.), maps. 26cm.

BUSS, Ernst
SCHWEIZER ALPEN-CLUB
Die ersten 25 Jahre des Schweizer Alpenclub:
Denkschrift; im Auftrag des Centralcomites verfasst
von Ernst Buss. Glarus: Bäschlin, 1889. 244p.,
fold. plates. 20cm.

BUSS, Ernst
SCHWEIZER ALPEN-CLUB
[Die ersten 25 Jahre ...]. Les vingt-cinq
premières années du Club Alpin Suisse: ouvrage
commémoratif ..., par Ernest Buss; traduit par Jean
Cevey et Alfred Richon. Genève: Le Club,[1889?].
280p., fold. plates. 20cm.

BUSSON, Paul
BENESCH, Fritz
Der Semmering und seine Berge: ein Album der
Semmering Landschaft von Gloggnitz bis Mürz-
zuschlag; mit ... Abbildungen nach Photograph-
ischen aufnahmen von Fritz Benesch; und einem
Begleitwort von Paul Busson. Wien: C. Reisser,
1913. 88p., col. plates, illus. 25cm.

BUTLER, Arthur John
QUILLER-COUCH, Sir Arthur
Memoir of Arthur John Butler. Murray, 1917.
vi, 261p., plates, illus. 23cm.

BUTLER, Frank Hedges
Fifty years of travel by land, water and air.
Unwin, 1920. 421p., illus. 22cm.

BUTLER, Frank Hedges
Through Lapland with ski and reindeer, with
some account of ancient Lapland and the Murman
coast. Unwin, 1917. 286p., plates (1 fold.),
illus., map. 24cm.

BUTLER, Samuel
Alps and sanctuaries of Piedmont and the Canton
Ticino (op.6.) 2nd ed. D. Bogue, 1882. viii,
376p., plates, illus., music. 23cm.

- - New and enl. ed., with author's revisions and
index; and an introduction by R.A. Streatfield.
A.C. Fifield, 1913.

BUTLER, Sir William Francis
The great lone land: a narrative of travel and
adventure in the north-west of America. 5th ed.
Sampson Low, Marston, Low & Searle, 1873. xi,
386p., plates (1 fold. col.), illus., map.
19cm.

BUTT, Mary Martha
See
SHERWOOD, Mary Martha

BUXTON, Edward North
Short stalks; or, Hunting camps north, south,
east and west. 2nd. ed. Stanford, 1893. xiii,
405p., illus. 24cm.

BUXTON, Hannah Maude
On either side of the Red Sea, with illustrations
of the granite ranges of the eastern desert of
Egypt, by H.M.B., C.E.B., and T.B.; with an
introduction by E.N. Buxton. Stanford, 1895.
viii, 163p., plates, illus. 22cm.

BUXTON, Harold
Trans-Caucasia. Faith Press, [1925]. xi, 99p.,
plates (1 col.), illus., map, bibl. 19cm.

BUXTON, Hon. Noel
See
NOEL-BUXTON, Noel, Baron Buxton

BUZZETTI, Pietro
CLUB ALPINO ITALIANO. Sezione in Chiavenna di
Sondrio
Il passo dello Spluga e strade chiavennasche,
[da] Pietro Buzzetti. [Chiavenna di Sondrio]:
La Sezione, 1928. 45p. 22cm.

BYERS, Samuel Hawkins Marshall
Switzerland and the Swiss, by an American resident [i.e. Samuel H.M. Byers]. Zurich: Orell
Füssli, 1875. xxvi, 203p., plates, illus., maps.
21cm.

BYLES, Marie Beuzeville
By cargo boat and mountain: the unconventional
experiences of a woman on tramp round the world.
Seeley, Service, 1931. 315p., plates, illus.
23cm.

BYNE, Eric
A climbing guide to Brassington rocks; with
photographs by J.A. Best and F.H. Restall.
Birmingham: Midland Association of Mountaineers,
1950. 35p., plates, illus. 14cm.

BYNE, Eric and WHITE, Wilfred B
Further developments in the Peak District;
edited by Eric Byne and Wilfred B. White.
Birkenhead: Willmer & Haram, 1957. iv, 205p.,
plates, illus. 16cm. (Climbs on gritstone,
v.4)

BYNE, Eric and SUTTON, Geoffrey
High peak: the story of walking and climbing in
the Peak District; with a foreword by Patrick
Monkhouse. Secker & Warburg, 1966. 256p.,
plates, illus., bibl. 23cm.

BYNE, Eric
The Saddleworth-Chew Valley area; edited by Eric
Byne. [N.p.]: Cade, [1965]. 210p., plates,
illus., bibl. 16cm. (Rock climbs in the Peak,
v.2)
Produced for and by British Mountaineering
Council, Peak Committee.

BYNE, Eric
The Sheffield area, by members of the Valkyrie
Mountaineering Club, Sheffield University
Mountaineering Club, "Oread" Mountaineering
Club, Midland Association of Mountaineers and
the Peak Climbing Club; edited by Eric Byne.
Rev. ed. Birkenhead: Willmer, 1956. 171p.,
plates, illus., bib. 16cm.

BYNE, Eric
The Sheffield-Stanage area; edited by Eric Byne.
[N.p.]: Cade, [1963?]. 214p., plates, illus.
16cm. (Rock climbs in the Peak, v.1)
Produced for and by British Mountaineering
Council, Peak Committee.

BYRON, George Gordon, Baron Byron
Childe Harold's pilgramage. Canto the third.
Murray, 1816. 79p. 22cm.

BYRON, George Gordon, Baron Byron
[Childe Harold's pilgrimage]. Childe Harold;
texte anglais publié avec une notice des arguments et des notes en français par Émile Chasles.
Paris: Hachette, 1883. xxvi, 264p. 16cm.

BYRON, George Gordon, Baron Byron
Letters and journals of Lord Byron, with notices
of his life, by Thomas Moore. Murray, 1830.
2.v., 1 plate, port. 30cm.

BYRON, George Gordon, Baron Byron
ENGEL, Claire Éliane
Byron et Shelley en Suisse et en Savoie, mai-
octobre 1816. Chambéry: Dardel, 1930. vii,
111p, plates, illus. 26cm.

C*******, Charles
See
CUCHETET, Charles

C., G., Esq.
See
CLOWES, George

C., G., Junr.
See
CLOWES, George

C., G.C.
See
CARREL, Georges

C., M.
Guide-itinéraire à Chamonix et autour du Mont-
Blanc ... par M.C. 2e éd. Genève: Imprimerie
V. Blanchard, 1873. 32p., map. 15cm.

C., T.H.
See
TOWNSHEND, Chauncy Hare

C., W.A.B.
See
COOLIDGE, William Augustus Brevoort

CABLE, Mildred and FRENCH, Francesca
The Gobi desert. Hodder & Stoughton, 1942.
303p., plates (1 fold., 3 col.), illus., map.
bibl. 24cm.

CADART, Charles
CLUB ALPIN FRANÇAIS. Section du Sud-Ouest
La Concession Russell du Vignemale, [par] Ch.
Cadart; édité par la Section du Sud-Ouest du
Club Alpin Français, Commission Scientifique.
Bordeaux, 1943. 24p., 2 plates (1 fold.), illus.,
map, bibl. 22cm.
Supplément au Bulletin no.43, avril 1943.

CADBY, Will and CADBY, Carine
Switzerland in winter (discursive information for
visitors); illustrated with ... photographs by
the authors. Mills & Boon, 1914. xii, 232p.,
plates (1 fold. col.), illus., map. 20cm.

CADIER FRÈRES
Au pays des Isards. le ptie. De l'Aneto à la
Munia. 2e éd. rev., accompagnée d'une préface du
Comte Henry Russell. Osse: Les Auteurs, 1903.
104p., illus., maps. 21cm.

CADIER FRÈRES
Au pays des Isards: un grand pic, Marmuré ou
Balaitous (le massif de Batlaytouse), par un des
cinq frères Cadier; avec une préface du Comte de
Saint-Saud. Osse: Izarda, 1913. 247p., plates
(1 fold. col.), illus., map. 22cm.

CADISCH, Joos
Der Bau der Schweizeralpen; räumlich dargestellt
und kurz erläutert. Zürich: Füssli, 1926. 61p.,
illus., map (fold. col. in pocket), bibl. 25cm.

CADOUX, Jean
[Operation 1000]. One thousand metres down, by
Jean Cadoux and others; preface by André Bourgin;
translated by R.L.G. Irving. Allen and Unwin,
1957. 179p., xii, plates, illus., maps. 24cm.

CADUFF, Christian
SCHWEIZER ALPEN-CLUB
Alpine Skitouren: eine Auswahl. Zollikon:
S.A.C., 1962. 2v., plates, illus. 19cm.
Bd.1. Zentralschweiz; bearb. von Fritz Ineichen.
Bd.2. Graubünden; bearb. von Christian Caduff.

CAFLISCH, Toni
Firn und Eis der Schweizer Alpen: Gletscher-
inventar, von Fritz Müller, Toni Caflisch,
Gerhard Müller. Zürich: Geographisches Institut,
1976. 2v., 1 fold. plate, illus., maps. 30cm.
(Geographisches Institut. Publ., Nr. 57)
At head of title: ETH: Eidgenössische Technische
Hochschule Zürich.

CAINE, W S
A trip round the world in 1887-8; illustrated by
John Pedder [and others]. Routledge, 1888.
xxiv, 398p., illus. 23cm.

CAIRNES, D D
Upper White River district, Yukon. Ottawa:
Government Printing Bureau, 1915. vi, 191p.,
plates (3 fold., 2 col.), illus., maps (in pocket).
26cm. (Canada. Department of Mines. Geological
Survey. Memoir, 50; Geological series, no.51)

CAIRNES, D D
The Yukon-Alaska international boundary, between
Porcupine and Yukon rivers. Ottawa: Government
Printing Bureau, 1914. v, 161p., 3 fold plates,
illus., maps (in pocket). 26cm. (Canada. Depart-
ment of Mines. Geological Survey. Memoir, 67;
Geological series, no.49)

CALAME, Alexandre
RAMBERT, Eugène
Alexandre Calame: sa vie et son oeuvre d'âpres
les sources originales. Paris: Fischbacher, 1884.
vii, 568p., port. 22cm.

CALDWELL, Johnny
The cross-country ski book. Brattleboro
(Vermont): S. Greene Press, 1964. 80p., illus.
23cm.

CALIFORNIA. Geological Survey of California
See
GEOLOGICAL SURVEY OF CALIFORNIA

CALVERT, J
Vazeeri Rupi, the silver country of the Vazeers
in Kulu: its beauties, antiquities and silver
mines, including a trip over the lower Himalayah
range and glaciers. Spon, 1873. xii, 102p.,
col. plates (1 fold.), illus., map. 25cm.

CAMBRAY DIGNY, Tommaso, conte de
See
DE CAMBRAY DIGNY, Tommaso, conte

CAMBRENSIS, Giraldus
See
GIRALDUS CAMBRENSIS

The Cambrian tourist; or, Post-chaise companion
through Wales; containing cursory sketches of the
Welsh territories... 5th ed... corr. and considerably enl. Edwards & Knibb, 1821. xvi,
467p., plates (2 fold.), illus. 19cm.

- - 6th ed... corr. and considerably enl. Geo.
B. Whitaker, 1828.

- - 7th ed... corr. and considerably enl. Whitaker,
Treacher, 1830.

CAMBRIDGE GARHWAL HIMALAYA EXPEDITION, 1977
Report; edited by J.C. Williams. Marlborough
(Wilts.): The Expedition, [1978]. 46 leaves,
illus., maps. 30cm.

CAMBRIDGE HINDU-KUSH EXPEDITION, 1966
Cambridge Hindu-Kush Expedition 1966, [by John
Ashburner, Henry Edmundson, Paul Newby]. [Cam-
bridge]: The Expedition, [1967]. 66p., plates
(2 fold.), illus., maps. 25cm.

CAMBRIDGE HINDU KUSH EXPEDITION, 1972
Report of the Cambridge Hindu Kush Expedition
1972, 20th June - 10th September; [R.C. Pelly,
editor]. Haslemere: The Expedition, [1973?].
83p., plates, illus., maps. 30cm.

CAMBRIDGE HINDU-KUSH EXPEDITION, 1976
Preliminary report. Cambridge: The Expedition,
[1976]. 13p., map. 30cm.

CAMBRIDGE-REYKJAVIK UNIVERSITIES EXPEDITION TO
VATNAJOKULL, ICELAND, 1976
The 1976 Cambridge-Reykjavik Universities Expedi-
tion to Vatnajokull, Iceland, [by] R.L. Ferrari,
K.J. Miller, G. Owen. Cambridge: The University,
1976. 34 leaves, plates, illus., maps. 29cm.
(University of Cambridge. Department of Engin-
eering. Special reports, 5)

CAMBRIDGE STAUNINGS EXPEDITION, 1970
The Cambridge Staunings Expedition 1970. Vol.1.
General report and the glaciological projects;
editor, K.J. Miller. Cambridge: University of
Cambridge, Department of Engineering, 1971. 66
leaves, illus., 1 fold. map. 30cm.

CAMENA D'ALMEIDA, P
Les Pyrénées: développement de la connaissance
géographique de la chaîne. Paris: Colin, [1893].
328p. 24cm.

CAMENISCH, Carl
Graubünden in der deutschen Dichtung, Auswahl und
Einleitung von Carl Camenisch. Leipzig: H.
Haessel, 1923. 95p. 16cm. (Die Schweiz im
deutschen Geistesleben, 21)

CAMERON, Una
A good line, written and illustrated by Una
Cameron. [The Author], 1932. 97p., plates,
illus., map. 23cm.

CAMINADE-CHATENAY, A
Souvenirs de Suisse: nouvelles; suivis de Autres
temps, autres moeurs: comédie de salon en trois
actes et en vers. Paris: F. Sartorius, 1862.
319p. 20cm.

CAMMANN, Schuyler
Trade through the Himalayas: the early British
attempts to open Tibet. Princeton: Princeton
University Press, 1951. x, 186p., plates, illus.,
maps, bibl. 23cm.

CAMMEL, Gustave Émile
Les pérégrinations d'un alpiniste à travers les
Alpes-Maritimes, les Basses-Alpes, le Dauphiné,
la Savoie, la Suisse, l'Italie septentrionale et
la Principauté de Monaco, par un Alsacien [i.e.
Gustave Émile Cammel]. Nice: Visconti, 1883.
315p. 22cm.

CAMPANILE, Vincent
Calendrier alpin avec des notices sur les éruptions volcaniques, explorations polaires, etc.
5e éd. Naples: [The Author], 1902. xv, 390p.
17cm.

CAMPBELL, Alexander
A journey from Edinburgh through parts of North
Britain, containing remarks on Scottish landscape
... T.N. Longman & O. Rees, 1802. 2v., 44 plates,
illus. 28cm.

- - New ed. J. Stockdale, 1810.

CAMPBELL, Bruce and CAMPBELL, Margaret
Brathay: the first twenty-five years, 1947-72;
appendixes compiled by Brian Ware. Ambleside:
Brathay Hall Trust, 1972. 80p., illus. 22cm.

CAMPBELL, Bruce
Snowdonia: the National Park of North Wales, by
F.J. North, Bruce Campbell, Richenda Scott.
Collins, 1949. 469p., plates (some col.), illus.,
maps, bibl. 22cm. (New naturalist series)

CAMPBELL, J I
A bibliography of mountains and mountaineering in
Africa; compiled by J.I. Campbell. Cape Town:
School of Librarianship, University of Cape Town,
1945. 48 leaves. 33cm.
Typescript.

CAMPBELL, John Douglas Sutherland, 9th Duke of
Argyll
See
ARGYLL, John Douglas Sutherland Campbell, 9th
Duke of

CAMPBELL, John Francis
Frost and fire: natural engines, toolmarks and
chips, with sketches taken at home and abroad by
a traveller. Edinburgh: Edmondston & Douglas,
1865. 2v., illus., col. map. 23cm.
Preface signed: J.F. Campbell.

CAMPBELL, John Robert
How to see Norway. Longmans, Green, 1871.
viii, 84p., plates, illus., map. 19cm.

CAMPBELL, Bruce and CAMPBELL, Margaret
Brathay: the first twenty-five years, 1947-72;
appendixes compiled by Brian Ware. Ambleside:
Brathay Hall Trust, 1972. 80p., illus. 22cm.

CAMPBELL, Wilfred
Canada; painted by T. Mower Martin; described by
Wilfred Campbell. Black, 1907. xviii, 272p.,
col. plates (1 fold.), illus., map. 24cm.

CAMPBELL-KELLY, Ben
PATAGONIAN MOUNTAINEERING EXPEDITION, 1974
A Patagonia handbook: Cerro Stanhardt 1974/5:
the report of the 1974 Patagonian Mountaineering
Expedition; compiled by Ben Campbell-Kelly with
assistance from Brian Wyvill. Manchester: The
Expedition, 1975. 30 leaves, plates, illus.,
maps. 30cm.

CAMUS, Théodore
De la montagne au désert: récits d'ascensions et
correspondance. Paris: Ch. Delagrave, [1912].
xv, 313p., 1 plate, port. 21cm.
Abridged ed., published in 1930 under title:
Oeuvres alpines.

CAMUS, Théodore
Oeuvres alpines. Chambéry: Dardel, 1930. xv,
247p., 1 plate, port. 20cm.
Abridged ed. of De la montagne au désert.

CANADA. Commission appointed to Delimit the
Boundary between the Provinces of Alberta and
British Columbia
Report, from 1913 to [1924]. Ottawa: Office of
the Surveyor General, 1917-25. 3pts., 1 col.
plate, illus., map. 26cm.

- - Atlas. 3pts.

CANADA. Defence Research Board
HATTERSLEY-SMITH, Geoffrey
North of latitude eighty: the Defence Research
Board in Ellesmere Island. Ottawa: Defence
Research Board, 1974. ix, 121p., plates (1 col.
fold.), bibl. 22cm.

CANADA. Department of the Interior
Description of & guide to Jasper Park. Ottawa:
The Department, 1917. 97p., illus., map. 26cm.

CANADA. Department of the Interior
Jasper National Park, by M.B. Williams. Ottawa:
The Department, 1928. 176p., 2 fold. plates,
illus., maps, bibl. 24cm.

CANADA. Geological Survey
See
GEOLOGICAL SURVEY OF CANADA

CANDLER, Edmund
On the edge of the world. Cassell, 1919. 278p.,
plates, illus., map. 22cm.

CANDLER, Edmund
The unveiling of Lhasa. Arnold, 1905. xvi,
304p., plates (1 fold.), illus., map. 24cm.

- - Another issue. Nelson, [1906?].

CANDLER, Edmund
A vagabond in Asia. Greening, 1900. 294p.,
plates, illus., map. 20cm.

CANE, Claude
Summer and fall in western Alaska: the record of
a trip to Cook's Inlet after big game. Cox,
1903. viii, 191p., plates, illus. 23cm.

CANE, Felice Giulio
Storia di Chesio e cenni storici della Valle
Strona. Chesio: Società Pro-Chesio, 1907. xvii,
246p., plates (1 fold., 2 col.), illus., maps,
bibl. 23cm.

CANETTA, Nemo and CORBELLINI, Giancarlo
Valmalenco: itinerari storici etnografici
naturalistici, Alta Via della Valmalenco, itinerari sci-escursionistici. Bologna: Tamari, 1976.
278p., 1 fold. col. plate, illus., map (in
pocket), bibl. 16cm. (Guide storiche etnografiche
naturalistiche, 1)

CANNING, Charles John Spencer George, Lord Garvagh
See
GARVAGH, Charles John Spencer George Canning, Baron
Garvagh

CANNON, Le Grand
Look to the mountain. Cassell, 1943. 410p., map.
20cm.

CANTÙ, C
Guida al Lago di Como ed alle strade di Stelvio e
Spluga. Como: Ostinelli, 1847. 129p., map. 16cm.

CANZIANI, Estella
Costumes, moeurs et légendes de Savoie; adapté
de l'anglais par A. Van Gennep. Chambéry: Dardel,
1920. ix, 105p., 47 col. plates, illus. 30cm.

CANZIO, E
In Valpellina: escursioni e studi, [da] E. Canzio,
F. Mondini, N. Vigna. Torino: Club Alpino
Italiano, 1899. 176p., plates (1 fold. col.),
illus., map. 25cm.

CAPPELLER, Moritz Anton
Pilati Montis historia, in pago Lucernensi
Helvetiae siti. Basileae: Typis & Sumptibus Joh.
Rodolphi Im-Hof, 1757 [i.e. 1767]. 188p., plates,
illus. 21cm.

CAPPELLERIUS, Mauricius Antonius
See
CAPPELLER, Moritz Anton

CAPPER, Samuel John
The shores and cities of the Boden See: rambles
in 1879 and 1880; with ... numerous original
etchings on stone by H. Schmidt-Pecht. Thos. de
la Rue, 1881. xxxvi, 452p., plates, illus., map.
23cm.

CAPRIN, Giuseppe
Alpi Giulie; disegni originali di: Barison,
Giuseppe [and others]. Trieste: G. Caprin, 1895.
439p., illus. 24cm.

CARBONNIÈRES, Louis François Élizabeth Ramond,
baron de
See
RAMOND, Louis

CARDONNE, Pierre de
Le retour éternel. Chambéry: Dardel, [19--].
147p. 17cm.

CARDUCCI, Giosue
Poesie, 1850-1900. 4a ed. Bologna: Zanichelli,
1905. xvi, 1075p., plates, ports. 20cm.

CAREGA DI MURICCE, F
Un'estate a Cutigliano: escursioni e ascensioni
nell'alto Appennino pistoiese. Pistoia: Tipografia Niccolai, 1878. 167p., 1 fold. plate,
illus., map. 16cm.

CARELLI DE ROCCA CASTELLO, Jacques
Une ascension au Mont-Blanc en 1843. Varallo:
Caligaris, 1843. 32p. 23cm.

CAREY, David
Picturesque scenes; or, A guide to the beauties
of the Highlands... 2nd ed. Cradock & Joy, 1812.
225p. 24cm.

CAREZ, L
La géologie des Pyrénées françaises. Paris:
Imprimerie Nationale, 1903-09. 6v., 39 plates
(some fold., some col.), illus., maps, bibl.
33cm. (Mémoires pour servir à l'explication de
la carte géologique détaillée de la France)

CARLE, Dr.
Sur les routes des Alpes en automobile: le massif
de la Chartreuse, le Vercors et la Forêt de
Lente, l'Oisans, la vallée des Arves, la haute
route des Alpes. Paris: Hachette, [1914].
241p., plates, illus., maps. 20cm.

CARLISLE, Henry E
HAYWARD, Abraham
A selection from the correspondence of Abraham
Hayward from 1834 to 1884, with an account of his
early life; edited by Henry E. Carlisle. Murray,
1886. 2v. 21cm.

CARLO ALBERTO, King of Sardinia
Relation du voyage en Savoie du roi et de la
reine de Sardaigne, leurs majestés Charles-Albert
et Marie-Thérèse, en 1834. Chambéry: L'Imprimerie du gouvernement, 1834. 127p. 22cm.

CARNE, John
Letters from Switzerland and Italy, during a late
tour, by the author of 'Letters from the East' &
'Travels in the East' [i.e. John Carne].
Published for Henry Colburn by Richard Bentley,
1834. xii, 472p. 24cm.

CARNE, John
Reise durch die Schweiz; aus dem Englischen übersetzt von Wilhelm Adolf Lindau. Dresden: Arnold,
1828. 192p. 17cm.

CAROLINE, Queen, consort of George IV, King of Great
Britain
Voyages and travels of Her Majesty, Caroline,
Queen of Great Britain ..., by one of Her
Majesty's Suite. Jones, 1822. x, 755p., plates,
illus., maps. 22cm.

CAROLINE, Queen, consort of George IV, King of Great
Britain
[Voyage and travels of Her Majesty, Caroline,
Queen of Great Britain ...]. Voyages de Caroline,
reine d'Angleterre, en Allemagne, en Suisse, en
Italie, en Grèce et en Palestine; traduits de
l'anglais par J. Dubar. Ostende: P. Scheldewaert,
1825. 3v., plates, illus. 18cm.

CARR, Alfred
Adventures with my alpenstock and knapsack: or,
A five weeks' tour in Switzerland, in 1874, with
some notes on Paris, Strasbourg, and other places.
York: The Author, 1875. 76p. 19cm.

CARR, Herbert Reginald Culling and CARR, Evelyn
A village antique shop in the Cotswolds, 1960-
1975. Cirencester: E. & H. Carr, 1975. [12p.],
illus. 21cm.

CARR, Glyn
See
STYLES, Showell

CARR, Herbert Reginald Culling
A climbers' guide to Snowdon and the Beddgelert
district... The Climbers' Club, 1926. 143p.,
plates (3 fold. col.), illus., maps, bibl. 16cm.

CARR, Herbert Reginald Culling
The Irvine diaries: Andrew Irvine and the enigma
of Everest 1924. Goring, Reading: Gastons-West
Col, 1979. 143., illus., map, ports., bibl.
22cm.

CARR, Herbert Reginald Culling and LISTER, George A
The mountains of Snowdonia in history, the
sciences, literature and sport; edited by Herbert
R.C. Carr and George A. Lister. Bodley Head, 1925.
xvix, 405p., plates (some col.), illus., maps (some
fold.). 23cm.

- - 2nd ed. Crosby, Lockwood, 1948.

CARR, Herbert Reginald Culling and CARR, Evelyn
A village antique shop in the Cotswolds, 1960-
1975. Cirencester: E. & H. Carr, 1975. [12p.],
illus. 21cm.

CARR, Herbert Reginald Culling
A walker's guide to Snowdon and the Beddgelert
district ..., by Herbert R.C. Carr, George A.
Lister and Paul Orkney Work. Newcastle upon
Tyne: Listers (Printers), 1949. vi, 60p., plates
(1 fold.), illus., bibl. 14cm.
Reprint, rev. and enl. from the walkers' section
of A climbers' guide to Snowdon... 1926.

CARR-SAUNDERS, Sir Alexander Morris
BROWN, Henry Phelps
Sir Alexander Carr-Saunders, 1886-1966. London,
1967. 379-389p., 1 plate, port. 25cm.
Offprint from Proceedings of the British Academy,
v.53, 1967.

CARREL, Georges
Les Alpes pennines dans un jour; soit, Panorama
boréal de la Becca de Nona, depuis le Mont-Blanc
jusqu'au Mont-Rose. Aoste: Lyboz, 1855. 61p.,
1 fold. col plate, illus. 19cm.

CARREL, Georges
Ascensions du Mont-Cervin en 1868. Aoste, 1868.
7p. 19cm.
Offprint from Feuille d'Aoste, no.49.

CARREL, Georges
Chaîne de la Grivola, (Alpes graies), vue de la
Becca de Nona. Aoste: Lyboz, 1860. 20cm.
Panorama.

- - 3e éd. corr. 1863.

CARREL, Georges
Le Col de Saint-Théodule: lettre à M.B. Gastaldi.
Torino, 1866. 15p. 22cm.
Offprint from Bulletino trimestrale del Club
Alpino di Torino, no.3.

CARREL, Georges
Nouvelle ascension du Mont-Cervin, [par Georges
Carrel?]. Aoste: Lyboz, [1867]. [1p.]. 22cm.

CARREL, Jean Antione
VIRIGLIO, Attilio
Jean Antione Carrel (il "Padre" di tutte le
guide). Bologna: Cappelli, 1948. 332p.,
plates, illus. 20cm. (Collana d'oro "le Alpi",
3)

CARRINGTON, Rab
BRITISH SOUTH AMERICA MOUNTAINEERING EXPEDITION,
1976-77
[Report]. [Sheffield]: The Expedition, [1977].
37 leaves, 1 plate, maps. 30cm.
Expedition leader: Rab Carrington.

CARSON, William English
Mexico: the wonderland of the south. Rev. ed.
with new chapters. New York: Macmillan, 1914.
xiii, 449p., plates (1 col.), illus., map. 23cm.

CARTELLIERI, Walther
Die römischen Alpenstrassen über den Brenner,
Reschen-Scheideck und Plöckenpass, mit ihren
Nebenlinien. Leipzig: Dieterich, 1926. 186p.,
8 fold. plates, maps. 24cm. (Philologus,
Supplementband 18, Heft 1)

CARTWRIGHT, J E
ROYAL AIR FORCE GREENLAND EXPEDITION, 1975
Report on the Royal Air Force Expedition to
Søndre Sermilik Fjord in south west Greenland,
10th June - 8th July 1975, by Flight Lieut. J.E.
Cartwright, expedition leader. [R.A.F.M.A.],
[1976]. 63p., illus., maps. 29cm.

CARUS, C G
Reise durch Deutschland, Italien und die Schweiz,
im Jahre 1828. Leipzig: Fleischer, 1835. 2v.
18cm.

CARVER, Toni
Climbing in Cornwall: a climber's guide to north,
south and east Cornwall; compiled and edited by
Toni Carver; written jointly by Toni Carver,
Peter Stanier & Pat Littlejohn; with foundation
work by the T.S.R.C.C. Minions Group. St. Ives:
J. Pike, 1973. 84p., illus., maps. 19cm.

CASANOVA, Oscar
Escursioni nei parchi alpini: 60 incontri con la
natura protetta dall'Argentera alle Alpi Giulie.
Torino: Centro di Documentazione Alpina, 1977.
178p., illus. (some col.), maps, bibl. 22cm.
(Biblioteca della montagna, 5)

CASELLA, Georges
L'alpinisme; préfaces de E. Sauvage, Léon
Auscher. Paris: Lafitte, 1913. xxiii, 428p.,
illus. 22cm. (Sports-bibliothèque)

CASELLA, Georges
Les deux routes. Paris: Flammarion, 1919.
251p. 20cm.

CASELLA, Georges
Le vertige des Cimes: roman d'aventures. Paris:
Ollendorff, [19--]. 272p. 19cm.

CASELLI, Carlo
Speleologia: studio delle caverne. Milano:
Hoepli, 1906. xii, 163p., bibl. 16cm. (Manuale
Hoepli. Serie scientifica, 358)

CASSAS, Louis Françoise
Travels in Istria and Dalmatia; drawn up from the
itinerary of L.F. Cassas by Joseph Lavallée;
translated from the French. R. Phillips, 1805.
iv, 124p., fold. plates, illus., map. 22cm. (In
A collection of modern and contemporary voyages...
v.1. London, 1805)

CASSIN, Riccardo and NANGERONI, Giuseppe
Lhotse '75: spedizione alpinistico-scientifica del
C.A.I. all'Himalaya del Nepal; relazioni del
gruppo alpinistico e del gruppo scientifico raccolte da Riccardo Cassin e da Giuseppe Nangeroni;
coordinazione e allestimento di Mario Fantin.
Milano: Club Alpino Italiano, 1977. 171p., plates
(some col.), illus., maps, bibl. 28cm.

CASTERET, Norbert
[Dix ans sous terre]. Ten years under the earth;
translated and edited by Barrows Mussey. Dent,
1939. xv, 240p., plates, illus., maps. 23cm.

CASTERET, Norbert
[Mes cavernes]. My caves; translated by R.L.G.
Irving. Dent, 1947. xi, 172p., plates, illus.
22cm.
Sequel to: Dix ans sous terre and Au fond des
gouffres.
CASTIGLIONI, Bruno
Il gruppo della Civetta (Alpi Dolomitiche).
Padova: Società Cooperativa Tipografica, 1931.
85p., 3 plates (1 fold.), illus., maps (1 fold.
col. in pocket). 34cm. (Memorie dell'Istituto
Geologico della R. Università di Padova, v.9)

CASTIGLIONI, Ettore
Alpi Carniche; con la collaborazione di Michele
Gortani [and others]; a cura di Silvio Saglio.
Milano: Club Alpino Italiano, Touring Club
Italiano, 1954. 709p., plates (some fold., some
col.), illus., maps. 17cm. (Guida dei monti
d'Italia)
CASTIGLIONI, Ettore
Dolomiti di Brenta. Milano: Club Alpino Italiano,
Touring Club Italiano, 1949. 498p., plates (some
col.), illus., maps, bibl. 17cm. (Guida dei
monti d'Italia)

BUSCAINI, Gino and CASTIGLIONI, Ettore
Domomiti di Brenta. 2a ed. Milano: Club Alpino
Italiano, Touring Club Italiano, 1977. 510p.,
plates (some col.), illus., maps, bibl. 17cm.
(Guida dei monti d'Italia)

CASTIGLIONI, Ettore
Odle, Sella, Marmolada. Roma: Club Alpino
Italiano; Milano: Touring Club Italiano, 1937.
778p., plates (some fold. col.), illus., maps,
bibl. 17cm. (Guida dei monti d'Italia)

CASTIGLIONI, Ettore
Pale di S. Martino: gruppo dei Feruc, Alpi
Feltrine. Roma: Club Alpino Italiano; Milano:
Touring Club Italiano, 1935. 484p., plates (some
fold., some col.), illus., maps, bibl. 17cm.
(Guida dei monti d'Italia)

CATELIN, Camille, vicomte de
See
ARVE, Stéphen d'

CATELIN, Edmond, vicomte de
See
ARVE, Stéphen d'

CATHCART, J   F
HOOKER, Sir Joseph Dalton
Illustrations of Himalayan plants, chiefly selected
from drawings made for J.F. Cathcart; the descriptions and analyses by J.D. Hooker; the plates
executed by W.H. Fitch. Lovell Reeve, 1855. 1v.
(chiefly illus.). 52cm.

CATLOW, Agnes and CATLOW, Maria E
Sketching rambles; or, Nature in the Alps and
Appennines; illustrated from sketches by the
authors. J. Hogg, [1861]. 2v., plates, illus.
22cm.

CATTANI, C
Das Alpenthal Engelberg und seine Berg-, Wasser-,
Milch-, und Molkenkuren. Luzern: Räber, 1852.
vi, 30p., plates (1 fold.), illus. 22cm.

CAULFIELD, Vivian
How to ski and how not to. 3rd ed. rev.
Nisbet, 1913. viii, 286p., plates, illus. 22cm.

CAULFIELD, Vivian
Ski-ing turns. 2nd ed. (rev.). Nisbet, 1924.
279p., illus. (some in pocket). 21cm.

CAUMERY, M   L   and PINCHON, J
Bécassine alpiniste, texte de M.-L. Caumery;
illustrations de J. Pinchon. Paris: Gautier et
Languereau, 1923. 64p., col. illus. 33cm.
(Édition de la semaine de Suzette)

CAVAZZANI, Francesco
Uomini del Cervino. Vol.1. Firenze: Olimpia,
1946. 239p., plates, illus., bibl. 27cm.

CAVE RESEARCH GROUP OF GREAT BRITAIN
A volume of essays presented to Brigadier E.A.
Glennie on the occasion of his 80th birthday,
July 18th 1969. Ledbury: C.R.G.G.B., 1969.
69-137p., plates, illus., map, bibl. 30cm.
(Cave Research Group of Great Britain. Trans-
actions, v.11, no.2, July 1969)

CAVENDISH, Georgiana, Duchess of Devonshire
See
DEVONSHIRE, Georgiana Cavendish, Duchess of

CAVIÉZEL, Michael
Das Oberengadin: ein Führer auf Spaziergängen
kleinen und grossen Touren. Chur: Im Selbstverlag des Verfassers, 1876. vi, 227p. 16cm.

-- 2. veränderte und verm. Aufl. Chur: Sprecher
& Plattner, 1881.

CAVIÉZEL, Michael
[Das Oberengadin ...]. Tourist's guide to the
Upper Engadine; translated ... by A.M.H.
Stanford, 1877. vii, 204p., map. 18cm.

CAVIÉZEL, Michael
[Das Oberengadin ...]. The Upper Engadine: a
guide to walks and tours, short and long. 5th
enl. and improved ed. Samaden: Tanner, 1891.
xii, 236p., maps (in pocket). 16cm.

CAYROL, René
Montagnes des Pyrénées-Orientales. T.1. De la
Méditerranée au Costabonne, par René Cayrol,
Pierre Roule, André Vinas. 3e éd. Perpignan:
Club Alpin Français, Section de Perpignan, 1973.
123p., fold. plates, maps. 15cm.

CAZIN, Jeanne
Les petits montagnards; illustré de ... vignettes
par G. Vuillier. Paris: Hachette, 1881. 303p.,
plates, illus. 19cm.

CELLINI, Benvenuto
Memoirs written by himself; translated by Thomas
Roscoe. Unit Library, 1903. xviii, 527p. 17cm.
(Unit Library, 24)

CENISE, Charles Rochat-
See
ROCHAT-CENISE, Charles

CENTRAL COUNCIL OF PHYSICAL RECREATION
The mountain code. C.C.P.R., 1968. [12p.],
illus. 19cm.

CENTRAL COUNCIL OF PHYSICAL RECREATION
Safety on mountains, by John Jackson and other members of the staff of Plas y Brenin, the Snowdonia National Recreation Centre; illustrated by Gordon F. Mansell. 7th ed. C.C.P.R., 1968. 48p., illus. 15cm.

CENTRE D'ESTUDIS I REALITZACIONS DE LES VALLS D'ANDORRA
Andorra pocket guide: tourism, shopping, real estate; editor: Luis S. Valdes. Andorra: The Centre, 1971. 122p.,1 fold. col. plate, illus., map. 16cm.

CENTRE EXCURSIONISTA DE CATALUNYA
Colección de guias.

    5. Cerdana, Andorra, Puigpedrós, Cadi, Puigmal, Carlit, por A. Jolis Felisart y A. Simó de Jolis. 2a ed. 1959.
    6. Posets-Maladeta, por A. Armengaud y A. Jolis. 1958.
    7. Pallars-Aran, por A. Jolis y M.A. Simó de Jolis. 1961.

CENTRE EXCURSIONISTA DE LA COMARCA DE BAGES
Expedición española Himalaya - 76: Makalu - 8481 mts.,24 de mayo 1976, [por José Ma. Montfort Fabrega]. Manresa: C.E.C.B., [13p.], illus. 28cm.

CENTRE EXCURSIONISTA DE LA COMARCA DE BAGES
[Expedición española Himalaya - 76]. Report ... [of] the Spanish Himalaya Expedition 1976: Makalu (8,481 mts.), south-east ridge, [by José Ma. Montfort]. Manresa: C.E.C.B., 1976. 4 leaves, illus., map. 29cm.

CENTRE EXCURSIONISTA DE LA COMARCA DE BAGES
Expedición espanola Hindu Kush - 73 (Himalaya). (In C.E.C.B. Butleti, no.19, 2a època, 2-3 trimestre, p.5-26, 2 fold. plates, illus., maps)

CENTRE EXCURSIONISTA DE LA COMARCA DE BAGES
77-Alaska operation. Manresa: C.E.C.B., [1977]. 2 leaves. 29cm.

CENTRO ALPINISTICO ITALIANO
  See
CLUB ALPINO ITALIANO

CENTRO EXCURSIONISTA DE CATALUNA
  See
CENTRE EXCURSIONISTA DE CATALUNYA

CENTRO EXCURSIONISTA DE LA COMARCA DE BAGES
  See
CENTRE EXCURSIONISTA DE LA COMARCA DE BAGES

CENTRO ITALIANO STUDIO DOCUMENTAZIONE ALPINISMO EXTRAEUROPEO
FANTIN, Mario
Alpinismo italiano extraeuropeo (al 112o anno): saggio di cronologia ed analisi critica; elabora- zione dall'Archivio del CISDAE in Bologna. Bologna: Tamari, 1967. 133p., plates, illus., bibl. 25cm.

Cents vues suisses, remarquables par leur situation, ou par des faits historiques, dessinées et gravées par Meyer, König [and others]. Zurich: Orell, Füssli, [ca 1820]. 1v. of illus. 14 x 21cm.

CENTURY ASSOCIATION. King Memorial Committee
  See
KING MEMORIAL COMMITTEE

CERESA, G   F
Escursioni alpine; ossia, Breve descrizione topo- grafica dei passi alpestri più frequentati ... cioè dal Colle ... Frejus al Brenner. Torino: C. Favale, 1869. 104p. 19cm.
At head of title: 600 kilometri alle Alpi.

CÉRÉSOLE, Alfred
Légendes des Alpes vaudoises; illustrations de Eugène Burnand. Lausanne: A. Imer, 1885. 380p., plates, illus. 27cm.

WOLF, F O and CÉRÉSOLE, Alfred
Valais and Chamonix. Zurich: Orell & Füssli, [18--]. vii, 826p., illus., maps. 19cm.

CÉRÉSOLE, Alfred
Zermatt et ses environs: description, histoire et légendes. Zurich: J.-A. Preuss, [ca 1891]. 80p., plates (some fold.), illus., maps. 19cm.

CERMENATI, Mario
Cose di alpinismo. Roma: Società editrice Dante Alighieri, 1901. 365p. 21cm.

CERRETELLI, Paolo
MONZINO, Guido
Kanjut Sar: atti della Spedizione G.M. '59 al Kanjut Sar, Karakorum; con monografia storico geo- grafica del Karakorum a cura di Pietro Meciani; osservazioni fisiologiche cliniche e psicologiche a cura di Paolo Cerretelli; note dal diario di Lorenzo Marimonti. Milano: A. Martello, 1961. 342p., illus., maps. 30cm.

CERRETELLI, Paolo
MONZINO, Guido
La Spedizione Italiana all'Everest 1973; con il resoconto scientifico di Paolo Cerretelli. [Milano]: La Spedizione, 1976. 256p., col. plates, illus., maps, bibl. 38cm.
In slip-case.

CERRO STANHARDT, 1974/1975
  See
PATAGONIAN MOUNTAINEERING EXPEDITION, 1974

CESSOLE, Victor de
CLUB ALPIN FRANÇAIS. Section des Alpes Maritimes
Manifestation organisée par la Section des Alpes Maritimes le 4 avril 1925, en l'honneur de Victor de Cessole, à l'occasion du 25me anniversaire de sa présidence. Nice: La Section, 1925. 40p., plates, port. 22cm.

CHABOD, Renato and GERVASUTTI, Giusto
Alpinismo; per cura di R. Chabod e G. Gervasutti. Roma: C.A.I., 1935. xxxviii, 222p., illus. 16cm. (Manuali del Club Alpino Italiano, 2)

CHABOD, Renato
La Cima di Entrelor; illustrato con disegni e dipinti dell'autore. Bologna: Zanichelli, 1969. 364p., col. plates, illus. 24cm. (Montagne, 6)

CHABOD, Renato
Monte Bianco [di] Renato Chabod [and others]. Milano: Club Alpino Italiano, Touring Club Italiano, 1963-68. 2v., col. plates (2 fold.), illus., maps (2 in pocket), bibl. 17cm. (Guida dei monti d'Italia)

CHAIX, B
Préoccupations statistiques, géographiques, pittoresques et synoptiques du Département des Hautes-Alpes. Grenoble: F. Allier, 1845. 979p., plates, illus. 23cm.

CHALBAUD CARDONA, Carlos
Expediciones a la Sierra Nevada de Merida. Caracas: Paraguachoa, 1959. 407p., 1 fold. col. plate, illus., map. 17cm.

CHALMERS, Charles
Electro-chemistry with positive results, and notes for inquiry on the sciences of geology and astro- nomy... J. Churchill, 1858. 100p., plates, illus. 23cm.

CHALONER, John
The Vale of Chamouni: a poem, by the author of "Rome" [i.e. John Chaloner]. J. Warren, 1822. xix, 176p. 22cm.

CHAMBERS'S JOURNAL
Up and down Mont Blanc: a Christmas extra double number of Chambers's Journal. Edinburgh: Chambers, 1866. 32p., illus. 27cm.

CHAMIER, Capt.
My travels; or, An unsentimental journey through
France, Switzerland and Italy. Hurst & Blackett,
1855. 3v. 21cm.

CHAMONIX. Musée
See
MUSÉE DE CHAMONIX

Chamonix, Mont-Blanc et sa vallée: guide illustré;
édité sous le patronage du Syndicat d'Initiative
de Chamonix. Grenoble: Dardelet, 1933. 62p.,
illus. 18cm.

CHANDEKAR, A   R
The god that did not fail: expedition to Hanuman
(19,930 ft.) May-June 1966. Bombay: Giri-Vihar,
[1966]. [48p.], plates, illus., map. 24cm.

CHANTRE, Mme B
À travers l'Arménie russe. Paris: Hachette, 1893.
368p., illus., maps. 29cm.

FAISAN, Albert and CHANTRE, E
Monographie géologique des anciens glaciers et du
terrain erratique de la partie moyenne du Basin du
Rhône. Lyon, 1879-80. 2v., fold. plates (1 col.),
illus. 28cm.

CHAPIN, Frederick H
The land of the cliff-dwellers. Boston: Appalachian Mountain Club, 1892. 188p., plates (1
fold.), illus., maps. 20cm.

CHAPIN, Frederick H
Mountaineering in Colorado: the peaks about Estes
Park. Boston: Appalachian Mountain Club, 1889.
168p., plates, illus. 21cm.

CHAPIUS, Thomas
Dans les montagnes de la Norvège.
(In Bibliothèque universelle... v.38-39, 1888,
3 pts.)

CHAPMAN, Abel and BUCK, Walter J
Unexplored Spain. Arnold, 1910. xvi, 416p.,
plates, illus. 27cm.

CHAPMAN, Abel
Wild Norway: with chapters on Spitzbergen,
Denmark... Arnold, 1897. xiii, 358p., plates,
illus. 23cm.

CHAPMAN, Frederick Spencer
Helvellyn to Himalaya, including an account of the
first ascent of Chomolhari; with an introduction
by the Marquis of Zetland. Chatto & Windus, 1940.
xv, 285p., plates (1 fold.), illus., maps. 23cm.

CHAPMAN, Frederick Spencer
Lhasa, the holy city; with an introduction by Sir
Charles Bell. Chatto & Windus, 1938. xiv, 342p.,
plates (1 fold., some col.), illus., map. 25cm.

CHAPMAN, Frederick Spencer
Living dangerously. Chatto & Windus in association with the Outward Bound Trust, 1953. 190p.,
plates, illus., maps. 21cm.

CHAPMAN, Frederick Spencer
Memoirs of a mountaineer: 'Helvellyn to Himalaya'
and 'Lhasa: the Holy City'. Reprint Society,
1945. 446p., plates, illus., maps (on lining
papers). 20cm.

CHAPMAN, Frederick Spencer
Watkins' last expedition; with an introduction by
Augustine Courtauld. Vanguard, 1953. 244p.
19cm.

CHAPMAN, Frederick Spencer
BARKER, Ralph
One man's jungle: a biography of F. Spencer
Chapman, D.S.O. Chatto & Windus, 1975. x, 374p.,
plates, illus. 23cm.

CHAPPAZ, Maurice
La haute route. Lausanne: Galland, 1974. 179p.
22cm.

CHAPPAZ, Maurice
Verdures de la nuit; lithographies de René Creux.
Lausanne: H.-L. Mermod, 1945. 41p., illus. 29cm.

CHARLES
Mémoire d'une toute petite tournée en Suisse, à
vol d'hirondelle dedié à mon ami Sept-Croix.
Harlem: Imprimé chez Joh. Enschedé, 1863. 91p.
21cm.
Signed: Charles.

CHARLES ALBERT, King of Sardinia
See
CARLO ALBERTO, King of Sardinia

CHARLET, Armand
Vocation alpine; souvenirs d'un guide de montagne; préface du Dr. Azema. Neuchatel: Attinger,
1949. 209p., plates, illus. 20cm. (Montagne)

CHARLET, Armand
BUSK, Sir Douglas
Armand Charlet: portrait d'un guide; préface de
Lucien Devies; traduit ... par Félix et Jeanne
Germain; illustré ... [par] Bridget Busk. Paris:
Arthaud, 1974. 279p., 10 plates, illus. 20cm.
(Collection sempervivum, no.61)

CHARNOCK, Richard Stephen
Guide to the Tyrol: comprising pedestrian tours
made in Tyrol, Styria, Carinthia, and Salzkammergut, during the summers of 1852 and 1853
... W.J. Adams, 1857. 112p., map. 17cm.

CHARPENTIER, Jean de
Essai sur les glaciers et sur le terrain erratique du Bassin du Rhône. Lausanne: M. Ducloux,
1841. x, 363p., plates, map. 24cm.

CHARPENTIER, Jean de
Notice sur la cause probable du transport des
blocs erratiques de la Suisse. Paris, 1835.
20p. 21cm.
Offprint from Annales des mines, t.8, 1835.

CHARPENTIER, Jean de
Quelques conjectures sur les grandes révolutions
qui ont changé la surface de la Suisse, et particulièrement celle du Canton de Vaud, pour
l'amener à son état actuel. Lausanne: M.
Ducloux, 1836. 12p. 21cm.

CHASE, Charles H
Alpine climbers. Society for Promoting Christian
Knowledge, [1888?]. 63p. 16cm.

CHASE, J   Smeaton
Yosemite trails: camp and pack-train in the
Yosemite region of the Sierra Nevada. Unwin,
1912. xi, 354p., plates, illus., map. 22cm.

CHASLES, Émile
BYRON, George Gordon, Baron Byron
[Childe Harold's pilgrimage]. Childe Harold;
texte anglais publié avec un notice des arguments
et des notes en français par Émile Chasles.
Paris: Hachette, 1883. xxvi, 264p. 16cm.

CHASTONAY, Paul de
Au Val d'Anniviers; traduction par André Favre.
St.-Maurice: Édition de l'oeuvre St.-Augustin,
[1939]. 93p., plates, illus., bibl. 19cm.

CHASTONAY, Paul de
[Kardinal Schiner]. Le Cardinal Schiner; adaptation française d'André Favre. Lausanne: F. Rouge,
[1943]. 135p., 6 plates, illus., bibl. 20cm.

CHASTONAY, Paul de
Sierre et son passé. Sierre: Amacker-Exquis,
1942. 77p., plates, illus. 19cm.

CHASTONAY, Paul de
Vercorin: le vieux village. Sierre: Tabin,
[1943]. 109p., plates, illus., bibl. 19cm.

Château of Leaspach; or, The stranger in Switzerland: a tale. Newman, 1827. 3v. 20cm.

CHATALAIN, Clara de
Handbook of the miniature Mont Blanc; edited by
Madame de Chatelain. 2nd ed. A.N. Myers, 1855.
42p. 18cm.
Based on Albert Smith's Hand-book.

CHATELLUS, Alain de
Alpiniste, est-ce toi? Paris: Arthaud, 1953.
174p., 15 plates, illus. 21cm. (Collection
sempervivum, 20)
Author's presentation inscription.

CHATELLUS, Alain de
De l'Eiger à l'Iharen; illustré de photographies
de l'auteur; préface de Lucien Devies. Paris:
J. Susse, 1947. 205p., plates, illus. 25cm.

CHATENAY, A   Caminade
See
CAMINADE-CHATENAY, A

CHATTERTON, Henrietta Georgiana, Lady
The Pyrenees, with excursions into Spain.
Saunders & Otley, 1843. 2v., plates, illus.
23cm.

CHAUSENQUE, Vincent de
Les Pyrénées; ou Voyages pédestres dans toutes
les régions de ces montagnes depuis l'Ocean
jusqu'à la Méditerranée. Paris: Lecointe et
Pougin, 1834. 2v., fold plates, illus. 22cm.

MILTON, William Fitzwilliam, Viscount and CHEADLE,
Walter Butler
The North-West passage by land, being the narra-
tive of an expedition from the Atlantic to the
Pacific, undertaken with a view of exploring a
route across the continent... 3rd ed. Cassell,
Petter and Galpin, 1865. xxiv, 400p., plates (2
fold. col.), illus., maps. 23cm.

- - 5th ed. 1866.

CHEEVER, George B
The pilgrim in the shadow of the Jungfrau Alp.
New York, London: Wiley, 1848. xii, 214p. 20cm.

- - Another ed. 1852.

CHEEVER, George B and HEADLEY, J   T
Travels among Alpine scenery. Blackwood, 1855.
396p., plates, illus. 18cm.

CHEEVER, George B
Wanderings of a pilgrim in the shadow of Mont
Blanc. Wiley & Putnam, 1845. x, 166p. 20cm.

- - Another ed. 1848.

- - Another ed. 1852.

CHEEVER, George B
Wanderings of a pilgrim in the shadow of Mont
Blanc and the Jungfrau Alp. Glasgow, London:
William Collins, [1847]. 367p., plates, illus.
20cm.

- - New ed., [with engravings by W.H. Bartlett].
[1848?].

- - New ed. Blackwood, [1859?].

Chemin de Fer du Simplon: Genève-Lausanne-Milan et
Turin, Oberland Bernois. Milan: Lampugnani,
[19--]. 200p., illus., maps, plans. 18cm.
(Guides Lampugnani, 61)

CHENEY, Michael John
HIMALAYAN CLUB
Expedition reports: Nepal Himalayas, pre-monsoon
season 1976, by M.J. Cheney. Kathmandu: The
Himalayan Club, 1976. 6 leaves. 33cm.
Typescript.

CHERBULIEZ, A   E
De la démocratie en Suisse. Paris: Ab. Cherbuliez,
1843. 2v. 23cm.

CHEREPOV, Ivan Aleksandrovich
Alpinisme soviétique; traduit du russe par Paul
Sulfourt. Paris: Amiot-Dumont, 1957. 203p.,
plates, illus., maps. 22cm. (Bibliothèque de
l'alpinisme)

CHEREPOV, Ivan Aleksandrovich
Obuchenie al'pinistov ... izdanie vtoroe, isprav-
lennoe i dopolnennoe; pod obshchei redaktsiei...
I.A. Cherepova. Moskva: Izd Vtssps Profizdat,
1957. 335p., bibl. 18cm.

CHEREPOV, Ivan Aleksandrovich
Pamiatka nachinaiushchego al'pinista. Moskva:
Izd. Vtssps Profizdat, 1955. 147p., illus.,
bibl. 17cm.

CHEREPOV, Ivan Aleksandrovich
Zagadki Tian'-shania. Moskva: Gos. Izd. Geograficheskoi Literatury, 1951. 148p., fold.
plates, illus., maps. 20cm.

CHERRY-GARRARD, Apsley
The worst journey in the world: Antarctic 1910-
13. Chatto & Windus, 1937. lxiv, 585p., plates
(some fold.), illus., maps. 23cm.

CHESSEX, Albert
Les Alpes vaudoises. Neuchatel: Éditions du
Griffon, 1949. 52p., illus. 25cm. (Trésors de
mon pays, 37)

CHEVALIER, Marcel
Andorra. Chambéry: Dardel, 1925. 112p., plates
(some fold., some col.), illus., maps, bibl.
26cm.

CHEVALIER, Pierre
Subterranean climbers: twelve years in the
world's deepest chasm; translated by E.M. Hart.
Faber, 1951. 223p., plates, illus., maps. 24cm.

CHEVALLEY, Gabriel
Avant-premières à l'Everest, [par] Gabriel
Chevalley, René Dittert, Raymond Lambert; introduction du Ed. Wyss-Dunant. Paris: Arthaud,
1953. 310p., plates (1 fold. col.), illus., maps.
22cm. (Collection sempervivum, 21)

CHEVALLEY, Gabriel
[Avant-premières à l'Everest]. Forerunners to
Everest: the story of the two Swiss expeditions
of 1952, by René Dittert, Gabriel Chevalley,
Raymond Lambert; preface by Sir John Hunt; English
version by Malcolm Barnes. Allen & Unwin, 1954.
256p., plates (1 col.), illus., maps. 23cm.

CHEZY, Helmina Wittwe von
Norika: neues ausführliches Handbuch für Alpenwanderer und Reisende... München: Fleischmann,
1833. xxiii, 278p., plates, illus., map. 21cm.

CHIANG, Yee
The silent traveller: a Chinese artist in Lake-
land; with a preface by Herbert Read. Country
Life, 1937. 67p., plates, illus. 23cm.

CHIANG, Yee
The silent traveller in the Yorkshire Dales;
written and illustrated by Chiang Yee. Methuen,
1941. xiii, 90p., plates (some col.), illus.
20cm.

CHILE
ARGENTINA
Argentine-Chilean Boundary: report presented to
the Tribunal appointed by H.B. Majesty's Government ... to justify the Argentine claims for the
boundary in the summit of the Cordillera de los
Andes... Government of Argentine Republic, 1900.
4v. (xlix, 1181p), plates, illus., maps. 34cm.

- - Maps (in portfolio).

CHILE
Statement presented on behalf of Chile in reply to
the Argentine Report submitted to the Tribunal
constituted by H.B. Majesty's Government acting as
arbitrator in pursuance of the Agreement dated
April 17, 1896. Government of Chile, 1901-2.
4v. in 3, fold. plates, maps. 26cm.

- - Appendix to the Statement. 1902.

- - Maps (in portfolio).

CHILE. Oficina de Límites
La Cordillera de los Andes entre las latitudes
30°40' i 35° S.: trabajos i estudios de la Segunda
Sub-Comision Chilena de Límites con la República
Arjentina, [por] Luis Riso Patron. Santiago de
Chile: La Oficina, 1903. xv, 258p., plates (some
fold. col.), illus., maps. 29cm.

CHILE. Oficina de Límites
La Cordillera de los Andes entre las latitudes 46° i
50° S., [por] Luis Riso Patron. Santiago de Chile:
La Oficina, 1905. x, 233p., plates (some fold.,
col.), illus., maps. 29cm.

CHILVERS, Hedley A
The seven wonders of southern Africa. Johannesburg: S.A. Railways and Harbours, 1929. xiii,
395p., col. plates, illus., maps. 22cm.

CHIROL, Sir Valentine
With pen and brush in eastern lands when I was
young. Cape, 1929. 203p., plates (1 col.), illus.
27cm.

CHISHOLM, George G
GSELL-FELS, Theodor
Switzerland: its scenery and people, pictorially
represented by eminent Swiss and German artists;
with historical and descriptive text based on the
German of Dr. Gsell-Fels. Blackie, 1881. xvi,
472p., plates, illus. 36cm.
Translation and adaptation are the work of George
G. Chisholm.

CHMIELOWSKI, Janusz and SWIERZ, Mieczysław
Tatry Wysokie (przewodnik szczegółowy). Tom 1.
Cześć Ogólna-Doliny. Kraków: Wydawnictw Sekcji
Turyst. Pol. Tow. Tatrz., 1925. 118p., illus.
16cm.

CHOLLEY, André
Les Préalpes de Savoie (Genevois, Bauges) et leur
avant-pays: étude de géographie régionale. Paris:
Colin, 1925. 755p., plates, illus., maps, bibl.
25cm.

CHOLLIER, Antoine
Ceux de l'Alps: types et coutumes; dessins
originaux de Th.-J. Delaye. Paris: Éditions des
Horizons de France, 1937. 133p., col. illus.
29cm.

CHORLEY, Katharine Campbell, Baroness Chorley
Hills and Highways; decorated with wood-engravings
by Margaret Pilkington. Dent, 1928. 232p., illus.
20cm.

CHOUINARD, Yvon
Climbing ice. Hodder and Stoughton, 1978. 192p.,
illus. (some col.). 29cm.

CHOUINARD, Yvon
BERNSTEIN, Jeremy
Profiles: ascending: [biographical article on
American climber Yvon Chouinard].
(In The New Yorker, January 31, 1977, p.36-52,
port.)

CHOULOT, Paul, comte de
Huit jours au pas de charge en Savoie et en
Suisse, par Paul de Kick [i.e. comte Paul de
Choulot]. Chambéry: J. Aubert, [1845?]. 78p.,
plates, illus. 30 x 43cm.

CHRIST, H
Ob dem Kernwald: Schilderungen aus Obwaldens
Natur und Volk. Basel: H. Georg, 1869. 205p.
18cm.

CHRIST, H
Das Pflanzenleben der Schweiz. Zürich: F.
Schulthess, 1879. xv, 488p., plates, illus.,
col. maps. 24cm.

CHRIST, H
Ueber die Verbreitung der Pflanzen der alpinen
Region der europäischen Alpenkette. [Basel],
[1866]. 85p., 1 fold. col. plate, map. 28cm.

CHRISTEN, Ernest
Sur l'Alpe; illustré par Albert Gos; préface de
Émile Yung. Genève: Atar, [1916]. xvii, 233p.,
illus. 20cm.

- - 2e éd. [1917].

CHRISTENSEN, Lars
My last expedition to the Antarctic 1936-37,
with a review of the research work done on the
voyages in 1927-1937: a lecture delivered before
the Norwegian Geographical Society, September
22nd, 1937. Oslo: G. Tanum, 1938. 16p.,plates,
illus., maps (on lining papers). 25cm.

CHRISTIE, MANSON & WOODS LTD.
ALPINE CLUB
Paintings, drawings and sculpture, c.1800 -
c.1920, the properties of the Alpine Club and
others, which will be sold at auction by Christie,
Manson & Woods ... on Friday, June 11, 1965.
Christie, Manson & Woods, 1965. 30p. 25cm.
Catalogue.

CHRISTOFFEL, Ulrich
La montagne dans la peinture: le Club Alpin
Suisse à ses membres à l'occasion du centenaire
1963; traduit par Henry-Jean Bolle. Genève:
C.A.S., 1963. 141p., 56 plates (some col.),
illus. 26cm.

CHRISTOMANNOS, Theodor
Christomannos-Gedenkbuch: Erinnerungen an
Theodor, von ... Tony Grubhofer; Rund um den
Rosengarten, nachgelassenes Manuskript von
Theodor Christomannos. Meran: F.W. Ellmenreichs,
1912. 72p., plates (some col.), illus. 26cm.

CHRISTOMANNOS, Theodor
Die neue Dolomitenstrasse: Bozen, Cortina,
Toblach und ihre Nebenlinien. Wien: C. Reisser,
1909. 71p., 1 plate, illus., map. 26cm.

CHRISTOMANNOS, Theodor
[Die neue Dolomitenstrasse ...]. The new
Dolomite road: Bozen, Cortina, Toblach and its
branches. Vienna: C. Reisser, [1910]. 71p.,
1 plate, illus., map. 26cm.

CHRISTOMANNOS, Theodor
Sulden-Trafoi: Schilderungen aus dem Ortler-
gebiete; mit Illustrationen nach Originalen von
E.T. Compton [and others]. Innsbruck: A.
Edlinger, 1895. vii, 175p., illus. 33cm.

CHROUSCHOFF, Michel de
Pau: souveniers et impressions. Pau: Aréas,
1891. 113p. 20cm.

CHUQUET, Arthur
DESAIX DE VEYGOUX, Louis Charles Antoine
Journal de voyage du Général Desaix: Suisse et
Italie, 1797; publié avec introduction et notes
par Arthur Chuquet. Paris: Plon-Nourrit, 1907.
lxxxviii, 305p., 2 plates, illus. 19cm.

CHURCH, Percy W
Chinese Turkestan with caravan and rifle.
Rivingtons, 1901. xii, 207p., plates (1 fold.),
illus., map. 23cm.

CHURCH, Richard
News from the mountain. Dent, 1932. x, 76p.,
plates, illus. 19cm.

CHURCH OF ENGLAND. Diocese of New Zealand
Annals of the Diocese of New Zealand. Society
for Promoting Christian Knowledge, 1856. xvi,
247p., plates, illus., map. 18cm.

GILBERT, Josiah and CHURCHILL, George Cheetham
The Dolomite mountains: excursions through Tyrol,
Carinthia, Carniola, & Friuli in 1861, 1862, &
1863; with a geological chapter... Longman, Green,
Longman, Roberts, & Green, 1864. xx, 576p., plates
(some fold., some col.), illus., maps. 22cm.

GILBERT, Josiah and CHURCHILL, George Cheetham
[The Dolomite mountains ...]. Die Dolomitberge:
Ausflüge ..., aus dem Englischen von Gustav Adolf
Zwanziger. Klagenfurt: F. v. Kleinmayr, 1865-68.
2v. 24cm.

CICERI, Eugène
Les Pyrénées, dessinées d'après nature et lithographiées par Eugène Ciceri. Luchon: Lafont,
[1871]. 2v. in l. (chiefly illus., map).
31 x 44cm.

CIMA, Claudio
Scalate nelle Grigne; cartine e schizzi
dell'Autore. Bologna: Tamari, 1975. 319p., fold.
plates, illus., map (in pocket). 16cm.

CINGRIA, Charles Albert
Le parcours du Haut Rhône; ou, La Julienne et
l'ail sauvage, textes et croquis pris sur la
route par Charles-Albert Cingria et Paul Monnier.
Fribourg: W. Egloff, 1944. 129p., col. illus.,
map. 25cm.

CITY UNIVERSITY - BRUNEL UNIVERSITY KISHTWAR
HIMALAYA EXPEDITION, 1978
Report ..., written by Paul Belcher; appendices by
Anthony Wheaton. The Expedition, [1979]. 54p.,
plates, illus., map. 31cm.

CIVIALE, A
Les alpes au point de vue de la géographie
physique et de la géologie: voyages photographiques
dans la Dauphiné, la Savoie, le nord de l'Italie,
la Suisse et le Tyrol. Paris: Rothschild, 1882.
vii, 619p., plates, illus. 25cm.

CLAPARÈDE, Arthur de
Champéry et le Val d'Illiez: histoire et description. Genève: H. Georg, 1886. 184p. 19cm.

- - 2e éd. rev. et augm. 1890.

CLARE, Constance Leigh
The Brenner Pass: Tirol from Kufstein to Riva;
illustrations by J.F. Leigh Clare. J. & J.
Bennett, 1912. 310p., plates (some col.), illus.,
map. 23cm.

CLARIS DE FLORIAN, Jean Pierre
See
FLORIAN, Jean Pierre Claris de

CLARK, Edmund
SHERWILL, Markham
Ascent of Captain Markham Sherwill (accompanied by
Dr. E. Clark) to the summit of Mont Blanc, 25th,
26th and 27th of August, 1825, in letters addressed
to a friend. The Author, 1826. 26p. 25cm.

CLARK, Edmund
SHERWILL, Markham
[Ascent of Captain Markham Sherwill ...]. Ascension du Docteur Edmund Clark et du Capitaine
Markham Sherwill à la première sommité du Mont
Blanc, les 25, 26 et 27 août 1825: relation
adressée à l'un de ses amis; traduit de l'anglais
par Alexandre P...r. Melun: Michelin, 1827. 81p.
20cm.

CLARK, Edmund and SHERWILL, Markham
Narrative of an excursion to the summit of Mont
Blanc, August 26th, 1825, by Edmund Clark and
Markham Sherwill. [London, 1826]. 434-449, 590-
600, 289-296p. 21cm.
Offprint from New Monthly Magazine, 1826.

CLARK, Edmund
SHERWILL, Markham
A visit to the summit of Mont Blanc, by Captain
Markham Sherwill [and Dr. Edmund Clark], 25th,
26th, and 27th of August, 1825, in letters
addressed to a friend, by Markham Sherwill.
[London, 1826]. 533-541, 40-47, 150-155p.
Offprint from New Monthly Magazine, 1826.

CLARK, Geoffrey and THOMPSON, W Harding
The Lakeland landscape. Black, 1938. xii,
136p., plates, illus., maps (1 fold. in pocket).
21cm. (The county landscapes)

CLARK, Jane Inglis
Pictures and memories. Edinburgh, London:
Moray Press, 1938. 91p., plates (some col.),
illus. 26cm.

CLARK, Leonard
The marching wind. Hutchinson, 1955. 347p.,
plates, illus., maps. 24cm.

CLARK, Ronald William
The Alps. Weidenfeld & Nicholson, 1973.
288p., illus. (some col.), maps, bibl. 26cm.

CLARK, Ronald William
The day the rope broke: the story of a great
Victorian tragedy. Secker & Warburg, 1965.
221p., plates, illus., map, bibl. 23cm.

CLARK, Ronald William
The early alpine guides. Phoenix House, 1949.
208p., plates, illus., maps, bibl. 23cm.

CLARK, Ronald William
An eccentric in the Alps: the story of the Rev.
W.A.B. Coolidge, the great Victorian mountaineer.
Museum Press, 1959. 224p., plates, illus. 24cm.

CLARK, Ronald William
Men, myths and mountains. Weidenfield & Nicholson, 1976. viii, 292p., illus., maps, bibl.
26cm.

CLARK, Ronald William and PYATT, Edward Charles
Mountaineering in Britain: a history from the
earliest times to the present day. Phoenix
House, 1957. 288p., 72 plates, illus., bibl.
26cm.

CLARK, Ronal William
A picture history of mountaineering. Hulton
Press, 1956. [162p.], illus. 29cm. (Hulton's
Picture histories)

CLARK, Ronald William
Six great mountaineers: E. Whymper, A.F. Mummery,
J.N. Collie, G. Leigh-Mallory, G.W. Young, Sir
John Hunt. Hamish Hamilton, 1956. 203p., plates,
port. 20cm.

CLARK, Ronald William
The splendid hills: the life and photographs of
Vittorio Sella, 1859-1943. Phoenix House, 1948.
x, 35p., 79 plates, illus. 30cm.

CLARK, Ronald William
The true book about mountaineering; illustrated
by F. Stocks May. F. Muller, 1957. 143p.,
illus. 20cm.

CLARK, Ronald William
The Victorian mountaineers. Batsford, 1953.
232p., plates, illus. 23cm.

CLARK, Simon
The Puma's Claw; with an introduction by Sir John
Hunt. Hutchinson, 1959. 223p., plates, illus.,
maps. 22cm.

CLARK, Syd
Borrowdale; illustrated by W. Heaton Cooper.
Stockport: Fell and Rock Climbing Club, 1978.
257p., 1 col. plate, illus., maps (on lining
papers). 16cm. (Climbing guides to the English
Lake District, [5th ser.], 3)

CLARK, W   A
Alpine plants: a practical method for growing the
rarer and more difficult alpine flowers; with
illustrations from photographs by Clarence
Elliott. On behalf of the Author by L. Upcott
Gill, 1901. vi, 108p., 9 plates, illus. 19cm.

LEWIS, Meriwether and CLARK, William
WHEELER, Olin D
The trail of Lewis and Clark 1804-1904: a story
of the great exploration across the continent in
1804-06; with a description of the old trail
based upon actual travel over it, and of the
changes found a century later. New York, London:
Putnam, 1904. 2v., col. plates (1 fold.), illus.,
maps. 22cm.

CLARK-SCHWARZENBACH, Annemarie
Ein Leben für die Berge: Lorenz Saladin; Geleitwort von Sven Hedin. Bern: Hallwag, 1938.
138p., plates, illus., map. 23cm.

CLARKE, Andrew
Tour in France, Italy, and Switzerland, during
the years 1840 and 1841. Whittaker, 1843. viii,
374p. 21cm.

CLARKE, C   C
The hundred wonders of the world, and of the
three kingdoms of nature, described according to
the best and latest authorities, and illustrated
by engravings. 18th ed. enl. and improved.
Whittaker, 1825. xii, 668p., plates, illus.
18cm.

CLARKE, Charles
Mountain medicine and physiology: proceedings of a
symposium for mountaineers, expedition doctors and
physiologists, sponsored by the Alpine Club;
edited by Charles Clarke, Michael Ward, Edward
Williams. Alpine Club, 1975. 143p., plates,
illus., bibl. 21cm.

CLARKE, J   V   C
The Essex Way. Colne Engaine: J.V.C. Clarke, 1977.
24p., illus., map. 21cm.

CLARKE, James
A survey of the Lakes of Cumberland, Westmorland,
and Lancashire; together with an account ... of
the adjacent country. The Author, 1787. xlii,
190p., plates, maps. 46cm.

CLARKSON, J   R
Rock-climbing, by T.S.Y.A. [i.e. Capt. J.R.
Clarkson]. 288-298p., illus. 25cm.
Offprint from Journal of the Royal Indian Army
Service Corps, v.9, n.s. no.3, Aug. 1941.

CLAVARINO, Luigi, marchese di
Saggio di corografia, statistica e storica delle
Valli di Lanzo. Torino: Stamperia della Gazzetta
del Popolo, 1867. 304p. 25cm.

CLAYTON, J   W
Il pellegrino: wanderings in Switzerland & Italy.
T. Cautley Newby, [1863]. 2v. in 1, plates,
illus. 20cm.

CLEARE, John
Collins guide to mountains and mountaineering.
Collins, 1979. 208p., illus., (some col.), maps,
bibl. 31cm.

CLEARE, John
Mountains. Macmillan, 1975. 256p., illus. (some
col.), bibl. 24cm.

CLEARE, John
SMYTHE, Tony
Rock climbers in action in Snowdonia, written by
Tony Smythe; illustrated by John Cleare; captions/
descriptions and layout by Robin G. Collomb.
Secker & Warburg, 1966. 127p., plates, illus.,
map. 25cm.

CLEARE, John and COLLOMB, Robin Gabriel
Sea cliff climbing in Britain. Constable, 1973.
189p., illus., maps. 25cm.

CLEAVER, Reginald
A winter-sport book; with an introduction by
Edward Lyttelton. Black, 1911. 62p., 21 plates,
illus. 25cm.

CLEGG, William
Great Langdale, by William Clegg, A.R. Dolphin &
J.W. Cook; with illustrations by W. Heaton Cooper.
Stockport: Fell & Rock Climbing Club, 1950.
(1954 reprint). 162p., 1 col. plate, illus.
16cm. (Rock-climbing guides to the English Lake
District, 2nd [i.e. 3rd] ser., 3)

CLEMENS, Samuel Leghorn
See
TWAIN, Mark

CLEMENTI, Mrs. Cecil
Through British Guiana to the summit of Roraima.
Unwin, 1920. 236p., plates (1 fold.), illus.,
map. 20cm.

CLERC, C
Les Alpes françaises: études de géologie militaire.
Paris: Berger-Levrault, 1882. 224p., plates (1
fold. col.), illus., map. 22cm.

CLERGET, Pierre
La Suisse au XXe siècle: études économique et
sociale. Paris: Colin, 1908. 268p., map. 20cm.

CLERICI, Idelfonso
In alta montagna. Milano: "Amatrix", 1929.
237p., illus. 20cm.

CLEVELAND MOUNTAINEERING CLUB
WILSON, M   F
Climbs in Cleveland; edited by M.R. Wilson.
Billingham: Cleveland Mountaineering Club, [1956].
83p., illus. 16cm.

CLIFFE, Charles Frederick
The book of North Wales. Longman, Brown, Green,
& Longmans, 1850. 302p., plates, illus. 18cm.

- - 2nd ed. Hamilton, Adams, 1851.

CLIFFE, John Henry
Notes and recollections of an angler: rambles
among the mountains, valleys and solitudes of
Wales; with sketches of some of the lakes,
streams, mountains... Hamilton, Adams, 1970.
xii, 254p. 20cm.

CLIFFORD, Sir Charles Cavendish
Travels by 'Umbra' [i.e. Charles C. Clifford].
Edinburgh: Edmonston & Douglas, 1865. vi, 278p.
22cm.

CLIMBERS' CLUB
Climbing guides to the Snowdon district; edited
by G.R. Speaker. 1936-39.

1. Cwm Idwal group. New and rev. ed., by J.M.
   Edwards. 1936.
2. Tryfan group, by J.M. Edwards and C.W.F.
   Noyce. 1937.
3. Glyder Fach group. New and rev. ed., by
   C.F. Kirkus. 1937.
4. Lliwedd group. New and rev. ed., by C.W.F.
   Noyce and J.M. Edwards. 1939.

CLIMBERS' CLUB
Climbing guides to the Snowdon district; edited
by H.E. Kretschmer. 1946-49.

1. Cwm Idwal. 2nd rev. ed., by J.M. Edwards.
   1940 (1946 reprint).
2. Tryfan, by J.M. Edwards and C.W.F. Noyce.
   1937 (1949 reprint).
4. Lliwedd, by C.W.F. Noyce and J.M. Edwards.
   1939 (1946 reprint).

CLIMBERS' CLUB
Climbing guides to the Snowdon district [and to
Cornwall]; edited by C.W.F. Noyce. 1949-61.

1. Cwm Idwal. New ed., by A.J.J. Moulem. 1958.
2. Tryfan and Glyder Fach, by A.J.J. Moulam. 1956
   (1959 reprint).
3. Glyder Fach, by C.F. Kirkus. 1937 (1949
   reprint).
4. Llanberis north, by D.T. Roscoe. 1961.
5. Cornwall, by A.W. Andrews and E.C. Pyatt.
   1950.
6. Llanberis Pass, by P.R.J. Harding. 1955.
7. The Carneddau, by A.J.J. Moulam. [1951].
8. Snowdon south, by J. Neill and T. Jones. 1960.

CLIMBERS' CLUB
Guides.

A climbers' guide to Snowdon and the Beddgelert
   district, by H.R.C. Carr. 1926.
A climbers' guide to South-East England, by
   E.C. Pyatt. 1956 (1960 reprint).
Climbing in the Ogwen district, by J.M.A.
   Thomson. 1910.
- - Appendix, by H.E.L. Porter. 1921.
The climbs on Lliwedd, by J.M.A. Thomson and
   A.W. Andrews. 1909.
Cornwall. Vol.1, by P.H. Biven and M.B.
   McDermott. 1968.
Cornwall. Vol.2, by V.N. Stevenson. 1966.
A guide to Black rocks and Cratcliffe Tor, by
   P.R.J. Harding and A.J.J. Moulam. 1949.
South-East England, by E.C. Pyatt. 2nd rev. ed.,
   by L.R. and L.E. Holliwell. 1969.

CLIMBERS' CLUB
Guides to Wales; edited by John Neill. 1963-66.

1. Carneddau. 2nd ed., by A.J.J. Moulam. 1966.
2. Cwm Idwal. New ed. rev., by A.J.J. Moulam.
   1964.
3. Tryfan and Glyder Fach. Rev. ed., by
   A.J.J. Moulam. 1964.
5. Llanberis south, by P. Crew. 1966.
6. Clogwyn du'r Arddu, by H.I. Banner and
   P. Crew. 1963.
8. Snowdon south. 2nd ed., by T. Jones and
   J. Neill. 1966.

   Moelwynion: an interim guide, by J.R. Lees.
   1962.

CLIMBERS' CLUB
Guides to Wales; edited by Trevor Jones.
1970-74.

2. Cwm Idwal. 3rd ed., by K. Wilson and Z.
   Leppert. 1974.
4. The Three Cliffs, by P. Hatton. 1974.
5. Cwm Glas. 2nd ed., by P. Crew and I. Roper.
   1970.
9. Snowdon east, by A.J.J. Moulam. 1970.
11. Cwm Silwyn and Cwellyn, by M. Yates and
   J. Perrin. 1971.

CLIMBERS' CLUB
Guides to Wales; edited by Pete Hatton. 1970-

8. Snowdon south. 3rd ed., by T. Jones and
   L. Holliwell. 1970.

CLIMBERS' CLUB
Guides to Wales; edited by Robert Moulton. 1975-

1. Carneddau. 3rd ed., by L. Holliwell. 1975.
3. Llanberis Pass. 2nd ed., by G. Milburn.
   1978
4. Clogwyn du'r Arddu. 3rd ed., by A. Sharp.
   1976.
7. Gogarth, by A. Sharp. 1977.

CLIMBERS' CLUB
Guides to West Penwith.

2. Chair Ladder and the south coast, by R.D.
   Moulton and T.D. Thompson, 1975.

Climbers of the Caucasus 1888-1889: [a commemorative
volume in memory of W.F. Donkin, H. Fox, K.
Streich and J. Fischer, 1888]. [Alpine Club],
[1890?]. 1v. (various pagings), plates (some
fold.), illus., maps. 26cm.
Articles by C. Dent and others from Alpine
Journal and Proceedings of the Royal Geographical
Society.

Climbs in Cumbria. Manchester: Cicerone Press.

The northern Lake District. Pt. 1, by G.A.
   Hassall. 1969.
The southern Lake District. Pt. 1, by R.B. Evans
   and W. Unsworth. 1971.

CLINKER, Charles
An unconventional guide for tourists: a fortnight
in Switzerland: a free-and-easy account of a
first visit to the Rigi, the Bernese Oberland,
Chamouny, &c., by the editor of "Western Gazette"
[i.e. Charles Clinker]. T. Cook, 1880. vi,
108p. 22cm.

CLINT, Alfred
BENNETT, G   J
The pedestrian's guide through North Wales: a
tour performed in 1837; with ... etchings, by A.
Clint. Colburn, [1838]. viii, 391p., plates
(some fold.), illus., music. 24cm.

CLISSOLD, Frederick
Narrative of an ascent to the summit of Mont
Blanc, August 18th, 1822; with an appendix, upon
the sensations experienced at great elevations.
Rivingtons & Cochran, 1823. 56p. 23cm.

CLOWES, George
Forty-Six days in Switzerland and the north of
Italy, by G.C., Junr. [i.e. George Clowes].
Printed by Clowes, 1856. 102p., 5 plates (4
fold.), illus., map. 21cm.

CLOWES, George
A picturesque tour by the new road from Chiavenna,
over the Splügen, and along the Rhine, to Coira,
in the Grisons; [with thirteen views, taken on
the spot by G.C. Esq., i.e. George Clowes, and
lithographed by F. Calvert]. W. Cole, 1826.
35p., plates, illus. 33cm.

CLUB ALPIN BELGE
Guide des rochers belges et luxembourgeois.
Bruxelles: C.A.B., [1972]. 1v. (loose-leaf),
fold. plates, illus., maps. 23cm.

CLUB ALPIN FRANÇAIS
Guides des Alpes Maritimes.

Alpinisme, par V. Paschetta. 1937.
Environs de Saint-Martin-Vésubie, par V.
   Paschetta [and others]. [1934?].

CLUB ALPIN FRANÇAIS
Manuel d'alpinisme; rédigé sous les auspices du
Club Alpin Français. Paris: L. Laveur, 1904.
vii, 694p., illus. 15cm.

CLUB ALPIN FRANÇAIS
Manuel d'alpinisme; publié avec la collaboration
du Groupe de Haute Montagne. Chambéry: Dardel,
1934. 2v., plates, illus. 23cm.

CLUB ALPIN FRANÇAIS
Manuel technique de camping et de bivouac en
montagne. Paris: C.A.F., 1936. 116p., illus.
19cm.

CLUB ALPIN FRANÇAIS
JOURNÉE MÉDICALE DE LA MONTAGNE, Paris, Bordeaux,
1944
Médecine et montagne: compte-rendu de la Journée
médicale de la montagne; organisée par le Club
Alpin Français le 28 juin 1944; avec le concours
de la Fédération Française de la Montagne.
Paris: C.A.F., [1945?]. 28p., illus. 27cm.

65

CLUB ALPIN FRANÇAIS
Refuges de montagnes françaises et zones limitrophes, par Jacques Meynieu; avec la collaboration de Claude Bourleaux [and others]. Paris: C.A.F., 1967. 273, xxvp., plates (some fold. col.), illus., maps (1 in pocket). 17cm.

CLUB ALPIN FRANÇAIS. Comité Scientifique
RIVOLIER, Jean
Expéditions françaises à l'Himalaya: aspect médical; avec la collaboration de P. Biget [and others]. Paris: Hermann, 1959. 229p., illus., bibl. 24cm. (Actualités scientifiques et industrielles, 1266)
At head of title: Comité de l'Himalaya, Comité Scientifique du Club Alpin Français.

CLUB ALPIN FRANÇAIS. Commission des Travaux Scientifiques
Les noms de lieux des montagnes françaises, par Léon Maury. Paris: C.A.F., 1929. viii, 325p., bibl. 26cm.

CLUB ALPIN FRANÇAIS. Commission des Travaux Scientifiques
L'oeuvre scientifique du Club Alpin Français (1874-1922); [les documents ... recueillis ... et annotés par Léon Maury]. Paris: C.A.F., 1936. vi, 518p., plates (some fold., some col.), illus., maps. 26cm.

CLUB ALPIN FRANÇAIS. Groupe de Haute Montagne
See
GROUPE DE HAUTE MONTAGNE

CLUB ALPIN FRANÇAIS. Section Ardennes
Ardennes: sentier de grande randonnée numéro 12 les sentiers pédestres dans les Ardennes. [Charleville-Mézières]: Comité departemental du Tourisme des Ardennes, 1976. [59p.], maps. 21cm.

CLUB ALPIN FRANÇAIS. Section d'Avignon
Guide des Dentelles de Montmirail. Avignon: La Section, 1970. 98p., 2 fold. plates, illus. 17cm.

CLUB ALPIN FRANÇAIS. Section de Barcelonnette
Barcelonnette & ses environs: [album photographique de la Vallée de Barcelonnette]; [execute par [C.] Rava; sous la direction ... de la Section de Barcelonnette du Club Alpin Français]. [Barcelonnette]: La Section, [1879?]. 1v. of illus. 25 x 34cm.

CLUB ALPIN FRANÇAIS. Section de Barcelonnette
Guide de l'alpiniste dans la Vallée de l'Ubaye; suivi de La région du Chambeyron, par W.A.B. Coolidge; édité par la Section de Barcelonnette à l'occasion du Congrès du C.A.F. en 1898. Barcelonnette: La Section, 1898. 120p., plates, illus. 19cm.

CLUB ALPIN FRANÇAIS. Section de Briançon
Guide du touriste dans le Briançonnais ...: histoire, promenades et excursions, aperçus botaniques et géologiques, études sur la faune ...; édité par le Club Alpin Français, Section de Briançon. Paris: X. Rondelet, 1898. 176p., plates, illus., maps, plans. 19cm. (Itinéraires illustrés Miriam)

CLUB ALPIN FRANÇAIS. Section de Côte d'Or
TURBEAUX, Jacques
Saffres (Côte-d'Or): groupe des Rochers de Miraude; edité avec l'appui de la Fédération de la Montagne. Côte d'Or: La Section, 1964. 55p., 1 fold. plate, illus., map. 22cm.

CLUB ALPIN FRANÇAIS. Section de l'Isère
Une cérémonie alpestre à La Pinéa: inauguration du sentier et de la plaque Lucien Vermorel, face nord-ouest de La Pinéa, le 13 mai 1926. Maçon: Protat, 1926. 41p., plates, illus., port. 21cm.

CLUB ALPIN FRANÇAIS. Section de l'Isère
Panorama circulaire du sommet de la Tête de la Maye (2522), (Oisans). [Grenoble]: La Section, [ca 1880]. 19cm.

CLUB ALPIN FRANÇAIS. Section du Mont Blanc and Section de l'Isère
Sur le toit du monde: l'ascension du Pic du Communisme (7495 mètres) point culminant de l'Union Soviétique. Combloux: Section du Mont Blanc, 1978. 56p., plates, illus., maps, bibl. 30cm.

CLUB ALPIN FRANÇAIS. Section de l'Orléanais
PELLÉ, Gilbert and RICHARD, Guy
Escalades à Surgy, Nievre. Orléans: La Section, 1974. 55p., illus. 22cm.

CLUB ALPIN FRANÇAIS. Section de la Lozère et des Causses
Les Causses et les Canons du Tarn ...; édité à Mende en 1892 par la Section de la Lozère & des Causses du C.A.F. Mende: La Section [1892]. 230, cxx, xiip., plates (some fold.), illus., maps, bibl. 18cm. (Itinéraires Miriam, 1)

CLUB ALPIN FRANÇAIS. Section de Paris-Chamonix
TAUPIN, D and BROT, M
Cormot: topo guide d'escalade. Paris: La Section, 1964. 64p., fold. plates, illus., maps. 22cm.

CLUB ALPIN FRANÇAIS. Section de Paris-Chamonix
EXPÉDITION FRANÇAISE AU GROENLAND SUD/LINDENOWS FJORD, 1971
Groenland 71, [par l'Équipe du Groenland]. [Paris, 1972]. 5-6p., plates, map. 30cm. Offprint from Bulletin de la Section de Paris du Club Alpin Français, fév. 1972.

CLUB ALPIN FRANÇAIS. Section de Paris-Chamonix
Pérou 1973; [édité par Jacques Davignon]. Paris: La Section, 1974. 162p., illus., maps. 21cm.

CLUB ALPIN FRANÇAIS. Section de Pau
De Pau au Pic d'Ossau et à Gavarnie; préface du comte Henry Russel. Pau: La Section, [1897]. 156p., 1 fold. plate, illus., map. 20cm.

CLUB ALPIN FRANÇAIS. Section de Perpignan
CAYROL, René
Montagnes des Pyrénées -Orientales. T.1. De la Méditerranée au Costabonne, par René Cayrol, Pierre Roule, André Vinas. 3e éd. Perpignan: La Section, 1973. 123p., fold. plates, maps. 15cm.

CLUB ALPIN FRANÇAIS. Section de Perpignan
SOL, René and CAYROL, René
Montagnes des Pyrénées Orientales. T.2. Le Massif du Canigou. Perpignan: La Section, 1974. 91p., fold. plates, illus., map. 15cm.

CLUB ALPIN FRANÇAIS. Section de Perpignan
SOL, René and CAYROL, René
Montagnes des Pyrénées-Orientales. T.3. Du Pla Guillem au Puigmal: Massifs de Carença et de Cerdagne-Sud. Perpignan: La Section, 1975. 119p., fold. col. plates, maps. 16cm.

CLUB ALPIN FRANÇAIS. Section de Provence
Les Calanques des Goudes à Cassis: excursions, centres d'escalades, spéléologie dans les massifs de Marseilleveyre et de Puget et de Cassis à la Ciotat. 2e éd. Marseille: Librairie de la Bourse, 1960. 45p., plates (1 fold. col.), illus., map. 22cm.

CLUB ALPIN FRANÇAIS. Section de Provence
Centre d'escalade du Devenson. Marseille: La Section, 1964. 45 leaves (some fold.)., illus. 22cm. (Massif des Calanques)

CLUB ALPIN FRANÇAIS. Section de Provence
Centres d'escalades des Goudes-St. Michel. Aix-en-Provence: Maison des Jeunes, [195-?]. 100p., illus., map. 21cm. (Massif des Calanques)

CLUB ALPIN FRANÇAIS. Section de Provence
La Grande Candelle. Marseille: La Section, 1959. 64p., illus., map. 22cm. (Les Calanques escalades)

CLUB ALPIN FRANÇAIS. Section de Provence
    Sormiou, Morgiou, Sugiton. Marseille: La Section,
    1961. 79p., illus., map. 22cm. (Les Calanques
    escalades)

CLUB ALPIN FRANÇAIS. Sections de Savoie
    Randonnées et ascensions: Maurienne: Grand Arc,
    Lauzière, Encombres, Peclet-Polset, Thabor,
    Arves, Grandes Rousses. Chambéry: Les Sections,
    1975. 314p., illus., maps, bibl. 20cm.

CLUB ALPIN FRANÇAIS. Sections de Savoie et de
Maurienne
    Randonnées et ascensions: Haute-Maurienne: Alpes
    Grées méridionales. Chambéry: Les Sections,
    1973. 255p., illus., maps. 20cm.

CLUB ALPIN FRANÇAIS. Section des Alpes Maritimes
    Manifestation organisée par la Section des Alpes
    Maritimes le 4 avril 1925 en l'honneur de Victor
    de Cessole à l'occasion du 25me anniversaire de sa
    présidence. Nice: La Section, 1925. 40p., 1
    plate, port. 22cm.

CLUB ALPIN FRANÇAIS. Section des Hautes-Pyrénées
MASSIE, F
    La cartographie des Pyrénées: étude; documentation
    illustrée de cartes et photographies de l'Exposi-
    tion de Cartographie des Pyrénées organisée par le
    Capitaine Massie, du 15 au 30 décembre 1933...
    Tarbes: La Section, 1934. 127p., plates (2 fold.),
    illus., maps, bibl. 23cm.

CLUB ALPIN FRANÇAIS. Section des Hautes Vosges
    Ballon d'Alsace, Bussang, St-Maurice, Vosges
    méridionales. 2e éd. rev. & augm. Belfort: La
    Section, [1905]. 167p., 2 fold. col. plates,
    illus., maps. 19cm. (Guides du touriste)

CLUB ALPIN FRANÇAIS. Section des Pyrénées Centrales
    Autour du Pic de Midi d'Ossau et du Balaïtous:
    trois semaines de campement, racontées et illus-
    trées par vingt campeurs... Toulouse: La Section,
    1928. 144p., plates, illus., maps. 27cm.

CLUB ALPIN FRANÇAIS. Section du Caroux
FÉDÉRATION FRANÇAISE DE LA MONTAGNE
    Escalades au Caroux. Saint-Pons Hérault: La
    Section, 1963. 334p., 1 fold. col. plate, illus.,
    maps. 17cm.
    "Edité sous le patronage de la Fédération Française
    de la Montagne et du Club Alpin Français".

CLUB ALPIN FRANÇAIS. Section du Mont Blanc and
Section de l'Isère
    Sur le toit du monde: l'ascension du Pic du
    Communisme (7495 mètres) point culminant de l'Union
    Soviétique. Combloux: Section du Mont Blanc, 1978.
    56p., plates, illus., maps, bibl. 30cm.

CLUB ALPIN FRANÇAIS. Section du Sud-Ouest
    Camp du Col d'Aran, 15-25 juillet 1943: compte-
    rendu publié par la Commission Scientifique de la
    Section du Sud-Ouest ...; préface de Colonel
    Pascot. [Bordeaux]: La Commission, 1943. 124p.,
    illus., maps, bibl. 22cm.
    At head of title: Fédération Française de la
    Montagne.
    Supplément au Bulletin n.45, oct. 1943.

CLUB ALPIN FRANÇAIS. Section du Sud-Ouest
    Le centenaire de Franz Schrader; publié par la
    Commission Scientifique de la Section du Sud-
    Ouest. Bordeaux: La Commission, 1944. 40p.,
    illus., port. 22cm.
    Supplément au Bulletin no.47, avril 1944.

CLUB ALPIN FRANÇAIS. Section du Sud-Ouest
    La Concession Russell du Vignemale, [par] Ch.
    Cadart; édité par la Section du Sud-Ouest du Club
    Alpin Français, Commission Scientifique.
    Bordeaux: La Commission, 1943. 24p., plates
    (1 fold.), illus., map, bibl. 22cm.
    Supplément au Bulletin no.43, avril 1943.

CLUB ALPIN FRANÇAIS. Section lyonnaise
LECLERC, Jeanne and LECLERC, Bernard
    Petit guide de la Haute-Maurienne: promenades,
    excursions, ascensions hivernales. 2e éd. (rev.
    et augm.). Lyon: La Section, [1937]. 38p.,
    plates, illus. 16cm.

CLUB ALPIN SUISSE
    See
SCHWEIZER ALPEN-CLUB

CLUB ALPINO ITALIANO
CONTI, Alfredo and LAENG, Walther
    Le Alpi di Val Grosina: guida alpina; illustrata
    ... da W. Laeng. Brescia: C.A.I., Gruppo
    Lombardo Alpinisti senza guide, 1909. ix,
    106p., plates (1 fold. col.), illus., map, bibl.
    16cm.

CLUB ALPINO ITALIANO
CONGRESSO SPELEOLOGICO NAZIONALE, 1st, Trieste, 1933
    Atti del 1o Congresso Speleologico Nazionale;
    organizzato del Club Alpino Italiano in occasione
    del conquantenario di fondazione della Sezione di
    Trieste (Società Alpina delle Giulie); sotto gli
    auspici delle Regie Grotte Demaniali di Postumia
    e dell'Istituto Italiano di Speleologia, Trieste
    10-14 giugno 1933 - XI. Trieste: C.A.I., 1933.
    252p., fold. plates, illus., maps. 25cm.

CLUB ALPINO ITALIANO
    Da rifugio a rifugio.

    3. Alpi Graie; a cura di S. Saglio. 1952.
    4. Alpi Pennine; a cura di S. Saglio. 1951.
    6. Alpi Retiche occidentali; a cura di S. Saglio.
       1953.
  10. Dolomiti occidentali; a cura di S. Saglio.
       1953.

CLUB ALPINO ITALIANO
    Guida dei monti d'Italia.

    Adamello, [di] S. Saglio, G. Laeng. 1954.
    Alpi Carniche, [di] E. Castiglioni; a cura di
      S. Saglio. 1954.
    Alpi Cozie settentrionali; per cura di E.
      Ferreri. 1923-27. 3v.
    Alpi Marittime, [di] G. Bobba. 1908.
    - - [Nuova ed.], [di] A. Sabbadini. 1934.
    Alpi Orobie [di] S. Saglio, A. Corti, B. Credaro.
      1957.
    Alpi Pennine, [di] G. Buscaini. 1970-71. 2v.
    Alpi Retiche occidentali. 1911.
    Alpi Venoste, Passirie, Breonie ... [di] S.
      Saglio. 1939.
    Appennino centrale, [di] C. Landi Vittorj. 1955.
    Bernina, [di] S. Saglio. 1959.
    Dolomiti di Brenta [di] E. Castiglioni. 1949.
    - - 2a ed. [di] G. Buscaini, E. Castiglioni.
      1977.
    Le Dolomiti orientali. 3a ed. [di] A. Berti.
      1950-61. 2v.
    Gran Paradiso: Parco Nazionale, [di] E. Andreis,
      R. Chabod, M.C. Santi. 2a ed. 1963.
    Gran Sasso d'Italia. 2a ed. [di] C. Landi
      Vittorj, S. Pietrostefani. 1962.
    Le Grigne, [di] S. Saglio. 1937.
    Monte Bianco, [di] R. Chabod [and others].
      1963-68. 2v.
    Monte Rosa, [di] S. Saglio, F. Boffa. 1960.
    Odle, Sella, Marmolada, [di] E. Castiglioni.
      1937.
    Pale di S. Martino, [di] E. Castiglioni. 1935.
    Prealpi Comasche, Varesine, Bergamasche, [di]
      S. Saglio. 1948.
    Regione dell'Ortler, [di] A. Bonacossa. 1915.
    Regione Màsino, Bregáglia, Disgrázia, [di]
      A. Bonacossa. 1936.
    - - 2a ed. di A. Bonacossa, G. Rossi. 1977. 2v.
    Sassolungo, Catinaccio, Latemar, [di] A.
      Tanesini. 1942.

CLUB ALPINO ITALIANO
CASSIN, Riccardo and NANGERONI, Giuseppe
Lhotse '75: spedizione alpinistico-scientifica
del C.A.I. all'Himalaya del Nepal; relazioni del
gruppo alpinistico e del gruppo scientifico raccolte da Riccardo Cassin e da Giuseppe Nangeroni;
coordinazione e allestimento di Mario Fantin.
Milano: C.A.I., 1977. 171p., plates (some col.),
illus., maps, bibl. 28cm.

CLUB ALPINO ITALIANO
Manuale della montagna; a cura del C[entro]
A[lpinistico] I[taliano]. Roma: Ulpiano, 1939.
xvi, 433p., illus., maps. 25cm.

CLUB ALPINO ITALIANO
L'opera del Club Alpino Italiano nel primo suo
cinquantennio, 1863-1913; pubblicato per cura del
Consiglio Direttivo. Torino: C.A.I., 1913.
282p., illus., bibl. 33cm.

CLUB ALPINO ITALIANO
SAGLIO, Silvio
I rifugi del C.A.I. Milano: C.A.I., 1957. 503p.,
illus. 17cm.

CLUB ALPINO ITALIANO
ARZANI, Carlo
I rifugi del Club Alpino Italiano e le stazioni del
Corpo Nazionale di Soccorso Alpino. 2a ed. Lecco:
Agielle, 1977. 159p., illus., maps, bibl. 21cm.

CLUB ALPINO ITALIANO
I rifugi del Club Alpino Italiano: storia e des-
crizione illustrata con elenco dei refugi costruiti
in Italia da altre società alpine, [da] Agostino
Ferrari; collaboratori: A. Bossi [and others].
Torino: 1905. vii, 287p., illus., plans. 26cm.
Offprint from Bolletino del C.A.I., vol.37, n.70,
1904-05.

CLUB ALPINO ITALIANO
Vade mecum dell'alpinista: cenni sulla costituzione
e sull'andamento del Club Alpino Italiano ...,
guida dei rifugi ed alberghi alpini. Torino:
Paravia, 1900. 159p., illus. 16cm.

CLUB ALPINO ITALIANO. Comitato Nazionale per le
Onoranze ad Emilio Comici
Emilio Comici: alpinismo eroico; a cura del
Comitato Nazionale del C.A.I. per le Onoranze ad
Emilio Comici; prefazione di Angelo Manaresi.
Milano: Hoepli, 1942. xxvii, 307p., 120 plates,
illus. 26cm.
Memorial volume of Comici's writings, and tributes
to him.

CLUB ALPINO ITALIANO. Comitato Scientifico
Alpinismo italiano nel mondo; a cura del Comitato
Scientifico del Club Alpino Italiano. Milano:
C.A.I., Touring Club Italiano, 1953. 363p., 60
plates, illus., maps. 28cm.

CLUB ALPINO ITALIANO. Comitato Scientifico
Manualetto di istruzioni scientifiche per
alpinisti. Milano: C.A.I., 1934. 308p., illus.
16cm.

CLUB ALPINO ITALIANO. Commissione Centrale per la
Protezione della Natura Alpina
[Come si distrugge un parco:] osservazioni e
proposte in difesa dei ghiacciai del Carè Alto e
del Parco Naturale Adamello-Brenta; [edito dal]
Club Alpino Italiano, Commissione Centrale per la
Protezione della Natura Alpina [e] Italia Nostra,
Sezione di Trento. Trento: C.A.I., 1973. 44p.,
1 plate, illus. (some col.), maps. 24cm.
English, German and French summaries.

CLUB ALPINO ITALIANO. Commissione per il Centenario
1863-1963: i cento anni del Club Alpino Italiano;
a cura della Commissione per il Centenario.
Milano: C.A.I., 1963. 949p., plates (1 fold,
some col.), illus., maps. 27cm.

- - 2a ed. 1964.

CLUB ALPINO ITALIANO. Sezione A. Locatelli
SUGLIANI, L   B
Guida sciistica delle Orobie. 2a ed. Bergamo:
La Sezione, 1971. xxiii, 330p., plates (some
fold.), illus., col. maps. 17cm.

CLUB ALPINO ITALIANO. Sezione Belluno
Il viaggiatore nel Bellunese: ricordo del XXV
Congresso degli Alpinisti Italiano, 1893.
Belluno: La Sezione, 1893. 120p., illus., maps.
17cm.

CLUB ALPINO ITALIANO. Sezione di Agordo
Rapida escursione alpina nel Bellunese; edita
a cura del C.A.I. Sezione di Agordo. Trento:
La Sezione, 1888. 120p., plates, illus.
17 x 22cm.

CLUB ALPINO ITALIANO. Sezione di Bergamo
Guida-itinerario alle prealpi Bergamasche, com-
presa la Valsassina ed i passi alla Valtellina
ed alla Valcamonica; colla prefazione... [di]
A. Stoppani ... T. Taramelli. 3a ed. rifatta
per cura della Sezione di Bergamo, C.A.I.
Milano: Hoepli, 1900. xlviii, 241p., plates,
maps. 16cm. (Manuali Hoepli)

- - Carte.

CLUB ALPINO ITALIANO. Sezione di Biella
Il Biellese; edito a cura della Sezione di
Biella del Club Alpino Italiano nel centenario
dalla nascita di Quintino Sella. Ivrea: F.
Viassone, 1927. 365p., plates (1 fold. col.),
illus., map. 31cm.

CLUB ALPINO ITALIANO. Sezione di Biella
Il Biellese: pagine raccolte e pubblicate dalla
Sezione di Biella del Club Alpino Italiano in
occasione del XXX Congresso Nazionale in Biella.
Biella: La Sezione, 1898. 279, livp., plates,
illus. 31cm.

CLUB ALPINO ITALIANO. Sezione di Bologna
L'Appennino bolognese: descrizioni e itinerari.
Bologna: Fava & Garagnani, 1881. xix, 887p.,
plates (some fold., some col.), illus., maps.
19cm.

CLUB ALPINO ITALIANO. Sezione di Bologna
Fiori del nostro Appennino: primavera, estate,
autunno nell'Appennino tosco-emiliano; hanno
collaborato: Alfonso Bernardi [and others].
Bologna: La Sezione, 1964. 48p., col. illus.
21cm.

CLUB ALPINO ITALIANO. Sezione di Bologna
BOSCHI, Luigi, marchese and BONORA, Alfredo
Itinerari dell'Appennino (dal Cimone al Catria).
Bologna: La Sezione, 1888. 62p., plates,
illus., maps. 18cm.

CLUB ALPINO ITALIANO. Sezione di Brescia
Guida alpina della provincia di Brescia. 2a ed.
riv. ed aug. Brescia: La Sezione, 1889. xvi,
371p., maps. 16cm.

CLUB ALPINO ITALIANO. Sezione di Cuneo
Montagne nostre. Cuneo: La Sezione, 1976.
423p., plates (some fold., some col.), illus.,
maps, bibl. 24cm.

CLUB ALPINO ITALIANO. Sezione di Milano
Dizionario alpino italiano. Milano: Hoepli, 1892.
xxi, 309p. 16cm. (Manuali Hoepli)

CLUB ALPINO ITALIANO. Sezione di Milano
Itinerari di gite effettuabili da Milano in 1,2,
e 3 giorni. Milano: La Sezione, 1921. xx,
170p. 17cm.

CLUB ALPINO ITALIANO. Sezione di Milano
Ricordo del XXXVII Congresso del Club Alpino
Italiano, indetto dalla Sezione di Milano, 3-8
settembre 1906. Milano: La Sezione, 1906. lv.
of illus. 25 x 33cm.

CLUB ALPINO ITALIANO. Sezione di Padova
Il Comelico ed il gruppo del Popera. Agosto:
La Sezione, 1924. 109p., plates, illus., map.
17cm.

CLUB ALPINO ITALIANO. Sezione di Roma
Da Brescia a Trento per le Alpi Retiche, relazione di E. Abbate; illustrata da A. Zoppi.
[Rome]: La Sezione, 1884. 56p., plates, illus.,
maps. 28cm.

CLUB ALPINO ITALIANO. Sezione di Roma
Tra i monti del Lazio e dell'Abruzzo; a cura della
Sezione di Roma del Club Alpino Italiano, a
ricordo del cinquantenario della sua fondazione;
[pubblicazione ... curata ...da Roberto Almagià
and others]. Roma: La Sezione, 1924. 111p.,
plates, illus. 26cm.

CLUB ALPINO ITALIANO. Sezione di Torino
Guida del Monviso, di Severino Bessone; con la
collaborazione ... [di] Felice Burdino. Torino:
La Sezione, 1957. xvi, 213p., plates (some fold.),
illus., maps, bibl. 17cm.

CLUB ALPINO ITALIANO. Sezione di Torino
MARTELLI, A   E   and VACCARONE, Luigi
Guida delle Alpi occidentali. Torino: La
Sezione, 1889-96. 2v. in 3, fold plates (some
col.), illus., maps, bibl. 17cm.
Vol.2, pt.2 is by G. Bobba and L. Vaccarone.

CLUB ALPINO ITALIANO. Sezione di Torino
MARTELLI, A   E   and VACCARONE, Luigi
Guida delle Alpi occidentali del Piemonte, dal
Colle dell'Argentera ... al Colle Girard...
Torino: La Sezione, 1880. xxxix, 480p., plates
(some fold.), illus., bibl. 17cm.

CLUB ALPINO ITALIANO. Sezione di Torino
Le valli di Lanzo (Alpi Graie); Club Alpino
Italiano, Sezione di Torino. Torino: La
Sezione, 1904. 547p., illus., fold. maps (in
pocket). 28cm.

CLUB ALPINO ITALIANO. Sezione di Torino.
Sottosezione GEAT
MOTTI, Gian Piero
Rocca Sbarua e M. Tre Denti. Torino: Sezione di
Torino, Sottosezione GEAT, 1969. 166p., 1 fold.
col. plate, illus., map. 16cm.

CLUB ALPINO ITALIANO. Sezione di Varallo
DURIO, Alberto
Bibliografia alpinistica-storica e scientifica
del Gruppo del Monte Rosa (dal Colle del Théodule
al Passo del Monte Moro) dei monti della Valesia
e della Sezione di Varallo del C.A.I. Novara:
Istituto Geografico de Agostini, 1925. 84p.
25cm.

CLUB ALPINO ITALIANO. Sezione di Varallo
I cento anni della Sezione di Varallo del Club
Alpino Italiano. Varallo: Sede Centrale, 1967.
[44p.], illus. (some col.), col. map. 27cm.

CLUB ALPINO ITALIANO. Sezione di Verona
Attraverso le Prealpi Veronesi e sul Lago di
Garda: 40o Congresso degli Alpinisti Italiani
Verona 5-11 settembre, 1909. Verona: La
Sezione, 1909. viii, 225p., illus. 19cm.
(Guida-itinerario)

CLUB ALPINO ITALIANO. Sezione di Vicenza
NEGRI, Arturo
Carta geologica della provincia di Vicenza;
pubblicata per cura della Sezione di Vicenza del
C.A.I. Vicenza: La Sezione, 1901. 110p., fold.
col. plate, map. 22cm.
Bibliography.

CLUB ALPINO ITALIANO. Sezione di Vigevano
RAINOLDI, Luciano
Antrona, Bognanco, Sempione. Vigevano: La
Sezione, 1976. 239p., illus., col. map, bibl.
21cm.

CLUB ALPINO ITALIANO. Sezione fiorentina
C.A.I. Sezione fiorentina, 1868-1968; a cura della
Sezione fiorentina del C.A.I. nel centenario della
fondazione. [Firenze]: La Sezione, 1969. 462p.,
plates (some fold., some col.), illus., maps.
24cm.

CLUB ALPINO ITALIANO. Sezione in Chiavenna di
Sondrio
Il Passo dello Spluga e strade Chiavennasche,
[di] Pietro Buzzetti. [Chiavenna di Sondrio]: La
Sezione, 1928. 45p. 22cm.

CLUB ALPINO ITALIANO. Società Alpina delle Giulie
See
SOCIETÀ ALPINA DELLE GIULIE

CLUB ALPINO ITALIANO. Società Alpinisti Tridentini
See
SOCIETÀ ALPINISTI TRIDENTINI

CLUB ALPINO SVIZZERO
See
SCHWEIZER ALPEN-CLUB

CLUB ANDINO VENEZOLANO
CONVENCION NACIONAL DE TURISMO, 1st, Mérida,
Venezuela, 1961
Itinerarios turisticos-alpinisticos en la Sierra
Nevada de Mérida; trabajo del Club Andino
Venezolano a cargo de ... Carlos Lacruz y Franco
Anzil. Mérida: Club Andino Venezolano, 1961.
9 leaves. 35cm.

CLUB DES GRIMPEURS DE GENÈVE
Chansonnier du Club des Grimpeurs de Genève.
Genève: Le Club, [n.d.] 62p. 15cm.

CLUB EXCURSIONISTA DE GRACIA
Alpamayo 72: Andes del Peru. [Barcelona]: Club
Excursionista de Gracia, [1973?]. [11p.],
illus. 22cm.

CLUTTERBUCK, Walter
Three in Norway, by two of them [i.e. J.A. Lees
and W. Clutterbuck]. Longmans, Green, 1882.
xv, 341p., plates, illus., map. 20cm.

COAZ, J
Die Lawinen der Schweizeralpen. Bern: Dalp,
1881. 147p., plates (some fold.), illus., maps.
25cm.

COAZ, J
Statistik und Verbau der Lawinen in den Schweizeralpen. Bern: Stämpfli, 1910. 126p., plates,
illus., maps, bibl. 31cm.

COBBETT, James P
Journal of a tour in Italy, and also in part of
France and Switzerland ... from October, 1828, to
September, 1829. [The Author?], 1830. 392p.
19cm.

COBBOLD, Ralph P
Innermost Asia: travel and sport in the Pamirs.
Heinemann, 1900. xviii, 354p., plates (1 fold.
col.), illus., map, bibl. 24cm.

COCHE, Raymond
ALPINUS
Alpinus, conteur dauphinois: nouveaux récits;
précédés d'une Vie d'Alpinus par Raymond Coche.
[Paris]: Flammarion, 1946. 189p., plates, illus.
22cm. (La vie en montagne)

COCKBURN, James
Swiss scenery from drawings by Major Cockburn.
Rodwell & Martin, 1820. vii, 200p., plates,
illus. 32cm.

COCKBURN, James
Views in the valley of Aosta, drawn from nature
by Major Cockburn, and on stone by A. Aglio and
T.M. Baynes. D. Walther, [1823]. 1v. of illus.
44cm.

COCKBURN, James
Views to illustrate the route of Mont Cenis,
drawn from nature by Major Cockburn; [and on
stone, by C. Hullmandel]. Rodwell & Martin,
[1822]. 1v. of illus. 51cm.

COCKBURN, James
Views to illustrate the route of the Simplon,
drawn from nature, by Major Cockburn; [and on
stone, by J. Harding]. Rodwell & Martin, [1822].
10 pts. of illus. 51cm.

COELLN, Ernst von
Das Buch vom Schöckel; verfasst auf Anregung des
Steirischen Gebirgsvereines. Graz: Leykam,
[1911]. 158p., plates, illus. 21cm.

COGHLAN, Francis
Guide through Switzerland and Chamounix; or,
Tourist's companion to the most interesting
objects in the cities... A.H. Baily, [183-].
xxxvi, 360p., map. 15cm.

- - New ed., rev., improved and completed until
1850. H. Hughes, 1850.

COHEN, Saul B
Oxford world atlas; Saul B. Cohen geographic
editor; prepared by the Cartographic Department
of the Clarendon Press. Oxford: University
Press, 1973. xii, 190p., chiefly col. maps.
39cm.

Un coin des Himalayas, par un missionaire. Paris:
Lefort, [1903?]. 166p., illus. 23cm.

COLE, Mrs. Henry Warwick
A lady's tour round Monte Rosa; with visits to
the Italian valleys ... in a series of excursions
in the years 1850-56-58, [by Mrs. H. Warwick
Cole]. Longman, Brown, Green, Longmans, &
Roberts, 1859. xi, 402p., col. plates (1 fold.),
illus., map. 21cm.

COLEMAN, Arthur Philemon
The Canadian Rockies: new and old trails. Unwin,
1911. 383p., plates (2 fold. col.), illus., maps.
24cm.

COLEMAN, Edmund Thomas
Scenes from the snow-fields, being illustrations
of the upper ice-world of Mont Blanc, from
sketches made ... in the years 1855, 1856, 1857,
1858; with historical and descriptive remarks
...; the views lithographed and printed in colours
by Vincent Brooks. Longman, Brown, Green,
Longmans & Roberts, 1859. viii, 47p., 12 col.
plates, illus. 57cm.

COLERIDGE, Gilbert
Some and sundry. Constable, 1931. 276p., port.
21cm.

COLES, John, F.R.G.S.
FRESHFIELD, Douglas William and WHARTON, W   J   L
Hints to travellers, scientific and general;
edited by Douglas W. Freshfield and W.J.L. Wharton.
8th ed. rev. and enl.; edited by John Coles.
Royal Geographical Society, 1901. 2v., plates
(some fold., some col.), illus., maps. 18cm.

COLES, John, F.R.G.S.
Summer travelling in Iceland, being the narrative
of two journeys across the island by unfrequented
routes ...; with a chapter on Askja by E. Delmer
Morgan. Murray, 1882. xxii, 269p., plates (2
fold. col.), illus., maps. 26cm.

COLES-FINCH, William and HAWKS, Ellison
Water in nature. Jack, [1911]. 308p., 1 col.
plate, illus. 22cm. ("Romance of reality"
series)

COLES-FINCH, William
Water its origin and use; illustrations of mountain and glacier scenery by Mrs. Aubrey Le Blond.
Alston Rivers,1908. xxi, 483p., plates, illus.
22cm.

COLIJN, A   H
Naar de eeuwige sneeuw van tropisch Nederland:
de bestijging van het Carstenszgebergte in
Nederlandsch Nieuw Guinee. Amsterdam: Scheltens
& Giltay, [1937?]. 286p., plates (1 fold. col.),
illus., map, bibl. 26cm.

A collection of modern and contemporary voyages and
travels; [compiled by Sir Richard Phillips].
Printed for Richard Phillips, by J.G. Barnard,
1805-06. 3v. 23cm.
No more published?

A collection of Welsh tours; or, A display of the
beauties of Wales; selected principally from
celebrated histories and popular tours ...; to
which is added, A tour of the River Wye. 3rd
ed., corr. G. Sael, 1798. xix, 456p. 18cm.

COLLEONI, Guardino
Leggenda e storia del Monte Summano. Vicenza:
The Author, 1890. 107p., plates, illus., map
(on lining paper). 16cm.

COLLET, Léon W
Description générale du Massif du Mont-Blanc.
Fasc.2. Aperçu sur la géologie du Massif du
Mont-Blanc et des Aiguilles Rouges. Paris:
Fischbacher, 1924. 53p., 15 plates, illus.,
maps, bibl. 18cm. (Guides Vallot)

COLLET, Léon W
Étude géologique de la Chaîne Tour Saillère -
Pic de Tanneverge. Berne: A. Francke, 1904. iv,
32, xip., 4 plates (some fold., some col.),
illus., map, bibl. 33cm. (Beiträge zur geologischen Karte der Schweiz = Matériaux pour
la carte géologique de la Suisse, 49, N.S., 19)

COLLET, Léon W   and PAREJAS, Edouard
Géologie de la Chaîne de la Jungfrau. Bern:
A. Francke, 1931. ix, 64p., 10 plates (some
fold., some col.), illus., bibl. 32cm.
(Beiträge zur geologischen Karte der Schweiz =
Matériaux pour la carte géologique de la Suisse,
93, N.S., 63)

COLLET, Léon W
Geology of the Swiss Alps; edited by A.K. Wells.
Stanford, 1926. 45p., plates (1 fold.), illus.,
bibl. 23cm.
Cover title.

COLLET, Léon W
Les lacs: leur mode de formation, leurs eaux,
leur destin: éléments d'hydrogeologie. Paris:
G. Doin, 1925. xi, 320p., 28 plates, illus.,
bibl. 25cm.

COLLET, Léon W
The structure of the Alps; foreword by O.T.
Jones. Arnold, 1927. xii, 289p., plates (some
fold.), illus., maps, bibl. 23cm.

- - 2nd ed. 1935.

COLLETT, John
A guide for visitors to Kashmir; enlarged, revised and corrected up to date by A. Mitra.
Calcutta: Newman, 1898. 205p., fold. col.
plates, map. 20cm.

COLLIE, John Norman
Climbing on the Himalaya and other mountain
ranges. Edinburgh: Douglas, 1902. xi, 315p.,
plates (3 fold. col.), illus., maps. 23cm.

COLLIE, John Norman
Climbing on the Nanga Parbat Range, Kashmir
(read before the Alpine Club, February 4, 1896).
London, 1896. 16p., plates, illus. 22cm.
Offprint from Alpine Journal, v.18, 1896.

STUTFIELD, Hugh Edward Millington and COLLIE,
John Norman
Climbs & exploration in the Canadian Rockies.
Longmans, Green, 1903. xii, 343p., plates (1
fold. col.), illus., maps. 23cm.

COLLIER, E C F
MONKSWELL, Mary, Baroness Monkswell
A Victorian diarist: extracts from the journals
of Mary, Lady Monkswell, 1875-95; edited by the
Hon. E.C.F. Collier. Murray, 1944. xxv, 284p.,
plates, illus. 23cm.

COLLINGS, Henry
Switzerland as I saw it. J. Weir & Knight,
[18--]. 44p. 19cm.
Lecture delivered in London.

COLLINGWOOD, William Gershom
The Lake counties. Dent, 1902. xii, 392p.,
plates, illus., maps (1 fold. in pocket). 17cm.
(Dent's county guides)

COLLINGWOOD, William Gershom
The life of John Ruskin. 7th ed. Methuen, 1911.
viii, 314p. 18cm. (Methuen's shilling books)

COLLINGWOOD, William Gershom
Limestone alps of Savoy: a study in physical
geology; with an introduction by J. Ruskin.
Orpington, Kent: Allen, 1884. xxiii, 206p.,
plates, illus., maps. 25cm.

COLLINGWOOD, William Gershom and STEFANSSON, Jón
A pilgrimage to the saga-steads of Iceland.
Ulverston: W. Holmes, 1899. x, 187p., col.
plates, illus., maps. 29cm.

COLLINGWOOD, William Gershom
RUSKIN, John
The poems of John Ruskin; now first collected
... and edited with notes ... by W.G.
Collingwood; with facsimiles of mss. and
illus. by the author. Orpington, London: Allen,
1891. 2v., plates, illus. 30cm.

COLLINS, Francis Arnold
Mountain climbing. J. Long, 1924. vi, 314p.,
plates, illus., bibl. 20cm.

Collins guide to mountains and mountaineering, by
John Cleare. Collins, 1979. 208p., illus.
(some col.), maps, bibl. 31cm.

MARTINS, Charles and COLLOMB, Édouard
Essai sur l'ancien glacier de la Vallée
d'Argelès (Hautes Pyrénées). Montpellier, 1868.
34p., 1 fold. col. plate, illus., map. 28cm.
Offprint from Mémoires de l'Académie des Sciences
de Montpellier, t.7, 1867.

COLLOMB, Édouard
Preuves de l'existence d'anciens glaciers dans
les vallées des Vosges, du terrain erratique de
cette contrée. Paris: Masson, 1847. 246p.,
illus., maps. 24cm.

COLLOMB, Robin Gabriel
Alpine points of view; or, Contemporary scenes
from the Alps including some observations and
opinions of an itinerant alpinist. Spearman,
1961. 239p., illus., maps. 24cm.

COLLOMB, Robin Gabriel
Bernese Alps central: Blümlisalp, Lauterbrunnen,
Jungfrau, Lötschental, Baltschieder, Oberaletsch,
Aletsch Basin west; compiled and edited by Robin
G. Collomb. Alpine Club, 1978. 199p., illus.
17cm. (Alpine Club guide books)
Revised and re-written version of part of the
author's Selected climbs in the Bernese Alps.

COLLOMB, Robin Gabriel
Bernese Alps east: Mönch, Eiger, Fiescher,
Finsteraar, Schreck, Lauteraar, Wetterhörner,
Oberaar, Grimsel; compiled and edited by Robin
G. Collomb. Alpine Club, 1978. 174p., illus.
17cm. (Alpine Club guide books)
Revised and re-written version of part of the
author's Selected climbs in the Bernese Alps.
1968.

COLLOMB, Robin Gabriel
Bernese Alps west from the Col du Pillon to the
Lötschenpass: Les Diablerets, Wildhorn, Wild-
strubel, Gemmi, Altels, Balmhorn: a selection of
popular walking and climbing routes; compiled by
Robin G. Collomb. Goring, Reading: West Col,
1970. 73p., plates, illus. 17cm. (West Col
alpine guides)

COLLOMB, Robin Gabriel
Bernina Alps: a selection of climbs; compiled and
edited by Robin G. Collomb. 2nd ed. Goring,
Reading: West Col, 1976. 127p., illus., map.
17cm. (West Col alpine guides)

COLLOMB, Robin Gabriel
Bregaglia east: Maloja, Forno, Albigna, Allievi,
Disgrazia: a selection of climbs; compiled and
edited by Robin G. Collomb. Goring, Reading: West
Col, 1971. 120p., illus., map, bibl. 17cm.
(West Col alpine guides)

COLLOMB, Robin Gabriel and CREW, Peter
Bregaglia west: [Sciora, Cengalo, Badile]: a
selection of popular and recommended climbs; compiled by Robin G. Collomb and Peter Crew. Goring,
Reading: West Col, 1967. 86p., illus., maps,
bibl. 17cm. (West Col alpine guides)

- - 2nd ed., by Robin G. Collomb. 1974.

COLLOMB, Robin Gabriel
A dictionary of mountaineering. Glasgow, London:
Blackie, 1957. 175p., illus. 20cm.

COLLOMB, Robin Gabriel
Grians east: Gran Paradiso area: a selection of
popular and recommended climbs. compiled by Robin
G. Collomb. Goring, Reading: West Col, 1969.
84p., plates, illus., map, bibl. 17cm. (West
Col alpine guides)

COLLOMB, Robin Gabriel
Graians west: Tarentaise and Maurienne: a selection of popular and recommended climbs; compiled
by Robin G. Collomb. Goring, Reading: West Col,
1967. 128p., illus., map, bibl. 16cm. (West
Col alpine guides)

COLLOMB, Robin Gabriel
Julian Alps: mountain walking and outline climbing guide; compiled by Robin G. Collomb; assisted
by M. Anderson. Goring, Reading: West Col, 1978.
136p., illus., maps, bibl. 18cm. (West Col
alpine guides)

COLLOMB, Robin Gabriel
Maritime Alps: Vésubie basin and Argentera: a
selection of popular and recommended climbs; compiled by Robin G. Collomb; based on the works of
Vincent Paschetta. Goring, Reading: West Col,
1968. 100p., illus., map, bibl. 17cm. (West
Col alpine guides)

COLLOMB, Robin Gabriel and O'CONNOR, William H
Mont Blanc range. Vol.1. Trélatête, Mont Blanc,
Maudit, Tacul, Brenva. Alpine Club, 1976.
221p., illus., bibl. 16cm. (Alpine Club guide
books)

COLLOMB, Robin Gabriel
Mountains of the Alps: tables of summits over
3500 metres with geographical and historical notes
and tables of selected lesser heights. Vol.1.
Western Alps: Mediterranean to the Simplonpass
and Grimselpass. Goring, Reading: West Col, 1971.
96p., illus. 23cm.

COLLOMB, Robin Gabriel
Pennine Alps central: Weisshorn, Dent Blanche,
Monte Rose, Matterhorn chains, Italian valley
ranges, Valpelline south; compiled and edited by
Robin G. Collomb. Alpine Club, 1975. 373p.,
illus., map, bibl. 17cm. (Alpine Club guide
books)

COLLOMB, Robin Gabriel
  Pennine Alps east: Saas and Mischabel chains;
  compiled and edited by Robin G. Collomb. Alpine
  Club, 1975. 169p., illus., bibl. 17cm. (Alpine
  Club guide books)

COLLOMB, Robin Gabriel
  Pennine Alps west: Grandes Dents, Bouquetins,
  Collon ...; compiled and edited by Robin G.
  Collomb. Alpine Club, 1979. 232p., illus. 17cm.
  (Alpine Club guide books)

CLEARE, John and COLLOMB, Robin Gabriel
  Sea cliff climbing in Britain. Constable, 1973.
  189p., illus. 25cm.

COLLOMB, Robin Gabriel
  Selected climbs in the Bernese Alps: from the
  Lötschenpass to the Grimselpass; compiled with
  the aid of the "Berner Alpen" guidebook series of
  the Swiss Alpine Club, and adapted with additional
  material by Robin G. Collomb. Alpine Club, 1968.
  223p., illus., bibl. 16cm. (Alpine Club guide
  books; selected climbs, 5)

COLLOMB, Robin Gabriel and CREW, Peter
  Selected climbs in the Mont Blanc range. Vol.1.
  From the Col de la Seigne to the Col du Géant;
  translated and adapted from the Guide Vallot and
  compiled with additional material by Robin G.
  Collomb and Peter Crew. Alpine Club, 1967.
  241p., illus., maps, bibl. 16cm. (Alpine Club
  guide books; selected climbs, 1)

COLLOMB, Robin Gabriel
  Selected climbs in the Mont Blanc range. Vol.2.
  From the Col du Géant to the Petit Col Ferret
  and Fenêtre d'Arpette; translated and adapted
  from the Guide Vallot and compiled with additional
  material by Robin G. Collomb and Peter Crew.
  Alpine Club, 1967. 185p., illus. 16cm. (Alpine
  Club guide books; selected climbs, 1)

COLLOMB, Robin Gabriel
  Selected climbs in the Pennine Alps. Vol. 2.
  Arolla and western ranges; translated and adapted
  from the "Guide des Alpes valaisannes" and compiled with additional material by Robin G.
  Collomb. 2nd ed. Alpine Club, 1968. 150p.,
  illus. 16cm. (Alpine Club guide books; selected
  climbs, 2)

COLLOMB, Robin Gabriel
  Zermatt and district, including Saas Fee.
  Constable, 1969. xiv, 242p., illus., maps, bibl.
  21cm. (Alpine guides, 2)

COLLOGUE MÉDICINE & HAUTE MONTAGNE, Grenoble, 1976
  Colloque ... organisé sous la présidence du prof.
  Tanche dans le cadre de la Commission Médicale de
  la Fédération Française de la Montagne, les 11 et
  12 juin 1976 à la Faculté de Médecine de Grenoble.
  Paris: Fédération Française de la Montagne,
  [1977]. 4v., illus., forms., bibl. 30cm.

COLORADO MOUNTAIN CLUB
HART, John L   Jerome
  Fourteen thousand feet: a history of the naming
  and early ascents of the high Colorado peaks.
  2nd ed. and A climber's guide to the high
  Colorado peaks, by Elinor Eppich Kingery. Denver:
  C.M.C., 1931. 71p., plates, illus., map. 23cm.

COLORADO MOUNTAIN CLUB
  Front Range panorama; edited by Louisa Ward Arps.
  Denver: C.M.C., 1962. 7 sheets and map in
  folder. 23 x 32cm.

COLSTON, Marianne
  Journal of a tour in France, Switzerland, and
  Italy, during the years 1819, 20, and 21; illus-
  trated by fifty lithographic prints... Paris:
  A. & W. Galignani, 1822. 2v. 22cm.

 - - Plates.

COMBA, E
  Histoire des Vaudois. Nouv. éd. Paris: Fischbacher, 1898. xvi, 208p., plates, illus., map.
  20cm.

ARMENGAUD, André and COMET, François
  Pyrénées. T.4. Guide de la région d'Aure et de
  Luchon (du Port de Barosa au Val d'Aran); sous le
  patronage de ... F.F.M. Toulouse:Privat, 1953.
  360p., fold. col. plates, illus., maps, bibl.
  16cm.

COMETTANT, Oscar
  De haut en bas: impression pyrénéennes. Paris:
  Degorce-Cadot, 1868. 311p. 20cm.

Comicalities of travel, for the Tarvin Bazaar, [by
  T. Brooke]. Chester: J. Seacome, 1836. 126p.,
  plates, illus. 20cm.

COMICI, Emilio
CLUB ALPINO ITALIANO. Comitato Nazionale per le
Onoranze ad Emilio Comici
  Emilio Comici: Alpinismo eroico; a cura del
  Comitato Nazionale del C.A.I. per le Onoranze ad
  Emilio Comici; prefazione di Angelo Manaresi.
  Milano: Hoepli, 1942. xxvii, 307p., 120 plates,
  illus. 26cm.
  Memorial volume of Comici's writings, and tributes
  to him.

COMISARÍA DE PARQUES NACIONALES
  See
SPAIN. Ministerio de Agricultura. Comisaría de
Parques Nacionales

COMITÉ DE L'HIMALAYA
  See
FÉDÉRATION FRANÇAISE DE LA MONTAGNE. Comité de
l'Himalaya

COMITÉ NATIONAL FRANÇAIS DES RECHERCHES ANTARCTIQUES
  Catalogue of publications. Paris: Le Comité:
  1971. 21p. 24cm.
  Contains abstracts.

COMMISSION APPOINTED TO DELIMIT THE BOUNDARY BE-
TWEEN THE PROVINCES OF ALTERTA AND BRITISH COLUMBIA
  See
CANADA. Commission Appointed to Delimit the
Boundary between the Provinces of Alberta and
Columbia

COMPAGNIE DES CHEMINS DE FER DU MIDI
  Les Pyrénées. Paris: Beauchamp, 1903-04. 4pts.
  in 1, illus. 15 x 24cm.

COMPAGNIE DES CHEMINS DE FER JURA-SIMPLON
  De Bale à Brigue et Zermatt: guide officiel du
  Jura-Simplon: IIIme sér. des guides illustrés de
  J. Boillot-Robert. Neuchatel: F. Wohlgrath,
  [ca 1893]. 74, 54p., plates (some fold., some col.),
  illus., maps. 23 x 32cm.

COMPAGNIE DES GUIDES DE CHAMONIX
  See
SYNDICAT DES GUIDES DE CHAMONIX - MONT-BLANC

COMPAGNIE DU CHEMIN DE FER DU GORNERGRAT
  Initiation au Gornergrat; édité par la Compagnie
  du Chemin de Fer du Gornergrat. Brigue: La
  Compagnie, 1948. 85p., illus. 22cm.

COMPAGNONI, Achille
  Il tricolore sul K2. Milano: Mondadori, 1965.
  85p., illus. (some col.). 21cm.

COMPTON, E   Harrison
FARRER, Reginald
  The Dolomites: King Laurin's garden; painted by
  E. Harrison Compton; described by Reginald Farrer.
  Black, 1913. vii, 207p., 21 col. plates (1 fold.),
  illus., map. 23cm.

COMPTON, E   Harrison
BAILLIE-GROHMAN, William Adolphus
  Tyrol; painted by E. Harrison Compton; described
  by W.A. Baillie-Grohman. Black, 1908. x, 208p.,
  col. plates, illus., maps. 20cm.

COMPTON, Edward T
Die Hohe Tatra: sieben Farbendrucke und sechsund-
zwanzig Holzschnitte nach Aquarellen von E.T.
Compton; Text von Paul Habel. Leipzig: J.J.
Weber, [ca 1905]. [6]p., plates (some col.),
illus., map. 44cm.
In portfolio.

COMPTON, Edward T
ZSIGMONDY, Emil
Im Hochgebirge: Wanderungen; mit Abbildungen von
E.T. Compton; hrsg. von K. Schulz. Leipzig:
Duncker & Humblot, 1899. xv, 365p., plates,
illus. 28cm.

COMPTON, Thomas
The northern Cambrian mountains; or, A tour
through North Wales describing the scenery and
general characters of that romantic country, and
embellished with ... coloured views, engraved
from original drawings. Printed for the Author,
by C. Corrall, 1817. 1v. (chiefly illus.).
25 x 34cm.

- - Another issue. T. Clay. 1820.

CONFÉRENCE INTERNATIONALE DES CLUBS ALPINS,
Geneva, 1879
Conférence internationale des clubs alpins, XVme
assemblée générale et fête du Club Alpin Suisse
tenues à Genève les 1,2,3 & 4 août 1879. Genève:
J. Jullien, H. Georg, 1880. 188p. 19cm.
Cover title: Compte-rendu de la réunion des clubs
alpins à Genève.

CONFÉRENCE INTERNATIONALE DES SOCIÉTÉS DE TOURISME
ALPIN, Zakopane, 1930
Conférence internationale des sociétés de
tourisme alpin, Zakopane, Pologne, 5-7 août 1930:
compte-rendu, protocole, rapports, résolutions.
Kraków: Société Polonaise de Tatra, 1931. 40p.,
plates, illus. 24cm.

CONGRÈS DE L'ALPINISME
See
CONGRÈS INTERNATIONAL DE L'ALPINISME

CONGRÈS DE MONACO. Congrès de l'alpinisme
See
CONGRÈS INTERNATIONAL DE L'ALPINISME, Monaco, 1920

CONGRÈS DE MONACO POUR FAVORISER LE DÉVELOPPEMENT
DES STATIONS HYDRO-MINÉRALES MARITIMES, CLIMATIQUES
& ALPINES DES NATIONS ALLIÉES, 1920
See
CONGRÈS INTERNATIONAL DE L'ALPINISME, MONACO, 1920

CONGRÈS GÉOLOGIQUE INTERNATIONAL, 6th, Zurich, 1894
Livret-guide géologique dans le Jura et les Alpes
de la Suisse; publié par le Comité d'organisation
en vue de la 6e session, à Zurich. Paris: Alcan,
1894. vii, 307p., fold. plates, illus., maps (fold.
col. in pockets). 22cm.

CONGRÈS INTERNATIONAL DE GÉOGRAPHIE
See
INTERNATIONAL GEOGRAPHIC CONGRESS

CONGRÈS INTERNATIONAL DE L'ALPINISME, Paris, 1900
Congrès international de l'alpinisme tenu à Paris
du 11 au 15 août 1900: compte rendu. Clermont:
Imprimerie Daix, 1902. ix, 256p., plates, illus.
23cm.

CONGRÈS INTERNATIONAL DE L'ALPINISME, Monaco, 1920
Congrès de Monaco ... Monaco - ler au 10 mai
1920, Congrès de l'alpinisme: comptes rendus.
Paris: Expansion Scientifique Française, 1921.
2 v. in 1, plates, illus., maps. 24cm.

CONGRÈS INTERNATIONAL DE L'ALPINISME, Monaco, 1920
Manuel d'alpinisme scolaire, [par] Jean Gotteland;
avec une introduction de Gaston Vidal. Chambery:
l'Association Sportive du Lycée de Monaco, Dardel,
1921. xvi, 105p. 22cm.

CONGRÈS INTERNATIONAL DES SCIENCES GÉOGRAPHIQUES
See
INTERNATIONAL GEOGRAPHIC CONGRESS

CONGRESSO SPELEOLOGICO NAZIONALE, 1st, Trieste, 1933
Atti del lo Congresso Speleologico Nazionale;
organizzato del Club Alpino Italiano in occasione
del cinquantenario di fondazione della Sezione di
Trieste (Società Alpina delle Giulie); sotto gli
auspici delle Regie Grotte Demaniali di Postumia
e dell'Istituto Italiano di Speologia, Trieste
10-14 giugno 1933 - XI. Trieste: C.A.I., 1933.
252p., fold. plates, illus., maps. 25cm.

CONRAD, Heinrich
TÖPFER, Rodolphe
[Voyages en zigzag]. Reisen im Zickzack; ueber-
setz und hrsg. von Heinrich Conrad. München:
G. Müller, 1912. vi, 405p., illus. 19cm.
(Lebenskunst, 4)

Le conservateur suisse; ou, Recuil complet des
étrennes helvétiennes. Ed. augm. Lausanne: L.
Knab, B. Corbaz, 1813-31. 13v. 18cm.

CONSTANT, Lucien
Quelques jours en Suisse. Paris: Imprimerie D.
Jouaust, 1872. 134p. 16cm.

CONTI, Alfredo and LAENG, Walther
Le alpi di Val Grosina: guida alpina; illustrata
... da W. Laeng. Brescia: Club Alpino Italiano,
Gruppo Lombardo Alpinisti Senza Guide, 1909.
ix, 106p., plates (1 fold. col.), illus., map,
bibl. 16cm.

Continental adventures: a novel. Hurst, Robinson,
1826. 3v. 20cm.

The continental traveller, being the journal of an
economical tourist to France, Switzerland, and
Italy ...; by a Travelling Lawyer; to which is
added A tour in Spain ... by a Travelling Artist.
M.A. Leigh, 1833. 122p, 1 fold plate, map.
18cm.
Flyleaf signed E. Gardner & F. Wilder.

CONTI, Henry A   de
Suisse française, Oberland bernois; guide pratique et illustré. Paris: A. Faure, [n.d.].
252p., illus., map. 15cm. (Guides pratiques &
circulaires Conty)

- - 12e éd. Paris: Administration des Guides
Conty, [n.d.].

CONVENCION NACIONAL DE TURISMO, 1st, Mérida,
Venezuela, 1961
Itinerarios turisticos-alpinísticos en la Sierra
Nevada de Mérida; trabajo del Club Andino
Venezolano a cargo de ... Carlos Lacruz y Franco
Anzil. Mérida: Club Andino Venezolano, 1961.
9 leaves. 35cm.

CONWAY, Derwent
A personal narrative of a journey through Norway,
part of Sweden and the islands ... of Denmark.
Edinburgh: Constable, 1829. xiv, 315p. 17cm.
(Constable's miscellany, 38)

CONWAY, Derwent
Switzerland, the south of France, and the
Pyrenees in MDCCCXXX. Vol.1. Switzerland.
Edinburgh: Constable; London: Hurst, Chance, 1831.
xviii, 284p., map. 16cm.

CONWAY, Sir Martin
See
CONWAY, William Martin, Baron Conway

CONWAY, William Martin, Baron Conway
Aconcagua and Tierra del Fuego: a book of climbing, travel and exploration. Cassell, 1902.
xii, 252p., plates, illus. 23cm.

CONWAY, William Martin, Baron Conway
The Alps; described by W. Martin Conway; painted
by A.D. McCormick. Black, 1904. x, 294p., 70
col. plates, illus. 25cm.

CONWAY, William Martin, Baron Conway
The Alps, described by Sir Martin Conway; with
illustrations from photographs by L. Edna
Walter. Black, 1910. 294p., plates, illus. 21cm.

CONWAY, William Martin, <u>Baron Conway</u>
   The Alps from end to end; with ... illustrations
   by A.D. M'Cormick. Constable, 1895. xii, 403p.,
   plates, illus. 25cm.

- - 2nd ed. 1895.

CONWAY, William Martin, <u>Baron Conway</u>
   The Alps from end to end; with ... illustrations
   by A.D. M'Cormick; and a chapter by W.A.B.
   Coolidge. Constable, 1900. viii, 300p., plates,
   illus. 22cm.

- - Another ed. 1904.

- - Another ed. 1905.

- - Another ed. Nelson, [1910].

- - Another ed. Nelson, [1917].

CONWAY, William Martin, <u>Baron Conway</u>
   The autobiography of a mountain climber
   <u>See his</u>
   <u>Mountain memories</u>

CONWAY, William Martin, <u>Baron Conway</u>
   The Bolivian Andes: a record of climbing &
   exploration in the Cordillera Real in the years
   1898 and 1900. Harper, 1901. ix, 403p., plates,
   illus., bibl. 23cm.

CONWAY, William Martin, <u>Baron Conway</u>
   Climbers' guide to the central Pennine Alps.
   Fisher Unwin, 1890. viii, 158p. 14cm. [Conway
   and Coolidge's climbers' guides, 1]

CONWAY, William Martin, <u>Baron Conway</u>
   Climbers' guide to the eastern Pennine Alps.
   Fisher Unwin, 1891. xii, 152p. 14cm. [Conway
   and Coolidge's climbers' guides, 2]

CONWAY, William Martin, <u>Baron Conway</u>
   Climbing and exploration in the Karakoram-
   Himalayas; with ... illustrations by A.D.
   McCormick and maps. Fisher Unwin, 1894. 2v.
   (xix, 709p.), plates, illus. 26cm.

- - Maps (3 fold col. in portfolio).
- - Scientific reports.
- - Another issue. New York: Appleton, 1894.

CONWAY, William Martin, <u>Baron Conway</u>
   [Climbing and exploration in the Karakoram-
   Himalayas]. Ascensions et explorations à sept
   mille mètres dans l'Himalaya; traduit et
   abrégé par Henri Jacottet. Paris: Hachette,
   1898. v, 242p., illus. 20cm.

CONWAY, William Martin, <u>Baron Conway</u>
   Episodes in a varied life, by Lord Conway of
   Allington. Country Life, 1932. viii, 276p.,
   plates, illus., ports. 23cm.

CONWAY, William Martin, <u>Baron Conway</u>
   The first crossing of Spitsbergen, being an
   account of an inland journey of exploration and
   survey, with descriptions of several mountain
   ascents ...; with contributions by J.W. Gregory
   [and others]. Dent, 1897. xii, 371p., plates
   (2 fold., some col.), illus., maps. 25cm.

CONWAY, William Martin, <u>Baron Conway</u> and COOLIDGE,
William Augustus Brevoort
   The Lepontine Alps. Fisher Unwin, 1892. xix,
   106p. 14cm. (Conway and Coolidge's climbers'
   guides, 3)

CONWAY, William Martin, <u>Baron Conway</u>
   Mountain memories: a pilgrimage of romance, by
   Sir Martin Conway. Cassell, 1920. 282p., plates,
   illus. 25cm.

CONWAY, William Martin, <u>Baron Conway</u>
   [Mountain memories]. The autobiography of a
   mountain climber. Abridged ed.Cape, 1933. 246p.
   18cm. (Travellers' library, 195)

CONWAY, William Martin, <u>Baron Conway</u>
   No man's land: a history of Spitsbergen from its
   discovery in 1596 to the beginning of the
   scientific exploration of the country. Cambridge:
   University Press, 1906. xii, 377p., plates,
   illus., maps, bibl. 25cm.

CONWAY, William Martin, <u>Baron Conway</u>
   Notes on a survey and map of part of the Karakoram
   Himalayas, made and constructed by W.M. Conway.
   Royal Geographical Society, 1894. 7p. 25cm.
   In slipcase with the two sheets of the map.

CONWAY, William Martin, <u>Baron Conway</u>
   [Zermatt pocket book: a guide to the Pennine Alps].
   Die Pennischen Alpen: ein Führer für Bergsteiger
   durch das Gebiet der Pennischen Alpen zwischen
   Simplon und Grossen St. Bernhard; bearb. und hrsg.
   von August Lorria. Zürich: Orell Füssli, 1891.
   vii, 204p. 17cm.

CONWAY, William Martin, <u>Baron Conway</u>
   With ski and sledge over arctic glaciers. Dent,
   1898. 235p., plates (1 fold. col.), illus., map.
   21cm.

CONWAY FAMILY
EVANS, Joan
   The Conways: a history of three generations.
   Museum Press, 1966. 308p., plates, illus. 23cm.

Conway and Coolidge's climbers' guides.

   1. Climbers' guide to the central Pennine
      Alps, by W.M. Conway. 1890.
   2. Climbers' guide to the eastern Pennine
      Alps, by W.M. Conway. 1891.
   3. The Lepontine Alps, by W.M. Conway and
      W.A.B. Coolidge. 1892.
   4. The central Alps of the Dauphiny, by W.A.B.
      Coolidge, H. Duhamel and F. Perrin. 1892.
      - - 2nd ed. 1905.
   5. The chain of Mont Blanc, by L. Kurz. 1892.
   6. The Adula Alps, by W.A.B. Coolidge. 1893.
   7. The mountains of Cogne, by G. Yeld and
      W.A.B. Coolidge. 1893.
   8. The range of the Tödi, by W.A.B. Coolidge.
      1894.
   9. The Bernese Oberland. Vol.1. From the
      Gemmi to the Mönchjoch, by G. Hasler.
      1902.
   9-10. The Bernese Oberland. Vol.1. From the
      Gemmi to the Mönchjoch, by W.A.B. Coolidge.
      New ed. 2 pts. 1909-10.
   11. The Bernese Oberland. Vol.2. From the
      Mönchjoch to the Grimsel, by W.A.B.
      Coolidge. 1904.
   12. The Bernese Oberland. Vol.3. Dent de
      Morcles to the Gemmi, by H. Dübi. 1907.
   13-14. The Bernese Oberland. Vol.4. Grimsel to
      the Uri Rothstock, by H. Dübi. 2 pts.
      1908.
   15-16. The Alps of the Bernina W. of the Bernina
      Pass, by E.L. Strutt. 1910. 2pts.

COOK, <u>Mrs.</u> E T
   <u>See</u>
COOK, Emily Constance

COOK, <u>Sir</u> Edward Tyas
COOK, Emily Constance
   From a holiday journal; illustrated with sketches
   and photographs by the author; [edited by E.T.
   Cook]. Allen, 1904. 217p., plates, illus.
   23cm.

COOK, <u>Sir</u> Edward Tyas
   Homes and haunts of John Ruskin; with ... illustrations by E.M.B. Warren. Allen, 1912. xvi,
   218p., plates, illus. 26cm.

COOK, <u>Sir</u> Edward Tyas
   The life of John Ruskin. Allen, 1911. 2v.,
   plates (1 fold.), illus. 23cm.

COOK, Emily Constance
   From a holiday journal; illustrated with sketches
   and photographs by the author; [edited by E.T.
   Cook]. Allen, 1904. 217p., plates, illus. 23cm.

COOK, Frederick Albert
To the top of the continent: discovery, exploration and adventure in sub-arctic Alaska, the
first ascent of Mt. McKinley, 1903-1906. Hodder
and Stoughton, 1909. xxiii, 321p., plates (1
col.), illus., maps. 25cm.

COOK, Theodore Andrea
Ice sports, by Theodore Andrea Cook [and
others]. Ward, Lock, 1901. 335p., plates (1
fold. col.), illus. 21cm. (Isthmian Library)

COOK, Theodore Andrea
Notes on tobogganing at St. Moritz. 2nd ed. rev.
and corr. up to March 1895. Rivington, Percival,
1896. xv, 118p., illus., bibl. 20cm.

COOK, Thomas & Sons
See
THOMAS COOK LTD.

COOKE, Charles
The tourist's and traveller's companion to the
Lakes of Cumberland, Westmorland, and Lancashire
... Sherwood, Jones, [ca 1825]. x, 140p.,
plates, illus., fold. map. 16cm.

COOKE, E   W
Leaves from my sketch-book, with descriptive
letterpress. Murray, 1876. 53 leaves, 34
plates, illus. 25 x 34cm.

COOKE, George Alexander
Topographical and statistical description of
North Wales... J. Robins, [ca 1830]. 200p.,
plates, illus., fold. col. map. 16cm.(Cooke's
topographical library of Great Britain.

COOKE, George Alexander
Topographical and statistical description of the
County of Cumberland... C. Cooke, [ca 1810].
160p., 1 fold. plate, map. 15cm. (Cooke's
topography of Great Britain, 27)

COOLIDGE, William Augustus Brevoort
The Adula Alps. Fisher Unwin, 1893. xix, 192p.
14cm. (Conway and Coolidge's climbers' guides, 6)

COOLIDGE, William Augustus Brevoort
Alp.(In: The Encyclopaedia Britannica. 11th ed.,
v.1, pt.4: Alex to Alum. Cambridge, 1910. 32cm.
p.721)
Article signed W.A.B.C.

COOLIDGE, William Augustus Brevoort
The alpine career (1868-1914) of Frederick
Gardiner described by his friend W.A.B. Coolidge.
[Woolton]: [Mrs. Gardiner], 1920. 75p., 1 plate,
port., bibl. 23cm.

COOLIDGE, William Augustus Brevoort
Alpine studies. Longmans, Green, 1912. xiii,
307p., plates, illus. 24cm.

COOLIDGE, William Augustus Brevoort
Alps.
(In: The Encyclopaedia Britannica. 11th ed.,
v.1, pt.4: Alex to Alum. Cambridge, 1910. 32cm.
p.737-754, illus., maps)
Article signed W.A.B.C., with section 10: Geology
signed P.La, i.e. Philip Lake, & sections 11, 12:
Flora & Fauna signed H.V.K., i.e. Howard V. Knox.

COOLIDGE, William Augustus Brevoort
CONWAY, William Martin, Baron Conway
The Alps from end to end; with ... illustrations
by A.D. M'Cormick, and a chapter by W.A.B.
Coolidge. Constable, 1900. viii, 300p., plates,
illus. 22cm.

- - Another ed. 1904.
- - Another ed. 1905.
- - Another ed. Nelson, [1910].
- - Another ed. Nelson, [1917].

COOLIDGE, William Augustus Brevoort
The Alps in nature and history. Methuen, 1908.
xx, 440p., plates (some fold. 1 col.), illus.,
maps, bibl. 23cm.

COOLIDGE, William Augustus Brevoort
[The Alps in nature and history]. Les Alpes dans
la nature et dans l'histoire; éd. française par
Edouard Combe. Lausanne: Payot, 1913. xi, 547p.,
plates, maps, bibl. 23cm.

COOLIDGE, William Augustus Brevoort
Die älteste Schulzhütte im Berner Oberland: ein
Beitrag zur Geschichte der bernischen Touristik:
Jubiläumsschrift. Bern: G. Grunau, 1915. 77p.,
1 plate, illus. 23cm.

COOLIDGE, William Augustus Brevoort
Belgium, Italy, and Switzerland, by G. Edmundson,
H. Wickham Steed, W.A.B. Coolidge. Encyclopaedia
Britannica, 1914. iv, 201p., plates, illus.
23cm.
Reproduced from the 11th edition of the Encyclo-
paedia Britannica.

COOLIDGE, William Augustus Brevoort
The Bernese Oberland. Vol.1. From the Gemmi to
the Mönchsjoch.Pt.1. The main ridge. New ed.
Fisher Unwin, 1909. xxiv, 155p. 14cm. (Conway
and Coolidge's climbers' guides, 9)

COOLIDGE, William Augustus Brevoort
The Bernese Oberland. Vol.1. From the Gemmi to
the Mönchjoch. Pt.2. The groups N. and S. of the
main ridge. New ed. Fisher Unwin, 1910. xxiv,
214p. 14cm. (Conway and Coolidge's climbers'
guides, 10)

COOLIDGE, William Augustus Brevoort
The Bernese Oberland. Vol.2. From the Mönchjoch
to the Grimsel. Fisher Unwin, 1904. xxix,
196p. 14cm. (Conway and Coolidge's climbers'
guides, 11)

COOLIDGE, William Augustus Brevoort
[The Bernese Oberland]. Hochgebirgsführer durch
die Berner Alpen. Bd.2. Von der Gemmi bis zum
Mönchjoch; übersetzt ... von H. Dübi. Bern:
Schweizer Alpen-Club, Sektion Bern, 1910. xx,
259p., bibl. 17cm.

COOLIDGE, William Augustus Brevoort
[The Bernese Oberland]. Hochgebirgsführer durch
die Berner Alpen. Bd.3. Vom Mönchsjoch bis zur
Grimsel; uebersetzt ... von H. Dübi. Bern:
Schweizer Alpen-Club, Sektion Bern, 1909. 199p.,
bibl. 17cm.

COOLIDGE, William Augustus Brevoort
La catena della Levanna (Alpi Graie centrali).
Torino, 1901. 44p., plates, illus. 25cm.
Offprint from Bollettino del C.A.I., v.34,
no.67, 1901.

COOLIDGE, William Augustus Brevoort
The central Alps of the Dauphiny, by W.A.B.
Coolidge, H. Duhamel and F. Perrin. Fisher
Unwin, 1892. xix, 248p. 14cm. (Conway and
Coolidge's climbers' guides, 4)

- - 2nd ed. thoroughly rev. 1905.

COOLIDGE, William Augustus Brevoort
Charles the Great's passage of the Alps in 773.
London, 1906. 493-505p. 25cm.
Offprint from the English historical review,
July 1906.

COOLIDGE, William Augustus Brevoort
Climbs in the Alps made in the years 1865 to
1900. The Author, [1900]. 23p. 21cm.

COOLIDGE, William Augustus Brevoort and
DUHAMEL, Henry
Le Col de Galest et le Col de la Galise. Lyon,
1905. 16p., 1 plate, illus. 24cm.
Offprint from Revue alpine, nov. 1905.

COOLIDGE, William Augustus Brevoort and
DUHAMEL, Henry
Le Col de la Leisse et les Quecées de Tignes.
Lyon: Imp. Geneste, 1905. 13p., 1 plate, illus.
24cm.

COOLIDGE, William Augustus Brevoort
Le Col Lombard et les passages avoisinants dans
l'histoire. Lyon, 1913. 10p. 24cm.
Offprint from Revue alpine, mars 1913.

COOLIDGE, William Augustus Brevoort
Le "Col Major" et le Col du Géant. Lyon, 1913.
24p. 25cm.
Offprint from Revue alpine, juillet 1913.

COOLIDGE, William Augustus Brevoort
Il Colle Clapier nella storia. Torino, 1911.
7p. 25cm.
Offprint from Rivista del Club Alpino Italiano,
v.30, n.6, 1911.

COOLIDGE, William Augustus Brevoort
Il Colle di San Teodulo nella storia. Torino,
1911. 11p. 25cm.
Offprint from Rivista del Club Alpino Italiano,
v.30, n.10, 1911.

COOLIDGE, William Augustus Brevoort
I Colli di Fenêtre e di Crête Sèche nella storia.
Torino, 1914. 7p. 25cm.
Offprint from Rivista del Club Alpino Italiano,
v.32, n.12, 1913.

COOLIDGE, William Augustus Brevoort
Les colonies vallaisannes de l'Oberland bernois.
[Berne?], [1906]. 15p. 23cm.
Offprint from Blätter für bernische Geschichte,
1906.

COOLIDGE, William Augustus Brevoort
Les Cols de la Chambre et de la Montée du Fond.
Lyon, 1911. 7p. 24cm.
Offprint from Revue alpine, juin 1911.

COOLIDGE, William Augustus Brevoort
Dix jours dans le Valgodemar et le Val Champoléon.
Grenoble: Imp. Allier, [1886?]. 24p. 24cm.

COOLIDGE, William Augustus Brevoort
Entre Arc et Stura. Lyon, 1908. 38p. 24cm.
Offprint from Revue alpine nov.-déc. 1908.

COOLIDGE, William Augustus Brevoort
Entre Isère et Doire. Lyon, 1912. 42p. 24cm.
Offprint from Revue alpine, juin, juillet et août
1912.

COOLIDGE, William Augustus Brevoort
Entre Valloire et Briançonnais. Grenoble, 1914.
46p. 24cm.
Offprint from Revue des Alpes dauphinoises, t.16,
1913.

COOLIDGE, William Augustus Brevoort
Les grands sommets des Alpes de la Tarantaise dans
l'histoire. Lyon, 1911. 15p. 24cm.
Offprint from Revue alpine, avril 1911.

COOLIDGE, William Augustus Brevoort
Il gruppo del Gran Paradiso... Torino, 1909.
72p., illus. 25cm.
Offprint from Bollettino del C.A.I. v.39, n.72,
1908.

COOLIDGE, William Augustus Brevoort
Guide du Haut-Dauphiné, par W.A.B. Coolidge,
H. Duhamel, F. Perrin. Grenoble: A. Gratier,
1887. lix, 442p., maps. 16cm.

- - Supplement. Grenoble: Imprimerie Breynat, 1890.

COOLIDGE, William Augustus Brevoort
[Guide du Haut-Dauphiné]. Das Hochgebirge des
Dauphiné, von W.A.B. Coolidge, H. Duhamel und F.
Perrin. 4. durchgesehene und 1. autorisierte
deutsche Ausg.; hrsg. von Österreichischen Alpenklub. Wien: Österreichischer Alpenklub, 1913.
351p. 17cm. (Alpenklub-Ausgabe, 1)

COOLIDGE, William Augustus Brevoort
Guide to Switzerland; with cycling supplement by
Chas. L. Freeston. Black, 1901. xxx, 245p.,
plates, maps, plans. 18cm. (Black's guide books)

COOLIDGE, William Augustus Brevoort
La Haute-Engadine et le Bregaglia à travers les
siècles: histoire et bibliographie. Zurich:
Orel Füssli, 1894. 67p., illus. 30cm.
Offprint from Lorria, A. and Martel, E.A. Le
Massif de la Bernina. 1894.

COOLIDGE, William Augustus Brevoort
BALL, John
Hints and notes practical and scientific for
travellers in the Alps, being a revision of the
general Introduction to the 'Alpine guide'. New
ed. prepared on behalf of the Alpine Club by
W.A.B. Coolidge. Longmans, Green, 1899. clxivp.
bibl. 19cm. (Alpine guide)

COOLIDGE, William Augustus Brevoort
History of the Swiss Confederation, with appen-
dices on Tell and Winkelried: a sketch.
[London], 1887. 84p. 19cm.
Reprinted from the Encyclopaedia Britannica.

COOLIDGE, William Augustus Brevoort
Johann Madutz, 1800-1861: ein Pionier der
Schweizer Alpen: eine biographische Skizze.
Bern: G. Grunau, 1917. 50p. 24cm.

COOLIDGE, William Augustus Brevoort
Josias Simler et les origines de l'alpinisme
jusqu'en 1600. Grenoble: Imprimerie Allier, 1904.
1v. (various pagings), plates, illus., map. 28cm.

COOLIDGE, William Augustus Brevoort and CONWAY,
William Martin, Baron Conway
The Lepontine Alps, by William Martin Conway and
W.A.B. Coolidge. Fisher Unwin, 1892. xix, 106p.
14cm. (Conway and Coolidge's climbers' guides, 3)

COOLIDGE, William Augustus Brevoort
A list of the writings (not being reviews of books)
dating from 1868 to 1912 and relating to the Alps
or Switzerland, of W.A.B. Coolidge. [Oxford]:
The Author, 1912. 37p. 21cm.
Unbound photocopy.

COOLIDGE, William Augustus Brevoort
Le massif de Bellecote. Paris, 1905. 19p.,
plates, illus., map. 23cm.
Offprint from La Montagne, v.1, 20 juillet 1905.

COOLIDGE, William Augustus Brevoort
LORRIA, August and MARTEL, Édouard Alfred
Le massif de la Bernina, par August Lorria et
É.A. Martel; avec la collaboration de W.A.B.
Coolidge et J. Caviezel. Zurich: Orell Füssli,
1894. 163p., 50 plates, illus., map, bibl.
33 x 42cm. (Les grandes Alpes)

COOLIDGE, William Augustus Brevoort
Le "Mont Alban". Lyon, 1911. 6p. 25cm.
Offprint from Revue alpine, fév. 1911.

COOLIDGE, William Augustus Brevoort
Le "Mont Coupeline". Lyon, 1903. 8p. 25cm.
Offprint from Revue alpine, no.7, 1903.

YELD, George and COOLIDGE, William Augustus
Brevoort
The mountains of Cogne. Fisher Unwin, 1893.
xvi, 176p., 1 fold col. plate, map (in pocket).
14cm. (Conway and Coolidge's climbers' guides, 7)

COOLIDGE, William Augustus Brevoort
Les origines du Grand Combin et du Mont Collon et
la légende de la "Crete à Collon". Aoste, 1913.
16p. 25cm.
Offprint from Bulletin de la Société de la flore
valdôtaine, no.9.

COOLIDGE, William Augustus Brevoort
Il Passo di Pagarì nella storia. Torino, 1913.
4p. 25cm.
Offprint from Rivista del Club Alpino, v.32, n.5,
1913.

COOLIDGE, William Augustus Brevoort
Die Petronella-Kapelle in Grindelwald. Grindelwald: J. Jakober-Peter, 1911. vii, 31p., plates,
illus., maps. 23cm.

COOLIDGE, William Augustus Brevoort
The range of the Tödi. Fisher Unwin, 1894. xxxi, 167p. 14cm. (Conway and Coolidge's climbers' guides, 8)

COOLIDGE, William Augustus Brevoort. La région du Chambeyron.
CLUB ALPIN FRANÇAIS. Section de Barcelonnette
Guide de l'alpiniste dans la Vallée de l'Ubaye; suivi de La région du Chambeyron, par W.A.B. Coolidge; édité par la Section de Barcelonnette à l'occasion du Congrès du C.A.F. en 1898. Barcelonnette: La Section, 1898. 120p., plates, illus. 19cm.

COOLIDGE, William Augustus Brevoort
A run through the Dolomites in 1876. York: B. Johnson, 1902. 14p. 23cm.
Offprint from Yorkshire Ramblers' Club, journal 4, 1902.

COOLIDGE, William Augustus Brevoort
Souvenirs de mon voyage en 1879 à travers les Alpes Maritimes. Nice, 1904. 39p. 24cm.
Offprint from Club Alpin Français. Section des Alpes Maritimes, bulletin, 24.

COOLIDGE, William Augustus Brevoort
Swiss travel and Swiss guide-books. Longmans, Green, 1889. xi, 336p., bibl. 20cm.

COOLIDGE, William Augustus Brevoort
Le tour de l'Oisans. Grenoble, 1887. 25p. 24cm.
Offprint from Annuaire des touristes du Dauphiné, 1886.

COOLIDGE, William Augustus Brevoort
Die Ueberschreitung des Berner Hochgebirges im Jahre 1712. Bern, 1913. 8p. 24cm.
Offprint from Blätter für bernische Geschichte, Kunst und Altertumskunde, Bd.9, 1913.

COOLIDGE, William Augustus Brevoort
BALL, John
The western Alps. New ed., reconstructed and revised on behalf of the Alpine Club by W.A.B. Coolidge. Longmans, Green, 1898. li, 612p., fold. col. plates, illus., maps. 19cm. (Alpine guide, pt.1)

COOLIDGE, William Augustus Brevoort
CLARK, Ronald William
An eccentric in the Alps: the story of the Rev. W.A.B. Coolidge the great Victorian mountaineer. Museum Press, 1959. 224p., plates, illus. 24cm.

COOLIDGE, William Augustus Brevoort
GODEFROY, René
W.A.B. Coolidge, 1850-1926. Chambéry: Dardel, 1926. 24p., plates, ports. 19cm.
Offprint from Revue alpine, 3e trimestre, 1926.

COOPER, Alfred Heaton
PALMER, William T
The English Lakes; painted by A. Heaton Cooper; described by Wm. T. Palmer. Black, 1905. ix, 230p., 75 col. plates, illus., map. 23cm.

- - 2nd ed. 1908.

COOPER, Alfred Heaton
The Norwegian fjords. Black, 1907. 178p., col. illus. 21cm.

COOPER, Alfred Heaton
MACBRIDE, Mackenzie
Wild Lakeland; painted by A. Heaton Cooper; described by Mackenzie MacBride. Black, 1922. viii, 229p., 32 col. plates, map. 22cm.

COOPER, C J Astley
Great Gable, Borrowdale, Buttermere, by C.J. Astley Cooper, E. Wood-Johnson and L.H. Pollitt; with illustrations by W. Heaton Cooper. Manchester: Fell & Rock Climbing Club, 1937. 153p., 1 plate, illus. 16cm. (Climbing guides to the English Lake District, [2nd ser.], 3)

COOPER, C J Astley
Great Gable, Geeen Gable, Kirkfell, Yewbarrow, Buckbarrow, by C.J. Astley Cooper, W. Peascod & A.P. Rossiter; with illustrations by W. Heaton Cooper. Manchester: Fell & Rock Climbing Club, 1948. 129p., 1 plate, illus. 16cm. (Rock-climbing guides to the English Lake District, 2nd [i.e. 3rd] ser., 1)

COOPER, Courtney Ryley
High country: the Rockies yesterday and to-day. Boston: Little, Brown, 1926. x, 294p., plates, illus. 22cm.

COOPER, Edward H
The monk wins. Duckworth, 1900. 351p. 20cm.

COOPER, Edward H
Wyemarke and the mountain-fairies; illustrated by "Wyemarke" and G.P. Jacomb-Hood. Duckworth, 1900. 84p., plates, illus. 23cm.

COOPER, James Fenimore
Excursions in Switzerland. Bentley, 1836. 2v. 20cm.

- - Another issue. Paris: A. & W. Galignani, 1836.
- - New ed. 1836. 2v. in 1.

COOPER, James Fenimore
[Excursions in Switzerland]. Excursions d'une famille américaine en Suisse; traduit par A.J.B. Defauconpret. Bruxelles: Wahlen, 1837. x, 259p. 15cm.

COOPER, James Fenimore
A residence in France; with an excursion up the Rhine, and a second visit to Switzerland. R Bentley, 1836. 2v. 20cm.

COOPER, T T
The Mishmee hills: an account of a journey made in an attempt to penetrate Thibet from Assam to open new routes for commerce. King, 1873. viii, 270p., plates (1 fold, some col.), illus., map, 21cm.

COOPER, William Heaton
The hills of Lakeland. 2nd ed. Warne, 1946. xviii, 126p., 52 plates (some col.), illus., maps. 25cm.

COPELAND, Fanny S
Beautiful mountains: in the Jugoslav Alps; illustrated by Edo Deržaj. Split: Jugoslav Bureau, [1934]. 120p., illus. 26cm.

COPELAND, Fanny S and DEBELAKOUA, M M
A short guide to the Slovene Alps (Jugoslavia) for British and American tourists. Ljubljana: Kleinmayr & Bamberg,1936. 128p., plates (2 fold.), illus., map. 16cm.

COPPIER, André Charles
Au Lac d'Annecy, aquarelles, dessins au roseau et au brou de noix et texte par André-Charles Coppier. Chambéry: Dardel, 1923. 119p., illus. (some col.). 33cm.

COPPIER, André Charles
De Tarantaise en Maurienne, aquarelles, dessins au brou de noix et au roseau, peintures, eau-forte et texte de André-Charles Coppier. Chambéry: Dardel, 1931. 111p., illus. (some col.). 33cm.

COPPIER, André Charles
Les portraits du Mont-Blanc, aquarelles, pastels, dessins au roseau et brou de noix et texte par André-Charles Coppier. Chambéry: Dardel, 1924. 128p., col. plates, illus. (some col.). 34cm.

COPPING, Harold
Canadian pictures: thirty-six plates in colour ... from original drawings by Harold Copping; with descriptive letterpress by E.P. Weaver. Religious Tract Society, 1912. 1v. (chiefly col. illus.). 41cm.

COQUOZ, Louis
Histoire et description de Salvan-Fins-Hauts, avec
petite notice sur Trient. Lausanne: Imprimerie
C. Pache, 1899. 271p. 19cm.

CANETTA, Nemo and CORBELLINI, Giancarlo
Valmalenco: itinerari storici etnografici
naturalistici, Alta Via della Valmalenco, itinerari
sci-escursionistici. Bologna: Tamari, 1976.
278p., 1 fold. col. plate, illus., map (in pocket),
bibl. 16cm. (Guide storiche etnografiche
naturalistiche, 1)

CORBETT, Edmund Victor
Great true mountain stories; selected and introduced
by Edmund V. Corbett. Arco, 1957. ix, 227p.
23cm.

CORBETT, John Rooke
The northern Highlands. Edinburgh: Scottish
Mountaineering Club, 1932. 87p., plates (some
fold., some col.), illus., maps. 22cm.
(Scottish Mountaineering Club guides)

- - 2nd ed. rev., edited by W.N. Ling and John Rooke
Corbett. 1936.

RÉVIL, Joseph and CORCELLE, Joseph
La Savoie: guide du touriste, du naturaliste et
de l'archéologue. Paris: Masson, [18--]. vi,
280p., illus., maps. 19cm.

CORDEIRO, F   J   B
The barometrical determination of heights: a
practical method of barometrical levelling and
hypsometry for surveyors and mountain climbers.
New York: Spon & Chamberlain; London: Spon, 1898.
28p. 18cm.

CORDILLERA BLANCA SEATTLE EXPEDITION, 1964
Ascent of Nevado Huascaran, [by] Hans A. Zogg
[and others]. Seattle: The Expedition, 1964.
55p., illus., map. 25cm.

COREAN ALPINE CLUB
See
KOREAN ALPINE CLUB

CORIN, Joseph
Escalades et escapades dans les Alpes, par un
magistrat, un professeur et un vagabond. Liège:
C. Desoer, 1904. 129p., illus. 23cm.

CORNAZ-VULLIET, C
En pays fribourgeois: manuel du voyageur.
Fribourg: Librarie de l'Université [1892?].
352p., 2 fold. plates, illus., plan, bibl. 20cm.
(La Suisse Romande en zig-zag, le ptie., 3e
section)

CORNWALL, Nellie
Hallvard Halvorsen; or, The avalanche: a story
of the Fjeld fjord and Fos. Partridge, [1888].
316p., illus. 20cm.

CORONA, Giuseppe
Aria di monti. Roma: Capaccini e Ripamonti, 1880.
ii, 211p. 14cm.

CORONA, Giuseppe
Manuel de l'alpiniste et de l'excursionniste dans
la Vallée d'Aoste... Rome: Imprimerie Romaine,
1880-81. 224p., illus. 16cm.

CORONA, Giuseppe
Mont Blanc or Simplon? Rome, 1880. 28p. 24cm.
Offprint from Minerva, March 1880.

CORONA, Giuseppe
Picchi e burroni: escursioni nelle Alpi. Torino:
Bocca, 1876. 348p. 20cm.

CORREVON, Henry and ROBERT, Philippe
La flore alpine. Genève: Atar, [1909]. 440p.,
col. illus. 22cm.

CORREVON, Henry and ROBERT, Philippe
[La flore alpine]. The alpine flora; translated
... and enlarged under the author's sanction, by
E.W. Clayforth. Geneva: Atar, [1911?]. 436p.,
1 plate, col. illus., port. 22cm.

- - Another issue. Methuen, [1912].

CORREVON, Henry
Flore coloriée de poche à l'usage du touriste
dans les montagnes ...; dessins par A. Jobin.
Paris: Klincksieck, [1894]. xv, 163p., col.
plates, illus. 17cm. (Bibliothèque de poche du
naturaliste, 2)

CORREVON, Henry
Par monts et vaux; avec nombreuses illustrations
de Mlle Adèle Correvon. Genève: A. Jullien,
1904. xiv, 232p., illus. 24cm.

CORREVON, Henry
Les plantes des Alpes. Genève: Imprimerie J.
Carey, 1885. 264p. 20cm.

CORREVON, Henry
Les plantes des montagnes et des rochers: leur
acclimation et leur culture dans les jardins.
Genève: L'Auteur, 1914. xx, 491p., illus. 20cm.

CORTÈS, Louis
L'Oisans: recherches historiques, tourisme;
préface de Henri Ferrand. Grenoble: Allier,
1926. 368p., 2 fold. plates, geneal. table,
plan. 26cm.

Cortina: official list of hotel & pension terms,
information regarding reduced railway fares ...
Cortina: [N.pub.], [1929]. [10p.], maps. 20cm.

CORYAT, Thomas
Coryat's crudities, hastily gobled up in five
months travells in France, Savoy, Italy, Rhetia
commonly called the Grisons country, Helvetia
alias Switzerland, some parts of High Germany
and the Netherlands ... Glasgow: James MacLehose,
1905. 2v., plates (some fold.), illus., facsms.
23cm.

HAYDEN, Sir Henry Hubert and COSSON, César
Sport and travel in the highlands of Tibet; with
an introduction by Sir Francis Younghusband.
R. Cobden-Sanderson, 1927. xvi, 262p., plates
(1 fold. col.), illus., map (in pocket). 23cm.

COSTE, Jean
Âme d'alpiniste: pensées extraites de la correspondance et des écrits de Jean Coste; préface de
Paul Helbronner. Grenoble: Arthaud, 1929.
203p., port. 20cm.

COSTE, Jean
Dernières campagnes; notes et impressions d'alpinisme. Gap: V. Vollaire, 1928. 219p., plates,
illus. 20cm.

COSTE, Jean
Mes quatre premières années de montagne; préface
de Paul Helbronner. Paris: G. Ficker, 1927.
xiii, 172p., plates, illus. 20cm.

COSTELLO, Dudley
Piedmont and Italy from the Alps to the Tiber;
illustrated in a series of views taken on the
spot; with a descriptive and historical narrative
by Dudley Costello. J.S. Virtue, 1861. 2v.,
plates, illus. 28cm.

COSTELLO, Louisa Stuart
Béarn and the Pyrenees: a legendary tour to the
country of Henri Quatre. R. Bentley, 1844. 2v.,
plates, illus. 23cm.

COSTELLO, Louisa Stuart
The falls, lakes and mountains of North Wales;
with illustrations by Thomas and Edward
Gilks, from original sketches by D.H. McKewan.
Longman, Brown, Green, & Longmans, 1845. xviii,
221p., plates, illus., fold map. 19cm.

COSTELLO, Louisa Stuart
Venice and the Venetians, with a glance at the
Vaudois and the Tyrol. New ed. J. & D.A. Darling,
1851. vi, 453p., plates, illus. 22cm.

COTESWORTH, W
Idle days in the Vorarlberg and its neighbourhood,
[by W. Cotesworth]. Printed at the Free School-
Press, 1887. 96p., plates, illus. 17cm.

COTTA, Bernhard von
Geologische Briefe aus den Alpen. Leipzig:
Weigel, 1850. 328p., plates (chiefly col.),
illus., bibl. 23cm.

COTTA, Bernhard von
Rocks classified and described: a treatise on
lithology. English ed. by Philip Henry Lawrence
with English, German and French synonyms; revised
by the author. Longmans, Green. 1866. xii,
425p. 21cm.
Translation of 3rd ed.

The cottages of the Alps; or Life and manners in
Switzerland, by a lady [i.e. Anna C. Johnson].
Sampson Low, 1860. 2v., plates, illus. 21cm.

COUCH, Stata B
In the shadow of the peaks: a novel. Greening,
1909. 320p., plates, illus. 20cm.

COULTER, Henry and MCLANE, Merrill F
Mountain climbing guide to the Grand Tetons.
Hanover (N.H.): Dartmouth Mountaineering Club,
1947. 67p., 1 fold. plate, illus., map. 18cm.

COULTER, John M
New manual of botany of the central Rocky
Mountains (vascular plants); revised by Aven
Nelson. New York: American Book Co., 1909.
646p. 22cm.

COUPÉ, Serge
Escalades du Vercors et de la Chartreuse. Paris:
Fédération Française de la Montagne, 1963. 167p.,
illus., maps. 17cm.

COUPÉ, Serge
Escalades en Chartreuse et Vercors. [Paris]:
Arthaud, 1972-73. 2v. in 1. (481p.), illus., maps.
17cm.

Course à l'éboulement du Glacier de Gétroz et au Lac
de Mauvoisin, au fond de la Vallée de Bagnes, 16
mai 1818, [par Philippe S. Bridel]. Vevey:
Loertscher, [1818]. 16p., 1 fold. plate, illus.
20cm.

Course de Bale à Vienne par les vallées du Jura, [par
Philippe S. Bridel]. Bale: Ch. Aug. Serini, 1789.
256p., plates, map. 17cm.

Courses alpestres en Suisse et en Savoie. Genève,
[1852]. iv. (various pagings). 22cm.
Six articles by J. Jullien, C. Peschier, Albert
Smith and L. Gentin.
Offprint from Nouvelle bibliothèque littéraire
1851-52.

COURTEN, Philippa de
Un jour d'autonne. Winterthur, 1946. 241-244p.,
illus. 25cm.
Offprint from Nos montagnes, 25. Jahrgang, Nr.257,
Nov. 1946.

COURTEN, Philippa de
GOS, Charles
Philippa de Courten, 1926-1946: an obituary, by
Charles Gos.
(In Almanach du Valais, 49e année, 1949, p.52-53,
illus.)

COURTEN, Philippa de
GOS, Charles
Tour était si beau là-haut ...: [la silhouette de
Philippa de Courten].
(In Bulletin paroissial d'Aigle, 29e année, no.2,
avril 1948. p.15-18, illus.)

COURTHION, L
Champéry, summer and winter resort, text by L.
Courthion; photographic views from Jullien Frères,
Geneva. Neuchatel: Delachaux & Niestlé, [19--].
32p., illus., map. 12 x 17cm.

COURVOISIER, Emile
SCHWEIZER ALPEN-CLUB
Les cabanes du Club Alpin Suisse en décembre 1895,
par Emile Courvoisier. Berne: Schmid, Francke,
1896. 40p., 1 fold. col. plate, map. 22cm.
Annexe to l'Annuaire du S.A.C., 31e année.

COURVOISIER, Emile
SCHWEIZER ALPEN-CLUB
Les cabanes du Club Suisse en 1899, par Emile
Courvoisier. Berne: Schmid, Francke, 1899. 19p.
23cm.
Annexe to l'Annuaire du S.A.C., 34e année.

COUTAGNE, Aimé
La Muse à la montagne: petite anthologie poétique
à l'usage des alpinistes. Lyon: G. Neveu, 1925.
145p. 21cm.

COUTAGNE, Aimé
Les trophées alpestres. Lyon: G. Neveu, 1925.
156p. 21cm.

COUTTET, Alfred
L'enchantement du ski, [par] Alfred Couttet,
Arnold Lunn, Emil Petersen; introduction de Henry
Cuénot ... Paris: Alpina, 1930. 159p., col.
plates, illus. 25cm.

COUTTET, Alfred and FRISON-ROCHE, Roger
63 itinéraires à ski dans la région de Chamonix
et le massif du Mont Blanc. Chamonix: J. Landru,
[19--]. 48p. 16cm.

COUTTET, Armand
DIDIER, Richard
Ailes de mouches et tricounis: récits d'Armand
Couttet. Paris: J. Vitiano, 1946. 241p., illus.,
20cm. (Sport, amour, idéal)

COUTTET, Joseph Marie
Chamonix, le Mont-Blanc, Courmayeur et le Grand-
Saint-Bernard: court itinéraire descriptif...
Genève: J.-G. Fick, 1851. 47p. 15cm.

COUZY, Jean
SÉGOGNE, Henry de
Les alpinistes célèbres; publié sous la direction
de Henry de Ségogne et Jean Couzy. Paris: L.
Mazenod, 1956. 416p., plates, illus. 30cm. (La
galerie des hommes célèbres, 9)

COVERLEY-PRICE, Victor
An artist among mountains; with ... illustrations
from drawings by the author. Hale, 1957. 231p.,
plates, illus. 23cm.

BOURDILLON, Jennifer and COVERLEY-PRICE, Victor
The Sherpas of Nepal. Oxford University Press,
[1959]. 32p., illus. 21cm. (People of the
world)

COVINO, Andrea
De Turin à Chambéry; ou, Les vallées de la Dora
Riparia et de l'Arc, et le tunnel des Alpes
cottiennes; traduction de Noemi Gachet. Turin:
L. Beuf, 1871. 152p., plates (some fold., 1
col.), illus., maps. 20cm.

COWLEY, Bill
Lyke Wake Walk: forty miles across the north
Yorkshire moors, described by Bill Cowley.
Clapham (Yorks.): Dalesman, 1968. 88p., illus.,
maps. 21cm. (Dalesman paperbacks)

COX, Ross
The Columbia river; or Scenes and adventures
during a residence of six years on the western
side of the Rocky Mountains among various tribes
of Indians hitherto unknown; together with a
journey across the American continent. 3rd ed.
Colburn and Bentley, 1832. 2v. 23cm.

COXE, Henry
The traveller's guide in Switzerland, being a
complete picture of that interesting country ...
and a narrative of the various attempts to ascend
Mont Blanc. Printed for Sherwood, Neely and
Jones, 1816. xxxvi, 210p. 15cm.

COXE, William
STILLINGFLEET, Benjamin
Literary life and select works of Benjamin
Stillingfleet ...; [edited by W. Coxe]. Longman,
Hurst, Rees, Orme and Brown, 1811. 3v. in 1,
plates, illus. 22cm.

COXE, William
Sketches of the natural, civil, and political
state of Swisserland, in a series of letters to
William Melmoth. J. Dodsley, 1779. viii, 533p.
22cm.

- - 2nd ed. 1780.

COXE, William
[Sketches of the natural, civil, and political
state of Swisserland ...]. Lettres de M. William
Coxe à M. W. Melmoth, sur l'état politique, civil
et naturel de la Suisse ...; augmentées des Observations faites ... par le traducteur [L. Ramond].
Paris: Belin, 1781. 2v. 21cm.

- - Another issue. 1782.
- - Another issue. 1787.

COXE, William
[Sketches of the natural, civil, and political
state of Swisserland ...]. Briefe über den
naturlichen, bügerlichen und politischen Züstand
der Schweiz, von Wilhelm Coxe an Wilhelm Melmoth.
Zürich: Orell, Gessner Füssli, 1781-91. 2v. 19cm.

COXE, William
La Svizzera secondo il Coxe, l'Ebel ed altri piu
moderni viaggiatori, si aggiumgono alcuni cenni
sulla storia, i monumenti, le leggi ed i costumi.
Milano: Vallardi, [ca 1820]. 230, 88p., plates,
illus. 13cm.
Cover title: Itinerario postale; o, Manuale della
Svizzera...

COXE, William
Travels in Switzerland, in a series of letters to
William Melmoth. T. Cadell, 1789. 3v., plates,
illus., maps. 22cm.

- - 3rd ed. 1794.
- - 3rd ed., with maps and views from drawings by
J. Smith. Printed for J. Edwards, 1796.

COXE, William
Travels in Switzerland, and in the country of the
Grisons, in a series of letters to William Melmoth.
4th ed. T. Cadell & W. Davies, 1801. 3v., plates
(some fold.), illus., map. 23cm.
Library's copy of v.1. lacks map.

COXE, William
Travels in Switzerland, and in the country of the
Grisons, in a series of letters to William Melmoth
...; to which are added the notes and observations
of Mr. Ramond, translated from the French. New
ed... with ... six views drawn by Birmann. Basil:
J. Decker, 1802. 3v., 6 plates, illus., map, bibl.
24cm. Library's copy lacks map.
COXE, William
[Travels in Switzerland ...]. Voyage en Suisse...
Paris: Letellier, 1790. 3v., fold. plates, illus.,
maps. 20cm.

- - Another issue. Lausanne: Grasset, 1790.

COXHEAD, Elizabeth
June in Skye: a novel. Cassel, 1938. 292p. 20cm.

COXHEAD, Elizabeth
One green bottle. Faber, 1951. 281p. 19cm.

CRAIG, Robert W
Storm and sorrow in the high Pamirs. Seattle:
The Mountaineers, 1977. xiii, 171p., col. plates,
illus., maps. 21cm.

CRAM, Alan Geoffrey
Pillar group; illustrated by W. Heaton Cooper.
Stockport: Fell & Rock Climbing Club, 1968.
148p., 1 col. plate, illus., map (on lining
papers). 16cm. (Climbing guides to the English
Lake District, [4th ser.], 5)

CRAM, Alan Geoffrey
Rock climbing in the Lake District: an illustrated
guide to selected climbs in the Lake District [by]
Geoff Cram, Chris Eilbeck, Ian Roper. Constable,
1975. xiii, 250p., illus., maps (on lining
papers). 18cm.

WICKHAM, Henry L   and CRAMER, J   A
A dissertation on the passage of Hannibal over
the Alps, by a member of the University of Oxford.
Oxford: Printed by W. Baxter for J. Parker, 1820.
xxii, 183p., plates (1 fold. col.), maps. 22cm.

- - 2nd ed., by Henry L. Wickham and J.A. Cramer.
Whittaker, 1828.

CRANE, Jane Miriam
HAVERGAL, Frances Ridley
Swiss letters and alpine poems, by the late Frances
Ridley Havergal; edited by her sister, J. Miriam
Crane. J. Nisbet, 1882. vii, 356p., plates,
illus. 21cm.

CRANFIELD, Ingrid
The challengers: British & Commonwealth adventure
since 1945. Weidenfeld and Nicolson, 1976.
xvii, 298p., plates, illus. 23cm.

CRANZ, H
Bettelwurf- und Speckkarspitze. Stuttgart:
Deutsche Verlags-Anstalt, 1906. 104p., plates,
illus., map. 18cm. (Alpine Gipfelführer, 6)

CRAVEN, Steven A
A brief review of Himalayan speleology. [Knares-
borough], 1971. 281-283p. 23cm.
Offprint from J. Craven Pothole Club, 4(5), 1971.

CRAVEN, Steven A
Some medical aspects of caving accidents, illus-
trated by a case history [of J. Miller].
[London], [1973?]. 94-99p., illus. 25cm.
Offprint from Injury: the British Journal of
accident surgery, v.5, no.2, [1973].

CRAWFORD, E   May
By the equator's snowy peak; a record of medical
missionary work and travel in British East Africa;
with a preface by the Bishop of Mombasa; and a
foreword by Eugene Stock. Church Missionary
Society, 1913. 176p., plates, illus., map. 23cm.

CRAWFORD, Robert
Across the pampas and the Andes. Longmans, Green,
1884. xxiii, 344p., plates (1 fold. col.),
illus., map. 20cm.

EVE, A   S   and CREASEY, C   H
Life and work of John Tyndall, by A.S. Eve and
C.H. Creasey, with a chapter on Tyndall as a
mountaineer by Lord Schuster... Macmillan, 1945.
xxxii, 404p., plates, illus. 25cm.

CRÉPIN, François
DUBOIS, Albert
Croquis alpins: promenades en Suisse et au pays
des Dolomites; avec une notice sur la flore alpestre par François Crépin. Mons: Byr & Loret,
1883. 526p. 25cm.

GAULIS, Louis and CREUX, René
Swiss hotel pioneers. Paudex: Éditions de
Fontainemore, Swiss National Tourist Office, 1976.
223p., illus., bibl. 25cm.

CREUX, René
CHAPPAZ, Maurice
Verdures de la nuit; lithographies de René Creux.
Lausanne: H.-L. Mermod, 1945. 41p., illus. 29cm.

CREW, Peter
Anglesey-Gogarth: Craig Gogarth, South Stack,
Holyhead Mountain; Gogarth Upper Tier by Les
Holliwell; photography by Ken Wilson. Goring,
Reading: West Col, 1969. 107p., plates, illus.,
map. 17cm. (West Col coastal climbing guides)

CREW, Peter
SOPER, Jack
The Black Cliff: the history of rock climbing on
Clogwyn du'r Arddu, by Jack Soper, Ken Wilson
and Peter Crew; based on the original research
of Rodney Wilson; foreword by A.D.M. Cox. Kaye
& Ward, 1971. 159p., illus., bibl. 22cm.

COLLOMB, Robin Gabriel and CREW, Peter
Bregaglia West: [Sciora, Cengalo, Badile]: a
selection of popular and recommended climbs;
compiled by Robin G. Collomb and Peter Crew.
Gording, Reading: West Col, 1967. 86p., illus.,
maps, bibl. 17cm. (West Col alpine guides)

BANNER, H I and CREW, Peter
Clogwyn Du'r Arddu; with a geological note by
N.J. Soper; a natural history note by Evan
Roberts; and diagrams by R.B. Evans. Stockport:
Climbers' Club, 1963. ix, 103p., illus., maps
(on lining papers). 16cm. (Climbers' Club
guides to Wales, 6)

CREW, Peter and ROPER, Ian
Cwm Glas; with a geological note by N.J. Soper;
a natural history note by Evan Roberts;
diagrams by R.B. Evans; and photographs by K.J.
Wilson and L.R. Holliwell. 2nd ed. Stockport:
Climbers' Club, 1970. ii, 157p., illus., maps.
16cm. (Climbers' Club guides to Wales, 5)

CREW, Peter
Encyclopaedic dictionary of mountaineering.
Constable, 1968. 140p., plates, illus. 23cm.

CREW, Peter
Llanberis south; with a geological note by N.J.
Soper; a natural history note by Evan Roberts;
photographs by K. Wilson; and diagrams by R.B.
Evans. Stockport: Climbers' Club, 1966. ix,
158p., illus., maps. 16cm. (Climbers' Club
guides to Wales, 5)

CREW, Peter
Selected climbs in the Dolomites; edited by P.
Crew; diagrams by R.B. Evans. Alpine Club, 1963.
214p., illus., maps, bibl. 16cm. (Alpine [Club]
guide books; selected climbs, 3)

COLLOMB, Robin Gabriel and CREW, Peter
Selected climbs in the Mont Blanc Range. Vol.1.
From the Col de la Seigne to the Col du Géant;
translated and adapted from the Guide Vallot; and
compiled with additional material by Robin G.
Collomb and Peter Crew. Alpine Club, 1967. 241p.,
illus., maps, bibl. 16cm. (Alpine Club guide
books; selected climbs, 1)

COLLOMB, Robin Gabriel and CREW, Peter
Selected climbs in the Mont Blanc Range. Vol.2.
From the Col du Géant to the Petit Col Ferret and
Fenêtre d'Arpette; translated and adapted from
the Guide Vallot; and compiled with additional
material by Robin G. Collomb and Peter Crew.
Alpine Club, 1967. 185p., illus. 16cm. (Alpine
Club guide books; selected climbs, 1)

CREW, Peter and HARRIS, Alan
Tremadoc area: Tremadoc Rocks, Craig y Gelli and
Carreg Hylldrem. Goring, Reading: West Col, 1970.
106p., 16plates, illus., map. 17cm. (West Col
coastal climbing guides)

CREWE, Richard J
Dorset; edited by R.J. Crewe. Rev. ed. Leicester:
R.J. Crewe, 1977. xxi, 232p., illus., maps.
16cm.

CRIRIE, James
Scottish scenery; or, Sketches in verse, descriptive of scenes chiefly in the Highlands ...
accompanied with notes and illustrations; and
ornamented with engravings by W. Byrne from views
painted by G. Walker. T. Cadell jr. & W. Davies,
1803. xxxiv, 412p., 20 plates, illus. 31cm.

CROCKET, S R
Ione March. 3rd ed. Hodder & Stoughton, 1899.
xii, 419p., plates, illus. 21cm.

CROFT, Andrew
Polar exploration. 2nd ed. Black, 1947. xii,
268p., plates, illus., maps, bibl. 22cm.

CROSBY, Oscar Terry
Tibet and Turkistan: a journey through old lands
and a study in new conditions. New York, London:
Putnam, 1905. xvii, 331p., plates (1 fold. col.).
illus., map. 22cm.

CROSFIELD, George
An excursion from Warrington to the English Lakes
in 1795. Warrington, 1873. 16p. 18cm.
Offprint from the Warrington Examiner.

CROSSE, Andrew F
Round about the Carpathians. Edinburgh, London:
Blackwood, 1878. viii, 375p., 1 fold. plate,
map. 21cm.

CROUCHER, Norman
High hopes. Hodder & Stoughton, 1976. 160p.,
plates, illus. 21cm.

CROUCHER, Norman
NORMAN CROUCHER PERUVIAN ANDES EXPEDITION, 1978
Report. The Expedition, [1979]. [16p.], illus.,
bibl. 21cm.

TABOR, R W and CROWDER, D F
Routes and rocks in the Mt. Challenger Quadrangle;
drawings by Ed Hanson. Seattle: The Mountaineers,
1968. 47p., plates, illus., maps (1 fold. col.
in pocket), bibl. 19cm. (Hiker's map of the
north Cascades)

CROWLEY, Aleister
The spirit of solitude: an autohagiography, sub-
sequently re-antichristened The Confessions of
Aleister Crowley. Mandrake Press, 1929
Plates, illus. 29cm.
Library has vols. 1 and 2 only.

CROWLEY, Aleister
SYMONDS, John
The great beast: the life of Aleister Crowley.
Rider, 1951. 316p., plates, illus. 24cm.

CROZIER, Anita
Beyond the southern lakes: the explorations of
W.G. Grave; edited by Anita Crozier; foreword by
Sir Thomas Hunter. Wellington: Reed, 1950.
124p., plates, illus., map (on lining papers).
23cm.

CS. EXPEDICE DOBYVÁ HINDUKUS, 1965
Soubor 12 fotografií Viléma Heckela. Praha: The
Expedition, [1965?]. 15cm.
Twelve photographs with explanatory leaflet in
folder.

CUCHETET, Charles
Souvenirs d'une promenade en Suisse, pendant
l'année 1827; recueillis pour ses amis, par
Charles C****** [i.e. Cuchetet]. Paris: Imprimerie de E. Duverger, 1828. 247p. 22cm.

CULBERT, Dick
Alpine guide to southwestern British Columbia.
Vancouver: The Author, 1974. 441p., illus. (some
col.), bibl. 17cm.

CULBERT, Dick
A climber's guide to the Coastal Ranges of British
Columbia (International Border to Nass River).
2nd ed. Vancouver: Alpine Club of Canada, 1969.
vi, 426p., plates, (some fold.), illus., maps.
18cm.

CUMBERLAND, C   S
Sport on the Pamirs and Turkistan steppes.
Edinburgh, London: Blackwood, 1895. x, 278p.,
plates (1 fold.), illus., map. 21cm.

Cumberland, Westmorland and Furness. Blackie, 1905.
128p., col. plates, illus., maps. 18cm. (The
English counties: a series of supplementary
readers)

CUMMING, Constance F   Gordon
From the Hebrides to the Himalayas: a sketch of
eighteen months' wanderings in Western Isles
and eastern highlands. Sampson Low, Marston,
Searle and Rivington, 1876. 2v., plates, illus.
23cm.

CUMMING, Constance F   Gordon
Granite crags. Edinburgh, London: Blackwoods,
1884. ix, 384p., plates (1 fold.), illus.,
map. 22cm.

- - Cheap ed. with title: Granite crags of
California. 1901. 21cm.

CUMMING, Constance F   Gordon
In the Himalayas and on the Indian plains.
Chatto & Windus, 1884. xvi, 608p., plates,
illus. 22cm.
Originally published in abridged form as v.2 of
the Author's From the Hebrides to the Himalayas.

CUNCHE, Gabriel
La renommée de A. de Haller en France: influence
du poème Des Alpes sur la littérature descriptive
du XVIIIe siècle. Neuchatel: Delachaux &
Niestlé, [ca 1918]. 155p., bibl. 25cm.

CUNNINGHAM, Alexander
Ladak, physical, statistical and historical; with
notices of the surrounding countries. Allen, 1854.
xiv, 485p., plates (some col.), illus., map. 27cm.

CUNNINGHAM, Allan
The life of Sir David Wilkie, with his journals,
tours, and critical remarks on works of art and a
selection from his correspondence. Murray, 1843.
3v., port. 23cm.

CUNNINGHAM, Carus Dunlop
ALMER, Christian
[Führerbuch]. A facsimile of Christian Almer's
Führerbuch 1856-1894; reproduced under the super-
intendence of C.D. Cunningham and W. de W. Abney.
Sampson Low, Marston, 1896. xxxii, 261p., 1 plate,
port. 20cm.

CUNNINGHAM, Carus Dunlop and ABNEY, Sir William
de Wyveleslie
The pioneers of the Alps. Sampson Low, Marston,
Searle, & Rivington, 1887. x, 287p., plates,
illus. 34cm.

- - Large paper ed. 1887.
- - 2nd ed. 1888.

ADAMS, Sir Francis Ottiwell and CUNNINGHAM, Carus
Dunlop
The Swiss Confederation. Macmillan, 1889. xx,
289p., col. plate, map. 24cm.

CUNYNGHAME, Sir Arthur Thurlow
Travels in the eastern Caucasus, on the Caspian and
Black Seas, especially in Daghestan and on the
frontiers of Persia and Turkey, during the summer
of 1871. Murray, 1872. xvi, 367p., plates (some
fold.), illus., maps. 23cm.

Curiosities of modern travel: a year-book of adventure. D. Bogue, 1847. vii, 312p., plates, illus.
18cm.

The curious traveller, being a choice collection of
very remarkable histories, voyages, travels, &c,
digested into familiar letters and conversations...
J. Rowland, 1742. 388p., 7 plates, illus. 21cm.

CURRAN, Mick
Antrim coast rockclimbs: interim guide; edited by
Mick Curran; additional information by Calvin
Torrans. Dublin: Federation of Mountaineering
Clubs of Ireland, 1975. 32p., maps. 16cm.
(F.M.C.I. guides)

Cursory notes of a nine weeks' tour, [by William
Dodd?]. Newcastle-upon-Tyne: J. Hernaman, 1834.
140p. 23cm.

CURZON, George Nathaniel, Marquess Curzon
Leaves from a Viceroy's note-book and other
papers, by the Marquess Curzon of Kedleston;
edited by F.W. Pember, Ian Malcolm. Macmillan,
1926. x, 414p., plates, illus. 24cm.

CURZON, George Nathaniel, Marquess Curzon
The Pamirs and the source of the Oxus. Royal
Geographical Society, 1896 (1899 reprint). 83p.,
1 fold. col. plate, illus., map. 26cm.

CUTTING, Suydam
The fire ox and other years. Collins, 1947.
xix, 393p., plates (some col.), illus., maps.
25cm.

CYSARZ, Herbert
Berge über uns: ein kleines Alpenbuch. München:
Müller, 1935. 85p. 19cm.

CYSAT, Johann Leopold
Bes chreibung dess Beruhmsten Lucerner-oder
4. Waldstatten Sees/und dessen Furtrefflichen
Qualiteten und Sonderbaaren Engenschafften...
Lucern: Bey David Hautten, 1661. 272p., fold.
plates, illus. 20cm.

CZANT, Herman
Alpinismus: Massentouristik, Massenskilauf,
Wintersport, Militäralpinistik und die 9700
Kilometer Gebirgsfronten im Weltkrieg. Berlin:
Verlag für Kulturpolitik, 1926. 336p., illus.,
maps. 26cm.

D., J.
See
DORNFORD, Joseph

D. & D., Messieurs
See
LUC, Jean André and DENTAND, Pierre Gédéon

DÄNDLIKER, Karl
A short history of Switzerland; translated by
E. Salisbury. Swan Sonnenschein, 1899. xvi,
322p., maps. 23cm.

DAHL, Eilif
On the vascular plants of eastern Svalbard,
chiefly based on material brought home from the
"Heimland" Expedition 1936. Oslo: J. Dybwad,
1937. 50p., maps, bibl. 27cm. (Norges Svalbard-
og Ishavs-Undersøkelser. Skrifter om Svalbard og
Ishavet, 75)

DAINELLI, Giotto
Il mio viaggio nel Tibet occidentale. Milano:
Mondadori, 1932. xvi, 403p., plates, illus.
27cm.

DAINELLI, Giotto
[Il mio viaggio nel Tibet occidentale.].
Buddhists and glaciers of western Tibet. Kegan
Paul, Trench, Trubner, 1933. xiii, 304p., plates,
illus., map. 26cm.

DAINELLI, Giotto
Mondo alpino: numero di primavera de "L'Illustrazione italiana". Milano: Treves, 1930.
130p., 2 col. plates, illus. 40cm.
Supplement to L'Illustrazione italiana, n.16,
20 aprile 1930.

DAINELLI, Giotto
SPEDIZIONE ITALIANA DE FILIPPI, 1913-14
[Relazioni scientifiche della] Spedizione Italiana
De Filippi, nell'Himàlaia, Caracorùm e Turchestàn
Cinese (1913-1914). Serie 2. Resultati geologici
e geografici; ... sotto la direzione di Giotto
Dainelli. Bologna: Zanichelli, 1922-25. 12v.,
plates, illus., maps.
Vol.3. Studi sul glaciale, [da] Giotto Dainelli.
1922. 2v. - v.8. Le condizioni delle genti, [da]
Giotto Dainelli. 1924. - v.9.I tipi umani, [da]
R. Biasutti e G. Dainelli. 1925.

DAKIN, Susanna Bryant
The published writings of Francis Peloubet
Farquhar; together with an introduction to FPF by
Susanna Bryant Dakin. San Francisco: [K.K.
Bechtel], 1954. vii, 17p. 27cm.

DALLA TORRE, Karl Wilhelm von
Die Alpenflora der österreichischen Alpenländer,
Südbaierns und der Schweiz; bearb. von K.W. v.
Dalla Torre. München: J. Lindauer, 1899. xvi,
271p. 21cm.

DALLA TORRE, Karl Wilhelm von
Tirol, Vorarlberg und Liechtenstein. Berlin:
W. Junk, 1913. xxiv, 486p., map. 17cm. (Junk's
Natur-Führer)

DALLA TORRE, Karl Wilhelm von
The tourist's guide to the flora of the Alps;
translated and edited by Alfred W. Bennett.
Swan Sonnenschein, Le Bas & Lowrey, 1886. vii,
392p. 14cm.
Issued under the auspices of the German and
Austrian Alpine Club.

DALLOZ, Pierre
Description de la haute montagne dans le Massif
du Mont-Blanc. Fasc. 6 bis. Groupes du Chardonnet
et du Tour entre les cols du Chardonnet et de
Balme, par Pierre Dalloz, Marcel Ichac, Pierre
Henry. Paris: Fischbacher, 1937. 137p., plates,
illus. 17cm. (Guides Vallot)

DALLOZ, Pierre
Haute montagne. [Paris]: P. Hartmann, 1931.
1v. (chiefly illus.) 27cm.

DALLOZ, Pierre
La pointe Lagarde; ou, Les plaisirs d'un alpiniste
au cours d'une première ascension; avec frontispice et culs-de-lampe de Robert Sara. Strasbourg:
Nuée- Bleue, 1926. 39p., illus. 20cm.

DALLOZ, Pierre
Zénith. Paris: Wahl, 1951. 21p. 21cm.
(Bibliophiles de la montagne, 1)

DALTON, Hugh
With British guns in Italy: a tribute to Italian
achievement. Methuen, 1919. xiv, 267p., plates,
illus., maps. 20cm.

DALY, Reginald Aldworth
A geological reconnaissance between Golden and
Kamloops, B.C., along the Canadian Pacific
Railway. Ottawa: Government Printing Bureau, 1915.
viii, 260p., plates (some fold., some col. in
pocket), illus., maps. 26cm. (Canada. Depart-
ment of Mines. Geological Survey. Memoir, no.68;
Geological series, no.59)

DALY, Reginald Aldworth
Geology of the North American Cordillera at the
49th parallel. Ottawa: Government Printing
Bureau, 1912. 3pts., plates (some fold.), illus.,
maps (some fold. col.), bibl. 26cm. (Canada.
Department of Mines. Geological Survey. Memoir
no. 38)
Pt.3 contains maps.

DANA, James Dwight
Problems of American geology: a series of lectures
dealing with some of the problems of the Canadian
Shield and of the Cordilleras, delivered at Yale
University and on the Silliman Foundation in 1913.
New Haven: Yale University Press; London: Oxford
University Press, 1915. xix, 505p., plates (some
fold.), illus., maps. 25cm. (Dana commemorative
lectures)

D'ANCONA, Alessandro
MONTAIGNE, Michel de
[Journal du voyage ...]. L'Italia alla fine del
secolo XVI: giornale del viaggio di Michel de
Montaigne in Italia nel 1580 e 1581. Nuova ed.
del testo francese ed italiano con note ... [di]
Alessandro d'Ancona. Città di Castello: S.
Lapi, 1895. xli, 719p. 20cm.

DANDOLO, Tullio
Guida storica, poetica e pittoresca per la
Svizzera. Milano: Guglielmini, 1857. 509p.
19cm.
DANDOLO, Tullio
Prospetto della Svizzera; ossia, Ragionamenti
da servire d'introduzione alle lettere sulla
Svizzera di Tullio Dandolo. Milano: A.F. Stella,
1832. 2v. in 1., maps. 16cm.

DANDOLO, Tullio
Saggio di lettere sulla Svizzera, Il Cantone
de' Grigioni, [da T. Dandolo]. Milano: Stella,
1829. 232p., map. 17cm.

DANDOLO, Tullio
La Svizzera considerata nelle sue vaghezze
pittoresche, nella storia, nelle leggi e ne'
costumi: Lettere. Milano: Stella, 1829-33.
10v. in 5., fold. col. plates, maps. 16cm.

DANDOLO, Tullio
La Svizzera pittoresca; o, Corse per le Alpi e
pel Jura; a comentario del medio evo elvetico.
Milano: Tipografia Valentini, 1846. 309p. 23cm.

DANDOLO, Tullio
Viaggio per la Svizzera orientale. Milano:
Stella, 1836. 2v. 17cm.

DANIEL, Hermann Adalbert
RICHTER, Eduard
Die Alpen nach H.A. Daniel's Schilderung; neu
bearbeitet. Leipzig: Fues, 1885. viii, 96p.,
1 plate, map. 24cm.

DARGAUD, J   M
Voyage aux Alpes. Paris: Hachette, 1857.
414p. 18cm.

DARLING, F   Fraser
Natural history in the Highlands & Islands.
Collins, 1947. xv, 303p., plates (some col.),
illus., maps, bibl. 23cm. (The new naturalist)

DARRAH, Henry Zouch
Sport in the highlands of Kashmir, being a narrative of an eight months' trip in Baltistan and
Ladak, and a lady's experiences in the latter
country; together with hints for the guidance of
sportsmen. Rowland Ward, 1898. xviii, 506p.,
fold. plates, illus., maps (in pocket). 24cm.

DARTMOUTH MOUNTAINEERING CLUB
COULTER, Henry and MCLANE, Merrill F
Mountain climbing guide to the Grand Tetons.
Hanover (N.H.): Dartmouth Mountaineering Club,
1947. 67p., 1 fold. plate, illus., map. 18cm.

DARWIN, Charles
Journal of researches into the natural history
and geology of the countries visited during the
voyage of HMS 'Beagle' round the world; with a
biographical introduction. Ward, Lock, [1897].
492p., plates, illus., port. 21cm. (Minerva
library)

DARWIN, Charles
A naturalist's voyage: journal of researches into
the natural history and geology of the countries
visited during the voyage of HMS 'Beagle' round
the world. Murray, 1889. x, 519p., illus.,
port. 20cm.

DARWIN, Sir Francis Sacheverell
Travels in Spain and the East, 1808-1810.
Cambridge: University Press, 1927. ix, 121p.,
plates (1 fold.), illus., maps (on lining papers),
port. 20cm.

DAS, Sarat Chandra
Journey to Lhasa and central Tibet; edited by
W.W. Rockhill. Murray, 1902. xi, 285p., fold.
col. plates, illus., maps. 23cm.

Dates and distances, showing what may be done in a
tour of sixteen months through various parts of
Europe, as performed in the years 1829 and 1830.
Murray, 1831. viii, 358p., map. 21cm.

DAUDET, Alphonse
Tartarin of Tarascon; translated by Edward Wilson.
Maclaren, [1907?]. 89p. 22cm.

DAUDET, Alphonse
Tartarin sur les Alpes: nouveaux exploits du
héros tarasconnais; illustré d'aquarelles par
Aranda, de Beaumont, Montenard, de Myrbach &
Rossi. Paris: Calmann-Levy, 1885. 338p., illus.,
(some col.). 25cm. (Édition du 'Figaro')

DAUDET, Alphonse
Tartarin sur les Alpes: roman; with introduction
notes and vocabulary by Walter Peirce. New York:
H. Holt, 1917. xix, 263p. 18cm.

DAUDET, Alphonse
[Tartarin sur les Alpes]. Tartarin on the Alps.
Routledge, 1887. 370p., illus. 21cm.

DAUDET, Alphonse
[Tartarin sur les Alpes]. Tartarin on the Alps;
translated by Horace Watt. Maclaren, [1907?].
128p. 22cm.

DAUDET, Alphonse
[Tartarin sur les Alpes]. Tartarin in den Alpen:
neue Thaten des Helden von Tarascon. Halle: O.
Hendel, [1897?]. vi, 179p. 18cm.

DAULLIA, Émile
Au pays des Pyrénées. Paris: Mendel, 1903.
314p., plates, illus. 26cm. (Alpes et Pyrénées)

DAULLIA, Émile
Le tour du Mont-Blanc. Paris: Mendel, 1899.
307p., plates, illus. 26cm. (Alpes et Pyrénées)

DAULLIA, Émile
Voyage impressioniste en Suisse (huit jours au
pas de course). Paris: E. Dentu, 1887. 271p.
18cm.

DAUMAS, J
La péninsule du Sinai. Le Caire: Royal Automobile
Club d'Egypte, 1951. 459p., plates (some fold.),
illus., maps. 18cm.

DAUNT, Achilles
Crag, glacier and avalanche: narratives of daring
and disaster. Nelson, 1889. 212p., plates,
illus. 19cm.

Dauphiné; introduction de M.R.de La Sizeranne.
[Paris]: Hachette, [1926]. 70p., illus. (1 col.).
32cm. (Le pays de France, v.2, ptie.12)

D'AUVERNE, Edmund B
Switzerland in sunshine and snow. T. Werner
Laurie, [1912]. viii, 307p., plates (some col.),
illus. 23cm.

- - Another ed. [1916].

DAUZAT, A and LOUDEMER
En vacances: Plaisirs & curiosités de la montagne,
par A. Dauzat; Pêche & chase au bord de la mer,
par Loudemer. Paris: Hetzel, 1909. viii, 128p.,
illus. 27cm.

DAUZAT, Albert
Le Rhône des Alpes à la mer: le Rhône à travers
les âges, le Valais, le Lac Léman, la traversée
du Jura, Lyon, le Rhône dauphinois, le Rhône
provençal. Paris: Alpina, 1928. 157p., illus.
33cm.

DAUZAT, Albert
La Suisse illustrée. Paris: Larousse, [1913].
vii, 283p., plates (some col.), illus., maps.
35cm.
Published in 24 pts.

DAUZAT, Albert
Toute la montagne. Paris: Charpentier, 1924.
324p. 20cm.

DAVID-NEEL, Alexandra
My journey to Lhasa: the personal story of the
only white woman who succeeded in entering the
Forbidden City. Heinemann, 1927. xix, 310p.,
plates, illus. 24cm.

DAVID-NEEL, Alexandra
With mystics and magicians in Tibet; with an
introduction by A. d'Arsonval. J. Lane, 1931.
xv, 320p., plates, illus. 23cm.

DAVIDSON, Art
The coldest climb: the winter ascent of Mt.
McKinlay. Bodley Head, 1970. 218p., plates,
illus. 23cm.

DAVIDSON, Gordon Charles
The North West Company. Berkeley: University of
California Press, 1918. xi, 349p., fold. plates,
maps. 25cm. (University of California. Publications in history, v.7)

DAVIDSON, L   Marion
Gates of the Dolomites; with a chapter on the
flora of the Dolomites by F.M. Spencer Thomson
...; with an introduction by Sir Melvill
Beachcroft. Bodley Head, 1912. xix, 332p.,
plates (1 fold.), illus., maps. 20cm.

- - 2nd ed. 1914.

HEWITT, L   Rodney and DAVIDSON, Mavis M
The mountains of New Zealand. Wellington: A.H.
& A.W. Reed, 1954. 128p., illus., maps. 26cm.

DAVIDSON, Mavis M
HEWITT, L   Rodney
The Southern Alps. Pt.2. Mount Cook alpine
regions. Christchurch (N.Z.): Pegasus Press,
1953. 56p., plates, illus. 18cm. (New Zealand
holiday guides, no.8)

DAVIES, Joseph Sanger
Dolomite strongholds: the last untrodden alpine
peaks: an account of ascents of the Croda di Lago,
the Little and Great Zinnen, the Cinque Torri,
the Fünffingerspitze, and the Langkofel; with map
and illustrations by the author. Bell, 1894.
vii, 176p., plates (3 col.), illus., map. 20cm.

- - Another ed. 1896.

DAVIGNON, Jacques
CLUB ALPIN FRANÇAIS.   Section Paris-Chamonix
Pérou 1973; [édité par Jacques Davignon]. Paris:
La Section, 1974. 162p., illus., maps. 21cm.

DAVIS, E   J
Pyrna: a commune; or, Under the ice, [by E.J.
Davis]. Bickers, 1875. 142p. 20cm.

SHALER, Nathaniel Southgate and DAVIS, William Morris
Glaciers. Boston: J.R. Osgood, 1881. vi, 196p.,
25 plates, illus., bibl. 36cm. (Illustrations
of the earth's surface)

Davos as health-resort: a handbook containing contributions by A.F. Bill [and others]; and introduction by W.R. Huggard. Davos: Davos Printing
Co., 1906. iv, 316p., plates, illus. 21cm.

Davos-Platz: a new alpine resort for sick and sound
in summer and winter, by one who knows it well
[i.e. Mrs. MacMorland]. Stanford, 1878. 239p.,
map. 17cm.

DAWSON, George M
Preliminary report on the physical and geological
features of that portion of the Rocky Mountains
between latitudes 49° and 51°30'. Montreal:
Dawson, 1886. 169p., plates (2 fold. col.),
illus., maps. 25cm.
At head of title: Geological and Natural History
Survey of Canada.

DEACOCK, Antonia
No purdah in Padam: the story of the Women's
Overland Himalayan Expedition 1958; with a foreword by Dame Isobel Cripps. Harrap, 1960.
207p., plates, illus., map. 22cm.

DE AGOSTINI, A   M
Ande Patagoniche: viaggi di esplorazione alla
cordigliera Patagonica australe. Torino:
Agostini, 1949. 381p., plates (some col.),
illus., maps, bibl. 28cm.

DE AMICIS, Edmondo
Alle porte d'Italia; illustrato da ... disegni di
Gennaro Amato. Milano: Treves, 1892. 419p.,
illus. 31cm.

DE AMICIS, Edmondo
Nel regno del Cervino: nuovi bozzetti e raconti.
Milano: Treves, 1905. 330p. 20cm.

DE AMICIS, H
See
DE AMICIS, Ugo

DE AMICIS, Ugo
Alpe mistica. Milano: Treves, 1926. 311p. 19cm.

DE AMCIS, Ugo
Piccoli uomini e grandi montagne. Milano, Treves,
1924. 247p., illus. 33cm.

DE AMICIS, Ugo
[Piccoli uomini e grandi montagne]. Petits hommes,
grandes montagnes; traduit de l'italien par E.
Gaillard. Chambéry: Dardel, 1927. 199p., plates,
illus. 20cm.

DEAN, John Fred
The tourists; or, Continental travelling; edited
by John Fred Dean. Leeds: C. Goodall, 1878. 70p.,
plates, illus. 19cm.

DEASY, H   H   P
In Tibet and Chinese Turkestan, being the record
of three years' exploration. Fisher Unwin, 1901.
xvi, 420p., plates (1 fold. col.), illus., map.
24cm.

DE BEER, Dora H
Yunnan 1938: account of a journey in S.W. China.
The Author, 1971. 88p., plates, illus., map.
24cm.

DE BEER, Sir Gavin
Alps and elephants: Hannibal's march; illustrated
by Audrey Weber. Bles, 1955. xv, 123p., plates,
illus., map (1 fold.). 19cm.

DE BEER, Sir Gavin
Alps and men: pages from forgotten diaries of
travellers and tourists in Switzerland. Arnold,
1932. 256p., 16 plates, illus., maps, bibl. 23cm.

DE BEER, Sir Gavin
Early travellers in the Alps. Sidgwick & Jackson,
1930. xx, 204p., 40 plates, illus., fold. map,
bibl. 22cm.

DE BEER, Sir Gavin
Escape to Switzerland. Services ed. Harmondsworth: Penguin, 1945. 159p., music, bibl. 18cm.

DE BEER, Sir Gavin and HEY, Max H
The first ascent of Mont Blanc. London, 1953.
236-255p., plates, illus. 26cm.
Offprint from Notes and records of the Royal
Society of London, v.2, no.2, March 1955.

BROWN, Thomas Graham and DE BEER, Sir Gavin
The first ascent of Mont Blanc; with a foreword
by Sir John Hunt. Oxford University Press, 1957.
460p., 13 plates (some col.), illus., maps,bibl.
23cm.
Published on the occasion of the centenary of
the Alpine Club.

BROWN, Thomas Graham and DE BEER, Sir Gavin
[The first ascent of Mont Blanc]. La prima
ascensione del Monte Bianco; con una prefazione
di Sir John Hunt. Milano: Martello, 1960. viii,
638p., plates (some col., 1 fold.), illus.,
maps, bibl. 25cm.

DE BEER, Sir Gavin
On Shelley. Oxford University Press, 1938. vi,
99p. 20cm.
Contents: Shelley is expelled, by E. Blunden. -
The atheist: an incident at Chamonix, by G.
De Beer. - Mary Shelley: novelist and dramatist,
by S. Norman.

DE BEER, Sir Gavin
Publications 1952-1960, [1960-1965]. The Author,
[1960-65?]. 2v. 25cm.

DE BEER, Sir Gavin
Speaking of Switzerland. Eyre & Spottiswoode,
1952. 216p., col. plates, illus., bibl. 23cm.
(New alpine library)

DE BEER, Sir Gavin
Travellers in Switzerland. Oxford University
Press, 1949. xvii, 584p., plates, illus., bibl.
23cm.

DE BEER, Sir Gavin
ROLAND DE LA PLATIÈRE, Marie Jeanne
Voyage en Suisse, 1787. Éd. collationée, annot.
et accompagnée d'un aperçu sur les débuts
touristiques féminins dans les Alpes, par G.R.
De Beer. Neuchatel: La Baconnière, 1937. 207p.,
illus. 20cm.

DEBELAKOVA, M   M
Plezalna tehnika. Ljubljana: Slovensko Planinsko
Drustvo, 1933. 89p., illus. 19cm. (Planinska
knjiznica, 2)

COPELAND, Fanny S   and DEBELAKOVA, M   M
A short guide to the Slovene Alps (Jugoslavia),
for British and American tourists. Ljubljana:
Kleinmayr & Bamberg, 1936. 128p., plates (2
fold.), illus., map. 16cm.

DEBRIGES, E
Les Alpes du Dauphiné. Paris: G. Chamerot,
1885. 47p., illus. 23cm.

DE CAMBRAY DIGNY, Tommaso, conte
[Monte Bianco]. Mont Blanc: Italian ode;
translated into English verse by an Italian
alpinist [i.e. Sebastiano Fenzi]; and dedicated
to the members of the British Alpine Club.
Firenze: Arte della Stampa, 1879. 13p. 17cm.

DÉCHY, Moriz von
Kaukasus: Reisen und Forschungen im kaukasischen
Hochgebirge. Berlin: Reimer, 1905-07. 3v.,
plates (some fold., some col.), illus., maps.
31cm.

DECOMBLE, Clément
Les chemins de fer transpyrénéens: leur histoire
diplomatique, leur avenir économique: un episode
des relations franco-espagnols. Paris: A.
Pedone, 1913. 367p., 5 fold. plates, maps.
26cm.

DE FILIPPI, Filippo
[Notizie historiche del Regno del Thibet ...].
An account of Tibet: the travels of Ippolito
Desideri of Pistola, S.J., 1712-1727; edited by
Filippo de Filippi; with an introduction by C.
Wessels. Routledge, 1932. xviii, 475p., plates
(1 fold col.), illus., map, bibl. 23cm.
(Broadway travellers)

DE FILIPPI, Filippo
SPEDIZIONE ITALIANA DE FILIPPI
[Relazioni scientifiche della] Spedizione
Italiana De Filippi, nell'Himàlaia, Caracorùm e
Turchestàn Cinese (1913-1914). Serie 1.
Geodesia e geofisica; ... sotto la direzione di
Filippo De Filippi. Vol.1. Astronomia geodetica,
geodesia e topografia, [da] G. Abetti [and
others]. Bologna: Zanichelli, 1925. xxxv,
419p., plates (some fold., some col.), illus.
33cm.

DE FILIPPI, Filippo
SPEDIZIONE ITALIANA DE FILIPPI
[Relazioni scientifiche della] Spedizione
Italiana De Filippi, nell'Himàlaia, Caracorùm e
Turchestàn Cinese (1913-1914). Serie 2.
Resultati geologici e geografici; ... sotto la
direzione di Giotto Dainelli. Bologna:
Zanichelli, 1922-25. 12v., plates, illus., maps.
33cm.
Vol.3. Studi sul glaciale, [da] Giotto Dainelli.
1922. 2v. - v.8. Le condizioni delle genti, [da]
G. Dainelli. 1924. - v.9. I tipi umani, [da]
R. Biasutti e G. Dainelli. 1925.

DE FILIPPI, Filippo
Il Ruwenzori: viaggio di esplorazione e prime
ascensioni delle più alte vette nella catena
nevosa ..., relazione ... [di] Filippo De Filippi;
illustrata da Vittorio Sella. Milano: Hoepli,
1908. xii, 358p., plates (some fold., some col.),
illus., maps. 26cm.
At head of title: S.A.R. il Principe Luigi Amedeo
di Savoia, leader of the expedition.

DE FILIPPI, Filippo
[Il Ruwenzori: viaggio di esplorazione ...].
Ruwenzori: an account of the expedition of H.R.H.
Prince Luigi Amedeo of Savoy, Duke of the
Abruzzi; with a preface by the Duke; [transla-
tion ... by Caroline De Filippi; illustrations
... from photographs taken by Vittorio Sella].
Constable, 1908. xvi, 408p., plates (some fold.,
some col.), illus., maps. 27cm.

DE FILIPPI, Filippo
La spedizione di Sua Altezza Reale il Principe
Luigi Amedeo di Savoia, Duca degli Abruzzi al
Monte Sant'Elia (Alaska) 1897; illustrata da
Vittorio Sella. Milano: Hoepli, 1900. xvii,
284p., plates (some fold., some col.), illus.,
maps, bibl. 29cm.

DE FILIPPI, Filippo
[La spedizione di Sua Altezza Reale ...]. The
ascent of Mount St. Elias (Alaska) by H.R.H.
Prince Luigi Amedeo di Savoia, Duke of the
Abruzzi, narrated by Filippo De Filippi; illus-
trated by Vittorio Sella; and translated by Linda
Villari with the author's supervision.
Constable, 1900. xvi, 241p., plates (some fold.,
1 col.), illus., maps, bibl. 28cm.

DE FILIPPI, Filippo
[La spedizione nel Karakoram e nell'Himalaya
occidentale 1909]. Karakoram and western
Himalaya 1909: an account of the expedition of
H.R.H. Prince Luigi Amedeo of Savoy, Duke of the
Abbruzzi; with a preface by the Duke; [put into
English by Caroline De Filippi and H.T. Porter;
the illustrations from photographs taken by
Vittorio Sella]. Constable, 1912. 2v., plates,
illus., maps. 29cm.

DE FILIPPI, Filippo
Storia della spedizione scientifica italiana nel
Himàlaia Caracorùm e Turchestàn Cinese (1913-
1914); con capitoli aggiuntivi di Giotto Dainelli
e J.A. Spranger. Bologna: Zanichelli, 1924. xv,
541p., plates (some fold., some col.), illus.,
maps. 28cm.

DE FILIPPI, Filippo
[Storia della spedizione scientifica italiana...].
The Italian expedition to the Himalaya, Karakoram
and eastern Turkestan (1913-1914); with chapters
by G. Dainelli and J.A. Spranger. Arnold, 1932.
xvi, 528p., plates (some fold., some col.), illus.,
maps (2 in pocket). 26cm.

D'EGVILLE, Alan Hervey
The game of ski-ing: a book for beginners; illustrated by the author. Arnold, 1936. 76p.,
illus. 22cm.

D'EGVILLE, Alan Hervey
Modern ski-ing. Arnold, 1927. xvi, 173p.,
illus. 23cm.

- - 2nd ed. 1929.

D'EGVILLE, Alan Hervey
Slalom: its technique, organisation and rules.
Arnold, 1934. 159p., illus. 23cm.

DEHANSY, Charles
La Suisse à pied: souvenirs de vacances offerts
aux jeunes touristes. Paris: Fonteney & Peltier,
[1861]. vii, 408p., 1 plate, map. 26cm.

DE INFANTI, Sergio
Dalle ferrate al 60 grado: le più belle scalate
sull Carniche. Udine: Arti Grafiche Friulane,
1976. 157p., illus. 24cm.

DELAGO, Hermann
Dolomiten-Wanderbuch. 2 verb. Aufl. Innsbruck:
Tyrolia, 1931. 368p., plates, maps. 18cm.

DELAGO, Hermann
Die Zillertaler Alpen. Innsbruck: Wagner, 1925.
viii, 392p., illus., maps. 16cm. (Wagners
Alpine Spezialführer, 3)

DELAIRE, Alexis
Genève et le Mont Blanc: notes de science et de
voyage. Paris: C. Douniol, 1876. 62p. 26cm.

DELAYE, Th   J
CHOLLIER, Antoine
Ceux de l'Alpe: types et coutumes; dessins
originaux de Th.-J. Delaye. Paris: Éditions des
Horizons de France, 1937. 138p., col. illus.
29cm.

DELCROS, François Joseph
Notice sur les altitudes du Mont-Blanc et du
Mont-Rose, determinées par des mesures baro-
métriques et géodesiques. Paris, 1851.
263-297p. 29cm.
Offprint from Annuaire météorologique de la
France, 1851, 3e année.

DELEBECQUE, André
Alluvions anciennes de Chambéry et de la Vallée
de l'Isère. [Paris?], 1895-96. 4p. 23cm.
Offprint from Bulletin des services de la Carte
géologique détaillée de la France et des topo-
graphies souterraines, t.7, 1895-96.

DELEBECQUE, André
Lac du Mont-Cenis, lacs du massif de Belledonne,
les eaux du Rhône et de la Dranse du Chablais.
Genève, 1893. 12p. 23cm.
Offprint from Archives des Sciences physiques
et naturelles, t.30, décembre 1893.

DELEBECQUE, André
Les lacs français. Paris: Typographie Chamerot
& Renouard, 1898. xii, 436p., 22 plates (1
fold.), illus., maps, bibl. 33cm.

- - Atlas

DELEBECQUE, André
La moraine d'Yvoire. Genève, 1894. 3p. 23cm.
Offprint from Archives des Sciences physiques et
naturelles, t.31, 15 juin 1894.

DELEBECQUE, André
Sur l'âge des alluvions anciennes du bois de la
Bâtie, de Bougy et de la Dranse et leurs relations
avec le lac de Genève. Genève, 1894. 4p. 23cm.
Offprint from Archives des Sciences physiques
et naturelles, t.32, décembre 1894.

TAMINI, Jean Émile and DELÈZE, Pierre
Essai d'histoire de la Vallée d'Illiez. 2e éd.
St.-Maurice: Imprimerie St.-Augustin, 1924.
420p., illus., bibl. 24cm.

Les délices de la Suisse, une des principales
républiques de l'Europe; ... avec un memoire
instructif sur les causes de la guerre arrivée en
Suisse l'an 1712, par Gottlieb Kypseler de
Munster [i.e. Abraham Ruchat]. Leide: P. Vander,
1714. 4v., plates (some fold.), illus., maps.
17cm.

DELILLE, Jacques
See
LILLE, Jacques de

DELKESKAMP, Friedrich Wilhelm
Relief pittoresque du sol classique de la Suisse =
Malerisches Relief ... dessiné d'après nature et
gravé ... par Frédéric Guillaume Delkeskamp.
Frankfurt a/M: The Author, [1830]. 1v. of fold.
plates, illus. 33 x 16cm.

DELLENBAUGH, Frederick S
Frémont and '49: the story of a remarkable career
and its relation to the exploration and development of our western territory, especially of
California. New York, London: Putnam, 1914.
xxiii, 547p., plates (some fold.), illus., maps,
bibl. 24cm.

DELLEPIANE, Giovanni
Guida per escursioni nell' Apennino ligure e nelle
sue adiacenze... Ligure: Club Alpino Italiano,
Sezione Ligure, 1892. xiv, 308p., plates, illus.,
maps, plans. 17cm.

- - 4a ed. 1914.

DELMARD, Sophia Duberly
Village life in Switzerland. Longman, Green,
Longman, Roberts, & Green, 1865. x, 323p. 21cm.

DE LUC, Jean André
See
LUC, Jean André de

DEL ZOTTO, Giancarlo
[Alpinismo moderno]. Alpinisme moderne;[collabora-
teurs: Mario Bisaccia [and others]; sous la direction de Giancarlo del Zotto]. Paris: Arthaud,
1971. 235p., plates, illus. 22cm. (Sempervivum,
no.51)

DEMIDOFF, Elim Pavlovich, principe di San Donato
After wild sheep in the Altai and Mongolia.
Rowland Ward, 1900. xii, 324p., col. plates (1
fold.), illus., map (in pocket). 24cm.

DEMIDOFF, Elim Pavlovich, principe di San Donato
Hunting trips in the Caucasus. Rowland Ward, 1898.
xvi, 319p., illus., map (in pocket). 24cm.
The 2nd and 3rd expeditions are described by
H.D. Levick.

DEMIDOV, Elim, Prince San Donato
See
DEMIDOFF, Elim Pavlovich, principe di San Donato

DE MINERBI, Leonardo
Formazza sciistica: itinerari; a cura di Leonardo
de Minerbi. Milano: Sci Club C.A.I., 1950.
167p., plates (1 fold.col.), illus., map (in
pocket). 17cm.

DEMPSTER, Charlotte L
The Maritime Alps and their seaboard, by the
author of 'Vera', 'Blue roses' &c. [i.e.
Charlotte L. Dempster]. Longmans, Green, 1885.
x, 384p., plates, illus. 24cm.

DEN DOOLAARD, A
See
DOOLAARD, A   den

DENHOLM, James
A tour to the principal Scotch and English lakes.
Glasgow: A. Macgoun, 1804. 306p., 1 fold. plate,
map. 22cm.

- - New ed. Glasgow: Printed by R. Chapman, 1817.

DENIWA, Ch
Tableau historique, statistique et moral de la
Haute-Italie, et des alpes qui l'entourent...
Paris: L. Fantin, 1805. xxviii, 412p. 22cm.

DENMAN, Earl
Alone to Everest. Collins, 1954. 255p., plates,
illus., maps. 23cm.

DENNIS, John
Views in Savoy, Switzerland and on the Rhine,
from drawings made upon the spot. The Author,
[1822]. 1v. (chiefly illus.). 43cm.

DENNYS, Joyce
A water sports alphabet; pictures by Joyce
Dennys; verses by "Evoe". John Lane, 1926.
57p. 28cm.

DENT, Clinton Thomas
Above the snow line: mountaineering sketches
between 1870 and 1880; with two engravings by
Edward Whymper and an illustration by Percy
Macquoid. Longmans, Green, 1885. xiv, 327p.,
plates, illus. 20cm.

DENT, Clinton Thomas
ASSOCIATION OF BRITISH MEMBERS OF THE SWISS
ALPINE CLUB
Inauguration of the Cabane Britannia on the
Klein Allalinhorne Saas Fee,August 17th, 1912,
and obituary notices and portrait of Clinton
Dent. A.B.M.S.A.C., 1913. 52p., plates,
illus. 22cm.

DENT, Clinton Thomas
Mountaineering, by C.T. Dent; with contributions
by W.M. Conway [and others]. Longmans, Green,
1892. xxii, 481p., plates, illus. 26cm.
(Badminton library)

- - 2nd ed. 1892.

DENT, Clinton Thomas
Mountaineering, by C.T. Dent; with contributions
by J. Bryce [and others]. 3rd ed. Longmans,
Green, 1900. xx, 464p., plates, illus. 20cm.

DENT, Clinton Thomas
[Mountaineering]. Hochtouren: ein Handbuch für
Bergsteiger; deutsch hrsg. von Walther Schulze.
Leipzig: Duncker & Humblot, 1893. xi, 532p.,
illus. 20cm.

LUC, Jean André de and DENTAND, Pierre Gédéon
Relation différents voyages dans les Alpes du
Faucigny, par Messieurs D. & D. [i.e. J.A. de
Luc, et P.G. Dentand]. Maestricht: J.E. Dufour
& Ph. Roux, 1776. xxi, 138p. 17cm.

LUC, Jean André de and DENTAND, Pierre Gédéon
[Relation de different voyages ...]. Reisen nach
den Eisgebürgen von Faucigny in Savoyen, [von]
J.A. de Luc [und P.G. Dentand]; aus dem Französ-
ischen übersetzt [von J.S. Wyttenbach]. Leipzig:
Weidmann, 1777. 174p. 21cm.

DENTON, J   W
A climbing guide to Dartmoor. Torquay: The
Author, [1957]. 17 leaves. 35cm.
Typescript.

DENTON, W
Montenegro, its people and their history. Daldy,
Isbister, 1877. 292p. 20cm.

DENVER AND RIO GRANDE RAILROAD COMPANY
Rocky Mountain scenery: a brief description of
prominent places of interest along the line of
the Denver and Rio Grande Railroad. [Denver]:
The Company, [1888?]. 79p., plates, illus., maps.
24 x 31cm.

DEPONS, F
Travels in parts of South America, during the
years 1801, 1802, 1803, & 1804... Phillips,
1806. 160p., 2 fold. plates, map, plan. 23cm.
(In A collection of modern and contemporary
voyages... v.3, 1806)

DEPPING, Georg Bernhard
La Suisse; ou, Tableau historique, pittoresque et
moral des cantons helvétiques... Paris: Librarie
D'Education D'Al. Eymery, 1822. 4v., plates,
illus. 14cm.

DERENNES, Gustave
À travers les Alpes françaises: carnet d'un
touriste. Paris: Gedalge, [1890]. 270p., illus.,
music. 29cm.

DERICHSWEILER, W
[Clubführer durch die Bündner Alpen]. Clubführer
durch die Graubündner-Alpen. Bd.2. Bündner Oberland und Rheinwaldgebiet; verfasst von W.
Derichsweiler, Ed. Imhof und Ed. Imhof, jun.
Genf: Schweizer Alpen-Club, 1918. 332p., illus.
17cm. (Clubführer des Schweizer Alpen-Club)

DERICHSWEILER, W
Clubführer durch die Bündner Alpen. Bd.2. Bündner
Oberland and Rheinwaldgebiet; verfasst von W.
Derichsweiler, Ed. Imhof und Ed. Imhof jun. 2
Aufl. Luzern: Schweizer Alpenclub, 1951. 431p.,
illus., maps (on lining papers), bibl. (Club-
führer des Schweizer Alpen-Club)

- - 3. Aufl., neu bearb. von Bernard Condrau. 1970.

DERICHSWEILER, W
Führer durch das Medelser-Gebirge: das Gebiet der
Medelserhütte der Sektion Uto des Schweizer Alpen
Club. Frauenfeld: Huber, 1910. 84p., illus.,
maps. 19cm.

DERRY, J   D
Some rock climbs near Plymouth: a climbing guide;
compiled by J.D. Derry. West Byfleet: The Author,
1950. 17 leaves, illus. 32cm.
Typescript.

DESAIX DE VEYGOUX, Louis Charles Antoine
Journal de voyage du général Desaix: Suisse et
Italie, 1797; publié avec introduction et notes
par Arthur Chuquet. Paris: Plon-Nourrit, 1907.
lxxxviii, 305p., 2 plates, illus. 19cm.

DESBAROLLES, Adolphe
Un mois de voyage en Suisse pour 200 francs...
Paris: Bohaire, 1840. viii, 239p. 20cm.

DESBAROLLES, Adolphe
Voyage d'un artiste en Suisse à 3 francs 50 par
jour. Paris: Librarie Nouvelle, [1861?].
362p. 20cm.

- - 2e éd. Paris: M. Lévy, 1862.
- - 3e éd. Paris: M. Lévy, 1865.

DESBUISSONS, Léon
La vallée de Binn, Valais: étude géographique,
géologique, minéralogique et pittoresque ...;
préface par M.A. Lacroix; suivi d'une Étude sur
la flore du Binnental par A. Binz. Lausanne:
Bridel, 1909. viii, 328p., plates, illus., maps.

DESBUISSONS, Léon
Vallées perdues. Lausanne: Spes, 1947. 3 pts.
in 1, plates, illus., maps. 24cm.
Contents: 1. Tourtemagne, texte d'après L.
Meyer [and others]. - 2. Binn, texte de L.
Desbuisson et E. Bohy. - 3. Le Lötschental,
texte de Jos. Siegen.

A descriptive tour to the lakes of Cumberland and
Westmorland, in the autumn of 1804, [by Benjamin
Travers]. T. Ostell, 1806. viii, 164p. 18cm.

Descrizione della Valtellina e delle grandiose
strade di Stelvio e di Spluga, [da] D.A.M.M.
Milano: Società Tipografia de' Classici Italiani,
1823. 96p. 21cm.

DE SELINCOURT, Ernest
WORDSWORTH, Dorothy
Journals of Dorothy Wordsworth; edited by E. de
Selincourt. Macmillan, 1941. 2v., plates,
illus., maps. 23cm.

DE SELINCOURT, Ernest
WORDSWORTH, William
Wordsworth's Guide to the Lakes.5th ed.(1835)...
an introduction, appendices, and notes textual
and illustrative by Ernest de Sélincourt.
Frowde, 1906. xxviii, 203p., plates (1 fold.),
illus., map. 18cm.

DESGODINS, Auguste
La mission du Thibet de 1855 à 1870, comprenant
l'exposé des affaires religieuses et divers docu-
ments sur ce pays ... d'après les lettres de
M. l'abbé Desgodins, par C.-H. Desgodins.
Verdun: Laurent, 1872. viii, 419p., map. 24cm.
Library's copy lacks map.

DESGODINS, C   H
La mission du Thibet de 1855 à 1870, comprenant
l'exposé des affaires religieuses et divers documents sur ce pays... d'après les lettres de M.
l'abbé Desgodins; par C.H. Desgodins. Verdun:
Laurent, 1872. viii, 419p., map. 24cm.
Library's copy lacks map.

DESIDERI, Ippolito
[Notizie historiche del Regno del Thibet ...].
An account of Tibet: the travels of Ippolito
Desideri of Pistola, S.J., 1712-1727; edited by
Filippo De Filippi; with an introduction by C.
Wessels. Routledge, 1932. xviii, 475p., plates
(1 fold. col.), illus., map, bibl. 23cm.

DESIDERI, Ippolito
PUINI, Carlo
Il Tibet (geografia, storia, religione, costumi),
secondo la relazione del viaggio del P. Ippolito
Desideri (1715-1721). Roma: Società Geografica
Italiana, 1904. lxiv, 402p. 25cm. (Società
Geografica Italiana.Memorie, v.10)

DESIO, Ardito
La conquista del K2, seconda cima del mondo.
Milano: Garzanti, 1954. xx, 250p., plates (some
fold., some col.), illus., maps. 23cm.

DESIO, Ardito
[La conquista del K2 ...]. Ascent of K2, second
highest peak in the world; translated by D.
Moore. Elek Books, 1955. 239p., illus. 23cm.

DESIO, Ardito and ZANETTIN, Bruno
Geology of the Baltoro Basin. Leiden: Brill,
1970. xx, 308p., fold. col. plates, illus.,
maps (in pocket), bibl. 28cm. (Italian expeditions to the Karakorum (K2) and Hindu Kush.
Scientific reports, 3. Geology, petrology,
v.2)

DESIO, Ardito
Results of half-a-century investigation on the glaciers of the Ortles-Cevedale mountain group (central Alps) = Risultati ..., [by] A. Desio; with the collaboration of S. Belloni [and others]. Roma: Il Consiglio, 1973. 107, 107p., 10 plates (2 fold.), illus., maps, bibl. 30cm. (Consiglio Nazionale delle Ricerche. Pubblicazioni, n.6)

AIMONE, Duke of Spoleto and DESIO, Ardito
La spedizione geografica italiana al Karakoram (1929...), storia del viaggio e risultati geografici. Milano: Arti Grafiche Bertarelli, 1936. xxiv, 568, lip., plates, illus., maps. 30cm.

- - Maps (in portfolio).

DESLYS, Ch
Nos Alpes: Le muet de Brides, Légendes d'Évian, La Dent du Chat, Drumette: nouvelles; illustré ... par Jules David et Taylor. Paris: Hachette, 1882. 312p., illus. 25cm.

DESMARETZ, Yves Marie, comte de Maillebois
See
MAILLEBOIS, Jean Baptiste François Desmarets, marquis de

DESMONTS, Oreste
Les Dolomites; ouvrage orné de 8 aquarelles de Jungreuthmayer. Paris: Alpina, 1928. 110p., 8 col. plates, illus. 34cm. (Visions d'Italie)

DESOR, Édouard
L'ascension de la Jungfrau, effectuée le 28 août 1841, par MM. Agassiz, Forbes, du Chatelier et Desor, précédée du récit de leur traversée de la Mer de Glace, du Grimsel à Viesch en Valais. [Genève], 1841. 56p., plate, illus. 21cm. Offprint from Bibliothèque universelle de Genève, nov. 1841.

DESOR, Édouard
Compte rendu des recherches de M. Agassiz pendant ses deux derniers séjours à l'Hotel des Neuchatelois, sur le glacier inferieur de l'Aar, en 1841 et 1842. Genève, 1843. 79p. 22cm. Offprint from Bibliothèque universelle de Genève, t.44, mars 1843.

DESOR, Édouard
De l'orographie des Alpes dans ses rapports avec la géologie. Neuchatel: Wolfrath et Metzner, 1862. 70p., fold. map. 22cm.

DESOR, Édouard
Une dernière ascension. Neuchatel, 1854. 25p. 24cm. Offprint from Revue Suisse, janvier 1854.

DESOR, Édouard and LORIOL, P   de
Échinologie helvétique: description des oursins fossiles de la Suisse. Wiesbade: C.W. Kreidel, 1868-69. 5 pts. (in portfolios), plates, illus. 37cm.

DESOR, Édouard
Excursions et séjour de M. Agassiz sur la Mer de Glace du Lauteraar et du Finsteraar, en société de plusieurs naturalistes. [Genève], 1841. 102p., 2 plates (1 fold., 1 col.), illus. 21cm. Offprint from Bibliothèque universelle de Genève, mars, avril 1841.

DESOR, Édouard
Excursions et séjours dans les glaciers et les hautes regions des Alpes, de M. Agassiz et de ses compagnons de voyage. Neuchatel: Kissling, 1844. 638p, illus., map. 19cm.

DESOR, Édouard
Der Gebirgsbau der Alpen. Wiesbaden: Kreidel, 1865. 151p., plates, illus., fold. col. map. 22cm.

DESOR, Édouard
Journal d'une course faite aux glaciers du Mont Rose et du Mont Cervin en société de MM. Studer, Agassiz, Lardy, Nicolet et autres. Genève, 1840. 63p., illus. 22cm. Offprint from Bibliothèque universelle de Genève, t.27, 1840.

DESOR, Édouard
Nouvelles excursions et séjours dans les glaciers et les hautes régions des Alpes, de M. Agassiz et de ses compagnons de voyage; accompagnées d'une notice sur les glaciers ... par M. Agassiz et d'un aperçu sur la structure géologique des Alpes par M. Studer. Neuchatel: Kissling, 1845. 266p., illus., maps. 19cm.

DESOR, Édouard
Récit d'une course faite aux glaciers en hiver, par MM. Agassiz et E. Desor. [Genève], 1842. 36p. 21cm. Offprint from Bibliothèque universelle de Genève, t.38, 1842.

DESOR, Édouard
Le Val d'Anniviers. Neuchatel, 1855. 36p. 24cm. Offprint from Revue Suisse, t.18, 1855.

DESPAUX, Léon
Notre vieux Marcadau: l'amitié d'un paysage pyrénéen. Toulouse: Privat, 1956. 302p., plates, illus., music, bibl. 20cm. (Sites de France)

DESROCHES
Les ascensions au Mont-Blanc, racontées par un de ses grimpeurs. Grenoble: X. Drevet, [1894]. 111p. 20cm. (Bibliothèque du touriste dans les Alpes)
(In Drevet, L. La Vallée de Chamonix et le Mont Blanc. Grenoble, [1908].)

DESSAUER, A
Bergwanderungen in den Ostalpen. München: C. Kuhn, 1912. xvi, 202p., plates, illus. 23cm.

DESSAUER, A
Mit krummer Feder auf grünem Hut: ernste und heitere Erzählungen. Innsbruck: A. Edlinger, 1905. 145p., illus. 19cm.

DETTLI, J
Clubführer durch die Bündner Alpen. Bd.3. Avers, Misox, Calanca. 2. Aufl. revidiert von J. Dettli und P. Carmine. Zürich: Schweizer Alpen-Club, 1956. 298p., illus., maps (on lining papers), bibl. 17cm. (Clubführer des Schweizer Alpen-Club)

DEUTSCH-AKADEM. GEOGRAPHENVEREIN GRAZ
Zur Geographie der deutschen Alpen: Professor Dr. Robert Sieger zum 60. Geburtstage gewidmet von Freunden und Schülern. Wien: Seidel, 1924. 234p., plates, illus., port. 26cm.

Deutsche Alpen. 10. Aufl. Leipzig: Bibliographisches Institut, 1899-1908. 3v., illus., maps, plans. 16cm. (Meyers Reisebücher) Vol.3 is 4. Aufl.

DEUTSCHE ARKTISCHE ZEPPELIN-EXPEDITION, 1910
Mit Zeppelin nach Spitzbergen: Bilder von der Studienreise der deutschen arktischen Zeppelin-Expedition; mit einem Vorwort des Prinzen Heinrich von Preussen; hrsg. von A. Miethe und H. Hergesell. Berlin: Bong, 1911. 291p., col. plates, illus. 27cm.

DEUTSCHE HIMALAJA-EXPEDITION, 1934
Himalaja-Bibliographie, 1801-1933; hrsg. von der Deutschen Himalaja-Expedition 1934; mit Unterstützung des Vereins der Freunde der Alpensvereinsbücherei; [compiled by Willy Merkl]. München: Die Expedition, 1934. 48p. 18cm.

DEUTSCHE HIMALAYA EXPEDITION, 1973
Besteigung des Dhaulagiri III, 7715m., August
1973 bis Februar 1974. München: Die Expedition,
[1974]. 20p., illus., map, bibl. 25cm.

DEUTSCHE SKIVERBAND
Der Deutsche Skilauf und 25 Jahre Deutscher
Skiverband; bearb. von Carl J. Luther. München:
Rother, 1930. 195p., illus. 25cm.

DEUTSCHER ALPENVEREIN
Alpenvereinsfünrer.

Ötztaler Alpen: ein Führer für Täler, Hütten und
Berge, [von] H.E. Klier und H. Prochaska. 1953.
Stubaier Alpen: ein Führer für Täler, Hütten und
Berge, [von] W. Rabensteiner und H.E. Klier.
1953.

DEUTSCHER ALPENVEREIN
HAUSER, Günter
Die Hütten des Deutschen Alpenvereins ...; bearb.
von Günter Hauser und Marianne Klotz. München:
D.A.V., 1969. 361p., 1 fold. col. plate, illus.,
map (in pocket). 15cm.

DEUTSCHER ALPENVEREIN
Die Kartographie im Alpenverein, von Erik
Arnberger; hrsg. vom Deutschen Alpenverein und
vom Österreichischen Alpenverein. München:
D.A.V.; Innsbruck: Ö.A.V., 1970. 253p., plates
(some fold., some col.), illus., maps, bibl.
29cm. (Wissenschaftliche Alpenvereinshefte,
Heft 22)

DEUTSCHER ALPENVEREIN
Sicherheitskreis im DAV: Ausschuss für Sicherheit
am Berg, Tätigkeitsbericht 1969-1970. München:
D.A.V., 1971. 123p., plates (some fold.), illus.
30cm.

DEUTSCHER ALPENVEREIN. Sektion Bayerland
Bergsteigen als Lebensform; hrsg. von der Sektion
Bayerland des Alpenvereins zum fünfzigjährigen
Bestehen, 1895-1945. München: F. Schmitt, 1949.
63p., plates, illus. 25cm.

DEUTSCHER ALPENVEREIN. Sektion Hochland
Festschrift der Sektion Hochland des Deutschen
Alpenvereins zum 50 jährigen Bestehen, 1902-1952.
München: Rother, 1952. 96p., 1 plate, illus.
22cm.

DEUTSCHER ALPENVEREIN
For 1874-1938 see
DEUTSCHER UND ÖSTERREICHISCHER ALPENVEREIN

DEUTSCHER UND ÖSTERREICHISCHER ALPENVEREIN
Die Alpenflora der österreichischen Alpenländer,
Südbaierns und der Schweiz; bearb. von K.W. v.
Dalla Torre. München: J. Lindauer, 1899. xvi,
271p. 21cm.

DEUTSCHER UND ÖSTERREICHISCHER ALPENVEREIN
FINSTERWALDER, R
Alpenvereinskartographie und die ihr dienenden
Methoden; mit Beiträgen von E. Ebster [and
others]. Berlin: H. Wichmann, 1935. 81p.,
plates (1 fold., some col.), illus., maps. 25cm.
(Sammlung Wichmann, Bd. 3)

DEUTSCHER UND ÖSTERREICHISCHER ALPENVEREIN
BÜHLER, Hermann
Alpine Bibliographie für das Jahr 1931
[-1935]; bearb. von Hermann Bühler; [hrsg. vom
Verein der Freunde der Alpenvereinsbücherei mit
Unterstützung des Hauptausschusses des Deutschen
und Österreichischen Alpenvereins]. München:
Gesellschaft Alpiner Bücherfreunde, 1932-37.
18cm.
Publisher varies.
- - Gesamtregister für die Jahr 1931-1938. München:
Münchner Verlag, 1949.

DEUTSCHER UND ÖSTERREICHISCHER ALPENVEREIN
Alpines Handbuch; unter Mitarbeit von Georg Blab
[and others]. Leipzig: Brockhaus, 1931. 2v.,
col. plates, illus., 2 fold. col. maps. 28cm.

DEUTSCHER UND ÖSTERREICHISCHER ALPENVEREIN
Alpines Rettungswesen des D. u. Ö.Alpenvereins:
Handbüchlein zum Gebrauch der Landesstellen für
alpines Rettungswesen ...; hrsg. vom Hauptaus-
schuss des D. u. Ö.Alpenvereins. München:
D.u.Ö.A.V., 1926. 83p., illus. 17cm.

DEUTSCHER UND ÖSTERREICHISCHER ALPENVEREIN
Anleitung zu wissenschaftlichen Beobachtungen
auf Alpenreisen; hrsg. vom Deutschen und
Oesterreichischen Alpenverein; bearb. von C. von
Sonklar [and others]. Wien: D.u.Ö.A.V., 1882.
2v. in 1., plates, illus., fold. map. 20cm.
(Beilagen zur Zeitschrift des D.u.Ö.A.V.)

DEUTSCHER UND ÖSTERREICHISCHER ALPENVEREIN
An leitung zum Kartenlesen im Hochgebirge; mit
besonderer Berücksichtigung der vom D.u.Ö.Alpen-
verein hrsg. Spezialkarten, von Josef Moriggl;
hrsg. vom Zentralausschuss des D.u.Ö. Alpenvereins. München, 1909. 93p., plates (1 fold.,
some col.), illus., maps, bibl. 23cm.

DEUTSCHER UND ÖSTERREICHISCHER ALPENVEREIN
Anleitung zur Ausübung des Bergführer-Berufes;
hrsg. vom Deutschen und Österreichischen Alpenverein. 3. Aufl. Graz: D.u.Ö.A.V., 1896.
151p., illus., maps(in pocket). 23cm.

- - 4. Aufl. 1906.

DEUTSCHER UND ÖSTERREICHISCHER ALPENVEREIN
Atlas der Alpenflora; hrsg. vom Deutschen und
Oesterreichischen Alpenverein. 2. neubearb.
Aufl. Wissenschaftlicher Redacteur: Dr. Palla;
Ausführung der Farbentafeln nach Naturaufnamen
und Originalvorlagen von A. Hartinger. Graz: J.
Lindauer, 1897. 10 pts. in 5v. in 7 portfolios,
col. plates, illus. 21cm.

DEUTSCHER UND ÖSTERREICHISCHER ALPENVEREIN
RICHTER, E
Die Erschliessung Ostalpen; unter redaction von
E. Richter; hrsg. vom Deutschen und Oesterreichen
Alpenverein. Berlin: D.u.Ö.A.V., 1893-94. 3v.,
plates, illus. 30cm.

DEUTSCHER UND ÖSTERREICHISCHER ALPENVEREIN
Führer-Tarife; [hrsg. vom Zentralausschuss des
D.u.Ö. Alpenvereins]. München: J. Lindauer,
1904-06. 3 pts. 17cm.

DEUTSCHER UND ÖSTERREICHISCHER ALPENVEREIN
Geschichte des Deutschen und Oesterreichischen
Alpenvereins; aus der Festschrift zur Feier des
fünfundzwanzigjährigen Bestehens ... von
Johannes Emmer. Berlin: D.u.Ö.A.V., 1894. iv,
263p., illus., maps (fold. col. in pocket).
23cm.

DEUTSCHER UND ÖSTERREICHISCHER ALPENVEREIN
Lichtbilder verzeichnis des D.und Ö. Alpenvereins. München: Alpenvereinsbucherèi, 1927-
28. 223p. 19cm.

- - Suppl. 1931.
- - Suppl. 1935.

DEUTSCHER UND ÖSTERREICHISCHER ALPENVEREIN
BLETZACHER, J
Lieder-buch des Deutschen u-Österreichischen
Alpen-Vereines... Hannover: A. Nagel, 1887.
256p., music. 17cm. (Words and music)

DEUTSCHER UND ÖSTERREICHISCHER ALPENVEREIN
Ratgeber für Alpenwanderer mit Schutzhütten-
verseichnis der Ostalpen, von J. Moriggl; hrsg.
vom Hauptausschuss des D.u.Ö. Alpenvereins.
München: D.u.Ö.A.V., 1924. viii, 296p. 19cm.

- - 2. Aufl. 1928.

DEUTSCHER UND ÖSTERREICHISCHER ALPENVEREIN
Die Schutzhütten des Deutschen und Österreichischen Alpenvereins; hrsg. vom Hauptausschuss. München: D.u.Ö.A.V., [1933]. xxvii,
130p., 298 plates, illus., maps. 27cm.

DEUTSCHER UND ÖSTERREICHISCHER ALPENVEREIN
Ski-Taschenbuch der Alpensvereinsmitglieder;
hrsg. im Einvernehmen mit dem Hauptausschuss des
Deutschen und Österreichischen Alpenvereins;
redigiert durch W. v. Schmidt zu Wellenburg.
Innsbruck: Alpiner Verlag, 1932. 286p., plates,
illus. 21cm.

DEUTSCHER UND ÖSTERREICHISCHER ALPENVEREIN
Taschenbuch für Alpenvereins-Mitglieder; hrsg.
im Einverständnis mit dem Hauptausschuss des
Deutsches und Österreichischen Alpen-Vereins;
redigiert durch W. v. Schmidt zu Wellenburg,
1930/31, [1933]. München: Alpiner Verlag,
1930-33. 2v., illus. 21cm.

DEUTSCHER UND ÖSTERREICHISCHER ALPENVEREIN
Verfassung und Verwaltung des Deutschen und
Oesterreichischen Alpenvereins: ein Handbuch
zum Gebrauch für die Sectionen ...; zusammengestellt und erläutert von Johannes Emmer.
Berlin: D.u.Ö.A.V., 1893. iv, 115p., plates,
plans. 23cm.

- - 4. Ausg. ... zuzammengestellt und erläutert
von J. Moriggl. 1928.

DEUTSCHER UND ÖSTERREICHISCHER ALPENVEREIN
Das Villnöstal und seine Umgebung unter
besonderer Berücksichtigung von St. Peter,
Gufidaun, Bad Froy, Brixen und Klausen, Schlüter-,
Plose- und Regensburgerhütte ...; hrsg. ...
D.u.Ö.A.V. Sektionen, Dresden, Regensburg und
Brixen. Giessen: Emil Roth, [n.d.]. 116p.,
illus. 21cm. (Roth's illustrierte Führer, 9)

DEUTSCHER UND ÖSTERREICHISCHER ALPENVEREIN. Sektion
'Austria'
PICHL, Eduard
Hoch vom Dachstein an! Hrsg. unter Förderung
durch den Deutschen und Österreichischen Alpen-
verein, Zweig Austria. 2. Aufl. München: F.
Bruckmann, 1936. xvi, 319p., illus., map, bibl.
24cm.

DEUTSCHER UND ÖSTERREICHISCHER ALPENVEREIN. Sektion
Bayerland
Anwendung des Seiles. 14 neubearb. Aufl.
München: Alpenvereinsektion Bayerland, 1930.
31p., illus. 15cm.

DEUTSCHER UND ÖSTERREICHISCHER ALPENVEREIN. Sektion
Bayerland
[Anwendung des Seiles]. L'uso della corda; ed-
ito dalla Sezione Bayerland E.V. del D.-Ö.-A.-V.,
Monaco (Baviera); ed. italiana a cura della casa
Merlet; traduzione dal tedesco, F. Terschak.
Bolzano: J.F. Amonn, 1931. 43p., illus. 17cm.

DEUTSCHER UND ÖSTERREICHISCHER ALPENVEREIN. Sektion
Berchtesgaden
Die Grill aus der Ramsau: eine deutsche Führer-
familie, zum fünfzigjährigen Führer-Jubiläum
Johann Grills des Jüngeren; von W.F. hrsg. von
der Sektion Berchtesgaden des Deutschen und
Österr. Alpenvereins. Berchtesgaden: L. Vonder-
thann, [1931?]. 20p., ports. 23cm.

DEUTSCHER UND ÖSTERREICHISCHER ALPENVEREIN. Sektion
Berlin
Verzeichniss der autorisirten Führer in den
deutschen und oesterreichischen Alpen; hrsg. von
der Sektion Berlin des D.u.Ö. Alpen-Vereins.
Jahrgang 1885-1903. Berlin: Sektion Berlin,
1903. 17v. in 2. 17cm.

DEUTSCHER UND ÖSTERREICHISCHER ALPENVEREIN. Sektion
Gröden
Das Grödner Thal; verfasst von Franz Moroder;
hrsg. von der Section Gröden des Deutschen u.
Oesterreichischen Alpenvereins... St. Ulrich in
Gröden: Sektion Gröden, 1891. 201p., map (in
pocket). 18cm.

DEUTSCHER UND ÖSTERREICHISCHER ALPENVEREIN. Sektion
Halle
Vierzig Jahre Sektion Halle des Deutschen und
Oesterreichischen Alpenvereins: Festschrift zum 14.
Mai 1926. Halle a.d.S.: Karras & Koennecke, 1926.
222p., col. plates, illus., map. 28cm.

DEUTSCHER UND ÖSTERREICHISCHER ALPENVEREIN. Sektion
Hochland
Die Nördliche Karwendelkette; hrsg. von der
Sektion Hochland des Deutschen und Österreichischen
Alpenvereins in München. München: J. Lindauer,
1913. vi, 107p., 2 plates, illus., map. 18cm.

DEUTSCHER UND ÖSTERREICHISCHER ALPENVEREIN. Sektion
Jena
Bücher- und Kartenverzeichnis der Bücherei der
Sektion Jena des Deutschen- und Oesterreichischen
Alpenvereins; bearb. von O. Knorr. Jena:
D.u.Ö.A.V., 1930. 23cm.

DEUTSCHER UND ÖSTERREICHISCHER ALPENVEREIN. Sektion
Küstenland
Chronik der Section Küstenland des Deutschen und
Österreichischen Alpenvereins, 1873-1892: Fest-
Publication zur Vollendung des 20. Vereinsjahres;
aus den Veröffentlichungen der Section zusammen-
gestellt von P.A. Pazze. Triest: Section Küsten-
land, 1893. 372p., plates, illus. 23cm.

DEUTSCHER UND ÖSTERREICHISCHER ALPENVEREIN. Sektion
Kufstein
50 Jahre Alpenvereinssektion Kufstein, 1877-1927;
[hrsg. von F. Nieberl]. Innsbruck: Sektion
Kufstein, 1927. 215p., plates, illus. 25cm.

DEUTSCHER UND ÖSTERREICHISCHER ALPENVEREIN. Sektion
München
Geschichte der Alpenvereinssection München; als
Denkschrift nach dreissigjährigen Bestehen hrsg.
München: Section München, 1900. xii, 401p.,
plates (some fold., 1 col.), illus., map (in
pocket). 28cm.
Contains Geschichte der Section von 1869-99, von
Nepomuk Zwickh.

DEUTSCHER UND ÖSTERREICHISCHER ALPENVEREIN. Sektion
Passau
Führer durch Passau & Umgebung: zugleich Fest-
schrift für die General-Versammlung des Deutschen
& Österr. Alpenvereins in Passau... 1899, von K.
Eckart, und einem Anhang über das alpine Arbeits-
Gebiet der Sektion von [F.] Lucas. Passau:
Sektion Passau, 1899. 75, 30p., plates (1 fold.
col.), illus., plan. 21cm.

DEUTSCHER UND ÖSTERREICHISCHER ALPENVEREIN. Sektion
Pforzheim
Ski und Winterführer durch die Münstertaler Alpen
und angrenzenden Gebiete: Westl. Ortlergruppe,
Malser Heide, Unterengadin und Alpen von Livigno;
unter Mitwirkung des D.u.Oe. Alpenvereins, hrsg.
... von Fr. Berger. München: Kommissionsverlag
der Deutschen Alpenzeitung, 1912. 180p., fold.
col. maps (in pocket). 17cm.

DEUTSCHER UND ÖSTERREICHISCHER ALPENVEREIN. Sektion
Rosenheim
Rosenheim: Berge und Vorland; hrsg. von der
Sektion Rosenheim des Deutschen und Öster-
reichischen Alpenvereins. Rosenheim: Sektion
Rosenheim, 1902. 174p., plates (2 fold.), illus.,
maps, plan. 20cm.

DEUTSCHER UND ÖSTERREICHISCHER ALPENVEREIN. Sektion
Wien
Die Schutzhütten und Unterkunfthäuser in den
Ostalpen; hrsg. von der Sektion Wien des Deutschen
und Österreichischen Alpenvereins. Dresden:
Kunstanstalt Stengel, [1909-10]. 3v., plates,
illus. 39cm.
Published in 43 pts.

DEUTSCHER UND ÖSTERREICHISCHER ALPENVEREIN. Zweig
Austria
See
DEUTSCHER UND ÖSTERREICHISCHER ALPENVEREIN. Sektion
'Austria'

DEVIES, Lucien
La chaîne du Mont Blanc. 1. Mont Blanc,
Trélatête, par Lucien Devies, Pierre Henry,
Jacques Lagarde. 2e éd. Paris: Arthaud [pour]
Groupe de Haute Montagne, 1951. 354p., illus.,
bibl. 17cm. (Guide Vallot)

DEVIES, Lucien and HENRY, Pierre
La chaîne du Mont Blanc. 1. Mont Blanc,
Trélatête. 3e éd. [Paris]: Arthaud [pour]
Groupe de Haute Montagne, 1973. 445p., illus.,
map. 17cm. (Guides Vallot)

- - 4e éd. 1978.

DEVIES, Lucien
La chaîne du Mont Blanc. 2. Aiguilles de
Chamonix, Grandes Jorasses. Grenoble: Arthaud
[pour] Groupe de Hauge Montagne, 1947. 387p.,
illus., maps. 17cm. (Guides Vallot)

- - Addendum. 1948.
- - 2e éd. 1951.

DEVIES, Lucien and HENRY, Pierre
La chaîne du Mont Blanc. 2. Les Aiguilles de
Chamonix. 3e éd. Paris: Arthaud [pour] Groupe
de Haute Montagne, 1977. 317p., illus., maps.
17cm. (Guides Vallot)

DEVIES, Lucien and HENRY, Pierre
La chaîne du Mont Blanc. 3. Aiguille Verte,
Dolent, Argentière, Trient. Grenoble: Arthaud
[pour] Groupe de Haute Montagne, 1949. 381p.,
illus. 17cm. (Guides Vallot)

- - 3e éd. 1966.
- - 4e éd. 1975.

DEVIES, Lucien and LALOUE, Maurice
Guide du Massif des Écrins (Meije, Écrins,
Ailefroide, Pelvoux, Bans, Olan, Muzelle). 2e
éd. Paris: Arthaud [pour] Groupe de Haute
Montagne, 1951. 2v., illus., bibl. 17cm.
Later eds. published under title: Le massif des
Écrins.

DEVIES, Lucien and TERRAY, Lionel
Joies de la montagne; réalisé sous la direction
de Lucien Devies et Lionel Terray. Paris:
Hachette, 1965. 255p., illus. (some col.).
29cm. (Collection joies et réalités)

DEVIES, Lucien
Le massif des Écrins. 1. Meije, Rateau,
Soreiller, par Lucien Devies, François Labande,
Maurice Laloue. 4e éd. Paris: Arthaud, 1976.
301p., illus., bibl. 17cm.
Originally published under title: Guide du
massif des Écrins.

DEVIES, Lucien
Le massif des Écrins. 2. Ailefroide, Pelvoux,
Bans, Olan, Muzelle, par Lucien Devies, François
Labande, Maurice Laloue. Paris: Arthaud, 1971.
662p., illus., bibl. 17cm.
Originally published under title: Guide du
massif des Écrins.

DEVIES, Lucien
Le massif des Écrins. 2. Écrins, Grande Ruine,
Roche Faurio, Agneaux, Glouzis, par Lucien Devies,
François Labande, Maurice Laloue. 4e éd. Paris:
Arthaud, 1976. 305p., illus. 17cm.
Originally published under title: Guide du
massif des Écrins.

DEVIES, Lucien
Le massif des Écrins. 3. Ailefroide, Pelvoux,
Bans, Sirac, par Lucien Devies, François Labande,
Maurice Laloue. 4e éd. Paris: Arthaud, 1978.
313p., illus. 17cm.
Originally published under title: Guide du
massif des Écrins.

DEVONSHIRE, Georgiana Cavendish, Duchess of
Memorandums of the face of the country in
Switzerland, [by the Duchess of Devonshire].
Cooper & Graham, 1799. 103p. 17cm.

DEVONSHIRE, Georgiana Cavendish, Duchess of
[The passage of the mountain of Saint Gothard].
Passage du Mont saint-Gothard: poème; traduit
de l'anglais par M. l'Abbé de Lille. [Paris]:
Imprimerie Lithographique de C. de Lasteyrie,
[18--]. ix, 44p., plates, illus. 31cm.
Text and notes in English and French.

DEVONSHIRE, Georgiana Cavendish, Duchess of
[The passage of the mountain of Saint Gothard].
Passage du St.-Gothard: poème; traduit de
l'anglais par Jacques Delille.
(In Lille, Jacques de. Dithyrambe ... Paris,
1802. 14cm. p.35-123)

DEVONSHIRE, Georgiana Cavendish, Duchess of
LASCELLES, Rowley
Sketch of a descriptive journey through Switzerland, [by R. Lascelles], to which is added The
passage of S. Gotthard, a poem by the Duchess
of Devonshire. Berne: J.J. Burgdorfer, 1816.
iv, 92p., plates, illus. 21cm.

DHEULLAND, G   and JULIEN, R
Théâtre de la guerre en Italie; ou, Carte nouvelle
des principauté de Piemont, République de Gênes,
Duchés de Milan, Plaisance et confins. Paris:
The Authors, 1748. 24 maps with gazeteer.
26cm.

Diary of a fortnight's trip through the English
Lake District and Scotland, in July, 1867, by a
few friends; written by one of the party, for
private circulation. Birmingham: M. Billing,
[1867]. 93p. 17cm.

The diary of a solitaire; or, Sketch of a pedestrian excursion through part of Switzerland,
[by E.S. Rickman]; with a prefatory address,
and notes, personal and general. Smith, Elder,
1835. liii, 111p. 23cm.

The diary of a traveller over Alps and Appenines;
or, Daily minutes of a circuitous excursion,
[by Murray Forbes]. Printed by W. Smith, 1824.
viii, 170p. 23cm.

DIAS, John
The Everest adventure: story of the second
Indian expedition. Delhi: Ministry of Information and Broadcasting, 1965. 63p., plates
(some col.), illus. 29cm.

Dictionnaire géographique de la Suisse; publié
sous les auspices de la Société Neuchateloise
de Géographie, et sous la direction de Charles
Knapp [and others]; avec des collaborateurs de
tous les cantons. Neuchatel: Attinger, 1902-10.
6v., plates (some fold., some col.), illus.,
maps. 29cm.

Dictionnaire géographique, historique et politique
de la Suisse. Neuchatel: J.P. Jeanrenaud, 1775.
2v. 20cm.
Extracts compiled by J.S. Wyttenbach from de
Felice's "Encyclopédie", 1770-76.

- - Nouv. éd. corr. et augm. Genève: Grasset, 1776.
- - Nouv. éd. corr.et augm. Genève: Nouffer &
Bassompierre, 1777.
- - Nouv. éd. augm. Genève: Barde, Manget, 1788.
3v., map.

[Dictionnaire géographique, historique et politique ...]. Historische, geographische und
physikalische Beschreibung des Schweizerlandes
...; aus dem Französischen übersezt, und mit
vielen Zusätzen vermehrt; [compiled and enlarged
by J.S. Wyttenbach]. Bern: E. Hortin, 1782-83.
3v. 21cm.

DIDIER, Richard
Ailes de mouches et tricounis: récits d'Armand
Couttet. Paris: J. Vitiano, 1946. 243p.,
illus. 20cm. (Sport, amour, idéal)

DIEMBERGER, Kurt
[Imaka - Leben zwischen 0 und 8000]. Summits and
secrets; translated by Hugh Merrick. Allen &
Unwin, 1971. 344p., plates, illus., maps. 25cm.

DIEMBERGER, Kurt
[Imaka - Leben zwischen 0 und 8000]. Tra zero e
ottomila. Bologna: Zanichelli, 1970. 428p.,
illus. (some col.), maps. 24cm.

DIENER, Carl
Der Gebirgsbau der Westalpen. Prag: Tempsky,
1891. v, 243p., fold. col. plates, maps. 26cm.

DIERICX DE TEN-HAMME, Joë
See
TEN-HAMME, Joë Diericx de

DIETERLEN, Jacques
Le chemineau de la montagne; préface de Henry
Ripert. [Paris]: Flammarion, 1938. 262p., 16
plates, illus. 22cm. (La vie en montagne)

DIETERLEN, Jacques
Ski de printemps. Paris: Flammarion, 1937.
125p., plates, illus. 22cm. (La vie en montagne)

HERMANN, André and DIETERLEN, Jacques
Le ski pour tous: ce que tout skieur doit savoir.
Paris: Flammarion, 1936. 268p., illus., bibl.
22cm. (La vie en montagne)

DIETZEL, Karl Heinrich
REISS, Wilhelm
Reisebriefe aus Südamerika 1868-1876; aus dem
Nachlasse hrsg. und bearb. von Karl Heinrich
Dietzel. München: Duncker & Humblot, 1921.
232p., col. plates, maps. 24cm. (Wissen-
schaftliche Veröffentlichungen der Gesellschaft
für Erdkunde zu Leipzig, Bd.9)

DIGNY, conte Tommaso de Cambray
See
DE CAMBRAY DIGNY, conte Tommaso

DILL, David Bruce
Life, heat, and altitude: physiological effects
of hot climates and great heights. Cambridge
(Mass.): Harvard University Press, 1938. xiv,
211p., plates, illus. 21cm.

DILL, J   R
Panorama d'une partie des Alpes bernoises pris
sur l'Aeggischhorn dans le Canton du Valais;
dessiné d'après nature et lithographié par J.R.
Dill. Berne: Dalp, [ca 1855]. 29cm.

DILL, J   R
Panorama des Alpes, pris sur les Gornergrat près
Zermatt, au Canton du Valais, dessiné d'après
nature et lithographié par J.R. Dill. Berne:
Dalp, [ca 1855]. 23cm.

DISLEY, John
Expedition guide, Duke of Edinburgh's Award: the
scheme for boys; edited by John Disley; illustrated by Gordon F. Mansell. Duke of Edinburgh's
Award Office, 1965. 110p., illus., maps. 15cm.

DISLEY, John
Tackle climbing this way; line drawings by Gordon
Mansell. Stanley Paul, 1959. 127p., plates,
illus., maps, bibl. 20cm.

A dissertation on the passage of Hannibal over the
Alps, by a member of the University of Oxford.
Oxford: Printed by W. Baxter for J. Parker, 1820.
xxiii, 183p., plates (1 fold. col.), maps. 22cm.

- - 2nd ed. by Henry L. Wickham and J.A. Cramer.
Whittaker, 1828.

DITSON, George Leighton
Circassia; or, A tour to the Caucasus. New York:
Stringer & Townsend; London: Newby, 1850. 455p.,
plates, illus. 23cm.

DITTERT, René
Avant-premières à l'Everest, [par] Gabriel
Chevalley, René Dittert, Raymond Lambert; intro-
duction du Ed. Wyss-Dunant. Paris: Arthaud,
1953. 310p., plates (1 fold. col.), illus., maps.
(Collection sempervivum, 21)

DITTERT, René
[Avant-premières à l'Everest]. Forerunners to
Everest: the story of the two Swiss expeditions
of 1952, by René Dittert, Gabriel Chevalley,
Raymond Lambert; preface by Sir John Hunt; English
version by Malcolm Barnes. Allen & Unwin, 1954.
256p., plates (1 col.), illus., maps. 23cm.

DITTERT, René
Passion des hautes cimes; préface d'André Roch.
Lausanne: F. Rouge, 1945. 248p., plates, illus.,
maps (1 fold.). 22cm. (Collection alpine, 4)

DITTMAR, Franz
Dittmar's Führer für die Strecke München-Brenner-
bahn nach Bozen-Gries, Meran, Trient, Arco und
an den Gardasee, nach Verona und Venedig. 2 verm.
und verb. Aufl. München: M. Kellerer, 1905.
74p., map. 17cm.

DI VALLEPIANA, Ugo
Ricordi di vita alpina; prefazione di Emilio
Orsini; fotografie dell'autore. Bologna: Tamari,
1972. 131p., plates, illus. 19cm. (Voci dai
monti, 3)

DIX, Edwin Asa
A midsummer drive through the Pyrenees. New
York, London: Putnam, 1891. 332p., 1 plate,
illus., map. 23cm.

DIXIE, Lady Florence
Waifs and strays; or, The pilgrimage of a
Bohemian abroad. Griffith, Farran, Okeden &
Welsh, 1884. 60p. 16cm.

DIXON, William Hepworth
The Switzers. Berlin: F. Duncker, 1872. x,
281p. 18cm.

DOCHARTY, William McKnight
A selection of some 900 British and Irish mountain tops; compiled and arranged by William
McKnight Docharty. Edinburgh: The Compiler, 1954.
124p., plates (9 fold.), illus. 26cm.

- - Supplement. 1962. 2v.

DODD, William
Cursory notes of a nine weeks' tour [by William
Dodd?]. Newcastle-upon-Tyne: J. Hernaman, 1834.
140p. 23cm.

DODDERIDGE, M
WHYMPER, Edward
Man on the Matterhorn; edited by M. Dodderidge
from Edward Whymper's Scrambles amongst the Alps.
Murray, 1940. 135p., illus., map. 18cm.
(Journeys and adventures)
For children

DODDS, David Allison
A cradle of rivers: the Natal Drakensberg. Cape
Town, London: Purnell, 1975. 128p., col. plates,
illus., map, bibl. 32cm.

DÖHLEMANN, C
Skiführer; hrsg. von Schneeschuhverein München
von 1893 e. V. Bd.2. Inntal-Chiemgau; bearb. von
C. Döhlemann. München: M. Steinbach, 1914. 110p.,
illus. 17cm.

HILLARY, Sir Edmund and DOIG, Desmond
High in the thin cold air. Hodder & Stoughton,
1963. 287p., plates, illus., maps (on lining
papers). 23cm.

DOLE, Nathan Haskell
The spell of Switzerland; illustrated from photographs and original paintings by Woldemar Ritter.
Boston (Mass.): Page, 1914. x, 489p., plates,
illus., map. 21cm. (The spell series)

DOLIN, H
Routes des Alpes françaises: itinéraires avec
profils des pentes ... á l'usage des alpinistes,
cyclistes et voituristes... Chambéry: Syndicat
d'Initiative, [1909]. 2v., maps. 16 x 26cm.

DOLLÉ, Frédéric
Souvenirs de voyage: Suisse, Savoie, France.
3e éd. Paris: Dentu, 1843. 360p., illus. 18cm.

DOLLFUS, Charles
À travers monts. 2e éd. Paris: P. Ollendorff,
1900. 324p. 19cm.

DOLLFUS, Gustave
DOLLFUS-AUSSET, Daniel
Photographies alpines, glaciers; [edited by
Gustave Dollfus]. [Paris]: Braun, Clement,
[1893]. 40p., plates, illus. 42cm.
Binding title.

DOLLFUS-AUSSET, Daniel
Matériaux pour l'étude des glaciers. Paris:
Savy, 1864- ... 12v. in 16, illus. 27cm.
Library has vols. 1-8 only.

DOLLFUS-AUSSET, Daniel
Photographies alpines, glaciers; [edited by
Gustave Dollfus]. [Paris]: Braun, Clement,
[1893]. 40p., plates, illus. 42cm.
Binding title.

DOLOMIEU, Déodat Guy S   T   de Gratet de
BRUUN-NEERGAARD, Tønnes Christian
Journal du dernier voyage du Gen. Dolomieu dans
les Alpes. Paris: Solvat, 1802. 154p. 21cm.
Half-title: Journal d'un Danois.

Dolomiten-Kletterführer. München: Rother.

1. [Westliche Dolomiten], von G. Langes.
   4. Aufl. 1959.
   - - 5. Aufl. 1964.
2. [Ostliche Dolomiten], von G. Langes. 1959.
3. Brenta-Gruppe, von H. Wels. 1963.

[Dolomitenland]. The Dolomites. Thames & Hudson,
1955. 1v. (chiefly illus., maps). 25cm.
(Beautiful highways)

The Dolomites: a practical guide. Berlin: A.
Goldschmidt; London: Williams & Norgate, 1911-12.
149p., 3 fold. plates, maps (1 in pocket).
(Grieben's guide books, v.154)

Dolomiti = Dolomitenland = Land of the Dolomits
[sic] ...: 160 foto artistiche in rotocalco ...
Bozen: L. Fränzl, 1948. 1v. of illus. 25cm.
Introduction in Italian, German, English, French.

DOMVILLE-FIFE, Charles W
Things seen in Switzerland in winter: a description of many of the winter sport centres of the
High Alps... Seeley, Service, 1926. 157p.,
plates, illus., map. 16cm.

DONALDSON, Florence
Lepcha Land; or, Six weeks in the Sikhim Himalayas.
Sampson Low Marston, 1900. xii, 213p., plates
(1 fold. col.), illus., map. 23cm.

DONALDSON, J   C
MUNRO, Sir Hugh
Munro's tables of the 3000-feet mountains of
Scotland and other tables of lesser heights; re-
vised by J.C. Donaldson and W.L. Coats. Rev. ed.
Edinburgh: Scottish Mountaineering Trust, 1969.
96p., illus. 22cm. (Scottish Mountaineering
Club district guide books)

- - Metric ed. edited and rev. by J.C. Donaldson.
1974.

DONCOURT, A   S   de
Le Mont Blanc et ses explorations précécé d'une
notice historique sur H.B. de Saussure. Paris:
Lefort, 1887. 224p., illus. 28cm.

DONNÉ, Alphonse
Change of air and scene: a physician's hints;
with notes of excursions for health amongst the
watering-places of the Pyrenees, France... H.S.
King, 1872. xi, 313p. 21cm.

DONNE, Benjamin John Merrifield
Colloquy & song; or, Sport in leash of the Muses.
Kegan Paul, Trench, Trübner, 1898. xiii, 212p.
19cm.

DONNE, Benjamin John Merrifield
Scattered poems, [by B.J.M. Donne]. Yeovil:
Western Gazette, 1895. 56p. 16cm.

DONOUGHUE, Carol
Everest; compiled by Carol Donoughue. Jackdaw
Publications, 1975. 10 leaves (9 fold.), illus.,
bibl. 23 x 35cm. (Jackdaw, no.128)

DONVITO, Lino
VIRGIL
Moretum (o delle origini della pizza); [tradu-
zione di Lino Donvito]; testo latino: "Appendix
Vergiliano". Torino: The Author [1973].
[12p.], plates, illus. 22cm.
Text in Latin & Italian, signed by the translator.

DOOLARD, A   den
Van camera, ski en propeller: filmavonturen en
ski-onderricht in het Mont-Blanc-gebied.
Amsterdam: "Die Spieghel", [1930?]. 101p.,
plates, illus. 22cm.

DOPOSCHEG, Josef
Die Zugspitze: Ersteigungs-Geschichte, Orographie,
Klima und touristisch-geologisch-botanischer
Führer auf den Zugangswegen und Anstiegslinien.
Garmisch: A. Adam, 1921. 168p., illus., map.
19cm.

DORANGE, J
Quinze excursions en Savoie et Dauphiné, texte
et itinéraires de J. Dorange. Paris: [N.pub.],
1911. 1v. (chiefly illus., map). 23cm.

DORÉ, Gustave
Des-agréments d'un voyage d'agrément. Paris:
Féchoz & Letouzey, [ca 1860]. 24p. of illus.
27 x 36cm.

DORÉ, Gustave
TENNYSON, Alfred, Baron Tennyson
Genièvre: poème traduit de l'anglais par
Francisque Michel; avec neuf gravures sur acier
d'après les dessins de Gustave Doré. Paris:
Hachette, 1868. 25p., 9 plates, illus. 45cm.

DORÉ, Gustave
TAINE, Hippolyte
Voyage aux Pyrénées. 3e éd., illustrée par G.
Doré. Paris: Hachette, 1860. vi, 354
(i.e. 554)p., illus. 25cm.

- - 14e éd. 1897.

DOREN, David MacNeil
Winds of Crete. Murray, 1974. 249p., plates,
illus. 23cm.

DORNFORD, Joseph
Mont Blanc: [account of a late attempt to reach
the summit of Mont Blanc], by J.D. [i.e. Joseph
Dornford]. [London, 1821]. 451-462, 505-517p.
22cm.
Offprint from New monthly magazine, v.1, 1821.

DORST, Jean
[Guide du naturaliste dans les Alpes]. Guida
del naturalista nelle Alpi, [da] J. Dorst [and
others]. Bologna: Zanichelli, 1973. xiv, 332p.,
illus. (some col.), maps, bibl. 24cm.

DOUBLET, Victor
SABINE, chanoine de
Les nouveaux voyageurs en Suisse et en Italie:
beautés et merveilles de ces delicieuses contrées,
par le chanoine de Sabine; ouvrage rev. corr. et
augm., par Victor Doublet. Nouv. éd. Paris: P.C.
Lehuby, [1847]. 351p., plates, illus. 22cm.

DOUDOU, Ernest
Exploration scientifique dans les cavernes, les abimes et les trous qui fument de la province de Liège. Liège: M. Thome, [1906?]. 342p., illus. 20cm.

DOUGHTY, C   M
On the Jöstedal-brae glaciers in Norway, with some general remarks. Stanford, 1866. 14p., 1 col. plate, map. 22cm.

DOUGHTY, Joseph Henry
Hill-writings of J.H. Doughty; collected by H.M. Kelly. Manchester: Rucksack Club, 1937. xix, 150p., plates, ports. 22cm.

DOUGHTY, Marion
Afoot through the Kashmir valleys. Sands, 1901. xxxii, 276p., plates, illus. 24cm.

DOUGLAS, Charles Edward
Mr. Explorer Douglas; edited by John Pascoe. Wellington: Reed, 1957. xx, 331p., plates, illus., maps, bibl. 25cm.

DOUGLAS, David
Journal kept by David Douglas during his travels in North America 1823-1827, together with a particular description of ... specimens of American oaks and ... species of Pinus. Wesley, 1914. 364p., plates, illus., port. 26cm.

DOUGLAS, John Scott
Summits of adventure: the story of famous mountain climbs and mountain climbers. Muller, 1955. xii, 227p., 16 plates, illus., bibl. 21cm.

DOUGLAS, John Sholto, 8th Marquis of Queensbury
The spirit of the Matterhorn,by Lord Queensbury. Watts, [1881]. 30p. 22cm.
Poem with prefatory essay.

DOUGLAS, R   de Breugel
See
BREUGEL DOUGLAS, R   de

DOUGLAS, William Orville
Beyond the high Himalayas. Gollancz, 1953. 352p., maps (on lining papers), music. 21cm.

DOUGLAS, William Orville
Of men and mountains. Gollancz, 1951. xiv, 338p., map (on lining papers). 23cm.

DOUIE, Charles
Beyond the sunset. Murray, 1935. 314p. 20cm.

DOUIE, Sir James
The Panjab, North-West frontier province and Kashmir. Cambridge: University Press, 1916. xiv, 373p., 2 fold. plates, illus., maps. 21cm. (Provincial geographies of India)

DOVE, H   W
Der Schweizer Fön: Nachtrag zu Eiszeit, Föhn und Scirocco. Berlin: Reimer, 1868. 34p. 23cm.

DOVE, H   W
Über Eiszeit, Föhn und Scirocco. Berlin: Reimer, 1867. 116p., illus. 23cm.

DOWNER, Arthur Cleveland
Mountaineering ballads. C. Murray, [1905]. 47p. 12 x 15cm.

DOWNES, G
Guide through Switzerland and Savoy; or, A new and complete geographical, historical and picturesque description of every remarkable place in these countries ... forming a complete itinerary. New ed. Paris: A. and W. Galignani, [ca 1830]. lxiv, 560p. 15cm.

DOWSING, William
Rambles in Switzerland, with reminiscences of the Great St. Bernard, Mont Blanc, and the Bernese Alps. Kingston-upon-Hull: J.W. Leng; London: Hamilton, Adams, 1869. 139p., plates, illus. 23cm.

DOYLE, Richard
The foreign tour of Messrs. Brown, Jones and Robinson. Routledge, 1904. 1v. of illus. 30cm.

D'OYLEY, Elizabeth
Great travel stories of all nations; edited by Elizabeth D'Oyley. Harrap, 1932. 1030p. 23cm.

DRÄGER, Anton
Deutsche Reisen für die reisere Jugend unternommen und beschrieben. Th.1. Die Wunder des Hochgebirges. Berlin: Winckelmann, 1853. 126p., plates, illus. 20cm.

DRÄGER, Anton
Die Natur des Hochgebirges, mit besonderer Rücksicht auf die Gletscher. Leipzig: E. Reil, 1857. viii, 190p., col. plates, illus. 19cm.

DRAKE, Samuel Adams
The heart of the White Mountains: their legend and scenery; with illustrations by W. Hamilton Gibson. Chatto & Windus, 1882. xiii, 318p., plates, illus., map. 31cm.

DRASDO, Harold and SOPER, N   Jack
Eastern crags; illustrated by W. Heaton Cooper. Stockport: Fell & Rock Climbing Club, 1969. 233p., 1 col. plate, illus., maps (on lining papers). 16cm. (Climbing guides to the English Lake District, [4th ser.], 2)

DRESCH, Jean and LÉPINEY, Jacques de
Le Massif du Toubkal; avec le concours de Théophile Jean Delaye. Rabat: Office Chérifien du Tourisme, 1938. 233p., fold. plates (1 col.), illus., maps. 16cm. (Guide alpin de la montagne morocaine)

DRESELI, J   B
Alpenröslein; oder, Vierundzwanzig malerische Ansichten, [von J.B. Dreseli]; verschiedener Burgen, Gegenden, Seen u. im Salzkammergute dann in den Salzburger-, Berchtesgadener- und Tyroler-Gebirgen ..., mit erläuterndem deutschen und französischen Texte... München: J. Lindauer, 1836. 21p., plates, illus. 21 x 26cm.

DREVET, Joanny
SCIZE, Pierre
En altitude; eaux-fortes et héliogravures de Joanny Drevet. Grenoble: Didier & Richard, 1930. 169p., plates, illus. 23cm. (Cites, paysages,2)

DREVET, Louise
La Vallée de Chamonix et le Mont Blanc; suivi de Les ascensions au Mont Blanc, racontées par un de ses grimpeurs [i.e. Desroches]. Nouv. éd. Grenoble: X. Drevet, [1908]. 70, 111p. 20cm.

DREW, Frederic
The Jummoo and Kashmir territories: a geographical account. Stanford, 1875. xv, 568p., plates (some fold. col.), illus., maps (1 in pocket). 25cm.

DREW, Frederic
The northern barrier of India: a popular account of the Jummoo and Kashmir territories. Stanford, 1877. xii, 336p., plates (2 fold.), illus., maps. 21cm.

DREYER, Aloys
Bergsteigerbrevier: eine Blütenlese aus den Werken alpiner Dichtkunst und Erfahrungsweisheit; gesammelt und hrsg. von A. Dreyer; mit farbigem Umschlagbild von Ernst Platz... München: Parcus, [1922]. 155p., plates, illus. 18cm.

- - 2. Aufl. [1927].

DREYFUS, Paul
Sylvain Saudan, skieur de l'impossible. Paris: Arthaud, 1970. 219p., plates, illus. 21cm. (Collection sempervivum, no. 50)

DRIELING, F H C
Aanteekeningen op eene Reize naar Zwitserland en
Lombardijen in 1829. Utrecht: N. van der Monde,
1833. viii, 314p., plates, illus. 23cm.

DRINKWATER, Maria
Poetische reise, [by Maria Drinkwater]. [N.p.]:
[n.pub.], 1837. 125p. 26cm.

DRUMMOND, D T K
Scenes and impressions in Switzerland and the
north of Italy ... taken from the notes of a four
months' tour during the summer of 1852.
Edinburgh: P. Kennedy, 1853. xii, 218p., col.
plates, illus. 20cm.

DUBOIS, Albert
Croquis alpins: promenades en Suisse et au pays
des Dolomites; avec une notice sur la flore
alpestre par François Crépin. Mons: Byr & Loret,
1883. 526p. 25cm.

DUBOIS, Jean
Souvenirs de la Suisse: cent vues les plus remarquables, [dessiné d'après nature par J.
Dubois]. Genève: Briquet & Dubois, [ca 1845].
1v. of illus. 14 x 18cm.

- - Another collection. [ca 1850]. 1v. of illus.
(some col.).
- - Another collection. [ca 1855]. 1v. of col.
illus.

DUBOIS, Mary R J
Poems of travellers; compiled by M.R.J. Dubois.
Bell, 1909. xvi, 496p. 17cm.

DU CHOUL, Joannes
GESNER, Conrad
De raris et admirandis herbis, quae ... Lunariae
nominantur, commentariolus: & obiter de aliis
etiam rebus quae in tenebris lucent ...; eiusdem
descriptio Montis Fracti, sive Montis Pilati,
iuxta Lucernam in Helvetia; his accedunt Jo. Du
Choul... Pilati Montis in Gallia descriptio; Jo.
Rhellicani Stockhornias, qua Stockhornus mons
altissimus in Bernensium Helvetiorum agro,
versibus heroicis describitur. Tiguri: Apud
Andream Gesnerum & Jacobum Gesnerum, [1555].
95p., illus. 19cm.

DUCIS, C A
Les Alpes graies, poenines & cottiennes. Annecy,
1872. 23p. 22cm.
Offprint from Revue savoisienne.

DUCKWORTH, F R G
Swiss fantasy. Benn, 1948. 128p., plates, illus.
19cm.

DUCOMMUN, Jules César
Une excursion au Mont-Blanc. Genève: Imprimerie
Vaney, 1858. 31p., 3 fold. plates, illus. 22cm.
Signed J.-C. Ducommun.

- - 2e éd. Genève: H. Georg, 1859.

DUCOMMUN, Jules César
Taschenbuch für den schweizerischen Botaniker;
bearb. von J.C. Ducommun. Solothurn: Selbstverlag
des Verfassers, 1869. xxxvi, 1024p., illus.
19cm.

- - 2. Ausg. Luzern: C.F. Prell, 1881.

DÜBI, Heinrich
LA HARPE, Eugène de
Les Alpes bernoises; illustrations par Fréd.
Boissonnas; texte par Eugène de la Harpe avec la
collaboration du Dr. H. Dübi. Lausanne: Bridel,
1915. viii, 152p., illus. 34cm.

DÜBI, Heinrich
The Bernese Oberland. Vol.3. Dent de Morcles to
the Gemmi. T. Fisher Unwin, 1907. xxiv, 136p.
14cm. (Conway and Coolidge's climbers' guides,
12)

DÜBI, Heinrich
The Bernese Oberland. Vol.4. Grimsel to the Uri
Rothstock. Pt.1. Grimsel to the Sustenlimmi.
T. Fisher Unwin, 1908. xx, 111p. 14cm.
(Conway and Coolidge's climbers' guides, 13)

DÜBI, Heinrich
The Bernese Oberland. Vol.4. Grimsel to the Uri
Rothstock. Pt.2. Sustenlimmi to the Uri Rothstock.
T. Fisher Unwin, 1908. xxiii, 132p. 14cm.
(Conway and Coolidge's climbers' guides, 14)

DÜBI, Heinrich
[The Bernese Oberland]. Hochgebirgsführer durch
die Berner Alpen. Bd.1. Von der Dent de Morcles
bis zur Gemmi. Bern: Schweizer Alpen-Club,
Sektion Bern, 1907. xvi, 111p., bibl. 17cm.

DÜBI, Heinrich
COOLIDGE, William Augustus Brevoort
[The Bernese Oberland]. Hochgebirgsführer durch
die Berner Alpen. Bd.2. Von der Gemmi bis zum
Mönchjoch; übersetzt ... von H. Dübi. Bern:
Schweizer Alpen-Club, Sektion Bern, 1910. xx,
259p., bibl. 17cm.

DÜBI, Heinrich
COOLIDGE, William Augustus Brevoort
[The Bernese Oberland]. Hochgebirgsführer durch
die Berner Alpen. Bd.3. Vom Mönchsjoch bis zur
Grimsel; übersetzt ... von H. Dübi. Bern:
Schweizer Alpen-Club, Sektion Bern, 1909.
199p., bibl. 17cm.

DÜBI, Heinrich
[The Bernese Oberland]. Hochgebirgsführer durch
die Berner Alpen. Bd.4. Von der Grimsel bis zum
Uri-Rotstock. Bern: Schweizer Alpen-Club,
Sektion Bern, 1908. 200p., bibl. 17cm.

DÜBI, Heinrich
Clubführer durch die Walliser-Alpen. Bd.2. Vom
Col de Collon bis zum Theodulpass. Aarau:
Schweizer Alpen-Club, 1921. xxi, 380p., illus.,
bibl. 17cm.

DÜBI, Heinrich
Clubführer durch die Walliser-Alpen. Bd.3b.
Vom Strahlhorn bis zum Simplon. St. Gallen:
Schweizer Alpen-Club, 1916. viii, 185-381p.,
illus. 17cm.

DÜBI, Heinrich
[Clubführer durch die Walliser-Alpen]. Guide
des Alpes valaisannes. Vol.2. Du Col de Collon
au Col du Théodule; traduit de l'allemand,
revisé et complété par A. Wohnlich... Aarau:
Club Alpin Suisse, 1922. xxvii, 374p., illus.,
bibl. 17cm.

DÜBI, Heinrich
[Clubführer durch die Walliser-Alpen]. Guide
des Alpes valaisannes. Vol.3. Du Col du
Théodule au Schwarzenberg-Weisstor et du
Strahlhorn au Simplon; traduit de l'allemand par
E. Steinmann. Genève: Club Alpin Suisse, 1919.
xxxv, 388p., illus., map, bibl. 17cm.

DÜBI, Heinrich
SCHWEIZER ALPEN-CLUB
Die ersten fünfzig Jahre des Schweizer Alpenclub:
Denkschrift; im Auftrag des Centralcomitees
verfasst von Heinrich Dübi. Bern: S.A.C., 1913.
vi, 304p., 4 fold. plates, illus. 27cm.

DÜBI, Heinrich
SCHWEIZER ALPEN-CLUB
[Die ersten fünfzig Jahre ...]. Les cinquante
premières années du Club Alpin Suisse: notice
historique, par Henri Dübi ...; traduction par
D. Delétra. Berne: C.A.S., 1913. vi, 303p.,
4 fold. plates, illus. 27cm.

DÜBI, Heinrich
Gesammelte Alpine Schriften. Bern, 1886-1904.
4v. 21-28cm.
Binding title.
Collection of offprints.

DÜBI, Heinrich
Paccard wider Balmat, oder die Entwicklung einer
Legende: ein Beitrag zur Besteigungsgeschichte
des Mont Blanc. Bern: Francke, 1913. 298p.,
plates, illus., port. 26cm.

DÜBI, Heinrich
Saas-Fee und Umgebung: ein Führer durch Geschichte,
Volk und Landschaft des Saastales. Bern: A.
Francke, 1902. viii, 160p., illus., map (in
pocket). 20cm.

- - 2 Aufl., neu bearb. von Alice Zimmermann. 1946.

DÜBI, Heinrich
STUDER, Gottlieb
Über Eis und Schnee: die höchsten Gipfel der
Schweiz und die Geschichte ihrer Besteigung.
2. Aufl. umgearb. und ergänzt von A. Wäber und
H. Dübi. Bern: Schmid, Francke, 1896-99. 3v.,
1 plate, port. 19cm.

DU FAUR, Freda
The conquest of Mount Cook and other climbs:
an account of four seasons' mountaineering on
the Southern Alps of New Zealand. Allen & Unwin,
1915. 250p., plates, illus. 27cm.

DUFFERIN AND AVA, Frederick Temple Hamilton-
Temple-Blackwood, Marquess of
ST. JOHN, Molyneux
The sea of mountains: an account of Lord
Dufferin's tour through British Columbia in 1876.
Hurst and Blackett, 1877. 2v., plates, port.
20cm.

DUFOUR, Guillaume Henri
SWITZERLAND. Eidgenössisches Topographisches
Bureau
La topographie de la Suisse, 1832-1864: histoire
de la Carte Dufour; publié par le Bureau Topographique Fédéral. Berne: The Bureau, 1898. viii,
270p., plates, maps (some col.), port. 25cm.

DUFRANC, Michel and LUCCHESI, Alexis
Escalades dans les Alpes de Provence: Verdon,
Cadières, Teillon, Aiglun. Pau: Marrimpouey, 1975.
159p., 1 fold. plate, illus., maps. 16cm.

DUFRANC, Michel
Massif de l'Argentera. Nice: C.A.F., Section des
Alpes-Maritimes, 1970. 217p., illus. 17cm.
(Guides Paschetta des Alpes-Maritimes, 2)

COOLIDGE, William Augustus Brevoort and DUHAMEL,
Henry
Le Col de Galest et le Col de la Galise. Lyon,
1905. 16p., plates, illus. 24cm.
Offprint from Revue alpine, nov. 1905.

COOLIDGE, William Augustus Brevoort and DUHAMEL,
Henry
Le Col de la Leisse et les Quecées de Tignes.
Lyon: Imp. Geneste, 1905. 13p., plates, illus.
24cm.

DUHAMEL, Henry
COOLIDGE, William Augustus Brevoort
Guide du Haut-Dauphiné, par W.A.B. Coolidge, H.
Duhamel, F. Perrin. Grenoble: A. Gratier, 1887.
lix, 442p., maps. 16cm.

- - Suppl. Grenoble: Imprimerie Breynat, 1890.

DUHAMEL, Henry
COOLIDGE, William Augustus Brevoort
[Guide du Haut-Dauphiné]. Das Hochgebirge des
Dauphiné, von W.A.B. Coolidge, H. Duhamel und F.
Perrin. 4. durchgesehene und 1. autorisierte
deutsche Ausg. hrsg. von Österreichischen Alpen-
klub. Wien: Ö.A.K., 1913. 351p., 17cm.
(Alpenklub-Ausgabe, 1)

DUHAMEL, Henry
PAULMY, Antoine René de Voyer d'Argenson, marquis
de
Voyage d'inspection de la frontière des Alpes
en 1752 par le marquis de Paulmy; [edited by]
Henry Duhamel. Grenoble: H. Falque & F. Perrin,
1902. 236p., plates, illus., maps, port. 26cm.

DUJARDIN, Victor
Voyages aux Pyrénées, Souvenirs du Midi, par un
homme du Nord... Le Rousillon. Ceret: L. Lamiot,
1890. 571p., 1 fold. plate, map. 19cm.

DUKE, Joshua
Kashmir and Jammu: a guide for visitors.
Calcutta: Thacker, Spink, 1903. xi, 613p., fold.
plates (some col.), illus., maps. 16cm.

DUKE OF EDINBURGH'S AWARD SCHEME
DISLEY, John
Expedition guide, Duke of Edinburgh's Award: the
scheme for boys; edited by John Disley; illus-
trated by Gordon F. Mansell. Duke of Edinburgh's
Award Office, 1965. 110p., illus., maps. 15cm.

DUMAS, Alexandre, 1802-1870
Impressions de voyage: le Caucase. Paris: M.
Lévy, 1865. 3v. 18cm.

DUMAS, Alexandre, 1802-1870
Impressions de voyage - Suisse. Nouv. éd.
Paris: C. Lévy, 1880-81, [v.1, 1881]. 3v. 19cm.
(Oeuvres complètes)

DUMAS, Alexandre, 1802-1870
[Impressions de voyage - Suisse]. The glacier
land; from the French ... by Mrs. W.R. Wilde.
Simms & M'Intyre, 1852. 272p. 18cm.
Translation of the first part.

DUMAS, Alexandre, 1802-1870
[Impressions de voyage - Suisse]. Swiss travel,
being chapters from 'Dumas' Impressions de
voyage'; edited by C.H. Parry. Longmans, Green,
1890. viii, 254p. 18cm.

- - New ed. 1895.

DUMLER, Helmut
PAULCKE, Wilhelm
[Die Gefahren der Alpen]. Hazards in mountaineering; [rev. by] Helmut Dumler, translated from
the German by E. Noel Bowman. Kaye & Ward, 1973.
161p. (1 fold., col.), illus., bibl. 21cm.

DUNAND, Léon
PORTIER, Francis
Grimenz, village valaisan: 10 planches fac-
similés des peintures de Francis Portier, texte
de Léon Dunand. Genève: Éditions "SADAG",
[1919?]. [6]p., col. plates, illus. 28 x 36cm.
In portfolio.

DUNANT, David
Le touriste à Chamonix en 1853. Genève: [The
Author], 1853. 295p. 24cm.

DUNANT, Édouard Wyss-
See
WYSS-DUNANT, Édouard

DUNCAN, Jane Ellen
A summer ride through western Tibet. Collins,
[1913?]. 316p., plates, illus. 16cm. (Illustrated pocket classics, no.211)

DUNDAS, Anne
Beneath African glaciers: the humours, tragedies
and demands of an East African Government station.
Witherby, 1924. 238p., plates, illus. 23cm.

DUNKIN, Robert
See
SNAFFLE

DUNMORE, Charles Adolphus Murray, 7th Earl of
The Pamirs, being a narrative of a year's expedition on horseback and on foot through Kashmir,
western Tibet, Chinese Tartary, and Russian
central Asia. Vol.1. 2nd ed. Murray, 1893. xx,
360p., plates (1 fold. col.), illus., map. 21cm.

DUNN, Robert
The shameless diary of an explorer. New York:
Outing Publishing, 1907. viii, 297p., plates
(2 fold.), illus., maps. 19cm.

DUNSHEATH, Joyce and BAILLIE, Eleanor
Afghan quest: the story of their Abinger
Afghanistan Expedition 1960. Harrap, 1961.
236p., plates, illus., map. 22cm.

DUNSHEATH, Joyce
Guests of the Soviets: Moscow and the Caucasus
1957. Constable, 1959. vii,183p., plates, illus.,
map (on lining paper), bibl. 22cm.

DUNSHEATH, Joyce
Mountains and memsahibs, by members of the Abinger
Himalayan Expedition 1956; foreword by Mrs.
Pandit. Constable, 1958. x, 198p., plates,
illus., maps. 22cm.

DUNSTAN, Mary
Jagged skyline: a novel. Constable, 1935. 20cm.

HEGI, Gustav and DUNZINGER, Gustav
Alpenflora: die verbreitetsten Alpenflanzen von
Bayern, Tirol und der Schweiz. München: J.F.
Lehmann, 1905. 66p., 30 col. plates, illus. 21cm.

- - 3. verb. Aufl. 1913.

HEGI, Gustav and DUNZINGER, Gustav
[Alpenflora]. Alpine flowers: the most common
alpine plants of Switzerland, Austria, and Bavaria,
by Gustav Hegi [and Gustav Dunzinger]. Authorised
translation by Winifred M. Deans. Blackie, 1930.
74p., 38 plates (chiefly col.), illus. 21cm.

HEGI, Gustav and DUNZINGER, Gustav
[Alpenflora]. Atlas colorié de la flore alpine:
Jura, Pyrénées, Alpes françaises, Alpes suisse;
[traduit] par J. Beauverie et L. Faucheron d'après
Hegi et Dunzinger; préface de R. Gérard. Paris:
J.-B. Baillière, 1906. 98p., 30 col. plates,
illus. 22cm.

DUPAIGNE, Albert
Les montagnes. 2e éd. rev. et augm. Tours: Mame,
1874. 581p., plates, illus., col. maps. 25cm.

DUPARC, Louis and RITTER, Étienne
Carbonifère alpin. Genève, 1894. 5p. 23cm.
Offprint from Archives des Sciences physiques et
naturelles, t.31, 15 jan. 1894.

DUPARC, Louis and RITTER, Étienne
Eclogites et Amphibolites du massif du Grand-Mont.
[Genève], 1894. 3p. 23cm.
Offprint from Archives des Sciences physiques et
naturelles, t.31, avril 1894.

DUPARC, Louis and RITTER, Étienne
Étude pétrographique des schistes de Casanna du
Valais: première note. Genève, 1896. 13p. 23cm.
Offprint from Archives des Sciences physiques et
naturelles, t.2 (4e période), juillet, 1896.

DUPARC, Louis and RITTER, Étienne
Formation quaternaire d'éboulis au Mont Salève.
Lausanne, 1893. 4p. 23cm.
Offprint from Archives des Sciences physiques et
naturelles, déc. 1893.

DUPARC, Louis and RITTER, Étienne
Le grès de Taveyannaz et ses rapports avec les
formations du flysch. Genève, 1895. 48p., illus.
23cm.
Offprint from Archives des Sciences physiques et
naturelles, t.33, mai et juin 1895.

DUPARC, Louis
Le lac d'Annecy: monographie. Genève, 1894.
33p., 1 fold. col. plate, map. 23cm.
Offprint from Archives des Sciences physiques et
naturelles, t.31, 15 jan. 1894.

DUPARC, Louis and MRAZEC, Ludovic
Le massif de Trient: étude pétrographique.
Lausanne, 1894. 16p., fold. plates, illus.
23cm.
Offprint from Archives des Sciences physiques et
naturelles, t.32, 15 sept. 1894.

DUPARC, Louis and RITTER, Étienne
Les massifs cristallins de Beaufort et Cevines:
étude pétrographique. Genève, 1893. 30p., fold.
plates, illus. 23cm.
Offprint from Archives des Sciences physiques et
naturelles, t.30, 1893.

DUPARC, Louis
Le Mont-Blanc au point de vue géologique et
pétrographique. Genève, 1896. 8p. 23cm.
Offprint from Archives des Sciences physiques et
naturelles, t.2 (4e période), sept. 1896.

DUPARC, Louis and MRAZEC, Ludovic
Note sur la serpentine de la vallée de Binnen
(Valais). Paris, 1894. 8p. 23cm.
Offprint from Bulletin de la Société française
de Mineralogie, t.16, no.8, 1894.

DUPARC, Louis and MRAZEC, Ludovic
Note sur les roches amphiboliques du Mont-Blanc.
Genève, 1893. 22p. 23cm.
Offprint from Archives des Sciences physiques et
naturelles, t.30, sept. 1893.

DUPARC, Louis
Notices pétrographiques. Genève, 1896. 4p.
23cm.
Offprint from Archives des Sciences physiques et
naturelles, t.1 (4e période), mai 1896.

DUPARC, Louis and MRAZEC, Ludovic
Nouvelles recherches sur le massif du Mont-Blanc.
Genève, 1895. 39p. 23cm.
Offprint from Archives des Sciences physiques et
naturelles, t.34, oct. 1895.

DUPARC, Louis
Prolongement supposé de la chaîne de Belledonne
vers le nord. Genève, 1894. 4p. 23cm.
Offprint from Archives des Sciences physiques et
naturelles, t.31, 15 juin 1894.

DUPARC, Louis
Publications scientifiques de M. le professeur
Duparc. [Genève]: [The Author], [1895]. 5p.
23cm.

DUPARC, Louis and MRAZEC, Ludovic
Recherches géologiques et pétrographiques sur le
massif du Mont-Blanc. Genève: Georg, 1898.
227p., plates (some fold, some col.), illus.,
map (in pocket). 32cm. (Mémoires de la Société
de physique et d'histoire naturelle de Genève,
t.33, no.1)

DUPARC, Louis and MRAZEC, Ludovic
La structure du Mont-Blanc. Genève, 1893. 13p.,
fold. col. plates, illus. 23cm.
Offprint from Archives des Sciences physiques et
naturelles, t.29, 15 jan. 1893.

DUPARC, Louis and MRAZEC, Ludovic
Sur quelques bombes de l'Etna, provenant des
éruptions de 1886 et 1892. Genève: [The Authors],
[1895?]. 3p. 27cm.

DUPARC, Louis and MRAZEC, Ludovic
Sur quelques bombes volcaniques de l'Etna des
éruptions de 1886 et 1892. Genève, 1892. 7p.,
plates, illus. 23cm.
Offprint from Archives des Sciences physiques et
naturelles, t.29, 15 mars 1893.

DU PLESSIS, J , comte
L'Alpe enchanteresse: Salzbourg, le Salzkammergut,
les Hauts Tauern. Paris: Hachette, 1913. vi,
232p., 33 plates (1 fold.), illus., map. 20cm.
(Collection des voyages illustrés)

DUPPA, Richard
Miscellaneous observations and opinions on the
continent, by the author of "The life of
Michel'Angelo" ... [i.e. Richard Duppa]. Longman,
Hurst, Rees, Orme, Brown, & Green, 1825. 214p.,
plates, illus. 26cm.

DU PREL, Carl, Freiherr
Unter Tannen und Pinien: Wanderungen in den Alpen,
Italien, Dalmatien und Montenegro. Berlin:
Denicke, 1875. vi, 312p. 22cm.

DURAND, Algernon
The making of a frontier: five years' experiences
and adventures in Gilgit, Hunza, Nagar, Chitral,
and the eastern Hindu-Kush. Murray, 1899. xvi,
298p., plates (1 fold.col.), illus., maps. 23cm.

DURAND, Sir Edward
Rifle, rod, and spear in the East: being sporting reminiscences. Murray, 1911. vii, 200p.,
plates, illus. 23cm.

DURBIN, John P
Observations in Europe, principally in France and
Great Britain. New-York: Harper, 1844. 2v.,
plates, maps. 21cm.

DURGNAT-JUNOD, Clara
Pinceaux et piolet: autobiographie anecdotique.
Lausanne: Éditions Held, 1943. 209p., plates,
illus. 20cm.

DURHAM, William Edward
Summer holidays in the Alps, 1898-1914. T. Fisher
Unwin, 1916. 207p., plates, illus. 28cm.

DURHEIM, C J
Sammlung trigonometrischer oder barometrisch-
bestimmter absoluter Höhen der Schweiz und ihrer
nähern Umgebung = Hypsométrie de la Suisse...
Bern: Haller, 1850. xxi, 705p. 26cm.
Introduction in German & French.

DURIER, Charles
Histoire du Mont-Blanc: conférences faites à
Paris les 23 et 30 mai 1873 à la salle du Boule-
vard des Capucines. Paris: Sandoz et Fischbacher,
1873. 97p. 17cm.

DURIER, Charles
Le Mont-Blanc. Paris. Sandoz & Fischbacher, 1877.
x, 488p., plates, illus., fold. maps. 25cm.

- - 2e éd. 1880.
- - 3e éd. Paris: Fischbacher, [1881].
- - 4e éd. rev. et augm. d'un supplément. 1897.
- - 5e éd. [1912].
- - 7e éd. annot. et illus., par Joseph Vallot et
Charles Vallot. 1923.

DURIO, Alberto
Bibliografia alpinistica-storica e scientifica
del Gruppo del Monte Rosa (dal Colle del Théodule
al Passo del Monte Moro) dei monti della Valesia
e della Sezione di Varallo del C.A.I., 1527-1924.
Novara: Istituto Geografico de Agostini, 1925.
84p. 25cm.

DURST, Carola
Im Zauberreich der Berge: Märchen und Sagen; dem
Freunden der Bergwelt für ihre Jugend gewidmet
von Carola Durst. Stuttgart: Horster, 1906.
144p., col. plate, illus. 22cm.

DURUZ, A
See
SOLANDIEU

DUSAULX, J
Voyage à Barège et dans les Hautes Pyrénées, fait
en 1788. Paris: Didot Jeune, 1796. 2v. in 1.
21cm.

DUTENS, L
Itinéraire des routes les plus fréquentées; ou,
Journal de plusieurs voyages aux villes princi-
pales de l'Europe, depuis 1768 jusqu'en 1783...
Paris: Barreis, 1783. xxxii, 271p., maps. 18cm.

DUTOIT, Sigismond
Tour du Mont-Blanc: descriptions de 12 itinéraires
avec profils, croquis et photographies. Berne:
Kümmerly & Frey, 1962. 60p., plates (1 col.),
illus., maps. 18cm. (Guides suisses de tourisme
pédestre. Série internationale, guide pédestre,
1)

DUTTON, Clarence E
Tertiary history of the Grand Canon District.
Washington: Government Printing Office, 1882.
xiv, 264p., 42 plates (1 col.), illus. 31cm.
(Monographs of the United States Geological
Survey, 2)

- - Atlas.

DUTTON, E A T
Kenya Mountain; with an introduction by Hilaire
Belloc. Cape, 1929. xv, 219p., 56 plates (1
fold.col.), illus., maps. 27cm.

DUVAL, M
La grande caravane: seize jours dans l'Oberland
(12-27 juillet 1854). Genève: Duchamp, 1855.
435p., 1 plate, illus. 20cm.

DUVERNEY, Jacques
Un tour en Suisse: histoire, science, monuments,
paysages; illustrations par Karl Girardet.
Tours: Mame, 1866. 2v. in 1., illus. 18cm.

DUVOTENAY, Ch
Atlas géographique, historique, statistique, et
itinéraire de la Suisse, divisé en vingt-deux
cantons, et de la Vallée de Chamouny, avec une
carte générale de la Suisse, dressé par Ch.
Duvotenay ...; gravé... par Ch. Dyonnet...
Delloye, 1837. xx, 104p., plates (1 col.),
illus., maps. 31cm.

DYHRENFURTH, Günter Oskar
Baltoro: ein Himalaya-Buch; mit Beiträgen von
Hettie Dyhrenfurth, Hans Ertl und André Roch.
Basel: Schwabe, 1939. 195p., plates, illus.,
bibl. 26cm.

- - Beilagen-Mappe.

DYHRENFURTH, Günter Oskar
Das Buch vom Kantsch: die Geschichte seiner
Besteigung. München: Nymphenburger Verlagshandlung, 1955. 190p., plates, illus., maps, bibl.
22cm.

DYHRENFURTH, Günter Oskar
Das Buch vom Nanga Parbat: die Geschichte seiner
Besteigung 1895-1953. München: Nymphenburger
Verlagshandlung, 1954. 199p., plates, illus.,
maps, bibl. 21cm.

DYHRENFURTH, Günter Oskar
Dämon Himalaya: Bericht der Internationalen
Karakoram-Expedition 1934; unter Mitarbeit von
Gustav Diessl, Hettie Dyhrenfurth, Hans Ertl,
André Roch und Hans Winzeler; hrsg. von Günter
O. Dyhrenfurth. Basel: Schwabe, 1935. vii,
111p, plates (1 fold.), illus., map. 26cm.

DYHRENFURTH, Günter Oskar
Der dritte Pol: die Achttausender und ihre
Trabanten. München: Nymphenburger Verlagshandlung, 1960. 263p., plates, illus., maps. bibl.
25cm.

DYHRENFURTH, Günter Oskar
Himalaya: unsere Expedition 1930; unter Mitarbeit
von Ch. Duvanel [and others]; hrsg. von Günter
O. Dyhrenfurth. Berlin: Scherl, 1931. 380p.,
plates (some fold., some col.), illus., bibl.
24cm.

- - Das Massiv des Kangchendzönga (Himalaya), von
Marcel Kurz. [Map].

DYHRENFURTH, Günter Oskar
HAGEN, Toni
   Mount Everest: Aufbau, Erforschung und Be-
   völkerung des Everest-Gebietes, [von] Toni Hagen,
   Günter-Oskar Dyhrenfurth, Christoph von Führer-
   Haimendorf, Erwin Schneider. Zürich: Orell
   Füssli, 1959. 234p., plates, illus., maps.
   24cm.

DYHRENFURTH, Günter Oskar
HAGEN, Toni
   [Mount Everest: Aufbau ...]. Mount Everest:
   formation, population and exploration of the
   Everest region, [by] Toni Hagen, Günter-Oskar
   Dyhrenfurth, Christoph von Führer-Haimendorf,
   Erwin Schneider; translated by E. Noel Bowman.
   Oxford University Press, 1963. xiv, 195p.,
   plates, illus., maps. 24cm.

DYHRENFURTH, Günter Oskar
   Zum dritten Pol: die Achttausender der Erde;
   mit Beiträgen von Erwin Schneider. München:
   Nymphenburger Verlagshandlung, 1952. 286p.,
   plates, illus., maps. 25cm.

DYHRENFURTH, Günter Oskar
   [Zum dritten Pol]. To the third pole: the
   history of the High Himalaya; with contributions
   by Erwin Schneider; translated by Hugh Merrick.
   Werner Laurie, 1955. xxvii, 233p., plates,
   illus., maps. 26cm.

DYHRENFURTH, Günter Oskar
   Memsahb im Himalaja: [die einzige weisse Frau auf
   der Internationalen Himalaja-Expedition 1930].
   Leipzig: Deutsche Buchwerkstätten, 1931. 71p.,
   plates, illus. 21cm.

DYKE, John C   van
   See
VAN DYKE, John Charles

DYKE, Thomas
   Travelling mems, during a tour through Belgium,
   Rhenish Prussia, Germany, Switzerland, and France,
   in the summer and autumn of 1832, including an
   excursion up the Rhine. Longman, Rees, Orme,
   Brown, Green, & Longman, 1834. 2v. 21cm.

E., T.
VEITCH, Sophie F   F
   Views in central Abyssinia; with portraits of the
   natives of the Galla tribes, taken in pen and ink
   under circumstances of peculiar difficulty by
   T.E., a German traveller ...; with descriptions
   by Sophie F.F. Veitch. J.C. Hotten, 1868. 1v.
   (chiefly illus.). 23 x 29cm.

EAGLE SKI CLUB
SKI CLUB OF GREAT BRITAIN
   Handbook on ski-touring and glacier ski-ing. Ski
   Club of Great Britain in conjunction with the
   Alpine Ski Club and the Eagle Ski Club, 1954.
   78p. 16cm.

- - 2nd ed. completely rev. 1961.

EASON, T   W   and HAMILTON, R
   A portrait of Michael Roberts; edited by T.W.
   Eason and R. Hamilton. College of S. Mark and
   S. John, 1949. xii, 72p., plates, ports, bibl.
   23cm.

EAST GREENLAND EXPEDITION, 1972
   A photographic album of the 1972 East Greenland
   Expedition from Cambridge University [by] K.J.
   Miller. Cambridge: University of Cambridge,
   Department of Engineering, 1974. 1v. (chiefly
   illus.). 30cm. (CUED Special project report,
   no.3)

EASTLAKE, Elizabeth, Lady
RIGBY, Edward
   Dr. Rigby's letters from France &c.in 1789; edited
   by his daughter, Lady Eastlake. Longmans, Green,
   1880. xviii, 232p. 20cm.

EASTMAN, S   C
   The White Mountain guide book. 10th ed. Concord:
   C. Eastman, 1872. 248p., 2 fold. plates, illus.,
   maps. 17cm.

EASTON, John
   An unfrequented highway through Sikkim and Tibet
   to Chumolaori. Scholartis Press, 1928. xii,
   133p., plates, illus. 27cm.

EBEL, Johann Gottfried
   Anleitung auf die nützlichste und genussvollste
   Art in der Schweitz zu reisen. Zürich: Orell,
   Gessner, Füssli, 1793. 2v., plates, illus., maps.
   19cm.

- - 2. ganz umgearb. und sehr verm. Aufl. 1804-05.
   4v.
- - 3. Aufl. 1809-10. 4v. in 3.
- - 7. Original Aufl., im auszuge ganz neu bearb.
   von G. von Escher. 1840. iv, 655p.
- - 8. Original Aufl. 1843. iv, 634p.

EBEL, Johann Gottfried
   [Anleitung auf die nützlichste und genussvollste
   Art...]. Instructions pour un voyageur qui se
   propose de parcourir la Suisse de la manière la
   plus utile... Basle: J.J. Tourneisen, 1795.
   2v., plates, illus., maps. 18cm.

EBEL, Johann Gottfried and HEIDEGGER, Heinrich
   Handbuch für Reisende in der Schweiz, [von J.G.
   Ebel und H. Heidegger]:[edited by R. Glutz-
   Blotzheim]. 4. verb. Aufl. Zürich: Orell,
   Füssli, 1818. viii, 520p. 20cm.

- - 5. verb. Aufl. 1823.
- - 6. verb. Aufl., hrsg. von J. Schoch. 1830.

EBEL, Johann Gottfried
   [Handbuch für Reisende in der Schweiz]. The
   traveller's guide through Switzerland, in four
   parts ..., by M.J.G. Ebel. New ed., arranged and
   improved by Daniel Wall with a complete atlas.
   Leigh, 1818. xxvii, 548p. and atlas, plates,
   illus. 15cm.

EBEL, Johann Gottfried
   [Handbuch für Reisende in der Schweiz]. Manuel
   du voyageur en Suisse: ouvrage où l'on trouve
   les directions necessaires pour recueillir tout
   le fruit et toutes les jouissances ...; traduit
   pour la seconde fois de l'allemand, sur la
   seconde éd. ... Zurich: Orell, Füssli, 1805.
   4v., plates, illus. 19cm.

- - 2e éd. ... de la 3e éd. originale. 1810-11.
- - 3e éd. 1818. 3v.
- - 4e éd. 1819. viii, 465p.
- - [Another ed.]. 1827. 566p.

EBEL, Johann Gottfried
   [Handbuch für Reisende in der Schweiz]. Manuel
   du voyageur en Suisse. Nouv. éd., aug. de
   l'Itineraire des Bords du Rhin par Schreiber et
   de la grande carte de Keller. Paris: Audin,
   1826. 620p., map. 18cm.

- - Nouv. éd. 1831.
- - Nouv. éd. 1834.

EBEL, Johann Gottfried
   [Handbuch für Reisende in der Schweiz]. Le
   nouvel Ebel: manuel du voyageur en Suisse et dans
   le Tyrol ...; revue d'après Murray. Paris:
   Maison, 1841. xxxi, 596p., plates, illus., maps.
   18cm.

- - 11e éd. 1853.

EBEL, Johann Gottfried
MEYER, J   J
Les nouvelles routes par le pays des Grisons
jusqu'aux lacs Majeur et de Como en 32 vues, par
J.J. Meyer; accompagnés de texte par J.G. Ebel.
Zurich: J.J. Meyer, 1827. 169p., plates, illus.,
map. 18 x 25cm.

EBEL, Johann Gottfried
Schilderung der Gebirgsvölker der Schweiz.
Leipzig: Pet. Phil. Wolf., 1798-1802. 2v., plates
(some fold.), illus. 22cm.

EBEL, Johann Gottfried
MEYER, J   J
Voyage pittoresque dans le Canton des Grisons en
Suisse vers le Lac Majeur et le Lac de Como à
travers les cols de Splugen et de St. Bernard;
accompagné d'une introduction et explication de
J.G. Ebel. Zurich: J.J. Meyer, 1827. 336p.,
plates, map. 22cm.

EBERHARD, Otto
Heures de liberté de Lionel Morton, publiées par
Otto Eberhard. Zurich: Orell, Füssli, [1916].
147p., plates, map. 20cm.

EBERL, Anton, Freiherr von
Erinnerung an Tirol. Innsbruck: Wagner, 1840.
81p., plates, illus. 14cm.

EBERLI, Henry
Switzerland poetical and pictorial: a collection
of poems by English and American poets; compiled
by Henry Eberli. Zurich: Orell, Füssli, 1893.
xvi, 537p., illus. 24cm.

ECKART, K
Führer durch Passau & Umgebung: zugleich Fest-
schrift für die General-Versammlung des Deutschen
& Österr. Alpenvereins in Passau ... 1899, von
K. Eckart; und einem Anhang über das alpine
Arbeits-Gebiet der Sektion von [F.] Lucas.
Passau: Sektion Passau, 1899. 75,30p., plates,
(1 fold.col.), illus., plan. 21cm.

ECKENSTEIN, Oscar and LORRIA, August
The Alpine portfolio: the Pennine Alps, from the
Simplon to the Great St. Bernard; edited by Oscar
Eckenstein & August Lorria. The Editors, [1889].
33p., 100 plates, illus. 42cm.
Photographs by V. Sella, E. Le Bland, W.F. Donkin,
and others, with an introductory text.

ECKENSTEIN, Oscar
The Karakorams and Kashmir: an account of a
journey. Fisher Unwin, 1896. xvi, 253p. 20cm.

ECKERT, Max
Das Gottesackerplateau, ein Karrenfeld im Allgäu:
Studien zur Lösung das Karrenproblems. Innsbruck:
D.u.Ö.A.V., 1902. vi, 108p., plates, illus., map.
30cm. (Wissenschaftliche Ergänzungshefte zur
Zeitschrift des D.u.Ö. Alpenvereins)

ECKSTEIN, Oskar
Seitenpfade um Saas-Fee. 3. Aufl. Zürich: Orell
Füssli, 1941. 81p., plates, illus., bibl. 23cm.

EDGAR, John Ware
Report on a visit to Sikhim and the Thibetan
frontier in October, November, and December, 1873.
Calcutta: Bengal Secretariat Press, 1874. 103p.,
illus. 25cm.

EDGCUMBE, Richard
SHELLEY, Frances, Lady
The diary of Frances Lady Shelley, 1787-1817;
edited by her grandson Richard Edgcumbe. Murray,
1912. vii, 406p., plates, illus. 23cm.

EDHOLM, O   G   and BACHARACH, A   L
Exploration medicine, being a practical guide for
those going on expeditions; edited by O.G. Edholm
and A.L. Bacharach; with an introduction by Sir
Raymond Priestly, Bristol: J. Wright, 1965.
xvi, 410p., illus., bibl. 23cm.

EDINBURGH. National Library of Scotland
See
NATIONAL LIBRARY OF SCOTLAND

EDMUNDSON, G
ENCYCLOPAEDIA BRITANNICA
Belgium, Italy and Switzerland, by G. Edmundson,
H. Wickham Steed, W.A.B. Coolidge. Encyclopaedia
Britannica, 1914. iv, 201p., plates. 23cm.
Reproduced from the 11th edition of the Encyclo-
paedia Britannica.

EDWARDS, Amelia Blandford
A midsummer ramble in the Dolomites
See her
Untrodden peaks and unfrequented valleys

EDWARDS, Amelia Blandford
Untrodden peaks and unfrequented valleys: a midsummer ramble in the Dolomites. Longmans Green,
1873. xxvi, 385p., plates (1 fold.col.), illus.,
map. 24cm.

- - [2nd ed.] published under title: A midsummer
ramble in the Dolomites. Routledge, 1889.
- - 2nd ed. published under title: Untrodden
peaks ... Routledge, 1890.
- - 3rd ed. Routledge,[ca 1900].

EDWARDS, Francis
Mountaineering, arctic travel, including a few
books from the late Mr. Edward Whymper's Library,
offered by Francis Edwards, Bookseller. F.
Edwards, 1913. 15p. 22cm.

EDWARDS, John Menlove and BARFORD, John Edward
Quintus
Clogwyn du'r Arddu. Manchester, 1942. 24p.,
plates, illus., bibl. 22cm.
Offprint from the Climbers' Club journal, 1942.

EDWARDS, John Menlove
Cwm Idwal. 2nd rev. ed. Manchester: Climbers'
Club, 1940 (1946 reprint). vii, 145p., plates,
illus. 16cm. (Climbing guides to the Snowdon
District, 1)

- - New ed., by A.J.J. Moulam. 1958.

EDWARDS, John Menlove
Cwm Idwal group; with illustrations by the
author. New and rev. ed. Barrow-in-Furness:
Climbers' Club, 1936. 135p., plates, illus.
16cm. (Climbing guides to the Snowdon District,
1)

NOYCE, Wilfrid and EDWARDS, John Menlove
Lliwedd group. New and rev. ed. Climbers' Club,
1939. vii, 173p., plates, illus., map. 16cm.
(Climbing guides to the Snowdon District, 4)

EDWARDS, John Menlove
Samson: the life and writings of Menlove
Edwards; edited with biographical memoir by
Geoffrey Sutton and Wilfrid Noyce. Stockport:
Cloister Press, 1960. ix, 122p., plates, illus.
22cm.

EDWARDS, John Menlove and NOYCE, Wilfrid
Tryfan group; with photographs by J.M. Edwards;
and diagrams by C.H. French. Climbers' Club,
1937. ix, 122p., plates, illus. 16cm.
(Climbing guides to the Snowdon District, 2)

EDWARDS, M   Betham-
See
BETHAM-EDWARDS, M

EDWARDS, Rowland
Climbs on North Wales limestone: the Little Orme,
the Great Orme, Craig y Forwyn. Leicester:
Cordee, 1976. 56p., illus. 18cm. (Interim rock
climbers guide to North Wales limestone)

EDY, John William
Boydell's Picturesque scenery of Norway; with the principal towns from the Naze ... to the ... Swinesund; from original drawings made on the spot, and engraved by John William Edy; with remarks and observations made in a tour through the country, and rev. and corr. by William Tooke. Hurst, Robinson, 1820. xlv p., 80 plates, illus. 42cm.

EGAN, Christopher P
Resumé of the 1962 field season of the Michigan State University Glaciological Institute, Juneau Icefield, Alaska. 61-69p., illus., map. 24cm. Offprint from The Compass, Sigma Gamma Epsilon, vol.41, no.1, Nov. 1963.

EGELER, Cornelius Geoffrey
[Maar onbestegen Andes toppen]. The untrodden Andes: climbing adventures in the Cordillera Blanca, Peru, by C.G. Egeler in co-operation with T. de Booy; translated from the Dutch by W.E. James. Faber, 1955. 203p., plates, illus., maps. 22cm.

EGERTON, Philip Henry
Journal of a tour through Spiti, to the frontier of Chinese Thibet; with photographic illustrations. Cundall, Downes, 1864. vi, 68p., plates, illus., map. 39cm.

EGGER, Carl
Aiguilles: ein Bergbüchlein. Zürich: Orell Füssli, 1924. 74p., 24 plates, illus. 22cm.

EGGER, Carl
Die Eroberung des Kaukasus. Basel: Schwabe, 1932. 311p., plates, illus., maps. 24cm.

EGGER, Carl
Höhenluft: Erlebtes und Erfühltes. München: Rother, 1930. 244p., plates, illus. 21cm. (Grosse Bergsteiger)

EGGER, Carl
Im Kaukasus: Bergbesteigungen und Reiseerlebnisse im Sommer 1914. Basel: Frobenius, 1915. 144p., plates (1 fold.), illus. 23cm.

EGGER, Carl
Michel-Gabriel Paccard und der Montblanc. Basel: Gaiser & Haldimann, 1943. 103p., plates, illus., bibl. 23cm.

EGGER, Carl
Pioniere der Alpen: 30 Lebensbilder der grossen Schweizer Bergführer von Melchior Anderegg bis Franz Lochmatter, 1837 bis 1933; hrsg. von der Schweizerischen Stiftung für Alpine Forschungen. Zürich: Amstutz, Herdeg, 1946. 371p., ports, bibl. 21cm.

EGGER, Carl
Vorübergang. Zürich: Orell Füssli, 1926. 128p. 19cm.

EGGERLING, Carl
See
EGGERLING-JÄGER, Carl

EGGERLING-JÄGER, Carl and TAUBER, Carl
Clubführer durch die Bündner Alpen. Bd. 8. Silvretta-Samnaun. Baden: S.A.C., 1934. 468p., illus., maps, bibl. 17cm. (Clubführer des Schweizer Alpen-Club)

- - 2. Aufl., revidiert von Carl Eggerling-Jäger und Jakob Schmid-Maron. 1961.

EGGLER, Albert
[Gipfel über den Wolken]. The Everest-Lhotse adventure; translated by Hugh Merrick. Allen & Unwin, 1957. 222p., plates (1 col.), illus., map. 24cm.
The third Swiss expedition of climbers and scientists, 1956.

EGLI, Emil
Swiss life and landscape; translated from the German by Eleanor Brockett. Elek, [1949]. 161p., illus, map (on lining papers). 22cm.

EGLI, Johann Jakob
Praktische Schweizerkunde für Schule und Haus. 3. vielverb. Aufl. St. Gallen: Huber, 1865. vi, 193p., 1 plate, map. 21cm.

LÜTHI, Gottlieb and EGLOFF, Carl
Das Säntis-Gebiet: illustrierter Touristenführer; mit einem naturgeschichtlichen Anhang von E. Bächler... 3. neurev. Aufl. St. Gallen: Fehr, 1913. 200p., illus., map (in pocket). 19cm.

- - 6. Aufl. neu bearb. von Karl Kleine. 1946.

EGMOND D'ARCIS, C
See
ARCIS, C   Egmond d'

EGVILLE, Alan Hervey d'
See
D'EGVILLE, Alan Hervey

EHMER, W
Um den Gipfel der Welt: die Geschichte des Bergsteigers Mallory. Stuttgart: J. Engelhorn, 1936. 186p., plates, port, map. 20cm.

EHRMANN, Theophil Friedrich
Neuste Kunde der Schweiz und Italiens; nach ihrem jetzigen Zustande aus den besten Quellen darge-stellt von Theophil Friedrich Ehrmann. Weimar: im Verlage des Geographischen Instituts, 1908. 578p., 11 plates, illus., maps, plans, bibl. 20cm. (Neueste Länder- und Völkerkunde, 5)

EICHENBERGER, Ad
Die Schweiz: illustriertes Reisehandbuch. 7.Aufl. von Sommer in der Schweiz; hrsg. unter dem Patronat der schweizerischen Verkehrszentrale Zürich ...; neu bearb. und erweitert von Ad. Eichenberger. Zürich: Wagner, 1927. xxvii, 438p., plates, illus., maps, plans. 19cm.

EICHERT, Wilhelm
Touristen-Führer für Wanderungen im Rosalien-Gebirge bei Wiener-Neustadt. 4.Aufl. Wiener-Neustadt: S. Meixner und F. Valentin, 1926. 46p., illus., map. 15cm. (Führer durch die Berg-gebiete bei Wiener-Neustadt, 2)

EICHHORN, Karl
Die Rigi und ihre nächste Umgebung: Führer für Kurgäste und Touristen. Luzern: C.J. Bucher, [19--]. 122p., illus., map. 17cm.

EIDGENOSSISCHE LANDESTOPOGRAPHIE
See
SWITZERLAND. Eidgenossisches Topographisches Bureau

EIDGENOSSISCHES TOPOGRAPHISCHES BUREAU
See
SWITZERLAND. Eidgenossisches Topographisches Bureau

EILBECK, Chris
Cram, Alan Geoffrey
Rock climbing in the Lake District: an illus-trated guide to selected climbs in the Lake District, [by] Geoff Cram, Chris Eilbeck, Ian Roper. Constable, 1975. xiii, 250p., illus., maps (on lining papers). 18cm.

Einsame Wanderungen in der Schweiz im Jahr 1809, [von Carl Theodor von Uklanski]. Berlin: Im Kunst- und Industrie-Comptoir, 1810. 387p. 17cm.

EISELIN, Max
Erfolg am Dhaulagiri: die Erstbesteigung des Achttausanders durch die Schweizerische Himalaya-Expedition 1960. Zürich: Orell Füssli, 1960. 204p., plates (some col.), illus., maps. 24cm.

EISELIN, Max
  [Erfolg am Dhaulagiri]. The ascent of Dhaulagiri;
  translated ... by E. Noel Bowman. Oxford University Press, 1961. xi, 159p., plates (some
  col.), illus., maps. 24cm.

ELCOURT, A   d'
  Au pied des Pyrénées. Paris: Hachette, 1864.
  215p. 20cm.

ELIAS, Ney
MORGAN, Gerald
  Ney Elias, explorer and envoy extraordinary in High
  Asia. Allen & Unwin, 1971. 294p., plates, illus.,
  7 maps, bibl. 23cm.

ÉLIE DE BEAUMONT, L
  See
BEAUMONT, L   Élie de

ELIOVSON, Sima
  Discovering wild flowers in Southern Africa; colour
  photographs by Ezra Eliovson; with a foreword by
  R. Allen Dyer. Cape Town: H. Timmins, 1962. 253p.,
  col. illus., map (on lining papers). 29cm.

ELLERMAN, J   R
BRITISH MUSEUM (NATURAL HISTORY)
  Checklist of Palaearctic and Indian mammals 1758
  to 1946, by J.R. Ellerman and T.C.S. Morrison-Scott.
  British Museum, 1951. 810p., bibl. 26cm.

ELLIOT, Daniel Giraud
WOLF, Joseph
  The life and habits of wild animals; illustrated
  by designs by Joseph Wolf; engraved by J.W. & Edward
  Whymper, with descriptive letterpress by Daniel
  Giraud Elliot. Macmillan, 1874. 72p., 20 plates,
  illus. 49cm.

ELLIOT, G   F   Scott
  A naturalist in mid-Africa, being an account of a
  journey to the mountains of the Moon and Tanganyika.
  Innes, 1896. xvi, 413p., plates (some fold.col.),
  illus., maps. 24cm.

ELLIOT, Robert
ROBERTS, Emma
  Hindostan: its landscapes, palaces, temples, tombs,
  the shores of the Red Sea, and the sublime and
  romantic scenery of the Himalaya Mountains illustrated in a series of views; drawn ... from
  original sketches by Robt. Elliot, & Geo. Francis
  White; with descriptions by Emma Roberts. Fisher,
  [1847?]. 2v., plates, illus. 28cm.

ELLIOTT, Henry Venn
BATEMAN, Josiah
  The life of the Rev. Henry Venn Elliott; with ...
  an appendix containing a short sketch of the life
  of the Rev. Julius Elliott. 3rd ed. Macmillan,
  1872. xv, 347p., port. 20cm.

ELLIOTT, Julius Marshall
  Memoir of the Rev. Julius M. Elliott. [Brighton?]:
  [N.pub.], [1870?]. 19p. 18cm.

ELLIOTT, Julius Marshall
BATEMAN, Josiah
  The life of the Rev. Henry Venn Elliott; with ...
  an appendix containing a short sketch of the life
  of the Rev. Julius Elliott. 3rd ed. Macmillan,
  1872. xv, 347p., port. 20cm.

ELLIS, R   H   U
  Alpine profile road book of Switzerland and the
  adjacent portions of the Tyrol and the Italian
  lake district ...; compiled and edited by R.H.U.
  Ellis. Cyclists' Touring Club, 1910. 148p.,
  illus., map (on lining papers). 11 x 19cm.

ELLIS, Robert
  An enquiry into the ancient routes between Italy
  and Gaul; with an examination of the theory of
  Hannibal's passage of the Alps by the Little St.
  Bernard. Cambridge: Deighton, Bell, 1867. viii,
  136p., fold. col. plates, maps. 24cm.

ELLIS, Robert
  A treatise on Hannibal's passage of the Alps, in
  which his route is traced over the Little Mont
  Cenis. Cambridge: Deighton, 1853. 188p., plates
  (some fold., some col.),illus., maps. 24cm.

ELLIS, S   M
HARDMAN, Sir William
  The letters and memoirs of Sir William Hardman.
  Second series, 1863-65; annotated and edited by
  S.M. Ellis. C. Palmer, 1925. ix, 286p., plates,
  illus. 23cm.

ELLIS, Sarah
  Summer and winter in the Pyrenees, by the author
  of "The women of England" ... [i.e. Sarah Ellis].
  Fisher, [1841]. xii, 393p., 1 plate, illus.
  21cm.

- - [Another ed.], by Mrs. Ellis. [1847].

ELLMENREICH, F   W
  Meran und Umgebung; herausgeber: F.W. Ellmenreich.
  Meran: F.W. Ellmenreich, 1909. xv, 229p., plates,
  illus., map. 17cm.

ELSNER, Eleanor
  The romance of the Basque country and the
  Pyrenees. Jenkins, 1927. 319p., plates, illus.
  23cm.

ELTON, Charles Isaac
  An account of Shelley's visits to France, Switzerland, and Savoy, in the years 1814 and 1816; with
  extracts from "The history of a six weeks' tour"
  and "Letters descriptive of a sail round the Lake
  of Geneva ..." Bliss, Sands, & Foster, 1894.
  viii, 200p., plates, illus., port., bibl. 20cm.

ELTON, Charles Isaac
  Norway: the road and the fell. J. Henry & J.
  Parker, 1864. vi, 285p.

ELTON, James Frederic
  Travels and researches among the lakes and mountains of eastern and central Africa; edited and
  compiled by H.B. Cotterill. Murray, 1879. xxii,
  417p., plates (some fold.,1 col.), illus., maps.
  24cm.

ELTON, Oliver
  C.E. Montague: a memoir. Chatto & Windus, 1929.
  xiii, 335p., plates, illus. 23cm.

ELZINGRE, Ed
  Swiss dress: 22 colour plates; paintings from
  Ed. Elzingre; text by E. Briner. Geneva: "L'Art
  en Suisse", 1931. 1v. (chiefly col. illus.).
  28cm. (Éditions de "L'Art en Suisse", no.7)
  Cover title.

EMERSON, William
  Papers from my desk and other poems. Longmans,
  Green, 1873. ix, 274p. 18cm.

EMERY, M   S
  Mont Blanc: a part of Underwood and Underwood's
  stereoscopic tour through Switzerland, personally
  conducted by M.S. Emery. New York, London:
  Underwood and Underwood, 1902. 27-34, 228-274p.,
  1 fold.col. plate, map. 19cm.

EMMER, Johannes
DEUTSCHER UND ÖSTERREICHISCHER ALPENVEREIN
  Geschichte des Deutschen und Oesterreichischen
  Alpenvereins; aus der Festschrift zur Feier des
  fünfundzwanzigjährigen Bestehens ... von Johannes
  Emmer. Berlin: D.u.Ö.A.V., 1894. iv, 263p.,
  illus., maps (fold.col. in pocket). 23cm.

EMMER, Johannes
DEUTSCHER UND ÖSTERREICHISCHER ALPENVEREIN
  Verfassung und Verwaltung des Deutschen und
  Oesterreichischen Alpenvereins: ein Handbuch zum
  Gebrauch für die Sectionen ...; zusammengestellt
  und erläutert von Johannes Emmer. Berlin:
  D.u.Ö.A.V., 1893. iv, 115p., plates, plans.
  23cm.

BURDSALL, Richard Lloyd and EMMONS, Arthur Brewster
Men against clouds: the conquest of Minya Konka;
with contributions by Terris Moore and Jack
Theodore Young. Lane, 1935. xv, 272p., plates
(some fold.), illus., maps, bibl. 23cm.

ÉNAULT, Louis
La Norvège. Paris: Hachette, 1857. 447p. 19cm.

Encyclopaedia Britannica. 11th ed. Vol.1, pt.4.
Alex to Alum. Cambridge: University Press, 1910.
577-768p., plates, illus. 32cm.
Contains articles on Alp and Alps.

ENCYCLOPAEDIA BRITANNICA
Belgium, Italy, and Switzerland, by G. Edmundson,
H. Wickham Steed, W.A.B. Coolidge. Encyclopaedia
Britannica, 1914. iv, 201p., plates, illus.
23cm.
Reproduced from the 11th ed. of the Encyclopaedia
Britannica.

Encyclopaedia of mountaineering; compiled by Walt
Unsworth. Hale, 1975. 272p., plates, illus.
24cm.

- - Another issue. Harmondsworth: Penguin, 1977.

[Encyclopaedia of world mountains]. Tokyo; Yama to
Keikoku, 1971. 766, 253p., col. plates, illus.,
maps. 27cm.
In Japanese.

Das Engadine und die Engadiner: Mittheilungen an
dem Sauerbrunnen bei St. Moritz im Kanton Bünden
... Freiburg im Breisgau: Herders, 1837. viii,
278p. 19cm.

ENGEL, Claire Éliane
Alpinistes d'autrefois: le major Roger et son
baromètre. Neuchatel: Attinger, 1935. 215p., 8
plates, illus., port. 19cm.

ENGEL, Claire Éliane
Les batailles pour l'Himalaya, 1783-1936. [Paris]:
Flammarion, 1936. 159p., plates, illus., maps,
bibl. 22cm. (La vie en montagne)

ENGEL, Claire Éliane
Byron et Shelley en Suisse et en Savoie, mai-octobre
1816. Chambéry: Dardel, 1930. vii, 113p., plates,
illus. 26cm.

ENGEL, Claire Éliane and VALLOT, Charles
"Ces monts affreux ...", 1650-1810; [edited by]
Claire Éliane Engel et Charles Vallot; avec seize
compositions originales de Samivel. Paris:
Delagrave, 1934. 320p., plates, illus., bibl.
24cm. (Les écrivains à la montagne)

ENGEL, Claire Éliane and VALLOT, Charles
"Ces monts sublimes ...", 1803-1895; [edited by]
Claire-Éliane Engel et Charles Vallot; avec huit
compositions originales de Samivel. Paris:
Delagrave, 1936. 320p., plates, illus., bibl.
23cm. (Les écrivains à la montagne)

ENGEL, Claire Éliane
A history of mountaineering in the Alps; with a
foreword by F.S. Smythe. Allen & Unwin, 1950.
296p., 24 plates, illus., bibl. 25cm.

ENGEL, Claire Éliane
[A history of mountaineering in the Alps].
Histoire de l'alpinisme des origines à nos jours.
Paris: Éditions "Je sers", 1950. 251p., plates,
illus., bibl. 22cm.

ENGEL, Claire Éliane
La littérature alpestre en France et an Angleterre
aux XVIIIe et XIXe siècles. Chambéry: Dardel,
1930. xi, 287p., 12 plates, illus., bibl. 26cm.

ENGEL, Claire Éliane
Mont Blanc: an anthology; compiled by Claire Éliane
Engel. Allen and Unwin, 1965. 232p., plates,
illus., bibl. 26cm.

ENGEL, Claire Éliane
Le Mont-Blanc: route classique et voies nouvelles.
Neuchatel: Attinger, [1939]. 163p., plates,
illus., maps. 21cm. (Montagne)

- - Ed. rev. et augm. [1946].

ENGEL, Claire Éliane
Le Mont-Blanc, lieu dit. Paris: Éditions du
Temps, 1961. [80]p., illus. (some col.), map.
16 x 23cm. (Lieu dit, 3)

ENGEL, Claire Éliane
La Suisse et ses amis. Neuchatel: Éditions de
la Baconnière, 1943. 269p., plates, illus.
20cm.

ENGEL, Claire Éliane
They came to the hills. Allen & Unwin, 1952.
275p., plates, illus., bibl. 23cm.

ENGEL, Claire Éliane
La vallée de Saas. Neuchatel: Attinger, 1948.
224p., plates, illus., map, bibl. 19cm.

ENGELHARDT, Christian Moritz
Das Monte-Rosa- und Matterhorn- (Mont-Cervin)-
Gebirg, aus der Inseite seines Erhebungsbogens
gen Nord... Paris: Treuttel & Würtz, 1852.
xxviii, 247p. and atlas, fold.col. plates,
illus., map. 22cm.

ENGELHARDT, Christian Moritz
Naturschilderungen, Sittenzüge und wissen-
schaftliche Bemerkungen aus den höchsten
Schweizer-Alpen, besonders in Sud-Wallis und
Graubünden... Basel: Schweighauser, 1840. xxv,
381p., plates, illus. 23cm.

- - Another issue. Paris: Treuttel & Würtz, 1840.

SAZERAC, Hilaire Léon and ENGELMANN, Gustav
Lettres sur la Suisse; accompagnées de vues
dessinées ... & lithographiées par [F.] Villeneuve.
Paris: G. Engelmann, 1823-32. 5v., plates, illus.
46cm.
Vols.2-3 by D. Raoul-Rochette and G. Engelmann,
v.4-5 by M. de Golbéry and G. Engelmann.

England's Lakeland: a tour therein; illustrated by
coloured pictures and woodcuts. Windermere: J.
Garnett; London: Simpkin, Marshall, [1877]. 76p.,
col. plates, illus. 23cm.

ENGLER, A
Monographie der Gattung Saxifraga L., mit besonderer Berücksichtigung der geographischen
Verhältnisse. Breslau: J.U. Kern, 1872. iv,
292p., 1 fold. plate, map. 22cm.

ENOCK, C   Reginald
The great Pacific coast: twelve thousand miles
in the Golden West... Richards, 1909. xi, 356p.,
plates (1 fold.col.), illus., map (in pocket).
24cm.

ENTE NAZIONALE INDUSTRIE TURISTICHE
Residencias en los Alpes italianos. Roma:
E.N.I.T., 1954. 400p., illus., maps. 17cm.

ENTE PROVINCIALE PER IL TURISMO, Bolzano
Skier's guide to the Dolomites, South Tyrol, Italy.
Bolzano: Ente Provinciale, [1957]. 398p., illus.
17cm.

ENTRESS, Ernst
Das Zuckerhütl und seine Nachbarn. Stuttgart:
Deutsche Verlags-Anstalt, 1909. 76p., 1 plate,
map. 18cm. (Alpine Gipfelführer, 19)

ENZENSPERGER, Ernst
Alpenfahrten der Jugend. München: J. Lindauer,
1911-12. 2v., plates, illus. 20cm.

ENZENSPERGER, Ernst
Bergsteigen; unter Mitwirkung von Eugen Roeckl,
Wilhelm Welzenbach und Anton Ziegler. Berlin:
Wiedmann, [1924]. xx, 369p., 2 fold. plates,
illus., maps. 22cm. (Handbuch der Liebesübungen,
Bd.6)

ENZENSPERGER, Ernst
Die Gruppe der Mädelegabel. Kempten: Jos. Kösel,
1909. iv, 104p., plates (1 fold.), illus., map
(in pocket). 20cm.

ENZENSPERGER, Ernst
Wie sollen unsere Mittelschüler die Alpen bereisen?
Technische Anleitungen und wissenschaftliche
Anregungen; umbearb. nach einem Programm des Kgl.
Wilhelmsgymnasiums in München 1908. Kempten: Jos.
Kösel, 1909. 123p., plates, illus. 20cm.

ENZENSPERGER, Josef
Josef Enzensperger: ein Bergsteigerleben; eine
Sammlung von alpinen Schilderungen nebst einem
Anhang Riesebriefe und Kerguelen-Tagebuch; hrsg.
vom Akademischen Alpenverein München. München:
Kommissionsverlag der Vereinigten Kunstanstalten,
1905. xv, 276p., plates (2 fold.), illus., maps.
29cm.

ERLER, Heinrich
NOLL-HASENCLEVER, Eleonore
Den Bergen verfallen: Alpenfahrten von Eleonore
Noll-Hasenclever; mit Geleitwort und Lebensbild
versehen und mit Beiträgen von G. Dyhrenfurth,
W. Martin, Hermann Trier und Willi Welzenbach;
hrsg. von Heinrich Erler; mit ... einem fak-
similierten Briefe Alexander Burgeners. Berlin:
Union Deutsche Verlagsgesellschaft Zweignieder-
lassung, 1932. 213p., plates, illus. 22cm.

ERSKINE, Angus B
ROYAL NAVY ELLESMERE ISLAND EXPEDITION, 1972
Expedition report, by A.B. Erskine. [Dunfermline]:
The Expedition, [1972]. 1v. (various pagings),
illus., maps. 30cm.

ERSKINE, Angus B
BANKS, Mike
High Arctic: the story of the British North Green-
land Expedition; with four chapters by Angus
Erskine; drawings by Lilias Stirling. Dent, 1957.
xi, 276p., plates (1 col.), illus., maps. 22cm.

ESCARRA, Jean
EXPÉDITION FRANÇAISE À L'HIMALAYA, 1936
L'Expédition française à l'Himalaya 1936, par Jean
Escarra [and others]; préface de M. Franchet
D'Espérey. Paris: Le Comité d'Organisation, 1937.
260p., plates, illus., map. 26cm.

- - Abridged ed. published under title: Karakoram:
Expédition française... Paris: Flammarion, 1938.

ESCARRA, Jean
EXPÉDITION FRANÇAISE À L'HIMALAYA, 1936
Himalayan assault: the French Himalayan Expedition
1936, [by Jean Escarra and others]; translated by
Nea Morin; with an introduction by C.G. Bruce.
Methuen, 1938. xv, 203p., plates, illus., map.
23cm.

ESCHER, G von
EBEL, Johann Gottfried
Anleitung auf die nützlichste und genussvollste
Art die Schweiz zu bereisen; im auszuge ganz neu
bearb. von G. von Escher. 7. original Aufl...
Zürich: Orell, Füssli, 1840. iv, 655p., plates,
illus., maps. 18cm.

- - 8. original Aufl. 1843.

ESCHER, Hans Caspar Hirzel
See
HIRZEL-ESCHER, Hans Caspar

ESCHER, Hans Erhard
Beschreibung des Zürich Sees: wie auch von Erbauung, Zunemmen, Stand und Wesen loblicher Statt
Zürich: Joh. R. Simler, 1692. 438p., 1 fold.
plate, map. 17cm.

ESCHER, H C
See
ESCHER VON DER LINTH, Hans Conrad

ESCHER VON DER LINTH, Arnold
Die Sentis-Gruppe: Text zur Specialkarte des
Sentis. Bern: Dalp, 1878. xix, 262p., illus.,
bibl. 33cm. (Beiträge zur Geologischen Karte
der Schweiz, Lfg.13. Geologische Beschreibung
der Sentis-Gruppe)

ESCHER VON DER LINTH, Arnold
HEER, Oswald
Arnold Escher von der Linth: Lebensbild eines
Naturforschers. Zürich: F. Schulthess, 1873.
385p., 1 plate, illus., port. 23cm.

ESCHER VON DER LINTH, Hans Conrad
Reise aus dem Linththal über den Kistenpass ins
vordere Rheinthal.; durchs Sunwixerthal ...;
durchs Val Cananria ..., vom 24. bis 30. August
1816. [Zürich, 1836]. 537-588p. 19cm.
Offprint from the Author's Beiträge zur Gebirgs-
kunde der Schweiz.

ESCHER VON DER LINTH, Hans Conrad
Relation succincte de l'écroulement de la montagne
au-dessus de Goldau, Canton de Schwytz le 2.
septembre 1806, [par H.C. Escher von der Linth].
Zuric: Orell, Fussli, 1806. 7p., 3 plates,
illus., map. 24 x 31cm.

ESCHMANN, Ernst
Der Geisshirt von Fiesch: eine Geschichte aus dem
Oberwallis: der reiseren Jugend ...; erzählt von
Ernst Eschmann. Zürich: Orell Füssli, 1919.
268p., illus. 21cm.

ESCHMANN, Ernst
Gian Caprez: eine Geschichte aus dem Engadin: der
reiseren Jugend; erzählt von Ernst Eschmann.
Zürich: Orell Füssli, 1923. 261p., illus. 21cm.

ESCUDIER, Jean
L'Aneto et les hommes. Pau: Marrimpouey, 1977.
183p., plates, illus., maps (1 fold.). 23cm.

Essais sur les montagnes, par le C. de N***.
Amsterdam: [n.pub.], 1785. 2v. 22cm.
Vol.2 has title: Suite des essais sur les
montagnes.

L'étape libératrice: scène de la vie des soldats
alliés internés en Suisse; texte de G. Jaccottet
[and others]. Genève: SADAG, 1918. 289p.,
illus. 23cm.
At head of title: Au soleil et sur les monts.

L'état de la Suisse écrit en 1714; traduit de
l'anglais. Amsterdam: J. Garrel, 1714. 232p.
17cm.

L'état et les délices de la Suisse, en forme de
relation critique ..., [par Abraham Ruchat,
Abraham Stanyan and others]. Amsterdam: Wetsteins
et Smith, 1730. 4v., plates, illus., maps. 20cm.

L'état et les délices de la Suisse; ou, Description
helvetique historique et géographique ..., [par
Abraham Ruchat, Abraham Stanyan & others].
Nouvelle éd. corr. & considérablement augm. par
plusiers auteurs célèbres. Basle: E. Tourneisen,
1764. 4v., fold. plates, illus., maps. 19cm.

- - Nouvelle ed. 1776.

État et délices de la Suisse; ou, Description historique et géographique des treize cantons
suisses et de leurs alliés, [par Abraham Ruchat,
Abraham Stanyan and others]. Nouv. [5e] éd.,
corr. & considérablement augm... Neuchatel: S.
Fauche, 1778. 2v., plates (some fold.), illus.,
maps. 27cm.

ETHERTON, P T
Across the roof of the world: a record of sport
and travel through Kashmir, Gilgit, Hunza, the
Pamirs, Chinese Turkistan, Mongolia and Siberia.
Constable, 1911. xvi, 437p., 1 fold.col. plate,
illus., map. 25cm.

ETHERTON, P   T
Adventures in five continents. Hutchinson, [1928].
320p., plates, illus. 24cm.

ETHERTON, P   T
In the heart of Asia. Constable, 1925. xii,
305p., 1 fold. plate. map. 23cm.

ETHERTON, P   T
The last strongholds. Jarrolds, 1934. 297p.,
plates, illus. 24cm.

ETNA, Donato
Memoriale per l'Ufficiale sulle Alpi. Torino: F.
Casanova, 1900. 159p., plates, illus. 16cm.

EUSTACE, John Chetwode
A classical tour through Italy. 8th ed., with an
additional preface, and translation of the various
quotations... T. Tegg, 1841. 3v., 1 fold. plate,
map. 21cm.

EVANS, Sir Charles
Eye on Everest: a sketch book from the great
Everest expedition. Dobson, 1955. 123p., illus.
26cm.

EVANS, Sir Charles
Kangchenjunga: the untrodden peak. Hodder &
Stoughton, 1956. xx, 187p., plates (some col.),
illus., maps. 23cm.

EVANS, Sir Charles
[Kangchenjunga ...]. Neprikosnovennaia Kanchendzhanga. Moskva: Gos. Izd. Fizkultura i Sport,
1961. 144p., illus., map. 20cm.

EVANS, Sir Charles
On climbing. Museum Press, 1956. 191p., plates,
illus., maps. 24cm.

EVANS, Harold
We learned to ski: [the Sunday Times tells you all
you need to know], by Harold Evans, Brian Jackman
and Mark Ottaway. 2nd paperback ed. Collins,
1977. 255p., illus. (some col.). 24cm.

EVANS, J
Letters written during a tour through North Wales
... C. & R. Baldwin, 1804. 3rd. ed. xix, 415p.
22cm.
First published in 1800 under title: A tour through
part of North Wales...

EVANS, J
A tour through part of North Wales, in the year
1798, and at other times; principally undertaken
with a view to botanical researches... J. White,
1800. viii, 417p. 22cm.
Third ed. published in 1804 under title: Letters
written during a tour through North Wales...

EVANS, Joan
The Conways: a history of three generations.
Museum Press, 1966. 308p., plates, illus. 23cm.

EVANS, Joan and WHITEHOUSE, John Howard
The diaries of John Ruskin; selected and edited by
Joan Evans and John Howard Whitehouse. Oxford:
Clarendon Press, 1956. 3v., plates, illus. 25cm.
Vol.1. 1835-1847. 1956. - v.2. 1848-1873. 1958. -

EVANS, R   B   and UNSWORTH, Walter
The southern Lake District. Pt.1. Difficult to
Hard Severe; illustrated by R.B. Evans. Manchester:
Cicerone Press, 1971. 55p., illus., map. 17cm.
(Climbs in Cumbria)

EVANS, Sir Robert Charles
See
EVANS, Sir Charles

EVE, A   S   and CREASEY, C   H
Life and work of John Tyndall; with a chapter on
Tyndall as a mountaineer by Lord Schuster...
Macmillan, 1945. xxxii, 404p., plates illus. 25cm.

EVEREST, Robert
A journey through Norway, Lapland and part of
Sweden, with some remarks on the geology of the
country, its climate and scenery, the ascent of
some of its principal mountains... Underwood,
1829. xi, 383p., charts, maps. 24cm.

EVOE
DENNYS, Joyce
A winter sports alphabet; pictures by Joyce
Dennys; verses by "Evoe". Lane, 1926. 57p.
28cm.

EWEN, William A
ALEXANDER, Sir Henry
The Cairngorms. 3rd ed. rev. by William A. Ewen.
Edinburgh: Scottish Mountaineering Club, 1950.
ix, 298p., plates (some fold.), illus., map (on
lining papers), bibl. 23cm. (Scottish Mountaineering Club guides)

Exhortation aux Suisses en générale pour leur conservation, contre les esmeutes & dangers du temps
présent. [Genève]: J. Planchant, 1639. 25, 3p.
15cm.

EXPEDÍCIA NANGA PARBAT ČSSR, 1971
II. Expedícia Nanga Parbat 8125m. Himaláje
Československo 1971, 10 IV - 18 VIII.
[Bratislava]: The Expedition, [1973?]. [48]p.,
illus. (some col.), map. 25cm.
Contains a summary in English.

EXPEDICIÓN ESPAÑOLA HIMALAYA, 1976
CENTRE EXCURSIONISTA DE LA COMARCA DE BAGES
Expedición española Himalaya - 76: Makalu -
8,481 mts., 24 de mayo 1976, [por Jose Ma.
Montfort Fabrega]. Manresa: C.E.C. Bages, 1976.
[13]p., illus. 28cm.

EXPEDICIÓN ESPANOLA HIMALAYA, 1976
CENTRE EXCURSIONISTA DE LA COMARCA DE BAGES
[Expedición espanola Himalaya - 76]. Report to
the Spanish Himalaya Expedition 1976: Makalu
(8,481 mts.), south east ridge, [by Jose Ma.
Montford]. Manresa: C.E.C. Bages, 1976.
4 leaves, illus., map. 29cm.

EXPEDICIÓN ESPANOLA HINDU KUSH, 1973
CENTRE EXCURSIONISTA DE LA COMARCA DE BAGES
Expedición espanola Hindu Kush - 73 (Himalaya).
(In C.E.C. Bages Butletti, no.19, 2a època,
2-3 trimestre, p5-26, 2 fold. plates, illus.,
maps)

EXPEDITION FRANÇAISE À L'HIMALAYA, 1936
L'Expédition française à l'Himalaya 1936, par
Jean Escarra [and others]; préface de M. Franchet
D'Espérey. Paris: Le Comité d'Organisation,
1937. 260p., plates, illus., map. 26cm.

- - Abridged ed. published under title: Karakoram:
Expédition française... Paris: Flammarion, 1938.

EXPEDITION FRANÇAISE À L'HIMALAYA, 1936
Himalayan assault: the French Himalayan Expedition 1936, [by Jean Escarra and others];
translated by Nea Morin; with an introduction by
C.G. Bruce. Methuen, 1938. xv, 203p., plates,
illus., map. 23cm.

EXPÉDITION FRANÇAISE À L'HIMALAYA, 1971
Makalu 8481m pilier ouest. [Paris]: L'Expédition, [1971?]. [9]p., illus. 27cm.

EXPÉDITION FRANÇAISE AU GROENLAND SUD/LINDENOWS
FJORD, 1971
Groenland 71, [par l'Equipe du Groenland].
[Paris, 1972]. 5-6p., 1 plate, map. 30cm.
Offprint from Bulletin de la Section de Paris du
Club Alpin Français, fév. 1972.

EXPÉDITION FRANÇAISE AU PILIER OUEST DU MAKALU
See
EXPÉDITION FRANÇAISE À L'HIMALAYA. 1971

EXPÉDITION PÉROU 77 - CORDILLÈRE BLANCHE, 1977
Compte-rendu d'activités. Paris: L'Expédition,
1977. 10p., plates, illus., map, plans. 30cm.
Chef d'expédition: Nicolas Jaeger.

Expeditions on the glaciers: including an ascent of
Mont Blanc, Monte Rosa, Col du Géant, and Mont
Buet, by a private of the Thirty-Eighth Artists',
and a member of the Alpine Club [i.e. John
Barrow]. Spon, 1864. 122p., plates, illus. 20cm.

EXPOSITION NATIONALE SUISSE
See
SCHWEIZERISCHE LANDESAUSSTELLUNG

EYRE, Donald C
John Sikander. Hale, 1954. 224p. 20cm.

EYRE, Mary
Over the Pyrenees into Spain. Bentley, 1865. ix,
361p. 21cm.

F., C.G.
See
FLOYD, C   G

F.J.M.
See
MARTIN, F   J

F., W
DEUTSCHER UND ÖSTERREICHISCHER ALPENVEREIN. Sektion
Berchtesgaden
Die Grill aus der Ramsau: eine deutsche Führer-
familie, zum fünfzigjährigen Führer-Jubiläum
Johann Grills des Jüngeren; von W.F. hrsg. von der
Sektion Berchtesgaden des Deutschen und Österr.
Alpenvereins. Berchtesgaden: L. Vonderthann,
[1931?]. 20p., ports. 23cm.

FA-HSIEN
The travels of Fa-Hsien (399-414 A.D.); or, Record
of the Buddhistic kingdoms; re-translated by H.A.
Giles. Cambridge: University Press, 1923. xvi,
96p., plates, illus., map (on lining paper). 18cm.

FABRIKANT, Michel
Guide des montagnes corses. 1. Le massif du Cinto.
2e éd. Paris: M. Fabrikant, 1974. 271p., fold.
plates, illus., maps. 18cm.

FABRIKANT, Michel
Guide des montagnes corses. 2. Montagnes de Corse
centrale et méridionale. Paris: M. Fabrikant,
1971. 319p., fold. plates, illus., maps. 17cm.

FABRIKANT, Michel
Les topo-guides de l'alpiniste et du randonneur en
Corse. Paris: M. Fabrikant, 1959-64. 5v., 1 fold.
plate, illus., maps. 21cm.
Library lacks v.2. Le massif du Cinto.

FABRIS, Peter
HAMILTON, Sir William
Campi Phlegraei: observations on the volcanoes of
the two Sicilies as they have been communicated to
the Royal Society of London; to which ... a new
and accurate map is annexed, with ... plates
illuminated from drawings ... by the editor Peter
Fabris. Naples [n.pub.], 1776. 90p., 54 plates,
illus. 46cm.
Text in English and French.

- - Supplement ... being an Account of the great
eruption of Mount Vesuvius in ... August 1779.
1779.

FAES, Henry and MERCANTON, Paul L
Le manuel du skieur, suivi des itinéraires recom-
mandables en Suisse occidentale. Lausanne:
Imprimeries Réunies, [1917]. 116p., illus. 22cm.

- - 2e éd. rev. et complétée... Lausanne: Payot,
1925.

FAIGE-BLANC, Henry Frédéric
See
ALPINUS

FAIN, Piero and SANMARCHI, Toni
Alta Via n.7: "sulle orme del Patéra nelle Prealpi
dell'Alpago", "passeggiata d'autunno nelle Prealpi
della Val Belluna". Bologna: Tamari, 1976.
160p., illus., bibl. 16cm. (Itinerari alpini:
itinerari per alpinisti ed escursionisti, 31)

FAIRBANKS, Harold Wellman
The geography of California. San Francisco:
Whitaker & Ray-Wiggin, 1912. 190p., 1 plate, map.
20cm.

FAIRBANKS, Harold Wellman
The western wonder-land: half-hours in the western
United States. Heath, 1905. vi, 302p., illus.,
maps. 20cm.

FALCONNET, Jean
Une ascension au Mont-Blanc et études scientfiques
sur cette montagne. Annecy, 1887. 160p. 26cm.
Offprint: Documents de l'Académie Salésienne,
t.9.

FALKE, Konrad
Im Banne der Jungfrau. Zürich: Rascher, 1909.
250p., plates, illus. 25cm.

FALSAN, Albert
Les Alpes françaises: la flore et la faune, le
role de l'homme dans les Alpes, la transhumance.
Paris: J.-B. Baillière, 1893. 356p., illus.
19cm.

FALSAN, Albert
Les Alpes françaises: les montagnes, les eaux,
les glaciers, les phénomenes de l'atmosphère.
Paris: J.-B. Baillière, 1893. 289p., illus. 19cm.
(Bibliothèque scientifique contemporaine)

FALSAN, Albert and CHANTRE, E
Monographie géologique des anciens glaciers et du
terrain erratique de la partie moyenne du Basin
du Rhône. Lyon, 1879-80. 2v., fold. plates (1
col.), illus. 28cm.
Offprint from Annales de la Société d'agriculture
..., t.7, 10 (4e série) et 1 (5e série)

Familien-Statistik der löblichen Pfarrei von St.
Niklaus; gesammelt und geordnet von Peter Joseph
Ruppen. Sitten: Eduard Läderich, 1861. vii,
132p. 18cm.

Familien-Statistik der löblichen Pfarrei von Zermatt,
mit Beilagen; gesammelt und geordnet von Joseph
Ruden. Ingenbohl: Buchdruckerei der Waisenanstalt,
1869. 184p., 1 plate, illus. 20cm.
Later ed., by Stanislaus Kronig published in 1927
under title: Familien-Statistik und Geschichtliches
über die Gemeinde Zermatt.

Familien-Statistik und Geschichtliches über die
Gemeinde Zermatt. [New ed.] von Stanislaus Kronig.
Ingenbohl: B. Theodosius-Buchdruckerei, 1927.
356p. 21cm.
Previous ed., by Joseph Ruden published in 1869
under title: Familien-Statistik der löblichen
Pfarrei von Zermatt...

FANCK, Arnold and SCHNEIDER, Hannes
Wunder des Schneeschuhs: ein System des richtigen
Skilaufens und seine Anwendung im alpinen Gelände-
lauf; Photographie: Arnold Fanck und Sepp
Allgeier. Hamburg: Enoch, 1925. 218, xxii p.,
fold. plates (in pocket), illus. 30cm.

FANCK, Arnold and SCHNEIDER, Hannes
[Wunder des Schneeschuhs]. The wonders of ski-
ing: a method of correct ski-ing and its applications to alpine running; translated from the ...
2nd ed. 1928 by George Gallowhur; photography by
Arnold Fanck & Sepp Allgeier. Allen & Unwin,
1933. 234p., plates, illus. 29cm.

FANE, Henry Edward
  Five years in India, comprising a narrative of
  travels in the presidency of Bengal, a visit to
  the court of Runjeet Sing, a residence in the
  Himalayah mountains... Colburn, 1842. 2v.,
  illus. 21cm.

FANTIN, Mario
  A settemila metri: gli Inca precursori d'alpinismo. Bologna, 1969. 23p., illus. (some col.),
  map. 25cm.
  Offprint from Rivista mensile del CAI, n.8,
  agosto 1969.

FANTIN, Mario
  A tu per tu con: Jivaros e Colorados, Amazzonia
  Ecuador. Bolzano: Manfrini, 1967. 125p., 78
  plates (some col.), illus. 28cm. (Alle soglie
  della civiltà)

FANTIN, Mario
  Alpinismo italiano extraeuropeo (al 112o anno):
  saggio di cronologia ed analisi critica;
  elaborazione dall'Archivio del CISDAE in Bologna.
  Bologna: Tamari, 1967. 138p., plates, illus.,
  bibl. 25cm.

FANTIN, Mario
  Alta via delle Alpi. Bologna: Tamari, [1957].
  155p., illus., maps. 29cm.

FANTIN, Mario
  Cervino, 1865/1965: Matterhorn - Mont Cervin,
  fotografie e testi di Mario Fantin; con una prefazione di Giuseppe Mazzotti. Bologna: Tamari,
  1965. 153p., illus., bibl. 29cm.

FANTIN, Mario
  Le "Dolomiti" del Sahara (l'alpinismo nel Tibesti
  e nell'Hoggar); I monti dell'Africa. Verona,
  1966. 11-320p., illus., maps. 30cm.
  Offprint from Monzino, G. Spedizioni d'alpinismo
  in Africa. 1966.

FANTIN, Mario
  Himàlaya e Karakorùm: sintesi monografica, geo-
  grafico-biologico etnografico-esplorativo-storico-
  alpinistica. Torino: Club Alpino Italiano, 1978.
  248p., illus., maps, bibl. 30cm.

FANTIN, Mario
  Italiani sulle montagne del mondo. Bologna:
  Cappelli, 1967. 354p., plates, illus., maps.
  29cm.

FANTIN, Mario
  K2: sogno vissuto. Bologna: Tamari, 1958. 246p.,
  illus., maps. 29cm.

FANTIN, Mario
  Montagne de Groenlandia: monografia-storico-
  esplorativa e geografico-alpinistica. Bologna:
  Tamari, 1969. 374p., plates, illus., maps (some
  col.). 29cm.

FANTIN, Mario
  I quattordici "8000": antologia. Bologna:
  Zanichelli, 1964. 302p., plates, illus., col.
  maps. 24cm.

FANTIN, Mario
  Sherpa, Himalaya, Nepal. Bologna: Tamari, 1971.
  137p., illus., maps. 28cm.

FANTIN, Mario
  Sui ghiacciai dell'Africa (Kilimangiaro, Kenya,
  Ruwenzori). Bologna: Cappelli, 1968. 395p.,
  plates (some col.), illus. 29cm.

FANTIN, Mario
  Tra i ghiacci della "Terra Verde" (l'alpinismo in
  Groenlandia). Verona, 1966. 64p., illus., col.
  maps. 29cm.
  Offprint from Monzino G. Spedizioni d'alpinismo in
  Groenlandia. 1966.

FANTIN, Mario
  I tre "Grandi" africani: Kilimangiaro, Kenya,
  Ruwenzori (l'alpinismo nell'Africa centro-
  orientale). Verona, 1966. 49-184p., illus.
  (some col.), maps. 29cm.
  Offprint from Monzino, G. Spedizioni d'alpinismo
  in Africa. 1966.

FANTIN, Mario
  Tuareg, Tassili, Sahara. Bologna: Tamari, 1971.
  208p., illus. (some col.), maps. 28cm. (Genti
  e montagne, 2)

FANTIN, Mario
  Uomini e montagne del Sahara: monografia
  alpinistico-esplorativa e storico-geografica con
  antologia. 2a ed. Bologna: Tamari, 1970.
  521p., plates, illus. (some col.), maps. 30cm.

FANTIN, Mario
  Yucay, montagna degli Incas: la Spedizione
  comasca alle Ande peruviane 1958; prefazione di
  Luigi Binaghi. Bologna: Tamari, 1958. 183p.,
  illus. (some col.), maps. 29cm.

FARINGTON, Joseph
HORNE, Thomas Hartwell
  The Lakes of Lancashire, Westmorland, and Cumberland; delineated in forty-three engravings, from
  drawings by Joseph Farington; with descriptions
  ... the result of a tour made in the summer of ...
  1816. T. Cadell & W. Davies, 1816. vii, 96p.,
  plates, illus., map. 39cm.

FARINGTON, Joseph
  Views of the Lakes, &c. in Cumberland and West-
  morland, engraved from drawings made by Joseph
  Farington. W. Byrne, 1789. 1v. of illus.
  45 x 59cm.
  Captions in English and French.

FARIS, John T
  Seeing the Far West. Philadelphia:Lippincott, 1920.
  304p., plates (2 fold.), illus., maps. 23cm.

FARQUHAR, Francis Peloubet
  Exploration of the Sierra Nevada. San Francisco,
  1925. 58p., plates, illus., bibl. 27cm.
  Offprint from the Quarterly of the California
  Historical Society, March 1925.

FARQUHAR, Francis Peloubet
  History of the Sierra Nevada. Berkeley: University
  of California Press, in collaboration with the
  Sierra Club, 1965. xvi, 262p., 1 col.plate, illus.,
  maps, bibl. 28cm.

FARQUHAR, Francis Peloubet and PHOUTRIDES, Aristides
Evangelus
  Mount Olympus. San Francisco: Johnck & Seeger,
  1929. xiii, 46p., plates, illus., map, bibl.
  29cm.

FARQUHAR, Francis Peloubet
  Mount Olympus revisited. [San Francisco], 1953.
  43-50p., plates, illus. 25cm.
  Offprint from Sierra Club Bulletin, v.38, no.8,
  Oct. 1953.

FARQUHAR, Francis Peloubet
KING, Clarence
  Mountaineering in the Sierra Nevada; edited and
  with a preface by Francis P. Farquhar. Black,
  1947. 320p., plates, illus., bibl. 23cm.

FARQUHAR, Francis Peloubet
  Place names of the High Sierra. San Francisco:
  Sierra Club, 1926. xi, 128p., bibl. 25cm.
  (Sierra Club. Publications, no.62)

FARQUHAR, Francis Peloubet
BREWER, William H
  Up and down California in 1860-1864: the journal
  of William H. Brewer, Professor of Agriculture in
  the Sheffield Scientific School from 1864 to 1903;
  edited by Francis P. Farquhar; with a preface by
  Russell H. Chittenden. New Haven: Yale University
  Press; London: Oxford University Press, 1930. xxx,
  601p., plates (1 fold.), illus., map. 24cm.

FARQUHAR, Francis Peloubet
Yosemite, the Big Trees, and the High Sierra:
a selective bibliography. Berkeley: University of
California Press, 1948. xii, 104p., illus. 28cm.

FARQUHAR, Francis Peloubet
DAKIN, Susanna Bryant
The published writings of Francis Peloubet
Farquhar; together with an introduction to FPF by
Susanna Bryant Dakin. San Francisco: [K.K.
Bechtel], 1954. vii, 17p. 27cm.

FARRAR, John Percy
On ropes and knots; edited by J.P. Farrar.
[Bedford]: The Author, 1913. 8p., plates, illus.
22cm.

FARRER, Reginald
Among the hills: a book of joy in high places.
Headley, [1911]. 326p., plates (some col.),
illus., fold. map. 22cm.

FARRER, Reginald
The Dolomites: King Laurin's garden; painted by
E. Harrison Compton; described by Reginald Farrer.
Black, 1913. vii, 207p., 21 col. plates (1 fold.),
illus., map. 23cm.

FARRER, Reginald
On the eaves of the world. Arnold. 1917. 2v.,
plates (1 fold.), illus., map. 23cm.

FARRER, Reginald
The Rainbow Bridge. Arnold, 1921. xi, 383p.,
plates (1 fold.), illus., maps. 23cm.

FASANA, Eugenio
Il Monte Rosa: vicende, uomini e imprese. Milano:
Rupicapra, 1931. 464p., plates (1 fold.), illus.,
map, bibl. 20cm.

FASANA, Eugenio
Uomini di sacco e di corda: pagine di alpinismo;
raccolte a cura di Giovanni Nato. Milano: Società
Escursionisti Milanesi, 1926. xxiv, 401p., plates,
illus. 27cm.

FATIO, Victor
Faune des vertébrés de la Suisse. Genève: H.
Georg, 1869-99 [v.2., 1899]. 3v., plates (some
col.), illus., map. 24cm.

FAUNA AND FLORA RESEARCH SOCIETY
Scientific results of the Japanese expeditions to
Nepal Himalaya, 1952-1953; edited by H. Kihara.
Kyoto: The Society, 1955-57. 3v., plates (some
fold., some col.), illus., maps. 27cm.

FAUR, Freda du
See
DU FAUR, Freda

FAURE, Gabriel
Les Alpes françaises, texte de Gabriel Faure;
photos de G.L. Arland. Paris: Éditions des
Horizons de France, [1925]. 97-128p., plates,
illus. 44cm. (Le visage de la France, fasc.4)

FAURE, Gabriel
The Dolomites. Medici Society, 1925. 143p., 1
fold. plate, illus., map. 21cm. (Picture guides)

FLEMING, Jon W   and FAUX, Ronald
Soldiers on Everest: the joint Army Mountaineering
Association/Royal Nepalese Army Mount Everest
Expedition 1976. H.M.S.O., 1977. xvi, 239p.,
plates (some col.), illus., maps. 18cm.

FAVRE, Alphonse
Explication de la carte géologique des parties de
la Savoie, du Piémont et de la Suisse voisines du
Mont Blanc. Genève, 1862. 37p. 25cm.
Offprint from Biblioth. universelle, nov. 1862.

FAVRE, Alphonse
H.-B. de Saussure et les Alpes: [fragments tirés
de documents en partie inédits]. Lausanne, 1870.
15p. 22cm.
Offprint from Bibliothèque universelle et revue
suisse.

FAVRE, Alphonse
On the origin of the alpine lakes and valleys:
a letter addressed to Sir Roderick I. Murchison.
[London], 1865. 10p. 22cm.
Offprint from Philosophical magazine, March 1865.

FAVRE, Alphonse
Recherches géologiques dans les parties de la
Savoie, du Piémont et de la Suisse voisines du
Mont-Blanc. Paris: Masson, 1867. 3v. and atlas.
24cm.

FAVRE, Alphonse
Sur la structure en éventail du Mont-Blanc;
extrait d'un travail présenté à la Société helvetique des sciences naturelles... [Genève],
1865. 6p. 22cm.
Offprint from Bibliothèque universelle et revue
suisse, nov. 1865.

FAVRE, Alphonse
Texte explicatif de la carte du phénomène
erratique et des anciens glaciers du versant nord
des Alpes suisses et de la chaîne du Mont-Blanc;
précédé d'une introduction par Ernest Favre; et
suivi d'une biographie de Léon du Pasquier par
Maurice de Tribolet, avec les portraits... Berne:
Schmid & Francke, 1898. 77p., plates, ports.
33cm. (Beiträge zur geologischen Karte der
Schweiz = Matériaux pour la carte géologique de
la Suisse, livr. 28)

FAVRE, André
CHASTONAY, Paul de
[Kardinal Schiner]. Le Cardinal Schiner; adaptation d'André Favre. Lausanne: F. Rouge, [1943].
135p., 6 plates, illus., bibl. 20cm.

FAVRE, Ernest and SCHARDT, Hans
Description géologique des préalpes du Canton
de Vaud et du Chablais jusqu'à la Dranse et de
la chaîne des Dents du Midi ... Berne: Schmid &
Francke, 1887. xx, 636p. and atlas, bibl. 33cm.
(Beiträge zur geologischen Karte der Schweiz =
Matériaux pour la carte géologique de la Suisse,
livr. 22)

FAWCETT, Douglas
From Heston to the high Alps: a chat about joy-
flying. Macmillan, 1936. 74p., plates, illus.
22cm.

FAWCETT, Douglas
The Zermatt dialogues, constituting the outlines
of a philosophy of mysticism mainly on problems
of cosmic import. Macmillan, 1931. xxix,
541p., plates, illus. 23cm.

FAZY, Robert
L'exploration du Karakoram: essai de synthèse
et de bibliographie raisonnée. Berne, 1942.
17p., plates, illus., map. 27cm.
Offprint from Les Alpes, fasc.1, 2, 3.

FEARNEHOUGH, Pat L
Great Gable, Wasdale and Eskdale; illustrated
by W. Heaton Cooper. Stockport: Fell & Rock
Climbing Club, 1969. 151p., 1 col. plate,
illus., maps (on lining papers). 16cm.
(Climbing guides to the English Lake District,
[4th ser.], 6)

FEATHERSTONE, B K
An unexplored pass: a narrative of a thousand-
mile journey to the Kara-koram Himalayas;
introduction by C.G. Bruce. Hutchinson, [1926].
295p., plates (1 fold.), illus., map. 25cm.

FEDDEN, Robin
Alpine ski tour: an account of the High Level
Route; with photographs by A. Costa and others.
Putnam, 1956. 93p., 24 plates, illus., fold.
map. 29cm.

FEDDEN, Robin
A bibliographical note on the early literature
of ski-ing in English. [London, 1961]. 203-
209p. 22cm.
Offprint from the British ski year book, 1961.

FEDDEN, Robin
The enchanted mountains: a quest in the Pyrenees.
Murray, 1962. 124p., plates, illus., maps. 23cm.

FEDDEN, Robin
Ski-ing in the Alps; in collaboration with Peter
Waddell; with a chapter on Norway by C.A. de
Linde. E. Hulton, 1958. 168p., illus. 23cm.

FEDERACIÓN ESPAÑOLA DE MONTAÑISMO
Alta montaña normas. Madrid: Delegacíon Nacional
de Educacíon Fisica y Deportes, 1960. 207p.,
illus. 17cm.

FÉDÉRATION FRANÇAISE DE LA MONTAGNE
CLUB ALPIN FRANÇAIS. Section du Sud-Ouest
Camp du Col d'Aran, 15-25 juillet 1943: compte-
rendu; publié par la Commission Scientifique de la
Section du Sud-Ouest ...; préface de Colonel
Pascot. [Bordeaux]: La Commission, 1943. 124p.,
illus., maps, bibl. 22cm.
At head of title: Fédération Française de la
Montagne.
Supplément au Bulletin n.45, oct. 1943.

FÉDÉRATION FRANÇAISE DE LA MONTAGNE
COLLOQUE MEDICINE & HAUTE MONTAGNE, Grenoble, 1976
Colloque ...; organisée sous la présidence du
prof. Tanche dans le cadre de la Commission
Médicale de la Fédération Française de la Mon-
tagne, les 11 et 12 juin 1976 à la Faculté de
Médecine de Grenoble. Paris: F.F.M., [1977].
4v., illus., forms., bibl. 30cm.

FÉDÉRATION FRANÇAISE DE LA MONTAGNE
CLUB ALPIN FRANÇAIS. Section du Caroux
Escalades au Caroux... Saint-Pons Hérault: La
Section, 1963. 334p., 1 fold.col. plate, illus.,
maps. 17cm.
"Edité sous le patronage de la Fédération Française
de la Montagne et du Club Alpin Français."

FÉDÉRATION FRANÇAISE DE LA MONTAGNE
COUPÉ, Serge
Escalades du Vercors et de la Chartreuse. Paris:
F.F.M., 1963. 167p., illus., maps. 17cm.

FÉDÉRATION FRANÇAISE DE LA MONTAGNE
LECLERC, Jeanne and LECLERC, Bernard
Guide de Tarentaise et Maurienne. Lyon: Audin
[pour] F.F.M., C.A.F. Section Lyonnaise, 1949.
2v., illus. 17cm.

FÉDÉRATION FRANÇAISE DE LA MONTAGNE
JOURNÉE MÉDICALE DE LA MONTAGNE, Paris, Bordeaux,
1944
Médecine et montagne: compte-rendu de la Journée
Médicale de la Montagne; organisée par le Club
Alpin Français le 28 juin 1944; avec le concours
de la Fédération Français de la Montagne. Paris:
C.A.F., [1945?]. 28p., illus. 27cm.

FÉDÉRATION FRANÇAISE DE LA MONTAGNE
Pyrénées. T.3. Bigorre, Arbizon, Néouvielle,
Troumouse, par Robert Ollivier et Xavier Defos du
Rau. Pau: R. Ollivier [pour] F.F.M., Société des
Amis du Musée Pyrénéen, 1959. xx, 272p., illus.,
maps. 16cm.

FÉDÉRATION FRANÇAISE DE LA MONTAGNE
Pyrénées. T.4. Guide de la région d'Aure et de
Luchon (du Port de Barosa au Val d'Aran),
par André Armengaud et François Comet; sous le
patronage de ... F.F.M. Toulouse: Privat, 1953.
360p., fold.col. plates, illus., maps, bibl. 16cm.

FÉDÉRATION FRANÇAISE DE LA MONTAGNE
Pyrénées centrales. 1. Cauterets, Vignemale,
Gavarnie, Canons Espagnols, par Dr. Minvielle [and
others]. Pau: R. Ollivier [pour] F.F.M., Groupe
Pyrénéiste de Haute Montagne, 1965. xv, 352p.,
1 fold. plate, illus., maps. 17cm.

FÉDÉRATION FRANÇAISE DE LA MONTAGNE
Pyrénées centrales. 2. Bigorre, Arbizon, Néouvielle, Troumouse, [par]Xavier Defos du Rau [and
others]. Pau: R. Ollivier [pour] F.F.M., Groupe
Pyrénéiste de Haute Montagne, 1974. xvi, 324p.,
1 fold. plate, illus., maps. 16cm.

FÉDÉRATION FRANÇAISE DE LA MONTAGNE
Pyrénées centrales. 3. Vallées d'Aure et de
Luchon: Batoua, Grand Batchimale, Gourgs-Blancs,
Spijeoles, Quayrat, Lézat, Crabioules, Maupas,
Sauvegarde, [par] André Armengaud, François Comet;
révue ... par Robert Ollivier [and others]. Pau:
R. Ollivier [pour] F.F.M., Groupe Pyrénéiste de
Haute Montagne, 1969. xv, 371p., fold. plates,
illus. 17cm.

FÉDÉRATION FRANÇAISE DE LA MONTAGNE
Pyrénées occidentales, par Dr. Boisson [and
others]. Pau: R. Ollivier pour F.F.M., 1960-63.
2v., 1 fold. plate, illus., maps. 17cm.

FÉDÉRATION FRANÇAISE DE LA MONTAGNE
Secourisme en montagne ...; réalisé par les
membres de la Commission Médicale de la Fédération Française de la Montagne ...; et sous la
haute autorité du professeur Merle-d'Aubigne.
Paris: Serpic, 1969. 197p., illus. 21cm.

FÉDÉRATION FRANÇAISE DE LA MONTAGNE
Le secours en montagne de France. Grenoble:
F.F.M., 1960. 192p., illus. 18cm.

- - 2e éd. 1967.

FÉDÉRATION FRANÇAISE DE LA MONTAGNE. Comité de
l'Himalaya
RIVOLIER, Jean
Expéditions françaises à l'Himalaya: aspect
médical; avec la collaboration de P. Biget [and
others]. Paris: Hermann, 1959. 229p., illus.,
bibl. 24cm. (Actualités scientifiques et industrielles, 1266)
At head of title: Comité de l'Himalaya, Comité
Scientifique du Club Alpin Français.

FEDERATION OF MOUNTAINEERING CLUBS OF IRELAND
Guides.

Antrim coast rockclimbs: interim guide; edited
by Mick Curran. 1975.
Bray Head and minor crags around Dublin; edited
by Joss Lynam and Liam Convery. 1978.
Burren Sea Cliff, Ailladie rock-climbs; edited
by Tom Ryan. 1978.
Coum Gowlaun: interim ... guide; compiled by
Joss Lynam. 1969.
Mountaineering in Ireland; revised by Joss Lynam.
1976.
Mourne rock-climbs; edited by John Forsythe.
1973.
S.W. Donegal: Malinbeg and other sea cliffs;
edited by Jim Leonard. 1979.
Wicklow rock-climbs (Glendalough and Luggala);
edited by Pat Redmond. 1973.

FEDERATSIIA AL'PINIZMA SSSR
Skalolazanie: pravila sorevnovanii. Moskva:
Izd. "Fizkultura i sport", 1968. 24p. 20cm.

FEDERER, Heinrich
Berge und Menschen: Roman. Berlin: G. Grote,
1911. 654p. 20cm. (Grote'sche Sammlung von
Werken zeitgenössischer Schriftsteller, 103)

FEDERER, Heinrich
Pilatus: eine Erzählung aus den Bergen. Berlin:
G. Grote, 1912. 360p. 20cm. (Grote'sche Sammlung von Werken zeitgenössischer Schriften-
steller, 109)

FEHRMANN, Rudolf
Der Bergsteiger in der sächsischen Schweiz:
Führer durch die Kletterfelson des Elbsandsteingebirges. Dresden: J. Siegel, 1908. viii, 285p.,
plates, illus. 16cm.

- - Nachtrag, 1927... Dresden: W. Volkmann, 1927.

FEIERABEND, August
Die schweizerische Alpenwelt; für junge und alte
Freunde der Alpen dargestellt von August Feiera-
band. Bielefeld: Velhagen & Klasing, 1873.
347p., plates, illus. 22cm.

FEIGL, Leo
Die Rax: ein Bergsteiger-Roman. Wien: Knepler, 1924. 180p. 19cm.

FELISART, Agustín Jolis
See
JOLIS, Agustín

FELL AND ROCK CLIMBING CLUB OF THE ENGLISH LAKE DISTRICT
Catalogue of the Library; compiled by Muriel Files. Lancaster: F. & R.C.C., 1972. vi, 81p. 26cm.

- - Additions, June 1972 to May 1975.
- - Additions, June 1975 to March 1979.
- - Section 4: Maps. 1978.

FELL AND ROCK CLIMBING CLUB OF THE ENGLISH LAKE DISTRICT
Guides. [1st series].

1. Doe Crags and climbs round Coniston, by G.S. Bower. [1922].
2. Pillar Rock and neighbouring climbs, by H.M. Kelly. [1923].
3. Climbs on the Scawfell group, by C.F. Holland. [1924].
4. Climbs on Great Gable, by H.S. Gross; and Rock climbing in Borrowdale, by A.R. Thomson. [1925].
5. Crags for climbing in and around Great Langdale, by G. Basterfield; and Rock climbing in Buttermere, by A.H. Thomson. [1926].

FELL AND ROCK CLIMBING CLUB OF THE ENGLISH LAKE DISTRICT
Guides. [2nd series].

1. Pillar Rock and neighbourhood, by H.M. Kelly. 1935.
2. Scafell group, by A.T. Hargreaves. 1936.
3. Great Gable, Borrowdale, Buttermere, by C.J. Astley Cooper, E. Wood-Johnson and L.H. Pollitt. 1937.
4. Dow Crag, Great Langdale and outlying crags, by A.T. Hargreaves [and others]. 1938.

FELL AND ROCK CLIMBING CLUB OF THE ENGLISH LAKE DISTRICT
Guides. [3rd series].

1. Great Gable, Green Gable, Kirkfell, Yewbarrow, Buckbarrow, by C.J. Astley Cooper [and others]. 1948.
2. Buttermere and Newlands area, by W. Peascod and G. Rushworth. 1949.
3. Great Langdale, by W. Clegg, A.R. Dolphin and J.W. Cook. 1950.
4. Pillar Rock and neighbourhood, by H.M. Kelly and W. Peascod. 1952.
5. Borrowdale, by B. Beetham. 1953.
6. Scafell group, by A.T. Hargreaves, A.R. Dolphin and R. Miller. 1956.
7. Dow Crag and other climbs, by A.T. Hargreaves [and others]. 1957.

FELL AND ROCK CLIMBING CLUB OF THE ENGLISH LAKE DISTRICT
Guides. [4th series].

1. Great Langdale, by J.A. Austin and R. Valentine. 1973.
2. Eastern crags, by H. Drasdo and N.J. Soper. 1969.
3. Borrowdale, by P.J. Nunn and O. Woolcock. 1968.
4. Buttermere and Newlands area, by N.J. Soper, N. Allinson. 1970.
5. Pillar group, by A.G. Cram. 1968.
6. Great Gable, Wasdale and Eskdale, by P.L. Fearnemough. 1969.
7. Scafell group, by G. Oliver and I.J. Griffin. 1967.
8. Dow Crag area, by D. Miller. 1968.

FELL AND ROCK CLIMBING CLUBS OF THE ENGLISH LAKE DISTRICT
Guides. [5th series].

3. Borrowdale, by Syd Clark. 1978.
7. Scafell group, by M. Burbage and W. Young. 1974.

FELL AND ROCK CLIMBING CLUB OF THE ENGLISH LAKE DISTRICT
FITZGIBBON, Mary Rose
Lakeland scene; edited by Mary Rose Fitzgibbon. Chapman and Hall, 1948. 240p., plates, illus. 23cm.
Essays selected from the Journal of the Fell and Rock Climbing Club.

FELLENBERG, Edmund von and MOESCH, Casimir
Geologische Beschreibung des Westlichen Theils des Aarmassivs, enthalten auf dem nördlich der Rhone ...; mit petrographischen Beiträgen von Carl Schmidt. Bern: Schmid, Francke, 1893. 2v. in 1. and atlas, fold.col. plates, illus., bibl. 32cm. (Beiträge zur geologischen Karte der Schweiz, Lfg.21)

FELLENBERG, Edmund von
Das Hochgebirge von Grindelwald: Naturbilder aus der schweizerischen Alpenwelt; von Christoph Aeby, Edm. von Fellenberg und Pfarrer Gerwer. Coblenz: Baedeker, 1865. lxv, 151p., plates (chiefly col., 2 fold.), illus. 28cm.

FELLENBERG, Edmund von
Der Ruf der Berge: die Erschliessung der Berner Hochalpen. Erlenbach-Zürich: Rentsch, 1925. 358p., plates (1 fold.col.), illus. 21cm.

FELLENBERG, Edmund von
ROTH, Abraham
Doldenhorn und Weisse Frau, zum ersten Mal ersteigen und geschildert von Abraham Roth und Edmund von Fellenberg, [von Abraham Roth]. Coblenz: Baedeker, 1863. 86p., col. plates (1 fold.), illus., map. 26cm.

FELLENBERG, Edmund von
ROTH, Abraham
The Doldenhorn and Weisse Frau, ascended for the first time by Abraham Roth and Edmund von Fellenberg. Coblenz: Baedeker; London: Williams & Norgate, 1863. 82p., col. plates (1 fold.), illus., map. 26cm.

A FELLOW OF THE CARPATHIAN SOCIETY
See
MAZUCHELLI, Nina Elizabeth

FELLOWES, Peregrine Forbes Morant
First over Everest: the Houston-Mount Everest expedition 1933, by P.F.M. Fellowes [and others]; with a foreword by John Buchan; and an account of the filming of the flight by Geoffrey Barkas. Lane, 1933. 279p., plates (some fold.), illus., maps. 25cm.

FELLOWS, Sir Charles
A narrative of an ascent to the summit of Mont Blanc [made by Charles Fellows and William Hawes]. [The Author], 1827. viii, 35p., plates, illus. 33cm.

FELLOWS, Sir Charles
A narrative of the late ascent to the summit of Monte Blanc by Mr. C.Fellows and Mr. W. Hawes contained in a letter from one of the parties; to which is prefixed a letter from Wilkie, the artist, and a short description of Monte Blanc and the glaciers. Nottingham, 1827. 12p. 18cm. Offprint from Nottingham and Newark Mercury, Aug. 25, 1827.

FELLOWS, Sir Charles
HAWES, Sir Benjamin
A narrative of an ascent to the summit of Mont Blanc, made during the summer of 1827 by Mr. William Hawes and Mr. Charles Fellows. Printed for Benjamin Hawes by Arthur Taylor, 1828. 35p., plates (1 fold.), illus. 25cm.

FELS, Theodor Gsell
 See
GSELL-FELS, Theodor

FELTHAM, John
 A guide to all the watering and sea bathing places,
 descriptions of the lakes, tour in Wales, &c. &c.,
 [by J. Feltham]. Longman, Hurst, Rees, Orme &
 Brown, [1825?]. iv, 492p., plates (6 fold.),
 illus., maps. 15cm.

FENAROLI, Luigi
 Flora delle Alpi: vegetazione e flora delle Alpi
 e degli altri monti d'Italia. Milano: A. Martello,
 1955. xiv, 370p., col. plates, illus., maps (on
 lining papers), bibl. 24cm.

FENDRICH, Anton
 Les sports de la neige; adaptation française par
 René Auscher. Paris: Hachette, 1912. vii, 134p.,
 illus. 21cm.

FENN, G   Manville
 In an alpine valley. Hurst & Blackett, 1894. 3v.
 20cm.
 Library lacks v.2.

FENWICK, G
 From east to west and west to east: some fine
 Dominion scenery. Dunedin: Otago Daily Times &
 Witness Newspapers, 1912. 44p.,plates, illus.
 16cm.

FERGUSON, Fergus
 Wanderings in France and Switzerland. Elliot
 Stock, 1869. 230p. 18cm.

WHITE, James and FURGUSON, George H
 Altitudes in the Dominion of Canada. 2nd ed.
 Ottawa: Commission of Conservation Canada, 1915.
 xxiv, 603p., fold.col. plates (some in pocket),
 illus., map. 26cm.

FERGUSON, Robert
 Swiss men and Swiss mountains. Longman, Brown,
 Green, & Longmans, 1853. viii, 143p. 19cm.
 (Traveller's library, 45)

FERGUSON, Robert
 [Swiss men and Swiss mountains]. Leute und Berge:
 Reisebilder aus der Schweiz; aus dem Englischen
 von I. Senbt. Leipzig: J.J. Weber, 1855. 175p.,
 illus. 18cm. (Weber's Illustrirte Reise-
 Bibliothek)

FERGUSSON, W   N
 Adventure sport and travel on the Tibetan steppes.
 Constable, 1911. xvi, 343p., plates (2 fold.col.),
 illus., maps. 25cm.

FERLET, Réné and POULET, Guy
 Aconcagua: south face; translated from the French
 by E. Noel Bowman. Constable, 1956. xii, 209p.,
 plates, illus., maps. 23cm.

FERRAND, Henri
 L'accident de la Meidje, 20 août 1896; [à la
 memoire de M.A. Payerne]. Grenoble, 1897. 30p.,
 25cm.
 Offprint from Annuaire de la Société des Touristes
 du Dauphiné, année 1896.

FERRAND, Henri
 Autour du Mont Blanc: Chamouni, la vallée d'Aoste,
 le grand et le petit Saint-Bernard. Grenoble:
 Rey, 1920. 158p., illus. 32cm.

FERRAND, Henri
 Autour du Pelvoux: le tour du Pelvoux, de la Grave
 au Pelvoux. Grenoble, 1885. 97p. 26cm.
 Offprint from Annuaire de la Société des Touristes
 du Dauphiné, années 1883 et 1884.

FERRAND, Henri
 Belledone et les Sept-Laux: montagnes d'Uriage et
 d'Allevard. Grenoble: Gratier, 1901. 122p.,
 plates, illus. 34cm.

FERRAND, Henri
 Le circuit de Chartreuse au départ de Grenoble.
 Paris: P. Bricet, 1924. 45p., illus., maps (in
 pocket). 17cm. (Guides Bricet)

FERRAND, Henri
 Le col du Lautaret au départ de Grenoble. Paris:
 P. Bricet, [n.d.]. 46p., illus., maps (1 fold.
 in pocket). 17cm. (Guides Bricet)

FERRAND, Henri
 D'Aix-les-Bains à la Vanoise: la Savoie méridionale. Grenoble: Gratier & Rey, 1907. 124p.,
 illus. 34cm. (Les Alpes de Savoie)

FERRAND, Henri
 Grenoble: capitale des Alpes françaises; préface de Léon Auscher. Grenoble: Rey, 1923.
 156p., illus. 22cm. (Les Beaux pays", 3)

FERRAND, Henri
 [Grenoble: capitale des Alpes françaises].
 Grenoble and thereabouts: Chartreuse, Oisans,
 Vercors... Medici Society, 1923. 154p., illus.
 21cm. (Picture guides)

FERRAND, Henri
 Guide pratique de l'Oisans et du Briançonnais.
 Valence: G. Toursier, [n.d.] 136p., illus.,
 maps, plans. 16cm. (Collection des guides Pol)

FERRAND, Henri
 Itinéraire descriptif, historique et archéologique de la Maurienne et de la Tarentaise;
 avec une carte & plusieurs illustrations par
 Abel Vellot. Grenoble: Dauphin & Dupont, 1879.
 88p., plates (1 fold.), illus., map. 24cm.

FERRAND, Henri
 L'Oisans: la Meidje, le Pelvoux, la Grave, le
 Lautaret, la Bérarde. Grenoble: Gratier &
 Rey, 1903. 124p., plates, illus. 34cm. (Les
 Alpes dauphinoises)

FERRAND, Henri
 La route des Alpes françaises. Grenoble: Rey,
 1925. 149p., 1 fold. plate, illus., map. 23cm.
 (Les "Beaux pays", 8)

FERRAND, Henri
 Les routes des Alpes du Dauphiné, Isère, Drôme,
 Hautes-Alpes: itinéraires avec profils des
 pentes ... à l'usage des cyclistes & automobilistes; avec le concours de Georges Faure et
 Émile Duchemin. Grenoble: Gratier, 1899. 92p.,
 illus., maps. 16 x 25cm.

FERRAND, Henri
 La route des Alpes françaises du Léman à la mer.
 Grenoble: Rey, 1912. 169p., illus., maps.
 34cm.

FERRAND, Henri
 Le Vercors: le Royannais et les Quatre Montagnes,
 région du Mont-Aiguille, du Villard-de-Lans et
 des Grands-Goulets. Grenoble: Gratier & Rey,
 1904. 93p., plates, illus. 34cm. (Les montagnes dauphinoises)

FERRARI, Agostino
 Nella catena del Monte Bianco: impressioni e
 ricordi di ascensioni. Torino: Club Alpino
 Italiano, 1912. 251p., plates (2 fold.), illus.
 27cm.

 - - Nuova ed. riv. e aum. Torino: A. Formica,
 1929.

FERRARI, Agostino
 Nelle gloria delle altezze: impressioni e ricordi
 di ascensioni nei dintorni di Ceresole, Valsava-
 ranche e Cogne. Torino: F. Casanova, 1931.
 359p., illus., bibl. 23cm.

FERRARI, Agostino
 I rifugi alpini d'Italia. Monza: Club Alpino
 Italiano, 1925. 171p. 19cm.

FERRARI, Agostino
CLUB ALPINO ITALIANO
I rifugi del Club Alpino Italiano: storia e descrizione; illustrata con elenco dei rifugi
costruiti in Italia da altre Società alpine [da]
Agostino Ferrari; collaboratori: A. Bossi [and
others]. Torino, 1905. vii, 287p., illus.,
plans. 26cm.
Offprint from Bollettino del C.A.I., v.37, n.70,
1904-05.

FERRARI, Agostino
La Valle di Viù: impressioni e ricordi di escursioni, storia e leggende, usi e costumi.
Torino: S. Lattes, 1912. viii, 239p., plates,
illus. 21cm.

FERRERI, Eugenio
Alpi Cozie settentrionali. Pt.1. Granero-Frioland,
Boucier-Cornour, Queyron-Albergian-Sestrières,
Assietta-Rocciavrè. Torino: Club Alpino
Italiano, 1923. xii, 510p., plates (some col.),
illus., maps, bibl. 17cm. (Guida dei monti
d'Italia; Alpi occidentali, 3)

FERRERI, Eugenio
Alpi Cozie settentrionali. Pt. 2. Sezione 1.
Ramière- Merciantàira, Chaberton-Clotesse, Le
Dolomiti di Valle Stretta. Torino: Club Alpino
Italiano, 1926. 271p., col. plates, illus., maps,
bibl. 17cm. (Guida dei monti d'Italia; Alpi
occidentali, 3)

FERRERI, Eugenio
Alpi Cozie settentrionali. Pt. 2. Sezione 2.
Le Dolomiti di Valle Stretta (Massiccio del Tàbor;
Costiera Bernàuda-Re Magi); Sarrasins-Marches;
Fréjus, Pierre Menue-Etiache; Ambin-Vallonetto-
Moncenisio. Torino: Club Alpino Italiano, 1927.
256p., plates, illus., maps, bibl. 17cm. (Guida
dei monti d'Italia; Alpi occidentali, 3)

FERRERO, Felice
The Valley of Aosta: a descriptive and historical
sketch of an Alpine valley... New York, London:
Putnam, 1910. xvi, 336p., plates (some fold., 1
col.), illus., maps, bibl. 22cm.

FERUGLIO, G
Guida touristica del Cadore, Zoldano ed Agordino.
Tolmezzo: G.B. Ciani, 1910. vii, 470p., illus.
18cm.

FEUZ, Ernst
Führer und Heimatkunde von Mürren; bearb. von
Ernst Feuz... Mürren: E. Feuz, 1934. 87p., illus.
19cm.

FIALA, Ivan
Makalu 1976: trasa Ceskoslovenskej horolezeckej
expedicie Himaláje. Bratislava: Pressfoto, 1977.
33 leaves of col. illus. in folder. 22cm.
Picture captions in Czech, Russion, English, German
and French.

FICKER, Heinrich von and AMPFERER, Otto
Aus Innsbrucks Bergwelt: Wanderbilder aus Inns-
brucks Bergen; mit ... Kunst beilagen ... nach
Originalaufnahmen von Otto Melzer; Text von
Heinrich von Ficker und Otto Ampferer. Innsbruck:
H. Schwick, 1902. 229p., plates, illus. 30cm.

FIELD, Alfred Ernest
ALPINE CLUB
Peaks, passes and glaciers, by members of the
Alpine Club. 3rd series; edited by A.E. Field and
Sydney Spencer. Methuen, 1932. xi, 307p., plates,
illus. 23cm.

FIELD, Edgar Stanley and PELLS, Edward G
A mountaineer's paradise: a guide to the mountains
of the Worcester district... Worcester (C.P.):
Mountain Club of South Africa, [1925]. [134]p.,
1 fold. plate, illus., maps. 21cm.

FIGARI, Bartolomeo
Montagna: fonte di gioia e di vita, scuola d'altruismo e di bontà: impressioni e ricordi di un
alpinista. Bologna: Tamari, 1956. 176p. 25cm.

FIGUIER, Louis
La terre et les mers, ou; Description physique du
globe. Paris: Hachette, 1864. viii, 508p., col.
plates, illus., maps. 25cm.

FIGUIER, Louis
[La terre et les mers]. Earth and sea; [with
additions by W.H. Davenport Adams]. Nelson, 1875.
13-715p., illus. 26cm.

FILEK, Egid
JAHN, Gustav
Gustav Jahn: ein Maler- und Bergsteigerleben; mit
28 meist farbigen Abbildungen nach Werken des
Künstlers; begleitende Worte von Egid Filek. Wien:
A. Luser, [1931]. [24]p., col. plates, illus.
(some col.). 31cm.

FILES, Muriel
FELL AND ROCK CLIMBING CLUB OF THE ENGLISH LAKE
DISTRICT
Catalogue of the Library; compiled by Muriel Files.
Lancaster: F. & R.C.C., 1972. vi, 81p. 26cm.

- - Additions, June 1972 to May 1975.
- - Additions, June 1975 to March 1979.
- - Section 4: Maps. 1978.

FILIPPI, Filippo de
See
DE FILIPPI, Filippo

La fin d'une conquête; préface de M. Barrault.
Lyon: Guiron-Perichon, 1953. 1v. (chiefly illus).
25cm.

FINCH, George Ingle
Climbing Mount Everest. Philip, 1930. 72p.,
illus. 19cm. (Philips' "New prospect" readers)

FINCH, George Ingle
Der Kampf um den Everest; Deutsch von Walter
Schmidkung. Leipzig: Brockhaus, 1925. 206p.,
plates, illus., maps. 24cm.

FINCH, George Ingle
The making of a mountaineer. Arrowsmith, 1924.
340p., plates, illus. 26cm.

FINCH, George Ingle
[The making of a mountaineer]. Comment on devient
alpiniste; traduit ... par R. de Malherbe et É.
Gaillard. Chambéry: Dardel, 1926. 327p., plates,
illus. 20cm.

FINCH, George Ingle
BLACKMAN, M
George Ingle Finch, 1888-1970, elected F.R.S.
1938. [London, 1972]. 223-239p., 1 plate, port.
26cm.
Offprint from Biographical Memoirs of Fellows of
the Royal Society, vol. 18, Nov. 1972.

FINDEN, Edward
ACLAND, Hugh Dyke
Illustrations of the Vaudois, in a series of views;
engraved by Edward Finden from drawings by Hugh
Dyke Acland; accompanied with descriptions [by
H.D. Acland]. C. Tilt, 1831. 34p., plates, map.
25cm.
Extract from Arnaud, H. The glorious recovery by
the Vaudois of their valleys. 1827.

FINLAY, Ian
The Highlands. Batsford, 1963. 208p., illus.,
maps. 23cm.

FINNEMORE, John
Switzerland; with ... illustrations in colour by
A.D. McCormick, J. Hardwicke Lewis and others.
Black, 1908. viii, 86p., col. plates, illus.,
map. 20cm. (Peeps at many lands)

FINSTERWALDER, Richard
Alpenvereinskartographie und die ihr dienenden
Methoden; mit Beiträgen von E. Ebster [and others].
Berlin: H. Wichmann, 1935. 81p., plates (1 fold.,
some col.), illus., maps. 25cm. (Sammlung
Wichmann, Bd.3)

FINSTERWALDER, Richard
Forschung am Nanga Parbat: Deutsche Himalaya-Expedition 1934, von Richard Finsterwalder [and others]. Hannover: Helwing, 1935. v, 143p., plates (2 fold.col.), illus., maps (in pocket). 26cm. (Geographische Gesellschaft zu Hannover. Sonderveröffentlichung)

FINSTERWALDER, S
Der Vernagtferner: seine Geschichte und seine Vermessung in den Jahren 1888 und 1889. Graz: D.U.Ö.A.V., 1897. 96p., fold. plates, illus., maps. 30cm. (Wissenschaftliche Ergänzungshefte zur Zeitschrift des D.U.Ö. Alpenvereins, Bd.1, Heft 1)

FIRBANK, Thomas
Bride to the mountain: a romance. Harrap, 1940. 256p., illus. 20cm.

FIRBANK, Thomas
I bought a mountain. Harrap, 1940. 320p. 23cm.

FIRSOFF, Valdemar Axel
Arran with camera and sketchbook; illustrated by the author with photographs and line drawings. Hale, 1951. 230p., 49 plates (1 fold.), illus., map. 23cm.

FIRSOFF, Valdemar Axel
The Cairngorms on foot and ski. Hale, 1949. 279p., plates (11fold.), illus., map. 23cm.

FIRSOFF, Valdemar Axel
In the hills of Breadalbane; illustrated from the author's photographs and drawings. Hale, 1954. 270p., plates, illus., maps (1 fold.). 23cm.

FIRSOFF, Valdemar Axel
Ski track on the battlefield. L. Drummond, [1944]. x, 158p., plates, illus., bibl. 24cm.

FIRSOFF, Valdemar Axel
The Tatra mountains. L. Drummond, [1942]. 128p., illus., map, music. 24cm.

FIRST AID COMMITTEE OF MOUNTAINEERING CLUBS
First aid: North Wales, Lake District, Scotland. Stockport: First Aid Committee of Mountaineering Clubs, 1938. 19p., plan. 16cm.

FIRST AID COMMITTEE OF MOUNTAINEERING CLUBS
For publications of this body after 1946
See
MOUNTAIN RESCUE COMMITTEE

FISCHER, Andreas
Hochgebirgswanderungen in den Alpen und im Kaukasus; hrsg., mit Lebensbild und Bericht von Ernst Jenny. Frauenfeld: Huber, 1913. vii, 311p., plates, illus. 21cm.

- - Neue Folge; hrsg. von Ernst Jenny. 1919.

FISCHER, Andreas
Zwei Kaukasus-Expeditionen. Bern: Schmidt, Francke, 1891. 150p., plates (1 fold.col.), illus., map. 20cm.

FISCHER, Christian August
Bergreisen; hrsg. von Christian August Fischer. Leipzig: J.F. Hartknoch, 1804-05. 2v. in 1, 2 fold. plates, maps. 17cm.
No more published?

FISCHER, Ernst
Der kartographische Standpunkt der Schweiz: ein Vortrag. München: E.A. Fleischmann, 1870. 49p., plates (some col.), illus., 2 maps (1 col.). 23cm.

FISCHER, Eugen
Mein Wallis: Festgabe zum Walliser Herbstfest in Zürich, 29. und 30. Oktober 1921; hrsg. im Auftrage des Festkomitees von Eugen Fischer. Zürich: H. Börsig, 1921. 72p., illus. 24cm.

FISCHER, H
Souvenir de l'Oberland bernois: vues & costumes d'après nature, dess. et lith. par H. Fischer. Berne: J. Dalp, [ca 1850]. 1v. of col. illus. 16 x 21cm.
Cover title.

FISCHER, Hans
Abfahrten, die man gemacht haben muss: 100 schöne Abfahrten der Ost- und Westalpen; zusammengestellt von Hans Fischer. München: Rother, [1932]. 81p., 100 plates, illus., 5 maps. 17 x 25cm.

FISCHER, Hans
Dolomiten: Worte und Bilder; hrsg. von Hans Fischer. München: Rother, 1928. 159p., plates (some col.), illus., maps. 25cm.

FISCHER, Hans
Der Grossglockner: das Buch des Königs der deutschen Berge; hrsg. von Hans Fischer. 2. Aufl. München: Rother, 1929. 166p., plates (some col.), illus., maps. 25cm.

FISCHER, Hans
In die Berge: ein Lehr- und Leitbuch für die reifere Jugend. München: Rother, 1927. 224p., plates, illus. 21cm.

FISCHER, L
Taschenbuch der Flora von Bern: systematische Uebersicht der in der Gegend von Bern wildwachsenden und zu öconomischen Zwecken allgemein cultiverten phanerogamischen Pflanzen. Bern: Huber, 1855. xx, 139p., 1 fold. plate, map. 19cm.

FISCHER, Walther
Oskar Schuster und sein Geist: ein Strauss bergsteigerischen Erlebens; mit Originalberichten der Erstbesteigungen von Oskar Schuster [and others]; im Auftrage der A.S.D. hrsg. von Walther Fischer. Dresden: Dressel, 1926. 88p., plates, illus. 27cm.
"Eine Festgabe der Akademischen Sektion Dresden des D. und Oe. Alpenvereins".

FISCHLI, Albert
Schweizer Balladen; ausgewählt und eingeleitet von Albert Fischli. Leipzig: H. Haessel, 1924. 102p. 17cm. (Die Schweiz im deutsche Geistesleben)

FISHER, H A L
James Bryce, Viscount Bryce of Dechmont. Macmillan, 1927. 2v., port. 22cm.

FISHER, Margery and FISHER, James
Shackleton; drawings by W.E. How. Barrie, 1957. 559p., plates, illus., maps, ports., bibl. 23cm.

FISHER, Joel E
Bibliography of Alaskan and Pacific Coast states mountain ascents. [New York?]: The Author, 1945. 85p. 22cm.

FISHER, Joel E
Bibliography of Canadian mountain ascents. [New York?]: The Author, 1945. 103p. 22cm.

FISHER, Joel E
Bibliography of eastern seaboard mountain ascents. [New York?]: The Author, 1945. 16p. 22cm.

FISHER, Joel E
Bibliography of Mexican, Central and South American mountain ascents. [New York?]: The Author, 1945. 25p. 22cm.

FISHER, Joel E
Bibliography of United States mountain ascents (except Pacific Coast states and the eastern seaboard). [New York?]: The Author, 1945. 64p. 22cm.

FISHER, Joel E
Problems in the geology of mountains: five thesis; collected, re-edited and privately published [N.p.]: [n.pub.], 1944. 80p., illus., bibl. 25cm.

FISHER, Margery and FISHER, James
  Shackleton; drawings by W.E. How. Barrie, 1957.
  559p., plates, illus., maps, ports., bibl. 23cm.

FISHER, Ruth B
  On the borders of Pigmy land. Marshall, [1905?].
  ix, 215p., plates, illus. 23cm.

FITTER, Richard
  Britain's wildlife: rarities and introductions;
  with 35 paintings by John Leigh-Pemberton; fore-
  word by the Duke of Edinburgh; preface by Peter
  Scott. Nicholas Kaye in association with Midland
  Bank, 1966. 95p., illus. (some col.), map. 30cm.

FITZGERALD, Edward Arthur
  Climbs in the New Zealand Alps, being an account
  of travel and discovery; ... with contributions
  by Sir Martin Conway [and others]. Fisher Unwin,
  1896. xvi, 363p., plates (1 fold.col.), illus.,
  map (in pocket). 26cm.

- - 2nd ed. 1896.

FITZGERALD, Edward Arthur
  The highest Andes: a record of the first ascent
  of Aconcagua and Tupungato in Argentina, and the
  exploration of the surrounding valleys; with
  chapters by Stuart Vines; and contributions by
  Professor Bonney [and others]. Methuen, 1899.
  xvi, 390p., plates (2 fold.col.), illus., maps.
  25cm.

FITZGERALD, Kevin
  The Chilterns. Batsford, 1972. 184p., illus.,
  map, bibl. 23cm.

FITZGIBBON, Mary Rose
  Lakeland scene; edited by Mary Rose Fitzgibbon.
  Chapman & Hall, 1948. 240p., plates, illus. 23cm.
  Essays selected from the Journal of the Fell and
  Rock Climbing Club.

FITZPATRICK, Thomas Cecil
RACKHAM, H
  Thomas Cecil Fitzpatrick: a memoir; edited by H.
  Rackham at the request of Mrs. Fitzpatrick.
  Cambridge: University Press, 1937. 47p., plates,
  illus. 22cm.

FITZSIMONS, Raymund
  The Baron of Piccadilly: the travels and enter-
  tainments of Albert Smith, 1816-1860. Bles, 1967.
  192p., plates, illus., bibl. 23cm.

FLAIG, Hermine and FLAIG, Walther
  Burgen an der Grenze: Erinnerungen und Bilder,
  Sagen und Geschichten aus dem Rhätikon zwischen
  Sulzfluh und Schesaplana. Dornbirn: Im Selbst-
  verlage der Verfasser, [1928?]. 140p., 24 plates,
  illus. 22cm.

FLAIG, Walther
  Arlberg: Ski und Schnee. München: F. Bruckmann,
  1933. 22p., 88 plates, illus., map. 26cm.

FLAIG, Walther
  Der Arlberg und die Klostertaler Alpen mit den
  Grenzgebieten des südlichen Bregenzer Waldes: ein
  Hochgebirgsführer. Innsbruck: Wagner, 1929.
  xxxiii, 360p., plates, illus., maps. 16cm.
  (Wagner's alpine Spezialführer, 1)

FLAIG, Walther
  Bernina: Erfahrungen und Erlebnisse. Stuttgart,
  1934-36. 3v., plates, illus., map. 26cm.
  Offprint from Zeitschrift des Deutschen und Österreichischen Alpenvereins, 1934-36.

FLAIG, Hermine and FLAIG, Walther
  Burgen an der Grenze: Erinnerungen und Bilder,
  Sagen und Geschichten aus dem Rhätikon zwischen
  Sulzfluh und Schesaplana. Dornbirn; Im Selbst-
  verlage der Verfasser, [1928?]. 140p., 24 plates,
  illus. 22cm.

FLAIG, Walther
  Eistechnik des Bergsteigers in Bildern und Merkworten. 2. Aufl. Stuttgart: Dieck, 1925. 4v.,
  fold. plates, illus. 16cm.

FLAIG, Walther
  Felsklettern in Bildern und Merkworten. Stuttgart:
  Dieck, 1924. 2v., fold. plates, illus. 15cm.

FLAIG, Walther
  Das Gletscherbuch: Rätsel und Romantik, Gestalt
  und Gesetz der Alpengletscher. Leipzig:
  Brockhaus, 1938. 196p., fold. plates, illus.,
  bibl. 24cm.

FLAIG, Walther
  Hoch über Tälern und Menschen: im Banne der
  Bernina. Stuttgart: Dieck, 1925. 151; viiip.,
  85 plates (1 fold.col.), illus., map. 28cm.
  (Stuttgarter Sportbücher)

FLAIG, Walther
  Hochgebirgsführer durch die Nordrhaetischen
  Alpen. Dornbirn: Vorarlberger Verlagsanstalt,
  1924. 4v., fold. plates, illus., maps. 16cm.
  Library has v. 1 and 2 only.

FLAIG, Walther
  Im Kampf um Tschomo-lungma den Gipfel der Erde:
  der Himalaja und sein höchster Gipfel, Mount
  Everest oder Tschomo-lungma. 16. Aufl. Stuttgart: Kosmos, 1923. 78p., illus., maps, bibl.
  22cm.

FLAIG, Walther
  Lawinen! Abenteuer und Erfahrung, Erlebnis und
  Lehre. Leipzig: Brockhaus, 1935. 173p., illus.,
  bibl. 24cm.

- - 2. vollständig neubearb. Aufl. Wiesbaden:
  Brockhaus, 1955.

FLAIG, Walther
  Das Silvretta-Buch: Volk und Gebirg über drei
  Ländern: Errrinerungen und Erkenntnisse eines
  Bergsteigers und Skitouristen. 4. verm. und verb.
  Aufl. Konstanz: Echo-Verlag, 1954. 240p.,
  plates (1 fold., 1 col.), illus., maps. 21cm.

FLAIG, Walther
  Silvretta-Skiführer, mit Paznaun und Montafon,
  Unterengadin und Prätigau, Ost-Rätikon und Verwall.
  8. Aufl. München: Rother, 1965. 266p., plates
  (2 fold.col.), illus., maps (in pocket). 17cm.

FLAIG, Walther
  Skiführer Rätikon und Bregenzerwaldgebirge, mit
  Fürstentum Liechtenstein, Walgau, Grosswalsertal,
  Klostertaler Alpen. München: Rother, 1961. 268p.,
  plates (2 fold.), illus., maps (in pocket). 17cm.

FLAIG, Walther
  Die Skiparadiese der Schweiz; hrsg. und eingeleitet von Walther Flaig. München: F. Bruckmann,
  1932. 108p. (chiefly illus.), bibl. 29cm.

FLAIG, Walther and ZWEIGELT, Sepp
  Vorarlberger Schieführer in mehreren Heften mit
  Schiekarten und Anstiegsbildern. Heft. 1; hrsg.
  von Walther Flaig und Sepp Zweigelt. Allgäu:
  Zumstein, Grünenbach, Bahern, 1928. 76p., map (in
  pocket). 16cm.

FLAUBERT, Gustave
  Par les champs et par les grèves; Pyrénées; Corse.
  Paris: L. Conard, 1910. 479p. 22cm. (Oeuvres
  complètes)

FLEINER, Albert
  Engelberg: Streifzüge durch Gebirg und Tal; unter
  Mitwirkung von X. Imfeld [and others]; geschildert
  von Albert Fleiner. Zürich: Hofer & Burger,
  [1890]. 226p., col. plates (some fold.), illus.,
  maps. 22cm.

FLEMING, John
LEIGHTON, John M
  The lakes of Scotland: a series of views, from
  paintings taken expressly for the work by John
  Fleming; engraved by Joseph Swan; with historical
  & descriptive illustrations by John M. Leighton.
  Glasgow: J. Swan, 1834. xiii, 223p., plates,
  illus. 28cm.

FLEMING, Jon W
JOINT BRITISH ARMY MOUNTAINEERING ASSOCIATION/
ROYAL NEPALESE ARMY NUPTSE EXPEDITION, 1975
   Nuptse 1975: preliminary report, [by J.W. Fleming
   and others]. Warminster: The Expedition, 1976.
   1v. (various pagings), plates, illus., map. 30cm.

FLEMING, Jon W
ARMY MOUNTAINEERING ASSOCIATION HIMACHAL PRADESH
EXPEDITION, 1973
   Preliminary report [by J.W. Fleming]. Aldershot:
   The Expedition, 1973. [19] leaves. 30cm.

FLEMING, Jon W
ARMY MOUNTAINEERING ASSOCIATION HIMACHAL PRADESH
EXPEDITION, 1973
   Report, [by the leader J.W. Fleming, and other
   expedition members]. Aldershot: The Expedition,
   [1974]. xii, 92p., illus., maps. 30cm.

FLEMING, Jon W   and FAUX, Ronald
   Soldiers on Everest: the joint Army Mountaineering
   Association/Royal Nepalese Army Mount Everest
   Expedition 1976. H.M.S.O., 1977. xvi, 239p.,
   plates (some col.), illus., maps. 18cm.

FLEMING, Peter
   Bayonets to Lhasa: the first full account of the
   British invasion of Tibet in 1904. Hart-Davis,
   1961. 319p., plates, illus., maps, bibl. 23cm.

FLEMING, Peter
   Brazilian adventure. New cheap ed. Cape, 1942.
   376p., plates, illus., maps. 21cm.

FLEMING, Peter
   News from Tartary: a journey from Peking to
   Kashmir. Cape, 1936. 384p., plates (1 fold.col.),
   illus., map. 21cm.

FLEMING, Sandford
   England and Canada: a summer tour between old and
   new Westminster. Montreal: Dawson, 1884. xi,
   449p., 1 fold.col. plate, map. 20cm.

FLEMING, Sandford
   Report on surveys and preliminary operations on the
   Canadian Pacific Railway up to January 1877.
   Ottawa: MacLean, Roger, 1877. xvi, 431p., fold.
   plates (some col.), illus., maps, plans. 27cm.

FLEMING, Sandford
GRANT, George M
   Ocean to ocean: Sandford Fleming's expedition
   through Canada in 1872, being a diary kept during
   a journey from the Atlantic to the Pacific with
   the expedition of the Engineer-in-chief of the
   Canadian Pacific and Intercolonial Railways.
   Sampson Low, Marston, Low & Searle, 1873. xv,
   371p., plates, illus. 21cm.

FLEMWELL, George
   Alpine flowers and gardens; painted and described
   by G. Flemwell. Black, 1910. xiv, 167p., col.
   plates, illus. 23cm.

FLEMWELL, George
   [Alpine flowers and gardens]. Sur l'alpe fleurie:
   promenades poétiques et philosophiques dans les
   Alpes; adapté de l'anglais par L. Marret et L.
   Capitaine. Paris: Société d'Édition des Sciences
   Naturelles, 1914. xi, 248p., plates (some col.),
   illus. 26cm.

FLEMWELL, George
   Chamonix; pictured and described by G. Flemwell.
   Blackie, 1913. 64p., col. plates, illus. 24cm.
   (Beautiful Switzerland)

FLEMWELL, George
   The flower-fields of alpine Switzerland: an appreciation and a plea; painted and written by G.
   Flemwell. Hutchinson, 1911. xviii, 195p., col.
   plates, illus. 23cm.

FLEMWELL, George
   Lausanne and its environs; painted and described
   by G. Flemwell. Blackie, 1914. 64p., col. plates,
   illus. 24cm. (Beautiful Switzerland)

FLEMWELL, George
   Lucerne; pictured and described by G. Flemwell.
   Blackie, 1913. 64p., col. plates, illus. 24cm.
   (Beautiful Switzerland)

FLEMWELL, George
THOMPSON, Harold Stuart
   Sub-alpine plants; or, Flowers of the Swiss woods
   and meadows; with ... coloured plates ... by
   George Flemwell. Routledge, 1912. iv, 325p.,
   col. plates, illus. 23cm.

FLEMWELL, George
   Villars and its environs; painted and described
   by G. Flemwell. Blackie, 1914. 64p., col.
   plates, illus. 24cm. (Beautiful Switzerland)

FLENDER, Walther
BLODIG, Karl
   Zur Erinnerung an Walther Flender, 11.Jan. 1880-
   26. Feb. 1902: ein Lebensabriss. Leipzig: [The
   Author], [19--]. 168p., plates, illus. 24cm.

FLETCHER, Betty
RAMBLERS' ASSOCIATION. Northern Area
   Ramblers' Cheviot: twelve walks in the Cheviot
   Hills. [Rev. ed., edited by Betty Fletcher].
   Newcastle-upon-Tyne: H. Hill, 1976. 84p.,
   illus., maps. 22cm.

FLETCHER, C R L
GODLEY, Alfred Denis
   Reliquiae; edited by C.R.L. Fletcher. Oxford
   University Press, 1926. 2v., plates (1 fold.),
   illus. 20cm.

FLETCHER, David Wilson
   The children of Kanchenjunga. Constable, 1955.
   ix, 251p., plates, illus. 23cm.

FLETCHER, Hanslip
   Changing London. Henry T. Wood, 1933. 1v.
   (chiefly illus.). 39cm.

FLETCHER, Hanslip
   Changing London (third series): a book of
   sketches; with an introduction and notes by A.E.
   Richardson. Methuen, 1928. 1v. (chiefly illus.).
   39cm.

FLETCHER, J S
   The enchanting North. E. Nash, 1908. xi, 253p.,
   plates (1 fold., some col.), illus., map. 23cm.

FLEURIAU, Jérome Charlemagne, marquis de Langle
   See
LANGLE, marquis de

FLEURIOT, Jean Marie Jérome
   See
LANGLE, marquis de

FLORIAN, Jean Pierre Claris de
   Guillaume Tell; ou, La Suisse libre: ouvrage
   posthume; précédé de son discours de réception à
   l'Académie Française, de la Vie de l'auteur, par
   Jauffret, de quelques pièces fugitives inédites.
   Paris: Briand, 1810. lvi, 94p., plates, illus.
   16cm. (Oeuvres de Florian)

FLORIAN, Jean Pierre Claris de
   Nouvelles de Florian. T.2. Paris: Briand, 1810.
   143p., plates, illus. 16cm. (Oeuvres de
   Florian)
   Contains: Camiré, Claudine, Sélico, Selmours,
   Valerie & Zulbar.

FLORIANT, V de
   À travers les Andes équatoriales: souvenirs personnels.
   (In Bibliothèque universelle ... v.49, 1891,
   p.54-81)

FLOYD, C G
   As ascent of Mont Blanc. London, 1855. 20p.
   22cm.
   Signed C.G.F. i.e, C.G. Floyd.
   Offprint from Fraser's Magazine, July 1855.

FLÜCKIGER, Alfred
SCHWEIZERISCHER SKI-VERBAND
Offizieller Ski Tourenführer der Schweiz; hrsg.
vom Schweizerischen Ski-Verband; Redaktion:
Alfred Flückiger. Bern: Kümmerly & Frey, 1933.
367p., plates, illus., maps. 21cm.

FLÜCKIGER, Otto
Die Schweiz aus der Vogelschau; hrsg. und eingeleitet von Otto Flückiger. Erlenbach-Zürich:
E. Rentsch, 1924. xxxxiii p., 172 plates,
illus., maps. 30cm.

FLÜCKIGER, Otto
[Die Schweiz aus der Vogelschau]. Switzerland
from the air; with ... illustrations from the collection of Walter Mittelholzer; edited and
prefaced by Otto Flückiger; translated by A.W.P.
Allan. Erlenbach-Zürich: E. Rentsch, 1926.
xxxii p., 176 plates, illus., maps. 30cm.

KILLAN, W and FLUSIN, G
Observations sur les variations des glaciers et
l'enneigement dans les Alpes dauphinoises; organisées par la Société des Touristes du Dauphiné.
Grenoble: Allier, 1900. 231p., plates, illus.
29cm.

Focus on Switzerland. Lausanne: Swiss Office for the
Development of Trade, 1975. 4v., illus. (some
col.), map and statistical pamphlet in folder.
21cm.
Sponsored by the Coordinating Committee for the
Presence of Switzerland Abroad.

FODERÉ, F E
Voyage aux Alpes Maritimes; ou, histoire naturelle,
agraire, civile et médicale, du comté de Nice et
pays limitrophes... Paris: F.G. Levrault, 1821.
2v. 22cm.

FÜRDERREUTHER, Max
Die Allgäuer Alpen: Land and Leute. Kempten: Jos.
Kösel, 1907. xvi, 525p., plates (1 fold., some
col.), illus., map. 26cm.

FOLLONIER, Jean
Peuple des montagnes; préface de Pierre Vallette;
illustrations d'Albert Chavaz. Sierre: Éditions
des Treize Étoiles, 1945. 97p., col. plates, illus.
22cm.

FOLTIN, Arthur
Tiroler Alpensagen; illustriert von Adolf
Schlabitz. Stuttgart: Greiner & Pfeiffer, [189-].
x, 301p., illus. 21cm.

FONDATION SUISSE D'EXPLORATION ALPINE
See
SCHWEIZERISCHE STIFTUNG FÜR ALPINE FORSCHUNGEN

FONTAINE, E
L'Aiguille du Dru et sa niche. Lyon: A. Geneste,
1913. 78p., plates, illus, bibl. 25cm.

FONTAINE, E
Alpinisme et volcanisme: l'éruption de Vésuve en
1906. Tours: Imprimerie R. & P. Deslis, 1928.
91p., plates, illus., bibl. 22cm.

FONTAINE, E
La fin d'une pierre: Groupe Triolet-Isabella,
chaîne du Mont Blanc. Tours: Imprimerie R. & P.
Deslis, 1926. 28p., plates, illus. 23cm.

FONTAINE, E
Notes sur l'alpinisme:massif du Mont-Blanc. Tours:
Imprimerie R. & P. Deslis, 1930. 105p., plates
(some fold.), illus. 22cm.

- - Suite à la publication de 1930. 1932.

FONTANA, Carlo
Guida storico, alpina di Valdagno, Recoaro, Schio,
Arisiero ... Schio: Club Alpino Italiano, Sezione
di Schio, 1898. xviii, 153p., plates, illus.
17cm.

FONTANET, Jean Claude
La montagne: roman. Paris: La Table Ronde, 1970.
257p. 21cm.

FONTANNAZ, Charles
Ascension du Mont-Blanc par l'Aiguille du Gouter.
Genève: Imprimerie H. Koch, 1893. 11p. 22cm.

FORBES, Alexander
Northernmost Labrador mapped from the air; with
contributions from O.M. Miller, N.E. Odell and
Ernest C. Abbe. New York: American Geographical
Society, 1938. xx, 255p., illus., maps. 26cm.
(American Geographical Society. Special publica-
tions, no.22)

- - Plates and navigational notes.
Booklet and 6 fold.col. maps in slip-case.

FORBES, Charles S
Iceland: its volcanoes, geysers and glaciers.
Murray, 1860. viii, 335p., plates (1 fold.),
illus., map. 22cm.

FORBES, George
RENDU, Louis
[Théorie des glaciers de la Savoie]. Theory of
the glaciers of Savoy; translated by Alfred Wills;
to which are added the original memoir and supplementary articles by P.G. Tait and John Ruskin;
edited with introductory remarks by George Forbes.
Macmillan, 1874. 216p., illus., map. 23cm.
Text in English and French.

FORBES, H   F   Gordon
The road from Simla to Shipki in Chinese Thibet
and various minor routes, with a few hints for
travellers. Calcutta: Thacker, Spink, 1893.
45p., fold. plate, map (in pocket). 18cm.

FORBES, James David
Description of some volcanic formations... 1.
On the volcanic geology of the Vivarais (Ardèche).
[Edinburgh]: [Royal Society], [1853]. 38p., 6
plates (1 fold., 1 col.), illus., map. 28cm.
(Transactions of the Royal Society of Edinburgh,
v.20, pt.1, 1853)

FORBES, James David
Historical remarks on the first discovery of the
real structure of glacier ice. Edinburgh, 1843.
20p. 23cm.
Offprint from Edinburgh new philosophical journal,
1843.

FORBES, James David
Illustrations of the viscous theory of glacier
motion. London, 1846. 143-210p., plates (2
fold., 1 col.), illus. 30cm.
Offprint from Philosophical transactions, pt.2,
1846.

FORBES, James David
[Letters on recent observations on glaciers].
Edinburgh, 1842-1851. 1v. (various pagings),
plates, illus. 23cm.
Offprint from Edinburgh new philosophical journal,
1842-51.

FORBES, James David
Norway and its glaciers visited in 1851; followed
by journals of excursions in the High Alps of
Dauphiné, Berne, and Savoy. Edinburgh: Black,
1853. xxiv, 349p., plates (1 fold., some col.),
illus., map. 27cm.

FORBES, James David
[Norway and its glaciers ...]. Norwegen und
seine Gletscher; nebst Reisen in den Hochalpen
der Dauphiné, von Bern und Savoyen; aus dem
englischen von Ernst A. Zuchold. Leipzig: A.Abel,
1855. x, 312p., 2 fold. plates, illus., map.
20cm.

FORBES, James David
Notes on the topography and geology of the
Cuchullin hills in Skye and on the traces of
ancient glaciers which they present. Edinburgh,
1845. 26p., 2 plates, illus., map. 22cm.
Offprint from Edinburgh new philosophical journal,
Jan. 1846.

FORBES, James David
Notice respecting Mr. Reilly's topographical
survey of the chain of Mont Blanc. Edinburgh,
1865. 335-338p. 22cm.
Offprint from Proceedings of the Royal Society,
Edinburgh, v.5, 1865.

FORBES, James David
Occasional papers on the theory of glaciers, now
first collected and chronologically arranged...
Edinburgh: Black, 1859. xxix, 278p., plates (1
fold., 1 col.), illus., map. 24cm.

FORBES, James David
On a remarkable structure observed by the author in
the ice of glaciers. Edinburgh, 1842. 8p., col.
plates, illus. 23cm.
Offprint from Edinburgh new philosophical journal,
Jan. 1842.

FORBES, James David
On some properties of ice near its melting point.
Edinburgh, 1858. 4p., illus. 23cm.
Offprint from Proceedings of the Royal Society,
Edinburgh, 1858.

FORBES, James David
On the geological relations of the secondary and
primary rocks of the chain of Mont Blanc.
Edinburgh, 1856. 189-203p., fold.col. plates,
illus. 22cm.
Offprint from Edinburgh new philosophical journal,
new ser., v.3., no.2, April 1856.

FORBES, James David
Remarks on a paper "On ice and glaciers" in the
last number of the Philosophical Magazine in a
letter to Prof. Tyndall. [London, 1859]. 6p. 23cm.
Offprint from Philosophical Magazine, March 1859.

FORBES, James David
Reply to Professor Tyndall's remarks in his work
"On the glaciers of the Alps" relating to Rendu's
"Théorie des glaciers". Edinburgh: Black, 1860.
28p. 22cm.

FORBES, James David
Sur l'eclipse totale de soleil du 8 juillet 1842:
extrait d'une lettre à M. le prof. Gautier.
[Genève, 1843]. 8p. 23cm.
Offprint from Bibliothèque universelle de Genève,
déc. 1843.

FORBES, James David
Topography of the chain of Mont Blanc. [Edinburgh,
1865]. 137-157p., plates, illus., maps. 23cm.
Extended review article from North British Review,
March 1865.

FORBES, James David
The tour of Mont Blanc and of Monte Rosa ...
See his
Travels through the Alps of Savoy ...

FORBES, James David
Travels through the Alps of Savoy and other parts
of the Pennine chain, with observations on the
phenomena of glaciers. Edinburgh: Black, 1843.
x, 424p., plates (some col.), illus., maps (1
fold). 27cm.

- - 2nd ed. rev. 1845.
- - New ed. rev. and annotated by W.A.B. Coolidge,
1900.

FORBES, James David
[Travels through the Alps of Savoy...]. The tour
of Mont Blanc and of Monte Rosa, being a personal
narrative, abridged from the author's "Travels in
the Alps of Savoy". Edinburgh: Black, 1855. xl,
320p., 2 fold plates (1 col.), illus., maps. 18cm.

FORBES, James David
[Travels through the Alps of Savoy ...]. Reisen
in den Savoyer Alpen und in anderen Theilen der
Penninen-Kette, nebst Beobachtungen über die
Gletscher; bearb. von Gustav Leonhard. Stuttgart:
Schweizerbart, 1845. 386p., illus., 2 maps. 23cm.

FORBES, James David
GEIKIE, Archibald
Memoir of the late James David Forbes, read to the
Geological Society of Edinburgh, 21st January 1869.
Edinburgh: Printed by T. Constable, 1869. 38p.,
23cm.

FORBES, James David
SHAIRP, John Campbell
Life and letters of James David Forbes, FRS., by
John Campbell Shairp, Peter Guthrie Tait and A.
Adams-Reilly. Macmillan, 1873. xv, 598p., plates,
illus., fold. map, bibl. 24cm.

FORBES, James David
TYNDALL, John
Principal Forbes and his biographers. Longmans,
Green, 1873. x, 35p. 19cm.

FORBES, Sir John
A physician's holiday; or, A month in Switzerland
in the summer of 1848. Murray, 1849. xii, 520p.,
plates (1 fold.), illus., map. 20cm.

- - 2nd ed. rev. and corr. 1850.
- - 3rd ed. entitled: The physician's holiday...
Wm. S. Orr, 1852.

FORBES, Sir John
Sight-seeing in Germany and the Tyrol in the
autumn of 1855. Smith, Elder, 1856. xix, 378p.,
plates (1 fold.), illus., map. 20cm.

FORBES, Murray
The diary of a traveller over Alps and Appenines;
or, Daily minutes of a circuitous excursion, [by
Murray Forbes]. Printed by W. Smith, 1824.
viii, 170p. 23cm.

FORBES, Rosita
Forbidden road - Kabul to Samarkand. Cassell,
1937. xii, 289p., plates, illus., map. 22cm.

FORD, William
A description of scenery in the Lake District,
intended as a guide to strangers. 2nd ed., carefully rev. throughout. Carlisle: Thurnam, 1840.
xi, 190p., plates (1 fold., 4 col.), maps. 19cm.

- - 3rd ed. 1844.
- - 4th ed. R. Groombridge, 1845.

FORDHAM, Derek and FORDHAM, Jennifer
THULE-GRISE FIORD EXPEDITION, 1976
General report, [by] Derek and Jennifer Fordham.
Greenwich: Thule-Grise Fiord Expedition, 1976.
34 leaves, illus., maps. 30cm.

FORESTER, Thomas
PRICE, Edward
Norway and its scenery, comprising the journal of
a tour by Edward Price, with considerable additions and a Road-book for tourists ...; edited
and compiled by Thomas Forester. Bohn, 1853.
xi, 470p., 21 plates, illus. 19cm. (Bohn's
illustrated library)

FORESTER, Thomas
Norway in 1848 and 1849, containing Rambles
among the fjelds and fjords of the central and
western districts; and including remarks on its
political, military, ecclesiastical, and social
organisation; with extracts from the journals of
Lieut. M.S. Biddulph. Longman, Brown, Green and
Longmans, 1850. xv, 484p., plates, illus., maps.
23cm.

FORESTER, Thomas
Rambles in Norway, among the fjelds and fjords of
the central and western districts, with remarks
on its political, military, ecclesiastical, and
social conditions... Longman, Brown, Green, &
Longmans, 1855. xv, 296p. 18cm.

FORESTER, Thomas
Rambles in the islands of Corsica and Sardinia,
with notices of their history, antiquities, and
present condition. Longman, Brown, Green, Longmans and Roberts, 1858. xvii, 450p., plates,
illus., maps. 27cm.

FORESTIER, Alcide, vicomte de
Alpes pittoresques: description de la Suisse, par
MM. de Chateauvieux, Dubochet [and others];
publiée sous la direction de Mr. le vte. Alcide de
Forestier. Paris: Delloye, 1837-38. 2v., plates,
maps. 31cm.

FORESTRY COMMISSION
See
GREAT BRITIAN. Forestry Commission

FORNIER, Marcellin
Histoire générale des Alpes maritimes ou cottiénes,
et particulière de leur metropolitaine Ambrun...
Paris: H. Champion, 1890. 2v. 26cm.

FORREST, Archibald S   and BAGGE, Henry
Switzerland, revisited by A.S. Forrest and Henry
Bagge. F. Griffiths, [1914]. 92p., illus., maps.
22cm.

FORRESTER, J   Campbell
A four weeks' tramp through the Himalayas: a guide
to the Pindari glacier. Calcutta: Thacker, Spink,
1911. 49p., plates, illus. 17cm.

FORSTER, George
Travels in the northern part of India, Kashmire,
Afghanistan, and Persia, and into Russia by the
Caspian Sea, performed in the years 1782, 83, and
84.
(In Sonnini de Manoncourt, Charles Nicolas.
Travels in Upper & Lower Egypt. London, [ca 1805].
15cm. p.111-284, plates, illus.)

FORSTMANN, Carl
Himatschal: die Throne der Götter: 25 Jahre im
Himalaya. Berlin: Scherl, 1926. 432p., plates (1
fold.), illus., map, bibl. 24cm.

FORSYTH, Sir Douglas
Autobiography and reminiscences of Sir Douglas
Forsyth; edited by his daughter [i.e. Ethel
Forsyth]. R. Bentley, 1887. vii, 283p., plates
(1 fold.col.), map, port. 23cm.

FORSYTHE, John
Mourne rock-climbs; edited by John Forsythe.
Dublin: Federation of Mountaineering Clubs of
Ireland, 1973. 88p., illus., map. 16cm.
(F.M.C.I. guides)

FORTESCUE, Winifred
Mountain madness. Blackwood, 1943. 176p., plates,
illus. 20cm.

A fortnight's ramble to the Lakes in Westmorland,
Lancashire, and Cumberland, by a rambler [i.e.
Joseph Budworth]. Hookham & Carpenter, 1792.
xxvii, 267p. 22cm.

- - 2nd ed. J. Nicholas, 1795.

Forty-six views of Tyrolese scenery ...
See
Ansichten von Tyrol

FOSCA, François
H.-H. Newton; illustré de dessins ... et de ...
planches... Paris: H. Floury, 1928. 22p., 40
plates, illus. 21cm.

FOSSEL, Annemarie
Blumen der Berge: ein Bilderbuch mit Begleitworten;
mit einem Nachwort von Franz Fischer. München:
Rother, 1935. 48p., plates, illus. 24cm.

FOSSEL, Marta E
WOLF, Karl
Alpentrachten unserer Zeit; Begleitworte von Karl
Wolf; Bilder von Marta E. Fossel. Graz: Verlag
Styria, 1937. 41p., 24 col. plates, illus. 19cm.
(Die deutschen Bergbücher, Bd.7)

FOTHERGILL, Claud F
A doctor in many countries. Pickering & Inglis,
1945. 168p., plates (2 col.), illus. 22cm.

FOUNTAIN, Paul
The eleven eaglets of the West. Murray, 1906.
xi, 362p. 23cm.

FOUNTAIN, Paul
The great mountains and forests of South America.
Longmans Green, 1902. 306p., plates, illus. 24cm.

FOUNTAIN, Paul
The river Amazon from its sources to the sea.
Constable, 1914. xi, 321p., plates (1 fold.),
illus., map. 24cm.

FOURNIER, E
Description géologique du Caucase central.
Marseille: Barthelet, 1896. 296p., plates (some
fold., some col.), illus., maps, bibl. 29cm.
(Thèses présentées à la Faculté des Sciences de
Paris, no. 880)

FOX, Sir Frank
Switzerland; with 32 illustrations in colour by
J. & M. Hardwicke Lewis, A.D. McCormick & others.
2nd ed. Black, 1930. xi, 197p., col. plates,
illus., map. 23cm.

FOX, Joseph Holroyd
Holiday memories. Wellington (Somerset):
Privately printed by L. Tozer, 1908. 147p. 28cm.

FR., J.F.
Reise eines Lehrers mit seinen Zöglingen aus
Isserten in einige romantische Gegenden der
Schweiz: ein nützliches und unterhaltendes
Lesebuch für die heranwachsende Jugend. München:
C.A. Fleischmann, 1821-23. 2v., plates, illus.
18cm.
Vol.2 signed: J.F. Fr.

FRAAS, Eberhard
Scenerie der Alpen. Leipzig: Weigel, 1892.
352p., plates (1 fold.col.), illus., map. 25cm.

FRACCARO, Plinio
Guida alpina del Bassanese e delle montagne
limitrofe. Bassano: Club Alpino Bassano, 1903.
189p., plates, illus. 16cm.

- - Another ed. 1909.

FRAENKEL, Peter
Overland. Newton Abbot, London: David & Charles,
1975. 156p., illus., map, bibl. 22cm.

FRANCE. Ministère de l'agriculture. Service
d'études des grandes forces hydrauliques (Région
des Alpes)
Études glaciologiques: Tirol autrichien, massif
des Grandes Rousses. Grenoble: Rey, 1909.
112p., plates (some fold.), illus., col. maps.
30cm.

FRANCE. Ministère de la guerre
Manuel de montagne et d'alpinisme militaire:
annexe à l'Instruction provisoire sur les opérations en montagne. Paris: Imprimerie Nationale,
1931. 189p., illus. 19cm.

FRANCE. Secrétariat d'état à la guerre
Instruction sur la pratique de l'alpinisme et du
ski. Paris: Berger-Levrault, 1953. 325p., illus.
21cm.

FRANCÉ, R   H
Die Alpen; gemeinverständlich dargestellt. Leipzig:
Thomas, [1912]. 964p., plates, illus., maps.
28cm.

FRANCÉ, R   H
BERLEPSCH, Hermann Alexander von
Die Alpen in Natur- und Lebensbildern: ausgewählte
Abschnitte ...; mit einem Bild und einer bio-
graphischen Skizze von F. v. Berlepsch-Valendas;
hrsg. von R.H. Francé. Leipzig: Theod. Thomas,
[1910]. 78p., illus. 16cm. (Natur-Bibliothek,
Nr.11)

FRANCÉ, R   H
BARTH, Hermann von
  Aus den nördlichen Kalkalpen: Ersteigungen und
  Erlebnisse; mit einer Einleitung und Anmerkungen
  hrsg. von R.H. Francé. Leipzig: Theod. Thomas,
  [1910]. 2v. 16cm. (Natur-Bibliothek, Nr.20/21,
  22)

FRANCÉ, R   H
SCHAUBACH, Adolph
  Die deutschen Alpen; mit einer Einleitung und
  Anmerkungen hrsg. von R.H. Francé. Leipzig:
  Theod. Thomas, [1911]. 2v. 16cm. (Natur-
  Bibliothek, Nr.37/38,39)

FRANCIS, Godfrey
  Mountain climbing; the diagrams drawn by Erik
  Thorn. English Universities Press, 1958. 192p.,
  8 plates, illus., bibl. 19cm. (Teach yourself
  books)
  Published with the sponsorship of the British
  Mountaineering Council and of the Association of
  Scottish Climbing Clubs.

FRANCO, Jean and TERRAY, Lionel
  Bataille pour le Jannu; préface de L. Devies.
  Paris: Gallimard, 1965. 293p., illus., maps.
  21cm.

FRANCO, Jean and TERRAY, Lionel
  [Bataille pour le Jannu]. At grips with Jannu;
  with a preface by Lucien Devies; translated by
  Hugh Merrick. Gollancz, 1967. 192p., plates,
  illus., maps. 23cm.

FRANCO, Jean
  Makalu; préface de Lucien Devies. Paris: Arthaud,
  1955. 225p., plates (some fold., some col.),
  illus., maps. 22cm. (Collection sempervivum, 29)

FRANCO, Jean and MORA, Marius
  Ski de France; avec la collaboration de Léon
  Fourès. Paris: Arthaud, 1962. 318p., illus. (1
  fold.). 24cm.

Frank's Ranche; or, My holiday in the Rockies, being
  a contribution to the inquiry into what we are to
  do with our boys, by the author of "An amateur
  angler's days in Dovedale" [i.e. Edward Marston].
  Sampson Low, Marston, Searle, & Rivington, 1886.
  xvi, 214p., plates illus., map. 18cm.

FRANKE, Hans
  Alpenvögel: ein Wonderbuch zum Bestimmen unserer
  Alpenvögel nach Aussehen, Stimme, Ausenthalt, mit
  ... farbigen Tafeln von Franz Käserbek. Leipzig:
  Deuticke, 1935. 51p., 16 col. plates, illus.
  19cm.

FRANKLIN, Sir John
M'DOUGALL, George Frederick
  The eventful voyage of H.M. Discovery ship
  "Resolute" to the Arctic regions in search of Sir
  John Franklin and the missing crews of H.M.
  Discovery ships "Erebus" and "Terror", 1852, 1853,
  1854... Longman, Brown, Green, Longmans & Roberts,
  1857. xl, 530p., col. plates, illus. 24cm.

FRANSCINI, Stefano
  Der Kanton Tessin, historisch, geographisch,
  statistisch geschildert ...: ein Hand- und Haus-
  buch für Cantonsbürger und Reisende; nach der
  Italienischen Handschrift von G.Hagnauer. St.
  Gallen: Huber, 1835. xii, 436p., 18cm.
  (Gemälde der Schweiz, 18)

FRANSCINI, Stefano
  Statistica della Svizzera. Lugano: Ruggia, 1827.
  xix, 482p., map. 23cm.

FRANZ, Hans
MAIR, Kurt
  Der Mensch am Berg: von der Freude, dem Kampf und
  der Kameradschaft der Bergsteiger: ein Bildbericht
  von Hans Franz mit Worten von Kurt Mair. München:
  F. Bruckmann, 1935. 150p., illus. 23cm.

FRANZ, Leonhard
  Vorgeschichtliches Leben in den Alpen. Wien: A.
  Schroll, 1929. 95p., 23 plates, illus. 28cm.

FRASER, Colin
  The avalanche enigma; [foreword by Sir Arnold
  Lunn]. Murray, 1966. xvi, 301p., plates, illus.,
  bibl. 24cm.

FRASER, Colin
  [The avalanche enigma]. L'enigma della valanghe;
  traduzione a cura di Roberto Agostini [and
  others]. Bologna: Zanichelli, 1970. 236p.,
  illus., bibl. 25cm.

FRASER, Colin
  Avalanches and snow safety. Murray, 1978. xiii,
  269p., plates, illus., bibl. 23cm.

FRASER, David
  The marches of Hindustan, the record of a journey
  in Thibet, Trans-Himalayan India, Chinese
  Turkestan, Russion Turkestan and Persia. Edinburgh, London, Blackwood: 1907. xvi, 521p.,
  plates (some fold., 1 col.), illus., maps. 24cm.

FRASER, Mrs. Hugh and FRASER, Hugh C
  Seven years on the Pacific slope. Laurie,
  [1916?]. xiii, 391p., plates, illus. 23cm.

FRASER, Sir Hugh
  Amid the high hills. Black, 1923. xv, 224p.,
  plates (some col.), illus. 23cm.

FRASER, James Baillie
  Journal of a tour through part of the snowy
  range of the Himālā mountains, and to the sources
  of the rivers Jumna and Ganges. Rodwell &
  Martin, 1820. xx, 548p. 31cm.

FRASER, James Baillie
  Views in the Himālā Mountains. Rodwell & Martin,
  1820. lv. of col. illus. 59 x 82cm.

FRASER, Maxwell
  Companion into Lakeland. Methuen, 1937. xii,
  290p., plates, illus., map. 20cm. ('Companion'
  books)

FRASS, Hermann
  [Dolomiten, berühmte Bergwelt...]. Dolomites,
  mountains of magic: discovery and conquest.
  Bolzano: Athesia, 1977. 127p., illus. (some
  col.). 30cm.

FRECH, Fritz
  Über den Gebirgsbau der tiroler Zentralalpen
  mit besonderer Rucksicht auf den Brenner.
  Innsbruck: D.u.Ö.A.V., 1905. 98p., plates (some
  fold., 1 col.), illus., map. 28cm. (Wissenschaftliche Ergänzungshefte zur Zeitschrift des
  D.u.Ö. Alpenvereins. Bd.2, Heft 1)

FREEMAN, Lewis R
  On the roof of the Rockies: the great Columbia
  icefield of the Canadian Rockies. Heinemann,
  1926. xv, 270p., plates, illus. 25cm.

FREEMAN, G   J
  Sketches in Wales; or, A diary of three walking
  excursions in that principality, in the years
  1823, 1824, 1825. Longman, Rees, Orme, Brown, &
  Green, 1826. xvi, 272p., plates, illus. 23cm.

FREESTON, Charles L
  The Alps for the motorist. Cassell and the
  Automobile Association, [ca 1926]. xii, 176p.,
  illus., maps. 22cm.

FREESTON, Charles L
  Cycling in the Alps with some notes on the chief
  passes. Richards, 1900. viii, 249p., illus.
  20cm.

FREESTON, Charles L
 The high-roads of the Alps: a motoring guide to one
 hundred mountain passes. Paul, Trench, Trübner,
 [1910]. xvi, 388p., plates, illus., maps (some
 fold.). 23cm.

- - 2nd ed. rev. and enl. 1911.

FREESTON, Charles L
 The passes of the Pyrenees: a practical guide to
 the mountain roads of the Franco-Spanish frontier.
 Kegan Paul, 1912. xiii, 196p., plates (1 fold.
 1 col.), illus., maps. 22cm.

FREI, Hermann
 Davoser Skitouren: illustrieter Führer. Davos: Ski-
 Club Davos, 1919. 116p., plates, illus. 21cm.

FREI, Hermann
 [Davoser Skitouren]. The best ski-tours of Davos;
 compiled by Henry Hoek, being an adaptation of
 Hermann Frei's "Davoser Skitouren"; English by
 W.G. and L.M. Lockett. Hamburg: Enoch, 1927. viii,
 96p. 18cm.

FREI, Hermann and HOEK, Henry
 Ski-Touren in den Bergen um Davos: ein Führer.
 Davos: Verkehrsverein Davos, 1932. 174p. 17cm.

FREMDENVERKEHRSVEREIN KUFSTEIN
 Kufstein und seine Umgebung: ein Führer für Fremde
 und Einheimische; Aquarelle von E.H. Compten und
 J. Wischniewsky ...; hrsg. von Fremdenverkehrsverein Kufstein. 2. Aufl. Kufstein: Ed. Lippett,
 1909. 173p., plates, illus. 20cm.

FRÉMONT, John Charles
 The life of Col. John Charles Frémont, and his
 narrative of explorations and adventures in Kansas,
 Nebraska, Oregon and California; the memoir by
 S.M. Smucker. New York: Miller, Orton and
 Mulligan, 1856. 493p., plates, illus. 20cm.

FRÉMONT, John Charles
 Narrative of the exploring expedition to the Rocky
 Mountains in the year 1842, and to Oregon and
 North Carolina in the years 1843-44. Wiley and
 Putnam, 1846. 324p., plates (1 fold.), illus.,
 map. 24cm.

FRÉMONT, John Charles
 Report of the exploring expedition to the Rocky
 Mountains in the year 1842, and to Oregon and
 North Carolina in the years 1843-'44. Washington:
 Gales and Seaton, 1845. 693p., plates (some fold.),
 illus., maps. 25cm.

FRÉMONT, John Charles
DELLENBAUGH, Frederick S
 Frémont and '49: the story of a remarkable career
 and its relation to the exploration and development
 of our western territory, especially of California.
 New York, London: Putnam, 1914. xxiii, 547p.,
 plates (some fold.), illus., maps, bibl. 24cm.

FRENCH HIMALAYAN EXPEDITION, 1936
 See
EXPÉDITION FRANÇAISE À L'HIMALAYA, 1936

FRENDO, Édouard
 La face nord des Grandes Jorasses; préface de
 Lucien Devies. Lausanne: F. Rouge, 1946. 141p.,
 plates (1 fold.), illus, plan. 21cm. (Collection
 alpine, 6)

POURCHIER, M   and FRENDO, Édouard
 La technique de l'alpinisme; avec le concours du
 Groupe de Haute Montagne ... publié sous le patron-
 age de la Fédération Française de la Montagne.
 Grenoble: Arthaud, 1943. 232p., illus. 19cm.

FRERE, Richard Burchmore
 "Rock climbs": a guide to the crags in the neigh-
 bourhood of Inverness. Inverness: "Northern
 Chronicle", 1938. 70p., plates, illus. 19cm.

FRERE, Richard Burchmore
 Thoughts of a mountaineer. Edinburgh, London:
 Oliver & Boyd, 1952. vi, 177p., plates, illus.
 19cm.

FRESHFIELD, Douglas William
 Across country from Thonon to Trent: rambles and
 scrambles in Switzerland and the Tyrol.
 Spottiswoode, 1865. 135p. 23cm.

FRESHFIELD, Douglas William
ALPINE CLUB
 Alpine Club exhibition: catalogue of a collection
 of mountain paintings and photographs exhibited
 at the XIXth Century Art Gallery ...; with a preliminary note by Douglas W. Freshfield. A.C.,
 1894. 64p. 22cm.

FRESHFIELD, Douglas William
 Below the snow line. Constable, 1923. viii,
 270p., maps. 23cm.

FRESHFIELD, Douglas William
 The exploration of the Caucasus; with illustrations by Vittorio Sella. Arnold, 1896. 2v.,
 plates (some fold.), illus., maps (1 in pocket),
 bibl. 29cm.

FRESHFIELD, Douglas William
 Hannibal once more. Arnold, 1914. 120p., plates
 (some fold.), illus., maps, bibl. 24cm.

FRESHFIELD, Douglas William and WHARTON, W   J   L
 Hints to travellers, scientific and general;
 edited for the Council of the Royal Geographical
 Society by Douglas W. Freshfield and W.J.L.
 Wharton. 6th ed. rev. and enl. Royal Geographical Society, 1889. xii, 430p., plates (some
 fold.col.), illus., maps. 18cm.

- - 7th ed. rev. and enl. 1893.
- - 8th ed. rev. and enl., edited by John Coles.
 1901.
- - 9th ed. rev. and enl., edited by E.A. Reeves.
 1906. 2v.
- - 10th ed. rev. and corr., edited by E.A. Reeves.
 1921. 2v.
- - 11th ed., [by] E.A. Reeves. 1935-38. 2v.

FRESHFIELD, Douglas William
 Italian Alps: sketches in the mountains of
 Ticino, Lombardy, the Trentino, and Venetia.
 Longmans, Green, 1875. xvii, 385p., plates (some
 fold., some col.), illus., maps. 21cm.

- - Another issue. Oxford: Blackwell, 1937.

FRESHFIELD, Douglas William
 [Italian Alps ...]. Le Alpi italiane: schizzi
 delle montagne del Trentino; traduzione di
 Giovanni Strobele. Trento: Società degli
 Alpinisti Tridentini, 1971. 365p., illus. 22cm.
 English text and Italian translation of chapters
 7 to 12 of the 1875 ed.

FRESHFIELD, Douglas William
 The life of Horace Benedict de Saussure, by
 Douglas W. Freshfield; with the collaboration of
 Henry F. Montagnier. Arnold, 1920. xii, 479p.,
 plates, illus., map, bibl. 25cm.

FRESHFIELD, Douglas William
 [The life of Horace Benedict de Saussure].
 Horace-Benedict de Saussure, par D.W. Freshfield;
 avec la collaboration de H.F. Montagnier; ...
 traduit de l'anglais par Louise Plan; préface de
 L.-W. Collet. Genève: Atar, 1924. 434p.,
 plates, illus., map, bibl. 25cm.

FRESHFIELD, Douglas William
 Quips for cranks and other trifles. The Author,
 1923. x, 112p. 17cm.

FRESHFIELD, Douglas William
 Round Kangchenjunga: a narrative of mountain
 travel and exploration. Arnold, 1903. xvi,
 367p., plates, illus., maps, bibl. 26cm.

FRESHFIELD, Douglas William
 Travels in the central Caucasus and Bashan, including visits to Ararat and Tabreez and ascents
 of Kazbek and Elbruz. Longmans, Green, 1869.
 xv, 509p., plates (some fold., some col.), illus.,
 maps. 22cm

FRESHFIELD, Douglas William
Unto the hills. Arnold, 1914. viii, 119p. 18cm.

FRESHFIELD, Mrs. Henry
Alpine byways; or, Light leaves gathered in 1859
and 1860, by a lady [i.e. Mrs. Henry Freshfield].
Longman, Green, Longman, & Roberts, 1861. ix,
232p., plates (some col.), maps. 21cm.

FRESHFIELD, Mrs. Henry
A summer tour in the Grisons and Italian valleys
of the Bernina. Longman, Green, Longman, &
Roberts, 1862. 292p., col. plates (2 fold.),
illus., maps. 21cm.

FRESIA, Camillo
Cuneo e le sue vallate. Cuneo: E. Fresia, 1905.
viii, 133p., plates, illus., map, plan. 18cm.

FREUCHEN, Peter
Ice floes and flaming water; translated from the
Danish by Johan Hambro. Landsborough Publica-
tions, 1959. 222p. 19cm. (Four square books)

FREY, Jakob
Das Schweizerland in Bild und Wort; dargestellt
in malarischen Original-Ansichten ... mit
geschichtlich- , topo- und orographisch-
physikalisch- und ethnographisch-erläuterndem
Text von Jakob Frey. Basel: Chr. Krüsi;
London: Williams & Norgate, [1873?]. 300 col.
plates, illus. 31cm.

FREY, Wolfgang
Zwischen Munjan und Bashgal (Zentraler
Afghanischer Hindukusch). Göppingen:"Klettern
und Bergsteigen", 1967-1968. 2v., 1 fold. plate,
illus., maps, bibl. 21cm.

FREYGANG, Frederika von
Lettres sur le Caucase et la Géorgie, suivies
d'une relation d'un Voyage en Perse en 1812.
Hambourg: Perthes & Besser, 1816. 353p., maps.
23cm.

FREYGANG, Frederika von
[Lettres sur le Caucase et la Géorgie ...].
Letters from the Caucasus and Georgia; to which
are added, the account of a journey into Persia
in 1812, and an abridged history of Persia since
the time of Nadir Shah; translated from the
French. Murray, 1823. xvi, 414p., plates (1
fold.), illus., maps. 24cm.

FREYGANG, Frederika von
[Lettres sur le Caucase et la Géorgie ...].
Briefe über den Kaukasus und Georgien, nebst
angehängtem Reisebericht über Persien vom Jahre
1812; aus dem Französischen übersetzt von
Heinrich von Struve. Hamburg: Perthes und Besser,
1817. vii, 331p., plates (1 fold.), illus., maps.
23cm.

FRICKER, P E
Geology of the expedition area, western central
Axel Heiberg Island, Canadian Arctic Archipelago.
Montreal: McGill University, 1963. x, 156p., 3
fold.plates, illus., maps (in pocket), bibl. 29cm.
(Axel Heiberg Island Research Reports, Geology,
no.1; Jacobsen-McGill Arctic Research Expedition
1959-1962)

FRICKER, P E and TRETTIN, H P
Pre-Mississippian succession of northernmost Axel
Heiberg Island, Canadian Arctic Archipelago.
Montreal: McGill University, 1963. iv, 27p., 1
fold. plate, maps (1 in pocket), bibl. 29cm.
(Axel Heiberg Island Research Reports, Geology,
no.3; Jacobsen-McGill Arctic Research Expedition
1959-62)

Fridolin Plant's Reise-Führer durch Vinschgau,
Oberinntal bis Landeck und die Seitentäler ...
2. verm. und verb. Aufl. Meran: Fridolin Plant,
1909. 160p., illus. 17cm.

FRIEDLAENDER, Ludwig
Darstellungen aus der Sittengeschichte Roms in der
Zeit von August bis zum Ausgang der Antonine. 6.
neu bearb. und verm. Aufl. 2. Theil. Das Verkehrs-
wesen, Die Reisen der Touristen... Leipzig: S.
Hirzel, 1889. xiii, 652p. 24cm.

FRIEDLAENDER, Ludwig
Ueber die Entstehung und Entwicklung des Gefühls
für das Romantische in der Natur; Herrn Professor
K. Lehrs zu seinem 50 jährigen Doctorjubiläum am
7. März 1873 überreicht von Ludwig Friedlaender.
Leipzig: S. Hirzel, 1873. 45p. 24cm.

FRIEDMANN, Louis
Die Ortler Gruppe. Berlin, 1893. 112p., plates
(1 col.), illus., map. 28cm.
Offprint from Erschliessung der Ostalpen, Bd.2.

FRIENDS OF THE LAKE DISTRICT
A road policy for the Lake District. Ulverston:
The Friends, [1961]. 31p., plates, illus., map.
22cm.

FRIENDS OF THE NATIONAL LIBRARIES
Thomas Sydney Blakeney: [an obituary].
(In Friends of the National Libraries. Annual
report, 1976, pp.5-6)

Friendship's offering of sentiment and mirth.
Smith, Elder, 1844. viii, 240p., plates, illus.
22cm.

FRIES, Rob E
Zur Kenntnis der alpinen Flora im nördlichen
Argentinien. Upsala: Akademische Buchdruckerei,
1905. 205p., plates (1 fold.), illus., map,
bibl. 29cm. (Nova acta Regiae Societatis
Scientiarum Upsaliensis, ser.4, v.1, no.1)

FRIIS, I A
Sporting life on the Norwegian fjelds ...;
translated from the Norwegian with Jottings on
sport in Norway by W.G. Lock. Lock, 1878. viii,
375p., map. 20cm.

FRISCHAUF, Johannes
Aus den Schladminger Tauern. Graz: Leuschner &
Lubensky, 1892. 79p., illus. 21cm.

FRISCHAUF, Johannes
Ein Ausflug auf den Monte Baldo. Wien: Oesterr.
Touristen-Club, 1883. iv, 33p., illus. 18cm.
(O.T.C. Touristen-Führer, 11)

FRISCHAUF, Johannes
Die Sannthaler Alpen. Wien: Brockhausen & Brauer,
1877. viii, 282p., illus., map. 17cm.

FRISON-ROCHE, Roger
L'appel du Hoggar. Paris: Flammarion, 1936.
141p., illus., map. 22cm. (La vie en montagne)

FRISON-ROCHE, Roger
La grande crévasse: roman; photographies de
Georges Tairraz. Lausanne: Fred. Gilliard, 1948.
303p., plates, illus. 19cm.

FRISON-ROCHE, Roger
[La grande crévasse]. The last crevasse;
translated by Janet Adam Smith and Nea Morin.
Methuen, 1952. 234p. 19cm.

FRISON-ROCHE, Roger and TAIRRAZ, Pierre
Mont Blanc aux sept vallées. Paris: Arthaud,
1959. 269p., illus. 24cm.

FRISON-ROCHE, Roger and TAIRRAZ, Pierre
[Mont Blanc aux sept vallées]. Mont Blanc and
the seven valleys; translated and adapted by R.
le Grand; with the cooperation of Wilfrid Noyce.
Kaye, 1961. 267p., illus. 24cm. (Les beaux
pays)

FRISON-ROCHE, Roger
Les montagnes de la terre. Paris: Flammarion,
1964. 2v., col. plates, illus., maps. 29cm.

FRISON-ROCHE, Roger
Premier de cordée. Grenoble: Arthaud, 1941.
380p., plates, illus. 19cm.

FRISON-ROCHE, Roger
Premier de cordée (naissance d'une vocation);
edited by P.E. Thompson. Harrap, 1953. 203p.,
plates, illus., map. 18cm.
School text.

FRISON-ROCHE, Roger
[Premier de cordée]. First on the rope: a novel;
translated by Janet Adam Smith. Methuen, 1949.
xi, 268p. 20cm.

FRISON-ROCHE, Roger
[Retour à la montagne]. Return to the mountains;
translated by H. Charteris. Methuen, 1961. 239p.
22cm.

COUTTET, Alfred and FRISON-ROCHE, Roger
63 itinéraires à ski dans la région de Chamonix
et le massif du Mont Blanc. Chamonix: J. Landru,
[19--]. 48p. 16cm.

FRITH, Henry
Ascents and adventures: a record of hardy mountaineering in every quarter of the globe. Routledge,
1884. 320p., illus. 19cm.

FRITZSCH, Magnus
Über Hohengrenzen in den Ortler-Alpen: Inaugural-
Dissertation zur Erlangung der Doktorwürde der
hohen philosophischen Fakultät der Universität
Leipzig. Leipzig: The Author, 1894. 189p., 3
fold. plates (2 col.), illus., map. 25cm.

FRITZSCH, Magnus
Verzeichniss der bis zum Sommer 1896 in den Ost-
alpen gesetzten Gletschermarken. Wien: Verlag des
D.u.Ö.A.V., 1898. 131p. 13 x 19cm.

FROBEL, Julius
Reise in die weniger bekannten Thäler auf der
Nordseite der pennischen Alpen. Berlin: G. Reimer,
1840. iv, 196p., 1 plate, map. 22cm.

FRÖLICH, H
Militärgeographie der Schweiz, nebst kurzer
Schilderung der Entstehung der Neutralität Savoyens
und historischer Notizen über verschiedene Alpen-
pässe; bearb. von Major Frölich. Aarau: H.R.
Sauerländer, 1906. 119p. 21cm.

From Calcutta to the snowy range, being the narrative
of a trip through the upper provinces of India to
the Himalayas, containing an account of Monghyr,
Benares, Allahabad, Cawnpore, Lucknow, Agra, Delhi
and Simla, by an old Indian [i.e. Frederick F.
Wyman]. Tinsley, 1866. viii, 264p., col. plates
(1 fold.), illus., map. 22cm.
Preface signed F.F.W.

From the Equator to the Pole: adventures of recent
discovery, by eminent travellers. Wm. Isbister,
[1886]. 254p., illus., map. 18cm.
Contents: 1. In the heart of Africa, by Joseph
Thomson. - 2. Climbing the Himalayas, by W.W.
Graham. - 3. On the road to the Pole, by A.H.
Markham.

FROMMEL, C
Tyrol scenery after paintings by C. Frommel.
Dresden: Published ... by A.H. Payne, [1851?].
16p., plates, illus. 45cm.

FROSSARD, Emilien
Tableau pittoresque des Pyrénées françaises:
Vallées du Lavédan, de Barèges, et de Gavarnie.
Paris: J.J. Risler, 1839. vi, 42p., plates (some
col.), illus. 28cm.

FROSSARD, Emilien
Vue des Hautes-Pyrénées, prise du sommet du Pic du
Midi en Bigorre. Toulouse: Delor, [1851?]. 1v.
of illus. 34cm.
Lithographed panorama.

FROSSARD, Emilien
JOURDAN, J
Vues prises dans les Pyrénées françaises;dessinées
par J. Jourdan; et accompagnées d'un teste des-
criptif par Emilien Frossard. Paris: Treuttel &
Würtz, 1828. 1v. (chiefly illus.). 50cm.

The frozen stream; or, An account of the nature,
properties, dangers and uses of ice, in various
parts of the world, [by Charles Tomlinson].
Society for Promoting Christian Knowledge, 1846.
150p., illus. 15cm.

- - Another ed. [ca 1862].

FRÜH, J
Geographie der Schweiz. Bd.3. Die Einzelland-
schaften der Schweiz. St. Gallen: Fehr, 1938.
145-720p., illus., maps, bibl. 28cm.

FRYXELL, Fritiof
The Teton peaks and their ascents. Wyoming:
Crandall Studios, 1932. xiii, 106p., plates (1
fold.), illus., map. 21cm.

FRYXELL, Fritiof
The Tetons: interpretations of a mountain landscape. Berkeley: University of California Press,
1938. xiv, 77p., plates (1 fold.), illus., map.
20cm.

FUCHS, Friedrich
Die Central-Karpathan mit den nächsten Voralpen:
Handbuch für Gebirgsreisende. Pest: G.
Heckenast, 1863. 318p., map. 19cm.

FUCHS, Wilhelm
Die Venetianer Alpen: ein Beitrag zur Kenntniss
der Hochgebirge. Solothurn: Jent & Gassmann,
1844. 61p., 18 col. plates, illus., maps.
32 x 37cm.

FÜHRER-VEREIN PONTRESINA
Statuten des Führer-Vereins Pontresina.
Pontresina: Der Verein, [1892]. 16p. 15cm.

Führer von Montana und Umgebung, [von A.H.M.L. i.e
Arnold Lunn]. Neuenburg: Delachaux & Niestlé,
1908. 80p., illus. 19cm.

FUNFSTÜCK, M
Taschenatlas der Gebirgs- und Alpenpflanzen, für
Touristen und Pflanzenfreunde in der Schweiz ...
Stuttgart: E. Ulmer, 1896. xxiii, 150p., plates,
illus. 16cm.

FÜRER-HAIMENDORF, Christoph von
Mount Everest: Aufbau, Erforschung und Bevölker-
ung des Everest-Gebietes, [von] Toni Hagen,
Günter-Oskar Dyhrenfurth, Christoph von Fürer-
Haimendorf, Erwin Schneider. Zürich: Orell
Füssli, 1959. 234p., plates, (1 fold.col.),
illus., maps. 24cm.

FÜRER-HAIMENDORF, Christoph von
Mount Everest: formation, population and ex-
ploration of the Everest region, [by] Toni Hagen,
Günter-Oskar Dyhrenfurth, Christoph von Fürer-
Haimendorf, Erwin Schneider; translated by E.
Noel Bowman. Oxford University Press, 1963.
xiv, 195p., plates, illus., maps. 24cm.

FÜRER-HAIMENDORF, Christoph von
The naked Nagas. Methuen, 1939. xv, 243p.,
plates, illus., map, bibl. 23cm.

FÜRER-HAIMENDORF, Christoph von
The Sherpas of Nepal, Buddhist highlanders.
Murray, 1964. xix, 298p., plates (1 fold.),
illus., maps, bibl. 23cm.

FULLERTON, James Alexander
Views in the Himalaya and Neilgherry hills, from
drawings by Lieut.-Colonel Fullerton, taken
during ... 1845-47. Dickinson, [1848]. 1v. of
col. illus. 19 x 28cm.

FULTON, John Henry Westropp
  With ski in Norway & Lapland; with introduction by
  G. Herbert Fowler; and numerous illustrations from
  photographs taken by the author and others. Philip
  Lee Warner, 1911. xv, 254p., plates, illus., maps
  (on lining papers). 20cm.

FURRER, Ernst
  Kleine Pflanzengeographie der Schweiz. Zürich:
  Beer, 1923. viii, 331p., plates, illus., maps.
  20cm.

FURSE, Katharine
  Ski-running. Longmans, Green, 1924. x, 134p.,
  plates, illus., map. 19cm.

The further adventures of the little traveller;
  [edited by G.F.P.]. J. Blackwood, 1857. 112p.,
  plates, illus. 18cm.

FYFFE, A   F
  Cairngorms area. Vol.5. South-east Cairngorms,
  Creag an Dubh-Loch, Glen Clova. Edinburgh:
  Scottish Mountaineering Trust, 1971. 113p.,
  illus., map. 17cm. (Scottish Mountaineering
  Club climbers' guide books)

G., H.B.
  See
  GEORGE, Hereford Brooke

G., U.B. von
  See
  UKLANSKI, Carl Theodor von, Baron

GABERELL, J
  Gaberell's Album of Switzerland; introduction
  by Maurice Jaton. Thalwil-Zurich: J. Gaberell,
  [1927]. 288p., 16 col. plates, illus. 30cm.

GACHOT, Edouard
  À travers les Alpes. Paris: Flammarion, [n.d.].
  310p., illus. 19cm.

GAILLARD, Émile
  L'aiguille de Bionnassay. Chambéry. 1929.
  55p., plates, illus., bibl. 25cm.
  Offprint from Revue alpine, 3e trimestre, 1928.

GAILLARD, Émile
  Les Alpes de Savoie. Chambéry: Dardel, [1912]-38.
  6v. in 10, fold. plates, maps. 18cm.
  T.1, ptie. 1 is 2nd ed.
  T.2, Macon: C. Faure.

GAILLARD, Émile
  Les Alpes du Dauphiné. T.1. Les massifs de
  Belledonne et des Sept-Laux: guide pour
  l'alpiniste. Chambéry: Dardel, [1924]. xv,
  199p., plates, illus., maps. 16cm.

GAILLARD, Émile
  Les Alpes du Dauphiné. T.2. Le Haut Dauphiné.
  Ptie.1. La Meije et les Écrins (du Signal de
  Pied-Montet au Col de la Temple): guide pour
  l'alpiniste. Chambéry: Dardel, 1929. xvi,
  343p., fold. plates, illus., maps. 16cm.

GAILLARD, Émile
  Une ascension romantique en 1838: Henriette
  d'Angeville au Mont-Blanc. Chambéry: Éditions
  Lire, 1947. 158p., plates, ports. 18cm. (Le
  roc et l'eau, 1)

GAILLARD, Émile
SAUSSURE, Horace Bénédict de
  Journal d'un voyage à Chamouni & à la cime du
  Mont-Blanc, en juillet et aoust 1787; [edited by
  E. Gaillard and H.F. Montagnier]. Lyon: Audin,
  1926. xvii, 53p., plates, illus. 30cm.

GAILLARD, Émile and MONTAGNIER, Henry Fairbanks
  Lettres de H.-B. de Saussure à sa femme; commentées par E. Gaillard et H.F. Montagnier.
  Chambéry: Imprimerie Réunies, 1937. 129p., 1
  plate, port. 24cm.

GAILLARD, Émile
SAUSSURE, Horace Bénédict de
  Le Mont-Blanc et le Col du Géant; annoté par E.
  Gaillard et Henry-F. Montagnier. Lyon: M. Audin,
  1927. 95p., plates (some fold.), illus. 30cm.

GALFY, Ivan and KRISSAK, Milan
  Makalu. Bratislava: Sport, 1978. 1v. (chiefly
  illus., map). 28cm.
  Summaries in Russian, German, English and French.

Galignani's Paris guide for 1894. Paris: Galignani,
  1894. iv, 316p., map, plans. 17cm.
  Library's copy lacks map.

Galignani's traveller's guide through Switzerland;
  chiefly compiled from ... works of Ebel and Coxe:
  with numerous additions and improvements from
  recent observations... Paris: Galignani, 1818.
  xxxvi, 593p. 15cm.

GALLAY, Marcel
  Une tragique aventure au Mont-Blanc: récit de la le
  traversée hivernale des Aiguilles du Diable du 7
  au 15 février 1938: [étude médicale sur les con-
  gélations]. 2e éd. Genéve: The Author, [1940].
  64p., illus. 22cm.

GALLENGA, Antonio
  Country life in Piedmont. Chapman & Hall, 1858.
  xvi, 279p. 21cm.

Gallery of the celebrated landscapes of Switzerland. Zurich: J.A. Preuss; London: H. Rothe,
  [1880]. 1v. (chiefly illus.). 27cm.

GALLET, Julien
  Dans l'Alpe ignorée: explorations et souvenirs.
  Lausanne: Imprimeries Réunies, 1910. 374p.,
  plates, illus. 24cm.

GALLET, Julien
  Derniers souvenirs de l'Alpe: suite au volume
  "Dans l'Alpe ignorée". Lausanne: Payot, 1927.
  207p. 24cm.

GALLHUBER, Julius
  Die Dolomiten: ein Landschafts- und Bergsteigerbuch; hrsg. von Julius Gallhuber. München: F.
  Bruckmann, 1934. 185p., col. plates, illus.
  26cm.

GALLHUBER, Julius
  Das Gesäuse und seine Berge: ein Landschafts-
  und Bergsteigerbuch; hrsg. von Julius Gallhuber.
  Wien: Reichenstein, 1928. 196p., plates (1 col.),
  illus. 25cm.

GALLI-VALERIO, B
  Guide du massif de Naye: souvenirs de courses et
  notes scientifiques. Lausanne: E. Frankfurter,
  [1930?]. 80p., illus., map. 16cm. (Collection
  tabula, 4)

GALLICUS
  Voyage en Suisse: notes humoristiques au jour le
  jour. Lyon: A. Vingtrinier, 1866. vii, 110p.
  19cm.

GALLOWAY, C   F   J
  The call of the West: letters from British
  Columbia. Unwin, 1916. 328p., plates (1 fold.),
  illus., map. 24cm.

GALSWORTHY, John
  The little dream: an allegory in six scenes.
  Duckworth, [1911]. 38p. 18cm.

GALTON, Francis
The art of travel; or, Shifts and contrivances
available in wild countries. Murray, 1855. viii,
196p., illus. 19cm.

- - 2nd ed. rev. and enl. 1856.
- - 3rd ed. rev. and enl.1860.
- - 4th ed. entirely recast and much enl. Murray,
1867.
- - 8th ed. 1893.

GALTON, Francis
Narrative of an explorer in tropical South Africa,
being an account of a visit to Damaraland in 1851;
with ... an appendix, bringing up the history ...
to a recent date; also Vacation tours in 1860 and
1861... [New ed.]. Ward, Lock, 1889. xx, 320p.,
plates, illus., map. 19cm. (Minerva library of
famous books)

GALTON, Francis
Vacation tourists and notes of travel in 1860
[1861, 1862-3]; edited by Francis Galton.
Cambridge, London: Macmillan, 1861-64. 3v.,
plates, illus., maps. 24cm.

GALWAN, Ghulam Rassul
Servant of sahibs: a book to be read aloud; with
an introduction by Sir Francis Younghusband.
Cambridge: Heffer, 1923. xix, 282p., plates,
port. 23cm.

Gamle Norge = Old Norway; or,Our holiday in
Scandinavia, [by Miss Blundell]. Hamilton, Adams,
1862. xi, 312, vii p., map. 18cm.

GANPAT
See
GOMPERTZ, M   L   A

GANSS, Ortwin
Erläuterungen zur geologischen Karte der Dachstein-
gruppe; aufgenommen 1936-1940 im Auftrage des
Alpenvereins ... von O. Ganss, F. Kümel und E.
Spengler. Innsbruck: Wagner, 1954. 82p., 6 plates
(2 fold., 1 col.), illus., map (in pocket). 28cm.
(Wissenschaftliche Alpenvereinshefte, Heft 15)

GANSSER, August
Geology of the Himalayas. Interscience, 1964.
xvi, 289p., fold. plates (4 col.), illus., maps
(in pocket), bibl. 31cm. (Regional geology
series)

HEIM, Arnold and GANSSER, August
Thron der Götter: Erlebnisse der ersten
schweizerischen Himalaya-Expedition. Zürich:
Morgarten, 1938. 270p., plates (some fold.),
illus., map (in pocket). 24cm.

HEIM, Arnold and GANSSER, August
[Thron der Götter]. The throne of the Gods: an
account of the first Swiss expedition to the
Himalayas; translated by Eden and Cedar Paul.
Macmillan, 1939. xxv, 235p., plates (some fold.),
illus., map (in pocket). 25cm.

GARBELY, Leo
Die Pfarrkirche von Münster (Goms): Monographie.
Sitten, 1949. 28p., 8 plates, illus. 26cm.
Offprint from Vallesia IV, 1949.

GARCÍA BELLIDO, J
Una aventura en la pedriza: novela. Madrid:
Rivadeneyra, 1923. 180p. 20cm.

GARD
BLANC,   chanoine
Réflexions sur la réponse de M. l'ingénieur Venetz
à deux lettres concernant les travaux du glacier
du Giétroz, Vallée de Bagnes, en Valais, écrites
par le chanoine Blanc à M. Gard, président du
Dixain d'Entre-mont, séant en Diète à Sion, en
décembre 1824. Lausanne: E. Vincent, 1825. 24p.
19cm.

GARDINER, Frederick
Courses et ascensions: nouvelles expéditions dans
le district de Zermatt (Suisse). Paris, 1876.
6p. 23cm.
Offprint from Annuaire du Club Alpin Français,
année 1876.

GARDINER, Frederick
COOLIDGE, William Augustus Brevoort
The alpine career (1868-1914) of Frederick
Gardiner; described by his friend W.A.B. Coolidge.
[Woolton]: [Mrs. Gardiner], 1920. 75p., 1 plate,
port., bibl. 23cm.

GARDINER, Kate
Canadian climbs, 1937. [Banff, 1938]. 19-29p.,
plates, illus., map. 23cm.
Offprint from Canadian alpine journal, v.25, 1937.

GARDINER, Kate
A climbing trip to the Freshfield Group and some
other ascents. [Banff, 1940]. 39-44p., plates,
illus. 23cm.
Offprint from Canadian alpine journal, v.27, 1939.

GARDINER, Kate
A pack train trip to the French Military group.
[Banff, 1931]. 63-72p., plates, illus. 23cm.
Offprint from Canadian alpine journal, v.19, 1930.

GARDINIER, Jean Paul
La montagne; illustrations de Maurice Parent.
Tournai: Encyclopédie Casterman, 1961. 92p.,
illus. 30cm.

GARDNER, Mrs. Alan
See
GARDNER, Nora

GARDNER, Arthur
The art and sport of alpine photography; described and illustrated with photographs by Arthur
Gardner. H.F. & W. Witherby, 1927. 224p., 150
plates, illus. 23cm.

GARDNER, Arthur
Britain's mountain heritage and its preservation
as national parks; illustrated by ... photographs
by the author. Batsford, 1942. xii, 51p.,
plates (1 fold.), illus., map. 23cm.

GARDNER, Arthur
The peaks, lochs & coasts of the western Highlands; penned by Arthur Gardner. H.F. & G.
Witherby, 1924. xi, 169p., 100 plates, illus.
23cm.

- - 2nd ed. rev. and enl. Edinburgh: R. Grant,
1928.

GARDNER, Arthur
Sun, cloud & snow in the western highlands from
Glencoe to Ardnamurchan, Mull and Arran.
Edinburgh: Grant & Murray, 1933. 122p., plates,
illus., map. 24cm.

GARDNER, E
The continental traveller, being the journal of
an economical tourist to France, Switzerland,
and Italy ..., by a travelling lawyer; to which
is added A tour in Spain ..., by a travelling
artist. M.A. Leigh, 1833. 122p., 1 fold. plate,
map. 18cm.
Flyleaf signed E. Gardner & F. Wilder, 1833.

GARDNER, John Dunn
Ascent and tour of Mont Blanc and passage of the
Col du Géant between Sept. 2nd and 7th 1850.
Chiswick: The Author, 1851. 60p. 15cm.

GARDNER, Nora
Rifle and spear with the Rajpoots, being the
narrative of a winter's travel and sport in
northern India; illustrated from photographs and
sketches by the author... Chatto & Windus, 1895.
xvi, 336p., illus. 28cm.

GARDNER, W   Biscombe
The peak country; painted by W. Biscombe Gardner;
described by A.R. Hope Moncrieff. Black, 1908.
xii, 182p., 24 plates, illus. 21cm.

GARF, B   A
Bezingiiskoe ushchel'e. Moskva: Gos. Izd.
Geograficheskoi Literatury, 1952. 114p., fold
plates, illus., map. 20cm.

GAROBBIO, Aurelio
Il grande libro delle montagne; a cura di Aurelio
Garobbio. Lainate (Mi.):Vallardi, 1976. 232p.,
illus. (some col.), maps. 32cm.

GAROBBIO, Aurelio
Montagne. Varese: La "Varesina Grafica", 1929.
205p. 24cm.

GAROLA, Ruggiero
Il Monte Bianco ed il Sempione: studii di confronto.
Torino, 1881. 32p., 2 plates, illus. 23cm.
Offprint from Atti della Società degli Ingegneri
e degli Industriali di Torino, 1880.

GARVAGH, Charles John Spencer George Canning,
Baron Garvagh
The pilgrim of Scandinavia. Sampson Low, Marston,
Low & Searle, 1875. vii, 219p., 7 plates, illus.
21cm.

GARVE, Andrew
The ascent of D.12. Collins, 1939. 191p. 21cm.
(Crime Club choice)

GARWOOD, E   J
Features of alpine scenery due to glacial protec-
tion. 310-339p., plates, illus., maps. 25cm.
Offprint from Geographical journal, Sept. 1910.

GASQUET, Francis Aidan
His Holiness Pope Pius XI: a pen portrait by ...
Cardinal Gasquet and The Pope as alpine climber;
translated from an article written by himself.
D. O'Connor, 1922. 30p., plates, illus., port.
26cm.
Originally published in Review of reviews.

GASTALDI, Bartolomeo
Alcuni dati sulle punte alpine situate fra la
Levanna ed il Rocciamelone. Torino, 1868. 49p.,
3 fold.col. plates, illus. 25cm.
Offprint from Bulletino trimestrale del Club Alpino
Italiano, v.2. n.10 and 11.

GASTALDI, Bartolomeo
Deux mots sur la géologie des Alpes cottiennes.
Turin, 1872. 22p. 24cm.
Offprint from Comptes rendus de l'Académie des
Sciences de Turin, v.7, 28 avril 1872.

GASTALDI, Bartolomeo
Studii geologici sulle Alpi occidentali; con
appendice mineralogica di G. Strüver. Firenze,
1871-74. 2 pts., plates (some fold., some col.),
illus. 36cm. (Memorie per servire alla descrizione della Carta geologica d'Italia)
Offprint from Memorie del R. Comitato geologico
d'Italia, v.1, 1871.

GASTALDI, Bartolomeo
Sui rilevamenti geologici fatti nelle Alpi
piemontesi durante la Campagna del 1877: lettera
del socio Bartolomeo Gastaldi al presidente
Quintino Sella. Roma, 1878. 11p., 2 col. plates,
illus., map. 31cm.
Offprint from Reale Accademia dei Lincei, ser.3.
Memorie della classe dei scienze fisiche... v.2,
1878.

GASTALDI, Bartolomeo
Sulla esistenza del serpentino in posto nelle
colline del Monferrato. Torino, 1866. 7p. 25cm.
Offprint from Atti dell'Accademia delle Sc. di
Torino, aprile 1866.

GASTINEAU, Henry
Wales illustrated, in a series of views, comprising the picturesque scenery, towns, castles
...; engraved ... from original drawings by Henry
Gastineau; accompanied by historical and topographical descriptions. Jones, 1830. 1v.
(chiefly illus.). 29cm.

GAUDIN, A
Switzerland in miniature: description of the grand
model of Switzerland, by Professor Gaudin, of
Geneva ... now exhibiting at the Egyptian Hall,
Piccadilly. Printed for the Proprietor, 1825.
32p. 21cm.

GAUDIN, Jean
Synopsis florae helveticae; opus posthumum con-
tinuatum et editum a I.P. Monnard. Turici:
Apud Orellium Fuesslinum & Socios, 1836. xvi,
827p. 17cm.

GAULIS, Louis and CREUX, René
Swiss hotel pioneers. Paudex: Éditions de
Fontainemore, Swiss National Tourist Office, 1976.
223p., illus., bibl. 25cm.

GAULLIEUR, J
Genève et le pays de Vaud après la mort de
Voltaire et de Rousseau: commencements de l'école
littéraire des physiciens et des naturalistes, et
de la littérature alpestre...
(In Sur l'histoire litteraire de la Suisse
française. [Geneva, 1856?]. 22cm. Chapitre XI,
p.187-211)

GAUSSEN, H
Les Pyrénées de la Catalogne au Pays basque;
illustré de ... bois gravés originaux par L.
Thiriat; avec un texte par H. Gaussen; H. Martin,
graveur. Toulouse: Éditions Argra, 1933. 83p.,
illus. (some col.). 28cm.

GAUTHIER, Gilbert and VACHEZ, Michel
Ski court: ski évolutif, ski sans peine. Paris:
Arthaud, 1972. 116p., plates, illus. 21cm.

GAUTHIER, J
En montagne: articles extraits de la collection
du "Moniteur Dauphinois" ..., 1895-97, [1897-98].
Grenoble: [Librarie Dauphinoise], 1897-98. 2v.,
illus. 21cm.
Vol.2 by J.Gauthier and others.

GAUTIER, Théophile
Les vacances du lundi: tableaux de montagnes.
Paris: Charpentier, 1881. 315p. 20cm.

GAY, Hilaire
Histoire du Vallais depuis les temps les plus
anciens jusqu'à nos jours. 2e éd. rev. Genève:
A. Jullien, 1903. 327p., bibl. 22cm.

GAYET-TANCREDE, Paul
See
SAMIVEL

GAZE, Henry
Switzerland: how to see it for ten guineas. 3rd
ed. W. Kent, 1863. 97p., illus. 19cm.

GEARING, Julian
The supreme challenge: a chronicle of all the
attempts to climb Mount Everest. Ham (Surrey):
The Author, 1976. 189 leaves, illus., maps. 31cm.
Photocopy of typescript.
Looseleaf.

GEBAUER, A   K
Um den Mount Everest: Fahrten und Abenteuer.
Wien: Deutscher Verlag für Jugend und Volk, 1925.
213p., illus., map. 19cm.

GEDDIE, John
Beyond the Himalayas: a story of travel and adventure in the wilds of Thibet. Nelson, 1882. vi,
256p., plates, illus. 19cm.

Gedichte über die Schweiz und über Schweizer. Bern:
E. Haller, 1793. 2v. 18cm.

GEDYE, G E R
A wayfarer in Austria. Methuen, 1928. xv, 223p.,
plates, illus., map (on lining paper). 20cm.

GEIGER, Hermann
Geiger and the Alps. Geneva: Atar, [1958?]. 37p.,
plates (some col.), illus., col. map. 29cm.

GEIGER, Hermann
Geiger: pilote des glaciers; récit recueilli par
André Guex; préface de Félix Germain. Paris:
Arthaud, 1955. 153p., plates, illus. 22cm.
(Collection sempervivum, no.26)

GEIGER, Hermann
[Geiger: pilote des glaciers]. Alpine pilot;
translated by Alan Tuppen. Cassel, 1956. 104p.,
plates, illus. 21cm.

GEIKIE, Archibald
MURCHISON, Sir Roderick Impey
Life of Sir Roderick I. Murchison based on his
journals and letters; with notices of his scientific contemporaries and a sketch of the rise and
growth of palaeozoic geology in Britain by
Archibald Geikie. Murray, 1875. 2v., plates,
illus., ports., bibl. 23cm.

GEIKIE, Archibald
Memoir of the late James David Forbes, read to the
Geological Society of Edinburgh, 21st January
1869. Edinburgh: Printed by T. Constable, 1869.
38p., bibl. 23cm.

GEIKIE, Archibald
On the phenomena of the glacial drift of Scotland.
Glasgow: J. Gray, 1863. viii, 190p., 1 fold.
plate, illus., map. 24cm.
Offprint from Transactions of the Geological
Society of Glasgow, v.1, pt.2.

GEIKIE, James
Earth sculpture; or, The origin of land-forms.
Murray, 1898. xvi, 320p., illus. 22cm. (Pro-
gressive science series)

GEILINGER, Walter
Der Kilimandjaro: sein Land und seine Menschen.
Bern: Huber, [1930]. 182p., plates (1 fold., 1
col.), illus., map, bibl. 23cm.

GEISER, Karl
HALLER, Albrecht von
Die Alpen; mit einer Beilage und Kupfern; dem
Andenken Hallers gewidmet von Karl Geiser. Bern:
U. Francke, 1902. 40p., plates, illus. 32cm.

GEISTBECK, Alois
Die Seen der Deutschen Alpen: eine geographische
Monographie; hrsg. von dem Verein für Erdkunde zu
Leipzig. Leipzig: Duncker & Humblot, 1885. 46p.,
8 plates, maps. 44cm.

Gelegenheit und heutiger Zustand dess Herzogthums
Savoyen und Fürstenthums Piemont ..., beschrieben
durch J.G.D.T. Nürnberg: In Verlegung Joh. Andreae
Endters, Seel, 1690. 706p., fold. plates, illus.,
maps. 21cm.

KROUTIL, F V and GELLNER, J
Vysoké Tatry, horolezecký pruvodce. Dil 1. Praha:
Orbis, 1935. xv, 116p., illus., maps. 17cm.

KROUTIL, F V and GELLNER, J
Vysoké Tatry, horolezecký pruvodce. 2. vydani v
cervnu. Praha: Orbis, 1947. 2v., illus., maps.
17cm.

Gemsen-Eier: Alpin-Humoristisches in Wort & Bild.
Kempten: Jos. Kösel, 1895-99. 4v., illus. 18cm.
Editor's preface signed: E. Bayberger.

A general outline of the Swiss landscapes, [by Rowley
Lascelles]; with miscellaneous notes and illustrations from M. de Saussure and others. 3rd. ed.
rev. and considerably enl. Murray, 1812. xii,
312p. 20cm.

Genfer See und Chamonix: praktischer Reiseführer.
2. Neubearb. Aufl. Berlin: Goldschmidt, 1911.
98p., maps. 17cm. (Griebens Reiseführer, 114)

GENNEP, Arnold van
CANZIANI, Estella
Costumes, moeurs et légendes de Savoie; adapté
de l'anglais par A. van Gennep. Chambéry: Dardel,
1920. ix, 105p., 47 col. plates, illus. 30cm.

GENNEP, Arnold van
La Savoie, vue par les écrivains et les artistes
...: guide pratique des curiositées artistiques
et naturelles de la Savoie et de la Haute-Savoie
... Paris: Louis-Michaud, [n.d.]. 392p., illus.,
bibl. 17cm. (La France pittoresque et artistique)

GENTIL, H
Le Brec de Chambeyron. Gap: Ophrys, 1976. 37p.,
illus., maps. 14cm. (Alpes et Midi; Guides
d'escalades, 1)

GENTIL, P F
A short manual of mountaineering training by W.C.
Burns, F. Shuttleworth and J.E.B. Wright. 6th ed.
rev. by P.F. Gentil. Mountaineering Association,
1964. 80p. 18cm.

GENTINETTA, Richard
Das alte schöne Wallis: Skizze mit Bildern.
Emmenbrücke: Selbstverlag des Verfassers, 1943.
63p., 32 plates, illus. 22cm.

GEOLOGICAL SURVEY OF CALIFORNIA
Geology. Vol.1. Report of proceedings and
synopsis of the field-work, from 1860 to 1864.
[San Francisco?]: Published by authority of the
Legislature of California, 1865. xxvii, 498p.,
plates, illus. 28cm.

GEOLOGICAL SURVEY OF CALIFORNIA
The Yosemite guide-book: a description of the
Yosemite valley and the adjacent region of the
Sierra Nevada, and of the Big Trees of California.
[San Francisco?]: Published by authority of the
Legislature, 1870. 155p., plates (2 fold.),
illus., maps (in pockets). 24cm.

GEOLOGICAL SURVEY OF CANADA
Guide book. No.8. Transcontinental excursion C1,
Toronto to Victoria and return... Ottawa: Government Printing Bureau, 1913. 3 pts. in 1.
(386p.), col. fold. plates, illus., maps, bibl.
22cm.

GEOLOGICAL SURVEY OF CANADA
Guide book. No.9. Transcontinental excursion C2,
Toronto to Victoria and return... Ottawa: Government Printing Bureau, 1913. 164p., col. fold.
plates, illus., maps, bibl. 22cm.

GEOLOGICAL SURVEY OF CANADA
Guide book. No.10. Excursions in Northern British
Columbia and Yukon territory... Ottawa: Government
Printing Bureau, 1913. 179p., fold. plates (some
col.), illus., maps, bibl. 22cm.

GEORGE, Hereford Brooke and MATHEWS, Charles Edward
Munchausen on the Jungfrau. Printed by
Spottiswoode, [ca 1870]. 6p. 22cm.
Signed H.B.G.-C.E.M. i.e. H.B. George and C.E.
Mathews.

GEORGE, Hereford Brooke
The Oberland and its glaciers explored and illustrated with ice-axe and camera; with twenty-eight
photographic illustrations by Ernest Edwards.
A.W. Bennett, 1866. xii, 243p., plates, illus.,
map. 28cm.

GEORGE, Marian M
A little journey to France and Switzerland, for
home and school ...; edited by Marian M. George.
Chicago: A. Flanagan, 1902. 100, 104p., 2 col.
plates, illus., map. 20cm.

GEORGES, Joseph
THOMPSON, Dorothy E
   Climbing with Joseph Georges. [Ladies Alpine
   Club], 1962. 159p., 13 plates, illus. 22cm.

GEORGI, Johannes
   Im Eis vergraben: Erlebnisse auf Station "Eismitte"
   der letzten Grönland-Expedition Alfred Wageners.
   München: Müller, 1933. 224p., illus. 23cm.

GERARD, Alexander
   Account of Koonawur, in the Himalayas ... by the
   late Alexander Gerard; edited by George Lloyd. J.
   Madden, 1841. xiii, 308, xxvi p., 1 fold. plate,
   map (in pocket). 24cm.

GERARD, Alexander
LLOYD, Sir William
   Narrative of a journey from Caunpoor to the
   Boorendo Pass in the Himalaya mountains, via
   Gwalior, Agra, Delhi and Sirhind, by Sir William
   Lloyd; and Alexander Gerard's Account of an attempt
   to penetrate by Bekhur to Garoo ... with a letter
   from the late J.G. Gerard detailing a visit to the
   Shatool and Boorendo Passes ...; edited by George
   Lloyd. J. Madden, 1840. 2v., fold. plates, maps.
   23cm.

GERARD, J   G
   Narrative of a journey from Caunpoor to the
   Boorendo Pass in the Himalaya mountains, via
   Gwalior, Agra, Delhi and Sirhind, by Sir William
   Lloyd; and Alexander Gerard's account of an attempt
   to penetrate by Bekhur to Garoo ... with a letter
   from the late J.G. Gerard detailing a visit to the
   Shatool and Boorendo Passes ...; edited by George
   Lloyd. J. Madden, 1840. 2v., fold. plates, maps.
   23cm.

GERLACH, Heinrich
   Erläuterung zu den Arbeiten von H. Gerlach in den
   Blättern ... südlich von der Rhone. Bern: J. Dalp,
   1883. 159, 79p., 1 fold.col. plate, illus. 33cm.
   (Beiträge zur Geologischen Karte der Schweiz,
   Lfg. 27)
   Contents: 1. Heinrich Gerlach: sein Leben und
   Wirken. - 2. Die Penninischen Alpen. - 3. Bericht
   über den Bergbau im Kanton Wallis.

GERLACH, Heinrich
   Das südwestliche Wallis mid den angrenzenden Landes-
   theilen von Savoien und Piemont... Bern: J. Dalp,
   1871. 175p., plates (1 fold.col.), illus. 29cm.
   (Beiträge zur geologischen Karte der Schweiz,
   Lfg. 9)

GERMAIN, Félix
   Cimes et visages du Haut Dauphiné; ... photographies ... vignettes de Jeanne Germain. [Paris]:
   Arthaud, 1955. 188p., plates (some fold., some
   col.), illus. 26cm. (Belles pages, belles
   couleurs, 24)

GERMAIN, Félix
   Les Dolomites. Grenoble: Arthaud, 1950. 199p.,
   illus., map (fold. in pocket). 23cm. (Les beaux
   pays, 95)

GERMAIN, Félix
   Escalades choisies (du Léman à la Méditerranée).
   Grenoble: Arthaud [pour] Groupe de Haute Montagne,
   1947. 2v., illus., maps, bibl. 17cm.

GERMAIN, Félix
   Sommets: 100 photographies en noir. [Paris]:
   Arthaud, 1959. 266p., illus. (some fold.). 26cm.

GERVAIS, Paul
   Le guide des Ormonts [Jean Lancerod]: élégie.
   (In Bibliothèque universelle ... v.34, 1887,
   p.25-43)

CHABOD, Benato and GERVASUTTI, Giusto
   Alpinismo; per cura di R. Chabod e G. Gervasutti.
   Roma: C.A.I., 1935. xxxviii, 222p., illus. 16cm.
   (Manuali del Club Alpino Italiano, 2)

GERVASUTTI, Giusto
   [Scalate nelle Alpi]. Gervasutti's climbs;
   translated by Nea Morin and Janet Adam Smith.
   Hart-Davis, 1957. 201p., plates, illus. 23cm.

- - Another issue. Diadem books, 1978.

GERVASUTTI, Giusto
   [Scalate nelle Alpi]. Montagnes, ma vie ...;
   préface de Lucien Devies. Grenoble: Arthaud,
   1949. 295p.,plates (2 fold.), illus., maps.
   21cm. (Collection sempervivum)

GERWER, R
   Das Hochgebirge von Grindelwald: Naturbilder aus
   der schweizerischen Alpenwelt, von Christoph
   Aeby und Edm. von Fellenberg und Pfarrer Gerwer.
   Coblenz: Baedeker, 1865. lxv, 151p., plates
   (chiefly col., 2 fold.), illus. 28cm.

GESCHICHTSFORSCHENDE VEREIN VON OBERWALLIS
   Walliser Sagen; hrsg. von dem Historischen
   Verein von Oberwallis. 1. Bd. Brig: Tscherrig &
   Tröndle, 1907. ix, 289p., port. 21cm.

GESCHICHTSFORSCHENDE VEREIN VON OBERWALLIS
   [Walliser Sagen]. Blätter aus der Walliser
   Geschichte. 9. Bd. 4. Jahrgang. Festschrift zum
   75. Geburtstag von Dionys Imesch. Brig: Der
   Verein, 1943. 327-506p., plates, illus. 21cm.

GESCHICHTSFORSCHENDE VEREIN VON OBERWALLIS
   [Walliser Sagen]. Légendes valaisannes, d'après
   les "Walliser Sagen" de la Société d'Histoire du
   Haut-Valais; traduction enrichie et illustrée par
   J.-B. Bouvier; préface de Jules Gross. Paris:
   Attinger, 1931. xviii, 206p., illus. 22cm.

GESELLSCHAFT VON FREUNDEN DES STUBEITHALES
   Stubei: Thal und Gebirg, Land und Leute; hrsg.
   durch die Gesellschaft von Freunden des
   Stubeithales. Leipzig: Duncker & Humblot, 1891.
   xx, 742p., plates (some fold, 1 col.), illus.,
   maps. 26cm.

GESELLSCHAFT VON FREUNDEN DES STUBEITHALES
   Das Stubeithal: eine topographisch-touristiche
   Darstellung von Thal und Gebirg, von Carl Gsaller.
   Leipzig: Duncker & Humblot, 1891. viii, 308p.,
   plates (some fold.), illus., maps. 26cm.
   First section of: Stubei: Thal und Gebirg ...

GESNER, Conrad
   De raris et admirandis herbis, quae... Lunariae
   nominantur, commentariolus: & obiter de aliis
   etiam rebus quae in tenebris lucent ...; eiusdem
   descriptio Montis Fracti, sive Montis Pilati,
   iuxta Lucernam in Helvetia; his accedunt Jo. Du
   Choul... Pilati Montis in Gallia descriptio; Jo.
   Rhellicani Stockhornias, qua Stockhornus mons
   altissimus in Bernensium Helvetiorum agro,
   versibus heroicis describitur. Tiguri: Apud
   Andream Gesnerum & Jacobum Gesnerum, [1555].
   95p., illus. 19cm.

GESNER, Conrad
   On the admiration of mountains, the prefatory
   letter addressed to Jacob Avienus ... in ... "On
   milk and substances prepared from milk", first
   printed at Zürich in 1543; A description of the
   Riven Mountain, commonly called Mount Pilatus ...
   1555; translated by H.B.D. Soulé; together with,
   On Conrad Gesner and The mountaineering of
   Theuerdank, by J. Monroe Thorington; bibliographical notes by W. Dock and J. Monroe
   Thorington. San Francisco: Grabhorn Press, 1937.
   54p., illus. 30cm.

GEX, F
   La Haute-Savoie, aujourd'hui et il y a 100 ans:
   receuil de notes administratives inédites.
   Chambéry: Dardel, 1923. lv., 190p. 19cm.

GEX, F
   Le Petit-Saint-Bernard: le "Mystère", le Col, les
   routes, l'Hospice, les voyageurs. Chambéry:
   Dardel, 1924. 172p., plates, illus. 19cm.

GEYER, Georg
Führer durch das Dachsteingebirge und die angren-
zenden Gebiete des Salzkammergutes und Ennsthales.
Wien: R. Lechner, Deutscher und Oesterreichischer
Alpenverein. Section 'Austria', 1886. xii,
125p. 17cm.

GHIGLIONE, Piero
Nelle Ande del sud Peru. Milano: Garzanti, 1953.
171p., plates (1 fold.col.), illus., map, bibl.
23cm.

GHIGLIONE, Piero
Lo sci e la tecnica moderna. Bergamo: Istituto
Italiano d'Arti Grafiche, Sci Club Torino, 1928.
278p., plates, illus. 26cm.

GHIKA, Elena, Kniaginia
See
ISTRIA, Dora d'

GHIRINGHELLI, Paolo
Alpe buona: novelle e versi della montagna. Como:
Omarini Vittorio, 1912. 246p. 17cm.

GIANNITRAPANI, Luigi
La Valle d'Aosta: monografia geografica. Firenze,
1933. 4pts. in 1, plates (some fold., some col.),
illus., maps. 25cm.
Offprint from L'Universo, anno 14, 1933.

GIBBON, Edward
Miscellaneous works of Edward Gibbon ..., with
memoirs of his life and writings composed by himself; illustrated from his letters with occasional
notes and narrative by John, Lord Sheffield. A
Strahan, T. Cadell, jun. & W. Davies, 1796. 2v.
29cm.

GIBBS AUTO TOURS
Touring East Africa with Gibbs Auto Tours.
Nairobi: Gibbs, [1947]. [54]p., map. 21cm.

GIBSON, Harry
Tobogganing on crooked runs; with contributions
by F. de B. Strickland and 'Lady Tobogganer'.
Longmans, Green, 1894. xiv, 255p., plates, illus.
20cm.

GIERTSEN, Ed B   and HALVORSEN, Adolph
Norway illustrated 1888; editors: Ed. B. Giertsen
and Adolph Halvorsen. Bergen: Ed. B. Giertsen,
1888. 112p., illus. 34cm.

GIESENHAGEN, Karl
HOFFMANN, Julius
Alpen-Flora für Touristen und Pflanzenfreunde; mit
... farbigen Abbildungen ... nach Aquarellen von
Hermann Friese; nebst textlicher Beschriebung ...
von Jul. Hoffmann. Stuttgart: Verlag für Naturkunde, 1902. 86p., 40 col. plates, illus. 22cm.

GIESENHAGEN, Karl
HOFFMANN, Julius
Alpenflora für Alpenwanderer und Pflanzenfreunde.
2. Aufl., mit neuem Text hrsg. von K. Giesenhagen.
Stuttgart: E. Schweizerbart, 1914. 147p., 43 col.
plates, illus. 21cm.

ALLAIS, Émile and GIGNOUX, Paul
Ski français, par Émile Allais et Paul Gignoux;
en collaboration avec Georges Blanchon; photographies de A. Vigneau. Grenoble: Arthaud, 1937.
154p., illus. 20cm.
At head of title:Méthode officielle d'enseignement de ski de descente de la Fédération
Française de Ski.

GIGON, Fernand
Histoires d'en haut. Neuchatel: Attinger, 1933.
115p. 19cm.

GIGON, Fernand
Voix de l'alpe; avec un portrait de l'auteur
dessiné par F.H. Paris: Attinger, 1931. 75p.,
port. 20cm.

GILBERT, Josiah
Cadore; or, Titian's country. Longmans, Green,
1869. xiv, 322p., plates, illus. 28cm.

GILBERT, Josiah and CHURCHILL, George Cheetham
The Dolomite mountains: excursions through Tyrol,
Carinthia, Carniola, & Friuli in 1861, 1862, &
1863; with a geological chapter... Longman,
Green, Longman, Roberts, & Green, 1864. xx,
576p., plates (some fold., some col.), illus.,
maps. 22cm.

GILBERT, Josiah and CHURCHILL, George Cheetham
[The Dolomite mountains ...]. Die Dolomitberge:
Ausflüge ...; aus dem Englischen von Gustav
Adolf Zwanziger. Klagenfurt: Ferdinand v.
Kleinmayr, 1865-68. 2v. 24cm.

GILBERT, Josiah
Landscape in art before Claude & Salvator.
Murray, 1885. xviii, 461p., plates, illus. 23cm.

GILBERT, Josiah
Six letters relating to travel, 1865-1869.
[Fairview (N.C.)?]: Edward C. Porter, 1954. 41p.
19cm.

GILBERT, Linney
The beauties and wonders of nature and science:
a collection of curious, interesting and valuable
information for the improvement of the enquiring
mind; edited by Linney Gilbert. Hutchinson,
[184-]. iv, 280p., plates, illus. 23cm.

GILBERT, Richard
Memorable Munros: an account of the ascent of the
3,000 ft. peaks in Scotland. Easingwold (York):
Printed by G.H. Smith, 1976. 100p., illus. 22cm.

GILES, H   A
FA-HSIEN
The travels of Fa-Hsien (399-414 A.D.); or,
Record of the Buddhistic kingdoms; re-translated
by H.A.Giles. Cambridge: Cambridge University
Press, 1923. xvi, 96p., plates, illus., map (on
lining paper). 18cm.

GILKISON, W   Scott
Aspiring, New Zealand: the romantic story of the
"Matterhorn of the Southern Alps". Christchurch:
Printed by Whitcombe & Tombs, 1951. 80p., plates,
illus., maps. 19cm.

GILL, Michael
Mountain midsummer: climbing in four continents.
Hodder & Stoughton, 1969. 220p., plates, illus.,
maps. 23cm.

GILL, William
The river of golden sand, being the narrative of a
journey through China and eastern Tibet to Burmah;
condensed by Edward Colborne Baber; edited ... by
Henry Yule. Murray, 1883. 332p., plates (2 fold.
col.), illus., map. 21cm.

SPENCER, Sir Baldwin and GILLEN, F   J
Across Australia. 2nd ed. Macmillan, 1912. 2v.,
plates (2 fold.), illus., maps. 22cm.

GILLI, A
Panorama delle Alpi viste dall'Osservatorio
Astronomico di Torino; disegno ... [di] A. Gilli.
[Torino]: C.A.I., [1884]. 7p., fold.col. plates,
illus. 24cm. (Bollettino del Club Alpino
Italiano, no.18)

GILLIÉRON, V
Aperçu géologique sur les Alpes de Fribourg en
général, et description spéciale du Monsalvens.
Berne: J. Dalp, 1873. viii, 273p., 10 plates
(some col.), illus., map, bibl. 29cm. (Beiträge
zur geologischen Karte der Schweiz = Matériaux
pour la carte géologique de la Suisse, livr. 12)

GILLIÉRON, V
Description géologique des territoires de Vaud,
Fribourg et Berne compris dans la Feuille 12 entre
le Lac de Neuchatel et la Crête du Niesen. Berne:
Schmidt, Francke, 1885. viii, 532, 10p., 13
plates (some fold., some col.), illus. 33cm.
(Beiträge zur geologischen Karte der Schweiz =
Matériaux pour la carte géologique de la Suisse,
livr. 18)

GILLMAN, Peter and HASTON, Dougal
Eiger direct; photographed by Christian Bonington.
Collins, 1966. 183p., plates (some col.), illus.
24cm.

GILLY, William Stephen
A memoir of Felix Neff, pastor of the high Alps;
and of his labours among the French protestants
of Dauphiné, a remnant of the primitive christians
of Gaul. 3rd ed. J.G. & F. Rivington, 1833. xvi,
351p., 1 fold. plate, map. 17cm.

GILLY, William Stephen
Narrative of an excursion to the mountains of
Piedmont, and researches among the Vaudois, or
Waldenses... C. & J. Rivington, 1824. xxi, 279,
ccxxiv p., plates (some fold.), illus., maps.
31cm.

- - 2nd ed. 1825.
- - 3rd ed. 1826.
- - 4th ed. 1827.

GILLY, William Stephen
MONSON, Frederick John, Baron Monson
Views in the Department of the Isère and the high
Alps, chiefly designed to illustrate the Memoir
of Felix Neff by Dr. Gilly; lithographed by Louis
Haghe, from sketches [and with descriptive text]
by Lord Monson. W.H. Dalton, 1840. 16p., 22
plates, illus., map. 64cm.
Introduction in English and French.

- - Another ed. Day, [ca 1845]

GILLY, William Stephen
Waldensian researches during a second visit to the
Vaudois of Piedmont; with an introductory inquiry
into the antiquity and purity of the Waldensian
Church... C.J.G. & F. Rivington, 1831. x, 560p.,
plates (some fold.), illus., map. 23cm.

GILPIN, William
Observations on several parts of the counties of
Cambridge, Norfolk, Suffolk, and Essex, also on
several parts of North Wales, relative chiefly to
picturesque beauty, in two tours ... 1769 ... 1773.
T. Cadell & W. Davies, 1809. x, 208p., plates
(chiefly col.), illus. 24cm.

GILPIN, William
Observations relative chiefly to picturesque
beauty, made in the year 1772, on several parts of
England, particularly the mountains, and Lakes of
Cumberland, and Westmoreland. Blamire, 1786.
2v., plates (some fold., some col.), illus., maps.
22cm.

- - 2nd ed. 1788.
- - 3rd ed. 1792.

GILPIN, William
[Observations relative chiefly to picturesque
beauty ...]. Voyage en différentes parties de
l'Angleterre, et particulièrement dans les montagnes & sur les Lacs ...; traduit de l'anglois
sur la 3e éd., par M. Guedon de Berchere. Paris:
Defer de Maisonneuve; Londres: Blamire, 1789.
2v., plates, illus., maps. 20cm.

GILPIN, William
Observations relative chiefly to picturesque
beauty, made in the year 1776, on several parts of
Great Britain, particularly the High-Lands of
Scotland. Blamire, 1789. 2v., col. plates,
illus., maps. 23cm.

GILPIN, William
Three essays: on picturesque beauty; on picturesque
travel; and on sketching landscape; with a poem on
landscape painting, to these are now added two
essays giving an account of the principles and mode
in which the author executed his own drawings. 3rd
ed. T. Cadell and W. Davies, 1808. xvi, 182p.,
plates, illus. 25cm.

GIORDANO, Felice
Ascensione del Monbianco partendo dal versante
italiano ed escursione nelle Alpi Pennine. Torino:
[The Author], 1864. 35p. 21cm.

GIORDANO, Felice
Esame geologico della catena alpina del San
Gottardo che deve essere attraversata dalla grande
galleria della ferrovia italo-elvetica. [Firenze],
[1872]. 63-95p., fold.col. plates, illus., map.
36cm.
Offprint from Memorie d. R. Comitato Geol.Italiano.

GIORDANO, Felice
Notice sur la constitution géologique du Mont
Cervin. [Genève, 1869]. 13p., 1 fold. plate,
illus. 22cm.
Offprint from Archives des sciences de la biblio-
thèque universelle, mars 1869.

GIRALDUS CAMBRENSIS
The itinerary through Wales and The description of
Wales; [edited by W. Llewelyn Williams]. J.M.
Dent, [1908]. xxiii, 210p. 18cm. (Everyman's
library)

GIRARD, Georges F
A pic: Dolomites. Paris: Éditions O.E.T., [1936].
1v. of illus., map. 22cm.

GIRARD, Raymond de
Le chemin de fer du Cervin au point de vue de
l'alpinisme, des intérêts locaux, de l'esthétique
naturelle et de la science. Fribourg (Suisse):
Librarie de l'Université, 1907. 23p., 1 plate,
illus. 23cm.

GIRARD, Raymond de
La conquête des Gastlosen (Alpes fribourgeoises).
Genève: Atar, [1921]. 83p., plates, illus. 22cm.
At head of title: Publié sous les auspices de la
section "Moléson" du Club Alpin Suisse, à l'occa-
sion de son cinqantenaire.

GIRDLESTONE, Arthur Gilbert
The high Alps without guides, being a narrative
of adventures in Switzerland, together with chapters on the practicability of such mode of
mountaineering, and suggestions for its accomplishment. Longmans, Green, 1870. x, 181p., plates
(some fold.), illus., maps. 22cm.

GIVERHOLT, Helge
Jotunheimens Erobring: 150 års fjellferder i
Jotunheimen og Vestheimen. Oslo: Cappelens, 1946.
344p., illus., maps, bibl. 24cm.

GLANVELL, Victor Wolf, Edler von
Führer durch die Pragser Dolomiten. Wien: R.
Lechner, 1890. ix, 168p. 17cm.

GLARDON, August
Louis Agassiz: étude biographique.
(In Bibliothèque universelle ... v.30-31, juin-
juillet, 1886. 2pts.)

Gleanings after "Grand tour-ists". Bosworth &
Harrison, 1856. vi, 415p. 21cm.
Preface signed R.

Gleanings of a wanderer, in various parts of
England, Scotland, & North Wales, made during an
excursion in the year 1804; illustrated with
various engravings, from the original drawings of
the author. R. Phillips, 1805. 182 (i.e. 172p.),
1 plate, illus. 23cm.
(In A collection of modern and contemporary
voyages... v.2, 1806)

GLEN, Alexander R
Young men in the Arctic: the Oxford University
Arctic Expedition to Spitzbergen 1933. Faber and
Faber, 1935. 329p., plates (1 fold.col.), illus.,
map. 23cm.

GLEN, Edwin F   and ABERCROMBIE, W   R
Reports of explorations in the territory of Alaska
(Cooks Inlet, Sushitna, Copper and Tanana Rivers)
1898; made under the direction of the Secretary of
War by Edwin F. Glen and W.R. Abercrombie.
Washington: Government Printing Office, 1899.
464p., 1 fold. plate, map. 25cm.

GLENNIE, Aubrey
See

GLENNIE, Edward Aubrey

GLENNIE, Edward Aubrey
CAVE RESEARCH GROUP OF GREAT BRITAIN
A volume of essays presented to Brigadier E.A.
Glennie on the occasion of his 80th birthday, July
18th 1969. Ledbury: The Group, 1969. 69-137p.,
plates, illus., map, bibl. 30cm. (Cave Research
Group of Great Britain. Transactions, v.11, no.2,
July 1969)

GLETSCHER-KOMMISSION
See
SCHWEIZERISCHE NATUFORSCHENDE GESELLSCHAFT.
Gletscher Kommission

GLOUTZ-BLOZHEIM, Robert
See
GLUTZ-BLOTZHEIM, Robert

GLOVER, Samuel
A description of the valley of Chamouni in Savoy.
Printed for the author by T. Harvey, 1819. 42p.,
1 plate, illus. 28cm.

- - [2nd ed.]. [1821].

GLUTZ-BLOTZHEIM, Robert
EBEL, Johann Gottfried
Handbuch für Reisende in der Schweiz, [von J.G.
Ebel und H. Heidegger]; [edited by R. Glutz-
Blotzheim]. 4. verb. Aufl. Zürich: Orell,
Füssli, 1818. viii, 520p. 20cm.

- - 5. verb. Aufl. 1823.
- - 6. verb. Aufl., hrsg. von J. Schoch. 1830.

GLUTZ-BLOTZHEIM, Robert
EBEL, Johann Gottfried
[Handbuch für Reisende in der Schweiz]. Manuel du
voyageur en Suisse, [par J.G. Ebel et H. Heidegger];
[edited by Robert Glutz-Glotzheim]. 4e éd.
originale; traduite de l'allemand. Zurich: Orell,
Fussli, 1819. viii, 465p. 19cm.

- - 3e éd. française, considérablement augm.,
[par J.C. Schoch]. 1827.

GLUTZ-BLOTZHEIM, Robert
MULLER, Jean de
Histoire de la Confédération suisse, par Jean de
Muller, Robert Gloutz-Blotzheim et J.-J. Hottinger;
traduit de l'allemand, et continuée jusqu'à nos
jours par Charles Monnard et Louis Vulliemin,
Paris: Ballimore, 1837-51. 18v. 24cm.

GMELCH, Jos.
Das Birnhorn und seiner Umgebung. Stuttgart:
Deutsche Verlags-Anstalt, 1909. 76p., 1 plate,
map. 18cm. (Alpine Gipfelführer, 18)

GMELCH, Jos.
Der Grossglockner. Stuttgart: Deutsche Verlags-
Anstalt, 1906. 79p., plates, illus., maps. 18cm.
(Alpine Gipfelführer, 7)

GNECCHI, A
Le montagne dell' alta valle Camenca: guida alpina.
Brescia: Club Alpino Italiano, Sezione Brescia,
1908. xvii, 154p., plates, maps. 16cm.

GOBAT, Dr.
Winter life in Switzerland: its sports and health
cures, by M.L. & Winifred M.A. Brooke; translated
from the German compilation of Dr. Gobat. Pitman,
[1911]. 276, 60p., illus. 20cm.

GODDARD, George F
The Dolomites of the Tyrol. [London, 1875]. 14p.
22cm.
Offprint from New quarterly magazine, v.5.

GODEFFROY, C
Notice sur les glaciers, les moraines et les blocs
erratiques des Alpes. Paris: Cherbuliez, 1840.
112p. 24cm.

GODEFROY, René
Géographie de la Savoie. Chambéry: Dardel, 1930.
186p., 2 fold. plates, illus., maps. 24cm.

GODEFROY, René
La nature alpine: exposé de géographie physique.
Grenoble: Arthaud, 1940. 445p., illus., maps.
26cm.

- - 2e éd. rev. et augm. Paris: Presses Univer-
sitaires de France, 1948.

GODEFROY, René
W.A.B. Coolidge, 1850-1926. Chambéry, 1926.
24p., plates, ports. 19cm.
Offprint from Revue alpine, 3e trimestre, 1926.

GODLEY, Alfred Denis
Reliquiae; edited by C.R.L. Fletcher. Oxford
University Press, 1926. 2v., plates (1 fold.),
illus. 20cm.

GODLEY, Alfred Denis
Second strings. Methuen, 1902. 99p. 18cm.

GODLINGTON, Douglas
Tackle ski-ing. S. Paul, 1973. 165p., illus.
20cm.

GRENIER, Ch. and GODRON, D   A
Flore de France; ou, Description des plantes qui
croissent naturellement en France et en Corse.
Paris: Baillière. 1848-56. 3v. 23cm.

GOETHE, Johann Wolfgang von
Goethes Sämtliche Werke. Neu durchgesehene und
erg. Ausg. Stuttgart: J.G. Cotta, [ca 1881].
19cm.
Contains: Briefe aus der Schweiz.
Library has vols. 15 and 21 only.

GOETZ, E
[Klein Edelweiss].
Little edelweiss in Switzerland; adapted from the
Swiss verses of Mdlle. Goetz by Marion Rivett-
Carnac; with Mdlle. E. Goetz's original illustra-
tions. Duckworth, 1902. 48p., plates, illus.
23cm.

GOLAY, H   C
Guide pratique du Salève d'Annemasse à
Cruseilles, à l'usage des promeneurs et des varappeurs. Genève: Echo Montagnard, 1928. 128p.,
illus., map. 20cm.

GOLBÉRY, Marie Philippe de
Histoire et description de la Suisse et du Tyrol.
Paris: Firmin Didot, 1838. 460p., plates, illus.,
map. 22cm. (L'univers. Histoire et description
de tous les peuples)

GOLBÉRY, Marie Philippe de
[Histoire et description de la Suisse ...]. Storia
e descrizione della Svizzera e del Tirolo; traduzione a cura di A. Francesco Falconetti.
Venezia: G. Antonelli, 1840. 468p., plates,
illus., map. 23cm.

GOLBÉRY, Marie Philippe de
SAZERAC, Hilaire Léon and ENGELMANN, Gustav
Lettres sur la Suisse par H. Sazerac et G.
Engelmann; accompagnées de vues dessinées ... &
lithographiées par [F.] Villeneuve. Paris: G.
Engelmann, 1823-32. 5v., plates, illus. 46cm.
Vols.4-5 by M. de Golbéry & G. Engelmann.

WASHBURN, Bradford and GOLDTHWAIT, Richard P
The Harvard-Dartmouth Alaskan expeditions, 1933-
1934. London, 1936. 481-517p., plates (1 fold.),
illus., map. 25cm.
Offprint from Geographical journal, v.87, no.6.
1936.

GOLOVIN, Ivan
The Caucasus. Trübner, 1854. 191p., 1 col. plate,
map. 24cm.

GOMIS, Cels
Botánica popular, ab gran nombre de confrontacions.
Barcelona: Álvar Verdaguer, 1891. 157p. 18cm.
(Folk-lore Catalá. Biblioteca popular de la
Associació d'Excursions Catalana, v.6)

GOMPERTZ, M L A
Magic ladakh: an intimate picture of a land of
topsy-turvy customs and great natural beauty.
Seeley, Service, 1928. 291p., plates, illus., map.
23cm.

GOMPERTZ, M L A
The road to Lamaland: impressions of a journey to
western Thibet. Hodder and Stoughton, [1926].
x, 246p., plates, illus. 24cm.

GOMPERTZ, M L A
The voice of Dashin: a romance of wild mountains,
by "Ganpat" [i.e. M.L.A. Gompertz]. Hodder and
Stoughton, [1919]. 319p. 20cm.

GONTARD, Jean
Dans les Sierras de California. Paris: Roger,
1923. 250p., plates, illus. 20cm. (Collection
"Les pays modernes")

GONZALES LLUBERA, Miguel
Les altes valls de l'Ariège. Barcelona, 1924.
48p., 8 plates, illus., maps, bibl. 25cm.
Offprint from Butlleti del Centre Excursionista
de Catalunya, no.348.

GOODMAN, Edward John
The best tour in Norway. Sampson Low, Marston,
1892. xvi, 336p., 34 plates, illus., map. 20cm.

- - 3rd ed. 1896.
- - Cheap ed. 1903.

GOODMAN, Edward John
Western Norway: notes to accompany Paul Lange's
photogravures. Sampson Low, Marston, 1893. 14p.,
51 plates, illus., map. 31 x 40cm.

GOODWIN, Buster
Life among the Pathans (Khattaks). 2nd ed. [J.
Pott?], [1975]. 191p., 12 plates (1 fold.),
illus., map. 22cm.

GOODWIN, Eric
See
GOODWIN, Buster

GOODWIN, Harry
KNIGHT, William
Through the Wordsworth country; [drawings] by
Harry Goodwin; [text by] Professor Knight. Swan
Sonnenschein, Lowrey, 1887. xix, 268p., plates,
illus. 30cm.

- - 5th ed. 1906.

GORDON, Mrs.
See
GORDON, Elizabeth Oke

GORDON, Elizabeth Oke
The life and correspondence of William Buckland ...
by his daughter Mrs. Gordon. Murray, 1894. xvi,
288p., plates, illus. 21cm.

GORDON, George Byron
In the Alaskan wilderness. Philadelphia: Winston,
1917. 247p., plates (some fold.), illus., maps.
24cm.

GORDON, Maria M   Ogilvie
Geologisches Wanderbuch der westlichen Dolomiten.
Wien: G. Freytag & Berndt, 1928. xv, 258p.,
plates (1 fold.), illus., col. map (in pocket).
22cm.

GORDON, Seton
Amid snowy wastes: wild life on the Spitsbergen
Archipelago. Cassell, 1922. xiv, 206p., plates
(1 fold.), illus., map. 25cm.

GORDON, Seton
The charm of the hills; with ... illustrations
from photographs by the author. Cassell, 1912.
xiv, 248p., plates, illus. 24cm.

GORDON, Sir Thomas Edward
The roof of the world, being the narrative of a
journey over the high plateau of Tibet to the
Russian frontier and the Oxus sources on Pamir.
Edinburgh: Edmonston and Douglas, 1876. xiv,
172p., plates (some fold., some col.), illus.,
map. 27cm.

GORDON, Sir Thomas Edward
A varied life: a record of military and civil
service, of sport and of travel in India, Central
Asia and Persia, 1849-1902. Murray, 1906. xvi,
357p., plates, illus., maps. 23cm.

GORE, F St. John
Lights and shades of hill life in the Afghan and
Hindu Highlands of the Punjab: a contrast.
Murray, 1895. xxi, 269p., plates (2 fold.col.),
illus., maps. 24cm.

GORE, F St. John
A tour to the Pindari glacier. Calcutta: Thacker
Spink, 1898. iv, 102p., 1 fold. plate, map. 19cm.

GORGEON, Bernard
Escalades dans le massif de la Sainte-Victoire:
partie centrale: les Deux Aiguilles, le Signal,
par Bernard Gorgeon, Christian Guyomar, Alexis
Lucchesi. Pau: Marrimpouey, 1978. 117p., 1 fold.
plate, illus., maps. 21cm.

GORNERGRAT-DERBY ZERMATT, 1950
Gornergrat-Derby, Zermatt, 17-18-19 mars 1950:
liste officielle des résultats. [Zermatt]:
[G.D.Z.], 1950. 19 leaves. 30cm.
Typescript.

GORRET, Amé and BICH, Claude, baron
Guide de la Vallée d'Aoste. Turin: F. Casanova,
1876. x, 443p., illus., map. 20cm.

GORRET, Amé
VICTOR-EMMANUEL II, King of Italy
Victor-Emmanuel sur les Alpes: notices et souvenirs, par Amé Gorret. Turin: F. Casanova, 1878.
99p., col. plates, illus., maps. 17cm.

- - 2e éd. rev. et augm. 1879.

GORSSE, Pierre de
Les anglais aux Pyrénées. Pau, 1956. 28p., 1
fold. plate, illus. 24cm.
Offprint from Revue regionaliste des Pyrénées,
nos. 131-132, juillet-déc. 1956.

GORTANI, Michele
Gorizia con le vallate dell'Isonzo e del Vipacco,
di Michele Gortani [and others]. Udine: Società
Alpina Friulana, 1930. 683p., plates, maps (in
pocket). 19cm. (Club Alpino Italiano, S.A.F.
Guida del Friuli, 5)

GOS, Albert
Souvenirs d'un peintre de montagne. Genève: J.-H.
Jeheber, 1942. xv, 188p., plates, illus., music.
20cm.

GOS, Albert
GOS, Charles
Albert Gos, 1852-1942. [Geneva?]: The Author,
1942. 16p., 2 plates, ports. (as inserts). 22cm.

GOS, Charles
Alpinisme anecdotique. Neuchatel: Attinger, 1934.
314p. 19cm. (Montagne)

GOS, Charles
Au point 510: notes d'un observateur ...; préface
du Colonel Divisionnaire de Diesbach. Neuchatel:
Attinger, 1932. 135p., plates, illus. 20cm.

GOS, Charles
L'autre horizon: histoire d'un volontaire suisse de
la Grande Guerre. Paris: Attinger, 1931. xxvii,
167p. 19cm.

GOS, Charles
Le Cervin. Neuchatel: Attinger, 1948. 2v.,
plates, illus., bibl. 21cm. (Montagne)

GOS, Charles
La Croix du Cervin. Lausanne: Payot, 1919. 255p.
20cm.

- - Nouv. éd. Paris: Attinger, 1933.

GOS, Charles
L'épopée alpestre: histoire abrégée de la montagne
et de l'alpinisme de l'antiquité à nos jours.
Neuchatel: Attinger, [1944]. 182p. 17cm.
(Montagne)

GOS, Charles
Généraux suisses: commandants en chef de l'Armée
Suisse de Marignan à 1914; préface du Colonel
Commandant de Corps Guisan. [Neuchatel]: Attinger,
1932. 312p., plates, illus., bibl. 26cm.

GOS, Charles
Le Groupe Franc de Girouc. Lausanne: Payot, 1942.
186p. 19cm.

GOS, Charles
Histoire du Cervin par l'image. Vol.1. Chambéry:
Dardel, 1923. 40p., plates, illus., maps, bibl.
19cm.

GOS, Charles
L'Hôtel des Neuchatelois: un épisode de la conquête des Alpes. Lausanne: Payot, 1928. 170p.,
plates, illus., map, bibl. 19cm.

GOS, Charles
Notre-Dame des neiges: roman. Neuchatel: Attinger,
1947. 319p., plates, illus. 20cm.

GOS, Charles
[Notre Dame des neiges]. Song of the high hills;
translated by Malcolm Barnes. Allen & Unwin, 1949.
224p. 21cm.

GOS, Charles
La nuit des Drus. Lausanne: Payot, 1929. 187p.
19cm.
Also contains: Le dialogue au refuge: les valeurs
morales de l'alpinisme.

- - Another issue. Paris: Attinger, [1934?].

GOS, Charles
On tourne au Cervin
See his
Pour Miss Cynthia

GOS, Charles
Philippa de Courten, 1926-1946: an obituary, by
Charles Gos.
(In Almanach du Valais, 49e année, 1949, p52-53,
illus.)

GOS, Charles
Pour Miss Cynthia; [et On tourne au Cervin]. Paris:
Attinger, [1934?]. 168p. 19cm.

- - Nouv. éd. entitled: Pour Miss Cynthia; On tourne
au Cervin. [ca 1939].

GOS, Charles
Près des névés et des glaciers: impressions
alpestres; ouvrage illustré de ... dessins à la
plume par Albert Gos; préface de Guido Rey.
Paris: Fischbacher, 1912. xiv, 276p., plates,
illus. 24cm.

- - 2e éd. [1912].
- - 4e éd. [ca 1915].

GOS, Charles
Propos d'un alpiniste. Lausanne: Payot, 1922.
239p. 19cm.

GOS, Charles
Solitude montagnarde. Neuchatel: Attinger, 1943.
287p. 21cm. (Montagne)

GOS, Charles
Song of the high hills
See his
Notre-Dame des neiges

GOS, Charles
Sous le drapeau: récits militaires; préface du
Colonel Divisionnaire, Ed. Secretan; avec ...
dessins à la plume par François Gos. Lausanne:
Payot, 1918. 256p., illus., music. 20cm.

GOS, Charles
Tout était si beau là-haut ...: [la silhouette de
Philippa de Courten].
(In Bulletin paroissial d'Aigle, 29e année, no.2,
avril 1948. p.15-18, illus.)

GOS, Charles
Tragédies alpestres. Lausanne: Payot, 1940. v,
402p., plates, illus. 21cm.

- - 2e éd. 1946.

GOS, Charles
[Tragédies alpestres]. Alpine tragedy; translated
by Michael Barnes. Allen & Unwin, 1948. x,
282p., plates, illus., map. 24cm.

GOS, Charles
Véronica: pièce en cinq actes. Neuchatel:
Attinger, [1934?]. 205p. 19cm.

GOS, Charles
Vie d'un grand guide: Joseph Pollinger. Berne,1944.
13p., plates, illus. 26cm.
Offprint from Les Alpes, 1944, fasc. 11 and 12.

GOS, Charles
Voyage de Saussure hors des Alpes. Neuchatel:
Attinger, [1934]. 144p., plates, illus., ports.
19cm.

GOS, Charles
Voyageurs illustres en Suisse; dessins au lavis
originaux par Frédéric Traffelet; préface de
Guiseppe Motta. Berne: Staempfli, 1937. viii,
119p., plates, illus., bibl. 34cm.
Éditions du Pavilion suisse, Paris 1937.
In slip-case.

GOS, Émile
SEYLAZ, Louis
Alpes vaudoises: quatre-vingt-une photographies
originales de Émile Gos. Lausanne: J. Marguerat,
1948. 100p., illus. 29cm. (Merveilles de la
Suisse)

GOS, François
Les Alpes de la Haute-Savoie; introduction de
Henry Bordeaux; préface de F. Regaut. Genève:
J.-H. Jeheber, 1926. 173p., illus. 24cm. (Au
pays de Savoie)

GOS, François
[Les Alpes de la Haute-Savoie]. Rambles in high
Savoy; with a preface by Geoffrey Winthrop Young;
and an introduction by F. Regaut, translated by
Frank Kemp. Longmans, Green, 1927. 169p.,
illus. 25cm.

GOS, François
Au Pays des Muverans (les Alpes vaudoises), texte
et vignettes de François Gos; illustrations photographiques d'Émile Gos. Lausanne: Spes, 1924.
160p., illus. 22cm. (L'Alpe suisse)

GOS, François
Zermatt et sa vallée; introduction de J. Musy.
Genève: Alpina, 1925. 180p., 1 fold.col. plate,
illus., map. 24cm.

GOS, François
[Zermatt et sa vallée]. Zermatt and its valley;
recast in English by F.F. Roget; preface by J.
Musy... Geneva: Alpina, 1926. 180p., 1 fold.col.
plate, illus., map. 25cm.

- - Another issue. Cassell, [1926].

GOS, François
[Zermatt et sa vallée]. Zermatt und seiner Tal;
Einführung von J. Musy. Genf: Alpina, 1925.
180p., 1 fold.col. plate, illus., map. 24cm.

GOSSE, Edmund W
Studies in the literature of northern Europe.
Kegan Paul, 1879. 375p. 20cm.

GOSSE, Henri-Albert
PLAN, Danielle
Un Genevois d'autrefois: Henri-Albert Gosse,
(1753-1816), d'après les lettres et les documents
inédits. Paris: Fischbacher, 1909. 522, 59p.,
plates, illus. 23cm.

GOSWAMI, S M
Everest, is it conquered? Calcutta: The Author,
[1954]. xvii, 122p., 2 plates, illus., map. 19cm.

GOTH, Jean S
Elle et lui à la montagne; dessinés et commentés
par Jean S. Goth. Genève: Cercle Littéraire, 1944.
1v. of illus. 16cm.

GOTH, Jean S
Elle et lui en ski; dessinés et commentés par Jean
S. Goth. Genève: Cercle Littéraire, 1945. 1v. of
illus. 16cm.

GOTTA, Salvator
Piccolo Alpino: romanzo. Milano: Mondadori, 1930.
257p., plates, illus. 24cm.

GOTTELAND, Jean
CONGRÈS INTERNATIONAL DE L'ALPINISME, Monaco, 1920
Manuel d'alpinisme scolaire, [par] Jean Gotteland;
avec une introduction de Gaston Vidal. Chambéry:
Association Sportive du Lycée de Monaco; Dardel,
1921. xvi, 105p. 22cm.

GOTTHARD, P
Rigyberg der Himmelsköniginn eingeweiht unter dem
Titel: Maria zum Schnee; oder, Ursprung der heiligen
Kapelle ... mit beygesetzter marianischen
Wochenandacht... Verm. Aufl. Zug: Joh. Michael
Aloys Blunschi, 1802. 136p., plates, illus. 17cm.

GOULBURN, Edward Meyrick
A rudimentary treatise on the philosophy of grammar,
with especial reference to the doctrine of the
cases. Longman, Brown, Green, & Longmans, 1852.
vii, 64p. 15cm.

GOULD, Sir Basil J
The jewel in the lotus: recollections of an Indian
political; foreword by Sir Ernest Barker. Chatto
& Windus, 1957. xiv, 252p., plates, illus., maps.
22cm.

GOULD, Sabine Baring
See
BARING-GOULD, Sabine

GOURDAULT, Jules
La Suisse pittoresque. 5e éd. Paris: Hachette,
1887. 320p., illus. 26cm. (Bibliothèque des
écoles et des familles)

GOURDON, Maurice
Au pays d'Aran. Saint-Gaudens, 1924. 224p.,
plates, illus. 27cm.
Offprint from Revue de Comminges, 1921 to 1924.

GRABEIN, Paul
Firnenrausch: Roman. Leipzig: Grethlein, [1897].
269p. 22cm.

GRABER, Alfred
Berge: Fahrten und Ziele. München: Bergland,
[1907]. 232p., plates, illus. 21cm.

GRABER, Alfred and SCHÄTZ, Josef Julius
Walliser Alpen. Bielefeld: Velhagen & Klasing,
1931. viii, 124p., plates, illus. 18cm.
(Velhagen & Klasings Bildführer ..., 6)

GRABER, Hans
Schweizer Maler. Königstein im Taunus: K.R.
Langewiesche, [1913]. 1v.(chiefly illus). 27cm.

GRABMAYR, Karl von
Süd-Tirol: Land und Leute vom Brenner bis zur
Salurner Klause; eingeleitet und hrsg. unter
Mitwirkung hervorragender tirolischer Gelehrter
und Schriftsteller von Karl von Grabmayr. Berlin:
Ullstein, 1919. 255p. 17cm.

GRABOW, H
Savoyen und die Dauphiné: ein Führer durch die
nördlichen Westalpen und ein Teil der französischen Voralpen. Freiburg: P. Lorenz, 1907-08.
88p., maps. 16cm. (Lorenz Reiseführer)

GRAF, Ferdinand
Die Alpenflanzen; nach der Natur gemalt von Jos.
Seboth [und Jenny Schermaul]; mit Text von
Ferdinand Graf; und einer Anleitung zur Cultur der
Alpenpflanzen... Prag: F. Tempsky, 1880-86. 4v.,
col. plates, illus. 16cm.
Vol.1 is 2 verb. Aufl. 1886.

GRAF, Ferdinand
[Alpenpflanzen]. Some alpine flowers: twenty-six
coloured illustrations; selected from Seboth's
"Alpine plants, painted from nature". London:
[n.pub.], 1893. 1v. of col. illus. 17cm.

GRAF, J H and BRANDSTETTER, Josef Leop.
Bibliographische Vorarbeiten, Kataloge der Bibliotheken, Gesellschaftsschriften, Zeitungen und
Kalender; zusammengestellt von J.H. Graf und J.L.
Brandstetter. Bern: K.J. Wyss, 1896. 2v. in 1.
22cm. (Bibliographie der Schweizerischen Landeskunde, Fasc.1)

GRAF, J H
Litteratur der Landesvermessung, Kataloge der
Kartensammlungen, Karten, Pläne, Reliefs, Pano-
ramen; hersg. von Eidgenössischen Topographischen
Büreau; redigirt von J.H. Graf. Bern: K.J. Wyss,
1896. 712p. 23cm. (Bibliographie der
Schweizerischen Landeskunde, Fasc.2)

GRAF, J H
[Litteratur der Landesvermessung ...]. Cartes de
parcelles plus ou moins grandes du territoire
Suisse; publié par le Bureau Topographique
Fédéral; rédigé par J.H. Graf. Berne: K.J. Wyss,
1892. 171-335p. 23cm. (Bibliographie nationale
suisse, Fasc.2b)

GRAHAM, J D
Rock climbing in Malta. Goring, Reading: West
Col, [1970]. v, 103p., illus. 17cm.

GRAHAM, Peter
Peter Graham, mountain guide; an autobiography;
edited by H.B. Hewitt; foreword and epilogue by
John Pascoe. Wellington: Reed; London: Allen &
Unwin, 1965. xiv, 245p., plates, illus., maps.
24cm.

GRAHAM, Stephen
A vagabond in the Caucasus, with some notes of
his experiences among the Russians. Lane, 1911.
vii, 311p., plates, illus., maps. 23cm.

GRAHAM, William Woodman
Climbing the Himalayas.
(In From the Equator to the Pole. London, [1886].
18cm. p.51-131, illus.)

GRAHAM, William Woodman
Up the Himalayas: mountaineering on the Indian
Alps. [London], 1885. 3 pts. in 1, illus. 25cm.
Offprint from Good words, 1885.

GRAINER, Franz
Aus freier Wildbahn: Thierstudien aus den Hochalpen, in Momentaufnahmen von Franz Grainer;
begleittert von Arthur Achleitner. Berlin: Rud.
Schuster, 1898. 1v. (chiefly illus.). 43cm.

GRAND-CARTERET, John
La montagne à travers les âges; rôle joué par elle:
façon dont elle a été vue. Grenoble: Librairie
Dauphinoise, 1903-04. 2v., illus. 31cm.

GRANDE, Julian
The Bernese Oberland in summer and winter; a guide.
Nelson, 1911. viii, 201p., illus., maps. 17cm.

GRANDJEAN, Maurice
À travers les Alpes autrichiennes. Tours: A. Mame,
1896. 287p., illus. 32cm. (Bibliothèque
illustré, 2e série)

GRANDJEAN, Valentin
Flâneries dans les Alpes:la chaîne des Aravis, les
Alpes de Taninges, les rochers des Fiz, le massif
de Platé. Genève: A. Jullien, 1908. 231p.,
plates, illus., bibl. 19cm.

GRANT, George M
Ocean to ocean: Sandford Fleming's expedition
through Canada in 1872, being a diary kept during
a journey from the Atlantic to the Pacific, with
the expedition of the Engineer-in-chief of the
Canadian Pacific and Intercolonial Railways.
Sampson Low, Marston, Low & Searle, 1873. xv,
371p., plates, illus. 21cm.

GRANT, James
Records of a run through continental countries,
embracing Belgium, Holland, Germany, Switzerland,
Savoy, and France. Routledge, 1853. 2v. 21cm.

GRANT, Richard
Annapurna II. Kimber, 1961. 192p., plates,
illus., map, bibl. 24cm.

GRATET DE DOLOMIEU, Déodat Guy S   T   de
See
DOLOMIEU, Déodat Guy S   T   de Gratet de

GRATRIX, Dawson
He and ski. Jenkins, [1929]. 312p. 20cm.

GRAVE, William George
CROZIER, Anita
Beyond the southern lakes: the explorations of
W.G. Grave; edited by Anita Crozier; foreword by
Sir Thomas Hunter. Wellington: Reed, 1950. 124p.,
plates, illus., map (on lining papers). 23cm.

GRAVES, Charles
Swiss summer. Nicholson & Watson, 1938. xi,
278p., plates (1 fold.), illus., map. 23cm.

GRAVES, Charles
Switzerland revisited. Bles, 1947. 226p., plates,
illus., map (on lining papers). 22cm.

GRAVESON, William
WRIGHT, Walter P
Alpine flowers and rock gardens, illustrated in
colour; described by Walter P. Wright; with notes
on "Alpine plants at home" by William Graveson.
Headley, [1910]. 292p., col. plates, illus. 24cm.

GRAY, Dennis
Rope boy. Gollancz, 1970. 320p., plates, illus.,
maps. 23cm.

GRAY, Robert
Letters during the course of a tour through
Germany, Switzerland and Italy, in the years 1791,
and 1792, with reflections on the manners, litera-
ture, and religion of those countries. F. & C.
Rivington, 1794. xiii, 468p. 22cm.

GRAY, Thomas
The works of Thomas Gray, containing his poems,
and correspondence with several eminent literary
characters; to which are added Memoirs of his life
and writings by W. Mason. F.C. & J. Rivington,
1821. 545p. 41cm.

GRAZ. Techniker-Alpenclub
See
TECHNIKER-ALPENCLUB IN GRAZ

GREAT BRITAIN. Air Ministry
Mountain rescue: training handbook for mountain
rescue teams. Air Ministry, 1953. v, 114p.,
illus., bibl. 22cm. (A.M. Pamphlet,299)

GREAT BRITAIN. Army. Axel Heiberg Expedition, 1972
See
BRITISH ARMY AXEL HEIBERG EXPEDITION, 1972

GREAT BRITAIN. Army. East Greenland Expedition,1968
See
ARMY EAST GREENLAND EXPEDITION, 1968

GREAT BRITAIN. Army Mountaineering Association
See
ARMY MOUNTAINEERING ASSOCIATION

GREAT BRITAIN. Army. West Greenland Expedition,1971
See
BRITISH ARMY WEST GREENLAND EXPEDITION, 1971

GREAT BRITAIN. Forestry Commission
SYMONDS, H   H
Afforestation in the Lake District: a reply to
the Forestry Commission's White Paper of 26th
August 1936; foreword by Lord Howard of Penrith.
Dent, 1936. xxi, 97p., plates, illus., map.
19cm.

GREAT BRITAIN. Forestry Commission
Snowdonia. H.M.S.O., 1948. 72p., 2 fold.col.
plates, illus., maps. 25cm. (National forest
park guides)

GREAT BRITAIN. Parliament
East India (Tibet): papers relating to Tibet,
presented to both Houses of Parliament by Command
of His Majesty. H.M.S.O., 1904-10. 4v. in 3.
34cm. (Cd. 1920, 2054, 2370, 5240)

GREAT BRITAIN. Royal Air Force
Mountain rescue: training handbook for mountain
rescue teams. Air Ministry, 1953. v, 114p.,
illus., bibl. 22cm. (A.M. Pamphlet,299)

GREAT BRITAIN. Royal Air Force. Expedition to the
Sierra Nevada de Santa Marta in Colombia, 1974
See
ROYAL AIR FORCE EXPEDITION TO THE SIERRA NEVADA DE
SANTA MARTA IN COLOMBIA, 1974

GREAT BRITAIN. Royal Air Force. Greenland
Expedition, 1975
See
ROYAL AIR FORCE GREENLAND EXPEDITION, 1975

GREAT BRITAIN. Royal Marines. Royal Navy and Royal
Marines Mountaineering Club
See
ROYAL NAVY AND ROYAL MARINES MOUNTAINEERING CLUB

GREAT BRITAIN. Royal Navy and Royal Marines
Mountaineering Club
See
ROYAL NAVY AND ROYAL MARINES MOUNTAINEERING CLUB

GREAT BRITAIN. Royal Navy. East Greenland
Expedition, 1966
See
ROYAL NAVY EAST GREENLAND EXPEDITION, 1966

GREAT BRITAIN. Royal Navy. Ellesmere Island
Expedition, 1972
    See
ROYAL NAVY ELLESMERE ISLAND EXPEDITION, 1972

GREAT BRITAIN. Royal Navy Ski and Mountaineering
Club
    See
ROYAL NAVY SKI AND MOUNTAINEERING CLUB

GREAT TRIGONOMETRICAL SURVEY OF INDIA
    See
SURVEY OF INDIA

GRÉBAUVAL, Armand
    Au pays alpin, d'Aix à Aix. Paris: Combet, [1902].
    234p., illus. 26cm. (Voyages en tous pays)

La Grèce immortelle [par] Th. Homolle [and others]:
    [sept conférences faites à Paris, Salle de la
    Boëtie, à l'occasion d'une exposition de vues de
    Grèce recueillies par Fréd. Boissonas]. Genève:
    Éditions d'Art Boissonnas, 1919. xii, 263p.,
    plates, illus. 20cm.
    Contains: "Le plus haut sommet de l'Olympe", par
    Daniel Baud-Bovy.

GREEN, John Richard
    Stray studies from England and Italy. Macmillan,
    1876. viii, 421p. 19cm.

GREEN, Roger Lancelyn
    A.R.W. Mason. Parrish, 1952. 272p., 1 plate,
    illus., bibl. 23cm.

GREEN, Vivian H
    The Swiss Alps. Batsford, 1961. 240p., illus.,
    maps. 23cm.

GREEN, William
    A description of a series of sixty small prints,
    etched by William Green, of Ambleside, from draw-
    ings made by himself. Ambleside: W. Green, 1814.
    34p., 60 plates, illus. 14 x 22cm.

GREEN, William
    A description of sixty studies from nature; etched
    in the soft ground by William Green of Ambleside,
    after drawings made by himself in Cumberland, West-
    morland, and Lancashire; comprising a general guide
    to the beauties of the North of England. Longman,
    Hurst, Rees and Orme, 1810. x, 122p. 20cm.
    Text only, no illustrations.

GREEN, William
    The tourist's new guide, containing a description
    of the lakes, mountains, and scenery, in Cumberland,
    Westmorland, and Lancashire ... Kendal: R. Lough,
    1819. 2v., plates, illus., fold. map. 24cm.

GREEN, William Spotswood
    Among the Selkirk glaciers, being the account of a
    rough survey in the Rocky Mountain regions of
    British Columbia. Macmillan, 1890. xvi, 251p.,
    plates (1 fold.col.), illus., map. 20cm.

GREEN, William Spotswood
    The high Alps of New Zealand; or, A trip to the
    glaciers of the Antipodes with an ascent of Mount
    Cook. Macmillan, 1883. xv, 350p., plates (1
    fold.), illus., maps. 20cm.

GREENBANK, Anthony
    Climbing, canoeing, ski-ing and caving. Kingswood
    (Surrey):Elliot Right Way Books, 1964. 156p.,
    plates, illus., bibl. 19cm.

GREENBANK, Anthony
    Instructions in mountaineering. Museum Press,
    1967. 125p., plates, illus. 23cm. (Brompton
    library)

GREENBANK, Anthony
    Instructions in rock climbing. Museum Press, 1963.
    159p., plates, illus. 23cm. (Brompton library)
GREENE, Raymond
    Moments of being: the random recollections of
    Raymond Greene. Heinemann, 1974. ix, 180p.,
    plates, illus. 25cm.

GREGORII, Johann Gottfried
    Die curieuse Orographia; oder, Accurate Bes-
    chreibung derer berühmtesten Berge, in Europa,
    Asia, Africa und America; mit denen auserlesensten
    theologischen, politischen, physicalischen,
    moralischen und andern notablen Anmerckungen...
    Franckfurth: Hieronymo Philippo Ritscheln, 1715.
    743p., plates, illus. 19cm.

GREGORIN, Janez
    Blagoslov gorá: sbrano delo. Ljubljana: Slovensko
    Planisko Drustvo, 1944. xxxi, 287p., illus. 22cm.

GREGOROVIUS, Ferdinand
    Corsica in its picturesque, social and historical
    aspects: the record of a tour in the summer of
    1852; translated from the German by Russell
    Martineau. Longman, Brown, Green & Longmans,
    1855. viii, 493p. 19cm.

GREGORY, Alexander Tighe
    Practical Swiss guide: Anglo-American hand-book
    for Switzerland, Savoy, North Italy, the routes
    from England by France, Belgium, Holland and the
    Rhine... 53rd issue, [by A.T. Gregory]. Kegan,
    Paul, Trench, Trübner, 1909. lxix, 200p.,
    plates, illus., maps, plans. 18cm. (English red
    books)

GREGORY, Alexander Tighe
    Practical Swiss guide, illustrated: the whole of
    Switzerland, Mont Blanc, Monte Rosa, Mont Cervin
    ..., by an Englishman in Switzerland [i.e. A.T.
    Gregory]. Longman, Brown, Green & Longmans, 1856.
    xxxvii, 124p., illus., map. 18cm.

GREGORY, Alfred
    The picture of Everest: [a book of full-colour
    reproductions of photographs of the Everest scene,
    chosen and explained by Alfred Gregory; with an
    introduction by Sir John Hunt]. Hodder &
    Stoughten, 1954. 1v. (chiefly col. illus.). 28cm.

GREGORY, John Walter and GREGORY, C   J
    To the Alps of Chinese Tibet: an account of a
    journey of exploration up to and among the snow-
    clad mountains of the Tibetan frontier. Seeley,
    Service, 1923. 321p., plates (1 fold.), illus.,
    maps. 23cm.

GREGORY, John Walter
CONWAY, William Martin, Baron Conway
    The first crossing of Spitsbergen, being an
    account of an inland journey of exploration and
    survey, with descriptions of several mountain
    ascents ...; with contributions by J.W. Gregory
    [and others]. Dent, 1897. xii, 371p., plates,
    illus., maps. 25cm.

GREGORY, John Walter
    The great Rift valley; being the narrative of a
    journey to Mount Kenya and Lake Baringo, with
    some account of the geology, natural history,
    anthropology, and future prospects of British
    East Africa. Murray, 1896. xxi, 422p., plates
    (some fold.col.), illus., maps. 25cm.

GREGORY, John Walter and GREGORY, C   J
    To the Alps of Chinese Tibet: an account of a
    journey . . . among the snow-clad mountains
    of the Tibetan frontier. Seeley, Service, 1923.
    321p., plates (1 fold.), illus., maps. 23cm.

GREIG, B   D   A
TARARUA TRAMPING CLUB
    Tararua story; edited by B.D.A. Greig.
    Wellington: The Club, 1946. 108p., plates (1
    fold.), illus., map. 25cm.

GREITBAUER, Karl
    Das Ganze der alpinen Idee: eine geistige Analyse
    des Bergsteigens. Wien: W. Braumüller, 1973.
    75p., bibl. 19cm.

GREITBAUER, Karl
    Die Gestalt des Bergsteigers: das alpine
    Geschehen im Lichte der Psychologie. Wien: W.
    Braumüller, 1956. xi, 415p. 24cm.

GREITBAUER, Karl
Das unverstandene Bergsteigen: zum geistigen Umfeld
des Bergsteigens, mit einem Beitrag zur Verhütung
der Unfälle durch subjektive Gefahren. Wien: W.
Braumüller, 1977. 95p. 19cm.

GREMLI, August
The flora of Switzerland for the use of tourists
and field-botanists; translated from the 5th ed.
by Leonard W. Paitson. D. Nutt, 1889. xxiv,
454p. 18cm.

BURNAT, Émile and GREMLI, August
Les roses des Alpes maritimes: études sur les roses
qui croissent spontanément dans la chaine des Alpes
maritimes et le département français de ce nom.
Genève: H. Georg, 1879. 136p., bibl. 23cm.

GRENARD, Fernand
Le Tibet: le pays et ses habitants. Paris: Colin,
1904. vii, 387p., 1 fold.col. plate, map. 20cm.

GRENARD, Fernand
[Le Tibet: le pays et les habitants]. Tibet: the
country and its inhabitants;translated by A.T.
Teixeira de Mattos. Hutchinson, 1904. viii,
373p., 1 fold.col. plate, map. 24cm.

GRENIER, Ch. and GODRON, D   A
Flore de France; ou, Description des plantes qui
croissent naturellement en France et en Corse.
Paris: Baillière, 1848-56. 3v. 23cm.

Grenoble et le Dauphiné: publié par MM. Audebrand,
Maurice Bergès [and others]. Grenoble: A. Gratier
& J. Rey, [1904]. 396p., plates, illus., map.
25cm.

GRENOBLE UNIVERSITÉ MONTAGNE
Hommes et montagnes du Kurdistan Turc, Sat Dag
1973: expédition organisée par le Grenoble
Université Montagne avec la participation
d'alpinistes du Club Alpin Français... [Grenoble]:
G.U.M., 1974. 64p., plates, illus., maps, bibl.
30cm.

GREPPIN, J   B
Description géologique du Jura bernois et de quelques districts adjacents... Berne: J. Dalp, 1870.
xx, 357p., plates (some fold., 1 col.), illus.
30cm. (Beiträge zur geologischen Karte der Schweiz
= Matériaux pour la carte géologique de la Suisse,
livr. 8)

GRETSCHMANN, Emil
Der Felsgeher und seine Technik. München: Verlag
der Alpenfreund, [1923]. 48p., plates, illus.
17cm. (Alpenfreund-Bücherei, Bd.5)

GREW, J   C
Sport and travel in the Far East; with ... illustrations from photographs by the author. Constable,
1910. xiv, 264p., illus. 22cm.

GREY, Rowland
In sunny Switzerland: a story of six weeks. Kegan
Paul, Trench, 1884. ix, 274p. 19cm.

GREYERZ, Otto von
Die Mundartdichtung der deutschen Schweiz,
geschichtlich dargestellt. Leipzig: H. Haessel,
1924. 117p. 16cm. (Die Schweiz im deutschen
Geistesleben, 33)

GRIBBLE, Francis
The early mountaineers. T. Fisher Unwin, 1899.
xiv, 338p., plates, illus. 23cm.

GRIBBLE, Francis
Geneva; painted by J. Hardwicke Lewis & May
Hardwicke Lewis; described by Francis Gribble.
Black, 1908. x, 135p., 20 col.plates, illus. 23cm.

GRIBBLE, Francis
Lausanne; painted by J. Hardwicke Lewis and May
Hardewicke Lewis;described by Francis Gribble.
Black, 1909. viii, 110p., 20 col. plates, illus.
23cm.

GRIBBLE, Francis
Montreux; painted by J. Hardwicke Lewis & May
Hardwicke Lewis; described by Francis Gribble.
Black, 1908. viii, 112p., 20 col. plates, illus.
24cm.

GRIBBLE, Francis
The story of alpine climbing. Newnes, 1904.
180p., plates, illus., bibl. 16cm.

GRIEBEN, Theobald
Illustriertes Handbüch für Reisende in der
Schweiz, Ober-Italien, Turin und Genua... 3.
verm. Aufl. Berlin: Grieben, 1861. 490p.,
illus., maps, plans. 17cm. (Grieben's Reise-
Bibliothek, 23)

GREIBEN, Theobald
München, Südbayern, Salzburg, Tirol: illustrirtes Handbüch für Reisende. 8 verb. Aufl.
Berlin: Grieben, 1861. viii, 149p., illus.,
map, plan. 16cm. (Grieben's Reise-Bibliothek,
20)

GREIBEN, Theobald
La Suisse et les Lacs de la Haute-Italie: guide
illustré du voyageur... 7e éd. rev. et corr.
Berlin: Grieben, 1859. viii, 179p., illus.,
map, plans. 17cm. (Guides-Grieben; Bibliothèque
du voyageur, 37)

GRIERSON, Thomas
Autumnal rambles among the Scottish mountains;
or, Pedestrian tourist's friend. Edinburgh:
Paton & Ritchie, 1850. xii, 122p., 1 plate,
illus. 18cm.

- - 2nd ed. greatly enl. Edinburgh: J. Hogg, 1851.

GRIESBACH, C   L
Geology of the central Himalayas. Calcutta:
Geological Survey of India, 1891. xi, 232, xix p.,
plates (some fold, 2 col.), illus., maps, bibl.
28cm. (Memoirs of the Geological Survey of
India, v.23)

GRIFFIN, Arthur Harold
In mountain Lakeland. Preston: Guardian Press,
1963. 216p., plates, illus. 24cm.

GRIFFIN, Arthur Harold
Inside the real Lakeland. Preston: Guardian
Press, 1961. 240p., plates, illus., maps (on
lining papers). 24cm.

GRIFFIN, Arthur Harold
Long days in the hills. Robert Hale, 1974.
188p., plates, illus. 23cm.

OLIVER, Geoffrey and GRIFFIN, L   Joe
Scafell group; illustrated by W. Heaton Cooper.
Stockport: Fell & Rock Climbing Club, 1967.
172p., 1 col.plate, illus., maps (on lining
papers). 16cm. (Climbing guides of the English
Lake District, [4th ser.], 7)

GRIFFIN, Lindsay N
Mont Blanc range. Vol.2. Chamonix Aiguilles,
Rochefort, Jorasses, Leschaux; compiled by Lindsay
N. Griffin. Alpine Club, 1978. 219p., illus.,
bibl. 17cm. (Alpine Club guide books)

GRIFFIN, Lindsay N
Mont Blanc range. Vol.3. Triolet, Verte/Drus,
Argentière, Chardonnet, Trient; compiled by
Lindsay N. Griffin. Alpine Club, 1980. 228p.,
illus. 17cm. (Alpine Club guide books)

GRIFFIN, Margaret
Tiquimani. Stellenbosch: Kosmo, 1965. 164p.,
plates (1 col.), illus., map (on lining papers).
23cm.

GRILL FAMILY
DEUTSCHER UND ÖSTERREICHISCHER ALPENVEREIN. _Sektion Berchtesgaden_
Die Grill aus der Ramsau: eine deutsche Führer-familie, zum fünfzigjährigen Führer-Jubiläum Johann Grills des Jüngeren, von W.F.; hrsg. von der Sektion Berchtesgaden des Deutschen und Österr. Alpenvereins. Berchtesgaden: L. Vonderthann, [1931?]. 20p., ports. 23cm.

GRILLET, Jean Louis
Dictionnaire historique, littéraire et statistique des départements du Mont-Blanc et du Léman; contenant l'histoire ancienne et moderne de la Savoie ... Chambéry: J.F. Puthod, 1807. 3v. 23cm.

GRINNELL, George Bird
ROOSEVELT, Theodore
American big-game hunting: the book of the Boone and Crockett Club;editors, Theodore Roosevelt, George Bird Grinnell. D. Douglas, 1893. 343p., plates, illus. 22cm.

GRINNELL, George Bird
Harper's Camping and scouting: an outdoor guide for American boys; consulting editors, George Bird Grinnell, Eugene L. Swan. New York, London: Harper, 1911. xvi, 398p., illus. 21cm.

GRINNELL, George Bird
ROOSEVELT, Theodore
Hunting in many lands: the book of the Boone and Crockett Club; editors, Theodore Roosevelt, George Bird Grinnell. New York: Forest and Stream Publishing Co., 1895. 447p., plates, illus. 22cm.

The Grisons, Switzerland. Coire: Grisons Public Interests Association, [1922]. 56p., 49 plates (1 fold.), illus., map. 16 x 24cm.
"To commemorate the completion of the electrification of all the narrow-guage railways ... and of the construction of the great electric power works in the Grisons."

GRITSTONE GUIDE COMMITTEE
Climbs on gritstone.

1. Laddow area; edited by H.C. Parker. 1948.
2. The Sheffield area; edited by E. Byne. Rev. ed.
3. Kinder, Roches and northern areas; edited by A. Allsopp. 1951.
4. Further developments in the Peak district; edited by E. Byne and W.B. White. 1957.

GRÜGER, Gustav and RABL, Josef
Die Entwicklung der Hochtouristik in den österreichischen Alpen; hrsg. vom Oesterreichischen Touristen-Club. Wien: R. Leckner, 1890. xi, 258p., plates, illus. 23cm.

GROHMAN, W A Baillie
See
BAILLIE-GROHMAN, William Adolphus

GROSS, Anton Johann
Handbuch für Reisende durch die österreichische Monarchie, mit besonderer Rücksicht auf die südlichen und Gebirgsländer, nämlich: Oesterreich, Salzburg, Steiermark, Illirien, Tirol, das lombardisch-venetianische Königreich und Dalmatien ...; nach eigenen Erfahrungen ... bearb. von Anton Johann Gross. 2. verm. Aufl. München: J. Lindauer, 1834. 2pts. in 1, 1 fold. plate, illus. 22cm.

GROSS, H S
Climbs on Great Gable, by H.S. Gross; and Rock climbing in Borrowdale, by A.R. Thomson. Barrow-in-Furness: Fell & Rock Climbing Club, [1925]. 63p., plates, illus. 21cm. (Climbers' guides, [1st ser.], 4)

GROSS, Jules
Le héros des Alpes, Au Grand-Saint-Bernard: drame et poésies alpestres. 2e éd. Paris: Fischbacher, [1904]. viii, 301p. 17cm.

GROSS, Jules
L'Hospice du Grand Saint-Bernard. Paris: Attinger, [1935?]. 151p., 1 plate, illus. 20cm. (Institutions et traditions de la Suisse Romande)

GROSS, Rudolf
Karte und Panorama vom Rigi. Zürich: C. Honnegger-Schmid, 1855. 17cm.
Map & circular panorama, mounted & folded.

GROSSE, Carl, _marchese von Grosse_
Die Schweiz. Halle: I.C. Hendels, 1791. iv, 400p. 2v. in 1. 18cm.

GROTE, George
Seven letters concerning the politics of Switzerland, pending the outbreak of the civil war in 1847... Murray, 1876. xii, 171p. 23cm.

GROUPE DE HAUTE MONTAGNE
DEVIES, Lucien
La chaîne du Mont Blanc. 1. Mont Blanc-Trélatête, par Lucien Devies, Pierre Henry, Jacques Lagarde. 2e éd. Paris: Arthaud [pour] G.H.M., 1951. 354p., illus., bibl. 17cm. (Guides Vallot)

- - 3e éd., par Lucien Devies et Pierre Henry. 1973.

GROUPE DE HAUTE MONTAGNE
DEVIES, Lucien
La chaine du Mont Blanc. 2. Aiguilles de Chamonix, Grandes Jorasses. Grenoble: Arthaud [pour] G.H.M., 1947. 387p., illus., maps. 17cm. (Guides Vallot)

- - Addendum. 1948.
- - 2e éd. 1951.
- - 3e éd., par Lucien Devies et Pierre Henry. 1974.

GROUPE DE HAUTE MONTAGNE
DEVIES, Lucien and HENRY, Pierre
La chaîne du Mont Blanc. 3. Aiguille Verte, Dolent, Argentière, Trient. Grenoble: Arthaud [pour] G.H.M., 1949. 381p., illus. 17cm.

- - 3e éd. 1966.
- - 4e éd. 1975.

GROUPE DE HAUTE MONTAGNE
GERMAIN, Félix
Escalades choisies (du Léman à la Méditerranée). Grenoble: Arthaud [pour] G.H.M., 1947. 2v., illus., maps, bibl. 17cm.

GROUPE DE HAUTE MONTAGNE
DEVIES, Lucien and LALOUE, Maurice
Guide du massif des Écrins... 2e éd. Paris: Arthaud [pour] G.H.M., 1951. 2v., illus., bibl. 17cm.
Later eds. published under title: Le massif des Écrins.

GROUPE DE HAUTE MONTAGNE
CLUB ALPIN FRANÇAIS
Manuel d'alpinisme; publié avec la collaboration du Groupe de Haute Montagne. Chambéry: Dardel, 1934. 2v., plates, illus. 23cm.

GROUPE DE HAUTE MONTAGNE
DEVIES, Lucien
Le massif des Écrins. 1. Meije, Rateau, Soreiller, par Lucien Devies, François Labande, Maurice Laloue. 4e éd. Paris: Arthaud, G.H.M., 1976. 301p., illus., bibl. 17cm.
Originally published under title: Guide du massif des Écrins.

GROUPE DE HAUTE MONTAGNE
DEVIES, Lucien
Le massif des Écrins. 2. Ailefroide, Pelvoux, Bans, Olan,Muzelle, par Lucien Devies, François Labande, Maurice Laloue. Paris: Arthaud, G.H.M., 1971. 662p., illus., bibl. 17cm.
Originally published under title: Guide du massif des Écrins.

GROUPE DE HAUTE MONTAGNE
DEVIES, Lucien
    Le massif des Écrins. 2. Écrins, Grande Ruine,
    Roche Faurio, Agneaux, Glouzis, par Lucien Devies,
    François Labande, Maurice Laloue. 4e éd. Paris:
    Arthaud, G.H.M., 1976. 305p., illus. 17cm.

GROUPE DE HAUTE MONTAGNE
DEVIES, Lucien
    Le massif des Écrins. 3. Ailefroide, Pelvoux,
    Bans, Sirac, par Lucien Devies, François Labande,
    Maurice Laloue. 4e éd. Paris: Arthaud, G.H.M.,
    1978. 313p., illus. 17cm.
    Originally published under title: Guide du massif
    des Écrins.

GROUPE PYRÉNÉISTE DE HAUTE MONTAGNE
LE BRETON, Henry and OLLIVIER, Robert
    Haute montagne Pyrénéenne: guide des ascensions
    difficiles aux Pyrénées: les Pyrénées occidentales,
    des Aiguilles d'Ansabère au Pic Long. Pau: Groupe
    Pyrénéiste de Haute Montagne, [1937]. xix, 317p.,
    plates (1 fold.), illus., maps. 17cm.

GROVE, Florence Crauford
    'The frosty Caucasus': an account of a walk
    through part of the range and of an ascent of
    Elbruz in the summer of 1874. Longmans, Green,
    1875. x, 341p., plates (1 fold.col.), map. 20cm.

GROVE, Florence Crauford
    ['The frosty Caucasus' ...]. Le Caucase glacé:
    promenade à travers une partie de la chaîne et
    ascension du Mont Elbrouz; ouvrage traduit ...
    par Jules Leclercq. Paris: A. Quantin, 1881.
    340p. 19cm.

GRUBE, A   W
    Alpenwanderungen: Fahrten auf hohe und höchste
    Alpenspitzen; nach der Originalberichten ausgewählt,
    bearb. und gruppiert für junge und alte Freunde
    der Alpenwelt. Leipzig: E. Kummer, 1874. 2v. in 1,
    col. plates, illus. 23cm.

- - 3. Aufl., neu bearb. und ergänzt von C. Benda.
    1886.

GRUBER, Hans
    Die Goldberg-, Sennblick-, gruppe in den Hohen
    Tauern: touristischer Spezialführer. Innsbruck:
    A. Edlinger, 1904. 76p., map. 17cm.

GRUBHOFER, Tony
CHRISTOMANNOS, Theodor
    Christomannos-Gedenkbuch: Erinnerungen an Theodor,
    von ... Tony Grubhofer; Rund um den Rosengarten,
    nachgelassenes Manuskript von Theodor Christomannos.
    Meran: F.W. Ellmenreichs, 1912. 72p., plates
    (some col.), illus. 26cm.

GRÜTTER, J   B
    Meine Matterhornbesteigung. St. Gallen: Th.
    Wirth, 1893. 48p., plates, illus. 20cm.

GRUNER, Gottlieb Sigmund
    Die Eisgebirge des Schweizerlandes. Bern: Verlag
    der neuen Buchhandlung, 1760. 3v. in 1, fold.
    plates, illus., maps. 21cm.

GRUNER, Gottlieb Sigmund
    [Die Eisgebirge des Schweizerlandes]. The icy
    mountains of Swisserland ...; translated from the
    German. [ca 1800]. 3 v. 38cm.
    Unpublished ms. in two hands, with some corrections
    & omissions.

GRUNER, Gottlieb Sigmund
    [Die Eisgebirge des Schweizerlandes]. Histoire
    naturelle des glaciers de Suisse; traduction libre
    de l'allemand ... par M. de Kéralio. Paris:
    Panckoucke, 1770. xvi, 359p., fold. plates,
    illus., maps. 26cm.

GRUNER, Gottlieb Sigmund
    Reisen durch die merkwürdigsten Gegenden Helvetiens,
    [von G.S. Gruner]. London: Bey der typographischen
    Gesellschaft, 1778. 2v., plates, illus., maps.
    18cm.
    A new version of the Author's Die Eisgebirge des
    Schweizerlandes.

GRUNNE, Xavier, comte de
MISSION SCIENTIFIQUE BELGE POUR L'EXPLORATION DU
RUWENZORI, 1932
    Vers les glaciers de l'équateur: le Ruwenzori:
    Mission scientifique belge 1932, par Xavier de
    Grunne [and others]; aquarelles de James Thiriar.
    Bruxelles: R. Dupriez, 1937. 300p., illus .(some
    fold., some col.), maps, bibl. 28cm.

GRUPPO TRENTINO DI LAVORO PER LA DIFESA
DELL'AMBIENTE NATURALE
    Perchè siamo contrari all'autostrada Trento -
    Vicenza - Rovigo. Trento: Il Gruppo, 1973.
    39p., plan. 19cm.

GSALLER, Carl
    Das Stubeithal: eine topographisch-touristische
    Darstellung von Thal und Gebirg, von Carl
    Gsaller. Leipzig: Duncker & Humblot, 1891.
    viii, 308p., plates (some fold.), illus., maps.
    26cm.
    First section of "Stubei: Thal und Gebirg ...";
    edited by the Gesellschaft von Freunden des
    Stubeithales.

GSELL-FELS, Theodor
    Die Schweiz. 2. umgearb. Aufl. Volks-Ausg.
    Zürich: Schmidt, 1883. 381p., plates, illus.
    33cm.

GSELL-FELS, Theodor
    [Die Schweiz]. Switzerland: its scenery and
    people, pictorially represented by eminent Swiss
    and German artists; with historical and descrip-
    tive text based on the German of Dr. Gsell-Fels.
    Blackie, 1881. xvi, 472p., plates, illus. 36cm.

GUÉCA, Catherine
    Massif des Lefka Ori de Crête: monts Guiguilos
    et Volakias. Athènes: Club Alpin Hellénique,
    1972. 16p., illus., maps. 25cm.
    Text in French and Greek.

GÜNTHER, Marie, comtesse von
    Tales and legends from the Tyrol; collected and
    arranged by La Comtesse von Günther. Chapman &
    Hall, 1874. xii, 219p. 20cm.

GÜNTHER, Walter
SCHWEIZER ALPEN-CLUB. Sektion Pilatus
    Zentralschweizerische Voralpen: Zürichsee, Vier-
    waldstättersee, Brünigpass; für die Sektion
    Pilatus des Schweizer Alpen-Clubs 1930 bearb.
    von Oskar Allgäuer; neu bearb. von Walter Günther.
    Zürich: Schweizer Alpen-Club, 1969. 204p.,
    plates, illus., maps (on lining papers). 17cm.
    (Clubführer des Schweizer Alpen-Club)

GÜSSFELDT, Paul
    In den Hochalpen: Ergebnisse aus den Jahren 1859-
    1885. 2. Aufl. Berlin: Allgemeiner Verein für
    deutsche Literatur, 1886. iv, 349p., plates,
    illus. 23cm.

GÜSSFELDT, Paul
    Der Montblanc. Berlin, 1892. 73-98, 206-239p.
    22cm.
    Offprint from Deutsche Rundschau, 19. Jahrg.,
    Heft 1/2 Okt.-Nov. 1892.

GÜSSFELDT, Paul
    Der Montblanc: Studien im Hochgebirge, vornehm-
    lich in der Montblanc-Gruppe. Berlin: Paetel,
    1894. xii, 280p., plates (1 fold.col.), illus.,
    maps. 25cm.

GÜSSFELDT, Paul
    [Der Montblanc ...]. Le Mont Blanc: ascensions
    d'hiver et d'été: études dans la haute montagne;
    traduction de D. Delétra; préface de Joseph
    Vallot. Genève: P.G. Drehmann, 1899. xviii,
    3-344p., plates (2 fold., 1 col.), maps. 21cm.

GÜSSFELDT, Paul
    Reise in den Andes von Chile und Argentinien.
    Berlin: Paetel, 1888. xv, 480p., fold.col.
    plates, maps. 26cm.

GUEX, André
  Geiger: pilote des glaciers; récit recueilli par
  André Guex; préface de Félix Germain. Paris:
  Arthaud, 1955. 153p., plates, illus. 22cm.
  (Collection sempervivum, no.26)

GUEX, Jules
  Dans la trace de Javelle: nombreux documents
  inédits, notes, croquis, dessins et photographies
  de Javelle. Lausanne: F. Rouge, 1947. 111p.,
  24 plates, illus., bibl. 22cm. (Collection
  alpine, 7)

GUEX, Jules
  La montagne et ses noms: études de toponymie
  alpine. Lausanne: F. Rouge, 1946. 235p., plates,
  illus., map, bibl. 22cm. (Collection alpine, 5)

GUGLIERMINA, G   B
GUGLIERMINA, Giuseppe F
  Vette: ricordi di esplorazioni e nuove ascensioni
  sulle Alpi, nei gruppi del Monte Rosa, del Cervino
  e del Monte Bianco dal 1896 al 1921, [da] G.F. e
  G.B. Gugliermina, Giuseppe Lampugnani.
  [Borgosesia]: Sezione di Varallo del Club Alpino
  Italiano, 1927. 361p., plates, illus. 30cm.

BERTOLINI, Amilcare and GUGLIERMINA, Giuseppe F
  Gruppo Monte Bianco; fra il Colle del Miage,
  il Col du Midi e il Col de la Tour Ronde; disegni
  Angelo Calegari. Monza: Club Alpino Italiano,
  1924. 77p., maps. 18cm. (C.A.I. Sez. Universitaria. Manuali. Guida Sucai)

BERTOLINI, Amilcare and GUGLIERMINA, Giuseppe F
  Gruppo Monte Rosa; schizzi di Angelo Calegari.
  Monza: Club Alpino Italiano, 1925. 75p., illus.
  19cm. (C.A.I. Sez. Universitaria. Guida Sucai)

GUGLIERMINA, Giuseppe F
  Il Monte Bianco esplorato, 1760-1948: notizie
  storico-alpinistiche e relazioni originali dei
  primi salitori; raccolte e ordinate da Guiseppe F.
  Gugliermina. Bologna: Tamari, 1973. 274p.,
  plates, illus., maps. 29cm.

GUGLIERMINA, Giuseppe F
  Vette: ricordi di esplorazioni e nuove ascensioni
  sulle Alpi, nei gruppi del Monte Rosa, del Cervino
  e del Monte Bianco dal 1896 al 1921, [da] G.F. e
  G.B. Gugliermina, Giuseppe Lampugnani.
  [Borgosesia]: Sezione di Varallo del Club Alpino
  Italiano, 1927. 361p., plates, illus. 30cm.

GUIBAUT, André
  Tibetan venture in the country of the Ngolo-Setas:
  second Guibaut-Liotard expedition; translated by
  Lord Sudley. Readers Union, 1949. 206p., plates,
  illus., maps (on lining papers). 21cm.

GUIBERT, Jacques Antoine, comte de
  Voyages de Guibert dans diverses parties de la
  France et en Suisse, faits en 1775, 1778, 1784, et
  1785; ouvrage posthume publié par sa veuve. Paris:
  d'Hautel, 1806. 414p. 22cm.

Guida al Sacro Monte di Varallo. Varallo: Colleoni,
  1857. 56p., illus. 17cm.

Guida da Milano a Ginevra pel Sempione. Milano: F.
  Artaria, 1822. xi, 175p., plates (1 fold.), illus.,
  map. 28cm.

Guida del naturalista nelle Alpi
    See
  Guide du naturaliste dans les Alpes

Guida illustrata della Valle d'Aosta... Pt.1. Valle
  Inferiore. 4a ed., interamente rifatta. Torino:
  Casanova, 1899. 247p., plates, illus., maps,
  plans. 19cm. (Collezione guide Casanova)

[Guida illustrata della Valle d'Aosta...]. Guide-
  manuel du touriste dans la vallée d'Aoste; la
  vallée de Gressoney et le massif du Mont-Rose.
  Turin: Casanova, [18--]. xii, 64p., plates,
  illus., maps, plans. 16cm. (Collection guides
  Casanova)

Guide à Chamouni, aux deux St-Bernard, Sixte et
  toutes les vallées autour du Mont-Blanc. Genève:
  Briquet & Dubois, [1846?]. 144p., plates (1
  fold.), maps. 19cm.

Le guide des voyageurs en Suisse ..., précédé d'un
  discours sur l'état politique du pays, [par
  J.L.A. Reynier]. 2e éd. Paris: Buisson, 1791.
  1x, 391p. 18cm.

[Guide du naturaliste dans les Alpes]. Guida del
  naturalista nelle Alpi, [da] J. Dorst [and
  others]. Bologna: Zanichelli, 1973. xvi, 332p.,
  illus. (some col.), maps, bibl. 24cm.

Guide du voyageur à la Vallée de Chamouni et à la
  Grande-Chartreuse... Chambéry: Puthod, 1836.
  93p., plates (1 fold.), map. 12 x 16cm.

Guide du voyageur de Genève à Milan par le Simplon.
  Milan: F. Artaria, [ca 1822]. xii, 167p., 1
  plate, map. 22cm.

Guide du voyageur en Suisse, [by Thomas Martyn and
  others]. Lausanne: J. Mourer, 1794. 203p. 19cm.

Guide-itinéraire à Chamonix et autour du Mont-Blanc
  ..., par M.C. 2e éd. Genève: Imprimerie V.
  Blanchard, 1873. 32p., map. 15cm.

Guide pratique de Saint-Gervais-les-Bains, Chamonix,
  Argentière, le Mont-Blanc. 5e éd. Lyon: G.
  Toursier, [n.d.]. 108p., illus., maps, plans.
  16cm. (Guides Pol)

Guide pratique du Vercors et Royans. Valence: G.
  Toursier, [n.d.]. 80p., plates, maps, plans.
  16cm. (Guides Pol)

A guide to all the watering and sea bathing places,
  descriptions of the lakes, tour in Wales, &c. &c.,
  [by J. Feltham]. Longman, Hurst, Rees, Orme &
  Brown, [1825?]. iv, 492p., plates (6 fold.),
  illus., maps. 15cm.

Guide to Montana and district. H. Marshall, 1907.
  79p., 1 fold. plate (in pocket), illus. 19cm.
  Preface signed: A.H.M.L. i.e.,Arnold Lunn.

[Guide to Montana ...]. Guide de Montana et des
  environs. Neuchatel: Delachaux & Niestlé, 1908.
  79p., illus. 19cm.
  Preface signed: A.H.M.L. i.e., Arnold Lunn.

Guide to Switzerland. Macmillan, 1903. cvi, 235p.,
  maps, plans. 18cm. (Macmillan's guides)

A guide to the Lakes, dedicated to the lovers of
  landscape studies ... by the author of The
  antiquities of Furness [i.e. Thomas West].
  Richardson & Urquhart, 1778. 204p. 19cm.

- - 2nd ed. rev. throughout and greatly enl.,
  entitled: A guide to the Lakes, in Cumberland,
  Westmorland, and Lancashire. 1780.
- - 3rd ed. rev. B. Law, 1784.
- - 4th ed. W. Richardson, 1789.
- - 5th ed. 1793.
- - 6th ed. 1796.
- - 7th ed. 1799.
- - 9th ed. Kendal: Printed by W. Pennington, 1807.
- - 10th ed. 1812.
- - 11th ed. 1821.

Guides Vallot. Paris: Arthaud [pour] Groupe de
  Haute Montagne.

  La chaîne du Mont Blanc.
  1. Mont Blanc-Trélatête, par L. Devies [and
     others]. 2e éd. 1951.
     - - 3e éd., par L. Devies et P. Henry. 1973.
  2. Aiguilles de Chamonix, Grandes Jorasses, par
     L. Devies. 1947.
     - - Addendum. 1948.
     - - 2e éd. 1951.
     - - 3e éd., par L. Devies et P. Henry. 1977.
     - - 4e éd. 1978.
  3. Aiguille Verte, Dolent, Argentière, Trient, par
     L. Devies et P. Henry. 1949.
     - - 3e éd. 1966.
     - - 4e éd. 1975.

Guides Vallot.   Paris: Arthaud [for] Groupe de
Haute Montagne.

La chaîne du Mont Blanc. (Cont.)
4. Grandes Jorasses, Géant, Rochefort. Leschaux,
Talèfre, par Gino Buscaini et Lucien Devies.
1979.

Guides Vallot.   Paris: Fischbacher.

Description de la haute montagne dans le massif
du Mont-Blanc.
1. Les Aiguilles de Chamonix, par J. de Lépiney
[and others]. 1925.
- - 2e éd. 1926.
2. La chaîne de l'Aiguille Verte, par H. de
Ségogne [and others]. 1926.
4. Groupes du Mont-Blanc et de la Tour Ronde, par
J. Lagarde. 1930.
5. Les Aiguilles Rouges, par J. de Lépiney. 1928.
- - Nouv. éd. par A. Charlet [and others].
1946.
6 bis. Groupes du Chardonnet et du Tour entre les
cols du Chardonnet et de Balme, par P. Dalloz
[and others]. 1937.
7. Groupes de Trélatête et de Miage, par P. Henry
et M. Ichac. 1933.

Guides Vallot.   Paris: Fischbacher.

Description de la moyenne montagne dans le massif
du Mont-Blanc.
1. Chamonix, Mont-Blanc, par C. Vallot. 1927.

Guides Vallot.   Paris: Fischbacher.

Description générale du Mont-Blanc.
1. Tableau historique ..., par C. Vallot [and
others]. 1925.

Guides Vallot.   Grenoble: Arthaud.

Tourisme en montagne dans le massif du Mont-Blanc,
par C. Vallot. 1950.

GUIDETTI, Étienne
L'homme et le Mont Blanc. [Paris]: Hachette,
1957. 195p., plates (1 fold.), illus., maps,
bibl. 22cm. (Bibliothèque des guides bleus)

GUIGUES, Émile
En montagne: bêtes et gens de l'Embrunais; ...
eaux-fortes de Guigues d'Embrun. Grenoble: Didier
& Richard, 1929. 1v. (chiefly illus.). 47cm.
In portfolio.

GUIGUES, Émile
Séchot et Poulard; fantaisie alpestre. Grenoble:
E. Baratier, 1886. 97p., illus. 28cm.

GUILD, Curtis
Over the ocean; or, Sights and scenes in foreign
lands. Boston: Lee & Shepard, 1889. viii, 558p.
21cm.

GUILERA, Josep M
See
GUILERA I ALBINYANA, Josep María

GUILERA I ALBINYANA, Josep María
Carnet d'un esquiador, 1915-1930. Barcelona:
Llibreria Catalonia, 1931. xiv, 246p., plates,
illus. 20cm.

GUILERA I ALBINYANA, Josep María
Excursions pels Pireneus i els Alps; proleg d'En
F. Maspons i Anglasell; 56 fotografies dibuixos
de Joan Queralt. Barcelona: Llibreria Catalonia,
1927. 281p., plates, illus. 22cm.

GUILLARMOD, Charles Jacot
See
JACOT-GUILLARMOD, Charles

GUILLARMOD, J   Jacot
Six mois dans l'Himalaya, le Karakorum et L'Hindu-
Kush: voyages et explorations aux plus hautes montagnes du monde. Neuchatel: Sandoz, [1903?].
363p., plates (some fold., some col.), illus,
maps. 25cm.

GUILLEMIN, Amédée
La neige, la glace et les glaciers. Paris:
Hachette, 1891. xv, 275p., illus. 19cm. (Petite
encyclopédie populaire des sciences et de leurs
applications)

GUILLERMET, Jean
Lucien Vermorel, 12 décembre 1893 - 2 octobre
1921, 27 ans: [discours prononcés aux funerailles
de M. Lucien Vermorel ..., par Jean Guillermet and
others]. Macon: Printed by Protat, [1921]. 26p.
21cm.

BETTEX, Gustave and GUILLON, Édouard
Les Alpes suisses dans la littérature et dans
l'art. Lausanne: F. Rouge, 1915. 335p., plates,
illus. 22cm.

GUITON, Paul
Au coeur de la Savoie; préface de Henri Béraud.
Grenoble: J. Rey, 1926. 150p., 1 fold. plate,
illus., map. 22cm. (Les beaux pays)

GUITON, Paul
Le livre de la montagne: essai d'une esthétique du
paysage. Grenoble: Arthaud, 1943. 274p. 21cm.

GUITON, Paul
La Suisse. Grenoble: Arthaud, 1929-30. 2v., 2
fold. plates, illus., maps. 22cm. (Les beaux
pays)

GUITON, Paul
[La Suisse]. Switzerland, western and southern,
Neuchatel & Geneva to Ticino. Medici Society,
1929. 224p., illus., map (on lining papers).
21cm. (Picture guides)

GULLY, John
New Zealand scenery; chromo-lithographed after
original water-colour drawings; with descriptive
letterpress by Julius von Haast. Marcus Ward,
1877. 1v. (chiefly illus.). 55cm.

GUNNENG, Asbjørn and SCHLYTTER, Boye
Fører for bestigninger i Horungtindene; utarbeidet
av Norsk Tindeklub ved Asbjørn Gunneng og Boye
Schlytter. Oslo: Grøndahl, 1928. 19p., illus.
23cm.

GUNNENG, Asbjørn and SCHLYTTER, Boye
[Fører for bestigninger i Horungtindene]. Climbs
in the Horungtinder, Norway; edited [for] Norsk
Tindeklub by Asbjørn Gunneng and Boye Schlytter.
Oslo: Grøndahl, 1933. 23p., 1 fold.col. plate,
illus., map (in pocket). 23cm.

GUNTHER, A   E
A week on ski among the Silvretta, February-March
1932. Oxford, 1933. 11p., plates, illus., map.
30cm.
Offprint from Draconian, 1933.

GUROWSKI, Adam
Impressions et souvenirs: promenade en Suisse en
1845. Lausanne: Librarie Française et Étrangère,
1846. 308p. 18cm.

GURTNER, Othmar
Das besinnliche Wanderbüchlein: auf alten Pfaden
im Lauterbrunnental. Zürich: Orell Füssli, [1924].
105p., plates, illus., map. 19cm.

GURTNER, Othmar
Grindelwald: Festgabe zum 17. Grossen Skirennen
der Schweiz, 1923; im Auftrag des S.C. Grindelwald
hrsg. von Othmar Gurtner. Meiringen: Kunstanstalt
Brügger, 1923. 63p., illus. 24cm.

GURTNER, Othmar
Der Jungfrauführer: ein Ratgeber für Bergsteiger.
Oberländer: Wengen, 1925. 110p., illus., maps.
16cm.

GURTNER, Othmar
Schlechtwetter Fahrten; mit Federzeichnungen vom
Verfasser. Bern: G.U. Bäschlin, 1917. 94p.,
illus. 19cm.

KURZ, K   J   and GURTNER, Othmar
Zwischen Aare und Rhone. Bern: Pochon-Jent &
Bühler, 1920. 144p., illus. 19cm.

GURUNG, Harka
Annapurna to Djaulagiri: a decade of mountaineer-
ing in Nepal Himalaya, 1950-1960. Kathmandu:
Ministry of Information & Broadcasting, Dept. of
Information, 1968. 122p., plates (1 fold., some
col.), illus., maps, bibl. 23cm.

GUSEV, A   M
El'brus. Moskva: Gos. Izd. Geograficheskoi
Literatury, 1948. 70p., 1 fold. plate, illus.,
maps. 20cm.

MUKHIN, A   S   and GUSEV, V   F
Fanskie gory. Moskva: Gos. Izd. Geograficheskoi
Literatury, 1949. 152p., fold. plates, illus.,
maps, bibl. 21cm.

GUTMANN, Bruno
Kipo Kilja: ein Buch vom Kobo. Leipzig: Verlag der
Evangelisch-lutherischen Mission, [1922?]. 63p.,
plates, illus. 21cm.

GUYER, Gebhard A
Im Ballon über die Jungfrau nach Italien: Natur-
aufnahmen aus dem Freiballon; mit einem Anhang
Himmelfahrt, traversierung der Alpen im Ballon
"Cognac" von K. Falke. Berlin: Braunbeck &
Gutenberg, [1909]. 46p., plates, illus. 27cm.

GUYER, Gebhard A
Le project du chemin de fer de la Jungfrau, examiné
au point de vue scientifique, technique et
financier. Zürich: Imprimerie F. Schulthess, 1897.
80p. 35cm.
Signed Guyer-Zeller.
In portfolio with 10 maps.

GUYER, Gebhard A
[Le projet du chemin de fer...]. The proposed
Jungfrau Railway, rising to an altitude of 13670
feet, considered from its scientific, technical, and
financial aspects; [translated by Murray Jackson and
Charles King]. Zürich: Printed by F. Schulthess,
1897. 87p. 35cm.
Signed Guyer-Zeller.
In portfolio with 10 maps.

GUYER, Rosie
Hallo, die Berge! Eine Geschichte für Kinder; mit
5 Bildern von L.B. Strasser-Tappolet. Zürich:
Orell Füssli, 1921. 96p., illus. 18cm. (Schweizer
Jugendbücher, 10)

GUYER-ZELLER, Gebhard A
See
GUYER, Gebhard A

GWERCHER, Franz
Das Oetzthal in Tirol: eine statistisch-
topographische Studie. Innsbruck: Wagner, 1886.
vii, 136p., map. 20cm.

GYGER, W   J
Guide to climbs in the Upper Engadine. 3rd ed.
Samaden, St. Moritz: Engadin Press, 1925. 101p.,
illus., maps. 17cm.

GYPSY DAVY
See
BARRETT, Robert Le Moyne

H., Professeur
Nouveau guide du voyageur dans les XXII cantons
suisses; traduit d'un manuscrit allemand du Prof.
H. par R.W.; avec la nouvelle carte de la Suisse
de Weiss. Berne: J.J. Bourgdorfer, 1822. xxxvi,
434p., fold.col. map (as insert). 18cm.
In slip-case.

H., A.A.
Where the world ends: a description of Arosa as a
centre for summer holidays or winter sport and as
a health resort for convalescents and invalids, by
A.A.H. Arosa: [N.pub.], 1911. 95p., plates,
illus. 19cm.

H. A. L.
See
LEVESON, Henry Astbury

H., E.R.
See
HILL, E   R

H., G
See
HOFFMANN, Georg

H., K.
See
HEWAT, Kirkwood

H., S.M.
See
HOLWORTHY, Sophia Matilda

HAAS, Rudolf
Leuchtende Gipfel: Roman. Leipzig: Staackmann,
1925. 241p. 20cm.

HAAS, Rudolf
Die Stimme des Berges: Novelle. München: Rother,
1924. 84p. 23cm.

HAAST, Julius von
Geology of the provinces of Canterbury and
Westland, New Zealand: a report comprising the
results of official explorations. Christchurch:
Printed at the "Times" office, 1879. xi, 486p.,
plates (some fold., some col.), illus., maps.
24cm.

HAAST, Julius von
GULLY, John
New Zealand scenery; chromo-lithographed after
original water-colour drawings; with descriptive
letterpress by Julius von Haast. Marcus Ward,
1877. 1v. (chiefly illus.). 55cm.

HABEL, Jean
Ansichten aus Südamerika: Schilderung einer Reise
am La Plata, in den argentinischen Anden und an der
Westküste. Berlin: Reimer, 1897. xii, 76p.,
plates (some fold.), illus., map. 29cm.

HABEL, Jean
The North Fork of the Wapta (British Columbia).
[Boston], 1898. 327-336p., plates, illus., map.
25cm.
Offprint from Appalachia, v.8, 4 March 1898.

HABEL, Paul
COMPTON, Edward T
Die Hohe Tatra: sieben Farbendrucke und suchsund-
zwanzig Holzschnitte nach Aquarellen von E.T.
Compton; Text von Paul Habel. Leipzig: J.J. Weber,
[ca 1905]. [6]p., plates (some col.), illus., map.
44cm.
In portfolio.

HABELER, Peter
Everest, impossible victory. Arlington Books,
1979. 223p., col. plates, illus., map. 25cm.

HACKEL, Heinrich
Führer durch die Tennengebirge... Wien: Artaria,
1925. vii, 167p., plates, illus. 17cm.

HACQUET, Balthasar
Hacquet's Mineralogisch-botanische Lustreise, von dem Berg Terglou in Krain, zu dem Berg Glockner in Tyrol, im Jahr 1779 und 81. 2. veränderte und verm. Aufl. Wien: Kraus, 1784. 149p., 4 fold. plates,illus., map. 21cm.

HACQUET, Balthasar
Reise durch die Norischen Alpen physikalischen und andern Inhants, unternommen in den Jahren 1784 bis 1786. Nürnberg: In der Raspischen Handlung, 1791. 2 pts.in 1, fold. plates, illus., maps. 21cm.

HADFIELD, John
Modern stories of the open air, by H.E. Bates [and others]; edited by John Hadfield. Dent, 1936. v, 407p. 21cm.

HAENDCKE, Berthold
Architecture, sculpture et peinture. Berne: K.J. Wyss, 1892. 100p. 22cm. (Bibliographie nationale suisse)

HAENSEL, Carl
Der Kampf ums Matterhorn: Tatsachenroman. Stuttgart: J. Engelhorns Nachf., 1929. 275p. 18cm. (Lebendige Welt)

- - Ungekurzte Neuausg. [1929?].

HAENSEL, Carl
[Der Kampf ums Matterhorn]. La lutte pour le Cervin: roman de faits. Éd. française autorisé, traduction de Marcel Travey. Genève: J.-H. Jeheber, [ca 1930]. 212p., 1 plate, port. 20cm.

HÄRRY, A
Die historische Entwicklung der schweizerischen Verkehrswege, mit besonderer Berücksichtigung des Transits und der Fluss-Schiffahrt. 1. Teil. Die Grundlagen des Verkehrs und die historische Entwicklung des Landverkehrs. Frauenfeld: Huber, 1911. xv, 276p., plates, illus., maps. 26cm. (Nordostschweizerischer Verband für Schiffahrt Rhein-Bodensee. Verbandsschrift, 12)

HÄUFLER, Joseph
Panorama vom Schneeberge in Nieder-Oesterreich, und Hemiorama vom Wechsel an der österreichisch-steiermärkischen Grenze; nebst Andentungen zur Ersteigung dieser Berge und einer Karte des Schneeberges. Wien: P. Rohrmann, 1841. 36p., fold.plates, illus., map. 21cm.

HÄUSSER, Ludwig
Die Sage vom Tell aufs neue kritisch untersucht: eine... Preisschrift. Heidelberg: J.C.B. Mohr, 1840. xiv, 110p. 22cm.

HAGEN, Gunther
Die Schweiz: ein Bildwerk, gestaltet von Gunther Hagen; die Begleitworte schrieb Jaques Heffe. München-Pullach: L. Simon [1960?]. 1v. (chiefly illus.). 27cm.

HAGEN, Helge
Fører for bestigninger i Sunnmøre, Romsdal og Inderdal; utarbeidet av Norsk Tindeklub ved Helge Hagen ... G.N. Sabro... Oslo: Grøndahl, 1936. 22p., illus., map. 23cm.

HAGEN, Toni
Mount Everest: Aufbau, Erforschung und Bevölkerung des Everest-Gebietes, [von] Toni Hagen [and others]. Zürich: Orell Füssli, 1959. 234p., plates, illus., maps. 24cm.

HAGEN, Toni
Mount Everest: formation, population and exploration of the Everest region [by] Toni Hagen [and others]; translated by E. Noel Bowman. Oxford University Press, 1963. xiv, 195p., plates, illus., maps. 24cm.

HAGNAUER, G
FRANSCINI, Stefano
Der Kanton Tessin, historisch, geographisch, statistisch geschildert ...; ein Hand- und Hausbuch für Cantonsbürger und Reisende; nach der italienischen Handschrift von G. Hagnauer. St. Gallen, Bern: Huber, 1835. xii, 436p. 18cm. (Gemälde der Schweiz, 18)

HAGUE, James D
Clarence King memoirs [and] The Helmet of Mambrino, [by Clarence King]. New York: Putnam for the King Memorial Committee of the Century Association, 1904. vii, 429p., plates, ports. 22cm.
Produced under the direction of the King Memorial Committee, chairman, James D. Hague.

HAHN, C
Aus dem Kaukasus: Reisen und Studien: Beiträge zur Kenntnis des Landes. Leipzig: Duncker & Humblot, 1892-96. 2v. in 1. 25cm.
[Vol.2] has title: Kaukasische Reisen und Studien: neue Beiträge zur Kenntnis des kaukasischen Landes.

HAIG-THOMAS, David
Tracks in the snow. Hodder & Stoughton, 1939. 292p., plates, illus., maps. 21cm.

HALAŠA, Ján and MARTON, Štefan
Liptovské hole a Chočské pohorie. Martin. Vydavatel'stvo Osveta, 1958. [15]p., 148 plates, illus. 30cm.
In Czech, German and Slovak.

HALDER, Arnold
Bergluft: Sonntagsstreifereien eines alten Clubisten; mit einem Vorwort von Abraham Roth. Bern: J. Dalp, 1869. vi, 221p., illus. 19cm.

HALEM, G A
Blicke auf einem Theil Deutschlands, der Schweiz und Frankreichs bey einer Reise vom Jahr 1790. Hamburg: C.E. Bohn, 1791. 2v. in 1. 18cm.

HALEY, Frank
Fifty week-end walks in the Lake District; [selected and described by] Frank Haley. Hodder & Stoughton, 1954. xi, 116p., maps. 19cm.

Half hours in air and sky: marvels of the universe. W. Isbister, 1880. xiv, 375p., plates, illus. 18cm. (Half hour library of travel, nature and science for young readers)

Half hours in many lands. Nisbet [ca 1880]. xii, 372p., illus. 20cm. (Half hour library, 7)

HALL, Arthur Vine
"Table Mountain": pictures with pen and camera. Cape Town, London: Juta, []1897]. 23p., plates (some col.), illus. 23cm.

- - 3rd ed. Cape Town: Miller; London: Sampson Low, Marston, [1900].

HALL, Basil
Patchwork. E. Moxon, 1841. 3v. 20cm.
Essays on travel in Switzerland, Italy and France.

HALL, Charles A
The Isle of Arran. Black, 1912. 64p., col. plates, illus., map. 23cm. (Beautiful Britain)

HALL, Charlotte
Through the Tyrol to Venice. Nisbet, 1860. 388p., plates, illus. 20cm.

HALL, Henry S
The Coast Range from the north and east. [Banff, 1933]. 93-110p., plates (1 fold.), illus., map. 23cm.
Offprint from Canadian alpine journal, v.21, 1932.

HALL, Marshall
  The cruise of the Norna. London, 1871. 32p.
  18cm.
  Offprint from Field quarterly magazine and review.

HALL, Richard Watson
  The art of mountain tramping: practical hints for
  both walker and scrambler among the British peaks.
  H.F. & G. Witherby, 1932. 191p., plates, illus.
  23cm. (Sports and pastimes library)

HALL, Richard Watson
  Some Cumbrian climbs and equipment. Cockermouth:
  The Author, [1923?]. 35p. 19cm.

HALLAM, Julia Clark
  The story of a European tour. 2nd ed. Sioux City
  (Iowa): [The Author], 1901. 329p., illus. 21cm.

HALLBERG, F   and MÜCKENBRUNN, H
  Le ski par la technique moderne; avec une étude sur
  la physiologie du ski et une préface par A.
  Latarjet. 3e éd. Grenoble: Arthaud, 1932. 430p.,
  illus. 22cm.

HALLBERG, F   and MÜCKENBRUNN, H
  [Le ski par la technique moderne]. The complete
  book of ski-ing; English translation by Brian Lunn.
  Arnold, 1936. 317p., col. plates, illus. 24cm.

HALLER, Albrecht von
  [Die Alpen]. Alpengedicht; nebst einer natur-
  historischen Beschreibung der Alpen, von
  ebendemselben = Les Alpes... Berne: Société
  Typographique, 1795. 87p., illus. 21cm.
  Text in German and French.

HALLER, Albrecht von
  Die Alpen; mit einer Beilage und Kupfern; dem
  Andenken Hallers gewidmet von Karl Geiser. Bern:
  U. Francke, 1902. 40p., plates, illus. 32cm.

HALLER, Albrecht von
  [Die Alpen]. Les Alpes: poème de M. Haller;
  traduit en prose françoise par M. de T[scharner].
  [Gottingen, 1749]. 16p. 21cm.
  Offprint from Nouvelle bibliothèque germanique.

HALLER, Albrecht von
  [Die Alpen]. Ode sur les Alpes, par M. Albert de
  Haller; ornée d'une vignette pour chaque strophe
  par Mons. Herrliberguer. Berne: Brounner & Haller,
  1773. 76p., 27 plates, illus. 22cm.

HALLER, Albrecht von
  [Die Alpen]. Les Alpes; 16 lithographies originales
  de Victor Surbek. Lausanne: A. Gonin, 1944.
  113p., plates, illus. 28cm. (Collection des
  flambeaux, 4)
  Text and notes in French and German.

HALLER, Albrecht von
  Icones plantarum Helvetiae, ex ipsius Historia
  stirpium helveticarum denuo racusae ...; additis
  notis editoris [Jac. Sam. Wyttenbach]. Bernae:
  Sumptibus Societatis Typographicae, 1795. xxxviii,
  68p., 52 plates, illus. 44cm.

HALLER, Albrecht von
  Iter Helveticum anni MDCCXXXVIIII. Gottingae:
  Sumtu Reg. Univers. Offic. Librariae,1740. 120,
  72p., fold. plates, illus. 22cm.

HALLER, Albrecht von
  Poésies de Monsieur de Haller; traduites de
  l'allemand. Zuric: Heidegger, 1752. 228p. 17cm.

  - - Nouvelle éd. retouchée et augm. Berne: Wagner,
  1760. 2v.

HALLER, Albrecht von
  Versuch schweizerischer Gedichte. 11. verm. und
  verb. Aufl. Bern: Bey Typographischen Gesellschaft, 1777. 343p., illus. 19cm.

HALLER, Albrecht von
CUNCHE, Gabriel
  La renommée de A. de Haller en France: influence
  du poème Des Alpes sur la littérature descriptive
  du XVIIIe siècle. Neuchatel: Delachaux & Niestlé,
  [ca 1918]. 155p., bibl. 25cm.

HALLER, Gottlieb Emanuel von
  Bibliothek der Schweizer-Geschichte und aller
  Theile so dahin Bezug haben. Bern: Haller, 1785-
  88. 7v. 21cm.

HALLER, Gottlieb Emanuel von
  Erster Versuch einer kritischen Verzeichniss,
  aller Schriften, welche die Schweiz ansehen.
  Bern: Wagner, 1759. 246p. 18cm.

HALLIER, Ernst
KOCH, Wilhelm Daniel Joseph
  Taschenbuch der Deutschen und Schweizer Flora,
  enthaltend die genauer bekannten Pflanzen, welche
  in Deutschland, der Schweiz, in Preussen und
  Istrien ...; bearb. von Wilh. Dan. Jos. Koch.
  4. Aufl. Leipzig: Gebhardt & Reisland, 1856.
  lxxx, 583p. 18cm.

  - - Another ed. Nach der Original-Ausgabe ...
  gänzlich umgearb., von Ernst Hallier. Leipzig:
  Fues, 1878.

HALLIWELL, J   O
  Notes of family excursions in North Wales, taken
  chiefly from Rhyl, Abergele, Llandudno, and
  Bangor. The Author, 1860. 231p. 20cm.

HALLWORTH, Rodney
  The last flowers on earth. Maidstone: Angley
  Books, 1966. 167p., plates, illus., map. 21cm.

GIERTSEN, Ed B   and HALVORSEN, Adolph
  Norway illustrated 1888; editors: Ed. B. Giertsen
  and Adolph Halvorsen. Bergen: Ed. B. Giertsen,
  1888. 112p., illus. 34cm.

HAMEL, J
  Rélation de deux tentatives récentes pour monter
  sur le Mont-Blanc, par Mr le Docteur Hamel...
  Genève, 1820. 40p. 22cm.
  Offprint from Bibliothèque universelle, août 1820.

HAMEL, J
  [Rélation de deux tentatives ...]. Reisen auf
  den Montblanc im August 1820. Basel: J.G. Neukirk,
  1820. 29p. 20cm.
  Originally published in French in Bibliothèque
  universelle, août 1820.

HAMER, Samuel H
  The Dolomites; with ... illustrations in colour
  by Harry Rountree. Methuen, 1910. xi, 305p.,
  col. plates, illus., map (on lining paper). 23cm.
  2nd ed. rev., published in 1926 under title: A
  wayfarer in the Dolomites.

HAMER, Samuel H
  A wayfarer in the Dolomites. 2nd ed. rev.
  Methuen, 1926. xv, 207p., plates, illus., map
  (on lining paper). 20cm.
  First ed. published in 1910 under title: The
  Dolomites.

HAMERTON, Philip Gilbert
  The Saône: a summer voyage; with ... illustrations
  by Joseph Pennell and the author... Seeley, 1887.
  xix, 368p., plates, illus., maps. 30cm.

HAMILTON, Francis
  An account of the Kingdom of Nepal and of the
  territories annexed to this dominion by the House
  of Gorkha. Edinburgh: Constable; London: Hurst
  Robinson, 1819. viii, 365p., fold. plates, illus.
  28cm.

HAMILTON, Helen
  Mountain madness. Collins, 1922. ix, 274p.,
  plates, illus. 19cm.

HAMILTON, John
Angelica's ladies library; or Parental present;
[edited by John Hamilton]. [Shakespeare Library],
1794. vi, 440p. 21cm.

HAMILTON, Sir William
Campi Phlegraei: observations on the volcanoes of
of the two Sicilies as they have been communicated
to the Royal Society of London; to which ... a new
and accurate map is annexed, with ... plates
illuminated from drawings ... by the editor Peter
Fabris. Naples: [N.pub.], 1776. 90p., 54 plates,
illus. 46cm.
Text in English and French.

- - Supplement ... being An account of the great
eruption of Mount Vesuvius in ... August 1779.
1779.

HAMILTON, Sir William
Observations on Mount Vesuvius, Mount Etna, and
other volcanoes in a series of letters addressed
to the Royal Society; to which are added explanatory notes by the author. T. Cadell, 1772. iv,
179p., 5 plates, illus., map. 20cm.

- - 2nd ed. 1773.

HAMMER, Wilhelm
Geologischer Führer durch die Westtiroler Zentralalpen. Berlin: Berntraeger, 1922. viii, 150p.,
plates, illus. 16cm. (Reihe der Ostalpen-Führer.
Sammlung geologischer Führer, 22)

HAMSA, Bhagwān
The Holy Mountain, being the story of a pilgrimage
to Lake Mānas and of initiation of Mount Kailās in
Tibet; by Bhagwān Shri Hamsa; translated from the
Marāthi by Shri Purohit Swāmi; with an introduction
by W.B. Yeats. Faber & Faber, 1934. 203p.,
plates, illus. 21cm.

HANAUSEK, Ernst
Skiland zwischen Grossglockner und Rax. München:
Bruckmann, 1933. 68p., fold. plates, illus., map.
30cm.

HANBURY-TRACY, John
Black river of Tibet; foreword by Sir William
Goodenough. Muller, 1938. 305p., plates, illus.,
map (on lining papers). 23cm.

A hand-book for travellers in Denmark, Norway, Sweden,
and Iceland. 3rd. ed. rev. and corr. Murray,
1858. xxiv, 394p., 3 fold. plates, map, plans.
17cm.

A handbook for travellers in North Wales. 4th ed.
Murray, 1874. xxxviii, 216p., map (in pocket).
18cm.

Handbook for travellers in Norway. 5th ed. rev.
Murray, 1874. 232p., fold.col. plates, maps,
plans. 18cm.

- - 7th ed. rev. 1880.
- - 9th ed. rev. 1897.

Handbook for travellers in Russia, Poland, and
Finland, including the Crimea, Caucasus, Siberia,
and Central Asia. 5th ed. thoroughly rev. Murray,
1893. xiii, 84, 500p., fold. plates, maps (1 in
pocket), plans. 18cm.

A hand-book for travellers in Switzerland and the
Alps of Savoy and Piedmont, including the Protestant valleys of the Waldenses. Murray, 1838.
lx, 367p., maps. 19cm.

- - New ed. enl. 1839.
- - 16th ed. rev. 1879.
- - 19th ed. ... rev. Stanford, 1904.

A handbook to the English Lakes... Murray, 1889.
xliii, 161p., plates (2 fold.), maps (in pockets).
18cm. (Murray's English handbooks)

Handbuck für Reisende durch die Schweiz, [von H.
Heidegger]. Zürich: Orell, Gessner, Fuesli,
1787-90. 2 pts. in 1, fold.col. plate, map.
19cm.

- - 2. stark verm. und verb. Aufl. 1790-91.

Handbuch für Touristik und Fremdenverkehr. Wien:
Österreichische Bergsteiger-Zeitung, 1948. 558p.,
illus. 20cm.

HANKE, Hans
ÖSTERREICHISCHER ALPENVEREIN
100 Jahr Österreichischer Alpenverein, 1862-1962,
von Hans Hanke. Wien: Ö.A.V., 1962. 76p.,
plates (some fold., some col.), illus. 25cm.

HANKINSON, Alan
Camera on the crags: a portfolio of early rock
climbing photographs by the Abraham brothers;
selected and written by Alan Hankinson. Heinemann,
1975. 39p., 99 plates, illus., maps (on lining
papers). 29cm.

HANKINSON, Alan
Changabang, by Chris Bonington [and others];
[edited by Alan Hankinson]. Heinemann, 1975.
118p., col. plates, illus., maps. 26cm.

HANKINSON, Alan
The first tigers: the early history of rock climbing in the Lake District; [with a foreword by C.
Bonington]. Dent, 1972. xviii, 196p., plates,
illus., maps. 23cm.

HANKINSON, Alan
The mountain men: an early history of rock climbing in North Wales. Heinemann Educational, 1977.
ix, 202p., illus., map, bibl. 23cm.

Hannibal's passage of the Alps, by a member of the
University of Cambridge [i.e. Henry Lawes Long].
Whittaker, Treacher, & Arnot, 1830. vi, 158p.,
1 fold. plate, map. 19cm.

HANSJAKOB, Heinrich
Alpenrosen mit Dornen: Reiseerinnerungen. 4.
Aufl. Stuttgart: A. Bonz, 1911. 604p., illus.
18cm.

HARA, Makoto and ASAMI, Masao
Makalu 1970: Harukanaru mitoono one. Tokyo:
Meikeido, 1972. 404p., col. plates (some fold.),
illus., maps, bibl. 27cm.
The Japanese Makalu Expedition 1970, organised by
the Japanese Alpine Club.
In Japanese with an English summary.

HARCOURT, A   F   P
The Himalayan districts of Kooloo, Lahoul and
Spiti. Allen, 1871. viii, 381p., plates (1
fold., some col.), illus., map. 20cm.

HARDIE, Martin
NORGATE, Edward
Miniatura; or, The art of limning; edited from
the ms. in the Bodleian Library and collated with
other mss. by Martin Hardie. Oxford: Clarendon
Press, 1919. xxix, 111p. 20cm.

HARDIE, Martin
ALLEN, Warner
Our Italian front; painted by Martin Hardie; described by Warner Allen. Black, 1920. ix, 203p.,
col. plates (1 fold.), illus., map. 23cm.

HARDIE, Norman
In highest Nepal: our life among the Sherpas.
Allen & Unwin, 1957. 191p., plates (1 col.),
illus., maps. 22cm.

HARDING, Peter R   J   and MOULAM, Anthony J   J
A guide to Black rocks and Cratcliffe Tor.
Malvern: Climbers' Club, 1949. x, 27p., plates,
illus., bibl. 22cm. (Climbers' Club guides)
HARDING, Peter R   J
Llanberis Pass. Stockport: Climbers' Club 1950
(1955 reprint). 228p., plates, illus., map. 16cm.
(Climbing guides to the Snowdon District, 6)

HARDMAN, Sir William
   The letters and memoirs of Sir William Hardman.
   2nd series, 1863-65; annotated and edited by S.M.
   Ellis. C. Palmer, 1925. ix, 286p., plates,
   illus. 23cm.

HARDMEYER, J
   Locarno und seine Täler; neu bearb. von Hermann
   Aellen. 5. Aufl. Zürich: Orell Füssli, [1923].
   108p., plates (1 fold.), illus., maps. 20cm.

HARDMEYER, J
   Lugano und Umgebung; neu bearb. von Ed. Platzhoff-
   Lejeune. 5. Aufl. Zürich: Orell Füssli, [1916].
   125p., plates, illus., maps. 20cm. (Wanderbilder
   114, 115, 116)

HARDY, Joseph
   A picturesque and descriptive tour in the mountains of the high Pyrenees, comprising twenty-four
   views of the most interesting scenes, from
   original drawings taken on the spot... Ackermann,
   1825. vii, 84p., col. plates, illus. 26cm.

HARE, Augustus J   C
   South-eastern France. Allen, 1890. viii, 598p.,
   illus. 20cm.

HARE, Augustus J   C
   South-western France. Allen, 1890. viii, 664p.,
   1 fold.col. plate, illus., map. 20cm.

HAREUX, Ernest
   La Meije et les Écrins: ... gravures en couleurs.
   Grenoble: A. Gratier & J. Rey, [1907]. 1v. of
   col. illus. 34cm. (Les maîtres de la montagne)

HAREUX, Ernest
BAUD-BOVY, Daniel
   La Meije et les Écrins; ouvrage illustré de ...
   vignettes et ...planches hors texte en couleurs
   ... par Ernest Hareux. Grenoble: A. Gratier &
   J. Rey, [1907]. 119p., col. illus. 34cm.

HARGREAVES, A   T
   Dow Crag and other climbs, by A.T. Hargreaves [and
   others]; with illustrations by W. Heaton Cooper.
   Stockport: Fell & Rock Climbing Club, 1957.
   135p., 1 plate, illus. 16cm. (Rock-climbing
   guides to the English Lake District, 2nd [i.e.
   3rd] ser., 7)

HARGREAVES, A   T
   Dow Crag, Great Langdale and outlying crags, by
   A.T. Hargreaves [and others]; with illustrations by
   W. Heaton Cooper. Manchester: Fell & Rock Climbing
   Club, 1938. 176p., 1 col. plate, illus. 16cm.
   (Climbing guides to the English Lake District,
   [2nd ser.], 4)

HARGREAVES, A   T
   Scafell Group; with illustrations by W. Heaton
   Cooper. Manchester: Fell & Rock Climbing Club,
   1936. 115p., 1 col. plate, illus. 16cm. (Climbing
   guides to the English Lake District, [2nd ser.],2)

HARGREAVES, A   T
   Scafell Group, by A.T. Hargreaves, A.R. Dolphin
   and R. Miller; with illustrations by W. Heaton
   Cooper. Stockport: Fell & Rock Climbing Club,
   1956. 154p., 1 col. plate, illus. 16cm. (Rock-
   climbing guides to the English Lake District, 2nd
   [i.e. 3rd] ser., 6)

HARKER, George
   Easter climbs (the British Alpine Club). Sherratt
   & Hughes, 1913. 141p., 1 plate, port. 20cm.

HARMON, Byron
   128 views of the Canadian Rockies ... specially
   selected, the results of five years' wandering in
   the Rockies ...; photographed by Byron Harmon.
   Banff: The Author, 1911. 1v. of illus. 18 x 26cm.

HARPER, Andrew
   Tour of Mont Blanc: [walking guide]. Manchester:
   Cicerone Press, 1977. 99p., illus., map, bibl.
   19cm.
   Cover title: Walking guide to the tour of Mont
   Blanc.

HARPER, Arthur Paul
   Memories of mountains and men. Christchurch
   (N.Z.): Simpson & Williams, 1946. 208p., plates,
   illus. 24cm.

HARPER, Arthur Paul
   Pioneer work in the Alps of New Zealand: a record
   of the first exploration of the chief glaciers and
   ranges of the Southern Alps. Fisher Unwin, 1896.
   xvi, 336p., plates (1 fold.col.), illus., map.
   23cm.

HARPER, Arthur Paul
   Southern Alps of New Zealand. Wellington (N.Z.):
   Government Publicity Office, [191-?]. 24p.,
   illus., map, bibl. 25cm.
   Cover title: New Zealand's alpine wonders.

HARPER, Walter
STUCK, Hudson
   The ascent of Denali: first complete ascent of Mt.
   McKinley, highest peak in North America; contain-
   ing the original diary of Walter Harper, first man
   to achieve Denali's true summit. Seattle: The
   Mountaineers, 1977. xiii, xix, 188, A-Z, AA-FFp.,
   plates, illus., maps. 22cm.

Harper's Camping and scouting: an outdoor guide for
   American boys; consulting editors, George Bird
   Grinnell, Eugene L. Swan. New York, London: Harper,
   1911. xvii, 398p., illus. 21cm.

HARRER, Heinrich
   [Sieben Jahre in Tibet...]. Seven years in Tibet;
   translated from the German by Richard Graves; with
   an introduction by Peter Fleming. Hart-Davis,
   1953. xv, 288p., plates (1 col.), illus., map.
   23cm.

HARRER, Heinrich
   [Sieben Jahre in Tibet...]. Sept ans d'aventures
   au Tibet; traduction de Henri Daussy. Paris:
   Arthaud, 1953. 275p., plates (1 fold.), illus.,
   map. 23cm. (Collection "Les clefs de l'aventure",
   4)

HARRER, Heinrich
   [Die Weisse Spinne]. The White Spider; the history
   of the Eiger's North Face; translated by Hugh
   Merrick. Hart-Davis, 1959. 240p., plates (1
   fold.), illus. 24cm.

- - Rev. ed., with additional chapters by Heinrich
   Harrer and Kurt Maix. 1965.

HARRIMAN ALASKA EXPEDITION, 1899
   Alaska, giving the results of the Harriman Alaska
   Expedition carried out with the co-operation of
   the Washington Academy of Sciences, by John
   Burroughs [and others]. Murray, 1902- . Plates
   (some fold., some col.), illus., maps. 27cm.
   Vol.1. Narratives, glaciers, natives. 1902.-
   v.2. History, geography, resources. 1902-
   v.3. Glaciers and glaciation. New York: Doubleday,
   Page, 1904.-

CREW, Peter and HARRIS, Alan
   Tremadoc area: Tremadoc Rocks, Craig y Gelli and
   Carreg Hylldrem. Goring, Reading: West Col, 1970.
   106p., 16 plates, illus., map. 17cm.

HARRIS, George and HASLER, Graeme
   A land apart: the Mount Cook alpine region.
   Wellington (N.Z.): Reed, 1971. 224p., illus.
   (some col.), map (on lining paper), bibl. 30cm.

HARRIS, Walter B
   Tafilet: the narrative of a journey of exploration
   in the Atlas mountains and the oases of the north-
   west Sahara; illustrated by Maurice Romberg from
   sketches and photographs by the author. Edinburgh,
   London: Blackwood, 1895. xii, 386p., plates,
   illus., maps. 22cm.

HARRISON, Frederic
   My alpine jubilee 1851-1907. Smith, Elder, 1908.
   viii, 141p., 1 plate, port. 20cm.

HARRISSON, F
Among the mountains. The Author, [1892]. 62p.
19cm.

HARROP, A   J
Touring in New Zealand. Allen & Unwin, 1935.
295p., plates (1 fold.), illus., maps, bibl. 22cm.

HARSTER, Hermann
Kampf und Sieg in Schnee und Eis: Winterolympia
1936; hrsg., von Hermann Harster, Baron Peter Le
Fort. München: Knorr & Hirth, 1936. 111p.,
illus. 27cm.

HART, Henry C
SMITH, Walter Parry Haskett
Climbing in the British Isles,by W.P. Haskett
Smith [and H.C. Hart]; illustrations by Ellis Carr.
Longmans, Green, 1894-95. 3v., illus., maps.
16cm.
Vol.3 not published.

HART, John L   Jerome
Fourteen thousand feet: a history of the naming
and early ascents of the high Colorado peaks. 2nd
ed. and A climber's guide to the high Colorado
peaks, by Elinor Eppich Kingery. Denver: Colorado
Mountain Club, 1931. 71p., plates, illus., map.
23cm.

HARTMAN, C   J
C.J. Hartmans Handbok i Skandinaviens Flora,
innefattande Sveriges och Norges Växter, till och
med Mossorna. 11. helt och hallet omarbetade
Upplagan, utgifven af Carl Hartman. Stockholm:
Z. Haeggström, 1879. lxxxiii, 616p., bibl. 23cm.

HARTMAN, Carl
HARTMAN, C   J
C.J. Hartmans Handbok i Skandinaviens Flora,
innefattande Sveriges och Norges Växter, till och
med Mossorna. 11. helt och hallet omarbetade
Upplagan, utgifven af Carl Hartman. Stockholm:
Z. Haeggström, 1879. lxxxiii, 616p., bibl. 23cm.

HARTMANN, B   Blazidus
Firnenglühn neue gedichte. Luzern: E. Haag, 1923.
91p., illus. 21cm.

HARTMANN, G
Alpiner Hochleistungstest: eine interdisziplinäre
Studie; hrsg. von G. Hartmann ... unter dem
Patronat der Schweizerischen Stiftung für Alpine
Forschungen. Bern: Huber, 1973. [8], 152p.,
plates (1 fold.), illus., map, bibl. 23cm.

HARTMANN, Otto
Im Zauber des Hochgebirges: alpine Stimmungsbilder.
Regensburg: G.J. Manz, [1914]. vii, 436p., illus.
29cm.

HARTWIG, E   von
Briefe aus und über Tirol geschrieben in den Jahren
1843 bis 1845: ein Beitrag zur näheren Charakteristik dieses Alpenlandes im Allgemeinen und der
Meraner Gegend. Berlin: Duncker und Humblot, 1846.
xiv, 650p., plates, illus. 25cm.

HARVARD TRAVELLERS CLUB
Handbook of travel; [edited by Glover M. Allen].
Cambridge (Mass.): Harvard University Press, 1917.
544p., illus., bibl. 19cm.

HARVEY, Edmund George
MARRACK, Richard
How we did them in seventeen days! To wit: Belgium,
the Rhine, Switzerland, & France; described and
illustrated by one of ourselves [i.e. Richard
Marrack]; aided, assisted, encouraged, and abetted
by the other [i.e. Edmund G. Harvey]. Truro:
Printed by Lake & Lake, [1875]. 68p., plates,
illus. 20cm.
Cover title: Our rapid run.

Harwood's Illustrations of the Lakes. Harwood,
[1852?]. 1v. of illus. 15 x 23cm.
Cover title.

HASENCLEVER, Eleonore Noll
See
NOLL-HASENCLEVER, Eleonore

HASKETT-SMITH, Walter Parry
See
SMITH, Walter Parry Haskett

HASLEHUST, Ernest W
BRADLEY, Arthur Granville
The English Lakes; described by A.G. Bradley;
pictured by E.W. Haslehust. Blackie, 1910.
56p., col. plates, illus. 24cm. (Beautiful
England)

HASLER, G
The Bernese Oberland. Vol.1. From the Gemmi to
the Mönchjoch. Fisher Unwin, 1902. xxvii, 164p.,
14cm. (Conway and Coolidge's climbers' guides, 9)

HARRIS, George and HASLER, Graeme
A land apart: the Mount Cook alpine region.
Wellington (N.Z.): Reed, 1971. 224p., illus.
(some col.), map (on lining paper), bibl. 30cm.

HASLER (Firm)
Hasler, 1852-1952: hundert Jahre Fernmeldetechnik
und Präzisionsmechanik. Bern: Hasler, 1952.
250p., illus. 26cm.

HASLUND, Henning
Mongolian journey; translated from the Danish by
F.H. Lyon. Routledge & Kegan Paul, 1949. 232p.,
plates, illus., map. 23cm.

HASSALL, G   A
The northern Lake District. Part 1. Difficult to
Hard Severe; illustrated by R.B. Evans.
Manchester: Cicerone Press, 1969. 40p., illus.,
map. 17cm. (Climbs in Cumbria)

HASSE, Dietrich
Cordillera Real: Berliner Jubiläumsexpedition
1969. [Berlin]: Die Expedition, 1969. 64p.,
illus., maps. 22cm.
Summaries in English and Spanish.

HASSE, Dietrich and STUTTE, Heinz Lothar
Meteora Felsen: Wander- und Kletterführer;
verfasst nach den Richtlinien der UIAA. München:
Geo-Buch Verlag, 1977. 127p., illus., maps,
bibl. 17cm. (Wander- und Kletterführer, 1)

HASSELBRINK, F
Führer durch Graubündens Kurorte, Sommerfrischen
und Sportplätze; unter Mitwirkung der bündn.
Verkehrsvereine bearb. von F. Hasselbrink. Chur:
Der Verband, [1907]. 183p., 1 fold.col. plate,
illus., map. 18cm.

HASSELBRINK, F
[Führer durch Graubündens Kurorte ...]. Guide to
the health, pleasure, and sport resorts of the
Grisons [Graubünden]: compiled by F. Hasselbrink
in co-operation with the Grisons Public Interests
Associations;[translated by W.G. Lockett].
Davos: United Public Interests Associations of
the Canton of the Grisons, [1907]. 190p., illus.,
map. 18cm.

PETERMANN, A   and HASSENSTEIN, Bruno
Inner-Afrika nach dem Stande der geographischen
Kenntniss in den Jahren 1861 bis 1863. Gotha:
Perthes, 1863. 50, 164p., fold.col. plates,
illus., maps. 28cm.

HASTINGS, Somerville
Summer flowers of the high Alps. Dent, [1910].
xxvi, 85p., 39 col. plates, illus. 23cm.

HASTON, Dougal
The Eiger. Cassell, 1974. 170p., plates, illus.
23cm.

GILLMAN, Peter and HASTON, Dougal
Eiger direct; photographed by Christian Bonington.
Collins, 1966. 183p., plates (some col.), illus.
24cm.

HASTON, Dougal
In high places. Cassell, 1972. 168p., plates, illus. 23cm.

HATCHER, J   B
SCOTT, William B
Reports of the Princeton University Expeditions to Patagonia, 1896-1899; J.B. Hatcher in charge; edited by William B. Scott. Vol.1. Narrative and geography, by J.B. Hatcher. Princeton (N.J.): The University, 1903. 314p., plates, illus., map. 34cm.

HATTERSLEY-SMITH, Geoffrey
North of latitude eighty: the Defence Research Board in Ellesmere Island. Ottawa: Defence Research Board, 1974. ix, 121p., plates, illus., maps, bibl. 22cm.

HATTON, Pete
The Three Cliffs; diagrams by Brian Evans; photography by Ken Wilson. Manchester: Climbers' Club, 1974. x, 140p., illus., maps. 16cm. (Climbers' Club guides to Wales, 4)

HAUGHTON, Henry Lawrence
Sport and folklore in the Himalaya. Arnold, 1913. ix, 332p., plates, illus. 23cm.

HAUSER, Fritz, Baron
OEHNINGER, C   J
Die Alpenflora: 130 Abbildungen ... auf 24 Tafeln; mit besonderer Berücksichtigung der Ostalpen; nach der Natur gemalt von Baron Fritz Hauser; hrsg., mit Einleitung und begleitendem Text versehen von C.J. Oehninger. Graz: Selbstverlag von C.J. Oehninger, 1908. 79p., 24 col. plates, illus. 23cm.

- - 5. vollständig umgearb. Aufl. Reichenhall (Münster): C.J. Oehniger, 1922.

HAUSER, Günter
Die Hütten des Deutschen Alpenvereins ...; bearb. von Günter Hauser und Marianne Klotz. München: Deutscher Alpenverein, 1969. 361p., 1 fold.col. plate, illus., map (in pocket). 15cm.

HAUSER, Günter
[Ihr Herren Berge]. White mountain and tawny plain; translated from the German by Richard Rickett. Allen & Unwin, 1961. 224p., plates, illus., maps. 22cm.

HAUSHOFER, Albrecht
Pass-Staaten in den Alpen. Berlin: Vowinckel, 1928. 200p., plates (some fold.), maps, bibl. 22cm.

HAUSHOFER, Max
Tirol. Bielefeld: Velhagen & Klasing, 1899. 198p., plates, illus., map. 26cm. (Land und Leute: Monographien zur Erdkunde, 4)
In slip-case.

HAUSSEZ, Charles Le Mercher de Longpré, baron d'
Alpes et Danube; ou, Voyage en Suisse, Styrie, Hongrie et Transylvanie, pour faire suite au Voyage d'un exile. Paris: A. Dupont, 1837. 2v. 23cm.

HAVERGAL, Frances Ridley
Life chords, comprising "Zenith", "Loyal responses" and other poems. Nisbet, 1883. xii, 300p., plates, illus. 21cm.

HAVERGAL, Frances Ridley
Life mosaic, The ministry of song and Under the surface. Nisbet, 1879. x, 315p., plates, illus. 21cm.

HAVERGAL, Frances Ridley
Swiss letters and alpine poems, by the late Frances Ridley Havergal; edited by her sister, J. Miriam Crane. Nisbet, 1882. vii, 356p., plates, illus. 21cm.

HAWES, Sir Benjamin
A narrative of an ascent to the summit of Mont Blanc, made during the summer of 1827 by Mr. William Hawes and Mr. Charles Fellows. Printed for Benjamin Hawes by Arthur Taylor, 1828. 35p., 2 plates (1 fold.), illus., 25cm.

HAWES, William
FELLOWS, Sir Charles
A narrative of an ascent to the summit of Mont Blanc [made by Charles Fellows and William Hawes]. The Author, 1827. vii, 35p., plates, illus. 33cm.

HAWES, William
HAWES, Sir Benjamin
A narrative of an ascent to the summit of Mont Blanc, made during the summer of 1827 by Mr. William Hawes and Mr. Charles Fellows. Printed for Benjamin Hawes by Arthur Taylor, 1828. 35p., 2 plates (1 fold.), illus. 25cm.

COLES-FINCH, William and HAWKS, Ellison
Water in nature. Jack, [1911?]. 308p., 1 col. plate, illus. 22cm. ("Romance of reality" series)

HAXTHAUSEN, August Baron von
Transcaucasia: sketches of the nations and races between the Black Sea and the Caspian. Chapman and Hall, 1854. xxiv, 448p., plates (1 fold., some col.), illus., map. 24cm.

HAYATA, B
The vegetation of Mt. Fuji; with a complete list of plants found on the mountain and a botanical map showing their distribution. Tokyo: Maruzen-Kabushiki-Kaisha, 1911. 125p., plates (1 col.), illus., maps. 23cm.

HAYDEN, F   V
Sun pictures of Rocky Mountain scenery, with a description of the geographical and geological features, and some account of the resources of the Great West; containing ... photographic views along the line of the Pacific rail road, from Omaha to Sacramento. New York: J. Bien, 1870. viii, 150p., 30 plates, illus. 32cm.

BURRARD, Sir Sidney Gerald and HAYDEN, Sir Henry Hubert
A sketch of the geography and geology of the Himalaya mountains and Tibet. Calcutta: Superintendent Government Printing, India, 1907-1908. 4 pts. in 1. (vi, 308p.), plates, illus., maps. 4 pts. in 1. 32cm.

- - 2nd ed. Rev. by Sir Sidney Burrard and A.M. Heron. Delhi: Manager of Publications, 1933-34.

HAYDEN, Sir Henry Hubert and COSSON, César
Sport and travel in the highlands of Tibet; with an introduction by Sir Francis Younghusband. R. Cobden-Sanderson, 1927. xvi, 262p., plates (1 fold.col.), illus., map (in pocket). 23cm.

HAYDEN, John
A sketch of a tour in Switzerland in a series of letters to a friend. Jackson & Walford, 1959. viii, 105p. 14cm.

HAYWARD, Abraham
A selection from the correspondence of Abraham Hayward from 1834 to 1884, with an account of his early life; edited by Henry E. Carlisle. Murray, 1886. 2v. 21cm.

HAYWARD, Abraham
Some account of a journey across the Alps, in a letter to a friend, [by A. Hayward]. [The Author], [1834?]. 44p. 18cm.

THURMAN, John and HAZLEWOOD, Rex
The Gilwell camp fire book; collected, arranged, and on occasion invented by John Thurman and Rex Hazlewood; tunes arranged by A. Mackintosh. Rucsac ed. E. Pearson, 1964. 96p., music. 19cm.

HAZLEWOOD, Rex and THURMAN, John
The second Gilwell camp fire book: a further collection of songs and yells from fifty years of
scouting; collected, arranged, and on occasion
invented by Rex Hazlewood and John Thurman; tunes
arranged by A. Mackintosh. C.A. Pearson, 1962.
136p., music. 21cm.

HEAD, F   B
Rough notes taken during some rapid journeys
across the pampas and among the Andes. Murray,
1826. xii, 309p. 22cm.

- - 2nd ed. 1826.

HEADLEY, J   T
The Alps and the Rhine: a series of sketches.
Wiley & Putnam, 1846. vii, 138p. 20cm.

HEADLEY, J   T
Rambles and sketches: [a biographical sketch of
J.T. Headley]. New York: J.S. Taylor, 1852. ix,
312p. 20cm.

CHEEVER, George B   and HEADLEY, J   T
Travels among alpine scenery. Blackwood, 1855.
396p., plates, illus. 18cm.

HEADLEY, J   T
Travels in Italy, the Alps, and the Rhine. Dublin:
J. M'Glashan, 1849. 350p. 18cm.

HEATH, Charles
BLESSINGTON, Marguerite, Countess of
Heath's book of beauty; with beautifully finished
engravings from drawings by the first artists;
edited by the Countess of Blessington. Longman,
Brown, Green and Longmans, [18--]. vi, 280p.,
plates, illus. 25cm.

HEATH, Charles
BLESSINGTON, Marguerite, Countess of
The keepsake 1846; with ... engravings ... under
the superintendence of Charles Heath; edited by the
Countess of Blessington. Longman, Brown, Green and
Longmans, 1846. iv, 278p., plates, illus. 25cm.

HEATHCOTE, Evelyn D
Flowers of the Engadine; drawn from nature by
Evelyn D. Heathcote. Winchester: The Author, 1891.
32p., 224 col. plates, illus. 29cm.

HEATHMAN, W   G
Switzerland in 1854-5: a book of travel, men, &
things. Hope, 1855. vi, 408p. 23cm.

HEBER, A   Reeve and HEBER, Kathleen M
In Himalayan Tibet: a record of 12 years spent in
the topsy-turvy land of lesser Tibet with a description of its cheery folk... Seeley Service,
1926. 283p., plates (1 fold.), illus., map. 23cm.

HECKEL, Vilém
Climbing in the Caucasus, text by Josef Styrsa;
foreword by Sir John Hunt; translated by Till
Gottheiner. Spring Books, [1958?]. 208p., illus.
(some col.). 29cm.

HECKMAIR, Anderl
Bergsteigen für Anfänger und Fortgeschrittene.
München: Nymphenburger Verlagshandlung, 1975.
132p., illus., bibl. 22cm.

HECKMAIR, Anderl
[Mein Leben als Bergsteiger]. My life as a mountaineer; translated by Geoffrey Sutton. Gollancz,
1975. 224p., plates, illus., map. 23cm.

HECKMAIR, Anderl
Les trois derniers problèmes des Alpes: la face
nord du Cervin, la face nord des Grandes Jorasses,
la face nord de l'Eiger; avec un chapitre inédit
relatif à l'escalade de la Pointe Walker, (août
1951); traduction de Loulou Boulaz. Paris:
Arthaud, 1951. 177p., 39 plates, illus., map.
21cm. (Collection sempervivum, no. 15)

HECKMAIR, Anderl
Um die Eiger-Nordwand, [von] Heckmair [and
others]. 2. Aufl. München: Zentralverlag der
NSDAP, 1938. 159p., 2 plates (1 fold. in pocket),
illus., plan. 25cm.

HECKMAIR, Andreas
See
HECKMAIR, Anderl

HEDIN, Sven
Adventures in Tibet. Hurst and Blackett, 1904.
487p., illus. 23cm.

HEDIN, Sven
Central Asia and Tibet: towards the holy city of
Lassa. Hurst and Blackett, 1903. 2v., plates
(2 fold.col.), illus., maps. 25cm.

HEDIN, Sven
Mount Everest. Leipzig: Brockhaus, 1923. 194p.,
plates, illus., maps. 20cm.
In German.

HEDIN, Sven
My life as an explorer; with ... illustrations ...
by the author. Cassell, 1926. xii, 498p., 1 col.
plate, illus. 25cm.

HEDIN, Sven
Southern Tibet: discoveries in former times com-
pared with my own researches in 1906-1908.
Stockholm: Lithographic Institute of the General
Staff of the Swedish Army, 1917-22. 9v., plates
(some fold.), illus., maps. 28cm.

- - Atlas of Tibetan panoramas. 1917.
- - Maps. 1922. 2v. in 3.

HEDIN, Sven
Through Asia. Methuen, 1898. 2v., illus., map.
25cm.

HEDIN, Sven
Trans-Himalaya: discoveries and adventures in
Tibet. Macmillan, 1909-13. 3v., plates (some
fold.col.), illus., maps. 24cm.

HEDIN, Sven
MARGERIE, Emmanuel de
L'oeuvre de Sven Hedin et l'orographie du Tibet.
Paris, 1929. 139p., plates (some fold.), illus.,
maps. 26cm.
Offprint from Bulletin de la Section de Géo-
graphie du Comité des Travaux historiques et
scientifiques, 1928.

HEER, J   C
An heiligen Wassern: Roman aus dem schweizerischen
Hochgebirge. 6. Aufl. Stuttgart: Cotta, 1901.
399p. 21cm.

HEER, J   C
Ein Besuch der Jungfrau-Bahn, 4.-8. Juni 1898.
Zürich, 1898. 25p. 19cm.
Offprint from Neue Zürcher Zeitung.

HEER, J   C
Guide to Lucerne, the lake, and its envirens ...;
issued by the Official Committee of Local Development, Lucerne. 14th ed. Lucerne: Keller's Foreign
Printing Office, 1905. 188p., plates, illus.,
maps. 17cm.

HEER, J   C
Der König der Bernina: Roman aus dem
schweizerischen Hochgebirge. 4. Aufl. Stuttgart:
Cotta, 1900. 361p. 21cm.

HEER, J   C
The Lake of Lucerne and the Forest Cantons: album.
[Ed. de luxe], descriptive chapters by J.C. Heer;
translated from the German by John C. Milligan.
Zürich: Th. Schröter, 1900. 331p., plates, illus.
34cm.

HEER, J   C
Schweiz. Bielefeld: Velhagen & Klasing, 1899.
192p., plates, illus., maps. 27cm. (Land und
Leute, 5)

-- - 3. Aufl. 1907.
- - 4. Aufl., von Leo Wehrli. 1913.

HEER, J   C
Sommer in der Schweiz: illustrierter Reiseführer;
hrsg. unter Mitwirkung von J.C. Heer [and others].
Zürich: Bürgi, [1911]. 432p., plates, illus.,
maps. 20cm.

HEER, J   C
Streifzüge im Engadin. Frauenfeld: Huber, 1907.
202p. 19cm.

HEER, J   C
Winter in der Schweiz: Wintersport und Winterkuren;
unter mitwirkung von J.C. Heer [and others]; bearb.
von Edwin Furrer. Zürich: Bürgi, [1911]. 382p.,
illus., maps. 20cm.

HEER, Oswald
Arnold Escher von der Linth: Lebensbild eines
Naturforschers. Zürich: F. Schulthess, 1873.
385p., 1 plate, illus., port. 23cm.

HEER, Oswald
Contributions to the fossil flora of North Green-
land, being a description of the plants collected
by Mr. Edward Whymper during the summer of 1867.
London, 1869. 445-488p., col. plates, illus. 30cm.
Offprint from Philosophical Transactions of the
Royal Society, 1869.

HEER, Oswald
HEGETSCHWEILER, Johann
Flora der Schweiz; fortgesetzt und hrsg. von Osw.
Heer. Zürich: F. Schulthess, 1840. xxviii,
1139p., 8 plates, illus. 18cm.

HEER, Oswald
Ueber die nivale Flora der Schweiz. [Basel]: [The
Author], [1883]. 114p. 28cm.

HEER, Oswald
Die Urwelt der Schweiz. 2. Subscriptions-Ausg. der
2. umgearb. ... Aufl. Zürich: F. Schulthess, 1883.
xix, 713p., col. plates, illus. 25cm.

HEGER, Thomas
A tour through a part of the Netherlands, France,
and Switzerland, in the year 1817; containing a
variety of incidents, with the author's reflections... Longman, Hurst, Rees, Orme, & Browne, 1820.
xi, 250p., plates, illus. 24cm.

HEGETSCHWEILER, Johann
Flora der Schweiz; fortgesetzt und hrsg. von Osw.
Heer. Zürich: F. Schulthess, 1840. xxviii,
1139p., 8 plates, illus. 18cm.

HEGETSCHWEILER, Johann
SUTER, Joh. Rudolf
Helvetiens flora enthaltend die Phänerogamischen
Gewächse Helvetiens. Vol.2; zuerst bearb. Joh.
Rudolf Suter; verm. hrsg., von Joh. Hegetschweiler.
Zürich: Orell, Füssli, 1822. 504p. 15cm.

HEGETSCHWEILER, Johann
Reisen in den Gebirgstock zwischen Glarus und
Graubünden in den Jahren 1819, 1820 und 1822.
Zürich: Orell, Füssli, 1825. 193p., plates, illus.,
map. 22cm.

HEGETSCHWEILER, Johann
Sammlung von Schweizer Pflanzen; nach der Natur
und auf Stein gezeichnet von J.D. Labram; Text von
Joh. Hegetschweiler. Basel: H. Bienz, [1826-34].
8v., col. plates, illus. 18cm.

HEGI, Gustav and DUNZINGER, Gustav
Alpenflora: die verbreitetsten Alpenflanzen von
Bayern, Tirol und der Schweiz. München: J.F.
Lehmann, 1905. 66p., 30 col. plates, illus. 21cm.

- - 3. verb. Aufl. 1913.

HEGI, Gustav and DUNZINGER, Gustav
[Alpenflora]. Alpine flowers: the most common
alpine plants of Switzerland, Austria, and Bavaria,
by Gustav Hegi [and Gustav Dunzinger]. Authorized
translation by Winifred M. Deans. Blackie, 1930.
74p., 38 plates (chiefly col.), illus. 21cm.

HEGI, Gustav and DUNZINGER, Gustav
[Alpenflora]. Atlas colorié de la flore alpine...
Alpes suisses; [traduit] par J. Beauverie et L.
Faucheron d'après Hegi et Dunzinger; préface de R.
Gérard. Paris: Baillière, 1906. 98p., 30 col.
plates, illus. 22cm.

HEGNER, Johann Huldric
SCHEUCHZER, Johann Jacob
Στοιχειολογιαν ad Helvetiam applicatam ...
praeses J. Jac. Scheuchzerus, et respondens Joh.
Huldricus Hegnerus. Tiguri: Typis Davidis
Gessneri, 1700. 20p. 22cm.

HEIDEGGER, Heinrich
Handbuch für Reisende durch die Schweiz, [von H.
Heidegger]. Zürich: Orell, Gessner, Fuesli,
1787-90. 2 pts. in 1., 1 fold.col. plate, map.
19cm.

- - 2. stark verm. und verb. Aufl. 1790-91.
- - 3. stark verm. und verb. Aufl. 1796.
- - 4. verb. Aufl., [von J.G. Ebel und H. Heidegger];
[hrsg. von R. Glutz-Blotzheim]. 1918.
- - 5. verb. Aufl. 1823.
- - 6. verb. Aufl., hrsg. von J. Schoch. 1830.

HEIDEGGER, Heinrich
[Handbuch für Reisende in der Schweiz]. Manuel
de l'étranger qui voyage en Suisse, [par H.
Heidegger]. Zürich: Orell, Gessner, Füssli, 1790.
2 pts. in 1., 1 fold.col. plate, map. 19cm.

- - 4e éd. originale, [par J.G. Ebel et H.Heidegger];
[edited by Robert Glutz-Blotzheim]. 1819.

- - 3e éd. française, ... augm. [par J.C. Schoch].
1827.

HEILMANN, A
A. Heilmann's Alpine-Zeichen-Studien: lose Blätter
aus seinem Skizzenbuche zum Studium und zur Ver-
vollkommnung im landschaftlichen Zeichnen. Wien:
G. Freytag & Berndt, [1910]. 1v. of illus. 43cm.
In portfolio.

HEILPRIN, Angelo
The eruption of Pelée: a summary and discussion
of the phenomena and their sequels. Philadelphia:
Printed for the Geographical Society of
Philadelphia by J.B. Lippincott, 1908. 72p.,
plates, illus. 36cm.

HEIM, Albert
Die Alpen und ihr Vorland: Rundsicht vom Gipfel
des Sentis ...; im Auftrag der Section St. Gallen
des Schweizer-Alpen-Club aufgenommen & in Stein
gestochen von Albert Heim. St. Gallen: S.A.C.,
1871. 24cm.
Later eds. published under title: Rundsicht vom
Gipfel des Säntis...

BUSS, Ernst and HEIM, Albert
Der Bergsturz von Elm den 11. September 1881:
Denkschrift. Zürich: J. Wurster, 1881. 163p.,
plates (1 fold., some col.), maps. 26cm.

HEIM, Albert
Geologie der Hochalpen zwischen Reuss und Rhein
...; mit einem Anhang von petrographischen
Beiträgen von Carl Schmidt. Bern: Schmid,
Francke, 1891. xx, 503,77p., 8 plates (some fold.,
some col.), illus., bibl. 33cm. (Beiträge zur
geologischen Karte der Schweiz, Lfg. 25)

HEIM, Albert
Geologie der Schweiz. Leipzig: Tauchnitz, 1919-
22. 2v. in 3, plates (some fold., some col.),
illus., maps. 28cm.

HEIM, Albert
Die Gipfelflur der Alpen. Zürich, 1927. 25p.,
fold. plates, illus. 30cm.
Neujahrsblatt der Naturforschenden Gesellschaft
in Zürich, 1927, Stuck 129.

HEIM, Albert
Handbuch der Gletscherkunde. Stuttgart:
Engelhorn, 1885. xvi, 560p., 1 fold.col. plate,
map. 22cm. (Bibliothek geographischer
Handbücher)

HEIM, Albert
Panorama vom Pizzo Centrale; od., Tritthorn Sanct
Gotthard ...; aufgenommen u. auf Steingezeichnet
von Albert Heim. Zürich: Orell, Füssli, 1868.
8p., 1 fold.col. plate, illus. 19cm.

HEIM, Albert
Panorama vom Ruchen Glärnisch; für die Section
"Todi" des S.A.C. aufgenommen und auf Stein
gezeichnet von Albert Heim. Glarus: Senn &
Stricker, 1870. 20cm.

HEIM, Albert
Panorama von der grossen Mythe ...; für die
Mythengesellschaft aufgenommen & lithographiert
von Albert Heim. Schaffhausen, 1867. 7p., 1
fold. plate, illus. 20cm.

HEIM, Albert
Rundsicht vom Gipfel des Säntis ...; im Auftrag
der Sektion St. Gallen des Schweizer Alpenclub
aufgenommen und in Stein gestochen von Albert
Heim. 8. Aufl., Revision und Relieffton von Ed.
Imhof. Zürich: S.A.C., 1929. 26cm.
First ed. published in 1871 under title: Die
Alpen und ihr Vorland...

HEIM, Albert
Das Säntisgebirge; untersucht und dargestellt von
Alb. Heim; Mitarbeiter: Marie Jerosch [and others].
Bern: A. Francke, 1905. 2v., plates (some fold.,
col.), illus., map, bibl. 33cm. (Beiträge zur
geologischen Karte der Schweiz, Lfg. 46, N.F.
Lfg. 16)

HEIM, Arnold
Minya Gongkar: Forschungsreise ins Hochgebirge
von chinesisch Tibet, Erlebnisse und Entdeckungen
von Arnold Heim. Bern: Huber, 1933. 244p.,
plates (some fold., some col.), illus., maps.
24cm.

HEIM, Arnold
Negro Sahara, von der Guineaküste zum Mittelmeer.
Bern: Huber, 1934. 160p., plates (1 fold.),
illus., map, bibl. 25cm.

HEIM, Arnold and GANSSER, August
Thron der Götter: Erlebnisse der ersten
schweizerischen Himalaya-Expedition. Zürich:
Morgarten-Verlag, 1938. 270p., plates (some
fold.), illus., map (in pocket). 24cm.

HEIM, Arnold and GANSSER, August
[Thron der Götter]. The throne of the Gods: an
account of the first Swiss expedition to the
Himalayas; translated by Eden and Cedar Paul.
Macmillan, 1939. xxv, 235p., plates (some fold.),
illus., map (in pocket). 25cm.

HEIM, Maurice
Sur les pentes du Pamir. 2e éd. Paris: Sansot,
1922. 334p. 19cm.

HEINIGER, E   A
Nos quatre mille mètres; avant-propos d'Émile
Blanchet. Lausanne: J. Marguerat, [1943]. 1v.
(chiefly illus.). 29cm.

HEINRICH, Fritz
Manual for ski-babies. Oxford University Press
for National Union of Students, 1935. x, 94p.,
plates, illus. 20cm.

HEINRICH, G   A
TONNELLÉ, Alfred
Fragments sur l'art et la philosophie, suivis de
notes et pensées diverses, recueillis dans les
papiers de Alfred Tonnellé; publiés par G.-A.
Heinrich. 2e éd. Paris: Ch. Douniol, 1860.
411p. 24cm.

HELBRONNER, Paul
Description géométrique détaillée des Alpes
françaises. T.1. Chaîne méridienne de Savoie.
Paris: Gauthier-Villars, 1910. 508p., plates
(some fold.), illus. 34cm.

HELBRONNER, Paul
Une semaine au Mont Blanc, août 1893. Paris: G.
Steinheil, 1894. 61p. 22cm.

HELLENIC ALPINE CLUB
Olympos. Athens: The Club [1972]. Folder, map.
24cm.
Contains information about huts.

MILNE, Malcolm and HELLER, Mark
The book of European skiing; edited by Malcolm
Milne and Mark Heller. Barker, 1966. 304p.,
illus. (some col.). 30cm.

HELLER, Mark
Ski guide - Austria. Quartet Books, 1973. 215p.,
col. maps. 21cm. (Guardian/Quartet guides)

HELLMICH, Walter
Tiere der Alpen: ein Webweiser für Bergsteiger;
mit Zeichnungen des Verfassers ...; hrsg. vom
Hauptausschuss des Deutschen und Österreichischen
Alpenvereins. München: F. Bruckmann, 1936.
126p., 12 plates (some col.), illus., bibl. 19cm.

HELMHOLTZ, Hermann
TYNDALL, John
[The forms of water in clouds & rivers, ice &
glaciers]. Les glaciers et les transformations
de l'eau; suivis d'une conférence sur le même
sujet par M. Helmholtz, avec la réponse de M.
Tyndall. Paris: Germer Baillière, 1873. 264p.,
8 plates, illus. 22cm. (Bibliothèque scientifique internationale)

Helvetiorum Respublica; diversorum autorum quorum
nonnulli nunc primum in lucem prodeunt. Lugd.
Bat.: ex Officina Elzeviriana, 1627. 552p. 12cm.
Contains De Republica Helvetiorum, by Josias
Simler.

HÉMANN, N   J
Beautés et merveilles de la nature en Suisse.
Paris: Corbet, 1837. 233p., plates, illus. 18cm.

HEMINGWAY, J
Panorama of the beauties, curiosities, & antiquities of North Wales ... intended as a pocket
companion to the tourist and traveller. 2nd ed.
R. Groombridge, 1835. viii, 314, vip., plates
(1 fold.), illus., map. 16cm.

- - 3rd ed. corr. and improved. 1842.
- - 4th ed. corr. and improved. 1844.

HENDERSON, Ebenezer
Biblical researches and travels in Russia; including a tour in the Crimea, and the passage of the
Caucasus... Nisbet, 1826. xii, 537p., plates (2
fold.), illus., maps. 22cm.

HENDERSON, Ebenezer
Iceland; or, The journal of a residence in that
island, during the years 1814 and 1815, containing
observations on the natural phenomena... 2nd ed.
Edinburgh: Waugh & Innes, 1819. xv, 576p.,
plates (2 fold. col.), illus., map. 23cm.

HENDERSON, Ebenezer
The Vaudois, comprising observations made during
a tour to the Valleys of Piedmont, in the summer
of 1844... J. Snow, 1845. xii, 262p., 1 fold.
plate, map. 21cm.

HENDERSON, Kenneth Atwood
The American Alpine Club's handbook of American mountaineering. Boston: Houghton Mifflin, 1942. 239p., illus., bibl. 19cm.

HENRY, abbé
Guide du Valpelline: Valpelline, Ollomont, Oyace, Bionaz, Prarayé. 2e éd. Aoste: Société Éditrice Valdotaine, 1925. 134p., map. 19cm.

HENRY, J
Alpinisme. Aoste: Éditions "Augusta Praetoria", 1925. 70p., illus. 18cm.

DEVIES, Lucien and HENRY, Pierre
La chaîne du Mont Blanc. 1. Mont Blanc, Trélatête. 3e éd. [Paris]: Arthaud [pour] Groupe de Haute Montagne, 1973. 445p., illus., map. 17cm. (Guides Vallot)

- - 4e éd. 1978.

DEVIES, Lucien and HENRY, Pierre
La chaîne du Mont Blanc. 2. Les Aiguilles de Chamonix. 3e éd. Paris: Arthaud [pour] Groupe de Haute Montagne, 1977. 317p., illus., maps. 17cm. (Guides Vallot)

DEVIES, Lucien and HENRY, Pierre
La chaîne du Mont Blanc. 3. Aiguille Verte, Dolent, Argentière, Trient. Grenoble: Arthaud [pour] Groupe de Haute Montagne, 1949. 381p., illus. 17cm. (Guides Vallot)

- - 3e éd. 1966.
- - 4e éd. 1975.

HENRY, Pierre and ICHAC, Marcel
Description de la haute montagne dans le massif du Mont-Blanc. Fasc. 7. Groupes de Trélatête et de Miage (entre les cols de Miage, de la Seigne et du Bonhomme); avec la collaboration de Paul Gayet-Tancrède. Paris: Fischbacher, 1933. 117p., plates, illus., maps. 17cm. (Guides Vallot)

HENSHAW, Julia W
Mountain wild flowers of America: a simple and popular guide to the names and descriptions of the flowers that bloom above clouds. Boston (Mass.): Ginn, 1906. xxi, 384p., illus. 22cm.
Also published under title Mountain wild flowers of Canada. Revised version published in 1915 under title: Wild flowers of the North American mountains.

HENSHAW, Julia W
Mountain wild flowers of Canada. Toronto: W. Briggs, 1906. xxvii, 384p., illus. 22cm.
Also published under title: Mountain wild flowers of America. Revised version published in 1915 under title: Wild flowers of the North American mountains.

HENSHAW, Julia W
Wild flowers of the North American mountains. New York: R.M. McBride, 1915. 383p., col. plates, illus. 22cm.
Revised version of: Mountain wild flowers of America. Boston (Mass.): Ginn, 1906.

- - [Another ed.]. McBride, Nast, 1916.

HERBAGE, Gastón San Román
See
SAN ROMÁN HERBAGE, Gastón

HERBERT, Agnes
Casuals in the Caucasus: the diary of a sporting holiday. Lane, 1912. xi, 331p., plates, illus. 23cm.

HERBERT, Henry
A fortnight's journal, with a short account of the manner of his death on one of the Jura mountains, August 2, 1837. R. & W. Swale, 1838. 64p., 1 fold. plate, illus. 20cm.

HERBIG, Friedrich August
REICHARD, Heinrich August Ottakar
Passagier auf der Reise in Deutschland und der Schweiz, nach Amsterdam, Brüssel ...: Reisehandbuch für Jedermann. 12 Aufl. von neuem durchgesehen, berichtigt und ergänzt von F.A. Herbig. Berlin: F.A. Herbig, 1843. viii, 773p., plates, maps, plans. 18cm.
In slip-case.

Herbst-Tage im Berner Oberlande. Gera: E. Amthor, 1872. 211p. 16cm.

HERGESELL, H
DEUTSCHE ARKTISCHE ZEPPELIN-EXPEDITION, 1910
Mit Zeppelin nach Spitzbergen: Bilder von der Studienreise der deutschen arktischen Zeppelin-Expedition; mit einem Vorwort des Prinzen Heinrich von Preussen; hrsg. von A. Miethe und H. Hergesell. Berlin: Bong, 1911. 291p., col. plates, illus. 27cm.

HERING, George E
The mountains and lakes of Switzerland, the Tyrol, and Italy; from drawings made during a tour through those countries. M.A. Nattali, 1847. 1v. (chiefly illus.). 38cm.

HERITSCH, Franz
The Nappe theory in the Alps (alpine tectonics, 1905-1928); translated by P.G.H. Boswell. Methuen, 1929. xxxi, 228p., plates, illus., maps, bibl. 21cm.

HERLIBERGER, David
See
HERRLIBERGER, David

HERMAN, André
Vallons de l'Helvétie: impressions de voyage. Paris: Ollendorff, 1882. ii, 205p., 1 fold. plate, illus., map. 20cm.

HERMAN, Karel
Německo-Český Slovník pro horolezce = deutschtzchechisches Wörterbuch für Bergsteiger. Praha: Horolezecký Svaz, 1972. 432p. 25cm.

HERMANN, André and DIETERLEN, Jacques
Le ski pour tous: ce que tout skieur doit savoir. Paris: Flammarion, 1936. 268p., illus., bibl. 22cm. (La vie en montagne)

HERNÁNDEZ-PACHECO, Eduardo
SPAIN. Ministerio de Agricultura. Comisaría de Parques Nacionales
Guías de los sitios naturales de interés nacional; publicadas bajo la dirección de Eduardo Hernández-Pacheco. Madrid: La Comisaría, 1931-33. 3v., fold. plate (some col.), illus., maps, bibl. 20cm.

HEROLD, J Christopher
The Swiss without halos. New York: Columbia University Press, 1948. 271p., illus., maps, bibl. 24cm.

HERON, A M
BURRARD, Sir Sidney Gerald and HAYDEN, Sir Henry Hubert
A sketch of the geography and geology of the Himalaya mountains and Tibet. Calcutta: Superintendent Government Printing, India, 1907-08. 4 pts. in 1. (vi, 308p.), plates (some fold., some col.), illus., maps. 32cm.

- - 2nd ed. rev. by Sir Sidney Burrard and A.M. Heron. Delhi: Manager of Publications, 1933-34.

HERRENSCHWAND, colonel and JACOT-GUILLARMOD, Charles
Études du terrain: lecture des cartes reconnaissances et croquis. 2e éd. Berne: Erben, 1925. 60p., col. plates, illus., map. 28cm.

HERRLIBERGER, David
Abhandlung von den Eisgebirgen und Gletschern des Helvetier-Landes, als eine General-Einleitung zu der Alp-Topographie. Zürich: D. Herrliberger, 1774. xx, viii, 38p., plates (some fold.), illus. 22cm. (Neue Topographie Helvetischer Gebirge..., 1)

HERRLIBERGUER, David
HALLER, Albrecht von
[Die Alpen]. Ode sur les Alpes; ornée d'une
vignette pour chaque strophe par Mons.
Herrliberguer. Berne: Brounner & Haller, 1773.
76p., 27 plates, illus. 22cm.

HERRLIGKOFFER, Karl Maria
Im Banne des Nanga Parbat: Bildband der deutsch-
österreichischen Willy-Merkl-Gedächtnisexpedition
1953 zum Nanga Parbat; hrsg. von Karl M.
Herrligkoffer. München: Lehmann, 1953. 80p.,
illus., maps. 26cm.

HERRLIGKOFFER, Karl Maria
Nanga Parbat, incorporating the official report
of the Expedition of 1953; translated and
additional material supplied by Eleanor Brockett
and Anton Ehrenzweig. Elek, 1954. 254p.,
plates (some col.), illus., maps. 24cm.

HERRLIGKOFFER, Karl Maria
Nanga Parbat 1953. München: Lehmann, 1954.
xvi, 192p., plates (some col.), illus., map.
24cm.

HERRLIGKOFFER, Karl Maria
MERKL, Willy
Willy Merkl: ein weg zum Nanga Parbat; Leben,
Vortrage und nachgelassene Schriften hrsg., von
seinem Bruder Karl Herrligkoffer; unter Mitarbeit
von Fritz Schmitt. 2. Aufl. München: Rother,
1936. 235p., plates, illus. 26cm.

HERVIEU, Paul
L'Alpe homicide. Nouv. éd. Paris: A. Lemerre,
1903. 282p. 20cm.

HERVIEU, Sosthène
Souvenirs d'un touriste. Bayeux: Nicolle, 1841.
iv, 239p. 22cm.

HERZ, Mar
Oesterreichs Berge und Thäler: Kund- und Bade-
Reisebuch. Wien: F. Meyer, 1876. 326p., illus.
18cm.

HERZEN, Sergio
Entre rocas y nieves; ilustraciones de Néstor de
Basterrechea. Buenos Aires: Peuser, 1945.
159p., illus. 23cm.

HERZOG, Maurice
Annapurna premier 8,000; préface de Lucien Devies.
Paris: Arthaud, 1952. 302p., plates (1 fold., 1
col.), illus., maps. 20cm. (Collection
sempervivum, 16)

HERZOG, Maurice
[Annapurna premier 8,000]. Annapurna: conquest
of the first 8000-metre peak (26,493 feet);
translated by Nea Morin and Janet Adam Smith; with
an introduction by Eric Shipton. Cape, 1952.
288p., plates (1 fold., 1 col.), illus., maps.
21cm.

- - Another issue. Reprint Society, 1954.

HERZOG, Maurice
La montagne; ouvrage publié sous la direction de
Maurice Herzog [and others]. Paris: Larousse,
1956. 476p., col.plates, illus., maps. 30cm.

HERZOG, Maurice and ICHAC, Marcel
Regards vers l'Annapurna; préface de Lucien
Devies. Paris: Arthaud, 1951. xv, 96p., illus.
(some col.), map (as insert). 27cm.

HERZOG, Theodor
Bergfahrten in Südamerika. Stuttgart: Strecker
und Schröder, 1925. xvi, 212p., plates, illus.,
maps, bibl. 23cm.

HERZOG, Theodor
Der Kampf um die Weltberge; hrsg. von Th. Herzog
unter Mitarbeit führender Bergsteiger. München:
F. Bruckmann, 1934. 318p., 96 plates, illus.,
maps. 22cm.

HERZOG, Theodor
Rings um die Jungfraubahn: Naturbeobachtungen.
Zürich: J. Frey, 1926. 70p., plates, illus.,
bibl. 18cm.

HERZOG, Theodor
Vom Urwald zu den Gletschen der Kordillere: zwei
Forschungsreisen in Bolivia. Stuttgart:
Strecker & Schröder, 1913. xi, 270p., plates,
illus., maps, bibl. 26cm.

- - 2. neubearb. Aufl. 1923.

HESS, Adolfo
Indicatore, turistico, alpinistico, sciistico
del Piemonte. Torino: Ente Provinciale per il
Turismo, 1938. xv, 344p., map. 16cm.

HESS, Adolfo
Saggi sulla psicologia dell'alpinista: raccolta
di autobiografie psicologiche di alpinisti
viventi; con introduzione di Enrico Steinitzer:
La psicologia dell'alpinismo. Torino: S. Lattes,
1914. xii, 613p., ports, bibl. 21cm.

HESS, Adolfo
Trent'anni di alpinismo nella catena del Monte
Bianco. Novara: Istituto Geografico de Agostini,
1929. 182p., plates, illus. 33cm.

HESS, Hans
Die Gletscher. Braunschweig: Vieweg, 1904. xi,
426p., 4 fold.col. plates, illus., maps, bibl.
25cm.

BLÜMCKE, Adolf and HESS, Hans
Die Nachmessungen am Vernagtferner in den Jahren
1891, 1893 and 1895. Graz: D.u.Ö.A., 1897.
97-112p., 2 col. plates (1 fold.), maps. 29cm.
(Wissenschaftliche Ergänzungshefte zur Zeitschrift des D.u.Ö. Alpenvereins. Bd. 1, Heft 1,
Anhang)

BLÜMCKE, Adolf and HESS, Hans
Untersuchungen am Hintereisferner. München:
D.u.Ö.A., 1899. 87p., plates (some fold., 1 col),
illus., maps. 29cm. (Wissenschaftliche
Ergänzungshefte zur Zeitschrift des D.u.Ö Alpen-
vereins. Bd. 1, Heft 2)

PURTSCHELLER, Ludwig and HESS, Heinrich
Der Hochtourist in den Ostalpen. 5. Aufl.
begründet von Ludwig Purtscheller und Heinrich
Hess; neu hrsg. ... von Hanns Barth. Leipzig:
Bibliographisches Institut, 1925-30. 8v.,
plates, illus., maps. 16cm. (Meyers Reisebücher)

HESS, Heinrich
Spezialführer durch das Gesäuse und durch die
Ennstaler Gebirge, zwishen Admont und Eisenerz.
3 ... verm. Aufl... Wien: Artaria, 1895. xvi,
211p., plates,illus., maps. 18cm.

HESS, Heinrich
PURTSCHELLER, Ludwig
Uber Fels und Firn: Bergwanderungen; hrsg. von
H. Hess. München: F. Bruckmann, 1901. xxii,
362p., plates, illus. 28cm.

HETTNER, Alfred
Reisen in den columbianischen Anden. Leipzig:
Duncker & Humblot, 1888. x, 398p., 1 fold.col.
plate, map. 23cm.

HEUGLIN, Th. von
Die Tinne'sche Expedition im westlichen Nil-
Quellgebiet 1863 und 1864, aus dem Tagebuche von
Th. von Heuglin. Gotha: Perthes, 1865. viii,
46p., 1 fold.col. plate, map. 28cm.
(Ergänzungsheft zu Petermann's "Geographischen
Mittheilungen", no.15)

HEUSER, Emil
Neuer Pfalzführer: ein Reisehandbuch für die
banerische Pfalz und angrenzende Gebiete. 3...
Aufl. Neustadt an der Hardt: L. Witter, 1905.
3v., illus., maps. 21cm.
In slip-case.

HEUSSER, Chr
Das Erdbeben im Visperthal, Kanton Wallis, vom
Jahr 1855. 2. Ausg. Zürich: Orell, Füssli, 1856.
31p., 4 col. plates, illus. 26cm.
Cover title.

HEWAT, Kirkwood
My diary, being notes of a continental tour, from
the Mersey ... to the crater of Mount Vesuvius ...
to the top of Mont Blanc ... from Paris to the
Firth of Forth, by K[irkwood] H[ewat]. [Ayr?]:
[The Author], [1878]. 146p. 18cm.

HEWITT, H   B
GRAHAM, Peter
Peter Graham, mountain guide: an autobiography;
edited by H.B. Hewitt; foreword and epilogue by
John Pascoe. Wellington (N.Z.): Reed; London:
Allen & Unwin, 1965. xiv, 245p., plates, illus.,
maps. 24cm.

HEWITT, L   Rodney and DAVIDSON, Mavis M
The mountains of New Zealand. Wellington (N.Z.):
Reed, 1954. 128p., illus., maps. 26cm.

HEWITT, L   Rodney and DAVIDSON, Mavis M
The Southern Alps. Pt. 2. Mount Cook alpine
regions. Christchurch (N.Z.): Pegasus Press, 1953.
56p., plates, illus. 18cm. (New Zealand holiday
guides, no.8)

DE BEER, Sir Gavin and HEY, Max H
The first ascent of Mont Blanc. London, 1955.
236-255p, plates, illus. 26cm.
Offprint from Notes and records of the Royal
Society of London, v.2, no.2, March 1955.

HEY, Rebecca
Recollections of the Lakes and other poems, by the
author of "The moral of flowers ..." Tilt & Bogue,
1841. xvi, 284p. 19cm.

HEY, Wilson
The News Chronicle guide to mountaineering...
London, 1951. A single sheet poster, with illus.
65cm.
In question and answer form, the questions by
Wilson Hey, the answers by A.S. Pigott.
Reprinted from the News Chronicle, March, 1951.

HEYERDAHL, Thor
The Kon-Tiki Expedition: by raft across the South
Seas; translated by F.H. Lyon. Allen & Unwin,
1950. 235p., plates, illus. 23cm.

HEYN, Carl
BAUMBACH, Rudolf
Schildereien aus dem Alpenlande; ... Lichtdruck-
bilder nach Gemälden von Carl und Ernst Heyn;
Gedichte, von Rudolf Baumbach; Randzeichnungen von
Johann Stauffacher. Leipzig: A.G. Liebeskind,
1882. [84]p., illus. 49cm.

HICKLIN, John
Excursions in North Wales: a complete guide to the
tourist ...; edited by John Hicklin. Whittaker,
1847. ix, 208p., plates (1 fold.col.), illus.,
map. 16cm.

HICKLIN, John
The illustrated hand-book of North Wales: a guide
for the tourist, the antiquarian, and the angler.
Whittaker, [ca 1862]. 250p., plates (1 fold.),
illus., map. 19cm.

HICKS, James
Description of an improved mercurial barometer.
London, [1864]. 2p., illus. 23cm.
Offprint from Proceedings of the Royal Society,
no.62, 1864.

HIEBELER, Toni
Combats pour l'Eiger; traduction de Monique
Bittebierre. Paris: Arthaud, 1965. 306p., plates,
illus. 21cm. (Collection sempervivum, no.41)

HIEBELER, Toni
[Im Banne der Spinne]. North face in winter: the
first winter climb of the Eiger's north face,
March 1961; introduced and translated by Hugh
Merrick. Barrie & Rockliff, 1962. 121p., plates,
illus. 23cm.

HIELY, Ph
Escalades dans les Calanques: Marseilleveyre,
Vallon des Aiguilles. Marseille: Librarie de la
Bourse, [196-?]. 37p., 46 plates, illus., maps.
22cm.

HIELY, Ph
Escalades dans les Calanques: en Vau, Vallon de
Rampes. Marseille: Librarie de la Bourse,
[196-?]. 36p., 44 plates, illus., map. 22cm.

HIGGINS, Vera
SCHACHT, Wilhelm
[Der Steingarten und zeine Welt]. Rock gardens
and their plants; edited and translated by Vera
Higgins. Blandford Press, 1963. xv, 215p.,
plates (some col.), illus. 23cm.

HIGHTON, Hugh P
Shooting trips in Europe and Algeria, being a
record of sport in the Alps, Pyrenees, Norway,
Sweden, Corsica and Algeria. Witherby, 1921.
237p., plates, illus. 23cm.

Highways and by-ways; or, Tales of the roadside,
picked up in the French provinces by a walking
gentleman. 2nd ser. Vol.1. Printed for Henry
Colburn, 1825. 293p. 20cm.

HILL, E   R
Rambles and scrambles in the Tyrol, by E.R.H.
[i.e. E.R. Hill]. T. Woolmer, 1885. 141p.,
illus. 19cm.
Chapters 4 and 5 are by Henry Hill.

HILL, Henry
HILL, E   R
Rambles and scrambles in the Tyrol, by E.R.H.
[i.e. E.R. Hill]. T. Woolmer, 1885. 141p.,
illus. 19cm.
Chapters 4 and 5 are by Henry Hill.

Hill and dale: sketches of wild nature and country
life, [by various authors]. Hodder & Stoughton,
[1912]. 127p. 19cm. (Open air books)

HILLARY, Sir Edmund and LOWE, George
East of Everest: an account of the New Zealand
Alpine Club Himalayan Expedition to the Barun
Valley in 1954. Hodder & Stoughton, 1956. 70p.,
48 plates, illus., maps. 25cm.

HILLARY, Sir Edmund
From the ocean to the sky: [jet boating up the
Ganges]. Hodder and Stoughton, 1979. 272p.,
plates (some col.), illus., map (on lining
papers). 25cm.

HILLARY, Sir Edmund
High adventure. Hodder & Stoughton, 1955.
224p., plates (1 col.), illus., maps. 22cm.

HILLARY, Sir Edmund
[High adventure]. L'aventure est sur les cimes
...; traduit de l'anglais par André Cubzac.
Paris: Amiot Dumont, 1955. 211p., plates, illus.,
2 maps. 22cm. (Collection étoile filante;
bibliothèque de l'alpinisme)

HILLARY, Sir Edmund and DOIG, Desmond
High in the thin cold air. Hodder & Stoughton,
1963. 287p., plates, illus., maps (on lining
papers). 23cm.

HILLARY, Sir Edmund
No latitude for error. Hodder & Stoughton, 1961.
255p., illus., maps. 24cm.

HILLARY, Sir Edmund
  Nothing venture, nothing win. Hodder and
  Stoughton, 1975. 319p., plates (some col.),
  illus., maps. 25cm.

HILLARY, Sir Edmund
  [Nothing venture, nothing win]. Arrischiare per
  vincere; traduzione ... e introduzione di Luciano
  Serra. [Milano]: dall'Oglio, 1976. 405p.,
  plates (some col.), illus. 21cm. (Exploits)

HILLARY, Sir Edmund
  Schoolhouse in the clouds. Hodder & Stoughton,
  1964. xi, 180p., plates, illus., map. 22cm.

HILLS, Denis
  My travels in Turkey. Allen & Unwin, 1964. 252p.,
  plates (1 col.), illus., maps (on lining papers),
  bibl. 23cm.

HILTBRUNNER, Hermann
WOLGENSINGER, Michael
  L'Engadine: terra Ladina, texte de Hermann
  Hiltbrunner. Lausanne: J. Marguerat, 1944. 71p.,
  illus. 29cm.

HILTBRUNNER, Hermann
  Graubünden; illustriert von Christian u. Hans
  Meisser; hrsg. von Christian Meisser. Genf:
  SADAG, [1928]. 3v., illus., maps. 25cm.
  Library lacks v.2.

HILTBRUNNER, Hermann
  [Graubünden]. Les Grisons. [T.1]. Le Rhin: la
  contrée de sa naissance; adapté ... par J. Volmar;
  illustrations de Christian et Jean Meisser; préface
  de Félix Calonder. Paris: Éditions Pittoresques,
  [1928]. 220p., illus., map. 25cm.

HIMALAYAN CLUB
  Classified catalogue of books, with alphabetical
  index of authors. Simla: The Club, 1929. 66p.
  25cm.
  Cover title.

HIMALAYAN CLUB
  A climber's guide to Sonamarg, Kashmir. New Delhi:
  The Club [1945]. vii, 51p., plates (1 fold.),
  illus., map. 23cm.

HIMALAYAN CLUB
  Expedition reports: Nepal Himalayas, pre-monsoon
  season 1976, by M.J. Cheney. Kathmandu: The Club,
  1976. 6 leaves. 33cm.
  Typescript.

HIMALAYAN MOUNTAINEERING INSTITUTE, Darjeeling
  Himalayan Mountaineering Institute. Darjeeling:
  The Institute [1977]. [32]p., illus. (some col.).
  21cm.

HINCHLIFF, Thomas Woodbine
  Over the sea and far away, being a narrative of
  wanderings round the world. Longmans, Green, 1876.
  xv, 416p., plates, illus. 24cm.

HINCHLIFF, Thomas Woodbine
  South American sketches; or, A visit to Rio
  Janeiro, the Organ Mountains, La Plata, and the
  Paraná. Longman, Green, Longman, Roberts, & Green,
  1863. xix, 414p., plates (1 fold., some col.),
  illus., map. 21cm.

HINCHLIFF, Thomas Woodbine
  Summer months among the Alps: with the ascent of
  Monte Rosa. Longman, Brown, Green, Longmans, &
  Roberts, 1857. xvi, 312p., fold.col. plates,
  maps. 21cm.

HIND, Henry Youle
  Narrative of the Canadian Red River exploring
  expedition of 1857 and of the Assinniboine and
  Saskatchewan exploring expedition of 1858.
  Longman, Green, Longman & Roberts, 1860. 2v., col.
  plates (1 fold.), illus., maps. 24cm.

HIND, Henry Youle
  North-west Territory: reports of progress; together with a preliminary and general report on
  the Assiniboine and Saskatchewan exploring expedition... Toronto: Lovell, 1859. xii, 201p.,
  plates (some fold., some col.), illus., maps.
  32cm.

HINGSTON, R   W   G
  A naturalist in Himalaya. H.F. & G. Witherby,
  1920. xii, 300p., plates, illus., map. 23cm.

HINKS, Arthur Robert
  Hints to travellers. 11th ed. Royal Geographical Society, 1935-38. 2v., fold plates (some
  col.), illus., maps. 18cm.
  Vol.1 by E.A. Reeves. - v.2, edited by the
  Secretary [i.e. A.R. Hinks] with the help of many
  travellers.

HINKS, Arthur Robert
BLAKENEY, Thomas Sydney
  A.R. Hinks and the first Everest Expedition,
  1921. London, 1970. 333-343p., plates, illus.,
  bibl. 25cm.
  Offprint from Geographical journal, v.136, pt. 3,
  September 1970.

HINTERBERGER, Fritz
  Bergsteigerschule. Wien: H. Kapri, [1936]. 96p.,
  illus. 17cm.

HIRSCHBERGER, Hermann
  See
SCHWAIGHOFER, Hermann

HIRST, John
RUCKSACK CLUB
  The songs of the mountaineers; collected and
  edited by John Hirst, for the Rucksack Club.
  Manchester: Rucksack Club, [1922]. 124p. 19cm.

HIRZEL, Heinrich
  Eugenias Briefe an ihre Mutter, geschrieben auf
  einer Reise nach den Bädern von Leuk im Sommer
  1806; hrsg. von Heinrich Hirzel. Zürich: Orell
  Füssli, 1809-20. 3v. 23cm.

HIRZEL-ESCHER, Hans Caspar
  Wanderungen in weniger besuchte Alpengegenden der
  Schweiz und ihrer nächsten Umgebungen. Zürich:
  Orell, Füssli, 1829. 168p. 17cm.

HISSEY, J   J
HUSON, T
  Round about Snowdon: thirty plates by T. Huson;
  with notes by J.J. Hissey. Seeley, 1894. 1v.
  (chiefly illus.). 33cm.

Historische, geographische und physikalische
Beschreibung des Schweizerlandes ...
  See
Dictionnaire géographique, historique et politique
de la Suisse

Historische, topographische und oekonomische Merkwürdigkeit des Kantons Luzern, seinen Mitbürgern
  gewidmet, von [J.] von Balthasar. Luzern: J.A.
  Salzmann, 1785-89. 3v. 17cm.

HISTORISCHER VEREIN VON OBERWALLIS
  See
GESCHICHTSFORSCHENDE VEREIN VON OBERWALLIS

The history of Switzerland, [by John Wilson].
  Longman, Brown, Green & Longmans, [1832]. xx,
  360p. 18cm. (Cabinet cyclopaedia)

HOBBS, William Herbert
  Characteristics of existing glaciers. New York:
  Macmillan, 1911. xxiv, 301p., plates, illus.,
  maps, bibl. 24cm.

HOBBS, William Herbert
  Les glaciers du mond actuel; traduit de l'anglais
  par A. Allix et J. Blache. Grenoble, 1922.
  99p., plates, illus. 26cm.
  Offprint from Revue de géographie alpine
  (Université de Grenoble) v.10, 1922.

HOBSON, John A
LLOYD, Henry Demarest
  The Swiss democracy: the study of a sovereign
  people; edited by John A. Hobson. Fisher Unwin,
  1908. xvi, 273p., plates, illus. 21cm.

HOCHALPINE FORSCHUNGSSTATION JUNGFRAUJOCH
  See
JUNGFRAUJOCH SCIENTIFIC STATION

HOCKING, Silas K
  The great hazard. Fisher Unwin, 1915. 383p.
  20cm.

HOCKING, Silas K
  Up the Rhine and over the Alps. Crombie, [1886].
  iv, 187p., plates, illus. 19cm.

HODDER, Edwin
  John MacGregor ("Rob Roy")... Hodder, 1894. xiv,
  458p., plates, illus. 23cm.

- - Popular ed. 1895.

HODGE, Edmund W
  Enjoying the Lakes: from post-chaise to National
  Park. Edinburgh, London: Oliver & Boyd, 1957. x,
  221p., plates, illus., maps. 23cm.

HODGE, Edmund W
NAISMITH, W   W
  The Islands of Scotland (excluding Skye); edited
  by W.W. Naismith. Edinburgh: Scottish Mountaineering Club, 1934. 135p., plates (some fold., some
  col.), illus., maps, bibl. 23cm. (Scottish
  Mountaineering Club guides)
- - 2nd ed., edited by W.W. Naismith and E.W. Hodge.
  1952.

HODGE, Edmund W
  The Northern Highlands. 3rd ed. Edinburgh:
  Scottish Mountaineering Club, 1953. 162p., plates
  (1 fold.), illus., maps. 23cm. (Scottish
  Mountaineering Club guides)

HODGKIN, Robin A
  Reconnaisance on an educational frontier. Oxford
  University Press, 1970. xi, 108p., illus., bibl.
  21cm.

HODGKINSON, George C
  Actinometrical observations among the Alps with
  the description of a new actinometer. London,
  1867. 321-330p. 23cm.
  Offprint from Proceedings of the Royal Society,
  no.89, 1867.

HODGSON, Randolph L
  On plain and peak: sporting and other sketches of
  Bohemia and Tyrol. Constable, 1898. viii, 254p.,
  plates, illus. 24cm.

HÜCKER, Paul Oskar
  Die Sonne von St. Moritz: Roman. Berlin: Allstein,
  1910. 304p. 16cm. (Allstein-Bucher)

HOEGEL, Hugo
  Führer in das Lavantthal in Kärnten; hrsg. von der
  Section Wolfsberg des Deutschen und
  Österreichischen Alpenvereins. Wolfsberg: Die
  Section, 1884. 84p., plates, map. 18cm.

Höhenklima und Bergwanderungen in ihrer Wirkung auf
  den Menschen: Ergebnisse experimenteller
  Forschungen im Hochgebirge und Laboratorium, von
  N. Zuntz [and others]. Berlin: Bong, 1906. xvi,
  494p., plates (some fold., 1 col.), illus. 31cm.

HÖHNEL, Ludwig von
  Discovery of Lakes Rudolf and Stephanie: a narrative of Count Samuel Teleki's exploring and hunting
  expedition in eastern equatorial Africa in 1887
  and 1888. Longmans, Green, 1894. 2v., 2 fold.col.
  plates, illus., maps. 26cm.

HOEK, Henry
  Alpine Wetterkunde. Leipzig, [1931]. 83-104p. 27cm.
  Offprint from Alpines Handbuch; hrsg. vom Deutschen
  und Österreichischen Alpenverein, 1.

HOEK, Henry
  Am Hüttenfeuer: erlebte und erlogene Abenteuer;
  mit ... Zeichnungen von Hella Jacobs. Hamburg:
  Enoch, 1935. 207p., illus. 18cm.

HOEK, Henry
  Aus Bolivias Bergen. Leipzig: Brockhaus, 1927.
  159p., plates, illus., maps. 20cm. (Reisen und
  Abenteuer, 39)

HOEK, Henry
  [Aus Bolivias Bergen]. Por las montañas de
  Bolivia; traducion por Emilio R. Sadía. Madrid:
  Bruno del Amo, 1929. 159p., plates, illus., map.
  18cm. (Viajes y aventuras, 4)

HOEK, Henry
  Die Aussicht vom Berge. [Bern, 1944]. 15p.
  26cm.
  Offprint from Die Alpen, Hefte 3-5, 1944.

HOEK, Henry
  Berg- und Wanderlieder. Wien: J. Gallhuber,
  [1926]. 47p. 17cm.

HOEK, Henry
  Davos: ein Berg- und Wanderbuch. Hamburg: Enoch,
  1934. 183p., illus. 19cm.

HOEK, Henry
  Davos, Parsenn: Sommerwanderungen im Parsenn-
  gebiet. [Davos]: Davos-Parsennbahn, [1939].
  12p., plates, illus., map. 18cm.
  Cover title.

HOEK, Henry
FREI, Hermann
  [Davoser Skitouren]. The best ski-tours of
  Davos; compiled by Henry Hoek, being an adapta-
  tion of Hermann Frei's "Davoser Skitouren";
  English by W.G. and L.M. Lockett. Hamburg:
  Enoch, 1927. viii, 96p. 18cm.

HOEK, Henry
  Der denkende Wanderer. Wien: Reichenstein-Verlag,
  1929. 190p., plates, illus. 18cm.

HOEK, Henry
  "Dir ...": ein Band Gedichte. 2.Aufl. München:
  Rother, 1925. 126p. 19cm.

HOEK, Henry
  Geologische Untersuchungen im Plessurgebirge um
  Arosa. Freiburg i.Br., 1903. 56p., fold plates,
  illus., bibl. 24cm.
  Offprint from Berichte der Naturforschenden
  Gesellschaft zu Freiburg i.Br., Bd.13, 1903.

HOEK, Henry
  Hans Beat Wieland, der Mahler der Berge.
  München, 1928. 13p., plates (1 col.), illus.
  27cm.
  Offprint from Zeitschrift des Deutschen und
  Österreichischen Alpenvereins, Bd.59, 1928.

HOEK, Henry
  Ma bella Engiadina: Ski und Schnee im Engadin.
  Hamburg: Enoch, 1933. 224p., illus., maps. 20cm.

HOEK, Henry
  Merkbuch für Schiläufer in 500 Sätzen. München:
  Rother, 1921. 46p. 19cm.

HOEK, Henry
  Moderne Wintermärchen. München: Rother, 1926.
  115p. 19cm.

HOEK, Henry
  Parsenn: berühmte Abfahrten in Bildern und Buch-
  staben. Hamburg: Enoch, 1932. 192p., illus.,
  plans. 20cm.

- - New and rev. ed. Zürich: Fretz & Wasmuth, 1939.

HOEK, Henry
  St. Moritz: Dorf, Bad, Campfèr; ein Führer und
  Reisebegleiter im Auftrag ... des Kur- und
  Verkehrs-Vereins ...; bearb. von H.Hoek. Zürich:
  Orell Füssli, [1931]. 291p., fold. plates (1
  col.), illus., map. 17cm.

HOEK, Henry
Schnee, Sonne und Ski: ein Buch über den Frühling
im Hochgebirge. Leipzig: Brockhaus, 1926. 166p.,
illus. 20cm.

HOEK, Henry and WALLAU, Heinrich
Schi-Fahrten im südlichen Schwarzwald. München:
G. Lammers, 1908. xx, 71p., maps. 17cm.

- - 2. verm. und verb. Aufl. München: Deutsche
Alpenzeitung, 1911.

HOEK, Henry and RICHARDSON, E   C
Der Schi und seine sportliche Benutzung
See their
Der Ski und seine sportliche Benutzung

HOEK, Henry
Schussfahrt und Schwung: ein brevier alpiner
Abfahrten. Hamburg: Enoch, 1931. 126p., plates,
illus. 19cm.

FREI, Hermann and HOEK, Henry
Ski-Touren in den Bergen um Davos: ein Führer.
Davos: Verkehrsverein Davos, 1932. 174p. 17cm.

HOEK, Henry
Ski-tours round Lenzerheide. Munich: Hochalpen-
Verlag, 1925. 63p. 18cm.

HOEK, Henry and RICHARDON, E   C
Der Ski und seine sportliche Benutzung ...,
besorgt von Henry Hoek. München: G. Lammers, 1906.
viii, 196p., plates, illus. 20cm.
Based on the 2nd ed. of E.C. Richardon's Ski-
running.

- - 3. deutsche Aufl. 1908.
- - 4. deutsche Aufl. 1910.
- - 5. Aufl. München: Deutsche Alpenzeitung, 1911.

HOEK, Henry
Skiheil, Kamerad! Skikurs für eine Freundin; mit
Zeichnungen von Hella Jacobs. 3 Aufl. Hamburg:
Enoch, 1934. 79p., illus. 20cm.

HOEK, Henry
Sport, Sporttrieb, Sportbetrieb. Leipzig:
Brockhaus, 1927. 223p. 20cm.

HOEK, Henry
Über Berge und Bergsteigen: drei kritische
Aufsätze; mit Vor- und Schlusswort. München:
Bergverlag, 1920. 71p. 20cm.

HOEK, Henry
Wanderbriefe an eine Frau. Hamburg: Enoch, 1925.
188p. 20cm.

HOEK, Henry
Wanderungen und Wandlungen. München: Rother, 1924.
159p. 24cm.

HOEK, Henry
Weg und Umweg einer Liebe: neue Wanderbriefe an
eine Frau. Hamburg: Enoch, 1929. 255p. 20cm.

HOEK, Henry
Wege und Weggenossen. München: Dreiländerverlag,
1919. 184p. 16cm.

- - 2.Aufl. München: Bergverlag, 1920.

HOEK, Henry
Wetter, Wolken, Wind: ein Buch für jedermann.
Leipzig: Brockhaus, 1926. 253p., plates, illus.
20cm.

HOEK, Henry
Wetterkunde. Bern: Hallwag, [1945]. 104p., illus.
16cm.

HOEK, Henry
Wie lerne ich Schi-laufen. 4.Aufl. München:
Deutsche Alpenzeitung, 1911. 39p., illus. 20cm.
- - 7. umgearb. und stark erweiterte Aufl. München:
W. Schmidkung, 1917.
- - 11.Aufl., bearb. von Carl J. Luther. München:
Rother, 1924.

HOEK, Henry
[Wie lerne ich Schi-laufen]. L'école du ski; rev.
par Max Winkler; traduit par Armand Pierhal.
Paris: S. Bornemann, 1933. 63p., illus. 19cm.

HOEK, Henry
Eine Winterfahrt in den Schweizer Bergen(Göschenen,
Oberalppass, Disentis, Lukmanier, Scopi, Olivone,
Biasca). [Wien, 1900]. 16p. 20cm.
Offprint from Oesterreichische Alpen-Zeitung, 7
Juni 1900.

HOEK, Henry
Das zentrale Plessurgebirge: geologische Unter-
suchungen. Freiburg i.Br., 1906. 82p., fold.
plates (1 col.), illus., maps, bibl. 24cm.
Offprint from Berichte der Naturforschenden
Gesellschaft zu Freiburg i.Br., Bd.16, 1906.

HOEK, Henry
Zermatt, zwischen Matterhorn und Monterosa,
zwischen Weisshorn und Dom: ein Buch für Berg-
Freunde. Hamburg: Enoch, 1936. 191p., illus.,
maps. 20cm. (Hoek-Enoch Bergbücher, 4)

HOEL, Adolf and WERENSKIOLD, Werner
Glaciers and snowfields in Norway. Oslo:
University Press, 1962. 291p., fold. plates,
illus., maps (some in folder). 27cm. (Norsk
Polarinstitutt, Skrifter, Nr.114)
At head of title: Kongelige Dept. for Industri og
Handverk.

HÖLDER, Chr. G   von
Meine Reise über den Gotthard nach den Borromäischen Inseln und Mailand; und von da zurük
über das Val Formazza,die Grimsel und das Oberland,
[von Chr. G. von Hölder]. Stuttgart: J.F.
Steinkopf, 1803-04. 2v. 17cm.

HOEN, Ernst W
The anhydrite diapirs of central western Axel
Heiberg Island. Montreal: McGill University, 1964.
vii, 102p., 1 fold. plate, illus., maps (in
pocket), bibl. 29cm. (Axel Heiberg Island
Research Reports, Geology, no.2; Jacobsen-McGill
Arctic Research Expedition 1959-1962)

HÖPFNER, Albrecht
Magazin für die Naturkunde Helvetiens; hrsg. von
Albrecht Höpfner. Zürich: Orell Füssli,1788-89.
4v., plates, illus. 20cm.

HÖRMANN, Ludwig von
Wanderungen durch Tirol und Vorarlberg; geschildert
von Ludwig von Hörmann [and others]; illustrirt
von Franz Defregger [and others]. Stuttgart:
Kröner, [1879]. 284p., plates, illus. 37cm.
(Unser Vaterland)

HÖRTNAGL, F
Der Monte Rosa. Stuttgart: Deutsche Verlags-
Anstalt, 1905. 37p., plates, illus., map. 18cm.
(Alpine Gipfelführer, 4)

HOFER, Andreas
MANNING, Anne
The year nine: a tale of the Tyrol, by the author
of "Mary Powell" [i.e. Anne Manning]. A. Hall,
Virtue, 1858. iv, 282p., plates, illus. 21cm.

HOFER, Andreas
THOMAS, Elizabeth
Hofer, the Tyrolese, by the author of "Claudine",
"Always happy" &c. [i.e. Elizabeth Thomas].
Harris, 1824. xii, 156p., plates, illus. 18cm.

HOFER, H   Berger-
See
BURGER-HOFER, H

HOFERER, Erwin
Bergsteigen im Winter. Berlin: W. Limpert, [1935].
78p., plates, illus. 19cm.

HOFERER, Erwin and SCHÄTZ, Josef Julius
Münchner Kletterführer: 250 der lohnendsten
Kletterfahrten in den Verbergen und im bayerisch-
tirolischen Grenzgebiet ...; hrsg. von Erwin
Hoferer und Jos. Jul. Schätz. München: Rother,
1923. 247p., plates, illus. 17cm.

HOFERER, Erwin
Winterliches Bergsteigen alpine Schilauftechnik.
München: Rother, 1925. 304p., illus. 21cm.

HOFFMAN, Eric Alfred
TOBIAS, Michael Charles
Dhaulagirideon; edited and with an introduction by
Eric Alfred Hoffman. Yellow Springs (Ohio):
International Mountaineering Arts Journal, 1973.
xiv, 97,25p., plates, illus. 22cm.

HOFFMANN, Georg
Wanderungen in der Gletscherwelt, von G.H. [i.e.
G. Hoffmann]. Zürich: Orell, Füssli, 1843.
160p., plates, illus. 17cm.

HOFFMANN, Julius
Alpen-Flora für Touristen und Pflanzenfreunde; mit
... farbigen Abbildungen ... nach Aquarellen von
Hermann Friese; nebst textlicher Beschriebung
..., von Jul. Hoffmann. Stuttgart: Verlag für
Naturkunde, 1902. 86p., 40 col. plates, illus.
22cm.

HOFFMANN, Julius
Alpenflora für Alpenwanderer und Pflanzenfreunde;
mit ... farbigen Abbildungen ... nach Aquarellen
von Hermann Friese. 2. Aufl., mit neuem Text hrsg.
von K. Giesenhagen. Stuttgart: E. Schweizerbart,
1914. 147p., 43 col. plates, illus. 21cm.

HOFFMEISTER, Werner
Travels in Ceylon and continental India; including
Nepal and other parts of the Himalayas, to the
borders of Thibet, with some notices of the over-
land route ...; translated from the German.
Edinburgh: Kennedy, 1848. xii, 527p. 22cm.

HOFMANN, Egon
Die Ausrüstung für Hochturen; mit Zeichnungen von
Ernst Platz. München: Verlag der Alpenfreund,
[1923]. 46p., illus. 16cm. (Alpenfreund-
Bücherei, Bd.6)

HOFMANN, Ernst
IMPERATORSKOE RUSSKOE GEOGRAFICHESKOE OBSHCHESTVO
Der nördliche Ural und das Küstengebirge Pai-Choi,
untersucht und beschrieben von einer in den Jahren
1847, 1848 und 1850 durch die Kaiserlich-Russische
Geographische Gesellschaft ausgerüsteten Expedition. St. Petersburg: Die Akademie der Wissenschaften, 1855-56. 2v., plates (some fold.),
illus. 32cm.
Bd.2 verfasst von dem Leiter der Ural-Expedition,
Ernst Hofmann.

HOFMANN, Karl and STÜDL, Johann
Wanderungen in der Glockner-Gruppe; mit einem
botanischen Anhang... München: J. Lindauer, 1871.
393p., plates (some fold.col.), illus. 22cm.

HOFMEIER, Walter
Bergsteigen im Winter. München: Alpenfreund-
Verlag, 1925. 193p., plates, illus., bibl. 22cm.

HOG, Roger
Tour on the continent in France, Switzerland, and
Italy, in the years 1817 and 1818. Whittaker,
1824. viii, 259p., plates, illus. 23cm.

HOGAN, Jim M
Impelled into experiences: the story of the
Outward Bound Schools. Wakefield: Educational
Productions, 1968. 118p., plates, illus. 20cm.

HOGARD, Henri
Principaux glaciers de la Suisse, imprimés en
lavis-aquarelle, d'après les originaux dessinés
et peints d'après nature par Henri Hogard.
Strasbourg: E. Simon, 1854. 31p., plates, illus.
(in portfolio). 27cm. (Matériaux pour servir à
l'étude des glaciers)

HOGG, Thomas Jefferson
Two hundred and nine days; or The journal of a
traveller on the continent. Hunt & Clarke, 1827.
2v. 21cm.

Die hohe Salve im Brirenthale in Tyrol, mit einer
Bergsilhouette. München: C. Wolf, 1859. 38p.
17cm.

HOHENLEITNER, Siegfried
Skiführer durch die Tuxer Vorberge. Innsbruck:
Wagner, 1933. 123p., 1 fold. plate, map. 18cm.

HOHENLEITNER, Siegfried
Die Stubaier Alpen. Innsbruck: Wagner, 1925.
viii, 205p., illus., maps. 16cm. (Wagners
Alpine Spezialführer, 4)

HOHLE, Per
Himalayas Helter: beromte ekspedisjoner til
jordens hoyeste tinder. Oslo: J. Dybwads, 1948.
251p., plates (1 fold.), illus., maps, bibl.
22cm.

HOHLE, Per
Til fjells med tau og isøks. Oslo: Gyldendal
Norsk Forlag, 1973. 143p., illus. 18cm.
(Gyldendals Ferie-og Fritidsbøker)

HOLDEN, Peter
TRENT POLYTECHNIC HINDU KUSH EXPEDITION, 1975
Report; edited by Peter Holden. [Nottingham]:
The Expedition, [1977]. 32, xxxvip., plates,
illus., map. 30cm.

HOLDICH, Sir Thomas Hungerford
The countries of the King's award. Hurst and
Blackett, 1904. xv, 420p., 1 fold. plate,
illus., map. 23cm.

HOLDICH, Sir Thomas Hungerford
The gates of India, being an historical narrative. Macmillan, 1910. xv, 555p., col. plates
(some fold.), maps. 24cm.

HOLDICH, Sir Thomas Hungerford
The Indian borderland 1880-1900. Methuen, 1901.
xii, 402p., plates (1 fold.col.), illus., map.
24cm.

HOLDICH, Sir Thomas Hungerford
Tibet, the mysterious. Rivers, [1907]. xii,
356p., 1 fold.col. plate, illus., maps, bibl.
24cm.

HOLDING, T H
The camper's handbook. Simpkin, Marshall,
Hamilton, Kent, 1908. 412p., illus. 19cm.

Holiday rambles in ordinary places, by a wife with
her husband [i.e. Richard Holt Hutton]. Daldy,
Isbister, 1877. 332p. 21cm.
Originally published in the Spectator.

HOLLAND, C F
Climbs on the Scawfell group: a climbers' guide.
Barrow-in-Furness: Fell & Rock Climbing Club,
[1924]. 66p., plates, illus. 21cm. (Climbers'
guides, [1st ser.], 3)

HOLLAND, Clive
Tyrol and its people; with ... illustrations in
colour by Adrian Stokes. Methuen, 1909. xiii,
336p., plates (some col.), illus. 23cm.

HOLLAND, Henry Scott
Henry Scott Holland: memoir and letters; edited
by Stephen Paget. Murray, 1921. xii, 336p.,
plates, illus. 23cm.

HOLLAND, P
Select views of the Lakes in Cumberland, West-
moreland, and Lancashire, from drawings made by
P. Holland; engraved by C. Rosenberg. Liverpool:
J. Peeling, 1792. [20] leaves, 20 plates,
illus. 21 x 28cm.

HOLLIWELL, Laurie
PYATT, Edward Charles
South-east England. 2nd rev. ed., by L.R. and
L.E. Holliwell; diagrams by L. Balding...
Stockport: Climbers' Club, 1969. xvi, 147p.,
illus., bibl. 16cm. (Climbers' Club guides)

HOLLIWELL, Les
Carneddau; diagrams by A.C. Cain and R.B. Evans;
Manchester: Climbers' Club, 1975. 151p., illus.,
maps (on lining papers). 18cm. (Climbers' Club
guides to Wales, 1)

HOLLIWELL, Les
JONES, Trevor and NEILL, John
Snowdon south; with a geological note by N.J.
Soper; natural history notes by R. Goodier; and
diagrams by R.B. Evans. 2nd ed. Stockport:
Climbers' Club, 1966. x, 142p., illus., maps.
16cm. (Climbers' Club guides to Wales, 8)

- - 3rd ed. including Moel Y Gest Quarry, by Les
Holliwell. 1970.

HOLLIWELL, Les
PYATT, Edward Charles
South-east England. 2nd rev. ed., by L.R. and
L.E. Holliwell; diagrams by L. Balding...
Stockport: Climbers' Club, 1969. xvi, 147p.,
illus., bibl. 16cm. (Climbers' Club guides)

HOLLWAY, John George
A month in Norway. Murray, 1853. viii, 160p.
18cm.

HOLME, Daryl
The young mountaineer; or, Frank Miller's lot in
life: the story of a Swiss boy. Nimmo, 1874.
vi, 282p., plates, illus. 18cm.

HOLMES, D   T
A Scot in France and Switzerland. Paisley: A.
Gardner, 1910. xii, 398p. 20cm.

HOLMES, Oliver Wendell
POLLOCK, Sir Frederick
The Pollock-Holmes letters: correspondence of Sir
Frederick Pollock and Mr. Justice Holmes, 1874-
1932; edited by Mark DeWolfe Howe; with an intro-
duction by Sir John Pollock. Cambridge: Cambridge
University Press, 1942. 2v., plates, illus. 23cm.

HOLMES, Peter
Mountains and a monastery. Bles, 1958. 191p.,
plates (some fold.), illus., maps. 23cm.

HOLTZ, Mathilda Edith and BEMIS, Katharine Isabel
Glacier National Park: its trails and treasures.
New York: Doran, 1917. 263p., plates, illus.,
map (on lining papers). 21cm.

HOLWAY, Edward W   D
PALMER, Howard
Edward W.D. Holway: a pioneer of the Canadian Alps.
Minneapolis: University of Minnesota Press, 1931.
xiv, 81p., plates, illus., map, bibl. 22cm.

HOLWORTHY, Sophia Matilda
Alpine scrambles and classic rambles: a gipsy tour
in search of summer snow and winter sun, a pocket
companion for the unprotected, by the author of
"Scylla & Charybdis"... Nisbet, [1882]. 114p.
16cm.
Preface signed: S.M.H. i.e. Sophia M. Holworthy.

HOMER, A   N
The imperial highway. Causton, for the Canadian
Pacific Railway, [1912]. 118p., illus. 30cm.

HONE, J   F
Switzerland and other poems. Gloucester: E. Nest,
1878. 122p. 19cm.

HONG KONG MOUNTAINEERING CLUB EXPEDITION TO THE
SNOW MOUNTAINS OF NEW GUINEA, 1972
[Report], narrative section ... by Jack Baines.
Hong Kong: The Expedition, [1973]. 27p., illus.,
maps. 26cm.

HOOFT, Jenny Visser
See
VISSER-HOOFT, Jenny

HOOKER, Sir Joseph Dalton
Himalayan journals; or, Notes of a naturalist in
Bengal, the Sikkim and Nepal Himalayas, the
Khasia Mountains, &c. Murray, 1854. 2v., col.
plates (some fold.), illus., maps. 23cm.

- - New ed., carefully rev. and condensed. 1855.
- - Another issue. Ward, Lock, Bowden, 1891.
- - Another issue. Ward, Lock, 1905.

HOOKER, Sir Joseph Dalton
Illustrations of Himalayan plants chiefly selected
from drawings made for J.F. Cathcart; the descriptions and analyses by J.D. Hooker; the plates
executed by W.H. Fitch. Lovell Reeve, 1855.
lv. (chiefly illus.). 52cm.

HOOKER, Sir Joseph Dalton and BALL, John
Journal of a tour in Marocco and the Great Atlas;
with an appendix including A sketch of the geology
of Marocco... Macmillan, 1878. xvi, 499p.,
plates (some fold.), illus., map. 23cm.

HOOKER, Sir Joseph Dalton
HUXLEY, Leonard
Life and letters of Sir Joseph Dalton Hooker, OM,
GCSI; based on materials collected and arranged
by Lady Hooker. Murray, 1918. 2v., plates (1
fold.), illus., map, port. 23cm.

HOOKER, William Dawson
Notes on Norway; or, A brief journal of a tour
made to the northern parts of Norway, in the
summer of 1836. Glasgow: The Author, 1837.
127p., plates, illus. 22cm.

HOOKER, William Jackson
Journal of a tour in Iceland in the summer of
1809. Halesworth: The Author, 1811. lxii,
503p., 3 plates (2 fold., 1 col.), illus. 22cm.

- - 2nd ed., with additions. Longman, Hurst, Rees,
Orme and Brown, 1813.

HOOKEY, M
The romance of Tasmania; with illustrations by
J. Connor [and others]. Hobart: W.E. Fuller &
J. Boa, 1921. 54p., illus. (some col.). 25cm.

HOOLE, Henry
Das Trainieren zum Sport: ein Handbuch für
Sportsleute jeder Art ...; für deutsche Ver-
hältnisse bearb., Uebersetzung von C.A. Neufeld.
Wiesbaden: J.F. Bergmann, 1899. xi, 170p. 22cm.

HOPE, Ascott R
See
MONCRIEFF, Ascott Robert Hope

WILLSON, John and HOPE, David E
Wye Valley. Vol. 1. Wintour's Leap, Symonds Yat
Western Cliffs. Leicester: Cordee, 1977. 123p.,
illus., maps. 18cm. (Rock climbs in the South-
West)

HOPE, Robert Philip
KIRKPATRICK, William Trench
Alpine days and nights, with a paper by R. Philip
Hope; and a foreword by E.L. Strutt. Allen &
Unwin, 1932. 198p., plates, illus. 21cm.

HORIZON MAGAZINE
Mountain conquest; by the editors of Horizon
magazine, author, Eric Shipton. New York:
American Heritage Publishing Co., 1966. 153p.,
illus. (some col.). 27cm. (Horizon Caravel
books)

HORMAYR ZU HORTENBURG, Josef, Freiherr von
[Ansichten von Tyrol]. Tombleson's Ansichten
von Tyrol; nach T. Allom's Zeichnungen und
Johanna v. Isser's Skizzen; [Text von Josef
Hormayr]. Tombleson, [ca 1840]. 127p., plates,
illus., map. 23cm.

HORMAYR ZU HORTENBURG, Josef, Freiherr von
[Ansichten von Tyrol]. Views in the Tyrol; from
drawings by T. Allom, after original sketches by
Johanna v. Isser ...; with letterpress descrip-
tions by a companion of Hofer [i.e. Josef
Hormayr]. Black & Armstrong, [ca 1837]. 72p.,
plates (1 fold.), illus., map. 28cm.
Second title page has title: Forty-six views of
Tyrolese scenery...
Cover title: Tyrolese scenery.

- - Another ed. of the text, with different plates,
entitled: Tyrolese scenery; or, Continental
travels. [ca 1840].

HORNADAY, William T
Camp-fires in the Canadian Rockies. Werner
Laurie, 1906. xix, 353p., plates, illus., map.
25cm.

HORNADAY, William T
Camp-fires on desert and lava. Werner Laurie,
[1906]. xx, 366p., plates (some col.), illus.,
maps. 24cm.

HORNBEIN, Thomas Frederick
Everest: the west ridge; photographs from the
American Mount Everest Expedition and by its
leader, Norman G. Dyhrenfurth; introduction by
William E. Siri; edited by David Brower. San
Francisco: Sierra Club, 1965. 205p., col. illus.
35cm. (Sierra Club Exhibit-format series, 12)

- - Another issue. Allen & Unwin, 1966.
- - Cheap ed. Allen & Unwin, 1971.

HORNBY, Emily
Mountaineering records, [by] E.H. [i.e. E.
Hornby]. Liverpool: J.A. Thompson, 1907. vii,
352p. 23cm.

HORNE, Thomas Hartwell
The Lakes of Lancashire, Westmorland, and Cumberland; delineated in ... engravings from drawings
by Joseph Farington; with descriptions ... the
result of a tour made in the summer of ... 1816.
T. Cadell & W. Davies, 1816. viii, 96p., plates,
illus., map. 39cm.

HORNE AND THORNTHWAITE (Firm)
Altitude tables and how to use them. Horne and
Thornthwaite, [ca 1870]. 32p. 13cm.

HORNUNG, Moise
En Savoie. Genève: Imprimerie J.-G. Fick, 1872.
145p. 18cm.

HORT, Arthur Fenton
Life and letters of Fenton John Anthony Hort.
Macmillan, 1896. 2v., 1 plate, port. 22cm.

HORT, Fenton John Anthony
HORT, Arthur Fenton
Life and letters of Fenton John Anthony Hort.
Macmillan, 1896. 2v., 1 plate, port. 22cm.

HORTENBURG, Josef Hormayr, Freiherr von
See
HORMAYR ZU HORTENBURG, Josef, Freiherr von

HOTEL MIRAVALLE
Hotel Miravalle, Gressoney Saint-Jean. Torino:
[The Hotel], [18--].
67p., illus. 12 x 16cm. (Guide illustrate
Reynaudi)

HOTELS SEILER, Zermatt
Einweihung der Gedenktafel am Hotel Monte Rosa
und des Hallenbades beim Hotel Mont Cervin im
Rahmen eines Presse-Empfanges vom 22. bis 24.
April 1970. [Zermatt]: [Hotels Seiler], 1970.
1v. of illus. 24cm.

HOTELS SEILER, Zermatt
Hotels Seiler, Zermatt, 1855-1930: [Festschrift
... im Rahmen des diamantenen Jubiläums]. Zürich:
Orell Füssli, 1930. 40p., plates, illus. 28cm.

HOTTINGER, J J
MULLER, Jean de
Histoire de la Confédération Suisse, par Jean de
Muller, Robert Gloutz-Blozheim et J.-J. Hottinger;
traduite de l'allemand, et continuée jusqu'à nos
jours par Charles Monnard et Louis Vulliemin.
Paris: Ballimore, 1837-51. 18v. 24cm.

HOUSEMAN, John
See
HOUSMAN, John

HOUSMAN, John
A descriptive tour, and guide to the Lakes, caves,
mountains, and other natural curiosities, in
Cumberland, Westmoreland, Lancashire, and a part
of the West Riding of Yorkshire. Carlisle:
Printed by F. Jollie, 1800. vii, 226p., plates
(some fold., some col.), illus., maps. 23cm.
Extract from the Author's A topographical description of Cumberland...

- - 2nd ed. 1802.
- - 6th ed. 1814.
- - 9th ed. 1821.

HOUSMAN, John
A topographical description of Cumberland, Westmorland, Lancashire, and a part of the West
Riding of Yorkshire... Carlisle: F. Jollie, 1800.
xii, 538p., plates (some fold.), illus., maps.
23cm.

HOUSTON, Charles Sneed and BATES, Robert Hicks
K2: the savage mountain. Collins, 1955. 192p.,
plates, illus., maps. 23cm.

- - Another issue. Diadem Books, 1979.

HOUSTON, Charles Sneed and BATES, Robert Hicks
[K2: the savage mountain]. K2: montagne sans
pitié, [par] Charles S. Houston, Robert H. Bates
et les membres de la troisième expédition
américaine au Karakorum; traduit par J. et F.
Germain. Paris: Arthaud, 1954. 234p., plates,
illus., map. 22cm. (Collection sempervivum, 25)

HOUSTON, Charles Sneed
K2, 8611m: [troisième expédition américaine au
Karakorum], par Charles S. Houston, Robert H.
Bates, George I. Bell. Paris: Arthaud, 1954.
100p., 1 fold. plate, illus. (some col.), map.
26cm.

How we did them in seventeen days! To wit:
Belgium, the Rhine, Switzerland, & France; des-
cribed and illustrated by one of ourselves [i.e.
Richard Marrack]; aided, assisted, encouraged,
and abetted by the other [i.e. Edmund G. Harvey].
Truro: Printed by Lake & Lake, [1875]. 68p.,
plates, illus. 20cm.
Cover title: Our rapid run.

How we spent the summer, or; A "Voyage en zigzag"
in Switzerland and Tyrol, with some members of
the Alpine Club, from the sketch book of one of
the party [i.e. Elizabeth Tuckett]. Longman,
Green, Longman, Roberts & Green, 1864. 40 leaves
of illus. 27 x 36cm.

- - 2nd ed. 1864.
- - 3rd ed, 1866.
- - 6th ed. 1874.

HOWARD, Tony
Walks and climbs in Romsdal, Norway, written and
illustrated by Tony Howard. Manchester: Cicerone
Press, 1970. 174p., illus., maps (on lining
papers). 16cm. (Cicerone Press guides)

HOWARD, W D and LLOYD, F H
Photographs among the Dolomite mountains. The
Authors, 1865. 1v. of illus. 39cm.

HOWARD-BURY, Charles Kenneth
Mount Everest: the reconnaisance, 1921, by C.K.
Howard-Bury and other members of the Mount Everest
Expedition. Arnold, 1922. xi, 350p., plates (3
fold.col.), illus., maps. 26cm.

HOWARD-BURY, Charles Kenneth
[Mount Everest...]. À la conquête du Mont Everest; traduction française par G. Moreau; précédé d'une introduction de Sir Francis Younghusband; préface du Prince Roland Bonaparte. Paris: Payot, 1923. 415p., plates (1 fold.), illus., map. 24cm.

HOWARTH, O J R
The scenic heritage of England and Wales; with a foreword by the Earl of Crawford and Balcarres and an introduction by Vaughan Cornish. Pitman, 1937. xxv, 190p., 48 plates (1 fold.), illus., map. 23cm.

HOWE, Mark DeWolfe
POLLOCK, Sir Frederick
The Pollock-Holmes letters; correspondence of Sir Frederick Pollock and Mr. Justice Holmes 1874-1932; edited by Mark DeWolfe Howe; with an introduction by Sir John Pollock. Cambridge: Cambridge University Press, 1942. 2v., plates, illus. 23cm.

HOWELL, Frederick W W
Icelandic pictures drawn with pen and pencil. Religious Tract Society, 1893. 176p., illus., map. 29cm.

HOWELL, George O
Recollections of a visit abroad, being notes of a scamper through Switzerland, with a ride down the Rhine, and a bound through Brussels, during the month of August 1894: a lecture... Plumstead: G.O. Howell, 1895. 73p. 21cm.

HOWELL, James
Instructions for forreine travell, 1642; collated with the 2nd ed. of 1650; carefully edited by Edward Arber. English reprints, 1868. 88p. 18cm.

- - Large paper ed. 1869.

HOWELLS, William Dean
A little Swiss sojourn. New York, London: Harper, 1892. 119p., illus. 14cm.

HOYS, Dudley
Below Scafell; with drawings by Lynton Lamb. Oxford University Press, 1955. 186p., plates, illus. 19cm.

HOYTE, John
Trunk road for Hannibal: with an elephant over the Alps. Bles, 1960. 191p., plates, illus., maps, bibl. 21cm.

HUBER, Eddie and ROGERS, Norman
The complete ski manual: how to begin, how to improve, how to excel. Allen & Unwin, 1949. xi, 129p., illus. 25cm.

HUBER, Ferd.
Sammlung von Schweizer-Kühreihen und Volkslieden = Recueil de ranz de vaches et chansons nationales. 4. verm. u. verb. Ausg. Bern: I.I. Burgdorfer, 1826. viii, 100p., plates, illus., music. 24 x 33cm.
Preface names Ferd. Huber, and preface signatory, W., as editors.

HUBER, Sepp
Führer durch das Tote Gebirge einschliesslich Warscheneck, Höllengebirge und Sengsengebirge. Wien: Artaria, 1927. 156p., plates, illus. 17cm.

HUC, Régis Évariste
Souvenirs d'un voyage dans la Tartarie, le Thibet et la Chine, pendant les années 1844, 1845 et 1846. Paris: Le Clere, 1850. 2v., 1 fold. plate, map. 23cm.

- - Nouv. éd. de [t.] 1. Paris: Plon, 1925.

HUC, Régis Évariste
[Souvenirs d'un voyage dans la Tartarie...]. Travels in Tartary, Thibet, and China during the years 1844-5-6; translated ... by W. Hazlitt. 2nd ed. National Illustrated Library, [1855?]. 2v., plates (1 fold.), illus., map. 21cm.

- - 3rd ed. Nelson, 1856.

HUC, Régis Évariste
[Souvenirs d'un voyage dans la Tartarie...]. Recollections of a journey through Tartary, Thibet, and China, during the years 1844, 1845, and 1846; a condensed translation by Mrs. Percy Sinnett. Longman, Brown, Green and Longmans, 1852. viii, 313p. 18cm.

HUCK, J Ch
Enzian und Edelweiss: Erinnerungen an meine Alpenfahrten. Konstanz a.B.: A.-G. Oberbad, 1925. vii, 160p., plates, illus. 21cm.

HUDSON, Charles and KENNEDY, Edward Shirley
Where there's a will there's a way: an ascent of Mont Blanc by a new route and without guides. Longman, Brown, Green, & Longmans, 1856. xvi, 95p., plates (1 fold.col.), illus., map. 21cm.

- - 2nd ed. 1856.

HUDSON, John
A complete guide to the Lakes ...; with Mr. Wordsworth's description of the scenery ...; and three letters on the geology ... by Professor Sedgwick; edited by the publisher. 2nd ed. Kendal: J. Hudson; London: Longman, 1843. vii, 259p., plates, illus., map. 19cm.

- - 3rd ed. 1846.
- - 4th ed. 1853.

HÜBEL, Paul
Führerlose Gipfelfahrten. München: C.H. Beck, 1927. xv, 248p., plates, illus. 24cm.

HUBER, William
Les glaciers. Paris: Challamel, 1867. viii, 266p., plates, illus., maps. 19cm.

HÜGLI, Emil
Die Jungfrau: Dichtung. Schkendik bei Leipzig: W. Schäfer, 1909. 187p. 19cm.

HÜRZELER, Jerome
Panorama du Napf (Righi d'Emmenthal); dessinés d'après nature par Jerome Hürzeler. [N.p.]: Soleure, 1883. 20cm.

HÜTTIG, Robert and KORDON, Frido
Führer durch die Ankogelgruppe einschliesslich Hochalmspitz, Hasner-und Reisseckgruppe. Wien: Artaria, 1926. xii, 313p., plates, illus., map (in pocket). 17cm.

HUF, Hans
English mountaineers: A. Wills, J. Tyndall, E. Whymper, C. Dent, A.F. Mummery, hrsg. von Hans Huf. Bamberg: C.C. Buchner, 1926. 87p., illus. 19cm. (Neusprachliche Klassiker mit fortlaufenden Präparationen, 51)

HUG, Lina and STEAD, Richard
Switzerland. Fisher Unwin, [1891]. xxiv, 430p., illus., maps. 21cm. (The story of the nations, 26)

- - 2nd ed. rev. and enl. 1920.

HUG, Oscar A
Die Ostwand des Tödi. [Bern, 1921]. 41-52p., illus. 26cm.
Offprint from Jahrbuch des Schweizer Alpenclub, 55 Jahrg. 1920.

HUGI, Franz Joseph
Die Gletscher und die erratischen Blöcke.
Solothurn: Jent & Gassmann, 1843. xvi, 256p. 22cm.

HUGI, Franz Joseph
NATURFORSCHENDE GESELLSCHAFT IN SOLOTHURN
Naturhistorische Alpenreise; vorgelesen der Naturforschenden Gesellschaft in Solothurn von ihrem
Vorsteher Fr. Jos. Hugi. Solothurn: Amiet-Lutiger,
1830. xviii, 378p., plates (some fold., some
col.), illus., maps. 21cm.

HUGO, Victor
En voyage: Alpes et Pyrénées. 3e éd. Paris:
J. Hetzel, 1890. 343p. 25cm. (Oeuvres inédites
de Victor Hugo)

HUGO, Victor
[En voyage: Alpes et Pyrénées]. The Alps and
Pyrenees; translated by John Manson. Bliss,
Sands, 1898. xvi, 354p. 20cm.

HUGO, Victor
France et Belgique, Alpes et Pyrénées. Paris:
Nelson, [1913]. 571p., plates, illus. 17cm.
(Oeuvres complètes de Victor Hugo, 24)

HUITFELDT, F
Das Skilaufen. Berlin: Manning, 1907. 59p.,
plates, illus. 20cm.

HULME, F   Edward
Familiar Swiss flowers; figured and described by
F. Edward Hulme. Cassell, 1908. viii, 224p.,
100 col. plates, illus. 20cm.

HULME, F   Edward
That rock-garden of ours. Fisher Unwin, 1909.
328p., 50 plates (1 col.), illus. 23cm.

HUMBLE, Benjamin Hutchison
The Cuillin of Skye. Hale, 1952. xv, 144p.,
plates, illus., map, bibl. 26cm.

HUMBLE, Benjamin Hutchison
On Scottish hills; foreword by Geoffrey Winthrop
Young; ... photographs by the author. Chapman &
Hall, 1946. 128p., illus., map. 26cm.

HUMBLE, Benjamin Hutchison and MCLELLAN, W   M
Songs for climbers; edited by B.H. Humble and
W.M. McLellan. Glasgow: Wm. McLellan, [1938].
33p., illus. 23cm.

HUMBLE, Benjamin Hutchison
The songs of Skye: an anthology; edited by B.H.
Humble; with introduction by Lauchlan Maclean Watt.
Stirling: E. Mackay, 1934. 176p., 5 plates (4
fold.), illus., bibl. 18cm.

HUMBOLDT, Alexander, Freiherr von
Ansichten der Natur, mit wissenschaftlichen
Erläuterungen. 3. verb. und verm. Ausg.
Stuttgart & Tübingen: J.G. Cotta, 1849. 2v. 19cm.

HUMBOLDT, Alexander, Freiherr von
[Ansichten der Natur]. Views of nature; or, con-
templations on the sublime phenomena of creation;
translated by E.C. Otté and Henry G. Bohn. Bohn,
1850. xxx, 452p., plates (1 col.), facsim. 20cm.
(Bohn's scientific library)

HUMBOLDT, Alexander, Freiherr von
Essai politique sur le royaume de la Nouvelle-
Espagne. Paris: Schoell, 1811. 5v., 1 fold.
plate, map. 22cm.

HUMBOLDT, Alexander, Freiherr von
Humboldt's travels and discoveries in South
America. 2nd. ed. J.W. Parker, 1846. viii,
278p., illus. 15cm.

HUMBOLDT, Alexander, Freiherr von
[Kosmos]. Cosmos: sketch of a physical description
of the universe; translated under the superinten-
dence of Edward Sabine. Longman, Brown, Green and
Longmans, 1846- . 5v. 21cm.
Library has v.1 and 2 only, v.2. is 2nd ed.

HUMBOLDT, Alexander, Freiherr von
[Kosmos]. Cosmos: a sketch of a physical descrip-
tion of the universe; translated ... by E.C.
Otté. Bohn, 1849-86. 5v., plates, port. 20cm.
(Bohn's scientific library)
Library lacks v.4.

HUMBOLDT, Alexander, Freiherr von
Personal narrative of travels to the equinoctial
regions of America during the years 1799-1804 by
Alexander von Humboldt and Aimé Bonpland, written
in French by Alexander von Humboldt; translated
and edited by Thomasina Ross. Henry G. Bohn,
1852-53. 3v. 20cm. (Bohn's scientific library)

HUMBOLDT, Alexander, Freiherr von
BAUER, Juliette
Lives of the brothers Humboldt, Alexander and
William; translated and arranged from the German
of Klencke & Schlesier by Juliette Bauer. Ingram,
Cooke, 1852. vii, 431p., 2 plates, ports. 20cm.

HUMBOLDT, Wilhelm, Freiherr von
BAUER, Juliette
Lives of the brothers Humboldt, Alexander and
William; translated and arranged from the German
of Klencke & Schlesier by Juliette Bauer. Ingram,
Cooke, 1852. vii, 431p., 2 plates, ports. 20cm.

HUMPELER, Louis
Der Grossvenediger. Stuttgart: Deutsche Verlags-
Anstalt, 1907. 74p., plates, illus., maps.
18cm. (Alpine Gipfelführer, 12)

HUNGARIAN TOURIST SOCIETY
See
MAGYAR TURISTA SZÖVETSÉG

HUNT, Sir Henry Cecil John
See
HUNT, John, Baron Hunt

HUNT, John, Baron Hunt
The ascent of Everest. Hodder & Stoughton, 1953.
xx, 300p., plates (some col.), illus., maps.
23cm.

HUNT, John, Baron Hunt
[The ascent of Everest]. The conquest of Everest;
with a chapter on the final assault by Sir Edmund
Hillary; foreword by the Duke of Edinburgh. New
York: Dutton, 1954. xx, 300p., plates, illus.,
maps. 23cm.
American ed. of the author's Ascent of Everest.

HUNT, John, Baron Hunt
The ascent of Everest; edited and abridged for
schools, with the assistance of the author, under
the direction of Leonard Brooks. University of
London Press, 1954. 160p., plates, illus., maps.
20cm.

- - Abridged ed. retold for younger readers ...
1954.

HUNT, John, Baron Hunt
[The ascent of Everest]. Victoire sur l'Everest
...; traduit par Bernard Pierre; dessins de
Charles Evans; avant-propos de S.A.R. le Duc
d'Edimbourg; préface de Maurice Herzog. Paris:
Amiot-Dumont, 1953. 350p., plates, illus., maps.
22cm. (Bibliothèque de l'alpinisme)

HUNT, John, Baron Hunt
[The ascent of Everest]. Mount Everest: Kampf
und Sieg. Wien: Ullstein, 1954. 314p., plates,
illus., maps. 23cm.

HUNT, John, Baron Hunt
[The ascent of Everest]. La ascension al Everest;
traducion de Francis Maclennan. Barcelona:
Juventud, 1953. 344p., plates, illus., maps.
23cm.

HUNT, John, Baron Hunt
[The ascent of Everest]. La conquista
dell'Everest; con un capitolo sull'assalto finale
di Sir Edmund Hillary; traduzione ... di Donato
Barbone; revisione alpinistica di Pietro Meciani.
Bari: "Leonardo da Vinci", 1954. 292p., plates,
illus., maps. 24cm. (All'insegna dell'orizzonte,
6)

HUNT, John, Baron Hunt
[The ascent of Everest]. Voskhozhdenie na
Iverest... Moskva: Izd. Inostrannoi Literatury,
1956. 293p., plates, illus., maps. 23cm.

HUNT, John, Baron Hunt
[The ascent of Everest]; retold for younger
readers in Bengali. [N.p.]: [n.pub.], [1954?].
109p., illus. 20cm.

HUNT, John, Baron Hunt
[The ascent of Everest]. Výstup na Everest;
přeložil Antonín Filanovský. Praha: Sportnovní a
Turistické Nakladatelství, 1957. 274p., plates,
illus., maps. 21cm.

HUNT, John, Baron Hunt
[The ascent of Everest]. De beklimming van de
Mount Everest, de hoogste top der aarde bereikt;
vertaling J.F. Kliphuis. Amsterdam: Scheltens &
Giltay, [1953]. 270p., plates, illus., maps.
24cm.

HUNT, John, Baron Hunt
[The ascent of Everest]. Mount Everestin
valloitus. Helsinki: Kustannusosakeyhtiö Tammi,
1953. 308p., plates, illus., maps. 24cm.
(Maailman ympäri, 4)

HUNT, John, Baron Hunt
[The ascent of Everest]. Junior Hindi [ed.].
[N.p.]: [n.pub.], 1956, (1957 reprint). 102p.,
illus. 20cm.

HUNT, John, Baron Hunt
[The ascent of Everest]. Á haesta tindi jardar;
inngangsord eftir Sigurd Þórarinsson. Reykjavik:
Heimskringla, 1954. xvi, 260p., plates, illus.,
maps. 22cm. (Mal og menning, 1)

HUNT, John, Baron Hunt
The ascent of Everest. Tokyo: Asahi Shimbun,
1954. 290,57,12p., plates, illus., maps. 22cm.
In Japanese.

HUNT, John, Baron Hunt
[The ascent of Everest]. Sekai nomeityo.
Japanese language juvenile ed. Tokyo: Kaiseisya,
1965. 262p., plates, illus., maps. 22cm.

HUNT, John, Baron Hunt
[The ascent of Everest]. Everest: seieren over
jordans høyeste fjell. Oslo: J.W. Cappelen, 1953.
289p., plates, illus., maps. 23cm.

HUNT, John, Baron Hunt
[The ascent of Everest]. Pobeda nad Everestom.
Subotica: Minerva, 1954. 276p., plates, illus.,
maps. 23cm.

HUNT, John, Baron Hunt
[The ascent of Everest]. [Colombo?]: M.D.
Gunasena, 1958. 236p., plates, illus. 19cm.
In Sinhalese.

HUNT, John, Baron Hunt
[The ascent of Everest]. Erövringen av Mount
Everest. Stockholm: P.A. Norstedt, 1954. 337p.,
plates, illus., maps. 23cm.

HUNT, John, Baron Hunt
The conquest of Everest
    See his
The ascent of Everest
HUNT, John, Baron Hunt
Life is meeting. Hodder and Stoughton, 1978.
286p., 16 plates, illus., maps. 25cm.

HUNT, John, Baron Hunt
My favourite mountaineering stories; edited by
John Hunt. Guildford, London: Lutterworth Press,
1978. 127p., illus., map. 23cm.

HUNT, John, Baron Hunt
Our Everest adventure: the pictorial history from
Kathmandu to the summit. Leicester: Brockhampton
Press, 1954. 128p., illus., map. 26cm.

HUNT, John, Baron Hunt and BRASHER, Christopher
The red snows: an account of the British Caucasus
Expedition 1958. Hutchinson, 1960. 176p.,
plates (1 col.), illus., map. 22cm.

- - Another issue. Travel Book Club, 1960.

HUNTER, J   de Graaff
STEIN, Sir Marc Aurel
Memoir on maps of Chinese Turkistan and Kansu
from the surveys made during Sir Aurel Stein's
explorations, 1900-1, 1906-8, 1913-5; with
appendices by K. Mason and J. de Graaff Hunter.
Dehra Dun: Trigonometrical Survey Office, 1923.
xv, 208p., 30 plates, illus. 35cm. (Records of
the Survey of India, 17)

HURSTON, Zora
The man of the mountain. Dent, 1941. 319p.
19cm.

HUSON, Thomas
Round about Helvellyn: twenty-four plates; with
notes by the artist and descriptive passages from
Wordsworth's poems. Seeley, 1895. 51p., 24
plates, illus. 41cm.

HUSON, Thomas
Round about Snowdon: thirty plates by T. Huson;
with notes by J.J. Hissey. Seeley, 1894. 1v.
(chiefly illus.). 33cm.

HUTCHINGS, James M
In the heart of the Sierras: the Yo Semite
Valley, both historical and descriptive and
scenes by the way, Big Tree groves, the High
Sierra with its magnificent scenery, ancient and
modern glaciers and other objects of interest.
Yo Semite Valley: Old Cabin, 1886. 496p.,
plates (1 fold.), illus., maps. 23cm.

HUTCHINGS, James M
Scenes of wonder and curiosity in California.
Chapman and Hall, 1865. 267p., illus. 23cm.

HUTCHINSON, Alexander H
Try Cracow and the Carpathians. 2nd ed. Chapman
& Hall, 1872. vii, 256p., plates (1 fold.col.),
illus., map. 20cm.

HUTCHINSON, H   N
The story of the hills: a popular account of
mountains and how they were made. Seeley, 1892.
xi, 357p., plates, illus. 20cm.

HUTCHINSON, Horace G
Big game shooting; edited by Horace G. Hutchinson.
Country Life, 1905. 2v., plates, illus. 24cm.
(Country Life library of sport)

HUTCHINSON, W
An excursion to the Lakes in Westmorland and
Cumberland; with a tour through part of the
northern counties in the years 1773 and 1774. J.
Wilkie, 1776. 386p., plates (some fold.), illus.
22cm.

HUTTON, Richard Holt
Holiday rambles in ordinary places, by a wife
with her husband [i.e. Richard Holt Hutton].
Daldy, Isbister, 1877. 332p. 21cm.
Originally published in the Spectator.

HUTTON, William
Remarks upon North Wales, being the result of
sixteen tours through that part of the principality. Birmingham: Knott & Lloyd, 1803. 226p.,
plates (2 fold.), illus. 22cm.

HUXLEY, Anthony
Mountain flowers in colour; illustrated by Daphne
Barry and Mary Grierson. Blandford Press, 1967.
428p., illus. (some col.), maps, bibl. 19cm.

HUXLEY, Anthony
Standard encyclopedia of the world's mountains;
edited by Anthony Huxley. Weidenfeld & Nicolson,
1962. 383p., 16 col. plates, illus., maps. 25cm.

HUXLEY, Leonard
Life and letters of Sir Joseph Dalton Hooker, OM,
GCSI; based on materials collected and arranged
by Lady Hooker. Murray, 1918. 2v., plates (1
fold.), illus, map, ports. 23cm.

HYDE, Walter Woodburn
Roman alpine routes (with map showing chief Roman
passes). Philadelphia: The Society, 1935. xvi,
248p., 1 fold. plate, map, bibl. 25cm. (Memoirs
of the American Philosophical Society, v.2)

I.U.A.A.
See
INTERNATIONAL UNION OF ALPINIST ASSOCIATIONS

IATSENKO, V   S
V gorakh Pamira: pumevye zapiski uchastnika
Pamirskoi al'pinistskoi ekspeditsii 1940 g.
Moskva: Gos. Izd. Geograficheskoi Literatury,
1950. 187p., 2 fold. plates, illus., map. 21cm.

Ice sports, by Theodore Andrea Cook [and others].
Ward, Lock, 1901. 335p., fold.col. plates, illus.
21cm. (Isthmian library)

ICEFIELD RANGES RESEARCH PROJECT
BUSHNELL, Vivian C and RAGLE, Richard H
Icefield Ranges Research Project: scientific
results; edited by Vivian C. Bushnell and Richard
H. Ragle; foreword and introduction by Walter A.
Wood. New York: American Geographical Society;
Montreal: Arctic Institute of North America,
1969-72. 3v., fold. plates (1 col.), illus., map.
29cm.

ICHAC, Marcel
L'assaut des Aiguilles du Diable: une arête, une
ascension, un film; illustré de ... photos
extraites du film et du 10 croquis de l'auteur.
Paris: J. Susse, 1945. 93p., illus., maps, bibl.
24cm.

HENRY, Pierre and ICHAC, Marcel
Description de la haute montagne dans le massif
du Mont-Blanc. Fasc. 7. Groupes de Trélatête et
de Miage (entre les cols de Miage, de la Seigne
et du Bonhomme); avec la collaboration de Paul
Gayet-Tancrède. Paris: Fischbacher, 1933. 117p.,
plates, illus., maps. 17cm. (Guides Vallot)

ICHAC, Marcel
Quand brillent les étoiles de midi; photographies
de Henri Leblanc, Marcel Ichac, Jacques Ertaud.
Paris: Arthaud, 1960. 123p., illus. (some col.),
map. 24cm.
"Realisé d'après le film: Les étoiles de midi."

Idle days in the Vorarlberg and its neighbourhood,
[by W. Cotesworth]. Printed at the Free School-
Press, 1887. 96p., plates, illus. 17cm.

An idyl of the Alps, by the author of "Mary Powell"
[i.e. Anne Manning]. Hall, 1876. vi, 312p.
20cm.

IGGULDEN, H   A
The 2nd Battalion Derbyshire Regiment in the
Sikkim Expedition of 1888; with an introduction
by Sir Steuart Bayley. Swan Sonnenschein, 1900.
xii, 116p., plates (1 fold.), illus., map. 21cm.

IGLESIAS, José Maria and JANNA, Mario Della
Andinismo y campamentos en el Parque Nacional
Nahuel Huapi; con la colaboración de Lillian
Canova, Sandra Della Janna, Vojslav Arko y Carlos
Sonntag. Buenos Aires: Ediciones Mundonuevo,
1959. 178p., col. plates (1 fold.), illus.,
maps. 18cm. (Colección Alpamayo. Guida, no.1)

ILLINGWORTH, Frank
Camping questions answered. Jordan, 1946.
118p., illus. 14cm.

ILLINGWORTH, Robin N
BRATHAY EXPLORATION GROUP
Expedition medicine: a planning guide, by R.N.
Illingworth. Ambleside (Cumbria): Brathay Hall
Trust, 1976. 27p., 1 fold. plate, bibl. 22cm.

ILLUSTRAZIONE ITALIANA
DAINELLI, Giotto
Mondo alpino: numero di primavera de
"L'Illustrazione Italiana". Milano: Treves, 1930.
130p., 2 col.plates, illus. 40cm.
Supplement to l'Illustrazione Italiana, n.16,
20 aprile 1930.

Illustrierter Führer auf die Gipfel der Schweizeralpen. Luzern: G. Speck-Jost, [19-?]. 2v.,
illus. 12 x 17cm.

Im Bann der Berge: Bergsteiger-Erlebnisse. Zürich:
Orell Füssli, 1935. 197p., 8 plates, illus.
21cm.

Im Kampf um den Berg: spannende Berglebnisse.
Zürich: Orell Füssli, 1934. 189p., plates,
illus. 22cm.

IM THURN, Sir Everard
Thoughts, talks and tramps: a collection of
papers by Sir Everard Im Thurn; edited with a
memoir by R.R. Marett. Oxford University Press,
1934. xxiii, 285p., map, port. 23cm.

IMESCH, Dionys
Blätter aus der Walliser Geschichte. 9.Bd. 4.
Jahrg. Festschrift zum 75. Geburtstag von Dionys
Imesch; hrsg. vom Geschichtsforschenden Verein
von Oberwallis. Brig: Der Verein, 1943. 327-
506p., plates, illus. 21cm.
Cover title.

IMFELD, X
Panorama vom Monte Rosa: vollständige Rundsicht
von der Dufourspitze (4638m), dem höchsten Gipfel
der Schweizeralpen, aufgenommen im September
1878 von X. Imfeld. Zürich: J. Wurster, 1878.
Col.fold. plates, illus. 21cm.
Cover title.

IMHOF, Eduard
Clubführer durch die Bündner Alpen. Bd.7.
Rätikon. Baden: Schweizer Alpenclub, 1936.
358p., illus., maps, bibl. 17cm. (Clubführer
des Schweizer Alpen-Club)

IMHOF, Eduard
Die grossen kalten Berge von Szetschuan:
Erlebnisse, Forschungen und Kartierungen im
Minya-Konka-Gebirge; hrsg. von der Schweizerischen
Stiftung für alpine Forschungen... Zürich: Orell
Füssli, 1974. 228p., col plates (1 fold.),
illus., maps, bibl. 31cm. (Montes mundi, 1)

IMHOF, Eduard
HEIM, Albert
Rundsicht vom Gipfel des Säntis ...; im Auftrag
der Sektion St. Gallen des Schweizer Alpenclub
aufgenommen und in Stein gestochen von Albert
Heim. 8. Aufl., Revision und Reliefton von Ed.
Imhof. Zürich: S.A.C., 1929. 26cm.

IMPERATORSKOE RUSSKOE GEOGRAFISCHESKOE OBSHCHESTVO
Der nördliche Ural und das Küstengebirge Pai-Choi,
untersucht und beschrieben von einer in den Jahren
1847, 1848 und 1850 durch die Kaiserlich-Russische
Geographische Gesellschaft ausgerüsteten Expedition. St. Petersburg: Die Akademie der Wissenschaften, 1853-56. 2v., plates (some fold.),
illus. 32cm.
Bd.2, verfasst von dem Leiter der Ural-Expedition,
Ernst Hofmann.

IMPERIAL JAPANESE GOVERNMENT RAILWAYS
An official guide to Eastern Asia: trans-
continental connections between Europe and Asia.
Tokyo: I.J.G.R. Plates (some fold., some col.),
illus., maps. 16cm.
Vol.2. South-western Japan. 1914. -v.4. China. 1915.

IMSENG, Johann Joseph
RUPPEN, Peter Joseph
Die Chronik des Thales Saas, für die Thalbewohner;
bearb. und hrsg. von Peter Joseph Ruppen. Sitten:
Calpini-Albertazzi, 1851. 187, iii p. 17cm.
Contains: Wissenschaftliche Bemerkungen ... by
Pfarrer Imseng.

INDIA. Survey of India
See
SURVEY OF INDIA

The Indian Alps and how we crossed them, being a
narrative of two years' residence in the Eastern
Himalaya and two months' tour into the interior,
by a lady pioneer [i.e. Nina E. Mazucelli];
illustrated by herself. Longmans, Green, 1876.
xiii, 612p., plates, illus., map. 27cm.

INDIAN EXPEDITION TO MOUNT EVEREST, 1962
Second Indian Expedition to Mount Everest February
- June, 1962 ...: souvenir brochure. Delhi:
Published on behalf of the Indian Mountaineering
Foundation by the Armed Forces Information Office,
[1962]. 24p., illus. 24cm.

INDIAN MOUNT EVEREST EXPEDITION, 1965
Indian Mount Everest Expedition 1965. New Delhi:
Published on behalf of the Indian Mountaineering
Foundation by the Armed Forces Information
Officer, Ministry of Defence, [1965]. 44p.,
illus. 27cm.

INDIAN MOUNTAINEERING FOUNDATION
Indian Mount Everest Expedition 1965. New Delhi:
Published on behalf of the Indian Mountaineering
Foundation by the Armed Forces Information
Officer, Ministry of Defence, [1965]. 44p.,
illus. 27cm.

INDIAN MOUNTAINEERING FOUNDATION
Second Indian Expedition to Mount Everest
February - June, 1962 ...: souvenir brochure.
Delhi: Published on behalf of the Indian Mountain-
eering Foundation by the Armed Forces Information
Office, [1962]. 24p., illus. 24cm.

INDO-JAPANESE NANDA DEVI EXPEDITION, 1976
Nanda Devi Travers 1976: preliminary report of
Indo-Japanese Nanda Devi expedition. [Tokyo]:
The Expedition, 1976. 18p., plates, illus., plans.
26cm.
In Japanese.

INDO-JAPANESE WOMEN'S JOINT HIMALAYAN EXPEDITION,
1976
[Report]. [Tokyo]: The Expedition, [1977]. 72p.,
plates, illus., maps, plans. 26cm.
In Japanese with summaries in English.

Die industrielle und kommerzielle Schweiz, beim
Eintritt ins 20. Jahrhundert. No.3. und 4.
Schweizerische Bergbahnen. Zürich: Polygraphisches
Institut, 1901. xii, 151-328p., plates, illus.,
maps. 35cm.

INEICHEN, Fritz
SCHWEIZER ALPEN-CLUB
Alpine Skitouren: eine Auswahl. Zollikon:
S.A.C., 1962. 2v., plates, illus. 19cm.
Bd.1. Zentralschweiz; bearb. von Fritz Ineichen.
-Bd.2. Graubünden; bearb. von Christian Caduff.

INGERSOLL, Ernest
The crest of the continent: a record of a summer's
ramble in the Rocky mountains and beyond.
Chicago: Donnelley, 1885. 344p., 1 fold. plate,
illus., map. 22cm.

INGERSOLL, Ernest
Knocking round the Rockies. New York: Harper,
1883. viii, 220p., illus. 24cm.

INGLIS, Henry D
Switzerland, the south of France, and the Pyrenees.
Whittaker, 1837. 370p. 21cm.

- - 4th ed. 1840

INGLIS, Henry D
The Tyrol; with a glance at Bavaria. 2nd ed.
Whittaker, Treacher, 1834. 2v. 21cm.

- - 3rd ed. 1837.

INNERLEITHEN ALPINE CLUB
Principal excursions of the Innerleithen Alpine
Club during the years 1889-94; with a memoir of
... Robert Mathison, first President of the Club.
Galashiels: John McQueen for the Club, 1895.
311p., plates, illus. 20cm.

- - 2nd ed. 1897.

INSTITUTE OF ARCTIC AND ALPINE RESEARCH, University
of Colorado
See
UNIVERSITY OF COLORADO. Institute of Arctic and
Alpine Research

Instruction pour les voyageurs qui vont voir les
glaciers & les Alpes du Canton de Berne, [par
J.S. Wyttenbach]. [2e éd.]. Berne: E. Haller,
1787. 40p. 22cm.

INTERNATIONAL GEOGRAPHIC CONGRESS, 4th, Paris, 1889
4e Congrès international des sciences géographiques tenu à Paris en 1889. Paris:
Bibliothèque des Annales Économiques, 1890. 2v.,
2 fold.col. plates, illus., maps. 25cm.

INTERNATIONAL GEOGRAPHIC CONGRESS, 8th, St. Louis,
1904
Report of the eighth International Geographic
Congress held in the United States, 1904.
Washington: Government Printing Office, 1905.
1064p., plates (some fold., some col.), illus.,
maps. 24cm. (House of Representatives. 58th
Congress, 3rd Session. Document no.460)

INTERNATIONAL GEOGRAPHIC CONGRESS, 9th, Geneva,
1908
Compte rendu des travaux du [neuvième] congrès
[international de géographie, Genève, 27 juillet
- 6 août 1908]; publié au nom du Comité
d'organisation par Arthur de Claparède. Genève:
Societé Générale d'Imprimerie, 1910. 2v.,
plates, illus., maps. 25cm.
T.2: Travaux scientifiques.
Library lacks t.1.

INTERNATIONAL UNION OF ALPINIST ASSOCIATIONS
UIAA climbing classification system. Genève:
U.I.A.A., 1973. 12p. 24cm.

INTERNATIONALER SKI-VERBAND
Internationale Wettkampf-Ordnung für Slalom- und
Abfahrtsrennen; beim XI. Internationalen Ski-
Kongress in Oslo und Finse ... 1930 festgesetzt.
Lausanne: Imprimerie Populaire, 1930. 14p. 22cm.
Supplement to Schneehase, No.4.

MACKENZIE, Georgina Muir and IRBY, Adelina Paulina
Across the Carpathians, [by Georgina M. Mackenzie
and Adelina P. Irby]. Cambridge, London:
Macmillan, 1862. 299p., 1 fold. plate, map. 20cm.

IRISH MOUNTAINEERING CLUB
Guide to the mountains of Connemara and Murrisk.

3. Twelve Bens, by J. Lynam. 1953.
4. Ben Corr rock-climbs, by J. Lynam. 1951.

IRISH MOUNTAINEERING CLUB
KENNY, Peter
A guide to the rock climbs of Dalkey Quarry. 2nd
ed., edited by Barry O'Flynn. Dublin: Irish
Mountaineering Club, 1964. 48p., illus., map.
13cm.

IRISH MOUNTAINEERING CLUB
Rock-climber's guide to Donegal. Dublin: Irish
Mountaineering Club, 1962. 56p., illus., map.
14cm.

IRISH MOUNTAINEERING CLUB
A rock-climber's guide to Glendalough. Dublin:
Irish Mountaineering Club, 1957. 38p., illus.
13cm.

IRISH MOUNTAINEERING CLUB
Rock-climbers' guide to the sea cliffs around
Dublin.

1. Bray Head, by J. Lynam. 1951.

Irish walk guides. Dublin: Gill and Macmillan.

3. The north west: Donegal/Sligo, by Patrick Simms,
Gerald Foley. 1979.
5. The east: Dublin/Wicklow, by David Herman [and
others]. 1979.
6. The south east: Tipperary/Waterford, by Frank
Martindale. 1979.

IRVINE, Andrew Comyn
CARR, Herbert Reginald Culling
The Irvine diaries: Andrew Irvine and the enigma of
Everest 1924. Goring, Reading: Gastons-West Col,
1979. 143p., illus., map, ports, bibl. 22cm.

IRVING, Robert Lock Graham
The Alps. Batsford, 1939. viii, 120p., plates
(1 col.), illus., maps (on lining papers). 23cm.

- - 2nd ed. rev. 1942.
- - 3rd ed. rev. 1947.

IRVING, Robert Lock Graham
A history of British mountaineering. Batsford,
1955. xv, 240p., plates, illus. 23cm.

IRVING, Robert Lock Graham
REY, Guido
[Il Monte Cervino]. The Matterhorn; translated by
J.E.C. Eaton; revised and two additional chapters
by R.L.G. Irving. Oxford: Blackwell, 1946. x,
278p., plates, illus. 22cm.

IRVING, Robert Lock Graham
The mountain way: an anthology in prose and verse;
collected by R.L.G. Irving. Dent, 1938. xii, 655p.
20cm.

IRVING, Robert Lock Graham
The romance of mountaineering. Dent, 1935. xiv,
320p., plates, illus. 24cm.

IRVING, Robert Lock Graham
[The romance of mountaineering]. La conquête de
la montagne; traduit par Clare-Éliane Engel. Paris:
Payot, 1936. 411p., 32 plates, illus. 23cm.
(Bibliothèque géographique)

IRVING, Robert Lock Graham
[The romance of mountaineering]. Werden und Wandlungen des Bergsteigens. Wien: A. Holzhausens
Nachfolger, 1949. xv, 343p., plates, illus., map.
27cm.

IRVING, Robert Lock Graham
Ten great mountains. Dent, 1940. xii, 213p.,
plates, illus., maps. 22cm.

- - Another ed. Travel Book Club, 1942.

IRVING, Robert Lock Graham
[Ten great mountains]. Dix grandes montagnes ...;
traduit par Claire-Éliane Engel. Neuchatel:
Attinger, 1945. 215p., plates, illus. 21cm.
(Montagne)

IRVING, Washington
Adventures of Captain Bonneville; or, Scenes
beyond the Rocky mountains of the Far West.
Bentley, 1835. 3v. in 1, plates, illus. 21cm.

IRVING, Washington
Astoria; or, Enterprise beyond the Rocky
mountains. Bentley, 1836. 3v. 19cm.

IRWIN, William Robert
Challenge: an anthology of the literature of
mountaineering; edited by William R. Irwin.
New York: Columbia University Press, 1950. xx,
444p., bibl. 24cm.

ISAACS, A   C
An ascent of Mount Shasta, 1856; introduction by
Francis P. Farquhar. Los Angeles, 1952. 22p.
19cm. (Early California travels series, 11)
Offprint from California Daily Chronicle, April
9, 1856.

ISAIA, Cesare
Al Monviso per Val di Po e Val di Varaita:
reminiscenze alpine. Torino: L. Beuf, 1874.
viii, 287p., plates (2 fold.), illus., 20cm.

ISELIN, Christof
Die Ski-Schaufel. Bern, 1928. 9p., illus. 22cm.
Offprint from Jahrbuch des Schweizer Ski-
Verbandes, 1928.

ISELIN, Fred and SPECTORSKY, A   G
Invitation to skiing; with action photographs by
Lloyd Arnold; drawings by S. Fleishman. Allen &
Unwin, 1952. xiii, 157p., illus. 26cm.

AUDEN, Whystan and ISHERWOOD, Christopher
The ascent of F6: a tragedy in two acts. 2nd ed.
Faber and Faber, 1937. 123p. 24cm.

ISSARTIER, Paul
Notice sur un projet d'ascenseur pour le Mont-
Blanc. Marseille, 1896. 27p., plates, illus.,
col. map. 26cm.
Offprint from Bulletin de la Société scientifique
de Marseille, 1895.

ISSELIN, Henri
La Barre des Écrins (4,102 m.). Paris: Arthaud,
1954. 233p., 18 plates, illus., maps, bibl.
22cm. (Collection sempervivum, 23)

ISSELIN, Henri
La Meije; croquis de Jeanne Germain. [Grenoble]:
Arthaud, 1956. 263p., plates, illus., map, bibl.
22cm. (Collection sempervivum, 31)

ISTRIA, Dora d'
La Suisse allemande et l'ascension du Moench.
Paris: J. Cherbuliez, 1856. 4v., plates, illus.
19cm.

ISTRIA, Dora d'
[La Suisse allemande ...]. Switzerland the
pioneer of the Reformation ...; translated ...
and comprising the chapter suppressed by order of
the Imperial Government in the Parisian edition
of the work, by H.G. A. Fullerton, 1858. 2v.,
port. 22cm.

ITALIA NOSTRA. Sezione di Trento
CLUB ALPINO ITALIANO. Commissione Centrale per la
Protezione della Natura Alpina
[Come si distrugge un parco]: osservazioni e
proposte in difesa dei ghiacciai del Carè Alto e
del Parco Naturale Adamello-Brenta; [edito dal]
Club Alpino Italiano, Commissione Centrale per
la Protezione della Natura Alpina [e] Italia
Nostra, Sezione di Trento. Trento: C.A.I., 1973.
44p., 1 plate, illus (some col.), maps. 24cm.
English, German and French summaries.

ITALY. Army. Corpo degli Alpini
I Verdi: cinqunt'anni di storia alpina, 1872-1922;
sotto gli auspici della Associazione Nazionale
Alpini; a cura di Renzo Boccardi. Roma: Alfieri
& Lacroix, [1922]. 133p., plates, illus., music.
25cm.

ITALY. Commissione Reale del Parco
Il Parco Nazionale del Gran Paradiso; pubblicazione edita a cura della Commissione Reale del
Parco. Torino: La Commissione, 1925. 111p., 1
fold. plate, illus., map. 27cm.

Iter helveticum,being a journal of the doings of a
cabinet ... of five fellow-travellers in Switzerland, during the last three weeks of September,
1866 ..., by their Lord Chancellor [i.e. William
A. Brigg]. Keighley: Printed privately by S.
Billows, 1887. 89p. 19cm.

Itinéraire de Genève à Chamouny et aux environs du
Mont-Blanc. Genève: de Chateauvieux, 1825. 16p.
21cm.

Itinéraire du Pays de Vaud, du Gouvernement d'Aigle,
et du Comte de Neuchatel et Vallengin. Berne:
Nouvelle Société Typographique, 1794. 116p. 19cm.

Itinéraire du voyage à Chamouny, autour du Mont-
Blanc, au Grand et au Petit St. Bernard, et autour
du Lac de Genève ... [par Baron de Malhem?].
Genève: Jullien, [18--]. xxxviii, 160p. 14cm.

Itinéraire général de la Suisse, on y a joint les
principales routes ..., par H.M. Genève: L.
Sestié, 1810. x, 141p., map. 18cm.

Itinerari alpini: guide per alpinisti ed
escursionisti. Bologna: Tamari.

    30. Escursioni in Val d'Ansiei, [di] G. Pais
        Becher. 1976.
    31. Alta Via n.7: "sulle orme del Patéra..." [di]
        P. Fain, T. Sanmarchi. 1976.

ITTLINGER, Josef
Ewige Berge: Erlebnisse und Geschichte. München:
Rösl, 1924. 239p. 20cm.

ITTLINGER, Josef
Führerloses Bergsteigen: das Gehen auf Fels,
Schnee und Eis. Leipzig: Grethlein, [1922].
301p., illus. 21cm. (Bibliothek für Sport und
Spiel)

ITTLINGER, Josef
Handbuch des Alpinismus. Leipzig: Grethlein,
[1913]. 217p., illus. 20cm. (Bibliothek für
Sport und Spiel)

ITTLINGER, Josef
Von Menschen, Bergen und anderen Dingen. München:
Rosl, 1922. 223p. 21cm.

IVATT, Albert
RERESBY, Sir John
Memoirs & travels of Sir John Reresby; [edited by
Albert Ivatt]. Kegan Paul, Trench, Trubner, 1904.
xix, 396p., plates, illus. 18cm. (Dryden House
memoirs)

IVIANI, Antonio
Guida delle grotte del Timavo a S. Canziano presso
Divaccia e della grotta Gigante presso Villa
Opicina, Trieste. Trieste: Società Alpina delle
Giulie, Sezione di Trieste, Club Alpino Italiano,
1934. 42p., illus., maps. 18cm.

IZZARD, Ralph
[The abominable snowman adventure]. Sur la piste
de l'abominable homme des neiges "The abominable
snowman"; compte rendu officiel de l'expédition
du Daily Mail dans l'Himalaya; traduit de
l'anglais par Henri Thies et Micheline Morin.
Paris: Amiot-Dumont, 1955. 199p., plates, illus.
22cm. (Bibliothèque de l'alpinisme)
Library's copy lacks p.49-64.

IZZARD, Ralph
The innocent on Everest. Hodder and Stoughton,
1955. 256p., plates, illus., bibl. 22cm.

J.G.D.T.
See
T., J.G.D.

J., K.C.A.
The sportsman's vade-mecum for the Himalayas,
containing notes on shooting, outfit, camp equipment, sporting yarns, etc. ..., by K.C.A.J.
H. Cox, 1891. 120p., illus. 23cm.

JACCARD, Auguste
Description géologique du Jura vaudois et
neuchatelois, et de quelques districts adjacents
du Jura français... Berne: J. Dalp, 1869. viii,
342p., 8 plates (some fold., some col.), illus.,
bibl. 29cm. (Beiträge zur geologischen Karte
der Schweiz = Matériaux pour la carte géologique
de la Suisse, livr.6)

- - Supplement. 1870.

JACCARD, H   A
BOREL, Maurice
Atlas cantonal, politique et économique de la
Suisse, par Maurice Borel, cartographe; textes de
H.-A. Jaccard. Neuchatel: Administration des
Publications du Dictionnaire Géographique de la
Suisse, [ca 1912]. iv, 76p., 76 col. plates,
illus., maps. 30cm.

JACCOTTET, G
L'étape libératrice: scènes de la vie des soldats
alliés internés en Suisse; texte de G. Jaccottet
[and others]. Genève: SADAG, 1918. 289p., illus.
32cm.
At head of title: Au soleil et sur les monts.

JACKMAN, Brian
EVANS, Harold
We learned to ski: [the Sunday Times tells you all
you need to know], by Harold Evans, Brian Jackman
and Mark Ottaway. 2nd paperback ed. Collins,
1977. 255p., illus. (some col.). 24cm.

JACKSON, Eileen Montague
Switzerland calling: a true tale of a boy and
girl's wonderful summer holidays climbing in the
Alps; announcer: "Miss Tarzan", Eileen Montague
Jackson. Black, 1927. vii, 237p., plates,
illus. 22cm.
For children.

JACKSON, F   Hamilton
Rambles in the Pyrenees and the adjacent districts, Gascony, Pays de Foix and Roussillon.
Murray, 1912. 419p., plates (1 fold.), illus.,
map. 25cm.

JACKSON H   H
A narrative of an ascent to the summit of Mont
Blanc ... Sept. 4, 1823. London [1827]. 458-
469p. 21cm.
Offprint from Colburn's New monthly magazine,
v.19, no.77, May 1827.

JACKSON, John Angelo
More than mountains. Harrap, 1955. 213p.,
plates, illus., maps. 22cm.

JACKSON, John Angelo
PLAS Y BRENIN NATIONAL MOUNTAINEERING CENTRE
Safety on mountains, by the staff of Plas y
Brenin, the Snowdonia National Recreation Centre;
illustrated by Gordon F. Mansell. 3rd ed.
Central Council of Physical Recreation, 1962.
40p., illus. 16cm.

- - 7th ed., by John Jackson and other members of
the staff of Plas y Brenin ... 1968.
- - 8th ed. 1972.

JACKSON, Monica and STARK, Elizabeth
  Tents in the clouds: the first women's Himalayan
  expedition. Collins, 1956. 255p., plates, illus.,
  maps. 22cm.

JACKSON, Monica
  The Turkish time machine. Hodder and Stoughton,
  1966. 159p., plates, illus., map (on lining
  papers). 22cm.

JACOBI, Georg Arnold
  Taschenbuch von J.G. Jacobi und seinen Freunden für
  1795. Königsberg: F. Nicolovius, [1794]. 186p.,
  plates, illus. 13cm.
  Includes Jacobi, G.A. Beschreibung einer Reise an
  den Fuss des Mont Blanc.

JACOBI, J   G
  Taschenbuch von J.G. Jacobi und seinen Freunden für
  1795. Königsberg: F. Nicolovius, [1794]. 186p.,
  plates, illus. 13cm.
  Includes Jacobi, G.A. Beschreibung einer Reise an
  den Fuss des Mont Blanc.

JACOBSEN-MCGILL ARCTIC RESEARCH EXPEDITION TO AXEL
HEIBERG ISLANDS, 1959-1962
  HOEN, Ernst W
  The anhydrite diapirs of central western Axel
  Heiberg Island. Montreal: McGill University, 1964.
  vii, 102p., 1 fold plate, illus., maps (1 in
  pocket), bibl. 29cm. (Axel Heiberg Island research
  reports, Geology, no.2; Jacobsen-McGill Arctic
  Research Expedition, 1959-1962)
JACOBSEN-MCGILL ARCTIC RESEARCH EXPEDITION TO AXEL
HEIBERG ISLANDS, 1959-1962
  FRICKER, P   E
  Geology of the expedition area, western central
  Axel Heiberg Island, Canadian Arctic Archipelago.
  Montreal: McGill University, 1963. x, 156p., 3
  fold. plates, illus., maps (in pocket), bibl.
  29cm. (Axel Heiberg Island research reports,
  Geology, no.1; Jacobsen-McGill Arctic Research
  Expedition, 1959-1962)

JACOBSEN-MCGILL ARCTIC RESEARCH EXPEDITION TO AXEL
HEIBERG ISLANDS, 1959-1962
  ANDREWS, Rodney H
  Meteorology and heat balance of the Ablation area,
  White Glacier, Canadian Arctic Archipelago -
  summer 1960. Montreal: McGill University, 1964.
  viii, 107p., illus., maps, bibl. 29cm. (Axel
  Heiberg Island research reports, Meteorology, no.1;
  Jacobsen-McGill Arctic Research Expedition,
  1959-1962)

JACOBSEN-MCGILL ARCTIC RESEARCH EXPEDITION TO AXEL
HEIBERG ISLANDS, 1959-1962
  Photogrammetric and cartographic results of the
  Axel Heiberg expedition. [N.p.], 1963. 79-122p.,
  illus., maps, bibl. 26cm.
  Offprint from Canadian surveyor, v.17, no.2, June
  1963.
JACOBSEN-MCGILL ARCTIC RESEARCH EXPEDITION TO AXEL
HEIBERG ISLANDS, 1959-1962
  FRICKER, P   E   and TRETTIN, H   P
  Pre-Mississippian succession of northernmost Axel
  Heiberg Island, Canadian Arctic Archipelago.
  Montreal: McGill University, 1963. iv, 27p., 1
  fold. plate, maps (1 in pocket), bibl. 29cm.
  (Axel Heiberg Island research reports, Geology,
  no.3; Jacobsen-McGill Arctic Research Expedition,
  1959-1962)

JACOBSEN-MCGILL ARCTIC RESEARCH EXPEDITION TO AXEL
HEIBERG ISLANDS, 1959-1962
  MÜLLER, Fritz
  Preliminary report 1961-1962, by F. Müller and
  others. Montreal: McGill University, 1963. xiv,
  241p., illus., maps, bibl. 29cm. (Axel Heiberg
  Island research reports; Jacobsen-McGill Arctic
  Research Expedition, 1959-1962)

  - - Map supplement.

JACOT-GUILLARMOD, Charles
  Chaîne de la Dent du Midi aux Dents Blanches de
  Champéry, vue de la Croix de Culet à l'altitude de
  1966m.   Berne, 1926. 26cm.
  Annexe to "Les Alpes" juin, 1926.
  Panorama.

HERRENSCHWAND, colonel and JACOT-GUILLARMOD, Charles
  Étude du terrain, lecture des cartes, reconnaissances et croquis. 2e éd. Berne: Erben, 1925.
  60p., col. plates, illus., maps. 28cm.

JACOTTET, Henri
  Le Jura français; notes de voyage en France.
  (In Bibliothèque universelle ... v.42, 1889,
  p.543-567)

JACQUEMONT, Victor
  Correspondance de V. Jacquemont avec sa famille
  et plusieurs de ses amis pendant son voyage dans
  l'Inde (1828-1832). 4e éd. Paris: Garnier,
  1846. 2v., 1 fold. plate, map. 20cm.

JACQUES, A
  Ski de descente (technique française). Paris:
  Arthaud, 1950. 238p., illus., bibl. 21cm.

JACQUES, A
  [Ski de descente]. Downhill skiing (the French
  technique); translated by Audrey Woodburn. Kaye,
  [1952]. 233p., illus. 22cm.

JACQUES, André
VAILLAT, Léandre
  Paysages d'Annecy; dessins d'André Jacques.
  Chambéry: Dardel, 1931. 149p., illus. 29cm.

JÄGER, Gustav
  Der Donatiberg bei Rohitsch in Unter-Steiermark.
  Wien: M. Auer, 1867. 105p., illus., map. 21cm.

JAEGER, Nicolas
EXPEDITION PEROU 77 - CORDILLÈRE BLANCHE, 1977
  Compte-rendu d'activités. Paris: Expédition
  Perou, 1977. 10p., plates, illus., map, plans.
  30cm.
  Chef d'expédition: Nicolas Jaeger.

JAHN, Gustav
  Gustav Jahn: ein Maler- und Bergsteigerleben; mit
  ... meist farbigen Abbildungen nach Werken des
  Künstlers; begleitende Worte von Egid Filek.
  Wien: A. Luser, [1931]. [24]p., col. plates,
  illus. (some col.). 31cm.

JAHNE, Ludwig
  Karawankenführer. 2. vollstandig ... Aufl.
  Klagenfurt: J. Henn, 1931. 158p., illus. 17cm.

JAHNE, Ludwig
  Ost- und Mittelkarawanken Saantaler (Steiner)
  Alpen... 2... Aufl. Berlin: Geuters Reiseführer-
  verlag, 1924-25. 86p., illus., map. 17cm.
  (Geuters Reiseführer, 10)

JAKŠIC, Dusan
  Planinarski kalendar; Izdaje u vlastitoj nakladi
  H.P.D. Podruznica'Sljeme' u Zagrebu. Godina:
  Tisak Tiskare Oljevac I Janzon, 1924. 105p.
  15cm.

JALEK, Maria
  En campant sur l'Alpe: au-dessus de la plus haute
  route d'Europe des Aiguilles d'Arves au Gran
  Paradiso; photos et croquis de l'auteur. Paris:
  Stock, 1937. 251p., illus., maps. 20cm. (Livres
  de nature, 39)

JAMES, Hugo
  A volunteer's scramble through Scinde, the Punjab,
  Hindostan, and the Himalayah mountains. W.
  Thacker, 1854. 2v. 20cm.

JAMES, J   F   W
  The skirts of Nanda Devi, by the Vice-President
  [of the Bihar and Orissa Research Society].
  [Patna, 1932-33]. 2pts., plates, illus., col.
  map. 25cm.
  Offprint from the Journal of the Bihar and Orissa
  Research Society, v.18, 1932 and v.19, 1933.

JAMES, Norman G   Brett
  The charm of Switzerland: an anthology; compiled
  by Norman G. Brett James. Methuen, 1910. xviii,
  304p. 20cm.

JAMES, Ron
Rock climbing in Wales. Constable, 1970. 241p.,
illus. 22cm.

JAMIESON, Mrs.
Popular voyages and travels throughout the continent & islands of Europe, in which the geography,
character, customs and manner of nations are described... Whittaker, 1820. viii, 506p., plates
(1 col.), illus. 20cm.

JANEBA, Josef
Horolezecká cvičení v Prachovských skalách,
1930-34. Praha: Klub Alpistu ČSL Praha, 1934.
163p., plates (1 fold.), illus. 24cm.

INGLESIAS, José Maria and JANNA, Mario Della
Andinismo y campamentos en el Parque Nacional
Nahuel Huapi; con la colaboración de Lillian
Canova, Sandra Della Janna, Vojslav Arko y
Carlos Sonntag. Buenos Aires: Ediciones
Mundonuevo., 1959. 178p., col. plates (1 fold.),
illus., maps. 18cm. (Colección Alpamayo.
Guia, no.1)

JAPAN CLIMBING EXPEDITION TO WEST WALL OF MANASLU,
1971
Manaslu west-wall, 1971. Tokyo: The Expedition,
1974. 300p., plates (some col.), illus., maps.
27cm.
In Japanese with an English summary by Akira
Takahasi.

JAPAN WALKING CLUB
Sangaku-bi (mountain beauty): a collection of
photos, narratives, descriptions and poems, with a
list of the principal mountains in Japan; compiled
and published by the Japan Walking Club and the
Japan Ladies' Walking Club. Hyogo-ken: The Club,
1922. 216p., illus. 26cm.
In Japanese with English introduction, contents
list and captions.

- - Supplement.

JAPANESE ALPINE CLUB
Exhibition of alpine literature, May, 1935. Tokyo:
The Club, 1935. 56p., plates, illus. 23cm.
Commemoration of the 30th year of foundation of the
Japanese Alpine Club.

JAPANESE ALPINE CLUB
Fujiyama. 2nd ed. Tokyo: The Club, 1931. 119p.,
plates, illus. 27cm.
In Japanese.

JAPANESE ALPINE CLUB
HARA, Makoto and ASAMI, Masao
Makalu 1970: Harukanaru mitoono one. Tokyo:
Meikeido, 1972. 404p., col. plates (some fold.),
illus., maps, bibl. 27cm.
The Japanese Makalu Expedition 1970, organised by
the Japanese Alpine Club.
In Japanese with an English summary.

JAPANESE ALPINE CLUB
Manaslu 1952/3-[1954/6]. Tokyo: Mainichi, 1954-58.
2v., plates (some fold., some col.), illus., maps.
27cm.
In Japanese with English summaries.

JAPANESE ANTARCTIC RESEARCH EXPEDITION, 1968-69
Report of the Japanese traverse Syowa-South Pole,
1968-69; edited by Masayoshi Murayama. Tokyo:
Polar Research Center, National Science Museum,
1971. xii, 279p., plates (1 fold., some col.),
illus., maps, bibl. 27cm. (Scientific reports.
Special issue, no. 2)

JAPANESE EXPEDITION TO NEPAL HIMALAYA, 1969
Gurja Himal: Japanese Expedition to Nepal Himalaya
1969; edited by Yoshimi Yakushi. Toyama: The
Expedition, 1970. vi, 168p., plates (1 fold.,
some col.), illus., map. 25cm.
In Japanese with an Engish summary.

JAPANESE MOUNT EVEREST EXPEDITION, 1970
Everest. Tokyo: Mainichi, 1970. 202p., 1 fold.
col. plate, col. illus., maps. 31cm.
In Japanese with an English summary and captions.

JAPANESE MOUNT EVEREST EXPEDITION, 1970
The official report. Tokyo: Japanese Alpine Club,
1972. 2v., plates (some fold.), illus., maps.
27cm.
In Japanese.

JARDINE, Effie
MACKINDER, H   J
The Rhine its valley & history; with illustrations
in colour after Mrs. James Jardine... Chatto &
Windus, 1908. 226p., col. plates (2 fold.),
illus., maps. 24cm.

JARDINE, Effie
ROOK, Clarence
Switzerland, the country and its people, written
by Clarence Rook; painted by Effie Jardine.
Chatto & Windus, 1907. x, 270p., plates (some
col.), illus. 25cm.

JASIEŃSKI, Stefan
Bildhafte alpine Photographie. Berlin: G.
Hackebeil, 1928. 69p., 20 plates, illus., bibl.
18cm. (Photofreund Bücherei, 12)

JAUFFRET, Louis François
FLORIAN, Jean Pierre Claris de
Guillaume Tell; ou, La Suisse libre: ouvrage
posthume; précédé de son discours de réception à
l'Académie Française, de la Vie de l'auteur, par
Jauffret, de quelques pieces fugitives inédites.
Paris: Briand, 1810. lvi, 94p., plates, illus.
16cm. (Oeuvres de Florian)

JAVELLE, Émile
Souvenirs d'un alpiniste; avec une notice biographique et littéraire par Eugène Rambert.
Lausanne: A. Imer, 1886. xlvii, 404p., 1 plate,
port. 20cm.

- - 3e éd. Lausanne: Payot, 1897.
- - 4e éd. Lausanne: Payot, 1906.
- - Another ed. Lausanne: Payot, 1920.
- - Another ed. Paris: Payot, 1929.

JAVELLE, Émile
[Souvenirs d'un alpiniste]. Alpine memories; with
a biographical and literary notice by Eugène
Rambert; translated and with an introduction by
W.H. Chesson. Fisher Unwin, 1899. vi, 444p.,
plates, illus. 21cm.

JAVELLE, Émile
GUEX, Jules
Dans la trace de Javelle: nombreux documents
inédits, notes, croquis, dessins et photographies
de Javelle. Lausanne: F. Rouge, 1947. 111p., 24
plates, illus., bibl. 22cm. (Collection alpine,7)

JEAN, Louis
Fleurs des Alpes les plus belles et les plus rares:
où et quand les cueillir? Préface de Joseph Pons;
présentation d'Émile Roux-Parassac. Gap: Édition
Ophrys, 1937. xvi, 296p., plates, illus. 18cm.

JEANDRÉ, René D
Contes des cabanes et des sommets. Genève: La
Petite Fusterie, 1925. 185p. 17cm.

JEANNEL, Maurice
Heures pyrénéennes; préface de Robert Ollivier.
Pau: Marrimpouey, 1972. 172p., illus. 22cm.

JEFFERS, Le Roy
The call of the mountains: rambles among the mountains and canyons of the United States and Canada.
New York: Dodd, Mead, 1922. xvii, 282p., plates
(1 col.), illus. 25cm.

- - Another ed. Unwin, 1923.

JEFFREYS, Harold
Earthquakes and mountains. Methuen, 1935. x,
183p., plates, illus., maps. 20cm.

JEGERLEHNER, Johannes
Alp legends; collected by Johannes Jegerlehner;
translated by I.M. Whitworth; black and white
illustrations by Rudolf Munger; coloured illustrations by M. Todhunter. Manchester: Sherratt &
Hughes, 1926. xxiii, 205p., col. plates, illus.
23cm.

JEGERLEHNER, Johannes
La route du Loetschberg; illustrations de Fréd.
Boisonnas. Genève: SADAG, [1917]. 158p., illus.
34cm.

JEGERLEHNER, Johannes
Die Todesfahrt auf das Matterhorn. Berlin: G.
Grote, 1928. 120p. 19cm. (Grote'sche Sammlung
von Werken zeitgenössischer Schriftsteller,
Bd. 171)
A fictionalised account.

JEGERLEHNER, Johannes
Das Val d'Anniviers, Eivischtal, nebst einem
Streifzug ins Val d'Herens, Evolena: Führer durch
Landschaft, Geschichte Volk und Sage eines Walliser
Hochtales. Bern: A. Francke, 1904. vii, 156p.,
plates, illus., bibl. 21cm.

JEMELIN, Erika
Die Wand: Tagebuch eines jungen Bergsteigers.
Zürich: Orell Füssli, 1936. 59p. 20cm

JEMIMA, Miss
Miss Jemima's Swiss journal: the first conducted
tour of Switzerland, the proceedings of the Junior
United Alpine Club, 1863, written for private circulation by 'Miss Jemima'. Putnam, 1963. xiii,
114p., 32 plates, illus., map. 19cm.

JENKINS, G   Gordon
Hill views from Aberdeen, with articles, maps,
diagrams & scientific notes. Aberdeen: D. Wyllie,
1917. x, 39p., plates (some fold., 1 col.), illus.
23cm.

JENKINS, Lady Minna
Sport and travel in both Tibets. Blades, East and
Blades, [1909]. 87p., col.plates, illus., map.
29cm.

JENKINSON, Henry Irwin
Jenkinson's Practical guide to North Wales.
Stanford, 1878. cxxii, 437p., fold. plates, maps
(1 in pocket). 17cm.

JENKINSON, Henry Irwin
Practical guide to the English Lake District. 7th
ed. Stanford, 1881. xcv, 364p., col.plates (some
fold.), illus., maps. 17cm.

JENNI-ZÜBLIN, Mathias
NAEF-BLUMER, Ed
Clubführer durch die Glarner-Alpen. 6.Aufl., neu
überarbeitet von Mathias Jenni-Züblin. Anhang:
Skiführer durch die Glarner Alpen; redigeirt von
P. Tschudi und Mathias Jenni. Biel: S.A.C., 1949.
vii, 488p. 17cm.

- - 7.Aufl., neu überarbeitet von Mathias Jenni-
Züblin, Walter Wild-Merz. 1963.

JENNY, Ernst
KLUCKER, Christian
Erinnerungen eines Bergführers; hrsg. und mit
Lebensbild versehen von Ernst Jenny. Erlenbach-
Zürich: E. Rentsch, 1930. 305p., plates, illus.
21cm.

- - 3. verb. Aufl. 1931.

JENNY, Ernst
FISCHER, Andreas
Hochgebirgswanderungen in den Alpen und im
Kaukasus; hrsg., mit Lebensbild und Bericht ...
von Ernst Jenny. Frauenfeld: Huber, 1913. vii,
311p., plates, illus. 21cm.

- - Neue Folge; hrsg. von Ernst Jenny. 1919.

JENSEN, Johannes
Der Gletscher: ein neuer Mythos vom ersten
Menschen. Berlin: Fischer, 1912. 291p. 19cm.

JEROSCH, Heinrich Brockmann
See
BROCKMANN-JEROSCH, Heinrich

JEROSCH, Marie
HEIM, Albert
Das Säntisgebirge; untersucht und dargestellt von
Alb. Heim; Mitarbeiter: Marie Jerosch [and others].
Bern: A. Francke, 1905. 2v., plates (some fold.
col.), illus., map. 33cm. (Beiträge zur geo-
logischen Karte der Schweiz, Lfg.46, N.F. Lfg.16)

JERVIS, Guglielmo
I tesori sotterranei dell'Italia... Torino:
Loescher, 1873-89. 4v., plates (1 col.), illus.
20cm.

JERVIS, W   P
The mineral resources of central Italy, including
a description of the mines and marble quarries.
Stanford, 1862-68. 2v. in 1. (132p.), plates
(some fold.), illus., maps. 22cm.
At head of title: International Exhibition, 1862.
Includes supplement.

JOANNE, Adolphe
Géographie du Département de l'Isère. 11e éd.
Paris: Hachette, 1901. 76p., 1 fold.col. plate,
illus., map. 19cm.

JOANNE, Adolphe
Géographie du Département de la Haute-Savoie.
8e éd. Paris: Hachette, 1902. 64p., 1 fold.col.
plate, illus., map. 19cm.

JOANNE, Adolphe
Géographie du Département des Hautes-Pyrénées...
6e éd. Paris: Hachette, 1897. 72p., illus.,
map. 19cm.

- - 8e éd., par Paul Joanne. 1907.

JOANNE, Adolphe
EBEL, Johann Gottfried
[Handbuch für Reisende in der Schweiz]. Nouvel
Ebel: manuel du voyageur en Suisse et dans la
vallée de Chamonix... 11e éd., revue par Adolphe
Joanne. Paris: Maison, 1853. xxxvi, 544p.,
maps. 17cm.

JOANNE, Adolphe
Itinéraire descriptif et historique de l'Allemagne; l'Allemagne du Sud... Paris: Maison, 1855.
liv, 756p., maps. 19cm.

JOANNE, Adolphe
Itinéraire descriptif et historique de la Savoie.
Paris: Hachette, 1860. xcix, 279p., illus.,
maps. 19cm. (Collection des guides-Joanne)

JOANNE, Adolphe
Itinéraire descriptif et historique de la Suisse
... du Mont Blanc, de la vallée de Chamouni, du
Grand-St.-Bernard et du Mont-Rose... Paris:
Paulin, 1841. 635p., plates, maps. 19cm.

JOANNE, Adolphe
Itinéraire descriptif et historique des Pyrénées
de l'océan à la Méditerranée. Paris: Hachette,
1858. xlvii, 683p., illus., maps, plans. 18cm.

JOANNE, Adolphe
Itinéraire général de la France. 1. Jura et
Alpes françaises. 2e éd. Paris: Hachette, 1882.
lv, 1091p., illus., maps, plans. 18cm.
(Collection des guides-Joanne)

JOANNE, Adolphe
Itinéraire général de la France. 2. Provence,
Alpes maritimes, Corse. 2e éd. Paris: Hachette,
1877. xxxv, 590p., maps, plans. 18cm.
(Collection guides-Joanne)

JOANNE, Adolphe and JOANNE, Paul
Pyrénées. 3e éd. Paris: Hachette, 1875. xxxix,
411p., maps, plans. 15cm. (Collection des
guides-Joanne; guides diamant)

JOANNE, Adolphe and JOANNE, Paul
Suisse. 4e éd., entièrement refondue. Paris:
Hachette, 1875. xxxvi, 498p., 11 maps. 15cm.
(Collection des guides-Joanne; guides diamant)

JOANNE, Paul
Austriche-Hongrie; Tyrol, Bavière méridionale.
Paris: Hachette, 1885. xxvii, 394p., maps, plans.
15cm. (Collection Joanne; guides diamant)

JOANNE, Paul
Géographie du Département des Alpes-maritimes.
9e éd. Paris: Hachette, 1910. 65p., 1 fold.col.
plate, illus., map. 19cm.

JOANNE, Paul
Géographie du Département des Basses-Pyrénées...
8e éd. Paris: Hachette, 1907. 76p., 1 fold.col.
plate, illus., map. 19cm.

JOANNE, Paul
Géographie du Département des Hautes-Alpes. 6e
éd. Paris: Hachette, 1909. 64p., 1 fold.col.
plate, illus., map. 19cm.

JOANNE, Paul
JOANNE, Adolphe
Géographie du Département des Hautes-Pyrénées...
6e éd. Paris: Hachette, 1897. 72p., illus.,
map. 19cm.

- - 8e éd., par Paul Joanne. 1907.

JOANNE, Paul
Géographie du Département des Pyrénées-orientales
... 7e éd. Paris: Hachette, 1910. 65p., 1 fold.
col. plate, illus., map. 19cm.

JOANNE, Paul
Italie. 1. Italie du Nord: Turin, Gênes, Milan,
Venise, les lacs et les vallées méridionales des
Alpes; collaborateurs: Ernest Franco, A. Le
Pileur. Éd. de 1891 ... mis au courant... Paris:
Hachette, 1891. lxxiv, 662p., maps, plans. 19cm.
(Collection des guides-Joanne)

JOANNE, Paul
Italie. 2. Italie du Centre: Bologne,
Florence, et Rome; collaborateur, Ernest Franco.
Paris: Hachette, 1893. xxii, 579p., maps, plans,
19cm. (Collection des guides-Joanne)

JOANNE, Paul
Itinéraire général de la France: Bourgogne, Morvan,
Jura, Lyonnais. Paris: Hachette, 1909. 64, xvii,
505p., maps (1 fold. in pocket), plans. 16cm.
(Collection des guides-Joanne)

JOANNE, Paul
Itinéraire général de la France: Corse. [Nouvelle
éd., mise à jour par Henri Boland]. Paris:
Hachette, 1892. lxiii, 180p., 4 maps. 18cm.
(Collection des guides-Joanne)

JOANNE, Paul
Itinéraire général de la France: Provence. Paris:
Hachette, 1903. 66, xxv, 486p., maps, plans.
16cm. (Collection des guides-Joanne)

JOANNE, Paul
Itinéraire général de la France: Savoie: revisée
par Maurice Paillon. Paris: Hachette, 1910.
xxxii, 477p., illus., maps, plans. 17cm.
(Collection des guides-Joanne)

JOANNE, Adolphe and JOANNE, Paul
Pyrénées. 3e éd. Paris: Hachette, 1875. xxxix,
411p., maps, plans. 15cm. (Collection des
guides-Joanne; guides diamant)

JOANNE, Adolphe and JOANNE, Paul
Suisse. 4e éd., entièrement refondue. Paris:
Hachette, 1875. xxxvi, 498p., 11 maps. 15cm.
(Collection des guides-Joanne; guides diamant)

JOHN, D H O
Photography on expeditions: recommended techniques
for difficult surroundings. Focal Press, 1965.
176p., plates, illus., bibl. 25cm. (Focal
library)

JOHNSON, A E
POCOCK, Noel
Below zero: a travesty of winter sport; with
verses adapted to the occasion by A.E. Johnson.
Hodder & Stoughton, [1911]. 61p., col. plates,
illus. 29cm.

JOHNSON, Anna C
The cottages of the Alps; or, Life and manners in
Switzerland, by a lady [i.e. Anna C. Johnson].
Sampson Low, 1860. 2v., plates, illus. 21cm.

JOHNSON, Clifton
Highways and byways of the Rocky mountains. New
York, London: Macmillan, 1910. xiv, 279p.,
plates, illus. 21cm. (American highways and
byways)

- - New ed. 1913.

JOHNSON, Fred. H
A winter's sketches in the South of France and
the Pyrenees, with remarks upon the use of the
climate and mineral waters in the cure of disease.
Chapman and Hall, 1857. 336p. 21cm.

JOHNSON, James
Changes of air; or, The pursuit of health and
recreation... 4th ed., with additions. S.
Highley, 1837. iv, 311p. 24cm.

JOHNSON, T Broadwood
Tramps round the mountains of the moon and through
the back gate of the Congo State; with an introduction by T.F.Victor Buxton. Unwin, 1908.
xxiii, 316p., plates (1 fold.), illus., maps.
21cm.

JOHNSTON, Alexander Keith
The physical atlas of natural phenomena.
Edinburgh, London: Blackwood, 1850. 122p., 24
col. plates, maps. 38cm.

JOHNSTON, Sir Harry H
The Kilima-Njaro expedition: a record of scientific exploration in eastern equatorial Africa.
Kegan Paul, Trench, 1886. xv, 572p., plates (2
fold.col.), illus., maps. 24cm.

JOHNSTON, Sir Harry H
The Uganda protectorate: an attempt to give some
description of the physical geography, botany,
zoology, anthropology ... of the territories ...
between the Congo Free State and the Rift valley
... Hutchinson, 1902. 2v. (1018p), col. plates
(some fold.), illus., maps. 26cm.

JOHNSTON, Hugh
Travel films, being pen pictures of Europe. H.
Kelly, [19--]. vii, 167p., plates, illus. 22cm.

JOHNSTON, Marjorie Scott
The mountain speaks. Cassell, 1938. v, 272p.
20cm.

JOHNSTON, Marjorie Scott
Pilgrim and the phoenix. Hamilton, 1940. 303p.
19cm.

JOHNSTONE, G Scott
PARKER, James A
The Western Highlands. 3rd. ed. rev. Edinburgh:
Scottish Mountaineering Club, 1947. 136p.,
plates (some fold.), illus., map (on lining
papers). 22cm. (Scottish Mountaineering Club
guides)

- - 4th ed. rev., by G. Scott Johnstone. Edinburgh:
Scottish Mountaineering Trust, 1964.

JOHNSTONE, J   M
Rock climbs in Arran. Edinburgh: Scottish Mountaineering Club, 1958. 84p., illus., map. 16cm.
[Scottish Mountaineering Club climbers' guide
books]

JOINT ARMY MOUNTAINEERING ASSOCIATION/ROYAL NEPALESE
ARMY MOUNT EVEREST EXPEDITION, 1976
FLEMING, Jon W   and FAUX, Ronald
Soldiers on Everest: the joint Army Mountaineering
Association/Royal Nepalese Army Mount Everest
Expedition 1976. H.M.S.O., 1977. xvi, 239p.,
plates (some col.), illus., maps. 18cm.

JOINT BRITISH ARMY MOUNTAINEERING ASSOCIATION/ROYAL
NEPALESE ARMY NUPTSE EXPEDITION, 1975
Nuptse 1975: preliminary report, [by J.W. Fleming
and others]. Warminster: The Expedition, 1976.
1v. (various pagings), plates, illus., map. 30cm.

JOINT SERVICES EXPEDITION TO CHILEAN PATAGONIA,
1972-73
The general report, by C.H. Agnew of Lochnaw yr.
The Expedition Trust Committee, 1974. ix, 70p.,
1 fold. plate, illus., map, bibl. 30cm.

JOINT SERVICES EXPEDITION TO CHILEAN PATAGONIA,
1972-73
Preliminary report. The Expedition, [1973].
[30]p., plates, illus., maps. 30cm.

JOINT SERVICES EXPEDITION TO ELEPHANT ISLAND, 1970-71
[Report]. The Expedition, 1971. 1v. (various
pagings), plates, illus., maps. 30cm.

JOINT SERVICES EXPEDITION TO NORTH PEARY LAND, 1969
Preliminary report. The Expedition, 1969. 7p.,
plates, maps. 30cm.

JOINT SERVICES EXPEDITION TO NORTH PEARY LAND, 1969
[Report]. The Expedition, 1972. 1v. (various
pagings), plates, illus., maps. 30cm.

JOINT SERVICES MOUNTAINEERING ASSOCIATION
MARSDEN, A   D
Climbing guide to Gibralter. Yeovil: David M.
Haynes for Joint Services Mountaineering Asso-
ciation, [1963?]. 82p., illus. 21cm.

JOKINEN, Matti A
Alppien seinämillä. Porvoo, Helsinki: W.S.
Osakeyhtiö, 1961. 173p., 1 plate, illus., col.
map. 24cm.

JOLIS, Agustín and SIMÓ DE JOLIS, María Antonia
Cerdaña, Andorra, Puigpedrós, Cadí, Puigmal, Carlit.
2a ed. Barcelona: Centro Excursionista de
Cataluña, 1959. xxiv, 286p., plates, illus., maps
(1 in pocket), bibl. 17cm. (Club Alpino Catalán.
Centro Excursionista de Cataluña. Coleccion de
guias, 5)

JOLIS, Agustín and SIMÓ DE JOLIS, María Antonia
Pallars-Aran (del Garona y Noguera Ribagorzana al
Noguera Pallaresa): Besiberri, Montarto, Colomes,
Peguera, Encantats, Mauberme. Barcelona: Centro
Excursionista de Cataluña, 1961. xxxi, 474p.,
plates (some fold., some col.), illus., maps, bibl.
17cm. (Club Alpino Catalán. Centro Excursionista
de Cataluña. Coleccion de guias, 7)

ARMENGAUD, André and JOLIS, Agustín
Posets-Maladeta (del Cinca al Noguera Ribagorzana):
Cotiella, Bachimala, Perdiguero, Eriste, Aneto,
Vallibierna, Forcanada. Barcelona: Centro
Excursionista de Cataluña, 1958. xxviii, 476p.,
fold plates, illus., maps. 16cm. (Club Alpino
Catalán. Centro Excursionista de Cataluña.
Coleccion de guias, 6)

ARMENGAUD, André and JOLIS, Agustín
Posets-Maladeta (du Cinca à la Noguera Ribagorzana):
Pena Montanesa, Cotiella, Turbón ...; traduit de
l'espagnol par Bernard Clos. Pau: R. Ollivier
[pour] Centre Excursioniste de Catalogne, 1967.
xvi, 307p., fold. plates (1 col.), illus., maps,
bibl. 17cm.

JOLY, John
The birth-time of the world and other scientific
essays. Unwin, 1915. 307p., illus., maps. 24cm.

JONAS, Rudolf
Frohsein Sonne und die schöne weite Welt: Junge
Menschen aus vieler Herren Ländern in Freundschaft
verbunden auf Fahrten und Abenteuern in Europa,
Afrika und Asien; ein Buch ... zusammengefasst von
Rudolf Jonas. Wien: L.W. Seidel, 1949. 199p.,
80 plates (some col.), maps. 24cm.

JONAS, Rudolf
Im Garten der göttlichen Nanda: Bergfahrten im
Garhwalhimalaya; mit einem Geleitwort des
österreichischen Alpenklubs. Wien: Seidel, 1948.
168p., plates (1 fold., some col.), illus, maps.
24cm.

JONES, C   A
The foreign freaks of five friends. Kegan Paul,
Trench, 1882. ix, 167p., illus. 20cm.

JONES, Chris
Climbing in North America. Berkeley, London:
University of California Press for the American
Alpine Club, 1976. xi, 392p., illus., bibl.
22 x 22cm.

- - Another issue. Diadem Books, 1979.

WIMPERIS, Edmond Monson and JONES, F
Snowdonia illustrated. Cooper & Hodson, [ca
1890]. 2v. of col. illus. 15 x 22cm.

JONES, Harry
The regular Swiss round in three trips. Strahan,
1865. vii, 393p., plates, illus., map. 17cm.

- - 2nd ed. 1866.

JONES, Harry Longueville
Illustrations of the natural scenery of the
Snowdonian mountains; accompanied by a description, topographical and historical of the County
of Caernarvon. C. Tilt, 1829. viii, 54p.,
plates, illus. 42cm.

JONES, Humphrey Owen
SHORTER, John
Humphrey Owen Jones, F.R.S. (1878-1912): chemist
and mountaineer. London, 1979. 261-277p.,
plates, illus. 25cm.
Offprint from Notes and records of the Royal
Society of London, v.33, no.3, March 1979.

JONES, Humphrey Owen
SHORTER, John
Humphrey Owen Jones (1878-1912): profile of a
pioneer climber and scientist. Glasgow, 1979.
18-20, 23p., illus. 30cm.
Offprint from Climber and rambler, Feb. 1979.

JONES, John Viriamu
JONES, Katherine Viriamu
Life of John Viriamu Jones. Smith, Elder, 1915.
vi, 400p., plates, ports. 23cm.

JONES, John Viriamu
POULTON, Edward Bagnall
John Viriamu Jones and other Oxford memories.
Longmans, Green, 1911. xii, 339p., plates, illus.
24cm.

JONES, Katherine Viriamu
Life of John Viriamu Jones. Smith, Elder, 1915.
vi, 400p., plates, ports. 23cm.

JONES, Mike
Canoeing down Everest. Hodder and Stoughton,
1979. 192p., plates (some col.), illus., map.
23cm.

JONES, Owen Glynne
Rock-climbing in the English Lake District.
Longmans, Green, 1897. xxvi, 284p., plates,
illus. 24cm.
- - 2nd ed., with a memoir ... of the author ...and
an appendix by George and Ashley Abraham. Keswick:
G.P. Abraham, 1900.

JONES, Trevor
LOVELOCK, James
   Climbing; with a chapter on artificial climbing by
   Trevor Jones. Batsford, 1971. 185p., plates,
   illus. 23cm.

NEIL, John and JONES, Trevor
   Snowdon south. Stockport: Climbers' Club, 1960.
   xii, 109p., plates, illus. 16cm. (Climbing
   guides to the Snowdon district, 8)

JONES, Trevor and NEILL, John
   Snowdon south; with a geological note by N.J.
   Soper; natural history notes by R. Goodier; and
   diagrams by R.B. Evans. 2nd ed. Stockport:
   Climbers' Club, 1966. x, 142p., illus., maps.
   16cm. (Climbers' Club guides to Wales, 8)

   - - 3rd ed., including Moel Y Gest Quarry, by Les
   Holliwell. 1970.

JORDAN, David Starr
   The Alps of the King-Kern Divide. San Francisco:
   Robertson, 1907. 22p., plates, illus. 18cm.

JORDAN, William Leighton
   Essays in illustration of the action of astral
   gravitation in natural phenomena. Longmans, Green,
   1900. xvi, 192p., 1 fold. plate, illus. 24cm.

Joseph A. Seiler, 1896-1948: zum Gedächtnis; [der
   Gattin und den Kindern des Verstorbenen zugedacht
   von seinen Geschwistern]. Zermatt: [n.pub.], 1949.
   38p., 1 plate, port. 30cm.

JOUBERT, Georges and VUARNET, Jean
   How to ski the new French way; translated by Sim
   Thomas and John Fry. Kaye & Ward, 1967. 208p.,
   27 plates, illus. 21cm.

JOUBERT, Georges
   Pour apprendre soi-meme à skier; préface, Jean
   Vuarnet; en collaboration avec les entraineurs du
   GUC ... [et] les membres de l'AUS... Paris:
   Arthaud, 1970. 208p., plates, illus. 21cm.

JOURDAN, J
   Vues prises dans les Pyrénées françaises; dessinées
   par J. Jourdan; et accompagnées d'un texte descriptif par Emilien Frossard. Paris: Treuttel &
   Würtz, 1829. 1v. (chiefly illus.). 50cm.

A journal kept during a summer tour, for the children
   of a village school, by the author of "Amy Herbert",
   "Gertrude" ... [i.e. Elizabeth M. Sewell].
   Longman, Brown, Green, & Longmans, 1852. 3v.,
   maps. 18cm.

Journal of a short excursion among the Swiss landscapes, made in the summer of the year ninety-four,
   [by Rowley Lascelles]. Murray, 1803. 132p.,
   1 fold.plate, music. 19cm.

Journal of a tour in France, Switzerland, and
   Lombardy, crossing the Simplon, and returning by
   Mont Cenis to Paris, during the Autumn of 1818.
   Brentford: P. Norbury; London: Baldwin, Cradock &
   Joy, 1821. 2v., plates, illus. 18cm.

Journal of a tour through the Highlands of Scotland
   during the summer of 1829, [by B. Botfield].
   Norton Hall: The Author, 1830. xvi, 376, 23p.,
   plates, illus., map. 18cm.

Journal of a tour to the northern parts of Great
   Britain, [by John Henry Manners, Duke of Rutland].
   Printed for J. Triphook, 1813. 300p., col.plates,
   illus. 24cm.

JOURNÉE MÉDICALE DE LA MONTAGNE, Paris, Bordeaux,1944
   Médecine et montagne: compte-rendu de la Journée
   médicale de la montagne; organisée par le Club
   Alpin Français le 28 juin 1944; avec le concours
   de la Fédération Française de la Montagne. Paris:
   C.A.F., [1945?]. 28p., illus. 27cm.

JOYCE, Ernest E   Mills
   The South Polar trail: the log of the Imperial
   Trans-Antarctic Expedition; with an introduction
   by Hugh Robert Mill. Duckworth, 1929. 220p.,
   plates, illus. 22cm.

JUDSON, David
   Ghar Parau. Cassell, 1973. 216p., plates (some
   col.), illus., map. 25cm.

JUGE, Stéphane
   Guide bleu illustré des Alpes françaises. 1.
   Dauphiné-Savoie... Paris: Librarie du Service
   Central de la Presse, 1894. 457p., illus., map.
   19cm.

JULEN, Hieronymus
   Die Gletscher-Theorie. [N.p.]: [n.pub.], [192-?].
   38p., plates, illus. 19cm.

DHEULLAND, G and JULIEN, R
   Théâtre de la guerre en Italie; ou, Carte nouvelle
   des principauté de Piemont, République de Gênes,
   Duchés de Milan, Plaisance et confins. Paris:
   The Authors, 1748. 24 maps with gazeteer. 26cm.

JULLIEN, Louis Antoine
   L'écho du Mont-Blanc: polka dedicated to his
   friend Albert Smith. Jullien, [1853?]. 9p.
   34cm.

Jungfrau-Bahn: Übersichtskarte. Bern: Hubacher &
   Biedermann, [ca 1900]. 21cm.
   In portfolio.

JUNGFRAUJOCH SCIENTIFIC STATION
   Hochalpine Forschungsstation Jungfraujoch...
   Internationale Stiftung. Zürich: H.F.J., 1931.
   100p., plates, illus. 30cm.
   Contributions in German, French and English.

JUNGMAN, Beatrix
   Norway, by Nico Jungman; text by Beatrix Jungman.
   Black, 1905. x, 199p., 75 plates, illus. 23cm.

JUNGMAN, Nico
JUNGMAN, Beatrix
   Norway, by Nico Jungman; text by Beatrix Jungman.
   Black, 1905. x, 199p., 75 plates, illus. 23cm.

JUNIOR MOUNTAINEERING CLUB OF YORKSHIRE
   Guide to the Island of Rhum; editors; W.H.
   Craven, S.A. Craven. Horbury: The Club, [1946].
   [16]p., illus., maps. 18cm.

JUNIOR UNITED ALPINE CLUB
JEMINA, Miss
   Miss Jemima's Swiss journal: the first conducted
   tour of Switzerland, the Proceedings of the Junior
   United Alpine Club, 1863 written for private
   circulation by 'Miss Jemima'. Putnam, 1963.
   xiii, 114p., 32 plates, illus., map. 19cm.

JUNK, W
   Meine Alpenfahrt; mit Zeichnungen von Lucien
   Bernhard. Berlin: Modern Humoristischer Verlag,
   [1905]. [63]p., col.plates, illus. 32cm.

JUNTA DE PARQUES NACIONALES
   See
SPAIN. Ministeria de Agricultura. Comisaría de
Parques Nacionales

JUSTICE FOR THE TYROL COMMITTEE
   Austria's just claim to South Tyrol. [London?]:
   [Justice for the Tyrol Committee], [1944?].
   84p., plates (some fold., some col.), illus.,
   maps (1 in pocket). 30cm.

The juvenile miscellany of amusement and instruction. Smith, Elder, 1842. vi, 320p., plates,
   illus. 18cm.

JUVENIS, Olim
   See
OLIM JUVENIS

K., H.V.
  See
KNOX, Howard V

KADEN, Woldemar
  Das Schweizerland: eine Sommerfahrt durch Gebirg
  und Thal ...; Holzschnitte von A. Closs.
  Stuttgart: J. Engelhorn, [1877]. viii, 421p.,
  plates, illus. 40cm.

KADEN, Woldemar
  [Das Schweizerland...].Switzerland and the
  Bavarian highlands. Virtue, [1879]. 2v., (xiv,
  628p.), plates, illus. 35cm.
  Translated from "Das Schweizerland", by Woldemar
  Kaden and "Wanderungen im Bayerischen Gebirge und
  Salzkammergut", by Herman von Schmid and Karl
  Stieler.

KADEN, Woldemar
  [Das Schweizerland...]. Switzerland: its mountains
  and valleys; described by Woldemar Raden [sic -
  i.e. Kaden]; with ... illustrations ... engraved
  by A. Closs. Bickers, 1878. xiv, 487p., plates,
  illus. 36cm.

KADEN, Woldemar
  [Das Schweizerland...]. Switzerland: its mountains, valleys, lakes and rivers... New and rev.
  ed. J.S. Virtue, 1889. xi, 388p., illus. 25cm.

- - New and rev. ed. W. Glaisher, 1903.

KADEN, Woldemar
  [Das Schweizerland...]. La Svizzera; descritta
  da Voldemaro Kaden; con illustrazioni di
  Alessandro Calame [and others]. Milano: Treves,
  1878. 512p., plates, illus. 39cm.

KADICH, Hanns Maria von
  Aus Österreichs Bergen: Tagd- und Waldfahrten.
  Neudamm: J. Neumann, 1913. 266p. 19cm.

KADNER, Herbert
  Leberle Führer durch das Wettersteingebirge ...
  4... Aufl. von H. Schwaigers Führer; hrsg. von
  Herbert Kadner. München: Lindauer, 1921. xx,
  244p. 16cm.

KÄMPFEN, Peter Joseph
  Freiheitskämpfe der Oberwalliser in den Jahren
  1778 & 1799; mit einem Anhang der neuesten
  Geschichte von Wallis; Dokumentensammlung von
  Sigismund Furrer. Stans: Caspar von Matt, 1867.
  271p. 23cm.

KÄMPFEN, Werner
  Alexander Seiler der Jüngere: sein Wirken für
  Zermatt, das Wallis und die Schweiz. Zürich:
  Benziger, 1945. 247p., plates, illus. 23cm.

KÄMPFEN, Werner
  Ein Burgerrechtsstreit im Wallis, rechtlich und
  geschichtlich betrachtet; mit einem Überblick über
  das Walliser Geteilschafts-, Burgerschafts- und
  Gemeindewesen. Zürich: [The Author], 1942. x,
  279p., plates, illus., bibl. 24cm.
  Thesis.

BUDRY, Paul and KÄMPFEN, Werner
  Le chemin de Zermatt: petite encyclopédie pratibornienne à l'usage des touristes curieux; dessins
  de Géa Augsbourg; édité par la Compagnie du
  Chemin de Fer Viège-Zermatt, Brigue et Lausanne,
  [en l'honneur de son cinquantième anniversaire].
  Lausanne: La Compagnie, 1941. xvi, 160p., 7
  plates, illus. 17cm.

KAIN, Conrad
  Where the clouds can go; edited, with additional
  chapters by J.Monroe Thorington. New York: The
  American Alpine Club, 1935. xxiii, 456p., plates,
  illus. 24cm.

- - Reprint. Boston: C.T. Bradford, 1954.

KAISER, J   and KAISER, A
  Clubführer durch die Bündner Alpen. Bd.10.
  Mittleres Engadin und Puschlav: Spöl bis Bernina-
  pass und Puschlav beidseitig. Montreux:
  Schweizer Alpenclub, 1947. 280p., illus., col.
  maps (on lining papers), bibl. 17cm.

KAISER, Isabelle
  La vierge du Lac: roman des montagnes
  d'Unterwalden. Paris: Perrin, 1914. 290p. 20cm.

KAISER, J   and KAISER, A
  Clubführer durch die Bündner Alpen. Bd.10.
  Mittleres Engadin und Puschlav: Spöl bis Bernina-
  pass und Puschlav beidseitig. Montreux:
  Schweizer Alpenclub, 1947. 280p., illus., col.
  maps (on lining papers), bibl. 17cm.

KAISERLICH-RUSSISCHE GEOGRAPHISCHE GESELLSCHAFT
  See
IMPERATORSKOE RUSSKOE GEOGRAFICHESKOE OBSHCHESTVO

KALIDASA
  Méchadúta; or, Cloud messenger; translated into
  English verse with annotations by H.H. Wilson.
  Calcutta: Vasáka, 1872. 70p. 24cm.

KALLEN, Urs
  A climbers guide to Yamnuska. 2nd ed.
  [Calgary?]: [The Author?], 1977. 43p., illus.
  14 x 22cm.

KALTBRUNNER, D
  Aide-mémoire du voyageur: notions générales de
  géographie mathématique, ... à l'usage des
  étudiants et des gens du monde. Zurich: Wurster,
  1881. 525p., col. plates, illus., maps. 23cm.
  Supplement to the Author's Manuel du voyageur.

KALTBRUNNER, D
  Manuel du voyageur. Zurich: Wurster, 1879. 1v.
  (various pagings), plates (some col.), illus.,
  maps. 23cm.

KAMBARA, Tatsu
  Nepal bibliography 1959; [compiled by Tatsu
  Kambara]. Tokyo: [The Author], 1959. 121p.
  22cm.
  Text in English and Japanese.
  Compiled from index cards covering 1955-1959.

KAMMER FÜR ARBEITER UND ANGESTELLTE FÜR SALZBURG
KAPRUNER GESPRÄCH, 1968
  Bericht vom Kapruner Gespräch, 1968 über
  Sicherung vor Berggefahren, 10. bis 12. Oktober
  1968 in Kaprun. [Salzburg]: K.A.A.S., [1968?].
  106p. 30cm.

KAMMER FÜR ARBEITER UND ANGESTELLTE FÜR SALZBURG
  Sicherung vor Berggefahren. Salzburg: K.A.A.S.,
  [1967?]. 192p., illus. 25cm.

KAMPEN, N   G van
  Zwitserland en de Alpen van Savoije, naar
  afbeeldingen op de plaats zelve geteekend; in
  tafereelen beschreven door N.G. van Kampen.
  Amsterdam: G.J.A. Beijerinck, [1837]. 2v. in 1,
  plates, illus. 28cm.
  Based on Beattie, William. Switzerland, 1836.

KANO, Ichiro
  The exploration of polar regions. Tokyo: Jiji
  Press, 1959-60 [v.1, 1960]. 2v., plates, illus.,
  maps. 19cm.
  In Japanese.

KANTONAL-BERNISCHE NATURSCHUTZKOMMISSION
  Geschützte Pflanzen im Kanton Bern; hrsg. von der
  Kantonal-Bernischen Naturschutzkommission. Thun:
  Kommissionsverlag W. Krebser, [1938]. 1v.
  (chiefly col. illus.). 19cm.

KAPFF, S   C
  Eine Schweizer-Reise... Stuttgart: J.F. Steinkopf,
  1843. viii, 254p., 12 plates, illus. 19cm.

KAPRUNER GESPRÄCH, 1968
Bericht vom Kapruner Gespräch, 1968 über Sicherung
vor Berggefahren, 10. bis 12. Oktober 1968 in
Kaprun. [Salzburg]: Kammer für Arbeiter und
Angestellte für Salzburg, [1968?]. 106p. 30cm.

KARPATENVEREIN. Sektion Schlesien
MÜLLER, Johannes
Wegweiser für die Hohe Tatra. Breslau: Müller &
Seiffert [für] Karpatenverein, Sektion Schlesien,
1905. 66p., 1 fold.col. plate, illus., map.
18cm.

KARR, Heywood W   Seton
See
SETON-KARR, Heywood W

KASSNER, Theo
My journey from Rhodesia to Egypt, including an
ascent of Ruwenzori and a short account of the
route from Cape Town to Broken Hill...
Hutchinson, 1911. xiv, 309p., plates, illus.,
maps. 23cm.

KASTHOFER, Karl
Bemerkungen auf einer Alpen-Reise über den Brünig,
Bragel, Kirenzenberg, und über die Flüela, den
Maloya und Splügen. Bern: Chr. Albr. Jenni, 1825.
xiv, 303p. 21cm.

KASTHOFER, Karl
Bemerkungen auf einer Alpen-Reise über den Susten,
Gotthard, Bernardin, und über die Oberalp, Furka
und Grimsel; mit Erfahrungen über die Kultur der
Alpen... Aarau: H.R. Sauerländer, 1822. 354p.,
plates, illus. 21cm.

KASTHOFER, Karl
[Bemerkungen auf einer Alpen-Reise über den
Susten ...]. Voyage dans les petits cantons et
dans les Alpes rhétiennes; traduit ... par E.J.
Fazy-Cazal. Genève: Barbezat & Delarue, 1827.
viii, 390p. 23cm.

KASTHOFER, Karl
Bemerkungen über die Wälder und Alpen des
bernerischen Hochgebirgs: ein Beitrag zur
Bestimmung der Vegetationsgrenze schweizerischer
Holzarten... 2. verm. und verb. Aufl. Aarau:
H.R. Sauerländer, 1818. xvi, 200p. 21cm.

KAUFMANN, Franz Joseph
BALTZER, A
Centralgebiet der Schweiz ...; bearb. von A.
Baltzer, F.J. Kaufmann und C. Moesch. Bern:
Schmid, Francke, 1886-94. 4v. in 6, plates (some
fold., some col.), illus. 33cm. (Beiträge zur
geologischen Karte der Schweiz, Lfg.25)
Library lacks v.2.

KAUFMANN, Franz Joseph
Der Pilatus, geologisch untersucht und beschrieben.
Bern: J. Dalp, 1867. xii, 169p. 29cm. (Beiträge
zur geologischen Karte der Schweiz, Lfg.5)

- - Tafeln und Karte.

KAUFMANN, Franz Joseph
Rigi und Molassegebiet der Mittelschweiz,
geologisch aufgenommen und beschrieben; Beilage:
Systematisches Verzeichniss der marinen Arten ...,
von Karl Mayer. Bern: J. Dalp, 1872. viii,
534p., 6 plates (some fold., some col.), illus.
29cm. (Beiträge zur geologischen Karte der
Schweiz, Lfg.11. Gebiete der Kantone Bern,
Luzern, Schwyz und Zug)

KAUKASICHES MUSEUM
See
KAVKAZSKII MUZEI I TIFLISSKAIA PUBLICHNAIA
BIBLIOTEKA

KAULBACK, Ronald
Salween. Hodder and Stoughton, 1938. xi, 331p.,
plates (1 fold.col.), illus., maps. 24cm.

KAVKAZSKII MUZEI I TIFLISSKAIA PUBLICHNAIA
BIBLIOTEKA
Die Sammlungen des Kaukasischen Museums; im
Vereine mit Special-Gelehrten bearb.und hrsg. von
Gustav Radde. Tiflis: Das Museum, 1899-   .
Plates (some fold.col.), illus., maps. 31cm.
Second title page in Russian.
Bd.1. Zoologie, von Gustav Radde. -Bd.2. Botanik,
von Gustav Radde. -Bd.5. Archaeologie; bearb.
von Gräfin P.S. Uvarov.

KAWAGUCHI, Ekai
Three years in Tibet; with the original Japanese
illustrations. Madras: Theosophist Office;
London: Theosophical Publishing Society, 1909.
xv, 719p., plates (2 fold.), illus., map. 25cm.

KAZAKOVA, Elena Alekseevna
K vershinam Altaia. Moskva: Izd. Vtssps
Profizdat, 1955. 150p., 2 fold. plates, illus.,
maps. 21cm.

KAZAKOVA, Elena Alekseevna
Tekhnika strakhovki v gorakh. Moskva: Izd.
Vtssps Profizdat, 1950. 215p., illus. 18cm.

KEANE, A   H
Asia. Vol.1. Northern and eastern Asia. 2nd
ed. rev. and corr. Stanford, 1906. xxvi,
528p., fold.col. plates, illus., maps. 21cm.
(Stanford's Compendium of geography and travel)

KEATE, George
The Alps: a poem. R. & J. Dodsley, 1763. 27p.,
illus. 26cm.

KEATE, George
A short account of the ancient history, present
government, and laws of the Republic of Geneva.
R. & J. Dodsley, 1761. xv, 218p., fold. plate,
map. 18cm.

KEENLYSIDE, Francis
Peaks and pioneers: the story of mountaineering;
preface by Lord Hunt. Elek, 1975. 248p.,
illus. (some col.), maps, bibl. 31cm.

KEHLING, Johannes
Im Hochgebirge: ein Büchlein für Alpenwanderer
und Bergsteiger. 3. Aufl. Leipzig: Quelle &
Meyer, [1926]. 79p., plates, illus. 19cm.
(Sport-Bibliothek)

PLANTA, A   von and KEKULÉ, A
Chemische Untersuchung der Heilquellen zu St.
Moritz im Kanton Graubünden. Chur: F. Wassali,
1854. 30p. 19cm.

KELLER, C
Im Hochgebirge: tierographische Charakterbilder.
Leipzig: Quelle & Meyer, [1911]. 144p., illus.
21cm. (Naturwissenschaftliche Bibliothek für
Jugund und Volk)

KELLER, C
Schweiz. Berlin: W. Junk, 1921. vii, 475p.,
plates, illus., maps. 18cm. (Junk's Natur-
Führer)

KELLER, F   C
Die Gemse: ein monografischer Beitrag zur Jagdzoologie. Klagenfurt: Joh. Leon, 1887. viii,
516p., plates, illus. 23cm.

KELLER, Heinrich
Panorama vom Rigi Berg; gezeichnet und hrsg. von
Heinrich Keller... Éd. originale corr. jusqu'à
1836. Zürich: H. Keller, 1836. 20cm.
In slip-case.
Accompanied by leaflet entitled: Description du
Mont-Rigi...

KELLER, Heinrich
[Panorama vom Rigi Berg]. Panorama of Switzerland
as viewed from the summit of Mont Righi; drawn
from nature by Henry Keller ...; also a circular
view of the country by General Pfyffer; with descriptive notices of the most remarkable objects.
S. Leigh, [ca 1830]. 28cm.
Accompanied by leaflet entitled: A companion to
Keller's panorama of Switzerland.

KELLER, Henry
See
KELLER, Heinrich

SCHINZ, Hans and KELLER, Robert
Flore de la Suisse. Ptie. 1. Flore d'excursion.
Éd. française rev. par E. Wilczek et Hans Schinz.
Lausanne: F. Rouge, 1909. xxiii, 690p., illus.
19cm.

KELLER, W A
Über die Schweiz und die Schweizer, [von Dr. W.A.
Keller?]. Berlin: Friedrich Vieweg, 1795-96.
2v. in 1. 18cm.

KELLY, Christine
ROYAL GEOGRAPHICAL SOCIETY
The RGS archives: a handlist. Pt.1, compiled by
Christine Kelly. [London, 1975]. 99-107p. 25cm.
Offprint from the Geographical journal v.141,
pt.1, March 1975.

KELLY, Harry M
DOUGHTY, Joseph Henry
Hill-writings of J.H. Doughty; collected by H.M.
Kelly. Manchester: Rucksack Club, 1937. xix,
150p., plates, ports. 22cm.

KELLY, Harry M
Pillar Rock and neighbourhood; with illustrations
by W. Heaton Cooper. New and rev. ed. Manchester:
Fell & Rock Climbing Club, 1935. 121p., 1 plate,
illus. 16cm. (Climbing guides to the English
Lake District,[2nd ser.], 1)

KELLY, Harry M   and PEASCOD, W
Pillar Rock and neighbourhood; with illustrations
by W. Heaton Cooper. Stockport: Fell & Rock
Climbing Club, 1952. 130p., 1 plate, illus.
16cm. (Rock-climbing guides to the English Lake
District, 2nd [i.e. 3rd] ser., 4)

KELLY, Harry M
Pillar Rock and neighbouring climbs: a climbers'
guide. Barrow-in-Furness: Fell & Rock Climbing
Club, [1923]. 68p., plates, illus. 21cm.
(Climbers' guides [1st ser.], 2)

KEMP, Dennis
Photography on expeditions.
(In Kodak News for education, winter '70. p.2-6,
illus.)

KEMPF, Bertrand
Guide pratique de la montagne; préface de Samivel.
Paris: Flammarion, 1962. 268p., illus., maps,
bibl. 21cm.

KEMPF, H
Das Berner Oberland: praktischer Reiseführer.
2. neubearb. Aufl., von H. Kempf. Berlin:
Goldschmidt, 1911. 100p., 3 maps. 16cm.
(Griebens Reiseführer, 110)

KENNEDY, Sir Alexander B   W
MOORE, Adolphus Warburton
The Alps in 1864: a private journal; edited by
Alex. B.W. Kennedy. Edinburgh: D. Douglas, 1902.
xxxv, 444p., plates, illus., maps. 26cm.

KENNEDY, Sir Alexander B   W
Petra: its history and monuments. Country Life,
1925. xiv, 88p., plates (some fold.), illus.,
maps. 32cm.

KENNEDY, Bart
A tramp in Spain from Andalusia to Andorra.
Newnes, 1904. viii, 319p., plates, illus., map.
23cm.

KENNEDY, Benjamin E
My old playground revisited: a tour in Italy in
the spring of 1881. Hurst & Blackett, 1882.
xiii, 241p. 20cm.

KENNEDY, Edward Shirley
ALPINE CLUB
Peaks, passes, and glaciers, being excursions by
members of the Alpine Club. 2nd series; edited
by Edward Shirley Kennedy. Longman, Green,
Longman, & Roberts, 1862. 2v., plates (some
fold., some col.), illus., maps. 22cm.

HUDSON, Charles and KENNEDY, Edward Shirley
Where there's a will there's a way: an ascent of
Mont Blanc by a new route and without guides.
Longman, Brown, Green, & Longmans, 1856. xvi,
95p., plates (1 fold.col.), illus., map. 21cm.

- - 2nd ed. 1856.

KENNEY, James
The Alaid; or, The secrets of office. T. Dolby,
[18--]. 58p., plates, illus. 15cm. (Dolby's
British Theatre)

KENNION, R L
Sport and life in the further Himalaya; with
photographs by the author. Edinburgh, London:
Blackwood, 1910. xii, 350p., plates, illus.
21cm.

KENNY, Peter
A guide to the rock climbs of Dalkey Quarry. 2nd
ed., edited by Barry O'Flynn. Dublin: Irish
Mountaineering Club, 1964. 48p., illus., map.
13cm.

KEPHART, Horace
Camping and woodcraft: a handbook for vacation
campers and for travelers in the winderness. New
ed. New York: Macmillan, 1922. 2v. in 1, illus.
18cm.

KEPHART, Horace
RUXTON, George Frederick
Wild life in the Rocky mountains: a true tale of
rough adventure in the days of the Mexican War;
edited by Horace Kephart. New York: Outing
Publishing Co., 1916. 303p., 2 plates, map.
20cm. (Outing adventure library)

KERAUDREN-AYMONIN, Monique
READER'S DIGEST
Guide des plantes sauvages en couleurs: un peu de
botanique ...; une réalisation de Sélection du
Reader's Digest; les textes sont de Monique
Keraudren-Aymonin. Paris: Sélection du Reader's
Digest, 1969. 64p., col. illus. 19cm.

KERN, Emil
SCHWEIZER ALPEN-CLUB. Sektion Uto
Technique de l'alpinisme; traduit de l'allemand
par Albert Roussy et Paul Schnaidt. Genève:
Section Genevoise du Club Alpin Suisse, [1932].
95p., illus. 16cm.
Pt. 1, by Emil Kern, pt. 2, by A.E. Roussy.
Originally published by Sektion Uto.

KERN, Emil
SCHWEIZER ALPEN-CLUB. Sektion Uto
The technique of alpine mountaineering, [by Emil
Kern]. English ed., adapted by members of the
Association of British Members of the S.A.C.
[1935]. 74p., illus. 16cm.
Originally published by Sektion Uto.

KESSER, Hermann
Luzern der Vierwaldstätter See und der St.
Gotthard. Leipzig: Klinkhardt & Biermann, [1908].
168p., plates, illus. 21cm. (Stätten der
Kultur, 7)

KESTER, Friedl
Der Falkenstein bei Füssen-Pfronten und seine
Umgebung. München: Im Selvstverlag des Verfassers,
1904. 81p., illus. 21cm.

KEW. Royal Botanic Gardens
See
ROYAL BOTANIC GARDENS, Kew

KEYSERLING, Hermann
The travel diary of a philosopher; translated by
J. Holroyd Reece. Cape, 1927. 735p. 23cm.

KEYSLER, John George
Travels through Germany, Bohemia, Hungary,
Switzerland, Italy, and Lorrain ...; carefully
translated from the 2nd ed. of the German. 2nd ed.
Linde, 1756. 4v., plates (2 fold.), illus., map.
28cm.

- - 3rd ed. G. Keith, 1760.

KICK, Paul de
See
CHOULOT, Paul, comte de

KICK, Wilhelm
Schlagintweits Vermessungsarbeiten am Nanga Parbat
1856. München: Verlag der Bayerischen Akademie
der Wissenschaften, 1967. 146p., illus., maps,
bibl. 30cm. (Deutsche Geodätische Kommission.
Dissertationen, Nr.97)

KIHARA, Hitoshi
FAUNA AND FLORA RESEARCH SOCIETY
Scientific results of the Japanese expeditions to
Nepal Himalaya, 1952-1953; edited by H. Kihara.
Kyoto: The Society, 1955-57. 3v., plates (some
fold., some col.), illus., maps. 27cm.

KILGOUR, William T
Twenty years on Ben Nevis, being a brief account of
the life, work, and experiences of the observers at
the highest meteorological station in the British
Isles. Paisley: A. Gardner, [1905]. 154p., plates
(1 fold.), illus., map. 20cm.

KILIAN, W   and FLUSIN, G
Observations sur les variations des glaciers et
l'enneigement dans les Alpes dauphinoises;
organisées par la Société des Touristes du Dauphiné.
Grenoble: Allier, 1900. 231p., plates, illus.
29cm.

KIMBALL, Edwin Coolidge
Midnight sunbeams; or, Bits of travel through the
land of the Norsemen. A. Gardner, [18--]. 279p.
21cm.

KING, Alfred Castner
Mountain idylls and other poems. Chicago: F.H.
Revell, 1901. 120p., illus. 19cm.

KING, Clarence
Mountaineering in the Sierra Nevada. Sampson Low,
Marston, Low & Searle, 1872. 292p. 24cm.

- - New ed. 1874.
- - 6th ed. Boston: Ticknor, 1886.
- - Another issue. Unwin, 1903.
- - Another issue. Black, 1947.

KING, Clarence
KING MEMORIAL COMMITTEE
Clarence King memoirs [and] The Helmet of Mambrino,
[by Clarence King]. New York: Putnam, for the King
Memorial Committee of the Century Association,
1904. vii, 429p., plates, ports. 22cm.
Produced under the direction of the King Memorial
Committee, chairman, James D. Hague.

WATSON, Sir Norman and KING, Edward J
Round mystery mountain: a ski adventure; with a
foreword by F.S. Smythe. Arnold, 1935. xii,
246p., plates (1 col.), illus., map. 23cm.
An expedition to the Coast Range and Mount
Waddington.

KING, Rin-Chen
We Tibetans: an intimate picture, by a woman of
Tibet, of an interesting and distinctive people...
Seeley Service, 1926. 228p., plates, illus. 23cm.

KING, Samuel William
The Italian valleys of the Pennine Alps: a tour
through all the romantic and less-frequented
"vals" of northern Piedmont, from the Tarentaise
to the Gries; with illustrations from the author's
sketches. Murray, 1858. ix, 558p., plates (some
fold.col.), illus., maps. 22cm.

KING MEMORIAL COMMITTEE
Clarence King memoirs [and]The Helmet of Mambrino,
[by Clarence King]. New York: Putnam, for the
King Memorial Committee of the Century Associa-
tion, 1904. vii, 429p., plates, ports. 22cm.
Produced under the direction of the King Memorial
Committee, chairman, James D. Hague.

KINGDON-WARD, Francis
The mystery rivers of Tibet: a description of the
little-known land where Asia's mightiest rivers
gallop in harness through the narrow gateway of
Tibet; its people, fauna & flora. Seeley Service,
1923. 316p., plates (1 fold.), illus., maps.
23cm.

KINGDON-WARD, Francis
A plant hunter in Tibet. Cape, 1934. 317p.,
plates (1 fold.), illus., map. 21cm.

KINGDON-WARD, Francis
The riddle of the Tsangpo gorges; with contributions by Earl Cawdor. Arnold, 1926. xv, 328p.,
plates (1 fold.col.), illus., map. 24cm.

KINGERY, Elinor Eppich
Fourteen thousand feet: a history of the naming
and early ascents of the high Colorado peaks, by
John L. Jerome Hart. 2nd ed.; and A climber's
guide to the high Colorado peaks, by Elinor Eppich
Kingery. Denver: Colorado Mountain Club, 1931.
71p., plates, illus., map. 23cm.

KINLOCH, Alexander A
Large game shooting in Thibet, the Himalayas, and
northern India. Calcutta: Thacker, Spink,1885.
vii, 237p., plates (1 fold.col.), illus., map.
30cm.

KINZEL, Karl and LUCKWALD, Christine von
Tiroler Bergwanderungen: noch ein Buch zum
Lustmachen; mit Bildern von F. Völkner. Schwerin
i. M.: Fr. Bahn, 1911. 211p., illus. 20cm.

KIRKPATRICK, William J
An account of the Kingdom of Nepaul, being the
substance of observations made during a mission
to that country, in the year 1793. W. Miller,
1811. xix, 386p., plates, illus., map. 30cm.

KIRKPATRICK, William Trench
Alpine days and nights; with a paper by R. Philip
Hope; and a foreword by E.L. Strutt. Allen &
Unwin, 1932. 198p., plates, illus. 21cm.

KIRKUS, Colin F
Glyder Fach group; with diagrams by C.H. French.
New and rev. ed. Climbers' Club, 1937. ix,
113p., plates, illus., map. 16cm. (Climbing
guides to the Snowdon District, 3)

KIRKUS, Colin F
"Let's go climbing!" Nelson, 1941. 201p.,
plates, illus. 21cm. (Nelsonian library)

KITTO, H   D   F
In the mountains of Greece. Methuen, 1933. ix,
150p., plates, illus., map. 20cm.

KITTO, John
Uncle Oliver's travels in Persia, giving a complete picture of eastern manners, customs ... and
history; adapted to the capacity of youth... H.G.
Bohn, 1846. 2v. in 1, plates, illus. 16cm.

KLAMMET, Gerhard
KNIGHT, Max
Return to the Alps; photographs by Gerhard Klammet;
edited with a foreword and selection from alpine
literature, by David R. Brower. San Francisco:
Friends of the Earth, 1970. 160p., illus. 36cm.

KLAPROTH, Jules
See
KLAPROTH, Julius

KLAPROTH, Julius
Tableau historique, géographique, ethnographique et politique du Caucase et des provinces limitrophes entre la Russie et la Perse. Paris: Ponthieu, 1827. 188p. 21cm.

KLAPROTH, Julius
Voyage au Mont Caucase et en Géorgie. Paris: Gosselin, 1823. 2v., map. 21cm.
Library's copy lacks map.

- - Nouv. éd. 1835.

KLEBELSBERG, R   von
Südtiroler Mittelgebirgswanderungen. München: F. Bruckmann, 1936. 32p., 24 plates, illus. 25cm.

KLEINE, Karl
Führer durch das Säntis-Gebiet von G. Lüthi und K. Egloff. 6. Aufl., neu bearb. von Karl Kleine. St. Gallen: Fehr, 1946. 190p., illus., map. 19cm.

Kleiner Führer durch die Glockner- und Venediger-Gruppe... München: Rother, [19--]. 70p., plates, illus., maps. 17cm.

Kleiner Führer durch die Schweiz. 3. Aufl. Freiburg: P. Lorenz, 1907-08. 127p., maps. 16cm. (Lorenz Reiseführer)

KLIER, Heinrich E   and PROCHASKA, Henriette
Ötztaler Alpen: ein Führer für Täler, Hütten und Berge. München: Rother, 1953. 453p., plates (1 fold.), illus., map. 17cm. (Deutscher und Österreichischer Alpenvereins. Alpenvereins-führer)

RABENSTEINER, Wolfgang and KLIER, Heinrich E
Stubaier Alpen: ein Führer für Täler, Hütten und Berge. München: Rother, 1953. 428p., plates (2 fold.), illus., maps. 17cm. (Deutscher und Österreichischer Alpenvereins. Alpenvereins-führer)

KLINGER, Enrico
Nel paese dei Grigioni: impressioni e note di viaggio... Firenze: Bemporad, 1902. 249p., illus. 20cm.

NICOLAS, R   and KLIPSTEIN, A
Die schöne alte Schweiz: die Kunst der Schweizer Kleinmeister; hrsg. von R. Nicolas und A. Klipstein. Zürich: A. Müller, 1926. 102p., 73 plates (some col.), illus. 32cm.

KLUB WYSOKOGÓRSKI
Himalaya Karakoram: [Polish Expedition Himalaya Karakoram, 1971]. Warszawa: K.W., 1971. [4]p., illus. 25cm.
Contains: Short history of Polish alpinism.

KLUB WYSOKOGÓRSKI
Ostatni atak na Kunyang Chhish [of the Klub Wysokogórski]; opracowanie: Józef Nyka [and others]. Warszawa: Wydawnictwo Sport i Turystyka, 1973. 255p., plates (some col.), illus., maps. 22cm.

KLUB WYSOKOGÓRSKI
NYKA, Józef
[Ostatni atak na Kunyang Chhish]. Gipfelsturm im Karakorum; hrsg. von Józef Nyka [and others]. Leipzig: Brockhaus, 1977. 162p., plates (some col.), illus., map. 24cm.

KLUCKER, Christian
Erinnerungen eines Bergführers; hrsg. und mit Lebensbild versehen von Ernst Jenny. Erlenbach-Zürich: E. Rentsch, 1930. 305p., plates, illus. 21cm.

- - 3. verb. Aufl. 1931.

KLUCKER, Christian
[Erinnerungen eines Bergführers]. Adventures of an alpine guide; translated from the 3rd German ed. by Erwin and Pleasaunce von Gaisberg; edited and with additional chapters by H.E.G. Tyndale. Murray, 1932. xiv, 329p., plates, illus., map. 23cm.

KNAPP, Charles
Dictionnaire géographique de la Suisse; publié sous les auspices de la Société Neuchateloise de Géographie, et sous la direction de Charles Knapp [and others]; avec des collaborateurs de tous les cantons. Neuchatel: Attinger, 1902-10. 6v., plates (some fold., some col.), illus., maps. 29cm.

The knapsack guide for travellers in Switzerland. Murray, 1864. 555p., maps, plans. 17cm.

- - New ed. 1867.

The knapsack guide for travellers in Tyrol and the eastern Alps. Murray, 1867. xi, 636 columns, illus., maps. 17cm.

The knapsack guide to Norway. Murray, 1864. xxviii, 196p., map. 18cm.

KNIGHT, Edward Frederick
Where three empires meet: a narrative of recent travel in Kashmir, western Tibet, Gilgit and the adjoining countries. New ed. Longmans, Green, 1897. 528p., illus., map. 19cm.

KNIGHT, Max
Return to the Alps; photographs by Gerhard Klammet; edited with a foreword and selection from alpine literature, by David R. Brower. San Francisco: Friends of the Earth, 1970. 160p., illus. 36cm. (The earth's wild places, 2)

KNIGHT, William
WORDSWORTH, Dorothy
Journals of Dorothy Wordsworth; edited by William Knight. Macmillan, 1934. xvii, 544p., plates, illus. 19cm.

KNIGHT, William
Through the Wordsworth country; [drawings] by Harry Goodwin, and [text by] Professor Knight. Swan Sonnenschein, Lowrey, 1887. xix, 268p., plates, illus. 30cm.

- - 5th ed. 1906.

KNORR, Otto
DEUTSCHER UND ÖSTERREICHISCHER ALPENVEREIN.
Sektion Jena
Bücher- und Kartenverzeichnis der Bücherei der Sektion Jena des Deutschen- und Oesterreichischen Alpenvereins; bearb. von O. Knorr. Jena: D.u.Ö.A.V., 1930. 23cm.

KNORR, Otto
Der Grossvenediger in der Geschichte des Alpinismus. München: Gesellschaft Alpiner Bücherfreunde, 1932. 60p., plates, illus., map. 27cm.

KNOWLES, Archibald Campbell
Adventures in the Alps. Philadelphia: G.W. Jacobs, [1913]. xi, 176p., plates, illus. 20cm.

KNOWLES, James Sheridan
William Tell: a play in five acts. J. Cumberland, [18--]. 86p. 15cm.

KNOWLTON, Elizabeth
The naked mountain. New York, London: Putnam, 1933. 335p., plates, illus., map. 24cm.

KNOX, Howard V
COOLIDGE, William Augustus Brevoort
Alps.
(In The Encyclopaedia Britannica. 11th ed. v.1, pt.4: Alex to Alum. Cambridge, 1910. 32cm. p.737-754, illus., maps)
Article signed W.A.B.C., with section 10: Geology signed P.La, i.e. Philip Lake, & sections 11, 12: Flora & Fauna signed H.V.K., ie. Howard V. Knox.

KOBE UNIVERSITY KARAKORUM EXPEDITION, 1976
Sherpi Kangri 1976: [report of the] Kobe University Karakorum Expedition. [Kobe]: The Expedition, 1976. 8p., plates (some col.), illus., maps. 26cm.
Four page summary in English as insert.

KOBER, L
Das Werden der Alpen: eine erdgeschichtliche Einführung. Karlsruhe: Braun, 1927. 86p., plates, illus., map. 22cm.

KOCH, Karl
Die kaukasischen Länder und Armenien in Reiseschilderungen von Curzon, K. Koch, Macintosh, Spencer und Wilbraham; hrsg. von Karl Koch. Leipzig: C.B. Lorck, 1855. xi, 335p. 20cm.

KOCH, Wilhelm Daniel Joseph
Synopsis florae germanicae et helveticae... Francofurti a.M.: Sumptibus Friederici Wilmans, 1837. lx, 844p. 22cm.

- - Index generum, specierum et synonymorum. 1838.
- - Ed. 2a. 1843.
- - Ed. 3a. Lipsiae: Gebhardt & Reisland, 1857.

KOCH, Wilhelm Daniel Joseph
Taschenbuch der deutschen und Schweizer Flora, enthaltend die genauer bekannten Pflanzen, welche in Deutschland, der Schweiz, in Preussen und Istrien ...; bearb. von Wilh. Dan. Jos. Koch. 4. Aufl. Leipzig: Gebhardt & Reisland, 1856. lxxx, 584p. 18cm.

- - Another ed. Nach der Original-Ausgabe ... gänzlich umgearb. von Ernst Hallier. Leipzig: Fues, 1878.

KOECHLIN-SCHWARTZ, A
Un touriste au Caucase: Volga, Caspienne, Caucase. Paris: Hetzel, [1882]. 353p., 1 fold.col. plate, map. 19cm.

KÖDER, G   W   and TSCHARNER, Peter Conradin von
Der Kanton Graubünden, historisch, geographische, statistisch geschildert... G.W. Köder und P.C. von Tscharner. St. Gallen: Huber, 1838. 381p. 18cm. (Gemälde der Schweiz, 15)

KÖHLER, Max
Gefahren und erste Hilfe in den Bergen. Wien: Österreichischer Bundesverlag, 1928. 88p., illus. 19cm.

KÖLL, Lois
Führer durch die Ortler-Gruppe: Täler, Hütten, Berge. München: Rother 1959. 258p., plates (1 fold.col.), illus., map (in pocket). 16cm.

KÖLLIKER, Alfred
In den einsamkeiten Patagoniens. Stuttgart: Strecker und Schröder, 1926. viii, 186p., plates, illus., map. 23cm.

RADDE, Gustav and KOENIG, E
Das Ostufer des Pontus und seine kulturelle Entwickelung im Verlaufe der letzten dreissig Jahre: vorläufiger Bericht über die Reisen im kolchischen Tieflande, Adsharien ... im Sommer 1893. Gotha: Perthes, 1894. iv, 120p., 2 fold. col. plates, maps. 28cm. (Ergänzungsheft zu "Petermanns Mitteilungen", 112)

KÖNIG, Erich
Mit Rucksack und Eispickel: Bergerinnerungen. Schw. Hall: F. Staib, [1896]. vii, 240p., port. 19cm.

KOENIG, Franz Nikolaus
[Neue Sammlung von Schweizertrachten...]. Alte Schweizer Trachten, nach Zeichnungen von F.N. König, Lory und Anderen; mit einer Einleitung von R. Nicolas. Zürich-Rüschlikon: Montana-Verlag, 1924. 277p., col. illus. 16cm.
Facsimile reprint of 1816 ed.

KOENIG, Franz Nikolaus
[Neue Sammlung von Schweizertrachten...]. Nouvelle collection de costumes suisses, d'après les dessins de F.N. Koenig. Zuric: Fuessli, 1813. 183p., col. plates, illus. 16cm.
Text in French and German.

KOENIG, Franz Nikolaus
Reise in die Alpen; begleitet mit naturhistorischen Beyträgen von Kuhn [and others]. Bern: Bey dem Verfasser, 1814. xii, 150p., plates, illus. 19cm.

KOENIG, Franz Nikolaus
MANDACH, Conrad de
F.-N. Koenig, 1765-1832. Genève: A. Ciana, 1923. 43p., illus. 27cm.

KOENIG, Hans
SCHWEIZER ALPEN-CLUB. Sektion Uto
Ratgeber für Bergsteiger; hrsg. von der Sektion "Uto". Zürich: Art. Institut Orel Füssli, 1916. 2v., illus., map. 21cm.
Bd.2. Die Technik des Bergsteigens, bearb. von Hans Koenig.

- - 2. verb. und verm. Aufl. 1920.

KOENIG, Hans
SCHWEIZER ALPEN-CLUB. Sektion Uto
[Ratgeber für Bergsteiger]. Le conseiller de l'ascensionniste. Vol.2. Technique de l'alpinisme, en tenant compte de nombreux cas d'accidents, par Hans Koenig; traduit par E. Corrévon et C. Brossy; dessins de C. Meili. Genève: C.A.S., 1918. 166p., illus. 21cm.
Translation of v.2 of "Ratgeber für Bergsteiger", originally published by the Section Uto, 1916.

KOENIGSMARCK, Hans, Graf von
The Markhor: sport in Cashmere; translated from the German by Norah Bashford. Kegan Paul, Trench, Trübner, 1910. xv, 151p., plates, illus. 20cm.

LAMBERT, Raymond and KOGAN, Claude
[Record à l'Himalaya]. White fury: Gaurisankar and Cho Oyu; translated by Showell Styles. Hurst & Blackett, 1956. 176p., plates, illus., map. 22cm.

KOGAN, Georges and LEININGER, Nicole
Cordillère Blanche: Expédition franco-belge à la cordillère des Andes, 1951; récit précédé d'un poème de Jacques Prévert à la mémoire de Georges Kogan; préface de Maurice Herzog. Paris: Arthaud, 1952. 155p., plates, illus. 21cm. (Collection sempervivum, 17)

KOGAN, Georges and LEININGER, Nicole
[Cordillère Blanche...]. The ascent of Alpamayo: an account of the Franco-Belgian Expedition to the Cordillera Blanca in the high Andes; with a foreword by Maurice Herzog; translated by Peter E. Thompson. Harrap, 1954. 135p., plates (1 col.), illus., maps. 21cm.

KOHL, Johann Georg
Alpenreisen. Dresden: Arnold, 1949-51. 3v. in 2. 22cm.
Vol.3 has title: Naturansichten aus den Alpen and is published Leipzig, 1851.

KOHL, Johann Georg
Austria, Vienna, Prague, Hungary, Bohemia and the Danube, Galicia, Styria, Moravia, Bukovina and the military frontier. Chapman & Hall, 1943. 532p. 22cm.

BERLEPSCH, Hermann Alexander von and KOHL, Johann Georg
Switzerland and the principal parts of southern Germany: handbook for travellers. Zürich: C. Schmidt, 1874. xxiv, 504p., plates, illus., maps, plans. 16cm.

KOHLI, M   S
Himalayan treks and climbs. Bombay: Air-India, [1971?]. 48p., plates, illus. 23cm.

KOHLI, M   S
The last of the Annapurnas; foreword by S.
Radhakrishnan. Delhi: Government of India,
Ministry of Information and Broadcasting, 1962.
143p., plates (some col.), illus., map. 23cm.

KOHLI, M   S
Nine atop Everest: story of the Indian ascent;
foreword by Indira Gandhi. Bombay: Orient
Longmans, 1969. xxvii, 384p., plates (some col.),
illus., maps. 25cm.

KOLB, Fritz
Himalaya venture; translated by Lawrence Wilson.
Lutterworth Press, 1959. 148p., plates, illus.,
maps, bibl. 23cm.

KOLB, Fritz
Pfade zur Hohe: Zehnjahrbuch der Alpinistengilde;
geleite von Fritz Kolb. Wien: Alpinistengilde,
[1931]. 205p., plates, illus., maps. 25cm.

KOLENATI, F   A
Die Bereisung Hocharmeniens und Elisabethopols der
Schekinschen Provinz und des Kasbek im Central-
Kaukasus. Dresden: R. Kuntze, 1858. 289p, vi p.
25cm.

KOLLBACH, Karl
Von der Tatra bis zur sachsischen Schweiz. Köln
a. Rh.: P. Neubner, [1897]. ix, 304p., plates,
illus. 24cm. (Wanderungen durch die deutschen
Gebirge, 2)

KOLLER, Engelbert
Das Höllengebirge. Vöcklabruck: Deutscher und
Oesterreichischer Alpenvereins, 1933. 64p., plates,
illus. 16cm.

KOLLER, Willy
Skiführer für Zell am See mit den östlichen
Kitzbühelern, Saalbach, Steinernem Meer, Gross-
glockner- und Venedigegruppe; bearb. Willy Koller.
2 Aufl. München: Rother, 1932. 98p., illus.
5 fold. maps (as inserts). 17cm.
Cover title: Skiführer der Hohen Tauern...

KOL'TSOVA-MASAL'SKAIA, Elena, Kniaginia
See
ISTRIA, Dora d'

KOMARNICKI, Gyula v.
Hochgebirgsführer der Hohen Tatra. Budapest:
Turistik und Alpinismus, 1918. 4v., fold.col.
plates, illus., maps. 16cm.
Library lacks v.1.

KONGSBERG TURISTFORENING
Kongsberg, with routes and map; compiled by Joh.
L. Alver; translated by Laura Poulsson. Kongsberg:
Tourist Club of Kongsberg and vicinity, 1890.
59p., map. 16cm.

KONNIGER, Karl
Försters Touristenführer in Wiens Umgebungen:
Wegweiser bei Ausflügen im Wiener Walde, im
österreichisch-steirischen Alpenlande und in der
Wachau. 12. neu bearb. Aufl. Wien: A. Hölder,
1903. 5v., illus., maps. 17cm.
In slip-case.

KONODY, P   G
Through the Alps to the Apennines; with ... illustrations from photographs and from pencil sketches
by E.A. Rickards. Kegan Paul, Trench, Trübner,
1911. xii, 370p., plates, illus. 23cm.

KONOW, Sten
NORWAY. Kirke- og Undervisningsdepartement
Norway: official publication for the Paris Exhibi-
tion 1900; [edited under the direction of the
Ecclesiastical and Educational Department by Sten
Konow and Karl Fischer]. Kristiania: The
Department, 1900. 626], xxxiv p., illus., maps.
27cm.

HÜTTIG, Robert and KORDON, Frido
Führer durch die Ankogelgruppe einschliesslich
Hochalmspitz, Hasner- und Reisseckgruppe. Wien:
Artaria, 1926. xii, 313p., plates, illus., map
(in pocket). 17cm.

KOREAN ALPINE CLUB
Korean Alpine Club. Seoul: The Club, [1973].
[8]p., illus. 26cm.

KOŘISTKA, Carl
Die Hohe Tatra in den Central-Karpaten: eine
geographische Skizze verfasst auf Grundlage einer
Bereisung. Gotha: Perthes, 1864. 36p., col.
plates (1 fold.), illus., map. 28cm.
(Ergänzungsheft zu Petermann's Geographischen
Mittheilungen, No.12)

KORRODI, Eduard
SCHWARZENBACH, Annemarie and SCHMID, Hans Rudolf
Das Buch von der Schweiz; hrsg. von Eduard
Korrodi. München: R. Piper, 1932-33. 2v.,
illus. 19cm. (Was nicht im Baedeker steht)
15-16)

KOVALEV, Pavel Vasil'evich
Kavkaz: ocherk prirody. Moskva: Gos. Izd.
Geograficheskoi Literatury, 1954. 78p., plates,
illus., map. 21cm.

KRANZ, C   A
WEBER, J   C
Die Alpen-Pflanzen Deutschlands und der Schweiz
in colorirten Abbildungen ...; mit einem
erläuternden Text von J.C. Weber. München: C.
Kaiser, [1843-56]. 3v., col. plates, illus.
14cm.

- - 4. Aufl., systematisch geordnet mit Text von
C.A. Kranz. 1880.

KRAPF, J   Lewis
Travels, researches, and missionary labours,
during an eighteen years' residence in eastern
Africa ...; with an appendix respecting the snow-
capped mountains of eastern Africa ... and ...
the discovery of the Uyenyesi by Dr. Livingstone
in September last, by E.G. Ravenstein. Trüber,
1860. liii, 566p., plates (2 fold., some col.),
illus., maps. 24cm.

KRAUS, Erwin
RITTERBUSH, Philip C
Report of the 1970 expedition to the Nevado del
Huila, central Andean Cordillera, Colombia, July
1970, by Philip C. Ritterbush and other members
of the expedition; with an account of the original
ascent by Erwin Kraus. Cali: Museo Departmental
de Historia Natural, [1970?]. 43p., plates,
illus., maps, bibl. 27cm. (Occasional publications of the Museo Departmental de Historia
Natural)

VARESCHI, Volkmar and KRAUSE, Ernst
Mountains in flower; photographs by Ernst Krause.
Lindsay Drummond, 1939. 159p., illus. (1 col.).
25cm.

KRAWCZYK, Chess
Mountaineering: a bibliography of books in
English to 1974. Metuchen (N.J.): Scarecrow P.,
1977. xii, 180p. 23cm.

KREBS, Norbert
Landerkunde der österreichischen Alpen.
Stuttgart: Engelhorn, 1913. 556p., illus., col.
maps, bibl. 25cm.
Second ed. published in 1928 under title: Die
Ostalpen und das heutige Österreich...

KREBS, Norbert
Die Ostalpen und das heutige Österreich: eine
Länderkunde. 2. wesentlich erw. Aufl. Stuttgart:
Engelhorn, 1928. 2v., plates, illus., maps, bibl.
24cm. (Bibliothek länderkundlicher Handbücher)
First ed. published in 1913 under title:
Länderkunde der österreichischen Alpen.

KREIDOLF, Ernst
Alpenblumenmärchen. Zürich: Rotapfelverlag, 1922.
36p., illus. 27 x 32cm.

GALFY, Ivan and KRISSAK, Milan
Makalu. Bratislava: Sport, 1978. 1v. (chiefly
illus., map). 28cm.
Summaries in Russian, German, English and French.

KRONECKER, Franz
Wanderungen in den südlichen Alpen Neu-Seelands.
Berlin: Pasch, 1898. 119p., plates (1 fold.),
illus., map. 25cm.

KRONIG, Stanislaus
Familien-Statistik und Geschichtliches über die
Gemeinde Zermatt. [New ed.] von Stanislaus
Kronig. Ingenbohl: B. Theodosius-Buchdruckerei,
1927. 356p. 21cm.
Previous ed., by Joseph Ruden, published in 1869
under title: Familien-Statistik der löblichen
Pfarrei von Zermatt...

KROPF, Ferdinand Noizovich
Spasatel'n'ye raboty v gorakh. Moskva: Izd.
"Fizkul'tura i sport", 1966. 120p., illus. 20cm.

KROUTIL, F   V   and GELLNER, J
Vysoké Tatry, horolezecký průvodce. Dil 1. Praha:
Orbis, 1935. xv, 116p., illus., maps. 17cm.

KROUTIL, F   V   and GELLNER, J
Vysoké Tatry, horolezecký průvodce. 2.vydani v
cervnu. Praha: Orbis, 1947. 2v., illus., maps.
17cm.

KRUSZYNA, Robert and PUTNAM, William Lowell
A climber's guide to the interior ranges of British
Columbia south. 6th ed. [New York]: American
Alpine Club, 1977. 226p., illus., maps. 17cm.

KUCHAR, Radovan
Deset velkých sten. Praha: Sportovní a Turistické
Nakladatelství, 1963. 174p., plates, illus., maps.
22cm.

KUCHLER, Carl
Unter der Mitternachtssonne durch die Vulkan- und
Gletscherwelt Islands. Leipzig: Abel & Müller,
1906. 174p., illus., map. 23cm.

KÜHNEL, Max
See
KNIGHT, Max

KÜMEL, Friedrich
GANSS, Ortwin
Erläuterungen zur geologischen Karte der Dachstein-
gruppe; aufgenommen 1936-1940 im Auftrage des
Alpenvereins ... von O. Ganss, F. Kümel und E.
Spengler. Innsbruck: Wagner, 1954. 82p., 6 plates
(2 fold., 1 col.), illus., map (in pocket). 28cm.
(Wissenschaftliche Alpenvereinshefte, Heft 15)

KÜRSINGER, Ignaz von and SPITALER, Franz
Der Gross-Venediger in der norischen Central-
Alpenkette, seine erste Ersteigung am 3. September
1841, und sein Gletscher ...; mit einem Anhange:
Die zweite Ersteigung am 6. September 1842, von Dr.
Spitaler. Innsbruck: Wagner, 1843. 310p., plates
(1 fold.), illus., map. 24cm.

KÜSCH, Gabriel
Der Kanton Appenzell, historisch, geographisch,
statistisch geschildert: ein Hand- und Hausbuch für
Kantonsbürger und Reisende; hrsg. von Gabriel Küsch.
St. Gallen: Huber, 1835. ix, 249p. 18cm. (Gemälde
der Schweiz, 13)

KÜTTNER, Carl Gottlob
Travels through Denmark, Sweden, Austria, and part
of Italy in 1798 & 1799; translated from the
German. iv, 200p., 1 fold. plate, map. 22cm.
(In A collection of modern and contemporary
voyages... v.1. London, 1805)

KUGY, Julius
Anton Oitzinger: ein Bergführerleben. Graz: Leykam,
1935. 159p., plates, illus., ports. 23cm.

KUGY, Julius
[Anton Oitzinger: ein Bergführerleben]. Son of
the mountains: the life of an alpine guide;
translated by H.E.G. Tyndale. Nelson, 1938.
200p., plates, illus., map. 21cm.

KUGY, Julius
Arbeit, Musik, Berge: ein Leben. München: Rother,
[1931]. 374p. 21cm.

KUGY, Julius
Aus dem Leben eines Bergsteigers. München:
Rother, 1925. xi, 340p., plates, illus., bibl.
27cm.

- - 2. Aufl. [1928].
- - 3. Aufl. [1930].
- - 4. Aufl. [ca 1932].
- - Another ed. 1935.

KUGY, Julius
[Aus dem Leben eines Bergsteigers]. Alpine pilgrimage; translated by H.E.G. Tyndale. Murray,
1934. xxii, 374p., plates (1 fold.), illus., map.
23cm.

KUGY, Julius
Fünf Jahrhunderte Triglav. Graz: Leykam, 1938.
xi, 378p., plates, illus. 25cm.

KUGY, Julius
Im göttlichen Lächeln des Monte Rosa. Graz:
Leykam, 1940. 2v. (xi, 372p.), plates (1 fold.),
illus., map. 25cm.

KUGY, Julius
Die Julischen Alpen im Bilde. Graz: Leykam, 1934.
1v. of illus. 24cm.

KUGY, Julius
Das Kugybuch: Dr. Julius Kugy's Lebenswerk "Aus
dem Leben eines Bergsteigers": eine Auswahl von
Besprechungen. München: Rother, [192-?]. 113p.
16cm.

KUHNS, Oscar
Switzerland: its scenery, history, and literary
associations. 2nd ed. New York: Crowell, 1910.
xii, 294p., plates (1 fold.), illus., map. 22cm.

KUKAČKA, Miroslav
Nízke Tatry, zostavil Miroslav Kukačka.
Bratislava: Vydavatel'stvo Osveta, 1962. 1v.
(chiefly illus.). 30cm.
Summaries in English, German and Russian.

KUMMER, K   W
Tableau géographico-topographique pour servir
d'explication au relief du Montblanc dans les
Alpes Suisses, de la vallée de Chamounix, du
passage du grand St. Bernhard... Berlin: Kummer,
[18--]. 8p. 22cm.
In French and German.

KUMMER, K   W
RITTER, C
Geographisch-historisch-topographische
Beschreibung zu K.W. Kummer's Stereorama oder
Relief des Montblanc-Gebirges und dessen nachster
Umgebung. Berlin: Kummer, 1824. 107p. 21cm.

LECHNER, Sigmund and KUNTSCHER, Karl
Skiführer durch die Ötztaler Alpen. Wien: Artaria,
1925. viii, 89p., plates (1 fold.), illus., map
(in pocket). 17cm.

KUPFFER, Adolf Theodor von
Voyage dans les environs du Mont Elbrouz dans le
Caucase, entrepris ... en 1829: rapport fait à
l'Académie Impériale des Sciences de St.-Péters-
bourg. St.-Pétersbourg: L'Académie, 1830. 126p.,
plates (1 fold.), illus. 27cm.

KURZ, Fritz
Bergklänge: gedichte. Wien: Verlag des
Österreichischen Alpenklubs, 1922. 76p. 18cm.

KURZ, Heinrich
Die Schweiz: Land, Volk und Geschichte in ausgewählten Dichtungen. Bern: J. Dalp, 1853. xvii,
499p. 24cm.

KURZ, K   J   and GURTNER, Othmar
Zwischen Aare und Rhone. Bern: Pochon-Jent &
Bühler, 1920. 144p., illus. 19cm.

KURZ, Louis
Guide de la chaîne du Mont-Blanc à l'usage des
ascensionnistes. Neuchatel: Attinger, 1892. xvi,
210p., bibl. 14cm.

- - 2e éd. Neuchatel: L'Auteur, 1914.
- - 3e éd., rev. et mise à jour par Marcel Kurz.
Lausanne: Payot, 1927.
- - 4e éd. Lausanne: Payot, 1935.

KURZ, Louis
[Guide de la chaîne du Mont-Blanc...]. The chain
of Mont Blanc. Fisher Unwin, 1892. xx, 143p.
14cm. (Conway and Coolidge's climbers' guides, 5)

KURZ, Marcel
Alpes valaisannes
See his
Clubführer durch die Walliser Alpen

KURZ, Marcel
Alpinisme hivernal: le skieur dans les Alpes;
préface de Édouard Sauvage. Paris: Payot, 1925.
xvi, 395p., plates, illus. 24cm.

KURZ, Marcel
[Alpinisme hivernal]. Alpinismo invernale.
Pinerolo: Casa Sociale Editrice, 1928. 499p.,
plates, illus. 21cm. (Classici della montagna)

KURZ, Marcel
Clubführer durch die Bünder Alpen. Bd.5. Bernina-
Gruppe. Zürich: Schweizer Alpenclub, 1932. 368p.,
1 fold. plate, illus., maps, bibl. 17cm. (Clubführer des Schweizer Alpen-Club)

- - 2. Aufl. Revision: H. Tgetgel. 1955.
- - 3. Aufl., neu bearb. von Otto Kaiser. 1973.

KURZ, Marcel
Clubführer durch die Walliser-Alpen. Bd.2. Vom
Col Collon bis zum Col de Théodule. 2.Aufl.
Zürich: Schweizer Alpen-Club, 1930. xliii, 372p.,
illus., bibl. 17cm.

- - 3.Aufl. 1955.
- - 4.Ausg.: Vom Col Collon zum Theodulpass, durchgesehen und erweitert von Maurice Brandt. 1971.

KURZ, Marcel
[Clubführer durch die] Walliser Alpen. Bd.3. Vom
Theodulpass zum Monte Moro. 4.Ausg., durchgesehen
und erweitert von Maurice Brandt. Zürich:
Schweizer Alpen-Club, 1970. 220p., illus., maps
(on lining papers). 17cm. (Clubführer des
Schweizer Alpen-Club)

KURZ, Marcel
[Clubführer durch die] Walliser Alpen. Bd.4. Vom
Strahlhorn zum Simplon. 4. Ausg., durchgesehen
und erweitert von Maurice Brandt. Zürich:
Schweizer Alpen-Club, 1970. 339p., 1 fold. plate,
illus., maps (on lining papers). 17cm. (Clubführer des Schweizer Alpen-Club)

KURZ, Marcel
[Clubführer durch die Walliser Alpen]. Guide des
Alpes valaisannes. Vol.1. Du Col Ferret au Col
de Collon. Aarau: Club Alpin Suisse, 1923. xxxix,
304p., illus., maps, bibl. 17cm.

- - 2e éd. Lucerne, 1937.
- - 2e éd. [avec] supplément. 1963.
- - 3e éd., rev. et augm. par Maurice Brandt. [1977].

KURZ, Marcel
[Clubführer durch die Walliser Alpen]. Guide des
Alpes valaisannes. Vol.2. Du Col Collon au Col
de Théodule. 2e éd. Club Alpin Suisse, 1930.
xxxviii, 347, 32p., illus., bibl. 17cm.

- - 3e éd. 1947.
- - 4e éd.: Col Collon au Théodulpass, rev. et augm.
par Maurice Brandt. 1970.

KURZ, Marcel
[Clubführer durch die Walliser Alpen]. Guide des
Alpes valaisannes. Vol.3a. Du Col de Théodule au
Monte Moro. 3e éd. Lucerne: Club Alpin Suisse,
1952. 280p., illus., map (on lining papers),
bibl. 17cm.

KURZ, Marcel
[Clubführer durch die Walliser Alpen]. Guide des
Alpes valaisannes. Vol.3b. Du Strahlhorn au
Simplon. 2e éd. Lucerne: Club Alpin Suisse,
1937. 271-680p., illus., maps (on lining papers).
17cm.

- - 3e éd. 1952.

KURZ, Marcel
[Clubführer durch die Walliser Alpen. Guide des]
Alpes valaisannes. Vol.3. Du Théodulpass au
Monte Moro. 4e éd. rev. et augm. par Maurice
Brandt. Zurich: Club Alpin Suisse, 1970. 236p.,
illus., maps (on lining papers). 17cm. (Guides
du Club Alpin Suisse)

KURZ, Marcel
[Clubführer durch die Walliser Alpen]. Guide des
Alpes valaisannes. Vol.4. Du Col du Simplon au
Col de la Furka. Genève: Club Alpin Suisse, 1920.
xxvii, 242p., illus., maps, bibl. 17cm.

- - 4e éd.: Du Strahlhorn au Simplon, rev. et augm.
par Maurice Brandt. 1970.

KURZ, Marcel
Essai de chronologie des records d'altitude
atteinte par l'homme en montagne. [Lausanne,
1947?]. 2pts. in 1, illus. 25cm.
Offprint from Montagnes du monde.

KURZ, Marcel
KURZ, Louis
Guide de la chaîne du Mont Blanc à l'usage des
ascensionnistes. 3e éd.,rev. et mise à jour par
Marcel Kurz. Lausanne: Payot, 1927. 408p., 1
fold. plate, illus., bibl. 17cm.

- - 4e éd. 1935.

KURZ, Marcel
Guide des Alpes valaisannes
See his
Clubführer durch die Walliser Alpen

KURZ, Marcel
Himalaya, 1933[-1936]. Paris, 1936-38. 2 pts. in
1, illus., maps. 29cm.
Offprint from Alpinisme, v.4-5, 1935-38.

KURZ, Marcel
Himalaya, 1939-1946. [Zürich, 1947-50]. 2 pts.
in 1, plates, illus. 25cm.
Offprint from Berge der Welt, Bde. 2 & 5, 1947-50.

KURZ, Marcel
Himalaya, 1939-1946. Ptie.1. [Lausanne, 1947?].
146-177p., plates, illus. 25cm.
Offprint from Montagnes du monde.

KURZ, Marcel
Himalaya, 1947-1950. [Zürich], 1952. 155-218p.,
illus., map. 25cm.
Offprint from Berge der Welt, Bd.7, 1952.

KURZ, Marcel
Himalaya, 1951-1952. [Lausanne], 1954. 205-
240p., plates, illus. 25cm.
Offprint from Montagnes du monde, v.9, 1954.

KURZ, Marcel
DYHRENFURTH, Günter Oskar
  Himalaya: unsere Expedition 1930; unter Mitarbeit
  von Charles Duvanel [and others]; hrsg. von
  Günter Oskar Dyhrenfurth. Berlin: Scherl, 1931.
  380p., plates (some fold., some col.), illus.,
  bibl. 24cm.

- - Das Massiv des Kangchendzönga (Himalaya), von
  Marcel Kurz.
  Map.

KURZ, Marcel
  Le Mont Olympe (Thessalie): monographie. Paris:
  Attinger, 1923. x, 232p., plates (some fold.),
  illus., maps (2 in pocket). 26cm.

KURZ, Marcel
  Le problème himalayen: étude géographique et
  historique. [Paris], 1934. 75p., fold. plates,
  illus., maps, bibl. 28cm.
  Offprint from Alpinisme, 1933-34.

KURZ, Marcel
  [Le problème himalayen...]. Die Erschliessung
  des Himalaya: eine Skizze; übersetzt von Paul
  Montandon. Bern, 1933. 68p., plates (2 fold.),
  illus., maps. 26cm.
  Offprint from Die Alpen, Jahrg. 9, Hfte.
  7, 9-11, 1933.

KURZ, Marcel
  Versuch einer Chronologie der Höhenrekorde im
  Gebirge. [Zürich, 1947]. 2 pts. in 1, plates,
  illus. 25cm.
  Offprint from Berge der Welt, Bde.1-2, 1946,
  1947.

KURZ, Marcel
  Walliser Alpen
  See his
  Clubführer durch die Walliser Alpen

KURZ, Marcel
  [Walliser-Skiführer]. Guide du skieur dans les
  Alpes valaisannes... Berne: Club Alpin Suisse,
  1924-30. 3 v., fold.col. plates, maps (in
  pocket). 20cm.
  Vols. 2-3 have title and text in German.

KUZ'MIN, Nikolai Ivanovich and RUKODEL'NIKOV, Boris
Leonidovich
  Obuchenie al'pinistov. Moskva: Izd. "Fizkul'tura
  i Sport", 1965. 192p., illus. 20cm.

KYOTO. University. Academic Alpine Club of Kyoto
  See
ACADEMIC ALPINE CLUB OF KYOTO

KYOTO. University. Fauna and Flora Research
Society
  See
FAUNA AND FLORA RESEARCH SOCIETY

KYPSELER DE MUNSTER, Gottlieb
  See
RUCHAT, Abraham

L., A.H.M.
  See
LUNN, Sir Arnold

L., H.A.
  See
LEVESON, Henry Astbury

L.N.R.R.
  See
R., L.N.R.

L., W.
  See
LONGMAN, William

La, P.
  See
LAKE, Philip

LABANDE, François
  100 sommets. Grenoble: Arthaud, 1975. 223p.,
  illus., maps. 24cm.

LA BEDOYÈRE, Henri, comte de
  Voyage en Savoie et dans le Midi: la France en
  1804 et 1805. Paris: Giguet et Michaud, 1808.
  439p. 22cm.

LABORATOIRE SCIENTIFIQUE INTERNATIONAL DU MONT ROSA
  See
LABORATORII SCIENTIFICI "A.MOSSO" SUL MONTE ROSA

LABORATORII SCIENTIFICI "A.MOSSO" SUL MONTE ROSA
  Travaux [des années 1903-1911]; publiés par A.
  Mosso. Turin: H. Loescher, 1904-1912. 3v.,
  illus. 25cm.
  Title in v.2 as: Atti ... sul Monte Rosa.
  Vols. 2 and 3, published V. Bona.

LABORDE, Jean Benjamin de
  Lettres sur la Suisse, adressées à Madame de
  M*** par un voyageur françois [i.e. Jean B.
  Laborde] en 1781... Genève: Jombert, 1783. 2v.,
  plates, map, plans. 23cm.

LABORDE, Jean Benjamin de
  Tableaux topographiques, pittoresques, physiques,
  historiques, moraux, politiques, littéraires, de
  la Suisse. Paris: Lamy, 1780-[88]. 2v. in 4,
  plates, illus. 51cm.
  Additional engraved title page: Tableaux de la
  Suisse; ou, Voyage pittoresque fait dans les
  XIII. cantons...
  Preface signed: Laborde.

- - 2e éd. entitled: Tableaux de la Suisse; ou,
  Voyage pittoresque... 1784-88. 12v.

LA BOULINIÈRE, P
  Itinéraire descriptif et pittoresque des Hautes-
  Pyrénées françoises, jadis territoires du Béarn,
  du Bigorre... Paris: Gide, 1825. 3v., plates
  (1 fold.), illus., map. 21cm.

LABRAM, Jonas David
HEGETSCHWEILER, Johann
  Sammlung von Schweizer Pflanzen; nach der Natur
  und auf Stein gezeichnet von J.D. Labram; Text
  von Joh. Hegetschweiler. Basel: H. Bienz,
  [1826-34]. 8v., col.plates, illus. 18cm.

LABRANA, Ferran
RODÉS, Josep M
  Roques, parets i agulles de Montserrat.
  1. Regió d'Agulles, [por] Josep M. Rodés i Ferran
  Labrana. Montserrat: L'Abadia de Montserrat,
  1972. 201p., illus., maps. 22cm.

LABROUE, E
  À travers les Pyrénées; illustrations d'après les
  photographies de Lacarme [and others]. Paris:
  C. Tallandier, [1900]. viii, 255p., illus. 30cm.

LACMANN, Otto
  Geleitworte zu den Blättern Claveringöya, Jordan
  Hill und Geographical Society-öya der Karte von
  Nordostgrönland. Oslo: Norges Svalbard- og
  Ishavs-Undersökelser, 1937. 57p., 3 fold.col.
  plates, illus., maps. 30cm.

LA CONDAMINE, Charles Marie de
  Journal of a tour to Italy... T. Lewis & G.
  Kearsly, 1763. xxii, 235p. 19cm.

LACROIX, Joseph
  Nouveau guide général du voyageur en Suisse; suivi
  du Tour du Mont Blanc par Joseph Lacroix. Paris:
  Garnier, [n.d.]. 405p., plates, illus., maps.
  19cm. (Guides Garnier Frères)

LACRUZ, Carlos
CONVENCION NACIONAL DE TURISMO, 1st, Mérida,
Venezuela, 1961
Itinerarios turisticos-alpinísticos en la Sierra
Nevada de Mérida; trabajo del Club Andino
Venezolano a cargo de ... Carlos Lacruz y Franco
Anzil. Mérida: Club Andino Venezolano, 1961.
9 leaves. 35cm.

Les lacs italiens: Cöme, Lugano, Majeur, et la
Vallée d'Intelvi. Milan: Lampugnani, [1906].
86p., illus., maps, plans. 19cm. (Guides
Lampugnani, 12)

LACUSTRIAN
Guidal hints to lake visitors. Queenstown (N.Z.):
Lake Wakatip Mail, [n.d.]. 18p., map. 18cm.

LADNER, Joh. Bapt.
Languard-Rundschau: ein hypsometrisches
Verzeichniss von Tausend über 8000' hohen Gipfeln
und Gräten der Alpenkette zwischen Montblanc und
Grossglockner, welche vom 10,887' hohen Piz-
Languard im Ober-Engadin aus gesehen werden...
Chur: Senti & Hummel, 1858. 32p. 20cm.

LADOUCETTE, J   C   F
Histoire, topographie, antiquités, usages,
dialectes des Hautes-Alpes, avec un atlas. 2e éd.,
rev. et considérablement augm. Paris: Ancienne
Librarie de Fantin, 1834. xvi, 664p., fold.
plates, illus., maps. 22cm.

- - 3e éd., rev. et augm. Paris: Gide, 1848. 2v.

A LADY
Alpine byways
See
FRESHFIELD, Mrs. Henry

A LADY
Autumn rambles; or, Fireside recollections...
See
STALEY, Mrs.

A LADY
Old stories of Switzerland; selected and
translated from the works of different German and
Swiss poets by a lady. Berne: R.F. Haller,
[1864]. viii, 304p. 16cm.

LADY BA
See
BARRETT, Katharine

A LADY PIONEER
See
MAZUCHELLI, Nina Elizabeth

A lady's tour round Monte Rosa; with visits to the
Italian valleys ... in a series of excursions in
the years 1850-56-58, [by Mrs. Henry Warwick
Cole]. Longman, Brown, Green, Longmans, &
Roberts, 1859. xi, 402p., col. plates (1 fold.),
illus., map. 21cm.

SAGLIO, Silvio and LAENG, Gualtiero
Adamello; con la collaborazione di Arrigo
Giannantonj. Milano: Club Alpino Italiano,
Touring Club Italiano, 1954. 694p., plates (some
fold., some col.), illus., maps, bibl. 17cm.
(Guida dei monti d'Italia)

LA FARINA, Giuseppe
La Svizzera storica ed artistica, descritta da
Giuseppe La Farina. Ed. illustrata da una serie
di ... incisioni in acciaio [da W.H. Bartlett].
Firenze: L. Bardi, 1842-43. 2v., plates, illus.
31cm.
Based on Beattie, William. Switzerland. 1836.

LAGARDE, Jacques
Description de la haute montagne dans le massif
du Mont-Blanc. Fasc.4. Groupes du Mont-Blanc et
de la Tour Ronde (Col du Géant, Col du Midi, Col
de Miage). Paris: Fischbacher, 1930. 269p.,
plates (some fold.), illus., maps. 17cm.
(Guides Vallot)

Lago di Garda e suoi dintorni: Brescia, Verona, Lago
d'Iseo. Milano: Lampugnani, [ca 1905]. 80p.,
illus., maps, plans. 18cm. (Guides Lampugnani,
34).

LA GRANDVILLE,   comtesse de
Voyage aux Pyrénées, par l'auteur des Souvenirs
de voyage [i.e. the Comtesse de la Grandville].
2e éd. Lille: L. Lefort, 1842. 286p., 1 plate,
illus. 18cm.

- - 3e éd., with subtitle: Fragments de l'ouvrage
intitulé: De la Loire aux Pyrénées. 1854.

LA HARPE, Charles de
Pourquoi aimons-nous la montagne? Genève, 1901.
55p., illus. 23cm.
Offprint from l'Echo des Alpes, juillet 1901.

LA HARPE, Eugène de
Les Alpes bernoises; illustrations par Fréd.
Boissonnas; texte par Eugène de La Harpe avec la
collaboration du Dr. H. Dübi. Lausanne: Bridel,
1915. viii, 152p., illus. 34cm.

LA HARPE, Eugène de
Les Alpes valaisannes; illustrations par Fréd.
Boissonnas; texte par Eugène de La Harpe avec la
collaboration de Henry Correvon [and others].
Lausanne: Bridel, 1911. vi, 216p., illus. 33cm.

LAING, Samuel
Journal of a residence in Norway during the years
1834, 1835 & 1836, made with a view to enquire
into the moral and political economy of that
country, and the condition of its inhabitants.
2nd ed. Longman, Orme, Brown, Green and Longmans,
1837. xii, 482p. 23cm.

LAING, Samuel
Notes of a traveller, on the social and political
state of France, Prussia, Switzerland, Italy, and
other parts of Europe, during the present
century. 2nd ed. Longman, Brown, Green, &
Longmans, 1842. xl, 496p. 24cm.

LAIRD, E   K
The rambles of a globe trotter in Australasia,
Japan, China, Jarva, India and Cashmere. Chapman
& Hall, 1875. 2v., fold. plates, illus., maps.
22cm.

LAISSUS, C
En Savoie: La Tarentaise, guide du baigneur, du
touriste et du naturaliste. Moutiers: F. Ducloz,
1894. 526p., illus. 15cm.

LAJARRIGA, Vimal de
Souvenirs de Sixt: itinéraire complet de la
vallée ..., par V.-L. [i.e. Vimal de Lajarriga].
Genève: Duchamp, 1856. xii, 220p., map. 17cm.

LAKE, Philip
COOLIDGE, William Augustus Brevoort
Alps.
(In The Encyclopaedia Britannica. 11th ed., v.1,
pt.4: Alex to Alum. Cambridge, 1910. 32cm.
p.737-754, illus., maps)
Article signed W.A.B.C., with section 10: Geology
signed P.La., i.e. Philip Lake, & sections 11,12:
Flora & Fauna signed H.V.K., i.e. Howard V. Knox.

LALANDE, Jérome de
Voyage en Italie, contenant l'histoire & les
anecdotes les plus singulières de l'Italy... 2e
éd., rev., corr. et augm. Yverdon: [n.pub.],
1787-88. 7v. 19cm.
Library has v.1 and 2 only.

DEVIES, Lucien and LALOUE, Maurice
Guide du massif des Écrins (Meije, Écrins, Ailefroide, Pelvoux, Bans, Olan, Muzelle). 2e éd.
Paris: Arthaud, pour Groupe de Haute Montagne,
1951. 2v., illus., bibl. 17cm.

LAMARTINE, Alphonse de
Harmonies poétiques et religieuses. Paris:
Hachette, 1904. xxxiv, 409p. 20cm.

LAMARTINE, Alphonse de
Jocelyn, épisode. [Nouv. éd.]. Paris: Hachette,
1903. xxi, 326p. 20cm.

LAMARTINE, Alphonse de
Premières méditations poétiques avec commentaires
... Paris: Hachette, 1903. lxix, 267p. 19cm.
(Oeuvres de Lamartine)

LAMBE, R   E
Craig Cowarch: a guide to the rock climbs on the
crags of Craig Cowarch; with a foreword by Eric
Byne. Stafford: The Mountain Club, 1958. v,
72p., plates, illus. 17 x 21cm.

LAMBER, Juliette
Dans les Alpes: nouveaux récits. Paris: Levy,
[1898]. 311p. 19cm.

LAMBERT, Cowley
A trip to Cashmere and Ladak. King, 1877. viii,
199p., plates, illus. 20cm.

LAMBERT, Léon
Au pays blanc: voyages. Bruxelles: Office de
Publicité, 1922. 276p. 19cm.

LAMBERT, Raymond
À l'assaut des "quatre mille": dix récits de haute
montagne; recueillis par Claude Varennes. Genève:
Éditions de la Frégate, 1946. 164p., plates,
illus. 23cm.

- - 2e éd. Genève: Éditions Jeheber, 1953.

LAMBERT, Raymond
Avant-premières à l'Everest, [par] Gabriel
Chevalley, René Dittert, Raymond Lambert; introduc-
tion du Ed. Wyss-Dunant. Paris: Arthaud, 1953.
310p., plates (1 fold.col.), illus., maps. 22cm.
(Collection sempervivum, 21)

LAMBERT, Raymond
[Avant-premières à l'Everest]. Forerunners to
Everest: the story of the two Swiss expeditions of
1952, by René Dittert, Gabriel Chevalley, Raymond
Lambert; preface by Sir John Hunt; English version
by Malcolm Barnes. Allen & Unwin, 1954. 256p.,
plates (1 col.), illus., maps. 23cm.

LAMBERT, Raymond and KOGAN, Claude
[Record à l'Himalaya]. White fury: Gaurisankar
and Cho Oyu; translated by Showell Styles. Hurst
& Blackett, 1956. 176p., plates, illus., map.
22cm.

LAMBOSSY, François E
Vents des crêtes; préface de Charles Gos; illus-
trations de P. Desaules et L. Furer. Lausanne:
The Author, 1941. 103p., illus., bibl. 20cm.

LAMI, Marcel
Ver les cimes; préface de Édouard Conte. Paris:
Louis-Michaud, [1912]. 318p. 20cm.

LAMMER, Eugen Guido
Jungborn: Bergfahrten und Höhengedanken eines
einsamen Pfadsuchers. Wien: Verlag des
Österreichischen Alpenklubs, 1922. 367p. 25cm.

- - 2. stark verm und veränderte Aufl. München:
Rother, 1923.
- - 3. Aufl. 1929.

LAMMER, Eugen Guido
[Jungborn ...]. Fontaine de jouvence, "Jungborn":
ascensions et reflections d'un alpiniste solitaire.
T.1; traduit et adapté ... par Ch. Sénéchal et E.
Gaillard. Chambéry: Dardel, 1931. 214p., plates,
illus. 20cm.

LAMMER, Eugen Guido
Wie anders ist das Besteigen der Alpen geworden!
Wien: Allgemeine Bergsteiger-Zeitung, [1937].
79p., plates, illus. 18cm.

LAMONT, Martha Macdonald
Impressions, thoughts, and sketches, during two
years in France and Switzerland. E. Moxon, 1844.
iv, 343p. 18cm.

LAMOTTE, A
Voyage dans le nord de l'Europe; consistant
principalement de promenades en Norwège, et de
quelques courses en Suède, dans l'année 1807 ...;
suivie d'un appendice contenant des remarques
historiques et physiques ... et des itinéraires
du pays. J. Hatchard, 1813. 244p., plates (1
fold.), illus., map. 30cm.

LAMPEN, Ernest Dudley
Chateau d'Oex: life and sport in an alpine valley;
illustrations in colour by Alice E. Prangley.
Methuen, 1910. xiv, 291p., plates (some col.),
illus. 20cm.

LAMPUGNANI, Giuseppe
GUGLIERMINA, Giuseppe F
Vette: ricordi di esplorazioni e nuove ascensioni
sulle Alpi, nei gruppi del Monte Rosa, del
Cervino e del Monte Bianco dal 1896 al 1921, [da]
G.F. e G.B. Gugliermina, Giuseppe Lampugnani.
[Borgosesia]: Sezione di Varallo del Club Alpino
Italiano, 1927. 361p., plates, illus. 30cm.

LAMY, J   P
Choix de vues en Suisse. Berne: J.P. Lamy, 1819.
1v. of col. illus. 41cm.

LANCEROD, Jean
GERVAIS, Paul
Le guide des Ormonts: élégie.
(In Bibliothèque universelle ... v.34, 1887,
p.25-43)

LANÇON, Xavier
See
GALLICUS

Das Land Tirol, mit einem Anhange: Vorarlberg:
ein Handbuch für Reisende. Innsbruck: Wagner,
1838. 3v. 19cm.

LANDESVERBAND FÜR FREMDENVERKEHR, Karlsbad
Wintersportplätze in Böhmen, Mähren und
Schlesien; bearb. vom Landesverband für Fremden-
verkehr. Karlsbad: Weltbader-Reklame- und
Verlagsunternehmen, [1922]. 114p., illus. 17cm.
At head of title: Tschechoslowakische Republik.

LANDI VITTORJ, Carlo
Appennino centrale (escluso il Gran Sasso
d'Italia). Milano: Club Alpino Italiano, Touring
Club Italiano, 1955. 519p., plates (1 fold.,
some col.), illus., maps, bibl. 17cm. (Guida
dei monti d'Italia)

LANDI VITTORJ, Carlo and PIETROSTEFANI, Stanislao
Gran Sasso d'Italia. 2a ed. Milano: Club Alpino
Italiano, Touring Club Italiano, 1962. 254p.,
plates (1 fold., some col.), illus., maps, bibl.
17cm. (Guida dei monti d'Italia)

LANDON, Perceval
Lhasa: an account of the country and people of
central Tibet and of the progress of the mission
sent there by the English Government in the year
1903-4. Hurst and Blackett, 1905. 2v., plates
(1 fold., some col.), illus., maps. 25cm.

LANDON, Perceval
Nepal. Constable, 1928. 2v., plates (some fold.,
some col.), illus., maps. 27cm.

LANDOR, A   Henry Savage
In the forbidden land: an account of a journey in
Tibet, capture by the Tibetan authorities,
imprisonment, torture, and ultimate release.
Heinemann, 1898. 2v., plates, illus., map. 24cm.

LANDOR, A   Henry Savage
Tibet & Nepal painted & described by A. Henry
Savage Landor. Black, 1905. x, 233p., plates
(1 fold., some col.), illus., map. 23cm.

LANDSEER, John
Some account of the dogs and of the Pass of the
Great Saint Bernard, intended to accompany an
engraving after a picture by Edwin Landseer ... of
alpine mastiffs extricating an overwhelmed
traveller from the snow. Printed for John Landseer,
[1831]. 47p. 24cm.

LANE, Ferdinand C
The story of mountains. New York: Doubleday, 1950.
xxi, 488p., plates, illus. 24cm.

LANG, P   S
Where the Soldanella grows. Heath, Cranton &
Ouseley, [1908]. 318p. 21cm.

LANGE, Paul
GOODMAN, Edward John
Western Norway: notes to accompany Paul Lange's
photogravures. Sampson Low, Marston, 1893. 14p.,
50 plates, illus., map. 31 x 40cm.

LANGES, Gunther
Dolomiten-Skiführer. 5. verm. Aufl. München:
Rother, 1938. 288p. 16cm.

- - Map.

LANGES, Gunther
Front in Fels und Eis: der Weltkrieg im Hochgebirge; mit einer Einleitung von Konrad Krafft
von Dellmensingen. München: F. Bruckmann, 1933.
xv, 143p., plates, illus. 25cm.

LANGES, Gunther
[Ostliche Dolomiten]; Anhang: Civetta- und
Monfalconi-Gruppe, von Toni Hiebeler. München:
Rother, 1959. 494p., plates, illus., maps (2 on
lining papers). 16cm. (Dolomiten-Kletterführer,
Bd.2)

LANGES, Gunther
[Westliche Dolomiten]. 4. Aufl. München: Rother,
1959. 416p., plates (1 fold.), illus., maps.
16cm. (Dolomiten-Kletterführer, Bd.1)

- - 5. Aufl. 1964.

LANGHANS, Daniel
Beschreibung verschledener Merkwürdigkeiten des
Siementhals, eines Theils des Bernergebiets...
Zürich: Heidegger, 1753. 132p. 18cm.

LANGLE, marquis de
Tableau pittoresque de la Suisse. Nouv. éd.
Paris: Desenne & Maret, [1791?]. 107p. 22cm.

LANGLE, marquis de
[Tableau pittoresque de la Suisse]. A picturesque
description of Switzerland; translated from the
French. Dublin: Printed by William Porter, for
P. Byrne, J. Moore, & W. Jones, 1792. xii, 201p.
18cm.

- - Another ed. [1798].

LANGMUIR, Eric
Mountain leadership: the official handbook of the
Mountain Leadership Training Boards of Great
Britain; [produced by the Scottish Mountain
Leadership Training Board]. Edinburgh: Scottish
Council of Physical Recreation, 1969. 88p.,
illus., bibl. 25cm.

LANGUEPIN, Jean Jacques and PAYAN, Louis
Nanda Devi: 3e expédition française a l'Himalaya;
préface de Jean Montel. Paris: Arthaud, 1952.
xvi, 13p., 72 plates (some col.), illus., maps.
20cm. (Collection belles pages, belles couleurs)

LANOYE, Ferdinand de
Les grandes scènes de la nature d'après les descriptions de voyageurs et d'écrivains célèbres.
Nouv. éd., rev. avec soin. Paris: Hachette, 1864.
376p., illus. 19cm.

LANTIER, E   F
Les voyageurs en Suisse. Paris: F. Buisson, 1803.
3v., 1 plate, port. 20cm.

LANTIER, E   F
[Les voyageurs en Suisse]. Travellers in Switzerland; comprising descriptions ... conversations ...
anecdotes of the principal literary characters
resident in that country and France ...; translated
by Frederic Shoberl. J. Badcock, 1804. 6v. 18cm.

LAPORTE, Albert
En Suisse, le sac au dos. 3e éd. Paris: T.
Lefevre, [ca 1875]. 400p., illus. 25cm.

LAPWORTH, Charles
PAGE, David
Introductory text-book of geology; rev. and in
great part rewritten by Charles Lapworth. 12th
and enl. ed. Edinburgh, London: Blackwood, 1888.
316p., illus. 19cm.

LARDEN, Walter
Argentine plains and Andine glaciers: life on an
estancia, and an expedition into the Andes.
Unwin, 1911. 320p., plates, illus., map. 23cm.

LARDEN, Walter
Guide to the walks & climbs around Arolla. S.
Chick, 1908. x, 138p., plates, illus. 15cm.

LARDEN, Walter
Inscriptions from Swiss chalets: a collection of
inscriptions found outside and inside Swiss
chalets, storehouses, and sheds. Oxford: Printed
for the Author at the University Press, 1913.
208p., plates, illus. 23cm.

LARDEN, Walter
Recollections of an old mountaineer. Arnold, 1910.
xv, 320p., plates, illus. 24cm.

LARDNER, Dionysius
History of Switzerland. Printed for Longman,
Rees, Orme, Brown, Green & Longman and J. Taylor,
1832. xx, 360p. 18cm. (Cabinet cyclopaedia,
cabinet of history)

LARGIADER, Anton
RAHN, Johann Rudolf
Wanderungen im Tessin: zur Erinnerung an der
Grenzdienst der 5. Division in Tessin 1915/16; neu
hrsg. von Lt. Largiadèr; mit einer Uebersicht über
die Geschichte des Kantons Tessin von Hptm.
Nabholz und einem Vorwort von Oberstdivisionär
Steinbuch. Zürich: A. Bopp, 1917. 174p., plates
(1 col.), illus. 18cm.

LASCELLES, Rowley
A general outline of the Swiss landscapes, [by
Rowley Lascelles]; with miscellaneous notes and
illustrations from M. de Saussure and others.
3rd ed., rev. and considerably enl. Murray, 1812.
xii, 312p. 20cm.

LASCELLES, Rowley
Journal of a short excursion among the Swiss
landscapes, made in the summer of the year ninety-
four, [by Rowley Lascelles]. Murray, 1803.
132p., 1 fold. plate, music. 19cm.

LASCELLES, Rowley
Sketch of a descriptive journey through Switzerland, [by Rowley Lascelles]; to which is added The
passage of S. Gotthard: a poem, by the Duchess of
Devonshire. Berne: J.J. Burgdorfer, 1816. iv,
92p., plates, illus. 21cm.

LASCELLES, Rowley
[Sketch of a descriptive journey...]. Scizze
einer mahlerischen Reise durch die Schweiz; aus
dem Englischen [of Rowley Lascelles]; hrsg. mit
einigen Anmerkungen u. einem doppellen Anhange,
von Joh. Rud. Wyss. Bern: J.J. Burgdorfer, 1816.
154p., plates, illus. 22cm.

LASSALLE, L
Costumes suisses des 22 cantons; dessinés par L.
Lassalle. Genève: S. Morel, [ca 1868]. 1v. of
col. illus. 22cm.
Cover title.

LASSELS, Richard
  Tne voyage of Italy; or, A compleat journey through
  Italy... Newly printed at Paris[by V. du Moutier
  for] John Starkey, 1670. 2 pts. in 1, plates,
  illus. 16cm.

LATROBE, Charles Joseph
  The alpenstock; or, Sketches of Swiss scenery and
  manners, 1825-1826. R.B. Seeley & W. Burnside,
  1829. x, 388p., plates, illus. 23cm.
- - 2nd ed. 1839.
LATROBE, Charles Joseph
  The pedestrian: a summer's ramble in the Tyrol,
  and some of the adjacent provinces, 1830. R.B.
  Seeley & W. Burnside, 1832. iv, 349p., map. 21cm.

LATZINA, Francisco
  Diccionario geográfico argentino, con ampliaciones
  enciclopédicas rioplatenses. 3a ed. Buenos Aires:
  J. Peuser, 1899. vi, 814p., 1 plate, port. 32cm.

LAULAGNET, Henri
SÉGOGNE, Henry de
  Le massif du Mont-Blanc: vallées et sommets; photo-
  graphies de Henri Laulagnet. Marseille: H.
  Laulagnet, 1947. 1v. (chiefly illus.). 27cm.

LAUNAY, Adrien
  Histoire de la mission du Thibet. Lille: Société
  Saint-Augustin, [1903]. 2v., 2 fold.plates, illus.
  27cm.

LAUNAY, L de
  La vie des montagnes. Paris: Fayard, [1926].
  126p., illus., maps. 25cm. (Les mystères de
  l'univers)

LAUR-BELART, R
  Studien zur Eröffnungsgeschichte des Gotthard-
  passes, mit einer Untersuchung über Stiebende
  Brücke und Teufelsbrücke. Zürich: Orell Füssli,
  1924. 171p., illus. 23cm.

LAUSANNE. Musée Cantonal des Beaux-Arts
  See
  MUSÉE CANTONAL DES BEAUX-ARTS, Lausanne

LAUSBERG, Carl
  Mit Stock und Pickel: Bergfahrten in den Alpen und
  Norwegen. Düsseldorf: Schmitz & Olbertz, 1910.
  218p. 24cm.

LAUT, Agnes C
  Enchanted trails of Glacier Park. New York:
  McBride, 1926. ix, 251p., plates, illus., maps
  (on lining papers). 23cm.

LAUTH, G
  Précis d'un voyage botanique, fait en Suisse, dans
  les Grisons, aux sources du Rhin ... en juillet,
  aout et septembre 1811; précédé de quelques réflexions sur l'utilité des voyages pour les
  naturalistes, par D. Villars, G. Lauth et A.
  Nestler. Paris: Lenormant, 1812. 66p., 4 fold.
  plates, illus. 20cm.

LAVALLÉE, Joseph, marquis de Bois-Robert
  Travels in Istria and Dalmatia; drawn up from the
  itinerary of L.F. Cassas, by Joseph Lavallée;
  translated from the French. R. Phillips, 1805.
  iv, 124p., fold. plates, illus., map. 22cm.
  (In A collection of modern and contemporary
  voyages... v.1. London, 1805)

LAVATER, Johann Rudolf
SCHEUCHZER, Johann Jacob
  Historiae Helveticae naturalis prolegomena ...;
  praeside J. Jacobo Scheuchzero, respondente Johanne
  Rodolfo Lavatero. Tiguri: Typis D. Gessneri, 1700.
  30p. 22cm.

LAVELEYE, Émile de
  Le Mont-Rose et les Alpes pennines: souvenirs de
  voyage. [Paris, 1865]. 819-857p. 25cm.
  Offprint from Revue des deux mondes, t.57, 1865.

LAVIANO, Enzo Valentini, conte di
  See
  VALENTINI, Enzo, conte di Laviano

LAVIS-TRAFFORD, M   A   de
  Le col alpin franchi par Hannibal: son identification topographique. Saint-Jean-de-Maurienne
  (Savoie): Termignon, 1956. 95p., plates (some
  fold.), illus., maps. 23cm.
  Originally published in the Bulletin commémorant
  la centenaire de Maurienne, t.13, 1956.

LAVIS-TRAFFORD, Marc A   de
  Commentaire sur l'oeuvre relative aux Alpes des
  topographes, cartographes et écrivains au cours
  de la deuxième moitié du XVIe siècle... Chambéry:
  Dardel, 1950. 16p. 27cm.

LAVIS-TRAFFORD, Marc A   de
  L'évolution de la cartographie de la région du
  Mont-Cenis et de ses abords au XVe siècles: étude
  critique des méthodes de travail des grands cartographes du XVIe siècle... Chambéry: Dardel,
  [1950]. 125p., 12 plates (1 fold.), maps. 28cm.

LAVIS-TRAFFORD, Marc A   de
  Mémorial du docteur Marc de Lavis-Trafford.
  [St-Jean-de-Maurienne]: Société d'histoire et
  d'archéologie de Maurienne, 1962. 224p., plates,
  illus., port. 22cm. (Société d'histoire et
  d'archéologie. Travaux, t.14, année 1962)

LAW, William John
  The Alps of Hannibal. Macmillan, 1866. 2v.,
  2 fold. plates, maps. 25cm.

LAWDER, K   M
  Climbing guide to Dartmoor and south west Devon;
  edited by K.M. Lawder. Portsmouth: The Royal
  Navy Ski and Mountaineering Club, [196-]. 70p.,
  1 plate, illus., map. 16cm.

LAWSON, Andrew C
  The geomorphogeny of the Upper Kern Basin.
  Berkeley: University Press, 1904. 291-376p.,
  plates, illus. 25cm. (University of California.
  Publications, v.3, no.15)

LAWSON, John Parker
  Scotland delineated: a series of views of the
  principal cities and towns ... mountains and
  rivers ..., accompanied by copious letterpress.
  Day, [ca 1855]. 285p., col. plates, illus. 34cm.

LAWSON, W   and OSBORNE, R   E
  Les Écrins et la Meije; traduit par H. Ferrand.
  Grenoble, 1908. 12p., plates, illus. 24cm.
  Offprint from Annuaire de la Société des touristes
  du Dauphiné, 1907.

LAYARD, Arthur
MAUNDEVILE, Sir John
  The marvellous adventures of Sir John Maundevile
  ...; edited and profusely illustrated by Arthur
  Layard, with a preface by John Cameron Grant.
  Constable, 1895. xxx, 414p., plates, illus. 22cm.

LAYCOCK, John
  Some shorter climbs (in Derbyshire and elsewhere).
  Manchester: Refuge Printing Department, 1913. ix,
  116p., plates, illus., bibl. 16cm. (Some gritstone climbs)

LAZZARINI, C   F
  Escursione nelle Alpi Cozie. Ivrea: Tipografia
  di F.L. Curbis, 1868. 70p. 18cm.

LAZZARINO, A
  Le nostre Alpi: gite ed escursioni alpine.
  Firenze: Bemporad, 1924. iv, 98p., illus. 20cm.

LEAR, Edward
  Journal of a landscape painter in Corsica. R.J.
  Bush, 1870. xvi, 272p., plates, illus., map.
  28cm.

LEBLANC, Henri
ICHAC, Marcel
  Quand brillent les étoiles de midi; photographies
  de Henri Leblanc, Marcel Ichac, Jacques Ertaud.
  Paris: Arthaud, 1960. 123p., illus. (some col.),
  map. 24cm.
  "Realisé d'après le film: Les étoiles de midi".

LE BLOND, Mrs.Aubrey
See
LE BLOND, Elizabeth

LE BLOND, Elizabeth
Adventures on the roof of the world. Fisher Unwin,
1904. xvi, 333p., plates, illus. 23cm.

LE BLOND, Elizabeth
Day in, day out. Lane, 1928. 264p., plates,
illus., ports. 23cm.

LE BLOND, Elizabeth
The high Alps in winter; or, Mountaineering in
search of health, by Mrs. Fred Burnaby. Sampson
Low, Marston, Searle, & Rivington, 1883. xix,
204p., plates (1 fold.), illus., maps. 20cm.

LE BLOND, Elizabeth
High life and towers of silence, by the author
of "The high Alps in winter" ... Sampson Low,
Marston, Searle, & Rivington, 1886. xii, 195p.,
plates, illus. 19cm.

LE BLOND, Elizabeth
Hints on snow photography, by Mrs. Main. Sampson
Low, Marston, 1894.   15p., 14 plates, illus.
22cm.

LE BLOND, Elizabeth
Mountaineering in the land of the midnight sun.
Fisher Unwin, 1908. xii, 304p., plates (1 fold.),
illus., map. 23cm.

LE BLOND, Elizabeth
My home in the Alps, by Mrs. Main. Sampson Low,
Marston, 1892. vii, 131p. 20cm.

LE BLOND, Elizabeth
The story of an alpine winter. Bell, 1907. vii,
289p. 19cm.

LE BLOND, Elizabeth
True tales of mountain adventure for non-climbers
young and old. Fisher Unwin, 1903. xvii, 299p.,
plates, illus. 23cm.

LE BONDIDIER, L
SOCIÉTÉ RAMOND
L.-F.-E. Ramond, 1755-1827: commémoration.
Bagnères-de-Bigorre: La Société, 1927 [printed
1930]. 163p., plates, illus., ports. 23cm.
Edited by L. Le Bondidier.

LE BRETON, Henry and OLLIVIER, Robert
Haute montagne pyrénéenne: guide des ascensions
difficiles aux Pyrénées, Les Pyrénées occidentales,
des Aiguilles d'Ansabère au Pic Long. Pau: Groupe
Pyrénéiste de Haute Montagne [1937]. xix, 317p.,
plates (1 fold.), illus., maps. 17cm.

LECHNER, Ernst
Graubünden: illustrierter Reisebegleiter durch alle
Talschaften. Chur: Manatschal Ebner, 1903. 232p.,
plates, illus., map. 21cm.

- - 5. verb. Aufl. 1920.

LECHNER, Ernst
Piz Languard und die Bernina-Gruppe bei Pontresina,
Oberengadin: Skizzen aus Natur und Bevölkerung,
zugleich als Wegweiser für Wanderungen. Leipzig:
Engelmann, 1858. x, 121p., plates (1 fold.col.),
illus., map. 20cm.

- - 2.Aufl. 1865.
- - 3.Aufl. 1900.

LECHNER, Ernst
Das Thal der Maira, Bergell: Wanderbild von Maloja
bis Chiavenna und historische Skizze. Samaden:
Engadin Press, 1903. 76p., illus., map. 19cm.

LECHNER, Sigmund and KUNTSCHER, Karl
Skiführer durch die Ötztaler Alpen. Wien: Artaria,
1925. viii, 89p., plates (1 fold.), illus., map
(in pocket). 17cm.

LECLERC, Jeanne and LECLERC, Bernard
Guide de Tarentaise et Maurienne. Lyon: Audin,
[pour] Fédération Française de la Montagne, Club
Alpin Français, Section Lyonnaise, 1949. 2v.,
illus. 17cm.

LECLERC, Jeanne and LECLERC, Bernard
Petit guide de la Haute-Maurienne: promenades,
excursions, ascensions hivernales. 2e éd. (rev.
et augm.). Lyon: Club Alpin Français, Section
Lyonnaise, [1937?]. 38p., plates, illus. 16cm.

LECLERC, Bernard
Ski en Tarentaise et Maurienne: guide itinéraire,
par J. et B. Leclerc et A. Steiner et la Section
Lyonnaise du C.A.F. Paris: J. Susse [1948?].
240p., fold. plates, maps. 18cm. (Guide Susse)
Publié sous le patronage officiel de Fédération
Française de la Montagne, Fédération Française de
Ski, Club Alpin Français.

LECLERC, Jeanne and LECLERC, Bernard
Guide de Tarentaise et Maurienne. Lyon: Audin,
[pour] Fédération Française de la Montagne, Club
Alpin Français, Section Lyonnaise, 1949. 2v.,
illus. 17cm.

LECLERC, Jeanne and LECLERC, Bernard
Petit guide de la Haute-Maurienne: promenades,
excursions, ascensions hivernales. 2e éd. (rev.
et augm.). Lyon: Club Alpin Français, Section
Lyonnaise, [1937]. 38p., plates, illus. 16cm.

LECLERC, Jeanne
Ski en Tarentaise et Maurienne: guide itinéraire,
par J. et B. Leclerc et A. Steiner et la Section
Lyonnaise du C.A.F. Paris: J. Susse, [1948?].
240p., fold. plates, maps. 18cm. (Guide Susse)
Publié sous le patronage officiel de Fédération
Française de la Montagne, Fédération Française
de Ski, Club Alpin Français.

LECLERCQ, Jules
Promenades et escalades dans les Pyrénées:
Lourdes, Luz, Barèges... 2e éd. Tours: Mame,
1877. 239p., plates, illus. 25cm.

LECLERCQ, Jules
Le Tyrol et le pays des Dolomites. Paris: A.
Quantin, 1880. 273p., 1 fold.col. plate, map.
19cm.

LECLERCQ, Jules
Voyage au Mont Ararat. Paris: Plon, 1892. 328p.,
plates, illus., map. 19cm.

LE COMTE, Jean
Étude monographique de la vallée de Saas. Viège:
The Author, 1926 [cover 1928]. 88p., plates
(some fold.), illus., plans. 23cm.

LECONTE, Joseph
A journal of ramblings through the high Sierra of
California by the University Excursion Party.
San Francisco: Sierra Club, 1930. xv, 152p.,
plates, illus., bibl. 23cm.
Originally published, San Francisco: Francis &
Valentine, 1875.

LECOQ, Henri
Des glaciers et des climats; ou, Des causes atmos-
phériques et géologie: recherches sur les forces
diluviennes, indépendantes de la chaleur centrale,
sur les phénomènes glaciaire et erratique. Paris:
Bertrand, 1847. 566p. 23cm.

BLANC, Pierre and LECOULTRE, Gérald
Ski: 67 itinéraires détaillés, établis par Pierre
Blanc, Gérald Lecoultre en collaboration avec O.
Treyvaud. Lausanne: Payot, 1936. 116p. 17cm.
(Les petits guides Schaefer sports)

LEDISCRET, Anatole
COMPAGNIE DES CHEMINS DE FER JURA-SIMPLON
De Bale à Brigue et Zermatt: guide officiel du
Jura-Simplon: IIIme sér. des guides illustrés de
J. Boillot-Robert. Neuchatel: F. Wohlgrath,
[ca 1893]. 74, 54p., plates (some fold., some
col.), illus., maps. 23 x 32cm.
Contains: Le Jura-Simplon en dix jours, par
Anatole Lediscret.

LEDORMEUR, Georges
Massif du Balaïtous: ascensions autour du Refuge
du Balaïtous. Tarbes: L'Auteur, 1928. 22p.,
illus., map. 22cm. (Guide Ledormeur. Supplément)

LEDORMEUR, Georges
Les Pyrénées centrales du Val d'Aran à la Vallée
d'Aspe. Tarbes: Imprimerie Lesbordes, 1928.
400p., maps. 19cm. (Guide Ledormeur)

LEDUC, Pierre Etienne Denis
See
LEDUC, Saint-Germain

LEDUC, Saint-Germain
Les vacances en Suisse: journal du voyage d'un
collegien; publié par St. Germain Leduc. Paris:
Levrault, 1837. 2v. in 1., plates, illus. 15cm.

LEE, Edwin
Memoranda on France, Italy, and Germany, with
remarks on climates, medical practice, mineral
waters, ... to which is added an appendix on some
of the predisposing causes of disease, and on the
advantages of travel and a residence abroad.
Saunders & Otley, [1841]. xii, 342p., plates,
illus. 20cm.

LEE, Frank Harold
The lure of the hills; selected by F.H. Lee.
Harrap, 1928. 223p., plates, illus. 19cm.
(Harrap library, 46)

LEE, Jonathan S
OUNDLE SCHOOL EXPEDITION TO ECUADOR, 1975
[Report]. [Peterborough]: Oundle School, 1975.
94 leaves. 32cm.
Expedition leader: Jonathan S. Lee.

LEE, Katharine
In the Alsatian mountains: a narrative of a tour
in the Vosges. R. Bentley, 1883. xv, 282p., 1
fold. plate, illus., map. 21cm.

LEE, Theresa Melville
The story of Switzerland; with preface by Mrs.
Lionel Tollemache. Rivingtons, 1885. viii, 294p.,
plates, illus. 18cm.

LEES, J   R
Moelwynion: an interim guide to the lower crags.
[N.p.], 1962. 329-355p. 22cm. (Climbers' Club
guides to Wales)
Offprint from the Climbers' Club journal, 1962.

LEES, James Arthur
Peaks and pines: another Norway book. Longmans,
Green, 1899. xii, 378p., illus. 21cm.

LEES, James Arthur and CLUTTERBUCK, Walter
Three in Norway, by two of them [i.e. J.A. Lees
and W. Clutterbuck]. Longmans, Green, 1882. xv,
341p., plates, illus., map. 20cm.

LEFEBURE, Charles
Mes étapes d'alpinisme; avant-propos de Pierre
Puiseux. Paris: Club Alpin Français, 1904.
241p., illus. 26cm.

- - 2e éd. 1904.

LEFEBURE, Molly
Cumberland heritage. Gollancz, 1970. 272p.,
plates, illus., bibl. 24cm.

LEFEBURE, Molly
Scratch & Co.: the great cat expedition. Gollancz,
1968. 158p., illus. 21cm.

LE FORT, Peter, Baron
HARSTER, Hermann
Kampf und Sieg in Schnee und Eis: Winterolympia
1936; hrsg. von Hermann Harster, Baron Peter Le
Fort. München: Knorr & Hirth, 1936. 111p.,
illus. 27cm.

LE GALLAIS, A
Chroniques du Mont Saint-Bernard. Tours: Ad.
Mame, 1860. 236p., 1 plate, illus. 23cm.

LEGGETT, Benjamin F
A tramp through Switzerland. New York: J.B.
Alden, 1887. 90p. 20cm.

LEGWARTH, Franz
Heiteres Touristen-Vademecum nebst einem unfehl-
baren Touristen-Wetter-Anzeiger: Allen Wand'rern
ein treuer Wegwart. Wien: Bediene Dich Selbst,
1906. 26p., illus. 14cm.

LEHNER, Albert
En ski avec Albert Lehner; préface du capitaine
R. Bonvin-Haenni. Lausanne: F. Roth, 1944.
44p., plates, illus. 21cm.

LEHNER, Karl
Kleine Zermatter Chronik, von Peterjosi [i.e.
Karl Lehner]. Zermatt, 1949. 36p. 19cm.
Offprint from Walliser Nachrichten.

LEHNER, Karl
[Kleine Zermatter Chronik]. A pocket history of
Zermatt; translated by Cicely Williams; paintings
by Edo de Handel-Mazzetti. Zermatt: Wega, [1952].
32p., col. plates, illus. 21cm.

LEHNER, Wilhelm
Die Eroberung der Alpen. München: Hochalpenverlag,
1924. xi, 727p., plates (some fold.), illus.
27cm.

LEHNER, Wilhelm
Julius Payers Bergfahrten: Erschliessungsfahrten
in den Ortler-, Adamello- und Presanella-Alpen
(1864-1868); hrsg. von Wilhelm Lehner. München:
Manz, 1920. vii, 190p., plates, illus., port.
27cm.

LEHRS, Karl
FRIEDLAENDER, Ludwig
Ueber die Entstehung und Entwicklung des Gefühls
für das Romantische in der Natur; Herrn Professor
K. Lehrs zu seinem 50 jährigen Doctorjubiläum am
7. März 1873 überreicht von Ludwig Frielaender.
Leipzig: S. Hirzil, 1873. 45p. 24cm.

LEIBING, Franz
Natur, Kunst und Menschen in Ober-Italien und der
Schweiz: psychologische Skizzen. Leipzig: A.
Fritsch, 1866. viii, 198p. 19cm.

LEICESTER ASSOCIATION OF MOUNTAINEERS
VICKERS, Ken S
Rock climbs in Leicestershire: interim guide.
Leicester: Leicester Association of Mountaineers,
1966. 46p., illus. 18cm.

LEICESTER POLYTECHNIC STUDENTS GREENLAND EXPEDITION,
1972
Kûgssuatziaq, Søndre Sermilik, southern Greenland:
[the official report]; edited by Andrew Barbier.
Leicester: City of Leicester Polytechnic, 1973.
v, 159p., plates, illus., maps, bibl. 30cm.

LEICESTER POLYTECHNIC STUDENTS ØKSFJORD EXPEDITION,
1970
The official report of Leicester Polytechnic
Students Øksfjord Expedition 1970: [Loppa
Peninsular, Finnmark, Arctic Norway]. Leicester:
City of Leicester Polytechnic, 1971. 95 leaves,
plates, illus., maps. 30cm.

LEIFER, Walter
Himalaya: mountains of destiny; translated by
Ursula Prideaux. Galley Press, 1962. x, 176p.,
plates, illus. 24cm.

LEIGH, Chandos
The view. W. Sams, 1819. 28p. 22cm.

Leigh's Guide to the lakes and mountains of Cumberland, Westmorland, and Lancashire. 2nd ed., enl.
and improved. Leigh, 1832. viii, 160p., col.
plates (1 fold.), maps. 19cm.

- - 3rd ed., carefully rev. and corr. 1835.
- - 4th ed., carefully rev. and corr. 1840.

Leigh's Guide to Wales & Monmouthshire... 6th ed.,
with considerable additions and improvements.
G. Biggs, 1841. viii, 386p., plates (1 fold.
col.), illus., map. 19cm.

LEIGHTON, John M
The lakes of Scotland: a series of views, from
paintings taken expressly for the work by John
Fleming; engraved by Joseph Swan; with historical
& descriptive illustrations by John M. Leighton.
Glasgow: J. Swan, 1834. xiii, 223p., plates,
illus. 28cm.

KOGAN, Georges and LEININGER, Nicole
Cordillère Blanche: Expédition franco-belge à la
cordillère des Andes, 1951; récit précédé d'un
poème de Jacques Prévert à la mémoire de Georges
Kogan; préface de Maurice Herzog. Paris: Arthaud,
1952. 155p., plates, illus. 21cm. (Collection
sempervivum, 17)

KOGAN, Georges and LEININGER, Nicole
[Cordillère Blanche...]. The ascent of Alpamayo:
an account of the Franco-Belgian Expedition to the
Cordillera Blanca in the high Andes; with a foreword by Maurice Herzog; translated by Peter E.
Thompson. Harrap, 1954. 135p., plates (1 col.),
illus., maps. 21cm.

LEITMEIER, Hans
Die österreichischen Alpen: eine zusammenfassende
Darstellung; bearb. von O. Abel [and others]; hrsg.
von Hans Leitmeier. Leipzig: F. Deuticke, 1928.
414p., plates (some fold.), illus., maps, music.
25cm.

LEMAITRE, Hélène
Les pierres dans l'oeuvre de Ruskin. Caen:
Association des Publications, 1965. 246p., plates,
illus., maps, bibl. 26cm. (Publications de la
Faculté des lettres et sciences humaines de
l'Université de Caen)

LE MERCHER DE LONGPRÉ, Charles, baron d' Haussez
See
HAUSSEZ, Charles Le Mercher de Longpré, baron d'

LEMERCIER, Abel
Ascensions au Mont Rose et au Mont Blanc: excursion
de quinzaine d'un Parisien, 14-29 août 1872.
Paris, 1873. 15p. 23cm.
Cover title.
Offprint from Bulletin de la Société de géographie,
juillet, 1873.

LE MESURIER, W H
An impromptu ascent of Mont Blanc. Stock, 1882.
76p., plates, illus. 24cm.

LEMPRIERE, William
A tour from Gibralter to Tangier, Sallee, Mogodore,
Santa Cruz, Tarudant, and thence over Mount Atlas
to Morocco... Printed for the author and sold by
J. Walter, J. Johnson & J. Sewell, 1791. xl,
464p., plates (1 fold.), map. 22cm.

LEMPRUCH, Moritz Erwin, Freiherr von
Der König der deutschen Alpen und seine Helden
(Ortlerkämpfe 1915/1918). Stuttgart: C. Belser,
1925. 153p., col. plates (1 fold.), illus., map
(in pocket). 36cm.

LENDENFELD, Robert von
Aus den Alpen; illustriert von E.T. Compton und
Paul Hey. Wien: F. Tempsky, 1896. 2v., 2 col.
plates, illus. 28cm.

LENDENFELD, Robert von
Australische Reise. Innsbruck: Wagner, 1892. xi,
325p., plates, illus. 26cm.

LENDENFELD, Robert von
Die Hochgebirge der Erde. Freiburg im Breisgau:
Herdersche Verlagshandlung, 1899. xiii, 531p.,
plates (1 fold.), illus., col. maps. 26cm.

LENDENFELD, Robert von
Neuseeland. Berlin: Schall, [1900?]. viii,
186p., 1 col. plate, illus., map, bibl. 26cm.
(Bibliothek der Länderkunde, Bd.9)

LENTHÉRIC, Charles
L'homme devant les Alpes. Paris: Plon, 1896.
480p., fold.col. plates, maps. 23cm.

LEONARD, R M
Poems on travel; selected by R.M. Leonard. Oxford
University Press, 1914. 128p. 17cm. (Oxford
garlands)

LEONARDO DA VINCI
RICCI, Virgilio
L'andata di Leonardo da Vinci al Monboso, oggi
Monte Rosa, e la teoria dell'azzurro del cielo.
Roma: Printed by Palombi, 1977. x, 82p., col.
plates, illus., bibl. 24cm.

LEONHARDI, Georg
Der Comersee und seine Umgebungen. Leipzig: W.
Engelmann, 1862. viii, 148p., map. 20cm.

LEONHARDI, Georg
Das Veltlin nebst einer Beschreibung der Bäder
von Bormio: ein Beitrag zur Kenntniss der
Lombardei, zugleich als Wegweiser für Wanderungen
vom Stilfser Joch bis zum Splügen. Leipzig: W.
Engelmann, 1860. viii, 198p., map. 20cm.

LEPILEUR, A
Ascension au Mont Blanc, par MM. Martins, Bravais
et Lepileur. [Paris? 1844]. 68-74p., illus.
37cm.
Offprint from L'Illustration, journal universel,
no.84, v.4, 5 oct. 1846.

LE PILEUR, A
ZURCHER, Frédéric and MARGOLLÉ, Élie
Les ascensions célèbres aux plus hautes montagnes
du globe; fragments de voyages; recuillis,
traduits et mis en ordre par Zurcher et Margollé.
5e éd., rev. par A. Le Pileur. Paris: Hachette,
1891. 309p., illus. 19cm. (Bibliothèque des
merveilles)

LÉPINAY, Jacques de
See
LÉPINEY, Jacques de

LÉPINEY, Jacques de
Les Aiguilles Rouge de Chamonix, Les Fis, Le Buet,
Les Perrons; rédaction nouvelle par Ar. Charlet,
L. Devies, F. Germain, R. Perret avec le concours
du G.H.M. Paris: Fischbacher, 1946. 103p.,
plates, illus., maps. 17cm. (Guides Vallot)

LÉPINEY, Jacques de
Description de la haute montagne dans le massif
du Mont-Blanc. Fasc.1. Les Aiguilles de Chamonix,
par Jacques de Lépiney, E. de Gigord et A. Migot.
Paris: Fischbacher, 1925. xv, 215p., plates (some
fold.), illus., maps. 19cm. (Guides Vallot)

- - 2e éd. 1926.

LÉPINEY, Jacques de
Description de la haute montagne dans le massif
du Mont-Blanc. Fasc.5. Les Aiguilles Rouges;
suivies de Les Fis, Le Buet, Les Perrons. Paris:
Fischbacher, 1928. 139p., plates (1 fold.col.),
illus., maps. 17cm. (Guides Vallot)

LÉPINEY, Jacques de
VALLOT, Henri
  Massif du Mont Blanc: les Aiguilles Rouges et la
  chaîne du Brévent. Paris, 1921. 52p., 5 plates
  (1 fold.), illus., maps. 23cm.
  Ptie.1. Description topographique, par Henri
  Vallot.- ptie.2. Itinéraires des Aiguilles Rouges,
  par Jacques de Lépinay.
  Offprint from La Montagne, 1921.

DRESCH, Jean and LÉPINEY, Jacques de
  Le massif du Toubkal; avec le concours de Théophile
  Jean Delaye. Rabat: Office Chérifien du Tourisme,
  1938. 233p., fold. plates (1 col.), maps. 16cm.
  (Guide alpin de la montagne morocaine)

LÉPINEY, Jacques de and LÉPINEY, Tom de
  Sur le crêtes du Mont Blanc: récits d'ascensions.
  Chambéry: Dardel, 1929. vii, 179p., 24 plates,
  illus. 20cm.

LÉPINEY, Jacques de and LÉPINEY, Tom de
  [Sur les cretes du Mont Blanc...]. Climbs on Mont
  Blanc; translated by Sydney Spencer. Arnold, 1930.
  xii, 179p., plates, illus. 22cm.

WILSON, Ken and LEPPERT, Zdzislaw
  Cwm Idwal; with notes on rare flora by Martin
  Boysen and illustrations by Brian Evans and A.C.
  Cain. 3rd ed. Climbers' Club, 1974. iii, 197p.,
  illus., maps. 16cm. (Climbers' Club guides to
  Wales, 2)

LERCHENFELD, Amand, Freiherr von Schweiger-
  See
SCHWEIGER-LERCHENFELD, Amand, Freiherr von

LERESCHE, J L B
LUTZ, Markus
  [Vollstandige Beschreibung des Schweizerlandes...].
  Dictionnaire géographique-statistique de la Suisse;
  traduit et revu par J.L.B. Leresche. Lausanne:
  Imprimerie de S. Delisle, 1836-37. 2v. 23cm.

LE ROUX, Marc
  La Haute-Savoie: guide du touriste, du naturaliste
  et de l'archéologue. Paris: Masson, [n.d.].
  340p., plates, illus., maps. 18cm. (Collection...
  Marcellin Boule)

LE ROUX, Marc. Vaud, Valais, Haute-Savoie...
  Guide pratique de Genève, son lac et ses environs,
  par Edm. W. Viollier; and Vaud, Valais, Haute-
  Savoie ... par Marc Le Roux. Lyon: G. Toursier,
  [n.d.]. 184p., illus., maps, plans. 17cm.
  (Collection des guides Pol)

LEROY, A L
  Nos fils et nos filles en voyage; préface de M.E.
  Bouty. Paris: Vuibert et Nony, [19--]. xv,
  263p., plates, illus. 24cm.

LESCHEVIN, P X
  Voyage à Genève et dans la Vallée de Chamouni, en
  Savoie. Paris: A.A. Renouard, 1812. 385p., 1
  plate, port. 17cm.

LESSER, Friedrich Christian
  Anmerckungen von der Baumanns-Höhle wie er sie
  selbst Anno 1734 den 21. May befunden; nebst
  Beyfügung derer natürlichen Ursachen ...; begleitet
  von Johann Gottlieb Lessern. 4. weit verm. Aufl.
  Nordhaussen: J.H. Gross, 1745. 78p. 18cm.

Letters, after a tour through some parts of France,
  Italy, Switzerland, and Germany, in 1816; with
  incidental reflections on some topics connected
  with religion, [by John Sheppard]. Edinburgh:
  Oliphant, Waugh, & Innes, 1817. xvii, 353p. 22cm.

- - Another issue entitled: Letters, descriptive of
  a tour... 1817.

Letters from an absent brother. S. Gosnell,
  printer, 1823. 265p. 22cm.
  Signed: D.W. i.e. Daniel Wilson.

- - 2nd ed., entitled: Letters from an absent
  brother, containing some account of a tour through
  parts of the Netherlands, Switzerland, Northern
  Italy, and France, in the summer of 1823. G.
  Wilson, 1824. 2v.
- - 3rd ed., very considerably enl. 1825. 2v.
- - 4th ed. 1827. 2v.

Letters from Switzerland, 1833. Carlsruhe: Printed
  by W. Hasper, 1834. 160p. 20cm.
  Unpublished.

Letters from Switzerland and Italy, during a late
  tour, by the author of 'Letters from the East',
  & 'Travels in the East' [i.e. John Carne].
  Published for H. Colburn by R. Bentley, 1834.
  xii, 472p. 24cm.

Lettres sur la Suisse, adressées à Madame de M***
  par un voyageur françois, [i.e. Jean B. Laborde]
  en 1781... Genève: Jombert, 1783. 2v., plates,
  map, plans. 23cm.

Lettres sur la Suisse, écrites en 1820, suivies d'un
  voyage à Chamouny et au Simplon. Paris: N.
  Nepveu, 1822. xx, 417p. 20cm.
  Preface signed: Raoul-Rochette.

Lettres sur quelques cantons de la Suisse, écrites
  en 1819, [par Désiré Raoul-Rochette]. Paris: H.
  Nicolle, 1820. vi, 494p. 22cm.

LEUCHS, Georg
  Führer durch das Kaisergebirge... 4. Aufl.
  München: J. Lindauer, 1922. xi, 254p., map (in
  pocket). 16cm. (Leuchs Führer)

LEUTHOLD, H F
  Cinquantes principales vues pittoresques en
  mignature de la Suisse, accompagnés d'un texte
  explicatif ...; publié par H.F. Leuthold. Zürich:
  The Author, [ca 1838]. 1v. of illus. 14 x 17cm.
  Captions in French and German.

LEUTHOLD, Heinrich
  Gedichte; mit Einleitung und Anmerkungen hrsg.
  von Max Mendheim. Leipzig: P. Reclam, [18--].
  320p. 15cm.

LEVASSEUR, E
  Les Alpes et les grandes ascensions, par E.
  Levasseur; avec la collaboration de membres des
  clubs alpins. Paris: Delagrave, 1889. viii,
  456p., plates (1 fold.), illus., col. maps, bibl.
  30cm.

LEVER, Charles
  The Dodd family abroad. Chapman & Hall, 1859.
  2v., plates, illus. 21cm.
  Library has vol.2 only.

LEVESON, Henry Astbury
  Sport in many lands, by H.A.L. "The Old Shekarry".
  Chapman & Hall, 1877. 2v., 1 plate, illus., port.
  23cm.

LEVICK, H D
DEMIDOFF, Elim Pavlovich, Principe di San Donato
  Hunting trips in the Caucasus. Ward, 1898. xvi,
  319p., illus., map (in pocket). 24cm.
  The 2nd and 3rd expeditions are described by H.D.
  Levick.

LEVIER, Émile
  À travers le Caucase: notes et impressions d'un
  botaniste. Neuchatel: Attinger, [1894]. 347p.,
  plates (1 fold.), illus., map. 26cm.

- - 2e éd. 1907.

LEVIER, Émile
Au coeur du Caucase: notes et impressions d'un
botaniste.
(In Bibliothèque universelle ... v.54-56, 1892,
6 pts.)

LEVIER, Emile
De Livourne à Batoum: notes et impressions d'un
botaniste.
(In Bibliothèque universelle ... v.48, oct.-déc.,
1890, 3pts.)

LEVIER, Émile
Retour du Caucase: notes et impressions d'un
botaniste.
(In Bibliothèque universelle ... v.57-58, mars-
mai, 1893, 3pts.)

LEVSTEK, Igor
V nasih stenah: izbrani plezalni vzponi v
Slovenskih Alpah, [by] Igor Levstek, Rado Kocevar,
Mitja Kilar. Ljublijana: Planinska zveza Slovenije,
1954. 123p., plates (1 fold.), illus. 20cm.

LEVY, Friedrich
Ostalpine Formenstudien; hrsg. von Friedrich Levy.
Berlin: Borntraeger, 1920-23. 8 pts. in 2, plates
(some fold.), illus., maps, bibl. 28cm.

LEWIN, Walter Henry
Climbs. The Author, [1933]. xvii, 226p., plates,
illus. 23cm.

LEWIS, A   G
Sport, travel and adventure; edited by A.G. Lewis.
Fisher Unwin, 1915. 352p., plates, illus., bibl.
23cm.

LEWIS, Meriwether and CLARK, William
THWAITES, Reuben Gold
A brief history of Rocky Mountain exploration with
especial reference to the expedition of Lewis and
Clark. New York: Appleton, 1904. xiii, 276p.,
plates (1 fold.), illus., map. 20cm.

LEWIS, Meriwether and CLARK, William
WHEELER, Olin D
The trail of Lewis and Clark 1804-1904: a story of
the great exploration across the continent in
1804-06; with a description of the old trail based
upon actual travel over it, and of the changes
found a century later. New York, London: Putnam,
1904. 2v., col. plates (1 fold.), illus., maps.
22cm.

LEYDEN, John
Journal of a tour in the Highlands and Western
Islands of Scotland in 1800; edited with a biblio-
graphy by James Sinton. Edinburgh, London:
Blackwood, 1903. xviii, 318p., bibl. 20cm.

LEYLAND, Peter
The naked mountain. Heinemann, 1951. xix, 83p.
19cm. (New Heinemann poetry)

LHOSTE, Jean Marc and AULARD, Claude
Guide des escalades du Hoggar; avec la collaboration de J. Boissonnas. Paris: Club Alpin Français,
[1962?]. xiv, 154p., illus., maps, bibl. 28cm.

LHOTZKY, Heinrich
Im Reiche der Sennerinnen: Roman. Ludwigshafen am
Bodensee: Hans Lhotzky, 1913. 197p. 18cm.
(Naturgeheimnisse, 1)

LIBERTY, Arthur Lasenby
Springtime in the Basque mountains; with illustrations by Emma Louise Liberty and others. G.
Richards, 1901. xx, 299p., plates, illus., maps.
22cm.

LIBRARY ASSOCIATION. County Libraries Group
Reader's guide to books on mountaineering. 2nd ed.
Newtown, (Mon.): The Group, 1972. 39p. 19cm.
(Readers' guides, new series, no.127)

LIDDIARD, William
The legend of Einsidlin: a tale of Switzerland,
with poetical sketches of Swiss scenery... Saunders
and Otley, 1829. xvi, 283p. 21cm.

LIDDIARD, William
A three months' tour in Switzerland and France;
illustrated with plates, descriptive of mountain
scenery, and interspersed with poetry; with a
route to Chamouni, the Bernese Alps, &c. Smith,
Elder, 1832. xvi, 263p., plates, illus., map.
22cm.

Liébana y los Picos de Europa: ligera resena
histórica, datos geográficos y estadísticos,
itinerarios, monumentos y santuarios... Santander:
"La Atalaya", 1913. 207p., 1 fold.col. plate,
illus., map. 25cm.

Liedersammlung für alpine vereinigungen; hrsg. von
der Alpinen Gesellschaft "Ybbstaler". Wien:
A.G.Y., 1910. 192p. 13cm.

LIENBACHER, Vera
Glockner-Gruppe: ein Führer für Täler, Hütten und
Berge. 4. Aufl. München: Rother, 1962. 219p.,
plates (1 fold.), illus., map (in pocket), bibl.
16cm. (Deutscher und Österreichischer Alpen-
vereine. Alpenvereinsführer. Ostalpen)

LILLE, Jacques de
Dithyrambe sur l'immortalité de l'âme, suivi du
Passage du St.-Gothard: poème traduit de l'anglais
[de Georgiana Cavendish, Duchess of Devonshire].
Paris: Giguet & Michaud; Londres: Prosper, 1802.
123p., plates, illus. 14cm.

LIND-AF-HAGEBY, L
Mountain meditations and some subjects of the day
and the war. Allen & Unwin, 1917. 217p. 19cm.

LINDAU, Paul
Im Fluge: gelegentliche Aufzeichnungen. 2.Aufl.
Leipzig: H. Dürselen, [1886?]. 243p. 20cm.

LINDAU, Wilhelm Adolf
Albina: ein Taschenbuch für Wanderer in der
sächsischen Schweiz, enthaltend eine Beschreibung
des meissnischen Hochlands ..., [von Wilhelm A.
Lindau]. Pirna: C. Diller, 1818. iv, 185p.,
plates, illus., map. 13cm.
In slip-case.

LINDER, Toni
Über Fels und Firn: Liederbuch für Hochtourischen,
enthaltend die schönsten Alpennationale und Volkslieder Chöre und ein-und mehrstimmige Gefänge.
Lahr: M. Schauenburg, 1895. 305p., music. 17cm.

LINDNER, Werner
Vom Reisen und Wandern in alter und neuer Zeit.
Berlin: Furche-Verlag, 1921. 144p., illus. 21cm.
(Werk und Feier, 2)

LINDSAY, William Lauder
The flora of Iceland. Edinburgh, 1861. 40p.
22cm.
Offprint from Edinburgh new philosophical journal,
new ser., July 1861.

LINDSAY, William Lauder
Observations on the lichens collected by Dr. Robert
Brown in West Greenland in 1867 [on Edward
Whymper's expedition]. London, 1869. 305-368p.,
plates, illus. 31cm.
Offprint from Transactions of the Linnean Society,
v.27.

LINER, Carl
Panorama vom Hohen Kasten; nach der Natur ge-
zeichnet ... von Carl Liner, 1904-1905. St.
Gallen: Selbstverlag, [1905]. 24cm.

LING, W   N
The Northern Highlands. Edinburgh: Scottish
Mountaineering Club, 1932. 87p., plates (some
fold., some col.), illus., maps. 22cm. (Scottish
Mountaineering Club guides)

- - 2nd ed. rev., edited by W.N. Ling and John
Rooke Corbett. 1936.

LINGSTROM, Freda
This is Norway; with a preface by Sir Karl Knudsen.
Howe, 1933. 152p., plates (some col.), illus. 22cm.

LINK, Ulrich
  Nanga Parbat: Berg des Schicksals im Himalaya.
  München: Rother, 1953. 52p., plates, illus., maps.
  25cm.

LINTH, Arnold Escher von der
  See
  ESCHER VON DER LINTH, Arnold

LINTH, Hans Conrad Escher von der
  See
  ESCHER VON DER LINTH, Hans Conrad

LINTON, E   Lynn
  The Lake country; with a map and one hundred illus-
  trations drawn and engraved by W.J. Linton. Smith,
  Elder, 1864. 351p., plates, illus., map. 25cm.

Lion hunting; or, A summer's ramble through parts of
  Flanders, Germany, and Switzerland in 1825, with
  some remarks on men, manners, and things, at home
  and abroad. Edinburgh: Black; London: Longman,
  Rees, Orme, Brown, & Green, 1826. iv, 272p. 20cm.

LIOTARD, André Frank and POMMIER, Robert
  Terre Adélie, 1949-1952; préface de Paul-Émile
  Victor. Paris: Arthaud, 1952. 48p., plates (some
  col.), illus. 26cm. (Collection belles pages-
  belles couleurs)

LIOTIER, Max
  Les seigneurs de la neige; couverture et dessins
  de Patrice Legrand. Paris: Arthaud, 1970. 274p.,
  illus. 21cm. (Collection sempervivum, no.49)

LIPSKII, Vladimir Ippolitovich
  Gornaia Bukharà: rezul'taty trekhl'tnikh"
  puteshestvii v" sredniuiu Asiiu v" 1896, 1897 i
  1899 godu. Chast' 2. Gissar", Khrebet" Petra
  Velikago, Alai 1897 g. S.-Peterburg": Izd.
  Imperatorskago Russkago Geograficheskago
  Obshchestva, 1902. 321-541p., plates, illus. 29cm.

LISIBACH, L
  Clubführer durch die Tessiner-Alpen, verfasst von
  L. Lisibach, G. End und J. Kutzner. [Zürich]:
  Schweizer Alpen-Club, [1908]. 2v., illus., bibl.
  17cm.

A list of the heights of nearly two hundred of the
  principal mountains of England and Wales.
  Birmingham: White & Pike, 1860. 8p. 18cm.

CARR, Herbert Reginald Culling and LISTER, George A
  The mountains of Snowdonia in history, the sciences,
  literature and sport; edited by Herbert R.C. Carr
  and George A. Lister. Bodley Head, 1925. xvix,
  405p., plates (some col.), illus., maps (some
  fold.). 23cm.

- - 2nd ed. Crosby, Lockwood, 1948.

LISTER, George A
CARR, Herbert Reginald Culling
  A walker's guide to Snowdon and the Beddgelert
  district ..., by Herbert R.C. Carr, George A.
  Lister and Paul Orkney Work. Newcastle upon Tyne:
  Listers (Printers), 1949. vi, 60p., plates (1
  fold.), illus., bibl. 14cm.
  Reprint, rev. and enl. from the walkers' section
  of A climbers' guide to Snowdon... 1926.

Literary souvenirs; [collected by Alaric A. Watts].
  [Longmans], 1827. xxiv, 402p., plates, illus.
  14cm.

- - Another [i.e. 9th] ed. 1833.

LITTLE, Archibald John
  Mount Omi and beyond: a record of travel on the
  Thibetan border. Heinemann, 1901. xv, 272p.,
  plates (1 fold.col.), illus., map. 24cm.

A little journey to Switzerland. Cassel, 1910.
  64p., col. plates, illus. 19cm.

LITTLEJOHN, Pat R
  South Devon: Chudleigh, Torbay, Torquay, Brixham,
  Berry Head, [by] Pat Littlejohn in association
  with Peter Biven. Goring, Reading: West Col
  Productions, 1971. 172p., illus., maps. 17cm.
  (West Col coastal climbing guides)

LIVANOS, Georges
  Au dela de la verticale. Paris: Arthaud, 1958.
  270p., plates, illus. 21cm. (Collection
  sempervivum, no.35)

LIVERPOOL INSTITUTE MOUNTAINEERING CLUB ICELAND
EXPEDITION, 1975
  Official report, by E.H. Anderson, A. Boyle, D.
  Brown & R.J. Cooke. Liverpool, 1975. 44 leaves,
  plates, illus., col. maps. 35cm.

LIVERSIDGE, Douglas
  The last continent. Travel Book Club, 1958.
  248p., plates, illus., map. 23cm.

Llanberis area guide: a guide to Llanberis, Nant
  Peris, Llanberis Pass and Snowdon. Dinorwic:
  Vector, 1971. 63p., illus., maps. 19cm.

LLANBERIS PROTECTION SOCIETY
  Park power: a memorandum on the proposed pumped
  storage scheme, Dinorwic, Llanberis in
  Caernarvonshire. Brynrefail: The Society, 1972.
  12p. 25cm.

LLIBOUTRY, Luis
  Nieves y glaciares de Chile: fundamentos de
  glaciologia. Santiago de Chile: Universidad de
  Chile, 1956. 471p., fold plates, illus., maps.
  28cm.

HOWARD, William D   and LLOYD, F   H
  Photographs among the Dolomite mountains.
  [London?]: The Authors, 1865. 1v. of illus. 39cm.

LLOYD, Francis
  The physiography of the Upper Engadine. Stanford,
  1881. 62p., illus., map. 14cm.

LLOYD, George
GERARD, Alexander
  Account of Koonawur, in the Himalaya ... by the
  late Alexander Gerard; edited by George Lloyd.
  Madden, 1841. xiii, 308, xxvip., 1 fold. plate,
  map (in pocket). 24cm.

LLOYD, George
  Narrative of a journey from Caunpoor to the
  Boorendo Pass in the Himalaya mountains, via
  Gwalior, Agra, Delhi and Sirhind, by Sir William
  Lloyd; and Alexander Gerard's Account of an
  attempt to penetrate by Bekhur to Garoo ...; with
  a letter from the late J.G. Gerard detailing a
  visit to the Shatool and Boorendo Passes ...;
  edited by George Lloyd. Madden, 1840. 2v., fold.
  plates, maps. 23cm.

LLOYD, Henry Demarest
  The Swiss democracy: the study of a sovereign
  people; edited by John A. Hobson. Fisher Unwin,
  1908. xvi, 273p., plates, illus. 21cm.

LLOYD, Robert Wylie
NATIONAL LIBRARY OF SCOTLAND
  Shelf-catalogue of the Lloyd collection of alpine
  books. Boston (Mass.): G.K. Hall, 1964. 1v.
  (various pagings). 21 x 26cm.
  Photocopy.

LLOYD, Robert Wylie
  A traverse of the Dent Blanche and the first
  direct ascent of the Aiguille de Bionnassay by
  the north face, (read before the Rucksack Club,
  March 11, 1927) and The first direct ascent of
  the Aiguille de Bionnassay by the north face
  (read before the Alpine Club, December 13, 1926).
  [The Author], 1927. 16p., plates (2 col.), illus.
  23cm.

LLOYD, Sir William
Narrative of a journey from Caunpoor to the
Boorendo Pass in the Himalaya mountains, via
Gwalior, Agra, Delhi and Sirhind, by Sir William
Lloyd; and Alexander Gerard's Account of an
attempt to penetrate by Bekhur to Garoo ...; with
a letter from the late J.G. Gerard detailing a
visit to the Shatool and Boorendo Passes ...;
edited by George Lloyd. Madden, 1840. 2v., fold.
plates, maps. 23cm.

LLUBERA, Miquel Gonzalez
See
GONZALEZ LLUBERA, Miquel

LOCK, W   G
FRIIS, I   A
Sporting life on the Norwegian fjelds ...;
translated from the Norwegian with jottings on
sport in Norway by W.G. Lock. Lock, 1878. viii,
375p., map. 20cm.

LÖBL, Robert
MERRICK, Hugh
The Alps in colour, text by Hugh Merrick; photographs by Robert Löbl. Constable, 1970. 237p.,
illus. 29cm.

LÖHRER, Hans
Die Schweiz im Spiegel englischer Literatur, 1849-
1875. Zürich: Juris-Verlag, 1952. 147p., bibl.
23cm. (Zürcher Beiträge zur vergleichenden
Literaturgeschichte, Bd.1)

LOEWENBERG, Julius
Schweizer Bilder. Berlin: J.G. Hasselberg, 1834.
v, 224p., plates, illus., map. 23cm.

LÖWL, Ferdinand
Aus dem Zillerthaler Hochgebirge. Gera: Amthor,
1878. vii, 436p. 18cm.

LOGES, Chretien de
Essais historiques sur le Mont St. Bernard.
[Genève?]: [The Author?], 1789. 230p. 19cm.

LONCHAMP, F   C
J.-L. Aberli, 1723-86: son temps, sa vie et son
oeuvre; avec un catalogue complet méthodique et
raisonné. Paris: Librairie des Bibliophiles, 1927.
3v. in 1., plates, illus. 24cm.

LONG, Henry Lawes
Hannibal's passage of the Alps, by a member of the
University of Cambridge [i.e. Henry Lawes Long].
Whittaker, Treacher, & Arnot, 1830. vi, 158p.,
1 fold. plate, map. 19cm.

LONGFELLOW, Henry Wadsworth
Hyperion: a romance; illustrated with 24 photographs ... by Francis Frith. A.W. Bennett, 1865.
x, 270p., plates, illus. 24cm.

LONGHI, Stefano
SKOCZYLAS, Adam
Stefano we shall come tomorrow. Poets' & Painter's
Press, 1962. 33p., plates, illus. 24cm.

LONGMAN, William and TROWER, Henry
Journal of six weeks' adventures in Switzerland,
Piedmont, and on the Italian lakes, by W.L[ongman]
and H.T[rower], June, July, August, 1856. Printed
by Spottiswoode, 1856. 123p., 1 fold.col. plate,
map. 21cm.

LONGMAN, William
A lecture on Switzerland. [The Author], 1857.
94p. 21cm.

LONGMAN, William
Suggestions for the exploration of Iceland: an
address delivered to the members of the Alpine
Club on April 4, 1861. Alpine Club, 1861. 39p.,
1 fold.col. plate. 23cm.

LONGMORE, John
Pencillings by the way, being a tour on the Rhine
and in Switzerland. Worcester: A.M. Baylis, 1872.
132p. 19cm.

LONGPRÉ, Charles Lemercher de, baron d'Haussez
See
HAUSSEZ, Charles Le Mercher de Longpré, baron d'

LONGSTAFF, Tom George
Mountain sickness and its probable causes.
Spottiswoode, 1906. 56p. 22cm.

LONGSTAFF, Tom George
This my voyage. Murray, 1950. 324p., 23 plates,
illus., maps, bibl. 23cm.

LONGSTAFF, Tom George
[This my voyage]. Mon odyssée montagnarde;
traduit par J. et F. Germain. Paris: Arthaud,
1955. 283p., plates, illus., maps. 22cm.
(Collection sempervivum,28)

LONGSTAFF, Tom George
[This my voyage]. Ein Alpinist in aller Welt;
übersetzt von Carl Bach. Zürich: Orell Füssli,
1951. 285p., plates, illus., maps. 24cm.

LONGSTAFF, Tom George
[This my voyage]. Recuerdos de viaje, del
Himalaya al Ártico; versión espanola por José
Casán Herrera. Barcelona: Labor, 1952 (1954
reprint). xv, 361p., plates, illus., maps. 23cm.
(Libros de viajes)

LONGSTAFF, Tom George
[This my voyage]. Sui tetti del mondo; traduzione
di Bruno Oddera. Milano: Bompiani, 1954. 281p.,
plates, illus. 22cm. (Uomini e paesi)

LONGSTAFF, Tom George
[This my voyage]. Japanese ed. Tokyo:
Hakusuisha, [1950?]. xxxvi, 412p., plates, illus.
20cm.

LONGSTAFF, Tom George
SHERRING, Charles A
Western Tibet and the British borderland: the
sacred country of Hindus and Buddhists, with an
account of the government, religion and customs
of its peoples; with a chapter by T.G. Longstaff
describing an attempt to climb Gurla Mandhata.
Arnold, 1906. xv, 367p., illus., maps. 26cm.

LONGWORTH, J   A
A year among the Circassians. Colburn, 1840.
2v., plates, illus. 22cm.

LONGYEAR, Burton O
Rocky Mountain wild flower studies: an account of
the ways of some plants that live in the Rocky
Mountain region; with illustrations from nature
by the author. Fort Collins (Colo.): The Author,
1909. xv, 156p., illus. 20cm.

LORENTZ, H   A
Zwarte menschen, witte bergen: verhaal van den
tocht naar het sneeuwgebergte van Nieuw-Guinea.
Leiden: E.J. Brill, 1913. xii, 262p., plates (1
fold.col.), illus., map (in pocket). 26cm.

LORENZONI, Antonio
Cadore. Bergamo: Istituto Italiano d'Arti
Grafiche, 1907. 138p., illus. 27cm. (Collezione
di monografie illustrate, ser. 1a. Italia
artistica, 33)

LORIMER, E   O
Language hunting in the Karakoram. Allen & Unwin,
1939. 310p., plates, illus., map. 23cm.

DESOR, Édouard and LORIOL, P   de
Échinologie helvétique: description des oursins
fossiles de la Suisse. Wiesbade: C.W. Kreidel,
1868-69. 5 pts. in 3 portfolios, plates, illus.
37cm.

LORNE, John Douglas Sutherland Campbell, Marquis of
See
ARGYLL, John Douglas Sutherland Campbell, 9th Duke of

ECKENSTEIN, Oscar and LORRIA, August
The Alpine portfolio: the Pennine Alps, from the
Simplon to the Great St. Bernard; edited by Oscar
Eckenstein & August Lorria. London: Published by
the Editors, 1889. 33p., 100 plates, illus. 42cm.
Photographs by V. Sella, E. Le Bland, W.F. Donkin
and others.
In portfolio with an introductory text.

LORRIA, August and MARTEL, Édouard Alfred
Le massif de la Bernina, par August Lorria et
É.A. Martel; avec la collaboration de W.A.B.
Coolidge et J. Caviezel. Zurich: Orell Füssli,
1894. 163p., 50 plates, illus., map, bibl.
33 x 42cm. (Les grandes Alpes)

LORRIA, August
CONWAY, William Martin, Baron Conway
Die pennischen Alpen: ein Führer für Bergsteiger
durch das Gebiet der pennischen Alpen zwischen
Simplon und Grossen St. Bernhard; bearb. und hrsg.
von August Lorria. Zürich: Orell Füssli, 1891.
vii, 204p. 17cm.

LORY, Gabriel, 1763-1840
Guida da Milano a Ginevra pel Sempione; [illus-
trazioni da G. Lory]. Milano: Artaria, 1822. xi,
175p., plates, map. 28cm.

LORY, Gabriel, 1763-1840 and LORY, Gabriel, 1784-1846
Schweizerland vor hundert Jahren: sechzehn farbige
Tafeln nach Originalstichen von Gabriel Lory, père
et fils; Einführung von C. von Mandach. Bern:
Iris, 1935. 11p., 16 col. plates,illus. 35cm.

LORY, Gabriel, 1763-1840 and LORY, Gabriel, 1784-1846
Voyage pittoresque aux glaciers de Chamouni;
[illustrations par G. Lory, père et fils]. Paris:
P. Didot, 1815. 1v. (chiefly col. illus.). 24cm.

LORY, Gabriel, 1763-1840 and LORY, Gabriel, 1784-1846
Voyage pittoresque de Genève à Milan par le
Simplon; [illustrations par G. Lory, père et fils].
Paris: P. Didot, 1811. 1v. (chiefly col. illus.).
43cm.

LORY, Gabriel, 1763-1840 and LORY, Gabriel, 1784-1846
[Voyage pittoresque de Genève à Milan par le
Simplon]. Picturesque tour from Geneva to Milan
by way of the Simplon; illustrated with thirty six
coloured views ... engraved from designs by J. and
J. Lory ... and accompanied with particulars
historical and descriptive, by Frederic Schoberl.
R. Ackermann, 1820. 136p., 36 col. plates, illus.,
map. 28cm.

LORY, Gabriel, 1763-1840 and LORY, Gabriel, 1784-1846
[Voyage pittoresque de Genève à Milan par le
Simplon]. Viaggio pittorico fatto da Ginevra a
Milano per la strada del Sempione; [illustrazioni
da G. Lory, padre e figlio]. Milano: Ferrario,
1821. 1v. (chiefly col. illus.). 48cm.
Text in Italian and French.

LORY, Gabriel, 1763-1840 and LORY, Gabriel, 1784-1846
12 Schweizertrachtenbilder, nach den alten
Originalen, von Gabriel Lory, Vater und Sohn.
Esslingen: Fingerle, [ca 1930]. 12 col. plates in
folder. 28cm.
Cover title.

LORY, J
See
LORY, Gabriel, 1763-1840 and LORY, Gabriel, 1784-1846

LOUGHBOROUGH COLLEGE OF EDUCATION
Loughborough rock climbing series: programmes 1-6,
by John Brailsford; editor John Leedham. Longman,
1969. 6v., illus. 20cm.

LOUGHBOROUGH UNIVERSITY MOUNTAINEERING CLUB KISHTWAR
HIMALAYAN EXPEDITION, 1976
L.U.M.C. 1976 Kishtwar Himalayan Expedition;
[edited by S.W. Pollington]. Loughborough: The
Expedition, [1978]. 36p., plates, illus. 30cm.

LOVAT, L S
Climbers' guide to Glencoe and Ardgour. Vol.1.
Buachaille Etive Mor. 2nd ed. Edinburgh:
Scottish Mountaineering Club, 1959. xvii, 99p.,
illus., map. 16cm. [Scottish Mountaineering
Club climbers' guide books]

LOVELACE, Mary, Countess of
LOVELACE, Ralph Milbanke, 2nd Earl of
Ralph Earl of Lovelace: a memoir, by Mary
Countess of Lovelace. Christophers, 1920. ix,
170p., plates, ports. 23cm.

LOVELACE, Ralph Milbanke, 2nd Earl of
Ralp Earl of Lovelace: a memoir, by Mary Countess
of Lovelace. Christophers, 1920. ix, 170p.,
plates, ports. 23cm.

LOVELOCK, James
Climbing, by James Lovelock; with a chapter on
artificial climbing by Trevor Jones. Batsford,
1971. 185p., plates, illus. 23cm.

LOVETT, Richard
Norwegian pictures drawn with pen and pencil con-
taining also a glance at Sweden and the Gotha
Canal. New ed. rev. and partly rewritten.
Religious Tract Society, 1890. 224p., 1 fold.col.
plate, illus., map. 29cm.

LOVETT, Richard
Welsh pictures drawn with pen and pencil, by J.E.
Lloyd [and others]; edited by Richard Lovett.
Religious Tract Society, [ca 1892]. 192p., illus.
29cm.

LOVEY-TROILLET, Ernest
La Val Ferret; préface de Charles Gos. Neuchatel:
Attinger, [1945]. 191p., plates, illus. 19cm.

LOVINS, Amory
Eryri, the mountains of longing; with photographs
by Philip Evans; introduction by Sir Charles
Evans; edited with a foreword, by David R. Brower.
San Francisco: Friends of the Earth, [1972].
176p., illus., map. 36cm.

LOVSIN, Evgen
V Triglavu in v njegovi sosescini. Ljubljana:
Slovensko Planinsko Drustvo, 1944. 339p., plates
(1 col.), illus., bibl. 25cm.

LOW, Sidney
Italy in the war. Longmans, Green, 1916. xii,
316p., plates (3 fold.), illus., maps. 20cm.

LOWE, Emily
Unprotected females in Norway; or, The pleasantest
way of travelling there, passing through Denmark
and Sweden; with Scandinavian sketches from
nature, [by Emily Lowe]. Routledge, 1857. viii,
295p., illus. 20cm.

- - [Later ed.]. 1859.

LOWE, Emily
Unprotected females in Sicily, Calabria, and on
the top of Mount Aetna, [by the author of
"Unprotected females in Norway", i.e. Emily Lowe].
Routledge, Warne, & Routledge, 1864. xi, 265p.,
plates, illus. 17cm.

HILLARY, Sir Edmund and LOWE, George
East of Everest: an account of the New Zealand
Alpine Club Himalayan Expedition to the Barun
Valley in 1954. Hodder & Stoughton, 1956. 70p.,
48 plates, illus., maps. 25cm.

LUBBOCK, John, Baron Avebury
See
AVEBURY, John Lubbock, Baron

LUBLINK WEDDIK, Bartholomeus T
See
WEDDIK, Bartholomeus T   Lublink

LUC, Jean André de
Histoire du passage des Alpes par Annibal...
Genève: J.J. Paschoud, 1818. xvi, 303p., 1 fold.
plate, map. 21cm.

- - 2e éd. corr. et augm. 1825.

LUC, Jean André de
Lettres physiques et morales sur l'histoire de la
terre et de l'homme, addressées à la reine de la
Grande Bretagne. La Haye: de Tune, 1779-80
[v.2., 1780]. 5v. in 6. 21cm.

LUC, Jean André de
Lettres physiques et morales, sur les montagnes et
sur l'histoire de la terre et de l'homme... La
Haye: de Tune, 1778. xxviii, 226p. 21cm.

LUC, Jean André de and DENTAND, Pierre Gédéon
Relation de différents voyages dans les Alpes du
Faucigny, par Messieurs D. & D. [i.e. J.A. de Luc
et P.G. Dentand]. Maestricht: J.E. Dufour, & Ph.
Roux, 1776. xxi, 138p. 17cm.

LUC, Jean André de and DENTAND, Pierre Gédéon
[Relation de différents voyages...]. Reisen nach
den Eisgebürgen von Faucigny in Savoyen, [von]
J.A. de Luc [und P.G. Dentand]; aus dem
Französischen übersetzt [von J.S. Wyttenbach].
Leipzig: Weidmann, 1777. 174p. 21cm.

LUCAS, E   V
Outposts of mercy: the record of a visit ... to the
various units of the British Red Cross in Italy.
Methuen, 1917. 60p., plates, illus. 18cm.

LUCAS, Franz
Führer durch Passau & Umgebung: zugleich Fest-
schrift für die General-Versammlung des Deutschen
& Österr. Alpenvereins in Passau... 1899, von K.
Eckart, und einem Anhang über das alpine Arbeits-
Gebiet der Sektion von [F.] Lucas. Passau: Sektion
Passau, 1899. 75,30p., plates (1 fold.col.),
illus., plan. 21cm.

LUCCHESI, Alexis
Escalades dans le massif de la Sainte-Baume:
Bartagne, Beguines. Pau: Marrimpouey, 1976.
147p., fold. plates, illus., maps. 21cm.

LUCCHESI, Alexis
GORGEON, Bernard
Escalades dans le massif de la Sainte-Victoire:
partie centrale: les Deux Aiguilles, le Signal, par
Bernard Gorgeon, Christian Guyomar, Alexis
Lucchesi. Pau: Marrimpouey, 1978. 117p., 1 fold.
plate, illus., maps. 21cm.

LUCCHESI, Alexis
Escalades dans le massif des Calanques: chaîne de
Marseilleveyre. Ptie. 3. Mounine-Callot, Plan des
Cailles, les Îles. Pau: Marrimpouey, 1977. 118p.,
illus., maps. 21cm.

LUCCHESI, Alexis
Escalades dans le massif des Calanques: chaîne de
Marseilleveyre. Ptie. 4. Bougie-Melette Walkyries.
Pau: Marrimpouey, 1978. 123p., illus., maps. 21cm.

LUCCHESI, Alexis
Escalades dans le massif des Calanques: Devenson,
Gardiole. Pau: Marrimpouey, 1976. 195p., fold.
plates, illus., maps. 21cm.

LUCCHESI, Alexis
Escalades dans le massif des Calanques en Vau.
Pau: Éditions Marrimpouey Jeune, 1972. 136p.,
illus., map. 22cm.

LUCCHESI, Alexis
Escalades dans le massif des Calanques: les Goudes,
St-Michel. Pau: Marrimpouey, 1977. 173p., illus.,
maps. 21cm.

LUCCHESI, Alexis
Escalades dans le massif des Calanques: Sormiou.
Pau: Marrimpouey, 1977. 104p., illus., maps.
21cm.

DUFRANC, Michel and LUCCHESI, Alexis
Escalades dans les Alpes de Provence: Verdon,
Cadières, Teillon, Aiglun. Pau: Marrimpouey, 1975.
159p., 1 fold. plate, illus., maps. 16cm.

KINZEL, Karl and LUCKWALD, Christine von
Tiroler Bergwanderungen: noch ein Buch zum Lustmachen; mit Bildern von F. Völkner. Schwerin
i.M.: Fr. Bahn, 1911. 211p., illus. 20cm.

LUDWIG, A
SCHWEIZER ALPEN-CLUB. Sektion St. Gallen
Festschrift zur fünfzigjährigen Jubiläums-Feier
der Sektion St. Gallen S.A.C., 1863-1913; nach
den Protokollen und anderen Quellen zusammengestellt von A. Ludwig. St. Gallen: Zollikofer,
1913. 128p., plates, illus. 24cm,

LUDWIG, J   M
Pontresina and its neighbourhood. 4th [i.e. 2nd
English] ed., translated by F.S. Reilly.
Stanford, 1879. x, 148p., map (in pocket). 14cm.

LUTHER, Carl J   and LÜCKE, G   P
Der Skitourist. München: J. Lindauer, 1913. vi,
169p., plates, illus. 16cm.

- - 2. Aufl., von Carl J. Luther. 1921.

LUERSSEN, Heinrich
Das Lahnthal von der Lahnquelle bis zur Mündung
nebst den Seitenthälern in ihren unteren und
mittleren Stufen. Giessen: Roth, 1902. xiv,
228p., plates, illus., maps (1 in pocket). 17cm.
(Roth's illustrierter Lahnführer)

LÜTHI, Gottlieb
Excelsior: Lieder eines Bergwanderers; illustriert
von Adolf Thierstein. Samaden: Engadin Press,
[n.d.]. 93p., plates, illus. 20cm.

LÜTHI, Gottlieb and EGLOFF, Carl
Das Säntis-Gebiet: illustrierter Touristenführer;
mit einem naturgeschichtlichen Anhang von E.
Bächler... 3. neurev. Aufl. St. Gallen: Fehr,
1913. 200p., illus., map (in pocket). 19cm.

- - 6. Aufl., neu bearb. von Karl Kleine. 1946.

LÜTSCHG, Otto
Der Märjelensee und seine Abflussverhältnisse:
eine hydrologische Studie unter Mitberück-
sichtigung hydrographischer Erscheinungen in
anderen Flussgebieten. Bern: Abteilung für
Wasserwirtschaft, 1915. xx, 358p., plates (some
fold., some col.), illus., maps, bibl. 32cm.
(Annalen der Schweiz. Landeshydrographie, Bd.1)

LÜTSCHG, Otto
[Der Märjelensee...]. Le Lac de Märjelen. Genève,
1916. 32p., 12 plates, illus. 23cm.
Summary in French of Der Märjelensee.
Offprint from Echo des Alpes.

LÜTSCHG, Otto
Über Niederschlag und Abfluss im Hochgebirge:
Sonderdarstellung des Mattmarkgebietes: ein
Beitrag zur Fluss- und Gletscherkunde der
Schweiz. Zürich: Schweizerischer Wasserwirt-
schaftsverband, 1926. 480p., plates (some fold.,
some col.), illus., maps, bibl. 31cm.

LUIGI AMEDEO, Duke of the Abruzzi
Il Ruwenzori, parte scientifica: resultati delle
osservazioni e studi ... [della] spedizione.
Milano: Hoepli, 1909. 2v., plates (1 fold., some
col.), illus., maps. 26cm.

LUIGI AMEDEO, Duke of the Abruzzi
DE FILIPPI, Filippo
Il Ruwenzori: viaggio di esplorazione e prime
ascensioni delle più alte vette nella catena
nevosa ..., relazione ... [di] Filippo De Filippi;
illustrata da Vittorio Sella. Milano: Hoepli,
1908. xii, 358p., plates (some fold., some col.),
illus., maps. 26cm.
At head of title: S.A.R. il Principe Luigi Amedeo
di Savoia, leader of the expedition.

LUIGI AMEDEO, Duke of the Abruzzi
DE FILIPPI, Filippo
[Il Ruwenzori: viaggio di esplorazione...].
Ruwenzori: an account of the expedition of H.R.H.
Prince Luigi Amedeo of Savoy, Duke of the Abruzzi;
with a preface by the Duke; [translation ... by
Caroline De Filippi; the illustrations from photo-
graphs taken by Vittorio Sella]. Constable, 1908.
xvi, 408p., plates (some fold., some col.), illus.,
maps. 27cm.

LUIGI AMEDEO, Duke of the Abruzzi
DE FILIPPI, Filippo
La spedizione di Sua Altezza Reale il Principe
Luigi Amedeo di Savoia, Duca degli Abruzzi al
Monte Sant'Elia (Alaska), 1897; illustrata da
Vittorio Sella. Milano: Hoepli, 1900. xvii,
284p., plates (some fold., some col.), illus.,
maps, bibl. 29cm.

LUIGI AMEDEO, Duke of the Abruzzi
DE FILIPPI, Filippo
[La spedizione di Sua Altezza Reale...]. The
ascent of Mont St. Elias (Alaska)by H.R.H. Prince
Luigi Amedeo di Savoia, Duke of the Abruzzi,
narrated by Filippo De Filippi; illustrated by
Vittorio Sella and translated by Linda Villari
with the author's supervision.
Constable, 1900. xvi, 241p., plates (some fold.,
1 col.), illus., maps, bibl. 28cm.

LUIGI AMEDEO, Duke of the Abruzzi
DE FILIPPI, Filippo
[La spedizione nel Karakoram e nell'Himalaya
occidentale, 1909]. Karakoram and Western Himalaya
1909: an account of the expedition of H.R.H. Prince
Luigi Amedeo of Savoy, Duke of the Abbruzzi; with
a preface by the Duke; [put into English by
Caroline de Filippi and H.T. Porter; the illustra-
tions from photographs taken by Vittorio Sella].
Constable, 1912. 2v., plates, illus., maps. 29cm.

LUIGI AMEDEO, Duke of the Abruzzi
La "Stella Polare" nel mare artico, 1899-1900, [da]
Luigi Amedeo di Savoia, U. Cagni, A. Cavalli
Motinelli. Milano: Hoepli, 1903. xii, 592p.,
plates (some fold.), illus., maps. 27cm.

LUKAN, Karl
[Die Alpen von Mont Ventoux zum Kahlenberg]. The
Alps; [introduction and notes ... by Wilfrid Noyce;
with descriptive essays by Karl Lukan]. Thames &
Hudson, 1961. 312p., illus., maps. 29cm.

LUKAN, Karl
[Alpinismus in Bildern]. The Alps and alpinism;
edited by Karl Lukan,translated by Hugh Merrick;
with an introduction by Christian Bonington.
Thames & Hudson, 1968. 184p., illus. (some col.).
29cm.

LUKAS, Hans
Der Krieg an Kärntens Grenze, 1915-1917, vom Hochweissstein bis zum Predil: ein Erinnerungsbuch.
Graz: Leykam-Verlag, 1938. 125p., plates (some
fold.), illus. 23cm.

LUND, T   W   M
The Lake of Como: its history, art and archaeology.
Kegan Paul, Trench, Trübner, 1910. x, 212p.,
plates (1 fold.col.), illus., map. 18cm.

LUNN, Sir Arnold
Alpine memories. [Berne, 1959]. 45-52p. 30cm.
Offprint from Swissair's "Across the Alps".

LUNN, Sir Arnold
Alpine ski-ing at all heights and seasons. 2nd ed.
rev. Methuen, 1926. xiv, 106p., plates, illus.
18cm.

LUNN, Sir Arnold
[Alpine ski-ing]. Le ski en hiver, au printemps,
sur les glaciers; traduit de l'anglais par A.G.
[i.e. A. de Gennes]. Chambéry: Dardel, 1924.
xv, 172p., plates, illus. 19cm.

LUNN, Sir Arnold
The Alps. Williams & Norgate, 1914. 256p., bibl.
18cm. (Home University library of modern
knowledge, 91)

- - Another issue. Thornton Butterworth, [1930].

LUNN, Sir Arnold
And the floods came: a chapter of war-time autobiography. Eyre & Spottiswoode, 1942. 237p.
23cm.

LUNN, Sir Arnold
The Bernese Oberland. H. Marshall, [1910]-20.
2v. 17cm.
Published on behalf of the Federal Council of
British Ski Clubs.

LUNN, Sir Arnold
The Bernese Oberland. Eyre & Spottiswoode, 1958.
215p., 16 plates (1 fold col.), illus. 21cm.

- - Rev. and enl. ed. Allen & Unwin, 1973.

LUNN, Sir Arnold
A century of mountaineering, 1857-1957; [centen-
ary tribute to the Alpine Club from the Swiss
Foundation for Alpine Research]. Allen & Unwin,
1957. 263p., plates (some col.), illus. 25cm.

LUNN, Sir Arnold
Come what may: an autobiography. Eyre &
Spottiswoode, 1940. 482p. 23cm.

- - Another issue. Boston: Little, Brown, 1941.

LUNN, Sir Arnold
The complete ski-runner. Methuen, 1930. 213p.,
plates, illus. 23cm. (The Complete series)

LUNN, Sir Arnold
[The complete ski-runner]. Le ski alpin:
tourisme et courses; traduit de l'anglais par A.
de Gennes. Chambéry: Dardel, 1930. ix, 221p.,
20 plates, illus. 19cm.

LUNN, Sir Arnold
The cradle of Switzerland. Hollis & Carter, 1952.
xiii, 226p., plates, illus. 19cm.

LUNN, Sir Arnold
Cross-country ski-ing. Methuen, 1920. viii,
118p., plates, illus. 16cm.

LUNN, Sir Arnold
COUTTET, Alfred
L'enchantement du ski, [par] Alfred Couttet,
Arnold Lunn, Emil Petersen; introduction de Henry
Cuénot. Paris: Alpina, 1930. 159p., col. plates,
illus. 25cm.

LUNN, Sir Arnold
The Englishman in the Alps, being a collection of
English prose and poetry relating to the Alps;
edited by Arnold Lunn. Oxford University Press,
1913. xx, 294p. 18cm.

LUNN, Sir Arnold
Family name. Methuen, 1931. 282p. 20cm.

LUNN, Sir Arnold
Guide to Montana and district. H. Marshall, 1907.
79p., 1 fold. plate (in pocket), illus. 19cm.
Preface signed: A.H.M.L. i.e. Arnold Lunn.

LUNN, Sir Arnold
[Guide to Montana...]. Guide de Montana et des
environs. Neuchatel: Delachaux & Niestlé, 1908.
79p., illus. 19cm.
Preface signed: A.H.M.L. i.e. Arnold Lunn.

LUNN, Sir Arnold
[Guide to Montana...]. Führer von Montana und
Umgebung. Neuenburg: Delachaux & Niestlé, 1908.
80p., illus. 19cm.
Preface signed: A.H.M.L. i.e. Arnold Lunn.

LUNN, Sir Arnold
The Harrovians. 6th ed. Methuen, 1926. vii,
312p. 20cm.

LUNN, Sir Arnold
A history of ski-ing. Oxford University Press,
1927. xv, 492p., plates, illus. 23cm.

LUNN, Sir Arnold
The Italian lakes and lakeland cities. Harrap,
1932. 156p., plates (1 fold, 1 col.), illus.,
map. 18cm. (Kitbag travel books)

LUNN, Sir Arnold
Matterhorn centenary. Allen & Unwin, 1965. 144p.,
25 plates (1 col.), illus. 23cm.

LUNN, Sir Arnold
Memory to memory. Hollis & Carter, 1956. 268p.,
plates, illus., port. 23cm.

LUNN, Sir Arnold
Mountain jubilee. Eyre & Spottiswoode, 1943.
xii, 287p., plates, illus. 23cm.

LUNN, Sir Arnold
[Mountain jubilee]. Ich gedenke der Berge; übersetzt von Henry Hoek. Zürich: Amstutz, Herdeg,
1945. 367p. 21cm.

LUNN, Sir Arnold
[Mountain jubilee]. Recuerdos de montaña;
traducción de José Lleonart e Ignacio Rodrigo.
Barcelona: Juventud, 1949. 157p., plates, illus.
23cm.

LUNN, Sir Arnold
Mountains of memory. Hollis & Carter, 1948.
xii, 248p., plates (1 col.), illus. 23cm.

LUNN, Sir Arnold
The mountains of youth. Oxford University Press,
1925. 192p., col. plates, illus. 23cm.

- - 2nd ed. Eyre & Spottiswoode, 1949.

LUNN, Sir Arnold
[The mountains of youth]. Les montagnes de ma
jeunesse; traduit par Claire-Éliane Engel.
Neuchatel: Attinger, 1943. 217p., plates, illus.
21cm. (Collection montagne)

LUNN, Sir Arnold
Oxford mountaineering essays; edited by Arnold
H.M. Lunn. Arnold, 1912. xi, 237p. 20cm.

LUNN, Sir Arnold
Ski-ing. E. Nash, 1913. 256p., plates, illus.
20cm.

LUNN, Sir Arnold
Ski-ing for beginners. Methuen, 1924. xi, 127p.,
plates, illus. 18cm.

- - 2nd ed., rev. 1926.

LUNN, Sir Arnold
The story of ski-ing. Eyre and Spottiswoode, 1952.
224p. 24cm.

LUNN, Sir Arnold
[The story of ski-ing]. Histoire du ski, avec un
sommaire chronologique; traduit par François
Vaudou. Paris: Payot, 1953. 251p. 23cm.

LUNN, Sir Arnold
The Swiss and their mountains: a study of the
influence of mountains on man. Allen & Unwin,
1963. 167p., 24 plates (some col.), illus. 23cm.

LUNN, Sir Arnold
Switzerland and the English. Eyre & Spottiswoode,
1944 (1945 reprint). x, 258p., plates, illus.
22cm.

LUNN, Sir Arnold
Switzerland in English prose and poetry; [edited]
by Arnold Lunn. Eyre & Spottiswoode, 1947. xxvii,
262p., plates (1 col.), illus. 22cm. (New alpine
library)

LUNN, Sir Arnold
'Unkilled for so long'. Allen & Unwin, 1968.
175p., 1 plate, port. 23cm.

LUNN, Sir Arnold
Zermatt and the Valais. Hollis & Carter, 1955.
x, 211p., plates, illus. 20cm.

LUNN, Sir Arnold
The Kandahar Review, v.5, no.9, Oct. 1974.
London, 1947. 101p., illus. 22cm.
Memorial issue for Sir Arnold Lunn, and golden
jubilee issue.

LUNN, Brian
Letters to young winter sportsmen. Allan, 1927.
xi, 148p., plates, illus. 20cm.

LUNN, Henry S
How to visit Switzerland: a new guide-book to the
chief scenes of interest in Switzerland, with the
programme of the Grindlewald Conference, 1895.
H. Marshall, 1895. 270p., illus., maps. 19cm.

LUNN, Peter
Evil in high places. Methuen, 1947. 255p. 20cm.

LUNN, Peter
A ski-ing primer. Methuen, 1948. 110p., plates,
illus. 20cm.

LURANI CERNUSCHI, Francesco, conte
In memoria di Francesco Lurani Cernuschi.
[Milano?]: [La contessa Lurani], [1913]. 86p.,1
plate, port. 25cm.

LUSI, comte de
Voyage sur le Mont-Blanc, entrepris le 15
septembre 1816. Vienne: C. Gerold, 1816. 54p.
18cm.

LUTHER, Carl J
DEUTSCHE SKIVERBAND
Der Deutsche Skilauf und 25 Jahre Deutscher
Skiverband; bearb. von Carl J. Luther. München:
Rother, 1930. 195p., illus. 25cm.

LUTHER, Carl J
Der moderne Wintersport: ein Handbuch und Nach-
schlagebuch für Anfänger und Sportleute. 2. Aufl.
Leipzig: Weber, 1912. viii, 152p., plates, illus.,
bibl. 18cm.

LUTHER, Carl J
Die Skiparadiese der Alpen; hrsg. von C.J. Luther.
München: F. Bruckmann, 1932. 1v. (various pagings),
plates, illus., maps. 30cm.

LUTHER, Carl J   and LÜCKE, G   P
Der Skitourist. München: J. Lindauer, 1913. vi,
169p., plates, illus. 16cm.

- - 2. Aufl., von Carl J. Luther. 1921.

LUTHER, Carl J
HOEK, Henry
Wie lerne ich Schi-laufen. 4. Aufl. München:
Verlag der Deutschen Alpenzeitung, 1911. 39p.,
illus. 20cm.

- - 7. umgearb. und stark erweiterte Aufl. München:
W. Schmidkung, 1917.
- - 11. Aufl., bearb. von Carl J. Luther. München:
Rother, 1924.

LUTZ, Markus
Vollstandige Beschreibung des Schweizerlandes;
oder, Geographischen-statistischen Hand-Lexicon...
2. Ausg. Aarau: H.R. Sauerlander, 1827-28. 4v.
20cm.

- - Supplement. 1835.

LUTZ, Markus
[Vollstandige Beschreibung des Schweizerlandes...].
Dictionnaire géographique-statistique de la Suisse;
traduit et revu par J.L.B. Leresche. Lausanne:
Imprimerie de Delisle, 1836-37. 2v. 23cm.

LYALL, Robert
    Travels in Russia, the Krimea, the Caucasus and
    Georgia. Cadell, 1825. 2v., illus. 22cm.

LYCOSTHENES, Conradus
TSCHUDI, Aegidius
    De prisca ac vera Alpina Rhaetia, cum caetero
    Alpinarum gentium tractu ... descriptio. Basileae:
    Apud Mich. Isingrinium, 1538. 134p. 23cm.

LYDON, A   F
    English Lake scenery; illustrated with a series of
    coloured plates from drawings by A.F. Lydon. J.
    Walker, 1880. 48p., col. plates, illus. 26cm.

LYELL, Sir Charles, Bart
    Life, letters and journals of Sir Charles Lyell,
    Bart; edited by his sister-in-law Mrs. Lyell.
    Murray, 1881. 2v., plates, illus., ports. 24cm.

LYMAN, William Denison
    The Columbia river: its history, its myths, its
    scenery, its commerce. New York: Putnam, 1909.
    xx, 409p., plates (2 fold.col.), illus., maps.
    26cm.

LYNAM, C   C
    The log of the Blue Dragon, 1892-1904, written by
    various hands and now revised and set forth by
    C.C. Lynam. A.H. Bullen, 1907. xxi, 299p.,
    plates, illus. 25cm.

LYNAM, C   C
    The log of the 'Blue Dragon II' in Orkney and
    Shetland 1909-10... Sidgwick & Jackson, 1911. xvi,
    176p., plates, illus., maps. 25cm.

LYNAM, C   C
    To Norway and the North Cape in 'Blue Dragon II',
    1911-12. Sidgwick & Jackson, 1913. xxiv, 232p.,
    plates (some fold.), illus., maps. 25cm.

LYNAM, Joss
    Ben Corr rock-climbs. [Dublin]: Irish Mountain-
    eering Club, 1951. 29p., illus., map. 13cm.
    (Guide to the mountains of Connemara and Murrisk,4)

LYNAM, Joss
    Bray Head. [Dublin]: Irish Mountaineering Club
    1951. 23p., illus. 13cm. (Rock-climbers' guide
    to the sea cliffs around Dublin, 1)

LYNAM, Joss
    Twelve Bens. [Dublin]: Irish Mountaineering Club,
    1953. 29p., illus., bibl. 13cm. (Guide to the
    mountains of Connemara and Murrisk, pt.3)

LYNCH, H   F   B
    Armenia: travels and studies. Longmans, Green,
    1901. 2v., plates (some fold., some col.), illus.,
    maps. 25cm.

LYTTON, Edward Robert Bulwer,1st Earl Lytton
    Glenaveril; or, The metamorphoses. Murray, 1885.
    2v. 19cm.

LYTTON, Hon. Neville
    Winter sports by Viscount Knebworth [and others];
    edited by the Hon. Neville Lytton. Seeley,
    Service, 1930. 254p., plates, illus. 23cm.
    (Lonsdale library, 8)

M.....
    Ma promenade au delà des Alpes. Berne: J.J.
    Bourgdorfer, 1819. 109p. 17cm.
    Dedication signed: M.....

M., C.E.
    See
MATHEWS, Charles Edward

M., D.A.M.
    Descrizione della Valtellina e delle grandiose
    strade di Stelvio e di Spluga, [da] D.A.M.M.
    Milano: Societé Tipografia de' Classici Italiani,
    1823. 96p. 21cm.

M., F   J
    See
MARTIN, F   J

M., H
    Itinéraire général de la Suisse, on y a joint les
    principales routes... Genève: L. Sestié, 1810.
    x, 141p., map. 18cm.

M., Helen
    Reminiscences of a continental tour. Briscoe,
    1871. 74p. 18cm.
    Cover title: Nellie's tour.

M., V.D.
    See
MUSSET PATHAY, Victor Donatien de

Ma promenade au delà des Alpes. Berne: J.J.
    Bourgdorfer, 1819. 109p. 17cm.
    Dedication signed: M.....

MACAULAY, James
PICKEN, Andrew
    Madeira illustrated by Andrew Picken; with a des-
    cription of the island edited by James Macaulay.
    Day & Haghes, 1840. 4,21p., plates, illus., map.
    56cm.

MACBRIDE, Mackenzie
    Arran of the bens, the glens & the brave; with
    illustrations in colour by J. Lawton Wingate.
    T.N. Foulis, 1910. xi, 231p., col.plates, illus.
    21cm.

MACBRIDE, Mackenzie
    Wild Lakeland; painted by A. Heaton Cooper; des-
    cribed by Mac Kenzie Mac Bride. Black, 1922.
    viii, 229p., 32 col. plates, illus., map. 22cm.

MCCABE, James D
    Our young folks abroad: the adventures of four
    American boys and girls in a journey through
    Europe to Constantinople. Philadelphia: J.B.
    Lippincott, 1881. 344p., plates, illus. 24cm.

MCCABE, Joseph
    Ice ages: the story of the earth's revolutions.
    Watts, 1922. vii, 112p., plates, illus. 19cm.

MCCLYMONT, W   G
    The exploration of New Zealand. Wellington [N.Z.]:
    Department of Internal Affairs, 1940. xv, 202p.,
    plates (2 fold.), illus., maps, bibl. 22cm.
    (New Zealand centennial surveys, 3)

- - 2nd ed. Oxford University Press, 1959.

MCCONNELL, R   G
    Report on the geological structure of a portion
    of the Rocky Mountains, accompanied by a section
    measured near the 51st parallel. Montreal:
    Dawson, 1887. 156p., plates (2 fold.col.),
    illus., maps. 25cm.
    At head of title: Geological and Natural History
    Survey of Canada.

MCCORMICK, Arthur David
CONWAY, William Martin, Baron Conway
    The Alps; described by W. Martin Conway; painted
    by A.D. McCormick. Black, 1904. x, 294p., 70
    col. plates, illus. 23cm.

MCCORMICK, Arthur David
CONWAY, William Martin, Baron Conway
The Alps from end to end; with ... illustrations
by A.D. M'Cormick. Constable, 1895. xii, 403p.,
plates, illus. 25cm.

- - 2nd ed. 1895.

MCCORMICK, Arthur David
An artist in the Himalayas; illustrated by over
100 original sketches made on the journey. Fisher
Unwin, 1895. xii, 306p., 1 fold. plate, illus.,
map. 23cm.

MCCORMICK, Arthur David
CONWAY, William Martin, Baron Conway
Climbing and exploration in the Karakoram-Himalayas;
with ... illustrations by A.D. McCormick and maps.
Fisher Unwin, 1894. 2v. (xix, 709p.), plates,
illus. 26cm.

- - Maps (3 fold.col. in portfolio).
- - Scientific reports.

M'CORMICK, R
Narrative of a boat expedition up the Willington
Channel in the year 1852 ... in search of Sir John
Franklin. Eyre and Spottiswoode, 1854. 60p.,
plates (1 fold.col.), illus., chart. 31cm.

MCCOSH, John
Nuova Italia; or, Tours and retours through France,
Switzerland, Italy, and Sicily: a poem in ten
cantos; by Nomentino [i.e. John McCosh]. Longmans,
Green, 1872-75. 2v. 18cm.
Vol.2, 2nd series, Chapman and Hall.

MCCRACKAN, William D
Romance Switzerland. Boston: J. Knight, 1894.
xiv, 270p. 14cm.

MCCRACKAN, William D
The spell of Tyrol; illustrated from photographs
and original paintings by Woldemar Ritter. Boston:
Page, 1914. xx, 328p., plates (some col.), illus.,
map (on lining paper). 21cm. (Spell series)

MCCRACKAN, William D
Teutonic Switzerland. Boston: J. Knight, 1894.
viii, 315p. 14cm.

MCCRACKAN, William D
The Tyrol. Duckworth, 1905. xx, 328p., plates,
illus. 20cm.

MACCULLOCH, J   A
The misty Isle of Skye: its scenery, its people,
its story. Edinburgh, London: Oliphant, Anderson
& Ferrier, 1905. 320p., 20 plates, illus., map.
20cm.

MCDERMOTT, F
How to be happy in Switzerland: winter sports.
Arrowsmith, 1928. 224p., plates, illus., map.
20cm. (Happy holiday series)

BIVEN, Peter H   and MCDERMOTT,M   B
Cornwall. Vol.I; with diagrams by C. Fishwick;
geological notes by M. Springett; notes on mining
and natural history by Ruth Neill; and notes on
birds by J. Braven. Sidcup: Climbers' Club, 1968.
xi, 209p., plates (1 fold.), illus., maps. 16cm.
(Climbers' Club guides)

MACDONALD, A
TYRWHITT, R   St John
A handbook of pictorial art; with a chapter on
perspective by A. Macdonald. 2nd ed. Oxford:
Clarendon Press, 1875. x, 384p., plates (some
col.), illus. 23cm. (Clarendon Press series)

MACDONALD, Alexander
Through the heart of Tibet. Blackie, 1910. 384p.,
col. plates, illus. 22cm.

MACDONALD, Hugh
On foot: an anthology selected by Hugh Macdonald.
Oxford University Press, 1942. 320p. 16cm.

MACDONNELL, Alice C
Songs of mountain and the burn. J. Ouseley,
[n.d.]. 128p. 20cm.

M'DOUGALL, George Frederick
The eventful voyage of H.M. Discovery ship
"Resolute" to the Arctic regions in search of Sir
John Franklin and the missing crews of H.M.
Discovery ships "Erebus" and "Terror", 1852, 1853,
1854... Longman, Brown, Green, Longmans & Roberts,
1857. xl, 530p., col. plates, illus. 24cm.

MCDOWALL, Arthur
Peaks & frescoes: a study of the Dolomites; illustrations from lino-cuts by Mary McDowall. Oxford
University Press,1928. 123p., 13 col. plates,
illus., map (on lining paper). 27cm.

M'GAVIN, William
Notes of a short tour through parts of France,
Switzerland, and Rhenish Germany, including a few
remarks on gambling. Ayr: Printed at the Ayr-
shire Express Office, 1860. 160p. 17cm.

MCGOVERN, William Montgomery
To Lhasa in disguise: an account of a secret
expedition through mysterious Tibet. Butterworth,
1924. 352p., plates, illus., maps. 23cm.

MACGREGOR, Alasdair Alpin
Over the sea to Skye; or, Rambles in an elfin
isle; foreword by James Ramsay Macdonald.
Chambers, [1926]. xxiv, 353p., plates, illus.,
map. 20cm.

MACGREGOR, John
The ascent of Mont Blanc: a series of four views;
printed in oil colours by George Baxter; the
original sketches and the description by J.
Macgregor. [G. Baxter], [1855]. 4p., 4 col.
plates, illus. 19 x 27cm.

MACGREGOR, John
My note book. J. Macrone, 1835. 3v., 3 plates,
illus. 21cm.
Description of a tour in the Netherlands, Germany,
and Switzerland.

MACGREGOR, John
My note book: Switzerland. Frankfort o. M,:
Jugel, 1837. 296p. 14cm.

MACGREGOR, John
HODDER, Edwin
John MacGregor ("Rob Roy")... Hodder, 1894. xiv,
458p., plates, illus. 23cm.

- - Popular ed. 1895.

MCGUIRE, J   A
In the Alaska-Yukon gamelands; introduction by
W.T. Hornaday. Cincinnati: Kidd, 1921. 215p.,
plates, illus. 22cm.

MACHAČEK, Fritz
Die Alpen. Leipzig: Quelle & Meyer, 1908.
146p., illus. 19cm. (Wissenschaft und Bildung,
29)

MACHAČEK, Fritz
Gletscherkunde. Leipzig: Goschen, 1902. 125p.,
plates, illus. 16cm. (Sammlung Goschen)

MACHETTO, Guido
Sette anni contro il Tirich, di Guido Machetto,
Maria Ludovica e Riccardo Varvelli. [Milano]:
dall'Oglio, 1976. 269p., plates (some col.),
illus., maps. 21cm.

MACINNES, Hamish
Call-out. Hodder & Stoughton, 1973. 190p.,
plates, illus., map. 23cm.

MACINNES, Hamish
Climb to the Lost World. Hodder & Stoughton,
1974. 224p., plates, illus., maps. 23cm.

- - Another issue. Harmondsworth: Penguin Books,
1976.

MACINNES, Hamish
International mountain rescue handbook. Constable,
1972. 218p., illus., bibl. 23cm.

MACINNES, Hamish
Scottish climbs: a mountaineer's pictorial guide
to climbing in Scotland. Constable, 1971. 2v.,
illus., maps, bibl. 18cm.

MACINTYRE, Donald
Hindu-Koh: wanderings and wild sport on and beyond
the Himalayas. Edinburgh, London: Blackwood,
1899. xx, 464p., plates (some col.), illus. 24cm.

- - New ed. [rev.]. 1891.

MACINTYRE, Neil
Attack on Everest. Methuen, 1936. vii, 172p.,
1 plate, map. 20cm.

MACKAY, Charles
The scenery & poetry of the English Lakes: a
summer ramble. Longman, 1846. xvi, 234p., plates,
illus. 21cm.

- - 2nd ed. 1852.

MACKENZIE, Alexander
Voyages from Montreal, on the river St. Laurence,
through the continent of North America, to the
frozen and Pacific oceans, in the years 1789 and
1793; with a preliminary account of the rise, progress, and present state of the fur trade of that
country. T. Cadell & W. Davies, 1801. viii,
cxxxii, 412p., plates (some fold. col.), maps,
port. 29cm.

MACKENZIE, Alexander
WOOLLACOTT, Arthur P
Mackenzie and his voyageurs: by canoe to the
Arctic and the Pacific, 1789-93. Dent, 1927. x,
237p., plates, illus., map, bibl. 22cm.

MACKENZIE, Sir George Steuart
Travels in the Island of Iceland, during the
summer of the year 1810. 2nd ed. Edinburgh:
Constable, 1812. xix, 491p., plates (1 fold.,
some col.), illus., maps, music. 31cm.

- - New ed., rev. by the author. Edinburgh:
Chambers, 1851.

MACKENZIE, Georgina Muir and IRBY, Adelina Paulina
Across the Carpathians, [by Georgina M. Mackenzie
and Adelina P. Irby]. Cambridge, London:
Macmillan, 1862. 299p., 1 fold. plate, map. 20cm.

MACKENZIE, William M
Climbing guide to the Cuillin of Skye; edited by
William M. MacKenzie. Edinburgh: Scottish
Mountaineering Club, 1958. 160p., illus., map.
17cm. [Scottish Mountaineering Club climbers'
guide books]

MACKINDER, H J
The Rhine: its valley & history; with illustrations in colour after Mrs. James Jardine...
Chatto & Windus, 1908. 226p., col. plates (2
fold.), illus., maps. 24cm.

MACKINTOSH, A J
Mountaineering clubs, 1857-1907. London, 1908.
31p. 23cm.
Reprinted with corrections and additions, from
the Alpine Journal, Aug. 1907.

MACKINTOSH, D
The scenery of England and Wales, its character
and origin, being an attempt to trace the nature
of the geological causes ... by which the physical
features ... have been produced. Longmans, Green,
1869. xxiii, 399p., illus. 21cm.

MCLANE, Merrill F
COULTER, Henry
Mountain climbing guide to the Grand Tetons.
Hanover (N.H.): Dartmouth Mountaineering Club,
1947. 67p., 1 fold. plate, illus., map. 18cm.

MCLAREN, Amy
From a Davos balcony. Duckworth, 1903. 307p.
20cm.

HUMBLE, Benjamin Hutchison and MCLELLAN, W M
Songs for climbers; edited by B.H. Humble and
W.M. McLellan. Glasgow: Wm. McLellan, [1938].
33p., illus. 23cm.

MACLEOD, Fred. T
Eilean a' Cheð, the Isle of Mist, comprising
articles on Skye by Skyemen; edited with an introduction by Fred. T. Macleod. 2nd ed. Edinburgh:
G. Wilson, [1917]. xv, 133p., plates, illus. 23cm.

MACLEOD, Norman
Mountain, loch and glen; illustrating "our life in
the Highlands" from paintings executed ... for
this work by Joseph Adam; with an essay on the
characteristics of Scottish scenery by Norman
Macleod; prepared under the superintendence of
Arthur Helps. 2nd ed. rev. Bell & Daldy, 1870.
1v. (chiefly illus.). 38cm.

MACMILLAN, Hugh
Holidays on high lands; or, Rambles and incidents
in search of alpine plants. Macmillan, 1869. vii,
300p. 19cm.

MACMORLAND, Mrs.
Davos-Platz; a new alpine resort for sick and
sound in summer and winter, by one who knows it
well [i.e. Mrs. MacMorland]. Stanford, 1878.
239p., map. 17cm.

NOYCE, Wilfrid and MCMORRIN, Ian
World atlas of mountaineering; edited by Wilfrid
Noyce and Ian McMorrin. Nelson, 1969. 224p., col.
plates, illus., maps. 28cm.

MCMORRIS, William Bruce
The real book of mountaineering. Dobson, 1961.
192p., illus., bibl. 21cm. (Real books)

MACNAIR, Peter
The geology and scenery of the Grampians and the
valley of Strathmore. Glasgow: MacLehose, 1908.
2v., fold. plates (some col.), maps, bibl. 24cm.

MACNEVEN, William James
A ramble through Swisserland in the summer and
autumn of 1802. Dublin: J. Stockdale, 1803.
280p. 22cm.
Title page damaged.

MACNEVIN, William James
See
MACNEVEN, William James

MACPHEE, G Graham
Ben Nevis; edited by G.Graham MacPhee. Rev. ed.
Edinburgh: Scottish Mountaineering Club, 1936.
viii, 101p., plates (some fold.), illus. 22cm.
(Scottish Mountaineering Club guides)

MACPHEE, G Graham
Climbers' guide to Ben Nevis. Edinburgh:
Scottish Mountaineering Club, 1954. xii, 156p.,
illus., maps. 16cm. [Scottish Mountaineering
Club climbers' guide books]

MACQUOID, Gilbert S
Up and down: sketches of travel; illustrations by
Thomas R. Macquoid. Ward and Downey, 1890. xi,
211p., plates, illus. 23cm.

MACQUOID, Katharine S
In the Ardennes; illustrations by Thomas R.
Macquoid. Chatto & Windus, 1881. xi, 351p.,
illus., map. 20cm.

MACROBERT, Harry
Ben Nevis; edited by H. MacRobert. Edinburgh:
Scottish Mountaineering Club, 1920. 42p., plates
(some fold.), illus., map. 23cm. (Scottish
Mountaineering Club guides, v.1., S.E.)

MACROBERT, Harry
The central Highlands; edited by H. MacRobert.
Edinburgh: Scottish Mountaineering Club, 1934.
158p., plates (2 fold.col.), illus., maps. 22cm.
(Scottish Mountaineering Club guides)

- - 2nd ed. 1952.

MADUSCHKA, Leo
Die Jüngste Erschliessungsgechichte des Wilden
Kaisers; mit einer Einleitung und durchgesehen von
Franz Nieberl. München: Sektion Bayerland des
Deutschen und Österreichischen Alpenvereins, 1933.
39p., plates, ports. 25cm.

MADUSCHKA, Leo
Junger Mensch im Gebirg: Leben, Schriften, Nachlass.
München: Gesellschaft Alpiner Bucherfreunde, 1936.
xxxv, 206p., plates, illus. 23cm.

MADUSCHKA, Leo
Neuzeitliche Felstechnik. 2. Aufl. München:
Rother, [1932]. 56p., illus. 17cm.

MADUSCHKA, Leo
[Neuzeitliche Felstechnik]. Le technique moderne
du rocher; traduit par Armand Pierhal. Paris: S.
Bornemann, 1948. 61p., illus. 18cm.

MADUSCHKA, Leo
Die Technik schwerster Eisfahrten. 2. Aufl.
München: Rother, [1932]. 55p., illus. 17cm.

MADUTZ, Johann
COOLIDGE, William Augustus Brevoort
Johann Madutz, 1800-1861: ein Pionier der Schweizer
Alpen: eine biographische Skizze. Bern: G. Grunau,
1917. 50p. 24cm.

MAEDER, Herbert
[Die Berge der Schweiz]. The mountains of Switzerland; the adventure of the High Alps; edited with
photographs and commentary by Herbert Maeder; with
an introduction by Werner Kämpfen and contributions by Georges Grosjean and Ricco Bianchi;
translated by Hendrik P.B. Betlem. Allen and
Unwin, 1968. 288p., illus. (some col.). 30cm.

MAEDER, Herbert
[Lockende Berge]. The lure of the mountains;
edited and selection of photos by Herbert Maeder.
Elsevier-Phaidon, 1975. 138p., col. illus. 30cm.

MAEL, Pierre
Terre de Fauves; roman. 6e éd. Paris: Société
d'Éditions Littéraires et Artistiques, 1905.
313p. 19cm.

MAGENDIE, A
MORILLOT, Paul
A travers nos Alpes; Dauphiné, par MM. Morillot,
R. Rey, Magendie; sous le patronage de M. Boirac.
Grenoble: A. Gratier, 1902. viii, 297p., illus.
19cm.
An anthology.

MAGGS, J
Round Europe with the crowd. W.H. Allen, 1880.
vii, 362p. 19cm.

MAGNI, Fermo
Guida illustrata della Valsassina. Lecco:
Tipografia Magni, 1904. viii, 243p., plates, maps.
17cm.

MAGNIN, J
Saint-Gervais-les-Bains et ses environs: guide
itinéraire historique, pittoresque... Paris: R.
Godfroy, [1898]. 113p., illus., map. 19cm.

MAGNONE, Guido
La face W des Drus. Paris: Amiot-Dumont, 1953.
207p., plates, illus. 22cm. (Bibliothèque de
l'alpinisme)

MAGNONE, Guido
[La face W des Drus]. The west face; translated...
by J.F. Burke. Museum Press, 1955. 166p., plates,
illus. 24cm.

MAGNUSSON, A   H
The Lichen-genus Acarospora in Greenland and
Spitsbergen. Oslo, 1935. 21p., illus. 23cm.
(Norges Svalbard- og Ishavs-Undersøkelser.
Meddelese, Nr. 27)
Offprint from Nyt Magazin for Naturvidenskaberne,
B.75, 1935)

MAGYAR TURISTA SZÖVETSÉG
Nemzetözi Alpin képkiállítása, Budapest, 1930
Marcius 22 - Aprilis 22. Budapest: M.T.S., 1930.
71p., plates, illus. 19cm.
Exhibition catalogue of alpine paintings. General
editor Zsitvay Tibor.

MAGYAR TURISTA SZÖVETSÉG
Orszagos Magyar turista kiállitas ismertetoje, az
1931, május 16 - június 21, Budapest ...;
Szerkesztette: Vörös Tihamér es Papp László.
Budapest: Magyar Turista Szövetség, 1931. 144p.,
plates, illus. 17cm.

"Magyarland", being the narrative of our travels
through the highlands and lowlands of Hungary, by
a fellow of the Carpathian Society [i.e. Nina E.
Mazuchelli]. Sampson Low, Marston, Searle, &
Rivington, 1881. 2v., plates, illus. 24cm.

MAGYARORSZÁGI KÁRPÁTEGYLET
Bibliotheca Carpatica; a "Magyarországi
Kárpátegylet" megbizásából összeállitotta Payer
Hugo. Késmárk: A "Magyarországi Kárpátegylet"
kiadványa, 1880. 378p. 23cm.

MAHTAB, B   C
Impressions: the diary of a European tour. St.
Catherine Press, [1908]. 273p., plates, illus.,
port. 24cm.

MAILLART, Ella K
The cruel way. Heinemann, 1947. 217p., plates,
illus. 23cm.

MAILLART, Ella K
Cruises & caravans. Dent, 1942 (1944 reprint).
vi, 161p., plates, illus., map (on lining papers).
23cm. (Travellers' tales)

MAILLART, Ella K
Forbidden journey - from Peking to Kashmir;
[translated from the French by Thomas McGreevy].
Heinemann, 1937. xvi, 312p., plates (1 fold.),
illus., maps. 23cm.

MAILLART, Ella K
The land of the Sherpas. Hodder & Stoughton,
1955. 61p., plates, illus., map. 23cm.

MAILLART, Ella K
'Ti-Puss'. Heinemann, 1951. 213p., plates,
illus., map. 23cm.

MAILLART, Ella K
Turkestan solo: one woman's expedition from the
Tien Shan to the Kizil Kum; translated from the
French by John Rodker. Putnam, 1934. xi, 307p.,
plates, illus., maps, bibl. 24cm.

MAILLEBOIS, Jean Baptiste François Desmarets,
marquis de
PEZAY, Alexandre Frédéric Jacques de Masson,
marquis de
Noms, situation et détails des vallées de la
France le long des grandes Alpes dans le Dauphiné
et la Provence, et de celles qui descendent des
Alpes en Italie depuis la Savoye jusqu'à celle de
Saint Étienne au Comté de Nice; extraits des
campagnes du Maréchal de Maillebois par le marq.
de Pesay. Turin: Reycends, 1793. 171p. 17cm.

MAILLY, Roger
Villes et montagnes marocaines... Montagnes
marocaines, par Roger Mailly... Rabat: "La Porte",
1964. 244p., plates (some fold.), illus., maps.
19cm. (Guides touristiques, 1964-1965)

MAIN, Mrs. D.F.
See
LE BLOND, Elizabeth

MAIN, Elizabeth
See
LE BLOND, Elizabeth

MAIR, Kurt
Der Mensch am Berg, von der Freude, dem Kampf und
der Kameradschaft der Bergsteiger: ein Bildbericht,
von Hans Franz; mit worten von Kurt Mair. München:
F. Bruckmann, 1935. 150p., illus. 23cm.

MAIRAN, D   de
Dissertation sur la glace; ou, Explication physique
de la formation de la glace et de ses divers phénomènes. Paris: Imprimerie Royale, 1749. xxix,
384p., plates, illus. 18cm.

MAITLAND, Frederic William
The life and letters of Leslie Stephen. Duckworth,
1906. ix, 510p., plates, ports., bibl. 24cm.

MAITLAND, Harry
The dash for winter sports; with sixteen illustrations by Alfred Leete. J. Ouseley, [1912].
160p., illus. 18cm.

MAIX, Kurt
Bergler, Bauern, Kameraden. Wien: Deutscher
Verlag für Jugend und Volk, 1943. 109p., illus.
19cm.

MAIX, Kurt
HARRER, Heinrich
[Die Weisse Spinne]. The White Spider: the
history of the Eiger's North Face; translated by
Hugh Merrick. Hart-Davis, 1959. 240p., plates
(1 fold.), illus. 24cm.

- - Rev. ed., with additional chapters by Heinrich
Harrer and Kurt Maix. 1965.

MIYOSHI, M   and MAKINO, T
Pocket-atlas of alpine plants of Japan. 2nd rev.
ed. Tokyo: Seibido, 1907. 2v. (140p.), 70 col.
plates, illus. 18cm.

MALARTIC, Yves
La conquête de l'Everest par le Sherpa Tensing,
récit d'Yves Malartic. Paris: Éditions du
Scorpion, 1953. 303p., plates, illus., maps, bibl.
20cm.

MALBY, Reginald A
With camera and rücksack in the Oberland and
Valais; with over seventy photographic studies by
the author. Headley, [1913]. 310p., plates (some
col.), illus. 22cm.

MALDINI WILDENHAINSKI, Rudolf, Barun
Bosna i Hercegovina, napisao Rudolf Barun Maldini
Wildenhainski; uredio Vjekoslav Novotni. Zagreb:
Tisak Antuna Scholza, 1908. xx, 157, vii p.,
illus. 33cm.

MALEINOV, A   A   and TUSHINSKII, G   K
Puteshestvie v gorakh. Moskva: Izd. Geograficheskoi
Literatury, 1950. 334p., plates (1 fold.), illus.
21cm.

MALHEN, Baron de
Itinéraire du voyage à Chamouny, autour du Mont-
Blanc, au Grand et au Petit St. Bernard, et autour
du Lac de Genève... [par Baron de Malhen?].
Genève: Jullien, [18--]. xxxviii, 160p. 14cm.

MALLESON, F   A
Holiday studies of Wordsworth: by rivers, woods,
and Alps, the Wharfe, the Duddon, and the Stelvio
pass. Cassell, 1890. 115p., illus. 24cm.

MALLESON, G   B
Captain Musafir's rambles in alpine lands; illustrated by G. Strangman Handcock. W.H. Allen, 1884.
xvi, 150p., plates, illus. 26cm.

- - 2nd ed. 1885.

MALLET, Édouard
BAULACRE, Léonard
Oeuvres historiques et littéraires de Léonard
Baulacre ...; recueillies et mises en ordre par
Édouard Mallet. Genève: Jullien, 1857. 2v. in 1,
plates, illus. 23cm.

MALLET, H
Description de Genève, ancienne et moderne ...;
suivie de la Relation de l'ascension de Mr. de
Saussure sur la cime du Mont-Blanc. Genève:
Manget & Cherbuliez, 1807. x, 481p., 1 fold.
plate, map. 18cm.

MALLIEUX, René
Le roi Albert, alpiniste. Brussels: La
Renaissance du livre, 1956. 197p., plates, illus.
23cm.

MALLORY, George Leigh
EHMER, Wilhelm
Um den Gipfel der Welt: die Geschichte des Bergsteigers Mallory. Stuttgart: J. Engelhorn, 1936.
186p., plates, map, port. 20cm.

MALLORY, George Leigh
PEYRÉ, Joseph
Mallory et son Dieu. Genève: Éditions du Milieu
du Monde, 1947. 310p., map. 19cm.

MALLORY, George Leigh
PYE, Sir David Randall
George Leigh Mallory: a memoir. Oxford University
Press, 1927. 183p., illus. 22cm.

MALLORY, George Leigh
ROBERTSON, David
George Mallory. Faber & Faber, 1969. 279p.,
plates, illus., maps, bibl. 23cm.

MALVERN COLLEGE ICELAND EXPEDITION, 1978
Preliminary report; [compiled by R.S.D. Smith,
expedition leader]. Malvern: The Expedition, 1978.
8p., illus., maps. 30cm.

- - Annexe.

MANARESI, Angelo
Parole agli alpinisti; con illustrazioni di V.
Grassi. Roma: Edizioni del C.A.I., 1932. 150p.,
26 plates, illus. 23cm.

MANCHESTER KARAKORUM EXPEDITION, 1968
Report; edited by John Allen. [Manchester]: The
Expedition, [1969?]. 21p., 1 fold. plate, illus.,
map, bibl. 25cm.

MANCHESTER NEPALESE EXPEDITION, 1970
Report, written by members of the expedition;
edited by John Allen. Manchester: The Expedition,
[1971]. 25p., 1 fold. plate, illus., map, bibl.
26cm.

MANCHESTER TOURING CLUB
Two on a tour, by one of the two for the other one,
being an accurate account, more or less, of the
first Swiss trip of the Manchester Touring Club,
Whitsuntide, 1892. Ardwick: Riley's Printing
Office, [1892]. 65p., port. 21cm.

MANCHESTER UNIVERSITY HINDU KUSH EXPEDITION, 1977
[Final report]. Enfield (Middlesex): The
Expedition, [1978]. 14p., illus., map. 30cm.

MANDACH, Conrad von
F.-N. Koenig, 1763-1832. Genève: Ciana, 1923.
43p., plates, illus. 27cm.

MANDACH, Conrad von
Schweizerland vor hundert Jahren: sechzehn farbige
Tafeln nach Originalstichen von Gabriel Lory, père
et fils; Einführung von C. von Mandach. Bern:
Iris, 1935. 11p., 16 col. plates, illus. 35cm.

MANER, Eduard and OBERSTEINER, Ludwig
Hochschwabführer. Wien: Artaria, 1922. xxiv,
239p., 1 plate, illus. 17cm.

MANGET, J   L
Chamonix, le Mont-Blanc et les deux Saint-Bernard:
nouvel itinéraire descriptif des Alpes centrales
et de leurs vallées... Genève: Combe, 1844. 182p.,
19cm.

MANGET, J   L
Chamonix, le Mont-Blanc, les deux Saint-Bernard et
la vallée de Sixt; nouvel itinéraire descriptif...
4e éd., rev. et augm. Genève: Gruaz, 1851.
260p., plates (some fold.), illus., maps. 19cm.

MANGET, J   L
[Itinéraire du voyage à Chamouny...]. Taschenbuch
für Reisende nach Chamouny, um den Mont-Blanc, auf
den Grossen und Kleinen Bernhard ...; nach der
Handschrift der 2. Ausgabe in französischer
Sprache, [von J.L. Manget], verm. und verb. Aarau:
H.R. Sauerländer, 1829. 198p., plates, maps,
plans. 15cm.

MANGET, J   L
La vallée de Sixt en 1843. Genève: Combe, 1843.
51p., 1 fold. plate, map. 18cm.
"Complément de l'ouvrage intitulé: Chamonix, le
Mont-Blanc et les deux St-Bernard".

MANN, Josefine
Was man für eine Schweizer-Reise wissen muss:
Anhaltspunkte für Reiselust und Kulturinteressen.
Zürich: Orell Füssli, 1913. 139p., plates, illus.
18cm.

MANNERING, George Edward
Eighty years in New Zealand, embracing fifty years
of New Zealand fishing. Christchurch (N.Z.):
Simpson & Williams, 1943. 255p., plates, illus.
23cm.

MANNERING, George Edward
Mount Cook and its surrounding glaciers. Auckland,
London: Whitcombe and Tombs, [192-?]. 1v. (chiefly
illus., map). 22 x 29cm.

MANNERING, George Edward
With axe and rope in the New Zealand Alps.
Longmans, Green, 1891. xi, 139p., plates (1 fold.
col.), illus., map. 25cm.

MANNERS, John Henry, Duke of Rutland
See
RUTLAND, John Henry Manners, 5th Duke of

MANNING, Anne
An idyl of the Alps, by the author of "Mary Powell"
[i.e. Anne Manning]. Hall, 1876. vi, 312p. 20cm.

MANNING, Anne
The year nine: a tale of the Tyrol, by the author
of "Mary Powell" [i.e. Anne Manning]. Hall,
Virtue, 1858. iv, 282p., plates, illus. 21cm.

MANNING, Samuel
American pictures drawn with pen and pencil.
Religious Tract Society, [1876]. 224p., illus.,
map. 29cm.

MANNING, Samuel
Swiss pictures drawn with pen and pencil, [by
Samuel Manning]; the illustrations by E. Whymper.
Religious Tract Society, [1866]. 214p., plates,
illus. 29cm.

- - New and enl. ed. [3rd ed.]. [1971].
- - New and enl. ed. [ca 1875].
- - New and enl. ed. [1880].
- - New ed., rev. and partly re-written with
illustrations by Edward Whymper. 1891.

MANNING, Thomas
BOGLE, George
Narratives of the mission of George Bogle to Tibet
and of the journey of Thomas Manning to Lhasa;
edited with notes, an introduction and lives of
Mr. Bogle and Mr. Manning by Clements R. Markham.
Trübner, 1876. clxiii, 354p., plates (some fold.,
some col.), illus., maps. 23cm.

MANSFIELD, T   C
Alpines in colour and cultivation. Rev. ed.
Collins, 1945 (1947 reprint). 283p., col. plates,
illus. 22cm.

BRIQUET, Moïse and MAQUELIN, L
Ascensions du Mont-Rose et du Mont-Blanc en juillet
1863. Genève, 1864. 36p. 22cm.
Offprint from Journal de Genève.

MARAINI, Fosco
Gasherbrum 4°, Baltoro, Karakorùm. 2a ed. Bari:
Leonardo da Vinci, 1960. xix, 334p., plates (some
col.), illus., maps, bibl. 24cm.

MARAINI, Fosco
[Gasherbrum 4°, Baltoro, Karakorùm]. Karakoram:
the ascent of Gasherbrum IV; translated from the
Italian by J. Cadell. Hutchinson 1961. 320p.,
plates (some col.), illus., maps, bibl. 25cm.

MARAINI, Fosco
Hindu Kush (mountains). 1974. 29cm.
Offprint from Encyclopaedia Britannica. 15th ed.
1974.

MARAINI, Fosco
Secret Tibet; with an introductory letter by
Bernard Berenson; illustrated from photographs by
the author; translated by Eric Mosbacher.
Hutchinson, 1952. 251p., plates, illus., map,
bibl. 25cm.

- - Another issue. New York: Viking Press, 1953.

MARAINI, Fosco
Where four worlds meet: Hindu Kush 1959; translated
from the Italian by Peter Green. Hamilton, 1964.
xii, 290p, plates (some fold., some col.), illus.,
maps, bibl. 24cm.

MARCET, William
The principal southern and Swiss health resorts,
their climate and medical aspect. J. & A.
Churchill, 1883. viii, 408p., plates, illus. 19cm.

MARCH, Bill
Modern snow & ice techniques. Manchester: Cicerone
Press, 1974 (1976 reprint). 66p., plates, illus.
17cm.

MARCO POLO
See
POLO, Marco

MARCOU, J
Une ascension dans les montagnes rocheuses.
[Paris], [1867]. 462-492p. 23cm.
Offprint from Bulletin de la Société de géographie,
1867.

MARCUS, Rebecca B
The first book of glaciers. E. Ward, 1963. 65p.,
illus. 24cm.

MARETT, R   R
SPENCER, Sir Baldwin
Spencer's last journey, being the Journal of an
expedition to Tierra del Fuego, by the late Sir
Baldwin Spencer; with a memoir edited by R.R.
Marett and T.K. Penniman; with contributions by Sir
James Frazer and H. Balfour. Oxford: Clarendon
Press, 1931. xii, 153p., plates (some fold.),
illus., maps, bibl. 23cm.

MARETT, R   R
IM THURN, Sir Everard
Thoughts, talks and tramps: a collection of papers,
by Sir Everard Im Thurn; edited with a memoir by
R.R. Marett. Oxford University Press, 1934.
xxiii, 285p., port, map. 23cm.

MARGERIE, Emmanuel de
L'oeuvre de Sven Hedin et l'orographie du Tibet.
Paris, 1929. 139p., plates (some fold.), illus.,
maps. 26cm.
Offprint from Bulletin de la Section de géographie
du Comité des travaux historiques et scientifiques,
1928.

ZURCHER, Frédéric and MARGOLLÉ, Elie
Les ascensions célèbres aux plus hautes montagnes
du globe: fragments de voyages recueillis; traduit
et mis en ordre par Zurcher et Margollé. 2e éd.
Paris: Hachette, 1869. 348p., illus. 18cm.
(Bibliothèque des merveilles)

- - 4e éd.,rev. et augm. 1879.
- - 5e éd., rev. par A. Le Pileur. 1891.

ZURCHER, Frédéric and MARGOLLÉ, Elie
[Les ascensions célèbres...]. Mountain adventures
in the various countries of the world; selected
from the narratives of celebrated travellers.
Seeley, Jackson, & Halliday, 1869. viii, 320p.,
plates, illus. 19cm.
"Founded on a compilation made by M.M. Zurcher and
Margollé... In several instances ... the narra-
tives of English travellers have been substituted".
- Prefatory note.

ZURCHER, Frédéric and MARGOLLÉ, Elie
Les glaciers, par Zurcher et Margollé; illustrée
... par L. Sabatier. Paris: Hachette, 1868.
323p., plates, illus. 20cm. (Bibliothèque des
merveilles)

- - 3e éd., rev. et augm. 1875.

MARGUERITTE, Paul
Le poste des neiges: roman inédit... Barcelona:
Richardin, Lamm, 1899. 203p, illus. 19cm.

MARIÉTAN, Ignace
Âme et visages du Valais; préface de Pierre Grellet.
Lausanne: F. Rouge, 1949. 257p., plates, illus.,
bibl. 21cm. (Collection alpine, 9)

MARIÉTAN, Ignace
Val d'Anniviers, Val d'Herens: descriptions de 42
itinéraires avec profils, croquis et photographies.
Berne: Kümmerly & Frey, 1954. 140p., plates,
illus., maps, bibl. 18cm. (Guides suisses de
tourisme pédestre, 12)

MARINELLI, Giovanni
Guida del Canal del Ferro o Valle del Fella,
Tagliamento. Udine: Società Alpina Friulana, 1894.
326p., li p., plates, maps (in pocket). 18cm.
(Guida del Friuli, 2)

MARINELLI, Giovanni
Guida della Carnia... Udine: Società Alpina
Friulana, 1898. xiii, 556p., plates, illus. 19cm.
(Guida del Friuli, 3)

- - 2a ed., con aggiunte e modificazioni. 1906.

MARINELLI, Olinto
Guida delle Prealpi Giulie; distretta di Gemona,
Tarcento, S. Daniele, Cividale e S. Pietro ... di
Olinto Marinelli [and others]. Udine: Società
Alpina Friulana, 1912. xxiii, 803p., plates,
illus., maps (in pocket), plans. 19cm. (Guida
del Friuli, 4)

MARINER, Wastl
Neuzeitliche Bergrettungstechnik: ein Leitfaden für
die Ausbildung des Rettungsmannes. 2.Aufl.
Herausgeber: Österr. Alpenverein. Innsbruck:
Tiroler Graphik, 1959. 191p., illus. 21cm.

MARINER, Wastl
[Neuzeitliche Bergrettungstechnik]. Mountain
rescue techniques; drawings by Fritz and Gert
Ebster; first aid instructions by Hans Heinz
Seidel; revised by Otto T. Trott and Kurt G. Beam.
1st English-language ed. Innsbruck:
Oesterreichischer Alpenverein, 1963. 200p.,
illus., bibl. 21cm.

MARIO***
See
TROLLIET, Marie

The Maritime Alps and their seaboard, by the author
of 'Vera', 'Blue roses' &c. [i.e. Charlotte L.
Dempster]. Longmans, Green, 1885. x, 384p.,
plates, illus. 24cm.

MARKHAM, Albert Hastings
On the road to the Pole.
(In From the Equator to the Pole. London, [1886].
18cm. p.133-254, illus., map)

MARKHAM, Sir Clements R
A memoir on the Indian surveys. W.H. Allen, 1871.
xxv, 303p., fold.col. plates, maps. 29cm.

- - 2nd ed. 1878.

MARKHAM, Sir Clements R
BOGLE, George
Narratives of the mission of George Bogle to
Tibet, and of the journey of Thomas Manning to
Lhasa; edited with notes, an introduction and
lives of Mr. Bogle and Mr. Manning by Clements R.
Markham. Trübner, 1876. clxiii, 354p., plates
(some fold., some col.), illus., maps. 23cm.

MARKHAM, Fred.
Shooting in the Himalayas: a journal of sporting
adventures and travel in Chinese Tartary, Ladac,
Thibet, Cashmere, etc. Bentley, 1854. xii,
375p., plates (1 fold., some col.), illus., map.
27cm.

MARMIER, Xavier
Voyage en Suisse; illustrations de MM. Rouargue
Frères. Paris: Morizot, [1862]. xxiii, 468p.,
plates, illus. 27cm.

MAROGNA, Nicolò
PONA, Giovanni
Monte Baldo, descritto da Giovanni Pona, Veronese,
in cui si figurano & descrivono molte rare piante
...; et due Commenti ... [di Nicolò Marogna
sopra l'amomo de gli antichi. Venetia: Roberto
Meietti, 1617. 248 [15], [4], 132p., illus.
22cm.

MARR, Anthony
North York moors; edited by Anthony Marr. Goring,
Reading: West Col for Cleveland Mountaineering
Club, 1970. 158p., illus., map. 17cm. (West
Col regional climbing guides)

MARR, John E
Cumberland. Cambridge: University Press, 1910.
xii, 169p., illus., maps (2 col.). 19cm.
(Cambridge County geographies)

MARR, John E
The scientific study of scenery. Methuen, 1899.
xi, 368p., plates, illus. 20cm.

MARRACK, Richard
How we did them in seventeen days! To wit:
Belgium, the Rhine, Switzerland, & France; des-
cribed and illustrated by one of ourselves [i.e.
Richard Marrack]; aided, assisted, encouraged,
and abetted by the other [i.e. Edmund G. Harvey].
Truro: Printed by Lake & Lake, [1875]. 68p.,
plates, illus. 20cm.
Cover title: Our rapid run.

MARRIOTT, Constance
See
SUTCLIFFE, Constance

MARSDEN, A D
Climbing guide to Gibralter. Yeovil: D.M. Haynes
for Joint Services Mountaineering Association,
[1963?]. 82p., illus. 21cm.

MARSDEN, William
POLO, Marco
The travels of Marco Polo, the Venetian; the
translation of Marsden revised with a selection
of his notes; edited by Thomas Wright. Bell,
1892. xxviii, 508p. 19cm. (Bohn's antiquarian
library)

MARSH, Herbert
Two seasons in Switzerland; with illustrations
from photographs by O. Williamson. Fisher Unwin,
1895. 261p., plates, illus. 21cm.

MARSHALL, Howard
Men against Everest. Country Life, 1954. 64p.,
plates, illus., maps. 23cm.

MARSHALL, J   R
Ben Nevis. Edinburgh: Scottish Mountaineering
Trust, 1969. 224p., illus. 17cm. (Scottish
Mountaineering Club climbers' guide books)

- - Rev. ed., with supplement. 1979.

MARSHALL, Robert
Arctic wilderness; edited with an introduction by
George Marshall; foreword by A. Starker Leopold.
Berkeley: University of California Press, 1956.
xxvi, 171p.,plates (1 fold.), illus., maps. 25cm.

MARSTON, Annie W
The great closed land: a plea for Tibet; with a
preface by B. La Trobe. Partridge, [1894?].
112p., illus., map. 23cm.

MARSTON, Edward
Frank's Ranche; or, My holiday in the Rockies,
being a contribution to the inquiry into what we
are to do with our boys, by the author of "An
amateur angler's days in Dovedale" [i.e. Edward
Marston]. Sampson Low, Marston, Searle, &
Rivington, 1886. xvi, 214p., plates, illus., map.
18cm.

MARTAGON
Montagnes et montagnards. le série. Pyrénées,
Catalogne, Île de Majorque, Provence. Paris:
Lemerre, 1901. ii, 407p. 20cm.

MARTEL, Édouard Alfred
Les abîmes, les eaux souterraines, les cavernes,
les sources, la spéléologie: explorations souterraines effectuées de 1888 à 1893 en France,
Belgique, Autriche et Grèce. Paris: Delagrave,
1894. 578p., illus., maps. 31cm.

MARTEL, Édouard Alfred
Les Cevennes et la région des Causses, Lozère,
Aveyron, Hérault, Gard, Ardèche. 3e éd., rev.
corr. et augm. Paris: Delagrave, 1891. viii,
407p., plates, illus., maps. 30cm.

MARTEL, Édouard Alfred
La Côte d'Azur russe (Riviera du Caucase): voyage
en Russie méridionale, au Caucase occidental et en
Transcaucasie (mission du gouvernement russe,
1903). Paris: Delagrave, [1908?]. 358p., 1 fold.
col. plate, illus., maps. 31cm.

MARTEL, Édouard Alfred
Le gouffre et la rivière souterraine de Padirac
(Lot): historique, description, exploration,
aménagement, (1889-1900). Paris: Delagrave, [1900].
180p., plates, illus., maps. 21cm.

MARTEL, Édouard Alfred
Irlande et cavernes anglaises. Paris: Delagrave,
1897. 403p., plates (3 fold.)., illus., maps,
bibl. 23cm.

LORRIA, August and MARTEL, Édouard Alfred
Le massif de la Bernina, par August Lorria et É.A.
Martel; avec la collaboration de W.A.B. Coolidge
et J. Caviezel. Zurich: Orell Füssli, 1894.
163p., 50 plates, illus., map, bibl. 33 x 42cm.
(Les grandes Alpes)

MARTEL, Édouard Alfred
Nouveau traité des eaux souterraines. Paris: Doin,
1921. 840p., illus., maps, bibl. 27cm.

MARTEL, Édouard Alfred
La spéléologie; ou, Science des cavernes. Paris:
G. Carré & C. Naud, 1900. 126p., illus. 20cm.
(Scientia. Biologie, no.8)

MARTEL, Peter
    See
MARTEL, Pierre

WINDHAM, William and MARTEL, Pierre
Relations de leurs deux voyages aux glaciers de
Chamonix (1741-1742); texte original français ...
avec une introduction et des notes par Théophile
Dufour. Genève: Bonnant, 1879. 69p. 26cm.

WINDHAM, William and MARTEL, Pierre
[Relations de leurs deux voyages...]. An account
of the glaciers or ice alps in Savoy, in two
letters, one from an English gentleman [i.e.
William Windham] to his friend at Geneva; the
other from Peter Martel ... as laid before the
Royal Society. Printed for Peter Martel, 1744.
28p., 2 plates, illus. 28cm.

- - Another ed. Ipswich: Printed by W. Craighton,
1747.

MARTELLI, A   E   and VACCARONE, Luigi
Guida delle Alpi occidentali. Torino: Club Alpino
Italiano, Sezione di Torino, 1889-96. 2v. in 3,
fold. plates (some col.), illus., maps, bibl.
17cm.

MARTELLI, A   E   and VACCARONE, Luigi
Guida delle Alpi occidentali del Piemonte, dal
Colle dell'Argentera ... al Colle Girard...
Torino: Club Alpino Italiano, Sezione di Torino,
1880. xxxix, 480p., plates (some fold.), illus.,
bibl. 17cm.

MARTIGNON, Andrée
Montagne. Paris: Stock, 1930. 261p. 20cm.
(Les livres de nature)

MARTIN, Alexandre
La Suisse pittoresque et ses environs: tableau
général, descriptif, historique et statistique
des 22 cantons, de la Savoie, d'une partie du
Piemont et du pays de Bade. Paris: Souverain,
1835. viii, 374p., 1 plate, map. 28cm.

MARTIN, Alexandre
[La Suisse pittoresque...]. La Svizzera
pittoresca e suoi dintorni... Mendrisio: Tipografia della Minerva Ticinese, 1836. 296p., 1
plate, map. 28cm.

MARTIN, F   J
Itinéraire descriptif de la vallée de Sixt, pro-
vince de Faucigny, en Savoie, par F.J.M. [i.e.
F.J. Martin]. Genève: Manget & Cherbuliez, 1821.
vi, 155p. 17cm.
Library's copy lacks illus.

TARR, Ralph Stockman and MARTIN, Lawrence
Alaskan glacier studies of the National Geographic
Society in the Yakutat Bay, Prince William Sound
and Lower Copper River regions, based upon the
field work in 1909, 1910, 1911 and 1913 by
National Geographic Society expeditions.
Washington (D.C.): National Geographic Society,
1914. xxvii, 498p., plates (some fold., col.),
maps (in pocket). 27cm.

MARTIN, Maurice
Note sur l'Expédition française 1957 au Groenland-
Sud: renseignements, communiqués par Maurice
Martin. [Paris]: The Author, [1957?]. [3]
leaves, maps. 30cm.
Photocopy of typescript.

MARTIN, Wilhelm
ÖSTERREICHISCHER ALPENKLUB
Führer durch die Mont-Blanc-Gruppe; im Auftrage
des Österreichischen Alpenklubs verfasst von
Wilhelm Martin [and others]. Wien: Ö.A.K., 1913.
2v., fold. plates, maps, bibl. 17cm.
In case with fold. map.

MARTIN-FRANKLIN, J   and VACCARONE, Luigi
Notice historique sur l'ancienne route de Charles-
Emmanuel II et les Grottes des Echelles. Chambéry:
Perrin, 1887. xvi, 235p. 24cm.

MARTINEAU, Harriet
A complete guide to the English Lakes. Windermere:
J. Garnett, 1855. iv, 233p., 1 plate, map. 18cm.

- - 3rd ed., edited and enlarged by Maria Martineau.
[ca 1865].

MARTINEAU, Harriet
Guide to Windermere, with tours to the neighbouring lakes... Windermere: J. Garnett, [ca 1855].
103p., plates (1 fold.), illus., map. 17cm.

MARTINEAU, Maria
MARTINEAU, Harriet
A complete guide to the English Lakes. Windermere:
J. Garnett, 1855. iv, 233p., 1 plate, map. 18cm.

- - 3rd ed., edited and enlarged by Maria Martineau.
[ca 1865].

MARTINS, Charles
Ascension au Mont Blanc, par MM. Martins, Bravais
et Lepileur. [Paris? 1844]. 68-74p., illus. 37cm.
Offprint from l'Illustration, journal universel,
no.84, v.4, 5 oct. 1844.

MARTINS, Charles
De l'ancienne extension des glaciers de Chamonix
depuis le Mont-Blanc jusqu'au Jura. [Paris],
[1847]. 919-943p. 23cm.
Offprint from La Revue des deux mondes, t.17, mars
1847.

MARTINS, Charles
Deux ascensions scientifiques au Mont-Blanc: leurs
résultats immédiats pour la météorologie, la physique du globe et les sciences naturelles. Paris,
1865. 38p. 25cm.
Offprint from Revue des deux mondes, t.15, mars
1865.

MARTINS, Charles
Du retrait et de l'ablation des glaciers de la
Vallée de Chamonix, constatés dans l'automne de
1865. [Genève], 1866. 22p. 22cm.
Offprint from Archives des sciences de la biblio-
thèque universelle, juillet, 1866.

MARTINS, Charles and COLLOMB, Édouard
Essai sur l'ancien glacier de la Vallée d'Argelès
(Hautes Pyrénées). Montpellier, 1868. 34p., 1
fold.col. plate, illus., map. 28cm.
Offprint from Mémoires de l'Académie des sciences
de Montpellier, v.7, 1867.

MARTINS, Charles
La réunion de la Société helvétique des sciences
naturelles en août 1863 à Samaden, dans la Haute-
Engadine... Paris, 1864. 35p. 24cm.
Offprint from Revue des deux mondes.

MARTINS, Charles and PLANTAMOUR, E
Sur l'influence de la distance et la correction
horaire des différences de niveau obtenues à l'aide
de deux baromètres correspondants. [Paris], 1860.
185-194p., illus. 24cm.
Offprint from Archives des sciences, v.9, nov. 1860.

HALAŠA, Ján and MARTON, Štefan
Liptovské hole a Chočské pohorie. Martin:
Vydavateľstvo Osveta, 1958. [15]p., 148 plates,
illus. 30cm.
In Czech, German and Slovak.

MARTONNE, Emmanuel de
Les Alpes (géographie générale). Paris: Colin,
1926. 217p., illus., maps. 18cm. (Collection
Armand Colin, no.76)

MARTYN, Thomas
An appendix to the Gentleman's guide through Italy,
containing catalogues of the paintings, statues,
busts etc., [by T. Martyn]. Printed for G.
Kearsley, 1787. 159p. 18cm.

MARTYN, Thomas
Guide du voyageur en Suisse, [by Thomas Martyn and
others]. Lausanne: J. Mourer, 1794. 203p. 19cm.

MARTYN, Thomas
Sketch of a tour through Swisserland with an
accurate map; also an appendix containing Catalogues of paintings, statues, busts etc. in
different parts of Italy. Printed for G.
Kearsley, 1787. 95, 159p., map. 18cm.

- - New ed., to which is added A short account of
an expedition to the summit of Mont Blanc by M. de
Saussure. 1788.

MASON, Alfred Edward Woodley
The broken road. 2nd ed. Smith, Elder, 1908.
352p. 21cm.

MASON, Alfred Edward Woodley
A romance of Wastdale. Hodder & Stoughton, 1914.
160p., plates, illus. 16cm. (Sevenpenny library)

MASON, Alfred Edward Woodley
Running water. Collins, [19--]. 282p., col.
plates, illus. 16cm. (Collins modern fiction,55)

MASON, Alfred Edward Woodley
GREEN, Roger Lancelyn
A.E.W. Mason. Parrish, 1952. 272p., 1 plate,
illus., bibl. 23cm.

MASON, B   R
Safety in the mountains: a handbook for trampers,
skiers, stalkers and mountaineers. 5th ed.,
editor: B.R. Mason. Wellington (N.Z.): Federated
Mountain Clubs of New Zealand, 1963. 120p.,
illus., bibl. 19cm.

MASON, Kenneth
Abode of snow: a history of Himalayan exploration
and mountaineering. Hart-Davis, 1955. xi, 372p.,
plate, illus., maps, bibl. 23cm.

MASON, Kenneth
Exploration of the Shaksgam valley and Aghil
ranges 1926. Dehra Dun: Survey of India: 1928.
182p., plates (1 fold.col.), illus., map (in
pocket). 26cm. (Records of the Survey of India,
v.22)

MASON, Kenneth
STEIN, Sir Marc Aurel
Memoir on maps of Chinese Turkistan and Kansu
from the surveys made during Sir Aurel Stein's
explorations, 1900-1, 1906-8, 1913-5; with appendices by K. Mason, and J. de Graaf Hunter. Dehra
Dun: Trigonometrical Survey Office, 1923. xv,
208p., illus.   35cm. (Records of the Survey
of India., v.17)

MASON, Kenneth
The representation of glaciated regions on maps
of the Survey of India. Dehra Dun: Survey of
India, 1929. 18p., plates (2 fold., 1 col.),
illus., map. 25cm. (Survey of India. Professional
paper, no. 25)

MASON, Kenneth
Routes in the western-Himalaya, Kashmir, etc.,
with which are included Montgomerie's routes revised and rearranged. Vol.1. Punch, Kashmir and
Ladakh. Dehra Dun: Trigonometrical Survey of
India, 1922. xvii, 273p., fold.col. plates, maps
(in pocket). 26cm.

- - 2nd ed. Calcutta: Government of India Press,
1929.

MASON, W
GRAY, Thomas
The works of Thomas Gray, containing his poems,
and correspondence with several eminent literary
characters; to which are added Memoirs of his life
and writings by W. Mason. F.C. & J. Rivington,
1821. 545p. 14cm.

MASSAM, J   A
The cliff dwellers of Kenya: an account of a
people ... their ways of living ... their magic &
superstitions. Seeley, Service, 1927. 268p.,
plates (1 fold.), illus., maps. 23cm.

MASSANO, Gino
Canti della montagna... 2a ed. Roma: Morpurgo, 1931. 62p., illus., music. 17cm. (Parole e musica)

MASSIE, F
La cartographie des Pyrénées: étude; documentation illustrée de cartes et photographies de l'Exposition de Cartographie des Pyrénées organisée par le Capitaine Massie, du 15 au 30 décembre 1933... Tarbes: La Section des Hautes-Pyrénées du Club Alpin Français, 1934. 127p., plates (2 fold.), illus., maps (2 fold.), bibl. 23cm.

MASSIE, J   W
Recollections of a tour: a summer ramble in Belgium, Germany, and Switzerland. J. Snow, 1846. xii, 548p. 21cm.

MASSON, Alexandre Frédéric Jacques de, marquis de Pezay
    See
PEZAY, Alexandre Frédéric Jacques de Masson, marquis de

MASSOW, Wilhelm von
Aus Krim und Kaukasus: Reiseskizzen. Leipzig: Wigand, 1902. viii, 142p., 1 fold.col. plate, illus., map. 22cm.

MATHEWS, Charles Edward
The annals of Mont Blanc: a monograph; with a chapter on the geology of the mountain by T.G. Bonney. Fisher Unwin, 1898. xxiv, 368p., plates (1 fold.col.), illus., map, bibl. 23cm.

MATHEWS, Charles Edward
Ascent of the Jungfrau. [Birmingham, 1860]. 3p. 23cm.
Offprint from Birmingham Gazette, 21st July, 1860.

MATHEWS, Charles Edward
The earlier and less-known poems of Alfred Tennyson ...; an address delivered before the members of the Harborne and Edgbaston Institute by C.E. Mathews, 30th January 1883. Birmingham: [n.pub.], 1883. 34p. 22cm.

GEORGE, Hereford Brooke and MATHEWS, Charles Edward
Munchausen on the Jungfrau. Printed by Spottiswoode, [ca 1870]. 6p. 22cm.
Signed H.B.G. - C.E.M. i.e. H.B. George and C.E. Mathews.

MATHEWS, Charles Edward
Narrative of an excursion on the chain of Mont Blanc. Birmingham, 1862.
Offprint from Birmingham Daily Gazette, July 10th, 1862.

MATHEWS, Charles Edward
Personal reminiscences of great climbs: [a lecture]. [Leeds?], 1902.   Offprint from Yorkshire Ramblers' Club journal, v.4, 1902.

MATHEWS, Charles Edward
The recollections of a mountaineer. London, 1892. 32p., illus. 24cm.
Offprint from Mountaineering, Badminton series.

MATHEWS, Charles Edward
Reminiscences of Pen-y-Gwryd. [Birmingham?], 1902. 25p., plates, illus. 22cm.
Offprint from Climber's Club journal.

MATHEWS, F   Schuyler
Field book of American wild flowers, being a short description of their character and habits ...; with ... reproductions of ... studies from nature by the author. New York, London: Putnam, 1903. xx, 552p., col. plates, illus. 18cm.

MATHEWS, William
The flora of Algeria, considered in relation to the physical history of the Mediterranean region, and supposed submergence of the Sahara. Stanford, 1880. 55p., 1 fold.col. plate, map. 23cm.

MATHIAS, H   V
Five weeks' sport in the interior of the Himalayas, together with a description of the game found there, also a few hints regarding equipment, &c. F. Thimm, 1865. 132p. 17cm.

MATHISON, Robert
INNERLEITHEN ALPINE CLUB
Principal excursions of the Innerleithen Alpine Club during the years 1889-94; with a memoir of Robert Mathison, first President of the Club. Galashiels: John McQueen for the Club, 1895. 311p., plates, illus. 20cm.

- - 2nd ed. 1897.

Matterhorn-Jubiläumsfestwoche = Centennial Festival of the Matterhorn. Zermatt: [Centennial Committee], 1965. 24p. 21cm.
At head of title: 1965 Jahr der Alpen = Year of the Alps.

MATTHEW, George King
The English Lakes, peaks and passes, from Kendal to Keswick. Kendal: J. Richardson, 1866. ix, 207, iiii p., plates (1 fold.), illus., map. 19cm.

MATTHEWS, Henry
The diary of an invalid, being the journal of a tour in pursuit of health, in Portugal, Italy, Switzerland, and France, in the years 1817, 1818, and 1819. Murray, 1820. xv, 515p. 23cm.

MATTHEY, André
Ascension du Mont-Blanc. Genève: 1834. 44-58p. 23cm.
Offprint from Bibliothèque universelle... t.2, 1834.

MATTHEY, André
Les bains de Saint-Gervais, près du Mont-Blanc (en Savoie). Paris: J.J. Paschoud, 1818. xvi, 240p., 1 fold. plate, illus. 22cm.

MATTHIAS, Eugen and TESTA, Giovanni
Natürliches Skilaufen: die Methode der einfachsten Fahrweise; mit einem sportärzlichen Beitrag von Paul Gut. München: Rother, 1936. 107p., plates, illus. 26cm.

MATTHIAS, Eugen and TESTA, Giovanni
[Natürliches Skilaufen...]. Sciare: tecnica moderna semplificata e razionalizzata; traduzione del conte Ugo di Vallepiana ... [e di] L.Ricotti. Milano: Sperling & Kupfer, 1938. 131p.,illus. 24cm.

MATTHISSON, Friedrich von
Briefe. Zürich: Orell, Gesner, Füssli, 1795. 2v. 19cm.

MATTHISSON, Friedrich von
Gedichte. Leipzig: P. Reclam, [1867]. 115p. 15cm. (Universal- Bibliothek, 140)

MAUGHAN, William Charles
The Alps of Arabia: travels in Egypt, Sinai, Arabia and the Holy Land. King, 1873. xvi, 374p., plates, map. 24cm.

- - New ed. 1875.

MAUND, J   Oakley
Mountaineering.
(In Morgan, W.A. The "House" on sport, by members of the London Stock Exchange; compiled and edited by W.A. Morgan. Gale & Polden, 1898. 24cm. p.259-285, illus.)

MAUNDEVILLE, Sir John
The marvellous adventures of Sir John Maundeville ...; edited and profusely illustrated by Arthur Layard; with a preface by John Cameron Grant. Constable, 1895. xxx, 414p., plates, illus. 22cm.

MAURER, Konrad
Isländische Volkssagen der Gegenwart, vorwiegend
nach mündlicher Überlieferung gesammelt und
verdeutscht. Leipzig: Hinrichs, 1860. xii,
352p. 24cm.

MAUROIS, Gérald
BONNET, Honoré
[Ski à la française]. Ski - the experts' way;
with photographs by Gérald Maurois; English technical adviser Robin Brock-Hollinshead. Newnes,
1966. 237p., illus. 25cm.

MAURY, Léon
Les noms de lieux des montagnes françaises. Paris:
C.A.F., 1929. viii, 325p., bibl. 26cm.

MAURY, Luc
Les ultimes ascensions d'Henri Brulle; [récits
recueillis et présentés par Luc Maury]. [Bordeaux],
1969. 21p., illus. 25cm.
Offprint from Revue pyrénéenne, no.18, juin 1969
et no.19, sept. 1969.

MAUS, Octave
Savoie; bois en couleurs de Louis Moret. Paris:
H. Floury, 1911. 37p., col. illus. 33cm.

MAVOR, William Fordyce
A tour in Wales, and through several counties of
England, including both the universities, per-
formed in the summer of 1805, [by William F.
Mavor]. R. Phillips, 1806. 184p., 1 fold. plate,
illus. 23cm.
(In A collection of modern and contemporary
voyages... Vol.3. 1806)

MAWMAN, J
An excursion to the Highlands of Scotland and the
English Lakes, with recollections, descriptions,
and references to historical facts. The Author,
1805. xv, 291p., plates (1 fold.), illus., map.
22cm.

MAXIMILIAN II, King of Bavaria
BODENSTEDT, Friedrich
Eine Königsreise. 3.Aufl. Leipzig: J. Lehmann,
[1883]. 295p. 20cm.

MAXWELL, D   C
Tables giving all the 3000-ft. mountains of
England, Wales and Ireland; compiled by D.C.
Maxwell. [Dundee?]: The Author, 1959. 8p. 23cm.

BEETHAM, George and MAXWELL, Joseph Prime
The first ascent of Mount Ruapehu, New Zealand and
a holiday jaunt to Mounts Ruapehu, Tongariro and
Ngauruhoe. Harrison, 1926. 40p., plates, illus.
22cm.

MAY, Étienne
La montagne: catalogue de la Bibliothèque léguée
au Touring-Club de France 1881-1962. Paris: Le
Club, 1965. 94 leaves. 27cm.

MAYER, Charles Joseph de
Voyage de M. de Mayer en Suisse en 1784; ou,
Tableau historique, civil, politique et physique de
la Suisse. Amsterdam: Leroy, 1786. 2v. 23cm.

MAYER, Erich August
O, ihr Berge! Funf Novellen. Berlin: Luser, 1931.
377p. 20cm.

MAYER, Karl
KAUFMANN, Franz Joseph
Rigi und Molassegebiet der Mittelschweiz, geo-
logisch aufgenommen und beschrieben; Beilage:
Systematisches Verzeichniss der marinen Arten ...,
von Karl Mayer. Bern: J. Dalp, 1872. viii, 534p.,
6 plates (some fold., some col.), illus. 29cm.
(Beiträge zur geologischen Karte der Schweiz,
Lfg.11. Gebiete der Kantone Bern, Luzern, Schwyz
und Zug)

MAYER-PFANNHOLZ, Anton
Deutsches Alpenland: ein Heimatbuch; hrsg. von
Anton Mayer-Pfannholz; mit Zeichnungen von Adolf
Geitz. Leipzig: F. Brandstetter, 1920. xvi,
464p., illus. 22cm.

MAYR, Julius
Auf stillen Pfaden: Wanderbilder aus Heimat und
Fremde. München: Rother, 1924. 247p. 22cm.

MAYRHOFER, Joseph K
Ueber den Brenner: von Innsbruck nach Botzen und
in die Seiten Thäler: topographisch-
kulturhistorische Schilderung; mit Illustrationen
von Friedrich Mayer und Philipp Sporrer. München:
C. Merhoff, 1868. xii, 236p., illus. 16cm.

MAZÉ, Jules
La grande montagne. Paris: Bloud et Gay, 1921.
141p., plates, illus. 24cm.

MAZEAUD, Pierre
[Montagne pour un homme nu]. Naked before the
mountain; with a preface by Walter Bonatti;
translated by Geoffrey Sutton. Gollancz, 1974.
256p., plates, illus. 23cm.

MAZEL, Anton
Künstlerische Gebirgs-Photographie. Autorisierte
deutsche Uebersetzung von E. Hegg. Berlin: G.
Schmidt, 1903. 176p., 12 plates, illus. 25cm.

MAZUCHELLI, Nina Elizabeth
The Indian Alps and how we crossed them, being a
narrative of two years' residence in the Eastern
Himalaya and two months' tour into the interior,
by a lady pioneer [i.e. Nina E. Mazuchelli],
illustrated by herself. Longmans, Green, 1876.
xvii, 612p., plates, illus., map. 27cm.

MAZUCHELLI, Nina Elizabeth
"Magyarland", being the narrative of our travels
through the highlands and lowlands of Hungary, by
a fellow of the Carpathian Society [i.e. Nina E.
Mazuchelli]. Sampson Low, Marston, Searle, &
Rivington, 1881. 2v., plates, illus. 24cm.

MAZZOTTI, Giuseppe
Il giardino delle rose: guida spirituale delle
Dolomiti. Torino: Edizioni "Montes", 1931. 210p.,
plates, illus. 24cm. (La piccozza e la penna, 7)

MAZZOTTI, Giuseppe
La grande parete. Milano: L'Eroica, 1938. 189p.
18cm. (Montagna, 18)

MAZZOTTI, Giuseppe
[La grande parete]. La grande Paroi; traduit par
É. Gaillard. Chambéry: Lire, 1948. 189p., plates,
illus. 19cm. (Le roc et l'eau)

MAZZOTTI, Giuseppe
Grandi imprese sul Cervino. Milano: L'Eroica,
1934. 245p., plates, illus., map, bibl. 18cm.
(Montagna, 10)

MAZZOTTI, Giuseppe
[Grandi imprese sul Cervino]. Dernières victoires
au Cervin; traduit ... par É. Gaillard. Neuchatel:
Attinger, 1934. 202p., plates, illus., map, bibl.
19cm.

MAZZOTTI, Giuseppe
[Grandi imprese sul Cervino]. Das Buch vom
Matterhorn: die Erstersteigungen; Übersetzung ...
von Heinrich Erler. Berlin: Union Deutsche
Verlagsgesellschaft, [1935]. 156p., plates,
illus., bibl. 22cm.

MAZZOTTI, Giuseppe
La montagna presa in giro: sollazzevole spas-
sosissimo libro, scritto da Giuseppe Mazzotti e
istoriato da Sante Cancian. Torino: Rivista
"Alpinismo", 1931. xi, 148p., illus. 19cm.

- - 2a ed., rifatta e raddoppiata. 1933.

MAZZOTTI, Giuseppe
[La montagna presa in giro...]. A chacun sa montagne; traduit ... par É. Gaillard; illustré par
G. Mazzotti. Chambéry: Lire, 1948. 207p., plates,
illus. 19cm. (Le roc et l'eau)

MAZZOTTI, Giuseppe
Trionfo della tecnica e decadenza dell'ideale:
studio su vari caratteri dell'alpinismo dolomitico.
[Torino, 1932]. 24p., illus. 25cm.
Offprint from Rivista del Club Alpino Italiano,
ott. 1932-X, n.10.

MEADE, Charles Francis
Approach to the hills. Murray, 1940. 265p.,
plates, illus., maps. 23cm.

MEADE, Charles Francis
High mountains. Harvill Press, 1954. 136p.,
plates, illus. 23cm.

MEANY, Edmond Stephen
Mount Rainier: a record of exploration; edited by
Edmond S. Meany. New York: Macmillan, 1916. xi,
325p., plates, illus. 23cm.

MEANY, Edmond Stephen
Mountain camp fires. Seattle: Lowman & Hanford,
1911. viii, 90p., plates, illus. 19cm.

MECHEL, Chrétien de
Itinéraire du St. Gothard, d'une partie du Vallais
et des contrées de la Suisse que l'on traverse ...
pour se rendre au Gothard, publié par Chrétien de
Mechel. Basle: The Author, 1795. 144p., 1 fold.
plate, map. 21cm.

MECIANI, Pietro
Le Ande: monografia geografico-alpinistica.
Bologna: Tamari, [1964?]. 158p., illus., maps,
bibl. 25cm.

MECIANI, Pietro
MONZINO, Guido
Kanjut Sar: atti della Spedizione G.M. '59 al
Kanjut Sar, Karakorum; con monografia storico geografica del Karakorum a cura di Pietro Meciani;
osservazioni fisiologiche cliniche e psicologiche
a cura di Paolo Cerretelli; note dal diario di
Lorenzo Marimonti. Milano: A. Martello, 1961.
342p., illus., maps. 30cm.

MEDLICOTT, H   B
On the geological structure and relations of the
southern portions of the Himalayan ranges, between
the rivers Ganges and Ravee. Calcutta: Geological
Survey of India, 1864. 210p., col. plates (2
fold.), illus., map. 26cm. (Memoirs of the
Geological Survey of India, v.3, pt.2)

MEERSCH, W   J   Ganshof van der
Une mission scientifique belge dans le massif du
Ruwenzori. Paris, 1933. [9]p., plates, illus.,
maps. 38cm.
Offprint from L'Illustration, 28 jan. and 4 fev.
1933.

MEIER, Mark F
AMERICAN ALPINE CLUB. Research Committee
Surface features of Dinwoody Glacier, Wind River
Mountains, Wyoming, geology by Mark F. Meier,
1950-1952; sponsored by the Research Committee,
American Alpine Club. New York: The Club, [1953].
Broadsheet, illus., map. 22cm.

MEILLON, Alphonse
Esquisse toponymique sur la Vallée de Cauterets,
Hautes-Pyrénées. Cauterets: Cazaux, 1908. 396p.
26cm.

MEILLON, Alphonse
Essai d'un glossaire des noms topographiques les
plus usités dans la Vallée de Cauterets et la
région montagneuse des Hautes-Pyrénées. 2e éd.
Cauterets: Thalabot, 1911. 33-98p. 26cm.

MEILLON, Alphonse
Excursions autour du Vignemale dans les hautes
vallées de Cauterets, de Gavarnie et du Rio Ara en
Aragon; l'origine du Pyrénéisme; contribution à
l'histoire de ces vallées. Pau: Garet-Haristoy,
1928. xii, 379p., plates (some fold.), illus.,
maps. 26cm.

MEILLON, Alphonse
Excursions topographiques dans la Vallée de
Cauterets (Hautes-Pyrénées). Cauterets: Cazaux,
1920. 3 pts., plates (some fold.), illus., map.
26-28cm.
Title in pt.3 as: Triangulation géodésique com-
plémentaire de la région de Cauterets...

Meine Reise über den Gotthard nach den borromäischen
Inseln und Mailand; und von da zurük über das Val
Formazza, die Grimsel und das Oberland, [von Chr.
G. von Hölder]. Stuttgart: J.F. Steinkopf, 1803-04.
2v. 17cm.

MEINERS, C
Briefe über die Schweiz. 2. und verm. Aufl.
Tübingen: Cotta, 1791. 4v. in 2. 18cm.

MEISNER, Friedrich
Friedrich Meisners Alpenreise mit seinem Zöglingen,
für Jugend beschrieben. Bern: E. Haller, 1801.
212p., plates, illus. 18cm.

MEISNER, Friedrich
Reise durch das Berner Oberland, nach Unterwalden
... Bern: J.J. Burgdorfer, 1821. 251p., plates,
illus. 18cm.

MEISSER, Christian
HILTBRUNNER, Hermann
Graubünden; illustriert von Christian u. Hans
Meisser; hrsg. von Christian Meisser. Genf: SADAG,
[1928]. 3v., illus., maps. 25cm.
Library lacks v.2.

MEISSER, Christian
Die schöne Schweiz in 92 Kunstblättern; Begleitwort von Heinrich Federer ...; gesammelt und hrsg.
von Christian Meisser. Genf: Édition des "Mille
et une vues de la Suisse", 1925. 1v. (chiefly
illus.). 29cm.
Multilingual captions.

MEISSNER, Alfred
Ein Ausflug zum Monte Rosa. [Leipzig, 1858].
57-64p. 26cm.
Offprint from Illustrirte deutsche Monatshefte,
v.4. 1858.

MEISTER, Leonard
Kleine Reisen durch einige Schweizer-Cantone: ein
Auszug aus zerstreuten Briefen und Tagregistern.
Basel: J. Schweighaufer, 1782. 220p. 18cm.

MELA, Pomponius
De orbis situ libri tres, accuratissime emendati,
unà cū Commētariis Ioachimi Vadiani Heluetii
castigatioribus... Adiecta... Rursum, Epistola
Vadiani... Basileae: Apud Andream Cratandrum,
1522. 1v. (various pagings). 31cm.
Contains Watt's account of the ascent of Pilatus,
with contemporary ms. notes.

Mélanges helvétiques de 1782 à 1786; [par P.S. and
J.P.L. Bridel]. Lausanne: H. Vincent, 1787. x,
370p. 15cm.

- - Des années 1787, 1788, 1789, 1790. Basle:
C.A. Serini, 1791.

PARKER, Terry M   and MELDRUM, Kim I
Outdoor education. Dent, 1973. 204p., plates,
illus., bibl. 22cm.

MELISSANTES
See
GREGORII, Johann Gottfried

MELMOTH, William
COXE, William
[Sketches of the natural civil and political state
of Swisserland...]. Lettres de William Coxe à
W. Melmoth, sur l'état politique, civil et naturel
de la Suisse ...; augmentées des observations
faites ... par le traducteur [L. Ramond]. Paris:
Belin, 1781. 2v. 21cm.

- - Another issue. 1782.
- - Another issue. 1787.

MELMOTH, William
COXE, William
[Sketches of the natural, civil and political state
of Swisserland...]. Briefe über den naturlichen,
bürgerlichen und politischen Zustand der Schweiz,
von Wilhelm Coxe an Wilhelm Melmoth. Zürich:
Orell, Gessner, Füssli, 1781-91. 2v. 19cm.

MÉLON, Pierre
Chasseurs de chamois. Paris: Attinger, [1935].
175p. 19cm. (Montagne)

MÉLON, Pierre
Montagnards. Lyon: Audin, 1949. 209p., 8 plates,
illus. 20cm. ("Vertige")

MELTZER, Charles
Guide autour du Mont-Blanc. Nouvelle éd. Genève:
Atar, [19--]. 196p., illus. 17cm.

MELZER, Otto
FICKER, Heinrich von and AMPFERER, Otto
Aus Innsbrucks Bergwelt: Wanderbilder aus Inns-
brucks Bergen; mit ... kunst Beilagen ... nach
Originalaufnahmen von Otto Melzer; Text von
Heinrich von Ficker und Otto Ampferer. Innsbruck:
H. Schwick, 1902. 229p., plates, illus. 30cm.

MELZERKNAPPEN
Die Lechtaler Alpen; bearb. von der deutsch.
alpinen Gesellschaft Melzerknappen... Innsbruck:
Wagner, 1924. 208p., maps. 16cm. (Wagners Alpine
Spezialführer, 2)

Mémoire d'une toute petite tournée en Suisse, à vol
d'hirondelle, dedié à mon ami Sept-Croix. Harlem:
Imprimé chez Joh. Enschedé, 1863. 91p. 21cm.
Signed: Charles.

Memorandums of the face of the country in Switzerland,
[by the Duchess of Devonshire]. Cooper & Graham,
1799. 103p. 17cm.

MÉNARD, Léon
Histoire des antiquités de la ville de Nismes et
de ses environs. Nouv. éd. Nismes: Gaude, 1819.
59p., plates (some fold.), illus. 20cm.

MENDELSSOHN, Felix
Reisebriefe, aus den Jahren 1830 bis 1832, von
Felix Mendelssohn Bartholdy. 2 unveränd. Aufl.
Leipzig: H. Mendelssohn, 1862. 340p. 21cm.

MENDELSSOHN, Felix
[Reisebriefe aus den Jahren 1830 bis 1832].
Letters from Italy and Switzerland; translated from
the German by Lady Wallace. 3rd ed. Longman,
Green, Longman, Roberts, & Green, 1864. xxiv,
356p., illus. 19cm.
Contains: Life of Mendelssohn, by H.F. Chorley.

MENDELSSOHN-BARTHOLDY, Felix
See
MENDELSSOHN, Felix

MENDEZ, Felix
Expedicion española a los Andes del Peru, 1961.
Madrid: Publicaciones del Comité Olimpico Español,
1962. [36]p., illus., maps. 22cm.

MENSIO, Luigi
Guida di Courmayer, Valle d'Aosta. Aosta: L.
Mensio, 1895. 78p. 12cm.

MENSIO, Luigi
Guida di Pré St. Didier, Valle d'Aosta. Aosta:
L. Mensio, 1895. 56p. 12cm.

MENSIO, Luigi
Guide de la ville d'Aoste. Aoste: L. Mensio, 1894.
48p. 12cm.

FAES, Henry and MERCANTON, Paul L
Le manuel du skieur, suivi des itinéraires re-
commandables en Suisse occidentale. Lausanne:
Imprimeries Réunies, [1917]. 116p., illus. 22cm.

- - 2e éd. rev. et complétée. Lausanne: Payot,
1925.
- - Another issue, 1925.

MERCANTON, Paul L
Vermessungen am Rhonegletscher = Mensurations au
Glacier du Rhone, 1874-1915; geleitet und hrsg.
von der Gletscher-Kommission der Schweizerischen
Naturforschenden Gesellschaft; [bearb. und
verfasst... von P.-L. Mercanton]. Basel: The
Society, 1916. 190p., plates, illus., maps.
32cm. (Neue Denkschriften, 52)

MERCEY, Frédéric
Le Tyrol et le nord de l'Italie: journal d'une
excursion dans ces contrées en 1830. 2e éd.
Paris: A. Bertrand, 1845. 2v. 23cm.

MERCIER, Jerome J
Mountains and lakes of Switzerland and Italy:
Sixty-four picturesque views ... from original
sketches, by C. Pyne; with descriptive notes by
Jerome J. Mercier. Bell & Daldy, 1871. 130p.,
col. illus., fold.col. map. 27cm.

MERCIER, Joachim
Aus der Urgeschichte des schweiz. Skilaufes:
Jubiläums-Schrift des Ski-Club Glarus, 1893-1928.
Glarus: Ski-Club Glarus, [1928]. 112p., plates,
illus. 24cm.

MEREDITH, Brian
Escape on skis. Hurst & Blackett, [1928]. 255p.,
plates, illus. 23cm.

MEREDITH, Louisa Anne
Over the Straits: a visit to Victoria ...; with
illustrations from photographs and the author's
sketches. Chapman & Hall, 1861. xii, 284p.,
illus. 20cm.

MERIAN, Matthaeus
Topographia Helvetiae, Rhaetiae, et Valesiae: das
ist Beschreibung und eygentliche Abbildung der
vornehmsten Stätte ...; in dieser andern Edition
... corrigirt, vermehrt und gebessert [von M.Z.,
i.e. Martin Zeiller]. Franckfurt am Mayn: Von
denen Merianischen Erben, 1654. 90p., plates
(some fold.), illus. 32cm.

- - Facsimile ed. [Basle?]: [n.pub.], [ca 1900].

MERKH, R
"Es war einmal": deutsche Wanderungen in Südtirol
und Oberitalien. Innsbruck: Wagner, 1913.
340p. 20cm.

MERKL, Willy
Himalaja-Bibliographie, 1801-1933; hrsg. von der
Deutschen Himalaja-Expedition 1934; mit Unter-
stützung des Vereins der Freunde der Alpens-
vereinsbücherei; [compiled by Willy Merkl].
München: Die Expedition, 1934. 48p. 18cm.

MERKL, Willy
Willy Merkl: ein weg zum Nanga Parbat; Leben,
Vortrage und nachgelassene Schriften hrsg. von
seinem Bruder Karl Herrligkoffer; unter Mitarbeit
von Fritz Schmitt. 2.Aufl. München: Rother,
1936. 235p., plates, illus. 26cm.

MERLE-D'AUBIGNE, Robert
Secourisme en montagne ...; réalisé par les
membres de la Commission médicale de la Fédération
Française de la Montagne ...; et sous la haute
autorité du professeur Merle-d'Aubigne. Paris:
Serpic, 1969. 197p., illus. 21cm.

MERRICK, Hugh
The Alps in colour, text by Hugh Merrick; photographs by Robert Löbl. Constable, 1970. 237p.,
col. illus. 29cm.

MERRICK, Hugh
Andreas at sundown. Hale, 1944. 320p. 20cm.

MERRICK, Hugh
The breaking strain. Constable, 1950. 312p.
19cm.

MERRICK, Hugh
Companion to the Alps. Batsford, 1974. 280p.,
illus., map. 23cm.

MERRICK, Hugh
The great motor highways of the Alps. Hale, 1958.
272p., plates, illus., maps, bibl. 25cm.

- - Rev. ed. 1961.

MERRICK, Hugh
Out of the night. Hale, 1957. 19cm.

MERRICK, Hugh
The perpetual hills: a personal anthology of
mountains. Newnes, 1964. 247p., plates, illus.
26cm.

MERRICK, Hugh
Pillar of the sky. Eyre & Spottiswoode, 1941.
304p. 20cm.

MERRICK, Hugh
Rambles in the Alps, written and illustrated by
Hugh Merrick. Country Life, 1951. 128p., illus.,
maps. 29cm.

MERRICK, Hugh
Savoy episode. Hale, 1946. 192p., 31 plates,
illus. 23cm.

MERRILL, Bill
See
MERRILL, W K

MERRILL, John N
Walking in Derbyshire: thirty-two walks in the
Peak District; described by John N. Merrill.
Clapham (Yorks.): Dalesman, 1969. 68p., illus.,
maps. 21cm. (Dalesman paperbacks)

MERRILL, W K
The survival handbook. New York: Winchester Press,
1972. 312p., illus. 20cm.

MERSEYSIDE HIMALAYAN EXPEDITION, 1977
Report, by B.C. Stroude. Wirral: The Expedition,
[1978?]. 34p., illus. 21cm.

MERTEL, Hans
BARTH, Hermann von
Einsame Bergfahrten; [edited with a postscript by
Hans Mertel]. München: A. Langen, [1925]. 230p.
20cm. (Bücher der Bildung, 21)

MERZBACHER, Gottfried
Aus den Hochregionen des Kaukasus: Wanderungen,
Erlebnisse, Beobachtungen. Leipzig: Duncker &
Humblot, 1901. 2v., plates (some fold.), illus.,
maps (in pockets). 26cm.

MERZBACHER, Gottfried
The central Tian-Shan mountains, 1902-1903.
Published under the authority of the Royal
Geographical Society, [by] Murray, 1905. ix,
285p., plates (1 fold.col.), illus., map. 24cm.

MESSISCHES INSTITUT, Neuwied
Die Schweizer-Reise des Messischen Instituts, 1845.
Neuwied: Buchdruckerei der Fürstl. Wied. Hof-Buch-
und kunsthandlung, 1847. 126p., col. plates,
illus. 16cm.

MESSNER, Reinhold
The big walls: history, routes, experiences;
translated by Audrey Salkeld. Kaye & Ward, 1978.
143p., illus. (some col.). 27cm.

MESSNER, Reinhold
The challenge; translated by Noel Bowman & Audrey
Salkeld. Kaye & Ward, 1977. 205p., illus. (some
col.), maps. 24cm.

MESSNER, Reinhold
Everest: expedition to the ultimate; translated
by Audrey Salkeld. Kaye & Ward, 1979. 254p.,
illus. (some col.). 24cm.

MESSNER, Reinhold
The seventh grade: most extreme climbing. New
York: Oxford University Press, 1974. 160p. 3 col.
plates, illus., map. 21cm.

MESSNER, Reinhold
Vita fra le pietre: popoli montanari nel mondo,
prima che soccombano; traduzione a cura ... [di]
Giuseppe Richebuono. Bolzano: Athesia, 1976.
136p., col. illus., maps. 26cm.

METCALFE, Frederick
The Oxonian in Iceland; or, Notes of travel in
that island in the summer of 1860, with a glance
at Icelandic folk-lore and sagas. Longman, Green,
Longman and Roberts, 1861. 424p., plates (1 fold.
col.), illus., maps. 22cm.

METCALFE, Frederick
The Oxonian in Norway; or, Notes of excursions
in that country in 1854-55. Hurst & Blackett,
1856. 2v., illus. 21cm.

- - 2nd ed., rev. 1857.

METCALFE, Frederick
The Oxonian in Thelemarken; or, Notes of travel
in south-western Norway in the summers of 1856
and 1857... Hurst & Blackett, 1858. 2v., illus.
21cm.

METHUEN, A
An alpine ABC and list of easy rock plants.
Methuen, 1922. x, 35p. 16cm.

METTIER, Peter
Die Bergüner Berge. Chur: Im Selbstverlage des
Verfassers, 1897. 157p., port. 19cm.

- - Neue Aufl. Samaden: Engadin Press, 1924.

MEULEN, M E van der
Mijne reis door Zwitserland, naar de Waldenzen,
in Piemont's valleijen. Utrecht: W.H. van
Heijningen, 1852. xxviii, 295p. 24cm.

MEUNIER, Stanislas
Les glaciers et les montagnes. Paris: Flammarion,
1920. 262p. 20cm. (Bibliothèque de philosophie
scientifique)

MEURER, Julius
Alpenlandschaften: Ansichten aus der deutschen,
österreichischen und Schweizer Gebirgswelt, [text
by Julius Meurer]. Leipzig: J.J. Weber, [1891].
2v. (chiefly illus.). 42cm.

MEURER, Julius and RABL, Josef
Der Bergsteiger im Hochgebirge: Alpin-touristische
Schilderungen nach den Berichten hervorragender
Hochtouristen; zusammengestellt und erläutert von
Julius Meurer und Josef Rabl. Wien: Hartleben,
1893. viii, 264p., illus. 25cm.

MEURER, Julius
Führer durch die Dolomiten. 4.Aufl. Gera:
Amthor, 1885. v, 228p., maps. 17cm. (Amthor's
Reisebücher)

MEURER, Julius
Handbuch des alpinen Sport. Wien: Hartleben,
1882. 280, xxxixp., illus., bibl. 19cm.

MEURER, Julius
A handy illustrated guide to Vienna and its
environs. Vienna: Hartleben, 1891. viii, 103p.,
plates, illus., maps. 16cm.

- - 2nd ed., rev. and enl. 1906.

MEURER, Julius
Katechismus für Bergsteiger, Gebirgtouristen,
Alpenreisende. Leipzig: J.J. Weber, 1892. viii,
261p., illus. 18cm. (Weber's illustrierte
Katechismen)

MEURER, Julius
Madonna di Campiglio, Arco, Riva und Garda-See,
mit Touren in die Brenta-Dolimiten und in die
Presanella-Adamello-Gruppe... Wien: Oesterr.
Touristen-Club, 1889. viii, 160p., plates, illus.,
maps. 17cm. (O.T.C. Touristen-Führer, 25)

MEURER, Julius
Weltreisebilder. Leipzig: Teubner, 1906. viii,
394p., plates, illus., maps. 25cm.

MEUTA, P   and RIVA, J
La Vallée d'Aoste monumentale; photographiée et
annotée historiquement par Meuta et Riva. Ivrea:
The Authors, 1869. 74p., plates, illus. 15 x
22cm.

MEYER, Hans
Hochtouren im tropischen Afrika. Leipzig:
Brockhaus, 1923. 159p., plates, illus., maps.
20cm.

MEYER, Hans
In den Hoch-Anden von Ecuador, Chimborazo, Cotopaxi
etc.: Reisen und Studien. Berlin: Reimer, 1907.
14, 552p., plates (some fold., some col.), illus.,
maps. 26cm.

- - Plates, illus. (in portfolio). Williams &
Norgate, 1908.

MEYER, Hans
Der Kilimandjaro: Reisen und Studien. Berlin:
Reimer, 1900. 436p., illus., map (in pocket).
30cm.

MEYER, Hans
Ostafrikanische Gletscherfahrten: Forschungsreisen
im Kilimandscharo-Gebiet. Leipzig: Duncker &
Humblot, 1890. xiv, 376p., plates (1 fold.col.),
illus., maps, bibl. 27cm.

MEYER, Hans
[Ostafrikanische Gletscherfahrten...]. Across
East African glaciers: an account of the first
ascent of Kilimanjaro; translated by E.H.S. Calder.
G. Philip, 1891. xx, 404p., plates (some fold.
col.), illus., maps, bibl. 26cm.

MEYER, Harold Albert
See
MERRICK, Hugh

MEYER, J   J
Les nouvelles routes par le pays des Grisons
jusqu'aux lacs Majeur et de Como en 32 vues, par
J.J. Meyer, accompagnés de texte par J.G. Ebel.
Zurich: J.J. Meyer, 1827. 169p., plates, illus.,
map. 18 x 25cm.

MEYER, J   J
Voyage pittoresque dans le canton des Grisons en
Suisse vers le Lac Majeur et le Lac de Como à
travers les cols de Splugen et de St. Bernard;
accompagné d'une introduction et explication de
J.G. Ebel. Zurich: J.J. Meyer, 1827. 336p.,
plates, illus, map. 22cm.

MEYER, Johann Rudolf and MEYER, Hieronymus
Reise auf den Jungfrau-Gletscher und Ersteigung
seines Gipfels, von Joh. Rudolf Meyer und
Hieronymus Meyer im Augustmonat 1811 unternommen.
[Aarau]: [The Authors], [1812]. 31p. 21cm.

MEYER, Johann Rudolf and MEYER, Hieronymus
Reise auf die Eisgebirge des Kantons Bern und
Ersteigung ihrer höchsten Gipfel, im Sommer 1812;
[hrsg. von Heinrich Zschokke]. Aarau: H.R.
Sauerländer, 1813. 45p., 1 fold.col. plate, map.
21cm.

MEYER, Leo
Vallées perdues.   Lausanne: Spes, 1947. 47, 47,
81p., plates, illus., maps. 24cm.
Contents: 1. Tourtemagne, texte d'après L. Meyer
[and others].-2. Binn, texte de L. Desbuisson et
E. Bohy.-3. Le Lötschental, texte de Jos. Siegen.

MEYER, Louis
Ls. Meyer's toposcopisches Panorama vom Rigi-Kulm.
2. umgearb. Aufl. Luzern: J. Kaiser, 1854. 21cm.

MEYER, Oskar Erich
Berg und Mensch: ein Buch der Andacht. Berlin:
Union Deutsche Verlagsgesellschaft, [1938].
63p., 1 plate, port. 19cm.

MEYER, Oskar Erich
Die Braut des Montblanc. Berlin: Union Deutsche
Verlagsgesellschaft, [1933]. 54p., illus., bibl.
19cm.

MEYER, Oskar Erich
Das Erlebnis des Hochgebirges. Berlin: Union
Deutsche Verlagsgesellschaft Zweigniederlassung,
1932. 165p., 1 plate, port. 22cm.

MEYER, Oskar Erich
Tat und Traum: ein Buch alpinen Erlebens.
München: Rother, 1920. 234p. 22cm.

- - 2. verm. Aufl. 1922.
- - 3. Aufl. 1928.

MEYER, Rudolf
See
MEYER, Johann Rudolf

Meyer's Volksbibliothek für Länder-, Völker- und
Naturkunde... Hindburghausen: Bibliographisches
Institut, [n.d.]. 60v. in 30, illus., maps.
14cm.

MEYERS, George
Yosemite climbs: topographic drawings of the best
rockclimbing routes in Yosemite Valley. Modesto
(Calif.): Mountain Letters, [1977]. 114p., 15
plates, illus. 22 x 28cm.

MEYERSTEIN, E   H   W
The climbers: an ode on the Eton masters who lost
their lives descending the Piz Roseg on August
17th, 1933. Metcalfe & Cooper, 1934. 5p. 28cm.

MEYNIEU, Jacques
Refuges des montagnes françaises et zones limitrophes, par Jacques Meynieu; avec la collaboration de Claude Bourleaux [and others]. Paris:
C.A.F., 1967. 273, xxvp., fold.col. plates,
illus., maps (1 in pocket). 17cm.

MICHAUD, S   Stelling
See
STELLING-MICHAUD, S

MICHAUX, F   A
Travels to the westward of the Allegany Mountains,
in the States of Ohio, Kentucky, and Tennessee,
in the year 1802... translated from the French.
R. Phillips, 1805. iv, 96p. 23cm.
(In A collection of modern and contemporary
voyages... Vol.1. 1805)

MICHEL, Albert
Bergtod und andere Gedichte. München: M.
Steinebach, [19--]. 30p. 20cm.

MICHEL, Hans
La Jungfrau; version française d'André Jaquemard.
Neuchatel: Éditions du Griffon, 1946. 48p.,
illus. 26cm. (Trésors de mon pays, 12)

MICHELET, Athénaïs
Nature; or, The poetry of earth and sea;
[translated] from the French [by W.H. Davenport
Adams]; with designs ... by Giacomelli. Nelson,
1872. xxxi, 431p., illus. 26cm. (Nelson's art
gift books)

MICHELET, Jules
La montagne; étude par André Theuriet. 3e éd.
Paris: Levy, 1899. xiii, iv, 388p. 20cm.
(Oeuvres complètes de Michelet)

MICHELET, Jules
[La montagne]. The mountain; from the French of
Michelet by the translator of 'The Bird' [W.A.D.
Adams]; with ... illustrations from designs by
Percival Skelton. Nelson, 1872. xvi, 323p.,
illus. 26cm.

MICHELET, Jules
[La montagne]. The mountain. Nelson, 1886.
260p., illus. 21cm.

MICHELET, Mme. Jules
See
MICHELET, Athénaïs

MICHIELS, Alfred
Les chasseurs de chamois. Paris: Hachette, 1860.
322p. 18cm.

MICHIGAN STATE UNIVERSITY. Glaciological Institute
EGAN, Christopher P
Resumé of the 1962 field season of the Michigan
State University Glaciological Institute, Juneau
Icefield, Alaska. 1963. 61-69p., illus., map.
24cm.
Offprint from The Compass, Sigma Gamma Epsilon,
v.41., no.1, Nov. 1963.

MIDDLETON, Dorothy
Victorian lady travellers. Routledge & Kegan Paul,
1965. xiii, 182p., 12 plates, illus., map, bibl.
23cm.

MIDLAND ASSOCIATION OF MOUNTAINEERS
BYNE, Eric
A climbing guide to Brassington rocks; with photo-
graphs by J.A. Best and F.H. Restall. Birmingham:
Midland Association of Mountaineers, 1950. 35p.,
plates, illus. 14cm.

MIDLANDS HINDU KUSH EXPEDITION, 1967
Report, written by D.K. Scott & W. Cheverst.
Nottingham: The Expedition, [1968]. 62p., plates
(some fold.), illus., maps. 25cm.

MIDOWICZ, W and AUGUSTYNOWICZ, M
Przewodnik Narciarski po beskidzie zachodnim (Babia
Gora, Pasmo Jalowieckie, Beskid Zywiecki, Beskid
Maly...). Krakow: Oddziele Polsk. Tow. Tatrz,
1928. 92p., plates (1 fold.), illus. 14cm.

MIETHE, A
DEUTSCHE ARKTISCHE ZEPPELIN-EXPEDITION, 1910
Mit Zeppelin nach Spitzbergen: Bilder von der
Studienreise der deutschen arktischen Zeppelin-
Expedition; mit einem Vorwort des Prinzen Heinrich
von Preussen; hrsg. von A. Miethe und H.Hergesell.
Berlin: Bong, 1911. 291p., col. plates, illus.
27cm.

MIÉVILLE, Sir Walter F
Letters from Norway. Brighton: Combridge;
London: Simpkin & Marshall, [1904?]. 200p., 1
plate, illus. 18cm.

MIGNAN, R
A winter journey through Russia, the Caucasion
Alps, and Georgia; thence across Mount Zagros, by
the Pass of Xenophon and the Ten Thousand Greeks,
into Koordistaun. Bentley, 1839. 2v., plates,
illus. 22cm.

MIGOT, André
Tibetan marches; translated from the French by
Peter Fleming. Hart-Davis, 1955. 288p., plates
(some col.), illus., maps. 23cm.

MILA, Massimo and TENZING NORGAY
Gli eroi del Chomolungma. Torino: Einaudi, 1954.
191p., col. plates, illus., maps. 26cm. (Nuova
Atlantide, 2)

MILBURN, Geoff
Llanberis Pass. Manchester: Climbers' Club, 1978.
160p., illus., maps (on lining papers). 18cm.
(Climbers' Club guides to Wales, 3)

MILES, Edwin J
Byeways in the southern Alps: sketches of spring
and summer resorts in Italy and Switzerland.
Zurich: Orell Füssli; London: H.K. Lewis, [1893].
120p., illus. 21cm.

MILFORD, John
Observations, moral, literary, and antiquarian,
made during a tour through the Pyrenees, South of
France, Switzerland, the whole of Italy, and the
Netherlands, in the years 1814 and 1815. Longman,
Hurst, Rees, Orme and Brown, 1818. 2v., illus.
22cm.

MILLAR, J Halket
ALACK, Frank
Guide aspiring; edited by J. Halket Millar.
Auckland: Oswald-Sealy, [1963]. 229p., plates,
illus. 23cm.

MILLAR, T G
Long distance paths of England and Wales. Newton
Abbot, London: David & Charles, 1977. 160p.,
illus., maps, bibl. 24cm.

MILLER, David
Dow Crag area; illustrated by W. Heaton Cooper.
Stockport: Fell & Rock Climbing Club, 1968. 133p.,
1 plate, illus., maps (on lining papers). 16cm.
(Climbing guides to the English Lake District,
[4th ser.],8)

MILLER, Keith J
The Cambridge Staunings Expedition, 1970. Vol.1.
General report and the glaciological projects;
editor, K.J. Miller. Cambridge: University of
Cambridge, Department of Engineering, 1971. 66
leaves, illus., 1 fold. map. 30cm.

MILLER, Keith J
A photographic album of the 1972 East Greenland
Expedition from Cambridge University, [by] K.J.
Miller. Cambridge: University of Cambridge,
Department of Engineering, 1974. 1v. (chiefly
illus.). 30cm. (CUED Special project report,
no.3)

MILLER, Leo E
In the wilds of South America: six years of ex-
ploration in Columbia, Venezuela, British Guiana,
Peru, Bolivia, Argentina, Paraguay and Brazil.
New York: Scribner, 1919. xiv, 428p., plates
(1 fold., 1 col.), illus., map. 24cm.

MILLER, Maynard M
A field institute of glaciological and expeditionary sciences in Alaska. Boston, 1963.
499-508p., illus. 24cm.
Offprint from Appalachia, June 1963.

MILLER, Maynard M
The geological and glaciological program of the
American Mt. Everest expedition, 1963. [Boston],
1963. 71-75p. 24cm.
Offprint from Harvard Mountaineering, no.16, May
1963.

MILLER, Warren H
Camp craft: modern practice and equipment; with
introduction by Ernest Thompson Seton. Batsford,
1915. xiii, 282p., plates, illus. 21cm.

MILLIN, A L
Voyage en Savoie, en Piémont, à Nice, et à Gênes.
Paris: C. Wassermann, 1816. 2v. 20cm.

MILLINGTON, Powell
To Lhassa at last. Smith, Elder, 1905. x, 200p.,
plates, illus. 20cm.

MILLS, Enos A
The Rocky Mountain wonderland. Boston: Houghton
Mifflin, [1915]. xiv, 363p., plates, illus. 21cm.

MILLS, Enos A
The spell of the Rockies. Constable, 1912. xii,
356p., plates, illus. 22cm.

MILLS, Enos A
Wild life on the Rockies. Boston: Houghton
Mifflin, 1909. xii, 263p., plates, illus. 21cm.

MILLS, James
Airborne to the mountains. Jenkins, 1961. 202p.,
plates, illus., maps. 23cm.

MILNE, Malcolm and HELLER, Mark
The book of European skiing; edited by Malcolm
Milne and Mark Heller. Barker, 1966. 304p.,
illus. (some col.). 30cm.

MILNE, Malcolm
The book of modern mountaineering; edited by
Malcolm Milne. Barker, 1968. 304p., illus. 30cm.

MILNER, Cyril Douglas
WEDDERBURN, Ernest Alexander Maclagan
Alpine climbing on foot and with ski. Manchester:
Open Air Publications, [1936]. 118p., illus.
18cm.

- - 2nd rev. ed., rev. by C. Douglas Milner.
Manchester & London: Countrygoer Books, 1954.

MILNER, Cyril Douglas
The Dolomites. Hale, 1951. xiv, 105p., plates
(1 col.), illus., maps (on lining papers),
bibl. 26cm.

MILNER, Cyril Douglas
Mont Blanc and the Aiguilles; with 70 illustrations by the author. Hale, 1955. xvi, 176p.,
65 plates (1 col.), illus., maps, bibl. 24cm.

MILNER, Cyril Douglas
Mountain photography: its art and technique in
Britain and abroad. Focal Press, 1945. 238p.,
illus., bibl. 25cm.

MILNER, Cyril Douglas
The photoguide to mountains for the backpacker
and climber. 2nd impression. Focal Press, 1978.
184p., illus. (some col.), bibl. 19cm. (Focal
photoguides)

MILNER, Cyril Douglas
[The photoguide to mountains...]. La fotografia
en la montaña: una guía para escaladores, excur-
sionistas y aficionados en general; traducido por
Antonio Juarez. Barcelona: Omega, 1980. 219p.,
illus. (some col.). 19cm.

MILNER, Cyril Douglas
Rock for climbing; illustrated with 97 photographs
by the author. Chapman & Hall, 1950. viii,
128p., illus. 26cm.

MILNER, Thomas
The gallery of nature: a pictorial and descriptive
tour through creation, illustrative of the wonders
of astronomy, physical geography and geology. New
ed. carefully rev. Orr, 1855. xii, 803p., plates,
illus. 28cm.

MILTON, William Fitzwilliam, Viscount and CHEADLE,
Walter Butler
The North-West passage by land, being the narra-
tive of an expedition from the Atlantic to the
Pacific, undertaken with a view of exploring a
route across the continent... 3rd ed. Cassell,
Petter and Galpin, 1865. xxiv, 400p.,plates (2
fold.col.), illus., maps. 23cm.

- - 5th ed. 1866.

MINELLE, Pierre
Le climat de montagne et l'ensoleillement, le ski
de compétition; leurs effets physiologiques.
Paris: A. Legrand, 1927. 106p., plates, illus.
20cm.
At head of title: Cours superieur d'éducation
physique de l'Université de Paris...

MINNEY, R   J
Midst Himalayan mists. Calcutta, London:
Butterworth, 1920. 80p., plates, illus., map.
23cm.

MINVIELLE, Pierre
À la découverte de la Sierra de Guara. Pau:
Marrimpouey, 1974. 136p., illus., maps. 22cm.

MIRBEAU, Octave
Les vingt et un jours d'un neurasthénique. Paris:
Charpentier, 1901. 435p. 19cm.

Miscellaneous observations and opinions on the
continent, by the author of "The life of Michel
Angelo" ... [i.e. Richard Duppa]. Longman, Hurst,
Rees, Orme, Brown, & Green, 1825. 214p., plates,
illus. 26cm.

MISSION SCIENTIFIQUE BELGE POUR L'EXPLORATION DU
RUWENZORI, 1932
MEERSCH, W   J   Ganshof van der
Une mission scientifique belge dans le massif du
Ruwenzori. Paris, 1933. [9]p., plates, illus.,
maps. 38cm.
Offprint from L'Illustration, 28 jan. and 4 fév.
1933.

MISSION SCIENTIFIQUE BELGE POUR L'EXPLORATION DU
RUWENZORI, 1932
Vers les glaciers de l'équateur: le Ruwenzori,
Mission scientifique belge 1932, par Xavier de
Grunne [and others]; aquarelles de James Thiriar.
Bruxelles: R. Dupriez, 1937. 300p., illus. (some
fold., some col.), maps, bibl. 28cm.

UN MISSIONNAIRE
Un coin des Himalayas, par un missionnaire.
Paris: Lefort, [1903?]. 166p., illus. 23cm.

MISSON, Maximilien
Nouveau voyage d'Italie, avec un mémoire contenant des avis utiles à ceux qui voudront faire
le mesme voyage. 4ieme éd... La Haye: H. van
Bulderen, 1702. 3v., plates, illus. 17cm.

MITCHELL, Benjamin Wiestling
Trail life in the Canadian Rockies. New York:
Macmillan, 1924. xiii, 269p., plates, illus.
21cm.

MITCHELL, Elyne
Australia's alps. Sydney, London: Angus and
Robertson, 1946. xii, 185p., plates, illus.,
maps. 25cm.

MITCHELL, Sir Harold P
Downhill ski-racing; with a preface by C.E.W.
Mackintosh. Allen and Unwin, 1931. 125p., plates,
illus. 21cm.

MITCHELL, Sir Harold P
In my stride. W. & R. Chambers, 1951. 250p.,
plates, illus. 23cm.

MITCHELL, John
Guide book to Mount Kenya and Kilimanjaro; edited
by John Mitchell. 3rd ed., completely rev.
Nairobi: Mountain Club of Kenya, 1971. 240p.,
illus., maps. 16cm.

MITCHELL, Michael A
Climbs on Yorkshire limestone; edited by Michael
A. Mitchell. Clapham (Yorks.): Dalesman, 1963.
40p., illus., maps. 22cm.

MITTELHOLZER, Walter
Alpenflug; unter Mitarbeit von H. Kempf. Zürich:
Orell Füssli,1928. 156p., 191 plates, illus.
24cm.

MITTELHOLZER, Walter
[Alpenflug]. Les ailes et les Alpes; ouvrage
publié avec la collaboration de H. Kempf; adaptation de René Gouzy. Paris: Éditions Pittoresques,
1929. 108p., 191 plates, illus. 25cm.

MITTELHOLZER, Walter
Im Flugzeug dem Nordpol entgegen: Junkers'sche
Hilfsexpedition für Amundsen nach Spitzbergen 1923;
hrsg. von Walter Mittelholzer... Zürich: Orell
Füssli, 1924. 106p., plates, illus., maps. 24cm.

MITTELHOLZER, Walter
Kilimandjaro Flug. 2.Aufl. Zürich: Orell Füssli,
1930. 102p., plates, illus. 23cm.

MITTELHOLZER, Walter
Persienflug; mit einem Nachwort von O. Flückiger;
96 Tiefdruckbildern nach Photographien vom Verfasser... Zürich: Orell Füssli, 1926. 212p.,
plates, illus., maps. 25cm.

MITTON, G   E
Austria-Hungary. Black, 1915. viii, 214p., plates,
illus., map. 23cm.

MIYOSHI, M   and MAKINO, T
Pocket-atlas of alpine plants of Japan. 2nd rev.
ed. Tokyo: Seibido, 1907. 2v. (140p.), 70 col.
plates, illus. 18cm.

MOBERLY, Walter
ROBINSON, Noel
Blazing the trail through the Rockies: the story
of Walter Moberly and his share in the making of
Vancouver, by Noel Robinson and the old man himself. Vancouver: News-Advertiser, [ca 1910].
118p., illus. 24cm.

MODLMAYR, H
Bunte Bilder aus dem obern Allgäu, Text von H.
Modlmayr; illustriert von W. Irlinger. Memmingen:
Th. Otto, 1903. 68p., plates (some col.), illus.
30cm.

MÖLLHAUSEN, Balduin
Tagebuch einer Reise vom Mississippi nach den
Küsten der Südsee; eingeführt von Alexander von
Humboldt. Leipzig: H. Mendelssohn, 1858. xv,
496p., 14 col. plates (1 fold.), illus., map.
32cm.

MÖLLHAUSEN, Balduin
[Tagebuch einer Reise...]. Diary of a journey
from the Mississippi to the coasts of the Pacific
with a United States Government expedition...;
introduction by Alexander von Humboldt; translated
by Mrs. Percy Sinnett. Longman, Brown, Green,
Longmans, & Roberts, 1858. 2v., col. plates (1
fold.), illus., map. 24cm.

MOESCH, Casimir
Der Aargauer-Jura und die nördlichen Gebiete des
Kantons Zürich: geologisch Untersucht und
Beschrieben. Bern: J. Dalp, 1867. xv, 321p.,
plates (some fold.col.), illus., bibl. 29cm.
(Beiträge zur geologischen Karte der Schweiz,
Lfg. 4)

MOESCH, Casimir
BALTZER, A
Centralgebiet der Schweiz ...; bearb. von A.
Baltzer, F.J. Kaufmann und C. Moesch. Bern:
Schmid, Francke, 1886-94. 4v. in 6, plates (some
fold., some col.), illus. 33cm. (Beiträge zur
geologischen Karte der Schweiz, Lfg. 24)
Library lacks vol.2

FELLENBERG, Edmund von and MOESCH, Casimir
Geologische Beschreibung des Westlichen Theils des
Aarmassives,enthalten auf dem nördlich der Rhone
...; mit petrographischen Beiträgen von Carl
Schmidt. Bern: Schmid, Francke, 1893. 2v. in 1.
and atlas, fold.col. plates, illus., bibl. 32cm.
(Beiträge zur geologischen Karte der Schweiz,
Lfg. 21)

MOESCH, Casimir
Geologischer Führer durch die Alpen, Passe und
Thäler der Centralschweiz. 2.Aufl. Zürich:
Raustein, 1897. iv, 120p. 16cm.

MOFFAT, Gwen
Hard option: a novel. Gollancz, 1975. 222p. 21cm.

MOFFAT, Gwen
On my home ground. Hodder & Stoughton, 1968.
256p., plates, illus. 23cm.

MOFFAT, Gwen
Over the sea to death. Gollancz, 1976. 192p.,
map. 21cm.

MOFFAT, Gwen
Space below my feet. Hodder & Stoughton, 1961.
286p., plates, illus. 21cm.

- - Another issue. Boston: Houghton Mifflin, 1961.
- - Another issue. Harmondsworth: Penguin, 1976.

MOFFAT, Gwen
Two star red: a book about R.A.F. mountain
rescue; with sketch maps and diagrams by the
author. Hodder & Stoughton, 1964. xviii, 206p.,
plates, maps. 21cm.

MOJSISOVICS VON MOJSVÁR, Edmund
Die Dolomit-Riffe von Südtirol und Venetien:
Beiträge zur Bildungsgeschichte der Alpen. Wien:
A. Hölder, 1879. xv, 552p., plates, illus., maps.
24cm.

- - Beilage: Geologische Uebersichtskarte tirolisch-
venetianischen Hochlandes zwischen Etsch und Piave.

MOLENAAR, Dee
The challenge of Rainier: a record of the explora-
tions and ascents, triumphs and tragedies, on the
Northwest's greatest mountain. Seattle: The
Mountaineers, 1971. xix, 332p., illus.; bibl.
27cm.

MOLONY, Eileen
Portraits of mountains; edited by Eileen Molony.
Dobson, 1950. 117p., plates, illus. 23cm.

MONCRIEFF, Ascott Robert Hope
The Peak country; painted by W. Biscombe Gardner;
described by A.R. Hope Moncrieff. Black, 1908.
xii, 182p., 24 plates, illus. 21cm.

MONCRIEFF, Ascott Robert Hope
Romance of the mountains, by Ascott R. Hope [i.e.
A.R. Hope Moncrieff]. J. Hogg, [1888]. viii,
376p., plates, illus. 20cm.

MONCRIEFF, Ascott Robert Hope
Seeing the world: the adventures of a young
mountaineer. Wells Gardner, Darton, 1909. vii,
296p. 22cm.

MONDINI, F
CANZIO, E
In Valpellina: escursioni e studi, [da] E. Canzio,
F. Mondini, N. Vigna. Torino: Club Alpino
Italiano, 1899. 176p., plates (1 fold.col),
illus., map. 25cm.

MONELLI, Paolo
Le scarpe al sole: cronaca di gaie e di tristi
avventure d'alpini di muli e di vino. Nuova ed.
Milano: Treves, 1930. xxiv, 269p. 20cm.

MONGLOND, André
RAMOND, Louis
[Observations faites dans les Pyrénées...].
Voyage dans les Pyrénées, précédé de La jeunesse
de Ramond par André Monglond. Lyon: H.
Lardanchet, 1927. cxlviii, 206p., plates, ports.
21cm. (Bibliothèque du bibliophile (anciens), 5)

MONITEUR DAUPHINOIS
GAUTHIER, J
En montagne: articles extraits de la collection
du "Moniteur Dauphinois" ..., 1895-97, [1897-98].
Grenoble: [Librarie Dauphinoise], 1897-8. 2v.,
illus. 21cm.

MONKHOUSE, Frank and WILLIAMS, Joe
Climber and fellwalker in Lakeland. Newton
Abbot (Devon): David & Charles, 1972. 214p., 1
col. plate, illus., maps, bibl. 24cm.

MONKHOUSE, Patrick
    On foot in the Peak. Maclehose, 1932. 196p., 9
    plates, illus. 19cm.

MONKSWELL, Mary, Baroness Monkswell
    A Victorian diarist: extracts from the journals of
    Mary, Lady Monkswell, 1873-95; edited by the Hon.
    E.C.F. Collier. Murray, 1944. xxv, 284p., plates,
    illus. 23cm.

MONMARCHÉ, Marcel
MUIRHEAD, Findlay
    The French alps; edited by Findlay Muirhead and
    Marcel Monmarché. Macmillan, 1923. xxxiv, 255p.,
    maps, plans. 16cm. (Blue guides)

MONMARCHÉ, Marcel
    Pyrénées ...; collaborateur, A. Dauzat; avec une
    introduction par F. Schrader. Nouv. éd. Paris:
    Hachette, 1919. lxxvi, 514p., illus., maps, plans.
    17cm. (Guides bleus)

MONMARCHÉ, Marcel
MUIRHEAD, Findlay
    Southern France; edited by Findlay Muirhead and
    Marcel Monmarché. Macmillan, 1926. xxxviii,
    488p., maps, plans. 16cm. (Blue guides)

MONNARD, Charles
MULLER, Jean de
    Histoire de la Confédération suisse, par Jean de
    Muller, Robert Gloutz-Blozheim et J.-J. Hottinger;
    traduite de l'allemand et continuée jusqu'à nos
    jours par Charles Monnard et Louis Vulliemin.
    Paris: Ballimore, 1837-51. 18v. 24cm.

MONNARD, Jean Pierre
GAUDIN, Jean
    Synopsis florae helveticae; opus posthumum con-
    tinuatum et editum a I.P. Monnard. Turici: Apud
    Orellium Fuesslinum, 1836. xvi, 827p. 17cm.

CINGRIA, Charles Albert and MONNIER, Paul
    Le parcours du Haut Rhône; ou, La Julienne et
    l'ail sauvage, textes et croquis pris sur la route
    par Charles-Albert Cingria et Paul Monnier.
    Fribourg: W. Egloff, 1944. 120p., col. illus.,
    map. 25cm.

MONOD, Jules
    Chamonix and Mont-Blanc; official guide book.
    Geneva: R. Burkhardt, 1913. 138p., illus., maps.
    18cm.

MONOD, Jules
    Sion, Les Mayens, Val d'Hérens, Vallée d'Hérémence,
    Evolène, Arolla; histoire, descriptions, excur-
    sions, monographie illustrée. Sion: C. Mussler,
    [1907?]. 48p., illus. 19cm. (Le Valais)

MONOD, Jules
    Zermatt et Saas-Fée: descriptions, histoire, ascen-
    sions, excursions... Genève: E. Haissly, [1904?].
    127p., 1 fold. plate, illus., map. 19cm. (Les
    hautes vallées des Alpes suisses)

MONSON, Frederick John, Baron Monson
    Views in the Department of the Isère and the High
    Alps; chiefly designed to illustrate the Memoir of
    Felix Neff by Dr. Gilly; lithographed by Louis
    Haghe, from sketches [and with descriptive text]
    by Lord Monson. W.H. Dalton, 1840. 16p., 22
    plates, illus., map. 64cm.
    Introduction in English and French.

- - Another ed. Day, [ca 1845].

MONTAGNIER, Henry Fairbanks
    A bibliography of the ascents of Mont Blanc from
    1786-1853. London, 1911. 35p. 23cm.
    Offprint from Alpine journal, v.25, no.193. Aug.
    1911.
- - A further contribution to the bibliography of
    Mont Blanc, 1786-1853. London, 1916.
    Offprint from Alpine journal, v.30, no.212, May
    1916.

MONTAGNIER, Henry Fairbanks
BAUD-BOVY, Daniel
    La Dent du Midi, Champéry et le Val d'Illiez; avec
    la collaboration de H.-F. Montagnier ...; illustra-
    tions d'après les photographies de Fred. Boissonnas.
    Genève: Art Boissonnas, 1923. 173p., plates,
    illus. 25cm.

MONTAGNIER, Henry Fairbanks
A further contribution to the bibliography of Mont
Blanc...
    See his
A bibliography of the ascents of Mont Blanc...

MONTAGNIER, Henry Fairbanks
SAUSSURE, Horace Bénédict de
    Journal d'un voyage à Chamouni & à la cime du
    Mont-Blanc, en juillet et aoust 1787, [edited by
    E. Gaillard and H.F. Montagnier]. Lyon: Audin,
    1926. xvi, 53p., plates, illus. 30cm.

GAILLARD, Émile and MONTAGNIER, Henry Fairbanks
    Lettres de H.-B. de Saussure à sa femme, commentées
    par E. Gaillard et H.F. Montagnier. Chambéry:
    Imprimeries Réunies, 1937. 129p., 1 plate, port.
    24cm.

MONTAGNIER, Henry Fairbanks
FRESHFIELD, Douglas William
    The life of Horace Benedict de Saussure, by Douglas
    W. Freshfield; with the collaboration of Henry F.
    Montagnier. Arnold, 1920. xii, 479p., plates,
    illus., maps, bibl. 25cm.

MONTAGNIER, Henry Fairbanks
SAUSSURE, Horace Bénédict de
    Le Mont-Blanc et le Col du Géant; annoté par É.
    Gaillard et Henry-F. Montagnier. Lyon: M. Audin,
    1927. 95p., plates (some fold.), illus. 30cm.

MONTAGNIER, Henry Fairbanks
    Note sur la relation de Paccard perdue. Lyon,
    1921. 24p., 1 plate, illus. 24cm.
    Offprint from Revue alpine, 4e trimestre, 1920.

MONTAGNIER, Henry Fairbanks
    Thomas Blaikie and Michel-Gabriel Paccard.
    [London], 1933. 34p., 1 col. plate, illus. 23cm.
    Offprint from Alpine journal, v.45, May 1933.

MONTAGU, Lady Mary Wortley
    Letters from the Right Honourable Lady Mary Wortley
    Montagu, 1709 to 1762; [introduction by R. Brimley
    Johnson]. Dent, 1906. xiii, 551p. 18cm.
    (Everymans Library)

MONTAGU, Lady Mary Wortley
    Letters of the Right Honourable Lady M--y W---y
    M----e, written during her travels in Europe,
    Asia and Africa ... accounts of the policy and
    manners of the Turks... A. Homer and P. Milton,
    1766. viii, 232p. 18cm.

MONTAGUE, Charles Edward
    The morning's war. Methuen, 1913. 308p. 21cm.

MONTAGUE, Charles Edward
ELTON, Oliver
    C.E. Montague: a memoir. Chatto & Windus, 1929.
    xiii, 335p., plates, illus. 23cm.
    Contains passages from his letters and war diaries.

MONTAGUE, Lady Mary Wortley
    See
MONTAGU, Lady Mary Wortley

MONTAIGNE, Michel de
    Journal du voyage de Michel de Montaigne en Italie,
    par la Suisse & l'Allemagne en 1580 & 1581, avec
    des notes par M. de Querlon. Rome: Le Jay, 1775.
    3v. 15cm.

MONTAIGNE, Michel de
    [Journal du voyage...]. The journal of Montaigne's
    travels in Italy by way of Switzerland and Germany
    in 1580 and 1581; translated and edited with an
    introduction and notes by W.G. Waters. Murray,
    1903. 3v., plates, illus. 17cm.

MONTAIGNE, Michel de
[Journal du voyage...]. L'Italia alla fine del secolo XVI: giornale del viaggio di Michele de Montaigne in Italia nel 1580 e 1581. Nuova ed. del testo francese ed italiano con note ... [di] Alessandro D'Ancona. Città di Castello: S. Lapi, 1895. xli, 719p. 20cm.

MONTANARI, Tommaso
Annibale, l'uomo, la traversata delle alpi e le prime campagne d'Italia fino al trasimeno, secondo gli antichi e la verità storica. Rovigo: The Author, 1901. 780p., fold. plates, illus., maps (some col.), bibl. 23cm.

MONTANDON, Paul
Die ersten fünfzig Jahre des Alpenklub Thun und der Sektion Blümlisalp des Schweizer Alpenklub, 3. Juni 1874 bis 2. Juni 1924: Denkschrift; verfasst in ihrem Auftrag von einigen ihrer Mit-glieder [i.e. Paul Montandon]. Glockenthal-Thun: S.A.C., [1924]. 127p., illus. 23cm.

MONTAYEUR, Charles
Voyage sentimental autour du Mont Blanc. Ptie.1. Paris: Duc, 1900. iv, 499p., plates, illus., map. 25cm.

MONTCEL, Robert Tézenas du
See
TÉZENAS DU MONTCEL, Robert

MONTÉMONT, Albert
Voyage aux Alpes et en Italie; ou, Description nouvelle de ces contrées. 4e éd., entièrement re-fondue... Paris: Bertrand, 1860. 364p. 24cm.

MONTÉMONT, Albert
[Voyage aux Alpes et en Italie] · Tour over the Alps and in Italy; translated from the French. R. Phillips, 1823. 1-78, 81-112p. 22cm.

MONTESSUS DE BALLORE, Fernand, comte de
La science séismologique: les tremblements de terre; avec une préface par Ed. Suess. Paris: Colin, 1907. vii, 579p., plates (some fold.), illus., maps, bibl. 27cm.

MONTESSUS DE BALLORE, Fernand, comte de
La sismologie moderne: les tremblements de terre. Paris: Colin, 1911. x, 284p.,plates (2 fold.), illus., maps. 20cm.

MONTESSUS DE BALLORE, Fernand, comte de
Les tremblements de terre: géographie séismolo-gique; avec une préface par A. de Lapparent. Paris: Colin, 1906. v, 475p., fold. plates, illus., maps. 27cm.

MONTFORT FABREGA, José Maria
Expedicion española Himalaya - 76: Makalu - 8,481mts., 24 de mayo 1976, [por José Ma Montfort Fabrega]. Manresa: C.E.C. Bages, 1976. [13]p., illus. 28cm.

MONTFORT FABREGA, José Maria
[Expedicion española Himalaya - 76]. Report to the Spanish Himalaya Expedition 1976: Makalu (8,481 mts.), south-east ridge, [by José Ma. Montford]. Manresa: C.E.C. Bages, 1976. 4 leaves, illus., map. 29cm.
Typescript with photographs.

MONTGOMERY, James
The wanderer of Switzerland, and other poems. 8th ed. Longman, Hurst, Rees, Orme and Brown, 1819. 167p. 17cm.

- - 9th ed. 1823.

A month at Gastein; or, Footfalls in the Tyrol, [by Walter White]. R. Bentley, [18--]. viii, 317p., illus. 19cm.

MONTIS, Robert
Kampf um den Berg: historische Bergfahrten; aus-gewählt und mit einem Vorwort versehen von Robert Montis. Graz: Styria, 1937. 239p., plates, _ illus., bibl. 19cm.

MONTOLIEU, Isabelle, baronne de
The avalanche; or, The old man of the Alps: a tale; translated from the French [of Isabelle de Montolieu]. H.N. Batten, 1829. 78p., plates, illus. 18cm.

MONTOLIEU, Isabelle, baronne de
Recueil de nouvelles. Paris, London: Colburn, 1813. 3v. 19cm.
Library has v.2 only.

MONY, A
Ascension au Pic de Néthou (Maladetta) 21 août 1859. Paris: Hennuyer, 1861. 107p. 20cm.

MONZINO, Guido
Grandes Murailles: cronaca di una spedizione alpina. Milano: Martello, 1957. 192p., illus. (some col.), maps (on lining papers). 30cm.

MONZINO, Guido
Italia in Patagonia: Spedizione italiana alle Ande patagoniche, 1957-1958. Milano: Martello, 1958. 173p., plates, illus. 30cm.

MONZINO, Guido
Kanjut Sar: atti della Spedizione G.M. '59 al Kanjut Sar, Karakorum; con monografia storico-geografica del Karakorum a cura di Pietro Meciani; osservazioni fisiologiche cliniche e psicologiche a cura di Paolo Cerretelli; note dal diario di Lorenzo Marimonti. Milano: Martello, 1961. 342p., illus., maps. 30cm.

MONZINO, Guido
La Spedizione italiana all'Everest 1973; con il resconto scientifico di Paolo Cerretelli. [Milano]: La Spedizione, 1976. 256p., col. plates, illus., maps, bibl. 38cm.

MONZINO, Guido
Spedizioni d'alpinismo in Africa: atti delle spedizioni G.M., 1959-1965. [Milano]: Mondadori, 1966. 348p., illus. (some col.), maps, bibl. 30cm.

MONZINO, Guido
Spedizioni d'alpinismo in Groenlandia: atti delle spedizioni G.M., 1960-1964. [Milano]: Mondadori, 1966. 426p., illus. (some col.), maps, bibl. 30cm.

MOORCROFT, William
Travels in the Himalayan provinces of Hindustan and the Panjab; in Ladakh and Kashmir; in Peshawar, Kabul, Kunduz and Bokhara, from 1819 to 1825, by William Moorcroft and George Trebeck; prepared for the press from original journals ... by Horace Hayman Wilson. Murray, 1841. 2v., plates (1 fold.), illus., map. 24cm.

MOORE, Adolphus Warburton
The Alps in 1864: a private journal. [N.p.]: [The Author], 1867. ix, 360p., plates, maps. 24cm.

- - Another issue; edited by Alex. B.W. Kennedy. Edinburgh: D. Douglas, 1902.
- - Another issue; edited by E.H. Stevens. Oxford: Blackwell, 1939. 2v.

MOORE, J   E   S
The Tanganyika problem:an account of the researches undertaken concerning the existence of marine animals in central Africa. Hurst and Blackett, 1903. xxiii, 371p., plates (some fold., some col.) illus., maps, bibl. 25cm.

MOORE, J   E   S
To the mountains of the moon, being an account of the modern aspect of Central Africa ... traversed by the Tanganyika expedition in 1899 and 1900. Hurst and Blackett, 1901. xvi, 350p., 1 fold.col. plate, illus., maps. 24cm.

MOORE, John
A view of the society and manners in France, Switzerland, and Germany, with anecdotes relating to some eminent characters. 4th ed., corr. W. Strahan, 1781. 2v. 22cm.

MOORE, Terris
Mt. KcKinley: the pioneer climbs. College
(Alaska): University of Alaska Press, 1967. xv,
202p., illus., maps, bibl. 25cm.

MOORE, Thomas
BYRON, George Gordon, Baron Byron
Letters and journals of Lord Byron; with notices
of his life by Thomas Moore. Murray, 1830. 2v.,
plates, port. 30cm.

MOOSER, R   Aloys and BOURGEOIS, Max
Itinéraires pour skieurs en Haute-Savoie. Genève:
Éditions de la Petite-Fusterie, 1925-29. 2v. in 1,
illus. 15cm.

FRANCO, Jean and MORA, Marius
Ski de France; avec la collaboration de Léon
Fourès. Paris: Arthaud, 1962. 318p., illus. (1
fold.). 24cm.

MORALES ARNAO, Cesar
Andinismo en la Cordillera Blanca. [Lima]:
Turismo Andino, 1968. 54p., plates, illus., maps,
bibl. 23cm.

MORDECAI, D
The Himalayas: an illustrated summary of the
world's highest mountain ranges. Calcutta: Daw
Sen, 1966. [58]p., 1 fold. plate, illus. 19 x
30cm.

MORDEN, William J
Across Asia's snows and deserts; introduction by
Roy Chapman Andrews. New York, London: Putnam,
1927. xiv, 415p., illus., maps. 25cm.

MORELAND, A   Maud
Through south Westland: a journey to the Haast and
Mount Aspiring, New Zealand. Witherby, 1911.
xix, 222p., plates (2 fold.), illus., maps. 23cm.

MORELL, J   R
Scientific guide to Switzerland. Smith, Elder,
1867. xvi, 411p, illus. 21cm.

MORENO, Francisco P
MUSEO DE LA PLATA
Notes préliminaires sur une excursion aux territoires du Nequen, Rio Negro, Chubut et Santa Cruz;
effectuées par les Sections topographique et géologique, sous la direction de Francisco P. Moreno.
La Plata: El Museo, 1897. 186p., plates (some
fold.), illus., maps. 29cm.
(Reconnaissance de la region andine, 1)

MORET, Louis
MAUS, Octave
Savoie; bois en couleurs de Louis Moret. Paris:
H. Floury, 1911. 37p., col. illus. 33cm.

MORF, C
Les pionniers du Club Alpin: étude historique.
Lausanne: Rouge & Dubois, 1875. 165p. 18cm.

MORGAN, E   Delmer
COLES, John, F.R.G.S.
Summer travelling in Iceland, being the narrative
of two journeys across the island by unfrequented
routes ...; with a chapter on Askja, by E. Delmer
Morgan. Murray, 1882. xxii, 269p., plates (2
fold.col.), illus., maps. 26cm.

MORGAN, Gerald
Ney Elias, explorer and envoy extraordinary in
High Asia. Allen & Unwin, 1971. 294p., plates,
illus., maps, bibl. 23cm.

MORGAN, John Minter
Letters to a clergyman, during a tour through
Switzerland and Italy, in the years 1846-1847.
Longman, Brown, Green, & Longmans, 1849. xi,
250p. 20cm. (Phoenix library)

MORGAN, Sydney, Lady
Italy. 3rd ed. Colburn, 1821. 3v. 22cm.

MORGAN, W   A
The "House" on sport, by members of the London
Stock Exchange; compiled and edited by W.A. Morgan.
Gale & Polden, 1898. 2v., plates, illus. 24cm.

MORGENTHALER, Hans
Ihr Berge: Stimmungsbilder aus einem Bergsteiger-
Tagebuch; mit 33 Federzeichnungen vom Verfasser.
Zürich: Orell Füssli, 1916. 144p., illus. 20cm.

MORIGGL, Josef
Anleitung zum Kartenlesen im Hochgebirge; mit besonderer Berücksichtigung der vom D.u.Ö. Alpenverein hrsg. Spezialkarten, von Josef Moriggl;
hrsg. vom Zentralausschusz des D.u.Ö. Alpenvereins.
München: D.u.Ö.A.V., 1909. 93p., plates (1 fold.
some col.), illus., maps, bibl. 23cm.

MORIGGL, Josef
Ratgeber für Alpenwanderer mit Schutzhütten-
verzeichnis der Ostalpen, von J. Moriggl; hrsg.
vom Hauptausschuss des D.u.Ö. Alpenvereins.
München: D.u.Ö.A.V., 1924. viii, 296p. 19cm.

- - 2.Aufl. 1928.

MORIGGL, Josef
Verfassung und Verwaltung des Deutschen und
Österreichischen Alpenvereins: ein Handbuch zum
Gebrauch für die Vereinsleitung und die Sektionen.
4. Ausg. ... zusammengestellt und erläutert von J.
Moriggl. München: D.u.Ö.A.V., 1928. xv, 356p.
23cm.

MORIGGL, Josef
Von Hütte zu Hütte: Führer zu den Schutzhütten der
deutschen und österreichischen Alpen ...; hrsg.
von Josef Moriggl. Leipzig: Hirzel, 1911-14.
6v., maps. 16cm.

MORIGGL, Josef
Von Hütte zu Hütte: Führer zu den Schutzhütten der
Ostalpen... 3. erw. und verb. Aufl. Leipzig:
Hirzel, 1925. xv, 378p., maps. 16cm.

MORILLOT, Paul
A travers nos Alpes: Dauphiné, par MM. Morillot,
R. Rey, Magendie; sous le patronage de M. Boirac.
Grenoble: A. Gratier, 1902. viii, 297p., illus.
19cm.
An anthology.

MORIN, Jean Antoine
Dix poèmes alpins; préface de Micheline Morin.
[N.p.]: M. Morin, [1965]. [17]p. 23cm.

MORIN, Micheline
L'alpe enchantée. Paris: Delagrave, 1951. 141p.,
col. plates, illus. 24cm.

MORIN, Micheline
Encordées; avec ... une préface de Henry de
Ségogne. Neuchatel: Attinger, 1936. xii, 187p.,
8 plates, illus. 21cm. (Montagne)

MORIN, Micheline
Everest: du premier assaut à la victoire; illustré
de A.J. Veilhan d'après les documents authentiques
des expéditions. Grenoble: Arthaud, 1953. 201p.,
illus. (some col.), maps. 21cm.

MORIN, Micheline
Everest: from the first attempt to the final
victory. Harrap, 1955. 205p., illus (some col.),
maps. 21cm.

MORIN, Micheline
Trag, le chamois; dessins de Samivel. [Paris]:
Delagrave, 1948. 125p., illus. 23cm.

MORIN, Nea
A woman's reach: mountaineering memoirs; with a
foreword by Eric Shipton. Eyre & Spottiswoode,
1968. 288p., plates, illus., maps. 23cm.

MORIS, Henri
Au pays bleu: Alpes-Maritimes; préface d'André Theuriet; illustré d'aquarelles d'Émile Costa [and others]. Paris. Plon, Nourrit, 1900. 222p., plates, illus. 34cm.

MORISON, Margaret Cotter
A lonely summer in Kashmir. Duckworth, 1904. x, 281p., plates, illus. 23cm.

MORITZI, Alexander
Die Flora der Schweiz, mit besonderer Berücksichtigung ihrer Vertheilung nach allgemein physischen und geologischen Momenten. Zürich: Verlag des Literarischen Comptoirs, 1844. xxii, 640p., 1 fold.col. plate, map. 17cm.

MORNET, Daniel
Le sentiment de la nature en France de J.-J. Rousseau à Bernardin de Saint-Pierre: essai sur les rapports de la littérature et des moeurs. Paris: Hachette, 1907. 578p., bibl. 24cm.

MORODER, Franz
Das Grödner Thal, verfasst von Franz Moroder; hrsg. von der Section Gröden des Deutschen u. Oesterreichischen Alpenvereins. St. Ulrich in Gröden: Die Sektion, 1891. 201p., map (in pocket). 18cm.

MORRELL, Jemima
See
JEMIMA, Miss

MORRIS, C   John
See
MORRIS, John

MORRIS, James
Coronation Everest. Faber & Faber, 1958. 146p., plates, illus., maps. 23cm.

NORTHEY, W   B   and MORRIS, John
The Gurkhas: their manners, customs and country; with a foreword by C.G. Bruce. Lane, 1928. xxxix, 282p., plates (1 fold.col.), illus., map. 24cm.

MORRIS, John
Hired to kill: some chapters of autobiography. Hart-Davis, 1960. 272p., maps. 23cm.

MORRIS, John
Living with Lepchas: a book about the Sikkim Himalayas. Heinemann, 1938. xiii, 312p., plates, illus., map (on lining papers). 23cm.

MORRIS, John
Traveller from Tokyo. Cresset Press, 1943. 163p. 21cm.

MORRIS, John
A winter in Nepal. Hart-Davis, 1963. 232p., plates, illus., maps, bibl. 23cm.

MORRISON-SCOTT, T   C   S
BRITISH MUSEUM (NATURAL HISTORY)
Checklist of palaearctic and Indian mammals 1758 to 1946, by J.R. Ellerman and T.C.S. Morrison-Scott. British Museum, 1951. 810p., bibl. 26cm.

MORROW, Ian F   D
The Austrian Tyrol: the land in the mountains. Faber & Faber, 1931. 336p., plates, illus., map, bibl. 23cm.

MORSE, Randy
The mountains of Canada; introduction by Andy Russell. Edmonton (Alberta): Hurtig, 1978. 144p., col. illus., bibl. 31cm.

MORTILLET, Gabriel de
Guide de l'étranger dans les départements de la Savoie et de la Haute-Savoie. Chambéry: Perrin, 1861. 479p., plates (1 fold.)., illus., map. 19cm.

MORTILLET, Gabriel de
Guide de l'étranger en Savoie. Chambéry: Perrin, 1855. xii, 479p., map. 20cm.

MORTON, John Bingham
Pyrenean, being the adventures of Miles Walker on his journey from the Mediterranean to the Atlantic. Longmans, Green, 1938. 212p., plates, illus. 23cm.

MORY, Emil
SCHWEIZERISCHE GESELLSCHAFT FÜR BALNEOLOGIE UND KLIMATOLOGIE
Health resorts of Switzerland: spas, mineral water, climatic resorts and sanatoria; edited under the auspices of the Swiss Society for Balneology and Climatology by E. Mory [and others]... 3rd ed. Zurich: Wagner, [ca 1925]. vi, 164p., plates, illus. 19cm.

MORYSON, Fynes
An itinerary, containing his ten yeeres travell through the twelve dominions of Germany,Bohmerland, Sweitzerland, Netherland, Denmarke, Poland, Italy, Turky, France, England, Scotland & Ireland. Glascow: James MacLehose, 1907. 4v., fold. plates, illus., facs. 23cm.

MOSNA, Ezio
SAT - CAI 1872-1952: pubblicazione commemorativa; edita dalla Società Alpinisti Tridentini del Club Alpino Italiano nel suo LXXX anniversario, riunendosi a Trento il LXIV Congresso Nazionale del CAI - Trento, settembre 1952; a cura di Ezio Mosna. Trento: La Società. 1952. 232p., plates (some fold.), illus., maps. 30cm.

MOSNA, Ezio
Visioni alpine III. Trento: "Trentino", 1933. 106p., illus., maps. 28cm. (Quaderno della rivista "Trentino")

MOSSO, Angelo
Fisiologia dell'uomo sulle Alpi: studi fatti sul Monte Rosa. Milano: Treves, 1897. 375p., illus. 27cm.

MOSSO, Angelo
[Fisiologia dell'uomo sulle Alpi]. Life of man on the high Alps; translated from the 2nd ed. of the Italian by E. Lough Kiesow. Fisher Unwin, 1898. xv, 342p., illus. 26cm.

MOSSO, Angelo
LABORATORII SCIENTIFICI "A. MOSSO" SUL MONTE ROSA
Travaux [des années 1903-11]; publiés par A. Mosso. Turin: H.Loescher, 1904-1912. 3v., illus. 25cm.
Title in v.2 as: Atti ... sul Monte Rosa.
Vols.2 and 3, published V. Bona.

MOTTI, Gian Piero
Rocca Sbarua e M. Tre Denti. Torino: Club Alpino Italiano, Sezione di Torino, Sottosezione GEAT, 1969. 166p., 1 fold.col. plate, illus., map. 16cm.

MOTTU, Henri
BOSSOLI, Carlo
Souvenirs de la Suisse: le Mont-Blanc et ses environs; dessinés d'après nature par Bossoli et Mottu. Genève: S. Morel, [ca 1860]. 1v. (chiefly illus.). 15 x 22cm.

MOUGIN, P
Études glaciologiques en Savoie. Paris: Imprimerie Nationale, 1925. 224p., plates (some fold.), illus., maps. 29cm. (France. Ministère de l'agriculture. Direction générale des eaux et forêts... Études glaciologiques, t.5)

MOUGIN, P   and BERNARD, C
Glacier de Tête-Tousse, les avalanches en Savoie. Paris: Imprimerie Nationale, 1922. 322p., fold. plates, illus., col. maps (in pocket), bibl. 29cm. (France. Ministère de l'agriculture. Direction générale des eaux et forêts... Études glaciologiques, t.4)

MOULAM, Anthony J   J
The Carneddau. Stockport: Climbers' Club, [1950].
123p., plates, illus., map. 16cm. (Climbing
guides to the Snowdon district, 7)

- - 2nd ed. 1966.

MOULAM, Anthony J   J
Cwm Idwal. New ed. Stockport: Climbers' Club,
1958. ix, 126p., plates, illus. 16cm. (Climbing
guides to the Snowdon district, 1)
- - Rev. and repr. ed. 1964.
MOULAM, Anthony J   J
Dartmoor. Goring, Reading: West Col, 1976. 68p.,
illus., maps. 17cm. (West Col regional climbing
guides)

HARDING, Peter R   J and MOULAM, Anthony J   J
A guide to Black rocks and Cratcliffe Tor.
Malvern: Climbers' Club, 1949. x, 27p., plates,
illus., bibl. 22cm. (Climbers' Club guides)

MOULAM, Anthony J   J
Snowdon east; natural history notes by R. Goodier;
diagrams by Steve Knott and L. Barker. Stockport:
Climbers' Club, 1970. vii, 191p., illus., maps.
16cm. (Climbers' Club guides to Wales, 9)

MOULAM, Anthony J   J
Tryfan and Glyder Fach; diagrams by A.J.J. Moulam
and J.M. Edwards. Stockport: Climbers' Club, 1956.
(1959 reprint). xi, 153p., plates, illus. 16cm.
(Climbing guides to the Snowdon district, 2)

·· ·· Rev. and repr. ed. 1964. (Climbers' Club guides
to Wales, 3)

MOULD, Daphne Desirée Charlotte Pochin
The mountains of Ireland. Batsford, 1955. 160p.,
plates, illus., map. 23cm.

MOULINIÉ, C   E   F
Promenades philosophiques et religieuses aux
environs du Mont-Blanc, précédées d'un itinéraire.
Genève: L. Sestié, 1817. xxiv, 385p. 18cm.

- - Nouv. éd., augm. d'une Promenade au Jura, et
d'une autre à l'hospice du Grand St. Bernard. 1820.

MOULTON, Louise Chandler
Lazy tours in Spain and elsewhere. Ward, Lock,
1896. x, 377p. 22cm.

MOULTON, Robert D and THOMPSON, Terry D
Chair Ladder and the south coast. Leicester:
Climbers' Club, 1975. 154p. 17cm. (Climbers'
Club guides to West Penwith, 2)
MOULTON, Robert D
Lundy rock climbs: a guide book to rock climbing
on Lundy. 2nd ed. Buckhurst Hill: The Author for
Royal Navy and Royal Marines Mountaineering Club,
1974. 122p., illus. 18cm.

MOUNSEY, Augustus H
A journey through the Caucasus and the interior of
Persia. Smith, Elder, 1872. xi, 336p., 1 fold.
plate, map. 24cm.

MOUNT EVEREST COMMITTEE
Catalogue of the exhibition of photographs and
paintings from the Mount Everest expedition 1922;
arranged by the Mount Everest Committee of the
Royal Geographical Society and the Alpine Club,
[Jan. 21 to Feb. 6, 1923]. The Committee, 1923.
16p., plates, illus. 19cm.

MOUNT PILATUS RAILWAY CO.
See
PILATUSBAHN-GESELLSCHAFT

Mountain adventures in the various countries of the
world; selected from the narratives of celebrated
travellers. Seeley, Jackson, & Halliday, 1869.
viii, 320p., plates, illus. 19cm.
"Founded on a compilation made by M.M. Zurcher and
Margollé... Les ascensions célèbres. In several
instances ... the narratives of English travellers
have been substituted".- Prefatory note.

Mountain climbing, by Edward L. Wilson [and others].
[New York]: Scribner, 1897. xi, 358p., illus.
21cm. (Out of door library)

MOUNTAIN CLUB OF KENYA
Guide book to Mount Kenya and Kilimanjaro. 2nd
ed., completely rev., edited by Ian C. Reid.
Nairobi: M.C.K., 1963. 192p., illus., map. 16cm.

- - 3rd ed., completely rev., edited by John
Mitchell. 1971.

MOUNTAIN CLUB OF KENYA
POWELL, Colin G
Guide to Ndeiya. 2nd ed. Nairobi: M.C.K., [1968].
84p., illus. 11 x 17cm.

MOUNTAIN CLUB OF KENYA
ROBSON, Peter
Mountains of Kenya. Nairobi: East African
Publishing House for M.C.K., 1969. 80p., col.
plates, illus., map, bibl. 23cm.

MOUNTAIN CLUB OF SOUTH AFRICA
FIELD, Edgar Stanley and PELLS, Edward G
A mountaineer's paradise: a guide to the mountains
of the Worcester district... Worcester (C.P.):
M.C.S.A., [1925]. [134]p., 1 fold. plate, illus.,
maps. 21cm.

MOUNTAIN CLUB OF SOUTH AFRICA. Cape Town Section
Table Mountain guide: walks and easy climbs on
Table Mountain, Devil's Peak and Lion's Head. 3rd
ed. Cape Town: The Section, 1966. 81p., plates,
illus., maps (on lining papers). 19cm.

MOUNTAIN CLUB OF UGANDA
OSMASTON, Henry A   and PASTEUR, David
Guide to the Ruwenzori: the Mountains of the Moon.
Kampala: M.C.U.; Goring, Reading: West Col, 1972.
200p., illus., maps, bibl. 18cm.

Mountain medicine and physiology: proceedings of a
symposium for mountaineers, expedition doctors
and physiologists; sponsored by the Alpine Club;
edited by Charles Clarke, Michael Ward, Edward
Williams. Alpine Club, 1975. 143p., plates,
illus., bibl. 21cm.
Cover title.

MOUNTAIN RESCUE ASSOCIATION
Mountain rescue equipment and techniques; co-
ordinated by the Mountain Rescue Association.
[New York]: American Alpine Club, 1967. 15p.,
illus. 28cm. (Mountain rescue and safety education program, article 6)

MOUNTAIN RESCUE COMMITTEE
For publications of this body before 1946 see
FIRST AID COMMITTEE OF MOUNTAINEERING CLUBS

MOUNTAINEER
See
WILSON, W

MOUNTAINEERING ASSOCIATION
The permanent school idea: a history of the progress towards a British mountaineering training
school, by J.E.B. Wright. [Mountaineering Asso-
ciation], [1963?]. [4]p., illus. 27cm.

MOUNTAINEERING ASSOCIATION
A short manual of mountaineering training, by W.C.
Burns, F. Shuttleworth and J.E.B. Wright. 6th ed.,
rev. by P.F. Gentil. The Association, 1964. 80p.
18cm.

Mountaineering in China; compiled by the People's
Physical Culture Publishing House. Peking:
Foreign Languages Press, 1965. [95]p., illus.
(some col.). 26cm.

Mountains and mountain-climbing: records of adventure
and enterprise among the famous mountains of the
world, by the author of "The Mediterranean
illustrated" ... [i.e. W.H.D. Adams]. Nelson,
1883. 415p., illus. 21cm.

MOURIER, J
Guide au Caucase. Paris: Maisonneuve, 1894.
xxiii, 202p., plates (some fold.), illus., maps.
18cm.

MOURRAL, Daniel
Glossaire des noms topographiques les plus usités
dans le sud-est de la France et les Alpes occidentales. Grenoble: X. Drevet, [18--]. 124p.
23cm. (Bibliothèque scientifique du Dauphiné)

MOUSSON, Albert
Die Gletscher der Jetztzeit: eine Zusammenstellung
und Prüfung ihrer Erscheinungen und Gesetze.
Zürich: Schulthess, 1854. 216p. 22cm.

MOXON, Margaret Louisa
Catalogue of Miss M.L. Moxon's alpine flower
studies and other paintings. [Royal Botanic
Gardens, Kew], [1924]. iv, 50 leaves. 33cm.

DUPARC, Louis and MRAZEC, Ludovic
Le massif de Trient: étude pétrographique.
Lausanne, 1894. 16p., fold. plates, illus. 23cm.
Offprint from Archives des sciences physiques et
naturelles, t.32, 15 sept. 1894.

DUPARC, Louis and MRAZEC, Ludovic
Note sur la serpentine de la Vallée de Binnen
(Valais). Paris, 1894. 8p. 23cm.
Offprint from Bulletin de la Société française de
minéralogie, t.16, no.8, 1894.

DUPARC, Louis and MRAZEC, Ludovic
Note sur les roches amphiboliques du Mont-Blanc.
Genève, 1893. 22p. 23cm.
Offprint from Archives des sciences physiques et
naturelles, t.30, sept. 1893.

DUPARC, Louis and MRAZEC, Ludovic
Nouvelles recherches sur le massif du Mont-Blanc.
Genève, 1895. 39p. 23cm.
Offprint from Archives des sciences physiques et
naturelles, t.34, oct. et nov. 1895.

DUPARC, Louis et MRAZEC, Ludovic
Recherches géologiques et pétrographiques sur le
massif du Mont-Blanc. Genève: Georg, 1898. 227p.,
plates (some fold., some col.), illus., map (in
pocket). 32cm. (Mémoires de la Société de
physique et d'histoire naturelle de Genève, t.33,
no.1)

DUPARC, Louis and MRAZEC, Ludovic
La structure du Mont-Blanc. Genève, 1893. 13p.,
fold.col. plates, illus. 23cm.
Offprint from Archives des sciences physiques et
naturelles, t.29, 15 jan. 1893.

DUPARC, Louis and MRAZEC, Ludovic
Sur quelques bombes de l'Etna, provenant des éruptions de 1886 et 1892. Genève: [The Authors],
[1895?]. 3p. 27cm.

DUPARC, Louis and MRAZEC, Ludovic
Sur quelques bombes volcaniques de l'Etna des
éruptions de 1886 et 1892. Genève, 1892. 7p.,
plates, illus. 23cm.
Offprint from Archives des sciences physiques et
naturelles, t.29, 15 mars 1893.

MUDDOCK, J E
The "J.E.M." guide to Switzerland: the Alps and
how to see them; edited by J.E. Muddock. 2nd ed.
London: [N.pub.], 1882. 20, cxxx, 274p., plates,
illus., maps. 18cm.

- - 6th ed., rev. and corr. 1886.
- - 8th ed., rev. and corr. 1890.

HALLBERG, F and MUCKENBRUNN, H
Le ski par la technique moderne; avec une étude
sur la physiologie du ski et une préface par A.
Latarjet. 3e. éd. Grenoble: Arthaud, 1932.
430p., illus. 22cm.

HALLBERG, F and MUCKENBRUNN, H
[Le ski par le technique moderne]. The complete
book of ski-ing; English translation by Brian
Lunn. Arnold, 1936. 317p., col. plates, illus.
24cm.

MÜHRY, Adalbert Adolf
Die Schweiz: Notizen über ihre Bereisung, ihre
wissenschaftlich-geographische Erforschung und
ihre Abbildung in Karte und Bild; [Bemerkungen
über die ersten Ergebnisse des Schweizer meteoro-
logischen Beobachtungs-Systems in Winter-Trimester
1863/64 von A. Mühry]. [Gotha]: [J. Perthes],
1864. 361-384p., plates, illus. 28cm.

MÜLLER, Albert
Geognostische Skizze des Kantons Basel und der
angrenzenden Gebiete... Neuenburg: F. Marolf,
1862. v, 71p., 2 fold. plates, illus. 29cm.
(Beiträge zur geologischen Karte der Schweiz, 1)

MÜLLER, Fred
SCHWEIZER ALPEN-CLUB. Sektion Bern
Hochgebirgsführer durch die Berner Alpen. Bd.2.
Gemmi bis Petersgrat. 6 Aufl., bearb. von Fred
Müller und W. Diehl. Zürich: S.A.C., 1976.
128p., illus., maps (on lining papers), bibl.
17cm. (Clubführer des Schweizer Alpen-Club)

MÜLLER, Fritz
Firn und Eis der Schweizer Alpen: Gletscher-
inventar, von Fritz Müller, Toni Caflisch, Gerhard
Müller. Zürich: Geographisches Institut, 1976.
2v., 1 fold. plate, illus., maps. 30cm.
(Geographisches Institut. Publ. nr.57)
At head of title: ETH: Eidgenössische Technische
Hochschule Zürich.

MÜLLER, Fritz
Preliminary report 1961-1962 by F. Müller and
others. Montreal: McGill University, 1963. xiv,
241p., illus., maps, bibl. 29cm. (Axel Heiberg
Island research reports; Jacobsen-McGill arctic
research expedition 1959-1962)

- - Map supplement.

MÜLLER, Hermann
Alpenblumen, ihre Befruchtung durch Insekten und
ihre Anpassungen an dieselban. Leipzig: Engelmann,
1881. iv, 612p., illus. 25cm.

MÜLLER, Johannes
Wegweiser für die Hohe Tatra. Breslau: Müller &
Seiffert, [for] Karpatenverein, Sektion Schlesien,
1905. 66p., 1 fold.col. plate, illus., map. 18cm.

MÜLLER, Karl
Ansichten aus den deutschen Alpen: ein Lehrbuch
für Alpenreisende, ein Naturgemälde für alle
Freunde der Natur. Halle: G. Schwetschke, 1858.
xvi, 452p., plates (1 fold.col.), illus., map.
21cm.

MÜLLER, Wilhelm
Topographical and military description of Germany
and the surrounding country. The Author, 1813.
vii, 114p., map. 16cm.

MÜNTER, Friederike Brun
Tagebuch einer Reise durch die östliche, südliche
und italienische Schweiz; ausgearbeitet in den
Jahren 1798 und 1799 von Friederike Brun geb.
Münter. Kopenhagen: F. Brummer, 1800. 540p., 3
plates, illus. 19cm.

MÜNZER, Kurt
Der gefühlvolle Baedeker: auch ein Handbuch für
Reisende durch Deutschland, Italien, die Schweiz
u. Tirol; mit zwölf Faksimile-Wiedergaben ... und
Zeichnungen von Hermann Struck. Berlin: Vita,
1911. 333p., plates, illus. 20cm.

MUIR, John
The mountains of California. Unwin, 1894. xv,
381p., illus., maps. 21cm.

- - Another issue. New York: Century, 1894.

MUIR, John
My first summer in the Sierra. Constable, 1911.
viii, 354p., plates, illus. 22cm.

MUIR, John
Steep trails; edited by William Frederic Badè.
Boston, Houghton Mifflin, 1919. xi, 391p., plates,
illus. 22cm.

MUIR, John
Stickeen. Boston: Houghton Mifflin, 1909. 74p.
20cm.

MUIR, John
Travels in Alaska. Boston: Houghton Mifflin, 1915.
329p., plates, illus. 22cm.

MUIR, John
WOLFE, Linnie Marsh
John of the mountains: the unpublished journals of
John Muir; edited by Linnie Marsh Wolfe. Boston:
Houghton Mifflin, 1938. xxiii, 459p., plates,
illus. 23cm.

MUIR, John
YOUNG, S   Hall
Alaska days with John Muir. New York, London:
Revell, 1915. [4th ed.]. 226p., plates, illus.,
map. 20cm.

MUIRHEAD, Findlay and MONMARCHE, Marcel
The French alps; edited by Findlay Muirhead and
Marcel Monmarché. Macmillan, 1923. xxxiv, 255p.,
maps, plans. 16cm. (Blue guides)

MUIRHEAD, Findlay
Ireland; edited by Findlay Muirhead. Benn, 1932.
lxxx, 279, 31p., plates (some col.), illus., maps.
16cm. (Blue guides)

MUIRHEAD, Findlay
Northern Spain, with the Balearic Islands; edited
by Findlay Muirhead. Macmillan, 1930. cxix,
345p., plates (some fold., some col.), maps. 16cm.
(Blue guides)

MUIRHEAD, Findlay and MONMARCHE, Marcel
Southern France; edited by Findlay Muirhead and
Marcel Monmarché. Macmillan, 1926. xxxviii,
488p., maps, plans. 16cm. (Blue guides)

MUIRHEAD, Findlay
BERTARELLI, L   V
Southern Italy including Rome, Sicily and Sardinia,
by L.V. Bertarelli; edited by Findlay Muirhead.
Macmillan, 1925. lxxii, 531p., maps, plans. 16cm.
(Blue guides)

MUIRHEAD, Findlay
Switzerland with Chamonix and the Italian lakes;
edited by Findlay Muirhead. Macmillan, 1923.
lviii, 512p., maps, plans. 17cm. (Blue guides)

MUIRHEAD, Findlay
Wales; edited by Findlay Muirhead. Macmillan,
1922. lvi, 260p., plates (some fold., some col.),
maps, plans. 16cm. (Blue guides)

MUIRHEAD, James F
A wayfarer in Switzerland. 3rd ed., rev. Methuen,
1930. x, 236p., plates, illus. 20cm.

MUIRHEAD, Litellus Russell
Bernese Oberland and Lucerne; edited by L. Russell
Muirhead. Benn, 1963. l, 110p., maps, plans.
17cm. (Blue guides)

MUIRHEAD, Litellus Russell
Northern Italy, from the Alps to Florence; edited
by L.Russell Muirhead. 3rd ed. Benn, 1937.
xlviii, 517p., plates, maps, plans. 16cm. (Blue
guides)

MUIRHEAD, Litellus Russell
Switzerland; edited by L. Russell Muirhead. 3rd
ed. Benn, 1952. lxiv, 473p., maps. 17cm. (Blue
guides)

MUKHIN, A   S   and GUSEV, V   F
Fanskie gory. Moskva: Gos. Izd. Geograficheskoi
Literatury, 1949. 152p., fold.plates, illus.,
maps, bibl. 21cm.

MULGREW, Peter
No place for men. N. Vane, 1965. 199p., plates,
illus. 23cm.

MULLER, August
A travers l'Oberland bernois. Mulhouse: H.
Stuckelberger, 1891. 355p. 20cm.

MULLER, August
Suisse et Lombardie: souvenirs de vacances, août
1865. Mulhouse: H. Stuckelberger, 1890. 497p.
20cm.

MULLER, Edwin
They climbed the Alps. New York: Cape & Harrison
Smith, 1930. 217p., plates, illus., bibl. 23cm.

- - Another issue. London: Cape, 1930.

MULLER, J   W
First aid to naturers. New York: Platt & Peck,
[1913]. 240p., illus. 19cm.

MULLER, Jean de
Histoire de la Confédération suisse, par Jean de
Muller, Robert Gloutz-Blozheim et J.-J. Hottinger;
traduite de l'allemand, et continuée jusqu'à nos
jours par Charles Monnard et Louis Vulliemin.
Paris: Ballimore, 1837-51. 18v. 24cm.

MUMELTER, Hubert
Berg-Fibel; die Zeichnungen stammen von Hubert
Mumelter. Berlin: Rowohlt, 1934. 96p., col.
illus. 21cm.

MUMM, Arnold Louis
The Alpine Club register, 1857-[1890], Arnold,
1923-28. 3v. 23cm.

MUMM, Arnold Louis
Five months in the Himalaya: a record of mountain
travel in Garhwal and Kashmir. Arnold, 1909.
xv, 263p., plates (some fold.), illus., maps.
26cm.

MUMMERY, Albert Frederick
My climbs in the Alps and Caucasus. Fisher
Unwin, 1895. xii, 360p., plates, illus. 28cm.

- - 2nd ed., 4th impression; with an introduction
by Mrs. Mummery and an appreciation by J.A.
Hobson. 1908.
- - Another issue. Nelson, [1908].
- - Another issue. Oxford: Blackwell, 1936.

MUMMERY, Albert Frederick
[My climbs in the Alps and Caucasus]. Mes escalades dans les Alpes et le Caucase; ouvrage
traduit ... par Maurice Paillon. Paris: L.
Laveur; Londres: Fisher Unwin, 1903. xl, 327p.,
plates, maps. 25cm.

- - Another ed. Grenoble: Didier & Richard, 1936.

MUMMERY, Albert Frederick
UNSWORTH, Walter
Tiger in the snow: the life and adventures of
A.F. Mummery. Gollancz, 1967. 126p., plates,
illus., maps, bibl. 23cm.

MUNCHAUSEN, Baron
GEORGE, Hereford Brooke and MATHEWS, Charles Edward
Munchausen on the Jungfrau. Printed by Spottis-
woode, [ca 1870]. 6p. 22cm.
Signed H.B.G.-C.E.M. i.e. H.B. George and C.E.
Mathews.

MUNDAY, Don
Mt. Garibaldi Park: Vancouver's alpine playground.
Vancouver: The Author, 1922. 47p., illus. 18cm.

MUNDAY, Don
The unknown mountain. Hodder & Stoughton, 1948.
xx, 268p., plates (1 fold.), illus., map. 23cm.
The ascent of Mount Waddington.

- - Another issue. Seattle: The Mountaineers, 1975.

MUNDELL, Frank
Stories of alpine adventure. Sunday School Union,
[1898]. 158p., illus. 19cm.

MUNRO, Sir Hugh
Munro's tables of the 3000-feet mountains of
Scotland, and other tables of lesser heights.
[New ed.]. Edinburgh: Scottish Mountaineering
Club, [1953]. 80p. 23cm. (Scottish Mountaineer-
ing Club guides)

MUNRO, Sir Hugh
Munro's tables of the 3000-feet mountains of
Scotland and other tables of lesser heights;
revised by J.C. Donaldson and W.L. Coats. Rev.
ed. Edinburgh: Scottish Mountaineering Trust,
1969. 96p., illus. 22cm. (Scottish
Mountaineering Club district guide books)

- - Metric ed., edited and revised by J.C. Donaldson.
1974.

MUNRO, Sir Hugh
GILBERT, Richard
Memorable Munros: an account of the ascent of the
3,000 ft. peaks in Scotland. Easingwold, York:
Printed by G.H. Smith, 1976. 100p., illus. 22cm.

MUNSTER, Gottlieb Kypseler de
See
RUCHAT, Abraham

MUNTER, Werner
Moderne Seilsicherung in der Experimentierphase:
zur Problematik der dynamischen Sicherungsmethoden.
Bern: Akademischer Alpenclub, 1971. 24p., illus.,
bibl. 21cm.
Beilage zum 66. Jahresbericht des Akademischen
Alpenclubs Bern.

MUNTHE, Axel
Memories & vagaries. Murray, 1908. vii, 227p.
20cm.
Contains: Mont Blanc, King of the Mountains.

MURAYAMA, Masayoshi
JAPANESE ANTARCTIC RESEARCH EXPEDITION, 1968-69
Report of the Japanese traverse Syowa-South Pole,
1968-1969; edited by Masayoshi Murayama. Tokyo:
Polar Research Center, National Science Museum,
1971. xii, 279p., plates (1 fold., some
col.), illus., maps, bibl. 27cm. (Scientific
reports. Special issue, no.2)

MURCHISON, Sir Roderick Impey
On the distribution of the superficial detritus of
the Alps, as compared with that of northern Europe.
[London, 1850]. 4p. 22cm.
Offprint from Quarterly journal of the Geological
Society of London, v.6, 1850.

MURCHISON, Sir Roderick Impey
On the earlier volcanic rocks of the papal states
and the adjacent parts of Italy. London, 1850.
282-310p., illus. 22cm.
Offprint from Quarterly journal of the Geological
Society of London, v.6, 1850.

MURCHISON, Sir Roderick Impey
On the former changes of the Alps. [London, 1851].
7p. 22cm.
Offprint from Royal Institution of Great Britain.
Weekly evening meeting, March 7, 1851.

MURCHISON, Sir Roderick Impey
On the geological structure of the Alps, Apennines
and Carpathians, more especially to prove a tran-
sition from secondary to tertiary rocks and the
development of Eocene deposits in southern Europe.
London, [1849]. 157-312p., plates, illus. 23cm.
Offprint from Quarterly journal of the Geological
Society of London, Dec., 1848.

MURCHISON, Sir Roderick Impey
On the vents of hot vapour in Tuscany and their
relations to ancient lines of fracture and erup-
tion. London, 1850. 18p., illus. 22cm.
Offprint from Quarterly journal of the Geological
Society of London, v.6, Nov. 1850.

SEDGWICK, Adam and MURCHISON, Sir Roderick Impey
A sketch of the structure of the eastern Alps;
with sections through the newer formations on the
northern flanks of the chain and through the
tertiary deposits of Styria. [London, 1831].
301-424p., plates (some fold., some col.), illus.,
map. 30cm.
Offprint from Geol. trans., 2nd series, v.3, 1831.

MURCHISON, Sir Roderick Impey
GEIKE, Archibald
Life of Sir Roderick I. Murchison based on his
journals and letters, with notices of his scientific contemporaries and a sketch of the rise and
growth of palaeozoic geology in Britain. Murray,
1875. 2v., illus., ports., bibl. 23cm.

MURDOCH, Nina
Tyrolean June: a summer holiday in Austrian Tyrol;
with 32 photographic studies by Adalbert Defner.
Harrap, 1936. 280p., plates, illus. 23cm.

MURICCE, F   Carega di
See
CAREGA DI MURICCE, F

MURILLO, Gerardo
See
ATL, Dr.

MURITH, Laurent Joseph
Le guide du botaniste qui voyage dans le Valais,
avec un catalogue des plantes de ce pays et de ses
environs... Lausanne: H. Vincent, 1810. viii,
108p. 26cm.

MURPHY, Arthur
Comedy of the way to keep him; with a critique by
R. Cumberland. Cooke's ed. C. Cooke, [18--].
102p. 15cm.

MURPHY, Lady Blanche
Down the Rhine. Cleveland (Ohio), [1890?].
75p., illus. 24cm.
(In Whymper, Edward. Scrambles amongst the Alps)

MURPHY, Dervla
The waiting land: a spell in Nepal. Murray, 1967.
ix, 216p., plates, illus., map. 23cm.

MURPHY, Dervla
Where the Indus is young: a winter in Baltistan.
Murray, 1977. 266p., plates, illus., map, bibl.
23cm.

MURPHY, Thomas D
Three wonderlands of the American West, being the
notes of a traveler concerning the Yellowstone
Park, the Yosemite National Park... Boston (Mass.):
Page, 1912. 180p., plates (some col.), illus.,
maps. 25cm.

MURRAY, Charles Adolphus, 7th Earl of Dunmore
See
DUNMORE, Charles Adolphus Murray, 7th Earl of

MURRAY, Geoffrey
The gentle art of walking; with illustrations by
Clifford Webb. Blackie, 1939. x, 307p., illus.,
bibl. 21cm.

MURRAY, George William
Dare me to the desert. Allen & Unwin, 1967.
214p., plates, illus., maps. 23cm.

MURRAY, H
Historical account of discoveries and travels in
Asia from the earliest ages to the present time.
Edinburgh: Constable, 1820. 3v., maps. 24cm.

MURRAY, James Erskine
A summer in the Pyrénées. J. Macrone, 1837. 2v.,
plates, illus. 23cm.

- - 2nd ed. 1837.

MURRAY, John
A glance at some of the beauties and sublimities
of Switzerland, with excursive remarks on the
various objects of interest, presented during a
tour through its picturesque scenery. Longman,
Rees, Orme, Brown & Green, 1829. xi, 282p. 20cm.

MURRAY, William Hutchison
ULLMAN, James Ramsey
The age of mountaineering; with a chapter on
British mountains by W.H. Murray. Collins, 1956.
384p., plates, illus., maps, bibl. 22cm.
Based on the author's High conquest.

MURRAY, William Hutchison
The companion guide to the West Highlands of
Scotland: the seaboard from Kintyre to Cape Wrath.
2nd ed. Collins, 1969. 415p., plates, illus.,
maps, bibl. 22cm. (Companion guides)

MURRAY, William Hutchison and WRIGHT, Jeremiah
Ernest Benjamin
The craft of climbing. N. Kaye, 1964. 77p.,
plates, illus. 23cm.

- - Another issue. Mountaineering Association, 1964.

MURRAY, William Hutchison
Mountaineering in Scotland. Dent, 1947. xiii,
252p., plates, illus., maps. 23cm.

- - New ed. 1962.

MURRAY, William Hutchison
Mountaineering in Scotland and Undiscovered
Scotland. Diadem Books, 1979. 2v. in 1, plates,
illus., maps. 23cm.
"A compilation of two books ... originally
published in 1947 and 1951". - t.p.

MURRAY, William Hutchison
Rock climbs: Glencoe and Ardgour. Edinburgh:
Scottish Mountaineering Club, 1949. 164p., illus.,
maps. 17cm. (Scottish Mountaineering Club
[climbers' guide books])

MURRAY, William Hutchison
The Scottish Highlands. Edinburgh: Scottish
Mountaineering Trust, 1976. 301p., plates, illus.,
maps, bibl. 22cm. (Scottish Mountaineering Club
district guide books)

MURRAY, William Hutchison
The Scottish Himalayan Expedition. Dent, 1951.
xiii, 282p., plates (some col.), illus., maps.
22cm.

MURRAY, William Hutchison
The story of Everest. Dent, 1953. ix, 193p.,
plates, illus., maps, bibl. 23cm.

- - 3rd ed. 1953.

MURRAY, William Hutchison
Undiscovered Scotland: climbs on rock, snow, and
ice; illustrated by Robert Anderson. Dent, 1951.
viii, 232p., plates, illus., maps. 22cm.

MUSÉE ALPIN SUISSE
See
SCHWEIZERISCHES ALPINES MUSEUM

MUSÉE CANTONAL DES BEAUX-ARTS, Lausanne
5e Exposition suisse d'art alpin; organisée par le
Club Alpin Suisse, du 26 mai au 23 juin 1946.
Lausanne: C.A.S., 1946. 32p., 8 plates, illus.
21cm.

MUSÉE DE CHAMONIX
Catalogue descriptif illustré. [Chamonix]: Le
Musée, 1927. 57p., illus. 18cm.

MUSEO DE LA PLATA
Notes préliminaires sur une excursion aux territoires du Nequen, Rio Negro, Chubut et Santa Cruz;
effectuée par les Sections topographique et géologique, sous la direction de Francisco P. Moreno.
La Plata: El Museo, 1897. 186p., plates (some
fold.), illus., maps. 29cm. (Reconnaissance de
la région andine, 1)

MUSGRAVE, George M
A pilgrimage into Dauphiné; comprising a visit to
the monastery of the Grand chartreuse; with
anecdotes, incidents, and sketches from twenty
departments of France. Hurst & Blackett, 1857.
2v., plates, illus. 20cm.

MUSGROVE, Charles D
Holidays and how to use them. Bristol: J.W.
Arrowsmith; London: Simpkin, Marshall, Hamilton,
Kent, 1914. viii, 205p. 19cm.

MUSSET, Alfred de
Poésies nouvelles, 1836-52. Nouv. éd. Paris:
Bibliothèque Charpentier, 1905. 324p. 19cm.

MUSSET PATHAY, Victor Donatien de
Voyage en Suisse et en Italie, fait avec l'Armée
de Réserve, par V.D.M. [i.e. V.D. Musset Pathay].
Paris: Moutardier, 1800. viii, 320p. 22cm.

MUSSON, Spencer C
The Engadine. Black, 1924. 64p., 7 col. plates,
illus., maps. 23cm. (Beautiful Europe)

MUSSON, Spencer C
The Upper Engadine; painted by J. Hardwicke Lewis;
described by Spencer C. Musson. Black, 1907.
xii, 212p., 25 plates (1 fold., some col.),
illus., map. 21cm. (Black's smaller series of
beautiful books)

MUSTON, A   J
[Report of the] British Army Axel Heiberg Expedition, [by A.J. Muston and others]. Donnington:
The Expedition, [1972]. 1v. (various pagings),
1 fold. plate, illus., maps. 30cm.

MUSTON, A   J
Report of the British Army West Greenland Expedition, 1971, [by A.J. Muston and others].
[Donnington]: The Expedition, [1971?]. 1v.
(various pagings), illus., maps. 30cm.

MUSTON, Alexis
The Israel of the Alps: a history of the persecu-
tions of the Waldenses; translated from the
French. 2nd ed. Ingram, Cooke, 1853. viii,
312p., plates, illus., map. 20cm.

MYRBACH, Otto
Wanderers Wetterbuch: Einführung in das Verständnis
der Wettervorgänge; mit einem Beitrag von Peter
Lautner. Leipzig: Berg & Buch, [1931]. 184p.,
illus., chart (in pocket). 18cm.

N***, comte de
Essais sur les montagnes par le C. de N***.
Amsterdam: [n.pub.], 1785. 2v. 22cm.
Vol.2 has title: Suite des essais sur les montagnes.

N., D.J.F.
See
NEWALL, David J   F

NAC, Paul and TOURS, Constant de
Vingt jours en Suisse: 160 dessins ...; par Paul
Nac. Paris: May & Motteroz, [1892]. 160p.,
illus., maps. 14 x 23cm. (Collection des guides-
albums du touriste)

NAEF-BLUMER, Ed
Clubführer durch die Glarner-Alpen. Schwanden:
Schweizer Alpen-Club, 1902. x, 228p., illus.
18cm.

- - 2. Aufl. 1912.
- - 3. Aufl. 1913.
- - 4. Aufl. 1920.
- - 6. Aufl., neu überarbeitet von Mathias Jenni-
Züblin; Anhang: Skiführer durch die Glarneralpen,
redigiert von P. Tschudi und Mathias Jenni. 1949.
- - 7. Aufl., neu überarbeitet von Mathias Jenni-
Züblin, Walter Wild-Merz; Anhang: Skiführer durch
die Glarner Alpen. 1963.

NAES, Arne
Opp stupet til Osttoppen av Tirich Mir. Oslo:
Gyldendal Norsk Forlag, 1964. 127p., plates (some
col.), illus., maps. 24cm.

NAGANO MOUNTAINEERING ASSOCIATION
Informe de la expedicion a los Andes peruanos de
la Asociacion Alpinista de Nagano 1967. Nagano:
The Association, 1970. 444p., illus., maps,
music. 25cm.
In Japanese with a summary in English.

- - Maps.

NAILLEN, A   van der
On the heights of Himalay. 6th ed. New York:
R.F. Fenno, 1900. 272p. 20cm.

NAISMITH, W   W
The islands of Scotland (excluding Skye); edited
by W.W. Naismith. Edinburgh: Scottish
Mountaineering Club, 1934. 135p., plates (some
fold., some col.), illus., maps, bibl. 23cm.
(Scottish Mountaineering Club guides)

- - 2nd ed., edited by W.W. Naismith and E.W. Hodge.
1952.

NAKAO, Sasuke
Living Himalayan flowers; the introduction by Siro
Kitamura. Tokyo: Mainichi, 1964. 194p., col.
illus., map. 27cm.
In Japanese and English.

NAMUR, Paul Franz
SCHWARTZ, Myrtil
Vers l'idéal par la montagne: souvenir de mes escalades de haute montagne en Europe et en Amérique;
illustrations de Paul-Franz Namur; préface de Mme
P.-F. Namur-Vallot. Paris: Dupont, 1924. 167p.,
plates, illus. 29cm.

NANSEN, Fridtjof
Durch den Kaukasus zur Wolga. Leipzig: Brockhaus,
1930. 184p., plates, illus., maps. 24cm.

NANSEN, Fridtjof
"Farthest North", being the record of a voyage of
exploration of the ship, Fram, 1893-96 and of a
fifteen months' sleigh journey... Constable, 1897.
2v., plates (some fold., some col.), illus. 26cm.

NATIONAL GEOGRAPHIC SOCIETY
TARR, Ralph Stockman and MARTIN, Lawrence
Alaskan glacier studies of the National Geographic
Society in the Yakutat Bay, Prince William Sound
and lower Copper River regions, based upon the
field work in 1909, 1910, 1911 and 1913 by National
Geographic Society Expeditions. Washington (D.C.):
National Geographic Society, 1914. xxvii, 498p.,
plates (some fold.col.), illus., maps (in pocket).
27cm.

NATIONAL LIBRARY OF SCOTLAND
Shelf-catalogue of the Lloyd Collection of alpine
books. Boston (Mass.): G.K. Hall, 1964. 1v.
(various pagings). 21 x 26cm.
Photocopy.

NATIONAL MOUNTAINEERING CENTRE
See
PLAS Y BRENIN NATIONAL MOUNTAINEERING CENTRE

NATIONAL TRUST FOR SCOTLAND
Glencoe and Dalness ...: guide book. Edinburgh:
National Trust for Scotland, 1951. 64p., illus.,
maps, bibl. 19cm.

NATO, Giovanni
FASANA, Eugenio
Uomini di sacco e di corda: pagine di alpinismo;
raccolte a cura di Giovanni Nato. Milano: Società
Escursionisti Milanesi, 1926. xxiv, 401p., plates,
illus. 27cm.

NATURFORSCHENDE GESELLSCHAFT IN SOLOTHURN
Naturhistorische Alpenreise; vorgelesen der
Naturforschenden Gesellschaft in Solothurn von
ihrem Vorsteher Fr. Jos. Hugi. Solothurn: Amiet-
Lutiger, 1830. xviii, 378p., plates (some fold.,
some col.), illus., maps. 21cm.

NAU, Norbert
Der Krieg in der Wischberggruppe: Berichte
einstiger Mitkämpfer; hrsg. von Norbert Nau.
Graz: Leykam, 1937. 100p., plates (1 fold.),
illus. 23cm.

NAUMOV, Aleksandr Fedorovich
Tsentral'nyi Kavkaz, raion Bezengi. Moskva: Izd.
"Fizkul'tura i Sport", 1967. 231p., maps. 21cm.

NAVEZ, Louis
En Suisse: Davos - Montreux. Bruxelles: A.-N.
Lebègue, [1881?]. 161p. 20cm.

NAWRATH, Alfred
Im Reiche der Medea: kaukasische Fahrten und
Abenteuer. Leipzig: Brockhaus, 1924. x, 254p.,
plates, illus., maps. 20cm.

NAZAROFF, Pavel Stepanovich
Hunted through central Asia; rendered into English
from the Russian ... by Malcolm Burr. Blackwood,
1932. xi, 332p., 1 plate, map (on lining paper),
port. 21cm.

NEALE, Erskine
Sunsets and sunshine; or, Varied aspects of life.
Longman, Green, Longman and Roberts, 1862. xii,
376p. 20cm.

NEAME, J   Armstrong
Among the meadow and alpine flowers of Northern
Italy. Mortiboy's, 1937. 192p., col. plates,
illus. 22cm.

Near home; or, The countries of Europe described,
with anecdotes and numerous illustrations, by the
author of "The peep of day", &c. [i.e. Favell L.
Bevan]. J. Hatchard, 1849. xvi, 386p., plates,
illus., map. 18cm.

- - 6th ed., carefully rev. Longmans, Green, 1902.

NEATE, William R
Mountaineering and its literature: a descriptive
bibliography of selected works published in the
English language, 1744-1976. Milnthorpe (Cumbria):
Cicerone Press, 1978. 165p., illus. 25cm.

NEBESKY-WOJKOWITZ, René von
Where the gods are mountains: three years among
the people of the Himalayas; translated from the
German by Michael Bullock. Weidenfeld and
Nicolson, 1956. 256p., plates,illus., maps. 24cm.

NEDERLANDSCHE ALPEN-VEREENIGING
Een halve eeuw Nederlands alpinisme, 1902-1952.
Leiden: N.A.V., 1952. 129p., 16 plates, illus.
27cm.

NEERGAARD, Tønnes Christian Bruun-
See
BRUUN-NEERGAARD, Tønnes Christian

NEFF, Felix
GILLY, William Stephen
A memoir of Felix Neff, pastor of the High Alps,
and of his labours among the French protestants of
Dauphiné, a remnant of the primitive christians of
Gaul. 3rd ed. J.G. & F. Rivington, 1833. xvi,
351p., 1 fold. plate, map. 17cm.

NEFF, Felix
MONSON, Frederick John, Baron Monson
Views in the Department of the Isère and the high
Alps, chiefly designed to illustrate the Memoir
of Felix Neff by Dr. Gilly; lithographed by Louis
Haghe, from sketches [and with descriptive text]
by Lord Monson. W.H. Dalton, 1840. 16p., 22
plates, illus., map.
Introduction in English and French.

- - Another ed. Day, [ca 1845].

NÈGRE, R
Petite flore des régions arides du Maroc occidental. Paris: C.N.R.S., 1961-62. 2v., col.
plates (1 fold.), illus., maps. 24cm.

NEGRI, Arturo
Carta geologica della provincia di Vicenza;
pubblicata per cura della Sezione di Vicenza del
C.A.I. Vicenza: C.A.I., 1901. 110p., fold.col.
map, bibl. 22cm.

NEGRI, N   C
The valley of shadows: the story of an Arctic
expedition. F. Muller, 1956. vii, 196p., 17
plates, illus., maps. 21cm.

NEIGEBAUR, Dr.
Neuestes Gemälde der Schweiz. Wien. A. Doll, 1831.
vi, 498p., plates, illus. 20cm. (Schuss's
allgemeine Erdkunde ..., Bd. 21)

NEILL, John
[Report of the] British Caucasus Expedition, 1958,
[by John Neill]. [The Expedition], [1958]. 7
leaves. 34cm.
Typescript.

NEILL, John
Selected climbs in the Pennine Alps; translated
and adapted from the Guide des Alpes valaisannes,
published by the Swiss Alpine Club and other
sources; edited by J. Neill. Alpine Club, 1962.
246p., illus., bibl. 16cm. (Alpine Club guide
books)

NEILL, John and JONES, Trevor
Snowdon South. Stockport: Climbers' Club, 1960.
xii, 109p., plates, illus. 16cm. (Climbing
guides to the Snowdon district, 8)

JONES, Trevor and NEILL, John
Snowdon south; with a geological note by N.J.
Soper; natural history notes by R. Goodier; and
diagrams by R.B. Evans. 2nd ed. Stockport:
Climbers' Club, 1966. x, 142p., illus., maps.
16cm. (Climbers' Club guide to Wales, 8)

- - 3rd ed., including Moel Y Gest Quarry, by Les
Holliwell. 1970.

NELSON, Aven
COULTER, John M
New manual of botany of the central Rocky
Mountains (vascular plants); revised by Aven
Nelson. New York: American Book Co., 1909. 646p.
22cm.

NERUDA, Ludwig Norman
See
NORMAN-NERUDA, Ludwig

NERUDA, May Norman
See
NORMAN-NERUDA, May

NESBIT, Paul W
Longs Peak: its story and a climbing guide. 5th
ed., rev. and enl. Colorado Springs: The Author,
1963. 64p., illus. 23cm.

NESTLER, A
VILLARS, Dominique
Précis d'un voyage botanique, fait en Suisse, dans
les Grisons, aux sources du Rhin ... en juillet,
août et septembre 1811; précédé de quelques réflexions sur l'utilité des voyages pour les
naturalistes, par D. Villars, G. Lauth et A.
Nestler. Paris: Lenormant, 1812. 66p., 4 fold.
plates, illus. 20cm.

NEUDEGG, Rudolf Freisauff von
Das Salkammergut, Salzburg, Oberbayern und Tirol.
22. Aufl. Berlin: Goldschmidt, 1900. 2v. in 1,
maps. 17cm. (Griebens Reiseführer, 20)

Die neue Dolomitenstrasse: Toblach, Ampezzo, Bozen
... 3. Aufl. Berlin: Geuters Reiseführerverlag,
1924. 112p., illus., map. 17cm. (Geuters Reiseführer, 13)

Neuer und vollstandiger Wegweiser durch die ganze
schweizerische Eidsgenossenschaft und die benachbarten Länder. Aarau: H.R. Sauerlander, 1828.
184p. 19cm.

Neuester Führer durch Innsbruck und Umgebung.
Innsbruck: A. Edlinger, [n.d.]. 94p., illus.,
maps. 18cm.

Neuestes Gemälde der Erde und ihrer Bewohner; oder,
Schilderung der vorzüglichsten Merkwürdigkeitn,
der Sitten und Gebräuche ... der Völkerschaften
aller Welttheile ... die Schweiz: [hrsg. von Carl
Friedrich Stuckart]. Schweidnitz, 1824. 199,
133p. 24cm.

NEUFELD, C   A
HOOLE, Henry
Das Trainieren zum Sport: ein Handbuch für Sports-
leute jeder Art ...; für deutsche Verhältnisse
bearb., Uebersetzung von C.A. Neufeld. Wiesbaden:
J.F. Bergmann, 1899. xi, 170p. 22cm.

NEUFFER, Hans
Erste Hilfe in den Bergen: ein Taschenbuch für den
Bergsteiger. Wien: R. Lechner, [1931]. 104p.,
plates, illus. 18cm.

NEVE, Arthur
Picturesque Kashmir. Sands, 1900. xvi, 163p.,
plates, illus. 26cm.

NEVE, Arthur
Thirty years in Kashmir. Arnold, 1913. viii,
316p., plates (1 fold.col.), illus., map. 24cm.

NEVE, Arthur
The tourists guide to Kashmir, Ladakh, Skardo
etc.; edited by Arthur Neve. 16th ed. rev., by
E.F. Neve. Lahore: Civil and Military Gazette
Press, 1938. vii, 2, x, 200p., 2 fold.col. plates,
maps. 20cm.

NEVE, Ernest F
Beyond the Pir Panjal: life among the mountains
and valleys of Kashmir. Fisher Unwin, 1912.
320p., plates (1 fold.col.), illus., map. 23cm.

NEVE, Ernest F
The tourist's guide to Kashmir, Ladakh, Skardo,
etc.; edited by Arthur Neve. 16th ed. rev., by
E.F. Neve. Lahore: Civil and Military Gazette
Press, 1938. vii, 2, x, 200p., 2 fold.col. plates,
maps. 20cm.

NEW, Charles
Life, wanderings and labours in Eastern Africa;
with an account of the first successful ascent of
the equatorial snow mountain, Kilima Njaro; and
remarks upon east African slavery. Hodder and
Stoughton, 1874. xiii, 528p., plates (1 fold.
col.), illus., map. 22cm.

NEW ZEALAND HIMALAYAN EXPEDITION, 1953
Himalayan holiday: an account of the New Zealand
Himalayan Expedition 1953. Christchurch: Whitcombe
and Tombs, 1954. 44p., plates, illus., map. 22cm.
Expedition leader: Athol R. Roberts.

NEWALL, David J F
The highlands of India. Harrison, 1882-87. 2v.,
plates (1 fold.), illus., map. 22cm.

NEWALL, David J F
Preliminary sketches in Cashmere; or, Scenes in
"cuckoo-cloud-land", by D.J.F.N. Isle of Wight:
The Author, 1882. xxx, 86p., plates, illus. 22cm.

NEWBIGIN, Marion I
Frequented ways: a general survey of the land
forms, climates and vegetation of Western Europe,
considered in their relation to the life of man;
including a detailed study of some typical regions.
Constable, 1922. xi, 321p., 31 plates, illus.
23cm.

NEWBIGIN, Marion I
BROADBENT, Ellinor Lucy
Under the Italian Alps; with a geographical essay
by Marion I. Newbigin. Methuen, 1925. xi, 251p.,
plates (1 fold.col.), illus., map. 20cm.

NEWBY, Eric
Great ascents: a narrative history of mountaineering. Newton Abbot: David & Charles, 1977.
208p., illus. (some col.), maps, plans, bibl.
26cm.

NEWBY, Eric
A short walk in the Hindu Kush. Secker & Warburg,
1958. 247p., plates (2 fold.), illus., maps. 23cm.

NEWELL, R H
Letters on the scenery of Wales; including a
series of subjects for the pencil ... and instructions to pedestrian tourists. Baldwin, Cradock,
& Joy, 1821. xv, 192p., plates, illus. 25cm.

NEWLAND, Henry
Forest life in Norway and Sweden, being extracts
from the journal of a fisherman. New ed.
Routledge, 1859. vi, 418p., plates, illus. 17cm.

NEWTH, J D
Austria. Black, 1930. v, 89p., 12 plates, illus.
20cm. (Peeps at many lands)

NEWTON, H H
FOSCA, François
H.-H. Newton; illustré de dessins ... et de ...
planches...Paris: H. Floury, 1928. 22p., 40
plates, illus. 21cm.

NICCOLAI, Francesco
Mugello e Val di Sieve: guida topografica, storico-
artistica, illustrata. Mugello: Touring Club
Italiano, 1914. xviii, 752p., illus., map. 18cm.

NICHOLS, Starr H
Monte Rosa: the epic of an Alp. Boston: Houghton,
Mifflin, 1883. 148p. 19cm.

NICHOLSON, Emilius
NICHOLSON, George
The Cambrian traveller's guide, and pocket com-
panion ...,[by George Nicholson]. Stourport:
George Nicholson, 1808. viii, 720 columns, illus.
21cm.

- - 2nd ed., corr. and considerably enl. Longmans,
Hurst, Rees, Orme & Brown, 1813.
- - 3rd ed., rev. and corr. by ... Emilius Nicholson.
1840.

NICHOLSON, Francis
Views in the Tyrol. Engelmann, Graf, Coindet,
[1829]. 1v. of illus. 36cm.
Cover title.

NICHOLSON, George
The Cambrian traveller's guide, and pocket
companion ..., [by George Nicholson]. Stourport:
George Nicholson, 1808. viii, 720 columns,
illus. 21cm.

- - 2nd ed., corr. and considerably enl. Longman,
Hurst, Rees, Orme & Brown, 1813.
- - 3rd ed., rev. and corr. by ... Emilius Nicholson.
1840.

NICOLAS, R
KOENIG, Franz Nikolaus
[Neue Sammlung von Schweizertrachten...]. Alte
Schweizer Trachten, nach Zeichnungen von F.N.
König, Lory und Anderen; mit einer Einleitung von
R. Nicolas. Zürich-Rüschlikon: Montana-Verlag,
1924. 277p., col. illus. 16cm.
Facsimile reprint of 1816 ed.

NICOLAS, R   and KLIPSTEIN, A
Die schöne alte Schweiz: die Kunst der Schweizer
Kleinmeister; hrsg. von R. Nicolas und A.
Klipstein. Zürich: A. Müller, 1926. 102p., 73
plates (some col.), illus. 32cm.

NICOLLE, Henri
Courses dans les Pyrénées: la montagne et les
eaux. Nouv. éd. Paris: Nouvelle, 1860. 355p.
20cm.

NICOLUSSI, Eduard Reut
See
REUT-NICOLUSSI, Eduard

NIEBERL, Franz
Erlebtes und Erdachtes. München: Rother, 1925.
139p. 24cm.

NIEBERL, Franz
DEUTSCHER UND ÖSTERREICHISCHER ALPENVEREIN.
Sektion Kufstein
50 Jahre Alpenvereinssektion Kufstein, 1877-1927;
[hrsg. von F. Nieberl]. Innstruck: Sektion
Kufstein, 1927. 215p., plates, illus. 25cm.

NIEBERL, Franz
Das Gehen auf Eis und Schnee; unter Mitwirkung
von Karl Blodig. München: Rother, 1923. 93p.,
plates, illus. 21cm.

NIEBERL, Franz
MADUSCHKA, Leo
Die jüngste Erschliessungsgeschichte des Wilden
Kaisers; mit einer Einleitung und durchgesehen
von Franz Nieberl. München: Sektion Bayerland
des Deutschen und Österreichischen Alpenvereins,
1933. 39p., 1 plate, ports. 25cm.

NIEBERL, Franz
Das Klettern im Fels; mit 50 Zeichnungen von Carl
Moos. München: G. Lammers, 1909. 92p., illus.
20cm.

- - 6. verm. Aufl., mit Zeichnungen von Carl Moos
und Prof. Zeliner. München: Rother, 1926.

NIEBERL, Franz
Das Totenkirchl. 2. Aufl. München: Rother, 1923.
48p., illus., bibl. 21cm.

NIEDERMAYR, F
Der Hochtourist: ein Handbuch für Anfänger. Wien:
A. Hartleben, 1908. 95p., plates, illus., bibl.
18cm.

NIELSEN, Yngvar
Handbook for travellers in Norway; translated
from the original 4th ed. Kristiania: Alb.
Cammermeyer, 1886. xiv, 738 columns, fold.col.
plates, maps. 19cm.

NIELSON, Yngvar
RUGE, Sophus
Norwegen. 2 Aufl., bearb. von Yngvar Nielsen.
Bielefeld: Velhagen & Klasing, 1905. 151p., 1
fold.col. plate, illus., map, bibl. 26cm.
(Land und Leute. Monographien zur Erdkunde, 3)

NIEPCE, B
Guide das les Alpes du Dauphiné, vallée d'Allevard
...; suivi des propriétés thérapeutiques et
médicales des eaux d'Uriage et de La Motte, et excursions dans leurs environs. Grenoble: Alph.
Merle, [1860?]. vii, 305p., plates, illus. 20cm.

NIEPMANN, Dr.
Der Ortler. Stuttgart; Deutsche Verlags-Anstalt,
1905. 73p., plates, illus., map. 18cm. (Alpine
Gipfelführer, 3)

NIESNER, Hans
Die alpinen Gefahren, ihre Verhütung und Bekämp-
fung; im Auftrage der Bergwacht bearb. von Hans
Niesner. München: Im Bergwacht-Verlag, 1926.
36p., bibl. 17cm. (Bergwacht-Bücherei, Heft 4)

NIEVELT, C   van
Een Alpenboek: Wandelingen in de Zwitsersche en
Tiroler Bergen. Leiden: S.C. van Doesburgh, 1886.
349p. 20cm.

NIEVELT, C   van
Bergstudien: een omgang in het land der Dolomieten.
Leiden: S.C. van Doesburgh, 1888. 195p. 20cm.

The night climber's guide to Trinity. 3rd ed.
Cambridge: Weatherhead, 1960. 60p., illus., plan.
22cm.

NIKHAZI, Friedrich
Tatraführer: Wegweiser in die Hohe Tatra und in
die Bäder der Tatragegent; unter Mitwirkung des
Ungar, Karpathen Vereins von Nikolaus Szontagh;
aus dem Ungarischen von Friedrich Nikhazi. 2...
Aufl. Budapest: Singer & Wolfner, 1904. 227p.,
map. 17cm.

NIKOPOULOS, Ilias
Mount Olympos, text and illustrations by Ilias
Nikopoulos; with a foreword by Ilias Venezis.
Athens: The Author, 1957. 31p., plates (1 fold.),
illus., map. 26cm.

NISARD, Désire
Promenades d'un artiste. Vol.2. Tyrol-Suisse,
Nord de l'Italie, [par Désire Nisard]. Paris: J.
Renouard, 1835. 406p., 26 plates, illus. 24cm.

NISSON, Claude
La conquête du Mont-Blanc. Paris: Spes, 1930.
215p., plates, illus. 24cm. (Des fleurs et des
fruits)

NIXON, John
Climbing guide to the Avon gorge. Bristol:
University of Bristol Mountaineering Club, 1959.
45p., illus. 17cm.

NOCK, Peter
Rock climbing. W. & G. Foyle, 1963. 96p., plates,
illus., bibl. 19cm. (Foyles Handbooks for
sportsmen)

NODIER, Charles
Promenade from Dieppe to the mountains of Scotland;
translated from the French. Edinburgh: Blackwood;
London: T. Cadell, 1822. xii, 211p. 18cm.

NOE, R
Die Schweiz in 15 Tagen mit Generalabonnement
genussreich und billig zu Bereisen. 4. verm. und
verb. Aufl. Freiburg im Breisgau, Leipzig: P.
Lorenz, 1907-8. 74p., maps, plans. 16cm.
(Lorenz' Reiseführer)

NOE, R
Tirol und die angrenzenden Alpengebiete von
Vorarlberg, Salzburg und Salzkammergut, sowie das
bayerische Hochland nebst München, in 20 Tagen.
2. verm. und verb. Aufl. Freiburg: P. Lorenz,
1907-08. 92p., maps. 16cm. (Lorenz Reiseführer)

NOEL, Baptist W
Notes of a tour in Switzerland, in the summer of
1847. J. Nisbet, 1848. viii, 308p., plates,
illus. 21cm.

NOEL, Baptist W
Notes of a tour in the valleys of Piedmont, in the
summer of 1854. J. Nisbet, 1855. 175p., map.
19cm.

NOEL, Gerard Thomas
Arvendel; or, Sketches in Italy and Switzerland,
[by Gerard T. Noel]. J. Nisbet, 1826. 123p. 24cm.

NOEL, John Baptist Lucius
Through Tibet to Everest. Arnold, 1927. 302p.,
plates, illus. 22cm.

NOEL-BUXTON, Noel, Baron Buxton
Travels and reflections. Allen & Unwin, 1929.
223p. 22cm.

NOLL-HASENCLEVER, Eleonore
Den Bergen verfallen: Alpenfahrten von Eleonore
Noll-Hasenclever; mit Geleitwort und Lebensbild
versehen und mit Beiträgen von G. Dyhrenfurth,
W. Martin, Hermann Trier und Willi Welzenbach;
hrsg. von Heinrich Erler; mit ... einem fak-
similierten Briefe Alexander Burgeners. Berlin:
Union Deutsche Verlagsgesellschaft Zweigniederlassung, 1932. 213p., plates, illus. 22cm.

NOMENTINO
See
MCCOSH, John

NORDMANN, Johannes
Meine Sonntage: Wanderbuch aus den Bergen des
österreichischen Hochlandes. 2. verm. Aufl.
Wien: Klinkhardt, 1880. 328p. 20cm.

NORGATE, Edward
Miniatura: or, The art of limning; edited from the
ms. in the Bodleian Library and collated with
other mss. by Martin Hardie. Oxford: Clarendon
Press, 1919. xxix, 111p. 20cm.

NORGAY, Tenzing
See
TENZING NORGAY

NORGES SKIFORBUND
Rules for ski-ing competitions, etc. Kristiania:
Printed by Grøndahl, 1923. 58p., fold. plates,
illus. 23cm.

NORGES STATSBANER
Sunlit Norway, nature's wonderland. B & N
Steamship Line, Norwegian State Railways, 1912.
205p., illus., maps. 18cm.

NORMAN CROUCHER PERUVIAN ANDES EXPEDITION, 1978
Report. The Expedition, [1979]. [16]p., illus.,
bibl. 21cm.

NORMAN-NERUDA, Ludwig
The climbs of Norman-Neruda; edited and with an
account of his last climb, by May Norman-Neruda.
Fisher Unwin, 1899. 12, 335p., plates, illus.
23cm.

NORMAN-NERUDA, Ludwig
[The climbs of Norman-Neruda]. Bergfahrten von
Norman-Neruda; hrsg. von May Norman-Neruda.
München: F. Bruckmann, [1901]. 245p., port. 22cm.

NORSK TINDEKLUB
GUNNENG, Asbjørn and SCHLYTTER, Boye
Fører for bestigninger i Horungtindene; utarbeidet
av Norsk Tindeklub ved Asbjørn Gunneng og Boye
Schlytter. Oslo: Grøndahl, 1928. 19p., illus.
23cm.

NORSK TINDEKLUB
GUNNENG, Asbjørn and SCHLYTTER, Boye
[Fører for bestigninger i Horungtindene]. Climbs
in the Horungtinder, Norway; edited [for] Norsk
Tindeklub by Asbjørn Gunneng and Boye Schlytter.
Oslo: Grøndahl, 1933. 23p., 1 fold.col. plate,
illus., map (in pocket). 23cm.

NORSK TINDEKLUB
HAGEN, Helge
  Fører for bestiginger i Sunnmøre, Romsdal og
  Inderdal; utarbeidet av Norsk Tindeklub ved Helge
  Hagen... G.N. Sabro... Oslo: Grøndahl, 1936.
  22p., illus., map. 23cm.

NORSK TINDEKLUB
  Klatrefører for Norge. Oslo: Norge Tindeklub,
  1970. 1v. (loose-leaf), illus., maps. 23cm.

NORSKE HIMALAIA-EKSPEDISJONEN, 1950
  Tirich Mir til topps: den Norske Himalaia-
  Ekspedisjonen. Oslo: Gyldendal Norsk Forlag, 1950.
  176p., plates (1 col.), illus., maps. 24cm.

NORSKE HIMALAIA-EKSPEDISJONEN, 1950
  Tirich Mir: the Norwegian Himalaya Expedition;
  translated by Sölvi and Richard Bateson. Hodder
  & Stoughton, 1952. 192p., plates, illus., maps.
  23cm.

NORTH, F   J
  Snowdonia: the National Park of North Wales by
  F.J. North, Bruce Campbell, Richenda Scott.
  Collins, 1949. 469p., plates (some col.), illus.,
  maps, bibl. 22cm. (The New naturalist series)

NORTH OF ENGLAND HIMALAYAS EXPEDITION, 1975
  The roof of the world: the report of the 1975
  North of England Himalayas Expedition. Stockton:
  The Expedition, 1975. [28]p., illus., maps. 30cm.
  Expedition leader: Paul Bean.

NORTH OF ENGLAND HIMALAYAN EXPEDITION, 1977
  A return to the roof of the world and the story of
  a Himalayan trilogy. Stockton: The Expedition,
  1977. 31p., illus., maps. 30cm.
  At head of title: For the Royal Jubilee. Expedition leader: Paul Bean.

NORTH OF ENGLAND KISHTWAR EXPEDITION, 1978
  [Report]. [Bakewell]: The Expedition, [1979].
  40p., maps. 22cm.

The northern Cambrian mountains; or, A tour through
  North Wales describing the scenery and general
  characters of that romantic country, [by Thomas
  Compton] and embellished with ... coloured views,
  engraved from original drawings. Printed for The
  Author by C. Corrall, 1817. 1v. (chiefly illus.).
  25 x 34cm.

  - - Another issue. T. Clay. 1820.

NORTHEY, W   Brook and MORRIS, John
  The Gurkhas: their manners, customs and country;
  with a foreword by C.G. Bruce. Lane, 1928. xxxix,
  282p., plates (1 fold.col.), illus., map. 24cm.

NORTHUMBRIAN MOUNTAINEERING CLUB
  A rock-climber's guide to Northumberland; compiled
  by members of the Northumbrian Mountaineering Club.
  2nd ed. Clapham, via Lancaster: Dalesman, 1964.
  68p., illus. 19cm.

NORTON, Basil P
  Ang Tharkay: memoires d'un Sherpa; recueillis par
  Basil P. Norton; traduits de l'anglais par H.
  Delgrove. Paris: Amiot-Dumont, 1954. 210p.,
  plates, illus., maps. 22cm.

NORTON, Edward Felix
  The fight for Everest: 1924. Arnold, 1925. xi,
  372p., plates (1 fold.col.), illus., map. 26cm.

NORWAY. Ecclesiastical and Educational Department
  See
NORWAY. Kirke- og Undervisningsdepartement

NORWAY. Kirke- og Undervisningsdepartement
  Norway: official publication for the Paris Exhibi-
  tion 1900; [edited under the direction of the
  Ecclesiastical and Educational Department by Sten
  Konow and Karl Fischer]. Kristiania: The Depart-
  ment, 1900. 626, xxxiv p., illus., maps. 27cm.

NORWAY TRAVEL ASSOCIATION
  Rock climbs in Norway. The Association, [1953].
  5v. in 1, 1 fold.plate, illus., map. 21cm.

NORWEGIAN HIMALAYA EXPEDITION
  See
NORSKE HIMALAIA-EKSPEDISJONEN

A Norwegian ramble among the fjords, fjelds, mountains and glaciers, by one of the ramblers. New
  York, London: Putnam, 1904. ix, 232p., 16 plates,
  illus. 18cm.

NORWEGIAN STATE RAILWAYS
  See
NORGES STATSBANER

Nos Alpes: poésies [par] Mme D.B.; illustré par Hans
  Wieland. Genève: Briquet, [n.d.]. 7p., illus.
  25cm.

BÜHM, Otto and NOSSBERGER, Adolf
  Führer durch die Schobergruppe. Wien: Artaria,
  1925. xv, 224p., 1 fold. plate, map (in pocket).
  17cm.

Notes abroad and rhapsodies at home, by a veteran
  traveller [i.e. W. Rae Wilson]. Longman, Rees,
  Orme, Brown, Green, & Longman, 1837. 2v., plates,
  illus. 22cm.

Notes and reflections during a ramble in Germany,
  by the author of "Recollections in the Peninsula",
  "Sketches of India" ... [i.e. Moyle Sherer].
  Longman, Rees, Orme, Brown, & Green, 1826. 400p.
  22cm.

Notes of a ramble through France, Italy, Switzerland, Germany, Holland, and Belgium; and of a
  visit to the scenes of "The Lady of the Lake",
  &c. &c., by a lover of the picturesque. Hamilton,
  Adams, 1836. ix, 464p. 24cm.

Notes on a tour in America, [by] R.W.T.   Wyman,
  [ca 1885]. 30p. 24 x 29cm.

Notes on a yacht voyage to Hardanger Fjord and the
  adjacent estuaries, by a yachting dabbler.
  Longman, Brown, Green, and Longman, [19--].
  xxvii, 110p., plates (1 fold., some col.), illus.
  23cm.

NOTOVITCH, Nicolas
  The unknown life of Christ; translated from the
  French by Violet Crispe. Hutchinson, 1895. lii,
  257p., plates, illus., maps. 20cm.

NOTTINGHAM UNIVERSITY HINDU KUSH EXPEDITION, 1972
  1972 Nottingham University Hindu Kush Expedition,
  [by Peter D. Boardman]. [Nottingham]: The
  Expedition, [1973?]. 37p., plates, illus., maps.
  23cm.

Nouveau guide de Bordeaux aux Pyrénées. Paris: N.
  Chaix, [1853]. xxxii, 256p., plates, map. 16cm.
  (Guide-Chaix; Bibliothèque du voyageur)

Nouveau guide du voyageur dans les XXII cantons
  suisses; traduit d'un manuscrit allemand du Prof.
  H. par R.W.; avec la nouvelle carte de la Suisse
  de Weiss. Berne: J.J. Bourgdorfer, 1822. xxxvi,
  434p., 1 fold.col. plate, map. 18cm.
  In slip-case.

Nouveau guide du voyageur en Italie. 6e éd.
  originale. Milan: Artaria, 1841. xxxii, 365p.,
  plates, maps, plans. 19cm.

Nouveau guide général du voyageur en Suisse; suivi
  du Tour du Mont Blanc par Joseph Lacroix. Paris:
  Garnier [n.d.] 405p., plates, illus., maps.
  19cm. (Guides Garnier Frères)

Nouvelle ascension du Mont-Cervin, [par Georges
  Carrel?]. Aoste: Lyboz, [1867]. [1]p. 22cm.

Nouvelle description de l'Oberland bernois à l'usage
  des voyageurs, [par R. Walthard]. Berne: J.J.
  Burgdorfer, 1838. xii, 40p., plates (some col.),
  maps. 23cm.

NOVARESE, Vittorio
REY, Guido
Il Monte Cervino; illustrazioni di Edoardo Rubino; prefazione di Edmondo de Amicis; nota geologica di Vittorio Novarese. Milano: Hoepli, 1904. xvi, 287p., plates. 31cm.

NOVOTNI, Vjekoslav
MALDINI WILDENHAINSKI, Rudolf, Barun
Bosna i Hercegovina, napisao Rudolf Barun Maldini Wildenhainski; uredio Vjekoslav Novotni. Zagreb: Tisak Antuna Scholza, 1908. xx, 157, vii p., illus. 33cm.

NOWILL, Sidney Edward Payn
See
ASHENDEN

NOWOPACKÝ, Jan
Alpine Kunstblätter: [40 Bilder aus Oesterreichs und Deutschlands Alpen: Original-Faksimile nach Oelgemälden von Jan Nowopicky]. Prag: B. Kocí, 1903. 10 pts. in 1, col. plates, illus. 32 x 39cm.

NOYCE, C   W   F
See
NOYCE, Wilfrid

NOYCE, Wilfrid
The Alps; with descriptive essays by Karl Lukan. Thames & Hudson, 1961. 312p., illus., maps. 29cm.

PYATT, Edward Charles and NOYCE, Wilfrid
British crags and climbers: an anthology; chosen by Edward C. Pyatt and Wilfrid Noyce. Dobson, [1952]. 235p., plates, illus. 23cm.

NOYCE, Wilfrid
The climber's fireside book; compiled by Wilfrid Noyce. Heinemann, 1964. xv, 268p., plates, illus. 22cm.

NOYCE, Wilfrid
Climbing the Fish's Tail. Heinemann, 1958. xiii, 150p., plates (1 col.), illus., maps. 21cm.

NOYCE, Wilfrid
The gods are angry. Heinemann, 1957. 198p., map (on lining papers). 21cm.

NOYCE, Wilfrid and EDWARDS, John Menlove
Lliwedd group. New and rev. ed. Climbers' Club, 1939. xii, 173p., plates, illus., map. 16cm. (Climbing guides to the Snowdon district, 4)

NOYCE, Wilfrid
Mountains and men. Bles, 1947. 160p., plates, illus., maps. 24cm.

NOYCE, Wilfrid
Poems. Heinemann, 1960. 98p. 23cm.

SUTTON, Geoffrey and NOYCE, Wilfrid
Samson: the life and writings of Menlove Edwards; edited with biographical memoir by Geoffrey Sutton and Wilfrid Noyce. Stockport: Cloister Press, 1960. ix, 122p., plates, illus. 22cm.

NOYCE, Wilfrid
Scholar mountaineers: pioneers of Parnassus; with wood engravings by R. Taylor. Dobson, 1950. 164p., plates, illus., bibl. 22cm.

NOYCE, Wilfrid
YOUNG, Geoffrey Winthrop
Snowdon biography by Geoffrey Winthrop Young, Geoffrey Sutton, and Wilfrid Noyce; edited by Wilfrid Noyce. Dent, 1957. xiii, 194p., plates, illus., maps (on lining papers), bibl. 22cm.

NOYCE, Wilfrid
South Col: one man's adventure on the ascent of Everest, 1953; foreword by Sir John Hunt. Heinemann, 1954. xx, 303p., plates (some col.), illus., maps. 23cm.

- - Abridged New Windmill ed. 1956 (1962 reprint).

NOYCE, Wilfrid
The springs of adventure. Murray, 1958. xii, 240p., plates, illus., bibl. 23cm.

NOYCE, Wilfrid
To the unknown mountain: ascent of an unexplored twenty-five thousander in the Karakoram. Heinemann, 1962. xii, 183p., plates, illus., maps. 23cm.

EDWARDS, John Menlove and NOYCE, Wilfrid
Tryfan group; with photographs by J.M. Edwards; and diagrams by C.H. French. Climbers' Club, 1937. ix, 122p., plates, illus. (Climbing guides to the Snowdon district, 2)

NOYCE, Wilfrid and MCMORRIN, Ian
World atlas of mountaineering; edited by Wilfrid Noyce and Ian McMorrin. Nelson, 1969. 224p., col. plates, illus., maps. 28cm.

NÜNLIST, Hugo
Spitsbergen: the story of the 1962 Swiss-Spitsbergen expedition; translated from the German by Oliver Coburn. Kaye, 1966. 191p., plates, illus., maps. 24cm.

NUNN, Paul J and WOOLCOCK, Oliver
Borrowdale; illustrated by W. Heaton Cooper. Stockport: Fell & Rock Climbing Club, 1968. 219p., 1 plate, illus., maps (on lining papers). 16cm. (Climbing guides to the English Lake District, [4th ser.], 3)

NUNN, Paul J
The Kinder area; edited by P.J. Nunn; produced for and by the Peak Committee of the British Mountaineering Council. B.M.C., [1971?]. 208p., illus., bibl. 16cm. (Rock climbs in the Peak, v.7)

NUNN, Paul J
The northern limestone area; compiled and arranged by Paul Nunn. Climbers' Club for British Mountaineering Council, Peak District Committee, 1969. xiv, 265p., plates, illus., map, bibl. 16cm. (Climbers' Club guides; Rock climbs in the Peak, 5)

NUNN, Paul J
Rock climbing in the Peak District: a photographic guide for rockclimbers. Constable, 1975. xx, 304p., illus., maps, bibl. 18cm. (Constable guides)

Nuova guida illustrata della Valle d'Aosta... Pt.2. Valle superiore. Torino: F. Casanova, 1882. xii, 400p., plates, illus., maps, plans. 18cm. (Collezione guide Casanova)

NYKA, Józef
Ostatni atak na Kunyang Chhish [of the Klub Wysokogórski]; opracowanie: Józef Nyka [and others]. Warszawa: Wydawnictwo Sport i Turystyka, 1973. 255p., plates (some col.), illus., maps. 22cm.

NYKA, Józef
[Ostatni atak na Kunyang Chhish]. Gipfelsturm im Karakorum; hrsg. von Józef Nyka [and others]. Leipzig: Brockhaus, 1977. 162p., plates (some col.), illus., map. 24cm.

OAKLEY, E   Sherman
Holy Himalaya: the religion, traditions and scenery of a Himalayan province (Kumaon and Garhwal). Edinburgh, London: Oliphant Anderson & Ferrier, 1905. 319p., plates, illus. 21cm.

OBER, P
Interlacren et ses environs. Berthoud: C. Langlois, 1841. 163p. 19cm.

- - 3e éd. Berne: C.J. Wyss, 1861.

OBER, P
L'Oberland bernois sous les rapports historique, scientifique et topographique: journal d'un voyageur. Berne: C.J. Wyss, 1858. 2v. 20cm.

OBERHOLZER, Jakob
Monographie einiger prähistorischer Bergstürze in der Glarneralpen. Bern: Schmid & Francke, 1900. ix, 209p., plates (some fold., some col.), illus., map. 33cm. (Beiträge zur geologischen Karte der Schweiz, Lfg. 39, N.F. Lfg. 9)

Oberland bernois. Zurich: Photoglob, [ca 1900]. 1v. of col. illus. 25 x 32cm.
Cover title.

OBERSTEINER, Ludwig
Führer durch die Otztaler Alpen. 2 Aufl. Innsbruck: Wagner, 1937. viii, 319p., plates, maps. 16cm. (Wagner's alpine Führer, 5)

MANER, Eduard and OBERSTEINER, Ludwig
Hochschwabführer. Wien: Artaria, 1922. xxiv, 239p., 1 plate, illus. 17cm.

OBERZINER, Giovanni
Le guerre di Augusto contro i popoli alpini. Roma: E. Loescher, 1900. 2v. in 1, col. maps. 34cm.

OCCIONI-BONAFFONS, G
Illustrazione del Commune di Udine. Udine: Società Alpina Friulana, 1886. xix, 482p., plates, illus., maps, plans. 19cm. (Guida del Friuli, 1)

O'CONNOR, Sir Frederick
On the frontier and beyond: a record of thirty years' service. Murray, 1931. xiv, 355p., plates, illus., map. 23cm.

O'CONNOR, Vincent Clarence Scott
The charm of Kashmir. Longmans, Green, 1920. xii, 182p., plates (some col.), illus. 30cm.

O'CONNOR, Vincent Clarence Scott
Travels in the Pyrenees, including Andorra and the coast from Barcelona to Carcassonne. J. Long, 1913. 348p., plates (1 fold., 1 col.), illus., map. 23cm.

O'CONNOR, William F
Routes in Sikkim; compiled in the Intelligence Branch of the Quartermaster General's Department in India. Calcutta: Office of the Superintendent of Government Printing, 1900. 90p. 34cm.

COLLOMB, Robin Gabriel and O'CONNOR, William H
Mont Blanc range. Vol.1. Trélatête, Mont Blanc, Maudit, Tacul, Brenva. Alpine Club, 1976. 221p., illus., bibl. 16cm. (Alpine Club guide books)

O'CONOR, Matthew
Picturesque and historical recollections during a tour through Belgium, Germany, France, and Switzerland, in the summer vacation of 1835. Wm. S. Orr, 1837. ii, 260, iii p., plates, illus. 19cm.

ODELL, Noel Ewart
Frequented and unfrequented ways in the Selkirks and Rockies. [New York], 1931. 268-276p., plates, illus. 23cm.
Offprint from American alpine journal, v.1, no.3, 1931.

ODELL, Noel Ewart
Geology of part of the central St. Elias range, Alaska-Yukon Territory, Mount Vancouver in particular. Cambridge: The Author, 1978. 13p., illus., map, bibl. 24cm.

ODELL, Noel Ewart
On the occurrence of granite in the Himalayan mountains. Milano, 1974. p375-391, illus. 24cm.
Offprint from Rivista italiana di paleontologia e stratigrafia, memoria, 14.

ODELL, Noel Ewart
The supposed Tibetan or Nepalese name of Mount Everest. [London], [1935]. 5p. 21cm.
Offprint from Alpine journal, v.47, no.250, May 1935.

ODERMATT, Madeleine
Madeleine Odermatt; ou, Le canton d'Uri. Genève: Ch. Gruaz, 1858. 333p. 19cm.
A series of letters written by or to or about Madeleine Odermatt.

OEHLMANN, E
Die Alpenpasse im Mittelalter. [Zürich, 1878-79]. 1v. (various pagings). 24cm.
Offprint from Jahrbuch für Schweiz. Geschichte, 3 & 4.

OEHLMANN, E
SEYDLITZ, Ernst von
Handbuch der Geographie. Jubiläums-Ausg. "Der Grosse Seydlitz" 25. Bearbeitung under Mitwirkung vieler Fachmänner besorgt von E. Oehlmann. Breslau: F. Hirt, 1908. xv, 848p., plates (some fold., some col.), illus., maps. 23cm.

OEHNINGER, C J
Die Alpenflora: 130 Abbildungen ... auf 24 Tafeln; nach der Natur gemalt von Baron Fritz Hauser; hrsg., mit Einleitung und begleitendem Text versehen von C.J. Oehninger. Graz: Selbstverlag von C.J. Oehninger, 1908. 79p., 24 col. plates, illus. 23cm.

- - 5. vollständig umgearb. Aufl. 1922.

ÖSTERREICHISCHE ALPENZEITUNG
Bergsteigen: Festschrift des Österreichischen Alpenklubs zu seiner Hundert-Jahr-Feier, 1878-1978; gestaltet von S. Walcher. Wien:Ö.A.V., 1979. 231p., ports. 27cm.
Sonderfolge der Österreichischen Alpenzeitung, Jan./Feb. 1979, Folge 1423.

ÖSTERREICHISCHE BUNDESBAHNEN
Winter sport in Austria. Vienna: Published by the Administration of the I.R. Austrian State Railways and the Austrian South Railway, [ca 1905]. [84]p., 1 fold. plate, illus., map. 16cm.

ÖSTERREICHISCHER ALPENKLUB
Bergsteigen: Festschrift des Österreichischen Alpenklubs zu seiner Hundert-Jahr-Feier,1878-1978; gestaltet von S. Walcher. Wien: Ö.A.V., 1979. 231p., ports. 27cm.
Sonderfolge der Österreichischen Alpenzeitung, Jan./Feb. 1979, Folge 1423.

ÖSTERREICHISCHER ALPENKLUB
Führer durch die Mont-Blanc-Gruppe; im Auftrage des Österreichischen Alpenklubs verfasst von Wilhelm Martin [and others]. Wien: Ö.A., 1913. 2v., fold. plates, maps, bibl. 18cm.

ÖSTERREICHISCHER ALPENVEREIN
For 1874-1938 see
DEUTSCHER UND ÖSTERREICHISCHER ALPENVEREIN

ÖSTERREICHISCHER ALPENVEREIN
Alpenbilder aus 150 Jahren: 100 Jahre Österreichischer Alpenverein, 1862-1962, Künstlerhaus Wien, 16. September - 14. Oktober, 1962. Wien: Ö.A.V., 1962. 24p., illus. 24cm.

ÖSTERREICHISCHER ALPENVEREIN
Alpenvereinsführer.

Glockner-Gruppe: ein Führer für Täler, Hütten und Berge ..., von Vera Lienbacher. 4. Aufl. 1962.
Ötzaler Alpen: ein Führer für Täler, Hütten und Berge, von H.E. Klier und H. Prochaska. 1953.
Stubaier Alpen: ein Führer für Täler, Hütten und Berge, von W. Rabensteiner und H.E. Klier. 1953.

ÖSTERREICHISCHER ALPENVEREIN
100 Jahre Österreichischer Alpenverein, 1862-1962, von Hans Hanke. Wien: Ö.A.V., 1962. 76p., plates (some fold., some col.), illus. 25cm.

ÖSTERREICHISCHER ALPENVEREIN
Die Kartographie im Alpenverein, von Erik Arnberger;
hrsg. vom Deutschen Alpenverein und vom
Österreichischen Alpenverein. München: D.A.V.;
Innsbruck: Ö.A.V., 1970. 253p., plates (some fold.,
some col.), illus., maps, bibl. 29cm. (Wissenschaftliche Alpenvereinshefte, Heft 22)

ÖSTERREICHISCHER ALPENVEREIN
MARINER, Wastl
Neuzeitliche Bergrettungstechnik: ein Leitfaden
für die Ausbildung des Rettungsmannes; Herausgeber:
Österr. Alpenverein. Innsbruck: Tiroler Graphik,
1959. 191p., illus. 21cm.

ÖSTERREICHISCHER ALPENVEREIN
MARINER, Wastl
[Neuzeitliche Bergrettungstechnik]. Mountain
rescue techniques; drawings by Fritz and Gert
Ebster; first aid instructions by Hans Heinz
Seidel; rev. by Otto T. Trott and Kurt G. Beam.
1st English-language ed. Innsbruck:
Oesterreichischer Alpenverein, 1963. 200p.,
illus., bibl. 21cm.

ÖSTERREICHISCHER ALPENVEREIN. U.K. Branch
Members handbook. London: Austrian Alpine Club,
[1951]. 204p. 18cm.

OESTERREICHISCHER TOURING-CLUB
See
OESTERREICHISCHER TOURISTEN-CLUB

OESTERREICHISCHER TOURISTEN-CLUB
GRÖGER, Gustav and RABL, Josef
Die Entwicklung der Hochtouristik in den
österreichischen Alpen; hrsg. vom Oesterreichischen
Touristen-Club. Wien: R. Leckner, 1890. xi,
258p., plates, illus. 23cm.

OESTERREICHISCHER TOURISTEN-CLUB
Gründung und Entwicklung des Oesterreichischen
Touristen-Club: Festschrift zur Gedenkfeier des
zehnjährigen Bestandes des Oesterreichischen
Touristen-Club im Mai 1879. Wien: Selbstverlag,
1879. 23p., plates (1 fold.), illus. 23cm.

OESTERREICHISCHER TOURISTEN-CLUB. Skilauf-Sektion
Skisport im Oesterr. Touring-Club; hrsg. von der
Skilauf-Sektion des Oesterr. Touring-Club. Wien:
Ö.T.C., 1914. 99p., illus. 16 x 24cm.

OFFENBRÜGGEN, Eduard
Wanderstudien aus der Schweiz. Schaffhausen: C.
Baader, [186-]. 5v. 18cm.

OFFICE NATIONAL SUISSE DU TOURISME
See
SCHWEIZERISCHE VERKEHRSZENTRALE

OFFLER, Hilary S
A short history of Switzerland, by E. Bonjour, H.S.
Offler and G.R. Potter. Oxford: Clarendon Press,
1952. 388p., maps, bibl. 23cm.

O'FLYNN, Barry
KENNY, Peter
A guide to the rock climbs of Dalkey Quarry. 2nd
ed., edited by Barry O'Flynn. Dublin: Irish
Mountaineering Club, 1964. 48p., illus., map.
13cm.

OGGIONI, Andrea
Le mani sulla roccia: il diario alpinistico di
Andrea Oggioni; a cura di Carlo Graffigna; con
scritti di W. Bonatti, B. Ferrario, R. Gallieni, P.
Mazeaud. Bologna: Tamari, 1964. 299p., plates,
illus. 19cm. (Collana "Voci dai monti")

OITZINGER, Anton
KUGY, Julius
Anton Oitzinger: ein Bergführerleben. Graz:
Leykam, 1935. 159p., plates,illus., port. 23cm.

OITZINGER, Anton
KUGY, Julius
[Anton Oitzinger: ein Bergführerleben]. Son of the
mountains: the life of an alpine guide; translated
by H.E.G. Tyndale. Nelson, 1938. 200p., plates,
map. 21cm.

OLAFSEN, Eggert
See
OLAFSSON, Eggert

OLAFSSON, Eggert and PALSSON, Bjarni
Travels in Iceland, performed by order of His
Danish Majesty, containing observations on ...
the inhabitants, a description of the lakes ...;
translated from the Danish. R. Phillips, 1805.
162p., plates (1 fold.), illus., map. 23cm.
(In A collection of modern and contemporary voyages
... Vol.2. 1806)

OLD INDIAN
See
WYMAN, Frederick F

OLD SHEKARRY
See
LEVESON, Henry Astbury

Old stories of Switzerland; selected and translated
from the works of different German and Swiss
poets by a lady. Berne: R.F. Haller, [1864].
viii, 304p. 16cm.

OLDHAM, Kenneth
The Pennine Way: Britain's longest continuous
footpath. Rev. [ed.]. Clapham (Yorks.): Dalesman,
1968. 80p., illus., maps, bibl. 21cm. [Dalesman
paperbacks]

OLDHAM, R D
The structure of the Himalayas, and of the
Gangetic plain, as elucidated by geodetic observations in India. Calcutta: Geological Survey of
India, 1917. 153p., 2 fold.col. plates, maps (in
pocket). 26cm. (Memoirs of the Geological Survey
of India, v.42, pt.2)

OLIM JUVENIS
Vacation rambles on the continent, told so as to
be a complete guide to the most interesting places
in Switzerland, Belgium, and the Rhine, by olim
juvenis. 5th ed. Thomas Cook, 1869. viii, 155p.
16cm.

OLIVER, Geoffrey and GRIFFIN, L Joe
Scafell group; illustrated by W. Heaton Cooper.
Stockport: Fell & Rock Climbing Club, 1967.
172p., 1 col. plate, illus., maps (on lining
papers). 16cm. (Climbing guides to the English
Lake District, [4th ser.], 7)

LE BRETON, Henry and OLLIVIER, Robert
Haute montagne pyrénéenne: guide des ascensions
difficiles aux Pyrénées, les Pyrénées occidentales, des Aiguilles d'Ansabère au Pic Long.
Pau: Groupe Pyrénéiste de Haute Montagne, [1937].
xix, 317p., plates (1 fold.), illus., maps. 17cm.

OLLIVIER, Robert and DEFOS DU RAU, Xavier
Pyrénées. T.3. Bigorre, Arbizon, Néouvielle,
Troumouse. Pau. R. Ollivier pour Fédération
Française de la Montagne, Société des Amis du
Musée Pyrénéen, 1959. xx, 272p., illus., maps.
16cm.

OLSEN, Jack
The climb up to hell; with an introduction by
Christopher Brasher. Gollancz, 1962. 191p.,
plates, illus. 23cm.

OLSEN, John Edward
See
OLSEN, Jack

OLSVIG, Viljam
Beyer's Guide to western Norway, with the coast-
route to the North Cape and overland routes to
Christiania, by Viljam Olsvig. Bergen: F. Beyer;
London: G. Philip, [1887]. 199p., fold.col.
plates, illus., bibl. 18cm.

- - Special supplement for 1890.

OLUFSEN, Ole
Through the unknown Pamirs: the second Danish
Pamir expedition 1898-99. Heinemann, 1904.
xviii, 238p., fold.plates, illus., maps. 23cm.

OLYMPIC MOUNTAIN RESCUE
Climber's guide to the Olympic Mountains. Seattle:
The Mountaineers, 1972. xvi, 222p., illus., maps.
19cm.
Based on a previous ed. published by the American
Alpine Club.

OMANG, S   O   F
Über einige Hieracium-Arten aus Grönland. Oslo:
J. Dybwad, 1937. 12p., 3 plates, illus. 25cm.
(Norges Svalbard- og Ishavs-Undersøkelser.
Meddelelse, nr. 40)

OMPTEDA, Georg, Freiherr von
Excelsior! Ein Bergsteigerleben. Berlin: E.
Fleischel, 1909. 424p. 21cm.

OMPTEDA, Georg, Freiherr von
Der jungfräuliche Gipfel: Roman. Stuttgart:
Deutsche Verlags-Anstalt, 1927. 308p. 20cm.

OMPTEDA, Georg, Freiherr von
Die kleine Zinne: Roman aus den Bergen. Berlin:
Ullstein, 1931. 314p. 18cm.

On Shelley. Oxford University Press, 1938. vi,
99p. 20cm.
Contents: Shelley is expelled, by E. Blunden. -
The Atheist: an incident at Chamonix, by G. De
Beer. -Mary Shelley: novelist and dramatist, by
S. Norman.

O'NEIL, Joseph Patrick
WOOD, Robert L
Men, mules and mountains: Lieutenant O'Neil's
Olympic expeditions. Seattle: The Mountaineers,
1976. xx, 483p., plates, illus., maps, bibl.
21cm.

Opérations géodésiques et astronomiques pour la
mesure d'un arc du parallèle moyen, exécutées en
Piémont et en Savoie par une commission composée
d'officiers ... piémontais et autrichiens en 1821,
1822, 1823. Milan: Imprimerie Impériale et Royale,
1825-27. 2v., fold. plates, illus., maps. 32cm.

OPPENHEIM, Edwin Camillo
New climbs in Norway: an account of some ascents
in the Sondmore district; illustrated by A.D.
McCormick, and from photographs. Fisher Unwin,
1898. x, 257p., illus. 21cm.

OPPENHEIM, Edwin Camillo
'The reverberate hills'. Constable, 1914. viii,
56p. 20cm.

OPPENHEIMER, Lehmann J
The heart of Lakeland. Sherratt & Hughes, 1908.
196p., plates, illus. 24cm.

OREGON WRITERS' PROJECT
Mount Hood: a guide; compiled by workers of the
Writers' Program of the Work Projects Administra-
tion in the State of Oregon. New York: Duell,
Sloan and Pearce, 1940. xxvii, 132p., plates,
illus., maps, bibl. 21cm.

ORIENT LINE
The Norwegian fjords. Produced for the Orient Line
by the Medici Society, [1912]. 114p., illus.,
maps (on lining papers). 24cm.

Original Tyrolean costumes in ten-colour reproductions of four-hundred standard specimens of
national costumes from private and public collections; preface by Baron Georg Franckenstein.
Vienna: H. Reichner, 1937. 60p., col. illus.
23cm.
Text in German, English & French.

ORŁOWICZ, Mieczysław
Guide illustré de la Pologne; [traduit en français
par Anna Domaniewska]. Varsovie: Ministère des
Travaux Publics à Varsovie, Office du Tourisme,
1927. viii, 285p., illus., map (in pocket). 17cm.

WHILLANS, Don and ORMEROD, Alick
Don Whillans: portrait of a mountaineer. Heinemann,
1971. ix, 266p., plates, illus. 23cm.

- - Another issue. Harmondsworth: Penguin, 1973.

ORTENBURGER, Leigh
A climber's guide to the Teton range; illustrated
by Eldon N. Dye. San Francisco: Sierra Club, 1956.
xi, 159p., plates, illus., maps, bibl. 19cm.

ORTH, Donald J
Dictionary of Alaska place names. Washington:
Government Printing Office, 1967. xi, 1084p.,
col. plates, illus., maps, bibl. 29cm. (Geo-
gical Survey. Professional paper, no.567)

ORTON, James
The Andes and the Amazon; or, Across the continent
of South America. New York: Harper, 1870.
356p., plates (1 fold.), illus. 22cm.

LAWSON, W   and OSBORNE, R   E
Les Écrins dt la Meije; traduit par H. Ferrand.
Grenoble, 1908. 12p., plates, illus. 24cm.
Offprint from Annuaire de la Société des touristes
du Dauphiné, 1907.

OSENBRÜGGEN, Eduard
Der Gotthard und das Tessin mit den Oberitalischen
Seen. Basel: Schwabe, 1877. viii, 232p. 22cm.

OSENBRÜGGEN, Eduard
Das Hochgebirge der Schweiz ...; Originalzeichnungen in Stahl radirt von C. Huber; mit topo-
graphischem Text von Ed. Osenbrüggen. 2. völlig
umgearb. Aufl. Basel: Chr. Krüsi; London: Williams
& Norgate, [1875]. 376 columns, 64 plates, illus.
31cm.

- - 3. erweiterte Aufl. [ca 1880].

OSENBRÜGGEN, Eduard
[Das Hochgebirge der Schweiz...]. Alpes et
glaciers de la Suisse ...; soixante vues pittoresque; et un texte topographique traduit de
l'allemand de Ed. Osenbrüggen par C-F. Girard.
Bâle: Chr. Krüsi, [1875]. 376 columns, plates,
illus. 31cm.

OSMASTON, Henry A   and PASTEUR, David
Guide to the Ruwenzori: the Mountains of the Moon.
Kampala: Mountain Club of Uganda; Goring, Reading:
West Col, 1972. 200p., illus., maps, bibl. 18cm.

OSMOND, Th   , comte d'
Dans la montagne, le Tyrol autrichien: Le
Salzkammergut, le Pongau, la Styrie, le Pâtre du
Moser. Paris: C. Lévy, 1878. 239p. 20cm.

OSWALD, E   J
By fell and fjord; or, Scenes and studies in
Iceland. Edinburgh: Blackwood, 1882. 282p., 1
fold. plate, illus., map. 22cm.

OTLEY, Jonathan
A concise description of the English Lakes, the
mountains in their vicinity, and the roads by
which they may be visited; with remarks on the
mineralogy and geology of the district. Keswick:
The Author, 1823. 130p., 1 fold. plate, map.
19cm.

- - 4th ed. 1830.
- - 5th ed. 1834.
- - 6th ed. 1837.

OTT, Adolf
Der Bergführer: hochgebirgs-Roman. Berlin: Schall,
[1900]. 255p. 20cm.

OTTAWAY, Mark
We learned to ski: [The Sunday Times tells you all
you need to know], by Harold Evans, Brian Jackman
and Mark Ottaway. 2nd paperback ed. Collins,
1977. 255p., illus. (some col.). 24cm.

OTTLEY, W   J
   With mounted infantry in Tibet. Smith, Elder,
   1906. xiii, 275p., plates, illus. 23cm.

OTTO, Dr.
   Die Hohe Tatra: praktischer Führer; neu bearb. von
   Dr. Otto. 2. Aufl. Berlin: Goldschmidt, 1895.
   143p., fold.plates (1 col.), illus., maps. 16cm.
   (Griebens Reisebücher, Bd.47)

OUNDLE SCHOOL EXPEDITION TO ECUADOR, 1975
   [Report]. [Peterborough]: Oundle School, 1975.
   94 leaves. 32cm.
   Expedition leader: Jonathan S. Lee

Our native land, its scenery and associations: a
   series of 36 water-colour sketches ... with descriptive notes, [by Jean L. Watson]. Ward, 1879.
   120p., plates, illus. 28cm.

OUSTON, T   G
RENWICK, George
   Romantic Corsica: wanderings in Napoleon's isle;
   with a chapter on climbing by T.G. Ouston. Fisher
   Unwin, 1909. 333p., plates (1 fold.col.), illus.,
   map. 23cm.

OUTRAM, Sir James, Bart
   In the heart of the Canadian Rockies. New York:
   Macmillan, 1905. xii, 466p., 3 col. plates (1
   fold.), illus., maps. 23cm.

OWEN, John
   Travels into different parts of Europe, in the
   years 1791 and 1792... T. Cadell, Jun. and W.
   Davies, 1796. 2v. 22cm.

OXFORD EXPEDITION TO THE HINDU KUSH, 1977
   [Report]. The Expedition, 1978. 31 leaves, maps.
   30cm.

OXFORD HIMALAYAN EXPEDITION, 1973
   [Report]. East Hanney: The Expedition, [1974].
   36p., illus., maps. 30cm.

OXFORD UNIVERSITY BAFFIN EXPEDITION, 1976
   [Report]. Oxford: The Expedition, [1977]. 40p.,
   illus. 30cm.

Oxford world atlas, Saul B. Cohen geographic editor;
   prepared by the Cartographic Department of the
   Clarendon Press. Oxford University Press, 1973.
   xii, 190p., chiefly col. maps. 39cm.

OXLEY, J   MacDonald
   L'hasa at last. Philadelphia: American Baptist
   Publication Society, 1900. 269p., plates, illus.
   19cm.

OXLEY, T   Louis
   Jacques Balmat; or, The first ascent of Mont Blanc:
   a true story. Kerby & Endean, 1881. 38p. 19cm.

OXONIAN
   See
WESTON, Stephen

ØYEN, P   A
   Variations of Norwegian glaciers. [Christiania],
   1901. 73-116p., illus. 26cm.
   Offprint from Nyt Magazin f. Naturvidenskab., b.39.

OYLEY, Elizabeth d'
   See
D'OYLEY, Elizabeth

P***, M. l'A.
   See
PALASSOU, M. l'A

P***, J.P.
   See
PICQUET, J   P

PACCARD, Michel Gabriel
   Dr. Paccard's 'Lost narrative': an attempted reconstruction, by E.H. Stevens. [London, 1929-30].
   2 pts., plates (some col.), illus. 23cm.
   Offprint from Alpine journal, v.41, 1929 and v.42,
   1930.

PACCARD, Michel Gabriel
EGGER, Carl
   Michel-Gabriel Paccard und der Montblanc. Basel:
   Gaiser & Haldimann, 1943. 103p., plates, illus.,
   bibl. 23cm.

PACCARD, Michel Gabriel
MONTAGNIER, Henry Fairbanks
   Note sur la relation de Paccard perdue. Lyon,
   1921. 24p., 1 plate, illus. 24cm.
   Offprint from Revue alpine, 4e trimestre, 1920.

PACCARD, Michel Gabriel
MONTAGNIER, Henry Fairbanks
   Thomas Blaikie and Michel-Gabriel Paccard.
   [London], 1933. 34p., 1 col. plate, illus. 23cm.
   Offprint from Alpine journal, v.45, 1933.

PACCARD, Michel Gabriel
STEVENS, Ernest H
   Dr. Paccard's diary. [London], 1934. 13p.,
   plates (1 col.), illus. 23cm.
   Offprint from Alpine journal, v.46, 1934.

PACCARD, Michel Gabriel
STEVENS, Ernest H
   In the footsteps of Dr. Paccard. [London],
   1935-37. 2 pts., plates (1 col.), illus., map.
   23cm.
   Offprint from Alpine journal, v.47, 1935 and v.49,
   1937.

PACHECO, Eduardo Hernandez
   See
HERNANDEZ-PACHECO, Eduardo

PACKE, Charles
   A guide to the Pyrenees, especially intended for
   the use of mountaineers. Longman, Green, Longman,
   Roberts & Green, 1862. xiv, 130p., plates (2
   fold., some col.), illus., maps. 18cm.

- - 2nd ed. rewritten and much enlarged. 1867.

PACKE, Charles
   The spirt of travel. Chapman & Hall, 1857. iv,
   160p. 19cm.

PAGE, David
   Introductory text-book of geology; revised and in
   great part rewritten by Charles Lapworth. 12th
   and enl. ed. Edinburgh, London: Blackwood, 1888.
   316p., illus. 19cm. (Blackwood's class books:
   natural science series)

PAGET, Stephen
HOLLAND, Henry Scott
   Henry Scott Holland: memoir and letters; edited
   by Stephen Paget. Murray, 1921. xii, 336p.,
   plates, illus. 23cm.

PAILLON, Mary
   L'Aiguille du Dru. Lyon, 1902. 12p., plates,
   illus., bibl. 25cm.
   Offprint from Revue alpine, nov. 1902.

PAILLON, Mary
   L'Album de Mlle d'Angeville. Paris: The Author,
   1909. 8p. 23cm. (Les femmes alpinistes)
   Reprinted with additions from La Montagne, 20
   avril 1909.

PAILLON, Mary
En souvenir de Miss Katharine Richardson,1854-1927.
[Paris], 1927. 12p., ports. 21cm.
Offprint from Montagne, déc., 1927.

PAILLON, Mary
Miss Kate Richardson: une grande alpiniste: liste
de courses et souvenirs. Lyon: "L'Écho de Savoie",
[1943?]. 55p., illus. 19cm.

PAILLON, Maurice
Alpes de France: régions naturelles, massifs
alpestres, préalpes et chaînes subalpines; illustrations en couleur par Albert Doran; photographies
de Jean Roubier. Paris: Alpina, 1938. 2v., col.
plates, illus., maps. 35cm.

PAILLON, Maurice
Chamonix et le Mont-Blanc, Saint-Gervais-les-
Bains, Argentière. Paris: Hachette, 1913. 71p.,
plates, illus., maps, plans. 17cm. (Guides
diamant)

PAILLON, Maurice
Dauphiné ...; rédigé par Maurice Paillon ..., mis
à jour pour 1911. Paris: Hachette, 1910. 588p.,
illus., plans. 16cm. (Collection des guides-
Joanne)

PAILLON, Maurice,
Exploration du massif de Séguret. Paris, 1901.
54p., illus. 24cm. (Études sur les massifs
alpestres)
Offprint with corrections and addititions from
Annuaire du C.A.F., v.26, 1899.

PAILLON, Maurice
JOANNE, Paul
Itinéraire général de la France: Savoie; revisée
par Maurice Paillon. Paris: Hachette, 1910.
xxxii, 477p., illus., maps, plans. 17cm.
(Collection des guides-Joanne)

PAIS BECHER, Gianni
Escursioni in Val d'Ansiei: le Dolomiti di Auronzo
di Cadore. Bologna: Tamari, 1976. 150p., 1 fold.
col. plate, illus., map (in pocket), bibl. 16cm.
(Itinerari alpini: guide per alpinisti ed escursionisti, 30)

PAKENHAM, Thomas
The mountains of Rasselas: an Ethiopian adventure.
Weidenfeld & Nicolson, 1959. 192p., plates, illus.,
maps. 23cm.

PALASSOU, M. l'A.
Essai sur la minéralogie des Monts-Pyrénées; suivi
d'un catalogue des plantes observées dans cette
chaîne de montagnes ..., [par M. l'A.P***, i.e.
Palassou]. Paris: Didot, 1781. xx, 346p., plates
(some fold.), illus., maps. 26cm.

PALLA, Eduard
DEUTSCHER UND ÖSTERREICHISCHER ALPENVEREIN
Atlas der Alpenflora; hrsg. vom Deutschen und
Oesterreichischen Alpenverein. 2. neubearb. Aufl.
Wissenschaftlicher Redacteur: Dr. Palla; Ausführung
der Farbentafeln nach Naturaufnamen und Originalvorlagen von A. Hartinger. Graz: J. Lindauer,
1897. 10 pts. in 5v. in 7 portfolios, col. plates,
illus. 21cm.

PALLAS, P   S
Travels through the southern provinces of the
Russian Empire in the years 1793 and 1794;
translated from the German. Longman & O. Rees,
1802-03. 2v., plates (some fold., some col.),
illus., maps. 28cm.

- - 2nd ed. Stockdale, 1812.

PALLIN, H   N
Andréegatan. Uppsala: J.A. Lindblad, 1934. 196p.,
maps. 23cm.

PALLIN, H   N
Kebnekaise: färder och äventyr i Lappland. Stockholm: Bonnier, 1927. 251p., illus., maps. 24cm.

PALLIS, Marco
Peaks and lamas. Cassell, 1939. xx, 428p.,
plates, illus., maps. 25cm.

PALLISER, John
Progress of the British North American Exploring
Expedition. London, 1859. 267-314p., 1 fold.
plate, map. 24cm.
Offprint from Journal of the Royal Geographical
Society, v.30, 1859.

PALMER, Francis H   E
Austro-Hungarian life in town and country.
Newnes, [19--]. x, 251p., 1 plate, illus. 19cm.

PALMER, Howard and THORINGTON, James Monroe
A climber's guide to the Rocky Mountains of
Canada. New York: Knickerbocker Press for the
American Alpine Club, 1921. xvii, 183p., plates
(some fold.), illus., maps, bibl. 18cm.

-- - 2nd ed. 1930.
- - 3rd ed. 1940.

PALMER, Howard
Edward W.D. Holway: a pioneer of the Canadian
Alps. Minneapolis: University of Minnesota Press,
1931. xiv, 81p., plates, illus., map, bibl.
22cm.

PALMER, Howard
Mountaineering and exploration in the Selkirks: a
record of pioneer work among the Canadian Alps,
1908-1912. New York, London: Putnam, 1914.
xxvii, 439p., plates, illus., maps. 24cm.

PALMER, William Thomas
The complete hill walker, rock climber and cave
explorer. Pitman, 1934. xi, 219p., illus. 22cm.
PALMER, William Thomas
The English Lakes; painted by A. Heaton Cooper;
described by Wm. T. Palmer. Black, 1905. ix,
230p., 75 col. plates, illus., map. 23cm.

- - 2nd ed. 1908.

PALMER, William Thomas
The English lakes: their topographical, historical
and literary landmarks. Harrap, 1930. 304p.,
plates (1 fold., 1 col.), illus., map. 18cm.

PALMER, William Thomas
In Lakeland dells and fells. Chatto & Windus,
1903. vi, 351p., plates, illus. 20cm.

PALMER, William Thomas
Lake-country rambles. Chatto & Windus, 1902.
viii, 334p., plates, illus. 20cm.

PALMER, William Thomas
Odd corners in English Lakeland: rambles,
scrambles, climbs and sport. Skeffington, 1913.
viii, 186p., 15 plates, illus. 20cm.

PALMER, William Thomas
Odd yarns of English Lakeland: narratives of
romance, mystery and superstition told by the
Dalesfolk; with a preface by Mrs. Humphry Ward.
Skeffington, 1914. x, 160p., 1 plate, illus.
20cm.

PALMER, William Thomas
Tramping in Lakeland. Country Life, 1934. xii,
220p., maps. 18cm.

PALMER, William Thomas
Wanderings in Lakeland; with fifteen illustrations
by John Hardman. Skeffington, [1945?]. 143p.,
plates, illus. 19cm.

OLAFSSON, Eggert and PALSSON, Bjarni
Travels in Iceland, performed by order of His
Danish Majesty, containing observations on ... the
inhabitants, a description of the lakes ...;
translated from the Danish. R. Phillips, 1805.
162p., plates (1 fold.), illus., map. 23cm.
(In A collection of modern and contemporary
voyages... Vol.2. 1806)

Panorama des Alpes pris sur la sommité du Galm près des Bains de Loëche. Sion: M. Müller, 1845. 21cm.

Panorama des Vierwaldstätter-see's und seinen Umgebungen = Plan pittoresque... Lucerne: H. Däniker, [ca 1850]. 17cm.

Panorama du Mont Righi. Zurich: R. Dickenmann, [ca 1850]. 17cm.

Panorama vom Piz Languard. [Zürich]: [N.pub.], [ca 1900]. 25 x 31cm.

PANOV, D   G
Geomorfologicheskii ocherk Poliarnykh Uralid i zapadnoi chasti Poliarnogo Shel'fa. Moskva: Akademia Nauk, 1937. 151p., 1 fold. plate, illus., maps, bibl. 26cm. (Akademia Nauk SSSR. Trudy Instituta Geografii, Vypusk 26. Geomorfologicheskie ocherki SSSR, no.4)
Summary in French.

PAPON, Jakob
Engadin: Zeichnungen aus der Natur und dem Volksleben eines unbekannten Alpenlandes. St. Gallen: Scheitlin & Zollikofer, 1857. xii, 219p. 16cm.

PARAGOT, Robert and SEIGNEUR, Yannick
Makalu pilier ouest; préface de Lucien Devies. [Paris]: Arthaud, 1972. 263p., plates (some col.), illus., maps. 21cm. (Collection sempervivum, no.57)

PARAGOT, Robert and BÉRARDINI, Lucien
Vingt ans de cordée; préface de Lucien Devies. Paris: Flammarion, 1974. 226p., plates, illus. 22cm. (L'aventure vécue)

COLLET, Léon W   and PAREJAS, Édouard
Géologie de la chaîne de la Jungfrau. Bern: A. Francke, 1931. ix, 64p., 10 plates (some fold., some col.), illus., bibl. 32cm. (Beiträge zur geologischen Karte der Schweiz, 93, N.F.63)

PAREJAS, Édouard
Géologie de la zone de Chamonix comprise entre le Mont-Blanc et les Aiguilles Rouges. Genève, 1922. 373-442p., 1 fold.col. plate, illus., map. 31cm. Offprint from Mémoires de la Société de physique et d'histoire naturelle de Genève, v.39, fasc.7, 1922.

PARES, Bip
Himalayan honeymoon. Hodder and Stoughton, 1940. 301p., plates (some col.), illus., maps. 23cm.

PARIBHRAMAN
Gujarat expedition to 'Shrirange' of Himalayas, 1963. Ahmedabad: Paribhraman, [1964]. [36]p., illus. 21 x 23cm.

PARIS, T   Clifton
Letters from the Pyrenees during three months' pedestrian wanderings amidst the wildest scenes of the French and Spanish mountains in the summer of 1842. Murray, 1843. xv, 314p., 1 plate, illus. 21cm.

UN PARISIEN
Voyage épisodique et anecdotique dans les Alpes, par un Parisien. Paris: Gagniard, 1830. 223p. 21cm.

PARKE, Thomas Heazle
My personal experiences in equatorial Africa as medical officer of the Emin Pasha relief expedition. Sampson Low, Marston, 1891. xxvii, 526p., plates (1 fold.col.), illus., map (in pocket). 24cm.

PARKER, H   C
Laddow area: edited by H.C. Parker; with sketches by C.N. Brayshaw. Birkenhead: Willmer, 1948. 68p., plates, illus., map, bibl. 16cm. (Climbs on gritstone, 1)

PARKER, James A
The Western Highlands. Edinburgh: Scottish Mountaineering Club, 1931. vi, 133p., plates (1 fold.), illus., bibl. 22cm. (Scottish Mountaineering Club guides)

- - 3rd ed., rev. 1947.
- - 4th ed., rev. by G. Scott Johnstone. Edinburgh: Scottish Mountaineering Trust, 1964.

PARKER, Samuel
Journal of an exploring tour beyond the Rocky Mountains, under the direction of the A.B.C.F.M., performed in the years 1835, '36 and '37; containing a description of the geography ... with a map of Oregon territory. Ithaca (New York): The Author, 1838. 371p., plates (1 fold.), illus., map. 20cm.

PARKER, Terry M   and MELDRUM, Kim I
Outdoor education. Dent, 1973. 204p., plates, illus., bibl. 22cm.

PARLATORE, Filippo
Viaggio alla catena del Monte Bianco e al Gran San Bernardo. Firenze: Le Monnier, 1850. xi, 219p., 1 fold. plate, illus. 25cm.

PARROT, Friedrich
Reise zum Ararat... Berlin: In der Haude & Spenerschen Buchhandlung, 1834. 2v., 1 fold. plate, illus., map. 24cm.

PARROT, Friedrich
[Reise zum Ararat...]. Journey to Ararat; translated by W.D. Cooley. Longman, Brown, Green and Longmans, 1845. xii, 375p., 1 fold. plate, illus., map. 24cm.

PARRY, C   H
DUMAS, Alexandre, 1802-1870
[Impressions de voyage-Suisse]. Swiss travel, being chapters from Dumas' 'Impressions de voyage'; edited by C.H. Parry. Longmans, Green, 1890. viii, 254p. 18cm.

- - New ed. 1895.

PARRY, Edward
Cambrian mirror; or, A new tourist companion through North Wales... 2nd ed. Simpkin, 1846. 353p., plates (1 fold.), illus., map. 16cm.

- - Another issue. Whittaker, 1850.

PARRY, John
Ridiculous things, scraps and oddities, some with, and many without meaning. T. M'Lean, 1854. 1v. of illus. 42cm.
Contains 32 lithographed plates of cartoons of contemporary events, etc. including Albert Smith's Mont Blanc lecture.

PARRY, John
A trip to North Wales, made in 1839; containing much information relative to that interesting alpine country... J. Limbird, 1840. 67p., plates (some fold.), illus. 15cm.

PARSONS, Alfred
Notes in Japan. Osgood, McIlvaine, 1896. xiv, 226p., illus. 22cm.

PARSONS, William
A poetical tour in the years 1784, 1785, and 1786, by a member of the Arcadian Society at Rome [i.e. W. Parsons], J. Robson and W. Clarke, 1787. iii, 208p. 19cm.

PASCAL, César
De glacier en glacier en Suisse et en Savoie: souvenirs de voyage précédés d'une notice biographique. Paris: Dentu, [1884]. 356p. 19cm.
Contains a biographical note on Olive H. Cutler.

PASCHETTA, Vincent
Alpes de Provence, Tinée, Ubaye: randonnées et
escalades faciles. Grenoble: Didier & Richard,
1977. 158p., illus. 18cm. (Guide Paschetta des
Alpes-Maritimes)
"La 4e éd. entièrement refondue du Guide Paschetta
Haute-Tinée-Barcelonnette". - Introduction.

PASCHETTA, Vincent
Alpinisme. Nice: C.A.F., Section des Alpes
Maritimes, 1937. viii, 339p., plates, illus.,
bibl. 16cm. (Guide des Alpes Maritimes, 2)

PASCHETTA, Vincent
Les Collines niçoises: circuits automibiles et
promenades à pied. 7e éd. Nice: Syndicat
d'Initiative, 1971. 130p., col. plates, illus.,
maps. 21cm. (Guides Paschetta des Alpes-
Maritimes, 3. Nice, Riviera, Côte d'Azur, 2)

PASCHETTA, Vincent
Environs de Breuil: guide pour skieurs. Paris:
C.A.F., Section des Alpes Maritimes, [19--].
114p., illus., map. 16cm. (Guide des Alpes-
Maritimes, 4)

PASCHETTA, Vincent
Environs de Saint-Martin-Vésubie: guide pour
touristes, alpinistes et skieurs, par Vincent
Paschetta [and others]. Nice: C.A.F., Section des
Alpes Maritimes [1934?]. 189p., 1 fold. plate,
maps, bibl. 16cm. (Guide des Alpes Maritimes, 2)

PASCHETTA, Vincent
Haute Tinée, Barcelonnette: Auron, Isola 2000,
Saint-Étienne-de-Tinée, Saint-Dalmas-le-Selvage,
Pra-Loup, Le Sauze. 3e éd. Grenoble: Didier-
Richard, 1973. 168p., 1 fold plate, illus. 21cm.
(Guides Paschetta des Alpes-Maritimes, 2. Ran-
données et alpinisme, 4)

PASCHETTA, Vincent
COLLOMB, Robin Gabriel
Maritime Alps: Vésubie basin and Argentera: a selection of popular and recommended climbs; compiled by Robin G. Collomb; based on the works of
Vincent Paschetta. Goring, Reading: West Col,
1968. 100p., illus., map, bibl. 17cm. (West Col
alpine guides)

PASCHETTA, Vincent
Merveilles, Tende, Gordolasque. 10e éd. Grenoble:
Didier et Richard, 1976. 110p., plates (some
col.), illus., maps, bibl. 21cm. (Guides
Paschetta des Alpes-Maritimes, 2. Randonnées et
alpinisme, 1)

PASCHETTA, Vincent
Nice et sa region: arts, histoire, tourisme. 9e
éd. Grenoble: Didier-Richard, [1973?]. 223p.,
plates (some col.), illus., bibl. 21cm. (Guides
du Syndicat d'Initiative; guides Paschetta des
Alpes-Maritimes, 3)

PASCHETTA, Vincent
Saint-Martin-Vésubie, Valdeblore. 10e éd.
Grenoble: Didier et Richard, 1976. 173p., col.
plates, illus., maps. 21cm. (Guides Paschetta
des Alpes-Maritimes, 2. Randonnées et ascensions,
circuits automobiles)

PASCHETTA, Vincent
Le ski dans les Alpes-Maritimes. 5e éd. Nice:
Fédération des Syndicats d'Initiative, 1967. 75p.,
col. plates, illus. 21cm. (Guides Paschetta des
Alpes-Maritimes)

PASCHETTA, Vincent
Valberg (Beuil, Guillaumes, Péone), Haut-Var
(Esteng, Pélens). 3e éd. Nice: Fédération des
Syndicats d'Initiative, 1972. 96p., 2 col. plates,
illus., maps. 21cm. (Guides Paschetta des Alpes-
Maritimes, 2. Randonnées et alpinisme, 3)

PASCHINGER, Viktor
Pasterzenstudien. Klagenfurt: Kleinmayr, 1948.
119p., plates, illus. 24cm. (Festschrift zum
hundertjährigen Bestand des Naturwissenschaftlichen
Vereins für Kärnten, T.2)

PASCOE, John
Great days in New Zealand mountaineering; foreword
by Sir Edmund Hillary. Bailey and Swinfen, 1958.
199p., plates, illus., maps, bibl. 23cm.

PASCOE, John
Land uplifted high. Christchurch (N.Z.): Whitcombe
& Tombs, 1952. xii, 235p., plates, illus., maps.
23cm.

PASCOE, John
The mountains, the bush and the sea: a photographic
report. Christchurch (N.Z.): Whitcombe & Tombs,
1950. 100p. (chiefly illus., map). 28cm.

PASCOE, John
Mr. Explorer Douglas; edited by John Pascoe.
Wellington: Reed, 1957. xx, 331p., plates, illus.,
maps, bibl. 25cm.

PASCOE, John
The Southern Alps. Part 1. From the Kaikouras to
the Rangitata. Christchurch (N.Z.): Pegasus Press,
1951. 96p., plates, illus., maps. 18cm. (New
Zealand holiday guides, no.3)

PASCOE, John
Unclimbed New Zealand: alpine travel in the
Canterbury and Westland ranges, Southern Alps.
Allen & Unwin, 1939. 238p., plates (some fold.,
some col.), illus., maps, bibl. 25cm.

PASQUIER, Léon du
FAVRE, Alphonse
Texte explicatif de la carte du phénomène erra-
tique et des anciens glaciers du versant nord des
Alpes suisses et de la chaîne du Mont-Blanc;
précédé d'une introduction par Ernest Favre; et
suivi d'une biographie de Léon du Pasquier par
Maurice de Tribolet; avec les portraits... Berne:
Schmid & Francke, 1898. 77p., plates, ports.
33cm. (Beiträge zur geologischen Karte der
Schweiz = Matériaux pour la carte géologique de la
Suisse, livr. 28)

PASQUIN, Antoine Claude
See
VALÉRY

PASSARGE, L
Sommerfahrten in Norwegen: Reiseerinnerungen,
Natur-und Kulturstudien. 3. Aufl. Leipzig: B.
Elischer Nachfolger, [189-]. 2v. in 1. 22cm.

PASSERI, Giovanni Battista
Dissertazione epistolare ... sopra un'antica
statuetta di marmo trovata nel distretto di
Perugia, ed ora esistente nel Museo dell'Istituto
di Bologna. Bologna: Lelio dalla Volpe, 1776.
14p., plates, illus. 26cm.

PASSMORE, T   H
In further Ardenne: a study of the Grand Duchy of
Luxembourg. Dent, 1905. xiii, 316p., plates,
illus., map. 24cm.

OSMASTON, Henry A   and PASTEUR, David
Guide to the Ruwenzori: the Mountains of the Moon.
Kampala: Mountain Club of Uganda; Goring, Reading:
West Col, 1972. 200p., illus., maps, bibl. 18cm.

PASUMOT, François
Voyages physiques dans les Pyrénées en 1788 et
1789: histoire naturelle d'une partie de ces montagnes... Paris: Le Clere, 1797. 423p., 3 fold.
plates, maps, plan. 21cm.

PATAGONIAN MOUNTAINEERING EXPEDITION, 1974
A Patagonia handbook: Cerro Stanhardt 1974/5: the
report of the 1974 Patagonian Mountaineering
Expedition; compiled by Ben Campbell-Kelly with
assistance from Brian Wyvill. Manchester: The
Expedition, 1975. 30 leaves, plates, illus., maps.
30cm.

PATERA, Lothar
Führer durch die Lienzer Dolomiten. Wien: Guberner
& Hierhammer, 1909. 176p., plates, illus., map.
17cm.

Paterfamilias's Diary of everybody's tour: Belgium and the Rhine, Munich, Switzerland, Milan, Geneva and Paris, [by Martin Tupper]. T. Hatchard, 1856. 385p., plates, illus. 18cm.

PATERSON, M
Mountaineering below the snow-line; or, The solitary pedestrian in Snowdonia and elsewhere; with etchings by Mackaness. G. Redway, 1886. viii, 307p., plates, illus. 19cm.

Paterson's guide to Switzerland. Edinburgh: Paterson; London: Stanford, 1885. xiv, 162p., maps, plans. 18cm.

- - 8th ed. [n.d.].

PATEY, Tom
One man's mountains: essays and verses; with a foreword by Christopher Brasher. Gollancz, 1971. 287p., plates, illus. 23cm.

PATON, William Agnew
Down the Islands: a voyage to the Caribees; with illustrations from drawings by M.J. Burns. New York: Scribner, 1896. xiii, 301p., plates, illus., map. 22cm.

PATRON, Luis Riso
See
RISO PATRON, Luis

PATRONI, Alfredo
La conquista dei ghiacciai, 1915-1918; prefazione di Filiberto di Savoia, Duca di Pistoia. Milano: L'Eroica, 1924. 195p., col. plates (1 fold.), illus., map. 25cm.

PATTERSON, George Neil
God's fool. Faber and Faber, 1956. 251p., plates, illus. 23cm.

PATTERSON, George Neil
Tibetan journey. Faber and Faber, 1954. 232p., plates, illus., maps. 23cm.

PAULCKE, Wilhelm
Berge als Schicksal. München: F. Bruckmann, 1936. 271p., plates, illus., map. 22cm.

PAULCKE, Wilhelm
ZSIGMONDY, Emil
Die Gefahren der Alpen: Erfahrungen und Ratschläge; neu bearb. und ergänst von W. Paulcke. 4. Aufl. Innsbruck: A. Edlinger, 1908. xv, 348p., plates, illus. 23cm.

- - 5. Aufl. Wien: A. Edlinger, 1911.
- - 7. Aufl. München: Rother, 1922.
- - 8. Aufl. München: Rother, 1927.
PAULCKE, Wilhelm
[Die Gefahren der Alpen]. Hazards in mountain-eering; [rev. by] Helmut Dumler, translated from the German by E. Noel Bowman. Kaye & Ward, 1973. 161p. (1 fold., col.), col. illus., bibl. 21cm.

PAULCKE, Wilhelm
Gefahrenbuch des Bergsteigers und Skiläufers: Katechismus für Bergfreunde in Sommer und Winter. Berlin: Union Deutsche Verlagsgesellschaft, 1942. 233p., illus. 20cm.

PAULCKE, Wilhelm
Lawinengefahr, ihre Entstehung und Vermeidung: eine Darlegung für Bergsteiger und Skiläufer. München: Lindauer, 1926. 60p., 1 fold. plate, illus., map. 22cm.

PAULIC, Dragutin
Vodic na Plitvicka Jezera. Zagreb: Zaklada Tiskare "Narodnih Novina", 1923. 120p., plates (2 fold, 1 col.), illus., maps. 17cm.

PAULMY, Antoine René de Voyer d'Argenson, marquis de
Voyage d'inspection de la frontière des Alpes en 1752 par le marquis de Paulmy; [edited by] Henry Duhamel. Grenoble: H. Falque & F. Perrin, 1902. 236p., plates, illus., maps, port. 26cm.

PAUSE, Walter
[Berg Heil]. Salute the mountains: the hundred best walks in the Alps; translated by Ruth Michaelis-Jena and Arthur Ratcliff. Harrap, 1962. 211p., illus., maps. 20cm.

PAUSE, Walter and WINKLER, Jürgen
100 scalate estreme (V e VI grado). Milano: Görlich, 1975. 207p., illus., maps (on lining papers), bibl. 26cm. (I volumi della montagna)

PAUSE, Walter
[Ski Heil]. Salute the skier: the hundred best ski runs in the Alps; translated by Ruth Michaelis-Jena and Arthur Ratcliff. Harrap, 1963. 211p., illus. 26cm.

LANGUEPIN, Jean Jacques and PAYAN, Louis
Nanda Devi: 3e expédition française à l'Himalaya; préface de Jean Montel. Paris: Arthaud, 1952. xvi, 13p., 72 plates (some col.), illus., maps. 20cm. (Collection Belles pages, belles couleurs)

PAYER, Hugo
MAGYARORSZÁGI KÁRPÁTEGYLET
Bibliotheca Carpatica; a "Magyarországi Kárpátegylet" megbizásából összeállította Payer Hugo. Késmárk: A "Magyarországi Kárpátegylet" kiadványa, 1880. 378p. 23cm.

PAYER, Julius
Die Adamello-Presanella-Alpen nach den Forschungen und Aufnahmen. Gotha: Perthes, 1865. 36p., 2 col. plates, illus., map. 28cm. (Ergänzungs-Heft zu Petermann's 'Geographischen Mittheilungen', No.17)

PAYER, Julius
[Bergfahrten]. Julius Payers Bergfahrten: Erschliessungsfahrten in den Ortler-, Adamello- und Presanella-Alpen (1864-1868); hrsg., von Wilhelm Lehner. München: Manz, 1920. vii, 190p., plates, illus., port. 27cm.

PAYER, Julius
Die centralen Ortler-Alpen (Gebiete: Martell, Laas und Saent), nebst einem Anhange zu den Adamello-Presanella-Alpen. Gotha: Perthes, 1872. 36p., 2 plates (1 fold.), illus., map. 29cm. (Ergänzungsheft zu Petermann's "Geographischen Mittheilungen", No.31)

PAYER, Julius
Die Ortler-Alpen (Sulden-Gebiet und Monte Cevedale) nach den Forschungen und Aufnamen. Gotha: Perthes, 1867. 15p., 2 plates (1 col.), illus., map. 28cm. (Ergänzungsheft zu Petermann's "Geographischen Mittheilungen", No.18)

WEYPRECHT, A and PAYER, Julius
Die Polar-Expedition von A. Weyprecht & Julius Payer im Jahre 1871. Wien, 1872. 24p. 22cm. Offprint from Mittheilungen der Geographischen Gesellschaft.

PAYER, Julius
Die südlichen Ortler-Alpen... Gotha: Perthes, 1869. 30p., 2 plates (1 fold., 1 col.), illus., map. 29cm. (Ergänzungsheft zu Petermann's "Geographischen Mittheilungen", No.27)

PAYER, Julius
Die westlichen Ortler-Alpen (Trafoier Gebiet)... Gotha: Perthes, 1868. 30p., col. plates, illus., map. 29cm. (Ergänzungsheft zu Petermann's "Geographischen Mittheilungen", No.23)

PAYER, Julius
Die zweite Deutsche Nordpol-Expedition, 1869-70. Gotha, 1871 2v., 1 plate, illus. 28cm. (Geographie u. Erforschung der Polar-Regionen, Nr. 45, 50)
Offprint from Petermann's Geogr. Mittheilungen, 1871.

PAYERNE, A
FERRAND, Henri
L'accident de la Meidje, 20 août 1896: [à la
mémoire de M.A. Payerne]. Grenoble, 1897. 30p.
25cm.
Offprint from Annuaire de la Société des Touristes
du Dauphiné, année 1896.

PAYN, James
The Lakes in sunshine, being photographic and
other pictures of the Lake District; with descriptive letterpress by James Payn. Simpkin, Marshall,
1873. 99, 92p., plates, illus. 29cm.

PAYNTER, Thomas
The ski and the mountain. Hurst and Blackett,
1954. 212p., plates, illus. 22cm.

PAYOT, Paul
Au royaume du Mont-Blanc. Bonneville (Haute-
Savoie): Plancher, 1950. 305p., plates, illus.
22cm.

PAYOT, Paul
La connaissance de la montagne; texte et photos de
Paul Payot. Bonneville (Haute Savoie): Plancher,
1944. 127p., illus. 24cm.

PAYOT, Venance
Catalogue des fougères, prêles et Lycopodiacées
des environs du Mont-Blanc ..., suivi d'un catalogue des mousses et des lichens... Paris, Genève:
J. Cherbuliez, 1860. 70p., 1 plate, map. 22cm.

PAYOT, Venance
Guide-itinéraire au Mont-Blanc et dans les vallées
comprises entre les deux Saint-Bernard et le Lac
de Genève... 2e éd. Genève: N. Ghisletty, 1869.
240p., 1 fold. plate, map. 18cm.

Paysages suisses. Paris: Wild, [ca 1860]. 1v. of
col. illus. 15 x 19cm.
Cover title.

PAZZE, Peter August
Chronik der Section Küstenland des Deutschen und
Österreichischen Alpenvereins, 1873-1892: Fest-
Publication zur Vollendung des 20. Vereinsjahres;
aus den Veröffentlichungen der Section zusammen-
gestellt von P.A. Pazze. Triest: Section
Küstenland, 1893. 372p., plates, illus. 23cm.

PEACOCKE, Thomas Arthur Hardy
Mountaineering. Black, 1941. viii, 212p., plates,
illus. 19cm. (The sportsman's library, v.29)

- - 3rd ed. 1953.

Peaks, passes and glaciers
See
ALPINE CLUB

PEARSALL, William H
Mountains and moorlands. Collins, 1950. xv,
312p., plates (some col.), illus., maps, bibl.
23cm. (The new naturalist)

PEARSE, Reginald O
Barrier of spears: drama of the Drakensberg;
illustrated by Malcolm L. Pearse. [Cape Town]:
H. Timmins, 1973. xxi, 304p., col. plates,
illus., maps, bibl. 29cm.

The peasants of Chamouni, containing an attempt to
reach the summit of Mont Blanc; and a delineation
of the scenery among the Alps. Baldwin, Cradock,
& Joy, 1823. 164p., plates, illus. 15cm.

- - 2nd ed. 1826.

PEASCOD, W   and RUSHWORTH, G
Buttermere and Newlands area; with illustrations
by W. Heaton Cooper. Manchester: Fell & Rock
Climbing Club, 1949. 125p., 1 col.plate, illus.
16cm. (Rock-climbing guides to the English Lake
District, 2nd [i.e. 3rd] ser., 2)

KELLY, Harry M   and PEASCOD, W
Pillar rock and neighbourhood; with illustrations
by W. Heaton Cooper. Stockport: Fell & Rock
Climbing Club, 1952. 130p., 1 plate, illus. 16cm.
(Rock-climbing guides to the English Lake
District, 2nd [i.e. 3rd] ser., 4)

PEATTIE, Roderick
The Friendly Mountains: Green, White and
Adirondacks; edited by Roderick Peattie. New
York: Vanguard Press, 1942. 341p., plates, illus.
24cm.

PEATTIE, Roderick
Mountain geography: a critique and field study.
Cambridge (Mass.): Harvard University Press,
1936. xiv, 257p., plates, illus., bibl. 25cm.

PEATTIE, Roderick
The Sierra Nevada: the range of light; with an
introduction by Donald Culross Peattie. New
York: Vanguard Press, 1947. 398p., plates (1
fold.), illus., map. 24cm.

PECK, Annie Smith
High mountain climbing in Peru & Bolivia: a
search for the apex of America, including the
conquest of Huascarán; with some observations on
the country and people below. Fisher Unwin,
1912. xix, 370p., plates (1 fold.), illus., map.
24cm.

PECK, Annie Smith
The South American tour: a descriptive guide.
New and rev. ed. Hurst & Blackett, 1924. xviii,
379p., plates (1 fold.col.), illus., map, bibl.
22cm.

PEEL, Sir Robert
A correct report of the speeches delivered by Sir
Robert Peel on his inauguration into the office
of Lord Rector of the University of Glasgow,
January 11, 1837... 4th ed. Murray, 1837. 100p.,
1 plate, port. 15cm.

A peep at the Pyrenees, by a pedestrian [i.e. Henry
Baden Pritchard], being a tourist's note-book.
Whittaker, 1867. viii, 147p., 1 fold.col. plate,
map. 17cm.

PEISSEL, Michel
Lords and lamas: a solitary expedition across the
secret Himalayan kingdom of Bhutan. Heinemann,
1970. xi, 180p., plates, illus., maps (on lining
papers). 23cm.

PELLÉ, Gilbert and RICHARD, Guy
Escalades à Surgy, Nievre. Orléans: Club Alpin
Français, Section de l'Orléannais, Section
Nivernais-Yonne, 1974. 55p., illus. 22cm.

FIELD, Edgar Stanley and PELLS, Edward G
A mountaineer's paradise: a guide to the mountains
of the Worcester district... Worcester (C.P.):
Mountain Club of South Africa, [1925]. [134]p.,
1 fold.plate, illus., maps. 21cm.

PELLY, Richard C
Report of the Cambridge Hindu Kush Expedition
1972, 20th June - 10th September; [R.C. Pelly,
editor]. Haslemere: The Expedition, [1973].
83p., plates, illus., maps. 30cm.

PEMBER, F   W
CURZON, George Nathaniel, Marquess Curzon
Leaves from a Viceroy's note-book and other
papers by the Marquess Curzon of Kedleston;
edited by F.W. Pember, Ian Malcolm. Macmillan,
1926. x, 414p., plates, illus. 24cm.

PEMBERTON, John Leigh
See
LEIGH-PEMBERTON, John

Pen & pencil sketches of the Lakes. Windermere:
J. Garnett; London: Hamilton, Adams, [ca 1860].
[16]p., col.plates, illus. 19cm.

PENBERTHY, Larry
Acute mountain sickness - Type R, including suggestions on climbing Mt. Rainier. Seattle: Altitude Medical Publishing, 1977. 48p., illus. 21cm.

PENCK, Albrecht and BRÜCKNER, Eduard
Die Alpen im Eiszeitalter. Leipzig: Tauchnitz, 1909. 3v. in 1, plates (some fold., 1 col.), illus., maps (some fold.). 29cm.

PENCK, Albrecht
Festband: Albrecht Penck zur Vollendung des sechzigsten Lebensjahrs Gewidmet von seinen Schülern und der Verlagsbuchhandlung. Stuttgart: J. Engelhorn, 1918. xii, 438p., plates, illus., maps. 24cm. (Bibliothek geographischer Handbücher, neue Folge)

PENCK, Albrecht
Gletscher und Eiszeit. Prag: [n.pub.], 1880. 20p. 23cm. (Sammlung Gemeinnütziger Vorträge, 59)

PENCK, Albrecht
Die Vergletscherung der deutschen Alpen, ihre Ursachen, periodische Wiederkehr und ihr Einfluss auf die Bodengestaltung. Leipzig: Barth, 1882. 484p., plates (1 fold., 3 col.), illus., maps. 24cm.

PENNANT, Thomas
The journey to Snowdon. Printed by H. Hughes, 1781. ii, 218p., plates, illus. 26cm.

PENNELL, Joseph
HAMERTON, Philip Gilbert
The Saône: a summer voyage; with ... illustrations by Joseph Pennell and the author... Seeley, 1887. xix, 368p., plates, illus., maps. 30cm.

PENNINGTON, Thomas
Continental excursions; or, Tours into France, Switzerland and Germany, in 1782, 1787, and 1789; with a description of ... the glacieres of Savoy ... F.C. & J. Rivington, 1809. 2v. 22cm.

PENNINGTON, Thomas
A journey into various parts of Europe and a residence in them, during the years 1818, 1819, 1820, and 1821; with notes, historical and classical... Geo. B. Whittaker, 1825. 2v. 23cm.

PENSIONNAT JANIN, Geneva
Voyage à Schaffhouse, retour par Zurich, le Righi et l'Oberland; rédigé par les élèves du Pensionnat Janin. Genève: Le Pensionnat, 1845. 107p., 1 plate, illus. 16 x 24cm.
Ms. facsimile.

PENZIG, O
Flora delle Alpi illustrata. Milano: Hoepli, 1902. xiv, 98p., 40 col.plates, illus. 22cm.

PEOPLE'S PHYSICAL CULTURE PUBLISHING HOUSE, Peking
Mountaineering in China; compiled by the People's Physical Culture Publishing House. Peking: Foreign Languages Press, 1965. [95]p., illus. (some col.). 26cm.

PERCY, Henry Algernon George, Earl Percy
Highlands of Asiatic Turkey. Arnold, 1901. xi, 338p., plates (some fold.col.), illus., maps. 24cm.

PEREDA, José M de
[Penas arriba]. Dans la montagne ...: roman; traduction de Henri Collet, Maurice Perrin; préface de René Bazin. Paris: Delagrave, 1918. 337p. 20cm.

Les pérégrinations d'un alpiniste à travers les Alpes-Maritimes, les Basses-Alpes, le Dauphiné, la Savoie, la Suisse, l'Italie septentrionale et la Principauté de Monaco, par un Alsacien [i.e. Gustave E. Cammel]. Nice: Visconti, 1883. 315p. 22cm.

PEREIRA, George
Peking to Lhasa: the narrative of journeys in the Chinese empire made by the late Brigadier-General George Pereira; compiled by Sir Francis Younghusband from notes and diaries supplied by Sir Cecil Pereira. Constable, 1925. x, 293p., plates (some fold.), illus., maps. 24cm.

PEREIRA, Michael
Across the Caucasus. Bles, 1973. 272p., plates, illus., maps, bibl. 22cm.

PERKONIG, Josef Friedrich
Mein Herz ist im Hochland. Graz: Lenkam, 1937. 161p., 100 plates, illus. 24cm.

PERLA, Ronald I   MARTINELLI, M
Avalance handbook. Washington (D.C.): U.S. Department of Agriculture, Forest Service, 1976. vi, 238p., illus., bibl. 26cm. (Agriculture handbooks, 489)

PERREAU, Joseph
L'épopée des Alpes: épisodes de l'histoire militaire des Alpes en particulier des Alpes françaises; avec une préface de M. le général Borson. Paris: Berger-Levrault, 1903-12. 3v., illus., plates (some fold.), illus., maps. 24cm.

PERRET, Paul
Les Pyrénées françaises; illustrations de E. Sadoux. Paris: H. Oudin, 1881. 3v., plates, illus., music. 27cm.
1. Lourdes - Argelès... Barèges. -2. Le Pays basque et la Basse-Navarre.
Library lacks v.3.

PERRET, Robert
L'évolution morphologique du Faucigny (Vallées du Giffre et de l'Arve; vallées du Trient et de la Viège en Bas Valais). Paris: Andriveau-Goujon, 1931. 166p., plates (1 fold.col.), illus., map, bibl. 24cm.

PERRET, Robert
Les panoramas du Mont Blanc. Chambéry: Dardel, 1929. 1v. (chiefly illus., map). 29cm.

PERRIN, André
PRIEURÉ DE CHAMONIX
Documents relatifs au Prieuré et a la vallée de Cahmonix [sic]; recueillis par J.-A. Bonnefoy; publiés et annotés par A. Perrin. Chambéry: Chatelain, 1879-83. 2v. 25cm.

PERRIN, André
Le Prieuré de Chamonix: histoire de la vallée et du Prieuré de Chamonix du Xe au XVIIIe siècle; d'après les documents recueillis par A. Bonnefoy. Chambéry: A. Perrin, 1887. 253p., 1 fold. plate, map. 25cm.

PERRIN, F
Guide du Haut-Dauphiné, par W.A.B. Coolidge, H. Duhamel, F. Perrin. Grenoble: Gratier, 1887. lix, 442p., maps. 16cm.

- - Supplement. Grenoble: Breynat, 1890.

PERRIN, F
[Guide du Haut-Dauphiné]. Das Hochgebirge des Dauphiné, von W.A.B. Coolidge, H. Duhamel and F. Perrin. 4. durchgesehene und 1 autorisierte deutsche Ausg., hrsg. von Österreichischen Alpenklub. Wien: Österreichischer Alpenklub, 1913. 351p. 17cm. (Alpenklub-Ausg., 1)

YATES, Mike and PERRIN, Jim
Cwm Silyn and Cwellyn; geological notes by Dave Thomas; diagrams by Steve Knott; photographs by K. Wilson and E. Siddall. Stockport: Climbers' Club, 1971. xiii, 173p., illus., maps (on lining papers). 16cm. (Climbers' Club guides to Wales, 11)

PERROTIN, Monsieur
Tableau des positions géographiques et hauteurs
absolues au-dessus du niveau de la mer des points
principaux du Département de l'Isère ... [par M.
Perrotin]. Grenoble, 1853. 25p. 24cm.
Offprint from Bulletin de la Société de statistique de l'Isère, 2e sér., v.2.

PERRY, Alexander W
Welsh mountaineering: a practical guide to the
ascent of all the principal mountains in Wales.
L. Upcott Gill, 1896. 172p., plates (1 fold.),
maps. 18cm.

PERTUSI, Luigi and RATTI, Carlo
Guida illustrata pel villeggiante del Biellese;
santuari ed ospizi stabilimenti idroterapici,
passeggiate ed escursioni ...; compilata da Luigi
Portusi e Carlo Ratti. Torino: Casanova, 1901.
xii, 282p., plates, illus., maps. 19cm.

PERTUSI, Luigi and RATTI, Carlo
Guida pel villeggiante nel Biellese. Torino: F.
Casanova, 1886. xv, 436p., plates, illus., map.
16cm.

PERU-BOLIVIA BOUNDARY COMMISSION
Peru-Bolivia Boundary Commission, 1911-1913:
reports of the British officers of the Peruvian
Commission, diplomatic memoranda and maps of the
boundary zone; edited for the Government of Peru
by the Royal Geographical Society of London.
Cambridge: Printed at the University Press, 1918.
xi, 242p., plates (some fold., some col.), illus.,
maps (3 in pocket). 30cm.

PERU HIGH-ALTITUDE COMMITTEE
Observations upon the effect of high altitude on
the physiological processes of the human body,
carried out in the Peruvian Andes, chiefly at
Cerro de Pasco: report to the Peru High-Altitude
Committee, 1922, by J. Barcroft [and others].
[London], 1923. p.351-480, plates, illus. 31cm.
Offprint from Philosophical transactions of the
Royal Society of London, v.211.

PESAY, Alexandre F   Masson, marquis de
See
PEZAY, Alexandre Frédéric Jacques de Masson,
marquis de

PETER, Ernst
Die Zugspitze. Stuttgart: Deutsche Verlags-
Anstalt, 1905. 66p., plates, illus., maps. 18cm.
(Alpine Gipfelführer, 1)

PETERJOSI
See
LEHNER, Karl

PETERMANN, A   and HASSENSTEIN, Bruno
Inner-Afrika nach dem Stande der geographischen
Kenntniss in den Jahren 1861 bis 1863. Gotha:
Perthes, 1863. 50, 164p., fold.col. plates,
illus., maps. 28cm.

PETERMANN, Reinhard E
Wanderungen in den östlichen Niedern Tauern:
Führer im Gebiete des Grossen Bösenstein bis zum
Seckauer Zinken, nebst einem Anhang über den
Zeyritzkampel. Wien: Alpine Gesellschaft Edel-
raute, 1903. 169p., illus. 18cm.

PETERS, Carl
New light on dark Africa, being the narrative of
the German Emin Pasha expedition, its journeyings
...; translated by H.W. Dulcken. Ward Lock, 1891.
xviii, 597p., plates (1 fold.col.), illus., map
(in pocket). 26cm.

PETERSEN, Emil
L'enchantement du ski, [par] Alfred Couttet,
Arnold Lunn, Emil Petersen; introduction de Henry
Cuénot... Paris: Alpina, 1930. 159p., col. plates,
illus. 25cm.

PETERSEN, Theodor
Ein Ausflug auf den Grossvenediger: Reiseskizze.
[Offenbach], [1865?]. 15p. 22cm.
Offprint from Jahresberichte des Offenbacher
Vereins für Naturkunde.

PETERSEN, Theodor
Haupthöhenpunkte in den österreichischen Hochalpen;
zusammengestellt von Theodor Petersen.
[Offenbach]. [ca 1865]. 59-64p. 22cm.
Offprint from Jahrberichte des Offenbacher Vereins
für Naturkunde.

PETERSEN, Theodor
Das Klönthal und der Glärnisch, Kanton Glarus.
[Offenbach], [ca 1865]. 93-98p. 22cm.
Offprint from Jahrberichte des Offenbacher Vereins
für Naturkunde.

PETIT, Victor
Souvenirs de Cauterets et de ses environs.
Bagnères-de-Luchon: Dulon, [ca 1850]. 1v. of
illus. 28 x 40cm.

PETIT, Victor
Souvenirs des Pyrénées: vues prises aux environs
des eaux thermales de Bagnères de Bigorre,
Bagnères de Luchon, Cauteretz, Saint-Sauveur,
Barèges, les Eaux Bonnes, les Eaux Chaudes & Pau;
dessinées ... et lithog. par Victor Petit. Pau:
A. Bassy, [ca 1850]. 5pts. in 1. (chiefly illus.).
29 x 41cm.

PETITHUGUENIN, Jean
A l'assaut de la cime du monde. Paris: Rouff,
[ca 1922]. 24p. 20cm. (La collection "Progrès")
Cover title.

PETRIE, Peter J   W   de C
Farewell to the mountains. Printed for private
circulation by Morton Burt, 1940. xii, 34p.,
plates, illus., port. 23cm.
Diary of a Himalayan journey.

PETROCOKINO, A
Along the Andes. Gay and Bird, 1903. viii,
147p., plates (some fold.), illus., maps. 24cm.

PETZENDORFER, Ludwig
Humoristische Naturgeschichte des alpinen
Menschen. 2. Aufl., mit 10 Illus. von G.
Sundblad. Stuttgart: R. Lutz, 1888. 60p., illus.
19cm.

PETZHOLDT, Alexander
Beiträge zur Geognosie von Tyrol: Skizzen auf
einer Reise durch Sachsen, Bayern, Salzkammergut,
Salzburg, Tyrol, Ostreich. Leipzig: Weber, 1843.
372p., illus. 24cm.

PETZOLDT, Patricia
On top of the world. Hamilton, 1956. 190p. 19cm.
(Mountaineering series, no.1; Panther book)

PEYER, Gustav
Geschichte des Reisens in der Schweiz: eine cul-
turgeschichtliche Studie. Basel: C. Detloff,
1885. viii, 248p. 19cm.

PEYRÉ, Joseph
Mallory et son Dieu. Genève: Éditions du Milieu
du Monde, 1947. 310p., map. 19cm.

PEYRÉ, Joseph
Matterhorn: roman. Paris: Grasset, 1939. 285p.
19cm.

PEYRÉ, Joseph
Mont Everest: roman. Paris: Grasset, 1942.
301p. 20cm.

PEZAY, Alexandre Frédéric Jacques de Masson,
marquis de
Noms, situation et détails des vallées de la
France le long des grandes Alpes dans le Dauphiné
et la Provence, et de celles qui descendent des
Alpes en Italie depuis la Savoye jusqu'à celle de
Saint Étienne au comté de Nice; extraits des cam-
pagnes du Maréchal de Maillebois par le marq. de
Pesay. Turin: Reycends, 1793. 171p. 17cm.

PFAFF, Friedrich
Mt. Blanc-Studien: ein Beitrag zur mechanischen
Geologie der Alpen. [N.p.], 1876. 2 pts., illus.
23cm.
Offprint from Zeitschr. d. Deutschen geologischen
Gesellschaft, Jahrg. 1876.

PFAFF, Friedrich
Die Naturkräfte in den Alpen; oder, Physikalische
Geographie des Alpengebirges. München: R.
Oldenbourg, 1877. x, 281p., illus. 19cm.

PFANN, Hans
Führerlose Gipfelfahrten in den Hochalpen, dem
Kaukasus, dem Tian-Schan und den Anden. Berlin:
Union Deutsche Verlagsgesellschaft, 1941. 255p.,
plates, illus. 22cm.

PFANN, Hans
Menschen im Hochgebirge: Festgabe für Hans Pfann
zum 60 Geuurtstage August 1933; bearb. von Hans
Baumeister; hrsg. von der Sektion Bayerland des
Deutschen und Österreichischen Alpenvereins.
München: Alpenvereinssektion Bayerland, 1933.
253p., plates, illus., port. 25cm.

PFANN, Paul
Bilder aus Tyrol: 20 Federzeichnungen. München:
Georg D.W. Callwey, [1912]. 20 plates, illus. (in
portfolio). 45cm.

PFANNHOLZ, Anton Mayer
See
MAYER-PFANNHOLZ, Anton

PFANNL, Heinrich
Was bist du mir, Berg? Schriften und Reden. Wien:
Österreichischer Alpenklub, 1929. 190p., plates,
illus. 25cm.

BARTH, L   and PFAUNDLER, L
Die Stubaier Gebirgsgruppe; hypsometrisch und orografisch bearb. und mit Unterstützung der kaiserlichen Akademie der Wissenschaften. Innsbruck:
Wagner, 1865. 147p., plates (some fold., 1 col.),
illus., map. 23cm.

PFEIFER, Gottfried
Die räumliche Gliederung der Landwirtschaft im
nördlichen Kalifornien. Leipzig: Hirt, 1936.
309p., plates (1 fold.), illus., maps, bibl. 26cm.
(Wissenschaftliche Veröffentlichungen der Gesell-
schaft für Erdkunde zu Leipzig, Bd. 10)
Festschrift zum 75 jährigen Bestehen der
Gesellschaft.

PFEIFFER, G
À la montagne: croquis montagnards; suivis d'une
notice sur la photographie à la montagne par E.
Potterat. Genève, Ch. Eggimann, [1897]. 197p.,
illus. 30cm.

PFISTER, Otto von
Das Montavon mit dem oberen Paznaun: ein Taschenbuch für Fremde und Einheimische. 2 Aufl., neu
bearb. und ergänzt von Franz Winsauer. München:
J. Lindauer, 1911. vii, 224p. 16cm.

PFYFFER VON WYHER, Ludwig
[Panorama vom Rigi Berg]. Panorama of Switzerland
as viewed from the summit of Mont Righi, drawn
from nature by Henry Keller ...; also a circular
view of the country, by General Pfyffer; with descriptive notices of the most remarkable objects.
S. Leigh, [ca 1830]. 28cm.
Accompanied by a leaflet entitled: A companion to
Keller's panorama of Switzerland...

PHILIPS, Francis
A reading party in Switzerland, with an account of
the ascent of Mont Blanc on the 12th and 13th of
August 1851. Manchester: The Author, 1851. 49p.
19cm.

PHILLIMORE, R   H
Historical records of the Survey of India;
collected and compiled by R.H. Phillimore. Dehra
Dun: Survey of India, 1945-58. Plates (some
fold.), illus. 30cm.
Library has v. 1 to 4.

PHILLIPPS-WOLLEY, Clive
Savage Svânetia. R. Bentley, 1883. 2v., plates,
illus. 20cm.

PHILLIPPS-WOLLEY, Clive
Sport in the Crimea and Caucasus. R. Bentley,
1881. x, 370p. 23cm.

PHILLIPS, John
Black's Picturesque guide to the English Lakes,
including an essay on the geology of the district,
by John Phillips. 4th ed. Edinburgh: Black, 1850.
xxiv, 240p., plates (2 fold.)., illus., maps.
18cm.

- - 17th ed. 1872.
- - 18th ed. 1874.

PHILLIPS, Sir Richard
A collection of modern and contemporary voyages
and travels ...; [compiled by Sir Richard Phillips].
Printed for Richard Phillips, by J.G. Barnard,
1805-06. 3v. 23cm.
No more published?

FARQUHAR, Francis Peloubet and PHOUTRIDES, Aristides
Evangelus
Mount Olympus. San Francisco: Johnck & Seeger,
1929. xiii, 46p., plates, illus., map, bibl.
29cm.

PHYTHIAN, J   C
Scenes of travel in Norway. Cassell, Petter &
Galpin, 1877. 176p. 19cm.

PIACHAUD, Dr
Une ascension au Mont-Blanc en 1864. Genève, 1865.
45p.
Offprint from Bibliothèque universelle et revue
suisse, mai 1865.

PIACHAUD, René Louis
Le Salève; préface de M. Planta Joerimann. Genève;
A. Ciana, 1924. 188p., illus. 25cm. (Le trésor
de l'alpiniste, 1)

PIAZ, Tita
Le diable des Dolomites; traduit de l'italien par
F. Germain. [Paris]: Arthaud, 1963. 245p.,
plates, illus., map. 21cm. (Collection semper-
vivum, no.39)
Originally published in Italian as two works:
"Mezzo secolo d'alpinismo" and "A tu per tu con le
crode".

PICHL, Eduard
Hoch vom Dachstein an! Hrsg. unter Förderung
durch den Deutschen und Österreichischen Alpenverein, Zweig Austria. 2. Aufl. München: F.
Bruckmann, 1936. xvi, 319p., illus., map, bibl.
24cm.

PICHL, Eduard
Wiens Bergsteigertum. Wien: Verlag der
Österreichischen Staatsdruckerei, 1927. vii,
192p., 6 plates, illus. 25cm.

PICHLER, Fritz
Wanderungen durch Steiermark und Kärnten; geschildert von P.K. Rosegger, Fritz Pichler und U.
von Rauschenfels; illustrirt von Richard Püttner
[and others]. Stuttgart: Kröner, [1880]. ix,
242p., plates, illus. 28cm. (Unser Vaterland)

PICKEN, Andrew
Madeira illustrated by Andrew Picken; with a description of the island edited by James Macaulay.
Day & Hughes, 1840. 4, 21p., plates, illus., map.
56cm.

PICKERING, G
ALLOM, Thomas
Lake and mountain scenery: Westmorland and Cumber-
land; from drawings on the spot, by T. Allom and
G. Pickering. P. Jackson, [184-]. 1v. of illus.
14 x 23cm.

PICOT, J
Statistique de la Suisse; ou, État de ce pays des vingt-deux Cantons dont il se compose... Genève: J.J. Paschoud, 1819. iii, 575p. 18cm.

PICQUET, J P
Voyage aux Pyrénées françaises et espagnoles ..., par J.P.P***. 2e éd., entièrement refondue et augm. Paris: E. Babeuf, 1828. viii, 432p. 21cm.
Previous ed. published in 1789 under title: Voyage dans les Pyrénées françoises...

PICQUET, J P
Voyage dans les Pyrénées françoises, dirigé principalement vers le Bigorre & les vallées ..., [par J.P. Picquet]. Paris: Le Jay, 1789. viii, 327p. 20cm.
2nd ed. published in 1828 under title: Voyage aux Pyrénées françaises et espagnoles...

PICTET, J P and PICTET, F J
Itinéraire de Chamouni, de Sixt, des deux Saint-Bernard et des vallées autour du Mont-Blanc. [Nouv. éd.]. Genève: Ab. Cherbuliez, 1840. xxxvi, 372p., 2 fold. plates, illus., map. 20cm.
First ed. published in 1808 under title: Nouvel itinéraire des vallées autour du Mont-Blanc.

- - Another ed. 1845.

PICTET, J P
Nouvel itinéraire des vallées autour du Mont-Blanc. Genève: Manget & Cherbuliez, 1808. xxiii 272p., 1 fold. plate, map. 17cm.

Pictorial New Zealand; with a preface by Sir W.B. Perceval. Cassell, 1895. xvi, 301p., illus., maps. 25cm.

Pictorial sport and adventure, being a record of deeds of daring and marvellous escapes by field and flood... F. Warne, [190-]. vii, 312p., plates, illus. 26cm.

Pictures in Tyrol and elsewhere, from a family sketch-book, by the author of "Voyage en zigzag" &c. [i.e. Elizabeth Tuckett]. Longmans, Green, 1867. 313p., plates, illus. 21cm.

- - 2nd ed. 1869.

Picturesque Europe; with illustrations on steel and wood by the most eminent artists. [Popular ed.]. Cassell, [1890?]. 5v., plates, illus. 32cm.
Articles by various authors.

Picturesque scenery in North Wales. Carnarvon: H. Humphreys, [ca 1855]. [30] leaves of illus. (some col.). 14 x 22cm.
Cover title: Humphreys's Book of views in North Wales.

A picturesque tour by the new road from Chiavenna, over the Splügen, and along the Rhine, to Coira, in the Grisons; [with thirteen views, taken on the spot by G.C. Esq., i.e. George Clowes, and lithographed by F. Calvert]. W. Cole, 1826. 35p., plates, illus. 33cm.

Picturesque tour from Geneva to Milan, by way of the Simplon
See
Voyage pittoresque de Genève à Milan par le Simplon

Picturesque tour from Geneva to the Pennine Alps; translated from the French [of Albanis Beaumont]. Printed by J. Nichols for J. Bate, 1792. 16p., 12 plates, illus. 53cm.

A picturesque tour of the English Lakes; containing a description of the most romantic scenery of Cumberland, Westmoreland, and Lancashire, etc. [R. Ackermann], [1821]. vi, 288p., plates, illus. 27cm.
Preface signed R. Ackermann.

A picturesque tour through France, Switzerland, on the banks of the Rhine and through parts of the Netherlands in the year 1816. [J. Mawman], [1817]. xiii, 379p., maps. 22cm.

Picturesque tour through the Oberland in the Canton of Berne, in Switzerland. R. Ackermann's Repository of Arts, 1823. viii, 120p., 17 plates (some col.), illus., map. 29cm.

PIDAL, Pedro and ZABALA, José F
Picos de Europa: contribución al estudio de las montañas españolas. Madrid: Club Alpino Español, 1918. 120p., plates (some fold., some col.), illus., maps. 29cm.

ROCH, André and PIDERMAN, Guido
Quer durchs "Schweizerland": Grönland-expedition des Akademischen Alpenclub Zürich. Zürich: Amstutz & Herdeg, 1941. 251p., illus., maps. 24cm.

PIDGEON, Daniel
An engineer's holiday; or, Notes of a round trip from long. 0' to 0'. Kegan Paul, Trench, 1882. 2v. 21cm.

PIERRE, Bernard
La conquête du Salcantay, géant des Andes. Paris: Amiot, Dumont, 1953. 191p., plates, illus., maps. 22cm. (Bibliothèque de l'alpinisme)

PIERRE, Bernard
Escalades au Hoggar. Paris: Arthaud, 1952. 183p., plates, illus., maps, bibl. 21cm. (Collection sempervivum, 18)

PIERRE, Bernard
SHIPTON, Eric
Face à l'Everest: l'Expédition Anglaise de Reconnaissance 1951, avec Les batailles pour l'Everest par Bernard Pierre. Paris: Amiot-Dumont, 1953. 156p., plates, illus., maps. 22cm. (Bibliothèque de l'alpinisme)

PIERRE, Bernard
Une montagne nommée Nun-Kun; préface de Sir John Hunt. Paris: Amiot-Dumont, 1954. 203p., plates, illus., map. 22cm. (Bibliothèque de l'alpinisme)

PIERRE, Bernard
[Une montagne nommée Nun-Kun]. A mountain called Nun Kun; translated by Nea Morin and Janet Adam Smith. Hodder & Stoughton, 1955. 189p., plates, illus., maps. 21cm.

PIERRE, Bernard
Montagnes de la lune. [Paris]: Hachette, 1959. 95p., col. plates, illus., maps. 24cm.

PIERRE, Bernard
Le petit Sherpa aux yeux bleus. Paris: Nathan, 1969. [28]p., illus. 33cm.

PIERRE, Bernard
Victoire sur les Andes; illustrations de Jean Reschofsky. Paris: Éditions G.P., 1976. 188p., illus.(some col.), maps. 18cm. (Collection spirale, 243)
For children.

PIERREPONT, Edward
Fifth Avenue to Alaska; with maps by Leonard Forbes Beckwith. New York, London: Putnam, 1884. vi, 329p., 4 fold.plates, maps. 21cm.

PIETH, Friedrich and HAGER, P Karl
Pater Placidus a Spescha: sein Leben und seine Schriften; unter der Aufsicht der Naturforschenden Gesellschaft Graubündens ... und der Sektion Rätia des Schweizerischen Alpenklubs ... hrsg., von Friedrich Pieth und P. Karl Hager. Bümpliz-Bern: Bentoli, 1913. cxiii, 515p., plates (1 col.), illus., map. 28cm.

LANDI VITTORJ, Carlo and PIETROSTEFANI, Stanislao
Gran Sasso d'Italia. 2a ed. Milano: Club Alpino Italiano, Touring Club Italiano, 1962. 254p., plates (1 fold., some col.), illus., maps, bibl. 17cm. (Guida dei monti d'Italia)

PIGEON, Anna and ABBOT, Ellen
Peaks and passes: [particulars of six mountaineering tours ... between the years 1869 and 1876]. [The Authors], 1885. 31p. 18cm.

PIGGOTT, Percy J
Burrow's Guide to North Wales: a practical handbook for the tourist ...; with a special article
upon mountain walks and rock climbs by Dora Benson.
Cheltenham, London: Ed. J. Burrow, [ca 1920].
162p., plates (1 fold.col.), illus., maps. 19cm.

PIGGOTT, Percy J
Burrow's Guide to the Lake District: a practical
handbook for the tourist; with a special article
upon mountain passes, walks & rock climbs by Dora
Benson. Cheltenham, London: Ed. J. Burrow, [ca
1920]. 120p., plates (1 fold.col.), illus., maps.
19cm.

PIKE, Warburton
The barren ground of northern Canada. Macmillan,
1892. xi, 300p., fold.col. plates, 2 maps. 24cm.

PILATUSBAHN-GESELLSCHAFT
Mount Pilatus: Switzerland's far-famed mountain
peak. Alpnachstad: Mt. Pilatus Railway Co., [ca
1965]. 31p., plates, illus. 21cm.
Cover title.

PILGRIM
Notes of wanderings in the Himmala containing des-
criptions of some of the grandest scenery of the
Snowy Range; among others of Nainee Tal, by
Pilgrim, with an appendix and map. Agra: Brown,
1844. viii, 199, xxxip., 1 fold.plate, map. 23cm.

PILKINGTON, Charles
Mountaineering without guides: the conclusion of a
lecture to the Yorkshire Ramblers' Club, given on
October 27th, 1896. Leeds: J. Whitehead, 1897.
[3]p. 24cm.

PILKINGTON, Lawrence
An alpine valley and other poems; wood engravings
by Margaret Pilkington. Longmans, Green, 1924.
70p., illus. 23cm.

PILKINGTON, Lawrence
Armathwaite. Longmans, Green, 1936. 27p. 19cm.

PILKINGTON, Lawrence
The hills of peace and other poems. Longmans,
Green, 1930. 48p. 20cm.

PILLEY, Dorothy E
Climbing days. Bell, 1935. xiii, 352p., plates,
illus., maps (on lining papers). 23cm.

- - 2nd rev. ed. Secker & Warburg, 1965.

PIMLOTT, J   A   R
The Englishman's holiday: a social history. Faber
& Faber, 1947. 318p., 24 plates, illus., bibl.
21cm.

CAUMERY, M   L   and PINCHON, J
Bécassine alpiniste, texte de M.-L. Caumery;
illustrations de J. Pinchon. Paris: Gautier et
Languereau, 1923. 64p., col. illus. 33cm.
(Édition de la Semaine de Suzette)

PINGRET, Édouard
SAZERAC, Hilaire Léon
Un mois en Suisse; ou, Souvenirs d'un voyageur;
recuillis par Hilaire Sazerac; et ornés de croquis
lithographiés d'après nature par Édouard Pingret.
Paris: Sazerac & Duval, 1825. 4 pts., 40 plates,
illus. 43cm.

PIPEROFF, Chr.
Géologie des Calanda... Bern: Schmid & Francke,
1897. x, 66p., 1 fold.col. plate, map, bibl.
33cm. (Beiträge zur geologischen Karte der
Schweiz, Lfg. 37, N.F., Lfg. 7)

PITSCHNER, W
Der Mont-Blanc: Darstellung der Besteigung
desselben am 31 Juli, 1. und 2 August 1859: ein
Blick in die Eislandschaften der europäischen
Hochalpen. Berlin: A. Hirschwald, 1860. 154p.
and atlas, plates, illus. 25cm.

PITTON DE TOURNEFORT, Joseph
Relation d'un voyage du Levant ... contenant
l'histoire ancienne & moderne de plusiers isles
de l'archipel, de Constantinople, des côtes de la
Mer Noire, de l'Armenie, de la Georgie, des
frontières de Perse & de l'Asie Mineure...
Amsterdam: Aux depens de la Compagnie, 1718. 2v.,
plates, illus., maps. 30cm.

PITTON DE TOURNEFORT, Joseph
[Relation d'un voyage du Levant...]. A voyage
into the Levant ... to which is prefix'd, the
author's Life ... adorn'd with an accurate map of
the author's travels... D. Midwinter, 1741. 3v.,
plates, illus., maps. 21cm.

PIUS II, Pope
WURTISEN, Christian
Epitome historiae Basiliensis, praeter totius
Rauricae descriptionem ...; accessit his, Aeneae
Sylvii... Basilea, nuspiam antehac edita.
Basileae: Per Sebastianum Henric Petri, 1577.
308, 30p., 1 fold. plate, illus. 17cm.

PIUS XI, Pope
Scritti alpinistici ... [de] Achille Ratti (ora
S.S. Pio Papa XI); raccolti e pubblicati in
occasione del cinquantenario della Sezione di
Milano del Club Alpino Italiano ... [da] Giovanni
Bobba e Francesco Mauro. Milano: Bertieri e
Vanzetti, 1923. xxiii, 189p., illus. 26cm.

PIUS XI, Pope
[Scritti alpinistici]. Climbs on alpine peaks,
by Achille Ratti; translated by J.E.C. Eaton;
with a foreword by Douglas Freshfield; and an
introduction by L.C. Casartelli. T. Fisher Unwin,
1923. 136p., plates, illus., map. 23cm.

- - Another issue. Benn, 1929.

PIUS XI, Pope
[Scritti alpinistici]. Ascensions: Mont Rose,
Cervin, Mont Blanc, [par] Achille Ratti (s.s.
Pie XI); traduit par Émile Gaillard. Chambéry:
Dardel, 1922. 121p., plates, illus. 22cm.

PIUS XI, Pope
[Scritti alpinistici]. Alpine Schriften des
Priesters Achille Ratti ...; gesammelt und hrsg.
[von] Giovanni Bobba und Francesco Mauro; ins
Deutsche übertragen von Leopold von Schlözer.
Berlin: R. Mosse, 1925. xxiii, 196p., plates,
illus. 26cm.

PIUS XI, Pope
GASQUET, Francis Aidan
His Holiness Pope Pius XI: a pen portrait, by
Cardinal Gasquet and The Pope as alpine climber;
translated from an article written by himself.
D. O'Connor, 1922. 30p., plates, illus., port.
26cm.
Originally published in Review of reviews.

PIUS XI, Pope
WILLIAMSON, Benedict
The story of Pope Pius XI. Alexander-Ouseley,
1931. 174p., plates, illus. 23cm.

PIZZI, Giovanni
Alpinismo. Milano: Hoepli, 1926. xix, 287p.,
illus. 16cm. (Manuali Hoepli)

PLACIDUS A SPESCHA, Pater
See
SPESCHA, Pater Placidus a

PLAN, Danielle,
Un Genevois d'autrefois: Henri Albert Gosse,
(1753-1816), d'après des lettres et des documents
inédits. Paris: Fischbacher, 1909. 522, 59 p.,
plates, illus. 23cm.

PLANTA, A   von and KEKULÉ, A
Chemische Untersuchung der Heilquellen zu St.
Moritz im Kanton Graubünden. Chur: F. Wassali,
1854. 30p. 19cm.

PLANTA, Frédéric, baron de
BERALDI, Henri
En marge du pyrénéisme: notes d'un bibliophile;
L'affaire Rilliet-Planta. Paris: The Author, 1931.
160p. 23cm.

PLANTIN, Jean Baptiste
Helvetia antiqua et nova; seu, Opus describens I.
Helvetiam... II. Antiquiora Helvetiae loca...
III. Populos Helvetiis finitimos... Bernae: G.
Sonnleitnerus, 1656. 368p., 2 fold. plates. 17cm.

PLANTINUS, Joh. Bapt.
See
PLANTIN, Jean Baptiste

PLAS Y BRENIN NATIONAL MOUNTAINEERING CENTRE
Safety on mountains, by the staff of Plas y Brenin,
the Snowdonia National Recreation Centre; illustrated by Gordon F. Mansell. 3rd ed. Central
Council of Physical Recreation, 1962. 40p.,
illus. 16cm.

- - 8th ed., by John Jackson and other members of
the staff of the Plas y Brenin National Mountaineering Centre. 1972.

PLATT, William
The joy of mountains. Bell, 1921. 80p., plates,
illus. 18cm.

PLATTNER, Felix Alfred
Jesuits go east; translated from the German by
Lord Sudley and Oscar Blobel. Dublin: Clonmore &
Reynolds, 1950. 283p., map (on lining papers).
23cm.

PLATZ, Ernst
ROTHPLETZ, August
Alpine Majestäten und ihr Gefolge: die Gebirgswelt
der Erde in Bildern... Ansichten ... mit einleitendem Text ..., von A. Rothpletz, [Ernst Platz
- Walther Bauer]. München: Vereinigte Kunstanstalten, 1901-04. 4v. (chiefly illus., maps).
46cm.

PLATZ, Ernst
Heinrich Schwaigers Führer durch das Karwendel-
gebirge. 3.Aufl. neubearb. ... Akademischen Alpenklub, Innsbruck; ausgestaltet mit Illustrationen
... von Ernst Platz. München: J. Lindauer, 1907.
xvi, 182p., plates, illus., maps. 16cm.

PLIETZ, Samuel
Vom Montblanc zum Wilden Kaiser. Erlenbach-Zürich:
E. Rentsch, 1936. 234p., plates, illus. 23cm.

PLUNKET, Frederica
Here and there among the Alps. Longmans, Green,
1875. 195p. 20cm.

POCOCK, Noel
Below zero: a travesty of winter sport; with
verses adapted to the occasion by A.E. Johnson.
Hodder & Stoughton, [1911]. 61p., col. plates,
illus. 29cm.

POCOCKE, Richard
A description of the East, and some other countries.
Printed for the Author by W. Bowyer, 1743-45. 2v.
in 3, plates (some fold.), illus., maps. 41cm.

POESCHEL, Erwin
Das Burgenbuch von Graubünden. Zürich: Orell
Füssli, 1930. 312p., 101 plates (1 fold.col.),
illus., map, plans. 30cm.

Poésies helvétiennes, par Mr. B. [i.e. P.S. Bridel].
Lausanne: Mourer, 1782. xvi, 248p., illus. 20cm.

A poetical tour in the years 1784, 1785, and 1786,
by a member of the Arcadian Society at Rome [i.e.
W. Parsons]. J. Robson and W. Clarke, 1787. iii,
208p. 19cm.

Poetische Reise, [von Maria Drinkwater]. [N.p.]:
[n.pub.], 1837. 125p. 26cm.

POISSON, Bernard
Escalades: guide des parois, région de Montréal.
Montréal: La Cordée, 1971. 121p., illus. 18cm.

POLARIS MOUNTAINEERING CLUB. Library
Polaris Mountaineering Club Library list.
[Nottingham?]: The Club, 1973. 3 leaves. 33cm.
Duplicated typescript.

POLASEK, Ollie
Skiing. Kaye, 1960. 120p., illus. 27cm.

Poles and tails; or, English vagabondism in
Switzerland, in the summer of 1854, by two of the
vagabonds. London: [N.pub.], 1855. 81p., 3 fold.
plates, illus. 19cm.

POLISH MOUNTAINEERING CLUB
See
KLUB WYSOKOGÓRSKI

POLJAK, Josip
Planinarski vodič po Velebitu. Zagreb: Izd.
Hrvatsko Planinarsko Drustvo, 1929. 277p., plates
(some fold.), illus., maps (in pocket). 19cm.

POLLINGER, Joseph
GOS, Charles
Vie d'un grand guide: Joseph Pollinger. Berne,
1944. 13p., plates, illus. 26cm.
Offprint from Les Alpes, 1944, fasc. 11 and 12.

POLLINGTON, Steve W
LOUGHBOROUGH UNIVERSITY MOUNTAINEERING CLUB KISHTWAR
HIMALAYAN EXPEDITION, 1976
L.U.M.C. 1976 Kishtwar Himalayan Expedition;
[edited by S.W. Pollington]. Loughborough: The
Expedition, [1978]. 36p., plates, illus. 30cm.

POLLOCK, Sir Frederick
The Pollock-Holmes letters: correspondence of Sir
Frederick Pollock and Mr. Justice Holmes, 1874-
1932; edited by Mark DeWolfe Howe; with an intro-
duction by Sir John Pollock. Cambridge: Cambridge
University Press, 1942. 2v., plates, illus. 23cm.

POLO, Marco
The travels of Marco Polo, the Venetian; the
translation of Marsden revised with a selection of
his notes; edited by Thomas Wright. Bell, 1892.
xxviii, 508p. 19cm. (Bohn's antiquarian library)

POLSKIE TOWARZYSTWO TATRZAŃSKIE
Conférence internationale des sociétés de tourisme
alpin, Zakopane, Pologne, 5-7 août 1930: compte-
rendu, protocole, rapports, résolutions. Kraków:
Société Polonaise de Tatra, 1931. 40p., plates,
illus. 24cm.

POLUNIN, Oleg
The concise flowers of Europe [by] Oleg Polunin,
assisted by Robin S. Wright. Oxford University
Press, 1972. xix, 107p., 192 col. illus. 23cm.

LIOTARD, André Frank and POMMIER, Robert
Terre Adélie, 1949-1952; préface de Paul-Émile
Victor. Paris: Arthaud, 1952. 48p., plates
(some col.), illus. 26cm. (Collection belles
pages - belles couleurs)

PONA, Giovanni
Monte Baldo descritto da Giovanni Pona, Veronese,
in cui si figurano & descrivono molte rare piante
... et due commenti ... [di] Nicolò Marogna sopra
l'amomo de gli antichi. Venetia: R. Meietti,
1617. 248, [15], [4], 132 p., illus. 22cm.

PONTING, Herbert G
The great white south; or, With Scott in the
Antarctic, being an account of experiences with
Captain Scott's South Pole expedition and of the
nature life of the Antarctic; introduction by Lady
Scott. 3rd. ed. Duckworth, 1923. xxvi, 306p.,
plates, illus., map. 23cm.

POPHAM, R   Brooks
Zig-zag ramblings; or, Further notes by the way,
by a nomad on the prowl, author of "Reminiscences
of many lands", etc. [i.e. R. Brooks Popham].
H.J. Drane, 1906. 158p., plates, illus. 19cm.
Anecdotes from Italy, Switzerland, etc.

ARBEZ, Victor and PORTE, Pierre
Vos premiers pas en ski de fond. [Paris]: Arthaud,
1975. 72p., illus. 19cm.

PORTER, Eliot
The place no one knew: Glen Canyon on the Colorado;
edited by David Brower. San Francisco: Sierra
Club, 1963. 170p., illus. 35cm. (Sierra Club
books)

PORTER, Harold Edward L
THOMSON, James Merriman Archer
Climbing in the Ogwen District; [issued by The
Climbers' Club]. Arnold, 1910. xx, 124p., plates,
illus. 16cm.

- - Appendix, containing accounts of many new climbs,
by H.E.L. Porter. 1921.

PORTIER, Francis
Évolène: dix planches en couleurs de Francis
Portier, texte et poème de Pierre Vallette.
Genève: Atar, 1942. [7]p., col. plates, illus.
36cm.
In portfolio.

PORTIER, Francis
Grimenz, village valaisan: 10 planches fac-similés
des peintures de Francis Portier, texte de Léon
Dunand. Genève: "SADAG", [1919?]. [6]p., col.
plates, illus. 28 x 36cm.
In portfolio.

POSEWITZ, Theodor
Reisehandbuch durch Zipsen, Hohe Tatra und Zipser
Mittelgebirge. Budapest: Franklin-Verein, 1898.
xvi, 336p., plates, illus., maps (1 in pocket).
17cm.

POTOMAC APPALACHIAN TRAIL CLUB
Guide to paths in the Blue Ridge: the Appalachian
Trail and side trails. Supplement, rev.
Washington (D.C.): The Club, 1937. 485p. 17cm.

POTOMAC APPALACHIAN TRAIL CLUB. Mountaineering
Section
ROBINSON, F   R
A climber's guide to Seneca Rocks, West Virginia.
Washington (D.C.): The Section, 1971. 122p.,
illus. 14cm.

POTTER, G   R
A short history of Switzerland, by E. Bonjour,
H.S. Offler and G.R. Potter. Oxford: Clarendon
Press, 1952. 388p., maps, bibl. 23cm.

POTTER, Stephen
One-upmanship. Hart-Davies, 1952. 160p., illus.
20cm.

POTTERAT, E
PFEIFFER, G
À la montagne: croquis montagnards; suivis d'une
notice sur la photographie à la montagne par E.
Potterat. Genève: Ch. Eggimann, [1897]. 197p.,
illus. 30cm.

POTTINGER, George
St. Moritz: an alpine caprice. Jarrolds, 1972.
163p., plates, illus. 23cm.

POUCHER, W.A.
The backbone of England; with photographs by the
author. Country Life, 1946. 208p., illus. 29cm.

POUCHER, W.A.
A camera in the Cairngorms; with ninety-three
photographs by the author. Chapman & Hall, 1947.
144p., illus., maps (on lining papers). 26cm.

POUCHER, W.A.
Escape to the hills; with photographs by the
author. Country Life, [1943]. viii, 216p.,
illus. 30cm.

POUCHER, W.A.
Highland holiday: Arran to Ben Cruachan; with
seventy-six photographs by the author. Chapman
& Hall, 1945. 104p., illus., maps (on lining
papers). 26cm.

POUCHER, W.A.
Lakeland holiday; with seventy photographs by the
author. Chapman & Hall, 1942. 112p., illus.
28cm.

POUCHER, W.A.
Lakeland journey; with 90 photographs by the
author. Chapman & Hall, 1945. 128p., illus.
29cm.

POUCHER, W.A.
The Lakeland peaks: a pictorial guide to walking
in the district and to the safe ascent of its
principal mountain groups. 5th ed. Constable,
1971. 420p., illus., maps. 18cm.

POUCHER, W.A.
Lakeland scrapbook; with one hundred and forty-
one photographs by the author. Chapman & Hall,
1950. 136p., illus. 29cm.

POUCHER, W.A.
Lakeland through the lens: a ramble over fell and
dale; with one hundred and twenty-two photographs
by the author. Chapman & Hall, 1940. 152p.,
illus. 29cm.

POUCHER, W.A.
The magic of Skye; with one hundred and forty-
eight photographs by the author. Chapman & Hall,
1949. 223p., illus., maps (on lining papers).
29cm.

POUCHER, W.A.
The magic of the Dolomites, written and illustrated by W.A. Poucher. Country Life, 1951.
144p., illus. 29cm.

POUCHER, W.A.
Over Lakeland fells; with 110 photographs by the
author. Chapman & Hall, 1948. 152p., illus.,
maps. 29cm.

POUCHER, W.A.
Peak panorama: Kinder Scout to Dovedale; with
eighty-five photographs by the author. Chapman
& Hall, 1946. 120p., illus. 29cm.

POUCHER, W.A.
Scotland through the lens: Loch Tulla to Lochaber;
with eighty photographs by the author. Chapman &
Hall, 1943. 119p., illus., maps (on lining
papers). 26cm.

POUCHER, W.A.
Snowdon holiday; with seventy-six photographs by
the author. Chapman & Hall, 1943. 127p., illus.
29cm.

POUCHER, W.A.
Snowdonia through the lens: mountain wanderings
in wildest Wales; with sixty-two photographs by
the author. Chapman & Hall, 1941. 124p., illus.
29cm.

FERLET, René and POULET, Guy
Aconcagua: south face; translated from the French
by E. Noel Bowman. Constable, 1956. xii, 209p.,
plates, illus., maps. 23cm.

POULTON, Edward Bagnall
John Virianu Jones and other Oxford memories.
Longmans, Green, 1911. xii, 339p., plates, illus.
24cm.

POURCHIER, M   and FRENDO, Édouard
La technique de l'alpinisme; avec le concours du
Groupe de Haute Montagne ...; publiée sous le
patronage de la Fédération Française de la Montagne.
Grenoble: Arthaud, 1943. 232p., illus. 19cm.

POVELSEN, Bjarni
See
PALSSON, Bjarni

POWELL, Addison M
Trailing and camping in Alaska. Hurst & Blackett,
1910. 379p., plates, illus. 22cm.

POWELL, Colin G
Guide to Ndeiya. 2nd ed. Nairobi: Mountain Club
of Kenya, [1968]. 84p., illus. 11 x 17cm.

POWELL, Colin G
Outlying crags. [Nairobi?]: The Author, [1970?].
29p., col. plates, illus. 33cm.

POWELL, Paul
Just where do you think you've been? Wellington
(N.Z.): Reed, 1970. 211p., plates, illus., maps.
26cm.

POWELL, Paul
Men aspiring. Wellington (N.Z.): Reed, 1967.
183p., plates, illus., maps. 25cm.

POWYS, Llewelyn
Swiss essays. Bodley Head, 1947. 165p., plates,
illus. 22cm.

Practical Swiss guide: Anglo-American hand-book for
Switzerland, Savoy, North Italy, the routes from
England by France, Belgium, Holland and the Rhine
... 53rd issue, [by A.T. Gregory]. Kegan, Paul,
Trench, Trübner, 1909. lxix, 200p., plates,
illus., maps, plans. 18cm. (English red books)

A practical Swiss guide, illustrated: the whole of
Switzerland, Mont Blanc, Monte Rosa, Mont Cervin
..., by an Englishman in Switzerland [i.e. A.T.
Gregory]. Longman, Brown, Green & Longmans, 1856.
xxxvii, 124p., illus., map. 18cm.

PRANAVANANDA, Swami
Exploration in Tibet; with a foreword by S.P.
Chatterjee. Calcutta: University Press, 1939.
xxi, 161p., plates (some fold.col.), illus., maps
(in pocket). 23cm.

PRANAVANANDA, Swami
Pilgrim's companion to the Holy Kailas and
Manasarovar, containing elaborate descriptions of
11 routes to the Holy Kailas and Manasarovar and
also to the "Sources of the four great rivers"...
Allahabad: Ram Dayal Agarwala, 1938. xviii, 178p.,
plates (2 fold.), illus., maps. 19cm.

WYON, Reginald and PRANCE, Gerald
The land of the Black Mountain: the adventures of
two Englishmen in Montenegro. Methuen, 1903.
xviii, 300p., plates, illus., map. 20cm.

PRATER, Gene
Snowshoeing. Seattle: The Mountaineers, 1974. x,
109p., illus., bibl. 22cm.

PRATI, Pino
Dolomiti di Brenta. Trento: Arti Grafiche
Tridentum, 1926. x, 318p., plates, illus., maps.
18cm. (Guida dei monti d'Italia: Alpi Tridentine)

PRATT, A   E
To the snows of Tibet through China. Longmans,
Green, 1892. xviii, 268p., plates (1 fold.),
illus., map. 25cm.

PRATTEN, Mary A
My hundred Swiss flowers, with a short account of
Swiss ferns. W.H. Allen, 1887. iv, 147p., 56
plates, illus. 21cm.

PREJEVALSKY, Nicholas Michailovitch
From Kulja, across the Tian Shan to Lob-Nor;
translated by E. Delmar Morgan; with introduction
by Sir T. Douglas Forsyth. Sampson Low, Marston,
Searle & Rivington, 1879. xii, 251p., 2 fold.col.
plates, maps. 24cm.

PREJEVALSKY, Nicholas Michailovitch
Mongolia, the Tangut country, and the solitudes of
northern Tibet, being a narrative of three years'
travel in eastern High Asia; translated by E.
Delmar Morgan. Sampson Low, Marston, Searle &
Rivington, 1876. 2v., plates (1 fold.col.),
illus., map. 24cm.

PREL, Carl, Freiherr du
See
DU PREL, Carl, Freiherr

PRELLER, C S   Du Riche
Italian mountain geology. Pt. 3. The Gran Sasso
d'Italia group, Abruzzi, Central Apennines; the
volcanoes of central and southern Italy. Wheldon
& Wesley, 1923. 162p., plates (2 fold.), maps.
23cm.

PRESCOTT, William H
History of the conquest of Mexico, with a preliminary view of the ancient Mexican civilization
and the life of the conqueror, Hernando Cortez.
New ed. Routledge, 1857. 2v. 18cm.

PRESTON-THOMAS, Herbert
The work and play of a government inspector; with
a preface by John Burns. Blackwood, 1909. xiii,
387p., plates, illus. 23cm.

PREUSS, Rudolf
Landschaft und Mensch in den Hohen Tauern: Beiträge zur Kulturgeographie. Würzburg-Aumühle: K.
Triltsch), 1939. xv, 326p., illus., maps (in
pocket). 25cm.

PRICE, Edward
Norway: views of wild scenery and journal.
Hamilton, Adams, 1834. vi, 85p., 21 plates, illus.
29cm.

PRICE, Edward
[Norway: views of wild scenery...]. Norway and
its scenery, comprising the journal of a tour by
Edward Price, with considerable additions and a
Road-book for tourists ...; edited and compiled by
Thomas Forester. Bohn, 1853. xi, 470p., 21
plates, illus. 19cm. (Bohn's illustrated library)

PRICE, Julius M
Six months on the Italian Front from the Stelvio
to the Adriatic, 1915-1916. Chapman & Hall, 1917.
xxiv, 300p., plates, illus. 23cm.

PRICE, Nancy
Vagabond's way: haphazard wanderings on the fells;
with illustrations by A.S. Hartrick. Murray,
1914. xi, 247p., plates, illus., map. 22cm.

PRICE, Victor Coverley
See
COVERLEY-PRICE, Victor

PRICE WOOD, J N
Travel & sport in Turkestan. Chapman & Hall, 1910.
xix, 201p., plates (1 fold.col.), illus., map.
25cm.

PRIEM, Fernand
La terre avant l'apparition de l'homme: périodes
géologiques, faunes et flores fossiles, géologie
régionale de la France. Paris: Baillière, 1893.
vi, 716p., illus., maps. 30cm. (Brehm, A.E.
Merveilles de la nature)

WRIGHT, C S   and PRIESTLEY, R E
Glaciology [of the Victoria land sector of the
Antarctic continent]. Harrison for the Committee
of the Captain Scott Antarctic Fund, 1922. xx,
581p., fold plates (some col.), illus., maps (some
in pocket). 31cm.

PRIEURÉ DE CHAMONIX
Documents relatifs au Prieuré et à la vallée de
Cahmonix [sic]; recueillis par J.-A. Bonnefoy;
publiés et annotés par A. Perrin. Chambéry:
Imprimerie Chatelain, 1879-83. 2v. 25cm.

PRIEURÉ DE CHAMONIX
PERRIN, André
Le Prieuré de Chamonix: histoire de la vallée et
du Prieuré de Chamonix du Xe au XVIII siècle;
d'après les documents recueillis par A. Bonnefoy.
Chambéry: A. Perrin, 1887. 253p., 1 fold. plate,
map. 25cm.

PRIME, Samuel Irenaeus
Letters from Switzerland. New York: Sheldon, 1860.
viii, 264p., illus. 19cm.

PRINZINGER, A
Die Höhen-Namen in der Ungebung von Salzburg und
Reichenhall: ein Beitrag zur Orts- Sprach- und
Volkskunde... Salzburg: Mayrische Buchhandlung,
1861. 23p. 23cm.

PRIOR, Herman
Ascents and passes in the Lake District of England,
being a new pedestrian and general guide to the
district. Simpkin, Marshall, [1865]. ix, v, 269,
v p., 1 fold. plate, map. 17cm.

PRIOR, Herman
Guide to the Lake District of England. 4th,
nonpareil, ed. Windermere: J. Garnett; London:
Simpkin, Marshall, [ca 1880]. x, 350, viii p.,
2 fold.col. plates, illus., maps (2 in pockets).
12cm.

- - 5th ed. [ca 1885].

PRITCHARD, Henry Baden
Beauty spots of the continent; with illustrations
by John Proctor and R.P. Leitch. Tinsley, 1875.
320p., plates, illus. 20cm.

PRITCHARD, Henry Baden
A peep at the Pyrenees, by a pedestrian [i.e.
Henry Baden Pritchard], being a tourist's note-
book. Whittaker, 1867. viii, 147p., 1 fold.col.
plate, map. 17cm.

PRITCHARD, Henry Baden
Tramps in the Tyrol. Tinsley, 1874. xii, 267p.,
illus. 20cm.

PRITCHETT, Robert Taylor
Gamle Norge: old Norway; or, Our holiday in
Scandinavia [by Robert Taylor Pritchett]. Hamilton,
Adams, 1862. xi, 312, vii p., map. 18cm.

PRITCHETT, Robert Taylor
"Gamle Norge": rambles and scrambles in Norway.
Virtue, 1879. x, 210p., plates, illus. 32cm.

Problems of American geology: a series of lectures
dealing with some of the problems of the Canadian
Shield and of the Cordilleras, delivered at Yale
University on the Silliman Foundation in 1913.
New Haven: Yale University Press; London: Oxford
University Press, 1915. xix, 505p., plates (some
fold.), illus., maps. 25cm.

KLIER, Heinrich E   and PROCHASKA, Henriette
Ötztaler Alpen: ein Führer für Täler, Hütten und
Berge. München: Rother, 1953. 453p., plates (1
fold.), illus., map. 17cm. (Deutscher und
Österreichischer Alpenverein. Alpenvereinsführer)

PROCTOR, Robert
Narrative of a journey across the cordillera of
the Andes, and of a residence in Lima, and other
parts of Peru, in the years 1823 and 1824.
Constable, 1825. xx, 374p. 22cm.

Promenade au Mont-Blanc et autour du Lac de Genève,
[par F. Vernes?]. Londres: [n.pub.], [ca 1790].
252p. 22cm.
"Promenade ... en l'année 178*".

Promenade durch die Schweiz, [von Braunschweiger].
Hamburg: G. Hoffmann, 1793. 270p. 20cm.

Promenades d'un artiste. Vol.2. Tyrol-Suisse, Nord
de l'Italie [par Désiré Nisard]. Paris: J.
Renouard, 1835. 406p., 26 plates, illus. 24cm.

PROPIAC, chevalier de
Beautés de l'histoire de la Suisse depuis l'époque
de la confédération jusqu'à nos jours... Paris: A.
Eymery, 1817. 435p., plates, illus. 18cm.

Protected wild flowers of the Cape Province. Cape
Town: Cape Provincial Administration, Department
of Nature Conservation, 1958. xii, 210p., col.
illus. 15cm.
Title page in English and Afrikaans.

PROUT, Samuel
ROSCOE, Thomas
The tourist in Switzerland and Italy; illustrated
from drawings by S. Prout. R. Jennings, 1830.
278p., plates, illus. 21cm. (Landscape annual
for 1830)

PROVINS, Marguerite Burnat
See
BURNAT-PROVINS, Marguerite

PROVINZIALVERBAND FÜR DEN FREMDENVERKEHR BOZEN
See
ENTE PROVINCIALE PER IL TURISMO, Bolzano

PRUSIK, Karl
Gymnastik für Bergsteiger; Buchschmuck von Rudolf
Lehnert. München: Rother, [1926]. 64p., illus.
16cm.

PRUSIK, Karl
Ein Wiener Kletterlehrer. Wien: Artaria, 1929.
124p., illus. 18cm.

PÜCKLER-MUSKAU, Hermann, Fürst von
[Briefe eines Verstorbenen]. Mémoires et voyages
du Prince Puckler Muskau: lettres posthumes sur
l'Angleterre, l'Irlande, la France, la Hollande
et l'Allemagne; traduites de l'éd. allemande par
J. Cohen. Bruxelles: J.P. Meline, 1833-34. 6v.
16cm.
Library lacks vols. 1 and 2.

PUINI, Carlo
Il Tibet (geografia, storia, religione, costumi),
secondo la relazione del viaggio del P. Ippolito
Desideri (1715-1721). Roma: Società Geografica
Italiana, 1904. lxiv, 402p. 25cm. (Società
Geografica Italiana. Memorie, v.10)

PUISEUX, Pierre
Où le père a passé ... au berceau de l'alpinisme
sans guide. Paris: Argo, 1928. 319p., plates,
illus. 25cm.

PURSLOW, Richard
Sleep till noon day. Heinemann, 1963. 221p.,
map. 21cm.

PURTSCHELLER, Ludwig
ZSIGMONDY, Emil
Die Gefahren der Alpen: praktische Winke für Berg-
steiger. 3. unter Mitwirkung Ludwig Purtscheller's
von Otto Zsigmondy besorgte Aufl. Augsburg:
Lampart, [ca 1900]. 188p., illus. 17cm.

PURTSCHELLER, Ludwig and HESS, Heinrich
Der Hochtourist in den Ostalpen. 5.Aufl. begründet
von Ludwig Purtscheller und Heinrich Hess; neu
hrsg. ... von Hanns Barth. Leipzig: Bibliographisches Institut, 1925-30. 8v., plates,
illus., maps. 16cm. (Meyers Reisebücher)

PURTSCHELLER, Ludwig
Über Fels und Firn: Bergwanderungen; hrsg. von H.
Hess. München: F. Bruckmann, 1901. xxii, 362p.,
plates, illus. 28cm.

- - Another issue. München: Rother, 1929.

PURVIS, J   B
  Through Uganda to Mount Elgon. Unwin, 1909.
  371p., 1 fold plate, illus., map. 22cm.

PUSKAS, Arno
  Nanga Parbat 8125m;fotografoval Ivan Urbanovic.
  Bratislava: Sport, 1976. 1v. (chiefly illus.,
  maps). 28cm.
  Pamphlet containing picture captions in Russian,
  German and English as insert.

PUTNAM, George Palmer
  In the Oregon country: out-doors in Oregon,
  Washington and California, together with some
  legendary lore and glimpses of the modern West in
  the making. New York: Putnam, 1915. xxi, 169p.,
  plates, illus. 20cm.

PUTNAM, William Lowell
  A climber's guide to the interior ranges of
  British Columbia. 5th ed. New York: American
  Alpine Club, 1971. 323p., plates, illus., maps,
  bibl. 17cm.

PUTNAM, William Lowell
  A climber's guide to the interior ranges of
  British Columbia North. 6th ed. [New York]:
  American Alpine Club, 1975. 210p., illus., maps.
  17cm.

KRUSZYNA, Robert and PUTNAM, William Lowell
  A climber's guide to the interior ranges of British
  Columbia South. 6th ed. [New York]: American
  Alpine Club, 1977. 226p., illus., maps. 17cm.

PUTNAM, William Lowell
THORINGTON, James Monroe
  A climber's guide to the Rocky Mountains of Canada.
  6th ed., with collaboration of William Lowell
  Putnam. New York: American Alpine Club, 1966.
  xx, 381p., bibl. 18cm.

PUTNAM, William Lowell
  Climber's guide to the Rocky Mountains of Canada
  North 1974, by William L. Putnam, Chris Jones,
  Robert Kruszyna. 6th ed. [New York]: American
  Alpine Club, 1974. 289p., illus., maps. 17cm.
  Based on previous eds. by James Monroe Thorington.

PUTNAM, William Lowell and BOLES, Glen W
  Climber's guide to the Rocky Mountains of Canada
  South. 6th ed. [New York]: American Alpine
  Club, 1973. 330p., illus., maps. 17cm.
  Based on earlier eds. by James Monroe Thorington.

PYATT, Edward Charles and NOYCE, Wilfrid
  British crags and climbers: an anthology; chosen
  by Edward C. Pyatt and Wilfrid Noyce. Dobson,
  [1952]. 235p., plates, illus. 23cm.

PYATT, Edward Charles
  Chalkways of south and south-east England; maps
  compiled by Gillian Pyatt. Newton Abbot (Devon):
  David & Charles, [1974]. 190p., illus., maps,
  bibl. 23cm.

PYATT, Edward Charles
  A climber in the West Country. Newton Abbot
  (Devon): David & Charles, 1968. 204p., illus.,
  bibl. 23cm.

PYATT, Edward Charles
  A climber's guide to south-east England; plans by
  L. Balding. Stockport: Climbers' Club,1956,
  (1960 reprint). 100p., plates, illus. 15cm.
  (Climbing guides to England & Wales, 8)

PYATT, Edward Charles
  Climbing and walking in south-east England.
  Newton Abbot (Devon): David & Charles, 1970.
  173p., illus., plans, bibl. 23cm.

ANDREWS, Arthur Westlake and PYATT, Edward Charles
  Cornwall. Stockport: Climber's Club, 1950. 164p.,
  plates, illus., maps. 16cm. (Climbing guides to
  the Snowdon district and to Cornwall, 5)

CLARK, Ronald William and PYATT, Edward Charles
  Mountaineering in Britain: a history from the
  earliest times to the present day. Phoenix House,
  1957. 288p., 72 plates, illus., bibl. 26cm.

PYATT, Edward Charles
  Mountains of Britain. Batsford, 1966. 216p.,
  illus., maps. 23cm. (Batsford Britain series)

PYATT, Edward Charles
  South-east England. 2nd rev. ed., by L.R. and
  L.E. Holliwell; diagrams by L. Balding. Stockport:
  Climbers' Club, 1969. xvi, 147p., illus., bibl.
  16cm. (Climbers' Club guides)

PYATT, Edward Charles
  Where to climb in the British Isles. Faber &
  Faber, 1960. 287p., 16 plates, illus., maps, bibl.
  19cm.

PYE, Sir David Randall
  George Leigh Mallory: a memoir. Oxford University
  Press, 1927. 183p., illus. 22cm.

PYNE, C
  Mountains and lakes of Switzerland and Italy:
  sixty-four picturesque views ... from original
  sketches, by C. Pyne; with descriptive notes by
  Jerome J. Mercier. Bell & Daldy, 1871. 130p.,
  1 fold.col. plate, col. illus., map. 27cm.

PYNE, J   B
  Lake scenery of England; drawn on stone by T.
  Picken. Day, [1859]. ixp., 50 leaves, col.
  plates, illus. 30cm.

Pyrna: a commune; or, Under the ice, [by E.J. Davis].
  Bickers, 1875. 142p. 20cm.

TAMINI, Jean Émile and QUAGLIA, Lucien
  Châtellenie de Granges, Lens, Grône, St-Léonard
  avec Chalais-Chippis. St-Maurice: Édition Oeuvre
  St-Augustin, 1942. 248p., plates, illus., bibl.
  25cm.

QUEENSBURY, John Sholto Douglas, 8th Marquis of
  See
DOUGLAS, John Sholto, 8th Marquis of Queensbury

QUERLON, Anne Gabriel Meusnier de
MONTAIGNE, Michel de
  Journal du voyage de Michel de Montaigne en
  Italie, par la Suisse & l'Allemagne en 1580 & 1581;
  avec des notes par M. de Querlon. Rome: Le Jay,
  1775. 3v. 15cm.

QUESTA, Emilio
  Guida delle Alpi Apuane, [da] L. Bozano, E. Questa,
  G. Rovereto. Genova: Club Alpino Italiano, Sezione
  Ligure, 1905. x, 370p., plates, illus., map.
  18cm.

- - 2a ed., con la collaberazione di Bartolomeo
  Figari, 1921.

QUIGLEY, Hugh
  Lombardy, Tyrol and the Trentino. Methuen, 1925.
  xii, 276p., plates, illus., maps (on lining
  papers). 20cm.

QUILLER-COUCH, Sir Arthur
  Memoir of Arthur John Butler. Murray, 1917. vi,
  261p., plates, illus. 23cm.

Quinze jours en Suisse: promenades d'un jeune peintre
  français dans les Cantons du Midi. Paris: L.
  Janet, [1820]. iv, 146p. 12cm.
  A series of letters.

R., J   A
    Fahrten in den Hohen Tauern. Innsbruck: Wagner,
    1875-77. 2v. 18cm.

R., L.N.R.
    A short account of our trip to the Sierra Nevada
    mountains. J. Martin [1884?]. 49p. 18cm.

R., W.v.
    See
RHETZ, Wilhelm von

R. F. [République Française]. Paris: Le Gouvernement
    français, 1938. [ca 250]p., illus. 39cm.
    "Cet ouvrage a été édité par le Gouvernement
    français à l'occasion de la visite en France de
    Leurs Majestés britanniques, le roi Georve VI et la
    reine Elizabeth, 19-22 juillet, 1938".
    In portfolio.

RABAJOLI, G
    Guida alle Terme di Vinadio. Torino: F. Casanova,
    1877. viii, 122p., map. 17cm.

RABENSTEINER, Wolfgang and KLIER, Heinrich E
    Stubaier Alpen: ein Führer für Täler, Hütten und
    Berge. München: Rother, 1953. 428p., plates,
    illus., maps. 17cm. (Deutscher und
    Österreichischer Alpenverein. Alpenvereinsführer)

MEURER, Julius and RABL, Josef
    Der Bergsteiger im Hochgebirge: alpin-touristische
    Schilderungen nach den Berichten hervorragender
    Hochtouristen; zusammengestellt und erläutert von
    Julius Meurer und Josef Rabl. Wien: Hartleben,
    1893. viii, 264p., illus. 25cm.

GRÖGER, Gustav and RABL, Josef
    Die Entwicklung der Hochtouristik in den
    österreichischen Alpen; hrsg. vom Oesterreichischen
    Touristen-Club. Wien: R. Leckner, 1890. xi,
    258p., plates, illus. 23cm.

RABL, Josef
    Illustrierter Führer auf den Tauernbahn und ihren
    Zugangslinien... Wien: Hartleben, 1906. xiv,
    280p., plates, maps. 16cm. (Hartleben's Illus-
    trierter Führer, 57)

RABL, Josef
    Illustrirter Führer durch Kärnten mit besonderer
    Berücksichtigung der Städte Klagenfurt und Villach
    ... Wien: Hartleben, 1884. xv, 279p., plates,
    illus. 17cm. (Hartleben's Illustrirter Führer,
    19)

RABL, Josef
    Illustrirter Führer durch Steiermark und Krain mit
    besonderer Berücksichtigung der Alpengebeite von
    Obersteiermark und Oberkrain. Wien: Hartleben,
    1885. xxx, 285p., plates, maps. 16cm.
    (Hartleben's Illustrirter Führer, 20)

RABL, Josef
    Meine Lebenserinnerungen. Wien: Sektion
    "Donauland" des Deutschen und Österreichischen
    Alpen-Vereins, 1923. 32p., port. 21cm.

RABL, Josef
    Traisenthal und das Pielachthal: ein Führer auf
    den Linien, St. Pölten-Scheibmühl, Scheibmühl-
    Hainfeld und Scheibmühl-Schrambach... 2 Abtheilung.
    Wien: Oesterreichischer Touristen-Club, 1884.
    102p. 18cm. (Touristen-Führer, 4)

RABL, Josef
    Wachau-Führer: ein Führer im Donauthale zwischen
    Krems und Melk und in den anschliessenden Theilen
    des Waldviertels... Wien: Oesterreichischer
    Touristen-Club, 1890. xv, 346p., plates, illus.
    17cm. (Touristen-Führer, 16)

RABOT, Charles
    Au Cap Nord: itinéraires en Norvège, Suède,
    Finlande. Paris: Hachette, 1898. 326p., 1 fold.
    plate, illus., maps. 21cm.

RABOT, Charles
    Aux fjords de Norvège et aux forets de Suède.
    Paris: Hachette, 1898. 300p., illus., maps. 18cm.

RABUT, Laurent
    Habitations lacustres de la Savoie. Premier
    mémoire. [Chambéry]: [n.pub.], 1863. 79-145p.
    23cm.

-- Album. Chambéry: Jh. Perrin, 1864.
-- Deuxième mémoire. Chambéry: F. Puthod, 1868.
-- Album. Chambéry: Jh. Perrin, 1867.

RACKHAM, H
    Thomas Cecil Fitzpatrick: a memoir; edited by
    H. Rackham at the request of Mrs. Fitzpatrick.
    Cambridge: University Press, 1937. 47p., plates,
    illus. 22cm.

RADCLIFFE, Ann
    A journey made in the summer of 1794, through
    Holland and the western frontier of Germany, with
    a return down the Rhine; to which are added obser-
    vations during a tour to the Lakes of Lancashire,
    Westmoreland, and Cumberland. G.G. & J. Robinson,
    1795. x, 500p. 26cm.

RADDE, Gustav
    Aus den dagestanischen Hochalpen vom Schah-dagh
    zum Dulty und Bogos: Reisen, asugeführt im Sommer
    1885. Gotha: Perthes, 1887. vi, 64p., col.
    plates (2 fold.), illus. 29cm. (Ergänzungsheft
    No.85 zu "Petermanns Mitteilungen")

RADDE, Gustav and KOENIG, E
    Das Ostufer des Pontus und seine kulturelle Ent-
    wickelung im Verlaufe der letzten dreissig Jahre:
    vorläufiger Bericht über die Reisen im kolchischen
    Tieflande, Adsharien ... im Sommer 1893. Gotha:
    Perthes, 1894. iv, 120p., 2 fold.col. plates,
    maps. 28cm. (Ergänzungsheft zu "Petermanns
    Mitteilungen", 112)

RADDE, Gustav
    Die Sammlungen des Kaukasischen Museums; im
    Vereine mit Special-Gelehrten bearb. und hrsg. von
    Gustav Radde. Tiflis: Das Museum, 1899-   .
    Plates (some fold.col.), illus., maps. 31cm.
    Second title page in Russian.
    Bd. 1. Zoologie, von Gustav Radde. -Bd.2. Botanik,
    von Gustav Radde. -Bd.5. Archaeologie; bearb. von
    Gräfin P.S. Uvarov.

RADDE, Gustav
    Vier Vorträge über den Kaukasus gehalten im Winter
    1873/4 in den grösseren Städten Deutschlands.
    Gotha: Perthes, 1874. vi, 71p., col. plates (1
    fold.), maps. 28cm.

RADEN, Woldemar
    See
KADEN, Woldemar

RADICS, P   von
    Bergfahrten in Oesterreich einst und jetzt, 1363-
    1887. Augsburg: Amthor, [1887]. 134p. 18cm.

RADIO-RADIIS, Alfred von
    Der Dachstein. Stuttgart: Deutsche Verlags-
    Anstalt, 1906. 79p., plates, illus., maps. 18cm.
    (Alpine Gipfelführer, 5)

RADIO-RADIIS, Alfred von
    Der Rosengarten. Stuttgart: Deutsche Verlags-
    Anstalt, 1907. 69p., 15 plates, illus., map.
    18cm. (Alpine Gipfelführer, 16)

BIENDL, Hans and RADIO-RADIIS, Alfred von
    Skitouren in den Ostalpen; über auftrag des
    Österreichischen Alpenklubs; hrsg. von Hans Biendl
    und Alfred v. Radio-Radiis. Wien: A. Holzhausen,
    1906. 3v., maps. 17cm.

RADIO-RADIIS, Alfred von
    Spezial-Führer durch das Dachsteingebirge und die
    angrenzenden Gebiete des Salzkammergutes und
    Ennstales. Wien: A. Holzhausen, 1908. xli, 248p.,
    plates, illus., map. 19cm.

RAEBURN, Harold
    Mountaineering art. Fisher Unwin, 1920. xii,
    274p., plates, illus., bibl. 20cm.

RAFFLES, Thomas
    Letters, during a tour through some parts of
    France, Savoy, Switzerland, Germany,and the
    Netherlands, in the summer of 1817. Liverpool:
    T. Taylor, 1818. xii, 336p. 19cm.

    - - 2nd ed. 1819.
    - - 3rd ed. 1820.

RAFFLES, W   Winter
    Zermatt, with the Cols d'Erin and de Collon; and
    an ascent to the summit of Mont Blanc: two letters
    addressed to the editor of the Liverpool Times.
    [Liverpool]: [The Author], 1854. 22p. 19cm.

BUSHNELL, Vivian C   and RAGLE, Richard H
    Icefield Ranges Research Project: scientific
    results; edited by Vivian C. Bushnell and Richard
    H. Ragle; foreword and introduction by Walter A.
    Wood. New York: American Geographical Society;
    Montreal: Arctic Institute of North America,
    1969-72. 3v., fold.plates (1 col.), illus., map.
    29cm.

RAHN, Johann Rudolf
    Wanderungen im Tessin: zur Erinnerung an der
    Grenzdienst der 5. Division im Tessin 1915/16; neu
    hrsg. von Lt. Largiader; mit einer Uebersicht über
    die Geschichte des Kantons Tessin von Hptm.
    Nabholz; und einem Vorwort von Oberstdivisionär
    Steinbuch. Zürich: Arnold Bopp, 1917. 174p.,
    plates (1 col.), illus. 18cm.

RAINOLDI, Luciano
    Antrona, Bognanco, Sempione. Vigevano: C.A.I.,
    Sezione di Vigevano, 1976. 239p., illus., col.
    map, bibl. 21cm.

RAITMAYR, Erich
    Kleiner Führer durch die Zillertaler Alpen und die
    Tuxer Voralpen: Talorte, Hütten, Übergänge, Gipfel.
    München: Rother 1953. 95p., 16 plates, maps.
    17cm.

RAMBERT, Eugène
    Alexandre Calame: sa vie et son oeuvre d'après les
    sources originales. Paris: Fischbacher, 1884.
    vii, 568p., port. 22cm.

RAMBERT, Eugène
    Les Alpes et la Suisse: oeuvres choisies; avec ...
    une notice sur l'auteur par V. Rossel; ouvrage
    publié par la Section des Diablerets du Club Alpin
    Suisse à l'occasion du centenaire d'Eugène Rambert.
    Lausanne: F. Rouge, 1930. 347p., 12 plates,
    illus. 25cm.

RAMBERT, Eugène
    Les Alpes suisses. Paris: Librarie de la Suisse
    Romande, 1866-75. 5v., illus., music. 20cm.
    Vol.2 is 2nd ed.
    Vols.2-5 published Bale: H. Georg.

RAMBERT, Eugène
    [Les Alpes suisses]. Ascensions et flaneries.
    Lausanne: Rouge, 1888. 369p. 21cm.

RAMBERT, Eugène
    [Les Alpes suisses]. Études d'histoire naturelle:
    Les plantes alpines, La question du foehn, Le
    voyage du glacier, La flore suisse et ses origines.
    Lausanne: Rouge, 1888. 379p. 20cm.

RAMBERT, Eugène
    [Les Alpes suisses]. Études de littérature
    alpestre et La marmotte au collier. Lausanne:
    Rouge, 1889. 429p. 20cm.

RAMBERT, Eugène
    [Les Alpes suisses]. Aus den Schweizer Bergen:
    Land und Leute, geschildert von E. Rambert.
    Deutsche Ausg., mit zweiundsechzig Illus. von G.
    Roux. Basel: H. Georg, 1874. 347p., plates,
    illus. 28cm.

RAMBERT, Eugène
    Bex et ses environs: guide et souvenir. Lausanne:
    Bureau de la Bibliothèque Universelle, 1871.
    304p., plates, illus. 18cm.

RAMBERT, Eugène
JAVELLE, Émile
    Souvenirs d'un alpiniste; avec une notice bio-
    graphique et littéraire par Eugène Rambert.
    Lausanne: A. Imer, 1886. xlvii, 404p., 1 plate,
    port. 20cm.

    - - 3e éd. Lausanne: F. Payot, 1897.
    - - 4e éd. Lausanne: F. Payot, 1906.

RAMBERT, Eugène
JAVELLE, Émile
    [Souvenirs d'un alpiniste]. Alpine memories; with
    a biographical and literary notice by Eugène
    Rambert; translated and with an introduction by
    W.H. Chesson. Fisher Unwin, 1899. vii, 444p.,
    plates, illus. 21cm.

RAMBERT, Eugène
TALLICHET, Éd.
    Eugène Rambert: souvenirs personnels.
    (In Bibliothèque universelle... v.33, 1887,
    p.111-134)

RAMBERT, Eugène
WARNERY, Henri
    Eugène Rambert: études contemporaines.
    (In Bibliothèque universelle...v.36, oct.-déc.,
    1887, 3pts.)

A RAMBLER
    See
BUDWORTH, Joseph

RAMBLERS' ASSOCIATION. Northern Area
    Ramblers' Cheviot: twelve walks in the Cheviot
    Hills. [Rev. ed., edited by Betty Fletcher].
    Newcastle-upon-Tyne: H. Hill, 1976. 84p., illus.,
    maps. 22cm.

RAMEAU, Jean
    L'ami des montagnes. Paris: Société d'Éditions
    Littéraires et Artistiques, 1908. 321p. 21cm.

RAMOND, Louis
    Carnets pyrénéens; préface de L. Le Bondidier.
    Lourdes: Éditions de l'Echauguette 1931-39.
    23cm. (Collection de l'Echauguette).
    Library has 1er Carnet, t. 1-2., 2e Carnet, t.3-4,
    only.

RAMOND, Louis
    Observations faites dans les Pyrénées, pour
    servir de suite à des observations sur les Alpes
    ... Paris: Belin, 1789. viii, 452p., 3 fold.
    plates, illus., maps. 21cm.

RAMOND, Louis
    [Observations faites dans les Pyrénées...].
    Reise nach den höchsten französischen und
    spanischen Pyrenaen, oder physikalische, geo-
    logische und moralische Beschreibung der Pyrenaen
    ... Strasburg: Akademische Buchhandlung, 1789.
    2v. in 1, illus., 2 maps. 21cm.

RAMOND, Louis
    [Observations faites dans les Pyrénées...].
    Voyage dans les Pyrénées, précédé de La jeunesse
    de Ramond, par André Monglond. Lyon: H. Lardanchet,
    1927. cxlviii, plates, ports. 21cm. (Biblio-
    thèque du bibliophile (anciens), 5)
    "Voyage dans les Pyrénées" is pt.1 of "Observations
    faites..."

RAMOND, Louis
    [Observations faites dans les Pyrénées...].
    Travels in the Pyrenees; containing a description
    of the principal summits, passes, and vallies;
    translated by F. Gold. Longman, Hurst, Rees, Orme,
    & Browne, 1813. viii, 324p. 24cm.
    "Travels in the Pyrenees" is a translation of pt.1
    of "Observations faites..."

RAMOND, Louis. [Observations sur les Alpes...].
COXE, William
    Lettres de M. William Coxe à M. W. Melmoth, sur
    l'état politique, civil et naturel de la Suisse...;
    augmentées des Observations faites ... par le tra-
    ducteur [L. Ramond]. Paris: Belin, 1781. 2v.
    21cm.

  - - Another issue. 1782.
  - - Another issue. 1787.

RAMOND, Louis. [Observations sur les Alpes...].
COXE, William
    Travels in Switzerland, and in the country of the
    Grisons, in a series of letters to William Melmoth
    ...; to which are added the notes and observations
    of Mr. Ramond, translated from the French. New
    ed... with ... six views drawn by Birmann. Basil:
    J. Decker, 1802. 3v., 6 plates, illus., map, bibl.
    24cm.
    Library's copy lacks map.

RAMOND, Louis
    Travels in the Pyrenees
    See his
    Observations faites dans le Pyrénées...

RAMOND, Louis
    Voyage dans les Pyrénées
    See his
    Observations faites dans les Pyrénées...

RAMOND, Louis
    Voyages au Mont-Perdu et dans la partie adjacente
    des Hautes-Pyrénées. Paris: Belin, 1801. iv,
    392p., fold. plates, illus., map. 21cm.

RAMOND, Louis
BERALDI, Henri
    La carrière posthume de Ramond, 1827-1868: notes
    d'un bibliophile. Paris: The Author, 1927.
    191p. 24cm.

RAMOND, Louis
BERALDI, Henri
    Le passé du pyrénéisme: notes d'un bibliophile.
    Paris: The Author. 23cm.
    Library has v.2-5 only.

RAMOND, Louis
SOCIÉTÉ RAMOND
    L.-F.-E. Ramond, 1755-1827: commémoration.
    Bagnères-de-Bigorre: La Société, 1927, printed
    1930. 163p., plates, illus., ports. 23cm.
    Edited by L. Le Bondidier.

RAMOND DE CARBONNIÈRES, Louis François Élizabeth,
baron
    See
RAMOND, Louis

RAMSAY, Andrew Crombie
    The excavation of the valleys of the Alps. 4p.
    23cm.
    Offprint from Philosophical magazine, Nov. 1862.

RAMSAY, Andrew Crombie
    The old glaciers of Switzerland and North Wales.
    Longman, Green, Longman, & Roberts, 1860. 116p.,
    plates (1 fold.col.), illus., map. 18cm.

RAMSAY, Andrew Crombie
    On the glacial origin of certain lakes in Switzer-
    land, the Black Forest, Great Britain, Sweden,
    North America and elsewhere. 185-204p., plates,
    2 maps. 23cm.
    Offprint from Quarterly journal of the Geological
    Society, Aug. 1862.

RAMUZ, C   F
    [Derborence]. When the mountain fell; English
    translation by Sarah Fisher Scott. Eyre &
    Spottiswoode, 1949. 221p. 19cm.

RAMUZ, C   F
    La Suisse Romande; couverture de Théophile-Jean
    Delaye. Grenoble: Arthaud, 1936. 197p., 1 fold.
    plate, illus., map. 24cm. (Les beaux pays)

RAMUZ, C   F
    Le village dans la montagne, [par] C.-F. Ramuz; et
    [illustré par] Edm. Bille. Lausanne: Payot,
    [1908]. 260p., plates (some col.), illus. 37cm.

RAMUZ, C   F
    Vues sur le Valais; illustré de photographies de
    différents auteurs. Bale: Urs Graf, 1943. 114p.,
    illus., bibl. 32cm. (L'heritage populaire de la
    Suisse, 2)

RANDALL, John Chace
THORINGTON, James Monroe
    The high adventure of Mr. Randall. [New York],
    1945. 333-348p., plates, illus. 23cm.
    Offprint from American alpine journal, v.5, no.3.,
    1945.
    On a fatal accident on Mont Blanc in 1870.

RANDERS, Kristofer
    Søndmøre: Reisehaandbog. 2den omarb. og forøgedᵃ
    udg. Kristiania: Alb. Cammermeyer, 1898. 210p.,
    fold. plates, maps. 18cm.

  - - 3dje rev. og forøkede utg. with title: Sunnmøre:
    reisehandbok. Alesund: Sunnmøre Turistforening,
    1930.

RANKIN, Sir Reginald
    A tour in the Himalayas and beyond. Lane: Bodley
    Head, 1930. 297p. 23cm.

RANKINE, Yve M
    Winter sports do's and dont's. Methuen, 1925.
    54p., illus. 19cm.

RAOUL-ROCHETTE, Désiré
SAZERAC, Hilaire Léon and ENGELMANN, Gustav
    Lettres sur la Suisse; accompagnées de vues
    dessinées ... & lithographiées par [F.] Villeneuve.
    Paris: G. Engelmann, 1823-32. 5v., plates, illus.
    46cm.
    Vols.2-3, by D. Raoul-Rochette and G. Engelmann,
    v.4-5, by M. de Golbéry and G. Engelmann.

RAOUL-ROCHETTE, Désiré
    Lettres sur la Suisse, écrites en 1820, suivis d'un
    voyage à Chamouny et au Simplon. Paris: N. Nepveu,
    1822. xx, 417p. 20cm.
    Preface signed: Raoul-Rochette.

  - - 2e éd., soigneusement rev. et corr. 1823.
  - - 3e éd. 1823. 6v.
  - - Another issue. Turin: Imprimerie Alliana, 1829.
    6v.

RAOUL-ROCHETTE, Désiré
    Lettres sur quelques cantons de la Suisse, écrites
    en 1819, [par Désiré Raoul-Rochette]. Paris: H.
    Nicolle, 1820. vi, 494p. 22cm.

RAOUL-ROCHETTE, Désiré
    Voyage pittoresque dans la Vallée de Chamouni et
    autour du Mont-Blanc; [illustré par G. Lory,
    père et fils...]; avec un texte explicatif par M.
    Raoul-Rochette. Paris: J.F. Ostervald, 1826. 1v.
    (chiefly illus.). 34cm.

RAPIN, D
    Le guide du botaniste dans le Canton de Vaud...
    Lausanne: [The Author], 1842. xxiii, 488p. 18cm.

Rapport sur l'état actuel de la Vallée de Bagne dans
    le Canton du Valais, relativement aux mesures
    propres à la prémunir contre l'effet destructeur du
    glacier inferieur de Giétroz; présenté au L.
    Gouvernement du Canton du Valais par la Commission
    chargée de cet examen. Zurich: La Commission, 1821.
    59p. 19cm.

RASCH, Gustav
    Touristen-Lust und Lied in Tirol: Tiroler Reisebuch.
    Stuttgart: C.F. Simon, 1874. x, 405p. 19cm.

RASPE, R   E
An account of some German volcanoes, and their
productions, with a new hypothesis of the prismatical basaltes, established upon facts, being an
essay of physical geography for philosophers and
miners, published as supplementary to Sir William
Hamilton's observations on the Italian volcanoes.
Davis, 1777. 136p., 2 plates, illus. 20cm.

RAST, Benedikt
ZERMATTEN, Maurice
Le Valais; 80 photographies originales de Benedikt
Rast. Lausanne: J. Marguerat, 1941. 98p., illus.
29cm. (Les merveilles de la Suisse)

RAST, Pius
St. Gallen, Fotografien von Pius Rast; [text by
Emile Anderegg and others]. Genf: Éditions
Générales, 1960. 245p., illus. (some col.).
29cm. (Städte und Landschaften der Schweiz, 15)

RATTI, Achille
See
PIUS XI, Pope

PERTUSI, Luigi and RATTI, Carlo
Guida illustrata pel villeggiante del Biellese:
santuari ed ospizi, stabilimenti idroterapici,
passeggiate ed escursioni ...; compilata da Luigi
Pertusi e Carlo Ratti. Torino: F. Casanova, 1901.
xii, 282p., plates, illus., maps. 19cm.
(Collezione guide Casanova)

PERTUSI, Luigi and RATTI, Carlo
Guida pel villeggiante nel Biellese. Torino:
F. Casanova, 1886. xv, 436p., plates, illus.,
map. 16cm.

RATTI, Carlo
Guida per il villeggiante e l'alpinista nelle
Valli di Lanzo. Torino: F. Casanova, 1904. 2v.,
illus., maps. 19cm. (Collezione guide-Casanova)

RAUCH, Andrea
Der Steinbock weider in den Alpen Zürich: Orell
Füssli, 1937. 150p., plates, illus. 24cm.

RAUCH, Andrea
[Der Steinbock weider in den Alpen]. Le bouquetin
dans les Alpes; traduit par L. Lanoix; préface du
Dr. A. Pfaehler. Paris: Payot, 1941. 191p.,
plates, illus. 23cm. (Bibliothèque géographique)

RAUCH, Rudolf
Der Ruf vom Nanga Parbat. Graz: Verlag Styria,
1935. 80p. 19cm. (Die deutsche Bergbücherei)

RAUSCHENFELS, U von
Wanderungen durch Steiermark und Kärnten; geschildert von P.K. Rosegger, Fritz Pichler und U.
von Rauschenfels; illustrirt von Richard Püttner
[and others]. Stuttgart: Kröner, [1880]. ix,
242p., plates, illus. 38cm. (Unser Vaterland)

RAVA, C
Barcelonette & ses environs: [album photographique
de la vallée de Barcelonnette]; [execute par [C.]
Rava; sous la direction ... de la section de
Barcelonnette du Club Alpin Français].
[Barcelonnette]: La Section, [1879?]. 1v. of
illus. 25 x 34cm.

RAVELLI, Luigi
Nuovissima guida illustrata turistica, artistica,
storica della Valle Sesia. Varallo: Unione
Tipografica Valsesiana, [1913]. 602p., illus.,
maps. 18cm.

RAVELLI, Luigi
La Val Grande del Sesia... Varallo-Sesia: Unione
Tipografica Valsesiana, [19--]. 176p., illus.,
maps. 18cm.

RAVELLI, Luigi
Varallo e dintorni: guida del villeggiante.
Varallo-Sesia: Unione Tipografica Valsesiana,
[19--]. 150p., illus. 18cm.

RAVERAT, Achille, baron
Haute-Savoie: promenades historiques, pittoresques
& artistiques en Genevois, Sémine, Faucigny et
Chablais. Lyon: L'Auteur, 1872. 672p. 22cm.

RAVERAT, Achille, baron
Savoie: promenades, historiques, pittoresques &
artistiques en Maurienne, Tarentaise, Savoie-Propre
et Chautagne. Lyon: L'Auteur, 1872. iv, 695p.
22cm.

RAWICZ, Slavomir
The long walk. Constable, 1956. 241p., maps.
23cm.
Describes a journey from Siberia, through China and
Tibet into India.

RAWLING, Cecil Godfrey
The great plateau, being an account of exploration in central Tibet, 1903, and of the Gartok
expedition, 1904-1905. Arnold, 1905. xii, 324p.,
plates (2 fold.col.), illus., maps. 24cm.

RAWNSLEY, Hardwicke Drummond
By fell and dale at the English Lakes. Glasgow:
J. MacLehose, 1911. xii, 233p., 8 plates, illus.
20cm.

RAWNSLEY, Hardwicke Drummond
A coach-drive at the Lakes: Windermere to Keswick;
and the Buttermere round. 3rd ed. Keswick: T.
Bakewell, 1902. 147p. 17cm.

RAWNSLEY, Hardwicke Drummond
Flower-time in the Oberland; with illustrations
from pencil sketches by Edith Rawnsley. Glasgow:
J. MacLehose, 1904. xiii, 337p., plates, illus.
20cm.

RAWNSLEY, Hardwicke Drummond
Lake country sketches. Glasgow: J. MacLehose,
1903. xii, 241p., plates, illus. 20cm.

RAWNSLEY, Hardwicke Drummond
Life and nature at the English Lakes. Glasgow:
J. MacLehose, 1899. viii, 192p. 20cm.

RAWNSLEY, Hardwicke Drummond
Months at the Lakes. Glasgow: J. MacLehose, 1906.
xii, 244p., plates, illus. 21cm.

RAWNSLEY, Hardwicke Drummond
Past and present at the English Lakes. Glasgow:
J. MacLehose, 1916. ix, 283p., plates, illus.
20cm.

RAWNSLEY, Hardwicke Drummond
Sonnets in Switzerland and Italy. Dent, 1899.
xvi, 167p. 21cm.

RAYMANN, Arthur
Évolution de l'alpinisme dans les Alpes françaises:
thèse pour le Doctorat d'Université de Grenoble.
Brunswick: The Author, 1912. 581p., bibl. 27cm.

RAYMOND, Diana
The climb. Cassell, 1962. 217p. 21cm.

READE, Herbert Vincent
Equipment for mountaineers. [N.p.]: [n.pub.],
[1910?]. [15]leaves. 22cm.

READE, John Edmund
Prose from the South. Ollier, 1846. 2v. 21cm.
A tour of France, Switzerland and Italy.

READE, T Mellard
The origin of mountain ranges considered experi-
mentally, structurally, dynamically and in relation to their geological history. Taylor & Francis,
1886. xviii, 359p., plates (some fold.), illus.
24cm.

READER'S DIGEST
Les Alpes: sélection du Reader's Digest. Paris:
Reader's Digest, 1969. 307p., illus. (chiefly
col.), map. 31cm.

READER'S DIGEST
Guide des plantes sauvages en couleurs: un peu de
botanique ...; une réalisation de Sélection du
Reader's Digest; les textes sont de Monique
Keraudren-Aymonin. Paris: Reader's Digest, 1969.
64p., col. illus. 19cm.

REBMANN, Hans Rudolph
See
REBMANN, Johann Rudolph

REBMANN, Johann Rudolph
Natures magnalia: ausführrliche Beschreibung der
Natur, Wundergeschopffen... Bern: A. Werli, 1620.
659p. 17cm.

RÉBUFFAT, Gaston
L'apprenti montagnard: les cinquante plus belles
courses graduées du massif du Mont-Blanc; préface
de J.-L. Babelay. Paris: Vasco, 1946. 129p.,
plates, illus. 23cm.

RÉBUFFAT, Gaston
[L'apprenti montagnard]. The Mont Blanc massif:
the 100 finest routes; translated from the French
by Jane and Colin Taylor. Kaye & Ward, 1975.
239p., illus. (some col.), maps (on lining papers),
plans. 27cm.
Translation of 1973 French ed.

RÉBUFFAT, Gaston
Cervin: cime exemplaire. [Paris]: Hachette, 1965.
223p., illus (some col.). 25cm.

RÉBUFFAT, Gaston
[Cervin: cime exemplaire]. Men and the Matterhorn;
translated by Eleanor Brockett. Vane, 1967.
222p., illus (some col.). 25cm.

RÉBUFFAT, Gaston
[Du Mont Blanc à l'Himalaya]. Mont Blanc to
Everest; with a preface by Wilfrid Noyce. Thames
& Hudson, 1956. 158p., illus. (some col.). 26cm.

RÉBUFFAT, Gaston
Entre terre et ciel, par Gaston Rébuffat et [photo-
graphies de] Pierre Tairraz. Paris: Arthaud, 1962.
183p., illus. (some fold., some col.). 24cm.
"Commentaire du film".

RÉBUFFAT, Gaston
[Entre terre et ciel]. Between heaven and earth,
by Gaston Rébuffat and [photographs by] Pierre
Tairraz; translated ... by Eleanor Brockett. Vane,
1965. 183p., illus. (some fold., some col.). 24cm.
"The film commentary".

RÉBUFFAT, Gaston
Étoiles et tempêtes (six faces nord). Paris:
Arthaud, 1954. 167p., plates, illus., map. 22cm.
(Collection sempervivum, 24)

RÉBUFFAT, Gaston
[Étoiles et tempêtes]. Starlight and storm: the
ascent of six great north faces of the Alps;
translated by Wilfrid Noyce & Sir John Hunt. Dent,
1956. xxi, 122p., plates, illus., map. 22cm.

RÉBUFFAT, Gaston
Glace, neige et roc. Paris: Hachette, 1970.
189p., illus. (some col.). 29cm.

RÉBUFFAT, Gaston
[Glace, neige et roc]. On ice and snow and rock;
translated ... by Patrick Evans. Kaye & Ward,
1971. 191p., illus. (some col.). 29cm.

RÉBUFFAT, Gaston
[Glace, neige et roc]. Ghiaccio, neve, roccia;
traduzione di Rosalba Donvito Gossi. Bologna:
Zanichelli, 1972. 191p., illus. (some col.).
28cm. (Montagne, 9)

RÉBUFFAT, Gaston
Les horizons gagnés. Paris: Denoël, 1975. 140p.,
col. illus. 32cm.

RÉBUFFAT, Gaston
[Les horizons gagnés]. Gli orizzonti conquistati.
Bologna: Zanichelli, 1976. 140p., col. illus.
32cm.

RÉBUFFAT, Gaston
[Neige et roc]. On snow and rock; translated
from the French by Eleanor Brockett, with technical assistance from J.E.B. Wright. Kaye, 1963.
191p., col. plates, illus. 24cm.

RECKE, Elisa, Baronin von der
Tagebuch einer Reise durch einen Theil Deutschlands und durch Italien, in den Jahren 1804 bis
1806; hrsg. vom Hofrath Böttiger. Berlin: In der
Nicolaischen Buchhandlung, 1815-17. 4v., 1
plate, map. 21cm.

RECKE, Elisa, Baronin von der
[Tagebuch einer Reise...]. Voyage en Allemagne
dans le Tyrol et en Italie, pendent les années
1804, 1805 et 1806; traduit de l'allemand par
Baronne de Montolieu. Paris: A. Berthrand, 1819.
3v. 20cm.

RECLUS, Elisée
The history of a mountain; translated from the
French by Bertha Ness and John Lillie; illustrated
by L. Bennett. Sampson Low, Marston, Searle, &
Rivington, 1881. iv., 262p., plates, illus. 20cm.

REDMOND, Pat
Wicklow rock-climbs (Glendalough and Luggala);
edited by Pat Redmond. Dublin: Federation of
Mountaineering Clubs of Ireland, 1973. 86p.,
illus. 16cm. (F.M.C.I. guides)

REED, A H and REED, A W
Farthest west afoot and afloat; together with
E.H. Wilmot's Journal of the Pioneer survey of
the Lake Manapouri-Dusky Sound area. Wellington
(N.Z.): Reed, 1950. 192p., plates, illus., maps.
23cm.

REES, Ioan Bowen
Galwad y mynydd: chwe dringwr enwog. Llandybie:
Llyfrau'r Dryw, 1961. 111p., plates, maps. 22cm.

REES, Ioan Bowen
Mynyddoedd: ysgrifau a cherddi; ynghyd a darluniau
gan John Wright. Llandysul: Gwasg Gomer, 1975.
102p., illus., maps, bibl. 21cm.

REEVES, E A
Hints to travellers, scientific and general;
edited for the Council of the Royal Geographical
Society by Douglas W. Freshfield and W.J.L.
Wharton. 6th ed., rev. and enlarged. Royal
Geographical Society, 1889. xii, 430p., plates
(some fold. col.), illus., maps. 18cm.

- - 7th ed. rev. and enl. 1893.
- - 8th ed. rev. and enl., edited by John Coles,
1901. 2v.
- - 9th ed. rev. and enl., edited by E.A. Reeves.
1906. 2v.
- - 10th ed. rev. and corr., edited by E.A. Reeves.
1921. 2v.
- - 11th ed., [by] E.A. Reeves. 1935-38. 2v.

REEVES, William Pember
New Zealand; painted by F. and W. Wright; described by William Pember Reeves. Black, 1908.
ix, 241p., col. plates (1 fold.), illus., map.
24cm.

REGAUD, Claudius
Autour de Bonneval (Haute-Maurienne). Paris,
1897. 51p., plates, illus. 23cm.
Offprint from Annuaire du Club Alpin Français,
v.23, 1896.

REICHARD, Heinrich August Ottakar
Malerische Reise durch einem grossen Theil der
Schweiz vor und nach der Revolution. Neue Ausg.,
mit spätern Nachträgen und Zusätzen; hrsg. vom
Kriegsdirektor Reichard. Gotha: Hennings, 1827.
xvi, 508p., plates, illus. 21cm.

REICHARD, Heinrich August Ottaker
Passagier auf der Reise in Deutschland und der
Schweiz, nach Amsterdam, Brüssel ...: ein Reise-
handbuch für Jedermann. 12 Aufl.von neuem durch-
geschen, berichtigt und ergänzt von F.A. Herbig.
Berlin: F.A. Herbig, 1843. viii, 773p., plates,
maps, plans. 18cm.
In slip-case.

REICHARD, Heinrich August Ottaker
[Passagier auf der Reise in Deutschland...].
Itinéraire de poche de l'Allemangne et de la
Suisse, avec les routes de Paris et de Pétersbourg
... Francfort: Wilmans, 1809. xiv, 494p., plates,
map. 17cm.

REICHARDT, A
Die Hohe Tatra und die Niedere Tatra, nebst einem
Ausflug in das Tokajer Weinland. Dresden: A.
Köhler, 1911. 223p., 3 fold.col. plates, maps.
16cm. (Köhlers Karpatenführer, Bd. 1. Zentral-
karpaten)

REICHENWALLNER, Leopold
Alpenzauber: Berglegende und Volksschauspiel in
vier Auszügen. Wien: Bereins Buchdruckerie,1906.
118p. 18cm.

REID, Ian C
Guide book to Mount Kenya and Kilimanjaro; edited
by Ian C. Reid. 2nd ed., completely rev. Nairobi:
Mountain Club of Kenya, 1963. 192p., illus., map.
16cm.

REID, John T
Art rambles in the Highlands and Islands of
Scotland; with 156 sketches ... drawn on wood by
the author, engraved by Dalziel Brothers.
Routledge, 1878. 183p., plates, illus. 26cm.

REID, Mayne
The plant hunters; or, Adventures among the
Himalaya mountains. Routledge, [1890]. vii,
482p., plates, illus. 17cm.

REIK, Henry Ottridge
A tour of America's national parks. New York:
Dutton, 1920. 209p., plates (1 col.), illus., map
(on lining papers). 22cm.

REINHARD, Raphael
Pässe und Strassen in den Schweizer Alpen: topo-
graphisch-historische Studien. Luzern: Eisenring,
1903. 203p., bibl. 26cm.

REINHARDT, Johann Christian
A collection of Swiss costumes, in miniature,
designed by Reinhardt...; to which is added a description in French and English. J. Goodwin,
[1822]. 1v. (chiefly col. illus.). 26cm.

REINL, Hans
Skiführer durch das Salzkammergut. 2.Aufl. Wien:
Artaria, 1925. xii, 117p., plates, illus., maps.
17cm.

REISCH, Franz
Skitouren um Kitzbuhel. München: G. Lammers, 1908.
42p., fold. plates, illus., map. 14 x 19cm.

REISCHEK, Andreas
Sterbende Welt: zwölf Jahre Forscherleben auf
Neuseeland; hrsg. von seinem Sohn. 2.Aufl.
Leipzig; Brockhaus, 1924. 334p., plates (1 fold.
col.), illus., map. 24cm.

Reise eines Lehrers mit seinen Zöglingen aus Isserten
in einige romantische Gegenden der Schweiz: ein
nützliches und unterhaltendes Lesebuch für die
heranwachsende Jugend. München: C.A. Fleischmann,
1821-23. 2v., plates, illus. 18cm.

Reisen durch die merkwürdigsten Gegenden Helvetiens,
[von G.S. Gruner]. London [i.e. Bern]: Bey der
typographischen Gesellschaft, 1778. 2v. 18cm.
A new version of the author's 'Die Eisgebirge des
Schweizerlandes'.

REISHAUER, Hermann
Die Alpen. Leipzig: Teubner, 1909. 140p., 1
plate, illus., map. 19cm. (Aus Natur und
Geisteswelt)

REISS, Wilhelm
Reisebriefe aus Südamerika 1868-1876; aus dem
Nachlasse hrsg. und bearb. von Karl Heinrich
Dietzel. München: Duncker & Humblot, 1921.
232p., col. plates, maps. 24cm. (Wissenschaftliche Veröffentlichungen der Gesellschaft
für Erdkunde zu Leipzig, Bd.9)

Relation succincte de l'écroulement de la montagne
au-dessus de Goldau, Canton de Schwytz le 2.
septembre 1806, [par H.C. Escher von der Linth].
Zuric: Orell, Füssli, 1806. 7p., 3 plates, illus.,
map. 24 x 31cm.

REMMEL, Walter
Fotografieren und filmen im Hochgebirge; unter
Mitwirkung von Walter Remmel [and others]; hrsg.
von Karl Weiss. Berlin: Union Deutsche Verlagsgesellschaft, 1934. 180p., illus. 23cm.

REMY, Claude and REMY, Yves
St. Loup, Vallorbe, Covatanne: 3 écoles d'escalades vaudoises. Renens: Bauer, 1975. 72p.,
illus. 21cm.

RENARD, Georges and RENARD, Louise
Autour des Alpes: contes roses et noirs.
Lausanne: Payot, 1892. 293p., illus. 20cm.

RENAUD, André
Les glaciers. Neuchatel: Éditions du Griffon,
1949. 52p., illus. 26cm. (Trésors de mon
pays, 38)

RENDU, Louis
[Théorie des glaciers de la Savoie]. Theory of
the glaciers of Savoy; translated by Alfred Wills;
to which are added the original memoir and supplementary articles by P.G. Tait and John Ruskin;
edited with introductory remarks by George Forbes.
Macmillan, 1874. 216p., illus., map. 23cm.
Text in English and French.

RENEVIER, E
Monographie géologique des Hautes-Alpes vaudoises
et parties avoisinantes du Valais. Berne:
Schmid, Francke, 1890. viii, 563p., 7 plates
(some fold., some col.), illus., bibl. 33cm.
(Beiträge zur geologischen Karte der Schweiz =
Matériaux pour la carte géologique de la Suisse,
livr. 16)

RENKER, Gustav
Als Bergsteiger gegen Italien. München: W.
Schmidkunz, 1918. 115p. 21cm.

RENNIE, David Field
Bhotan and the story of the Dooar war including
sketches of a three months' residence in the
Himalayas, and narrative of a visit to Bhotan in
May 1865. Murray, 1866. xxv, 408p., plates (1
fold.), illus., map. 20cm.

RENWICK, George
Romantic Corsica: wanderings in Napoleon's isle;
with a chapter on climbing by T.G. Ouston.
Fisher Unwin, 1909. 333p., plates (1 fold.col.),
illus., map. 23cm.

RERESBY, Sir John
Memoirs & travels of Sir John Reresby; [edited by
Albert Ivatt]. Kegan Paul, Trench, Trubner, 1904.
xix, 396p., plates, illus. 18cm. (Dryden House
memoirs)

REUEL, Fritz
Neue Möglichkeiten im Skilauf: ein Buch zur
Förderung der Fahrtechnik. 4.Aufl. Stuttgart:
Dieck & Coin, 1926. 262p., illus. 21cm.

RÉUNION DES CLUBS ALPINS, Geneva, 1879
See
CONFÉRENCE INTERNATIONALE DES CLUBS ALPINS, Geneva
1879

REUSS, A E
Paläontologische Studien über die älteren
Tertiärschichten der Alpen. 1. Abteilung. Die
Fossilen Anthozoen der Schichten von Castelgom-
berto. Wien, 1868. 56p., 16 plates, illus. 32cm.
Offprint from Denkschriften d.k. Akad. d.
Wissensch. math.-naturw. Cl., Bd.28.

REUT-NICOLUSSI, Eduard
Tirol unterm Beil. München: C.H. Beck, 1928.
244p., plates, illus., port. 23cm.

REVELLI, Mariz
Il canto della montagna: romanzo. Foligno:
Campitelli, 1924. 295p. 21cm.

RÉVIL, Joseph and CORCELLE, Joseph
La Savoie: guide du touriste, du naturaliste et de
l'archéologue. Paris: Masson, [18--]. vi, 280p.,
illus., maps. 19cm. (Collection ... de Marcellin
Boule)

REY, Guido
Alba alpina. [Monza]: [S.U.C.A.I.], [1915]. 32p.
18cm.

REY, Guido
[Alba alpina]. Aube alpine; traduit de l'italien
par Émile Gaillard; dessins de André Jacques.
Chambéry: Dardel, 1925. 61p., illus. 24cm.

SARAGAT, Giovanni and REY, Guido
Alpinismo a quattro mani. Torino: Roux Frassati,
1898. 238p. 20cm.

REY, Guido
Alpinismo acrobatico. Torino: Lattes, 1914.
314p., illus. 25cm.

- - Nuova ed. Torino: Montes, 1932.

REY, Guido
[Alpinismo acrobatico]. Peaks and precipices:
scrambles in the Dolomites and Savoy; translated
by J.E.C. Eaton. Fisher Unwin, 1914. 238p.,
plates, illus. 27cm.

REY, Guido
[Alpinismo acrobatico]. Alpinisme acrobatique;
traduit par Émile Gaillard. Chambéry: Dardel,
1919. xvi, 336p., illus. 22cm.

- - 2e éd. 1929.

REY, Guido
[Alpinismo acrobatico]. Bergakrobaten: Kletterfahrten an Montblanc-Nadeln und Dolomiten-Türmen;
übertragung ... von Heinrich Erler. Erfurt:
Richter, [19--]. 304p., plates, illus., port.
20cm.

SARAGAT, Giovanni and REY, Guido
Famiglia alpinistica: tipi e paesaggi. Torino:
Lattes, 1904. 365p., plates, facsims. 21cm.

REY, Guido
Il Monte Cervino; illustrazioni di Edoardo Rubino;
prefazione di Edmondo de Amicis; nota geologica di
Vittorio Novarese. Milano: Hoepli, 1904. xvi,
287p., plates (some col.), illus. 31cm.

REY, Guido
[Il Monte Cervino]. The Matterhorn; with an
introduction by Edmondo de Amicis; translated by
J.E.C. Eaton. Fisher Unwin, 1907. 336p., plates
(some col.), illus. 29cm.

- - Another issue, rev. and with two additional
chapters by R.L.G. Irving. Oxford: Blackwell,1946.

REY, Guido
[Il Monte Cervino]. Le Mont Cervin; ouvrage
traduit de l'italien par L. Espinasse-Mongenet.
Paris: Hachette, 1905. xx, 411p., plates, illus.,
bibl. 20cm.

- - Another issue. Chambéry: Dardel, 1925.
- - Another issue. Lausanne: Spes, 1925.
- - Nouv. éd. Lausanne: Spes, 1937.

REY, Guido
Récits et impressions d'alpinisme; traduit de
l'italien par Émile Gaillard; préface par Henry
Bordeaux. Macon: C. Faure, 1913. xxix, 266p.
25cm.

REY, Guido
Souvenirs de visions d'alpinisme; traduit de
l'italien par E. Gaillard. Chambéry: Dardel,
1937. 175p., 1 plate, port. 23cm.

REY, Raymond
A travers nos Alpes: Dauphiné, par MM. Morillot,
R. Rey, Magendie; sous le patronage de M. Boirac.
Grenoble: A. Gratier, 1902. viii, 297p., illus.
19cm.
An anthology.

REYNIER, Jean Louis Antoine
Le guide des voyageurs en Suisse, précédé d'un
discours sur l'état politique du pays, [par
J.L.A. Reynier]. Paris: Buisson, 1790. lx,
391p. 18cm.

- - 2e éd. 1791.

REYNOLDS, Kev
Walks and climbs in the Pyrenees. Milnthorpe:
Cicerone Press, 1978. 127p., illus., maps.
19cm.

REZNICEK, Felicitas von
Das Buch von Engelberg: Vergangenheit und Gegenwart eines Kurortes. Bern: P. Haupt, 1964.
148p., illus., map. 25cm. (Schweizer Heimat-
bücher, 118/119)

REZNICEK, Felicitas von
Von der Krinoline zum sechsten Grad. Salzburg:
Bergland-Buch, 1967. 273p., plates, illus. 24cm.

RHAM, Georges de
L'Argentine: description de vingt itinéraires
d'escalade, précédée de quelques considérations
sur leurs difficultés et leurs dangers. Lausanne:
E. Roth, 1944. 38p., plates (1 fold.), illus.,
map, bibl. 19cm.

RHEDEN, J
TERSCHAK, Emil
Die Photographie im Hochgebirge: ein Ratgeber für
Bergwanderer. 4.Aufl., gänzlich neu bearb. von
J. Rheden. Berlin: Union Deutsche Verlagsgesell-
schaft, 1921. 110p., plates, illus. 21cm.

RHELLICANUS, Joannes
GESNER, Conrad
De raris et admirandis herbis, quae ... Lunariae
nominantur, commentariolus: & obiter de aliis
etiam rebus quae in tenebris lucent ...; eiusdem
descriptio Montis Fracti, sive Montis Pilati,
iuxta Lucernam in Helvetia; his accedunt Jo. Du
Choul... Pilati Montis in Gallia descriptio; Jo.
Rhellicani Stockhornias, qua Stockhornus mons
altissimus in Bernensi Helvetiorum agro,
versibus heroicis describitur. Tiguri: Apud
Andream Gesnerum & Jacobum Gesnerum, [1555].
95p., illus. 19cm.

RHETZ, Wilhelm von
Reise eines Norddeutschen durch die Hochpyrenäen
in den Jahren 1841 und 1842, von W. v. R[hetz].
Leipzig: Brockhaus & Avonarius, 1843. 2v. in 1.
20cm.

RHIND, William
The Scottish tourist, and itinerary; or, A guide
to the scenery and antiquities of Scotland and the
Western Islands... 2nd ed., with considerable
additions. Edinburgh: Stirling & Kenney, 1827.
xiv, 403p., plates (some fold., 1 col.), illus.,
maps. 19cm.

- - 9th ed., edited by William Rhind. Edinburgh:
W.H. Lizars, 1845.

RHODES, Daniel P
A pleasure-book of Grindelwald. New York:
Macmillan, 1903. xv, 235p., illus., map. 21cm.

RICCI, Virgilio
L'andata di Leonardo da Vinci al Monboso, oggi
Monte Rosa, e la teoria dell'azzurro del cielo.
Roma: Printed by Palombi, 1977. x, 82p., col.
plates, illus., bibl. 24cm.

RICHARD
Guide aux Pyrénées: itinéraire pédestre des
montagnes ..., par Richard. Paris: Audin, 1834.
xvi, 420p., plates, illus., maps. 15cm.

RICHARD
Guide du voyageur en Suisse, par Richard. Paris:
Audin, 1824. liii, 718p., plates, illus. 18cm.

RICHARD
EBEL, Johann Gottfried
[Handbuch für Reisende in der Schweiz]. Manuel du
voyageur en Suisse... Nouv. éd., entièrement rev...
et augm... mis en ordre par Richard. Paris: Audin,
1834. 692p., maps. 20cm.

- - Another ed. Paris: Maison, 1841.

RICHARD
Merveilles et beautés de la nature en Suisse; ou,
Description de tout ce que la Suisse offre de
curieux et d'intéressant ... par J.B. Richard.
Paris: Audin, 1824. 2v., plates, illus. 17cm.

RICHARD
Promenades dans l'Oberland, par Wyss et Lutz;
revues par Richard. 3e éd. Paris: Maison, [1836?].
153p., map. 15cm.

RICHARD, Colette
Climbing blind; translated by Norman Dale; with a
foreword by Maurice Herzog; and a preface by
Norbert Casteret. Hodder & Stoughton, 1966. 159p.,
plates, illus. 21cm.

PELLE, Gilbert and RICHARD, Guy
Escalades à Surgy, Nievre. Orléans: Club Alpin
Français, Section de l'Orléanais, Section Nivernais-
Yonne, 1974. 55p., illus. 22cm.

RICHARD, J   B
See
RICHARD

RICHARDS, Dorothy
See
PILLEY, Dorothy E

HOEK, Henry and RICHARDSON, E   C
Der Schi und seine sportliche Benutzung
See their
Der Ski und seine sportliche Benutzung

RICHARDSON, E   C
The 'shilling' ski-runner. 2nd ed. Richardson &
Wroughton, 1911. 36p., illus. 20cm.

RICHARDSON, E   C
The ski-runner. The Author, [1910]. 240p., col.
plates, bibl. 23cm.

RICHARDSON, E   C
Ski-running, by D.M.M. Crichton Somerville, W.R.
Rickmers, and E.C. Richardson; edited by E.C.
Richardson. H. Cox, 1904. 76p., plates, illus.,
bibl. 23cm.

- - 2nd ed. 1905.

HOEK, Henry and RICHARDSON, E   C
Der Ski und seine sportliche Benutzung ...;
besorgt von Henry Hoek. München: G. Lammers, 1906.
viii, 196p., plates, illus. 20cm.
Based on the 2nd ed. of E.C. Richardson's Ski-
running.

- - 3. deutsche Aufl. 1908.
- - 4. deutsche Aufl. 1910.
- - 5.Aufl. München: Verlag der Deutschen Alpenzeitung, 1911.

RICHARDSON, Katharine
PAILLON, Mary
En souvenir de Miss Katharine Richardson, 1854-
1927. [Paris], 1927. 12p., ports. 21cm.
Offprint from Montagne, déc. 1927.

RICHARDSON, Katharine
PAILLON, Mary
Miss Kate Richardson, une grande alpiniste: liste
de courses et souvenirs. Lyon: "L'echo de
Savoie", [1943?]. 55p., illus. 19cm.
Contains drawings by Kate Richardson.

RICHARDSON, Ralph
Corsica: notes on a recent visit, with a map of
the forests and the mines of Corsica. Edinburgh,
1894. 21, 15p., illus., map. 25cm.
Offprint from Scottish geographical magazine,1894.

RICHARDSON, W   R
From London Bridge to Lombardy by a macadamised
route. Sampson Low, & Marston, 1869. xii, 202p.,
illus., map. 22cm.

RICHMOND, William Kenneth
Climber's testament. A. Redman, 1950. 246p.,
plates, illus. 23cm.

RICHTER, Eduard
Die Alpen nach H.A. Daniel's Schilderung neu
bearb. Leipzig: Fues, 1885. 96p., 1 plate, map.
24cm.

RICHTER, Eduard
Die Erschliessung Ostalpen; unter Redaction von
E. Richter; hrsg. vom Deutschen und Oesterr.
Alpenverein. Berlin: D.u.O.A.V., 1893-94. 3v.,
plates, illus. 30cm.

RICHTER, Eduard
Die Gletscher der Ostalpen. Stuttgart: Engelhorn,
1888. 306p., plates (some fold.), illus., maps.
25cm. (Handbücher zur deutschen Landes- und
Volkskunde, Bd.3)

RICKER, John F
Yuraq Janka:guide to the Peruvian Andes. Pt.1.
Cordilleras Blanca and Rosko. Banff (Alberta):
Alpine Club of Canada, 1977. xi,180p., plates
(some fold.), illus., maps (4 fold.col. as
inserts). 23cm.

RICKMAN, E   S
The diary of a solitaire; or, Sketch of a pedestrian excursion through part of Switzerland,[by
E.S. Rickman]; with a prefatory address, and notes
personal and general. Smith, Elder, 1835. liii,
111p. 23cm.

RICKMERS, Willi Rickmer
Alai! Alai! Arbeiten und Erlebnisse der Deutsch-
Russischen Alai-Pamir-Expedition. Leipzig:
Brockhaus, 1930. 300p., plates (2 fold.), illus.,
map. 24cm.

RICKMERS, Willi Rickmer
The Duab of Turkestan: a physiographic sketch and
account of some travels. Cambridge: University
Press, 1913. xv, 564p., fold. plates (some col.),
illus., maps. 29cm.

RICKMERS, Willi Rickmer
Querschnitt durch mich. München: Gesellschaft
Alpiner Bücherfreunde, 1930. 544p., plates,
illus., port. 20cm.

RICKMERS, Willi Rickmer
Ski-ing for beginners and mountaineers. Unwin,
1910. 175p., plates, illus., bibl. 20cm.

RICKMERS, Willi Rickmer
Ski-running, by D.M.M. Crichton Somerville, W.R.
Rickmers, and E.C. Richardson; edited by E.C.
Richardson. H. Cox, 1904. 76p., plates, illus.,
bibl. 23cm.

- - 2nd ed. 1905.

RICKMERS, Willi Rickmer
Die Wallfahrt zum Wahren Jacob: Gebirgswanderungen
in Kantabrien. Leipzig: Brockhaus, 1926. 159p.,
plates, illus., maps. 20cm.

RIDDELL, James and RIDDELL, Jeanette
Ski holidays in the Alps. Harmondsworth: Penguin
Books, 1961. 400p., illus., maps. 18cm.

RIDDELL, James
The ski runs of Austria, by James Riddell assisted
by Jeanette Oddie. M. Joseph, 1958. 262p.,
plates, illus., maps. 24cm.

RIDDELL, James
The ski runs of Switzerland; with a foreword by
Sir Arnold Lunn. M. Joseph, 1957. 360p., illus.,
maps. 24cm.

RIDDELL, James and RIDDELL, Jeanette
Ski holidays in the Alps. Harmondsworth: Penguin
Books, 1961. 400p., illus., maps. 18cm.

RIDDELL, Robert Andrew
WILSON, Joseph
A history of mountains, geographical and minera-
logical; accompanied by A picturesque view of the
principal mountains of the world, in their res-
pective proportions ..., by Robert Andrew Riddell.
Nicol, 1807-10. 3v., plates, illus. 31cm.

RIDGWAY, John
Cockleshell journey: the adventures of three men
and a girl. Hodder & Stoughton, 1974. 213p.,
plates, illus., map (on lining papers). 23cm.

RIDLEY, Norman M
ROYAL AIR FORCE EXPEDITION TO THE SIERRA NEVADA DE
SANTA MARTA IN COLOMBIA, 1974
Report, by N.M. Ridley. The Expedition, [1975?].
1v. (various pagings), illus., maps. 30cm.

RIENCOURT, Amaury de
Lost world: Tibet, key to Asia. Gollancz, 1951.
317p., plates, illus., map (on lining papers).
23cm.

RIGBY, Edward
Dr. Rigby's letters from France &c. in 1789;
edited by his daughter, Lady Eastlake. Longmans,
Green, 1880. xviii, 232p. 20cm.

RIGELE, Fritz
50 Jahre Bergsteiger: Erlebnisse und Gedanken.
Berlin-Wilmersdorf: "Sport und Spiel", 1935.
373p., plates, illus. 23cm.

RIJNHART, Susie Carson
With the Tibetans in tent and temple: narrative of
four years' residence on the Tibetan border and of
a journey into the far interior. 4th ed.
Edinburgh, London: Oliphant, Anderson & Ferrier,
1904. 406p., plates (1 fold.), illus., map. 22cm.

RIKLI, M
Natur-und Kulturbilder aus den Kaukasusländern und
Hocharmenien von Teilnehmern der schweizerischen
naturwissenschaftlichen Studienreise, Sommer 1912;
unter Leitung von M. Rikli. Zürich: Füssli, 1914.
viii, 317p., plates, illus., maps, bibl. 24cm.

RILEY, C Graham
Place names in Mount Cook National Park. Christ-
church (N.Z.), 1968. 24p., bibl. 22cm.
Offprint from New Zealand alpine journal, 22, 1967.

RILLIET, Albert
Les origines de la Confédération Suisse: histoire
et légende. 2e éd. rev. et corr. Genève: H.
Georg, 1869. xi, 438p., map. 22cm.

RILLIET, Théodore
BERALDI, Henri
En marge du pyrénéisme: notes d'un bibliophile;
L'affaire Rilliet-Planta. Paris: The Author, 1931.
160p. 23cm.

RINEHART, Mary Roberts
Tenting to-night: a chronicle of sport and adventure in Glacier Park and the Cascade Mountains.
Boston: Houghton Mifflin, 1918. ix, 188p., plates,
illus. 21cm.

RINEHART, Mary Roberts
Through Glacier Park: seeing America first with
Howard Eaton. Boston: Houghton Mifflin, 1916.
x, 92p., plates illus. 20cm.

RION, Alphonse
Guide du botaniste en Valais; publié sous les
auspices de la Section Monte-Rosa du C.A.F. par
R. Ritz et F.-O. Wolf. Sion: A. Galerini, 1872.
xxxii, 252p. 18cm.

RISO PATRON, Luis
CHILE. Oficina de Límites
La Cordillera de los Andes entre las latitudes
30°40' i 35° S.; trabajos i estudios de la Segunda
Sub-Comision Chilena de Límites con la República
Arjentina, [por] Luis Riso Patron. Santiago de
Chile: La Oficina, 1903. xv, 258p., plates (some
fold.col.), illus., maps. 29cm.

RISO PATRON, Luis
CHILE. Oficina de Límites
La Cordillera de los Andes entre las latitudes
46° i 50° S., [por] Luis Riso Patron. Santiago
de Chile: La Oficina, 1905. x, 233p., plates
(some fold.col.), illus., maps. 29cm.

RITA
Edelweiss: a romance. Spencer Blackett, 1890.
160p. 19cm.

RITCHIE, Leitch
Travelling sketches in the north of Italy, the
Tyrol, and on the Rhine; with ... engravings,
from drawings by Clarkson Stanfield. Longman,
Rees, Orme, Brown, & Green, 1832. vii, 256p.,
plates, illus. 21cm. (Heath's picturesque
annual for 1832)

RITTER, C
Geographisch-historisch-topographische
Beschreibung zu K.W. Kummer's Stereorama; oder,
Relief des Montblanc-Gebirges und dessen nächster
Umgebung. Berlin: Kummer, 1824. 107p. 21cm.

DUPARC, L and RITTER, Étienne
Carbonifère alpin. Genève, 1894. 5p. 23cm.
Offprint from Archives des sciences physiques et
naturelles, t.31, 15 jan. 1894.

DUPARC, L and RITTER, Étienne
Eclogites et Amphibolites du massif du Grand-Mont.
[Genève], 1894. 3p. 23cm.
Offprint from Archives des sciences physiques et
naturelles, t.31, avril 1894.

DUPARC, L and RITTER, Étienne
Étude pétrographique des schistes de Casanna du
Valais: première note. Genève, 1896. 13p. 23cm.
Offprint from Archives des sciences physiques et
naturelles, t.2 (4e période), juillet, 1896.

DUPARC, L and RITTER, Étienne
Formation quaternaire d'éboulis au Mont Salève.
Lausanne, 1893. 4p. 23cm.
Offprint from Archives des sciences physiques et
naturelles, déc. 1893.

DUPARC, L and RITTER, Étienne
Le grès de Taveyannaz et ses rapports avec les
formations du Flysch. Genève, 1895. 48p., illus.
23cm.
Offprint from Archives des sciences physiques et
naturelles, t.33, mai et juin 1895.

DUPARC, L and RITTER, Étienne
Les massifs cristallins de Beaufort et Cevins:
étude pétrographique. Genève, 1893. 30p., fold.
plates, illus. 23cm.
Offprint from Archives des sciences physiques et
naturelles, t.30, 1893.

RITTER, Hermann
  Bergfahrten: Erinnerung an die Hochalpen.
  Bamberg: Handels-Druckerei, [1896]. 201p.,
  illus. 19cm. (Für Sommer und Winter,3)

RITTERBUSH, Philip C
  Report of the 1970 expedition to the Nevado del
  Huila, Central Andean Cordillera, Colombia, July,
  1970, by Philip C. Ritterbush and other members
  of the expedition; with an account of the
  original ascent by Erwin Kraus. Cali: Museo
  Departmental de Historia Natural, [1970?]. 43p.,
  plates, illus., maps, bibl. 27cm. (Occasional
  publication of the Museo Departmental de Historia
  Natural)

MEUTA, P   and RIVA, J
  La Vallée d'Aoste monumentale; photographiée et
  annotée historiquement par Meuta et Riva. Ivrea:
  The Authors, 1869. 74p., plates, illus. 15 x
  22cm.

BUDRY, Paul and RIVAZ, Paul de
  Villes et régions d'art de la Suisse =
  Schweizerische Kunststätten. Neuchatel: Éditions
  de la Baconnière, [1943]. 3v., plates, illus.
  18cm.

RIVETT-CARNAC, Marion
GOETZ, E
  [Klein Edelweiss]. Little edelweiss in Switzer-
  land; adapted from the Swiss verses of Mdlle
  Goetz by Marion Rivett-Carnac; with Mdlle E.
  Goetz's original illustrations. Duckworth, 1902.
  48p., plates, illus. 23cm.

RIVINGTON, Alexander
  Notes of travels in Europe in the years 1856-64.
  Printed by Gilbert & Rivington, 1865. xxxix,
  276p., plates, illus. 16cm.

RIVOLIER, Jean
  Expéditions françaises à l'Himalaya: aspect
  médical; avec la collaboration de P. Biget [and
  others]. Paris: Hermann, 1959. 229p., illus.,
  bibl. 24cm. (Actualités scientifiques et industrielles, 1266)
  At head of title: Comité de l'Himalaya, Comité
  Scientifique du Club Alpin Français.

RIVOLIER, Jean
  Médicine et montagne; préface de Lucien Devies.
  Paris: Arthaud, Masson, 1956. 201p., illus.
  22cm. (Collection sempervivum, 30)

Roadside sketches in the South of France and Spanish
  Pyrenees, by three wayfarers; with twenty-
  four illustrations by Touchstone [i.e. M. Booth]. Bell
  & Daldy, 1859. vi, 113p., plates, illus. 27cm.

ROB ROY
  See
MACGREGOR, John

ROBBINS, Royal
  Advanced rockcraft; illustrated by Sheridan
  Anderson. Glendale (Calif.): La Siesta Press,
  1973. 95p., illus. 21cm.

ROBBINS, Royal
  Basic rockcraft; illustrated by Sheridan Anderson.
  Glendale (Calif.): La Siesta Press, 1971. 70p.,
  illus. 21cm.

ROBERT, François
  Voyage dans les XIII cantons suisses, les Grisons,
  le Valais, et autres pays et états alliés ou
  sujets des Suisses. Paris: Hotel d'Aubeterre,
  1789. 2v. 21cm.

ROBERT, J   Boillot
  See
BOILLOT-ROBERT, J

ROBERT, Paul A
BORDEAUX, Henry
  Les fleurs des Alpes;18 planches en dix couleurs
  d'apres les acquarelles de Paul A. Robert; texte
  de Henry Bordeaux. Paris: Plon, 1938. 15p., 18
  col. plates, illus. 28cm. (Collection "Iris")

CORREVON, Henry and ROBERT, Philippe
  La flore alpine. Genève: Atar, [1909]. 440p.,
  col. illus. 22cm.

CORREVON, Henry and ROBERT, Philippe
  [La flore alpine]. The alpine flora; translated
  and enlarged under the author's sanction, by
  E.W. Clayforth. Geneva: Atar, [1911?]. 436p.,
  1 plate, col. illus., port. 22cm.

- - Another issue. Methuen, [1912].

ROBERTS, Askew and WOODALL, Edward
  Gossiping guide to Wales, North Wales and
  Aberystwyth. Traveller's ed. Simpkin, Marshall,
  Hamilton, Kent, 1914. xcvi, 328p., plates (some
  fold.col.), illus. (1 fold. in pocket), maps.
  17cm.

ROBERTS, Athol R
  Himalayan holiday: an account of the New Zealand
  Himalayan Expedition, 1953. Christchurch (N.Z.):
  Whitcombe and Tombs, 1954. 44p., plates, illus.,
  map. 22cm.
  Expedition leader: Athol R. Roberts.

ROBERTS, David
  The mountain of my fear. Souvenir Press, 1969.
  157p., plates, illus., maps. 23cm.

ROBERTS, Dennis
  I'll climb Mount Everest alone: the story of
  Maurice Wilson. Hale, 1957. 158p., plates,
  illus., maps. 23cm.

ROBERTS, Emma
  Hindostan: its landscapes, palaces, temples,
  tombs, the shores of the Red Sea, and the sublime
  and romantic scenery of the Himalaya mountains;
  illustrated in a series of views drawn ... from
  original sketches by Robt. Elliot, & Geo. Francis
  White; with descriptions by Emma Roberts. Fisher,
  [1847]. 2v., plates, illus. 28cm.

ROBERTS, Emma
WHITE, George Francis
  Views in India, chiefly among the Himalaya
  mountains, taken during tours ... in 1829-31-32;
  with notes and descriptive illustrations. Fisher,
  1836-37. 2v., plates, illus. 37cm.

- - Another ed.; edited by Emma Roberts. 1838.

ROBERTS, Eric
  Glockner Region. Goring, Reading: West Col,
  1976. 135p., plates, illus., map, bibl. 17cm.
  (West Col alpine guides)

ROBERTS, Eric
  High level route: Chamonix, Zermatt, Saas: ski
  mountaineering in the Mont Blanc Range and
  Pennine Alps. Goring, Reading: West Col, 1973.
  136p.,plates, illus., maps. 19cm.

ROBERTS, Eric
  Stubai Alps: a survey of popular walking and
  climbing routes; compiled by Eric Roberts.
  Goring, Reading: West Col, 1972. 156p., illus.,
  map, bibl. 17cm. (West Col alpine guides)

ROBERTS, Harry
  The tramp's hand-book; illustrated by William
  Pascoe. Lane, 1903. xi, 175p., illus.,bibl. 18cm.

ROBERTS, Michael
  Orion marches: poems. Faber & Faber, 1939. 96p.
  23cm.

ROBERTS, Michael
  Poems. Jonathan Cape, 1936. 64p. 21cm.

ROBERTS, Michael
  A portrait of Michael Roberts; edited by T.W.
  Eason and R. Hamilton. Chelsea: College of S.
  Mark and S. John, 1949. xii, 72p., plates,
  ports., bibl. 23cm.

ROBERTS, Morley
On the old trail through British Columbia after
forty years. Nash & Grayson, 1927. xiv, 242p.,
plates, illus. 24cm.

ROBERTS, Morley
The Western Avernus: three years' autobiography
in western America. New ed. Brown, Langham,
1904. ix, 277p., plates (1 fold.col.), map, port.
21cm.

ROBERTSON, Alexander
Through the Dolomites from Venice to Toblach.
Allen, 1896. xii, 264p., 42 plates, illus., map.
19cm.

- - 2nd ed. rev., with a supplementary chapter.
1903.

ROBERTSON, David
George Mallory. Faber & Faber, 1969. 279p.,
plates, illus., maps, bibl. 23cm.

ROBERTSON, Eric
Wordsworthshire: an introduction to a poet's
country ...; illustrated with forty-seven drawings
by Arthur Tucker. Chatto & Windus, 1911. 352p.,
plates, illus., bibl. 23cm.

ROBERTSON, Sir George Scott
The Kafirs of the Hindu-Kush. Lawrence and
Bullen, 1896. xx, 658p., 1 fold.col. plate,
illus., map. 26cm.

ROBERTSON, James
Arachnia: occasional verses. Macmillan, 1904. xi,
212p., port. 18cm.
Contains three alpine poems and translated poems.

ROBERTSON, Max
Mountain panorama: a book of winter sports and
climbing; edited by Max Robertson. Parrish, 1955.
128p., illus. 25cm.

ROBERTSON, William
TAINE, Hippolyte
Voyage aux Pyrénées; edited by William Robertson.
Oxford: Clarendon Press, 1905. xvi, 211p., 1
plate, map. 20cm. (Oxford modern French series)

ROBINSON, Anthony Melland
Alpine roundabout. Chapman & Hall, 1947. ix,
214p., plates (1 col.), illus. 23cm.

ROBINSON, F   R
A climber's guide to Seneca Rocks, West Virginia.
Washington (D.C.): Potomac Appalachian Trail Club,
Mountaineering Section, 1971. 122p., illus. 14cm.

ROBINSON, J   Wilson
RUMNEY, A   Wren
The way about the English Lake District; together
with appendices on crag climbing and fishing by
J. Wilson Robinson and G.E. Lowthian... Iliffe, &
Sturmey, [1898]. 160p., 1 fold. plate, illus.,
maps. 17cm. (Way-about series of gazetteer
guides, no.12)

ROBINSON, John
A guide to the Lakes in Cumberland, Westmorland,
and Lancashire... Lackington, Hughes, Harding,
Mavor, and Jones, 1819. x, 328p., plates (1 fold.
col.), illus., map. 21cm.

ROBINSON, Noel
Blazing the trail through the Rockies: the story
of Walter Moberly and his share in the making of
Vancouver, by Noel Robinson and the old man
himself. Vancouver: News-Advertiser, [ca 1910].
118p., illus. 24cm.

ROBINSON, W
Alpine flowers for English gardens. Murray, 1870.
xviii, 392p., illus. 21cm.

- - New ed., rev. 1875.

ROBINSON, W
Alpine flowers for gardens: rock, wall, marsh
plants, and mountain shrubs. 4th ed., rev.
Murray, 1910. xix, 344p., plates, illus. 23cm.

ROBSON, E   I
A wayfarer in the Pyrenees. Methuen, 1929. xi,
216p., plates, illus., map (on lining paper).
21cm.

ROBSON, George Fennell
Scenery of the Grampian Mountains; illustrated by
forty-one plates, representing the principal
hills... Longman, Hurst, Rees, Orme, & Brown,
1819. 1v. (chiefly col. illus., map). 58cm.

ROBSON, Peter
Mountains of Kenya. Nairobi: East African
Publishing House for Mountain Club of Kenya, 1969.
80p., col. plates, illus., map, bibl. 23cm.

ROBY, John
Seven weeks in Belgium, Switzerland, Lombardy,
Piedmont, Savoy, &c. &c; with ... engravings on
wood from the author's sketches. Longman, Orme,
Brown, Green, & Longmans, 1838. 2v., illus., map.
21cm.

ROCH, André
Belles ascensions alpines: ascensions classiques;
80 photographies originales d'André Roch.
Lausanne: J. Marguerat, [1951]. 19p., 80 plates,
illus., map (on lining papers). 29cm.

ROCH, André
Les conquêtes de ma jeunesse; préface de Charles
Gos. Neuchatel: Attinger, 1942. xi, 177p., 16
plates, illus. 21cm.

ROCH, André
[Les conquêtes de ma jeunesse]. Climbs of my
youth. Lindsay Drummond, 1949. 159p., 16 plates,
illus. 23cm.

ROCH, André
Everest 1952; préface ... de E.F. Norton; introduction ... [de] Ed. Wyss-Dunant; avec le concours
des membres de l'expédition: J.-J. Asper [and
others]. Genève: Jeheber, 1952. 110p. (chiefly
illus., map). 26cm.

ROCH, André
La Haute-Route: Chamonix, Zermatt, Saas-Fée: 77
photographies originales présentées par André
Roch. Lausanne: J. Marguerat, 1943 [i.e. 1944].
1v. (chiefly illus.). 29cm.

ROCH, André
Images d'escalades: 88 photographies; publié sous
les auspices de la Fondation Suisse d'Exploration
Alpine. Lausanne: J. Marguerat, 1946. 1v.
(chiefly illus.). 25cm.

ROCH, André
In Fels und Eis: ein Photo-Tourenbuch ...; hrsg.
von der Schweizerischen Stiftung für Alpine
Forschungen. Zürich: Herdeg, 1946. xv, 81p.,
illus. 25cm.

ROCH, André
[In Fels und Eis...]. On rock and ice: mountain-
eering in photographs; with a foreword by Frank
S. Smythe. Black, 1947. xv, 80p., illus. 26cm.

ROCH, André
Karakoram Himalaya: sommets de 7000; préface de
Marcel Kurz; publié sous les auspices de la
Fondation Suisse d'Explorations Alpines.
Neuchatel: Attinger, 1945. 185p., plates (1 col.),
illus., map. 22cm. (Montagne)

ROCH, André
Mon carnet de courses; préface d'André Guex.
Lausanne: F. Rouge, 1948. 205p., plates, illus.
22cm. (Collection alpine, 8)

ROCH, André and PIDERMAN, Guido
Quer durchs "Schweizerland": Grönlandexpedition des Akademischen Alpenclub Zürich. Zürich: Amstutz & Herdeg, 1941. 251p., illus., maps. 24cm.

ROCH, André
Taeschhorn, face sud (4498m.), (3e ascension). (In Akademischer Alpen-Club Zürich, 48. Jahresbericht, 1943, p.23-31)

ROCHAS, Albert de
La campagne de 1692 dans le Haut Dauphiné: documents inédits relatifs à l'histoire et la topographie militaire des Alpes, lettres de Catinat, de Vauban ...; [edited by Albert de Rochas]. Paris, 1874. 181p., plates, maps. 26cm. Offprint from Bulletin de la Société de statistique de l'Isère.

ROCHAS D'AIGLUN, Albert de
See
ROCHAS, Albert de

ROCHAT-CENISE, Charles
Jacques Balmat du Mont-Blanc. Paris: E. Malfère, 1929. 189p. 19cm. (Bibliothèque du hérisson)

ROCHAT-CENISE, Charles
Pays de glace et de granit: images; bois gravés de Maurice Sauvayre. Grenoble: Arthaud, 1931. 188p., illus. 21cm.

ROCHE, Roger Frison
See
FRISON-ROCHE, Roger

ROCHETTE, Raoul
See
RAOUL-ROCHETTE, Désiré

ROCK, Joseph F
The Amnye ma-chhen range and adjacent regions: a monographic study. Roma: Istituto Italiano per il Medio ed Estremo Oriente, 1956. xi, 194p., plates (some fold., some col.), illus., maps. 26cm. (Serie orientale Roma, v.12)

ROCK CLIMBING CLUB, Japan
Everest 8848m: the Japanese expedition to Mt. Everest, 1973: the preliminary report. [Tokyo?]: The Club, 1974. 43p., illus. 26cm.
In Japanese with diary and captions in English.

ROCKHILL, William Woodville
Diary of a journey through Mongolia and Tibet in 1891 and 1892. Washington (D.C.): Smithsonian Institution, 1894. xx, 413p., plates (1 fold. col.), illus., map. 25cm.

ROCOFFORT, L
Le secret de l'avalanche. Lyon: J. Desvigne, 1922. 119p. 19cm.

ROCOFFORT, L
Sur les trois versants du Mont-Blanc: Suisse, France, Italie. Lyon: J. Desvigne, 1925. 98p., illus. 34cm.

ROD, Édouard
Là-haut. Paris: Perrin, 1897. vi, 364p. 19cm.

ROD, Édouard
Notes sur la peinture alpestre. (In Bibliothèque universelle... v.62, 1894, p.318-337)

ROD, Édouard
L'ombre s'étend sur la montagne. Paris: Nelson, [1916]. 288p., plates, illus. 17cm.

RODÉS, Josep M
Roques, parets i agulles de Montserrat. 1. Regió d'Agulles, [per] Josep M. Rodés i Ferran Labraña. Montserrat: L'Abadia de Montserrat, 1972. 201p., illus., maps. 22cm.

ROEFFEL, Albin
Sportliches Bersteigen. Wien: The Author, 1922. 89p., illus. 15cm.

ROEGNER, Otto
Der Schilauf im Hochgebirge. München: Alpenfreund-Verlag, 1924. 96p., plates, illus. 11cm. (Alpenfreundbucherei, Bd.14)

ROEGNER, Otto
Schwarzwaldwinter: Schnee - Sport - Sonne; mit einem Wegweiser für Verkehr und Reiseziele von Willi Romberg. München: F. Bruckmann, 1934. viii, 88p., illus., map. 25cm.

RÜLLIN, Albert and TÄUBER, Carl
Clubführer durch die Bündner-Alpen. Bd.3. Calanca, Misox, Avers. Aarau: Schweizer Alpen-Club, 1921. 248p., illus. 17cm. (Clubführer des Schweizer Alpen-Club)

ROERICH, George N
Trails to inmost Asia: five years of exploration with the Roerich Central Asian Expedition; with a preface by Louis Marin. New Haven: Yale University Press; London: Oxford University Press, 1931. 504p., plates, illus., map. 26cm.

ROERICH, Nicholas
Himalayas: abode of light; by Nicholas Roerich; with illustrations from his paintings. Bombay: Nalanda Publications; London: D. Marlowe, 1947. 176p., col. plates, illus (1 col.). 25cm.

ROESSEL, Albin
Sportliches Bergsteigen. Wien: The Author, 1922. 95p., illus. 15cm.

ROGER, Alexandre Salomon
ENGEL, Claire Éliane
Alpinistes d'autrefois: le major Roger et son baromètre. Neuchatel: Attinger, 1935. 215p., 8 plates, illus., port. 19cm.

ROGER, Noelle
Saas-Fée et la Vallée de la Viège de Saas; illustrations de Lacombe & Arlaud. Bale: Georg, 1902. 109p., plates, illus. 34cm.

ROGER-SMITH, Hugh
Plant hunting in Europe. Bedford: Rush & Warwick; [Woking]: Alpine Garden Society, [1950]. 80p., plates, illus. 22cm.

HUBER, Eddie and ROGERS, Norman
The complete ski manual: how to begin, how to improve, how to excel. Allen & Unwin, 1949. xi, 129p., illus. 25cm.

ROGERS, Samuel
Italy: a poem. Murray, 1823. 198p. 21cm.

- - Another issue. E. Moxon, 1840.

ROGET, F   F
Altitude and health. Constable, 1919. xii, 186p. 23cm. (Chadwick library)
Three lectures delivered in London for the Chadwick Trust.

ROGET, F   F
Hints on alpine sports; with a supplement on mountaineering and winter sports clothing. Burberrys, [1912]. 55p., illus. 23cm.

ROGET, F   F
Ski-runs in the High Alps; with 25 illustrations by L.M. Crisp. Fisher Unwin, 1913. 312p., plates, illus., maps. 23cm.

ROHRDORF, Caspar
Reise über die Grindelwald-Viescher-Gletscher auf den Jungfrau-Gletscher und Ersteigung des Gletschers des Jungfrau-Berges, unternommen und beschrieben im August und September 1828, durch Caspar Rohrdorf. Bern: L.A. Haller, 1828. 48p., plates (1 col.), illus., map. 21cm.

ROLAND, Mme.
See
ROLAND DE LA PLATIÈRE, Marie Jeanne

ROLAND DE LA PLATIÈRE, Marie Jeanne
Voyage en Suisse, 1787. Éd. collationée, annot. et accompagnée d'un aperçu sur les débuts touristiques féminins dans les Alpes, par G.R. De Beer. Neuchatel: La Baconnière, 1937. 207p., illus. 20cm.

ROLLE, Friedrich
Erläuterungen und Profile zur geologischen Karte der Umgebungen von Bellinzona im Kanton Tessin und von Chiavenna in Italien. Bern: J. Dalp, 1881. 59p., 9 plates (some col.), illus. 33cm. (Beiträge zur geologischen Karte der Schweiz, Lfg. 23. Das südwestliche Graubünden und nordöstliche Tessin)

ROLLINS, Alice W
From palm to glacier, with an interlude: Brazil, Bermuda and Alaska. New York: Putnam, 1892. ix, 145p., plates, illus. 24cm.

ROMBERG, Willi
ROEGNER, Otto
Schwarzwaldwinter: Schnee - Sport - Sonne; mit einem Wegweiser für Verkehr und Reiseziele von Willi Romberg. München: F. Bruckmann, 1934. viii, 88p., illus., map. 25cm.

ROMM, Michael
The ascent of Mount Stalin; translated by Alec Brown. Lawrence and Wishart, 1936. xii, 270p., plates (1 fold.), illus., map. 23cm.

RONALDSHAY, Lawrence John Lumley Dundas, Earl of
Lands of the thunderbolt: Sikkim, Chumbi & Bhutan. Constable, 1923. xvii, 267p., plates (1 fold.), illus., map. 23cm.

RONALDSHAY, Lawrence John Lumley Dundas, Earl of
On the outskirts of empire in Asia. Blackwood, 1904. xxii, 408p., plates (1 fold.col.), illus., map. 25cm.

RONALDSHAY, Lawrence John Lumley Dundas, Earl of
Sport and politics under an eastern sky. Blackwood, 1902. xxiv, 423p., plates (2 fold. col.), illus., map. 24cm.

RONEY, Sir Cusack P
The Alps and the Eastern mails. Effingham Wilson, 1867. 59p., 1 fold.plate, map. 22cm.

The roof-climber's guide to Trinity, containing a practical description of all routes, [by G. Winthrop Young]. Cambridge: W.P. Spalding, [1900]. 35p., illus. 18cm.

- - New ed. 1930.

ROOK, Clarence
Switzerland, the country and its people, written by Clarence Rook; painted by Effie Jardine. Chatto & Windus, 1907. x, 270p., plates (some col.), illus. 25cm.

ROOSEVELT, Theodore, 1858-1919 and GRINNELL, George Bird
American big-game hunting: the book of the Boone and Crockett Club; editors, Theodore Roosevelt, George Bird Grinnell. D. Douglas, 1893. 343p., plates, illus. 22cm.

ROOSEVELT, Theodore, 1858-1919 and GRINNELL, George Bird
Hunting in many lands: the book of the Boone and Crockett Club; editors, Theodore Roosevelt, George Bird Grinnell. New York: Forest and Stream Publishing Co., 1895. 447p., plates, illus. 22cm.

ROOSEVELT, Theodore, 1887-1944 and ROOSEVELT, Kermit
East of the sun and west of the moon. Scribner, 1926. xi, 284p., plates, illus., maps. 23cm.

CREW, Peter and ROPER, Ian
Cwm Glas; with a geological note by N.J. Soper; a natural history note by Evan Roberts; diagrams by R.B. Evans; and photographs by K.J. Wilson and L.R. Holliwell. 2nd ed. Stockport: Climbers' Club, 1970. ii, 157p., illus., maps. 16cm. (Climbers' Club guides to Wales, 5)

ROPER, Ian
Rock climbing in the Lake District: an illustrated guide to selected climbs in the Lake District, [by] Geoff Cram, Chris Eilbeck, Ian Roper. Constable, 1975. xiii, 250p., illus., maps (on lining papers). 18cm.

ROPER, Steve
The climber's guide to the High Sierra. San Francisco: Sierra Club, 1976. 380p., illus., maps. 16cm. (Sierra Club totebooks)

ROPER, Steve
A climber's guide to Yosemite valley; drawings by Al MacDonald. San Francisco: Sierra Club, 1964. 190p., illus. 19cm.

- - [New ed.]. 1971 (1975 repr.). (Sierra Club totebooks)

ROSA, G Titta
See
TITTA ROSA, G

ROSCHNIK, Rudolf
Der Triglav. Stuttgart: Deutsche Verlags-Anstalt, 1906. 84p., plates, illus., maps. 18cm. (Alpine Gipfelführer, 8)

ROSCOE, Don Thomas
Llanberis north. Stockport: Climbers' Club, 1961. 108p., plates, illus. 16cm. (Climbing guides to the Snowdon district)

ROSCOE, Don Thomas
Mountaineering: a manual for teachers & instructors. Faber & Faber, 1976. 181p., plates, illus., bibl. 23cm.

ROSCOE, Thomas and THORNTON, Cyril
Rambles in France and Switzerland; illustrated with ... steel engravings of drawings by S. Prout and J.D. Harding. Allman, [n.d.]. 78p., 27 plates, illus. 26cm.

ROSCOE, Thomas
The tourist in Switzerland and Italy; illustrated from drawings by S. Prout. R. Jennings, 1830. 278p., plates, illus. 21cm. (Landscape annual for 1830)

ROSCOE, Thomas
Wanderings and excursions in North Wales. C.Tilt, [1836?]. 264p., plates, illus. 25cm.

- - Another issue. H.G. Bohn, 1853.
- - Another ed. 1862.

ROSE, George
See
SKETCHLEY, Arthur

ROSE, Thomas
The British Switzerland; or, Picturesque rambles in the English Lake District, comprising a series of views ..., by Thomas Allom; with descriptive letterpress, by Thomas Rose. London Printing and Publishing Co. [1856-60]. 2v., plates (1 fold. col.), illus., map. 28cm.

ROSE, Thomas
The northern tourist: seventy-three views of lake and mountain scenery, etc. in Westmorland, Cumberland, Durham, & Northumberland, [by Thomas Rose]. Fisher, 1836. 149-220p., plates, illus. 28cm.
Also published as v.3 of the author's Westmorland, Cumberland, Durham...

ROSE, Thomas
Westmorland, Cumberland, Durham, and Northumberland; illustrated from original drawings by Thomas Allom, and George Pickering, &c; with descriptions by T. Rose. H. Fisher, R. Fisher, & P. Jackson, 1832-[35]. 3v., plates, illus. 28cm.

ROSEGGER, P   K
Wanderungen durch Steiermark und Kärnten; geschildert von P.K. Rosegger, Fritz Pichler und U. von Rauschenfels; illustrirt von Richard Püttner [and others]. Stuttgart: Kröner, [1880]. ix, 242p., plates, illus. 38cm. (Unser Vaterland)

ROSENBERG, C
HOLLAND, P
Select views of the Lakes in Cumberland, Westmoreland, and Lancashire, from drawings made by P. Holland; engraved by C. Rosenberg. Liverpool, J. Peeling, 1792. [20] leaves, 20 plates, illus. 21 x 28cm.

ROSENOW, Hermann
Der Wintersport: ein Handbuch. Leipzig: Grethlein, [1912]. 174p., illus., bibl. 21cm.

ROSIÈRE, J
Chamonix: station d'altitude. Paris: Société d'éditions scientifiques, 1898. vii, 82p., plates, illus. 18cm.

ROSS, Alexander
Adventures of the first settlers on the Oregon or Columbia River, being a narrative of the expedition fitted out by John Jacob Astor, to establish the "Pacific Fur Company"; with an account of some Indian tribes on the coast of the Pacific. Smith, Elder, 1849. xvi, 352p., 1 fold. plate, map. 21cm.

ROSS, Alexander
The fur hunters of the Far West: a narrative of adventures in the Oregon and Rocky Mountains. Smith, Elder, 1855. 2v. in 1, plates (1 fold.), illus., map. 20cm.

ROSS, Colin
Südamerika die aufsteigende Welt. 3.Aufl. Leipzig: Brockhaus, 1923. 319p., plates, illus., map. 20cm.

ROSS, Mrs. Forrest and ROSS, Noel
Mixed grill. Auckland (N.Z.): Whitcombe and Tombs, 1934. 282p. 22cm.

BAKER, Ernest Albert and ROSS, Francis Edward
The voice of the mountains; edited by Ernest A. Baker and Francis E. Ross. Routledge, [1905]. xxii, 294p. 17cm.

ROSS, Helen E
Behaviour and perception in strange environments. Allen & Unwin, 1974. 171p., 6 plates, illus., bibl. 23cm. (Advances in psychology series, 5)

ROSS, Malcolm
A climber in New Zealand; illustrated from photographs by the author. Arnold, 1914. xx, 316p., plates, illus. 23cm.

ROSS, Mrs. Malcolm
See
ROSS, Mrs. Forrest

ROSS, Mars and STONEHEWER-COOPER, H
The highlands of Cantabria; or, Three days from England. Sampson Low, Marston, Searle & Rivington, 1885. xvi, 378p., 1 plate, illus., map. 24cm.

ROSS, Martin and SOMERVILLE, E   OE
Beggars on horseback: a riding tour in North Wales; with numerous illustrations by E.OE. Somerville. Edinburgh, London: Blackwood, 1895. vi, 186p., illus. 20cm.

ROSS, Mrs. Forrest and ROSS, Noel
Mixed grill. Auckland (N.Z.): Whitcombe and Tombs, 1934. 282p. 22cm.

ROSS, Thomasina
HUMBOLDT, Alexander, Freiherr von
Personal narrative of travels to the equinoctial regions of America during the years 1799-1804, by Alexander von Humboldt and Aimé Bonpland, written in French by Alexander von Humboldt; translated and edited by Thomasina Ross. Bohn, 1852-53. 3v. 20cm.

ROSS, W   A
A yacht voyage to Norway, Denmark and Sweden. 2nd ed. H. Colburn, 1849. viii, 432p., 1 plate, illus. 21cm.

ROSSIER, Edmond
L'Aiguille Verte. Lausanne: [The Author], [1935?]. 12p. 24cm.

ROTH, Abraham
Doldenhorn und Weisse Frau, zum ersten Mal ersteigen und geschildert von Abraham Roth und Edmund von Fellenberg, [von Abraham Roth]. Coblenz: Baedeker, 1863. 86p., col. plates (1 fold.), illus., map. 26cm.

ROTH, Abraham
[Doldenhorn und Weisse Frau...]. The Doldenhorn and Weisse Frau, ascended for the first time by Abraham Roth and Edmund von Fellenberg. Coblenz: Baedeker; London: Williams & Norgate, 1863. 82p., col. plates (1 fold.), illus., map. 26cm.

ROTH, Abraham
Finsteraarhornfahrt. Berlin: Springer, 1863. 112p., 2 plates (1 fold., 1 col.), illus., map. 20cm.

ROTH, Abraham
Gletscherfahrten in den Berner Alpen, unternommen und geschildert von Abraham Roth. Berlin: Springer, 1861. vii, 175p., 1 plate, illus. 17cm.

ROTHER, Rudolf
Berner Oberland: Bilder von den Bergen, Seen und Tälern zwischen Aare, Rhone und Simme. München: Rother, 1924. 63p., plates (some col.), illus. 32cm.

ROTHPLETZ, August
Alpine Majestäten und ihr Gefolge: die Gebirgswelt der Erde in Bildern ... Ansichten ... mit einleitendem Text ..., von A. Rothpletz, [Ernst Platz - Walther Bauer]. München: Vereinigte Kunstanstalten, 1901-04. 4v. (chiefly illus., maps). 46cm.
Published in parts, containing a few views outside the Alps.

ROTHPLETZ, August
Geologischer Führer durch die Alpen. 1. Das Gebiet der zwei grossen rhätischen Uerberschiebungen zwischen Bodensee und dem Engadin. Berlin: Borntraeger, 1902. xiv, 256p., illus. 16cm. (Sammlung geologischer Führer, 10)

ROTOTAEV, P   S
Pobezhdennaia Ushba. Moskva: Gos. Izd. Geograficheskoi Literatury, 1948. 135p., 1 fold. plate, illus., map. 21cm.

ROUCH, Monique
Wakhan: victoires pyrénéennes dans l'Himalaya; préface de Robert Ollivier. Pau: Marrimpouey, 1970. 101p., plates (1 col.), illus., maps. 19cm.

ROUFF, Marcel
L'homme et la montagne. Paris: Émile-Paul, 1925. 303p. 20cm.

Rough notes of an excursion to the Soonderdoongee glacier in the Himalaya mountains during the autumn of 1848, by H.B.T. Couchman, 1858. 47p. 22cm.

ROUSSEAU, Jean Jacques
[Les Confessions]. Jean-Jacques Rousseau en Savoie: Annecy - Chambéry - Les Charmettes; extraits des "Confessions" situés et commentés par F. Vermale. Chambéry: Dardel, 1922. 221p. 20cm.

ROUSSEAU, Jean Jacques
La nouvelle Héloise, ou; Lettres de deux amants,
habitants d'une petite ville au pied des Alpes.
Genève: J.J. Rousseau, 1783. 3v., plates, illus.
17cm.

ROUX, Xavier
Les Alpes: histoire et souvenirs. Paris: Téqui,
1897. 271p. 20cm.

ROUX-PARASSAC, Émile
Les poèmes de l'Alpe... Paris: H. Falque, 1910.
266p. 20cm.

ROVERETO, Gaetano
Guida delle Alpi apuane, [da] L. Bozano, E. Questa,
G. Rovereto. Genova: Club Alpino Italiano,
Sezione Ligure, 1905. x, 370p., plates, illus.,
map. 18cm.

- - 2a ed.: con la collaborazione di Bartolomeo
Figari, 1921.

ROWBOTHAM, J F
The epic of the Swiss lake-dwellers: an epic poem
in twelve cantos. Cromwell, 1913. 55p. 22cm.

ROWE, I G
Northern Highlands area. Vol.1 Letterewe and
Easter Ross. Edinburgh: Scottish Mountaineering
Trust, 1969. 192p., illus., maps. 17cm.
(Scottish Mountaineering Club climbers' guide
books)

ROWELL, F E
ROWELL, Robert
Recollections of our midsummer ramble, by the
Printer [i.e. Robert Rowell and] by his wife.
Ventnor: Robert Rowell, [1873]. 39p., plates,
illus. 19cm.

ROWELL, Galen A
In the throne room of the mountain gods. Allen &
Unwin, 1977. x, 326p., illus. (some col.), maps,
bibl. 29cm.

ROWELL, Galen A
The vertical world of Yosemite: a collection of
photographs and writings on rock climbing in
Yosemite; edited by Galen A. Rowell. Berkeley:
Wilderness Press, 1974. xiv, 207p., illus. (some
col.). 29cm.

ROWELL, Robert
Recollections of our midsummer ramble ..., by the
Printer [i.e. Robert Rowell and] by his wife.
Ventnor: Robert Rowell, [1873]. 39p., plates,
illus. 19cm.

ROWLAND, E G
The ascent of Snowdon; illustrated by Jonah Jones;
foreword by John Disley. Criccieth: Cidron Press,
1956. 21, iiip., illus., map. 20cm.

ROWLAND, E G
Hill walking in Snowdonia; camera studies by W.A.
Poucher. Camping & Open Air Press, 1951 (1952
reprint). 83p., plates, illus., map. 22cm.

- - New and fully rev. ed. Criccieth: Cidron Press,
1958.

ROYAL AIR FORCE EXPEDITION TO THE SIERRA NEVADA DE
SANTA MARTA IN COLOMBIA, 1974
Report, by N.M. Ridley. The Expedition, [1975?].
1v. (various pagings), plates, illus., maps. 30cm.

ROYAL AIR FORCE GREENLAND EXPEDITION, 1975
Report on the Royal Air Force Expedition to Søndre
Sermilik Fjord in South West Greenland 10th June -
8th July 1975, by J.E. Cartwright, Expedition
Leader. [R.A.F.M.A.], [1976]. 63p., illus., maps.
29cm.

ROYAL BOTANIC GARDENS, Kew
Catalogue of Miss M.L. Moxon's alpine flower
studies and other paintings. [Royal Botanic
Gardens, Kew], [1924]. iv, 50 leaves. 33cm.

ROYAL GEOGRAPHICAL SOCIETY
Hints to travellers, scientific and general;
edited for the Council of the Royal Geographical
Society by Douglas W. Freshfield and W.J.L.
Wharton. 6th ed., rev. and enl. Royal
Geographical Society, 1889. xii, 430p., plates
(some fold.col.), illus., maps. 18cm.

- - 7th ed. rev. and enl. 1893.
- - 8th ed. rev. and enl., edited by John Coles.
1901. 2v.

ROYAL GEOGRAPHICAL SOCIETY
Hints to travellers, scientific and general...
(Cont.)

- - 9th ed. rev. and enl., edited by E.A. Reeves.
1906. 2v.
- - 10th ed. rev. and corr., edited by E.A. Reeves.
1921. 2v.
- - 11th ed., [by] E.A. Reeves. 1935-38. 2v.

ROYAL GEOGRAPHICAL SOCIETY
Peru-Bolivia Boundary Commission, 1911-1913:
reports of the British officers of the Peruvian
Commission, diplomatic memoranda and maps of the
boundary zone; edited for the Government of Peru
by the Royal Geographical Society of London.
Cambridge: Printed at the University Press, 1918.
xi, 242p., plates (some fold., some col.), illus.,
maps (3 in pocket). 30cm.

ROYAL GEOGRAPHICAL SOCIETY
The RGS archives: a handlist. Pt.1, compiled by
Christine Kelly. [London, 1975]. 99-107p. 25cm.
Offprint from Geographical journal, v.141, pt. 1,
March 1975.

ROYAL GOEGRAPHICAL SOCIETY. Mount Everest Committee
See
MOUNT EVEREST COMMITTEE

ROYAL MILITARY COLLEGE OF SCIENCE SHRIVENHAM ANDEAN
EXPEDITION, 1972
[Report of] the RMCS Andean expedition to the
Sierra Nevada de Santa Marta, Colombia, South
America. Shrivenham: The Expedition, [1973?].
1v. (various pagings), plates, maps. 30cm.

ROYAL NAVY AND ROYAL MARINES MOUNTAINEERING CLUB
MOULTON, Robert D
Lundy rock climbs: a guide book to rock climbing
on Lundy. 2nd ed. Buckhurst Hill: The Author for
Royal Navy and Royal Marines Mountaineering Club,
1974. 122p., illus. 18cm.

ROYAL NAVY AND ROYAL MARINES MOUNTAINEERING CLUB
NORDLAND EXPEDITION, 1978
Report. The Expedition, [1979]. [32]p., plates,
illus. 31cm.

ROYAL NAVY EAST GREENLAND EXPEDITION, 1966
Report on the Royal Navy East Greenland Expedition
1966, by M.B. Thomas, R.H. Wallis and members of
the expedition. [Plymouth]: The Expedition,
[1967]. [64]p., plates, illus., maps. 34cm.

ROYAL NAVY ELLESMERE ISLAND EXPEDITION, 1972
Expedition report, by A.B. Erskine. [Dunfermline]:
The Expedition, [1972]. 1v. (various pagings),
illus., maps. 30cm.

ROYAL NAVY SKI AND MOUNTAINEERING CLUB
LAWDER, K M
Climbing guide to Dartmoor and south west Devon;
edited by K.M. Lawder. Portsmouth: The Royal Navy
Ski and Mountaineering Club, [196-]. 70p., 1
plate, illus., map. 16cm.

RUBENSON, C W
Med telt og husbaat i Kashmir. Kristiania:
Steenske Forlag, 1923. 115p., illus. 25cm.

RUCHAT, Abraham
Les delices de la Suisse, une des principales républiques de l'Europe ...; avec un memoire instructif sur les causes de la guerre arrivée en
Suisse l'an 1712, par Gottlieb Kypseler de Munster
[i.e.Abraham Ruchat]. Leide: P. Vander, 1714. 4v.,
plates (some fold.), illus., maps. 17cm.

RUCHAT, Abraham
L'état dt les delices de la Suisse, en forme de
relation critique ..., [par Abraham Ruchat,
Abraham Stanyan and others]. Amsterdam: Wetsteins
et Smith, 1730. 4v., plates, illus., maps. 20cm.

- - Nouv. éd. Basle: E. Tourneisen, 1764.
- - Nouv. éd. Basle: E. Tourneisen, 1776.
- - Nouv. éd. Neuchatel: S. Fauche, 1778.

RUCKSACK CLUB
The songs of the mountaineers; collected and
edited by John Hirst, for the Rucksack Club.
Manchester: Rucksack Club, [1922]. 124p. 19cm.

RUDATIS, Domenico
Das Letzte im Fels; mit einer Einführung von Paul
Hübel; und einem Nachwort von Oskar Krammer.
München: Gesellschaft Alpiner Bücherfreunde, 1936.
249p., illus. 19cm.

RUDDER, May de
Un montagnard grison [Nicolaus Sererhard] raconte
en 1742. Bruxelles, 1939. 19p., 2 plates, illus.
25cm.
Offprint from Revue d'alpinisme, t.4, année 1938,
n.1.

RUDDER, May de
Les vingt ans du Refuge Solvay au Cervin.
Bruxelles, 1938. 10p., 1 col. plate, illus. 25cm.
Offprint from Revue d'alpinisme, t.3, 1937.

RUDEN, Joseph
Familien-Statistik der löblichen Pfarrei von
Zermatt, mit Beilagen; gesammelt und geordnet von
Joseph Ruden. Ingenbohl: Buchdruckerei der
Waisenanstalt, 1869. 184p., 1 plate, illus. 20cm.
New ed. published in 1927 under title: Familien-
Statistik und Geschichtliches über die Gemeinde
Zermatt, von Stanislaus Kronig.

RUDGE, E   C   W
Mountain days near home; illustrated with photographs by the author and drawings by his wife.
Wellingborough: Printed by W.D. Wharton, 1941.
vii, 75p., plates, illus. 23cm.

RÜBEL, E
Pflanzengeographische Monographie des Bernina-
gebietes. Leipzig, 1912. x, 615p., 37 plates (1
fold., 2 col.), illus., map. 25cm.
Offprint from Botanische Jahrbücher Bd.47, Heft
1/4.

RÜTIMEYER, L
Der Rigi: Berg, Thal und See: naturgeschichtliche
Darstellung der Landschaft. Basel: H. Georg,
1877. vii, 160p., plates (1 col.), illus., map.
30cm.

RÜTIMEYER, L
Über Thal- und See-Bildung: Beiträge zum Ver-
ständniss der Oberfläche der Schweiz. Basel: C.
Schultze, 1869. 95p., fold.col. plates, illus.,
map. 28cm.

RÜTTER, H
Clubführer durch die Bündner-Alpen. Bd.4. Die
südlichen Bergellerberge und Monte Disgrazia.
Aarau: Schweizer Alpen-Club, 1922. xvi, 182p.,
illus. 17cm. (Clubführer des Schweitzer Alpen-
Club)

- - 2. Aufl. 1935.
- - 3. Aufl., rev. von H. Grimm und M. Zisler. 1966.

RUGE, Sophus
Norwegen. Bielefeld: Velhagen & Klasing, 1899.
140p., 1 fold.col. plate, illus., map, bibl.
26cm. (Land und Leute. Monographien zur
Erdkunde, 3)

- - 2. Aufl., bearb. von Yngvar Nielson. 1905.

KUZ'MIN, Nikolai Ivanovich and RUKODEL'NIKOV, Boris
Leonidovich
Obuchenie al'pinistov. Moskva: Izd. "Fizkul'tura
i Sport", 1965. 192p., illus. 20cm.

RUMNEY, A   Wren
The Dalesman. Kendal: T. Wilson, 1911. 219p.,
plates, illus. 24cm.

RUMNEY, A   Wren
The way about the English Lake District; together
with appendices on crag climbing and fishing by
J. Wilson Robinson and G.E. Lowthian. Iliffe &
Sturmey, [1898]. 160p., 1 fold.plate, illus.,
maps. 17cm. (Way-about series of gazetteer
guides, no.12)

RUNDALL, L   B
The ibex of Shā-ping and other Himalayan studies;
with numerous pen and ink sketches and coloured
plates by the author. Macmillan, 1915. xiv,
152p., col. plates, illus. 26cm.

Rundreisen in der Schweiz; einschliesslich des
Bodensees, dar oberitalienischen Seen und Mailand,
27.Aufl. München: A. Bruckmann, 1913. 367p.,
plates, maps. 17cm. (Bruckmann's illustrierte
Reiseführer, 54-59)

RUNGE, H
La Suisse: collection de vues pittoresques avec
texte historique-topographique; traduit de
l'allemand par J.T. Thévenot. Darmstadt: G.G.
Langé, 1866. 3v., plates, illus. 27cm.

RUPPEN, Peter Joseph
Die Chronik des Thales Saas, für die Thalbewohner;
bearb. und hrsg. von Peter Joseph Ruppen. Sitten:
Calpini-Albertazzi, 1851. 187, iii p. 17cm.
Contains: Wissenschaftliche Bernerkungen ..., by
Pfarrer Imseng.

RUPPEN, Peter Joseph
SANKT NIKLAUS (Parish)
Familien-Statistik der löblichen Pfarrei von St.
Niklaus; gesammelt und geordnet von Peter Joseph
Ruppen. Sitten: Eduard Läderich, 1861. vii,
132p. 18cm.

RUPRECHT, F   J
Flora boreali-uralensis: ueber die Verbreitung der
Pflanzen im nördlichen Ural. 50p., plates (1
fold.), illus. 32cm.
(In Imperatorskoe Russkoe Geograficheskoe
Obshchestvo. Der nördliche Ural... St. Petersburg,
1853-56)

RUSCH, J   B   E
Wanderspiegel. Leipzig: A.G. Liebeskind, 1873.
vi, 224p. 18cm.

PEASCOD, W   and RUSHWORTH, G
Buttermere and Newlands area; with illustrations
by W. Heaton Cooper. Manchester: Fell & Rock
Climbing Club, 1949. 128p., 1 col.plate, illus.
16cm. (Rock-climbing guides to the English Lake
District, 2nd [i.e. 3rd] ser., 2)

RUSK, C   E
Tales of a western mountaineer: a record of
mountaineering experiences on the Pacific coast.
Boston: Houghton Mifflin, 1924. xiii, 309p.,
plates, illus. 22cm.

RUSKIN, John
Deucalion: collected studies of the lapse of
waves, and life of stones. Orpington: Allen,
1879-80. 2v. in 1, plates (1 col.), illus. 23cm.

RUSKIN, John
The diaries of John Ruskin; selected and edited
by Joan Evans and John Howard Whitehouse. Oxford:
Clarendon Press, 1956- . 3v., plates, illus.
25cm.
Vol.1. 1835-1847. 1956. -v.2. 1848-1873. 1958. -

RUSKIN, John
In montibus sanctis: studies of mountain form and
of its visible causes; collected and completed out
of 'Modern painters'. Orpington: Allen, 1884-85.
85p. 27cm.

RUSKIN, John
Modern painters. Smith, Elder, 1856-60 (v.1,
1857). 5v., plates (some col.), illus. 28cm.
Vol.1 is 6th ed., v.2. Of mountain beauty, 4th ed.

RUSKIN, John
The poems of John Ruskin; now first collected ...
and edited ... with notes ... by W.G. Collingwood;
with facsimiles of mss. and illus. by the author.
Orpington, London: Allen, 1891. 2v., plates,
illus. 30cm.

RUSKIN, John
Praeterita: outlines of scenes and thoughts perhaps
worthy of memory in my past life. Allen, 1887.
2v., plates, illus. 25cm.

RUSKIN, John
RENDU, Louis
[Théorie des glaciers de la Savoie]. Theory of the
glaciers of Savoy; translated by Alfred Wills; to
which are added the original memoir and supplementary articles by P.G. Tait and John Ruskin;
edited with introductory remarks by George Forbes.
Macmillan, 1874. 216p., illus., map. 23cm.
Text in English and French.

RUSKIN, John
COLLINGWOOD, William Gershom
The life of John Ruskin. 7th ed. Methuen, 1911.
viii, 314p. 18cm. (Methuen's shilling books)

RUSKIN, John
COOK, Sir Edward Tyas
Homes and haunts of John Ruskin; with ... illustrations by E.M.B. Warren. Allen, 1912. xvi, 218p.,
plates, illus. 26cm.

RUSKIN, John
COOK, Sir Edward Tyas
The life of John Ruskin. Allen, 1911. 2v., plates
(1 fold.), illus. 23cm.

RUSKIN, John
LEMAITRE, Hélène
Les pierres dans l'oeuvre de Ruskin. Caen:
Association des Publications, 1965. 246p., plates,
maps, bibl. 26cm. (Publications de la Faculté
des Lettres et sciences humaines de l'Université
de Caen)

RUSSELL, Andrew
Oxford Himalayan Expedition, 1973. East Hanney:
The Expedition, [1974]. 36p., illus., maps. 30cm.

RUSSELL, Henry, Count
Biarritz and Basque countries. Stanford, 1873.
192p., 1 fold.col. plate, map. 21cm.

RUSSELL, Henry, Count
Les grandes ascensions des Pyrénées d'une mer à
l'autre: guide spécial du piéton. Paris: Hachette,
[1866]. 297p., plates, maps. 20cm.

RUSSELL, Henry, Count
Pau and the Pyrenees. Longmans, Green, 1871.
82p., 3 fold.plates, illus., maps. 19cm.

RUSSELL, Henry, Count
Pau, Biarritz, Pyrenees. 2nd ed. Pau: Vignancour,
1890. 156p., 1 plate, map. 20cm.

RUSSELL, Henry, Count
Pyrenaica. Pau: Vignancour, 1902. 250p. 20cm.

RUSSELL, Henry, Count
Les Pyrénées, les ascensions et la philosophie de
l'exercice. Pau: Vignancour, 1865. 62p. 23cm.

RUSSELL, Henry, Count
Souvenirs d'un montagnard. Pau: Vignancour, 1878.
416p. 20cm.

RUSSELL, Henry, Count
Souvenirs d'un montagnard, 1858-1888. Pau:
Vignancour, 1888. xx, 508p. 19cm.

- - 2e éd., rev. et corr. 1908.

RUSSELL, Henry, Count
CLUB ALPIN FRANÇAIS. Section du Sud-Ouest.
La Concession Russell du Vignemale, [par] Ch.
Cadart; édité par la Section du Sud-Ouest du Club
Alpin Français, Commission Scientifique.
Bordeaux: La Commission, 1943. 24p., plates (1
fold.), illus., map, bibl. 22cm.
Supplément au Bulletin no.43, avril 1943.

RUSSELL, Israel C
Glaciers of North America: a reading lesson for
students of geography and geology. Boston
(Mass.): Ginn, 1897. x, 210p., plates, illus.,
map. 24cm.

SCHWATKA, Frederick and RUSSELL, Israel C
Two expeditions to Mount St. Elias. [New York]:
1891. 865-884p., illus., maps. 25cm.
Offprint from Century magazine, v.41, April 1891.

RUSSELL, John and WILTON, Andrew
Turner in Switzerland. Dubendorf (Zurich): De
Clivo Press, 1976. 148p., illus. (some col.),
maps. 32cm.
Sponsored by the Swiss National Tourist Office and
the Swiss Foundation for Alpine Research.

RUSSELL, R   Scott
Mountain prospect. Chatto & Windus, 1946. xvi,
248p., 46 plates, illus., maps. 22cm.

RUSSELL-KILLOUGH, Henry, comte
See
RUSSELL, Henry, Count

RUTHNER, Anton von
Die Alpenländer Oesterreichs und die Schweiz:
eine Parallele der Naturschönheiten des
österreichischen und Schweizer Hochlandes. Wien:
Braumüller & Seidel, 1843. 36p. 23cm.

RUTHNER, Anton von
Aus dem oesterreich. Hochgebirge: Ersteigung der
Hohen Wildspitze im Oetzthale. Wien, 1863. 28p.
27cm.
Offprint from Mittheilungen der K.K. Geographischen
Gesellschaft, 6.Jahrgang.

RUTHNER, Anton von
Aus Tirol: Berg- und Gletscher-Reisen in den
österreichischen Hochalpen. Neue Folge. Wien:
C. Gerold, 1869. viii, 464p., col.plates (1
fold.), illus., map. 23cm.

RUTHNER, Anton von
Berg-und Gletscher-Reisen in den österreichischen
Hochalpen. Wien: C. Gerold, 1864. xvii, 414p.,
col.plates (1 fold.), illus., map. 22cm.

RUTHNER, Anton von
Höhenmessungen aus der Tauernkette. Wien, 1862.
3p. 26cm.
Offprint from Mittheilungen der K.K. Geographischen
Gesellschaft, 5.Jahrgang.

RUTHNER, Anton von
Das Maltathal in Kärnthen: Ersteigung des
Hochalpenspitzes. Wien, 1861. 28p. 26cm.
Offprint from Mittheilungen der K.K. Geographischen
Gesellschaft, 5.Jahrgang.

RUTHNER, Anton von
Übergang aus dem Ötzthale in das Pitzthal über den
Hochvernagt- und Sechsegertenferner. Wien, 1859.
28p. 27cm.
Offprint from Mittheilungen der K.K. Geographischen
Gesellschaft, 3.Jahrgang.

RUTHNER, Anton von
Wanderungen auf dem Glocknergebiete. Wien, 1857.
38p. 26cm.
Offprint from Mittheilungen der K.K. Geographischen
Gesellschaft, 1.Jahrgang.

- - Neue Folge. 1863.
Offprint from Mittheilungen ... 6.Jahrgang.

RUTLAND, John Henry Manners, 5th Duke of
Journal of a tour to the northern parts of Great
Britain, [by John Henry Manners, Duke of Rutland].
Printed for J. Triphook, 1813. 300p., col. plates,
illus. 24cm.

RUTTLEDGE, Hugh
Attack on Everest; [foreword by Sir Francis
Younghusband]. New York: McBride, 1935. 339p.,
plates (1 col.), illus., map. 25cm.
Based on the author's Everest 1933. London:
Hodder & Stoughton, 1934.

RUTTLEDGE, Hugh
Everest 1933. Hodder & Stoughton, 1934. xv,
390p., 59 plates (3 fold.col.), illus., maps.
27cm.

- - Popular ed. 1936.
- - Black jacket ed. 1938.

RUTTLEDGE, Hugh
[Everest 1933]. Mount Everest; oversatt av Bjarne
Kroepelien. Oslo: Gyldendal Norsk Forlag, 1938.
191p., plates, illus., map. 22cm.

RUTTLEDGE, Hugh
Everest: the unfinished adventure. Hodder &
Stoughton, 1937. 295p., plates (2 fold.col.),
illus., maps, ports. 27cm.

RUXTON, George Frederick
Adventures in Mexico and the Rocky Mountains.
Murray, 1847. viii, 332p. 19cm.

RUXTON, George Frederick
Wild life in the Rocky Mountains: a true tale of
rough adventure in the days of the Mexican War;
edited by Horace Kephart. New York: Outing
Publishing Co., 1916. 303p., 1 plate, map. 20cm.
(Outing adventure library)

RYDBERG, Per Axel
Flora of the Rocky Mountains and adjacent plains:
Colorado, Utah, Wyoming, Idaho, Montana, Saskatchewan, Alberta... New York: The Author, 1917.
xii, 1110p. 24cm.

RYDER, C   H   D
SURVEY OF INDIA
Annual reports of parties and offices, 1919-20:
prepared under the direction of C.H.D. Ryder.
Dehra Dun: Survey of India, 1921. 134p., plates
(some fold.col.), illus., maps. 35cm. (Records
of the Survey of India, v.15, supplementary to
General Report 1919-20)

RYDZEWSKI, Anton von
Zehn Jahre Bergführer Kluckers "Herr": Erlebnisse
A. von Rydzewskis Naturschilderungen und Anderes;
redigiert, gruppiert, z. T. verfasst, und hrsg.
von Hermann Tanner. 1. Buch. Anton von Rydzewski
als Künstler, eine alpine Bildergalerie in Prosa.
Bern: Liter.-Art. Bureau, 1934. 119p., 1 plate,
illus. 19cm.

RYFFEL, Alfred
Bilder von Vierwaldstätter-See; Begleitwort von
Isabelle Kaiser. Zürich: Orell Füssli, [1916].
12p., plates, illus. 20cm. (Wanderbilder, 318-
320)

RYN, Zdzisław
Medycyna i alpinizm. Warszawa: Państwowe
Wydawnictwo Naukowe, 1973. 44p. 19cm. (Polska
Akademia Nauk. Oddział w Krakowie. Nauka dla
wszystkich, nr.189)

RYN, Zdzisław
Motivation and personality in high-mountain climbing. Cracow: Psychiatrical Clinic, Medical Academy,
[1978]. 9 leaves, bibl. 31cm.
Translation of article in Psychiatria Polska, 1969,
v.3, no.4.

RYTZ, W
AMSTUTZ, Eveline
Wiesenblumenfibel; mit Farbenphotos der ...
schönsten Wiesenblumen nach der Natur aufgenommen;
eingeleitet von Eveline Amstutz; mit botanischen
Erläuterungen von W. Rytz. München: F.
Bruckmann, 1938. 1v. (chiefly col. illus.).
11 x 13cm.

RZIHA, Adolf
Der Rodelsport mit Berucksichtigung der ubrigen
Schlittensporte; hrsg., vom Wintersport-Club des
Oe. T.C. Wien. München: Lammers, 1908. xi,
134p., plates, illus. 21cm.

S., G.
See
SACCHI, Giuseppe

SABBADINI, Attilio
Alpi Marittime (dal Colle di Tenda al Colle della
Maddalena). Roma: Club Alpino Italiano; Milano:
Touring Club Italiano, 1934. 604p., plates (1
fold., some col.), illus., maps, bibl. 17cm.
(Guida dei monti d'Italia)

SABINE, chanoine de
Les nouveaux voyageurs en Suisse et en Italie:
beautés et merveilles de ces delicieuses
contrées, par le chanoine de Sabine; ouvrage rev.
corr. et augm., par Victor Doublet. Nouv. éd.
Paris: P.C. Lehuby, [1847]. 351p., plates,
illus. 22cm.

SABRO, G   N
Fører for bestigninger i Sunnmøre, Romsdal og
Inderdal; utarbeidet av Norsk Tindeklub ved Helge
Hagen ... G.N. Sabro... Oslo: Grøndahl, 1936.
22p., illus., map. 23cm.

SACCHI, Giuseppe
Le ghiacciaje della Svizzera ed i vulcani.
Bologna: Tipografia di s. Tommaso d'Aquino, 1837.
288p. 15cm.
Preface signed: Giuseppe Sacchi.

SACCHI, Giuseppe
Viaggio in Francia e nella Svizzera occidentale.
Bologna: Tipografia di s. Tommaso d'Aquino, 1838.
252p. 15cm.
Editor's preface signed: G.S. i.e. Giuseppe
Sacchi.
Adapted from the writings of Dumas and Janin.

SACCO, Federico
Sull'origine delle vallate e dei laghi alpini in
rapporto coi sollevamenti delle Alpi e coi
terreni pliocenici e quaternari della Valle
Padana. Torino, 1885. 26p., fold.col. plates,
illus. 25cm.
Offprint from Atti della R. Accademia delle
Scienze di Torino, v.20, marzo 1885.

SACK, John
The ascent of Yerupaja. H. Jenkins, 1954. 191p.,
plates, illus., map. 20cm.

SAGET, P
Description du Chateau de Pau et de ses dépen-
dances. Pau: Vignancour, 1831. 96p., 1 fold.
plate, plan. 21cm.

SAGLIO, Silvio and LAENG, Gualtiero
Adamello; con la collaborazione di Arrigo
Giannantonj. Milano: Club Alpino Italiano,
Touring Club Italiano, 1954. 694p., plates (some
fold., some col.), illus., maps, bibl. 17cm.
(Guida dei monti d'Italia)

SAGLIO, Silvio
Alpi Graie. Milano: Touring Club Italiano, Club Alpino Italiano, 1952. 432p., plates (some fold. col.), illus., maps. 17cm. (Da rifugio a rifugio, 3)

SAGLIO, Silvio
Alpi Orobie, [da] Silvio Saglio, Alfredo Corti, Bruno Credaro. Milano: Club Alpino Italiano, Touring Club Italiano, 1957. 591p., plates (some fold., some col.), illus., maps, bibl. 17cm. (Guida dei monti d'Italia)

SAGLIO, Silvio
Alpi Pennine. Milano: Touring Club Italiano, Club Alpino Italiano, 1951. 448p., plates (some fold., some col.), illus., maps. 17cm. (Da rifugio a rifugio, 4)

SAGLIO, Silvio
Alpi Retiche occidentali. Milano: Touring Club Italiano, Club Alpino Italiano, 1953. 350p., plates (1 fold., some col.), illus., maps. 17cm. (Da rifugio a rifugio, 6)

SAGLIO, Silvio
Alpi Venoste, Passirie, Breonie, Giogaia di Tessa, Monti Sarentini dal Passo di Resia al Passo del Brénnero. Roma: Centro Alpinistico Italiano; Milano: Consociazione Turistica Italiana, 1939. 795p., plates (1 fold., some col.), illus., maps, bibl. 17cm.

SAGLIO, Silvio
Bernina. Milano: Club Alpino Italiano, Touring Club Italiano, 1959. 562p., plates (1 fold., some col.), illus., maps, bibl. 17cm. (Guida dei monti d'Italia)

SAGLIO, Silvio
Dolomiti occidentali. Milano: Touring Club Italiano, Club Alpino Italiano, 1953. 270p., plates (some fold., some col.), illus., maps. 17cm. (Da rifugio a rifugio, 10)

SAGLIO, Silvio
Le Grigne. Roma: Club Alpino Italiano; Milano: Touring Club Italiano, 1937. 492p., plates (1 col.), illus., maps, bibl. 17cm. (Guida dei monti d'Italia)

SAGLIO, Silvio and BOFFA, F
Monte Rosa. Milano: Club Alpino Italiano, Touring Club Italiano, 1960. 575p., plates, illus., map (on lining papers), bibl. 17cm. (Guida dei monti d'Italia)

SAGLIO, Silvio
Ortles-Cevedale: itinerari sciistici. Milano: Sci Club, 1935. 127p., plates, illus., map. 21cm. In slip-case.

SAGLIO, Silvio
Prealpi Comasche, Varesine, Bergamasche. Milano: Club Alpino Italiano, Touring Club Italiano, 1948. 379p., plates (some fold.)., illus., maps, bibl. 17cm. (Guida dei monti d'Italia)

SAGLIO, Silvio
I rifugi del C.A.I. Milano: Club Alpino Italiano, 1957. 503p., illus. 17cm.

SAILER, Toni
Ski with Toni Sailer. Oak Tree Press, 1964. 172p., illus. 20cm.

SAINSBURY, George R
Climber's guide to the Cascade and Olympic Mountains of Washington, by a committee of the Cascade Section of the American Alpine Club; under the Chairmanship of George R. Sainsbury. [New York]: A. A.C., 1961. xii, 386p., plates (1 fold.col.), illus, maps. 17cm.
Based on a previous ed. by Fred Becky.

ST. HELENS MOUNTAINEERING CLUB ANDEAN EXPEDITION, 1977
[Report]. St. Helens (Lancs.): St. Helens Mountaineering Club, [1978]. 18 leaves. 30cm.

ST. JOHN, Bayle
The subalpine kingdom; or, Experiences and studies in Savoy, Piedmont, and Genoa. Chapman & Hall, 1856. 2v., plates, illus. 20cm.

ST. JOHN, James Augustus
There and back again in search of beauty. Longman, Brown, Green & Longmans, 1853. 2v. 21cm.

ST. JOHN, Molyneux
The sea of mountains: an account of Lord Dufferin's tour through British Columbia in 1876. Hurst and Blackett, 1877. 2v., 1 plate, port. 20cm.

SAINT LOUP
Face nord: roman. Grenoble: Arthaud, 1947. 384p., plates, illus. 19cm.

SAINT LOUP
La montagne n'a pas voulu. Grenoble: Arthaud, 1949. 209p., plates, illus. 19cm.

SAINT LOUP
Montagne sans Dieu: roman. Paris: Amiot-Dumont, 1955. 230p. 19cm.

SAINT LOUP
Monts pacifique de l'Aconcagua au Cap Horn. Paris: Arthaud, 1951. 277p., plates, illus. 21cm. (Collection sempervivum, 10)

SAINT-MARTIN, Louis Vivien de
See
VIVIEN DE SAINT-MARTIN, Louis

SAINT-ROMME, député
L'Oisans et la Bérade: huit jours dans les glaciers; photographies d'Eugène Charpenay. Paris: Blot, 1893. 56p., illus. 25cm. (Conférences sur les Alpes françaises faites à la Section de Paris de la Société des Touristes du Dauphiné; Le Dauphiné pittoresque, 1)

SAINT-ROMME, député
Le Pelvoux: voyage en zig-zag dans les Hautes-Alpes. Paris: Berthaud, 1896. 80p., 1 fold. plate, illus., map. 25cm. (Le Dauphiné pittoresque, 2)

SAINT-SAUD, Aymard d'Arlot, comte de
Cinquante ans d'excursions et d'études dans les Pyrénées espagnoles et françaises: mémorandum publié à l'occasion du cinquantenaire du Club Alpin. Bordeaux: l'Auteur, 1924. 62p., plates, illus. 26cm.

SAINT-SAUD, Aymard d'Arlot, comte de
Monographie des Picos de Europa (Pyrénées cantabriques et asturiennes): études et voyages; cartes dressées et dessinées par L. Maury ...; préface par F. Schrader. Paris: H. Barrère, 1922. xiii, 271p., 1 plate, illus., maps (in portfolio). 26cm.

SAINT-SÉVERIN, Hector Tredicini, marquis de
See
TREDICINI DE SAINT-SÉVERIN, Hector, marquis de

SALADIN, Lorenz
CLARK-SCHWARZENBACH, Annemarie
Ein Leben für die Berge: Lorenz Saladin; Geleitwort von Sven Hedin. Bern: Hallwag, 1938. 138p., plates, illus., map. 23cm.

SALISBURY, F S
Rambles in the Vaudese Alps; with eight illustrations from photographs by Somerville Hastings. Dent, 1916. x, 154p., plates, illus. 19cm.

SALSAS, Albert
La Cerdagne espagnole. Perpignan: Imprimerie-Librarie de l'Indépendant, 1899. 231p., plates, illus., bibl. 20cm. (Pyrénées inconnues)

SALT, David
  The Staffordshire Gritstone area; compiled by David
  Salt; produced for and by the Peak Committee of
  the British Mountaineering Council. B.M.C.,
  [1973]. 231p., illus., bibl. 16cm. (Rock climbs
  in the Peak, v.9)

SALT, Henry Stephen
  On Cambrian and Cumbrian hills: pilgrimages to
  Snowdon and Scawfell. A.C. Fifield, 1908. 128p.,
  plates, illus. 18cm.

SALVANESCHI, Nino
  Sports invernali: pattinaggio, slitta, bobsleigh,
  skeleton, skis. Milano: Hoepli, 1911, xv, 171p.,
  illus. 16cm.

SALZBURG. Kammer für Arbeiter und Angestellte für
Salzburg
  See
KAMMER FÜR ARBEITER UND ANGESTELLTE FÜR SALZBURG

SAMAZEUILH, J   F
  Souvenirs des Pyrénées. Agen: Noubel, 1827-29.
  2v. in 1, plates (1 fold.), illus., map. 20cm.

A'BECKETT, Arthur and SAMBOURNE, Linley
  Our holiday in the Scottish Highlands. Bradbury,
  Agnew, [1876]. 144p., plates, illus. 26 x 41cm.

SAMIVEL
  L'amateur d'abîmes: récit; illustrations de
  l'auteur. Paris: Stock, 1940. 243p., illus.
  19cm. (Les livres de nature, 53)

- - 4e éd. 1951.

SAMIVEL
  Ayorpok et Ayounghila: conte eskimo. Lyon: IAC,
  1950. 31p., col. illus. 23 x 28cm.

SAMIVEL
  Canard; ou, Le songe d'un jour de neige. Paris:
  Delagrave, 1938. [40]p., illus. (some col.).
  33cm.

SAMIVEL
  Cimes et merveilles. [Paris]: Arthaud, 1952.
  40p., plates (some col.), illus. 26cm. (Belles
  pages - belles couleurs)

- -[Nouv. éd.]. 1975.

SAMIVEL
  Contes à pic; ouvrage orné de 10 lavis de l'auteur.
  Paris: Arthaud, 1951. 285p., plates, illus. 21cm.
  (Collection sempervivum, 14)

SAMIVEL
  Le fou d'Edenberg: roman. Paris: A. Michel, 1967.
  493p. 20cm.

SAMIVEL
  Hommes, cimes et dieux: les grandes mythologies de
  l'altitude et la légende dorée des montagnes à
  travers le monde. Paris: Arthaud, 1973. 467p.,
  plates, illus., bibl. 23cm.

SAMIVEL
  -10°: quatre-vingt dix images sur les sports
  d'hiver. Paris: Delagrave, 1933. 63p., illus.
  33cm.

SAMIVEL
  M. Dumullot sur le Mont-Blanc: les aventures surprenantes de M. Dumollet (de Saint-Malo) durant
  son voyage de 1837 aux glacières de Savoie et
  d'Helvétie; extraites du cahier de ses mémoires,
  recueillies, annotées et corrigées par Samivel, et
  illustrées par le même... Lyon: Imprimerie
  Artistique en Couleurs, 1946. 157p., col. illus.
  23cm.

SAMIVEL
  Neiges: dix estampes de Samivel; d'après les
  aquarelles originales et précédées d'une introduction de l'artiste. Paris: Delagrave, 1937. 1v.
  (chiefly col. illus.). 42cm.
  In portfolio.

SAMIVEL
  L'opéra de pics: cinquante compositions; prédédées
  de La réponse des hauteurs. Grenoble: Arthaud,
  1945. 59p. (chiefly col. illus.). 30cm.

SAMIVEL
  Sous l'oeil des choucas; ou, Les plaisirs de
  l'alpinisme: quatre-vingts dessins alpins de
  Samivel; précédés d'une adresse de Guido Rey.
  Paris: Delagrave, 1932. 63p. (chiefly illus.).
  33cm.

SAMIVEL
MORIN, Micheline
  Trag, le chamois; dessins de Samivel. [Paris]:
  Delagrave, 1948. 125p., illus. 23cm.

Sammlung von Schweizer-Kühreihen und Volksliedern =
  Recueil de ranz de vaches et chansons nationales.
  4. verm. u. verb. Ausg. Bern: I.I. Burgdorfer,
  1826. viii, 100p., plates, illus., music. 24 x
  33cm.
  Preface names Ferd. Huber, and preface signatory,
  W., as editors.

SAND, George
  Lettres d'un voyageur. Nouv. éd. Paris: M.Lévy,
  1869. viii, 344p. 19cm.

SANDBERG, Graham
  The exploration of Tibet: its history and particulars from 1623 to 1904. Calcutta: Thacker,
  Spink, 1904. vi, 324p., fold.col. plates, maps.
  23cm.

SANDBERG, Graham
  An itinerary of the route from Sikkim to Lhasa,
  together with a plan of the capital of Tibet and
  a new map of the route from Yamdok Lake to
  Lhasa. Calcutta: The Author, 1901. 29p., 1
  fold.col. plate, map (in pocket), plan. 26cm.

SANDEMAN, R   G
  A mountaineer's journal. Carmarthen: Druid Press,
  1948. 168p., plates, illus. 23cm.

SAN DONATO, Elim Pavlovich Demidoff, principe di
  See
DEMIDOFF, Elim Pavlovich, principe di San Donato

SANKT NIKLAUS (Parish)
  Familien-Statistik der löblichen Pfarrei von St.
  Niklaus; gesammelt und geordnet von Peter Joseph
  Ruppen. Sitten: E. Läderich, 1861. vii, 132p.
  18cm.

FAIN, Piero and SANMARCHI, Toni
  Alta Via n.7: "sulle orme del Patéra nelle
  Prealpi dell'Alpago", "passeggiata d'autunno nelle
  Prealpi della Val Belluna". Bologna: Tamari,
  1976. 160p., illus., bibl. 16cm. (Itinerari
  alpini: itinerari per alpinisti ed escursionisti,
  31)

SAN-ROBERTO, Paolo, conte di
  Gita al Gran Sasso d'Italia, luglio 1871. Torino:
  Bona, 1871. 32p., plates, illus. 32cm.

SAN-ROBERTO, Paolo, conte di
  Mémoires scientifiques; réunis et mis en ordre.
  T.3. Mécanique, hypsométrie. Turin: V. Bona,
  1874. ix, 413p., illus. 24cm.

SAN-ROBERTO, Paolo, conte di
  Una salita alla Torre d'Ovarda, agosto 1872, [da]
  Paolo di St-Robert [and others]. Torino: Bocca,
  1873. 75p., 2 fold. plates, illus. 25cm.

SAN ROMÁN HERBAGE, Gastón
  Guia de excursionismo para la Cordillera de
  Santiago. Santiago de Chile: Federacion de
  Andinismo de Chile, 1977. 132p., illus. 23cm.

SANS-TERRE, Robert
  Les sensations extraordinaires: à travers les
  périls de l'Alpe. Genève: R.A. Durwang, [1925].
  263p. 22cm.

SANTI, E
   Itinerari skiistici della Val Formazza. Busto
   Arsizio: Club Alpino Italiano, Sezione di Busto
   Arsizio, 1927. 43p., illus., maps. 18cm.

ZOLFANELLI, Cesare and SANTINI, Vincenzo
   Guida alle Alpi Apuane, compilata dal Professore
   Cesare Zolfanelli e Vincenzo Santini. Firenze:
   Tipografia di G. Barbera, 1874. vii, 228p.,
   plates, illus., bibl. 20cm.

SANUKI, Matao and YAMADA, Keiichi
   The Alps. Tokyo: Kodansha International, 1969
   (1972 reprint)   146p., col. illus. (1
   fold.), maps. 19cm.   (This beautiful world, 11)

SAPOZHNIKOV, V   V
   Katun' i eia istoki: puteshestviia 1897-1899
   godov. Tomsk: Parovaia Tipo-litografiia, 1901.
   vii, 271, 15p., plates (some fold., some col.),
   illus., maps, bibl. 27cm.
   Summary in French.

SAPOZHNIKOV, V   V
   Mongol'skii Altai v istokakh Irtysha i Kobdo.
   Tomsk: Tipo-litografiia Sibirskago, 1911. xvii,
   408, 8p., plates (some fold.col.), illus., bibl.
   28cm.
   Summary in French.

SARAGAT, Giovanni and REY, Guido
   Alpinismo a quattro mani. Torino: R. Frassati,
   1898. 233p. 20cm.

SARAGAT, Giovanni and REY, Guido
   Famiglia alpinistica: tipi e paesaggi. Torino: S.
   Lattes, 1904. 365p., plates, facsims. 21cm.

SARENNE, Jean
   Trois curés en montagne. Paris: Arthaud, 1950.
   235p., plates, illus. 21cm. (Collection
   sempervivum)

SARKAR, Bidyut Kumar
   Report of the Trans Himalayan trekking. Calcutta:
   Y.H.A.I., South Calcutta District Committee,
   [1978]. 34p., 1 fold.plate, illus., map. 22cm.

SARS, Michael
   Beretning om en i Sommeren 1861 foretagen Reise i
   en Deel af Christianas Stift for at fortsaette
   Undersøgelsen af de i vor Glacial-formation
   indeholdte organiske Levninger. [Christiania],
   [1861]. 18p. 23cm.
   Offprint from Mag. f. Naturvid, B.11.

SAUDAN, Sylvain
DREYFUS, Paul
   Sylvain Saudan, skieur de l'impossible. Paris:
   Arthaud, 1970. 219p., plates, illus. 21cm.
   (Collection sempervivum, no.50)

SAUNDERS, I   J
   See
   PILGRIM

SAUSSURE, Horace Bénédict de
   Journal d'un voyage à Chamouni & à la cime du
   Mont-Blanc, en juillet et aoust 1787; [edited by
   E. Gaillard and H.F. Montagnier]. Lyon: Audin,
   1926. xvii, 53p., plates, illus. 30cm.

SAUSSURE, Horace Bénédict de
   Lettres de H.-B. de Saussure à sa femme; commentées
   par E. Gaillard et H.F. Montagnier. Chambéry:
   Imprimeries Réunies, 1937. 129p., 1 plate, port.
   24cm.

SAUSSURE, Horace Bénédict de
   Relation abrégée d'un voyage à la cime du Mont-
   Blanc en août 1787. Genève: Barde, Manget, [1787].
   31p. 22cm.

SAUSSURE, Horace Bénédict de
   Relation abrégée d'un voyage à la cime du Mont-
   Blanc en août 1787 = Kurzer Bericht von einer
   Reise auf den Gipfel des Montblanc, im August
   1787. München: Gesellschaft Alpiner Bücher-
   freunde in München, 1928. 2v. 22cm.
   Facsimiles of the Geneva ed. of 1787, and the
   Strasburg ed. of 1788.

SAUSSURE, Horace Bénédict de
   [Relation abrégée...]. An appendix to the sketch
   of a tour through Swisserland, containing a short
   account of an expedition to the summit of Mont
   Blanc ... in order to ascertain the height of
   that celebrated mountain... G. Kearsley, 1788.
   101-127p. 19cm.

SAUSSURE, Horace Bénédict de
   Voyages dans les Alpes, précédés d'un essai sur
   l'histoire naturelle des environs de Genève.
   Neuchatel: S. Fauche, 1779-96. 4v., plates (some
   fold.), illus., map. 26cm.

- - Another issue. 1780-86.
- - Another issue. Genève: Barde, Manget, 1787-96.
8v.

SAUSSURE, Horace Bénédict de
   [Voyages dans les Alpes]. Reisen durch die Alpen,
   nebst einem Versuch über die Naturgeschichte der
   Gegenden von Genf; aus dem Franzosischen übersetzt. Leipzig: Junius, 1781-88. 4v.,illus. 21cm.

SAUSSURE, Horace Bénédict de
   Voyages dans les Alpes: partie pittoresque des
   ouvrages de H.B. de Saussure. Genève: Cherbuliez,
   1834. xxvii, 396p. 21cm.

- - 2e éd. Paris: Cherbuliez, 1852.
- - 6e éd. Paris: Fischbacher, [1898].

SAUSSURE, Horace Bénédict de
   [Voyages dans les Alpes]. L'ascension du Mont-
   Blanc; précédés d'une notice par Léon Chauvin.
   Limoges: Ardant, [1895]. 239p., illus. 25cm.

SAUSSURE, Horace Bénédict de
   [Voyages dans les Alpes]. Saussure aux Alpes.
   1. Portrait de H.-B. de Saussure, par Charles
   Vallot [et] Autour du Mont-Blanc: extrait des
   "Voyages dans les Alpes", de H.-B. de Saussure.
   Paris: Fischbacher, 1938. 190p. 19cm.

SAUSSURE, Horace Bénédict de
   [Voyages dans les Alpes]. La cime du Mont-Blanc;
   pages extraites et annotées a l'usage des écoles
   du Quatrième voyage dans les Alpes , par R.L.G.
   Irving et R.L.A. Du Pontet. Oxford University
   Press, 1933. 87p. 18cm. (Modern French authors)

SAUSSURE, Horace Bénédict de
   [Voyages dans les Alpes]. Grotte de Balme, située
   entre Cluse et Maglan sur la route de Chamonix =
   The Grotto of Balme ...; [description de Mr. de
   Saussure ... de Mr. Bourrit ... de Mr. J.F.
   Albanis Beaumont]. Genève: J.J. Paschoud, 1827.
   34p. 15cm.
   Parallel texts in French & English.

SAUSSURE, Horace Bénédict de
   [Voyages dans les Alpes]. Le Mont-Blanc et le Col
   du Géant; annoté par E. Gaillard et Henry-F.
   Montagnier. Lyon: Audin, 1927. 95p., plates
   (some fold.), illus. 30cm.

SAUSSURE, Horace Bénédict de
   [Voyages dans les Alpes]. Le Montblanc et sa
   première ascension aus Voyages dans les Alpes;
   für die Schule bearb. von Eugene Peschier.
   Berlin: Gaertner, 1895. 155p., 1 plate, map.
   21cm. (Schulbibliothek französischer und
   englischer Prosaschriften...)

SAUSSURE, Horace Bénédict de
[Voyages dans les Alpes]. La première ascension du
Mont Blanc. Neuchatel: Delachaux & Niestlé,
[1908]. 94p. 15cm. (Bibliothèque de la plume de
paon)

SAUSSURE, Horace Bénédict de
[Voyages dans les Alpes]. Viaggio al Monte
Bianco ...; a cura di Pietro Meciani. Milano:
Club Alpino Italiano, 1955. 101p., plates, illus.
16cm.

SAUSSURE, Horace Bénédict de
FAVRE, Alphonse
H.-B. de Saussure et les Alpes: [fragments tirés
de documents en partie inédits]. Lausanne, 1870.
15p. 22cm.
Offprint from Bibliothèque universelle et revue
suisse.

SAUSSURE, Horace Bénédict de
FRESHFIELD, Douglas William
The life of Horace Benedict de Saussure, by Douglas
W. Freshfield; with the collaboration of Henry
F. Montagnier. Arnold, 1920. xii, 479p., plates,
illus., map, bibl. 25cm.

SAUSSURE, Horace Bénédict de
FRESHFIELD, Douglas William
[The life of Horace Benedict de Saussure]. Horace-
Bénédict de Saussure, par D.W. Freshfield; avec la
collaboration de H.F. Montagnier ...; traduit de
l'anglais par Louise Plan; préface de L.-W. Collet.
Genève: Atar, 1924. 434p., plates, illus., map,
bibl. 25cm.

SAUSSURE, Horace Bénédict de
GOS, Charles
Voyage de Saussure hors des Alpes. Neuchatel:
Attinger, [1934]. 144p., plates, illus., ports.
19cm.

SAUSSURE, Horace Bénédict de
SENEBIER, Jean
Mémoire historique sur la vie et les écrits de
Horace Bénédict Desaussure ... lu à la Société de
physique et d'histoire naturelle de Genève, le 23
Prairial an VIII. Genève: Paschoud, IX [1801].
219p. 23cm.

SAVAGE-LANDOR, A   Henry
Everywhere: the memoirs of an explorer. Fisher
Unwin, 1924. 586p., plates, illus., maps. 25cm.

SAVI-LOPEZ, Maria
Leggende delle Alpi; illustrazioni di Carlo Chessa.
Torino: Paravia, 1889. 358p., illus. 20cm.

SAVIGNY, Laurence de
Le Robinson des Alpes. Paris: Arnauld de Vresse,
[1868?]. 283p., 16 plates, illus. 26cm.

Savoie; introduction de M. Henry Bordeaux. [Paris]:
Hachette, [1926]. 70p., illus. (1 col.). 32cm.
(Le pays de France, v.2, ptie.11)

SAVORY, Isabel
A sportswoman in India: personal adventures and
experiences of travel in known and unknown India.
Hutchinson, 1900. ix, 408p., plates, illus. 23cm.

SAYRE, Woodrow Wilson
Four against Everest. Barker, 1964. 251p.,
illus., maps. 24cm.

SAYSSE-TOBICZYK, Kazimierz
Himalaje-Karakorum; dzielo zespolowe pod redakcja
naczelna Kazimierza Saysse-Tobiczyka. Warsaw:
Wiedza Powszechna, 1974. 471p., col. plates,
illus. 25cm. (W skalach i lodach swiata, t.5)
Summaries in Russian and English.

SAZERAC, Hilaire Léon and ENGELMANN, Gustav
Lettres sur la Suisse; accompagnées de vues dessinées ... & lithographiées par [F.] Villeneuve.
Paris: G. Engelmann, 1823-32. 5v., plates, illus.
46cm.
Vols. 2-3, by D. Raoul-Rochette and G. Engelmann,
v.4-5, by M. de Golbéry and G. Engelmann.

SAZERAC, Hilaire Léon
Un mois en Suisse; ou, Souvenirs d'un voyageur;
recuillis par Hilaire Sazerac; et ornés de
croquis lithographiés d'après nature par Édouard
Pingret. Paris: Sazerac & Duval, 1825. 4 pts.,
40 plates, illus. 43cm.

SCACCHI, D
Scanno e la valle del Sagittario, Abruzzo. Roma:
Loescher, 1899. 82p., illus., map. 17cm.

SCAPINELLI, Carl, conte
Gipfelsturmer: Roman. Leipzig; Grethlein, 1910.
334p. 23cm.

SCARR, Josephine
Four miles high. Gollancz, 1966. 188p., plates,
illus., maps. 23cm.

La Scava; or, Some account of an excavation of a
Roman town on the hill of Chatelet, in Champagne
... discovered in the year 1772; to which is
added, A journey to the Simplon, by Lausanne,
and to Mont Blanc, through Geneva, by the author
of "Letters from Paris in 1791-2" [i.e. Stephen
Weston]. Baldwin, Cradock, & Joy, 1818. vi,
133p., 1 plate, illus. 24cm.

Scenes of modern travel and adventure. Nelson,
1848. vi, 342p. 18cm.

SCHACHT, Wilhelm
[Der Steingarten und seine Welt]. Rock gardens
and their plants; edited and translated by Vera
Higgins. Blandford Press, 1963. xv, 215p.,
plates (some col.), illus. 23cm.

SCHADEN, Adolph von
Neustes Taschenbuch für Reisende durch Bayerns
und Tyrols Hochlande ...; humoristisch, topo-
graphisch und statistisch bearb. von Adolph von
Schaden. München: [The Author?], 1833. xiv,
184p., plates, illus. 20cm. (Humoristischer
Rösselsprung)
In slip-case.

SCHAEBERLE, J   M
Report on the total eclipse of the sun, observed
at Mina Bronces, Chile, on April 16, 1893.
Sacramento: State Office, A.J. Johnston, 1895.
[8], 127p., plates, illus. 24cm. (Contributions
from the Lick Observatory, no.4)

SCHÄFER, Raimund
Hochtouren in den Alpen, Spanien, Nordafrika,
Kalifornien und Mexico; ausgeführt und beschrieben
von Raimund Schäfer. Leipzig: J.J. Weber, 1903.
ix, 176p., col. plates, illus. 28cm.

SCHÄFFER, Mary T   S
Old Indian trails: incidents of camp and trail
life covering two years exploration through the
Rocky Mountains of Canada. New York, London:
Putnam, 1911. xv, 364p., plates(1 fold.col.),
illus., map. 21cm.

SCHAER, Alfred
Die Arth-Rigi-Bahn. 3. neu bearb. Aufl. Zürich:
Orell Füssli, [1916]. 38p., 14 plates, illus.,
map. 20cm. (Wanderbilder, 324-325)

SCHÄTZ, Josef Julius
Berge und Bergsteiger. Bielefeld: Velhagen &
Klasing, 1929. 56p., 48 plates, illus. 26cm.
(Monographien zur Erdkunde, Nr.41)

HOFERER, Erwin and SCHÄTZ, Josef Julius
Münchner Kletterführer: 250 der lohnendsten
Kletterfahrten in den Vorbergen und im bayerisch-
tirolischen Grenzgebiet ...; hrsg. von Erwin
Hoferer und Jos. Jul. Schätz. München: Rother,
1923. 247p., plates, illus. 17cm.

SCHÄTZ, Josef Julius
Südtirol vom Brenner bis Salurn: ein Buch von
Menschen, Bergen und der Schönheit des Landes;
Herausgeber Jos. Jul Schätz. Bozen: Joh. Amonn,
1923. 94p., plates (1 col.), illus. 33cm.

GRABER, Alfred and SCHÄTZ, Josef Julius
Walliser Alpen. Bielefeld: Velhagen & Klasing,
1931. viii, 124p., plates, illus. 18cm.
(Velhagen & Klasings Bildführer ..., 6)

SCHÄTZ, Josef Julius
Wanderfahrten in den Bergen; mit acht Original-
radierungen von Walter Sandstein und vielen Text-
bildern von U. Bitterlich. 2. Aufl. Stuttgart:
Levy & Müller, [1925?]. viii, 212p., plates,
illus. 23cm.

SCHÄTZ, Josef Julius
Wunder der Alpen; hrsg. v. Jos. Jul. Schätz.
München: F. Bruckmann, [1926]. 6v. in 1. (chiefly
illus.). 31cm.

- - 2. Aufl. 1949.

SCHÄTZ, Josef Julius
[Wunder der Alpen]. Alpine wonderland: a collection of photographs, made by J.J. Schätz;
introduced by Sir Claud Schuster. Chapman & Hall,
1936. xxiv, 256p., illus. 30cm.

SCHAFFRAN, E
Hochgebirgs-Fantasien: ... origin. Lithographien.
Wien: Rablbund Mödling, 1924. 8 plates, illus.
41cm.
In portfolio.

FAVRE, Ernest and SCHARDT, Hans
Description géologique des préalpes du Canton de
Vaud et du Chablais jusqu'à la Dranse et de la
chaîne des Dents du Midi... Berne: Schmid, Francke,
1887. xx, 636p. and atlas (15p., 29 plates),
illus., map, bibl. 33cm. (Beiträge zur geologischen Karte der Schweiz = Matériaux pour la
carte géologique de la Suisse, livr.22, 1)

SCHAUB, Charles and BRIQUET, Moïse
Guide practique de l'ascensionniste sur les montagnes qui entourent le Lac de Genève... 3e éd.,
rev. et augm. Genève: J. Jullien, 1893. vi,
240p. 18cm.

SCHAUB, Charles
La Suisse historique et pittoresque... Ptie.2
La Suisse pittoresque. Genève: Grand-Mézel, 1856.
584p., plates (some col.), illus. 27cm.

SCHAUBACH, Adolph
Die deutschen Alpen: ein Handbuch für Reisende
durch Tyrol, Oesterreich, Steyermark, Illyrien,
Oberbayern und die anstossenden Gebiete. Jena:
Frommann, 1845-46. 4v. 23cm.

SCHAUBACH, Adolph
Die deutschen Alpen für Einheimische und Fremde
geschildert. 2. Aufl. Jena: Frommann, 1865-71
[v.1, 1871]. 6v. in 5. 18cm.

SCHAUBACH, Adolph
Die deutschen Alpen; mit einer Einleitung und
Anmerkungen hrsg. von R.H. Francé. Leipzig: T.
Thomas, [1911]. 2v. 16cm. (Natur-Bibliothek,
37/38, 39)
Selections.

SCHEFFEL, Joseph Viktor von
Mountain psalms; translated from the German by
Mrs. Francis Brünnow. Trübner, 1882. 62p.,
plates, illus. 17cm.

SCHEFFEL, Joseph Viktor von
Reise-Bilder; mit einem Vorwort von Johannes
Proelss. Stuttgart: A. Bonz, 1887. xiv, 408p.
17cm.

SCHEFFEL, P   H
Verkehrsgeschichte der Alpen. Berlin: Reimer,
1908-14. 2v. in 1. 27cm.

SCHERMAUL, Jenny
Die Alpenpflanzen; nach der Natur gemalt von Jos.
Seboth [und Jenny Schermaul]; mit Text von
Ferdinand Graf; und einer Anleitung zur Cultur der
Alpenpflanzen. Prag: F.Tempsky, 1880-86 [v.1,
1886]. 4v., col.plates, illus. 16cm.
Vol.1 is 2nd ed.

SCHERZER, Carl
Travels in the free states of Central America:
Nicaragua, Honduras and San Salvador. Longman,
Brown, Green, Longmans & Roberts, 1857. 2v., 2
fold.col. plates, illus., map. 21cm.

SCHERZER, Hans
Geologisch-botanische Wanderungen durch die Alpen.
1.Bd. Das Berchtesgadener Land. München: Kösel
& Pustet, 1927. 218p., plates (1 fold., 1 col.),
illus., maps. 19cm.

SCHEUCHZER, D
See
SCHEUCHZER, Johann Jacob

SCHEUCHZER, Johann Jacob
Aepoypaøias Helveticae, praeside Joh. Jacobo
Scheuchzero; pro consequendo examine philosophico
defendent Johannes Schmuzius [et al.]. Tiguri:
Gessner, 1723-25. 2v. 22cm.

SCHEUCHZER, Johann Jacob
Beschreibung der Natur-Geschichten des Schweizerlands. Zürich: In Verlegung des Authoris, 1706-08.
3v. in 1, fold. plates, illus. 22cm.

SCHEUCHZER, Johann Jacob
Beschreibung des Wetter-Jahrs MDCCXXXI: Besonders
aber des Traurigen-Himmels, der ob unseren
Häubteren geschwebet, den 1. Heumonat. Zürich:
J.H. Bürckli, 1732. 30p., 2 fold. plates, charts.
22cm.

SCHEUCHZER, Johann Jacob
Cataclysmographiam Helvetiae, censurae publicae
subiicient Joh. Jacobus Scheuchzer; & pro consequendo examine philosophico Conradus Mullerus
[et al.]. Tiguri: Typis Marci Rordorfi, 1733.
52p. 22cm.

SCHEUCHZER, Johann Jacob
Coelum triste ad Julias calendas anni MDCCXXXI,
publicae eruditorum censurae subiicient Joh.
Jacobus Scheuchzer; et pro consequendo examine
philosophico Abrahamus Hegius [et al.]. [Zürich]:
Typis J. H. Byrcklini, [1732]. 41p. 22cm.

SCHEUCHZER, Johann Jacob
De Helvetiae aeribus, aquis, locis: specimen I
[-II], defendent Joh. Jacobus Scheuchzerus; et pro
consequendo examine philosophico Joh. Casparus
Ammianus [et al.]. Tiguri: Typis H. Byrcklini,
1728-29. 2v. 22cm.

SCHEUCHZER, Johann Jacob
Einladungs-Brief zu Erforschung natürlicher
Wunderen so sich im Schweitzer-Land befinden.
[Zürich]: [n.pub.], [ca 1700]. 16p. 22cm.
Introduction signed: D. Scheuchzer.

SCHEUCHZER, Johann Jacob
Helvetiae stoicheiographia, orographia, et oreo-
graphia; oder, Beschreibung der Elementen...
Zürich: In der Bodmerischen Truckeren, 1716-18.
3v. in 1, fold.plates, illus. 21cm. (Der Natur-
Histori des Schweizerlands, 1-3)

SCHEUCHZER, Johann Jacob
Historia Helvetiae. [Zürich]: [n.pub.], [1727?].
[4]p. 29cm.

SCHEUCHZER, Johann Jacob
Historiae Helveticae naturalis prolegomena ...,
praeside J. Jacobo Scheuchzero; respondente
Johanne Rodolfo Lavatero. Tiguri: Gessner, 1700.
30p. 22cm.

SCHEUCHZER, Johann Jacob
Natur-Geschichte des Schweitzerlandes, samt seinen
Reisen über die schweizerische Gebürge; aufs neue
hrsg., und mit einigen Anmerkungen versehen von
Joh. Georg. Sulzern. Zürich: Gessner, 1746. 2v.
in 1, plates (some fold.), illus., maps. 22cm.

SCHEUCHZER, Johann Jacob
Ονρεοιφοίτης Helviticus; sive, Itinera alpina
tria; in quibus incolae, animalia, plantae, montium
altitudines barometricae ... exponitur. Londini:
Impensis Henrici Clements, 1708. 3v. in 1, plates
(some fold.), illus. 25cm.

SCHEUCHZER, Johann Jacob
Ονρεοιφοίτης Helviticus; sive, Itinera per
Helvetiae alpinas regiones facta annis MDCCII ...
- MDCCXI. Lugduni Batavorum: Typis ac sumptibus
Petri Vander Aa, 1723. 4v. in 1, (635p.), plates
(some fold., some col.), illus., maps. 26cm.

SCHEUCHZER, Johann Jacob
Specimen lithographiae Helveticae curiosae quo
lapides ex figuratis Helveticis selectissimi aeri
incisi sistuntur & describuntur. Tiguri: Gessner,
1702. 67p., fold.plates, illus. 19cm.

SCHEUCHZER, Johann Jacob
Στοιχειολογιαν ad Helvetiam applicatam ...,
praeses J. Jac. Scheuchzerus, et respondens Joh.
Huldricus Hegnerus. Tiguri: Gessner, 1700. 20p.
22cm.

SCHEUCHZER, Johann Jacob
Vernunfftmässige Untersuchung des Bads zu Baden,
dessen Eigenschafften und Würckungen. Zürich:
M. Rordorf, 1732. 68p., plates. 22cm.

SCHIDER, Eduard
Gastein für Kurgäste und Touristen. 12. verm. und
verb. Aufl. ..., von Oskar Gerke... Salzburg:
Mayrische Buch- und Kunsthandlung, 1906. 104p.,
map. 15cm.

SCHILLER, Friedrich von
Schillers Gedichte. Schulausgabe mit Anmerkungen.
Stuttgart: J.C. Cotta, 1894. viii, 315p. 18cm.
(Schul-Ausgaben Deutsche Klassiker)

SCHILLER, Friedrich von
Wilhelm Tell: Schauspiel. Halle a.d.S.: O.
Hendel, [ca 1880]. 124p., 1 plate, port. 19cm.

SCHILLER, Hans von
Im Zeppelin über der Schweiz; 55 Bilder eingeleitet
von Hans von Schiller. Zürich: Orell Füssli, 1930.
16p., plates, illus. 20cm. (Schaubücher, 36)

SCHILLING, R   E
Nachricht von der unterhalb der Stadt Bremen im
Hornung des 1771. Jahres erfolgten Verstopfung
des Weser-Stroms und nachher geschehener Aufeisung
desselben. Bremen: J.H. Cramer, 1772. 36p.,
1 fold. plate, illus. 21cm.

SCHINER, Hildebrand
Description du Département du Simplon, ou de la
ci-devant République du Valais. Sion: Antoine
Advocat, 1812. x, 558p. 20cm.

SCHINER, Matthäus
CHASTONAY, Paul de
[Kardinal Schiner]. Le Cardinal Schiner; adaptation française d'André Favre. Lausanne: F. Rouge,
[1934]. 135p., plates, illus., bibl. 20cm.

SCHINZ, Hans and KELLER, Robert
Flore de la Suisse. Ptie. 1. Éd. française rev.
par E. Wilczek et Hans Schinz. Lausanne: F. Rouge,
1909. xxiii, 690p., illus. 19cm.

SCHINZ, Rudolf
Ventrage zur nähern Kenntniss des Schweizerlandes.
Zürich: Füessly, 1783-87. 5v. in 2, illus., maps.
20cm.

SCHIRMER, Gustav
Die Schweiz im Spiegel englischer und
amerikanischer Literatur bis 1848; hrsg. von der
Stiftung von Schnyder von Wartensee. Zürich:
Orell Füssli, 1929. xvi, 460p. 23cm.

SCHJELDERUP, Ferdinand
Med norsk flag i Nordland: saortryk av den norske
turistforenings aarbok for 1911. Kristiania:
Grøndahl, 1911. 50p., plates, illus. 23cm.

SCHLAGINTWEIT BROTHERS
Schlagintweits Vermessungsarbeiten am Nanga Parbat
1856. München: Bayerische Akademie der Wissen-
schaften, 1967. 146p., illus., maps. 30cm.
(Deutsche Geodätische Kommission. Bayerische
Akademie der Wissenschaften. Dissertationen, 97)

SCHLAGINTWEIT, Adolph and SCHLAGINTWEIT-SAKÜNLÜNSKI,
Hermann
Neue Untersuchungen über die physicalische
Geographie und die Geologie der Alpen. Leipzig:
T.O. Weigel, 1854. xvi, 630p. and atlas (22p.,
8 plates). 28cm.

SCHLAGINTWEIT, Adolph
Official reports on the last journeys and the
death of Adolphe Schlagintweit in Turkistán;
collected by Hermann and Robert Schlagintweit.
Berlin: The Editors, 1859. 19p. 29cm.

SCHLAGINTWEIT-SAKÜNLÜNSKI, Hermann and SCHLAGINTWEIT,
Adolph
Untersuchungen über die physicalische Geographie
der Alpen in ihren Beziehungen zu den Phaenomenen
der Gletscher, zur Geologie, Meteorologie und
Pflanzengeographie. Leipzig: Barth, 1850. xv,
600p., plates (some fold., some col.), illus.,
maps. 29cm.

SCHLAGINTWEIT, Hermann
See
SCHLAGINTWEIT-SAKÜNLÜNSKI, Hermann

SCHLAGINTWEIT-SAKÜNLÜNSKI, Hermann and SCHLAGINTWEIT,
Robert
Official reports on the last journeys and the
death of Adolphe Schlagintweit in Turkistán;
collected by Hermann and Robert Schlagintweit.
Berlin: The Editors, 1859. 15p. 29cm.

SCHLAGINTWEIT, Adolph and SCHLAGINTWEIT-SAKÜNLÜNSKI,
Hermann
Neue Untersuchungen über die physicalische Geo-
graphie und die Geologie der Alpen. Leipzig:
T.O. Weigel, 1854. xvi, 630p. and atlas (22p.,
8 plates). 28cm.

SCHLAGINTWEIT-SAKÜNLÜNSKI, Hermann and SCHLAGINTWEIT,
Robert
Official reports on the last journeys and the death
of Adolphe Schlagintweit in Turkistán;
collected by Hermann and Robert Schlagintweit.
Berlin: The Editors, 1859. 19p. 29cm.

SCHLAGINTWEIT-SAKÜNLÜNSKI, Hermann von
Reisen in Indien und Hochasien: eine Darstellung
der Landschaft, der Cultur und Sitten der Bewohner,
in Verbindung mit klimatischen und geologischen
Verhaltnissen, basirt auf die ... Mission ...
1854-1858. Jena: Costenoble, 1869-80. 4v.,
illus., maps. 25cm.

SCHLAGINTWEIT-SAKÜNLÜNSKI, Hermann and SCHLAGINTWEIT,
Adolph
Untersuchungen über die physicalische Geographie
der Alpen in ihren Beziehungen zu den Phaenomenen
der Gletscher, zur Geologie, Meteorologie und
Pflanzengeographie. Leipzig: Barth, 1850. xv,
600p., plates (some fold., some col.), illus.,
maps. 29cm.

SCHLEIDT, Wilhelm
Triomphaler Festzug zur Erinnerung an die Ein-
weihung der Jungfraubahn (1. Section Eiger-
gletscher) im Juli 1898: Op.31. Hannover:
Oertel, [1898]. 7p. 35cm.
Piano score in portfolio.

SCHLINCKE, L
Der Rigi: Handbüchlein für Reisende; nach eigener
Anschauung und den besten Quellen bearb. von L.
Schlincke. 3. verb. und verm. Aufl. Luzern:
Kaiser, 1857. 123p., plates (1 fold.), illus.,
map. 16cm.

SCHLINK, Herbert H
Ski-ing from Kiandra to Kosciusko, July 28, 29, 30,
1927. [Sydney]: Ski Club of Australia, 1927.
[12]p, illus., map. 23cm.
Originally published in Sydney Mail, Aug. 31st,
1927.

GUNNENG, Asbjørn and SCHLYTTER, Boye
Fører for bestiginger i Horungtindene; utarbeidet
av Norsk Tindeklub ved Asbjørn Gunneng og Boye
Schlytter. Oslo: Grøndahl, 1928. 19p., illus.
23cm.

GUNNENG, Asbjørn and SCHLYTTER, Boye
[Fører for bestiginger i Horungtindene]. Climbs
in the Norungtinder, Norway; edited [for] Norsk
Tindeklub by Asbjørn Gunneng and Boye Schlytter.
Oslo: Grøndahl, 1933. 23p., 1 fold.col. plate,
illus., map (in pocket). 23cm.

SCHMID, Franz
SCHWETZER, J   J
Das Faulhorn im Grindelwald: ein Topographie- und
Panoram-Gemälde; entworfen von mehreren Alpen-
Freunden und hrsg. von J.J. Schwetzer; mit einem
Panorama von Franz Schmid. Bern: C.A. Jenni, 1832.
viii, 56p., 1 fold. plate, illus., panorama. 21cm.

SCHMID, Franz
Die Gletscher und Alpengebirge des Bern-Oberlandes
vom Nordosten der Stadt Bern angesehen; gezeichnet
von F. Schmid. Bern: J.J. Burgdorfer, 1824. 21cm.
Hand coloured panorama.

SCHMID, Hans
Bündnerfahrten: Engadin und südliche Täler; mit
Federzeichnungen von Chr. Conradin. Frauenfeld:
Huber, 1923. 257p., illus. 19cm.

SCHMID, Hans
Spaziergänge im Tessin. 2.Aufl. Frauenfeld:
Huber, 1909. 201p. 19cm.

SCHMID, Hans
Wallis: ein Wanderbuch. 3. verb. Aufl.
Frauenfeld: Huber, 1935. 265p. 19cm.

SCHWARZENBACH, Annemarie and SCHMID, Hans Rudolf
Das Buch von der Schweiz; hrsg. von Eduard Korrodi.
München: R. Piper, 1932-33. 2v., illus. 19cm.
(Was nicht im Baedeker steht, 15-16)

SCHMID, Herman von and STIELER, Karl
[Aus deutschen Bergen]. The Bavarian Highlands
and the Salzkammergut; profusely illustrated by
G. Closs [and others]; with an account of the
habits and manners of the hunters, poachers, and
peasantry of these districts. Chapman & Hall,
1874. ix, 205p., plates, illus. 36cm.

SCHMID, Herman von and STIELER, Karl
Wanderungen im bayerischen Gebirge und
Salzkammergut; geschildert von Herman von Schmid
und Karl Steiler; illustrirt von Gustav Closs
[and others]. 2.Aufl. Stuttgart: Kröner, [1878].
vii, 215p., plates, illus. 38cm. (Unser Vaterland)
First ed. published under title: Aus deutschen
Bergen.

SCHMID, Herman von. [Wanderungen im bayerischen
Gebirge und Salzkammergut].
KADEN, Woldemar
Switzerland and the Bavarian Highlands. Virtue
[1879]. 2v. (xiv, 628p.), plates, illus. 35cm.
Translated from "Das Schweizerland", by Woldemar
Kaden and "Wanderungen im bayerischen Gebirge und
Salzkammergut" by Herman von Schmid and Karl
Stieler.

SCHMID, Toni
BAUMEISTER, Hans
Jugend in Fels und Eis: ein Ehrenmal gewidmet dem
Helden von Matterhorn: Toni Schmid von seinen
Kameraden; bearb. von Hans Baumeister... München:
Alpenkränzchen Berggeist, 1934. 293p., 52 plates,
illus. 25cm.

- - 3.Aufl. [ca 1940].

SCHMID, Walter
Komm mit mir ins Wallis; mit 112 Aufnahmen des
Verfassers. 2. Aufl. Bern: Hallwag, [1945].
248p., illus. 25cm.

SCHMID, Walter
Romantic Switzerland, mirrored in the literature
and graphic art of the 18th and 19th centuries.
Zurich: Swiss National Tourist Office, 1952.
[48]p., col. illus. 18cm.

SCHMID, Walter
Wer die Berge liebt: kleine alpine Trilogie; die
Schönheit der Berge, die Liebe zu den Bergen, die
Macht der Berge; gesammelt und hrsg. von Walter
Schmid. 2.Aufl. Bern: Hallwag, [1945]. 80p.,
illus. 20cm.

SCHMID, Walter
Wetter: praktische Winke zur Wettervoraussage.
3.Aufl. Bern: Hallwag, [1904]. 108p., illus.
17cm.

TRENKER, Luis and SCHMIDKUNZ, Walter
Berge und Heimat: das Buch von den Bergen und
ihren Menschen. Berlin: Th. Knaur, 1939. 138p.,
plates, illus. 26cm.

SCHMIDKUNZ, Walter
Der Kampf über den Gletschern: ein Buch von der
Alpenfront. Erfurt: Richter, 1934. 287p.,
plates, illus. 20cm.

SCHMIDKUNZ, Walter
Kletterführer durch die bayerischen Voralpen.
München: Deutsche Alpenzeitung, 1910. vii,
148p., plates, illus. 17cm. (Kletterführer der
Deutschen Alpenzeitung, 1)

SCHMIDKUNZ, Walter
Das quietschvergnugte Skibrevier; mit zeichnungen
von Hans Jorg Schuster. Erfurt: Richter, 1935.
191p., illus. 13cm.

SCHMIDKUNZ, Walter
Zwischen Himmel und Erde: alpine Anekdoten; mit
12 Bildern von Otto Linnekogel. München: P.
Stangl, 1925. 319p., illus. 18cm.

SCHMIDL, A   Adolf
Das Bihar-Gebirge an der Grenze von Ungarn und
Siebenbürgen; (mit einer geodätischen Abhandlung,
Karte ... von Josef Wastler). Wien: Förster &
Bartelmus, 1863. xvi, 442p., plates (some fold.,
some col.), illus., maps. 27cm.

SCHMIDL, A   Adolf
Reisehandbuch durch das Erzherzogthum Oesterreich
mit Salzburg, Obersteyermark und Tirol. Güns:
Reichard, 1834. xviii, 504p. 19cm.

SCHMIDL, A   Adolf
Reisehandbuch durch das Herzogthum Steiermark,
Illnrein, Venedig und die Lombardie. Wien: C.
Gerold, 1836. x, 331p. 19cm.

SCHMIDL, A   Adolf
Der Schneeberg in unter Oesterreich mit seinen
Umgebungen von Wien bis Mariazell. Wien: A. Doll,
1831. 309p. 19cm.

SCHMIDT, Albert
Führer durch die Fichtelgebirge und den Steinwald
... 2 neubearb. Aufl. Wunsiedel im Fichtelgebirge: G. Kohler, 1899. viii, 200p., maps. 17cm.

SCHMIDT, Carl
HEIM, Albert
Geologie der Hochalpen zwischen Reuss und Rhein
...; mit einem Anhang von petrographischen
Beiträgen von Carl Schmidt. Bern: Schmid Francke,
1891. 503, 77p., 8 plates (some fold., some col.),
illus., bibl. 33cm. (Beiträge zur geologischen
Karte der Schweiz, Lfg. 25)

SCHMIDT, Carl
FELLENBERG, Edmund von and MOESCH, Casimir
   Geologische Beschreibung des Westlichen Theils des
   Aarmassivs, enthalten auf dem nördlich der Rhone
   ...; mit petrographischen Beiträgen von Carl
   Schmidt. Bern: Schmid, Francke, 1893. 2v. in 1
   and atlas (18 plates), illus., map, bibl. 32cm.
   (Beiträge zur geologischen Karte der Schweiz, 21)

SCHMIDT, Theodor
   Aus goldener Ferienzeit: ein Strauss fröhlicher
   Berglieder. Breslau: Mar Wonwod, 1908. 147p.,
   illus. 20cm.

SCHMIDT ZU WELLENBURG, W   von
   Ski-Taschenbuch der Alpensvereinsmitglieder; hrsg.
   im Einvernehmen mit dem Hauptausschuss des
   Deutschen und Österreichischen Alpenvereins;
   redigiert durch W. v. Schmidt zu Wellenburg.
   Innsbruck: Alpiner Verlag, 1932. 286p., plates,
   illus. 21cm.

SCHMIDT ZU WELLENBURG, W   von
   Taschenbuch für Alpenvereins-Mitglieder; hrsg.
   im Einverständnis mit dem Hauptausschuss des
   Deutschen und Österreichischen Alpenvereins;
   redigiert durch W. v. Schmidt zu Wellenburg.
   1930/31, [1933]. München: Alpiner Verlag, 1930-33.
   2v., illus. 21cm.

SCHMIEDER, Oscar
   The east Bolivian Andes south of the Rio Grande or
   Guapay. Berkeley (Calif.): University of
   California Press, 1926. 85-166p., plates (1
   fold.), illus., maps. 28cm. (University of
   California.Publications in geography, v.2, no.5,
   1926)

SCHMITHALS, Hans
   Die Alpen; hrsg. von Hans Schmithals; mit einer
   Einleitung von Eugen Kalkschmidt. Berlin: E.
   Wasmuth, 1926. xxviii, 319p., plates (1 fold.
   col.), illus., map. 32cm.

SCHMITT, Fritz
   Der Bergsteiger von heute: Entwicklung, Technik
   und Grundlagen des neuzeitlichen Bergsteigens.
   München: Rother, 1937. 349p., 16 plates, illus.,
   bibl. 21cm.

Der Schnee und seine Metamorphose: erste Ergebnisse
   und Anwendungen einer systematischen Untersuchung
   der alpinen Winterschneedecke ... 1934-1938, von
   H. Bader [and others]. Bern: Kümmerly & Frey,
   1939. xxiii, 340p., plates (some fold.), illus.
   30cm. (Beiträge zur Geologie der Schweiz, Geotechnische Serie, Hydrologie, Lfg., 3)

SCHNEESCHUHVEREIN, München
   Skiführer; hrsg. vom Schneeschuhverein München von
   1893 e. V. Bd.1. Schliersee-Bayreischzell; bearb.
   von Mitgliedern der Vereins. München: M.
   Steinebach, 1913. 76p., illus. 17cm.

SCHNEESCHUHVEREIN, München
   Skiführer; hrsg. von Schneeschuhverein München von
   1893 e. V. Bd.2. Inntal-Chiemgau; bearb. von C.
   Döhlemann. München: M. Steinebach, 1914. 110p.,
   illus. 17cm.

FANCK, Arnold and SCHNEIDER, Hannes
   Wunder des Schneeschuhs: ein System des richtigen
   Skilaufens und seine Anwendung im alpinen Gelände-
   lauf; Photographie: Arnold Franck und Sepp Allgeier.
   Hamburg: Enoch, 1925. 218, xxii p., fold. plates
   (in pocket), illus. 30cm.

FANCK, Arnold and SCHNEIDER, Hannes
   [Wunder des Schneeschuhs...]. The wonders of ski-
   ing: a method of correct ski-ing and its applications to alpine running, by Hannes Schneider and
   Arnold Fanck; translated from the ... [2nd ed.,
   1928] by George Gallowhur; photography by Arnold
   Fanck & Sepp Allgeier. Allen & Unwin, 1933.
   234p., plates, illus. 29cm.

SCHNELLER, Christian
   Südtirolische Landschaften: Nons- und Sulzberg,
   Civezzano und Pine, Vergine, Valsugana. Innsbruck:
   Wagner, 1899. iv, 342p., plates, illus. 20cm.

- - 2. Reihe. Das Lagerthan - La Valle Lagarina.
   1900.

SCHOBERL, Frederic
   See
SHOBERL, Frederick

SCHOCH, J   C
EBEL, Johann Gottfried and HEIDEGGER, Heinrich
   Handbuch für Reisende in der Schweiz, [von J.G.
   Ebel und H. Heidegger]; [edited by] Robert
   Glutz-Blotzheim. 6. verb. Aufl., hrsg. von J.
   Schoch. Zürich: Orell, Füssli, 1830. 595p., map.
   19cm.

SCHOCH, J   C
EBEL, Johann Gottfried and HEIDEGGER, Heinrich
   [Handbuch für Reisende in der Schweiz]. Manuel
   du voyageur en Suisse, [par J.G. Ebel et H.
   Heidegger]; [edited by] Robert Glutz-Blotzheim.
   3e éd. française, considérablement augmentée
   [par J.C. Schoch]. Zurich: Orell, Fussli, 1827.
   566p., map. 19cm.

SCHÖNER, Hellmut
ZELLER, Max
   Berchtesgadener Alpen: ein Führer für Täler,
   Hütten und Berge. 10. neubearb. Aufl., von
   Hellmut Schöner. München: Rother 1962. 387p.,
   plates (1 fold.), illus., map (in pocket). 16cm.

SCHÖNER, Hellmut
   Julische Alpen: die wichtigsten und schönsten
   Bergfahrten jeden Schwierigkeitsgrades. München:
   Rother, 1956. 171p., plates (1 fold.), illus.,
   map. 20cm.

SCHOFIELD, Stuart J
   Geology of Cranbrook map area, British Columbia.
   Ottawa: Government Printing Bureau, 1915. vii,
   245p., plates (some fold., 1 col.), illus., maps
   (1 in pocket). 26cm. (Canada. Department of
   Mines. Geological Survey. Memoir, no.76; Geological series, no.62)

SCHOMBERG, Reginald Charles Francis
   Between the Oxus and the Indus. Hopkinson, 1935.
   275p., plates (1 fold.), illus., map. 23cm.

SCHOMBERG, Reginald Charles Francis
   Kafirs and glaciers: travels in Chitral.
   Hopkinson, 1938. 287p., plates (1 fold., 1 col.),
   illus., map. 23cm.

SCHOMBERG, Reginald Charles Francis
   Peaks and plains of central Asia. Hopkinson,
   1933. 288p., plates (some col.), illus., maps.
   23cm.

SCHOMBERG, Reginald Charles Francis
   Unknown Karakoram. Hopkinson, 1936. 244p.,
   plates (1 fold.col.), illus., map (in pocket).
   23cm.

SCHOMBURG, Hugo
   Auf Schneeschuhen und zu Fuss durchs Sauerland.
   Berlin-Wilmersdorf: H. Paetel, 1912. 108p.,
   plates, illus., map. 19cm. (Sammlung belehrender
   Unterhaltungsschriften, 41)

SCHOPENHAUER, Johanna
   Reise von Paris durch das südliche Frankreich bis
   Chamouny. 2.verb. und verm. Aufl. Leipzig:
   F.A. Brockhaus, 1824. 2v. in 1. 18cm.

SCHOTT, Albert
   Die deutschen Colonien in Piedmont, ihr Land ihre
   Mundart und Herkunft: ein Beitrag zur Geschichte
   der Alpen. Stuttgart: J.G. Cotta, 1842. xvi,
   348p. 23cm.

SCHOTTKY, Julius Mar
Bilder aus der süddeutschen Alpenwelt. Innsbruck:
Wagner, 1834. 275p. 18cm.

SCHRADER, Franz
CLUB ALPIN FRANÇAIS. Section du Sud-Ouest
Le centenaire de Franz Schrader; publié par la
Commission scientifique de la Section du Sud-Ouest.
Bordeaux: La Commission, 1944. 40p., illus.,
port. 22cm.
Supplément au Bulletin no.47, avril 1944.

SCHREIBER, A
Manuel du voyageur par la Suisse, le Wurtenberg,
la Bavière, le Tyrol, le Pays de Salzbourg et au
Lac de Constance... Heidelberg: J. Engelmann,
[1835?]. 258p. 16cm.
"Suite et supplément du Guide du voyageur sur le
Rhin" - title page.

SCHRÖTER, Carl
Kleine Führer durch die Pflanzenwelt der Alpen.
Zürich: A. Raustein, 1932. viii, 80p., 2 fold.
plates, illus. 21cm.

SCHRÖTER, Carl
Das Pflanzenleben der Alpen: ein Schilderung der
Hochgebirgsflora, von C. Schroeter; unter Mitwirkung von A. Günthart [and others]; Zeichnungen
von Ludwig Schroeter. Zürich: A. Raustein, 1908.
xvi, 806p., plates, illus. 26cm.

- - 2. durchgearb. und verm. Aufl.,unter Mitwirkung
von H. und M. Brockmann-Jerosch [and others].
1923-26.

SCHRÖTER, Carl
Taschenflora des Alpen-Wanderers; colorirte
Abbildungen ... nach der Natur gemalt von Ludwig
Schröter; mit Vorwort und kurzem botanischem Text
... von C. Schröter. Zürich: Meyer & Zeller, 1889.
1v. (chiefly col. illus). 22cm.

- - 3. vollständig umgearb. und verm. Aufl. 1892.
- - 10. und 11. Aufl. A. Raustein, [1905?].

SCHRÖTER, Carl
[Taschenflora des Alpen-Wanderers]. Coloured vade-
mecum to the alpine flora for the use of tourists
in Switzerland, by L. Schröter and C. Schröter.
4th ed. Zurich: A. Raustein; London: D. Nutt,
[1894]. 1v. (chiefly col. illus.)
Text in English, French and German.

- - 7th ed., entirely rewritten and greatly enl.
1900.
- - 8th ed. 1903.
- - 12th and 13th ed. [1906?].

SCHRÖTER, Carl
[Taschenflora des Alpen-Wanderers]. Flore coloriée
portative du touriste dans les Alpes; 207 fleurs
coloriées ... par L. Schröter; avec texte par C.
Schröter. 12e et 13e éd. Zurich: A. Raustein,
[1906?]. 1v. (chiefly col. illus.). 21cm.

SCHUBERT, S H
Wanderbüchlein eines reisenden Gelehrten nach
Salzburg, Tirol und der Lombardey. Erlangen: J.J.
Palm & E. Enke, 1823. viii, 278p. 15cm.

SCHUCHT, Richard
Die Wildspitze. Stuttgart: Deutsche Verlags-
Anstalt, 1906. 66p., plates, illus., maps. 18cm.
(Alpine Gipfelführer, 11)

SCHUDI, Aegidius
See
TSCHUDI, Aegidius

SCHÜCKING, L
Helvetia: Natur, Geschichte, Sage im Spiegel
deutscher Dichtung; hrsg. von L. Schücking.
Frankfurt: K. Fügel, 1857. viii, 509p. 19cm.

SCHÜTZ WILSON, Henry
See
WILSON, Henry Schütz

SCHULER, Johann Melchior
Die Linth-Thäler, beschrieben von Johann Melchior
Schuler. Zürich: Orell, Füssli, 1814. xvi,
306p. 22cm.

SCHULTES, J A
Reise auf den Glockner. Wien: J.V. Degen, 1804.
4v. in 3, plates, illus. 18cm.
Th. 3-4 have second title page with title: Reise
durch Salzburg und Berchtesgaden.

SCHULTHESS, Emil
Top of Switzerland: 360° Panorama vom höchsten
Punkt der Schweiz. Zürich: Artemis, 1970. 1v.
(chiefly col. illus.). 37 x 43cm.
Folded photographic panorama with explanatory
note in German, English & French.

SCHULZ, Friedrich
Alpenlicht: Gornergrat, Furka, Maloja. St.
Gallen: Honegger, 1910. 79p., plates, illus.,
port. 23cm.

SCHULZ, K
ZSIGMONDY, Emil
Im Hochgebirge: Wanderungen; mit Abbildungen vom
E.T. Compton; hrsg. von K. Schulz. Leipzig:
Duncker & Humblot, 1889. xv, 365p., plates,
illus. 28cm.

SCHUMACHER, August
Bilder aus den Alpen der Steyermark. Wien: C.
Schaumburg, 1822. vi, 103p., plates, illus.
21cm.

SCHUPPLI, Ad.
BERTHOLD, Theodor
Die schönsten Alpen-Blumen: 12 chromolith Tafeln
in getreuester Wiedergabe; nach der Natur gemalt
von Ad. Schuppli; mit begleitendem Text von Th.
Berthold. Einsiedeln: Benziger, [ca 1895]. 16p.,
12 col. plates, illus. 27cm.
Library's copy imperfect.

SCHUSTER, Sir Arthur
Biographical fragments. Macmillan, 1932. 268p.,
plates, illus., map. 22cm.

SCHUSTER, Sir Arthur
Indian sketches. [N.p.]: The Author, 1908. 1v.
of col. illus. 27cm.

SCHUSTER, August
Führer durch die Ammergauer Alpen für Bergsteiger,
Wanderer und Besucher der bayer. Konigsschlösser.
München: Verlag der Alpenfreund, 1922. 148p.,
illus., map. 16cm. (D.u.Ö.A.V. Sektion Bergland.
Alpenfreund Führer, 1)

SCHUSTER, Claud, Baron Schuster
Men, women and mountains: days in the Alps and
Pyrenees; foreword by Lord Sankey. Ivor Nicholson
& Watson, 1931. xv, 143p., plates, illus. 25cm.

SCHUSTER, Claud, Baron Schuster
Mountaineering: the Romanes lecture, delivered in
the Sheldonian Theatre, 21 May 1948. Oxford:
Clarendon Press, 1948. 32p. 23cm.

SCHUSTER, Claud, Baron Schuster
Peaks and pleasant pastures. Oxford: Clarendon
Press, 1911. 227p., plates, maps. 24cm.

SCHUSTER, Claud, Baron Shuster
Postscript to adventure. Eyre & Spottiswoode,
1950. 214p., plates, illus. 23cm. (New alpine
library)

SCHUSTER, Karl
Weisse Berge, schwarze Zelte: eine Persienfahrt.
München: Gesellschaft Alpiner Bücherfreunde, 1932.
196p., illus., map. 19cm.

SCHUSTER, Oskar
FISCHER, Walther
Oskar Schuster und sein Geist: ein Strauss berg-
steigerischen Erlebens; mit Originalberichten der
Erstbesteigungen von Oskar Schuster Sattler,
Israel, Pfeilschmidt, Spielhagen und Lamprecht;
im Auftrage der A.S.D. hrsg. von Walther Fischer.
Dresden: Dressel, 1926. 88p., plates, illus. 27cm.
"Eine Festgabe der Akademischen Sektion Dresden
des D.u.Oe. Alpenvereins".

SCHWABIK, Aurel
Switzerland in real life; English version by R.A.
Langford. Zurich: Orell Füssli, 1938. 1v.
(chiefly illus.). 25cm.

SCHWAIGER, Heinrich
Heinrich Schwaigers Führer durch das Karwendel-
gebirge. 3.Aufl., neubearb. ... Akademischen
Alpenklub, Innsbruck; ausgestattet mit Illustrationen ... von Ernst Platz. München: J. Lindauer,
1907. xvi, 182p., plates, illus., maps. 16cm.

SCHWAIGHOFER, Hermann
Bergwanderbuch: gesammelte Schilderungen aus
Nordtirol, von Hermann Schwaighofer-Hirschberger.
München: Im Hochalpenverlag, 1924. 167p. 16cm.

SCHWAIGHOFER, Hermann
Die Stubaier- und Otztaler-Alpen. Innsbruck:
Wagner, [19--]. viii, 188p., map. 16cm.
(Wagner's Alpine Spezialführer, 1)

SCHWAIGHOFER-HIRSCHBERGER, Hermann
See
SCHWAIGHOFER, Hermann

SCHWARTZ, Myrtil
Drei Giganten des Hochgebirges: meine Erinnerungen
an deren Besteigung. Basel: Basler Druck- &
Verlags-Anstalt, 1921. 98p., illus. 22cm.

SCHWARTZ, Myrtil
... et la montagne conquit l'homme: histoire du
développement de l'alpinisme; préface de Henry
Bregeault; introduction du colonel A. Brocard.
Paris: Fischbacher, 1931. v, 329p., 58 plates,
illus., bibl. 25cm.

SCHWARTZ, Myrtil
Vers l'idéal par la montagne: souvenir de mes
escalades de haute montagne en Europe et en
Amérique; illustrations de Paul-Franz Namur; préface de Mme P.-F. Namur-Vallot. Paris: P. Dupont,
1924. 167p., plates, illus. 29cm.

SCHWARZ, Bernhard
Die Erschliessung der Gebirge von der ältesten
Zeiten bis auf Saussure (1787) ... 2.Ausg.
Leipzig: E. Baldamus, 1888. viii, 475p. 24cm.

SCHWARZ, F   W
Kleiner Ratgeber des Alpenwanderers mit besonderer
Berücksichtigung der Verhältnisse in der Schweiz.
Frauenfeld: Huber, [1906]. 67p. 10cm.

SCHWARZ, Th.
Über Fels und Firn: die Bezwingung der mächtigsten
Hochgipfel der Erde durch den Menschen; nach
Berichten aus früherer und späterer Zeit für junge
wie alte Freunde der Berge dargestellt von Th.
Schwarz. Leipzig: P. Frohberg, 1884. vii, 418p.
23cm.

SCHWARZENBACH, Annemarie and SCHMID, Hans Rudolf
Das Buch von der Schweiz; hrsg. von Eduard Karrodi.
München: R. Piper, 1932-33. 2v., illus. 19cm.
(Was nicht im Baedeker steht, 15-16)

SCHWATKA, Frederick and RUSSELL, Israel C
Two expeditions to Mount St. Elias. [New York],
1891. 865-884p., illus., maps. 25cm.
Offprint from Century magazine, v.41, April 1891.

SCHWEICHEL, Robert
Aus den Alpen: Erzählungen. 2. mit einem Vorwort
des Verfassers verm. Aufl. Berlin: O. Janke, 1872.
2v. in 1. 18cm.

SCHWEIGER-LERCHENFELD, Amand, Freiherr von
Alpenglühen: Naturansichten und Walderbilder: ein
Hausbuch für das deutsche Volk. Stuttgart: Union
Deutsche Verlagsgesellschaft, [1893]. xii, 388p.,
plates, illus. 33cm.

Schweiz. 14.Aufl. Leipzig: Bibliographisches
Institut, 1895. xii, 403p., illus., maps, plans.
16cm. (Meyers Reisebücher)

Die Schweiz: geographische, demographische,
politische, volkswirtschaftliche und geschichtliche
Studie, von Aug. Aeppli [and others];Redaktion:
Heinrich Brunner. Neuenburg: Administration der
Bibliothek des Geographischen Lexikons der
Schweiz, 1909. viii, 711p., 1 fold. plate, illus.,
maps. 32cm.

Die Schweiz: Notizen über ihre Bereisung, ihre
wissenschaftlich-geographische Erforschung und
ihre Abbildung in Karte und Bild; [Bemerkungen
über die ersten Ergebnisse des Schweizer meteo-
rologischen Beobachtungs-Systems in Winter-
Trimester 1863/64 von A. Mühry]. [Gotha]:
[Perthes], 1864. 361-384p., plates, illus. 28cm.
Offprint from Petermann's Geographisches
Mittheilungen.

SCHWEIZER, Heinrich
Emmental 1 (Unteremmental): Lueggebiet, Ober-
waldgebiet, Lüdern - Napfgebiet; 30 Routen-
beschreibungen ... bearb. von Heinrich Schweizer.
Bern: Kümmerly & Frey, 1947. 142p., illus., maps.
18cm. (Berner Wanderbuch, 2)

SCHWEIZER ALPEN-CLUB
Album der Clubhütten des S.A.C. [Bern]: S.A.C.,
[1896]. 56 leaves of illus. 22cm.

SCHWEIZER ALPEN-CLUB
Alpine Skitouren: eine Auswahl. Zollikon: S.A.C.,
1962. 2v., plates, illus. 19cm.
Bd.1. Zentralschweiz; bearb. von Fritz Ineichen.-
Bd.2. Graubünden; bearb. von Christian Caduff.

SCHWEIZER ALPEN-CLUB
[Bergsteigen]. Mountaineering handbook: a complete and practical guide for beginner or expert;
published for the Association of British Members
of the Swiss Alpine Club. Paternoster Press,
1950. 168p., illus. 19cm.
Translation of work originally published by the
Swiss Alpine Club.

SCHWEIZER ALPEN-CLUB
Les cabanes du Club Alpin Suisse, par Julius
Becker-Becker; traduction de A. Bernoud. Genève:
C.A.S., 1892. 63p., 16 plates, illus., map.
25 x 34cm.

SCHWEIZER ALPEN-CLUB
Les cabanes du Club Alpin Suisse en décembre 1895,
par Émile Courvoisier. Berne: Schmid, Francke,
1896. 40p., 1 fold.col. plate, map. 22cm.
Annexe to Annuaire du S.A.C., 31e année.

SCHWEIZER ALPEN-CLUB
Les cabanes du Club Alpin Suisse en 1899, par
Émile Courvoisier. Berne: Schmid, Francke, 1899.
19p. 23cm.
Annexe to Annuaire du S.A.C., 34e année.

SCHWEIZER ALPEN-CLUB
Cabanes; édité par le Comité central du C.A.S.
Lausanne: C.A.S., 1928. 1v. (chiefly illus.),
maps. 21 x 30cm.
Text in French and German.

- - Suppléments. 1-4. 1930-46.

SCHWEIZER ALPEN-CLUB
MUSÉE CANTONAL DES BEAUX-ARTS, Lausanne
5e Exposition suisse d'art alpin; organisée par
le Club Alpin Suisse, du 26 mai au 23 juin 1946.
Lausanne: C.A.S., 1946. 32p., 8 plates, illus.
21cm.

SCHWEIZER ALPEN-CLUB
SCHWEIZERISCHE LANDESAUSSTELLUNG, 1896
  Club Alpin Suisse, Groupe XLIII: Catalogue spécial.
  Genève: Exposition Nationale Suisse, 1896. 55p.
  21cm.

SCHWEIZER ALPEN-CLUB
  Clubführer
    See its
  Führer

SCHWEIZER ALPEN-CLUB
  Clubhütten
    See its
  Cabanes
  Klubhütten

SCHWEIZER ALPEN-CLUB
  Die ersten 25 Jahre des Schweizer Alpenclub:
  Denkschrift; im Auftrag des Centralcomites verfasst
  von Ernst Buss. Glarus: Bäschlin, 1889. 244p.,
  fold. plates. 20cm.

SCHWEIZER ALPEN-CLUB
  [Die ersten 25 Jahre...]. Les vingt-cinq premières
  années du Club Alpin Suisse: ouvrage commemoritif
  ..., par Ernest Buss; traduit par Jean Cavey et
  Alfred Richon. Genève: C.A.S. [1889?]. 280p.,
  fold. plates. 20cm.

SCHWEIZER ALPEN-CLUB
  Die ersten fünfzig Jahre des Schweizer Alpenclub:
  Denkschrift; im Auftrag des Centralcomitees
  verfasst von Heinrich Dübi. Bern: S.A.C., 1913.
  vi, 304p., 4 fold. plates, illus. 27cm.

SCHWEIZER ALPEN-CLUB
  [Die ersten fünfzig Jahre...]. Les cinquante
  premières années du Club Alpin Suisse: notice
  historique, par Henri Dübi; traduction par D.
  Delétra. Berne, C.A.S., 1913. vi, 303p., 4 fold.
  plates, illus. 27cm.

SCHWEIZER ALPEN-CLUB
  Führer

  Clubführer durch die Bündner Alpen
  1. [Tamina- und Plessurgebirge], von F.W. Sprecher
    und E. Naef-Blumer. 1916.
    - - 2.Aufl., von F.W. Sprecher und C.
    Eggerling. 1925.
    - - 3.Aufl., rev. von H. Schmid und C.
    Eggerling-Jäger. 1958.
  2. Bündner Oberland und Rheinwaldgebiet, von W.
    Derichsweiler, Ed. Imhof und Ed. Imhof, jun.
    1918.
    - - 2.Aufl. 1951.
    - - 3.Aufl., neu bearb. von B. Condrau. 1970.
  3. Calanca, Misox, Avers, von A. Röllin und
    C. Täuber. 1921.
    - - 2.Aufl., rev. von J. Dettli und P. Carmine.
    1956.
  4. Die südlichen Bergellerberge und Monte
    Disgrazia, von H. Rütter. 1922.
    - - 2.Aufl. 1935.
    - - 3.Aufl., rev. von H. Grimm und M. Zisler.
    1966.
  5. Bernina-Gruppe, von M. Kurz. 1932.
    - - 2.Aufl. Revision: H. Tgetgel. 1955.
    - - 3.Aufl., neu bearb. von O. Kaiser. 1973.
  6. Albula (Septimer bis Flüela), von E. Wenzel.
    1934.
  7. Rätikon, von Ed. Imhof. 1936.
  8. Silvretta-Samnaun, von C. Eggerling und
    C. Täuber. 1934.
    - - 2.Aufl., rev. von C. Eggerling-Jäger und
    J. Schmid-Maron. 1961.
  9. Unter-Engadin, von H. Tgetgel. 1946.
  10. Mittleres Engadin und Puschlav, von J. und
    A. Kaiser. 1947.

SCHWEIZER ALPEN-CLUB
  Führer. (Contd.)

  Clubführer durch die Glarner-Alpen, von Ed.
  Naef-Blumer. 1902.
  - - 2.Aufl. 1912.
  - - 3.Aufl. 1913.
  - - 4.Aufl. 1920.
  - - 6.Aufl., neu überarbeitet von M. Jenni-Züblin
  [mit] Anhang: Skiführer durch die Glarneralpen;
  red. von P. Tschudi und M. Jenni. 1949.
  - - 7.Aufl., neu überarbeitet von M. Jenni-Züblin,
  W. Wild-Merz [mit] Anhang. 1963.

  Clubführer durch die Tessiner-Alpen, von L.
  Lisibach, G. End und J. Kutzner. 1908. 2v.
  - - 2.Bearb. 1931.
  - - 3.Aufl.: Tessiner und Misoxer Alpen; neu
  bearb. von E. Borioli. 1973.
  - - 3a ed.: Alpi ticinesi e mesolcinesi. 1973.

  Clubführer durch die Walliser-Alpen
  2. Vom Col de Collon bis zum Theodulpass, von
    H. Dübi. 1921.
    - - 2.Aufl., von M. Kurz. 1930.
    - - 3.Aufl., von M. Kurz. 1955.
    - - 4.Ausg., erweitert von M. Brandt. 1971.
  3. Vom Theodulpass zum Monte Moro, von M. Kurz.
    4.Ausg., erweitert von M. Brandt. 1970.
  3b. Vom Strahlhorn bis zum Simplon, von H. Dübi.
    1916.
  4. Vom Strahlhorn zum Simplon, von M. Kurz.
    4.Ausg., erweitert von M. Brandt. 1970.

  [Clubführer durch die Walliser Alpen]. Guide des
  Alpes valaisannes.
  1. Du Col Ferret au Col de Collon, par K. Kurz.
    1923.
    - - 2e éd. 1937.
    - - 2e éd. [avec] supplément. 1963.
    - - 3e éd., rev. et augm. par Maurice Brandt.
    [1977].
  2. Du Col de Collon au Col du Théodule, par H.
    Dübi; rev. et complété par A. Wohnlich. 1922.
    - - 2e éd., par M. Kurz. 1930.
    - - 3e éd., par M. Kurz. 1947.
    - - 4e éd.: Du Col Collon au Théodulpass;
    rev. et augm. par M. Brandt. 1970.
  3. Du Col du Théodule au Schwarzenberg-Weisstor
    et du Strahlhorn au Simplon, par H. Dübi. 1919.
  3a. Du Col de Théodule au Monte Moro. 3e éd.,
    par M. Kurz. 1952.
  3b. Du Strahlhorn au Simplon. 2e éd., par M.
    Kurz. 1937.
    - - 3e éd. 1952.
  3. Du Théodulpass au Monte Moro. 4e éd., rev.
    et augm. par M. Brandt. 1970.
  4. Du Col du Simplon au Col de la Furka, par
    M. Kurz. 1920.
    - - 4e éd.: Du Strahlhorn au Simplon; rev.
    et augm. par M. Brandt. 1970.
  5. Du Simplon à la Furka. 2e éd., par M. Brandt.
    1976.

  Führer durch die Urner-Alpen. 1905. 2v.
  - - 3.Aufl. 1930-32.
  - - 4.Aufl. of Bd.1. 1954.
  - - 5.Aufl. of Bd.1: Urner Alpen Ost. 1970.
  - - 6.Aufl. of Bd.2: Urner Alpen West. 1966.

  Guide d'escalades dans le Jura, par M. Brandt.
  1966. 2v.

  Guide de la chaîne frontière entre la Suisse et
  la Haute Savoie. 1928-30. 2v.
  - - [Nouv. éd.]: Guide des Préalpes franco-suisses,
  [par] P. Bossus. 1964.

  Guides des Alpes fribourgeoises. 1951.
  - - Nouv. éd. modernisée ... révisée et ...
  agrandie: Préalpes fribourgeoises, par M.
  Brandt. 1972.

  Guide des Alpes vaudoises. 1946.
  - - [Nouv. éd.]: Alpes vaudoises, par P. Vittoz.
  1970.

SCHWEIZER ALPEN-CLUB
Führer. (Contd.)

Hochgebirgsführer durch die Berner Alpen.
1. Von der Dent de Morcles bis zur Gemmi: hrsg.
    von H. Dübi. 1907.
    - - 3.neubearb. Aufl, von H. Baumgartner [and
    others]. 1951.
    - - 4.durchgesehene Aufl. bearb., von A.
    Oberli. 1976.
2. Von der Gemmi bis zum Mönchsjoch, von W.A.B.
    Coolidge; hrsg. von H. Dübi. 1910.
    - - 2.neubearb. Aufl., von K. Bürgi [and
    others]. 1937.
    - - 3.neubearb. Aufl., von F. Müller und W.
    Diehl. 1949.
    - - 6.Aufl. bearb., von F. Müller und W.
    Diehl. 1976.
3. Vom Mönchsjoch bis Grimsel, von W.A.B.
    Coolidge; hrsg. von H. Dübi. 1909.
    - - 2.neubearb. Aufl. 1931.
    - - 3.neubearb. Aufl. 1948.
    - - 4.neubearb. Aufl. 1972.
4. Von der Grimsel bis zum Uri-Rotstock; hrsg.
    von H. Dübi. 1908.
    - - 2.neubearb. Aufl.: Petersgrat,
    Finsteraarjoch, Unteres Studerjoch. 1931.
    - - 3.neubearb. Aufl. 1956.
    - - 6.ergänzte Aufl. 1975.
5. Grindelwald, Meiringen, Grimsel, Münster;
    bearb. von R. Wyss. 1955.
    - - 3.Aufl. 1975.

Zentralschweizerische Voralpen; neu bearb. von
    W. Günther. 1969.

SCHWEIZER ALPEN-CLUB
Führer in die Excursionsgebiete
    See its
    Itinéraire

SCHWEIZER ALPEN-CLUB
BAUMGARTNER, Heinrich
Die Gefahren des Bergsteigens; hrsg. vom Schweizer
Alpenclub. Zürich: S.A.C., 1886. 64p. 22cm.

SCHWEIZER ALPEN-CLUB
Instruction für die Gletscher-Reisenden des
Schweizerischen Alpenclubs. Bern: Dalp., 1871.
40p., 1 plate, illus. 19cm.

SCHWEIZER ALPEN-CLUB
Itinéraire, 1865-1901. Chur: Club Alpin Suisse,
1865-1900. 26v. in 5, fold.plates, illus., maps.
21cm.

SCHWEIZER ALPEN-CLUB
Klubhütten-Album des Schweizer Alpen-Club.
Freiburg: Zentral-Komitee S.A.C., 1911. 119p.,
plates, illus., maps. 19 x 27cm. (Beilage zum
Jahrbuch S.A.C., Bd.46)

- - Nachtrag. 1913.

SCHWEIZER ALPEN-CLUB
Liederbuch für Schweizer Alpenklubisten ...; hrsg.
vom Zentral-Komitee des Schweizer Alpenklubs.
Aarau: A. Trüb, 1921. 116p. 18cm.

SCHWEIZER ALPEN-CLUB
Manuel d'alpinisme. [Zurich]: C.A.S., 1943.
150p., illus. 19cm.

SCHWEIZER ALPEN-CLUB
CHRISTOFFEL, Ulrich
La montagne dans la peinture: le Club Alpin Suisse
à ses membres à l'occasion du centenaire 1963;
traduit par Henry-Jean Bolle. Genève: C.A.S.,
1963. 141p., 56 plates (some col.), illus. 26cm.

SCHWEIZER ALPEN-CLUB
Der Pilatus: zur Erinnerung an die fünfte Jahresversammlung des Schweizer-Alpenclub in Luzern...
1867. Luzern: F.J. Schiffmann, 1868. 52p.,
1 plate, illus. 22cm.

SCHWEIZER ALPEN-CLUB
SCHWEIZERISCHE LANDESAUSSTELLUNG, 1883
Special-Catalog der Gruppen 27, 28 und 42:
Forstwirthschaft, Jagd und Fischerei, Schweizer
Alpen Club. Zürich: Verlag des Centralcomité
der Schweiz. Landesausstellung, 1883. 139p.
22cm.

SCHWEIZER ALPEN-CLUB
Statuten des Schweizer-Alpen-Club; angenommen von
der Generalversammlung am 2. September 1866 ...
abgeändert ... 1869. Zürich, 1869. 7p., 1 fold.
plate. 20cm.

SCHWEIZER ALPEN-CLUB
Tarif général pour les guides et porteurs des
Alpes suisses, établi par le Comité central du
Club Alpin Suisse avec le concours des sections.
Neuchatel: C.A.S., 1897-99. 3v. in 1. 18cm.
Vols. 2-3 are in German.

SCHWEIZER ALPEN-CLUB
Verzeichnis der Clubhütten des S.A.C. Stand
ende Februar 1952; hrsg. vom Central-Comité
Glarus. Kriens: S.A.C., [1952]. 79p., 1 fold.
col. plate, illus., map (in pocket). 17cm.

- - Stand Sommer 1961.

SCHWEIZER ALPEN-CLUB. Association of British
Members
    See
ASSOCIATION OF BRITISH MEMBERS OF THE SWISS ALPINE
CLUB

SCHWEIZER ALPEN-CLUB. Sektion Bern
Hochgebirgsführer durch die Berner Alpen. Bern:
Die Sektion, 1907-55. 5v., bibl. 17cm.

- - 2.Aufl. of Bde. 2-4. 1931-37.
- - 3.Aufl. 1948-75. 5v.
- - 4.Aufl. of Bde. 1,3. 1972-76.
- - 6.Aufl. of Bde. 2,4. 1975-76.

SCHWEIZER ALPEN-CLUB. Sektion Bern
[Hochgebirgsführer durch die Berner Alpen].
Suisu Beruna Arupusu. Abridged Japanese ed.
Zürich: S.A.C., [1977]. 248p., illus., map. 19cm.

SCHWEIZER ALPEN-CLUB. Sektion Bern
STUDER, Gottlieb
Pontresina und Engelberg: Aufzeichnungen aus den
Jahren 1826-1863: Festgabe der Sektion Bern des
S.A.C. an die Theilnehmer des Clubfestes in Bern
21.-23. September 1907. Bern: U. Francke, 1907.
63p., plates (1 col.), illus. 19cm.
In slip-case.

SCHWEIZER ALPEN-CLUB. Sektion Blümlisalp
Die ersten fünfzig Jahre des Alpenklub Thun und
der Sektion Blümlisalp des Schweizer Alpenclub,
3.Juni 1874 bis 2.Juni 1924: Denkschrift; verfasst
in ihrem Auftrag von einigen ihrer Mitglieder
[i.e. Paul Montandon]. Glockenthal-Thun; Die
Sektion, [1924]. 127p., illus. 23cm.

SCHWEIZER ALPEN-CLUB. Sektion Davos.
Chronik 1886-1896; hrsg. zur Feier ihres zehnjährigen Bestehens. Davos: Richter, 1896. 32p.,
plates, illus. 26cm.

SCHWEIZER ALPEN-CLUB. Sektion Diablerets
RAMBERT, Eugène
Les Alpes et la Suisse; oeuvres choisies avec ...
une notice sur l'auteur par V. Rossel; ouvrage
publié par la Section des Diablerets du Club Alpin
Suisse à l'occasion du centenaire d'Eugène Rambert.
Lausanne: F. Rouge, 1930. 347p., 12 plates, illus.
25cm.

SCHWEIZER ALPEN-CLUB. Sektion Diablerets
Chansonnier des Sections romandes du Club Alpin
Suisse; édité par la Section des Diablerets.
Lausanne: A. Duvoisin, 1902. 87p., music. 18cm.

- - 3e éd. 1909.

SCHWEIZER ALPEN-CLUB. Sektion Diablerets
Club Alpin Suisse, Section des Diablerets,
Lausanne, 1863-1963, [par Louis Seylaz]. Lausanne:
La Section, 1963. 118p., illus. 22cm.

SCHWEIZER ALPEN-CLUB. Sektion Geneva
Guide de la chaîne frontière entre la Suisse et
la Haute Savoie. Vol.1. Massif Oche-Bise, Massif
Arvouin-Bellevue, Massif Ouzon-Grange, Massif
Géant-Hautforts. Genève: La Section, 1928. viii,
123p., illus. 17cm.

SCHWEIZER ALPEN-CLUB. Sektion Geneva
Guide de la chaîne frontière entre la Suisse et la
Haute Savoie. Vol.2. Dent du Midi, Dents Blanches,
Avoudrues, Tour Sallière, Tenneverge, Feniva, Buet
Salantin, Perrons, Croiz de Fer, Arpille. Genève:
La Section, 1930. xvi, 204p., illus., bibl. 17cm.

SCHWEIZER ALPEN-CLUB. Sektion Geneva
Le Salève: description scientifique et pittoresque;
publié par la Section genevoise du Club Alpin
Suisse. Genève: H. Kündig, 1899. vii, 448p.,
1 fold.col. plate, illus., bibl. 27cm.

SCHWEIZER ALPEN-CLUB. Sektion Geneva
Technique de l'alpinisme; traduit de l'allemand
par Albert Roussy et Paul Schnaidt. Genève:
Section genevoise du Club Alpin Suisse, [1932].
95p., illus. 16cm.
Pt.1, by Emil Kern, pt.2, by A.E. Roussy.
Originally published by Sektion Uto.

SCHWEIZER ALPEN-CLUB. Sektion Leventina
Clubführer durch die Tessiner-Alpen. 2.Bearb.
Zürich: S.A.C., 1931. xvii, 581p., illus., bibl.
17cm.

SCHWEIZER ALPEN-CLUB. Sektion Moléson
Guide des Alpes fribourgeoises. Zürich: Club
Alpin Suisse, 1951. 239p., illus., bibl. 17cm.

SCHWEIZER ALPEN-CLUB. Sektion Monte Rosa
Monte Rosa, 1865-1965. Sion: Die Sektion, 1965.
197p., illus., bibl. 25cm.

SCHWEIZER ALPEN-CLUB. Sektion Montreux
Guide des Alpes vaudoises: des Dents de Morcles au
Sanetsch. Lucerne: Club Alpin Suisse, 1946.
136p., illus., maps, bibl. 17cm.

SCHWEIZER ALPEN-CLUB. Sektion Oberland
Verzeichniss der patentirten Berg-Führer im Berner
Oberland. Interlaken: Selbstverlag der Herausgeber,
[1882]. 28p. 16cm.

SCHWEIZER ALPEN-CLUB. Sektion Pilatus
Zentralschweizerische Voralpen: Zürichsee,
Vierwaldstättersee, Brünigpass; für die Sektion
Pilatus des Schweizer Alpen-Clubs 1930 bearb. von
Oskar Allgäuer; neu bearb. von Walter Günther.
Zürich: S.A.C., 1969. 204p., plates, illus., maps
(on lining papers). 17cm. (Clubführer des
Schweizer Alpen-Club)

SCHWEIZER ALPEN-CLUB. Sektion St. Gallen
Festschrift zur fünfzigjährigen Jubiläums-Feier
der Sektion St. Gallen S.A.C., 1863-1913; nach den
Protokollen und anderen Quellen zuzammengestellt
von A. Ludwig. St. Gallen; Zollikofer, 1913.
128p., plates, illus. 24cm.

SCHWEIZER ALPEN-CLUB. Sektion Uto
Ratgeber für Bergsteiger; hrsg. von der Sektion
"Uto". Zürich: Orell Füssli, 1916. 2v. col.,
plates, illus., map. 21cm.

- - 2.verb. und verm. Aufl. 1920.

SCHWEIZER APLEN-CLUB. Sektion Uto
[Ratgeber für Bergsteiger]. Le conseiller de
l'ascensionniste. Vol.2. Technique de l'alpinisme,
en tenant compte de nombreux cas d'accidents, par
Hans Koenig; traduit ... par E. Corrévon et C.
Brossy; desins de C. Meili. Genève: C.A.S. 1918.
166p., illus. 21cm.
Translation of v.2 of "Ratgeber für Bergsteiger",
originally published by the Sektion Uto, 1916.

SCHWEIZER ALPEN-CLUB. Sektion Uto
Technique de l'alpinisme; traduit de l'allemand
par Albert Roussy et Paul Schnaidt. Genève:
Section genevoise du Club Alpin Suisse, [1932].
95p., illus. 16cm.
Pt. 1, by Emil Kern, pt. 2, by A.E. Roussy.
Originally published by Sektion Uto.

SCHWEIZER ALPEN-CLUB. Sektion Uto
[Technique de l'alpinisme]. The technique of
alpine mountaineering, [by Emil Kern]. English
ed., adapted by members of the Association of
British members of the S.A.C. A.B.M.S.A.C.,
[1935]. 74p., illus. 16cm.
Originally published by Sektion Uto.

SCHWEIZER ALPEN-CLUB. Sektion Uto
Das Unglück an der Jungfrau vom 15. Juli 1887;
auf Veranlassung des Vorstandes der Section Uto,
S.A.C. dargestellt von F. Becker, A. Fleiner.
Zürich: Hofer & Burger, [1887]. 48p., col.
plates, illus., map. 22cm.

SCHWEIZER ALPEN-CLUB. Zentralstelle für Alpine
Projektionsbilder
Katalog, 1908 [-Katalog IV, 1917] der Zentralstelle für alpine Projektionsbilder, Lanternbilder
[des] S.A.C. [vom Schweiz. Alpinen Museum in Bern
verwaltet]. Bern: S.A.C., 1911-18. 4v. in 1, 1
fold.col. plate, map. 22cm.

SCHWEIZER ALPENKLUB
See
SCHWEIZER ALPEN-CLUB

Schweizer Balladen; ausgewählt und eingeleitet von
Albert Fischli. Leipzig: H. Haessel, 1924.
102p. 17cm. (Die Schweiz im deutsche Geistesleben)

Schweizer Bergführer erzählen; Ausstattung und 29
Zeichnungen von Ernst Buss. Zürich: Orell Füssli,
1936. 205p., ports. 21cm.

- - 3.Aufl. [1936?]
- - 4.Aufl. 1950.

SCHWEIZERISCHE BERGBAHNEN
Die industrielle und kommerzielle Schweiz, beim
Eintritt ins 20. Jahrhundert. No.3 und 4.
Schweizerische Bergbahnen. Zürich: Polygraphisches
Institut, 1901. xii, 151-328p., plates, illus.,
maps. 35cm.

SCHWEIZERISCHE BUNDESBAHNEN
Summer in Switzerland; edited by the Publicity
Office of the Swiss Federal Railways. Berne:
Swiss Federal Railways, 1924. 79p., illus. 19cm.

SCHWEIZERISCHE GEODÄTISCHE COMMISSION
Das Schweizerische Dreiecknetz. 1.Bd.: Die
Winkelmessungen und Stationsausgleichungen; hrsg.
von der Schweizerischen geodätischen Commission.
Zürich: S. Höhr, 1881. xxiv, 268p., illus. 30cm.
At head of title Europäische Gradmessung.

SCHWEIZERISCHE GESELLSCHAFT FÜR BALNEOLOGIE UND
KLIMATOLOGIE
Health resorts of Switzerland: spas, mineral
waters, climatic resorts and sanatoria; edited
under the auspices of the Swiss Society for
Balneology and Climatology by E. Mory [and
others]... 3rd ed. Zurich: J. Wagner, [ca
1925]. vi, 164p., plates, illus. 19cm.

SCHWEIZERISCHE LANDESAUSSTELLUNG, 1883
Special-Catalog der Gruppen 27, 28 und 42:
Forstwirthschaft, Jagd und Fischerei, Schweizer
Alpen Club. Zürich: Verlag des Centralcomité der
Schweiz. Landesausstellung, 1883. 139p. 22cm.

SCHWEIZERISCHE LANDESAUSSTELLUNG, 1896
Club Alpin Suisse, Groupe XLIII: Catalogue
spécial. Genève: Exposition National Suisse,
1896. 55p. 21cm.

SCHWEIZERISCHE NATURFORSCHENDE GESELLSCHAFT
MARTINS, Charles
La réunion de la Société helvétique des sciences
naturelles en aout 1863 à Samaden, dans la Haute-
Engadine. Paris, 1864. 35p. 24cm.
Offprint from Revue des deux mondes.

SCHWEIZERISCHE NATURFORSCHENDE GESELLSCHAFT.
Gletscher-Kommission
Vermessungen am Rhonegletscher: Mensurations au
Glacier du Rhône, 1874-1915; geleitet und hrsg.
von der Gletscher-Kommission der Schweizerischen
Naturforschenden Gesellschaft; [bearb. und
verfasst ... von P.-L. Mercanton]. Basel: The
Society, 1916. 190p., plates, illus. 32cm.
Bound with a folder containing 11 maps and plans.

SCHWEIZERISCHE OBERPOSTDIREKTION
See
SWITZERLAND. Post-, Telegraphen- und
Telephonverwaltung

SCHWEIZERISCHE POSTVERWALTUNG
See
SWITZERLAND. Post-, Telegraphen- und
Telephonverwaltung

SCHWEIZERISCHE STIFTUNG FÜR ALPINE FORSCHUNGEN
HARTMANN, G
Alpiner Hochleistungstest: eine interdisziplinäre
Studie; hrsg. von G. Hartmann ... unter dem Patronat
der Schweizerischen Stiftung für Alpine Forschungen.
Bern: Huber, 1973. [8], 152p., plates (1 fold.),
illus., bibl. 23cm.

SCHWEIZERISCHE STIFTUNG FÜR ALPINE FORSCHUNGEN
LUNN, Sir Arnold
A century of mountaineering, 1857-1957: [a cen-
tenary tribute to the Alpine Club from the Swiss
Foundation for Alpine Research]. Allen & Unwin,
1957. 263p., plates (some col.), illus. 25cm.

SCHWEIZERISCHE STIFTUNG FÜR ALPINE FORSCHUNGEN
Everest: relation photographique [de l'expedition
Suisse de 1952]. Genève: Jeheber, 1953. xx,
148p., col. plates, illus., maps. 28cm.

SCHWEIZERISCHE STIFTUNG FÜR ALPINE FORSCHUNGEN
Everest: the Swiss expeditions [of 1952]. Hodder
& Stoughton, 1954. xx, 148p., col. plates, illus.,
map. 28cm.

SCHWEIZERISCHE STIFTUNG FÜR ALPINE FORSCHUNGEN
Everest: ein Bilderbericht [of the Swiss Expedition
of 1952]. Zürich: Büchergilde Gutenberg, 1953.
xx, 148p., col. plates, illus., map. 28cm.

SCHWEIZERISCHE STIFTUNG FÜR ALPINE FORSCHUNGEN
The first ten years, Swiss Foundation for Alpine
Research. Zurich: S.F.A.R., 1951. 48p., 1 fold.
plate, illus. (1 col.), map. 30cm.

SCHWEIZERISCHE STIFTUNG FÜR ALPINE FORSCHUNGEN
ROCH, André
Images d'escalades: 88 photographies; publié sous
les auspices de la Fondation suisse d'exploration
alpine. Lausanne: J. Marguerat, 1946. 1v.
(chiefly illus.). 25cm.

SCHWEIZERISCHE STIFTUNG FÜR ALPINE FORSCHUNGEN
ROCH, André
Karakoram Himalaya: sommets de 7000; préface de
Marcel Kurz; publié sous les auspices de la
Fondation suisse d'explorations alpines.
Neuchatel: Attinger, 1945. 185p., plates (1 col.),
illus., map. 22cm. (Montagne)

SCHWEIZERISCHE STIFTUNG FÜR ALPINE FORSCHUNGEN
EGGER, Carl
Pioniere der Alpen: 30 Lebensbilder der grossen
Schweizer Bergführer von Melchior Anderegg bis
Franz Lochmatter, 1827 bis 1933; hrsg. von der
Schweizerischen Stiftung für Alpine Forschungen.
Zürich: Amstutz, Herdeg, 1946. 371p., ports,
bibl. 21cm.

SCHWEIZERISCHE STIFTUNG FÜR ALPINE FORSCHUNGEN
STEPHEN, Leslie
[The playground of Europe]. Der Spielplatz
Europas; mit einer Einleitung von G. Winthrop
Young; übersetzt und bearb. von Henry Hoek; hrsg.
von der Schweizerischen Stiftung für Ausseralpine
Forschungen. Zürich: Amstutz, Herdeg, 1942.
272p., plates, illus. 22cm.

SCHWEIZERISCHE STIFTUNG FÜR ALPINE FORSCHUNGEN
Schweizer im Himalaja; hrsg. von der
Schweizerischen Stiftung für Ausseralpine
Forschungen; mit einem Geleitwort von R. Schöpfer.
Zürich: Amstutz & Herdeg, 1939. 152p., illus.,
maps. 24cm.

- - 2.Aufl. 1940.

SCHWEIZERISCHE STIFTUNG FÜR ALPINE FORSCHUNGEN
Schweizerische Stiftung für Alpine Forschungen
1939 bis 1970: Rückblick auf ihre 30 jährige
Tätigkeit; [edited by Karl Weber and Ernst Feuz].
Zürich: S.S.A.F., 1972. 159p., 8 plates, illus.,
ports., bibl. 28cm.

SCHWEIZERISCHE STIFTUNG FÜR AUSSERALPINE FORSCHUNGEN
See
SCHWEIZERISCHE STIFTUNG FÜR ALPINE FORSCHUNGEN

SCHWEIZERISCHE VERKEHRSZENTRALE
Bibliographie der Reiseliteratur der
Schweizerischen Verkehrszentrale, Schweizerischen
Transportanstalten, Verkehrs-Kur- und Hotelier-
vereine. Zürich: Schweizerische Verkehrszentrale,
1926. 64p. 20cm.

SCHWEIZERISCHE VERKEHRSZENTRALE
On the Swiss alpine roads = Sur les routes
alpestres suisses. Goldswil-Interlaken: H.A.
Gurtner, [1927?]. 52p., col. plates, illus.
27cm.
In French and English.

SCHWEIZERISCHER FREMDENVERKEHRSVERBAND
Gegenwarts- und Zukunftsprobleme des
Schweizerischen Fremdenverkehrs: Festgabe für
Hermann Seiler; hrsg. vom Schweizerischen
Fremdenverkehrsverband. Zürich: Buchdruckerei
vormals J. Rüegg, 1946. 175p., 1 plate, port.
23cm.

SCHWEIZERISCHER SKI-VERBAND
Offizieller Ski Tourenführer der Schweiz; hrsg.
vom Schweizerischen Ski-Verband; Redaktion: Alfred
Flückiger. Bern: Kümmerly & Frey, 1933. 367p.,
plates, illus., maps. 21cm.

SCHWEIZERISCHES ALPINES MUSEUM
Katalog, 1908 [- Katalog IV, 1917] der Zentralstelle für alpine Projektionsbilder, Lanternbilder
[des] S.A.C. [vom Schweiz. Alpinen Museum in Bern
verwaltet]. Bern: S.A.C., 1911-18. 4v. in 1,
1 fold.col. plate, map. 22cm.

SCHWEIZERISCHES ALPINES MUSEUM
Ein Rundgang durch das Schweizerische Alpine
Museum in Bern, von R. Zeller. Bern: The Museum,
1934. 32p., illus. 21cm.

SCHWEIZERISCHES ALPINES MUSEUM
[Ein Rundgang...]. Une visite au Musée Alpin
Suisse à Berne, par R. Zeller; traduction du Dr.
A. Lang. Berne: The Museum, 1935. 32p., illus.
21cm.

SCHWERIN, Detlof, Freiherr von
Führer durch die Tannheimer Berge und für die
umliegenden Talerte. München: Verlag der Alpenfreund, 1922. 160p., illus. 16cm. (D.u.Ö.A.V.
Sektion München. Alpenfreund-Führer, 2)

SCHWETZER, J J
Das Faulhorn im Grindelwald: ein Topographie- und
Panoram-Gemälde; entworfen von mehreren Alpen-
Freunden und hrsg. von J.J. Schwetzer; mit einem
Panorama von Franz Schmid. Bern: C.A. Jenni, 1832.
viii, 56p., 1 fold. plate, illus. 21cm.

SCI CLUB MILANO
    468 itinerari sciistici: dal Colle di Tenda a S.
    Candido; raccolti dallo Sci Club Milano. Milano:
    S.C.M., 1932. 435p. 17cm.

SCI CLUB TORINO
GHIGLIONE, Piero
    Lo Sci e la tecnica moderna. Bergamo: Istituto
    Italiano d'Arti Grafiche, Sci Club Torino, 1928.
    278p., plates, illus. 26cm.

SCIOBERET, P
    Abdallah Schlatter; ou, Les curieuses aventures
    d'un Suisse au Caucase. Lausanne: Blanc, Imer &
    Lebet, 1370. 74p. 19cm.

SCIZE, Pierre
    En altitude; eaux-fortes et héliogravures de
    Joanny Drevet. Grenoble: Didier & Richard, 1930.
    169p., plates, illus. 23cm. (Cites, paysages, 2)

SCOLARI, Carlo
CLUB ALPINO ITALIANO. Sezione di Milano
    Dizionario alpino italiano. Milano: Ulrico Hoepli,
    1892. 309p. 16cm. (Manuali Hoepli)
    Pt.1, by Emilio Bignami-Sormani, Pt.2, by Carlo
    Scolari.

SCOTT, Alexander
MONTEMONT, Albert
    [Voyage aux Alpes et in Italie]. Tour over the
    Alps and in Italy; translated from the French.
    Sir Richard Phillips, 1823. 1-78, 81-112p. 22cm.

SCOTT, Daniel
    Cumberland and Westmorland. Methuen, 1920. xii,
    227p., plates (1 fold.col.), illus., map, bibl.
    16cm. (The little guides)

SCOTT, Douglas K
    Big wall climbing: [development, techniques and
    aids]. Kaye & Ward, 1974. xii, 348p., illus.,
    maps. 21cm.

SCOTT, Douglas K
    The Cilo Dag mountains of S.E. Turkey: [report ...
    of an expedition organised by the Nottingham
    Climbers' Club]. [Nottingham]: [The Club], [1966].
    72p., plates, illus., maps. 26cm.

SCOTT, Douglas K
MIDLANDS HINDU KUSH EXPEDITION, 1967
    Report, written by D.K. Scott & W. Cheverst.
    Nottingham: The Expedition, [1968]. 62p., plates
    (some fold.),illus., maps. 25cm.

SCOTT, Douglas K
    Tibesti. [Nottingham]: The Author, [1965]. 78p.,
    plates, illus., map. 25cm.
    Account of the Nottingham Tibesti Expedition, 1965.

SCOTT, Hugh
    In the high Yemen. Murray, 1942. xix, 260p.,
    plates (some fold.), illus., maps, bibl. 24cm.

SCOTT, J M
    Gino Watkins. Hodder & Stoughton, 1935. xviii,
    317p., plates (1 col.), illus., maps. 23cm.

SCOTT, John
    Sketches of manners, scenery, &c. in the French
    provinces, Switzerland, and Italy. Longman, Hurst,
    Rees, Orme, & Brown, 1821. vi, 519p. 22cm.

SCOTT, Richenda
    Snowdonia: The National Park of North Wales, by
    F.J. North, Bruce Campbell, Richenda Scott.
    Collins, 1949. 469p., plates (some col.), illus.,
    maps, bibl. 22cm. (The new naturalist series)

SCOTT, T C S Morrison
    See
MORRISON-SCOTT, T C S

SCOTT, Mrs. W L L
    Views in the Himalayas, drawn on the spot. H.
    Graves, 1852. 1v. (chiefly illus.). 63cm.

SCOTT, Sir Walter
    Anne of Geierstein, [by Sir Walter Scott].
    Edinburgh: Black, 1854. 2v., plates, illus.
    17cm. (Waverley novels, 44-45)

SCOTT, William B
    Reports of the Princeton University Expeditions
    to Patagonia, 1896-1899; J.B. Hatcher in charge;
    edited by William B. Scott. Vol.1. Narrative and
    geography, by J.B. Hatcher. Princeton (N.J.):
    The University, 1903. 314p., plates, illus.,
    map. 34cm.

SCOTT JOHNSTON, Marjorie
    See
JOHNSTON, Marjorie Scott

SCOTT RUSSELL, R
    See
RUSSELL, R   Scott

SCOTTI, Ranutio
    Helvetia profana, e sacra. Macerata: Grisei,
    1642. 2v. 22cm.

SCOTTISH BAFFIN ISLAND EXPEDITION, 1976
    Report. [N.p.]: The Expedition, [1977]. [8]p.,
    maps, bibl. 30cm.

SCOTTISH HINDU KUSH EXPEDITION, 1968
    Report. [Edinbugh]: The Expedition, [1968?].
    [26]p., illus., maps. 35cm.

SCOTTISH HINDU KUSH EXPEDITION, 1970
    Scottish expedition to the roof of the world.
    Aberdeen: The Expedition, [1971?]. 20p., illus.,
    maps. 30cm.

SCOTTISH MOUNTAIN LEADERSHIP TRAINING BOARD
LANGMUIR, Eric
    Mountain leadership: the official handbook of the
    Mountain Leadership Training Boards of Great
    Britain; [produced by the Scottish Mountain
    Leadership Training Board]. Edinburgh: Scottish
    Council of Physical Recreation, 1969. 88p.,
    illus., bibl. 25cm.

SCOTTISH MOUNTAINEERING CLUB
    Climbers' guide books.

    Climbers' guide to Ben Nevis, by G.G. MacPhee.
    1954.
    Climbers' guide to Glencoe and Ardgour. Vol.1.
    Buachaille Etive Mor. 2nd ed., by L.S. Lovat.
    1959.
    Climbers' guide to the Cairngorms area, by M.
    Smith. 1961-62. 2v.
    Climbing guide to the Cuillin of Skye; edited by
    W.M. MacKenzie. 1958.
    Rock climbs in Arran, by J.M. Johnstone. 1958.
    Rock climbs: Glencoe and Ardgour, by W.H. Murray.
    1949.

SCOTTISH MOUNTAINEERING CLUB
    Climbers' guide books. New series.

    Ben Nevis, by J.R. Marshall. 1969.
    - - Rev. ed. with supplement. 1979.
    Cairngorms area. Vols. 4 and 5. Lochnagar and
    Creag an Dubh-Loch, by G.S. Strange and D.S.
    Dinwoodie. 1978.
    Cairngorms area. Vol. 5. South-east Cairngorms,
    Creag an Dubh-Loch, Glen Clova, by A.F. Fyffe.
    1971.
    Cuillin of Skye. 3rd ed. by J.W. Simpson. 1969.
    Northern Highlands area. Vol.1. Letterewe and
    Easter Ross, by I.G. Rowe. 1969.

SCOTTISH MOUNTAINEERING CLUB
    District guide books

    The Cairngorms. 5th ed., by A. Watson. 1975.
    The island of Skye, by M. Slesser. 1970.
    - - 2nd ed. 1975.
    The islands of Scotland, by N. Tennent. 1971.
    Munro's tables of the 3000-feet mountains of
    Scotland and other tables of lesser heights.
    Rev. ed., by J.C. Donaldson and W.L. Coats. 1969.
    - - Metric ed., by J.C. Donaldson. 1974.

SCOTTISH MOUNTAINEERING CLUB
District guide books. (Contd.)

The northern Highlands by T. Strang. 1970.
- - 2nd ed. 1975.
The southern uplands, by K.M. Andrew and A.A.
  Thrippleton. 1972.

SCOTTISH MOUNTAINEERING CLUB
Guides.
[General guide-book]; edited by J.R. Young. 1921.
- - New ed. rev. 1933.

Ben Nevis; edited by H. MacRobert. 1920.
- - Rev. ed. by G.G. MacPhee. 1936.
The Cairngorms, by H. Alexander. 1928.
- - 2nd ed. 1938.
- - 3rd ed., rev. by W.A. Ewen. 1950.
The central Highlands; edited by H. MacRobert.
  1934.
- - 2nd ed. 1952.
Island of Skye; edited by E.W. Steeple, G. Barlow
  and H. MacRobert. 1923.
- - 2nd ed. rev. 1948.
- - 3rd ed. 1954.
The islands of Scotland (excluding Skye); edited
  by W.W. Naismith. 1934.
- - 2nd ed., edited by W.W. Naismith and E.W.
  Hodge. 1952.
Munro's tables of the 3000-feet mountains of
  Scotland and other tables of lesser heights.
  [New ed.]. [1953].
The northern Highlands, by W.N. Ling. 1932.
- - 2nd ed. rev., edited by W.N. Ling and J.R.
  Corbett. 1936.
- - 3rd ed., by E.W. Hodge. 1953.
The southern Highlands; edited by J.D.B. Wilson.
  1949.
The western Highlands, by J.A. Parker. 1931.
- - 3rd ed. rev. 1947.
- - 4th ed., rev. by G. Scott Johnstone. 1964.

SCOTTISH MOUNTAINEERING CLUB
The Scottish Mountaineering Club guide; edited by
James Reid Young. Vol.1., Section A. Edinburgh:
S.M.C., 1921. 144p., plates, illus. 23cm.
- - New ed. rev. to 1933 entitled: General guide-
book. 1933.

SCOTTISH PERUVIAN ANDES EXPEDITION, 1976
Report. The Expedition, [1977?]. [41]p., illus.,
map. 30cm.

The Scottish tourist, and itinerary; or, A guide to
the scenery and antiquities of Scotland and the
Western Islands... 2nd ed., with considerable
additions. Edinburgh: Stirling & Kenney, 1827.
xiv, 403p., plates (some fold., 1 col.), illus.,
maps. 19cm.

- - 9th ed. entitled: The Scottish tourist, being a
guide to the picturesque scenery and antiquities
of Scotland; edited by William Rhind. Edinburgh:
W.H. Lizars, 1845.

SCUOLA NAZIONALE DI ALPINISMO A. PARRAVICINI
SPEDIZIONE MONTE API, 1978
[Report]. Milano: La Spedizione, 1979. 2 leaves,
plates, illus., maps. 30cm.

SEATTLE EXPEDITION, 1964
  See
CORDILLERA BLANCA SEATTLE EXPEDITION, 1964

SEAVER, George
Edward Wilson: nature-lover. Murray, 1937. xi,
221p., col. plates, illus. 22cm.

SEAVER, George
Edward Wilson of the Antarctic: naturalist and
friend; together with a memoir of Oriana Wilson;
with an introduction by Apsley Cherry-Garrard.
Murray, 1937 (1950 reprint). xxxiv, 310p., plates
(1 fold., 1 col.), illus., maps. 23cm.

SEAVER, George
The faith of Edward Wilson. Murray, 1953. 48p.,
1 plate, illus. 21cm.

SEAVER, George
Francis Younghusband; explorer and mystic. Murray,
1952. 391p., plates, illus., maps. 22cm.

SEBOTH, Joseph
Die Alpenpflanzen; nach der Natur gemalt von Jos.
Seboth [und Jenny Schermaul]; mit Text von
Ferdinand Graf; und einer Anleitung zur Cultur der
Alpenpflanzen. Prag: F. Tempsky, 1880-86. [v.1,
1886]. 4v., col. plates, illus. 16cm.
Vol.1 is 2nd ed.

SEBOTH, Joseph
[Die Alpenpflanzen]. Some alpine flowers: twenty-
six coloured illustrations selected from Seboth's
"Alpine plants, painted from nature". London:
[n.pub.], 1893. 1v. of col. illus. 17cm.

SECRET, Jean
L'alpiniste: essai critique; préface de Jacques
Chevalier; hors-texte de Samivel. Bordeaux:
Delmas, 1937. xii, 199p., plates, illus. 20cm.

SEDGWICK, Adam
HUDSON, John
A complete guide to the Lakes ...; with Mr.
Wordsworth's description of the scenery ...; and
three letters on the geology ... by Professor
Sedgwick; edited by the publisher. 2nd ed.
Kendal: J. Hudson; London: Longman, 1843. vii,
259p., plates, illus., map. 19cm.

- - 3rd ed. 1846.
- - 4th ed. 1853.

SEDGWICK, Adam and MURCHISON, Sir Roderick Impey
A sketch of the structure of the eastern Alps;
with sections through the newer formations on the
northern flanks of the chain, and through the
tertiary deposits of Styria. [London, 1831].
301-424p., plates (some fold., some col.), illus.,
map. 30cm.
Offprint from Geol. trans., 2nd series, v.3, 1831.

SEE, Thomas Jefferson Jackson
WEBB, W L
Brief biography and popular account of the un-
paralleled discoveries of T.J.J. See. Lynn
(Mass.): Ths. P. Nichols; London: Wm. Wesley,
1913. xii, 298p., plates, illus., maps. 25cm.

SEGANTINI, Giovanni
VILLARI, L
Giovanni Segantini: the story of his life; together with seventy five reproductions of his
pictures. Fisher Unwin, 1901. 207p., plates,
illus. 30cm.

SÉGOGNE, Henry de
Les alpinistes célèbres; publié sous la direction
de Henry de Ségogne et Jean Couzy. Paris: L.
Mazenod, 1956. 416p., plates, illus. 30cm.
(La galerie des hommes célèbres, 9)

SÉGOGNE, Henry de
Description de la haute montagne dans le massif du
Mont-Blanc. Fasc.2. La Chaîne de l'Aiguille Verte,
par Henry de Ségogne, E. de Gigord, J. de Lépiney,
Jean-A. Morin. Paris: Fischbacher, 1926. 245p.,
plates (some fold.), illus., maps. 17cm. (Guides
Vallot)

SÉGOGNE, Henry de
Le massif du Mont-Blanc: vallées et sommets; photo-
graphies de Henri Laulagnet. Marseille: H.
Laulagnet, 1947. 1v. (chiefly illus.). 27cm.

SEGUIN, L G
A picturesque tour in picturesque lands: France,
Switzerland, Tyrol, Spain, Holland... Strahan,
1881. viii, 312p., illus. 40cm.

SEGUIN, L G
Walks in Bavaria: an autumn in the country of the
passion-play. Strahan, 1884. 361p., plates (1
fold.), illus., map (on lining papers). 20cm.

SEHRIG, Othmar
  Skiführer durch Tirol: Wegweiser für alpine
  Wintertouren. Innsbruck: A. Edlinger, 1906. xi,
  55p. 16cm.

SEIDL, Joh. Gabr.
  Wanderungen durch Tyrol und Steyermark. Leipzig:
  G. Wigand, [18--]. 2v., plates, illus. 24cm.
  Vol.1 only in Library.

SEIDLITZ, Wilfried von
  Entstehen und Vergehen der Alpen... Stuttgart;
  Enke, 1926. xvi, 267p., 2 fold. plates, illus.,
  maps, bibl. 23cm.

SEIGNEUR, Yannick
  À la conquete de l'impossible. Paris: Flammarion,
  1977. 203p., plates, illus. 21cm.

PARAGOT, Robert and SEIGNEUR, Yannick
  Makalu pilier ouest; préface de Lucien Devies.
  [Paris]: Arthaud, 1972. 263p., plates (some col.),
  illus., maps. 21cm. (Collection sempervivum,
  no.57)

SEILER FAMILY
HOTELS SEILER, Zermatt
  Hotels Seiler, Zermatt, 1855-1930: [Festschrift ...
  im Rahmen des diamantenen Jubiläums]. Zürich:
  Orell Füssli, 1930. 40p., plates, illus. 28cm.

SEILER, Alexander
KÄMPFEN, Werner
  Alexander Seiler der Jüngere: sein Wirken für
  Zermatt, das Wallis und die Schweiz. Zürich:
  Bensiger, 1945. 247p., plates, illus. 23cm.

SEILER, Hermann
  Gegenwarts- und Zukunftsprobleme des schweizerischen
  Fremdenverkehrs: Festgabe für Hermann Seiler; hrsg.
  vom Schweizerischen Fremdenverkehrsverband.
  Zürich: Buckdruckerei vormals J. Rüegg, 1946.
  175p., 1 plate, port. 23cm.

SEILER, Joseph A
  Joseph A. Seiler, 1896-1948: zum Gedächtnis; [der
  Gattin und den Kindern des Verstorbenen zugedacht
  von seinen Geschwistern]. Zermatt, 1949. 38p.,
  1 plate, port. 30cm.

SEIPPEL, Paul
  La Suisse au dix-neuvième siècle; ouvrage publié
  par un groupe d'écrivains suisses; sous le
  direction de Paul Seippel. Lausanne: F. Payot,
  1899-1901. 3v., illus. 26cm.

SEIVE, F
BLANCHARD, Raoul
  Les Alpes françaises à vol d'oiseau, [par] Raoul
  Blanchard, F. Seive ...; photographies aériennes
  du capitaine Seive [and others]. Grenoble:
  Arthaud, 1928. 187p., illus. 22cm. (Beaux
  pays, 22)

Select views of the antiquities and harbours in the
  South of France; with topographical and historical
  descriptions, by the author of the Rhaetian Alps
  [i.e. J.F. Albanis Beaumont]. Printed by T.
  Bensley, 1794. 56p., 15 plates, maps. 44cm.

SELIGMAN, Gerald
  Snow structure and ski fields, being an account of
  snow and ice forms met with in nature, and a study
  on avalanches and snowcraft; with an appendix on
  alpine weather by C.K.M. Douglas. Macmillan, 1936.
  xii, 555p., fold. plates, illus., bibl. 23cm.

SELLA, Quintino
CLUB ALPINO ITALIANO. Sezione di Biella
  Il Biellese; edito a cura della Sezione di Biella
  del Club Alpino Italiano nel centenario dalla
  nascita di Quintino Sella. Ivrea: F. Viassone,
  1927. 365p., plates (1 fold.col.), illus., map.
  31cm.

SELLA, Quintino
  Una salita al Monviso: lettera di Quintino Sella a
  B. Gastaldi. Torino: Tipografia dell'Opinione,
  1863. 63p. 16cm.

SELLA, Vittorio
AITKEN, Samuel
  Among the Alps: a narrative of personal ex-
  periences; the illustrations by Vittorio Sella.
  Northwood: The Author, 1900. 119p., 73 plates,
  illus. 29 x 39cm.

SELLA, Vittorio
FRESHFIELD, Douglas William
  The exploration of the Caucasus; with illustrations by Vittorio Sella. Arnold, 1896. 2v-
  plates (some fold.), illus., maps. 29cm.

SELLA, Vittorio and VALLINO, Domenico
  Monte Rosa & Gressoney. Biella: G. Amosso,
  [1890]. 62p., plates, illus. 25 x 33cm.

SELLA, Vittorio
DE FILIPPI, Filippo
  Il Ruwenzori: viaggio di esplorazione e prime
  ascensioni delle più alte [di] vette nella catena
  nevosa ..., relazione ... [di] Filippo De Filippi;
  illustrata da Vittorio Sella. Milano: Hoepli,
  1908. xii, 358p., plates (some fold., some col.),
  illus., maps. 26cm.
  At head of title: S.A.R. il Principe Luigi Amedeo
  di Savoia, leader of the expedition.

SELLA, Vittorio
DE FILIPPI, Filippo
  [Il Ruwenzori: viaggio di esplorazione...].
  Ruwenzori: an account of the expedition of H.R.H.
  Prince Luigi Amedeo of Savoy, Duke of the Abruzzi;
  with a preface by the Duke; [translation ... by
  Caroline De Filippi; illustrations from photo-
  graphs taken by Vittorio Sella]. Constable, 1908.
  xvi, 408p., plates (some fold., some col.), illus.,
  maps. 27cm.

SELLA, Vittorio
DE FILIPPI, Filippo
  La spedizione di Sua Altezza Reale il Principe
  Luigi Amedeo di Savoia, Duca degli Abruzzi al
  Monte Sant'Elia (Alaska), 1897; illustrata da
  Vittorio Sella. Milano: Hoepli, 1900. xvii,
  284p., plates (some fold., some col.), illus.,
  maps, bibl. 29cm.

SELLA, Vittorio
DE FILIPPI, Filippo
  [La spedizione di Sua Altezza Reale...]. The
  ascent of Mount St. Elias (Alaska)by H.R.H. Prince
  Luigi Amedeo di Savoia, Duke of the Abruzzi,
  narrated by Filippo De Filippi; illustrated by
  Vittorio Sella; and translated by Linda Villari
  with the author's supervision. Constable, 1900.
  xvi, 241p., plates (some fold., 1 col.), illus.,
  maps, bibl. 28cm.

SELLA, Vittorio
DE FILIPPI, Filippo
  [La spedizione nel Karakoram e nell'Himalaya
  occidentale 1909]. Karakoram and western Himalaya
  1909: an account of the expedition of H.R.H.
  Prince Luigi Amedeo of Savoy, Duke of the
  Abbruzzi; with a preface by the Duke; [put into
  English by Caroline De Filippi and H.T. Porter;
  the illustrations from photographs taken by
  Vittorio Sella]. Constable, 1912. 2v., plates,
  illus., maps. 29cm.

SELLA, Vittorio
CLARK, Ronald William
  The splendid hills: the life and photographs of
  Vittorio Sella, 1859-1943. Phoenix House, 1948.
  x, 35p., 79 plates, illus. 30cm.

SELOUS, Henry C
BURFORD, Robert
  Description of a view of the Bernese Alps, taken
  from the Faulhorn mountain, and part of Switzerland, now exhibiting at the Panorama, Leicester
  Square, painted by Robert Burford; assisted by
  H.C. Selous, from drawings taken by himself in
  1852. W.J. Golbourn, [1852]. 16p., fold. plates,
  illus. 21cm.

SELOUS, Percy
  Travel and big game, by Percy Selous; with two
  chapters by H.A. Bryden... Bellairs, 1897. 195p.,
  plates, illus. 26cm.

SEMINAR ON THE CAUSES AND MECHANICS OF GLACIER
SURGES, St. Hilaire, Quebec, 1968
  Papers presented at the Seminar on the Causes and
  Mechanics of Glacier Surges, St. Hilaire, Quebec
  ... Sept., 10-11, 1968 and the Symposium on Surging
  Glaciers, Banff, Alberta ..., June 6-8, 1968.
  (In Canadian Journal of Earth Sciences, v.6, no.4,
  pt.2, Aug. 1969. iv, 807-1018p., illus., maps,
  bibl.)

SENDEN, G   H   van
  Alpenrozen. 2.druk met aanteekeningen vermeerderd
  en nagezien door B.T. Lublink Weddik en P.H.
  Witkamp. Amsterdam: C.L.B. Brinkman, [ca 1858].
  iv, 502p., 1 plate, map. 19cm.

SENEBIER, Jean
  Mémoire historique sur la vie et les écrits de
  Horace Bénédict Desaussure ... lu à la Société de
  physique et d'histoire naturelle de Genève, le 23
  Prairial an VIII. Genève: Paschoud, IX [1801].
  219p. 23cm.

SENGER, Max
  Wie die Schweizer Alpen erobert wurden. Zürich:
  Büchergilde Gutenberg, 1945. 327p., illus., bibl.
  24cm.

SENNETT, A   R
  Across the Great Saint Bernard: the modes of nature
  and the manners of man; with original drawings by
  Harold Percival. Bemrose, 1904. xvi, 444, 111p.,
  plates, illus. 22cm.

SENNETT, A   R
  Fragments from continental journeyings. Whittaker,
  1903. 515p. 20cm.

SERAND, François and SERAND, Joseph
  Massif de la Tournette: rive droite du Lac d'Annecy.
  Annecy: Imprimerie Commerciale, 1926. 48p.,
  illus., map. 17cm. (Topo-guides Serand)

SERAND, François and SERAND, Joseph
  Mont Veyrier: rive droite du Lac d'Annecy. Annecy:
  Imprimerie Commerciale, 1926. 30p., illus., map.
  17cm. (Topo-guides Serand)

SERAND, François and SERAND, Joseph
  Pointe-Percée: massif des Aravis. Annecy: Impri-
  merie Commerciale, 1926. 30p., illus., map. 17cm.
  (Topo-guides Serand)

SERAND, Joseph
  Guide de l'alpiniste dans la région d'Annecy.
  Fasc.1. Massif des Dents d'Alex, Lanfon, Lanfonnet,
  Cruet. Annecy: Hérisson, 1910. 102p., plates,
  illus., maps. 17cm.

SERAND, François and SERAND, Joseph
  Massif de la Tournette: rive droite du Lac
  d'Annecy. Annecy: Imprimerie Commerciale, 1926.
  48p., illus., map. 17cm. (Topo-guides Serand)

SERAND, François and SERAND, Joseph
  Mont Veyrier: rive droite du Lac d'Annecy.
  Annecy: Imprimerie Commerciale, 1926. 30p.,
  illus., map. 17cm. (Topo-guides Serand)

SERAND, François and SERAND, Joseph
  Pointe-Percée: massif des Aravis. Annecy:
  Imprimerie Commerciale, 1926. 30p., illus., map.
  17cm. (Topo-guides Serand)

SERAO, Matilde
  Evviva la vita! Romanzo. Roma: Nuova Antologia,
  [19--]. 454p. 20cm. (Biblioteca romantica, 19)

SERERHARD, Nicolaus
  Einfalte Delineation aller Gemeinden gemeiner
  dreien Bünden nach der Ornung der Hochgerichten
  eines jeden Bunds ..., beschrieben ... im Jahr ...
  1742. Cur: Verlag der Antiquariatsbuchhandlung,
  1872. viii, 126,60,134p. 22cm. (Bündnerische
  Geschichtschreiber und Chronisten, 8)

SERERHARD, Nicolaus
RUDDER, May de
  Un montagnard grison [Nicolaus Sererhard] raconte
  en 1742. Bruxelles, 1939. 19p., 2 plates, illus.
  25cm.
  Offprint from Revue d'alpinisme, t.4, année 1938,
  n.1.

SERRES, Marcel de
  Voyage dans le Tyrol, et une partie de la Bavière,
  pendant l'année 1811. Paris: Nepveu, 1823. 2v.,
  plates (some fold., some col.), illus. 21cm.

SETON-KARR, Heywood W
  Bear-hunting in the White Mountains; or, Alaska
  and British Colombia revisited; with illustrations
  direct from the author's sketches... Chapman &
  Hall, 1891. vii, 156p., plates (1 fold.col.),
  illus., map. 21cm.

SETON-KARR, Heywood W
  Shores and Alps of Alaska. Sampson Low, Marston,
  Searle, & Rivington. 1887. xv, 248p., 2 col.
  plates (1 fold.), illus., maps. 23cm.

SETON-KARR, Heywood W
  Ten years travel & sport in foreign lands; or,
  Travels in the eighties. 2nd ed., with additions.
  Chapman & Hall, 1890. xi, 445p., 1 plate, port.
  21cm.

SEUE, C   de
  Le Névé de Justedal et ses glaciers; publié par...
  S.A.Sexe. Christiania: Université Royale de
  Christiania, 1870. 55p., plates (2 fold.), illus.,
  maps. 29cm.

SEWELL, Elizabeth M
  A journal kept during a summer tour, for the
  children of a village school, by the author of
  "Amy Herbert", "Gertrude" ... [i.e. Elizabeth M.
  Sewell]. Longman, Brown, Green, & Longmans, 1852.
  3v., maps. 18cm.

SEWERZOW, N
  Erforschung des Thian-Schan-Gebirgs-Systems 1867.
  Gotha: Perthes, 1875. 2 pts. in 1, 2 fold.col.
  plates, maps. 29cm. (Ergänzungsheft No.42, 43 zu
  Petermann's "Geographischen Mittheilungen")

SEXE, S   A
  Boiumbraeen 1 July 1868. Christiania: [Université
  Royale de Christiania], 1869. 40p., 1 fold. plate,
  illus. 29cm.
  Contains French translation.

SEXE, S   A
  Maerker efter en Iistid i Omegnen af Hardangerf-
  jorden. Christiania: [Université Royale de
  Christiania], 1866. 34p., 1 fold.col. plate,
  illus., map. 29cm.
  Contains French translation.

SEXE, S   A
SEUE, C   de
  Le Névé de Justedal et ses glaciers; publié par ...
  S.A. Sexe. Christiania: Université Royal de
  Christiania, 1870. 55p., plates (2 fold.),
  illus., maps. 29cm.

SEXE, S   A
  Om Sneebraeen Folgefon. Christiania: [Université
  Royale de Christiania], 1864. xii, 36p., 1 fold.
  col. plate, illus., map. 30cm.
  Contains a summary in French.

SEYDLITZ, Ernst von
  Geographie. Ausg. D ...; für höhere Lehranstalten
  bearb. von A. Rohrmann. 2. Heft. Europe ohne das
  Deutsche Reich. 12.Aufl. Breslau: F. Hirt, 1912.
  71p., plates, illus., maps. 23cm.

SEYDLITZ, Ernst von
  Handbuch der Geographie. Jubiläums-Ausg. "Der
  Grosse Seydlitz", 25. Bearbeitung unter Mitwirkung
  vieler Fachmänner besorgt von E. Oehlmann. Breslau:
  F. Hirt, 1908. xvi, 848p., plates (some fold.,
  some col.), illus., maps. 23cm.

SEYLAZ, Louis
Alpes vaudoises; ... photographies originales de
Émile Gos. Lausanne: J. Marguerat, 1948. 102p.,
illus. 29cm. (Merveilles de la Suisse)

SEYLAZ, Louis
Ascensions dans le massif du Trient. Lausanne:
Novos, 1941. 160p., illus. 28cm.

SEYLAZ, Louis
Club Alpin Suisse, Section des Diablerets,
Lausanne, 1863-1963, [par Louis Seylaz].
Lausanne: La Section, 1963. 118p., illus. 22cm.

SEYLAZ, Louis
BLAIKIE, Thomas
[Diary of a Scotch gardener...]. Journal de
Thomas Blaikie: excursions d'un botaniste écossais
dans les Alpes et le Jura en 1775; traduit et
publié avec une introduction et des notes par L.
Seylaz. Neuchatel: La Baconnière, 1935. 159p.,
plates, illus. 20cm.

SEYLAZ, Louis
Nos Alpes vaudoises, texte de Louis Seylaz.
Lausanne: Librairie Centrale et Universitaire,
1924. 168p., illus. 22cm. (Notre beau pays)

SHACKLETON, Sir Ernest Henry
The heart of the Antarctic, being the story of the
British Antarctic Expedition, 1907-1909; with an
introduction by Hugh Robert Mill; an account of
the first journey to the south magnetic pole by
T.W. Edgeworth David. Heinemann, 1909. 2v.,
plates (some col.), illus., maps (in pocket).
26cm.

SHACKLETON, Sir Ernest Henry
FISHER, Margery and FISHER, James
Shackleton; drawings by W.E. How. Barrie, 1957.
xvi, 559p., plates, illus., maps, ports., bibl.
23cm.

SHAIRP, John Campbell
Life and letters of James David Forbes, F.R.S., by
John Campbell Shairp, Peter Guthrie Tait and A.
Adams-Reilly. Macmillan, 1873. xv, 598p., plates
(1 fold.), illus., map, bibl. 24cm.

SHALER, Nathaniel Southgate and DAVIS, William Morris
Glaciers. Boston: J.R. Osgood, 1881. vi, 196p.,
25 plates, illus., bibl. 36cm. (Illustrations of
the earth's surface)

SHAND, Alexander Innes
Old-time travel: personal reminiscences of the
continent forty years ago compared with experiences
of the present day. Murray, 1903. xii, 426p.,
plates, illus. 21cm.

SHARP, Alec
Clogwyn du'r Arddu; diagrams by R.B. Evans and map
by Ken Wilson. Manchester: Climbers' Club, 1976.
99p., illus., maps (on lining papers). 17cm.
(Climbers' Club guides [rev.], 4)

SHARP, Alec
Gogarth. Manchester: Climbers' Club, 1977. 136p.,
illus., maps (on lining papers). 17cm. (Climbers'
Club guides to Wales, 7)

SHARP, Samuel
Letters from Italy, describing the customs and
manners of that country, in the years 1765 and
1766; to which is annexed an admonition to gentle-
men who pass the Alps in their tour through Italy.
2nd ed. R. Cave, 1767. iv, 315p. 21cm.

- - 3rd ed. [17--].

SHARPE, C F Stewart
Landslides and related phenomena: a study of mass-
movements of soil and rock. New York: Columbia
University Press, 1938. xv, 137p., plates, illus.,
bibl. 25cm.

SHAW, Robert
Visits to high Tartary, Yarkand, and Kashghar
(formerly Chinese Tartary) and return journey over
the Karakoram Pass. Murray, 1871. xvi, 486p.,
plates (some fold., some col.), illus., maps.
24cm.

SHELDON, Charles
The wilderness of the Upper Yukon: a hunter's
explorations for wild sheep in sub-arctic mountains. Fisher Unwin, 1911. xxi, 354p., plates
(1 fold., 1 col.), illus., maps, bibl. 24cm.

SHELLEY, Frances, Lady
The diary of Frances Lady Shelley, 1787-1817;
edited by her grandson Richard Edgcumbe. Murray,
1912. vii, 406p., plates, illus. 23cm.

SHELLEY, Mary
SHELLEY, Percy Bysshe
Essays, letters from abroad, translations and
fragments; edited by Mrs. Shelley. New ed. E.
Moxon, 1852. 2v. in 1. 17cm.
Vol.2 contains Journal of a six weeks' tour.

SHELLEY, Mary
SHELLEY, Percy Bysshe
On Shelley. Oxford University Press, 1938. vi,
99p. 20cm.
Contents: Shelley is expelled, by E. Blunden.
-The atheist: an incident at Chamonix, by G.
De Beer. -Mary Shelley: novelist and dramatist,
by S. Norman.

SHELLEY, Percy Bysshe
Essays, letters from abroad, translations and
fragments; edited by Mrs. Shelley. New ed. E.
Moxon, 1852. 2v. in 1. 17cm.
Vol.2 contains Journal of a six weeks' tour.

SHELLEY, Percy Bysshe
Prometheus unbound, with Adonis, the Cloud, Hymn
to intellectual beauty and An exhortation.
Cassell, 1894. 192p. 15cm. (Cassell's national
library)

SHELLEY, Percy Bysshe
ELTON, Charles Isaac
An account of Shelley's visits to France,
Switzerland, and Savoy, in the years 1814 and
1816; with extracts from "The history of a six
weeks' tour" and "Letters descriptive of a sail
round the Lake of Geneva...". Bliss, Sands, &
Foster, 1894. viii, 200p., plates, illus., port.,
bibl. 20cm.

SHELLEY, Percy Bysshe
ENGEL, Claire Éliane
Byron et Shelley en Suisse et en Savoie, mai-
octobre 1816. Chambéry: Dardel, 1930. vii,
113p., plates, illus. 26cm.

SHELLEY, Percy Bysshe
On Shelley. Oxford University Press, 1938. vi,
99p. 20cm.
Contents:Shelley is expelled, by E. Blunden.
-The atheist: an incident at Chamonix, by G. De
Beer. -Mary Shelley: novelist and dramatist, by
S. Norman.

SHEPARD, J S
Over the Dovrefjelds. H.S. King, 1873. 217,
viii p., plates, illus. 19cm.

SHEPPARD, John
Letters, after a tour through some parts of
France, Italy, Switzerland, and Germany, in 1816;
with incidental reflections on some topics connected with religion, [by John Sheppard].
Edinburgh: Oliphant, Waugh, & Innes, 1817. xvii,
353p. 22cm.

- - Another issue, entitled: Letters, descriptive
of a tour... 1817. 23cm.

SHERER, Moyle
  Notes and reflections during a ramble in Germany,
  by the author of "Recollections in the Peninsula",
  "Sketches of India" ... [i.e. Moyle Sherer].
  Longman, Rees, Orme, Brown, & Green, 1826. 400p.
  22cm.

SHERIDAN, James
  The school for scandal: a comedy in five acts.
  Dublin: [J. Cumberland], 1800. 72p., plates,
  illus. 15cm.

SHERLOCK, Martin
  Nouvelles lettres d'un voyageur anglois. Esprit,
  1780. 248p. 21cm.

SHERMAN, Paddy
  Cloud walkers: six climbs on major Canadian peaks;
  maps by John A. Hall. Toronto: Macmillan, 1965.
  161p., plates, illus., maps. 23cm.

SHERRING, Charles A
  Western Tibet and the British borderland: the
  sacred country of Hindus and Buddhists, with an
  account of the government, religion and customs of
  its people; with a chapter by T.G. Longstaff describing an attempt to climb Gurla Mandhata. Arnold,
  1906. xv, 376p., plates (2 fold.col.), illus.,
  maps. 26cm.

SHERWILL, Markham
  Ascent of Captain Markham Sherwill (accompanied by
  Dr. E. Clark) to the summit of Mont Blanc, 25th,
  26th and 27th of August, 1825, in letters addressed
  to a friend. The Author, 1826. 26p. 25cm.

SHERWILL, Markham
  [Ascent of Captain Markham Sherwill...]. Ascension
  du docteur Edmund Clark et du capitaine Markham
  Sherwill à la première sommité du Mont Blanc, les
  25, 26, et 27 août 1825; traduit de l'anglais par
  Alexandre P---r. Genève: De Chateauvieux, 1827.
  81p. 21cm.

- - Another issue. Melun: Michelin, 1827.

CLARK, Edmund and SHERWILL, Markham
  Narrative of an excursion to the summit of Mont
  Blanc, August 26th, 1825, by Edmund Clark and
  Markham Sherwill. [London, 1826]. 434-449,
  590-600, 289-296p. 21cm.
  Offprint from New monthly magazine, 1826.

SHERWILL, Markham
  A visit to the summit of Mont Blanc, by Captain
  Markham Sherwill [and Dr. Edmund Clark], 25th,
  26th, and 27th August, 1825, in letters addressed
  to a friend, by Markham Sherwill. [London, 1826].
  533-541, 40-47, 150-155p. 22cm.
  Offprint from New monthly magazine, 1826.

SHERWILL, Walter Stanhope
  Notes upon a tour in the Sikkim Himalayah mountains
  undertaken for the purpose of ascertaining the
  geological formation of Kunchinjinga and of the
  perpetually snow-covered peaks in its vicinity.
  Calcutta: The Author, [1852?]. 59p., plates (1
  fold.col.), illus. 23cm.

SHERWOOD, Mary Martha
  Aleine; or, Le Bächen Hölzli. 2nd ed. Berwick:
  T. Melrose, 1833. 40p., illus. 15cm.

SHIPTON, Diana
  The antique land; decorations by Jill Davis.
  Hodder & Stoughton, 1950. 219p., plates, illus.,
  map (on lining papers). 23cm.

SHIPTON, Eric
  Blank on the map; with a foreword by T.G. Longstaff.
  Hodder & Stoughton, 1938. xvi, 299p., plates (1
  fold.col.), illus., maps. 23cm.

SHIPTON, Eric
  Land of tempest: travels in Patagonia, 1958-62.
  Hodder & Stoughton, 1963. 224p., plates, illus.,
  maps. 23cm.

SHIPTON, Eric
  The Mount Everest Reconnaissance Expedition 1951,
  [by] Eric Shipton (on behalf of the Joint
  Himalayan Committee of the Royal Geographical
  Society and the Alpine Club). Hodder & Stoughton,
  1952. 128p., illus., maps. 27cm.

SHIPTON, Eric
  [The Mount Everest Reconnaissance Espedition...].
  Face à l'Everest: l'Expédition anglaise de Reconnaissance 1951; avec Les batailles pour l'Everest
  par Bernard Pierre. Paris: Amiot-Dumont, 1953.
  156p., plates, illus., maps. 22cm. (Bibliothèque
  de l'alpinisme)

SHIPTON, Eric
  Mountain conquest; by the editors of Horizon
  Magazine; author Eric Shipton. New York: American
  Heritage Publishing Co., 1966. 153p., illus.
  (some col.). 27cm. (Horizon Caravel books)

SHIPTON, Eric
  Mountains of Tartary; photographs by the author.
  Hodder & Stoughton, [1951]. 224p., plates,
  illus., map. 23cm.

SHIPTON, Eric
  Nanda Devi; with a foreword by Hugh Ruttledge.
  Hodder & Stoughton, 1936. xvi, 310p., plates,
  illus., map (on lining papers). 23cm.

SHIPTON, Eric
  That untravelled world: an autobiography; line
  illustrations by Biro. Hodder & Stoughton, 1969.
  286p., plates, illus., maps. 23cm.

SHIPTON, Eric
  Tierra del Fuego: the fatal lodestone. C. Knight,
  1973. viii, 175p., plates, illus., map. 24cm.
  (Latin American adventure series)

SHIPTON, Eric
WHYMPER, Edward
  Travels amongst the Great Andes of the Equator;
  edited and introduced by Eric Shipton. C. Knight,
  1972. xxii, 214p., 1 fold. plate, illus., maps.
  24cm. (Latin American adventure series)

SHIPTON, Eric
  The true book about Everest; illustrated by F.
  Stocks May. F. Muller, 1955 (1958 reprint).
  142p., illus., maps. 20cm. (True books, 15)

SHIPTON, Eric
  Upon that mountain; with a foreword by Geoffrey
  Winthrop Young. Hodder & Stoughton, 1943. 222p.,
  plates, illus., maps. 21cm.

SHIPTON, Eric
  [Upon that mountain]. "Sur cette montagne...";
  traduction de J. et F. Germain. Grenoble:
  Arthaud, 1950. 297p., plates (1 fold.), illus.,
  maps. 21cm.

SHIRAKAWA, Yoshikazu
  Alps. Tokyo: Kodansha, 1969. 149p., 1 plate,
  col. illus., map. 36cm.
  Text in Japanese.

SHOBERL, Frederic
  Switzerland; containing a description of the
  character, manners, customs ... of the inhabitants
  of the twenty-two cantons in particular; [edited
  by Frederic Shoberl]. R. Ackermann, [1827].
  viii, 287p., 18 col. plates, illus. 15cm. (The
  world in miniature)

SHOBERL, Frederic
  Tibet, and India beyond the Ganges; containing a
  description of the character, manners, customs ...
  of the nations inhabiting those countries; [edited
  by Frederic Shoberl]. R. Ackermann, [1824]. xi,
  352p., 12 plates, illus. 15cm. (The world in
  miniature)

SHOBERL, Frederic
[Voyage pittoresque de Genève à Milan par le Simplon]. Picturesque tour from Geneva to Milan, by way of the Simplon; illustrated with thirty six coloured views ... engraved from designs by J. and J. Lory ... and accompanied with particulars historical and descriptive by Frederick Schoberl. R. Ackermann, 1820. 136p., 36 col. plates, illus., map. 28cm.

SHORTER, John
Humphrey Owen Jones (1878-1912): profile of a pioneer climber and scientist. Glasgow, 1979. 18-20, 23p., illus. 30cm.
Offprint from Climber and rambler, Feb. 1979.

SHORTER, John
Humphrey Owen Jones, F.R.S. (1878-1912): chemist and mountaineer. London, 1927. 261-277p., plates, illus. 25cm.
Offprint from Notes and records of the Royal Society of London, v.33, no.3, March 1979.

SHUCKBURGH, Sir George
Observations made in Savoy, in order to ascertain the height of mountains by means of the barometer, being an examination of Mr. De Luc's rules... 1777. 513-596p., 1 fold.plate, map. 23cm.
Offprint from Philosophical transactions v.67, 1777.

SHUTTLEWORTH, F
A short manual of mountaineering training, by W.C. Burns, F. Shuttleworth and J.E.B. Wright. 6th ed., rev. by P.F. Gentil. Mountaineering Association, 1964. 80p. 18cm.

SIDGWICK, Arthur Hugh
Walking essays. Arnold, 1912. xi, 275p. 20cm.

SIEGEN, Johann
Gletschermärchen für Gross und Klein aus dem Lötschenthal; mit 34 illus. von Eug. Reichlen. Bern: E. Kuhn, [ca 1919]. 79p., illus. (some col.). 18cm.

SIEGEN, Johann
[Gletschermärchen...]. Les légendes du glacier; recueillies dans le Lötschental; traduction française de J. Bohy. Lausanne: Spes, [1919]. 80p. col. illus. 18cm.

SIEGEN, Johann
Das Lötschental: Führer für touristen, Abhandlung über eines der eigentümlichsten Täler der Schweizer Alpen; mit 44 Federzeichnungen ... von Eug. Reichlen. Lausanne: Spes, [1929]. 104p., illus. 18cm.

SIEGEN, Johann
The Lötschental; translated by Ida M. Whitworth; with a foreword by Katharine C. Chorley. Kendal: Titus Wilson, 1960. xi, 75p., plates, illus., map. 23cm.

SIEGEN, Johann
Vallées perdues. Lausanne: Spes, 1947. 47, 47, 81p., plates, illus., maps. 24cm.
Contents: 1. Tourtemagne, texte d'après L. Meyer [and others]. -2. Binn, texte de L. Desbuisson et E. Bohy. -3. Le Lötschental, texte de Jos. Siegen.

SIEGER, Robert
Die Alpen. Leipzig: Göschen, 1900. 170p., plates (1 fold.col.), illus., map. 17cm.

SIEGER, Robert
DEUTSCH-AKADEM. GEOGRAPHENVEREIN GRAZ
Zur Geographie der deutschen Alpen: Professor Dr. Robert Sieger zum 60. Geburtstage gewidmet von Freunden und Schülern. Wien: Seidel, 1924. 234p., plates, illus., port. 26cm.

SIEGHARDT, August
Der Wendelstein: eine Monographie. München: Alpenfreund-Verlag, [1924]. 156p., plates, illus. 18cm.

SIEMENS, Werner von
Kaukasusreisen; hrsg. von Kurt Fleischhack. Zeulenrode: Sporn, 1943. 62p. 19cm.

SIERRA CLUB
ORTENBURGER, Leigh
A climber's guide to the Teton range; illustrated by Eldon N. Dye. San Francisco: Sierra Club, 1956. xi, 159p., plates, illus., maps, bibl. 19cm.

SIERRA CLUB
Totebooks.

A climber's guide to the High Sierra, by S. Roper. 1976.
A climber's guide to Yosemite valley, by S. Roper. 1971 (1975 reprint)

SIEVERS, Wilhelm
Die Cordillerenstaaten. Berlin: Göschen, 1913. 2v., illus., plates (some fold.col.), maps. 10cm. (Sammlung Göschen)

SIEVERS, Wilhelm
Reise in Peru und Ecuador ausgeführt 1909. München: Duncker & Humblot, 1914. xii, 411p., plates (some fold., some col.), illus., maps (in pocket). 26cm. (Wissenschaftliche Veröffentlichungen der Gesellschaft für Erdkunde zu Leipzig, Bd.8)

SIGNOT, Jacques
La totale et vraie descriptiö de toʒ les passaiges, lieux & destroictz, par lesʠlz on peut passer & entrer des Gaules es Ytalies ..., [par Jacques Signot]. Paris: Toussains Denys, 1518. 40 leaves, 1 fold.plate, map. 20cm.

SILESTUS, Eduard
Spaziergang durch die Alpen. Wien: C. Gerold, 1844. 3v. in 1. 19cm.

SILIUS ITALICUS, Cajius
Punicorum; libri septemdecim ad optimas editiones collati; praemittur notitia literaria studiis Societatis Bipontinae. Biponti: Ex Typographia Societatis, 1784. xxvii, 440p. 21cm.

SILVA, P
Le ascensioni sull'Everest: loro difficoltà pericoli, deduzioni e utilità per le scienze. Roma, 1926. 51p., illus., map. 24cm.
Offprint from Civiltà cattolica, v.4, 1926.

SIM, Charles Henry
The pyrenees: a poem. [N.p.]: [n.pub.], 1887. 14p., plates, illus. 22cm.

SIMLER, Josias
De Alpibus commentarius = die Alpen. München: Gesellschaft Alpiner Bucherfreunde, 1931. xxxiv, 217p., 1 plate, illus., map. 17cm.

SIMLER, Josias
De republica helvetiorum, libri duo... Tiguri: C. Froschouerus, 1577. 211 leaves. 17cm.

SIMLER, Josias
[De republica helvetiorum]. Helvetiorum respublica; diversorum autorum quorum nonulli nunc primum in lucem prodeunt. Lugd. Bat.: Ex Officina Elzeviriana, 1627. 552p. 12cm.
Largely the De republica helvetiorum of Josias Simler.

SIMLER, Josias
Respublica helvetiorum: hoc est exacta tum communis totius Helvetiae, et singulorum pagorum, politiae; tum rerum ab initio foedere gestarum, descriptio... Tiguri: In Officina Wolphiana, 1608. 211 leaves, 13 fold. plates, illus. 13cm.
Originally published as De republica helvetiorum.

SIMLER, Josias
[Respublica helvetiorum]. La République des Suisses, comprinse en deux livres, descrite en latin ... & mise en françois. 6e éd. rev. et nouvellement augm. Genève: J. Planchant, 1639. 485p., 1 fold.plate, map. 15cm.

SIMLER, Josias
Vallesiae descriptio, libri duo, De alpibus
commentarius. Tiguri: C. Froschouerus, 1574. 152
leaves. 16cm.

SIMLER, Josias
Vallesiae et Alpium descriptio. Lugduni Batavorum:
Officina Elzeviriana, 1633. 377p. 11cm.

SIMLER, Josias
COOLIDGE, William Augustus Brevoort
Josias Simler et les origines de l'alpinisme
jusqu'en 1600. Grenoble: Imprimerie Allier, 1904.
1v. (various pagings), plates, illus., map. 28cm.

SIMLER, Rudolf Theodor
Botanischer Taschenbegleiter des Alpenclubisten:
eine Hochalpenflora der Schweiz und des alpinen
Deutschlands... Zürich: C. Schmidt, [1870?].
xxviii, 164p., 4 plates, illus. 16cm.

- - Another issue. Zürich: Schabelitz, 1871.

SIMLER, Rudolf Theodor
Der Tödi-Rusein und die Excursion nach Obersandalp:
Beschreibung der am 30. Juli 1861 von Stachelberg
aus unternommenen Ersteigung. Bern: Haller, 1863.
viii, 64p., col. plates (1 fold.), illus., map.
22cm.

SIMMEL, Eugen
Spaziergänge in den Alpen. Leipzig: A.G.
Liebeskind, 1880. vi, 122p., plates, illus. 21cm.

JOLIS, Agustin and SIMÓ DE JOLIS, María Antonia
Cerdaña, Andorra, Puigpedrós, Cadi, Puigmal,
Carlit. 2a ed. Barcelona: Centro Excursionista de
Cataluña, 1959. xxiv, 286p., plates, illus., maps
(in pocket), bibl. 17cm. (Club Alpino Catalan.
Centro Excursionista de Cataluña. Colección de
Guias, 5)

JOLIS, Agustin and SIMÓ DE JOLIS, María Antonia
Pallars-Aran (del Garona y Noguera Ribagorzana al
Noguera Pallaresa): Besiberri, Montarto, Colomes,
Peguera, Encantats, Mauberme. Barcelona: Centro
Excursionista de Cataluña, 1961. xxxi, 474p.,
plates (some fold., some col.), illus, maps, bibl.
17cm. (Colección de Guias, 7)

SIMON, Charles
Erlibnisse und Gedanken eines alten Bergsteigers,
1880-1930. Zürich: Orell Füssli, 1932. 224p.,
plates, illus. 23cm.

SIMON, S
Rundsicht vom Schrankogl; aufgenommen von S. Simon.
Amberg: Verlag der Sect. Amberg d. D.Ö.A.V., 1894.
27cm.
Panorama.

SIMOND, Charles F
A pedaller abroad, being an illustrated narrative
of the adventures and experiences of a cycling
twain during a 1,000 kilométre ride in and around
Switzerland. J. Causton, 1897. 199p., illus.
18cm.

SIMOND, L
Voyage en Suisse fait dans les années 1817, 1818
et 1819... Paris: Treuttel et Würtz, 1822. 2v.,
plates, illus. 21cm.

SIMOND, L
[Voyage en Suisse...]. Switzerland; or, A journal
of a tour and residence in that country, in the
years 1817, 1818, and 1819; followed by an
historical sketch... Murray, 1822. 2v. 22cm.

- - 2nd ed. 1823.

SIMOND, L
[Voyage en Suisse...]. Travels in Switzerland, in
1817, 1818, and 1819; translated from the French.
R. Phillips, 1822. 128p. 24cm.

SIMONY, Friedrich
Auf dem hohen Dachstein. Wien: Österreichischer
Schulbücherverlag, 1921. 97p., plates, illus.,
map. 19cm.

SIMONY, Friedrich
Charakterbiler aus den österreichischen Alpen
See his
Physiognomischer Atlas der österreichischen Alpen

SIMONY, Friedrich
Das Dachsteingebiet: ein geographisches Charakter-
bild aus den österreichischen Nordalpen. Lfg. 1.
Wien: E. Hölzel, 1889. 24p., plates, illus. 35cm.

SIMONY, Friedrich
Physiognomischer Atlas der österreichischen Alpen.
Gotha: Perthes, 1862. 1v. (chiefly illus., maps).
46 x 60cm.

- - Charakterbilder aus den österreichischen Alpen:
Begleitworte zu dem Physiognomischen Atlas. 1862.

Le Simplon: promenade pittoresque de Genève à Milan.
Paris: L. Janet, [181-]. 207p., plates, illus.
14cm.

SIMPSON, H
Rambles in Norway. Mills & Boon, 1912. 243p.,
illus. (some col.). 21cm.

SIMPSON, J W
Cuillin of Skye. 3rd ed. Edinburgh: Scottish
Mountaineering Trust, 1969. 2v., illus., maps.
17cm. (Scottish Mountaineering Club climbers'
guide books)

SIMPSON, Myrtle
Due north. Gollancz, 1970. 191p., plates,
illus., map. 23cm.

SIMPSON, Myrtle
White horizons; with an appendix by Hugh Simpson.
Gollancz, 1967. 191p., plates, illus., maps.
23cm.

SIMSON, Alfred
Travels in the wilds of Ecuador and the exploration of the Putumayo river. Sampson, Low, Marston,
Searle and Rivington, 1886. v, 270p., 1 fold.col.
plate, map. 20cm.

SINCLAIR, Catherine
Hill and valley; or, Hours in England and Wales.
Edinburgh: W. Whyte, 1838. v, 454p., plates,
illus. 22cm.

Sing' ma oans! Alpenliederbuch; hrsg. von E.
Banberger, M. Förderrenther und A. Geiftbeck.
Passau: Rudolf, 1891. vii, 144p. 17cm.

- - 5.Aufl. Passau: Kleiter, 1901.
- - 6.Aufl. Passau: Rudolf, [19--].

SINGH, Gyan
Lure of Everest: story of the first Indian expedi-
tion; foreword by Jawaharlal Nehru. Delhi:
Government of India, Ministry of Information and
Broadcasting, 1961. xiii, 212p., plates, illus.,
maps, bibl. 22cm.

SINIGAGLIA, Leone
[Ricordi alpini delle Dolomiti]. Climbing
reminiscences of the Dolomites: with introduction
by Edmund J. Garwood; translated by Mary Alice
Vialls. Fisher Unwin, 1896. xxiii, 224p., plates
(1 fold.col.), illus., map. 26cm.

SINTON, James
LEYDEN, John
Journal of a tour in the Highlands and Western
Islands of Scotland in 1800; edited with a biblio-
graphy by James Sinton. Edinburgh, London:
Blackwood, 1903. xviii, 318p., bibl. 20cm.

SIXTY-ONE
A trip to Norway in 1873; with illustrations by
Frederick Milbank and Alice Milbank. Bickers,
1874. xii, 111p., plates, illus. 20cm.

SKEAT, E G
The principles of geography, physical & human.
Oxford: Clarendon Press, 1923. 432p., illus.,
maps, bibl. 19cm.

SKELTON, John
Essays in romance and studies from life. Edinburgh,
London: Blackwood, 1878. 369p. 22cm.

Sketch of a descriptive journey through Switzerland,
[by Rowley Lascelles]; to which is added The
passage of S. Gotthard: a poem, by the Duchess
of Devonshire. Berne: J.J. Burgdorfer, 1816. iv,
92p., plates, illus. 21cm.

[Sketch of a descriptive journey...]. Scizze einer
mahlerischen Reise durch die Schweiz; aus dem
Englischen [of Rowley Lascelles] ... hrsg., mit
einigen Anmerkungen u. einem doppellen Anhange,
von Joh. Rud. Wyss. Bern, J.J. Burgdorfer: 1816.
154p., plates, illus. 22cm.

Sketches descriptive of Italy in the years 1816 and
1817 with a brief account of travels in various
parts of France and Switzerland in the same years,
[by Jane Waldie]. Murray, 1820. 4v. 17cm.

Sketches in the Pyrenees; with some remarks on
Languedoc, Provence, and the Cornice, by the author
of "Slight reminiscences of the Rhine" ... [i.e.
Mary Boddington]. Longman, Rees, Orme, Brown,
Green, & Longman, 1837. 2v. 21cm.

SKETCHLEY, Arthur
Mrs. Brown on tne Grand Tour. Routledge, [18--].
152p. 17cm.

SKETCHLEY, Arthur
Out for a holiday with Cook's excursion, through
Switzerland and Italy. Routledge, [1871]. 140p.
17cm.

SKI CLUB OF GREAT BRITAIN
Handbook on ski-touring and glacier ski-ing.
Ski Club of Great Britain in conjunction with the
Alpine Ski Club and the Eagle Ski Club, 1954.
78p. 16cm.

- - 2nd ed., completely rev. 1961.

Skiführer durch das Ost-Allgäu: Gebiet von Wertach
bis zum Hochvogel. 2.Aufl. München: Rother, 1935.
40p., map. 16cm.

Skiführer durch die Ortlergruppe. München: Rother,
1937. 104 (i.e.140)p., plates, illus., map. 17cm.

SKI-ING UNION OF NORWAY
See
NORGES SKIFORBUND

SKINNER, Thomas
Excursions in India; including a walk over the
Himalaya mountains, to the sources of the Jumna and
Ganges. Colburn and Bentley, 1832. 2v., plates,
illus. 24cm.

SKOCZYLAS, Adam
Stefano we shall come tomorrow. Poets' &
Painters' Press, 1962. 33p., plates, illus. 24cm.

SKREDE, Wilfred
Across the roof of the world; translated from the
Norwegian by M.A. Michael. Staples, 1954. 255p.,
illus., map (on lining papers). 21cm.

SKRINE, C P
Chinese central Asia; with an introduction by Sir
Francis Younghusband. Methuen, 1926. xvi, 306p.,
plates (some fold., some col.),illus., maps. 24cm.

SKRINE, Henry
Two successive tours throughout the whole of Wales,
with several of the adjacent English counties...
Elmsley & Bremner, 1798. xxviii, 280p. 23cm.

- - 2nd ed., with a map, and additions. T. Turner,
1812.

SLEEN, W G N van der
Four months' camping in the Himalayas; translated
by M.W. Hoper. P. Allan, 1929. xiii, 213p.,
plates, illus. 25cm.

SLESSER, Malcolm
The Andes are prickly. Gollancz, 1966. 254p.,
plates, illus., maps. 23cm.

SLESSER, Malcolm
The island of Skye. Edinburgh: Scottish
Mountaineering Trust, 1970. 176p., 52 plates,
illus., maps, bibl. 22cm. (Scottish Mountaineering Club district guide books)

- - 2nd ed. 1975.

SLESSER, Malcolm
Red Peak: a personal account of the British-Soviet
Pamir Expedition 1962. Hodder & Stoughton, 1964.
256p., plates (some col.), illus., map (on lining
papers). 23cm.

SLINGSBY, William Cecil
The Justedalsbrae revisited. [N.p.]: The Author,
[1889?]. 31p., plates (1 fold.col.), illus.,
map. 24cm.

SLINGSBY, William Cecil
Norway, the northern playground: sketches of
climbing and mountain exploration in Norway between
1872 and 1903. Edinburgh: D. Douglas, 1904. xix,
425p., plates (some fold.), illus., maps. 24cm.

- - Another issue, with a biographical notice by
Geoffrey Winthrop Young. Oxford: Blackwell, 1941.

SLINGSBY, William Cecil
[Norway, the northern playground]. Til fjells i
Norge; til norsk ved Thor Bryn. Oslo: Cappelen,
1966. 202p., illus. 20cm.
Translation of part only of original work.

SLOCUM, Joshua
Sailing alone around the world; illustrated by
Thomas Fogarty and George Varian. 3rd ed.
Sampson, Low, Marston, 1902. xvi, 294p., plates,
illus., maps. 21cm.

SMAILL, Gordon
Squamish chief guide. Vancouver: B. Lupul and
M. Smaill, 1975. 114p., illus. (some fold.).
19cm.

SMALL, John
A hundred wonders of the world in nature and art,
described according to the latest authorities;
edited by John Small. Nimmo, 1876. 607p., illus.
20cm. (Nimmo's national library)

SMILAX, H
Près des sommets. Lausanne: H. Mignot, [1890].
317p., illus. 20cm.

SMITH, Albert
The adventures of Mr. Ledbury and his friend Jack
Johnson. King, [19--]. 381p. 19cm. (Home
instructor library)

SMITH, Albert
A boy's ascent of Mont Blanc
See his
The story of Mont Blanc

SMITH, Albert
A hand-book of Mr. Albert Smith's ascent of Mont
Blanc; illustrated by Mr. William Beverley ...
first represented at the Egyptian Hall, Piccadilly
... March 15, 1852. The Author, 1852. 31p.,
illus. 13 x 21cm.

- - 4th ed. 1853.
- - 5th ed. 1853.
- - 6th ed. 1855.

SMITH, Albert
[A hand-book of Mr. Albert Smith's ascent of Mont
Blanc]. Exercise in colouring Mont Blanc. [The
Author], [ca 1852]. 1v. of illus. 16 x 20cm.
Lithographs of William Beverley's drawings for the
Hand-book.

SMITH, Albert
CHATELAIN, Clara de
  Handbook of the miniature Mont Blanc; edited by
  Madame de Chatelain. 2nd ed. A. & S. Joseph
  Myers, 1955. 42p. 18cm.
  Based on Albert Smith's Hand-book.

SMITH, Albert
  The miscellany: a book for the field or the fireside, amusing tales and sketches; written and
  edited by Albert Smith. D. Bogue, 1850. v, 236p.
  21cm.

SMITH, Albert
  Mont Blanc. London, 1852. 88p. 18cm.
  Offprint from Blackwood's magazine, Jan. 1852.

SMITH, Albert
  [Mont Blanc]. Albert Smith's ascent of Mont Blanc.
  (In Travel, adventure and sport from Blackwood's
  magazine, p.1-61)

SMITH, Albert
  Le Mont Blanc; traduit de l'anglais de M. Albert
  Smith par M. John Coindet. London, 1854. 47p.,
  illus. 19cm.
  Translation of an article originally published in
  Blackwood's magazine, Jan. 1852.

SMITH, Albert
  Mr. Albert Smith's Mont Blanc to China is now open
  ... Egyptian Hall, Piccadilly. [The Author],
  [1858]. [6]p. 23cm.
  A programme.

SMITH, Albert
  The new game of the ascent of Mont Blanc. C.Warren,
  [1854?]. 22cm.
  Child's game on a single sheet, mounted on linen
  and folded in a slipcase, inspired by Albert Smith's
  lecture and exhibition.

SMITH, Albert
  Programme of Mr. Albert Smith's ascent of Mont
  Blanc (August 12th & 13th, 1851) as represented
  every evening at the Egyptian Hall. The Author,
  1851. 11p., illus. 23cm.

SMITH, Albert
  The story of Mont Blanc. D. Bogue, 1853. xii,
  219p., 1 col. plate, illus. 21cm.

- - Another issue. New York: G.P. Putnam, 1853.
- - 2nd ed., enl. 1854 (1857 reprint).

SMITH, Albert
  [The story of Mont Blanc]. Mont Blanc; with a
  memoir of the author by Edmund Yates. Ward & Lock,
  [1860]. xxxvi, 299p., illus. 17cm.

- - Another ed. [1871?].

SMITH, Albert
  The story of Mont Blanc, and a diary To China and
  back. The Author, 1859-60. 2v. in 1, 1 plate,
  illus. 18cm.
  Contains 2nd ed. of The Story of Mont Blanc bound
  up with a copy of To China and back.

SMITH, Albert
  [The story of Mont Blanc]. A boy's ascent of Mont
  Blanc; with a memoir of the author by Edmund Yates.
  Ward, Lock and Tyler, [ca 1871]. xxxvi, 299p.,
  1 plate, illus. 17cm.

SMITH, Albert
  The struggles and adventures of Christopher Tadpole
  at home and abroad; illustrated by Leech.
  Willoughby, [1849?]. viii, 512p., plates, illus.
  21cm.

SMITH, Albert
  To China and back: being a diary kept, out and
  home...
    See
  The story of Mont Blanc, and A diary To China and
  back...

SMITH, Albert
FITZSIMONS, Raymund
  The Baron of Piccadilly: the travels and enter-
  tainments of Albert Smith, 1816-1860. Bles, 1967.
  192p., plates, illus., bibl. 23cm.

SMITH, Albert
THORINGTON, James Monroe
  Mont Blanc sideshow: the life and times of Albert
  Smith. Philadelphia: J.C. Winston, 1934. xv,
  255p., plates, illus., bibl. 23cm.

SMITH, Alexander
  A summer in Skye. A. Strahan, 1865. 2v. 21cm.

- - Popular ed. 1866.
- - Another ed. Edinburgh: N.R. Mitchell, 1880.
- - Another ed. Edinburgh: W.P. Nimmo, Hay &
  Mitchell, 1912.
- - Another ed. [ca 1913].

SMITH, Alfred
  Sketches in Norway and Sweden; drawn on stone
  from the original sketches by Henry Warren. T.
  Maclean, 1847. 1v. of illus. 56cm.

SMITH, B   Webster
  Pioneers of mountaineering. Blackie, [1933].
  223p., plates, illus., maps. 20cm. (Pioneer
  library)

SMITH, George Adam
SMITH, Lilian Adam
  George Adam Smith: a personal memoir and a family
  chronicle. Hodder and Stoughton, 1943 (1944
  reprint). 272p., plates, illus. 20cm.

SMITH, George Alan and SMITH, Carol D
  The armchair mountaineer: a gathering of wit,
  wisdom & idolatry; edited by George A. Smith,
  Carol D. Smith. New York, London: Pitman, 1968.
  xv, 361p., col. plates, illus., bibl. 27cm.

SMITH, George Alan
  Introduction to mountaineering. New and rev. ed.;
  introduction by James R. Ullman. South Brunswick:
  A.S. Barnes, T. Yoseloff, 1967. xiv, 134p.,
  illus., bibl. 27cm.

SMITH, H   Llewellyn
SPENDER, Harold
  Through the High Pyrenees; with illustrations and
  supplementary sections by H. Llewellyn Smith.
  A.D. Innes, 1898. xii, 370p., plates (1 fold.,
  some col.), illus., maps, bibl. 24cm.

SMITH, Walter George and SMITH, Helen Grace
  Fidelis of the Cross: James Kent Stone. 2nd ed.
  New York, London: Putnam, 1927. xvi, 467p.,
  plates, illus. 24cm.

SMITH, Hubert
  Tent life with English gipsies in Norway. H.S.
  King, 1873. xxii, 540p., plates, illus., map,
  music. 23cm.

- - 2nd ed. 1874.

SMITH, Hugh Roger
  See
ROGER-SMITH, Hugh

SMITH, James Edward
  A sketch of a tour on the continent. 2nd ed.,
  with additions and corrections. Longman, Hurst,
  Rees, & Orme; J. White, 1807. 3v., bibl. 23cm.

SMITH, Janet Adam
  Mountain holidays. Dent, 1946. xii, 194p., 32
  plates, illus., maps. 22cm.

SMITH, John, Lecturer on Education
  A guide to Bangor, Beaumaris, Snowdonia and other
  parts of North Wales. 3rd ed., improved. Liverpool: E. Smith, 1833. 89p., plates (1 fold.),
  illus., map. 19cm.

SMITH, John, of Gray's Inn
A month in France and Switzerland, during the autumn of 1824. Kingsbury, Parbury, & Allen, 1825. 304p. 23cm.

SMITH, Joseph Denham
A voice from the Alps; or, The Vaudois valleys, with scenes by the way of lands and lakes historically associated. Dublin: J. Robertson, 1854. xv, 253p. 18cm.

SMITH, Lilian Adam
George Adam Smith: a personal memoir and a family chronicle. Hodder and Stoughton, 1943 (1944 reprint). 272p., plates, illus. 20cm.

SMITH, Malcolm
Climbers' guide to the Cairngorms area. Edinburgh: Scottish Mountaineering Club, 1961-62. 2v., illus., maps. 16cm. [Scottish Mountaineering Club climbers' guide books]

SMITH, Roger S   D
MALVERN COLLEGE ICELAND EXPEDITION, 1978
Preliminary report; [compiled by R.S.D. Smith (expedition leader)]. Malvern: The Expedition, 1978. 8p., illus., maps. 30cm.

SMITH, Roger S   D
A synopsis of mountaineering in south Greenland. Belper (Derbys): The Author, [1972]. 16 leaves, maps. 31cm.

SMITH, Walter A
The hill paths, drove roads & 'cross country' routes in Scotland from the Cheviots to Sutherland. Edinburgh: Macniven & Wallace, 1924. 104p. 19cm.

SMITH, Walter George and SMITH, Helen Grace
Fidelis of the Cross: James Kent Stone. 2nd ed. New York, London: Putnam, 1927. xvi, 467p., plates, illus. 24cm.

SMITH, Walter Parry Haskett
Climbing in the British Isles; illustrations by Ellis Carr. Longmans, Green, 1894-95. 3v., illus., maps. 16cm.
Vol.3 not published.
1. England, by W.P. Haskett Smith. -2. Wales and Ireland, by W.P. Haskett Smith and H.C. Hart.

SMITH, William
Adventures with my alpen-stock and carpet-bag; or, A three weeks' trip to France and Switzerland. Pitman, 1864. xvi, 120p., 1 plate, port. 18cm.

SMUCKER, Samuel M
The life of Col. John Charles Fremont, and his narrative of explorations and adventures in Kansas, Nebraska, Oregon and California; the memoir by Samuel M. Smucker. New York: Miller, Orton and Mulligan, 1856. 493p., plates, illus. 20cm.

SMUTEK, Ray
Light weight stoves for mountaineering, text by Ray Smutek; tests by Steve Sabel. Renton (Washington): Off Belay, 1975. [29]p., illus. 22cm.

SMUTEK, Ray
Mount St. Helens Washington: a climber's guide. Renton (Washington): Off Belay, 1969. Broadsheet, illus., maps. 23cm.

SMYTH, C   Piazzi
Teneriffe, an astronomer's experiment; or, Specialities of a residence above the clouds. Lovell Reeve, 1858. xvi, 451p., 21 plates, illus., map. 20cm.

SMYTHE, Frank S
The adventures of a mountaineer. Dent, 1940. viii, 228p., plates, illus., bibl. 23cm. (Travellers' tales)

SMYTHE, Frank S
[The adventures of a mountaineer]. L'aventure alpine...; traduction de J. et F. Germain. Paris: Arthaud, 1951. 260p., plates, illus., bibl. 21cm. (Collection sempervivum, 11)

SMYTHE, Frank S
Again Switzerland; photographs by the author. Hodder & Stoughton, 1947. viii, 248p., plates (1 col.), illus., map (on lining papers). 23cm.

SMYTHE, Frank S
An alpine journey; with fifty-three photographs by the author. Gollancz, 1934. 351p., plates, (1 fold.), illus., map. 24cm.

SMYTHE, Frank S
Alpine ways ... from photographs by the author. Black, 1942. 106p., 1 plate, illus., map. 28cm.

SMYTHE, Frank S
Behold the mountains: climbing with a color camera; with fifty-seven color photographs by the author. New York: Chanticleer Press, 1949. 155p., col. illus. 29cm.
American ed. of the author's Mountains in colour.

SMYTHE, Frank S
British mountaineers. Collins, 1942. 48p., 8 col. plates, illus., bibl. 23cm. (Britain in pictures)

SMYTHE, Frank S
A camera in the hills. Black, 1939. 147p., 1 plate, illus. 28cm.

- - 3rd ed. 1946.
- - 4th ed. 1948.

SMYTHE, Frank S
Camp Six: an account of the 1933 Mount Everest Expedition. Hodder & Stoughton, 1937. xi, 307p., plates, illus., map. 23cm.

- - Another ed. Black, 1956.

SMYTHE, Frank S
Climbs and ski runs: mountaineering and ski-ing in the Alps, Great Britain and Corsica; with a foreword by Geoffrey Winthrop Young. Edinburgh, London: Blackwood, 1929. xx, 307p., plates (1 fold.), illus. 23cm.

- - Another ed. Black, 1957.

SMYTHE, Frank S
Climbs in the Canadian Rockies. Hodder and Stoughton, 1950. ix, 260p., plates (some col.), illus., maps. 24cm.

SMYTHE, Frank S
Edward Whymper. Hodder & Stoughton, 1940. xiv, 330p., plates (2 fold.), illus., map. 23cm.

SMYTHE, Frank S
Edward Whymper: ein Bergsteiger- und Forscherleben; bearb. und hrsg. von Walter Schmid. Bern: Hallweg, 1940. 328p., plates, illus. 23cm.

SMYTHE, Frank S
Edward Whymper; translated into Japanese by Ichiro Yoshizawa. Tokyo: Akane, 1966. 327p., plates (2 fold.), illus., maps. 22cm.

SMYTHE, Frank S
Kamet conquered. Gollancz., 1932. xvi, 420p., plates (1 fold.col.), illus., maps. 24cm.

- - Another issue. Hodder and Stoughton, 1938.

SMYTHE, Frank S
The Kangchenjunga adventure. Gollancz, 1930. 464p., plates, illus. 24cm.

- - Another issue. Black jacket ed. Hodder & Stoughton, 1946.

SMYTHE, Frank S
The mountain scene. Black, 1937. ix, 153p., illus. 28cm.

SMYTHE, Frank S
The mountain top: an illustrated anthology from the prose and pictures of Frank S. Smythe. St. Hugh's Press, 1947. 45p., illus. 16cm.

SMYTHE, Frank S
 The mountain vision. Hodder & Stoughton, 1941.
 xi, 308p., plates, illus. 23cm.

SMYTHE, Frank S
 Mountaineering holiday. Hodder & Stoughton, 1940.
 xiii, 229p., plates, illus. 23cm.

SMYTHE, Frank S
 [Mountaineering holiday]. Vacances d'alpiniste
 ...; traduction de J. et F. Germain. Grenoble:
 Arthaud, 1948. 279p., plates, illus. 21cm.

SMYTHE, Frank S
 Mountains in colour; with fifty-seven colour photographs by the author. Parrish, 1949. 155p.,
 col. illus. 29cm.

SMYTHE, Frank S
 My alpine album. 2nd ed. Black, 1947. 147p.,
 illus., map. 28cm.

SMYTHE, Frank S
 Over Tyrolese hills; photographs by the author.
 Hodder & Stoughton, 1936. xv, 292p., plates (1
 fold.), illus., map. 23cm.

SMYTHE, Frank S
 Over Welsh hills; with fifty-one ... photographs
 by the author. Black, 1941. 101p., illus., map.
 28cm.

SMYTHE, Frank S
 Peaks and valleys; with ... reproductions of photographs by the author. Black,1938. xi, 129p., 1
 col. plate, illus. 28cm.

SMYTHE, Frank S
 Rocky Mountains; with forty-eight monochrome
 plates and sixteen plates in colour from photographs
 by the author. Black, 1948. 149p., 1 col. plate,
 illus. (some col.), map. 29cm.

SMYTHE, Frank S
 Secret mission. Hodder & Stoughton, 1942. 256p.,
 map. 20cm.

SMYTHE, Frank S
 Snow on the hills; with forty-seven photographs by
 the author. Black, 1946. 119p., plates, illus.
 33cm.

SMYTHE, Frank S
 The spirit of the hills; photographs by the author.
 Hodder & Stoughton, 1935. xiv, 308p., plates,
 illus. 23cm.

SMYTHE, Frank S
 Swiss winter ... from photographs by the author.
 Black, 1948. 125p., illus (some col.). 29cm.

SMYTHE, Frank S
 The valley of flowers. Hodder & Stoughton, 1938.
 xiii, 322p., plates (1 fold., some col.), illus.,
 maps. 23cm.

- - Uniform ed. 1947.

SMYTHE, Tony
 Rock climbers in action in Snowdonia, written by
 Tony Smythe; illustrated by John Cleare; captions/
 descriptions and layout by Robin G. Collomb.
 Secker & Warburg, 1966. 127p., plates, illus.,
 map. 25cm.

SMYTHE, William and LOWE, Frederick
 Narrative of a journey from Lima to Para, across
 the Andes and down the Amazon; undertaken with a
 view of ascertaining the practicability of a
 navigable communication with the Atlantic by the
 rivers Pachitea, Ucayali and Amazon. Murray, 1836.
 viii, 305p., plates (some fold.), illus., maps.
 23cm.

SNAFFLE
 In the land of the Bora; or, Camp life and sport in
 Dalamatia and the Herzegovina, 1894-5-6, by
 "Snaffle"; illustrated by Harry Dixon from sketches
 by the author. Kegan Paul, Trench, Trübner, 1897.
 viii, 406p., plates, illus. 24cm.

SNAITH, Stanley
 Alpine adventure. Percy Press, 1944 (1946
 reprint). v, 153p., 8 plates, illus. 20cm.

SNOECK, C A
 Promenade aux Alpes. [Renaix]: The Author,
 [1824?]. iii, 108p., plates (some col.), illus.,
 maps. 27cm.

SNOW, Robert
 Memorials of a tour on the continent, to which are
 added miscellaneous poems. W. Pickering, 1845.
 vii, 311p. 21cm.

The snow-storm; or,An account of the nature, properties, dangers, and uses of snow, in various
 parts of the world, [by Charles Tomlinson].
 Society for Promoting Christian Knowledge, 1845.
 116p., illus. 15cm.

SNOWDONIA NATIONAL RECREATION CENTRE
 See
 PLAS Y BRENIN NATIONAL MOUNTAINEERING CENTRE

SOCIETA ALPINA DELLE GIULIE
 Guida dei dintorni di Trieste. Trieste: La
 Società, 1909. 239p., plates, illus., maps (1
 in pocket). 16cm.

SOCIETA ALPINISTI TRIDENTINI
 Monografia del gruppe di Sella. Trento: Società
 Alpinisti Tridentini, 1925. 120p., illus., map.
 17cm. (S.A.T. Annuario, 24)

SOCIETA ALPINISTI TRIDENTINI
 SAT - CAI 1872-1952: pubblicazione commemorativa
 edita dalla Società Alpinisti Tridentini del Club
 Alpino Italiano nel suo LXXX anniversario,
 riunendosi a Trento il LXIV Congresso Nazionale
 del CAI - Trento, settembre 1952; a cura di Ezio
 Mosna. Trento: La Società, 1952. 232p., plates
 (some fold.), illus., maps. 30cm.

SOCIETA DI SCIENZE E LETTERE DI GENOVA
 Catalogo delle memorie edite negli "Atti" sociali
 dal 1890 al 1939, nel cinquantesimo della
 fondazione della Società. Pavia: La Società,
 1939. 109p. 26cm.

SOCIETA ESCURSIONISTI OSSOLANI
 L'Ossola e le sue valli; edizione per cura della
 Società Escursionisti Ossolani. Milano:
 Lampugnani, [ca 1904]. 50p., 1 fold.col. plate,
 illus., map. 25 x 37cm.

SOCIETA ESCURSIONISTI OSSOLANI
 [L'Ossola e le sue valli]. L'Ossola et ses
 vallées; edition publiée par la Société des
 Excursionnistes de l'Ossola. Milan: Lampugnani,
 [ca 1904]. 51p., 1 fold.col. plate, illus., map.
 26 x 37cm.

SOCIÉTÉ D'HISTOIRE DU HAUT-VALAIS
 See
 GESCHICHTSFORSCHENDE VEREIN VON OBERWALLIS

SOCIÉTÉ DE GUIDES PYRÉNÉES
BELLEFON, Patrice de
 Excursions et escalades aux Pyrénées. Luchon:
 Société de Guides Pyrénées, 1969. 64p., 1 fold.
 plate, illus., map, bibl. 16cm.

SOCIÉTÉ DES EXCURSIONNISTES DE L'OSSOLA
 See
 SOCIETA ESCURSIONISTI OSSOLANI

SOCIÉTÉ DES TOURISTES DU DAUPHINÉ
 Guides, porteurs et muletiers de la Société:
 règlements et tarifs, chalets et refuges.
 Grenoble: La Société, 1901. 95p. 19cm.

SOCIÉTÉ HELVÉTIQUE DES SCIENCES NATURELLES
 See
 SCHWEIZERISCHE NATURFORSCHENDE GESELLSCHAFT

SOCIÉTÉ POLONAISE DE TATRA
 See
 POLSKIE TOWARZYSTWO TATRZAŃSKIE

SOCIÉTÉ RAMOND
L.-F.-E. Ramond, 1755-1827: commémoration ... 1927. Bagnères-de-Bigorre: La Société, 1927 [i.e. 1930]. 163p., plates, illus., ports. 23cm. Edited by L. Le Bondidier.

SOCIÉTÉ SUISSE DES HOTELIERS
Les hôtels de la Suisse: guide pour les voyageurs; publié au nom de la Société suisse des hôteliers. Basle: Schweizerische Verlag-Druckerei, 1896. xxiv, 150p., illus., map. 20cm.

SOCIÉTÉ SUISSE DES HOTELIERS
[Les hôtels de la Suisse]. The hotels of Switzerland: a tourist's guide; published by the Association of Swiss Hotel Proprietors and Managers. Basle: Swiss Publishing and Printing Office, 1896. xxiv, 150p., illus., map. 20cm.

SOCIÉTÉ VAUDOISE D'UTILITÉ PUBLIQUE
Guide des vallées vaudoises du Piémont; publié par la Société vaudoise d'utilité publique. Torre Pellice: Typographie Besson, 1898. 338p., plates, illus., map (in pocket). 18cm.

- - 2e éd. Torre Pellice: Albarin & Coisson, 1907.

SOCIETY OF FRIENDS
The Aurora Borealis: a literary annual; edited by the members of the Society of Friends. Newcastle upon Tyne: C. Empson: London: C.Tilt, 1833. xiv, 174p. 18cm.

SODIRO, Luis
Relacion sobre la erupcion del Cotopaxi, acaecida el dia 26 de junio de 1877. Quito: Imprenta Nacional, 1877. 40p. 21cm.

SÖDERBERG, E A Bo
Reserapport: Svenska Himalaya Expeditionen 1973; [rapporten sammanställd av Bo Söderberg]. [Västeras]: The Expedition, [1974]. 67p., plates, illus., maps. 21cm. Summary in English.

SÖLCH, Johann
Die Ostalpen. Breslau: F. Hirt, 1930. 116p., 20 plates, illus., maps. 20cm. (Jedermanns Bücherei: Erdkunde)

SOHN, Kyongsuk
Introduction to mountaineering: method and technique. [Seoul?]: Cultural Press, 1962. 462p., illus., maps. 19cm. In Korean.

SOL, René and CAYROL, René
Montagnes des Pyrénées Orientales. T.2. Le massif du Canigou. Perpignan: Club Alpin Français, Section de Perpignan, 1974. 91p., fold. plates, illus., map. 15cm.

SOL, René and CAYROL, René
Montagnes des Pyrénées-Orientales. T.3. Du Pla Guillem au Puigmal: massifs de Carenca et de Cardagne-Sud. Perpignan: Club Alpin Français, Section de Perpignan, 1975. 119p., fold. col. plates, maps. 16cm.

SOLANDIEU
Légendes valaisannes; recueillies et adaptées par Solandieu; avec 61 illustrations de Eug. Reichlen; préface de Sigismond de Courten. Lausanne: Spes, [1919]. 112p., illus. 24cm.

SOLANDIEU
Le Valais pittoresque, [par] Solandieu; ouvrage orné de 330 photographies inédites par S.A. Schnegg. Lausanne: L. Martinet, 1910. 163p., illus. 33cm.

SOLER Y SANTALÓ, Juli
La Vall d'Aran: guia monografica de la comarca. Barcelona: Tipografia l'Avenc, 1906. 403p., plates, illus., maps (1 in pocket), plans. 19cm. (Alts Pireneus Catalans)

SOLIS, Antonio de
Historia de la conquista de Mejico: poblacion y progresos de la América Setentrional, conocida por el nombre de Nueva España. Paris: Bossange Padre, 1826. 3v. 13cm. (Clásicos españoles)

Some protected birds of the Cape Province. [Rev. ed.]. Cape Town: Cape Provincial Administration, Department of Nature Conservation, 1962. 13, xivp., 172 col. plates, illus. 15cm.

SOMERVELL, Theodore Howard
After Everest: the experiences of a mountaineer and medical missionary. Hodder & Stoughton, 1936. xiii, 339p., plates (1 fold., 1 col.), illus., maps. 23cm.

SOMERVILLE, D M M Crichton
RICHARDSON, E C
Ski-running, by D.M.M. Crichton Somerville, W.R. Rickmers and E.C. Richardson; edited by E.C. Richardson. H. Cox, 1904. 76p., plates, illus., bibl. 23cm.

- - 2nd ed. 1905.

ROSS, Martin and SOMERVILLE, E OE
Beggars on horseback: a riding tour in North Wales; with numerous illustrations by E. OE. Somerville. Edinburgh, London: Blackwood, 1895. vi, 186p., illus. 20cm.

SOMERVILLE, Mary
Physical geography. New ed., thoroughly rev. Murray, 1849. 2v., port. 19cm.

SOMIS, Ignazio
A true and particular account of the most surprising preservation, and happy deliverance of three women who were buried, thirty-seven days, in the ruins of a stable, by a heavy fall of snow from the mountains, at the village of Bergemoletto, in Italy; translated from the Italian. H. Serjeant, 1768. vi, 208p., plates, illus. 17cm.

Sommer in der Schweiz: illustrierter Reiseführer; hrsg. unter Mitwirkung von J.C. Heer [and others]. Zürich: Bürgi, [1911]. 432p., plates, illus., maps. 20cm.

SONKLAR, Carl von
See
SONKLAR, Karl, Edler von Innstädten

SONKLAR, Karl, Edler von Innstädten
Anleitung zu wissenschaftlichen Beobachtungen auf Alpenreisen; hrsg. vom Deutschen und Oesterreichischen Alpenverein; bearb. von C. von Sonklar [and others]. Wien: D.u.Ö.A.V., 1882. 2v. in 1, plates (1 fold.), illus., map. 20cm. (Beilagen zur Zeitschrift des D.u.Ö.A.V.)

SONKLAR, Karl, Edler von Innstädten
Die Eintheilung der Schweizer und der deutschen Alpen. [Gotha], 1870. 313-320p., fold.col. plates, maps. 27cm. Offprint from Petermann's Geographische Mittheilungen, Heft 9, 1870.

SONKLAR, Karl, Edler von Innstädten
Die Gebirgsgruppe der Hohen-Tauern, mit besonderer Rücksicht auf Orographie, Gletscherkunde, Geologie und Meteorologie. Wien: Beck, 1866. 408p., fold. plates (some col.), maps. 27cm.

SONKLAR, Karl, Edler von Innstädten
Lehrbuch der Geographie für die k.k. Militär-Real- und Kadetenschulen. Wien: Seidel, 1880. 2v. in 1, fold. plates, maps, bibl. 23cm. 1.Th., 2.verb. Aufl.; 2.Th., 4. verb. Aufl.

SONKLAR, Karl, Edler von Innstädten
Die Oetzthaler Gebirgsgruppe mit besonderer Rücksicht auf Orographie und Gletscherkunde. Gotha: Perthes, 1860. xvi, 292p., 1 col. plate, illus. 23cm.

SONKLAR, Karl, Edler von Innstädten
Reiseskizzen aus den Alpen und Karpathen. Wien:
Seidel, 1857. vi, 350p. 22cm.

SONKLAR EDLER VON INNSTÄDTEN, Karl A
See
SONKLAR, Karl, Edler von Innstädten

SONNIER, Georges
Un médicin de montagne: roman. Paris: A. Michel.
1963. 244p. 20cm.

SONNIER, Georges
Meije: récit; frontispice de Maxime Vibert. Paris:
A. Wahl, 1952. 118p., illus. 19cm. (Bibliophiles
de la montagne, 2)

SONNIER, Georges
La montagne et l'homme. Paris: A. Michel, 1970.
332p., 48 plates, illus. 22cm.

SONNIER, Georges
Où régne la lumière. Paris: A. Michel, 1946.
206p., 16 plates, illus. 19cm.

SONNIER, Georges
Terre du ciel. Paris: A. Michel, 1959. 235p.
19cm.

SOPER, N   Jack
The Black Cliff: the history of rock climbing on
Clogwyn du'r Arddu, by Jack Soper, Ken Wilson and
Peter Crew; based on the original research of
Rodney Wilson; foreword by A.D.M. Cox. Kaye &
Ward, 1971. 159p., illus., bibl. 22cm.

SOPER, N   Jack and ALLINSON, Neil
Buttermere and Newlands area. Stockport: Fell &
Rock Climbing Club, 1970. 151p., 1 col. plate,
illus., maps (on lining papers). 16cm. (Climbing
guides to the English Lake District, [4th ser.],
4)

DRASDO, Harold and SOPER, N   Jack
Eastern crags; illustrated by W. Heaton Cooper.
Stockport: Fell & Rock Climbing Club, 1969. 233p.,
1 col. plate, illus., maps (on lining papers).
16cm. (Climbing guides to the English Lake
District, [4th ser.], 2)

SORA, Gennaro
Con gli Alpini all'80° parallelo. Milano:
Mondadori,1929. 239p., plates (2 fold.), illus.,
maps. 23cm.

SORENSEN, Henrick Lauritz
Norsk flora for skoler. 4. Oplag. Christiania:
Alb. Cammermeyer, 1882. xv, 126p., illus. 19cm.

SORMANI, Emilio Bignami
See
BIGNAMI-SORMANI, Emilio

SORRE, M
Les Pyrénées. Paris: Colin, 1922. 216p., 3 fold.
plates, illus., maps. 18cm. (Collection Armand
Colin)

SOTHEBY, William
Italy and other poems. Murray, 1828. 342p. 18cm.

SOTHEBY, WILKINSON AND HODGE
[The library of the late Edward Whymper...] sold by
order of the executors. Sotheby, Wilkinson and
Hodge, [1912]. 58-94p. 25cm.
Section of a catalogue.

SOUBIRON, Pierre
Espingo et le Cirque d'Oô: 12 itinéraires nouveaux
aux alentours du Refuge d'Espingo. Toulouse:
l'Auteur, 1925. 38p., illus., maps. 19cm.
Supplément au "Guide Soubiron" - t.p.

SOUBIRON, Pierre
Les Pyrénées du Pic d'Anie au Canigou en 30 excur-
sions. Toulouse, [ca 1920]. 19-380p., maps. 19cm.
Offprint from Guide Soubiron.

South Devon for the most beautiful holiday resorts
in Great Britain. Torquay: M. Fisher, 1949.
[150]p. of illus., map. 29cm.

SOUTH OF ENGLAND EAST KULU EXPEDITION, 1978
[Report]. The Expedition, [1979]. 16p., illus.,
maps. 32cm.

SOUTH WEST FACE BRITISH EVEREST EXPEDITION, 1975
Everest conquered! Expedition fact sheet.
Barclays Bank International, 1975. 4 leaves,
4 illus. (in pocket). 31cm.

SOUTHAMPTON UNIVERSITY MOUNTAINEERING CLUB
ANNETTE, Barrie M
Limestone climbs on the Dorset coast. 2nd ed.
Southampton: Southampton University Mountaineering
Club, 1960. 36 leaves, 1 plate, illus. 21cm.

SOUTHESK, James Carnegie, Earl of
Saskatchewan and the Rocky Mountains: a diary and
narrative of travel, sport and adventure during
a journey through the Hudson's Bay Company's
territories in 1859 and 1860. Edinburgh:
Edmonston and Douglas, 1875. xxx, 448p., plates
(2 fold.col.), illus., maps. 23cm.

Souvenir de Chamonix. [Chamonix?]: [n.pub.],
[ca 1890]. 1v. (chiefly illus.). 12 x 18cm.
Souvenir de l'Oberland bernois = Album vom Berner
Oberland. Interlaken: Prell & Eberle, [ca 1890].
1v. of col. illus. 15 x 21cm.

Souvenir de la Suisse. Schaffhouse: L. Bleuler,
[1830?]. 1v. (chiefly illus.). 30cm.

Souvenir de Loëche, la Ghemmi et les environs.
Vevey: G. Blanchoud, [1851]. 1v. of col. illus.
16 x 23cm.

Souvenir du Mont-Blanc et de Chamonix. Genève:
Impr. de P.-A. Bonnant, [ca 1840]. 1v. (chiefly
illus.). 13 x 17cm.

Souvenir du Mont-Blanc et de Chamonix. Chamonix:
Payot, [ca 1860]. 1v. (chiefly illus.).
17 x 23cm.
A collection of coloured lithographs by A.
Cuvillier.

Souvenir du Righi. Zurich: D. Herter, [ca 1860].
1v. (chiefly illus.). 11 x 14cm.

Souvenirs d'un voyage par le Stilvio au Lac de Côme
en 1825. [N.p.]: Imprimerie de G.L. Wesché,
[182-]. 88p. 18cm.

Souvenirs de la Suisse. Genève: Bécherat, [ca 1860].
1v. of col. illus. 16 x 22cm.
Coloured lithographs, many drawn by Loppé, and
printed by Lemercier in Paris.

Souvenirs de Sixt: itinéraire complet de la vallée
..., par V.-L. [i.e. Vimal de Lajarriga]. Genève:
Duchamp, 1856. xii, 220p., map. 17cm.

Souvenirs du Mont Blanc. Paris: Wild, [ca 1860].
1v. (chiefly illus.). 27 x 35cm.

Souvenirs du Mont-Blanc et de la vallée de Chamonix.
Genève: Schmid, [ca 1840]. 1v. (chiefly illus.).
14 x 19cm.

Souvenirs photographiques de la Suisse: Chamonix.
Genève: Briquet, [ca 1900]. 1v. (chiefly illus.).
14cm.

Souvenirs pittoresques des glaciers de Chamouny;
ornés de dix-huit dessins coloriés. Genève: J.J.
Luc Sestié, [ca 1825]. 39p., 18 plates, illus.
22 x 30cm.

SOUVESTRE, Émile
Scènes et récits des Alpes: Le chasseur de
chamois, La fillole des Allemagnes, l'Hospice de
Selisberg. Nouv. éd. Paris: Calmann Lévy, 1877.
260p. 18cm. (Oeuvres complètes)

SOWERBY, J
   The forest cantons of Switzerland: Lucerne, Schwyz,
   Uri, Unterwalden. Percival, 1892. viii, 288p.,
   map. 19cm.

SOYER, Daniel
BLAINVILLE, J   de
   Travels through Holland, Germany, Switzerland, but
   especially Italy ...; translated from the author's
   manuscript ... by Dr. Turnbull, [Mr. Guthrie, Mr.
   Lockman and the editor, Daniel Soyer]. J. Noon,
   1757. 3v., maps. 26cm.

SPAIN. Ministerio de Agricultura. Comisaría de
Parques Nacionales
   Guías de los sitios naturales de interés nacional;
   publicadas bajo la dirección de Eduardo Hernández-
   Pacheco. Madrid: La Comisaría, 1931-33. 3v.,
   fold. plates (some col.), illus., maps, bibl.
   20cm.

SPAIN. Ministerio de Fomento. Junta de Parques
Nacionales
   See
SPAIN. Ministerio de Agricultura. Comisaría de
Parques Nacionales

SPAZIER, Karl
   Wanderungen durch die Schweiz. Gotha: Ettinger,
   1790. iv, 488p. 17cm.

Special practical guide for Geneva, the Lake of
   Geneva, Chamouny and Mont Blanc. Simpkin,
   Marshall, 1872. 137-168p., plates (1 fold.),
   illus., map. 17cm.
   Offprint from Practical continental guide: France,
   Belgium ..., by Englishmen abroad.

ISELIN, Fred and SPECTORSKY, A   G
   Invitation to skiing; with action photographs by
   Lloyd Arnold; drawings by S. Fleishman. Allen and
   Unwin, 1952. xiii, 157p., illus. 26cm.

SPEDIZIONE ITALIANA DE FILIPPI, 1913-14
   Explorations in the eastern Kara-korum and the
   Upper Yarkand valley: narrative report of the
   Survey of India detachment with the De Filippi
   Scientific Expedition 1914, [by H. Wood]. Dehra
   Dun: Survey of India, 1922. iii, 42p., plates
   (some fold., some col.), illus., maps (in pocket).
   44cm.

SPEDIZIONE ITALIANA DE FILIPPI, 1913-14
   [Relazioni scientifiche della] Spedizione Italiana
   De Filippi, nell'Himàlaia, Caracorùm e Turchestàn
   Cinese (1913-1914). Serie 1. Geodesia e geofisica
   ...; sotto la direzione di Filippo De Filippi.
   Vol.1. Astronomia, geodetica, geodesia e topografia,
   [da] G. Abetti [and others]. Bologna: Zanichelli,
   1925. xxxv, 419p., plates (some fold., some col.),
   illus. 33cm.

SPEDIZIONE ITALIANA DE FILIPPI, 1913-14
   [Relazioni scientifiche della] Spedizione Italiana
   De Filippi, nell'Himàlaia, Caracorùm e Turchestàn
   Cinese (1913-1914). Serie 2. Resultati geologici
   e geografici ...; sotto la direzione di Giotto
   Dainelli. Bologna: Zanichelli, 1922-25. 12v.,
   plates, illus., maps. 33cm.
   Vol.3. Studi sul glaciale, [da] Giotto Dainelli.
   1922. 2v. -v.8. Le condizioni delle genti, [da]
   Giotto Dainelli. 1924. -v.9. I tipi umani, [da]
   R. Biasutti e G. Dainelli. 1925.

SPEER, Stanhope T
   On the physiological phenomena of the mountain
   sickness, as experienced in the ascent of the
   higher Alps. London, 1853. 51p. 20cm.
   Offprint from Association medical journal.

SPELTERINI, Eduard
   Über den Wolken = Par dessus les nuages; Geleit-
   wort von Albert Heim und Emile Gautier. Zürich:
   Brunner, [1928]. 94p., illus. (some col.). 31cm.

Spemanns goldenes Buch des Sports: eine Hauskunde für
   jedermann; hrsg. unter Mitwirkung von Mar Ahles
   [and others]. Berlin: Spemann, 1910. 1v. (various
   pagings), plates, illus. 18cm. (Spemanns
   Hauskunde, 8)

SPENCE, James Mudie
   The land of Bolivar; or, War, peace and adventure
   in the Republic of Venezuela. 2nd ed. Sampson
   Low, Marston, Searle & Rivington, 1878. 2v.,
   plates (1 fold.col.), illus., maps, bibl. 24cm.

SPENCER, Sir Baldwin and GILLEN, F   J
   Across Australia. 2nd ed. Macmillan, 1912. 2v.,
   plates (2 fold.), illus., maps. 22cm.

SPENCER, Sir Baldwin
   Spencer's last journey, being the Journal of an
   expedition to Tierra del Fuego, by the late Sir
   Baldwin Spencer, with a memoir; edited by R.R.
   Marett and T.K. Penniman; with contributions by
   Sir James Frazer and H. Balfour. Oxford:
   Clarendon Press, 1931. xii, 153p., plates (some
   fold.), illus., maps, bibl. 23cm.

SPENCER, Edmund
   Travels in the western Caucasus, including a tour
   through Imeritia, Mingrelia, Turkey, Moldavia,
   Calicia, Silesia and Moravia. Colburn, 1838.
   2v., plates, illus. 23cm.

SPENCER, Sydney
   Mountaineering, by Sydney Spencer, editor, [and
   others]. Seeley Service, 1934. 383p., plates
   (some fold., some col.), maps, bibl. 23cm.
   (Lonsdale library, v.18)

SPENCER, Sydney
   Peaks, passes and glaciers, by members of the
   Alpine Club. 3rd series; edited by A.E. Field
   and Sydney Spencer. Methuen, 1932. xi, 307p.,
   plates, illus. 23cm.

SPENDER, A   Edmund
   Two winters in Norway, being an account of two
   holidays spent on snow-shoes, and in sleigh-
   driving, and including an expedition to the Lapps.
   Longmans, Green, 1902. xiv, 270p., plates, illus.
   23cm.

SPENDER, Harold
   In praise of Switzerland, being the Alps in prose
   and verse. Constable, 1912. xv, 291p. 23cm.

SPENDER, Harold
   Through the High Pyrenees; with illustrations and
   supplementary sections by H. Llewellyn Smith.
   A.D. Innes, 1898. xii, 370p., plates (1 fold.,
   some col.), illus., maps, bibl. 24cm.

SPENGLER, E
GANSS, Ortwin
   Erläuterungen zur geologischen Karte der Dachstein-
   gruppe; aufgenommen 1936-1940 im Auftrage des
   Alpenvereins ... von O. Ganss, F. Kümel und E.
   Spengler. Innsbruck: Wagner, 1954. 82p., 6
   plates (2 fold., 1 col.), map (in pocket). 28cm.
   (Wissenschaftliche Alpenvereinshefte, Heft 15)

SPESCHA, Pater Placidus a
PIETH, Friedrich and HAGER, P   Karl
   Pater Placidus a Spescha: sein Leben und seine
   Schriften; unter der Aufsicht der Naturforschenden
   Gesellschaft Graubündens ... und der Sektion Rätia
   des Schweizerischen Alpenklubs, hrsg., von
   Friedrich Pieth und P. Karl Hager. Bümpliz-Bern:
   Bentoli, 1913. cxiii, 515p., plates (1 col.),
   illus., map. 28cm.

SPINDLER, Robert
   Die Alpen in der englischen Literatur und Kunst.
   Leipzig: B. Tauchnitz, 1932. 31p., illus., bibl.
   24cm. (Beiträge zur englischen Philologie,
   Heft 21)

SPIRO, Louis
   L'Alpe inspiratrice. Lausanne; Payot, 1942.
   168p., illus. 20cm.

SPIRO, Louis
   Guides de montagne. Nouv. éd. Lausanne: Payot,
   1944. 158p., plates, ports. 20cm.

SPIRO, Louis
    [Guides de montagne]. La guida alpina; traduzione
    di Ademaro Barbiellini Amidei; prefazione di
    Camillo Giussani. Bergamo: U. Tavecchi, [1931].
    xvi, 199p., plates, illus., ports. 21cm.

SPIRO, Louis
    Histoire de l'alpinisme. [Geneva, 1916?]. 202p.
    24cm.
    Offprint from l'Echo des Alpes.

KÜRSINGER, Ignaz von and SPITALER, Franz
    Der Gross-Venediger in der norischen Central-
    Alpenkette, seine erste Ersteigung am 3. September
    1841, und sein Gletscher ...; mit einem Anhange:
    Die zweite Ersteigung am 6. September 1842, von
    Dr. Spitaler. Innsbruck: Wagner, 1843. 310p.,
    plates (1 fold.), illus., maps. 24cm.

SPITTELER, Carl
    Der Gotthard. Frauenfeld: J. Huber, 1897. 250p.
    19cm.

SPOHR, Gregory
    Selected climbs in the Canmore area. Banff: Alpine
    Club of Canada, 1976. 37p., illus., map. 15cm.

SPOLETO, Duca di
    See
    AIMONE, Duke of Spoleto

SPON, Isaac
    Histoire de Genève; rectifiée et considérablement
    augm. par d'amples notes... Genève: Fabri &
    Barrillot, 1730. 4v., plates, illus., maps. 17cm.

SPON, Isaac
    Histoire de la ville et de l'état de Genève, depuis
    les premiers siècles de la fondation de la ville
    jusqu'à present... 2e éd. rev. et corr. Lyon:
    T. Amaulry, 1682. 2v., plates, illus. 16cm.

SPON, Isaac
    [Histoire de la ville et de l'état de Genève...].
    The history of the city and state of Geneva, from
    its first foundation to this present time. B.
    White, 1687. 250p., plates, illus., maps. 33cm.

SPONT, Henry
    Sur la montagne (les Pyrénées). Paris: Plon,
    Nourrit, 1898. 221p., illus. 22cm.

Sport in Europe; edited by F.G. Aflalo. Sands, 1901.
    xii, 483p., plates, illus. 29cm.

The sportsman's vade-mecum for the Himalayas: con-
    taining notes on shooting, outfit, camp equipment,
    sporting yarns ..., by K.C.A.J. H. Cox, 1891.
    120p., illus. 23cm.

SPRECHER, F   W   and NAEF-BLUMER, E
    [Clubführer durch die Bündner Alpen]. Clubführer
    durch die Graubündner-Alpen. (Tamina- und
    Plessurgebirge). Bd.1. St. Gallen: Schweizer
    Alpen-Club, 1916. 488p., illus., bibl. 17cm.
    (Clubführer des Schweizer Alpen-Club)

- - 2.Aufl., verfasst von F.W. Sprecher und C.
    Eggerling. 1925.
- - 3.Aufl., revidiert von Hans Schmid und Carl
    Eggerling-Jäger, 1958.

SPRECHER VON BERNEGG, Fortunat
    Rhetia, ubi eius verus situs, politia, bella,
    foedera, et alia memorabilia accuratissime des-
    cribuntur. Lugd. Batavorum: Ex officina
    Elzeviriana, 1633. 429p. 12cm.

SPRING, Ira and EDWARDS, Harvey
    100 hikes in the Alps. Leicester: Cordee, 1979.
    224p., illus., maps, bibl. 22cm.

SPRINGENSCHMID, Karl
    Bauern in den Bergen; in Worten von Karl
    Springenschmid; in Bildern von Peterpaul Atzwanger.
    München: F. Bruckmann, 1936. 175p., illus. 24cm.

SPRINGENSCHMID, Karl
    Da lacht Tirol: Geschichten aus dem Tiroler Volks-
    leben. Stuttgart: Kosmos, 1935. 125p. 21cm.

SPRUCE, Richard
    Notes of a botanist on the Amazon & Andes, being
    records of travel on the Amazon ... the Orinoco,
    along the eastern side of the Andes of Peru and
    Ecuador, and the shores of the Pacific, during
    the years 1849-1864; edited and condensed by
    Alfred Russel Wallace; with a biographical intro-
    duction. Macmillan, 1908. 2v., plates (some
    fold.col.), illus., maps. 23cm.

SPYRI, Johanna
    Heidi; illustrated by Leonard Weisgard; introduc-
    tion by May Lamberton Becker. World Publishing
    Co., 1946. 334p., col. plates, illus. 22cm.
    (Rainbow classics)

SPYRI, Johanna
    [Kurze Geschichten]. Swiss stories for children
    and those who love children; from the German of
    Madam Johanna Spyri by Lucy Wheelock; illustrated
    by Horace Petherick. Blackie, 1889. 208p.,
    plates, illus. 19cm.

STALDER, Franz Joseph
    Die Landessprachen der Schweiz; oder,
    Schweizerische Dialektologie, mit kritischen
    Sprachbemerkungen beleuchtet; nebst der Gleichniss-
    rede von dem verlorenen Sohne in allen Schweizer-
    mundarten. Aarau: H. Sauerländer, 1819. xii,
    424p. 22cm.

STALEY, Mrs.
    Autumn rambles; or, Fireside recollections of
    Belgium, the Rhine, the Moselle, German spas,
    Switzerland, the Italian lakes, Mont Blanc, and
    Paris, written by a lady [i.e. Mrs. Staley].
    Rochdale: Printed by E. Wrigley, 1863. vii,
    217p. 19cm.

STAMP, L   Dudley
    Britain's structure and scenery. Collins, 1946.
    xvi, 255p., plates (some col.), illus., maps,
    bibl. 23cm. (New naturalist)

Standard encyclopedia of the world's mountains;
    edited by Anthony Huxley. Weidenfeld & Nicholson,
    1962. 383p., 16 col. plates, illus., maps. 25cm.

STANDEN, R   S
    Continental way-side notes: the diary of a seven
    months' tour in Europe. [London]: Printed for
    private circulation, 1865. viii, 344p. 19cm.

STANDEN, R   S
    A trip to the Harz Mountains in the summer of
    1860. Oxford: [The Author], [1862]. 41p. 16cm.

STANLEY, Arthur Penrhyn
    Sinai and Palestine in connection with their
    history. Murray, 1856. 1v., 535p., maps. 24cm.

STANLEY, Henry M
    In darkest Africa; or, The quest rescue and
    retreat of Emin, Governor of Equatoria. Sampson
    Low, Marston, Searle and Rivington, 1890. 2v.,
    plates (some fold.col.), illus., maps. 24cm.

STANYAN, Abraham
    An account of Switzerland, written in the year
    1714, [by Abraham Stanyan]. J. Tonson, 1714.
    247p. 20cm.

STANYAN, Abraham
    L'état et les délices de la Suisse, en forme de
    relation critique ... [par Abraham Ruchat, Abraham
    Stanyan and others]. Amsterdam: Wetsteins et
    Smith, 1730. 4v., plates, illus., maps. 20cm.

STANYAN, Abraham
    L'état et les délices de la Suisse; ou, Descrip-
    tion helvetique, historique et géographique ...
    [par Abraham Ruchat, Abraham Stanyan and others].
    Nouv. éd., corr. & considérablement augm. par
    plusiers auteurs célèbres. Basle: E. Tourneisen,
    1764. 4v., fold. plates, illus., maps. 19cm.

- - Nouv. éd. ... Basle: Emanuel Tourneisen, 1776.

STANYAN, Abraham
État et délices de la Suisse; ou, Description
historique et géographique des treize cantons
suisses et de leurs alliés, [par Abraham Ruchat,
Abraham Stanyan and others]. Nouv. [5e] éd.,
corr. & considérablement augm... Neuchatel:
S. Fauche, 1778. 2v., plates, maps. 27cm.

STAPFER, Philipp Albert
Voyage pittoresque de l'Oberland; ou, Description
de vues prises dans l'Oberland, district du
Canton de Berne [par S. Weibel]; accompagné de
notices historiques et topographiques [par Philipp
A. Stapfer]. Paris: Treuttel & Würz, 1812. 90p.,
15 col. plates, illus., map. 35cm.

JACKSON, Monica and STARK, Elizabeth
Tents in the clouds: the first Women's Himalayan
Expedition. Collins, 1956. 255p., illus., maps.
22cm.

STARK, Freya
The southern gates of Arabia: journey in the
Hadhramaut. Murray, 1936. xii, 328p., plates
(some fold.), illus., maps, bibl. 25cm.

STARK, Freya
Traveller's prelude. Murray, 1950. xiii, 346p.,
plates, illus., map. 23cm.

STARK, Freya
The valleys of the assassins and other Persian
travels. Murray, 1934. 365p., plates (some fold.),
illus., maps. 23cm.

STARKE, Mariana
Information and directions for travellers on the
continent. 7th ed., thoroughly rev. Murray, 1829.
615p., plan. 21cm.

STARKE, Mariana
Letters from Italy; containing a view of the revolutions in that country... 2nd ed., rev. corr. and
considerably enl. by an itinerary of Chamouni, and
all the most frequented passes of the Alps... G. &
S. Robinson, 1815. 2v., 1 fold. plate, map. 24cm.

STARKLOF, L
Durch die Alpen; Kreuz- und Quer-Züge. Leipzig:
J.J. Weber, 1850. xv, 360p. 18cm.

STARR, Walter A
Guide to the John Muir trail and the high Sierra
region. San Francisco: Sierra Club, 1934. xiii,
145p., plates (1 fold.col.), map, port. 22cm.

STAUFFACHER, Johann
BAUMBACH, Rudolf
Schildereien aus dem Alpenlande: 30 Lichtdruck-
bilder nach Gemälden von Carl und Ernst Heyn;
Gedichte, von Rudolf Baumbach; Randzeichnungen von
Johann Stauffacher. Leipzig: A.G. Liebeskind,
1882. [84]p., illus. 49cm.

STEAD, Richard
Adventures on the high mountains: romantic incidents
& perils of travel, sport, and exploration throughout the world. Seeley, 1908. 327p., plates,
illus. 21cm.

HUG, Lina and STEAD, Richard
Switzerland. Fisher Unwin, [1891]. xxiv, 430p.,
illus., maps. 21cm. (The story of the nations,
26)

- - 2nd ed., rev. and enl. 1920.

STEBBING, E P
Stalks in the Himalaya: jottings of a sportsman-
naturalist ...; with ... illustrations by the
author & others. Bodley Head, 1912. xxviii,
321p., plates, illus. 23cm.

STEBLER, F G
Alp- und Weidewirtschaft: ein Handbuch für
Viehzüchter und Alpwirte. Berlin: P. Parey, 1903.
xii, 471p., illus., bibl. 25cm.

STEED, H Wickham
Belgium, Italy, and Switzerland, by G. Edmundson,
H. Wickham Steed, W.A.B. Coolidge. Encyclopaedia
Britannica, 1914. iv, 201p., plates, illus. 23cm.
Reproduced from the 11th ed. of the Encyclopaedia
Britannica.

STEEL, Charles
The Ben Nevis race. Fort William: C. Steel,
[1956]. 40p., plan. 18cm.

STEEL, W G
The mountains of Oregon. Portland (Oregon): D.
Steel, 1890. 112p., plates, illus., bibl. 24cm.

STEELE, Peter
Doctor on Everest: a personal account of the 1971
expedition. Hodder and Stoughton, 1972. 222p.,
plates, maps. 23cm.

STEELE, Peter
Medical care for mountain climbers. Heinemann
Medical Books, 1976. xi, 220p., illus. 19cm.

STEELE, Peter
Two and two halves to Bhutan: a family journey in
the Himalayas; line drawings by Phoebe Bullock.
Hodder & Stoughton, 1970. 191p., plates, illus.,
map (on lining papers). 23cm.

STEEPLE, E W
Island of Skye; edited by E.W. Steeple, G. Barlow
and H. MacRobert. Edinburgh: Scottish Mountaineering Club, 1923. 126p., plates (some fold.),
illus., map (in pocket). 23cm. (Scottish
Mountaineering Club guides, v.3., section A)

- - 2nd ed. rev. 1948.
- - 3rd ed. 1954.

COLLINGWOOD, William Gershom and STEFANSSON, Jón
A pilgrimage to the saga-steads of Iceland.
Ulverston: W. Holmes, 1899. x, 187p., col.
plates, illus., map. 29cm.

STEFANSSON, Vilhjalmur
Greenland. Harrap, 1943. 240p., plates, illus.,
map, bibl. 25cm.

STEIGER, Willy
Unserer Alpenfahrt: ein Schülerbriefwechsel im
Spiegel einer Schulfahrt ins österreichische
Alpenland; zusammengestellt von Willy Steiger.
Wien: Oesterreichischer Bunderverlag, 1925. 67p.,
plates (some col.), illus. 20cm.

STEIN, Christian Gottfried Daniel
Reise durch Baiern, Salzburg, Tirol, die Schweiz
und Württemberg. Leipzig; J.C. Hinrichs, 1829.
viii, 275p., plates, illus. 18cm.

STEIN, Sir Marc Aurel
Memoir on maps of Chinese Turkistan and Kansu from
the surveys made during Sir Aurel Stein's explorations, 1900-1, 1906-8, 1913-5; with appendices by
K. Mason and J. de Graaff Hunter. Dehra Dun:
Trigonometrical Survey Office, 1923. xv, 208p.,
30 plates, illus. 35cm. (Records of the Survey
of India, v.17)

STEIN, Sir Marc Aurel
Mountain panoramas from the Pamirs and Kwen Lun;
photographed and annotated by M. Aurel Stein.
Royal Geographical Society, 1908. 36p., fold.
plate, illus., map. 34cm.

STEIN, Sir Marc Aurel
On ancient Central-Asian tracks: brief narrative
of three expeditions in innermost Asia and northwestern China. Macmillan, 1933. xxiv, 342p.,
plates (some fold., some col.), illus., map.
25cm.

STEIN, Sir Marc Aurel
Ruins of desert Cathay: personal narrative of
explorations in central Asia and westernmost
China. Macmillan, 1912. 2v., plates (some fold.,
some col.), maps. 25cm.

STEIN, Sir Marc Aurel
Sand-buried ruins of Khotan: personal narrative of
a journey of archaeological and geographical exploration in Chinese Turkestan. Unwin, 1903.
xliii, 524p., plates (1 fold.col.), illus., map.
24cm.

STEINAUER, Ludwig
Der weisse Berg: meine Erlebnisse am Montblanc.
München: F. Bruckmann, 1941. 139p., plates (some
col.), illus. 23cm.

STEINBRÜCHEL, Ernst
Praktische Winke für den photographierenden
Bergfreund ...; zusammengestellt von Ernst
Steinbrüchel. 2., neu bearb., Ausg. München:
P. Müller, [1935]. 28p. 15cm.

STEINBRÜCK, J H T
Recueil d'études sur Nice et ses environs. Leipzig:
F.A. Brockhaus, 1891. viii, 413p. 23cm.
Extracts in French, English and German.

STEINER, André
Ski en Tarentaise et Maurienne: guide itinéraire,
par J. et B. Leclerc et A. Steiner et la Section
Lyonnaise du C.A.F. Paris: J. Susse [1948?].
240p., fold. plates, maps. 18cm. (Guide Susse)
Publié sous le patronage officiel de Fédération
Française de la Montagne, Fédération Française de
Ski, Club Alpin Français.

STEINER, Johann
Der Reise-Gefährte durch die oesterreichische
Schweiz; oder, Das obderennsische Salzkammergut ...
2. verm. und verb. Aufl. Linz: J. Fink, 1829.
xxiv, 450p., plates, illus. 17cm.

STEINER, Leonhard
Jungfraubahn: Festspiel zur Einweihung der 1.
Sektion Scheidegg-Gletscher. Zürich: [n.pub.],
[1898]. 7p. 22cm.
In portfolio.

STEINER, Louis
Mélanges alpestres; [tirés du Fédéral, du Tribune
et du Journal de Genève et recueillis par Louis
Steiner]. Genève, 1869 [-1901]. 1v. (various
pagings). 23cm.
Press cuttings.

STEINITZER, Alfred
Der Alpinismus in Bildern. München: R. Piper,
1913. x, 482p., 8 col. plates, illus. 31cm.

- - 2. ergänzte Aufl. 1924.

STEINITZER, Alfred
Geschichtliche und kulturgeschichtliche
Wanderungen durch Tirol und Vorarlberg. Innsbruck:
Wagner, 1905. xvi, 530p., plates, illus., map,
bibl. 22cm.

STEINITZER, Alfred
Das Land Tirol: Geschtliche, Kulture und Kunst-
geschichliche Wanderungen. Innsbruck: Wagner, 1922.
xvi, 610p., illus. 18cm.

STEINITZER, Enrico
See
STEINITZER, Heinrich

STEINITZER, Heinrich
HESS, Adolfo
Saggi sulla psicologia dell'alpinista: raccolta di
autobiografie psicologiche di alpinisti viventi;
con introduzione di Enrico Steinitzer: La
psicologia dell'alpinismo. Torino: S. Lattes,
1914. xii, 613p., ports., bibl. 21cm.

STEINITZER, Wilhelm
Japanische Bergfahrten: Wanderungen fern von
Touristenpfaden. München: E. Reinhardt, 1918.
120p., 33 plates (1 fold.), illus., maps. 24cm.

STELLING-MICHAUD, S
Visage de la Perse; préface du général Sir Percy
Sykes. Lausanne: C. Bonnard, 1931. 104p. 23cm.

STEPHEN, Sir Leslie
The playground of Europe. Longmans, Green, 1871.
xii, 321p., plates, illus. 20cm.

- - New ed. 1894.
- - New ed. 1895.
- - Another issue. 1899.
- - Another issue. Oxford: Blackwell, 1936.

STEPHEN, Sir Leslie
[The playground of Europe]. Le terrain de jeu de
l'Europe; traduit par Claire-Éliane Engel.
Neuchatel: Attinger, 1935. 269p., plates, illus.
21cm. (Montagne)

STEPHEN, Sir Leslie
[The playground of Europe]. Der Spielplatz
Europas; mit einer Einleitung von G. Winthrop
Young; Ubersetzt und bearb. von Henry Hoek; hrsg.
von der Schweizerischen Stiftung für Ausseralpine
Forschungen. Zürich: Amstutz, Herdeg, 1942.
272p., plates, illus. 22cm.

STEPHEN, Sir Leslie
ANNAN, Noel Gilroy
Leslie Stephen; his thought and character in relation to his time. Macgibbon and Kee, 1951.
viii, 342p., plates, illus., bibl. 23cm.

STEPHEN, Sir Leslie
MAITLAND, Frederick William
The life and letters of Leslie Stephen. Duckworth,
1906. ix, 510p., plates, ports., bibl. 24cm.

STERN, Bernhard
Vom Kaukasus zum Hindukusch: Reisemomente; mit ...
einem Anhang: Kaukasische Marschrouten. Berlin:
Cronbach, 1893. vii, 322p., illus. 19cm.

STEUB, Ludwig
Kleinere Schriften. Bd.1. Reiseschilderungen.
Stuttgart: J.G. Cotta, 1873. iv, 276p. 18cm.

STEUB, Ludwig
Wanderungen im bayerischen Gebirge. 2.verm. Aufl.
München: G.A. Fleischmann, 1864. 332p. 19cm.

STEUB, Ludwig
Zur Namens- und Landeskunde der deutschen Alpen.
Nördlingen: C.H. Beck, 1885. iv, 174p. 21cm.

STEVEN, Campbell
The island hills. Hurst & Blackett, 1955. 190p.,
plates, illus., maps. 22cm.

STEVEN, Campbell
The story of Scotland's hills. Hale, 1975.
192p., plates, illus., map. 23cm.

STEVENS, Ernest H
MOORE, Adolphus Warburton
The Alps in.1864: a private journal; edited by
E.H. Stevens. Oxford: Blackwell, 1939. 2v.,
plates, illus., maps. 21cm. (Blackwell's
mountaineering library, 5)

STEVENS, Ernest H
Dr. Paccard's diary. [London], 1934. 13p.,
plates (1 col.), illus. 23cm.
Offprint from Alpine journal, v.46, May 1934.

STEVENS, Ernest H
Dr. Paccard's "Lost narrative": an attempted
reconstruction, by E.H. Stevens. [London,
1929-30]. 2pts., plates (some col.), illus.
23cm.
Offprint from Alpine journal, v.41, 1929 and
v.42, 1930.

STEVENS, Ernest H
In the footsteps of Dr. Paccard. [London],
1935-37. 2pts., plates (1 col.), illus., map.
23cm.
Offprint from Alpine journal v.47, 1935 and v.49,
1937.

STEVENSON, Seth William
A tour in France, Savoy, Northern Italy,
Switzerland, Germany and the Netherlands, in the
summer of 1825; including some observations on the
scenery of the Neckar and the Rhine. C. & J.
Rivington, 1827. 2v. 24cm.

STEVENSON, Vivian N
Cornwall. Vol.2; with diagrams by C. Fishwick.
Stockport: Climbers' Club. 1966. x, 150p., plates,
illus., maps. 16cm. (Climbers' Club guides)

SCHMID, Herman von and STIELER, Karl
[Aus deutschen Bergen]. The Bavarian Highlands and
the Salzkammergut; profusely illustrated by G.
Closs [and others]; with an account of the habits
and manners of the hunters, poachers, and peasantry
of these districts. Chapman & Hall, 1874. ix,
205p., plates, illus. 36cm.

SCHMID, Herman von and STIELER, Karl
Wanderungen im bayerischen Gebirge und
Salzkammergut; geschildert von Herman von Schmid
und Karl Steiler; illustrirt von Gustav Closs [and
others]. 2.Aufl. Stuttgart: Kröner, [1878]. vii,
215p., plates, illus. 38cm. (Unser Vaterland)
First ed. published under title: Aus deutschen
Bergen.

STIELER, Karl. [Wanderungen im bayerischen Gebirge
und Salzkammergut].
KADEN, Woldemar
Switzerland and the Bavarian Highlands. Virtue,
[1879]. 2v. (xiv, 628p.), plates, illus. 35cm.
Translated from "Das Schweizerland" by Woldemar
Kaden, and "Wanderungen im Bayerischen Gebirge und
Salzkammergut" by Herman von Schmid and Karl
Stieler.

STILES, William F   and WAY, H   John
Austria; line illustrations by Reg Gammon. Vane,
1954. 110p., 1 fold. plate, illus., maps. 16cm.
("Good companion" guides, no.1)

STILLINGFLEET, Benjamin
Literary life and select works of Benjamin
Stillingfleet ...; [edited by W. Coxe]. Longman,
Hurst, Rees, Orme and Brown, 1811. 3v. in 1,
plates, illus. 22cm.

STOBART, Tom
Adventurer's eye: the autobiography of Everest
film-man Tom Stobart. Odhams Press, 1958. 256p.,
plates, illus. 23cm.

STOCK, E   Elliot
Scrambles in storm and sunshine among the Swiss
and English alps. J. Ouseley, [1910]. 210p.,
plates, illus. 24cm.

ASHTON, John R   and STOCKS, F   Arnold
The open air guide, for wayfarers of all kinds.
Heywood, 1928. 209p., 1 fold. plate, illus., map.
18cm.

STODDARD, Frederick Wolcott
Tramps through Tyrol: life, sport, and legend.
Mills & Boon, 1912. x, 299p., plates (1 fold.,
some col.), illus., map. 23cm.

STODDART, John
Remarks on local scenery & manners in Scotland
during the years 1799 and 1800. W. Miller, 1801.
2v. 25cm.

STÖLKER, Carl
Die Alpenvögel der Schweiz. Ser.1., dargestellt
von Carl Stölker; photographirt von Gebrüder
Taeschler. St. Fiden bei St. Gallen: The Author,
[1876]. 1v. (chiefly illus.). 34cm.

STOFFEL, Joh. Rud.
Das Hochtal Avers, Graubünden: die höchstgelegene
Gemeinde Europas; dargestellt von Joh. Rud. Stoffel.
Zofingen: Zofinger Tagblatt, 1938. x, 260p.,
plates, illus. 24cm.

STOLBERG, Friedrich Leopold, Graf zu
Travels through Germany, Switzerland, Italy, and
Sicily; translated by Thomas Holcroft. 2nd ed.
G.G. & J. Robinson, 1797. 4v., plates, illus.,
map. 22cm.

STONE, James Kent
SMITH, Walter George and Helen Grace
Fidelis of the Cross; James Kent Stone. 2nd ed.
New York, London: Putnam, 1927. xvi, 467p.,
plates, illus. 24cm.

STONE, Olivia M
Norway in June; with illustrations from photographs taken during the tour... Ward, 1882. xv,
448p., plates, illus., map. 20cm.

STONE, S   J
In and beyond the Himalayas: a record of sport
and travel in the abode of snow; illustrated by
Charles Whymper. Arnold, 1896. xix, 330p.,
plates, illus. 24cm.

ROSS, Mars and STONEHEWER-COOPER, H
The highlands of Cantabria; or, Three days from
England. Sampson Low, Marston, Searle &
Rivington, 1885. xvi, 378p., 1 plate, illus.,
map. 24cm.

STONER, Charles
The Sherpa and the snowman; with a foreword by
Sir John Hunt. Hollis & Carter, 1955. xii,
209p., plates, illus. 23cm.

STOPPANI, Antonio
Il bel paese: conversazioni sulle bellezze
naturali, la geologia e la geografia fisica
d'Italia. 4a ed. Milano: Agnelli, 1883. xv,
645p., illus., maps. 23cm.

STOPPANI, P
Come d'autunno... Milano: L.F. Cogliati, 1903.
x, 294p., plates (1 fold.), illus. 24cm.

Stories from Switzerland and the Tyrol. Nelson,
1853. viii, 494p., plates, illus. 17cm.

STORR, G   K   Ch
Alpenreise vom Jahre 1781. Leipzig: J. Müller,
1784-86. 2v., 7 plates, illus. 21cm.

STORY, Alfred Thomas
North Wales. Methuen, 1907. viii, 289p., plates
(1 fold.col.), illus., map. 16cm. (Little
guides)

STOWE, Harriet Beecher
Sunny memories of foreign lands. Author's ed.
with illustrations. Sampson Low, 1854. x, 539p.,
plates, illus. 19cm.

STRACHEY, Henry
Narrative of a journey to Cho Lagan (Rákas Tal),
Cho Mapan (Mánasarówar) and the valley of Pruang
in Gnari, Húndés, in September and October 1846.
[London], 1848. 3pts. in 1., 1 fold.col. plate,
map. 23cm.
Offprint from Journal of the Asiatic Society,
1848.

STRAHL, Adolph
Ein Sommer in der Schweiz: Reisebilder aus den
Alpen. Wien: Tendler & Schaefer, 1840. 224p.
20cm.

STRANG, John
Travelling notes in France, Italy and Switzerland
of an invalid in search of health, [i.e. John
Strang]. Glasgow: D. Robertson; London: Longman,
1863. xix, 266p. 20cm.

STRANG, Tom
The northern Highlands. Edinburgh: Scottish
Mountaineering Trust, 1970. 222p., plates, illus.,
maps, bibl. 22cm. (Scottish Mountaineering Club
district guide books)

- - 2nd ed. 1975.

Strange tales of peril and adventure. Religious
Tract Society, [18--]. 332p., plates, illus.
21cm.

STRASSER, Gottfried
Der Napf: der Rigi des Emmenthals (1408m).
Langnau: F. Wyss, 1883. 22p., illus. 20cm.

STRATZ, Rudolph
Montblanc: Roman. Stuttgart: Cotta, 1899. 250p.
21cm.

STRATZ, Rudolph
Die Thörichte Jungfrau: Roman. 4.Aufl. Stuttgart:
Cotta, 1901. 409p. 21cm.

STRAWBRIDGE, Anne West
Shadows of the Matterhorn. Zurich: The Author,
[ca 1950]. 19p. 19cm.

STREIFF-BECKER, R
Altes und Neues über den Glarner-Föhn. Glarus,
1930. 52p., plates, illus., bibl. 23cm.
Offprint from Mitteilungen der Naturforschenden
Gesellschaft des Kantons Glarus, 1930.

STREIT, Conrad
Souvenir Schweiz = Souvenirs de Suisse = Souvenir
book of Switzerland = Visioni svizzere; preface by
Werner Kämpfen; text by Conrad Streit. Wabern:
Souvenir Book Publishers, 1968. 228p., illus.
19 x 25cm.
Text in German, French, Italian and English.

STRICKLAND, F   de Beauchamp
The Engadine: a guide to the district; with
articles by John Addington Symonds [and others].
2nd ed. Sampson Low, Marston, Searle & Rivington,
1891. vi, 339p., 3 fold. plates (2 col.), maps.
15cm.

STRONG, John H
Mountaineering: a solace to sedate old age. [New
York], 1949. 165-171p., plates, illus. 23cm.
Offprint from American alpine journal, v.7, no.2,
1949.

STROUDE, Ben C
MERSEYSIDE HIMALAYAN EXPEDITION, 1977
Report, by B.C. Stroude. Wirral: The Expedition,
[1978?]. 34p., illus. 21cm.

STRÜVER, G
GASTALDI, Bartolomeo
Studii geologici sulle Alpi occidentali; con
appendice mineralogica di G. Strüver. Firenze,
1871-74. 2pts., plates (some fold., some col.),
illus. 36cm. (Memorie per servire alla descrizione della Carte geologica d'Italia)
Offprint from Memorie del R. Comitato geologico
d'Italia, v.1, 1871.

STRUTT, Edward Lisle
The Alps of the Bernina W. of the Bernina Pass.
Fisher Unwin, 1910. 2v., 1 fold. plate, map (in
pocket). 14cm. (Conway and Coolidge's climbers'
guides)

STRUTT, Elizabeth
Domestic residence in Switzerland. T.C. Newby,
1842. 2v., col. plates, illus. 22cm.

STUART, A   A   Verrijn
See
VERRIJN STUART, Xander

STUART-WATT, Eva
Africa's dome of mystery: comprising the first descriptive history of the Wachagga people of
Kilimanjaro ... and a girl's pioneer climb to the
crater of their 19,000ft snow shrine; preface by
Sir H.H. Stileman. Marshall, Morgan & Scott,
[1930]. 215p., plates (1 fold.), illus., map.
26cm.

STUCK, Hadson
The ascent of Denali (Mt. McKinley): a narrative of
the first complete ascent of the highest peak in
North America. Bickers, 1914. 188p., illus. 22cm.

STUCK, Hudson
The ascent of Denali: first complete ascent of
Mt. McKinley, highest peak in North America; containing the original diary of Walter Harper, first
man to achieve Denali's true summit. Seattle: The
Mountaineers, 1977. xiii, xix, 188, A-Z, AA-FFp.,
plates, illus., maps. 22cm.

STUCK, Hudson
Ten thousand miles with a dog sled: a narrative
of winter travel in interior Alaska. T. Werner
Laurie, [1914]. xix, 420p., plates (1 fold.col.),
illus., map. 24cm.

STUCKART, Carl Friedrich
Neuestes Gemälde der Erde und ihrer Bewohner;
oder, Schilderung der vorzüglichsten Merkwürdigkeitn, der Sitten und Gebräuche ... der Völkerschaften aller Welttheile ... die Schweiz; [hrsg.
von Carl Friedrich Stuckart]. Schweidnitz, 1824.
199, 133p. 24cm.

STUCKI, G
Schülerbüchlein für den Unterricht in der
Schweizer-Geographie. 7.Aufl... Zürich: Orell
Füssli, 1919. ix, 137p., illus. 21cm.

STUDER, Bernhard
Geologie der Schweiz. Bern: Stämpflischer Verlag,
1851-53. 2v., 1 fold.col. plate, illus., map.
20cm.

STUDER, Bernhard
Geschichte der physischen Geographie der Schweiz
bis 1815. Bern: Stämpflische Verlagshandlung,
1863. 696p. 23cm.

STUDER, Bernhard
Index der Petrographie und Stratigraphie der
Schweiz und ihrer Umgebungen. Bern: Dalp, 1872.
v, 272p. 24cm.

STUDER, Bernhard
STUDER, Gottlieb
Topographische Mittheilungen aus dem Alpengebirge.
1. Die Eiswüsten und selten betretenen Hochalpen
und Bergspitzen des Kantons Bern und angrenzender
Gegenden; eingeführt von Bernard Studer. Bern:
Huber, 1843. 172p. and atlas. 19cm.
No more published.

- - 2.Ausg. 1844.

STUDER, Gottlieb
Berg- und Gletscher-Fahrten in den Hochalpen der
Schweiz, von G. Studer, M. Ulrich, J.J. Weilenmann.
Zürich: F. Schulthess, 1859-63. 2v., plates,
illus. 19cm.

STUDER, Gottlieb
Der Kampf um die Gipfel. Zürich: Füssli, [1920].
90p., plates, illus. 19cm. (Schweizer Jugendbücher, Bd.8)

STUDER, Gottlieb
Panorama vom Mänlichen (Berner Oberland) 2345m.,
aufgenommen von G. Studer; gezeichnet von W.
Benteli. Bern: Dalp, [1874]. 13p., 1 fold.col.
plate, illus. 29cm.

STUDER, Gottlieb
Panorama vom Mattwald oder Simmelihorn im Wallis
(3270m...); nach der Natur gezeichnet den 16. Juli
1840 von G. Studer. Bern: [n.publ], [1840].
22cm.

STUDER, Gottlieb
Das Panorama von Bern: Schilderung der in Berns
Umgebungen sichtbaren Gebirge; mit einer vom
Eichplatz in der Enge aufgenommen Alpenansicht.
Bern: L.R. Walthard, 1850. iv, 252p., 1 fold.
plate, illus. 18cm.

STUDER, Gottlieb
Pontresina und Engelberg: Aufzeichnungen aus den
Jahren 1826-1863: Festgabe der Sektion Bern des
S.A.C. an die Theilnehmer des Clubfestes in Bern
21.-23. September 1907. Bern: Francke, 1907.
63p., plates (1 col.), illus. 19cm.
In slip-case.

STUDER, Gottlieb
Topographische Mittheilungen aus dem Alpengebirge.
1. Die Eiswüsten und selten betretenen Hochalpen
und Bergspitzen des Kantons Bern und angrenzender
Gegenden; eingeführt von Bernhard Studer. Bern:
Huber, 1843. 172p. and atlas. 19cm.
No more published.

- - 2.Ausg. 1844.

STUDER, Gottlieb
Ueber Eis und Schnee: die höchsten Gipfel der
Schweiz und die Geschichte ihrer Besteigung. Bern:
Dalp, 1869. 4v. in 2. 18cm.

- - 2.Aufl., umgearb. und ergänzt von A. Wäber und
H. Dübi. Bern: Schmid, Francke, 1896-99. 3v.

STUDER, Gottlieb
Über Gletscher und Gipfel; hrsg. und mit Lebensbild versehen von Ernst Jenny. Erlenbach-Zürich:
Rentsch, 1931. 447p., plates (1 fold.), illus.
21cm.

HOFMANN, Karl and STÜDL, Johann
Wanderungen in der Glockner-Gruppe; mit einem
botanischen Anhang... München: J. Lindauer, 1871.
393p., plates (some fold.col.), illus., map. 22cm.

STURM, August
Deutsches Liederbuch. 3.verm. Aufl. Halle a. S.:
O. Hendel, 1911. xv, 256p. 19cm.

STURM, Günter
Erfolg am Kantsch 8438m: die Himalaya-Expedition
des Deutschen und Österreichischen Alpenvereins.
München: BLV, 1975. 142p., illus. (some col.),
maps, bibl. 21cm.

STUTFIELD, Hugh Edward Millington
The brethren of Mount Atlas, being the first part
of an African Theosophical story. Longmans, Green,
1891. iv, 313p. 20cm.

STUTFIELD, Hugh Edward Millington and COLLIE, John
Norman
Climbs & exploration in the Canadian Rockies.
Longmans, Green, 1903. xii, 342p., plates (1 fold.
col.), illus., maps. 23cm.

HASSE, Dietrich and STUTTE, Heinz Lothar
Meteora Felsen: Wander- and Kletterführer; verfasst
nach den Richtlinien der UIAA. München: Geo-Buch
Verlag, 1977. 127p., illus., maps, bibl. 17cm.
(Wander- und Kletterführer, 1)

STYLES, Showell
The Arrow book of climbing. Arrow Books, 1967.
192p., plates, illus. 18cm.

STYLES, Showell
Backpacking: a comprehensive guide. Macmillan,
1976. 91p., illus. (some col.), bibl. 23cm.

STYLES, Showell
Backpacking in Alps and Pyrenees. Gollancz, 1976.
191p., plates, illus., maps. 23cm.

STYLES, Showell
A climber in Wales; with a foreword by L.S. Amery.
Birmingham: Cornish Bros., [ca 1948]. 85p., plates,
illus., maps (on lining papers), bibl. 22cm.

STYLES, Showell
The climber's bedside book. Faber & Faber, 1968.
256p., illus. 21cm.

STYLES, Showell
Death on Milestone buttress. Bles, 1951. 285p.,
illus. 20cm.

STYLES, Showell
Death under Snowdon. Bles, 1954. 238p. 19cm.

STYLES, Showell
First on the summits; with diagrams by R.B. Evans.
Gollancz, 1970. 157p., plates, illus., maps, bibl.
23cm.

STYLES, Showell
Introduction to mountaineering. Seeley Service,
[1954]. 159p., plates, illus., bibl. 22cm.
(Beaufort library v.4)

STYLES, Showell
The ladder of snow. Gollancz, 1962. 189p. 21cm.

STYLES, Showell
The moated mountain. Hurst and Blackett, 1955.
255p., plates (1 col.), illus., maps. 23cm.

STYLES, Showell
Modern mountaineering. Faber & Faber, 1964.
189p., 8 plates, illus. 23cm.

STYLES, Showell
The mountaineer's week-end book; decorated by
Thomas Beck. Seeley Service, 1950. 408p., illus.
20cm. (Week-end series)

STYLES, Showell
Mountains of the midnight sun. Hurst and Blackett,
1954. 208p., plates, illus. 23cm.

STYLES, Showell
On top of the world: an illustrated history of
mountaineering and mountaineers; with an introduction by Fosco Maraini. Hamish Hamilton, 1967.
xx, 278p., 32 col. plates, illus. 27cm.

STYLES, Showell
Rock and rope. Faber & Faber, 1967. 174p.,
plates, illus. 21cm.

STYLES, Showell
The shop in the mountain. Gollancz, 1961. 191p.,
illus., map. 21cm.

STYLES, Showell
Snowdon range; diagrams by Brian Evans. Goring,
Reading: Gaston's Alpine Books, West Col, 1973.
94p., illus., maps (on lining papers), bibl.
22cm. (Snowdonia district guide books)

STYLES, Showell
Swing away, climber. Bles, 1959. 256p., illus.
19cm.

SUBIRÁ, José
Mi valle pirenaico: cuadros novelescos. Madrid:
Paez, 1927. 159p. 20cm.

SUESS, Eduard
[Das Antlitz der Erde]. The face of the earth;
translated by Hertha B.C. Sollas, under the direction of W.J. Sollas. Oxford: Clarendon Press,
1904-09. 4v., plates (some col.), illus., maps.
20cm.
Library lacks v.2.

SUESS, Eduard
[Das Antlitz der Erde]. La face de la terre.
T.1. Les montagnes; traduit de l'allemand ... et
annoté sous la direction de Emm. de Margerie;
avec une préface par Marcel Bertrand. Paris:
Colin, 1905. xv, 835p., plates (some col.),
illus., maps. 26cm.

SUESS, Eduard
Die Entstehung der Alpen. Wien: Braumuller, 1875.
iv, 168p. 25cm.

SUGLIANI, L B
Guida sciistica delle Orobie. 2a ed. Bergamo:
Club Alpino Italiano, Sezione A. Locatelli, 1971.
330p., plates (some fold.), illus., col. maps.
17cm.

La Suisse: étude géographique, démographique,
politique, économique et historique, par A. Aeppli
[and others]. Neuchatel: Direction du dictionnaire géographique de la Suisse, [1908]. ix,
709p., 1 fold. plate, illus., maps. 30cm.

La Suisse illustrée. Genève: F. Margueron, [1856?].
lv. (chiefly col. illus.). 16 x 23cm.
Cover title: Souvenirs de la Suisse et des Alpes.

SULZER, Johann Georg
SCHEUCHZER, Johann Jacob
  Natur-Geschichte des Schweitzerlandes, samt seinen
  Reisen über die schweitzerische Gebürge; aufs neue
  hrsg., und mit Anmerkungen versehen von Joh. Georg
  Sulzern. Zürich: Gessner, 1746. 2v. in 1, plates
  (some fold.), illus., maps. 22cm.

SULZER, Johann Georg
  Untersuchung von dem Ursprung der Berge, und andrer
  damit verknüpsten Dinge. Zürich: Gessner, 1746.
  44p., plates, illus. 22cm.

Summer and winter in the Pyrenees, by the author of
  "The women of England" ... [i.e. Sarah Ellis].
  Fisher, [1841]. xii, 393p., 1 plate, illus. 21cm.

- - [Another ed.] by Mrs. Ellis. [1847].

The summer tour of an invalid. Saunders, Otley,
  1860. vii, 120p. 18cm.
  Describes a tour in Switzerland.

SUMNER, John
  Central Wales: Craig Cowarch and the Arans.
  Goring, Reading: West Col, 1973. 153p., plates,
  illus., maps. 17cm. (West Col regional climbing
  guides)

SUMNER, John
  Dolgellau area: Cader Idris and the Rhinog Range;
  sketches by R. Thorndyke. Goring, Reading: West
  Col, 1975. 139p., illus., map. 17cm. (West Col
  regional climbing guides)

SUNDSTRÖM, Lennart
  Scandinavia in pictures: a pictorial rhapsody in
  collaboration with Scandinavia's foremost photographers; compiled and edited by Lennart
  Sundström; English text by Burnett Andersson.
  Stockholm: A.B. Lindqvists Förlag, 1949. 1v. of
  illus. 31cm.

SUNDT, Eilert
  The first winter-ascent of the Aconcagua, September
  1915. [Buenos Aires]: The Author, [1915]. 8p.,
  plates, illus. 28cm.

SUNDT, Eilert
  Patagonia: pa kryss og tvers. [Oslo]: Raabe, 1942.
  157p., plates (1 fold.), illus., maps, bibl. 23cm.

SUPF, Peter
  Flieger erobern die Berge der Welt. München:
  Nymphenburger Verlagshandlung, 1956. 175p., plates,
  illus., bibl. 21cm.

SURBEK, Victor
HALLER, Albrecht von
  [Die Alpen]. Les Alpes; 16 lithographies
  originales de Victor Surbek. Lausanne: A. Gonin,
  1944. 113p., illus. 28cm. (Collection des
  flambeaux, 4)

SURVEY OF INDIA
  Annual reports of parties and offices, 1919-20;
  prepared under the direction of C.H.D. Ryder.
  Dehra Dun: Survey of India, 1921. 134p., plates
  (some fold.col.), illus., maps. 35cm. (Records of
  the Survey of India, v.15)

SURVEY OF INDIA
  Catalogue of maps. Parts 1 and 2, corrected up to
  31st March 1928; published under the direction of
  E.A. Tandy. Calcutta: Survey of India, 1928. vii,
  37p., col. plates, maps. 35cm.

SURVEY OF INDIA
  Completion of the link connecting the triangula-
  tions of India and Russia, 1913; prepared under the
  direction of Sir S.G. Burrard. Dehra Dun: Survey
  of India, 1914. 121p., plates (some fold.), illus.,
  maps. 33cm. (Records of the Survey of India, v.6)

SURVEY OF INDIA
  Descriptions and co-ordinates of the principal
  and secondary stations and other fixed points of
  North-West Himalaya series (or Series C of the
  N.W. Quadrilateral) and the triangulation of the
  Kashmir Survey, by J.T. Walker and his assistants.
  Dehra Dun: Survey of India, 1879. xiii, lxxiii,
  293p., fold. plates, maps. 32cm. (Synopsis of
  the results of the operations of the Great Trigo-
  nometrical Survey of India, v.7)

SURVEY OF INDIA
  Descriptions and co-ordinates of the principal and
  secondary stations and other fixed points of the
  North-East longitudinal series of triangulation
  (or Series I of the N.E. Quadrilateral); prepared
  under the direction of S.G. Burrard. Dehra Dun:
  Survey of India, 1909. 2v., plates, maps. 31cm.
  (Synopsis of the results of the operations of the
  Great Trigonometrical Survey of India, v.35)

SURVEY OF INDIA
  Explorations in the eastern Kara-korum and the
  upper Yārkand valley: narrative report of the
  Survey of India detachment with the De Filippi
  Scientific Expedition 1914, [by H. Wood]. Dehra
  Dun: Survey of India, 1922. iii, 42p., plates
  (some fold., some col.), illus., maps (in pocket).
  44cm.

SURVEY OF INDIA
  Historical records of the Survey of India; col-
  lected and compiled by R.H. Phillimore. Dehra
  Dun: Survey of India, 1945-58. Plates (some
  fold.), illus., maps. 30cm.
  Vol.1. 18th century. 1945. -v.2. 1800 to 1815.
  1950. -v.3. 1815-1830. 1954. -v.4. 1830-1843:
  George Everest. 1958.

SURVEY OF INDIA
  Map catalogue, corrected up to 30 Nov. 1931;
  published under the direction of R.H. Thomas.
  Calcutta: Survey of India, 1931. 35p., plates
  (some fold.col.), maps. 35cm.

SUTCLIFFE, Constance
  Our lady of the ice: a story of the Alps.
  Greening, 1909. 128p. 22cm. (Greening's popu-
  lar "sixpennies")

SUTER, Joh. Rudolf
  Helvetiens flora enthaltend die Phänerogamischen
  Gewächse Helvetiens. Vol.2; zuerst bearb. Joh.
  Rudolf Suter; verm. hrsg., von Joh. Hegetschweiler.
  Zürich: Orell, Füssli, 1822. 504p. 15cm.

SUTTON, Geoffrey
  Artificial aids in mountaineering. Kaye, 1962.
  64p., illus. 19cm.
  Published under the auspices of the Mountaineering
  Association.

BYNE, Eric and SUTTON, Geoffrey
  High Peak: the story of walking and climbing in
  the Peak District; with a foreword by Patrick
  Monkhouse. Secker & Warburg, 1966. 256p., plates,
  illus., bibl. 23cm.

SUTTON, Geoffrey and NOYCE, Wilfrid
  Samson: the life and writings of Menlove Edwards;
  edited with biographical memoir by Geoffrey Sutton
  and Wilfrid Noyce. Stockport: Cloister Press,
  1960. ix, 122p., plates, illus. 22cm.

SUTTON, Geoffrey
  Snowdon biography, by Geoffrey Winthrop Young,
  Geoffrey Sutton, and Wilfrid Noyce; edited by
  Wilfrid Noyce. Dent, 1957. xiii, 195p., plates,
  illus., maps (on lining papers), bibl. 22cm.

SUTTON, Graham
  Fell days. Museum Press, 1948. 221p., plates,
  illus., map. 22cm.

SVENONIUS, Fredric
Lappland, samt öfriga delar af Väster- och
Norrbottens län; utarb. af Fredr. Svenonius. 3.
uppl. Stockholm: S.T., 1904. xi, 195p., 1 fold.
col. plate, map (in pocket). 17cm. (Resehand-
böcker, 9)

SVENSKA HIMALAYA EXPEDITIONEN, 1973
Reserapport: Svenska Himalaya Expeditionen 1973;
[rapporten sammenställd av Bo Söderberg].
[Västeras]: The Expedition, [1974]. 67p., plates,
illus., maps. 21cm.
Summary in English.

SVENSKA TURISTFÖRENINGEN
Lappland, samt öfriga delar af Väster- och
Norbottens län; utarb. af Fredr. Svenonius. 3.
uppl. Stockholm: S.T., 1904. xi, 195p., 1 fold.
col. plate, map (in pocket). 17cm. (Resehand-
böcker, 9)

SVENSKA TURISTFÖRENINGEN
The Swedish Touring Club's Guide to Sweden.
Philip, 1898. xlii, 244p., fold.col. plates, maps.
17cm.

SVENSKA TURISTTRAFIKFÖRBUNDET
A book about Sweden. Stockholm: Swedish Traffic
Association, 1922. 183p., 1 fold.col. plate,
illus., maps. 21cm.

La Svizzera. Nouva. ed. Milano: Treves, 1909. xxi,
254p., plates, maps, plans. 16cm. (Guides Treves,
N.S.)

La Svizzera secondo il Coxe, l'Ebel ed altri piu
moderni viaggiatori, si aggiungono alcuni cenni
sulla storia, i monumenti, le leggi ed i costumi.
Milano: Vallardi, [ca 1820]. 230, 88p., plates,
illus. 13cm.
Cover title: Manuale della Svizzera...

SWAN, Eugene L
Harper's Camping and scouting: an outdoor guide
for American boys; consulting editors George Bird
Grinnell, Eugene L. Swan. New York, London:
Harper, 1911. xvi, 398p., illus. 21cm.

SWAYNE, H   G   C
Through the highlands of Siberia. Rowland Ward,
1904. xiv, 259p., 1 fold. plate, illus., map.
24cm.

SWEDISH TOURING CLUB
See
SVENSKA TURISTFÖRENINGEN

SWEDISH TRAFFIC ASSOCIATION
See
SVENSKA TURISTTRAFIKFÖRBUNDET

CHMIELOWSKI, Janusz and SWIERZ, Mieczysław
Tatry Wysokie (przewodnik szczegółowy). Tom 1.
Cześć Ogólna-Doliny, Kraków: Wydawnictw Sekcji
Turyst. Pol. Tow. Tatrz., 1925. 118p., illus.
16cm.

SWINBURNE, T   R
A holiday in the happy valley with pen and pencil.
Smith, Elder, 1907. xii, 342p., col. plates (1
fold.), illus., map. 24cm.

SWISS FEDERAL RAILWAYS
See
SCHWEIZERISCHE BUNDESBAHNEN

SWISS FOUNDATION FOR ALPINE RESEARCH
See
SCHWEIZERISCHE STIFTUNG FÜR ALPINE FORSCHUNGEN

SWISS NATIONAL TOURIST OFFICE
See
SCHWEIZERISCHE VERKEHRSZENTRALE

Swiss notes, by five ladies. Leeds: Inchbold & Beck,
1875. vii, 136p., plates, illus. 25cm.

Swiss pictures drawn with pen and pencil, [by Samuel
Manning]; the illustrations by E. Whymper.
Religious Tract Society, [1866]. 214p., plates,
illus. 29cm.

- - New and enl. ed. [3rd ed.]. 1871.
- - New and enl. ed. [ca 1875].
- - New and enl. ed. [1880].
- - New ed., rev. 1891.

SWISS SOCIETY FOR BALNEOLOGY AND CLIMATOLOGY
See
SCHWEIZERISCHE GESELLSCHAFT FÜR BALNEOLOGIE UND
KLIMATOLOGIE

SWISS TOURIST INFORMATION OFFICE
See
SCHWEIZERISCHE VERKEHRSZENTRALE

SWISSAIR
Across the Alps: aerial views between Nice and
Vienna ...; texts by Hans Annaheim, Paul Eggenberg,
Arnold Lunn, Erich Schwabe. Berne: Kümmerly &
Frey, 1959. 54p., plates (some col.), illus.,
maps (on lining papers). 31cm.

SWITZERLAND. Administration des Postes et
Telegraphes suisses
See
SWITZERLAND. Post-, Telegraphen- und Telephon-
verwaltung

SWITZERLAND. Bureau topographique fédéral
See
SWITZERLAND. Eidgenössisches Topographisches Bureau

SWITZERLAND. Commission fédérale du parc national
See
SWITZERLAND. Eidgenössische Nationalparkkommission

SWITZERLAND. Departement des Innern. Inspektion
für Forstwesen, Jagd und Fischerei.See its Inspektion
...

SWITZERLAND. Departement des Innern. Statistisches
Bureau
See
SWITZERLAND. Eidgenössisches Statistisches Bureau

SWITZERLAND. Département fédéral de l'intérieur
See
SWITZERLAND. Departement des Innern

SWITZERLAND. Eidgenössische Nationalparkkommission
Le parc national suisse: guide officiel pour
touristes. [Bern?]: La Commission fédérale du
parc national, 1970. 46p., col. illus., maps.
14 x 19cm.

SWITZERLAND. Eidgenössische Postverwaltung
See
SWITZERLAND. Post-, Telegraphen- und Telephon-
verwaltung

SWITZERLAND. Eidgenössisches Statistisches Bureau
Die Alpenwirthschaft der Schweiz im Jahre 1864;
hrsg. vom Statistischen Bureau des Eidg. Departement des Innern. Bern: Orell, Fuessli, 1868.
xxi, 432p. 29cm. (Schweizerische Statistik)

SWITZERLAND. Eidgenössisches Topographisches Bureau
Hundert Jahre Eidg. Landestopographie, ehemaliges
Eidg. Topographisches Bureau, 1838-1938: Erinnerungsmappe. Bern: Eidg. Landestopographie, 1938.
3v. 31cm.

SWITZERLAND. Eidgenössisches Topographisches Bureau
Litteratur der Landesvermessung, Kataloge der
Kartensammlungen, Karten, Pläne, Reliefs, Panoramen;
hrsg. vom Eidgenössischen Topographischen Bureau;
redigirt von J.H. Graf. Bern: K.J. Wyss, 1896.
712p. 23cm. (Bibliographie der Schweizerischen
Landeskunde, fasc.2)

SWITZERLAND. Eidgenössisches Topographisches Bureau
[Litteratur der Landesvermessung...]. Cartes de
parcelles plus ou moins grandes du territoire
suisse; publié par le Bureau topographique fédéral;
rédigé par J.H. Graf. Berne: K.J. Wyss, 1892.
171-335p. 23cm. (Bibliographie nationale suisse,
fasc. 2b)

SWITZERLAND. Eidgenössisches Topographisches Bureau
La topographie de la Suisse, 1832-1864: histoire
de la Carte Dufour; publiée par le Bureau topographique fédéral. Berne: The Bureau, 1898. viii,
270p., plates, maps (some col.), port. 25cm.

SWITZERLAND. Inspection fédérale des forêts
See
SWITZERLAND. Inspektion für Forstwesen, Jagd und
Fischerei

SWITZERLAND. Inspektion für Forstwesen, Jagd und
Fischerei
Arbres et forêts de la Suisse. le série; publié
par le Département fédéral de l'intérieur, Division
forestière (Inspection fédérale des forets).
Berne: A. Francke, 1908. 23p., plates, illus.
33cm.
In portfolio.

SWITZERLAND. Post-, Telegraphen- und Telephonverwaltung
Le centenaire des postes alpestres suisses.
Genève: L'Art en Suisse, 1932. 82p., col. plates
(2 fold.), illus., maps (2 in pocket). 28cm.

SWITZERLAND. Post-, Telegraphen- und Telephonverwaltung
[Le centenaire des postes...]. A century of Swiss
alpine postal coaches. Geneva: L'Art en Suisse,
1932. 82p., col. plates (2 fold.), illus., maps
(2 in pocket). 28cm.

SWITZERLAND. Post-, Telegraphen- und Telephonverwaltung
Grimselpass: Poststrasse Meiringen-Grimsel-Gletsch;
hrsg. von der Eidgenössischen Postverwaltung.
Bern: Kümmerly & Frey, [1934?]. 92p., col. plates
(1 fold.), illus., map (in pocket). 17cm.
(Schweizerische Alpenposten. Routenführer)

SWITZERLAND. Post-, Telegraphen- und Telephon-
verwaltung
Schönheiten der Alpenstrassen: eine Auswahl
Schweizerischer Graphik ...; hrsg. von der
Schweiz. Oberpostdirektion. Bern: Oberpost-
direktion [1930?]. 3v., plates, illus. 43cm.
Text in German, French, Italian and English.

SWITZERLAND. Post-, Telegraphen- und Telephonverwaltung
Die Schweizerischen Alpenpässe und die Postkurse
im Gebirge: offizielles illustriertes Posthandbuch; [hrsg. von der Schweiz. Postverwaltung;
illustr... v. J.M. Steiger]. 2.verm. Aufl. Bern:
Schweiz. Postverwaltung, 1893. xv, 369p., plates
(1 fold.), illus., maps. 19cm.

SWITZERLAND. Schweizerische Geodätische Commission
See
SCHWEIZERISCHE GEODÄTISCHE COMMISSION

Switzerland, a practical guide. 2nd ed. Berlin,
London: Goldschmidt, Williams & Norgate, 1912-13.
184p., maps. 16cm. (Grieben's guide books, 123)

Switzerland: a series of narratives of personal
visits to places therein famous for natural beauty
or historical association. Cambridge (Mass.):
W.M. Griswold, 1892. lv. (various pagings). 21cm.

Switzerland and Savoy. D. Bogue, 1852. vi, 338p.,
map. 15cm. (Bogue's guides for travellers, 2)

Switzerland and the Swiss, by an American resident
[i.e. Samuel H.M. Byers]. Zurich: Orell, Füssli,
1875. xxvi, 203p., plates, illus., maps. 21cm.

Switzerland and the Swiss: sketches of the country
and its famous men, by the author of "Knights of
the frozen sea". Seeley, Jackson & Halliday,
1877. viii, 291p., plates, illus. 19cm.

Switzerland, containing a description of the
character, manners, customs ... of the inhabitants
of the twenty-two cantons in particular; [edited
by Frederic Shober]. R. Ackermann, [1827].
viii, 287p., 18 col. plates, illus. 15cm. (The
world in miniature)

Switzerland in miniature: description of the grand
model of Switzerland, by Professor Gaudin, of
Geneva ... now exhibiting at the Egyptian Hall,
Piccadilly. Printed for the Proprietor, 1825.
32p. 21cm.

Switzerland: its mountains, valleys, lakes, and
rivers... New and rev. ed., [by Woldemar Kaden].
J.S. Virtue & Co., 1889. xi, 388p., illus. 25cm.

- - New and rev. ed. Glaisher, 1903.

SYDNEY ROCK-CLIMBING CLUB
The rock-climbs of N.S.W.; compiled by members
of the Sydney Rock-Climbing Club. Sydney:
S.R.C.C., [1963]. 112p., illus. 26cm.

SYDOW, Albrecht von
Bemarkungen auf einer Reise im Jahre 1827 durch
die Beskiden über Krakau und Wieliczka nach den
Central-Karpathen, als Beitrag zur Characteristik
dieser Gebirgsgegenden und ihrer Bewohner. Berlin:
F. Dümmler, 1830. xxv, 406p., 1 fold. plate,
map. 22cm.

SYERS, Ernest and SYERS, Madge
The book of winter sports; edited by Ernest Syers
and Madge Syers with an introduction by the Earl
of Lytton. Arnold, 1908. 336p., plates, illus.
24cm.

SYKES, Ella and SYKES, Sir Percy
Through deserts and oases of central Asia.
Macmillan, 1920. xii, 340p., plates (1 fold.
col.), illus., map (in pocket). 23cm.

SYKES, Sir Percy
A history of exploration from the earliest times
to the present day. 2nd ed., (rev.). Routledge,
1935. xiv, 374p., plates (some fold.), illus.,
maps. 26cm.

SYKES, Ella and SYKES, Sir Percy
Through deserts and oases of central Asia.
Macmillan, 1920. xi, 340p., plates (1 fold.
col.), illus., map (in pocket). 23cm.

SYLVIUS, Aeneas
See
PIUS II, Pope

SYMES-THOMPSON, Edmund
SYMES-THOMPSON, Lilla
Memories of Edmund Symes-Thompson ... a follower
of St. Luke, by his wife [Lilla Symes-Thompson];
with a preface by the Lord Bishop of Wakefield.
Elliot Stock, 1908. vii, 195p., plates, illus.
21cm

SYMES-THOMPSON, Lilla
Memories of Edmund Symes-Thompson ... a follower
of St. Luke, by his wife [Lilla Symes-Thompson];
with a preface by the Lord Bishop of Wakefield.
Elliot Stock, 1908. vii, 195p., plates, illus.
21cm.

SYMINGTON, Noel Howard
See
WHIPPLESNAITH

SYMONDS, H H
Afforestation in the Lake District: a reply to
the Forestry Commission's White Paper of 26th
August 1936; foreword by Lord Howard of Penrith.
Dent, 1936. xxi, 97p., plates, illus., map.
19cm.

SYMONDS, John
The great beast: the life of Aleister Crowley.
Rider, 1951. 316p., plates, illus. 24cm.

SYMONDS, John Addington and SYMONDS, Margaret
Our life in the Swiss highlands. Black, 1892. x,
366p., plates, illus. 20cm.

- - 2nd ed. 1907.

SYMONDS, John Addington
BROWN, Horatio F
John Addington Symonds: a biography; compiled
from his papers and correspondence. 2nd ed.
Smith, Elder, 1908. xxiv, 495p., plates, illus.
21cm.

SYMONDS, John Addington
SYMONDS, Margaret
Out of the past; with an account of Janet Catherine
Symonds by Mrs. Walter Leaf. Murray, 1925. xv,
318p., plates, illus. 23cm.

SYMONDS, Margaret
A child of the alps. Fisher Unwin, 1920. 364p.
20cm. (The first novel library)

SYMONDS, John Addington and SYMONDS, Margaret
Our life in the Swiss highlands. Black, 1892. x,
366p., plates, illus. 20cm.

- - 2nd ed. 1907.

SYMONDS, Margaret
Out of the past; with an account of Janet Catherine
Symonds by Mrs. Walter Leaf. Murray, 1925. xv,
318p., plates, illus. 23cm.

SYMPOSIUM ON GLACIER MAPPING, Ottawa, 1965
[Papers presented at a] symposium on glacier
mapping, [Sept. 20 to 22, 1965].
(In Canadian journal of earth sciences, special
issue, v.3.,no.6, Nov. 1966, 737-915p., plates,
illus., maps (including 14 in portfolio), bibl.)

SYMPOSIUM ON SURGING GLACIERS, Banff, Alberta, 1968
Papers presented at the Seminar on the Causes and
Mechanics of Glacier Surges, St. Hilaire, Quebec
... Sept. 10-11, 1968 and the Symposium on Surging
Glaciers, Banff, Alberta ..., June 6-8, 1968.
(In Canadian journal of earth sciences, v.6, no.4,
pt.2, Aug. 1969. iv, 807-1018p., illus., maps,
bibl.)

SYNDICAT DES GUIDES DE CHAMONIX-MONT-BLANC
Règlement et tarif de la Compagnie des Guides de
Chamonix (Haute-Savoie). [Chamonix]: [La
Compagnie], 1872. 35p. 16cm.

- - Another ed. 1889.

SYNDICAT DES GUIDES DE CHAMONIX-MONT-BLANC
Règlement et tarif des guides de Chamonix. Annecy:
Imprimerie de L. Thésio, 1862. 28p. 17cm.

- - Another ed. 1872.

SYNDICAT DES GUIDES DE CHAMONIX-MONT-BLANC
Tarif des courses et ascensions. [Chamonix]: Le
Syndicat, 1936. [25]p. 11 x 18cm.

SYNGE, Georgina M
A ride through wonderland. Sampson Low, Marston,
1892. iv, 166p., 1 fold.col. plate, illus., map.
20cm.

SYNGE, Patrick M
Mountains of the Moon: an expedition to the equatorial mountains of Africa. Drummond, 1937. xxiv,
221p., plates (1 fold., some col.), maps. 24cm.

SZONTAGH, Nikolaus
Tatraführer; Wegweiser in die Hohe Tatra und in
die Bäder der Tatragegend; unter Mitwirkung des
Ungar Karpathen-Vereins von Nikolaus Szontagh; aus
dem Ungarischen von Friedrich Nikhazi. 2.Aufl.
Budapest: Singer & Wolfner, 1904. 227p., map.
17cm.

T., F.
See
THIOLY, François

T., F.M.
See
TRENCH, Fanny Maria

T., G.
What may be done in two months: a summer's tour,
through Belgium, up the Rhine, and to the lakes
of Switzerland; also to Chamouny... Chapman &
Hall, 1834. 188p., map. 19cm.
Letters, signed: G.T.

T., H.
See
TROWER, Henry

T., H.B.
Rough notes of an excursion to the Soonderdoongee
glacier in the Himalaya mountains during the
autumn of 1848, by H.B.T. Couchman, 1858. 47p.
22cm.

T., J.G.D.
Gelegenheit und heutiger Zustand dess Hertsogthums
Savoyen und Fürstenthums Piemont ..., beschrieben
durch J.G.D.T. Nürnberg: In Verlegung Joh.
Andreae Endters, Seel, 1690. 706p., 1 fold.
plate, illus., maps. 21cm.

T., R.
See
TÖPFFER, Rodolphe

T., R.W.
Notes on a tour in America, [by] R.W.T. Wyman,
[ca 1885]. 30p. 24 x 29cm.

T.S.Y.A.
See
CLARKSON, J   R

Tableau des positions géographiques et hauteurs
absolues au-dessus du niveau de la mer, des points
principaux du Département de l'Isère ... [par M.
Perrotin]. Grenoble, 1853. 25p. 24cm.
Offprint from Bulletin de la Societé de Statis_
tique de l'Isère, 2e sér. 2e vol.

TABOR, R   W   and CROWDER, D   F
Routes and rocks in the Mt. Challenger Quadrangle;
drawings by Ed Hanson. Seattle: The Mountaineers,
1968. 47p., plates (1 fold.col.), illus., maps
(1 in pocket), bibl. 19cm. (Hiker's map of the
north Cascades)

TAUBER, Carl
Auf fremden Bergpfaden. Zürich: Orell Füssli,
[1916]. 513p., illus. 21cm.

TAUBER, Carl
Die Berner Hochalpen. 2.Aufl. Zürich: Poli-
graphisches Institut, [1908]. 119p., plates (1
fold.), illus. 19cm.

TAUBER, Carl
Il Ticino. Zurigo: Orell Füssli, 1918. 156p.,
plates (1 col.), illus., map, music, bibl. 20cm.

Tagebuch einer Reise auf den bis dahin unersteigenen
Berg Gross-Glockner an den Gränzen Cärntens,
Salzburgs und Tirols im Jahre 1799, [von Johann
Zopoth]. Salzburg: Mayer, 1800. 88p., 1 fold.
plate, illus., map. 22cm.
Besonderer Abdruk aus des Froyherrn von Moll
Jahrbüchern der Berg- und Hüttenkunde.

TAINE, Hippolyte
Voyage aux Pyrénées. 3e éd.; illustrée par G.
Doré. Paris: Hachette, 1860. vi, 354 (i.e.
554)p., illus. 25cm.

- - 14e éd. 1897.

TAINE, Hippolyte
Voyage aux Pyrénées; edited by William Robertson.
Oxford: Clarendon Press, 1905. xvi, 211p., 1
plate, map. 20cm. (Oxford modern French series)

TAIRRAZ, Pierre
RÉBUFFAT, Gaston
Entre terre et ciel; par Gaston Rébuffat et
[photographies de] Pierre Tairraz. Paris:
Arthaud, 1962. 183p., illus. (some fold., some
col.). 24cm.
"Commentaire du film".

TAIRRAZ, Pierre
RÉBUFFAT, Gaston
[Entre terre et ciel]. Between heaven and earth,
by Gaston Rébuffat and [photographs by] Pierre
Tairraz; translated by Eleanor Brockett. Vane,
1965. 183p., illus.(some fold., some col.). 24cm.
Film commentary.

FRISON-ROCHE, Roger and TAIRRAZ, Pierre
Mont Blanc aux sept vallées. Paris: Arthaud, 1959.
269p., illus. 24cm.

FRISON-ROCHE, Roger and TAIRRAZ, Pierre
[Mont Blanc aux sept vallées]. Mont Blanc and the
seven valleys; translated and adapted by R. Le
Grand; with the cooperation of Wilfrid Noyce.
Kaye, 1961. 267p., illus. 24cm. (Les beaux pays)

TAIT, P   G
RENDU, Louis
[Théorie des glaciers de la Savoie]. Theory of
the glaciers of Savoy; translated by Alfred Wills;
to which are added the original memoir and supplementary articles by P.G. Tait and John Ruskin;
edited with introductory remarks by George Forbes.
Macmillan, 1874. 216p., illus., map. 23cm.
Text in English and French.

TAKATOU, S
Nippon sangaku-shi. Tokyo: Hakubunan, 1906.
674p, 37, 130p., plates, illus., maps. 23cm.
In Japanese.

TAKEBUSHI, S
Nandakot Tohan; or, The ascent of Nanda Kot: the
Rikkyo University Himalaya Expedition 1936. 101p.,
plates, illus., plans. 27cm.
In Japanese.

TAKEDA, H
Alpine flora. Tokyo: Azusa-Shobo, 1933. 4, 80p.,
322 plates, illus. 15cm.
Text in Japanese, with Latin nomenclature in
captions.

TALBERT, Émile
Les Alpes: études et souvenirs. Paris: Hachette,
1880. 224p., illus. 23cm. (Bibliothèque des
écoles et des familles)

TALBOT, Daniel
A treasury of mountaineering stories; edited by
Daniel Talbot. P. Davies, 1955. ix, 282p. 21cm.

TALBOT, Frederick A
The making of a great Canadian railway: the story
of the search for and discovery of the route and
the construction of the nearly completed grand
trunk Pacific railway... Seeley, Service, 1912.
349p., plates (1 fold.), illus., map. 23cm.

TALBOT, I   T. The ascent of Mont Blanc
BARTOL, C   A
Pictures of Europe, framed in ideas. 2nd ed.
Boston: Crosby, Nichols, 1856. 407p. 21cm.
Also contains: Talbot, I.T. The ascent of Mont
Blanc.

TALBOT, Jeremy O
Central Switzerland: Grimsel, Furka, Susten: a
guide for walkers and climbers. Goring, Reading:
West Col, 1969. 181p., illus., maps, bibl. 16cm.
(West Col alpine guides)

TALBOT, Jeremy O
Engelhorner and Salbitschijen, including Wellhörner
and Scheideggwetterhorn: a selection of popular
and recommended climbs; compiled by Jeremy O.
Talbot. Goring, Reading: West Col, 1968. 107p.,
illus., map, bibl. 17cm. (West Col alpine
guides)

TALBOT, Jeremy O
Gower Peninsula: Caswell Bay to Worms Head, Burry
Holms to Tor Gro. Goring, Reading: West Col,
1970. 160p., plates, illus., map. 17cm. (West
Col coastal climbing guides)

- - Supplement 1973.

TALBOT, Jeremy O
Kaisergebirge: a selection of climbs; compiled by
Jeremy Talbot. Goring, Reading: West Col, 1971.
96p., illus., map, bibl. 17cm. (West Col alpine
guides)

Tales from Switzerland. [New ed.]. Printed for
Edgerley, 1827. 4v. 18cm.
Library lacks v.1.

Tales in rhyme. [N.p.]: [n.pub.], 1863. 32p. 23cm.

Tales of adventure from the old annuals... New ed.
Sampson Low, Marston, 1895. xiv, 181p., plates,
illus. 21cm.

Tales of the Great Saint Bernard. H. Colburn, 1828.
3v. 21cm.

TALFOURD, Sir Thomas Noon
Recollections of a first visit to the Alps, in
August and September 1841. [The Author], [1842].
xi, 193p. 15cm.

TALFOURD, Sir Thomas Noon
Three speeches delivered in the House of Commons
in favour of a measure for an extension of copyright; to which are added, The petitions in favour
of the Bill... Moxon, 1840. xxxi, 148p. 15cm.

TALFOURD, Sir Thomas Noon
Vacation rambles and thoughts; comprising the
recollections of three continental tours in the
vacations of 1841, 1842, and 1843. Moxon, 1845.
2v. 22cm.

- - 2nd ed. 1845.
- - 3rd ed. 1851.
- - Supplement. 1854.

TALLANTIRE, Philip
'Felix Austria' (hut-to-hut touring guides).
Eden, Banff: The Author, 1964-68. 4v., plates
(some fold., some col.), illus., maps. 18cm.

TALLICHET, Ed.
Eugène Rambert: souvenirs personnels.
(In Bibliothèque universelle... v.33, 1887,
p.111-134.)

TAMINI, Jean Émile and QUAGLIA, Lucien
Châtellenie de Granges, Lens, Grône, St-Léonard
avec Chalais-Chippis. St-Maurice: Édition Oeuvre
St-Augustin, 1942. 248p., plates, illus., bibl.
25cm.

TAMINI, Jean Émile and DELEZE, Pierre
Essai d'histoire de la Vallée d'Illiez. 2e éd.
St-Maurice: Imprimerie St-Augustin, 1924. 422p.,
illus., bibl. 24cm.

TANDY, E   A
SURVEY OF INDIA
Catalogue of maps. Parts 1 and 2, corrected up to
31st March 1928; published under the direction of
E.A. Tandy. Calcutta: Survey of India, 1928.
vii, 37p., col. plates, maps. 35cm.

TANESINI, Arturo
Sassolungo, Catinaccio, Latemar. Milano: Club
Alpino Italiano, Touring Club Italiano, 1942.
503p., plates, illus., maps, bibl. 18cm. (Guida
dei monti d'Italia)

TANNER, Beryl
Salute to the early mountaineer [H.C.B. Tanner]:
six short articles on the Himalayas. Bovey Tracey
(Devon): B. Tanner, [n.d]. 32p., plates, illus.,
port. 22cm.

TANNER, H   A
Beiträge zur Erschliessung der südlichen Bergeller
Berge und Führer für Forno-Albigna-Bondasca.
Basel: The Author, 1906. viii, 158p., illus.,
bibl. 17cm.

TANNER, Henry C   B
TANNER, Beryl
Salute to the early mountaineer [H.C.B. Tanner]:
six short articles on the Himalayas. Bovey Tracey
(Devon): B. Tanner, [n.d.]. 32p., plates, illus.,
port. 22cm.

TANNER, Hermann
Zehn Jahre Bergführer Kluckers "Herr": Erlebnisse
A. von Rydzewskis Naturschilderungen und Anderes;
redigiert, gruppiert, z. T. verfasst, und hrsg.
von Hermann Tanner. 1. Buch. Anton von Rydzewski
als Künstler, eine alpine Bildergalerie in Prosa.
Bern: Liter.-Art. Bureau, 1934. 119p., 1 plate,
illus. 19cm.

TAPERNOUX, Ph
Nouveau guide en Suisse. Lausanne: Jaquenod,
[n.d.]. xxvii, 204p., maps. 17cm.

TARAMELLI, Torquato
Il Canton Ticino meridionale ed i paesi finitimi:
spiegazione del Foglio 24 ... da Spreafico, Negri
e Stoppani. Berna: J. Dalp, 1880. 232, 42p., 4
col. plates (3 fold.), illus., map, bibl. 32cm.
(Beiträge zur geologischen Karte der Schweiz =
Materiali per la carta geologica della Svizzera,
vol.17)

TARARUA TRAMPING CLUB
Tararua story; edited by B.D.A. Greig. Wellington
(N.Z.): The Club, 1946. 108p., plates, illus.,
map. 25cm.
Published in commemoration of the silver jubilee of
the Tararua Tramping Club, 1919-1944.

TARBUCK, Kenneth
Nylon rope and climbing safety. Edinburgh: British
Ropes, [1961]. 35p., illus. 14cm. (British Ropes
publication, no.37)

TARGA, Spartaco
La guerra di montagna e la difesa delle Alpi.
Torino: E. Schioppo, 1926. 176p., plates, illus.,
bibl. 18cm. (Breviari Schioppo, ser. la, n.2)

TARNUZZER, Chr.
THEOBALD, Gottfried
Naturbilder aus den Rätischen Alpen: ein Führer
durch Graubünden. 4.umgearb. Aufl., von Chr.
Tarnuzzer. Chur: Manatschal Ebner, 1920. vi, 335p.
21cm.

TARR, Ralph Stockman and MARTIN, Lawrence
Alaskan glacier studies of the National Geographic
Society in the Yakutat Bay, Prince William Sound
and Lower Copper River regions, based upon the
field work in 1909, 1910, 1911 and 1913 by National
Geographic Society expeditions. Washington (D.C.):
National Geographic Society, 1914. xxvii, 498p.,
plates (some fold. col.), illus., maps (in pocket).
27cm.

Taschenbuch für Reisende im Berner Oberlande, um und
auf den Seen von Thun und Brienz... Aarau: H.R.
Sauerländer, 1829. 276p., maps. 16cm.

Taschenbuch für Reisende nach Chamouny, um den Mont-
Blanc, auf den Grossen und Kleinen Bernhard ...
nach der Handschrift der 2.Ausg. in französischer
Sprache [von J.L. Manget] verm. und verb. Aarau:
H.R. Sauerländer, 1829. 198p., plates, maps, plans.
15cm.
Translation of: Itinéraire du voyage à Chamouny...

Taschenbuch von J.G. Jacobi und seinen Freunden für
1795. Königsberg: F. Nicolovius, [1794]. 186p.,
plates, illus. 13cm.
Includes Jacobi, G.A. Beschreibung einer Reise
an den Fuss des Mont Blanc.

Taschenbuch zu Schweizer-Reisen, mit hinweisung auf
alle Sehens und Merkwurdigkeiten der Schweiz;
eines Theils von Savonen und anderer Benachbarten
Orte. Glarus: F. Schmid, 1832. xxiv, 327p. 17cm.

- - 3. verb. Aufl. 1841.

TASSE, Père
VINCENT, Henri
Les vingt-deux années du Père Tasse à Chambrousse.
Grenoble: Baratier, 1891. 296p., illus. 19cm.

TASSIN, Nicolas
Description de tous les cantons, villes, bourgs,
villages, et autres particularitez du pays des
suisses, avec une brieve forme de leur République
... Paris: S. Cramoisy, 1639. 65p., 35 plates,
illus. 20 x 26cm.

TASTU, Mme Amable
See
TASTU, Sabine Amable

TASTU, Sabine Amable
Alpes et Pyrénées: arabesques littéraires, com-
posées de nouvelles historiques, anecdotes, descriptions, chroniques et récits divers, par Mme
Amable Tastu [and others]. Paris: P.C. Lehury,
1842. viii, 392p., plates, illus. 23cm.

TASTU, Sabine Amable
Voyage en France. Tours: Ad. Mame, 1852. 535p.,
plates, illus., map. 25cm.

- - Nouv. éd., rev. et augm. 1879.

TATHAM, H   F   W
The footprints in the snow and other tales; with
a memoir by A.C. Benson. Macmillan, 1910. xxvii,
187p., plates, illus. 22cm.

TATRANSKÁ EXPEDÍCIA HIMALÁJE, 1969
Tatranská Expedícia Himaláje 1969 = The High
Tatras Expedition, Himalaya 69; [issued in English
by the participants... English version: Lida
Pokorna]. Stary Smokovec: The Expedition, 1968.
[33]p., illus. (some col.). 25cm.
Preliminary brochure.

TATTERSALL, George
The Lakes of England. Sherwood, 1836. xii,
165p., 43 plates (1 fold. col.), illus., map.
21cm.

TAUPIN, D   and BROT, M
Cormot: topo guide d'escalade. Paris: Club Alpin
Français, Section de Paris-Chamonix, 1964. 64p.,
fold. plates, illus., maps. 22cm.

TAYLOR, Bayard
Northern travel: summer and winter pictures of
Sweden, Lapland and Norway. Sampson Low, 1858.
xvi, 389p. 21cm.

TAYLOR, Bayard
Views afoot; or, Europe seen with knapsack and
staff; revised by the author. Sampson Low, &
Marston, 1869. xvi, 318p. 16cm. (Low's copyright series of American authors)

TAYLOR, Isodore Justin, baron
Les Pyrénées. Paris: Gide, 1843. viii, 618p.
26cm.

TAYLOR, J   E
Mountain and moor. Society for Promoting
Christian Knowledge, 1880. 256p., illus. 18cm.
(Natural history rambles)

TAYLOR, Neville
Ibex shooting on the Himalayas. Sampson Low,
Marston, 1903. xi, 146p., plates, illus. 19cm.

TAYLOR, Peter
Coopers Creek to Langtang II. Angus and Robertson,
1965. 239p., plates, illus., maps (on lining
papers). 23cm.

TAYLOR, Rebe P
Pyrenean holiday. Hale, 1952. 224p., plates,
illus., maps, bibl. 23cm.

TCHEREPOV, I   A
See
CHEREPOV, Ivan Aleksandrovich

TCHERNINE, Odette
The snowman and company; foreword by Eric Shipton;
postscript by H.W. Tilman. Hale, 1961. 174p.,
plates, illus., maps, bibl. 22cm.

TECHNIKER-ALPENCLUB IN GRAZ
Denkschrift zur Feier des 25 jährigen Bestehens
des Techniker-Alpenclub in Graz. Graz: Im Selbstverlage des Vereines, 1898. 156p., 1 plate, illus.
24cm.

TEDESCHI, Renato
Alpinismo e sci. Roma: Murpurgo, 1930. 52p.,
plates, illus., bibl. 20cm.

TEGERNSEE, Otto von
See
HARTMANN, Otto

TEICHMAN, Sir Eric
Journey to Turkistan. Hodder and Stoughton, 1937.
221p., plates (1 fold.col.), illus., maps. 24cm.

TELEKI, Samuel, Count
HÖHNEL, Ludwig von
Discovery of Lakes Rudolf and Stephanie: a narrative of Count Samuel Teleki's exploring and hunting
expedition in eastern equatorial Afrida in 1887
and 1888. Longmans, Green, 1894. 2v., 2 fold.col.
plates, illus. 26cm.

TELFER, J   Buchan
The Crimea and Transcaucasia, being the narrative
of a journey in the Kouban, in Gouria, Georgia,
Armenia, Ossety, Imeritia. ... King, 1876. 2v.,
plates (2 fold.col.), illus., maps. 25cm.

TELL, Wilhelm
BORDIER, Henri L
Le Grütli et Guillaume Tell; ou, Défense de la
tradition vulgaire sur les origines de la Confédération Suisse. Genève: H. Georg, 1869. 92p. 23cm.

TELL, Wilhelm
COOLIDGE, William Augustus Brevoort
History of the Swiss Confederation, with appendices
on Tell and Winkelried: a sketch. [Edinburgh],
1887. 84p. 19cm.
Reprinted from Encyclopaedia Britannica.

TELL, Wilhelm
FLORIAN, Jean Pierre Claris de
Guillaume Tell; ou, La Suisse libre: ouvrage
posthume, précédé de son discours de réception à
l'Académie Française, de la Vie de l'auteur, par
Jauffret, de quelques pièces fugitives inédites.
Paris: Briand, 1810. lvi, 94p., plates, illus.
16cm. (Oeuvres de Florian)

TELL, Wilhelm
HÄUSSER, Ludwig
Die Sage vom Tell aufs neue kritisch untersucht:
eine... Preisschrift. Heidelberg: J.C.B. Mohr,
1840. xiv, 110p. 22cm.

TELMANN, Konrad
Die Lawine: ein Roman. Berlin: Verlag Neues Leben
W. Borngraeber, [1925]. 259p. 20cm.

TELMANN, Konrad
Unter den Dolomiten: Roman. Dresden: Reiszner,
1911. 8.Aufl. 431p. 21cm.

TELVENBURG, Josef von Trentinaglia
See
TRENTINAGLIA-TELVENBURG, Josef, Ritter von

TEMPLE, John and WALKER, Alan
Kirinyaga: a Mount Kenya anthology; edited by
John Temple and Alan Walker. Nairobi: Mountain
Club of Kenya, [1974]. 61p. 33cm.

TEMPLE, Philip
Nawok! The New Zealand expedition to New Guinea's
highest mountains. Dent, 1962. xiii, 189p.,
plates (1 col.), illus., maps. 23cm.

TEMPLE, Philip
The sea and the snow: the South Indian Ocean
Expedition to Heard Island; foreword by Sir Edmund
Hillary. Melbourne: Cassell Australia, 1966.
188p., plates, illus., maps. 22cm.

TEMPLE, Philip
The world at their feet: the story of New Zealand
mountaineers in the great ranges of the world.
Christchurch (N.Z.): Whitcombe & Tombs, 1969.
250p., plates, illus., maps, bibl. 25cm.

TEMPLE, Sir Richard
Journals kept in Hyderabad, Kashmir, Sikkim and
Nepal; edited with introductions by his son,
Richard Carnac Temple. Allen, 1887. 2v., plates
(some fold., some col.), illus., maps. 24cm.

TEN-HAMME, Joë Diericx de
Vingt-cinq Belges au Mont-Blanc: itinéraires
détaillés de 12 et de 15 jours en Suisse.
Bruxelles: Delevingne & Callewaert, 1869. iv,
192p., plates (1 fold.), illus., map. 24cm.
"Guide du touriste".

TENNANT, Charles
A tour through parts of the Netherlands, Holland,
Germany, Switzerland, Savoy, and France, in the
year 1821-2, including a description of ... the
stupendous scenery of the Alps in the depth of
winter. Longman, Hurst, Rees, Orme, Brown, &
Green, 1824. 2v., 8 plates, facsims. 22cm.

TENNENT, Norman
The Islands of Scotland. Edinburgh: Scottish
Mountaineering Trust, 1971. 172p., plates (1
fold.), illus. 22cm. (Scottish Mountaineering
Club district guide books)

TENNYSON, Alfred, Baron Tennyson
[Guinevere]. Genièvre: poème traduit de l'anglais
par Francisque Michel; avec neuf gravures sur
acier d'après les dessins de Gustave Doré. Paris:
Hachette, 1868. 25p., 9 plates, illus. 45cm.

TENNYSON, Alfred, Baron Tennyson
MATHEWS, Charles Edward
The earlier and less-known poems of Alfred
Tennyson ...: an address delivered before the
members of the Harborne and Edgbaston Institute,
by C.E. Mathews, 30th January 1883. Birmingham:
[n.pub.], 1883. 34p. 22cm.

TENSING
See
TENZING NORGAY

TENZING
See
TENZING NORGAY

TENZING NORGAY
After Everest: an autobiography, by Tenzing Norgay
Sherpa; as told to Malcolm Barnes. Allen & Unwin,
1977. 184p., plates (some col.), illus., map.
23cm.

TENZING NORGAY
Le conquête de l'Everest, par le Sherpa Tensing,
récit d'Yves Malartic. Paris: Éditions du
Scorpion, 1953. 303p., plates, illus., maps, bibl.
20cm.

TENZING NORGAY
Gli eroi del Chomolungma, [da] Massimo Mila,
Tensing Norkey. Torino: Einaudi, 1954. 191p.,
col. plates, illus., maps. 26cm. (Nuova
Atlantide, 2)

TENZING NORGAY
  Man of Everest: the autobiography of Tenzing told
  to J.R. Ullman. Harrap, 1955. 320p., plates (some
  col.), illus., maps. 23cm.

TENZING NORGAY
  [Man of Everest]. Tenzing de l'Everest: autobio-
  graphie raconté à James Ramsay Ullman. [Paris]:
  Arthaud, 1955. 277p., plates, illus., maps. 22cm.
  (Collection sempervivum, 27)

TERCINOD, G
  Recueil de pages valdotaines à l'occasion du
  centenaire de la première ascension du Mont Cervin
  ... Aoste: [The Author], 1965. 147p., plates,
  illus., bibl. 21cm.

FRANCO, Jean and TERRAY, Lionel
  Bataille pour le Jannu; préface de Lucien Devies.
  Paris: Gallimard, 1965. 293p., illus., maps. 21cm.

FRANCO, Jean and TERRAY, Lionel
  [Bataille pour le Jannu]. At grips with Jannu;
  with a preface by Lucien Devies; translated by Hugh
  Merrick. Gollancz, 1967. 192p., plates, illus.,
  maps. 23cm.

TERRAY, Lionel
  [Les conquérants de l'inutile]. Conquistadors of
  the useless: from the Alps to Annapurna; translated
  by Geoffrey Sutton. Gollancz, 1963. 351p.,
  plates, illus., maps. 23cm.

DEVIES, Lucien and TERRAY, Lionel
  Joies de la montagne; réalisé sous la direction de
  Lucien Devies et Lionel Terray. Paris: Hachette,
  1965. 255p., illus. (some col.). 29cm. (Collection joies et réalités).

TERRAZ, Claude
  À la découverte du ski de fond. Paris: Arthaud,
  1972. 158p., plates, illus., bibl. 21cm.

TERRE, Robert Sans
  See
  SANS-TERRE, Robert

TERRY, H
  WEY, Francis
  La Haute Savoie: récits de voyage et d'histoire.
  Éd. illustrée de cinquante grandes lithographies
  dessinées ... par H. Terry. Paris: Hachette, 1866.
  119p., plates, illus. 54cm.

TERSCHAK, Emil
  Die Photographie im Hochgebirg: praktische Winke in
  Wort und Bild. Berlin: G. Schmidt, 1900. 83p.,
  illus. 21cm.

  - - 2. durchgesehene Aufl. 1905.
  - - 4.Aufl. gänzlich neu bearb. von J. Rheden.
  Berlin: Union Deutsche Verlagsgesellschaft, 1921.

MATTHIAS, Eugen and TESTA, Giovanni
  Natürliches Skilaufen: die Methode der einfachsten
  Fahrweise; mit einem sportärztlichen Beitrag von
  Paul Gut. München: Rother, 1936. 107p., plates,
  illus. 26cm.

MATTHIAS, Eugen and TESTA, Giovanni
  [Natürliches Skilaufen...]. Sciare: tecnica
  moderna semplificata e razionalizzata; traduzione
  del Conte Ugo di Vallepiana colla collaborazione
  ... [di] L. Ricotti. Milano: Sperling & Kupfer,
  1938. 131p., 18 plates, illus. 24cm.

TESTER, Ch.
  Unter den Adlernestern: Erlebtes und Geschautes aus
  den Bergtälern Rheinwald und Savien. Rorschach:
  E. Löpfe-Benz, 1912. 291p. 21cm.

TÉZENAS DU MONTCEL, Robert
  Ce monde qui n'est pas le nôtre... [Paris]:
  Gallimard, 1965. 203p. 19cm.

TGETGEL, H
  Clubführer durch die Bündner Alpen. Bd.5.
  Bernina-Gruppe, verfasst von Marcel Kurz; revision
  der 2.Aufl. H. Tgetgel. Zürich: Schweizer Alpen-
  Club, 1955. 408p., 1 plate, illus. 17cm.

TGETGEL, H
  Clubführer durch die Bündner Alpen. Bd.9. Unter-
  Engadin, Spöl-Fuorn-Val Müstair bis Punt Martina.
  Montreux: Schweizer Alpenclub, 1946. 380p.,
  illus., col. maps (on lining papers), bibl. 17cm.

TH., F.
  See
  THIOLY, François

THARKAY, Ang
  Ang Tharkay: mémoires d'un Sherpa: recueillis par
  Basil P. Norton; traduits de l'anglais par H.
  Delgove. Paris: Amiot-Dumont, 1954. 210p.,
  plates, illus., maps. 22cm.

THEOBALD, Gottfried
  Das Bündner Oberland; oder, Der Vorderrhein mit
  seinen Seitenthälern. Chur: L. Hitz, 1861.
  215p., plates, illus., map. 19cm.

THEOBALD, Gottfried
  Geologische Beschreibung ... von Graubünden.
  Bern: J. Dalp, 1865. viii, 374p., plates (some
  fold., some col.), illus., bibl. 29cm. (Beiträge
  zur geologischen Karte des Schweiz, Lfg.2.
  Geologische Beschreibung der nordöslichen Gebirge
  von Graubünden)

THEOBALD, Gottfried
  Geologische Beschreibung ... von Graubünden.
  Bern: J. Dalp, 1866. xii, 359p., plates (some
  fold., some col.), illus., bibl. 29cm. (Beiträge
  zur geologischen Karte des Schweiz, Lfg.3. Die
  südöstlichen Gebirge von Graubünden und dem
  angrenzenden Veltlin)

THEOBALD, Gottfried
  Naturbilder aus den rhätischen Alpen. Chur: L.
  Hitz, 1860. iv, 296p. 17cm.

  - - 2.verm. und verb. Aufl. 1862.
  - - 4.umgearb. Aufl., Führer durch Graubünden von
  Chr. Tarnuzzer. Chur: Manatschal Ebner, 1920.

THEOTOKY, C   , comte
  Vie de montagne. Paris: Perrin, 1895. 315p.
  23cm.

THEYTAZ, Aloys
  Le Président de Viouc: pièce valaisanne en 6
  tableaux; illustrations d'Alfred Wicky. Sierre:
  Imprimerie E. Schoechli, [1942]. 96p., illus.
  20cm.

THIELE, Ludwig
  Bilder aus den Alpen: Erinnerungen eines Malers.
  Leipzig: C.B. Lorck, 1857. vi, 139p. 17cm.

THIELMANN, Max, Baron von
  Journey in the Caucasus, Persia, and Turkey in
  Asia; translated by Charles Heneage. Murray, 1875.
  2v., plates (1 fold.col.), illus., map. 20cm.

THIERS, Adolphe
  Les Pyrénées et le Midi de la France, pendant les
  mois de novembre et décembre 1822. Paris:
  Ponthieu, 1823. 222p. 20cm.

THIOLY, François
  Ascension des Dents-d'Oche et du Midi, par F.
  T[hioly]. [Genève]: [The Author], 1863. 45p.,
  plates, illus. 23cm.

THIOLY, François
  Ascension du Mont-Cervin (Matterhorn). Genève:
  [The Author], 1871. 37p. 20cm.

THIOLY, François
  De Genève à Zermatt par le Val d'Anniviers et le
  Col du Trift. Genève: [The Author], 1867. 23p.
  24cm.

THIOLY, François
Excursion dans le Val d'Illiers par Samoëns, le col
de Golèze et le col de Couz. [Genève?]: [The
Author], 1858. 31p., illus. 22cm.
Signed: F.Th. scripsit.
Ms. facsimile.

THIOLY, François
Excursion en Savoie et en Suisse. [Genève?]: [The
Author], 1858. 64p., illus. 22cm.
Signed: F.T. scripsit.
Ms. facsimile.

THIOLY, François
Voyage aux glaciers de Savoie. Genève: [The
Author], 1861. 15p., illus. 22cm.
Signed: F.Th.
Ms. facsimile.

THIOLY, François
Voyage en Suisse et ascension du Mont Rose.
[Genève?]: [The Author], 1860. 96p., illus. 22cm.
Signed: F.Th. scripsit.
Ms. facsimile.

THIOLY, François
Zermatt et l'ascension du Mont Rose, par F.
T[hioly]. Genève: Imprimerie Pferrer & Puky, 1860.
34p., plates, illus. 24cm.

THIRIAT, L
GAUSSEN, H
Les Pyrénées de la Catalogne au Pays basque;
illustré de 57 bois gravés originaux par L. Thiriat;
avec un texte par H. Gaussen; H. Martin, graveur.
Toulouse: Argra, 1933. 83p., illus. (some col.).
28cm.

THIRLMERE, Rowland
Alpine and other lyrics. Stratford-upon-Avon:
Shakespeare Head Press, 1926. vii, 46p. 20cm.

THIRRING, Gustav
Führer durch Sopron (Oedenburg) und die ungarischen
Alpen. Sopron: Dunántúli Turista-Egyesület, 1912.
xix, 283p., plates (some col.), illus., maps,
plans. 16cm.

THOMAS, David Haig
See
HAIG-THOMAS, David

THOMAS, Elizabeth
Hofer, the Tyrolese, by the author of "Claudine",
"Always happy" &c. [i.e. Elizabeth Thomas]. Harris,
1824. xii, 156p., plates, illus. 18cm.

THOMAS, George Powell
Views of Simla. Dickinson, 1846. 11, ii p., 24
plates, illus., map. 53cm.

THOMAS, M   B   and WALLIS, R   H
Report on the Royal Navy East Greenland Expedition
1966, by M.B. Thomas, R.H. Wallis and members of
the expedition. [Plymouth]: The Expedition, [1967].
[64]p., plates, illus., maps. 34cm.

THOMAS, R   H
SURVEY OF INDIA
Map catalogue, corrected up to 30 Nov. 1931;
published under the direction of R.H. Thomas.
Calcutta: Survey of India, 1931. 35p., plates
(some fold.col.), maps. 35cm.

THOMAS COOK LTD.
Cook's tourist's handbook for Switzerland. Thomas
Cook, 1884. vii, 236p. 18cm.

THOMAS COOK LTD.
India, Burma, and Ceylon: information for
travellers and residents. Thos. Cook, 1926. vi,
238p., fold.col. plates, maps. 16cm.

THOMAS COOK LTD.
The Swiss School of Mountaineering. Thos. Cook,
[1935]. 16p., illus. 15cm.

THOMASSET, Ch.
La Vallée d'Aoste: vue à vol d'oiseau, exécuté
par Ch. Thomasset d'aprè le plan relief de Louis
Desco. Aoste: J. Vittaz, [1911]. 1v. of illus.
15 x 21cm.

THOMÉ, Otto Wilhelm
Flora von Deutschland, Österreich und der Schweiz.
2.verm und verb. Aufl. Gera: F. von Zezschwitz,
1903-05. 4v. in 8, col. plates, illus. 24cm.

THOMPSON, Arthur J
Ortler Alps: Ortles, Zebru, Trafoier Wall,
Cevedale: a selection of popular and recommended
climbs; compiled by Arthur J. Thompson. Goring,
Reading: West Col, 1968. 98p., illus., map, bibl.
17cm. (West Col alpine guides)

THOMPSON, C   J   S
"The best thing to do.": first aid in simple
ailments & accidents, for travellers and tourists,
at home and abroad. Record Press, [ca 1905].
53p. 19cm.

THOMPSON, Dorothy E
Climbing with Joseph Georges. [Ladies Alpine
Club], 1926. 159p., 13 plates, illus. 22cm.

THOMPSON, Harold Stuart
Alpine plants of Europe, together with cultural
hints. Routledge, [1911]. xvi, 287p., col.
plates (1 fold.), illus., map. 23cm.

THOMPSON, Harold Stuart
Sub-alpine plants; or, Flowers of the Swiss
woods and meadows; with 33 coloured plates ...
by Geoge Flemwell. Routledge, 1912. xv, 325p.,
col. plates, illus. 23cm.

THOMPSON, Jane Dee
The Great Saint Bernard Pass and Hospice and the
life of Saint Bernard de Menthon. Epworth Press,
1929. 60p., plates, illus. 19cm.

MOULTON, Robert D   and THOMPSON, Terry D
Chair ladder and the south coast. Leicester:
Climbers' Club, 1975. 154p., illus., maps. 17cm.
(Climbers' Club guides to West Penwith, 2)

CLARK, Geoffrey and THOMPSON, W   Harding
The Lakeland landscape. Black, 1938. xii, 136p.,
plates, illus., maps (1 fold. in pocket). 21cm.
(The county landscapes)

THOMSON, A   R   . Rock climbing in Borrowdale
Climbs on Great Gable, by H.S. Gross and Rock
climbing in Borrowdale, by A.R. Thomson. Barrow-
in-Furness: Fell & Rock Climbing Club, [1925].
63p., plates, illus. 21cm. (Climbers' guides,
[1st ser.], 4)

THOMSON, A   R   . Rock climbing in Buttermere
Crags for climbing in and around Great Langdale,
by George Basterfield and Rock climbing in
Buttermere, by A.R. Thomson. Barrow-in-Furness:
Fell & Rock Climbing Club, [1926]. 68p., plates
(1 fold.), illus., map. 21cm. (Climbers' guide,
[1st ser.], 5)

THOMSON, F   M   Spencer
DAVIDSON, L   Marion
Gates of the Dolomites; with a chapter on the
flora of the Dolomites by F.M. Spencer Thomson
...; with an introduction by Sir Melvill
Beachcroft. Bodley Head, 1912. xix, 332p.,
plates (1 fold.), illus., map. 20cm.

- - 2nd ed. 1914.

THOMSON, J   Arthur
Mountain and moorland. Society for Promoting
Christian Knowledge, 1921. 176p., plates (1 col.),
illus. 19cm. (Nature lover's series)

THOMSON, J   B
Joseph Thomson, African explorer: a biography, by
his brother J.B. Thomson. 2nd ed. Sampson Low,
Marston, 1897. x, 358p., plates, illus., maps.
20cm.

THOMSON, James Merriman Archer
Climbing in the Ogwen District; [issued by the
Climbers' Club]. Arnold, 1910. xx, 124p., plates,
illus. 16cm.

- - Appendix, containing accounts of many new climbs,
by H.E.L. Porter. 1921.

THOMSON, James Merriman Archer and ANDREWS, Arthur
Westlake
The climbs on Lliwedd; issued by the Climbers'
Club. Arnold, 1909. xv, 99p., plates, illus.
16cm.

THOMSON, Joseph
Through Masai land: a journey of exploration among
the snowclad volcanic mountains and strange tribes
of eastern equatorial Africa. New and rev. ed.
Sampson Low, Marston, [1897?]. xvi, 364p., 1 fold.
col. plate, illus., map. 19cm.

THOMSON, Joseph
[Through Masai land...]. Au pays des Masai:
voyage d'exploration à travers les montagnes
neigeuses et volcaniques et les tribus étranges de
l'Afrique équatoriale... Paris: Hachette, 1886.
388p., 1 fold. plate, illus., map. 19cm.

THOMSON, Joseph
Travels in the Atlas and southern Morocco: a
narrative of exploration. Philip, 1889. xviii,
488p., plates (2 fold.col.), illus., maps. 20cm.

THOMSON, Joseph
THOMSON, J   B
Joseph Thomson, African explorer: a biography, by
his brother J.B. Thomson. 2nd ed. Sampson Low,
Marston, 1897. x, 358p., plates, illus., maps.
20cm.

THOMSON, Thomas
Western Himalaya and Tibet: a narrative of a
journey through the mountains of northern India
during the years 1847-8. Reeve, 1852. xii, 501p.,
plates (1 fold.), illus., maps. 24cm.

THORINGTON, James Monroe
American Alpine Club annals; [compiled by] J.
Monroe Thorington. [New York], [1947]. 115p.
23cm.
Offprint from American alpine journal, v.6, no.1,
1946 and no.3, 1947.

THORINGTON, James Monroe
A climber's guide to the Interior Ranges of British
Columbia. New York: American Alpine Club, 1937.
xii, 149p., 1 plate, map, bibl.

- - 2nd ed. 1947.

PALMER, Howard and THORINGTON, James Monroe
A climber's guide to the Rocky Mountains of Canada.
New York: Knickerbocker Press for the American
Alpine Club, 1921. xvii, 183p., plates (some
fold.), illus., maps, bibl. 18cm.

- - 2nd ed. Philadelphia: J.C. Winston, 1930.
- - 3rd ed. New York: American Alpine Club, 1940.
- - 6th ed. with the collaboration of William Lowell
Putnam. New York: American Alpine Club, 1966.

THORINGTON, James Monroe
PUTNAM, William Lowell
Climber's guide to the Rocky Mountains of Canada
North 1974, by William L. Putnam, Chris Jones,
Robert Kruszyna. 6th ed. [New York]: American
Alpine Club, 1974. 289p., illus., maps. 17cm.
Based on earlier eds. by James Monroe Thorington.

THORINGTON, James Monroe
PUTNAM, William Lowell and BOLES, Glen W
Climber's guide to the Rocky Mountains of Canada
South. 6th ed. [New York]: American Alpine Club,
1973. 330p., illus., maps. 17cm.
Based on earlier eds. by James Monroe Thorington.

THORINGTON, James Monroe
The glittering mountains of Canada: a record of
exploration and pioneer ascents in the Canadian
Rockies 1914-1924. Philadelphia: Lea, 1925.
310p., illus., maps. 24cm.

THORINGTON, James Monroe
The high adventure of Mr. Randall. [New York],
1945. 333-348p., plates, illus. 23cm.
Offprint from American alpine journal, v.5, no.3.
1945.

THORINGTON, James Monroe
John Auldjo, fortunate traveller: [John Auldjo,
1805-86; collected and arranged for the Alpine
Club by J. Monroe Thorington]. [Philadelphia?]:
[The Author], 1953. 1v. (various pagings). 42cm.

THORINGTON, James Monroe
Mont Blanc sideshow: the life and times of Albert
Smith. Philadelphia: J.C. Winston, 1934. xv,
255p., plates, illus., bibl. 23cm.

THORINGTON, James Monroe
Mountains and mountaineering: a list of the
writings, 1917-1947 of J. Monroe Thorington.
[Philadelphia?]: [The Author], 1947. 12p. 23cm.

THORINGTON, James Monroe
GESNER, Conrad
On the admiration of mountains, the prefatory
letter addressed to Jacob Avienus ... in ... "On
milk and substances prepared from milk", first
printed at Zurich in 1543; A description of the
Riven Mountain, commonly called Mount Pilatus ...
1555; translated by H.B.D. Soulé; together with,
On Conrad Gesner and The mountaineering of
Theuerdank, by J. Monroe Thorington; bibliographical notes by W. Dock and J. Monroe Thorington.
San Francisco: Grabhorn Press, 1937. 54p., illus.
30cm.

THORINGTON, James Monroe
Once in the Eastern Alps. [Boston], [1948].
16-20p., plates, illus. 23cm.
Offprint from Appalachia, June 1948.

THORINGTON, James Monroe
The Purcell Range of British Columbia. New York:
American Alpine Club, 1946. 152p., plates,
illus., maps, bibl. 24cm.

THORINGTON, James Monroe
A survey of early American ascents in the Alps in
the nineteenth century. [New York]: American
Alpine Club, 1943. vii, 83p., illus., bibl. 24cm.

THORNBER, J   J
ARMSTRONG, Margaret
Field book of western wild flowers, by Margaret
Armstrong; in collaboration with J.J. Thornber.
New York, London: Putnam, 1915. xx, 596p., col.
plates, illus. 18cm.

THORNBER, Norman
The Three Peaks. Clapham (Lancs.): Dalesman,
1949. 30p., plates, illus., map. 22cm. (Dalesman pocket books, 7)

THORNE, Guy
The greater power: [a story of the present campaign in Italy]. Gale & Polden, [1915]. 184p.
19cm.

ROSCOE, Thomas and THORNTON, Cyril
Rambles in France and Switzerland; illustrated
with ... steel engravings of drawings by S. Prout
and J.D. Harding. Allman, [ca 1880]. 78p., 27
plates, illus. 26cm.

Three in Norway, by two of them   [i.e. J.A. Lees
and W. Clutterbuck]. Longmans, Green, 1882. xv,
341p., plates, illus., map. 20cm.

THREE WAYFARERS
Roadside sketches in the south of France and
Spanish Pyrenees, by three wayfarers; with twenty-
four illustrations by Touchstone [i.e. M. Booth].
Bell & Daldy, 1859. vi, 113p., plates, illus.
27cm.

A three weeks tour in Savoy and Switzerland, written with the intention of showing a cheap and agreeable manner of travelling in those countries, with a list of the best hotels... Geneva: P.G. Ledouble, 1844. 68p. 18cm.

ANDREW, Ken M   and THRIPPLETON, Alan A
The southern Uplands. Edinburgh: Scottish Mountaineering Trust, 1972. 231p., plates (1 col.), illus., bibl. 22cm. (Scottish Mountaineering Club district guide books)

THULE-GRISE FIORD EXPEDITION, 1976
General report, [by] Derek and Jennifer Fordham. Greenwich: Thule-Grise Fiord Expedition, 1976. 34 leaves, illus., map. 30cm.

THURMAN, John
Fun with ropes and spars: more pioneering projects; illustrated by Kenneth Brookes and John Sweet. 2nd ed. C.A. Pearson, 1964. 127p., plates, illus. 21cm.
Publication approved by the Boy Scouts Association.

THURMAN, John and HAZLEWOOD, Rex
The Gilwell camp fire book; collected, arranged, and on occasion invented by John Thurman and Rex Hazlewood; tunes arranged by A. Mackintosh. Rucsac ed. C.A. Pearson, 1964. 96p., music. 19cm.

THURMAN, John
Pioneering principles. C.A. Pearson, 1962. 128p., plates, illus. 21cm.

HAZLEWOOD, Rex and THURMAN, John
The second Gilwell camp fire book: a further collection of songs and yells from fifty years of scouting; collected, arranged, and on occasion invented by Rex Hazlewood and John Thurman; tunes arranged by A. Mackintosh. C.A. Pearson, 1962. 136p., music. 21cm.

THURN, Sir Everard im
See
IM THURN, Sir Everard

THURWIESER, Peter Carl
Ausgewählte Schriften; mit Bildern von Joseph Riedl. München: Verlag der Alpenfreund, [1924]. 88p., 1 fold. plate, illus. 17cm. (Alpenfreund-Bücherei, Bd.1)

Thusis, via Mala-Schyn. Dresden: Römmler & Jonas, 1893. 1v. of illus. 18cm.

THWAITES, Reuben Gold
A brief history of Rocky Mountain exploration with especial reference to the expedition of Lewis and Clark. New York: Appleton, 1904. xiii, 276p., plates (1 fold.), illus., map. 20cm.

TIBALDI, Tancredi
La regione d'Aosta attraverso i secoli: studi critici di storia. Torino: Roux e Viarengo, 1900-10. 4v. 21cm.

Tibet, and India beyond the Ganges; containing a description of the character, manners, customs ... of the nations inhabiting those countries; [edited by Frederic Shoberl]. R. Ackermann, [1824]. xi, 352p., 12 plates, illus. 15cm. (The world in miniature)

TICHY, Herbert
Cho Oyu, by favour of the gods; translated by Basil Creighton; with a foreword by Sir John Hunt. Methuen, 1957. 196p., plates, illus., maps. 23cm.

TICHY, Herbert
Zum heiligsten Berg der Welt: auf Landstrassen und Pilgerfahrten in Afghanistan, Indien und Tibet; Geleitwort von Sven Hedin. Wien: Seidel, 1937. 192p., plates (2 fold.), illus., maps. 24cm.

TIFFIN, Walter Francis
Sketches, principally in Switzerland and the Genoese Riviera, drawn from nature & lithographed by Walter F. Tiffin. Salisbury: Walter F. Tiffin. [ca 1870]. 1v. of illus. 38cm.

TIGRI, Giuseppe
Guida della montagna pistoiese. 3a ed. corr. Pistoia: Club Alpino Italiano, 1878. 183p., illus. 18cm.

TILLOTSON, John
Picturesque scenery in Wales; illustrated by thirty-seven engravings on steel, by H. Adlard, Allen, Gastineau and others; with descriptions by John Tillotson. T.J. Allman, [1860]. vi, 80p., plates, illus. 26cm.

TILLY, Henri, comte de
Ascensions aux cimes de l'Etna et du Mont Blanc. Genève: Berthier-Guers, 1835. 114p., plates, illus. 22cm.

TILMAN, Harold William
The ascent of Nanda Devi; with a foreword by T.G. Longstaff. Cambridge: University Press, 1937. xii, 235p., plates, illus., maps. 23cm.

- - Another issue. Readers' Union, 1937.

TILMAN, Harold William
China to Chitral; with 69 photographs taken by the author. Cambridge: University Press, 1951. xii, 124p., plates, illus., maps. 24cm.

TILMAN, Harold William
Mischief among the penguins. Hart-Davis, 1961. 192p., plates, illus., maps. 23cm.

TILMAN, Harold William
Mount Everest 1938. Cambridge: University Press, 1948. x, 169p., 34 plates, illus., maps, bibl. 23cm.

TILMAN, Harold William
[Mount Everest 1938]. Everest 1938; traduit par J. et F. Germain. Paris: Arthaud, 1952. 252p., plates, illus., maps. 21cm. (Collection sempervivum, 19)

TILMAN, Harold William

Nepal Himalaya; with 61 photographs taken by the author. Cambridge: University Press, 1952. xii, 272p., plates, illus., maps. 23cm.

TILMAN, Harold William
Snow on the Equator. G. Bell, 1937. xi, 265p., plates, illus., maps. 23cm.

TILMAN, Harold William
Triumph and tribulation. Lymington (Hants.): Nautical, 1977. 153p., illus., maps. 23cm.

TILMAN, Harold William
Two mountains and a river. Cambridge: University Press, 1949. xii, 233p., plates (1 fold.), illus., maps. 23cm.

TILMAN, Harold William
[Two mountains and a river]. Deux montagnes et une rivière ...; traduction de Thérèse Sermorens. Paris: Arthaud, 1953. 240p., plates, illus. 22cm. (Collection sempervivum, 22)

TILMAN, Harold William
When men & mountains meet. Cambridge: University Press, 1946. x, 232p., plates, illus., maps. 23cm.

TIROLER LANDESVERKEHRSAMT
Tirol: Natur, Kunst, Volk, Leben; hrsg. und verlegt vom Tiroler Landesverkehrsamte. Innsbruck: Tiroler Landesverkehrsamt, 1927. 404, 195p., 1 plate, illus. 31cm.

Tirolerführer: Reisehandbuch für Deutsch- und Wälschtirol... Gera: Amthor, 1868. xiv, 470p., plates, maps, plans. 17cm. (Führer in die deutschen Alpen, 1)

TISCHLER, Ernst and WILKE, Viktor
Skitourenführer durch die östl. Beskiden von der Weichsel bis zur Waag ...; hrsg. von Ernst Tischler und Viktor Wilke. Bielitz: Im Selvstverlage des Wintersportklubs, 1912. 42p., 1 plate, map. 18cm.

TISSOT, Roget
Mont Blanc; with a preface by Geoffrey Winthrop
Young. Medici Society, 1924. 142p., 1 fold. plate,
illus., map. 22cm. (Picture guides)

TISSOT, Victor
[La Suisse inconnue]. Au pays des glaciers:
vacances en Suisse; illustrations de Regamey [and
others]. 2e éd. Paris: Delagrave, 1895. 235p.,
illus. 26cm.
Extract from the Author's La Suisse inconnue.

- - 3e éd. 1898.

TISSOT, Victor
[La Suisse inconnue]. Unknown Switzerland;
translated from the 12th ed. by Mrs. Wilson.
Hodder & Stoughton, 1889. x, 361p. 20cm.

- - Another ed. New York: A.D.F. Randolph, [1890].
- - Another ed. New York: J. Pott, 1900.

BORGOGNONI, A   and TITTA ROSA, G
Scalatori: le più audaci imprese alpinistiche da
Whymper al "sesto grado", raccontate dai
protagonisti; a cura di A. Borgognono, G. Titta
Rosa. 2a ed., riv. e aggiornata. Milano: Hoepli,
1941. xv, 403p., plates, illus., bibl. 21cm.

TOBIAS, Michael Charles
Dhaulagirideon; edited and with an introduction by
Eric Alfred Hoffman. Yellow Springs (Ohio):
International Mountaineering Arts Journal, 1973.
xiv, 97, 25p., plates, illus. 22cm.

TOBIAS, Michael Charles
Tsa; with a foreword by Eric Alfred Hoffman.
[Yellow Springs (Ohio)]: International Mountain-
eering Arts Institute, 1974. [79]p. 17 x 19cm.

TÖPFFER, Rodolphe
Derniers voyages en zigzag; ou, Excursions d'un
pensionnat en vacances dans les cantons suisses et
sur le revers italien des Alpes. Genève: A.
Jullien, 1910. 2v. in 1, 1 plate, illus., port.
20cm.

TÖPFFER, Rodolphe
Mélanges. Paris: Cherbuliez, 1852. 355p. 18cm.

TÖPFFER, Rodolphe
Nouveaux voyages en zigzag, à la Grande Chartreuse,
autour du Mont Blanc, dans les vallées d'Herenz
...;précédés d'une notice par Sainte-Beuve;
illustrés d'après les dessins originaux de Töpffer
... Paris: V. Lecou, 1854. xvii, 454p., plates,
illus. 28cm.

- - 2e éd. Paris: Garnier, 1858.
- - 3e éd. 1864.
- - 4e éd. 1877.

TÖPFFER, Rodolphe
Nouvelles génevoises; précédées d'une lettre ...
par le comte Xavier de Maistre. Paris: Charpentier,
1846. 491p. 18cm.

- - Another éd. 1848.
- - Nouv. éd. Paris: Hachette, 1855.

TÖPFFER, Rodolphe
Premiers voyages en zigzag... 4e éd. Paris: V.
Lecou, 1855. 457p., plates, illus. 28cm.
Earlier eds. published under title: Voyages en
zigzag...

TÖPFFER, Rodolphe
Voyage autour du Mont Blanc, dans les vallées
d'Herens, de Zermatt et au Grimsel, autographié
par R.T. [i.e. Rodolphe Töpffer]. Genève: Schmid,
1843. 1v. (chiefly illus.). 20 x 26cm.
Texts in ms. facsimile.

TÖPFFER, Rodolphe
Voyages en zigzag; ou, Excursions d'un pensionnat
en vacances dans les cantons suisses et sur le
revers italien des Alpes. Paris: J.-J. Dubochet,
1844. viii, 542p., plates, illus. 28cm.

- - 2e éd. 1846.
Later eds. published under title: Premiers voyages
en zigzag...

TÖPFFER, Rodolphe
[Voyages en zigzag...]. Reisen im Zickzack;
uebersetzt und hrsg. von Heinrich Conrad. München:
G. Müller, 1912. vi, 405p., illus. 19cm.
(Lebenskunst, 4)

TOGA-RASA
See
SARAGAT, Giovanni

TOLLEMACHE, Beatrix L
Engelberg and other verses. 2nd ed. Rivingtons,
1898. xi, 105p. 19cm.

TOLLEMACHE, Beatrix L
Grisons incidents in olden times. Percival, 1891.
79p. 20cm.

TOLSTOY, Leo, Count
The Cossacks and other tales of the Caucasus;
translated by Louise and Aylmer Maude. Oxford
University Press, 1916. viii, 371p. 17cm.
(World's classics)

TOMBAZI, N   A
Account of a photographic expedition to the
southern glaciers of Kangchenjunga in the Sikkim
Himalaya. Bombay: The Author, 1925. 73, 3, 5p.,
plates (some fold.), illus., map (in pocket).
20cm.

Tombleson's Ansichten von Tyrol
See
Ansichten von Tyrol

Tombleson's Upper Rhine; [edited by W.G. Fearnside].
Black & Armstrong, [185-]. viii, 181p., plates,
illus. 24cm.

TOMLIN, James
Notes from a traveller's journal, during an
excursion in Norway and Sweden. [The Author],
1852. 204p. 21cm.

TOMLINSON, Charles
The frozen stream; or, An account of the nature,
properties, dangers and uses of ice, in various
parts of the world, [by Charles Tomlinson].
Society for Promoting Christian Knowledge, 1846.
150p., illus. 15cm.

- - Another ed. [ca 1862].

TOMLINSON, Charles
The snow-storm; or, An account of the nature,
properties, dangers, and uses of snow, in various
parts of the world, [by Charles Tomlinson].
Society for Promoting Christian Knowledge, 1845.
116p., illus. 15cm.

TONELLA, Guido
Skiing at Sestrières; translated by Katherine
Natzio. Sestrières: Ski Club, 1934. 148p.,
illus., map (in pocket). 18cm.

TONETTI, Federico
Guida illustrata della Valsesia e del Monte Rosa.
Varallo: Tipografia Camaschella e Zanfa, 1891.
xv, 532p., illus. 19cm.

TONIOLO, A   R
Revisione critica delle partizioni del sistema
alpino occidentale. Firenze: I.G.M., 1925. 169p.,
fold.plates, illus., col. map, bibl. 25cm.
(Istituto Geografico Militare. Pubblicazioni)

TONNEAU, Alfred
Alpages et sommets: courses en Haute-Savoie.
Genève: Labarthe, [1903?]. viii, 162p., illus.
33cm.

TONNELLÉ, Alfred
Fragments sur l'art et la philosophie, suivis de
notes et pensées diverses; recueillis dans les
papiers de Alfred Tonnellé; publié par G.-A.
Heinrich. 2e éd. Paris: Ch. Douniol, 1860.
411p. 24cm.

TOOKE, William
Boydell's Picturesque scenery of Norway; with the
principal towns from the Naze ... to the ...
Swinesund; from original drawings made on the spot,
and engraved by John William Edy; with remarks and
observations made in a tour through the country,
and rev. and corr. by William Tooke. Hurst,
Robinson, 1820. xlv p., 80 plates, illus. 42cm.

TOPALI, Constantin P
Constantin P. Topali, 1898-1924. Payot, 1926.
87p., illus. 22cm.

- - 2nd ed. Lausanne: Imprimeries Réunies, 1931.

TOPHAM, W   F
The Lakes of England; illustrated with eighteen
coloured etchings. T.J. Allman, 1869. 40p., col.
plates, illus. 22cm.

TORLIK, J H A
Reise in der Schweiz und einem Theile italiens, in
Jahre 1803. Kopenhagen: J.H. Schubothe, 1807.
374p. 18cm.

TORNQUIST, A
Geologischer Führer durch Ober-Italien. 1. Das
Gebirge der ober-italienischen Seen... Berlin:
Borntraeger, 1902. xvi, 302p., illus., maps.
16cm. (Sammlung geologischer Führer, 9)

TORR, Cecil
Hannibal crosses the Alps. Cambridge: University
Press, 1924. viii, 40p., map. 19cm.

- - 2nd ed. 1925.

TORRAS, César August
Pirineu Català: guia itinerari del excursionista a
Camprodon... Barcelona: Tip. "L'Avenç", 1902.
xxviii, 643p., fold.col. plates, illus., maps.
19cm.

- - Another ed. in 8v. 1905-18.
Library has v. 1-2, 5-7 only.

TORRE, Karl Wilhelm von dalla
See
DALLA TORRE, Karl Wilhelm von

TORRENS, Henry D
Travels in Ladak, Tartary and Kashmir. Saunders,
Otley, 1862. iv, 367p., plates (some fold., some
col.), illus, map. 23cm.

La totale et vraie descriptiõ de toₓ les passaiges,
lieux & destroictz, par lesq̃lz on peut passer &
entrer des Gaules es Ytalies ..., [par Jacques
Signot]. Paris: Toussains Denys, 1518. 40 leaves,
1 fold. plate, map. 20cm.

TOUCHSTONE
See
BOOTH, M

TOULOUSE, Gilbert
Montagne retrouvée. Paris: Arthaud, 1957. 213p.
22cm. (Collection sempervivum, 32)

A tour in Wales, and through several counties of
England, including both the universities, performed
in the summer of 1805, [by William F. Mavor]. R.
Phillips, 1806. 184p., 1 fold. plate, illus. 23cm.
(In: A collection of modern and contemporary
voyages... Vol.3. 1806)

A tour through part of France, Switzerland, and
Italy, including a summary history of the principal
cities... Baldwin, Cradock, & Joy, 1827. 2v. 24cm.

A tour to Great St. Bernard's and round Mont Blanc;
with descriptions copied from a journal kept by
the author; and drawings taken from nature.
Harvey & Darton, 1827 [cover 1828]. iv, 144p.,
plates, illus., fold. map. 19cm.

TOURING-CLUB DE FRANCE
La montagne: catalogue de la Bibliothèque léguée
au Touring-Club de France par Étienne May,
1881-1962. Paris: The Club, 1965. 94 leaves.
27cm.

Le touriste à Chamonix en 1853, [par David Dunant].
Genève: Ch. Gruaz, 1853. 294p. 24cm.

The tourist's manual; or, An account of the principal pleasure tours in Scotland. 8th ed.
Edinburgh: J. Thomson, 1832. xi, 383p., plates
(2 fold.), illus., maps. 19cm.

The tourists; or, Continental travelling; edited by
John Fred Dean. Leeds: C. Goodall, 1878. 70p.,
plates, illus. 19cm.

TOURNEFORT, Joseph Pitton de
See
PITTON DE TOURNEFORT, Joseph

NAC, Paul and TOURS, Constant de
Vingt jours en Suisse; 160 dessins ... par Paul
Nac. Paris: May & Motteroz, [1892]. 160p.,
illus., maps. 14 x 23cm. (Collection des guides-
albums du touriste)

TOWNSHEND, Chauncy Hare
A descriptive tour in Scotland, by T.H.C. [i.e.
Chauncy Hare Townshend]. Brussels: Hauman,
London: Whitaker, 1840. x, 395p., plates, illus.
23cm.

TOZER, Henry Fanshawe
A history of ancient geography. Cambridge:
University Press, 1897. xvii, 387p., fold. plates
(some col.), maps. 21cm. (Cambridge geographical
series)

TOZER, Henry Fanshawe
Researches in the highlands of Turkey; including
visits to Mounts Ida, Athos, Olympus and Pelion...
Murray, 1869. 2v., plates (1 fold.), illus.,
maps. 21cm.

TOZER, Henry Fanshawe
Turkish Armenia and eastern Asia Minor. Longmans,
Green, 1881. xiv, 470p., plates (1 fold.col.),
illus., map. 23cm.

Tracks in Norway of four pairs of feet, delineated
by four hands with notes on the handiwork of each
by the others. Sampson Low, Marston, Searle &
Rivington, 1884. x, 95p., map. 19cm.

TRAFFORD, Marc A   de Lavis
See
LAVIS-TRAFFORD, Marc A   de

TRANTER, Philip
No tigers in the Hindu Kush; edited by Nigel
Tranter. Hodder & Stoughton, 1968. 155p., plates
(1 col.), illus., map, bibl. 23cm.

TRAUTWEIN, Th.
Das bayrische Hochland mit den Allgäu, das an-
grenzende Nordtirol, Vorarlberg, Salzburg nebst
Salzkammergut. 16.Aufl., bearb. von Anton
Edlinger. Wien: A. Edlinger, 1914. xxxii, 373p.,
maps, plans. 17cm.

TRAUTWEIN, Th.
Tirol Südbaiern und Salzburg nebst den angren-
zenden Alpenländern Oesterreichs: Wegweiser für
Reisende. 8.verm. Aufl. Augsburg: Lamparts
Alpiner Verlag, 1889. xx, 538p., maps, plans.
17cm.

TRAUTWEIN, Th.
Tirol und Vorarlberg, bayr. Hochland, Allgäu, Salzburg, Ober- und Nieder-Oesterreich, Steiermark, Kärnten und Krain: Wegweiser für Reisende; bearb. von Anton Edlinger und Heinrich Hess. 18.Aufl. Wien: A. Edlinger, 1913. 8v., maps, plans. 17cm. In slip-case.

The traveller's companion in an excursion from Chester through North Wales. Chester: Printed for G. Batenham by R. Evans, [1827]. 100p., plates (1 fold.col.), illus., map. 17cm.

The traveller's guide through Scotland, and its islands. 6th ed. Edinburgh: J. Thomson, 1814. 2v., plates (some fold.), illus., maps. 19cm.

A traveller's thoughts; or, Lines suggested by a tour on the continent. 2nd ed. Longman, Orme, Brown, Green & Longmans, 1837. 100p. 20cm.

Travelling notes in France, Italy and Switzerland of an invalid in search of health [i.e. John Strang]. Glasgow: D. Robertson; London: Longman, 1863. xix, 266p. 20cm.

Travels by 'Umbra' [i.e. Charles C. Clifford]. Edinburgh: Edmonston & Douglas, 1865. vi, 278p. 22cm.

Travels in Switzerland. Society for Promoting Christian Knowledge, [ca 1847]. viii, 324p., illus. 15cm.

Travels in Switzerland; compiled from the most recent authorities. Dublin: P.D. Hardy, 1830. 164p., plates, illus. 15cm.

TRAVERS, Benjamin
A descriptive tour to the Lakes of Cumberland and Westmoreland, in the autumn of 1804, [by Benjamin Travers]. T. Ostell, 1806. viii, 164p. 18cm.

TRAVERS, W   T   L
New Zealand, graphic and descriptive; the illustrations by C.D. Barraud; edited by W.T.L. Travers. Sampson Low, Marston, Searle & Rivington, 1877. 40p., plates, illus., map. 58cm.

TRAYNARD, Philippe and TRAYNARD, Claude
Cimes et neige: 102 sommets à ski. [Paris], Arthaud, 1971. [250]p., illus., maps. 24cm.

TRAYNARD, Claude and TRAYNARD, Philippe
Ski de montagne, [par] Paul Beylier [and others]; sous la direction de Claude et Philippe Traynard. [Grenoble]: Arthaud, 1974. 230p., plates, illus., bibl. 22cm. (Collection sempervivum, no.59)

TREBECK, George
MOORCROFT, William
Travels in the Himalayan provinces of Hindustan and the Panjab; in Ladakh and Kashmir; in Peshawar, Kabul, Kunduz and Bokhara, from 1819 to 1825, by William Moorcroft and George Trebeck; prepared for the press from original journals ... by Horace Hayman Wilson. Murray, 1841. 2v., plates (1 fold.), illus., map. 24cm.

TREDICINI DE SAINT-SÉVERIN, Hector, marquis de
La chasse au chamois; préface de Henry Bordeaux. Paris: Firmin-Didot, [1925]. xxiii, 285p., illus. 21cm.

- - Another issue. 1897.

TRENCH, Fanny Maria
A journal abroad in 1868, for young friends at home, by F.M.T. [i.e. Fanny M. Trench] aetat. 16; with a short preface by her father, Francis Trench. R. Bentley, [1868]. iv, 142p. 21cm.

TRENCH, Francis
A walk round Mont Blanc, etc. R. Bentley, 1847. 332p. 21cm.

- - Another issue. 1847.

TRENKER, Luis
Berge im Schnee: das Winterbuch. Berlin: Neufeld & Henius, 1932. 128p., plates, illus. 26cm.

TRENKER, Luis and SCHMIDKUNZ, Walter
Berge und Heimat: das Buch von den Bergen und ihren Menschen. Berlin: Th. Knaur, 1939. 138p., plates, illus. 26cm.

TRENKER, Luis
Kameraden der Berge. Berlin: Rowohlt, 1932. 203p., plates, illus. 21cm.

TRENKER, Luis
[Kameraden der Berge]. Brothers of the snow; translated by F.H. Lyon. Routledge, 1933. vii, 247p., plates, illus. 23cm.

TRENKER, Luis
Meine Berge: Das Bergbuch; unter Mitarbeit von Walter Schmidkunz. Berlin: Neufeld & Henius, 1931. 132p., plates, illus. 26cm.

TRENT POLYTECHNIC HINDU KUSH EXPEDITION, 1975
Report; edited by Peter Holden. Nottingham: The Expedition, [1977]. 32, xxxvip., plates, illus., map. 30cm.

TRENTINAGLIA-TELVENBURG, Josef, Ritter von
Das Gebiet der Rosanna und Trisanna (Sannengebiet in West-Tirol); mit besonderer Berücksichtigung der orographischen, glacialen... Verhältnisse, nach eigenen Untersuchungen dargestellt von Josef Ritter von Trentinaglia-Telvenburg. Wien: C. Gerold, 1875. 204p., col. plates (1 fold.), illus., map. 25cm.

TRENTINI, Albert von
Südtirol. Bielefeld: Velhagen & Klasing, [1912]. 34p., illus. (some col.), map. 26cm. (Velhagen & Klasings Volksbücher der Erdkunde, Nr.56)

TREPTOW, Leon
Schwartzenstein, Mörchner-Mösele. Stuttgart: Deutsche Verlags-Anstalt, 1909. 81p., plates, illus., map. 18cm. (Alpine Gipfelführer, 20)

TREVENA, John
Adventures among wild flowers. Arnold, 1914. vii, 304p., plates, illus. 21cm.

TREVES, Sir Frederick
The Lake of Geneva. Cassell, 1922. xii, 347p., plates (1 fold.col.), illus., map. 24cm.

TREVOR-BATTYE, Aubyn
Camping in Crete, with notes upon the animal and plant life of the island; including a description of certain caves and their ancient deposits, by Dorothea M.A. Bate. Witherby, 1913. xxi, 308p., plates (1 fold.col.), illus., map. 23cm.

TRIBOLET, Maurice de
FAVRE, Alphonse
Texte explicatif de la carte du phénomène erratique et des anciens glaciers du versant nord des Alpes suisses et de la chaîne du Mont-Blanc; précédé d'une introduction par Ernest Favre; et suivi d'une biographie de Léon du Pasquier par Maurice de Tribolet, avec les portraits... Berne: Schmid & Francke, 1898. 77p., plates, ports. 33cm. (Beiträge zur geologischen Karte der Schweiz = Matériaux pour la carte géologique de la Suisse, livr.28)

TRIGONOMETRICAL SURVEY OF INDIA
See
SURVEY OF INDIA

A trimester in France and Swisserland; or, A three months' journey in ... 1820, from Calais to Basle ... and from Basle to Paris, through Strasburg and Reims, by an Oxonian [i.e. Stephen Weston]. W. Clarke, 1821. 88p., plates, illus. 22cm.

TRINKLER, Emil
Tibet: sein geographisches Bild und seine Stellung
im asiatischen Kontinent. München, 1922. 146p.,
plates (1 fold.), illus., map, bibl. 25cm.
Offprint from Mitteilungen der Geographischen
Gesellschaft in München, Bd.15, 1922.

Trip to Paris and Switzerland. Leeds: Printed by
B.W. Sharp, 1867. 88p. 21cm.

TROIL, Uno von
Letters on Iceland, containing observations on the
civil ... and natural history; antiquities, volcanos, basalts, hot springs ... made during a
voyage undertaken in the year 1772, by Joseph
Banks, assisted by Dr. Solander, J. Lind, Uno von
Troil ..., written by Uno von Troil. W.Richardson,
1780. xxvi, 400p., plates (1 fold.), illus., map,
bibl. 21cm.

TROILLET, Ernest Lovey
See
LOVEY-TROILLET, Ernest

TROLLIET, Marie
Edelweiss: un roman dans les Alpes.
(In Bibliothèque universelle ... v.61-62, jan.-
juin, 1894, 6pts.)

TROLLIET, Marie
Un vieux pays: croquis valaisans, [par] Mario***
[i.e. Marie Trolliet]; illustrations de E. Ravel.
2e éd. Lausanne: Payot, 1892. 289p., plates,
illus. 20cm.

TROLLOPE, Anthony
British sports and pastimes; edited by A. Trollope.
Virtue, 1868. 322p. 20cm.
Reprinted from Saint Paul's magazine.

TROLLOPE, Anthony
Travelling sketches. Chapman & Hall, 1866. 112p.
20cm.
Reprinted from Pall Mall gazette.
Contains: The Alpine Club man.

TROLLOPE, T   Adolphus
Impressions of a wanderer in Italy, Switzerland,
France, and Spain. H. Colburn, 1850. viii, 408p.
21cm.

LONGMAN, William and TROWER, Henry
Journal of six weeks' adventures in Switzerland,
Piedmont, and on the Italian Lakes, by W. L[ongman]
and H. T[rower], June, July, August, 1856.
Printed by Spottiswoode, 1856. 123p., 1 fold.col.
plate, map. 21cm.

TROYE, J
A short account of Mont Blanc and the valley of
Chamouni; with an historical sketch of the city of
Geneva, serving to illustrate the models of these
two places. Whittingham and Rowland, 1817. 22p.,
plates, illus. 22cm.

TROYON, Frédéric
Habitations lacustres des temps anciens et modernes.
Lausanne: G. Bridel, 1860. xii, 495p., plates,
illus. 23cm.

TRUFFAUT, Roland
[Du Kenya au Kilimanjaro]. From Kenya to Kilimanjaro. Hale, 1957. 155p., illus., bibl. 23cm.

TRUTAT, Eugène
Les glaciers de La Maladetta et le Pic des Posets.
Toulouse, 1876. 27p., plates, illus. 24cm.
Offprint from Annuaire du Club Alpin Français, 1875.

TRUTAT, Eugène
La photographie en montagne. Paris: Gauthier-
Villars, 1894. ix, 137p., illus. 19cm.

TRUTAT, Eugène
Les Pyrénées: les montagnes, les glaciers, les eaux
minérales, les phénomènes de l'atmosphère, la
flore, la faune et l'homme. Paris: Baillière,
1896. 371p., illus. 19cm. (Bibliothèque
scientifique contemporaine)

TSCHARNER, Hans Fritz von
Auf wolkigen Höhen. Bern: Berna-Vorlag, [1936].
167p., plates, illus. 22cm.

TSCHARNER, Hans Fritz von
Gipfel und Grate. Bern: A. Scherz, 1943. 311p.
22cm.

TSCHARNER, Hans Fritz von
[Gipfel und Grate]. Cimes et arêtes; traduction
d'André Roch. Lausanne: F. Rouge, 1944. 246p.,
plates, illus. 22cm. (Collection alpine)

TSCHARNER, Johann Baptist von
Die Bernina (1786). München: Im Münchner Buch-
verlag, 1933. 43p., illus. 18 x 25cm.

TSCHARNER, J   K   von
Der Kanton Graubünden, historisch, statistisch,
geographisch, dargestellt für einheimische und
fremde Reisende. Chur: Grubenmann, 1842. 296p.,
plates, illus. 18cm.

KÖDER, G   W   and TSCHARNER, Peter Conradin von
Der Kanton Graubünden, historisch, geographisch,
statistisch geschildert ... G.W. Köder und P.C.
von Tscharner. St. Gallen: Huber, 1838. 381p.
18cm. (Gemälde der Schweiz, 15)

TSCHARNER, Peter Conradin von
Wanderungen durch die Rhätischen Alpen: ein
Beytrag zur Charakteristik dieses Theils des
schweizerischen Hochlandes und seiner Bewohner,
[von Peter C. von Tscharner]. Zürich: Orell,
Füssli, 1829-31. 2v., plates, maps. 21cm.

TSCHARNER, Vincent Bernhard von
HALLER, Albrecht von
Les Alpes: poème de M. Haller; traduit en prose
françoise par M. de T[scharner]. [Göttingen,
1749]. 16p. 21cm.
Offprint from Nouvelle bibliothèque germanique.

TSCHUDI FAMILY
TSCHUDI, Carlos
Ein dankesbuch. [N.p.]: The Author, [1930].
152p., plates (2 fold.), illus., port. 24cm.

TSCHUDI, Aegidius
De prisca ac vera Alpina Rhaetia, cum caetero
Alpinarum gentium tractu ... descriptio. Basileae:
Apud Mich. Isingrinium, 1538. 134p. 23cm.

- - Another ed., cui hac ed. accessit regula ... per
Conradum Lycosthenem. 1560.

TSCHUDI, Aegidius
[De prisca ac vera Alpina Rhaetia...]. Die vralt
warhafftig Alpisch Rhetia, sampt dem Tract der
anderen Alpgebirgen, nach Plinii, Ptolemei...
Basell: Gedrukt zu Basell, 1538. [134]p. 22cm.

TSCHUDI, Carlos
Ein dankesbuch. [N.p.]: The Author, [1930].
152p., plates (2 fold.), illus., port. 24cm.

TSCHUDI, Friedrich von
Das Thierleben der Alpenwelt: Naturansichten und
Thierzeichnungen aus dem schweizerischen Gebirge.
5.verb. Aufl. Leipzig: J.J. Weber, 1860. xv,
534p., 25 plates, illus. 24cm.

TSCHUDI, Friedrich von
[Das Thierleben der Alpenwelt...]. Les Alpes:
description pittoresque de la nature et de la
faune alpestres; traduction authorisée par
l'auteur. Berne: Dalp, 1859. 737p., plates,
illus. 24cm.

TSCHUDI, Friedrich von
[Das Thierleben der Alpenwelt...]. Le monde des
Alpes; ou, Description pittoresque des montagnes
de la Suisse et particulièrement des animaux qui
les peuplent. Genève: Jules, 1858. 3v. 19cm.

TSCHUDI, Friedrich von
[Das Thierleben der Alpenvelt...]. Sketches of
nature in the Alps... Longman, Brown, Green, &
Longmans, 1856. xii, 246p. 19cm. (Traveller's
library)
Selections.

- - Another ed. 1862.

TSCHUDI, Friedrich von
Tiere der Alpen. Zürich: Orell Füssli, [1917].
175p., illus. 18cm. (Schweizer Jugendbücher, 5)

TSCHUDI, Iwan von
Guide suisse: manuel du voyageur dans les cantons
avec détails plus particuliers sur les principales
villes, les lieux de cures et les Alpes. le éd.,
française. St. Gall: Scheitlin & Zollikofer, 1861.
vii, 278p., map. 16cm.

TSCHUDI, Iwan von
Savoyen und des angrenzende Piemont und Dauphiné:
Reisetaschenbuch. St. Gallen: Scheitlin &
Zollikofer, 1871. iv, 176p., maps, plans. 16cm.
(Schweizerführer)

TSCHUDI, Iwan von
Der Tourist in der Schweiz und den Grenzrayons:
Reisetaschenbuch. 4.Aufl. Zürich: Orell Füssli,
1899. 3v., maps, plans. 16cm.
In slip-case.

TSCHUDI, Iwan von
Der Turist in der Schweiz und dem angrenzenden Süd-
Deutschland, Ober-Italien und Savoyen: Reisetaschenbuch. 31.Aufl. Zürich: Orell Füssli 1890. xlv,
660p., plates, illus., maps, plans. 16cm.

TSCHUDI, Iwan von
Ur- und Südschweiz: Reisetaschenbuch für die Kantone
Luzern, Unterwalden, Zug, Schwyz, Uri, Wallis und
Tessin, die Walliner und die Grauen Alpen und
Ober-Italien... St. Gallen: Scheitlin und
Zollikofer, 1869. xv, 270p., plates, illus., maps,
plans. 16cm. (Schweizerführer)

TSCHUDI, J J von
Travels in Peru during the years 1838-1842, on the
coast, in the sierra, across the cordilleras and
the Andes, into the primeval forests; translated
from the German by Thomasina Ross. Bogue, 1847.
xii, 506p., plates, illus. 24cm.

TSCHUMI, Otto
Urgeschichte der Schweiz. Frauenfeld: Huber, 1926.
195p., 20 plates, illus. 22cm. (Die Schweiz im
deutschen Geistesleben, Bd.5)

TUBBY, Alfred Herbert
A consulting surgeon in the Near East.
Christophers, 1920. xv, 279p., plates, illus.
23cm.

TUCCI, Giuseppe
Nepal: the discovery of the Malla; translated from
the Italian by Lovett Edwards. Allen & Unwin,
1962. 96p., plates (some col.), illus., map.
20cm.

TUCKER, A R
Toro: visits to Ruwenzori "Mountains of the Moon".
Church Missionary Society, 1899. 51p., illus.,
map. 20 x 23cm.

TUCKER, John
Kanchenjunga; foreword by Sir John Hunt. Elek
Books, 1955. 224p., plates, illus., maps. 24cm.

TUCKETT, Elizabeth
Beaten tracks; or, Pen and pencil sketches in
Italy, by the authoress of "A voyage en zigzag"
[i.e. Elizabeth Tuckett]. Longmans, Green, 1866.
viii, 278p., plates, illus. 23cm.

TUCKETT, Elizabeth
How we spent the summer; or, A "Voyage en zigzag"
in Switzerland and Tyrol, with some members of the
Alpine Club, from the sketch book of one of the
party [i.e. Elizabeth Tuckett]. Longman, Green,
Longman, Roberts & Green, 1864. 40 leaves of
illus. 27 x 36cm.

- - 2nd ed. 1864.
- - 6th ed. 1874.

TUCKETT, Elizabeth
Pictures in Tyrol and elsewhere, from a family
sketch-book, by the author of a "Voyage en zigzag"
&c. [i.e. Elizabeth Tuckett]. Longmans, Green,
1867. 313p., plates, illus. 21cm.

- - 2nd ed. 1869.

TUCKETT, Elizabeth
Zigzagging amongst Dolomites, [by Elizabeth
Tuckett]. Longmans, Green, Reader & Dyer, 1871.
38 leaves of illus., map. 26 x 36cm.

TUCKETT, Francis Fox
Dauphiné Alps: heights and outlines. [Bristol]:
[n.pub.], [ca 1870]. lv. of illus. 37cm.

TUCKETT, Francis Fox
Hochalpenstudien: gesammelte Schriften; Uebersetzung von A. Cordes. Autorisirte Ausg. Leipzig:
Liebeskind, 1873-74. 2v., plates (some fold.),
illus. (some in pocket), map. 19cm.

TUCKETT, Francis Fox
A pioneer in the high Alps: alpine diaries and
letters of F.F. Tuckett, 1856-1874. Arnold, 1920.
xi, 372p., plates, illus. 23cm.

TUCKETT, Lizzie
See
TUCKETT, Elizabeth

TÜRLER, E A
Die Berge am Vierwaldstätter-See ...; für
Touristen und Alpenfreunde dargestellt von E.A.
Türler. Luzern: Doleschal, 1888. viii, 230p.,
plates, illus. 18cm.

TÜRLER, E A
Das malerische und romantische Emmenthal nebst
den angrenzenden Landestheilen: ein Wanderbuch...
Burgdorf: C. Langlois, 1887. viii, 203p., plates,
illus. 21cm.

TÜRLER, E A
St. Gotthard, Airolo und Val Piora; pittoreske
Beschreibung der Natur und Landschaft des St.
Gotthardgebirges ...; für Alpenfreunde dargestellt
von E.A. Türler. Bern: Kaeser, 1891. viii,
160p., plates, illus. 19cm.

TUGWELL, George
On the mountain, being the Welsh experiences of
Abraham Black & Jonas White, Esquires, moralists,
photographers, fishermen, and botanists. R.
Bentley, 1862. viii, 262p., col. plates, illus.
20cm.

TUMA, Henrik
Pomen in razvoj alpinizma. Zalozba: Turistični
Klub Skala, [1930?]. 296p., plates, illus. 25cm.

TUPPER, Martin
Paterfamilias's Diary of everybody's tour:Belgium
and the Rhine, Munich, Switzerland, Milan, Geneva
and Paris, [by Martin Tupper]. Hatchard, 1856.
385p., plates, illus. 18cm.

TURBEAUX, Jacques
Saffres (Côte-d'Or): groupe des Rochers de
Miraude; édité avec l'appui de la Fédération
Française de la Montagne. Côte d'Or: Club Alpin
Français, Section de Côte d'Or, 1964. 55p., 1
fold.plate, illus., map. 22cm.

TURIN. Università. Laboratorii Scientifici
"A. Mosso" sul Monte Rosa
  See
LABORATORII SCIENTIFICI "A. MOSSO" SUL MONTE ROSA

TURLERUS, Hieronymus
  De peregrinatione et agro neapolitano, libri II;
  omnibus peregrinantibus utiles ac necessarii: ac
  in eorum gratiam nunc primum editi. Argentorati:
  Per Bernhardum Iobinum, 1574. 107p. 16cm.

TURLETTI, Vittorio
  Attraverso le Alpi: storia aneddotica delle guerre
  di montagna combattutesi dal 1742 al 1748 in difesa
  dell'Italia; illustrata ... [di] Giuseppe Ricci.
  Torino: Paravia, 1897. 292p., illus. 25cm.

TURNER, Joseph Mallord William
RUSSELL, John and WILTON, Andrew
  Turner in Switzerland. Dubendorf (Zurich): De
  Clivo Press, 1976. 148p., illus. (some col.),
  maps. 32cm.
  Sponsored by the Swiss National Tourist Office and
  the Swiss Foundation for Alpine Research.

TURNER, Samuel, 1749? - 1802
  An account of an embassy to the court of Teshoo
  Lama in Tibet; containing a narrative of a journey
  through Bootan, and part of Tibet; to which are
  added, views taken on the spot by Lieutenant Samuel
  Davis; and observations botanical, mineralogical,
  and medical, by Mr. Robert Saunders. Nicol, 1800.
  xxviii, 473p., plates, illus. 30cm.

TURNER, Samuel, 1869 - 1929
  The conquest of the New Zealand Alps. Fisher
  Unwin, 1922. 291p., plates, illus. 23cm.

TURNER, Samuel, 1869 - 1929
  My climbing adventures in four continents. Fisher
  Unwin, 1911. 283p., plates, illus. 23cm.

TURNER, Samuel, 1869 - 1929
  Siberia: a record of travel, climbing and exploration; with an introduction by Baron Heyking;
  illustrated from photographs by the author. Fisher
  Unwin, 1905. xxiv, 420p., plates (2 fold.), illus.,
  maps. 23cm.

  - - 2nd ed. 1911.

TURSKY, Franz
  Führer durch die Glocknergruppe. 2.verb. und verm.
  Aufl. Wien: Artaria, 1925. xv, 184p., plates,
  illus., map (in pocket). 17cm.

TURSKY, Franz
  Führer durch die Goldberggruppe, Sonnblickgruppe.
  Wien: Artaria, 1927. 180p., plates, illus., map.
  17cm.

TURSKY, Franz
  Der Grossglockner und seine Geschichte. Wien: A.
  Hartleben, 1922. 143p., illus., maps. 19cm.

TURSKY, Franz
  Höhenzauber: Erlebnisse und Gedanken eines Berg-
  steigers und Schneeschuhläufers. München: Im
  Hochalpenverlag, 1924. 201p., plates, illus. 20cm.

TURSKY, Franz
  Skiführer durch die Kitzbüheler Alpen. Wien:
  Artaria, 1926. xii, 242p., plates, illus. 18cm.

TUSHINSKII, G   K
  Laviny: vozniknovenie i zashchita ot nikh; pod
  redaktsiei ... K.K. Markova. Moskva: Gos. Izd.
  Geograficheskoi Literatury, 1949. 212p., plates,
  illus., bibl. 23cm.

MALEINOV, A   A   and TUSHINSKII, G   K
  Puteshestvie v gorakh. Moskva: Gos. Izd.
  Geograficheskoi Literatury, 1950. 334p., fold.
  plates, illus. 21cm.

TUSHKAN, Geogi
  The hunter of the Pamirs: a novel of adventure in
  Soviet Central Asia; translated from the Russian by
  Gerard Shelley. Hutchinson, [1944]. 327p. 20cm.

TUTT, J   W
  Rambles in alpine valleys. Swan Sonnenschein, 1895.
  viii, 208p., plates, illus., map. 19cm.

TUTTON, Alfred Edwin Howard
  The high Alps: a natural history of ice and snow.
  Cheaper ed. K. Paul, Trench, Trubner, 1931. xvi,
  319p., 48 plates, illus., map. 23cm.

TUTTON, Alfred Edwin Howard
  The natural history of ice and snow, illustrated
  from the Alps. K. Paul, Trench, Trubner, 1927.
  xvi, 319p., plates (1 fold.), illus., map. 23cm.

TUVAR, Lorenzo
  Tales & legends of the English Lakes and mountains;
  collected from the best and most authentic sources
  by Lorenzo Tuvar. Longmans, [1852]. 312p.,
  plates, illus. 20cm.

TWAIN, Mark
  A tramp abroad; illustrated by W. Fr. Brown ... and
  other artists, with also three or four pictures
  made by the author... Hartford (Conn.): American
  Publishing Co.; London: Chatto & Windus, 1880.
  631p., illus. 23cm.

TWINING, Henry
  The elements of picturesque scenery; or, Studies
  of nature made in travel with a view to improvement in landscape painting. Longman, Brown, Green,
  & Longmans, 1853. xiv, 309p., plates, illus.
  27cm.

TWINING, Henry
  On the elements of picturesque scenery, considered
  with reference to landscape painting. Printed for
  private distribution by G. Barclay, 1846. xii,
  375p., plates (some col.), illus. 27cm.

TWITTERS, Peter
  How I went up the Jung-Frau, and came down again,
  by Peter Twitters, Philosopher, Camden Town, from
  his own private diary... The Author, [ca 1852].
  9-14p., illus. 17cm.

Two on a tour, by one of the two for the other one,
  being an accurate account, more or less, of the
  first Swiss Touring trip of the Manchester Touring Club,
  Whitsuntide, 1892. Ardwick: Riley's Printing
  Office, [1892]. 65p., port. 21cm.

TYACKE, R   H
  How I shot my bears; or, Two years' tent life in
  Kulu and Lahoul. Sampson Low, Marston, 1893.
  xii, 318p., 1 fold.col. plate, illus., map. 20cm.

TYLER, J   E
  The alpine passes: the Middle Ages (962-1250).
  Oxford: Blackwell, 1930. 188p., bibl. 23cm.

TYNDALE, Henry Edmund Guise
KLUCKER, Christian
  [Erinnerungen eines Bergführers]. Adventures of
  an alpine guide; translated from the 3rd German
  ed. by Erwin and Pleasaunce von Gaisberg; edited
  and with additional chapters by H.E.G. Tyndale.
  Murray, 1932. xiv, 329p., plates, illus., map.
  23cm.

TYNDALE, Henry Edmund Guise
  Mountain paths. Eyre & Spottiswoode, 1948. x,
  208p., plates, illus. 23cm. (New alpine library)

TYNDALE, Henry Edmund Guise
WHYMPER, Edward
  Scrambles amongst the Alps, with additional illustrations and material from the author's unpublished
  diaries. 6th ed., rev. and edited by H.E.G.
  Tyndale. Murray, 1936. xxii, 414p., plates (some
  fold.col.), illus., maps. 23cm.

TYNDALE-BISCOE, Cecil Earle
  Kashmir in sunlight and shade: a description of
  the beauties of the country, the life, habits and
  humour of its inhabitants ...; with an introduction
  by L.C. Dunsterville. Seeley, Service, 1922.
  315p., plates (1 fold.), illus., map. 22cm.

TYNDALL, John
The forms of water in clouds & rivers, ice &
glaciers. H.S. King, 1872. vii, 192p., plates,
illus. 20cm. (International scientific series,
v.1)
- - 11th ed. K. Paul, Trench, Trübner, 1892.

TYNDALE, John
[The forms of water in clouds & rivers, ice &
glaciers]. Les glaciers et les transformations de
l'eau; suivis d'une conférence sur le même sujet
par M. Helmholtz, avec la réponse de M. Tyndall.
Paris: Baillière, 1873. 264p., 8 plates, illus.
22cm. (Bibliothèque scientifique internationale)

TYNDALL, John
Fragments of science: a series of detached essays,
addresses and reviews. 8th ed. Longmans, Green,
1889-1892. 2v., illus., map. 20cm.
Vol.2 is 7th ed.

TYNDALL, John
The glaciers of the Alps, being a narrative of
excursions and ascents, an account of the origin
and phenomena of glaciers, and an exposition of the
physical principles to which they are related.
Murray, 1860. xxi, 444p., plates, illus. 21cm.

- - New ed. Longmans, Green, 1896.
- - Another issue. Routledge, [1905].
Contains pt.1 only.
- - Another issue. Longmans, Green, 1906.

TYNDALL, John
The glaciers of the Alps & Mountaineering in 1861.
Dent, [1906?]. xiii, 274p., illus. 18cm.
(Everyman's library, 98)

TYNDALL, John
[The glaciers of the Alps...]. Die Gletscher der
Alpen; autorisirte deutsche Ausg. mit einem Vorwort
von G. Wiedemann. Braunschweig: Vieweg, 1898.
550p., illus. (1 col.). 23cm.

TYNDALL, John
[The glaciers of the Alps...]. Al'piskie ledniki;
perevod" s angliskago S.A. Rachinskago. Moskva:
Izd. Knigoprodavtsa A.I. Glazunova, 1866. xix,
346p., plates (some col.), illus. 26cm.

TYNDALL, John
Haute montagne; traduction de Bernard Lemoine;
préface de Lord Schuster. Neuchatel: Attinger,
1946. xv, 275p., plates, illus. 21cm. (Montagne)
Selections from: The glaciers of the Alps, Hours
of exercise in the Alps and New fragments.

TYNDALL, John
Heat, a mode of motion. 3rd ed., with additions
and illustrations. Longmans, Green, 1868. xxiii,
520p., plates, illus. 21cm.

- - 6th ed. 1904.

TYNDALL, John
Hours of exercise in the Alps. Longmans, Green,
1871. x, 473p., plates, illus. 21cm.
Contains: Notes on ice and glaciers.

- - 2nd ed. 1871.
- - New ed. 1899 (1906 reprint).

TYNDALL, John
Mountaineering in 1861: a vacation tour. Longman,
Green, Longman, & Roberts, 1862. ix, 105p., 2
plates, illus. 22cm.
Also published as: A vacation tour in Switzerland.

TYNDALL, John
[Mountaineering in 1861]. Dans les montagnes; traduction par L. Lortet. Paris: Hetzel, [1869?].
viii, 356p., illus. 18cm. (Bibliothèque d'éducation et de récréation)

- - Another ed. [ca 1880].
- - Another issue. 1904.

TYNDALL, John
[Mountaineering in 1861]. In den Alpen.
Autorisirte deutsche Ausg.; mit einem Vorwort von
Gustav Wiedemann. Braunschweig: Vieweg, 1872.
xiv, 420p. 22cm.

TYNDALL, John
New fragments. 2nd ed. Longmans, Green, 1892.
500p. 20cm.

TYNDALL, John
Principal Forbes and his biographers. Longmans,
Green, 1873. x, 35p. 19cm.
Memoir of the late James David Forbes.

TYNDALL, John
A vacation tour in Switzerland. Longman, Green,
Longman, & Roberts. [1862]. ix, 105p., 2 plates,
illus. 22cm.
Also published as: Mountaineering in 1861.

TYNDALL, John
EVE, A   S   and CREASEY, C   H
Life and work of John Tyndall; with a chapter on
Tyndall as a mountaineer by Lord Schuster...
Macmillan, 1945. xxxii, 404p., plates, illus.
25cm.

Tyrolese scenery; or, Continental travels
See
Ansichten von Tyrol

TYRWHITT, R   St John
A handbook of pictorial art; with a chapter on
perspective by A. Macdonald. 2nd ed. Oxford:
Clarendon Press, 1875. xv, 384p., plates (some
col.), illus. 23cm. (Clarendon Press series)

TYSON, T
Trout fishing in Kulu; with a brief description of
rivers, routes and accommodation available for
visitors. 2nd ed. Lahore: Civil and Military
Gazette, 1941. viii, 71p., 1 fold.col. plate,
map. 23cm.

TYTLER, Alexander Fraser
A critical examination of Mr. Whitaker's "Course
of Hannibal over the Alps ascertained". Robinson,
1795. 139p., 1 fold. plate, map. 23cm.

U.I.A.A.
See
INTERNATIONAL UNION OF ALPINIST ASSOCIATIONS

ACHLEITNER, Arthur and UBL, Emil
Tirol und Vorarlberg: neue Schilderung von Land
und Leuten. 2.Aufl. Leipzig: A.H. Payne, [1905?].
400p., plates (1 fold., some col.), illus., map
(in pocket). 32cm.

Über die Schweiz und die Schweizer, [von Dr. W.A.
Keller?]. Berlin: Vieweg, 1795-96. 2v. in 1.
18cm.

UJFALVY-BOURDON, Marie de
Voyage d'une Parisienne dans l'Himalaya occidental.
Paris: Hachette, 1887. 452p., 1 fold. plate,
illus., maps. 20cm.

UKLANSKI, Carl Theodor, Baron von
Einsame Wanderungen in der Schweiz im Jahr 1809,
[von Carl Theodor von Uklanski]. Berlin: Im
Kunst- und Industrie-Comptoir, 1810. 387p. 17cm.

ULE, Otto
Bilder aus den Alpen und aus der mitteldeutschen
Gebirgswelt: Blicke in die Geschichte der Erde und
den Bau der Gebirge. Halle: G. Schwetschke'scher
Verlag, 1866. 240p., illus. 18cm.

ULLMAN, James Ramsey
The age of mountaineering; with a chapter on
British mountains by W.H. Murray. Collins, 1956.
384p., plates, illus., maps, bibl. 22cm.
Based on the author's High conquest.

ULLMAN, James Ramsey
Americans on Everest: the official account of the
ascent led by Norman G. Dyhrenfurth, by James
Ramsey Ullman and other members of the expedition.
Joseph, 1965. xxiii, 429p., plates, illus., maps.
25cm.

ULLMAN, James Ramsey
And not to yield. Collins, 1970. 444p. 22cm.

ULLMAN, James Ramsey
Banner in the sky. Collins, 1955. 254p. 21cm.

ULLMAN, James Ramsey
High conquest: the story of mountaineering.
Gollancz, 1942. 320p., plates, illus., maps, bibl.
23cm.

ULLMAN, James Ramsey
[High conquest]. La grande conquête ...;
traduction de J. et F. Germain. Grenoble: Arthaud,
1948. 372p., plates, illus., maps, bibl. 21cm.

ULLMAN, James Ramsey
Kingdom of adventure: Everest, a chronicle of man's
assault on the earth's highest mountain, narrated
by the participants ...; with an accompanying text
by James Ramsey Ullman. Collins, 1948. 320p.,
plates, illus., maps, bibl. 23cm.

- - American ed. New York: Sloane, 1947.

ULLMAN, James Ramsey
Man of Everest: the autobiography of Tenzing told
to J.R. Ullman. Harrap, 1955. 320p., plates
(some col.), illus., maps. 23cm.

ULLMAN, James Ramsey
[Man of Everest]. Tenzing de l'Everest: autobio-
graphie racontée à James Ramsay Ullman. [Paris]:
Arthaud, 1955. 277p., plates, illus., maps. 22cm.
(Collection sempervivum, 27)

ULLMAN, James Ramsey
Mass attack on the mighty peak: Americans make a
triple conquest of Everest.
(In Life, v.55, no.12, Sept. 20 1963, p.68-94,
illus.)

ULLMAN, James Ramsey
The white tower. Philadelphia: Lippincott, 1945.
479p. 21cm.

- - Another ed. Collins, 1946.

ULLOA, Antonio de
Noticias americanas: entretenimientos físico-
históricos sobre la América meridional, y la
septentrional oriental: comparacion general de los
territorios, climas y producciones en las tres
especies vegetal, animal y mineral... Madrid:
Imprenta Real, 1792. xvi, 342p. 21cm.

ULRICH, Melchior
Berg- und Gletscher-Fahrten in den Hochalpen der
Schweiz, von G. Studer, M. Ulrich, J.J. Weilenmann.
Zürich: F. Schulthess, 1859-63. 2v., plates,
illus. 19cm.
Vol.2. is also by H. Zeller.

ULRICH, Melchior
Die Ersteigung des Tödi. Zürich: F. Schulthess,
1859. 74p., 1 plate, illus. 18cm.

ULRICH, Melchior
Die Seitenthäler des Wallis und der Monterosa,
topographisch geschildert. Zürich: Orell, Füssli,
1850. 90p. 21cm.

UMBRA
See
CLIFFORD, Charles Cavendish

UMLAUFT, Friedrich
Die Alpen: Handbuch der gesammten Alpenkunde.
Wien: A. Hartleben, 1887. viii, 488p., plates
(some fold.), illus., col. maps. 25cm.

UMLAUFT, Friedrich
[Die Alpen]. The Alps; translated by Louisa
Brough. K. Paul, Trench, 1889. xii, 523p.,
plates (some fold.col.), illus., maps. 26cm.

An unconventional guide for tourists: a fortnight
in Switzerland: a free-and-easy account of a first
visit to the Rigi, the Bernese Oberland, Chamouny,
&c., by the editor of the "Western Gazette" [i.e.
Charles Clinker]. T. Cook, 1880. vi, 108p. 22cm.

UNDERHILL, Miriam
Give me the hills. Methuen, 1956. 252p., plates
(some col.), illus. 23cm.

- - [New ed.]. Riverside (Conn.): Chatham Press in
association with the Appalachian Mountain Club,
1971.

UNGAR, Karl
Die Alpenflora der Südkarpathen; hrsg. vom Sieben-
bürgischen Karpathenverein. Hermannstadt: Jos.
Drotleff, 1913. 92p., 24 col. plates (in pocket),
illus. 26cm.

UNGARISCHER KARPATHENVEREIN
See
MAGYARORSZÁGI KÁRPÁTEGLYLET

UNION INTERNATIONALE DES ASSOCIATIONS D'ALPINISME
See
INTERNATIONAL UNION OF ALPINIST ASSOCIATIONS

UNITED PUBLIC INTERESTS ASSOCIATIONS OF THE CANTON
OF THE GRISONS
See
VERBAND DER BÜNDNERISCHEN VERKEHRSVEREIN

UNITED STATES. Congress. House
Report of the eighth International Geographic
Congress held in the United States, 1904.
Washington: Government Printing Office, 1905.
1064p., plates (some fold., some col.), illus.,
maps. 24cm. (House of Representatives. 58th
Congress, 3rd Session. Document no.460)

UNITED STATES. Department of Agriculture. Forest
Service
Avalanche handbook. Washington: Government
Printing Office, 1953. iv, 146p., illus., bibl.
27cm.

UNITED STATES. Department of Agriculture. Forest
Service
Avalanche handbook, by Ronald I. Perla and M.
Martinelli. Washington: U.S. Department of
Agriculture, Forest Service, 1976. vi, 238p.,
illus., bibl. 26cm. (Agriculture handbooks, 489)

UNITED STATES. Geological Survey
ORTH, Donald J
Dictionary of Alaska place names. Washington:
Government Printing Office, 1967. xi, 1084p.,
col. plates, illus., maps, bibl. 29cm. (Geologi-
cal Survey. Professional Paper no.567)

UNITED STATES. Geological Survey
Twentieth annual report of the United States
Geological Survey to the Secretary of the Interior,
1898-99. Pt.7. Explorations in Alaska in 1898.
Washington: Government Printing Office, 1900. v,
509p., plates (some fold., some col.), illus.,
maps (5 in pocket). 30cm.

UNITED STATES. House of Representatives
See
UNITED STATES. Congress. House

UNITED STATES. National Park Service
National Parks portfolio by Robert Sterling Yard.
2nd ed. Washington: Government Printing Office,
1917. 11 leaflets, illus., maps. 24cm.

UNITED STATES. School of Aviation Medicine
Operation Everest. Pensacola (Fla.): School of
Aviation Medicine, U.S. Naval Air Station, 1946.
47p., plates, illus. 25cm.

UNITED STATES. War Department
Reports of explorations and surveys to ascertain
the most practicable and economical route for a
railroad from the Mississippi River to the Pacific
Ocean, made under the direction of the Secretary
of War, in 1853-4... Vol.3. Washington: B. Tucker,
printer, 1856. 1v. (various pagings), plates
(some fold., some col.), illus., map. 30cm.
(U.S. 33d Congress, 2d Session. Ex. Doc. no.78)

UNITED STATES. War Department
Reports of explorations in the territory of Alaska
(Cooks Inlet, Sushitna, Copper and Tanana rivers)
1898; made under the direction of the Secretary of
War by Edwin F. Glenn and W.R. Abercrombie.
Washington: Government Printing Office, 1899.
464p., 1 fold. plate, map. 25cm.

UNIVERSITÀ DI TORINO. Laboratorii Scientifici
"A. Mosso" sul Monte Rosa
See
LABORATORII SCIENTIFICI "A. MOSSO" SUL MONTE ROSA

UNIVERSITY OF BRISTOL MOUNTAINEERING CLUB
NIXON, John
Climbing guide to the Avon gorge. Bristol:
University of Bristol Mountaineering Club, 1959.
45p., illus. 17cm.

UNIVERSITY OF BRISTOL MOUNTAINEERING CLUB HIMALAYAN
EXPEDITION, 1976
Kulu 1976: the report of the University of Bristol
Mountaineering Club Himalayan Expedition. Bristol:
The Expedition, 1976. 12p., illus., maps. 30cm.

UNIVERSITY OF COLORADO. Institute of Arctic and
Alpine Research
List of publications of the Institute of Arctic and
Alpine Research, 1967-1974; compiled by Martha
Andrews. Boulder (Col.): University of Colorado,
1975. 45p. 28cm.

UNIVERSITY OF SOUTHAMPTON LADAKH EXPEDITION, 1976
Report. Southampton: The Expedition, 1977. 94p.,
plates (1 fold.), illus., maps. 30cm.

Unprotected females in Norway; or, The pleasantest
way of travelling there, passing through Denmark
and Sweden; with Scandinavian sketches from nature,
[by Emily Lowe]. Routledge, 1857. viii, 295p.,
illus. 20cm.

- - [Later ed.]. 1859.

Unprotected females in Sicily, Calabria, and on the
top of Mount Aetna, [by the author of "Unprotected
females in Norway", i.e. Emily Lowe]. Routledge,
Warne, & Routledge, 1864. xi, 265p., plates,
illus. 17cm.

UNSWORTH, Walter
Because it is there: famous mountaineers, 1840-
1940. Gollancz, 1968. 144p., plates, illus. 23cm.

UNSWORTH, Walter
The book of rock-climbing. Barker, 1968. 112p.,
illus., bibl. 24cm.

UNSWORTH, Walter
A climber's guide to Pontesford rocks. Shrewsbury:
Wilding, 1962. 35p., illus. 16cm.

UNSWORTH, Walter
Encyclopaedia of mountaineering; compiled by Walt
Unsworth. Hale, 1975. 272p., plates, illus.
24cm.

- - Another issue. Harmondsworth: Penguin, 1977.

UNSWORTH, Walter
The English outcrops; with a foreword by Jack
Longland. Gollancz, 1964. 192p., plates, illus.,
bibl. 23cm.

UNSWORTH, Walter
Matterhorn man: the life and adventures of Edward
Whymper. Gollancz, 1965. 127p., plates, illus.,
maps, bibl. 23cm.

UNSWORTH, Walter
North face: the second conquest of the Alps; with
a foreword by Chris Bonington. Hutchinson, 1969.
160p., 12 plates, illus., maps (on lining papers).
21cm. (Men in action series)

UNSWORTH, Walter
EVANS, R B
The southern Lake District. Part 1. Difficult to
Hard Severe; illustrated by R.B. Evans.
Manchester: Cicerone Press, 1971. 55p., illus.,
map. 17cm. (Climbs in Cumbria)

UNSWORTH, Walter
Tiger in the snow: the life and adventures of
A.F. Mummery. Gollancz, 1967. 126p., plates,
illus., maps, bibl. 23cm.

UNWIN, David J
Mountain weather for climbers. Leicester: Cordee,
1978. 60p., illus., maps, bibl. 15cm.

Unwin's chap book. Unwin, [1899]. 14p. 24cm.
Contains: The last climb of Norman-Neruda. -
Dragons in the Alps. - A crack Swiss Guide:
[Mattias Zurbriggen].

Up and down Mont Blanc: a Christmas extra double
number of Chambers's journal. Edinburgh: Chambers,
1866. 32p., illus. 27cm.

URBANOVIC, Ivan
PUSKAS, Arno
Nanga Parbat 8125m; fotografoval Ivan Urbanovic.
Bratislava: Sport, 1976. 1v. (chiefly illus.,
maps). 28cm.
Pamphlet containing picture captions in Russian,
German and English as insert.

URECH, Charles
Bernese Oberland, descriptive and narrative, by
Charles Urech and various collaborators.
Interlaken: Montana, 1926. 47p., plates (some
col.), illus. 33cm.

URSTISIUS, Christianus
See
WURTISEN, Christian

USMIANI, Toni
Roccia e ghiaccio: guida tecnico-didattica.
Bolzano: Arti Grafiche Manfrini, 1954. 159p.,
plates, illus. 23cm.

UVAROV, P S , Gräfin
Die Sammlungen des Kaukasischen Museums; im
Vereine mit Special-Gelehrten bearb. und hrsg. von
Gustav Radde. Tiflis: Das Museum, 1899-   .
Plates (some fold.col.), illus., maps. 31cm.
Second title page in Russian.
Bd.1. Zoologie, von Gustav Radde. -Bd.2. Botanik,
von Gustav Radde. -Bd.5. Archaeologie; bearb. von
Gräfin P.S. Uvarov.

UWAROW, P S
See
UVAROV, P S , Gräfin

V., J.
See
VIZARD, John

Vacation rambles on the continent, told so as to be
a complete guide to the most interesting places in
Switzerland, Belgium, and the Rhine, by olim
juvenis. 5th ed. T. Cook, 1869. viii, 155p.
16cm.

VACCARONE, Luigi
  Il Gruppo del Gran Paradiso. Torino: V. Bona,
  1894. 30p., 6 fold. plates, illus., map. 21cm.

MARTELLI, A   E   and VACCARONE, Luigi
  Guida delle Alpi occidentali. Torino: Club Alpino
  Italiano, Sezione di Torino, 1889-96. 2v. in 3,
  fold. plates (some col.), illus., maps, bibl.
  17cm.
  Vol.2., pt.2 is by G. Bobba and L. Vaccarone.

MARTELLI, A   E   and VACCARONE, Luigi
  Guida delle Alpi occidentali del Piemonte, dal Colle
  dell'Argentera ... al Colle Girard... Torino: Club
  Alpino Italiano, Sezione di Torino, 1880. xxxix,
  480p., plates (some fold.), illus., bibl. 17cm.

VACCARONE, Luigi
  Guida-itinerario per le valli dell'Orco, di Soana
  e di Chiusella. Torino: Club Alpino Italiano,
  1878. viii, 194p., map. 17cm.

MARTIN-FRANKLIN, J   and VACCARONE, Luigi
  Notice historique sur l'ancienne route de Charles-
  Emmanuel II et les Grottes des Échelles. Chambery:
  Perrin, 1887. xvi, 235p. 24cm.

VACCARONE, Luigi
  Le Pertuis du Viso: Étude historique, d'après des
  documents inédits, conservés aux Archives Nationales
  de Turin. Turin: Casanova, 1881. 127p., 1 plate,
  facsim. 25cm.

GAUTHIER, Gilbert and VACHEZ, Michel
  Ski court: ski évolutif, ski sans peine. Paris:
  Arthaud, 1972. 116p., plates, illus. 21cm.

VADIANUS, Joachimus
  See
  WATT, Joachim von

VAILLAT, Léandre
  Le coeur et la croix de Savoie: Chambery, Maurienne,
  Tarentaise. Paris: Perrin, 1914. 355p. 19cm.

VAILLAT, Léandre
  Notre Savoie; ouvrage publié sous la direction de
  Léandre Vaillat; dessins de Claire-Lise Monnier.
  Paris: Compagnie des Chemins de Fer Paris-Lyon-
  Mediterranée, 1920. 219p., illus., map. 20cm.

VAILLAT, Léandre
  Paysages d'Annecy; dessins d'André Jacques.
  Chambery: Dardel, 1931. 149p., illus. 29cm.

VAILLAT, Léandre
  La Savoie. Paris: Perrin, 1912. 351p. 20cm.

VAILLAT, Léandre
  La Savoie: Chambéry, la Maurienne, la Tarentaise;
  dessins de André Jacques. Chambéry: Dardel, 1913.
  121p., illus. 34cm.

VALAIS
  See
  WALLIS

VALBUSA, U
  Piante alpine. Torino: S. Lattes, [n.d.]. 1v.
  (chiefly col. illus.). 15cm. (Piccolo atlante
  popolare di storia naturale. Botanica, 2.)

VALDES, Luis S
CENTRE D'ESTUDIS I REALITZACIONS DE LES VALLS
D'ANDORRA
  Andorra pocket guide: tourism, shopping, real
  estate. Editor: Luis S. Valdes. Andorra: The
  Centre, 1971. 122p., 1 fold.col. plate, illus.,
  map. 16cm.

AUSTIN, J   Allan and VALENTINE, Rodney
  Great Langdale; illustrations by W. Heaton Cooper.
  Stockport: Fell & Rock Climbing Club, 1973. 256p.,
  1 col. plate, illus., map (on lining paper). 16cm.
  (Climbing guides to the English Lake District,
  [4th ser.], 1)

VALENTINE-RICHARDS, Alfred Valentine
BALL, John
  The Central Alps. Part 1. Including those portions
  of Switzerland to the north of the Rhone and the
  Rhine valleys. New ed.; reconstructed and revised
  on behalf of the Alpine Club under the general
  editorship of A.V. Valentine-Richards. Longmans,
  Green, 1907. xxviii, 326p., fold.col. plates,
  maps. 19cm. (Alpine guides, pt.2)

VALENTINI, Enzo, conte di Laviano
  Letters and drawings of Enzo Valentini, conte di
  Laviano, Italian volunteer and soldier; translated
  by Fernanda Bellachioma. Constable, 1917. vi,
  168p., plates, illus. 20cm.

VALERY
  Voyages historiques, littéraires et artistiques
  en Italie: guide raisonné et complet du voyageur
  et de l'artiste. 2e éd. Paris: Baudry, 1838.
  3v., 1 fold.col. plate, map. 22cm.

VALLA, François and ZUANON, Jean Paul
  Pamir: escalade d'un 7.000 au pays des Kirghizes;
  avec la participation des membres de l'expédition
  dauphinoise au Pamir 74. Domene: Segirep, 1976.
  301p., plates (1 fold.col.), illus., maps, bibl.
  22cm.

Vallées perdues. Lausanne: Spes, 1947. 47, 47,
  81p., plates, illus., maps. 24cm.
  Contents: 1. Tourtemagne, texte d'après L. Meyer
  [and others]. -2. Binn, texte de L. Desbuisson et
  E. Bohy. -3. Le Lötschental, texte de Jos. Siegen.

VALLENTIN, Florian
  Les Alpes Cottiennes et Graies: géographie gallo-
  romaine. Paris: Champion, 1883. 113p., 1 fold.
  plate, map, bibl. 26cm.

VALLETTE, Pierre
  Évolène; dix planches en couleurs de Francis
  Portier; texte et poème de Pierre Vallette,
  Genève: Atar, [1942]. [7]p., col. plates, illus.
  36cm.
  In portfolio.

VALLETTE, Pierre
  Le miracle des cloches: contes et poèmes
  valaisans; ornés d'une vignette et d'un hors-texte
  d'Éd. Elzingre. Genève: A. Jullien, 1937. 65p.,
  illus. 22cm.

VALLINO, Domenico
  Album d'un alpinista, [da Domenico Vallino].
  Biella: G. Amosso, 1878- . Illus., maps. 22 x
  30cm.
  Library has pts. 2-3 only.

SELLA, Vittorio and VALLINO, Domenico
  Monte Rosa & Gressoney. Biella: G. Amosso, [1890].
  62p., plates, illus. 25 x 33cm.

ENGEL, Claire Éliane and VALLOT, Charles
  "Ces monts affreux ...", 1650-1810; [edited by]
  Claire Éliane Engel et Charles Vallot; avec seize
  compositions originales de Samivel. Paris:
  Delagrave, 1934. 320p., plates, illus., bibl.
  24cm. (Les écrivains à la montagne)

ENGEL, Claire Éliane and VALLOT, Charles
  "Ces monts sublimes ...", 1803-1895; [edited by]
  Claire-Éliane Engel et Charles Vallot; avec huit
  compositions originales de Samivel. Paris:
  Delagrave, 1936. 320p., plates, illus., bibl.
  23cm.

VALLOT, Charles
  Description de la moyenne montagne dans le massif
  du Mont-Blanc. Fasc.1. Chamonix, Mont-Blanc.
  Paris: Fischbacher, 1927. 255p., plates (some
  fold.col.), maps. 17cm. (Guides Vallot)

VALLOT, Charles
  Description générale du massif du Mont-Blanc par
  Ch. Vallot [and others]. Paris: Fischbacher, 1925.
  8 pts. in 1, plates (1 fold.), illus., maps, bibl.
  19cm. (Guides Vallot)

VALLOT, Charles and VALLOT, Joseph
Le massif du Mont-Blanc: paysages characteristiques
et documentaires. Versailles: Dufay, [1914]-23.
2v., plates, illus. 20cm.

VALLOT, Charles
Saussure aux Alpes. 1. Portrait de H.-B. de
Saussure, par Charles Vallot [et] Autour du Mont-
Blanc; extrait des "Voyages dans les Alpes", de
H.-B. de Saussure. Paris: Fischbacher, 1938.
190p. 19cm.

VALLOT, Charles
Tourisme en montagne dans le massif du Mont-Blanc:
Chamonix, Mont-Blanc, Saint-Gervais-les-Bains.
173p., plates (some fold.), illus., maps. 17cm.
(Guides Vallot)

VALLOT, Henri and VALLOT, Joseph
Description générale du massif du Mont-Blanc:
répertoire des altitudes principales du massif du
Mont-Blanc. Paris: Fischbacher, 1924. 33p. 18cm.
(Guides Vallot)

VALLOT, Henri
Levés à la planchette en haute montagne. Paris:
H. Barrère, 1909. vii, 193p., illus. 18cm.

VALLOT, Henri
Manuel de topographie alpine. Paris: H. Barrère,
1904. xiv, 171p., illus. 18cm.

VALLOT, Henri
Massif du Mont Blanc: les Aiguilles Rouges et la
chaîne du Brévent. Paris: H. Barrère, 1921. 52p.,
5 plates (1 fold.), illus., maps. 23cm.
Offprint from La Montagne, 1921.
Ptie.1. Description topographiques, par Henri
Vallot. -Ptie.2. Itinéraires des Aiguilles Rouges,
par Jacques de Lépinay.

VALLOT, Henri
Réseau trigonométrique du massif du Mont-Blanc,
établi et calculé par Henri Vallot; d'après les
stationnements de Joseph Vallot pour les sommets
de la haute chaîne et de Henri Vallot pour le reste
du massif. Paris: Fischbacher, 1924. 55, 22p.,
1 fold. plate, illus., map. 30cm.

VALLOT, Henri and VALLOT, Joseph
Description générale du massif du Mont-Blanc:
répertoire des altitudes principales du massif du
Mont-Blanc. Paris: Fischbacher, 1924. 33p. 18cm.
(Guides Vallot)

VALLOT, Charles and VALLOT, Joseph
Le massif du Mont Blanc: paysages charactéristiques
et documentaires. Versailles: Dufay, [1914]-23.
2v., plates, illus. 20cm.
Vol.2, Paris: Fischbacher.

VALRÉAS, Henri
Une ascension dramatique au Mont Blanc. Paris:
Paulin, [1905?]. 248p., 1 plate, illus., map.
20cm.

VALSESIA, Teresio and BURGENER, Giuseppe
Macugnaga e il Monte Rosa. Trezzano: A. Fattorini,
1968. 101p., 1 fold.col. plate, illus. (some col.),
map (in pocket). 28cm.

VAN DER NAILLEN, A
See
NAILLEN, A   van der

VAN DYKE, John Charles
The mountain: renewed studies in impressions and
appearances. Werner Laurie, [1915]. xvii, 234p.,
plates, illus. 20cm.

VARENNES, Claude
LAMBERT, Raymond
À l'assaut des "quatre mille": dix récits de haute
montagne; recueillis par Claude Varennes. Genève:
Éditions de la Frégate, 1946. 164p., plates,
illus. 23cm.

- - 2e éd. Genève: Jeheber, 1953.

VARESCHI, Volkmar and KRAUSE, Ernst
Mountains in flower; photographs by Ernst Krause.
Lindsay Drummond, 1939. 159p., illus. (1 col.)
25cm.

VARVELLI, Maria Ludovica and VARVELLI, Riccardo
Sette anni contro il Tirich, di Guido Machetto,
Maria Ludovica e Riccardo Varvelli. [Milano]:
Dall'Oglio, 1976. 269p., plates (some col.),
illus., maps. 21cm.

VAUCHER, Charles
Chamois; illustré de 58 photographies de l'auteur.
Genève: Éditions de la Frégate, 1944. 140p.,
plates, illus. 23cm. (La vie sauvage)

VAUGHAN, Mrs. W.W.
See
SYMONDS, Margaret

VAUTIER, Auguste
Au pays des Bisses; avec 42 dessins de Eug.
Reichlen. Lausanne: Spes, 1928. 155p., 32
plates, illus., bibl. 20cm.

- - 2e éd., rev. et augm. 1942.

VAUTIER, Auguste
Gabrisse: journal d'un gardien de cabane. 2e éd.,
ornée. Lausanne: Spes, 1941. 171p., illus.,
port. 19cm.

VAUX, Frederic W
Rambles in the Pyrenees; and a visit to San
Sebastian. Longman, Orme, Brown, Green & Longmans,
1838. xi, 218p., 1 fold. plate, illus., map.
21cm.

VÁVRA, Karl and BRUNNER, Richard
Skisport: wie wir ihn betreiben; Herausgeber
Sportclub 'Die weissen Elf'. Wien: Frick, 1910.
vii, 82p., illus. 22cm.

- - 3.Aufl. 1910.

VEAZEY, Harry G
The epic of Adelboden ...: the silver jubilee
booklet of the Adelboden parties of S. Mark's,
Camberwell, S.E. 5. [The Author], [1951]. 47p.,
plates, illus. 21cm.

VEITCH, Sophie F   F
Views in central Abyssinia; with portraits of the
natives of the Galla tribes, taken in pen and ink
under circumstances of peculiar difficulty, by
T.E., a German traveller ...; with descriptions by
Sophie F.F. Veitch. J.C. Hotten, 1868. 1v.
(chiefly illus.). 23 x 29cm.

VENETZ, Ignace
Apologie des travaux du glacier de Giétroz contre
les attaques réitérées de M. le chanoine Blanc.
Sion: A. Advocat, 1825. 23p. 19cm.

VENETZ, Ignace
BLANC,   chanoine
Réflexions sur la réponse de M. l'ingénieur
Venetz à deux lettres concernant les travaux du
glacier du Giétroz, Vallée de Bagnes, en Valais,
écrites par le chanoine Blanc à M. Gard, président
du Dixain d'Entre-mont, séant en Diète à Sion, en
Décembre 1824. Lausanne: E. Vincent, 1825. 24p.
19cm.

Venezianer und Tridentiner Voralpen: Trient-Vicenza-
Padua. Mailand: Lampugnani, [19--]. 110p.,
illus., plans. 18cm. (Lampugnani's Reise Führer,
37)

VERBAND DER BÜNDNERISCHEN VERKEHRSVEREIN
HASSELBRINK, F
Führer durch Graubündens Kurorte, Sommerfrischen
und Sportplätze; unter Mitwirkung der bündn.
Verkehrsvereine, bearb. von F. Hasselbrink. Chur:
Der Verband, [1907]. 183p., 1 fold.col. plate,
illus., map. 18cm.

VERBAND DER BÜNDNERISCHEN VERKEHRSVEREIN
HASSELBRINK, F
  [Führer durch Graubündens Kurorte...]. Guide to
  the health, pleasure, and sport resorts of the
  Grisons [Graubünden]; compiled by F. Hasselbrink
  in co-operation with the Grisons Public Interests
  Associations; [translated by W.G. Lockett]. Davos:
  United Public Interests Associations of the Canton
  of the Grisons, [1907]. 190p., illus., map. 18cm.

VEREIN DER FREUNDE DER ALPENVEREINSBÜCHEREI
BÜHLER, Hermann
  Alpine Bibliographie für das Jahr 1931 [- 1935];
  bearb. von Hermann Bühler, [hrsg. vom Verein der
  Freunde der Alpenvereinsbücherei mit Unterstützung
  des Hauptausschusses des Deutschen und
  Österreichischen Alpenvereins]. München: Gesell-
  schaft Alpiner Bücherfreunde, 1932-37. 5v. 18cm.
  Publisher varies.

- - Gesamtregister für die Jahre 1931-1938. München:
  Münchner Verlag, 1949.

VEREIN DER FREUNDE UND GÖNNER, San Martino di
Castrozza
  Wege und Markirungen in der Umgebung von San
  Martino di Castrozza, Südtirol. 4. ... Aufl.
  Leipzig: Grimme & Trömel, 1911. 40p., map. 17cm.

VERGHESE, B   G
  Himalayan endeavour; edited by B.G. Verghese.
  Bombay: Times of India, 1962. x, 155p., plates
  (1 fold., 2 col.), illus., maps. 23cm.

VERGIL
  See
VIRGIL

VERGILIUS MARO, Publius
  See
VIRGIL

VERMALE, F
ROUSSEAU, Jean Jacques
  Jean-Jacques Rousseau en Savoie: Annecy- Chambéry-
  Les Charmettes; extraits des "Confessions" situés
  et commentés par F. Vermale. Chambéry: Dardel,
  1922. 221p., bibl. 20cm.

VERMOREL, Lucien
  À travers les Alpes: premier essais (1919-1921),
  notes d'ascensions et correspondances.
  Villefranche-en-Beaujolais: [n.pub.], 1927. 70p.,
  plates, illus. 22cm.

VERMOREL, Lucien
CLUB ALPIN FRANÇAIS. Section de l'Isère
  Une cérémonie alpestre à La Pinéa: inauguration du
  sentier et de la plaque Lucien Vermorel, face nord-
  ouest de La Pinéa, le 13 mai 1926. Mâcon: Protat,
  1926. 41p., plates, illus., port. 21cm.

VERMOREL, Lucien
GUILLERMET, Jean
  Lucien Vermorel, 12 décembre 1893 - 2 octobre,
  1921, 27 ans: [discours prononcés aux funerailles
  de M. Lucien Vermorel ..., par Jean Guillermet and
  others]. Mâcon: Protat, [1921]. 26p. 21cm.

VERNEILH PUIRASEAU, Joseph, baron de
  Statistique générale de la France, publiée par
  ordre de Sa Majesté l'empereur et roi... Paris:
  Testu, 1807. 560p., 1 fold. plate, map. 27cm.

VERNES, F
  Promenade au Mont-Blanc et autour du Lac de Genève,
  [par F. Vernes?]. Londres: [n.pub.], [ca 1790].
  252p. 22cm.
  "Promenade ... en l'année 178*".

VERNES, F
  Voyage épisodique et pittoresque aux glaciers des
  Alpes... Paris: Gautier & Bretin, 1807. xii, 302p.
  17cm.

- - 2e éd. 1808.

VERNET, Jean
  Au coeur des Alpes. Paris: Arthaud, 1951. 211p.,
  plates, illus., map. 21cm. (Collection
  sempervivum, 13)

VERRIJN STUART, Xander
  Annapurna, 8091 meter: Nederlandse klimmers in de
  Himalaya. Bussum: Van Holkema & Warendorf, 1978.
  298p., col. plates, illus., maps, bibl. 24cm.

Veteran traveller
  See
WILSON, W   Rae

VEUILLOT, Louis
  Les pélérinages de Suisse: Einsiedeln, Sachslen,
  Maria-Stein. Bruxelles: Société Nationale pour
  la Propagation des Bons Livres, 1839. 423p.
  18cm.

Viaggio in Francia e nella Svizzera occidentale.
  Bologna: Tipografia di s. Tommaso d'Aquino, 1838.
  252p. 15cm.
  Editor's preface signed: G.S., i.e. Giuseppe
  Sacchi.
  Adapted from the writings of Dumas and Janin.

Viaggio nella Svizzera. Milano: Tipografia e
  Libreria Pirotta, 1836. 2v. 14cm.

Viaggio pittorico fatto da Ginevra a Milano...
  See
Voyage pittoresque de Genève à Milan par le Simplon

VIAL, A   E   Lockington
  Alpine glaciers. Batchworth, 1952. 126p., illus.
  27cm.

VICARY, John Fulford
  An American in Norway. W.H. Allen, 1885. viii,
  283p. 20cm.

VICKERS, Ken S
  Rock climbs in Leicestershire: interim guide.
  Leicester: Leicester Association of Mountaineers,
  1966. 46p., illus. 18cm.

VICTOR, Paul Émile
  Groenland, 1948-1949. Paris: Arthaud, 1951.
  47p., plates (some col.), illus., map. 27cm.

VICTOR-EMMANUEL II, King of Italy
  Victor-Emmanuel sur les Alpes: notices et
  souvenirs, par Amé Gorret. Turin: Casanova, 1878.
  99p., col. plates, illus., maps. 17cm.

- - 2e éd., rev. et augm. 1879.

VICTORIA, Queen of Great Britain
MACLEOD, Norman
  Mountain, loch and glen; illustrating "Our life
  in the Highlands" from paintings executed ... for
  this work by Joseph Adam; with an essay on the
  characteristics of Scottish scenery by Norman
  Macleod; prepared under the superintendence of
  Arthur Helps. 2nd ed. rev. Bell & Daldy, 1870.
  1v. (chiefly illus.). 38cm.

VIDAL Y RIBA, Edouard
  El Montseny: guia monografica de la regio,
  itineraris-excursions. Barcelona: L'Avenc, 1912.
  156p., plates, illus., map. 16cm.

VIENNA. Alpen-Skiverein
  See
ALPEN-SKIVEREIN WIEN

VIEUSSEUX, A
  The history of Switzerland, from the first irrup-
  tion of the northern tribes to the present time
  ...; compiled from the best authorities. Bohn,
  1846. xxvi, 351p., 1 fold.plate, map. 23cm.

Views in North Wales. Chester: T. Catherall, [ca
  1851]. 1v. of illus. 14 x 22cm.

Views in the Tyrol
  See
Ansichten von Tyrol

VIGNA, N
In Valpellina: escursioni e studi, [da] E. Canzio,
F. Mondini, N. Vigna. Torino: Club Alpino Italiano,
1899. 176p., plates (1 fold.col.), illus., map.
25cm.

VIGNE, G   T
A personal narrative of a visit to Ghuzni, Kabul,
and Afghanistan, and of a residence at the court
of Dost Mohamed; with notices of Runjit Sing,
Khiva, and the Russion expedition. Whittaker,
1840. xv, 479p., plates, illus. 24cm.

VILLARI, L
Giovanni Segantini: the story of his life; together
with seventy five reproductions of his pictures.
Fisher Unwin, 1901. 207p., plates, illus. 30cm.

VILLARS, Dominique
Précis d'un voyage botanique, fait en Suisse, dans
les Grison, aux sources du Rhin ... en juillet,
aout et september 1811; précédé de quelques réflexions sur l'utilité des voyages pour les
naturalistes, par D. Villars, G. Lauth et A.
Nestler. Paris: Lenormant, 1812. 66p.,4 fold.
plates, illus. 20cm.

VILLENEUVE, F
SAZERAC, Hilaire Léon and ENGELMANN, Gustav
Lettres sur la Suisse; accompagnées de vues
dessinées ... & lithographiées par [F.] Villeneuve.
Paris: G. Engelmann, 1823-32. 5v., plates, illus.
46cm.

Villes et montagnes marocaines... Montagnes marocaines, par Roger Mailly... Rabat: "La Porte",
1964. 244p., plates (some fold.), illus., maps.
19cm. (Guides touristiques, 1964-1965)

VINCENT, A
Six mois dans les neiges, Tarantaise et Maurienne:
journal d'un officier. Moutiers-Tarentaise:
Ducloz, 1905. 263p., illus. 21cm.

VINCENT, Henri
Les vingt-deux années du Père Tasse à Chambrousse.
Grenoble: Baratier, 1891. 296p., illus. 19cm.

VINES, Stuart
FITZGERALD, Edward Arthur
The highest Andes: a record of the first ascent of
Aconcagua and Tupungato in Argentina, and the ex-
ploration of the surrounding valleys; with chapters
by Stuart Vines, and contributions by Professor
Bonney [and others]. Methuen, 1899. xvi, 390p.,
plates (2 fold.col.), illus., maps. 25cm.

VIOLLET-LE-DUC, Eugène
Le massif du Mont Blanc: étude sur sa constitution
géodésique et géologique, sur ses transformations
et sur l'état ancien et moderne de ses glaciers.
Paris: Baudry, 1876. xvi, 280p., plates, illus.,
map. 26cm.

VIOLLET-LE-DUC, Eugène
[Le massif du Mont Blanc...]. Mont Blanc: a
treatise on its geodesical and geological constitution, its transformations, and the ancient and
recent state of its glaciers; translated by B.
Bucknall. Sampson Low, Marston, Searle, &
Rivington, 1877. xvi, 378p., illus. 23cm.

VIOLLIER, Edmond W
Guide pratique de Genève, son Lac et les environs,
par Edm. W. Viollier and Vaud, Valais, Haute-Savoie
..., par Marc Le Roux. Lyon: G. Toursier, [n.d.].
184p., illus., maps, plans. 17cm. (Collection
des guides Pol)

VIOLLIER, Edmond W
Le Val de Bagnes, Chables, Lourtier, Fionnay,
Canton du Valais (Suisse). Vevey: E. de la Harpe,
[1902]. 24p., illus. 19cm.

VIRGIL
Moretum (o delle origini della pizza); traduzione
di Lino Donvito, testo latino: "Appendix
Vergiliana". Torino: The Author, [1973]. [12]p.,
plates, illus. 22cm.
Text in Latin and Italian, signed by the translator.

VIRGILIO, Francesco
Cenno geognostico-mineralogico sulla miniera
cuprifera di Champ de Praz in Valle d'Aosta.
Torino: The Author, 1879. 30p., 2 col. plates,
illus. 32cm.
Thesis (Laurea in scienze naturali) - R. Università degli studi di Torino.

VIRGILIUS MARO, Publius
See
VIRGIL

VIRIAMU JONES, John
See
JONES, John Viriamu

VIRIGLIO, Attilio
Jean Antoine Carrel (il "Padre" di tutte le
guide). Bologna: Cappelli, 1948. 332p., plates,
illus. 20cm. (Collana d'oro "le Alpi", 3)

VIRIGLIO, Attilio
Pastelli di monte. Torino: Anfossi, [1906].
137p. 23cm.

VISCONTI, Giammartino Arconati
See
ARCONATI VISCONTI, Giammartino

VISSER, Philips Christiaan
VISSER-HOOFT, Jenny
Among the Kara-Korum glaciers in 1925; with contributions by Ph.C. Visser. Arnold, 1926. xii,
303p., plates (1 fold.), illus., maps. 23cm.

VISSER, Philips Christiaan
Boven en beneden de sneeuwgrens. Utrecht: Honig,
1910. 376p., fold. plates, illus., maps, bibl.
26cm.

VISSER, Philips Christiaan and VISSER-HOOFT, Jenny
Naar Himalaya en Kara-korum. Bijlage bevattende
de wetenschappelijke uitkomsten der Karak-Korum
Expeditie 1922. Rotterdam: Nijgh & van Ditmar,
1925. 100p., plates (some fold.), illus. 23cm.

VISSER, Philips Christiaan
Winter in de Alpen; met een hoofdstuk voor
wintersport-beoefenaarsters door Jenny Visser-
Hooft. Schiedam: Roelants, 1913. viii, 114p.,
illus., bibl. 22cm.

VISSER, Philips Christiaan and VISSER-HOOFT, Jenny
Wissenschaftliche Ergebnisse der niederländischen
Expeditionen in den Karakorum und die angrenzenden
Gebiete in den Jahren 1922, 1925 und 1929/30;
hrsg. von Ph. C. Visser und Jenny Visser-Hooft.
Leipzig: F.A. Brockhaus, 1935-38. 2v., plates
(some fold.col.), illus., maps, bibl. 30cm.

VISSER-HOOFT, Jenny
Among the Kara-Korum glaciers in 1925; with contributions by Ph.C. Visser. Arnold, 1926. 303p.,
plates (1 fold.), illus., maps. 23cm.

VISSER, Philips Christiaan and VISSER-HOOFT, Jenny
Wissenschaftliche Ergebnisse der niederländischen
Expeditionen in den Karakorum und die angrenzenden
Gebiete in den Jahren 1922, 1925 und 1929/30;
hrsg. von Ph. C. Visser und Jenny Visser-Hooft.
Leipzig: F.A. Brockhaus, 1935-38. 2v., plates
(some fold.col.), illus., maps, bibl. 30cm.

VITTORJ, Carlo Landi
See
LANDI VITTORJ, Carlo

VITTOZ, Ed
Le Valais, texte de Prof. Ed. Vittoz; photo-
graphies de S.A. Schnegg [and others]. Lausanne:
Nouvelles Éditions Illustrées, [1928]. 24 pts.,
plates, illus. 22cm. (Les merveilles de la
Suisse: tourisme, 1)

VITTOZ, Pierre
Alpes vaudoises. Zürich: Club Alpin Suisse, 1970.
140p., illus., maps (on lining papers). 17cm.
(Guides du Club Alpin Suisse)

VIVIEN DE SAINT-MARTIN, Louis
Atlas dressé pour l'histoire de la géographie et
des découvertes géographiques depuis les temps les
plus reculés jusqu'à nos jours. Paris: Hachette,
1874. 4p., 12 col. plates, maps. 44cm.

VIZARD, John
Narrative of a tour through France, Italy, and
Switzerland, in a series of letters. Simpkin &
Marshall, 1872. iv, 132p. 19cm.
Preface signed: J.V., i.e. John Vizard.

VOGT, Carl
Agassiz' und seiner Freunde geologische Alpenreisen
in der Schweiz, Savoyen und Piemont ..., hrsg., von
Carl Vogt. 2. stark verm. Aufl. Frankfurt am
Main: Literarische Anstalt, 1847. xxxvi, 672p.,
1 fold.col. plate, map. 20cm.

VOGT, Carl
Im Gebirg und auf den Gletschern. Solothurn: Jent
& Gassmann, 1843. 259p. 19cm.

VOLKENS, Georg
Der Kilimandscharo: Darstellung der allgemeineren
Ergebnisse eines fünfzehnmonatigen Aufenthalts im
Dschaggalando. Berlin: Reimer, 1897. 388p.,
plates (1 fold.col.), illus., map. 27cm.

VONBUN, F   I
Alpenmärchen; gesammelt von F.I. Vonbun.
Stuttgart-Cannstatt: Holbein, 1910. 82p., illus.
21cm.

VOSS, Richard
Der Todesweg auf den Piz Palü: Roman. Berlin:
Ullstein, [1910]. 304p. 16cm. (Ullstein-Bücher,
10)

Voyage aux Pyrénées, par l'auteur des Souvenirs de
voyage [i.e. la comtesse de la Grandville]. 2e
éd. Lille: L. Lefort, 1842. 286p., 1 plate,
illus. 18cm.

- - 3e éd. 1854.

Voyage aux Pyrénées françaises et espagnoles ...,
par J.P.P***. 2e éd., entièrement ref. et augm.
Paris: E. Babeuf, 1828. viii, 432p. 21cm.
Previous ed. published in 1789 under title: Voyage
dans les Pyrénées françaises...

Voyage dans les Pyrénées françoises, dirigé
principalement vers le Bigorre & les vallées ...,
[par J.P. Picquet]. Paris: Le Jay, 1789. viii,
327p. 20cm.
2nd ed. published in 1828 under title: Voyage aux
Pyrénées françaises et espagnoles...

Voyage en Savoie et dans le Midi: la France en 1804
et 1805,[par La Bedoyère].Paris: Giguet et Michaud,
1808. 439p. 22cm.

Voyage épisodique et anecdotique dans les Alpes, par
un Parisien. Paris: Gagniard, 1830. 223p. 21cm.

Voyage pittoresque au Lac de Come; [illustré par
J.J. Wetzel]. Zurich: Orell, Fussli, 1822. 31p.,
15 plates, illus. 44cm.

Voyage pittoresque au Lac des Waldstettes ou des IV
Cantons; [illustré par J.J. Wetzel]. Zurich:
Orell, Fussli, 1817. 1v. (chielfy col. illus.).
45cm.

Voyage pittoresque aux glaciers de Chamouni;[illus-
trations par G. Lory, père et fils]. Paris: P.
Didot, 1815. 1v. (chiefly col. illus.). 48cm.

Voyage pittoresque aux Lacs Majeur et de Lugano;
[illustrations par J.J. Wetzel]. Zurich: Orell,
Fussli, 1823. 41p., col. plates, illus. 44cm.

Voyage pittoresque de Genève à Milan par le Simplon;
[illustrations par G. Lory, père et fils]. Paris:
P. Didot, 1811. 1v. (chiefly col. illus.). 43cm.

[Voyage pittoresque de Genève à Milan par le
Simplon]. Picturesque tour from Geneva to Milan,
by way of the Simplon; illustrated with thirty six
coloured views ... engraved from designs by J.
and J. Lory ... and accompanied with particulars
historical and descriptive by Frederic Schoberl.
R. Ackermann, 1820. 136p., 36 col. plates, illus.,
map. 28cm.

[Voyage pittoresque de Genève à Milan par le
Simplon]. Viaggio pittorico fatto da Ginevra a
Milano per la strada del Sempione; [illustrazioni
di G. Lory, padre e figlio]. Milano: Ferrario,
1821. 1v. (chiefly illus.). 48cm.
Texts in Italian and French.

Voyage pittoresque de l'Oberland; ou, Description
de vues prises dans l'Oberland, district du Canton
de Berne [par S. Weibel]; accompagné de notices
historiques et topographiques [par Philipp A.
Stapfer]. Paris: Treuttel & Würz, 1812. 90p.,
15 col. plates, illus., map. 35cm.

Voyages and travels of Her Majesty, Caroline Queen
of Great Britain ..., by one of Her Majesty's
Suite. Jones, 1822. x, 755p., plates, illus.,
maps. 22cm.

Le voyageur en Suisse; ou, Manuel instructif et
portatif à l'usage des étrangers qui se proposent
de parcourir ce pays; extrait des meilleurs
ouvrages de nos jours. Genève: l'Auteur, [ca
1816]. 75p. 22cm.
Editor's preface signed: F.B.

VOYER D'ARGENSON, Antoine Réné de, marquis de Paulmy
See
PAULMY, Antoine Réné de Voyer d'Argenson, marquis de

VOZ DE LIÉBANA
Liébana y los Picos de Europa; ligera resena
histórica, datos geográficos y estadísticos,
itinerarios, monumentos y santuarios... Santander:
"La Atalaya", 1913. 207p., 1 fold.col. plate,
illus., map. 25cm.

JOUBERT, Georges and VUARNET, Jean
How to ski the new French way; translated by Sim
Thomas and John Fry. Kaye & Ward, 1967. 208p.,
27 plates, illus. 21cm.

Vues de la Suisse. Paris: Wild, [ca 1860]. 1v. of
illus. 26 x 35cm.

Vues remarquables des montagnes de la Suisse, avec
leur description. Ptie.1; [dessinés par C. Wolf;
avec préface par A. von Haller, et Description
d'un voyage fait en 1776 ... par Jac. Sam.
Wyttenbach]. Berne: Wagner, 1776. 17p., col.
plates, illus. 43cm.

- - Another ed. Amsterdam: J. Yntema, 1785.

VULLIEMIN, L
Le doyen Bridel: essai biographique. Lausanne:
G. Bridel, 1855. 340p. 19cm.

VULLIET, C   Cornaz
See
CORNAZ-VULLIET, C

W.A.C.
See
WEST-ALPEN-CLUB

W., D
See
WILSON, Daniel

W., F.F.
See
WYMAN, Frederick F

W., H.C.
　See
WARD, H　C

W., J.
　See
WALLER, James

WADDELL, L　Austine
　Among the Himalayas. Constable, 1899. xvi, 452p.,
　plates (1 fold.col.), illus., maps. 25cm.

WADDELL, L　Austine
　Lhasa and its mysteries, with a record of the
　expedition of 1903-1904. 2nd ed. Murray, 1905.
　xxiii, 530p., plates (some fold., some col.),
　illus., maps. 24cm.

WADE, Mary Hazelton
　Our little Swiss cousin; illustrated by L.J.
　Bridgman. Boston: L.C. Page, 1903. vi, 125p.,
　plates, illus. 20cm.

WÄBER, A
　Descriptions géographiques et récits de voyages et
　excursions en Suisse: contribution à la biblio-
　graphie de la litterature suisse des voyages de
　1891 à 1900 avec des suppléments relatifs à la
　période antérieure à 1891. Berne: K.J. Wyss, 1909.
　172p. 22cm. (Bibliographie nationale suisse.
　Fasc. III, 2)

WÄBER, A
　Landes- und Reisebeschreibungen: ein Beitrag zur
　Bibliographie der schweizerischen Reiselitteratur,
　1479-1890; zusammengestellt von A. Wäber. Bern:
　K.J. Wyss, 1899. xxii, 440p. 22cm. (Biblio-
　graphie der schweizerischen Landeskunde, Fasc. 3)

WÄBER, A
STUDER, Gottlieb
　Uber Eis und Schnee: die höchsten Gipfel der
　Schweiz und die Geschichte ihrer Besteigung.
　2.Aufl., umgearb. und ergänzt von A. Wäber und H.
　Dübi. Bern: Schmid, Franke, 1896-99. 3v., 1
　plate, port. 19cm.

WÄHNER, Franz
　Das Sonnwendgebirge im Unterinnthal: ein typus
　alpinen Gebirgsbaues. Pt.1. Leipzig: Deuticke,
　1903. 356p., col. plates (some fold.), illus.
　31cm.

WAGNER, Bruno
　The alpine highways of Switzerland; with thirty-
　five photographs by Michael Wolgensinger; drawings
　by Paul Ceres. Stanford, 1950. 125p., plates,
　illus. 14 x 21cm.

WAGNER, Henry R
　The plains and the Rockies: a bibliography of
　original narratives of travel and adventure, 1800-
　1865. San Francisco: J. Howell, 1921. 193p.
　26cm.

WAGNER, Johann Jacob
　Historia naturalis Helvetiae curiosa, in VII.
　sectiones compendiose digesta. Tiguri: Impensis
　Joh. Henrici Lindinneri, 1680. 418p. 14cm.

WAGNER, Johann Jacob
　Mercurius Helveticus: fürstellend die Denk- und
　Schauwürdigsten vornemsten Sachen und Seltsamkeiten
　der Eidgnossschaft... Zürich: Joh. Heinrich
　Lindinner, 1701. 258p., 1 plate, map. 14cm.

WAGNER, Richard
BRAUNSTEIN, Josef
　Richard Wagner and the Alps; [translated by E.S.
　Tattersall]. [N.p.]: [n.pub.], [1929?]. 31p.
　21cm.
　English translation of an article originally
　published in Nachrichten des A.V. Donauland, 1928.

Wagner's Führer durch Nordtirol, Vorarlberg die
　angrenzenden Gebiete von Oberbayern und den Tauern;
　bearb. von Hermann Schwaighofer. Innsbruck:
　Wagner, 1922. 432p., maps, plans. 16cm.

WAGNON, Aug.
　Excursions et escalades de la Dent du Midi au Buet,
　autour de Salvan et de Fins-Hauts. 2e éd.
　Lausanne: C. Pache, 1895. 212p., plates, illus.
　18cm.

WAGNON, Aug.
　Finhaut et la Vallée du Trient: excursions - esca-
　lades de la Dent-du-Midi au Mont-Blanc. 3e éd.
　Lausanne: C. Pache, 1903. 213p., 1 fold.col.
　plate, illus., map. 20cm.

WAGNON, Aug.
　Guide de la Vallée du Trient: excursions, esca-
　lades de la Dent-du-Midi au Mont-Blanc. 3e éd.
　Genève: A. Jullien, 1903. 213p., illus., maps.
　20cm.

WAHLENBERG, Georg
　Bericht über Messungen und Beobachtungen zur
　Bestimmung der Höhe und Temperatur der lapp-
　ländischen Alpen unter dem 67sten Breitengrade
　angestellt im Jahre 1807; aus dem Schwedischen
　übersetzt. Göttingen: Dieterich, 1812. 61p.,
　plates (2 fold.), illus., map. 25cm.

WAINWRIGHT, A
　Fellwanderer: the story behind the guidebooks.
　Kendal: Westmorland Gazette, 1966. [70]p., plates,
　illus. 15 x 23cm.

WAINWRIGHT, A
　A pictorial guide to the Lakeland fells, being an
　illustrated account of a study and exploration of
　the mountains in the English Lake District. Book
　1. The eastern fells. Low Bridge, Kentmere: H.
　Marshall, 1955. 1v. (various pagings), maps. 18cm.

WAINWRIGHT, A
　A pictorial guide to the Lakeland fells, being an
　illustrated account of a study and exploration of
　the mountains in the English Lake District. Book
　2. The far eastern fells. Low Bridge, Kentmere:
　H. Marshall, 1957. 1v. (various pagings), illus.,
　maps. 18cm.

WAINTWRIGHT, A
　A pictorial guide to the Lakeland fells, being an
　illustrated account of a study and exploration of
　the mountains in the English Lake District. Book
　3. The central fells. Low Bridge, Kentmere: H.
　Marshall, 1958. 1v. (various pagings), illus.,
　maps. 18cm.

WAINWRIGHT, A
　A pictorial guide to the Lakeland fells, being an
　illustrated account of a study and exploration of
　the mountains in the English Lake District. Book
　4. The southern fells. Low Bridge, Kentmere: H.
　Marshall, 1960. 1v. (various pagings), illus.,
　maps. 18cm.

WAINWRIGHT, A
　A pictorial guide to the Lakeland fells, being an
　illustrated account of a study and exploration of
　the mountains in the English Lake District. Book
　5. The northern fells. Low Bridge, Kentmere: H.
　Marshall, 1962. 1v. (various pagings), illus.,
　maps. 18cm.

WAIS, Julius
　Allgäuführer: wanderfahrten. Stuttgart: Union
　Deutsche Verlagsgesellschaft, 1925-[28]. 2v.,
　plates (some fold.col.), illus., maps. 16cm.

WAKEFIELD, Priscilla
　The juvenile travellers, containing the remarks of
　a family during a tour through the principal states
　and kingdoms of Europe... 10th ed. Darton, Harvey,
　& Darton, 1814. 419p., map. 18cm.

WALA, Antoni and WALA, Jerzy
　Routes leading to Pik Kommunizma, 7495, Soviet
　Union, Pamir, 1933-1971. Kraków: The Authors,
　1971. 6 leaves, plates, illus., map. 30cm.
　Typescript.

WALA, Jerzy
Hindu Kush, mountain group: Hendukuse Zebak.
Krakow: Klub Wysokogorski, 1974. 24 leaves, fold.
plates, illus., maps (2 in pocket), bibl. 30cm.

WALA, Jerzy
Hindu Kush: the regional divisions. Krakow: Klub
Wysokogorski, 1973. 39 leaves, fold. plates,
illus., maps, bibl. 30cm.

- - 9 maps in portfolio.

WALA, Jerzy
Kohe Pamir - Wakhan: orographical sketch-map,
elaborated by Jerzy Wala. Krakow: Klub
Wysokogorski, 1975. 5 leaves, illus. (1 fold.),
maps (1 fold.). 25cm.

BIEL, Stanisław and WALA, Jerzy
The Polish Hindu Kush and Pamir Expedition, 1971.
[Krakow]: The Expedition, [1971?]. 18, 3 leaves,
plates, maps. 29cm.

WALA, Antoni and WALA, Jerzy
Routes leading to Pik Kommunizma, 7495, Soviet
Union, Pamir, 1933-1971. Krakow: The Authors,
1971. 6 leaves, plates, illus., map. 30cm.
Typescript.

WALA, Jerzy
Topography of the Hispar Mustagh mountain group,
Karakorum. Krakow: Klub Wysokogorski, 1974. 23,
10 leaves, fold. plates, illus., maps, bibl. 22cm.

WALA, Jerzy
W sprawie nomenklatury obiektow gorskich. [Warsaw],
1977. 177-179p. 26cm.
Offprint from Przeglad geograficzny, t.49, z.1,
1977.

WALCHER, Joseph
Nachrichten von den Eisbergen im Tyrol. Frankfurt:
[n.pub.], 1773. 98p., 5 plates, illus. 20cm.

WALCHER, S
Taschenbuch zu Schweizer-Reisen, mit hinweisung auf
alle Sehens und Merkwurdigkeiten der Schweiz; eines
Theils von Savonen und anderer benachbarten Orte.
Glarus: F. Schmid, 1832. xxiv, 327p. 17cm.

- - 3.verb. Aufl. 1841.

WALCHER, S
Touristenführer durch die Schweiz. Leipzig: J.J.
Weber, 1856. viii, 407p., plates, illus., maps.
16cm.

WALCOTT, Mackenzie E   C
A guide to the mountains, lakes, and north-west
coast of England, descriptive of natural scenery
historical, archaeological and legendary.
Stanford, 1860. xii, 243p., 1 fold.col. plate,
map. 17cm. (Stanford's series of pocket guide-
books, 12)

WALDIE, Jane
Sketches descriptive of Italy in the years 1816 and
1817, with a brief account of travels in various
parts of France and Switzerland in the same years,
[by Jane Waldie]. Murray, 1820. 4v. 17cm.

WALDIS, Alfred
Switzerland: the traveller's illustrated guide;
revised ... by Alfred Waldis. 4th rev. English ed.
Faber & Faber, 1965. 248p., plates (some fold.,
some col.), illus., maps, plans. 19cm.

WALES, Hubert
The thirty days. Cassell, 1915. 312p., col.
plates, illus. 24cm.

WALFORD, Thomas
The scientific tourist through England, Wales, &
Scotland ... arranged by counties... Vol.2. J.
Booth, 1818. [352]p., plates, maps. 17cm.

A walk through Switzerland in September 1816.
Printed for T. Hookham, Jun. and Baldwin, Cradock
& Joy, 1818. 242p., maps. 18cm.

WALKER, A
Remarks made in a tour from London to the Lakes of
Westmoreland and Cumberland, in the summer of
1791 ...; to which is annexed, a sketch of the
police, religion, arts, and agriculture of France,
made in an excursion to Paris in 1785. G. Nicol,
1792. 251p., illus. 24cm.

TEMPLE, John and WALKER, Alan
Kirinyaga: a Mount Kenya anthology; edited by
John Temple and Alan Walker. Nairobi: Mountain
Club of Kenya, [1974]. 61p. 33cm.

WALKER, James Hubert
Mountain days in the Highlands and Alps. Arnold,
1937. 320p., col. plates, illus., maps. 23cm.

WALKER, James Hubert
On hills of the north. Edinburgh, London: Oliver
& Boyd, 1948. xv, 182p., plates, illus., maps.
22cm.

WALKER, James Hubert
Walking in the Alps; with photographs and maps by
the author. Edinburgh, London: Oliver and Boyd,
1951. xii, 274p., plates, illus., maps. 24cm.

WALKER, J   T
Descriptions and co-ordinates of the principal
and secondary stations and other fixed points of
North-West Himalaya series (or Series C of the
N.W. Quadrilateral) and the triangulation of the
Kashmir Survey, by J.T. Walker and his assistants.
Dehra Dun: Survey of India, 1879. xiii, lxxiii,
293p., fold. plates, maps. 32cm. (Synopsis of
the results of the operations of the Great Trigo-
nometrical Survey of India, v.7)

WALL, Claud W
Mountaineering in Ireland; with an introduction
by R. Lloyd Praeger; revised by Joss Lynam.
Dublin: Federation of Mountaineering Clubs of
Ireland, 1976. 111p., map, bibl. (F.M.C.I.
guides)

WALL, Daniel
EBEL, Johann Gottfried
[Handbuch für Reisende in der Schweiz]. The
traveller's guide through Switzerland, in four
parts ..., by M.J.G. Ebel. New ed., arranged
and improved by Daniel Wall with a complete atlas.
Leigh, 1818. xxvii, 548p., and atlas, plates,
illus. 15cm.

WALL, David
Rondoy: an expedition to the Peruvian Andes;
with a foreword by Don Whillans. Murray, 1965.
xiv, 176p., plates, illus., maps. 23cm.

Wall and roof climbing, by the author of "The roof-
climber's guide to Trinity" [i.e. Geoffrey
Winthrop Young]. Eton College, Spottiswoode,1905.
viii, 109p. 23cm.

WALLACE, Alfred Russel
SPRUCE, Richard
Notes of a botanist on the Amazon & Andes, being
records of travel on the Amazon ... the Orinoco,
along the eastern side of the Andes of Peru and
Ecuador, and the shores of the Pacific, during
the years 1849-1864; edited and condensed by
Alfred Russel Wallace; with a biographical introduction. Macmillan, 1908. 2v., plates (some
fold., col.), illus., maps. 23cm.

WALLACE, Cornelia
Mountain monarchs. Swan Sonnenschein, 1887.
23p. 19cm.

WALLACE, Doreen
English Lakeland. Batsford, 1940. viii, 120p.,
plates (1 col.), illus., maps (on lining papers).
22cm. (The face of Britain)

HOEK, Henry and WALLAU, Heinrich
Schi-Fahrten im südlichen Schwarzwald. München:
G.Lammers, 1908. xx, 71p., maps. 17cm.

- - 2.verm und verb. Aufl. München: Deutsche
Alpenzeitung, 1911.

WALLER, James
  The everlasting hills. Edinburgh, London:
  Blackwood, 1939. xii, 190p., plates, illus., maps
  (on lining paper). 23cm.

WALLIS, C   S
  Sierre and Montana; illustrated by E.S. Norton.
  Zurich: Orell Füssli, [1894?]. 64p., plates (1
  fold.), illus. 19cm.

THOMAS, M   B   and WALLIS, R   H
  Report on the Royal Navy East Greenland Expedition
  1966 by M.B. Thomas, R.H. Wallis and members of
  the expedition. [Plymouth]: The Expedition,
  [1967]. [64]p., plates, illus., maps. 34cm.

WALLIS. Commission sur le glacier Giétroz
  Rapport sur l'état actuel de la Vallée de Bagne
  dans le Canton du Valais relativement aux mesures
  propres à la prémunir contre l'effet destructeur
  du glacier inférieur de Giétroz; présenté au
  Gouvernement du Canton du Valais par la Commission
  chargée de cet examen. Zurich: La Commission,
  1821. 59p. 19cm.

WALLIS. Département de Justice et Police
  Tarif général pour les guides et porteurs des
  Alpes valaisannes et Règlement des colonnes de
  secours. Sion: Le Département, 1933. 60p. 16cm.
  Text in French and German.

WALLISER HERBSTFEST
  Mein Wallis: Festgabe zum Walliser Herbstfest in
  Zürich, 29. und 30. Oktober 1921; hrsg. im Auftrage
  des Festkomitees von Eugen Fischer. Zürich: H.
  Börsig, 1921. 72p., illus. 24cm.

WALLROTH, Ernst
  Der Alpenstock: Wegweiser für Reisende in der
  Schweiz, Savoyen und Piemont. 2.Aufl. Stuttgart:
  P. Neff, [n.d.]. xxxi, 277p., map. 14cm.

WALSER, Hermann
  Landeskunde der Schweiz. Leipzig: G.J. Göschen,
  1908. 146p., 16 plates, illus., map. 16cm.
  (Sammlung Göschen)

- - 2.Aufl. 1914.
- - 3.verb. Aufl.,besorgt von Otto Flückiger.
  Berlin: W. de Grunter, 1926.

WALSH, Maurice
  The hill is mine. Chambers, 1940. 351p. 20cm.

WALSH, Maurice
  The key above the door. Chambers, 1928. 264p.
  19cm.

WALTENBERGER, A
  Allgäu, Vorarlberg und Westtirol nebst den angrenzenden Gebieten der Schweiz. 14.Aufl. bearb. von
  Eugen Waltenberger. Wien: A. Edlinger, 1914.
  xiii, 436p., maps. 17cm.

WALTENBERGER, A
  Orographie der Algäuer Alpen. Augsburg: Lampart,
  1872. 20p., 2 fold.col. plates, illus. 30cm.

WALTENBERGER, A
  Orographie des Wetterstein-Gebirges und der Miem-
  ingerkette: Orographie des Wetterstein- und
  Karwendel-Gebirges I; mit einem Vorwort und
  Ersteigungslinien von Hermann von Barth. Augsburg:
  Lampart, 1882. viii, 59p., fold. plates (some
  col.), illus., maps. 29cm.

WALTENBERGER, A
  Stubai, Oetzthaler- und Ortlergruppe nebst den
  angrenzenden Gebieten; mit besonderer Berücksichtigung der Brennerbahn, der Gegend von Meran
  und Bozen. Augsburg: Lampart, 1879. xii, 404p.,
  map. 17cm. (Special-Führer, 2)

WALTER, James Conway
  Stray leaves on travel, sport, animals and kindred
  subjects. K. Paul, Trench, Trübner, 1910. xii,
  295p. 23cm.

WALTER, L   Edna
  The fascination of Switzerland. Black, 1912.
  viii, 104p., 24 plates, illus. 17cm.

WALTER, Weever
  Letters from the Continent, containing sketches of
  foreign scenery and manners... Edinburgh:
  Blackwood; London: T. Cadell, 1828. 307p. 20cm.

WALTHARD, Rod.
  Nouvelle description de l'Oberland bernois à
  l'usage des voyageurs, [par R. Walthard]. Berne:
  J.J. Burgdorfer, 1838. xii, 40p., plates (some
  col.), maps. 23cm.

WALTON, Elijah
  Alpine flowers
    See his
  Flowers from the upper Alps...

WALTON, Elijah
  Alpine vignettes; with descriptive text by T.G.
  Bonney. 4th ed. W.M. Thompson, 1882. 1v.
  (chiefly col. illus.). 34cm.
  First ed. published in 1873 under title: Vignettes:
  alpine and eastern.

WALTON, Elijah
  The Bernese Oberland: twelve scenes among its
  peaks and lakes, by Elijah Walton; with descriptive text by T.G. Bonney. W.M. Thompson, 1874.
  1v. (chiefly col. illus.). 44cm.

WALTON, Elijah
  The coast of Norway, from Christiania to
  Hammerfest; the descriptive text by T.G. Bonney.
  W.M. Thompson, 1871. viii, 24p., 12 plates,
  illus. 35 x 44cm.

WALTON, Elijah
  English Lake scenery; with descriptive text by
  T.G. Bonney. W.M. Thompson, 1876. [102] leaves,
  col. plates, illus. 34cm.

WALTON, Elijah
  Flowers from the upper Alps, with glimpses of
  their homes; the descriptive text by T.G. Bonney.
  W.M. Thompson, 1869. 1v. (chiefly col. illus.).
  34cm.

- - 5th ed. 1882.
- - Alpine flowers after Elijah Walton. 1912.
  The plates, without text, in a portfolio.

WALTON, Elijah
  The peaks and valleys of the Alps; [chromolitho-
  graphed by J.H. Lowes]; with descriptive text by
  T.G. Bonney. Day, 1867. 1v. (chiefly illus.).
  57cm.

- - Reissue. Sampson Low, Son, & Marston, 1868.

WALTON, Elijah
  Peaks in pen and pencil for students of alpine
  scenery; edited by T.G. Bonney. Longmans, Green,
  1872. 1v. (chiefly illus.). 49cm.

WALTON, Elijah
  Vignettes: alpine and eastern; the descriptive
  text by T.G. Bonney. W.M. Thompson, 1873. 1v.
  (chiefly col. illus.). 34cm.
  Fourth ed. published in 1882 under title: Alpine
  vignettes.

- - Alpine series. 1873.

WALTON, Elijah
  Welsh scenery (chiefly in Snowdonia); with descriptive text by T.G. Bonney. W.M. Thompson,
  1875. 1v. (chiefly col. illus.). 34cm.

WALTON, William Howard Murray
  Scrambles in Japan and Formosa. Arnold, 1934.
  304p., plates (2 fold.col.), illus., maps. 23cm.

WANDERER
  Notes on the Caucasus. Macmillan, 1883. viii,
  280p. 23cm.

Wanderungen durch die Rhätischen Alpen: ein Beytrag
  zur Charakteristik dieses Theils des
  schweizerischen Hochlandes und seiner Bewohner,[von
  Peter C. von Tscharner]. Zürich: Orell, Füssli,
  1829-31. 2v., plates, maps. 21cm.

Wanderungen durch Tirol und Vorarlberg; geschildert
  von Ludwig von Hörmann [and others]; illustrirt von
  Franz Defregger [and others]. Stuttgart: Kröner,
  [1879]. 284p., plates, illus. 37cm. (Unser
  Vaterland)

The war in Italy. Milan: Treves, 1916. 3v. in 1,
  (193p.), fold.col. plates, illus., map. 33cm.

- - Soldier's ed. 1916.

WARBURTON, Lloyd E
  The steepest mountain: N.Z. Andes Expedition, 1960.
  Invercargill: R.J. Cuthill, 1964. 136p., plates,
  illus. 22cm.

WARD, A E
  The sportsman's guide to Kashmir & Ladak, &c.; reproduced with additions from letters which appeared
  in the "Asian". 2nd and rev. ed. Calcutta:
  Calcutta Central Press Co., 1883. vi, 90p., fold.
  plates, maps. 23cm.

- - 3rd and rev. ed. 1887.

BADDELEY, Mountford J B and WARD, C S
  Ireland. 4th ed. Dulau, 1901. 2v., col. plates
  (some fold.), maps. 17cm. (Thorough guides,
  12-13)
  Library has pt.2 only.

- - 5th ed., rev. 1902-09.

WARD, C S
  North Devon, including west Somerset, and north
  Cornwall... 8th ed., rev. Dulau, 1903. xvi,
  160p., plates (some fold.,some col.), maps. 17cm.
  (Thorough guides, 3)

BADDELEY, Mountford J B and WARD, C S
  North Wales. Pt.1. 7th ed., rev. Dulau, 1902.
  xxiv, 239p., fold.col. plates, illus., maps. 17cm.
  (Thorough guides, 8)

WARD, C S and BADDELEY, Mountford J B
  South Wales and the Wye district of Monmouthshire.
  4th ed., rev. Dulau, 1901. xvi, 192p., plates
  (some fold.col.), maps. 17cm. (Thorough guides,
  10)

WARD, F Kingdon
  See
  KINGDON-WARD, Francis

WARD, H C
  Wild flowers of Switzerland; or, A year amongst the
  flowers of the Alps, by H.C. W[ard]. Sampson Low,
  Marston, Searle, & Rivington, 1883. vi, 76p.,
  16 plates, illus. 40cm.

WARD, Julius H
  The White Mountains: a guide to their interpreta-
  tion. 2nd ed., rev. and enl. Boston: Houghton,
  Mifflin, 1896. ix, 311p., plates (1 fold.), illus.,
  map, bibl. 19cm.

WARD, Michael
  In this short span: a mountaineering memoir.
  Gollancz, 1972. 304p., plates, illus., maps, bibl.
  23cm.

WARD, Michael
  Mountain medicine: a clinical study of cold and
  high altitude. Crosby Lockwood Staples, 1975. x,
  376p., plates, illus., bibl. 23cm.

WARD, Michael
  Mountain medicine and physiology: proceedings of a
  symposium for mountaineers, expedition doctors and
  physiologists; sponsored by the Alpine Club; edited
  by Charles Clarke, Michael Ward, Edward Williams.
  A.C., 1975. 143p., plates, illus., bibl. 21cm.
  Cover title.

WARD, Michael
  The mountaineer's companion; edited by Michael
  Ward. Eyre & Spottiswoode, 1966. 598p., 24
  plates (some col.), illus. 23cm.

WARD-DRUMMOND, Edwin
  Extremely severe in the Avon gorge: [the 1967
  guide to the harder climbs]. Bristol: N.
  Crowhurst, 1967. 30p., illus., map. 21cm.

WARD, LOCK, AND CO.
  Handbook to North Wales. Complete ed. Ward,
  Lock, [ca 1920]. 2v. in 1, plates (some fold.
  col.), illus., maps. 18cm.

WARD, LOCK, AND CO.
  Ward and Lock's (late Shaw's) Pictorial and historical guide to the English Lakes; their scenery
  and associations; with an introduction by the poet
  Wordsworth. Ward, Lock, [ca 1889]. xvi, 202p.,
  col. plates (some fold.), illus., maps. 17cm.

WARDEN, Gertrude
  The crime in the Alps: a novel. White, 1908.
  vii, 311p. 21cm.

WARING, George E
  Tyrol and the skirt of the Alps. New York:
  Harper, 1880. 171p., illus. 24cm.

WARING, Samuel Miller
  The travellers' fire-side: a series of papers on
  Switzerland, the Alps... Baldwin, Cradock & Joy,
  1819. v, 309p. 19cm.

WARMINGTON, Annie
  Sport, by one who looked on (Annie Warmington).
  Simpkin, Marshall, 1910. vii, 78p., plates,
  illus. 21cm.

WARNER, Richard
  A walk through Wales in August 1797. Bath:
  Printed by R. Cruttwell; London: C. Dilly, 1798.
  viii, 236p., plates, illus., maps. 23cm.

- - A second walk ... in ... 1798. 1799.

WARNERY, Henri
  Eugène Rambert: études contemporaines.
  (In Bibliothèque universelle ... v.36, oct.-déc.
  1887, 3pts.)

WARNERY, Henri
  Sur l'alpe: poésies. Lausanne: Payot, 1895.
  127p., illus. 28cm.

WASHBURN, Bradford
  Among the Alps with Bradford; with a foreword by
  his brother; illustrated with sketches by the
  author and photographs. New York, London: Putnam,
  1927. xiv, 160p., plates, illus. 21cm.

WASHBURN, Bradford and GOLDTHWAIT, Richard P
  The Harvard-Dartmouth Alaskan expeditions, 1933-
  1934. London, 1936. 481-517p., plates (1 fold.
  col.), illus., map. 25cm.
  Offprint from Geographical journal, v.87, no.6,
  June 1936.

WASHBURN, Bradford
  Mount McKinley and the Alaska Range in literature:
  a descriptive bibliography. Boston (Mass.):
  Museum of Science, 1951. 88p. 23cm.

WASHBURN, Bradford
  A tourist guide to Mount McKinley: the story of
  "Denali", "the Great One", mile-by-mile through
  the park over the Denali Highway, the record of
  McKinley climbs. Anchorage: Alaska Northwest
  Publishing Company, 1971. 79p., illus., map (on
  lining papers), bibl. 29cm.

- - Rev. ed. 1974.

WASHBURN, Bradford
  The trails and peaks of the Presidential Range of
  the White Mountains. Worcester (Mass.): The
  Author, 1926. 79p., 1 fold. plate, illus., map.
  16cm.

WASHBURN, Henry Bradford, jr.
See
WASHBURN, Bradford

WASHINGTON ACADEMY OF SCIENCES
HARRIMAN ALASKA EXPEDITION, 1899
Alaska, giving the results of the Harriman Alaska
Expedition carried out with the co-operation of the
Washington Academy of Sciences, by John Burroughs
[and others]. Murray, 1902-   . Plates (some
fold., some col.), illus., maps. 27cm.
Vol.1. Narratives, glaciers, natives. 1902. -v.2.
History, geography, resources. 1902. -v.3.
Glaciers and glaciation. New York: Doubleday,
Page, 1904. -

WATERS, Helena L
From Dolomites to Stelvio. Methuen, 1926. xv,
272p., plates, illus., maps. 18cm.

WATERS, W   G
MONTAIGNE, Michel de
[Journal du voyage...]. The journal of Montaigne's
travels in Italy by way of Switzerland and Germany
in 1580 and 1581; translated and edited with an
introduction and notes by W.G. Waters. Murray,
1903. 3v., plates, illus. 17cm.

WATKINS, Gino
CHAPMAN, Frederick Spencer
Watkins' last expedition; with an introduction by
Augustine Courtauld. Vanguard, 1953. 244p. 19cm.

WATKINS, Gino
SCOTT, J   M
Gino Watkins. Hodder & Stoughton, 1935. xviii,
317p., plates (1 col.), illus., maps. 23cm.

WATKINS, Olga
Tales from Tyrol. Edinburgh: Blackwood, 1935.
331p. 21cm.

WATKINS, Thomas
Travels through Switzerland, Italy, Sicily, the
Greek Islands to Constantinople; through part of
Greece, Ragusa, and the Dalmatian Isles ...: a
series of letters to Pennoyre Watkins ... in the
years 1787, 1788, 1789. 2nd ed. Printed by J.
Owen, 1794. 2v. 23cm.

WATKINS MOUNTAINS EXPEDITION, 1969
Anglo-Danish mountain survey in East Greenland,
preliminary report, [by] Alastair Allan.
Cambridge: The Expedition, 1969. 9p, 1 plate,
map. 30cm.

WATSON, Adam
The Cairngorms: the Cairngorms, the Mounth,
Lochnager; map drawings by James Renny. 5th ed.,
rewritten. Edinburgh: Scottish Mountaineering
Trust, 1975. 302p., plates (1 col.), illus., maps,
bibl. 22cm. (Scottish Mountaineering Club
district guide books)

WATSON, G   C
Hints for pedestrians, practical and medical. New
ed. Bell & Daldy, 1862. xi, 116p. 18cm.

WATSON, Jean L
Our native land: its scenery and associations, a
series of 36 water-colour sketches ...; with descriptive notes [by Jean L. Watson]. Marcus Ward,
1879. 120p., col. plates, illus. 28cm.

WATSON, Sir Norman and KING, Edward J
Round mystery mountain: a ski adventure; with a
foreword by F.S. Smythe. Arnold, 1935. xii,
246p., plates (1 col.), illus., map. 23cm.
An expedition to the Coast Range and Mount
Waddington.

WATT, Joachim von
MELA, Pomponius
De orbis situ libri tres, accuratissime emendati,
unà cu Commetariis Ioachimi Vadiani Heluetii
castigatioribus... Adiecta... Rursum, Epistola
Vadiani... Basileae: Apud Andream Cratandrum, 1522.
1v. (various pagings). 31cm.
Contains Watt's account of the ascent of Pilatus,
with contemporary ms. notes.

WATTS, Alaric A
Literary souvenirs; [collected by Alaric A. Watts].
[Longmans], 1827. xxiv, 402p., plates, illus.
14cm.

- - Another,[i.e. 9th ed.].1833.

WATTS, William Lord
Across the Vatna Jökull; or, Scenes in Iceland,
being a description of hitherto unknown regions.
Longmans, 1876. 202p., plates (1 fold.col.),
illus., maps. 20cm.

WATTS, William Lord
Snioland; or, Iceland; its jokulls and fjalls.
Longmans, 1875. 183p., plates (1 fold.col.),
illus., map. 20cm.

WAUGH, Edwin
Rambles in the Lake country and its borders.
Whittaker, 1861. 267p. 18cm.

STILES, William F   and WAY, H   John
Austria; line illustrations by Reg Gammon. Vane,
1954. 110p., 1 fold. plate, illus., maps. 16cm.
("Good companion" guides, no.1)

WEAVER, E   P
COPPING, Harold
Canadian pictures: thirty-six plates in colour ...
from original drawings by Harold Copping; with
descriptive letterpress by E.P. Weaver. Religious
Tract Society, 1912. 1v. (chiefly col. illus.).
41cm.

WEBB, Frank
Switzerland of the Swiss. Pitman, 1909. x,
254p., plates, illus. 20cm.

WEBB, W   L
Brief biography and popular account of the un-
paralleled discoveries of T.J.J. See. Lynn
(Mass.): Ths. P. Nichols, London: Wm. Wesley,
1913. xii, 298p., plates, illus., maps. 25cm.

WEBER, E
Reise- und Handlexikon der Schweiz; hrsg. von E.
Weber. Zürich: H. Mahler, 1854. 1054p. 15cm.

WEBER, J   C
Die Alpen-Pflanzen Deutschlands und der Schweiz
in colorirten Abbildungen ...; mit einem
erläuternden Text von J.C. Weber. München: Kaiser,
[1843-56]. 3v., col. plates, illus. 14cm.

- - 4.Aufl., systematisch geordnet mit Text von
C.A. Kranz. 1880.

WEBER, Julius
Geologische Wanderungen durch die Schweiz: eine
Einführung in die Geologie; hrsg., von Schweizer
Alpen-Club. Zürich: S.A.C. Central-Comitee,
1911-15. 3v., illus., maps. 17cm. (Schweizer
Alpen-Club. Clubführer)

WEBER, Karl
Schweizerische Stiftung für Alpine Forschungen
1939 bis 1970: Rückblick auf ihre 30 jährige
Tätigkeit; [edited by Karl Weber and Ernst Feuz].
Zürich: S.S.A.F., 1972. 159p., plates, illus.,
ports., bibl. 28cm.

WEBER, P   X
Der Pilatus und seine Geschichte. Luzern: E.
Haag, 1913. xix, 379p., plates, illus., map,
bibl. 21cm.

WECHSBERG, Joseph
Avalanche. Weidenfeld and Nicolson, 1958. 190p.,
maps. 22cm.

WEDDERBURN, Ernst Alexander Maclagan
Alpine climbing on foot and with ski. Manchester:
Open Air Publications, [1936]. 118p., illus.
18cm.

- - 2nd rev. ed., revised by C. Douglas Milner.
Manchester, London: Countrygoer Books, 1954.

WEDDIK, Bartholomeus T   Lublink
SENDEN, G   H   van
  Alpenrozen. 2.druk met aanteekeningen vermeerderd
  en nagezien door B.T. Lublink Weddik en P.H.
  Witkamp. Amsterdam: C.L.B. Brinkman, [ca 1858].
  iv., 502p., 1 plate, map. 19cm.

WEDDIK, Bartholomeus T   Lublink
  Tafereelen, gedachten en beelden: impressions de
  voyage; Verzameld langs den Rijn en in Zwitserland
  ... Arnhem: D.A. Thieme, 1854. 259p., plates,
  illus. 23cm.

WEGMANN, Eugen
  Zur Geologie der St. Bernharddecke im Val d'Hérens
  (Wallis). Neuchatel, 1923. 66p., 1 fold.col.
  plate, illus., map, bibl. 24cm.
  Offprint from Bulletin de la Societé neuchateloise
  des sciences naturalles, t.47, année 1922.

WEHRLI, Leo
  Das Dioritgebiet von Schlans bis Disentis im
  Bündner Oberland: geologische-petrographische
  Studie. Bern: Schmid, Francke, 1896. vii, 67p.,
  plates (some col.), illus., map. 33cm. (Beiträge
  zur geologischen Karte der Schweiz, Lfg.36, N.F.,
  Lfg. 6)

WEHRLI, Leo
  Profils géologiques transversaux de la Cordillère
  argentino-chilienne: stratigraphie et tectonique.
  Ptie.1. Du rapport définitif sur une expédition
  géologique effectuée par Leo Wehrli et Carl
  Burckhardt. La Plata: Museo de La Plata, 1900.
  vii, 136p., plates (some fold., some col.),
  illus., map. 39cm. (Anales del Museo de La
  Plata. Sección geológica y mineralógica, 2)

WEHRLI, Leo
HEER, J   C
  Schweiz. 4.Aufl., von Leo Wehrli. Bielefeld:
  Velhagen, 1913. 222p., plates, illus., map.
  26cm. (Land und Leute, 5)

WEIBEL, Max
  Die Mineralien der Schweiz: ein Mineralogischer
  Führer. 4.erw.Aufl. Basel: Birkhäuser Verlag,
  1972. 185p., illus. (some col.), maps. 20cm.

WEIBEL, Max
  [Die Mineralien der Schweiz]. A guide to the
  minerals of Switzerland. Interscience, 1966. xi,
  123p., plates (some col.), illus., maps. 23cm.

WEIBEL, S
  Voyage pittoresque de l'Oberland; ou, Description
  de vues prises dans l'Oberland, district du Canton
  de Berne, [par S. Weibel]; accompagné de notices
  historiques et topographiques [par Philipp A.
  Stapfer]. Paris: Treuttel & Würtz, 1812. 90p.,
  15 col. plates, illus., map. 35cm.

WEIDMANN, F   C
  Alpengegenden Niederösterreichs und Obersteyer-
  marks im Bereiche der Eisenbahn von Wien bis
  Mürzzuschlag. 4.verm. ... versehene Aufl. Wien:
  Gerold, 1862. 269p., map. 14cm.

WEIDMANN, F   C
  Darstellungen aus dem Steyermärk'schen Oberlande.
  Wien: Gerold, 1834. xviii, 229p., 2 plates (1
  fold.), illus., map. 25cm.

WEILENMANN, Johann Jacob
  Aus der Firnenwelt: gesammelte Schriften. Leipzig:
  A.G. Liebeskind, 1872 [-77]. 3v., plates, port.,
  map. 18cm.

WEILENMANN, Johann Jacob
  Aus der Firnenwelt: gesammelte Schriften ...; mit
  einem Lebensbild Weilenmanns von Walter Flaig und
  mid Bildern ... von Toni Schönecker. München:
  Rother, 1923-24. 2v., illus. 21cm.

  - - 2.Aufl.[of Bd.] 1. 1929.

WEILENMANN, Johann Jacob
  Berg- und Gletscher-Fahrten in den Hochalpen der
  Schweiz, von G. Studer, M. Ulrich, J.J.Weilenmann,
  Zürich: F. Schulthess, 1859-63. 2v., illus. 19cm.

WEILENMANN, Johann Jacob
  Eine Ersteigung des Piz Linard im Unter-Engadin.
  St. Gallen: Scheitlin & Zollikofer, 1859. 49p.
  16cm.

WEINGARTNER, Josef
  Bozner Burgen. Innsbruck: Verlagsanstalt Tyrolia,
  1922. 228p., plates, illus. 25cm.

WEIR, Thomas
  Camps and climbs in Arctic Norway. Cassell, 1953.
  vii, 87p., plates, illus., maps. 23cm.

WEIR, Thomas
  East of Katmandu. Oliver and Boyd, 1955. 138p.,
  plates (2 col.), illus., maps. 23cm.

WEIR, Thomas
  Highland days; with 35 photographs by the author.
  Cassell, 1948. xi, 139p., plates, illus., maps.
  23cm.

WEIR, Thomas
  The ultimate mountains: an account of four months'
  mountain exploring in the central Himalaya; with
  ... photographs by Thomas Weir and Douglas Scott.
  Cassell, 1953. x, 98p., plates, illus., maps.
  23cm.

WEISS, Jurg
  Murailles et abîmes ...; traduit de l'allemand
  par Elizabeth A. Cuénod. Neuchatel: Attinger,
  1946. 174p., plates, illus. 20cm.

WEISS, Karl
  Fotografieren und filmen im Hochgebirge; unter
  Mirwirkung von Walter Remmel [and others]; hrsg.
  von Karl Weiss. Berlin: Union Deutsche Verlagsgesellschaft, 1934. 180p., illus. (1 col.).
  23cm.

WEISS, Richard
  Die Entdeckung der Alpen: eine Sammlung
  schweizerische und deutscher Alpenliteratur bis
  zum Jahr 1800; ausgewählt und bearb. von Richard
  Weiss. Frauenfeld: Huber, 1934. xvi, 232p.,
  plates, illus. 21cm.

WELCH, Ann
  Accidents happen: anticipation, avoidance,
  survival. Murray, 1978. xii, 240p., illus. 22cm.

WELD, Charles Richard
  Auvergne, Piedmont, and Savoy: a summer ramble.
  J.W. Parker, 1850. xi, 351p., illus. 21cm.

WELD, Charles Richard
  The Pyrenees, west and east. Longman, Brown,
  Green, Longmans, & Roberts, 1859. xvi, 410p.,
  plates, illus. 20cm.

WELD, Charles Richard
  Two months in the Highlands,Orcadia, and Skye.
  Longman, Green, Longman, & Roberts, 1860. xxi,
  404p., col. plates, illus. 21cm.

WELDEN, Ludwig, Freiherr von
  Der Monte-Rosa: eine topographische und naturhistorische Skizze, nebst einem Anhange der von
  Herrn Zumstein gemachten Reisen zur Ersteigung
  seiner Gipfel. Wien: Gerold, 1824. viii, 167p.,
  fold. plates, illus., map. 23cm.

WELLENBURG, W   von Schmidt zu
  See
  SCHMIDT ZU WELLENBURG, W   von

WELLS, Herbert George
  Ann Veronica. Newnes, [1913]. 318p., plates,
  illus. 23cm. (Sevenpenny novel)

WELS, Horst
  Brenta-Gruppe. München: Rother, 1963. 158p.,
  plates (1 fold.), illus., maps. 16cm.
  (Dolomiten-Kletterführer, Bd.3)

WELZENBACH, Willo
[Bergfahrten]. Willo Welzenbachs Bergfahrten;
unter Mitwirkung von Eugen Allwein, Fritz Bechtold
[and others]; hrsg. von Akademischen Alpenverein
München. Berlin: Union Deutsche Verlagsgesellschaft, 1935. 260p., plates, illus., bibl. 22cm.

WELZENBACH, Willo
[Bergfahrten]. Les ascensions de Willo Welzenbach:
Alpes orientales, Alpes valaisannes, Mont Blanc,
Oberland bernois, Himalaya; traduit par Mme A.
Cuénod. Paris: Éditions de France, 1939. xi,
232p., 12 plates, illus. 19cm.

WENTWORTH, Ralph Milbanke, Lord Wentworth
  See
LOVELACE, Ralph Milbanke, 2nd Earl of

WENZEL, Eugen
Clubführer durch die Bündner Alpen. Bd.6. Albula
(Septimer bis Flüela). Baden: Schweizer Alpenclub,
1934. 595p., illus., col. maps (on lining papers),
bibl. 17cm. (Clubführer des Schweizer Alpen-Club)

HOEL, Adolf and WERENSKIOLD, Werner
Glaciers and snowfields in Norway. Oslo: Univer-
sity Press, 1962. 291p., fold. plates, illus.,
maps (some in separate folder). 27cm. (Norsk
Polarinstitutt, Skrifter Nr.114)
At head of title: Kongelige Dept. for Industri og
Handverk.

WEST, Lionel F
The climber's pocket book: rock climbing accidents,
with hints on first aid to the injured, some uses
of the rope, methods of rescue, and transport.
Manchester: Scientific Publishing Co., [1907].
79p., illus. 17cm.

WEST, Thomas
A guide to the Lakes, dedicated to the lovers of
landscape studies ... by the author of The antiquities of Furness [i.e. Thomas West]. Richardson
& Urquhart, 1778. 204p. 19cm.

- - 2nd ed., rev. throughout and greatly enl.,
entitled "A guide to the Lakes, in Cumberland,
Westmorland, and Lancashire". 1780.
- - 3rd ed., rev. B. Law, 1784.
- - 4th ed. W. Richardson, 1789.
- - 5th ed. 1793.
- - 6th ed. 1796.
- - 7th ed. 1799.
- - 9th ed. Kendal: Printed by W. Pennington, 1807.
- - 10th ed. 1812.
- - 11th ed. 1821.

WEST-ALPEN-CLUB
Bergkameraden: Mitgleider des W.A.C. erzählen.
Zürich: Orell Füssli, 1939. 271p., plates, illus.
20cm.

West Col alpine guides. Goring, Reading: West Col
Productions.

Bernese Alps west from the Col du Pillon to the
Lötschenpass; compiled by R.G. Collomb. 1970.
Bernina Alps; compiled by R.G. Collomb. 2nd ed.
1976.
Bregaglia east; compiled by R.G. Collomb. 1971.
Bregaglia west; compiled by R.G. Collomb and P.
Crew. 1967.
- - 2nd ed. by R.G. Collomb. 1974.
Central Switzerland, [by] J.O. Talbot. 1969.
Dents du Midi region: an interim guide. 1967.
Engelhorner and Salbitschijen including Wellhörner
and Scheideggwetterhorn; compiled by J.O. Talbot.
1968.
Glockner region, by E. Roberts. 1976.
Grians east: Gran Paradiso area; compiled by R.G.
Collomb. 1969.
Grians west: Tarentaise and Maurienne; compiled by
R.G. Collomb. 1967.
Julian Alps; compiled by R.G. Collomb; assisted by
M. Anderson. 1978.
Kaisergebirge; compiled by J. Talbot. 1971.
Maritime Alps: Vésubie basin and Argentera; com-
piled by R.G. Collomb. 1968.
Ortler Alps; compiled by A.J. Thompson. 1968.
Stubai Alps; compiled by Eric Roberts. 1972.

West Col coastal climbing guides. Goring, Reading:
West Col Productions.

Anglesey-Gogarth: Craig Gogarth, South Stack,
Holyhead Mountain, Gogarth Upper Tier, by P.
Crew and L. Holliwell. 1969.
Gower Peninsula: Caswell Bay to Worms Head, Burry
Holms to Tor Gro, by J. Talbot. 1970.
- - Supplement. 1973.
South Devon: Chudleigh, Torbay, Torquay, Brixham,
Berry Head, by P. Littlejohn and P. Biven. 1971.
Tremadoc area: Tremadoc Rocks, Craig y Gelli and
Carreg Hylldrem, by P.Crew and A. Harris. 1970.

West Col regional climbing guides. Goring, Reading:
West Col. Productions.

Central Wales: Craig Cowarch and the Arans, by J.
Sumner. 1973.
Dartmoor, by A.J.J. Moulam. 1976.
Dolgellau area: Cader Idris and the Rhinog range,
by J. Sumner. 1975.

WESTALL, William
Tales and traditions of Switzerland. Tinsley,
1882. 334p. 20cm.

WESTER, Josip
Iz Domovine in Tujine: izbrani planinski in
popotni spisi. Ljubljana: Zalozilo in izdalo
Slovensko planinsko drustvo, 1944. 319p., plates,
illus. 21cm.

WESTMORLAND, Horace
  See
WESTMORLAND, Rusty

WESTMORLAND, Rusty
Adventures in climbing. Pelham Books, 1964.
124p., plates, illus. 20cm. (Pelham adventurers
library)

WESTON, Stephen
La Scava; or, Some account of an excavation of a
Roman town on the hill of Chatelet, in Champagne
... discovered in the year 1772; to which is
added, A journey to the Simplon, by Lausanne, and
to Mont Blanc, through Geneva, by the author of
"Letters from Paris in 1791-2", [i.e. Stephen
Weston]. Baldwin, Cradock, & Joy, 1818. vii,
133p., 1 plate, illus. 24cm.

WESTON, Stephen
A trimester in France and Swisserland; or, A
three months' journey in ... 1820, from Calais to
Basle ... and from Basle to Paris, through
Strasburg and Reims, by an Oxonian [i.e. Stephen
Weston]. W. Clarke, 1821. 88p., plates, illus.
22cm.

WESTON, Walter
Mountaineering and exploration in the Japanese
Alps. Murray, 1896. xvi, 346p., plates (2 fold.
col.), illus., maps. 25cm.

WESTON, Walter
The playground of the Far East. Murray, 1918.
xiii, 333p., plates (2 fold.col.), illus., maps.
23cm.

WESTON, Walter
A wayfarer in unfamiliar Japan. Methuen, 1925.
xi, 207p., plates, illus., map (on lining paper).
20cm.

WETZEL, Johann Jacob
Voyage pittoresque au Lac de Come; [illustrations
par J.J. Wetzel]. Zurich: Orell, Füssli, 1822.
31p., 15 plates, illus. 44cm.

WETZEL, Johann Jacob
Voyage pittoresque au Lac des Waldstettes ou des
IV Cantons; [illustrations par J.J. Wetzel].
Zurich: Orell, Füssli, 1817. 1v. (chiefly col.
illus.). 45cm.

WETZEL, Johann Jacob
Voyage pittoresque aux Lacs Majeur et de Lugano;
[illustrations par J.J. Wetzel]. Zurich: Orell,
Füssli, 1823. 41p., col. plates, illus. 44cm.

WEY, Francis
La Haute Savoie: récits d'histoire et de voyage...
2e éd., rev. par l'auteur. Paris: Hachette, 1865.
viii, 502p. 19cm.

WEY, Francis
La Haute Savoie: récits de voyage et d'histoire.
Éd. illustrée de cinquante grandes lithographies
dessinées ... par H. Terry. Paris: Hachette,
1866. 119p., plates, illus. 54cm.

WEYPRECHT, A   and PAYER, Julius
Die Polar-Expedition von A. Weyprecht & Julius
Payer im Jahre 1871. Wien, 1872. 24p. 22cm.
Offprint from Mittheilungen der geographischen
Gesellschaft.

WHALLEY, Thomas Sedgwick
Mont Blanc: an irregular lyric poem. Bath: J.
Marshall, 1788. 57p. 23cm.

FRESHFIELD, Douglas William and WHARTON, W   J   L
Hints to travellers, scientific and general;
edited for the Council of the Royal Geographical
Society by Douglas W. Freshfield and W.J.L.
Wharton. 6th ed., rev. and enl. Royal Geographical Society, 1889. xii, 430p., plates (some
fold.col.), illus., maps. 18cm.

- - 7th ed., rev. and enl. 1893.
- - 8th ed., rev. and enl.; edited by John Coles.
1901. 2v.
- - 9th ed., rev.,enl.; edited by E.A. Reeves. 1906.
2v.
- - 10th ed., rev. and corr.; edited by E.A. Reeves.
1921. 2v.
- - 11th ed., [by] E.A. Reeves. 1935-38. 2v.

What may be done in two months: a summer's tour,
through Belgium, up the Rhine, and to the lakes of
Switzerland; also to Chamouny... Chapman & Hall,
1834. 188p., map. 19cm.
Letters, signed: G.T.

WHEELER, Arthur Oliver
The Selkirk mountains: a guide for mountain
climbers and pilgrims. Winnipeg: Stovel Co., 1912.
199p., plates (some fold.), illus., maps, bibl.
20cm.

WHEELER, Arthur Oliver
The Selkirk range. Ottawa: Government Printing
Bureau, 1905. 2v., plates (some fold.), illus.,
maps. 25cm.

WHEELER, Olin D
The trail of Lewis and Clark 1804-1904: a story of
the great exploration across the continent in
1804-06; with a description of the old trail based
upon actual travel over it, and of the changes
found a century later. New York, London: Putnam,
1904. 2v., col. plates (1 fold.), illus., maps.
22cm.

WHEELOCK, Lucy
SPYRI, Johanna
[Kurze Geschichten]. Swiss stories for children
and those who love children; from the German of
Madam Johanna Spyri by Lucy Wheelock; illustrated
by Horace Petherick. Blackie, 1889. 208p.,
plates, illus. 19cm.

Where the world ends: a description of Arosa as a
centre for summer holidays or winter sport and as
a health resort for convalescents and invalids, by
A.A.H. Arosa: [n.pub.], 1911. 95p., plates,
illus. 19cm.

WHERRY, George
Alpine notes & the climbing foot. Cambridge:
Macmillan & Bowes, 1896. xvi, 174p., illus. 20cm.

WHERRY, George
Notes from a knapsack. Cambridge: Bowes & Bowes,
1909. ix, 312p., plates, illus., map. 20cm.

WHERRY, George
ALPINE CLUB
[Peaks, passes and glaciers]. Narratives selected
from Peaks, passes and glaciers; edited with intro-
duction and notes by George Wherry. Cambridge:
University Press, 1910. 156p., maps. 18cm.
Selected from the 1st series.

WHILLANS, Don and ORMEROD, Alick
Don Whillans: portrait of a mountaineer.
Heinemann, 1971. ix, 266p., plates, illus. 23cm.

- - Another issue. Harmondsworth: Penguin Books,
1973.
- - Reprint. 1976.

WHIPPLESNAITH
The night climbers of Cambridge. Chatto & Windus,
1937. vii, 183p., plates, illus. 23cm.

WHISTLER, Hugh
In the high Himalayas: sport and travel in the
Rhotang and Baralacha, with some notes on the
natural history of that area. Witherby, 1924.
223p., plates, illus., map. 24cm.

WHITAKER, John
The course of Hannibal over the Alps ascertained.
Stockdale, 1794. 2v. 23cm.

WHITBREAD, S   A
The silent hills. Hutchinson, [19--]. 191p.,
plates, port. 23cm.

WHITE, George Francis
ROBERTS, Emma
Hindostan: its landscapes, palaces, temples,
tombs, the shores of the Red Sea, and the sublime
and romantic scenery of the Himalaya mountains;
illustrated in a series of views drawn ... from
original sketches by Robt. Elliot & Geo. Francis
White; with descriptions by Emma Roberts. Fisher,
[1847?]. 2v., plates, illus. 28cm.

WHITE, George Francis
Views in India, chiefly among the Himalaya mountains, taken during tours ... in 1829-31-32; with
notes and descriptive illustrations. Fisher,
1836-37. 2v., plates, illus. 37cm.

- - Another ed; edited by Emma Roberts. 1838.

WHITE, James
Altitudes in the Dominion of Canada with a relief
map of North America. Ottawa: Geological Survey
of Canada, 1901. xii, 266p., map. 26cm.

- - 2nd ed. Ottawa: Commission of Conservation,
1915.

WHITE, James
Dictionary of altitudes in the Dominion of Canada
with a relief map of Canada. Ottawa: Department
of the Interior, 1903. x, 143p. 26cm.
Supplement to Author's Altitudes in ... Canada.

- - 2nd ed. Ottawa: Commission of Conservation,
1916.

WHITE, John Claude
Sikhim and Bhutan: twenty-one years on the North-
East frontier 1887-1908. Arnold, 1909. xix,
332p., plates (1 fold.col.), illus., map. 27cm.

WHITE, Stewart Edward
The mountains. Hodder and Stoughton, 1904. 282p.,
plates (1 col.), illus. 23cm.

WHITE, Walter
Holidays in Tyrol: Kufstein, Klobenstein, and
Paneveggio. Chapman & Hall, 1876. xvii, 361p.,
1 fold. plate, map. 22cm.

WHITE, Walter
A July holiday in Saxony, Bohemia, and Silesia.
Chapman & Hall, 1857. xiv, 305p. 21cm.

WHITE, Walter
A month at Gastein; or, Footfalls in the Tyrol,
[by Walter White]. R. Bentley, [18--]. viii,
317p., illus. 19cm.

WHITE, Walter
On foot through Tyrol in the summer of 1855.
Chapman & Hall, 1856. viii, 316p. 21cm.

WHITE, Walter
To Mont Blanc and back again. Routledge, 1854.
xvi, 208p. 18cm. (Routledge's new series)
Later ed. published in 1870 under title: To
Switzerland and back.

WHITE, Walter
To Switzerland and back. Birmingham: White & Pike,
1870. xvi, [208]p. 22cm.
Originally published in 1854 under title: To Mont
Blanc and back again.

BYNE, Eric and WHITE, Wilfred B
Further developments in the Peak District; edited
by Eric Byne and Wilfred B. White. Birkenhead:
Willmer & Haram, 1957. iv, 205p., plates, illus.
16cm. (Climbs on gritstone, v.4)

WHITEHEAD, John
Exploration of Mount Kina Balu, North Borneo.
Gurney & Jackson, 1893. x, 317p., col. plates,
illus. 37cm.

WHITING, Lilian
Canada, the spellbinder. Dent, 1917. x, 322p.,
plates (1 fold., 1 col.), illus., map. 21cm.

WHITING, Lilian
The land of enchantment: from Pike's Peak to the
Pacific. Siegle, Hill, 1910. xii, 347p., plates,
illus. 22cm.

WHITWORTH, I   M
JEGERLEHNER, Johannes
Alp legends; collected by Johannes Jegerlehner;
translated by I.M. Whitworth; black and white
illustrations by Rudolf Munger. Manchester.
Sherratt & Hughes, 1926. xxiii, 205p., col.
plates, illus. 23cm.

WHYMPER, Edward
The ascent of the Matterhorn. Murray, 1880.
xxiii, 325p., plates (2 fold.), illus., maps (1
col.). 24cm.

WHYMPER, Edward
Catalogue of books offered for sale by Mr. Whymper
about 1908. [N.p.]: [n.pub.], [1908]. [8]p.
22cm.

WHYMPER, Edward
Chamonix and the range of Mont Blanc: a guide.
5th ed. Murray, 1900. xxiv, 206p., plates,
illus., maps, plans. 19cm.

- - 8th ed. 1903.
- - 16th ed. 1911.

WHYMPER, Edward
How to use the aneroid barometer. Murray, 1891.
61p. 24cm.

WHYMPER, Edward
A letter addressed to the members of the Alpine
Club [on the controversy over a leap by Christian
Almer]. [The Author], 1900. 16p., 1 plate,
illus. 22cm.

WHYMPER, Edward
[The Library of the late Edward Whymper ... sold
by order of the executors]. [Sotheby Wilkinson
and Hodge], [1912]. 58-94p. 25cm.

WHYMPER, Edward
The life and habits of wild animals; illustrated
by designs by Joseph Wolf; engraved by J.W. &
Edward Whymper; with descriptive letterpress by
Daniel Giraud Elliot. Macmillan, 1874. 72p., 20
plates, illus. 49cm.

WHYMPER, Edward
Man on the Matterhorn
  See his
Scrambles amongst the Alps...

WHYMPER, Edward
Scrambles amongst the Alps in the years 1860-69.
Murray, 1871. xviii, 432p., plates (some fold.
col.), illus., maps. 24cm.

- - 2nd ed. 1871.
- - 4th ed. 1893.
- - 5th ed. 1900.
- - 6th ed., with additional illustrations and
material from the author's unpublished diaries;
revised and edited by H.E.G. Tyndale. 1936.

WHYMPER, Edward
Scrambles amongst the Alps in the years 1860-'69.
Philadelphia: J.B. Lippincott, 1873. 164p.,
plates, illus. 24cm.

WHYMPER, Edward
Scrambles amongst the Alps, by Edward Whymper;
and Down the Rhine, by Lady Blanche Murphy.
Cleveland (Ohio): Burrows, [1890?]. 164, 75p.,
plates, illus., map. 24cm.

WHYMPER, Edward
Scrambles amongst the Alps in the years 1860-69.
Nelson, [1908]. 480p., plates, illus. 17cm.
(Nelson's shilling library, 1)

WHYMPER, Edward
[Scrambles amongst the Alps...]. Man on the
Matterhorn; edited by M. Dodderidge. Murray, 1940.
135p., illus., map. 18cm. (Journeys and adventures)
"Edited ... from Edward Whymper's Scrambles amongst
the Alps".

WHYMPER, Edward
[Scrambles amongst the Alps...]. Escalades dans
les Alpes de 1860 à 1869; ouvrage traduit ...
avec l'autorisation de l'auteur par Adolphe
Joanne. Paris: Hachette, 1873. iv, 431p., illus.,
maps. 27cm.

WHYMPER, Edward
[Scrambles amongst the Alps...]. Escalades dans
les Alpes de 1860 à 1869. Nouv. éd., traduit ...
avec l'autorisation de l'auteur, et considérablement augm. Genève: A. Jullien, 1912. xiii,
284p., illus., maps, port. 24cm.

WHYMPER, Edward
[Scrambles amongst the Alps...]. Escalades;
introduction de Claire-Éliane Engel. Neuchatel:
Attinger, 1944. 249p., plates, illus. 21cm.
Selections from Scrambles amongst the Alps and
Travels amongst the Great Andes...

WHYMPER, Edward
[Scrambles amongst the Alpes...]. Edward
Whympers Berg- und Gletscherfahrten in den Alpen
in den Jahren 1860 bis 1869. Autorisirte deutsche
Bearb., von Friedrich Steger. 3.Aufl., mit einer
Einführung von Theodor Wundt. Braunschweig: G.
Westermann, 1909. xxiv, 536p., plates, illus.,
maps. 24cm.

- - 4.völlig unveränderte Aufl. 1922.

- - 5.völlig unveränderte Aufl. [1931].

WHYMPER, Edward
MANNING, Samuel
Swiss pictures drawn with pen and pencil, [by
Samuel Manning]; the illustrations by E. Whymper.
Religious Tract Society, [1866]. 214p., plates,
illus. 29cm.

- - New and enl. ed. [3rd ed.]. [1871].
- - New and enl. ed. [ca 1875].
- - New and enl. ed. [1880].
- - New ed., revised and partly re-written with
several additional illustrations by Edward Whymper
... 1891.

WHYMPER, Edward.
  Travels amongst the great Andes of the Equator.
  Murray, 1892. xxv, 456p., plates, illus., maps.
  24cm.

- - Supplementary appendix. 1891.
- - Special ed. 1892. 3v.
- - 2nd ed.

WHYMPER, Edward
  Travels amongst the great Andes of the Equator.
  Nelson, [1911]. 379p., plates, illus. 17cm.
  (Nelson library of notable books, 69)

WHYMPER, Edward
  Travels amongst the great Andes of the Equator;
  edited with an introduction by F.S. Smythe. J.
  Lehmann, 1949. 272p. 19cm. (Chiltern library)

WHYMPER, Edward
  Travels amongst the Great Andes of the Equator;
  edited and introduced by Eric Shipton. C. Knight,
  1972. xxii, 214p., 1 fold. plate, illus., maps.
  24cm. (Latin American adventure series)

WHYMPER, Edward
  The valley of Zermatt and the Matterhorn: a guide.
  7th ed. Murray, 1903. xiv, 224p., plates, illus.,
  maps, plans. 20cm.

- - 15th ed. 1911.

WHYMPER, Edward
CLARK, Ronald William
  The day the rope broke: the story of a great
  Victorian tragedy. Secker & Warburg, 1965. 221p.,
  plates, illus., map, bibl. 23cm.

WHYMPER, Edward
SMYTHE, Frank S
  Edward Whymper. Hodder & Stoughton, 1940. xiv,
  330p., plates (2 fold.), illus., maps. 23cm.

WHYMPER, Edward
SMYTHE, Frank S
  Edward Whymper: ein Bergsteiger- und Forscherleben;
  bearb. und hrsg. von Walter Schmid. Bern: Hallweg,
  1940. 328p., plates, illus. 23cm.

WHYMPER, Edward
SMYTHE, Frank S
  Edward Whymper; translated into Japanese by Ichiro
  Yoshizawa. Tokyo: Akane, 1966. 327p., plates (2
  fold.), illus. 22cm.

WHYMPER, Edward
UNSWORTH, Walter
  Matterhorn man: the life and adventures of Edward
  Whymper. Gollancz, 1965. 126p., plates, illus.,
  maps, bibl. 23cm.

WHYMPER, Edward
YOUNG, Bert Edward
  Edward Whymper: alpinist of the heroice age; a
  paper delivered before the Round Table of Nashville.
  Nashville (Tenn.), 1914. 9p. 31cm.
  Offprint from Popular science monthly, June, 1913.

WHYMPER, Frederick
  Travel and adventure in the territory of Alaska,
  formerly Russian America - now ceded to the United
  States - and in various other parts of the North
  Pacific. Murray, 1868. xx, 331p., plates (1
  fold.), illus., maps. 24cm.

WHYMPER, Frederick
  [Travels and adventure in ...]. Voyages et aventures dans l'Alaska (ancienne Amérique Russe)...;
  traduit avec l'autorisation de l'auteur par Émile
  Jonveaux. Paris: Hachette, 1871. vi, 412p., 1
  fold. plate, illus., map. 26cm.

WICKHAM, Henry L   and CRAMER, J   A
  A dissertation on the passage of Hannibal over the
  Alps, by a member of the University of Oxford.
  Oxford: Printed by W. Baxter for J. Parker, 1820.
  xxiii, 183p., plates (1 fold.col.), maps. 22cm.

- - 2nd ed., by Henry L. Wickham and J.A. Cramer.
  Whittaker, 1828.

WIDMANN, Joseph Viktor
  Spaziergänge in den Alpen: Wanderstudien und
  Plaudereien. 2.veränderte und verm. Aufl.
  Frauenfeld: J. Huber, 1892. 312p. 20cm.

WIELAND, Hans Beat
HOEK, Henry
  Hans Beat Wieland, der Mahler der Berge. München,
  1928. 13p., plates (1 col.), illus. 27cm.
  Offprint from Zeitschrift des D.u.Ö.A.V., Bd.59,
  1928.

WIELEITNER, H
  Schnee und Eis der Erde. Leipzig: Reclam, 1913.
  198p., 16 plates, illus. 15cm. (Bücher der
  Naturwissenschaft, Bd.16)

BORCHERS, Philipp and WIEN, Karl
  Bergfahrten im Pamir. Innsbruck, 1929. 64-160p.,
  1 fold. plate, illus., map. 26cm.
  Offprint from Zeitschrift des D.u.Ö.A.V., Bd.60,
  1929.

WIFFEN, J   H
  Julia Alpinula; with The captive of Stamboul and
  other poems. 2nd ed. Longman, Rees, Orme, Brown
  & Green, [182-]. xiii, 237p. 19cm.

WIGNALL, Sydney
  Prisoner in red Tibet. Hutchinson, 1957. 264p.,
  plates, illus., map (on lining papers). 23cm.

WIGRAM, Harriet Mary
  Memoirs of Woolmore Wigram, Canon of St. Albans,
  by his wife [Harriet Mary Wigram], 1831-1907.
  Swan Sonnenschein, 1908. 298p., port. 19cm.

WIGRAM, Woolmore and WIGRAM, Edgar T   A
  The cradle of mankind: life in eastern Kurdistan.
  Black, 1914. xii, 373p., plates (1 fold.), illus.,
  map. 24cm.

WIGRAM, Woolmore
WIGRAM, Harriet Mary
  Memoirs of Woolmore Wigram, Canon of St. Albans, by
  his wife [Harriet Mary Wigram], 1831-1907. Swan
  Sonnenschein, 1908. 298p., port. 19cm.

WILBRAHAM, Edward Bootle
  Narrative of an ascent of Mont-Blanc in August
  1830.
  (In The Keepsake for 1832; edited by Frederic
  Mansel Reynolds. Longman, Rees, Orme, Brown and
  Green, 1832. 20cm. p.1-16)

WILBRAHAM, Richard
  Travels in the Trans-Caucasian provinces of Russia,
  and along the southern shore of the Lakes of Van
  and Urumiah, in the autumn and winter of 1837.
  Murray, 1839. xviii, 477p., plates (1 fold.),
  illus., map. 24cm.

WILCOX, Walter Dwight
  Camping in the Canadian Rockies: an account of
  camp life in the wilder parts of the ... mountains
  ... and a sketch of the early explorations. New
  York, London: Putnam, 1896. xiii, 283p., plates,
  illus. 27cm.
  Revised ed. published in 1900 under title: The
  Rockies of Canada.

WILCOX, Walter Dwight
  The Rockies of Canada. New York, London: Putnam,
  1900. xi, 309p., plates (2 fold.), illus., maps
  (in pocket). 26cm.
  Revised and enlarged ed. of Camping in the Canadian
  Rockies.

- - 3rd ed. 1909.

WILCZEK, E
SCHINZ, Hans and KELLER, Robert
  Flore de la Suisse. Ptie.1. Flore d'excursion.
  Éd. française rev., par E. Wilczek et Hans Schinz.
  Lausanne: F. Rouge, 1909. xxiii, 690p., illus.
  19cm.

WILD, J   J
Reise nach Norwegen vom 27. Juni bis 9. August
1856. Stäfa am Zürichsee: Druck von Gebr. Gull,
1859. 97p. 19cm.

WILDENHAINSKI, Barun Rudolf Maldini
See
MALDINI WILDENHAINSKI, Rudolf, Barun

WILDER, F
The continental traveller, being the journal of
an economical tourist to France, Switzerland, and
Italy ..., by a travelling lawyer; to which is
added A tour in Spain ..., by a travelling artist.
M.A. Leigh, 1833. 122p., 1 fold. plate, map.
18cm.
Flyleaf signed E. Gardner & F. Wilder, 1833.

WILEY, William H   and WILEY, Sara King
The Yosemite, Alaska and the Yellowstone. London,
1893. xix, 230p., 1 fold. plate, illus., maps.
30cm.
Offprint from Engineering, 1892.

TISCHLER, Ernst and WILKE, Viktor
Skitourenführer durch die östl. Beskiden von der
Weichsel bis zur Waag ...; hrsg. von Ernst Tischler
und Viktor Wilke. Bielitz: In Selbstverlage des
Wintersportklubs, 1912. 42p., 1 fold.col. plate,
map. 18cm.

WILKERSON, James A
Medicine for mountaineering; edited by James A.
Wilkerson. 2nd ed. Seattle: The Mountaineers,
1975 (1978 reprint). 365p., illus., bibl. 20cm.

WILKES, Charles
Narrative of the United States' exploring expedition during the years 1838, 1839, 1840, 1841, 1842.
Condensed and abridged. Whittaker, [1845]. vii,
372p. 25cm.

WILKES, Charles
Narrative of the United States exploring expedi-
tion, during the years 1838, 1839, 1940, 1941, 1942.
Ingram, Cooke, 1852. 2v., plates, illus. 20cm.

WILKIE, Sir David
CUNNINGHAM, Allan
The life of Sir David Wilkie, with his journals,
tours, and critical remarks on works of art and a
selection from his correspondence. Murray, 1843.
3v., port. 23cm.

WILKINS, Charles Armar
Curiosities of travel; or, Glimpses of nature.
Tinsley, 1876. 2v. 20cm.

WILKINSON, Frank
Yorkshire limestone: a rock climber's guide; edited
by Frank Wilkinson. Bradford: Yorkshire Mountaineering Club, 1968. 169p., illus., maps. 16cm.

WILKINSON, Sir J   Gardner
Dalmatia and Montenegro, with a journey to Mostar
in Herzegovina and remarks on the slavonic nations
... Murray, 1848. 2v., plates, illus., map. 23cm.

WILKINSON, Joseph
Select views in Cumberland, Westmoreland and
Lancashire; [introduction by William Wordsworth].
R. Ackermann, 1817. 46p., 48 plates, illus. 49cm.

WILKINSON, Spenser
Hannibal's march through the Alps. Oxford:
Clarendon Press, 1911. 48p., plates (1 fold.),
illus., map. 24cm.

WILKINSON, T   E
Twenty years of continental work and travel; with
a preface by the Right Hon. Sir Edmund Monson,
Bart. Longmans, Green, 1906. xxiii, 438p., port.
23cm.

WILKINSON, Thomas
Tours to the British mountains, with descriptive
poems by Lowther, and Emont Vale. Taylor & Hessey,
1824. vii, 320p. 21cm.

WILLIAMS, Becket
The High Pyrenees, summer and winter. Wishart,
1928. 215p., plates, illus., map (on lining
papers). 19cm.

WILLIAMS, Becket
Winter sport in Europe. Bell, 1929. 256p.,
plates, illus. 20cm.

WILLIAMS, Charles
The Alps, Switzerland and the north of Italy.
Cassell, 1854. viii, 634p., plates, illus., map.
29cm.

WILLIAMS, Cicely
Bishop's wife - but still myself. Allen & Unwin,
1961. 226p., 8 plates, illus. 23cm.

WILLIAMS, Cicely
A church in the Alps: a century of Zermatt and the
English; foreword by Lord Hunt. Commonwealth &
Continental Church Society, 1970. 46p., illus.
(some col.). 19cm.

WILLIAMS, Cicely
Dear abroad. Allen & Unwin, 1967. 238p. 23cm.

WILLIAMS, Cicely
Diary of a decade: more memoirs of a Bishop's wife.
Allen & Unwin, 1970. 256p. 7 plates, illus. 23cm.

WILLIAMS, Cicely
Women on the rope: the feminine share in mountain
adventure. Allen & Unwin, 1973. 240p., 8 plates,
illus., bibl. 23cm.

WILLIAMS, Cicely
Zermatt saga; foreword by Sir Arnold Lunn. Allen
& Unwin, 1964. 197p., 9 plates, illus. 23cm.

WILLIAMS, Edward
Mountain medicine and physiology: proceedings of
a symposium for mountaineers, expedition doctors
and physiologists;sponsored by the Alpine Club;
edited by Charles Clarke, Michael Ward and Edward
Williams. A.C., 1975. 143p., plates, illus.,
bibl. 21cm.
Cover title.

WILLIAMS, Helen Maria
A tour in Switzerland; or, A view of the present
state of the government and manners of those cantons, with comparative sketches of the present
state of Paris. G.G. & J. Robinson, 1798. 2v.
22cm.
Vol.2 is 2nd ed.

WILLIAMS, Helen Maria
[A tour in Switzerland...]. Nouveau voyage en
Suisse, contenant une peinture de ce pays, de ses
moeurs et de ses gouvernemens actuels ...; traduit
par J.B. Say. Paris: C. Pougens, 1798. 2v. in 1.
21cm.

- - 2e éd. 1802.

WILLIAMS, Howel
Landscapes of Alaska: their geological evolution;
prepared by members of the United States Geological
Survey; published in cooperation with the National
Park Service U.S. Dept. of the Interior. Berkeley:
University of California Press, 1958. xii, 148p.,
plates (some fold., some col.), illus., maps. 27cm.

WILLIAMS, Ira A
The Columbia River gorge: its geological history
interpreted from the Columbia River Highway. 2nd.
ed. Portland (Oregon): Oregon Bureau of Mines and
Geology, 1923. 130p., fold. plates (1 col.),
illus., maps. 27cm.
Revised reprint of Mineral Resources of Oregon,
v.2., no.3.

WILLIAMS, Jenny C
CAMBRIDGE GARHWALL HIMALAYA EXPEDITION, 1977
Report; edited by J.C. Williams. Marlborough
(Wilts.): The Expedition, [1978]. 46 leaves,
illus., maps. 30cm.

MONKHOUSE, Frank and WILLIAMS, Joe
Climber and fellwalker in Lakeland. Newton Abbot
(Devon): David & Charles, 1972. 214p., 1 col.
plate, illus., map, bibl. 24cm.

WILLIAMS, John Harvey
The guardians of the Columbia: Mount Hood, Mount
Adams and Mount St. Helens. Tacoma: Williams,
1912. 144p., illus. (8 col.). 26cm.

WILLIAMS, John Harvey
The mountain that was "God", being a little book
about the great peak which the Indians called
"Tacoma" but which is officially named "Rainier".
Tacoma: The Author, 1910. 111p., illus. (some
col.), maps (on lining paper). 27cm.

- - 2nd ed., rev. and greatly enl. 1911.

WILLIAMS, John Harvey
Yosemite and its High Sierra. Tacoma: The Author,
1914. 147p., plates, illus., maps. 27cm.

WILLIAMS, Mabel Berta
Jasper National Park. Ottawa: Department of the
Interior, 1928. 176p., 2 fold. plates, illus.,
maps, bibl. 24cm.

WILLIAMS, Mabel Berta
Through the heart of the Rockies and Selkirks.
Ottawa: Ministry of the Interior, 1921. 105p.,
fold. plates, illus., maps. 24cm.

- - 4th ed. 1929.

WILLIAMS, W   Llewelyn
GIRALDUS CAMBRENSIS
The itinerary through Wales and The description of
Wales; [edited by W. Llewelyn Williams]. Dent,
[1908]. xxiii, 210p. 18cm. (Everyman's library)

WILLIAMS, William Mattieu
Through Norway with a knapsack. Smith, Elder,
1859. 332p., col. plates (1 fold.), illus., map.
22cm.

- - New and improved ed., with notes on recent
changes. Stanford, 1876.

WILLIAMS, William Mattieu
Through Norway with ladies. Stanford, 1877. xv,
380p., 30 plates, illus., map. 21cm.

WILLIAMS COLLEGE. Williams Outing Club
See
WILLIAMS OUTING CLUB

WILLIAMS OUTING CLUB
The Mountains of Eph: a guide book of the Williams
Outing Club. Williamstown (Mass.): W.O.C. Trail
Commission, 1927. 55p., plates (some fold.),
illus., maps. 18cm.

WILLIAMSON, Benedict
The story of Pope Pius XI. Alexander-Ouseley, 1931.
174p., plates, illus. 23cm.

WILLIAMSON, C   J
The Everest "message": [letter to the editor].
(In Journal of the Society for Psychical Research,
v.48, no.769, September 1976, p.318-320)

WILLIAMSON, C   N   and WILLIAMSON, A   M
The Princess passes: a romance of a motor.
Methuen, 1904. viii, 323p., plates, illus. 21cm.

WILLS, Sir Alfred
The ascent of Mont Blanc, together with some
remarks on glaciers. [The Author], 1858. 90p.
18cm.

WILLS, Sir Alfred
"The Eagle's Nest" in the valley of Sixt: a summer
home among the Alps; together with some excursions
among the great glaciers. Longman, Green, Longman,
& Roberts, 1860. xix, 327p., col. plates, illus.
20cm.

- - 2nd ed. 1860.

WILLS, Sir Alfred
["The Eagle's Nest"...]. Le Nid d'Aigle et
l'ascension du Wetterhorn: récits montagnards;
traduit par F.M. Paris: Ch. Meyrueis, 1864.
294p., 1 plate, map. 19cm.

WILLS, Sir Alfred
RENDU, Louis
[Théorie des glaciers de la Savoie]. Theory of
the glaciers of Savoy; translated by A. Wills; to
which are added the original memoir and supplementary articles by P.G. Tait and John Ruskin;
edited with introductory remarks by George Forbes.
Macmillan, 1874. 216p., illus., map. 23cm.
Text in English and French.

WILLS, Sir Alfred
Wanderings among the high Alps. R. Bentley, 1856.
xix, 384p., plates, illus. 19cm.

- - 2nd ed., rev. with additions. 1858.
- - Another issue. Oxford: Blackwell, 1937.

WILLSON, John and HOPE, David E
Wye Valley. Vol.1. Wintour's Leap, Symonds Yat,
Western Cliffs. Leicester: Cordee, 1977. 123p.,
illus., maps. 18cm. (Rock climbs in the South-
West)

WILLSON, Thomas B
The handy guide to Norway; with maps and an appendix on the flora and lepidoptera... Stanford, 1886.
viii, 183p., fold.col. plates, maps. 17cm.

- - 4th ed., rev. and enl., with ... appendices on
... glacier climbing... 1898.
- - 6th ed., thoroughly rev. 1911.

WILLSON, Thomas B
Norway at home. Newnes, [1910?]. xi, 228p.,
plates, illus. 20cm.

WILMOT, E   H   . Journal...
REED, A   H   and REED, A   W
Farthest west afoot and afloat; together with E.H.
Wilmot's Journal of the Pioneer survey of the Lake
Manapouri-Dusky Sound area. Wellington (N.Z.):
Reed, 1950. 192p., plates, illus., maps. 23cm.

WILMSEN, F   P
Merkwürdige Bergreisen, Seefahrten und Abentheuer
unserer Zeit, Der Jugend lehrreich; erzählt von
F.P. Wilmsen... Berlin: J.G. Hasselberg, [1823].
vi, 290p., 8 plates, illus. 18cm.

WILSON, Andrew
The abode of snow: observations on a journey from
Chinese Tibet to the Indian Caucasus, through the
upper valleys of the Himalaya. Edinburgh, London:
Blackwood, 1875. xxvi, 475p., col. plates (1
fold.), illus., map (in pocket). 24cm.

- - 2nd ed. 1876.

WILSON, Claude
The Aiguilles d'Arves: some notes and memories.
London, 1928. 10-21p., plates, illus. 22cm.
Offprint from the Alpine journal, v.40, 1928.

WILSON, Claude
An epitome of fifty years' climbing. [Tunbridge
Wells?]: The Author, 1933. 119p. 22cm.

WILSON, Claude
Mountaineering; with illustrations by Ellis Carr.
Bell, 1893. vi, 208p., illus. 17cm. (All-
England series)

WILSON, Daniel
Letters from an absent brother. S. Gosnell,
printer, 1823. 265p. 22cm.
Signed: D.W., i.e. Daniel Wilson.

- - 2nd ed., entitled: Letters from an absent brother,
containing some account of a tour through parts of
the Netherlands, Switzerland, Northern Italy, and
France, in the summer of 1823. G.Wilson, 1824. 2v.
- - 3rd ed., very considerably enl. 1825. 2v.
- - 4th ed. 1827. 2v.

WILSON, Edward
SEAVER, George
Edward Wilson: nature-lover. Murray, 1937. xi, 221p., col. plates, illus. 22cm.

WILSON, Edward
SEAVER, George
Edward Wilson of the Antarctic: naturalist and friend, together with a memoir of Oriana Wilson; with an introduction by Apsley Cherry-Garrard. Murray, 1937 (1950 reprint). xxxiv, 310p., plates (1 fold., 1 col.), illus., maps. 23cm.

WILSON, Edward
SEAVER, George
The faith of Edward Wilson. Murray, 1953. 48p., plates, illus. 21cm.

WILSON, Edward Livingstone
Mountain climbing, by Edward L. Wilson [and others]. [New York]: Scribner, 1897. xi, 358p., illus. 21cm. (Out of door library)

WILSON, Henry Schütz
Alpine ascents and adventures; or, Rock and snow sketches; with two illustrations by Marcus Stone and Edward Whymper. Sampson Low, Marston, Searle, & Rivington, 1878. xi, 319p., 1 plate, illus. 20cm.

- - 2nd ed. 1878.

WILSON, Henry Schütz
A quiet day in the Alps. The Author, [1878]. 16p. 21cm.

WILSON, Henry Schütz
Studies and romances. H.S. King, 1873. 384p. 20cm.

WILSON, Horace Hayman
Travels in the Himalayan provinces of Hindustan and the Panjab; in Ladakh and Kashmir; in Peshawar, Kabul, Kunduz and Bokhara, from 1819 to 1825; by William Moorcroft and George Trebeck; prepared for the press from original journals ... by Horace Hayman Wilson. Murray: 1841. 2v., plates (1 fold.), illus., map. 24cm.

WILSON, J   D   B
The Southern Highlands; edited by J.D.B. Wilson; including an appendix on the Rock climbs in the Arrachar district by B.H. Humble and J.B. Nimlin. Edinburgh: Scottish Mountaineering Club, 1949. xi, 204p., plates, illus., map (on lining papers). 23cm. (Scottish Mountaineering Club guides)

WILSON, Jim
Aorangi: the story of Mount Cook. Christchurch (N.Z.): Whitcombe & Tombs, 1968. 253p., plates (some col.), illus., maps. 23cm.

WILSON, John
The history of Switzerland, [by John Wilson]. Longman, Brown, Green & Longmans, [1832]. xx, 360p. 18cm. (Cabinet cyclopaedia)

WILSON, Joseph
A history of mountains, geographical and minera-logical; accompanied by A picturesque view of the principal mountains of the world, in their res-pective proportions ..., by Robert Andrew Riddell. Nicol, 1807-10. 3v., plates, illus. 31cm.

WILSON, Ken
The Black Cliff: the history of rock climbing on Clogwyn du'r Arddu, by Jack Soper, Ken Wilson and Peter Crew; based on the original research of Rodney Wilson; foreword by A.D.M. Cox. Kaye & Ward, 1971. 159p., illus., bibl. 22cm.

WILSON, Ken
Classic rock: great British rock-climbs; compiled by Ken Wilson; with editorial assistance from Mike Pearson. Granada Publishing, 1978. 256p., illus. (some col.). 29cm.

WILSON, Ken and LEPPERT, Zdzislaw
Cwm Idwal; with notes on rare flora by Martin Boysen and illustrations by Brian Evans and A.C. Cain. 3rd ed. Climbers' Club, 1974. iii, 197p., illus., maps. 16cm. (Climbers' Club guides to Wales, 2)

WILSON, Ken
The games climbers play; edited by Ken Wilson; with cartoons by Sheridan Anderson. Diadem Books, 1978. 688p., plates, illus. 23cm.

WILSON, Ken
Hard rock: great British rock-climbs; compiled by Ken Wilson; with editorial assistance from Mike and Lucy Pearson; diagrams by Brian Evans. Hart-Davis, MacGibbon, 1975. xix, 220p., illus. 29cm.

WILSON, Leigh
Do you go back dismayed? Methuen, 1949. 202p. 20cm.

WILSON, M   F
Climbs in Cleveland; edited by M.F. Wilson. Billingham: Cleveland Mountaineering Club, [1956]. 83p., illus. 16cm.

WILSON, Maurice
ROBERTS, Dennis
I'll climb Mount Everest alone: the story of Maurice Wilson. Hale, 1957. 158p., plates, illus., maps. 23cm.

WILSON, W
A summer ramble in the Himalayas, with sporting adventures in the Vale of Cashmere; edited by "Mountaineer" [i.e. W. Wilson]. Hurst & Blackett, 1860. iv, 358p., 1 plate, illus. 23cm.

WILSON, W   Rae
Notes abroad and rhapsodies at home, by a veteran traveller [i.e. W. Rae Wilson]. Longman, Rees, Orme, Brown, Green, & Longman, 1837. 2v., plates, illus. 22cm.

WILSTACH, Paul
Along the Pyrenees. Bles, 1925. 302p., plates, illus. 25cm.

RUSSELL, John and WILTON, Andrew
Turner in Switzerland. Dubendorf (Zurich): De Clivo Press, 1976. 148p., illus. (some col.), maps. 32cm.
Sponsored by the Swiss National Tourist Office and the Swiss Foundation for Alpine Research.

WIMPERIS, Edmond Monson and JONES, F
Snowdonia illustrated. Cooper & Hodson, [ca 1890]. 2v. of col. illus. 15 x 22cm.

WINDHAM, William and MARTEL, Pierre
Relations de leurs deux voyages aux glaciers de Chamonix (1741-1742); texte original français ... avec une introduction et des notes par Théophile Dufour. Genève: Bonnant, 1879. 69p. 26cm.

WINDHAM, William and MARTEL, Pierre
[Relations de leurs deux voyages...]. An account of the glacieres or ice alps in Savoy, in two letters, one from an English gentleman [i.e. William Windham] to his friend at Geneva; the other from Peter Martel ... as laid before the Royal Society. Printed for Peter Martel, 1744. 28p., 2 plates, illus. 28cm.

- - Another ed. Ipswich: Printed by W. Craighton, 1747.

WINGATE, J   Lawton
MACBRIDE, Mackenzie
Arran of the bens, the glens & the brave; with illustrations in colour by J. Lawton Wingate. T.N. Foulis, 1910. ix, 231p., col. plates, illus. 21cm.

WINGATE, John
Avalanche. Weidenfeld & Nicolson, 1977. 153p., map. 23cm.

WINKELRIED, Arnold von
COOLIDGE, William Augustus Brevoort
History of the Swiss Confederation, with appendices on Tell and Winkelried: a sketch. [London], 1887. 84p. 19cm.
Reprinted from the Encyclopaedia Britannica.

WINKLER, Georg
KÖNIG, Erich
Empor! Georg Winklers Tagebuch: in memoriam: ein Reigen von Bergfahrten hervorragender Alpinisten von heute. Leipzig: Grethlein, [1910]. xv, 325p., illus. 28cm.

WINKLER, Gustave Georg
Island: der Bau seiner Gebirge und dessen geologische Bedeutung. München: Gummi; London: D. Nutt, 1863. 303p., illus. 24cm.

PAUSE, Walter and WINKLER, Jürgen
100 scalate estreme (V e VI grado). Milano: Görlich, 1975. 207p., illus., maps (on lining papers), bibl. 26cm. (I volumi della montagna)

WINKLER, Max
La nouvelle technique du ski: méthode d'enseignement collectif et d'apprentissage individuel; traduit de l'allemand par Jacques Selz. Chambéry: Dardel, 1930. 131p., plates, illus. 19cm.

WINKLER, Max
HOEK, Henry
[Wie lerne ich Schi-laufen]. L'école du ski; rev. par Max Winkler; traduit par Armand Pierhal. Paris: S. Bornemann, 1933. 63p., illus. 19cm.

WINTER, J   B
From Switzerland to the Mediterranean on foot. Werner Laurie, 1922. 124p., plates, illus. 19cm.

Wintersport und Winterkuren in der Schweiz: praktischer Reiseführer. Berlin: Goldschmidt, 1910. 109p., maps. 17cm. (Griebens Reiseführer, 135)

WINTHROP, Theodore
The canoe and the saddle: adventures among the northwestern rivers and forests and Isthmiana. Edinburgh: Paterson, 1883. 266p. 18cm.

- - Another issue. Sampson Low, 1863.

WINTHROP, Theodore
The canoe and the saddle; or, Klalam and Klackatat; to which are now first added his western letters and journals; edited with an introduction and notes by J.H. Williams. Tacoma: Williams, 1913. xxvi, 332p., plates (some col.), illus. 25cm.

WISE, A   T   Tucker
The alpine winter cure, with notes on Davos Platz, Wiesen, St. Moritz, and the Maloja. New ed. Baillière, Tindall, & Cox, 1884. 85p., map. 22cm.

WITHERS, Percy
Friends in solitude. Cape, 1923. 256p. 21cm.

WITKAMP, P   H
SENDEN, G   H   van
Alpenrozen. 2.druk met aanteekeningen vermeerderd en nagezien door B.T. Lublink Weddik en P.H. Witkamp. Amsterdam: C.L.B. Brinkman, [ca 1858]. iv, 502p., 1 plate, map. 19cm.

WITTE, Karl
Alpenisches und Transalpinisches. Berlin: W. Hertz, 1858. 482p., plates, illus. 15cm.

WITTICH, William
Curiosities of physical geography. Knight, 1845-46. 2v. 15cm.

- - Another ed. Blackwood, [1869].

WITTING, A
Wenzels Führer durch Garmisch-Partenkirchen und Umgebung. 7.Aufl., bearb. von A. Witting. Partenkirchen-Garmisch: L. Wenzel, [n.d.]. 84p., illus., maps. 17cm.

WITZENMANN, Ad.
Sesvenna und Lischanna. Stuttgart: Deutsche Verlags-Anstalt, 1907. 80p., 14 plates, illus., map. 18cm. (Alpine Gipfelführer, 13)

WODEHOUSE, P. G.
William Tell told again; with illustrations in colour by Philip Dadd; described in verse by John W. Houghton. Black, 1904. vii, 106p., plates, illus. 23cm.

WÖDL, Hans
Führer durch die Schladminger Tauern. Wien: Artaria, 1924. iv, 196p., plates (some col.), illus., map. 17cm.

WOLF, C
Vues remarquables des montagnes de la Suisse, avec leur description. Ptie.1; [dessinés par C. Wolf, avec préface par A. von Haller et Description d'un voyage fait en 1776 ... par Jac. Sam. Wyttenbach]. Berne: Wagner, 1776. 17p., col. plates, illus. 43cm.

- - Another ed. Amsterdam: J. Yntema, 1785.

WOLF, Ferdinand Otto and CÉRÉSOLE, Alfred
Valais and Chamonix. Zurich: Orell & Füssli, [18--]. vii, 826p., illus., maps. 19cm.

WOLF, Ferdinand Otto
Valais et Chamounix. Zurich: Orell, Füssli, [ca 1900]. 2v., plates, illus., maps. 19cm. (L'Europe illustrée, nos. 100-102, 106-108)

WOLF, Joseph
The life and habits of wild animals; illustrated by designs by Joseph Wolf; engraved by J.W. & E. Whymper; with descriptive letterpress by Daniel Giraud Elliot. Macmillan, 1874. 72p., 20 plates, illus. 49cm.

WOLF, Karl
Alpentrachten unserer Zeit; Begleitworte von Karl Wolf; Bilder von Marta E. Fossel. Graz: Verlag Styria, 1937. 41p., 24 col. plates, illus. 19cm. (Die deutschen Bergbücher, Bd.7)

WOLF, Rudolf
Biographien zur Kulturgeschichte der Schweiz. Zürich: Orell, Fussli, 1858-62. 4v., plates, ports. 21cm.

WOLFE, Linnie Marsh
John of the mountains: the unpublished journals of John Muir; edited by Linnie Marsh Wolfe. Boston: Houghton Mifflin, 1938. xxiii, 459p., plates, illus. 23cm.

WOLFF, C   F
See
WOLFF, Karl Felix

WOLFF, Karl Felix
Guida practica delle Dolomiti. Bolzano: G. Ferrari, 1924. 100p., illus., map. 16cm.

WOLFF, Karl Felix
Monographie der Dolomitenstrasse und des von ihr durchzogenen Gebiets: ein Handbuch für Dolomitenfahrer ... Bd.1. Bozen: F. Moser, 1908. xvi, 396p., plates (some col.), illus., map (in pocket). 20cm.
No more published?

WOLFF, Karl Felix
Südtirol: Schenkers Führer und Hotel-Anzeiger für Südtirol. Bozen: Schenker, 1911. xxiv, 362p., 1 fold.col. plate, illus., map. 19cm.

WOLGENSINGER, Michael
L'Engadine: terra Ladina, texte de Hermann Hiltbrunner. Lausanne: J. Marguerat, 1944. 71p., illus. 29cm.
Photographs with introductory text.

WOLLASTON, Alexander Frederick Richmond
From Ruwenzori to the Congo: a naturalist's journey across Africa. Murray, 1908. xxv, 315p., plates (1 fold.), illus., maps. 23cm.

WOLLASTON, Alexander Frederick Richmond
Letters and diaries of A.F.R. Wollaston; selected and edited by Mary Wollaston; with a preface by Sir Henry Newbolt. Cambridge: University Press, 1933. xiii, 261p., plates, ports. 23cm.

WOLLASTON, Nicholas
Handles of chance: a journey from the Solomon Islands to Istanbul. Cape, 1956. 256p., plates (some col.), illus., map. 21cm.

WOLLEY, Clive Phillips
See
PHILLIPPS-WOLLEY, Clive

WOLTERSTORFF, Hermann
Aus dem Hochgebirge: Erinnerungen eines Berg-steigers. Magdeburg: Selbstverlag des Verfassers, 1902. xii, 212p., plates, illus., 2 maps (in pocket), bibl. 23cm.

- - 2.verm. und verb. Aufl. Teil 1. Zermatt und die Zermatter Bergwelt. 1909.

The wonders of creation, as pourtrayed [sic] by Humboldt, Livingstone, Ruskin and other great writers. Gall & Inglis,[18--]. xiv, 15-302p., plates, illus. 21cm.

Wonders of the physical world: the glacier, the ice-berg, the ice-field, and the avalanche [by W.H.D. Adams]. Nelson, 1875. 314p., illus. 19cm.

- - Another ed. 1880.

WOOD, Charles W
Norwegian by-ways. Macmillan, 1903. 384p., 9 plates, illus. 21cm.

WOOD, Edith Elmer
An Oberland chalet. Werner Laurie, [1911]. 285p., plates, illus. 21cm.

WOOD, H
Explorations in the eastern Kara-korum and the Upper Yārkand valley: narrative report of the Survey of India detachment with the De Filippi Scientific Expedition 1914, [by H. Wood]. Dehra Dun: Survey of India, 1922. iii, 42p., plates (some fold., some col.), illus., maps (in pocket). 44cm.

WOOD, H
Report on the identification and nomenclature of the Himalayan peaks as seen from Katmandu, Nepal; with preface by St. G. Gore; prepared under the direction of F.B. Longe. Calcutta: Office of the Superintendent of Government Printing, 1904. iii, 7, iv p., fold. plates, illus., map (in pocket). 34cm.

WOOD, Hugh
Views in France, Switzerland, the Tyrol, and Italy. Dickinson, [ca 1840]. 1v. of illus. 49 x 60cm.

WOOD, John
A journey to the source of the river Oxus. New ed., edited by his son; with an essay on the geography of the valley of the Oxus by H. Yule. Murray, 1872. 280p., plates (2 fold.), illus., maps. 24cm.

WOOD, John
Mountain trail: the Pennine Way from the Peak to the Cheviots; described by John Wood; decorated by Donald Foster. Allen & Unwin for the Blackfriars Press, 1947. 240p., illus. 23cm.

WOOD, Robert L
Men, mules and mountains: Lieutenant O'Neil's Olympic expeditions. Seattle: The Mountaineers, 1976. xx, 483p., plates, illus., maps, bibl. 21cm.

WOOD, Ruth Kedzie
The tourist's Northwest. New York: Dodd, Mead, 1917. xiv, 528p., plates (some fold.col.), illus., maps. 20cm.

ROBERTS, Askew and WOODALL, Edward
Gossiping guide to Wales (North Wales and Aberystwyth). Traveller's ed. Simpkin, Marshall, Hamilton, Kent, 1914. xcvi, 328p., plates (some fold.col.), illus. (1 fold.in pocket), maps. 17cm.

WOODS, E   G
See
SKEAT, E   G

NUNN, Paul J   and WOOLCOCK, Oliver
Borrowdale; illustrated by W. Heaton Cooper. Stockport: Fell & Rock Climbing Club, 1968. 219p., 1 plate, illus., maps (on lining papers). 16cm. (Climbing guides to the English Lake District, [4th ser.], 3)

WOOLLACOTT, Arthur P
Mackenzie and his voyageurs: by canoe to the Arctic and the Pacific, 1789-93. Dent, 1927. x, 237p., plates, illus., map, bibl. 22cm.

WOOSTER, David
Alpine plants: figures and descriptions of some of the most striking and beautiful of the alpine flowers; edited by David Wooster. Bell & Daldy, 1872. xii, 152p., 54 col. plates, illus. 26cm.

- - 2nd ed. 1874.
- - 2nd series. 1874.

WORDSWORTH, Dorothy
Journals of Dorothy Wordsworth; edited by E. de Selincourt. Macmillan, 1941. 2v., 2 plates, illus., maps. 23cm.

WORDSWORTH, Dorothy
Journals of Dorothy Wordsworth; edited by William Knight. Macmillan, 1934. xvii, 544p., plates, illus. 19cm.

WORDSWORTH, William
HUDSON, John
A complete guide to the Lakes ...; with Mr. Wordsworth's description of the scenery ... and three letters on the geology ... by Professor Sedgwick; edited by the publisher. 2nd ed. Kendal: J. Hudson; London: Longman, 1843. vii, 259p., plates, illus., map. 19cm.

- - 3rd ed. 1846.
- - 4th ed. 1853.

WORDSWORTH, William
The complete poetical works of William Wordsworth; with an introduction by John Morley. Macmillan, 1893. 928p., port. 20cm.

WORDSWORTH, William
A guide through the District of the Lakes in the North of England... 5th ed., with considerable additions. Kendal: Hudson & Nicholson, 1835. xxiv, 139p. 18cm.

WORDSWORTH, William
[Guide through the District of the Lakes...]. Wordsworth's Guide to the Lakes, fifth edition (1835); with an introduction, appendices and notes textual and illustrative by Ernest de Selincourt. H. Frowde, 1906. xxviii, 203p., plates (1 fold.) illus., map. 18cm.

WORDSWORTH, William
Our English lakes, mountains, and waterfalls as seen by William Wordsworth; photographically illustrated [by T. Ogle]. A.W. Bennett, 1864. 191p., plates, illus. 21cm.

WORDSWORTH, William
The prelude; or, Growth of a poet's mind... E. Moxon, 1850. 374p. 23cm.

WORDSWORTH, William
The River Duddon, a series of sonnets: Vaudracour and Julia and other poems ... to which is annexed a topographical description of the Country of the Lakes... Longman, Hurst, Rees, Orme and Brown, 1820. viii, 321p. 24cm.

WORDSWORTH, William
WILKINSON, Joseph
Select views in Cumberland, Westmoreland and Lancashire; [introduction by William Wordsworth]. R. Ackermann, 1817. 46p., 48 plates, illus. 49cm.

WORDSWORTH, William
KNIGHT, William
Through the Wordsworth country; [drawings] by Harry Goodwin and [text by] Professor Knight. Swan Sonnenschein, Lowrey, 1887. xix, 268p., plates, illus. 30cm.

- - 5th ed. 1906.

WORDSWORTH, William
MALLESON, F   A
Holiday studies of Wordsworth by rivers, woods and Alps, the Wharfe, the Duddon, and the Stelvio pass. Cassell, 1890. 115p., illus. 24cm.

WORDSWORTH, William
ROBERTSON, Eric
Wordsworthshire: an introduction to a poet's country ...; illustrated with forty-seven drawings by Arthur Tucker. Chatto & Windus, 1911. xii, 352p., plates, illus., bibl. 23cm.

WORK, Paul Orkney
CARR, Herbert Reginald Culling
A walker's guide to Snowdon and the Beddgelert district ..., by Herbert R.C. Carr, George A. Lister and Paul Orkney Work. Newcastle upon Tyne: Listers, (Printers), 1949. vi, 60p., plates (1 fold.), illus., bibl. 14cm.
Reprint, rev. and enl. from the walkers' section of A climbers' guide to Snowdon... 1926.

WORKMAN, William Hunter and WORKMAN, Fanny Bullock
The call of the snowy Hispar: a narrative of exploration and mountaineering on the northern frontier of India; with an appendix by Count Cesare Calciati and Mathias Koncza. Constable, 1910. xvi, 297p., plates, illus., maps. 24cm.

WORKMAN, Fanny Bullock and WORKMAN, William Hunter
Ice-bound heights of the Mustagh: an account of two seasons of pioneer exploration and high climbing in the Baltistan Himalaya. Constable, 1908. xv, 444p., plates (some fold., some col.), illus., maps. 25cm.

WORKMAN, Fanny Bullock and WORKMAN, William Hunter
In the ice world of Himalaya: among the peaks and passes of Ladakh, Nubra, Suru, and Baltistan. Fisher Unwin, 1900. xvi, 204p., plates (2 fold. col.), illus., maps. 24cm.

- - Another ed. 1901.

WORKMAN, Fanny Bullock and WORKMAN, William Hunter
Peaks and glaciers of Nun Kun: a record of pioneer-exploration and mountaineering in the Punjab Himalaya. Constable, 1909. xv, 204p., plates (1 fold., 1 col.), illus., map. 25cm.

WORKMAN, William Hunter and WORKMAN, Fanny Bullock
Through town and jungle: fourteen thousand miles a-wheel among the temples and people of the Indian plain. Fisher Unwin, 1904. xxiv, 380p., 1 fold. col. plate, illus., map. 26cm.

WORKMAN, Fanny Bullock and WORKMAN, William Hunter
Two summers in the ice-wilds of Eastern Karakoram: the exploration of nineteen hundred square miles of mountain and glacier; with ... illustrations by the authors. Fisher Unwin, 1917. 296p., plates (some fold.), illus., maps. 24cm.

The world of wonders: a record of things wonderful in nature, science, and art. New ed. Cassell, Petter, Galpin, 1882. vii, 416p., illus. 27cm.

WORMSER, C   W
Bergenweelde: [boek over Indisch alpinisme]. 3. druk. Bandoeng: Mij. Vorkink, 1931. 192p., plates (1 col.), illus. 31cm.

WORSFOLD, W   Basil
The valley of light: studies with pen and pencil in the Vaudois valleys of Piedmont. Macmillan, 1899. x, 335p., illus., map. 24cm.

WORTHAM, H   E
Victorian Eton and Cambridge, being the life of Oscar Browning. New ed. A. Baker, 1956. vii, 327p. 21cm.

WRANGHAM, E   A   and BRAILSFORD, John
Selected climbs in the Dauphiné and Vercors; translated and adapted from the GHM guide and other sources by E.A. Wrangham and J. Brailsford. Alpine Club, 1967. 176p., illus., map. 16cm. (Alpine Club guide books; selected climbs, 4)

WRANGHAM, E   A
Selected climbs in the range of Mont Blanc; translated and adapted by the Alpine Climbing Group from the Guide Vallot and other sources; edited by E.A. Wrangham. Allen & Unwin, 1957. 224p., illus. 17cm.

WRIGHT, C   S   and PRIESTLEY, R   E
Glaciology [of the Victoria Land sector of the Antarctic continent]. Harrison, for the Committee of the Captain Scott Antarctic Fund, 1922. xx, 581p., fold. plates (some col.), illus., maps (some in pocket). 31cm.

WRIGHT, G   N
Scenes in North Wales; with historical illustrations, legends, and biographical notices. T.T. & J. Tegg, 1833. viii, 160p., plates, illus. 20cm.

MURRAY, William Hutchison and WRIGHT, Jeremiah Ernest Benjamin
The craft of climbing. Kaye, 1964. 77p., plates, illus. 23cm.

- - Another issue. Mountaineering Association, 1964.

WRIGHT, Jeremiah Ernest Benjamin
Mountain days in the Isle of Skye. Edinburgh, London: Moray Press, 1934. 239p., plates, illus., map. 23cm.

WRIGHT, Jeremiah Ernest Benjamin
MOUNTAINEERING ASSOCIATION
The permanent school idea: a history of the progress towards a British Mountaineering Training School. [Mountaineering Association], [1963?]. 4p., illus. 27cm.

WRIGHT, Jeremiah Ernest Benjamin
Rock climbing in Britain. Kaye, 1958. 142p., plates, illus., maps. 22cm.

WRIGHT, Jeremiah Ernest Benjamin
The technique of mountaineering: a handbook of established methods. Kaye, under the auspices of the Mountaineering Association, 1955. 144p., plates, illus., maps. 21cm.

- - 2nd rev. ed. 1958.
- - 3rd rev. ed. 1964.

WRIGHT, Thomas
POLO, Marco
The travels of Marco Polo, the Venetian; the translation of Marsden revised, with a selection of his notes; edited by Thomas Wright. Bell, 1892. xxviii, 508p. 19cm. (Bohn's antiquarian library)

WRIGHT, Walter P
Alpine flowers and rock gardens, illustrated in colour, described by Walter P. Wright; with notes on "Alpine plants at home" by William Graveson. Headley, [1910]. 292p., col. plates, illus. 24cm.

WRIGHT, Walter W
  The White Mountains: an annotated bibliography,
  1918-1947; compiled by Walter W. Wright. [Boston],
  1948. 205-223p., plates, illus. 22cm.
  Offprint from Appalachia, Dec. 1948.

WROUGHTON, E   H
  Concerning winter sport; illustrated with drawings
  by A.H. d'Egville. Burberrys, [1928]. [48]p.,
  illus. 23cm.

Die wunder-volle Schnee-Koppe; oder, Beschreibung
  des Schlesischen Riesen-Gebirges, aus denen
  Nachrichten einiger Personen, welche diesen hohen
  Berg selbst überstiegen haben; zusammen getragen
  von einem bekannten Schlesier. Leipzig: [n.pub.],
  1736. 152p. 18cm.

WUNDT, Theodor and WUNDT, Maud
  Engadin - Ortler - Dolomiten; hrsg. von der Sektion
  Berlin des Deutschen und Österreichischen Alpenvereins. Stuttgart: Greiner & Pfeiffer, [ca 1898].
  276p., plates, illus., maps. 29cm.

- - 2.Aufl. [1900].

WUNDT, Theodor
  Die Besteigung des Cimone della Pala: ein Album
  für Kletterer und Dolomiten-Freunde. Stuttgart:
  Greiner & Pfeiffer, [1892]. 71p., 24 plates,
  illus. 24 x 32cm.

WUNDT, Theodor
  Das Diadem: Ideale und Illusionen: ein Höhenroman;
  mit photographischen Aufnahmen des Verfassers und
  Textillustrationen von R. Reschreiter. Berlin: R.
  Bong, [1926]. 290p., plates, illus. 22cm.

WUNDT, Theodor and WUNDT, Maud
  Engadin - Ortler - Dolomiten; hrsg. von der Sektion
  Berlin des Deutschen und Österreichischen Alpenvereins. Stuttgart: Greiner & Pfeiffer, [ca 1898].
  276p., plates, illus., maps. 29cm.

- - 2.Aufl. [1900].

WUNDT, Theodor
  Hinauf! Etwas zum Sinnieren für nachdenkliche
  Alpenwanderer; den Freundin von "Spemanns Alpen-
  Kalender" gewidmet von Theodor Wundt. Stuttgart:
  W. Spemann, 1913. 192p., illus. 26cm.

WUNDT, Theodor
  Ich und die Berge: ein Wanderleben. Berlin: R.
  Bong, 1917. 366p., plates, illus., maps. 21cm.

WUNDT, Theodor
  Die Jungfrau und das Berner Oberland; hrsg. von der
  Sektion Berlin des Deutschen und Österreichischen
  Alpenvereins. Berlin: R. Mitscher, [1898].
  248p., plates (1 fold.), illus., map. 29cm. (In
  luftigen Höh'n)

- - 2.Aufl. [ca 1900].

WUNDT, Theodor
  Matterhorn: ein Hochgebirgs-Roman. Berlin: R.
  Bong, [1916]. 286p., plates, illus. 21cm.

WUNDT, Theodor
  Das Matterhorn und seine Geschichte; hrsg. von der
  Sektion Berlin des Deutschen und Österreichischen
  Alpenvereins. Berlin: R. Mitscher, [1896]. 192p.,
  plates, illus. 29cm. (In luftigen Höh'n, 1)

- - 2.Aufl. [ca 1900].

WUNDT, Theodor
  Wanderbilder aus den Dolomiten; in Farben gesetzt
  von G. Herdtle; hrsg. von der Sektion Berlin des
  Deutschen und Österreichischen Alpenvereins.
  Stuttgart: Deutsche Verlags-Anstalt, [1894]. 1v.
  (chiefly illus.). 59cm.

WUNDT, Theodor
  Wanderungen in den Ampezzaner Dolomiten; hrsg. von
  der Sektion Berlin des Deutschen und
  Oesterreichischen Alpenvereins. Berlin: R.
  Mitscher, [1894]. 136p., plates (1 fold.col.),
  illus., map. 32cm.

- - 2.Aufl. Stuttgart: Deutsche Verlags-Anstalt,
  1895.

WUNDT, Theodor
  Zermatt und seine Berge. Neue ... Aufl. Zürich:
  Orell Füssli, 1930. xii, 140p., plates (1 fold.),
  illus., map. 26cm.

WURTISEN, Christian
  Epitome historiae Basiliensis, praeter totius
  Rauricae descriptionem ...; accessit his, Aeneae
  Sylvii... Basilea, nuspiam antehac edita.
  Basileae: Per Sebastianum Henric Petri, 1577.
  308, 30p., 1 fold. plate, illus. 17cm.

WYATT, Colin
  The call of the mountains. Thames & Hudson, 1952.
  96p., 75 plates, illus. 31cm.

WYLIE, James A
  Wanderings and musings in the valleys of the
  Waldenses. J. Nisbet, 1858. viii, 389p. 19cm.

WYLLIE, Marian Amy
  Norway and its fjords. Methuen, 1907. xii,
  315p., plates (some col.), illus. 21cm.

WYMAN, Frederick F
  From Calcutta to the snowy range, being the
  narrative of a trip through the upper provinces
  of India to the Himalayas, containing an account
  of Monghyr, Benares, Allahabad, Cawnpore, Lucknow,
  Agra, Delhi and Simla, by an old Indian [i.e.
  Frederick F. Wyman]. Tinsley, 1866. viii,
  264p., col. plates (1 fold.), illus., map. 22cm.
  Preface signed F.F.W.

WYNDHAM, Francis M
  Wild life on the fjelds of Norway. Longman,
  Green, Longman, & Roberts, 1861. xv, 273p.,
  plates, illus., maps. 21cm.

WYON, Reginald and PRANCE, Gerald
  The land of the Black Mountain: the adventures of
  two Englishmen in Montenegro. Methuen, 1903.
  xviii, 300p., plates, illus., map. 20cm.

WYSS, Édouard
  See
WYSS-DUNANT, Édouard

WYSS, Johann Rudolf
  Reise in das Berner Oberland. Bern: J.J.
  Burgdorfer, 1816-17. 2v. and atlas, plates,
  illus. 22cm.

WYSS, Johann Rudolf
  [Reise in das Berner Oberland]. Voyage dans
  l'Oberland bernois; traduit ... par H. de
  C[rousaz]. Berne: J.J. Bourgdorfer, 1817. 2v.
  and atlas, plates, illus. 22cm.

WYSS, Johann Rudolf
LASCELLES, Rowley
  [Sketch of a descriptive journey...]. Scizze
  einer mahlerischen Reise durch die Schweiz; aus
  dem Englischen [of Rowley Lascelles]. ...
  hrsg., mit einigen Anmerkungen u. einem doppellen Anhange, von Joh. Rud. Wyss. Bern: J.J.
  Burgdorfer, 1816. 154p., plates, illus. 22cm.

WYSS-DUNANT, Édouard
  L'appel des sommets. Paris: Attinger, 1931-33.
  2v., illus. 19cm.
  Vol.1, nouv. éd., remaniée par l'auteur.

WYSS-DUNANT, Édouard
  Au delà des cimes
    See his
  L'appel des sommets, v.2.

WYSS-DUNANT, Édouard
Mes ascensions en Afrique; préface ... [de E.] Grosselin. Paris: Payot, 1938. 255p., illus. 24cm.

WYTTENBACH, Jacob Samuel
Dictionnaire géographique, historique et politique de la Suisse. Neuchatel: J.P. Jeanrenaud, 1775. 2v. 20cm.
Extracts compiled by J.S. Wyttenbach from de Felice's 'Encyclopédie', 1770-76.

- - Nouv. éd. corr. et augm. Genève: Grasset, 1776.
- - Nouv. éd. corr. et augm. Genève: Nouffer & Bassompierre, 1777.
- - Nouv. éd. augm. Genève: Barde, Manget, 1788.

WYTTENBACH, Jacob Samuel
[Dictionnaire géographique, historique et politique...]. Historische, geographische und physikalische Beschreibung des Schweizerlandes ...; aus dem Französischen übersezt, und mit vielen Zusätzen vermehrt; [compiled and enlarged by J.S. Wyttenbach]. Bern: Hortin, 1782-83. 3v. 21cm.

WYTTENBACH, Jacob Samuel
HALLER, Albrecht von
Icones plantarum Helvetiae, ex ipsius Historia stirpium helveticarum denuo recusae ...; additis notis editoris [Jac. Sam. Wyttenbach]. Bernae: Sumptibus Societatis Typographicae, 1795. xxxviii, 68p., 52 plates, illus. 44cm.

WYTTENBACH, Jacob Samuel
Instruction pour les voyageurs qui vont voir les glaciers & les Alpes du Canton de Berne, [par J.S. Wyttenbach]. [2e éd.]. Berne: E. Haller, 1787. 40p. 22cm.

WYTTENBACH, Jacob Samuel
BESSON, H
Manuel pour les savans et les curieux qui voyagent en Suisse; avec des notes par Mr. W*** [Wyttenbach]. Lausanne: J.-P. Heubach, 1786. 2v. in 1. 20cm.

WYTTENBACH, Jacob Samuel
LUC, Jean André de and DENTAND, Pierre Gédéon
[Relation de différents voyages...]. Reisen nach den Eisgebürgen von Faucigny in Savoyen [von] J.A. de Luc [und P.G. Dentand]; aus dem Französischen übersetzt [von J.S. Wyttenbach]. Leipzig: Weidmann, 1777. 174p. 21cm.

WYTTENBACH, Jacob Samuel
Vues remarquables des montagnes de la Suisse, avec leur description. Ptie.1; [dessinés par C. Wolf, avec préface par A. von Haller, et Description d'un voyage fait en 1776 ... par Jac. Sam. Wyttenbach]. Berne: Wagner, 1776. 17p., col. plates, illus. 43cm.

- - Another ed. Amsterdam: J. Yntema, 1785.

X.......

YACHTING DABBLER
Notes on a yacht voyage to Hardanger Fjord and the adjacent estuaries, by a yachting dabbler. Longman, Brown, Green, and Longman, [19--]. xxvii, 110p., plates (1 fold., some col.), illus. 23cm.

YAKUSHI, Yoshimi
Catalogue of the Himalayan literature. Kyoto: The Author, 1972. 343p. 26cm.
Contains English translation of Japanese entries.

YAKUSHI, Yoshimi
Gurja Himal: Japanese Expedition to Nepal Himalaya 1969; edited by Yoshimi Yakushi. Toyama: The Expedition, 1970. vi, 168p., plates (1 fold., some col.), illus., map. 25cm.
In Japanese with an English summary.

SANUKI, Matao and YAMADA, Keiichi
The Alps. Tokyo: Kodansha International, 1969 (1972 reprint). 146p., col. illus. (1 fold.), maps. 19cm. (This beautiful world, v.11)

YAMADA, Keiichi
Weisses Heiligtum. Tokyo: The Author, 1966. ix, 64p. (chiefly illus.). 25cm.
Text in Japanese.

YAMAKEI COLOR DELUXE
Mountains of the world. [Tokyo?]: Yamakei, 1975. 350p. (chiefly col. illus., maps). 26cm.
Text in Japanese.

YATES, Edmund
SMITH, Albert
[The story of Mont Blanc]. Mont Blanc; with a memoir of the author by Edmund Yates. Ward and Lock, [1860]. xxxvi, 299p., illus. 17cm.

- - Another ed. [1871?].

YATES, Edmund
SMITH, Albert
[The story of Mont Blanc]. A boy's ascent of Mont Blanc; with a memoir of the author by Edmund Yates. Ward, Lock and Tyler, [ca 1871]. xxxvi, 299p., 1 plate, illus. 17cm.

YATES, F   M   L
Letters written during a journey to Switzerland in the autumn of 1841. Duncan & Malcolm, 1843. 2v. 20cm.

YATES, Mike and PERRIN, Jim
Cwm Silyn and Cwellyn; geological notes by Dave Thomas; diagrams by Steve Knott; photographs by K. Wilson and E. Siddall. Stockport: Climbers' Club, 1971. xiii, 173p., illus., maps (on lining papers). 16cm. (Climbers' Club guides to Wales, 11)

The year nine: a tale of the Tyrol, by the author of "Mary Powell" [i.e. Anne Manning]. Hall, Virtue, 1858. iv, 282p., plates, illus. 21cm.

YEATS, William Butler
HAMSA, Bhagwan
The Holy Mountain, being the story of a pilgrimage to Lake Manas and of initiation on Mount Kailas in Tibet, by Bhagwan Shri Hamsa; translated from the Marathi by Shri Purchit Swami; with an intro- duction by W.B. Yeats. Faber & Faber, 1934. 203p., plates, illus. 21cm.

YEE, Chiang
See
CHIANG, Yee

YEIGH, Frank
Through the heart of Canada. Unwin, 1910. 319p., plates, illus. 24cm.

YELD, George and COOLIDGE, William Augustus Brevoort
The mountains of Cogne. Fisher Unwin, 1893. xvi, 176p., 1 fold.col. plate, map (in pocket). 14cm. (Conway and Coolidge's climbers' guides)

YELD, George
Scrambles in the eastern Graians, 1878-1897. Fisher Unwin, 1900. xx, 279p., plates (1 fold.), illus., map. 21cm.

YODA, Takayoshi
Ascent of Manaslu in photographs, 1952-6. Tokyo: Mainichi, 1956. 1v. (various pagings), plates (some col.), illus., map. 30cm.
In Japanese, with English captions.

YORKSHIRE MOUNTAINEERING CLUB
Yorkshire limestone: a rock climber's guide;
edited by Frank Wilkinson. Bradford: Yorkshire
Mountaineering Club, 1968. 169p., illus., maps.
16cm.

YORKSHIRE RAMBLERS' CLUB. Library
Yorkshire Ramblers' Club library. Leeds: Central
Library, 1959. 154p. 25cm.
Catalogue of the Yorkshire Ramblers' Club library
and of the mountaineering collection of Leeds
Central Library.

YOSY, A
Switzerland, as now divided into nineteen cantons
...; with picturesque representations of the dress
and manners of the Swiss; illustrated in fifty
coloured engravings of the costume... J. Booth,
1815. 2v., col. plates, illus. 25cm.

YOUNG, Bert Edward
Edward Whymper; alpinist of the heroic age; a paper
delivered before the Round Table of Nashville.
Nashville (Tenn.), 1914. 9p. 31cm.
Offprint from Popular science monthly, June, 1913.

YOUNG, Eleanor Winthrop and YOUNG, Geoffrey Winthrop
In praise of mountains; compiled by Eleanor and
Geoffrey Winthrop Young. F. Muller, 1948. [59]p.,
illus. 15cm.

YOUNG, Geoffrey Winthrop
April and rain: poems. Sidgwick & Jackson, 1923.
64p. 20cm.

YOUNG, Geoffrey Winthrop
Collected poems of Geoffrey Winthrop Young.
Methuen, 1936. viii, 245p. 23cm.

YOUNG, Geoffrey Winthrop
Freedom: poems. Smith, Elder, 1914. viii, 146p.
23cm.

YOUNG, Geoffrey Winthrop
The grace of forgetting. Country Life, 1953.
352p., plates, illus., maps. 23cm.

YOUNG, Eleanor Winthrop and YOUNG, Geoffrey Winthrop
In praise of mountains: an anthology for friends;
compiled by Eleanor and Geoffrey Winthrop Young.
F. Muller, 1948. [59]p., illus. 15cm.

YOUNG, Geoffrey Winthrop
Mont Blanc by a new way.
(In Great hours of sport; edited by John Buchan.
London, 1921. 22cm. p.117-151, 6 plates, illus.,
map)

YOUNG, Geoffrey Winthrop
Mountain craft; edited by Geoffrey Winthrop Young.
Methuen, 1920. xvii, 603p., plates, illus., maps.
23cm.

- - 5th ed. 1946.
- - 7th ed., rev. 1949.

YOUNG, Geoffrey Winthrop
[Mountain craft]. Die Schule der Berge; Deutsch
von Rickmer Rickmers. Leipzig: Brockhaus, 1925.
334p., plates, illus. 24cm.

YOUNG, Geoffrey Winthrop
Mountains with a difference. Eyre & Spottiswoode,
1951. xi, 282p., plates, illus. 22cm. (New
alpine library)

YOUNG, Geoffrey Winthrop
SLINGSBY, William Cecil
Norway, the northern playground; with a bio-
graphical notice by G. Winthrop Young. Oxford:
Blackwell, 1941. xxvii, 227p., plates, illus.,
maps. 21cm. (Blackwell's mountaineering library)

YOUNG, Geoffrey Winthrop
On high hills; memories of the Alps. Methuen,
1927. xiv, 368p., plates, illus. 23cm.

- - 5th ed. 1947.

YOUNG, Geoffrey Winthrop
[On high hills]. Mes aventures alpines; traduit
par Bernard Lemoine. Neuchatel: Attinger, [1939].
301p. 21cm. (Montagne)
Contains the first part of On high hills.

YOUNG, Geoffrey Winthrop
[On high hills]. Nouvelles escalades dans les
Alpes, 1910-1914: premières du Taeschorn, face
sud, Grépon, Mer de Glace, Grandes Jorasses, Col
des Hirondelles ...;traduction de Bernard Lemoine.
Neuchatel: Attinger, [1939]. 275p. 21cm.
(Montagne)
Contains the second part of On high hills.

YOUNG, Geoffrey Winthrop
The roof-climber's guide to Trinity, containing
a practical description of all routes, [by G.
Winthrop Young]. Cambridge: W.P. Spalding,
[1900]. 35p., illus. 18cm.

YOUNG, Geoffrey Winthrop
Snowdon biography, by Geoffrey Winthrop Young,
Geoffrey Sutton, and Wilfrid Noyce; edited by
Wilfrid Noyce. Dent, 1957. xiii, 195p., plates,
illus., maps (on lining papers). 22cm.

YOUNG, Geoffrey Winthrop
Wall and roof climbing, by the author of "The
roof-climber's guide to Trinity" [i.e. Geoffrey
Winthrop Young]. Eton College, Spottiswoode,
1905. viii, 109p. 23cm.

YOUNG, Geoffrey Winthrop
Wind and hill: poems. Smith, Elder, 1909.
viii, 106p. 19cm.

YOUNG, P
Himalayan holiday: a trans-Himalayan diary, 1939;
with a foreword by Bentley Beauman. Jenkins,
[1944?]. 108p., plates (1 fold.), illus., maps.
23cm.

YOUNG, S   Hall
Alaska days with John Muir. [4th ed.]. New York,
London: Revell, 1915. 226p., plates, illus., map.
20cm.

BURBAGE, Mike and YOUNG, William
Scafell group. Stockport: Fell & Rock Climbing
Club, 1974. 201p., 1 col. plate, illus., map (on
lining papers). 16cm. (Climbing guides to the
English Lake District, [5th Ser.], 7)

YOUNGHUSBAND, Sir Francis
Among the celestials ...
See his
The heart of a continent ...

YOUNGHUSBAND, Sir Francis
The epic of Mount Everest. Arnold, 1926. 319p.,
plates, illus., maps. 22cm.

YOUNGHUSBAND, Sir Francis
[The epic of Mount Everest]. L'Épopée de
l'Éverest ...; traduction de J. et F. Germain.
Grenoble: Arthaud, 1947. 334p., plates, illus.,
maps. 21cm.

YOUNGHUSBAND, Sir Francis
[The epic of Mount Everest]. La epopeya del
Everest; traducido por M. Manent. Barcelona:
Juventud, 1946. 220p., plates, illus., maps.
23cm.

YOUNGHUSBAND, Sir Francis
Everest: the challenge. Nelson, 1936. ix, 243p.,
plates, illus., maps. 23cm.

YOUNGHUSBAND, Sir Francis
The heart of a continent: commemorating the
fiftieth anniversary of his journey from Peking
to India by way of the Gobi Desert and Chinese
Turkistan, and across the Himalaya by the Mustagh
Pass. Rev. ed. Murray, 1937. xvi, 243p.,
plates (1 fold.), illus., map. 23cm.

YOUNGHUSBAND, Sir Francis
The heart of a continent: a narrative of travels
in Manchuria, across the Gobi Desert, through the
Himalayas, the Pamirs, and Chitral, 1884-1894.
2nd ed. Murray, 1896. 409p., illus., maps. 24cm.

YOUNGHUSBAND, Sir Francis
[The heart of a continent...]. Among the
celestials: a narrative of travels in Manchuria,
across the Gobi Desert, through the Himalayas to
India. Murray, 1898. xi, 261p., plates (1 fold.
col.), illus., map. 22cm.
Abridged ed.

YOUNGHUSBAND, Sir Francis
The heart of nature; or, The quest for natural
beauty. Murray, 1921. xxviii, 235p. 23cm.

YOUNGHUSBAND, Sir Francis
India and Tibet: a history of the relations which
have subsisted between the two countries from the
time of Warren Hastings to 1910; with a particular
account of the Mission to Lhasa of 1904. Murray,
1910. xvi, 455p., plates (2 fold.col.), illus.,
maps. 24cm.

YOUNGHUSBAND, Sir Francis
Kashmir; paintings by Major E. Molyneux. Black,
1909. xv, 283p., col. plates (1 fold.), illus.,
map. 21cm.

YOUNGHUSBAND, Sir Francis
Peking to Lhasa: the narrative of journeys in the
Chinese Empire made by the late Brigadier-General
George Pereira; compiled by Sir Francis
Younghusband, from notes and diaries supplied by
Sir Cecil Pereira. Constable, 1925. x, 293p.,
plates (some fold.), illus., maps. 24cm.

YOUNGHUSBAND, Sir Francis
Wonders of the Himalaya. Murray, 1924. x, 210p.,
1 plate, illus., map. 23cm.

YOUNGHUSBAND, Sir Francis
SEAVER, George
Francis Younghusband: explorer and mystic. Murray,
1952. 391p., illus., maps. 22cm.

YOUNGHUSBAND, Sir George
A soldier's memories in peace and war. Jenkins,
1917. 355p., plates, illus., ports. 23cm.

YUNG, Émile
Zermatt et la vallée de la Viège. Genève: F.
Thévoz, 1894. 107p., illus., bibl. 32cm.

YUNG, Émile
[Zermatt et la vallée de la Viège]. Zermatt and
the Valley of the Viège; translated ... by Mrs.
Wharton Robinson. Geneva: F. Thévoz; London: J.R.
Gotz, 1894. 107p., illus., bibl. 32cm.

PIDAL, Pedro and ZABALA, José F
Picos de Europa: contribución al estudio de las
montañas españolas. Madrid: Club Alpino Espanol,
1918. 120p., plates (some fold., some col.),
illus., maps. 29cm.

ZABIROV, R D
Oledenenie Pamira. Moskva: Gos. Izd. Geograficheskoi Literatury, 1955. 372p., fold. plates,
illus., maps, bibl. 23cm.

ZACHARIAH, O
Travel in South Africa. 3rd ed. Johannesburg:
South African Railways and Harbours, 1927. 331p.,
illus., map. 19cm.

DESIO, Ardito and ZANETTIN, Bruno
Geology of the Baltoro Basin. Leiden: Brill, 1970.
xx, 308p., fold.col. plates, illus., maps (in
pocket), bibl. 28cm. (Italian expeditions to the
Karakorum (K2) and Hindu Kush. Scientific reports,
3. Geology, petrology, v.2)

ZARN, Adolf and BARBLAN, Peter
Der Skifahrer: Ski-Turnen und Ski-Fahrtechnik;
mit einem Kapitel ... von J.B. Masüger; einem
Vorwort von Sonderegger. Zürich: Bopp, 1920.
246p., illus. 22cm.

ZARN, Adolf and BARBLAN, Peter
[Der Skifahrer]. L'art du ski: gymnastique et
technique du ski; traduction par Felix
Krahnstoever. Zurich: Bopp, 1922. 258p., illus.
21cm.

ZAY, Karl
Goldau und seine Gegend: wie sie war und was sie
geworden, in Zeichnungen und Beschreibungen...
Zürich: Orell, Füssli, 1807. xii, 390p., plates,
illus., map. 20cm.

ZDARSKY, Mathias
Alpine (Lilienfelder) Skifahr-Technik: eine
Anleitung zum Selbstunterricht. 4., methodisch
umgearb. Aufl. Berlin: K.W. Mecklenburg, 1908.
98p., illus. 19cm.

ZDARSKY, Mathias
Beiträge zur Lawinenkunde; hrsg. vom Alpen-
Skiverein Wien. Wien: A.B.Z., [1929]. 127p.,
illus. 16cm.

ZDARSKY, Mathias
Skisport: gesammelte Aufsätze; hrsg. von Alpen-
Skiverein. Wien: C. Konegen, 1909. vi, 123p.
17cm.

ZDARSKY, Mathias
Das Wandern im Gebirge. Berlin: K.W. Mecklenburg,
1925. 254p., plates, illus. 23cm.

ZEILLER, Martin
MERIAN, Matthaeus
Topographia Helvetiae, Rhaetiae, et Valesiae: das
ist Beschreibung und eygentlich Abbildung der
vernehmsten Stätte ...; in dieser andern Edition
... corrigirt, vermehrt und gebessert [von M.Z.,
i.e. Martin Zeiller]. Franckfurt am Mayn; Von
denen Merianischen Erben, 1654. 90p., plates
(some fold.), map. 32cm.

- - Facsimile ed. [Basle?]: [n.pub.], [ca 1900].

ZELLER, Franz
Lese- und Sprachbuch für allgemeine Volkschulen
in Tirol. Vol.3. Innsbruck: Verlag der Vereins-
buchhandlung, 1909. 351p., plates, illus. 21cm.
Anthology for schoolchildren.

ZELLER, H
Gebirgsaussicht gezeichnet vom Gipfel des Titlis
den 15n. August 1832. [N.p.]: [n.pub.], 1832.
29cm.
Panorama.

ZELLER, Max
Berchtesgadner Alpen: ein Führer für Täler, Hütten
und Berge. 10 neubearb. Aufl., von Helmut
Schöner. München: Rother, 1962. 387p., plates
(1 fold.), illus., maps (in pocket). 16cm.

ZELLER, R
Ein Rundgang durch das Schweizerische Alpine
Museum in Bern. Bern: The Museum, 1934. 32p.,
illus. 21cm.

ZELLER, R
[Ein Rundgang...]. Une visite au Musée Alpin
Suisse à Berne; traduction du Dr. A. Lang. Berne:
The Museum, 1935. 32p., illus. 21cm.

ZENTRALSTELLE FÜR ALPINE PROJEKTIONSBILDER
See
SCHWEIZER ALPENCLUB. Zentralstelle für Alpine
Projektionsbilder

ZEPPELIN-EXPEDITION
See
DEUTSCHE ARKTISCHE ZEPPELIN-EXPEDITION, 1910

ZERMATT (Parish)
Familien-Statistik der löblichen Pfarrei von
Zermatt, mit Beilagen; gesammelt und geordnet von
Joseph Ruden. Ingenbohl: Buchdruckerei der
Waisenanstalt, 1869. 184p., 1 plate, illus. 20cm.

- - [New ed.] entitled: Familien-Statistik und
Geschichtliches über die Gemeinde Zermatt, von
Stanislaus Kronig. Ingenbohl: B. Theodosius-
Buchdruckerei, 1927.

Zermatt. Zürich: Photoglob, [19--]. 1v. of illus.
18cm.

ZERMATTEN, Maurice
Chapelles valaisannes: le visage pittoresque et
religieux du Valais. Neuchatel: Attinger, 1941.
214p., 32 plates, illus. 26cm.

ZERMATTEN, Maurice
Nourritures valaisannes: illustrations de Paul
Monnier. Fribourg: Librairie de l'Université,
1938. 58p., col. illus. 26cm.

ZERMATTEN, Maurice
Les saisons valaisannes. Neuchatel: Attinger,
1948. 238p., plates, illus. 26cm.

ZERMATTEN, Maurice
Le Valais; 80 photographies originales de Benedikt
Rast. Lausanne: J. Marguerat, 1941. 98p., illus.
29cm. (Les merveilles de la Suisse)

ZETTLER, Ernst
Skiführer durch das West-Allgau Gebiet von
Immenstadt-Oberstdorf bis zum Bregenzer Wald;
bearb. von Ernst Zettler. München: Rother, 1937.
40p., map. 17cm.

ZIAK, Karl
Balmat oder Paccard? Ein Mont-Blanc Roman. Wien:
Verlag Allegemeine Bergsteiger-Zeitung, 1930.
287p. 18cm.

ZIAK, Karl
Erwanderte Heimat: Land und Leute in Österreich.
3.Aufl. Wien: Wiener Volksbuchverlag, 1949.
192p., illus. 24cm.

ZIAK, Karl
Der Mensch und die Berge: eine Weltgeschichte des
Alpinismus. 2.Aufl. Salzburg: "Das Bergland-
Buch", 1956. 372p., illus. 22cm.

ZIEGLER, Anton
Erschliesser der Berge: zusammengestellt von Anton
Ziegler; hrsg. vom Hauptausschuss des Deutschen und
Österreichischen Alpenvereins. München: D.u.Ö.A.V.,
1926. 3v., plates, illus. 20cm.

ZIEGLER, J   M
Erläuterungen zur Karte der Schweiz=Eclaircisse-
ments... Zürich: Zürcher & Furrer, 1852. xi, 72p.
25cm.
Text in French and German.
Includes a gazetteer.

- - Erläuterungen zur neuen Karte... Winterthur: J.
Wurster, 1857.
- - Erläuterungen zur dritten Karte... 1866.

ZIEGLER, J   M
Sammlung absoluter Höhen der Schweiz und der
angrenzenden Gegenden der Nachbarländer, als
Ergänzung der Karte in Reduction von 1 : 380000=
Hypsometrie de la Suisse... Zürich: Zürcher &
Furrer, 1853. xiv, 398p. 26cm.
Introduction in German and French.

ZIEGLER, J   M
Zur Hypsometrie der Schweiz und zur Orographie der
Alpen: Erlauterungen für die hypsometrische Karte
der Schweiz. Winterthur: Wurster, 1866. 60p.
25cm.

Zig-zag ramblings; or, Further notes by the way, by
a nomad on the prowl, author of "Reminiscences of
many lands" etc. [i.e. R. Brooks Popham]. H.J.
Drane, 1906. 158p., plates, illus. 19cm.

Zigzagging amongst Dolomites, [by Elizabeth Tuckett].
Longmans, Green, Reader & Dyer, 1871. 38 leaves of
illus., map. 26 x 36cm.

ZIMMERMAN, John George
Solitude, written originally by J.G. Zimmerman; to
which are added The life of the author ... and
7 ... engravings by Ridley. Vernor & Hood,
1800-02. 2v., plates, illus. 18cm.
Vol.2 is 3rd ed.

ZIMMERMANN, Alice
DUBI, Heinrich
Saas-Fee und Umgebung: ein Führer durch Geschichte,
Volk und Landschaft des Saastales. 2.Aufl., neu
bearb. von Alice Zimmermann. Bern: A. Francke,
1946. 128p., plates, illus., bibl. 19cm.

ZINCKE, F   Barham
A month in Switzerland. Smith, Elder, 1873. xv,
271p. 20cm.

ZINCKE, F   Barham
Swiss allmends and a walk to see them, being a
second month in Switzerland. Smith, Elder, 1874.
ix, 367p. 20cm.

ZINCKE, F   Barham
A walk in the Grisons, being a third month in
Switzerland. Smith, Elder, 1875. xv, 368p. 19cm.

ZIRKEL, Ferdinand
Physiographische Skizzen aus den Pyrenäen.
Augsburg, 1867. 3pts. in 1. 32cm.
Offprint from Das Ausland, 1867.

ZOGG, Hans A
CORDILLERA BLANCA SEATTLE EXPEDITION, 1964
Ascent of Nevado Huascaran [by] Hans A. Zogg [and
others]. Seattle: The Expedition, 1964. 55p.,
illus., map. 25cm.

ZOLFANELLI, Cesare and SANTINI, Vincenzo
Guida alle Alpi Apuane; compilata dal professore
Cesare Zolfanelli e Vincenzo Santini. Firenze:
Tipografia di G. Barbera, 1874. vii, 228p.,
plates, illus., bibl. 20cm.

ZOLLER, Otto
Janpeter Bruns Abenteuer in den Tessiner und
Graubündner Berge, erzählt von Otto Zoller.
Zürich: Orell Füssli, [1910]. vii, 268p., plates,
illus. 20cm.

ZOPOTH, Johann
Tagebuch einer Reise auf den bis dahin uner-
steigenen Berg Gross-Glokner an den Gränzen
Cärntens, Salzburgs und Tirols im Jahre 1799, [von
Johann Zopoth]. Salzburg, 1800. 88p., 1 fold.
plate, illus., map. 22cm.
Besonderer Abdruk aus des Freyherrn von Moll Jahr-
büchern der Berg- und Hüttenkunde.

ZOPPI, Giuseppe
Das Buch von der Alp: über den Dörfern des Tessin.
Einsiedeln/Köln: Benziger, 1939. 176p., illus.
21cm.

ZORNLIN, Rosina M
Recreations in physical geography; or, The earth
as it is. 5th ed. Parker, 1855. vii, 424p.,
plates (2 fold.), illus., maps. 19cm.

ZSCHOKKE, Heinrich
Autobiography. Chapman & Hall, 1845. viii, 220p.
22cm.

ZSCHOKKE, Heinrich
Die klassischen Stellen der Schweiz und deren
Hauptorte in Originalansichten dargestellt;
gezeichnet von Gust. Adolph Müller ...; mit Er-
läuterungen von Heinrich Zschokke. Karlsruhe:
Kunst, 1836-38. 2v. (423p.), plates, illus. 24cm.

ZSCHOKKE, Heinrich
MEYER, Johann Rudolf and MEYER, Hieronymus
Reise auf die Eisgebirge des Kantons Bern und
Ersteigung ihrer höchsten Gipfel, in Sommer 1812;
[hrsg. von Heinrich Zschokke]. Aarau: H. R.
Sauerländer, 1813. 45p., 1 plate, map. 21cm.

ZSIGMONDY, Emil
Dr. Emil Zsigmondy; eine Auswahl; zusammengestellt von Anton Ziegler. München: D.u.Ö.A.V., 1926. 87p., plates, illus. 20cm. (Erschliesser der Berge, 3)

ZSIGMONDY, Emil
Die Gefahren der Alpen: praktische Winke für Bergsteiger. Leipzig: P. Frohberg, 1885. x, 214p., plates, illus. 24cm.

- - 2., von Otto Zsigmondy besorgte Aufl. Augsburg: Lampart, [1886].
- - 3., unter Mitwirkung Ludwig Purtscheller's von Otto Zsigmondy besorgte Aufl. Augsburg: Lampart, [ca 1900].
- - 4.Aufl., neu bearb. und ergänst von W. Paulcke. Innsbruck: A. Edlinger, 1908.
- - 5.Aufl. Wien: A. Edlinger, 1911.
- - 7.Aufl., bearb. seit der 4.Aufl. von W. Paulcke. München, Rother, 1922.
- - 8.Aufl., von Emil Zsigmondy und Wilhelm Paulcke. München: Rother, 1927.

ZSIGMONDY, Emil
[Die Gefahren der Alpen...]. Les dangers dans la montagne: indications pratiques pour les ascensionnistes; traduit de l'allemand; précédé d'une préface par Abel Lemercier. Paris: Fischbacher, 1886. 203p., plates, illus. 24cm.

ZSIGMONDY, Emil
Im Hochgebirge; Wanderungen; mit Abbildungen von E.T. Compton; hrsg., von K. Schulz. Leipzig: Duncker & Humblot, 1889. xv, 365p., plates, illus. 28cm.

VALLA, François and ZUANON, Jean Paul
Pamir: escalade d'un 7.000 au pays des Kirghizes; avec la participation des membres de l'expédition dauphinoise au Pamir 74. Domene: Segirep, 1976. 301p., plates (1 fold.col.), illus., maps, bibl. 22cm.

ZÜRCHER, Otto
Das Berner Oberland im Lichte der deutschen Dichtung; ausgewahlt und eingeleitet von Otto Zürcher. Leipzig: H. Haessel, 1923. 103p. 16cm. (Die Schweiz im deutschen Geistesleben, 18)

ZUMAGLINO, Vittorio
BERNARDI, Marziano
Il Cervino e la sua storia; a cura di Vittorio Zumaglino. Torino: S.A. Cervino, 1944. 71p., illus. 29cm.

ZUMSTEIN, Joseph
WELDEN, Ludwig, Freiherr von
Der Monte-Rosa: eine topographische und natur-historische Skizze, nebst einem Anhange der von Herrn Zumstein gemachten Reisen zur Ersteigung seiner Gipfel. Wien: Gerold, 1824. viii, 167p., fold. plates, illus., maps. 23cm.

ZUMSTEINS LANDKARTENHAUS
Zumstein Katalog mit Register. Grosse Ausg. München: Zumstein, 1964. 1v. (various pagings), illus. 24cm.

ZUNTZ, N
Höhenklima und Bergwanderungen in ihrer Wirkung auf den Menschen: Ergebnisse experimenteller Forschungen im Hochgebirge und Laboratorium, von N. Zuntz [and others]. Berlin: Bong, 1906. xvi, 494p., plates (some fold., 1 col.), illus. 31cm.

ZURBRIGGEN, Matthias
From the Alps to the Andes, being the autobiography of a mountain guide; [translated by Mary Alice Vialls]. Fisher Unwin, 1899. xvi, 269p., illus. 23cm.

ZURBRIGGEN, Matthias
[From the Alpes to the Andes]. Von den Alpen zu den Anden: Lebenserinnerungen eines Bergführers. Berlin: Union Deutsche Verlagsgesellschaft, [1938]. 167p., illus. 22cm.

ZURCHER, Frédéric and MARGOLLÉ, Élie
Les ascensions célèbres aux plus hautes montagnes du globe: fragments de voyages; recueillis, traduits et mis en ordre par Zurcher et Margollé. 2e éd. Paris: Hachette, 1869. 348p., illus. 18cm. (Bibliothèque des merveilles)

- - 4e éd., rev. et augm. 1897.
- - 5e éd., rev. par A. Le Pileur. 1891.

ZURCHER, Frédéric and MARGOLLÉ, Élie
[Les ascensions célèbres]. Mountain adventures in the various countries of the world; selected from the narratives of celebrated travellers. Seeley, Jackson, & Halliday, 1869. viii, 320p., plates, illus. 19cm.
"Founded on a compilation made by M.M. Zurcher and Margollé... In several instances ... the narratives of English travellers have been substituted". - Prefatory note.

ZURCHER, Frédéric and MARGOLLÉ, Élie
Les glaciers, par Zurcher et Margollé; illustrés ... par L. Sabatier. Paris: Hachette, 1868. 323p., plates, illus. 20cm. (Bibliothèque des merveilles)

- - 3e éd., rev. et augm. 1875.

ZWAHLEN, Otto
Der Kampf um die Eiger-Nordwand: illustrierter Bericht über die Bergtragödien im Sommer 1935 und 1936; bearb. von Otto Zwahlen. Basel: O. & A. Zwahlen, 1936. 48p., illus. 21cm.

FLAIG, Walther and ZWEIGELT, Sepp
Vorarlberger Schieführer in mehreren Heften mit Schiekarten und Anstiegsbildern. Heft 1. Schiefahrten um Gargellen; hrsg. von Walther Flaig und Sepp Zweigelt. Allgäu: Zumstein, Grünenbach, Bahern, 1928. 76p., map (in pocket). 16cm.

ZWICKH, Nepomuk
DEUTSCHER UND ÖSTERREICHISCHER ALPENVEREIN. Sektion München
Geschichte der Alpenvereinssection München als Denkschrift nach dreissigjährigem Bestehen hrsg. München: Die Section, 1900. xii, 401p., plates (some fold., 1 col.), illus., map (in pocket). 28cm. Contains: "Geschichte der Section von 1869-99", by Nepomuk Zwickh.

O M I S S I O N S

p.177, col.2.
KNIGHT, William Henry
  Diary of a pedestrian in Cashmere and Thibet.
  Bentley, 1863. xvi, 385p., plates (some col.),
  illus. 23cm.

p.178, col.1.
KÖNIG, Erich
  Empor! Georg Winklers Tagebuch: in memoriam:
  ein Reigen von Bergfahrten hervorragender
  Alpinisten von heute. Leipzig: Grethlein,
  [1910]. xv, 325p., illus. 28cm.

p.181, col.1.
KURZ, Marcel
  Chronique himalayenne: l'âge d'or 1940-1955.
  Zurich: Fondation Suisse pour Explorations
  Alpines, 1959. x, 441p., plates (1 fold.),
  illus., maps. 25cm.

- - Supplément. 1963.

p.209, col.2.
MELMOTH, William
COXE, William
  Sketches of the natural, civil and political
  state of Swisserland, in a series of letters to
  William Melmoth. J. Dodsley, 1779. viii,
  533p. 22cm.

- - 2nd ed. 1780.

p.228, col.2.
NOEL, Roden
  Songs of the heights and deeps. Elliot Stock,
  1885. viii, 214p. 20cm.

p.268, col.2.
SAINT-ROBERT, Paul de
  See
SAN-ROBERTO, Paolo, conte di

PART 2

CLASSIFIED CATALOGUES

CATALOGUE OF PERIODICALS

SECTION 1

CLASSIFIED CATALOGUE

(BOOKS)

CLASSIFICATION SCHEME

01   PHYSICAL SCIENCES

010   General works

BUCHANAN, John Young
   Comptes rendus of observation and reasoning.
   1917.

CAMPBELL, John Francis
   Frost and fire: natural engines, tool-marks and
   chips, with sketches taken at home and abroad, by
   a traveller. 1865.

CHALMERS, Charles
   Electro-chemistry with positive results, and notes
   for inquiry on the sciences of geology and
   astronomy... 1858.

DARWIN, Charles
   Journal of researches into the natural history and
   geology of the countries visited during the voyage
   of HMS 'Beagle' round the world; with a biographical introduction. [1897].

GEIKIE, James
   Earth sculpture; or, The origin of land-forms.
   1898.

JEFFREYS, Harold
   Earthquakes and mountains. 1935.

JUNGFRAUJOCH SCIENTIFIC STATION
   Hochalpine Forschungsstation Jungfraujoch...
   Internationale Stiftung. 1931.

LABORATORII SCIENTIFICI "A. MOSSO" SUL MONTE ROSA
   Travaux [des années 1903-1911]; publiés par A.
   Mosso. 1904-1912. 3v.

SOCIETÀ DI SCIENZE E LETTERE DI GENOVA
   Catalogo delle memorie edite negli "Atti" sociali
   dal 1890 al 1939, nella cinquantesime della
   fondazione della Società. 1939.

TYNDALL, John
   Fragments of science: a series of detached essays,
   addresses, and reviews. 8th ed. 1829-1892. 2v.

TYNDALL, John
   Heat, a mode of motion. 3rd ed. 1868.

- - 6th ed. 1904.

UNIVERSITY OF COLORADO. Institute of Arctic and
Alpine Research
   List of publications ..., 1967-1974; compiled by
   Martha Andrews. 1975.

The wonders of creation, as pourtrayed [sic] by
   Humboldt, Livingstone, Ruskin and other great
   writers. [18--].

The world of wonders: a record of things wonderful
   in nature, science, and art. New ed. 1882.

011   Earth formation

BALL, Sir Robert S
   The cause of an ice age. 1891.

BONNEY, Thomas George
   The story of our planet. 1893.

FIGUIER, Louis
   La terre et les mers; ou, Description physique du
   globe. 1864.

FIGUIER, Louis
   [La terre et les mers]. Earth and sea. 1875.

HUMBOLDT, Alexander, Freiherr von
   Ansichten der Natur. 3. verb. und verm. Ausg.
   1849.

HUMBOLDT, Alexander, Freiherr von
   [Ansichten der Natur...]. Views of nature... 1850.

HUMBOLDT, Alexander, Freiherr von
   [Kosmos]. Cosmos: a sketch of a physical description of the universe. 1886. 5v.

JOLY, John
   The birth-time of the world and other scientific
   essays. 1915.

JORDAN, William Leighton
   Essays in illustration of the action of astral
   gravitation in natural phenomena. 1900.

LUC, Jean André de
   Lettres physiques et morales sur l'histoire de
   la terre et de l'homme... 1779-80. 5v. in 6.

MCCABE, Joseph
   Ice ages: the story of the earth's revolutions.
   1922.

PRIEM, Fernand
   La terre avant l'apparition de l'homme: periodes
   géologiques... 1893.

SMALL, John
   A hundred wonders of the world in nature and art.
   1876.

SUESS, Eduard
   [Das Antlitz der Erde]. The face of the earth.
   1904-09. 4v.

SUESS, Eduard
   [Das Antlitz der Erde]. La face de la terre.
   T.1. Les montagnes. 1905.

011.3   Volcanic eruptions

ANDERSON, Tempest
   Volcanic studies in many lands... 1903.

- - 2nd series, the text by T.G. Bonney. 1917.

AULDJO, John
   Sketches of Vesuvius with short accounts of its
   principal eruptions, from the commencement of
   the Christian era to the present time. 1832.

- - Another ed. 1833.

BERGEAT, Alfred
   Die Vulkane. 1925.

BONNEY, Thomas George
   Volcanoes: their structure and significance.
   1899.

BROOKE, N
   Voyage à Naples et en Toscane, avant et pendant
   l'invasion des Français en Italie, avec ... des
   détails sur la terrible explosion du Mont-Vésuve,
   pris sur les lieux à minuit, en juin 1794. (1799).

BULLARD, Fred M
   Volcanoes in history, in theory, in eruption.
   1962.

CAMPANILE, Vincent
   Calendrier alpin avec des notices sur les éruptions volcaniques... 5e éd. 1902.

DUPARC, Louis and MRAZEC, Ludovic
   Sur quelques bombes de l'Etna, provenant des
   éruptions de 1886 et 1892. [1895?].

DUPARC, Louis and MRAZEC, Ludovic
   Sur quelques bombes volcaniques de l'Etna des
   éruptions de 1886 et 1892. 1893.

FONTAINE, E
   Alpinisme et volcanisme: l'éruption de Vésuve en
   1906. 1928.

HAMILTON, Sir William
   Campi Phlegraei: observations on the volcanoes of
   the two Sicilies... 1776.

- - Supplement ... being An account of the great
   eruption of Mount Vesuvius... 1779.

011.3 Volcanic eruptions (Cont.)

HAMILTON, Sir William
  Observations on Mount Vesuvius, Mount Etna, and
  other volcanoes... 1772.

- - 2nd ed. 1773.

HEILPRIN, Angelo
  The eruption of Pelée: a summary and discussion of
  the phenomena and their sequels. 1908.

PRELLER, C S Du Riche
  Italian mountain geology. Pt.3. The Gran Sasso
  d'Italia group, Abruzzi, central Apennines, the
  volcanoes of central and southern Italy. 1923.

SACCHI, Giuseppe
  Le ghiacciaje della Svizzera ed i vulcani. 1837.

SODIRO, Luis
  Relacion sobre la erupcion del Cotopaxi, acaecida
  el dia 26 de Junio de 1877. 1877.

012 Glaciology

ADAMS, William H Davenport
  Wonders of the physical world: the glacier, the
  iceberg, the ice-field, and the avalanche. 1875.

- - Another ed. 1880.

AGASSIZ, Louis
  Études sur les glaciers. 1840.

AGASSIZ, Louis
  [Études sur les glaciers]. Untersuchungen über
  die Gletscher. 1841.

AGASSIZ, Louis
  Nouvelles études et expériences sur les glaciers
  actuels, leur structure, leur progression et leur
  action physique sur le sol. 1847.

BALL, John
  On the cause of the motion of glaciers. 1871.

BARETTI, Martino
  I ghiacciai antichi e moderni. 1866.

BÖHM, August, Edler von Böhmersheim
  Geschichte der Moranenkunde. 1901.

BONNEY, Thomas George
  Ice-work present and past. 1896.

BONNEY, Thomas George
  On the formation of "cirques" and their bearing
  upon theories attributing the excavation of alpine
  valleys mainly to the action of glaciers. 1871.

FORBES, James David
  Historical remarks on the first discovery of the
  real structure of glacier ice. 1843.

FORBES, James David
  Illustrations of the viscous theory of glacier
  motion. 1846.

FORBES, James David
  [Letters on recent observations on glaciers].
  1842-51.

FORBES, James David
  Notes on the topography and geology of the
  Cuchullin hills in Skye and on the traces of
  ancient glaciers which they present. 1845.

FORBES, James David
  Notice respecting Mr. Reilly's topographical survey
  of the chain of Mont Blanc. 1865.

FORBES, James David
  Occasional papers on the theory of glaciers...
  1859.

FORBES, James David
  On a remarkable structure observed by the author
  in the ice of glaciers. 1842.

FORBES, James David
  On some properties of ice near its melting point.
  1858.

FORBES, James David
  Remarks on a paper "On ice and glaciers" ... in a
  letter to Prof. Tyndall. 1859.

FORBES, James David
  Reply to Professor Tyndall's remarks in his work
  "On the glaciers of the Alps" relating to Rendu's
  "Théorie des glaciers". 1860.

FORBES, James David
  Sur l'éclipse totale de soleil du 8 juillet 1842:
  extrait d'une lettre... 1843.

GUILLEMIN, Amédée
  La neige, la glace et les glaciers. 1891.

HEIM, Albert
  Handbuch der Gletscherkunde. 1885.

HESS, Hans
  Die Gletscher. 1904.

HOBBS, William Herbert
  Characteristics of existing glaciers. 1911.

HOBBS, William Herbert
  Les glaciers du mond actuel. 1922.

HUBER, William
  Les glaciers. 1867.

HUGI, Franz Joseph
  Die Gletscher und die erratischen Blöcke. 1843.

JULEN, Hieronymus
  Die Gletscher-Theorie. [1923?].

LECOQ, Henri
  Des glaciers et des climats. 1847.

MACHAČEK, Fritz
  Gletscherkunde. 1902.

MASON, Kenneth
  The representation of glaciated regions on maps
  of the Survey of India. 1929.

MEUNIER, Stanislas
  Les glaciers et les montagnes. 1920.

MOUSSON, Albert
  Die Gletscher der Jetztzeit: eine Zusammenstellung
  und Prüfung ihrer Erscheinungen und Gesetze.
  1854.

PENCK, Albrecht
  Gletscher und Eiszeit. 1880.

RAMSAY, Andrew Crombie
  On the glacial origin of certain lakes in
  Switzerland, the Black Forest, Great Britain,
  Sweden, North America and elsewhere. 1862.

RENDU, Louis
  [Théorie des glaciers de la Savoie]. Theory of
  the glaciers of Savoy. 1874.

SEMINAR ON THE CAUSES AND MECHANICS OF GLACIER
SURGES, St. Hilaire, Quebec, 1968
  Papers presented at the Seminar on the Causes and
  Mechanics of Glacier Surges and the Symposium on
  Surging Glaciers. 1968.

SHALER, Nathaniel Southgate and DAVIS, William
Morris
  Glaciers. 1881.

SYMPOSIUM ON GLACIER MAPPING, Ottawa, 1965
  [Papers]. [1965].

TYNDALL, John
  The forms of water in clouds & rivers, ice and
  glaciers. 1872.

- - 11th ed. 1892.

012 Glaciology (Cont.)
TYNDALL, John
  [The forms of water in clouds & rivers, ice &
  glaciers]. Les glaciers et les transformations de
  l'eau; suivis d'une conférence sur le même sujet
  par M. Helmholtz, avec la réponse de M. Tyndall.
  1873.

ZURCHER, Frédéric and MARGOLLÉ, Élie
  Les glaciers. 1868.

- - 3e éd., rev. et augm. 1875.

013 Physical geography

AVEBURY, John Lubbock, Baron
  The beauties of nature and the wonders of the
  world we live in. 1892.

GILBERT, Linney
  The beauties and wonders of nature and science.
  [184-].

INTERNATIONAL GEOGRAPHIC CONGRESS, 4th, Paris, 1889
  4e Congrès international des sciences géographiques.
  1890.

INTERNATIONAL GEOGRAPHIC CONGRESS, 8th, St. Louis,
1904
  Report. 1905.

INTERNATIONAL GEOGRAPHIC CONGRESS, 9th, Geneva, 1908
  Compte rendu des travaux du congrès. 1910.

JOHNSTON, Alexander Keith
  The physical atlas of natural phenomena. 1850.

LANOYE, Ferdinand de
  Les grandes scènes de la nature d'après les des-
  criptions de voyageurs et d'écrivains célèbres.
  Nouv. éd. 1864.

MARR, John E
  The scientific study of scenery. 1899.

MELA, Pomponius
  De orbis situ libri tres, accuratissime emendati,
  unà cù Commêtariis Ioachimi Vadiani Heluetii
  castigatioribus... Adiecta... Rursum, Epistola
  Vadiani... 1522.

MILNER, Thomas
  The gallery of nature: a pictorial and descriptive
  tour through creation, illustrative of the wonders
  of astronomy, physical geography and geology. New
  ed. 1855.

Oxford world atlas, Saul B. Cohen geographic editor;
  prepared by the Cartographic Department of the
  Clarendon Press. 1973.

SEYDLITZ, Ernst von
  Handbuch der Geographie. Jubiläums-Ausg.: 25.
  Bearb. 1908.

SKEAT, E G
  The principles of geography, physical & human.
  1923.

SOMERVILLE, Mary
  Physical geography. New ed., thoroughly rev.
  1849.

SONKLAR, Karl, Edler von Innstädten
  Lehrbuch der Geographie für die k.k. Militär-Real-
  und Kadetenschulen. 2nd improved ed. 1880.
  2v. in 1.

TOZER, Henry Fanshawe
  A history of ancient geography. 1897.

VIVIEN DE SAINT-MARTIN, Louis
  Atlas dressé pour l'histoire de la géographie et
  des découvertes géographiques... 1874.

WILKINS, Charles Armar
  Curiosities of travel; or, Glimpses of nature.
  1876.

WITTICH, William
  Curiosities of physical geography. 1845-46.

- - Another ed. [1869].

ZORNLIN, Rosina M
  Recreations in physical geography; or, The earth
  as it is. 5th ed. 1855.

013.3 Geology

COLLET, Léon W
  Les lacs: leur mode de formation, leurs eaux,
  leur destin: éléments d'hydro-géologie. 1925.

COTTA, Bernhard von
  Rocks classified and described: a treatise on
  lithology; revised by the author. 1866.

LEMAITRE, Hélène
  Les pierres dans l'oeuvre de Ruskin. 1965.

PAGE, David
  Introductory text-book of geology; revised and in
  great part rewritten by Charles Lapworth. 12th
  and enl. ed. 1888.

SENNETT, A R
  Across the Great Saint Bernard: the modes of
  nature and the manners of man. 1904.

013.4 Geomorphology

BUSS, Ernst and HEIM, Albert
  Der Bergsturz von Elm den 11. September 1881:
  Denkschrift. 1881.

ESCHER VON DER LINTH, Hans Conrad
  Relation succincte de l'Écroulement de la montagne
  au-dessus de Goldau, Canton de Schwytz le 2.
  septembre 1806. 1806.

HEUSSER, Chr.
  Das Erdbeben im Visperthat, Kanton Wallis, vom
  Jahr 1855. 2.Ausg. 1856.

SHARPE, C F Stewart
  Landslides and related phenomena: a study of mass-
  movements of soil and rock. 1938.

013.6 Cartography

BERALDI, Henri
  Balaïtous et Pelvoux: notes sur les officiers de
  la Carte de France. 1907-10. 2 v.

DEUTSCHER ALPENVEREIN
  Die Kartographie im Alpenverein, von Erik
  Arnberger; hrsg. vom Deutschen Alpenverein und vom
  Österreichischen Alpenverein. 1970.

DEUTSCHER UND ÖSTERREICHISCHER ALPENVEREIN
  Anleitung zum Kartenlesen im Hochgebirge; mit
  besonderer Berücksichtigung der vom D.u.Ö
  Alpenverein hrsg. Spezialkarten, von Josef Moriggl.
  1909.

FINSTERWALDER, Richard
  Alpenvereinskartographie und die ihr dienenden
  Methoden; mit Beiträgen von E. Ebster [and others].
  1935.

FISCHER, Ernst
  Der kartographische Standpunkt der Schweiz: ein
  Vortrag. 1870.

LAVIS-TRAFFORD, Marc A de
  L'évolution de la cartographie de la région du
  Mont-Cenis et de ses abords au XVe et XVIe siècles:
  étude critique des méthodes de travail des grands
  cartographes du XVIe siècle... [1950].

MASON, Kenneth
  The representation of glaciated regions on maps
  of the Survey of India. 1929.

013.6 Cartography (Cont.)

MASSIE, F
La cartographie des Pyrénées: étude; documentation
illustrée de cartes et photographies de l'Exposition de Cartographie des Pyrénées organisée par le
capitaine Massie. 1934.

Opérations géodésiques et astronomiques pour la
mesure d'un arc du parallèle moyen, exécutées en
Piémont et en Savoie par une commission composée
d'officiers ... piémontais et autrichiens en 1821,
1822, 1823. 1825-27. 2v.

SCHWEIZERISCHE GEODÄTISCHE COMMISSION.
Das Schweizerische Dreiecknetz. Bd.1. 1881.

SWITZERLAND. Eidgenössisches topographisches Bureau
Hundert Jahre Eidg. Landestopographie, ehemaliges
Eidg. topographisches Bureau, 1838-1938:
Erinnerungsmappe. 1938. 3v.

SWITZERLAND. Eidgenössisches topographisches Bureau
La topographie de la Suisse, 1832-1864: histoire
de la Carte Dufour. 1898.

SYMPOSIUM ON GLACIER MAPPING, Ottawa, 1965
[Papers]. [1965].

VALLOT, Henri
Levés à la planchette en haute montagne. 1909.

VALLOT, Henri
Manuel de topographie alpine. 1904.

014   Mountain formation

BAILEY, E   B
Tectonic essays, mainly alpine. 1935.

BEAUMONT, L   Élie de
Notice sur les systèmes de montagnes. 1852. 3v.

CLARKE, C   C
The hundred wonders of the world, and of the three
kingdoms of nature, described according to the
best and latest authorities. 8th ed. 1825.

DAUZAT, Albert
Toute la montagne. 1924.

DUPAIGNE, Albert
Les montagnes. 2e éd., rev. et augm. 1874.

FISHER, Joel E
Problems in the geology of mountains: five thesis.
1944.

HUTCHINSON, H   N
The story of the hills: a popular account of
mountains and how they were made. 1892.

LANE, Ferdinand C
The story of mountains. 1950.

LAUNAY, L   de
La vie des montagnes. [1926].

LENDENFELD, Robert von
Die Hochgebirge der Erde. 1899.

MICHELET, Jules
La montagne; [avec une] étude par André Theuriet.
[3e éd.]. 1899.

MICHELET, Jules
[La montagne]. The mountain. 1872.

N***,   , comte de
Essais sur les montagnes. 1785.

PEATTIE, Roderick
Mountain geography: a critique and field study.
1936.

READE, T   Mellard
The origin of mountain ranges considered experi-
mentally, structurally, dynamically and in relation
to their geological history. 1886.

RECLUS, Elisée
The history of a mountain. 1881.

RUSKIN, John
In montibus sanctis: studies of mountain form and
of its visible causes; collected and completed out
of 'Modern painters'. 1884-85.

SCHEUCHZER, Johann Jacob
Natur-Geschichte des Schweitzerlandes, samt seinen
Reisen über die Schweizerische Gebürge; aufs neue
hrsg., und mit einigen Anmerkungen versehen von
Joh. Georg Sulzern. 1746. 2v. in 1.

SULZER, Johann Georg
Untersuchung von dem Ursprung der Berge, und
andrer damit verknüpsten Dinge. 1746.

VAN DYKE, John Charles
The mountain: renewed studies in impressions and
appearances. [1915].

WILSON, Joseph
A history of mountains, geographical and minera-
logical; accompanied by A picturesque view of the
principal mountains of the world, in their res-
pective proportions ..., by Robert Andrew Riddell.
1807-10. 3v.

015   Spelaeology

BADIN, Adolphe
Grottes et cavernes. 1870.

BAKER, Ernest Albert and BALCH, Herbert E
The netherworld of Mendip: explorations in the
great caverns of Somerset, Yorkshire, Derbyshire,
and elsewhere. 1907.

BERTARELLI, L   V   and BOEGAN, Eugenio
Duemila grotte: quarant'anni di esplorazioni
nella Venezia Giulia. 1926.

BROWNE, George Forrest
Ice-caves of France and Switzerland: a narrative
of subterranean exploration. 1865.

CADOUX, Jean
[Operation-1000]. One thousand metres down, by
Jean Cadoux and others. 1957.

CASELLI, Carlo
Speleologia: studio delle caverne. 1906.

CASTERET, Norbert
[Dix ans sous terre]. Ten years under the earth.
1939.

CASTERET, Norbert
[Mes cavernes]. My caves. 1947.

CAVE RESEARCH GROUP OF GREAT BRITAIN
A volume of essays presented to Brigadier E.A.
Glennie on the occasion of his 80th birthday,
July 18th 1969. 1969.

CHEVALIER, Pierre
Subterranean climbers: twelve years in the world's
deepest chasm. 1951.

CONGRESSO SPELEOLOGICO NAZIONALE, 1st Trieste, 1933
Atti ...; organizzato del Club Alpino Italiano.
1933.

CRAVEN, Steven A
A brief review of Himalayan speleology. 1971.

DOUDOU, Ernest
Exploration scientifique dans les cavernes, les
abîmes et les trous qui fument de la province de
Liège. [1906?].

JERVIS, Guglielmo
I tesori sotterranei dell'Italia... 1873-89. 4v.

JUDSON, David
Ghar Parau. 1973.

015 Speleology (Cont.)

LESSER, Friedrich Christian
Anmerckungen von der Baumanns-Höhle wie er sie
selbst Anno 1734. den 21. May befunden; nebst
Beyfügung derer natürlichen Ursachen ...; begleitet
von Johann Gottlieb Lessern. 4. weit verm. Aufl.
1745.

MARTEL, Édouard Alfred
Les abîmes, les eaux souterraines, les cavernes,
les sources, la spéléologie: explorations souterraines effectuées de 1888 à 1893 en France,
Belgique, Autriche et Grèce. 1894.

MARTEL, Édouard Alfred
Les Cevennes et la région des Causses, Lozère,
Aveyron, Hérault, Gard, Ardèche. 3e éd., rev.
corr. et augm. 1891.

MARTEL, Édouard Alfred
Le gouffre et la rivière souterraine de Padirac
(Lot): historique, description, exploration,
aménagement, (1889-1900). [1900].

MARTEL, Édouard Alfred
Irlande et cavernes anglaises. 1897.

MARTEL, Édouard Alfred
Nouveau traité des eaux souterraines. 1921.

MARTEL, Édouard Alfred
La spéléologie; ou, Science des cavernes. 1900.

TREVOR-BATTYE, Aubyn
Camping in Crete, with notes upon the animal and
plant life of the island; including a description
of certain caves and their ancient deposits, by
Dorothea H.A. Bate. 1913.

016 Natural phenomena

SCHAEBERLE, J   M
Report on the total eclipse of the sun, observed
at Mina Bronces, Chile, on April 16, 1893. 1895.

016.1 Atmospheric pressure

CORDEIRO, F   J   B
The barometrical determination of heights: a practical method of barometrical levelling and hypsometry for surveyors and mountain climbers. 1898.

HICKS, James
Description of an improved mercurial barometer.
[1864].

HODGKINSON, George C
Actinometrical observations among the Alps with the
description of a new actinometer. 1867.

HORNE AND THORNTHWAITE (Firm)
Altitude tables and how to use them. [ca 1870].

MARTINS, Charles and PLANTAMOUR, E
Sur l'influence de la distance et la correction
horaire des différences de niveau obtenues à l'aide
de deux baromètres correspondants. 1860.

SAN-ROBERTO, Paolo, conte di
Mémoires scientifiques, réunis et mis en ordre.
T.3. Mécanique, hypsométrie. 1874.

WHYMPER, Edward
How to use the aneroid barometer. 1891.

016.2 Snow, ice, water

BADER, H
Der Schnee und seine Metamorphose: erste Ergebnisse
und Anwendungen einer systematischen Untersuchung
der alpinen Winterschneedecke ... 1934-1938, von
H. Bader [and others]. 1939.

BREND, William A
The story of ice in the present and past. 1902.

BUCHANAN, John Young
Comptes rendus of observation and reasoning. 1917.

COLES-FINCH, William and HAWKS, Ellison
Water in nature. [1911].

COLES-FINCH, William
Water its origin and use. 1908.

MAIRAN, D   de
Dissertation sur la glace; ou, Explication
physique de la formation de la glace et de ses
divers phénomènes. 1749.

SELIGMAN, Gerald
Snow structure and ski fields, being an account
of snow and ice forms met with in nature, and a
study on avalanches and snowcraft; with an appendix on Alpine weather by C.K.M. Douglas. 1936.

TOMLINSON, Charles
The frozen stream; or, An account of the nature,
properties, dangers and uses of ice, in various
parts of the world. 1846.

- - Another ed. [ca 1862].

TOMLINSON, Charles
The snow-storm; or, An account of the nature,
properties, dangers, and uses of snow, in various
parts of the world. 1845.

TUTTON, Alfred Edwin Howard
The high Alps: a natural history of ice and snow.
1931.

TUTTON, Alfred Edwin Howard
The natural history of ice and snow. 1927.

WIELEITNER, H
Schnee und Eis der Erde. 1913.

016.3 Avalanches

ATWATER, Montgomery M
The avalanche hunters. 1968.

BORDE, Josef
Achtung Lawine! Ratschläge und Hilfsmittel. 5.
verm. und verb. Aufl. 1946.

BORDE, Josef
Berge und Schnee [und] Achtung Lawine: Ratschlage
und Hilfsmittel. 8.verb. Aufl. 1952.

BUCHER, Edwin
Beitrag zu den theoretischen Grundlagen des
Lawinenverbaus. 1948.

COAZ, J
Die Lawinen der Schweizeralpen. 1881.

COAZ, J
Statistik und Verbau der Lawinen in den
Schweizeralpen. 1910.

FLAIG, Walther
Lawinen! Abenteuer und Erfahrung, Erlibnis und
Lehre. 1935.

- - 2. vollständig neubearb. Aufl. 1955.

FRASER, Colin
The avalanche enigma. 1966.

FRASER, Colin
[The avalanche enigma]. L'enigma delle valanghe.
1970.

FRASER, Colin
Avalanches and snow safety. 1978.

PAULCKE, Wilhelm
Lawinengefahr, ihre Entstehung und Vermeidung:
eine Darlegung für Bergsteiger und Skiläufer.
1926.

016.3 Avalanches (Cont.)
PERLA, Ronald I   and MARTINELLI, M
    Avalanche handbook. 1976.

TUSHINSKII, G   K
    Laviny: vizniknovenie i zashchita ot nikh. 1949.

UNITED STATES. Department of Agriculture, Forest
Service
    Avalanche handbook. 1953.

WECHSBERG, Joseph
    Avalanche. 1958.

ZDARSKY, Mathias
    Beiträge zur Lawinenkunde. [1929].

016.4 Earthquakes

MONTESSUS DE BALLORE, Fernand, comte de
    La science séismologique: les tremblements de
    terre. 1907.

MONTESSUS DE BALLORE, Fernand, comte de
    La sismologie moderne: les tremblements de terre.
    1911.

MONTESSUS DE BALLORE, Fernand, comte de
    Les tremblements de terre: géographie séismo-
    logique. 1906.

017 Climate, weather

BERNDT, Gustav
    Der Alpenföhn in seinem Einfluss auf Natur- und
    Menschenleben. 1886.

BERNDT, Gustav
    Der Föhn: ein Beitrag zur orographischen Meteo-
    rologie und comparativen Klimatologie. 1886.

DOVE, H   W
    Der Schweizer Fön: Nachtrag zu Eiszeit, Föhn und
    Scirocco. 1868.

DOVE, H   W
    Über Eiszeit, Föhn und Scirocco. 1867.

HOEK, Henry
    Wetter, Wolken, Wind: ein Buch für jedermann. 1926.

HOEK, Henry
    Wetterkunde. [1945].

MYRBACH, Otto
    Wanderers Wetterbuch: Einführung in das Verständ-
    nis der Wettervorgänge. [1931].

SCHMID, Walter
    Wetter: praktische Winke zur Wettervoraussage.
    [1904].

STREIFF-BECKER, R
    Altes und Neues über den Glarner-Föhn. 1930.

UNWIN, David J
    Mountain weather for climbers. 1978.

02 BIOLOGICAL SCIENCES

022 Anthropology, human geography

BLACHE, Jules
    L'homme et la montagne. 1933.

MESSNER, Reinhold
    Vita fra le pietre: popoli montanari nel mondo,
    prima che soccombano. 1976.

TROYON, Frédéric
    Habitations lacustres des temps anciens et
    modernes. 1860.

023 Agriculture, animal husbandry

STEBLER, F   G
    Alp- und Weidewirtschaft: ein Handbuch für Vieh-
    züchter und Alpwirte. 1903.

024 Natural history - general

BIESE, Alfred
    The development of the feeling for nature in the
    middle ages and modern times. 1905.

MICHELET, Athénaïs
    Nature; or, The poetry of earth and sea. 1872.

RUSKIN, John
    Deucalion: collected studies of the lapse of waves,
    and life of stones. 1879-80. 2v. in 1.

THOMSON, J   Arthur
    Mountain and moorland. 1921.

025 Fauna

BRITISH MUSEUM (NATURAL HISTORY)
    Checklist of Palaearctic and Indian mammals 1758
    to 1946, by J.R. Ellerman and T.C.S. Morrison-
    Scott. 1951.

KELLER, C
    Im Hochgebirge: tierographische Charakterbilder.
    [1911].

WOLF, Joseph
    The life and habits of wild animals; illustrated
    by designs by Joseph Wolf. 1874.

026 Flora

ENGLER, A
    Monographie der Gattung Saxifraga L., mit be-
    sonderer Berücksichtigung der geographischen
    Verhältnisse. 1872.

GOMIS, Cels
    Botánica popular, ab gran nombre de confrontacions.
    1891.

POLUNIN, Oleg
    The concise flowers of Europe. 1972.

PONA, Giovanni
    Monte Baldo descritto da Giovanni Pona, Veronese,
    in cui si figurano & descrivono molte rare piante...
    1617.

READER'S DIGEST
    Guide des plantes sauvages en couleurs. 1969.

027 Alpine gardens, gardening

CLARK, W   A
    Alpine plants: a practical method for growing the
    rarer and more difficult alpine flowers. 1901.

CORREVON, Henry
    Les plantes des Alpes. 1885.

CORREVON, Henry
    Les plantes des montagnes et des rochers: leur
    acclimatation et leur culture dans les jardins.
    1914.

HULME, F   Edward
    That rock-garden of ours. 1909.

MANSFIELD, T   C
    Alpines in colour and cultivation. Rev. ed.
    1945 (1947 reprint).

METHUEN, A
    An alpine ABC and list of easy rock plants. 1922.

027 Alpine gardens... (Cont.)

ROBINSON, W
Alpine flowers for English gardens. 1870.

- - New ed., rev. 1875.

ROBINSON, W
Alpine flowers for gardens: rock, wall, marsh
plants, and mountain shrubs. 4th ed., rev. 1910.

SCHACHT, Wilhelm
[Der Steingarten und zeine Welt]. Rock gardens
and their plants. 1963.

WRIGHT, Walter P
Alpine flowers and rock gardens. [1910?].

03 APPLIED SCIENCES

031 Medical aspects, research, survival

BARCROFT, Joseph
The respiratory function of the blood. Pt.1.
Lessons from high altitudes. [2nd ed.]. 1925.

BRATHAY EXPLORATION GROUP
Expedition medicine: a planning guide, by R.N.
Illingworth. 1976.

BRITISH-INDIAN-NEPALESE SERVICES HIMALAYAN
EXPEDITION, 1960
Oxygen report. 1960.

COLLOQUE MÉDECINE & HAUTE MONTAGNE, Grenoble, 1976
Colloque ... organisé sous la présidence du prof.
Tanche dans le cadre de la Commission médicale de
la Fédération Française de la Montagne. [1977].

DILL, David Bruce
Life, heat, and altitude: physiological effects of
hot climates and great heights. 1938.

EDHOLM, O   G   and BACHARACH, A   L
Exploration medicine, being a practical guide for
those going on expeditions. 1965.

HARTMANN, G
Alpiner Hochleistungstest: eine interdisziplinäre
Studie. 1973.

HILLARY, Sir Edmund and DOIG, Desmond
High in the thin cold air. 1963.

Höhenklima und Bergwanderungen in ihrer Wirkung auf
den Meschen: Ergebniss experimenteller Forschungen
im Hochgebirge und Laboratorium, von N. Zuntz [and
others]. 1906.

JOURNÉE MÉDICALE DE LA MONTAGNE, Paris, Bordeaux, 1944
Médicine et montagne: compte-rendu de la Journée
médicale de la montagne organisée par le Club Alpin
Français. [1945?].

JUNGFRAUJOCH SCIENTIFIC STATION
Hochalpine Forschungsstation Jungfraujoch...
Internationale Stiftung. 1931.

LABORATORII SCIENTIFICI "A. MOSSO" SUL MONTE ROSA
Travaux [des années 1903-1911]. 1904-1912.

LUCAS, E   V
Outposts of mercy: the record of a visit ... to
the various units of the British Red Cross in
Italy. 1917.

MERRILL, W   K
The survival handbook. 1972.

MINELLE, Pierre
Le climat de montagne et l'ensoleillement, le ski
de compétition: leurs effets physiologiques. 1927.

MOSSO, Angelo
Fisiologia dell'uomo sulle Alpi: studi fatti sul
Monte Rosa. 1897.

MOSSO, Angelo
[Fisiologia dell'uomo sulle Alpi]. Life of man on
the high Alps. 1898.

Mountain medicine and physiology: proceedings of a
symposium for mountaineers, expedition doctors and
physiologists, sponsored by the Alpine Club. 1975.

PERU HIGH-ALTITUDE COMMITTEE
Observations upon the effect of high altitude on
the physiological processes of the human body,
carried out in the Peruvian Andes, chiefly at
Cerro de Pasco. 1923.

RIVOLIER, Jean
Expéditions françaises à l'Himalaya: aspect
médical. 1959.

RIVOLIER, Jean
Médicine et montagne. 1956.

ROGET, F   F
Altitude and health. 1919.

RYN, Zdzisław
Medycyna i alpinizm. 1973.

SCHWEIZERISCHE STIFTUNG FÜR ALPINE FORSCHUNGEN
The first ten years. 1951.

SCHWEIZERISCHE STIFTUNG FÜR ALPINE FORSCHUNGEN
Schweizerische Stiftung für Alpine Forschungen
1939 bis 1970. 1972.

WARD, Michael
Mountain medicine: a clinical study of cold and
high altitude. 1975.

WATSON, G   C
Hints for pedestrians, practical and medical.
New ed. 1862.

WHERRY, George
Alpine notes & the climbing foot. 1896.

WILKERSON, James A
Medicine for mountaineering. 2nd ed. 1975 (1978
reprint).

031.1 Acclimatisation, physical fitness

HOOLE, Henry
Das Trainieren zum Sport: ein Handbuch für Sportsleute jeder Art. 1899.

PRUSIK, Karl
Gymnastik für Bergsteiger. [1926].

UNITED STATES. School of Aviation Medicine
Operation Everest. 1946.

031.2 Safety precautions, hazards

DEUTSCHER ALPENVEREIN
Sicherheitskreis im DAV: Ausschuss für Sicherheit
am Berg, Tätigkeitsbericht 1969-1970. 1971.

KAMMER FÜR ARBEITER UND ANGESTELLTE FÜR SALZBURG
Sicherung vor Berggefahren. [1967?].

KAPRUNER GESPRÄCH, 1968
Bericht. 1968.

KÖHLER, Max
Gefahren und erste Hilfe in den Bergen. 1928.

MASON, B   R
Safety in the mountains: a handbook for trampers,
skiers, stalkers and mountaineers. 5th ed. 1963.

NIESNER, Hans
Die alpinen Gefahren, ihre Verhütung und Bekämp-
fung. 1926.

PAULCKE, Wilhelm
[Die Gefahren der Alpen]. Hazards in mountaineering; [rev. by] Helmut Dumler. 1973.

031.2 Safety precautions... (Cont.)

PAULCKE, Wilhelm
  Gefahrenbuch des Bergsteigers und Skiläufers.
  1942.

PLAS Y BRENIN NATIONAL MOUNTAINEERING CENTRE
  Safety on mountains. 1962.

- - 7th ed. 1968
- - 8th ed. 1972.

ZSIGMONDY, Emil
  Die Gefahren der Alpen.
  Various editions.

ZSIGMONDY, Emil
  [Die Gefahren der Alpen...]. Les dangers dans la
  montagne. 1886.

031.4 Diseases, mountain sickness, hypothermia

BHATTACHARJYA, Bidypati
  Mountain sickness. 1964.

BRITISH MOUNTAINEERING COUNCIL. Safety Sub-Committee
  Mountain hypothermia. 1972.

GALLAY, Marcel
  Une tragique aventure au Mont-Blanc: le traversée
  hivernale des Aiguilles du Diable du 7 au 15
  février 1938: [étude médicale sur les congéla-
  tions]. 2e éd. [1940].

LONGSTAFF, Tom George
  Mountain sickness and its probable causes. 1906.

PENBERTHY, Larry
  Acute mountain sickness - Type R, including suggestions on climbing Mt. Rainier. 1977.

SPEER, Stanhope T
  On the physiological phenomena of the mountain
  sickness, as experienced in the ascent of the
  higher Alps. 1853.

031.5 First aid

BERNHARD, Oscar
  Die erste Hilfe bei Unglücksfällen im Hochgebirge,
  für Bergführer und Touristen. 5. verm. und verb.
  Aufl. 1913.

BERNHARD, Oscar
  [Die erste Hilfe ...]. First aid to the injured,
  with special reference to accidents occuring in
  the mountains. 1896.

BÜRLI, J
  Taschenbuch für die erste Hülfe bei Unglücksfällen
  und Erkrankungen, mit besonderer Berücksichtigung
  der Krankenpflege. 1903.

FIRST AID COMMITTEE OF MOUNTAINEERING CLUBS
  First aid: North Wales, Lake District, Scotland.
  1938.

NEUFFER, Hans
  Erste Hilfe in den Bergen: ein Taschenbuch für den
  Bergsteiger. [1931].

STEELE, Peter
  Medical care for mountain climbers. 1976.

THOMPSON, C J S
  "The best thing to do": first aid in simple ailments & accidents, for travellers and tourists, at
  home and abroad. [ca 1905].

031.6 Mountain rescue techniques and equipment

DEUTSCHER UND ÖSTERREICHISCHER ALPENVEREIN
  Alpines Rettungswesen. 1926.

FÉDÉRATION FRANÇAISE DE LA MONTAGNE
  Secourisme en montagne. 1969.

FÉDÉRATION FRANÇAISE DE LA MONTAGNE
  Le secours en montagne de France. 1960.

- - 2e éd. 1967.

GREAT BRITAIN. Air Ministry
  Mountain rescue: training handbook for mountain
  rescue teams. 1953.

KROPF, Ferdinand Aloizovich
  Spasatel'n'ye raboty v. gorakh. 1966.

MACINNES, Hamish
  International mountain rescue handbook. 1972.

MARINER, Wastl
  Neuzeitliche Bergrettungstechnik. 1959.

MARINER, Wastl
  [Neuzeitliche Bergrettungstechnik]. Mountain
  rescue techniques. 1963.

MOUNTAIN RESCUE ASSOCIATION
  Mountain rescue equipment and techniques. 1967.

WEST, Lionel F
  The climber's pocket book: rock climbing
  accidents, with hints on first aid to the injured
  some uses of the rope, methods of rescue, and
  transport. [1907].

031.7 Accidents

AMRHEIN, Max
  Halt aus oder stirb! [1928].

CRAVEN, Steven A
  Some medical aspects of caving accidents.
  [1973?].

FERRAND, Henri
  L'accident de la Meidje, 20 août 1896. 1897.

GOS, Charles
  Tragédies alpestres. 1940.

- - 2e éd. 1946.

GOS, Charles
  [Tragédies alpestres]. Alpine tragedy. 1948.

MACINNES, Hamish
  Call-out. 1973.

MOFFAT, Gwen
  Two star red: a book about R.A.F. Mountain Rescue
  1964.

SAINT LOUP
  La montagne n'a pas voulu. 1949.

SANS-TERRE, Robert
  Les sensations extraordinaires: à travers les
  périls de l'Alpe. [1925].

SCHWEIZER ALPEN-CLUB. Sektion Uto
  Das Unglück an der Jungfrau vom 15 Juli 1887.
  [1887].

SKOCZLAS, Adam
  Stefano we shall come tomorrow. 1962.

SOMIS, Ignazio
  A true and particular account of the most surprising preservation, and happy deliverance of
  three women who were buried ... by a heavy fall
  of snow from the mountains, at the village of
  Bergemoletto, in Italy. 1768.

STEINER, Louis
  Mélanges alpestres. 1869.

THORINGTON, James Monroe
  The high adventure of Mr. Randall. 1945.

THORINGTON, James Monroe
  The strange death of Dr. Bean. 1945.

031.7 Accidents (Cont.)
WELCH, Ann
 Accidents happen: anticipation, avoidance,
 survival. 1978.

032 Health cures, health resorts

DONNÉ, Alphonse
 Change of air and scene: a physician's hints; with
 notes of excursions for health amongst the
 watering-places of the Pyrenees, France... 1872.

JOHNSON, James
 Changes of air; or The pursuit of health and
 recreation... 4th ed. 1837.

LEE, Edwin
 Memoranda on France, Italy, and Germany, with
 remarks on climates, medical practice, mineral
 waters... [1841].

MARCET, William
 The principal southern and Swiss health resorts,
 their climate and medical aspect. 1883.

SCHWEIZERISCHE GESELLSCHAFT FÜR BALNEOLOGIE UND
KLIMATOLOGIE
 Health resorts of Switzerland: spas, mineral
 waters, climatic resorts and sanatoria. 3rd ed.
 [ca 1925].

WISE, A T Tucker
 The alpine winter cure, with notes on Davos Platz,
 Wiesen, St. Moritz, and the Maloja. New ed. 1884.

04 TRAVEL, EXPLORATION, MOUNTAINEERING

040 World travel, exploration - general

AFLALO, F G
 Behind the ranges: parentheses of travel. 1911.

AIR FRANCE
 Vacationing in five continents. [1963].

ANSTED, D T
 Scenery, science and art, being extracts from the
 note-book of a geologist and mining engineer.
 1854.

ASHTON, John R and STOCKS, F Arnold
 The open air guide, for wayfarers of all kinds.
 1928.

BATES, Henry Walter
 Illustrated travels: a record of discovery, geography, and adventure. [1870?].

BLACKWOOD'S MAGAZINE
 Travel, adventure, and sport from Blackwood's
 magazine. Vol.4. [186-].

BLASHFORD-SNELL, John and BALLANTINE, Alistair
 Expeditions the experts' way. 1977.

BROWN, Thomas
 The reminiscences of an old traveller throughout
 different parts of Europe. 2nd ed., greatly enl.
 1835.

BUCHAN, John
 The last secrets; The final mysteries of exploration. 1923 (1925 reprint).

CAINE, W S
 A trip round the world in 1887-8. 1888.

COOKE, E W
 Leaves from my sketch-book. 1876.

Curiosities of modern travel: a year-book of adventure. 1847.

The curious traveller, being a choice collection of
 very remarkable histories, voyages, travels...
 1742.

DARWIN, Charles
 A naturalist's voyage. 1889.

DARWIN, Sir Francis Sacheverell
 Travels in Spain and the East, 1808-1810. 1927.

FRAENKEL, Peter
 Overland. 1975.

FRESHFIELD, Douglas William and WHARTON, W J L
 Hints to travellers, scientific and general.
 Various editions.

FRIEDLAENDER, Ludwig
 Darstellungen aus der Sittengeschichte Roms in der
 Zeit von August bis zum Ausgang der Antonine. 6.
 neu bearb. und verm. Aufl. 2.Theil. Das Verkehrs-
 wesen, Die Reisen der Touristen... 1889.

GALTON, Francis
 The art of travel; or, Shifts and contrivances
 available in wild countries.
 Various editions.

GALTON, Francis
 Vacation tourists and notes on travel in 1860,
 [1861, 1862-3]. 1861-64. 3v.

Half hours in many lands. [ca 1880].

HALL, Marshall
 The cruise of the Norna. 1871.

HARVARD TRAVELLERS CLUB
 Handbook of travel. 1917.

HERRENSCHWAND, colonel and JACOT-GUILLARMOD, Charles
 Étude du terrain, lecture des cartes, reconnaissances et croquis. 2e éd. 1925.

HOWELL, James
 Instructions for forreine travell, 1642; collated
 with the 2nd ed. of 1650. 1868.

JOHNSTON, Hugh
 Travel films, being pen pictures of Europe.
 [19--].

KALTBRUNNER, D
 Aide-mémoire du voyageur: notions générales de
 géographie mathématique ..., à l'usage des
 étudiants et des gens du monde. 1881.

KALTBRUNNER, D
 Manuel du voyageur. 1879.

LEMPRIERE, William
 A tour from Gibralter to Tangier, Sallee, Mogodore,
 Santa Cruz, Tarudant, and thence over Mount Atlas
 to Morocco... 1791.

LEWIS, A G
 Sport, travel and adventure. 1915.

LINDAU, Paul
 Im Fluge: gelegentliche Aufzeichnungen. 2.Aufl.
 [1886?].

LINDNER, Werner
 Vom Reisen und Wandern in alter und neuer Zeit.
 1921.

MIDDLETON, Dorothy
 Victorian lady travellers. 1965.

MUSGROVE, Charles D
 Holidays and how to use them. 1914.

PHILLIPS, Sir Richard
 A collection of modern and contemporary voyages and
 travels. 1805-06. 3v.

PIMLOTT, J A R
 The Englishman's holiday: a social history. 1947.

POCOCKE, Richard
 A description of the East, and some other countries.
 1743-45. 2v. in 3.

040 World travel... (Cont.)

PRITCHARD, Henry Baden
Beauty spots of the continent. 1875.

ROYAL GEOGRAPHICAL SOCIETY
The RGS archives: a handlist. Pt.1 compiled by
Christine Kelly. [1975].

Scenes of modern travel and adventure. 1848.

SETON-KARR, Heywood W
Ten years travel & sport in foreign lands; or,
Travels in the eighties. 2nd ed. 1890.

SYKES, Sir Percy
A history of exploration from the earliest times
to the present day. 2nd ed., (rev.). 1935.

TROLLOPE, Anthony
Travelling sketches. 1866.

WILKES, Charles
Narrative of the United States exploring expedition, during the years 1838, 1839, 1840, 1841,
1842. 1852. 2v.

WILMSEN, F   P
Merkwürdige Bergreisen, Seefahrten und Abentheuer
unserer Zeit, Der Jugend lehrreich. [1823].

041 Mountaineering - general

AFLALO, F   G
The sports of the world. 1903.

ALDEBERT, Max
Conquète de la haute montagne. 1947.

ALPINE CLUB
Peaks, passes, and glaciers.
All series and editions.

BAUMGARTNER, Heinrich
Tausend Höhenangaben. 3.Aufl. 1892.

Bergsteigen: Festschrift des Österreichischen
Alpenklubs zu seiner Hundert-Jahr-Feier, 1878-1978.
1979.

BUELER, William M
Mountains of the world: a handbook for climbers &
hikers. 1977.

BYLES, Marie Beuzeville
By cargo boat & mountain: the unconventional experiences of a woman on tramp round the world.
1931.

CLARK, Ronald William
The splendid hills: the life and photographs of
Vittorio Sella, 1859-1943. 1948.

CLEARE, John
Mountains. 1975.

COLLIE, John Norman
Climbing on the Himalaya and other mountain ranges.
1902.

COLLOMB, Robin Gabriel
A dictionary of mountaineering. 1957.

CONGRÈS INTERNATIONAL DE L'ALPINISME, Paris, 1900
Compte rendu. 1902.

CONGRÈS INTERNATIONAL DE L'ALPINISME, Monaco, 1920
Congrès de Monaco. 1921. 2v. in 1.

[Encyclopaedia of world mountains]. 1971.
In Japanese.

FRESHFIELD, Douglas William.
Below the snow line. 1923.

FRISON-ROCHE, Roger
Les montagnes de la terre. 1964. 2v.

GARDINIER, Jean Paul
La montagne. 1961.

GAROBBIO, Aurelio
Il grande libro delle montagne. 1976.

GREGORII, Johann Gottfried
Die curieuse Orographia, oder, Accurate
Beschreibung derer berühmtesten Berge, in Europa,
Asia, Africa und America. 1715.

HERZOG, Maurice
La montagne. 1956.

HOEK, Henry
Die Aussicht vom Berge. [1944].

HUXLEY, Anthony
Standard encyclopedia of the world's mountains.
1962.

Im Kampf um den Berg: spannende Berglebnisse. 1934.

JAPAN WALKING CLUB
Sangaku-bi (mountain beauty): a collection of
photos, narratives, descriptions and poems, with
a list of the principal mountains in Japan. 1922.
In Japanese.

- - Supplement.

JONAS, Rudolf
Frohsein Sonne und die schöne weite Welt. 1949.

LEWIN, Walter Henry
Climbs. [1933].

MAIR, Kurt
Der Mensch am Berg. 1935.

MILNE, Malcolm
The book of modern mountaineering. 1968.

Mountain climbing, by Edward L. Wilson [and others].
1897.

NOYCE, Wilfrid and MCMORRIN, Ian
World atlas of mountaineering. 1969.

PFANN, Hans
Führerlose Gipfelfahrten in den Hochalpen, dem
Kaukasus, dem Tian-Schan und den Anden. 1941.

PLATT, William
The joy of mountains. 1921.

RÉBUFFAT, Gaston
[Du Mont Blanc à l'Himalaya]. Mont Blanc to
Everest. 1956.

RÉBUFFAT, Gaston
Les horizons gagnés. 1975.

RÉBUFFAT, Gaston
[Les horizons gagnés]. Gli orizzonti conquistati.
1976.

REES, Ioan Bowen
Mynyddoedd: ysgrifau a cherddi. 1975.

SCHÄFER, Raimund
Hochtouren in den Alpen, Spanien, Nordafrika,
Kalifornien und Mexico. 1903.

SCHWEIZERISCHE STIFTUNG FÜR ALPINE FORSCHUNGEN
The first ten years Swiss Foundation for Alpine
Research. 1951.

SCHWEIZERISCHE STIFTUNG FÜR ALPINE FORSCHUNGEN
Schweizerische Stiftung für Alpine Forschungen
1939 bis 1970. 1972.

SMYTHE, Frank S
Behold the mountains: climbing with a color camera.
1949.

SMYTHE, Frank S
The mountain scene. 1937.

SMYTHE, Frank S
Mountains in colour. 1949.

041 Mountaineering - general (Cont.)

SMYTHE, Frank S
 Peaks and valleys. Adam & Charles Black, 1938.

SMYTHE, Frank S
 Snow on the hills. 1946.

UNSWORTH, Walter
 Encyclopaedia of mountaineering. 1975.

WEST-ALPEN-CLUB
 Bergkameraden: Mitglieder des W.A.C. erzählen.
 1939.

WYATT, Colin
 The call of the mountains. 1952.

YAMAKEI COLOR DELUXE
 Mountains of the world. 1975.

042 Mountaineering - introduction to

ABRAHAM, George Dixon
 The complete mountaineer. 1907.

- - 2nd ed. 1908.

ABRAHAM, George Dixon
 Modern mountaineering. 1933.

- - 2nd ed. 1945.
- - 3rd ed., rev. 1948.

AMIGUET, Philippe
 Technique et poésie de la montagne. 1936.

ANUFRIKOV, M   I
 Sputnik al'pinista. 1970.

BANKS, Mike
 Mountaineering for beginners. 1977.

BURLINGHAM, Frederick
 How to become an alpinist. [1916?].

COLLINS, Francis Arnold
 Mountain climbing. 1924.

DAUZAT, A   and LOUDEMER
 En vacances: plaisirs & curiosités de la montagne,
 par A. Dauzat; Peche & chasse au bord de la mer,
 par Loudemer. 1909.

DENT, Clinton Thomas
 Mountaineering. 1892.

- - 2nd ed. 1892.
- - 3rd ed. 1900.

DENT, Clinton Thomas
 [Mountaineering]. Hochtouren: ein Handbuch für
 Bergsteiger. 1893.

DEVIES, Lucien and TERRAY, Lionel
 Joies de la montagne. 1965.

DISLEY, John
 Expedition guide, Duke of Edinburgh's Award: the
 scheme for boys. 1965 (1966 reprint).

EVANS, Sir Charles
 On climbing. 1956.

HENRY, J
 Alpinisme. 1925.

KIRKUS, Colin F
 "Let's go climbing!" 1941.

LEFEBURE, Charles
 Mes étapes d'alpinisme. 1904.

- - 2e éd. 1904.

MCMORRIS, William Bruce
 The real book of mountaineering. 1961.

MAUND, J   Oakley
 Mountaineering.
 (In Morgan, W.A. The "House" on sport. 1898)

RAEBURN, Harold
 Mountaineering art. 1920.

SCHMITT, Fritz
 Der Bergsteiger von heute. 1937.

SMITH, George Alan
 Introduction to mountaineering. New and rev. ed.
 1967.

SOHN, Kyongsuk
 Introduction to mountaineering: method and
 technique. 1962.
 In Korean.

SPENCER, Sydney
 Mountaineering. 1934.

STYLES, Showell
 Introduction to mountaineering. [1954].

STYLES, Showell
 Rock and rope. 1967.

WESTMORLAND, Rusty
 Adventures in climbing. 1964.

WILSON, Claude
 Mountaineering. 1893.

YOUNG, Geoffrey Winthrop
 Mountain craft. 1920.

- - 5th ed. 1946.
- - 7th ed., rev. 1949.

YOUNG, Geoffrey Winthrop
 [Mountain craft]. Die Schule der Berge. 1925.

ZDARSKY, Mathias
 Das Wandern im Gebirge. 1925.

043 Mountaineering manuals, - 1950

ABRAHAM, George Dixon
 First steps to climbing. 1923.

BALL, John
 Hints and notes practical and scientific for
 travellers in the Alps. New ed. 1899.

BARFORD, John Edward Quintus
 Climbing in Britain. 1946.

BAUDINO, Carlo
 Manuale popolare dell'alpinista. 1931.

BENSON, Claude Ernest
 British mountaineering. 1909.

- - 2nd ed., rev. and enl. 1914.

BONER, Charles
 Guide for travellers in the plain and on the
 mountain. [1866].

- - 2nd ed. 1876.

BROCHEREL, Giulio
 Alpinismo. 1898.

BRODBECK, E
 L'alpinisme: guide pratique. 1933.

BRUNNING, Carl
 Rock climbing and mountaineering. [1936].

- - New and rev. ed. 1946.

CASELLA, Georges
 L'alpinisme. 1913.

CHABOD, Renato and GERVASUTTI, Giusto
 Alpinismo. 1935.

CLUB ALPIN FRANÇAIS
 Manuel d'alpinisme. 1904.

- - [Nouv. éd.]. 1934. 2v.

043 <u>Mountaineering manuals</u> (Cont.)

CLUB ALPINO ITALIANO
  Manuale della montagna. 1939.

CLUB ALPINO ITALIANO. <u>Comitato Scientifico</u>
  Manualetto di istruzioni scientifiche per alpinisti.
  1934.

DEBELAKOVA, M   M
  Plezalna tehnika. 1933.

DEUTSCHER UND ÖSTERREICHISCHER ALPENVEREIN
  Anleitung zur Ausübung des Bergführer-Berufes.
  3.Aufl. 1896.

- - 4.Aufl. 1906.

ENZENSPERGER, Ernst
  Bergsteigen. [1924].

FISCHER, Hans
  In die Berge: ein Lehr- und Leitbuch für reifere
  Jugend. 1927.

FLAIG, Walther
  Eistechnik des Bergsteigers in Bildern und Merkworten. 2.Aufl. 1925. 4v.

FLAIG, Walther
  Felsklettern in Bildern und Merkworten. 1924.
  2v.

GOTTELAND, Jean
  Manuel d'alpinisme scolaire. 1921.

GRETSCHMANN, Emil
  Der Felsgeher und seine Technik. [1923].

HENDERSON, Kenneth Atwood
  The American Alpine Club's handbook of American
  mountaineering. 1942.

HINTERBERGER, Fritz
  Bergsteigerschule. [1936].

HOFERER, Erwin
  Bergsteigen im Winter. [1935].

HOFMEIER, Walter
  Bergsteigen im Winter. 1925.

ITTLINGER, Josef
  Führerloses Bergsteigen: das Gehen auf Fels, Schnee
  und Eis. [1922].

ITTLINGER, Josef
  Handbuch des Alpinismus. [1913].

KAZAKOVA, Elena Alekseevna
  Tekhnika strakhovki v gorakh. 1950.

KEHLING, Johannes
  Im Hochgebirge: ein Büchlein für Alpenwanderer und
  Bergsteiger. 3.Aufl. [1926].

MADUSCHKA, Leo
  Neuzeitliche Felstechnik. 2.Aufl. [1932].

MADUSCHKA, Leo
  [Neuzeitliche Felstechnik]. Le technique moderne
  du rocher. 1948.

MADUSCHKA, Leo
  Die Technik schwerster Eisfahrten. 2.Aufl. [1932].

MALEINOV, A   A   and TUSHINSKII, G   K
  Puteshevstvie v gorakh. 1950.

MEURER, Julius
  Katechismus für Bergsteiger...1892.

NIEBERL, Franz
  Das Gehen auf Eis und Schnee. 1923.

NIEBERL, Franz
  Das Klettern im Fels. 1909.

- - 6. verm. Aufl. 1926.

NIEDERMAYR, F
  Der Hochtourist: ein Handbuch für Anfänger. 1908.

PALMER, William Thomas
  The complete hill walker, rock climber and cave
  explorer. 1934.

PAYOT, Paul
  La connaissance de la montagne, texte et photos
  de Paul Payot. 1944.

PEACOCKE, Thomas Arthur Hardy
  Mountaineering. 1941.

- - 3rd ed. 1953.

PILKINGTON, Charles
  Mountaineering without guides. 1896.

PIZZI, Giovanni
  Alpinismo. 1926.

POURCHIER, M   and FRENDO, Édouard
  La technique de l'alpinisme. 1943.

PRUSIK, Karl
  Ein Wiener Kletterlehrer. 1929.

ROESSEL, Albin
  Sportliches Bergsteigen. 1922.

RUDATIS, Domenico
  Das Letzte im Fels. 1936.

SCHWARZ, F   W
  Kleiner Ratgeber des Alpenwanderers... [1906].

SCHWEIZER ALPEN-CLUB
  [Bergsteigen]. Mountaineering handbook: a
  complete and practical guide for beginner or
  expert; published for the Association of British
  Members of the Swiss Alpine Club. 1950.

SCHWEIZER ALPEN-CLUB
  Manuel d'alpinisme. 1943.

SCHWEIZER ALPEN-CLUB. <u>Sektion Uto</u>
  Ratgeber für Bergsteiger. 1916. 2v.

- - 2. verb. und verm. Aufl. 1920.

SCHWEIZER ALPEN-CLUB. Sektion Uto
  [Ratgeber für Bergsteiger]. Le conseiller de
  l'ascensionniste. Vol.2. Technique de l'alpinisme.
  1918.

SCHWEIZER ALPEN-CLUB. <u>Sektion Uto</u>
  Technique de l'alpinisme. [1932].

SCHWEIZER ALPEN-CLUB. <u>Sektion Uto</u>
  [Technique de l'alpinisme]. The technique of
  alpine mountaineering. [1935].

WEDDERBURN, Ernest Alexander Maclagan
  Alpine climbing on foot and with ski. [1936].

- - 2nd rev. ed., revised by C. Douglas Milner.
  1954.

044 <u>Mountaineering manuals, 1951</u> -

ALLAIN, Pierre
  L'art de l'alpinisme. 1956.

AMY, Bernard
  Technique de l'alpinisme. 1977.

BLACKSHAW. Alan
  Mountaineering, from hill walking to alpine
  climbing. 1965.

- - Rev. ed. 1970.

CHEREPOV, Ivan Aleksandrovich
  Obuchenie al'pinistov... 1957.

044 Mountaineering manuals (Cont.)

CHEROPOV, Ivan Aleksandrovich
   Pamiatka nachinaiushchego al'pinista. 1955.

CHOUINARD, Yvon
   Climbing ice. 1978.

DEL ZOTTO, Giancarlo
   [Alpinismo moderno]. Alpinisme moderne. 1971.

DISLEY, John
   Tackle climbing this way. 1959.

FEDERACIÓN ESPAÑOLA DE MONTAÑISMO
   Alta montana normas. 1960.

FRANCE. Secrétariat d'état à la guerre
   Instruction sur la pratique de l'alpinisme et du
   ski. 1953.

FRANCIS, Godfrey
   Mountain climbing. 1958.

GREENBANK, Anthony
   Climbing, canoeing, ski-ing and caving. 1964.

GREENBANK, Anthony
   Instructions in mountaineering. 1967.

GREENBANK, Anthony
   Instructions in rock climbing. 1963.

HECKMAIR, Anderl
   Bergsteigen für Anfänger und Fortgeschrittene.
   1975.

HOHLE, Per
   Til fjells med tau og isøks. 1973.

KEMPF, Bertrand
   Guide pratique de la montagne. 1962.

KUZ'MIN, Nikolai Ivanovich and RUKODEL'NIKOV, Boris
Leonidovich
   Obuchenie al'pinistov. 1965.

LOUGHBOROUGH COLLEGE OF EDUCATION
   Loughborough rock climbing series: programmes 1-6,
   by John Brailsford. 1969. 6v.

LOVELOCK, James
   Climbing. 1971.

MARCH, Bill
   Modern snow & ice techniques. 1974 (1976 reprint).

MESSNER, Reinhold
   The big walls: history, routes, experiences. 1978.

MESSNER, Reinhold
   The seventh grade: most extreme climbing. 1974.

MURRAY, William Hutchison and WRIGHT, Jeremiah Ernest
Benjamin
   The craft of climbing. 1964.

NOCK, Peter
   Rock climbing. 1963.

PEACOCKE, Thomas Arthur Hardy
   Mountaineering. 1941.

- - 3rd ed. 1953.

RÉBUFFAT, Gaston
   Glace, neige et roc. 1970.

RÉBUFFAT, Gaston
   [Glace, neige et roc]. On ice and snow and rock.
   1971.

RÉBUFFAT, Gaston
   [Glace, neige et roc]. Ghiaccio, neve, roccia.
   1972.

RÉBUFFAT, Gaston
   [Neige et roc]. On snow and rock. 1963.

ROBBINS, Royal
   Advanced rockcraft. 1973.

ROBBINS, Royal
   Basic rockcraft. 1971.

SCOTT, Douglas K
   Big wall climbing. 1974.

STYLES, Showell
   The Arrow book of climbing. 1967.

STYLES, Showell
   Modern mountaineering. 1964.

SUTTON, Geoffrey
   Artificial aids in mountaineering. 1962.

UNSWORTH, Walter
   The book of rock-climbing. 1968.

USMIANI, Toni
   Roccia e ghiaccio: guida tecnico-didattica.
   1954.

WEDDERBURN, Ernest Alexander Maclagan
   Alpine climbing on foot and with ski. [1936].

- - 2nd rev. ed., revised by C. Douglas Milner.
   1954.

WRIGHT, Jeremiah Ernest Benjamin
   The technique of mountaineering: a handbook of
   established methods. 1955.

- - 2nd rev. ed. 1958.
- - 3rd rev. ed. 1964.

045 Mountaineering - grading, training

045.1 Grading of climbs

INTERNATIONAL UNION OF ALPINIST ASSOCIATIONS
   UIAA climbing classification system. 1973.

045.2 Mountaineering - training

LANGMUIR, Eric
   Mountain leadership: the official handbook of
   the Mountain Leadership Training Boards of Great
   Britain. 1969.

MOUNTAINEERING ASSOCIATION
   A short manual of mountaineering training by
   W.C. Burns, F. Shuttleworth and J.E.B. Wright.
   6th ed. 1964.

ROSCOE, Don Thomas
   Mountaineering: a manual for teachers &
   instructors. 1976.

THOMAS COOK LTD.
   The Swiss School of Mountaineering.[1935].

WRIGHT, Jeremiah Ernest Benjamin
   The permanent school idea: a history of the
   progress towards a British Mountaineering Training
   School. [1963?].

045.4. Competition climbing

FEDERATSIIA AL'PINIZMA SSSR
   Skalolazanie: pravila sorevnovanii. 1968.

045.7 Military mountaineering

ALLEN, Warner
   Our Italian front. 1920.

ANGELINI, Giovanni
   La difesa della Valle di Zoldo nel 1848. 1948.

AUSTRIA. Gendarmerie. Zentraldirektion
   Alpin-Vorschrift für die österr. Bundesgendarmerie
   nebst einem Anhang über die Zentralmeldestelle für
   alpine Unfälle in Wien. [1926?].

045.7 Military mountaineering (Cont.)

BOELL, Jacques
S.E.S.: Éclaireurs-Skieurs au combat, 1940- 1944 -
1945. 1946.

BORDEAUX, P   E
À travers les Alpes militaires: quelques souvenirs.
1928.

BURTSCHER, Guido
Die Kämpfe in den Felsen der Tofana: Geschichte der
von Mai 1915 bis November 1917 heiss umstrittenen
Kampfabschnitte Travenanzes und Lagazuoi. 1933.

CZANT, Herman
Alpinismus: Massentouristik, Massenskilauf, Winter-
sport, Militäralpinistik und die 9700 Kilometer
Gebirgsfronten im Weltkrieg. 1926.

DALTON, Hugh
With British guns in Italy: a tribute to Italian
achievement. 1919.

L'étape libératrice: scène de la vie des soldats
alliés internés en Suisse; texte de G. Jaccottet
[and others]. 1918.

FIRSOFF, Valdemar Axel
Ski track on the battlefield. [1944].

FRANCE. Ministère de la Guerre
Manuel de montagne et d'alpinisme militaire. 1931.

GOS, Charles
Au point 510: notes d'un observateur. 1932.

GOS, Charles
L'autre horizon: histoire d'un volontaire suisse
de la Grande Guerre. 1931.

GOS, Charles
Généraux suisses; commandants en chef de l'Armée
Suisse de Marignan à 1914. 1932.

GOS, Charles
Le Groupe Franc de Girouc. 1942.

GOS, Charles
Sous le drapeau: récits militaires. 1918.

ITALY. Army. Corpo degli Alpini
I Verdi: cinquant'anni di storia alpina. 1872-1922.

KÄMPFEN, Peter Joseph
Freiheitskämpfe der Oberwalliser in den Jahren
1798 & 1799; mit einem Anhang der neuesten
Geschichte von Wallis. 1867.

LANGES, Gunther
Front in Fels und Eis: der Weltkrieg im Hochgebirge. 1933.

LEMPRUCH, Moritz Erwin, Freiherr von
Der König der deutschen Alpen und seine Helden
(Ortlerkämpfe 1915/1918). 1925.

LOW, Sidney
Italy in the war. 1916.

LUKAS, Hans
Der Krieg an Kärntens Grenze, 1915-1917: vom
Hochweissstein bis zum Predil: ein Erinnerungsbuch.
1938.

NAU, Norbert
Der Krieg in der Wischberggruppe: Berichte einstiger Mitkämpfer. 1937.

OBERZINER, Giovanni
Le guerre di Augusto contro i popoli alpini. 1900.
2v. in 1.

PATRONI, Alfredo
La conquista dei ghiacciai, 1915-1918. 1924.

PRICE, Julius M
Six months on the Italian Front from the Stelvio
to the Adriatic. 1917.

RENKER, Gustav
Als Bergsteiger gegen Italien. 1918.

ROCHAS, Albert de
La campagne de 1692 dans le Haut Dauphiné: documents inédits relatifs à l'histoire et à la topographie militaire des Alpes. 1874.

SCHMIDKUNZ, Walter
Der Kampf über den Gletschern: ein Buch von der
Alpenfront. 1934.

TARGA, Spartaco
La guerra di montagna e la difesa delle Alpi. 1926.

TURLETTI, Vittorio
Attraverso le Alpi: storia aneddotica delle guerre
di montagna combattutesi dal 1742 al 1748 in
difesa dell'Italia. 1897.

The war in Italy. 1916.

- - Soldier's ed. 1916.

046 Equipment

ALPINE CLUB
Catalogue of equipment for mountaineers. 1899.

ALPINE CLUB. Special Committee on Equipment for
Mountaineers
Equipment for mountaineers. 1892.

ALPINE CLUB. Special Committee on Equipment for
Mountaineers
Provisional report. 1891.

ALPINE CLUB. Special Committee on Ropes, Axes, and
Alpenstocks
Report. 1864.

ASHLEY, Clifford W
The Ashley book of knots. 1947.

BRITISH-INDIAN-NEPALESE SERVICES HIMALAYAN
EXPEDITION, 1960
Oxygen report. 1960.

BRITISH STANDARDS INSTITUTION
Nylon mountaineering ropes. 1959.

BURBERRYS (Firm)
Gabardine in peace and war. [ca 1911].

DEUTSCHER UND ÖSTERREICHISCHER ALPENVEREIN.
Sektion Bayerland
Anwendung des Seiles. 14 neubearb. Aufl. 1930.

DEUTSCHER UND ÖSTERREICHISCHER ALPENVEREIN.
Sektion Bayerland
[Anwendung des Seiles]. L'usage della corda.
1931.

FARRAR, John Percy
On ropes and knots. 1913.

HOFMANN, Egon
Die Ausrüstung für Hochturen. [1923].

MUNTER, Werner
Moderne Seilsicherung in der Experimentierphase:
zur Problematik der dynamischen Sicherungsmethoden.
1971.

READE, Herbert Vincent
Equipment for mountaineers. [1910?].

ROGET, F   F
Hints on alpine sports; with a supplement on
mountaineering and winter sports clothing. [1912].

SMUTEK, Ray
Light weight stoves for mountaineering. 1975.

TARBUCK, Kenneth
Nylon rope and climbing safety. [1961].

WROUGHTON, E   H
Concerning winter sport. [1928].

047 <u>Other mountain activities</u>

CENTRAL COUNCIL OF PHYSICAL RECREATION
  The mountain code. 1968.

HOGAN, Jim M
  Impelled into experiences: the story of the Outward
  Bound Schools. 1968.

PARKER, Terry M   and MELDRUM, Kim I
  Outdoor education. 1973.

047.1 <u>Walking</u>

ATTANOUX, J   Bernard d'
  La marche et la pratique du tourisme à pied. 2e
  éd., rev. et augm. 1913.

DISLEY, John
  Expedition guide, Duke of Edinburgh's Award: the
  scheme for boys; edited by John Disley. 1965.

HALL, Richard Watson
  The art of mountain tramping: practical hints for
  both walker and scrambler among the British peaks.
  1932.

MURRAY, Geoffrey
  The gentle art of walking. 1939.

ROBERTS, Harry
  The tramp's hand-book. 1903.

SIDGWICK, Arthur Hugh
  Walking essays. 1912.

STYLES, Showell
  Backpacking: a comprehensive guide. 1976.

047.3 <u>Camping, pioneering</u>

AMATEUR CAMPING CLUB
  The handbook of the Amateur Camping Club. [ca
  1909].

BONNAMAUX, H   and BONNAMAUX, Ch.
  Manuel pratique de camping. [1913].

CLUB ALPIN FRANÇAIS
  Manuel technique de camping et de bivouac en
  montagne. 1936.

Harper's Camping and scouting: an outdoor guide for
  American boys. 1911.

HOLDING, T   H
  The camper's handbook. 1908.

ILLINGWORTH, Frank
  Camping questions answered. 1946.

JALEK, Maria
  En campant sur l'Alpe: au-dessus de la plus haute
  route d'Europe des Aiguilles d'Arves au Gran
  Paradiso. 1937.

KEPHART, Horace
  Camping and woodcraft: a handbook for vacation
  campers and for travelers in the wilderness. New
  ed. 1922. 2v. in 1.

MILLER, Warren H
  Camp craft: modern practice and equipment. 1915.

THURMAN, John
  Fun with ropes and spars: more pioneering projects.
  2nd ed. 1964.

THURMAN, John
  Pioneering principles. 1962.

047.4 <u>Hunting</u>

ADAIR, F   E   S
  Sport in Ladakh. 1895.

ALPINUS
  La chasse alpestre en Dauphiné. 1873.

- - [New ed.]. 1925.

BAILLIE-GROHMAN, William Adolphus
  Sport in the Alps in the past and present: an
  account of the chase of the chamois, red-deer,
  bouquetin... 1896.

BAIRNSFATHER, P   R
  Sport and nature in the Himalayas. 1914.

BARNARD, M   R
  Sport in Norway, and where to find it... 1864.

BENNET, E
  Shots and snapshots in British East Africa. 1914.

BENSON, Claude Ernest
  Crag and hound in Lakeland. 1902.

BONER, Charles
  Chamois hunting in the mountains of Bavaria. 1853.

BONER, Charles
  Chamois hunting in the mountains of Bavaria and
  in the Tyrol. New ed. 1860.

BRINCKMAN, Arthur
  The rifle in Cashmere: a narrative of shooting
  expeditions in Ladak, Cashmere, Punjaub... 1862.

BURRARD, Gerald
  Big game hunting in the Himalayas and Tibet.
  1925.

BUXTON, Edward North
  Short stalks; or, Hunting camps north, south,
  east and west. 2nd ed. 1893.

CUMBERLAND, C   S
  Sport on the Pamirs and Turkistan steppes. 1895.

DARRAH, Henry Zouch
  Sport in the highlands of Kashmir... 1898.

DEMIDOFF, Elim Pavlovich, <u>Principe di San Donato</u>
  After wild sheep in the <u>Altai and Mongolia</u>. 1900.

DEMIDOFF, Elim Pavlovich, <u>Principe di San Donato</u>
  Hunting trips in the Caucasus. 1898.

DURAND, <u>Sir</u> Edward
  Rifle, rod, and spear in the East, being sporting
  reminiscences. 1911.

FRASER, <u>Sir</u> Hugh
  Amid the high hills. 1923.

GARDNER, Nora
  Rifle and spear with the Rajpoots, being the
  narrative of a winter's travel and sport in
  northern India. 1895.

GREW, J   C
  Sport and travel in the Far East. 1910.

HAUGHTON, Henry Lawrence
  Sport and folklore in the Himalaya. 1913.

HIGHTON, Hugh P
  Shooting trips in Europe and Algeria, being a
  record of sport in the Alps, Pyrenees, Norway,
  Sweden, Corsica and Algeria. 1921.

HUTCHINSON, Horace G
  Big game shooting. 1905. 2v.

J., K.C.A.
  The sportsman's vade-mecum for the Himalayas.
  1891.

047.4 Hunting (Cont.)
KELLER, F   C
    Die Gemse: ein monografischer Beitrag zur Jagd-
    zoologie. 1887.

KENNION, R   L
    Sport and life in the further Himalaya. 1910.

KINLOCH, Alexander A
    Large game shooting in Thibet, the Himalayas, and
    northern India. 1885.

KOENIGSMARCK, Hans, Graf von
    The Markhor: sport in Cashmere. 1910.

MACINTYRE, Donald
    Hindu-Koh: wanderings and wild sport on and beyond
    the Himalayas. 1899.

- - New ed. [rev.]. 1891.

MARKHAM, Fred.
    Shooting in the Himalayas. 1854.

MATHIAS, H   V
    Five weeks' sport in the interior of the Himalayas.
    ... 1865.

MELON, Pierre
    Chasseurs de chamois. [1935].

MICHIELS, Alfred
    Les chasseurs de chamois. 1860.

PHILLIPPS-WOLLEY, Clive
    Sport in the Crimea and Caucasus. 1881.

ROOSEVELT, Theodore, 1858-1919 and GRINNELL, George
Bird
    American big-game hunting: the book of the Boone
    and Crockett Club. 1893.

ROOSEVELT, Theodore, 1858-1919 and GRINNELL, George
Bird
    Hunting in many lands: the book of the Boone and
    Crockett Club. 1895.

RUNDALL, L   B
    The ibex of Sha-ping and other Himalayan studies.
    1915.

SAVORY, Isabel
    A sportswoman in India: personal adventures and
    experiences of travel in known and unknown India.
    1900.

SELOUS, Percy
    Travel and big game. 1897.

SETON-KARR, Heywood W
    Bear-hunting in the White Mountains; or, Alaska
    and British Colombia revisited. 1891.

SNAFFLE
    In the land of the Bora; or, Camp life and sport
    in Dalamatia and the Herzegovina, 1894-5-6. 1897.

STEBBING, E   P
    Stalks in the Himalaya: jottings of a sportsman-
    naturalist... 1912.

STONE, S   J
    In and beyond the Himalayas: a record of sport and
    travel in the abode of snow. 1896.

SWAYNE, H   G   C
    Through the highlands of Siberia. 1904.

TAYLOR, Neville
    Ibex shooting on the Himalayas. 1903.

TYACKE, R   H
    How I shot my bears; or, Two years' tent life in
    Kullu and Lahoul. 1893.

TYSON, T
    Trout fishing in Kulu. 2nd ed. 1941.

WARD, A   E
    The sportsman's guide to Kashmir & Ladak. 1883.

WHISTLER, Hugh
    In the high Himalayas: sport and travel in the
    Rhotang and Baralacha, with some notes on the
    natural history of that area. 1924.

WHITBREAD, S   A
    The silent hills. [19--].

WILSON, W
    A summer ramble in the Himalayas, with sporting
    adventures in the Vale of Cashmere. 1860.

047.5 Photography

ABNEY, Sir William de Wyveleslie
    The Barnet book of photography: a collection of
    practical articles by Capt. W. de W. Abney [and
    others]. 3rd ed. 1898.

CLARK, Ronald William
    The splendid hills: the life and photographs of
    Vittorio Sella, 1859-1943. 1948.

DOLLFUS-AUSSET, Daniel
    Photographies alpines, glaciers. [1893].

DOOLAARD, A   den
    Van camera, ski en propeller: filmavonturen en
    ski-onderricht in het Mont-Blanc-gebied. [1930?].

GARDNER, Arthur
    The art and sport of alpine photography. 1927.

HANKINSON, Alan
    Camera on the crags; a portfolio of early rock
    climbing photographs by the Abraham brothers.
    1975.

JASIEŃSKI, Stefan
    Bildhafte alpine Photographie. 1928.

JOHN, D   H   O
    Photography on expeditions: recommended techniques
    for difficult surroundings. 1965.

KEMP, Dennis
    Photography on expeditions.
    (In Kodak News for education, Winter '70)

LE BLOND, Elizabeth
    Hints on snow photography. 1894.

MAZEL, Anton
    Künstlerische Gebirgs-Photographie. 1903.

MILNER, Cyril Douglas
    Mountain photography: its art and technique in
    Britain and abroad. 1945.

MILNER, Cyril Douglas
    The photoguide to mountains for the backpacker and
    climber. 2nd impression. 1978.

MILNER, Cyril Douglas
    [The photoguide to mountains...]. La fotografia
    en la montana... 1980.

PFEIFFER, G
    À la montagne: croquis montagnards; suivis d'une
    notice sur la photographie à la montagne par E.
    Potterat. [1897].

STEINBRÜCHEL, Ernst
    Praktische Winke für den photographierenden
    Bergfreund. 2. neu bearb. Ausg. [1935].

TERSCHAK, Emil
    Die Photographie im Hochgebirg: Praktische Winke
    in Wort und Bild. 1900.

- - 2. durchgesehene Aufl. 1905.
- - 4.Aufl. 1921.

047.5 Photography (Cont.)

TRUTAT, Eugène
  La photographie en montagne. 1894.

WEISS, Karl
  Fotografieren und filmen im Hochgebirge. 1934.

047.6 Flying

MITTELHOLZER, Walter
  Persienflug. 1926.

SUPF, Peter
  Flieger erobern die Berge der Welt. 1956.

048 Winter sports

ABERDARE, Morys George Lyndhurst Bruce, 4th Baron
  The Lonsdale book of sporting records, 1937. 1937.

AFLALO, F   G
  The cost of sport, by the Earl of Coventry [and
  others]; edited by F.G. Aflalo. 1899.

AFLALO, F   G
  Sport in Europe. 1901.

BUCHAN, John
  Great hours in sport. 1921.

BUCHMÜLLER, Julius
  Bergsteiger- und Wintersport- Kalender, 1926.
  1926.

MORGAN, W   A
  The "House" on sport by members of the London Stock
  Exchange. 1898. 2v.

ROEFFEL, Albin
  Sportliches Bergsteigen. 1922.

Spemanns goldenes Buch des Sports: eine Hauskunde
  für jedermann. 1910.

TROLLOPE, Anthony
  British sports and pastimes. 1868.

WARMINGTON, Annie
  Sport, by one who looked on. 1910.

048.2 Ice and snow games

AKADEMISCHER TURNVEREIN GRAZ
  Zum 60. Stiftungsfest der A.T.V. Graz von 1914-
  1924. [1925].

BENSON, E   F
  Winter sports in Switzerland. 1913.

CLEAVER, Reginald
  A winter-sport book. 1911.

COOK, Theodore Andrea
  Notes on tobogganing at St. Moritz. 2nd ed., rev.
  and corr. 1896.

FENDRICH, Anton
  Les sports de la neige. 1912.

GIBSON, Harry
  Tobogganning on crooked runs. 1894.

HARSTER, Hermann
  Kampf und Sieg in Schnee und Eis: Winterolympia
  1936. 1936.

Ice sports, by Theodore Andrea Cook [and others].
  1901.

LUNN, Brian
  Letters to young winter sportsmen. 1927.

LUTHER, Carl J
  Der moderne Wintersport: ein Handbuch und Nach-
  schlagebuch für Anfänger und Sportleute. 2.Aufl.
  1912.

LYTTON, Hon. Neville
  Winter sports by Viscount Knebworth [and others];
  edited by the Hon. Neville Lytton. 1930.

MAITLAND, Harry
  The dash for winter sports. [1912].

MEURER, Julius
  Handbuch des alpinen Sport. 1882.

ÖSTERREICHISCHE BUNDESBAHNEN
  Winter sport in Austria. [ca 1905].

RANKINE, Yve M
  Winter sports do's and dont's. 1925.

ROBERTSON, Max
  Mountain panorama: a book of winter sports and
  climbing. 1955.

ROGET, F   F
  Hints on alpine sports. [1912].

ROSENOW, Hermann
  Der Wintersport: ein Handbuch. [1912].

RZIHA, Adolf
  Der Rodelsport mit Berücksichtigung der übrigen
  Schlittensporte. 1908.

SALVANESCHI, Nino
  Sports invernali: pattinaggio, slitta, bobsleigh,
  skeleton, skis. 1911.

SAMIVEL
  -10°: quatre-vingt dix images sur les sports
  d'hiver. 1933.

SYERS, Edgar and SYERS, Madge
  The book of winter sports. 1908.

TRENKER, Luis
  Berge im Schnee: das Winterbuch. 1932.

VISSER, Philips Christiaan
  Winter in de Alpen; met een hoofdstuk voor
  wintersport-beoefenaarsters door Jenny Visser-
  Hooft. 1913.

WILLIAMS, Becket
  Winter sport in Europe. 1929.

WROUGHTON, E   H
  Concerning winter sport. [1928].

048.4 Skiing

BARSIS, Max
  Bottoms up: an unreliable handbook for skiers.
  1939.

BARSIS, Max
  Ski whiz! Bottoms up, old and new. [1945].

COUTTET, Alfred
  L'enchantement du ski, [par] Alfred Couttet,
  Arnold Lunn, Emil Petersen. 1930.

DEUTSCHER UND ÖSTERREICHISCHER ALPENVEREIN
  Ski-Taschenbuch der Alpensvereinsmitglieder.
  1932.

DIETERLEN, Jacques
  Ski de printemps. 1937.

DOOLAARD, A   den
  Van camera, ski en propeller: filmavonturen en
  ski-onderricht in het Mont-Blanc-gebied. [1930?].

HOEK, Henry and RICHARDSON, E   C
  [Ski-running]. Der Ski und seine sportliche
  Benutzung. 1906.

- - 3. deutsche Aufl. 1908.
- - 4. deutsche Aufl. 1910.
- - 5. Aufl. 1911.

048.4 Skiing

HOEK, Henry
  Skiheil, Kamerad! Skikurs für eine Freundin.
  3.Aufl. 1934.

ISELIN, Christof
  Die Ski-Schaufel. 1928.

MILNE, Malcolm and HELLER, Mark
  The book of European skiing. 1966.

RICHARDSON, E   C
  Ski-running, by D.M.M. Crichton Somerville, W.R.
  Rickmers, and E.C. Richardson. 1904.

- - 2nd ed. 1905.

TEDESCHI, Renato
  Alpinismo e sci. 1930.

ZDARSKY, Mathias
  Skisport: gesammelte Aufsätze. 1909.

048.42 Skiing - history

ARCIS, C   Egmond d'
  Neiges éternelles. 1945.

DEUTSCHE SKIVERBAND
  Der Deutsche Skilauf und 25 Jahre Deutscher Skiverband. 1930.

FEDDEN, Robin
  A bibliographical note on the early literature of
  ski-ing in English. [1961].

GORNERGRAT-DERBY ZERMATT, 1950
  Liste officielle des résultats. [1950].

GUILERA I ALBINYANA, Josep María
  Carnet d'un esquiador, 1915-1930. 1931.

LUNN, Sir Arnold
  A history of ski-ing. 1927.

LUNN, Sir Arnold
  The story of ski-ing. 1952.

LUNN, Sir Arnold
  [The story of ski-ing]. Histoire du ski. 1953.

MERCIER, Joachim
  Aus der Urgeschichte des schweiz. Skilaufes;
  Jubiläums-Schrift des Ski-Club Glarus 1893-1928.
  [1928].

OESTERREICHISCHER TOURISTEN-CLUB. Skilauf-Sektion
  Skisport im Oesterr. Touring-Club. 1914.

048.43 Skiing - manuals, - 1950

ALLAIS, Émile and GIGNOUX, Paul
  Ski français. 1937.

AMSTUTZ, Walter
  Das Ski-ABC: ein Skischulfilm aus 450 Zeitlupen-
  Bildern. 1938.

AMSTUTZ, Walter
  [Das Ski-ABC]. Ski-ing from A-Z: an instructional
  film of 450 instantaneous movie photographs. 1939.

BAILLIE, G
  Ski-ing simplified for beginners. 1923.

BERNARD, G
  Guide du skieur: fabrication et théorie du ski, le
  ski dans la montagne. 1910.

BERNARD, M
  Marie-Rose; ou, Le ski sans entraves. 1931.

CAULFIELD, Vivian
  How to ski and how not to. 3rd ed., rev. 1913.

CAULFIELD, Vivian
  Ski-ing turns. 2nd ed. (rev.). 1924.

DAHINDEN, Josef
  [Die Ski-Schule]. The art of ski-ing. 1928.

D'EGVILLE, Alan Hervey
  The game of ski-ing: a book for beginners. 1936.

D'EGVILLE, Alan Hervey
  Modern ski-ing. 1927.

- - 2nd ed. 1929.

GHIGLIONE, Piero
  Lo sci e la tecnica moderna. 1928.

HALLBERG, F   and MÜCKENBRUNN, H
  Le ski par la technique moderne; avec une étude sur
  la physiologie du ski. 3e éd. 1932.

HALLBERG, F   and MÜCKENBRUNN, H
  [Le ski par la technique moderne]. The complete
  book of ski-ing. 1936.

HEINRICH, Fritz
  Manual for ski-babies. 1935.

HERMANN, André and DIETERLEN, Jacques
  Le ski pour tous: ce que tout skieur doit savoir.
  1936.

HOEK, Henry
  Merkbuch für Schiläufer in 500 Sätzen. 1921.

HOEK, Henry
  Wie lerne ich Schi-Laufen. 4.Aufl. 1911.

- - 7. umgearb. und stark erweiterte Aufl. 1917.
- - 11.Aufl. 1924.

HOEK, Henry
  [Wie lerne ich Schi-Laufen]. L'école du ski.
  1933.

HUBER, Eddie and ROGERS, Norman
  The complete ski manual: how to begin, how to
  improve, how to excel. 1949.

HUITFELDT, F
  Das Skilaufen. 1907.

LEHNER, Albert
  En ski avec Albert Lehner. 1944.

LUNN, Sir Arnold
  The complete ski-runner. 1930.

LUNN, Sir Arnold
  [The complete ski-runner]. Le ski alpin: tourisme
  et courses. 1930.

LUNN, Sir Arnold
  Ski-ing. 1913.

LUNN, Sir Arnold
  Ski-ing for beginners. 1924.

- - 2nd ed., rev. 1926.

LUNN, Peter
  A ski-ing primer. 1948.

MATTHIAS, Eugen and TESTA, Giovanni
  Natürliches Skilaufen, die Methode der einfachsten
  Fahrweise. 1936.

MATTHIAS, Eugen and TESTA, Giovanni
  [Natürliches Skilaufen]. Sciare: tecnica moderna
  semplificata e razionalizzata. 1938.

REUEL, Fritz
  Neue Möglichkeiten im Skilauf: ein Buch zur
  Förderung der Fahrtechnik. 4.Aulf. 1926.

RICHARDSON, E   C
  The 'shilling' ski-runner. 2nd ed. 1911.

RICHARDSON, E   C
  The ski-runner. [1910].

048.43 Skiing - manuals... (Cont.)
VÁVRA, Karl and BRUNNER, Richard
  Skisport: wie wir ihn betreiben. 1910.

- - 3.Aufl. 1910.

WINKLER, Max
  La nouvelle technique du ski: méthode d'enseignement collectif et d'apprentissage individuel.
  1930.

ZARN, Adolf and BARBLAN, Peter
  Der Skifahrer: Ski-Turnen und Ski-Fahrtechnik.
  1920.

ZARN, Adolf and BARBLAN, Peter
  [Der Skifahrer]. L'art du ski: gymnastique et
  technique du ski. 1922.

ZDARSKY, Mathias
  Alpine (Lilienfelder) Skifahr-Technik; eine
  Anleitung zum Selbstunterricht. 4. methodisch
  umgearb. Aufl. 1908.

048.44 Skiing - manuals, 1950 -

BEATTIE, Bob
  My ten secrets of skiing. 1968.

BONNET, Honoré
  [Ski à la française]. Ski - the experts' way.
  1966.

EVANS, Harold
  We learned to ski: [the Sunday Times tells you all
  you need to know], by Harold Evans, Brian Jackman
  and Mark Ottaway. 2nd paperback ed. 1977.

FEDDEN, Robin
  Ski-ing in the Alps. 1958.

FRANCE. Secrétariat d'état à la guerre
  Instruction sur la pratique de l'alpinisme et du
  ski. 1953.

FRANCO, Jean and MORA, Marius
  Ski de France. 1962.

GAUTHIER, Gilbert and VACHEZ, Michel
  Ski court, ski évolutif, ski sans peine. 1972.

GODLINGTON, Douglas
  Tackle ski-ing. 1973.

ISELIN, Fred and SPECTORSKY, A   G
  Invitation to skiing. 1952.

JACQUES, A
  Ski de descente (technique française). 1950.

JACQUES, A
  [Ski de descente]. Downhill skiing (the French
  technique). [1952].

JOUBERT, Georges and VUARNET, Jean
  How to ski the new French way. 1967.

JOUBERT, Georges
  Pour apprendre soi-meme à skier. 1970.

POLASEK, Ollie
  Skiing. 1960.

SAILER, Toni
  Ski with Toni Sailer. 1964.

048.45 Competition skiing, racing

D'EGVILLE, Alan Hervey
  Slalom: its technique, organisation and rules.
  1934.

INTERNATIONALER SKI-VERBAND
  Internationale Wettkampf-Ordnung für Slalom- und
  Abfahrtsrennen; beim XI. Internationalen Ski-
  Kongress in Oslo und Finse... 1930 festgesetzt.
  1930.

MINELLE, Pierre
  Le climat de montagne et l'ensoleillement, le ski
  de competition, leurs effets physiologiques.
  1927.

MITCHELL, Sir Harold P
  Downhill ski-racing. 1931.

NORGES SKIFORBUND
  Rules for ski-ing competitions. 1923.

048.47 Cross-country ski-running

ARBEZ, Victor and PORTE, Pierre
  Vos premiers pas en ski de fond. 1975.

BILGERI, Georg
  Der alpine Skilauf. 1910.

BILGERI, Georg
  [Ski-Handbuch]. Colonel Bilgeri's handbook on
  mountain skiing. 1929.

CALDWELL, Johnny
  The cross-country ski book. 1964.

FAES, Henry and MERCANTON, Paul L
  Le manuel du skieur, suivi des itinéraires re-
  commandables en Suisse occidentale. [1917].

- - 2e éd. rev. et complétée. 1925.

FANCK, Arnold and SCHNEIDER, Hannes
  Wunder des Schneeschuhs: ein System des richtigen
  Skilaufens und seine Anwendung im alpinen
  Geländelauf. 1925.

FANCK, Arnold and SCHNEIDER, Hannes
  [Wunder des Schneeschuhs]. The wonders of ski-
  ing: a method of correct ski-ing and its applications to alpine running. 1933.

FISCHER, Hans
  Abfahrten, die man gemacht haben muss: 100 schöne
  Abfahrten der Ost- und Westalpen. [1932].

FURSE, Katharine
  Ski-running. 1924.

HOEK, Henry
  Schnee, Sonne und Ski: ein Buch über den Früling
  im Hochgebirge. 1926.

HOEK, Henry
  Schussfahrt und Schwung: ein brevier alpiner
  Abfahrten. 1931.

HOFERER, Erwin
  Winterliches Bergsteigen alpine Schilauftechnik.
  1925.

KURZ, Marcel
  Alpinisme hivernal: le skieur dans les Alpes.
  1925.

KURZ, Marcel
  [Alpinisme hivernal]. Alpinismo invernale. 1928.

LUNN, Sir Arnold
  Alpine ski-ing at all heights and seasons. 2nd
  ed., rev. 1926.

LUNN, Sir Arnold
  [Alpine ski-ing...]. Le ski en hiver, au printemps, sur les glaciers. 1924.

LUNN, Sir Arnold
  The complete ski-runner. 1930.

LUNN, Sir Arnold
  [The complete ski-runner]. Le ski alpin:
  tourisme et courses. 1930.

LUNN, Sir Arnold
  Cross-country ski-ing. 1920.

048.47 Cross-country ski-running (Cont.)
LUTHER, Carl J   and LÜCKE, G   P
  Der Skitourist. 1913.

- - 2.Aufl. 1921.

MEREDITH, Brian
  Escape on skis. [1928].

PAUSE, Walter
  [Ski Heil]. Salute the skier; the hundred best
  ski runs in the Alps. 1963.

PAYNTER, Thomas
  The ski and the mountain. 1954.

PRATER, Gene
  Snowshoeing. 1974.

RICKMERS, Willi Rickmer
  Ski-ing for beginners and mountaineers. 1910.

ROEGNER, Otto
  Der Schilauf im Hochgebirge. 1924.

SKI CLUB OF GREAT BRITAIN
  Handbook on ski-touring and glacier ski-ing. 1954.

- - 2nd ed., completely rev. 1961.

SMYTHE, Frank S
  Climbs and ski runs: mountaineering and ski-ing
  in the Alps, Great Britain and Corsica. 1929.

- - Another ed. 1957.

TERRAZ, Claude
  À la découverte du ski de fond. 1972.

TRAYNARD, Claude and TRAYNARD, Philippe
  Ski de montagne, [par] Paul Beylier [and others];
  sous la direction de Claude et Philippe Traynard.
  1974.

TRAYNARD, Philippe and TRAYNARD, Claude
  Cimes et neige: 102 sommets à ski. 1971.

048.48 Regional ski-guides

AKADEMISCHER ALPEN-CLUB ZÜRICH
  Ski-Führer für die Silvretta- und Bernina-Gruppe.
  1913.

AKADEMISCHER SKICLUB MÜNCHEN
  Skiführer für das bayerische Hochland und angrenzende Gebiete. 2.Aufl. 1906.

ALLGÄUER SKIVERBAND
  Allgäuer Ski-Touren. 1913.

BIENDL, Hans and RADIO-RADIIS, Alfred von
  Schifahrten in den Ostalpen. Bd.3. Der Rhätikon
  ... 2.Aufl. 1923.

BIENDL, Hans and RADIO-RADIIS, Alfred von
  Skitouren in den Ostalpen. 1906. 3v.

BLANC, Pierre and LECOULTRE, Gérald
  Ski: 67 itinéraires détaillés. 1936.

BRESSY, M
  Itinerari sciistica di Valle Po e Valle Varaita.
  1928.

COUTTET, Alfred and FRISON-ROCHE, Roger
  63 itinéraires à ski dans la région de Chamonix
  et le massif du Mont Blanc. [19--].

DE MINERBI, Leonardo
  Formazza sciistica: itinerari. 1950.

DEUTSCHER UND ÖSTERREICHISCHER ALPENVEREIN. Sektion
Pforzheim
  Ski und Winterführer durch die Münstertaler Alpen
  und angrenzenden Gebiete. 1912.

ENTE PROVINCIALE PER IL TURISMO, Bolzano
  Skier's guide to the Dolomites, South Tyrol,
  Italy. [1957].

FEDDEN, Robin
  Alpine ski tour: an account of the High Level
  Route. 1956.

FLAIG, Walther
  Arlberg: Ski und Schnee. 1933.

FLAIG, Walther
  Silvretta-Skiführer, mit Paznaun und Montafon,
  Unterengadin und Prätigau, Ost-Rätikon und
  Verwall. 8.Aufl. 1965.

FLAIG, Walther
  Skiführer Rätikon und Bregenzerwaldgebirge mit
  Fürstentum Liechtenstein, Walgau, Grosswalsertal,
  Klostertaler Alpen. 1961.

FLAIG, Walther
  Die Skiparadiese der Schweiz. 1932.

FREI, Hermann
  Davoser Skitouren. 1919.

FREI, Hermann
  [Davoser Skitouren]. The best ski-tours of
  Davos; compiled by Henry Hoek. 1927.

FREI, Hermann and HOEK, Henry
  Ski-Touren in den Bergen um Davos. 1932.

FULTON, John Henry Westropp
  With ski in Norway & Lapland. 1911.

GUNTHER, A   E
  A week on ski among the Silvretta, February -
  March 1932. 1933.

HANAUSEK, Ernst
  Skiland zwischen Grossglockner und Rax. 1933.

HELLER, Mark
  Ski guide - Austria. 1973.

HOEK, Henry
  Ma bella Engiadina: Ski und Schnee im Engadin.
  1933.

HOEK, Henry and WALLAU, Heinrich
  Schi-Fahrten im südlichen Schwarzwald. 1908.

HOEK, Henry
  Ski-tours round Lenzerheide. 1925.

HOHENLEITNER, Siegfried
  Skiführer durch die Tuxer Vorberge. 1933.

KOLLER, Willy
  Skiführer für Zell am See mit den östlichen
  Kitzbühelern... 1932.

KURZ, Marcel
  [Walliser-Skiführer]. Guide du skieur dans les
  Alpes valaisannes... 1924-30. 3v.

LANDESVERBAND FÜR FREMDENVERKEHR, Karlsbad
  Wintersportplätze in Bömen, Mähren und Schlesien.
  [1922].

LANGES, Gunther
  Dolomiten-Skiführer. 5. verm. Aufl. 1938.

LECHNER, Sigmund and KUNTSCHER, Karl
  Skiführer durch die Ötztaler Alpen. 1925.

LECLERC, Jeanne
  Ski en Tarentaise et Maurienne; guide itinéraire.
  [1948?].

LUNN, Sir Arnold
  The Bernese Oberland. [1910]-20. 2v. (Alpine
  Ski Club guides)

LUTHER, Carl J
  Die Skiparadiese der Alpen. 1932.

MIDOWICZ, W   and AUGUSTYNOWICZ, M
  Przewodnik Narciarski po beskidzie zachodnim...
  1928.

048.48 Regional ski-guides (Cont.)

MOOSER, R   Aloys and BOURGEOIS, Max
Itinéraires pour skieurs en Haute-Savoie. 1925-29.
2v. in 1.

PASCHETTA, Vincent
Environs de Breuil; guide pour skieurs. [19--].

PASCHETTA, Vincent
Le ski dans les Alpes-Maritimes. 5e éd. 1967.

REINL, Hans
Skiführer durch das Salzkammergut. 2.Aufl. 1925.

REISCH, Franz
Skitouren um Kitzbühel. 1908.

RIDDELL, James and RIDDELL, Jeannette
Ski holidays in the Alps. 1961.

RIDDELL, James
The ski runs of Austria. 1958.

RIDDELL, James
The ski runs of Switzerland. 1957.

ROBERTS, Eric
High level route; Chamonix, Zermatt, Saas; ski
mountaineering in the Mont Blanc Range and Pennine
Alps. 1973.

ROGET, F   F
Ski-runs in the high Alps. 1913.

SCHLINK, Herbert H
Ski-ing from Kiandra to Kosciusko, July 28, 29,
30, 1927. 1927.

SCHNEESCHUHVEREIN, München
Skiführer. Bd.1. Schliersee-Bayrischzell. 1913.

SCHNEESCHUHVEREIN, München
Skiführer. Bd.2. Inntal-Chiemgau. 1914.

SCHWEIZER ALPEN-CLUB
Alpine Skitouren: eine Auswahl. 1962. 2v.

SCHWEIZERISCHER SKI-VERBAND
Offizieller Ski Tourenführer der Schweiz. 1933.

SCI CLUB MILANO
468 itinerari sciistici: dal Colle di Tenda a
S. Candido. 1932.

SEHRIG, Othmar
Skiführer durch Tirol: Wegweiser für alpine
Wintertouren. 1906.

Skiführer durch das Ost-Allgäu: Gebiet von
Wertach bis zum Hochvogel. 2.Aufl. 1935.

Skiführer durch die Ortlergruppe. 1937.

TISCHLER, Ernst and WILKE, Viktor
Skitourenführer durch die östl. Beskiden von der
Weichsel bis zur Waag... 1912.

TONELLA, Guido
Skiing at Sestrières. 1934.

TURSKY, Franz
Skiführer durch die Kitzbüheler Alpen. 1926.

05   MOUNTAINEERING PHILOSOPHY, MYTHOLOGY, ART,
MUSIC

050 Philosophy

ANDERSON, J   R   L
The Ulysses factor: the exploring instinct in man.
1970.

BARTOL, C   A
Pictures of Europe, framed in ideas. 2nd ed.
1856.

BERTRAND, E
Le Thevenon; ou, Les journées de la montagne.
1777.

- - Nouv. éd.,rev. corr.& augm. 1780.

CHATELLUS, Alain de
Alpiniste, est-ce toi? 1953.

CONFÉRENCE INTERNATIONALE DES SOCIÉTÉS DE TOURISME
ALPIN, Zakopane, 1930
Compte-rendu, protocole, rapports, résolutions.
1931.

DEUTSCHER ALPENVEREIN. Sektion Bayerland
Bergsteigen als Lebensform. 1949.

ENGEL, Claire Éliane
They came to the hills. 1952.

FAWCETT, Douglas
The Zermatt dialogues, constituting the outlines
of a philosophy of mysticism... 1931.

GESNER, Conrad
On the admiration of mountains... in 1543. 1937.

GOS, Charles
La nuit des Drus. 1929.

GRAND-CARTERET, John
La montagne à travers les ages: role joué par
elle... 1903-04. 2v.

GUITON, Paul
Le livre de la montagne: essai d'une esthétique
du paysage. 1943.

HODGKIN, Robin A
Reconnaisance on an educational frontier. 1970.

HOEK, Henry
Sport, Sporttrieb, Sportbetrieb. 1927.

LA HARPE, Charles de
Pourquoi aimons-nous la montagne? 1901.

LIND-AF-HAGEBY, L
Mountain meditations and some subjects of the day
and the war. 1917.

MAZZOTTI, Giuseppe
Trionfo della tecnica e decadenza dell'ideale:
studio su vari caratteri dell'alpinismo
dolomitico. [1932].

MEADE, Charles Francis
High mountains. 1954.

MORNET, Daniel
Le sentiment de la nature en France de J.-J.
Rousseau à Bernardin de Saint-Pierre: essai sur
les rapports de la littérature et des moeurs.
1907.

MULLER, Edwin
They climbed the Alps. 1930.

N***, comte de
Essais sur les montagnes. 1785. 2v.

NOYCE, Wilfrid
The springs of adventure. 1958.

PACKE, Charles
The spirit of travel. 1857.

RUSSELL, Henry, Count
Les pyrénées, les ascensions et la philosophie de
l'exercice. 1865.

SECRET, Jean
L'alpiniste: essai critique. 1937.

SMYTHE, Frank S
The mountain top: an illustrated anthology from
the prose and pictures of Frank S. Smythe. 1947.

050 Philosophy (Cont.)

SMYTHE, Frank S
The mountain vision. 1941.

SMYTHE, Frank S
The spirit of the hills. 1935.

SONNIER, Georges
La montagne et l'homme. 1970.

SPIRO, Louis
L'Alpe inspiratrice. 1942.

TUMA, Henrik
Pomen in razvoj alpinizma. [1930?].

VAN DYKE, John Charles
The mountain: renewed studies in impressions and
appearances. [1915].

YOUNGHUSBAND, Sir Francis
The heart of nature; or, The quest for natural
beauty. 1921.

051 Apologia

BALCH, Edwin Swift
Mountain exploration. 1893.

CLARKSON, J   R
Rock-climbing. 1941.

CLUB ALPIN FRANÇAIS. Section du Sud-Ouest
Camp du Col d'Aran, 15-25 juillet 1943: compte-
rendu. 1943.

CORONA, Guiseppe
Aria di monti. 1880.

COSTE, Jean
Âme d'alpiniste: pensées. 1929.

FRERE, Richard Burchmore
Thoughts of a mountaineer. 1952.

HOEK, Henry
Über Berge und Bergsteigen. 1920.

LAMMER, Eugen Guido
Jungborn: Bergfahrten und Höhengedanken eines
einsamen Pfadsuchers. 1922.

- - 2. stark verm. und veränderte Aufl. 1923.
- - 3.Aufl. 1929.

RICHMOND, William Kenneth
Climber's testament. 1950.

ROBERTS, David
The mountain of my fear. 1969.

SANS-TERRE, Robert
Les sensations extraordinaires: à travers les
périls de l'Alpe. [1925].

SCHUSTER, Claud, Baron Schuster
Mountaineering: the Romanes lecture. 1948.

SCHWARTZ, Myrtil
Vers l'idéal par la montagne: souvenir de mes
escalades de haute montagne en Europe et en
Amérique. 1924.

STRONG, John H
Mountaineering: a solace to sedate old age. 1949.

TOBIAS, Michael Charles
Dhaulagirideon. 1973.

TOBIAS, Michael Charles
Tsà. 1974.

WYSS-DUNANT, Édouard
L'Appel des sommets. 1931-33. 2v.

053 Psychology

GREITBAUER, Karl
Das Ganze der alpinen Idee: eine geistige Analyse
des Bergsteigens. 1973.

GREITBAUER, Karl
Dei Gestalt des Bergsteigers: das alpine Geschehen
im Lichte der Psychologie. 1956.

GREITBAUER, Karl
Das unverstandene Bergsteigen: zum geistigen
Umfeld des Bergsteigens, mit einem Beitrag zur
Verhütung der Unfälle durch subjektive Gefahren.
1977.

HESS, Adolfo
Saggi sulla psicologia dell'alpinista: raccolta
di autobiografie psicologiche di alpinisti
viventi. 1914.

ROSS, Helen E
Behaviour and perception in strange environments.
1974.

RYN, Zdzisław
Motivation and personality in high-mountain
climbing. [1978].

WILLIAMSON, C   J
The Everest "message": [letter to the editor].
(In Journal of the Society for Psychical Research,
v.48, 1976).

ZIMMERMAN, John George
Solitude. 1800-02. 2v.

054 Mythology, religion

BALLIANO, Adolfo and AFFENTRANGER, Irene
La strada à questa... 1957.

BRUNTON, Paul
A hermit in the Himalayas. [ca 1936].

CHASE, Charles H
Alpine climbers. [1888?].

HAMSA, Bhagwan
The Holy Mountain, being the story of a pilgri-
mage to Lake Mānas and of initiation on Mount
Kailās in Tibet. 1934.

PRANAVANANDA, Swami
Pilgrim's companion to the Holy Kailas and
Manasarovar. 1938.

ROERICH, Nicholas
Himalayas: abode of light. 1947.

SAMIVEL,
Hommes, cimes et dieux: les grandes mythologies
de l'altitude et la légende dorée des montagnes
à travers le monde. 1973.

055 Art

ALDEBERT, Max
Conquète de la haute montagne. 1947.

ALPINE CLUB
Alpine Club Exhibition: catalogue of a collection
of mountain paintings and photographs exhibited
at the XIXth Century Art Gallery. 1894.

ALPINE CLUB
Exhibition of Swiss coloured prints lent by
members of the Alpine Club and their friends.
1924.

BAILLIE-GROHMAN, William Adolphus
Sport in art: an iconography of sport during four
hundred years from the beginning of the fifteenth
to the end of the eighteenth centuries. [1913].

055 Art (Cont.)

BARNARD, George
The continental drawing book for the use of
advanced pupils, being views in Switzerland, the
Alps and Italian lakes. 1837.

BARNARD, George
Drawing from nature: a series of progressive
instructions in sketching ... with examples from
Switzerland and the Pyrenees... 1865.

- - New ed. 1877.

BARNARD, George
The theory and practice of landscape painting in
watercolours. New ed. 1871.

BETTEX, Gustave and GUILLON, Édouard
Les Alpes suisses dans la littérature et dans
l'art. 1915.

BREDT, E W
Die Alpen und ihre Maler. [1910].

CHRISTIE, MANSON & WOODS LTD.
Paintings, drawings and sculpture, c.1800 - c.1920,
the properties of the Alpine Club and others,
which will be sold at auction. 1965.

CHRISTOFFEL, Ulrich
La montagne dans la peinture: le Club Alpin Suisse
à ses membres a l'occasion du centenaire. 1963.

COVERLEY-PRICE, Victor
An artist among mountains. 1957.

DEUTSCHER UND ÖSTERREICHISCHER ALPENVEREIN
Lichtbilder verzeichnis. 1927-28.

- - Suppl. 1931.
- - Suppl. 1935.

DORÉ, Gustave
Des-agréments d'un voyage d'agrément. [ca 1860].

DOYLE, Richard
The foreign tour of Messrs. Brown, Jones &
Robinson. 1904.

DURGNAT-JUNOD, Clara
Pinceaux et piolet: autobiographie anecdotique.
1943.

FOSCA, François
H.-H. Newton. 1928.

GILBERT, Josiah
Cadore; or, Titian's country. 1869.

GILBERT, Josiah
Landscape in art before Claude & Salvator. 1885.

GILPIN, William
Three essays: on picturesque beauty; on picturesque
travel; and on sketching landscape... 1808.

GOS, Albert
Souvenirs d'un peintre de montagne. 1942.

GOS, Charles
Albert Gos, 1852-1942. 1942.

GOTH, Jean S
Elle et lui à la montagne, dessinés et commentés
par Jean S. Goth. 1944.

GOTH, Jean S
Elle et lui en ski, dessinés et commentés par
Jean S. Goth. 1945.

GRABER, Hans
Schweizer Maler. [1913].

HAENDCKE, Berthold
Architecture, sculpture et peinture. 1892.

HAREUX, Ernest
La Meije et les Écrins. [1907].

HOEK, Henry
Hans Beat Wieland der Mahler der Berge. 1928.

JAHN, Gustav
Gustav Jahn: ein Maler- und Bergsteigerleben.
[1931].

LEAR, Edward
Journal of a landscape painter in Corsica. 1870.

LEMAITRE, Hélène
Les pierres dans l'oeuvre de Ruskin. 1965.

LUKAN, Karl
[Alpinismus in Bildern]. The Alps and alpinism.
1968.

LUNN, Sir Arnold
The Swiss and their mountains: a study of the
influence of mountains on man. 1963.

MCCORMICK, Arthur David
An artist in the Himalayas. 1895.

MAGYAR TURISTA SZÖVETSÉG
Nemzetközi Alpin képkiállítása, Budapest, 1930
Marcius 22-Aprilis 22. 1930.

MUSÉE CANTONAL DES BEAUX-ARTS, Lausanne
5e Exposition suisse d'art alpin, organisée par
le Club Alpin Suisse. 1946.

NICOLAS, R and KLIPSTEIN, A
Die schöne alte Schweiz: die Kunst der Schweizer
Kleinmeister. 1926.

NORGATE, Edward
Miniatura; or, The art of limning; edited from
the ms. in the Bodleian Library and collated with
other mss. 1919.

ÖSTERREICHISCHER ALPENVEREIN
Alpenbilder aus 150 Jahren. 1962.

PARRY, John
Ridiculous things, scraps and oddities, some with,
and many without meaning. 1854.
Cartoons.

PASSERI, Giovanni Battista
Dissertazione epistolare ... sopra un'antica
statuetta di marmo trovata nel distretto di
Perugia. 1776.

POCOCK, Noel
Below zero: a travesty of winter sport. [1911].

ROD, Édouard
Notes sur la peinture alpestre.
(In Bibliothèque universelle... v.62, 1894)

RUSKIN, John
Modern painters. 1856-60. 5v.

SAMIVEL
Neiges: dix estampes de Samivel, d'après les
aquarelles originales. 1937.

SAMIVEL
L'opéra de pics: cinquante compositions; précédées de La réponse des hauteurs. 1945.

SAMIVEL
Sous l'oeil des choucas; ou, Les plaisirs de
l'alpinisme: quatre-vingts dessins alpins. 1932.

SCHAFFRAN, E
Hochgebirgs-Fantasien. 1924.

SPINDLER, Robert
Die Alpen in der englischen Literatur und Kunst.
1932.

STEINITZER, Alfred
Der Alpinismus in Bildern. 1913.

- - 2. ergänzte Aufl. 1924.

055 Art (Cont.)

TONNELLÉ, Alfred
Fragments sur l'art et la philosophie, suivis de notes et pensées diverses. 2e éd. 1860.

TWINING, Henry
The elements of picturesque scenery; or, Studies of nature made in travel with a view to improvement in landscape painting. 1853.

TWINING, Henry
On the elements of picturesque scenery, considered with reference to landscape painting. 1846.

TYRWHITT, R St John
A handbook of pictorial art. 1875. 2nd ed.

VILLARI, L
Giovanni Segantini: the story of his life. 1901.

WALTON, Elijah
Peaks in pen and pencil for students of alpine scenery. 1872.

057 Music

BRANTSCHEN, Gregor
Gesammelte Lieder im Volkston. [1946].

BRANTSCHEN, Gregor
Neue Volkslieder für zwei Singstimmen. 1926.

- - 3. verm Aufl. 1935.

BRAUNSTEIN, Josef
Richard Wagner and the Alps. [1929?].

JULLIEN, Louis Antoine
L'écho du Mont-Blanc: polka dedicated to his friend Albert Smith. [1853?].

Sammlung von Schweizer-Kühreihen und Volksliedern = Recueil de ranz de vaches et chansons nationales. 4. verm. u. verb. Ausg. 1826.

SCHLEIDT, Wilhelm
Triomphaler Festzug zur Erinnerung an die Einweihung der Jungfraubahn (1. Section Eigergletscher) im Juli 1898. [1898].

06 LITERATURE, LANGUAGE

060 General works

BETTEX, Gustave and GUILLON, Édouard
Les Alpes suisses dans la littérature et dans l'art. 1915.

CUNCHE, Gabriel
La renommée de A. de Haller en France: influence du poème Des Alpes sur la littérature descriptive du XVIIIe siècle. [ca 1918].

ENGEL, Claire Éliane
La littérature alpestre en France et en Angleterre aux XVIIIe et XIXe siècles. 1930.

FRIEDLAENDER. Ludwig
Ueber die Entstehung und Entwicklung des Gefühls für das Romantische in der Natur. 1873.

GAULLIEUR, J
Genève et le pays de Vaud après la mort de Voltaire et de Rousseau: commencements de l'école littéraire des physiciens et des naturalistes, et de la littérature alpestre...
(In Sur l'histoire littéraire de la Suisse française. [Geneva, 1856?])

GOULBURN, Edward Meyrick
A rudimentary treatise on the philosophy of grammar, with especial reference to the doctrine of the cases. 1852.

GRAF, J H and BRANDSTETTER, Josef Leop.
Bibliographische Vorarbeiten: Kataloge der Bibliotheken, Gesellschaftsschriften, Zeitungen und Kalender. 1896.

GREYERZ, Otto von
Die Mundartdichtung der deutschen Schweiz, geschichtlich dargestellt. 1924.

LÜHRER, Hans
Die Schweiz im Spiegel englischer Literatur, 1849-1875. 1952.

MACKAY, Charles
The scenery & poetry of the English Lakes: a summer ramble. 1846.

- - 2nd ed. 1852.

Meyer's Volksbibliothek für Länder-, Völker- und Naturkunde... [n.d.]. 60v. in 30.

MORNET, Daniel
Le sentiment de la nature en France de J.-J. Rousseau à Bernardin de Saint-Pierre: essai sur les rapports de la littérature et des moeurs. 1907.

RAMBERT, Eugène
[Les Alpes suisses]. Études de littérature alpestre et La marmotte au collier. 1889.

SCHIRMER, Gustav
Die Schweiz im Spiegel englischer und amerikanischer Literatur bis 1848. 1929.

SPINDLER, Robert
Die Alpen in der englischen Literatur und Kunst. 1932.

TALFOURD, Sir Thomas Noon
Three speeches delivered in the House of Commons in favour of a measure for an extension of copyright... 1840.

WOLF, Rudolf
Biographien zur Kulturgeschichte der Schweiz. 1858-62. 4v.

061 Anthologies

ALPINE GESELLSCHAFT D'VOISTHALER
Festschrift. 1910.

ANDERSON, William
Tales of discovery, enterprise, and adventure for the young. [187-].

Angelica's ladies library; or, Parental present. 1794.

Archiv kleiner zerstreuter Reisebeschreibungen durch Merkwürdige Gegenden der Schweiz. 1796.

BAKER, Ernest Albert and ROSS, Francis Edward
The voice of the mountains. [1905].

BAYBERGER, Emmeran
Gemsen-Eier: Alpin-Humoristisches in Wort & Bild. 1895-99. 4v.

BERTI, Antonio
Parlano i monti. 1948.

BLESSINGTON, Marguerite, Countess of
Heath's book of beauty. [18--].

BLESSINGTON, Marguerite, Countess of
The keepsake. 1846.

BOZMAN, Ernest Franklin
Mountain essays by famous climbers. [1928].

Die brieftasche aus den Alpen. 1789.

CLERICI, Idelfonso
In alta montagna. 1929.

061 Anthologies (Cont.)

DREYER, Aloys
Bergsteigerbrevier: eine Blütenlese aus den Werken
alpiner Dichtkunst und Erfahrungsweisheit. [1922].

- - 2.Aufl. [1927].

EBERLI, Henry
Switzerland poetical and pictorial: a collection
of poems by English and American poets. 1893.

ENGEL, Clair Éliane and VALLOT, Charles
"Ces monts affreux...", 1650-1810. 1934.

ENGEL, Claire Éliane and VALLOT, Charles
"Ces monts sublimes...", 1803-1895. 1936.

Friendship's offering of sentiment and mirth. 1844.

Gedichte über die Schweiz und über Schweizer. 1793.

GERMAIN, Félix
Sommets: 100 photographies en noir. 1959.

GURTNER, Othmar
Grindelwald: Festgabe zum 17. Grossen Skirennen
der Schweiz. 1923.

Half hours in air and sky: marvels of the universe.
1880.

HUNT, John, Baron Hunt
My favourite mountaineering stories; edited by
John Hunt. 1978.

IRVING, Robert Lock Graham
The mountain way: an anthology in prose and verse;
collected by R.L.G. Irving. 1938.

IRWIN, William Robert
Challenge: an anthology of the literature of
mountaineering; edited by William R. Irwin. 1950.

JAMES, Norman G   Brett
The charm of Switzerland: an anthology; compiled
by Norman G. Brett James. 1910.

The juvenile miscellany of amusement and instruction.
1842.

KURZ, Heinrich
Die Schweiz: Land, Volk und Geschichte in ausgewählten Dichtungen. 1853.

A LADY
Old stories of Switzerland; selected and translated
from the works of different German and Swiss poets
by a lady. [1864].

LEE, Frank Harold
The lure of the hills; selected by H.F. Lee. 1928.

Literary souvenirs; [collected by Alaric A. Watts].
1827.

- - Another [i.e. 9th] ed. 1833.

LUNN, Sir Arnold
The Englishman in the Alps, being a collection of
English prose and poetry relating to the Alps;
edited by Arnold Lunn. 1913.

LUNN, Sir Arnold
Oxford mountaineering essays; edited by Arnold
H.M. Lunn. 1912.

LUNN, Sir Arnold
Switzerland in English prose and poetry; [edited]
by Arnold Lunn. 1947.

MACDONALD, Hugh
On foot: an anthology selected by Hugh Macdonald.
1942.

MAYER-PFANNHOLZ, Anton
Deutsches Alpenland: ein Heimatbuch; hrsg. von
Anton Mayer-Pfannholz. 1920.

MERRICK, Hugh
The perpetual hills: a personal anthology of
mountains. 1964.

MEURER, Julius and RABL, Josef
Der Bergsteiger im Hochgebirge: Alpin-touristische
Schilderungen nach den Berichten hervorragender
Hochtouristen; zusammengestellt und erläutert von
Julius Meurer und Josef Rabl. 1893.

NOYCE, Wilfrid
The climber's fireside book; compiled by Wilfrid
Noyce. 1964.

Pictorial sport and adventure, being a record of
deeds of daring and marvellous escapes by field
and flood... [190-].

SCHMIDT, Walter
Wer die Berge liebt: kleine alpine Trilogie: die
Schönheit der Berge, die Liebe zu den Bergen, die
Macht der Berge; gesammelt und hrsg. von Walter
Schmid. 2.Aufl. [1945].

SCHÜCKING, L
Helvetia: Natur, Geschichte, Sage im Spiegel
deutscher Dichtung; hrsg. von L. Schücking. 1857.

SMITH, George Alan and SMITH, Carol D
The armchair mountaineer: a gathering of wit,
wisdom & idolatry; edited by George A. Smith,
Carol D. Smith. 1968.

SOCIETY OF FRIENDS
The Aurora Borealis: a literary annual; edited
by the members of the Society of Friends. 1833.

SPENDER, Harold
In praise of Switzerland, being the Alps in prose
and verse. 1912.

STYLES, Showell
The mountaineer's week-end book. 1950.

Tales in rhyme. 1863.

Tales of adventure from the old annuals... New ed.
1895.

Tales of the Great Saint Bernard. 1828.

WARD, Michael
The mountaineer's companion; edited by Michael
Ward. 1966.

WILSON, Ken
The games climbers play; edited by Ken Wilson.
1978.

YOUNG, Eleanor Winthrop and YOUNG, Geoffrey Winthrop
In praise of mountains: an anthology for friends;
compiled by Eleanor and Geoffrey Winthrop Young.
1948.

ZÜRCHER, Otto
Das Berner Oberland im Lichte der deutschen
Dichtung; ausgewahlt und eingeleitet von Otto
Zürcher. 1923.

062 Essays, letters, journals

ALPINUS
Alpinus, conteur dauphinois: nouveaux récits, précédés d'une Vie d'Alpinus, par Raymond Coche.
1946.

AMERY, Leopold Stennett
The stranger of the Ulysses. 1934.

ANDRÉ, August
Sur nos monts. 1895.

ARCIS, C   Egmond d'
En montagne: récits et souvenirs. [1936].

ARCIS, C   Egmond d'
Neiges éternelles; avec une préface de Charles
Gos. 1945.

BAULACRE, Léonard
Oeuvres historiques et littéraires. 1857. 2v.

062 Essays... (Cont.)

BAZIN, René
  Récits de la plaine et de la montagne. 11e éd.
  [1903?].

BENSON, Arthur Christopher.
  Along the road. 1913.

BERTRAM, Anthony
  To the mountains. 1929.

BORDEAUX, Henry
  Aventures en montagne. 1946.

BORDEAUX, Henry
  Paysages romanesques. 1906.

BRIDEL, Philippe Sirice and BRIDEL, J   L   Louis
  Mélanges Helvétiques des années 1787, 1788, 1789,
  1790. 1791.

- - 1782 à 1786. 1787.

CERMENATI, Mario
  Cose di alpinismo. 1901.

CHABOD, Renato
  La Cima di Entrelor. 1969.

CHORLEY, Katharine Campbell, Baroness Chorley
  Hills and highways. 1928.

CORREVON, Henry
  Par monts et vaux. 1904.

CYSARZ, Herbert
  Berge über uns. 1935.

DALLOZ, Pierre
  Zénith. 1951.

DE AMICIS, Ugo
  Alpe mistica. 1926.

DE AMICIS, Ugo
  Piccoli uomini e grandi montagne. 1924.

DI VALLEPIANA, Ugo
  Ricordi di vita alpina. 1972.

DOUGHTY, Joseph Henry
  Hill-writings. 1937.

EGGER, Carl
  Aiguilles: ein Bergbüchlein. 1924.

GIGON, Fernand
  Voix de l'alpe. 1931.

GODLEY, Alfred Denis
  Reliquiae. 1926.

GOETHE, Johann Wolfgang von
  Goethes Sämtliche Werke. Neu durchgesehene und
  erg. Ausg. [ca 1881].

GOS, Charles
  Le Groupe Franc de Girouc. 1942.

GOS, Charles
  Près des névés et des glaciers: impressions
  alpestres. 1912.

- - 2e éd. [1912].
- - 4e éd. [ca 1915].

GOS, Charles
  Solitude montagnarde. 1943.

GOSSE, Edmund W
  Studies in the literature of northern Europe.
  1879.

GREEN, John Richard
  Stray studies from England and Italy. 1876.

GREGORIN, Janez
  Blagoslov gorá: zbrano delo. 1944.

GURTNER, Othmar
  Schlechtwetter Fahrten. 1917.

HEADLEY, J   T
  Rambles and sketches. 1852.

HOEK, Henry
  Am Hüttenfeuer: erlebte und erlogene Abenteuer.
  1935.

HOEK, Henry
  Der denkende Wanderer. 1929.

HOEK, Henry
  Wanderbriefe an eine Frau. 1925.

HOEK, Henry
  Wanderungen und Wandlungen. 1924.

HOEK, Henry
  Weg und Umweg einer Liebe: neue Wanderbriefe an
  eine Frau. 1929.

HOEK, Henry
  Wege und Weggenossen. 1919.

- - 2.Aufl. 1920.

ITTLINGER, Josef
  Ewige Berge: Erlebnisse und Geschichte. 1924.

LAMBERT, Léon
  Au pays blanc: voyages. 1922.

LAMMER, Eugen Guido
  [Jungborn]. Fontaine de jouvence, "Jungborn":
  ascensions et reflections d'un alpiniste solitaire.
  1931.

MÉLON, Pierre
  Montagnards. 1949.

MEYER, Oskar Erich
  Berg und Mensch: ein Buch der Andacht. [1938].

MONTAGU, Lady Mary Wortley
  Letters from the Right Honourable Lady Mary
  Wortley Montagu 1709 to 1762. 1906.

MONTAGU, Lady Mary Wortley
  Letters of the Right Honourable Lady M--y W---y
  M----e, written during her travels in Europe,
  Asia and Africa ... accounts of the policy and
  manners of the Turks. 1766.

MORGENTHALER, Hans
  Ihr Berge: Stimmungsbilder aus einem Bergsteiger-
  Tagebuch. 1916.

MUNTHE, Axel
  Memories & vagaries. 1908.

NIEBERL, Franz
  Erlebtes und Erdachtes. 1925.

PATEY, Tom
  One man's mountains: essays and verses. 1971.

PETZENDORFER, Ludwig
  Humoristische Naturgeschichte des alpinen Menschen.
  2.Aufl. 1888.

PFANNL, Heinrich
  Was bist du mir, Berg? Schriften und Reden. 1929.

RAMBERT, Eugène
  Les Alpes et la Suisse; oeuvres choisies. 1930.

ROCHAT-CENISE, Charles
  Pays de glace et de granit: images. 1931.

ROSS, Mrs. Forrest and ROSS, Noel
  Mixed grill. 1934.

RUSKIN, John
  Praeterita: outlines of scenes and thoughts
  perhaps worthy of memory in my past life. 1887.

RYDZEWSKI, Anton von
  Zehn Jahre Bergführer Kluckers "Herr": Erlebnisse
  A. von Rydzewskis Naturschilderungen und Anderes.
  1. Buch. Anton von Rydzewski als Künstler, eine
  alpine Bildergalerie in Prosa. 1934.

062 Essays... (Cont.)

SAMIVEL
L'amateur d'abîmes: récit. 1940.

- - 4e éd. 1951.

SAVI-LOPEZ, Maria
Leggende delle Alpi. 1889.

SCHMIDKUNZ, Walter
Das quietschvergnugte Skibrevier. 1935.

SCHMIDKUNZ, Walter
Zwischen Himmel und Erde: alpine Anekdoten. 1925.

SCHUSTER, Claud, Baron Schuster
Men, women and mountains: days in the Alps and
Pyrenees. 1931.

SCHUSTER, Claud, Baron Schuster
Postscript to adventure. 1950.

SHELLEY, Percy Bysshe
Essays, letters from abroad, translations and
fragments. 1852. 2v. in 1.

SMITH, Albert
The miscellany: a book for the field or the fireside, amusing tales and sketches. 1850.

SONNIER, Georges
Où règne la lumière. 1946.

SONNIER, Georges
Terre du ciel. 1959.

STILLINGFLEET, Benjamin
Literary life and select works. 1811. 3v.

STOPPANI, P
Come d'autunno...1903.

STYLES, Showell
The climber's bedside book. 1968.

TEZENAS DU MONTCEL, Robert
Ce monde qui n'est pas le nôtre... 1965.

TÖPFFER, Rodolphe
Mélanges. 1852.

TOULOUSE, Gilbert
Montagne retrouvée. 1957.

TYNDALL, John
New fragments. 2nd ed. 1892.

Unwin's chap book. [1899].

VALENTINI, Enzo, conte di Laviano
Letters and drawings of Enzo Valentini, conte di
Laviano, Italian volunteer and soldier. 1917.

VIRIGLIO, Attilio
Pastelli di monte. [1906].

WEISS, Jurg
Murailles et abîmes... 1946.

WHERRY, George
Notes from a knapsack. 1909.

WILSON, Henry Schütz
Studies and romances. 1873.

WORDSWORTH, Dorothy
Journals; edited by E. de Selincourt. 1941. 2v.

WORDSWORTH, Dorothy
Journals; edited by William Knight. 1934.

YOUNG, Geoffrey Winthrop
Wall and roof climbing. 1905.

ZOPPI, Giuseppe
Das Buch von der Alp; über den Dörfern des Tessin.
1939.

063 Prose

POTTER, Stephen
One-upmanship. 1952.

064 Novels

An alpine tale, suggested by circumstances which
occurred towards the commencement of the present
century, by the author of Tales from Switzerland.
1823. 2v.

ARMANDY, André
Terre de suspicion: roman d'aventures. 1926.

AUBERT, Théodore
Émérentienne: roman. [1908].

AUBERT, Théodore
L'isole: roman. 1908.

AUDIBERT, Raoul
Montagnes. 1930.

BALLANTYNE, R   M
Rivers of ice: a tale illustrative of alpine
adventure and glacier action. 1875.

BALLANTYNE, R   M
The rover of the Andes: a tale of adventure in
South America. 1885.

BALLANTYNE, R   M
The world of ice. [1915?].

BARTROPP, John
Barbarian: a tale of the Roman wall. 1933.

BAUM, Vicki
Marion alive. 1943.

BECKFORD, William
Italy, with Sketches of Spain and Portugal. 1834.
Contains "Vathek: an Arabian tale".

BENSON, Robert Hugh
The coward. 1912.

BERNT, Ferdinand
Der Bund der Freien: Erzählung. 1910.

BOLT, Niklaus
Svizzero! Die Geschichte einer Jugend. 1913.

BORDEAUX, Henry
Les jeux dangereux. 1926.

BORDEAUX, Henry
[La maison morte]. The house that died. 1923.

BORDEAUX, Henry
La neige sur les pas: roman. 1912.

BORDEAUX, Henry
[La neige sur les pas]. La neve sulle orme:
romanzo. 1915.

BOWMAN, W   E
The ascent of Rum Doodle. 1956.

BOYLE, Kay
Avalanche: a novel. 1944.

BOZMAN, Ernest Franklin
X plus Y: a novel. 1936.

BRAY, Claude
Ivanda; or, The pilgrim's quest: a tale [of
Thibet]. 1894.

BRUHL, Etienne
Accident à la Meije: roman. 1947.

BURGBACHER, Kurt
[Pilot in der weissen Hölle]. White hell: a story
of the Search and Rescue Service in the Alps.
1963.

064 Novels (Cont.)

BURNAND, F   C
  Very much abroad. 1890.

CANNON, Le Grand
  Look to the mountain. 1943.

CARDONNE, Pierre de
  Le retour éternel. [19--].

CASELLA, Georges
  Les deux routes. 1919

CASELLA, Georges
  Le vertige des cimes: roman d'aventures. [19--].

CAZIN, Jeanne
  Les petits montagnards. 1881.

Chateau of Leaspach; or, The stranger in
  Switzerland: a tale. 1827. 3v.

Continental adventures: a novel. 1826. 3v.

COOPER, Edward H
  The monk wins. 1900.

CORNWALL, Nellie
  Hallvard Halvorsen; or, The avalanche: a story of
  the Fjeld, Fjord and Fos. [1888].

COUCH, Stata B
  In the shadow of the peaks: a novel. 1909.

COXHEAD, Elizabeth
  June in Skye: a novel. 1938.

COXHEAD, Elizabeth
  One green bottle. 1951.

CROCKETT, S   R
  Ione March. 3rd ed. 1899.

DAUDET, Alphonse
  Tartarin of Tarascon. [1907?].

DAUDET, Alphonse
  Tartarin sur les Alpes: nouveaux exploits du héros
  tarasconnais. 1885.

DAUDET, Alphonse
  Tartarin sur les Alpes: roman. 1917.

DAUDET, Alphonse
  [Tartarin sur les Alpes]. Tartarin on the Alps.
  1887.

DAUDET, Alphonse
  [Tartarin sur les Alpes]. Tartarin on the Alps.
  [1907?].

DAVIS, E   J
  Pyrna: a commune; or, Under the ice. 1875.

DUCKWORTH, F   R   G
  Swiss fantasy. 1948.

DUNSTAN, Mary
  Jagged skyline: a novel. 1935.

EGGER, Carl
  Vorübergang. 1926.

EYRE, Donald C
  John Sikander. 1954.

FEDERER, Heinrich
  Berge und Menschen: Roman. 1911.

FEDERER, Heinrich
  Pilatus: eine Erzählung aus den Bergen. 1912.

FEIGL, Leo
  Die Rax: ein Bergsteiger-Roman. 1924.

FENN, G   Manville
  In an alpine valley. 1894.   3v.

FIRBANK, Thomas
  Bride to the mountain: a romance. 1940.

FONTANET, Jean Claude
  La montagne: roman. 1970.

FRISON-ROCHE, Roger
  La grande crévasse: roman. 1948.

FRISON-ROCHE, Roger
  [La grande crevasse]. The last crevasse. 1952.

FRISON-ROCHE, Roger
  Premier de cordée. 1941.

FRISON-ROCHE, Roger
  Premier de cordée (naissance d'une vocation).
  1953.

FRISON-ROCHE, Roger
  [Premier de cordée]. First on the rope: a novel.
  1949.

FRISON-ROCHE, Roger
  [Retour à la montagne]. Return to the mountains.
  1961.

GARCÍA BELLIDO, J
  Una aventura en la pedriza: a novela. 1923.

GARVE, Andrew
  The ascent of D.13. 1939.

GEDDIE, John
  Beyond the Himalayas: a story of travel and
  adventure in the wilds of Thibet. 1882.

GOMPERTZ, M   L   A
  The voice of Dashin: a romance of wild mountains.
  [1919].

GOS, Charles
  Notre-Dame des neiges: roman. 1947.

GOS, Charles
  [Notre-Dame des neiges]. Song of the high hills.
  1949.

GOS, Charles
  La nuit des Drus. 1929.

GOS, Charles
  Pour Miss Cynthia [et On tourne au Cervin].
  [1934?].

- - Nouv. éd. [ca 1939].

GOTTA, Salvator
  Piccolo Alpino: romanzo. 1930.

GRABEIN, Paul
  Firnenrausch: Roman. [1897].

GRATRIX, Dawson
  He and ski. [1929].

HAAS, Rudolf
  Leuchtende Gipfel: Roman. 1925.

HAENSEL, Carl
  Der Kampf ums Matterhorn: Tatsachenroman. 1929.

- - Ungekurzte Neuausgabe. [1929?].

HAENSEL, Carl
  [Der Kampf ums Matterhorn]. La lutte pour le
  Cervin: roman de faits. [ca 1930].

HEER, J   C
  An heiligen Wassern: Roman aus dem schweizerischen
  Hochgebirge. 6.Aufl. 1901.

HEER, J   C
  Der König der Bernina: Roman aus dem
  schweizerischen Hochgebirge. 4.Aufl. 1900.

HOCKING, Silas K
  The great hazard. 1915.

064 Novels (Cont.)
HOCKER, Paul Oskar
   Die Sonne von St. Moritz: roman. 1910.

HURSTON, Zora
   The man of the mountain. 1941.

JENSON, Johannes V
   Der Gletscher: ein neuer Mythos vom ersten
   Menschen. 1912.

JOHNSTON, Marjorie Scott
   The mountain speaks. 1938.

JOHNSTON, Marjorie Scott
   Pilgrim and the phoenix. 1940.

KAISER, Isabelle
   La vierge du Lac: roman des montagnes
   d'Unterwalden. 1941.

LAMI, Marcel
   Ver les cimes. [1912].

LANG, P   S
   Where the Soldanella growns. [1908].

LE BLOND, Elizabeth
   The story of an alpine winter. 1907.

LEFEBURE, Molly
   Scratch & Co.: the great cat expedition. 1968.

LEVER, Charles
   The Dodd family abroad. 1859.   2v.

LHOTZKY, Heinrich
   Im Reiche der Sennerinnen: Roman. 1913.

LIOTIER, Max
   Les seigneurs de la neige. 1970.

LONGFELLOW, Henry Wadsworth
   Hyperion: a romance. 1865.

LUNN, Sir Arnold
   Family name. 1931.

LUNN, Sir Arnold
   The Harrovians. 6th ed. 1926.

LUNN, Peter
   Evil in high places. 1947.

MACDONALD, Alexander
   Through the heart of Tibet. 1910.

MCLAREN, Amy
   From a Davos balcony. 1903.

MAEL, Pierre
   Terre de Fauves: roman. 6e éd. 1905.

MANNING, Anne
   An idyl of the Alps. 1876.

MANNING, Anne
   The year nine: A tale of the Tyrol. 1858.

MARGUERITTE, Paul
   Le poste des neiges: roman inédit... 1899.

MASON, Alfred Edward Woodley
   The broken road. 2nd ed. 1908.

MASON, Alfred Edward Woodley
   A romance of Wastdale. 1914.

MASON, Alfred Edward Woodley
   Running water. [19--].

MAZZOTTI, Giuseppe
   La grande parete. 1938.

MAZZOTTI, Giuseppe
   [La grande parete]. La grande paroi. 1948.

MERRICK, Hugh
   Andreas at sundown. 1944.

MERRICK, Hugh
   The breaking strain. 1950.

MERRICK, Hugh
   Out of the night. 1957.

MERRICK, Hugh
   Pillar of the sky. 1941.

MIRBEAU, Octave
   Les vingt et un jours d'un neurasthénique.
   1901.

MOFFAT, Gwen
   Hard option: a novel. 1975.

MOFFAT, Gwen
   Over the sea to death. 1976.

MONELLI, Paolo
   Le scarpe al sole: cronaca di gaie e di tristi
   avventure d'alpini di muli e di vino. 1930.

MONTAGUE, Charles Edward
   The morning's war. 1913.

NAILLEN, A   van der
   On the heights of Himalay. 6th ed. 1900.

NOYCE, Wilfrid
   The gods are angry. 1957.

ODERMATT, Madeleine
   Madeleine Odermatt; or, Le canton d'Uri. 1858.

OMPTEDA, Georg, Freiherr von
   Excelsior! Ein Bergsteigerleben. 1909.

OMPTEDA, Georg, Freiherr von
   Der jungfräuliche Gipfel: Roman. 1927.

OMPTEDA, Georg, Freiherr von
   Die kleine Zinne: Roman aus den Bergen. 1931.

OTT, Adolf
   Der Bergführer: hochgebirgs-Roman. [1900].

PEREDA, José M   de
   [Peñas arriba]. Dans la montagne...: roman.
   1918.

PEYRE, Joseph
   Matterhorn: roman. 1939.

PEYRE, Joseph
   Mont Everest: roman. 1942.

PURSLOW, Richard
   Sleep till noon day. 1963.

RAMEAU, Jean
   L'ami des montagnes. 1908.

RAMUZ, C   F
   [Derborence]. When the mountain fell. 1949.

RAYMOND, Diana
   The climb. 1962.

REVELLI, Mariz
   Il canto della montagna: romanzo. 1924.

RITA
   Edelweiss: a romance. 1890.

ROCOFFORT, L
   Le secret de l'avalanche. 1922.

ROD, Édouard
   Là-haut. 1897.

ROD, Édouard
   L'ombre s'étend sur la montagne. [1916].

ROUFF, Marcel
   L'homme et la montagne. 1925.

RUMNEY, A   Wren
   The Dalesman. 1911.

064 Novels (Cont.)

SAINT LOUP
  Face nord: roman. 1947.

SAINT LOUP
  Montagne sans Dieu: roman. 1955.

SAMIVEL
  Le fou d'Édenberg: roman. 1967.

SCAPINELLI, Carl, conte
  Gipfelstürmer: Roman. 1910.

SCHWEICHEL, Robert
  Aus den Alpen: Erzählungen. 2. verm.
  Aufl. 1872. 2v. in 1.

SCIOBÉRET, P
  Abdallah Schlatter; ou, Les curieuses aventures
  d'un Suisse au Caucase. 1870.

SCOTT, Sir Walter
  Anne of Geierstein. 1854.

SERAO, Matilde
  Evviva la vita! Romanzo. [19--].

SKETCHLEY, Arthur
  Mrs. Brown on the Grand Tour. [18--].

SMITH, Albert
  The adventures of Mr. Ledbury and his friend Jack
  Johnson. [19--].

SMITH, Albert
  The struggles and adventures of Christopher
  Tadpole at home and abroad. [1849?].

SMYTHE, Frank S
  Secret mission. 1942.

SONNIER, Georges
  Un médecin de montagne: roman. 1963.

SONNIER, Georges
  Meije: récit. 1952.

STRATZ, Rudolph
  Montblanc. 1899.

STRATZ, Rudolph
  Die Thörichte Jungfrau. Roman. 4.Aufl. 1901.

STYLES, Showell
  Death on Milestone buttress. 1951.

STYLES, Showell
  Death under Snowdon. 1954.

STYLES, Showell
  Swing away, climber. 1959.

SUTCLIFFE, Constance
  Our Lady of the ice: a story of the Alps. 1909.

SYMONDS, Margaret
  A child of the Alps. 1920.

TELMANN, Konrad
  Die Lawine: ein Roman. [1925].

TELMANN, Konrad
  Unter den Dolomiten: Roman. 8.Aufl. 1911.

THÉOTOKY, C   comte
  Vie de montagne. 1895.

THORNE, Guy
  The greater power. [1915].

TROLLIET, Marie
  Edelweiss: un roman dans les Alpes.
  (In Bibliothèque universelle ... v.61-62, 1894)

TUGWELL, George
  On the mountain. 1862.

TUSHKAN, Georgi
  The hunter of the Pamirs: a novel of adventure in
  Soviet Central Asia. [1944].

ULLMAN, James Ramsey
  And not to yield. 1970.

ULLMAN, James Ramsey
  Banner in the sky. 1955.

ULLMAN, James Ramsey
  The white tower. 1945.

- - Another ed. 1946.

VALRÉAS, Henri
  Une ascension dramatique au Mont Blanc. [1905?].

VAUTIER, Auguste
  Gabrisse: journal d'un gardien de cabane. 2e éd.
  1941.

VOSS, Richard
  Der Todesweg auf den Piz Palü: Roman. [1910].

WALES, Hubert
  The thirty days. 1915.

WALSH, Maurice
  The hill is mine. 1940.

WALSH, Maurice
  The key above the door. 1926 (1940 reprint).

WARDEN, Gertrude
  The crime in the Alps: a novel. 1908.

WATKINS, Olga
  Tales from Tyrol. 1935.

WELLS, Herbert George
  Ann Veronica. [1913].

WILLIAMSON, C   N   and WILLIAMSON, A   M
  The Princess passes: a romance of a motor. 1904.

WILSON, Leigh
  Do you go back dismayed? 1949.

WINGATE, John
  Avalanche. 1977.

WUNDT, Theodor
  Das Diadem: Ideale und Illusionen: ein Höhenroman. [1926].

WUNDT, Theodor
  Matterhorn: ein Hochgebirgs-Roman. [1916].

ZIAK, Karl
  Balmat oder Paccard? Ein Mont-Blanc Roman.
  1930.

065 Short stories, legends, folk-tales

AUERBACH, Berthold
  Auerbach's Dorfgeschichten. 4.Aufl. 1848.

BÉRARD, Clément
  Au coeur d'un vieux pays: légendes et traditions
  du Valais. 2e éd. 1928.

BESSIÈRES, Albert
  L'empire de la paix: récits de la montagne
  suisse, empire des neiges. 1931.

BIRTT, W   Bridges
  By the roaring Reuss: idylls and stories of the
  Alps. 1898.

BLACKWOOD, Algernon
  Pan's garden: a volume of nature studies. 1912.

BLATTL, Josef
  Wenn die Lawinen donnern und Anderes: zwanzig
  Geschichten aus Tirol. 1931.

065 Short stories... (Cont.)

BORDEAUX, Henry
  Contes de la montagne. 1928.

CAMINADE-CHATENAY, A
  Souvenirs de Suisse: nouvelles; suivis de Autres
  temps, autres moeurs: comédie de salon en trois
  actes et en vers. 1862.

CÉRÉSOLE, Alfred
  Légendes des Alpes vaudoises. 1885.

DESLYS, Ch
  Nos Alpes: Le muet de Brides, Légendes d'Évian, La
  Dent du Chat, Drumette: nouvelles. 1882.

DESSAUER, A
  Mit krummer Feder auf grünem Hut: ernste und
  heitere Erzählungen. 1905.

FLORIAN, Jean Pierre Claris de
  Guillaume Tell; ou, La Suisse libre: ouvrage
  posthume. 1810.

FLORIAN, Jean Pierre Claris de
  Nouvelles de Florian. T.2. 1810.

GESCHICHTSFORSCHENDE VEREIN VON OBERWALLIS
  Walliser Sagen. Bd.1. 1907.

GESCHICHTSFORSCHENDE VEREIN VON OBERWALLIS
  [Walliser Sagen]. Légendes valaisannes. 1931.

GHIRINGHELLI, Paolo
  Alpe buona: novelle e versi della montagna. 1912.

GIGON, Fernand
  Histoires d'en haut. 1933.

GOS, Charles
  La Croix du Cervin. 1919.

- - Nouv. éd. 1933.

GOS, Charles
  Sous le drapeau: récits militaires. 1918.

GÜNTHER, Marie, comtesse von
  Tales and legends from the Tyrol. 1874.

GUIGUES, Émile
  Séchot et Poulard; fantaisie alpestre. 1886.

HAAS, Rudolf
  Die Stimme des Berges: Novelle. 1924.

HADFIELD, John
  Modern stories of the open air, by H.E. Bates [and
  others]; edited by John Hadfield. 1936.

HALDER, Arnold
  Bergluft: Sonntagsstreifereien eines alten
  Clubisten. 1869.

HERVIEU, Paul
  L'Alpe homicide. Nouv. éd. 1903.

Highways and by-ways; or, Tales of the roadside,
  picked up in the French provinces by a walking
  gentleman. 2nd series. Vol.1. 1825.

HOEK, Henry
  Moderne Wintermärchen. 1926.

ITTLINGER, Josef
  Von Menschen, Bergen und anderen Dingen. 1922.

JEANDRÉ, René D
  Contes des cabanes et des sommets. 1925.

JEGERLEHNER, Johannes
  Alp legends. 1926.

LAMBER, Juliette
  Dans les Alpes: nouveaux récits. [1898].

LAMBOSSY, François E
  Vents des crêtes. 1941.

MAYER, Erich August
  O, ihr Berge! Funf Novellen. 1931.

MONTOLIEU, Isabelle, baronne de
  Recueil de nouvelles. 1813. 3v.

RENARD, Georges and RENARD, Louise
  Autour des Alpes: contes roses et noirs. 1892.

SAMIVEL
  Contes à pic. 1951.

SCIZE, Pierre
  En altitude. 1930.

SIEGEN, Johann
  Gletschermärchen für Gross und Klein aus dem
  Lötschenthal. [ca 1919].

SKELTON, John
  Essays in romance and studies from life. 1878.

SOLANDIEU
  Légendes valaisannes. [1919].

SOUVESTRE, Émile
  Scènes et récits des Alpes: Le chasseur de
  chamois, La fillole des Allemagnes, l'Hospice de
  Selisberg. Nouv. éd. 1877.

SPRINGENSCHMID, Karl
  Da lacht Tirol: Geschichten aus dem Tiroler
  Volksleben. 1935.

Stories from Switzerland and the Tyrol. 1853.

Strange tales of peril and adventure. [18--].

STRAWBRIDGE, Anne West
  Shadows of the Matterhorn. [ca 1950].

SUBIRÁ, José
  Mi valle pirenaico: cuadros novelescos. 1927.

SUTTON, Graham
  Fell days. 1948.

TALBOT, Daniel
  A treasury of mountaineering stories. 1955.

Tales from Switzerland. [New ed.]. 1827. 4v.

TATHAM, H F W
  With footprints in the snow and other tales.
  1910.

TÖPFFER, Rodolphe
  Nouvelles génèvoises. 1846.

- - Another ed. 1848.
- - Nouv. éd. 1855.

TOLSTOY, Leo, Count
  The Cossacks and other tales of the Caucasus.
  1916.

TUVAR, Lorenzo
  Tales & legends of the English Lakes and mountains. [1852].

VALLETTE, Pierre
  Le miracle des cloches: contes et poèmes
  valaisans. 1937.

WESTALL, William
  Tales and traditions of Switzerland. 1882.

WITHERS, Percy
  Friends in solitude. 1923.

066 Children's stories

ABBOTT, Jacob
  Rollo in Switzerland. 1854.

ANDERSON, Hans Christian
  The ice-maiden. 1863.

066 Children's stories (Cont.)

BAKER, Olaf
Shasta of the wolves. 1921.

BETHELL, Augusta
Helen in Switzerland: a tale for young people.
[1887].

BING, Walter
Drei Jungens am Seil. 1932.

BLOBEL, Oscar
Little Herta's Christmas dream: a Christmas fairy-
tale of the mountains. 1911.

BOVET, Mar. Alex.
Légendes de la Gruyère. [1912].

CAUMERY, M   and PINCHON, J
Bécassine alpiniste. 1923.

COOPER, Edward H
Wyemarke and the mountain-fairies. 1900.

DURST, Carola
Im Zauberreich der Berge: Märchen und Sagen; dem
Freunden der Bergwelt für ihre Jugend. 1906.

ESCHMANN, Ernst
Der Geisshirt von Fiesch: eine Geschichte aus dem
Oberwallis... 1919.

ESCHMANN, Ernst
Gian Caprez: eine Geschichte aus dem Engadin...
1923.

FINCH, George Ingle
Climbing Mount Everest. 1930.

FOLTIN, Arthur
Tiroler Alpensagen. [189-].

The further adventures of the little traveller.
1857.

GEBAUER, A   K
Um den Mount Everest: Fahrten und Abenteuer. 1925.

GUYER, Rosie
Hallo, die Berge! Eine Geschichte für Kinder.
1921.

HOLME, Daryl
The young mountaineer; or, Frank Miller's lot in
life. 1874.

JEMELIN, Erika
Die Wand: Tagebuch eines jungen Bergsteigers.
1936.

MAIX, Kurt
Bergler, Bauern, Kameraden. 1943.

MONCRIEFF, Ascott Robert Hope
Seeing the world: the adventures of a young
mountaineer. 1909.

MONTOLIEU, Isabelle, baronne de
The avalanche; or, The old man of the Alps: a tale.
1829.

MORIN, Micheline
Trag, le chamois. 1948.

OXLEY, J   MacDonald
L'hasa at last. 1900.

The peasants of Chamouni, containing an attempt to
reach the summit of Mont Blanc; and a delineation
of the scenery among the Alps. 1823.

- - 2nd ed. 1826.

PETITHUGUENIN, Jean
À l'assaut de la cime du monde. [ca 1922].

PIERRE, Bernard
Le petit Sherpa aux yeux bleus. 1969.

RIVETT-CARNAC, Marion
Little Edelweiss in Switzerland. 1902.

SAMIVEL
Ayorpok et Ayounghila: conte eskimo. 1950.

SAMIVEL
Canard; ou, Le songe d'un jour de neige. 1938.

SAMIVEL
M. Dumollet sur le Mont-Blanc: les aventures surprenantes de M. Dumollet (de Saint-Malo) durant
son voyage de 1837 aux glacières de Savoie et
d'Helvétie. 1946.

SAVIGNY, Laurence de
Le Robinson des Alpes. [1868?].

SHERWOOD, Mary Martha
Aleine; or, Le Bächen Hölzli. 2nd ed. 1833.

SIEGEN, Johann
[Gletschermärchen...]. Les légendes du glacier.
[1919].

SPYRI, Johanna
Heidi. 1946.

SPYRI, Johanna
[Kurze Geschichten]. Swiss stories for children
and those who love children. 1889.

STEIGER, Willy
Unsere Alpenfahrt: ein Schülerbrief-wechsel im
Spiegel einer Schulfahrt ins österreichische
Alpenland. 1925.

STUDER, Gottlieb
Der Kampf um die Gipfel. [1920].

STYLES, Showell
The ladder of snow. 1962.

STYLES, Showell
The shop in the mountain. 1961.

TALBERT, Émile
Les Alpes: études et souvenirs. 1880.

VONBUN, F   I
Alpenmärchen. 1910.

WADE, Mary Hazelton
Our little Swiss cousin. 1903.

WODEHOUSE, P.G.
William Tell told again. 1904.

ZOLLER, Otto
Janpeter Bruns Abenteuer in den Tessiner und
Graubündner Berge. [1910].

067 Plays

AUDEN, Whystan Hugh and ISHERWOOD, Christopher
The ascent of F6: a tragedy in two acts. 2nd ed.
1937.

BICKERSTAFF, Isaac
Love in a village... 1791.

GALSWORTHY, John
The little dream: an allegory in six scenes.
[1911].

GOS, Charles
L'autre horizon: histoires d'un volontaire suisse
de la Grande Guerre. 1931.

GOS, Charles
Véronica: pièce en cinq actes. [1934?].

GROSS, Jules
Le héros des Alpes, Au Grand-Saint-Bernard: drame
et poésies alpestres. 2e éd. [1904].

KENNY, James
The Alaid; or The secrets of office. [18--].

067 Plays (Cont.)

KNOWLES, James Sheridan
   William Tell: a play in five acts. [18--].

MURPHY, Arthur
   Comedy of the way to keep him. [18--].

REICHENWALLNER, Leopold
   Alpenzauber:Berglegende und Volksschauspiel in
   vier Auszügen. 1906.

SCHILLER, Friedrich von
   Wilhelm Tell: Schauspiel [ca 1880].

STEINER, Leonard
   Jungfraubahn: Festspiel zur Einweihung der 1.
   Sektion Scheidegg-Gletscher. [1898].

THEYTAZ, Aloys
   Le Président de Viouc: pièce valaisanne. [1942].

068 Poems

ANDREWS, Arthur Westlake
   Poems. Vol.9. 1943.

ANDREWS, Arthur Westlake
   Selected poems on West Penwith and Reflections.
   Vol.1. 1957.

ANDREWS, Arthur Westlake
   Selected verse, 1939-1944. [1944?].

ANDREWS, Arthur Westlake
   Selected verse, 1940-2. [1942?].

ARNOULD, Joseph
   Hospice of St. Bernard: a prize poem. 1834.

AROSA, Hans Roelli
   Schnee: Verse für empfindsame Skileute. [n.d.].

ATL, Dr.
   Le sinfonie del Popocatepetl: poema messicano.
   1930.

AUDEN, Whystan Hugh
   Mountains. 1954.

B., Mme D.
   Les Alpes. [n.d.].

BAILLY, Rosa
   Fêtes de la terre. 1934-37. 3v.

BAILLY, Rosa
   Pastorale de la Maladette. 1939.

BAINBRIDGE, W
   Alpine lyrics. 1854.

BARA, Jakob
   Alpen im Feuer mit den Kärntner Achterjägern an
   der italienischen Front. [1918].

BARTH, Hanns
   Was Fels und Firn mir zugeraunt: Berg-, Zeit-, und
   Liebes-Lieder eines Alpinisten. 1926.

BARY, Alice de
   Rochers: poèmes. 1938.

BAUMBACH, Rudolf
   Schildereien aus dem Alpenlande... Gedichte, von
   Rudolf Baumbach. 1882.

BELL, William
   Mountains beneath the horizon. 1950.

BLAKENEY, Edward Henry
   Alpine poems. 1929.

BLAKENEY, Edward Henry
   Footsteps of autumn and other poems. 1912.

BOECK, Kurt
   Himalaya: Lieder und Bilder. 1927.

BRANTSCHEN, Gregor
Gesammelte Lieder im Volkston. [1946].

BRANTSCHEN, Gregor
   Neue Volkslieder für zwei Singstimmen. 1926.

- - 3. verm. Aufl. 1935.

BRIDEL, Philippe Sirice
   Poésies helvétiennes. 1782.

BROWNE, Mary A
   Mont Blanc and other poems... 1827.

BRYDGES, Sir Egerton
   The lake of Geneva: a poem, moral and descriptive.
   1832.

BYRON, George Gordon, Baron Byron
   Childe Harold's pilgrimage. Canto the third.
   1816.

BYRON, George Gordon, Baron Byron
   [Childe Harold's pilgrimage]. Childe Harold.
   1883.

CARDUCCI, Giosue
   Poesie, 1850-1900. 4a ed. 1905.

CAREY, David
   Picturesque scenes; or,A guide to the beauties
   of the Highlands... 2nd ed. 1812.

CHALONER, John
   The Vale of Chamouni: a poem. 1822.

CHAPPAZ, Maurice
   Verdures de la nuit. 1945.

CHURCH, Richard
   News from the mountain. 1932.

COUTAGNE, Aimé
   La Muse à la montagne: petite anthologie poétique
   à l'usage des alpinistes. 1925.

COUTAGNE, Aimé
   Les trophées alpestres. 1925.

CRIRIE, James
   Scottish scenery; or, Sketches in verse, descriptive of scenes chiefly in the Highlands...
   1803.

DEAN, John Fred
   The tourists; or, Continental travelling. 1878.

DE CAMBRAY DIGNY, Tommaso, conte
   [Monte Bianco]. Mont Blanc: Italian ode. 1879.

DENNYS, Joyce
   A winter sports alphabet: pictures by Joyce
   Dennys, verses by "Evoe". 1926.

DEVONSHIRE, Georgiana Cavendish, Duchess of
   [Passage of the Mountain of Saint Gothard].
   Passage du Mont saint-Gothard: poème. [18--]

DEVONSHIRE, Georgiana Cavendish, Duchess of
   [The passage of the Mountain of Saint Gothard].
   Passage du St.-Gothard: poème...
   (In Lille, Jacques de. Dithyrambe... 1802)

DIXIE, Lady Florence
   Waifs and strays; or, The pilgrimage of a
   Bohemian abroad. 1884.

DONNE, Benjamin John Merrifield
   Colloquy & song; or, Sport in the leash of the
   Muses. 1898.

DONNE, Benjamin John Merrifield
   Scattered poems. 1895.

DOUGLAS, John Sholto. 8th Marquis of Queensbury
   The spirit of the Matterhorn. [1881].

068 Poems (Cont.)

DOWNER, Arthur Cleveland
Mountaineering ballads. [1905].

DUBOIS, Mary R J
Poems for travellers. 1909.

DU LÉDO, Georges
Alpes fleuries. 1898.

EBERL, Anton, Freiherr von
Erinnerung an Tirol. 1840.

EMERSON, William
Papers from my desk and other poems. 1873.

FRESHFIELD, Douglas William
Quips for cranks and other trifles. 1923.

FRESHFIELD, Douglas William
Unto the hills. 1914.

GAROBBIO, Aurelio
Montagne. 1929.

GODLEY, Alfred Denis
Second strings. 1902.

GRAY, Thomas
The works of Thomas Gray. 1821.

HALLER, Albrecht von
[Die Alpen]. Alpengedicht. 1795.

HALLER, Albrecht von
Die Alpen. 1902.

HALLER, Albrecht von
[Die Alpen]. Les Alpes. [1749].

HALLER, Albrecht von
[Die Alpen]. Ode sur les Alpes. 1773.

HALLER, Albrecht von
[Die Alpen]. Les Alpes. 1944.

HALLER, Albrecht von
Poésies. 1752.

- - Nouv. éd. retouchée et augm. 1760.

HALLER, Albrecht von
Versuch schweizerischer Gedichte. 11. verm und
verb. Aufl. 1777.

HALLERS, Gottlieb Emanuel von
Bibliothek der Schweizer-Geschichte. 1785-88.
7v.

HARTMANN, B Blazidus
Firnenglühn neue Gedichte. 1923.

HAVERGAL, Frances Ridley
Life chords, comprising "Zenith", "Loyal responses"
and other poems. 1883.

HAVERGAL, Frances Ridley
Life mosaic, The ministry of song and Under the
surface. 1879.

HEY, Rebecca
Recollections of the Lakes and other poems. 1841.

HOEK, Henry
Berg- und Wanderlieder. [1926].

HOEK, Henry
"Dir...": ein Band Gedichte. 2.Aufl. 1925.

HONE, J F
Switzerland and other poems. 1878.

HÜGLI, Emil
Die Jungfrau: Dichtung. 1909.

HUMBLE, Benjamin Hutchison
The songs of Skye: an anthology. 1934.

JUNK, W
Meine Alpenfahrt. [1905].

KĀLIDĀSA
Méchadutz; or, Cloud messenger. 1872.

KEATE, George
The Alps: a poem. 1763.

KING, Alfred Castner
Mountain idylls and other poems. 1901.

KURZ, Fritz
Bergklänge: Gedichte. 1922.

LAMARTINE, Alphonse de
Harmonies poétiques et religieuses. 1904.

LAMARTINE, Alphonse de
Jocelyn: épisode. [New ed.]. 1903.

LAMARTINE, Alphonse de
Premières méditations poétiques avec commentaires
... 1903.

LEGWARTH, Franz
Heiteres Touristen-Vademecum nebst einem unfehl-
baren Touristen-Wetter-Anzeiger: Allen Wand'rern
ein treuer Wegwart. 1906.

LEIGH, Chandos
The view. 1819.

LEONARD, R M
Poems on travel. 1914.

LEUTHOLD, Heinrich
Gedichte. [18--].

LEYLAND, Peter
The naked mountain. 1951.

LIDDIARD, William
The legend of Einsidlin: a tale of Switzerland,
with poetical sketches of Swiss scenery. 1829.

LILLE, Jacques de
Dithyrambe sur l'immortalité de l'âme, suivi du
Passage du St.-Gothard: poème traduit de l'anglais
[de Georgiana Cavendish, Duchess of Devonshire].
1802.

LYTTON, Edward Robert Bulwer, 1st Earl Lytton
Glenaveril; or, The metamorphoses. 1885. 2v.

MCCOSH, John
Nuova Italia; or, Tours and retours through France,
Switzerland, Italy, and Sicily: a poem in ten
cantos. 1872-75. 2v.

MACDONNELL, Alice C
Songs of mountain and the burn. [n.d.].

MATTHISSON, Friedrich von
Gedichte. [1867].

MEYERSTEIN, E H W
The climbers: an ode on the Eton masters who lost
their lives descending the Piz Roseg on August
17th, 1933. 1934.

MICHEL, Albert
Bergtod und andere Gedichte. [19--].

MONTGOMERY, James
The wanderer of Switzerland, and other poems. 8th
ed. 1819.

- - 9th ed. 1823.

MORIN, Jean Antoine
Dix poèmes alpins. [1965].

MUMELTER, Hubert
Berg-Fibel. 1934.

MUSSET, Alfred de
Poésies nouvelles, 1836-52. 1905.

NICHOLS, Starr H
Monte Rosa: the epic of an Alp. 1883.

068 Poems (Cont.)

NOEL, Roden
Songs of the heights and deeps. 1885.

NOYCE, Wilfrid
Poems. 1960.

NOYCE, Wilfrid
Scholar mountaineers: pioneers of Parnassus.
1950.

OPPENHEIM, Edwin Camillo
'The reverberate hills'. 1914.

PARSONS, William
A poetical tour in the years 1784, 1785, and 1786.
1787.

PILKINGTON, Lawrence
An alpine valley and other poems. 1924.

PILKINGTON, Lawrence
Armathwaite. 1936.

PILKINGTON, Lawrence
The hills of peace and other poems. 1930.

RAWNSLEY, Hardwicke Drummond
Sonnets in Switzerland and Italy. 1899.

REBMANN, Johann Rudolph
Naturae magnalia: ausführliche Beschreibung der
Natur, Wundergeschopffen... 1620.

ROBERTS, Michael
Orion marches: poems. 1939.

ROBERTS, Michael
Poems. 1936.

ROBERTSON, James
Arachnia: occasional verses. 1904.

ROGERS, Samuel
Italy: a poem. 1823.

ROUX-PARASSAC, Émile
Les poèmes de l'Alpe... 1910.

ROWBOTHAM, J F
The epic of the Swiss lake-dwellers: an epic poem
in twelve cantos. 1913.

RUSKIN, John
The poems. 1891. 2v.

SCHEFFEL, Joseph Victor von
Mountain psalms. 1882.

SCHILLER, Friedrich von
Schillers Gedichte. 1894.

SCHMIDT, Theodor
Aus goldener Ferienzeit. 1908.

SCHULZ, Friedrich
Alpenlicht: Gornergrat, Furka, Maloja. 1910.

Schweizer Balladen. 1924.

SHELLEY, Percy Bysshe
Prometheus unbound, with Adonis, The cloud, Hymn
to intellectual beauty and An exhortation. 1894.

SHELLEY, Percy Bysshe
On Shelley. 1938.

SILIUS ITALICUS, Cajius
Punicorum. 1784.

SIM, Charles Henry
The Pyrenees: a poem. 1887.

SNOW, Robert
Memorials of a tour on the continent, to which are
added miscellaneous poems. 1845.

SOTHEBY, William
Italy and other poems. 1828.

STURM, August
Deutsches Liederbuch. 3.Aufl. 1911.

TENNYSON, Alfred, Baron Tennyson
[Guinevere]. Genièvre. 1868.

TENNYSON, Alfred, Baron Tennyson
MATHEWS, Charles Edward
The earlier and less-known poems of Alfred
Tennyson ...: an address delivered before the
members of the Harborne and Edgbaston Institute.
1883.

THIRLMERE, Rowland
Alpine and other lyrics. 1926.

TOLLEMACHE, Beatrix L
Engelbreg and other verses. 2nd ed. 1898.

A traveller's thoughts; or, Lines suggested by a
tour on the continent. 2nd ed. 1837.

TSCHARNER, Johann Baptist von
Die Bernina (1786). 1933.

VIRGIL
Moretum (o delle origini della pizza). [1973].

WALLACE, Cornelia
Mountain monarchs. 1887.

WARNERY, Henri
Sur l'alpe: peósies. 1895.

WHALLEY, Thomas Sedgwick
Mont Blanc: an irregular lyric poem. 1788.

WIFFEN, J H
Julia Alpinula; with The captive of Stamboul and
other poems. 2nd ed. [182-].

WILKINSON, Thomas
Tours to the British mountains, with descriptive
poems of Lowther, and Emont Vale. 1824.

WORDSWORTH, William
The complete poetical works. 1893.

WORDSWORTH, William
Our English lakes, mountains, and waterfalls as
seen by William Wordsworth. 1864.

WORDSWORTH, William
The prelude; or, Growth of a poet's mind... 1850.

WORDSWORTH, William
The River Duddon, a series of sonnets: Vaudracour
and Julia and other poems... 1820.

YOUNG, Geoffrey Winthrop
April and rain: poems. 1923.

YOUNG, Geoffrey Winthrop
Collected poems. 1936.

YOUNG, Geoffrey Winthrop
Freedom: poems. 1914.

YOUNG, Geoffrey Winthrop
Wind and hill: poems. 1909.

068.8. Songbooks - climbing, camping

Alpenröschen: schweizerisches Taschen-Liederbuch.
2.verm. Aufl. [1897].

BASTERFIELD, George
Songs of a cragsman. 1935.

BAUMBACH, Rudolf
Reise-und Wanderlieder. 1914.

BLETZACHER, J
Lieder-buch des Deutschen u-österreichischen Alpen-
Vereines... 1887.

BOTHMER, Heinrich
Das Schweizerland im Liede: eine anthologie. 1892.

068.8 Songbooks... (Cont.)

CLUB DES GRIMPEURS DE GENÈVE
  Chansonnier. [n.d.].

HAZLEWOOD, Rex and THURMAN, John
  The second Gilwell camp fire book. 1962.

HUMBLE, Benjamin Hutchison and MCLELLAN, W   M
  Songs for climbers. [1938].

Liedersammlung für alpine vereinigungen. 1910.

LINDER, Toni
  Über Fels und Firn: Liederbuch für
  Hochtourischen... 1895.

LÜTHI, Gottlieb
  Excelsior: Lieder eines Bergwanderers. [n.d.].

MASSANO, Gino
  Canti della montagna... 2a ed. 1931.

MEANY, Edmond Stephen
  Mountain camp fires. 1911.

RUCKSACK CLUB
  The songs of the mountaineers. [1922].

SCHWEIZER ALPEN-CLUB
  Liederbuch. 1921.

SCHWEIZER ALPEN-CLUB. Sektion Diablerets
  Chansonnier des Sections romandes du Club Alpin
  Suisse. 1902.

- - 3e éd. 1909.

Sing' ma oans! Alpenliederbuch. 1891.

- - 5.Aufl. 1901.
- - 6.Aufl. [19--].

THURMAN, John and HAZLEWOOD, Rex
  The Gilwell camp fire book. 1964.

07   HISTORY OF MOUNTAINEERING

070 History - general

ADAMS, William H   Davenport
  Celebrated women travellers of the nineteenth
  century. 1883.

ADAMS, William H   Davenport
  Mountains and mountain-climbing: records of adventure and enterprise among the famous mountains
  of the world. 1883.

BENSON, Claude Ernest
  Mountaineering ventures. [1928?].

CLARK, Ronald William
  The early alpine guides. 1949.

CLARK, Ronald William
  Men, myths and mountains. 1976.

CLARK, Ronald William
  A picture history of mountaineering. 1956.

CLARK, Ronald William
  Six great mountaineers: E. Whymper, A.F. Mummery,
  J.N. Collie, G. Leigh-Mallory, G.W. Young, Sir
  John Hunt. 1956.

CLARK, Ronald William
  The true book about mountaineering. 1957.

CLARK, Ronald William
  The Victorian mountaineers. 1953.

CLUB ALPINO ITALIANO. Comitato Scientifico
  Alpinismo italiano nel mondo. 1953.

COOLIDGE, William Augustus Brevoort
  Josias Simler et les origines de l'alpinisme
  jusqu'en 1600. 1904.

CORBETT, Edmund Victor
  Great true mountain stories. 1957.

CRANFIELD, Ingrid
  The challengers: British & Commonwealth adventure
  since 1945. 1976.

DOUGLAS, John Scott
  Summits of adventure: the story of famous
  mountain climbs and mountain climbers. 1955.

FANTIN, Mario
  Alpinismo italiano extraeuropeo... 1967.

FANTIN, Mario
  Italiani sulle montagne del mondo. 1967.

FRITH, Henry
  Ascents and adventures: a record of hardy
  mountaineering in every quarter of the globe.
  1884.

GRIBBLE, Francis
  The early mountaineers. 1899.

HERZOG, Theodor
  Der Kampf um die Weltberge. 1934.

HUF, Hans
  English mountaineers: A. Wills, J. Tyndall, E.
  Whymper, C. Dent, A.F. Mummery. 1926.

IRVING, Robert Lock Graham
  The romance of mountaineering. 1935.

IRVING, Robert Lock Graham
  [The romance of mountaineering]. La conquête de
  la montagne. 1936.

IRVING, Robert Lock Graham
  [The romance of mountaineering]. Werden und
  Wandlungen des Bergsteigens. 1949.

IRVING, Robert Lock Graham
  Ten great mountains. 1940.

- - Another ed. 1942.

IRVING, Robert Lock Graham
  [Ten great mountains]. Dix grandes montagnes...
  1945.

KEENLYSIDE, Francis
  Peaks and pioneers: the story of mountaineering.
  1975.

KURZ, Marcel
  Essai de chronologie des records d'altitude
  atteinte par l'homme en montagne. [1947?].

KURZ, Marcel
  Versuch einer Chronologie der Höhenrekorde im
  Gebirge. [1947].

LE BLOND, Elizabeth
  Adventures on the roof of the world. 1904.

LEHNER, Wilhelm
  Die Eroberung der Alpen. 1924.

LUNN, Sir Arnold
  A century of mountaineering, 1857-1957. 1957.

MIDDLETON, Dorothy
  Victorian lady travellers. 1965.

MONCRIEFF, Ascott Robert Hope
  Romance of the mountains. [1888].

MORIN, Micheline
  Encordées. 1936.

070 History... (Cont.)

Mountain adventures in the various countries of the
world; selected from the narratives of celebrated
travellers.
"Founded on a compilation made by M.M. Zurcher
and Margollé..."

NEWBY, Eric
Great ascents: a narrative history of mountaineering. 1977.

PIMLOTT, J A R
The Englishman's holiday: a social history. 1947.

REES, Ioan Bowen
Galwad y mynydd: chwe dringwr enwog. 1961.

REZNICEK, Felicitas von
Von der Krinoline zum sechsten Grad. 1967.

SCHWARTZ, Myrtil
... et la montagne conquit l'homme: histoire du
développement de l'alpinisme. 1931.

SCHWARZ, Bernhard
Die Erschliessung der Gebirge von der ältesten
Zeiten bis auf Saussure (1787)... 2.Ausg. 1888.

SCHWARZ, Th.
Über Fels und Firn: die Bezwingung der mächtigsten
Hochgipfel der Erde durch den Menschen. 1884.

SCOTT, Douglas K
Big wall climbing: [development, technique and
aids]. 1974.

SÉGOGNE, Henry de
Les alpinistes célèbres. 1956.

SHIPTON, Eric
Mountain conquest; by the editors of Horizon
Magazine, author Eric Shipton. 1966.

SMITH, B Webster
Pioneers of mountaineering. [1933].

SMYTHE, Frank S
British mountaineers. 1942.

SONNIER, Georges
La montagne et l'homme. 1970.

SPIRO, Louis
Histoire de l'alpinisme. [1916?].

STEAD, Richard
Adventures on the high mountains: romantic incidents & perils of travel, sport, and exploration
throughout the world. 1908.

STEINITZER, Alfred
Der Alpinismus in Bildern. 1913.

- - 2. ergänzte Aufl. 1924.

STYLES, Showell
First on the summits. 1970.

STYLES, Showell
On top of the world: an illustrated history of
mountaineering and mountaineers. 1967.

TEMPLE, Philip
The world at their feet: the story of New Zealand
mountaineers in the great ranges of the world.
1969.

TUMA, Henrik
Pomen in razvoj alpinizma. [1930?].

ULLMAN, James Ramsey
The age of mountaineering; with a chapter on
British mountains by W.H. Murray. 1956.

ULLMAN, James Ramsey
High conquest: the story of mountaineering. 1942.

ULLMAN, James Ramsey
[High conquest].La grande conquête... 1948.

UNSWORTH, Walter
Because it is there: famous mountaineers,
1840-1940. 1968.

WILLIAMS, Cicely
Women on the rope: the feminine share in mountain
adventure. 1973.

ZIAK, Karl
Der Mensch und die Berge: eine Weltgeschichte des
Alpinismus. 2. ... Aufl. 1956.

ZURCHER, Frédéric and MARGOLLÉ, Élie
Les ascensions célèbres aux plus hautes montagnes
du globe. 2e éd. 1869.

- - 4e éd. rev. et augm. 1879.
- - 5e éd., rev. par A. Le Pileur. 1891.

075 History - regional

IRVING, Robert Lock Graham
A history of British mountaineering. 1955.

LUNN, Sir Arnold
Switzerland and the English. 1944. (1945
reprint).

THORINGTON, James Monroe
A survey of early American ascents in the Alps
in the nineteenth century. 1943.

076 Mountaineering Clubs - history

AKADEMISCHER ALPEN-CLUB ZÜRICH
50 Jahre AACZ, 1896-1946: Festschrift zum fünfzigjährigen Bestehen des Akademischen Alpenclub
Zürich. 1946.

AKADEMISCHER ALPEN-CLUB ZÜRICH
75 Jahre Akademischer Alpen-Club Zürich. 1971.

ALPINE CLUB
The Alpine Club register, 1857-[1890], by A.L.
Mumm. 1923-28. 3v.

ALPINE CLUB
Record of expeditions in 1909 [-1913]. [1910-14].
5 pts. in 1.

BLAKENEY, Thomas Sidney
The Alpine Club. [1964].

CLUB ALPINO ITALIANO
L'opera del Club Alpino Italiano nel primo suo
cinquantennio, 1863-1913. 1913.

CLUB ALPINO ITALIANO. Commissione per il Centenario
1863-1963: i cento anni del Club Alpino Italiano.
1963.

- - 2a ed. 1964.

CLUB ALPINO ITALIANO. Sezione di Torino
Le valli di Lanzo (Alpi Graie). 1904.

CLUB ALPINO ITALIANO. Sezione di Varollo
I cento anni della Sezione di Varollo del Club
Alpino Italiano. 1967.

DEUTSCHER ALPENVEREIN. Sektion Bayerland
Bergsteigen als Lebensform. 1949.

DEUTSCHER UND ÖSTERREICHISCHER ALPENVEREIN
Geschichte des Deutschen und Oesterreichischen
Alpenvereins. 1894.

MACKINTOSH, A J
Mountaineering clubs, 1857-1907. 1908.

NEDERLANDSCHE ALPEN-VEREENIGING
Een halve eeuw Nederlands alpinisme. 1952.

08 MOUNTAINEERING BIBLIOGRAPHY

ALPINE CLUB. Library
Catalogue of books in the Library of the Alpine
Club. 1880.

- - Catalogue of books... 1888.
- - Catalogue of books... 1889.
- - [Lists of additions to the Alpine Club Library].
1903-17. 3v.
- - [List for Nov. 1932]. 1932.

BARKER, Clive S
Bibliography of exploration, mountaineering,
travel, history and nomenclature of the Gilgit-
Hunza River watershed, Haramosh Range and Basha
River watershed in the Eastern Hindu-Kush and
Western Karakoram. 1965-75. 3pts.

BENT, Allen H
A bibliography of the White Mountains. 1911.

- - Additions... [1918].

BRIDGE, George
Rock climbing in the British Isles, 1894-1970: a
bibliography of guidebooks. 1971.

BÜHLER, Hermann
Alpine Bibliographie für das Jahr 1931 [-1935].
1932-37.

- - Gesamtregister für die Jahre 1931-1938. 1949.

CAMPBELL, J I
A bibliography of mountains and mountaineering in
Africa. 1945.

COMITÉ NATIONAL FRANÇAIS DES RECHERCHES ANTARCTIQUES
Catalogue of publications. 1971.

COOLIDGE, William Augustus Brevoort
A list of the writings (not being reviews of
books) dated from 1868 to 1912 and relating to
the Alps or Switzerland. 1912.

COOLIDGE, William Augustus Brevoort
Swiss travel and Swiss guide-books. 1889.

DE BEER, Sir Gavin
Publications 1952-[1965]. [1960-65?]. 2v.

DEUTSCHE HIMALAJA-EXPEDITION, 1934
Himalaja-Bibliographie (1801-1933). 1934.

DEUTSCHER UND ÖSTERREICHISCHER ALPENVEREIN
Lichtbilder verzeichnis des D. und Ö. Alpenvereins. 1927-28.

- - Suppl. 1931.
- - Suppl. 1935.

DEUTSCHER UND ÖSTERREICHISCHER ALPENVEREIN.
Sektion Jena
Bücher- und Kartenverzeichnis. 1930.

DUPARC, Louis
Publications scientifiques. [1895].

DURIO, Alberto
Bibliografia alpinistica-storica e scientifica del
Gruppo del Monte Rosa (dal Colle del Théodule al
Passo del Monto Moro) dei monti della Valsesia e
della Sezione di Varallo del C.A.I., 1527-1924.
1925.

EDWARDS, Francis
Mountaineering, arctic travel, including a few
books from the late Mr. Edward Whymper's Library;
offered by Francis Edwards, Bookseller. 1913.

FAZY, Robert
L'exploration du Karakoram: essai de synthèse et
de bibliographie raisonnée. 1942.

FEDDEN, Robin
A bibliographical note on the early literature of
ski-ing in English. [1961].

FELL AND ROCK CLIMBING CLUB OF THE ENGLISH LAKE
DISTRICT
Catalogue of the Library; compiled by Muriel Files.
1972.

- - Additions June 1972 to May 1975. 1975.
- - Additions June 1975 to March 1979. 1979.
- - Section 4: Maps. 1978.

FISHER, Joel E
Bibliography of Alaskan and Pacific Coast states
mountain ascents. 1945.

FISHER, Joel E
Bibliography of Canadian mountain ascents. 1945.

FISHER, Joel E
Bibliography of eastern seaboard mountain ascents.
1945.

FISHER, Joel E
Bibliography of Mexican, Central and South
American mountain ascents. 1945.

FISHER, Joel E
Bibliography of United States mountain ascents
(except Pacific Coast states and the eastern
seaboard). 1945.

GRAF, J H and BRANDSTETTER, Josef Leop.
Bibliographische Vorarbeiten: Kataloge der Biblio-
theken, Gesellschaftsschriften, Zeitungen und
Kalender. 1896. 2v. in 1. (Bibliographie der
Schweizerischen Landeskunde, Fasc. 1)

HAENDCKE, Berthold
Architecture, sculpture et peinture. 1892.
(Bibliographie nationale suisse)

HALLER, Gottlieb Emanuel von
Bibliothek der Schweizer-Geschichte und aller
Theile so dahin Bezug haben. 1785-88. 7v.

HALLER, Gottlieb Emanuel von
Erster Versuch einer kritischen Verzeichniss,
aller Schriften, welche die Schweiz ansehen.
1759.

HIMALAYAN CLUB
Classified catalogue of books with alphabetical
index of authors. 1929.

JAPANESE ALPINE CLUB
Exhibition of alpine literature, May, 1935. 1935.

KAMBARA, Tatsu
Nepal bibliography 1959. 1959.

KRAWCZYK, Chess
Mountaineering: a bibliography of books in English
to 1974. 1977.

LIBRARY ASSOCIATION. County Libraries Group
Reader's guide to books on mountaineering. 2nd ed.
1972.

MAGYARORSZÁGI KÁRPÁTEGYLET
Bibliotheca Carpatica. 1880.

MONTAGNIER, Henry Fairbanks
A bibliography of the ascents of Mont Blanc from
1786-1853. 1911.

- - A further contribution to the bibliography of
Mont Blanc, 1786-1853. 1916.

NATIONAL LIBRARY OF SCOTLAND
Shelf-catalogue of the Lloyd Collection of alpine
books. 1964.

NEATE, William R
Mountaineering and its literature: a descriptive
bibliography of selected works published in the
English language, 1744-1976. 1978.

POLARIS MOUNTAINEERING CLUB. Library
Polaris Mountaineering Club Library list. 1973.

08 Bibliography (Cont.)

SCHWEIZERISCHE VERKHEHRSZENTRALE
  Bibliographie der Reiseliteratur der
  Schweizerischen Verkehrszentrale, Schweizerischen
  Transportanstalten, Verkehrs-Kur-und Hotelier-
  vereine. 1926.

SOCIETÀ DI SCIENZE E LETTERE DI GENOVA
  Catalogo delle memorie edite negli "Atti" sociali
  dal 1890 al 1939, nel cinquantesimo della
  fondazione della società. 1939.

SOTHEBY, WILKINSON AND HODGE
  [The Library of the late Edward Whymper ... sold
  by order of the executors]. 1912.

SURVEY OF INDIA
  Catalogue of maps. Parts 1 and 2. 1928.

SURVEY OF INDIA
  Map catalogue, corrected up to 30 Nov. 1931.
  1931.

SWITZERLAND. Eidgenössisches topographisches
Bureau
  Litteratur der Landesvermessung Kataloge der
  Kartensammlungen, Karten, Pläne, Reliefs,
  Panoramen. 1896. (Bibliographie der
  schweizerischen Landeskunde, Fasc.2)

SWITZERLAND. Eidgenössisches topographisches
Bureau
  [Litteratur der Landesvermessung...]. Cartes de
  parcelles plus ou moins grandes du territoire
  suisse. 1892. (Bibliographie nationale suisse,
  Fasc. 2)

THORINGTON, James Monroe
  Mountains and mountaineering: a list of the
  writings (1917-1947). 1947.

TOURING-CLUB DE FRANCE
  La montagne: catalogue de la bibliothèque léguée
  au Touring-Club de France par Étienne May, 1881-
  1962. 1965.

UNIVERSITY OF COLORADO. Institute of Arctic and
Alpine Research
  List of publications of the Institute of Arctic
  and Alpine Research. 1975.

WÄBER, A
  Descriptions géographiques et récits de voyages
  et excursions en Suisse: contribution à la bibliographie de la litterature suisse des voyages de
  1891 à 1900 avec des suppléments relatifs à la
  période antérieure à 1891. 1909. (Bibliographie
  nationale suisse, Fasc. III, 2)

WÄBER, A
  Landes-und Reisebeschreibungen: ein Beitrag zur
  Bibliographie der schweizerischen Reiselitteratur,
  1479-1890. 1899. (Bibliographie der
  schweizerischen Landeskunde, Fasc. 3)

WAGNER, Henry R
  The plains and the Rockies: a bibliography of
  original narratives of travel and adventure,
  1800-1865. 1921.

WASHBURN, Bradford
  Mount McKinley and the Alaska Range in literature:
  a descriptive bibliography. 1951.

WHYMPER, Edward
  Catalogue of books offered for sale by Mr. Whymper
  about 1908. [1908?].

WRIGHT, Walter W
  The White Mountains: an annotated bibliography,
  1918-1947. 1948.

YAKUSHI, Yoshimi
  Catalogue of the Himalayan literature. 1972.

YORKSHIRE RAMBLERS' CLUB. Library
  Yorkshire Ramblers' Club library: [catalogue]. 1959.

ZUMSTEINS LANDKARTENHAUS
  Zumstein Katalog mit Register. Grosse Ausg. 1964.

09 BIOGRAPHY, AUTOBIOGRAPHY

090 Collective Biography

CLARK, Ronald William
  The early alpine guides. 1949.

ENGEL, Claire Éliane
  They came to the hills. 1952.

HESS, Adolfo
  Saggi sulla psicologia dell'alpinista: raccolta
  di autobiografie psicologiche di alpinisti
  viventi. 1914.

NEALE, Erskine
  Sunsets and sunshine; or, Varied aspects of life.
  1862.

SÉGOGNE, Henry de
  Les alpinistes célèbres. 1956.

SPIRO, Louis
  [Guides de montagne]. La guida alpina. [1931].

WOLF, Rudolf
  Biographien zur Kulturgeschichte der Schweiz.
  1858-62. 4v.

ZIEGLER, Anton
  Erschliesser der Berge. 1926.

090 A - Z Individual Biography

ABERLI, Jean Louis
LONCHAMP, F   C
  J.-L. Aberli, 1723-86: son temps, sa vie et son
  oeuvre, avec un catalogue complet méthodique et
  raisonné. 1927.

ABRAHAM, Ashley Perry and ABRAHAM, George Dixon
HANKINSON, Alan
  Camera on the crags: a portfolio of early rock
  climbing photographs, by the Abraham brothers.
  1975.

AGASSIZ, Louis
AGASSIZ, Elizabeth Cary
  Louis Agassiz: his life and correspondence. 1885.

AGASSIZ, Louis
AGASSIZ, Elizabeth Cary
  Louis Agassiz: sa vie et sa correspondance. 1887.

AGASSIZ, Louis
GOS, Charles
  L'Hôtel des Neuchâtelois: un épisode de la
  conquête des Alpes. 1928.

AHLUWALIA, Hari Pal Singh
  Higher than Everest: memoirs of a mountaineer.
  1973.

ALBERT I, King of the Belgians
MALLIEUX, René
  Le roi Albert, alpiniste. 1956.

AMERY, Leopold Stennett
  Days of fresh air, being reminiscences of outdoor life. 1939.

AMERY, Leopold Stennett
  In the rain and the sun. 1946.

AMPFERER, Otto
  Bergtage: Gewalt und Glück der Höhen. 1930.

ANGENVILLE, Henriette d'
MEYER, Oskar Erich
  Die Braut des Montblanc. [1933].

ARANTHON, Jean d'
  La vie de Messire Jean D'Aranthon D'Alex, évèque
  et prince de Genève avec son directoire pour
  bien mourir... 2e éd., rev. & beaucoup augm. 1699.

090 A - C Biography (Cont.)

ASHENDEN
  The mountains of my life: journeys in Turkey and
  the Alps. 1954.

BAKER, George Percival
  Mountaineering memories of the past. 1951.

BANKS, Mike
  Commando climber. 1955.

BANKS, Mike
  Snow commando. 1961.

BEAUFOY FAMILY
BEAUFOY, Gwendolyn
  Leaves from a beech tree. 1930.

BELL, Gertrude
  The letters of Gertrude Bell. 1927. 2v.

BEST, Allena
  Abroad, and how to live there: a narrative of
  three years' residence in Germany and Switzerland.
  1860.

BLAKENEY, Thomas Sydney
FRIENDS OF THE NATIONAL LIBRARIES
  Thomas Sydney Blakeney: [an obituary].
  (In Friends of the National Libraries. Annual
  report, 1976, pp.5-6)

BLAZER, F
  Mes souvenirs de montagne. 1929.

BONATTI, Walter
  [I giorni grandi]. The great days. 1974.

BONATTI, Walter
  [Le mie montagne]. On the heights. 1964.

BONATTI, Walter
  [Le mie montagne]. A mes montagnes. 1962.

BONINGTON, Chris
  I chose to climb. 1966.

BONINGTON, Chris
  The next horizon: autobiography II. 1973.

BONNEY, Thomas George
  Memories of a long life. 1921.

BORTHWICK, Alastair
  Always a little further. 1969.

BRIDEL, Philippe Sirice
VULLIEMIN, L
  Le doyen Bridel: essai biographique. 1855.

BROOKE, Sir Victor
  Sir Victor Brooke, sportsman & naturalist: a
  memoir of his life and extracts from his letters
  and journals. 1894.

BROOKS, Phillips
  Letters of travel. 1893.

BROWN, Frederick Augustus Yeats
  Family notes. 1917.

BROWN, Joe
  The hard years: an autobiography. 1967.

BROWNE, George Forrest
  Off the mill: some occasional papers. 1895.

BROWNE, George Forrest
  The recollections of a bishop. 1915.

BROWNING, Oscar
WORTHAM, H   E
  Victorian Eton and Cambridge, being the life of
  Oscar Browning. New ed. 1956.

BRUCE, Hon. Charles Granville
  Himalayan wanderer. 1934.

BRULLE, Henri
  Souvenirs. 1930.

BRULLE, Henri
  Les ultimes ascensions. 1969.

BRUNNARIUS, Ernest
  Ernest Brunnarius, 1857-1901. 1903.

BRUNNER, Giorgio
  Un uomo va sui monti. 1957.

BRYCE, James, Viscount Bryce
  Memories of travel. 1923.

BRYCE, James, Viscount Bryce
FISHER, H   A   L
  James Bryce, Viscount Bryce of Dechmont. 2v.
  1927.

BUCKLAND, William
GORDON, Elizabeth Oke
  The life and correspondence of William Buckland
  ... 1894.

BUHL, Hermann
  Achttausend, drüber und drunter. 1954.

BUHL, Hermann
  [Achttausend, drüber und drunter]. Nanga Parbat
  pilgrimage. 1956.

BUHL, Hermann
  [Achttausend, drüber und drunter]. Buhl du
  Nanga Parbat. 1959.

BURTON, Reginald G
  Tropics and snows: a record of travel and
  adventure. 1898.

BUSK, Sir Douglas
  The delectable mountains. 1946.

BUTLER, Arthur John
QUILLER-COUCH, Sir Arthur
  Memoir of Arthur John Butler. 1917.

BUTLER, Frank Hedges
  Fifty years of travel by land, water and air.
  1920.

BYRON, George Gordon, Baron Byron
  Letters and journals of Lord Byron, with notices
  of his life, by Thomas Moore. 1830. 2v.

CALAME, Alexandre
RAMBERT, Eugène
  Alexandre Calame: sa vie et son oeuvre... 1884.

CAROLINE, Queen, Consort of George IV, King of
Great Britain
  Voyages and travels of her Majesty, Caroline
  Queen of Great Britain ..., by one of Her
  Majesty's Suite. 1822.

CARR, Herbert Reginald Culling and CARR, Evelyn
  A village antique shop in the Cotswolds, 1960-
  1975. 1975.

CARR-SAUNDERS, Sir Alexander Morris
BROWN, Henry Phelps
  Sir Alexander Morris Carr-Saunders, 1886-1966.
  1967.

CARREL, Jean Antoine
VIRIGLIO, Attilio
  Jean Antione Carrel (il "Padre" di tutte le
  guide). 1948.

CELLINI, Benvenuto
  Memoirs, written by himself. 1903.

CHAPMAN, Frederick Spencer
  Living dangerously. 1953.

CHAPMAN, Frederick Spencer
  Memoirs of a mountaineer: 'Helvellyn to Himalaya'
  and 'Lhasa: the Holy City'. 1945.

090 C - F Biography (Cont.)

CHAPMAN, Frederick Spencer
BARKER, Ralph
  One man's jungle: a biography of F. Spencer
  Chapman, D.S.O. 1975.

CHARLET, Armand
  Vocation alpine: souvenirs d'un guide de montagne.
  1949.

CHARLET, Armand
BUSK, Sir Douglas
  Armand Charlet: portrait d'un guide. 1974.

CHOUINARD, Yvon
BERNSTEIN, Jeremy
  Profiles: ascending: [biographical article on
  American climber Yvon Chouinard].
  (In New Yorker, January 31, 1977)

CHRISTOMANNOS, Theodor
  Christomannos-Gedenkbuch. 1912.

CLARK, Jane Inglis
  Pictures and memories. 1938.

CLUB ALPINO ITALIANO. Comitato Nazionale per le
Onoranze ad Emilio Comici
  Emilio Comici: alpinismo eroico. 1942.

COLERIDGE, Gilbert
  Some and sundry. 1931.

CONWAY, William Martin, Baron Conway
  Episodes in a varied life. 1932.

CONWAY, William Martin, Baron Conway
  Mountain memories: a pilgrimage of romance. 1920.

CONWAY, William Martin, Baron Conway
  [Mountain memories]. The autobiography of a
  mountain climber. Abridged ed. 1933.

CONWAY FAMILY
EVANS, Joan
  The Conways: a history of three generations. 1966.

COOLIDGE, William Augustus Brevoort
  Climbs in the Alps made in the years 1865 to 1900.
  [1900].

COOLIDGE, William Augustus Brevoort
CLARK, Ronald William
  An eccentric in the Alps: the story of the Rev.
  W.A.B. Coolidge the great Victorian mountaineer.
  1959.

COOLIDGE, William Augustus Brevoort
GODEFROY, Réné
  W.A.B. Coolidge, 1850-1926. 1926.

COSTE, Jean
  Dernières campagnes: notes et impressions
  d'alpinisme. 1928.

COSTE, Jean
  Mes quatre premières années de montagne. 1927.

COURTEN, Philippa de
GOS, Charles
  Tout était si beau là-haut ...: [la silhouette de
  Philippa de Courten].
  (In Bulletin paroissial d'Aigle, avril 1948)

CROUCHER, Norman
  High hopes. 1976.

CROWLEY, Aleister
  The spirit of solitude: an autohagiography, subse-
  quently re-antichristened The Confessions of
  Aleister Crowley. Vol.1. 1929. -Vol.2. 1929.

CROWLEY, Aleister
SYMONDS, John
  The great beast: the life of Aleister Crowley.
  1951.

CURZON, George Nathaniel, Marquess Curzon
  Leaves from a Viceroy's note-book and other papers.
  1926.

CUTTING, Suydam
  The fire ox and other years. 1947.

DIEMBERGER, Kurt
  [Imaka - Leben zwischen 0 und 8000]. Summits and
  secrets. 1971.

DIEMBERGER, Kurt
  [Imaka - Leben zwischen 0 und 8000]. Tra zero e
  ottomila. 1970.

DOUIE, Charles
  Beyond the sunset. 1935.

EDWARDS, John Menlove
  Samson: the life and writings of Menlove Edwards;
  edited with biographical memoir by Geoffrey
  Sutton and Wilfrid Noyce. [1960].

ELIAS, Ney
MORGAN, Gerald
  Ney Elias: explorer and envoy extraordinary in
  High Asia. 1971.

ELLIOTT, Henry Venn and ELLIOTT, Julius Marshall
BATEMAN, Josiah
  The life of the Rev. Henry Venn Elliott...; and
  an appendix, containing a short sketch of the
  life of the Rev. Julius Elliott. 3rd ed. 1872.

ELLIOTT, Julius Marshall
  Memoir of the Rev. Julius M. Elliott. [1870?].

ENZENSPERGER, Josef
  Josef Enzensperger: ein Bergsteigerleben; eine
  Sammlung von alpinen Schilderungen nebst einem
  Anhang Reisebriefe und Kerguelen-Tagebuch. 1905.

ESCHER VON DER LINTH, Arnold
HEER, Oswald
  Arnold Escher von der Linth: Lebensbild eines
  Naturforschers. 1873.

ETHERTON, P   T
  Adventures in five continents. [1928].

EVANS, Sir Charles
  On climbing. 1956.

FARQUHAR, Francis Peloubet
DAKIN, Susanna Bryant
  The published writings of Francis Peloubet
  Farquhar; together with an introduction to FPF by
  Susanna Bryant Dakin. 1954.

FINCH, George Ingle
  The making of a mountaineer. 1924.

FINCH, George Ingle
  [The making of a mountaineer]. Comment on devient
  alpiniste. 1926.

FINCH, George Ingle
BLACKMAN, M
  George Ingle Finch, 1888-1970. [1972].

FISCHER, Andreas
  Hochgebirgswanderungen in den Alpen und im
  Kaukasus. 1913.

- - Neue Folge. 1919.

FITZPATRICK, Thomas Cecil
RACKHAM, H
  Thomas Cecil Fitzpatrick: a memoir; edited by H.
  Rackham at the request of Mrs. Fitzpatrick. 1937.

FLENDER, Walther
BLODIG, Karl
  Zur Erinnerung an Walther Flender, 11.Jan. 1880-
  26.Feb. 1902: ein Lebensabriss. [19--].

090 F - K <u>Biography</u> (Cont.)

FORBES, James David
SHAIRP, John Campbell
  Life and letters of James David Forbes, F.R.S.,
  by John Campbell Shairp, Peter Guthrie Tait and
  A. Adams-Reilly. 1873.

FORBES, James David
TYNDALL, John
  Principal Forbes and his biographers. 1873.

FORSYTH, <u>Sir</u> Douglas
  Autobiography and reminiscences of Sir Douglas
  Forsyth; edited by his daughter [i.e. Ethel
  Forsyth]. 1887.

FORTESCUE, Winifred
  Mountain madness. 1943.

FOTHERGILL, Claud F
  A doctor in many countries. 1945.

FOX, Joseph Hoyland
  Holiday memories. 1908.

FREUCHEN, Peter
  Ice floes and flaming water. 1959.

GACHOT, Édouard
  À travers les Alpes. [n.d.].

GARDINER, Frederick
COOLIDGE, William Augustus Brevoort
  The alpine career (1868-1914) of Frederick
  Gardiner described by his friend W.A.B. Coolidge.
  1920.

GEIGER, Hermann
  Geiger: pilote des glaciers. 1955.

GEIGER, Hermann
  [Geiger: pilote des glaciers]. Alpine pilot.
  1956.

GIBBON, Edward
  **Miscellaneous works of Edward Gibbon ..., with
  memoirs of his life and writings composed by
  himself. 1796. 2v.**

GILBERT, Josiah
  Six letters relating to travel, 1865-1869. 1954.

GILL, Michael
  Mountain midsummer: climbing in four continents.
  1969.

GOS, Charles
  Au point 510: notes d'un observateur... 1932.

GOSSE, Henri Albert
PLAN, Danielle
  Un Genevois d'autrefois: Henri Albert Gosse,
  (1753-1816). 1909.

GRABER, Alfred
  Berge: Fahrten und Ziele. [1907].

GRAHAM, Peter
  Peter Graham, mountain guide: an autobiography.
  1965.

GRAY, Dennis
  Rope boy. 1970.

GREENE, Raymond
  Moments of being: the random recollections of
  Raymond Greene. 1974.

GRILL FAMILY
DEUTSCHER UND ÖSTERREICHISCHER ALPENVEREIN. <u>Sektion
Berchtesgaden</u>
  Die Grill aus der Ramsau: eine deutsche Führer-
  familie, zum fünfzigjährigen Führer-Jubiläum
  Johann Grills des Jüngeren. [1931?]

HARDMAN, <u>Sir</u> William
  The letters and memoirs of Sir William Hardman.
  2nd series, 1863-65. 1925.

HARPER, Arthur Paul
  Memories of mountains and men. 1946.

HARRISON, Frederic
  My alpine jubilee 1851-1907. 1908.

HASTON, Dougal
  In high places. 1972.

HAYWARD, Abraham
  A selection from the correspondence of Abraham
  Hayward from 1834 to 1884, with an account of
  his early life. 1886. 2v.

HECKMAIR, Anderl
  [Mein Leben als Bergsteiger]. My life as a
  mountaineer. 1975.

HEDIN, Sven
  My life as an explorer. 1926.

HILLARY, <u>Sir</u> Edmund
  High adventure. 1955.

HILLARY, <u>Sir</u> Edmund
  [High adventure]. L'aventure est sur les cimes.
  1955.

HILLARY, <u>Sir</u> Edmund
  Nothing venture, nothing win. 1975.

HILLARY, <u>Sir</u> Edmund
  [Nothing venture, nothing win]. Arrischiare per
  vincere. 1976.

HINCHLIFF, Thomas Woodbine
  Over the sea and far away, being a narrative of
  wanderings round the world. 1876.

HOLLAND, Henry Scott
  Henry Scott Holland: memoir and letters. 1921.

HOOKER, <u>Sir</u> Joseph Dalton
HUXLEY, Leonard
  Life and letters of Sir Joseph Dalton Hooker, OM,
  GCSI. 1918. 2v.

HORT, Fenton John Anthony
HORT, Arthur Fenton
  Life and letters of Fenton John Anthony Hort.
  1896. 2v.

HUMBOLDT, Alexander, <u>Freiherr von</u> and HUMBOLDT,
Wilhelm, <u>Freiherr von</u>
BAUER, Juliette
  Lives of the brothers Humboldt, Alexander and
  William. 1852.

IRVINE, Andrew Comyn
CARR, Herbert Reginald Culling
  The Irvine diaries: Andrew Irvine and the enigma
  of Everest 1924. 1979.

JAVELLE, Émile
GUEX, Jules
  Dans la trace de Javelle: nombreux documents
  inédits, notes, croquis, dessins et photographies
  de Javelle. 1947.

JONES, Humphrey Owen
SHORTER, John
  Humphrey Owen Jones (1878-1912): profile of a
  pioneer climber and scientist. 1979.

JONES, Humphrey Owen
SHORTER, John
  Humphrey Owen Jones, F.R.S. (1878-1912): chemist
  and mountaineer. 1979.

JONES, John Viriamu
JONES, Katherine Viriamu
  Life of John Viriamu Jones. 1915.

JONES, John Viriamu
POULTON, Edward Bagnall
  John Viriamu Jones and other Oxford memories.
  1911.

KAIN, Conrad
  Where the clouds can go. 1935.

090 <u>K - M</u> <u>Biography</u> (<u>Cont.</u>)

KEYSERLING, Hermann
  The travel diary of a philosopher. 1927.

KING, Clarence
  Clarence King memoirs [and] The Helmet of Mambrino.
  1904.

KLUCKER, Christian
  Erinnerungen eines Bergführers. 1930.

- - 3.verb. Aufl. 1931.

KLUCKER, Christian
  [Erinnerungen eines Bergführers]. Adventures of
  an alpine guide. 1932.

KOENIG, Franz Nikolaus
MANDACH, Conrad de
  F.-N. Koenig, 1765-1832. 1923.

KUGY, Julius
  Arbeit, Musik, Berge: ein Leben. [1931].

KUGY, Julius
  Aus dem Leben eines Bergsteigers. 1925.
  Various editions.

KUGY, Julius
  [Aus dem Leben eines Bergsteigers]. Alpine pilgrimage. 1934.

KUGY, Julius
  Das Kugybuch: Dr. Julius Kugy's Lebenswerk "Aus
  dem Leben eines Bergsteigers": eine Auswahl von
  Besprechungen. [192-?].

LAIRD, E   K
  The rambles of a globe trotter in Australasia,
  Japan, China, Jarva, India and Cashmere. 1875.
  2v.

LAMMER, Eugen Guido
  Wie anders ist das Besteigen der Alpen geworden!
  [1937].

LANCEROD, Jean
GERVAIS, Paul
  Le guide des Ormonts: élégie.
  (<u>In</u> Bibliothèque universelle... v.34, 1887)

LARDEN, Walter
  Recollections of an old mountaineer. 1910.

LAVIS-TRAFFORD, Marc de
  Mémorial du docteur Marc de Lavis-Trafford. 1962.

LE BLOND, Elizabeth
  Day in, day out. 1928.

LEVESON, Henry Astbury
  Sport in many lands. 1877. 2v.

LIVANOS, Georges
  Au dela de la verticale. 1958.

LONGSTAFF, Tom George
  This my voyage. 1950.

LONGSTAFF, Tom George
  [This my voyage]. Mon odyssée montagnarde. 1955.

LONGSTAFF, Tom George
  [This my voyage]. Ein Alpinist in aller Welt.
  1951.

LONGSTAFF, Tom George
  [This my voyage]. Recuerdos de viaje, del Himalaya
  al Ártico. 1952 (1954 reprint).

LONGSTAFF, Tom George
  [This my voyage]. Sui tetti del mondo. 1954.

LONGSTAFF, Tom George
  [This my voyage] Japanese ed. [1950?].

LOVELACE, Ralph Milbanke, <u>2nd Earl of</u>
LOVELACE, Mary, <u>Countess of</u>
  Ralph Earl of <u>Lovelace</u>: a memoir, by Mary
  Countess of Lovelace. 1920.

LUNN, <u>Sir</u> Arnold
  Alpine memories. [1959].

LUNN, <u>Sir</u> Arnold
  And <u>the</u> floods came: a chapter of war-time
  autobiography. 1942.

LUNN, <u>Sir</u> Arnold
  Come <u>what</u> may: an autobiography. 1940.

LUNN, <u>Sir</u> Arnold
  Memory to memory. 1956.

LUNN, <u>Sir</u> Arnold
  Mountain jubilee. 1943.

LUNN, <u>Sir</u> Arnold
  [Mountain jubilee]. Ich gedenke der Berge.
  1945.

LUNN, <u>Sir</u> Arnold
  [Mountain jubilee]. Recuerdos de montaña. 1949.

LUNN, <u>Sir</u> Arnold
  Mountains of memory. 1948.

LUNN, <u>Sir</u> Arnold
  The mountains of youth. 1925.

- - 2nd ed. 1949.

LUNN, <u>Sir</u> Arnold
  [The mountains of youth]. Les montagnes de ma
  jeunesse. 1943.

LUNN, <u>Sir</u> Arnold
  'Unkilled for so long'. 1968.

LUNN, <u>Sir</u> Arnold
  The Kandahar review, v.5, no.9, Oct. 1974.
  Memorial issue for Sir Arnold Lunn.

LURANI CERNUSCHI, Francesco, <u>conte</u>
  In memoria di Francesco Lurani Cernuschi.
  [1913].

LYELL, <u>Sir</u> Charles, <u>Bart.</u>
  Life, letters and journals of Sir Charles Lyell,
  Bart. 1881.

MACGREGOR, John
HODDER, Edwin
  John MacGregor ("Rob Roy")... 1894.

- - Popular ed. 1895.

MADUSCHKA, Leo
  Junger Mensch im Gebirg: Leben, Schriften,
  Nachlass. 1936.

MADUTZ, Johann
COOLIDGE, William Augustus Brevoort
  Johann Madutz, 1800-1861: ein Pionier der
  Schweizer Alpen: eine biographische Skizze. 1917.

MAHTAB, B   C
  Impressions: the diary of a European tour. [1908].

MAILLART, Ella K
  Cruises & caravans. 1942(1944 reprint).

MAILLART, Ella K
  'Ti-Puss'. 1951.

MALLORY, George Leigh
EHMER, Wilhelm
  Um den Gipfel der Welt: die Geschichte des Berg-
  steigers Mallory. 1936.

MALLORY, George Leigh
PEYRÉ, Joseph
  Mallory et son Dieu. 1947.

090 M-R <u>Biography</u> (Cont.)

MALLORY, George Leigh
PYE, <u>Sir</u> David Randall
  George Leigh Mallory: a memoir. 1927.

MALLORY, George Leigh
ROBERTSON, David
  George Mallory. 1969.

MANNERING, George Edward
  Eighty years in New Zealand... 1943.

MASON, Alfred Edward Woodley
GREEN, Roger Lancelyn
  A.E.W. Mason. 1952.

MAUNDEVILE, <u>Sir</u> John
  The marvellous adventures of Sir John Maundevile
  ... 1895.

MAZEAUD, Pierre
  [Montagne pour un homme nu]. Naked before the
  mountain. 1974.

MERKL, Willy
  Willy Merkl: ein weg zum Nanga Parbat; Leben
  Vortrage und nachgelassene Schriften. 1936.

MESSNER, Reinhold
  The big walls: history, routes, experiences.
  1978.

MESSNER, Reinhold
  The seventh grade: most extreme climbing. 1974.

MEURER, Julius
  Weltreisebilder. 1906.

MITCHELL, <u>Sir</u> Harold P
  In my stride. 1951.

MOFFAT, Gwen
  On my home ground. 1968.

MOFFAT, Gwen
  Space below my feet. 1961.

MONKSWELL, Mary, <u>Baroness Monkswell</u>
  A Victorian diarist: extracts from the journals
  of Mary, Lady Monkswell, 1873-95. 1944.

MONTAGUE, Charles Edward
ELTON, Oliver
  C.E. Montague: a memoir. 1929.

MORIN, Nea
  A woman's reach: mountaineering memoirs. 1968.

MORRIS, John
  Hired to kill: some chapters of autobiography.
  1960.

MUIR, John
  John of the mountains: the unpublished journals
  of John Muir. 1938.

MUIR, John
  Stickeen. 1909.

MUMMERY, Albert Frederick
UNSWORTH, Walter
  Tiger in the snow: the life and adventures of
  A.F. Mummery. 1967.

MURCHISON, <u>Sir</u> Roderick Impey
GEIKIE, Archibald
  Life of Sir Roderick I. Murchison based on his
  journals and letters, with notices of his
  scientific contemporaries... 1875. 2v.

NEFF, Felix
GILLY, William Stephen
  A memoir of Felix Neff, pastor of the High Alps...
  1833.

NOEL-BUXTON, Noel, <u>Baron Buxton</u>
  Travels and reflections. 1929.

NOYCE, Wilfrid
  Mountains and men. 1947.

OGGIONI, Andrea
  Le mani sulla roccia: il diario alpinistico di
  Andrea Oggioni. 1964.

OITZINGER, Anton
KUGY, Julius
  Anton Oitzinger: ein Bergführerleben. 1935.

OITZINGER, Anton
KUGY, Julius
  [Anton Oitzinger: ein Bergführerleben]. Son of
  the mountains: the life of an alpine guide.
  1938.

PAULCKE, Wilhelm
  Berge als Schicksal. 1936.

PAYER, Julius
  Julius Payers Bergfahrten: Erschliessungsfahrten
  in den Ortler-, Adamello- und Presanella-Alpen
  (1864-1868). 1920.

PENCK, Albrecht
  Festband: Albrecht Penck zur Vollendung des
  sechzigsten Lebensjahrs... 1918.

PERKONIG, Josef Friedrich
  Mein Herz ist im Hochland. 1937.

PETRIE, Peter J W de C
  Farewell to the mountains. 1940.

PETZOLDT, Patricia
  On top of the world. 1956.

PFANN, Hans
  Menschen im Hochgebirge: Festgabe für Hans Pfann
  zum 60 Geburtstage 4. August 1933. 1933.

PIAZ, Tita
  Le diable des Dolomites. 1963.

PIDGEON, Daniel
  An engineer's holiday; or, Notes of a round trip
  from long. 0' to 0'. 1882. 2v.

PILLEY, Dorothy E
  Climbing days. 1935.

- - 2nd rev. ed. 1965.

PIUS XI, <u>Pope</u>
GASQUET, Francis Aidan
  His Holiness Pope Pius XI: a pen portrait... and
  The Pope as alpine climber; translated from an
  article written by himself. 1922.

PIUS XI, <u>Pope</u>
WILLIAMSON, Benedict
  The story of Pope Pius XI. 1931.

POLLINGER, Joseph
GOS, Charles
  Vie d'un grand guide: Joseph Pollinger. 1944.

POLLOCK, <u>Sir</u> Frederick
  The Pollock-Holmes letters: correspondence of Sir
  Frederick Pollock and Mr. Justice Holmes, 1874-
  1932. 1942. 2v.

POLO, Marco
  The travels of Marco Polo, the Venetian. 1892.

POWELL, Paul
  Men aspiring. 1967.

PRESTON-THOMAS, Herbert
  The work and play of a government inspector.
  1909.

RABL, Josef
  Meine Lebenserinnerungen. 1923.

RAMBERT, Eugène
TALLICHET, Ed.
  Eugène Rambert: souvenirs personnels.
  (<u>In</u> Bibliothèque universelle ... v.33, 1887)

090 R - S Biography (Cont.)

RAMBERT, Eugène
WARNERY, Henri
    Eugène Rambert: études contemporaines.
    (In Bibliothèque universelle... v.36, 1887)

RAMOND, Louis
BERALDI, Henri
    La carrière posthume de Ramond, 1827-1868: notes
    d'un bibliophile. 1927.

RAMOND, Louis
BERALDI, Henri
    Le passé du pyrénéisme: notes d'un bibliophile.
    Library has v.2-5, 1913-20 only.

RAMOND, Louis
SOCIÉTÉ RAMOND
    L.-F.-E. Ramond, 1755-1827: commémoration. 1927
    [printed 1930].

RÉBUFFAT, Gaston
    Entre terre et ciel. 1962.
    "Commentaire du film".

RÉBUFFAT, Gaston
    [Entre terre et ciel]. Between heaven and earth.
    1965.

RÉBUFFAT, Gaston
    Étoiles et tempêtes (Six faces nord). 1954.

RÉBUFFAT, Gaston
    [Étoiles et tempêtes]. Starlight and storm: the
    ascent of six great north faces of the Alps.
    1956.

RERESBY, Sir John
    Memoirs & travels of Sir John Reresby. 1904.

REY, Guido
    Alba alpina. [1915].

REY, Guido
    [Alba alpina]. Aube alpine. 1925.

REY, Guido
    Alpinismo acrobatico. 1914.

- - Nuova ed. 1932.

REY, Guido
    [Alpinismo acrobatico]. Peaks and precipices:
    scrambles in the Dolomites and Savoy. 1914.

REY, Guido
    [Alpinismo acrobatico]. Alpinisme acrobatique.
    1919.

- - 2e éd. 1929.

REY, Guido
    [Alpinismo acrobatico]. Bergakrobaten: Kletter-
    fahrten an Montblanc-Nadeln und Dolomiten-Türmen.
    [19--].

REY, Guido
    Souvenirs et visions d'alpinisme. 1937.

RICHARD, Colette
    Climbing blind. 1966.

RICHARDSON, Katharine
PAILLON, Mary
    En souvenir de Miss Katharine Richardson, 1854-
    1927. 1927.

RICHARDSON, Katharine
PAILLON, Mary
    Miss Kate Richardson, une grande alpiniste: liste
    de courses et souvenirs. [1943?].

RICKMERS, Willi Rickmer
    Querschnitt durch mich. 1930.

RIGELE, Fritz
    50 Jahre Bergsteiger: Erlebnisse und Gedanken.
    1935.

ROBERTS, Michael
EASON, T   W   and HAMILTON, R
    A portrait of Michael Roberts. 1949.

ROBINSON, Anthony Melland
    Alpine roundabout. 1947.

ROCH, André
    Les conquétes de ma jeunesse. 1942.

ROCH, André
    [Les conquétes de ma jeunesse]. Climbs of my
    youth. 1949.

ROGER, Alexandre Salomon
ENGEL, Claire Éliane
    Alpinistes d'autrefois: le major Roger et son
    baromètre. 1935.

RUSKIN, John
    The diaries of John Ruskin.
    Vol.1: 1835-1847. 1956. -Vol.2: 1848-1873.
    1958. -

RUSKIN, John
COLLINGWOOD, William Gershom
    The life of John Ruskin. 7th ed. 1911.

RUSKIN, John
COOK, Sir Edward Tyas
    Homes and haunts of John Ruskin. 1912.

RUSKIN, John
COOK, Sir Edward Tyas
    The life of John Ruskin. 1911. 2v.

RUSSELL, Henry, Count
    Souvenirs d'un montagnard. 1878.

RUSSELL, Henry, Count
    Souvenirs d'un montagnard, 1858-1888. 1888.

- - 2e éd., rev. et corr. 1908.

SALADIN, Lorenz
CLARK-SCHWARZENBACH, Annemarie
    Ein Leben für die Berge: Lorenz Saladin. 1938.

SAND, George
    Lettres d'un voyageur. Nouv. éd. 1869.

SAUDAN, Sylvain
DREYFUS, Paul
    Sylvain Saudan, skieur de l'impossible. 1970.

SAUSSURE, Horace Bénédict de
    Lettres de H.-B. de Saussure à sa femme, com-
    mentées par E. Gaillard et H.F. Montagnier. 1937.

SAUSSURE, Horace Bénédict de
FRESHFIELD, Douglas William
    The life of Horace Bénédict de Saussure, by
    Douglas W. Freshfield with the collaboration of
    Henry F. Montagnier. 1920.

SAUSSURE, Horace Bénédict de
FRESHFIELD, Douglas William
    [The life of Horace Bénédict de Saussure]. Horace-
    Bénédict de Saussure, par Douglas W. Freshfield
    avec la collaboration de Henry F. Montagnier.
    1924.

SAUSSURE, Horace Bénédict de
SENEBIER, Jean
    Mémoire historique sur la vie et les écrits de
    Horace Bénédict Desaussure... [1801].

SAUSSURE, Horace Bénédict de
VALLOT, Charles
    Saussure aux Alpes. 1. Portrait de H.-B. de
    Saussure par Charles Vallot... 1938.

SAVAGE-LANDOR, A   Henry
    Everywhere: the memoirs of an explorer. 1924.

SCHINER, Matthäus
CHASTONAY, Paul de
    [Kardinal Schiner]. Le Cardinal Schiner. [1943].

090 S - T Biography (Cont.)

SCHMID, Toni
BAUMEISTER, Hans
  Jugend in Fels und Eis: ein Ehrenmal gewidmet dem
  Helden vom Matterhorn: Toni Schmid von seinen
  Kameraden. 1934.

- - 3.Aufl. [ca 1940].

SCHUSTER, Sir Arthur
  Biographical fragments. 1932.

SCHUSTER, Oskar
FISCHER, Walther
  Oskar Schuster und sein Geist. 1926.

SEE, Thomas Jefferson Jackson
WEBB, W   L
  Brief biography and popular account of the un-
  paralleled discoveries of T.J.J. See. 1913.

SEIGNEUR, Yannick
  À la conquête de l'impossible. 1977.

SEILER, Alexander
KÄMPFEN, Werner
  Alexander Seiler der Jüngere: sein Wirken für
  Zermatt, das Wallis und die Schweiz. 1945.

SEILER, Joseph A
  Joseph A. Seiler, 1896-1948: zum Gedächtnis.
  1949.

SELLA, Vittorio
CLARK, Ronald William
  The splendid hills: the life and photographs of
  Vittorio Sella, 1859-1943. 1948.

SHACKLETON, Sir Ernest Henry
FISHER, Margery and FISHER, James
  Shackleton. 1957.

SHELLEY, Frances, Lady
  The diary of Frances Lady Shelley, 1787-1817.
  1912.

SHIPTON, Eric
  That untravelled world: an autobiography. 1969.

- - New ed. 1977.

SHIPTON, Eric
  Upon that mountain. 1943.

SHIPTON, Eric
  [Upon that mountain]. "Sur cette montagne..."
  1950.

SIMON, Charles
  Erlebnisse und Gedanken eines alten Bergsteigers,
  1880-1930. 1932.

SLOCUM, Joshua
  Sailing alone around the world. 3rd ed. 1902.

SMITH, Albert
FITZSIMONS, Raymund
  The Baron of Piccadilly: the travels and enter-
  tainments of Albert Smith, 1816-1860. 1967.

SMITH, Albert
THORINGTON, James Monroe
  Mont Blanc sideshow: the life and times of Albert
  Smith. 1934.

SMYTHE, Frank S
  The adventures of a mountaineer. 1940.

SMYTHE, Frank S
  [The adventures of a mountaineer]. L'aventure
  alpine... 1951.

SMYTHE, Frank S
  [Mountaineering holiday]. Vacances d'alpiniste...
  1948.

SOMERVELL, Theodore Howard
  After Everest: the experiences of a mountaineer
  and medical missionary. 1936.

SPESCHA, Pater Placidus a
  Pater Placidus a Spescha; sein Leben und seine
  Schriften. 1913.

STARK, Freya
  Traveller's prelude. 1950.

STEPHEN, Sir Leslie
ANNAN, Noel Gilroy
  Leslie Stephen; his thought and character in re-
  lation to his time. 1951.

STEPHEN, Sir Leslie
MAITLAND, Frederic William
  The life and letters of Leslie Stephen. 1906.

STILLINGFLEET, Benjamin
  Literary life and select works of Benjamin
  Stillingfleet... 1811. 3v. in 1.

STOBART, Tom
  Adventurer's eye: the autobiography of Everest
  film-man Tom Stobart. 1958.

STONE, James Kent
SMITH, Walter George and SMITH, Helen Grace
  Fidelis of the Cross: James Kent Stone. 2nd ed.
  1927.

STYLES, Showell
  Rock and rope. 1967.

SYMES-THOMPSON, Edmund
SYMES-THOMPSON, Lilla
  Memories of Edmund Symes-Thompson ... a follower
  of St. Luke. 1908.

SYMONDS, John Addington
BROWN, Horatio F
  John Addington Symonds: a biography; compiled
  from his papers and correspondence. 2nd ed.
  1908.

SYMONDS, John Addington
SYMONDS, Margaret
  Out of the past; with an account of Janet
  Catherine Symonds by Mrs. Walter Leaf. 1925.

TANNER, Henry C   B
TANNER, Beryl
  Salute to the early mountaineer [H.C.B. Tanner]:
  six short articles on the Himalayas. [n.d.].

TASSE, Père
VINCENT, Henri
  Les vingt-deux années du Père Tasse à
  Chambrousse. 1891.

TENZING NORGAY
  After Everest: an autobiography, by Tenzing Norgay
  Sherpa; as told to Malcolm Barnes. 1977.

TENZING NORGAY
  La conquête de l'Everest par le Sherpa Tenzing;
  récit d'Yves Malartic. 1953.

TENZING NORGAY
  Gli eroi del Chomolungma, [da] Massimo Mila,
  Tensing Norkey. 1954.

TENZING NORGAY
  Man of Everest: the autobiography of Tenzing told
  to James Ramsey Ullman. 1955.

TENZING NORGAY
  [Man of Everest]. Tenzing de l'Everest: autobiographie racontée à James Ramsey Ullman. 1955.

TERRAY, Lionel
  [Les conquérants de l'inutile]. Conquistadors of
  the useless: from the Alps to Annapurna. 1963.

THARKEY, Ang
  Ang Tharkey: mémoires d'un Sherpa; recuillis par
  Basil P. Norton. 1954.

THOMSON, Joseph
THOMSON, J   B
  Joseph Thomson, African explorer: a biography, by
  his brother J.B. Thomson. 2nd ed. 1897.

090 T - Z Biography (Cont.)

TOPALI, Constantin P
  Constantin P. Topali, 1898-1924. 1926.

- - 2e éd. 1931.

TRENKER, Luis
  Kameraden der Berge. 1932.

TRENKER, Luis
  [Kameraden der Berge]. Brothers of the snow.
  1933.

TRENKER, Luis
  Meine Berge: Das Bergbuch. 1931.

TSCHUDI, Carlos
  Ein Dankesbuch. [1930].

TUBBY, Alfred Herbert
  A consulting surgeon in the Near East. 1920.

TUCKETT, Francis Fox
  A pioneer in the High Alps: alpine diaries and
  letters of F.F. Tuckett, 1856-1874. 1920.

TURNER, Samuel, 1869-1929
  My climbing adventures in four continents. 1911.

TYNDALL, John
EVE, A   S   and CREASEY, C   H
  Life and work of John Tyndall. 1945.

UNDERHILL, Miriam
  Give me the hills. 1956.

- - [New ed.]. 1971.

VERMOREL, Lucien
GUILLERMET, Jean
  Lucien Vermorel, 12 décembre 1893 - 2 octobre
  1921, 27 ans. [1921].

VICTOR-EMMANUEL II, King of Italy
GORRET, Amé
  Victor-Emmanuel sur les Alpes: notices et
  souvenirs. 1878.

- - 2e éd.,rev. et augm. 1879.

WALKER, James Hubert
  Mountain days in the Highlands and Alps. 1937.

WALTER, James Conway
  Stray leaves on travel, sport, animals and kindred
  subjects. 1910.

WATKINS, Gino
SCOTT, J   M
  Gino Watkins. 1935.

WHILLANS, Don and ORMEROD, Alick
  Don Whillans: portrait of a mountaineer. 1971.

WHITBREAD, S   A
  The silent hills. [19--].

WHYMPER, Edward
SMYTHE, Frank S
  Edward Whymper. 1940.

WHYMPER, Edward
SMYTHE, Frank S
  Edward Whymper: ein Bergsteiger- und Forscher-
  leben. 1940.

WHYMPER, Edward
SMYTHE, Frank S
  Edward Whymper; translated into Japanese. 1966.

WHYMPER, Edward
UNSWORTH, Walter
  Matterhorn man: the life and adventures of Edward
  Whymper. 1965.

WHYMPER, Edward
YOUNG, Bert Edward
  Edward Whymper: alpinist of the heroic age.
  1914.

WIGRAM, Woolmore
WIGRAM, Harriet Mary
  Memoirs of Woolmore Wigram, Canon of St. Albans.
  1908.

WILKIE, Sir David
CUNNINGHAM, Allan
  The life of Sir David Wilkie, with his journals,
  tours, and critical remarks on works of art and
  a selection from his correspondence. 1843. 3v.

WILKINSON, T   E
  Twenty years of continental work and travel.
  1906.

WILLIAMS, Cicely
  Bishop's wife - but still myself. 1961.

WILLIAMS, Cicely
  Dear abroad. 1967.

WILLIAMS, Cicely
  Diary of a decade: more memoirs of a Bishop's
  wife. 1970.

WILSON, Claude
  An epitome of fifty years' climbing. 1933.

WILSON, Edward
SEAVER, George
  Edward Wilson: nature-lover. 1937.

WILSON, Edward
SEAVER, George
  Edward Wilson of the Antarctic: naturalist and
  friend, together with a memoir of Oriana Wilson.
  1937.

WILSON, Edward
SEAVER, George
  The faith of Edward Wilson. 1953.

WINKLER, Georg
KÖNIG, Erich
  Empor! Georg Winklers Tagebuch. [1910].

WOLLASTON, Alexander Frederick Richmond
  Letters and diaries of A.F.R. Wollaston; selected
  and edited by Mary Wollaston. 1933.

WUNDT, Theodor
  Ich und die Berge: ein Wanderleben. 1917.

YOUNG, Geoffrey Winthrop
  The grace of forgetting. 1953.

YOUNG, Geoffrey Winthrop
  Mountains with a difference. 1951.

YOUNG, Geoffrey Winthrop
  On high hills: memories of the Alps. 1927.

- - 5th ed. 1947.

YOUNGHUSBAND, Sir Francis
SEAVER, George
  Francis Younghusband: explorer and mystic. 1952.

YOUNGHUSBAND, Sir George
  A soldier's memories in peace and war. 1917.

ZSCHOKKE, Heinrich
  Autobiography. 1845.

ZURBRIGGEN, Matthias
  From the Alps to the Andes, being the autobiography of a mountain guide. 1899.

ZURBRIGGEN, Matthias
  [From the Alps to the Andes]. Von den Alpen zu
  den Anden: Lebenserinnerungen eines Bergführers.
  [1938].

10   BRITISH ISLES

101   Geology, natural history

FITTER, Richard
   Britain's wildlife: rarities and introductions.
   1966.

MACKINTOSH, D
   The scenery of England and Wales, its character
   and origin, being an attempt to trace the nature
   of the geological causes ... by which the physical
   features ... have been produced. 1869.

PEARSALL, William H
   Mountains and moorlands. 1950.

STAMP, L   Dudley
   Britain's structure and scenery. 1946.

TAYLOR, J   E
   Mountain and moor. 1880.

102   Geography, description, travel

An account of the principal pleasure tours in
   England and Wales. 1822.

BELL, James Horst Brunnerman
   British hills and mountains, by J.H.B. Bell, E.F.
   Bozman and J. Fairfax Blakeborough. 1940.

BICKNELL, Peter
   British hills and mountains. 1947.

BOGG, Edmund
   Two thousand miles of wandering in the Border
   Country, Lakeland and Ribblesdale. 1898.

DENHOLM, James
   A tour to the principal Scotch and English lakes.
   1804.

- - New ed. 1817.

Diary of a fortnight's trip through the English Lake
   District and Scotland, in July, 1867, by a few
   friends; written by one of the party. [1867].

DURBIN, John P
   Observations in Europe, principally in France and
   Great Britain. 1844. 2v.

FELTHAM, John
   A guide to all the watering and sea bathing places:
   descriptions of the lakes, tour in Wales...
   [1825?].

GARDNER, Arthur
   Britain's mountain heritage and its preservation
   as National Parks. 1942.

GILPIN, William
   Observations on several parts of the counties of
   Cambridge, Norfolk, Suffolk, and Essex; also on
   several parts of North Wales... 1809.

Gleanings of a wanderer, in various parts of
   England, Scotland, & North Wales...
   (In A collection of modern and contemporary
   voyages... Vol.2. 1806)

HOWARTH, O   J   R
   The scenic heritage of England and Wales. 1937.

MAVOR, William Fordyce
   A tour in Wales, and through several counties of
   England, including both the universities...
   (In A collection of modern and contemporary
   voyages... Vol.3. 1806)

MAWMAN, J
   An excursion to the Highlands of Scotland and the
   English Lakes, with recollections, descriptions,
   and references to historical facts. 1805.

MOLONY, Eileen
   Portraits of mountains. 1950.

NODIER, Charles
   Promenade from Dieppe to the mountains of Scotland.
   1822.

POUCHER, W.A.
   Escape to the hills. [1943].

PYATT, Edward Charles
   Mountains of Britain. 1966.

RUTLAND, John Henry Manners, 5th Duke of
   Journal of a tour to the northern parts of Great
   Britain. 1813.

SALT, Henry Stephen
   On Cambrian and Cumbrian hills: pilgrimages to
   Snowdon and Scawfell. 1908.

SINCLAIR, Catherine
   Hill and valley; or, Hours in England and Wales.
   1838.

STOWE, Harriet Beecher
   Sunny memories of foreign lands. 1854.

WATSON, Jean L
   Our native land: its scenery and associations, a
   series of 36 water-colour sketches ... with descriptive notes. 1879.

WILKINSON, Thomas
   Tours to the British mountains, with descriptive
   poems of Lowther, and Emont Vale. 1824.

103   Climbing history, reminiscences

ABRAHAM, George Dixon
   Mountain adventures at home and abroad. 1910.

ABRAHAM, George Dixon
   On alpine heights and British crags. 1919.

BAKER, Ernest Albert
   The British highlands with rope & rucksack. 1933.

BRIDGE, George
   Rock climbing in the British Isles, 1894-1970: a
   bibliography of guidebooks. 1971.

CLARK, Ronald William and PYATT, Edward Charles
   Mountaineering in Britain: a history from the
   earliest times to the present day.
   1957.

PATERSON, M
   Mountaineering below the snow-line; or, The
   solitary pedestrian in Snowdonia and elsewhere.
   1886.

PYATT, Edward Charles and NOYCE, Wilfrid
   British crags and climbers: an anthology. [1952].

RUDGE, E   C   W
   Mountain days near home. 1941.

SANDEMAN, R   G
   A mountaineer's journal. 1948.

104   Climbs and climbing

ABRAHAM, George Dixon
   British mountain climbs. 1909.

BARFORD, John Edward
   Climbing in Britain. 1946.

BENSON, Claude Ernest
   British mountaineering. 1909.

- - 2nd ed., rev. and enl. 1914.

104 British Isles - climbs and climbing (Cont.)

BRIDGE, George
The mountains of England and Wales: tables of mountains of two thousand feet and more in altitude. 1973.

CLEARE, John and COLLOMB, Robin Gabriel
Sea cliff climbing in Britain. 1973.

DOCHARTY, William McKnight
A selection of some 900 British and Irish mountain tops. 1954.

- - Supplement. 1962. 2v.

A list of the heights of nearly two hundred of the principal mountains of England and Wales. 1860.

MAXWELL, D   C
Tables giving all the 3000-ft. mountains of England, Wales and Ireland. 1959.

MILNER, Cyril Douglas
Rock for climbing. 1950.

PYATT, Edward Charles
Where to climb in the British Isles. 1960.

RICHMOND, William Kenneth
Climber's testament. 1950.

SMITH, Walter Parry Haskett
Climbing in the British Isles..
1. England. 1894. -2. Wales and Ireland. 1895.

WILSON, Ken
Classic rock: great British rock-climbs. 1978.

WILSON, Ken
Hard rock: great British rock-climbs. 1975.

WRIGHT, Jeremiah Ernest Benjamin
Rock climbing in Britain. 1958.

108 Walking

HALL, Richard Watson
The art of mountain tramping: practical hints for both walker and scrambler among the British peaks. 1932.

MILLAR, T   G
Long distance paths of England and Wales. 1977.

109 Guide-books

WALFORD, Thomas
The scientific tourist through England, Wales, & Scotland ... arranged by counties... Vol.2. 1818.

11   ENGLAND
(excluding Lake District)

112 Geography, description, travel

BAKER, Ernest Albert and BALCH, Herbert E
The netherworld of Mendip: explorations in the great caverns of Somerset, Yorkshire, Derbyshire, and elsewhere. 1907.

GILPIN, William
Observations relative chiefly to picturesque beauty, made in the year 1772, on several parts of England... 1786. 2v.

- - 2nd ed. 1788.
- - 3rd ed. 1792.

Hill and dale: sketches of wild nature and country life. [1912].

MALLESON, F   A
Holiday studies of Wordsworth: by rivers, woods, and Alps, the Wharfe, the Duddon, and the Stelvio pass. 1890.

MARTEL, Édouard Alfred
Irlande et cavernes anglaises. 1897.

113 Climbs and climbing - general

UNSWORTH, Walter
The English outcrops. 1964.

114 East & South East

CLARKE, J   V   C
The Essex Way. 1977.

FITZGERALD, Kevin
The Chilterns. 1972.

The night climber's guide to Trinity. 3rd ed. 1960.

PYATT, Edward Charles
Chalkways of South and South-East England. [1974].

PYATT, Edward Charles
Climbing and walking in South-East England. 1970.

WHIPPLESNAITH
The night climbers of Cambridge. 1937.

YOUNG, Geoffrey Winthrop
The roof-climber's guide to Trinity, containing a practical description of all routes. [1900].

- - New ed. 1930.

115 South West

DENTON, J   W
A climbing guide to Dartmoor. [195-].

DERRY, J   D
Some rock climbs near Plymouth: a climbing guide. 1950.

PYATT, Edward Charles
A climber in the West Country. 1968.

117 Peaks, Pennines

BAKER, Ernest Albert
Moors, crags & caves of the High Peak and the neighbourhood. [1903].

BYNE, Eric and SUTTON, Geoffrey
High Peak: the story of walking and climbing in the Peak District. 1966.

MERRILL, John N
Walking in Derbyshire: thirty-two walks in the Peak District. 1969.

MONCRIEFF, Ascott Robert Hope
The Peak country. 1908.

MONKHOUSE, Patrick
On foot in the Peak. 1932.

OLDHAM, Kenneth
The Pennine Way: Britain's longest continuous footpath. Rev. [ed.]. 1968.

POUCHER, W.A.
The backbone of England. 1946.

POUCHER, W.A.
Peak panorama: Kinder Scout to Dovedale. 1946.

117 Peaks, Pennines (Cont.)

RAMBLERS ASSOCIATION. Northern Area
  Ramblers' Cheviot: twelve walks in the Cheviot
  Hills. [Rev. ed., edited by Betty Fletcher].
  1976.

WOOD, John
  Mountain trail: the Pennine Way from the Peak to
  the Cheviots. 1947.

118 North East, Yorkshire

CHIANG, Yee
  The silent traveller in the Yorkshire Dales. 1941.

COWLEY, Bill
  Lyke Wake Walk: forty miles across the north
  Yorkshire moors. 1968.

FLETCHER, J S
  The enchanting North. 1908.

ROSE, Thomas
  Westmorland, Cumberland, Durham, and
  Northumberland. 1832-[35]. 3v.

119 Guide-books

BADDELEY, Mountford J B
  The Peak District of Derbyshire and neighbouring
  counties... 7th ed., rev. and enl. 1899.

BADDELEY, Mountford J B
  Yorkshire... 4th ed., rev. 1901-02. 2v.

WARD, C S
  North Devon, including west Somerset, and north
  Cornwall... 8th ed., rev. 1903.

12 LAKE DISTRICT

122 Geography, description, travel

ABRAHAM, Ashley Perry
  Beautiful Lakeland. 1912.

ALLOM, Thomas
  Lake and mountain scenery: Westmorland and
  Cumberland. [184-].

BAINES, Edward
  A companion to the Lakes of Cumberland,
  Westmoreland, and Lancashire, in a descriptive
  account of a family tour... 1829.

- - 3rd ed. 1834.

BARON, Joseph
  All about the English Lakes: a cyclopedia of
  places, persons, myths and happenings. 1925.

BRADLEY, Arthur Granville
  The English Lakes. 1910.

BRADLEY, Arthur Granville
  Highways and byways in the Lake District. 1901.

- - Pocket ed. 1924.

BUDWORTH, Joseph
  A fortnight's ramble to the Lakes in Westmoreland,
  Lancashire, and Cumberland. 1792.

- - 2nd ed. 1795.
- - 3rd ed. 1810.

CAMPBELL, Bruce and CAMPBELL, Margaret
  Brathay: the first twenty-five years, 1947-72.
  1972.

CHIANG, Yee
  The silent traveller: a Chinese artist in
  Lakeland. 1937.

CLARK, Geoffrey and THOMPSON, W   Harding
  The Lakeland landscape. 1938.

CLARKE, James
  A survey of the Lakes of Cumberland, Westmorland,
  and Lancashire; together with an account ... of
  the adjacent country... 1787.

COLLINGWOOD, William Gershom
  The Lake counties. 1902.

COOPER, William Heaton
  The hills of Lakeland. 2nd ed. 1946.

CROSFIELD, George
  An excursion from Warrington to the English Lakes
  in 1795. 1873.

Cumberland, Westmorland and Furness. 1905.

England's Lakeland: a tour therein. [1877].

FARINGTON, Joseph
  Views of the Lakes, &c. in Cumberland and
  Westmorland. 1789.

FITZGIBBON, Mary Rose
  Lakeland scene. 1948.

FORD, William
  A description of scenery in the Lake District,
  intended as a guide to strangers. 2nd ed. 1840.

- - 3rd ed. 1844.
- - 4th ed. 1845.

FRASER, Maxwell
  Companion into Lakeland. 1937.

FRIENDS OF THE LAKE DISTRICT
  A road policy for the Lake District. [1961].

GILPIN, William
  Observations relative chiefly to picturesque
  beauty, made in the year 1772, on several parts
  of England, particularly the mountains, and Lakes
  of Cumberland, and Westmoreland. 1786. 2v.

- - 2nd ed. 1788.
- - 3rd ed. 1792.

GILPIN, William
  [Observations relative chiefly to picturesque
  beauty...]. Voyage en différentes parties de
  l'Angleterre, et particulièrement dans les montagnes & sur les Lacs. 1789. 2v.

GREEN, William
  A description of a series of sixty small prints,
  etched by William Green, of Ambleside, from drawings made by himself. 1814.

GREEN, William
  A description of sixty studies from nature;
  etched in the soft ground by William Green of
  Ambleside after drawings made by himself in
  Cumberland, Westmorland, and Lancashire... 1810.
  Text only, no illustrations.

GREEN, William
  The tourist's new guide, containing a description
  of the Lakes, mountains, and scenery, in
  Cumberland, Westmorland, and Lancashire... 1819.
  2v.

GRIFFIN, Arthur Harold
  Inside the real Lakeland. 1961.

GRIFFIN, Arthur Harold
  Long days in the hills. 1974.

Harwood's Illustrations of the Lakes. [1852?].

122 Lake District - geography ... (Cont.)

HODGE, Edmund W
   Enjoying the Lakes: from post-chaise to National
   Park. 1957.

HOLLAND, P
   Select views of the Lakes in Cumberland, Westmore-
   land, and Lancashire, from drawings made by P.
   Holland. 1792.

HORNE, Thomas Hartwell
   The Lakes of Lancashire, Westmorland, and
   Cumberland; delineated in forty-three engravings,
   from drawings by Joseph Farington. 1816.

HOUSMAN, John
   A descriptive tour, and guide to the Lakes, caves,
   mountains, and other natural curiosities, in
   Cumberland, Westmoreland, Lancashire, and a part
   of the West Riding of Yorkshire. 1800.

   - - 2nd ed. 1802.
   - - 6th ed. 1814.
   - - 9th ed. 1821.

HOUSMAN, John
   A topographical description of Cumberland,
   Westmorland, Lancashire, and a part of the West
   Riding of Yorkshire... 1800.

HOYS, Dudley
   Below Scafell. 1955.

HUSON, Thomas
   Round about Helvellyn: twenty-four plates; with
   notes by the artist and descriptive passages from
   Wordsworth's poems. 1895.

HUTCHINSON, W
   An excursion to the Lakes in Westmorland and
   Cumberland; with a tour through part of the
   Northern counties in the years 1773 and 1774.
   1776.

KNIGHT, William
   Through the Wordsworth country. 1887.

   - - 5th ed. 1906.

LEFEBURE, Molly
   Cumberland heritage. 1970.

LINTON, E   Lynn
   The Lake country. 1864.

LYDON, A   F
   The English Lake scenery. 1880.

MACBRIDE, Mackenzie
   Wild Lakeland. 1922.

MACKAY, Charles
   The scenery & poety of the English Lakes: a summer
   ramble. 1846.

   - - 2nd ed. 1852.

MARR, John E
   Cumberland. 1910.

MATTHEW, George King
   The English Lakes, peaks and passes, from Kendal
   to Keswick. 1866.

OTLEY, Jonathan
   A concise description of the English Lakes, the
   mountains in their vicinity, and the roads by
   which they may be visited; with remarks on the
   mineralogy and geology of the district. 1823.

   - - 4th ed. 1830.
   - - 5th ed. 1834.
   - - 6th ed. 1837.

PALMER, William Thomas
   The English Lakes. 1905.

   - - 2nd ed. 1908.

PALMER, William Thomas
   The English Lakes, their topographical,
   historical and literary landmarks. 1930.

PALMER, William Thomas
   In Lakeland dells and fells. 1903.

PALMER, William Thomas
   Lake-country rambles. 1902.

PALMER, William Thomas
   Odd yarns of English Lakeland: narratives of
   romance, mystery and superstition told by the
   Dalesfolk. 1914.

PALMER, William Thomas
   Wanderings in Lakeland. [1945?].

PAYN, James
   The Lakes in sunshine. 1873.

Pen & pencil sketches of the Lakes. [ca 1860].

A picturesque tour of the English Lakes; containing
   a description of the most romantic scenery of
   Cumberland, Westmoreland, and Lancashire...
   [1821].
   Preface signed R. Ackermann.

POUCHER, W.A.
   Lakeland holiday. 1942.

POUCHER, W.A.
   Lakeland journey. 1945.

POUCHER, W.A.
   Lakeland scrapbook. 1950.

POUCHER, W.A.
   Lakeland through the lens: a ramble over fell
   and dale. 1940.

POUCHER, W.A.
   Over Lakeland fells. 1948.

PYNE, J   B
   Lake scenery of England. [1859].

RADCLIFFE, Ann
   A journey made in the summer of 1794, through
   Holland and the western frontier of Germany, with
   a return down the Rhine; to which are added
   observations during a tour to the Lakes of
   Lancashire, Westmoreland, and Cumberland. 1795.

RAWNSLEY, Hardwicke Drummond
   By fell and dale at the English Lakes. 1911.

RAWNSLEY, Hardwicke Drummond
   A coach-drive at the Lakes: Windermere to
   Keswick; and the Buttermere round. 3rd ed. 1902.

RAWNSLEY, Hardwicke Drummond
   Lake country sketches. 1903.

RAWNSLEY, Hardwicke Drummond
   Life and nature at the English Lakes. 1899.

RAWNSLEY, Hardwicke Drummond
   Months at the Lakes. 1906.

RAWNSLEY, Hardwicke Drummond
   Past and present at the English Lakes. 1916.

ROBERTSON, Eric
   Wordsworthshire: an introduction to a poet's
   country... 1911.

ROBINSON, John
   A guide to the Lakes in Cumberland, Westmorland,
   and Lancashire... 1819.

ROSE, Thomas
   The British Switzerland; or, Picturesque rambles
   in the English Lake District, comprising a series
   of views... [1856-60]. 2v.

122 Lake District - geography ... (Cont.)

ROSE, Thomas
  The northern tourist: seventy-three views of lake
  and mountain scenery, etc. in Westmorland,
  Cumberland, Durham, & Northumberland. 1836.

ROSE, Thomas
  Westmorland, Cumberland, Durham, and Northumberland. 1832-[35]. 3v.

RUMNEY, A   Wren
  The Dalesman. 1911.

SYMONDS, H   H
  Afforestation in the Lake District: a reply to
  the Forestry Commission's White Paper of 26th
  August 1936. 1936.

TATTERSALL, George
  The Lakes of England. 1836.

TOPHAM, W   F
  The Lakes of England. 1869.

TRAVERS, Benjamin
  A descriptive tour to the Lakes of Cumberland and
  Westmoreland, in the autumn of 1804. 1806.

TUVAR, Lorenzo
  Tales & Legends of the English Lakes and mountains;
  collected from the best and most authentic
  sources. [1852].

WAINWRIGHT, A
  Fellwanderer: the story behind the guidebooks.
  1966.

WALKER, A
  Remarks made in a tour from London to the Lakes of
  Westmoreland and Cumberland, in the summer of
  1791... 1792.

WALLACE, Doreen
  English Lakeland. 1940.

WALTON, Elijah
  English Lake scenery. 1876.

WEST, Thomas
  A guide to the Lakes, dedicated to the lovers of
  landscape studies... 1778.
  Various editions.

WILKINSON, Joseph
  Select views in Cumberland, Westmoreland and
  Lancashire. 1817.

WORDSWORTH, William
  A guide through the District of the Lakes in the
  North of England... 5th ed., with considerable
  additions. 1835.

WORDSWORTH, William
  [A guide through the District of the Lakes...].
  Wordsworth's Guide to the Lakes. 5th ed. (1835);
  with an introduction, appendices, and notes
  textual and illustrative by Ernest de Sélincourt.
  1906.

123 Climbing history, reminiscences

BARROW, John, 1808-1898
  Mountain ascents in Westmoreland and Cumberland.
  1886.

- - Rev. and enl. ed. 1888.

GRIFFIN, Arthur Harold
  In mountain Lakeland. 1963.

HANKINSON, Alan
  The first tigers: the early history of rock
  climbing in the Lake District. 1972.

HARKER, George
  Easter climbs (the British Alpine Club). 1913.

OPPENHEIMER, Lehmann J
  The heart of Lakeland. 1908.

SUTTON, Graham
  Fell days. 1948.

124 Climbs and climbing

BENSON, Claude Ernest
  Crag and hound in Lakeland. 1902.

JONES, Owen Glynne
  Rock-climbing in the English Lake District. 1897.

- - 2nd ed. 1900.

MONKHOUSE, Frank and WILLIAMS, Joe
  Climber and fellwalker in Lakeland. 1972.

128 Walking

BAGLEY, Arthur L
  Holiday rambles in the English Lake District.
  [ca 1925].

BARBER, John B   and ATKINSON, George
  Lakeland passes, including some charming walks
  through the District. 2nd ed. 1928.

BROWN, Clare and BROWN, Marshall
  Fell walking from Wasdale. [1947?].

HALEY, Frank
  Fifty week-end walks in the Lake District. 1954.

PALMER, William Thomas
  Odd corners in English Lakeland: rambles,
  scrambles, climbs and sport. 1913.

PALMER, William Thomas
  Tramping in Lakeland. 1934.

POUCHER, W.A.
  The Lakeland peaks: a pictorial guide to walking
  in the district and to the safe ascent of its
  principal mountain groups. 1971.

PRICE, Nancy
  Vagabonds way: haphazard wanderings on the fells.
  1914.

PRIOR, Herman
  Ascents and passes in the Lake District of England,
  being a new pedestrian and general guide to the
  district. [1865].

RUMNEY, A   Wren
  The way about the English Lake District; together
  with appendices on crag climbing and fishing by
  J. Wilson Robinson and G.E. Lowthian... [1898].

WAUGH, Edwin
  Rambles in the Lake country and its borders. 1861.

129 Guide-books

BADDELEY, Mountford J   B
  The English Lake District...

  Various editions.

Black's Picturesque guide to the English Lakes,
  including an essay on the geology of the district,
  by John Phillips.
  Various editions.

BRABANT, F   G
  The English Lakes. 1902.

COOKE, Charles
  The tourist's and traveller's companion to the
  Lakes of Cumberland, Westmoreland, and Lancashire.
  [ca 1825].

129 Lake District - guide-books (Cont.)

COOKE, George Alexander
  Topographical and statistical description of the
  County of Cumberland... [ca 1810].

A handbook to the English Lakes... 1889.

HUDSON, John
  A complete guide to the Lakes ...; with Mr.
  Wordsworth's description of the scenery... 2nd ed.
  1843.

- - 3rd ed. 1846.
- - 4th ed. 1853.

JENKINSON, Henry Irwin
  Practical guide to the English Lake District.
  7th ed. 1881.

Leigh's Guide to the Lakes and mountains of Cumberland, Westmorland, and Lancashire. 2nd ed., enl.
  and improved. 1832.

- - 3rd ed., carefully rev. and corr. 1835.
- - 4th ed., carefully rev. and corr. 1840.

MARTINEAU, Harriet
  A complete guide to the English Lakes. 1855.

- - 3rd ed., edited and enlarged by Maria Martineau.
  [ca 1865].

MARTINEAU, Harriet
  Guide to Windermere, with tours to the neighbouring
  lakes... [ca 1855].

PIGGOTT, Percy J
  Burrow's Guide to the Lake District: a practical
  handbook for the tourist; with a special article
  upon mountain passes, walks & rock climbs by Dora
  Benson. [ca 1920].

PRIOR, Herman
  Guide to the Lake District of England. 4th,
  nonpareil, ed. [ca 1880].

- - 5th ed. [ca 1885].

SCOTT, Daniel
  Cumberland and Westmorland. 1920.

WALCOTT, Mackenzie E   C
  A guide to the mountains, lakes, and north-west
  coast of England, descriptive of natural scenery
  historical, archaeological and legendary. 1860.

Ward and Lock's (late Shaw's) Pictorial and
  historical guide to the English Lakes; their
  scenery and associations; with an introduction by
  the poet Wordsworth. [ca 1889].

13 WALES

131 Geology, natural history

RAMSAY, Andrew Crombie
  The old glaciers of Switzerland and North Wales.
  1860.

132 Geography, description, travel

AIKIN, Arthur
  Journal of a tour through North Wales and part of
  Shropshire; with observations in mineralogy, and
  other branches of natural history. 1797.

BATTY, Robert
  Welsh scenery. 1823.

BENNETT, G   J
  The pedestrian's guide through North Wales: a
  tour performed in 1837. [1838].

BINGLEY, William
  Excursions in North Wales, including Aberystwith
  and the Devil's Bridge, intended as a guide to
  tourists. 3rd ed. 1839.

BINGLEY, William
  North Wales, delineated from two excursions
  through all the interesting parts ... intended as
  a guide to future tourists. 2nd ed. 1814.

BINGLEY, William
  North Wales, including its scenery, antiquities,
  customs ... delineated from two excursions ...
  during the summers of 1798 and 1801. 1804. 2v.

BINGLEY, William
  A tour round North Wales, performed during the
  summer of 1798... 1800. 2v.

BRADLEY, Arthur Granville
  Highways and byways in North Wales. 1898 (1905
  reprint).

The Cambrian tourist; or, Post-chaise companion
  through Wales; containing cursory sketches of the
  Welsh territories... 5th ed. ... corr., and
  considerably enl. 1821.

- - 6th ed. ... corr., and considerably enl. 1828.
- - 7th ed. ... corr., and considerably enl. 1830.

CLIFFE, John Henry
  Notes and recollections of an angler: rambles
  among the mountains, valleys, and solitudes of
  Wales... 1870.

A collection of Welsh tours; or, A display of the
  beauties of Wales; selected principally from
  celebrated histories and popular tours ...; to
  which is added, A tour of the River Wye. 3rd ed.,
  corr. 1798.

COSTELLO, Louisa Stuart
  The falls, lakes, and mountains of North Wales.
  1845.

EVANS, J
  Letters written during a tour through North Wales
  ... 3rd ed. 1804.

EVANS, J
  A tour through part of North Wales, in the year
  1798, and at other times; principally undertaken
  with a view to botanical researches... 1800.

FREEMAN, G   J
  Sketches in Wales; or, A diary of three walking
  excursions in that principality, in the years
  1823, 1824, 1825. 1826.

GASTINEAU, Henry
  Wales illustrated, in a series of views, comprising
  the picturesque scenery, towns, castles... 1830.

GIRALDUS CAMBRENSIS
  The itinerary through Wales and The description of
  Wales. [1908].

HALLIWELL, J   O
  Notes of family excursions in North Wales, taken
  chiefly from Rhyl, Abergele, Llandudno, and Bangor.
  1860.

HUTTON, William
  Remarks upon North Wales, being the result of
  sixteen tours through that part of the principality.
  1803.

LOVETT, Richard
  Welsh pictures drawn with pen and pencil, by J.E.
  Lloyd [and others]; edited by Richard Lovett.
  [ca 1892].

NEWELL, R   H
  Letters on the scenery of Wales; including a
  series of subjects for the pencil ... and instructions to pedestrian tourists. 1821.

132 Wales - geography, description ... (Cont.)

NICHOLSON, George
    The Cambrian traveller's guide, and pocket com-
    panion. 1808.

- - 2nd ed., corr. and considerably enl. 1813.
- - 3rd ed., rev. and corr. 1840.

PARRY, John
    A trip to North Wales, made in 1839; containing
    much information relative to that interesting
    alpine country... 1840.

Picturesque scenery in North Wales. [ca 1855].

ROSCOE, Thomas
    Wanderings and excursions in North Wales. [1836?].

- - Another ed. 1862.

ROSS, Martin and SOMERVILLE, E   OE
    Beggers on horseback: a riding tour in North
    Wales. 1895.

SKRINE, Henry
    Two successive tours throughout the whole of Wales,
    with several of the adjacent English counties...
    1798.

- - 2nd ed. 1812.

SMITH, John, Lecturer on Education
    A guide to Bangor, Beaumaris, Snowdonia, and other
    parts of North Wales. 3rd ed., improved. 1833.

TILLOTSON, John
    Picturesque scenery in Wales. [1860].

Views in North Wales. [ca 1851].

WARNER, Richard
    A walk through Wales in August 1797. 1798.

- - A second walk ... in ... 1798. 1799.

WRIGHT, G   N
    Scenes in North Wales; with historical illustra-
    tions, legends, and biographical notices. 1833.

134 Climbs and climbing

PERRY, Alexander W
    Welsh mountaineering: a practical guide to the
    ascent of all the principal mountains in Wales.
    1896.

135 Snowdonia

BRANSBY, James Hews
    A description of Llanberis and the Snowdon
    district. 1845.

CARR, Herbert Reginald Culling and LISTER, George A
    The mountains of Snowdonia in history, the
    sciences, literature and sport. 1925.

- - 2nd ed. 1948.

COMPTON, Thomas
    The northern Cambrian mountains; or, A tour through
    North Wales describing the scenery and general
    characters of that romantic country. 1817.

FIRBANK, Thomas
    I bought a mountain. 1940.

GREAT BRITAIN. Forestry Commission
    Snowdonia. 1948.

HUSON, Thomas
    Round about Snowdon. 1894.

JONES, Harry Longueville
    Illustrations of the natural scenery of the
    Snowdonian mountains; accompanied by a description,
    topographical and historical of the County of
    Caernarvon. 1829.

LLANBERIS PROTECTION SOCIETY
    Park power: a memorandum on the proposed pumped
    storage scheme, Dinorwic, Llanberis in
    Caernarvonshire. 1972.

LOVINS, Amory
    Eryri, the mountains of longing. [1972].

MATHEWS, Charles Edward
    Reminiscences of Pen-y-Gwryd. 1902.

NORTH, F   J
    Snowdonia: the National Park of North Wales, by
    F.J. North, Bruce Campbell, Richenda Scott. 1949.

PENNANT, Thomas
    The journey to Snowdon. 1781.

POUCHER, W.A.
    Snowdon holiday. 1943.

POUCHER, W.A.
    Snowdonia through the lens: mountain wanderings
    in wildest Wales. 1941.

SMYTHE, Frank S
    Over Welsh hills. 1941.

TUGWELL, George
    On the mountain, being the Welsh experiences of
    Abraham Black & Jonas White, Esquires, moralists,
    photographers, fishermen, and botanists. 1862.

WALTON, Elijah
    Welsh scenery (chiefly in Snowdonia). 1875.

WIMPERIS, Edmond Monson and JONES, F
    Snowdonia illustrated. [ca 1890]. 2v.

136 Snowdonia - climbing, walking

ABRAHAM, George Dixon and ABRAHAM, Ashley Perry
    Rock-climbing in North Wales. 1906.

BAGLEY, Arthur L
    Holiday rambles in North Wales. [1920].

CARR, Herbert Reginald Culling
    A walker's guide to Snowdon and the Beddgelert
    district... 1949.

HANKINSON, Alan
    The mountain men: an early history of rock climb-
    ing in North Wales. 1977.

ROWLAND, E   G
    The ascent of Snowdon. 1956.

ROWLAND, E   G
    Hill walking in Snowdonia. 1951 (1952 reprint).

- - New and fully rev. ed. 1958.

SMYTHE, Tony
    Rock climbers in action in Snowdonia. 1966.

SOPER, N   Jack
    The Black Cliff: the history of rock climbing on
    Clogwyn du'r Arddu, by Jack Soper, Ken Wilson and
    Peter Crew. 1971.

STYLES, Showell
    A climber in Wales. [ca 1948].

YOUNG, Geoffrey Winthrop
    Snowdon biography, by Geoffrey Winthrop Young,
    Geoffrey Sutton, and Wilfrid Noyce. 1957.

139 Wales - guide-books

BADDELEY, Mountford J   B   and WARD, C   S
North Wales. Pt.1. 7th ed., rev. 1902.

BATENHAM, George
The traveller's companion in an excursion from
Chester through North Wales. [1827].

Black's picturesque guide through North and South
Wales and Monmouthshire. 1853.

Black's picturesque guide to Wales. 1872.

CLIFFE, Charles Frederick
The book of North Wales. 1850.

- - 2nd ed. 1851.

COOKE, George Alexander
Topographical and statistical description of
North Wales... [ca 1830].

A handbook for travellers in North Wales. 4th ed.
1874.

HEMINGWAY, J
Panorama of the beauties, curiosities, &
antiquities of North Wales ... intended as a
pocket companion to the tourist and traveller.
2nd ed. 1835.

- - 3rd ed., corr. and improved. 1842.
- - 4th ed., corr. and improved. 1844.

HICKLIN, John
Excursions in North Wales: a complete guide to the
tourist... 1847.

HICKLIN, John
The illustrated hand-book of North Wales: a guide
for the tourist, the antiquarian, and the angler.
[ca 1862].

JENKINSON, Henry Irwin
Jenkinson's Practical guide to North Wales. 1878.

Leigh's Guide to Wales & Monmouthshire... 6th ed.,
with considerable additions and improvements.
1841.

Llanberis area guide: a guide to Llanberis, Nant
Peris, Llanberis Pass and Snowdon. 1971.

MUIRHEAD, Findlay
Wales. 1922. (Blue guides)

PARRY, Edward
Cambrian mirror; or, A new tourist companion
through North Wales... 2nd ed. 1846.

PIGGOTT, Percy J
Burrow's guide to North Wales: a practical handbook for the tourist ...; with a special article
upon Mountain walks and rock climbs by Dora Benson.
[ca 1920].

ROBERTS, Askew and WOODALL, Edward
Gossiping guide to Wales (North Wales and
Aberystwyth). Traveller's ed. 1914.

STORY, Alfred Thomas
North Wales. 1907.

WARD, C   S   and BADDELEY, Mountford J   B
South Wales and the Wye district of Monmouthshire.
4th ed., rev. 1901.

WARD, LOCK, AND CO.
Handbook to North Wales. Complete ed. [ca 1920].
2v.

14   SCOTLAND

141 Geology, natural history

FORBES, James David
Notes on the topography and geology of the
Cuchullin hills in Skye and on the traces of
ancient glaciers which they present. 1845.

GEIKIE, Archibald
On the phenomena of the glacial drift of Scotland.
1863.

MACNAIR, Peter
The geology and scenery of the Grampians and the
valley of Strathmore. 1908. 2v.

142 Geography, description, travel

BEATTIE, William
Scotland; illustrated in a series of views...
1838-42. 2v.

CAMPBELL, Alexander
A journey from Edinburgh through parts of North
Britain, containing remarks on Scottish landscape
... 1802.

- - New ed. 1810.

GILPIN, William
Observations relative chiefly to picturesque
beauty, made in the year 1776, on several parts
of Great Britain; particularly the High-Lands of
Scotland. 1789. 2v.

GRIERSON, Thomas
Autumnal rambles among the Scottish mountains;
or, Pedestrian tourist's friend. 1850.

- - 2nd ed., greatly enl. 1851.

INNERLEITHEN ALPINE CLUB
Principal excursions of the Innerleithen Alpine
Club during the years 1889-94; with a memoir
of ... Robert Mathison, first President of the
Club. 1895.

- - 2nd ed. 1897.

LAWSON, John Parker
Scotland delineated: a series of views of the
principal cities and towns ... mountains and
rivers... [ca 1855].

LEIGHTON, John M
The lakes of Scotland: a series of views, from
paintings taken expressly for the work. 1834.

PEEL, Sir Robert
A correct report of the speeches delivered by Sir
Robert Peel on his inauguration into the office
of Lord Rector of the University of Glasgow...
1837.

SMYTHE, Frank S
A camera in the hills. 1939.

- - 3rd ed. 1946.
- - 4th ed. 1948.

STEVEN, Campbell
The story of Scotland's hills. 1975.

STODDART, John
Remarks on local scenery & manners in Scotland
during the years 1799 and 1800. 1801. 2v.

TOWNSHEND, Chauncy Hare
A descriptive tour in Scotland. 1840.

The traveller's guide through Scotland, and its
islands. 6th ed. 1814. 2v.

143 Scotland - climbing history, reminiscences

BELL, James Horst Brunnerman
  A progress in mountaineering: Scottish hills to
  alpine peaks. 1950.

FRERE, Richard Burchmore
  Thoughts of a mountaineer. 1952.

MURRAY, William Hutchison
  Mountaineering in Scotland. 1947.

- - New ed. 1962.

MURRAY, William Hutchison
  Mountaineering in Scotland and Undiscovered
  Scotland. 1979.
  "A compilation of two books ... originally
  published in 1947 and 1951". - t.p.

MURRAY, William Hutchison
  Undiscovered Scotland: climbs on rock, snow, and
  ice. 1951.

145 Highlands and Islands - general

A'BECKETT, Arthur and SAMBOURNE, Linley
  Our holiday in the Scottish Highlands. [1876].

BOTFIELD, B
  Journal of a tour through the Highlands of
  Scotland during the summer of 1829. 1830.

CRIRIE, James
  Scottish scenery; or, Sketches in verse, descriptive of scenes chiefly in the Highlands... 1803.

CUMMING, Constance F   Gordon
  From the Hebrides to the Himalayas: a sketch of
  eighteen months' wanderings in Western Isles
  and eastern highlands. 1876. 2v.

DARLING, F   Fraser
  Natural history in the Highlands & Islands. 1947.

FINLAY, Ian
  The Highlands. 1963.

FIRSOFF, Valdemar Axel
  Arran with camera and sketchbook. 1951.

FIRSOFF, Valdemar Axel
  In the hills of Breadalbane. 1954.

FRASER, Sir Hugh
  Amid the high hills. 1923.

GARDNER, Arthur
  The peaks, lochs & coasts of the western Highlands.
  1924.

- - 2nd ed., rev. and enl. 1928.

GARDNER, Arthur
  Sun, cloud & snow in the western Highlands from
  Glencoe to Ardnamurchan, Mull and Arran. 1933.

HALL, Charles A
  The Isle of Arran. 1912.

HUMBLE, Benjamin Hutchison
  The songs of Skye: an anthology. 1934.

KILGOUR, William T
  Twenty years on Ben Nevis, being a brief account
  of the life, work, and experiences of the observers
  at the highest meteorological station in the
  British Isles. [1905].

LEYDEN, John
  Journal of a tour in the Highlands and Western
  Islands of Scotland in 1800. 1903.

MACBRIDE, Mackenzie
  Arran of the bens, the glens & the brave. 1910.

MACCULLOCH, J   A
  The misty Isle of Skye: its scenery, its people,
  its story. 1905.

MACGREGOR, Alasdair Alpin
  Over the sea to Skye; or, Rambles in an elfin
  isle. [1926].

MACLEOD, Fred. T
  Eilean a' Cheò, the Isle of Mist, comprising
  articles on Skye by Skyemen. 2nd ed. [1917].

MACLEOD, Norman
  Mountain, loch and glen, illustrating "Our life
  in the Highlands" from paintings executed ... for
  this work by Joseph Adam. 1870.

MURRAY, William Hutchison
  The companion guide to the west Highlands of
  Scotland: the seaboard from Kintyre to Cape Wrath.
  2nd ed. 1969.

MURRAY, William Hutchison
  The Scottish Highlands. 1976.

NATIONAL TRUST FOR SCOTLAND
  Glencoe and Dalness ...: guide book. 1951.

POUCHER, W.A.
  Highland holiday: Arran to Ben Cruachan. 1945.

POUCHER, W.A.
  The magic of Skye. 1949.

POUCHER, W.A.
  Scotland through the lens: Loch Tulla to Lochaber.
  1943.

REID, John T
  Art rambles in the Highlands and Islands of
  Scotland. 1878.

ROBSON, George Fennell
  Scenery of the Grampian Mountains. 1819.

SMITH, Alexander
  A summer in Skye. 1865. 2v.

- - Popular ed. 1866.
- - Another ed. 1880.
- - Another ed. 1912.
- - Another ed. [ca 1913].

STEVEN, Campbell
  The Island hills. 1955.

WALKER, James Hubert
  On hills of the north. 1948.

WELD, Charles Richard
  Two months in the Highlands, Orcadia, and Skye.
  1860.

146 Highlands and Islands - climbing

ABRAHAM, Ashley Perry
  Rock-climbing in Skye. 1908.

BAGLEY, Arthur L
  Walks and scrambles in the Highlands. 1914.

BAKER, Ernest Albert
  The Highlands with rope and rucksack. 1923.

BROWN, Hamish M
  Hamish's mountain walk: the first traverse of all
  the Scottish Munros in one journey. 1978.

FRERE, Richard Burchmore
  "Rock climbs": a guide to the crags in the
  neighbourhood of Inverness. 1938.

GILBERT, Richard
  Memorable Munros: an account of the ascent of the
  3,000 ft. peaks in Scotland. 1976.

146 Highlands and Islands - climbing (Cont.)

HUMBLE, Benjamin Hutchison
  The Cuillin of Skye. 1952.

HUMBLE, Benjamin Hutchison
  On Scottish hills. 1946.

STEEL, Charles
  The Ben Nevis race. [1956].

WEIR, Thomas
  Highland days. 1948.

WRIGHT, Jeremiah Ernest Benjamin
  Mountain days in the Isle of Skye. 1934.

147 Cairngorms

BURTON, John Hill
  The Cairngorm mountains. 1864.

FIRSOFF, Valdemar Axel
  The Cairngorms on foot and ski. 1949.

GORDON, Seton
  The charm of the hills. 1912.

JENKINS, G   Gordon
  Hill views from Aberdeen. 1917.

POUCHER, W.A.
  A camera in the Cairngorms. 1947.

148 Walking

SMITH, Walter A
  The hill paths, drove roads & 'cross country'
  routes in Scotland from the Cheviots to Sutherland.
  1924.

149 Guide-books

ANDERSON, George and ANDERSON, Peter
  Guide to the Highlands and Islands of Scotland.
  1834.

- - 3rd ed., carefully rev. enl. and remodelled.
  1851.

BADDELEY, Mountford J   B
  Scotland. Pt.1. 7th ed. 1892.

Black's picturesque tourist of Scotland. 1840.

- - 3rd ed. 1843.
- - 15th ed. 1861.
- - 17th ed. 1865.

The Scottish tourist, and itinerary; or, A guide to
  the scenery and antiquities of Scotland and the
  Western Islands... 2nd ed. 1827.

- - 9th ed. 1845.

The tourist's manual; or, An account of the principal
  pleasure tours in Scotland. 8th ed. 1832.

15   IRELAND

152 Geography, description, travel

MARTEL, Édouard Alfred
  Irlande et cavernes anglaises. 1897.

MOULD, Daphne Desirée Charlotte
  The mountains of Ireland. 1955.

153 Climbing history, reminiscences

AIREY, Alan F
  Irish hill days. [1937].

BIGHAM, Hon. Richard
  The Caha Mountains. 1973.

159 Guide-books

BADDELEY, Mountford J   B   and WARD, C   S
  Ireland. 4th ed. 1901. 2v.
  Library has pt.2 only.

- - 5th ed., rev. 1902-09. 2v.

MUIRHEAD, Findlay
  Ireland. 1932. (Blue guides)

20   ALPINE EUROPE

201 Geology, climate

BALL, John
  On the formation of alpine lakes. 1863.

BONNEY, Thomas George
  The building of the Alps. 1912.

CLERC, C
  Les Alpes françaises: études de géologie militaire.
  1882.

COLLET, Léon W
  The structure of the Alps. 1927.

- - 2nd ed. 1935.

COTTA, Bernhard von
  Geologische Briefe aus den Alpen. 1850.

DELEBECQUE, André
  Alluvions anciennes de Chambéry et de la Vallée
  de l'Isère. 1895-96.

DELEBECQUE, André
  Lac du Mont-Cenis, Lacs du massif de Belledonne,
  Les eaux du Rhône et de la Dranse du Chablais.
  1893.

DELEBECQUE, André
  La moraine d'Yvoire. 1894.

DELEBECQUE, André
  Sur l'âge des alluvions anciennes du bois de la
  Bâtie, de Bougy et de la Dranse et leurs relations
  avec le lac de Genève. 1894.

DESOR, Édouard
  De l'orographie des Alpes dans ses rapports avec
  la géologie. 1862.

DESOR, Édouard
  Der Gebirgsbau der Alpen. 1865.

DEUTSCHER UND ÖSTERREICHISCHER ALPENVEREIN
  Anleitung zu wissenschaftlichen Beobachtungen auf
  Alpenreisen. 1882. 2v.

DIENER, Carl
  Der Gebirgsbau der Westalpen. 1891.

DOLLFUS-AUSSET, Daniel
  Matériaux pour l'étude des glaciers. 1864- .
  12v. in 16.

DOLLFUS-AUSSET, Daniel
  Photographies alpines, glaciers. [1893].

DUPARC, Louis and RITTER, Étienne
  Carbonifère alpin. 1894.

201   Alpine Europe - geology, climate (Cont.)

DUPARC, Louis and RITTER, Étienne
Étude pétrographique des schistes de Casanna du
Valais: première note. 1896.

DUPARC, Louis and RITTER, Étienne
Formation quaternaire d'éboulis au Mont Salève.
1893.

DUPARC, Louis and RITTER, Étienne
Le grès de Taveyannaz et ses rapports avec les
formations du Flysche. 1895.

DUPARC, Louis
Le lac d'Annecy: monographie. 1894.

DUPARC, Louis and MRAZEC, Ludovic
Le massif de Trient: étude pétrographique. 1894.

DUPARC, Louis and RITTER, Étienne
Les massifs cristallins de Beaufort et Cevins:
étude pétrographique. 1893.

DUPARC, Louis
Le Mont-Blanc au point de vue géologique et
pétrographique. 1896.

DUPARC, Louis and MRAZEC, Ludovic
Note sur la serpentine de la valée de Binnen
(Valais). 1894.

DUPARC, Louis and MRAZEC, Ludovic
Note sur les roches amphiboliques du Mont-Blanc.
1893.

DUPARC, Louis
Notices pétrographiques. 1896.

DUPARC, Louis and MRAZEC, Ludovic
Nouvelles recherches sur le massif du Mont-Blanc.
1895.

DUPARC, Louis
Prolongement supposé de la chaîne de Belledonne
vers le nord. 1894.

ENZENSPERGER, Ernst
Wie sollen unsere Mittelschüler die Alpen bereisen?
Technische Anleitungen und wissenschaftliche
Anregungen. 1908.

FAVRE, Alphonse
On the origin of the alpine lakes and valleys: a
letter addressed to Sir Roderick I. Murchison.
1865.

FLAIG, Walther
Das Gletscherbuch: Rätsel und Romantik, Gestalt
und Gesetz der Alpengletscher. 1938.

FORBES, James David
Travels through the Alps of Savoy and other parts
of the Pennine chain, with observations on the
phenomena of glaciers. 1843.

- - 2nd ed., rev. 1845.
- - New ed., rev. 1900.

FORBES, James David
[Travels through the Alps of Savoy...]. Reisen in
den Savoyer Alpen und in anderen Theilen der
Penninen-Kette, nebst Beobachtungen über die
Gletscher. 1845.

FRAAS, Eberhard
Scenerie der Alpen. 1892.

FRANCE. Ministère de l'agriculture. Service
d'études des grandes forces hydrauliques (Région
des Alpes)
Études glaciologiques: Tirol autrichien, massif
des Grandes Rousses. 1909.

GARWOOD, E   J
Features of alpine scenery due to glacial protection. 1910.

GODEFFROY, C
Notice sur les glaciers, les moraines et les
blocs erratiques des Alpes. 1840.

GODEFROY, René
La nature alpine: exposé de géographie physique.
1940.

- - 2e éd., rev. et augm. 1948.

HEIM, Albert
Die Gipfelflur der Alpen. 1927.

HERITSCH, Franz
The Nappe theory in the Alps (alpine tectonics,
1905-1928). 1929.

HOEK, Henry
Alpine Wetterkunde. [1931].

KOBER, L
Das Werden der Alpen: eine erdgeschichtliche
Einführung. 1927.

LENTHÉRIC, Charles
L'homme devant les Alpes. 1896.

MURCHISON, Sir Roderick Impey
On the distribution of the superficial detritus
of the Alps, as compared with that of northern
Europe. [1850].

MURCHISON, Sir Roderick Impey
On the former changes of the Alps. [1851].
Offprint from Royal Institution of Great Britain.
Weekly evening meeting, March 7, 1851.

MURCHISON, Sir Roderick Impey
On the geological structure of the Alps,
Apennines and Carpathians, more especially to
prove a transition from secondary to tertiary
rocks and the development of Eocene deposits in
southern Europe. [1840].

NEWBIGIN, Marion I
Frequented ways: a general survey of the land
forms, climates and vegetation of Western Europe,
considered in their relation to the life of man;
including a detailed study of some typical
regions. 1922.

PENCK, Albrecht and BRÜCKNER, Eduard
Die Alpen im Eiszeitalter. 1909. 3v.

PERRET, Robert
L'évolution morphologique du Faucigny (vallées
du Giffre et de l'Arve; vallées du Trient et de
la Viège en Bas Valais). 1931.

RAMSAY, Andrew Crombie
The excavation of the valleys of the Alps. 1862.

SAUSSURE, Horace Bénédict de
Voyages dans les Alpes, précédés d'un essai sur
l'histoire naturelle des environs de Genève.
1779-96. 4v.

SAUSSURE, Horace Bénédict de
[Voyages dans les Alpes]. Reisen durch die
Alpen, nebst einem Versuch über die Natur-
geschichte der Gegenden von Genf. 1781-82. 4v.

SCHLAGINTWEIT, Adolph and SCHLAGINTWEIT-SAKÜNLÜNSKI,
Hermann
Neue Untersuchungen über die physicalische
Geographie und die Geologie der Alpen. 1854.

SCHLAGINTWEIT-SAKÜNLÜNSKI, Hermann and SCHLAGINTWEIT
Adolph
Untersuchungen über die physicalische Geographie
der Alpen in ihren Beziehungen zu den Phaenomenen
der Gletscher, zur Geologie, Meteorologie und
Pflanzengeographie. 1850.

SUESS, Eduard
Die Entstehung der Alpen. 1875.

201 Alpine Europe - geology, climate (Cont.)

TUTTON, Alfred Edwin Howard
  The high Alps: a natural history of ice and snow.
  Cheaper ed. 1931.

TYNDALL, John
  The glaciers of the Alps, being a narrative of
  excursions and ascents, an account of the origin
  and phenomena of glaciers, and an exposition of
  the physical principles to which they are related.
  Various editions.

TYNDALL, John
  [The glaciers of the Alps...]. Die Gletscher der
  Alpen. 1898.

TYNDALL, John
  [The glaciers of the Alps...]. Al'piskie ledniki.
  1866.

ULE, Otto
  Bilder aus den Alpen und aus der mitteldeutschen
  Gebirgswelt: Blicke in die Geschichte der Erde
  und den Bau der Gebirge. 1866.

VIAL, A E Lockington
  Alpine glaciers. 1952.

VOGT, Carl
  Agassiz' und seiner Freunde geologische Alpenreisen in der Schweiz, Savoyen und Piemont...
  hrsg., von Carl Vogt. 2. stark verm. Aufl. 1847.

202 Geography, description

Alpenlandschaften: Ansichten aus der deutschen,
  österreichischen und Schweizer Gebirgswelt.
  [1891]. 2v.

BALL, John
  Le Alpi; traduzione... [from the Encyclopaedia
  Britannica]. 1888.

BANCK, Otto
  Alpenbilder: Schilderungen aus Natur und Leben in
  der Alpenwelt. 1863. 2v.

- - 2. verm. Aufl. 1869.

BARNARD, George
  The continental drawing book for the use of
  advanced pupils, being views in Switzerland, the
  Alps and Italian lakes... 1837.

BAUMBACH, Rudolf
  Schildereien aus dem Alpenlande. 1882.

BELLOC, Hilaire
  Many cities. 1928.

BERLEPSCH, Hermann Alexander von
  Die Alpen in Natur- und Lebensbildern: ausgewählte
  Abschnitte... [1910].

BERLEPSCH, Hermann Alexander
  [Die Alpen...]. Les Alpes: descriptions et récits.
  1869.

BONAPARTE, Roland, prince
  Le glacier de l'Aletsch et le Lac de Märjelen.
  1889.

BONNEY, Thomas George
  The alpine regions of Switzerland and the neighbouring countries: a pedestrian's notes on their
  physical features, scenery, and natural history.
  1868.

BREDT, E W
  Die Alpen und ihre Maler. [1910].

BROCKEDON, William
  Illustrations of the passes of the Alps, by which
  Italy communicates with France, Switzerland, and
  Germany. 1828-29. 2v.

- - Another ed. [1877].

CIVIALE, A
  Les Alpes au point de vue de la géographie
  physique et de la géologie: voyages photographiques dans le Dauphiné, la Savoie, le nord de
  l'Italie, la Suisse et le Tyrol. 1882.

CLOWES, George
  A picturesque tour by the new road from Chiavenna,
  over the Splügen, and along the Rhine, to Coira,
  in the Grisons. 1826.

CONWAY, William Martin, Baron Conway
  The Alps. 1904.

- - Another ed. 1910.

COOLIDGE, William Augustus Brevoort
  Alp.
  (In The Encyclopaedia Britannica. 11th ed. 1910)

COOLIDGE, William Augustus Brevoort
  Alps.
  (In The Encyclopaedia Britannica. 11th ed. 1910)

COOLIDGE, William Augustus Brevoort
  A list of the writings (not being reviews of books)
  dating from 1868 to 1912 and relating to the Alps
  or Switzerland, of W.A.B. Coolidge. 1912.

DAUZAT, Albert
  Le Rhône des Alpes à la mer: le Rhône à travers
  les âges, le Valais, le Lac Léman, la traversée
  du Jura, Lyon, le Rhône dauphinois, le Rhône
  provençal. 1928.

DENNIS, John
  Views in Savoy, Switzerland and on the Rhine, from
  drawings made upon the spot. [1822].

DEUTSCHER UND ÖSTERREICHISCHER ALPENVEREIN
  Alpines Handbuch unter Mitarbeit von Georg Blab,
  A. Dreyer [and others]. 1931. 2v.

EHRMANN, Theophil Friedrich
  Neuste Kunde der Schweiz und Italiens. 1908.

ENCYCLOPAEDIA BRITANNICA
  Belgium, Italy, and Switzerland, by G. Edmundson,
  H. Wickham Steed, W.A.B. Coolidge. 1914.

GEIGER, Hermann
  Geiger and the Alps. [1958?].

GERMAIN, Félix
  Sommets: 100 photographies en noir. 1959.

HERING, George E
  The mountains and lakes of Switzerland, the Tyrol,
  and Italy; from drawings made during a tour
  through those countries. 1847.

IRVING, Robert Lock Graham
  The Alps. 1939.

- - 2nd ed., rev. 1942.
- - 3rd ed., rev. 1947.

KNIGHT, Max
  Return to the Alps; photographs by Gerhard
  Klammet, edited with a foreword and selection
  from Alpine literature, by David R. Brower. [1970].

KNOWLES, Archibald Campbell
  Adventures in the Alps. [1913].

LAVIS-TRAFFORD, Marc A de
  Commentaire sur l'oeuvre relative aux Alpes des
  topographes, cartographes et écrivains au cours de
  la deuxième moitié du XVIe siècle... 1950.

LEE, Edwin
  Memoranda on France, Italy, and Germany, with
  remarks on climates, medical practice, mineral
  waters... [1841].

LENDENFELD, Robert von
  Aus den Alpen. 1896. 2v.

202 Alpine Europe - geography, description (Cont.)

LORY, Gabriel, 1763-1840 and LORY, Gabriel, 1784-1846
 Voyage pittoresque de Genève à Milan par le
 Simplon. 1811.

LORY, Gabriel, 1763-1840 and LORY, Gabriel, 1784-1846
 [Voyage pittoresque de Genève à Milan par le
 Simplon]. Picturesque tour from Geneva to Milan,
 by way of the Simplon. 1820.

LORY, Gabriel, 1763-1840 and LORY, Gabriel, 1784-1846
 [Voyage pittoresque de Genève à Milan par le
 Simplon]. Viaggio pittorico fatto da Ginevra a
 Milano per la strada del Sempione. 1821.

MACHAČEK, Fritz
 Die Alpen. 1908.

MARTONNE, Emmanuel de
 Les Alpes (géographie générale). 1926.

MERCIER, Jerome J
 Mountains and lakes of Switzerland and Italy:
 sixty-four picturesque views... 1871.

MERRICK, Hugh
 The Alps in colour. 1970.

MERRICK, Hugh
 Companion to the Alps. 1974.

MÜNZER, Kurt
 Der gefühlvolle Baedeker: auch ein Handbuch für
 Reisende durch Deutschland, Italien, die Schweiz
 u. Tirol. 1911.

NOYCE, Wilfrid
 The Alps. 1961.

Opérations géodésiques et astronomiques pour la
 mesure d'un arc du parallèle moyen, exécutées en
 Piémont et en Savoie par une Commission composée
 d'officiers ... piémontais et autrichiens en 1821,
 1822, 1823. 1825-27. 2v.

READER'S DIGEST
 Les Alpes: sélection du Reader's Digest. 1969.

REISHAUER, Hermann
 Die Alpen. 1909.

RICHTER, Eduard
 Die Alpen nach H.A. Daniel's Schilderung; neu
 bearbeitet. 1885.

ROSCOE, Thomas
 The tourist in Switzerland and Italy. 1830.

ROTHPLETZ, August
 Alpine Majestäten und ihr Gefolge: die Gebirgswelt
 der Erde in Bildern... 1901-04. 4v.

RUSSELL, John and WILTON, Andrew
 Turner in Switzerland. 1976.

SANUKI, Matao and YAMADA, Keiichi
 The Alps. 1969 (1972 reprint).

SCHÄTZ, Josef Julius
 Wunder der Alpen. [1926]. 6v. in 1.

- - 2.Aufl. 1949.

SCHÄTZ, Josef Julius
 [Wunder der Alpen]. Alpine wonderland: a collection of photographs. 1936.

SCHMITHALS, Hans
 Die Alpen. 1926.

SCHWEIGER-LERCHENFELD, Amand, Freiherr von
 Alpenglühen: Naturansichten und Wanderbilder: ein
 Hausbuch für das deutsche Volk. [1893].

SEGUIN, L   G
 A picturesque tour in picturesque lands: France,
 Switzerland, Tyrol, Spain, Holland... 1881.

SHIRAKAWA, Yoshikazu
 Alps. 1969.

SIEGER, Robert
 Die Alpen. 1900.

SIMLER, Josias
 De alpibus Commentarius = die Alpen. 1931.

SMYTHE, Frank S
 Alpine ways... 1942.

SMYTHE, Frank S
 A camera in the hills. 1939.

- - 3rd ed. 1946.
- - 4th ed. 1948.

SMYTHE, Frank S
 Peaks and valleys. 1938.

SONKLAR, Karl, Edler von Innstädten
 Die Eintheilung der Schweizer und der deutschen
 Alpen. 1870.

SPELTERINI, Eduard
 Über den Wolken = Par dessus les nuages. [1928].

SWISSAIR
 Across the Alps: aerial views between Nice and
 Vienna... 1959.

TIFFIN, Walter Francis
 Sketches, principally in Switzerland and the
 Genoese Riviera. [ca 1870].

TONIOLO, A   R
 Revisione critica delle partizioni del sistema
 alpino occidentale. 1925.

TRAYNARD, Philippe and TRAYNARD, Claude
 Cimes et neige: 102 sommets à ski. 1971.

TRENKER, Luis and SCHMIDKUNZ, Walter
 Berge und Heimat: das Buch von den Bergen und
 ihren Menschen. 1939.

UMLAUFT, Friedrich
 Die Alpen: Handbuch der gesammten Alpenkunde.
 1887.

UMLAUFT, Friedrich
 [Die Alpen]. The Alps. 1889.

Voyage pittoresque aux Lacs Majeur et de Lugano;
 [illustrations par J.J. Wetzel]. 1823.

WALTON, Elijah
 The peaks and valleys of the Alps. 1867.

WALTON, Elijah
 Vignettes: alpine and eastern. 1873.

- - Alpine series. 1873.
- - 4th ed. 1882.

WILLIAMS, Charles
 The Alps, Switzerland and the north of Italy.
 1854.

WOOD, Hugh
 Views in France, Switzerland, the Tyrol, and
 Italy. [ca 1840].

WUNDT, Theodor
 Hinauf! Etwas zum Sinnieren für nachdenkliche
 Alpenwanderer. 1913.

YAMADA, Keiichi
 Weisses Heiligtum. 1966.

202.5 A - Z Alpine Europe - panoramas

DILL, J R
Panorama d'une partie des Alpes bernoises pris sur
L'Aeggischhorn dans le canton du Valais.
[ca 1855].

CARREL, Georges
Les Alpes pennines dans un jour; soit Panorama
boréal de la Becca de Nona, depuis le Mont-Blanc
jusqu'au Mont-Rose. 1855.

CARREL, Georges
Chaîne de la Grivola, (Alpes graies), vue de la
Becca de Nona. 1860.

- - 3e éd., corr. 1863.

SCHMID, Franz
Die Gletscher und Alpengebirge des Bern-Oberlandes
vom Nordosten der Stadt Bern angesehen. 1824.

STUDER, Gottlieb
Das Panorama von Bern: Schilderung der in Berns
Umgebungen sichtbaren Gebirge. 1850.

JACOT-GUILLARMOD, Charles
Chaîne de la Dent du Midi aux Dents Blanches de
Champéry vue de la Croix de Culet à l'altitude de
1966m. 1926.

BURFORD, Robert
Description of a view of the Bernese Alps, taken
from the Faulhorn mountain... [1852].

BURGER-HOFER, H
Panorama vom Gäbris, 1250m. üb. Meer... [ca 1880].

Panorama des Alpes pris sur la sommité du Galm près
des Bains de Loëche. 1845.

DILL, J R
Panorama des Alpes, pris sur les Gornergrat près
Zermatt au Canton du Valais. [ca 1855].

BOSSHARD, Albert
Rundsicht vom Gipfel des Hörnli, 1133m ü.M. 1931.

LINER, Carl
Panorama vom Hohen Kasten. [1905].

STUDER, Gottlieb
Panorama vom Mänlichen (Berner Oberland) 2345m.
[1874].

STUDER, Gottlieb
Panorama vom Mattwald oder Simmelihorn im Wallis
(3270m...). [1840].

BOSSOLI, E F
Panorama du Monte Generoso, (1740m). [1890].

HEIM, Albert
Panorama von der grossen Mythe... 1867.

HÜRZELER, Jerome
Panorama du Napf (Righi d'Emmenthal). 1883.

Panorama vom Piz Languard. [ca 1900].

HEIM, Albert
Panorama vom Pizzo Centrale od. Tritthorn Sanct
Gotthard... 1868.

GROSS, Rudolf
Karte und Panorama vom Rigi. 1855.

KELLER, Heinrich
Panorama vom Rigi. 1836.

MEYER, Louis
Ls. Meyer's toposcopisches Panorama vom Rigi-Kulm
2. umgearb. Aufl. 1854.

Panorama du Mont Righi. [ca 1850].

HEIM, Albert
Panorama vom Ruchen Glärnisch. 1870.

HEIM, Albert
Die Alpen und ihr Vorland: Rundsicht vom Gipfel
des Sentis [Säntis]... 1871.

- - 8.Aufl. 1929.

HÄUFLER, Joseph
Panorama vom Schneeberge in Nieder-Oesterreich,
und Hemiorama vom Wechsel an der österreichisch-
steiermärkischen Grenze. 1841.

SIMON, S
Rundsicht vom Schrankogl. 1894.

CLUB ALPIN FRANÇAIS. Section de l'Isère
Panorama circulaire du sommet de la Tête de la
Maye (2522) (Oisans). [ca 1880].

ZELLER, H
Gebirgsaussicht gezeichnet vom Gipfel des Titlis
den 15n. August 1832. 1832.

GILLI, A
Panorama delle Alpi viste dall'Osservatorio
Astronomico di Torino. [1884].

202.7 The "Haute Route"

CHAPPAZ, Maurice
La haute route. 1974.

FANTIN, Mario
Alta via delle Alpi. [1957].

FEDDEN, Robin
Alpine ski tour: an account of the High Level
Route. 1956.

ROBERTS, Eric
High level route. 1973.

ROCH, André
La Haute-Route. 1943.

203 History

ALLAIS, Giovanni
Le Alpi occidentali nell'antichità: nuove
rivelazioni. 1891.

CARTELLIERI, Walther
Die Römischen Alpenstrassen über den Brenner,
Reschen-Scheideck und Plöckenpass, mit ihren
Nebenlinien. 1926.

CLARK, Ronald William
The early alpine guides. 1949.

CLUB ALPINO ITALIANO
Manuale della montagna. 1939.

CLUB ALPINO ITALIANO. Sezione in Chiavenna di
Sondrio
Il Passo dello Spluga e strade chiavennasche, [da]
Pietro Buzzetti. 1928.

COOLIDGE, William Augustus Brevoort
The Alps in nature and history. 1908.

COOLIDGE, William Augustus Brevoort
[The Alps in nature and history]. Les Alpes dans
la nature et dans l'histoire. 1913.

COOLIDGE, William Augustus Brevoort
Charles the Great's passage of the Alps in 773.
1906.

COOLIDGE, William Augustus Brevoort
Le "Col Major" et le Col du Géant. 1913.

COOLIDGE, William Augustus Brevoort
Josias Simler et les origines de l'alpinisme
jusqu'en 1600. 1904.

DE BEER, Sir Gavin
Early travellers in the Alps. 1930.

203 Alpine Europe - history (Cont.)

DUCIS, C   A
   Les Alpes graies, poenines & cottiennes. 1872.

FRANZ, Leonhard
   Vorgeschichtliches Leben in den Alpen. 1929.

GRAND-CARTERET, John
   La montagne à travers les àges: rôle joué par elle,
   façon dont elle a été vue. 1903-04. 2v.

HAUSHOFER, Albrecht
   Pass-Staaten in den Alpen. 1928.

LADOUCETTE, J   C   F
   Histoire, topographie, antiquités, usages,
   dialectes des Hautes-Alpes, avec un atlas. 2e éd.,
   rev. et considérablement augm. 1834.

- - 3e éd., rev. et augm. 1948. 2v.

LAUER-BELART, R
   Studien zur Eröffnungsgeschichte des Gotthard-
   passes mit einer Untersuchung über Stiebende
   Brücke und Teufelsbrücke. 1924.

LEHNER, Wilhelm
   Die Eroberung der Alpen. 1924.

LENTHÉRIC, Charles
   L'homme devant les Alpes. 1896.

OBERZINER, Giovanni
   Le guerre di Augusto contro i popoli alpini. 1900.

OEHLMANN, E
   Die Alpenpasse im Mittelalter. [1878-79].

PERREAU, Joseph
   L'épopée des Alpes: épisodes de l'histoire
   militaire des Alpes en particulier des Alpes
   françaises. 1903-12. 3v.

REINHARD, Raphael
   Pässe und Strassen in den Schweizer Alpen: topo-
   graphisch-historische Studien. 1903.

ROCHAS, Albert de
   La compagne de 1692 dans le Haut Dauphiné:
   documents inédits relatifs à l'histoire et la
   topographie militaire des Alpes... 1874.

RONEY, Sir Cusack P
   The Alps and the eastern mails. 1867.

SCHEFFEL, P   H
   Verkehrsgeschichte der Alpen. 1908-14. 2v. in 1.

SIGNOT, Jacques
   La totale et vraie descriptiŏ de toꝫ les
   passaiges, lieux & destroictz, par lesꝗlz on peut
   passer & entrer des Gaules es Ytalies... 1518.

TYLER, J   E
   The alpine passes: the Middle Ages (962-1250).
   1930.

VACCARONE, Luigi
   Le Pertuis du Viso: étude historique... 1881.

VALLENTIN, Florian
   Les Alpes cottiennes et graies: géographie Gallo-
   Romaine. 1883.

WEISS, Richard
   Die Entdeckung der Alpen: eine Sammlung
   schweizerische und deutscher Alpenliteratur bis
   zum Jahr 1800. 1934.

203.6 Hannibal

AZAN, Paul
   Annibal dans les Alpes. 1902.

BONUS, Arthur Rivers
   Where Hannibal passed. 1925.

DE BEER, Sir Gavin
   Alps and elephants: Hannibal's march. 1955.

ELLIS, Robert
   An enquiry into the ancient routes between Italy
   and Gaul; with an examination of the theory of
   Hannibal's passage of the Alps by the Little
   St. Bernard. 1867.

ELLIS, Robert
   A treatise on Hannibal's passage of the Alps, in
   which his route is traced over the Little Mont
   Cenis. 1853.

FRESHFIELD, Douglas William
   Hannibal once more. 1914.

HOYTE, John
   Trunk road for Hannibal: with an elephant over
   the Alps. 1960.

HYDE, Walter Woodburn
   Roman alpine routes (with map showing chief
   Roman passes). 1935.

LAVIS-TRAFFORD, Marc A   de
   Le col alpin franchi par Hannibal: son identification topographique. 1956.

LAW, William John
   The Alps of Hannibal. 1866. 2v.

LONG, Henry Hawes
   Hannibal's passage of the Alps. 1830.

LUC, Jean André de
   Histoire du passage des Alpes par Annibal. 1818.

- - 2e éd., corr. et augm. 1825.

MONTANARI, Tommaso
   Annibale: l'uomo, la traversata delle Alpi e le
   prime campagne d'Italia fino al trasimeno, secondo
   gli antichi e la verità storica. 1901.

TORR, Cecil
   Hannibal crosses the Alps. 1924.

- - 2nd ed. 1925.

TYTLER, Alexander Fraser
   A critical examination of Mr. Whitaker's "Course
   of Hannibal over the Alps ascertained". 1795.

WHITAKER, John
   The course of Hannibal over the Alps ascertained.
   1794. 2v.

WICKHAM, Henry L   and CRAMER, J   A
   A dissertation on the passage of Hannibal over
   the Alps. 1820.

- - 2nd ed. 1828.

WILKINSON, Spenser
   Hannibal's march through the Alps. 1911.

204 Natural history

BALFOUR, John Hutton
   Account of a botanical excursion to Switzerland,
   with pupils, in August 1858. 1859.

BERLEPSCH, Hermann Alexander von
   Die Alpen in Natur- und Lebensbildern. 1861.

- - 4. sehr verm. und verb. Aufl. 1871
- - 5. sehr verm. und verb. Aufl. 1885.

BERLEPSCH, Hermann Alexander von
   [Die Alpen in Natur- und Lebensbildern]. The
   Alps; or, Sketches of life and nature in the
   mountains. 1861.

204 Alpine Europe - natural history (Cont.)

BLAIKIE, Thomas
Diary of a Scotch gardener at the French Court at the end of the eighteenth century. 1931.

BUSCAGLIA, Italo
Il sentiero: pagine sulla montagna. 1934.

COOLIDGE, William Augustus Brevoort
The Alps in nature and history. 1908.

DRÄGER, Anton
Die Natur des Hochgebirges, mit besonderer Rücksicht auf die Gletscher. 1857.

FARRER, Reginald
Among the hills: a book of joy in high places. [1911].

FRANCÉ, R   H
Die Alpen, gemeinverständlich dargestellt. [1912].

[Guide du naturaliste dans les Alpes]. Guida del naturalista nelle Alpi, [da] J. Dorst [and others]. 1973.

KOHL, Johann Georg
Alpenreisen. 1849-51. 3v.

MACMILLAN, Hugh
Holidays on high lands; or, Rambles and incidents in search of alpine plants. 1869.

RAMBERT, Eugène
[Les Alpes suisses]. Études d'histoire naturelle: Les plantes alpines, La question du foehn, Le voyage du glacier, La flore suisse et ses origines. 1888.

SAMIVEL
Cimes et merveilles. 1952.

- - [Nouv. éd.]. 1975.

SCHERZER, Hans
Geologisch-botanische Wanderungen durch die Alpen. 1. Bd. Das Berchtesgadener Land. 1927.

SPINDLER, Robert
Die Alpen in der englischen Literatur und Kunst. 1932.

TSCHUDI, Friedrich von
Das Thierleben der Alpenwelt: Naturansichten und Thierzeichnungen aus dem schweizerischen Gebirge. 5. verb. Aufl. 1860.

TSCHUDI, Friedrich von
[Das Thierleben der Alpenwelt]. Les Alpes: description pittoresque de la nature et de la faune alpestres. 1859.

TSCHUDI, Friedrich von
[Das Thierleben der Alpenwelt]. Le monde des Alpes; ou, Description pittoresque des montagnes de la Suisse et particulièrement des animaux qui les peuplent. 1858. 3v.

TSCHUDI, Friedrich von
[Das Thierleben der Alpenwelt]. Sketches of nature in the Alps... 1856.
Selections.

- - Another ed. 1862.

TUTT, J   W
Rambles in alpine valleys. 1895.

VILLARS, Dominique
Précis d'un voyage botanique, fait en Suisse, dans les Grisons, aux sources du Rhin ... en juillet, août et septembre 1811; précédé de quelques réflexions sur l'utilité des voyages pour les naturalistes. 1812.

205 Flora and fauna

205.1 Flora

AMSTUTZ, Eveline
Wiesenblumenfibel. 1938.

AMSTUTZ, Walter
Alpenblumenfibel. [1936].

ANGREVILLE, J   E   d'
La flore vallaisanne. 1862.

ARBER, E A   Newell
Plant life in alpine Switzerland, being an account in simple language of the natural history of alpine plants. 1910.

BARNEBY, T   P
European alpine flowers in colour. 1967.

BENNETT, Alfred W
The flora of the Alps, being a description of all ... flowering plants indigenous to Switzerland; and of the alpine species of the adjacent mountain districts ... including the Pyrenees. 1896. 2v.

BORDEAUX, Henry
Les fleurs des Alpes. 1938.

BROCKMANN-JEROSCH, Heinrich
Die Flora des Puschlav (Bezirk Bernina, Kanton Graubünden) und ihre Pflanzengesellschaften. 1907.

BURNAT, Émile and GREMLI, August
Les roses des Alpes maritimes: études sur les roses qui croissent spontanément dans la chaîne des Alpes maritimes et le département français de ce nom. 1879.

CHRIST, H
Das Pflanzenleben der Schweiz. 1879.

CHRIST, H
Ueber die Verbreitung der Pflanzen der alpinen Region der europäischen Alpenkette. 1866.

CORREVON, Henry and ROBERT, Philippe
La flore alpine. [1909].

CORREVON, Henry and ROBERT, Philippe
[La flore alpine]. The alpine flora. [1911?].

CORREVON, Henry
Flore coloriée de poche à l'usage du touriste dans les montagnes... [1894].

DALLA TORRE, Karl Wilhelm von
Die Alpenflora der österreichischen Alpenländer, Südbaierns und der Schweiz. 1899.

DALLA TORRE, Karl Wilhelm von
The tourist's guide to the flora of the Alps. 1886.

DEUTSCHER UND ÖSTERREICHISCHER ALPENVEREIN
Atlas der Alpenflora. 2. neubearb. Aufl. 1897. 5v.

DUCOMMUN, Jules César
Taschenbuch für den schweizerischen Botaniker. 1869.

- - 2. Ausg. 1881.

FENAROLI, Luigi
Flora delle Alpi: vegetazione e flora delle Alpi e degli altri monti d'Italia. 1955.

FISCHER, L
Taschenbuch der Flora von Bern. 1855.

FLEMWELL, George
Alpine flowers and gardens. 1910.

205.1 Alpine Europe - flora (Cont.)

FLEMWELL, George
[Alpine flowers and gardens]. Sur l'alpe fleurie:
promenades poétiques et philosophiques dans les
Alpes. 1914.

FLEMWELL, George
The flower-fields of alpine Switzerland: an
appreciation and a plea. 1911.

FOSSEL, Annemarie
Blumen der Berge: ein Bilderbuch mit Begleitworten.
1935.

FÜNFSTÜCK, M
Taschenatlas der Gebirgs- und Alpenpflanzen, für
Touristen und Pflanzenfreunde in der Schweiz.
1896.

FURRER, Ernst
Kleine Pflanzengeographie der Schweiz. 1923.

GAUDIN, Jean
Synopsis florae helveticae. 1836.

GRAF, Ferdinand
Die Alpenpflanzen. 1880-86. 4v.

GREMLI, August
[Excursionsflora]. The flora of Switzerland for
the use of tourists and field-botanists. 1889.

GRENIER, Ch.   and GODRON, D   A
Flore de France; ou, Description des plantes qui
croissent naturellement en France et en Corse.
1848-56. 3v.

HALLER, Albrecht von
Icones plantarum Helvetiae, ex ipsius Historia
stirpium helveticarum denuo recusae... 1795.

HASTINGS, Somerville
Summer flowers of the high Alps. [1910].

HEATHCOTE, Evelyn D
Flowers of the Engadine. 1891.

HEER, Oswald
Ueber die nivale Flora der Schweiz. [1883].

HEGETSCHWEILER, Johann
Flora der Schweiz. 1840.

HEGETSCHWEILER, Johann
Sammlung von Schweizer Pflanzen nach der Natur und
auf Stein gezeichnet. [1826-34]. 8v.

HEGI, Gustav and DUNZINGER, Gustav
Alpenflora: die verbreitetsten Alpenpflanzen von
Bayern, Tirol und der Schweiz. 1905.

- - 3. verb. Aufl. 1913.

HEGI, Gustav and DUNZINGER, Gustav
[Alpenflora]. Alpine flowers: the most common
alpine plants of Switzerland, Austria, and Bavaria.
1930.

HEGI, Gustav and DUNZINGER, Gustav
[Alpenflora]. Atlas colorié de la flore alpine:
Jura, Pyrénées, Alpes françaises, Alpes suisses.
1906.

HOFFMANN, Julius
Alpen-Flora für Touristen und Pflanzenfreunde.
1902.

- - 2. Aufl. 1914.

HULME, F   Edward
Familiar Swiss flowers. 1908.

HUXLEY, Anthony
Mountain flowers in colour. 1967.

JEAN, Louis
Fleurs des Alpes les plus belles et les plus rares:
où et quand les cueillir? 1937.

KANTONAL-BERNISCHE NATURSCHUTZKOMMISSION
Geschützte Pflanzen im Kanton Bern. [1938].

KOCH, Wilhelm Daniel Joseph
Synopsis florae germanicae et helveticae... 1837.

- - Index generum, specierum et synonymorum. 1838.
- - Ed. 2a. 1843.
- - Ed. 3a. 1857.

KOCH, Wilhelm Daniel Joseph
Taschenbuch der deutschen und Schweizer Flora...
4. Aufl. 1856.

- - Another ed. 1878.

KREIDOLF, Ernst
Alpenblumenmärchen. 1922.

MORITZI, Alexander
Der Flora der Schweiz... 1844.

MÜLLER, Hermann
Alpenblumen... 1881.

MURITH, Laurent Joseph
Le guide du botaniste qui voyage dans le Valais,
avec un catalogue des plantes de ce pays et de
ses environs... 1810.

NEAME, J   Armstrong
Among the meadow and alpine flowers of northern
Italy. 1937.

OEHNINGER, C   J
Die Alpenflora. 1908.

- - 5., vollständig umgearb. Aufl. 1922.

PENZIG, O
Flora delle Alpi illustrata. 1902.

PONA, Giovanni
Monte Baldo descritto da Giovanni Pona, in cui si
figurano & descrivono molte rare piante... 1617.

PRATTEN, Mary A
My hundred Swiss flowers, with a short account of
Swiss ferns. 1887.

RAPIN, D
Le guide du botaniste dans le Canton de Vaud...
1842.

ROGER-SMITH, Hugh
Plant hunting in Europe. [1950].

ROYAL BOTANIC GARDENS, Kew
Catalogue of Miss M.L. Moxon's alpine flower
studies and other paintings. [1924].

RÜBEL, E
Pflanzengeographische Monographie des Bernina-
gebietes. 1912.

SCHINZ, Hans and KELLER, Robert
Flore de la Suisse. Ptie.1. Flore d'excursion.
1909.

SCHRÖTER, Carl
Kleine Führer durch die Pflanzenwelt der Alpen.
1932.

SCHRÖTER, Carl
Das Pflanzenleben der Alpen: eine Schilderung der
Hochgebirgsflora. 1908.

- - 2. durchgearb. und verm. Aufl. 1923-26. 2v.

SCHRÖTER, Carl
Taschenflora des Alpen-Wanderers. 1889.

- - 3. vollständig umgearb. und verm. Aufl. 1892.
- - 10. und 11. Aufl. [1905?].

205.1 Alpine Europe - flora (Cont.)

SCHRÖTER, Carl
[Taschenflora des Alpen-Wanderers]. Coloured vade-
mecum to the alpine flora... [1894].

- - 7th ed., entirely rewritten and greatly enl.
1900.
- - 8th ed. 1903.
- - 12th and 13th ed. [1906?].

SCHRÖTER, Carl
[Taschenflora des Alpen-Wanderers]. Flore coloriée
portative du touriste dans les Alpes. 12e et 13e
éd. [1906?].

SEBOTH, Joseph
Die Alpenpflanzen. 1880-86. 4v.

SEBOTH, Joseph
[Die Alpenpflanzen]. Some alpine flowers. 1893.

SIMLER, Rudolf Theodor
Botanischer Taschenbegleiter des Alpenclubisten:
eine Hochalpenflora der Schweiz und des alpinen
Duetschlands... [1870?].

SUTER, Joh. Rudolf
Helvetiens flora enthaltend die Phänerogamischen
Gewächse Helvetiens. Vol.2. 1822.

THOMÉ, Otto Wilhelm
Flora von Deutschland, Österreich und der Schweiz.
2. verm. und verb. Aufl. 1903-05. 4v. in 8.

THOMPSON, Harold Stuart
Alpine plants of Europe, together with cultural
hints. [1911].

THOMPSON, Harold Stuart
Sub-alpine plants; or, Flowers of the Swiss woods
and meadows. 1912.

TREVENA, John
Adventures among wild flowers. 1914.

VALBUSA, U
Piante alpine. [n.d.]

VARESCHI, Volkmar and KRAUSE, Ernst
Mountains in flower. 1939.

WALTON, Elijah
Flowers from the upper Alps, with glimpses of
their homes. 1869.

- - 5th ed. 1882.

WARD, H   C
Wild flowers of Switzerland; or, A year amongst
the flowers of the Alps. 1883.

WOOSTER, David
Alpine plants: figures and descriptions of some
of the most striking and beautiful of the alpine
flowers. 1872.

- - 2nd ed. 1874.
- - 2nd series. 1874.

205.2 Trees

SWITZERLAND. Inspektion für Forstwesen, Jagd und
Fischerei
Arbres et forêts de la Suisse. le série. 1908.

205.5 Fauna

FATIO, Victor
Faune des vertébrés de la Suisse. 1869-99. 3v.

FRANKE, Hans
Alpenvögel: ein Wanderbuch zum Bestimmen unserer
Alpenvögel nach Aussehen, Stimme, Ausenthalt.
1935.

GRAINER, Franz
Aus freier Wildbahn: Thierstudien aus den
Hochalpen... 1898.

HELLMICH, Walter
Tiere der Alpen: ein Wegweiser für Bergsteiger.
1936.

RAUCH, Andrea
Der Steinbock wieder in den Alpen. 1937.

RAUCH, Andrea
[Der Steinbock wieder in den Alpen]. Le bouquetin
dans les Alpes. 1941.

STÖLKER, Carl
Die Alpenvögel der Schweiz. 1. Serie. [1876].

TSCHUDI, Friedrich von
Tiere der Alpen. [1917].

VAUCHER, Charles
Chamois. 1944.

206 Travel - personal accounts, reminiscences

AMATI, Giacinto
Peregrinazione al Gran San Bernardo, Losanna,
Friburgo, Ginevra con una corsa a Lione, Parigi
e Londra. 1838.

BAILLIE, Marianne
First impressions on a tour upon the continent in
the summer of 1818, through parts of France,
Italy, Switzerland, the borders of Germany and a
part of French Flanders. 1819.

BAKEWELL, R
Travels, comprising observations made during a
residence in the Tarentaise, and various parts of
the Grecian and Pennine Alps, and in Switzerland
and Auvergne, in ... 1820, 1821, and 1822. 1823.
2v.

BARON, A
Pérégrinations en Suisse, en Savoie et sur les
bords du Rhin. 2e éd. [1867].

BARROW, John, 1808-1898
Tour on the Continent, by rail and road, in the
summer of 1852, through northern Germany, Austria,
Tyrol, Austrian Lombardy... 1853.

BAUMGARTNER, Joseph
Die neuesten und vorzüglichsten Kunst-Strassen
über die Alpen; beschrieben auf einer Reise durch
Östreich, Steyermark, Kärnthen, Krain und Tyrol,
das Küstenland und die Lombardie, einen Theil von
Piemont und der südlichen Schweiz. 1834.

BAXTER, William Edward
Impressions of central and southern Europe,
being notes of successive journeys in Germany,
Austria, Italy, Switzerland, and the Levant.
1850.

BEAUMONT, Jean François Albanis
Travels from France to Italy, through the
Lepontine Alps; or, An itinerary of the road from
Lyons to Turin, by the way of the Pays-de-Vaud,
the Vallais... 1800.

- - Another ed. 1806.

BEAUMONT, Jean François Albanis
Travels through the Maritime Alps, from Italy to
Lyons... 1795.

BEAUMONT, Jean François Albanis
Travels through the Rhaetian Alps, in the year
1786, from Italy to Germany, through Tyrol...
1792.

BECKFORD, William
The history of the Caliph Vathek; and European
travels... 1891.

206 <u>Alpine Europe - travel ...</u> (<u>Cont</u>.)

BELLOC, Hilaire
The path to Rome. 1902.

- - Another ed. [1910].

BERNARD, A   de
Les stations d'un touriste. 1861.

BERTRAND, E
Le Thevenon; ou, Les journées de la montagne.
1777.

- - Nouv. éd., rev. corr. & augm. 1780.

BITHRAY, Ebenezer
Switzerland and Italy, being personal notes of a
tour via Belgium and Germany, returning home
through France. [1883].

BLAINVILLE, J   de
Travels through Holland, Germany, Switzerland, but
especially Italy... 1757. 3v.

BONGHI, Ruggiero
In viaggio da Pontresina a Londra: impressioni
dolci, osservazioni amare. 1a ser. 1889.

BOURRIT, Marc Théodore
Description des Alpes pennines et rhetiennes.
1781. 2v.

BOURRIT, Marc Théodore
[Description des Alpes pennines et rhetiennes].
Beschreibung der penninischen und rhatischen
Alpen. 1782.

BOURRIT, Marc Théodore
Description des cols; ou, Passages des Alpes.
1803. 2v. in 1.

BOURRIT, Marc Théodore
Nouvelle description des glacieres, vallées de
glace et glaciers, qui forment la grande chaîne
des Alpes, de Savoye, de Suisse et d'Italie.
Nouv. éd., rev. et corr. 1787. 3v.

BOURRIT, Marc Théodore
Nouvelle description des vallées de glace et des
hautes montagnes, qui forment la chaîne des Alpes
pennines et rhetiennes. 1783. 2v. in 1.

BOURRIT, Marc Théodore
Nouvelle description générale et particulière des
glacieres, vallées de glace et glaciers, qui
forment la grande chaîne des Alpes de Suisse,
d'Italie & de Savoye. Nouv. éd., corr. & augm.
1785. 3v.

BOURRIT, Marc Théodore
[Nouvelle description générale et particulière
des glacieres...]. Beschreibung der savoyischen
Eisgeburge. 1786.

BRAUNSTEIN, Josef
Richard Wagner and the Alps. [1929?].

BREMER, Fredrika
Two years in Switzerland and Italy. 1861.

BRIDGES, George Windham
Alpine sketches, comprised in a short tour through
parts of Holland, Flanders, France, Savoy,
Switzerland and Germany, during the summer of
1814, by a member of the University of Oxford.
1814.

A Briton abroad, by the author of "Two years abaft
the mast". 1878.

BROCKEDON, William
Journals of excursions in the Alps: the Pennine,
Graian, Cottian, Rhetian, Lepontian, and Bernese.
1833.

- - 3rd ed. 1845.

BROOKE, T
Comicalities of travel; for the Tarvin Bazaar.
1836.

BRUEN, Matthias
Essays descriptive and moral, on scenes in Italy,
Switzerland and France, by an American. 1823.

BRUN, Friederika
Episoden aus Reisen durch das südliche
Deutschland, die westliche Schweiz, Genf und
Italien in den Jahren 1801, 1802, 1803, nebst
Anhängen vom Jahr 1805. Vol.1. 1806.

BUCKINGHAM, James Silk
Belgium, the Rhine, Switzerland, and Holland: an
autumnal tour. [1848]. 2v.

BUCKINGHAM, James Silk
France, Piedmont, Italy, Lombardy, the Tyrol,
and Bavaria: an autumnal tour. [1848]. 2v.

BURNET, Gilbert
Some letters containing, An account of what
seemed most remarkable in Switzerland, Italy, &c.
1686.

CARNE, John
Letters from Switzerland and Italy, during a
late tour. 1834.

CAROLINE, <u>Queen</u>, <u>consort of George IV</u>, <u>King of
Great Britain</u>
Voyages and travels of Her Majesty, Caroline
Queen of Great Britain ..., by one of Her
Majesty's Suite. 1822.

CAROLINE, <u>Queen</u>, <u>consort of George IV</u>, <u>King of
Great Britain</u>
[Voyages and travels of Her Majesty, Caroline
Queen of Great Britain]. Voyages de Caroline,
reine d'Angleterre, en Allemagne, en Suisse, en
Italie, en Grèce et en Palestine. 1825. 3v.

CATLOW, Agnes and CATLOW, Maria E
Sketching rambles; or, Nature in the Alps and
Appennines. [1861].

CERESA, G   F
Escursioni alpine; ossia, Breve descrizione topografica dei passi alpestri più frequentati ...
cioè dal Colle di Frejus al Brenner. 1869.

CHAMIER, <u>Capt</u>.
My travels; or, An unsentimental journey through
France, Switzerland and Italy. 1855. 3v.

CHEEVER, George B   and HEADLEY, J   T
Travels among alpine scenery. 1855.

CHOULOT, Paul, <u>comte de</u>
Huit jours au pas de charge en Savoie et en
Suisse. [1845?].

CLARKE, Andrew
Tour in France, Italy, and Switzerland, during
the years 1840 and 1841. 1843.

CLAYTON, J   W
Il pellegrino: wanderings in Switzerland & Italy.
[1863].

CLIFFORD, <u>Sir</u> Charles Cavendish
Travels. 1865.

COBBETT, James P
Journal of a tour in Italy, and also in part of
France and Switzerland ... from October, 1828,
to September, 1829. 1830.

COLSTON, Marianne
Journal of a tour in France, Switzerland, and
Italy, during the years 1819, 20, and 21. 1822.
2v.

The continental traveller, being the journal of an
economical tourist to France, Switzerland, and
Italy... 1833.

206 Alpine Europe - travel ... (Cont.)

CONWAY, Derwent
  Switzerland, the south of France, and the
  Pyrenees... Vol.1. Switzerland. 1831.

COOK, Emily Constance
  From a holiday journal. 1904.

COOPER, James Fenimore
  A residence in France; with an excursion up the
  Rhine, and a second visit to Switzerland. 1836.
  2v.

CORYAT, Thomas
  Coryat's crudities, hastily gobled up in five
  moneths travells in France, Savoy, Italy, Rhetia
  commonly called the Grisons country, Helvetia
  alias Switzerland, some parts of high Germany
  and the Netherlands... 1905. 2v.

Cursory notes of a nine weeks' tour, [by William
  Dodd?]. 1834.

DESAIX DE VEYGOUX, Louis Charles Antoine
  Journal de voyage du général Desaix: Suisse et
  Italie, 1797. 1907.

DOLLÉ, Frédéric
  Souvenirs de voyage: Suisse, Savoie, France. 3e
  éd. 1843.

DOLLFUS, Charles
  À travers monts. 2e éd. 1900.

DOYLE, Richard
  The foreign tour of Messrs. Brown, Jones &
  Robinson. 1904.

DRIELING, F H C
  Aanteekeningen op eene Reize naar Zwitserland en
  Lombardijen in 1829. 1833.

DRUMMOND, D T K
  Scenes and impressions in Switzerland and the
  north of Italy ... taken from the notes of a four
  months' tour during the summer of 1852. 1853.

DUBOIS, Albert
  Croquis alpins: promenades en Suisse et au pays
  des Dolomites. 1883.

DUPPA, Richard
  Miscellaneous observations and opinions on the
  continent. 1825.

DU PREL, Carl, Freiherr
  Unter Tannen und Pinien: Wanderungen in den Alpen,
  Italien, Dalmatien und Montenegro. 1875.

DURBIN, John P
  Observations in Europe, principally in France and
  Great Britain. 1844. 2v.

DYKE, Thomas
  Travelling mems, during a tour through Belgium,
  Rhenish Prussia, Germany, Switzerland, and France,
  in the summer and autumn of 1832: including an
  excursion up the Rhine. 1834. 2v.

ELTON, Charles Isaac
  An account of Shelley's visits to France,
  Switzerland, and Savoy, in the years 1814 and 1816;
  with extracts from "The history of a six weeks'
  tour" and "Letters descriptive of a sail round the
  Lake of Geneva..." 1894.

ENGEL, Claire Éliane
  Byron et Shelley en Suisse et en Savoie, mai-
  octobre 1816. 1930.

FAVRE, Alphonse
  H.-B. de Saussure et les Alpes. 1870.

FERGUSON, Fergus
  Wanderings in France and Switzerland. 1869.

FISCHER, Christian August
  Bergreisen. 1804-05. 2v. in 1.

FORBES, Murray
  The diary of a traveller over Alps and Appenines;
  or, Daily minutes of a circuitous excursion.
  1824.

FRESHFIELD, Mrs. Henry
  Alpine byways; or, Light leaves gathered in 1859
  and 1860. 1861.

GAUTIER, Théophile
  Les vacances du lundi: tableaux de montagnes.
  1881.

GEORGE, Marian M
  A little journey to France and Switzerland, for
  home and school. 1902.

Gleanings after "Grand tour-ists". 1856.

GOS, Charles
  Voyage de Saussure hors des Alpes. [1934].

GRANT, James
  Records of a run through continental countries,
  embracing Belgium, Holland, Germany, Switzerland,
  Savoy, and France. 1853. 2v.

GRAY, Robert
  Letters during the course of a tour through
  Germany, Switzerland and Italy, in the years
  1791, and 1792... 1794.

GUIBERT, Jacques Antoine, comte de
  Voyages de Guibert dans diverses parties de la
  France et en Suisse, faits en 1775, 1778, 1784,
  et 1785. 1806.

GUILD, Curtis
  Over the ocean; or, Sights and scenes in foreign
  lands. 1889.

HALEM, G A
  Blicke auf einem Theil Deutschlands, der Schweiz
  und Frankreichs bey einer Reise vom Jahre 1790.
  1791. 2v.

HALL, Basil
  Patchwork. 1841. 3v.

HALL, Charlotte
  Through the Tyrol to Venice. 1860.

HALLAM, Julia Clark
  The story of a European tour. 2nd ed. 1901.

HAUSSEZ, Charles Le Mercher de Longpré, baron d'
  Alpes et Danube; ou, Voyage en Suisse, Styrie,
  Hongrie et Transylvanie, pour faire suite au
  Voyage d'un exile. 1837. 2v.

HAYWARD, Abraham
  Some account of a journey across the Alps, in a
  letter to a friend. [1834?].

HEADLEY, J T
  The Alps and the Rhine: a series of sketches.
  1846.

HEADLEY, J T
  Travels in Italy, the Alps, and the Rhine. 1849.

HEGER, Thomas
  A tour through a part of the Netherlands, France,
  and Switzerland, in the year 1817: containing a
  variety of incidents, with the author's reflections... 1820.

HERBERT, Henry
  A fortnight's journal, with a short account of
  the manner of his death on one of the Jura mountains, August 2, 1837. 1838.

HERVIEU, Sosthène
  Souvenirs d'un touriste. 1841.

HEWAT, Kirkwood
  My diary, being notes of a continental tour from
  the Mersey ... to the crater of Mount Versuvius
  ... to the top of Mont Blanc ... from Paris to the
  Firth of Forth. [1878].

206 Alpine Europe - travel ... (Cont.)

HOCKING, Silas K
Up the Rhine and over the Alps. [1886].

HOLDER, Chr. G   von
Meine Reise über den Gotthard nach den
Borromäischen Inseln und Mailand; und von da
zurük über das Val Formazza, die Grimsel und das
Oberland. 1803-04. 2v.

HOG, Roger
Tour on the continent in France, Switzerland, and
Italy, in the years 1817 and 1818. 1824.

HOGG, Thomas Jefferson
Two hundred and nine days; or, The journal of a
traveller on the continent. 1827. 2v.

HOLMES, D   T
A Scot in France and Switzerland. 1910.

HOLWORTHY, Sophia Matilda
Alpine scrambles and classic rambles: a gipsy
tour in search of summer snow and winter sun, a
pocket companion for the unprotected. [1882].

HOWELL, George O
Recollections of a visit abroad, being notes of
a scamper through Switzerland, with a ride down
the Rhine, and a bound through Brussels, during
the month of August 1894. 1895.

HUCK, J   Ch.
Enzian und Edelweiss: Erinnerungen an meine
Alpenfahrten. 1925.

HUTTON, Richard Holt
Holiday rambles in ordinary places. 1877.

INGLIS, Henry D
Switzerland, the South of France, and the
Pyrenees. 1837.

- - 4th ed. 1840.

JAMIESON, Mrs.
Popular voyages and travels throughout the continent & islands of Europe: in which the
geography, character, customs and manner of
nations are described... 1820.

Journal of a tour in France, Switzerland, and
Lombardy, crossing the Simplon, and returning by
Mont Cenis to Paris, during the autumn of 1818.
1821. 2v.

KEYSLER, John George
Travels through Germany, Bohemia, Hungary,
Switzerland, Italy, and Lorrain. 2nd ed.
1756-57. 4v.

- - 3rd ed. 1760. 4v.

KOHL, Johann Georg
Alpenreisen. 1849-51. 3v. in 2.

LAING, Samuel
Notes of a traveller, on the social and political
state of France, Prussia, Switzerland, Italy, and
other parts of Europe, during the present century,
2nd ed. 1842.

LAMONT, Martha Macdonald
Impressions, thoughts, and sketches, during two
years in France and Switzerland. 1844.

LAMPEN, Ernest Dudley
Chateau d'Oex: life and sport in an alpine valley.
1910.

LEIBING, Franz
Natur, Kunst und Menschen in Ober-Italien und der
Schweiz: psychologische Skizzen. 1866.

LEROY, A   L
Nos fils et nos filles en voyage. [19--].

LIDDIARD, William
A three months' tour in Switzerland and France.
1832.

Lion hunting; or, A summer's ramble through parts
of Flanders, Germany, and Switzerland in 1825,
with some remarks on men, manners, and things, at
home and abroad. 1826.

LONGMAN, William and TROWER, Henry
Journal of six weeks' adventures in Switzerland,
Piedmont, and on the Italian lakes. 1856.

LUC, Jean André de
Lettres physiques et morales, sur les montagnes
et sur l'histoire de la terre et de l'homme...
1778.

M.....
Ma promenade au delà des Alpes. 1819.

M., Helen
Reminiscences of a continental tour. 1871.

MCCABE, James D
Our young folks abroad: the adventures of four
American boys and girls in a journey through
Europe to Constantinople. 1881.

M'GAVIN, William
Notes of a short tour through parts of France,
Switzerland, and Rhenish Germany... 1860.

MACGREGOR, John
My note book. 1835. 3v.

MACQUOID, Gilbert S
Up and down: sketches of travel. 1890.

MAGGS, J
Round Europe with the crowd. 1880.

MALLESON, F   A
Holiday studies of Wordsworth: by rivers, woods,
and Alps, the Wharfe, the Duddon, and the Stelvio
pass. 1890.

MALLESON, G   B
Captain Musafir's rambles in alpine lands. 1884.

- - 2nd ed. 1885.

MARCET, William
The principal southern and Swiss health resorts,
their climate and medical aspect. 1883.

MARRACK, Richard
How we did them in seventeen days! To wit:
Belgium, the Rhine, Switzerland, & France, des-
cribed and illustrated. [1875].

MASSIE, J   W
Recollections of a tour: a summer ramble in
Belgium, Germany, and Switzerland. 1846.

MATTHEWS, Henry
The diary of an invalid, being the journal of a
tour in pursuit of health; in Portugal, Italy,
Switzerland, and France, in the years 1817, 1818,
and 1819. 1820.

- - 2nd ed. 1820.
- - 4th ed. 1824.
- - 5th ed. 1835.

MATTHISSON, Friedrich von
Briefe. 1795. 2v.

MENDELSSOHN, Felix
Reisebriefe aus den Jahren 1830 bis 1832. 2
unveränderte Aufl. 1862.

MENDELSSOHN, Felix
[Reisebriefe aus den Jahren 1830 bis 1832].
Letters... 3rd ed. 1864.

MEULEN, M   E   van der
Mijne reis door Zwitserland, naar de Wandenzen,
in Piemont's valleijen. 1852.

206 Alpine Europe - travel ... (Cont.)

MILES, Edwin J
   Byeways in the southern Alps: sketches of spring
   and summer resorts in Italy and Switzerland.
   [1893].

MILFORD, John
   Observations, moral, literary, and antiquarian,
   made during a tour through the Pyrenees, South of
   France, Switzerland, the whole of Italy, and the
   Netherlands, in the years 1814 and 1815. 1818.
   2v.

MILLIN, A   L
   Voyage en Savoie, en Piémont, à Nice, et à Gênes.
   1816. 2v.

MONTAIGNE, Michel de
   [Journal du voyage...]. The journal of Montaigne's
   travels in Italy by way of Switzerland and Germany
   in 1580 and 1581. 1903. 3v.

MONTÉMONT, Albert
   Voyage aux Alpes et en Italie; ou, Description
   nouvelle de ces contrées. 4e éd., entièrement
   refondue... 1860.

MONTÉMONT, Albert
   [Voyage aux Alpes et en Italie]. Tour over the
   Alps and in Italy. 1823.

MOORE, John
   A view of the society and manners in France,
   Switzerland, and Germany, with anecdotes relating
   to some eminent characters. 4th ed., corr. 1781.
   2v.

MORGAN, John Minter
   Letters to a clergyman, during a tour through
   Switzerland and Italy, in the years 1846-1847.
   1849.

MORYSON, Fynes
   An itinerary, containing his ten yeeres travell
   through the twelve dominions of Germany,
   Bohmerland, Sweitzerland, Netherland, Denmarke,
   Poland, Italy, Turky, France, England, Scotland &
   Ireland. 1907. 4v.

MOULTON, Louise Chandler
   Lazy tours. 1896.

MULLER, August
   Suisse et Lombardie: souvenirs de vacances, août
   1865. 1890.

MUSSET PATHAY, Victor Donatien de
   Voyage en Suisse et en Italie, fait avec l'Armée
   de Réserve. 1800.

NIEVELT, C   van
   Een Alpenboek: Wandelingen in de Zwitsersche en
   Tiroler Bergen. 1886.

NISARD, Désiré
   Promenades d'un artiste. Vol.2. 1835.

NOEL, Gerard Thomas
   Arvendel; or, Sketches in Italy and Switzerland.
   1826.

Notes of a ramble through France, Italy, Switzerland,
   Germany, Holland, and Belgium... 1836.

O'CONOR, Matthew
   Picturesque and historical recollections during a
   tour through Belgium, Germany, France, and
   Switzerland, in the summer vacation of 1835. 1837.

OWEN, John
   Travels into different parts of Europe, in the
   years 1791 and 1792... 1796. 2v.

PASCAL, César
   De glacier englacier en Suisse et en Savoie:
   souvenirs de voyage précédés d'une notice biographique. [1884].

PENNINGTON, Thomas
   Continental excursions; or, Tours into France,
   Switzerland and Germany, in 1782, 1787, and 1789...
   1809. 2v.

PENNINGTON, Thomas
   A journey into various parts of Europe; and a
   residence in them, during the years 1818, 1819,
   1820, and 1821. 1825. 2v.

A picturesque tour through France, Switzerland, on
   the banks of the Rhine and through parts of the
   Netherlands in the year 1816. [1817].

POPHAM, R   Brooks
   Zig-zag ramblings; or, Further notes by the way.
   1906.

PÜCKLER MUSKAU, Hermann, Fürst von
   [Briefe eines Verstorbenen]. Mémoires et voyages
   du Prince Pückler Muskau: lettres posthumes sur
   l'Angleterre, l'Irlande, la France, la Hollande
   et l'Allemagne. 1833-34. 6v.
   Library lacks vols. 1 and 2.

RAFFLES, Thomas
   Letters, during a tour through some parts of
   France, Savoy, Switzerland, Germany, and the
   Netherlands, in the summer of 1817. 1818.

- - 2nd ed. 1819.
- - 3rd ed. 1820.

READE, John Edmund
   Prose from the south. 1846. 2v.

RECKE, Elisa, Baronin von der
   Tagebuch einer Reise durch einen Theil Deutschlands und durch Italien, in den Jahren 1804 bis
   1806. 1815-17. 4v.

RECKE, Elisa, Baronin von der
   [Tagebuch einer Reise...]. Voyage en Allemagne
   dans le Tyrol et en Italie, pendant les années
   1804, 1805 et 1806. 1819. 3v.

RIGBY, Edward
   Dr. Rigby's letters from France &c. in 1789.
   1880.

RITCHIE, Leitch
   Travelling sketches in the North of Italy, the
   Tyrol, and on the Rhine. 1832.

RIVINGTON, Alexander
   Notes of travels in Europe in the years 1856-64.
   1865.

ROBY, John
   Seven weeks in Belgium, Switzerland, Lombardy,
   Piedmont, Savoy, &c. &c. 1838. 2v.

ROSCOE, Thomas and THORNTON, Cyril
   Rambles in France and Switzerland. [n.d.].

ROWELL, Robert
   Recollections of our midsummer ramble... [1873].

RUSCH, J   B   E
   Wanderspiegel. 1873.

SACCHI, Giuseppe
   Viaggio in Francia e nella Svizzera occidentale.
   1838.

ST. JOHN, James Augustus
   There and back again in search of beauty. 1853.
   2v.

SAUSSURE, Horace Bénédict de
   Voyages dans les Alpes, précédés d'un essai sur
   l'histoire naturelle des environs de Genève.
   1779-96. 4v.

SAUSSURE, Horace Bénédict de
   [Voyages dans les Alpes]. Reisen durch die
   Alpen, nebst einem Versuch über die Natur-
   geschichte der Gegenden von Genf. 1781-88. 4v.

206 <u>Alpine Europe - travel ...</u> (<u>Cont.</u>)

SAUSSURE, Horace Bénédict de
Voyages dans les Alpes: partie pittoresque des
ouvrages de H.B. de Saussure. 1834.

- - 2e éd., augm. 1852.
- - 6e éd., augm. [1898].

SCHEFFEL, Joseph Viktor von
Reise-Bilder. 1887.

SCOTT, John
Sketches of manners, scenery, &c. in the French
provinces, Switzerland, and Italy. 1821.

SENNETT, A   R
Fragments from continental journeyings. 1903.

SEWELL, Elizabeth M
A journal kept during a summer tour, for the
children of a village school. 1852. 3v.

SHAND, Alexander Innes
Old-time travel: personal reminiscences of the
continent forty years ago compared with experiences
of the present day... 1903.

SHELLEY, Percy Bysshe
Essays, letters from abroad, translations and
fragments. New ed. 1852. 2v.

SHEPPARD, John
Letters, after a tour through some parts of France,
Italy, Switzerland, and Germany, in 1816. 1817.

SHERLOCK, Martin
Nouvelles lettres d'un voyageur anglois. 1780.

SKETCHLEY, Arthur
Out for a holiday with Cook's excursion, through
Switzerland and Italy. [1871].

SMITH, James Edward
A sketch of a tour on the continent. 2nd ed.,
with additions and corrections. 1807. 3v.

SMITH, John, <u>of Gray's Inn</u>
A month in France and Switzerland, during the
autumn of 1824. 1825.

SMITH, Joseph Denham
A voice from the Alps; or, The Vaudois valleys,
with scenes by the way of lands and lakes
historically associated. 1854.

SMITH, William
Adventures with my alpen-stock and carpet-bag; or
A three weeks' trip to France and Switzerland.
1864.

STALEY, <u>Mrs.</u>
Autumn rambles; or, Fireside recollections of
Belgium, the Rhine, the Moselle, German spas,
Switzerland, the Italian lakes, Mont Blanc, and
Paris. 1863.

STANDEN, R   S
Continental way-side notes: the diary of a seven
months' tour in Europe. 1865.

STARKLOF, L
Durch die Alpen; Kreus- und Quer-Züge. 1850.

STEIN, Christian Gottfried Daniel
Reise durch Baiern, Salzburg, Tirol, die Schweiz
und Württemberg. 1829.

STEUB, Ludwig
Kleinere Schriften. Bd.1. Reiseschilderungen.
1873.

STEVENSON, Seth William
A tour in France, Savoy, Northern Italy,
Switzerland, Germany and the Netherlands, in the
summer of 1825. 1827. 2v.

STOLBERG, Friedrich Leopold, <u>Graf zu</u>
Travels through Germany, Switzerland, Italy, and
Sicily. 1797. 4v.

STOWE, Harriet Beecher
Sunny memories of foreign lands. 1854.

STRANG, John
Travelling notes in France, Italy and Switzerland
of an invalid in search of health. 1863.

T., G.
What may be done in two months: a summer's tour,
through Belgium, up the Rhine, and to the lakes
of Switzerland; also to Chamouny... 1834.

TALFOURD, <u>Sir</u> Thomas Noon
Recollections of a first visit to the Alps, in
August and September 1841. [1842].

TALFOURD, <u>Sir</u> Thomas Noon
Vacation rambles and thoughts; comprising the
recollections of three continental tours in the
vacations of 1841, 1842, and 1843. 1845. 2v.

- - 2nd ed. 1845.
- - 3rd ed. 1851.
- - Supplement. 1854.

TAYLOR, Bayard
Views afoot; or, Europe seen with knapsack and
staff. 1869.

TENNANT, Charles
A tour through parts of the Netherlands, Holland,
Germany, Switzerland, Savoy, and France, in the
year 1821-2, including a description of ... the
stupendous scenery of the Alps in the depth of
winter. 1824. 2v.

A three weeks tour in Savoy and Switzerland, written
with the intention of showing a cheap and agreeable
manner of travelling in those countries, with a
list of the best hotels... 1844.

TÖPFFER, Rodolphe
Derniers voyages en zigzag; ou, Excursions d'un
pensionnat en vacances dans les cantons suisses
et sur le revers italien des Alpes. 1910. 2v.in 1.

TÖPFFER, Rodolphe
Nouveaux voyages en zigzag, à la Grande Chartreuse,
autour du Mont Blanc, dans les vallées d'Herenz...
1854.

- - 2e éd. 1858.
- - 3e éd. 1864.
- - 4e éd. 1877.

TÖPFFER, Rodolphe
Voyage autour du Mont Blanc, dans les vallées
d'Herens, de Zermatt et au Grimsel, autographié
par R.T. (i.e. Rodolphe Töpffer). 1843.

TÖPFFER, Rodolphe
Voyages en zigzag; ou, Excursions d'un pensionnat
en vacances dans les cantons suisses et sure le
revers italien des Alpes. 1844.

- - 2e éd. 1846.
- - 4e éd. 1855.
- - 6e éd. 1860.

TÖPFFER, Rodolphe
[Voyages en zigzag...]. Reisen im Zickzack. 1912.

A tour through part of France, Switzerland, and
Italy, including a summary history of the principal
cities. 1827. 2v.

TRENCH, Francis
A walk round Mont Blanc, etc. 1847.

Trip to Paris and Switzerland. 1867.

TROLLOPE, T   Adolphus
Impressions of a wanderer in Italy, Switzerland,
France, and Spain. 1850.

TUCKETT, Elizabeth
Beaten tracks; or, Pen and pencil sketches in
Italy. 1866.

206 Alpine Europe - travel ... (Cont.)

TUPPER, Martin
Paterfamilias's Diary of everybody's tour: Belgium
and the Rhine, Munich, Switzerland, Milan, Geneva
and Paris. 1856.

TWAIN, Mark
A tramp abroad. 1880.

- - Another ed. 1880.

VIZARD, John
Narrative of a tour through France, Italy, and
Switzerland, in a series of letters. 1872.

WALTER, Weever
Letters from the Continent, containing sketches
of foreign scenery and manners... 1828.

WATKINS, Thomas
Travels through Switzerland, Italy, Sicily, the
Greek Islands to Constantinople; through part of
Greece, Ragusa, and the Dalmatian Isles... 2nd
ed. 1794. 2v.

WEDDIK, Bartholomeus T   Lublink
Tafereelen, gedachten en beelden: impressions de
voyage; Verzameld langs den Rijn en in Zwitserland
... 1854.

WELD, Charles Richard
Auvergne, Piedmont, and Savoy: a summer ramble.
1850.

WESTON, Stephen
A trimester in France and Swisserland; or, A three
months' journey in ... 1820, from Calais to Basle
... and from Basle to Paris, through Strasburg
and Reims. 1821.

WILSON, Daniel
Letters from an absent brother. 1823.

- - 2nd ed. 1824. 2v.
- - 3rd ed. 1825.
- - 4th ed. 1827.

WILSON, W   Rae
Notes abroad and rhapsodies at home. 1837. 2v.

WINTER, J   B
From Switzerland to the Mediterranean on foot.
1922.

WITTE, Karl
Alpinisches und Transalpinisches. 1858.

206.2 Walking

CASANOVA, Oscar
Escursioni nei parchi alpini: 60 incontri con la
natura protetta dall'Argentera alle Alpi Giulie.
1977.

COLLOMB, Robin Gabriel
Alpine points of view; or, Contemporary scenes
from the Alps including some observations and
opinions of an itinerant alpinist. 1961.

GRANDJEAN, Valentin
Flâneries dans les Alpes: la chaîne des Aravis,
les Alpes de Taninges, les rochers des Fiz, le
massif de Platé. 1908.

MERRICK, Hugh
Rambles in the Alps. 1951.

PAUSE, Walter
[Berg Heil]. Salute the mountains: the hundred
best walks in the Alps. 1962.

SPRING, Ira and EDWARDS, Harvey
100 hikes in the Alps. 1979.

WALKER, James Hubert
Walking in the Alps. 1951.

206.4 Cycling, motoring

CARLE, Dr.
Sur les routes des Alpes en automobile. [1914].

FREESTON, Charles L
The Alps for the motorist. [ca 1926].

FREESTON, Charles L
Cycling in the Alps with some notes on the chief
passes. 1900.

FREESTON, Charles L
The high-roads of the Alps: a motoring guide to
one hundred mountain passes. [1910].

- - 2nd ed., rev. and enl. 1911.

MERRICK, Hugh
The great motor highways of the Alps. 1958.

- - Rev. ed. 1961.

206.5 Railways

Die industrielle und kommerzielle Schweiz, beim
Eintritt ins 20. Jahrhundert. No. 3 und 4.
Schweizerische Bergbahnen. 1901.

206.6 Flying

BURGBACHER, Kurt
[Pilot in der weissen Hölle]. White hell: a
story of the Search and Rescue Service in the
Alps. 1963.

FAWCETT, Douglas
From Heston to the high Alps: a chat about joy-
flying. 1936.

GEIGER, Hermann
Geiger and the Alps. [1958?].

GEIGER, Hermann
Geiger: pilote des glaciers. 1955.

GEIGER, Hermann
[Geiger: pilote des glaciers]. Alpine pilot.
1956.

GUYER, Gebhard A
Im Ballon über die Jungfrau nach Italien.
[1909].

MITTELHOLZER, Walter
Alpenflug. 1928.

MITTELHOLZER, Walter
[Alpenflug]. Les ailes et les Alpes. 1929.

SCHILLER, Hans von
Im Zeppelin über der Schweiz. 1930.

206.7 Hunting

BAILLIE-GROHMAN, William Adolphus
Sport in the Alps in the past and present: an
account of the chase of the chamois, red-deer,
bouquetin... 1896.

COTESWORTH, W
Idle days in the Vorarlberg and its neighbourhood. 1887.

HODGSON, Randolph L
On plain and peak: sporting and other sketches of
Bohemia and Tyrol. 1898.

KELLER, F   C
Die Gemse: ein monografischer Beitrag zur
Jagdzoologie. 1887.

MELON, Pierre
Chasseurs de chamois. [1935].

206.7 Alpine Europe - hunting (Cont.)

TREDICINE DE SAINT-SÉVERIN, Hector, marquis de
La chasse au chamois. [1925].

208 Route books, itineraries

BRASCA, Luigi
Itinerari alpini. Ser.1. 1917.

BROCKEDON, William
The hand-book for travellers in Italy, from London
to Naples. [1831].

BROCKEDON, William
Road-book from London to Naples. 1835.

DOWNES, G
Guide through Switzerland and Savoy; or, A new and
complete geographical, historical, and picturesque
description of every remarkable place in these
countries ... forming a complete itinerary. New
ed. 1825-26.

DUTENS, L
Itinéraire des routes les plus fréquentées; ou,
Journal de plusieurs voyages aux villes principales
de l'Europe, depuis 1768 jusqu'en 1783... 1783.

ELLIS, R H U
Alpine profile road book of Switzerland and the
adjacent portions of the Tyrol and the Italian
lake district. 1910.

Guida da Milano a Ginevra pel Sempione. 1822.

Guide du voyageur de Genève à Milan par le Simplon.
[ca 1822].

Itinéraire du voyage à Chamouny, autour du Mont-
Blanc, au Grand et au Petit St. Bernard, et
autour du Lac de Genève... [18--].

LAJARRIGA, Vimal de
Souvenirs de Sixt: itinéraire complet de la vallée
... 1856.

MEYER, J J
Les nouvelles routes par le pays des Grisons
jusqu'aux Lacs Majeur et de Como. 1827.

REICHARD, Heinrich August Ottakar
Passagier auf der Reise in Deutschland und der
Schweiz, nach Amsterdam, Brüssel ...: ein Reise-
handbuch für Jedermann. 12 Aufl. 1843.

REICHARD, Heinrich August Ottakar
[Passagier auf der Reise in Deutschland...].
Itinéraire de poche de l'Allemagne et de la Suisse.
1809.

SCHREIBER, A
Manuel du voyageur par la Suisse, le Wurtenberg,
la Bavière, le Tyrol, le pays de Salzbourg et au
Lac de Constance... [1835?].

SILESTUS, Eduard
Spaziergang durch die Alpen. 1844. 3v. in 1.

Le Simplon: promenade pittoresque de Genève à Milan.
[181-].

STUDER, Gottlieb
Topographische Mittheilungen aus dem Alpengebirge.
1. Die Eiswüsten und selten betretenen Hochalpen
und Bergspitzen des Kantons Bern und angrenzender
Gegenden. 1843.

- - 2.Ausg. 1844. 2v.

209 Guide-books

AUGUSTIN FAMILY
Streifzüge durch die norischen Alpen. 1840.

BALL, John
Hints and notes practical and scientific for
travellers in the Alps, being a revision of the
general introduction to the 'Alpine guide'. New
ed. 1899.

BALL, John
Introduction to 'The alpine guide'. New ed.
1873.

BLAB, Georg
Aus der Frühzeit der Bergsteigerei. 1926.

BRADSHAW, B
B. Bradshaw's dictionary of mineral waters,
climatic health resorts, sea baths, and hydropathic establishments... 1902.

CARUS, C G
Reise durch Deutschland, Italien und die Schweiz,
im Jahre 1828. 1835. 2v.

GRIEBEN, Theobald
Illustriertes Handbüch für Reisende in der
Schweiz, Ober-Italien, Turin und Genua... 1861.

GRIEBEN, Theobald
La Suisse et les lacs de la Haute-Italie: guide
illustré du voyageur... 7e éd., rev. et corr.
1859.

MORIGGL, Josef
Von Hütte zu Hütte: Führer zu den Schutzhütten
der deutschen und österreichischen Alpen...
1911-14. 6v.

OLIM JUVENIS
Vacation rambles on the continent, told so as to
be a complete guide to the most interesting
places in Switzerland, Belgium, and the Rhine.
5th ed. 1869.

STARKE, Mariana
Information and directions for travellers on the
continent. 7th ed., thoroughly rev. 1829.

WALLROTH, Ernst
Der Alpenstock: Wegweiser für Reisende in der
Schweiz, Savoyen und Piemont. 2.Aufl. [n.d.].

210 Alpine climbing - general

ADAMS, William H Davenport
Alpine adventure; or, Narratives of travel and
research in the Alps. 1878.

ADAMS, William H Davenport
Alpine climbing: narratives of recent ascents of
Mont Blanc, the Matterhorn, the Jungfrau, and
other lofty summits of the Alps. 1881.

AEBY, Christoph
Das Hochgebirge von Grindelwald: Naturbilder
aus der schweizerischen Alpenwelt. 1865.

ALPINE CLUB
Peaks, passes, and glaciers: a series of excur-
sions by members of the Alpine Club; edited by
John Ball. 1859.

2nd ed. 1859.
4th ed. 1859.
5th ed. 1860.

ALPINE CLUB
Peaks, passes, and glaciers, being excursions
by members of the Alpine Club. 2nd series; by
Edward Shirley Kennedy. 1862. 2v.

ALPINE CLUB
Peaks, passes and glaciers, by members of the
Alpine Club. 3rd series; edited by A.F. Field
and Sydney Spencer. 1932.

210 Alpine Europe - climbing - general (Cont.)

ALPINE CLUB
  [Peaks, passes and glaciers]. Narratives selected
  from Peaks, passes and glaciers; edited with
  introduction and notes by George Wherry. 1910.
  Selected from the 1st series.

ALPINE CLUB
  Peaks, passes & glaciers; selected and annotated
  by E.H. Blakeney. [1926].

ALPINE CLUB
  [Peaks, passes and glaciers]. Les grimpeurs des
  Alpes = Peaks, passes and glacies [sic]. 1862.

- - Another ed. 1886.

Archiv kleiner zerstreuter Reisebeschreibungen durch
  Merkwürdige Gegenden der Schweiz. 1796. 2v.

BALLIANO, Adolfo and AFFENTRANGER, Irene
  La strada è questa... 1957.

BORGOGNONI, A   and TITTA ROSA, G
  Scalatori: le più audaci imprese alpinistiche da
  Whymper al "sesto grado", raccontate dai protagonisti; a cura di A. Borgognoni, G. Titta Rosa.
  2a ed., riv. e aggiornata. 1941.

CLARK, Ronald William
  The Alps. 1973.

COOLIDGE, William Augustus Brevoort
  Alpine studies. 1912.

COOLIDGE, William Augustus Brevoort
  The Alps in nature and history. 1908.

CUNNINGHAM, Carus Dunlop and ABNEY, Sir William de
Wyveleslie
  The pioneers of the Alps. 1887.

- - 2nd ed. 1888.

DIDIER, Richard
  Ailes de mouches et tricounis: récits d'Armand
  Couttet. 1946.

DÜBI, Heinrich
  Gesammelte alpine Schriften. 1886-1904. 4v.

EGGER, Carl
  Pioniere der Alpen: 30 Lebensbilder der grossen
  Schweizer Bergführer von Melchior Anderegg bis
  Franz Lochmatter, 1827 bis 1933. 1946.

ENGEL, Claire Éliane
  A history of mountaineering in the Alps. 1950.

ENGEL, Claire Éliane
  [A history of mountaineering in the Alps].
  Histoire de l'alpinisme des origines à nos jours.
  1950.

ENZENSPERGER, Ernst
  Alpenfahrten der Jugend. 1911-12. 2v.

GOS, Charles
  Alpinisme anecdotique. 1934.

GOS, Charles
  L'épopée alpestre: histoire abrégé de la montagne
  et de l'alpinisme de l'antiquité à nos jours.
  [1944].

GOS, Charles
  Propos d'un alpiniste. 1922.

GOS, Charles
  Tragédies alpestres. 1940.

- - 2e éd. 1946.

GOS, Charles
  [Tragédies alpestres]. Alpine tragedy. 1948.

GRIBBLE, Francis
  The story of alpine climbing. 1904.

GRUBE, A   W
  Alpenwanderungen: Fahrten auf hohe und höchste
  Alpenspitzen. 1874. 2v. in 1.

- - 3.Aufl. 1886.

LE BLOND, Elizabeth
  True tales of mountain adventure for non-climbers
  young and old. 1903.

LEVASSEUR, E
  Les Alpes et les grandes ascensions. 1889.

LUKAN, Karl
  [Alpinismus in Bildern]. The Alps and alpinism.
  1968.

LUNN, Sir Arnold
  The Alps. 1914.

MATHEWS, Charles Edward
  The recollections of a mountaineer. 1892.

MAZZOTTI, Giuseppe
  La montagna presa in giro. 1931.

- - 2a ed., rifatta e raddoppiata. 1933.

MAZZOTTI, Giuseppe
  [La montagna presa in giro]. À chacun sa
  montagne. 1948.

MEADE, Charles Francis
  Approach to the hills. 1940.

MILNER, Cyril Douglas
  Rock for climbing. 1950.

MULLER, Edwin
  They climbed the Alps. 1930.

MUNDELL, Frank
  Stories of alpine adventure. [1898].

RICHTER, Eduard
  Die Erschliessung Ostalpen. 1893-94. 3v.

SARAGAT, Giovanni and REY, Guido
  Famiglia alpinistica: tipi e paesaggi. 1904.

SCHÄTZ, Josef Julius
  Berge und Bergsteiger. 1929.

SEIDLITZ, Wilfried von
  Entstehen und Vergehen der Alpen... 1926.

SNAITH, Stanley
  Alpine adventure. 1944 (1946 reprint).

SPIRO, Louis
  Guides de montagne. Nouv. éd. 1944.

SPIRO, Louis
  [Guides de montagne]. La guida alpina. [1931].

STEINER, Louis
  Mélanges alpestres. 1869 [-1901].

STUDER, Gottlieb
  Über Gletscher und Gipfel. 1931.

THORINGTON, James Monroe
  A survey of early American ascents in the Alps
  in the nineteenth century. 1943.

VERNET, J
  Au coeur des Alpes. 1951.

WILMSEN, F   P
  Merkwürdige Bergreisen, Seefahrten und Abentheuer
  unserer Zeit... [1823].

WUNDT. Theodor and WUNDT, Maud
  Engadin - Ortler - Dolomiten. [ca 1898].

- - 2.Aufl. [1900].

211 Alpine Europe - climbing, up to 1854

Courses alpestres en Suisse et en Savoie. [1852].

FORBES, James David
  Norway and its glaciers visited in 1851; followed
  by Journals of excursions in the high Alps of
  Dauphiné, Berne, and Savoy. 1853.

FORBES, James David
  [Norway and its glaciers...]. Norwegen und seine
  Gletscher; nebst Reisen in den Hochalpen der
  Dauphiné, von Bern und Savoyen. 1855.

MONTIS, Robert
  Kampf um den Berg: historische Bergfahrten. 1937.

SACCHI, Giuseppe
  Le ghiacciaje della Svizzera ed i vulcani. 1837.

THURWIESER, Peter Carl
  Ausgewählte Schriften. [1924].

212 Alpine climbing, 1854-1884, Golden Age

ALMER, Christian
  [Führerbuch]. A facsimile of Christian Almer's
  Führerbuch 1856-1894. 1896.

CAMMEL, Gustave Émile
  Les pérégrinations d'un alpiniste à travers les
  Alpes-Maritimes, les Basses-Alpes, le Dauphiné, la
  Savoie, la Suisse, l'Italie septentrionale et la
  Principauté de Monaco. 1883.

COOLIDGE, William Augustus Brevoort
  Alpine studies. 1912.

CORONA, Giuseppe
  Picchi e burroni: escursioni nelle Alpi. 1876.

DAUNT, Achilles
  Crag, glacier and avalanche: narratives of daring
  and disaster. 1889.

DENT, Clinton Thomas
  Above the snow line: mountaineering sketches
  between 1870 and 1880. 1885.

FELLENBERG, Edmund von
  Der Ruf der Berge: die Erschliessung der Berner
  Hochalpen. 1925.

FRESHFIELD, Douglas William
  Across country from Thonon to Trent: rambles and
  scrambles in Switzerland and the Tyrol. 1865.

GIRDLESTONE, Arthur Gilbert
  The high Alps without guides, being a narrative of
  adventures in Switzerland, together with chapters
  on the practicability of such mode of mountaineering, and suggestions for its accomplishment. 1870.

GÜSSFELDT, Paul
  In den Hochalpen: Ergebnisse aus den Jahren
  1859-1885. 2.Aufl. 1886.

HINCHLIFF, Thomas Woodbine
  Summer months among the Alps, with the ascent of
  Monte Rosa. 1857.

HORNBY, Emily
  Mountaineering records. 1907.

HUF, Hans
  English mountaineers: A. Wills, J. Tyndall, E.
  Whymper, C. Dent, A.F. Mummery. 1926.

JAVELLE, Émile
  Souvenirs d'un alpiniste.
  Various editions.

JAVELLE, Émile
  [Souvenirs d'un alpiniste]. Alpine memories.
  1899.

JONES, Harry
  The regular Swiss round in three trips. 1865.

- - 2nd ed. 1866.

LE BLOND, Elizabeth
  The high Alps in winter; or, Mountaineering in
  search of health. 1883.

LE BLOND, Elizabeth
  High life and towers of silence. 1886.

LE BLOND, Elizabeth
  My home in the Alps. 1892.

MATHEWS, Charles Edward
  Personal reminiscences of great climbs: [a
  lecture]. 1902.

MOORE, Adolphus Warburton
  The Alps in 1864: a private journal. 1867.

MUMMERY, Albert Frederick
  My climbs in the Alps and Caucasus. 1895.

- - 2nd ed. 1905.

MUMMERY, Albert Frederick
  [My climbs in the Alps and Caucasus]. Mes
  escalades dans les Alpes et le Caucase. 1903.

- - Another ed. 1936.

PIGEON, Anna and ABBOT, Ellen
  Peaks and passes: [particulars of six mountaineering tours ... between the years 1869 and
  1876]. 1885.

PLUNKET, Frederica
  Here and there among the Alps. 1875.

PUISEUX, Pierre
  Où le père a passé ... au berceau de l'alpinisme
  sans guide. 1928.

PURTSCHELLER, Ludwig
  Über Fels und Firn: Bergwanderungen. 1901.

ROTH, Abraham
  Doldenhorn und Weisse Frau, zum ersten Mal
  ersteigen und geschildert... 1863.

ROTH, Abraham
  [Doldenhorn und Weisse Frau...]. The Dolderhorn
  and Weisse Frau, ascended for the first time...
  1863.

SIMMEL, Eugen
  Spaziergänge in den Alpen. 1880.

STEPHEN, Sir Leslie
  The playground of Europe.
  Various editions.

STEPHEN, Sir Leslie
  [The playground of Europe]. Le terrain de jeu
  de l'Europe. 1935.

STEPHEN, Sir Leslie
  [The playground of Europe]. Der Spielplatz
  Europas. 1942.

THIOLY, François
  Ascension des Dents-d'Oche et du Midi. 1863.

THIOLY, François
  Excursion dans le Val d'Illiers par Samoëns, le
  col de Golèze et le col de Couz. 1858.

THIOLY, François
  Excursion en Savoie et en Suisse. 1858.

TUCKETT, Francis Fox
  Hochalpenstudien: gesammelte Schriften. 1873.
  2v.

TYNDALL, John
  The glaciers of the Alps: a narrative of excursions and ascents. [1905].

212 Alpine Europe - climbing, 1854-1884 ... (Cont.)

TYNDALL, John
  Haute montagne. 1946.

TYNDALL, John
  Hours of exercise in the Alps. 1871.

- - 2nd ed. 1871.
- - New ed. 1899 (1906 reprint).

TYNDALL, John
  Mountaineering in 1861: a vacation tour. 1862.
  Also published as: A vacation tour in Switzerland.

TYNDALL, John
  [Mountaineering in 1861]. Dans les montagnes.
  [1869].

- - Another ed. [ca 1880].

TYNDALL, John
  [Mountaineering in 1861]. In den Alpen. 1872.

TYNDALL, John
  A vacation tour in Switzerland. [ca 1862].
  Also published as: Mountaineering in 1861.

VICTOR-EMMANUEL II, King of Italy
  Victor-Emmanuel sur les Alpes. 1878.

- - 2e éd., rev. et augm. 1879.

VINCENT, Henri
  Les vingt-deux années du Père Tasse à Chambrousse.
  1891.

WEILENMANN, Johann Jacob
  Aus der Firnenwelt: gesammelte Schriften.
  1872 [-1877]. 3v.

WHYMPER, Edward
  A letter addressed to the members of the Alpine
  Club [on the controversy over a leap by Christian
  Almer]. 1900.

WHYMPER, Edward
  Scrambles amongst the Alps in the years 1860-69.
  Various editions.

WHYMPER, Edward
  [Scrambles amongst the Alps]. Escalades dans les
  Alpes de 1860 à 1869. 1873.

- - Nouv. éd. 1912.
- - [Nouv. éd., rev.]. 1944.

WHYMPER, Edward
  [Scrambles amongst the Alps]. Edward Whympers
  Berg- und Gletscherfahrten in den Alpen in den
  Jahren 1860 bis 1869. 3.Aufl. 1909.

- - 4.völlig unveränderte Aufl. 1922.
- - 5.völlig unveränderte Aufl. [1931].

WILLS, Sir Alfred
  "The Eagle's Nest" in the valley of Sixt; a summer
  home among the Alps; together with some excursions
  among the great glaciers. 1860.

- - 2nd ed. 1860.

WILLS, Sir Alfred
  ["The Eagle's Nest..."]. Le Nid d'Aigle et
  l'ascension du Wetterhorn: récits montagnards.
  1864.

WILLS, Sir Alfred
  Wanderings among the high Alps. 1856.

- - 2nd ed., rev. with additions. 1858.

WILSON, Henry Schütz
  Alpine ascents and adventures; or, Rock and snow
  sketches. 1878.

- - 2nd ed. 1878.

WOLTERSTORFF, Hermann
  Aus dem Hochgebirge: Erinnerungen eines Bergsteigers. 1902.

ZSIGMONDY, Emil
  Im Hochgebirge: Wanderungen. 1889.

213 Alpine climbing, 1885-

Im Bann der Berge: Bergsteiger-Erlebnisse. 1935.

Schweizer Bergführer erzählen. 1936.

- - 3.Aufl. 1936.
- - 4.Aufl. 1950.

UNSWORTH, Walter
  North face: the second conquest of the Alps.
  1969.

213.1 Alpine climbing, 1885-1919

ABRAHAM, George Dixon
  Mountain adventures at home and abroad. 1910.

ABRAHAM, George Dixon
  On Alpine heights and British crags. 1919.

AITKEN, Samuel
  Among the Alps: a narrative of personal
  experiences. 1900.

BACCELLI, Alfredo
  Vette e ghiacci: impressioni e ricordi. 1901.

BALAVOINE, Hippolyte
  Dans les Alpes et le Jura: souvenirs d'un
  alpiniste. 1911.

BAURON, Pierre
  Courses dans les Alpes. 2e éd. 1906.

BLODIG, Karl
  Die Viertausender der Alpen. 1923.

CAMUS, Théodore
  De la montagne au désert: récits d'ascensions et
  correspondance. [1912].

CAMUS, Théodore
  Oeuvres alpines. 1930.

CHRISTEN, Ernest
  Sur l'Alpe. [1916].

- - 2e éd. [1917].

CONWAY, William Martin, Baron Conway
  The Alps from end to end.
  Various editions.

CORIN, Joseph
  Escalades et escapades dans les Alpes, par un
  magistrat, un professeur et un vagabond. 1904.

DE AMICIS, Ugo
  Piccoli uomini e grandi montagne. 1924.

DE AMICIS, Ugo
  [Piccoli uomini e grandi montagne]. Petits
  hommes, grandes montagnes. 1927.

DURHAM, William Edward
  Summer holidays in the Alps, 1898-1914. 1916.

EGGER, Carl
  Höhenluft: Erlebtes und Erfühltes. 1930.

FONTAINE, E
  Alpinisme et volcanisme: l'éruption de Vésuve en
  1906. 1928.

GALLET, Julien
  Dans l'Alpe ignorée: explorations et souvenirs.
  1910.

213.1 Alpine Europe - climbing, 1885-1919 (Cont.)

GALLET, Julien
    Derniers souvenirs de l'Alpe: suite au volume
    "Dans l'Alpe ignorée". 1927.

GUGLIERMINA, Giuseppe F
    Vette: ricordi di esplorazioni e nuove ascensioni
    sulle Alpi, nei gruppi del Monte Rosa, del Cervino
    e del Monte Bianco dal 1896 al 1921. 1927.

HAMILTON, Helen
    Mountain madness. 1922.

HÜBEL, Paul
    Führerlose Gipfelfahrten. 1927.

KIRKPATRICK, William Trench
    Alpine days and nights. 1932.

KOLB, Fritz
    Pfade zur Hohe: Zehnjahrbuch der Alpinistengilde.
    [1931].

LAMMER, Eugen Guido
    Jungborn: Bergfahrten und Höhengedanken eines
    einsamen Pfadsuchers. 1922.

- - 2. stark verm. und veränderte Aufl. 1923.
- - 3.Aufl. 1929.

LAUSBERG, Carl
    Mit Stock und Pickel: Bergfahrten in den Alpen und
    Norwegen. 1910.

LEFEBURE, Charles
    Mes étapes d'alpinisme. 1904.

- - 2e éd. 1904.

MARSH, Herbert
    Two seasons in Switzerland. 1895.

MARTIN-FRANKLIN, J   and VACCARONE, Luigi
    Notice historique sur l'ancienne route de Charles-
    Emmanuel II et les Grottes des Échelles. 1887.

MEYER, Oskar Erich
    Tat und Traum: ein Buch alpinen Erlebens. 1920.

- - 2. verm. Aufl. 1922.
- - 3. Aufl. 1928.

NORMAN-NERUDA, Ludwig
    The climbs of Norman-Neruda. 1899.

NORMAN-NERUDA, Ludwig
    [The climbs of Norman-Neruda]. Bergfahrten von
    Norman-Neruda. [1901].

PIUS XI, Pope
    Scritti alpinistici... 1923.

PIUS XI, Pope
    [Scritti alpinistici]. Climbs on alpine peaks.
    1923.

PIUS XI, Pope
    [Scritti alpinistici]. Ascensions... 1922.

PIUS XI, Pope
    [Scritti alpinistici]. Alpine Schriften. 1925.

REY, Guido
    Alpinismo acrobatico. 1914.

- - Nuova ed. 1932.

REY, Guido
    [Alpinismo acrobatico]. Peaks and precipices:
    scrambles in the Dolomites and Savoy. 1914.

REY, Guido
    [Alpinismo acrobatico]. Alpinisme acrobatique.
    1919.

- - 2e éd. 1929.

REY, Guido
    [Alpinismo acrobatico]. Bergakrobaten. Kletter-
    fahrten an Montblanc-Nadeln und Dolomiten-Türmen.
    [19--].

REY, Guido
    Récits et impressions d'alpinisme. 1913.

- - Another ed. 1920.

SARAGAT, Giovanni and REY, Guido
    Alpinismo a quattro mani. 1898.

SCHÄTZ, Josef Julius
    Wanderfahrten in den Bergen. [1925?].

SCHUSTER, Claud, Baron Schuster
    Peaks and pleasant pastures. 1911.

STOCK, E   Elliot
    Scrambles in storm and sunshine among the Swiss
    and English alps. [1910].

TÄUBER, Carl
    Auf fremden Bergpfaden. [1916].

TUTTON, Alfred Edwin Howard
    The high Alps: a natural history of ice and snow.
    1931.

VISSER, Philips Christiaan
    Boven en beneden de sneeuwgrens. 1910.

WHERRY, George
    Alpine notes & the climbing foot. 1896.

YOUNG, Geoffrey Winthrop
    On high hills: memories of the Alps. 1927.

- - 5th ed. 1947.

YOUNG, Geoffrey Winthrop
    [On high hills]. Mes aventures alpines. [1939].

YOUNG, Geoffrey Winthrop
    [On high hills]. Nouvelles escalades dans les
    Alpes, 1910-1914... [1939].

213.2 Alpine climbing, 1919-1945

ALBERTAS, Sylvia d'
    Des Calanques aux faces nord. 1948.

BELL, James Horst Brunnerman
    A progress in mountaineering: Scottish hills to
    alpine peaks. 1950.

BLANCHET, Émile Robert
    Au bout d'un fil: douze ascensions nouvelles dans
    les Alpes suisses et françaises. 1937.

BLANCHET, Émile Robert
    [Au bout d'un fil...]. Als Letzter am Seil: zwölf
    Erstbesteigungen in den Schweizer und in den
    französischen Alpen... [1938].

BLANCHET, Émile Robert
    Hors des chemins battus: ascensions nouvelles dans
    les Alpes. 1932.

- - Nouv. éd. 1946.

BLANCHET, Émile Robert
    [Hors des chemins battus...]. Jenseits begangener
    Pfade: neue Bergfahrten in den Alpen. [1939?].

BLANCHET, Émile Robert
    [Hors des chemins battus...]. Fuori delle strade
    battute. 1935.

CHATELLUS, Alain de
    De l'Eiger à l'Iharen. 1947.

DALLOZ, Pierre
    Haute montagne. 1931.

213.2 Alpine Europe - climbing, 1919-1945 (Cont.)

DIDIER, Richard
    Ailes de mouches et tricounis: récits d'Armand
    Couttet. 1946.

DIETERLEN, Jacques
    Le chemineau de la montagne. 1938.

DITTERT, René
    Passion des hautes cimes. 1945.

FASANA, Eugenio
    Uomini di sacco e di corda: pagine di alpinismo.
    1926.

FERRARI, Agostino
    Nella gloria delle altezze: impressioni e ricordi
    di ascensioni nei dintorni di Ceresole, Valsava-
    ranche e Cogne. 1931.

GERVASUTTI, Giusto
    [Scalate nelle Alpi]. Gervasutti's climbs. 1957.

GERVASUTTI, Giusto
    [Scalate nelle Alpi]. Montagnes, ma vie... 1949.

GUILERA I ALBINYANA, Josep María
    Excursions pels Pireneus i els Alps. 1927.

HECKMAIR, Anderl
    Les trois derniers problèmes des Alpes... 1951.

HERZEN, Sergio
    Entre rocas y nieves. 1945.

JACKSON, Eileen Montague
    Switzerland calling: a true tale of a boy and
    girl's wonderful summer holidays climbing in the
    Alps... 1927.

LAMBERT, Raymond
    À l'assaut des "quatre mille": dix récits de
    haute montagne. 1946.

- - 2e éd. 1953.

MEYER, Oskar Erich
    Das Erlebnis des Hochgebirges. 1932.

MORIN, Micheline
    Encordées. 1936.

NOLL-HASENCLEVER, Eleonore
    Den Bergen verfallen: Alpenfahrten. 1932.

PLIETZ, Samuel
    Vom Montblanc zum Wilden Kaiser. 1936.

ROBINSON, Anthony Melland
    Alpine roundabout. 1947.

ROCH, André
    Belles ascensions alpines: ascensions classiques.
    [1951].

ROCH, André
    Les conquêtes de ma jeunesse. 1942.

ROCH, André
    [Les conquêtes de ma jeunesse]. Climbs of my
    youth. 1949.

ROCH, André
    Images d'escalades. 1946.

ROCH, André
    In Fels und Eis: ein Photo-Tourenbuch. 1946.

ROCH, André
    [In Fels und Eis...]. On rock and ice: mountain-
    eering in photographs. 1947.

ROCH, André
    Mon carnet de courses. 1948.

SCHWARTZ, Myrtil
    Drei Giganten des Hochgebirges: meine Erinnerungen
    an deren Besteigung. 1921.

SCHWARTZ, Myrtil
    Vers l'idéal par la montagne: souvenir de mes
    escalades de haute montagne en Europe et en
    Amérique. 1924.

SMITH, Janet Adam
    Mountain holidays. 1946.

SMYTHE, Frank S
    An alpine journey. 1934.

SMYTHE, Frank S
    Climbs and ski runs: mountaineering and ski-ing
    in the Alps, Great Britain and Corsica. 1929.

- - Another ed. 1957.

SMYTHE, Frank S
    Mountaineering holiday. 1940.

SMYTHE, Frank S
    My alpine album. 2nd ed. 1947.

THOMPSON, Dorothy E
    Climbing with Joseph Georges. 1962.

TSCHARNER, Hans Fritz von
    Auf wolkigen Höhen. [1936].

TSCHARNER, Hans Fritz von
    Gipfel und Grate. 1943.

TSCHARNER, Hans Fritz von
    [Gipfel und Grate]. Cimes et arêtes. 1944.

TYNDALE, Henry Edmund Guise
    Mountain paths. 1948.

VERMOREL, Lucien
    À travers les Alpes: premier essais (1919-1921),
    notes d'ascensions et correspondances. 1927.

WASHBURN, Bradford
    Among the Alps with Bradford. 1927.

WEISS, Jurg
    Murailles et abîmes... 1946.

WELZENBACH, Willo
    [Bergfahrten]. Willo Welzenbachs Bergfahrten.
    1935.

WELZENBACH, Willo
    [Bergfahrten]. Les ascensions de Willo Welzenbach:
    Alpes orientales, Alpes valaisannes, Mont Blanc,
    Oberland bernois, Himalaya. 1939.

WYSS DUNANT, Édouard
    L'appel des sommets. 1931-33. 2v.

213.3. Alpine climbing, 1945-

ALLAIN, Pierre
    Alpinisme et compétition. 1949.

JOKINEN, Matti A
    Alppien seinämillä. 1961.

KUCHAŘ, Radovan
    Deset velkých stěn. 1963.

LABANDE, François
    100 sommets. 1975.

MONZINO, Guido
    Grandes Murailles: cronaca di una spedizione
    alpina. 1957.

PARAGOT, Robert and BÉRARDINI, Lucien
    Vingt ans de cordée. 1974.

PAUSE, Walter and WINKLER, Jürgen
    100 scalate estreme (V e VI grado). 1975.

RÉBUFFAT, Gaston
    Entre terre et ciel. 1962.

213.3 Alpine Europe - climbing, 1945- (Cont.)

RÉBUFFAT, Gaston
[Entre terre et ciel]. Between heaven and earth.
1965.

RÉBUFFAT, Gaston
Étoiles et tempêtes (six faces nord). 1954.

RÉBUFFAT, Gaston
[Étoiles et tempêtes]. Starlight and storm: the
ascent of six great north faces of the Alps. 1956.

215.1 Mont Blanc - general

BERNARDI, Alfonso
Il Monte Bianco: dalle esplorazioni alla conquista
(1091-1786); antologia. 1965.

CORONA, Giuseppe
Mont Blanc or Simplon? 1880.

ENGEL, Claire Éliane
Mont Blanc: an anthology. 1965.

GAROLA, Ruggiero
Il Monte Bianco ed il Sempione: studii di
confronto. 1881.

ISSARTIER, Paul
Notice sur un projet d'ascenseur pour le Mont-
Blanc. 1896.

MAZÉ, Jules
La grande montagne. 1921.

PAYOT, Paul
Au royaume du Mont-Blanc. 1950.

215.11 Mont Blanc - geology, natural history

BARETTI, Martino
Aperçu géologique sur la chaîne du Mont Blanc en
rapport avec le trajet probable d'un tunnel pour
une nouvelle ligne de chemin de fer. 1881.

DELCROS, François Joseph
Notice sur les altitudes du Mont-Blanc et du Mont-
Rose, determinées par des mesures barométriques
et géodesiques. 1851.

DUPARC, Louis and MRAZEC, Ludovic
Recherches géologiques et pétrographiques sur le
massif du Mont-Blanc. 1898.

DUPARC, Louis and MRAZEC, Ludovic
La structure du Mont-Blanc. 1893.

FAVRE, Alphonse
Explication de la carte géologique des parties de
la Savoie, du Piémont et de la Suisse voisines du
Mont Blanc. 1862.

FAVRE, Alphonse
Recherches géologiques dans les parties de la
Savoie, du Piémont et de la Suisse voisines du
Mont-Blanc. 1867. 3v.

FAVRE, Alphonse
Sur la structure en éventail du Mont-Blanc. 1865.

FORBES, James David
On the geological relations of the secondary and
primary rocks of the chain of Mont Blanc. 1856.

GAULLIEUR, J
Genève et le pays de Vaud après la mort de
Voltaire et de Rousseau: commencements de l'école
littéraire des physiciens et des naturalistes, et
de la littérature alpestre...
(In Sur l'histoire littéraire de la Suisse
française. [1856?])

MARTINS, Charles
De l'ancienne extension des glaciers de Chamonix
depuis le Mont-Blanc jusqu'au Jura. [1847].

MARTINS, Charles
Du retrait et de l'ablation des glaciers de la
vallée de Chamonix, constatés dans l'automne de
1865. 1866.

PAREJAS, Édouard
Géologie de la zone de Chamonix comprise entre le
Mont-Blanc et les Aiguilles Rouges. 1922.

PAYOT, Venance
Catalogue des fougères, prèles et lycopodiacées
des environs du Mont-Blanc... 1860.

PFAFF, Friedrich
Mt. Blanc-Studien: ein Beitrag zur mechanischen
Geologie der Alpen. 1876.

RENDU, Louis
[Théorie des glaciers de la Savoie]. Theory of
the glaciers of Savoy. 1874.

VALLOT, Henri
Réseau trigonométrique du massif du Mont-Blanc,
établi et calculé par Henri Vallot; d'après les
stationnements de Joseph Vallot pour les sommets
de la haute chaîne et de Henri Vallot pour tout le
reste du massif. 1924.

VIOLLET-LE-DUC, Eugène
Le massif du Mont Blanc: étude sur sa constitution
géodésique et géologique sur ses transformations
et sur l'état ancien et moderne de ses glaciers.
1876.

VIOLLET-LE-DUC, Eugène
[Le massif du Mont Blanc...]. Mont Blanc: a
treatise on its geodesical and geological constitution; its transformations; and the ancient and
recent state of its glaciers. 1877.

215.12 Mont Blanc - geography, description, travel

APPLES, H   d'
Croquis chamoniards et le tour du Mont-Blanc.
[19--].

Au pays du Mont-Blanc. [1910].

BAUD-BOVY, Daniel
Le Mont-Blanc de près et de loin. [1903].

BERTHOUD VAN BERCHEM, Jacob Pierre
Itinéraire de la vallée de Chamonix, d'une partie
du Bas-Vallais et des montagnes avoisinantes.
1790.

- - [New ed.]. 1805.
- - [New ed.]. 1816.

BIOLEY, B
Le pont mystérieux du gouffre de la Tête-Noire =
The mysterious bridge on the abyss to be seen from
the Tete-Noire... 1893.

BOSSOLI, Carlo
Souvenirs de la Suisse: le Mont-Blanc et ses
environs. [ca 1860].

BRAVAIS, Auguste
Le Mont Blanc; ou, Description de la vue et des
phénomènes que l'on peut apercevoir du sommet du
Mont Blanc. [1854].

BRÉGEAULT, Henry
La chaîne du Mont Blanc. 1928.

BURFORD, Robert
Description of a view of Mont Blanc, the valley of
Chamonix, and the surrounding mountains, now ex-
hibiting at the Panorama, Leicester Square. 1837.

COPPIER, André Charles
Les portraits du Mont-Blanc. 1924.

DAULLIA, Émile
Le tour du Mont-Blanc. 1899.

215.12   Mont Blanc-geography, description... (Cont.)

DREVET, Louise
  La vallée de Chamonix et le Mont Blanc; suivi de
  Les ascensions au Mont Blanc, racontées par un de
  ses grimpeurs. [1908].

FERRAND, Henri
  Autour du Mont Blanc... 1920.

La fin d'une conquête. 1953.

FLEMWELL, George
  Chamonix. 1913.

FORBES, James David
  Notice respecting Mr. Reilly's topographical
  survey of the chain of Mont Blanc. 1865.

FORBES, James David
  Topography of the chain of Mont Blanc. [1865].

FRISON-ROCHE, Roger and TAIRRAZ, Pierre
  Mont Blanc aux sept vallées. 1959.

FRISON-ROCHE, Roger and TAIRRAZ, Pierre
  [Mont Blanc aux sept vallées]. Mont Blanc and the
  seven valleys. 1961.

GLOVER, Samuel
  A description of the valley of Chamouni in Savoy.
  1819.

- - [2nd ed.]. [1821].

GRILLET, Jean Louis
  Dictionnaire historique, littéraire et sta-
  tistique des départemens du Mont-Blanc et du
  Léman... 1807. 3v.

KUMMER, K   W
  Tableau géographico-topographique pour servir
  d'explication au relief du Montblanc dans les
  Alpes suisses, de la vallée de Chamounix, du
  passage du Grand St. Bernhard. [18--].

MANGET, J   L
  Chamonix, le Mont-Blanc et les deux Saint-Bernard:
  nouvel itinéraire descriptif des Alpes centrales
  et de leurs vallées... 1844.

- - 4e éd., rev. et augm. 1851.

MANGET, J   L
  La vallée de Sixt en 1843. 1843.

MONTAYEUR, Charles
  Voyage sentimental autour du Mont Blanc. Ptie.1.
  1900.

PARLATORE, Filippo
  Viaggio alla catena del Monte Bianco e al Gran San
  Bernardo. 1850.

PERRET, Robert
  Les panoramas du Mont Blanc. 1929.

PICTET, J   P
  Nouvel itinéraire des vallées autour du Mont-Blanc.
  1808.

- - [Nouv. éd.]. 1840.
- - Another ed. 1845.

RITTER, C
  Geographisch-historisch-topographische Beschreibung
  zu K.W. Kummer's Stereorama; oder, Relief des
  Montblanc-Gebirges und dessen nachster Umgebung.
  1824.

ROCOFFORT, L
  Sur les trois versants du Mont-Blanc: Suisse,
  France, Italie. 1925.

ROSIÈRE, J
  Chamonix: station d'altitude. 1898.

SAUSSURE, Horace Bénédict de
  Grotte de Balme, située entre Cluse et Maglan sur
  la route de Chamonix... 1827.

SÉGOGNE, Henry de
  Le massif du Mont-Blanc: vallées et sommets.
  1947.

Souvenir de Chamonix. [ca 1890].

Souvenir du Mont-Blanc et de Chamonix. [ca 1840].

Souvenir du Mont-Blanc et de Chamonix. [ca 1860].

Souvenirs du Mont Blanc. [ca 1860].

Souvenirs du Mont-Blanc et de la vallée de Chamonix.
  [ca 1840].

Souvenirs photographiques de la Suisse: Chamonix.
  [ca 1900].

Souvenirs pittoresques des glaciers de Chamouny.
  [ca 1825].

TISSOT, Roger
  Mont Blanc. 1924.

TROYE, J
  A short account of Mont Blanc and the valley of
  Chamouni; with an historical sketch of the city of
  Geneva; serving to illustrate the models of these
  two places. 1817.

VALLOT, Charles and VALLOT, Joseph
  Le massif du Mont-Blanc: paysages charactéristiques
  et documentaires. [1914]-23. 2v.

VALLOT, Henri and VALLOT, Joseph
  Description générale du massif du Mont-Blanc:
  répertoire des altitudes principales du massif du
  Mont-Blanc. 1924.

VERNEILH PUIRASEAU, Joseph, baron de
  Statistique générale de la France, publiée par
  ordre de sa majesté l'empereur et roi... 1807.

VINCENT, A
  Six mois dans les neiges, Tarentaise et Maurienne:
  journal d'un officier. 1905.

Voyage pittoresque aux glaciers de Chamouni; [illus-
  trations par G. Lory, père et fils]. 1815.

WHALLEY, Thomas Sedgwick
  Mont Blanc: an irregular lyric poem. 1788.

215.13 Mont Blanc - climbing history

ARVE, Stéphen d'
  Les fastes du Mont-Blanc: ascensions célèbres et
  catastrophes depuis M. de Saussure jusqu'à nos
  jours. 1876.

DESROCHES,
  Les ascensions au Mont-Blanc, racontées par un de
  ses grimpeurs. [1908].

DONCOURT, A   S   de
  Le Mont Blanc et ses explorations précédé d'une
  notice historique sur H.B. de Saussure. 1887.

DURIER, Charles
  Histoire du Mont-Blanc. 1873.

DURIER, Charles
  Le Mont-Blanc.
  Various editions.

ENGEL, Claire Éliane
  Le Mont-Blanc. 1961.

ENGEL, Claire Éliane
  Le Mont-Blanc: route classique et voies nouvelles.
  [1939].

- - Éd., rev. et augm. [1946].

215.13 Mont Blanc - climbing history (Cont.)

FALCONNET, Jean
  Une ascension au Mont-Blanc et études scientifiques
  sur cette montagne. 1887.

FONTAINE, E
  L'Aiguille du Dru et sa niche. 1913.

FONTAINE, E
  La fin d'une pierre: Groupe Triolet-Isabella,
  chaîne du Mont Blanc. 1926.

FONTAINE, E
  Notes sur l'alpinisme:massif du Mont-Blanc. 1930.

- - Suite à la publication de 1930. 1932.

GAILLARD, Émile
  L'Aiguille de Bionnassay. 1929.

GUGLIERMINA, Giuseppe F
  Il Monte Bianco esplorato, 1760-1948: notizie
  storico-alpinistiche e relazioni originali dei
  primi salitori. 1973.

GUIDETTI, Étienne
  L'homme et le Mont Blanc. 1957.

MATHEWS, Charles Edward
  The annals of Mont Blanc: a monograph. 1898.

MILNER, Cyril Douglas
  Mont Blanc and the Aiguilles. 1955.

MONTAGNIER, Henry Fairbanks
  A bibliography of the ascents of Mont Blanc from
  1786-1853. 1911.

MUSÉE DE CHAMONIX
  Catalogue descriptif illustré. 1927.

NISSON, Claude
  La conquète du Mont-Blanc. 1930.

PAILLON, Mary
  L'Aiguille du Dru. 1902.

SEYLAZ, Louis
  Ascensions dans le massif du Trient. 1941.

215.14 Mont Blanc - visits, climbs, 18th century

BERTHOUD VAN BERCHEM, Jacob Pierre
  Excursion dans les mines du Haut Faucigny, et
  Description de deux nouvelles routes pour aller
  sur le Buet & le Breven, avec une notice sur le
  Jardin. 1787.

BORDIER, André César
  Voyage pitoresque aux glacieres de Savoye, fait en
  1772. 1773.

BOURRIT, Marc Théodore
  Description des aspects du Mont-Blanc, du côté de
  la Val-d'Aost, des glacieres qui en descendent, de
  l'Allée-Blanche... 1776.

BOURRIT, Marc Théodore
  Description des glacieres, glaciers &c amas de
  glace du Duché de Savoye. 1773.

BOURRIT, Marc Théodore
  [Description des glacieres...]. A relation of a
  journey to the glaciers, in the Dutchy of Savoy.
  1775.

- - 2nd ed. 1776.
- - 3rd ed. 1776.

BOURRIT, Marc Théodore
  Itinéraire de Genève, Lausanne et Chamouni. 1791.

- - Nouv. éd., rev. corr. et augm. 1792.
- - 3e éd. 1808.

BROOKE, N
  Voyage à Naples et en Toscane, avant et pendant
  l'invasion des Français en Italie... [1799].

BROWN, Thomas Graham and DE BEER, Sir Gavin
  The first ascent of Mont Blanc. 1957.

BROWN, Thomas Graham and DE BEER, Sir Gavin
  [The first ascent of Mont Blanc]. La prima ascensione del Monte Bianco. 1960.

DE BEER, Sir Gavin and HEY, Max H
  The first ascent of Mont Blanc. 1955.

DÜBI, Heinrich
  Paccard wider Balmat oder die Entwicklung einer
  Legende: ein Beitrag zur Besteigungsgeschichte
  des Mont Blanc. 1913.

EGGER, Carl
  Michel-Gabriel Paccard und der Montblanc. 1943.

JACOBI, J G
  Taschenbuch von J.G. Jacobi und seinen Freunden
  für 1795. [1794].

MONTAGNIER, Henry Fairbanks
  Note sur la relation de Paccard perdue. 1921.

MONTAGNIER, Henry Fairbanks
  Thomas Blaikie and Michel-Gabriel Paccard. 1933.

OXLEY, T Louis
  Jacques Balmat; or, The first ascent of Mont
  Blanc: a true story. 1881.

PACCARD, Michel Gabriel
  Dr. Paccard's 'Lost narrative': an attempted reconstruction, by E.H. Stevens. 1930.

Promenade au Mont-Blanc et autour du Lac de Genève.
  [ca 1790].

ROCHAT-CENISE, Charles
  Jacques Balmat du Mont-Blanc. 1929.

SAUSSURE, Horace Bénédict de
  Journal d'un voyage à Chamouni & à la cime du
  Mont-Blanc, en juillet et aoust 1787. 1926.

SAUSSURE, Horace Bénédict de
  Relation abregée d'un voyage à la cime du Mont-
  Blanc en août 1787. [1787].

SAUSSURE, Horace Bénédict de
  Relation abrégée d'un voyage à la cime du Mont-
  Blanc en août 1787 = Kurzer Berict von einer
  Reise auf den Gipfel des Montblanc, im August
  1787. 1928.

SAUSSURE, Horace Bénédict de
  [Relation abrégée...]. An appendix to the sketch
  of a tour through Swissserland, containing a short
  account of an expedition to the summit of Mont
  Blanc... 1788.

SAUSSURE, Horace Bénédict de
  Voyages dans les Alpes: partie pittoresque des
  ouvrages de M. H.-B. de Saussure. 6e éd.,
  augmentée des voyages en Valais, au Mont Cervin
  et autour du Mont Rose. [1898].

SAUSSURE, Horace Bénédict de
  [Voyages dans les Alpes]. L'ascension du Mont-
  Blanc. [1895].

SAUSSURE, Horace Bénédict de
  [Voyages dans les Alpes]. Saussure aux Alpes.
  1. Portrait, par H.-B. de Saussure, par Charles
  Vallot [et] Autour du Mont-Blanc, extrait des
  "Voyages dans les Alpes", de H.-B. de Saussure.
  1938.

SAUSSURE, Horace Bénédict de
  [Voyages dans les Alpes]. La cime du Mont-Blanc.
  1933.

215.14 Mont Blanc - visits, ... 18th century (Cont.)

SAUSSURE, Horace Bénédict de
 [Voyages dans les Alpes]. Le Mont-Blanc et le Col
 du Géant. 1927.

SAUSSURE, Horace Bénédict de
 [Voyages dans les Alpes]. Le Montblanc et sa
 première ascension aus Voyages dans les Alpes.
 1895.

SAUSSURE, Horace Bénédict de
 [Voyages dans les Alpes]. La première ascension
 du Mont Blanc. [1908].

SAUSSURE, Horace Bénédict de
 [Voyages dans les Alpes]. Viaggio al Monte
 Bianco... 1955.

STEVENS, Ernest H
 Dr. Paccard's diary. 1934.

STEVENS, Ernest H
 In the footsteps of Dr. Paccard. 1935-37. 2 pts.

WINDHAM, William and MARTEL, Pierre
 Relations de leurs deux voyages aux glaciers de
 Chamonix (1741-1742). 1879.

WINDHAM, William and MARTEL, Pierre
 [Relations de leurs deux voyages...]. An account
 of the glacieres or ice alps in Savoy, in two
 letters... 1744.

- - Another ed. 1747.

215.15 Mont Blanc - visits, climbs, 1801-1853

ATKINS, Henry Martin
 Ascent to the summit of Mont Blanc, on the 22nd
 and 23rd of August, 1837. 1838.

ATKINS, Henry Martin
 [Ascent to the summit of Mont Blanc...]. Ascension au sommet du Mont-Blanc le 22 et le 23 août
 1837. 1838.

AULDJO, John
 Narrative of an ascent to the summit of Mont Blanc,
 on the 8th and 9th August, 1827. 1828.

- - 2nd ed. 1830.
- - 3rd ed. 1856.
- - 4th ed. 1867.

BARRY, Martin
 Ascent to the summit of Mont Blanc, 16th-18th of
 9th Month (Septr), 1834. [1835].

- - Another ed. 1836.

BROWNE, J D H
 Ten scenes in the last ascent of Mont Blanc,
 including five views from the summit. 1853.

BULWER, James Redford
 Extracts from my journal, 1852. 1853.

CARELLI DE ROCCA CASTELLO, Jacques
 Une ascension au Mont-Blanc en 1843. 1843.

CHATELAIN, Clara de
 Handbook of the miniature Mont Blanc. 2nd ed.
 1855.

CHEEVER, George B
 Wanderings of a pilgrim in the shadow of Mont
 Blanc. 1848.

- - New ed. [1848?].
- - New ed. [1859?].

CLARK, Edmund and SHERWILL, Markham
 Narrative of an excursion to the summit of Mont
 Blanc, August 26th, 1825. 1826.

CLISSOLD, Frederick
 Narrative of an ascent to the summit of Mont
 Blanc, August 18th, 1822. 1823.

DORNFORD, Joseph
 Mont Blanc: [account of a late attempt to reach
 the summit of Mont Blanc]. [1821].

DUNANT, David
 Le touriste à Chamounix en 1853. 1853.

FELLOWS, Sir Charles
 A narrative of an ascent to the summit of Mont
 Blanc. 1827.

FELLOWS, Sir Charles
 A narrative of the late ascent to the summit of
 Mont Blanc by Mr. C. Fellows and Mr. W. Hawes
 contained in a letter from one of the parties...
 1827.

FORBES, James David
 [Travels through the Alps of Savoy...]. The tour
 of Mont Blanc and of Monte Rosa, being a personal
 narrative, abridged from the author's "Travels in
 the Alps of Savoy". 1855.

GAILLARD, Émile
 Une ascension romantique en 1838: Henriette
 d'Angeville au Mont-Blanc. 1947.

GARDNER, John Dunn
 Ascent and tour of Mont Blanc and passage of the
 Col du Géant between Sept 2nd and 7th 1850. 1851.

HAMEL, J
 Relation de deux tentatives récentes pour monter
 sur le Mont-Blanc... 1820.

HAMEL, J
 [Relation de deux tentatives...]. Reisen auf den
 Montblanc im August 1820. 1820.

HAWES, Sir Benjamin
 A narrative of an ascent to the summit of Mont
 Blanc, made during the summer of 1827. 1828.

Itinéraire de Genève à Chamouny et aux environs du
 Mont-Blanc. 1825.

JACKSON, H H
 A narrative of an ascent to the summit of Mont
 Blanc... Sept. 4, 1823. [1827].

LESCHEVIN, P X
 Voyage à Genève et dans la vallée de Chamouni, en
 Savoie. 1812.

LUSI, comte de
 Voyage sur le Mont-Blanc entrepris le 15 septembre
 1816. 1816.

MARTINS, Charles
 Ascension au Mont Blanc, par MM. Martins, Bravais
 et Lepileur. [1844].

MARTINS, Charles
 Deux ascensions scientifiques au Mont-Blanc:
 leurs résultats immédiats pour la météorologie,
 la physique du globe et les sciences naturelles.
 1865.

MATTHEY, André
 Ascension du Mont-Blanc. 1834.

MEYER, Oskar Erich
 Die Braut des Montblanc. [1933].

MOULINIÉ, C E F
 Promenades philosophiques et religieuses aux
 environs du Mont-Blanc... 1817.

- - Nouv. éd. 1820.

PAILLON, Mary
 L'album de Mlle d'Angeville. 1909.

215.15 <u>Mont Blanc - visits, ... 1801-1853</u> (<u>Cont</u>.)

The peasants of Chamouni, containing an attempt to reach the summit of Mont Blanc; and a delineation of the scenery among the Alps. 1823.

- - 2nd ed. 1826.

PHILIPS, Francis
A reading party in Switzerland, with an account of the ascent of Mont Blanc on the 12th and 13th of August 1851. 1851.

RAOUL-ROCHETTE, Désiré
Voyage pittoresque dans la vallée de Chamouni et autour du Mont-Blanc. 1826.

SAMIVEL
M. Dumollet sur le Mont-Blanc: les aventures surprenantes de M. Dumollet (de Saint-Malo) durant son voyage de 1837 aux glacières de Savoie et d'Helvétie. 1946.

SHERWILL, Markham
Ascent of Captain Markham Sherwill (accompanied by Dr. E. Clark) to the summit of Mont Blanc, 25th, 26th and 27th of August, 1825. 1826.

SHERWILL, Markham
[Ascent of Captain Markham Sherwill...]. Ascension du docteur Edmund Clark et du capitaine Markham Sherwill à la première sommité du Mont Blanc, les 25, 26, et 27 août 1825. 1827.

SHERWILL, Markham
A visit to the summit of Mont Blanc, by Captain Markham Sherwill [and Dr. Edmund Clark], 25th, 26th, and 27th of August, 1825. [1826].

SMITH, Albert
A hand-book of Mr. Albert Smith's ascent of Mont Blanc. 1852.

- - 4th ed. 1853.
- - 5th ed. 1853.
- - 6th ed. 1853.

SMITH, Albert
Mont Blanc. 1852.

SMITH, Albert
[Mont Blanc]. Albert Smith's ascent of Mont Blanc. (<u>In</u> Travel, adventure and sport from 'Blackwood's Magazine', v.4.)

SMITH, Albert
Le Mont Blanc. 1854.

SMITH, Albert
Mr. Albert Smith's Mont Blanc to China is now open... [1858].

SMITH, Albert
Programme of Mr. Albert Smith's ascent of Mont Blanc (August 12th & 13th, 1851) as represented every evening at the Egyptian Hall. 1851.

SMITH, Albert
The story of Mont Blanc. 1853.

- - 2nd ed., enl. 1854.

SMITH, Albert
[The story of Mont Blanc]. Mont Blanc; with a memoir of the author by Edmund Yates. [1860].

- - Another ed. [1871?].

SMITH, Albert
The story of Mont Blanc, and a diary, To China and back. 1860.

SMITH, Albert
[The story of Mont Blanc]. A boy's ascent of Mont Blanc; with a memoir of the author by Edmund Yates. [ca 1871].

THORINGTON, James Monroe
John Auldjo, fortunate traveller: [John Auldjo, 1805-86]. 1953.

THORINGTON, James Monroe
Mont Blanc sideshow: the life and times of Albert Smith. 1934.

TILLY, Henri, <u>comte de</u>
Ascensions aux cimes de l'Etna et du Mont Blanc. 1835.

TÖPFFER, Rodolphe
Nouveaux voyages en zigzag, à la Grande Chartreuse, autour du Mont Blanc, dans les vallées d'Herenz... 1854.

- - 2e éd. 1858.
- - 3e éd. 1864.
- - 4e éd. 1877.

A tour to Great St. Bernard's and round Mont Blanc... 1827 [cover 1828].

TRENCH, Francis
A walk round Mont Blanc, etc. 1847.

WESTON, Stephen
La scava; or, Some account of an excavation of a Roman town on the hill of Chatelet, in Champagne ... to which is added, A journey to the Simplon, by Lausanne, and to Mont Blanc, through Geneva. 1818.

WILBRAHAM, Edward Bootle
Narrative of an ascent of Mont-Blanc in August 1830.
(<u>In</u> The Keepsake for 1832)

215.16 <u>Mont Blanc - visits, climbs, 1854-1884</u>

ANDERSON, Eustace
Chamouni and Mont Blanc: a visit to the valley and an ascent of the mountain in the autumn of 1855. 1856.

ARVE, Stéphen d'
Le Mont-Blanc: deuxième ascension scientifique de ... W. Pitschner, du 30 août au 16 septembre 1861: relation sommaire... 1861.

ARVE, Stéphen d'
Première ascension photographique au sommet du Mont-Blanc par MM. Bisson frères... 1861.

BARROW, John, <u>1808-1898</u>
Expeditions on the glaciers: including an ascent of Mont Blanc, Monte Rosa, Col du Géant, and Mont Buét. 1864.

BAURON, Pierre
Autour du Mont-Blanc: étapes de la caravane minimoise, aout 1882. 1883.

BRIQUET, Moïse and MAQUELIN, L
Ascensions du Mont-Rose et du Mont-Blanc en juillet 1863. 1864.

COLEMAN, Edmund Thomas
Scenes from the snow-fields, being illustrations of the upper ice-world of Mont Blanc, from sketches made ... in the years 1855, 1856, 1857, 1858; with historical and descriptive remarks. 1859.

DE CAMBRAY DIGNY, Tommaso, <u>conte</u>
[Monte Bianco]. Mont Blanc: Italian ode. 1879.

DELAIRE, Alexis
Genève et le Mont Blanc: notes de science et de voyage. 1876.

DUCOMMUN, Jules César
Une excursion au Mont-Blanc. 1858.

- - 2e éd. 1859.

FALCONNET, Jean
Une ascension au Mont-Blanc et études scientifiques sur cette montagne. 1887.

215.16 Mont Blanc - visits, ... 1854-1884 (Cont.)

FLOYD, C   G
  An ascent of Mont Blanc. 1855.

GIORDANO, Felice
  Ascensione del Monbianco partendo dal versante
  italiano ed escursione nelle Alpi Pennine. 1864.

HUDSON, Charles and KENNEDY, Edward Shirley
  Where there's a will there's a way: an ascent of
  Mont Blanc by a new route and without guides.
  1856.

- - 2nd ed. 1856.

LEMERCIER, Abel
  Ascensions au Mont Rose et au Mont Blanc: excursion de quinzaine d'un Parisien, 14-29 août 1872.
  1873.

LE MESURIER, W   H
  An impromptu ascent of Mont Blanc. 1882.

MACGREGOR, John
  The ascent of Mont Blanc: a series of four views,
  printed in oil colours by George Baxter; the
  original sketches and the description, by J.
  Macgregor. [1855].

MATHEWS, Charles Edward
  Narrative of an excursion on the chain of Mont
  Blanc. 1862.

PIACHAUD, Dr
  Une ascension au Mont-Blanc en 1864. 1865.

PITSCHNER, W
  Der Mont-Blanc: Darstellung der Besteigung
  desselben am 31. Juli, 1. und 2. August 1859...
  1860.

RAFFLES, W   Winter
  Zermatt, with the Cols d'Erin and de Collon; and
  an ascent to the summit of Mont Blanc: two
  letters... 1854.

TALBOT, I   T
  The ascent of Mont Blanc.
  (In Bartol, C.A. Pictures of Europe, framed in
  ideas. 2nd ed. 1856)

THIOLY, François
  Voyage aux glaciers de Savoie. 1861.

THORINGTON, James Monroe
  The high adventure of Mr. Randall. 1945.

Up and down Mont Blanc: a Christmas extra double
  number of Chambers's journal. 1866.

WHITE, Walter
  To Mont Blanc and back again. 1854.

WHITE, Walter
  To Switzerland and back. 1870.

WILLS, Sir Alfred
  The ascent of Mont Blanc, together with some
  remarks on glaciers. 1858.

215.17 Mont Blanc - visits, climbs, 1885-

AUDOUBERT, Louis
  Peuterey, fantastique intégrale: récit. 1975.

BROWN, Thomas Graham
  Brenva. 1944.

DALLOZ, Pierre
  La pointe Lagarde; ou, Les plaisirs d'un alpiniste
  au cours d'une première ascension. 1926.

EGGER, Carl
  Aiguilles: ein Bergbüchlein. 1924.

EMERY, M   S
  Mont Blanc: a part of Underwood and Underwood's
  stereoscopic tour through Switzerland... 1902.

FERRARI, Agostino
  Nella catena del Monte Bianco: impressioni e
  ricordi di ascensioni. 1912.

- - Nuova ed., riv. e aum. 1929.

FONTANNAZ, Charles
  Ascension du Mont-Blanc par l'Aiguille du Goûter.
  1893.

FRENDO, Édouard
  La face nord des Grandes Jorasses. 1946.

GALLAY, Marcel
  Une tragique aventure au Mont-Blanc: récit de la
  1re traversée hivernale des Aiguilles du Diable du
  7 au 15 février 1938: [étude médicale sur les
  congélations]. 2e éd. [1940].

GÜSSFELDT, Paul
  Der Montblanc. 1892.

GÜSSFELDT, Paul
  Der Montblanc: Studien im Hochgebirge, vornehmlich
  in der Montblanc-Gruppe. 1894.

GÜSSFELDT, Paul
  [Der Montblanc...]. Le Mont Blanc: ascensions
  d'hiver et d'été, études dans la haute montagne.
  1899.

HELBRONNER, Paul
  Une semaine au Mont Blanc, août 1893. 1894.

HESS, Adolfo
  Trent'anni di alpinismo nella catena del Monte
  Bianco. 1929.

ICHAC, Marcel
  L'assaut des Aiguilles du Diable: une arête, une
  ascension, un film. 1945.

ICHAC, Marcel
  Quand brillent les étoiles de midi. 1960.

LÉPINEY, Jacques de and LÉPINEY, Tom de
  Sur les crêtes du Mont Blanc: récits d'ascensions.
  1929.

LÉPINEY, Jacques de and LÉPINEY, Tom de
  [Sur les crêtes du Mont Blanc]. Climbs on Mont
  Blanc. 1930.

LLOYD, Robert Wylie
  A traverse of the Dent Blanche and the first
  direct ascent of the Aiguille de Bionnassay by the
  north face... 1927.

MAGNONE, Guido
  La face W des Drus. 1953.

MAGNONE, Guido
  [La face W des Drus]. The West face. 1955.

ROSSIER, Edmond
  L'Aiguille Verte. [1935?].

STEINAUER, Ludwig
  Der weisse Berg: meine Erlebnisse am Montblanc.
  1941.

YOUNG, Geoffrey Winthrop
  Mont Blanc by a new way.
  (In Great Hours of Sport. 1921)

215.19 Mont Blanc - guide-books

BERTOLINI, Amilcare and GUGLIERMINA, Guiseppe F
  Gruppo Monte Bianco, fra il colle del Miage, il
  col du Midi e il col de la Tour Ronde. 1924.

215.19 Mont Blanc - guide-books (Cont.)

C., M.
Guide-itinéraire à Chamonix et autour du Mont-
Blanc... 2e éd. 1873.

COUTTET, Joseph Marie
Chamonix, le Mont-Blanc, Courmayeur et le Grand-
Saint-Bernard: court itinéraire descriptif...
1851.

DUTOIT, Sigismond
Tour du Mont-Blanc: descriptions de 12
itinéraires... 1962.

Guide à Chamouni, aux deux St-Bernard, Sixte et
toutes les vallées autour du Mont-Blanc. [1846?].

Guide du voyageur à la vallée de Chamouni et à la
Grande-Chartreuse... 1836.

HARPER, Andrew
Tour of Mont Blanc: [walking guide]. 1977.

MANGET, J   L
[Itinéraire du voyage à Chamouny...]. Taschenbuch
für Reisende nach Chamouny, um den Mont-Blanc,
auf den grossen und kleinen Bernhard... 1829.

MELTZER, Charles
Guide autour du Mont-Blanc. Nouv. éd. [19--].

MONOD, Jules
Chamonix and Mont-Blanc: official guide book.
1913.

ÖSTERREICHISCHER ALPENKLUB
Führer durch die Mont-Blanc-Gruppe. 1913. 2v.

PAYOT, Venance
Guide-itinéraire au Mont-Blanc et dans les vallées
comprises entre les deux Saint-Bernard et le Lac
de Genève... 2e éd. 1869.

RÉBUFFAT, Gaston
L'apprenti montagnard: les cinquante plus belles
courses graduées du massif du Mont-Blanc. 1946.

RÉBUFFAT, Gaston
[L'apprenti montagnard...]. The Mont Blanc
massif: the 100 finest routes. 1975.

Special practical guide for Geneva, the Lake of
Geneva, Chamouny and Mont Blanc. 1872.

VALLOT, Henri
Massif du Mont Blanc: les Aiguilles Rouges et la
chaîne du Brévant. 1921.

215.2 Matterhorn

BELLOWS, William
Zermatt and the Matterhorn. 1925.

BELLOWS, William
[Zermatt and the Matterhorn]. Der Berg meiner
Sehnsucht: Zermatt und das Matterhorn, eine
Traversierung. 1928.

BERNARDI, Alfonso
Il Gran Cervino: antologia. 1963.

BERNARDI, Marziano
Il Cervino e la sua storia. 1944.

BOBBA, Giovanni
Monte Cervino. 2a ed. 1924.

CARREL, George
Ascensions du Mont-Cervin en 1868. 1868.

CARREL, Georges
Le col de Saint-Théodule. 1866.

CAVAZZANI, Francesco
Uomini del Cervino. Vol. 1. 1946.

CLARK, Ronald William
The day the rope broke: the story of a great
Victorian tragedy. 1965.

DE AMICIS, Edmondo
Nel regno del Cervino: nuovi bozzetti e racconti.
1905.

ENGELHARDT, Christian Moritz
Das Monte-Rosa- und Matterhorn- (Mont-Cervin)-
Gebirg... 1852.

FANTIN, Mario
Cervino 1865/1965; Matterhorn - Mont Cervin. 1965.

GIORDANO, Felice
Notice sur la constitution géologique du Mont
Cervin. [1869].

GIRARD, Raymond de
Le chemin de fer du Cervin au point de vue de
l'alpinisme, des intérets locaux, de l'esthétique
naturelle et de la science. 1907.

GOS, Charles
Alpinisme anecdotique. 1934.

GOS, Charles
Le Cervin. 1948. 2v.

GOS, Charles
La Croix du Cervin. 1919.

- - Nouv. éd. 1933.

GOS, Charles
Histoire du Cervin par l'image. Vol.1. 1923.

GOS, Charles
Pour Miss Cynthia [et On tourne au Cervin].
[1934?].

- - Nouv. éd. [ca 1939].

GRÜTTER, J   B
Meine Matterhornbesteigung. 1893.

HAENSEL, Carl
Der Kampf ums Matterhorn: Tatsachenroman. 1929.

- - Ungekurzte Neuausg. [1929?].

HAENSEL, Carl
[Der Kampf ums Matterhorn]. La lutte pour le
Cervin: roman de faits. [ca 1930].

JEGERLEHNER, Johannes
Die Todesfahrt auf das Matterhorn. 1928.

LUNN, Sir Arnold
Matterhorn centenary. 1965.

Matterhorn-Jubiläumsfestwoche = Centennial Festival
of the Matterhorn. 1965.

MAZZOTTI, Giuseppe
Grandi imprese sul Cervino. 1934.

MAZZOTTI, Giuseppe
[Grandi imprese sul Cervino]. Dernières victoires
au Cervin. 1934.

MAZZOTTI, Giuseppe
[Grandi imprese sul Cervino]. Das Buch vom
Matterhorn: die Erstersteigungen. [1935].

Nouvelle ascension du Mont-Cervin. [1867].

PEYRÉ, Joseph
Matterhorn: roman. 1939.

RÉBUFFAT, Gaston
Cervin: cime exemplaire. 1965.

RÉBUFFAT, Gaston
[Cervin: cime exemplaire]. Men and the Matterhorn.
1967.

215.2 Matterhorn (Cont.)

REY, Guido
Il Monte Cervino. 1904.

REY, Guido
[Il Monte Cervino]. The Matterhorn. 1907.

REY, Guido
[Il Monte Cervino]. Le Mont Cervin. 1905.

RUDDER, May de
Les vingt ans du Refuge Solvay au Cervin. 1938.

TERCINOD, G
Recueil de pages valdôtaines à l'occasion du
centenaire de la première ascension du Mont
Cervin... 1965.

THIOLY, François
Ascension du Mont-Cervin (Matterhorn). 1871.

WHYMPER, Edward
The ascent of the Matterhorn. 1880.

WHYMPER, Edward
[Scrambles amongst the Alps...]. Man on the
Matterhorn. 1940.

WUNDT, Theodor
Das Matterhorn und seine Geschichte. [1896?].

- - 2.Aufl. [ca 1900].

215.3 Monte Rosa

ARCONATI VISCONTI, Giammartino
Ascensione al Monte Rosa nell' agosto 1864. 1872.

BARROW, John, 1808-1898
Expeditions on the glaciers, including an ascent
of Mont Blanc, Monte Rosa, col du Géant, and Mont
Buet... 1864.

BERTOLINI, Amilcare and GUGLIERMINA, Giuseppe F
Gruppo Monte Rosa. 1925.

COLE, Mrs. Henry Warwick
A lady's tour round Monte Rosa; with visits to the
Italian valleys... in a series of excursions in
the years 1850-56-58. 1859.

DURIO, Alberto
Bibliografia alpinistica-storica e scientifica del
Gruppo del Monte Rosa (dal colle del Théodule al
passo del Monte Moro) dei monti della Valesia e
della Sezione di Varallo del C.A.I., 1527-1924.
1925.

ENGELHARDT, Christian Moritz
Das Monte-Rosa- und Matterhorn- (Mont-Cervin)-
Gebirg... 1852.

FASANA, Eugenio
Il Monte Rosa: vicende, uomini e imprese. 1931.

FORBES, James David
[Travels through the Alps of Savoy...]. The tour
of Mont Blanc and of Monte Rosa, being a personal
narrative, abridged from the author's "Travels in
the Alps of Savoy", &c. 1855.

HÖRTNAGL, F
Der Monte Rosa. 1905.

IMFELD, X
Panorama vom Monte Rosa: vollständige Rundsicht
von der Dufourspitze (4638m.), dem höchsten Gipfel
der Schweizeralpen. 1878.

KUGY, Julius
Im göttlichen Lächeln des Monte Rosa. 1940. 2v.

LABORATORII SCIENTIFICI "A. MOSSO" SUL MONTE ROSA
Travaux des années 1903-[1911]. 1904-1912. 3v.

LAVELEYE, Émile de
Le Mont-Rose et les Alpes pennines: souvenirs de
voyage. [1865].

LEMERCIER, Abel
Ascensions au Mont Rose et au Mont Blanc: excursion de quinzaine d'un Parisien,14-29 août 1872.
1873.

MEISSNER, Alfred
Ein Ausflug zum Monte Rosa. [1858].

MOSSO, Angelo
Fisiologia dell'uomo sulle Alpi: studi fatti sul
Monte Rosa. 1897.

RICCI, Virgilio
L'andata di Leonardo da Vinci al Monboso, oggi
Monte Rosa, e la teoria dell'azzurro del cielo.
1977.

SCHWEIZER ALPEN-CLUB. Sektion Monte Rosa
Monte Rosa 1865-1965. 1965.

SELLA, Vittorio and VALLINO, Domenico
Monte Rosa & Gressoney. [1890].

THIOLY, François
Voyage en Suisse et ascension du Mont Rose. 1860.

THIOLY, François
Zermatt et l'ascension du Mont Rose. [1860].

ULRICH, Melchior
Die Seitanthäler des Wallis und der Monterosa,
topographisch geschildert. 1850.

VALSESIA, Teresio and BURGENER, Giuseppe
Macugnaga e il Monte Rosa. 1968.

WELDEN, Ludwig, Freiherr von
Der Monte-Rosa: ein topographische und naturhistorische Skizze... 1824.

215.6 Eiger

GILLMAN, Peter and HASTON, Dougal
Eiger direct. 1966.

HARRER, Heinrich
[Die Weisse Spinne]. The White Spider: the
history of the Eiger's North Face. 1959.

- - Rev. ed. 1965.

HASTON, Dougal
The Eiger. 1974.

HECKMAIR, Anderl
Um die Eiger-Nordwand. 2.Aufl. 1938.

HIEBELER, Toni
Combats pour l'Eiger. 1965.

HIEBELER, Toni
[Im Banne der Spinne]. North Face in winter: the
first winter climb of the Eiger's North Face,
March 1961. 1962.

OLSEN, Jack
The climb up to hell. 1962.

SKOCZYLAS, Adam
Stefano we shall come tomorrow. 1962.

ZWAHLEN, Otto
Der Kampf um die Eiger-Nordwand:... Bericht über
die Bergtragödien ... [in] 1935 und 1936. 1936.

215.7 Jungfrau

BIENDL, Hans
Die Jungfrau. 1907.

215.7 Jungfrau (Cont.)

CHEEVER, George B
   The pilgrim in the shadow of the Jungfrau Alp.
   1848.

- - Another ed. 1852.

CHEEVER, George B
   Wanderings of a pilgrim in the shadow of Mont
   Blanc and the Jungfrau Alp. [1847].

- - New ed. [1848?].
- - New ed. [1859?].

COLLET, Léon W   and PARÉJAS, Édouard
   Géologie de la chaîne de la Jungfrau. 1931.

DESOR, Édouard
   L'ascension de la Jungfrau, effectuée le 28 août
   1841, par MM. Agassiz, Forbes, du Chatelier et
   Desor... 1841.

DESOR, Édouard
   Excursions et séjour de M. Agassiz sur la Mer de
   Glace du Lauteraar et du Finsteraar, en société de
   plusieurs naturalistes... 1841.

FALKE, Konrad
   Im Banne der Jungfrau. 1909.

GEORGE, Hereford Brooke and MATHEWS, Charles Edward
   Munchausen on the Jungfrau. [ca 1870].

GUYER, Gebhard A
   Le projet du chemin de fer de la Jungfrau... 1897.

GUYER, Gebhard A
   [Le projet du chemin de fer...]. The proposed
   Jungfrau Railway... 1897.

HEER, J   C
   Ein Besuch der Jungfrau-Bahn, 4.-8. Juni 1898.
   1898.

HERZOG, Theodor
   Rings um die Jungfraubahn: Naturbeobachtungen.
   1926.

Jungfrau-Bahn: Übersichtskarte. [ca 1900].

JUNGFRAUJOCH SCIENTIFIC STATION
   Hochalpine Forschungsstation Jungfraujoch...
   Internationale Stiftung. 1931.

MATHEWS, Charles Edward
   Ascent of the Jungfrau. [1860].

MEYER, Johann Rudolf and MEYER, Hieronymus
   Reise auf den Jungfrau-Gletscher und Ersteigung
   seines Gipfels. [1812].

MEYER, Johann Rudolf and MEYER, Hieronymus
   Reise auf die Eisgebirge des Kantons Bern und
   Ersteigung ihrer höchsten Gipfel, im Sommer 1812.
   1813.

MICHEL, Hans
   La Jungfrau. 1946.

ROHRDORF, Caspar
   Reise über die Grindelwald-Viescher-Gletscher auf
   den Jungfrau-Gletscher und Ersteigung des Gletschers
   des Jungfrau-Berges, unternommen und beschrieben
   im August und September 1828. 1828.

ROTH, Abraham
   Finsteraarhornfahrt. 1863.

SCHLEIDT, Wilhelm
   Triomphaler Festzug zur Erinnerung an die Einweihung der Jungfraubahn, (1. Section Eigergletscher) im Juli 1898. Op.31. [1898].

SCHWEIZER ALPEN-CLUB. Sektion Uto
   Das Unglück an der Jungfrau vom 15. Juli 1887.
   [1887].

STEINER, Leonhard
   Jungfraubahn: Festspiel zur Einweihung der 1.
   Sektion Scheidegg-Gletscher. [1898].

TWITTERS, Peter
   How I went up the Jung-Frau, and came down again.
   [ca 1852].

WUNDT, Theodor
   Die Jungfrau und das Berner Oberland. [1898].

- - 2.Aufl. [ca 1900].

215.8 Pilatus

CAPPEILER, Moritz Anton
   Pilati Montis historia, in pago Lucernensi
   Helvetiae siti. 1757 [i.e. 1767].

GESNER, Conrad
   De raris et admirandis herbis... eiusdem
   descriptio Montis Fracti, sive Montis Pilati,
   iuxta Lucernam in Helvetia. [1555].

GESNER, Conrad
   On the admiration of mountains... a description
   of the Riven Mountain, commonly called Mount
   Pilatus... 1555. 1937.

KAUFMANN, Franz Joseph
   Der Pilatus: geologisch Untersucht und
   Beschrieben. 1867.

MELA, Pomponius
   Le orbis situ libri tres... 1522.
   Contains Watt's account of the ascent of Pilatus.

PILATUSBAHN-GESELLSCHAFT
   Mount Pilatus: Switzerland's far-famed mountain
   peak. [ca 1965].

SCHWEIZER ALPEN-CLUB
   Der Pilatus... 1868.

WEBER, P   X
   Der Pilatus und seine Geschichte. 1913.

215.9 Argentine
RHAM, Georges de
   L'Argentine: description de vingt itinéraires
   d'escalade, précédée de quelques considérations
   sur leurs difficultés et leurs dangers. 1944.

215.9 Barre des Écrins

ISSELIN, Henri
   La Barre des Écrins (4,102m). 1954.

215.9 Cimone della Pala

WUNDT, Theodor
   Die Besteigung des Cimone della Pala: ein Album
   für Kletterer und Dolomiten-Freunde. [1892].

215.9 Dent Blanche

LLOYD, Robert Wylie
   A traverse of the Dent Blanche and the first
   direct ascent of the Aiguille de Bionnassay by
   the North Face... 1927.

215.9 Dent du Midi

BREUGEL DOUGLAS, R
   La Dent du Midi. 1913.

215.9 Faulhorn

SCHWETZER, J   J
   Das Faulhorn im Grindelwald: ein Topographie-
   und Panoram-Gemälde. 1832.

215.9 Galenstock

DESOR, Édouard
   Une dernière ascension. 1854.

215.9 (Cont.)

215.9 Gastlosen

GIRARD, Raymond de
La conquête des Gastlosen (Alpes fribourgeoises).
[1921].

215.9 Gornergrat

COMPAGNIE DU CHEMIN DE FER DU GORNERGRAT
Initiation au Gornergrat. 1948.

215.9 Meidje

FERRAND, Henri
L'accident de la Meidje, 20 août 1896. 1897.

ISSELIN, Henri
La Meije. 1956.

SONNIER, Georges
Meije: récit. 1952.

215.9 Monviso

SELLA, Quintino
Una salita al Monviso. 1863.

VACCARONE, Luigi
Le Pertuis du Viso: étude historique. 1881.

215.9 Piz Languard

LECHNER, Ernst
Piz Languard und die Bernina-Gruppe bei Pontresina,
Oberengadin: Skizzen aus Natur und Bevölkerung,
zugleich als Wegweiser für Wanderungen. 1858.

- - 2.Aufl. 1865.
- - 3.Aufl. 1900.

215.9 Piz Linard

WEILENMANN, Johann Jacob
Eine Ersteigung des Piz Linard im Unter-Engadin.
1859.

215.9 Rigi

GOTTHARD, P
Rigyberg der Himmelsköniginn eingeweiht unter dem
Titel: Maria zum Schnee... 1802.

RÜTIMEYER, L
Der Rigi: Berg, Thal und See: naturgeschichtliche
Darstellung der Landschaft. 1877.

SCHLINCKE, L
Der Rigi: Handbüchlein für Reisende. 3.verb. Aufl.
1857.

Souvenir du Righi. [ca 1860].

215.9 Taeschhorn

ROCH, André
Taeschhorn, face sud (4498m.) (3e ascension).
(In Akademischer Alpen-Club Zürich, 48 Jahres-
bericht, 1943)

215.9 Tödi

HUG, Oscar A
Die Ostwand des Tödi. [1921].

SIMLER, Rudolf Theodor
Der Tödi-Rusein und die Excursion nach Obersandalp... 1863.

ULRICH, Melchior
Die Ersteigung des Tödi. 1859.

215.9 Torre d'Ovarda

SAN-ROBERTO, Paolo, conte di
Una salita alla Torre d'Ovarda. 1873.

22 SWITZERLAND

SCHWEIZERISCHE VERKEHRSZENTRALE
Bibliographie der Reiseliteratur der
Schweizerischen Verkehrszentrale, Schweizerischen
Transportanstalten, Verkehrs-Kur- und Hotelier-
vereine. 1926.

221 Geology, climate

ALTMANN, Johann Georg
Versuch einer historischen und physischen
Beschreibung der helvetischen Eisbergen. 1751.

AVEBURY, John Lubbock, Baron
The scenery of Switzerland and the causes to
which it is due. 1896.

- - 5th ed. 1913.

BALTZER, A
Das Berneroberland und Nachbargebiete: ein
geologischer Führer. 1906.

BALTZER, A
Centralgebiet der Schweiz... 1886-94. 4v. in 6.

BALTZER, A
Der Glärnisch, ein Problem alpinen Gebirgsbaues:
geologische Monographie über einen Gebirgsstock
der östschweizerischen Kalkalpen. 1873.

BALTZER, A
Der mechanische Contact von Gneiss und Kalk im
Berner-Oberland. 1880.

BRIDEL, Philippe Sirice
Course à l'éboulement du Glacier de Gétroz et au
Lac de Mauvoisin, au fond de la Vallée de Bagnes,
16 mai 1818. [1818].

BURCKHARDT, Carl
Monographie der Kreideketten zwischen Klönthal,
Sihl und Linth. 1896.

CADISCH, Joos
Der Bau der Schweizeralpen. 1926.

CHARPENTIER, Jean de
Essai sur les glaciers et sur le terrain
erratique du Bassin du Rhône. 1841.

CHARPENTIER, Jean de
Notice sur la cause probable du transport des
blocs erratiques de la Suisse. 1835.

CHARPENTIER, Jean de
Quelques conjectures sur les grandes révolutions
qui ont changé la surface de la Suisse, et particulièrement celle du Canton de Vaud, pour
l'amener à son état actuel. 1836.

COLLET, Léon W
Étude géologique de la chaîne Tour Saillère -
Pic de Tanneverge. 1904.

COLLET, Léon W and PARÉJAS, Édouard
Géologie de la chaîne de la Jungfrau. 1931.

COLLET, Léon W
Geology of the Swiss Alps. 1926.

CONGRÈS GÉOLOGIQUE INTERNATIONAL, 6th, Zurich, 1894
Livret-guide géologique dans le Jura et les Alpes
de la Suisse. 1894.

DESOR, Édouard
Compte rendu des recherches de M. Agassiz pendant
ses deux derniers séjours à l'Hôtel des
Neuchâtelois, sur le glacier inférieur de l'Aar,
en 1841 et 1842. 1843.

DESOR, Édouard and LORIOL, P de
Échinologie helvétique: description des oursins
fossiles de la Suisse. 1868-69. 5 pts.

221 Switzerland - geology, climate (Cont.)

DESOR, Édouard
Excursions et séjour de M. Agassiz sur la Mer de
Glace du Lauteraar et du Finsteraar, en société
de plusieurs naturalistes. 1841.

DESOR, Édouard
Excursions et séjours dans les glaciers et les
hautes regions des Alpes, de M. Agassiz et de ses
compagnons de voyage. 1844.

DESOR, Édouard
Journal d'une course faite aux glaciers du Mont
Rose et du Mont Cervin en société de MM. Studer,
Agassiz, Lardy, Nicolet et autres. 1840.

DESOR, Édouard
Nouvelles excursions et séjours dans les glaciers
et les hautes regions des Alpes, de M. Agassiz et
de ses compagnons de voyage... 1845.

DESOR, Édouard
Récit d'une course faite aux glaciers en hiver,
par MM. Agassiz et É. Desor. 1842.

ESCHER VON DER LINTH, Arnold
Die Sentis-Gruppe: Text zur Specialkarte des
Sentis. 1878.

FALSAN, Albert and CHANTRE, E
Monographie géologique des anciens glaciers et du
terrain erratique de la partie moyenne du Bassin
du Rhône. 1879-80. 2v.

FAVRE, Alphonse
Texte explicatif de la carte du phénomène
erratique et des anciens glaciers du versant nord
des Alpes suisses et de la chaîne du Mont-Blanc.
1898.

FAVRE, Ernest and SCHARDT, Hans
Description géologique des préalpes du Canton de
Vaud et du Chablais jusqu'à la Dranse et de la
chaîne des Dents du Midi... 1887.

FELLENBERG, Edmund von and MOESCH, Casimir
Geologische Beschreibung des westlichen Theils des
Aarmassivs, enthalten auf dem nördlich der Rhone...
1893.

GEORGE, Hereford Brooke
The Oberland and its glaciers explored and illustrated with ice-axe and camera. 1866.

GERLACH, Heinrich
Erläuterung zu den Arbeiten von H. Gerlach in den
Blättern ... sudlich von der Rhone. 1883.

GERLACH, Heinrich
Das südwestliche Wallis mit den angrenzenden
Landestheilen von Savoien und Piemont. 1871.

GILLIÉRON, V
Aperçu géologique sur les Alpes de Fribourg en
général, et description spéciale du Monsalvens.
1873.

GILLIÉRON, V
Description géologique des territoires de Vaud,
Fribourg et Berne... 1885.

GREPPIN, J   B
Description géologique du Jura bernois et de
quelques districts adjacents... 1870.

GRUNER, Gottlieb Sigmund
Die Eisbebirge des Schweizerlandes. 1760. 3v.

GRUNER, Gottlieb Sigmund
[Die Eisgebirge des Schweizerlandes]. The icy
mountains of Swisserland... [ca 1800]. 3v.

GRUNER, Gottlieb Sigmund
[Die Eisgebirge des Schweizerlandes]. Histoire
naturelle des glacieres de Suisse. 1770.

HALLER, Albrecht von
Iter Helveticum anni MDCCXXXVIIII. 1740.

HEER, Oswald
Die Urwelt der Schweiz. 2. Subscriptions-Ausg.
der 2., umgearb. und verm. Aufl. 1883.

HEIM, Albert
Geologie der Hochalpen zwischen Reuss und Rhein...
1891.

HEIM, Albert
Geologie der Schweiz. 1919-22. 2v. in 3.

HEIM, Albert
Das Säntisgebirge, untersucht und dargestellt von
Alb. Heim. 1905. 2v.

HERRLIBERGER, David
Abhandlung von den Eisgebirgen und Gletschern des
Helvetier-Landes, als eine General-Einleitung zu
der Alp-Topographie. 1774.

HOEK, Henry
Geologische Untersuchungen im Plessurgebirge um
Arosa. 1903.

HOEK, Henry
Das zentrale Plessurgebirge: geologische Untersuchungen. 1906.

HOGARD, Henri
Principaux glaciers de la Suisse. 1854.

JACCARD, Auguste
Description géologique du Jura Vaudois et
Neuchatelois, et de quelques districts adjacents
du Jura français... 1869.

- - Supplement. 1870.

KAUFMANN, Franz Joseph
Der Pilatus, geologisch Untersucht und
Beschrieben. 1867.

KAUFMANN, Franz Joseph
Rigi und Molassegebiet der Mittelschweiz. 1872.

LONGMAN, William
A lecture on Switzerland. 1857.

LÜTSCHG, Otto
Der Märjelensee und seine Abflussverhältnisse:
eine hydrologische Studie unter Mitberück-
sichtigung hydrographischer Erscheinungen in
anderen Flussgebieten. 1915.

LÜTSCHG, Otto
[Der Märjelensee...]. Le Lac de Märjelen. 1916.

LÜTSCHG, Otto
Über Niederschlag und Abfluss im Hochgebirge:
Sonderdarstellung des Mattmarkgebietes: ein
Beitrag zur Fluss- und Gletscherkunde der
Schweiz. 1926.

MARTINS, Charles
La réunion de la Société helvétique des sciences
naturelles en août 1863 à Samaden, dans la Haute-
Engadine... 1864.

MOESCH, Casimir
Der Aargauer-Jura und die nördlichen Gebiete des
Kantons Zürich: geologisch Untersucht und
Beschrieben. 1867.

MOESCH, Casimir
Geologischer Führer durch die Alpen, Passe und
Thäler der Centralschweiz. 2. Aufl. 1897.

MORELL, J   R
Scientific guide to Switzerland. 1867.

MÜLLER, Albert
Geognostische Skizze des Kantons Basel und der
angrenzenden Gebiete... 1862.

MÜLLER, Fritz
Firn und Eis der Schweizer Alpen: Gletscher-
inventar, von Fritz Müller, Toni Caflisch,
Gerhard Müller. 1976. 2v.

221 Switzerland - geology, climate (Cont.)

NATURFORSCHENDE GESELLSCHAFT IN SOLOTHURN
Naturhistorische Alpenreise. 1830.

OBERHOLZER, Jakob
Monographie einiger prähistorischer Bergstürze
in der Glarneralpen. 1900.

PIPEROFF, Chr.
Geologie des Calanda... 1897.

RAMSAY, Andrew Crombie
The old glaciers of Switzerland and North
Wales. 1860.

RENAUD, André
Les glaciers. 1949.

RENEVIER, E
Monographie géologique des Hautes-Alpes vaudoises
et parties avoisinantes du Valais. 1890.

ROLLE, Friedrich
Erläuterungen und Profile zur geologischen Karte
der Umgebungen von Bellinzona im Kanton Tessin
und von Chiavenna in Italien. 1881.

RÜTIMEYER, L
Über Thal- und See-Bildung: Beiträge zum Ver-
ständniss der Oberfläche der Schweiz. 1869.

SCHEUCHZER, Johann Jacob
Αερογραφιας Helveticae... 1723-25. 2v.

SCHEUCHZER, Johann Jacob
Beschreibung der Natur-Geschichten des
Schweizerlands. 1706-08. 3v. in 1.

SCHEUCHZER, Johann Jacob
Beschreibung des Wetter-Jahrs MDCCXXXI: Besonders
aber des Traurigen-Himmels, der ob unseren
Häubteren geschwebet, den 1. Heumonat. 1732.

SCHEUCHZER, Johann Jacob
Cataclysmographiam Helvetiae... 1733.

SCHEUCHZER, Johann Jacob
Coelum triste ad Julias calendas anni MDCCXXXI...
[1732].

SCHEUCHZER, Johann Jacob
De Helvetiae aeribus, aquis, locis... 1728-29.
2v.

SCHEUCHZER, Johann Jacob
Einladungs-Brief zu Erforschung natürlicher
Wanderen so sich im Schweitzer-Land befinden.
[ca 1700].

SCHEUCHZER, Johann Jacob
Helvetiae stoicheiographia, orographia, et
oreographia; oder, Beschreibung der Elementen...
1716-18. 3v. in 1.

SCHEUCHZER, Johann Jacob
Historiae Helveticae naturalis prolegomena...
1700.

SCHEUCHZER, Johann Jacob
Natur-Geschichte des Schweizerlandes, samt seinen
Reisen über die Schweitzerische Gebürge; aufs neue
hrsg., und mit einigen Anmerkungen versehen von
Joh. Georg Sulzern. 1746. 2v. in 1.

SCHEUCHZER, Johann Jacob
Ουρεσιφοίτης Helveticus; sive, Itinera alpina
tria... 1708. 3v. in 1.

SCHEUCHZER, Johann Jacob
Ουρεσιφοίτης Helviticus; sive, Itinera per
Helvetiae alpinas regiones... 1723. 4v.

SCHEUCHZER, Johann Jacob
Specimen lithographiae Helveticae curiosae, quo
lapides ex figuratis Helveticis selectissimi aeri
incisi sistuntur & describunter. 1702.

SCHEUCHZER, Johann Jacob
Στοιχειολογιαν ad Helvetiam applicatam...1700.

SCHWEIZER ALPEN-CLUB
Instruction für die Gletscher-Reisenden des
Schweizerischen Alpenclubs. 1871.

SCHWEIZERISCHE NATURSFORSCHENDE GESELLSCHAFT.
Gletscher-Kommission
Vermessungen am Rhonegletscher: Mensurations au
Glacier du Rhône, 1874-1915. 1916.

STUDER, Bernhard
Geologie der Schweiz. 1851-53. 2v.

STUDER, Bernhard
Geschichte der physischen Geographie der Schweiz
bis 1815. 1863.

STUDER, Bernhard
Index der Petrographie und Stratigraphie der
Schweiz und ihrer Umgebungen. 1872.

TARAMELLI, Torquato
Il Canton Ticino meridionale ed i paesi finitimi
... 1880.

THEOBALD, Gottfried
Geologische Beschreibung ... von Graubünden.
1864.

THEOBALD, Gottfried
Geologische Beschreibung ... von Graubünden.
1866

WAGNER, Johann Jacob
Historia naturalis Helvetiae curiosa. 1680.

WEBER, Julius
Geologische Wanderungen durch die Schweiz: eine
Einführung in die Geologie. 1911-15. 3v.
(Schweizer Alpen-Club. Clubführer)

WEGMANN, Eugen
Zur Geologie der St. Bernharddecke im Val
d'Hérens (Wallis). 1923.

WEHRLI, Leo
Das Dioritgebiet von Schlans bis Disentis im
Bündner Oberland: geologisch-petrographische
Studie. 1896.

WEIBEL, Max
Die Mineralien der Schweiz: ein Mineralogischer
Führer. 4. erw. Aufl. 1972.

WEIBEL, Max
[Die Mineralien der Schweiz]. A guide to the
minerals of Switzerland. 1966.

222 Geography, description

Album-Panorama suisse. 1re sér. 1902.

ALEXANDER, William Lindsay
Switzerland and the Swiss churches, being notes
of a short tour and notices of the principal religious bodies in that country. 1846.

ASHBY, Douglas
Things seen in Switzerland in summer: a description of a wonderful country... 1928.

Atlas géographique, économique, historique de la
Suisse. [1908].

BARNARD, George
Switzerland: scenes and incidents of travel in the
Bernese Oberland... [1843].

BAUER, J   P
Nomina alpium. 1. 1977.

BAUMGARTNER, Heinrich
Tausend Höhenangeben. 3.Aufl. 1892

BEATTIE, William
Switzerland. 1836. 2v.

BEATTIE, William
[Switzerland]. La Suisse pittoresque. 1836. 2v.

222 Switzerland - geography, description (Cont.)

BEATTIE, William
[Switzerland]. Die Schweiz nach William Beattie.
[1840].

BÉGIN, Émile
Voyage pittoresque en Suisse, en Savoie et sur les
Alpes. 1852.

BERLEPSCH, Hermann Alexander von
Schweizerkunde: Land, Volk und Staat, geographisch-
statistisch, übersichtlichvergleichand dargestellt.
1864.

- - 2. umgearb. Aufl. 1875.

Beschrijving van Zwitserland, met betrekking tot
deszelts aardrijkskundige ligging, natuurlijke
voortbrengsels, oudheden, geschiedenis en
koophandel. 1824. 2v.

BESSON, H
Manuel pour les savans et les curieux qui voyagent
en Suisse. 1786. 2v. in 1.

Bilder-Atlas der Schweiz: Sammlung von Landschafts-,
Städt-, und Typenbildern aus allen Kantonen mit
erklärendem Text zusammengestellt durch die Mitarbeiter am Geographischen Lexicon der Schweiz.
[1910?].

BONSTETTEN, Ch. Victor de
La Scandinavie et les Alpes [et Fragments sur
l'Islande]. 1826.

BOREL, Maurice
Atlas cantonal, politique et économique de la
Suisse. [ca 1912].

BOSSÉ, Fernand
Géographie de la Suisse. 2e éd. 1912 [i.e.
1913].

BOURRIT, Marc Théodore
Itinéraire de Genève, Lausanne et Chamouni. 1791.

- - Nouv. éd., rev., corr. et augm. 1792.
- - 3e éd. 1808.

BUDDEUS, Aurelio
Schweizerland: Natur und Menschenleben. 1853.
2v. in 1.

BYERS, Samuel Hawkins Marshall
Switzerland and the Swiss. 1875.

CADBY, Will and CADBY, Carine
Switzerland in winter (discursive information for
visitors). 1914.

Cents vues suisses, remarquables par leur situation,
ou par des faits historiques. [ca 1820].

COMPAGNIE DES CHEMINS DE FER JURA-SIMPLON
De Bale à Brigue et Zermatt: guide officiel du
Jura-Simplon. [ca 1893].

DANDOLO, Tullio
Prospetto della Svizzera; ossia, Ragionamenti da
servire d'introduzione alle lettere sulla
Svizzera. 1832. 2v. in 1.

DANDOLO, Tullio
Saggio di lettere sulla Svizzera, Il Cantone
de' Grigioni. 1829.

DANDOLO, Tullio
La Svizzera considerata nelle sue vaghezze pittoresche, nella storia, nelle leggi e ne' costumi:
lettere. 1829-33. 10v. in 5.

D'AUVERGNE, Edmund B
Switzerland in sunshine and snow. [1912].

- - Another ed. [1916].

DAUZAT, Albert
La Suisse illustrée. [1913].

DELKESKAMP, Friedrich Wilhelm
Relief pittoresque du sol classique de la Suisse.
[1830].

Dictionnaire géographique de la Suisse. 1902-10.
6v.

Dictionnaire géographique, historique et politique
de la Suisse. 1775. 2v.

- - Nouv.éd., corr. et augm. 1776. 2v. in 1.
- - Nouv.éd., corr. et augm. 1777. 2v.
- - Nouv.éd., augm. 1788. 3v.

[Dictionnaire géographique, historique et politique
...]. Historische, geographische und physikalische
Beschreibung des Schweizerlandes... 1782-83. 3v.

DIXON, William Hepworth
The Switzers. 1872.

DUBOIS, Jean
Souvenirs de la Suisse: cent vues les plus
remarquables. [ca 1845].

- - Another collection. [ca 1850].
- - Another collection. [ca 1855].

DURHEIM, C   J
Sammlung trigonometrischer oder barometrisch-
bestimmter absoluter Höhen der Schweiz und ihrer
nähern Umgebung = Hypsométrie de la Suisse...
1850.

DUVOTENAY, Ch.
Atlas géographique, historique, statistique, et
itinéraire de la Suisse, devisé en vingt-deux
cantons, et de la Vallée de Chamouny. 1837.

EBERLI, Henry
Switzerland poetical and pictorial: a collection
of poems by English and American poets. 1893.

EGLI, Emil
Swiss life and landscape. [1949].

EGLI, Johann Jakob
Praktische Schweizerkunde für Schule und Haus. 3.
vielverb. Aufl. 1865.

L'état et les délices de la Suisse, en forme de relation critique, [par Abraham Ruchat, Abraham
Stanyan & others]. 1730. 4v.

L'état et les délices de la Suisse; ou, Description
helvetique historique et géographique ..., [par
Abraham Ruchat, Abraham Stanyan and others]. Nouv.
éd., corr. & considérablement augm. 1764. 4v.

- - Nouv. éd. 1776.

État et délices de la Suisse; ou, Description
historique et géographique des treize cantons
suisses et de leurs alliés, [par Abraham Ruchat,
Abraham Stanyan and others]. [5e] éd., corr. &
considérablement augm... 1778. 2v.

FEIERABEND, August
Die schweizerische Alpenwelt; für junge und alte
Freunde der Alpen dargestellt. 1873.

FINNEMORE, John
Switzerland. 1908.

FISCHER, Ernst
Der kartographische Standpunkt der Schweiz: ein
Vortrag. 1870.

FLAIG, Walther
Die Skiparadiese der Schweiz. 1932.

FLÜCKIGER, Otto
Die Schweiz aus der Vogelschau. 1924.

FLÜCKIGER, Otto
[Die Schweiz aus der Vogelschau]. Switzerland from
the air. 1926.

Focus on Switzerland. 1975. 4v.

222 Switzerland - geography, description (Cont.)

FORESTIER, Alcide, vicomte de
Alpes pittoresques: description de la Suisse.
1837-38. 2v.

FOX, Sir Frank
Switzerland. 2nd ed. 1930.

FRANSCINI, Stefano
Statistica della Svizzera. 1827.

FREY, Jakob
Das Schweizerland in Bild und Wort. [1873?].

FRÖLICH, H
Militärgeographie der Schweiz, nebst kurzer
Schilderung der Entstehung der Neutralität
Savoyens und historischer Notizen über verschiedene
Alpenpässe. 1906.

FRÜH, J
Geographie der Schweiz. Bd.3. Die Enzelland-
schaften der Schweiz. 1938.

GABERELL, J
Gaberell's Album of Switzerland. [1927].

Gallery of the celebrated landscapes of Switzerland.
[1880].

GAUDIN, A
Switzerland in miniature: description of the grand
model of Switzerland, by Professor Gaudin, of
Geneva ... now exhibiting at the Egyptian Hall,
Piccadilly. 1825.

GAULIS, Louis and CREUX, René
Swiss hotel pioneers. 1976.

GOURDAULT, Jules
La Suisse pittoresque. 5e éd. 1887.

GRAF, J H
Litteratur der Landesvermessung Kataloge der
Kartensammlungen, Karten, Pläne, Reliefs,
Panoramen. 1896.

GREEN, Vivian H
The Swiss Alps. 1961.

GROSSE, Carl, Marchese von Grosse
Die Schweiz. 1791. 2v. in 1.

GSELL-FELS, Theodor
Die Schweiz. 2. umgearb. Aufl. Volks-Ausg. 1883.

GSELL-FELS, Theodor
[Die Schweiz]. Switzerland: its scenery and
people, pictorially represented by eminent Swiss
and German artists. 1881.

GUITON, Paul
La Suisse. 1929-30. 2v.

GUITON, Paul
[La Suisse]. Switzerland, western and southern:
Neuchatel & Geneva to Ticino. 1929.

HAGEN, Gunther
Die Schweiz: ein Bildwerk. [1960?].

HEER, J C
Schweiz. 1899.

- - 3.Aufl. 1907.
- - 4.Aufl. 1913.

HEINIGER, E A
Nos quatre mille mètres. [1943].

Helvetiorum Respublica, diversorum autorum quorum
nonulli nunc primum in lucem prodeunt. 1627.

HÉMANN, N J
Beautés et merveilles de la nature en Suisse.
1837.

HÜPFNER, Albrecht
Magazin für die Naturkunde Helvetiens. 1788-89. 4v.

JAMES, Norman G Brett
The charm of Switzerland: an anthology. 1910.

JEGERLEHNER, Johannes
La route du Loetschberg. [1917].

KADEN, Woldemar
Das Schweizerland: eine Sommerfahrt durch Gebirg
und Thal... [1877].

KADEN, Woldemar
[Das Schweizerland...]. Switzerland and the
Bavarian highlands. [1879].

KADEN, Woldemar
[Das Schweizerland...]. Switzerland: its mountains and valleys. 1878.

- - New and rev. ed. 1889.
- - New and rev. ed. 1903.

KADEN, Woldemar
[Das Schweizerland...]. La Svizzera. 1878.

KAMPEN, N G van
Switserland en de Alpen van Savoije. [1837].
2v. in 1.

KNOWLES, Archibald Campbell
Adventures in the Alps. [1913].

KUHNS, Oscar
Switzerland: its scenery, history, and literary
associations. 2nd ed. 1910.

KURZ, Heinrich
Die Schweiz: Land, Volk und Geschichte in
ausgewählten Dichtungen. 1853.

LABORDE, Jean Benjamin de
Tableaux topographiques, pittoresques, physiques,
historiques, moraux, politiques, littéraires, de
la Suisse. 1780-[88]. 2v. in 4.

- - 2e éd. 1784-88. 12v.

LA FARINA, Giuseppe
La Svizzera storica ed artistica. 1842-43. 2v.

LAMY, J P
Choix de vues en Suisse. 1819.

LASCELLES, Rowley
A general outline of the Swiss landscapes. 3rd
ed., rev. and considerably enl. 1812.

LEUTHOLD, H F
Cinquantes principales vues pittoresques en
mignature de la Suisse. [ca 1838].

A little journey to Switzerland. 1910.

LOEWENBERG, Julius
Schweizer Bilder. 1834.

LORY, Gabriel, 1763-1840
Schweizerland vor hundert Jahren: sechzehn farbige
Tafeln. 1935.

LUNN, Sir Arnold
The cradle of Switzerland. 1952.

LUTZ, Markus
Vollstandige Beschreibung des Schweizerlandes;
oder, Geographischen-statistischen Hand-Lexicon...
2. Ausg. 1827-28. 4v.

- - Supplement. 1835.

LUTZ, Markus
[Vollstandige Beschreibung des Schweizerlandes...].
Dictionnaire géographique-statistique de la Suisse.
1836-37. 2v.

MCCRACKAN, William D
Romance Switzerland. 1894.

MCCRACKAN, William D
Teutonic Switzerland. 1894.

222 Switzerland - geography, description (Cont.)

MAEDER, Herbert
[Die Berge der Schweiz]. The mountains of
Switzerland: the adventure of the high Alps. 1968.

MAEDER, Herbert
[Lockende Berge]. The lure of the mountains. 1975.

MANNING, Samuel
Swiss pictures drawn with pen and pencil.
Various eds.

MARTIN, Alexandre
La Suisse pittoresque et ses environs: tableau
general, descriptif, historique et statistique des
22 cantons, de la Savoie, d'une partie du Piemont
et du pays de Bade. 1835.

MARTIN, Alexandre
[La Suisse pittoresque...]. La Svizzera
pittoresca e suoi dintorni... 1836.

MEISSER, Christian
Die schöne Schweiz in 92 Kunstblättern. 1925.

MERIAN, Matthaeus
Topographia Helvetiae, Rhaetiae, et Valesiae: das
ist Beschreibung und eygentliche Abbildung der
vernehmsten Stätte... 1654.

- - Facsim. ed. [ca 1900].

MUIRHEAD, James F
A wayfarer in Switzerland. 3rd ed., rev. 1930.

NAC, Paul and TOURS, Constant de
Vingt jours en Suisse. [1892].

NICOLAS, R   and KLIPSTEIN, A
Die schöne alte Schweiz: die Kunst der Schweizer
Kleinmeister. 1926.

OSENBRÜGGEN, Eduard
Das Hochgebirge der Schweiz... 2. völlig umgearb.
Aufl. [1875].

- - 3.erweiterte Aufl. [ca 1880].

OSENBRÜGGEN, Eduard
[Das Hochgebirge der Schweiz...]. Alpes et
glaciers de la Suisse ...; soixante vues pittoresques... [1875].

Paysages suisses. [ca 1860].

PFAFF, Friedrich
Die Naturkräfte in den Alpen; oder, Physikalische
Geographie des Alpengebirges. 1877.

PICOT, J
Statistique de la Suisse; ou, État de ce pays des
vingt-deux Cantons dont il se compose... 1819.

PLANTIN, Jean Baptiste
Helvetia antiqua et nova; seu, Opus describens I.
Helvetiam... II. Antiquiora Helvetiae loca...
III. Populos Helvetiis finitimos... 1656.

POWYS, Llewelyn
Swiss essays. 1947.

RAMBERT, Eugène
Les Alpes suisses. 1866-75. 5v.

RAMBERT, Eugène
[Les Alpes suisses]. Aus den Schweizer Bergen:
Land und Leute. 1874.

RAMUZ, C   F
La Suisse Romande. 1936.

RICHARD
Merveilles et beautés de la nature en Suisse; ou,
Description de tout ce que la Suisse offre de
curieux et d'intéressant... 1824. 2v.

RION, Alphonse
Guide du botaniste en Valais. 1872.

ROOK, Clarence
Switzerland: the country and its people. 1907.

RUCHAT, Abraham
Les délices de la Suisse, une des principales
républiques de l'Europe. 1714. 4v.

RUNGE, H
La Suisse: collection de vues pittoresques avec
texte historique-topographique. 1866. 3v.

RUTHNER, Anton von
Die Alpenländer Oesterreichs und die Schweiz:
eine Parallele der Naturschönheiten des
österreichischen und Schweizer Hochlandes. 1843.

SAZERAC, Hilaire Léon and ENGELMANN, Gustav
Lettres sur la Suisse. 1823-32. 5v.

SCHMID, Walter
Romantic Switzerland mirrored in the literature
and graphic art of the 18th and 19th centuries.
1952.

SCHWABIK, Aurel
Switzerland in real life. 1938.

Die Schweiz: geographische, demographische,
politische, volkswirtschaftliche und
geschichtliche Studie, von Aug. Aeppli [and
others]. 1909.

Die Schweiz: Notizen über ihre Bereisung, ihre
wissenschaftlich-geographische Erforschung und
ihre Abbildung in Karte und Bild. 1864.

SCHWEIZERISCHE BUNDESBAHNEN
Summer in Switzerland. 1924.

SCHWEIZERISCHE GEODÄTISCHE COMMISSION
Das Schweizerische Dreiecknetz. 1. Bd. Die
Winkelmessungen und Stationsausgleichungen. 1881.

SCHWEIZERISCHE GESELLSCHAFT FÜR BALNEOLOGIE UND
KLIMATOLOGIE
Health resorts of Switzerland: spas, mineral
waters, climatic resorts and sanatoria. 3rd ed.
[ca 1925].

SCHWEIZERISCHE VERKEHRSZENTRALE
On the Swiss alpine roads = Sur les routes
alpestres suisses. [1927?].

SCHWEIZERISCHES ALPINES MUSEUM
Katalog, 1908 [- Katalog IV, 1917] der Zentralstelle für alpine Projektionsbilder, Lanternbilder [of the] S.A.C. 1911-18. 4v. in 1.

SCHWEIZERISCHES ALPINES MUSEUM
Ein Rundgang durch das Schweizerische Alpine
Museum in Bern. 1934.

SCHWEIZERISCHES ALPINES MUSEUM
[Ein Rundgang...]. Une visite au Musée Alpin
Suisse à Berne. 1935.

SEIPPEL, Paul
La Suisse au dix-neuvième siècle. 1899-1901. 3v.

SHOBERL, Frederic
Switzerland; containing a description of the
character, manners, customs ... of the inhabitants of the twenty-two cantons in particular.
[1827].

SIMLER, Josias
De republica Helvetiorum libri duo... 1577.

SIMLER, Josias
[De republica Helvetiorum]. Helvetiorum respublica; diversorum autorum quorum nonnulli nunc
primum in lucem prodeunt. 1627.

SIMLER, Josias
Respublica Helvetiorum: hoc est exacta tum
communis totius Helvetiae, et singulorum pagorum,
politiae; tum rerum ab initio foedere gestarum,
descriptio... 1608.

222 Switzerland - geography, description (Cont.)

SIMLER, Josias
[Respublica Helvetiorum]. La Republique des
Suisses. 6e éd., rev. et nouvellement augm. 1939.

SIMLER, Josias
Vallesiae descriptio, libri duo. De alpibus
commentarius. 1574.

SIMLER, Josias
Vallesiae et Alpium descriptio. 1633.

SMYTHE, Frank S
Swiss winter ... from photographs by the author.
1948.

Souvenir de la Suisse. [1830?].

Souvenirs de la Suisse. [ca 1860].

SOWERBY, J
The forest cantons of Switzerland. 1892.

STANYAN, Abraham
An account of Switzerland. 1714.

STREIT, Conrad
Souvenir Schweiz... 1968.

STUCKART, Carl Friedrich
Neuestes Gemälde der Erde und ihrer Bewohner;
oder, Schilderung der vorzüglichsten Merkwürdigkeitn, der Sitten und Gebräuche ... der Völkerschaften aller Welttheile ... die Schweiz. 1824.

STUCKI, G
Schülerbüchlein für den Unterricht in der
Schweizer-Geographie. 7.Aufl. 1919.

La Suisse: étude géographique, démographique,
politique, économique et historique, par A. Aeppli
[and others]. [1908].

La Suisse illustrée. [1856?].

SWITZERLAND. Eidgenössisches Statistisches Bureau
Die Alpenwirthschaft der Schweiz im Jahre 1864.
1868.

SWITZERLAND. Eidgenössisches Topographisches Bureau
Hundert Jahre Eidg. Landestopographie, ehemaliges
Eidg. Topographisches Bureau, 1838-1938.
Erinnerungsmappe. 1938.

SWITZERLAND. Eidgenössisches Topographisches Bureau
La topographie de la Suisse, 1832-1864: histoire
de la Carte Dufour. 1898.

SWITZERLAND. Post-, Telegraphen- und
Telephonverwaltung
Schönheiten der Alpenstrassen: eine Auswahl
Schweizerischer Graphik ... [1930?]. 3 pts.

SWITZERLAND. Post-, Telegraphen- und
Telephonverwaltung
Die Schweizerischen Alpenpässe und die Postkurse
im Gebirge: offizielles illustriertes Posthandbuch.
2. verm. Aufl. 1893.

Switzerland and the Swiss: sketches of the country
and its famous men, by the author of Knights of
the frozen sea. 1877.

TASSIN, Nicolas
Description de tous les cantons, villes, bourgs,
villages, et autres particularitez du pays des
suisses, avec une briève forme de leur République
... 1639.

TISSOT, Victor
[La Suisse inconnue]. Unknown Switzerland. 12th
ed. [1890].

- - Another ed. 1900.

Über die Schweiz und die Schweizer. 1795-96.
2v. in 1.

Vues de la Suisse. [ca 1860].

Vues remarquables des montagnes de la Suisse, avec
leur description; [dessinées par C. Wolf; avec
préface par A. von Haller...]. 1776.

- - Another ed. 1785.

WAGNER, Bruno
The alpine highways of Switzerland. 1950.

WAGNER, Johann Jacob
Mercurius Helveticus: fürstellend die Denk- und
Schauwürdigsten vornemsten Sachen urd Seltsam-
keiten der Eidgnossschaft... 1701.

WARING, Samuel Miller
The travellers' fire-side: a series of papers on
Switzerland, the Alps... 1819.

WEBB, Frank
Switzerland of the Swiss. 1909.

ZIEGLER, J   M
Erläuterungen zur Karte der Schweiz... 1852.

- - Erläuterungen zur neuen Karte... 1857.
- - Erläuterungen zur dritten Karte... 1866.

ZIEGLER, J   M
Sammlung absoluter Höhen der Schweiz und der
angrenzenden Gegenden der Nachberländer, als
Ergänzung der Karte in Reduction von 1 : 380000 =
Hypsometrie de la Suisse... 1853.

ZIEGLER, J   M
Zur Hypsometrie der Schweiz und zur Orographie der
Alpen: Erlauterungen für die hypsometrische Karte
der Schweiz. 1866.

ZSCHOKKE, Heinrich
Die klassischen Stellen der Schweiz und deren
Hauptorte in Originalansichten dargestellt.
1836-38. 2v.

222.5 People, living conditions, costume

BAUD-BOVY, Daniel
Peasant art in Switzerland. 1924.

ELZINGER, Ed.
Swiss dress. 1931.

KOENIG, Franz Nikolaus
[Neue Sammlung von Schweizertrachten...]. Alte
Schweizer Trachten. 1924.

KOENIG, Franz Nikolaus
[Neue Sammlung von Schweizertrachten...]. Nouvelle
collection de costumes suisses. 1813.

LARDEN, Walter
Inscriptions from Swiss chalets: a collection of
inscriptions found outside and inside Swiss
chalets, storehouses, and sheds. 1913.

LASSALLE, L
Costumes suisses des 22 cantons. [ca 1868].

LORY, Gabriel, 1763-1840 and LORY, Gabriel, 1784-1846
12 Schweizertrachtenbilder. [ca 1930].

RAMUZ, C   F
Le village dans la montagne. [1908].

REINHARDT, Johann Christian
A collection of Swiss costumes, in miniature.
[1822].

STALDER, Franz Joseph
Die Landessprachen der Schweiz; oder,
Schweizerische Dialektologie, mit kritischen Sprach-
bemerkungen beleuchtet; nebst der Gleichnissrede
von dem verlorenen Sohne in allen Schweizer-
mundarten. 1819.

222.5 Switzerland - people, ... costume (Cont.)

YOSY, A
Switzerland, as now divided into nineteen cantons
...; with picturesque representations of the dress
and manners of the Swiss. 1815. 2v.

223 Regions

223.1 Valais (Wallis)

ACHARD, Paul
Hommes et chiens du Grant-Saint-Bernard. 1937.

ANNELER, Hedwig
Lötschen, das ist: Landes- u. Volkskunde des
Lötschentales. 1917.

ARNOLD, P
Der Simplon: zur Geschichte des Passes und des
Dorfes. [1948].

BARBEY, Frédéric
La route du Simplon. 1906.

BAUD-BOVY, Daniel
À travers les Alpes: [de Brigue à l'Eggishorn et
au glacier d'Aletsch]. 1899.

BAUD-BOVY, Daniel
[À travers les Alpes...]. Wanderungen in den
Alpen: von Brieg auf das Eggischhorn, den Aletsch-
gletscher und Umgebung... 1899.

BAUD-BOVY, Daniel
La Dent du Midi, Champéry et le Val d'Illiez;
avec la collaboration de H.-F. Montagnier...
1923.

BAXTER, Wynne E
Quiet resting places in the Swiss highlands:
Evolena, Ferpècle, Arolla. [1898].

BÉRARD, Clément
Au coeur d'un vieux pays: légendes et traditions
du Valais. 2e éd. 1928.

BESSE, Eugène
Un voyage au Giétroz, vallée de Bagnes (Valais,
Suisse) en 1863. 1864.

BLANC,   chanoine
Examen de l'apologie des travaux du glacier du
Giétroz. 1825.

BLANC,   chanoine
Observations sur les travaux que le Gouvernement
du Valais fait exécuter au glacier de Giétroz,
vallée de Bagnes, dans le dessein de prévenir une
nouvelle débâcle. 1825.

BLANC,   chanoine
Réflexions sur la réponse de M. l'ingénieur Venetz
à deux lettres concernant les travaux du glacier
du Giétroz, vallée de Bagnes, en Valais, écrites
par le chanoine Blanc à M. Gard. 1825.

BOCCARD, François
Histoire du Vallais, avant et sous l'ère
chrétienne jusqu'à nos jours. 1844.

BRIDEL, Philippe Sirice
Course à l'éboulement du glacier de Gétroz et au
lac de Mauvoisin, au fond de la vallée de Bagnes,
16 mai 1818. [1818].

BRIDEL, Philippe Sirice
Essai statistique sur le canton de Vallais. 1820.

BUDRY, Paul and KÄMPFEN, Werner
Le chemin de Zermatt: petite encyclopédie pratibornienne à l'usage des touristes curieux. 1941.

BUDRY, Paul and RIVAZ, Paul de
Villes et régions d'art de la Suisse =
schweizerische Kunststätten. [1943]. 3v.

BÜHLER, Fritz
Der Gornergrat und die Walliser Alpenpässe, mit
geschichtlichen Notizen. 1894.

BURNAT-PROVINS, Marguerite
Petits tableaux valaisans. 1903.

CÉRÉSOLE, Alfred
Zermatt et ses environs: description, histoire et
légendes. [ca 1891].

CHASTONAY, Paul de
Au Val d'Anniviers. [1939].

CHASTONAY, Paul de
Sierre et son passé. 1942.

CHASTONAY, Paul de
Vercorin: le vieux village. [1943].

CINGRIA, Charles Albert
Le parcours du Haut Rhône; ou, La Julienne et
l'ail sauvage. 1944.

CLAPARÈDE, Arthur de
Champéry et le Val d'Illiez: histoire et description. 1886.

- - 2e éd., rev. et augm. 1890.

COCKBURN, James
Views to illustrate the route of the Simplon.
[1822].

CONWAY, William Martin, Baron Conway
[Zermatt pocket book: a guide to the Pennine
Alps...]. Die Penninischen Alpen: ein Führer für
Bergsteiger durch das Gebiet der Penninischen
Alpen zwischen Simplon und Grossen St. Bernhard.
1891.

COOLIDGE, William Augustus Brevoort
Les colonies vallaisannes de l'Oberland bernois.
[1906].

COQUOZ, Louis
Histoire et description de Salvan-Fins-Hauts,
avec petite notice sur Trient. 1899.

CORONA, Giuseppe
Mont Blanc or Simplon? 1880.

DESBUISSONS, Léon
La vallée de Binn, Valais: étude géographique,
géologique, minéralogique et pittoresque... 1909.

DESOR, Édouard
Le Val d'Anniviers. 1855.

DUBI, Heinrich
Saas-Fee und Umgebung: ein Führer durch Geschichte
Volk und Landschaft des Saastales. 1902.

- - 2.Aufl. 1946.

ECKENSTEIN, Oscar and LORRIA, August
The Alpine portfolio: the Pennine Alps, from the
Simplon to the Great St. Bernard. [1889].

ECKSTEIN, Oskar
Seitenpfade um Saas-Fee. 3.Aufl. 1941.

ENGEL, Claire Éliane
La vallée de Saas. 1948.

FEHRMANN, Rudolf
Der Bergsteiger in der sächsischen Schweiz: Führer
durch die Kletterfelson des Elbsandsteingebirges.
1908.

- - Nachtrag. 1927.

FISCHER, Eugen
Mein Wallis: Festgabe zum Walliser Herbstfest in
Zürich, 29. und 30. Oktober 1921. 1921.

FLEMWELL, George
Villars and its environs. 1914.

223.1 <u>Valais (Wallis)</u> (<u>Cont.</u>)

FOLLONIER, Jean
  Peuple des montagnes. 1945.

FRÖBEL, Julius
  Reise in die weniger bekannten Thäler auf der
  Nordseite der Pennischen Alpen. 1840.

GARBELY, Leo
  Die Pfarrkirche von Münster (Goms): Monographie.
  1949.

GAROLA, Ruggiero
  Il Monte Bianco ed il Sempione: studii di confronto. 1881.

GAY, Hilaire
  Histoire du Vallais depuis les temps les plus
  anciens jusqu'à nos jours. 2e éd., rev. 1903.

GENTINETTA, Richard
  Das alte schöne Wallis: Skizze mit Bildern. 1943.

GESCHICHTSFORSCHENDE VEREIN VON OBERWALLIS
  Walliser Sagen. 1.Bd. 1907.

GESCHICHTSFORSCHENDE VEREIN VON OBERWALLIS
  [Walliser Sagen]. Blätter aus der Walliser
  Geschichte. 9.Bd, 4. Jahrg. Festschrift zum 75.
  Geburtstag von Dionys Imesch. 1943.

GESCHICHTSFORSCHENDE VEREIN VON OBERWALLIS
  [Walliser Sagen]. Légendes valaisannes, d'après
  les "Walliser Sagen" de la Société d'Histoire du
  Haut-Valais. 1931.

GEX, F
  Le Petit-Saint-Bernard: le "Mystère", le Col, les
  routes, l'Hospice, les voyageurs. 1924.

GOS, François
  Zermatt et sa vallée. 1925.

GOS, François
  [Zermatt et sa vallée]. Zermatt and its valley.
  1926.

GOS, François
  [Zermatt et sa vallée]. Zermatt und seiner Tal.
  1925.

GRABER, Alfred and SCHÄTZ, Josef Julius
  Walliser Alpen. 1931.

GROSS, Jules
  L'Hospice du Grand Saint-Bernard. [1935?].

GUEX, Jules
  La montagne et ses noms: études de toponymie
  alpine. 1946.

HEUSSER, Chr.
  Das Erdbeben im Visperthal, Kanton Wallis, vom
  Jahr 1855. 2.Ausg. 1856.

HOEK, Henry
  Zermatt: zwischen Matterhorn und Monterosa,
  zwischen Weisshorn und Dom: ein Buch für Berg-
  Freunde. 1936.

HOTELS SEILER, <u>Zermatt</u>
  Einweihung der Gedenktafel am Hotel Monte Rosa und
  des Hallenbades beim Hotel Mont Cervin im Rahmen
  einer Presse-Empfanges vom 22. bis 24. April 1970.
  1970.

HOTELS SEILER, <u>Zermatt</u>
  Hotels Seiler, Zermatt, 1855-1930: [Festschrift
  ... im Rahmen des diamantenen Jubiläums]. 1930.

JEGERLEHNER, Johannes
  Das Val d'Anniviers, Eivischtal, nebst einem
  Streifzug ins Val d'Herens, Evolena: Führer durch
  Landschaft, Geschichte Volk und Sage eines Walliser
  Hochtales. 1904.

KÄMPFEN, Peter Joseph
  Freiheitskämpfe der Oberwalliser in den Jahren
  1798 & 1799. 1867.

KÄMPFEN, Werner
  Ein Burgerrechtsstreit im Wallis. 1942.

LA HARPE, Eugène de
  Les Alpes valaisannes. 1911.

LANDSEER, John
  Some account of the dogs and of the pass of the
  Great Saint Bernard. [1831].

LE COMTE, Jean
  Étude monographique de la vallée de Saas. 1926
  [cover 1928].

LE GALLAIS, A
  Chroniques du Mont Saint-Bernard. 1860.

LEHNER, Karl
  Kleine Zermatter Chronik. 1949.

LEHNER, Karl
  [Kleine Zermatter Chronik]. A pocket history of
  Zermatt. [1952].

LOGES, Chrétien de
  Essais historiques sur le Mont St. Bernard. 1789.

LOVEY-TROILLET, Ernest
  La Val Ferret. [1945].

LUNN, <u>Sir</u> Arnold
  Guide to Montana and district. 1907.

LUNN, <u>Sir</u> Arnold
  [Guide to Montana...]. Guide de Montana et des
  environs. 1908.

LUNN, <u>Sir</u> Arnold
  [Guide to Montana...]. Führer von Montana und
  Umgebung. 1908.

LUNN, <u>Sir</u> Arnold
  Zermatt and the Valais. 1955.

MALBY, Reginald A
  With camera and rücksack in the Oberland and
  Valais. [1913].

MARIÉTAN, Ignace
  Âme et visages du Valais. 1949.

MARIÉTAN, Ignace
  Val d'Anniviers, Val d'Herens: descriptions de 42
  itinéraires avec profils... 1954.

MONOD, Jules
  Sion, Les Mayens, Val d'Herens, vallée d'Héremence,
  Evolène, Arolla: histoire, descriptions, excur-
  sions. [1907?].

MONOD, Jules
  Zermatt et Saas-Fée: descriptions, histoire, ascensions, excursions... [1904?].

PORTIER, Francis
  Grimenz, village valaisan. [1919?].

RAMUZ, C F
  Vues sur le Valais. 1943.

Rapport sur l'état actuel de la vallée de Bagne dans
  le canton du Valais, relativement aux mesures
  propres à la prémunir contre l'effet destructeur
  du glacier inférieur de Gétroz; présenté au
  Gouvernement du canton du Valais par la Commission
  chargée de cet examen. 1821.

ROGER, Noelle
  Saas-Fée et la vallée de la Viège de Saas. 1902.

RUPPEN, Peter Joseph
  Die Chronik des Thales Saas, für die Thalbewohner.
  1851.

SANKT NIKLAUS (Parish)
  Familien-Statistik der löblichen Pfarrei von St.
  Niklaus; gesammelt und geordnet von Peter Joseph
  Ruppen. 1861.

223.1 Valais (Wallis) (Cont.)

SCHINER, Hildebrand
Description du Département du Simplon, ou de la
ci-devant République du Valais. 1812.

SCHMID, Hans
Wallis: ein Wanderbuch. 3.Aufl. 1935.

SCHMID, Walter
Komm mit mir ins Wallis. 2.Aufl. [1945].

SENNETT, A   R
Across the Great Saint Bernard: the modes of nature
and the manners of man. 1904.

SIEGEN, Johann
Gletschermärchen für Gross und Klein aus dem
Lötschenthal. [ca 1919].

SIEGEN, Johann
Das Lötschental: Führer für touristen, Abhandlung
über eines der eigentümlichsten Täler der
Schweizer Alpen. [1929].

SIEGEN, Johann
The Lötschental. 1960.

SOLANDIEU
Légendes valaisannes. [1919].

SOLANDIEU
Le Valais pittoresque. 1910.

Souvenir de Loëche, la Ghemmi et les environs. [1851].

STRAWBRIDGE, Anne West
Shadows of the Matterhorn. [ca 1950].

STYLES, Showell
Backpacking in Alps and Pyrenees. 1976.

TAMINI, Jean Émile and QUAGLIA, Lucien
Châtellenie de Granges, Lens, Gróne, St-Léonard
avec Chalais-Chippis. 1942.

TAMINI, Jean Émile and DELÈZE, Pierre
Essai d'histoire de la vallée d'Illiez. 2e éd.
1924.

THIOLY, François
De Genève à Zermatt par le Val d'Anniviers et le
col du Trift. 1867.

THOMPSON, Jane Dee
The Great Saint Bernard Pass and Hospice and the
life of Saint Bernard de Menthon. 1929.

TROLLIET, Marie
Un vieux pays: croquis valaisans. 2e éd. 1892.

ULRICH, Melchior
Die Seitenthäler des Wallis und der Monterosa.
1850.

Vallées perdues. 1947.

VALLETTE, Pierre
Évolène. [1942].

VALLETTE, Pierre
Le miracle des cloches: contes et poèmes
valaisans. 1937.

VAUTIER, Auguste
Au pays des Bisses. 1928.

- - 2e éd., rev. et augm. 1942.

VENETZ, Ignace
Apologie des travaux du glacier de Giétroz contre
les attaques réitérées de M. le chanoine Blanc.
1825.

VIOLLIER, Edmond W
Le Val de Bagnes, Chables, Lourtier, Fionnay,
canton du Valais (Suisse). [1902].

VITTOZ, Ed.
Le Valais. [1928]. 24 pts.

WAGNON, Aug.
Finhaut et la vallée du Trient: excursions -
escalades de la Dent-du-Midi au Mont-Blanc. 3e
éd... 1903.

WALLIS, C   S
Sierre and Montana. [1894?].

WESTON, Stephen
La Scava; or, Some account of an excavation of a
Roman town on the hill of Chatelet, in Champagne...
to which is added, A journey to the Simplon, by
Lausanne, and to Mont Blanc, through Geneva. 1818.

WILLIAMS, Cicely
A church in the Alps: a century of Zermatt and the
English. 1970.

WILLIAMS, Cicely
Zermatt saga. 1964.

WILSON, Henry Schütz
A quiet day in the Alps. [1878].

WOLF, Ferdinand Otto and CÉRÉSOLE, Alfred
Valais and Chamonix. [18--].

WOLF, Ferdinand Otto
Valais et Chamounix. [ca 1900]. 2v.

WUNDT, Theodor
Zermatt und seine Berge. Neue ... Aufl. 1930.

YUNG, Émile
Zermatt et la vallée de la Viège. 1894.

YUNG, Émile
[Zermatt et la vallée de la Viège]. Zermatt and
the valley of the Viège. 1894.

ZERMATT (Parish)
Familien-Statistik der löblichen Pfarrei von
Zermatt, mit Beilagen; gesammelt und geordnet von
Joseph Ruden. 1869.

ZERMATT (Parish)
Familien-Statistik und Geschichtliches über die
Gemeinde Zermatt. [New ed.] von Stanislaus Kronig.
1927.

Zermatt. [19--].

ZERMATTEN, Maurice
Chapelles valaisannes: le visage pittoresque et
religieux du Valais. 1941.

ZERMATTEN, Maurice
Nourritures valaisannes. 1938.

ZERMATTEN, Maurice
Les saisons valaisannes. 1948.

ZERMATTEN, Maurice
Le Valais. 1941.

223.2 Bernese Oberland

BAUD-BOVY, Daniel
L'Oberland bernois. 1926.

BONNEY, Thomas George
Lake and mountain scenery from the Swiss Alps.
1874.

Chemin de Fer du Simplon; Genève-Lausanne-Milan et
Turin; Oberland bernois. [19--].

COOLIDGE, William Augustus Brevoort
Die älteste Schutzhütte im Berner Oberland: ein
Beitrag zur Geschichte der bernischen Touristik:
Jubiläumsschrift. 1915.

COOLIDGE, William Augustus Brevoort
Die Petronella-Kapelle in Grindelwald. 1911.

223.2 Bernese Oberland (Cont.)

COOLIDGE, William Augustus Brevoort
  Die Ueberschreitung des Berner Hochgebirges im
  Jahre 1712. 1913.

DUVAL, M
  La grande caravane: seize jours dans l'Oberland
  (12-27 juillet 1854). 1855.

EBERHARD, Otto
  Heures de liberté de Lionel Morton. [1916].

FISCHER, H
  Souvenir de l'Oberland bernois: vues & costumes
  d'après nature. [ca 1850].

GEORGE, Hereford Brooke
  The Oberland and its glaciers explored and
  illustrated with ice-axe and camera. 1866.

GMELCH, Jos.
  Das Birnhorn und seine Umgebung. 1909.

GRANDE, Julian
  The Bernese Oberland in summer and winter: a
  guide. 1911.

GURTNER, Othmar
  Das besinnliche Wanderbüchlein: auf alten Pfaden
  im Lauterbrunnental. [1924].

GURTNER, Othmar
  Grindelwald: Festgabe zum 17. Grossen Skirennen
  der Schweiz, 1923. 1923.

Herbst-Tage im Berner Oberlande. 1872.

KASTHOFER, Karl
  Bemerkungen über die Wälder und Alpen des
  bernerischen Hochgebirgs: ein Beitrag zur
  Bestimmung der Vegetationsgrenze schweizerischer
  Holzarten... 2.verm. und verb. Aufl. 1818.

KEMPF, H
  Das Berner Oberland: praktischer Reiseführer.
  2.neubearb. Aufl. 1911.

LA HARPE, Eugène de
  Les Alpes bernoises. 1915.

LANGHANS, Daniel
  Beschreibung verschledener Merkwürdigkeiten des
  Siementhals, eines Theils des Bernergebiets...
  1753.

LUNN, Sir Arnold
  The Bernese Oberland. 1958.

- - Rev. and enl. ed. 1973.

MEISNER, Friedrich
  Friedrich Meisners Alpenreise mit seinem Zöglingen,
  für die Jugend beschrieben. 1801.

MEISNER, Friedrich
  Reise durch das Berner Oberland, nach Unterwalden
  ... 1821.

MULLER, August
  À travers l'Oberland bernois. 1891.

OBER, P
  Interlacren et ses environs. 1841.

- - 3e éd. 1861.

OBER, P
  L'Oberland bernois sous les rapports historique,
  scientifique et topographique: journal d'un
  voyageur. 1858. 2v.

Oberland bernois. [ca 1900].

Picturesque tour through the Oberland in the canton
  of Berne, in Switzerland. 1823.

RAWNSLEY, Hardwicke Drummond
  Flower-time in the Oberland. 1904.

RHODES, Daniel P
  A pleasure-book of Grindelwald. 1903.

ROTH, Abraham
  Gletscherfahrten in den Berner Alpen. 1861.

ROTHER, Rudolf
  Berner Oberland: Bilder von den Bergen, Seen und
  Tälern zwischen Aare, Rhone und Simme. 1924.

SCHWEIZER ALPEN-CLUB. Section Oberland
  Verzeichniss der patentirten Berg-Führer im
  Berner Oberland. [1882].

Souvenir de l'Oberland bernois. [ca 1890].

STAPFER, Philipp Albert
  Voyage pittoresque de l'Oberland; ou, Description
  de vues prises dans l'Oberland, district du canton
  de Berne. 1812.

STUDER, Gottlieb
  Panorama vom Mänlichen (Berner Oberland) 2345m.
  [1874].

STUDER, Gottlieb
  Das Panorama von Bern: Schilderung der in Berns
  Umgebungen sichtbaren Gebirge. 1850.

STUDER, Gottlieb
  Topographische Mittheilungen aus dem Alpengebirge.
  1. Die Eiswüsten und selten betretenen Hochalpen
  und Bergspitzen des Kantons Bern und angrenzender
  Gegenden. 1843.

- - 2.Ausg. 1844. 2v.

STYLES, Showell
  Backpacking in Alps and Pyrenees. 1976.

SWITZERLAND. Post-, Telegraphen- und
Telephonverwaltung
  Grimselpass: Poststrasse Meiringen-Grimsel-Gletsch.
  [1934?].

TÄUBER, Carl
  Die Berner Hochalpen. 2.Aufl. [1908].

Taschenbuch für Reisende im Berner Oberlande, um und
  auf den Seen von Thun und Brienz... 1829.

URECH, Charles
  Bernese Oberland, descriptive and narrative. 1926.

VEAZEY, Harry G
  The epic of Adelboden ...: the silver jubilee
  booklet of the Adelboden parties of S. Mark's,
  Camberwell, S.E. 5. [1951].

VOGT, Carl
  Im Gebirg und auf den Gletschern. 1843.

WALTHARD, Rod.
  Nouvelle description de l'Oberland bernois à
  l'usage des voyageurs. 1838.

WALTON, Elijah
  The Bernese Oberland: twelve scenes among its peaks
  and lakes. 1874.

WOOD, Edith Elmer
  An Oberland chalet. [1911].

WUNDT, Theodor
  Die Jungfrau und das Berner Oberland. [1897].

- - 2.Aufl. [ca 1900].

WYSS, Johann Rudolf
  Reise in das Berner Oberland. 1816-17. 2v.

WYSS, Johann Rudolf
  [Reise in das Berner Oberland]. Voyage dans
  L'Oberland bernois. 1817. 2v.

WYTTENBACH, Jacob Samuel
  Instruction pour les voyageurs qui vont voir les
  glaciers & les Alpes du canton de Berne. 1787.

223.2 Bernese Oberland (Cont.)

ZÜRCHER, Otto
  Das Berner Oberland im Lichte der deutschen
  Dichtung. 1923.

223.3 Forest Cantons (Waldstätten)

BALTHASAR, Joseph Anton Felix von
  Historische, topographische und oekonomische Merkwürdigkeit des Kantons Luzern, seinen Mitbürgern
  gewidmet. 1785-89. 3v.

BECKER, Fridolin
  Über den Klausen: auf neuer Gebirgsstrasse zwischen
  Ur- und Ost-Schweiz... 1900.

BRENNWALD, Alfred
  Vues pittoresques du lac des Quatre Cantons et de
  ses environs. [ca 1890].

BÜHLER, Alfred
  Das Meiental im Kanton Uri. 1928.

BUSINGER, Joseph Maria
  Itinéraire du Mont-Righi et du lac des 4 Cantons,
  précédé de la description de la ville de Lucerne
  et de ses environs. 1815.

CATTANI, C
  Das Alpenthal Engelberg und seine Berg-, Wasser-,
  Milch-, und Molkenkuren. 1852.

CHRIST, H
  Ob dem Kernwald: Schilderungen aus Obwaldens Natur
  und Volk. 1869.

CYSAT, Johann Leopold
  Beschreibung dess Beruhmsten Lucerner-oder 4.
  Waldstätten Sees und dessen Furtrefflichen
  Qualiteten und Sonderbaaren Engenschafften... 1661.

ESCHER VON DER LINTH, Hans Conrad
  Relation succincte de l'écroulement de la montagne
  au-dessus de Goldau, canton de Schwytz le 2. septembre 1806. 1806.

FLEINER, Albert
  Engelberg: Streifzüge durch Gebirg und Tal. [1890].

FLEMWELL, George
  Lucerne. 1913.

HEER, J   C
  Guide to Lucerne, the lake, and its environs...
  14th ed. 1905.

HEER, J   C
  The Lake of Lucerne and the Forest Cantons: album.
  1900.

KESSER, Hermann
  Luzern der Vierwaldstätter See und der St.
  Gotthard. [1908].

Panorama des Vierwaldstätter-See's und seinen
  Umgebungen. [ca 1850].

REZNICEK, Felicitas von
  Das Buch von Engelberg: Vergangenheit und Gegenwart eines Kurortes. 1964.

TÜRLER, E   A
  Die Berge am Vierwaldstätter-See... 1888.

Voyage pittoresque au lac des Waldstettes ou des IV
  Cantons. 1817.

ZAY, Karl
  Goldau und seine Gegend, wie sie war und was sie
  geworden. 1807.

223.4 Glarus

BUSS, Ernst and HEIM, Albert
  Der Bergsturz von Elm den 11. September 1881:
  Denkschrift. 1881.

EBEL, Johann Gottfried
  Schilderung der Gebirgsvölker der Schweitz.
  1798-1802. 2v.

HEGETSCHWEILER, Johann
  Reisen in den Gebirgstock zwischen Glarus und
  Graubünden in den Jahren 1819, 1820 und 1822.
  1825.

PETERSEN, Theodor
  Das Klönthal und der Glärnisch, Kanton Glarus.
  [ca 1865].

SCHULER, Johann Melchior
  Die Linth-Thäler. 1814.

223.5 St. Gall, Appenzell

Ansichten aus dem Alpstein, Kanton Appenzell,
  Schweiz. 1863.

EBEL, Johann Gottfried
  Schilderung der Gebirgsvölker der Schweiz. 1798-
  1802. 2v.

KUSCH, Gabriel
  Der Kanton Appenzell, historisch, geographisch,
  statistisch geschildert ...: ein Hand-und Hausbuch
  für Kantonsbürger und Reisende. 1835.

LÜTHI, Gottlieb and EGLOFF, Carl
  Das Säntis-Gebiet: illustrierter Touristenführer.
  3.neurev. Aufl. 1913.

- - 6.Aufl. neu bearb. von Karl Kleine. 1946.

RAST, Pius
  St. Gallen. 1960.

223.6 Grisons (Graubünden)

ALBANEDER, Joseph Theodor
  Der Sauerbrunnen zu Obladis, im Oberinnthal, k.k.
  Landgerichts Reid, als Trink- und Bad- kurort.
  1835.

AMSTUTZ, Walter
  Das goldene Buch vom Engadin. 1936.

ANDREA, Silvia
  Das Bergell: Wanderungen in der Landschaft und
  ihrer Geschichte. 1901.

BILL, A   F
  Davos as health-resort: a handbook containing contributions by A.F. Bill [and others]. 1906.

BRUNIES, Stephan
  Bilder aus dem Schweizerischen Nationalpark und
  seiner Umgebung. 1919.

BRUNIES, Stephan
  Der Schweizerische Nationalpark. 1914.

BRUNIES, Stephan
  [Der Schweizerische Nationalpark]. Le Parc
  national suisse. 1925.

CAMENISCH, Carl
  Graubünden in der deutschen Dichtung. 1923.

CAVIEZEL, Michael
  Das Oberengadin: ein Führer auf Spaziergängen
  kleinen und grossen Touren. 1876.

- - 2. veränderte und verm. Aufl. 1881.

CAVIEZEL, Michael
  [Das Oberengadin...]. Tourist's guide to the
  Upper Engadine. 1877.

223.6 Grisons (Graubünden) (Cont.)

CAVIEZEL, Michael
    [Das Oberengadin ...]. The Upper Engadine: a
    guide to walks and tours, short and long. 5th
    enl. and improved ed. 1891.

COOLIDGE, William Augustus Brevoort
    La Haute-Engadine et le Bregaglia à travers les
    siècles: histoire et bibliographie. 1894.

Das Engadine und die Engadiner: Mittheilungen an dem
    Sauerbrunnen bei St. Moritz im Kanton Bünden...
    1837.

FLAIG, Hermine and FLAIG, Walther
    Burgen an der Grenze: Erinnerungen und Bilder,
    Sagen und Geschichten aus dem Rhätikon zwischen
    Sulzfluh und Schesaplana. [1928?].

FLAIG, Walther
    Bernina: Erfahrungen und Erlebnisse. 1934-36. 3v.

FLAIG, Walther
    Hoch über Tälern und Menschen:im Banne der Bernina.
    1925.

FLAIG, Walther
    Das Silvretta-Buch: Volk und Gebirg über drei
    Ländern: Erinnerungen und Erkenntnisse eines Berg-
    steigers und Skitouristen. 4.verm und verb. Aufl.
    1954.

FRESHFIELD, Mrs. Henry
    A summer tour in the Grisons and Italian valleys
    of the Bernina. 1862.

The Grisons, Switzerland. [1922].

GYGER, W   J
    Guide to climbs in the Upper Engadine. 3rd ed.
    1925.

H., A.A.
    Where the world ends: a description of Arosa as a
    centre for summer holidays or winter sport and as
    a health resort for convalescents and invalids.
    1911.

HASSELBRINK, F
    Führer durch Graubündens Kurorte, Sommerfrischen
    und Sportplätze. [1907].

HEER, J   C
    Streifzüge im Engadin. 1907.

HILTBRUNNER, Hermann
    Graubünden. [1928]. 3v.

HILTBRUNNER, Hermann
    [Graubünden]. Les Grisons. [T.1.]. Le Rhin: la
    contrée de sa naissance. [1928].

HOEK, Henry
    Davos: ein Berg- und Wanderbuch. 1934.

HOEK, Henry
    Davos, Parsenn: Sommerwanderungen im Parsenn-
    gebiet. [1939].

HOEK, Henry
    Ma bella Engiadina: Ski und Schnee im Engadin.
    1933.

HOEK, Henry
    Parsenn: berühmte Abfahrten in Bildern und
    Buchstaben. 1932.

- - [New and rev. ed.]. 1939.

HOEK, Henry
    St. Moritz: Dorf, Bad, Campfèr; ein Führer und
    Reisebegleiter im Auftrag und unter Mitarbeit des
    Kur- und Verkehrs- Vereins St. Moritz. [1931].

KLINGER, Enrico
    Nel paese dei Grigioni: impressioni e note di
    viaggio... 1902.

KÜDER, G   W
    Der Kanton Graubünden, historisch, geographisch,
    statistisch geschildert... 1838.

LECHNER, Ernst
    Graubünden: illustrierter Reisebegleiter durch alle
    Talschaften. 1903.

- - 5.verb. Aufl. 1920.

LLOYD, Francis
    The physiography of the Upper Engadine. 1881.

LORRIA, August and MARTEL, Édouard Alfred
    Le massif de la Bernina. 1894.

METTIER, Peter
    Die Bergüner Berge. 1897.

- - Neue Aufl. 1924.

MEYER, J   J
    Voyage pittoresque dans le canton des Grisons en
    Suisse vers le Lac Majeur et le Lac de Come à
    travers les cols de Splugen et de St. Bernard.
    1827.

MUSSON, Spencer C
    The Engadine. 1924.

MUSSON, Spencer C
    The Upper Engadine. 1907.

PAPON, Jakob
    Engadin: Zeichnungen aus der Natur und dem Volks-
    leben eines unbekannten Alpenlandes. 1857.

PLANTA, A   von and KEKULÉ, A
    Chemische Untersuchung der Heilquellen zu St.
    Moritz im Kanton Graubünden. 1854.

POESCHEL, Erwin
    Das Burgenbuch von Graubünden. 1930.

POTTINGER, George
    St. Moritz: an alpine caprice. 1972.

ROTHPLETZ, A
    Geologischer Führer durch die Alpen. 1. Das Gebiet
    der zwei grossen rhätischen Uerberschiebungen
    zwischen Bodensee und dem Engadin. 1902.

RUDDER, May de
    Un montagnard grison [Nicolaus Sererhard] raconte
    en 1742. 1939.

SCHMID, Hans
    Bündnerfahrten: Engadin und südliche Täler. 1923.

SEREHARD, Nicolaus
    Einfalte Delineation aller Gemeinden gemeiner
    dreien Bünden nach der Ordnung der Hochgerichten
    eines jeden Bunds ... beschrieben ... im Jahr ...
    1742. 1872.

SPRECHER VON BERNEGG, Fortunat
    Rhetia, ubi eius verus situs, politia, bella,
    foedera, et alia memorabilia accuratissime des-
    cribuntur. 1633.

STOFFEL, Joh. Rud.
    Das Hochtal Avers, Graubünden: die höchstgelegene
    Gemeinde Europas. 1938.

STRICKLAND, F   de Beauchamp
    The Engadine: a guide to the district. 2nd ed.
    1891.

SWITZERLAND. Eidgenössische Nationalparkkommission
    Le Parc national suisse: guide officiel pour
    touristes. 1970.

SYMONDS, John Addington and SYMONDS, Margaret
    Our life in the Swiss highlands. 1892.

- - 2nd ed. 1907.

TESTER, Ch.
    Unter den Adlernestern: Erlebtes und Geschautes aus
    den Bergtälern Rheinwald und Safien. 1912.

223.6 Grisons (Graubünden) (Cont.)

THEOBALD, Gottfried
Das Bündner Oberland; oder, Der Vorderrhein mit
seinen Seitenthälern. 1861.

THEOBALD, Gottfried
Naturbilder aus den Rhätischen Alpen. 1860.

- - 2.verm. und verb. Aufl. 1862.
- - 4.umgearb. Aufl., von Chr. Tannuzzer. 1920.

Thusis, via Mala-Schyn. 1893.

TOLLEMACHE, Beatrix L
Grisons incidents in olden times. 1891.

TSCHARNER, J   K   von
Der Kanton Graubünden, historisch, statistisch,
geographisch, dargestellt für einheimische und
fremde Reisende. 1842.

TSCHARNER, Peter Conradin von
Wanderungen durch die Rhätischen Alpen: ein
Beytrag zur Charakteristik dieses Theils des
schweizerischen Hochlandes und seiner Bewohner.
1829-31. 2v.

TSCHUDI, Aegidius
De prisca ac vera Alpina Rhaetia, cum caetero
Alpinarum gentium tractu ... descriptio. 1538.

- - Another ed. 1560.

WISE, A   T   Tucker
The Alpine winter cure, with notes on Davos Platz,
Wiesen, St. Moritz, and the Maloja. New ed. 1884.

WOLGENSINGER, Michael
L'Engadine: terra Ladina. 1944.

ZINCKE, F   Barham
A walk in the Grisons, being a third month in
Switzerland. 1875.

223.7 Ticino, St. Gotthard

BERLEPSCH, Hermann Alexander von
Die Gotthard-Bahn, beschreibendes und
geschichtliches. 1881.

BRUSONI, Edmondo
Locarno, seine Umgebung und seine Thäler. 1899.

BUTLER, Samuel
Alps and sanctuaries of Piedmont and the Canton
Ticino (Op.6). 2nd ed. 1882.

- - New and enl. ed. 1913.

FRANSCINI, Stefano
Der Kanton Tessin, historisch, geographisch,
statistisch geschildert ...: ein Hand- und Hausbuch für Cantonsbürger und Reisende. 1835.

HARDMEYER, J
Locarno und seine Täler. 5.Aufl. [1923].

MECHEL, Chrétien de
Itinéraire du St. Gothard, d'une partie du Vallais
et des contrées de la Suisse que l'on traverse ...
pour se rendre au Gothard. 1795.

OSENBRÜGGEN, Eduard
Der Gotthard und das Tessin mit den Oberitalischen
Seen. 1877.

RAHN, Johann Rudolf
Wanderungen im Tessin: zur Erinnerung an der
Grenzdienst der 5. Division im Tessin 1915/16.
1917.

SCHMID, Hans
Spaziergänge im Tessin. 2.Aufl. 1909.

SPITTELER, Carl
Der Gotthard. 1897.

TÄUBER, Carl
Il Ticino. 1918.

TÜRLER, E   A
St. Gotthard, Airolo und Val Piora: pittoreske
Beschreibung der Natur und Landschaft des St.
Gotthardgebirges... 1891.

223.8 Emmental, Fribourg, Geneva, Zurich

BERLEPSCH, Hermann Alexander von
Der Rheinfall, der Zürich-See und der Wallen-See:
ein Führer für Fremde. 1858.

CORNAZ-VULLIET, C
En pays frigourgeois: manuel du voyageur. [1892?].

ESCHER, Hans Erhard
Beschreibung des Zürich Sees: wie auch von
Erbauung, Zunemmen, Stand und Wesen loblicher Statt
Zürich... 1692.

GALLI-VALERIO, B
Guide du massif de Naye: souvenirs de courses et
notes scientifiques. [1930?].

GRIBBLE, Francis
Geneva. 1908.

HÜRZELER, Jerome
Panorama du Napf (Righi d'Emmenthal). 1883.

KEATE, George
A short account of the ancient history, present
government, and laws of the Republic of Geneva.
1761.

KURZ, K   J   and GURTNER, Othmar
Zwischen Aare und Rhone. 1920.

LESCHEVIN, P   X
Voyage à Genève et dans la vallée de Chamouni, en
Savoie. 1812.

MALLET, H
Description de Genève, ancienne et moderne...
1807.

SCHWEIZER, Heinrich
Emmental 1 (Unteremmental): Lueggebiet, Oberwand-
gebiet, Lüdern - Napfgebiet. 1947.

SPON, Isaac
Histoire de Genève. 1730. 4v.

SPON, Isaac
Histoire de la ville et de l'état de Genève, depuis
les premiers siècles de la fondation de la ville
jusqu'à present. 2e éd., rev. & corr. 1682. 2v.

SPON, Isaac
[Histoire de la ville et de l'état de Genève...].
The history of the city and state of Geneva, from
its first foundation to this present time. 1687.

STRASSER, Gottfried
Der Napf: der Rigi des Emmenthals (1408m). 1883.

TREVES, Sir Frederick
The Lake of Geneva. 1922.

TÜRLER, E   A
Das malerische und romantische Emmenthal nebst den
angrenzenden Landestheilen: ein Wanderbuch...
1887.

223.9 Jura, Vaud, Lausanne, Montreux

BABILLOTTE, A
Führer durch die Vogesen und den elsässischen Jura.
3. ... Aufl. 1907-08.

BRIDEL, Philippe Sirice
Course de Bale à Vienne par les vallées du Jura.
1789.

223.9 Jura, Vaud, Lausanne, Montreux (Cont.)

BRIDEL, Philippe Sirice
Reise durch eine der romantischesten Gegenden der
Schweiz, 1788. 1789.

CÉRÉSOLE, Alfred
Légendes des Alpes vaudoises. 1885.

CHESSEX, Albert
Les Alpes vaudoises. 1949.

DELMARD, Sophia Duberly
Village life in Switzerland. 1865.

FLEMWELL, George
Lausanne and its environs. 1914.

GOS, François
Au pays des Muverans (les Alpes vaudoises). 1924.

GRIBBLE, Francis
Lausanne. 1909.

GRIBBLE, Francis
Montreux. 1908.

Itinéraire du pays de Vaud, du Gouvernement d'Aigle,
et du comte de Neuchatel et Vallengin. 1794.

RAMBERT, Eugène
Bex et ses environs: guide et souvenir. 1871.

SALISBURY, F S
Rambles in the Vaudese Alps. 1916.

SEYLAZ, Louis
Alpes vaudoises. 1948.

SEYLAZ, Louis
Nos Alpes vaudoises. 1924.

WURTISEN, Christian
Epitome historiae Basiliensis... 1577.

224 Switzerland - history, travel

ADAMS, Sir Francis Ottiwell and CUNNINGHAM, Carus
Dunlop
The Swiss Confederation. 1889.

BETTEX, Gustave and GUILLON, Édouard
Les Alpes suisses dans la littérature et dans
l'art. 1915.

BONJOUR, E
A short history of Switzerland. 1952.

BORDIER, Henri L
Le Grütli et Guillaume Tell; ou, Défense de la
tradition vulgaire su les origines de la
Confédération suisse. 1869.

BORDIER, Henri L
La querelle sur les traditions concernant l'origine
de la Confédération suisse. 1869.

BRAY, Anna Eliza
The mountains and lakes of Switzerland; with descriptive sketches of other parts of the continent.
1841. 3v.

CHASTONAY, Paul de
[Kardinal Schiner]. Le Cardinal Schiner. [1943].

CHERBULIEZ, A E
De la démocratie en Suisse. 1843. 2v.

CLERGET, Pierre
La Suisse au XXe siècle: étude économique et
sociale. 1908.

Le conservateur suisse; ou, Recueil complet des
étrennes helvétiennes. Ed. augm. 1813-31. 13v.

COOLIDGE, William Augustus Brevoort
History of the Swiss Confederation, with appendices
on Tell and Winkelried: a sketch. 1887.

COOLIDGE, William Augustus Brevoort
Swiss travel and Swiss guide-books. 1889.

DÄNDLIKER, Karl
A short history of Switzerland. 1899.

DAUDET, Alphonse
[Tartarin sur les Alpes...]. Tartarin in den
Alpen: neue Thaten des Helden von Tarascon.
[1897?].

DE BEER, Sir Gavin
Alps and men: pages from forgotten diaries of
travellers and tourists in Switzerland. 1932.

DE BEER, Sir Gavin
Escape to Switzerland. Services ed. 1945.

DE BEER, Sir Gavin
Speaking of Switzerland. 1952.

DE BEER, Sir Gavin
Travellers in Switzerland. 1949.

DEPPING, Georg Bernhard
La Suisse; ou, Tableau historique, pittoresque et
moral des cantons helvétiques. 1822. 4v.

ENGEL, Claire Éliane
La Suisse et ses amis. 1943.

L'état de la Suisse écrit en 1714. 1714.

Exhortation aux Suisses en générale pour leur conservation, contre les esmeutes & dangers du temps
présent. 1639.

GOLBÉRY, Marie Philippe de
Histoire et description de la Suisse et du Tyrol.
1838.

GOLBÉRY, Marie Philippe de
[Histoire et description de la Suisse...]. Storia
e descrizione della Svizzera e del Tirolo. 1840.

GOS, Charles
Au point 510: notes d'un observateur... 1932.

GOS, Charles
Généraux suisses: commandants en chef de l'Armée
Suisse de Marignan à 1914. 1932.

GOS, Charles
Voyageurs illustres en Suisse. 1937.

GROTE, George
Seven letters concerning the politics of Switzerland, pending the outbreak of the Civil War in
1847... 1876.

HARRY, A
Die historische Entwicklung der Schweizerischen
Verkehrswege, mit besonderer Berücksichtigung des
Transits und der Fluss-Schiffahrt. 1. Teil. Die
Grundlagen des Verkehrs und die historische Ent-
wicklung des Landverkehrs. 1911.

HÄUSSER, Ludwig
Die Sage vom Tell aufs neue kritisch untersucht:
eine... Preisschrift. 1840.

HALLER, Gottlieb Emanuel von
Erster Versuch einer kritischen Verzeichniss, aller
Schriften, welche die Schweiz ansehen. 1759.

HASLER (Firm)
Hasler, 1852-1952: hundert Jahre Fernmeldetechnik
und Präzisionsmechanik. 1952.

HEROLD, J Christopher
The Swiss without halos. 1948.

HUG, Lina and STEAD, Richard
Switzerland. [1891].

- - 2nd ed., rev. and enl. 1920.

ISTRIA, Dora d'
La Suisse allemande et l'ascension du Moench.
1856. 4v.

224 <u>Switzerland - history, travel</u> (<u>Cont</u>.)

ISTRIA, Dora d'
  [La Suisse allemande...]. Switzerland the pioneer
  of the Reformation... 1858. 2v.

JACCOTTET, G
  L'étape libératrice: scènes de la vie des soldats
  alliés internés en Suisse. 1918.

LANTIER, E   F
  Les voyageurs en Suisse. 1803. 3v.

LANTIER, E   F
  [Les voyageurs en Suisse]. Travellers in
  Switzerland; comprising descriptions ... conversations ... anecdotes of the principal literary
  characters resident in that country and France...
  1804. 6v.

LARDNER, Dionysius
  History of Switzerland. 1832.

LEE, Theresa Melville
  The story of Switzerland. 1885.

LLOYD, Henry Demarest
  The Swiss democracy: the study of a sovereign
  people. 1908.

LUNN, Sir Arnold
  The Englishman in the Alps, being a collection of
  English prose and poetry relating to the Alps.
  1913.

LUNN, Sir Arnold
  The Swiss and their mountains: a study of the
  influence of mountains on man. 1963.

LUNN, Sir Arnold
  Switzerland and the English. 1944 (1945 reprint).

LUNN, Sir Arnold
  Switzerland in English prose and poetry. 1947.

MULLER, Jean de
  Histoire de la Confédération suisse, par Jean de
  Muller, Robert Gloutz-Blozheim et J.-J. Hottinger.
  1837-51. 18v.

NEUGEBAUR, Dr.
  Neuestes Gemälde der Schweiz. 1831.

PEYER, Gustav
  Geschichte des Reisens in der Schweiz: eine cultur-
  geschichtliche Studie. 1885.

PROPIAC, <u>chevalier de</u>
  Beautés de l'histoire de la Suisse depuis l'époque
  de la confédération jusqu'à nos jours... 1817.

RILLIET, Albert
  Les origines de la Confédération suisse: histoire
  et légende. 2e éd., rev. et corr. 1869.

SCHAUB, Charles
  La Suisse historique et pittoresque... Ptie.2.
  La Suisse pittoresque. 1856.

SCHEUCHZER, Johann Jacob
  Historia Helvetiae. [1727?].

SCHINZ, Rudolf
  Ventrage zur nähern Kenntniss des Schweizerlandes.
  1783-87. 5v. in 2.

SCHIRMER, Gustav
  Die Schweiz im Spiegel englischer und
  amerikanischer Literatur bis 1848. 1929.

SCHWEIZERISCHER FREMDENVERKEHRSVERBAND
  Gegenwarts- und Zukunftsprobleme des
  Schweizerischen Fremdenverkehrs: Festgabe für
  Hermann Seiler. 1946.

SCOTTI, Ranutio
  Helvetia profana, e sacra. 1642. 2v.

SPENDER, Harold
  In praise of Switzerland, being the Alps in prose
  and verse. 1912.

STRAHL, Adolph
  Ein Sommer in der Schweiz: Reisebilder aus den
  Alpen. 1840.

SWITZERLAND. <u>Post-, Telegraphen- und
  Telephonverwaltung</u>
  Le centenaire des postes alpestres suisses. 1932.

SWITZERLAND. <u>Post-, Telegraphen- und
  Telephonverwaltung</u>
  [Le centenaire des postes...]. A century of Swiss
  alpine postal coaches. 1932.

TSCHUMI, Otto
  Urgeschichte der Schweiz. 1926.

VIEUSSEUX, A
  The history of Switzerland, from the first irrup-
  tion of the northern tribes to the present time...
  1846.

WÄBER, A
  Descriptions géographiques et récits de voyages et
  excursions en Suisse: contribution à la bibliographie de la littérature suisse des voyages de
  1891 à 1900 avec des suppléments relatifs à la
  période antérieure à 1891. 1909.

WALTER, L   Edna
  The fascination of Switzerland. 1912.

WILSON, John
  The history of Switzerland. [1832].

225 <u>Switzerland - visitors, up to 19th century</u>

ANDREAE, Johann Gerhard Reinhard
  Briefe aus der Schweiz nach Hannover geschrieben
  in dem Jare 1763. 1776.

BLAIKIE, Thomas
  [Diary of a Scotch gardener...]. Journal de
  Thomas Blaikie: excursions d'un botaniste écossais
  dans les Alpes et le Jura en 1775. 1935.

COXE, William
  Sketches of the natural, civil, and political state
  of Swisserland, in a series of letters to William
  Melmoth. 1779.

- - 2nd ed. 1780.

COXE, William
  [Sketches of the natural civil and political state
  of Swisserland]. Lettres de M. William Coxe à
  M.W. Melmoth, sur l'état politique, civil et
  naturel de la Suisse... 1781. 2v.

COXE, William
  [Sketches of the natural, civil, and political
  state of Swisserland...]. Briefe über den
  naturlichen, bürgerlichen und politischen Zustand
  der Schweiz, von Wilhelm Coxe an Wilhelm Melmoth.
  1781-91. 2v.

COXE, William
  Travels in Switzerland, in a series of letters to
  William Melmoth. 1789.

- - 3rd ed. 1794. 2v.
- - 4th ed. 1801. 3v.
- - New ed. 1802. 3v.

COXE, William
  [Travels in Switzerland]. Voyage en Suisse...
  1790. 3v.

DEVONSHIRE, Georgiana Cavendish, <u>Duchess of</u>
  Memorandums of the face of the country in
  Switzerland. 1799.

GRUNER, Gottlieb Sigmund
  Reisen durch die merkwürdigsten Gegenden Helvetiens.
  1778.

225 <u>Switzerland - visitors, to 19th century</u> (<u>Cont</u>.)

LABORDE, Jean Benjamin de
  Lettres sur la Suisse, adressées à Madame de M***
  par un voyageur françois. 1783. 2v.

LANGLE, <u>marquis de</u>
  Tableau pittoresque de la Suisse. Nouv. éd.
  [1791?].

LANGLE, <u>marquis de</u>
  [Tableau pittoresque de la Suisse]. A picturesque
  description of Switzerland. 1792.

- - Another ed. [1798].

LASCELLES, Rowley
  Journal of a short excursion among the Swiss landscapes, made in the summer of the year ninety-four.
  1803.

LASCELLES, Rowley
  Sketch of a descriptive journey through
  Switzerland, [by R. Lascelles] to which is added
  The passage of S. Gotthard, a poem by the Duchess
  of Devonshire. 1816.

LASCELLES, Rowley
  [Sketch of a descriptive journey...]. Scizze
  einer mahlerischen Reise durch die Schweiz. 1816.

MARTYN, Thomas
  Sketch of a tour through Swisserland with an
  accurate map. 1787.

- - New ed. 1788.

MAYER, Charles Joseph de
  Voyage de M. de Mayer en Suisse en 1784; ou,
  Tableau historique, civil, politique et physique
  de la Suisse. 1786. 2v.

MEINERS, C
  Briefe über die Schweiz. 2. und verm. Aufl. 1791.
  4v.

MEISTER, Leonard
  Kleine Reisen durch einige Schweizer-Cantone: ein
  Auszug aus zerstreuten Briefen und Tagregistern.
  1782.

MÜNTER, Friederike Brun
  Tagebuch einer Reise durch die östliche, südliche
  und italienische Schweiz, ausgearbeitet in den
  Jahren 1798 und 1799. 1800.

Promenade durch die Schweiz. 1793.

REICHARD, Heinrich August Ottakar
  Malerische Reise durch einem grossen Theil der
  Schweiz vor und nach der Revolution. Neue Ausg.
  1827.

ROBERT, François
  Voyage dans les XIII cantons suisses, les Grisons,
  le Valais, et autres pays et états alliés ou
  sujets des Suisses. 1789. 2v.

ROLAND DE LA PLATIÈRE, Marie Jeanne
  Voyage en Suisse, 1787. Éd. collationée, annot.
  et accompagnée d'un aperçu sur les débuts
  touristiques feminins dans les Alpes, par G.R. De
  Beer. 1937.

ROUSSEAU, Jean Jacques
  La nouvelle Héloise; ou, Lettres de deux amants,
  habitants d'une petite ville au pied des Alpes.
  1783. 3v.

SPAZIER, Karl
  Wanderungen durch die Schweiz. 1790.

STORR, G K Ch.
  Alpenreise vom Jahre 1781. 1784-86. 2v.

WILLIAMS, Helen Maria
  A tour in Switzerland; or, A view of the present
  state of the government and manners of those
  cantons, with comparative sketches of the present
  state of Paris. 1798. 2v.

WILLIAMS, Helen Maria
  [A tour in Switzerland...]. Nouveau voyage en
  Suisse, contenant une peinture de ce pays, de ses
  moeurs et de ses gouvernemens actuels... 1798.
  2v. in 1.

- - 2e éd. 1802.

226 <u>Switzerland - visitors, 19th century</u>

ABADIE, Louis d'
  Trente jours de voyage en Suisse par six écoliers
  en vacances. [18--].

AGASSIZ, Lewis
  A journey to Switzerland, and pedestrian tours in
  that country; including a sketch of its history...
  1833.

ARAGON, Anne Alexandrine
  Souvenirs d'un voyage en Suisse. 1843.

BENZENBERG, J F
  Briefe geschrieben auf einer Reise durch die
  Schweiz im Jahre 1810. 1811-12. 2v. in 1.

BERTHOUD, Fritz
  Sur la montagne. le ptie. Alpes et Jura. 1865.

BRIGG, William Anderton
  Iter helveticum, being a journal of the doings of
  a cabinet ... of five fellow-travellers in
  Switzerland... 1887.

BRUUN-NEERGAARD, Tønnes Christian
  Journal du dernier voyage du gen. Dolomieu dans
  les Alpes. 1802.

CARNE, John
  Reise durch die Schweiz. 1828.

CARR, Alfred
  Adventures with my alpenstock and knapsack; or, A
  five weeks' tour in Switzerland, in 1874. 1875.

CLINKER, Charles
  An unconventional guide for tourists: a fortnight
  in Switzerland: a free-and-easy account of a first
  visit to the Rigi, the Bernese Oberland... 1880.

CLOWES, George
  Forty-six days in Switzerland and the north of
  Italy. 1856.

COCKBURN, James
  Swiss scenery from drawings by Major Cockburn.
  1820.

COLLINGS, Henry
  Switzerland as I saw it. [18--].

CONSTANT, Lucien
  Quelques jours en Suisse. 1872.

COOPER, James Fenimore
  Excursions in Switzerland. 1836. 2v.

- - New ed. 1836.

COOPER, James Fenimore
  [Excursions in Switzerland]. Excursions d'une
  famille américaine en Suisse. 1837.

CUCHETET, Charles
  Souvenirs d'une promenade en Suisse, pendant
  l'année 1827. 1828.

DANDOLO, Tullio
  Viaggio per la Svizzera orientale. 1836. 2v.

DARGAUD, J M
  Voyage aux Alpes. 1857.

DAULLIA, Émile
  Voyage impressioniste en Suisse (huit jours au pas
  de course). 1887.

226 Switzerland - visitors, 19th century (Cont.)

DEHANSY, Charles
La Suisse à pied: souvenirs de vacances offerts aux jeunes touristes. [1861].

DESBAROLLES, Adolphe
Un mois de voyage en Suisse pour 200 francs... 1840.

DESBAROLLES, Adolphe
Voyage d'un artiste en Suisse à 3 francs 50 par jour. [1861?].

DORÉ, Gustave
Des-agréments d'un voyage d'agrément. [ca 1860].

DOWSING, William
Rambles in Switzerland, with reminiscences of the Great St. Barnard, Mont Blanc, and the Bernese Alps. 1869.

DUMAS, Alexandre, 1802-1870
Impressions de voyage - Suisse. Nouv. éd. 1880-81. 3v.

DUMAS, Alexandre, 1802-1870
[Impressions de voyage - Suisse]. The glacier land. 1852.

DUMAS, Alexandre, 1802-1870
[Impressions de voyage - Suisse]. Swiss travel, being chapters from Dumas' 'Impressions de voyage'. 1890.

- - New ed. 1895.

DUNANT, David
Le touriste à Chamounix en 1853. 1853.

DUVERNEY, Jacques
Un tour en Suisse: histoire, science, monuments, paysages. 1866. 2v. in 1.

ESCHER VON DER LINTH, Hans Conrad
Reise aus dem Linththal über den Kistenpass ins vordere Rheinthal... [1836].

FERGUSON, Robert
Swiss men and Swiss mountains. 1853.

FORBES, Sir John
A physician's holiday; or, A month in Switzerland in the summer of 1848. 1849.

- - 2nd ed., rev. and corr. 1850.
- - 3rd ed. 1852.

GALLICUS
Voyage en Suisse: notes humoristiques au jour le jour. 1866.

GREY, Rowland
In sunny Switzerland: a story of six weeks. 1884.

GUROWSKI, Adam
Impressions et souvenirs: promenade en Suisse en 1845. 1846.

HARRISSON, F
Among the mountains. [1892].

HAVERGAL, Frances Ridley
Swiss letters and alpine poems. 1882.

HAYDEN, John
A sketch of a tour in Switzerland in a series of letters to a friend. 1859.

HEATHMAN, W G
Switzerland in 1854-5: a book of travel, men, & things. 1855.

HERMAN, André
Vallons de l'Helvétie: impressions de voyage. 1882.

HIRZEL, Heinrich
Eugenias Briefe an ihre Mutter: geschrieben auf einer Reise nach den Bädern von Leuk im Sommer 1806. 1809-20. 3v.

HIRZEL-ESCHER, Hans Caspar
Wanderungen in weniger besuchte Alpengegenden der Schweiz und ihrer nächsten Umgebungen. 1829.

HOWELLS, William Dean
A little Swiss sojourn. 1892.

HUGO, Victor
En voyage: Alpes et Pyrénées. 3e éd. 1890.

HUGO, Victor
[En voyage: Alpes et Pyrénées]. The Alps and Pyrenees. 1898.

Itinéraire général de la Suisse, on y a joint les principales routes... 1810.

JEMIMA, Miss
Miss Jemima's Swiss journal: the first conducted tour of Switzerland, the proceedings of the Junior United Alpine Club, 1863. 1963.

JOHNSON, Anna C
The cottages of the Alps; or, Life and manners in Switzerland. 1860. 2v.

JONES, C A
The foreign freaks of five friends. 1882.

KASTHOFER, Karl
Bemerkungen auf einer Alpen-Reise über den Brünig, Bragel, Kirenzenberg, und über die Flüela, den Maloya und Splügen. 1825.

KASTHOFER, Karl
Bemerkungen auf einer Alpen-Reise über den Susten, Gotthard, Bernardin, und über die Oberalp, Furka und Grimsel. 1822.

KASTHOFER, Karl
[Bemerkungen auf einer Alpen-Reise über den Susten...]. Voyage dans les petits cantons et dans les Alpes rhétiennes. 1827.

KOENIG, Franz Nikolaus
Reise in die Alpen. 1814.

LAPORTE, Albert
En Suisse, le sac au dos. 3e éd. [ca 1875].

LATROBE, Charles Joseph
The alpenstock; or, Sketches of Swiss scenery and manners, 1825-1826. 1829.

- - 2nd ed. 1839.

LEDUC, Saint-Germain
Les vacances en Suisse: journal du voyage d'un collegien. 1837. 2v. in 1.

LEGGETT, Benjamin F
A tramp through Switzerland. 1887.

Letters from Switzerland, 1833. 1834.

LÜHRER, Hans
Die Schweiz im Spiegel englischer Literatur, 1849-1875. 1952.

LONGMORE, John
Pencillings by the way, being a tour on the Rhine and in Switzerland. 1872.

MACGREGOR, John
My note book: Switzerland. 1837.

MACNEVEN, William James
A ramble through Swisserland in the summer and autumn of 1802. 1803.

MAEDER, Herbert
[Lockende Berge]. The lure of the mountains; edited ... by Herbert Maeder. 1975.

226 Switzerland - visitors, 19th century (Cont.)

MARMIER, Xavier
  Voyage en Suisse. [1862].

Mémoire d'une toute petite tournée en Suisse, à vol
  d'hirondelle, dedié à mon ami Sept-Croix. 1863.

MESSISCHES INSTITUT, Neuwied
  Die Schweizer-Reise des Messischen Instituts,
  1845. 1847.

MURRAY, John
  A glance at some of the beauties and sublimities
  of Switzerland, with excursive remarks on the
  various objects of interest, presented during a
  tour through its picturesque scenery. 1829.

NAVEZ, Louis
  En Suisse: Davos-Montreux. [1881?].

NOEL, Baptist W
  Notes of a tour in Switzerland, in the summer of
  1847. 1848.

UN PARISIEN
  Voyage épisodique et anecdotique dans les Alpes.
  1830.

PENSIONNAT JANIN, Geneva
  Voyage à Schaffhouse, retour par Zurich, le Righi
  et l'Oberland. 1845.

Poles and tails; or, English vagabondism in
  Switzerland, in the summer of 1854, by two of the
  vagabonds. 1855.

PRIME, Samuel Irenaeus
  Letters from Switzerland. 1860.

Quinze jours en Suisse: promenades d'un jeune peintre
  français dans les cantons du Midi. [1820].

RAOUL-ROCHETTE, Désiré
  Lettres sur la Suisse, écrites en 1820... 1822.

- - 2e éd., soigneusement rev. et corr. 1823. 2v.
- - 3e éd. 1823. 6v.

RAOUL-ROCHETTE, Désiré
  Lettres sur quelques cantons de la Suisse, écrites
  en 1819. 1820.

Reise eines Lehrers mit seinen Zöglingen aus
  Isserten in einige romantische Gegenden der
  Schweiz: ein nützliches und unterhaltendes Lese-
  buch für die heranwachsende Jugend. 1821-23. 2v.

RICKMAN, E S
  The diary of a solitaire; or, Sketch of a pedestrian excursion through part of Switzerland. 1835.

SAZERAC, Hilaire Léon
  Un mois en Suisse; ou, Souvenirs d'un voyageur.
  1825. 4 pts.

SENDEN, G H van
  Alpenrozen. [ca 1858].

SIMOND, Charles F
  A pedeller abroad, being an illustrated narrative
  of the adventures and experiences of a cycling
  twain during a 1,000 kilomètre ride in and around
  Switzerland. 1897.

SIMOND, L
  Voyage en Suisse fait dans les années 1817, 1818
  et 1819... 1822. 2v.

SIMOND, L
  [Voyage en Suisse...]. Switzerland; or, A journal
  of a tour and residence in that country, in the
  years 1817, 1818, and 1819; followed by an historical sketch... 1822. 2v.

- - 2nd ed. 1823. 2v.

SIMOND, L
  [Voyage en Suisse...]. Travels in Switzerland,
  in 1817, 1818, and 1819. 1822.

SMILAX, H
  Près des sommets. [1890].

SNOECK, C A
  Promenade aux Alpes. [1824?].

STRUTT, Elizabeth
  Domestic residence in Switzerland. 1842. 2v.

The summer tour of an invalid. 1860.

Swiss notes, by five ladies. 1875.

Switzerland: a series of narratives of personal
  visits to places therein famous for natural
  beauty or historical association. 1892.

TEN-HAMME, Joë Diericx de
  Vingt-cinq Belges au Mont-Blanc: itinéraires
  détaillés de 12 et de 15 jours en Suisse. 1869.

TISSOT, Victor
  [La Suisse inconnue]. Au pays des glaciers:
  vacances en Suisse. 2e éd. 1895.

- - 3e éd. 1898.

TISSOT, Victor
  [La Suisse inconnue]. Unknown Switzerland.
  1889.

TORLIK, J H A
  Reise in der Schweiz und einem Theile Italiens,
  in Jahre 1803. 1807.

Travels in Switzerland. [ca 1847].

Travels in Switzerland; compiled from the most
  recent authorities. 1830.

TRENCH, Fanny Maria
  A journal abroad in 1868, for young friends at
  home. [1868].

TUCKETT, Elizabeth
  How we spent the summer;or, A "Voyage en zig-zag"
  in Switzerland and Tyrol, with some members of the
  Alpine Club... 1864.

- - 2nd ed. 1864.
- - 3rd ed. 1866.
- - 6th ed. 1874.

Two on a tour, by one of the two for the other one,
  being an accurate account, more or less, of the
  first Swiss trip of the Manchester Touring Club,
  Whitsuntide, 1892. [1892].

UKLANSKI, Carl Theodor, Baron von
  Einsame Wanderungen in der Schweiz im Jahr 1809.
  1810.

VERNES, F
  Voyage épisodique et pittoresque aux glaciers des
  Alpes... 1807.

- - 2e éd. 1808.

VEUILLOT, Louis
  Les pélérinages de Suisse: Einsiedeln, Sachslen,
  Maria-Stein. 1839.

Viaggio nella Svizzera. 1836. 2v.

A walk through Switzerland in September 1816. 1818.

WHITE, Walter
  To Mont Blanc and back again. 1854.

WIDMANN, Joseph Viktor
  Spaziergänge in den Alpen: Wanderstudien und
  Plaudereien. 2.veränderte und verm. Aufl. 1892.

226 Switzerland - visitors, 19th century (Cont.)

YATES, F   M   L
Letters written during a journey to Switzerland in
the autumn of 1841. 1843. 2v.

ZINCKE, F   Barham
A month in Switzerland. 1873.

ZINCKE, F   Barham
Swiss allmends and a walk to see them, being a
second month in Switzerland. 1874.

227 Switzerland - visitors, 20th century

DOLE, Nathan Haskell
The spell of Switzerland. 1914.

DOMVILLE-FIFE, Charles W
Things seen in Switzerland in winter: a descrip-
tion of many of the winter sport centres of the
High Alps... 1926.

FORREST, Archibald S   and BAGGE, Henry
Switzerland, revisited. [1914].

GRAVES, Charles
Swiss summer. 1938.

GRAVES, Charles
Switzerland revisited. 1947.

HANSJAKOB, Heinrich
Alpenrosen mit Dornen: Reiseerinnerungen. 4.Aufl.
1911.

SMYTHE, Frank S
Again Switzerland. 1947.

228 Climbing history, reminiscences

ASSOCIATION OF BRITISH MEMBERS OF THE SWISS ALPINE
CLUB
Inauguration of the Cabane Britannia on the Klein
Allalinhorne Saas Fee... 1913.

AZELINE
Carnet d'un touriste. 1884.

AZELINE
Par monts et vaux: souvenirs d'un alpiniste. 1879.

AZELINE
Récits d'un montagnard: Alpes et Jura. 1887.

COOLIDGE, William Augustus Brevoort
Die älteste Schutzhütte im Berner Oberland: ein
Beitrag zur Geschichte der bernischen Touristik:
Jubiläumschrift. 1915.

COURTEN, Philippa de
Un jour d'automne. 1946.

ENGELHARDT, Christian Moritz
Naturschilderungen, Sittenzüge und wissenschaftliche Bemerkungen aus den höchsten Schweizer-
Alpen, besonders in Sud-Wallis und Graubünden...
1840.

GARDINER, Frederick
Courses et ascensions: nouvelles expéditions dans
le district de Zermatt (Suisse). 1876.

HOEK, Henry
Eine Winterfahrt in den Schweizer Bergen...
[1900].

HOFFMANN, Georg
Wanderungen in der Gletscherwelt. 1843.

MORF, C
Les pionniers du Club Alpin: étude historique.
1875.

PFEIFFER, G
A la montagne: croquis montagnards. [1897].

PONTRESINA FÜHRER-VEREIN
Statuten des Führer-Vereins Pontresina. [1892].

RAMBERT, Eugène
[Les Alpes suisses]. Ascensions et flaneries.
1888.

SCHWEIZER ALPEN-CLUB
Album der Clubhütten des S.A.C. [1896].

SCHWEIZER ALPEN-CLUB
Les cabanes... 1892.

SCHWEIZER ALPEN-CLUB
Les cabanes... en décembre 1895. 1896.

SCHWEIZER ALPEN-CLUB
Les cabanes... en 1899. 1899.

SCHWEIZER ALPEN-CLUB
Cabanes. 1928.

- - Suppléments. 1-4. 1930-46.

SCHWEIZER ALPEN-CLUB
Die ersten 25 Jahre des Schweizer Alpenclub:
Denkschrift. 1889.

SCHWEIZER ALPEN-CLUB
[Die ersten 25 Jahre...]. Les vingt-cinq
premières années du Club Alpin Suisse. [1889?].

SCHWEIZER ALPEN-CLUB
Die ersten fünfzig Jahre des Schweizer Alpenclub:
Denkschrift. 1913.

SCHWEIZER ALPEN-CLUB
[Die ersten fünfzig Jahre...]. Les cinquante
premières années du Club Alpin Suisse: notice
historique. 1913.

SCHWEIZER ALPEN-CLUB
Itinéraire, 1865-1901. 1865-1900. 26v. in 5.

SCHWEIZER ALPEN-CLUB
Klubhütten-Album des Schweizer Alpen-Club. 1911.

- - Nachtrag. 1913.

SCHWEIZER ALPEN-CLUB
Statuten des Schweizer-Alpen-Club. 1869.

SCHWEIZER ALPEN-CLUB
Tarif général pour les guides et porteurs des
Alpes suisses. 1897-99. 3v. in 1.

SCHWEIZER ALPEN-CLUB. Sektion Blümlisalp
Die ersten fünfzig Jahre des Alpenklub Thun und
der Sektion Blümlisalp des Schweizer Alpenklub,
3. Juni 1874 bis 2. Juni 1924: Denkschrift.
[1924].

SCHWEIZER ALPEN-CLUB. Sektion Davos
Chronik 1886-1896. 1896.

SCHWEIZER ALPEN-CLUB. Sektion Diablerets
Club Alpin Suisse, Section des Diablerets,
Lausanne, 1863-1963. 1963.

SCHWEIZER ALPEN-CLUB. Sektion St. Gallen
Festschrift zur fünfzigjährigen Jubiläums-Feier
der Sektion St. Gallen S.A.C., 1863-1913. 1913.

SCHWEIZERISCHE LANDESAUSSTELLUNG, 1883
Special-Catalog der Gruppen 27, 28 und 42: Forstwirthschaft, Jagd und Fischerei. 1883.

SCHWEIZERISCHE LANDESAUSSTELLUNG, 1896
Club Alpin Suisse, Groupe XLIII: Catalogue spécial.
1896.

SENGER, Max
Wie die Schweizer Alpen erobert wurden. 1945.

STUDER, Gottlieb
Berg- und Gletscher-Fahrten in den Hochalpen der
Schweiz. 1859-63. 2v.

228 Switzerland - climbing history ... (Cont.)

STUDER, Gottlieb
Pontresina und Engelberg: Aufzeichnungen aus den
Jahren 1826-1863: Festgabe der Sektion Bern des
S.A.C. 1907.

STUDER, Gottlieb
Über Eis und Schnee: die höchsten Gipfel der
Schweiz und die Geschichte ihrer Besteigung.
1869. 4v. in 2.

- - 2.Aufl. umgearb. und ergänzt von A. Wäber und
H. Dübi. 1896-99. 3v.

WALLIS. Département de Justice et Police
Tarif général pour les guides et porteurs des
Alpes valaisannes et Reglement des colonnes de
secours. 1933.

WINTER, J   B
From Switzerland to the Mediterranean on foot.
1922.

229 Guide-books

ALLBUT, Robert
The tourist's handbook to Switzerland, with practical information as to routes, excursions, railway and diligence fares... 1884.

ANDRÉ, August
A guide for Champéry and its surroundings. [19--].

Avis aux voyageurs en Suisse, avec une nouvelle
carte des principales routes de la Suisse, où l'on
a marqué les distances d'un endroit à l'autre.
1796.

BAEDEKER, Karl
Die Schweiz: Handbüchlein für Reisende. 1844.

BAEDEKER, Karl
La Suisse et les parties limitrophes de la Savoie
et de l'Italie: manuel du voyageur. 30e éd. 1928.

BAEDEKER, Karl
La Suisse, les lacs italiens, Milan, Genes, Turin:
manuel du voyageur. 3e éd. 1857.

BAEDEKER, Karl
Switzerland together with Chamonix and the Italian
lakes: handbook for travellers. 27th rev. ed.
1928.

BECKER, Fridolin
Glarnerland mit Walensee und Klausenstrasse.
[1912?].

BERGEN, J   van
In Italiaansch Zwitserland en Grauwbunderland.
[19--].

BERGEN, J   van
In Zwitserland. 1908.

BERLEPSCH, Hermann Alexander von
Der Führer auf den Vereinigten Schweizerbahnen und
deren Umgebungen: ein Reisetaschenbuch für die
Ostschweiz. 1859.

BERLEPSCH, Hermann Alexander von
Lucerne, the lake of the Four Cantons and the
Gothard: a guide for visitors to the Alps. [18--].

BERLEPSCH, Hermann Alexander von
Neuestes Reisehandbuch für die Schweiz. 1862.

BERLEPSCH, Hermann Alexander von and KOHL, Johann
Georg
Switzerland and the principal parts of southern
Germany: handbook for travellers. 1874.

BINDER, Gottlieb
Der Utliberg und die Albiskette. [1916].

BLACK, C   B
Guide to Switzerland and the Italian lakes.
[n.d.].

BOLLMANN, Louis de
Die Schweiz: ein Handbuch zunächt für Reisende.
1837.

BOLLMANN, Louis de
Wegweiser der Schweiz, enthaltend die besuchtesten
Gegenden des Landes... 1836.

BRIDEL, Philippe Sirice
Kleine Fussreisen durch die Schweiz. 1797. 2v.

CAVIÉZEL, Michael
Das Oberengadin: ein Führer auf Spaziergängen
kleinen und grossen Touren. 1876.

- - 2.veränderte und verm. Aufl. 1881.

CAVIÉZEL, Michael
[Das Oberengadin...]. Tourist's guide to the
Upper Engadine. 1877.

Chamonix, Mont-Blanc et sa vallée: guide illustré.
1933.

COGHLAN, Francis
Guide through Switzerland and Chamounix; or,
Tourist's companion to the most interesting
objects in the cities... [183-].

- - New ed., rev. improved and completed until 1850.
1850.

CONTY, Henry A   de
Suisse française, Oberland bernois; guide pratique
et illustré. n.d.

- - 12e éd. [n.d.]. 2v.

Cook's tourist's handbook for Switzerland. 1884.

COOLIDGE, William Augustus Brevoort
Guide to Switzerland; with cycling supplement.
1901.

COURTHION, L
Champéry, summer and winter resort. [19--].

COXE, Henry
The traveller's guide in Switzerland, being a
complete picture of that interesting country...
and a narrative of the various attempts to ascend
Mont Blanc. 1816.

DANDOLO, Tullio
Guida storica, poetica e pittoresca per la
Svizzera. 1857.

DANDOLO, Tullio
La Svizzera pittoresca; o, Corse per le Alpi e pel
Jura; a comentario del Medio Evo elvetico. 1846.

Davos-Platz; a new alpine resort for sick and sound
in summer and winter. 1878.

DERICHSWEILER, W
Führer durch das Medelser-Gebirge: das Gebiet der
Medelserhütte der Sektion Uto des Schweizer Alpen
Club. 1910.

EBEL, Johann Gottfried
Anleitung auf die nützlichste und genussvollste
Art in der Schweitz zu reisen. 1793. 2v.

- - 2. ganz umgearb. und sehr verm. Aufl. 1804-05.
4v.
- - 3. Aufl. 1809-10. 4v. in 3.
- - 7. original Aufl. 1840.
- - 8. original Aufl. 1843.

EBEL, Johann Gottfried
[Anleitung auf die nützlichste und genussvollste
Art...]. Instructions pour un voyageur qui se
propose de parcourir la Suisse de la manière la
plus utile... 1795.

229 Switzerland - guide-books (Cont.)

EBEL, Johann Gottfried and HEIDEGGER, Heinrich
Handbuch für Reisende in der Schweiz. 4.verb.
Aufl. 1818.

- - 5. verb. Aufl. 1823.
- - 6. verb. Aufl. 1830.

EBEL, Johann Gottfried
[Handbuch für Reisende in der Schweiz]. The
traveller's guide through Switzerland. New ed.
1818.

EBEL, Johann Gottfried
[Handbuch für Reisende in der Schweiz]. Manuel du
voyageur en Suisse: ouvrage où l'on trouve les
directions necessaires pour recueillir tout le
fruit et toutes les jouissances...
Various editions.

EICHENBERGER, Ad.
Die Schweiz: illustriertes Reisehandbuch. 7.Aufl.
von Sommer in der Schweiz. 1927.

EICHHORN, Karl
Die Rigi und ihre nächste Umgebung: Führer für
Kurgäste und Touristen. [19--].

FERGUSON, Robert
Swiss men and Swiss mountains. 1853.

FERGUSON, Robert
[Swiss men and Swiss mountains]. Leute und Berge:
Reisebilder aus der Schweiz. 1855.

FEUZ, Ernst
Führer und Heimatkunde von Mürren. 1934.

FRISCHAUF, Johannes
Ein Ausflug auf den Monte Baldo. 1883.

Galignani's traveller's guide through Switzerland;
chiefly compiled from ... works of Ebel and Coxe;
with numerous additions and improvements from
recent observations... 1818.

GAZE, Henry
Switzerland: how to see it for ten guineas. 3rd
ed. 1863.

Genfer See und Chamonix: praktischer Reiseführer.
2. neubearb. Aufl. Goldschmidt, 1911.

GOLAY, H   C
Guide pratique du Salève d'Annemasse à Cruseilles
à l'usage des promeneurs et des varappeurs. 1928.

GRANDE, Julian
The Bernese Oberland in summer and winter: a guide.
1911.

GREGORY, Alexander Tighe
Practical Swiss guide: Anglo-American hand-book
for Switzerland, Savoy, North Italy, the routes
from England by France, Belgium, Holland and the
Rhine... 53rd issue. 1909.

GREGORY, Alexander Tighe
A practical Swiss guide, illustrated: the whole of
Switzerland, Mont Blanc, Monte Rosa, Mont Cervin...
1856.

Guide du voyageur en Suisse, [by Thomas Martyn and
others]. 1794.

Guide pratique de Saint-Gervais-les-Bains, Chamonix,
Argentière, le Mont-Blanc. 5e éd. Toursier,
[n.d.].

Guide to Switzerland. Macmillan, 1903.

A hand-book for travellers in Switzerland and the
Alps of Savoy and Piedmont, including the Protes-
tant valleys of the Waldenses. Murray.
Various editions.

HARDMEYER, J
Lugano und Umgebung. 5.Aufl. [1916].

HASSELBRINK, F
[Führer durch Graubündens Kurorte...]. Guide to...
the Grisons [Graubünden]. [1907].

HEER, J   C
Winter in der Schweiz: Wintersport und Winterkuren.
[1911].

HEIDEGGER, Heinrich
Handbuch für Reisende durch die Schweiz. 1787-90.
2 pts. in 1.

- - 2. stark verm. und verb. Aufl. 1790-91.
- - 3. stark verm. und verb. Aufl. 1796.

HEIDEGGER, Heinrich
[Handbuch für Reisende in der Schweiz]. Manuel de
l'étranger qui voyage en Suisse. 1790. 2pts. in 1.

- - 4e éd. originale. 1819.
- - 3e éd. française. 1827.

Illustrierter Führer auf die Gipfel der Schweizeralpen. Speck-Jost, [19-?].

JOANNE, Adolphe
Itinéraire descriptif et historique de la Suisse
... du Mont Blanc, de la vallée de Chamouni, du
Grand-St-Bernard et du Mont-Rose... 1841.

JOANNE, Adolphe and JOANNE, Paul
Suisse. 4e éd., entièrement refondue. 1875.

KAPFF, S   C
Eine Schweizer-Reise... 1843.

KELLER, C
Schweiz. 1921.

Kleiner Führer durch die Schweiz. 3.Aufl. 1907-08.

The knapsack guide for travellers in Switzerland.
1864.

- - New ed., rev. 1867.

LADNER, Joh. Bapt.
Languard-Rundschau: ein hypsometrisches
Verzeichniss von Tausend über 8000' hohen Gipfeln
und Gräten der Alpenkette zwischen Montblanc und
Grossglockner, welche vom 10,887' hohen Piz-
Languard im Ober-Engadin aus gesehen werden. 1858.

LECHNER, Ernst
Piz Languard und die Bernina-Gruppe bei Pontresina,
Oberengadin: Skizzen aus Natur und Bevölkerung,
zugleich als Wegweiser für Wanderungen. 1858.

- - 2. Aufl. 1865.
- - 3. Aufl. 1900.

LUNN, Henry S
How to visit Switzerland: a new guide-book to the
chief scenes of interest in Switzerland... 1895.

MCDERMOTT, F
How to be happy in Switzerland; winter sports.
1928.

MANN, Josefine
Was man für eine Schweizer-Reise wissen muss:
Anhaltspunkte für Reiselust und Kulturinteressen.
1913.

MUDDUCK, J   E
The "J.E.M." guide to Switzerland: the Alps and
how to see them. 2nd ed. 1882.

- - 6th ed., rev. and corr. 1886.
- - 8th ed., rev. and corr. 1890.

MUIRHEAD, Findlay
Switzerland with Chamonix and the Italian lakes.
1923.

MUIRHEAD, Litellus Russell
Bernese Oberland and Lucerne. 1963.

229 Switzerland - guide-books (Cont.)

MUIRHEAD, Litellus Russell
Switzerland. 3rd ed. 1952.

Neuer und vollstandiger Wegweiser durch die ganze
Schweizerische Eidsgenössenschaft und die
benachbarten Länder. 1828.

NOË, R
Die Schweiz in 15 Tagen mit Generalabonnement
genussreich und billig zu Bereisen. 4.verm. und
verb. Aufl. 1907-8.

Nouveau guide du voyageur dans les XXII cantons
suisses. Bourgdorfer, 1822.

Nouveau guide général du voyageur en Suisse; suivi
du Tour du Mont Blanc par Joseph Lacroix.
Garnier, [n.d.].

OFENBRÜGGEN, Eduard
Wanderstudien aus der Schweiz. [186-]. 5v.

PAILLON, Maurice
Chamonix et le Mont-Blanc, Saint-Gervais-les-
Bains, Argentière. 1913.

Paterson's guide to Switzerland. 1885.

- - 8th ed. [n.d.].

REYNIER, Jean Louis Antoine
Le guide des voyageurs en Suisse, précédé d'un
discours sur l'état politique du pays. 1790.

- - 2e éd. 1791.

RICHARD
Guide du voyageur en Suisse. 1824.

RICHARD
Promenades dans l'Oberland, par Wyss et Lutz;
revues par Richard. 3e éd. [1836?].

Rundreisen in der Schweiz, einschliesslich des
Bodensees, der oberitalienischen Seen und Mailand.
27.Aufl. 1913.

RYFFEL, Alfred
Bilder vom Vierwaldstätter-See. [1916].

SCHAER, Alfred
Die Arth-Rigi-Bahn. 3. neu bearb. Aufl. [1916].

SCHAUB, Charles and BRIQUET, Moïse
Guide pratique de l'ascensionniste sur les montagnes qui entourent le lac de Genève... 3e éd.,
rev. et augm. 1893.

SCHWARZENBACH, Annemarie and SCHMID, Hans Rudolf
Das Buch von der Schweiz. 1932-33. 2v.

Schweiz. 14.Aufl. 1895. (Meyers Reisebücher)

SOCIÉTÉ SUISSE DES HÔTELIERS
Les hôtels de la Suisse: guide pour les voyageurs.
1896.

SOCIÉTÉ SUISSE DES HÔTELIERS
[Les hôtels de la Suisse]. The hotels of
Switzerland: a tourist's guide. 1896.

Sommer in der Schweiz: illustrierter Reiseführer;
hrsg. unter Mitwirkung von J.C. Heer [and others].
[1911].

La Svizzera. Nouva ed. Treves, 1909.

La Svizzera secondo il Coxe, l'Ebel ed altri piu
moderni viaggiatori, si aggiungono alcuni cenni
sulla storia, i monumenti, le leggi ed i costumi.
[ca 1820].

Switzerland, a practical guide. 2nd ed.
Goldschmidt, Williams & Norgate, 1912-13.

Switzerland and Savoy. Bogue, 1852.

TAPERNOUX, Ph.
Nouveau guide en Suisse. Jaquenod, [n.d.].

TSCHUDI, Iwan von
Guide suisse: manuel du voyageur dans les cantons
avec détails plus particuliers sur les principales
villes, les lieux de cures et les Alpes. 1861.

TSCHUDI, Iwan von
Der Tourist in der Schweiz und den Grenzrayons:
Reisetaschenbuch. 4... Aufl. 1899. 3v.

TSCHUDI, Iwan von
Der Turist in der Schweiz und dem Angrenzenden
Süd-Deutschland, Ober-Italien und Savoyen: Reise-
taschenbuch. 31... Aufl. 1890.

TSCHUDI, Iwan von
Ur- und Südschweiz: Reisetaschenbuch für die
Kantone Luzern, Unterwalden, Zug, Schwyz, Uri,
Wallis and Tessin, die Walliner und die Grauen
Alpen und Ober-Italien... 1869.

VIOLLIER, Edmond W
Guide pratique de Genève, son lac et les environs,
par Edm. W. Viollier and Vaud, Valais, Haute-
Savoie..., par Marc Le Roux. [n.d.].

Le voyageur en Suisse; ou, Manuel instructif et
portatif à l'usage des étrangers qui se proposent
de parcourir ce pays; extrait des meilleurs
ouvrages de nos jours. [ca 1816].

WAGNON, Aug.
Excursions et escalades de la Dent du Midi au
Buet, autour de Salvan et de Fins-Hauts. 2e éd.
1895.

WAGNON, Aug.
Guide de la vallée du Trient: excursions, escalades
de la Dent-du-Midi au Mont-Blanc. 3e éd. 1903.

WALCHER, S
Taschenbuch zu Schweizer-Reisen, mit hinweisung
auf alle Sehens und Merkwurdigkeiten der Schweiz;
eines Theils von Savonen und anderer benachbarten
Orte. 1832.

- - 3. verb. Aufl. 1841.

WALCHER, S
Touristenführer durch die Schweiz. 1856.

WALDIS, Alfred
Switzerland: the traveller's illustrated guide.
1965.

WALSER, Hermann
Landeskunde der Schweiz. 1908.

- - 2.Aufl. 1914.
- - 3.verb. Aufl. 1926.

WEBER, E
Reise- und Handlexikon der Schweiz. 1854.

WHYMPER, Edward
Chamonix and the range of Mont Blanc: a guide.
5th ed. 1900.

- - 8th ed. 1903.
- - 16th ed. 1911.

WHYMPER, Edward
The valley of Zermatt and the Matterhorn: a guide.
7th ed. 1903.
- - 15th ed. 1911.

Wintersport und Winterkuren in der Schweiz:
praktischer Reiseführer. Goldschmidt, 1910.

23 FRANCE

231 Geology, climate

ALLIX, André
Observations glaciologiques faites en Dauphiné
jusqu'en 1924. 1927.

CLUB ALPIN FRANÇAIS. Commission des travaux
scientifiques
L'oeuvre scientifique du Club Alpin Français
(1874-1922). 1936.

COLLINGWOOD, William Gershom
Limestone Alps of Savoy: a study in physical
geology. 1884.

COLLOMB, Édouard
Preuves de l'existence d'anciens glaciers dans les
vallées des Vosges, du terrain erratique de cette
contrée. 1847.

DELEBECQUE, André
Les lacs français. 1898.

DUPARC, Louis and RITTER, Étienne
Eclogites et Amphibolites du massif du Grand-Mont.
1894.

FALSAN, Albert
Les Alpes françaises: les montagnes, les eaux, les
glaciers, les phénomènes de l'atmosphère. 1893.

FORBES, James David
Description of some volcanic formations... 1. On
the volcanic geology of the Vivarais (Ardèche).
[1853].

HELBRONNER, Paul
Description géométrique détaillée des Alpes
françaises. T.1. Chaîne méridienne de Savoie.
1910.

KILIAN, W and FLUSIN, G
Observations sur les variations des glaciers et
l'enneigement dans les Alpes dauphinoises. 1900.

MOUGIN, P
Études glaciologiques en Savoie. 1925.

MOUGIN, P and BERNARD, C
Glacier de Tête-Rousse, les avalanches en Savoie.
1922.

232 Geography, description

BUSH-ATKINS, Daisy
Through the Alps. 1963.

CLUB ALPIN FRANÇAIS. Commission des travaux
scientifiques
Les noms de lieux des montagnes françaises. 1929.

GRENIER, Ch. and GODRON, D A
Flore de France; ou, Description des plantes qui
croissent naturellement en France et en Corse.
1848-56. 3v.

HAMERTON, Philip Gilbert
The Saône: a summer voyage. 1887.

HARE, Augustus J C
South-eastern France. 1890.

HARE, Augustus J C
South-western France. 1890.

MOURRAL, Daniel
Glossaire des noms topographiques les plus usités
dans le Sud-Est de la France et les Alpes occidentales. [18--].

TASTU, Sabine Amable
Alpes et Pyrénées: arabesques littéraires... 1842.

TASTU, Sabine Amable
Voyage en France. 1852.

- - Nouv. éd., rev. et augm. 1879.

WALKER, A
Remarks made in a tour from London to the Lakes of
Westmoreland and Cumberland, in the summer of
1791 ..., to which is annexed, a sketch of the
police, religion, arts, and agriculture of France,
made in an excursion to Paris in 1785. 1792.

233 History

BLAIKIE, Thomas
Diary of a Scotch gardener at the French Court at
the end of the eighteenth century. 1931.

BOELL, Jacques
S.E.S.: Éclaireurs-Skieurs au combat, 1940-1944-
1945. 1946.

BORDEAUX, P E
À travers les Alpes militaires: quelques souvenirs.
1928.

BURCH, Lambert van der
Sabaudiae Respublica et historia. 1634.

RIGBY, Edward
Dr. Rigby's letters from France &c. in 1789. 1880.

T., J.G.D.
Gelegenheit und heutiger Zustand dess Hertzogthums
Savoyen und Fürstenthums Piemont... 1690.

234 Travel - personal accounts, reminiscences

BOLAND, Henri
Coins de France: Brie, Ardennes, Normandie,
Bretagne, Anjou, Massif Central, Pyrénées. 1910.

BRETON, J B J
Voyage en Piémont, contenant la description topographique et pittoresque, la statistique et
l'histoire des six départements réunis à la France,
par le Senatus-Consulte de l'an XI. 1803.

COSTELLO, Louisa Stuart
Béarn and the Pyrenees: a legendary tour to the
country of Henri Quatre. 1844.

FODERÉ, F E
Voyage aux Alpes Maritimes; ou, Histoire naturelle,
agraire, civile et médicale, du comté de Nice et
pays limitrophes... 1821. 2v.

HUGO, Victor
France et Belgique, Alpes et Pyrénées. [1913].

MUSGRAVE, George M
A pilgrimage into Dauphiné, comprising a visit to
the monastery of the Grand Chartreuse; with anecdotes, incidents, and sketches from twenty departments of France. 1857. 2v.

SCHOPENHAUER, Johanna
Reise von Paris durch das südliche Frankreich bis
Chamouny. 2.verb. und verm.Aufl. 1824. 2v. in 1.

235 French Alps - general

BLANCHARD, Raoul
Les Alpes françaises. 1925.

BLANCHARD, Raoul
Les Alpes françaises à vol d'oiseau. 1928.

CHOLLIER, Antoine
Ceux de l'Alpe: types et coutumes. 1937.

235 French Alps - general (Cont.)

DOLIN, H
Routes des Alpes françaises: itinéraires avec profils des pentes ... à l'usage des alpinistes, cyclistes et voituristes... [1909].

DORANGE, J
Quinze excursions en Savoie et Dauphiné. 1911.

FALSAN, Albert
Les Alpes françaises: la flore et la faune, le rôle de l'homme dans les Alpes, la transhumance. 1893.

FAURE, Gabriel
Les Alpes françaises. [1925].

GRÉBAUVAL, Armand
Au pays alpin, d'Aix à Aix. [1902].

JALEK, Maria
En campant sur l'Alpe: au-dessus de la plus haute route d'Europe des Aiguilles d'Arves au Gran Paradiso. 1937.

PAILLON, Maurice
Alpes de France: régions naturelles, massifs alpestres, préalpes et chaînes subalpines. 1938. 2v.

236 Regions

236.1 North-East

CLUB ALPIN FRANÇAIS. Section Ardennes
Ardennes: sentier de grande randonnée numéro 12 et les sentiers pédestres dans les Ardennes. 1976.

CLUB ALPIN FRANÇAIS. Section des Hautes Vosges
Ballon d'Alsace, Bussang, St-Maurice, Vosges méridionales. 2e éd., rev. & augm. [1905].

FERRAND, Henri
Le circuit de Chartreuse au départ de Grenoble. 1924.

LEE, Katharine
In the Alsatian mountains: a narrative of a tour in the Vosges. 1883.

MACQUOID, Katharine S
In the Ardennes. 1881.

WESTON, Stephen
La Scava; or, Some account of an excavation of a Roman town on the hill of Chatelet, in Champagne ... discovered in the year 1772... 1818.

236.2 Savoy, Jura, Mont Cenis

ANTHONIOZ, Charles
Maisons savoyardes. 1932.

BALTARD, Louis Pierre
Journal descriptif en croquis de vues pittoresques faits dans un voyage en Savoye du 10 au 21 août 1837. [1837?].

BEAUMONT, Jean François Albanis
Description des Alpes grecques et cottiennes; ou, Tableau historique et statistique de la Savoie. 2e ptie. 1806. 2v.

BEAUMONT, Jean François Albanis
Voyage pittoresque aux Alpes pennines; précédé de quelques observations sur les hauteurs des montagnes, glaciers... 1787.

BEAUMONT, Jean François Albanis
[Voyage pittoresque aux Alpes pennines]. Picturesque tour from Geneva to the Pennine Alps. 1792.

BELLET, Jean
Le col du Mont-Cenis, "Porte millenaire des Alpes"; bref historique. 1976.

BERLIOUX, E   F
Le Jura. 1880.

BERTOLOTTI, Davide
Viaggio in Savoia; ossia, Descrizione degli stati oltramontani di S.M. il Re di Sardegna. 1828. 2v. in 1.

BRUCHET, Max
La Savoie d'après les anciens voyageurs... 1908.

CANZIANI, Estella
Costumes, moeurs et légendes de Savoie. 1920.

CARLO ALBERTO, King of Sardinia
Relation du voyage en Savoie du roi et de la reine de Sardaigne, leurs majestés Charles-Albert et Marie-Thérèse, en 1834. 1834.

CHOLLEY, André
Les Préalpes de Savoie (Genevois, Bauges) et leur avant-pays: étude de géographie régionale. 1925.

COCKBURN, James
Views to illustrate the route of Mont Cenis. [1822].

COOLIDGE, William Augustus Brevoort and DUHAMEL, Henry
Le col de Galest et le col de la Galise. 1905.

COOLIDGE, William Augustus Brevoort and DUHAMEL, Henry
Le col de la Leisse et les Quecées de Tignes. 1905.

COOLIDGE, William Augustus Brevoort
Le col Lombard et les passages avoisinants dans l'histoire. 1913.

COOLIDGE, William Augustus Brevoort
Les cols de la Chambre et de la Montée du Fond. 1911.

COOLIDGE, William Augustus Brevoort
Dix jours dans le Valgodemar et le Val Champoléon. [1886?].

COOLIDGE, William Augustus Brevoort
Entre Arc et Stura. 1908.

COOLIDGE, William Augustus Brevoort
Les grands sommets des Alpes de la Tarentaise dans l'histoire. 1911.

COOLIDGE, William Augustus Brevoort
Le massif de Bellecôte. 1905.

COOLIDGE, William Augustus Brevoort
Le "Mont Alban". 1911.

COOLIDGE, William Augustus Brevoort
Le "Mont Coupeline". 1903.

COPPIER, André Charles
Au lac d'Annecy. 1923.

COPPIER, André Charles
De Tarentaise en Maurienne. 1931.

COVINO, Andrea
De Turin à Chambéry; ou, Les vallées de la Dora Riparia et de l'Arc, et le tunnel des Alpes cottiennes. 1871.

FERRAND, Henri
D'Aix-les-Bains à la Vanoise: la Savoie méridionale. 1907.

FERRAND, Henri
Itinéraire descriptif, historique et archéologique de la Maurienne et de la Tarentaise. 1879.

GEX, F
La Haute-Savoie, aujourd'hui et il y a 100 ans: receuil de notes administratives inédites. 1923.

GODEFROY, René
Géographie de la Savoie. 1930.

236.2 Savoy, Jura, Mont Cenis (Cont.)

GOS, François
Les Alpes de la Haute-Savoie. 1926.

GOS, François
[Les Alpes de la Haute-Savoie]. Rambles in high
Savoy. 1927.

GRAGOW, H
Savoyen und die Dauphiné: ein Führer durch die
nördlichen Westalpen und ein Teil der französischen
Voralpen. 1907-08.

GRANDJEAN, Valentin
Flâneries dans les Alpes: la chaîne des Aravis,
les Alpes de Taninges, les rochers des Fiz, le
massif de Platé. 1908.

GRILLET, Jean Louis
Dictionnaire historique, littéraire et statistique
des départements du Mont-Blanc et du Léman; contenant l'histoire ancienne et moderne de la Savoie
... 1807. 3v.

GUITON, Paul
Au coeur de la Savoie. 1926.

HELBRONNER, Paul
Description géometrique détaillée des Alpes
françaises. T.1. Chaîne méridienne de Savoie.
1910.

HORNUNG, Moise
En Savoie. 1872.

JACOTTET, Henri
Le Jura français: notes de voyage en France.
(Bibliothèque Universelle ... v.42, 1889, p.543-
567)

JOANNE, Adolphe
Géographie du département de la Haute-Savoie.
8e éd. 1902.

JOANNE, Adolphe
Itinéraires descriptif et historique de la Savoie.
1860.

JOANNE, Adolphe
Itinéraire général de la France. 1. Jura et Alpes
françaises. 2e éd. 1882.

JOANNE, Paul
Itinéraire général de la France: Savoie. 1910.

LA BEDOYÈRE, Henri, comte de
Voyage en Savoie et dans le Midi: la France en
1804 et 1805. 1808.

LAISSUS, C
En Savoie: la Tarentaise, guide du baigneur, du
touriste et du naturaliste. 1894.

LAVIS-TRAFFORD, Marc A   de
L'évolution de la cartographie de la région du
Mont-Cenis et de ses abords au XVe et XVIe siècles:
étude critique des méthodes de travail des grands
cartographes du XVIe siècle... 1950.

LUC, Jean André de and DENTANT, Pierre Gédéon
Relation de différents voyages dans les Alpes du
Faucigny. 1776.

LUC, Jean André de and DENTANT, Pierre Gédéon
[Relation de différents voyages...]. Reisen nach
den Eisgebürgen von Faucigny in Savoyen. 1777.

MAGNIN, J
Saint-Gervais-les-Bains et ses environs: guide
itinéraire historique, pittoresque... [1898].

MARTIN, F   J
Itinéraire descriptif de la vallée de Sixt,
province de Faucigny, en Savoie. 1821.

MATTHEY, André
Les bains de Saint-Gervais, près du Mont-Blanc
(en Savoie). 1818.

MAUS, Octave
Savoie. 1911.

MERRICK, Hugh
Savoy episode. 1946.

MORTILLET, Gabriel de
Guide de l'étranger dans les départements de la
Savoie et de la Haute-Savoie. 1861.

MORTILLET, Gabriel de
Guide de l'étranger en Savoie. 1855.

MUSÉE DE CHAMONIX
Catalogue descriptif illustré. 1927.

PERRIN, André
Le Prieuré de Chamonix: histoire de la vallée et
du Prieuré de Chamonix du Xe au XVIIIe siècle.
1887.

PIACHAUD, René Louis
Le Salève. 1924.

PRIEURÉ DE CHAMONIX
Documents relatifs au Prieuré et à la vallée de
Cahmonix [sic]. 1879-83. 2v.

RABUT, Laurent
Habitations lacustres de la Savoie. 1863-68. 4v.

RAVERAT, Achille, baron
Haute-Savoie: promenades historiques, pittoresques
& artistiques en Genevois, Sémine, Faucigny et
Chablais. 1872.

RAVERAT, Achille, baron
Savoie: promenades, historiques, pittoresques &
artistiques en Maurienne, Tarentaise, Savoie-Propre
et Chautagne. 1872.

REGAUD, Claudius
Autour de Bonneval (Haute-Maurienne). 1897.

RÉVIL, Joseph and CORCELLE, Joseph
La Savoie: guide du touriste, du naturaliste et de
l'archéologue. [18--].

ROUSSEAU, Jean Jacques
[Les confessions]. Jean-Jacques Rousseau en
Savoie: Annecy-Chambéry - Les Charmettes; extraits
des "Confessions". 1922.

Savoie; introduction de M. Henry Bordeaux.
Hachette, [1926].

SCHWEIZER ALPEN-CLUB. Sektion Geneva
Le Salève: description scientifique et pittoresque.
1899.

SERAND, François and SERAND, Joseph
Massif de la Tournette, rive droite du lac
d'Annecy. 1926.

SERAND, François and SERAND, Joseph
Mont Veyrier, rive droite du lac d'Annecy. 1926.

SERAND, François and SERAND, Joseph
Pointe-Percée: massif des Aravis. 1926.

TONNEAU, Alfred
Alpages et sommets: courses en Haute-Savoie.
[1903?].

VAILLAT, Léandre
Le coeur et la croix de Savoie: Chambéry,
Maurienne, Tarentaise. 1914.

VAILLAT, Léandre
Notre Savoie. 1920.

VAILLAT, Léandre
Paysages d'Annecy. 1931.

VAILLAT, Léandre
La Savoie. 1912.

VAILLAT, Léandre
La Savoie: Chambéry, la Maurienne, la Tarentaise.
1913.

236.2 Savoy, Jura, Mont Cenis (Cont.)

WEY, Francis
La Haute Savoie: récits d'histoire et de voyage...
2e éd., rev. 1865.

WEY, Francis
La Haute Savoie: récits de voyage et d'histoire.
1866.

WILLS, Sir Alfred
"The Eagle's Nest" in the valley of Sixt: a summer
home among the Alps; together with some excursions
among the great glaciers. 1860.

- - 2nd ed. 1860.

236.3 Dauphiné,Maritime Alps, Isère

ALPINUS
La chasse alpestre en Dauphiné. 1874.

- - [New ed.]. 1925.

ARNAUD, F
La vallée de Barcelonnette (l'Ubaye). 1900.

BAUD-BOVY, Daniel
La Meije et les Écrins. [1907].

BELL, Gertrude
Dauphiné and the Aiguille Méridionale d'Arves:
unpublished letters. 1928.

BERRET, Paul
Le Dauphiné: choix de textes précédés d'une étude.
1922.

BOELL, Jacques
Cimes d'Oisans: récits de courses en Dauphiné.
1937.

BOELL, Jacques
[Cimes d'Oisans...]. High heaven. 1947.

BONNEY, Thomas George
Outline sketches in the high Alps of Dauphiné.
1865.

CHAIX, B
Préoccupations statistiques, géographiques, pit-
toresques et synoptiques du département des Hautes-
Alpes. 1845.

CLUB ALPIN FRANÇAIS. Section de Barcelonnette
Barcelonette & ses environs: [album photographique
de la vallée de Barcelonnette]. [1879?].

CLUB ALPIN FRANÇAIS. Section de Barcelonnette
Guide de l'alpiniste dans la vallée de l'Ubaye;
suivi de La région du Chambeyron par W.A.B.
Coolidge. 1898.

COOLIDGE, William Augustus Brevoort
Entre Isère et Doire. 1912.

COOLIDGE, William Augustus Brevoort
Entre Valloire et Briançonnais. 1914.

COOLIDGE, William Augustus Brevoort
Guide du Haut-Dauphiné. 1887.

- - Supplément. 1890.

COOLIDGE, William Augustus Brevoort
[Guide du Haut-Dauphiné].
Das Hochgebirge des Dauphiné. 4. durchgesehene
und 1 autorisierte deutsche Ausg. 1913.

COOLIDGE, William Augustus Brevoort
Souvenirs de mon voyage en 1879 à travers les
Alpes Maritimes. 1904.

COOLIDGE, William Augustus Brevoort
Le tour de l'Oisans. 1887.

CORTES, Louis
L'Oisans: recherches historiques, tourisme. 1926.

Dauphiné; introduction de M.R. de La Sizeranne.
Hachette, [1926].

DEBRIGES, E
Les Alpes du Dauphiné. 1885.

DEMPSTER, Charlotte L
The Maritime Alps and their seaboard. 1885.

DERENNES, Gustave
À travers les Alpes françaises: carnet d'un
touriste. [1890].

DONNET, Gaston
Le Dauphiné. [1890].

FERRAND, Henri
Autour du Pelvoux: le tour du Pelvoux; De la Grave
au Pelvoux. 1885.

FERRAND, Henri
Belledone et les Sept-Laux: montagnes d'Uriage et
d'Allevard. 1901.

FERRAND, Henri
Grenoble: capitale des Alpes françaises. 1923.

FERRAND, Henri
[Grenoble: capitale des Alpes françaises].
Grenoble and thereabouts: Chartreuse, Oisans,
Vercors. 1923.

FERRAND, Henri
L'Oisans: la Meidge, le Pelvoux, la Grave, le
Lautaret, la Bérarde. 1903.

FERRAND, Henri
Le pays briançonnais: de Briançon au Viso, la
vallée de Névache et le Queyras. 1909.

FERRAND, Henri
La route des Alpes françaises. 1925.

FERRAND, Henri
La route des Alpes françaises du Léman à la mer.
1912.

FERRAND, Henri
Les routes des Alpes du Dauphiné, Isère, Drôme,
Hautes-Alpes: itinéraires avec profils des pentes
... à l'usage des cyclistes & automobilistes.
1899.

FERRAND, Henri
Le Vercors: le Royannais et les Quatre Montagnes,
région du Mont-Aiguille, du Villard-de-Lans et
des Grands-Goulets. 1904.

GAUTHIER, J
En montagne: articles extraits de la collection du
"Moniteur Dauphinois" ..., 1895-97, [1897-98].
1897-98. 2v.

GERMAIN, Félix
Cimes et visages du Haut Dauphiné. 1955.

Grenoble et le Dauphiné; publié par MM. Audebrand,
Maurice Bergès [and others]. [1904].

GUIGUES, Émile
En montagne: bêtes et gens de l'Embrunais. 1929.

JOANNE, Adolphe
Géographie du département de l'Isère. 11e éd.
1901.

JOANNE, Adolphe
Itinéraire général de la France. 2. Provence,
Alpes Maritimes, Corse. 2e éd. 1877.

JOANNE, Paul
Géographie du département des Alpes-Maritimes.
9e éd. 1910.

236.3 Dauphiné, Maritime Alps, Isère (Cont.)

JOANNE, Paul
  Géographie du département des Hautes-Alpes. 6e éd.
  1909.

LAWSON, W   and OSBORNE, R   E
  Les Écrins et la Meije. 1908.

MONSON, Frederick John, Baron Monson
  Views in the Department of the Isère and the High
  Alps. 1840.

- - Another ed. [ca 1845].

MORILLOT, Paul
  À travers nos Alpes: Dauphiné, par MM. Morillot,
  R. Rey, Magendie. 1902.

MORIS, Henri
  Au pays bleu: Alpes-Maritimes. 1900.

PAILLON, Maurice
  Dauphiné... 1910.

PAILLON, Maurice
  Exploration du massif de Séguret. 1901.

PASCHETTA, Vincent
  Alpes de Provence, Tinée, Ubaye: randonnées et
  escalades faciles. 1977.

PASCHETTA, Vincent
  Les Collines niçoises: circuits automobiles et
  promenades à pied. 7e éd. 1971.

PASCHETTA, Vincent
  Haute Tinée, Barcelonnette: Auron, Isola 2000...
  3e éd. 1973.

PASCHETTA, Vincent
  Merveilles, Tende, Gordolasque. 10e éd. 1976.

PASCHETTA, Vincent
  Nice et sa region: arts, histoire, tourisme. 9e
  éd. [1973?].

PASCHETTA, Vincent
  Saint-Martin-Vésubie, Valdeblore. 10e éd. 1976.

PASCHETTA, Vincent
  Valberg (Beuil, Guillaumes, Péone), Haut-Var
  (Esteng, Pélens). 3e éd. 1972.

PAULMY, Antoine René de Voyer d'Argenson, marquis de
  Voyage d'inspection de la frontière des Alpes en
  1752. 1902.

PERROTIN, Monsieur
  Tableau des positions géographiques et hauteurs
  absolues au-dessus du niveau de la mer des points
  principaux du département de l'Isère... 1853.

PEZAY, Alexandre Frédéric Jacques de Masson,
marquis de
  Noms, situation et détails des vallées de la
  France le long des grandes Alpes dans le Dauphiné
  et la Provence, et de celles qui descendent des
  Alpes en Italie depuis la Savoye jusqu'à celle de
  Saint Étienne au comté de Nice. 1793.

ROUX, Xavier
  Les Alpes: histoire et souvenirs. 1897.

SAINT-ROMME, député
  L'Oisans et la Bérarde: huit jours dans les
  glaciers. 1893.

SAINT-ROMME, député
  Le Pelvoux: voyage en zig-zag dans les Hautes-
  Alpes. 1896.

SARENNE, Jean
  Trois curés en montagne. 1950.

STEINBRÜCK, J   H   T
  Recueil d'études sur Nice et ses environs. 1891.

TUCKETT, Francis Fox
  Dauphiné Alps: heights and outlines. [ca 1870].

WILSON, Claude
  The Aiguilles d'Arves: some notes and memories.
  1928.

236.4 Languedoc, Cevennes, Tarn

BARING-GOULD, Sabine
  A book of the Cevennes. 1907.

BEAUMONT, Jean François Albanis
  Select views of the antiquities and harbours in
  the South of France. 1794.

BETHAM-EDWARDS, M
  The roof of France; or, The Causses of the Lozère.
  1889.

CLUB ALPIN FRANÇAIS. Section de la Lozère et des
Causses
  Les Causses et les Cañons du Tarn... 1892.

MARTEL, Édouard Alfred
  Les Cevennes et la région des Causses, Lozère,
  Aveyron, Hérault, Gard, Ardèche. 3e éd., rev.
  corr. et augm. 1891.

MÉNARD, Léon
  Histoire des antiquités de la ville de Nismes et
  de ses environs. Nouv. éd. 1819.

236.7 Brittany

BLACKBURN, Henry
  Artistic travel in Normandy, Brittany, the
  Pyrenees, Spain and Algeria. New ed. 1895.

FLAUBERT, Gustave
  Par les champs et par les grèves, Pyrénées; Corse.
  1910.

236.9 South-West (excluding Pyrenees: 331-335)

MARTEL, Édouard Alfred
  Le gouffre et la rivière souterraine de Padirac
  (Lot): historique, description, exploration,
  aménagement (1889-1900). [1900].

238 Climbing history, reminiscences

CLUB ALPIN FRANÇAIS. Section de l'Isère
  Une cérémonie alpestre à La Pinéa: inauguration
  du sentier et de la plaque Lucien Vermorel, face
  nord-ouest de La Pinéa, le 13 mai 1926. 1926.

CLUB ALPIN FRANÇAIS. Section des Alpes Maritimes
  Manifestation organisée par la Section des Alpes
  Maritimes le 4 avril 1925 en l'honneur de Victor
  de Cessole à l'occasion du 25me anniversaire de
  sa présidence. 1925.

CLUB ALPIN FRANÇAIS. Section du Sud-Ouest.
  Le centenaire de Franz Schrader. 1944.

LABANDE, François
  100 sommets. 1975.

RAYMANN, Arthur
  Évolution de l'alpinisme dans les Alpes françaises.
  1912.

SOCIÉTÉ DES TOURISTES DU DAUPHINÉ
  Guides, porteurs et muletiers de la Société: règlements et tarifs, chalets et refuges. 1901.

SYNDICAT DES GUIDES DE CHAMONIX-MONT-BLANC
  Règlement et tarif de la Compagnie des Guides de
  Chamonix (Haute-Savoie). 1872.

- - Another ed. 1889.

238 French Alpes - climbing ... (Cont.)

SYNDICAT DES GUIDES DE CHAMONIX-MONT-BLANC
Règlement et tarif des guides de Chamonix. 1862.

- - Another ed. 1872.

SYNDICAT DES GUIDES DE CHAMONIX-MONT-BLANC
Tarif des courses et ascensions. 1936.

239 Guide-books

Les Alpes françaises: Dauphiné, Savoie, Haute Savoie,
Hautes-Alpes. Flammarion, [n.d.].

ARDOUIN-DUMAZET, Victor Eugène
Voyage en France. 2e sér.: Anjou, Bas-Maine,
Nantes, Basse-Loire, Alpes mancelles, Suisse
normande. 1894.

ARDOUIN-DUMAZET, Victor Eugène
Voyage en France. 7e sér.:La région lyonnaise...
3e éd. 1911.

ARDOUIN-DUMAZET, Victor Eugène
Voyage en France. 9e sér.: Bas-Dauphiné... 2e éd.
1903.

ARDOUIN-DUMAZET, Victor Eugène
Voyage en France. 10e sér.: Les Alpes du Léman à
la Durance, nos chasseurs alpins. 1897.

- - 3e éd. 1910.

ARDOUIN-DUMAZET, Victor Eugène
Voyage en France. 12e sér.: Alpes de Provence et
Alpes Maritimes... 2e éd. 1904.

ARDOUIN-DUMAZET, Victor Eugène
Voyage en France. 39e sér.: Pyrénées, partie
orientale... 1904.

ARDOUIN-DUMAZET, Victor Eugène
Voyage en France. 40e sér.: Pyrénées centrales...
1904.

ARDOUIN-DUMAZET, Victor Eugène
Voyage en France. 41e sér.: Pyrénées, partie
occidentale... 1904.

ARNOLLET, François
Nos Alpes Isère et Dorons: guide d'excursions
autour de Brides, Salins... 1895.

BAEDEKER, Karl
Le Midi de la France, depuis l'Auvergne et y
compris les Alpes: manuel du voyageur. 4e éd.
1892.

BAEDEKER, Karl
Northern France from Belgium and the English
Channel to the Loire, excluding Paris and its
environs: handbook for travellers. 1889.

BAEDEKER, Karl
Paris and environs with routes from London to
Paris: handbook for travellers. 18th rev. ed.
1913.

BAEDEKER, Karl
The Riviera, south-eastern France and Corsica, the
Italian lakes and the lake of Geneva: handbook for
travellers. 1931.

BAEDEKER, Karl
South-western France from the Loire and the Rhone
to the Spanish frontier: handbook for travellers.
2nd ed. 1895.

BAEDEKER, Karl
Southern France from the Loire to the Spanish and
Italian frontiers including Corsica: handbook for
travellers. 1891.

BAEDEKER, Karl
Le sud-est de la France, du Jura à la Méditerranèe
y compris la Corse: manuel du voyageur. 1910.

CLUB ALPIN FRANÇAIS. Section de Briançon
Guide du touriste dans le Briançonnais...:
histoire, promenades et excursions, aperçus
botanique et géologique, étude sur la faune...
1898.

FERRAND, Henri
Le col du Lautaret au départ de Grenoble. [n.d.].

FERRAND, Henri
Guide pratique de l'Oisans et du Briançonnais.
[n.d.].

Galignani's Paris guide for 1894. 1894.

GENNEP, Arnold van
La Savoie, vue par les écrivains et les artistes
...: guide pratique des curositées artistiques et
naturelles de la Savoie et de la Haute-Savoie...
[n.d.].

Guide pratique du Vercors et Royans. Toursier,
[n.d.].

JOANNE, Paul
Itinéraire général de la France: Bourgogne, Morvan,
Jura, Lyonnais. 1909.

JOANNE, Paul
Itinéraire général de la France: Provence. 1903.

JOANNE, Paul
Itinéraire général de la France: Savoie. 1910.

JUGE, Stéphane
Guide bleu illustré des Alpes françaises. 1.
Dauphiné-Savoie... 1894.

LE ROUX, Marc
La Haute-Savoie: guide du touriste, du naturaliste
et de l'archéologue. [n.d.].

MUIRHEAD, Findlay and MONMARCHÉ, Marcel
The French Alps. 1923.

MUIRHEAD, Findlay and MONMARCHÉ, Marcel
Southern France. 1926.

NIEPCE, B
Guide dans les Alpes du Dauphiné, vallée
d'Allevard... [1860?].

SERAND, Joseph
Guide de l'alpiniste dans la région d'Annecy.
Fasc. 1. Massif des Dents d'Alex, Lanfon,
Lanfonnet, Cruet. 1910.

TSCHUDI, Iwan von
Savoyen und des angrenzende Piemont und Dauphiné:
Reisetaschenbuch. 1871.

24   ITALY

241 Geology, climate

BARETTI, Martino
Geologia della Provincia di Torino. 1893.

BARETTI, Martino
Il ghiacciaio del Miage: versante italiano del
gruppo del Monte Bianco (Alpi Pennine). 1880.

BARETTI, Martino
Relazione sulle condizioni geologiche del versante
destro della Valle della Dora Riparia tra
Chiomonte e Salbertrand. 1881.

BARETTI, Martino
Studi geologici sul Gruppo del Gran Paradiso.
1877.

BARETTI, Martino
Studi geologici sulle Alpi Graie settentrionali:
memoria. 1879.

241 Italy - geology, climate (Cont.)

BARETTI, Martino
Sui rilevamenti geologici fatti nelle Alpi
piemontesi durante la campagna 1877: nota. 1878.

CASTIGLIONI, Bruno
Il gruppo della Civetta (Alpi Dolomitiche). 1931.

DESIO, Ardito
Results of half-a-century investigation on the
glaciers of the Ortles-Cevedale mountain group
(central Alps) = Risultati... 1973.

FRITZSCH, Magnus
Über Hohengrenzen in den Ortler-Alpen. 1894.

FUCHS, Wilhelm
Die venetianer Alpen: ein Beitrag zur Kenntniss
der Hochgebirge. 1844.

GASTALDI, Bartolomeo
Alcuni dati sulle punte alpine situate fra la
Levanna ed il Rocciamelone. 1868.

GASTALDI, Bartolomeo
Deux mots sur la géologie des Alpes cottiennes.
1872.

GASTALDI, Bartolomeo
Studii geologici sulle Alpi occidentali; con
appendice mineralogica di G. Strüver. 1871-74.
2 pts.

GASTALDI, Bartolomeo
Sui rilevamenti geologici fatti nelle Alpi
piemontesi durante la Compagna del 1877. 1878.

GASTALDI, Bartolomeo
Sulla esistenza del serpentino in posto nelle
colline del Monferrato. 1866.

GIORDANO, Felice
Esame geologico della catena alpina del San
Gottardo che deve essere attraversata dalla grande
galleria della ferrovia italo-elvetica. [1872].

GORDON, Maria M   Ogilvie
Geologisches Wanderbuch der westlichen Dolomiten.
1928.

JERVIS, W   P
The mineral resources of central Italy... 1862-63.
2v. in 1.

MARTINS, Charles
Du retrait et de l'ablation des glaciers de la
vallée de Chamonix, constatés dans l'automne de
1865. 1866.

MOJSISOVICS VON MOJSVÁR, Edmund
Die Dolomit-Riffe von Südtirol und Venetien: Beiträge zur Bildungsgeschichte der Alpen. 1879.

PAYER, Julius
Die Adamello-Presanella-Alpen nach den Forschungen
und Aufnahmen. 1865.

PAYER, Julius
Die centralen Ortler-Alpen (Gebiete: Martell, Laas
und Saent), nebst einem Anhange zu den Adamello-
Presanella-Alpen. 1872.

PAYER, Julius
Die Ortler-Alpen (Sulden-Gebiet und Monte Cevedale)
nach den Forschungen und Aufnahmen. 1867.

PAYER, Julius
Die südlichen Ortler-Alpen... 1869.

PAYER, Julius
Die westlichen Ortler-Alpen (Trafoier Gebiet)...
1868.

PRELLER, C   S   Du Riche
Italian mountain geology. Pt.3. The Gran Sasso
d'Italia group, Abruzzi, Central Apennines; the
volcanoes of central and southern Italy. 1923.

REUSS, A   E
Paläontologische Studien über die älteren Tertiärschichten der Alpen. 1. Abtheilung. Die
Fossilen Anthozoen der Schichten von Castel-
gomberto. 1868.

SACCO, Federico
Sull'origine delle vallate e dei laghi alpini in
rapporto coi sollevamenti delle Alpi e coi
terreni pliocenici e quaternari della Valle Padana.
1885.

VIRGILIO, Francesco
Cenno geognostico-mineralogico sulla miniera cuprifera di Champ de Praz in Valle d'Aosta. 1879.

242 Geography, description, travel

ADDISON, Joseph
Remarks on several parts of Italy, &c. 3rd ed.
1726.

BATTY, Elizabeth Frances
Italian scenery from drawings made in 1817. 1820.

BECKFORD, William
Italy, with sketches of Spain and Portugal. 1834.

BROCKEDON, William
The hand-book for travellers in Italy, from
London to Naples. [1831].

BROCKEDON, William
Road-book from London to Naples. 1835.

COSTELLO, Dudley
Piedmont and Italy from the Alps to the Tiber.
1861. 2v.

DHEULLAND, G   and JULIEN, R
Théâtre de la guerre en Italie; ou, Carte
nouvelle des Principauté de Piemont, République
de Gênes, Duchés de Milan, Plaisance et confins.
1748.

EUSTACE, John Chetwode
A classical tour through Italy. 8th ed. 1841.
3v.

KENNEDY, Benjamin E
My old playground revisited: a tour in Italy in
the spring of 1881. 1882.

KONODY, P   G
Through the Alps to the Apennines. 1911.

LA CONDAMINE, Charles Marie de
Journal of a tour to Italy... 1763.

LALANDE, Jérome de
Voyage en Italie, contenant l'histoire & les anecdotes les plus singulières de l'Italie... 2e éd.,
rev. corr. et augm. 1787-88. 7v.

LASSELS, Richard
The voyage of Italy; or, A compleat journey
through Italy... 1670.

MISSON, Maximilien
Nouveau voyage d'Italie, avec un mémoire contenant des avis utiles à ceux qui voudront faire
le mesme voyage. 4e éd.... 1702. 3v.

MONTAIGNE, Michel de
Journal du voyage de Michel de Montaigne en
Italie, par la Suisse & l'Allemagne en 1580 &
1581. 1775. 3v.

MONTAIGNE, Michel de
[Journal du voyage...]. l'Italia alla fine del
secolo XVI: giornale del viaggio di Michele de
Montaigne in Italia nel 1580 e 1581. Nuova ed.
1895.

MORGAN, Sydney, Lady
Italy. 3rd ed. 1821. 3v.

242 Italy - geography, description, ... (Cont.)

ROGERS, Samuel
  Italy: a poem. 1823.

SABINE, chanoine de
  Les nouveaux voyageurs en Suisse et en Italie:
  beautés et merveilles de ces delicieuses contrées.
  Nouv. éd. [1847].

ST. JOHN, Bayle
  The subalpine kingdom; or, Experiences and studies
  in Savoy, Piedmont, and Genoa. 1856. 2v.

STARKE, Mariana
  Letters from Italy; containing a view of the revolutions in that country... 2nd ed., rev. corr.
  and considerably enl. 1815. 2v.

STOPPANI, Antonio
  Il bel paese: conversazioni sulle bellezze
  naturali, la geologia e la geografia fisica
  d'Italia. 4a ed. 1883.

WALDIE, Jane
  Sketches descriptive of Italy in the years 1816
  and 1817 with a brief account of travels in
  various parts of France and Switzerland in the
  same years. 1820. 4v.

243 History

ALBERTI, Leandro
  Descrittione di tutta l'Italia, et isole per-
  tinenti ad essa... Nuovamente ristampata, & con
  somma diligenza revista, & correta. 1596.

ALBERTI, Leandro
  Isole appartinenti all' Italia; di nuovo
  ricorrette, et con l'aggionta... 1596.

ALLEN, Warner
  Our Italian front. 1920.

AMATI, Pasquale
  Dissertazione ... sopra il passaggio dell'Apennino
  fatto da Annibale e sopra il Castello Mutilo degli
  antichi Galli. 1776.

BOCCARDI, Renzo
  I Verdi: conquant'anni di storia alpina, 1872-1922.
  [1922].

BURTSCHER, Guido
  Die Kämpfe in den Felsen der Tofana: Geschichte
  der von Mai 1915 bis November 1917 heiss umstrittenen Kampfabschnitte Travenanzes und
  Lagazuoi. 1933.

DALTON, Hugh
  With British guns in Italy: a tribute to Italian
  achievement. 1919.

DE AMICIS, Edmondo
  Alle porte d'Italia. 1892.

ETNA, Donato
  Memoriale per l'Ufficiale sulle Alpi. 1900.

LANGES, Gunther
  Front in Fels und Eis: der Weltkrieg im Hochgebirge. 1933.

LEMPRUCH, Moritz Erwin, Freiherr von
  Der König der deutschen Alpen und seine Helden
  (Ortlerkämpfe 1915/1918). 1925.

LOW, Sidney
  Italy in the war. 1916.

LUKAS, Hans
  Der Krieg an Kärntens Granze, 1915-1917: vom
  Hochweissstein bis zum Predil: ein Erinnerungsbuch.
  1938.

NAU, Norbert
  Der Krieg in der Wischberggruppe: Berichte einstiger Mitkämpfer. 1937.

PATRONI, Alfredo
  La conquista dei ghiacciai, 1915-1918. 1924.

PRICE, Julius M
  Six months on the Italian Front from the Stelvio
  to the Adriatic, 1915-1916. 1917.

RENKER, Gustav
  Als Bergsteiger gegen Italien. 1918.

SCHMIDKUNZ, Walter
  Der Kampf über den Gletschern: ein Buch von der
  Alpenfront. 1934.

SHARP, Samuel
  Letters from Italy, describing the customs and
  manners of that country, in the years 1765 and
  1766; to which is annexed an admonition to gentle-
  men who pass the Alps in their tour through Italy.
  2nd ed. 1767.

- - 3rd ed. [17--].

SILIUS ITALICUS, Cajius
  Punicorum; libri septemdecim ad optimas editiones
  collati. 1784.

T., J.G.D.
  Gelegenheit und heutiger Zustand dess Hertzogthums
  Savoyen und Fürstenthums Piemont... 1690.

TARGA, Spartaco
  La guerra di montagna e la difese delle Alpi.
  1926.

TILMAN, Harold William
  When men & Mountains meet. 1946.

TURLETTI, Vittorio
  Attraverso le Alpi: storia aneddotica delle guerre
  di montagna combattutesi dal 1742 al 1748 in
  difesa dell'Italia. 1897.

The war in Italy. Treves, 1916. 3v. in 1.

- - Soldier's ed. 1916.

244 Italian Alps - general

ABBA, Giuseppe Cesare
  Le Alpi nostri e il Monferrato. 1899. 5v.

Le Alpi che cingono l'Italia, considerate militarmente così nell'antica come nella presente loro
  condizione. Pt. la. 1845.

AMORETTI, Carlo
  Viaggio da Milano ai tre laghi, Maggiore, di
  Lugano e di Como, e ne' monti che li circondano.
  6a ed. corretta. 1824.

CLUB ALPINO ITALIANO. Sezione di Milano
  Dizionario alpino italiano. 1892.

CORONA, Guiseppe
  Picchi e burroni: escursioni nelle Alpi. 1876.

DAINELLI, Giotto
  Mondo alpino: numero di primavera de "L'Illustrazione italiana". 1930.

DENINA, Ch.
  Tableau historique, statistique et moral de la
  Haute-Italie, et des Alpes qui l'entourent...
  1805.

FRESHFIELD, Douglas William
  Italian Alps: sketches in the mountains of Ticino,
  Lombardy, the Trentino, and Venetia. 1875.

LAZZARINO, A
  Le nostre Alpi: gite ed escursioni alpine. 1924.

244 Italian Alps - general (Cont.)

LUNN, Sir Arnold
  The Italian lakes and lakeland cities. 1932.

MOSNA, Ezio
  Visioni alpine III. 1933.

QUIGLEY, Hugh
  Lombardy, Tyrol and the Trentino. 1925.

TUCKETT, Elizabeth
  Zigzagging amongst Dolomites. 1871.

245 Dolomites - general

ANGELINI, Giovanni
  Civetta per le vie del passato. 1977.

ANGELINI, Giovanni
  Contributi alla storia dei monti di Zoldo. [1953].

ANGELINI, Giovanni
  Salite in Moiazza. 1950.

BARTH, Hanns
  Gröden und seine Berge: ein Buch der Erinnerung
  und Dankbarkeit. 1927.

BENESCH, Fritz
  Bergfahrten in der Grödner Dolomiten. 1899.

BERNARDI, Alfonso
  La Grande Civetta. 1971.

BERTI, Antonio
  Le Dolomiti del Cadore: guida alpinistica. 1908.

BESOZZI, Manlio
  Dallo Stelvio al Tonale: Merano, Bolzano, Dolomiti
  di Brenta. 1928.

CASTIGLIONI, Bruno
  Il gruppo della Civetta (Alpi dolomitiche). 1931.

CHRISTOMANNOS, Theodor
  Christommanos-Gedenkbuch: Erinnerungen. 1912.

CHRISTOMANNOS, Theodor
  Die neue Dolomitenstrasse: Bozen, Cortina, Toblach
  und ihre Nebenlinien. 1909.

CHRISTOMANNOS, Theodor
  [Die neue Dolomitenstrasse...]. The new Dolomite
  road: Bozen, Cortina, Toblach and its branches.
  [1910].

CLUB ALPINO ITALIANO. Commissione Centrale per la
Protezione della Natura Alpina
  [Come si distrugge un parco:] osservazioni e
  proposte in difesa dei ghiacciai del Carè Alto e
  del Parco Naturale Adamello-Brenta. 1973.

COOLIDGE, William Augustus Brevoort
  A run through the Dolomites in 1876. 1902.

DAVIDSON, L Marion
  Gates of the Dolomites. 1912.

- - 2nd ed. 1914.

DAVIES, Joseph Sanger
  Dolomite strongholds: the last untrodden alpine
  peaks: an account of ascents of the Croda di Lago,
  the Little and Great Zinnen, the Cinque Torri, the
  Fünffingerspitze, and the Langkofel. 1894.

- - Another ed. 1896.

DELAGO, Hermann
  Dolomiten-Wanderbuch. 2 verb. Aufl. 1931.

DESMONTS, Oreste
  Les Dolomites. 1928.

DEUTSCHER UND ÖSTERREICHISCHER ALPENVEREIN.
Sektion Gröden
  Das Grödner Thal, verfasst von Franz Moroder.
  1891.

[Dolomitenland]. The Dolomites. Thames & Hudson,
  1955.

Dolomiti = Dolomitenland = Land of the Dolomits
  [sic]... L. Fränzl, 1948.

EDWARDS, Amelia Blandford
  Untrodden peaks and unfrequented valleys: a
  midsummer ramble in the Dolomites.
  Various editions.

FARRER, Reginald
  The Dolomites: King Laurin's garden. 1913.

FAURE, Gabriel
  The Dolomites. 1925.

FISCHER, Hans
  Dolomiten: Worte und Bilder. 1928.

FRASS, Hermann
  [Dolomieten, berühmte Bergwelt...]. Dolomites,
  mountains of magic: discovery and conquest. 1977.

FRESHFIELD, Douglas William
  [Italian Alps...]. Le Alpi italiane: schizzi delle
  montagne del Trentino. 1971.
  English text and Italian translation of chapters
  7 to 12 of the 1875 ed.

GALLHUBER, Julius
  Die Dolomiten: ein Landschafts- und Bergsteigerbuch. 1934.

GERMAIN, Félix
  Les Dolomites. 1950.

GILBERT, Josiah and CHURCHILL, George Cheetham
  The Dolomite mountains: excursions through Tyrol,
  Carinthia, Carniola, & Friuli in 1861, 1862, &
  1863. 1864.

GILBERT, Josiah and CHURCHILL, George Cheetham
  [The Dolomite mountains...]. Die Dolomitberge:
  Ausflüge... 1865-68. 2v.

GIRARD, Georges F
  À pic: Dolomites. [1936].

GLANVELL, Victor Wolf, Edler von
  Führer durch die Pragser Dolomiten. 1890.

GODDARD, George F
  The Dolomites of the Tyrol. [1875].

GORDON, Maria M Ogilvie
  Geologisches Wanderbuch der westlichen Dolomiten.
  1928.

HAMER, Samuel H
  The Dolomites. 1910.

- - 2nd ed., rev. 1926.

HOWARD, William D and LLOYD, F H
  Photographs among the Dolomite mountains. 1865.

LECLERCQ, Jules
  Le Tyrol et le pays des Dolomites. 1880.

MCDOWALL, Arthur
  Peaks & frescoes: a study of the Dolomites. 1928.

MAZZOTTI, Giuseppe
  Il giardino delle rose: guida spirituale delle
  Dolomiti. 1931.

MAZZOTTI, Giuseppe
  Trionfo della tecnica e decadenza dell'ideale:
  studio su vari caratteri dell'alpinismo dolomitico.
  [1932].

245 <u>Dolomites - general</u> (<u>Cont</u>.)

MEURER, Julius
Führer durch die Dolomiten. 4.Aufl. 1885.

MILNER, Cyril Douglas
The Dolomites. 1951.

MOJSISOVICS VON MOJSVÁR, Edmund
Die Dolomit-Riffe von Südtirol und Venetien;
Beiträge zur Bildungsgeschichte der Alpen. 1879.

Die neue Dolomitenstrasse: Toblach, Ampezzo, Bozen
... 3.Aufl. 1924.

NIEVELT, C   van
Bergstudien: een omgang in het land der Dolomieten.
1888.

PATERA. Lothar
Führer durch die Lienzer Dolomiten. 1909.

POUCHER, W. A.
The magic of the Dolomites. 1951.

PRATI, Pino
Dolomiti di Brenta. 1926.

ROBERTSON, Alexander
Through the Dolomites from Venice to Toblach.
1896.

- - 2nd ed., rev. 1903.

SINIGAGLIA, Leone
[Ricordi alpini delle Dolomiti]. Climbing
reminiscences of the Dolomites. 1896.

SOCIETÀ DEGLI APLINISTI TRIDENTINI
Monografia del gruppo di Sella. 1925.

VALENTINI, Enzo, <u>conte di Laviano</u>
Letters and drawings of Enzo Valentini, conte di
Laviano, Italian volunteer and soldier. 1917.

WATERS, Helena L
From Dolomites to Stelvio. 1926.

WOLFF, Karl Felix
Monographie der Dolomitenstrasse und des von ihr
durchzogenen Gebiets: ein Handbuch für Dolomitenfahrer... 1908.

WOLFF, Karl Felix
Südtirol: Schenkers Führer und Hotel-Anzeiger für
Südtirol. 1911.

WUNDT, Theodor
Wanderbilder aus den Dolomiten. [1894].

WUNDT, Theodor
Wanderungen in den Ampezzaner Dolomiten. [1894].

- - 2.Aufl. 1895.

246   <u>Regions</u>

246.1   <u>North-West</u>

ACLAND, Hugh Dyke
Illustrations of the Vaudois, in a series of views.
1831.

ALDROVANDI, Mario
Aosta: le sue valli e i suoi castelli ... = its
valleys and its castles. 1930.

ARGENTIER, Auguste
Courmayeur et Pré-St-Didier, Val d'Aoste: leurs
bains, leurs eaux & leurs environs. 1864.

ARNAUD, Henri
The glorious recovery by the Vaudois of their
valleys, from the original by Henri Arnaud; with a
compendious history of that people, previous and
subsequent to that event, by Hugh Dyke Acland.
1827.

BEATTIE, William
The Waldenses; or, Protestant valleys of Piedmont,
Dauphiny, and the Ban de la Roche. 1838.

BEATTIE, William
[The Waldenses...]. Les vallées vaudoises pittoresques; ou, Vallées protestantes du Piémont,
du Dauphiné, et du Ban de la Roche. 1838.

BETHA, Pierre Joseph
Valgrisanche: notices historiques. 1877.

BICKNELL, C
The prehistoric rock engravings in the Italian
Maritime Alps. 1902.

BROADBENT, Ellinor Lucy
Alpine valleys of Italy, from San Remo to Lake
Orta. 1928.

BROCHEREL, Giulio
Guida illustrata di Courmayeur e dintorni. 1895.

BROCHEREL, Giulio
La valle d'Aosta. 1932-33. 2v.

BUTLER, Samuel
Alps and sanctuaries of Piedmont and the Canton
Ticino (Op.6). 2nd ed. 1882.

- - New and enl. ed. 1913.

CANE, Felice Giulio
Storia di Chesio e cenni storici della Valle
Strona. 1907.

CANZIO, E
In Valpellina: escursioni e studi, [da] E.
Canzio, F. Mondini, N. Vigna. 1899.

CARREL, Georges
Les Alpes pennines dans un jour; soit, Panorama
boréal de la Becca de Nona, depuis le Mont-Blanc
jusqu'au Mont-Rose. 1855.

CLAVARINO, Luigi, <u>marchese di</u>
Saggio di corografia, statistica e storica delle
valli di Lanzo. 1867.

CLUB ALPINO ITALIANO. <u>Sezione di Bergamo</u>
Guida-itinerario alle prealpi Bergamasche, com-
presa la Valsassina ed i passa alla Valtellina ed
alla Valcamonica. 3a ed., rifatta. 1900.

CLUB ALPINO ITALIANO. <u>Sezione di Biella</u>
Il Biellese   ... nel centenario dalla nascita
di Quintino Sella. 1927.

CLUB ALPINO ITALIANO. <u>Sezione di Biella</u>
Il Biellese: pagine raccolte e pubblicate ...
in occasione del XXX Congresso nazionale in Biella.
1898.

CLUB ALPINO ITALIANO. <u>Sezione di Cuneo</u>
Montagne nostre. 1976.

COCKBURN, James
Views in the valley of Aosta. [1823].

COMBA, E
Histoire des Vaudois. Nouvelle éd. 1898.

COOLIDGE, William Augustus Brevoort
La catena della Levanna (Alpi Graie centrali).
1901.

COOLIDGE, William Augustus Brevoort
Il colle Clapier nella storia. 1911.

COOLIDGE, William Augustus Brevoort
Il colle di San Teodulo nella storia. 1911.

COOLIDGE, William Augustus Brevoort
I colli di Fenètre e di Crète Sèche nella storia.
1914.

COOLIDGE, William Augustus Brevoort
Il gruppo del Gran Paradiso... 1909.

246.1 <u>Italy - North-West</u> (Cont.)

COOLIDGE, William Augustus Brevoort
Les origines du Grand Combin et du Mont Collon et
la légende de la "Crête à Collon". 1913.

COOLIDGE, William Augustus Brevoort
Il Passo di Pagarì nella storia. 1913.

CORONA, Giuseppe
Manuel de l'alpiniste et de l'excursionniste dans
la vallée d'Aoste... 1880-81.

DE AMICIS, Edmondo
Alle porte d'Italia. 1892.

FERRARI, Agostino
La valle di Viù: impressioni e ricordi di escursioni, storia e leggende, usi e costumi. 1912.

FERRERO, Felice
The Valley of Aosta: a descriptive and historical
sketch of an alpine valley... 1910.

FORNIER, Marcellin
Histoire générale des Alpes Maritimes ou
Cottienes et particulière de leur metropolitaine
Ambrum. 1890. 2v.

GALLENGA, Antonio
Country life in Piedmont. 1858.

GIANNITRAPANI, Luigi
La valle d'Aosta: monografia geografica. 1933.

GILLY, William Stephen
Narrative of an excursion to the mountains of
Piemont, and researches among the Vaudois, or
Waldenses... 1824.

- - 2nd ed. 1825.
- - 3rd ed. 1826.
- - 4th ed. 1827.

GILLY, William Stephen
Waldensian researches during a second visit to the
Vaudois of Piedmont. 1831.

GORRET, Amé and BICH, Claude, <u>baron</u>
Guide de la vallée d'Aoste. <u>1876.</u>

HENDERSON, Ebenezer
The Vaudois, comprising observations made during a
tour to the valleys of Piedmont, in the summer of
1844... 1845.

HENRY, <u>abbé</u>
Guide du Valpelline: Valpelline, Ollomont, Oyace,
Bionaz, Prarayé. 2e éd. 1925.

HESS, Adolfo
Indicatore, turistico, alpinistico, sciistico del
Piemonte. 1938.

ISAIA, Cesare
Al Monviso per Val di Po e Val di Varaita:
reminiscenze alpine. 1874.

ITALY. <u>Commissione Reale del Parco</u>
Il Parco Nazionale del Gran Paradiso. 1925.

JOANNE, Paul
Italie. 1. Italie du Nord: Turin, Gênes, Milan,
Venise, les lacs et les vallées méridionales des
Alpes. 1891.

KING, Samuel William
The Italian valleys of the Pennine Alps: a tour
through all the romantic and less-frequented
"vals" of northern Piedmont, from the Tarentaise
to the Gries. 1858.

LAZZARINI, C   F
Escursione nelle Alpi Cozie. 1868.

LECHNER, Ernst
Das Thal der Maira, Bergell: Wanderbild von Maloja
bis Chiavenna und historische Skizze. 1903.

MENSIO, Luigi
Guida di Courmayer, valle d'Aosta. 1895.

MENSIO, Luigi
Guida di Pré St. Didier, valle d'Aosta. 1895.

MENSIO, Luigi
Guide de la ville d'Aoste. 1894.

MEUTA, P   and RIVA, J
La vallée d'Aoste monumentale. 1869.

MUSTON, Alexis
The Israel of the Alps: a history of the persecu-
tions of the Waldenses. 2nd ed. 1853.

NOEL, Baptist W
Notes of a tour in the valleys of Piedmont, in the
summer of 1854. 1855.

PERTUSI, Luigi and RATTI, Carlo
Guida pel villeggiante nel Biellese. 1886.

RAVELLI. Luigi
Nuovissima guida illustrata turistica, artistica,
storica della valle Sesia. [1913].

SCHOTT, Albert
Die deutschen Colonien in Piedmont, ihr Land ihre
Mundart und Herkunft: ein Beitrag zur Geschichte
der Alpen. 1842.

SMITH, Joseph Denham
A voice from the Alps; or, The Vaudois valleys...
1854.

SOCIETÀ ESCURSIONISTI OSSOLANI
L'Ossola e le sue valli.   [ca 1904].

SOCIETÀ ESCURSIONISTE OSSOLANI
[L'Ossola e le sue valli]. L'Ossola et ses vallées.
[ca 1904].

SOCIÉTÉ VAUDOISE D'UTILITÉ PUBLIQUE
Guide des vallées vaudoises du Piémont. 1898.

- - 2e éd. 1907.

THOMASSET, Ch.
La vallée d'Aoste: vue à vol d'oiseau. [1911].

TIBALDI, Tancredi
La regione d'Aosta attraverso i secoli: studi
critici di storia. 1900-1910. 4v.

TONETTI, Federico
Guida illustrata della Valsesia e del Monte Rosa.
1891.

TORNQUIST, A
Geologischer Führer durch Ober-Italien. 1. Das
Gebirge der ober-italienischen Seen... 1902.

VACCARONE, Luigi
Il gruppo del Gran Paradiso. 1894.

VALLINO, Domenico
Album d'un alpinista. 1878-80. Pts. 2-3.

WORSFOLD, W   Basil
The valley of light: studies with pen and pencil
in the Vaudois valleys of Piedmont. 1899.

WYLIE, James A
Wanderings and musings in the valleys of the
Waldenses. 1858.

YELD, George
Scrambles in the eastern Graians, 1878-1897. 1900.

246.2 <u>Lombardy</u>

ABEL, August
Zum Ortler nach Sulden und Tirol... 1898.

BONACOSSA, Aldo
Regione dell'Ortler. 1915.

246.2 Lombardy (Cont.)

CHRISTOMANNOS, Theodor
  Sulden-Trafoi:Schilderungen aus dem Ortlergebiete.
  1895.
CLUB ALPINO ITALIANO. Sezione di Milano
  Itinerari di gite effettuabili da Milano in 1, 2,
  e 3 giorni. 1921.

FRIEDMANN, Louis
  Die Ortler Gruppe. 1893.

Les lacs italiens: Côme, Lugano, Majeur, et la
  vallée d'Intelvi. Lampugnani, [1906].

Lago di Garda e suoi dintorni: Brescia, Verona, Lago
  d'Iseo. Lampugnani, [ca 1905].

LEONHARDI, Georg
  Der Comersee und seine Umgebungen. 1862.

LEONHARDI, Georg
  Das Veltlin nebst einer Beschreibung der Bäder von
  Bormio: ein Beitrag zur Kenntniss der Lombardei,
  zugleich als Wegweiser für Wanderungen vom Stilfser
  Joch bis zum Splügen. 1860.

LUND, T   W   M
  The Lake of Como: its history, art, and
  archaeology. 1910.

M., D.A.M.
  Descrizione della Valtellina e delle grandiose
  strade di Stelvio e di Spluga. 1823.

NIEPMANN, Dr.
  Der Ortler. 1905.

SAGLIO, Silvio
  Ortles-Cevedale: itinerari sciistici. 1935.

Souvenirs d'un voyage par le Stilvio au Lac de Come
  en 1825. G.L. Wesché, [182-].

Voyage pittoresque au Lac de Côme; [illustrée par
  J.J. Wetzel]. 1822.

246.3 Veneto, Trentino, Alto Adige

ANGELINI, Giovanni
  La difesa della Valle di Zoldo nel 1848: memorie
  e documenti. 1948.

BATTISTI, Cesare
  Il Trentino: cenni geografici, storici, economici;
  con un'appendice su l'Alto Adige. 1915.

- - 2a ed. 1917.

BROADBENT, Ellinor Lucy
  Under the Italian Alps. 1925.

BRUNIALTI, Attilio
  Il Trentino nella natura, nella storia, nell'arte
  e nella vita degli abitanti. 1919.

CLUB ALPINO ITALIANO. Sezione di Agordo
  Rapida escursione alpina nel Bellunese. 1888.

COLLEONI, Guardino
  Leggenda e storia del Monte Summano. 1890.

Cortina: official list of hotel & pension terms,
  information regarding reduced railway fares...
  [1929].

COSTELLO, Louisa Stuart
  Venice and the Venetians, with a glance at the
  Vaudois and the Tyrol. New ed. 1851.

ELLMENREICH, F   W
  Meran und Umgebung. 1909.

GILBERT, Josiah
  Cadore; or, Titian's country. 1869.

GRUPPO TRENTINO DI LAVORO PER LA DIFESA
DELL'AMBIENTE NATURALE
  Perchè siamo contrari all'autostrada Trento-
  Vicenza-Rovigo. 1973.

LORENZONI, Antonio
  Cadore. 1907.

NEGRI, Arturo
  Carta geologica della provincia di Vincenza. 1901.

SCHNELLER, Christian
  Südtirolische Landschaften: Nons- und Sulzberg,
  Civezzano und Pine, Vergine, Valsugana. 1899.

- - 2. Reihe. Das Lagerthal - La Valle Lagarina.
  1900.

Venezianer und Tridentiner Voralpen: Trient-Vicenza-
  Padua. Lampugnani, [19--].

246.4 Apennines, Emilia-Romagna

Brian, Alessandro
  Guida per escursioni nell'Appennino parmense.
  1903.

CLUB ALPINO ITALIANO. Sezione di Bologna
  L'Appennino bolognese: descrizioni e itinerari.
  1881.

CLUB ALPINO ITALIANO. Sezione di Bologna
  Fiori del nostro Appennino: primavera, estate,
  autunno nell'Appennino tosco-emiliano. 1964.

246.5 Apennines, Tuscany

BIENDL, Hans
  Der Monte Cristallo. 1906.

BOZANO, Lorenzo
  Guida delle Alpi Apuane, [da] L. Bozano, E.Questa,
  G. Rovereto. 1905.

- - 2a ed. 1921.

CAREGA DI MURICCE, F
  Un'estate a Cutigliano: escursioni e ascensioni
  nell'alto Appennino pistoiese. 1878.

ZOLFANELLI, Cesare and SANTINI,Vincenzo
  Guida alle Alpi Apuane. 1874.

246.6 Apennines, Central Italy, Gran Sasso

CLUB ALPINO ITALIANO. Sezione di Roma
  Tra i monti del Lazio e dell'Abruzzo. 1. 1924.

JOANNE, Paul
  Italie. 2. Italie du Centre: Bologne, Florence,
  et Rome. 1893.

SAN-ROBERTO, Paolo, conte di
  Gita al Gran Sasso d'Italia. 1871.

246.7 Apennines, Southern Italy, Vesuvius

AULDJO, John
  Sketches of Vesuvius with short accounts of its
  principal eruptions, from the commencement of the
  Christian era to the present time. 1832.

- - Another ed. 1833.

BROOKE, N
  Voyage à Naples et en Toscane, avant et pendant
  l'invasion des Français en Italie, avec ... des
  détails sur la terrible explosion du Mont-Vésuve,
  pris sur les lieux à minuit, en juin 1794...
  [1799].

246.7 Apennines, Southern Italy, Vesuvius (Cont.)

FONTAINE, E
  Alpinisme et volcanisme: l'éruption de Vésuve en
  1906. 1928.

HAMILTON, Sir William
  Campi Phlegraei: observations on the volcanoes of
  the two Sicilies... 1776.

- - Supplement... 1779.

HAMILTON, Sir William
  Observations on Mount Vesuvius, Mount Etna, and
  other volcanoes... 1772.

- - 2nd ed. 1773.

TURLERUS, Hieronymus
  De peregrinatione et agro neapolitano, libri II.
  1574.

246.8 Sicily

LOWE, Emily
  Unprotected females in Sicily, Calabria, and on
  the top of Mount Aetna. 1864.

TILLY, Henri, comte de
  Ascensions aux cimes de l'Etna et du Mont Blanc.
  1835.

246.9 Sardinia, Corsica

BLANCHARD, Raoul
  La Corse. 1927.

FLAUBERT, Gustave
  Par les champs et par les grèves; Pyrénées; Corse.
  1910.

FORESTER, Thomas
  Rambles in the island of Corsica and Sardinia,
  with notices of their history, antiquities, and
  present condition. 1858.

GREGOROVIUS, Ferdinand
  Corsica in its picturesque, social and historical
  aspects: the record of a tour in the summer of
  1852. 1855.

JOANNE, Paul
  Itinéraire général de la France: Corse. [Nouvelle
  éd.]. 1892.

LEAR, Edward
  Journal of a landscape painter in Corsica. 1870.

RENWICK, George
  Romantic Corsica: wanderings in Napoleon's isle.
  1909.

RICHARSON, Ralph
  Corsica: notes on a recent visit, with a map of
  the forests and the mines of Corsica. 1894.

248 Climbing history, reminiscences

CLUB ALPINO ITALIANO
  I rifugi del Club Alpino Italiano: storia e descrizione illustrata con elenco dei rifugi costruiti
  in Italia da altre Società alpine. 1905.

CLUB ALPINO ITALIANO. Sezione di Milano
  Ricordo del XXXVII Congresso del Club Alpino
  Italiano, indetto dalla Sezione di Milano. 1906.

CLUB ALPINO ITALIANO. Sezione di Roma
  Da Brescia a Trento per le Alpi Retiche. 1884.

CLUB ALPINO ITALIANO. Sezione fiorentina
  C.A.I. Sezione fiorentina 1868-1968. 1969.

FIGARI, Bartolomeo
  Montagna: fonte di gioia e di vita, scuola
  d'altruismo e di bontà: impressioni e ricordi di un
  alpinista. 1956.

MANARESI, Angelo
  Parole agli alpinisti. 1932.

RUDATIS, Domenico
  Das Letzte im Fels. 1936.

SOCIETÀ DEGLI ALPINISTI TRIDENTINI
  SAT - CAI 1872-1952. 1952.

249 Guide-books

ABBATE, Enrico
  Guida al Gran Sasso d'Italia. 1888.

ABBATE, Enrico
  Guida dell'Abruzzo. 1903.

BAEDEKER, Karl
  Italy from the Alps to Naples: abridged handbook
  for travellers. 3rd rev. ed. 1928.

BAEDEKER, Karl
  Italy: handbook for travellers. Pt.2. Central
  Italy and Rome. 9th rev. ed. 1886.

BAEDEKER, Karl
  Italy: handbook for travellers. Pt.3. Southern
  Italy and Sicily, with excursions to the Lipari
  islands, Malta, Sardinia, Tunis, and Corfu. 9th
  rev. ed. 1887.

BAEDEKER, Karl
  Northern Italy, including Ravenna, Florence, and
  Pisa: handbook for travellers. 15th rev. ed.
  1930.

BAEDEKER, Karl
  Tyrol and the Dolomites including the Bavarian
  Alps: handbook for travellers. 13th rev. ed.
  1927.

BATTISTI, Cesare
  Guida di Mezolombardo e dintorni: il distretto di
  Mezolombardo, da Mezolombardo a Campiglio, Peio,
  Rabbi, Mendola, il gruppo di Brenta. 1905.

BENI, Carlo
  Guida illustrata del Casentino. 1881.

BERNASCONI, Mario
  Itinerari sciistici della zona Formico-Grioni,
  Prealpi bergamasche, valle Seriana. 1929.

BERTARELLI, L V
  Southern Italy including Rome, Sicily and Sardinia.
  1925.

BERTI, Antonio
  Le Dolomiti della Val Talagona e il rifugio
  Padova in Prà di Toro: valli, forcelle e cime.
  1910.

BERTINI, Emilio
  Guida della Val di Bisenzio, Appennino di Monte-
  piano, Toscana. 1881.

BRENTARI, Ottone
  Guida del Cadore e della valle di Zoldo. 1896.

BRENTARI, Ottone
  Guida del Trentino. 1890-1900. 3v.

BRENTARI, Ottone
  Guida di Monte Baldo. 1893.

BRUSONI, Edmondo
  Guida alle Alpi centrali italiane e regioni
  adiacenti della Svizzera. 1892-1908. 3v.

BRUSONI, Edmondo
  Guida ciclo, alpina, itineraria, descrittiva della
  Valtellina e regioni adiacenti della Svizzera.
  1906.

249 Italy - guide-books (Cont.)

BRUSONI, Edmondo
Guida delle Alpi ossolane e regioni adiacenti.
Pt.1. Tra Locarno e il Sempione... 1901.

BRUSONI, Edmondo
Guida itinerario, alpina, descrittiva di Lecco...
1903.

CANTÙ, C
Guida al Lago di Como ed alle strade di Stelvio e
Spluga. 1847.

CLUB ALPINO ITALIANO
Vade mecum dell'alpinista: cenni sulla costituzione
e sull'andamente del Club Alpino Italiano...,
guida dei rifugi ed alberghi alpini. 1900.

CLUB ALPINO ITALIANO. Sezione Belluno
Il viaggiatore nel Bellunese: ricordo del XXV
Congresso degli Alpinisti Italiani. 1893.

CLUB ALPINO ITALIANO. Sezione di Brescia
Guida alpina della provincia di Brescia. 2a ed.,
rev. ed aug. 1889.

CLUB ALPINO ITALIANO. Sezione di Padova
Il Comelico ed il gruppo del Popera. 1924.

CLUB ALPINO ITALIANO. Sezione di Verona
Attraverso le Prealpi veronesi e sul Lago di
Garda: 40o Congresso degli Alpinisti Italiani,
Verona 5-11 settembre, 1909. 1909.

DELLEPIANE, Giovanni
Guida per escursioni nell'Appenino ligure e nelle
sue adiacenze... 1892.

- - 4a ed. 1914.

DITTMAR, Franz
Dittmar's Führer für die Strecke München-Brenner-
bahn nach Bozen-Gries, Meran, Trient, Arco und an
den Gardasee, nach Verona und Venedig. 2 verm.
und verb. Aufl. 1905.

FERRARI, Agostino
I rifugi alpini d'Italia. 1925.

FERUGLIO, G
Guida touristica del Cadore, Zoldano ed Agordino.
1910.

FONTANA, Carlo
Guida storico, alpina di Valdagno, Recoaro, Schio,
Arsiero... 1898.

FRACCARO, Plinio
Guida alpina del Bassanese e delle montagne
limitrofe. 1903.

- - Another ed. 1909.

FRESIA, Camillo
Cuneo e le sue vallate. 1905.

GNECCHI, A
Le montagne dell'alta valle Camonica: guida
alpina. 1908.

GORTANI, Michele
Gorizia con le vallate dell'Isonzo e del Vipacco.
1930.

Guida al Sacre Monte di Varallo. 1857.

Guida illustrata della valle d'Aosta... Pt.1.
Valle inferiore. 4a ed., interamente rifatta.
Casanova, 1899.

[Guida illustrata della valle d'Aosta...]. Guide-
manuel du touriste dans la vallée d'Aoste; la
vallée de Gressoney et le massif du Mont-Rose.
Casanova, [18--].

HOTEL MIRAVALLE
Hotel Miravalle, Gressoney Saint-Jean. [18--].

IVIANI, Antonio
Guida delle grotte del Timavo a S. Canziano presso
Divaccia e della grotto Gigante presso Villa
Opicina, Trieste. 1934.

LUDWIG, J M
Pontresina and its neighbourhood. 4th [2nd
English] ed. 1879.

MAGNI, Fermo
Guida illustrata della Valsassina. 1904.

MARINELLI, Giovanni
Guida del Canal del Ferro o Valle del Fella,
Tagliamento. 1894.

MARINELLI, Giovanni
Guida della Carnia... 1898.

- - 2a ed. 1906.

MARINELLI, Olinto
Guida delle Prealpi Giulie; distretta di Gemona,
Tarcento, S. Daniele, Cividale e S. Pietro...
1912.

MARTYN, Thomas
An appendix to the Gentleman's guide through Italy
containing catalogues of the paintings, statues,
busts etc. 1787.

MEURER, Julius
Madonna di Campiglio, Arco, Riva und Garda-See,
mit Touren in die Brenta-Dolimiten und in die
Presanella-Adamello-Gruppe... 1889.

MUIRHEAD, Litellus Russell
Northern Italy, from the Alps to Florence. 3rd ed.
1937.

NICCOLAI, Francesco
Mugello e Val di Sieve: guida topografica, storico-
artistica, illustrata. 1914.

Nouveau guide du voyageur en Italie. 6e éd.
Artaria, 1841.

Nuova guida illustrata della valle d'Aosta... Pt.2.
Valle superiore. Casanova, 1882.

OCCIONI-BONAFFONS, G
Illustrazione del commune di Udine. 1886.

PERTUSI, Luigi and RATTI, Carlo
Guida illustrata pel villeggiante del Biellese:
santuari ed ospizi stabilimenti idroterapici,
passeggiate ed escursioni... 1901.

RABAJOLI, G
Guida alle Terme di Vinadio. 1877.

RATTI, Carlo
Guida per il villeggiante e l'alpinista nelle
valli di Lanzo. 1904. 2v.

RAVELLI, Luigi
La Val Grande del Sesia... [19--].

RAVELLI, Luigi
Varallo e dintorni: guida del villeggiante.
[19--].

SANTI, E
Itinerari skiistici della Val Formazza. 1927.

SCACCHI, D
Scanno e la valle del Sagittario, Abruzzo. 1899.

SCHMIDL, A Adolf
Reisehandbuch durch das Herzogthum Steiermark,
Illnrein, Venedig und die Lombardie. 1836.

SOCIETÀ ALPINA DELLE GIULIE
Guida dei dintorni di Trieste. 1909.

TIGRI, Giuseppe
Guida della montagna pistoiese. 3a ed. corr.
1878.

249 Italy - guide-books (Cont.)

VACCARONE, Luigi
   Guida-itinerario per le valli dell'Orco, di Soana
   e di Chiusella. 1878.

VALERY
   Voyages historiques, littéraires et artistiques en
   Italie: guide raisonné et complet du voyageur et
   de l'artiste. 2e éd. 1838.

VEREIN DER FREUNDE UND GÖNNER, San Martino di
Castrozza
   Wege und Markirungen in der Umgebung von San
   Martino di Castrozza, Südtirol. 4.Aufl. 1911.

25   AUSTRIA

251 Geology, climate

BARTH, L   and PFAUNDLER, L
   Die Stubaier Gebirgsgruppe, hypsometrisch und
   orografisch bearbeitet... 1865.

BLÜMCKE, Adolf and HESS, Hans
   Die Nachmessungen am Vernagtferner in den Jahren
   1891, 1893 und 1895. 1897.

BLÜMCKE, Adolf and HESS, Hans
   Untersuchungen am Hintereisferner. 1899.

DALLA TORRE, Karl Wilhelm von
   Tirol, Vorarlberg und Liechtenstein. 1913.

ECKERT, Max
   Das Gottesackerplateau, ein Karrenfeld im Allgäu:
   Studien zur Lösung des Karrenproblems. 1902.

FINSTERWALDER, S
   Der Vernagtferner: seine Geschichte und seine
   Vermessung... 1897.

FRECH, Fritz
   Über den Gebirgsbau der Tiroler Zentralalpen mit
   besonderer Rücksicht auf den Brenner. 1905.

FRITZSCH, Magnus
   Verzeichniss der bis zum Sommer 1896 in den
   Ostalpen gesetzten Gletschermarken. 1898.

GANSS, Ortwin
   Erläuterungen zur geologischen Karte der Dachstein-
   gruppe. 1954.

HACQUET, Balthasar
   Hacquet's Mineralogisch-botanische Lustreise, von
   dem Berg Terglou in Krain, zu dem Berg Glokner in
   Tyrol... 1784.

LEVY, Friedrich
   Ostalpine Formenstudien. 1920-23. 8 pts. in 2.

PASCHINGER, Viktor
   Pasturzenstudien. 1948.

PENCK, Albrecht
   Die Vergletscherung der deutschen Alpen, ihre
   Ursachen, periodische Wiederkehr und ihr Einfluss
   auf die Bodengestaltung. 1882.

PETZHOLDT, Alexander
   Beiträge zur Geognosie von Tyrol: Skizzen auf
   einer Reise durch Sachsen, Bayern,Salzkammergut,
   Salzburg, Tyrol, Östreich. 1843.

RICHTER, Eduard
   Die Gletscher der Ostalpen. 1888.

SCHERZER, Hans
   Geologisch-botanische Wanderungen durch die Alpen.
   1. Bd. Das Berchtesgadener Land. 1927.

SEDGWICK, Adam and MURCHISON, Sir Roderick Impey
   A sketch of the structure of the eastern Alps; with
   sections through the newer formations on the
   northern flanks of the chain and through the
   tertiary deposits of Styria. [1831].

SONKLAR, Karl, Edler von Innstädten
   Die Oetzthaler Gebirgsgruppe mit besonderer Rücksicht auf Orographie und Gletscherkunde. 1860.

WÄHNER, Franz
   Das Sonnwendgebirge im Unterinnthal: ein Typus
   alpinen Gebirgsbaues. Pt. 1. 1903.

WALCHER, Joseph
   Nachrichten von den Eisbergen im Tyrol. 1773.

252 Geography, description, travel

Album von Salzburg, Salzkammergut und Berchtesgaden.
   J. Schoen, [ca 1850].

BARROW, John, 1808-1898
   Tour in Austrian Lombardy, the northern Tyrol, and
   Bavaria... 1841.

CHARNOCK, Richard Stephen
   Guide to the Tyrol: comprising pedestrian tours
   made in Tyrol, Styria, Carinthia, and Salzkammergut, during the summers of 1852 and 1853... 1857.

DEUTSCH-AKADEM. GEOGRAPHENVEREIN GRAZ
   Zur Geographie der deutschen Alpen. 1924.

DEUTSCHER ALPENVEREIN
   Die Kartographie im Alpenverein, von Erik
   Arnberger; hrsg. vom Deutschen Alpenverein und vom
   Österreichischen Alpenverein. 1970.

FINSTERWALDER, Richard
   Alpenvereinskartographie und die ihr dienenden
   Methoden. 1935.

GEDYE, G   E   R
   A wayfarer in Austria. 1928.

GEISTBECK, Alois
   Die Seen der deutschen Alpen: eine geographische
   Monographie. 1885.

GROSS, Anton Johann
   Handbuch für Reisende durch die österreichische
   Monarchie, mit besonderer Rücksicht auf die
   südlichen und Gebirgsländer... 2.verm. Aufl.
   1834. 2 pts. in 1.

HACQUET, Balthasar
   Reise durch die Norischen Alpen physikalischen und
   andern Inhalts, unternommen in den Jahren 1784
   bis 1786. 1791. 2 pts. in 1.

INGLIS, Henry D
   The Tyrol; with a glance at Bavaria. 2nd ed.
   1834. 2v.

- - 3rd ed. 1837.

LATROBE, Charles Joseph
   The pedestrian: a summer's ramble in the Tyrol,
   and some of the adjacent provinces. 1832.

NEWTH, J   D
   Austria. 1930.

OSMOND, Th., comte d'
   Dans la montagne, le Tyrol autrichien: le
   Salzkammergut, le Pongau, la Styrie, le Pâtre du
   Moser. 1878.

ROSEGGER, P   K
   Wanderungen durch Steiermark und Kärnten. [1880].

SCHULTES, J   A
   Reise auf den Glockner. 1804.

252 Austria - geography, description..., (Cont.)

SIMONY, Friedrich
Physiognomischer Atlas der österreichischen Alpen.
1862.

- - Charakterbilder aus den österreichischen Alpen
... 1862.

WEINGARTNER, Josef
Bozner Burgen. 1922.

WOLF, Karl
Alpentrachten unserer Zeit. 1937.

ZELLER, Franz
Lese- und Sprachbuch für allgemeine Volkschulen
in Tirol. Vol.3. 1909.

ZIAK, Karl
Erwanderte Heimat: Land und Leute in Österreich.
3.Aufl. 1949.

253 History

FRANZ, Leonhard
Vorgeschichtliches Leben in den Alpen. 1929.

JUSTICE FOR THE TYROL COMMITTEE
Austria's just claim to South Tyrol. [1944?].

MITTON, G E
Austria-Hungary. 1915.

PALMER, Francis H E
Austro-Hungarian life in town and country. [19--].

REUT-NICOLUSSI, Eduard
Tirol unterm Beil. 1928.

THOMAS, Elizabeth
Hofer, the Tyrolese. 1824.

255 Austrian Alps - general

Alpenröslein; oder, Vierundzwanzig malerische
Ansichten [von J.B. Dreseli]. 1836.

BARTH, Hermann von
Aus den nördlichen Kalkalpen: Ersteigungen und
Erlebnisse in den Gebirgen Berchtesgadens, des
Algäu, des Innthales, des Isar-Quellengebietes und
des Wetterstein. 1874.

BARTH, Hermann von
Aus den nördlichen Kalkalpen: Ersteigungen und
Erlebnisse...[1910]. 2v.

BARTH, Hermann von
Einsame Bergfahrten. [1925].

BENESCH, Erwin
Österreichs Alpenwelt: über Berg und Tal vom
Bodensee bis zum Wienerwald. 1937.

BURCKHARDT, Alexander
Bergfahrten und Spaziergänge. Vol.1. [1898].

DESSAUER, A
Bergwanderungen in den Ostalpen. 1912.

DRÄGER, Anton
Deutsche Reisen für die reisere Jugend unternommen
und beschrieben. Th.1. Die Wunder des Hochgebirges. 1853.

DU PLESSIS, J , comte
L'Alpe enchanteresse: Salzbourg, le Salzkammergut,
les Hauts Tauern. 1913.

GRANDJEAN, Maurice
À travers les Alpes autrichiennes. 1896.

HARTMANN, Otto
Im Zauber des Hochgebirges: alpine Stimmungsbilder.
[1914].

HEILMANN, A
A. Heilmann's Alpine-Zeichen-Studien: lose Blätter
aus seinem Skizzenbuche zum Studium und zur
Vervollkommnung im landschaftlichen Zeichnen.
[1910].

HERZ, Mar
Oesterreichs Berge und Thäler: Kund- und Bade-
Reisebuch. 1876.

KADICH, Hanns Maria von
Aus Österreichs Bergen. 1913.

KÖNIG, Erich
Mit Rucksack und Eispickel: Bergerinnerungen.
[1896].

KREBS, Norbert
Länderkunde der österreichischen Alpen. 1913.

KREBS, Norbert
Die Ostalpen und das heutige Österreich: eine
Länderkunde. 2. wesentlich erw. Aufl. 1928. 2v.

LEITMEIER, Hans
Die österreichischen Alpen: eine zusammenfassende
Darstellung. 1928.

MAYER-PFANNHOLZ, Anton
Deutsches Alpenland: ein Heimatbuch. 1920.

MAYR, Julius
Auf stillen Pfaden: Wanderbilder aus Heimat und
Fremde. 1924.

MÜLLER, Karl
Ansichten aus den deutschen Alpen: ein Lehrbuch
für Alpenreisende, ein Naturgemälde für alle
Freunde der Natur. 1858.

NORDMANN, Johannes
Meine Sonntage: Wanderbuch aus den Bergen des
österreichischen Hochlandes. 2.verm. Aufl. 1880.

NOWOPACKÝ, Jan
Alpine Kunstblätter. 1903.

PETERSEN, Theodor
Haupthöhenpunkte in den österreichischen Hochalpen. [ca 1865].

RITTER, Hermann
Bergfahrten: Erinnerung an die Hochalpen. [1896].

RUTHNER, Anton von
Die Alpenländer Oesterreichs und die Schweiz:
eine Parallele der Naturschönheiten des
österreichischen und Schweizer Hochlandes. 1843.

SCHADEN, Adolph von
Neustes Taschenbuch für Reisende durch Bayerns
und Tyrols Hochlande... 1833.

SCHAUBACH, Adolph
Die deutschen Alpen: ein Handbuch für Reisende
durch Tyrol, Oesterreich, Steyermark, Illyrien,
Oberbayern und die anstossenden Gebiete. 1845-46.
4v.

SCHAUBACH, Adolph
Die deutschen Alpen für Einheimische und Frende
geschildert. 2.Aufl. 1865-71. 6v. in 5.

SCHAUBACH, Adolph
Die deutschen Alpen... [1911]. 2v.

SCHUBERT, S H
Wanderbüchlein eines reisenden Gelehrten nach
Salzburg, Tirol und die Lombardey. 1823.

SÖLCH, Johann
Die Ostalpen. 1930.

THIELE, Ludwig
Bilder aus den Alpen: Erinnerungen eines Malers.
1857.

TURSKY, Franz
Höhenzauber: Erlebnisse und Gedanken eines Bergsteigers und Schneeschuhläufers. 1924.

256 Austria - regions

256.1 Tyrol, Vorarlberg

ACHLEITNER, Arthur and UBL, Emil
  Tirol und Vorarlberg: neue Schilderung von Land
  und Leuten. 2.Aufl. [1905?].

[Ansichten von Tyrol]. Views in the Tyrol, from
  drawings by T. Allom, after original sketches by
  Johanna v. Isser ...; with letterpress descrip-
  tions, by a companion of Hofer [i.e. Josef
  Hormayr].
  Various editions.

BAILLIE-GROHMAN, William Adolphus
  Gaddings with a primitive people, being a series
  of sketches of alpine life and customs. 1878. 2v.

BAILLIE-GROHMAN, William Adolphus
  The land in the mountains, being an account of the
  past & present of Tyrol, its people and its
  castles. 1907.

BAILLIE-GROHMAN, William Adolphus
  Tyrol. 1908.

BAILLIE-GROHMAN, William Adolphus
  Tyrol and the Tyrolese: the people and the land in
  their social, sporting, and mountaineering aspects.
  1876.

- - 2nd ed. 1877.

BARTH, Hanns
  Nord-Tirol bis zum Brenner und Vorarlberg. 29.
  Aufl. 1922.

BARTH, Hanns
  Tirol und Vorarlberg: praktischer Reiseführer.
  27.Aufl. 1911-12.

BAUMEISTER, Georg
  Das Bauernhaus des Walgaues und der walserischen
  Bergtäler Vorarlbergs einschliesslich des Montavon:
  Beiträge zur Hausforschung in Alemannisch-
  Romanischem Grenzgebiet. 1913.

BECKER, Gustav
  Die Hochwilde. 1907.

BENESCH, Fritz
  Führer auf den Schneeberg. 5.Aufl. 1924.

BERTRAM, Anthony
  Pavements and peaks: impressions of travel in
  Germany and Austria. 1933.

BEYRER, Magnus Bartholomaeus
  Guide des voyageurs dans la ville d'Innsbruck et
  des environs. [1826].

BLAAS, J
  Geologischer Führer durch die Tiroler und Vorarlberger Alpen. 1902. 7v.

BLAKE, J   M
  Joy of Tyrol: a human revelation. [19--].

BOHLIG, F
  Die Elmauer Haltspitze. 1905.

BONER, Charles
  Chamois hunting in the mountains of Bavaria and in
  the Tyrol. New ed. 1860.

BUSK, R   H
  The valleys of Tyrol: their traditions and customs,
  and how to visit them. 1874.

CLARE, Constance Leigh
  The Brenner Pass: Tirol from Kufstein to Riva.
  1912.

COTESWORTH, W
  Idle days in the Vorarlberg and its neighbourhood.
  1887.

CRANZ, H
  Bettelwurf- und Speckkarspitze. 1906.

DELAGO, Hermann
  Die Zillertaler Alpen. 1925.

DEUTSCHER UND ÖSTERREICHISCHER ALPENVEREIN.
Sektion Hochland
  Die Nördliche Karwendelkette. 1913.

ENTRESS, Ernst
  Das Zuckerhütl und seine Nachbarn. 1909.

ENZENSPERGER, Ernst
  Die Gruppe der Mädelegabel. 1909.

FICKER, Heinrich von and AMPFERER, Otto
  Aus Innsbrucks Bergwelt: Walderbilder aus
  Innsbrucks Bergen. 1902.

FLAIG, Walther
  Arlberg: Ski und Schnee. 1933.

FLAIG, Walther
  Der Arlberg und die Klostertaler Alpen mit den
  Grenzgebieten des südlichen Bregenzer Waldes: ein
  Hochgebirgsführer. 1929.

FROMMEL, C
  Tyrol scenery after paintings by C. Frommel.
  [1851?].

GESELLSCHAFT VON FREUNDEN DES STUBEITHALES
  Stubei: Thal und Gebirg, Land und Leute. 1891.

GOLBÉRY, Marie Philippe de
  Histoire et description de la Suisse et du Tyrol.
  1838.

GRABMAYR, Karl von
  Süd-Tirol: Land und Leute vom Brenner bis zur
  Salurner Klause. 1919.

GSALLER, Carl
  Das Stubeithal: eine topographisch-touristische
  Darstellung von Thal und Gebirg. 1891.

GWERCHER, Franz
  Das Oetzthal in Tirol: eine statistisch-
  topographische Studie. 1886.

HAMMER, Wilhelm
  Geologischer Führer durch die Westtiroler Zentralalpen. 1922.

HARTWIG, E   von
  Briefe aus und über Tirol geschrieben in den
  Jahren 1843 bis 1845: ein Beitrag zur näheren
  Charakteristik dieses Alpenlandes im Allgemeinen
  und der Meraner Gegend. 1846.

HAUSHOFER, Max
  Tirol. 1899.

HILL, E   R
  Rambles and scrambles in the Tyrol. 1885.

HOFERER, Erwin and SCHÄTZ, Josef Julius
  Münchner Kletterführer: 250 der lohnendsten
  Kletterfahrten in den Vorbergen und im bayerisch-
  tirolischen Grenzgebiet... 1923.

HOHENLEITNER, Siegfried
  Die Stubaier Alpen. 1925.

HOLLAND, Clive
  Tyrol and its people. 1909.

HUBER, Sepp
  Führer durch das Tote Gebirge einschliesslich
  Warscheneck, Höllengebirge und Sengsengebirge.
  1927.

JOANNE, Paul
  Austriche-Hongrie: Tyrol, Bavière méridionale.
  1885.

256.1 <u>Tyrol, Vorarlberg</u> (Cont.)

KADNER, Herbert
  Leberle Führer durch das Wettersteingebirge ...
  4... Aufl. 1921.

KINZEL, Karl and LUCKWALD, Christine von
  Tiroler Bergwanderungen: noch ein Buch zum
  Lustmachen. 1911.

KLEBELSBERG, R von
  Südtiroler Mittelgebirgswanderungen. 1936.

LECLERCQ, Jules
  Le Tyrol et le pays des Dolomites. 1880.

LEUCHS, Georg
  Führer durch das Kaisergebirge... 4.Aufl. 1922.

LÖWL, Ferdinand
  Aus dem Zillerthaler Hochgebirge. 1878.

MCCRACKAN, William D
  The spell of Tyrol. 1914.

MCCRACKAN, William D
  The Tyrol. 1905.

MADUSCHKA, Leo
  Die jüngste Erschliessungsgechichte des Wilden
  Kaisers. 1933.

MAYRHOFER, Joseph K
  Ueber den Brenner: von Innsbruck nach Botzen und
  die Seiten Thäler: topographisch-kulturhistorische
  Schilderung. 1868.

MELZERKNAPPEN
  Die Lechtaler Alpen. 1924.

MERCEY, Frédéric
  Le Tyrol et le nord de l'Italie: journal d'une excursion dans ces contrées en 1830. 2e éd. 1845.
  2v.

MERKH, R
  "Es war einmal": deutsche Wanderungen in Südtirol
  und Oberitalien. 1913.

MORROW, Ian F D
  The Austrian Tyrol: the land in the mountains.
  1931.

MURDOCH, Nina
  Tyrolean June: a summer holiday in Austrian Tyrol.
  1936.

Neuester Führer durch Innsbruck und Umgebung.
  A. Edlinger, [n.d.].

NICHOLSON, Francis
  Views in the Tyrol. [1829].

NIEBERL, Franz
  Das Totenkirchl. 2.Aufl. 1923.

NOE, R
  Tirol und die angrenzenden Alpengebiete von
  Vorarlberg, Salzburg und Salzkammergut sowie das
  bayerische Hochland nebst München in 20 Tagen.
  2.verm. Aufl. 1907-08.

OBERSTEINER, Ludwig
  Führer durch die Ötztaler Alpen. 2.Aufl. 1937.

Original Tyrolean costumes in ten-colour reproductions of four-hundred standard specimens of
  national costumes from private and public collections. 1937.

PFANN, Paul
  Bilder aus Tyrol. [1912].

PRITCHARD, Henry Baden
  Tramps in the Tyrol. 1874.

RADIO-RADIIS, Alfred von
  Der Rosengarten. 1907.

RASCH, Gustav
  Touristen-Lust und Lied in Tirol: Tiroler Reisebuch. 1874.

RUTHNER, Anton von
  Aus dem oesterreich. Hochgebirge: Ersteigung der
  Hohen Wildspitze im Oetzthale. 1863.

RUTHNER, Anton von
  Aus Tirol: Berg- und Gletscher-Reisen in den
  österreichischen Hochalpen. Neue Folge. 1869.

RUTHNER, Anton von
  Übergang aus dem Ötzthale in das Pitzthal über den
  Hochvernagt- und Sechsegertenferner. 1859.

SCHÄTZ, Josef Julius
  Südtirol vom Brenner bis Salurn: ein Buch von
  Menschen, Bergen und der Schönheit des Landes.
  1923.

SCHUCHT, Richard
  Die Wildspitze. 1906.

SCHWAIGER, Heinrich
  Heinrich Schwaigers Führer durch das Karwendel-
  gebirge. 3.Aufl. 1907.

SCHWAIGHOFER, Hermann
  Bergwanderbuch: gesammelte Schilderungen aus
  Nordtirol. 1924.

SCHWAIGHOFER, Hermann
  Die Stubaier- und Otztaler-Alpen. [19--].

SEIDL, Joh. Gabr.
  Wanderungen durch Tyrol und Steyermark. [18--].
  2v.

SERRES, Marcel de
  Voyage dans le Tyrol, et une partie de la Bavière,
  pendant l'année 1811. 1823. 2v.

SMYTHE, Frank S
  Over Tyrolese hills. 1936.

SPRINGENSCHMID, Karl
  Bauern in den Bergen. 1936.

STEINITZER, Alfred
  Geschichtliche und kulturgeschichtliche Wanderungen
  durch Tirol und Vorarlberg. 1905.

STEINITZER, Alfred
  Das Land Tirol: geschtliche, kulture und kunst-
  geschichliche Wanderungen. 1922.

STODDARD, Frederick Wolcott
  Tramps through Tyrol: life, sport, and legend.
  1912.

TIROLER LANDESVERKEHRSAMT
  Tirol: Natur, Kunst, Volk, Leben. 1927.

TRENTINAGLIA-TELVENBURG, Josef, <u>Ritter von</u>
  Das Gebiet der Rosanna und Trisanna (Sannengebiet
  in West-Tirol); mit besonderer Berücksichtigung
  der orographischen, glacialen ... Verhältnisse,
  nach eigenen Untersuchungen... 1875.

TRENTINI, Albert von
  Südtirol. [1912].

TUCKETT, Elizabeth
  Pictures in Tyrol and elsewhere, from a family
  sketch-book. 1867.

- - 2nd ed. 1869.

WALTENBERGER, A
  Orographie der Algäuer Alpen. 1872.

WALTENBERGER, A
  Orographie des Wetterstein-Gebirges und der
  Miemingerkette: Orographie des Wetterstein- und
  Karwendel-Gebirges I. 1882.

Wanderungen durch Tirol und Vorarlberg. [1879].

256.1 <u>Tyrol, Vorarlberg</u> (Cont.)

WARING, George E
  Tyrol and the skirt of the Alps. 1880.

WECHSBERG, Joseph
  Avalanche. 1958.

WHITE, Walter
  Holidays in Tyrol: Kufstein, Klobenstein, and
  Paneveggio. 1876.

WHITE, Walter
  A month at Gastein; or, Footfalls in the Tyrol.
  [18--].

WHITE, Walter
  On foot through Tyrol in the summer of 1855. 1856.

WITZENMANN, Ad.
  Sesvenna und Lischanna. 1907.

256.2 <u>Hohe Tauern, Gross Glockner, Gross Venediger</u>

BRANDENSTEIN, Wilhelm
  Glocknerfahrten. 1931.

BÜDEL, Julius and GLASER, Ulrich
  Neue Forschungen im Umkreis der Glocknergruppe.
  1969.

FISCHER, Hans
  Der Grossglockner: das Buch des Königs der
  deutschen Berge. 2.Aufl. 1929.

GMELCH, Jos.
  Der Grossglockner. 1906.

GRUBER, Hans
  Die Goldberg, Sonnblick- Gruppe in den Hohen
  Tauern: touristischer Spezialführer. 1904.

HOFMANN, Karl and STÜDL, Johann
  Wanderungen in der Glockner-Gruppe. 1871.

HUMPELER, Louis
  Der Grossvenediger. 1907.

KNORR, Otto
  Der Grossvenediger in der Geschichte des
  Alpinismus. 1932.

KÜRSINGER, Ignaz von and SPITALER, Franz
  Der Gross-Venediger in der norischen Central-
  Alpenkette, seine erste Ersteigung am 3. September
  1841, und sein Gletscher ...; mit einem Anhange:
  Die zweite Ersteigung am 6. September 1842. 1843.

PETERSEN, Theodor
  Ein Ausflug auf den Grossvenediger: Reiseskizze.
  [1865?].

PREUSS, Rudolf
  Landschaft und Mensch in den Hohen Tauern:
  Beiträge zur Kulturgeographie. 1939.

R., J.A.
  Fahrten in den Hohen Tauern. 1875-77. 2v.

RABL, Josef
  Illustrierter Führer auf den Tauernbahn und ihren
  Zugangslinien... 1906.

RUTHNER, Anton von
  Berg und Gletscher-Reisen in den österreichischen
  Hochalpen. 1864.

RUTHNER, Anton von
  Höhenmessungen aus der Tauernkette. 1862.

RUTHNER, Anton von
  Das Maltathal in Kärnthen: Ersteigung des Hochalpenspitzes. 1861.

RUTHNER, Anton von
  Wanderungen auf dem Glocknergebiete. 1857.

- - Neue Folge. 1863.

SONKLER, Karl, <u>Edler von Innstädten</u>
  Die Gebirgsgruppe der Hohen-Tauern, mit besonderer
  Rücksicht auf Orographie, Gletscherkunde, Geologie
  und Meteorologie. 1866.

TURSKY, Franz
  Führer durch die Glocknergruppe. 2.verb. und
  verm. Aufl. 1925.

TURSKY, Franz
  Führer durch die Goldberggruppe, Sonnblickgruppe.
  1927.

TURSKY, Franz
  Der Grossglockner und seine Geschichte. 1922.

ZOPOTH, Johann
  Tagebuch einer Reise auf den bis dahin uner-
  steigenen Berg Gross-Glokner an den Gränzen
  Cärntens, Salzburgs und Tirols... 1800.

256.3 <u>Salzburg</u>

Album vom Salzburger-Alpenlande. [ca 1850].

BOHLIG, F
  Der Watzmann. 1906.

PRINZINGER, A
  Die Höhen-Namen in der Umgebung von Salzburg und
  Reichenhall: ein Beitrag zur Orts- Sprach- und
  Volkskunde... 1861.

256.4 <u>Carinthia</u>

BENESCH, Fritz
  Führer auf die Karalpe. 8.verm. und verb. Aufl.
  1925.

FRISCHAUF, Johannes
  Aus den Schladminger Tauern. 1892.

RABL, Josef
  Illustrirter Führer durch Kärnten mit besonderer
  Berücksichtigung der Städte Klagenfurt und
  Villach... 1884.

256.5 <u>Styria</u>

BORDE, Josef and NOSSBERGER, Adolf
  Führer für Schneeschuläufer durch die Ennstaler
  Alpen... 1922.

COELLN, Ernst von
  Das Buch vom Schöckel. [1911].

GALLHUBER, Julius
  Das Gesäuse und seine Berge: ein Landschafts- und
  Bergsteigerbuch. 1928.

HESS, Heinrich
  Spezialführer durch das Gesäuse und durch die
  Ennstaler Gebirge, zwishen Admont und Eisenerz.
  3... verm. Aufl... 1895.

JÄGER, Gustav
  Der Donatiberg bei Rohitsch in Unter-Steiermark.
  1867.

RABL, Josef
  Illustrirter Führer durch Steiermark und Krain mit
  besonderer Berücksichtigung der Alpengebiete von
  Obersteiermark und Oberkrain. 1885.

SCHUMACHER, August
  Bilder aus den Alpen der Steyermark. 1822.

WEIDMANN, F C
  Alpengegenden Niederösterreichs und Obersteyer-
  marks im Bereiche der Eisenbahn von Wien bis
  Mürzzuschlag. 4.verm. ... versehene Aufl. 1862.

WEIDMANN, F C
  Darstellungen aus dem steyermärk'schen Oberlande.
  1834.

256.6 North-East, Lower Austria

BENESCH, Fritz
    Der Semmering und seine Berge: ein Album der
    Semmering Landschaft von Gloggnitz bis
    Mürzzuschlag. 1913.

BENESCH, Fritz
    Spezial-Führer auf den Schneeberg. 3.Aufl. 1913.

BENESCH, Fritz
    Spezialführer auf die Raxalpe. 5.verm. und verb.
    Aufl. 1914.

BODENSTEIN, Gustav
    Aus der Ostmark: ein Buch von Landschaft und
    alpinem Leben, Kultur und Geschichte. 1927.

MEURER, Julius
    A handy illustrated guide to Vienna and its
    environs. 1891.

- - 2nd ed., rev. and enl. 1906.

SCHMIDL, A   Adolf
    Der Schneeberg in unter Oesterreich mit seinen
    Umgebungen von Wien bis Mariazell. 1831.

256.7 Upper Austria

PICHL, Eduard
    Hoch vom Dachstein an! 2.Aufl. 1936.

RADIO-RADIIS, Alfred von
    Der Dachstein. 1906.

RADIO-RADIIS, Alfred von
    Spezial-Führer durch das Dachsteingebirge und die
    angrenzenden Gebiete des Salzkammergutes und
    Ennstales. 1908.

SCHMID, Herman von and STIELER, Karl
    [Aus deutschen Bergen]. The Bavarian Highlands
    and the Salzkammergut. 1874.

SCHMID, Herman von and STIELER, Karl
    Wanderungen im bayerischen Gebirge und Salz-
    kammergut. 2.Aufl. [1878].

SIMONY, Friedrich
    Auf dem hohen Dachstein. 1921.

SIMONY, Friedrich
    Das Dachsteingebiet: ein geographisches Charakter-
    bild aus den österreichischen Nordalpen. Lfg.1.
    1889.

258 Climbing history, reminiscences

DEUTSCHER UND ÖSTERREICHISCHER ALPENVEREIN
    Führer-Tarife. 1904-06. 3pts.

DEUTSCHER UND ÖSTERREICHISCHER ALPENVEREIN
    Ratgeber für Alpenwanderer mit Schutshütten-
    verzeichnis der Ostalpen. 1924.

- - 2.Aufl. 1928.

DEUTSCHER UND ÖSTERREICHISCHER ALPENVEREIN
    Die Schutzhütten des Deutschen und Österreichischen
    Alpenvereins. [1933].

DEUTSCHER UND ÖSTERREICHISCHER ALPENVEREIN
    Taschenbuch für Alpenvereins-Mitglieder. 1930-33.
    2v.

DEUTSCHER UND ÖSTERREICHISCHER ALPENVEREIN
    Verfassung und Verwaltung des Deutschen und
    Oesterreichischen Alpenvereins: ein Handbuch zum
    Gebrauch für die Sectionen... 1893.

- - 4.Ausg. 1928.

DEUTSCHER UND ÖSTERREICHISCHER ALPENVEREIN.
Sektion Berlin
    Verzeichniss der autorisirten Führer in den
    deutschen und oesterreichischen Alpen. 1885-1903.
    17v. in 2.

DEUTSCHER UND ÖSTERREICHISCHER APLENVEREIN.
Sektion Kufstein
    50 Jahre Alpenvereinssektion Kufstein, 1877-1927.
    1927.

DEUTSCHER UND ÖSTERREICHISCHER ALPENVEREIN.
Sektion Wien
    Die Schutzhütten und Unterkunfthäuser in den
    Ostalpen. [1909-10]. 3v.

GRÖGER, Gustav and RABL, Josef
    Die Entwicklung der Hochtouristik in den
    österreichischen Alpen. 1890.

Handbuch für Touristik und Fremdenverkehr. 1948.

ÖSTERREICHISCHER ALPENVEREIN
    100 Jahre Österreichischer Alpenverein, 1862-1962.
    1962.

OESTERREICHISCHER TOURISTEN-CLUB
    Gründung und Entwicklung des Oesterreichischen
    Touristen-Club: Festschrift. 1879.

PICHL, Eduard
    Wiens Bergsteigertum. 1927.

RADICS, P   von
    Bergfahrten in Oesterreich einst und jetzt,
    1363-1887. [1887].

TECHNIKER-ALPENCLUB IN GRAZ
    Denkschrift zur Feier des 25 jährigen Bestehens des
    Techniker-Alpenclub in Graz. 1898.

259 Guide-books

BAEDEKER, Karl
    Austria, together with Budapest, Prague, Karlsbad,
    Marienbad: handbook for travellers. 12th rev. ed.
    1929.

BAEDEKER, Karl
    The eastern Alps including the Bavarian Highlands,
    Tyrol, Salzburg, Upper and Lower Austria, Styria,
    Carinthia and Carniola: handbook for travellers.
    11th ed., rev. and augm. 1907.

BAEDEKER, Karl
    Südbayern Tirol und Salzburg, Ober- und Nieder-
    Österreich, Steiermark, Kärnten und Krain. 1910.

BAEDEKER, Karl
    Tyrol and the Dolomites including the Bavarian Alps:
    handbook for travellers. 13th rev. ed. 1927.

Bayrisches Hochland, Salzburg, Salzkammergut: prak-
    tischer Reiseführer. 27.Aufl. Goldschmidt,
    1911-12.

BÖHM, August, Edler von Böhmersheim
    Führer durch die Hochschwab Gruppe. 2. vollstandig
    neu bearb. Aufl. 1896.

BÖHM, Otto and NOSSBERGER, Adolf
    Führer durch die Schobergruppe. 1925.

CHARNOCK, Richard Stephen
    Guide to Tyrol: comprising pedestrian tours made in
    Tyrol, Styria, Carinthia, and Salzkammergut, during
    the summers of 1852 and 1853, together with a
    skeleton map of the country. 1857.

DEUTSCHER UND ÖSTERREICHISCHER ALPENVEREIN
    Das Villnöstal und seine Ungebung... [n.d.].

EICHERT, Wilhelm
    Touristen-Führer für Wanderungen in Rosalien-
    Gebirge bei Wiener-Neustadt. 4.Aufl. 1926.

259 Austria - guide-books (Cont.)

FLAIG, Walther and ZWEIGELT, Sepp
Vorarlberger Schieführer in mehreren Heften mit
Schiekarten und Anstiegsbildern. Heft 1. Schie-
fahrten um Gargellen. 1928.

FREMDENVERKEHRSVEREIN KUFSTEIN
Kufstein und seine Umgebung: ein Führer für Fremde
und Einheimische. 1909.

Fridolin Plant's Reise-Führer durch Vinschgau,
Oberinntal bis Landeck und die Seitentäler...
2.verm und verb. Aufl. 1909.

FRISCHAUF, Johannes
Die Sannthaler Alpen. 1877.

GEYER, Georg
Führer durch das Dachsteingebirge und die angrenzenden Gebiete des Salzkammergutes und Ennsthales.
1886.

GRIEBEN, Theobald
München, Südbayern, Salzburg, Tirol: illustrirtes
Handbuch für Reisende. 8.verb. Aufl. 1861.

HACKEL, Heinrich
Führer durch die Tennengebirge... 1925.

HOEGEL, Hugo
Führer in das Lavantthal in Kärnten. 1884.

Die hohe Salve im Brireathale in Tyrol, mit einer
Bergsilhouette. C. Wolf, 1859.

JAHNE, Ludwig
Karawankenführer. 2. vollstandig ... Aufl. 1931.

JAHNE, Ludwig
Ost- und Mittelkarawanken Saantaler (Steiner)
Alpen... 2.. Aufl. 1924-25.

Kleiner Führer durch die Glockner- und Venediger-
Gruppe... [19--].

The knapsack guide for travellers in Tyrol and the
eastern Alps. Murray, 1867.

KOHL, Johann Georg
Austria, Vienna, Prague, Hungary, Bohemia and the
Danube, Galicia, Styria, Moravia, Bukovina and the
military frontier. 1843.

KONNIGER, Karl
Försters Touristenführer in Wiens Umgebungen:
Wegweiser bei Ausflügen im Wiener Walde, im
österreichisch-steirischen Alpenlande und in der
Wachau. 12. neu bearb. Aufl. 1903. 5v.

Das Land Tirol, mit einem Anhange: Vorarlberg: ein
Handbuch für Reisende. 1838. 3v.

NEUDEGG, Rudolf Freisauff von
Das Salzkammergut, Salzburg, Oberbayern und Tirol.
22.Aufl. 1900. 2v. in 1.

PETERMANN, Reinhard E
Wanderungen in den östlichen Niedern Tauern:
Führer im Gebiete des Grossen Bösenstein bis zum
Seckauer Zinken nebst einem Anhang über den
Zeyritzkampel. 1903.

PFISTER, Otto von
Das Montavon mit dem oberen Paznaun: ein Taschenbuch für Fremde und Einheimische. 2.Aufl. 1911.

RABL, Josef
Traisenthal und das Pielachthal: ein Führer auf
den Linien: St. Pölten-Scheibmühl, Scheibmühl-
Hainfeld und Scheibmühl-Schrambach... 2. Abtheilung. 1884.

RABL, Josef
Wachau-Führer: ein Führer im Donauthale zwischen
Krems und Melk und in den anschliessenden Theilen
des Waldviertels... 1890.

RAITMAYR, Erich
Kleiner Führer durch die Zillertaler Alpen und die
Tuxer Voralpen: Talorte, Hütten, Übergänge, Gipfel.
1953.

SCHIDER, Eduard
Gastein für Kurgäste und Touristen. 12.verm und
verb. Aufl. 1906.

SCHMIDL, A   Adolf
Reisehandbuch durch das Erzherzogthum Oesterreich,
mit Salzburg, Obersteyermark und Tirol. 1834.

STEINER, Johann
Der Reise-Gefährte durch die oesterreichische
Schweiz: oder, Das obderennsische Salzkammergut...
2.verm und verb. Aufl. 1829.

STILES, William F   and WAY, H   John
Austria. 1954.

Tirolerführer: Reisehandbuch für Deutsch- und
Wälschtirol. Amthor, 1868.

TRAUTWEIN, Th.
Das bayrische Hochland mit den Allgäu das
angrenzende Nordtirol, Vorarlberg, Salzburg nebst
Salzkammergut. 16.Aufl. 1914.

TRAUTWEIN, Th.
Tirol Südbaiern und Salzburg nebst den angrenzenden
Alpenländern Oesterreichs: Wegweiser für Reisende.
8.verm. Aufl. 1889.

TRAUTWEIN, Th.
Tirol und Vorarlberg, bayr. Hochland, Allgäu,
Salzburg, Ober- und Nieder-Oesterreich, Steiermark,
Kärnten und Krain: Wegweiser für Reisende. 18.
Aufl. 1913.

Wagner's Führer durch Nordtirol, Vorarlberg die
angrenzenden Gebiete von Oberbayern und den
Tauern. 1922.

WALTENBERGER, A
Allgäu, Vorarlberg und Westtirol nebst den
angrenzenden Gebieten der Schweiz. 1914.

WALTENBERGER, A
Stubai, Oetzthaler- und Ortlergruppe nebst den
angrenzenden Gebieten; mit besonderer Berücksichtigung der Brennerbahn, der Gegend von Meran
und Bozen. 1879.

WITTING, A
Wenzels Führer durch Garmisch-Partenkirchen und
Umgebung. 7.Aufl. [n.d.].

WÖDL, Hans
Führer durch die Schladminger Tauern. 1924.

26 GERMANY

261 Geology, climate

RASPE, R   E
An account of some German volcanoes, and their productions with a new hypothesis of the prismatical
basaltes established upon essay, being an essay of
physical geography for philosophers and miners,
published as supplementary to Sir William
Hamilton's observations on the Italian volcanoes.
1777.

SCHEUCHZER, Johann Jacob
Vernunfftmässige Untersuchung des Bads zu Baden,
dessen Eigenschafften und Würckungen. 1732.

SCHILLING, R   E
Nachright von der Unterhalb der Stadt Bremen im
Hornung des 1771. Jahres erfolgten Verstopfung
des Weser-Stroms und nachher geschehener Aufeisung
desselben. 1772.

262 Germany - geography, description, travel

BERTRAM, Anthony
Pavements and peaks: impressions of travel in
Germany and Austria. 1933.

MÜLLER, Wilhelm
Topographical and military description of Germany
and the surrounding country. 1813.

RADCLIFFE, Ann
A journey made in the summer of 1794, through
Holland and the western frontier of Germany, with
a return down the Rhine... 1795.

SHERER, Moyle
Notes and reflections during a ramble in Germany.
1826.

THOMÉ, Otto Wilhelm
Flora von Deutschland, Österreich und der Schweiz.
2.verm. und verb. Aufl. 1903-05. 4v. in 8.

WHITE, Walter
A July holiday in Saxony, Bohemia, and Silesia.
1857.

265 German Alps - general

Deutsche Alpen. 10.Aufl. 1899-1908. 3v. (Meyers
Reisebücher)

STEUB, Ludwig
Zur Namens- und Landeskunde der deutschen Alpen.
1885.

266 Regions

266.1 Bavaria

BODENSTEDT, Friedrich
Eine Königsreise. 3.Aufl. [1883].

BONER, Charles
Chamois hunting in the mountains of Bavaria.
1853.

BONER, Charles
Chamois hunting in the mountains of Bavaria and in
the Tyrol. 1860.

DEUTSCHER UND ÖSTERREICHISCHER ALPENVEREIN.
Sektion Rosenheim
Rosenheim: Berge und Vorland. 1902.

DOPOSCHEG, Josef
Die Zugspitze: Ersteigungs-Geschichte, Orographie,
Klima und touristisch-geologisch-botanischer
Führer auf den Zugangswegen und Anstiegslinien.
1921.

ECKART, K
Führer durch Passau & Umgebung. 1899.

FÖRDERREUTHER, Max
Die Allgäuer Alpen: Land und Leute. 1907.

HÜTTIG, Robert and KORDOV, Frido
Führer durch die Ankogelgruppe einschliesslich
Hochalmspitz, Hasner-und Reisseckgruppe. 1926.

JOANNE, Adolphe
Itinéraire descriptif et historique de l'Allemagne:
l'Allemagne du Sud... 1855.

KADEN, Woldemar
[Das Schweizerland...]. Switzerland and the
Bavarian highlands. [1879]. 2v.

KESTER, Friedl
Der Falkenstein bei Füssen-Pfronten und seine
Umgebung. 1904.

MODLMAYR, H
Bunte Bilder aus dem obern Allgäu. 1903.

PETER, Ernst
Die Zugspitze. 1905.

SCHMID, Herman von and STIELER, Karl
[Aus deutschen Bergen]. The Bavarian Highlands and
the Salzkammergut. 1874.

SCHMID, Herman von and STIELER, Karl
Wanderungen in bayerischen Gebirge und Salzkammergut. 2.Aufl. [1878].

SCHMIDKUNZ, Walter
Kletterführer durch die bayerischen Voralpen.
1910.

SCHOTTKY, Julius Mar
Bilder aus der süddeutschen Alpenwelt. 1834.

SCHUSTER, August
Führer durch die Ammergauer Alpen für Bergsteiger,
Wanderer und Besucher der bayer. Konigsschlösser.
1922.

SCHWERIN, Detlof, Freiherr von
Führer durch die Tannheimer Berge und für die
umliegenden Talorte. 1922.

SEGUIN, L   G
Walks in Bavaria: an autumn in the country of the
passion-play. 1884.

SERRES, Marcel de
Voyage dans le Tyrol, et une partie de la Bavière.
1823. 2v.

SIEGHARDT, August
Der Wendelstein: eine Monographie. [1924].

STEUB, Ludwig
Wanderungen im bayerischen Gebirge. 2.verm. Aufl.

THORINGTON, James Monroe
Once in the eastern Alps. [1948].

266.3 South-West, Rhine, Black Forest, Sauerland

CAPPER, Samuel James
The shores and cities of the Boden See: rambles in
1879 and 1880. 1881.

MACKINDER, H   J
The Rhine: its valley & history. 1908.

MURPHY, Lady Blanche
Down the Rhine.
(In Whymper, Edward. Scrambles amongst the Alps.
[1890?])

ROEGNER, Otto
Schwarzwaldwinter: Schnee - Sport - Sonne. 1934.

SCHOMBURG, Hugo
Auf Schneeschuhen und zu Fuss durchs Sauerland.
1912.

Tombleson's Upper Rhine. [185-].

266.5 Central Germany, Hartz

ANDERSEN, Hans Christian
Rambles in the romantic regions of the Hartz mountains, Saxon Switzerland... 1848.

KOLLBACH, Karl
Von der Tatra bis zur sächsischen Schweiz. [1897].

LESSER, Friedrich Christian
Anmerckungen von der Baumanns-Höhle wie er sie
selbst Anno 1734 den 21. May befunden. 4. weit
verm. Aufl. 1745.

LINDAU, Wilhelm Adolf
Albina: ein Taschenbuch für Wanderer in der sächsischen Schweiz, enthaltend eine Beschreibung des
meissnischen Hochlands... 1818.

266.5 Central Germany, Hartz (Cont.)

STANDEN, R S
    A trip to the Harz Mountains in the summer of 1860.
    [1862].

TREPTOW, Leon
    Schwartzenstein, Mörchner-Mösele. 1909.

268 Climbing history, reminiscences

DEUTSCHER ALPENVEREIN. Sektion Hochland
    Festschrift der Sektion Hochland des Deutschen
    Alpenvereins zum 50 jährigen Bestehen, 1902-1952.
    1952.

DEUTSCHER UND ÖSTERREICHISCHER ALPENVEREIN.
Sektion Halle
    Vierzig Jahre Sektion Halle des Deutschen und
    Österreichischen Alpenvereins. 1926.

DEUTSCHER UND ÖSTERREICHISCHER ALPENVEREIN.
Sektion München
    Geschichte der Alpenvereinssection München; als
    Denkschrift nach dreissigjährigem Bestehen hrsg.
    1900.

269 Guide-books

BAEDEKER, Karl
    Northern Germany, as far as the Bavarian and
    Austrian frontiers: handbook for travellers. 15th
    rev. ed. 1910.

BAEDEKER, Karl
    The Rhine from Rotterdam to Constance: handbook
    for travellers. 16th rev. ed. 1906.

BAEDEKER, Karl
    Southern Germany: handbook for travellers. 9th
    rev. ed. 1902.

BERLEPSCH, Hermann Alexander von and KOHL, Johann
Georg
    Switzerland and the principal parts of southern
    Germany: handbook for travellers. 1874.

BLANK, Hans
    Illustrirter Führer durch Saalfelden im Pinzgau
    und seine Seitenthäler und Berge; mit besonderer
    Rücksichtnahme auf das Steinerne Meer. 1890.

FORBES, Sir John
    Sight-seeing in Germany and the Tyrol in the
    autumn of 1855. 1856.

GRIEBEN, Theobald
    München, Südbayern, Salzburg, Tirol: illustrirtes
    Handbuch für Reisende. 8.verb. Aufl. 1861.

HEUSER, Emil
    Neuer Pfalzführer: ein Reisehandbuch für die
    banerische Pfalz und angrenzende Gebiete. 3...
    Aufl. 1905. 3v.

KOLLER, Engelbert
    Das Höllengebirge. 1933.

LUERSSEN, Heinrich
    Das Lahnthal von der Lahnquelle bis zur Mündung
    nebst den Seitenthälern in ihren unteren und
    mittleren Stufen. 1902.

SCHMIDL, A   Adolf
    Reisehandbuch durch das Erzherzogthum Oesterreich
    mit Salzburg, Obersteyermark und Tirol. 1834.

SCHMIDT, Albert
    Führer durch die Fichtelgebirge und den Steinwald
    ... 2 neubearb. Aufl. 1899.

ZETTLER, Ernst
    Skiführer durch das West-Allgau Gebiet von
    Immenstadt-Oberstdorf bis zum Bregenzer Wald.
    1937.

27 YUGOSLAVIA

272 Geography, description, travel

SNAFFLE
    In the land of the Bora; or, Camp life and sport in
    Dalamatia and the Herzegovina, 1894-5-6. 1897.

WILKINSON, Sir J   Gardner
    Dalmatia and Montenegro, with a journey to Mostar
    in Herzegovina, and remarks on the slavonic
    nations... 1848. 2v.

275 Julian Alps

CAPRIN, Giuseppe
    Alpi Giulie. 1895.

COPELAND, Fanny S
    Beautiful mountains: in the Jugoslav Alps. [1934].

KUGY, Julius
    Fünf Jahrhunderte Triglav. 1938.

KUGY, Julius
    Die Julischen Alpen im Bilde. 1934.

LOVŠIN, Evgen
    V Triglavu in v njegovi soseščini. 1944.

ROSCHNIK, Rudolf
    Der Triglav. 1906.

WESTER, Josip
    Iz Domovine in Tujine: izbrani planinski in
    popotni spisi. 1944.

276 Regions

276.2 Croatia, Istria, Dalmatia

ALLASON, Thomas
    Picturesque views of the antiquities of Pola in
    Istria. 1819.

BAEDEKER, Karl
    Dalmatien und die Adria: westliches Südslawien,
    Bosnien, Budapest, Istrien, Albanien, Korfu: Hand-
    buch für Reisende. 1929.

CASSAS, Louis François
    Travels in Istria and Dalmatia. 1805.

PAULIC, Dragutin
    Vodič na Plitvička Jezera. 1923.

276.4 Bosnia, Herzegovina, Montenegro

DENTON, W
    Montenegro, its people and their history. 1877.

MALDINI WINDENHAINSKI, Rudolf, Barun
    Bosna i Hercegovina. 1908.

WYON, Reginald and PRANCE, Gerald
    The land of the Black Mountain: the adventures of
    two Englishmen in Montenegro. 1903.

278 Climbing history, reminiscences

DEUTSCHER UND ÖSTERREICHISCHER ALPENVEREIN.
Sektion Küstenland
    Chronik der Section Küstenland des Deutschen und
    Österreichischen Alpenvereins, 1873-1892: Fest-
    Publication... 1893.

28   NON-ALPINE EUROPE

ADAMS, W
   The modern voyager & traveller through Europe,
   Asia, Africa, & America. Vol.4. Europe. 1828.

BEVAN, Favell Lee
   Near home; or, The countries of Europe described.
   1849.

- - 6th ed., carefully rev. 1902.

Dates and distances, showing what may be done in a
   tour of sixteen months through various parts of
   Europe, as performed in the years 1829 and 1830.
   Murray, 1831.

Handbook for travellers in Russia, Poland, and
   Finland; including the Crimea, Caucasus, Siberia,
   and Central Asia. 5th ed., thoroughly rev.
   Murray, 1893.

KÜTTNER, Carl Gottlob
   Travels through Denmark, Sweden, Austria, and part
   of Italy, in 1798 & 1799.
   (In A collection of modern and contemporary
   voyages... Vol.1. 1805)

Picturesque Europe. Cassell, [1890?]. 5v.

SEYDLITZ, Ernst von
   Geographie. Ausg. D. 2.Heft. Europa ohne das
   Deutsche Reich. 12.Aufl. 1912.

WAKEFIELD, Priscilla
   The juvenile travellers; containing the remarks of
   a family during a tour through the principal
   states and kingdoms of Europe... 10th ed. 1814.

29   EASTERN EUROPE

291   Geology, climate

UNGAR, Karl
   Die Alpenflora der Südkarpathen. 1913.

292   Geography, description, travel

HAUSSEZ, Charles Le Mercher de Longpré, baron d'
   Alpes et Danube; ou, Voyage en Suisse, Styrie,
   Hongrie et Transylvanie. 1837. 2v.

MITTON, G   E
   Austria-Hungary. 1915.

WHITE, Walter
   A July holiday in Saxony, Bohemia, and Silesia.
   1857.

294   Carpathians

BONER, Charles
   Transylvania: its products and its people. 1865.

CROSSE, Andrew F
   Round about the Carpathians. 1878.

FUCHS, Friedrich
   Die Central-Karpathen mit den nächsten Voralpen:
   Handbuch für Gebirgsreisende. 1863.

KOLLBACH, Karl
   Von der Tatra bis zur Sächsischen Schweiz. [1897].

MACKENZIE, Georgina Muir and IRBY, Adelina Paulina
   Across the Carpathians. 1862.

MAGYARORSZÁGI KÁRPÁTEGYLET
   Bibliotheca Carpatica; a "Magyarországi
   Kárpátegylet" megbizásából összeállította Payer
   Hugo. 1880.

MAZUCHELLI, Nina Elizabeth
   "Magyarland", being the narrative of our travels
   through the highlands and lowlands of Hungary.
   1881. 2v.

SCHMIDL, A   Adolf
   Das Bihar-Gebirge an der Grenze von Ungarn und
   Siebenbürgen. 1863.

SONKLAR, Karl, Edler von Innstädten
   Reiseskizzen aus den Alpen und Karpathen. 1857.

SYDOW, Albrecht von
   Bemerkungen auf einer Reise im Jahre 1827 durch die
   Beskiden über Krakau und Wieliczka nach den
   Central-Karpathen, als Beitrag zur Characteristik
   dieser Gebirgsgegenden und ihrer Bewohner. 1830.

295   Tatra

COMPTON, Edward T
   Die Hohe Tatra: sieben Farbendrucke und sechsund-
   zwanzig Holzschnitte nach Aquarellen. [ca 1905].

FIRSOFF, Valdemar Axel
   The Tatra mountains. [1942].

HALAŠA, Ján and MARTON, Stefan
   Liptovské hole a Chočské pohorie. 1958.

HUTCHINSON, Alexander H
   Try Cracow and the Carpathians. 2nd ed. 1872.

KORISTKA, Carl
   Die Hohe Tatra in den Central-Karpaten: eine geo-
   graphische Skizze verfasst auf Grundlage einer
   Bereisung. 1864.

KUKACKA, Miroslav
   Nízke Tatry. 1962.

POSEWITZ, Theodor
   Reisehandbuch durch Zipsen, Hohe Tatra und Zipser
   Mittelgebirge. 1898.

SZONTAGH, Nikolaus
   Tátraführer: Wegweiser in die Hohe Tatra und in die
   Bäder der Tatragegend. 2... Aufl. 1904.

TATRANSKÁ EXPEDÍCIA HIMALÁJE, 1969
   Tatranská Expedícia Himaláje 1969 = the High Tatras
   Expedition, Himalaya 69. 1968.
   Preliminary brochure, largely on the High Tatras.

296.1   Bohemia

Die wunder-volle Schnee-Koppe; oder, Beschreibung des
   Schlesischen Riesen-Gebirges, aus denen Nachrichten
   einiger Personen, welche diesen hohen Berg selbst
   überstiegen haben; zusammen getragen von einem
   bekannten Schlesier. 1736.

296.7   Central Poland

ORŁOWICZ, Mieczysław
   Guide illustré de la Pologne. 1927.

298   Hungary

MAGYAR TURISTA SZÖVETSÉG
   Országos Magyar turista kiállitas ismertetöje, az
   1931, május 16-június 21, Budapest... 1931.

THIRRING, Gustav
   Führer durch Sopron (Oedenburg) und die ungarischen
   Alpen. 1912.

30 RUSSIA (EUROPEAN)

BRANDT, J   F
Bemerkungen über die Wirbelthiere des nördlichen
europäischen Russlands, besonders des nördlichen
Ural's. 1856.

HENDERSON, Ebenezer
Biblical researches and travels in Russia;
including a tour in the Crimea, and the passage of
the Caucasus... 1826.

IMPERATORSKOE RUSSKOE GEOGRAFICHESKOE OBSHCHESTVO
Der nördliche Ural und das Küstengebirge Pai-Choi.
1853-56. 2v.

PALLAS, P   S
Travels through the southern provinces of the
Russian Empire... 1802-03. 2v.

- - 2nd ed. 1812.

PANOV, D   G
Geomorfologicheskii ocherk Poliarnykh Uralid i
zapadnoi chasti Poliarnogo Shel'fa. 1937.

RUPRECHT, F   J
Flora boreali-uralensis: ueber die Verbreitung der
Pflanzen im nördlichen Ural. 1856.

31 SCANDINAVIA

BARROW, John, 1808-1898
Excursions in the north of Europe, through parts
of Russia, Finland, Sweden, Denmark, and Norway,
in the years 1830 & 1833. 1834.

- - New ed. 1835.

BONSTETTEN, Ch. Victor de
La Scandinavie et les Alpes [et Fragments sur
l'Islande]. 1826.

BROOKE, Sir Arthur de Capell
A winter in Lapland and Sweden, with various observations relating to Finmark and its inhabitants; made during a residence at Hammerfest,
near the North Cape. [1825].

BUNBURY, Selina
A summer in northern Europe, including sketches in
Sweden, Norway, Finland, the Aland Islands,
Gothland... 1856. 2v.

CONWAY, Derwent
A personal narrative of a journey through Norway,
part of Sweden and the islands and states of
Denmark. 1829.

EVEREST, Robert
A journey through Norway, Lapland and part of
Sweden, with some remarks on the geology of the
country, its climate and scenery, the ascent of
some of its principal mountains... 1829.

GARVAGH, Charles John Spencer George Canning,
Baron Carvagh
The pilgrim of Scandinavia. 1875.

HARTMAN, C   J
C.J. Hartmans Handbok i Skandinaviens Flora,
innefattande Sveriges och Norges Växter, till och
med Mossorna. 11., helt och hallet omarbetade
uppl. 1879.

LAMOTTE, A
Voyage dans le nord de l'Europe; consistant
principalement de promenades en Norwège, et de
quelques courses en Suède, dans l'année 1807...
1813.

RABOT, Charles
Au Cap Nord: itinéraires en Norwège, Suède... 1898.

RABOT, Charles
Aux fjords de Norwège et aux forets de Suède.
1898.

ROSS, W   A
A yacht voyage to Norway, Denmark and Sweden. 2nd
ed. 1849.

SMITH, Alfred
Sketches in Norway and Sweden. 1847.

SORENSEN, Henrick Lauritz
Norsk flora for skoler. 4.opl. 1882.

SUNDSTRÖM, Lennart
Scandinavia in pictures: a pictorial rhapsody in
collaboration with Scandinavia's foremost
photographers. 1949.

TAYLOR, Bayard
Northern travel: summer and winter pictures of
Sweden, Lapland and Norway. 1858.

TOMLIN, James
Notes from a traveller's journal, during an excursion in Norway and Sweden. 1852.

311 Norway - geology, climate

DOUGHTY, C   M
On the Jöstedal-brae glaciers in Norway, with
some general remarks. 1866.

HOEL, Adolf and WERENSKIOLD, Werner
Glaciers and snowfields in Norway. 1962.

LYNAM, C   C
To Norway and the North Cape in 'Blue Dragon II'...
1913.

ØYEN, P   A
Variations of Norwegian glaciers. 1901.

SARS, Michael
Beretning om en i Sommeren 1861 foretagen Reise
i en Deel af Christianas Stift for at fortsaette
Undersøgelsen af de i vor Glacial-formation
indeholdte organiske Levninger. [1861].

SEUE, C   de
Le Névé de Justedal et ses glaciers. 1870.

SEXE, S   A
Boiumbraeen 1 Juli 1868. 1869.

SEXE, S   A
Maerker efter en Iistid i Omegnen af Hardanger-
fjorden. 1866.

SEXE, S   A
Om Sneebraeen Folgefon. 1864.

WAHLENBERG, Georg
Bericht über Messungen und Beobachtungen zur
Bestimmung der Höhe und Temperatur der
Lappländischen Alpen unter dem 67sten Breitengrade
angestellt im Jaahre 1807. 1812.

312 Norway - geography, description

B AND N STEAMSHIP LINE
Sunlit Norway, nature's wonderland. 1912.

BARNARD, M   R
Sketches of life, scenery, and sport in Norway.
1871.

BARNARD, M   R
Sport in Norway, and where to find it; together
with ... a list of the Alpine flora of the Dovre
Fjeld and of Norwegian ferns... 1864.

BECKETT, Samuel J
The fjords and folk of Norway. 1915.

BOWDEN, J
The naturalist in Norway; or, Notes on the wild
animals, birds, fishes, and plants of that
country, with some account of the principal salmon
rivers. 1869.

312 Norway - geography, description (Cont.)

Boydell's Picturesque scenery of Norway; with the
principal towns from the Naze ... to the ...
Swinesund. 1820.

BRØGGER, W   C
Norge i det nittende Aarhundrede: Tekst og
billeder af Norske Forfattere og Kunstnere. 1900.
2v.

CHAPMAN, Abel
Wild Norway, with chapters on Spitsbergen,
Denmark... 1897.

COOPER, Alfred Heaton
The Norwegian fjords. 1907.

FRIIS, I   A
Sporting life on the Norwegian fjelds... 1878.

GIERTSEN, Ed. B   and HALVORSEN, Adolph
Norway illustrated... 1888.

GOODMAN, Edward John
Western Norway... 1893.

KONGSBERG TURISTFORENING
Kongsberg, with routes and map. 1890.

LAING, Samuel
Journal of a residence in Norway during the years
1834 & 1836, made with a view to enquire into the
moral and political economy of that country, and
the condition of its inhabitants. 2nd ed. 1837.

LINGSTROM, Freda
This is Norway. 1933.

LOVETT, Richard
Norwegian pictures drawn with pen and pencil, con-
taining also a glance at Sweden and the Gotha
Canal. New ed., rev. and partly rewritten. 1890.

NORWAY. Kirke- og Undervisningsdepartement
Norway: official publication for the Paris Exhibition 1900. 1900.

ORIENT LINE
The Norwegian fjords. [1912].

RUGE, Sophus
Norwegen. 1899.

- - 2.Aufl. 1905.

WALTON, Elijah
The coast of Norway, from Christiania to
Hammerfest. 1871.

WILLSON, Thomas B
Norway at home. [1910?].

313 Norway - travel

ANDERSON, Sir Charles
An eight week's journal in Norway... 1853.

BEAUCLERK, Lady Diana De Vere
A summer and winter in Norway. 1868.

BUCH, Leopold von, Freiherr
Travels through Norway and Lapland during the
years 1806, 1807 and 1808. 1813.

BUCH, Leopold von, Freiherr
Voyage en Norvège et en Laponie fait dans les
années 1806, 1807 et 1808. 1816.

FORBES, James David
Norway and its glaciers visited in 1851. 1853.

FORBES, James David
[Norway and its glaciers]. Norwegen und seine
Gletscher... 1855.

FORESTER, Thomas
Norway in 1848 and 1849, containing Rambles among
the fjelds and fjords of the central and western
districts; and including remarks on its political,
military, ecclesiastical, and social organisation.
1850.

FORESTER, Thomas
Rambles in Norway, among the fjelds and fjords of
the central and western districts, with remarks on
its political, military, ecclesiastical, and social
conditions. 1855.

FULTON, John Henry Westropp
With ski in Norway & Lapland. 1911.

GOODMAN, Edward John
The best tour in Norway. 1892.

- - 3rd ed. 1896.
- - Cheap ed. 1903.

HOLDWAY, John George
A month in Norway. 1853.

HOOKER, William Dawson
Notes on Norway; or, A brief journal of a tour
made to the northern parts of Norway, in the summer
of 1836. 1837.

JUNGMAN, Beatrix
Norway. 1905.

KIMBALL, Edwin Coolidge
Midnight sunbeams; or, Bits of travel through the
land of the Norsemen. [18--].

LEES, James Arthur
Peaks and pines: another Norway book. 1899.

LEES, James Arthur and CLUTTERBUCK, Walter
Three in Norway, by two of them. 1882.

LOWE, Emily
Unprotected females in Norway; or, The pleasantest
way of travelling there, passing through Denmark
and Sweden; with Scandinavian sketches from nature,
[by Emily Lowe]. 1857.

- - [Later ed.]. 1859.

METCALFE, Frederick
The Oxonian in Norway; or, Notes of excursions in
that country in 1854-55. 1856. 2v.

- - 2nd ed., rev. 1857.

METCALFE, Frederick
The Oxonian in Thelemarken; or, Notes of travel in
south-western Norway in the summers of 1856 and
1857... 1858. 2v.

MIÉVILLE, Sir Walter F
Letters from Norway. [1904?].

NEWLAND, Henry
Forest life in Norway and Sweden, being extracts
from the journal of a fisherman. New ed. 1859.

A Norwegian ramble among the fjords, fjelds, mountains and glaciers, by one of the ramblers. 1904.

PASSARGE, L
Sommerfahrten in Norwegen: Reiseerinnerungen,
Natur-und Kulturstudien. 3.Aufl. [189-]. 2v.
in 1.

PHYTHIAN, J   C
Scenes of travel in Norway. 1877.

PRICE, Edward
Norway: views of wild scenery and journal. 1834.

PRICE, Edward
[Norway: views of wild scenery...]. Norway and its
scenery, comprising the journal of a tour by Edward
Price, with considerable additions and a Road-book
for tourists... 1853.

313 Norway - travel (Cont.)

PRITCHETT, Robert Taylor
  Gamle Norge: old Norway; or, Our holiday in
  Scandinavia. 1862.

PRITCHETT, Robert Taylor
  "Gamle Norge": rambles and scrambles in Norway.
  1879.

SHEPARD, J   S
  Over the Dovrefjelds. 1873.

SIMPSON, H
  Rambles in Norway. 1912.

SIXTY-ONE
  A trip to Norway in 1873. 1874.

SMITH, Hubert
  Tent life with English gipsies in Norway. 1873.

- - 2nd ed. 1874.

SPENDER, A   Edmund
  Two winters in Norway, being an account of two
  holidays spent on snow-shoes, and in sleigh-
  driving, and including an expedition to the Lapps.
  1902.

STONE, Olivia M
  Norway in June. 1882.

Tracks in Norway of four pairs of feet, delineated
  by four hands with notes on the handiwork of each
  by the others. 1884.

VICARY, John Fulford
  An American in Norway. 1885.

WILD, J   J
  Reise nach Norwegen vom 27. Juni bis 9. August
  1856. 1859.

WILLIAMS, William Mattieu
  Through Norway with a knapsack. 1859.

- - New and improved ed. 1876.

WILLIAMS, William Mattieu
  Through Norway with ladies. 1877.

WOOD, Charles W
  Norwegian by-ways. 1903.

WYLLIE, Marian Amy
  Norway and its fjords. 1907.

WYNDHAM, Francis M
  Wild life on the fjelds of Norway. 1861.

YACHTING DABBLER
  Notes on a yacht voyage to Hardanger Fjord and the
  adjacent estuaries. [19--].

314 Norway - climbs, expeditions

BURCHARDT, D   B
  Fjell i Norge over 2000 m.o.h. = Norwegian mountains over 2000 metres high, altitudes, locations
  and first ascents. 1950.

CHAPIUS, Thomas
  Dans les montagnes de la Norvège. 1888. 3 pts.

GIVERHOLT, Helge
  Jotunheimens Erobring: 150 ars fjellferder i
  Jotunheimen og Vestheimen. 1946.

LAUSBERG, Carl
  Mit Stock und Pickel: Bergfahrten in den Alpen und
  Norwegen. 1910.

LE BLOND, Elizabeth
  Mountaineering in the land of the midnight sun.
  1908.

LEICESTER POLYTECHNIC STUDENTS ØKSFJORD EXPEDITION,
1970
  The official report of Leicester Polytechnic
  Students Øksfjord Expedition 1970: [Loppa
  Peninsular, Finnmark, Arctic Norway]. 1971.

NEGRI, N   C
  The valley of shadows: the story of an Arctic
  expedition. 1956.

ROYAL NAVY AND ROYAL MARINES MOUNTAINEERING CLUB
NORDLAND EXPEDITION, 1978
  Report. [1979].

OPPENHEIM, Edwin Camillo
  New climbs in Norway: an account of some ascents
  in the Sondmore district. 1898.

PATERSON, M
  Mountaineering below the snow-line; or, The
  solitary pedestrian in Snowdonia and elsewhere.
  1886.

SCHJELDERUP, Ferdinand
  Med norsk flag i Nordland... 1911.

SLINGSBY, William Cecil
  The Justedalsbrae revisited. [1889?].

SLINGSBY, William Cecil
  Norway, the northern playground: sketches of
  climbing and mountain exploration in Norway between
  1872 and 1903. 1904.

- - Another issue, with a biographical notice by
  G.W. Young. 1941.

SLINGSBY, William Cecil
  [Norway, the northern playground]. Til fjells i
  Norge. 1966.

STYLES, Showell
  Mountains of the midnight sun. 1954.

WEIR, Thomas
  Camps and climbs in Arctic Norway. 1953.

315 Lappland

BRAY, Reynold
  Five watersheds: a winter journey to Russian
  Lapland. 1935.

BUTLER, Frank Hedges
  Through Lapland with ski and reindeer with some
  account of ancient Lapland and the Murman coast.
  1917.

PALLIN, H   N
  Kebnekaise: färder och äventyr i Lappland. 1927.

316 Sweden

SVENSKA TURISTTRAFIKFÖRBUNDET
  A book about Sweden. 1922.

319 Scandinavia - guide-books

BAEDEKER, Karl
  Norway, Sweden, and Denmark: handbook for
  travellers. 6th ed. 1895.

- - 8th ed., rev. and augm. 1903.
- - 9th ed., rev. and augm. 1909.
- - 10th ed., rev. and augm. 1912.

Beyer's Guide to western Norway, with the coast-
  route to the North Cape and overland routes to
  Christiania. [1887].

- - Special supplement for 1890.

BRETON
  Scandinavian sketches; or, A tour in Norway;
  intended as the tourist's guide through the
  interior of that country. 2nd ed. 1837.

319 Scandinavia - guide-books (Cont.)

CAMPBELL, John Robert
  How to see Norway. 1871.

CHEZY, Helmina Wittwe von
  Norika: Neues ausführliches Handbuch für Alpenwanderer und Reisende... 1833.

ELTON, Charles Isaac
  Norway: the road and the fell. 1864.

ÉNAULT, Louis
  La Norvège. 1857.

A hand-book for travellers in Denmark, Norway,
  Sweden, and Iceland. 3rd ed., rev. and corr.
  Murray, 1858.

Handbook for travellers in Norway. 5th ed., rev.
  Murray, 1874.

- - 7th ed., rev. 1880.
- - 9th ed., rev. 1897.

The knapsack guide to Norway. Murray, 1864.

NIELSEN, Yngvar
  Handbook for travellers in Norway. 1886.

RANDERS, Kristofer
  Søndmøre: reisehaandbog. 2den omarb. og forøgede
  udg. 1898.

- - 3dje rev. og forøkede utg. 1930.

SVENSKA TURISTFÖRENINGEN
  Lappland, samt öfriga delar af Väster-och
  Norrbottens län. 3.uppl. 1904.

SVENSKA TURISTFÖRENINGEN
  The Swedish Touring Club's Guide to Sweden. 1898.

WILLSON, Thomas B
  The handy guide to Norway... 1886.

- - 4th ed., rev. and enl. 1898.
- - 6th ed., thoroughly rev. 1911.

32 SUB-ARCTIC REGIONS

322 Iceland

AHLMANN, Hans Wilhelmsson
  Land of ice and fire. 1938.

BADER, Paul Louis
  Notes sur le Massif des Kerlingarfjöll en Islande.
  1917.

BARING-GOULD, Sabine
  Iceland: its scenes and sagas. 1863.

CLIFFORD, Sir Charles Cavendish
  Travels by 'Umbra'. 1865.

COLES, John, F.R.G.S.
  Summer travelling in Iceland, being the narrative
  of two journeys across the island by unfrequented
  routes... 1882.

COLLINGWOOD, William Gershom and STEFANSSON, Jón
  A pilgrimage to the saga-steads of Iceland. 1899.

FORBES, Charles S
  Iceland: its volcanoes, geysers and glaciers.
  1860.

HENDERSON, Ebenezer
  Iceland; or, The journal of a residence in that
  island, during the years 1814 and 1815, containing
  observations on the natural phenomena... 2nd ed.
  1819.

HOOKER, William Jackson
  Journal of a tour in Iceland in the summer of 1809.
  1811.

- - 2nd ed., with additions. 1813.

HOWELL, Frederick W W
  Icelandic pictures drawn with pen and pencil.
  1893.

KÜCHLER, Carl
  Unter der Mitternachtssonne durch die Vulkan- und
  Gletscherwelt Islands. 1906.

LINDSAY, William Lauder
  The flora of Iceland. 1861.

LINDSAY, William Lauder
  Observations on the lichens collected by Dr. Robert
  Brown in West Greenland in 1867 (on Edward
  Whymper's expedition). 1869.

LONGMAN, William
  Suggestions for the exploration of Iceland...
  1861.

MACKENZIE, Sir George Steuart
  Travels in the Island of Iceland, during the summer
  of 1810. 2nd ed. 1812.

- - New ed., rev. 1851.

MALVERN COLLEGE ICELAND EXPEDITION, 1978
  Preliminary report. 1978.

MAURER, Konrad
  Isländische Volkssagen der Gegenwart, vorwiegend
  nach mundlicher Überlieferung gesammelt und
  verdeutscht. 1860.

METCALFE, Frederick
  The Oxonian in Iceland; or, Notes of travel in that
  island in the summer of 1860, with a glance at
  Icelandic folk-lore and sagas. 1861.

OLAFSSON, Eggert and PALSSON, Bjorni
  Travels in Iceland, performed by order of His
  Danish Majesty, containing observations on the
  inhabitants, a description of the lakes...
  (In A collection of modern and contemporary
  voyages... Vol.2. 1806)

OSWALD, E   J
  By fell and fjord; or, Scenes and studies in
  Iceland. 1882.

TROIL, Uno von
  Letters on Iceland, containing observations on the
  civil ... and natural history, antiquities,
  volcanos, basalts, hot springs... 1780.

WATTS, William Lord
  Snioland; or, Iceland; its jokulls and fjalls.
  1875.

WINKLER, Gustav Georg
  Island: der Bau seiner Gebirge und dessen geologische Bedeutung. 1863.

322.5 Vatnajökull

CAMBRIDGE-REYKJAVIK UNIVERSITIES EXPEDITION TO
VATNAJÖKULL, ICELAND, 1976
  The 1976 Cambridge-Reykjavik Universities Expedi-
  tion to Vatnajökull, Iceland. 1976.

LIVERPOOL INSTITUTE MOUNTAINEERING CLUB ICELAND
EXPEDITION, 1975
  Official report. 1975.

WATTS, William Lord
  Across the Vatna Jökull; or, Scenes in Iceland;
  being a description of hitherto unknown regions.
  1876.

324 Spitsbergen

CONWAY, William Martin, Baron Conway
The first crossing of Spitsbergen, being an account
of an inland journey of exploration and survey,
with descriptions of several mountain ascents...
1897.

CONWAY, William Martin, Baron Conway
No man's land: a history of Spitsbergen from its
discovery in 1596 to the beginning of the
scientific exploration of the country. 1906.

CONWAY, William Martin, Baron Conway
With ski and sledge over Arctic glaciers. 1898.

DAHL, Eilif
On the vascular plants of eastern Svalbard,
chiefly based on material brought home from the
"Heimland" Expedition 1936. 1937.

DEUTSCHE ARKTISCHE ZEPPELIN-EXPEDITION, 1910
Mit Zeppelin nach Spitzbergen: Bilder von der
Studienreise der deutschen arktischen Zeppelin-
Expedition. 1911.

GLEN, Alexander R
Young men in the Arctic: the Oxford University
Arctic Expedition to Spitzbergen 1933. 1935.

GORDON, Seton
Amid snowy wastes: wild life on the Spitsbergen
Archipelago. 1922.

LUIGI AMEDEO, Duke of the Abruzzi
La "Stella Polare" nel mare artico 1899-1900, [da]
Luigi Amedeo di Savoia, U. Cagni, A. Cavalli
Molinelli. 1903.

MAGNUSSON, A   H
The Lichen-genus Acarospora in Greenland and
Spitsbergen. 1935.

MITTELHOLZER, Walter
Im Flugzeug dem Nordpol entgegen: Junkers'sche
Hilfsexpedition für Amundsen nach Spitzbergen
1923. 1924.

NANSEN, Fridtjof
"Farthest North", being the record of a voyage
of exploration of the ship, Fram, 1893-96 and of a
fifteen months' sleigh journey... 1897. 2v.

NUNLIST, Hugo
Spirtsbergen: the story of the 1962 Swiss-
Spitsbergen expedition. 1966.

PALLIN, H   N
Andréegatan. 1934.

SORA, Gennaro
Con gli Alpini all'80° parallelo. 1929.

TILMAN, Harold William
Triumph and tribulation. 1977.

WEYPRECHT, A   and PAYER, Julius
Die Polar-Expedition. 1872.

33 SPAIN & PORTUGAL

331 Pyrenees - geology, climate

CAREZ, L
La géologie des Pyrénées françaises. 1903-09.
6v.

CLUB ALPIN FRANÇAIS. Commission des Travaux
Scientifiques
L'oeuvre scientifique du Club Alpin Français
(1874-1922). 1936.

MARTINS, Charles and COLLOMB, Édouard
Essai sur l'ancien glacier de la Vallée d'Argelès
(Hautes Pyrénées). 1868.

PALASSOU, M. l'A
Essai sur la minéralogie des Monts-Pyrénées; suivi
d'un catalogue des plantes observées dans cette
chaîne de montagnes... 1781.

TRUTAT, Eugène
Les glaciers de La Maladetta et le Pic des Posets.
1876.

TRUTAT, Eugène
Les Pyrénées: les montagnes, les glaciers, les eaux
minérales, les phénomènes de l'atmosphère, la flore,
la faune et l'homme. 1896.

332 Pyrenees - geography, description

ABADIE, A
Itinéraire topographique et historique des Hautes-
Pyrénées... 3e éd., corr. et augm. 1833.

Album des Pyrénées; drawn by T. Allom [ca 1850].

ARBANÈRE, Étienne
Tableau des Pyrénées françaises, contenant une
description complète de cette chaîne de montagnes
... 1828. 2v. in 1.

BARING-GOULD, Sabine
A book of the Pyrenees. 1907.

BELLOC, Hilaire
The Pyrenees. 1909.

CAMENA D'ALMEIDA, P
Les Pyrénées: développement de la connaissance
géographique de la chaîne. [1893].

CENTRE D'ESTUDIS I REALITZACIONS DE LES VALLS
D'ANDORRA
Andorra pocket guide: tourism, shopping, real
estate. 1971.

CHEVALIER, Marcel
Andorra. 1925.

CHROUSCHOFF, Michel de
Pau: souvenirs et impressions. 1891.

CICERI, Eugène
Les Pyrénées. [1871].

CLUB ALPIN FRANÇAIS. Section de Pau
De Pau au Pic d'Ossau et à Gavarnie. [1897].

COMPAGNIE DES CHEMINS DE FER DU MIDI
Les Pyrénées. 1903-04.

DUJARDIN, Victor
Voyages aux Pyrénées, Souvenirs du Midi, par un
homme du Nord... 1890.

FLAUBERT, Gustave
Par les champs et par les grèves; Pyrénées; Corse.
1910.

FREESTON, Charles L
The passes of the Pyrenees: a practical guide to
the mountain roads of the Franco-Spanish frontier.
1912.

FROSSARD, Emilien
Tableau pittoresque des Pyrénées françaises:
vallées du Lavédan, de Barèges, et de Gavarnie.
1839.

FROSSARD, Emilien
Vue des Hautes-Pyrénées, prise du sommet du Pic du
Midi en Bigorre... [1851?].

GAUSSEN, H
Les Pyrénées de la Catalogne au Pays basque. 1933.

JEANNEL, Maurice
Heures pyrénéennes. 1972.

332 <u>Pyrenees - geography, description</u> (<u>Cont</u>.)

JOANNE, Adolphe
  Géographie du Département des Hautes-Pyrénées...
  6e éd. 1897.

- - 8e éd. 1907.

JOANNE, Paul
  Géographie du Département des Basses-Pyrénées...
  8e éd. 1907.

JOANNE, Paul
  Géographie du Département des Pyrénées-orientales
  ... 7e éd. 1910.

JOURDAN, J
  Vues prises dans les Pyrénées françaises. 1829.

LA BOULINIÈRE, P
  Itinéraire descriptif et pittoresque des Hautes-
  Pyrénées françoises, jadis territoires du Béarn,
  du Bigorre... 1825. 3v.

LABROUE, E
  À travers les Pyrénées. [1900].

MARTIGNON, Andrée
  Montagne. 1930.

MASSIE, F
  La cartographie des Pyrénées: étude. 1934.

MEILLON, Alphonse
  Esquisse toponymique sur la vallée de Cauterets,
  Hautes-Pyrénées. 1908.

MEILLON, Alphonse
  Essai d'un glossaire des noms topographiques les
  plus usités dans la vallée de Cauterets et la
  région montagneuse des Hautes-Pyrénées. 2e éd.
  1911.

MEILLON, Alphonse
  Excursions topographiques dans la vallée de
  Cauterets. 1920. 3 pts.

PERRET, Paul
  Les Pyrénées françaises. 1881-. 3v.
  Library lacks v.3.

PETIT, Victor
  Souvenirs de Cauterets et de ses environs. [ca
  1850].

PETIT, Victor
  Souvenirs des Pyrénées: vues prises aux environs
  des eaux thermales de Bagnères de Bigorre...
  [ca 1850].

RUSSELL, Henry, <u>Count</u>
  Biarritz and Basque countries. 1873.

RUSSELL, Henry, <u>Count</u>
  Pau and the Pyrenees. 1871.

RUSSELL, Henry, <u>Count</u>
  Pau, Biarritz, Pyrenees. 2nd ed. 1890.

SAGET, P
  Description du Chateau de Pau et de ses dépen-
  dances. 1831.

SALSAS, Albert
  La Cerdagne espagnole. 1899.

SORRE, M
  Les Pyrénées. 1922.

SUBIRÁ, José
  Mi valle pirenaico: cuadros novelescos. 1927.

TASTU, Sabine Amable
  Alpes et Pyrénées: arabesques littéraires... 1842.

TAYLOR, Isidore Justin, <u>baron</u>
  Les Pyrénées. 1843.

TORRAS, César August
  Pirineu Català: guía itinerari del excursionista
  a Camprodon... 1902.

- - Another ed. 1905-18.

WILLIAMS, Becket
  The High Pyrénées, summer and winter. 1928.

ZIRKEL, Ferdinand
  Physiographische Skizzen aus den Pyrenäen. 1867.

333 <u>Pyrenees - history</u>

BERALDI, Henri
  Balaïtous et Pelvoux: notes sur les officiers de
  la Carte de France. 1907-10. 2v.

BERALDI, Henri
  La carrière posthume de Ramond, 1827-1868: notes
  d'un bibliophile. 1927.

BERALDI, Henri
  Cent ans aux Pyrénées. 1898-1902. 7v.

BERALDI, Henri
  En marge du pyrénéisme: notes d'un bibliophile,
  L'affaire Rilliet-Planta. 1931.

BERALDI, Henri
  Le passé du pyrénéisme: notes d'un bibliophile.
  1911-20. 5v.

BERALDI, Henri
  Le sommet des Pyrénées: notes d'un bibliophile.
  1923-25. 3v.

CLUB ALPIN FRANÇAIS. <u>Section du Sud-Ouest</u>
  Camp du Col d'Aran, <u>15-25 juillet 1943</u>. 1943.

CLUB ALPIN FRANÇAIS. <u>Section du Sud-Ouest</u>
  La Concession Russell du Vignemale. 1943.

ESCUDIER, Jean
  L'Aneto et les hommes. 1977.

GORSSE, Pierre de
  Les Anglais aux Pyrénées. 1956.

334 <u>Pyrenees - travel</u>

BATSÈRE, B
  Excursion dans les Hautes-Pyrénées: souvenirs
  historiques, rêveries. 2e éd. 1858.

BILBROUGH, E   Ernest
  'Twixt France and Spain; or, A spring in the
  Pyrenees. 1883.

BLACKBURN, Henry
  Artistic travel in Normandy, Brittany, the
  Pyrenees, Spain and Algeria. 1895.

BLACKBURN, Henry
  The Pyrenees: a description of summer life at
  French watering places. 1867.

BODDINGTON, Mary
  Sketches in the Pyrenees; with some remarks on
  Languedoc, Provence, and the Cornice. 1837. 2v.

BOOTH, M
  Roadside sketches in the South of France and
  Spanish Pyrenees. 1859.

CADIER FRÈRES
  Au pays des Isards. le ptie. De l'Aneto à la
  Munia. 1903.

CHATTERTON, Henrietta Georgiana, <u>Lady</u>
  The Pyrenees, with excursions into Spain. 1843.
  2v.

CHAUSENQUE, Vincent de
  Les Pyrénées: ou, Voyages pédestres dans toutes
  les régions de ces montagnes depuis l'Océan
  jusqu'à la Méditerranée. 1834. 2v.

334 Pyrenees - travel (Cont.)

COMETTANT, Oscar
De haut en bas: impressions pyrénéennes. 1868.

COSTELLO, Louisa Stuart
Béarn and the Pyrenees: a legendary tour to the
country of Henri Quatre. 1844. 2v.

DAULLIA, Émile
Au pays des Pyrénées. 1903.

DIX, Edwin Asa
A midsummer drive through the Pyrenees. 1891.

DUSAULX, J
Voyage à Barège et dans les Hautes Pyrénées, fait
en 1788. 1796. 2v. in 1.

ELCOURT, A   d'
Au pied des Pyrénées. 1864.

ELLIS, Sarah
Summer and winter in the Pyrenees. [1841].

- - [Another ed.]. [1847].

EYRE, Mary
Over the Pyrenees into Spain. 1865.

HARDY, Joseph
A picturesque and descriptive tour in the mountains of the High Pyrenees. 1825.

HUGO, Victor
En voyage: Alpes et Pyrénées. 3e éd. 1890.

HUGO, Victor
[En voyage: Alpes et Pyrénées]. The Alps and
Pyrenees. 1898.

HUGO, Victor
France et Belgique, Alpes et Pyrénées. [1913].

INGLIS, Henry D
Switzerland, the South of France, and the Pyrenees.
1837.

- - 4th ed. 1840.

JACKSON, F   Hamilton
Rambles in the Pyrenees and the adjacent districts,
Gascony, Pays de Foix and Roussillon. 1912.

JOHNSON, Fred. H
A winter's sketches in the South of France and the
Pyrenees, with remarks upon the use of the climate
and mineral waters in the cure of disease. 1857.

LA GRANDVILLE, comtesse de
Voyage aux Pyrénées. 2e éd. 1842.

- - 3e éd. 1854.

MORTON, John Bingham
Pyrenean, being the adventures of Miles Walker on
his journey from the Mediterranean to the Atlantic.
1938.

MURRAY, James Erskine
A summer in the Pyrénées. 1837. 2v.

- - 2nd ed. 1837.

NICOLLE, Henri
Courses dans les Pyrénées: la montagne et les
eaux. 1860.

O'CONNOR, Vincent Clarence Scott
Travels in the Pyrenees, including Andorra and the
coast from Barcelona to Carcassonne. 1913.

PARIS, T   Clifton
Letters from the Pyrenees during three months'
pedestrian wanderings amidst the wildest scenes of
the French and Spanish mountains in the summer of
1842. 1843.

PASUMOT, François
Voyages physiques dans les Pyrénées en 1788 et
1789: histoire naturelle d'une partie de ces
montagnes... 1797.

PICQUET, J   P
Voyage dans les Pyrénées françoises, dirigé
principalement vers le Bigorre & les vallées...
1789.

- - 2e éd., entièrement refondue et augm. 1828.

PRITCHARD, Henry Baden
A peep at the Pyrenees, by a pedestrian. 1867.

RAMOND, Louis
Carnets pyrénéens. 1931-39.

RAMOND, Louis
Observations faites dans les Pyrénées, pour servir
de suite à des observations sur les Alpes... 1789.

RAMOND, Louis
[Observations faites dans les Pyrénées...]. Reise
nach den höchsten französischen und spanischen
Pyrenaen... 1789. 2v. in 1.

RAMOND, Louis
[Observations faites dans les Pyrénées...].
Voyage dans les Pyrénées... 1927.
"Voyages dans les Pyrénées" is pt.1 of "Observa-
tions faites...".

RAMOND, Louis
[Observations faites dans les Pyrénées...].
Travels in the Pyrenees... 1813.
"Travels in the Pyrenees" is a translation of pt.1
of "Observations faites...".

RAMOND, Louis
Voyages au Mont-Perdu et dans la partie adjacente
des Hautes-Pyrénées. 1801.

RHETZ, Wilhelm von
Reise eines Norddeutschen durch die Hochpyrenäen
in den Jahren 1841 und 1842. 1843. 2v.

ROBSON, E   I
A wayfarer in the Pyrenees. 1929.

SAMAZEUILH, J   F
Souvenirs des Pyrénées. 1827-29. 2v. in 1.

TAINE, Hippolyte
Voyage aux Pyrénées. 3e éd. 1860.

- - 14e éd. 1897.

TAINE, Hippolyte
Voyage aux Pyrénées: edited by William Robertson.
1905.

TAYLOR, Rebe P
Pyrenean holiday. 1952.

THIERS, Adolphe
Les Pyrénées et le Midi de la France... 1823.

VAUX, Frederic W
Rambles in the Pyrenees; and a visit to San
Sebastian. 1838.

WELD, Charles Richard
The Pyrenees, west and east. 1859.

WILSTACH, Paul
Along the Pyrenees. 1925.

335 Pyrenees - climbing

BUHAN, Paul
Neiges et sommets pyrénéens: souvenirs d'excursions
dans les Pyrénées centrales. 1911.

CADIER FRÈRES
Au pays des Isards: un grand pic Marmuré ou
Balaïtous (le massif de Batlaytouse). 1913.

335 Pyrenees - climbing (Cont.)

CLUB ALPIN FRANÇAIS. Section des Pyrénées
Autour du Pic de Midi d'Ossau et du Balaïtous:
trois semaines de campement... 1928.

DESPAUX, Léon
Notre vieux Marcadau: l'amitié d'un paysage
pyrénéen. 1956.

FEDDEN, Robin
The enchanted mountains: a quest in the Pyrenees.
1962.

GONZALES LLUBERA, Miguel
Les altes valls de l'Ariège. 1924.

GOURDON, Maurice
Au pays d'Aran. 1924.

GUILERA I ALBINYANA, Josep María
Carnet d'un esquiador, 1915-1930. 1931.

GUILERA I ALBINYANA, Josep María
Excursions pels Pireneus i els Alps. 1927.

LECLERCQ, Jules
Promenades et escalades dans les Pyrénées: Lourdes,
Luz, Barèges... 2e éd. 1877.

MARTAGON
Montagnes et montagnards. le série. Pyrénées,
Catalogne, île de Majorque, Provence. 1901.

MEILLON, Alphonse
Excursions autour du Vignemale dans les hautes
vallées de Cauterets, de Gavarnie et du Rio Ara en
Aragon, l'origine du pyrénéisme, contribution à
l'histoire de ces vallées. 1928.

MONY, A
Ascension au Pic de Néthou (Maladetta) 21 août
1859. 1861.

PACKE, Charles
A guide to the Pyrenees especially intended for
the use of mountaineers. 1862.

- - 2nd ed., rewritten and much enlarged. 1867.

RUSSELL, Henry, Count
Les grandes ascensions des Pyrénées d'une mer à
l'autre: guide spécial du piéton. [1866].

RUSSELL, Henry, Count
Pyrenaica. 1902.

RUSSELL, Henry, Count
Les Pyrénées, les ascensions et la philosophie de
l'exercice. 1865.

RUSSELL, Henry, Count
Souvenirs d'un montagnard, 1858-1888. 1888.

- - 2e éd., rev. et corr. 1908.

SAINT-SAUD, Aymard d'Arlot, comte de
Cinquante ans d'excursions et d'études dans les
Pyrénées espagnoles et françaises... 1924.

SOUBIRON, Pierre
Espingo et le Cirque d'Oô: 12 itinéraires nouveaux
aux alentours du Refuge d'Espingo. 1925.

SOUBIRON, Pierre
Les Pyrénées du Pic d'Anie au Canigou en 30
excursions. [ca 1920].

SPENDER, Harold
Through the High Pyrenees. 1898.

SPONT, Henry
Sur la montagne (les Pyrénées). 1898.

STYLES, Showell
Backpacking in Alps and Pyrenees. 1976.

336 Regions

CHAPMAN, Abel and BUCK, Walter J
Unexplored Spain. 1910.

KENNEDY, Bart
A tramp in Spain from Andalusia to Andorra. 1904.

SPAIN. Ministerio de Agricultura. Comisaría de
Parques Nacionales
Guías de los sitios naturales de interés nacional.
1931-33. 3v.

336.1 Picos de Europa

BOADA, J
Picos de Europa. [19--].

Liébana y los Picos de Europa: ligera reseña
histórica, datos geográficos y estadísticos,
itinerarios, monumentos y santuarios... 1913.

PIDAL, Pedro and ZAVALA, José F
Picos de Europa: contribución al estudio de las
montañas españolas. 1918.

RICKMERS, Willi Rickmer
Die Wallfahrt zum Wahren Jacob: Gebirgswanderungen in Kantabrien. 1926.

ROSS, Mars and STONEHEWER-COOPER, H
The highlands of Cantabria; or, Three days from
England. 1885.

SAINT-SAUD, Aymard d'Arlot, comte de
Monographie des Picos de Europa (Pyrénées cantabriques et asturiennes): études et voyages. 1922.

336.2 Basque Provinces

ELSNER, Eleanor
The romance of the Basque country and the Pyrenees.
1927.

LIBERTY, Arthur Lasenby
Springtime in the Basque mountains. 1901.

336.6 Aragon

MINVIELLE, Pierre
A la découverte de la Sierra de Guara. 1974.

337 Madeira, Teneriffe

PICKEN, Andrew
Madeira illustrated. 1840.

SMYTH, C Piazzi
Teneriffe, an astronomer's experiment; or,
Specialities of a residence above the clouds.
1858.

339 Guide-books

BAEDEKER, Karl
Spain and Portugal: handbook for travellers. 2nd
ed. 1901.

DECOMBLE, Clément
Les chemins de fer transpyrénéens: leur histoire
diplomatique, leur avenir économique: épisode des
relations franco-espagnols. 1913.

JOANNE, Adolphe
Itinéraire descriptif et historique des Pyrénées
de l'océan à la Méditerranée. 1858.

JOANNE, Adolphe and JOANNE, Paul
Pyrénées. 3e éd. 1875.

MONMARCHÉ, Marcel
Pyrénées... 1919.

339 Spain & Portugal - guide-books (Cont.)

MUIRHEAD, Findlay
  Northern Spain, with the Balearic Islands. 1930.

Nouveau guide de Bordeaux aux Pyrénées. [1853].

RICHARD
  Guide aux Pyrénées: itinéraire pédestre des
  montagnes... 1834.

SOLER Y SANTALÓ, Juli
  La Vall d'Aran: guia monografica de la comarca.
  1906.

VIDAL Y RIBA, Edouard
  El Montseny: guia monografica de la regio,
  itineraris-excursions. 1912.

34   BALKANS

341 Greece

BOLLMANN, Louis de
  Remarques sur l'état moral, politique et militaire
  de la Grèce, écrites sur les lieux... [1823].

DOREN, David MacNeil
  Winds of Crete. 1974.

FARQUHAR, Francis Peloubet and PHOUTRIDES, Aristides
Evangelus
  Mount Olympus. 1929.

FARQUHAR, Francis Peloubet
  Mount Olympus revisited. 1953.

La Grèce immortelle, [par] Th. Homolle [and others].
  1919.

GUÉCA, Catherine
  Massif des Lefka Ori de Crète: monts Guiguilos et
  Volakias. 1972.

HELLENIC ALPINE CLUB
  Olympos. [1972].

KITTO, H   D   F
  In the mountains of Greece. 1933.

KURZ, Marcel
  Le Mont Olympe (Thessalie): monographie. 1923.

NIKOPOULOS, Ilias
  Mount Olympos. 1957.

TOZER, Henry Fanshawe
  Researches in the highlands of Turkey; including
  visits to Mounts Ida, Athos, Olympus, and Pelion...
  1869. 2v.

TREVOR-BATTYE, Aubyn
  Camping in Crete with notes upon the animal and
  plant life of the island; including a description
  of certain caves and their ancient deposits, by
  Dorothea M.A. Bate. 1913.

WATKINS, Thomas
  Travels through Switzerland, Italy, Sicily, the
  Greek Islands to Constantinople; through part of
  Greece, Ragusa, and the Dalmation Isles... 2nd
  ed. 1794. 2v.

342 Albania

L'Albanie: guide de montagne. 1958.

36   LOW COUNTRIES

361 Belgium

BAEDEKER, Karl
  Belgium and Holland: handbook for travellers. 7th
  ed.,rev. and augm. 1884.

DOUDOU, Ernest
  Exploration scientifique dans les cavernes, les
  abîmes et les trous qui fument de la province de
  Liège. [1906?].

362 Netherlands

BAEDEKER, Karl
  Belgium and Holland: handbook for travellers. 7th
  ed., rev. and augm. 1884.

BONAPARTE, Roland, prince
  Le premier établissement des Néerlandais à Maurice.
  1890.

363 Luxemburg

PASSMORE, T   H
  In further Ardenne: a study of the Grand Duchy of
  Luxembourg. 1905.

40   NORTH AMERICA & POLAR REGIONS

401 Geology, climate, flora

DALY, Reginald Aldworth
  Geology of the North American Cordillera at the
  49th parallel. 1912.

HENSHAW, Julia W
  Mountain wild flowers of America: a simple and
  popular guide to the names and descriptions of the
  flowers that bloom above the clouds. 1906.

HENSHAW, Julia W
  Wild flowers of the North American mountains.
  1915.

- - [Another ed.]. 1916.

LONGYEAR, Burton O
  Rocky Mountain wild flower studies: an account of
  the ways of some plants that live in the Rocky
  Mountain region. 1909.

Problems of American geology: a series of lectures
  dealing with some of the problems of the Canadian
  Shield and of the Cordilleras, delivered at Yale
  University on the Silliman Foundation in 1913.
  1915.

RUSSELL, Israel C
  Glaciers of North America: a reading lesson for
  students of geography and geology. 1897.

RYDBERG, Per Axel
  Flora of the Rocky Mountains and adjacent plains:
  Colorado, Utah, Wyoming, Idaho, Montana, Saskatche-
  wan, Alberta... 1917.

402 Geography, description, travel

AMERICAN GEOGRAPHICAL SOCIETY OF NEW YORK
  Memorial volume of the transcontinental excursion
  of 1912. 1915.

BAILLIE-GROHMAN, William Adolphus
  Fifteen years' sport and life in the hunting
  grounds of western America and British Columbia.
  1900.

402   North America - geography, description... (Cont.)

BODDAM-WHETHAM, J   W
    Western wanderings: a record of travel in the
    evening land. 1874.

DOUGLAS, David
    Journal kept by David Douglas during his travels
    in North America 1823-1827... 1914.

ENOCK, C   Reginald
    The great Pacific coast: twelve thousand miles in
    the Golden West... 1909.

IRVING, Washington
    Adventures of Captain Bonneville; or, Scenes
    beyond the Rocky Mountains of the Far West. 1835.
    3v. in 1.

IRVING, Washington
    Astoria;, or, Enterprise beyond the Rocky
    Mountains. 1836. 3v.

MANNING, Samuel
    American pictures drawn with pen and pencil.
    [1876].

MILTON, William Fitzwilliam, Viscount and CHEADLE,
Walter Butler
    The North-West Passage by land, being the narra-
    tive of an expedition from the Atlantic to the
    Pacific, undertaken with a view of exploring a
    route across the continent... 3rd ed. 1865.

- - 5th ed. 1866.

WOOD, Ruth Kedzie
    The tourist's Northwest. 1917.

405   Climbing history, reminiscences

FISHER, Joel E
    Bibliography of Alaskan and Pacific Coast States
    mountain ascents. 1945.

FISHER, Joel E
    Bibliography of Eastern Seaboard mountain ascents.
    1945.

JEFFERS, Le Roy
    The call of the mountains: rambles among the
    mountains and canyons of the United States and
    Canada. 1922.

- - Another ed. 1923.

JONES, Chris
    Climbing in North America. 1976.

SHERMAN, Paddy
    Cloud walkers: six climbs on major Canadian peaks.
    1965.

WHITE, Stewart Edward
    The mountains. 1904.

41   CANADA

411   Geology, climate

ALLAN, John A
    Geology of field map-area, B.C. and Alberta. 1914.

DALY, Reginald Aldworth
    A geological reconnaissance between Golden and
    Kamloops, B.C., along the Canadian Pacific Railway.
    1915.

DAWSON, George M
    Preliminary report on the physical and geological
    features of that portion of the Rocky Mountains
    between latitudes 49° and 51°30'. 1886.

HENSHAW, Julia W
    Mountain wild flowers of Canada. 1906.

MCCONNELL, R   G
    Report on the geological structure of a portion of
    the Rocky Mountains... 1887.

SCHOFIELD, Stuart J
    Geology of Cranbrook map-area, British Columbia.
    1915.

WHITE, James
    Altitudes in the Dominion of Canada with a relief
    map of North America. 1901.

- - 2nd ed. 1915.

WHITE, James
    Dictionary of altitudes in the Dominion of Canada
    with a relief map of Canada. 1903.

- - 2nd ed. 1916.

412   Geography, description, travel

ADAMS, Joseph
    Ten thousand miles through Canada: the natural
    resources, commercial industries, fish and game,
    sports and pastimes of the great Dominion. 3rd ed.
    1913.

AMI, Henry M
    North America. Vol.1. Canada & Newfoundland. 2nd
    ed. 1915.

ARGYLL, John Douglas Sutherland Campbell, 9th Duke of
    Canadian pictures, drawn with pen and pencil.
    [1884?].

BUTLER, Sir William Francis
    The great lone land: a narrative of travel and
    adventure in the north-west of America. 5th ed.1873.

- - 16th ed. 1917.

CAMPBELL, Wilfred
    Canada. 1907.

CANADA. Commission Appointed to Delimit the Boundary
between the Provinces of Alberta and British Columbia
    Report, from 1913 to [1924]. 1917-25. 3 pts.

DAVIDSON, Gordon Charles
    The North West Company. 1918.

FLEMING, Sandford
    England and Canada: a summer tour between old and
    new Westminster. 1884.

FLEMING, Sandford
    Report on surveys and preliminary operations on the
    Canadian Pacific Railway... 1877.

FORBES, Alexander
    Northernmost Labrador mapped from the air. 1938.

FRASER, Mrs. Hugh and FRASER, Hugh C
    Seven years on the Pacific slope. [1916?].

GALLOWAY, C   F   J
    The call of the West: letters from British Columbia.
    1916.

GRANT, George M
    Ocean to ocean: Sandford Fleming's expedition
    through Canada in 1872, being a diary kept during a
    journey from the Atlantic to the Pacific... 1873.

HIND, Henry Youle
    Narrative of the Canadian Red River exploring expe-
    dition of 1857 and of the Assinniboine and
    Saskatchewan exploring expedition of 1858. 1860.
    2v.

HIND, Henry Youle
    North-west Territory: reports of progess; together
    with a preliminary and general report on the Assini-
    boine and Saskatchewan exploring expedition... 1859.

412 Canada - geography, description, travel (Cont.)

HOMER, A   N
The imperial highway. [1912].

M'CORMICK, R
Narrative of a boat expedition up the Willington Channel in the year 1852... in search of Sir John Franklin. 1854.

MACKENZIE, Alexander
Voyages from Montreal, on the river St.Laurence, through the continent of North America, to the frozen and Pacific oceans, in the years 1789 and 1793. 1801.

PALLISER, John
Progress of the British North American Exploring Expedition. 1859.

PIKE, Warburton
The barren ground of northern Canada. 1892.

ROBERTS, Morley
On the old trail through British Columbia after forty years. 1927.

ROBINSON, Noel
Blazing the trail through the Rockies: the story of Walter Moberly and his share in the making of Vancouver. [ca 1910].

ST. JOHN, Molyneux
The sea of mountains: an account of Lord Dufferin's tour through British Columbia in 1876. 1877. 2v.

TALBOT, Frederick A
The making of a great Canadian railway: the story of the search for and discovery of the route and the construction of the nearly completed grand trunk Pacific railway... 1912.

WHITING, Lilian
Canada, the spellbinder. 1917.

WILLIAMS, John Harvey
The guardians of the Columbia: Mount Hood, Mount Adams and Mount St. Helens. 1912.

WINTHROP, Theodore
The canoe and the saddle: adventures among the northwestern rivers and forests and Isthmiana. 1883.

WINTHROP, Theodore
The canoe and the saddle; or, Klalam and Klickatat; to which are now first added his western letters and journals. 1913.

WOOLLACOTT, Arthur P
Mackenzie and his voyageurs: by canoe to the Arctic and the Pacific 1789-93. 1927.

YEIGH, Frank
Through the heart of Canada. 1910.

414 Rockies, Jasper National Park

ALPINE CLUB OF CANADA
The Alpine Club of Canada in Jasper National Park, Alberta. [1926?].

BINNIE, Alfred M
Western Canada in 1933. [1934].

BROWN, Stewardson
Alpine flora of the Canadian Rocky Mountains. 1907.

BURPEE, Lawrence J
Among the Canadian alps. 1915.

CANADA. Department of the Interior
Description of & guide to Jasper Park. 1917.

CANADA. Department of the Interior
Jasper National Park. 1928.

COLEMAN, Arthur Philemon
The Canadian Rockies: new and old trails. 1911.

COPPING, Harold
Canadian pictures... 1912.

FISHER, Joel E
Bibliography of Canadian mountain ascents. 1945.

FREEMAN, Lewis R
On the roof of the Rockies: the great Columbia icefield of the Canadian Rockies. 1926.

GARDINER, Kate
Canadian climbs, 1937. [1938].

GARDINER, Kate
A climbing trip to the Freshfield Group and some other ascents. [1940].

GARDINER, Kate
A pack train trip to the French Military Group. [1931].

HABEL, Jean
The North Fork of the Wapta (British Columbia). 1898.

HARMON, Byron
128 views of the Canadian Rockies... 1911.

HORNADAY, William T
Camp-fires in the Canadian Rockies. 1906.

MEREDITH, Brian
Escape on skis. [1928].

MITCHELL, Benjamin Wiestling
Trail life in the Canadian Rockies. 1924.

MORSE, Randy
The mountains of Canada. 1978.

ODELL, Noel Ewart
Frequented and unfrequented ways in the Selkirks and Rockies. 1931.

OUTRAM, Sir James, Bart
In the heart of the Canadian Rockies. 1905.

PALMER, Howard
Edward W.D. Holway: a pioneer of the Canadian alps. 1931.

PAYNTER, Thomas
The ski and the mountain. 1954.

SCHÄFFER, Mary T   S
Old Indian trails: incidents of camp and trail life covering two years' exploration through the Rocky Mountains of Canada. 1911.

SMYTHE, Frank S
Climbs in the Canadian Rockies. 1950.

SMYTHE, Frank S
Rocky Mountains. 1948.

SOUTHESK, James Carnegie, Earl of
Saskatchewan and the Rocky Mountains: a diary and narrative of travel, sport and adventure during a journey through the Hudson's Bay Company's territories in 1859 and 1860. 1875.

STUTFIELD, Hugh Edward Millington and COLLIE, John Norman
Climbs & exploration in the Canadian Rockies. 1903.

THORINGTON, James Monroe
The glittering mountains of Canada: a record of exploration and pioneer ascents in the Canadian Rockies 1914-1924. 1925.

WILCOX, Walter Dwight
Camping in the Canadian Rockies: an account of camp life in the wilder parts of the ... mountains ... and a sketch of the early explorations. 1896.

423 United States - White Mountains, ... (Cont.)

PEATTIE, Roderick
  The Friendly Mountains: Green, White and
  Adirondacks. 1942.

WARD, Julius H
  The White Mountains: a guide to their interpreta-
  tion. 2nd ed., rev. and enl. 1896.

WILLIAMS OUTING CLUB
  The Mountains of Eph: a guide book of the Williams
  Outing Club. 1927.

WRIGHT, Walter W
  The White Mountains: an annotated bibliography,
  1918-1947. 1948.

- - Additions. [n.d].

424 Western States - general

ALLEN, Edward Frank
  A guide to the national parks of America. 1915.

BREWER, William H
  Up and down California in 1860-1864: the journal
  of William H. Brewer, Professor of Agriculture in
  the Sheffield Scientific School from 1864 to 1903.
  1930.

CHAPIN, Frederick H
  The land of the cliff-dwellers. 1892.

CUMMING, Constance F   Gordon
  Granite crags. 1884.

- - Cheap ed. 1901.

DOUGLAS, William Orville
  Of men and mountains. 1951.

FAIRBANKS, Harold Wellman
  The geography of California. 1912.

FAIRBANKS, Harold Wellman
  The western wonder-land: half-hours in the western
  United States. 1905.

FARIS, John T
  Seeing the Far West. 1920.

FOUNTAIN, Paul
  The eleven eaglets of the West. 1906.

HORNADAY, William T
  Camp-fires on desert and lava. [1906].

HUTCHINGS, James M
  Scenes of wonder and curiosity in California.
  1865.

LYMAN, William Denison
  The Columbia River: its history, its myths, its
  scenery, its commerce. 1909.

MUIR, John
  Steep trails. 1919.

MURPHY, Thomas D
  Three wonderlands of the American West, being the
  notes of a traveler concerning the Yellowstone
  Park, the Yosemite National Park... 1912.

PARKER, Samuel
  Journal of an exploring tour beyond the Rocky
  Mountains... 1838.

PFEIFER, Gottfried
  Die räumliche Gliederung der Landwirtschaft im
  nördlichen Kalifornien. 1936.

PUTNAM, George Palmer
  In the Oregon country: outdoors in Oregon, Washington and California, together with some legendary
  lore and glimpses of the modern West in the making.
  1915.

REIK, Henry Ottridge
  A tour of America's national parks. 1920.

RINEHARD, Mary Roberts
  Tenting to-night: a chronicle of sport and adventure in Glacier Park and the Cascade Mountains.
  1918.

ROBERTS, Morley
  The Western Avernus: three years' autobiography in
  western America. New ed. 1904.

ROSS, Alexander
  Adventures of the first settlers on the Oregon or
  Columbia River, being a narrative of the expedition
  fitted out by John Jacob Astor, to establish the
  "Pacific Fur Company", with an account of some
  Indian tribes on the coast of the Pacific. 1849.

ROSS, Alexander
  The fur hunters of the Far West: a narrative of
  adventures in the Oregon and Rocky Mountains.
  1855. 2v. in 1.

RUSK, C   E
  Tales of a western mountaineer: a record of
  mountaineering experiences on the Pacific coast.
  1924.

STEEL, W   G
  The mountains of Oregon. 1890.

UNITED STATES. National Park Services
  National parks portfolio, by Robert Sterling Yard.
  2nd ed. 1917.

WHITING, Lilian
  The land of enchantment: from Pike's Peak to the
  Pacific. 1910.

WILEY, William H   and WILEY, Sara King
  The Yosemite, Alaska and the Yellowstone. [1893].

WILLIAMS, Ira A
  The Columbia River gorge: its geological history
  interpreted from the Columbia River Highway. 2nd
  ed. 1923.

425 Cascades, Olympics

BECKEY, Fred
  Challenge of the North Cascades. 1969 (1977
  reprint).

ISAACS, A   C
  An ascent of Mount Shasta, 1856. 1952.

MEANY, Edmond Stephen
  Mount Rainier: a record of exploration. 1916.

MOLENAAR, Dee
  The challenge of Rainier: a record of the explora-
  tions and ascents, triumphs and tragedies, on the
  Northwest's greatest mountain. 1971.

OREGON WRITERS' PROJECT
  Mount Hood: a guide. 1940.

WILLIAMS, John Harvey
  The mountain that was "God", being a little book
  about the great peak which the Indians called
  "Tacoma" but which is officially named "Rainier".
  1910.

- - 2nd ed., rev. and greatly enl. 1911.

WOOD, Robert L
  Men, mules and mountains: Lieutenant O'Neil's
  Olympic expeditions. 1976.

426 Rockies

AMERICAN ALPINE CLUB. Research Committee
Surface features of Dinwoody Glacier, Wind River
Mountains, Wyoming, geology by Mark F. Meier.
[1953].

ATWOOD, Wallace W
The Rocky Mountains. 1945.

BAILLIE-GROHMAN, William Adolphus
Camps in the Rockies, being a narrative of life on
the frontier, and sport in the Rocky Mountains,
with an account of the cattle ranches of the West.
1882.

BUELER, William M
Roof of the Rockies: a history of mountaineering
in Colorado. 1974.

CHAPIN, Frederick H
Mountaineering in Colorado: the peaks about Estes
Park. 1889.

COLORADO MOUNTAIN CLUB
Front Range panorama. 1962.

COOPER, Courtney Ryley
High country: the Rockies yesterday and to-day.
1926.

COULTER, John M
New manual of botany of the central Rocky Mountains (vascular plants). 1909.

DENVER AND RIO GRANDE RAILROAD COMPANY
Rocky Mountain scenery: a brief description of
prominent places of interest along the line of the
Denver and Rio Grande Railroad. [1888?].

FISHER, Joel E
Bibliography of United States mountain ascents
(except Pacific Coast states and the Eastern
Seaboard). 1945.

FRYXELL, Fritiof
The Teton peaks and their ascents. 1932.

FRYXELL, Fritiof
The Tetons: interpretations of a mountain landscape. 1938.

HAYDEN, F V
Sun pictures of Rocky Mountain scenery, with a
description of the geographical and geological
features, and some account of the resources of the
Great West. 1870.

HOLTZ, Mathilda Edith and BEMIS, Katharine Isabel
Glacier National Park: its trails and treasures.
1917.

INGERSOLL, Ernest
The crest of the continent: a record of a summer's
ramble in the Rocky Mountains and beyond. 1885.

INGERSOLL, Ernest
Knocking round the Rockies. 1883.

JOHNSON, Clifton
Highways and byways of the Rocky Mountains. 1910.

- - New ed. 1913.

LAUT, Agnes C
Enchanted trails of Glacier Park. 1926.

MARCOU, J
Une ascension dans les montagnes rocheuses.
[1867].

MARSTON, Edward
Frank's Ranche; or, My holiday in the Rockies,
being a contribution to the inquiry into what we
are to do with our boys. 1886.

MILLS, Enos A
The Rocky Mountain wonderland. [1915].

MILLS, Enos A
The spell of the Rockies. 1912.

MILLS, Enos A
Wild life on the Rockies. 1909.

PORTER, Eliot
The place no one knew: Glen Canyon on the
Colorado. 1963.

RINEHART, Mary Roberts
Through Glacier Park: seeing America first with
Howard Eaton. 1916.

RUXTON, George Frederick
Wild life in the Rocky Mountains: a true tale of
rough adventure in the days of the Mexican War.
1916.

SYNGE, Georgina M
A ride through wonderland. 1892.

THWAITES, Reuben Gold
A brief history of Rocky Mountain exploration with
especial reference to the expedition of Lewis and
Clark. 1904.

WAGNER, Henry R
The plains and the Rockies: a bibliography of
original narratives of travel and adventure,
1800-1865. 1921.

427 Sierra Nevada, Yosemite

ADAMS, Ansel
Sierra Nevada: the John Muir trail. 1938.

CHASE, J Smeaton
Yosemite trails: camp and pack-train in the Yosemite region of the Sierra Nevada. 1912.

FARQUHAR, Francis Peloubet
Exploration of the Sierra Nevada. 1925.

FARQUHAR, Francis Peloubet
History of the Sierra Nevada. 1965.

FARQUHAR, Francis Peloubet
Place names of the High Sierra. 1926.

FARQUHAR, Francis Peloubet
Yosemite, the Big Trees, and the High Sierra: a
selective bibliography. 1948.

GEOLOGICAL SURVEY OF CALIFORNIA
The Yosemite guide-book: a description of the
Yosemite Valley and the adjacent region of the
Sierra Nevada, and of the Big Trees of California.
1870.

GONTARD, Jean
Dans les Sierras de Californie. 1923.

HUTCHINGS, James M
In the heart of the Sierras: the Yo Semite Valley,
both historical and descriptive... 1886.

JORDAN, David Starr
The alps of the King-Kern Divide. 1907.

KING, Clarence
Mountaineering in the Sierra Nevada. 1872.

- - New ed. 1874.
- - 6th ed. 1886.

LECONTE, Joseph
A journal of ramblings through the High Sierra of
California. 1930.

MUIR, John
The mountains of California. 1894.

MUIR, John
My first summer in the Sierra. 1911.

PEATTIE, Roderick
The Sierra Nevada: the range of light. 1947.

427 United States - Sierra Nevada, Yosemite (Cont.)

R., L.N.R.
  A short account of our trip to the Sierra Nevada mountains. [1884?].

ROWELL, Galen A
  The vertical world of Yosemite: a collection of photographs and writings on rock climbing in Yosemite. 1974.

STARR, Walter A
  Guide to the John Muir trail and the High Sierra region. 1934.

WILLIAMS, John Harvey
  Yosemite and its High Sierra. 1914.

428 Climbing history, reminiscences

AMERICAN ALPINE CLUB
  American Alpine Club Annals; [compiled by] J. Monroe Thorington. [1947].

AMERICAN ALPINE CLUB
  By-laws and Register...   1919-40. 4v.

APPALACHIAN MOUNTAIN CLUB. Snow-shoe Section
  List of excursions, parties, mountain climbs, 1882-1911. 1911.

BANKS, Mike
  Shockly-Ghastly and others.
  (In Blackwood's magazine, 1973)
  On climbing in the United States.

429 Guide-books

BAEDEKER, Karl
  The United States, with an excursion into Mexico: handbook for travellers. 2nd rev. ed. 1899.

44 ALASKA

441 Geology, climate

BUSHNELL, Vivian C   and RAGLE, Richard H
  Icefield Ranges Research Project: scientific results. 1969-72. 3v.

EGAN, Christopher P
  Resumé of the 1962 season of the Michigan State University Glaciological Institute, Juneau Icefield, Alaska. 1963.

MILLER, Maynard M
  A field institute of glaciological and expeditionary sciences in Alaska. 1963.

ODELL, Noel Ewart
  Geology of part of the central St. Elias Range, Alaska-Yukon Territory: Mount Vancouver in particular. 1978.

TARR, Ralph Stockman and MARTIN, Lawrence
  Alaskan glacier studies of the National Geographic Society in the Yakutat Bay, Prince William Sound and Lower Copper River regions. 1914.

UNITED STATES. Geological Survey
  Twentieth annual report of the United States Geological Survey to the Secretary of the Interior, 1898-99. Pt.7. 1900.

WASHBURN, Bradford and GOLDTHWAIT, Richard P
  The Harvard-Dartmouth Alaskan expeditions, 1933-1934. 1936.

WILLIAMS, Howel
  Landscapes of Alaska: their geological evolution. 1958.

442 Geography, description, travel

ABERCROMBIE, W   R
  Alaska, 1899: Copper River exploring expedition. 1900.

ANDRASKO, Kenneth
  Alaska crude: visions of the last frontier. 1977.

AUER, Harry A
  Camp fires in the Yukon. 1916.

BOEHM, William D
  Glacier Bay. 1975.

BROKE, George
  With sack and stock in Alaska. 1891.

CAIRNES, D   D
  Upper White River district, Yukon. 1915.

CAIRNES, D   D
  The Yukon-Alaska international boundary, between Porcupine and Yukon Rivers. 1914.

CANE, Claude
  Summer and fall in western Alaska: the record of a trip to Cook's Inlet after big game. 1903.

GORDON, George Byron
  In the Alaskan winderness. 1917.

HARRIMAN ALASKA EXPEDITION, 1899
  Alaska: giving the results of the Harriman Alaska Expedition carried out with the co-operation of the Washington Academy of Sciences. 1902-04.

MCGUIRE, J   A
  In the Alaska-Yukon gamelands. 1921.

MARSHALL, Robert
  Arctic winderness. 1956.

MUIR, John
  Travels in Alaska. 1915.

ORTH, Donald J
  Dictionary of Alaska place names. 1967.

PIERREPONT, Edward
  Fifth Avenue to Alaska. 1884.

POWELL, Addison M
  Trailing and camping in Alaska. 1910.

ROBERTS, David
  The mountain of my fear. 1969.

SETON-KARR, Heywood W
  Bear-hunting in the White Mountains; or, Alaska and British Colombia revisited. 1891.

SETON-KARR, Heywood W
  Shores and alps of Alaska. 1887.

SHELDON, Charles
  The wilderness of the Upper Yukon: a hunter's explorations for wild sheep in sub-arctic mountains. 1911.

STUCK, Hudson
  Ten thousand miles with a dog sled: a narrative of winter travel in interior Alaska. [1914].

UNITED STATES. War Department
  Reports of explorations in the territory of Alaska (Cooks Inlet, Sushitna, Copper and Tanana Rivers), ... by Edwin F. Glenn and W.R. Abercrombie. 1899.

WHYMPER, Frederick
  Travel and adventure in the territory of Alaska, formerly Russian America - now ceded to the United States - and in various other parts of the North Pacific. 1868.

WHYMPER, Frederick
  [Travel and adventures in ... Alaska]. Voyages et aventures dans l'Alaska (ancienne Amérique Russe). 1871.

442 Alaska - geography, description, ... (Cont.)

YOUNG, S   Hall
  Alaska days with John Muir. [4th ed.].1915.

444 Mount McKinley

BALCH, Edwin Swift
  Mount McKinley and mountain climbers' proofs.
  1914.

BROWNE, Belmore
  The conquest of Mount McKinley: the story of three
  expeditions through the Alaskan wilderness to
  Mount McKinley... 1913.

- - New ed. 1956.

CENTRE EXCURSIONISTA DE LA COMARCA DE BAGES
  77-Alaska operation. [1977].

COOK, Frederick Albert
  To the top of the continent: discovery, exploration and adventure in sub-arctic Alaska, the first
  ascent of Mt. McKinley, 1903-1906. 1909.

DAVIDSON, Art
  The coldest climb: the winter ascent of Mt.
  McKinley. 1970.

DUNN, Robert
  The shameless diary of an explorer. 1907.

MILLS, James
  Airborne to the mountains. 1961.

MOORE, Terris
  Mt. McKinley: the pioneer climbs. 1967.

STUCK, Hudson
  The ascent of Denali (Mt. McKinley): a narrative
  of the first complete ascent of the highest peak
  in North America. 1914.

STUCK, Hudson
  The ascent of Denali: first complete ascent of Mt.
  McKinley, highest peak in North America; containing the original diary of Walter Harper, first man
  to achieve Denali's true summit. 1977.

WASHBURN, Bradford
  Mount McKinley and the Alaska Range in literature:
  a descriptive bibliography. 1951.

WASHBURN, Bradford
  A tourist guide to Mount McKinley: the story of
  "Denali", "the Great One", mile-by-mile through
  the park over the Denali Highway, the record of
  McKinley climbs. 1971.

- - Rev. ed. 1974.

445 Mount St. Elias

DE FILIPPI, Filippo
  La spedizione di Sua Altezza Reale il Principe
  Luigi Amedeo di Savoia, Duca degli Abruzzi al
  Monte Sant'Elia (Alaska). 1900.

DE FILIPPI, Filippo
  [La spedizione di Sua Altezza Reale...]. The
  ascent of Mount St. Elias (Alaska) by H.R.H.
  Prince Luigi Amedeo di Savoia, Duke of the
  Abruzzi. 1900.

SCHWATKA, Frederick and RUSSELL, Israel C
  Two expeditions to Mount St. Elias. 1891.

47 NORTH POLE

472 Geography, description, travel

BARROW, Sir John, 1764-1848
  A chronological history of voyages into the Arctic
  regions; undertaken chiefly for the purpose of
  discovering a north-east, north-west, or polar
  passage... 1818.

BARROW, Sir John, 1764-1848
  Voyages of discovery and research within the Arctic
  regions from the year 1818 to the present time...
  1846.

BERTRAM, Colin
  Arctic and Antarctic: the technique of polar
  travel. 1939.

CROFT, Andrew
  Polar exploration. 2nd ed. 1947.

HAIG-THOMAS, David
  Tracks in the snow. 1939.

KANO, Ichiro
  The exploration of polar regions. 1959-60. 2v.

M'DOUGALL, George Frederick
  The eventful voyage of H.M. Discovery ship
  "Resolute" to the Arctic regions in search of Sir
  John Franklin and the missing crews of H.M.
  Discovery ships "Erebus" and "Terror". 1857.

MARKHAM, Albert Hastings
  On the road to the Pole.
  (In From the Equator to the Pole. [1886])

SIMPSON, Myrtle
  Due north. 1970.

473 Axel Heiberg

ANDREWS, Rodney H
  Meteorology and heat balance of the Ablation area,
  White Glacier, Canadian Arctic Archipelago -
  summer 1960. 1964.

BRITISH ARMY AXEL HEIBERG EXPEDITION, 1972
  [Report]. [1972?].

FRICKER, P   E
  Geology of the expedition area, western central
  Axel Heiberg Island, Canadian Arctic Archipelago.
  1963.

FRICKER, P   E   and TRETTIN, H   P
  Pre-Mississippian succession of northernmost Axel
  Heiberg Island, Canadian Arctic Archipelago. 1963.

HOEN, Ernst W
  The anhydrite diapirs of central western Axel
  Heiberg Island. 1964.

JACOBSEN-MCGILL ARCTIC RESEARCH EXPEDITION TO AXEL
HEIBERG ISLANDS, 1959-1962
  Photogrammetric and cartographic results of the
  Axel Heiberg expedition. 1963.

MÜLLER, Fritz
  Preliminary report 1961-1962. 1963.

474 Ellesmere Island

HATTERSLEY-SMITH, Geoffrey
  North of latitude eighty: the Defence Research
  Board in Ellesmere Island. 1974.

ROYAL NAVY ELLESMERE ISLAND EXPEDITION, 1972
  Expedition report. [1972].

THULE-GRISE FIORD EXPEDITION, 1976
  General report. 1976.

475 Baffin Island

OXFORD UNIVERSITY BAFFIN EXPEDITION, 1976
[Report]. [1977].

SCOTTISH BAFFIN ISLAND EXPEDITION, 1976
Report. [1977].

48 GREENLAND

481 Geology, climate, flora

HEER, Oswald
Contributions to the fossil flora of North
Greenland, being a description of the plants
collected by Mr. Edward Whymper during the summer
of 1867. 1869.

MAGNUSSON, A   H
The Lichen-genus Acarospora in Greenland and
Spitsbergen. 1935.

OMANG, S   O   F
Über einige Hieracium-Arten aus Grönland. 1937.

482 Geography, description, travel

BANKS, Mike
Greenland. 1975.

BOYD, Louise A
The fiord region of East Greenland. 1935. 2v.

FANTIN, Mario
Montagne de Groenlandia: monografia storico-
esplorativa e geografico-alpinistica. 1969.

LACMANN, Otto
Geleitworte zu den Blättern Claveringöya, Jordan
Hill and Geographical Society-öya der Karte von
Nordostgrönland. 1937.

SIMPSON, Myrtle
White horizons. 1967.

STEFANSSON, Vilhjalmur
Greenland. 1943.

TILMAN, Harold William
Triumph and tribulation. 1977.

483 Expeditions

ARMY EAST GREENLAND EXPEDITION, 1968
Expedition report. [1968?].

BANKS, Mike
High Arctic: the story of the British North
Greenland Expedition. 1957.

BENNET, Donald J
Staunings Alps - Greenland: Scoresby Land and
Nathorsts Land. 1972.

BRITISH ARMY WEST GREENLAND EXPEDITION, 1971
Final scientific report. 1972.

BRITISH ARMY WEST GREENLAND EXPEDITION, 1971
Report. [1971?].

CAMBRIDGE STAUNINGS EXPEDITION, 1970
The Cambridge Staunings Expedition 1970. Vol.1.
General report and the glaciological projects.
1971.

CHAPMAN, Frederick Spencer
Watkins' last expedition. 1953.

EAST GREENLAND EXPEDITION, 1972
A photographic album... 1974.

EXPÉDITION FRANÇAISE AU GROENLAND SUD/LINDENOWS
FJORD, 1971
Groenland 71. [1972].

FANTIN, Mario
Tra i ghiacci della "Terra Verde" (l'alpinismo in
Groenlandia). 1966.

GEORGI, Johannes
Im Eis vergraben: Erlebnisse auf Station "Eismitte"
der letzten Grönland-Expedition Alfred Wegeners.
1933.

HALLWORTH, Rodney
The last flowers on earth. 1966.

JOINT SERVICES EXPEDITION TO NORTH PEARY LAND, 1969
Preliminary report. 1969.

JOINT SERVICES EXPEDITION TO NORTH PEARY LAND, 1969
[Report]. 1972.

LEICESTER POLYTECHNIC STUDENTS GREENLAND EXPEDITION,
1972
Kûgssuatsiaq, Søndre Sermilik, southern Greenland:
[the official report]. 1973.

MARTIN, Maurice
Note sur l'Expédition française 1957 au Groenland-
Sud... [1957?].

MONZINO, Guido
Spedizioni d'alpinismo in Groenlandia: atti delle
spedizioni G.M. 1960-1964. 1966.

PAYER, Julius
Die zweite Deutsche Nordpolar-Expedition, 1869-70.
1871. 2v.

ROCH, André and PIDERMAN, Guido
Quer durchs "Schweizerland": Grönlandexpedition
des Akademischen Alpenclub Zürich. 1941.

ROYAL AIR FORCE GREENLAND EXPEDITION, 1975
Report on the Royal Air Force Expedition to Søndre
Sermilik Fjord in south west Greenland... [1976].

ROYAL NAVY EAST GREENLAND EXPEDITION, 1966
Report. [1967].

SMITH, Roger S   D
A synopsis of mountaineering in south Greenland.
[1972].

THULE-GRISE FIORD EXPEDITION, 1976
General report. 1976.

VICTOR, Paul Émile
Groenland 1948-1949. 1951.

WATKINS MOUNTAINS EXPEDITION, 1969
Anglo-Danish mountain survey in east Greenland,
preliminary report. 1969.

50 CENTRAL & SOUTH AMERICA

501 Geology, climate, flora

SPRUCE, Richard
Notes of a botanist on the Amazon & Andes, being
records of travel on the Amazon ... the Orinoco,
along the eastern side of the Andes of Peru and
Ecuador, and the shores of the Pacific, during the
years 1849-1864. 1908. 2v.

502 Geography, description, travel

BINGLEY, William
Travels in South America from modern writers with
remarks and observations, exhibiting a connected
view of the geography and present state of that
quarter of the globe, designed for the use of
young persons. 1820.

BRYCE, James, Viscount Bryce
South America: observations and impressions.
1912.

502 <u>Central & South America - geography, ... (Cont.)</u>

FISHER, Joel E
  Bibliography of Mexican, Central and South
  American mountain ascents. 1945.

FOUNTAIN, Paul
  The great mountains and forests of South America.
  1902.

HERZOG, Theodor
  Bergfahrten in Südamerika. 1925.

HINCHLIFF, Thomas Woodbine
  South American sketches; or, A visit to Rio
  Janeiro, the Organ Mountains, La Plata, and the
  Paranà. 1863.

HUMBOLDT, Alexander, <u>Freiherr von</u>
  Essai politique sur <u>le royaume</u> de la Nouvelle-
  Espagne. 1811. 5v.

HUMBOLDT, Alexander, <u>Freiherr von</u>
  Humboldt's travels <u>and discoveries</u> in South
  America. 2nd ed. 1846.

HUMBOLDT, Alexander, <u>Freiherr von</u>
  Personal narrative <u>of travels</u> to the equinoctial
  regions of America during the years 1799-1804.
  1852-53. 3v.

MECIANI, Pietro
  Le Ande: monografia geografico-alpinistica.
  [1964?].

MILLER, Leo E
  In the wilds of South America: six years of
  exploration in Colombia, Venezuela, British
  Guiana, Peru, Bolivia, Argentina, Paraguay and
  Brazil. 1919.

ORTON, James
  The Andes and the Amazon; or, Across the continent
  of South America. 1870.

PECK, Annie Smith
  The South American tour: a descriptive guide. New
  and rev. ed. 1924.

REISS, Wilhelm
  Reisebriefe aus Südamerika 1868-1876. 1921.

ROSS, Colin
  Südamerika die aufsteigende Welt. 3.Aufl. 1923.

SCHERZER, Carl
  Travels in the free states of Central America:
  Nicaragua, Honduras and San Salvador. 1857. 2v.

ULLOA, Antonio de
  Noticias americanas: entretenimientos físico-
  históricos sobre la América meridional, y la
  septentrional oriental: comparacion general de los
  territorios, climas y producciones en las tres
  especies vegetal, animal y mineral... 1792.

51 <u>MEXICO</u>

512 <u>Geography, description, travel</u>

ATL, <u>Dr</u>.
  Le <u>sinfonie</u> del Popocatepetl: poema messicano.
  1930.

BROCKLEHURST, Thomas Unett
  Mexico to-day: a country with a great future, and
  a glance at the prehistoric remains and antiquities
  of the Montezumas. 1883.

CARSON, William English
  Mexico: the wonderland of the south. Rev. ed.
  1914.

PRESCOTT, William H
  History of the conquest of Mexico, with a preliminary view of the ancient Mexican civilization
  and the life of the conqueror, Hernando Cortez.
  New ed. 1857. 2v.

RUXTON, George Frederick
  Adventures in Mexico and the Rocky Mountains.
  1847.

SCHWARTZ, Myrtil
  Drei Giganten des Hochgebirges: meine Erinnerungen
  an deren Besteigung. 1921.

SCHWARTZ, Myrtil
  Vers l'idéal par la montagne: souvenir de mes escalades de haute montagne en Europe et en Amérique.
  1924.

SOLIS, Antonio de
  Historia de la conquista de Mejico; poblacion y
  progresos de la América Setentrional, conocida por
  el nombre de Nueva España. 1826. 3v.

52 <u>ANDES, CHILE, ARGENTINA, PATAGONIA, TIERRA
  DEL FUEGO</u>

521 <u>Geology, climate</u>

BERTONE, Mario
  Aspectos glaciologicos de la zona del Hielo
  Continental Patagónico. 1972.

BERTONE, Mario
  Inventario de los glaciares existentes en la
  vertiente Argentina entre los paralelos 47° 30' y
  51° S.

BURCKHARDT, Carl
  Coupe géologique de la Cordillère entre Las Lajas
  et Curacautin. 1900.

BURCKHARDT, Carl
  Profils géologiques transversaux de la Cordillère
  argentino-chilienne: stratigraphie et tectonique...
  1900.

FRIES, Rob E
  Zur Kenntnis der alpinen Flora im nördlichen
  Argentinien. 1905.

LLIBOUTRY, Luis
  Nieves y glaciares de Chile: fundamentos de
  glaciología. 1956.

MUSEO DE LA PLATA
  Notes préliminaires sur une excursion aux territoires du Nequen, Rio Negro, Chubut et Santa Cruz,
  effectuée par les Sections topographique et géologique. 1897.

522 <u>Geography, description, travel</u>

Across the Andes, from Buenos Ayres to the Pacific.
  [1904].

ARGENTINA
  Argentine-Chilean Boundary: report. 1900.

CHILE
  Statement presented on behalf of Chile in reply to
  the Argentine report. 1901-02. 4v.

- - Appendix. 1902. 2v. in 1.

CHILE. Oficina de Límites
  La Cordillera de los Andes entre las latitudes
  30° 40' i 35° S... 1903.

CHILE. Oficina de Límites
  La Cordillera de los Andes entre las latitudes
  46° i 50° S. 1905.

522 Andes, Chile, Argentina - geography, ... (Cont.)

CRAWFORD, Robert
Across the pampas and the Andes. 1884.

DE AGOSTINI, A   M
Ande patagoniche: viaggi di esplorazione alla
cordigliera patagonica australe. 1949.

GÜSSFELDT, Paul
Reise in den Andes von Chile und Argentinien.
1888.

HABEL, Jean
Ansichten aus Südamerika: Schilderung einer Reise
am La Plata, in den argentinischen Anden und an
der Westküste. 1897.

HEAD, F   B
Rough notes taken during some rapid journeys
across the pampas and among the Andes. 1826.

- - 2nd ed. 1826.

HERZEN, Sergio
Entre rocas y nieves. 1945.

HOLDICH, Sir Thomas Hungerford
The countries of the King's award. 1904.

KÖLLIKER, Alfred
In den einsamkeiten Patagoniens. 1926.

LARDEN, Walter
Argentine plains and Andine glaciers: life on an
estancia, and an expedition into the Andes. 1911.

LATZINA, Francisco
Diccionario geográfico argentino, con ampliaciones
enciclopédicas rioplatenses. 3a ed. 1899.

RIDGWAY, John
Cockleshell journey: the adventures of three men
and a girl. 1974.

SHIPTON, Eric
Land of tempest: travels in Patagonia, 1958-62.
1963.

SHIPTON, Eric
Tierra del Fuego: the fatal lodestone. 1973.

SPENCER, Sir Baldwin
Spencer's last journey, being the journal of an
expedition to Tierra del Fuego. 1931.

SUNDT, Eilert
Patagonia: pa kryss og tvers. 1942.

523 Climbs and climbing

AZÉMA, Marc Antonin
La conquête du Fitz-Roy. 1954.

AZÉMA, Marc Antonin
[La conquète du Fitz-Roy]. The conquest of
Fitzroy. 1957.

CONWAY, William Martin, Baron Conway
Aconcagua and Tierra del Fuego: a book of climbing,
travel and exploration. 1902.

FERLET, René and POULET, Guy
Aconcagua: south face. 1956.

FITZGERALD, Edward Arthur
The highest Andes: a record of the first ascent of
Aconcagua and Tupungato in Argentina, and the ex-
ploration of the surrounding valleys. 1899.

JOINT SERVICES EXPEDITION TO CHILEAN PATAGONIA,
1972-73
General report. 1974.

JOINT SERVICES EXPEDITION TO CHILEAN PATAGONIA,
1972-73
Preliminary report. [1973].

MONZINO, Guido
Italia in Patagonia: Spedizione Italiana alle Ande
patagoniche, 1957-1958. 1958.

PARAGOT, Robert and BÉRARDINI, Lucien
Vingt ans de cordée. 1974.

PATAGONIAN MOUNTAINEERING EXPEDITION, 1974
A Patagonia handbook: Cerro Stanhardt 1974/5: the
report of the 1974 Patagonian Mountaineering
Expedition. 1975.

SAINT-LOUP
Monts pacifique de l'Aconcagua au Cap Horn. 1951.

SAN ROMÁN HERBAGE, Gastón
Guia de excursionismo para la Cordillera de
Santiago. 1977.

SCOTT, William B
Reports of the Princeton University Expeditions to
Patagonia, 1896-1899. Vol.1. Narrative and geo-
graphy. 1903.

SUNDT, Eilert
The first winter-ascent of the Aconcagua, September
1915. [1915].

53   ANDES, BOLIVIA, PERU

532 Geography, description, travel

BINGHAM, Hiram
Inca land: explorations in the highlands of Peru.
1922.

BOWMAN, Isaiah
The Andes of southern Peru: geographical reconnaissance along the seventy-third meridian. 1916.

BRAND, Charles
Journal of a voyage to Peru: a passage across the
cordillera of the Andes, in the winter of 1827,
performed on foot in the snow; and a journey across
the pampas. 1828.

HERZOG, Theodor
Vom Urwald zu den Gletschen der Kordillere: zwei
Forschungsreisen in Bolivia. 1913.

PERU-BOLIVIA BOUNDARY COMMISSION
Peru-Bolivia Boundary Commission, 1911-1913:
reports of the British officers of the Peruvian
Commission, diplomatic memoranda and maps of the
boundary zone. 1918.

PETROCOKINO, A
Along the Andes. 1903.

PROCTOR, Robert
Narrative of a journey across the cordillera of the
Andes, and of a residence in Lima, and other parts
of Peru, in the years 1823 and 1824. 1825.

SCHMIEDER, Oscar
The east Bolivian Andes south of the Rio Grande or
Guapay. 1926.

SIEVERS, Wilhelm
Reise in Peru und Ecuador ausgeführt 1909. 1914.

SMYTHE, William and LOWE, Frederick
Narrative of a journey from Lima to Para, across
the Andes and down the Amazon: undertaken with a
view of ascertaining the practicability of a navigable communication with the Atlantic by the
rivers Pachitea, Ucayali and Amazon. 1836.

TSCHUDI, J   J   von
Travels in Peru during the years 1838-1842, on the
coast, in the sierra, across the cordilleras and
the Andes, into the primeval forests. 1847.

533 Andes, Bolivia, Peru - climbs and climbing

BORCHERS, Philipp
Die weisse Kordillere. 1935.

BRITISH SOUTH AMERICA MOUNTAINEERING EXPEDITION, 1976-77
[Report]. [1977].

CLARK, Simon
The Puma's Claw. 1959.

CLUB ALPIN FRANÇAIS. Section de Paris-Chamonix
Pérou 1973. 1974.

CLUB EXCURSIONISTA DE GRACIA
Alpamayo 72: Andes del Peru. [1973?].

CONWAY, William Martin, Baron Conway
The Bolivian Andes: a record of climbing & exploration in the Cordillera Real in the years 1898 and 1900. 1901.

CORDILLERA BLANCA SEATTLE EXPEDITION, 1964
Ascent of Nevado Huascaran. 1964.

EGELER, Cornelius Geoffrey
[Naar onbestegen Andes toppen]. The untrodden Andes: climbing adventures in the Cordillera Blanca, Peru. 1955.

EXPÉDITION PEROU 77 - CORDILLÈRE BLANCHE, 1977
Compte-rendu d'activités. 1977.

FANTIN, Mario
A settemila metri: gli Inca precursori d'alpinismo. 1969.

FANTIN, Mario
Yucay, montagna degli Incas: la Spedizione comasca alle Ande peruviane... 1958.

GHIGLIONE, Piero
Nelle Ande del sud Perù. 1953.

GRIFFIN, Margaret
Tiquimani. 1965.

HASSE, Dietrich
Cordillera Real: Berliner Jubiläumsexpedition. 1969.

HAUSER, Günter
[Ihr Herren Berge]. White mountain and tawny plain. 1961.

HOEK, Henry
Aus Bolivias Bergen. 1927.

HOEK, Henry
[Aus Bolivias Bergen]. Por las montañas de Bolivia. 1929.

KOGAN, Georges and LEININGER, Nicole
Cordillère Blanche: Expédition franco-belge à la cordillère des Andes, 1951. 1952.

KOGAN, Georges and LEININGER, Nicole
[Cordillère Blanche...]. The ascent of Alpamayo: an account of the Franco-Belgian Expedition to the Cordillera Blanca in the high Andes. 1954.

MENDEZ, Felix
Expedicion española a los Andes del Peru. 1962.

MORALES ARNAO, Cesar
Andinismo en la Cordillera Blanca. 1968.

NAGANO MOUNTAINEERING ASSOCIATION
Informe de la expedicion a los Andes peruanos. 1970.

NORMAN CROUCHER PERUVIAN ANDES EXPEDITION, 1978
Report. [1979].

PECK, Annie Smith
High mountain climbing in Peru & Bolivia: a search for the apex of America, inluding the conquest of Huascarán, with some observations on the country and people below. 1912.

PIERRE, Bernard
La conquéte du Salcantay, géant des Andes. 1953.

PIERRE, Bernard
Victoire sur les Andes. 1976.

RICKER, John F
Yuraq Janka: guide to the Peruvian Andes. Pt.1. Cordilleras Blanca and Rosko. 1977.

SACK, John
The ascent of Yerupaja. 1954.

ST. HELENS MOUNTAINEERING CLUB ANDEAN EXPEDITION, 1977
[Report]. [1978].

SCOTTISH PERUVIAN ANDES EXPEDITION, 1976
Report. [1977?].

SLESSER, Malcolm
The Andes are prickly. 1966.

WALL, David
Rondoy: an expedition to the Peruvian Andes. 1965.

WARBURTON, Lloyd E
The steepest mountain: N.Z. Andes Expedition. 1964.

54 ANDES, ECUADOR, COLOMBIA, VENEZUELA

542 Geography, description, travel

DEPONS, F
Travels in parts of South America, during the years 1801, 1802, 1803, & 1804...
(In A collection of modern and contemporary voyages... Vol.3. 1806)

FANTIN, Mario
A tu per tu con: Jivaros e Colorados Amazzonia Ecuador. 1967.

FLORIANT, V de
À travers les Andes équatoriales: souvenirs personnels. 1891.

HETTNER, Alfred
Reisen in den columbianischen Anden. 1888.

MEYER, Hans
In den Hoch-Anden von Ecuador: Chimborazo, Cotopaxi etc.: Reisen und Studien. 1907.

SIEVERS, Wilhelm
Die Cordillerenstaaten. 1913. 2v.

SIMSON, Alfred
Travels in the wilds of Ecuador and the exploration of the Putumayo river. 1886.

SODIRO, Luis
Relacion sobre la erupcion del Cotopaxi, acaecida el dia 26 de junio de 1877. 1877.

SPENCE, James Mudie
The land of Bolivar; or, War, peace and adventure in the Republic of Venezuela. 2nd ed. 1878. 2v.

WHYMPER, Edward
Travels amongst the great Andes of the Equator. Various editions.

543 Climbs and climbing

CHALBAUD CARDONA, Carlos
Expediciones a la Sierra Nevada de Mérida. 1959.

CONVENCION NACIONAL DE TURISMO, 1st, Mérida, Venezuela, 1961
Itinerarios turisticos-alpinísticos en la Sierra Nevada de Mérida. 1961.

OUNDLE SCHOOL EXPEDITION TO ECUADOR, 1975
[Report]. 1975.

543 Andes, Ecuador - climbs and climbing (Cont.)

RITTERBUSH, Philip C
Report of the 1970 expedition to the Nevado del
Huila, Central Andean Cordillera, Colombia, July,
1970. [1970].

ROYAL AIR FORCE EXPEDITION TO THE SIERRA NEVADA
DE SANTA MARTA IN COLOMBIA, 1974
Report. [1975?].

ROYAL MILITARY COLLEGE OF SCIENCE SHRIVENHAM ANDEAN
EXPEDITION, 1972
[Report of] the RMCS Andean Expedition to the
Sierra Nevada de Santa Marta, Colombia...
[1973?].

WHYMPER, Edward
Travels amongst the Andes of the Equator.
Various editions.

55   GUIANA

553   Climbs and climbing

CLEMENTI, Mrs. Cecil
Through British Guiana to the summit of Roraima.
1920.

MACINNES, Hamish
Climb to the Lost World. 1974.

56   BRAZIL, AMAZON

562   Geography, description, travel

BATES, Henry Walter
The naturalist on the River Amazons: a record of
adventures, habits of animals, sketches of
Brazilian and Indian life, and aspects of nature
under the Equator, during eleven years of travel.
2nd ed. 1864.

FLEMING, Peter
Brazilian adventure. New cheap ed. 1942.

FOUNTAIN, Paul
The river Amazon from its sources to the sea.
1914.

ROLLINS, Alice W
From palm to glacier with an interlude: Brazil,
Bermuda and Alaska. 1892.

58   WEST INDIES

582   Geography, description, travel

HEILPRIN, Angelo
The eruption of Pelée: a summary and discussion of
the phenomena and their sequels. 1908.

PATON, William Agnew
Down the islands: a voyage to the Caribees. 1896.

59   SOUTH PACIFIC

593   Expeditions

HEYERDAHL, Thor
The Kon-Tiki Expedition, by raft across the South
Seas. 1950.

60   ASIA (GENERAL)

602   Geography, description, travel

BONVALOT, Gabriel
Du Caucase aux Indes à travers le Pamir. 1888.

BONVALOT, Gabriel
[Du Caucase aux Indes...]. Through the heart of
Asia, over the Pamir to India. 1889.

CUMBERLAND, C   S
Sport on the Pamirs and Turkistan steppes. 1895.

DOUGLAS, William Orville
Beyond the high Himalayas. 1953.

ETHERTON, P   T
Across the roof of the world: a record of sport
and travel through Kashmir, Gilgit, Hunza, the
Pamirs, Chinese Turkistan, Mongolia and Siberia.
1911.

FORSTER, George
Travels in the northern part of India, Kashmire,
Afghanistan, and Persia, and into Russia by the
Caspian Sea, performed in the years 1782, 83, and
84. [ca 1805].

FRASER, David
The marches of Hindustan, the record of a journey
in Thibet, Trans-Himalayan India, Chinese Turkestan, Russian Turkestan and Persia. 1907.

GORDON, Sir Thomas Edward
The roof of the world, being the narrative of a
journey over the high plateau of Tibet to the
Russian frontier and the Oxus sources on Pamir.
1876.

GREW, J   C
Sport and travel in the Far East. 1910.

HEDIN, Sven
Through Asia. 1898. 2v.

HOFFMEISTER, Werner
Travels in Ceylon and continental India; including
Nepal and other parts of the Himalayas, to the
borders of Thibet, with some notices of the overland route. 1848.

MURRAY, H
Historical account of discoveries and travels in
Asia from the earliest ages to the present time.
1820. 3v.

PLATTNER, Felix Alfred
Jesuits go east. 1950.

RONALDSHAY, Lawrence John Lumley Dundas, Earl of
Sport and politics under an eastern sky. 1902.

SCHLAGINTWEIT-SAKUNLUNSKI, Hermann von
Reisen in Indien und Hochasien: eine Darstellung
der Landschaft, der Cultur und Sitten der Bewohner,
in Verbindung mit klimatischen und geologischen
Verhaltnissen... 1869-80. 4v.

SHOBERL, Frederic
Tibet, and India beyond the Ganges; containing a
description of the character, manners, customs ...
of the nations inhabiting those countries. [1824].

THOMAS COOK LTD.
India, Burma, and Ceylon: information for
travellers and residents. 1926.

YOUNGHUSBAND, Sir Francis
The heart of a continent: a narrative of travels
in Manchuria, across the Gobi Desert, through the
Himalayas, the Pamirs, and Chitral, 1884-1894.
2nd ed. 1896.

602 Asia - geography, description, ... (Cont.)

YOUNGHUSBAND, Sir Francis
The heart of a continent: commemorating the
fiftieth anniversary of his journey from Peking
to India by way of the Gobi Desert and Chinese
Turkistan, and across the Himalaya by the Mustagh
Pass. 1937.

YOUNGHUSBAND, Sir Francis
[The heart of a continent...]. Among the
celestials: a narrative of travels in Manchuria,
across the Gobi desert, through the Himalayas to
India. 1898.
Abridged ed.

61   HIMALAYAS (GENERAL)

BARKER, Clive S
Bibliography of exploration, mountaineering,
travel, history and nomenclature of the Gilgit-
Hunza River watershed, Haramosh Range and Basha
River watershed in the Eastern Hindu-Kush and
Western Karakoram. 1965-75. 3 pts.

BAUME, Louis Charles
Sivalaya: the 8000-metre peaks of the Himalaya: a
chronicle and bibliography of exploration. 1978.

DEUTSCHE HIMALAJA-EXPEDITION, 1934
Himalaja-Bibliographie. 1934.

HIMALAYAN MOUNTAINEERING INSTITUTE, Darjeeling
Himalayan Mountaineering Institute. [1977].

YAKUSHI, Yoshimi
Catalogue of the Himalayan literature. 1972.

611 Geology, climate, flora, fauna

ADAMS, Andrew Leith
Wanderings of a naturalist in India, the western
Himalayas and Cashmere. 1867.

BURRARD, Sir Sidney Gerald
The attraction of the Himalaya mountains upon the
plumb-line in India: considerations of recent data.
1901.

BURRARD, Sir Sidney Gerald
Investigations of isostasy in Himalayan and neighbouring regions. 1918.

BURRARD, Sir Sidney Gerald
On the origin of the Himalaya mountains: a con-
sideration of the geodetic evidence. 1912.

BURRARD, Sir Sidney Gerald and HAYDEN, Sir Henry
Hubert
A sketch of the geography and geology of the
Himalaya mountains and Tibet. 1907-08.

- - 2nd ed., rev. 1933-34.

GANSSER, August
Geology of the Himalayas. 1964.

GRIESBACH, C   L
Geology of the central Himaláyas. 1891.

HOOKER, Sir Joseph Dalton
Himalayan journals; or, Notes of a naturalist in
Bengal, the Sikkim and Nepal Himalayas, the Khasia
mountains... 1854. 2v.

- - New ed., carefully rev. and condensed. 1855.

HOOKER, Sir Joseph Dalton
Illustrations of Himalayan plants... 1855.

MASON, Kenneth
The representation of glaciated regions on maps of
the Survey of India. 1929.

MEDLICOTT, H   B
On the geological structure and relations of the
southern portions of the Himalayan ranges, between
the rivers Ganges and Ravee. 1864.

NAKAO, Sasuke
Living Himalayan flowers. 1964.

ODELL, Noel Ewart
On the occurrence of granite in the Himalayan
mountains. 1974.

OLDHAM, R   D
The structure of the Himalayas, and of the Gangetic
Plain, as elucidated by geodetic observations in
India. 1917.

REID, Mayne
The plant hunters; or, Adventures among the
Himalaya mountains. [1890].

SHERWILL, Walter Stanhope
Notes upon a tour in the Sikkim Himalayah mountains
undertaken for the purpose of ascertaining the
geological formation of Kunchinjinga and of the
perpetually snow-covered peaks in the vicinity.
[1852?].

TCHERNINE, Odette
The snowman and company. 1961.

612 Geography, description, travel

ANDERSON, C   W
To the Pindari Glacier: a sketch book and guide.
1921.

ASAHI SHIMBUN
The magnificence of the Himalayas. 1978.

ATKINSON, Edwin T
Notes on the history of the Himalaya of the N.W.P.,
India. [1883]. 2v.

BARRETT, Robert Le Moyne and BARRETT, Katharine
The Himalayan letters of Gipsy Davy and Lady Ba
written on pilgrimage to the high quiet places
among the simple people of an old folk tale. 1927.

BOECK, Kurt
Durch Indien ins verschlossene Land Nepal: ethnographische und photographische Studienblätter.
1903.

BOECK, Kurt
Himalaya-Album... [1894].

BOECK, Kurt
Himalaya: Lieder und Bilder. [1927].

BOECK, Kurt
Indische Gletscherfahrten: Reisen und Erlebnisse im
Himalaja. 1900.

BONIN, Charles Eudes
Les royaumes des neiges (états himalayens). 1911.

BRUNTON, Paul
A hermit in the Himalayas. [ca 1936].

BURRARD, Sir Sidney Gerald and HAYDEN, Sir Henry
Hubert
A sketch of the geography and geology of the
Himalaya mountains and Tibet. 1907-08. 4 pts.
in 1.

- - 2nd ed., rev. 1933-34. 4 pts.

CALVERT, J
Vazeeri Rupi, the silver country of the Vazeers in
Kulu: its beauties, antiquities and silver mines,
including a trip over the lower Himalayah range and
glaciers. 1873.

Un coin des Himalyas, par un missionnaire. [1903?].

CRAVEN, Steven A
A brief review of Himalayan speleology. 1971.

612 Himalayas - geography, description, ... (Cont.)

CUMMING, Constance F   Gordon
From the Hebrides to the Himalayas: a sketch of
eighteen months' wanderings in Western Isles and
eastern highlands. 1876. 2v.

CUMMING, Constance F   Gordon
In the Himalayas and on the Indian plains, 1884.

DOUIE, Sir James
The Panjab, North-West Frontier Province and
Kashmir. 1916.

ETHERTON, P   T
The last strongholds. 1934.

FA-HSIEN
The travels of Fa-Hsien (399-414 A.D.); or, Record
of the Buddhistic kingdoms. 1923.

FANE, Henry Edward
Five years in India; comprising a narrative of
travels in the presidency of Bengal, a visit to
the court of Runjeet Sing, a residence in the
Himalayah mountains... 1842. 2v.

FANTIN, Mario
Himàlaya e Karakorùm sintesi monografica, geo-
grafico-biologico etnografico-esplorativo-storico-
alpinistica. 1978.

FARRER, Reginald
On the eaves of the world. 1917. 2v.

FORBES, H   F   Gordon
The road from Simla to Shipki in Chinese Thibet and
various minor routes with a few hints for
travellers. 1893.

FORRESTER, J   Campbell
A four weeks' tramp through the Himalayas: a guide
to the Pindari Glacier. 1911.

FRASER, James Baillie
Journal of a tour through part of the snowy range
of the Himàlà mountains, and to the sources of the
rivers Jumna and Ganges. 1820.

FULLERTON, James Alexander
Views in the Himalaya and Neilgherry hills.
[1848].

GALWAN, Ghulam Rassul
Servant of sahibs: a book to be read aloud. 1923.

GERARD, Alexander
Account of Koonawur, in the Himalaya... 1841.

GORDON, Sir Thomas Edward
A varied life: a record of military and civil
service, of sport and of travel in India, Central
Asia and Persia, 1849-1902. 1906.

GORE, F   St. John
A tour to the Pindari Glacier. 1898.

HILLARY, Sir Edmund
From the ocean to the sky: [jet boating up the
Ganges]. 1979.

HOLDICH, Sir Thomas Hungerford
The gates of India, being an historical narrative.
1910.

HOLDICH, Sir Thomas Hungerford
The Indian borderland, 1880-1900. 1901.

JACQUEMONT, Victor
Correspondance de V. Jacquemont avec sa famille et
plusieurs de ses amis pendant son voyage dans
l'Inde (1828-1832). 4e éd. 1846. 2v.

JAMES, Hugo
A volunteer's scramble through Scinde, the Punjab,
Hindostan, and the Himalayah mountains. 1854. 2v.

KNIGHT, Edward Frederick
Where three empires meet: a narrative of recent
travel in Kashmir, western Tibet, Gilgit and the
adjoining countries. New ed. 1897.

LEIFER, Walter
Himalaya: mountains of destiny. 1962.

LLOYD, Sir William
Narrative of a journey from Caunpoor to the
Boorendo Pass in the Himalaya mountains... 1840.
2v.

MACINTYRE, Donald
Hindu-Koh: wanderings and wild sport on and beyond
the Himalayas. 1899.

- - New ed., [rev.]. 1891.

MARKHAM, Sir Clements R
A memoir on the Indian surveys. 1871.

- - 2nd ed. 1878.

MARKHAM, Fred.
Shooting in the Himalayas: a journal of sporting
adventures and travel in Chinese Tartary, Ladac,
Thibet, Cashmere, etc. 1854.

MOORCROFT, William
Travels in the Himalayan provinces of Hindustan and
the Panjab; in Ladakh and Kashmir; in Peshawar,
Kabul, Kunduz and Bokhara, from 1819 to 1825.
1841. 2v.

NEBESKY-WOJKOWITZ, René von
Where the gods are mountains: three years among the
people of the Himalayas. 1956.

NEWALL, David J   F
The highlands of India. 1882-87. 2v.

OAKLEY, E   Sherman
Holy Himalaya: the religion, traditions and scenery
of a Himalayan province (Kumaon and Garhwal). 1905.

PARES, Bip
Himalayan honeymoon. 1940.

RANKIN, Sir Reginald
A tour in the Himalayas and beyond. 1930.

ROERICH, Nicholas
Himalayas: abode of light. 1947.

Rough notes of an excursion to the Soonderdoongee
Glacier in the Himalaya mountains during the autumn
of 1848, by H.B.T. 1858.

SAVORY, Isabel
A sportswoman in India: personal adventures and
experiences of travel in known and unknown India.
1900.

SCHUSTER, Sir Arthur
Indian sketches. 1908.

SKINNER, Thomas
Excursions in India; including a walk over the
Himalaya mountains, to the sources of the Jumna and
the Ganges. 1832. 2v.

SLEEN, W   G   N   van der
Four months' camping in the Himalayas. 1929.

SMYTHE, Frank S
Peaks and valleys. 1938.

STONE, S   J
In and beyond the Himalayas: a record of sport and
travel in the abode of snow. 1896.

SURVEY OF INDIA
Annual reports of parties and offices, 1919-20.
1921.

SURVEY OF INDIA
Catalogue of maps. Parts 1 and 2. 1928.

612 Himalayas - geography, description, ... (Cont.)

SURVEY OF INDIA
Descriptions and co-ordinates of the principal and secondary stations and other fixed points of North-West Himalaya series. 1879.

SURVEY OF INDIA
Descriptions and co-ordinates of the principal and secondary stations and other fixed points of the North-East longitudinal series of triangulation. 1909.

SURVEY OF INDIA
Historical records of the Survey of India. 1945- .

SURVEY OF INDIA
Map catalogue. 1931.

TEMPLE, Sir Richard
Journals kept in Hyderabad, Kashmir, Sikkim and Nepal. 1887. 2v.

UJFALVY-BOURDON, Marie de
Voyage d'une Parisienne dans l'Himalaya occidental. 1887.

WADDELL, L   Austine
Among the Himalayas. 1899.

WALA, Jerzy
W sprawie nomenklatury obiektów górskich. 1977.

WHISTLER, Hugh
In the high Himalayas: sport and travel in the Rhotang and Baralacha, with some notes on the natural history of that area. 1924.

WILSON, Andrew
The abode of snow: observations on a journey from Chinese Tibet to the Indian Caucasus, through the upper valleys of the Himalaya. 1875.

- - 2nd ed. 1876.

WILSON, W
A summer ramble in the Himalayas, with sporting adventures in the Vale of Cashmere. 1860.

WOLLASTON, Nicholas
Handles of chance: a journey from the Solomon Islands to Istanbul. 1956.

WORKMAN, William Hunter and WORKMAN, Fanny Bullock
Through town and jungle... 1904.

WYMAN, Frederick F
From Calcutta to the snowy range, being the narrative of a trip through the upper provinces of India to the Himalayas... By an old Indian. 1866.

YOUNGHUSBAND, Sir Francis
Wonders of the Himalaya. 1924.

613 Climbing history, reminiscences

BRAHAM, Trevor
Himalayan odyssey. 1974.

BRUCE, Hon. Charles Granville
Twenty years in the Himalaya. 1910.

DYHRENFURTH, Günter Oskar
Der dritte Pol: die Achttausender und ihre Trabanten. 1960.

DYHRENFURTH, Günter Oskar
Zum dritten Pol: die Achttausender der Erde. 1952.

DYHRENFURTH, Günter Oskar
[Zum dritten Pol.]. To the third pole: the history of the High Himalaya. 1955.

EDGAR, John Ware
Report on a visit to Sikhim and the Thibetan frontier in October, November, and December, 1873. 1874.

ENGEL, Claire Éliane
Les batailles pour l'Himalaya, 1783-1936. 1936.

FANTIN, Mario
I quattordici "8000": antologia. 1964.

FORSTMANN, Carl
Himatschal: die Throne der Götter: 25 Jahre im Himalaya. 1926.

GUILLARMOD, J   Jacot
Six mois dans l'Himalaya, le Karakorum et l'Hindu-Kush: voyages et explorations aux plus hautes montagnes du monde. [1903?].

HOHLE, Per
Himalayas Helter: beromte ekspedisjoner til jordens hoyeste tinder. 1948.

JACKSON, John Angelo
More than mountains. 1955.

KURZ, Marcel
Chronique himalayenne: l'âge d'or 1940-1955. 1959.

- - Supplément. 1963.

KURZ, Marcel
Essai de chronologie des records d'altitude atteinte par l'homme en montagne. [1947?].

KURZ, Marcel
Himalaya 1933[-1954]. 1935-55. 8pts.

KURZ, Marcel
Le problème himalayen: étude géographique et historique. 1934.

KURZ, Marcel
[Le problème himalayen.]. Die Erschliessung des Himalaya: eine Skizze. 1933.

KURZ, Marcel
Versuch einer Chronologie der Höhenrekorde im Gebirge. [1947].

MASON, Kenneth
Abode of snow: a history of Himalayan exploration and mountaineering. 1955.

MEADE, Charles Francis
Approach to the hills. 1940.

MINNEY, R   J
Midst Himalayan mists. 1920.

MORDECAI, D
The Himalayas: an illustrated summary of the world's highest mountain ranges. 1966.

PILGRIM
Notes of wanderings in the Himmala containing descriptions of some of the grandest scenery of the Snowy Range; among others of Nainee Tal. 1844.

VERGHESE, B   G
Himalayan endeavour. 1962.

WARD, Michael
In this short span: a mountaineering memoir. 1972.

614 Climbing expeditions

ABINGER HIMALAYAN EXPEDITION, 1956
Mountains and memsahibs. 1958.

DYHRENFURTH, Günter Oskar
Himalaya: unsere Expedition 1930. 1931.

DYHRENFURTH, Hettie
Memsahb im Himalaja: [die einzige weisse Frau auf der Internationalen Himalaja-Expedition 1930]. 1931.

GRAHAM, William Woodman
Climbing the Himalayas.
(In From the Equator to the Pole. [1886])

614 Himalayas - climbing expeditions (Cont.)

GRAHAM, William Woodman
   Up the Himalayas: mountaineering on the Indian
   alps. 1885.

HEIM, Arnold and GANSSER, August
   Thron der Götter: Erlebnisse der ersten
   Schweizerischen Himalaya-Expedition. 1938.

HEIM, Arnold and GANSSER, August
   [Thron der Götter]. The throne of the Gods: an
   account of the first Swiss expedition to the
   Himalayas. 1939.

HIMALAYAN CLUB
   Expedition reports: Nepal Himalayas, pre-monsoon
   season 1976. 1976.

IZZARD, Ralph
   [The abominable snowman adventure]. Sur la piste
   de l'abominable homme des neiges "The abominable
   snowman": compte rendu officiel de l'expédition
   du Daily Mail dans l'Himalaya. 1955.

KOHLI, M   S
   Himalayan treks and climbs. [1971?].

MUMM, Arnold Louis
   Five months in the Himalaya: a record of mountain
   travel in Garhwal and Kashmir. 1909.

NEW ZEALAND HIMALAYAN EXPEDITION, 1953
   Himalayan holiday: an account of the New Zealand
   Himalayan Expedition 1953. 1954.

NORTH OF ENGLAND HIMALAYAS EXPEDITION, 1975
   The roof of the world: the report of the 1975
   North of England Himalayas Expedition. 1975.

PALLIS, Marco
   Peaks and lamas. 1939.

SARKAR, Bidyut Kumar
   Report of the Trans Himalayan trekking. [1978].

STONOR, Charles
   The Sherpa and the snowman. 1955.

TILMAN, Harold William
   China to Chitral. 1951.

WALLER, James
   The everlasting hills. 1939.

WORKMAN, Fanny Bullock and WORKMAN, William Hunter
   In the ice world of Himalaya: among the peaks and
   passes of Ladakh, Nubra, Suru, and Baltistan.
   1900.

- - Another ed. 1901.

615 Hunting

ADAIR, F   E   S
   Sport in Ladakh. 1895.

BAIRNSFATHER, P   R
   Sport and nature in the Himalayas. 1914.

BRINCKMAN, Arthur
   The rifle in Cashmere: a narrative of shooting expeditions in Ladak, Cashmere, Punjaub... 1862.

BURRARD, Gerald
   Big game hunting in the Himalayas and Tibet. 1925.

DARRAH, Henry Zouch
   Sport in the highlands of Kashmir... 1898.

DURAND, Sir Edward
   Rifle, rod, and spear in the East, being sporting
   reminiscences. 1911.

GARDNER, Nora
   Rifle and spear with the Rajpoots, being the narra-
   tive of a winter's travel and sport in northern
   India. 1895.

GREW, J   C
   Sport and travel in the Far East. 1910.

HAUGHTON, Henry Lawrence
   Sport and folklore in the Himalaya. 1913.

J., K.C.A.
   The sportsman's vade-mecum for the Himalayas.
   1891.

KENNION, R   L
   Sport and life in the further Himalaya. 1910.

KINLOCH, Alexander A
   Large game shooting in Thibet, the Himalayas, and
   northern India. 1885.

KOENIGSMARCK, Hans, Graf von
   The Markhor: sport in Cashmere. 1910.

MACINTYRE, Donald
   Hindu-Koh: wanderings and wild sport on and beyond
   the Himalayas. 1899.

- - New ed. [rev.]. 1891.

MARKHAM, Fred.
   Shooting in the Himalayas. 1854.

MATHIAS, H   V
   Five weeks' sport in the interior of the Himalayas
   ... 1865.

RUNDALL, L   B
   The ibex of Sha-ping and other Himalayan studies.
   1915.

SAVORY, Isabel
   A sportswoman in India: personal adventures and
   experiences of travel in known and unknown India.
   1900.

STEBBING, E   P
   Stalks in the Himalaya: jottings of a sportsman-
   naturalist... 1912.

STONE, S   J
   In and beyond the Himalayas: a record of sport and
   travel in the abode of snow. 1896.

TAYLOR, Neville
   Ibex shooting on the Himalayas. 1903.

TYACKE, R   H
   How I shot my bears; or, Two years' tent life in
   Kullu and Lahoul. 1893.

TYSON, T
   Trout fishing in Kulu. 2nd ed. 1941.

WARD, A   E
   The sportsman's guide to Kashmir & Ladak. 1883.

- - 3rd and rev. ed. 1887.

WHISTLER, Hugh
   In the high Himalayas: sport and travel in the
   Rhotang and Baralacha, with some notes on the
   natural history of that area. 1924.

WILSON, W
   A summer ramble in the Himalayas, with sporting
   adventures in the Vale of Cashmere. 1860.

62 HIMALAYA, KARAKORAM, HINDU KUSH,PAMIR EXPEDITIONS

621 Hindu Kush

AGRESTI, Henri
  Montagnes arides du Wakhan. [1970].

CAMBRIDGE HINDU-KUSH EXPEDITION, 1966
  [Report]. [1967?].

CAMBRIDGE HINDU KUSH EXPEDITION, 1972
  Report. [1973?].

CAMBRIDGE HINDU-KUSH EXPEDITION, 1976
  Preliminary report. [1976].

CENTRE EXCURSIONISTA DE LA COMARCA DE BAGES
  Expedición Española Hindu-Kush - 73. [1973].

ČS. EXPEDICE DOBYVÁ HINDÚKUŠ, 1965
  Soubor 12 fotografií Viléma Heckela. [1965?].

DUNSHEATH, Joyce and BAILLIE, Eleanor
  Afghan quest: the story of their Abinger
  Afghanistan Expedition 1960. 1961.

FREY, Wolfgang
  Zwischen Munjan und Bashgal (Zentraler
  Afghanischer Hindukusch). 1967-68. 2v.

MACHETTO, Guido
  Sette anni contro il Tirich, di Guido Machetto,
  Maria Ludovica e Riccardo Varvelli. 1976.

MANCHESTER UNIVERSITY HINDU KUSH EXPEDITION, 1977
  [Final report]. [1978].

MARAINI, Fosco
  Where four worlds meet: Hindu Kush 1959. 1964.

MIDLANDS HINDU KUSH EXPEDITION, 1967
  Report. [1968].

NAESS, Arne
  Opp stupet til Osttoppen av Tirich Mir. 1964.

NEWBY, Eric
  A short walk in the Hindu Kush. 1958.

NORSKE HIMALAIA-EKSPEDISJONEN, 1950
  Tirich Mir til topps: den Norske Himalaia-
  Ekspedisjonen. 1950.

NORSKE HIMALAIA-EKSPEDISJONEN, 1950
  Tirich Mir: the Norwegian Himalaya Expedition.
  1952.

NOTTINGHAM UNIVERSITY HINDU KUSH EXPEDITION, 1972
  [Report]. [1973?].

OXFORD EXPEDITION TO THE HINDU KUSH, 1977
  [Report]. 1978.

POLISH HINDU KUSH AND PAMIR EXPEDITION, 1971
  [Report]. [1971?].

ROUCH, Monique
  Wakhan: victoires pyrénéennes dans l'Himalaya.
  1970.

SCOTTISH HINDU KUSH EXPEDITION, 1968
  Report. [1968?].

SCOTTISH HINDU KUSH EXPEDITION, 1970
  Scottish expedition to the roof of the world.
  [1971?].

TRANTER, Philip
  No tigers in the Hindu Kush. 1968.

TRENT POLYTECHNIC HINDU KUSH EXPEDITION, 1975
  Report. [1977].

WALA, Jerzy
  Hindu Kush mountain group: Hendukuse Zebak. 1974.

WALA, Jerzy
  Hindu Kush: the regional divisions. 1973.

622 Pamirs

ACADEMIC ALPINE CLUB OF KYOTO
  Ascent of Noshaq: the Japanese Pamir expedition,
  1960. 1961.
  In Japanese.

BORCHERS, Philipp
  Berge und Gletscher im Pamir. 1931.

BORCHERS, Philipp and WIEN, Karl
  Bergfahrten im Pamir. 1929.

CLUB ALPIN FRANÇAIS. Section du Mont Blanc and
Section de l'Isère
  Sur le toit du monde: l'ascension du Pic du
  Communisme (7495 mètres) point culminant de l'Union
  Soviétique. 1978.

CRAIG, Robert W
  Storm & sorrow in the high Pamirs. 1977.

DUNMORE, Charles Adolphus Murray, 7th Earl of
  The Pamirs, being a narrative of a year's expedition on horseback and on foot through Kashmir,
  western Tibet, Chinese Tartary, and Russian central
  Asia. 2nd ed. 1893.

HEIM, Maurice
  Sur les pentes du Pamir. 2e éd. 1922.

IATSENKO, V   S
  V gorakh Pamira: pumevye zapiski uchastnika
  Pamirskoi al'pinistskoi ekspeditsii 1940 g. 1950.

MUKHIN, A   S   and GUSEV, V   F
  Fanskie gory. 1949.

OLUFSEN, Ole
  Through the unknown Pamirs: the second Danish Pamir
  expedition 1898-99. 1904.

RICKMERS, Willi Rickmer
  Alai! Alai! Arbeiten und Erlebnisse der Deutsch-
  Russischen Alai-Pamir-Expedition. 1930.

ROMM, Michael
  The ascent of Mount Stalin. 1936.

SLESSER, Malcolm
  Red Peak: a personal account of the British-Soviet
  Expedition 1962. 1964.

STEIN, Sir Marc Aurel
  Mountain panoramas from the Pamirs and Kwen Lun.
  1908.

VALLA, François and ZUANON, Jean Paul
  Pamir: escalade d'un 7,000 au pays des Kirghizes...
  1976.

WALA, Antoni and WALA, Jerzy
  Routes leading to Pik Kommunizma, 7495, Soviet
  Union, Pamir, 1933-1971. 1971.

WALA, Jerzy
  Kohe Pamir - Wakhan: orographical sketch-map. 1975.

ZABIROV, R   D
  Oledenenie Pamira. 1955.

623 Karakoram

ACADEMIC ALPINE CLUB OF KYOTO
  Chogolisa:the Japanese Chogolisa Expedition, 1958.
  1959.
  In Japanese.

ACADEMIC ALPINE CLUB OF KYOTO
  Saltoro Kangri: the Japan-Pakistan Joint Expedition
  1962. 1964.
  In Japanese.

623 Karakoram (Cont.)

AMERICAN KARAKORAM EXPEDITION, 1938
  Five miles high: the story of an attack on the
  second highest mountain in the world. 1939.

- - Another ed. 1940.

BAND, George
  Road to Rakaposhi. 1955.

BANKS, Mike
  Rakaposhi. 1959.

BARKER, Clive S
  Bibliography of exploration, mountaineering,
  travel, history and nomenclature of the Gilgit-
  Hunza River watershed, Haramosh range and Basha
  River watershed in the eastern Hindu Kush and
  western Karakoram. 1965.

BARKER, Ralph
  The last blue mountain. 1959.

COMPAGNONI, Achille
  Il tricolore sul K2. 1965.

CONWAY, William Martin, Baron Conway
  Climbing and exploration in the Karakoram-
  Himalayas. 1894.

CONWAY, William Martin, Baron Conway
  [Climbing and exploration in the Karakoram-
  Himalayas]. Ascensions et explorations à sept
  mille mètres dans l'Himalaya. 1898.

DESIO, Ardito
  La conquista del K2, seconda cima del mondo. 1954.

DESIO, Ardito
  [La conquista del K2...]. Ascent of K2, second
  highest peak in the world. 1955.

DYHRENFURTH, Günter Oskar
  Baltoro: ein Himalaya-Buch. 1939.

DYHRENFURTH, Günter Oskar
  Dämon Himalaya: Bericht der Internationalen
  Karakoram-Expedition 1934. 1935.

EXPÉDITION FRANÇAISE À L'HIMALAYA, 1936
  L'Expédition française à l'Himalaya 1936, par Jean
  Escarra. 1937.

- - Abridged ed. 1938.

EXPÉDITION FRANÇAISE À L'HIMALAYA, 1936
  Himalayan assault: the French Himalayan Expedition.
  1938.

FANTIN, Mario
  K2: sogno vissuto. 1958.

FAZY, Robert
  L'exploration du Karakoram: essai de synthèse et
  de bibliographie raisonnée. 1942.

FEATHERSTONE, B   K
  An unexplored pass: a narrative of a thousand-mile
  journey to the Kara-koram Himalayas. [1926].

HOUSTON, Charles Sneed and BATES, Robert Hicks
  K2: the savage mountain. 1955.

HOUSTON, Charles Sneed and BATES, Robert Hicks
  [K2: the savage mountain]. K2: montagne sans
  pitié. 1954.

HOUSTON, Charles Sneed
  K2, 8611m: [troisième expédition américaine au
  Karakorum]. 1954.

KLUB WYSOKOGÓRSKI
  Himalaya Karakoram: [Polish Expedition Himalaya
  Karakoram, 1971]. 1971.

KOBE UNIVERSITY KARAKORUM EXPEDITION, 1976
  Sherpi Kangri 1976: [report of the] Kobe
  University Karakorum Expedition. 1976.

MCCORMICK, Arthur David
  An artist in the Himalayas. 1895.

MANCHESTER KARAKORUM EXPEDITION, 1968
  Report. [1969?].

MARAINI, Fosco
  Gasherbrum 4o, Baltoro, Karakorum. 2a ed. 1960.

MARAINI, Fosco
  [Gasherbrum 4o, Baltoro, Karakorum]. Karakoram:
  the ascent of Gasherbrum IV. 1961.

MONZINO, Guido
  Kanjut Sar: atti della Spedizione G.M. '59 al
  Kanjut Sar, Karakorum. 1961.

NOYCE, Wilfrid
  To the unknown mountain: ascent of an unexplored
  twenty-five thousander in the Karakoram. 1962.

NYKA, Józef
  Ostatni atak na Kunyang Chhish [of the Klub
  Wysokogórski]. 1973.

NYKA, Józef
  [Ostatni atak na Kunyang Chhish]. Gipfelsturm im
  Karakorum. 1977.

ROCH, André
  Karakoram Himalaya: sommets de 7000. 1945.

ROWELL, Galen A
  In the throne room of the mountain gods. 1977.

SAYSSE-TOBICZYK, Kazimierz
  Himalaje-Karakorum. 1974.

SCHOMBERG, Reginald Charles Francis
  Unknown Karakoram. 1936.

SHIPTON, Eric
  Blank on the map. 1938.

TILMAN, Harold William
  Two mountains and a river. 1949.

TILMAN, Harold William
  [Two mountains and a river]. Deux montagnes et une
  rivière... 1953.

VISSER, Philips Christiaan
  Naar Himalaya en Kara-korum. 1925.

WALA, Jerzy
  Topography of the Hispar Mustagh mountain group,
  Karakorum. 1974.

WORKMAN, Fanny Bullock and WORKMAN, William Hunter
  Ice-bound heights of the Mustagh: an account of
  two seasons of pioneer exploration and high climbing in the Baltistan Himalaya. 1908.

WORKMAN, Fanny Bullock and WORKMAN, William Hunter
  Two summers in the ice-wilds of eastern Karakoram:
  the exploration of nineteen hundred square miles
  of mountain and glacier. 1917.

WORKMAN, William Hunter and WORKMAN, Fanny Bullock
  The call of the snowy Hispar: a narrative of exploration and mountaineering on the northern
  frontier of India. 1910.

YOUNG, Peter
  Himalayan holiday: a trans-Himalayan diary 1939.
  [1944?].

624 Kashmir

AMPLEFORTH COLLEGE HIMALAYAN EXPEDITION, 1977
  Report. [1978].

BAUER, Paul
  Auf Kundfahrt im Himalaja: Siniolchu und Nanga
  Parbat - Tat und Schicksal deutscher Bergsteiger.
  1937.

624 Kashmir (Cont.)

BAUER, Paul
[Auf Kundfahrt im Himalaja...]. Himalayan quest:
the German expeditions to Siniolchum and Nanga
Parbat. 1938.

BAUER, Paul
Das Ringen um den Nanga Parbat, 1856-1953: hundert
Jahre bergsteigerischer Geschichte. 1955.

BAUER, Paul
[Das Ringen um den Nanga Parbat...]. The seige of
Nanga Parbat, 1856-1953. 1956.

BECHTOLD, Fritz
Deutsche am Nanga Parbat: der Angriff 1934. 1935.

BECHTOLD, Fritz
[Deutsche am Nanga Parbat...]. Nanga Parbat adventure: a Himalayan expedition. 1935.

BRITISH BARNAJ HIMALAYAN EXPEDITION, 1977
Expedition report. [1978?].

CANDLER, Edmund
On the edge of the world. 1919.

CITY UNIVERSITY - BRUNEL UNIVERSITY KISHTWAR
HIMALAYA EXPEDITION, 1978
Report. [1979].

COLLIE, John Norman
Climbing on the Himalaya and other mountain ranges.
1902.

COLLIE, John Norman
Climbing on the Nanga Parbat Range, Kashmir. 1896.

DEACOCK, Antonia
No purdah in Padam: the story of the Women's Overland Himalayan Expedition, 1958. 1960.

DYHRENFURTH, Günter Oskar
Das Buch vom Nanga Parbat: die Geschichte seiner
Besteigung 1895-1953. 1954.

EXPEDÍCIA NANGA PARBAT ČSSR, 1971
II. Expedícia Nanga Parbat 8125m. Himaláje
Československo 1971. [1973?].

FINSTERWALDER, Richard
Forschung am Nanga Parbat: Deutsche Himalaya-
Expedition 1934. 1935.

HERRLIGKOFFER, Karl Maria
Im Banne des Nanga Parbat: Bildband der deutsch-
österreichischen Willy-Merkl-Gedächtnisexpedition
1953 zum Nanga Parbat. 1953.

HERRLIGKOFFER, Karl Maria
Nanga Parbat, incorporating the official report of
the expedition of 1953. 1954.

HERRLIGKOFFER, Karl Maria
Nanga Parbat 1953. 1954.

KICK, Wilhelm
Schlagintweits Vermessungsarbeiten am Nanga Parbat
1856. 1967.

KNOWLTON, Elizabeth
The naked mountain. 1933.

KOLB, Fritz
Himalaya venture. 1959.

LINK, Ulrich
Nanga Parbat: Berg des Schicksals im Himalaya.
1953.

LOUGHBOROUGH UNIVERSITY MOUNTAINEERING CLUB KISHTWAR
HIMALAYAN EXPEDITION, 1976
L.U.M.C. 1976 Kishtwar Himalayan Expedition.
[1978].

NORTH OF ENGLAND KISHTWAR EXPEDITION, 1978
[Report]. [1979].

PIERRE, Bernard
Une montagne nommée Nun-Kun. 1954.

PIERRE, Bernard
[Une montagne nommée Nun-Kun]. A mountain called
Nun Kun. 1955.

PUSKAS, Arno
Nanga Parbat 8125m. 1976.

RAUCH, Rudolf
Der Ruf vom Nanga Parbat. 1935.

TATRANSKÁ EXPEDÍCIA HIMALÁJE, 1969
Tatranská Expedícia Himaláje 1969 = the High Tatras
Expedition, Himalaya 69. 1968.

TILMAN, Harold William
Two mountains and a river. 1949.

TILMAN, Harold William
[Two mountains and a river]. Deux montagnes et une
rivière... 1953.

UNIVERSITY OF SOUTHAMPTON LADAKH EXPEDITION, 1976
Report. 1977.

WELZENBACH, Willo
[Bergfahrten]. Willo Welzenbachs Bergfahrten.
1935.

WELZENBACH, Willo
[Bergfahrten]. Les ascensions de Willo Welzenbach:
Alpes orientales, Alpes valaisannes, Mont Blanc,
Oberland Bernois, Himalaya. 1939.

WORKMAN, Fanny Bullock and WORKMAN, William Hunter
Peaks and glaciers of Nun Kun: a record of pioneer-
exploration and mountaineering in the Punjab
Himalaya. 1909.

625 Punjab

ARMY MOUNTAINEERING ASSOCIATION HIMACHAL PRADESH
EXPEDITION, 1973
Preliminary report. 1973.

ARMY MOUNTAINEERING ASSOCIATION HIMACHAL PRADESH
EXPEDITION, 1973
Report. [1974].

BRUCE, Hon. Charles Granville
Kulu and Lahoul. 1914.

MERSEYSIDE HIMALAYAN EXPEDITION, 1977
Report. [1978?].

NORTH OF ENGLAND HIMALAYAN EXPEDITION, 1977
A return to the roof of the world and the story of
a Himalayan trilogy. [1977].

SCARR, Josephine
Four miles high. 1966.

SOUTH OF ENGLAND EAST KULU EXPEDITION, 1978
[Report]. [1979].

SVENSKA HIMALAYA EXPEDITIONEN, 1973
Reserapport. [1974].

UNIVERSITY OF BRISTOL MOUNTAINEERING CLUB HIMALAYAN
EXPEDITION, 1976
Kulu 1976: the report of the University of Bristol
Mountaineering Club Himalayan Expedition. 1976.

626 Nepal

BONINGTON, Chris
Annapurna South Face. 1971.

BONINGTON, Chris
[Annapurna South Face]. Annapurna face sud. 1972.

BONINGTON, Chris
[Annapurna South Face]. Annapurna parete sud.
1973.

626 Nepal (Cont.)

BRITISH JANNU EXPEDITION, 1978
  [Report]. 1978.

BRITISH NEPALESE ARMY ANNAPURNA EXPEDITION, 1970
  The ascent of Annapurna 20th May 1970. [1970?].

CASSIN, Riccardo and NANGERONI, Giuseppe
  Lhotse '75: spedizione alpinistico-scientifica del
  C.A.I. all'Himalaya del Nepal. 1977.

CENTRE EXCURSIONISTA DE LA COMARCA DE BAGES
  Expedicion española Himalaya - 76: Makalu -
  8,481 mts. 1976.

CENTRE EXCURSIONISTA DE LA COMARCA DE BAGES
  [Expedicion española Himalaya - 76]. Report. 1976.

DEUTSCHE HIMALAYA EXPEDITION, 1973
  Besteigung des Dhaulagiri III 7715m. [1974].

EISELIN, Max
  Erfolg am Dhaulagiri: die Erstbesteigung des Acht-
  tausanders durch die Schweizerische Himalaya-
  Expedition 1960. 1960.

EISELIN, Max
  [Erfolg am Dhaulagiri]. The ascent of Dhaulagiri.
  1961.

EXPÉDITION FRANÇAISE À L'HIMALAYA, 1971
  Makalu 8481m pilier ouest. [1971?].

FIALA, Ivan
  Makalu 1976: trasa Ceskoslovenskej horolezeckej
  expedicie Himaláje. 1977.

FRANCO, Jean and TERRAY, Lionel
  Bataille pour le Jannu. 1965.

FRANCO, Jean and TERRAY, Lionel
  [Bataille pour le Jannu]. At grips with Jannu.
  1967.

FRANCO, Jean
  Makalu. 1955.

GALFY, Ivan and KRISSAK, Milan
  Makalu. 1978.

GRANT, Richard
  Annapurna II. 1961.

GURUNG, Harka
  Annapurna to Dhaulagiri: a decade of mountaineering in Nepal Himalaya, 1950-1960. 1968.

HARA, Makoto and ASAMI, Masao
  Makalu 1970: Harukanaru mitoono one. 1972.

HERZOG, Maurice
  Annapurna premier 8,000. 1952.

HERZOG, Maurice
  [Annapurna premier 8,000]. Annapurna: conquest of
  the first 8000-metre peak (26,493 feet). 1952.

HERZOG, Maurice and ICHAC, Marcel
  Regards vers l'Annapurna. 1951.

HILLARY, Sir Edmund and LOWE, George
  East of Everest: an account of the New Zealand
  Alpine Club Himalayan Expedition to the Barun
  Valley in 1954. 1956.

HILLARY, Sir Edmund and DOIG, Desmond
  High in the thin cold air. 1963.

JACKSON, Monica and STARK, Elizabeth
  Tents in the clouds: the first Women's Himalayan
  Expedition. 1956.

JAPAN CLIMBING EXPEDITION TO WEST WALL OF MANASLU,
1971
  Manaslu west-wall 1971. 1974.

JAPANESE ALPINE CLUB
  Manaslu 1952/3-[1954/6]. 1954-58. 2v.

JAPANESE EXPEDITION TO NEPAL HIMALAYA, 1969
  Gurja Himal: Japanese Expedition to Nepal Himalaya
  1969. 1970.

JOINT BRITISH ARMY MOUNTAINEERING ASSOCIATION/ROYAL
NEPALESE ARMY NUPTSE EXPEDITION, 1975
  Nuptse 1975: preliminary report. 1976.

KAMBARA, Tatsu
  Nepal bibliography 1959. 1959.

KOHLI, M S
  The last of the Annapurnas. 1962.

LAMBERT, Raymond and KOGAN, Claude
  [Record à l'Himalaya]. White fury: Gaurisankar and
  Cho Oyu. 1956.

MANCHESTER NEPALESE EXPEDITION, 1970
  Report. [1971].

MULGREW, Peter
  No place for men. 1965.

NOYCE, Wilfrid
  Climbing the Fish's Tail. 1958.

OXFORD HIMALAYAN EXPEDITION, 1973
  [Report]. [1974].

PARAGOT, Robert and SEIGNEUR, Yannick
  Makalu pilier ouest. 1972.

RIVOLIER, Jean
  Expéditions françaises à l'Himalaya: aspect
  médical. 1959.

SCARR, Josephine
  Four miles high. 1966.

SCUOLA NAZIONALE DI ALPINISMO A. PARRAVICINI
SPEDIZIONE MONTE API, 1978
  [Report]. 1979.

STYLES, Showell
  The moated mountain. 1955.

TAYLOR, Peter
  Coopers Creek to Langtang II. 1965.

TICHY, Herbert
  Cho Oyu, by favour of the gods. 1957.

TILMAN, Harold William
  Nepal Himalaya. 1952.

VERRIJN STUART, Xander
  Annapurna, 8091 meter: Nederlandse klimmers in de
  Himalaya. 1978.

YODA, Takayoshi
  Ascent of Manaslu in photographs 1952-6. 1956.

627 Sikkim, Bhutan

BAUER, Paul
  Im Kampf um den Himalaja: der erste deutsche
  Angriff auf den Kangchendzönga 1929. 1931.

BAUER, Paul
  [Im Kampf um den Himalaja...]. Himalayan campaign:
  the German attack on Kangchenjunga, the second
  [sic] highest mountain in the world. 1937.

BAUER, Paul
  [Kampf um den Himalaja]. Kanchenjunga challenge.
  1955.

BAUER, Paul
  Um den Kantsch: der zweite deutsche Angriff auf den
  Kangchendzönga 1931. 1933.

CHAPMAN, Frederick Spencer
  Helvellyn to Himalaya, including an account of the
  first ascent of Chomolhari. 1940.

DYHRENFURTH, Günter Oskar
  Das Buch vom Kantsch: die Geschichte seiner
  Besteigung. 1955.

627 Sikkim, Bhutan (Cont.)

EVANS, Sir Charles
Kangchenjunga: the untrodden peak. 1956.

EVANS, Sir Charles
[Kangchenjunga...]. Neprikosnovennaia
Kanchendzhanga. 1961.

FRESHFIELD, Douglas William
Round Kangchenjunga: a narrative of mountain
travel and exploration. 1903.

SMYTHE, Frank S
The Kangchenjunga adventure. 1930.

STURM, Günter
Erfolg am Kantsch 8438 m: die Himalaya-Expedition
des Deutschen und Österreichischen Alpenvereins.
1975.

TILMAN, Harold William
When men & mountains meet. 1946.

TUCKER, John
Kanchenjunga. 1955.

WARD, Michael
In this short span: a mountaineering memoir. 1972.

628 Garhwal

BOARDMAN, Peter
The Shining Mountain: two men on Changabang's west
wall. 1978.

CAMBRIDGE GARHWAL HIMALAYA EXPEDITION, 1977
Report. [1978].

CHANDEKAR, A   R
The god that did not fail: expedition to Hanuman
(19930 ft) May-June 1966. [1966].

HANKINSON, Alan
Changabang, by Chris Bonington [and others];
[edited by Alan Hankinson]. 1975.

INDO-JAPANESE NANDA DEVI EXPEDITION, 1976
Nanda Devi Travers 1976: preliminary report. 1976.

INDO-JAPANESE WOMEN'S JOINT HIMALAYAN EXPEDITION,
1976
[Report]. [1977].

JAMES, J   F   W
The skirts of Nanda Devi. 1933.

JONAS, Rudolf
Im Garten der göttlichen Nanda: Bergfahrten im
Garhwalhimalaya. 1948.

Languepin, Jean Jacques and PAYAN, Louis
Nanda Devi: 3e expédition française à l'Himalaya.
1952.

MURRAY, William Hutchison
The Scottish Himalayan Expedition. 1951.

PARIBHRAMAN
Gujarat expedition to 'Shrirange' of Himalayas,
1963. [1964].

SCHWEIZERISCHE STIFTUNG FÜR ALPINE FORSCHUNGEN
Schweizer im Himalaja. 1939.

- - 2.Aufl. 1940.

SHIPTON, Eric
Nanda Devi. 1936.

SMYTHE, Frank S
Kamet conquered. 1932.

SMYTHE, Frank S
The valley of flowers. 1938.

- - Uniform ed. 1947.

TAKABUSHI, S
Nandakot Tohan; or, The ascent of Nanda Kot: the
Rikkyo University Himalaya Expedition 1936. 1937.
In Japanese.

TILMAN, Harold William
The ascent of Nanda Devi. 1937.

WEIR, Thomas
The ultimate mountains: an account of four months'
mountain exploring in the central Himalaya. 1953.

629 Assam

TILMAN, Harold William
When men & mountains meet. 1946.

63   EVEREST

632 General works

BOECK, Kurt
Im Banne des Everest: Erlebnisse in Nepal, der für
Weisse verschlossenen Heimat der Gorkhas im Zentral-
Himalaja. 1923.

BRYANT, Leslie Vickery
New Zealanders and Everest. 1953.

BURRARD, Sir Sidney Gerald
Mount Everest and its Tibetan names: a review of
Sir Sven Hedin's book. 1931.

DONOUGHUE, Carol
Everest. 1975.

FINCH, George Ingle
Der Kampf um den Everest. 1925.

FLAIG, Walther
Im Kampf um Tschomo-lungma den Gipfel der Erde:
der Himalaja und sein höchster Gipfel Mount
Everest, oder, Tschomo-lungma. 16.Aufl. 1923.

GEARING, Julian
The supreme challenge: a chronicle of all the
attempts to climb Mount Everest. 1976.

HAGEN, Toni
Mount Everest: Aufbau, Erforschung und Bevölkerung
des Everest-Gebietes. 1959.

HAGEN, Toni
Mount Everest: formation, population and exploration of the Everest region. 1963.

HEDIN, Sven
Mount Everest. 1923.

MARSHALL, Howard
Men against Everest. 1954.

MILA, Massimo and TENZING NORGAY
Gli eroi del Chomolungma. 1954.

MORIN, Micheline
Everest: du premier assaut à la victoire. 1953.

MORIN, Micheline
Everest: from the first attempt to the final
victory. 1955.

MURRAY, William Hutchison
The story of Everest. 1953.

- - 3rd ed. 1953.

ODELL, Noel Ewart
The supposed Tibetan or Nepalese name of Mount
Everest. [1935].

PEYRÉ, Joseph
Mont Everest: roman. 1942.

632 Everest - general works (Cont.)

SHIPTON, Eric
[The Mount Everest Reconnaissance Expedition...].
Face à l'Everest: l'Expédition Anglaise de
Reconnaissance 1951, avec Les batailles pour
l'Everest par Bernard Pierre. 1953.

SHIPTON, Eric
The true book about Everest. 1955 (1958 reprint).

ULLMAN, James Ramsey
Kingdom of adventure: Everest; a chronicle of
man's assault on the earth's highest mountain.
1948.

YOUNGHUSBAND, Sir Francis
Everest: the challenge. 1936.

633 Expeditions, to 1939

BLAKENEY, Thomas Sydney
A.R. Hinks and the first Everest expedition, 1921.
1970.

BRUCE, Hon. Charles Granville
The assault on Mount Everest 1922. 1923.

BRUCE, Hon. Charles Granville
[The assault on Mount Everest 1922]. L'assaut du
Mont Everest 1922. [1923].

FELLOWES, Peregrine Forbes Morant
First over Everest; the Houston-Mount Everest
expedition 1933. 1933.

HOWARD-BURY, Charles Kenneth
Mount Everest: the reconnaisance, 1921. 1922.

HOWARD-BURY, Charles Kenneth
[Mount Everest...]. À la conquète du Mont
Everest. 1923.

MACINTYRE, Neil
Attack on Everest. 1936.

MOUNT EVEREST COMMITTEE
Catalogue of the exhibition of photographs and
paintings from the Mount Everest expedition 1922.
1923.

NOEL, John Baptist Lucius
Through Tibet to Everest. 1927.

NORTON, Edward Felix
The fight for Everest: 1924. 1925.

ROBERTS, Dennis
I'll climb Mount Everest alone: the story of
Maurice Wilson. 1957.

RUTTLEDGE, Hugh
Attack on Everest. 1935.

RUTTLEDGE, Hugh
Everest 1933. 1934.

RUTTLEDGE, Hugh
[Everest 1933]. Mount Everest. 1938.

RUTTLEDGE, Hugh
Everest: the unfinished adventure. 1937.

SILVA, P
Le ascensioni sull'Everest: loro difficoltà-
pericoli, deduzioni e utilità per le science.
1926.

SMYTHE, Frank S
Camp Six: an account of the 1933 Mount Everest
expedition. 1937.

SOMERVELL, Theodore Howard
After Everest: the experiences of a mountaineer
and medical missionary. 1936.

TILMAN, Harold William
Mount Everest 1938. 1948.

TILMAN, Harold William
[Mount Everest 1938]. Everest 1938. 1952.

YOUNGHUSBAND, Sir Francis
The epic of Mount Everest. 1926.

YOUNGHUSBAND, Sir Francis
[The epic of Mount Everest]. L'épopée de
l'Everest... 1947.

YOUNGHUSBAND, Sir Francis
[The epic of Mount Everest]. La epopeya del
Everest. 1946.

634 Expeditions, 1940-50

DENMAN, Earl
Alone to Everest. 1954.

635 Expeditions, 1951-60

CHEVALLEY, Gabriel
Avant-premières à l'Everest, [par] Gabriel
Chevalley, René Dittert, Raymond Lambert. 1953.

DITTERT, René
[Avant-premières à l'Everest]. Forerunners to
Everest: the story of the two Swiss expeditions of
1952, by René Dittert, Gabriel Chevalley, Raymond
Lambert. 1954.

EGGLER, Albert
[Gipfel über den Wolken]. The Everest-Lhotse
adventure. 1957.

EVANS, Sir Charles
Eye on Everest: a sketch book from the great
Everest expedition. 1955.

GOSWAMI, S   M
Everest is it conquered? [1954].

GREGORY, Alfred
The picture of Everest. 1954.

HILLARY, Sir Edmund
High adventure. 1955.

HILLARY, Sir Edmund
[High adventure]. L'aventure est sur les cimes.
1955.

HUNT, John, Baron Hunt
The ascent of Everest. 1953.

HUNT, John, Baron Hunt
[The ascent of Everest]. The conquest of Everest.
1954.

HUNT, John, Baron Hunt
The ascent of Everest; edited and abridged for
schools. 1954.

- - Abridged ed., retold for younger readers... 1954.

HUNT, John, Baron Hunt
[The ascent of Everest]. Victoire sur l'Everest...
1953.

HUNT, John, Baron Hunt
[The ascent of Everest]. Mount Everest: Kampf und
Sieg. 1954.

HUNT, John, Baron Hunt
[The ascent of Everest]. La ascension al Everest.
1953.

HUNT, John, Baron Hunt
[The ascent of Everest]. La conquista
dell'Everest. 1954.

HUNT, John, Baron Hunt
[The ascent of Everest]. Voskhozhdenie na
Iverest... 1956.

HUNT, John, Baron Hunt
[The ascent of Everest], retold for younger
readers in Bengali. [1954?].

635 Everest - expeditions, 1951-60 (Cont.)

HUNT, John, Baron Hunt
[The ascent of Everest]. Výstup na Everest. 1957.

HUNT, John, Baron Hunt
[The ascent of Everest]. De beklimming van de
Mount Everest, de hoogste top der aarde bereikt.
[1953].

HUNT, John, Baron Hunt
[The ascent of Everest]. Mount Everestin
valloitus. 1953.

HUNT, John, Baron Hunt
[The ascent of Everest]. Junior Hindi [ed.].
1956 (1957 reprint).

HUNT, John, Baron Hunt
[The ascent of Everest]. Á haesta tindi jardar.
1954.

HUNT, John, Baron Hunt
The ascent of Everest. 1954.
In Japanese.

HUNT, John, Baron Hunt
[The ascent of Everest]. Sekai no meityo.
Japanese language juvenile ed. 1965.

HUNT, John, Baron Hunt
[The ascent of Everest]. Everest: seieren over
jordans høyeste fjell. 1953.

HUNT, John, Baron Hunt
[The ascent of Everest]. Pobeda nad Everestom.
1954.

HUNT, John, Baron Hunt
[The ascent of Everest]. 1958.
In Sinhalese.

HUNT, John, Baron Hunt
[The ascent of Everest]. Erövringen av Mount
Everest. 1954.

HUNT, John, Baron Hunt
Our Everest adventure: the pictorial history from
Kathmandu to the summit. 1954.

IZZARD, Ralph
The innocent on Everest. 1955.

LAMBERT, Raymond
Á l'assaut des "quatre mille": dix récits de haute
montagne. 1946.

- - 2e éd. 1953.

MORRIS, James
Coronation Everest. 1958.

NOYCE, Wilfrid
South Col: one man's adventure on the ascent of
Everest, 1953. 1954.

- - Abridged ed. 1956 (1962 reprint).

PEOPLE'S PHYSICAL CULTURE PUBLISHING HOUSE, Peking
Mountaineering in China. 1965.

ROCH, André
Everest 1952. 1952.

SCHWEIZERISCHE STIFTUNG FÜR ALPINE FORSCHUNGEN
Everest: relation photographique [des expéditions
suisse de 1952]. 1953.

SCHWEIZERISCHE STIFTUNG FÜR ALPINE FORSCHUNGEN
Everest: the Swiss expeditions [of 1952]. 1954.

SCHWEIZERISCHE STIFTUNG FÜR ALPINE FORSCHUNGEN
Everest: ein Bildbericht [of the Swiss expeditions
of 1952]. 1953.

SHIPTON, Eric
The Mount Everest Reconnaissance Expedition 1951.
1952.

SINGH, Gyan
Lure of Everest: story of the first Indian expedition. 1961.

STOBART, Tom
Adventurer's eye: the autobiography of Everest
film-man Tom Stobart. 1958.

TENZING NORGAY
Man of Everest: the autobiography of Tenzing told
to J.R. Ullman. 1955.

636 Expeditions, 1961-70

DIAS, John
The Everest adventure: story of the second Indian
Expedition. 1965.

HORNBEIN, Thomas Frederick
Everest: the west ridge. 1965.

INDIAN EXPEDITION TO MOUNT EVEREST, 1962
Second Indian Expedition to Mount Everest February-
June, 1962...: souvenir brochure. [1962].

INDIAN MOUNT EVEREST EXPEDITION, 1965
Indian Mount Everest Expedition 1965. [1965].

JAPANESE MOUNT EVEREST EXPEDITION, 1970
Everest. 1970.

JAPANESE MOUNT EVEREST EXPEDITION, 1970
The official report. 1972. 2v.

KOHLI, M S
Nine atop Everest: story of the Indian ascent.
1969.

MILLER, Maynard M
The geological and glaciological program of the
American Mt. Everest expedition 1963. 1963.

SAYRE, Woodrow Wilson
Four against Everest. 1964.

ULLMAN, James Ramsey
Americans on Everest: the official account of the
ascent led by Norman G. Dyhrenfurth. 1965.

ULLMAN, James Ramsay
Mass attack on the mighty peak: Americans make a
triple conquest of Everest. 1963.

637 Expeditions, 1971-

BONINGTON, Chris
Everest, South West Face. 1973.

BONINGTON, Chris
[Everest, South West Face]. Everest parete sud-
ovest. 1975.

BONINGTON, Chris
Everest the hard way. 1976.

FLEMING, Jon W and FAUX, Ronald
Soldiers on Everest: the joint Army Mountaineering
Association/Royal Nepalese Army Mount Everest
Expedition 1976. 1977.

HABELER, Peter
Everest, impossible victory. 1979.

JONES, Mike
Canoeing down Everest. 1979.

MESSNER, Reinhold
Everest: expedition to the ultimate. 1979.

MONZINO, Guido
La Spedizione italiana all'Everest 1973. 1976.

ROCK CLIMBING CLUB, Japan
Everest 8848m: the Japanese expedition to Mt.
Everest, 1973: the preliminary report. 1974.

637 Everest - expeditions, 1971- (Cont.)

SOUTH WEST FACE BRITISH EVEREST EXPEDITION, 1975
    Everest conquered! Expedition fact sheet. 1975.

STEELE, Peter
    Doctor on Everest: a personal account of the 1971
    expedition. 1972.

66 HIMALAYA, KARAKORAM, HINDU KUSH, PAMIR (OTHER
    WORKS)

661 Afghanistan, Hindu Kush

ADAMEC, Ludwig W
    Badakhshan Province and northeastern Afghanistan.
    1972.

ADAMEC, Ludwig W
    Farah and southwestern Afghanistan. 1973.

ATKINSON, James
    The expedition into Affghanistan: notes and
    sketches descriptive of the country, contained in
    a personal narrative during the campaign of 1839
    & 1840, up to the surrender of Dost Mohamed Khan.
    1842.

DURAND, Algernon
    The making of a frontier: five years' experiences
    and adventures in Gilgit, Hunza, Nagar, Chitral,
    and the eastern Hindu-Kush. 1899.

FORBES, Rosita
    Forbidden road - Kabul to Samarkand. 1937.

MARAINI, Fosco
    Hindu Kush (mountains). 1974.

ROBERTSON, Sir George Scott
    The Kafirs of the Hindu-Kush. 1896.

SCHOMBERG, Reginald Charles Francis
    Kafirs and glaciers: travels in Chitral. 1938.

VIGNE, G   T
    A personal narrative of a visit to Ghuzni, Kabul,
    and Afghanistan, and of a residence at the court
    of Dost Mohamed; with notices of Runjit Sing,
    Khiva, and the Russian expedition. 1840.

662 Pamirs

BURRARD, Sir Sidney Gerald
    Completion of the link connecting the triangula-
    tions of India and Russia, 1913. 1914.

CURZON, George Nathaniel, Marquess Curzon
    The Pamirs and the source of the Oxus. 1896 (1899
    reprint).

WOOD, John
    A journey to the source of the river Oxus. New
    ed. 1872.

663 Karakoram

AIMONE, Duke of Spoleto and DESIO, Ardito
    La spedizione geografica italiana al Karakoram
    (1929...): storia del viaggio e risultati
    geografici. 1936.

CONWAY, William Martin, Baron Conway
    Notes on a survey and map of part of the Karakoram
    Himalayas. 1894.

DE FILIPPI, Filippo
    [La spedizione nel Karakoram e nell'Himalaya
    occidentale 1909]. Karakoram and Western Himilaya.
    1912. 2v.

DE FILIPPI, Filippo
    Storia della spedizione scientifica italiana nel
    Himàlaia Caracorùm e Turchestàn Cinese (1913-1914).
    1924.

DE FILIPPI, Filippo
    [Storia della spedizione scientifica italiana...].
    The Italian expedition to the Himalaya, Karakoram
    and eastern Turkestan (1913-1914). 1932.

DESIO, Ardito and ZANETTIN, Bruno
    Geology of the Baltoro Basin. 1970.

ECKENSTEIN, Oscar
    The Karakorams and Kashmir: an account of a
    journey. 1896.

LORIMER, E   O
    Language hunting in the Karakoram. 1939.

MASON, Kenneth
    Exploration of the Shaksgam valley and Aghil ranges
    1926. 1928.

SPEDIZIONE ITALIANA DE FILIPPI, 1913-14
    [Relazioni scientifiche della] Spedizione Italiana
    De Filippi, nell'Himàlaia, Caracorùm e Turchestàn
    Cinese (1913-1914). Ser.1. Geodesia e geofisica.
    1925.

SPEDIZIONE ITALIANA DE FILIPPI, 1913-14
    [Relazioni scientifiche della] Spedizione Italiana
    De Filippi, nell'Himàlaia, Caracorùm e Turchestàn
    Cinese (1913-1914). Ser.2. Risultati geologici
    e geografici. 1922-25.

SURVEY OF INDIA
    Explorations in the eastern Kara-korum and the
    Upper Yārkand valley: narrative report of the
    Survey of India detachment with the De Filippi
    Scientific Expedition 1914. 1922.

VISSER, Philips Christiaan and VISSER-HOOFT, Jenny
    Wissenschaftliche Ergebnisse der Niederländischen
    Expeditionen in den Karakorum und die angrenzenden
    Gebiete in den Jahren 1922, 1925 und 1929/30.
    1935-38. 2v.

VISSER-HOOFT, Jenny
    Among the Kara-Korum glaciers in 1925. 1926.

664 Kashmir

ADAIR, F   E   S
    Sport in Ladakh: five letters from "The Field".
    1895.

ARBUTHNOT, James
    A trip to Kashmir. 1900.

BOULNOIS, Helen Mary
    Into little Thibet. 1923.

BOURBEL, Raoul, marquis de
    Routes in Jammu and Kashmir arranged topographi-
    cally with descriptions of routes; distances by
    stages; and information as to supplies and
    transport. 1897.

BRINCKMAN, Arthur
    The rifle in Cashmere: a narrative of shooting ex-
    peditions in Ladak, Cashmere, Punjaub... 1862.

BRUCE, Hon. Mrs. Charles Granville
    Kashmir. 1911.

COLLETT, John
    A guide for visitors to Kashmir. 1898.

CUNNINGHAM, Alexander
    Ladak, physical, statistical and historical; with
    notices of the surrounding countries. 1854.

DARRAH, Henry Zouch
    Sport in the highlands of Kashmir... 1898.

664 Kashmir (other works) (Cont.)

DOUGHTY, Marion
Afoot through the Kashmir valleys. 1901.

DREW, Frederic
The Jummoo and Kashmir territories: a geographical account. 1875.

DREW, Frederic
The northern barrier of India: a popular account of the Jummoo and Kashmir territories. 1877.

DUKE, Joshua
Kashmir and Jammu: a guide for visitors. 1903.

GOMPERTZ, M L A
Magic Ladakh: an intimate picture of a land of topsy-turvy customs and great natural beauty. 1928.

HAUGHTON, Henry Lawrence
Sport and folklore in the Himalaya. 1913.

HEBER, A Reeve and HEBER, Kathleen M
In Himalayan Tibet: a record of 12 years spent in the topsy-turvy land of lesser Tibet with a description of its cheery folk... 1926.

KNIGHT, William Henry
Diary of a pedestrian in Cashmere and Tibet. 1863.

KOENIGSMARCK, Hans, Graf von
The Markhor: sport in Cashmere. 1910.

LAMBERT, Cowley
A trip to Cashmere and Ladak. 1877.

MASON, Kenneth
Routes in the western-Himalaya, Kashmir, etc., with which are included Montgomerie's routes revised and rearranged. Vol.1. Punch, Kashmir and Ladakh. 1922.

- - 2nd ed. 1929.

MORISON, Margaret Cotter
A lonely summer in Kashmir. 1904.

MURPHY, Dervla
Where the Indus is young: a winter in Baltistan. 1977.

NEVE, Arthur
Picturesque Kashmir. 1900.

NEVE, Arthur
Thirty years in Kashmir. 1913.

NEVE, Arthur
The tourist's guide to Kashmir, Ladakh, Skardo, etc. 16th ed. 1938.

NEVE, Ernest F
Beyond the Pir Panjal: life among the mountains and valleys of Kashmir. 1912.

NEWALL, David J F
Preliminary sketches in Cashmere; or, Scenes in "cuckoo-cloud-land". 1882.

O'CONNOR, Vincent Clarence Scott
The charm of Kashmir. 1920.

RUBENSON, C W
Med telt og husbaat i Kashmir. 1923.

SCHOMBERG, Reginald Charles Francis
Between the Oxus and the Indus. 1935.

SWINBURN, T R
A holiday in the happy valley with pen and pencil. 1907.

TAYLOR, Neville
Ibex shooting on the Himalayas. 1903.

TYNDALE-BISCOE, Cecil Earle
Kashmir in sunlight and shade: a description of the beauties of the country, the life, habits and humour of its inhabitants... 1922.

WARD, A E
The sportsman's guide to Kashmir & Ladak. 2nd and rev. ed. 1883.

- - 3rd and rev. ed. 1887.

YOUNGHUSBAND, Sir Francis
Kashmir. 1909.

665 Punjab

EGERTON, Philip Henry
Journal of a tour through Spiti, to the frontier of Chinese Thibet. 1864.

FRASER, James Baillie
Views in the Himāla Mountains. 1820.

FULLERTON, James Alexander
Views in the Himalaya and Neilgherry hills. [1848].

GOODWIN, Buster
Life among the Pathans (Khattaks). 2nd ed. [1975].

GORE, F St.John
Lights and shades of hill life in the Afghan and Hindu highlands of the Punjab. 1895.

HARCOURT, A F P
The Himalayan districts of Kooloo, Lahoul and Spiti. 1871.

HINGSTON, R W G
A naturalist in Himalaya. 1920.

HOLMES, Peter
Mountains and a monastery. 1958.

MATHIAS, H V
Five weeks' sport in the interior of the Himalayas ... 1865.

ROBERTS, Emma
Hindostan: its landscapes, palaces, temples, tombs ... [1847?]. 2v.

SCOTT, Mrs. W L L
Views in the Himalayas. 1852.

THOMAS, George Powell
Views of Simla. 1846.

TYSON, T
Trout fishing in Kulu; with a brief description of rivers, routes and accommodation available for visitors. 2nd ed. 1941.

WHITE, George Francis
Views in India, chiefly among the Himalaya mountains, taken during tours ... in 1829-31-32. 1836-37. 2v.

- - Another ed. 1838.

666 Nepal

BOECK, Kurt
Durch Indien ins verschlossene Land Nepal: ethnographische und photographische Studienblätter. 1903.

BORDET, Pierre
Recherches géologiques dans l'Himalaya du Népal, région du Makalu. 1961.

BOURDILLON, Jennifer and COVERLEY-PRICE, Victor
The Sherpas of Nepal. [1959].

BOURDILLON, Jennifer
Visit to the Sherpas. 1956.

666 Nepal (other works) (Cont.)

BROWN, Percy
  Picturesque Nepal. 1912.

FANTIN, Mario
  Sherpa, Himalaya, Nepal. 1971.

FAUNA AND FLORA RESEARCH SOCIETY
  Scientific results of the Japanese expeditions to
  Nepal Himalaya, 1952-1953. 1955-57. 3v.

FLEMING, Robert L   and FLEMING, Linda Firth
  Kathmandu Valley. 1978.

FÜRER-HAIMENDORF, Christoph von
  The Sherpas of Nepal, Buddhist highlanders. 1964.

HAMILTON, Francis
  An account of the Kingdom of Nepal and of the
  territories annexed to this dominion by the House
  of Gorkha. 1819.

HARDIE, Norman
  In highest Nepal: our life among the Sherpas.
  1957.

HILLARY, Sir Edmund
  Schoolhouse in the clouds. 1964.

KIRKPATRICK, William J
  An account of the Kingdom of Nepaul, being the
  substance of observations made during a mission to
  that country,in the year 1793. 1811.

LANDON, Perceval
  Nepal. 1928. 2v.

LANDOR, A   Henry Savage
  Tibet & Nepal. 1905.

MAILLART, Ella K
  The land of the Sherpas. 1955.

MORRIS, John
  A winter in Nepal. 1963.

MURPHY, Dervla
  The waiting land: a spell in Nepal. 1967.

NORTHEY, W   Brook and MORRIS, John
  The Gurkhas: their manners, customs and country.
  1928.

TUCCI, Giuseppe
  Nepal: the discovery of the Malla. 1962.

WEIR, Thomas
  East of Katmandu. 1955.

WOOD, H
  Report on the identification and nomenclature of
  the Himalayan peaks as seen from Katmandu, Nepal.
  1904.

667 Sikkim, Bhutan

BENGAL. Secretariat
  The gazetteer of Sikhim. 1894.

BROWN, Percy
  Tours in Sikhim and the Darjeeling district. 2nd
  ed. 1922.

DONALDSON, Florence
  Lepcha Land; or, Six weeks in the Sikhim Himalayas.
  1900.

EASTON, John
  An unfrequented highway through Sikkim and Tibet
  to Chumolaori. 1928.

FLETCHER, David Wilson
  The children of Kanchenjunga. 1955.

IGGULDEN, H   A
  The 2nd Battalion Derbyshire Regiment in the
  Sikkim Expedition of 1888. 1900.

MAZUCHELLI, Nina Elizabeth
  The Indian Alps and how we crossed them, being a
  narrative of two years' residence in the eastern
  Himalaya and two months' tour into the interior.
  1876.

MORRIS, John
  Living with Lepchas: a book about the Sikkim
  Himalayas. 1938.

O'CONNOR, William F
  Routes in Sikkim. 1900.

PEISSEL, Michel
  Lords and lamas: a solitary expedition across the
  secret Himalayan kingdom of Bhutan. 1970.

RENNIE, David Field
  Bhotan and the story of the Dooar war including
  sketches of a three months' residence in the
  Himalayas, and narrative of a visit to Bhotan...
  1866.

RONALDSHAY, Lawrence John Lumley Dundas, Earl of
  Lands of the thunderbolt: Sikhim, Chumbi & Bhutan.
  1923.

STEELE, Peter
  Two and two halves to Bhutan: a family journey in
  the Himalayas. 1970.

TOMBAZI, N   A
  Account of a photographic expedition to the
  southern glaciers of Kangchenjunga in the Sikkim
  Himalaya. 1925.

WHITE, John Claude
  Sikhim and Bhutan: twenty-one years on the North-
  East Frontier, 1887-1908. 1909.

669 Assam

ALLSUP, W
  Notes on walking around Shillong. 1934.

FÜRER-HAIMENDORF, Christoph von
  The naked Nagas. 1939.

67 TIBET

BELL, Sir Charles
  Tibet past and present. 1924.

CAMMANN, Schuyler
  Trade through the Himalayas: the early British
  attempts to open Tibet. 1951.

DESGODINS, Auguste
  La mission du Thibet de 1855 à 1870, comprenant
  l'exposé des affaires religieuses et divers documents sur ce pays... 1872.

FLEMING, Peter
  Bayonets to Lhasa: the first full account of the
  British invasion of Tibet in 1904. 1961.

GOULD, Sir Basil J
  The jewel in the lotus: recollections of an Indian
  political. 1957.

GREAT BRITAIN. Parliament
  East India (Tibet): papers relating to Tibet.
  1904-10. 4v. in 3.

LAUNAY, Adrien
  Histoire de la mission du Thibet. [1903]. 2v.

MARSTON, Annie W
  The great closed land: a plea for Tibet. [1894?].

NOTOVITCH, Nicolas
  The unknown life of Christ. 1895.

67 Tibet (Cont.)

TURNER, Samuel, 1749?-1802
An account of an embassy to the court of the
Teshoo Lama in Tibet; containing a narrative of a
journey through Bootan, and part of Tibet. 1800.

YOUNGHUSBAND, Sir Francis
India and Tibet: a history of the relations which
have subsisted between the two countries from the
time of Warren Hastings to 1910; with a particular
account of the Mission to Lhasa of 1904. 1910.

672 Geography, description, travel

BAILEY, Frederick Marshman
No passport to Tibet. 1957.

BOGLE, George
Narratives of the mission of George Bogle to Tibet,
and of the journey of Thomas Manning to Lhasa.
1876.

BOSSHARD, Walter
Durch Tibet und Turkistan: Reisen im unberührten
Asien. 1930.

BOWER, Hamilton
Diary of a journey across Tibet. 1894.

BURRARD, Sir Sidney Gerald
Explorations in Tibet and neighbouring regions,
1865-[1892]. 1915. 2v.

CLARK, Leonard
The marching wind. 1955.

COOPER, T   T
The Mishmee hills: an account of a journey made in
an attempt to penetrate Thibet from Assam to open
new routes for commerce. 1873.

CROSBY, Oscar Terry
Tibet and Turkistan: a journey through old lands
and a study in new conditions. 1905.

CUTTING, Suydam
The fire ox and other years. 1947.

DAINELLI, Giotto
Il mio viaggio nel Tibet occidentale. 1932.

DAINELLI, Giotto
[Il mio viaggio nel Tibet occidentale]. Buddhists
and glaciers of western Tibet. 1933.

DEASY, H   H   P
In Tibet and Chinese Turkestan, being the record
of three years' exploration. 1901.

DESIDERI, Ippolito
[Notizie historiche del Regno del Thibet...]. An
account of Tibet: the travels of Ippolito Desideri
of Pistola, S.J., 1712-1727. 1932.

DUNCAN, Jane Ellen
A summer ride through western Tibet. [1913?].

FERGUSSON, W   N
Adventure sport and travel on the Tibetan steppes.
1911.

GOMPERTZ, M   L   A
The road to Lamaland: impressions of a journey to
western Thibet. [1926].

GREGORY, John Walter and GREGORY, C   J
To the alps of Chinese Tibet: an account of a
journey of exploration up to and among the snowclad mountains of the Tibetan frontier. 1923.

GRENARD, Fernand
Le Tibet: le pays et les habitants. 1904.

GRENARD, Fernand
[Le Tibet: le pays et les habitants]. Tibet: the
country and its inhabitants. 1904.

GUIBAUT, André
Tibetan venture in the country of the Ngolo-Setas;
second Guibaut-Liotard expedition. 1949.

HANBURY-TRACY, John
Black river of Tibet. 1938.

HARRER, Heinrich
[Sieben Jahre in Tibet...]. Seven years in Tibet.
1953.

HARRER, Heinrich
[Sieben Jahre in Tibet...]. Sept ans d'aventures
au Tibet. 1953.

HAYDEN, Sir Henry Hubert and COSSON, César
Sport and travel in the highlands of Tibet. 1927.

HEDIN, Sven
Adventures in Tibet. 1904.

HEDIN, Sven
Central Asia and Tibet: towards the holy city of
Lassa. 1903. 2v.

HEDIN, Sven
Southern Tibet: discoveries in former times compared with my own researches in 1906-1908.
1917-22. 9v.

HEDIN, Sven
Trans-Himalaya: discoveries and adventures in
Tibet. 1909-13. 3v.

HOLDICH, Sir Thomas Hungerford
Tibet, the mysterious. [1907].

JENKINS, Lady Minna
Sport and travel in both Tibets. [1909].

KAULBACK, Ronald
Salween. 1938.

KAWAGUCHI, Ekai
Three years in Tibet, with the original Japanese
illustrations. 1909.

KING, Rin-Chen
We Tibetans: an intimate picture, by a woman of
Tibet, of an interesting and distinctive people...
1926.

KINGDON-WARD, Francis
The mystery rivers of Tibet: a description of the
little-known land where Asia's mightiest rivers
gallop in harness through the narrow gateway of
Tibet, its people, fauna & flora. 1923.

KINGDON-WARD, Francis
A plant hunter in Tibet. 1934.

KINGDON-WARD, Francis
The riddle of the Tsangpo gorges. 1926.

LANDOR, A   Henry Savage
In the forbidden land: an account of a journey in
Tibet, capture by the Tibetan authorities, imprisonment, torture, and ultimate release. 1898.
2v.

LANDOR, A   Henry Savage
Tibet & Nepal. 1905.

LITTLE, Archibald John
Mount Omi and beyond: a record of travel on the
Thibetan border. 1901.

MARAINI, Fosco
Secret Tibet. 1952.

- - Another ed. 1953.

MARGERIE, Emmanuel de
L'oeuvre de Sven Hedin et l'orographie du Tibet.
1928.

MIGOT, André
Tibetan marches. 1955.

672 Tibet - geography, description, travel (Cont.)

O'CONNOR, Sir Frederick
On the frontier and beyond: a record of thirty
years' service. 1931.

OTTLEY, W   J
With mounted infantry in Tibet. 1906.

PATTERSON, George Neil
God's fool. 1956.

PATTERSON, George Neil
Tibetan journey. 1954.

PRANAVANANDA, Swami
Exploration in Tibet. 1939.

PRATT, A   E
To the snows of Tibet through China. 1892.

PUINI, Carlo
Il Tibet (geografia, storia, religione, costumi),
secondo la relazione del viaggio del P. Ippolito
Desideri (1715-1721). 1904.

RAWLING, Cecil Godfrey
The great plateau, being an account of exploration
in central Tibet, 1903, and of the Gartok expedition, 1904-1905. 1905.

RIENCOURT, Amaury de
Lost world: Tibet, key to Asia. 1951.

RIJNHART, Susie Carson
With the Tibetans in tent and temple: narrative of
four years' residence on the Tibetan border and of
a journey into the far interior. 4th ed. 1904.

ROCK, Joseph F
The Amnye Ma-chhen range and adjacent regions: a
monographic study. 1956.

ROCKHILL, William Woodville
Diary of a journey through Mongolia and Tibet in
1891 and 1892. 1894.

SANDBERG, Graham
The exploration of Tibet: its history and particulars from 1623 to 1904. 1904.

STRACHEY, Henry
Narrative of a journey to Cho Lagan (Rákas Tal),
Cho Mapan (Mánasaròwar) and the valley of Pruang
in Gnari, Húndés. 1848.

THOMSON, Thomas
Western Himalaya and Tibet: a narrative of a
journey through the mountains of northern India
during the years 1847-8. 1852.

TICHY, Herbert
Zum heiligsten Berg der Welt: auf Landstrassen und
Pilgerfahrten in Afghanistan, Indien und Tibet.
1937.

TRINKLER, Emil
Tibet: sein geographisches Bild und seine Stellung
im asiatischen Kontinent. 1922.

TURNER, Samuel, 1749?-1802
An account of an embassy to the court of the
Teshoo Lama in Tibet; containing a narrative of a
journey through Bootan, and part of Tibet. 1800.

WIGNALL, Sydney
Prisoner in red Tibet. 1957.

YOUNGHUSBAND, Sir Francis
India and Tibet: a history of the relations which
have subsisted between the two countries from the
time of Warren Hastings to 1910; with a particular
account of the Mission to Lhasa of 1904. 1910.

673 Religion

BELL, Sir Charles
The religion of Tibet. 1931.

DAVID-NEEL, Alexandra
With mystics and magicians in Tibet. 1931.

HAMSA, Bhagwān
The Holy Mountain, being the story of a pilgrimage
to Lake Mānas and of initiation on Mount Kailās in
Tibet. 1934.

PALLIS, Marco
Peaks and lamas. 1939.

PRANAVANANDA, Swami
Pilgrim's companion to the Holy Kailas and
Manasarovar, containing elaborate descriptions of
11 routes to the Holy Kailas and Manasarovar and
also to the "Sources of the four great rivers".
1938.

SHERRING, Charles A
Western Tibet and the British borderland: the
sacred country of Hindus and Buddhists, with an
account of the government, religion and customs of
its peoples. 1906.

674 Language

BELL, Sir Charles
English-Tibetan colloquial dictionary. 2nd ed.
1920.

BELL, Sir Charles
Grammar of colloquial Tibetan. 3rd ed. 1939.

675 Lhasa

BELL, Sir Charles
Portrait of the Dalai Lama. 1946.

CANDLER, Edmund
The unveiling of Lhasa. 1905.

CHAPMAN, Frederick Spencer
Lhasa: the holy city. 1938.

DAS, Sarat Chandra
Journey to Lhasa and central Tibet. 1902.

DAVID-NEEL, Alexandra
My journey to Lhasa: the personal story of the
only white woman who succeeded in entering the
Forbidden City. 1927.

LANDON, Perceval
Lhasa: an account of the country and people of
central Tibet and of the progress of the mission
sent there by the English Government in the year
1903-4. 1905. 2v.

McGOVERN, William Montgomery
To Lhasa in disguise: an account of a secret expedition through mysterious Tibet. 1924.

MILLINGTON, Powell
To Lhassa at last. 1905.

OXLEY, J   MacDonald
L'hasa at last. 1900.

SANDBERG, Graham
An itinerary of the route from Sikkim to Lhasa,
together with a plan of the capital of Tibet and a
new map of the route from Yamdok Lake to Lhasa.
1901.

WADDELL, L   Austine
Lhasa and its mysteries, with a record of the expedition of 1903-1904. 2nd ed. 1905.

YOUNGHUSBAND, Sir Francis
Peking to Lhasa: the narrative of journeys in the
Chinese empire made by the late Brigadier-General
George Pereira. 1925.

70 ASIA (ALL OTHER AREAS)

702 Geography, description, travel

ATKINSON, Thomas Witlam
Travels in the regions of the upper and lower
Amoor and the Russian acquisitions on the confines
of India and China. 2nd ed. 1861.

CANDLER, Edmund
A vagabond in Asia. 1900.

CHIROL, Sir Valentine
With pen and brush in eastern lands when I was
young. 1929.

ETHERTON, P   T
Across the roof of the world: a record of sport
and travel through Kashmir, Gilgit, Hunza, the
Pamirs, Chinese Turkistan, Mongolia and Siberia.
1911.

FLEMING, Peter
News from Tartary: a journey from Peking to
Kashmir. 1936.

Handbook for travellers in Russia, Poland, and
Finland; including the Crimea, Caucasus, Siberia,
and Central Asia. 5th ed. Murray, 1893.

KEANE, A   H
Asia. Vol.1. Northern and eastern Asia. 2nd ed.,
rev. and corr. 1906.

LAIRD, E   K
The rambles of a globe trotter in Australasia,
Japan, China, Jarva, India and Cashmere. 1875.
2v.

MAILLART, Ella K
The cruel way. 1947.

MAILLART, Ella K
Forbidden journey - from Peking to Kashmir. 1937.

MORDEN, William J
Across Asia's snows and deserts. 1927.

PITTON DE TOURNEFORT, Joseph
Relation d'un voyage du Levant... 1718. 2v.

PITTON DE TOURNEFORT, Joseph
[Relation d'un voyage du Levant...]. A voyage
into the Levant.... 1741. 3v.

POLO, Marco
The travels of Marco Polo... 1892.

RONALDSHAY, Lawrence John Lumley Dundas, Earl of
On the outskirts of empire in Asia. 1904.

71 MIDDLE EAST

BEKE, Charles T
Mount Sinai, a volcano. 1873.

BUXTON, Hannah Maude
On either side of the Red Sea. 1895.

DAUMAS, J   ..
La péninsule du Sinai. 1951.

KENNEDY, Sir Alexander B   W
Petra: its history and monuments. 1925.

MAUGHAN, William Charles
The alps of Arabia: travels in Egypt, Sinai,
Arabia and the Holy Land. 1873.

- - New ed. 1875.

MURRAY, George William
Dare me to the desert. 1967.

PARROT, Friedrich
Reise zum Ararat... 1834. 2v.

PARROT, Friedrich
[Reise zum Ararat]. Journey to Ararat. 1845.

SCOTT, Hugh
In the high Yemen. 1942.

STANLEY, Arthur Penrhyn
Sinai and Palestine in connection with their
history. 1856.

STARK, Freya
The southern gates of Arabia: a journey in the
Hadhramaut. 1936.

WALTON, Elijah
Vignettes: alpine and eastern. 1873.

712 Turkey

AMY, Bernard
La montagne des autres: alpinisme en pays kurde.
1972.

BRIDGES, Shirley M
Two in Turkey: a mountain-climbing expedition.
[1967?].

BURNABY, Fred
On horseback through Asia Minor. 1877. 2v.

GRENOBLE UNIVERSITÉ MONTAGNE
Hommes et montagnes du Kurdistan turc, Sat Dag
1973: espédition... 1974.

HILLS, Denis
My travels in Turkey. 1964.

JACKSON, Monica
The Turkish time machine. 1966.

LECLERCQ, Jules
Voyage au Mont Ararat. 1892.

LYNCH, H   F   B
Armenia: travels and studies. 1901. 2v.

MONTAGU, Lady Mary Wortley
Letters of the Right Honourable Lady M--y W---y
M----e, written during her travels in Europe,
Asia and Africa ... accounts of the policy and
manners of the Turks... 1766.

PARROT, Friedrich
Reise zum Ararat... 1834. 2v.

PARROT, Friedrich
[Reise zum Ararat...]. Journey to Ararat. 1845.

PERCY, Henry Algernon George, Earl Percy
Highlands of Asiatic Turkey. 1901.

SCOTT, Douglas K
The Cilo Dag mountains of S.E. Turkey: [report ...
of an expedition organised by the Nottingham
Climbers' Club]. [1966].

TOZER, Henry Fanshawe
Turkish Armenia and Eastern Asia Minor. 1881.

WIGRAM, Woolmore and WIGRAM, Edgar T   A
The cradle of mankind: life in eastern Kurdistan.
1914.

714 Iran

BUSK, Sir Douglas
A map of the Central Elburz: note. 1958.

JUDSON, David
Char Parau. 1973.

KITTO, John
Uncle Oliver's travels in Persia: giving a complete
picture of eastern manners, customs ... and
history... 1846. 2v. in 1.

714 Iran (Cont.)

SCHUSTER, Karl
    Weisse Berge, schwarze Zelte: eine Persienfahrt.
    1932.

STARK, Freya
    The valleys of the assassins and other Persian
    travels. 1934.

STELLING-MICHAUD, S
    Visage de la Perse. 1931.

72 CAUCASUS

721 Geology, climate

FOURNIER, E
    Description géologique du Caucase central. 1896.

722 Geography, description, travel

BADDELEY, John F
    The rugged flanks of Caucasus. 1940. 2v.

BELL, James Stanislaus
    Journal of a residence in Circassia during the
    years 1837, 1838 and 1839. 1840. 2v.

BERNOVILLE, Raphaël
    La Souanétie libre: épisode d'un voyage à la
    chaîne centrale du Caucase. 1875.

BIERBAUM, Paul Willi
    Streifzüge im Kaukasus und in Hocharmenien, 1912.
    1913.

BRYCE, James, Viscount Bryce
    Transcaucasia and Ararat, being notes of a vaca-
    tion tour in the autumn of 1876. 1877.

BUXTON, Harold
    Trans-Caucasia. [1926].

CAMERON, Una
    A good line. 1932.

CHANTRE, Mme B
    À travers l'Arménie russe. 1893.

CUNYNGHAME, Sir Arthur Thurlow
    Travels in the eastern Caucasus, on the Caspian
    and Black Seas, especially in Daghestan and on the
    frontiers of Persia and Turkey, during the summer
    of 1871. 1872.

DÉCHY, Moriz von
    Kaukasus: Reisen und Forschungen im kaukasischen
    Hochgebirge. 1905-07. 3v.

DEMIDOFF, Elim Pavlovich, principe di San Donato
    Hunting trips in the Caucasus. 1898.

DITSON, George Leighton
    Circassia; or, A tour to the Caucasus. 1850.

DUMAS, Alexandre, 1802-1870
    Impressions de voyage: le Caucase. 1865. 3v.

EGGER, Carl
    Höhenluft: Erlebtes und Erfühltes. 1930.

FRESHFIELD, Douglas William
    The exploration of the Caucasus. 1896. 2v.

FREYGANG, Frederika von
    Lettres sur le Caucase et la Géorgie, suivies
    d'une rélation d'un Voyage en Perse en 1812. 1816.

FREYGANG, Frederika von
    [Lettres sur le Caucase et la Géorgie...]. Letters
    from the Caucasus and Georgia; to which are added,
    the account of a journey into Persia in 1812...
    1823.

FREYGANG, Frederika von
    [Lettres sur le Caucase et la Géorgie...]. Briefe
    über den Kaukasus und Georgien, nebst angehängtem
    Reisebericht über Persien vom Jahre 1812. 1817.

GARF, B A
    Bezingiiskoe ushchel'e. 1952.

GOLOVIN, Ivan
    The Caucasus. 1854.

GRAHAM, Stephen
    A vagabond in the Caucasus, with some notes of his
    experiences among the Russians. 1911.

GROVE, Florence Crauford
    'The frosty Caucasus': an account of a walk through
    part of the range and of an ascent of Elbruz in the
    summer of 1874. 1875.

GROVE, Florence Crauford
    ['The frosty Caucasus'...]. Le Caucase glacé: pro-
    menade à travers une partie de la chaîne et ascen-
    sion du Mont Elbrouz. 1881.

GUSEV, A M
    El'brus. 1948.

HAHN, C
    Aus dem Kaukasus: Reisen und Studien... 1892-96.
    2v. in 1.

HAXTHAUSEN, August, Baron von
    Transcaucasia; sketches of the nations and races
    between the Black Sea and the Caspian. 1854.

HENDERSON, Ebenezer
    Biblical researches and travels in Russia; in-
    cluding a tour in the Crimea, and the passage of
    the Caucasus... 1826.

HERBERT, Agnes
    Casuals in the Caucasus: the diary of a sporting
    holiday. 1912.

KAVKAZSKII MUZEI I TIFLISSKAIA PUBLICHNAIA BIBLIOTEKA
    Die Sammlungen des Kaukasischen Museums. 1899- .
    Second title page in Russian.
    Bd.1. Zoologie, von Gustav Radde. -Bd.2. Botanik,
    von Gustav Radde. -Bd.5. Archaeologie; bearb.
    von Gräfin P.S. Uvarov.

KLAPROTH, Julius
    Tableau historique, géographique, ethnographique
    et politique du Caucase et des provinces limi-
    trophes entre la Russie et la Perse. 1827.

KLAPROTH, Julius
    Voyage au Mont Caucase et en Géorgie. 1823. 2v.

- - Nouv. éd. 1835.

KOCH, Karl
    Die kaukasischen Länder und Armenien in Reise-
    schilderungen... 1855.

KOECHLIN-SCHWARTZ, A
    Un touriste au Caucase; Volga, Caspienne, Caucase.
    [1882?].

KOLENATI, F A
    Die Bereisung Hocharmeniens und Elisabethopols der
    Schekinschen Provinz und des Kasbek im Central-
    Kaukasus. 1858.

KOVALEV, Pavel Vasil'evich
    Kavkaz: ocherk prirody. 1954.

KUCHAR, Radovan
    Deset velkých stěn. 1963.

KUPFFER, Adolf Theodor von
    Voyage dans les environs du Mont Elbrouz dans le
    Caucase... 1830.

LEVIER, Émile
    À travers le Caucase: notes et impressions d'un
    botaniste. [1894].
- - 2e éd. 1907.

722 Caucasus - geography, description, ... (Cont.)

LEVIER, Émile
    Au coeur du Caucase: notes et impressions d'un botaniste. 1892.

LEVIER, Émile
    De Livourne à Batoum: notes et impressions d'un botaniste. 1890.

LEVIER, Émile
    Retour du Caucase: notes et impressions d'un botaniste. 1893.

LONGWORTH, J   A
    A year among the Circassians. 1840. 2v.

LYALL, Robert
    Travels in Russia, the Krimea, the Caucasus and Georgia. 1825. 2v.

MARTEL, Édouard Alfred
    La Côte d'Azur russe (Riviera du Caucase): voyage en Russie méridionale, au Caucase occidental et en Transcaucasie... [1908?].

MASSOW, Wilhelm von
    Aus Krim und Kaukasus: Reiseskizzen. 1902.

MIGNAN, R
    A winter journey through Russia, the Caucasian alps, and Georgia; thence across Mount Zagros, by the Pass of Xenophon and the ten thousand Greeks, into Koordistaun. 1839. 2v.

MOUNSEY, Augustus H
    A journey through the Caucasus and the interior of Persia. 1872.

NANSEN, Fridtjof
    Durch den Kaukasus zur Wolga. 1930.

NAWRATH, Alfred
    Im Reiche der Medea: kaukasische Fahrten und Abenteuer. 1924.

PALLAS, P   S
    Travels through the southern provinces of the Russian Empire in the years 1793 and 1794. 1802-03. 2v.

PEREIRA, Michael
    Across the Caucasus. 1973.

PHILLIPPS-WOLLEY, Clive
    Savage Svånetia. 1883. 2v.

PHILLIPPS-WOLLEY, Clive
    Sport in the Crimea and Caucasus. 1881.

RADDE, Gustav
    Aus den Dagestanischen Hochalpen vom Schah-dagh zum Dulty und Bogos: Reisen. 1887.

RADDE, Gustav and KOENIG, E
    Das Ostufer des Pontus und seine kulturelle Entwickelung im Verlaufe der letzten dreissig Jahre... 1894.

RADDE, Gustav
    Vier Vorträge über den Kaukasus gehalten im Winter 1873/4 in den grösseren Städten Deutschlands. 1874.

RIKLI, M
    Natur-und Kulturbilder aus den Kaukasusländern und Hocharmenien... 1914.

ROTOTAEV, P   S
    Pobezhdennaia Ushba. 1948.

SIEMENS, Werner von
    Kaukasusreisen. 1943.

SPENCER, Edmund
    Travels in the western Caucasus, including a tour through Imeritia, Mingrelia, Turkey, Moldavia, Galicia, Silesia and Moravia. 1838. 2v.

STERN, Bernhard
    Vom Kaukasus zum Hindukusch: Reisemomente. 1893.

TELFER, J   Buchan
    The Crimea and Transcaucasia, being the narrative of a journey in the Kouban, in Gouria, Georgia, Armenia, Ossety, Imeritia. 1876. 2v.

THIELMANN, Max, Baron von
    Journey in the Caucasus, Persia, and Turkey in Asia. 1875. 2v.

WANDERER,
    Notes on the Caucasus. 1883.

WILBRAHAM, Richard
    Travels in the Trans-Caucasian provinces of Russia, and along the southern shore of the Lakes of Van and Urumiah, in the autumn and winter of 1837. 1839.

724 Climbs and climbing

BRITISH CAUCASUS EXPEDITION, 1958
    [Report]. [1958].

BUSK, Sir Douglas
    The Central Caucasus: the main chain and subsidiary spurs from Elbruz to Kasbek, including the mountains north of the Shtuluvsek. [1948].

Climbers of the Caucasus 1888-1889: [a commemorative volume in memory of W.F. Donkin, H. Fox, K. Streich and J. Fischer, 1888]. [1890?].

DUNSHEATH, Joyce
    Guests of the Soviets: Moscow and the Caucasus 1957. 1959.

EGGER, Carl
    Die Eroberung des Kaukasus. 1932.

EGGER, Carl
    Im Kaukasus: Bergbesteigungen und Reiseerlebnisse im Sommer 1914. 1915.

FISCHER, Andreas
    Zwei Kaukasus-Expeditionen. 1891.

FRESHFIELD, Douglas William
    Travels in the central Caucasus and Bashan including visits to Ararat and Tabreez and ascents of Kazbek and Elbruz. 1869.

HECKEL, Vilém
    Climbing in the Caucasus. [1958?].

HUNT, John, Baron Hunt and BRASHER, Christopher
    The red snows: an account of the British Caucasus Expedition 1958. 1960.

MERZBACHER, Gottfried
    Aus den Hochregionen des Kaukasus: Wanderungen, Erlebnisse, Beobachtungen. 1901. 2v.

MUMMERY, Albert Frederick
    My climbs in the Alps and Caucasus. 1895.

- - 2nd ed. 1905.

MUMMERY, Albert Frederick
    [My climbs in the Alps and Caucasus.]. Mes escalades dans les Alpes et le Caucase. 1903.

729 Guide-books

MOURIER, J
    Guide au Caucase. 1894.

73 RUSSIA (IN ASIA)

732 Geography, description, travel

ALMÁSY, György
Vándor-utam Ázsia Szivébe. 1903.

ATKINSON, Thomas Witlam
Oriental and western Siberia: a narrative of seven
years' explorations and adventures in Siberia,
Mongolia, the Kirghis steppes, Chinese Tartary and
part of Central Asia. 1858.

CHEREPOV, Ivan Aleksandrovich
Alpinisme soviétique. 1957.

CHEREPOV, Ivan Aleksandrovich
Zagadki Tian'-shania. 1951.

COBBOLD, Ralph P
Innermost Asia: travel and sport in the Pamirs.
1900.

DEMIDOFF, Elim Pavlovich, principe di San Donato
After wild sheep in the Altai and Mongolia. 1900.

KAZAKOVA, Elena Alekseevna
K vershinam Altaia. 1955.

MERZBACHER, Gottfried
The central Tian-Shan mountains 1902-1903. 1905.

NAZÁROFF, Pavel Stepanovich
Hunted through Central Asia. 1932.

PALLAS, P S
Travels through the southern provinces of the
Russian Empire in the years 1793 and 1794.
1802-03. 2v.

- - 2nd ed. 1812.

PREJEVALSKY, Nicholas Michailovitch
From Kulja, across the Tian Shan to Lob-Nor. 1879.

RAWICZ, Slavomir
The long walk. 1956.

ROERICH, George N
Trails to inmost Asia: five years of exploration
with the Roerich Central Asian Expedition. 1931.

SAPOZHNIKOV, V V
Katun' i eia istoko: puteshestviia 1897-1899 godov.
1901.

SAPOZHNIKOV, V V
Mongol'skii Altai v istokakh Irtysha i Kobdo.
1911.

SEWERZOW, N
Erforschung des Thian-Schan-Gebirgs-Systems 1867.
1875.

SWAYNE, H G C
Through the highlands of Siberia. 1904.

TURNER, Samuel, 1869-1929
Siberia: a record of travel, climbing and exploration. 1905.

- - 2nd ed. 1911.

74 TARTARY

742 Geography, description, travel

BRUCE, Clarence Dalrymple
In the footsteps of Marco Polo, being the account
of a journey overland from Silma to Pekin. 1907.

CABLE, Mildred and FRENCH, Francesca
The Gobi desert. 1942.

HASLUND, Henning
Mongolian journey. 1949.

HUC, Régis Évariste
Souvenirs d'un voyage dans la Tartarie, le Thibet
et la Chine pendant les années 1844, 1845 et 1846.
1850. 2v.

- - Nouv. éd. [de t.] 1. 1925.

HUC, Régis Évariste
[Souvenirs d'un voyage dans la Tartarie...].
Travels in Tartary, Thibet, and China during the
years 1844-5-6. 2nd ed. [1855?].

HUC, Régis Évariste
[Souvenirs d'un voyage dans la Tartarie...].
Recollections of a journey through Tartary, Thibet,
and China, during the years 1844, 1845, and 1846:
a condensed translation. 1852.

PREJEVALSKY, Nicholas Michailovitch
Mongolia, the Tangut country, and the solitudes
of northern Tibet, being a narrative of three
years' travel in eastern High Asia. 1876. 2v.

SCHOMBERG, Reginald Charles Francis
Peaks and plains of Central Asia. 1933.

SHAW, Robert
Visits to high Tartary, Yârkand, and Kâshghar
(formerly Chinese Tartary) and return journey over
the Karakoram Pass. 1871.

TORRENS, Henry D
Travels in Ladâk, Tartary and Kashmir. 1862.

75 CHINA

752 Geography, description, travel

CHURCH, Percy W
Chinese Turkestan with caravan and rifle. 1901.

FARRER, Reginald
The Rainbow Bridge. 1921.

GILL, William
The river of golden sand, being the narrative of a
journey through China and eastern Tibet to Burmah.
1883.

IMPERIAL JAPANESE GOVERNMENT RAILWAYS
An official guide to eastern Asia: transcontinental
connections between Europe and Asia. 1914- .

SCHLAGINTWEIT-SAKÜNLÜNSKI, Hermann and SCHLAGINTWEIT,
Robert
Official reports on the last journeys and the
death of Adolphe Schlagintweit in Turkistán. 1859.

SHIPTON, Diana
The antique land. 1950.

SKREDE, Wilfred
Across the roof of the world. 1954.

SKRINE, C P
Chinese central Asia. 1926.

SMITH, Albert
The story of Mont Blanc, and a diary, To China and
back. 1859-60. 2v. in 1.

STEIN, Sir Marc Aurel
Memoir on maps of Chinese Turkistan and Kansu from
the surveys made during Sir Aurel Stein's explorations... 1923.

STEIN, Sir Marc Aurel
Mountain panoramas from the Pamirs and Kwen Lun.
1908.

752 China - geography, description, travel (Cont.)

STEIN, Sir Marc Aurel
  On ancient Central-Asian tracks: brief narrative
  of three expeditions in innermost Asia and northwestern China. 1933.

STEIN, Sir Marc Aurel
  Ruins of desert Cathay: personal narrative of explorations in Central Asia and westernmost China.
  1912. 2v.

STEIN, Sir Marc Aurel
  Sand-buried ruins of Khotan: personal narrative of
  a journey of archaeological and geographical
  exploration in Chinese Turkestan. 1903.

SYKES, Ella and SYKES, Sir Percy
  Through deserts and oases of Central Asia. 1920.

TEICHMAN, Sir Eric
  Journey to Turkistan. 1937.

TILMAN, Harold William
  China to Chitral. 1951.

756 Climbs and climbing

DE BEER, Dora H
  Yunnan 1938: account of a journey in S.W. China.
  1971.

756.3 Minya Konka

BURDSALL, Richard Lloyd and EMMONS, Arthur Brewster
  Men against the clouds: the conquest of Minya
  Konka. 1935.

HEIM, Arnold
  Minya Gongkar: Forschungsreise ins Hochgebirge von
  Chinesisch Tibet. 1933.

IMHOF, Eduard
  Die grossen kalten Berge von Szetschuan: Erleb-
  nisse, Forschungen und Kartierungen im Minya-
  Konka-Gebirge. 1974.

76 TURKISTAN

762 Geography, description, travel

BAILEY, Frederick Marshman
  Mission to Tashkent. 1946.

BLACKLER, L V Stewart
  On secret patrol in High Asia. 1922.

ETHERTON, P T
  In the heart of Asia. 1925.

FORBES, Rosita
  Forbidden road - Kabul to Samarkand. 1937.

LIPSKII, Vladimir Ippolitovich
  Gornaia Bukharà: rezul'taty trekhl'tnikh'
  puteshestvii v" sredniuiu Asiiu v" 1896, 1897 i
  1899 godu. Chast' 2. Gissar", Khrebet" Petra
  Velikago, Alai 1897 g. 1902.

MAILLART, Ella K
  Turkestan solo: one woman's expedition from the
  Tien Shan to the Kizil Kum. 1934.

PRICE WOOD, J N
  Travel & sport in Turkestan. 1910.

RICKMERS, Willi Rickmer
  The Duab of Turkestan: a physiographic sketch and
  account of some travels. 1913.

ROOSEVELT, Theodore, 1887-1944 and ROOSEVELT, Kermit
  East of the sun and west of the moon. 1926.

SHIPTON, Eric
  Mountains of Tartary. [1951].

77 JAPAN

771 Geology, climate, flora

HAYATA, B
  The vegetation of Mt. Fuji; with a complete list
  of plants found on the mountain and a botanical
  map showing their distribution. 1911.

MIYOSHI, M and MAKINO, T
  Pocket-atlas of alpine plants of Japan. 2nd rev.
  ed. 1907. 2v.

TAKEDA, H
  Alpine flora. 1933.

772 Geography, description, travel

JAPAN WALKING CLUB
  Sangaku-bi (mountain beauty): a collection of
  photos, narratives, descriptions and poems, with
  a list of the principal mountains in Japan. 1922.

MORRIS, John
  Traveller from Tokyo. 1943.

PARSONS, Alfred
  Notes in Japan. 1896.

TAKATOU, S
  Nippon sangaku-shi. 1906.

WESTON, Walter
  A wayfarer in unfamiliar Japan. 1925.

YAMADA, Keiichi
  Weisses Heiligtum. 1966.

775 Climbs and climbing

ARCHER, Clement Hugh
  Climbs in Japan and Korea: a photographic record
  and guide. [1936].

JAPANESE ALPINE CLUB
  Fujiyama. 2nd ed. 1931.

STEINITZER, Wilhelm
  Japanische Bergfahrten: Wanderungen fern von
  Touristenpfaden. 1918.

WALTON, William Howard Murray
  Scrambles in Japan and Formosa. 1934.

WESTON, Walter
  Mountaineering and exploration in the Japanese
  alps. 1896.

WESTON, Walter
  The playground of the Far East. 1918.

779 Guide-books

IMPERIAL JAPANESE GOVERNMENT RAILWAYS
  An official guide to Eastern Asia: transcontinental connections between Europe and Asia.
  1914.

78 KOREA

785 Climbs and climbing

ARCHER, Clement Hugh
  Climbs in Japan and Korea: a photographic record
  and guide. [1936].

80 AFRICA

801 Geology, climate, natural history

ELLIOT, G F Scott
A naturalist in mid-Africa, being an account of a journey to the mountains of the Moon and Tanganyika. 1896.

MOORE, J E S
The Tanganyka problem, an account of the researches undertaken concerning the existence of marine animals in central Africa. 1903.

WOLLASTON, Alexander Frederick Richmond
From Ruwenzori to the Congo: a naturalist's journey across Africa. 1908.

802 Geography, description, travel

BARNS, T Alexander
The wonderland of the eastern Congo: the region of snow-crowned volcanoes... 1922.

BENNET, E
Shots and snapshots in British East Africa. 1914.

BUSK, Sir Douglas
The fountain of the sun: unfinished journeys in Ethiopia and the Ruwenzori. 1957.

CRAWFORD, E May
By the equator's snowy peak: a record of medical missionary work and travel in British East Africa. 1913.

ELTON, James Frederic
Travels and researches among the lakes and mountains of eastern and central Africa. 1879.

FANTIN, Mario
Sui ghiacciai dell'Africa (Kilimangiaro, Kenya, Ruwenzori). 1968.

FISHER, Ruth B
On the borders of Pigmy land. [1905?].

GIBBS AUTO TOURS
Touring East Africa with Gibbs Auto Tours. [1947].

GREGORY, John Walter
The great Rift valley, being the narrative of a journey to Mount Kenya and Lake Baringo, with some account of the geology, natural history, anthropology, and future prospects of British East Africa. 1896.

HEUGLIN, Th. von
Die Tinne'sche Expedition im westlichen Nil-Quellgebiet 1863 and 1864. 1865.

HÖHNEL, Ludwig von
Discovery of Lakes Rudolf and Stephanie: a narrative of Count Samuel Teleki's exploring and hunting expedition in eastern equatorial Africa in 1887 and 1888. 1894. 2v.

JOHNSTON, Sir Harry H
The Uganda protectorate: an attempt to give some description of the physical geography, botany, zoology, anthropology ... of the territories ... between the Congo Free State and the Rift valley ... 1902. 2v.

KASSNER, Theo
My journey from Rhodesia to Egypt, including an ascent of Ruwenzori and a short account of the route from Cape Town to Broken Hill... 1911.

KRAPF, J Lewis
Travels, researches, and missionary labours, during an eighteen years' residence in eastern Africa... 1860.

MONTEMONT, Albert
[Voyage aux Alpes et en Italie]. Tour over the Alps and in Italy. 1823.
Contains: Narrative of a journey from Egypt to the western coast of Africa...

NEW, Charles
Life, wanderings and labours in eastern Africa, with an account of the first successful ascent of the equatorial snow mountain, Kilima Njaro; and remarks upon east African slavery. 1874.

PARKE, Thomas Heazle
My personal experiences in equatorial Africa as medical officer of the Emin Pasha relief expedition. 1891.

PETERMANN, A and HASSENSTEIN, Bruno
Inner-Afrika nach dem Stande der geographischen Kenntniss in den Jahren 1861 bis 1863. 1863.

PETERS, Carl
New light on dark Africa, being the narrative of the German Emin Pasha expedition, its journeyings ... 1891.

PURVIS, J B
Through Uganda to Mount Elgon. 1909.

SPELTERINI, Eduard
Über den Wolken = Par dessus les nuages. [1928].

STANLEY, Henry M
In darkest Africa; or, The quest, rescue and retreat of Emin, Governor of Equatoria. 1890. 2v.

THOMSON, J B
Joseph Thomson, African explorer: a biography, by his brother J.B. Thomson. 2nd ed. 1897.

THOMSON, Joseph
Through Masai land: a journey of exploration among tne snowclad volcanic mountains and strange tribes of eastern equatorial Africa. [1897].

THOMSON, Joseph
[Through Masai land...]. Au pays des Masai: voyage d'exploration à travers les montagnes neigeuses et volcaniques et les tribus étranges de l'Afrique équatoriale... 1886.

805 Climbs and climbing

CAMPBELL, J I
A bibliography of mountains and mountaineering in Africa. 1945.

MONZINO, Guido
Spedizioni d'alpinismo in Africa; atti delle spedizioni G.M. 1959-1965. 1966.

81 NORTH AFRICA (ATLAS, HOGGAR, SAHARA)

811 Geology, climate, flora

MATHEWS, William
The flora of Algeria, considered in relation to the physical history of the Mediterranean region, and supposed submergence of the Sahara. 1880.

NÈGRE, R
Petite flore des régions arides du Maroc occidental. 1961-62. 2v.

812 Geography, description, travel

AGRESTI, Henri
Aïr: montagnes de la soif. [1917?].

AGRESTI, Henri
Escalade au Hoggar, Noël 1967, Pâques 1970. [1971?].

812 North Africa - geography, description ... (Cont.)

BANSE, Ewald
  Die Atlasländer (Orient I): eine Länderkunde.
  1910.

BARCLAY, Edgar
  Mountain life in Algeria. 1882.

BRITISH CENTRAL SAHARAN EXPEDITION, 1978
  Provisional prospectus. 1978.

BRITISH HOGGAR MOUNTAINS AND BILMA SANDS EXPEDITION,
1976
  Technical report. 1977.

CAMUS, Théodore
  De la montagne au désert: récits d'ascensions et
  correspondence. [1912].

CHATELLUS, Alain de
  De l'Eiger à l'Iharen. 1947.

FANTIN, Mario
  Le "Dolomiti" del Sahara (l'alpinismo nel Tibesti
  e nell'Hoggar);I monti dell'Africa. 1966.

FANTIN, Mario
  Tuareg, Tassili, Sahara. 1971.

FANTIN, Mario
  Uomini e montagne del Sahara: monografia
  alpinistico-esplorativa e storico-geografica con
  antologia. 2a ed. 1970.

FRISON-ROCHE, Roger
  L'appel du Hoggar. 1936.

HARRIS, Walter B
  Tafilet: the narrative of a journey of exploration
  in the Atlas mountains and the oases of the north-
  west Sahara. 1895.

HEIM, Arnold
  Negro Sahara: von der Guineaküste zum Mittelmeer.
  1934.

HOOKER, Sir Joseph Dalton and BALL, John
  Journal of a tour in Marocco and the Great Atlas.
  1878.

LEMPRIERE, William
  A tour from Gibraltar to Tangier, Sallee, Mogodore,
  Santa Cruz, Tarudant, and thence over Mount Atlas
  to Morocco... 1791.

LHOSTE, Jean Marc and AULARD, Claude
  Guide des escalades du Hoggar. [1962?].

PIERRE, Bernard
  Escalades au Hoggar. 1952.

SCOTT, Douglas K
  Tibesti. [1965].

STUTFIELD, Hugh Edward Millington
  The brethren of Mount Atlas, being the first part
  of an African Theosophical story. 1891.

THOMSON, Joseph
  Travels in the Atlas and Southern Morocco: a
  narrative of exploration. 1889.

Villes et montagnes marocaines... Montaignes
  marocaines, par Roger Mailly... 1964.

82 ETHIOPIA

822 Geography, description, travel

PAKENHAM, Thomas
  The mountains of Rasselas: an Ethiopian adventure.
  1959.

VEITCH, Sophie F   F
  Views in central Abyssinia. 1868.

84 KENYA, KILIMANJARO

842 Geography, description, travel

BENUZZI, Felice
  [Fuga sul Kenya]. No picnic on Mount Kenya. 2nd
  ed. 1952.

BENUZZI, Felice
  [Fuga sul Kenya]. Kenya; ou, La fugure africaine.
  1950.

DUNDAS, Anne
  Beneath African glaciers: the humours, tragedies
  and demands of an East African Government station.
  1924.

DUTTON, E   A   T
  Kenya Mountain. 1929.

FANTIN, Mario
  I tre "Grandi" africani: Kilimangiaro, Kenya,
  Ruwenzori (l'alpinismo nell'Africa centro-
  orientale). 1966.

GEILINGER, Walter
  Der Kilimandjaro: sein Land und seine Menschen.
  [1930].

GUTMANN, Bruno
  Kipo Kilja: ein Buch vom Kibo. [1922?].

JOHNSTON, Sir Harry H
  The Kilima-Njaro expedition: a record of scientific
  exploration in eastern equatorial Africa. 1886.

MASSAM, J   A
  The cliff dwellers of Kenya: an account of a people
  ... 1927.

MEYER, Hans
  Hochtouren im tropischen Africa. 1923.

MEYER, Hans
  Der Kilimandjaro: Reisen und Studien. 1900.

MEYER, Hans
  Ostafrikanische Gletscherfahrten: Forschungsreisen
  im Kilimandscharo-Gebiet. 1890.

MEYER, Hans
  [Ostafrikanische Gletscherfahrten...]. Across
  east African glaciers: an account of the first
  ascent of Kilimanjaro. 1891.

MITTELHOLZER, Walter
  Kilimandjaro Flug. 2.Aufl. 1930.

STUART-WATT,Eva
  Africa's dome of mystery, comprising the first
  descriptive history of the Wachagga people of
  Kilimanjaro... and a girl's pioneer climb to the
  crater of their 19,000ft snow shrine. [1930].

TEMPLE, John and WALKER, Alan
  Kirinyaga: a Mount Kenya anthology. [1974].

TRUFFAUT, Roland
  From Kenya to Kilimanjaro. 1957.

VOLKENS, Georg
  Der Kilimandscharo: Darstellung der allgemeineren
  Ergebnisse eines fünfzehnmonatigen Aufenthalts im
  Dschaggalande. 1897.

WYSS-DUNANT, Édouard
  Mes ascensions en Afrique. 1938.

85 RUWENZORI

852 Geography, description, travel

BERE, Rennie
  The way to the Mountains of the Moon. 1966.

DE FILIPPI, Filippo
  Il Ruwenzori: viaggio di esplorazione e prime
  ascensioni delle più alte vette nella catena
  nevosa... 1908.

DE FILIPPI, Filippo
  [Il Ruwenzori: viaggio di esplorazione...].
  Ruwenzori: an account of the expedition of H.R.H.
  Prince Luigi Amedeo of Savoy, Duke of the Abruzzi.
  1908.

JOHNSON, T   Broadwood
  Tramps round the Mountains of the Moon and through
  the back gate of the Congo State. 1908.

LUIGI AMEDEO, Duke of the Abruzzi
  Il Ruwenzori, parte scientifica: risultati delle
  osservazioni e studi... 1909. 2v.

MEERSCH, W   J   Ganshof van der
  Une mission scientifique belge dans le massif du
  Ruwenzori. 1933.

MISSION SCIENTIFIQUE BELGE POUR L'EXPLORATION DU
RUWENZORI, 1932
  Vers les glaciers de l'équateur: le Ruwenzori,
  Mission scientifique belge 1932. 1937.

MOORE, J   E   S
  To the Mountains of the Moon, being an account of
  the modern aspect of Central Africa ... traversed
  by the Tanganyika expedition in 1899 and 1900.
  1901.

PIERRE, Bernard
  Montagnes de la Lune. 1959.

SYNGE, Patrick M
  Mountains of the Moon: an expedition to the equatorial mountains of Africa. 1937.

TILMAN, Harold William
  Snow on the Equator. 1937.

TUCKER, A   R
  Toro: visits to Ruwenzori "Mountains of the Moon".
  1899.

86 SOUTH AFRICA

861 Geology, climate, natural history

ELIOVSON, Sima
  Discovering wild flowers in southern Africa. 1962.

Protected wild flowers of the Cape Province. 1958.

Some protected birds of the Cape Province. [Rev.
  ed.]. 1962.

862 Geography, description, travel

CHILVERS, Hedley A
  The seven wonders of southern Africa. 1929.

GALTON, Francis
  Narrative of an explorer in tropical South Africa,
  being an account of a visit to Damaraland in 1851.
  1889.

ZACHARIAH, O
  Travels in South Africa. 3rd ed. 1927.

864 Climbing history, reminiscences

BURMAN, José
  A peak to climb: the story of South African
  mountaineering. 1966.

866 Drakensberg Mountains

DODDS, David Allison
  A cradle of rivers: the Natal Drakensberg. 1975.

PEARSE, Reginald O
  Barrier of spears: drama of the Drakensberg.
  1973.

867 Table Mountain

HALL, Arthur Vine
  "Table Mountain": pictures with pen and camera.
  [1897?].

- - 3rd ed. [1900?].

89 MAURITIUS

894 Climbs and climbing

The ascent of the Pieterboth Mountain, Mauritius,
13 October, 1864. 1864.

90 AUSTRALASIA

LAIRD, E   K
  The rambles of a globe trotter in Australasia,
  Japan, China, Jarva, India and Cashmere. 1875.
  2v.

91 AUSTRALIA

912 Geography, description, travel

LENDENFELD, Robert von
  Australische Reise. 1892.

MEREDITH, Louisa Anne
  Over the Straits: a visit to Victoria... 1861.

MITCHELL, Elyne
  Australia's alps. 1946.

SCHLINK, Herbert H
  Ski-ing from Kiandra to Kosciusko. 1927.

SPENCER, Sir Baldwin and GILLEN, F   J
  Across Australia. 2nd ed. 1912. 2v.

918 Tasmania

HOOKEY, M
  The romance of Tasmania. 1921.

92 NEW ZEALAND

921 Geology, climate

HAAST, Julius von
  Geology of the provinces of Canterbury and Westland, New Zealand: a report comprising the results
  of official explorations. 1879.

922 New Zealand - geography, description, travel

BARRAUD, Charles D
New Zealand, graphic and descriptive. 1877.

BAUGHAN, Blanche Edith
Glimpses of New Zealand scenery. [ca 1912].

BELL, James Mackintosh
The wilds of Maoriland. 1914.

FENWICK, G
From east to west and west to east: some fine
Dominion scenery. 1912.

GULLY, John
New Zealand scenery. 1877.

HARROP, A J
Touring in New Zealand. 1935.

KRONECKER, Franz
Wanderungen in den südlichen Alpen Neu-Seelands.
1898.

LENDENFELD, Robert von
Neuseeland. [1900?].

MORELAND, A Maud
Through south Westland: a journey to the Haast and
Mount Aspiring, New Zealand. 1911.

Pictorial New Zealand; with a preface by Sir W.B.
Perceval. 1895.

REED, A H and REED, A W
Farthest west afoot and afloat; together with
E.H. Wilmot's Journal of the Pioneer survey of
the Lake Manapouri-Dusky Sound area. 1950.

REEVES, William Pember
New Zealand. 1908.

REISCHEK, Andreas
Sterbende Welt: zwölf Jahre Forscherleben auf
Neuseeland. 2.Aufl. 1924.

923 History, exploration

ANDERSEN, Johannes C
Jubilee history of South Canterbury. 1916.

BEAGLEHOLE, J C
The discovery of New Zealand. 1961.

CHURCH OF ENGLAND. Diocese of New Zealand
Annals of the Diocese of New Zealand. 1856.

CROZIER, Anita
Beyond the southern lakes: the explorations of
W.G. Grave. 1950.

DOUGLAS, Charles Edward
Mr. Explorer Douglas. 1957.

MCCLYMONT, W G
The exploration of New Zealand. 1940.

- - 2nd ed. 1959.

924 Climbing history, reminiscences

ALACK, Frank
Guide aspiring. [1963].

ALACK, Frank
A priest wants to live in hell. [ca 1960].

FITZGERALD, Edward Arthur
Climbs in the New Zealand Alps, being an account
of travel and discovery. 1896.

- - 2nd ed. 1896.

GILKISON, W Scott
Aspiring, New Zealand: the romantic story of the
"Matterhorn of the Southern Alps". 1951.

GRAHAM, Peter
Peter Graham; mountain guide: an autobiography.
1965.

GREEN, William Spotswood
The high Alps of New Zealand; or, A trip to the
glaciers of the Antipodes with an ascent of Mount
Cook. 1883.

HARPER, Arthur Paul
Pioneer work in the Alps of New Zeland: a record
of the first exploration of the chief glaciers
and ranges of the Southern Alps. 1896.

HARPER, Arthur Paul
Southern Alps of New Zealand. [191-?].

HEWITT, L Rodney and DAVIDSON, Mavis M
The mountains of New Zealand. 1954.

MANNERING, George Edward
With axe and rope in the New Zealand Alps. 1891.

MASON, B R
Safety in the mountains: a handbook for trampers,
skiers, stalkers and mountaineers. 5th ed. 1963.

PASCOE, John
Great days in New Zealand mountaineering. 1958.

PASCOE, John
Land uplifted high. 1952.

PASCOE, John
The mountains, the bush and the sea: a photographic
report. 1950.

PASCOE, John
Unclimbed New Zealand: alpine travel in the
Canterbury and Westland ranges, Southern Alps.
1939.

- - 2nd ed. 1950.

POWELL, Paul
Just where do you think you've been? 1970.

POWELL, Paul
Men aspiring. 1967.

ROSS, Malcolm
A climber in New Zealand. 1914.

TARARUA TRAMPING CLUB
Tararua story. 1946.

TURNER, Samuel, 1869-1929
The conquest of the New Zealand Alps. 1922.

925 Mount Cook

BOWIE, Nan
Mick Bowie: the Hermitage years. 1969.

DU FAUR, Freda
The conquest of Mount Cook and other climbs: an
account of four seasons' mountaineering on the
Southern Alps of New Zealand. 1915.

HARRIS, George and HASLER, Graeme
A land apart: the Mount Cook alpine region. 1971.

MANNERING, George Edward
Mount Cook and its surrounding glaciers. [192-?].

RILEY, C Graham
Place names in Mount Cook National Park. 1968.

WILSON, Jim
Aorangi: the story of Mount Cook. 1968.

928 Ruapehu

BEETHAM, George and MAXWELL, Joseph Prime
The first ascent of Mount Ruapehu, New Zealand and
a holiday jaunt to Mounts Ruapehu, Tongariro and
Ngauruhoe. 1926.

93   INDONESIA, MALAYSIA, NEW GUINEA

934   Climbs and climbing

COLIJN, A   H
    Naar de eeuwige sneeuw van tropisch Nederland:
    de bestijging van het Carstenszgebergte in
    Nederlandsch Nieuw Guinee. [1937?].

HONG KONG MOUNTAINEERING CLUB EXPEDITION TO THE SNOW
MOUNTAINS OF NEW GUINEA, 1972
    [Report]. [1973].

LORENTZ, H   A
    Zwarte menschen, witte bergen: verhaal van den
    tocht naar het sneeuwgebergte van Nieuw-Guinea.
    1913.

TEMPLE, Philip
    Nawok! The New Zealand expedition to New Guinea's
    highest mountains. 1962.

WHITEHEAD, John
    Exploration of Mount Kina Balu, North Borneo.
    1893.

WORMSER, C   W
    Bergenweelde: [boek over Indisch alpinisme]. 1931.

97   SOUTH POLE, ANTARCTICA

COMITÉ NATIONAL FRANÇAIS DES RECHERCHES ANTARCTIQUES
    Catalogue of publications. 1971.

971   Geology, climate

WRIGHT, C   S   and PRIESTLEY, R   E
    Glaciology [of the Victoria Land sector of the
    Antarctic Continent]. 1922.

972   Geography, description, travel

BERTRAM, Colin
    Arctic and Antarctic: the technique of polar
    travel. 1939.

CROFT, Andrew
    Polar exploration. 2nd ed. 1947.

KANO, Ichiro
    The exploration of polar regions. 1959-60. 2v.
    In Japanese.

LIVERSIDGE, Douglas
    The last continent. 1958.

TILMAN, Harold William
    Mischief among the penguins. 1961.

974   South Pole - expeditions

BAGSHAWE, Thomas Wyatt
    Two men in the Antarctic: an expedition to Graham
    Land 1920-1922. 1939.

CHERRY-GARRARD, Apsley
    The worst journey in the world: Antarctic 1910-13.
    1937.

CHRISTENSEN, Lars
    My last expedition to the Antarctic 1936-1937,
    with a review of the research work done on the
    voyages in 1927-1937. 1938.

HILLARY, Sir Edmund
    No latitude for error. 1961.

JAPANESE ANTARCTIC RESEARCH EXPEDITION, 1968-69
    Report of the Japanese traverse Syowa-South Pole,
    1968-1969. 1971.

JOINT SERVICES EXPEDITION TO ELEPHANT ISLAND,
1970-71
    [Report]. 1971.

JOYCE, Ernest E   Mills
    The South Polar trail: the log of the Imperial
    Trans-Antarctic Expedition. 1929.

LIOTARD, André Frank and POMMIER, Robert
    Terre Adélie, 1949-1952. 1952.

PONTING, Herbert G
    The great white south; or, With Scott in the
    Antarctic, being an account of experiences with
    Captain Scott's South Pole expedition and of the
    nature life of the Antarctic. 1923.

SHACKLETON, Sir Ernest Henry
    The heart of the Antarctic, being the story of the
    British Antarctic Expedition, 1907-1909. 1909.
    2v.

TEMPLE, Philip
    The sea and the snow: the South Indian Ocean
    Expedition to Heard Island. 1966.

SECTION 2

CLASSIFIED CATALOGUE

(CLIMBING GUIDES)

CLASSIFICATION SCHEME
CLIMBING GUIDES

<u>1mg</u> <u>BRITISH ISLES</u>

<u>11mg</u> <u>LAKE DISTRICT</u>

AUSTIN, J   Allan and VALENTINE, Rodney
Great Langdale. F. & R.C.C., 1973. (Climbing
guides to the English Lake District, [4th ser.],1)

BASTERFIELD, George and THOMSON, A   R
Crags for climbing in and around Great Langdale,
by George Basterfield and Rock climbing in
Buttermere, by A.R. Thomson.   F. & R.C.C., [1926].
(Climbers' guides, [1st ser.], 5)

BEETHAM, Bentley
Borrowdale. F. & R.C.C., 1953. (Rock-climbing
guides to the English Lake District, 2nd [i.e.
3rd] ser., 5)

BOWER, George S
Doe Crags and climbs round Coniston: a climbers'
guide. F. & R.C.C., [1922]. (Climbers' guides,
[1st ser.], 1)

BURBAGE, Mike and YOUNG, William
Scafell group. F. & R.C.C., 1974. (Climbing
guides to the English Lake District, [5th ser.],7)

CLARK, Syd
Borrowdale. F. & R.C.C., 1978. (Climbing guides
to the English Lake District, [5th ser.], 3)

CLEGG, William
Great Langdale, by William Clegg, A.R. Dolphin &
J.W. Cook. F. & R.C.C., 1950 (1954 reprint).
(Rock-climbing guides to the English Lake
District, 2nd [i.e. 3rd] ser., 3)

COOPER, C   J   Astley
Great Gable, Borrowdale, Buttermere, by C.J.
Astley Cooper, E. Wood-Johnson and L.H. Pollitt.
F. & R.C.C., 1937. (Climbing guides to the
English Lake District [2nd ser.], 3)

COOPER, C   J   Astley
Great Gable, Green Gable, Kirkfell, Yewbarrow,
Buckbarrow, by C.J. Astley Cooper, W. Peascod &
A.P. Rossiter. F. & R.C.C., 1948. (Rock-climbing
guides to the English Lake District, 2nd [i.e.
3rd] ser., 1)

CRAM, Alan Geoffrey
Pillar group. F. & R.C.C., 1968. (Climbing
guides to the English Lake District [4th ser.], 5)

CRAM, Alan Geoffrey
Rock climbing in the Lake District: an illustrated
guide to selected climbs in the Lake District,
[by] Geoff Cram, Chris Eilbeck, Ian Roper. 1975.

DRASDO, Harold and SOPER, N   Jack
Eastern crags. F. & R.C.C., 1969. (Climbing
guides to the English Lake District, [4th ser.], 2)

EVANS, R   B   and UNSWORTH, Walter
The southern Lake District. Part 1. Difficult to
Hard Severe. 1971. (Climbs in Cumbria)

FEARNEHOUGH, Pat L
Great Gable, Wasdale and Eskdale. F. & R.C.C.,
1969. (Climbing guides to the English Lake
District, [4th ser.], 6)

GROSS, H   S   and THOMSON, A   R
Climbs on Great Gable, by H.S. Gross, and Rock
climbing in Borrowdale, by A.R. Thomson.
F. & R.C.C., [1925]. (Climbers' guides, [1st
ser.], 4)

HALL, Richard Watson
Some Cumbrian climbs and equipment. [1923?].

HARGREAVES, A   T
Dow Crag and other climbs, by A.T. Hargreaves [and
others]. F. & R.C.C., 1957. (Rock-climbing
guides to the English Lake District, 2nd [i.e. 3rd]
ser., 7)

HARGREAVES, A   T
Dow Crag, Great Langdale and outlying crags, by
A.T. Hargreaves [and others]. F. & R.C.C., 1938.
(Climbing guides to the English Lake District,
[2nd ser.], 4)

HARGREAVES, A   T
Scafell group. F. & R.C.C., 1936. (Climbing
guides to the English Lake District, [2nd ser.],2)

HARGREAVES, A   T
Scafell group, by A.T. Hargreaves, A.R. Dolphin
and R. Miller. F. & R.C.C., 1956. (Rock-climbing
guides to the English Lake District, 2nd [i.e.
3rd] ser., 6)

HASSALL, G   A
The northern Lake District. Part 1. Difficult
to Hard Severe. 1969. (Climbs in Cumbria).

HOLLAND, C   F
Climbs on the Scawfell group: a climbers' guide.
F. & R.C.C., [1924]. (Climbers' guides, [1st
ser.], 3)

KELLY, Harry M
Pillar Rock and neighbourhood. New and rev. ed.
F. & R.C.C., 1935. (Climbing guides to the
English Lake District, [2nd ser.], 1)

KELLY, Harry M   and PEASCOD, W
Pillar Rock and neighbourhood. F. & R.C.C., 1952.
(Rock-climbing guides to the English Lake District,
2nd[i.e. 3rd] ser., 4)

KELLY, Harry M
Pillar Rock and neighbouring climbs: a climbers'
guide. F. & R.C.C., [1923]. (Climbers' guides,
[1st ser.], 2)

MILLER, David
Dow Crag area. F. & R.C.C., 1968. (Climbing
guides to the English Lake District, [4th ser.],8)

NUNN, Paul J   and WOOLCOCK, Oliver
Borrowdale. F. & R.C.C., 1968. (Climbing guides
to the English Lake District [4th ser.], 3)

OLIVER, Geoffrey and GRIFFIN, L   Joe
Scafell group. F. & R.C.C., 1967. (Climbing
guides to the English Lake District, [4th ser.],7)

PEASCOD, W   and RUSHWORTH, G
Buttermere and Newlands area. F. & R.C.C., 1949.
(Rock-climbing guides to the English Lake
District, 2nd [i.e. 3rd] ser., 2)

SOPER, N   Jack and ALLINSON, Neil
Buttermere and Newlands area. F. & R.C.C., 1970.
(Climbing guides to the English Lake District,
[4th ser.], 4)

WAINWRIGHT, A
A pictorial guide to the Lakeland fells, being an
illustrated account of a study and exploration of
the mountains in the English Lake District.
Book 1. The eastern fells. 1955.
Book 2. The far eastern fells. 1957.
Book 3. The central fells. 1958.
Book 4. The southern fells. 1960.
Book 5. The northern fells. 1962.

<u>12mg</u> <u>ENGLAND (EXCEPT LAKE DISTRICT)</u>

<u>121mg</u> <u>South East</u>

BRYSON, H   Courtney
Rock climbs round London... 1936.

PYATT, Edward Charles
A climber's guide to south-east England.
Climbers' Club, 1956 (1960 reprint). (Climbing
guides to England & Wales, 8)

PYATT, Edward Charles
South-east England. 2nd rev. ed. by L.R. and
L.E. Holliwell. 1969. (Climbers' Club guides)

123mg England - South West

ANDREWS, Arthur Westlake and PYATT, Edward Charles
Cornwall. Climber's Club, 1950. (Climbing guides
to the Snowdon district and to Cornwall, 5)

ANNETTE, Barrie M
Limestone climbs on the Dorset coast. 2nd ed.
1960.

ARCHER, Clement Hugh
Coastal climbs in north Devon. [1961?].

- - Supplement for 1962.
- - Interim report on 1963.

BIVEN, Peter H   and MCDERMOTT, M   B
Cornwall. Vol.1. 1968. (Climbers' Club guides)

BROOMHEAD, Richard
Cheddar: Cheddar Gorge, Brean Down, The Mendips.
1977.

CARVER, Toni
Climbing in Cornwall: a climber's guide to north,
south and east Cornwall. 1973.

CREWE, Richard J
Dorset. 1977.

LAWDER, K   M
Climbing guide to Dartmoor and south west Devon.
[196-].

LITTLEJOHN, Pat R
South Devon: Chudleigh, Torbay, Torquay, Brixham,
Berry Head. 1971. (West Col coastal climbing
guides)

MOULAM, Anthony J   J
Dartmoor. 1976. (West Col regional climbing
guides)

MOULTON, Robert D   and THOMPSON, Terry D
Chair Ladder and the south coast. 1975. (Climbers'
Club guides to West Penwith, 2)

MOULTON, Robert D
Lundy rock climbs: a guide book to rock climbing
on Lunday. 2nd ed. 1974.

- - 3rd ed. 1980.

NIXON, John
Climbing guide to the Avon gorge. 1959.

STEVENSON, Vivian N
Cornwall. Vol.2. 1966. (Climbers' Club guides)

WARD-DRUMMOND, Edwin
Extremely Severe in the Avon gorge: [the 1967
guide to the harder climbs]. 1967.

WILLSON, John and HOPE, David E
Wye valley. Vol.1. Wintour's Leap, Symonds Yat,
Western Cliffs. 1977.

124mg Midlands

UNSWORTH, Walter
A climber's guide to Pontesford rocks. 1962.

VICKERS, Ken S
Rock climbs in Leicestershire: interim guide. 1966.

125mg Peaks, Pennines, North West

ALLSOPP, Allan
Kinder, Roches and northern areas. 1951. (Climbs
on gritstone, v.3)

BANCROFT, Steve
Recent developments. 1977. (Rock climbs in the
Peak)

BIRTLES, Geoff B
Stoney Middleton dale. 1966.

BYNE, Eric
A climbing guide to Brassington rocks. 1950.

BYNE, Eric and WHITE, Wilfred B
Further developments in the Peak District. 1957.
(Climbs on gritstone, v.4)

BYNE, Eric
The Saddleworth-Chew Valley area. [1965].
(Rock climbs in the Peak, v.2)

BYNE, Eric
The Sheffield area. 1956. (Climbs on gritstone,
v.2)

BYNE, Eric
The Sheffield-Stanage area. [1963?]. (Rock
Climbs in the Peak, v.1)

HARDING, Peter R   J   and MOULAM, Anthony   J J
A guide to Black Rocks and Cratcliffe Tor. 1949.
(Climbers' Club guides)

LAYCOCK, John
Some shorter climbs (in Derbyshire and elsewhere).
1913. (Some gritstone climbs)

MITCHELL, Michael A
Climbs on Yorkshire limestone. 1963.

NUNN, Paul J
The Kinder area. [1971?]. (Rock climbs in the
Peak, v.7)

NUNN, Paul J
The northern limestone area. 1969. (Climbers'
Club guides; Rock climbs in the Peak, 5)

NUNN, Paul J
Rock climbing in the Peak District: a photographic
guide for rockclimbers. 1975.

PARKER, H   C
Laddow area. 1948. (Climbs on gritstone, 1)

SALT, David
The Staffordshire gritstone area. [1973]. (Rock
climbs in the Peak, v.9)

THORNBER, Norman
The Three Peaks. 1949.

WILKINSON, Frank
Yorkshire limestone: a rock climber's guide.
1968.

127mg North East

NORTHUMBRIAN MOUNTAINEERING CLUB
A rock-climber's guide to Northumberland. 2nd
ed. 1964.

WILSON, M   F
Climbs in Cleveland. [1956].

13mg WALES

134mg North Wales, Snowdonia

BANNER, H   I   and CREW, Peter
Clogwyn du'r Arddu. 1963. (Climbers' Club
guides to Wales, 6)

CARR, Herbert Reginald Culling
A climbers' guide to Snowdon and the Beddgelert
district. Climbers' Club. 1926.

CREW, Peter
Anglesey-Gogarth: Craig Gogarth, South Stack,
Holyhead Mountain; Gogarth Upper Tier by Les
Holliwell. 1969. (West Col coastal climbing
guides)

CREW, Peter and ROPER, Ian
Cwm Glas. 2nd ed. 1970. (Climbers' Club guides
to Wales, 5)

134mg North Wales, Snowdonia (Cont.)

CREW, Peter
Llanberis south. 1966. (Climbers' Club guides to Wales, 5)

CREW, Peter and HARRIS, Alan
Tremadoc area: Tremadoc Rocks, Craig y Gelli and Carreg Hylldrem. 1970. (West Col coastal climbing guides)

EDWARDS, John Menlove and BARFORD, John Edward Quintus
Clogwyn du'r Arddu. 1942.

EDWARDS, John Menlove
Cwm Idwal. 2nd rev. ed. 1940 (1946 reprint). (Climbing guides to the Snowdon district, 1)

- - New ed., by A.J.J. Moulam. 1958.

EDWARDS, John Menlove
Cwm Idwal group. New and rev. ed. 1936. (Climbing guides to the Snowdon district, 1)

EDWARDS, John Menlove and NOYCE, Wilfrid
Tryfan group. 1937. (Climbing guides to the Snowdon district, 2)

EDWARDS, Rowland
Climbs on North Wales limestone: the Little Orme, the Great Orme, Craig y Forwyn. 1976.

HARDING, Peter R   J
Llanberis Pass. 1950 (1955 reprint). (Climbing guides to the Snowdon district,6)

HATTON, Pete
The Three Cliffs. 1974. (Climbers' Clug guides to Wales, 4)

HOLLIWELL, Les
Carneddau. 1975. (Climbers' Club guides to Wales, 1)

JAMES, Ron
Rock climbing in Wales. 1970.

- - 2nd ed. rev. 1975.

JONES, Trevor and NEILL, John
Snowdon south. 2nd ed. 1966. (Climbers' Club guides to Wales, 8)

- - 3rd ed. 1970.

KIRKUS, Colin F
Glyder Fach group. New and rev. ed. 1937. (Climbing guides to the Snowdon district, 3)

LAMBE, R   E
Craig Cowarch: a guide to the rock climbs on the crags of Craig Cowarch. 1958.

LEES, J   R
Moelwynion: an interim guide to the lower crags. 1962. (Climbers' Club guides to Wales)

MILBURN, Geoff
Llanberis Pass. 1978. (Climbers' Club guides to Wales, 3)

MOULAM, Anthony J   J
The Carneddau. [1950]. (Climbing guides to the Snowdon district, 7)

- - 2nd ed. 1966. (Climbers' Club guides to Wales, 1)

MOULAM, Anthony J   J
Cwm Idwal. New ed. 1958. (Climbing guides to the Snowdon district, 1)

- - Rev. and repr. ed. 1964.

MOULAM, Anthony J   J
Snowdon east. 1970. (Climbers' Club guides to Wales, 9)

MOULAM, Anthony J   J
Tryfan and Glyder Fach. 1956 (1959 reprint). (Climbing guides to the Snowdon district, 2)

- - Rev. and repr. ed. 1964.

NEILL, John and JONES, Trevor
Snowdon south. 1960. (Climbing guides to the Snowdon district, 8)

NOYCE, Wilfrid and EDWARDS, John Menlove
Lliwedd group. 1939. (Climbing guides to the Snowdon district, 4)

ROSCOE, Don Thomas
Llanberis north. 1961. (Climbing guides to the Snowdon district)

SHARP, Alec
Clogwyn du'r Arddu. 1976. (Climbers' Club guides to Wales, 4)

SHARP, Alec
Gogarth. 1977. (Climbers' Club guides to Wales,7)

STYLES, Showell
Snowdon range. 1973. (Snowdonia district guide books)

THOMSON, James Merriman Archer
Climbing in the Ogwen district. 1910.

- - Appendix, containing accounts of many new climbs, by H.E.L. Porter. 1921.

THOMSON, James Merriman Archer and ANDREWS, Arther Westlake
The climbs on Lliwedd. 1909.

WILSON, Ken and LEPPERT, Zdzislaw
Cwm Idwal. 3rd ed. 1974. (Climbers' Club guides to Wales, 2)

YATES, Mike and PERRIN, Jim
Cwm Silyn and Cwellyn. 1971. (Climbers' Club guides to Wales, 11)

137mg Central & South Wales

SUMNER, John
Central Wales: Craig Cowarch and the Arans. 1973. (West Col regional climbing guides)

SUMNER, John
Dolgellau area; Cader Idris and the Rhinog Range. 1975. (West Col regional climbing guides)

TALBOT, Jeremy O
Gower Peninsula: Caswell Bay to Worms Head, Burry Holms to Tor Gro. 1970. (West Col coastal climbing guides)

- - Supplement 1973.

14mg SCOTLAND

ALEXANDER, Sir Henry
The Cairngorms. 1928. (Scottish Mountaineering Club guides)

- - 2nd ed. 1938.
- - 3rd ed. 1950.

ANDREW, Ken M   and THRIPPLETON, Alan A
The southern uplands. 1972. (Scottish Mountaineering Club district guide books)

BROWN, Hamish M
The island of Rhum: a national nature reserve. 1972.

FYFFE, A   F
Cairngorms area. Vol.5. Cairngorms, Creag an Dubh-Loch, Glen Clova. 1971. (Scottish Mountaineering Club climbers' guide books)

14mg Scotland (Cont.)

HODGE, Edmund W
  The northern Highlands. 3rd ed. 1953. (Scottish
  Mountaineering Club guides)

JOHNSTONE, J   M
  Rock climbs in Arran. 1958. [Scottish Mountaineering Club climbers' guide books]

JUNIOR MOUNTAINEERING CLUB OF YORKSHIRE
  Guide to the island of Rhum. [1946].

LING, W   N
  The northern Highlands. 1932. (Scottish Mountaineering Club guides)

- - 2nd rev. ed. 1936.

LOVAT, L   S
  Climbers' guide to Glencoe and Ardgour. Vol.1.
  Buachaille Etive Mor. 2nd ed. 1959. [Scottish
  Mountaineering Club climbers' guide books]

MACINNES, Hamish
  Scottish climbs: a mountaineer's pictorial guide
  to climbing in Scotland. 1971. 2v.

MACKENZIE, William M
  Climbing guide to the Cuillin of Skye. 1958.
  [Scottish Mountaineering Club climbers' guide
  books]

MACPHEE, C   Graham
  Ben Nevis. Rev. ed. 1936. (Scottish Mountaineering Club guides)

MACPHEE, G   Graham
  Climbers' guide to Ben Nevis. 1954. [Scottish
  Mountaineering Club climbers' guide books]

MACROBERT, Harry
  Ben Nevis. 1920. (Scottish Mountaineering Club
  guide, v.1, S.E.)

MACROBERT, Harry
  The central Highlands. 1934. (Scottish Mountaineering Club guides)

- - 2nd ed. 1952.

MARSHALL, J   R
  Ben Nevis. 1969. (Scottish Mountaineering Club
  climbers' guide books)

- - Rev. ed. with supplement. 1979.

MUNRO, Sir Hugh
  Munro's tables of the 3000-feet mountains of
  Scotland, and other tables of lesser heights. [New
  ed.]. [1953]. (Scottish Mountaineering Club
  guides)

- - Rev. ed. 1969.
- - Metric ed. 1974.

MURRAY, William Hutchison
  Rock climbs: Glencoe and Ardgour. 1949. (Scottish
  Mountaineering Club [climbers' guide books])

NAISMITH, W   W
  The islands of Scotland (excluding Skye). 1934.
  (Scottish Mountaineering Club guides)

- - 2nd ed. 1952.

PARKER, James A
  The western Highlands. 1931. (Scottish Mountaineering Club guides)

- - 3rd ed., rev. 1947.
- - 4th ed., rev. 1964.

ROWE, I   G
  Northern Highlands area. Vol.1. Letterewe and
  Easter Ross. 1969. (Scottish Mountaineering Club
  climbers' guide books)

SCOTTISH MOUNTAINEERING CLUB
  The Scottish Mountaineering Club guide. Vol.1.,
  section A. 1921.

- - New ed.,rev. 1933.

SIMPSON, J   W
  Cuillin of Skye. 3rd ed. 1969. 2v. (Scottish
  Mountaineering Club climbers' guide books)

SLESSER, Malcolm
  The island of Skye. 1970. (Scottish Mountaineering Club district guide books)

- - 2nd ed. 1975.

SMITH, Malcolm
  Climbers' guide to the Cairngorms area. 1961-62.
  2v. [Scottish Mountaineering Club climbers' guide
  books]

STEEPLE, E   W
  Island of Skye. 1923. (Scottish Mountaineering
  Club guides)

- - 2nd ed., rev. 1948.
- - 3rd ed. 1954.

STRANG, Tom
  The northern Highlands. 1970. (Scottish Mountaineering Club district guide books)

- - 2nd ed. 1975.

TENNENT, Norman
  The islands of Scotland. 1971. (Scottish Mountaineering Club district guide books)

WATSON, Adam
  The Cairngorms. 5th ed. 1975. (Scottish Mountaineering Club district guide books)

WILSON, J   D   E
  The southern Highlands. 1949. (Scottish Mountaineering Club guides)

15mg IRELAND

CURRAN, Mick
  Antrim coast rockclimbs: interim guide. 1975.
  (F.M.C.I. guides)

FORSYTHE, John
  Mourne rock-climbs. 1973. (F.M.C.I. guides)

IRISH MOUNTAINEERING CLUB
  Rock-climber's guide to Donegal. 1962.

IRISH MOUNTAINEERING CLUB
  A rock-climber's guide to Glendalough. 1957.

KENNY, Peter
  A guide to the rock climbs of Dalkey Quarry.
  Irish Mountaineering Club, 1964.

LYNAM, Joss
  Ben Corr rock-climbs. 1951. (Guide to the
  mountains of Connemara and Murrisk, pt.4)

LYNAM, Joss
  Bray Head. 1951. (Rock-climbers' guide to the
  sea cliffs around Dublin, pt.1)

LYNAM, Joss
  Twelve Bens. 1953. (Guide to the mountains of
  Connemara and Murrisk, pt.3)

REDMOND, Pat
  Wicklow rock-climbs (Glendalough and Luggala).
  1973. (F.M.C.I. guides)

WALL, Claud W
  Mountaineering in Ireland. 1976. (F.M.C.I.
  guides)

<u>2mg</u>   <u>ALPINE EUROPE</u>

<u>22mg</u>   <u>ALPS</u>

ARZANI, Carlo
  I rifugi del Club Alpino Italiano e le stazioni
  del Corpo Nazionale di Soccorso Alpino. 2a ed.
  1977.

ASSOCIATION OF THE BRITISH MEMBERS OF THE SWISS
ALPINE CLUB
  A list and short guide to the huts of the Swiss
  Alpine Club, [with] addenda: huts belonging to the
  Academies Alpine Clubs of Bale, Bern and Zurich
  and to the French Alpine Club in the Mt. Blanc
  group. [195-?].

COLLOMB, Robin Gabriel
  Mountains of the Alps: tables of summits over
  3500 metres with geographical and historical notes
  and tables of selected lesser heights. Vol.1.
  Western Alps: Mediterranean to the Simplonpass and
  Grimselpass. 1971.

ENTE NAZIONALE INDUSTRIE TURISTICHE
  Residencias en los Alpes italianos. 1954.

HAUSER, Günter
  Die Hütten des Deutschen Alpenvereins... 1969.

MEYNIEU, Jacques
  Refuges des montagnes françaises et zones
  limitrophes. C.A.F., 1967.

ÖSTERREICHISCHER ALPENVEREIN. <u>U.K. Branch</u>
  Members handbook. [1951].

SAGLIO, Silvio
  I rifugi del C.A.I. 1957.

SCHWEIZER ALPEN-CLUB
  Verzeichnis der Clubhütten des S.A.C. [1952].

- - Stand Sommer 1961.

<u>221mg</u> <u>Western & Southwestern Alps</u>

ANDREIS, E
  Gran Paradiso: parco nazionale, [di] E. Andreis,
  R. Chabod, M.C. Santi. 2a ed., aggiornata,
  conpletata e illustrata. 1963. (Guida dei monti
  d'Italia)

BALL, John
  A guide to the western Alps. 1863. (Alpine guide,
  pt.1)

- - New [3rd] ed. 1870.

BALL, John
  [A guide to the western Alps]. South-western Alps,
  including Dauphiné and Piedmont from Nice to the
  Little St. Bernard. 1873. (Ball's alpine guides)

BALL, John
  The western Alps. New ed.; reconstructed and
  revised on behalf of the Alpine Club by W.A.B.
  Coolidge. 1898. (Alpine guide, pt.1)

BESSONE, Severino
  Guida del Monviso. C.A.I., 1957.

BOBBA, Giovanni
  Alpi Marittime. 1908. (Guida dei monti d'Italia)

BOSSUS, Pierre
  Guide des Préalpes franco-suisses: chaine
  frontière entre le Valais et la Haute-Savoie.
  C.A.S., 1964.

BRANDT, Maurice
  Guide d'escalades dans le Jura. C.A.S., 1966. 2v.

CLUB ALPIN FRANÇAIS. <u>Section d'Avignon</u>
  Guide des Dentelles de Montmirail. 1970.

CLUB ALPIN FRANÇAIS. <u>Sections de Savoie</u>
  Randonnées et ascensions: Maurienne. 1975.

CLUB ALPIN FRANÇAIS. <u>Sections de Savoie et de</u>
<u>Maurienne</u>
  Randonnées et ascensions: Haute-Maurienne. 1973.

COLLOMB, Robin Gabriel
  Graians east:Gran Paradiso area: a selection of
  popular and recommended climbs. 1969. (West
  Col alpine guides)

COLLOMB, Robin Gabriel
  Graians west: Tarentaise and Maurienne: a selec-
  tion of popular and recommended climbs. 1967.
  (West Col alpine guides)

COLLOMB, Robin Gabriel
  Maritime Alps: Vésubie basin and Argentera: a
  selection of popular and recommended climbs.
  1968. (West Col alpine guides)

COOLIDGE, William Augustus Brevoort
  The central Alps of the Dauphiny, by W.A.B.
  Coolidge, H. Duhamel and F. Perrin. 1892.
  (Conway & Coolidge's climbers' guides, 4)

- - 2nd ed., thoroughly rev. 1905.

COUPÉ, Serge
  Escalades du Vercors et de la Chartreuse.
  F.F.M., 1963.

COUPÉ, Serge
  Escalades en Chartreuse et Vercors. 1972-73.
  2v. in 1.

DEVIES, Lucien and LALOUE, Maurice
  Guide du massif des Écrins. 2e éd. 1951. 2v.

DEVIES, Lucien
  Le massif des Écrins. 1. Meije, Rateau,
  Soreiller, par Lucien Devies, François Labande,
  Maurice Laloue. 4e éd. 1976.

DEVIES, Lucien
  Le massif des Écrins. 2. Ailefroide, Pelvoux,
  Bans, Olan, Muzelle, par Lucien Devies, François
  Labande, Maurice Laloue. 1971.

DEVIES, Lucien
  Le massif des Écrins. 2. Écrins, Grande Ruine,
  Roche Faurio, Agneaux, Glouzis, par Lucien Devies,
  François Labande, Maurice Laloue. 4e éd. 1976.

DEVIES, Lucien
  Le massif des Écrins. 3. Ailefroide, Pelvoux,
  Bans, Sirac, par Lucien Devies, François Labande,
  Maurice Laloue. 4e éd. 1978.

DUFRANC, Michel and LUCCHESI, Alexis
  Escalades dans les Alpes de Provence: Verdon,
  Cadières, Teillon, Eiglun. 1975.

- - Nouv. éd. 1980.

DUFRANC, Michel
  Massif de l'Argentera. C.A.F. 1970.

FERRERI, Eugenio
  Alpi Cozie settentrionali. 1923-27. 3v. in 2.
  (Guida dei monti d'Italia: Alpi occidentali, 3)

GAILLARD, Émile
  Les Alpes de Savoie. [1912]-38. 6v. in 10.

GAILLARD, Émile
  Les Alpes du Dauphiné. T.1. Les massifs de
  Belledonne et des Sept-Laux: guide pour
  l'alpiniste. [1924].

GAILLARD, Émile
  Les Alpes du Dauphiné. T.2. Le Haut Dauphiné.
  Ptie. 1. La Meije et les Écrins (du Signal de
  Pied-Montet au Col de la Temple): guide pour
  l'alpiniste. 1929.

221mg <u>Western & Southwestern Alps</u> (<u>Cont.</u>)

GENTIL, H
  Le Brec de Chambeyron. 1976.

GERMAIN, Félix
  Escalades choisies (du Léman à la Méditerranée).
  1947. 2v.

GORGEON, Bernard
  Escalades dans le massif de la Sainte-Victoire:
  partie centrale: les Deux Aiguilles, le Signal,
  par Bernard Gorgeon, Christian Guyomar, Alexis
  Lucchesi. 1978.

LECLERC, Jeanne and LECLERC, Bernard
  Guide de Tarentaise et Maurienne. 1949. 2v.

LECLERC, Jeanne and LECLERC, Bernard
  Petit guide de la Haute-Maurienne: promenades,
  excursions, ascensions hivernales. 2e éd. (rev.
  et aug.). [1937?].

LUCCHESI, Alexis
  Escalades dans le massif de la Sainte-Baume:
  Bartagne, Beguines. 1976.

MARTELLI, A   E   and VACCARONE, Luigi
  Guida delle Alpi occidentali. C.A.I., 1889-96.
  2v. in 3.

MARTELLI, A   E   and VACCARONE, Luigi
  Guida delle Alpi occidentali del Piemonte, dal
  Colle dell'Argentera ... al Colle Girard. C.A.I.,
  1880.

MOTTI, Gian Piero
  Rocca Sbarua e M. Tre Denti. C.A.I., 1969.

PASCHETTA, Vincent
  Alpinisme. C.A.F., 1937. (Guide des Alpes
  Maritimes, 2)

PASCHETTA, Vincent
  Environs de Saint-Martin-Vésubie: guide pour
  touristes, alpinistes et skieurs, par Vincent
  Paschetta [and others]. C.A.F., [1934?]. (Guide
  des Alpes Maritimes, 2)

SABBADINI, Attilio
  Alpi Marittime (dal Colle di Tenda al Colle della
  Maddalena). 1934. (Guida dei monti d'Italia)

SAGLIO, Silvio
  Alpi Graie. 1952. (Da rifugio a rifugio, 3)

SCHWEIZER ALPEN-CLUB. <u>Sektion Geneva</u>
  Guide de la chaine frontière entre la Suisse et la
  Haute Savoie. C.A.S., 1928-30. 2v.

WEST COL PRODUCTIONS
  Dents du Midi region: an interim guide. 1967.
  (West Col alpine guides)

WRANGHAM, E   A   and BRAILSFORD, John
  Selected climbs in the Dauphiné Alps and Vercors.
  1967. (Alpine Club guide books;selected climbs,4)

222mg <u>Mont Blanc Massif</u>

ALPINE CLIMBING GROUP
  Selected climbs in the range of Mont Blanc.
  [1953]. 1v.

- - Re-issue, updated and corrected. [1954].

ALPINE CLIMBING GROUP
  Selected climbs in the range of Mont Blanc ...;
  adapted by the Alpine Climbing Group from the Guide
  Vallot and other sources; edited by E.A. Wrangham.
  1957.

BOSSUS, Pierre
  Les Aiguilles Rouges: Perrons, Fis, massifs de
  Colonné et de Platé. 1974.

CHABOD, Renato
  Monte Bianco, [di] Renato Chabod [and others].
  1963-68. 2v. (Guida dei monti d'Italia)

COLLET, Léon W
  Description général du massif du Mont-Blanc.
  Fasc.2. Aperçu sur la géologie du massif du Mont-
  Blanc et des Aiguilles Rouges. 1924. (Guides
  Vallot)

COLLOMB, Robin Gabriel and O'CONNOR, William H
  Mont Blanc range. Vol.1. Trélatête, Mont Blanc,
  Maudit, Tacul, Brenva. 1976. (Alpine Club guide
  books)

COLLOMB, Robin Gabriel and CREW, Peter
  Selected climbs in the Mont Blanc range. 1967.
  2v. (Alpine Club guide books; selected climbs, 1)

DALLOZ, Pierre
  Description de la haute montagne dans le massif
  du Mont-Blanc. Fasc. 6 bis. Groupes du Chardonnet
  et du Tour entre les cols du Chardonnet et de
  Balme, par Pierre Dalloz, Marcel Ichac, Pierre
  Henry. 1937. (Guides Vallot)

DEVIES, Lucien
  La chaîne du Mont Blanc. 1. Mont Blanc,
  Trélatête, par Lucien Devies, Pierre Henry,
  Jacques Lagarde. 2e éd. 1951. (Guides Vallot)

- - 3e éd. 1973.
- - 4e éd. 1978.

DEVIES, Lucien
  La chaîne du Mont Blanc. 2. Aiguilles de Chamonix,
  Grande Jorasses. 1947. (Guides Vallot)

- - Addendum. 1948.
- - 2e éd. 1951.
- - 3e éd. 1977.

DEVIES, Lucien and HENRY, Pierre
  La chaîne du Mont Blanc. 3. Aiguille Verte,
  Dolent, Argentière, Trient. 1949. (Guides
  Vallot).

- - 3e éd. 1966.
- - 4e éd. 1975.

GAILLARD, Émile
  Les Alpes de Savoie. T.6. Le massif du Mont
  Blanc. [1925]-33. 3pts.

GRIFFIN, Lindsay N
  Mont Blanc range. Vol.2. Chamonix Aiguilles,
  Rochefort, Jorasses, Leschaux. 1978. (Alpine
  Club guide books)

GRIFFIN, Lindsay N
  Mont Blanc range. Vol.3. Triolet, Verte/Drus,
  Argentière, Chardonnet, Trient. 1980. (Alpine
  Club guide books)

HENRY, Pierre and ICHAC, Marcel
  Description de la haute montagne dans le massif
  du Mont-Blanc. Fasc. 7. Groupes de Trélatête et
  de Miage. 1933.

KURZ, Louis
  Guide de la chaîne du Mont-Blanc à l'usage des
  ascensionnistes. 1892.

- - 2e éd. 1914.
- - 3e éd., rev. 1927.
- - 4e éd. 1935.

KURZ, Louis
  [Guide de la chaîne du Mont-Blanc...]. The chain
  of Mont Blanc. 1892. (Conway and Coolidge's
  climbers' guides, 5)

LAGARDE, Jacques
  Description de la haute montagne dans le massif du
  Mont-Blanc. Fasc.4. Groupes du Mont-Blanc et de
  la Tour Ronde. 1930. (Guides Vallot)

222mg Mont Blanc Massif (Cont.)

LÉPINEY, Jacques de
  Les Aiguilles Rouges de Chamonix,Les Fis, Le Buet,
  Les Perrons; rédaction nouvelle par Ar. Charlet
  [and others]. 1946. (Guides Vallot)

LÉPINEY, Jacques de
  Description de la haute montagne dans le massif du
  Mont-Blanc. Fasc.1. Les Aiguilles de Chamonix.
  1925. (Guides Vallot)

- - 2e éd. 1926.

LÉPINEY, Jacques de
  Description de la haute montagne dans le massif du
  Mont-Blanc. Fasc.5. Les Aiguilles Rouges;
  suivies de Les Fis, Le Buet, Les Perrons. 1928.
  (Guides Vallot)

SÉGOGNE, Henry de
  Description de la haute montagne dans le massif du
  Mont-Blanc. Fasc.2. La chaîne de l'Aiguille
  Verte, par Henry de Ségogne [and others]. 1926.
  (Guides Vallot)

VALLOT, Charles
  Description de la moyenne montagne dans le massif
  du Mont-Blanc. Fasc.1. Chamonix, Mont-Blanc.
  1927. (Guides Vallot)

VALLOT, Charles
  Description générale du massif du Mont-Blanc, par
  Ch. Vallot [and others]. 1925. 8pts. in l.
  (Guides Vallot)

VALLOT, Charles
  Tourisme en montagne dans le massif du Mont-Blanc:
  Chamonix, Mont-Blanc, Saint-Gervais-les-Bains.
  1950. (Guides Vallot)

223mg Pennine Alps

BALL, John
  [A guide to the western Alps]. Pennine Alps, including Mont Blanc and Monte Rosa. 1873. (Ball's
  alpine guides)

- - New ed. 1878.

BUSCAINI, Gino
  Alpi Pennine. Vol.1. Dal Col du Petit Ferret al
  Col d'Otemma. 1971. (Guida dei monti d'Italia)

BUSCAINI, Gino
  Alpi Pennine. Vol.2. Dal Col d'Otemma al Colle
  del Teodulo. 1970. (Guida dei Monti d'Italia)

COLLOMB, Robin Gabriel
  Pennine Alps central: Weisshorn, Dent Blanche,
  Monte Rosa, Matterhorn chains, Italian valley
  ranges, Valpelline south. 1975. (Alpine Club
  guide books)

COLLOMB, Robin Gabriel
  Pennine Alps east: Saas and Mischabel chains.
  1975. (Alpine Club guide books)

COLLOMB, Robin Gabriel
  Pennine Alps west: Grandes Dents, Bouquetins,
  Collon... 1979. (Alpine Club guide books)

COLLOMB, Robin Gabriel
  Selected climbs in the Pennine Alps. Vol.2.
  Arolla and western ranges. 2nd ed. 1968. (Alpine
  Club guide books; selected climbs 2)

COLLOMB, Robin Gabriel
  Zermatt and district, including Saas Fee. 1969.
  (Alpine guides, 2)

CONWAY, William Martin, Baron Conway
  Climbers' guide to the central Pennine Alps. 1890.

CONWAY, William Martin, Baron Conway
  Climbers' guide to the eastern Pennine Alps. 1891.

DÜBI, Heinrich
  Clubführer durch die Walliser-Alpen. Bd.2. Vom
  Col de Collon bis zum Theodulpass. S.A.C., 1921.

DÜBI, Heinrich
  Clubführer durch die Walliser-Alpen. Bd.3b. Vom
  Strahlhorn bis zum Simplon. S.A.C., 1916.

DÜBI, Heinrich
  [Clubführer durch die Walliser-Alpen]. Guide des
  Alpes valaisannes. Vol.2. Du Col de Collon au
  Col du Théodule. C.A.S., 1922.

DÜBI, Heinrich
  [Clubführer durch die Walliser-Alpen]. Guide des
  Alpes valaisannes. Vol.3. Du Col du Théodule au
  Schwarzenberg-Weisstor et du Strahlhorn au
  Simplon. C.A.S., 1919.

KURZ, Marcel
  Clubführer durch die Walliser-Alpen. Bd.2. Vom
  Col Collon bis zum Col de Théodule. 2.Aufl.
  S.A.C., 1930.

- - 3.Aufl. 1955.
- - 4.Ausg. ... von Maurice Brandt. 1971.

KURZ, Marcel
  [Clubführer durch die] Walliser Alpen. Bd.3.
  Vom Theodulpass zum Monte Moro. 4.Ausg., durch-
  gesehen und erweitert von Maurice Brandt. 1970.
  (Clubführer des Schweizer Alpen-Club)

KURZ, Marcel
  [Clubführer durch die] Walliser Alpen. Bd.4.
  Vom Strahlhorn zum Simplon. 4.Ausg., durch-
  gesehen und erweitert von Maurice Brandt. 1970.
  (Clubführer des Schweizer Alpen-Club)

KURZ, Marcel
  [Clubführer durch die Walliser Alpen]. Guide des
  Alpes valaisannes. Vol.1. Du Col Ferret au Col
  de Collon. C.A.S., 1923.

- - 2e éd. 1937.
- - 2e éd. [avec] supplément. 1963.
- - 3e éd., rev. et augm., par Maurice Brandt.
  [1977].

KURZ, Marcel
  [Clubführer durch die Walliser Alpen]. Guide des
  Alpes valaisannes. Vol.2. Du Col Collon au Col
  de Théodule. 2e éd. C.A.S., 1930.

- - 3e éd. 1947.
- - 4e éd., rev. et augm., par Maurice Brandt. 1970.

KURZ, Marcel
  [Clubführer durch die Walliser Alpen]. Guide des
  Alpes valaisannes. Vol.3a. Du Col de Théodule
  au Monte Moro. 3e éd. C.A.S., 1952.

KURZ, Marcel
  [Clubführer durch die Walliser Alpen]. Guide des
  Alpes valaisannes. Vol.3b. Du Strahlhorn au
  Simplon. 2e éd. C.A.S., 1937.

- - 3e éd. 1952.

KURZ, Marcel
  [Clubführer durch die Walliser Alpen. Guide des]
  Alpes valaisannes. Vol.3. Du Théodulpass au
  Monte Moro. 4e éd., rev. et augm., par Maurice
  Brandt. 1970. (Guides du Club Alpin Suisse)

KURZ, Marcel
  [Clubführer durch die Walliser Alpen]. Guide des
  Alpes valaisannes. Vol.4. Du Col du Simplon au
  Col de la Furka. C.A.S., 1920.

- - 4e éd., rev. et augm., par Maurice Brandt. 1970.

LARDEN, Walter
  Guide to the walks & climbs around Arolla. 1908.

NEILL, John
  Selected climbs in the Pennine Alps. 1962.
  (Alpine Club guide books; selected climbs, 2)

223mg Pennine Alps (Cont.)

RAINOLDI, Luciano
    Antrona, Bognanco, Sempione. C.A.I., 1976.

SAGLIO, Silvio
    Alpi Pennine. 1951. (Da rifugio a rifugio, 4)

SAGLIO, Silvio and BOFFA, F
    Monte Rosa. 1960. (Guida dei monti d'Italia)

YELD, George and COOLIDGE, William Augustus Brevoort
    The mountains of Cogne. 1893. (Conway and
    Coolidge's climbers' guides, 7)

224mg Bernese Oberland, Vaud, Fribourg

AKADEMISCHER ALPENCLUB BERN
    Clubführer durch die Engelhörner. 1914.

- - Nachtrag. 1927.
- - 3.Aufl. 1954.

BALL, John
    [The central Alps]. Bernese Alps, including the
    Oberland. 1873. (Ball's alpine guides)

- - New ed. 1875.

BRANDT, Maurice
    Préalpes fribourgeoises: Moléson, Vanil Noir,
    Gastlosen, Chemiflue, Gantrisch, Stockhorn. 1972.
    (Guides du Club Alpin Suisse)

COLLOMB, Robin Gabriel
    Bernese Alps central. 1978. (Alpine Club guide
    books)

COLLOMB, Robin Gabriel
    Bernese Alps east. 1978. (Alpine Club guide
    books)

COLLOMB, Robin Gabriel
    Bernese Alps west from the Col du Pillon to the
    Lötschenpass. 1970. (West Col alpine guides)

COLLOMB, Robin Gabriel
    Selected climbs in the Bernese Alps. 1968.
    (Alpine Club guide books; selected climbs, 5)

COOLIDGE, William Augustus Brevoort
    The Bernese Oberland. Vol.1. From the Gemmi to
    the Mönchjoch. 1909. 2pts. (Conway and
    Coolidge's climbers' guides, 9-10)

COOLIDGE, William Augustus Brevoort
    The Bernese Oberland. Vol.2. From the Mönchjoch
    to the Grimsel. 1904. (Conway and Coolidge's
    climbers' guides, 11)

DÜBI, Heinrich
    The Bernese Oberland. Vol.3. Dent de Morcles to
    the Gemmi. 1907. (Conway and Coolidge's climbers'
    guides, 12)

DÜBI, Heinrich
    The Bernese Oberland. Vol.4. Grimsel to the Uri
    Rothstock. 1908. 2pts. (Conway and Coolidge's
    climbers' guides, 13-14)

GURTNER, Othmar
    Der Jungfrauführer: ein Ratgeber für Bergsteiger.
    1925.

HASLER, G
    The Bernese Oberland. Vol.1. From the Gemmi to
    the Mönchjoch. 1902. (Conway and Coolidge's
    climbers' guides, 9)

REMY, Claude and REMY, Yves
    St. Loup, Vallorbe, Covatanne: 3 écoles d'escalades
    vaudoises. 1975.

SCHWEIZER ALPEN-CLUB. Sektion Bern
    Hochgebirgsführer durch die Berner Alpen. 5v.
    Various editions.

SCHWEIZER ALPEN-CLUB. Sektion Bern
    [Hochgebirgsführer durch die Berner Alpen]. Suisu
    Beruna Arupusu. Abridged Japenese ed. [1977].

SCHWEIZER ALPEN-CLUB. Sektion Moléson
    Guides des Alpes fribourgeoises. 1951.

SCHWEIZER ALPEN-CLUB. Sektion Montreux
    Guide des Alpes vaudoises: des Dents de Morcles
    au Sanetsch. 1946.

TALBOT, Jeremy O
    Engelhorner and Salbitschijen including Wellhörner
    and Scheideggwetterhorn. 1968. (West Col alpine
    guides)

VITTOZ, Pierre
    Alpes vaudoises. 1970. (Guides du Club Alpin
    Suisse)

225mg Central Alps

ABRAHAM, George Dixon
    Swiss mountain climbs. 1911.

AKADEMISCHER ALPEN-CLUB ZÜRICH
    Führer durch die Urner-Alpen. S.A.C., 1905. 2v.

- - 3.Aufl. 1930-32.
- - 4.Aufl. of Bd.1. 1954.

AKADEMISCHER ALPEN-CLUB ZÜRICH
    Urner Alpen West: Urner Alpen Bd.2. 6.Aufl.
    1966. (Clubführer des Schweizer Alpen-Club)

ANDERSON, Michael
    Mittel Switzerland. 1974. (Pilot alpine guides)

BALL, John
    The central Alps, including the Bernese Oberland,
    and all Switzerland excepting the neighbourhood
    of Monte Rosa and the Great St. Bernard; with
    Lombardy, and the adjoining portion of Tyrol.
    1864. (Alpine guide, pt.2)

- - New ed. 1876.
- - New ed. 1882.
- - New ed. 1907-11. 2v.

BALL, John
    [The central Alps]. East Switzerland, including
    the Engadine and Lombard valleys. 1873. (Ball's
    alpine guides)

BALL, John
    [The central Alps]. North Switzerland, including
    the Righi, Zurich and Lucerne. 1873. (Ball's
    alpine guides)

BALL, John
    [The central Alps]. The Pass of St. Gothard and
    the Italian lakes. 1873. (Ball's alpine guides)

BONACOSSA, Aldo
    Regione Másino, Brogáglia, Disgrázia. 1936.
    (Guida dei monti d'Italia)

- - 2a ed. 1977. 2v.

BORIOLI, Ermes
    Tessiner und Misoxer Alpen. 3.Aufl., neu bearb.
    von Ermes Borioli. 1973. (Clubführer des
    Schweizer Alpen-Club)

BRASCA, Luigi
    Alpi Retiche occidentali. 1911. (Guida dei monti
    d'Italia; Alpi centrali, v.1)

CANETTA, Nemo and CORBELLINI, Giancarlo
    Valmalenco: itinerari storici etnografici natural-
    istici, Alta Via della Valmalenco, itinerari sci-
    escursionistici. 1976.

CIMA, Claudio
    Scalate nelle Grigne. 1975.

225mg Central Alps (Cont.)

COLLOMB, Robin Gabriel
Bernina Alps: a selection of climbs. 2nd ed. 1976.
(West Col alpine guides)

COLLOMB, Robin Gabriel
Bregaglia east: Maloja, Forno, Albigna, Allievi,
Disgrazia; a selection of climbs. 1971. (West
Col alpine guides)

COLLOMB, Robin Gabriel and CREW, Peter
Bregaglia west: [Sciora, Cengalo, Badile]: a
selection of popular and recommended climbs. 1967.
(West Col alpine guides)

- - 2nd ed. 1974.

CONTI, Alfredo and LAENG, Walther
Le alpi di Val Grosina: guida alpina. C.A.I.,
1909.

CONWAY, William Martin, Baron Conway and COOLIDGE,
William Augustus Brevoort
The Lepontine Alps. 1892. (Conway and Coolidge's
climbers' guides, 3)

COOLIDGE, William Augustus Brevoort
The Adula Alps. 1893. (Conway and Coolidge's
climbers' guides, 6)

COOLIDGE, William Augustus Brevoort
The range of the Tödi. 1894. (Conway and
Coolidge's climbers' guides, 8)

FLAIG, Walther
Hochgebirgsführer durch die Nordrhaetischen Alpen.
1924. 4v.

LISIBACH, L
Clubführer durch die Tessiner-Alpen, von L.
Lisibach, G. End und J. Kutzner. S.A.C., [1908].
2v.

NAEF-BLUMER, Ed
Clubführer durch die Glarner-Alpen. S.A.C.
Various eds.

SAGLIO, Silvio and LAENG, Gualtiero
Adamello. 1954. (Guida dei monti d'Italia)

SAGLIO, Silvio
Alpi Orobie, [da] Silvio Saglio, Alfredo Corti,
Bruno Credaro. 1957. (Guida dei monti d'Italia)

SAGLIO, Silvio
Alpi Retiche occidentali. 1953. (Da rifugio a
rifugio, 6)

SAGLIO, Silvio
Bernina. 1959. (Guida dei monti d'Italia)

SAGLIO, Silvio
Le Grigne. 1937. (Guida dei monti d'Italia)

SAGLIO, Silvio
Prealpi Comasche, Varesine, Bergamasche. 1948.
(Guida dei monti d'Italia)

SCHWEIZER ALPEN-CLUB
Clubführer durch die Bündner Alpen. 10.v.
Various editions.

SCHWEIZER ALPEN-CLUB. Sektion Leventina
Clubführer durch die Tessiner-Alpen. 2. Bearb.
1931.

SCHWEIZER ALPEN-CLUB. Sektion Pilatus
Zentralschweizerische Voralpen: Zürichsee, Vier-
waldstättersee, Brünigpass; bearb. von Oskar
Allgäuer; neu bearb. von Walter Günther. 1969.
(Clubführer des Schweizer Alpen-Club)

STRUTT, Edward Lisle
The Alps of the Bernina W. of the Bernina Pass.
1910. 2v. (Conway and Coolidge's climbers'
guides, 15-16)

SUGLIANI, L   B
Guida sciistica delle Orobie. 2a ed. C.A.I.,
1971.

TALBOT, Jeremy O
Central Switzerland: Grimsel, Furka, Susten: a
guide for walkers and climbers. 1969. (West Col
alpine guides)

TANNER, H   A
Beiträge zur Erschliessung der südlichen Bergeller
Berge und Führer für Forno-Albigna-Bondasca. 1906.

226mg Tyrol

ANDERSON, Michael
Karwendel. 1971. (Pilot alpine guides)

BALL, John
[A guide to the eastern Alps]. Central Tyrol,
including the Gross Glockner. 1873. (Ball's
alpine guides)

BALL, John
[A guide to the eastern Alps]. North Tyrol,
Bavarian and Salzburg Alps. 1873. (Ball's alpine
guides)

BONACOSSA, Aldo
Regione dell'Ortler. 1915. (Guida dei monti
d'Italia; Alpi centrali)

KLIER, Heinrich E   and PROCHASKA, Henriette
Ötztaler Alpen: ein Führer für Täler, Hütten und
Berge. 1953. (Deutscher und Österreichischer
Alpenverein. Alpenvereinsführer)

KÜLL, Lois
Führer durch die Ortler-Gruppe: Täler, Hütten,
Berge. Rother, 1959.

LIENBACHER, Vera
Glockner-Gruppe: ein Führer für Täler, Hütten und
Berge. 4.Aufl. 1962. (Deutscher und
Österreichischer Alpenverein. Alpenvereinsführer.
Ostalpen)

MANER, Eduard and OBERSTEINER, Ludwig
Hochschwabführer. 1922.

RABENSTEINER, Wolfgang and KLIER, Heinrich E
Stubaier Alpen: ein Führer für Täler, Hütten und
Berge. 1953. (Deutscher und Österreichischer
Alpenverein. Alpenvereinsführer)

ROBERTS, Eric
Glockner region. 1976. (West Col alpine guides)

ROBERTS, Eric
Stubai Alps: a survey of popular walking and
climbing routes. 1972. (West Col alpine guides)

TALBOT, Jeremy O
Kaisergebirge: a selection of climbs. 1971.
(West Col alpine guides)

TALLANTIRE, Philip
'Felix Austria' (hut-to-hut touring guides).
1964-68. 4v.

THOMPSON, Arthur J
Ortler Alps: Ortles, Zebru, Trafoier Wall,
Cevedale; a selection of popular and recommended
climbs. 1968. (West Col alpine guides)

WAIS, Julius
Allgäuführer: Wanderfahrten. 1925-[28]. 2v.

227mg Dolomites

BALL, John
[A guide to the eastern Alps]. South Tyrol and
Venetian or Dolomite Alps. 1873. (Ball's alpine
guides)

227mg Dolomites (Cont.)

BERTI, Antonio
Le Dolomiti orientali. 3a ed. 1950-61. 2v.
(Guida dei monti d'Italia)

BRAILSFORD, John
Dolomites east. 1970. (Alpine Club guide books,
new series)

BRAILSFORD, John
Dolomites west. 1970. (Alpine Club guide books,
new series)

BUSCAINI, Gino and CASTIGLIONI, Ettore
Dolomiti di Brenta. 2a ed. 1977. (Guida dei
monti d'Italia)

CASTIGLIONI, Ettore
Dolomiti di Brenta. 1949. (Guida dei monti
d'Italia)

CASTIGLIONI, Ettore
Odle, Sella, Marmolada. 1937. (Guida dei monti
d'Italia)

CASTIGLIONI, Ettore
Pale di S. Martino: gruppo dei Feruc, Alpi
Feltrine. 1935. (Guida dei monti d'Italia)

CREW, Peter
Selected climbs in the Dolomites. 1963. (Alpine
[Club] guide books; selected climbs, 3)

The Dolomites: a practical guide. 1911-12.
(Grieben's guide books, v.154)

FAIN, Piero and SANMARCHI, Toni
Alta Via n.7: "sulle orme del Patéra nelle Prealpi
dell'Alpago", "Passeggiata d'autunno nelle Prealpi
della Val Belluna". 1976.

LANGES, Gunther
[Ostliche Dolomiten]; Anhang: Civetta- und
Monfalconi-Gruppe von Toni Hiebeler. 1959.
(Dolomiten-Kletterführer, Bd.2)

LANGES, Gunther
[Westliche Dolomiten]. 4.Aufl. 1959. (Dolomiten-
Kletterführer, Bd.1)

- - 5.Aufl. 1964.

PAIS BECHER, Gianni
Escursioni in Val d'Ansiei: le Dolomiti di Auronzo
di Cadore. 1976.

SAGLIO, Silvio
Alpi Venoste... 1939. (Guida dei monti d'Italia)

SAGLIO, Silvio
Dolomiti occidentali. 1953. (Da rifugio a rifugio,
110)

TANESINI, Arturo
Sassolungo, Catinaccio, Latemar. 1942. (Guida
dei monti d'Italia)

WELS, Horst
Brenta-Gruppe. 1963. (Dolomiten-Kletterführer,
Bd.3)

228mg Eastern Alps

BALL, John
A guide to the eastern Alps. 1868. (Alpine guide,
pt.3)

- - New ed. 1879

BALL, John
[A guide to the eastern Alps]. Styrian, Carnic
and Julian Alps. 1873. (Ball's alpine guides)

BRILEJ, A
Prirocnik za planince: zbirka pravil, navodil in
podaikov ter kratek vodnik po gorah Slovenije.
1950.

CASTIGLIONI, Ettore
Alpi Carniche. 1954. (Guida dei monti d'Italia)

COLLOMB, Robin Gabriel
Julian Alps: mountain walking and outline climbing
guide. 1978. (West Col alpine guides)

COPELAND, Fanny S   and DEBELAKOVA, M   M
A short guide to the Slovene Alps (Jugoslavia) for
British and American tourists. 1936.

DE INFANTI, Sergio
Dalle ferrate al 60 grado: le più belle scalate
sulle Carniche. 1976.

LEVSTEK, Igor
V naših stenah: izbrani plezalni vzponi v
Slovenskih Alpah, [by] Igor Levstek, Rado Kocevar,
Mitja Kilar. 1954.

MORIGGL, Josef
Von Hütte zu Hütte: Führer zu den Schutzhütten der
Ostalpen, Bd.3. 1925.

PURTSCHELLER, Ludwig and HESS, Heinrich
Der Hochtourist in den Ostalpen. 5.Aufl., von
Hans Barth. 1925-30. 8v. (Meyers Reisebücher)

SCHÖNER, Hellmut
Julische Alpen: die wichtigsten und schönsten
Bergfahrten jeden Schwierigkeitsgrades. Rother,
1956.

ZELLER, Max
Berchtesgadner Alpen: ein Führer für Täler, Hütten
und Berge. 10. neubearb. Aufl., von Hellmut
Schöner. Rother, 1962.

23mg   FRANCE (NON ALPINE)

CLUB ALPIN FRANÇAIS. Section de Provence
Les Calanques des Goudes à Cassis: excursions,
centres d'escalades, spéléologie dans les massifs
de Marseilleveyre et de Puget et de Cassis à la
Ciotat. 2e éd. 1960.

CLUB ALPIN FRANÇAIS. Section de Provence
Centre d'escalade du Devenson. 1964.

CLUB ALPIN FRANÇAIS. Section de Provence
Centres d'escalades des Goudes-St. Michel.
[195-?]. (Massif des Calanques)

CLUB ALPIN FRANÇAIS. Section de Provence
La Grande Candelle. 1959. (Les Calanques escalades)

CLUB ALPIN FRANÇAIS. Section de Provence
Sormiou, Morgiou, Sugiton. 1961. (Les Calanques
escalades)

CLUB ALPIN FRANÇAIS. Section du Caroux
Escalades au Caroux. 1963.

HIELY, Ph.
Escalades dans les Calanques:en Vau, Vallon de
Rampes. [196-?].

HIELY, Ph.
Escalades dans les Calanques: Marseilleveyre,
Vallon des Aiguilles. [196-?].

LUCCHESI, Alexis
Escalades dans le massif des Calanques: chaine de
Marseilleveyre. Ptie.3. Mounine-Callot, Plan des
Cailles, les Îles. 1977.

LUCCHESI, Alexis
Escalades dans le massif des Calanques: chaine de
Marseilleveyre. Ptie.4. Bougie-Melette
Walkyries. 1978.

LUCCHESI, Alexis
Escalades dans le massif des Calanques: Devenson,
Gardiole. 1976.

23mg France (Non Alpine) (Cont.)

LUCCHESI, Alexis
Escalades dans le massif des Calanques en Vau.
1972.

LUCCHESI, Alexis
Escalades dans le massif des Calanques: les Goudes,
St-Michel. 1977.

LUCCHESI, Alexis
Escalades dans le massif des Calanques: Sormiou.
1977.

PELLÉ, Gilbert and RICHARD, Guy
Escalades à Surgy, Nievre. C.A.F., 1974.

TAUPIN, D   and BROT, M
Cormot: topo guide d'escalade. C.A.F., 1964.

TURBEAUX, Jacques
Saffres (Côte-d'Or): groupe des Rochers de Miraude.
C.A.F., 1964.

236mg Corsica

FABRIKANT, Michel
Guide des montagnes corses. 1. Le massif du
Cinto. 2e éd. 1974.

FABRIKANT, Michel
Guide des montagnes corses. 2. Montagnes de
Corse centrale et méridionale. 1971.

FABRIKANT, Michel
Les topo-guides de l'alpiniste et du randonneur en
Corse. 1959-64. 5v.

24mg APENNINES

BOSCHI, Luigi, marchese and BONORA, Alfredo
Itinerari dell'Appennino (dal Cimone al Catria).
C.A.I., 1888.

LANDI VITTORJ, Carlo
Appennino centrale (escluso il Gran Sasso d'Italia).
1955. (Guida dei monti d'Italia)

LANDI VITTORJ, Carlo and PIETROSTEFANI, Stanislao
Gran Sasso d'Italia. 2a ed. 1962. (Guida dei
monti d'Italia)

27mg VELEBIT

POLJAK, Josip
Planinarski vodić po Velebitu. 1929.

29mg EASTERN EUROPE

291mg TATRA

CHMIELOWSKI, Janusz and ŚWIERZ, Mieczysław
Tatry Wysokie (przewodnik szczegółowy). Tom 1.
Część Ogólna-Doliny. 1925.

JANEBA, Josef
Horolezecká cvičení v Prachovských skalách,
1930-34. 1934.

KOMARNICKI, Gyula v.
Hochgebirgsführer der Hohen Tatra. 1918. 4v.
Library lacks v.1.

KROUTIL, F   V   and GELLNER, J
Vysoké Tatry, horolezecký průvodce. Díl 1. 1935.

KROUTIL, F   V   and GELLNER, J
Vysoké Tatry, horolezecký průvodce. 2 vydám v
červnu. 1947. 2v.

MÜLLER, Johannes
Wegweiser für Hohe Tatra. Karpatenverein, 1905.

OTTO, Dr.
Die Hohe Tatra: praktischer Führer. 2.Aufl. 1895.
(Griebens Reisebücher, Bd. 47)

REICHARDT, A
Die Hohe Tatra und die Niedere Tatra, nebst einem
Ausflug in das Tokajer Weinland. 1911. (Köhlers
Karpatenführer, Bd.1. Zentralkarpaten)

3mg EUROPE (OTHER AREAS)

312mg Norway

GUNNENG, Asbjørn and SCHLYTTER, Boye
Fører for bestigninger i Horungtindene; utarbeidet
av Norsk Tindeklub. 1928.

GUNNING, Asbjøorn and SCHLYTTER, Boye
[Fører for bestigninger i Horungtindene]. Climbs
in the Horungtinder, Norway. 1933.

HAGEN, Helge
Fører for bestigninger i Sunnmøre, Romsdal og
Inderdal; utarbeidet av Norsk Tindeklub. 1936.

HOWARD, Tony
Walks and climbs in Romsdal, Norway. 1970.
(Cicerone Press guides)

NORSK TINDEKLUB
Klatrefører for Norge. 1970.

NORWAY TRAVEL ASSOCIATION
Rock climbs in Norway. [1953].

33mg PYRENEES

ANGULO, Miguel
Guide des Pyrénées basques: promenades, ascensions,
escalades, sur les 2 versants des Pyrénées. 1977.

ARMENGAUD, André and JOLIS, Agustín
Posets-Maladeta (del Cinca al Noguera Ribagorzana).
1958. (Centro Excursionista de Cataluña.
Coleccion de guias, 6)

ARMENGAUD, André and JOLIS, Agustín
Posets-Maladeta (du Cinca à la Noguera
Ribagorzana)...; traduit de l'espagnol. 1967.

BATTAGEL, Arthur
Pyrenees east: a guide to the mountains for
walkers and climbers. West Col, 1975.

BATTAGEL, Arthur
Pyrenees west: a guide to the mountains for
walkers and climbers. Gastons-West Col, 1975.

BELLEFON, Patrice de
Excursions et escalades aux Pyrénées. Société de
Guides Pyrénées, 1969.

BOISSON, G
Guide des montagnes des Basses-Pyrénées. T.1.
Vallée d'Aspe, Chaîne Interaspossaloise. 1938.

CLUB ALPIN FRANÇAIS. Section de Perpignan
Montagnes des Pyrénées-Orientales. T.1. De la
Méditerranée au Costabonne, par René Cayrol,
Pierre Roule, André Vinas. 1973.

33mg Pyrenees (Cont.)

CLUB ALPIN FRANÇAIS. Section de Perpignan
  Montagnes des Pyrénées Orientales. T.2. Le
  massif du Canigou, par René Sol et René Cayrol.
  1974.

CLUB ALPIN FRANÇAIS. Section de Perpignan
  Montagnes des Pyrénées-Orientales. T.3. Du Pla
  Guillem au Puigmal, par René Sol et René Cayrol.
  1975.

FÉDÉRATION FRANÇAISE DE LA MONTAGNE
  Pyrénées. T.3. Bigorre, Arbizon, Néouvielle,
  Troumouse, par Robert Ollivier et Xavier Defos du
  Rau. 1959.

FÉDÉRATION FRANÇAISE DE LA MONTAGNE
  Pyrénées. T.4. Guide de la région d'Aure et de
  Luchon (du Port de Barosa au Val d'Aran), par
  André Armengaud et François Comet. 1953.

FÉDÉRATION FRANÇAISE DE LA MONTAGNE
  Pyrénées centrales. 1. Cauterets, Vignemale,
  Gavarnie, Canons Espagnols, par Dr. Minvielle [and
  others]. 1965.

FÉDÉRATION FRANÇAISE DE LA MONTAGNE
  Pyrénées centrales. 2. Bigorre, Arbizon,
  Néouvielle, Troumouse, [par] Xavier Defos du Rau
  [and others]. 1974.

FÉDÉRATION FRANÇAISE DE LA MONTAGNE
  Pyrénées centrales. 3. Vallées d'Aure et de
  Luchon, [par] André Armengaud, François Comet;
  revue ... par Robert Ollivier. 1969.

FÉDÉRATION FRANÇAISE DE LA MONTAGNE
  Pyrénées occidentales, par Dr. Boisson [and
  others]. 1960-63. 2v.

JOLIS, Agustín and SIMÓ DE JOLIS, María Antonia
  Cerdaña, Andorra, Puigpedrós, Cadí, Puigmal,
  Carlit. 2a ed. 1959. (Centro Excursionista de
  Cataluña. Coleccion de guias, 5)

JOLIS, Agustín and SIMÓ DE JOLIS, María Antonia
  Pallars-Aran (del Garona y Noguera Ribagorzana al
  Noguera Pallaresa). 1961. Centro Excursionista
  de Cataluña. Coleccion de guias, 7)

LE BRETON, Henry and OLLIVIER, Robert
  Haute montagne pyrénéenne: guide des ascensions
  difficiles aux Pyrénées; les Pyrénées occidentales.
  Groupe Pyrénéiste de Haute Montagne, [1937].

LEDORMEUR, Georges
  Massif du Balaïtous: ascensions autour du Refuge
  du Balaïtous. 1928.

LEDORMEUR, Georges
  Les Pyrénées centrales du Val d'Aran à la Vallée
  d'Aspe. 1928.

REYNOLDS, Kev
  Walks and climbs in the Pyrenees. 1978.

334mg Montserrat

RODÉS, Josep M   and LABRAÑA, Ferran
  Roques, parets i agulles de Montserrat. 1. Regió
  d'Agulles. 1972.

336mg Gibralter

MARSDEN, A   D
  Climbing guide to Gibralter.   Joint Services
  Mountaineering Association, [1963?].

34mg   GREECE

HASSE, Dietrich and STUTTE, Heinz Lothar
  Meteora Felsen: Wander- und Kletterführer. 1977.

349 Malta

GRAHAM, J   D
  Rock climbing in Malta. West Col, [1970].

36   LOW COUNTRIES

CLUB ALPIN BELGE
  Guide des rochers belges et luxembourgeois.
  [1972].

4mg   NORTH AMERICA

41mg CANADA

CULBERT, Dick
  Alpine guide to southwestern British Columbia.
  1974.

CULBERT, Dick
  A climber's guide to the Coastal Ranges of
  British Columbia (international Border to Nass
  River) 2nd ed. A.C.C., 1969.

KALLEN, Urs
  A climbers guide to Yamnuska. 2nd ed. 1977.

KRUSZYNA, Robert and PUTNAM, William Lowell
  A climber's guide to the interior ranges of
  British Columbia south. 6th ed. A.A.C., 1977.

PALMER, Howard and THORINGTON, James Monroe
  A climber's guide to the Rocky Mountains of Canada.
  A.A.C., 1921.

- - 2nd ed. 1930.
- - 3rd ed. 1940.

POISSON, Bernard
  Escalades: guide des parois, région de Montréal.
  1971.

PUTNAM, William Lowell
  A climber's guide to the interior ranges of
  British Columbia. 5th ed. A.A.C., 1971.

PUTNAM, William Lowell
  A climber's guide to the interior ranges of
  British Columbia north. 6th ed. A.A.C., 1975.

PUTNAM, William Lowell
  Climber's guide to the Rocky Mountains of Canada
  north 1974, by William L. Putnam, Chris Jones,
  Robert Kruszyna. 6th ed. A.A.C., 1974.

PUTNAM, William Lowell and BOLES, Glen W
  Climber's guide to the Rocky Mountains of Canada
  south. 6th ed. A.A.C., 1973.

SMAILL, Gordon
  Squamish chief guide. 1975.

SPOHR, Gregory
  Selected climbs in the Canmore area. A.C.C., 1976.

THORINGTON, James Monroe
  A climber's guide to the interior ranges of
  British Columbia. A.A.C., 1937.

- - 2nd ed. 1947.

THORINGTON, James Monroe
  A climber's guide to the Rocky Mountains of Canada.
  6th ed., with the collaboration of William Lowell
  Putnam. A.A.C., 1966.

WHEELER, Arthur Oliver
  The Selkirk mountains: a guide for mountain
  climbers and pilgrims. 1912.

42mg UNITED STATES

423mg Eastern States

APPALACHIAN MOUNTAIN CLUB
  The A.M.C. Maine mountain guide: a guide to trails
  in the mountains of Maine. 1961.

APPALACHIAN MOUNTAIN CLUB
  The A.M.C. Massachusetts and Rhode Island trail
  guide: a guide to hiking trails in Massachusetts and Rhode Island. 1964.

- - 2nd ed. 1967.

APPALACHIAN MOUNTAIN CLUB
  The A.M.C. New England canoeing guide: a guide to
  the canoeable waterways of New England. 1965.

- - 2nd ed. 1968.

APPALACHIAN MOUNTAIN CLUB
  [The A.M.C. White Mountain guide]. Guide to paths
  in the White Mountains and adjacent regions.
  Various editions.

EASTMAN, S   C
  The White Mountain guide book. 10th ed. 1872.

POTOMAC APPALACHIAN TRAIL CLUB
  Guide to paths in the Blue Ridge: the Appalachian
  Trail and side trails. Supplement, rev. 1937.

ROBINSON, F   R
  A climber's guide to Seneca Rocks, West Vieginia.
  Potomac Appalachian Trail Club, 1971.

WASHBURN, Bradford
  The trails and peaks of the Presidential Range of
  the White Mountains. 1926.

426mg Western States

AMERICAN ALPINE CLUB. Cascade Section
  Climber's guide to the Cascade and Olympic Mountains. 1961.

BECKEY, Fred
  Climber's guide to the Cascade and Olympic Mountains. A.A.C., 1949.

BECKEY, Fred
  Columbia River to Stevens Pass. The Mountaineers,
  1973. (Cascade alpine guide: climbing and high
  routes)

BECKEY, Fred
  Darrington & Index: rock climbing guide. The
  Mountaineers, 1976.

BECKEY, Fred and BJORNSTAD, Eric
  Guide to Leavenworth rock-climbing areas. The
  Mountaineers, 1965.

BECKEY, Fred
  Stevens Pass to Rainy Pass. The Mountaineers,
  1977. (Cascade alpine guide: climbing and high
  routes)

COULTER, Henry and MCLANE, Merrill F
  Mountain climbing guide to the Grand Tetons.
  Dartmouth Mountaineering Club, 1947.

HART, John L   Jerome
  Fourteen thousand feet: a history of the naming
  and early ascents of the high Colorado peaks. 2nd
  ed., and A climber's guide to the high Colorado
  peaks, by Elinor Eppich Kingery. Colorado Mountain Club, 1931.

MEYERS, George
  Yosemite climbs: topographic drawings of the best
  rockclimbing routes in Yosemite Valley. [1977].

NESBIT, Paul W
  Longs Peak; its story and a climbing guide. 5th
  ed., rev. and enl. 1963.

OLYMPIC MOUNTAIN RESCUE
  Climber's guide to the Olympic Mountains. The
  Mountaineers, 1972.

ORTENBURGER, Leigh
  A climber's guide to the Teton range. Sierra
  Club, 1956.

ROPER, Steve
  The climber's guide to the High Sierra. Sierra
  Club, 1976.

ROPER, Steve
  A climber's guide to Yosemite valley. Sierra
  Club, 1964.

- - [New ed.]. 1971 (1975 repr.).

SMUTEK, Ray
  Mount St. Helens Washington: a climber's guide.
  Off Belay, 1969.

TABOR, R   W   and CROWDER, D   F
  Routes and rocks in the Mt. Challenger Quadrangle.
  The Mountaineers, 1968. (Hiker's map of the north
  Cascades)

5mg CENTRAL & SOUTH AMERICA

51mg ANDES

IGLESIAS, José María and JANNA, Mario Della
  Andinismo y campamentos en el Parque Nacional
  Nahuel Huapi. 1959. (Colección Alpamayo.
  Guia, no.1)

6mg ASIA

61mg HIMALAYAS

HIMALAYAN CLUB
  A climber's guide to Sonamarg, Kashmir. [1945].

7mg ASIA (ALL OTHER AREAS)

72mg CAUCASUS

AFANASIEFF, Rostislav
  100 Kaukasus-Gipfel. 1913.

- - 1.Anhang. 1914.

NAUMOV, Aleksandr Fedorovich
  Tsentral'nyi Kavkaz, raion Bezengi. 1967.

75mg CHINA

759mg Hong Kong

BUNNELL, J   F
  Rock climbing guide to Hong Kong. 1959.

8mg   AFRICA

81mg   NORTH AFRICA

DRESCH, Jean and LÉPINEY, Jacques de
  Le massif du Toubkal. 1938. (Guide alpin de la
  montagne morocaine)

84mg   KENYA, KILIMANJARO

MITCHELL, John
  Guide book to Mount Kenya and Kilimanjaro. 3rd
  ed., completely rev. Mountain Club of Kenya, 1971.

POWELL, Colin G
  Guide to Ndeiya. 2nd ed. Mountain Club of Kenya,
  [1968].

POWELL, Colin G
  Outlying crags. [1970?].

REID, Ian C
  Guide book to Mount Kenya and Kilimanjaro. 2nd
  ed., completely rev. Mountain Club of Kenya, 1963.

ROBSON, Peter
  Mountains of Kenya. Mountain Club of Kenya, 1969.

85mg   RUWENZORI

OSMASTON, Henry A   and PASTEUR, David
  Guide to the Ruwenzori: the Mountains of the Moon.
  Mountain Club of Uganda, 1972.

86mg   SOUTH AFRICA

FIELD, Edgar Stanley and PELLS, Edward G
  A mountaineer's paradise: a guide to the mountains of the Worcester district. Mountain Club
  of South Africa, [1925].

MOUNTAIN CLUB OF SOUTH AFRICA. Cape Town Section
  Table Mountain guide: walks and easy climbs on
  Table Mountain, Devil's Peak and Lion's Head. 3rd
  ed. 1966.

9mg   AUSTRALASIA

91mg   AUSTRALIA

SYDNEY ROCK-CLIMBING CLUB
  The rock-climbs of N.S.W. [1963].

92mg   NEW ZEALAND

HEWITT, L   Rodney and DAVIDSON, Mavis M
  The Southern Alps. Pt.2. Mount Cook alpine
  regions. 1953. (New Zealand holiday guides, no.8)

PASCOE, John
  The Southern Alps. Pt.1. From the Kaikouras to
  the Rangitata. 1951. (New Zealand holiday
  guides, no.3)

I N D E X

to major mountain groups/regions represented in classified
catalogues of books and climbing guides in the Library.

SECTION 3

CATALOGUE OF PERIODICALS

Accidents in American Mountaineering
See
Accidents in North American Mountaineering

Accidents in North American Mountaineering including
Canada and the United States: report of the Safety
Committee of the American Alpine Club. New York:
A.A.C. 23cm.
5th, 1952 -
Library's holdings are incomplete.

Acta geographica. Paris: La Société de Géographie.
24cm.
No.3, 1947 - no.78, 1969; 3e sér., no.1, 1970 -
Frequency varies.
Library's holdings are incomplete.

Acta geographica sinica. Peking: Institute of
Geography. 26cm.
Vol.29, no.4, 1963 - v.32, no.2, 1966.
Quarterly.
In Chinese.

AKADEMISCHER ALPENCLUB BERN
Jahresbericht. Bern: A.A.C.B. 24cm.
1, 1905/06 - 5, 1909/10; 10, 1914 - 29, 1934;
43, 1947 -

AKADEMISCHER ALPEN-CLUB ZÜRICH
Jahresbericht. Zürich: A.A.C.Z. 24cm.
7, 1902 - 13, 1908; 21, 1916 -
Library's holdings are incomplete.

AKADEMISCHER ALPENKLUB INNSBRUCK
Jahresbericht. Innsbruck: A.A.K.I. 23cm.
4, 1896/97 - 19, 1911/12.

AKADEMISCHER ALPEN-VERIEN BERLIN
Jahresbericht. Berlin: A.A.V.B. 25cm.
1, 1904-7, 1910; 11, 1913-29, 1931/32.
Library's holdings are incomplete.

AKADEMISCHER ALPENVEREIN KWANSAI
Annalen. Kwansai: Der Alpenverein. 28cm.
1, 1930 - 1934.
In Japanese.

AKADEMISCHER ALPENVEREIN LEIPZIG
Jahres-Bericht. Leipzig: A.A.V.L. 23cm.
1901 - 1904.

AKADEMISCHER ALPENVEREIN MÜNCHEN
Jahresbericht. München: A.A.V.M. 23cm.
1, 1892/93; 7, 1898/99 - 46, 1937/38; 70,
1960/62 - 76, 1967/68.
Library's holdings are incomplete.

AKADEMISCHER ALPINE VEREIN INNSBRUCK
Bericht. Innsbruck: A.A.V.I. 24cm.
1920/21 - 1932/33.
Irregular.

AKADEMISCHER SKI-CLUB FREIBERG
Jahres-Bericht. Freiburg: A.S.C.F. 23cm.
Library has 1912/13 only.

AKADEMISCHER SKI CLUB MÜNCHEN
Jahresbericht. München: A.S.C.M. 23cm.
Library has 10, 1911 only.

AKADEMISCHER SKIKLUB STUTTGART
Jahresbericht. Stuttgart: A.S.K.S. 22cm.
1928/29; 1934 - 1934/35.

Allgemeine Bergsteiger-Zeitung. Wien: Die Zeitung.
47-50cm.
1.Jahrg., Nr.1, 1923 - 16.Jahrg., Nr.816, 1938.
Weekly.
Continued by: Österreichische Bergsteiger Zeitung.

ALLGEMEINE GESCHICHTFORSCHENDE GESELLSCHAFT DER
SCHWEIZ
Jahrbuch für schweizerische Geschichte. Zürich:
S. Höhr. 23cm.
Bd.3, 1878; Bd.15, 1890.

Almanacco dello sport: la vita sportiva dell'Italia
e dell'estero in tutte le sue manifestazioni.
Firenze: Bemporad. 19cm.
Library has 1914 only.

Almanach du Valais. Sion: L'Almanach. 25cm.
Library has 49e année, 1949 only.

l'Alpe: bollettino della Sezione Ossolana del
C.A.I. Domodossola: La Sezione. 26-36cm.
Anno 1, 1920 - anno 7, n.6, 1926.
Five issues a year.

Die Alpen: Monatschrift des Schweizer Alpenclub
See
Les Alpes ...: revue du Club Alpin Suisse.

Das Alpenbuch der Eidg. Postverwaltung. Bern:
Schweiz. Oberpostdirektion. 25cm.
Bd.1, [1929] - Bd.5, 1937.
Irregular.

Der Alpenfreund: Halbmonatschrift für Bergsteigen
und Bergwandern. München: Rother. 29-32cm.
Library has 9.Jahrg., 1928 only.

Der Alpenfreund: illustrierte Touristen-Zeitschrift
für das Alpengebeit. Innsbruck: A. Edlinger.
29cm.
Nr.1, 1891 - 6, 1896.

Der Alpenfreund: Monatshefte für Verbreitung von
Alpenkunde unter Jung und Alt; hrsg. von Ed.
Amthor. Gera: Amthor. 23cm.
Bd.1, 1870 - Bd.11, 1878.

Die Alpenpost... Glarus: Schmid. 28-30cm.
Bd.1, 1871 - Bd.7, 1874.

Alpenrosen, von A.E. Fröhlich [and others]. Aarau:
Christen. 18cm.
Library has 1852 only.

Alpenrosen: illustrirtes Familienblatt. Bern:
Haller. 31cm.
1.Jahrg., 1866 - 4.Jahrg., 1869.
Fortnightly.

ALPENVEREIN DONAULAND
Berg und Ski: Zeitschrift des Alpenvereins
Donauland. Wien: Der Alpenverein. 29cm.
14.Jahrg., Nr.148, 1934 - 17.Jahrg., Nr.187, 1937.
Eight issues a year.
Continues: Nachrichten des Alpenvereins Donauland
und des Deutschen Alpenvereins Berlin.

ALPENVEREIN DONAULAND
Donauland Nachrichten: Zeitschrift. Wien: Der
Alpenverein. 33cm.
Nr.42 - Nr.51, 1925.
Monthly.
Continues: Nachrichten der Sektion Donauland des
Deutschen und Österreichischen Alpenvereins.
Continued by: Nachrichten des Alpenvereins
Donauland und des Deutschen Alpenvereins Berlin.

ALPENVEREIN DONAULAND and DEUTSCHER ALPENVEREIN
BERLIN
Nachrichten. Wien: Der Alpenverein. 33cm.
Nr.52, 1925 - Nr.147, 1933.
Monthly.
Continues: Donauland Nachrichten.
Continued by: Berg und Ski.

Les Alpes = Le Alpi = Las Alps = Die Alpen:
bulletin mensuel du Club Alpin Suisse. Berne:
C.A.S. 25cm.
33e année, no.7, 1957 -

Les Alpes = Le Alpi = Las Alps = Die Alpen: revue
du Club Alpin Suisse. Berne: C.A.S. 27cm.
T.1, no.1, 1925 -
Quarterly.
Title varies: T.1. - t.33, 1925-1957: Die Alpen =
Les Alpes = Le Alpi...
Continues:Jahrbuch des S.A.C. and Echo des Alpes.
Index: Table générale des matières: t.1-18,
1925-42 (1v.).

Le Alpi: rivista del Club Alpino Svizzero
See
Les Alpes ...: revue du Club Alpin Suisse

Le Alpi: rivista mensile del Centro Alpinistico
Italiano. Roma: Il Centro. 24cm.
Vol.57, no.2, 1938 - v.58, no.5, 1938/39.

Alpi Giulie: rassegna della Sezione di Trieste del
Club Alpino Italiano Società Alpina delle Giuilie.
Trieste: La Società. 24cm.
Anno 1, 1896 - anno 63, 1968.
Frequency varies.
Library's holdings are incomplete.

Le Alpi illustrate: raccolta di vedute alpine ...
approvata dal C.A.I. Milano: A. Fusetti. 24cm.
Anno 1, 1897 - 1898.

Le Alpi Orobiche: bollettino mensile della Sezione
di Bergamo del Club Alpino Italiano. Bergamo: La
Sezione. 26cm.
Anno 4, 1923 - anno 5, 1924.
Continues: Bollettino mensile della Sezione di
Bergamo.

Le Alpi Venete: rassegna delle Sezioni Trivenete del
C.A.I. Venezia: Le Sezioni. 24-26cm.
Anno 1, 1947 - anno 7, n.1, 1953; anno 16, n.2,
1962 - anno 26, n.2, 1972.
Biennial.

Alpina: eine Schrift der genauern Kenntniss der
Alpen gewiedmet; hrsg. von Carl Ulisses von Salis
und Johann Rudolph Steinmüller. Winterthur:
Steiner. 20cm.
Bd.1, 1806 - Bd.4, 1809.
Alpina
Neue Alpina: eine Schrift der schweizerischen Natur-
geschichte, Alpen- und Landwirthschaft gewiedmet;
hrsg. von Johann Rudolf Steinmüller. Winterthur:
Steiner. 20cm.
Library has Bd.1, 1821 only.

Alpina: Mitteilungen des Schweizer Alpen-Club.
Zürich: Orell Füssli. 32cm.
1.Jahrg., 1893 - 32.Jahrg., 1924.
No more published.

Alpina: organo oficial del Club Alpino Español.
Madrid: C.A.E. 25cm.
Quarterly.
Library has 1918 only.

Alpina: Reise-Novellen, Wanderbriefe und
Schilderungen für Freunde und Besucher des
Schweizerlandes. St. Gallen: Scheitlin &
Bollikofer. 24cm.
Nro.1 - Nro.21, 1856.
Weekly.

Alpina Wintersport: illustriertes officielles und
obligatorisches Organ des Ski-Club Bern. Thun:
S.C.B. 33cm.
Nr.1, 1903 - Nr.16, 1904.
Issued weekly during the season.

Alpine annual; adapted from the Alpine journal.
Dent. 23cm.
Vol.1, 1950 - v.2, 1951.

Alpine Chronik. Wien: Österreichischer Touristen-
Club. 23cm.
1.Jahrg., 1880 - 1889.
Annual.

Alpine climbing: bulletin of the Alpine Climbing
Group. The Group. 30cm.
1954 -
Annual.
Not published for 1960, 1961.

ALPINE CLIMBING GROUP
Alpine climbing: bulletin of the Alpine Climbing
Group. The Group. 30cm.
1954 -
Annual.
Not published for 1960, 1961.

ALPINE CLUB
The Alpine journal: a record of mountain adventure
and scientific observation. Alpine Club. 23cm.
Vol.1, 1863 -
Annual.
Indexes: v.1 - 15, 1863-91 (1v.); v.16 - 38,
1892-1926 (1v.); v.39 - 58, 1927-52 (1v.);
v.59 - 73, 1953-68 (1v.).

ALPINE CLUB OF CANADA
The Canadian Alpine journal. Banff: Alpine Club
of Canada. 24-28cm.
Vol.1, no.1, 1907 -
Annual.

ALPINE CLUB OF CANADA
The gazette. Banff: The Club. 24cm.
No.1, 1921 - no.30, 1937; no.50, 1954 - no.53,
1957; no.86, 1975 -
Frequency varies.
Library's holdings are incomplete.

ALPINE CLUB OF CANADA. Kootenay Section
Kootenay karabiner: journal of the Kootenay
Section. Kootenay: The Section. 22-28cm.
Vol.2, May 1965 - v.8, spring 1968.
Two issues a year.

ALPINE GARDEN SOCIETY
Quarterly bulletin. Woking: The Society. 22cm.
Vol.1, 1930 -
Index: v.1 - 15, 1930 - 1947.

ALPINE GARDEN SOCIETY
Yearbook. Woking: The Society. 21cm.
1950 -

The Alpine journal: a record of mountain adventure
and scientific observation. Alpine Club. 23cm.
Vol.1, 1863 -
Annual.

The Alpine journal
Alpine annual; adapted from ... the Alpine journal.
Dent. 23cm.
Vol.1, 1950 - v.2, 1951.

ALPINE SKI CLUB
The Alpine Ski Club annual: a record of winter
mountaineering, by members of the Alpine Ski Club;
edited by Arnold Lunn. H. Marshall. 22cm.
Vol.1, no.1, 1908 - no.6, 1913.
Annual.
Amalgamated with: British ski year book.

ALPINE SKI CLUB
Alpine Ski Club review. A.S.C. 23cm.
Vol.2, no.8, 1933 - 1958.
Annual.

ALPINE SKI CLUB
British ski year book; editor Sir Arnold Lunn.
Pitman for Ski Club of G.B. and Alpine Ski Club.
22cm.
Vol.1, 1920 - v.23, 1971.
Amalgamated with Ski notes and queries to produce
Ski survey.

ALPINE SPORTS CLUB. Auckland Branch
Alpinesport. Auckland: The Club. 27cm.
Vol.1, no.1, 1930 - v.16, no.2, 1948.
Frequency varies.
Library's holdings are incomplete.

Alpinesport. Auckland: Alpine Sports Club, Auckland
Branch. 27cm.
Vol.1, no.1, 1930 - v.16, no.2, 1948.
Frequency varies.
Library's holdings are incomplete.

Alpinisme: revue trimestrielle; édité par le Club
Académique Français d'Alpinisme. Paris: Le Club.
29cm.
Année 1, 1926 - année 29, 1954.
Amalgamated with: La montagne.
Published by Groupe de Haute Montagne, no.25,
1932 -
Indexes: v.1 - 12, 1926 - 1954 (1v.).

Alpinisme et randonnée: le magazine de la montagne
et de la neige. Paris: S.N.E.P. 30cm.
No.7, 1979 -
Monthly.

Alpinismo: rivista mensile. Torino: La Sezione di
Torino del C.A.I. 28-30cm.
Anno 1, 1929 - anno 9, 1937.

Alpinismus: Magazin für Bergsteiger, Skifahren und
Kanusportler. München: Heering. 27-30cm.
1.Jahrg., 1. Okt. 1963 -
Monthly.

The Alpinist. Tokyo: The Journal. 27cm.
No.19, 1949 - no.68, 1953.
In Japanese.

L'Alpinista: periodico mensile del Club Alpino
Italiano. Torino: C.A.I. 24cm.
Anno 1, 1874 - anno 3, 1875.

L'Alpiniste: revue illustrée de l'alpinisme.
Genève: L'Alpiniste. 31cm.
1ère année, no.1, 1903 - 3e année, no.44, 1905.

Alpyský vestnik: orgán Českého odboru slovinského
alpského družstva. Praze: J. Otty. 24-29cm.
1, 1898 - 16, 1914.
Six issues a year.

AMERICAN ALPINE CLUB
The American Alpine journal. New York: American
Alpine Club. 24cm.
Vol.1, no.1, 1929 -
Annual.
Index: v.1 - 20, 1929 - 1976 (1v.).

AMERICAN ALPINE CLUB. Safety Committee
Accidents in North American mountaineering
including Canada and the United States: report of
the Safety Committee of the American Alpine Club.
New York: A.A.C. 23cm.
5th, 1952 -
Library's holdings are incomplete.

The American Alpine journal. New York: American
Alpine Club. 24cm.
Vol.1, no.1, 1929 -
Annual.
Index: v.1 - 20, 1929 - 1976 (1v.).

AMERICAN GEOGRAPHICAL SOCIETY OF NEW YORK
Bulletin of the American Geographical Society of
New York. New York: A.G.S. 26cm.
Vol.37, no.1, 1905 - v.47, no.12, 1915.
Monthly.
Continued by: the Geographical review.

AMERICAN GEOGRAPHICAL SOCIETY OF NEW YORK
The Geographical review. New York: A.G.S. 27cm.
Vol.1, no.1, 1916 - v.2., no.6, 1916; v.52, no.1,
1962 -
Quarterly.
Continues: Bulletin of the A.G.S.
Library's holdings are incomplete.
Index: v.29 - 51, 1939 - 61 (1v.).

Los Amigos del campo: revista deportiva ilustrada.
Madrid: La Revista. 26cm.
Año 1, núm.1, 1915 - año 4, núm.26, 1918.
Monthly.

AMIS DU VIEUX CHAMONIX
Assemblée générale. Chamonix: Les Amis. 29cm.
Année 1975 -
Annual.

Andinismo: publicación del Centro Andino Buenos
Aires. Buenos Aires: C.A.B.A. 27cm.
Año 27, no.1/1977 -

Annales de géographie: bulletin de la Société de
Géographie. Paris: Colin. 26cm.
T.50, 1941 - t.55, 1946.
Quarterly.
Library's holdings are incomplete.

Annales des Alpes: recueil périodique des archives
des Hautes-Alpes. Gap: Annales des Alpes. 26cm.
1897 - 1898.

Annuaire de la Suisse pittoresque et hygiénique:
stations de cures d'air, bains, belles excursions,
villes d'hiver de la Méditerranée. Lausanne:
Bureau de la Bibliothèque Universelle. 16cm.
Library has 1891 only.

Antarctic record: reports of the Japanese Antarctic
Expedition. Tokyo: Polar Research Center. 26cm.
No.11, 1961 - no.46, 1973.
Three issues a year.
Contributions in Japanese and English.

Appalachia: bulletin of the Appalachian Mountain
Club. Boston (Mass.): A.M.C. 21-27cm.
Vol.1, no.1, 1907 -
Eleven issues a year.
Library's holdings are incomplete.

Appalachia: register of the Appalachian Mountain
Club. Boston (Mass.): A.M.C. 16-20cm.
1890 - v.22, no.3, 1934.
- - New series. Vol.1, no.2, 1935 - v.11, no.5,
1945.
Set lacks v.9, 1943.

Appalachia: the journal of the Appalachian Mountain
Club. Boston (Mass.): The Club. 24cm.
Vol.1, no.1, 1876 -
Frequency varies.
Indexes: v.1 - 10, 1876 - 1904 (1v.); v.11 - 25,
1905-45 (1v.); v.36, 1966-67 (1v.); v.37, 1968-69
(1v.); v.38, 1970-71 (1v.); v.39, 1972-73 (1v.).

APPALACHIAN MOUNTAIN CLUB
Appalachia: bulletin of the Appalachian Mountain
Club. Boston (Mass.): A.M.C. 21-27cm.
Vol.1, no.1, 1907 -
Eleven issues a year.
Library's holdings are incomplete.

APPALACHIAN MOUNTAIN CLUB
Appalachia: register of the Appalachian Mountain
Club. Boston (Mass.): A.M.C. 16-20cm.
1890 - v.22, no.3, 1934.
- - New series. Vol.1, no.2, 1935 - v.11, no.5,
1945.
Set lacks v.9, 1943.

APPALACHIAN MOUNTAIN CLUB
Appalachia: the journal of the Appalachian Moun-
tain Club. Boston (Mass.): The Club. 24cm.
Vol.1, no.1, 1876 -
Frequency varies.
Indexes:v.1- 10, 1876 - 1904 (1v.); v.11 - 25,
1905-45 (1v.);v.36, 1966-67 (1v.); v.37, 1968-69
(1v.); v.38, 1970-71 (1v.); v.39, 1972-73 (1v.).

L'Appennino: notiziario bimestrale del C.A.I., Sez.
di Roma. Roma: La Sezione. 24cm.
Anno 24, n.1, 1976.

L'Appennino centrale: bollettino bimestrale del
Club Escursionisti e della Sezione di Iesi del
Club Alpino Italiano. Iesi: Il Club. 25cm.
Anno 1, 1904 - anno 4, 1907.

L'Appennino meridionale: bollettino trimestrale del
Club Alpino Italiano, Sezione di Napoli. Napoli:
La Sezione. 26cm.
Anno 7(1), 1899 - anno 4, 1902.
Continues: Bollettino of the Società Alpina
Meridonale.

Ardennes et Alpes: revue trimestrielle du Club
Alpin Belge. Bruxelles: C.A.B. 29cm.
10e année, no.3, 1965 - 12e année, no.3, 1967.
Library's holdings are incomplete.

Arête: Tuesday Climbing Club news. The Club. 33cm.
Vol.1, spring 1961 - winter/spring 1970.
Quarterly.
No more published.

L'Ascensionniste grenoblois: revue officielle du
Club Ascensionniste. Grenoble: Le Club. 25cm.
3e année, 1902 - 4e année, no.2, 1903.
Monthly.
Continues: Le Philanthrope.
Continued by: Revue montagnarde.

Ascent: Sierra Club mountaineering journal. San
Francisco: The Club. 28cm.
Vol.1, no.1, 1967 -
Annual.

ASSOCIACIÓ D'EXCURSIONS CATALANA
Anuari. Barcelona: La Associació. 23cm.
Library has v.1, 1881 only.

ASSOCIACIÓ D'EXCURSIONS CATALANA
Bulletí. Barcelona: La Associació. 22cm.
Any 1, num.2, 1878 - any 13, nos.145 - 147, 1890.
Three issues a year.
Continued by: Bulletí del Centre Excursionista de
Catalunya.

ASSOCIATED MOUNTAINEERING CLUBS OF NORTH AMERICA
Bulletin. New York: The Clubs. 17cm.
1916 - 1919.

ASSOCIATED OUTDOOR CLUBS OF AMERICA
Mountain magazine. Pleasantville (N.Y.):
Associated Outdoor Clubs of America, Adirondack
Mountain Club. 27cm.
Vol.6, no.1, 1927 - v.9, no.1, 1931.
Quarterly.

ASSOCIATION DES ALPINISTES HELLENES
Orivassia: revue. Athènes: L'Association. 25cm.
No.1, 1959; no.2, 1966.
Contributions in Greek and French.

ASSOCIATION OF BRITISH MEMBERS OF THE SWISS ALPINE
CLUB
Annual report, accounts, balance sheet, list of
members, office bearers... A.B.M.S.A.C. 18cm.
1909 - 1961/62.
Title varies: 1960/61 - 1961/62: Yearbook and
report.
Continued by: A.B.M.S.A.C. Journal.

ASSOCIATION OF BRITISH MEMBERS OF THE SWISS ALPINE
CLUB
Journal. A.B.M.S.A.C. 21cm.
1962/63 -
Annual.
Continues: Annual report ..., Yearbook and report.

ASSOCIAZIONE "PRO CADORE"
Cadore: rivista illustrata della regione delle
Alpi Dolomitiche. Padova: L'Associazione. 29cm.
Anno 1, 1906 - anno 2, 1908.
Irregular.

AUSTRIA. Bundesministerium für Handel und
Wiederaufbau
Österreich in Wort und Bild: Zeitschrift für
Fremdenverkehr und Wirtschaft. Wien: Bundes-
ministerium für Handel und Wiederaufbau. 25cm.
Library has Folge 12/13, 1949 only.

AUSTRIA. Bundesministerium für Heerwesen
Gebirgskrieg: militärwissenschaftliche und
technische Miteilungen. Wien: Bundesministerium
für Heerwesen. 23cm.
58.Jahrg., Sept.-Oct., 1927.

The B.C. Mountaineer: official organ of the British
Columbia Mountaineering Club. Vancouver: The Club.
23cm.
Vol.40, no.8, 1962 - v.41, no.5, 1963.
Monthly.
Library's holdings are incomplete.

Backpacker. New York: The Magazine. 28cm.
Vol. 1973 -
Six issues a year.

Der Bayerländer: Mitteilungen der Alpenverein-
sektion Bayerland. München: Die Sektion. 24cm.
Jahrg.1, 1914 - 1921; 1931 - 1938.
Irregular.

Der Berg:illustrierte Monatsschrift für Hochturistik.
München: Alpine Verlagsanstalt. 30cm.
1.Jahrg., 1923 - 5.Jahrg., 1927.

Berg und Buch... Mitteilungsblatt der Gesellschaft
Alpiner Bücherfreunde. München: G.A.B. 25cm.
1.Folge, 1936 - 7.Folge, 1937.
Three issues a year.

Berg und Mensch: internationales alpines Jahrbuch;
hrsg. von Toni Hiebeler. München: Fr. Bassermann. 25cm.
Library has 1961 only.

Berg und Ski: Zeitschrift des Alpenvereins
Donauland. Wien: Der Alpenverein. 29cm.
14.Jahrg., Nr.148, 1934 - 17.Jahrg., Nr.187,1937.
Eight issues a year.
Continues: Nachrichten des Alpenvereins Donauland
und des Deutschen Alpenvereins Berlin.

Berge der Welt; hrsg. von der Schweiz. Stiftung für
Alpine Forschungen. Zürich: Büchergilde
Gutenberg. 25cm.
Bd.1, 1946 - Bd.12, 1958/59.
Annual.
No more published.
Original version of Mountain World.
Index: Bde.1 - 17, 1946 - 1968/69 (1v.).

Berge der Welt
The Mountain world. Allen & Unwin for Swiss Founda-
tion for Alpine Research. 25cm.
1953 - 1968/69.
Annual.
No more published.
English version of Berge der Welt.

Berge und Heimat: alpine Monatsschrift; hrsg. vom
Österreichischen Alpenverein in Arbeitsgemein-
schaft mit dem Österreichischen Gebirgsverein und
Österreichischen Touristenklub. Wien: A.
Holzhausen. 25cm.
1.Jahrg., Heft 1, 1946 - 8.Jahrg., Heft 12, 1953.
Amalgamated with: Der Bergsteiger.

BERGENS FJELLMANNALAG
Bergens Fjellmannalags Ars-Oversyn. Bergen: B.F.
22cm.
1, 1895 - 5, 1899.

Bergflits: mededelingenblad van de Koninklijke
Nederlandse Alpen-Vereniging. The Hague:
K.N.A.V. 30cm.
1.Jaarg., nr.1, 1975 -
Six issues a year.

De Berggids: tweemaandelijks tijdschrift van de
Koninklijke Nederlandse Alpen-Vereniging. The
Hague: K.N.A.V. 27cm.
1.Jaarg., 1933 - 1953; 35.Jaarg., nr.1, 1967 -
Quarterly.

Bergheimat: Jahreschrift des Liechtensteiner Alpenvereins. Vaduz: L.A.V. 23cm.
Library has 1965 only.

Der Bergkamerad: Monatsschrift für Bergsteiger,
Skiläufer, Wanderer. München: Rother. 24cm.
30.Jahrg., Heft 4 - Heft 5, 1969.

Der Bergkamerad,der Bergsteiger, der Schiläufer,
der Jungwanderer: alpine Wochenschrift. München:
Rother. 32cm.
1.Jahrg., Nr.26, 1924 - 10.Jahrg., 1933.

Der Bergsteiger   [und] Berge und Heimat: Organ
des Österreichischen Alpenvereins. München:
Bruckmann. 27-33cm.
1.Jahrg., Nr.1, 1923 -
Monthly.
Incorporates Berge und Heimat from 1954 -

Bernese Oberland: winter sports journal. Interlaken:
J. Aemmer. 33cm.
No.1, 1912 - no.12, 1914.
Twelve issues during the season.

BIBLIOGRAFSKI INSTITUT FNRJ
Bibliografija Jugoslavije: Knjige, brosure i
muzikalije. Beograd: Bibl. Inst. 24cm.
Library has broj 10, 1951 only.

Bibliographie nationale Suisse: répertoire méthodique de ce qui a été publié sur la Suisse et ses
habitants; publiée avec le concours des authorités
fédérales, et d'administrations fédérales et
cantonales. Berne: K.J. Wyss. 22cm.
Fasc.1, 1892 -

Bibliotheca geographica; hrsg. von der Gesellschaft
für Erdkunde zu Berlin. Berlin: W.H. Kühl. 24cm.
Bd.6, Jahrg., 1897 - Bd.16, Jahrg., 1907.

B'LGARSKI ALPIISKI KLUB'
Annuaire du Club Alpin Bulgare. Sofia: The Club.
27cm.
Library has 1936/37 only.

B'lgarski Turist'. Sofia: The Journal. 31cm.
15, 1922 - 17, 1925.
Ten issues a year.

Bollettino dell'alpinista: rivista bimestrale.
Trento: Società degli Alpinisti Tridentini.
24-36cm.
Anno 1, 1904/05; anno 3, 1906 - anno 13, 1922.

BRITISH CHAMBER OF COMMERCE FOR SWITZERLAND
The English Herald abroad: the continental review
...: the official organ of the British Chamber of
Commerce for Switzerland. Montreux: The Chamber.
32-45cm.
28th year, new ser. no.21, 1921 - 30th year, no.
56, 1923.

BRITISH COLUMBIA MOUNTAINEERING CLUB
The B.C. Mountaineer: official organ. Vancouver:
The Club. 23cm.
Vol.40, no.8, 1962 - v.41, no.5, 1963.
Monthly.
Library's holdings are incomplete.

BRITISH MOUNTAINEERING COUNCIL
Annual report. Manchester: B.M.C. 21cm.
1968 -
Size varies.

BRITISH MOUNTAINEERING COUNCIL
Climber & rambler: the journal of the British
Mountaineering Council. Edinburgh: Holmes
McDougall. 30cm.
Vol.8, no.3, 1969 -
Monthly.
Continues: Climber.
Incorporates: Mountain life.
Library's holdings, 1969 - 1976, are incomplete.

BRITISH MOUNTAINEERING COUNCIL
Handbook. Manchester: B.M.C. 21cm.
1971/72 -
Biennial.

BRITISH MOUNTAINEERING COUNCIL
Mountain life & rocksport: official magazine of
the British Mountaineering Council. Richmond
(Surrey): The Magazine. 30cm.
No.1, April 1972 - Dec./Jan. 1976.
Six issues a year.
Continues: Mountaineering.
Amalgamated with: Climber & rambler.

BRITISH MOUNTAINEERING COUNCIL
Mountaineering: the official journal of the
British Mountaineering Council. B.M.C. 22cm.
Vol.1, June 1947 - v.6, no.5, 1971.
Frequency varies.
Subtitle varies.
Continued by: Mountain life ...

The British mountaineering journal
The Mountaineering journal. Birkenhead: Willmer.
26cm.
Vol.1, no.1, June 1932 - v.6, no.1, Dec. 1937/
Jan., Feb., 1938.
Quarterly.
Vol.1, no.1 published as The British Mountain-
eering journal.

BRITISH SKI ASSOCIATION
Skiing: the review of the British Ski Association.
H. Marshall. 23cm.
Vol.1, no.1, 1912 - v.1, no.2, 1913.
Amalgamated with: British ski year book.

British ski year book; editor Sir Arnold Lunn.
Pitman for Ski Club of G.B. and Alpine Ski Club.
22cm.
Vol.1, 1920 - v.23, 1971.
Amalgamated with Ski notes and queries to pro-
duce Ski survey.

Bulletin pyrénéen. Pau: Club Alpin Français,
Section de Pau. 24-26cm.
No.13, 1899 - no.234, 1939.
Quarterly.
Publishers vary: 1904 - published by Fédération
[Franco-Espagnole] des sociétés pyrénéistes.

C.H.A. MOUNTAINEERING CLUB
The journal. The Club. 23cm.
Vol.1, no.1, 1931.
Continues as: The journal of the Tricouni Club.

Cadore: rivista illustrata della regione delle
Alpi Dolomitiche. Padova: L'Associazione "Pro
Cadore". 29cm.
Anno 1, 1906 - anno 2, 1908.
Irregular.

CAIRNGORM CLUB
The Cairngorm Club journal. Aberdeen: The Club.
23cm.
Vol.1, no.1, 1893 -
Frequency varies.

Cambridge mountaineering: the journal of the
Cambridge University Mountaineering Club.
Cambridge: The Club. 23cm.
1925/26 -
Annual.

CAMBRIDGE UNIVERSITY MOUNTAINEERING CLUB
Cambridge mountaineering: the journal of the
Cambridge University Mountaineering Club.
Cambridge: The Club. 23cm.
1925/26 -
Annual.

CAMBRIDGE UNIVERSITY MOUNTAINEERING CLUB
Oxford and Cambridge mountaineering. Cambridge:
S.G. Marshall. 23cm.
1921 - 1928/29.
Frequency varies.

Camping & outdoor life. The Camping Club of Great
Britain and Ireland. 25cm.
Vol.31, no.1, 1935 - v.56, no.12, 1961.
Monthly.
Title varies: 1935 - 1945: Camping.

CAMPING CLUB OF GREAT BRITAIN AND IRELAND
Camping & outdoor life. The Club. 25cm.
Vol.31, no.1, 1935 - v.56, no.12, 1961.
Monthly.
Title varies: 1935 - 1945: Camping.

CANADA. National Research Council
See
NATIONAL RESEARCH COUNCIL OF CANADA

The Canadian alpine journal. Banff: Alpine Club of
Canada. 24-28cm.
Vol.1, no.1, 1907 -
Annual.

Canadian geographical journal. Ottawa: Canadian
Geographical Society. 26cm.
Vol.1, 1930; v.23, no.1, 1941; v.24, no.3, 1942;
v.38, no.2, 1949.
Monthly.

CANADIAN GEOGRAPHICAL SOCIETY
Canadian geographical journal. Ottawa: The
Society. 26cm.
Vol.1, 1930; v.23, no.1, 1941; v.24, no.3, 1942;
v.38, no.2, 1949.
Monthly.

Canadian journal of earth sciences. Ottawa:
National Research Council. 26cm.
Vol.3, no.6, 1966; v.6, no.4, 1969.
Six issues a year.

Canavese e Valle d'Aosta: rivista mensile illustrata.
Ivrea: Sezione Canavesana del C.A.I. 26cm.
Anno 1, n.1, 1909 - n.5, 1910.

The Canterbury mountaineer: journal of the
Canterbury Mountaineering Club. Christchurch
(N.Z.): The Club. 23-25cm.
No.1, 1931/32 -
Annual.

CANTERBURY MOUNTAINEERING CLUB
The Canterbury mountaineer: journal of the
Canterbury Mountaineering Club. Christchurch
(N.Z.): The Club. 23-25cm.
No.1, 1931/32 -
Annual.

CARLISLE MOUNTAINEERING CLUB
Annual journal. Carlisle: The Club. 22cm.
Library has v.1, no.1, 1954 only.

CENTRE EXCURSIONISTA ALIGA
Butlletí. Barcelona: C.E.A. 24cm.
Any 5, núm.30 - núm.40, 1935.
Monthly.

CENTRE EXCURSIONISTA DE CATALUNYA
Boletin de la Seccion de Montaña y C.A.D.E.
Barcelona: El Centre. 25cm.
Año 1, num.1, 1948 - año 4, num.16, 1951.
Quarterly.
Continued by: Montaña (now Muntanya).

CENTRE EXCURSIONISTA DE CATALUNYA
Butlletí del Centre Excursionista de Catalunya,
Club Alpí Catalá, Club d'Esquí de Catalunya.
Barcelona: El Centre. 23-27cm.
Any 3, no.10, 1893 - any 47, no.511, 1937.
Monthly.
Continues: Bulleti de la Associació d'Excursions
Catalana.

CENTRE EXCURSIONISTA DE CATALUNYA
Muntanya. Barcelona: Centre Excursionista de
Catalunya, Club Alpí Català. 24-30cm.
Año 5, num.17, 1952 -
Six issues a year.
Continues: Boletin de la Seccion de Montaña y
C.A.D.E.

CENTRE EXCURSIONISTA "SABADELL"
Butlletí. Sabadell: C.E.S. 25cm.
Vol.1, núm.7 - núm.8, 1926.
Six issues a year.

CENTRO ALPINISTICO ITALIANO
See
CLUB ALPINO ITALIANO

CENTRO ANDINO BUENOS AIRES
Andinismo: publicación del Centro Andino Buenos
Aires. Buenos Aires: C.A.B.A. 27cm.
Ano 27, no.1/1977.

CENTRO DOCUMENTAZIONE ALPINA
Rivista della montagna: trimestrale. Torino:
C.D.A. 24cm.
Anno 4, n.11, 1973 - n.15, 1974; anno 8, n.27,
1977.

CENTRO EXCURSIONISTA DE CATALUÑA
See
CENTRE EXCURSIONISTA DE CATALUNYA

ČESKY ODBOR SLOVINISKÉHO ALPSEKÉHO DRUŽSTVA
Alpský vestník: orgán Českého odboru slovinského
alpského druzstva. Praze: J. Otty. 24-29cm.
1, 1898 - 16, 1914.
Six issues a year.

The Chicago mountaineer. Chicago: The Chicago
Mountaineering Club. 22cm.
Library retains current year only.

CHICAGO MOUNTAINEERING CLUB
The Chicago mountaineer. Chicago: The Club. 22cm.
Library retains current year only.

CHICAGO MOUNTAINEERING CLUB
Newsletter. Chicago: The Club. 29cm.
Library has v.10, 1956 only.
Six issues a year.

Chronik der Wengernalp und Jungfraubahn. Bern: A.G.
Hallwag. 24cm.
Nr.1, 1923 - Nr.3, 1924.
Irregular.

CLEVELAND MOUNTAINEERING CLUB
Newsletter. Cleveland: The Club. 26cm.
No.1, Jan. 1959 - no.2, Feb. 1960.
Annual.

The Climber: the national monthly magazine for hill-
and fell-walkers, rock climbers and all mountaineers. Castle-Douglas: G. Outram. 25cm.
Vol.1, no.7, 1963; v.2, no.8, 1964; v.4, no.6,
1966; v.6, no.2, 1967.
Continued by: Climber & rambler.

Climber & rambler; the journal of the British
Mountaineering Cluncil. Edinburgh: Holmes
McDougall. 30cm.
Vol.8, no.3, 1969 -
Monthly.
Continues: Climber.
Incorporates: Mountain life.
Library's holdings, 1969 - 1976 are incomplete.

CLIMBERS' CLUB
The bulletin. New ser. Oxford: Hollywell Press.
26cm.
Vol.1, no.1, Aug. 1924 - no.26, May 1931.
Frequency varies.

CLIMBERS' CLUB
The Climbers' Club journal. The Club. 26cm.
Vol.1, no.1, Aug. 1898 - v.13, nos.49/50, Sept./
Dec. 1910.
Quarterly.
- - New ser. No.1, Feb. 1912 -
Annual.

CLIMBERS' CLUB
Rules, list of members and officers. The Club.
21-25cm.
1900 - 1912.
Irregular.

CLIMBERS CLUB, Bombay
The Climbers Club bulletin. Bombay: The Club.
26cm.
No.1, 1962 -
Biennial.

Climbing. Aspen (Colo.): Mountain States Communica-
tion. 28cm.
No.46, 1978 -
Six issues a year.

Clogwyn: University College of North Wales Mountaineering Club journal. Bangor: The Club. 24cm.
1967; 1970 - 1971.
Annual.

CLUB ACADÉMIQUE FRANÇAIS D'ALPINISME
 Alpinisme: revue trimestrielle; éditée par le Club
 Académique Français d'Alpinisme. Paris: Le Club.
 29cm.
 Vol.1, 1926 - v.29, 1954.
 Amalgamated with: La Montagne.
 No.25, 1932 - published by Groupe de Haute
 Montagne.
 Index: v.1 - 12, 1926 - 1954 (1v.).

CLUB ACADÉMIQUE FRANÇAIS D'ALPINISME
 Annuaire. Paris: Le Club. 22cm.
 Library has 1ère année, no.1, 1931 only.

CLUB ALPIN BELGE
 Ardennes et Alpes: revue trimestrielle.
 Bruxelles: C.A.B. 29cm.
 10e année, no.3, 1965 - 12e année, no.3, 1967.
 Library's holdings are incomplete.

CLUB ALPIN BELGE
 Bulletin. Bruxelles: C.A.B. 25cm.
 No.1, 1886 - no.18, 1893.
 Two issues a year.
 - - 2e sér. T.1, no.1, déc.,1925 - t.8, no.22,
 mars, 1931.
 Continued by: Revue alpine: bulletin du C.A.B.

CLUB ALPIN BELGE
 Bulletin trimestriel [nouv. sér.]. Bruxelles:
 C.A.B. 28cm.
 2e année, no.3, 1957 - 10e année, no.2, 1965.
 Quarterly.
 Continues: Revue d'alpinisme.

CLUB ALPIN BELGE
 Revue alpine: bulletin du Club Alpin Belge.
 Bruxelles: C.A.B. 26cm.
 T.8, nos.23/24, 1931 - t.10, 1933.
 - - 3e sér. T.1, 1934.
 Two issues a year.
 Continues: Bulletin du C.A.B., 2e sér.
 Continued by: Revue d'alpinisme.

CLUB ALPIN BELGE
 Revue d'alpinisme; éditée par le Club Alpin Belge.
 Bruxelles: C.A.B. 26cm.
 T.1, no.1, 1935 - 5e série, t.7, 1954/55.
 Annual.
 Continues: Revue alpine: bulletin du C.A.B.
 Continued by: Bulletin trimestriel [nouv. sér.].

CLUB ALPIN FRANÇAIS
 Annuaire. Paris: C.A.F. 23cm.
 1, 1874 - 30, 1903.
 Continued by: La Montagne.
 Indexes: v.1 - 5, 1874 - 1878 (1v.); v.1 - 15,
 1874 - 1888 (1v.); v.16 - 30, 1889 - 1903 (1v.).

CLUB ALPIN FRANÇAIS
 Bulletin mensuel. Paris: C.A.F. 22cm.
 No.1, 1874 - no.12, 1904.
 Title varies: 1874-81: Bulletin trimestriel.
 Continued by: La Montagne.

CLUB ALPIN FRANÇAIS
 La Montagne & alpinisme. Paris: C.A.F., Groupe de
 Haute Montagne. 24-30cm.
 Vol.1, 1904/05 -
 Quarterly.
 Continues: C.A.F. Annuaire and Bulletin.
 Incorporates Alpinisme du G.H.M., 1955 -

CLUB ALPIN FRANÇAIS. Section de Barcelonnette
 Bulletin. Barcelonnette: La Section. 26cm.
 2e année, no.2, 1924 - 3e année, no.3, 1925.
 Annual.

CLUB ALPIN FRANÇAIS. Section de Belfort
 Bulletin. Belfort: La Section. 23cm.
 No.16, 1907/08; 27e année, no.1, 1913.
 Frequency varies.

CLUB ALPIN FRANÇAIS. Section de l'Isère
 Bulletin trimestriel. Grenoble: La Section. 22cm.
 2e année, no.2, 1927 - 13e année, no.4, 1938.
 Title varies: 1927-29: Circulaire trimestrielle...
 Library's holdings are incomplete.

CLUB ALPIN FRANÇAIS. Section de la Côte d'Or et du
Morvan
 Bulletin. Dijon: La Section. 24-26cm.
 1, 1877 - 24, 1913.
 Annual.

CLUB ALPIN FRANÇAIS. Section de la Drôme
 Bulletin. Valence: La Section. 26cm.
 Library has no.2, 1905 only.

CLUB ALPIN FRANÇAIS. Section de Paris-Chamonix
 Paris-Chamonix. Paris: La Section. 28cm.
 Avril, 1969 - juin, 1970.
 Five issues a year.

CLUB ALPIN FRANÇAIS. Section de Pau
 Bulletin pyrénéen. Pau: La Section. 24-26cm.
 No.13, 1899 - no.234, 1939.
 Quarterly.
 Publishers vary: 1904 - published by the Fédération
 [Franco-Espagnole] des sociétés pyrénéistes.

CLUB ALPIN FRANÇAIS. Section de Provence
 Bulletin. Marseille: La Section. 23cm.
 2e sér., No.1, 1898 - 1924/25; 1933.
 Annual.
 Library's holdings are incomplete.

CLUB ALPIN FRANÇAIS. Section des Alpes Maritimes
 Annuaire. Nice: La Section. 21cm.
 27e année, 1906 - 31e année, 1910; 1916 - 1920.
 Continues: Bulletin.

CLUB ALPIN FRANÇAIS. Section des Alpes Maritimes
 Bulletin. Nice: La Section. 24cm.
 1, 1880 - 26, 1905.
 Annual.
 Continued by: Annuaire.

CLUB ALPIN FRANÇAIS. Section des Alpes Maritimes
 Bulletin trimestriel de la Section des Alpes
 Maritimes du Club Alpin Français et du Ski-Club-
 Alpin de Nice. Nouv. sér. Nice: La Section.
 23cm.
 3e année, no.9, 1932 - 9e année, no.6, 1939.

CLUB ALPIN FRANÇAIS. Section des Pyrénées Centrales
 Bulletin mensuel. Toulouse: La Section. 23cm.
 1ère année, no.1, 1911 - 3e année, no.31, 1913.

CLUB ALPIN FRANÇAIS. Section du Canigou
 Bulletin. Perpignan: La Section. 22cm.
 Library has 1894 only.

CLUB ALPIN FRANÇAIS. Section du Canigou
 Bulletin trimestriel. Perpignan: La Section.
 25cm.
 1ère année, no.1, 1907 - 4e année, no.16, 1910.

CLUB ALPIN FRANÇAIS. Section du Jura
 Bulletin. Besançon: La Section. 23cm.
 No.5, 1877 - no.7, 1879.
 Annual.

CLUB ALPIN FRANÇAIS. Section du Sud-Ouest
 Bulletin. Bordeaux: La Section. 24-27cm.
 No.27, 1890 - no.64, 1908.
 - - 2e sér. No.1, 1909 - no.3, 1910.
 - - 3e sér. No.1, 1911 - no.13, 1927/29.
 - - 4e sér. published with Ski-Club Bordelaise. No.1,
 1932 - no.29, 1939; no.48 - no.49, 1944.

CLUB ALPIN FRANÇAIS. Section lyonnaise
 Bulletin. Lyon: La Section. 23cm.
 1, 1878 - 8, 1892.
 Biennial.
 Continued by: Revue alpine.

CLUB ALPIN FRANÇAIS. Section lyonnaise
 Revue alpine. Lyon: La Section. 23-28cm.
 No.1, nov.-déc., 1894.
 Quarterly.
 Continues: Bulletin.

CLUB ALPIN FRANÇAIS. Section Saone-et-Loire
 Bulletin. Chalon-sur-Saone: La Section. 25cm.
 Library has 15, 1910 only.
 Annual.

CLUB ALPIN FRANÇAIS. Section Vosgienne
Bulletin. Malzéville-Nancy: La Section. 23cm.
19e année, 1900 - 50e année, 1931.
Two issues a year.
Continued by: Revue.
Library's holdings are incomplete.

CLUB ALPIN FRANÇAIS. Section Vosgienne
Revue. Nouv. sér. Nancy: La Section. 23cm.
No.1, 1932/33 - no.4, 1933.
Quarterly.
Continues: Bulletin.

CLUB ALPIN FRANÇAIS. Sections Pyrénéennes
Revue pyrénéenne: revue trimestrielle. Bordeaux:
Les Sections. 22-30cm.
No.87, avril 1954 -

CLUB ALPIN SUISSE
See
SCHWEIZER ALPEN-CLUB

CLUB ALPINO ACCADEMICO ITALIANO
Annuario. Torino: Il Club. 25cm.
1922/1923 - 1927/31.

CLUB ALPINO BASSANESE
Bollettino annuale. Bassano: Il Club. 24cm.
Vol.1893/94 - v.3, 1896.

CLUB ALPINO BASSANESE
Colonia alpina bassanese, Umberto 1o. Bassano:
Il Club. 19cm.
1901 - 1906.
Annual.

CLUB ALPINO ESPANOL
Alpina: organo oficial. Madrid: C.A.E. 25cm.
Library has 1918 only.
Quarterly.

CLUB ALPINO ESPAÑOL
Anuario. Madrid: C.A.E. 21-26cm.
1912; 1917 - 1920.

CLUB ALPINO ESPAÑOL
[Memoria]. Madrid: C.A.E. 26cm.
Library has 1912-13 only.

CLUB ALPINO FIUMANO
See
CLUB ALPINO ITALIANO. Sezione di Fiume

CLUB ALPINO ITALIANO
Le Alpi: rivista mensile. Roma: Centro Alpinistico
Italiano. 24cm.
Vol.57, n.2, 1938 - v.58, n.5, 1938/39.

CLUB ALPINO ITALIANO
Le Alpi illustrate: raccolta di vedute alpine ...
approvata dal C.A.I. Milano: A. Fusetti. 24cm.
Anno 1, 1897 - 1898.

CLUB ALPINO ITALIANO
L'Alpinista: periodico mensile. Torino: C.A.I.
24cm.
Anno 1, 1874 - anno 2, 1875.

CLUB ALPINO ITALIANO
Bollettino. Roma: C.A.I. 24-26cm.
Vol.1, no.1, 1865 - v.43, no.76, 1936.
Annual.
Index: 1865 - 1884 (1v.).

CLUB ALPINO ITALIANO
Cronaca. Torino: C.A.I. 25cm.
Library has 1863/88 only.

CLUB ALPINO ITALIANO
La Rivista. Torino: C.A.I. 25-31cm.
Vol.1, no.1, 1882 -
Title varies: v.1 - 3, 1882-84: Rivista alpina
italiana.
Index: v.1 - 10, 1882 - 1891 (1v.).
Frequency varies.

CLUB ALPINO ITALIANO. Sezione Cadore
Rassegna. Feltre: La Sezione. 25cm.
Library has 1925 only.

CLUB ALPINO ITALIANO. Sezione Canavesana
Canavese e Valle d'Aosta: rivista mensile
illustrata. Ivrea: La Sezione. 26cm.
Anno 1, n.1, 1909 - n.5, 1910.

CLUB ALPINO ITALIANO. Sezione di Bergamo
Le Alpi Orobiche: bollettino mensile. Bergamo:
La Sezione. 26cm.
Anno 4, 1923 - anno 5, 1924.
Continues: Bollettino mensile.

CLUB ALPINO ITALIANO. Sezione di Bergamo
Bollettino mensile. Bergamo: La Sezione. 26cm.
Anno 2, 1921 - anno 3, 1922.
Continued by: Le Alpi Orobiche.

CLUB ALPINO ITALIANO. Sezione di Bergamo
Relazione sull'andamento della Sezione. Bergamo:
La Sezione. 25cm.
1881 - 1900.
Irregular.

CLUB ALPINO ITALIANO. Sezione di Biella
Relazione sull'andemento sezionale. Biella: La
Sezione. 19cm.
1892 - 1901.
Irregular.

CLUB ALPINO ITALIANO. Sezione di Bolzano
Rivista dell' Alto Adige e bollettino mensile.
Bolzano: La Sezione. 32cm.
Anno 1, num.21, 1922 - anno 7, 1925.

CLUB ALPINO ITALIANO. Sezione di Fiume
Annuario del Club Alpino Fiumano. Fiume: Il Club.
23cm.
1, 1889 - 2, 1892.

CLUB ALPINO ITALIANO. Sezione di Fiume
Comunicato mensile ai soci. Fiume: La Sezione.
26cm.
Library has anno 1, 1923 only.

CLUB ALPINO ITALIANO. Sezione di Fiume
Liburnia: rivista trimestrale. Fiume: La Sezione.
26cm.
Anno 1, 1902 - 12, 1913; v.17, anno 1924 - v.19,
1926; v.23, 1930.

CLUB ALPINO ITALIANO. Sezione di Fiume
Relazione. Fiume: La Sezione. 26cm.
Library has 1930/31 only.

CLUB ALPINO ITALIANO. Sezione di Gorizia
Bollettino bimestrale. Gorizia: La Sezione.
24cm.
Library has anno 1, 1922 only.

CLUB ALPINO ITALIANO. Sezione di Iesi
L'Appennino centrale: bollettino bimestrale del
Club Escursionisti e della Sezione di Iesi.
Iesi: Il Club. 25cm.
Anno 1, 1904 - anno 4, 1907.

CLUB ALPINO ITALIANO. Sezione di Milano
Annuario. Milano: La Sezione. 18-25cm.
Anno 1, 1882 - anno 1913.
Library's holdings are incomplete.

CLUB ALPINO ITALIANO. Sezione di Milano
Bollettino mensile. Milano: La Sezione. 25cm.
Anno 1, 1952 - anno 6, 1957.

CLUB ALPINO ITALIANO. Sezione di Milano
Comunicato mensile ai soci. Milano: La Sezione.
26cm.
Anno 1, 1920 - anno 10, 1932.

CLUB ALPINO ITALIANO. Sezione di Napoli
L'Appennino meridionale: bollettino trimestrale.
Napoli: La Sezione. 26cm.
Anno 7(1) 1899 - anno 4, 1902.
Continues: Bollettino of the Società Alpina
Meridionale.

CLUB ALPINO ITALIANO. Sezione di Napoli
Bollettino mensile. Napoli: La Sezione. 26cm.
Anno 2, 1923 - anno 7, 1928.

CLUB ALPINO ITALIANO. Sezione di Napoli
Rivista trimestrale. Napoli: La Sezione. 26cm.
Nos.2 - 3, 1932.

CLUB ALPINO ITALIANO. Sezione di Palermo
Le montagne della Conca d'Oro. Palermo: La
Sezione. 24cm.
Library has anno 9, n.1, 1931 only.
Monthly.

CLUB ALPINO ITALIANO. Sezione di Roma
Annuario. Roma: La Sezione. 25cm.
Vol.1, 1886 - v.3, 1888/91.

CLUB ALPINO ITALIANO. Sezione di Roma
L'Appennino: notiziario bimestrale. Roma: La
Sezione. 24cm.
Anno 24, n.1, 1976 -

CLUB ALPINO ITALIANO. Sezione di Torino
Alpinismo: rivista mensile. Torino: La Sezione.
28-30cm.
Anno 1, 1929 - anno 9, 1937.

CLUB ALPINO ITALIANO. Sezione di Torino
Annuario. Torino: La Sezione. 26cm.
Library has 1926 only.

CLUB ALPINO ITALIANO. Sezione di Torino
Notiziario mensile. Torino: La Sezione. 25cm.
Anno 1, 1939 - anno 2, no.4, 1940.

CLUB ALPINO ITALIANO. Sezione di Torino. Gruppo
S.A.R.I.
Sari: rivista mensile. Torino: La Sezione. 26cm.
Anno 2, n.8, 1909 - anno 4, 1911; anno 7, 1914.

CLUB ALPINO ITALIANO. Sezione di Trieste. Società
Alpina delle Giulie
See
SOCIETÀ ALPINA DELLE GIULIE

CLUB ALPINO ITALIANO. Sezione di Udine. Società
Alpina Friulana
See
SOCIETÀ ALPINA FRIULANA

CLUB ALPINO ITALIANO. Sezione di Verona
[Annuario]. Verona: La Sezione. 19cm.
1901 - 1905.

CLUB ALPINO ITALIANO. Sezione di Verona
Bollettino mensile. Verona: La Sezione. 26cm.
Anno 1, 1921 - anno 9, 1929.
Frequency varies.

CLUB ALPINO ITALIANO. Sezione di Verona
Cronaca alpina. Verona: La Sezione. 19cm.
Library has 1879/80 only.

CLUB ALPINO ITALIANO. Sezione di Verona
Rivista mensile. Verona: La Sezione. 24cm.
Library has no.5, 1930 only.

CLUB ALPINO ITALIANO. Sezione di Vicenza
Bollettino. Vicenza: La Sezione. 19-25cm.
Vol.3, 1877 - v.4, 1878; v.7, 1884 - v.10, 1889;
1927.

CLUB ALPINO ITALIANO. Sezione Fiorentina
Annuario. Firenze: La Sezione. 20cm.
1886 - 1887.

CLUB ALPINO ITALIANO. Sezione Fiorentina
Bollettino. Firenze: La Sezione. 26cm.
Anno 1, 1910 - anno 13, 1922.
Six issues a year.

CLUB ALPINO ITALIANO. Sezione Ligure
Annuario. Genova: La Sezione. 21cm.
1902 - 1909.

CLUB ALPINO ITALIANO. Sezione Ossolana
L'Alpe: bollettino. Domodossola: La Sezione.
26-36cm.
Anno 1, 1920 - anno 7, n.6, 1926.
Five issues a year.

CLUB ALPINO ITALIANO. Sezione Verbano
Bollettino. Intra: La Sezione. 25cm.
1877 - 1884/86.
Irregular.

CLUB ALPINO ITALIANO. Sezioni Venete
Le Alpi Venete: rassegna. Venezia: Le Sezioni.
24-26cm.
Anno 1, 1947 - anno 7, n.1, 1953; anno 16, n.2,
1962 - anno 26, no.2, 1972.
Biennial.

CLUB ALPINO ITALIANO. Società Alpina delle Giulie
See
SOCIETÀ ALPINA DELLE GIULIE

CLUB ALPINO ITALIANO. Società Alpina Meridionale
See
SOCIETÀ ALPINA MERIDIONALE

CLUB ALPINO ITALIANO. Società Alpinisti Tridentini
See
SOCIETÀ ALPINISTI TRIDENTINI

CLUB ALPINO SARDO
Bollettino. Cagliari: Il Club. 26cm.
1893 - 1897.
Title varies: 1896 - 1897: Annuario.

CLUB ALPINO SICILIANO
Sicilia: rivista mensile. Palermo: Il Club.
29-35cm.
Library has anno 2, 1927 only.

CLUB ALPINO SICILIANO
Sicula: rivista trimestrale. Palermo: Il Club.
25-36cm.
Anno 1, 1896 - anno 16, 1925/26.

CLUB ALPINO SICILIANO. Sezione di Palermo
Bollettino mensile. Palermo: La Sezione. 25cm.
Anno 2, 1924 - anno 4, 1925.

CLUB ALPINO TICINESE
Annuario. Bellinzona: Il Club. 21cm.
1, 1886 - 5, 1894.

CLUB ANDINISTA CORDILLERA BLANCA
Revista Peruana de andinismo y glaciología:
organo oficial del Club Andinista Cordillera
Blanca de Huaraz. Huaraz: El Club. 22cm.
Año 4, no.2, 1954/55 -
Title varies: año 4 - 14, 1954/55 - 1964/65:
Revista Peruana de andinismo.

CLUB ANDINO BARILOCHE
Anuario. Bariloche: El Club. 22cm.
17, 1949 - 33/35, 1967.
Frequency varies.

CLUB ANDINO BARILOCHE
Memoria. Bariloche: El Club. 23cm.
Vol.5, 1936 - v.16, 1947.
Annual.

CLUB ANDINO OSORNO
Memoria. Osorno: El Club. 24cm.
Vol.1, 1935/36 - v.2, 1936/7.
Annual.

CLUB ASCENSIONNISTE GRENOBLOIS
L'Ascensionniste grenoblois: revue officielle.
Grenoble: Le Club. 25cm.
3e année, 1902 - 4e année, no.2, 1903.
Monthly.
Continues: Le Philanthrope.
Continued by: Revue montagnarde.

CLUB ASCENSIONNISTE GRENOBLOIS
Revue montagnarde. Grenoble: Le Club. 25cm.
1ère année, 1906 - 6e année, no.23, 1911.
Quarterly.
Continues: L'Ascensionniste grenoblois.

CLUB SUISSE DE FEMMES ALPINISTES
See
SCHWEIZERISCHER FRAUEN-ALPEN-CLUB

CLUB TOURISTI TRIESTINI
Il Tourista: bollettino trimestrale. Trieste:
C.T.T. 25-31cm.
Annata 1, 1894 - anno 10, 1903.

CLUBE DE CAMPISMO DE LISBOA
Companheiros: boletim. Lisboa: C.C.L. 24cm.
46, 1971 -
Six issues a year.

Colonia alpina bassanese, Umberto Io. Bassano: Club
Alpino Bassanese. 19cm.
1901 - 1906.
Annual.

COLORADO MOUNTAIN CLUB
Trail and timberline. Denver: Colorado Mountain
Club. 23-25cm.
No.76, 1925 - no.516, 1961.
Monthly.
Library now retains current year only.

COMITATO GLACIOLOGICO ITALIANO
Bollettino del Comitato Glaciologico Italiano;
[sotto cli auspici del C.A.I. e della S.I.P.S.].
Roma: Società Italiana per il Progresso delle
Scienze. 28cm.
Num.1, 1914 - num.13, 1933.
Irregular.
Imprint varies: 1927 - published by the Comitato.
Set lacks num.4, 6.

COMITÉ DES STATIONS FRANÇAISES DE SPORTS D'HIVER
Ski en montagnes de France: revue annuelle des
sports d'hiver ... du Comité des stations
françaises de sports d'hiver. Paris: Le Comité.
31cm.
Library has 1947 - 1948 only.

Companheiros: boletim do Clube de Campismo de
Lisboa. Lisboa: C.C.L. 24cm.
46, 1971 -
Six issues a year.

Le Conservateur suisse; ou, Recueil complet des
étrennes helvétiennes. Lausanne: B. Corbaz. 18cm.
T.1, 1813 - t.13, 1831.

La Cordée: bulletin mensuel de la Section Monte Rosa,
Sion, Club Alpin Suisse. Sion: La Section. 26cm.
1ère année, no.4, 1926 - 6e année, 1931.

Crag and canyon and national park gazette. Banff
Hot Springs: I. Byers. 28cm.
Vol.1, no.2, 1900 - no.9, 1901.
Weekly.
Library's holdings are incomplete.

Crags. Sheffield: Dark Peak. 30cm.
No.1, March 1976 -
Six issues a year.

CRAVEN POTHOLE CLUB
Journal. New ser. Skipton: The Club. 22cm.
Vol.1, no.1, 1949 - v.1, no.2, 1950.
Annual.

Cronaca alpina. Verona: La Sezione di Verona del
C.A.I. 19cm.
Library has 1879/80 only.

Cumberland review. Wilmslow: W. Parr. 30cm.
Vol.3, no.2, 1971 - v.4, no.3, 1973.
3 issues a year.

DARTMOUTH MOUNTAINEERING CLUB
Dartmouth mountaineering journal. Hanover (N.H.):
D.M.C. 24cm.
1962; 1965.

Dartmouth mountaineering journal. Hanover (N.H.):
D.M.C. 24cm.
1962; 1965.

Deutsche Alpenzeitung. München: Rother. 33cm.
1.Jahrg., 1901 - 34.Jahrg., 1939.
Monthly.
Imprint varies.
Set lacks Heft 2 - 3; 5 - 7; 9, 1939.

DEUTSCHER ALPENVEREIN
Alpenvereins-Jahrbuch; hrsg. vom Österreichischen
und vom Deutschen Alpenverein. Innsbruck:
O.E.A.V.; München: D.A.V. 25cm.
Bd.95, 1970 -
Continues: Jahrbuch des Deutschen Alpenvereins.

DEUTSCHER ALPENVEREIN
Jahrbuch des Deutschen Alpenvereins. München:
Rother. 26cm.
Bd. 76, 1951 - Bd.94, 1969.
Continued by: Alpenvereins-Jahrbuch; hrsg. vom
Österreichischen und vom Deutschen Alpenverein.
Index: Register, 1926 - 1968 (1v.).

DEUTSCHER ALPENVEREIN
Jugend am Berg: Zeitschrift der Jugend des
Deutschen Alpenvereins. München: D.A.V. 23cm.
1.Jahrg., 1955 - 13.Jahrg., 1967.
Quarterly.
Amalgamated with: Mitteilungen.

DEUTSCHER ALPENVEREIN
Mitteilungen: Jugend am Berg. München: D.A.V.
27-30cm.
3.Jahrg., 1951 -
Six issues a year.
Incorporates Jugend am Berg, 1968 -

DEUTSCHER ALPENVEREIN BERLIN
Monatsnachrichten. Berlin: D.A.V. 23cm.
1.Jahrg., 1926 - 9.Jahrg., 1934.

DEUTSCHER ALPENVEREIN BERLIN
Tätigkeitsbericht. Berlin: D.A.V. 23cm.
1928 - 1928/29.
Annual.

DEUTSCHER GEBIRGSVEREIN
Jahrbuch ... für das Jechken und Isergebirge.
Reichenberg: D.G.V. 25cm.
1.Jahrg., 1891 - 48.Jahrg., 1938.

DEUTSCHER UND ÖSTERREICHISCHER ALPENVEREIN
Mitteilungen des Deutschen und Oesterreichischen
Alpenvereins. Wien: D.Ö.A.V. 22-33cm.
Bd.1, 1875 - Bd.64 (neue Folge Bd.54., März 1938.
Monthly.
Continues as: Mitteilungen des Deutschen Alpen-
vereins.

DEUTSCHER UND ÖSTERREICHISCHER ALPENVEREIN
Register zu den Vereinsschriften des Deutschen
und Oesterreichischen Alpenvereins ..., 1863-1894,
von Johannes Emmer. Graz: Verlag des Vereins,
1896. 165p. 22cm.
- - Register ... 1895 - 1900.
- - Register ... 1863 - 1925. 2v. 28cm.

DEUTSCHER UND ÖSTERREICHISCHER ALPENVEREIN
Zeitschrift. München: J. Lindauer etc. 22-28cm.
Bd.1, 1869/70 - Bd.69, 1938.

DEUTSCHER UND ÖSTERREICHISCHER ALPENVEREIN.
Akademische Sektion Wien
Mitteilungen. Wien: Die Sektion. 24cm.
1.Jahrg., 1896 - 35.Jahrg., 1934; 38.Jahrg.,
1937 - 39.Jahrg., 1938.
6 issues a year.
Library's holdings are incomplete.

DEUTSCHER UND ÖSTERREICHISCHER ALPENVEREIN. Sektion
Allgäu-Immenstadt
Jahres-Bericht. Immenstadt: Die Sektion. 22cm.
1905 - 1909.

DEUTSCHER UND ÖSTERREICHISCHER ALPENVEREIN. Sektion
Ansbach
Bericht. Ansbach: Die Sektion. 24cm.
1897/1900 - 1904/1906.

DEUTSCHER UND ÖSTERREICHISCHER ALPENVEREIN. Sektion
Asch
   Jahresbericht. Asch: Die Sektion. 23cm.
   1904 - 1909.

DEUTSCHER UND ÖSTERREICHISCHER ALPENVEREIN. Sektion
Austria
   Nachrichten. Wien: Die Sektion. 28-32cm.
   1.Jahrg., 1892 - 16.Jahrg., 1907; 1923 - 1926.
   Quarterly.

DEUTSCHER UND ÖSTERREICHISCHER ALPENVEREIN. Sektion
Baden
   Jahresbericht. Baden: Die Sektion. 23cm.
   1905 - 1910.

DEUTSCHER UND ÖSTERREICHISCHER ALPENVEREIN. Sektion
Bamberg
   Jahres-Bericht. Bamberg: Die Sektion. 23cm.
   18, 1904 - 21, 1907; 23, 1909 - 26, 1912.

DEUTSCHER UND ÖSTERREICHISCHER ALPENVEREIN. Sektion
Bayerland
   Der Bayerländer: Mitteilungen. München: Die
   Sektion. 24cm.
   Jahrg.1, 1914 - 1921; 1931 - 1938.
   Irregular.

DEUTSCHER UND ÖSTERREICHISCHER ALPENVEREIN. Sektion
Bayerland
   Jahresbericht. München: Die Sektion. 22cm.
   6, 1901 - 15, 1911; 17, 1912 - 28, 1937.
   Library's holdings are incomplete.

DEUTSCHER UND ÖSTERREICHISCHER ALPENVEREIN. Sektion
Berchtesgaden
   Jahres-Bericht. Berchtesgaden: Die Sektion. 24cm.
   1902 - 1908/9.

DEUTSCHER UND ÖSTERREICHISCHER ALPENVEREIN. Sektion
Bergland
   Jahres-Bericht. München: Die Sektion. 23cm.
   1908/09 - 1910.

DEUTSCHER UND ÖSTERREICHISCHER ALPENVEREIN. Sektion
Berlin
   Jahresbericht. Berlin: Die Sektion. 23cm.
   1881 - 1911.

DEUTSCHER UND ÖSTERREICHISCHER ALPENVEREIN. Sektion
Berlin
   Mitteilungen. Berlin: Die Sektion. 25cm.
   1.Jahrg., 1900 - 15.Jahrg., 1914.
   Monthly.
   Library's holdings are incomplete.

DEUTSCHER UND ÖSTERREICHISCHER ALPENVEREIN. Sektion
Bludenz
   Jahresbericht. Bludenz: Die Sektion. 20cm.
   9, 1904 - 12, 1907.

DEUTSCHER UND ÖSTERREICHISCHER ALPENVEREIN. Sektion
Bozen
   Jahresbericht. Bozen: Die Sektion. 23cm.
   33, 1902 - 39, 1908.

DEUTSCHER UND ÖSTERREICHISCHER ALPENVEREIN. Sektion
Breslau
   Bericht. Breslau: Die Sektion. 23cm.
   4, 1901 - 6, 1903; 8, 1905 - 13, 1910.
   Annual.

DEUTSCHER UND ÖSTERREICHISCHER ALPENVEREIN. Sektion
Döbeln
   Jahres-Bericht. Döbeln: Die Sektion. 23cm.
   1, 1903/1904 - 2, 1905/1907.

DEUTSCHER UND ÖSTERREICHISCHER ALPENVEREIN. Sektion
Donauland
   Nachrichten. Wien: Die Sektion. 33cm.
   Nr.1, 1921 - Nr.41, 1925.
   Monthly.
   Continued by: Donauland-Nachrichten: Zeitschrift
   des Alpenvereins Donauland.

DEUTSCHER UND ÖSTERREICHISCHER ALPENVEREIN. Sektion
Dortmund
   Jahresbericht. Dortmund: Die Sektion. 23cm.
   1904 - 1910.

DEUTSCHER UND ÖSTERREICHISCHER ALPENVEREIN. Sektion
Dresden
   Jahres-Bericht. Dresden: Die Sektion. 24cm.
   1893/94 - 1911.

DEUTSCHER UND ÖSTERREICHISCHER ALPENVEREIN. Sektion
Frankfurt
   Bericht. Frankfurt: Die Sektion. 23cm.
   1905 - 1908.

DEUTSCHER UND ÖSTERREICHISCHER ALPENVEREIN. Sektion
Freiburg
   Nachrichten. Freiburg: Die Sektion. 24cm.
   1927 - 1935.
   Quarterly.

DEUTSCHER UND ÖSTERREICHISCHER ALPENVEREIN. Sektion
Fürth
   Bericht. Fürth: Die Sektion. 24cm.
   21, 1903 - 27, 1910.
   Annual.

DEUTSCHER UND ÖSTERREICHISCHER ALPENVEREIN. Sektion
Garmisch-Partenkirchen
   Jahres-Bericht. Garmisch-Partenkirchen: Die
   Sektion. 23cm.
   1905 - 1912.

DEUTSCHER UND ÖSTERREICHISCHER ALPENVEREIN. Sektion
Gera
   Jahresbericht. Gera: Die Sektion. 23cm.
   1905 - 1908.

DEUTSCHER UND ÖSTERREICHISCHER ALPENVEREIN. Sektion
Gleiwitz
   Tätigkeitsbericht. Gleiwitz: Die Sektion. 23cm.
   8, 1902 - 18, 1912.
   Annual.

DEUTSCHER UND ÖSTERREICHISCHER ALPENVEREIN. Sektion
Halle
   Bericht. Halle: Die Sektion. 24cm.
   1896 - 1913.
   Annual.

DEUTSCHER UND ÖSTERREICHISCHER ALPENVEREIN. Sektion
Hamburg
   Jahresbericht. Hamburg: Die Sektion. 23cm.
   31, 1908 - 36, 1913.

DEUTSCHER UND ÖSTERREICHISCHER ALPENVEREIN. Sektion
Hannover
   Jahresbericht. Hannover: Die Sektion. 23cm.
   16, 1900 - 24, 1908.

DEUTSCHER UND ÖSTERREICHISCHER ALPENVEREIN. Sektion
Heidelberg
   Jahresbericht. Heidelberg: Die Sektion. 23cm.
   1905 -1908.

DEUTSCHER UND ÖSTERREICHISCHER ALPENVEREIN. Sektion
Hildesheim
   Jahres-Bericht. Hildesheim: Die Sektion. 23cm.
   1907 - 1910.

DEUTSCHER UND ÖSTERREICHISCHER ALPENVEREIN. Sektion
Innsbruck
   Bericht. Innsbruck: Die Sektion. 23cm.
   1870 - 1906.
   Annual.

DEUTSCHER UND ÖSTERREICHISCHER ALPENVEREIN. Sektion
Konstanz
   Jahres-Bericht. Konstanz: Die Sektion. 23cm.
   28, 1901 - 30, 1903.

DEUTSCHER UND ÖSTERREICHISCHER ALPENVEREIN. Sektion
Küstenland
   Jahres-Bericht. Triest: Die Sektion. 24cm.
   1905/06 - 1907/08.

DEUTSCHER UND ÖSTERREICHISCHER ALPENVEREIN. Sektion
Lausitz
   Jahresbericht. Die Sektion. 23cm.
   1903 - 1909.

DEUTSCHER UND ÖSTERREICHISCHER ALPENVEREIN. Sektion
Leipzig
   Jahresbericht. Leipzig: Die Sektion. 23cm.
   1892 - 1908.

DEUTSCHER UND ÖSTERREICHISCHER ALPENVEREIN. Sektion
Leipzig
    Veröffentlichungen. Leipzig: Die Sektion.
    22-27cm.
    No.2, 1882 - no.19, 1902.

DEUTSCHER UND ÖSTERREICHISCHER ALPENVEREIN. Sektion
Linz
    Nachrichten. Linz: Die Sektion. 33cm.
    4.Jahrg., 1932 - 10.Jahrg., 1938.
    Six issues a year.

DEUTSCHER UND ÖSTERREICHISCHER ALPENVEREIN. Sektion
Männer-Turn-Verein München
    Jahresbericht. München: Die Sektion. 23cm.
    1, 1903 - 7, 1909.

DEUTSCHER UND ÖSTERREICHISCHER ALPENVEREIN. Sektion
Mark Brandenburg
    Bericht. Berlin: Die Sektion. 23cm.
    1899/1905 - 1910/12.
    Biennial.

DEUTSCHER UND ÖSTERREICHISCHER ALPENVEREIN. Sektion
Meissner Hochland
    Jahres-Bericht. Dresden: Die Sektion. 23cm.
    1907 - 1909.

DEUTSCHER UND ÖSTERREICHISCHER ALPENVEREIN. Sektion
Memmingen
    Jahresbericht. Memmingen: Die Sektion. 23cm.
    1897 - 1903.
    Library lacks 1901.

DEUTSCHER UND ÖSTERREICHISCHER ALPENVEREIN. Sektion
Mödling
    Nachrichten. Mödling: Die Sektion. 33cm.
    7.Jahrg., 1932 - 1933.
    Quarterly.

DEUTSCHER UND ÖSTERREICHISCHER ALPENVEREIN. Sektion
Moravia
    Jahres-Bericht. Brünn: Die Sektion. 23cm.
    1903 - 1910.

DEUTSCHER UND ÖSTERREICHISCHER ALPENVEREIN. Sektion
Oberland
    Jahresbericht. München: Die Sektion. 23cm.
    1, 1899 -
    Set lacks 2, 1900.

DEUTSCHER UND ÖSTERREICHISCHER ALPENVEREIN. Sektion
Pforzheim
    Nachrichten. Pforzheim: Die Sektion. 30-33cm.
    1925 - 1927; 1935.
    Frequency varies.

DEUTSCHER UND ÖSTERREICHISCHER ALPENVEREIN. Sektion
Prag
    Jahres-Bericht. Prag: Die Sektion. 23cm.
    1901 - 1908.
    Set lacks 1904.

DEUTSCHER UND ÖSTERREICHISCHER ALPENVEREIN. Sektion
Regensburg
    Jahresbericht. Regensburg: Die Sektion. 23cm.
    1905 - 1911.

DEUTSCHER UND ÖSTERREICHISCHER ALPENVEREIN. Sektion
Reichenau
    Bericht. Reichenau: Die Sektion. 22cm.
    19, 1904 - 24, 1909.
    Annual.

DEUTSCHER UND ÖSTERREICHISCHER ALPENVEREIN. Sektion
Reutlingen
    Jahresbericht. Reutlingen: Die Sektion. 23cm.
    1, 1906 - 6, 1911.

DEUTSCHER UND ÖSTERREICHISCHER ALPENVEREIN. Sektion
St. Pölten
    Nachrichten. St. Pölton: Die Sektion. 30cm.
    9.Jahrg., Nr.11, 1934; 10.Jahrg., Nr.4, 1935.
    Monthly.

DEUTSCHER UND ÖSTERREICHISCHER ALPENVEREIN. Sektion
Starkenburg zu Darmstadt
    Bericht. Darmstadt: Die Sektion. 23cm.
    1896/98 - 1906/08.
    Issued every three years.

DEUTSCHER UND ÖSTERREICHISCHER ALPENVEREIN. Sektion
Tübingen
    Jahres-Bericht. Tübingen: Die Sektion. 24cm.
    1906 - 1912.

DEUTSCHER UND ÖSTERREICHISCHER ALPENVEREIN. Sektion
Villach
    Jahresbericht. Villach: Die Sektion. 23cm.
    32, 1901 - 34, 1903; 38, 1907 - 41, 1910.

DEUTSCHER UND ÖSTERREICHISCHER ALPENVEREIN. Sektion
Vorarlberg
    Jahres-Bericht. Bregenz: Die Sektion. 24cm.
    25, 1894 - 42, 1911.

DEUTSCHER UND ÖSTERREICHISCHER ALPENVEREIN. Sektion
Warnsdorf
    Bericht. Zittau: Die Sektion. 23cm.
    1902/03 - 1909.
    Annual.

DEUTSCHER UND ÖSTERREICHISCHER ALPENVEREIN. Sektion
Wiesbaden
    Bericht. Wiesbaden: Die Sektion. 23cm.
    25, 1907 - 28, 1910.
    Annual.

DEUTSCHER UND ÖSTERREICHISCHER TOURISTEN-KLUB.
Sektion Dresden
    Bericht. Dresden: Die Sektion. 22cm.
    1904/05 - 1909.
    Annual.

Le Dolomiti. Bolzano: The Journal. 31cm.
    Library has estate 1949 only.

Donauland Nachrichten: Zeitschrift des Alpenvereins
    Donauland. Wien: Der Alpenverein. 33cm.
    Nr.42 - Nr.51, 1925.
    Monthly.
    Continues: Nachrichten der Sektion Donauland des
    Deutschen und Österreichischen Alpenvereins.
    Continued by: Nachrichten des Alpenvereins
    Donauland und des Deutschen Alpenvereins Berlin.

Downhill only, being the journal of the Downhill
    Only Club. Watford: D.O.C. 24cm.
    Vol.3, no.14, Nov. 1956 - Nov. 1961.
    Annual.
    Set lacks 1960.

DOWNHILL ONLY CLUB
    Downhill only, being the journal of the Downhill
    Only Club. Watford: D.O.C. 24cm.
    Vol.3, no.14, Nov. 1956 - Nov. 1961.
    Annual.
    Set lacks 1960.

EAGLE SKI CLUB
    Year book. The Club. 22cm.
    1969 -

L'Echo des Alpes: organe du Club Alpin Suisse pour
    les sections de langue française. Genève: Jullien.
    23cm.
    1ère année, 1865 - 60e année, 1924.
    Monthly.
    Continued by: Les Alpes ...: revue.
    Indexes: v.1 - 25, 1865 - 1889 (1v.); v.26 - 60,
    1890 - 1924 (2v. in 1).

L'Echo montagnard: organe officiel de la Fédération
    montagnarde genevoise et de l'Union montagnarde
    vaudoise. Genève: La Fédération. 26cm.
    6e année, no.1, 1928 - 15e année, no.11, 1937.
    Fortnightly.

L'Echo touristique de la Corse. Paris: A. Clavell.
    27cm.
    2e année, no.7, 1928 - 4e année, no.16, 1930.
    Six issues a year.
    Library's holdings are incomplete.

ÉCOLE NATIONALE DE SKI ET D'ALPINISME
Montagne et sports: revue de l'École nationale de ski et d'alpinisme. Chamonix: E.N.S.A. 27cm.
No.1, 1975 -
Annual.

Ekdromika: revue mensuelle illustrée d'alpinisme et de tourisme. Athènes: The Journal. 26-30cm.
8, 1930 - 86, 1936.
Monthly.

The English herald abroad: the continental review ... the official organ of the British Chamber of Commerce for Switzerland. Montreux: The Chamber.
32-45cm.
28th year, new ser., no.21, 1921 - 30th year, no.56, 1923.

L'Escursionista: notizia delle gite alpine ed artistiche dell'Unione Escursionisti Torino.
Torino: L'Unione. 25cm.
Anno 1, 1899 - anno 12, 1910.
Monthly.
Library's holdings are incomplete.

Étrennes helvétiennes et patriotiques. Lausanne:
C.H. Vincent. 11cm.
Library has no.6, 1788 only.

Étrennes helvétiques. [Published by and for the Swiss community in London]. 19cm.
Library has 1875 only.

LES EXCURSIONISTES MARSEILLAIS
See
SOCIÉTÉ DES EXCURSIONISTES MARSEILLAIS

Expedition: the magazine for the independent traveller. WEXAS. 30cm.
Irregular.
Library retains current year only.

Exploration review: journal of the Imperial College Exploration Society. The Society. 22cm.
Library has Feb. 1961 only.

Explorations pyrénéennes: bulletin trimestriel de la Société Ramond. Bagnères-de-Bigorre: La Société.
24-26cm.
No.1, 1866 - 51e année, 1916; 64e & 65e années, 1929/30.
Library's holdings are incomplete.
Index: Table générale, 1866 - 1915 (lv.).

FEDERACIÓN ARGENTINA DE MONTANISMO Y AFINES
La montana: organo de la Federación. Buenos Aires: F.A.M.A. 27cm.
Ano 2, no.2, 1960 - no.12, 1969.
Annual.

FEDERACIÓN DE ANDINISMO Y EXCURSIONISMO DE CHILE
Anuario de montana. Santiago: F.A.E.C. 18cm.
1956 - 1960.

FEDERACIÓN DE SKI Y ANDINISMO DE CHILE
Revista andina: organo oficial de la Federación de ski y andinismo de Chile. Santiago: Club Andino de Chile. 27cm.
Ano 10, no.56, 1947 -
Frequency varies.

FEDERACIÓN ESPANOLA DE MONTANISMO
Anuario. Madrid: F.E.M. 25cm.
1952 - 1973.

FEDERACIÓN VASCO-NAVARRA DE ALPINISMO
Pyrenaica: annales de la Federación Vasco-Navarra de Alpinismo. Bilbao: La Federación. 25cm.
Vol.1, num.1, 1926 - v.5, num.16, 1930.
Quarterly.

FEDERATED MOUNTAIN CLUBS OF N.Z.
F.M.C. bulletin. Wellington (N.Z.): F.M.C. 21cm.
No.46, 1973 -

FÉDÉRATION FRANCO-ESPAGNOLE DES SOCIÉTÉS PYRÉNÉISTES
Bulletin pyrénéen. Pau: C.A.F., Section de Pau.
26cm.
No.13, 1899 - no.234, 1939.
Quarterly.
Publishers vary: 1904 - published by Fédération [Franco-Espagnole] des sociétés pyrénéistes.

FÉDÉRATION MONTAGNARDE GENEVOISE
L'Écho montagnard: organe officiel de la Fédération montagnarde genevoise et de l'Union montagnarde vaudoise. Genève: La Fédération.
26cm.
6e année, no.1, 1928 - 15e année, no.11, 1937.
Fortnightly.

FEDERATION OF MOUNTAINEERING CLUBS OF IRELAND
Mountain log: FMCI newsletter. Dublin: F.M.C.I.
21cm.
No.1, 1978 -
Quarterly.

FEDERATION OF MOUNTAINEERING CLUBS OF IRELAND
New climbs. Dublin: Federation of Mountaineering Clubs of Ireland. 15-22cm.
1973 -
Annual.

FELL AND ROCK CLIMBING CLUB OF THE ENGLISH LAKE DISTRICT
Chronicle. [Stockport?]: The Club. 30cm.
Two issues a year.
Library retains current issue only.

FELL AND ROCK CLIMBING CLUB OF THE ENGLISH LAKE DISTRICT
The journal of the Fell and Rock Climbing Club of the English Lake District. Stockport: The Club.
21cm.
Vol.1, no.1, 1907 -
Frequency varies.

Fels und Firn: ein Jahrbuch für Alpinismus, Forschungsreise und Wanderung; geleitet von Jos. Jul. Schätz und Alfred Graber. München: Rother.
32cm.
Library has 1925 only.

FÖRENINGEN FÖR SKIDLÖPNINGENS FRÄMJANDE I SVERIGE
På Skidor: arsskrift. Stockholm: Färeningen.
23cm.
1909 - 1915.

FÖRENINGEN FÖR SKIDLÖPNINGENS FRÄMJANDE I SVERIGE
Svensk Skidkalender. Stockholm: F.S.F.S. 20cm.
Library has 4.argangen, 1935 only.

FÖRENINGEN TIL SKI-IDRAETTENS FREMME
Aarbok. Oslo: Foreningen. 23cm.
1909 - 1927.

Formes et couleurs: revue internationale des arts, du gout et des idées. Lausanne: The Journal.
31cm.
Library has 94e année,no.2, 1947 only.

FRANCE. Ministère de l'agriculture. Service des grandes forces hydrauliques (Régions des Alpes et du Sud-Ouest)
Compte rendu et résultats... Paris: Le Ministère.
30cm.
T.4, 1911 - t.9, 1920.
Library's holdings are incomplete.

Für die Sicherheit im Bergland: Jahrbuch; hrsg. vom Österreichischen Kuratorium für Alpine Sicherheit.
Wien: Das Kuratorium. 20cm.
1972 -

Gebirgsfreund: Mitteilungen der Sektion Österreichischer Gebirgsverein. Wien: Ö.A.V. 30cm.
66.Jahrg., 1955 - 72.Jahrg., 1961; 83.Jahrg., 1972 - 89.Jahrg., 1978.
Six issues a year.
No more published?

Der Gebirgsfreund: Zeitschrift des Niederöster-
reichischen Gebirgsvereins. Wien: Selbstverlag.
29cm.
6.Jahrg., 1895 - 12.Jahrg., 1901.
Monthly.

Gebirgskrieg: militärwissenschaftliche und technische
Miteilungen; hrsg. vom Österreichischen Bundesministerium für Heerwesen. Wien: Bundesministerium.
23cm.
58.Jahrg., Sept.-Okt. 1927.

GEOGRAPHICAL ASSOCIATION
The geographical teacher. London Geographical
Institute. 26cm.
No.11, v.3, pt.1, 1905 - no.14, v.3, pt.4, 1906.
Three issues a year.
Continued by: Geography.

GEOGRAPHICAL ASSOCIATION
Geography: the quarterly journal of the Geo-
graphical Association. London Geographical
Institute. 25cm.
No.131, v.26, pt.1, 1941 - no.202, v.43, pt.4,
1958.
Continues: The Geographical teacher.

The Geographical journal. Royal Geographical
Society. 25cm.
Vol.1, 1893-
Three issues a year.
Indexes: v.1-20, 1893-1902 (1v.); v.21-40,
1903-1912 (1v.); v.41-60, 1913-1922 (1v.);
v.61-80, 1923-1932 (1v.); v.81-100, 1933-
1942 (1v.); v.101-120, 1943-1954 (1v.)

The Geographical magazine. Times Publishing Co.
25cm.
Vol.7, no.5, 1938 - v.30, no.6, 1957.
Monthly.

The Geographical review. New York: American
Geographical Society. 27cm.
Vol.1, no.1, 1916 - v.2, no.6, 1916; v.52, no.1,
1962 -
Quarterly.
Continues: Bulletin of the A.G.S.
Library's holdings are incomplete.
Index: v.29 - 51, 1939 - 61 (1v.).

GEOGRAPHICAL SOCIETY OF PHILADELPHIA
The bulletin. Philadelphia: G.S.P. 26cm.
Vol.5, no.1, 1907 - v.13, no.4, 1915.
Quarterly.

The Geographical teacher: the organ of the Geo-
graphical Association. London Geographical
Institute. 26cm.
No.11, v.3, pt.1, 1905 - no.14, v.3, pt.4, 1906.
Three issues a year.
Continued by: Geography.

La Géographie: bulletin de la Société de géographie.
Paris: Masson. 29cm.
T.1, 1900 - t.29, 1914.
Annual.

Geography: the quarterly journal of the Geographical
Association. London Geographical Institute. 25cm.
No.131, v.26, pt.1, 1941 - no.202, v.43, pt.4,
1958.
Continues: The Geographical teacher.

GEOLOGICAL SURVEY OF CANADA
Annual report (new ser.). Ottawa: Government
Printing Bureau. 25cm.
Library has v.13, 1900 only.

GEOLOGICAL SURVEY OF INDIA
Records. Calcutta: Geological Survey of India.
28cm.
Vol.11, pt.2, 1878 - v.44, pt.4, 1914.

GESELLSCHAFT DER ALPINER BÜCHERFREUNDE
Berg und Buch ...: Mitteilungsblatt. München:
G.A.B. 25cm.
1.Folge, 1936 - 7.Folge, 1937.
Three issues a year.

GESELLSCHAFT FÜR ERDKUNDE ZU BERLIN
Bibliotheca geographica. Berlin: W.H. Kühl. 24cm.
Bd.6, Jahrg., 1897 - Bd.16, Jahrg., 1907.

GESELLSCHAFT FÜR ERDKUNDE ZU BERLIN
Zeitschrift. Berlin: E.S. Mittler. 27cm.
1907 - 1913.
Ten issues a year.

GESELLSCHAFT FÜR ERDKUNDE ZU LEIPZIG
Mitteilungen. Leipzig: F. Hirt. 24cm.
1923/25; 1929/30; 1937/39 - 1940/41.

Giornale delle Alpi degli Appennini e dei Vulcani.
Torino: G.T. Cimino. 25cm.
Anno 1, 1864 - anno 3, 1866.
Anno 3 has title: Rivista delle Alpi ...

Giovane montagna: rivista di vita alpina. Torino:
Fanton. 26cm.
Anno 10, 1924; anno 17, 1931 - anno 22, n.2,
1937; anno 34, n.1, 1948.
Monthly.

GLACIALISTS' ASSOCIATION
The Glacialists' magazine: a monthly magazine of
glacial geology, embodying the proceedings of the
Glacialists' Association. F.H. Butler. 24cm.
Vol.1, no.1, 1893 - v.2, no.7, 1895.
No more published?

The Glacialists' magazine: a monthly magazine of
glacial geology, embodying the proceedings of the
Glacialists' Association. F.H. Butler. 24cm.
Vol.1, no.1, 1893 - v.2, no.7, 1895.
No more published?

Glimpses of the wonderful: Christmas annual.
Harvey & Darton. 16cm.
Library has 1845 only.

GLOUCESTERSHIRE MOUNTAINEERING CLUB
Rope: the official journal. Cheltenham: The
Club. 20cm.
Library has v.1, no.1, 1957 only.

Gore in ljudije. Ljubljana: Odbor za Planinstvo
in Alpinistiko. 25cm.
Leto 1, 1, 1946 - leto 2, 12, 1947.
Irregular.

GRAMPIAN CLUB
The Grampian Club journal. Dundee: The Club.
22cm.
Library has v.1, no.1, 1937 only.

GRITSTONE CLUB
The Gritstone Club journal. Bradford: The Club.
26cm.
Vol.4, no.1, 1930 - v.4, no.2, 1933.

Le grotte d'Italia: rivista di speleologia: organo
ufficiale dell'Azienda autonoma di stato delle
R.R. Grotte Demaniali di Postumia. Trieste:
R.R.G.D.P. 26cm.
Anno 2, 1928 - anno 8, 1934.
Subtitle (1929 -): rivista trimestrale
dell'Istituto Italiano di Speleologia.
- - Ser. 2a. Vol.1, 1936 - v.3, 1938.

GROUPE DE HAUTE MONTAGNE
Alpinisme: revue trimestrielle; editée par le
Club Académique Français d'Alpinisme. Paris: Le
Club. 29cm.
Vol.1, 1926 - v.29, 1954.
Published by Groupe de Haute Montagne, no.25,
1932 -
Amalgamated with: La Montagne.
Index: v.1 - 12, 1926 - 1954 (1v.).

GROUPE DE HAUTE MONTAGNE
Annales. Paris: G.H.M. 28-30cm.
1960 -

GROUPE DE HAUTE MONTAGNE
Annuaire. C.A.F. 23cm.
No.1, 1926 - no.5, 1931.
Continued in: Alpinisme.

GROUPE DE HAUTE MONTAGNE
  La montagne & alpinisme. Paris: C.A.F., G.H.M.
  24-30cm.
  1ère année, no.1, 1905 -
  Four issues a year.
  Continues: C.A.F. Annuaire and Bulletin.
  Incorporates Alpinisme du G.H.H., 1955 -

GRUP EXCURSIONISTA JOVENTUT CATALANA
  Butlleti. Barcelona: G.E.J.C. 25cm.
  Any 3, no.11, 1927 - any 4, no.17, 1928.
  Six issues a year.

GRUPO ANDINISTA CORDILLERA BLANCA
  See
CLUB ANDINISTA CORDILLERA BLANCA

GRUPPO ITALIANO SCRITTORI DI MONTAGNA
  Montagna. Torino: Il Gruppo. 26cm.
  Anno 2, 1935 - anno 6, 1939.
  Monthly.

Harvard mountaineering. Cambridge (Mass.): The
  Club. 23-26cm.
  Vol.1, no.1, 1927 -
  Frequency varies.
  Library's holdings are incomplete.

HARVARD MOUNTAINEERING CLUB
  Bulletin. Cambridge (Mass.): The Club. 26cm.
  Vol.2, no.1, 1929 - v.3, no.7, 1931.
  Monthly.
  Library's holdings are incomplete.

HARVARD MOUNTAINEERING CLUB
  Harvard mountaineering. Cambridge (Mass.): The
  Club. 23-26cm.
  Vol.1, no.1, 1927 -
  Library's holdings are incomplete.

Heimatschutz: Zeitschrift der Schweizer.Vereinigung
  für Heimatschutz... Bümpliz: A. Benteli. 26-32cm.
  Jahrg.1, 1906 - Jahrg.12, 1917.
  Monthly.

HELLENIC ALPINE CLUB
  To vouno: édition bimestrielle. Athènes: Le Club.
  25cm.
  1, 1934 - 222, 1961.

HIMALAYAN ASSOCIATION
  Himalayan Association journal. Calcutta: The
  Association. 22-25cm.
  1970; 1974/75.

HIMALAYAN CLUB
  The Himalayan journal: records of the Himalayan
  Club. Calcutta: The Club. 23cm.
  Vol.1, 1929 -
  Annual.
  Indexes: v.1 - 21, 1929-58 (lv.); v.22 - 32,
  1959-73 (lv.); v.33, 1973-74 (lv.); v.34, 1974-75
  (lv.).

HIMALAYAN CLUB
  Newsletter. Bombay: The Club. 29cm.
  Library retains current issue only.

HIMALAYAN FEDERATION
  Himavanta. Calcutta: The Federation. 22-39cm.
  Vol.2, no.10, 1971 -
  Monthly.

The Himalayan journal: records of the Himalayan Club.
  Calcutta: The Club. 23cm.
  Vol.1, 1929 -
  Annual.
  Indexes: v.1 - 21, 1929-58 (lv.); v.22 - 32,
  1959-73 (lv.); v.33, 1973-74 (lv.); v.34, 1974-75
  (lv.).

HIMALAYAN MOUNTAINEERING INSTITUTE, Darjeeling
  Himalayan mountaineering journal. Darjeeling: The
  Institute. 23cm.
  Vol.8, 1973 - v.9, 1974.
  Annual.

HIMALAYAN MOUNTAINEERING INSTITUTE, Darjeeling
  Newsletter. Darjeeling: The Institute. 20-22cm.
  No.4, 1961 - no.10, 1964.
  Two issues a year.
  Library lacks no.5.

Himalayan mountaineering journal. Darjeeling.
  Himalayan Mountaineering Institute. 23cm.
  Vol.8, 1973 - v.9, 1974.
  Annual.

Himavanta. Calcutta: Himalayan Federation. 22-39cm.
  Vol.2, no.10, 1971 -
  Monthly.

Horolezec: vestnik Svazu československých horolezců.
  Praha: S.C.H. 24cm.
  Roč.5, 1938; roč.1(9), 1947 - roc.(2) 10, 1948.
  Roc.5, 1938, published by Klub alpistu
  československých.

Hrvatski planinar: glasilo Hrvatskog planinarskog
  drustva. Zagreb: The Society. 23-28cm.
  God.18, 1922 - god.36, 1940.

HRVATSKO PLANINARSKO DRUŠTVO
  Hrvatski planinar: glasilo Hrvatskog planinarskog
  drustva. Zagreb: The Society. 24-28cm.
  God.18, 1922 - god.36, 1940.

The Ice-cap, being the journal of the Mountain Club
  of East Africa. Moshi: The Club. 26cm.
  Library has no.1, 1932 only.

IMPERIAL COLLEGE EXPLORATION SOCIETY
  Exploration review: journal. The Society. 22cm.
  Library has Feb. 1961 only.

Inaka; or, Reminiscences of Rokkosan and other rocks;
  collected and compiled by the Bell Goat. Kobe:
  Kobe Herald. 24cm.
  Vol.1, 1915 - v.18, 1924.

INSTITUTE OF GEOGRAPHY, Peking
  Acta geographica sinica. Peking: Institute of
  Geography. 26cm.
  Vol.29, no.4, 1963 - v.32, no.2, 1966.
  Quarterly.
  In Chinese.

INTERNATIONAL UNION OF ALPINIST ASSOCIATIONS
  Bulletin. Genève: I.U.A.A. 24-30cm.
  No.16, juin 1965; no.18, nov. 1965; no.20,
  avril 1966 -
  Five issues a year.

The Iowa climber. Iowa: Iowa Mountaineers. 24-26cm.
  Vol.3, no.3, 1950 - v.10, no.5, 1961.
  Quarterly.
  Library's holdings are incomplete.

IOWA MOUNTAINEERS (CLUB)
  The Iowa climber. Iowa: Iowa Mountaineers.
  24-26cm.
  Vol.3, 1950 - v.10, no.5, 1961.
  Quarterly.
  Library's holdings are incomplete.

IOWA MOUNTAINEERS (CLUB)
  Iowa Mountaineers journal. Iowa: Iowa Mountaineers
  26cm.
  Vol.4, no.4, 1957; v.5, no.5, 1965.
  Frequency varies.

Iowa Mountaineers journal. Iowa: Iowa Mountaineers.
  26cm.
  Vol.4, no.4, 1957; v.5, no.5, 1965.
  Frequency varies.

Irish mountaineering: journal of the Irish Moun-
taineering Club. [Dublin]: The Club. 22cm.
Vol.1, no.1, Aug. 1950 -
Frequency varies.

IRISH MOUNTAINEERING CLUB
Irish mountaineering: journal of the Irish
Mountaineering Club. [Dublin]: The Club. 22cm.
Vol.1, no.1, Aug. 1950 -
Frequency varies.

ISTITUTO GEOGRAFICO MILITARE
L'Universo: rivista bimestrale. Firenze:
L'Istituto. 25cm.
Anno 42, n.5, 1962 - anno 55, n.1, 1975.

ISTITUTO ITALIANO DI SPELEOLOGIA
Le Grotte d'Italia: rivista di speleologia: organo
ufficiale dell'Azienda autonoma di stato delle
R.R. Grotte Demaniali di Postumia. Trieste:
R.R.G.D.P. 26cm.
Anno 2, 1928 - anno 8, 1934.
Subtitle (1929 -): rivista trimestrale
dell'Istituto Italiano di Speleologia.
- - Ser.2a. Vol.1, 1936 - v.3, 1938.

The Iwa to yuki. Tokyo: Yama-Kei. 26cm.
38, 1974 -
Six issues a year.
In Japanese with summaries in English.

JAPAN POLAR RESEARCH ASSOCIATION
Polar news. Tokyo: The Association. 26cm.
Vol.2, no.1, 3, 1966 -
Two issues a year.
In Japanese, with English list of contents.

JAPANESE ALPINE CLUB
Sangaku: the journal of the Japanese Alpine Club.
Tokyo: The Club. 22-27cm.
Vol.1, 1906 -
Annual
In Japanese.

Journal illustré des stations du Valais: organe de
l'industrie hotelière valaisanne. Genève: J.Monod.
33cm.
1ère année, 1903 - 2e année, mars 1904; 10e année,
1911 - 11e année, jan. 1913.
Cover title: La Vallée du Rhône: journal...
Fortnightly.

Jugend am Berg: Zeitschrift der Jugend des Deutschen
Alpenvereins. München: D.A.V. 23cm.
1.Jahrg., 1955 - 13.Jahrg., 1967.
Quarterly.
Amalgamated with: Mitteilungen des Deutschen
Alpenvereins.

The Kandahar review. The Journal. 22cm.
Library has v.5, no.9, Oct. 1974 only.

KARABINER MOUNTAINEERING CLUB
Journal. Manchester: The Club. 25cm.
Library has v.1, 1950 only.
Continues: News letter.

KARABINER MOUNTAINEERING CLUB
News letter. Manchester: The Club. 33cm.
No.4 July, 1946 - no.9, Feb. 1948.
Frequency varies.
Continued by: Journal.

Die Karpathen: Turistik, Alpinismus, Wintersport.
Kesmark: Karpathenverein. 24cm.
10.Jahrg., 1934 - 14.Jahrg. 1938.
Six issues a year.
Continues: Turistik, Alpinismus und Wintersport.

KARPATHENVEREIN
Die Karpathen: Turistik, Alpinismus, Wintersport.
Kesmark: Karpathenverein. 24cm.
10.Jahrg., 1934 - 14.Jahrg., 1938.
Six issues a year.
Continues: Turistik, Alpinismus und Wintersport.

KARPATHENVEREIN
Turistik, Alpinismus und Wintersport. Kesmark:
Karpathenverein. 26cm.
1924 - 1927.
Monthly
- - 2.Teil: Mitteilungen. 33cm.
1927 - 1933.
Continues: Turistik und Alpinismus.
Continued by: Die Karpathen...

KARPATHENVEREIN
Turistik und Alpinismus. Kesmark: Karpathenverein. 26cm.
1918 - 1923.
Monthly.
Continued by: Turistik, Alpinismus und Wintersport.
Also published in Hungarian by Magyar turista
szövetség as Turistaság es alpinismus, 1910-1935.

KAVKAZSKOE GORNOE OBSHCHESTVO
Ezhegodnik. Piatigorsk': The Society. 28cm.
No.2, 1904 - no.3, 1909.

KLUB ALPISTU ČESKOSLOVENSKÝCH
Horolezec: věstnik Klubu... = Bulletin.
Praha: K.A.C. 22-26cm.
Roč.5, 1938; roč.1(9), 1947 - roč.2(10),1948.
Roč.1(9), 1947 - roč.2(10), 1948 published by
Svaz československých horolezcu.
Continues: Věstnik.

KLUB ALPISTU ČESKOSLOVENSKÝCH
Věstnik = Bulletin. Praha: K.A.C. 25-30cm.
Roč.1, 1934 - roč.4, 1937.
Six issues a year.
Continued by: Horolezec.

KONINKLIJKE NEDERLANDSE ALPEN-VERENIGING
See
NEDERLANDSE ALPEN-VERENIGING

Krasy slovenska. Bratislava: The Journal. 24cm.
Roč.31, 1954 - roč.32, 1955.
Monthly.
Library's holdings are incomplete.

KRYMSKO-KAVKAZSKII GORNYI KLUB
Zapiski... = Bulletin du Club Alpin de Crimée et
du Caucase. Odessa: The Club. 25cm.
No.1, 1898 - 1915.

LADIES'ALPINE CLUB
Journal. The Club. 23cm.
1958 - 1975.
Annual.
Continues: Year book.
Amalgamated with: The Alpine journal.

LADIES' ALPINE CLUB
[Report]. The Club. 19cm.
1922: 1924 - 1926.
Annual.
Continued by: Year book.

LADIES' ALPINE CLUB
[Year book]. The Club. 22cm.
1927 - 1957.
Continues: Report.
Continued by: Journal.

LADIES' SCOTTISH CLIMBING CLUB
Ladies' Scottish Climbing Club journal. Howgate,
Falkirk: The Club. 23cm.
No.1, 1929 - no.5, 1968.
Frequency varies.

LADIES' SKI CLUB
  The Ladies' Ski Club bulletin. The Club.
  No.20, v.2, pt.12, 1950 - 1973.
  Set lacks 1955 - 1958; 1962 - 1968; 1972.

LAKE DISTRICT SKI CLUB
  Lake District ski journal. Kendal: The Club.
  22cm.
  Library has no.1, 1936-37 only.

Lake District ski journal. Kendal: Lake District
  Ski Club. 22cm.
  Library has no.1, 1936-37 only.

LANCASHIRE CAVING AND CLIMBING CLUB
  The journal. Chorley: The Club.
  Vol.1, no.1, 1949 - v.4, no.1, 1968.
  Annual.
  Continues: News bulletin.
  Library's holdings are incomplete.

LANCASHIRE CAVING AND CLIMBING CLUB
  News bulletin. Bolton: The Club. 22cm.
  Vol.1, no.2, [1946?] - v.1, no.3, spring 1947.
  Continued by: The Journal.

LANDESARBEITGEMEINSCHAFT DER ALPINEN VEREINE IN
BAYERN
  Mitteilungen. München: Alpiner Verlag. 30cm.
  1.Jahrg., Heft 1 - Heft 9, 1948.

LEEDS UNIVERSITY UNION CLIMBING CLUB
  Journal. Leeds: The Club. 24cm.
  Library has 1973 only.

Liburnia:rivista trimestrale della Sezione di Fiume
  del Club Alpino Italiano. Fiume: La Sezione.
  26cm.
  Anno 1, 1902 - 12, 1913; v.17, anno 1924 - v.19,
  1926; v.23, 1930.

LIECHTENSTEINER ALPENVEREIN
  Bergheimat: Jahreschrift des Liechtensteiner
  Alpenvereins. Vaduz: L.A.V. 23cm.
  Library has 1965 only.

MAGYAR TERMÉSZETBARÁT SZÖVETSÉG
  Természetbarat. Budapest: M.T.S. 28cm.
  27, 1947 - 30, 1950.

MAGYAR TURISTA EGYESÜLET
  Turisták lapja: folyóirat a turistásag és
  honismeret terjesztésére. Budapest: M.T.E. 25cm.
  1, 1889; 38, 1926 - 42, 1930; 48, 1936.

MAGYAR TURISTA SZÖVETSÉG
  Turistaság es alpinismus. Budapest: Magyar Turista
  Szövetség. 26cm.
  1, 1910/11 - 4, 1914; 22, 1932 - 25, 1935.
  Monthly.
  Also published in German by Karpathenverein as
  Turistik und Alpinismus, 1918 - 1923.

MAGYARORSZAGI KÁRPÁTEGYESÜLET
  Evkönyve = Jahrbuch. Igló: Selbstverlag. 24cm.
  1.Jahrg., 1874 - 44.Jahrg., 1917.
  In Hungarian and German.

MANCHESTER UNIVERSITY MOUNTAINEERING CLUB
  Journal. Manchester: The Club. 27cm.
  1929 - 1966/67.
  Library's holdings are incomplete.

Mazama: a record of mountaineering in the Pacific
  Northwest. Portland (Oregon): Mazamas. 26cm.
  Vol.1, no.1, 1896 -
  Annual.

MAZAMAS (CLUB)
  Mazama: a record of mountaineering in the Pacific
  Northwest. Portland (Oregon): Mazamas. 26cm.
  Vol.1, no.1, 1896 -
  Annual.

MECSEK EGYESÜLET
  A Mecsek-Egyesület évkönyve. Pecsett: Wessely
  & Horvath. 22cm.
  18, 1908 - 22, 1912.

MIDLAND ASSOCIATION OF MOUNTAINEERS
  Bulletin. Birmingham: The Association. 22cm.
  No.1, 1933 - no.6, 1939.
  Annual.
  Continued by: The Journal.

MIDLAND ASSOCIATION OF MOUNTAINEERS
  The journal. Birmingham: The Association. 22cm.
  Vol.2, no.1, 1947 -
  Biennial.
  Continues: Bulletin.

MIDLAND ASSOCIATION OF MOUNTAINEERS
  Reports. Birmingham: The Association. 22cm.
  1922 - 1924.

Montagna: organo del Gruppo Italiano Scrittori di
  Montagna. Torino: Il Gruppo. 26cm.
  Anno 2, 1935 - anno 6, 1939.
  Monthly.

Montagna: rivista mensile di vita alpina. Torino:
  La Rivista. 25cm.
  N.1, gen. - n.6, giugno 1940.

La Montagna: settimanale d'alpinismo. Torino:
  The Journal. 33cm.
  Library has anno 1,1922 only.

Le Montagne della Conca d'Oro. Palermo: La Sezione
  di Palermo del C.A.I. 24cm.
  Library has anno 9, n.1, 1931 only.
  Monthly.

La Montagne & alpinisme. Paris: C.A.F., Groupe de
  Haute Montagne. 24-30cm.
  1ère année, no.1, 1905 -
  Four issues a year.
  Continues: C.A.F. Annuaire and Bulletin.
  Incorporates Alpinisme du G.H.M. 1955 -

Montagne et sports: revue de l'École nationale de
  ski et d'alpinisme. Chamonix: E.N.S.A. 27cm.
  No.1, 1975 -
  Annual.

Montagnes magazine: le mensuel de la montagne.
  Grenoble: Sarl Symbiose. 28cm.
  No.4, 1979 -

MONTAÑA: anales del Centro Excursionista de Cataluña
  See
MUNTANYA

La Montaña: organo de la Federación Argentina de
  Montañismo y Afines. Buenos Aires: F.A.M.A.
  27cm.
  Año 2,no.2, 1960 - no.12, 1969.
  Annual.

MORAY MOUNTAINEERING CLUB
  The Moray Mountaineering Club journal. Elgin:The
  Club. 23cm.
  Vol.1, no.1, 1935 - v.1, no.3, 1950.
  Irregular.

Mount Kenya monthly magazine. Nanyuki: The Magazine. 33cm.
  No.1, 1936 - no.8, 1937.

Mountain. Sheffield: Mountain magazine. 32cm.
  No.1, Jan. 1969 -
  Six issues a year.
  Continues: Mountain craft.
  Nos. 1-26, published by the Youth Hostels
  Association (England and Wales).

Mountain and cave rescue, with lists of official
  teams and posts: the handbook of the Mountain
  Rescue Committee. Buxton (Derbys.): The
  Committee. 18cm.
  1947 -
  Title, size and frequency vary.

MOUNTAIN AND SKI CLUB OF JAPAN
The journal. Tokyo: The Club. 25cm.
No.15, 1922 - no.66, 1926.
Monthly.
In Japanese.

MOUNTAIN CLUB OF EAST AFRICA
The ice-cap, being the journal of the Mountain
Club of East Africa. Moshi: The Club. 26cm.
Library has no.1, 1932 only.

MOUNTAIN CLUB OF EAST AFRICA. Kenya Section
Bulletin. Nairobi: Kenya Section. 25-36cm.
No.1, 1946 - no.10, 1949.
Quarterly.
Continued by: Bulletin of the Mountain Club of
Kenya.

MOUNTAIN CLUB OF KENYA
Bulletin. Nairobi: The Club. 21-25cm..
No.11, June 1949 -
Frequency varies.
Continues: Bulletin of the Mountain Club of East
Africa (Kenya Section).

MOUNTAIN CLUB OF NATAL
Annual. Maritzburg: The Club. 23cm.
No.1, 1920 - no.2, 1922.

MOUNTAIN CLUB OF RHODESIA
Mountain Club of Rhodesia journal. Salisbury:
The Club. 22cm.
Vol.2, 1960 -
Irregular.

MOUNTAIN CLUB OF SOUTH AFRICA
The annual. Cape Town: The Cape Town Section.
25cm.
No.1, 1894 - no.33, 1930.
Continued by: The Journal.

MOUNTAIN CLUB OF SOUTH AFRICA
The journal. Cape Town: Cape Town Section. 23cm.
No.34, 1931 -
Annual.
Continues: The Annual.
Index: v.1 - 71, 1894-1968 (1v.).

MOUNTAIN CLUB OF UGANDA
Mountain Club of Uganda bulletin. Kampala: The
Club. 21cm.
No.6, 1959/60 - no.8, 1961/63.

Mountain craft. Mountaineering Association.
22-34cm.
No.14, 1952; no.18, 1953; no.79, 1968; no.81,
1968.
Continued by: Mountain.

Mountain gazette. Boulder (Colo.): Write-On
Publishing. 37cm.
No.8, April 1973; no.18, 1974 - no.76/7, 1978/79.
Eleven issues a year.
No more published.

Mountain life & rocksport: official magazine of the
British Mountaineering Council. Richmond (Surrey):
The Magazine. 30cm.
No.1, April 1972 - Dec./Jan. 1976.
Six issues a year.
Continues: Mountaineering.
Amalgamated with: Climber & rambler.

Mountain log: FMCI newsletter. Dublin: F.M.C.I.
21cm.
No.1, 1978 -
Quarterly.

Mountain magazine. Pleasantville (N.Y.): Associated
Outdoor Clubs of America, Adirondack Mountain
Club. 27cm.
Vol.6, no.1, 1927 - v.9, no.1, 1931.
Quarterly.

Mountain rescue
 See
Mountain and cave rescue

MOUNTAIN RESCUE COMMITTEE
Mountain and cave rescue, with lists of official
teams and posts: the handbook of the Mountain
Rescue Committee. Buxton (Derbys.): The
Committee. 18cm.
1947 -
Title, size and frequency vary.

MOUNTAIN RESCUE COMMITTEE
News letter. Buxton (Derbys.): The Committee.
23cm.
Library has Dec. 1976 only.

Mountain view: official journal of the Umtali
Mountain and Outdoor Club. Umtali: The Club.
21cm.
Library has 1952 only.

The Mountain world. Allen & Unwin for Swiss Foun-
dation for Alpine Research. 25cm.
1953 - 1968/69.
Annual.
No more published.
English version of Berge der Welt.

Mountain world: climbing, backpacking, skiing,
caving, expeditions and allied activities. Sidcup
(Kent): Stone Industrial Publications. 41cm.
April 1980 -
Monthly.

The Mountaineer. Seattle (Wash.): The Mountaineers.
23-29cm.
Vol.1, no.1, 1907 -
Annual.

Mountaineering: the official journal of the British
Mountaineering Council. 22cm.
Vol.1, June 1947 - v.6, no.5, 1971.
Frequency varies.
Subtitle varies.
Continued by: Mountain life ...

MOUNTAINEERING ASSOCIATION
Mountain craft. The Association. 22-34cm.
No.14, 1952; no.18, 1953; no.79, 1968; no.81,
1968.
Continued by: Mountain.

The Mountaineering journal. Birkenhead: Willmer.
26cm.
Vol.1, no.1, June 1932 - v.6, no.1, Dec. 1937/
Jan., Feb., 1938.
Quarterly.
Vol.1, no.1 published as The British mountain-
eering journal.

MOUNTAINEERS (CLUB)
The mountaineer. Seattle (Wash.): The
Mountaineers. 23-29cm.
Vol.1, no.1, 1907 -
Annual.

Mt. Kenya review. Nanyuki: The Review. 33cm.
Library has no.14, 1932 only.

MT. WHITNEY CLUB
Mt. Whitney Club journal. Visalia (Calif.): The
Club. 26cm.
Vol.1, no.1, 1902 - v.1, no.3, 1904.
Annual.

MULANJE MOUNTAIN CLUB
Mulanje Mountain Club journal. Blantyre: The
Club. 25cm.
Library has 1971 only.

Muntanya. Barcelona: Centre Excursionista de
Catalunya, Club Alpí Català. 24-30cm.
Año 5, num.17, 1952 -
Six issues a year.
Title varies.
Continues: Boletin de la Seccion de Montaña y
C.A.D.E.

NAINI TAL MOUNTAINEERING CLUB
Nanda: news bulletin. Naini Tal: The Club. 29cm.
Vol.1, no.1, 1979 -

NANDA: news bulletin. Naini Tal: The Naini Tal
Mountaineering Club. 29cm.
Vol.1, no.1, 1979 -
Monthly.

NATAL MOUNTAIN CLUB
Annual. Maritzburg: The Club. 24cm.
No.3, 1923 only.

NATIONAL RESEARCH COUNCIL OF CANADA
Canadian journal of earth sciences. Ottawa: The
Council. 26cm.
Vol.3, no.6, 1966; v.6, no.4., 1969.
Six issues a year.

NATIONAL SKI ASSOCIATION OF AMERICA
Year book. Bellows Falls (Vt.): N.S.A.A. 26cm.
Library has 1930 only.

NATIONAL SKI ASSOCIATION OF AMERICA. Eastern
Division
See
UNITED STATES EASTERN AMATEUR SKI ASSOCIATION

NEDERLANDSE ALPEN-VERENIGING
Bergflits: mededelingenblad. The Hague: K.N.A.V.
30cm.
1.Jaarg., nr.1, 1975 -
Six issues a year.

NEDERLANDSE ALPEN-VERENIGING
De berggids: tweemaandelijks tijdschrift. The
Hague: K.N.A.V. 27cm.
1.Jaarg., 1933 - 1935; 35.Jaarg., nr.1, 1967 -
Quarterly.

NEDERLANDSE ALPEN-VERENIGING
Jaarboek. Rotterdam: Nijgh & Ditmar. 25cm.
1911; 1913.

NEDERLANDSE ALPEN-VERENIGING
Mededeelingen. Rotterdam: Nijgh & Ditmar. 25cm.
1.Jaarg., 1903 - 30.Jaarg., 1932.
Two issues a year.

Neue Alpenpost. Zürich: Orell Füssli. 30cm.
Bd.3, 1876 - Bd.16, 1882.

Neue Alpina: eine Schrift der schweizerischen
Naturgeschichte, Alpen- und Landwirthschaft
gewiedmet; hrsg. von Johann Rudolf Steinmüller.
Winterthur: Steiner. 20cm.
Bd.1, 1821 only.

Neutouren. Bern: Schweizer Alpen-Club. 17cm.
1970 -
Annual.
Offprint from Die Alpen.

New climbs. Dublin: Federation of Mountaineering
Clubs of Ireland. 15-22cm.
1973 -
Annual.

NEW ZEALAND. Department of Lands and Survey
Report. Wellington (N.Z.): Government Printer.
34cm.
1892/93 - 1903/04.

NEW ZEALAND ALPINE CLUB
Bulletin. Wellington: N.Z.A.C. 21-28cm.
No.14, 1951 - no.31, 1958; no.47, 1966; no.50,
1967; no.63/4, 1976.
Two issues a year.

NEW ZEALAND ALPINE CLUB
New Zealand alpine journal. Dunedin: The Club.
22-25cm.
Vol.1, no.1, 1892 -
Annual.

New Zealand alpine journal. Dunedin: New Zealand
Alpine Club. 22-25cm.
Vol.1, no.1, 1892 -
Annual.

NIEDERÖSTERREICHISCHER GEBIRGSVEREIN
Der Gebirgsfreund: Zeitschrift. Wien: Der Verein.
29cm.
6.Jahrg., 1895 - 12.Jahrg., 1901.
Monthly.

Norsk fjellsport, utgitt av Norsk Tindeklub. Oslo:
Grøndahl. 25cm.
1914; 1933; 1948; 1958; 1968.

NORSK TINDEKLUB
Norsk fjellsport, utgitt av Norsk Tindeklub.
Oslo: Grøndahl. 25cm.
1914; 1933; 1948; 1958; 1968.

NORSKE TURISTFORENING
Den Norske Turistforenings årbok. Oslo: N.T.
23-25cm.
1869 - 1957.
Indexes: 1868-93 (1v.); 1868 - 1918 (1v.).

NORTH OF ENGLAND SKI CLUB
Year book. Newcastle-on-Tyne: The Club.
Vol.1, no.3, 1912 - v.1, no.4, 1913.
Amalgamated with: British ski year book.

NORWEGIAN CLUB
Year book. The Club. 23cm.
1897 - 1907.

Nos montagnes = Unsere Berge = Le Nostre vette =
Nossas muntagnas: revue du Club Suisse de Femmes
Alpinistes... Zürich: C.S.F.A. 24-29cm.
2e année, no 5, 1921 -
Monthly.
Library's holdings are incomplete.

Le Nostre vette
See
Nos montagnes

NOTTINGHAM UNIVERSITY MOUNTAINEERING CLUB
Journal. Nottingham: The Club. 26cm.
Library has no.6, July 1967 only.

OBSERVATOIRE MÉTÉOROLOGIQUE DU MONT BLANC
Annales ...; publiées sous la direction de J.
Vallot. Paris: G. Steinheil. 29cm.
1893 - 1917.

Österreich in Wort und Bild: Zeitschrift für Fremdenverkehr und Wirtschaft. Wien: Bundesministerium
für Handel und Wiederaufbau. 25cm.
Library has Folge 12/13, 1949 only.

Österreichische Alpenzeitung; hrsg. vom
Österreichischen Alpenklub. Wien: Ö.A.K. 29cm.
1.Jahrg., 1879 -
Six issues a year.

Österreichische Bergsteiger-Zeitung: offizielles
Organ des Österreichischen Kuratoriums für Alpine
Sicherheit. Wien: ABZ-Verlag. 30-54cm.
24.Jahrg., Nr.6, 1946 - 56.Jahrg., 1978.
Monthly.
Continues: Allgemeine Bergsteiger-Zeitung.

Österreichische touristen Zeitung. Wien:
Österreichischer Touristen-Club. 30cm.
Bd.1, 1881 - Jahrg.44, 1924; Jahrg.57, 1937 -
Jahrg.58, 1938; Jahrg.64, 1951.
Frequency varies.

ÖSTERREICHISCHER ALPENKLUB
Österreichische Alpenzeitung. Wien: Ö.A.K. 29cm.
1.Jahrg., 1879 -
Six issues a year.

ÖSTERREICHISCHER ALPENVEREIN
Alpenvereins-Jahrbuch; hrsg. vom Österreichischen
und vom Deutschen Alpenverein. Innsbruck:
OE.A.V.; München: D.A.V. 25cm.
Bd.95, 1970 -
Continues: Jahrbuch des Deutschen Alpenvereins.

ÖSTERREICHISCHER ALPENVEREIN
Berge und Heimat: alpine Monatsschrift; hrsg. vom
Österreichischen Alpenverein in Arbeitsgemeinschaft
mit dem Österreichischen Gebirgsverein und
Österreichischen Touristenklub. Wien: A.
Holzhausen. 25cm.
1.Jahrg., Heft 1, 1946 - 8.Jahrg., Heft 12, 1953.
Amalgamated with: Der Bergsteiger.

ÖSTERREICHISCHER ALPENVEREIN
Der Bergsteiger [und] Berge und Heimat: Organ des
Österreichischen Alpenvereins. München:
Bruckmann. 27-33cm.
L.Jahrg., Nr.1, 1923 -
Monthly.
Incorporates Berge und Heimat from 1954 -

ÖSTERREICHISCHER ALPENVEREIN
Jahrbuch. Innsbruck: Wagner. 26cm.
Bd.74, 1949 - Bd.75, 1950.

ÖSTERREICHISCHER ALPENVEREIN
Mitteilungen. Innsbruck: OE.A.V. 25cm.
1.Jahrg., 1946 -
Six issues a year.
Previously published as: Mittheilungen des
Deutschen und Oesterreichischen Alpenvereins,
1875 - 1938.

ÖSTERREICHISCHER ALPENVEREIN
Mittheilungen. Wien: W. Braumüller. 19cm.
Bd.1, 1863 - Bd.2, 1864.

ÖSTERREICHISCHER ALPENVEREIN.   Sektion
Österreichischer Gebirgsverein
Gebirgsfreund: Mitteilungen. Wien: Ö.A.V. 30cm.
66.Jahrg., 1955 - 72.Jahrg., 1961; 83.Jahrg.,
1972 - 89.Jahrg., 1978.
Six issues a year.
No more published?

ÖSTERREICHISCHER TOURISTEN-CLUB
Alpine Chronik. Wien: Der Club. 23cm.
1.Jahrg., 1880 - 1889.
Annual.

ÖSTERREICHISCHER TOURISTEN-CLUB
Jahrbuch. Wien: Der Club. 22cm.
1, 1869/70 - 12, 1881.

ÖSTERREICHISCHER TOURISTEN-CLUB
Österreichische touristen Zeitung. Wien: Der Club.
30cm.
Bd.1, 1881 - Jahrg.44, 1924; Jahrg.57, 1937 -
Jahrg.58, 1938; Jahrg.64, 1951.
Frequency varies.

ÖSTERREICHISCHER TOURISTEN-CLUB.   Sektion für
Naturkunde
Mittheilungen. Wien: Die Sektion. 29cm.
1.Jahrg., 1889 - 8.Jahrg., 1896.
Monthly.

ÖSTERREICHISCHER TOURISTEN-CLUB.   Sektion
Wiener-Neustadt
Jahres-Bericht. Wiener-Neustadt: Der Club. 24cm.
21, 1899 - 31, 1909.
Library's holdings are incomplete.

ÖSTERREICHISCHES KURATORIUM FÜR ALPINE SICHERHEIT
Für die Sicherheit im Bergland: Jahrbuch; hrsg.
vom Österreichischen Kuratorium für Alpine
Sicherheit. Wien: Das Kuratorium. 20cm.
1972 -

ÖSTERREICHISCHES KURATORIUM FÜR ALPINE SICHERHEIT
Österreichische Bergsteiger-Zeitung. Wien:
ABZ-Verlag. 30-54cm.
24.Jahrg., Nr.6, 1946 - 56.Jahrg., 1978.
Monthly.
Continues: Allgemeine Bergsteiger-Zeitung.

ÖSTERREICHISCHES KURATORIUM FÜR SICHERUNG VOR
BERGGEFAHREN
See
ÖSTERREICHISCHES KURATORIUM FÜR ALPINE SICHERHEIT

Off belay: the mountain magazine. Washington: Off
Belay. 26cm.
No.1, 1972 -
Six issues a year.

Orivassia: revue de l'Association des Alpinistes
Hellènes. Athènes: L'Association. 25cm.
No.1, 1959; no.2, 1966.
Contributions in Greek and French.

Oxford and Cambridge mountaineering. Cambridge:
S.G. Marshall. 23cm.
1921 - 1928/29.
Frequency varies.

Oxford mountaineering: the journal of the Oxford
University Mountaineering Club. Oxford: The Club.
21cm.
1935 -
Frequency varies.

OXFORD UNIVERSITY MOUNTAINEERING CLUB
Oxford and Cambridge mountaineering. Cambridge:
S.G. Marshall. 23cm.
1921 - 1928/29.
Frequency varies.

OXFORD UNIVERSITY MOUNTAINEERING CLUB
Oxford mountaineering: the journal of the Oxford
University Mountaineering Club. Oxford: The Club.
21cm.
1935 -
Frequency varies.

På skidor: årsskrift, utgifven af Föreningen for
Skidlöpningens Främjande i Sverige. Stockholm:
Föreningen. 23cm.
1909 - 1915.

La Paganella: bollettino bimestrale della Società
Paganella. Trento: La Società. 31cm.
Anno 1, 1910 - anno 2, 1911.

Paris-Chamonix. Paris: La Section de Paris-
Chamonix du C.A.F. 28cm.
Avril, 1969 - juin, 1970.
Five issues a year.

Passage: cahiers de l'alpinisme. Paris: F. Lanore.
21cm.
1, 1977 -
Irregular.

Patrie et montagne: bulletin semestriel. Genève:
Société Allobrogia. 24cm.
Vol.1, 1897 - v.26, 1912.
Irregular.
Library's holdings are incomplete.

La Patrie suisse: journal illustré. Genève:
Société suisse de publications illustrées. 30cm.
Vol.30, 1923 - v.33, 1926.
Fortnightly.

Peñalara; revista de alpinismo: organo de la R.
Sociedad Española de Alpinismo. Madrid: S.E.A.
23-28cm.
Núm.1, 1913 -
Frequency varies.
Library's holdings are incomplete.

Petermanns geographische Mitteilungen. Gotha: J.
Perthes. 28cm.
[1], 1855 - 1882.
Monthly.
Title varies: 1855-78: Mittheilungen aus Justus
Perthes' Geographischer Anstalt über Wichtige
neue Erforschungen auf dem Gesammtgebiete der
Geographie. - 1879 - 1937: Dr. A. Petermanns
Mitteilungen...

Der Pilatus: Mitteilungen der Sektion Pilatus des
Schweizer Alpenklub. Luzern: Die Sektion. 24cm.
4.Jahrg., 1926 - 28.Jahrg., Nr.10, 1950.

PINNACLE CLUB
The Pinnacle Club journal. Scunthorpe: The Club.
22cm.
No.1, 1924 -
Frequency varies.

Le Piolet: organe du Piolet-Club de Genève. Genève:
Le Club. 27cm.
1ère année, no 1, 1899 - 6e année, no 5, 1904.
Monthly.

PIOLET CLUB
Le Piolet: organe du Piolet-Club de Genève.
Genève: Le Club. 27cm.
1ère année, no 1, 1899 - 6e année, no 5, 1904.
Monthly.

PLANINSKA ZVEZA SLOVENIJE
Planinski vestnik: glasilo Planinske zveze
slovenije. Ljubljana: The Society. 25cm.
Leto 24, 1924 -
Monthly.
Library's holdings are incomplete.

Planinski vestnik: glasilo Planinske zveze
slovenije. Ljubljana: Planinska zveza slovenije.
25cm.
Leto 24, 1924 -
Monthly.
Library's holdings are incomplete.

Planinski zbornik. Ljubljana: Planinsko drustvo
slovenije. 24cm.
Library has 1945 only.

PLANINSKO DRUŠTVO SLOVENIJE
Planinski zbornik. Ljubljana: Planinsko društvo
slovenije. 24cm.
Library has 1945 only.

Pobezhdennye vershiny. Moskva: Izd. Mysl'. 21cm.
1954 - 1970/71.

Polar news. Tokyo: Japan Polar Research Association.
26cm.
Vol.2, no.1, 3, 1966 -
Two issues a year.
In Japanese, with English list of contents.

The Polar record. Cambridge: Scott Polar Research
Institute. 24cm.
No.1, Jan. 1931 -
Three issues a year.

POLAR RESEARCH CENTER
Antarctic record: reports of the Japanese Ant-
arctic Expedition. Tokyo: Polar Research Center.
26cm.
No.11, 1961 - no.46, 1973.
Three issues a year.
Contributions in Japanese and English.

POLSKI ZWIAZEK ALPINIZMU POSWIECONY SPRAWOM
TATERNICTWA ALPINIZMU I SPELEOLOGII
Taternik. Warszawa: The Society. 24cm.
Rok 1, 1907 -
Library's holdings are incomplete.

POLSKIE TOWARZYSTWO TATRZAŃSKIE
Pamietnik. Krakow: The Society. 23-33cm.
Tom.1, 1876 - t.2, 1877; t.23, 1902 - t.33, 1912.

POLSKIE TOWARZYSTWO TATRZAŃSKIE
Przeglad turystyczny: organ Polskiego Towarzystwa
Tatrzańskiego. Krakow: The Society. 26cm.
Rok 3, 1927 - r.4, 1928.

POLSKIE TOWARZYSTWO TATRZAŃSKIE
Turysta w. Polsce. Krakow: The Society. 36cm.
Rok 1, 1935 - r.2, 1936

POLSKIE TOWARZYSTWO TATRZAŃSKIE
Wierchy: Rocznik poswiecony górom i géralszcznie,
organ Polskiego Tow. Tatrzańskiego. Krakow: The
Society. 28cm.
5, 1927 -
Annual.
Subtitle varies.

Le Prealpi: rivista mensile della Società
Escursionisti Milanesi. Milano: La Società.
26-31cm.
Anno 1, 1902 - anno 34, 1934.
Frequency varies.
Library's holdings are incomplete.

PRESTON MOUNTAINEERING CLUB
Journal. Preston. The Club. 27cm.
Vol.3, 1947/1948 only.

Przeglad turystyczny: organ Polskiego Towarzystwa
Tatrzańskiego. Krakow: The Society. 26cm.
Rok 3, 1927 - r.4, 1928.

PUBLIC SCHOOLS ALPINE SPORTS CLUB
Year book. The Club. 19cm.
1907 - 1930.
Library's holdings are incomplete.

Pyrenaica: anales de la Federación Vasco-Navarra
de Alpinismo. Bilbao: La Federación. 25cm.
Vol.1, num.1, 1926 - v.5, num.16, 1930.
Quarterly.

Rassegna alpina due. Milano: La Rassegna. 30cm.
N.2, 1968 - n.43, 1974.
Irregular.
Library's holdings are incomplete.

Rassegna di alpinismo. Firenze: F.C. di Muricce.
24cm.
Library has anno 2, 1880 only.
Irregular.

Revista andina: organo oficial de la Federación de
Ski y Andinismo de Chile. Santiago: Club Andino
de Chile. 27cm.
Año 10, no.56, 1947 -
Frequency varies.

Revista peruana de andinismo y glaciología: organo
oficial del Club Andinista Cordillera Blanca de
Huaraz. Huaraz: El Club. 22cm.
Año 4, no.2, 1954/55 -
Frequency varies.
Title varies: años 4 - 14, 1954/55 - 1964/65:
Revista peruana de andinismo.

Revue alpine. Lyon: Club Alpin Français, Section
lyonnaise. 23-28cm.
No 1, nov.-déc. 1894 -
Quarterly.
Continues: Bulletin.

Revue alpine: bulletin du Club Alpin Belge.
Bruxelles: C.A.B. 26cm.
T.8, nos.23/24, 1931 - t.10, 1933.
- - 3e sér. T.1, 1934.
Two issues a year.
Continues: Bulletin du C.A.B., 2e sér.
Continued by: Revue d'alpinisme.

Revue d'alpinisme; éditée par le Club Alpin Belge.
Bruxelles: C.A.B. 26cm.
T.1, no 1, 1935 - 5e sér., t.7, 1954/55.
Annual.
Continues: Revue alpine: bulletin du C.A.B.
Continued by: Bulletin trimestriel [nouv. sér.].

Revue de géographie alpine. Grenoble: L'Institut
de géographie alpine (Université de Grenoble).
26cm.
T.11, fasc.2, 1923 - t.17, 1929; t.26, fasc.4,
1938 - t.28, 1940.
Quarterly.

Revue des Alpes dauphinoises: bulletin mensuel.
Grenoble: Société des alpinistes dauphinoises.
25cm.
1ère année, 1898/1899 - 16e année, 1913/1914.

Revue montagnarde: organe du Club ascensionniste
grenoblois. Grenoble: Le Club. 25cm.
1ère année, 1906 - 6e année, no 23, 1911.
Quarterly.
Continues: L'Ascensionniste grenoblois.

Revue pyrénéenne: revue trimestrielle des sections
pyrénéennes du C.A.F. Bordeaux: Les Sections.
22-30cm.
No 87, avril 1954 -

Rimmon journal. Oldham: Rimmon Mountaineering Club.
26cm.
Library has v.1, no.1, Dec. 1962 only.

RIMMON MOUNTAINEERING CLUB
Rimmon journal. Oldham: The Club. 26cm.
Library has v.1, no.1, Dec. 1962 only.

Rivista della montagna: trimestrale del Centro
Documentazione Alpina. Torino: C.D.A. 24cm.
Anno 4, n.11, 1973 - n.15, 1974; anno 8, n.27,
1977.

Roca y nieve: organo del montañismo en Mexico.
Mexico City: D.F. 24cm.
Año 1, nos.1-5, 1938.
Frequency varies.

Rock. Brighton (Vict.): Victorian Climbing Club.
30cm.
No.1, 1978 -
Annual.

Rocksport. Nottingham: P. Grainger. 30cm.
Oct./Nov. 1969 - April/May 1972.
Six issues a year.
Library's holdings are incomplete.

Rope: the official journal of the Gloucestershire
Mountaineering Club. Cheltenham: The Club. 20cm.
Library has v.1, no.1, 1957 only.

ROYAL GEOGRAPHICAL SOCIETY
The Geographical journal. R.G.S. 25cm.
Vol.1, 1893-
Three issues a year.
Indexes: v.1-20, 1893-1902 (1v.); v.21-40,
1903-1912 (1v.); v.41-60, 1913-1922 (1v.);
v.61-80, 1923-1932 (1v.); v.81-100, 1933-
1942 (1v.); v.101-120, 1943-1954 (1v.)

ROYAL GEOGRAPHICAL SOCIETY
Proceedings of the Royal Geographical Society and
monthly record of geography. New ser. R.G.S.
25cm.
Vol.1, 1879 - v.11, 1889.

ROYAL NAVY SKI AND MOUNTAINEERING CLUB
Year book. The Club. 22cm.
1961/62 - 1962/63.

ROYAL SCOTTISH GEOGRAPHICAL SOCIETY
The Scottish geographical magazine. Edinburgh:
The Society. 26cm.
Vol.1, 1885 - v.20, 1904.
Monthly.

RUCKSACK CLUB
Report. Manchester: The Club. 24cm.
1st, 1903 - 3rd, 1905.
Annual.
Continued by: The Rucksack Club journal.

RUCKSACK CLUB
The Rucksack Club journal. Manchester: The Club.
22cm.
Vol.1, no.1, 1907 -
Annual.
Continues: Report.

Rucksack magazine. Waverton (N.S.W.): The Magazine.
24cm.
March 1966; March 1968.

RUSSKOE GORNOE OBSHCHESTVO
Biulleten'. Moskva: The Society. 23cm.
No.1, 1911 - no.15, 1915.
Quarterly.

RUSSKOE GORNOE OBSHCHESTVO
Ezhegodnik. Moskva: The Society. 27cm.
1, 1901 - 12, 1912.

Sangaku: the journal of the Japanese Alpine Club.
Tokyo: The Club. 22-27cm.
Vol.1, 1906 -
Annual.
In Japanese.

Sari: rivista mensile. Torino: La Sezione di
Torino e Gruppo S.A.R.I. del C.A.I. 26cm.
Anno 2, n.8, 1909 - anno 4, 1911; anno 7, 1914.

SBORNIK SOVETSKOGO AL'PINIZMA
Pobezhdennye vershiny. Moskva: Izd. Mysl'. 21cm.
1954 - 1970/71.

Das Schnee Huhn: Korrespondenzblatt der
"Schneehühner", offizielles Organ des Ski-Club
Luzern. Luzern: G. Speck-Jost. 25-29cm.
1904 - 1907.
Irregular.

Der Schneehase: Jahrbuch des Schweizerischen
Akademischen Ski-Club. Zürich: S.A.S. 26-30cm.
Bd.1, No.1, 1924/27 - Bd.5, No.19, 1947; Nr.30,
1972/74.

Schweiz = Suisse = Svizzera = Switzerland. Foreign
ed. Zürich: Swiss National Tourist Office,
Schweizerische Verkehrszentrale. 31cm.
1965, Nr.1 -
Two issues a year.

SCHWEIZER ALPEN-CLUB
Les Alpes = Le Alpi = Las Alps = Die Alpen:
bulletin mensuel. Berne: C.A.S. 25cm.
33e année, no 7, 1957 -

SCHWEIZER ALPEN-CLUB
Les Alpes = Le Alpi= Las Alps = Die Alpen: revue.
Berne: C.A.S. 27cm.
T.1, no 1, 1925 -
Quarterly.
Title varies: T.1 - t.33, 1925 - 1957: Die Alpen =
Les Alpes = Le Alpi...
Continues: Jahrbuch des S.A.C. and Echo des Alpes.
Index: Table générale des matières: t.1-18,
1925-42 (1v.).

SCHWEIZER ALPEN-CLUB
Alpina: Mitteilungen. Zürich: Orell Füssli. 32cm.
1.Jahrg., 1893 - 32.Jahrg., 1924.
No more published.

SCHWEIZER ALPEN-CLUB
Annuaire. Bâle: H. Georg. 18-20cm.
1867/68 - 1868/69.

SCHWEIZER ALPEN-CLUB
L'Echo des Alpes: organe du Club Alpin Suisse pour
les sections de langue française. Genève:
Jullien. 23cm.
1ère année, 1865 - 60e année, 1924.
Monthly.
Continued by: Les Alpes ...: revue.
Indexes: v.1-25, 1865 - 1889 (1v.); v.26-60,
1890 - 1924 (2v. in 1).

SCHWEIZER ALPEN-CLUB
Jahrbuch. Bern: S.A.C. 19-27cm.
1.Jahrg., 1864 - 58.Jahrg., 1923.
Continued by: Les Alpes ...: revue.
Indexes: Repertorium und Ortsregister, v.1-20,
1864 - 1884/85 (1v.); v.21-44, 1885/86 - 1908/09
(1v.).

SCHWEIZER ALPEN-CLUB
Jahresversammlung. St. Gallen: S.A.C. 24cm.
4, 1866 - 15, 1879.
Library's holdings are incomplete.

SCHWEIZER ALPEN-CLUB
  Mitglieder-Verzeichniss. Bern: S.A.C. 24cm.
  1865 - 1892.
  Irregular.

SCHWEIZER ALPEN-CLUB
  Neutouren. Bern: S.A.C. 17cm.
  1970 -
  Annual.
  Offprint from Die Alpen.

SCHWEIZER ALPEN-CLUB
  Schweizer Alpen-Zeitung: Organ für die deutschen
  Sectionen des Schweizer Alpenclubs sowie für alle
  Freunde der Alpenwelt. Zürich: F. Schulthess.
  24cm.
  1.Jahrg., No.1, 1882 - 11.Jahrg., No.24, 1893.
  Fortnightly.

SCHWEIZER ALPEN-CLUB. Sektion Basel
  Jahresbericht. Basel: Die Sektion. 24cm.
  43, 1905 -

SCHWEIZER ALPEN-CLUB. Sektion Bern
  Jahresbericht. Bern: Die Sektion. 24cm.
  1911 - 1913.

SCHWEIZER ALPEN-CLUB. Sektion Geneva
  Bulletin. Genève: La Section. 24cm.
  1ère année, 1925 - 2e année, 1926.
  Monthly.

SCHWEIZER ALPEN-CLUB. Sektion La Chaux-de-Fonds
  Bulletin. La Chaux-de-Fonds: La Section. 22cm.
  No 1, 1892 - no 39, 1931; no 43, 1937.

SCHWEIZER ALPEN-CLUB. Sektion La Chaux-de-Fonds
  Rapport annuel. La Chaux-de-Fonds: La Section.
  20cm.
  1930 - 1936; 1938 - 1948.
  Library's holdings are incomplete.

SCHWEIZER ALPEN-CLUB. Sektion Moléson
  Bulletin mensuel. Fribourg: La Section. 25cm.
  1ère année, no 8, 1927 - 13e année, no 11, 1939.

SCHWEIZER ALPEN-CLUB. Sektion Monte-Rosa
  La cordée: bulletin mensuel. Sion: La Section.
  26cm.
  1ère année, no 4, 1926 - 6e année, 1931.

SCHWEIZER ALPEN-CLUB. Sektion Pilatus
  Der Pilatus: Mitteilungen. Luzern: Die Sektion.
  24cm.
  4.Jahrg., 1926 - 28.Jahrg., Nr.10, 1950.

SCHWEIZER ALPEN-CLUB. Sektion St. Gallen
  Club Nachrichten. St. Gallen: Die Sektion. 24cm.
  1.Jahrg., 1929 - 32.Jahrg., Nr.6, 1960.

SCHWEIZER ALPEN-CLUB. Sektion St. Gallen
  Jahresbericht. St. Gallen: Die Sektion. 24cm.
  58/59, 1921/22 - 65, 1927.

SCHWEIZER ALPEN-CLUB. Sektion Uto
  Der Uto: Nachrichten. Zürich: Die Sektion. 24cm.
  5.Jahrg., 1927 - 8.Jahrg., 1930.
  Monthly.

SCHWEIZER ALPEN-CLUB. Sektion Weissenstein
  Jahresbericht. Solothurn: Die Sektion. 24cm.
  18, 1904 - 23, 1909.

Schweizer Alpen-Zeitung: Organ für die deutschen
  Sectionen des Schweizer Alpenclubs sowie für alle
  Freunde der Alpenwelt. Zürich: F. Schulthess.
  24cm.
  1.Jahrg., No.1, 1882 - 11.Jahrg., No.24, 1893.
  Fortnightly.

Schweizerische jugendbücherei für Naturschutz.
  Basel: B. Schwabe. 21cm.
  Nos. 1, 8 - 13, [1919].

SCHWEIZERISCHE NATURSCHUTZKOMMISSION and
SCHWEIZERISCHER BUND FÜR NATURSCHUTZ
  Jahresbericht. Basel: Selbstverlag. 25cm.
  6, 1911/12 - 7, 1913/14.

SCHWEIZERISCHE STIFTUNG FÜR ALPINE FORSCHUNGEN
  Berge der Welt; hrsg. von der Schweiz. Stiftung
  für Alpine Forschungen. Zürich: Büchergilde
  Gutenberg. 25cm.
  Bd.1, 1946 - Bd.12, 1958/59.
  Annual.
  No more published.
  Original version of Mountain world.
  Index: Bde.1 - 17, 1946 - 1968/69 (1v.).

SCHWEIZERISCHE STIFTUNG FÜR ALPINE FORSCHUNGEN
  Journal. Zürich: Swiss Foundation for Alpine
  Research. 24cm.
  Vol.1, Nr.1, 1953 - V.4, Nr.11, 1962.

SCHWEIZERISCHE STIFTUNG FÜR ALPINE FORSCHUNGEN
  The mountain world. Allen & Unwin for Swiss
  Foundation for Alpine Research. 25cm.
  1953 - 1968/69.
  Annual.
  No more published.
  English version of Berge der Welt.

SCHWEIZERISCHE VEREINIGUNG FÜR HEIMATSCHUTZ
  Heimatschutz: Zeitschrift. Bümpliz: A. Benteli.
  26-32cm.
  Jahrg.1, 1906 - Jahrg.12, 1917.
  Monthly.

SCHWEIZERISCHE VERKEHRSZENTRALE
  Schweiz = Suisse = Svizzera = Switzerland.
  Zürich: Swiss National Tourist Office,
  Schweizerische Verkehrszentrale. 31cm.
  1965, Nr.1 -
  Two issues a year.

SCHWEIZERISCHE VERKEHRSZENTRALE
  Swiss tourist almanac. Zürich: Swiss Tourist
  Information Office. 21cm.
  Library has Winter season, 1921/22 only.
  Annual.

SCHWEIZERISCHE VERKEHRSZENTRALE
  Switzerland news. Swiss National Tourist Office.
  30cm.
  Thirteen issues a year.
  Library retains current year only.

SCHWEIZERISCHER AKADEMISCHER SKI-CLUB
  Der Schneehase: Jahrbuch. Zürich: S.A.S. 26-30cm.
  Bd.1, No.1, 1924/27 - Bd.5, No.19, 1947; Nr.30,
  1972/74.

SCHWEIZERISCHER FRAUEN-ALPEN-CLUB
  Nos montagnes = Unsere Berge = Le nostre vette =
  Nossas muntagnas: revue du Club Suisse de Femmes
  Alpinistes... Zürich: C.S.F.A. 24-29cm.
  2e année, no.5, 1921 -
  Monthly.
  Library's holdings are incomplete.

SCHWEIZERISCHER SKI-VERBAND
  Ski: illustriertes offizielles Organ des
  Schweizerischen Ski-Verbandes. Basel: H.A. Tanner.
  24cm.
  1.Jahrg., 1904/05 - 3.Jahrg., 1906/07.
  - - Beilage: Allgemeines Korrespondenzblatt...
  2.Jahrg., 1904/05 - 4.Jahrg., 1906/07.
  - - Alpiner Wintersport: Zeitschrift...
  2.Jahrg., 1904/05 - 4.Jahrg., 1906/07.
  Continued by: Ski: Jahrbuch...

SCHWEIZERISCHER SKI-VERBAND
  Ski: Jahrbuch. Bern: Selbstverlag. 23cm.
  6.Jahrg., 1910 - 18.Jahrg., 1923.
  Continues: Ski: illustriertes offizielles Organ...

SCOTT POLAR RESEARCH INSTITUTE
  The polar record. Cambridge: Scott Polar Research
  Institute. 24cm.
  No.1, Jan. 1931 -
  Three issues a year.

The Scottish geographical magazine. Edinburgh:
  Royal Scottish Geographical Society. 26cm.
  Vol.1, 1885 - v.20, 1904.
  Monthly.

SCOTTISH GEOGRAPHICAL SOCIETY
See
ROYAL SCOTTISH GEOGRAPHICAL SOCIETY

The Scottish Mountaineering Club journal. Edinburgh:
The Club. 23cm.
Vol.1, no.1, 1890 -
Annual. Indexes: v.1 - 10, 1890 - 1909 (1v.);
v.11 - 20, 1910 - 35 (1v.).
SCOTTISH SKI CLUB
Circular. Edinburgh: The Club. 25cm.
No.1, 1907 - no.2, 1908.
Annual.
Continued by: Scottish Ski Club magazine.

SCOTTISH SKI CLUB
Magazine. Edinburgh: The Club. 25cm.
Vol.1, no.1, 1909 - v.2, no.2, 1915.
Annual.
Continues: Scottish Ski Club circular.
Continued by: Scottish Ski Club journal.

SCOTTISH SKI CLUB
Scottish Ski Club journal. Glasgow: The Club.
20-22cm.
Vol.2, pt.1, 1930 - v.5, pt.5, 1950/51.
Annual.
Continues: Scottish Ski Club magazine.
Library's holdings are incomplete.

SHEFFIELD UNIVERSITY MOUNTAINEERING CLUB
Journal. Sheffield: The Club. 21cm.
Library has Dec. 1955 only.

Sicula: rivista trimestrale. Palermo: Club Alpino
Siciliano. 25-36cm.
Anno 1, 1896 - anno 16, 1925/26.

SIEBENBÜRGISCHE KARPATHENVEREIN
Jahrbuch. Hermannstadt: Selbstverlag. 25cm.
1.Jahrg., 1881 - 32.Jahrg., 1912.
Library's holdings are incomplete.

SIERRA CLUB
Ascent: Sierra Club mountaineering journal. San
Francisco: The Club. 28cm.
Vol.1, no.1, 1967 -
Annual.

SIERRA CLUB
The Sierra Club bulletin. San Francisco: The Club:
25-28cm.
Vol.1, no.1, Jan. 1893 -
Frequency varies.

Ski: illustriertes offizielles Organ des
Schweizerischen Ski-Verbandes. Basel: H.A.Tanner.
24cm.
1.Jahrg., 1904/05 - 3.Jahrg., 1906/07.
- - Beilage: Allgemeines Korrespondenzblatt...
2.Jahrg., 1904/05 - 4.Jahrg., 1906/07.
- - Alpiner Wintersport: Zeitschrift...
2.Jahrg., 1904/05 - 4.Jahrg., 1906/07.
Continued by: Ski: Jahrbuch...

Ski: Jahrbuch des Schweiz. Ski-Verbandes. Bern:
Selbstverlag. 23cm.
6.Jahrg., 1910 - 18.Jahrg., 1923.
Continues: Ski: illustriertes offizielles Organ...

Ski-Chronik: Jahrbuch des Mitteleuropäischen Ski-
Verbandes. Karlsruhe: Verlag Ski-Verbandes.
23cm.
1.Jahrg., 1908/09 - 4.Jahrg., 1912.

SKI-CLUB ACADÉMIQUE SUISSE
See
SCHWEIZERISCHER AKADEMISCHER SKI-CLUB

SKI-CLUB BERN
Alpina Wintersport: illustriertes officielles und
obligatorisches Organ. Thun: S.C.B. 33cm.
Nr.1, 1903 - Nr.16, 1904.
Issued weekly during the season.

SKI-CLUB LUZERN
Das Schnee Huhn: Korrespondenzblatt. Luzern: G.
Speck-Jost. 25-29cm.
1904 - 1907.
Irregular.

SKI CLUB OF GREAT BRITAIN
British ski year book; editor Sir Arnold Lunn.
Pitman for Ski Club of G.B. and Alpine Ski Club.
22cm.
Vol.1, 1920 - v.23, 1971.
Amalgamated with Ski notes and queries to produce
Ski survey.

SKI CLUB OF GREAT BRITAIN
Notices. The Club. 22cm.
Autumn 1958 - autumn 1959.

SKI CLUB OF GREAT BRITAIN
Ski notes and queries. The Club. 23-28cm.
Vol.3, no.32, 1927 - v.28 (8), no.141, 1970.
Three issues a year.
Amalgamated with British ski year book to produce
Ski survey.

SKI CLUB OF GREAT BRITAIN
Ski survey. The Club. 30cm.
Vol.1, no.1, Sept. 1972 -
Five issues a year.
Continues: British ski year book, Ski notes and
queries, The Alpine Ski Club annual.
Library's holdings are incomplete.

SKI CLUB OF GREAT BRITAIN
Year-book of the Ski Club of Great Britain and the
National Ski Union. The Clubs. 25cm.
Vol.1, no.1, 1905 - v.2, no.8, 1912.
Annual.
Vol.1 - v.2, no.7, published by Ski Club of Great
Britain only.
Amalgamated with: British ski year book.

Ski en montagnes de France: revue annuelle des
sports d'hiver ... du Comité des stations
françaises de sports d'hiver. Paris: Le Comité.
31cm.
Library has 1947 - 1948 only.

SKI-KLUB SALZBURG
Jahrbuch. München: D.A.Z. 23cm.
Library has 1912 only.

Ski notes and queries. Ski Club of Great Britain.
23-28cm.
Vol.3, no.32, 1927 - v.28 (8), no.141, 1970.
Three issues a year.
Amalgamated with British ski year book to produce
Ski survey.

Ski-sports d'hiver: revue mensuelle illustrée.
Paris: A. Saint Jacques. 28cm.
T.1, 1931/32 - t.4, no.61, 1939.

Ski survey. Ski Club of Great Britain. 30cm.
Vol.1, no.1, Sept. 1972 -
Five issues a year
Continues: British ski year book, Ski notes and
queries, The Alpine Ski Club annual.
Library's holdings are incomplete.

SKIDFRÄMJANDET
See
FÖRENINGEN FÖR SKIDLÖPNINGENS FRÄMJANDE I SVERIGE

Skiing: the review of the British Ski Association.
H. Marshall. 23cm.
Vol.1, no.1, 1912 - v.1, no.2, 1913.
Amalgamated with: British ski year book.

Snaplink: Wellingborough Mountaineering Club journal.
Wellingborough: The Club. 27cm.
Library has winter/spring 1966 only.

SOCIEDAD ESPAÑOLA DE ALPINISMO
Penalara: revista de alpinismo: organo de la R.
Sociedad Española de Alpinismo. Madrid: S.E.A.
23-28cm.
Núm.1, 1913 -
Frequency varies.
Library's holdings are incomplete.

SOCIETÀ ALPINA DEL TRENTINO
See
SOCIETÀ ALPINISTI TRIDENTINI

SOCIETÀ ALPINA DELLE GIULIE
  Alpi Giulie: rassegna. Trieste: La Società.
  24cm.
  Anno 1, 1896 - anno 63, 1968.
  Frequency varies.
  Library's holdings are incomplete.

SOCIETÀ ALPINA FRIULANA
  Cronaca. Udine: La Società. 20cm.
  Library has anno 1, 1881 only.

SOCIETÀ ALPINA FRIULANA
  In alto: cronaca semestrale della Società Alpina
  Friulana Sez. di Udine del Club Alpino Italiano.
  Udine: La Società. 24-33cm.
  Anno 1, 1890 - anno 38, 1927; anno 40, 1929 -
  anno 41/42, 1930/31.
  Irregular.

SOCIETÀ ALPINA MERIDIONALE
  Bollettino trimestrale. Napoli: La Società. 26cm.
  Anno 1, 1893 - anno 6, 1898.
  Continued by: L'Appennino meridionale ... del
  C.A.I., Sezione di Napoli.

SOCIETÀ ALPINISTI TRIDENTINI
  Annuario. Trento: La Società. 19-21cm.
  1874 - 1877; 1880/81 - 1903/04.
  From 1874 - 1877, published by Società Alpina del
  Trentino.

SOCIETÀ ALPINISTI TRIDENTINI
  Bollettino. Trento: La Società. 25cm.
  Anno 17, 1954 - anno 21, n.1-2, 1958; anno 28,
  n.4, 1965.
  Frequency varies.

SOCIETÀ ALPINISTI TRIDENTINI
  Bollettino dell'alpinista: rivista bimestrale.
  Trento: La Società. 24-36cm.
  Anno 1, 1904/05; anno 3, 1906 - anno 13, 1922.

SOCIETÀ ALPINISTI TRIESTINI
  Atti e memorie. Trieste: La Società. 24cm.
  1883/1885 - 1887/92.
  Irregular.

SOCIETÀ DEGLI ALPINISTI TRIDENTINI
  See
SOCIETÀ ALPINISTI TRIDENTINI

SOCIETÀ ESCURSIONISTI MILANESI
  Le prealpi: rivista mensile. Milano: La Società.
  26-31cm.
  Anno 1, 1902 - anno 34, 1934.
  Frequency varies.
  Library's holdings are incomplete.

SOCIETÀ PAGANELLA
  La Paganella: bollettino bimestrale. Trento: La
  Società. 31cm.
  Anno 1, 1910 - anno 2, 1911.

SOCIETÀ RODODENDRO
  Bollettino. Trento: La Società. 31cm.
  Anno 1, 1904 - anno 5, 1908.
  Irregular.

SOCIÉTÉ ALLOBROGIA
  Patrie et montagne: bulletin semestriel. Genève:
  La Société. 24cm.
  Vol.1, 1897 - v.26, 1912.
  Irregular.
  Library's holdings are incomplete.

SOCIÉTÉ DE GÉOGRAPHIE
  Acta geographica. Paris: La Société. 24cm.
  No 3, 1947 - no 78, 1969; 33 sér., no 1, 1970 -
  Frequency varies.
  Library's holdings are incomplete.

SOCIÉTÉ DE GÉOGRAPHIE
  Annales de géographie: bulletin. Paris: Colin.
  26cm.
  T.50, 1941 - t.55, 1946.
  Quarterly.
  Library's holdings are incomplete.

SOCIÉTÉ DE GÉOGRAPHIE
  Bulletin. 7e sér. Paris: La Société. 23cm.
  T.9, 1888 - t.20, 1899.
  Annual.

SOCIÉTÉ DE GÉOGRAPHIE
  Compte rendu des séances. Paris: La Société.
  24cm.
  1888 - 1899.
  Monthly.

SOCIÉTÉ DE GÉOGRAPHIE
  La géographie: bulletin de la Société. Paris:
  Masson. 29cm.
  T.1, 1900 - t.29, 1914.
  Annual.

SOCIÉTÉ DE SPÉLÉOLOGIE
  Mémoires. Paris: La Société. 26cm.
  T.1, 1896/97 - t.4, no 24, 1900.
  Irregular.
  Amalgamated with: Spelunca.

SOCIÉTÉ DE SPÉLÉOLOGIE
  Spelunca: bulletin [et mémoires] de la Société.
  Paris: La Société. 25cm.
  1ère année, 1895 - t.9, 1913.
  Quarterly.
  Contains Mémoires from 1901.

SOCIÉTÉ DES ALPINISTES DAUPHINOIS
  Annuaire. Grenoble: La Société. 23cm.
  1892 - 1897.
  Issue for 1892, published by Société des
  alpinistes grenoblois.

SOCIÉTÉ DES ALPINISTES DAUPHINOIS
  Revue des Alpes dauphinoises: bulletin mensuel.
  Grenoble: La Société. 25cm.
  1ère année, 1898/1899 - 16e année, 1913/1914.

SOCIÉTÉ DES ALPINISTES GRENOBLOIS
  See
SOCIÉTÉ DES ALPINISTES DAUPHINOIS

SOCIÉTÉ DES EXCURSIONNISTES MARSEILLAIS
  Bulletin annuel. Marseille: La Société. 22cm.
  3e année, 1899 - 13e année, 1909.
  Library's holdings are incomplete.

SOCIÉTÉ DES GRIMPEURS DES ALPES
  Annuaire. Grenoble: La Société. 25cm.
  1927 - 1928.

SOCIÉTÉ DES TOURISTES DU DAUPHINÉ
  Annuaire. Grenoble: La Société. 26cm.
  No 1, 1875 - t.48, 1950.
  Index: v.1 - 20, 1875-94 (1v.)

SOCIÉTÉ RAMOND
  Explorations pyrénéennes: bulletin trimestriel.
  Bagnères-de-Bigorre: La Société. 24-26cm.
  No 1, 1866 - 51e année, 1916; 64e & 65e années,
  1929/30.
  Index: Table générale, 1866 - 1915 (1v.).

Spelunca: bulletin [et mémoires] de la Société de
  spéléologie. Paris: La Société. 25cm.
  1ère année, 1895 - t.9, 1913.
  Quarterly.
  Contains Mémoires from 1901.

Les sports d'hiver en Suisse: annuaire de la Suisse
  hivernale. Neuchatel: Attinger. 20cm.
  1906/07; [1908/09].

Les Sports d'hiver et l'alpinisme: organe des sports
  de glace, de neige et de montagne. Paris: L.
  Magnus. 33cm.
  Library has 4e année, 1911/12 only.
  Weekly, October - March.
  Fortnightly, April - September.

STEIRISCHER GEBIRGSVEREIN
  Jahrbuch. Graz: S.G.V. 22-24cm.
  1873 - 1908.

SVAZ ČESKOSLOVENSKÝCH HOROLEZCŮ
Horolezec: vestnik Svazu československých
horolezců. Praha: S.C.H. 24cm.
Roč.5, 1938; roč.1 (9), 1947 - roč.2 (10), 1948.
Roc.5, 1938, published by Klub alpistů
československých.

SVAZ LYŽAŘU REPUBLIKY ČESKOSLOVENSKÉ
Zimní sport: orgán Svazu lyžařů republiky
československé. Praha: S.L. 31cm.
Library has roč.23, 1933/34 only.

Svensk skidkalender; utgiven av Föreningen för
Skidlöpningens Främjande i Sverige (Skidfrämjandet).
Stockholm: F.S.F.S. 20cm.
Library has 4. årgången, 1935 only.

Svensk turistkalender; utgiven av Svenska Turistföreningen. Stockholm: S.T.F. 19cm.
1929 - 1936; 1938 - 1939.

SVENSKA FJÄLLKLUBBEN
Till fjälls: Svenska Fjällklubbens årsbok.
Stockholm: S.F. 24-26cm.
1929 -

SVENSKA TURISTFÖRENINGEN
Svensk turistkalender; utgiven av Svenska Turistföreningen. Stockholm: S.T.F. 19cm.
1929 - 1936; 1938 - 1939.

SVENSKA TURISTFÖRENINGEN
Svenska Turistföreningens årsskrift. Stockholm:
S.T.F. 22cm.
1889 - 1940.

SVENSKA TURISTFÖRENINGEN
Svenska Turistföreningens tidning. Stockholm:
S.T.F. 29cm.
Årg.1, 1933 - Årg.26, 1958.
Six issues a year.

SVENSKA TURISTFÖRENINGEN
Turist: Svenska Turistföreningens tidning.
Stockholm: S.T.F. 29cm.
Årg.39, nr.6, 1971 -
Six issues a year.
Library's holdings are incomplete.

The Swiss advertiser: fortnightly review for the
furtherance of English travellers' interests in
Switzerland. 35cm.
Vol.1, no.1 - no.24, 1904.

SWISS NATIONAL TOURIST OFFICE
See
SCHWEIZERISCHE VERKEHRSZENTRALE

Swiss tourist almanac. Zurich: Swiss Tourist Infor-
mation Office. 21cm.
Library has Winter season, 1921/22 only.
Annual.

SWISS TOURIST INFORMATION OFFICE
See
SCHWEIZERISCHE VERKEHRSZENTRALE

SWITZERLAND. Eidgenössische Postverwaltung
See
SWITZERLAND. Post-, Telegraphen- und Telephon-
verwaltung

SWITZERLAND. Post-, Telegraphen- und Telephon-
verwaltung
Das Alpenbuch des Eidg. Postverwaltung. Bern:
Schweiz. Oberpostdirektion. 25cm.
Bd.1, [1929] - Bd.5, 1937.
Irregular.

Switzerland news. Swiss National Tourist Office.
30cm.
Thirteen issues a year.
Library retains current issue only.

Tararua. Wellington (N.Z.): Tararua Tramping Club.
22-28cm.
No.1, 1947 -
Annual.
Library's holdings are incomplete.

The Tararua tramper. Wellington (N.Z.): Tararua
Tramping Club. 21cm.
Vol.42, no.9, 1970 -
Monthly.

TARARUA TRAMPING CLUB
Tararua. Wellington (N.Z.): The Club. 22-28cm.
No.1, 1947 -
Annual.
Library's holdings are incomplete.

TARARUA TRAMPING CLUB
The Tararua tramper. Wellington (N.Z.): The Club.
21cm.
Vol.42, no.9, 1970 -
Monthly.

Taternik: organ Polskiego zwiazku alpinizmu
poswiecony sprawom taternictwa alpinizmu i
speleologii. Warszawa: The Society. 24cm.
Rok 1, 1907 -
Library's holdings are incomplete.

Természetbarát. Budapest: Magyar Termeszetbarát
szövetség. 28cm.
27, 1947 - 30, 1950.

Thrutch: The Australasian climbing magazine.
Annandale (N.S.W.): The Magazine. 25-27cm.
Vol.4, no.7, 1967 -
Quarterly.

Till fjälls: Svenska Fjällklubbens årsbok.
Stockholm: S.F. 24-26cm.
1929 -

Tiroler Wintersport. Innsbruck: Landesverkehrsrat.
32cm.
Library has 2.Jahrg., 1912-1913 only.
Weekly.

To vouno: édition bimestrielle. Athènes: Club Alpin
Hellénique. 25cm.
1, 1934 - 222, 1961.

TOURING CLUB ITALIANO. Commissione di turismo
invernale
Annuario di turismo e sports invernali. Milano:
Touring Club Italiano. 16cm.
Library has 1, 1911 only.

Der Tourist: illustrierte Zeitschrift zur Förderung
des Fremdenverkehrs in Deutschland; offizielles
Organ des Verbandes Deutscher Touristen und
Gebirgsvereine. Berlin: Der Tourist. 28cm.
Jahrg.14, 1897 - Jahrg.16, 1899.

Der Tourist: Organ für Natur- und Alpenfreunde;
redigirt von Gustav Jäger. Wien: W. Jäger.
22-32cm.
Jahrg.1, 1869 - Jahrg.23, 1891.

Il Tourista: bollettino trimestrale. Trieste: Club
Touristi Triestini. 25-31cm.
Annata 1, 1894 - anno 10, 1903.

Tourista: revue pratique de voyages. Paris: The
Journal. 32cm.
Library has 1903 only.
Fortnightly.

Touristische Blätter: Rundschau aus dem Gebiete der
Alpenkunde und Touristik. Wien: A. Cohn. 24cm.
Bd.1, 1876 - Bd.4, 1878.
Monthly.

The Town and country miscellany; [edited by Albert
Smith]. Bogue. 20cm.
No.1, April 1850 - no.5, Aug. 1850.
Monthly.
No more published.

Trail and timberline. Denver: Colorado Mountain
   Club. 23-25cm.
   No.76, 1925 - no.516, 1961.
   Monthly.
   Library now retains current year only.

Tramping and mountaineering: the journal of the
   Wellington Tramping and Mountaineering Club.
   Wellington (N.Z.): The Club. 28cm.
   Vol.1, no.2, 1948 - v.2, no.1, 1949.
   Three issues a year.

The Travel handbook & calendar. Continental Travel
   Ltd. 19cm.
   Library has summer 1911 only.

The Traveller. WEXAS. 30cm.
   Irregular.
   Library retains current year only.

TRICOUNI CLUB
   The Journal. Ilford: The Club. 23cm.
   Vol.2, no.1, 1935 - v.3, no.2, 1939.
   Frequency varies.
   Vol.1 published as The Journal of the C.H.A.
   Mountaineering Club.

TRONDHJEMS SKIKLUB
   Trondhjems Skiklubs årbok. Trondhjem: Trondhjem
   Skiklubs. 23cm.
   Library has 1929 only.

TUESDAY CLIMBING CLUB
   Arête: Tuesday Climbing Club news. The Club. 33cm.
   Vol.1, spring 1961 - winter/spring 1970.
   Quarterly.
   No more published.

Turist: Svenska Turistföreningens tidning.
   Stockholm: S.T.F. 29cm.
   Årg.39, nr.6, 1971 -
   Six issues a year.
   Library's holdings are incomplete.

Turisták lapja; folyóirat a turistásag és honismeret
   terjesztésére. Budapest: Magyar Turista Egyesület.
   25cm.
   1, 1889; 38, 1926 - 42, 1930; 48, 1936.

Turistasåg es alpinismus. Budapest: Magyar Turista
   Szövetség. 26cm.
   1, 1910/11 - 4, 1914; 22, 1932 - 25, 1935.
   Monthly.
   Also published in German by Karpathenverein as
   Turistik und Alpinismus, 1918 - 1923.

Turistik, Alpinismus und Wintersport. Kesmark:
   Karpathenverein. 26cm.
   1924 - 1927.
   Monthly.
- - 2. Teil: Mitteilungen. 33cm.
   1927 - 1933.
   Continues: Turistik und Alpinismus.
   Continued by: Die Karpathen.

Turistik und Alpinismus.Kesmark:Karpathenverein.26cm.
   1918 - 1923.
   Monthly.
   Continued by: Turistik, Alpinismus und Wintersport.
   Also published in Hungarian by Magyar turista
   szövetség as Turistasåg es alpinismus, 1910 - 1935.

Turysta w. Polsce. Krakow: Polskie Towarzystwo
   Tatrzanskie. 36cm.
   Rok 1, 1935 - r.2, 1936.
   Monthly.

Ueber Berg und Thal: Organ des Gebirgsvereins für
   die sächsische Schweiz. Dresden: C.C. Meinhold.
   33cm.
   Bd.2, 1882/85 - Bd.5, 1894/97; 23.Jahrg., 1900.
   Set lacks no.7, 1900.

UMTALI MOUNTAIN AND OUTDOOR CLUB
   Mountain view: official journal. Umtali: The
   Club. 21cm.
   Library has 1952 only.

UNIONE ALPINISTICA TORRE PELLICE
   Bollettino. Torre Pellice: L'Unione. 18cm.
   Anno 8, 1908 - 12, 1912.
   Annual.
   Library's holdings are incomplete.

UNIONE ESCURSIONISTI TORINO
   L'Escursionista: notizia delle gite alpine ed
   artistiche. Torino: L'Unione. 25cm.
   Anno 1, 1899 - anno 12, 1910.
   Monthly.
   Library's holdings are incomplete.

UNITED STATES. National Museum
   Annual report ... of the Smithsonian Institution
   ...: report of the U.S. National Museum.
   Washington: Government Printing Office. 24cm.
   Library has 1904 only.

UNITED STATES EASTERN AMATEUR SKI ASSOCIATION
   Year book. Bellows Falls (Vt.): U.S.E.A.S.A.
   26cm.
   Library has 1929 only.

The Universal magazine of knowledge and pleasure,
   containing letters, history... W. Bent. 22cm.
   Library has v.92, 1793 only.

UNIVERSITÉ DE GRENOBLE. Institut de géographie
alpine
   Recueil des traveaux. Grenoble: l'Institut.
   26cm.
   T.3, 1915 - t.7, 1919.
   Quarterly.
   Set lacks t.6, 1918.

UNIVERSITÉ DE GRENOBLE. Institut de géographie
alpine
   Revue de géographie alpine. Grenoble: L'Institut.
   26cm.
   T.11, fasc.2, 1923 - t.17, 1929; t.26, fasc.4,
   1938 - t.28, 1940.
   Quarterly.

UNIVERSITY COLLEGE OF NORTH WALES MOUNTAINEERING
CLUB
   Clogwyn: University College of North Wales
   Mountaineering Club journal. Bangor: The Club.
   24cm.
   1967; 1970 - 1971.
   Annual.

UNIVERSITY OF BIRMINGHAM MOUNTAINEERING CLUB
   Journal. Birmingham: U.B.M.C. 21cm.
   No.2, 1960 - no.6, 1964.
   Annual.
   Title varies: no.2: Handbook.

UNIVERSITY OF UPPSALA. Geological Institution
   Bulletin. Uppsala: The University. 27cm.
   Vol.9, 1908/09 - v.10, 1910/11; v.23, 1932 -
   v.31, 1946.

L'Universo: rivista bimestrale dell'Istituto
   Geografico Militare. Firenze: L'Istituto. 25cm.
   Anno 42, n.5, 1962 - anno 55, n.1, 1975.

Unsere Berge
   See
Nos montagnes

Der Uto: Nachrichten der Sektion Uto des Schweizer
   Alpenklub. Zürich: Die Sektion. 24cm.
   5.Jahrg., 1927 - 8.Jahrg., 1930.
   Monthly.

La Vallée du Rhône: journal ...
   See
Journal illustré des stations du Valais ...

VARSITY OUTDOOR CLUB
The Varsity Outdoor Club journal. Vancouver:
V.O.C. 22cm.
Library has v.1, 1958 only.

VERBAND DEUTSCHER TOURISTEN-VEREINE
Der Tourist: illustrierte Zeitschrift zur Förderung
des Fremdenverkehrs in Deutschland; offizielles
Organ des Verbandes Deutscher Touristen und
Gebirgsvereine. Berlin: Der Tourist. 28cm.
Jahrg.14, 1897 - Jahrg.16, 1899.

VEREIN ZUM SCHUTZ UND ZUR PFLEGE DER ALPENPFLANZEN
Bericht. Bamberg: Der Verein. 24cm.
1, 1901; 4, 1904 - 12, 1913.
Annual.

VICTORIAN CLIMBING CLUB
Rock. Brighton (Vict.): The Club. 30cm.
No.1, 1978 -
Annual.

La Vie alpine: revue du régionalisme dans les Alpes
françaises. Grenoble: G. Blanchon. 29cm.
1ère année, no.1, 1927 - 9e année, no.80, 1936.
Quarterly.

Der Wanderer in der Schweiz: eine malerische Zeitschrift; hrsg. von mehrern Freunden des Vater-
landes. Basel: Mählm & Schabelitz. 23cm.
1.Jahrg., No.1, 1834 - No.52, 1835.
Weekly.

Wandern und Reisen: illustrierte Zeitschrift für
Touristik, Landes- und Volkskunde Kunst und Sport.
Düsseldorf: L. Schwann. 32cm.
1.Jahrg., 1903 - 2.Jahrg., 1904.
Fortnightly.

WAYFARERS' CLUB
The wayfarers' journal. Liverpool: Wayfarers'
Club. 23cm.
No.1, 1928 -
Frequency varies.

The Wayfarers' journal. Liverpool: Wayfarers' Club.
23cm.
No.1, 1928 -
Frequency varies.

WELLINGBOROUGH MOUNTAINEERING CLUB
Snaplink: Wellingborough Mountaineering Club
journal. Wellingborough: The Club. 27cm.
Library has winter/spring 1966 only.

WELLINGTON TRAMPING AND MOUNTAINEERING CLUB
Tramping and mountaineering. Wellington (N.Z.):
The Club. 28cm.
Vol.1, no.2, 1948 - v.2, no.1, 1949.
Three issues a year.

WEXAS
Expedition: the magazine for the independent
traveller. WEXAS. 30cm.
Irregular.
Library retains current year only.

WEXAS
The traveller. WEXAS. 30cm.
Irregular.
Library retains current year only.

The White hare: the White Hare Ski Club magazine.
The Club. 23cm.
1961; 1969.
Annual.

WHITE HARE SKI CLUB
The white hare: the White Hare Ski Club magazine.
The Club. 23cm.
1961; 1969.
Annual.

Wierchy: rocznik poswiecony góróm i géralszczyznie;
organ Polskiego Tow. Tatrzańskiego. Krakow: The
Society. 28cm.
5, 1927 -
Annual.
Subtitle varies.

Der Winter. München: Rother. 22-28cm.
Jahrg.1, 1906/7 - Jahrg.8, 1913/14; Jahrg.12,
1926; Jahrg.21, 1927/28 - Jahrg.22, 1928/29;
Jahrg.37, 1949/50 - Jahrg.46, Heft 8, 1959.
Weekly.

WINTER SPORTS CLUB
The winter sports review. The Club. 22cm.
Oct.1911 - Sept. 1913.
Four issues a year.

The Winter sports review. The Club. 22cm.
Oct. 1911 - Sept. 1913.
Four issues a year.

WORLD EXPEDITIONARY ASSOCIATION
See
WEXAS

Yama to Keikoku (mountain & valley). Tokyo: Y.T.K.
26cm.
38 - 39; 169, 1953 - 178, 1954; 448, 1976 -
Monthly.
In Japanese.

YORKSHIRE MOUNTAINEERING CLUB
Journal. [Bradford]: The Club. 21cm.
1955 - v.5, no.1, 1962.
Frequency varies.

YORKSHIRE RAMBLERS' CLUB
Annual report, rules, list of members, etc.
Leeds: The Club. 24cm.
1892/93 - 1897/98.

YORKSHIRE RAMBLERS' CLUB
Syllabus. Leeds: The Club. 24cm.
1896/97 - 1898/99.
Annual.

YORKSHIRE RAMBLERS' CLUB
The Yorkshire Ramblers' Club journal. Leeds: The
Club. 24cm.
Vol.1, 1899 -
Frequency varies.

YOUTH HOSTELS ASSOCIATION (ENGLAND AND WALES)
Mountain. Sheffield: Mountain Magazine. 32cm.
No.1, Jan. 1969 -
Six issues a year.
Continues: Mountain craft.
Nos.1 - 26, published by the Youth Hostels
Association (England and Wales).

Zeitschrift für Gletscherkunde, für Eiszeit-
forschung und Geschichte des Klimas. Berlin:
Borntraeger. 26cm.
Bd.1, 1906/07 - Bd.7, 1912/13.
Annual.

Zimní sport: orgán Svazu lyžařu republiky československé. Praha: S.L. 31cm.
Library has roč.23, 1933/34 only.